KEY TO WORLD MAP PAGES

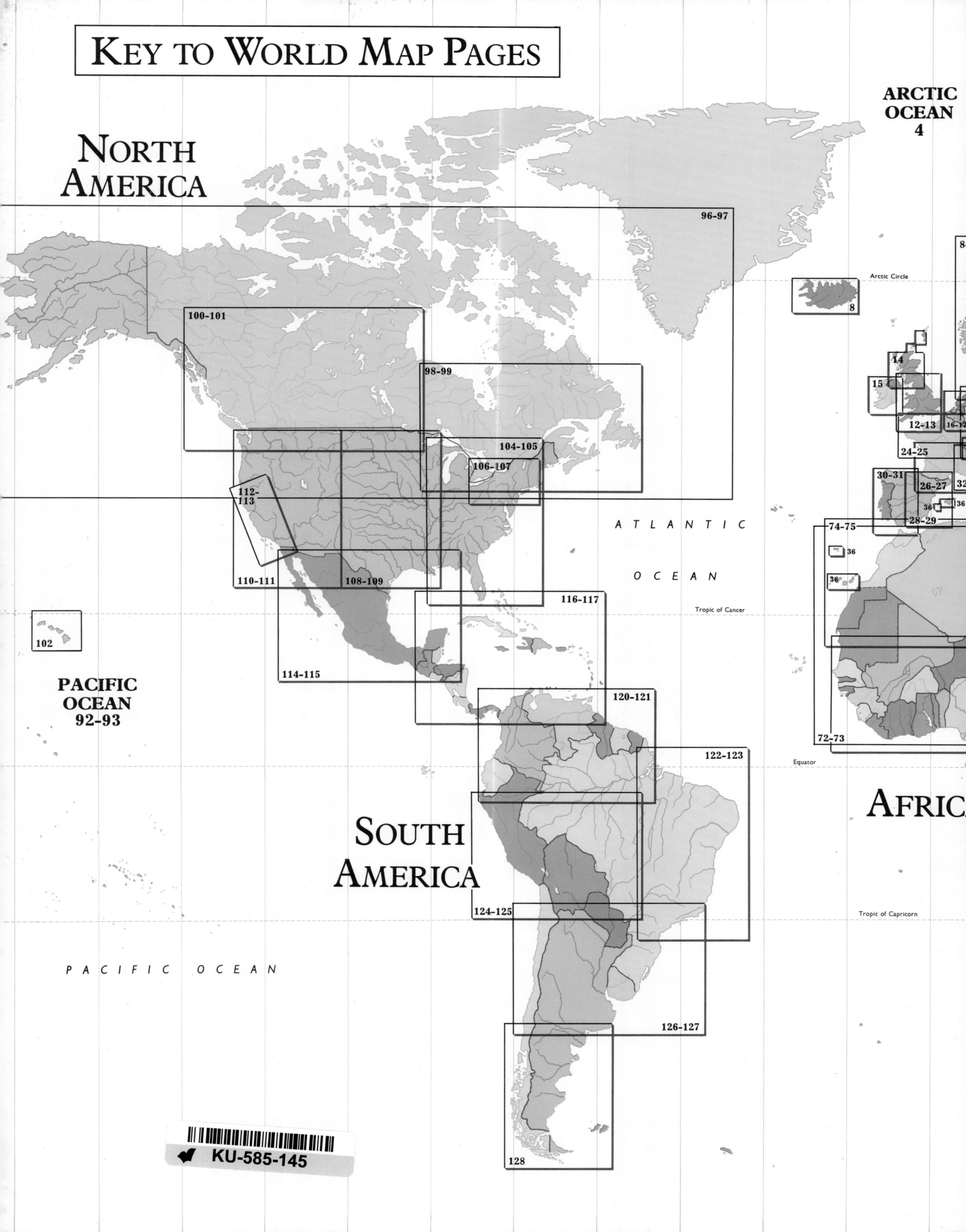

NORTH AMERICA

ARCTIC OCEAN 4

96-97

Arctic Circle

8

100-101

98-99

14

15

104-105

12-13

106-107

24-25

30-31

26-27

32

36

36

74-75

28-29

ATLANTIC

OCEAN

36

36

Tropic of Cancer

112-113

110-111

108-109

116-117

102

114-115

72-73

PACIFIC OCEAN 92-93

120-121

122-123

Equator

AFRICA

SOUTH AMERICA

124-125

Tropic of Capricorn

126-127

PACIFIC OCEAN

128

PHILIP'S

GREAT WORLD ATLAS

PHILIP'S

GREAT WORLD ATLAS

Published in Great Britain in 1995
by George Philip Limited,
an imprint of Reed Books,
Michelin House, 81 Fulham Road, London SW3 6RB,
and Auckland, Melbourne, Singapore and Toronto

Cartography by Philip's

Copyright © 1995 Reed International Books Limited

ISBN 0–540–06159–X

A CIP catalogue record for this book is available from
the British Library

Printed in Hong Kong

PHILIP'S WORLD MAPS

The reference maps which form the main body of this atlas have been prepared in accordance with the highest standards of international cartography to provide an accurate and detailed representation of the Earth. The scales and projections used have been carefully chosen to give balanced coverage of the world, while emphasizing the most densely populated and economically significant regions. A hallmark of Philip's mapping is the use of hill shading and relief colouring to create a graphic impression of landforms: this makes the maps exceptionally easy to read. However, knowledge of the key features employed in the construction and presentation of the maps will enable the reader to derive the fullest benefit from the atlas.

Map sequence

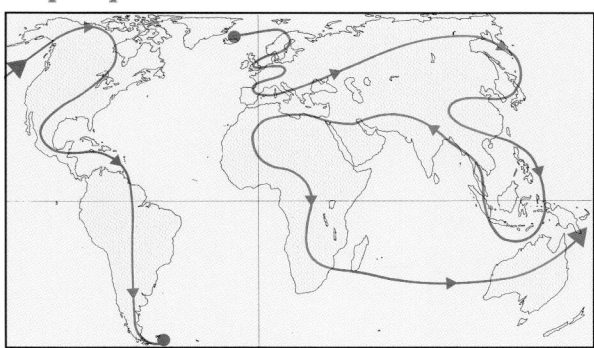

The atlas covers the Earth continent by continent: first Europe; then its land neighbour Asia (mapped north before south, in a clockwise sequence), then Africa, Australia and Oceania, North America and South America. This is the classic arrangement adopted by most cartographers since the 16th century. For each continent, there are maps at a variety of scales. First, physical relief and political maps of the whole continent; then a series of larger-scale maps of the regions within the continent, each followed, where required, by still larger-scale maps of the most important or densely populated areas. The governing principle is that by turning the pages of the atlas, the reader moves steadily from north to south through each continent, with each map overlapping its neighbours. A key map showing this sequence, and the area covered by each map, can be found on the endpapers of the atlas.

Map presentation

With very few exceptions (e.g. for the Arctic and Antarctic), the maps are drawn with north at the top, regardless of whether they are presented upright or sideways on the page. In the borders will be found the map title; a locator diagram showing the area covered and the page numbers for maps of adjacent areas; the scale; the projection used; the degrees of latitude and longitude; and the letters and figures used in the index for locating place names and geographical features. Physical relief maps also have a height reference panel identifying the colours used for each layer of contouring.

Map symbols

Each map contains a vast amount of detail which can only be conveyed clearly and accurately by the use of symbols. Points and circles of varying sizes locate and identify the relative importance of towns and cities; different styles of type are employed for administrative, geographical and regional place names. A variety of pictorial symbols denote landscape features such as glaciers, marshes and reefs, and man-made structures including roads, railways, airports, canals and dams. International borders are shown by red lines. Where neighbouring countries are in dispute, for example in the Middle East, the maps show the *de facto* boundary between nations, regardless of the legal or historical situation. The symbols are explained on the first page of the World Maps section of the atlas.

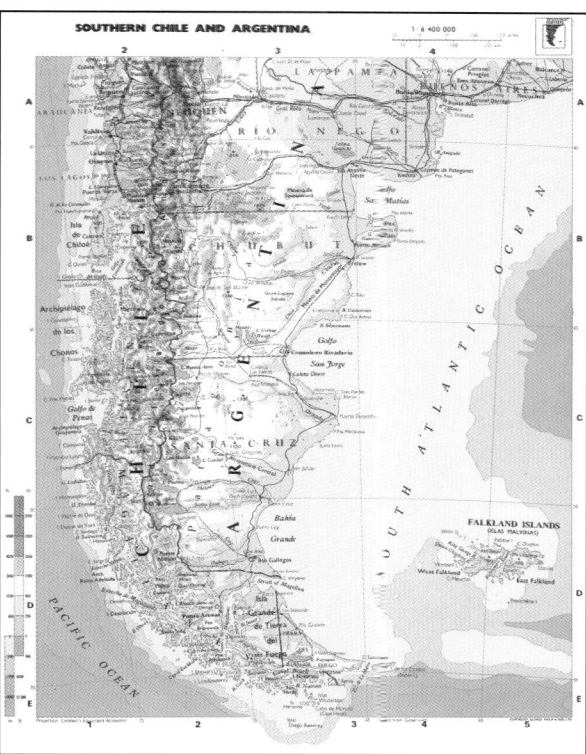

Map scales

> 1: 16 000 000
> 1 inch = 252 statute miles

The scale of each map is given in the numerical form known as the 'representative fraction'. The first figure is always one, signifying one unit of distance on the map; the second figure, usually in millions, is the number by which the map unit must be multiplied to give the equivalent distance on the Earth's surface. Calculations can easily be made in centimetres and kilometres, by dividing the Earth units figure by 100 000 (i.e. deleting the last five 0s). Thus 1:1 000 000 means 1 cm = 10 km. The calculation for inches and miles is more laborious, but 1 000 000 divided by 63 360 (the number of inches in a mile) shows that 1:1 000 000 means approximately 1 inch = 16 miles. The table below provides distance equivalents for scales down to 1:50 000 000.

	LARGE SCALE	
1: 1 000 000	1 cm = 10 km	1 inch = 16 miles
1: 2 500 000	1 cm = 25 km	1 inch = 39.5 miles
1: 5 000 000	1 cm = 50 km	1 inch = 79 miles
1: 6 000 000	1 cm = 60 km	1 inch = 95 miles
1: 8 000 000	1 cm = 80 km	1 inch = 126 miles
1: 10 000 000	1 cm = 100 km	1 inch = 158 miles
1: 15 000 000	1 cm = 150 km	1 inch = 237 miles
1: 20 000 000	1 cm = 200 km	1 inch = 316 miles
1: 50 000 000	1 cm = 500 km	1 inch = 790 miles
	SMALL SCALE	

Measuring distances

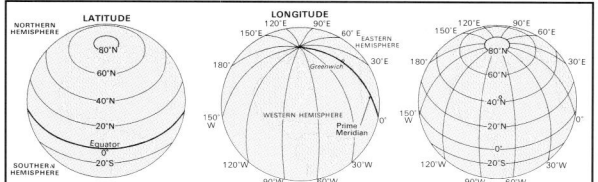

Although each map is accompanied by a scale bar, distances cannot always be measured with confidence because of the distortions involved in portraying the curved surface of the Earth on a flat page. As a general rule, the larger the map scale (i.e. the lower the number of Earth units in the representative fraction), the more accurate and reliable will be the distance measured. On small-scale maps such as those of the world and of entire continents, measurement may only be accurate along the 'standard parallels', or central axes, and should not be attempted without considering the map projection.

Map projections

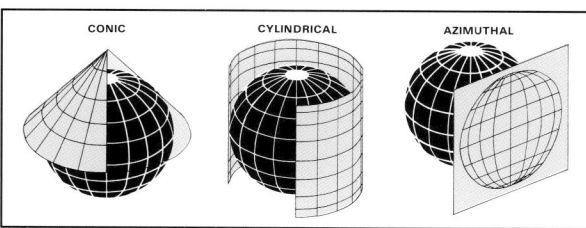

Unlike a globe, no flat map can give a true scale representation of the world in terms of area, shape and position of every region. Each of the numerous systems that have been devised for projecting the curved surface of the Earth on to a flat page involves the sacrifice of accuracy in one or more of these elements. The variations in shape and position of landmasses such as Alaska, Greenland and Australia, for example, can be quite dramatic when different projections are compared.

For this atlas, the guiding principle has been to select projections that involve the least distortion of size and distance. The projection used for each map is noted in the border. Most fall into one of three categories – conic, cylindrical or azimuthal – whose basic concepts are shown above. Each involves plotting the forms of the Earth's surface on a grid of latitude and longitude lines, which may be shown as parallels, curves or radiating spokes.

Latitude and longitude

Accurate positioning of individual points on the Earth's surface is made possible by reference to the geometrical system of latitude and longitude. Latitude *parallels* are drawn west–east around the Earth and numbered by degrees north and south of the Equator, which is designated 0° of latitude. Longitude *meridians* are drawn north–south and numbered by degrees east and west of the *prime meridian*, 0° of longitude, which passes through Greenwich in England. By referring to these co-ordinates and their subdivisions of minutes (1/60th of a degree) and seconds (1/60th of a minute), any place on Earth can be located to within a few hundred yards. Latitude and longitude are indicated by blue lines on the maps; they are straight or curved according to the projection employed. Reference to these lines is the easiest way of determining the relative positions of places on different maps, and for plotting compass directions.

Name forms

For ease of reference, both English and local name forms appear in the atlas. Oceans, seas and countries are shown in English throughout the atlas; country names may be abbreviated to their commonly accepted form (e.g. Germany, not The Federal Republic of Germany). Conventional English forms are also used for place names on the smaller-scale maps of the continents. However, local name forms are used on all large-scale and regional maps, with the English form given in brackets only for important cities – the large-scale map of Russia and Central Asia thus shows Moskva (Moscow). For countries which do not use a Roman script, place names have been transcribed according to the systems adopted by the British and US Geographic Names Authorities. For China, the Pin Yin system has been used, with some more widely known forms appearing in brackets, as with Beijing (Peking). Both English and local names appear in the index, the English form being cross-referenced to the local form.

CONTENTS

WORLD STATISTICS

Countries x
Cities xi
Distances xii
Climate xiii
Physical
Dimensions xiv–xv
Regions in the News xvi

INTRODUCTION TO WORLD GEOGRAPHY

The Universe 2–3
The Solar System 4–5

THE EARTH
Time and Motion 6–7
Geology 8–9
Oceans 10–11
Atmosphere 12–13
Climate 14–15
Water and
Land Use 16–17
Landscape 18–19
Environment 20–21

PEOPLE
Demography 22–23
Cities 24–25
The Human Family 26–27
Conflict and
Co-operation 28–29

PRODUCTION
Agriculture 30–31
Energy 32–33
Minerals 34–35
Manufacturing 36–37
Trade 38–39

QUALITY OF LIFE
Wealth 40–41
Standards 42–43
Health 44–45
Environment 46–47

WORLD MAPS

1–128

THE WORLD

Map Symbols

1

The World: Political
1:64 000 000

2–3

Arctic Ocean 1:28 000 000
Greenland

4

Antarctica 1:28 000 000

5

NOTE
The titles to the World Maps
list the main countries, states
and provinces covered by
each map. A name given in
italics indicates that only part
of the country is shown on
the map.

EUROPE

Europe: Physical
1:16 000 000
6

Europe: Political
1:16 000 000
7

Scandinavia 1:4 000 000
Norway, Sweden, *Finland*,
Iceland

8–9

**Denmark and Southern
Sweden** 1:2 000 000
Denmark, *Norway, Sweden*

10–11

England and Wales
1:1 600 000
Isle of Man, Channel Islands

12–13

Scotland 1:1 600 000

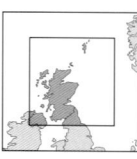

14

Ireland 1:1 600 000
Irish Republic, Northern Ireland

15

Netherlands, Belgium and Luxembourg 1:1 000 000

16–17

Germany 1:2 000 000

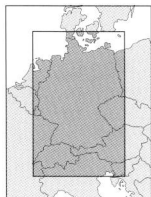

18–19

Middle Europe 1:2 800 000
Austria, Czech Republic, Slovak Republic, Hungary, Poland, Bosnia-Herzegovina, Croatia, Slovenia, Yugoslavia

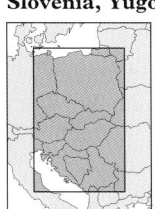

20–21

Switzerland 1:800 000
Liechtenstein

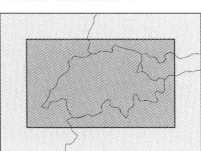

22–23

Northern France 1:2 000 000

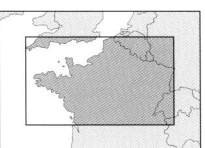

24–25

Southern France 1:2 000 000
Corsica, Monaco

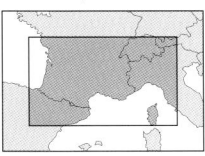

26–27

Eastern Spain 1:2 000 000
Andorra

28–29

Western Spain and Portugal 1:2 000 000

30–31

Northern Italy, Slovenia and Croatia
1:2 000 000
San Marino, Slovenia, *Croatia*

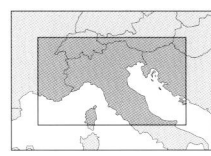

32–33

Southern Italy 1:2 000 000
Sardinia, Sicily

34–35

Balearics, Canaries and Madeira 1:800 000 / 1:1 040 000
Mallorca, Menorca, Ibiza, Tenerife

36

Malta, Crete, Corfu, Rhodes and Cyprus
1:800 000 / 1:1 600 000

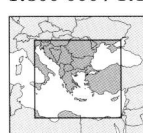

37

The Balkans 1:2 800 000
Yugoslavia, Romania, Bulgaria, Greece, Albania, Macedonia

38–39

Baltic States, Belarus and Ukraine 1:4 000 000
Russia, Estonia, Latvia, Lithuania, Belarus, Moldova, Ukraine

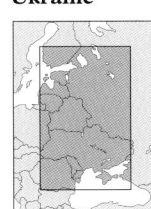

40–41

Volga Basin and the Caucasus 1:4 000 000
Russia, Georgia, *Armenia, Azerbaijan*

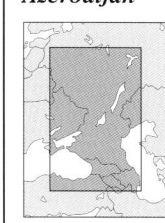

42–43

ASIA

Russia and Central Asia
1:16 000 000
Russia, Kazakhstan, Turkmenistan, Uzbekistan

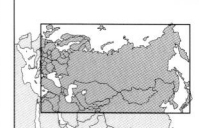

44–45

Asia: Physical
1:40 000 000

46

Asia: Political
1:40 000 000

47

Japan 1:4 000 000
Ryukyu Islands

48–49

Northern China and Korea
1:4 800 000
North Korea, South Korea

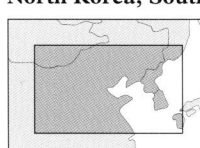

50–51

Southern China 1:4 800 000
Hong Kong, Taiwan, Macau

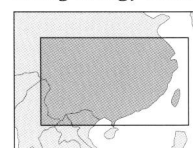

52–53

China 1:16 000 000
Mongolia

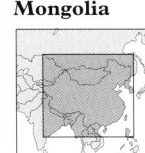

54

Philippines 1:6 000 000

55

Indonesia 1:10 000 000
Malaysia, Singapore, Brunei

56–57

Mainland South-East Asia
1:4 800 000
Thailand, Vietnam, Cambodia,
Laos

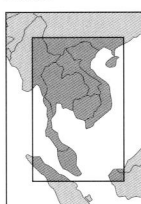

58–59

South Asia 1:8 000 000
India, Pakistan, Bangladesh,
Burma, Sri Lanka, Afghanistan

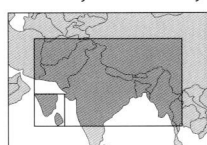

60–61

The Indo-Gangetic Plain
1:4 800 000
India, *Pakistan*, Nepal, Kashmir

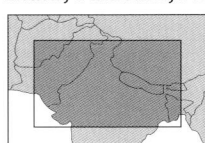

62–63

The Middle East 1:5 600 000
Iran, Iraq, *Saudi Arabia*, United
Arab Emirates, Kuwait, Qatar

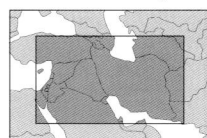

64–65

**Turkey and
Transcaucasia** 1:4 000 000
Turkey, Syria, Georgia,
Armenia, Azerbaijan, *Iraq*

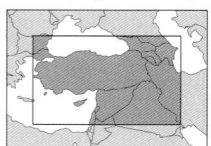

66–67

**Arabia and the Horn of
Africa** 1:12 000 000
Saudi Arabia, Oman, Yemen,
Somalia, Ethiopia, Eritrea,
Djibouti

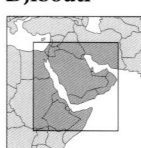

68

The Near East 1:2 000 000
Israel, Lebanon, *Jordan*

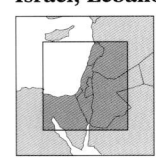

69

AFRICA

Africa: Physical
1:33 600 000

70

Africa: Political
1:33 600 000

71

Northern Africa 1:12 000 000
Libya, Chad, Niger

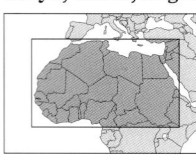

72–73

North-West Africa
1:6 400 000
Algeria, Morocco, Tunisia,
Mauritania, *Niger*, *Mali*

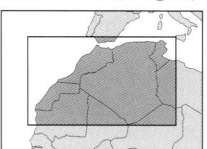

74–75

The Nile Valley 1:6 400 000
Egypt, Sudan, Eritrea, *Ethiopia*
The Nile Delta 1:3 200 000

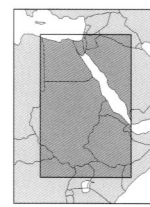

76–77

West Africa 1:6 400 000
Nigeria, Ivory Coast, Ghana,
Senegal, Guinea, Burkina Faso

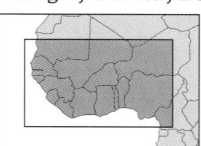

78–79

**Central and Southern
Africa** 1:12 000 000
Zaïre, Angola, Cameroon, Congo,
Gabon, Central African Republic

80–81

East Africa 1:6 400 000
Kenya, Tanzania, Zambia,
Uganda, Malawi

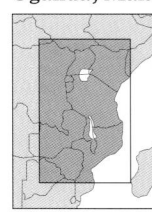

82–83

Southern Africa 1:6 400 000
South Africa, Zimbabwe,
Madagascar, *Mozambique*,
Botswana, Namibia

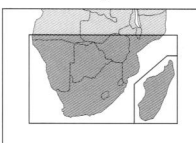

84–85

AUSTRALIA AND OCEANIA

Australia and Oceania: Physical and Political
1:40 000 000
86

New Zealand 1:4 800 000
Fiji, Tonga, Samoa

87

Western Australia
1:6 400 000
Northern Territory

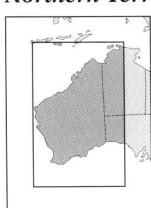

88–89

Eastern Australia 1:6 400 000
New South Wales, Queensland,
Victoria, *South Australia*,
Tasmania

90–91

Pacific Ocean 1:43 200 000
Kiribati, Vanuatu, New
Caledonia, Tuvalu, Micronesia,
French Polynesia
92–93

NORTH AMERICA

North America: Physical
1:28 000 000
94

North America: Political
1:28 000 000
95

Canada 1:12 000 000
Northwest Territories, Yukon
Alaska 1:24 000 000

96–97

Eastern Canada 1:5 600 000
Quebec, *Ontario*, Newfoundland

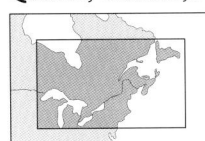

98–99

Western Canada 1:5 600 000
British Columbia, Alberta,
Saskatchewan, Manitoba

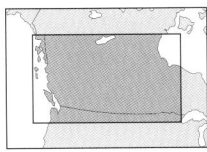

100–101

United States 1:9 600 000
Hawaii 1:8 000 000

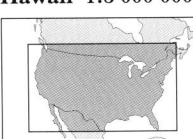

102–103

Eastern United States
1:4 800 000

104–105

**North-Eastern United
States** 1:2 000 000
New York, New England,
Pennsylvania

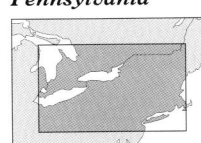

106–107

Middle United States
1:4 800 000

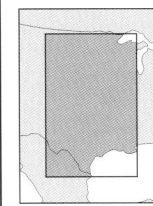

108–109

Western United States
1:4 800 000

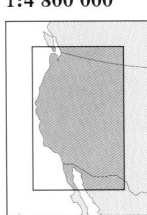

110–111

**Central and Southern
California and
Washington** 1:2 000 000

112–113

Mexico 1:6 400 000

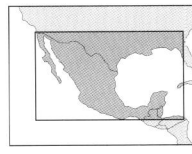

114–115

**Central America and the
West Indies** 1:6 400 000
Guatemala, Nicaragua, Cuba,
Jamaica, Panama, Haiti

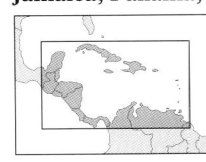

116–117

SOUTH AMERICA

South America: Physical
1:28 000 000
118

South America: Political
1:28 000 000
119

**South America –
North-West** 1:6 400 000
Colombia, Venezuela, *Brazil*,
Ecuador, Guyana

120–121

Eastern Brazil 1:6 400 000

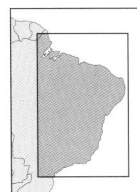

122–123

South America – West
1:6 400 000
Peru, *Brazil*, Bolivia

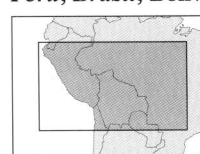

124–125

Central South America
1:6 400 000
Argentina, *Chile*, *Brazil*,
Paraguay, Uruguay

126–127

**Southern Chile and
Argentina** 1:6 400 000

128

INDEX TO WORLD MAPS

129–224

World Statistics: Countries

This alphabetical list includes all the countries and territories of the world. If a territory is not completely independent, then the country it is associated with is named. The area figures give the total area of land, inland water and ice. Units for areas and populations are thousands. The annual income is the Gross National Product per capita in US dollars. The figures are the latest available, usually 1994.

Country/Territory	Area km² Thousands	Area miles² Thousands	Population Thousands	Capital	Annual Income US $
Adélie Land (Fr.)	432	167	0.03	–	–
Afghanistan	652	252	18,879	Kabul	450
Albania	28.8	11.1	3,414	Tirana	820
Algeria	2,382	920	27,325	Algiers	1,840
American Samoa (US)	0.20	0.08	53	Pago Pago	6,000
Amsterdam Is. (Fr.)	0.05	0.02	0.03	–	–
Andorra	0.45	0.17	65	Andorra la Vella	14,000
Angola	1,247	481	10,674	Luanda	620
Anguilla (UK)	0.1	0.04	8	The Valley	6,800
Antigua & Barbuda	0.44	0.17	65	St John's	4,770
Argentina	2,767	1,068	34,182	Buenos Aires	2,780
Armenia	29.8	11.5	3,548	Yerevan	780
Aruba (Neths)	0.19	0.07	69	Oranjestad	6,000
Ascension Is. (UK)	0.09	0.03	1.5	Georgetown	–
Australia	7,687	2,968	17,847	Canberra	17,260
Australian Antarctic Territory	6,120	2,363	0	–	–
Austria	83.9	32.4	7,918	Vienna	22,380
Azerbaijan	86.6	33.4	7,472	Baku	740
Azores (Port.)	2.2	0.87	238	Ponta Delgada	–
Bahamas	13.9	5.4	272	Nassau	12,070
Bahrain	0.68	0.26	549	Manama	6,910
Bangladesh	144	56	117,787	Dhaka	220
Barbados	0.43	0.17	261	Bridgetown	6,540
Belarus	207.6	80.1	10,163	Minsk	2,930
Belgium	30.5	11.8	10,080	Brussels	20,880
Belize	23	8.9	210	Belmopan	2,220
Benin	113	43	5,246	Porto-Novo	410
Bermuda (UK)	0.05	0.02	63	Hamilton	27,800
Bhutan	47	18.1	1,614	Thimphu	180
Bolivia	1,099	424	7,237	La Paz/Sucre	680
Bosnia-Herzegovina	51	20	3,527	Sarajevo	2,454
Botswana	582	225	1,443	Gaborone	2,790
Bouvet Is. (Nor.)	0.05	0.02	0.02	–	–
Brazil	8,512	3,286	159,143	Brasília	2,770
British Antarctic Terr. (UK)	1,709	660	0.3	Stanley	–
British Indian Ocean Terr. (UK)	0.08	0.03	0	–	–
Brunei	5.8	2.2	280	Bandar Seri Begawan	14,120
Bulgaria	111	43	8,818	Sofia	1,330
Burkina Faso	274	106	10,046	Ouagadougou	300
Burma (Myanmar)	677	261	45,555	Rangoon	500
Burundi	27.8	10.7	6,209	Bujumbura	210
Cambodia	181	70	9,968	Phnom Penh	202
Cameroon	475	184	12,871	Yaoundé	820
Canada	9,976	3,852	29,141	Ottawa	20,710
Canary Is. (Spain)	7.3	2.8	1,494	Las Palmas/Santa Cruz	–
Cape Verde Is.	4	1.6	381	Praia	850
Cayman Is. (UK)	0.26	0.10	30	George Town	20,000
Central African Republic	623	241	3,235	Bangui	410
Chad	1,284	496	6,183	Ndjamena	222
Chatham Is. (NZ)	0.96	0.37	0.05	Waitangi	–
Chile	757	292	14,044	Santiago	2,730
China	9,597	3,705	1,208,841	Beijing (Peking)	470
Christmas Is. (Aus.)	0.14	0.05	2	The Settlement	–
Cocos (Keeling) Is. (Aus.)	0.01	0.005	0.6	West Island	–
Colombia	1,139	440	34,545	Bogotá	1,330
Comoros	2.2	0.86	630	Moroni	500
Congo	342	132	2,516	Brazzaville	1,030
Cook Is. (NZ)	0.24	0.09	19	Avarua	900
Costa Rica	51.1	19.7	3,347	San José	1,960
Croatia	56.5	21.8	4,504	Zagreb	1,800
Crozet Is. (Fr.)	0.51	0.19	35	–	–
Cuba	111	43	10,960	Havana	1,580
Cyprus	9.3	3.6	734	Nicosia	9,820
Czech Republic	78.9	30.4	10,295	Prague	2,450
Denmark	43.1	16.6	5,173	Copenhagen	26,000
Djibouti	23.2	9	566	Djibouti	1,000
Dominica	0.75	0.29	71	Roseau	2,520
Dominican Republic	48.7	18.8	7,684	Santo Domingo	1,050
Ecuador	284	109	11,220	Quito	1,070
Egypt	1,001	387	61,636	Cairo	640
El Salvador	21	8.1	5,641	San Salvador	1,170
Equatorial Guinea	28.1	10.8	389	Malabo	330
Eritrea	94	36	3,437	Asmara	150
Estonia	44.7	17.3	1,541	Tallinn	2,760
Ethiopia	1,128	436	53,435	Addis Ababa	110
Falkland Is. (UK)	12.2	4.7	2	Stanley	–
Faroe Is. (Den.)	1.4	0.54	47	Tórshavn	23,660
Fiji	18.3	7.1	771	Suva	2,010
Finland	338	131	5,083	Helsinki	21,970
France	552	213	57,747	Paris	22,260
French Guiana (Fr.)	90	34.7	141	Cayenne	2,500
French Polynesia (Fr.)	4	1.5	215	Papeete	6,000
Gabon	268	103	1,283	Libreville	4,450
Gambia, The	11.3	4.4	1,081	Banjul	370
Georgia	69.7	26.9	5,450	Tbilisi	850
Germany	357	138	80,278	Berlin/Bonn	23,030
Ghana	239	92	16,944	Accra	450
Gibraltar (UK)	0.007	0.003	28	Gibraltar Town	15,080
Greece	132	51	10,416	Athens	7,290
Greenland (Den.)	2,176	840	58	Godthåb (Nuuk)	9,000
Grenada	0.34	0.13	92	St George's	2,310
Guadeloupe (Fr.)	1.7	0.66	421	Basse-Terre	7,000
Guam (US)	0.55	0.21	147	Agana	6,000
Guatemala	109	42	10,322	Guatemala City	980
Guinea	246	95	6,501	Conakry	570
Guinea-Bissau	36.1	13.9	1,050	Bissau	220
Guyana	215	83	825	Georgetown	330
Haiti	27.8	10.7	7,035	Port-au-Prince	380
Honduras	112	43	5,493	Tegucigalpa	580
Hong Kong (UK)	1.1	0.40	5,838	Victoria	15,360
Hungary	93	35.9	10,161	Budapest	2,970
Iceland	103	40	266	Reykjavik	23,880
India	3,288	1,269	918,570	New Delhi	310
Indonesia	1,905	735	194,615	Jakarta	670
Iran	1,648	636	65,758	Tehran	2,200
Iraq	438	169	19,925	Baghdad	2,000
Ireland	70.3	27.1	3,539	Dublin	12,210
Israel	27	10.3	5,458	Jerusalem	13,220
Italy	301	116	57,157	Rome	20,460
Ivory Coast	322	125	13,780	Yamoussoukro	670
Jamaica	11	4.2	2,429	Kingston	1,340
Jan Mayen Is. (Nor.)	0.38	0.15	0.06	–	–
Japan	378	146	124,815	Tokyo	28,190
Johnston Is. (US)	0.002	0.0009	1	–	–
Jordan	89.2	34.4	5,198	Amman	1,120
Kazakhstan	2,717	1,049	17,027	Alma-Ata	1,680
Kenya	580	224	27,343	Nairobi	310
Kerguelen Is. (Fr.)	7.2	2.8	0.7	–	–
Kermadec Is. (NZ)	0.03	0.01	0.1	–	–
Kiribati	0.72	0.28	77	Tarawa	750
Korea, North	121	47	23,483	Pyongyang	1,040
Korea, South	99	38.2	44,563	Seoul	6,790
Kuwait	17.8	6.9	1,633	Kuwait City	16,150
Kyrgyzstan	198.5	76.6	4,667	Bishkek	820
Laos	237	91	4,742	Vientiane	250
Latvia	65	25	2,583	Riga	1,930
Lebanon	10.4	4	2,915	Beirut	1,400
Lesotho	30.4	11.7	1,996	Maseru	590
Liberia	111	43	2,941	Monrovia	400
Libya	1,760	679	5,225	Tripoli	5,800
Liechtenstein	0.16	0.06	30	Vaduz	33,000
Lithuania	65.2	25.2	3,706	Vilnius	1,310
Luxembourg	2.6	1	401	Luxembourg	35,160
Macau (Port.)	0.02	0.006	398	Macau	2,000
Macedonia	25.3	9.8	2,142	Skopje	1,812
Madagascar	587	227	14,303	Antananarivo	230
Madeira (Port.)	0.81	0.31	253	Funchal	–
Malawi	118	46	10,843	Lilongwe	210
Malaysia	330	127	19,695	Kuala Lumpur	2,790
Maldives	0.30	0.12	246	Malé	460
Mali	1,240	479	10,462	Bamako	254
Malta	0.32	0.12	364	Valletta	7,300
Marshall Is.	0.18	0.07	52	Dalap-Uliga-Darrit	1,500
Martinique (Fr.)	1.1	0.42	375	Fort-de-France	4,000
Mauritania	1,025	396	2,217	Nouakchott	530
Mauritius	2.0	0.72	1,104	Port Louis	2,700
Mayotte (Fr.)	0.37	0.14	101	Mamoundzou	–
Mexico	1,958	756	91,858	Mexico City	3,470
Micronesia, Fed. States	0.70	0.27	121	Palikir	1,500
Midway Is. (US)	0.005	0.002	2	–	–
Moldova	33.7	13	4,420	Kishinev	1,300
Monaco	0.002	0.0001	31	Monaco	16,000
Mongolia	1,567	605	2,363	Ulan Bator	112
Montserrat (UK)	0.10	0.04	11	Plymouth	5,800
Morocco	447	172	26,488	Rabat	1,030
Mozambique	802	309	15,527	Maputo	60
Namibia	825	318	1,500	Windhoek	1,610
Nauru	0.02	0.008	11	Yaren District	–
Nepal	141	54	21,360	Katmandu	170
Netherlands	41.5	16	15,397	Amsterdam/The Hague	20,480
Neths Antilles (Neths)	0.99	0.38	197	Willemstad	6,000
New Caledonia (Fr.)	19	7.3	178	Nouméa	4,000
New Zealand	269	104	3,531	Wellington	12,300
Nicaragua	130	50	4,275	Managua	340
Niger	1,267	489	8,846	Niamey	284
Nigeria	924	357	88,515	Abuja	320
Niue (NZ)	0.26	0.10	2	Alofi	–
Norfolk Is. (Aus.)	0.03	0.01	2	Kingston	–
Northern Mariana Is. (US)	0.48	0.18	47	Saipan	11,500
Norway	324	125	4,318	Oslo	25,820
Oman	212	82	2,077	Muscat	6,480
Pakistan	796	307	136,645	Islamabad	420
Palau	0.46	0.18	17	Koror	2,260
Panama	77.1	29.8	2,585	Panama City	2,420
Papua New Guinea	463	179	4,205	Port Moresby	950
Paraguay	407	157	4,830	Asunción	1,380
Peru	1,285	496	23,331	Lima	950
Peter 1st Is. (Nor.)	0.18	0.07	0	–	–
Philippines	300	116	66,188	Manila	770
Pitcairn Is. (UK)	0.03	0.01	0.07	Adamstown	–
Poland	313	121	38,341	Warsaw	1,910
Portugal	92.4	35.7	9,830	Lisbon	7,450
Puerto Rico (US)	9	3.5	3,646	San Juan	6,330
Qatar	11	4.2	540	Doha	15,860
Queen Maud Land (Nor.)	2,800	1,081	0	–	–
Réunion (Fr.)	2.5	0.97	644	Saint-Denis	4,000
Romania	238	92	22,922	Bucharest	1,130
Ross Dependency (NZ)	435	168	0	–	–
Russia	17,075	6,592	147,370	Moscow	2,510
Rwanda	26.3	10.2	7,750	Kigali	250
St Christopher & Nevis	0.36	0.14	41	Basseterre	3,960
St Helena (UK)	0.12	0.05	6	Jamestown	–
St Lucia	0.62	0.24	141	Castries	2,500
St Paul Is. (Fr.)	0.007	0.003	0	–	–
St Pierre & Miquelon (Fr.)	0.24	0.09	6	Saint Pierre	–
St Vincent & Grenadines	0.39	0.15	111	Kingstown	1,730
San Marino	0.06	0.02	25	San Marino	20,000
São Tomé & Príncipe	0.96	0.37	130	São Tomé	350
Saudi Arabia	2,150	830	17,451	Riyadh	7,510
Senegal	197	76	8,102	Dakar	780
Seychelles	0.46	0.18	73	Victoria	5,110
Sierra Leone	71.7	27.7	4,402	Freetown	160
Singapore	0.62	0.24	2,821	Singapore	15,730
Slovak Republic	49	18.9	5,333	Bratislava	1,930
Slovenia	20.3	7.8	1,942	Ljubljana	7,150
Solomon Is.	28.9	11.2	366	Honiara	690
Somalia	638	246	9,077	Mogadishu	150
South Africa	1,220	471	40,555	Pretoria/Cape Town	2,670
South Georgia (UK)	3.8	1.4	0.05	–	–
South Sandwich Is. (UK)	0.38	0.15	0	–	–
Spain	505	195	39,568	Madrid	13,970
Sri Lanka	65.6	25.3	18,125	Colombo	540
Sudan	2,506	967	27,361	Khartoum	277
Surinam	163	63	418	Paramaribo	4,280
Svalbard (Nor.)	62.9	24.3	4	Longyearbyen	–
Swaziland	17.4	6.7	832	Mbabane	1,090
Sweden	450	174	8,738	Stockholm	27,010
Switzerland	41.3	15.9	7,131	Bern	36,080
Syria	185	71	14,171	Damascus	1,170
Taiwan	36	13.9	20,659	Taipei	8,780
Tajikistan	143.1	55.2	5,933	Dushanbe	490
Tanzania	945	365	28,846	Dodoma	110
Thailand	513	198	58,183	Bangkok	1,840
Togo	56.8	21.9	4,010	Lomé	390
Tokelau (NZ)	0.01	0.005	2	Nukunonu	–
Tonga	0.75	0.29	98	Nuku'alofa	1,100
Trinidad & Tobago	5.1	2	1,292	Port of Spain	3,940
Tristan da Cunha (UK)	0.11	0.04	0.33	Edinburgh	–
Tunisia	164	63	8,733	Tunis	1,720
Turkey	779	301	60,771	Ankara	1,980
Turkmenistan	488.1	188.5	4,010	Ashkhabad	1,230
Turks & Caicos Is. (UK)	0.43	0.17	14	Cockburn Town	5,000
Tuvalu	0.03	0.01	9	Fongafale	600
Uganda	236	91	20,621	Kampala	170
Ukraine	603.7	233.1	51,465	Kiev	1,820
United Arab Emirates	83.6	32.3	1,861	Abu Dhabi	20,020
United Kingdom	243.3	94	58,091	London	17,790
United States of America	9,373	3,619	260,631	Washington, DC	23,240
Uruguay	177	68	3,167	Montevideo	3,340
Uzbekistan	447.4	172.7	22,349	Tashkent	850
Vanuatu	12.2	4.7	165	Port-Vila	1,120
Vatican City	0.0004	0.0002	1	–	–
Venezuela	912	352	21,378	Caracas	2,910
Vietnam	332	127	72,931	Hanoi	220
Virgin Is. (UK)	0.15	0.06	18	Road Town	–
Virgin Is. (US)	0.34	0.13	104	Charlotte Amalie	12,000
Wake Is.	0.008	0.003	0.30	–	–
Wallis & Futuna Is. (Fr.)	0.20	0.08	19	Mata-Utu	–
Western Sahara	266	103	272	El Aaiún	–
Western Samoa	2.8	1.1	169	Apia	940
Yemen	528	204	13,873	Sana	520
Yugoslavia	102.3	39.5	10,763	Belgrade	3,000
Zaïre	2,345	905	42,552	Kinshasa	220
Zambia	753	291	9,196	Lusaka	460
Zimbabwe	391	151	11,002	Harare	570

WORLD STATISTICS: CITIES

This list shows the principal cities with more than 500,000 inhabitants (for China and Japan, only cities with more than 1 million inhabitants are included). The figures are taken from the most recent census or estimate available, and as far as possible are the population of the metropolitan area, e.g. greater New York, Mexico or London. All the figures are in thousands. Local name forms have been used for the smaller cities (e.g. Kraków).

Afghanistan
Kabul — 1,424
Algeria
Algiers — 1,722
Oran — 664
Angola
Luanda — 1,544
Argentina
Buenos Aires — 11,256
Córdoba — 1,198
Rosario — 1,096
Mendoza — 775
La Plata — 640
San Miguel de Tucumán — 622
Mar del Plata — 520
Armenia
Yerevan — 1,254
Australia
Sydney — 3,657
Melbourne — 3,081
Brisbane — 1,302
Perth — 1,193
Adelaide — 1,050
Austria
Vienna — 1,560
Azerbaijan
Baku — 1,149
Bangladesh
Dhaka — 6,105
Chittagong — 2,041
Khulna — 877
Rajshahi — 517
Belarus
Minsk — 1,613
Gomel — 506
Belgium
Brussels — 954
Bolivia
La Paz — 1,126
Santa Cruz — 696
Bosnia-Herzegovina
Sarajevo — 526
Brazil
São Paulo — 9,480
Rio de Janeiro — 5,336
Salvador — 2,056
Belo Horizonte — 2,049
Fortaleza — 1,758
Brasília — 1,596
Curitiba — 1,290
Recife — 1,290
Nova Iguaçu — 1,286
Pôrto Alegre — 1,263
Belém — 1,246
Manaus — 1,011
Goiânia — 921
Campinas — 846
Guarulhos — 781
São Gonçalo — 748
São Luís — 695
Duque de Caxias — 665
Maceió — 628
Santo André — 614
Natal — 607
Teresina — 598
São Bernado de Campo — 565
Osasco — 563
Campo Grande — 526
São João de Meriti — 508
Bulgaria
Sofia — 1,141
Burkina Faso
Ouagadougou — 634
Burma (Myanmar)
Rangoon — 2,513
Mandalay — 533
Cambodia
Phnom Penh — 800
Cameroon
Douala — 884
Yaoundé — 750
Canada
Toronto — 3,893
Montréal — 3,127
Vancouver — 1,603
Ottawa-Hull — 921
Edmonton — 840
Calgary — 754
Winnipeg — 652
Québec — 646
Hamilton — 600
Central African Rep.
Bangui — 597

Chad
Ndjamena — 530
Chile
Santiago — 5,343
China
Shanghai — 12,320
Beijing (Peking) — 9,750
Tianjin — 7,790
Chongqing — 6,511
Wenzhou — 5,948
Guangzhou — 5,669
Hangzhou — 5,234
Shenyang — 5,055
Dalian — 4,619
Jinzhou — 4,448
Wuhan — 4,273
Qingdao — 4,205
Chengdu — 4,025
Jilin — 3,974
Nanjing — 3,682
Jinan — 3,376
Xi'an — 2,911
Harbin — 2,830
Yingkou — 2,789
Dandong — 2,574
Anshan — 2,517
Nanchang — 2,471
Zibo — 2,460
Lanzhou — 2,340
Lupanshui — 2,247
Taiyuan — 2,177
Fushun — 2,045
Changchun — 2,110
Kunming — 1,976
Tianshui — 1,967
Zhengzhou — 1,943
Fuxin — 1,693
Zigong — 1,673
Fuzhou — 1,652
Liaoyang — 1,612
Zhaozhuang — 1,612
Botou — 1,593
Hepei — 1,541
Guiyang — 1,530
Huainan — 1,519
Tangshan — 1,500
Linyi — 1,385
Qiqihar — 1,380
Tai'an — 1,370
Changsha — 1,330
Shijiazhuang — 1,320
Huaibei — 1,308
Pingxiang — 1,305
Xintao — 1,272
Yangcheng — 1,265
Yulin — 1,255
Dongguang — 1,230
Chao'an — 1,227
Hohhot — 1,206
Baotou — 1,200
Suining — 1,195
Luoyang — 1,190
Macheng — 1,190
Xintai — 1,167
Yichun — 1,167
Ürümqi — 1,160
Puyang — 1,125
Datong — 1,110
Handan — 1,110
Shaoxing — 1,091
Ningbo — 1,090
Zhongshan — 1,073
Nanning — 1,070
Huangshi — 1,069
Laiwu — 1,054
Leshan — 1,039
Heze — 1,017
Linhai — 1,012
Changshu — 1,004
Colombia
Bogotá — 4,921
Cali — 1,624
Medellin — 1,581
Barranquilla — 1,019
Cartagena — 688
Congo
Brazzaville — 938
Pointe-Noire — 576
Croatia
Zagreb — 931
Cuba
Havana — 2,119
Czech Republic
Prague — 1,216
Denmark
Copenhagen — 1,337

Dominican Rep.
Santo Domingo — 1,601
Ecuador
Guayaquil — 1,508
Quito — 1,101
Egypt
Cairo — 6,800
Alexandria — 3,380
El Gîza — 2,144
Shubra el Kheima — 834
El Salvador
San Salvador — 1,522
Ethiopia
Addis Ababa — 2,213
Finland
Helsinki — 977
France
Paris — 9,319
Lyons — 1,262
Marseilles — 1,087
Lille — 959
Bordeaux — 696
Toulouse — 650
Nice — 516
Georgia
Tbilisi — 1,279
Germany
Berlin — 3,446
Hamburg — 1,669
Munich — 1,229
Cologne — 957
Frankfurt — 654
Essen — 627
Dortmund — 601
Stuttgart — 592
Düsseldorf — 578
Bremen — 553
Duisburg — 537
Hanover — 517
Leipzig — 503
Ghana
Accra — 965
Greece
Athens — 3,097
Guatemala
Guatemala — 2,000
Guinea
Conakry — 705
Haiti
Port-au-Prince — 1,144
Honduras
Tegucigalpa — 679
Hong Kong
Kowloon — 2,031
Hong Kong — 1,251
Tsuen Wan — 690
Hungary
Budapest — 2,016
India
Bombay — 12,572
Calcutta — 10,916
Delhi — 8,081
Madras — 5,361
Hyderabad — 4,280
Bangalore — 4,087
Ahmadabad — 3,298
Pune — 2,485
Kanpur — 2,111
Nagpur — 1,661
Lucknow — 1,642
Surat — 1,517
Jaipur — 1,515
Kochi — 1,140
Coimbatore — 1,136
Vadodara — 1,115
Indore — 1,104
Patna — 1,099
Madurai — 1,094
Bhopal — 1,064
Vishakhapatnam — 1,052
Varanasi — 1,026
Ludhiana — 1,012
Agra — 956
Jabalpur — 887
Allahabad — 858
Meerut — 847
Vijayawada — 845
Jamshedpur — 834
Trivandrum — 826
Dhanbad — 818
Kozhikode — 801
Asansol — 764
Nasik — 722
Gwalior — 701
Tiruchchirappalli — 711
Amritsar — 709

Durg-Bhilai — 689
Mysore — 652
Jodhpur — 649
Hubli-Dharwad — 648
Solapur — 621
Faridabad — 614
Ranchi — 614
Bareilly — 608
Srinagar — 595
Aurangabad — 592
Guwahati — 578
Chandigarh — 575
Salem — 574
Cochin — 564
Kota — 536
Ghaziabad — 520
Jullundur — 520
Indonesia
Jakarta — 7,886
Surabaya — 2,224
Medan — 1,806
Bandung — 1,567
Semarang — 1,027
Palembang — 787
Ujung Pandang — 709
Malang — 512
Iran
Tehran — 6,476
Mashhad — 1,759
Esfahan — 1,127
Tabriz — 1,089
Shiraz — 965
Ahvaz — 725
Qom — 681
Bakhtaran — 624
Iraq
Baghdad — 3,841
Diyala — 961
As Sulaymaniyah — 952
Arbil — 770
Mosul — 644
Kadhimain — 521
Ireland
Dublin — 1,024
Israel
Tel Aviv-Jaffa — 1,844
Jerusalem — 544
Italy
Rome — 2,791
Milan — 1,432
Naples — 1,206
Turin — 992
Palermo — 734
Genoa — 701
Ivory Coast
Abidjan — 1,929
Jamaica
Kingston — 538
Japan
Tokyo — 11,936
Yokohama — 3,220
Osaka — 2,624
Nagoya — 2,155
Sapporo — 1,672
Kobe — 1,477
Kyoto — 1,461
Fukuoka — 1,237
Kawasaki — 1,174
Hiroshima — 1,086
Kitakyushu — 1,026
Jordan
Amman — 1,272
Az-Zarqa — 605
Kazakhstan
Alma-Ata — 1,147
Karaganda — 613
Kenya
Nairobi — 1,429
Korea, North
Pyongyang — 2,639
Hamhung — 775
Chongjin — 754
Chinnamp'o — 691
Sinuiju — 500
Korea, South
Seoul — 10,628
Pusan — 3,798
Taegu — 2,229
Inchon — 1,818
Kwangju — 1,145
Taejon — 1,062
Ulsan — 683
Puch'on — 668
Suwon — 645
Songnam — 541
Chonju — 517

Kyrgyzstan
Bishkek — 641
Latvia
Riga — 917
Lebanon
Beirut — 1,500
Tripoli — 500
Libya
Tripoli — 990
Lithuania
Vilnius — 593
Macedonia
Skopje — 563
Madagascar
Antananarivo — 802
Malaysia
Kuala Lumpur — 938
Mali
Bamako — 746
Mexico
Mexico City — 15,048
Guadalajara — 2,847
Monterrey — 2,522
Puebla — 1,055
León — 872
Ciudad Juárez — 798
Tijuana — 743
Culiacán Rosales — 602
Mexicali — 602
Acapulco de Juárez — 592
Mérida — 557
Chihuahua — 530
San Luis Potosí — 526
Aguascalientés — 506
Moldova
Kishinev — 667
Mongolia
Ulan Bator — 575
Morocco
Casablanca — 2,409
Rabat-Salé — 893
Fès — 562
Marrakesh — 549
Mozambique
Maputo — 1,070
Netherlands
Amsterdam — 1,091
Rotterdam — 1,069
The Hague — 694
Utrecht — 543
New Zealand
Auckland — 896
Nicaragua
Managua — 682
Nigeria
Lagos — 1,347
Ibadan — 1,295
Kano — 700
Ogbomosho — 661
Norway
Oslo — 746
Pakistan
Karachi — 5,181
Lahore — 2,953
Faisalabad — 1,104
Rawalpindi — 795
Hyderabad — 752
Multan — 722
Gujranwala — 659
Peshawar — 556
Paraguay
Asunción — 945
Peru
Lima-Callao — 6,415
Arequipa — 635
Trujillo — 532
Callao — 515
Philippines
Manila — 6,720
Quezon City — 1,667
Davao — 868
Cebu — 641
Caloocan — 629
Poland
Warsaw — 1,655
Lódz — 847
Kraków — 751
Wroclaw — 643
Poznan — 590
Portugal
Lisbon — 2,561
Oporto — 1,174
Romania
Bucharest — 2,064
Russia
Moscow — 8,957

St Petersburg — 5,004
Novosibirsk — 1,472
Nizhniy Novgorod — 1,451
Yekaterinburg — 1,413
Samara — 1,271
Omsk — 1,193
Chelyabinsk — 1,170
Perm — 1,108
Kazan — 1,107
Ufa — 1,100
Volgograd — 1,031
Rostov — 1,027
Voronezh — 958
Krasnoyarsk — 925
Saratov — 909
Togliatti — 677
Vladivostok — 675
Krasnodar — 671
Barnaul — 665
Izhevsk — 651
Irkutsk — 644
Simbirsk — 638
Yaroslavl — 637
Khabarovsk — 626
Novokuznetsk — 614
Tula — 591
Orenburg — 574
Kemerovo — 559
Penza — 553
Tyumen — 550
Ryazan — 533
Kirov — 525
Naberezhnyye-Chelny — 517
Astrakhan — 512
Tomsk — 506
Lipetsk — 504
Saudi Arabia
Riyadh — 2,000
Jedda — 1,400
Mecca — 618
Medina — 500
Senegal
Dakar — 1,730
Singapore
Singapore — 2,818
Somali Republic
Mogadishu — 1,000
South Africa
Cape Town — 1,912
Johannesburg — 1,726
East Rand — 1,038
Durban — 982
Pretoria — 823
Port Elizabeth — 652
West Rand — 647
Vereeniging — 540
Spain
Madrid — 3,121
Barcelona — 1,707
Valencia — 753
Seville — 659
Zaragoza — 586
Málaga — 512
Sri Lanka
Colombo — 1,863
Sudan
Khartoum — 561
Omdurman — 526
Sweden
Stockholm — 1,503
Gothenburg — 734
Switzerland
Zürich — 840
Syria
Damascus — 1,451
Aleppo — 1,445
Holms — 518
Taiwan
Taipei — 2,718
Kaohsiung — 1,396
Taichung — 774
Tainan — 690
Panchiao — 543
Tajikistan
Dushanbe — 602
Tanzania
Dar es Salaam — 1,361
Thailand
Bangkok — 5,876
Togo
Lomé — 500
Tunisia
Tunis — 1,395
Turkey
Istanbul — 7,309

Ankara — 3,022
Izmir — 2,665
Adana — 1,430
Bursa — 1,031
Konya — 1,015
Gaziantep — 760
Içel — 701
Kayseri — 588
Uganda
Kampala — 773
Ukraine
Kiev — 2,643
Kharkiv — 1,622
Dnipropetrovsk — 1,190
Donetsk — 1,121
Odessa — 1,096
Zaporizhya — 898
Lviv — 807
Kryvyy Rih — 729
Mariupol — 523
Mykolayiv — 515
Luhansk — 505
United Kingdom
London — 6,933
Birmingham — 1,012
Leeds — 725
Glasgow — 681
Sheffield — 532
United States
New York — 18,087
Los Angeles — 14,532
Chicago — 8,066
San Francisco — 6,253
Philadelphia — 5,899
Detroit — 4,665
Boston — 4,172
Washington, DC — 3,924
Dallas — 3,885
Houston — 3,711
Miami — 3,193
Atlanta — 2,834
Cleveland — 2,760
Seattle — 2,559
San Diego — 2,498
Minneapolis-SP. — 2,464
St Louis — 2,444
Baltimore — 2,382
Pittsburgh — 2,243
Phoenix — 2,122
Tampa — 2,098
Denver — 1,848
Cincinnati — 1,744
Milwaukee — 1,607
Kansas City — 1,566
Sacramento — 1,481
Portland — 1,478
Norfolk — 1,396
Columbus — 1,377
San Antonio — 1,303
Indianapolis — 1,250
New Orleans — 1,239
Buffalo — 1,189
Charlotte — 1,162
Hartford — 1,086
Salt Lake City — 1,072
Albany — 861
San Jose — 782
Jacksonville — 672
Memphis — 610
Uruguay
Montevideo — 1,384
Uzbekistan
Tashkent — 2,094
Venezuela
Caracas — 2,784
Maracaibo — 1,364
Valencia — 1,032
Maracay — 800
Barquisimeto — 745
Ciudad Guayana — 524
Vietnam
Ho Chi Minh — 3,924
Hanoi — 3,056
Haiphong — 1,448
Yugoslavia
Belgrade — 1,137
Zaïre
Kinshasa — 3,804
Lubumbashi — 739
Mbuji-Mayi — 613
Kolwezi — 544
Zambia
Lusaka — 982
Zimbabwe
Harare — 1,189
Bulawayo — 622

WORLD STATISTICS: DISTANCES

The table shows air distances in miles and kilometres between thirty major cities. Known as 'Great Circle' distances, these measure the shortest routes between the cities, which aircraft use where possible. The maps show the world centred on six individual cities, and illustrate, for example, why direct flights from Japan to northern America and Europe are across the Arctic regions, and Singapore is on the direct line route from Europe to Australia. The maps have been constructed on an Azimuthal Equidistant projection, on which all distances measured through the centre point are true to scale. The circular lines are drawn at 5,000, 10,000 and 15,000 km from the central city.

The table below gives distances in kilometres (lower-left triangle, labelled **Kms**) and in miles (upper-right triangle, labelled **Miles**); the diagonal cells hold the city names.

	Berlin	Bombay	Buenos Aires	Cairo	Calcutta	Caracas	Chicago	Copenhagen	Darwin	Hong Kong	Honolulu	Johannesburg	Lagos	Lisbon	London	Los Angeles	Mexico City	Moscow	Nairobi	New York	Paris	Peking	Reykjavik	Rio de Janeiro	Rome	Singapore	Sydney	Tokyo	Toronto	Wellington
Berlin	Berlin	3907	7400	1795	4370	5241	4402	222	8044	5440	7310	5511	3230	1436	557	5785	6047	1000	3958	3967	545	4860	1482	6230	734	6179	10002	5545	4037	11272
Bombay	6288	Bombay	9275	2706	1034	9024	8048	3990	4510	2683	8024	4334	4730	4982	4467	8700	9728	3126	2816	7793	4356	2956	5179	8332	3837	2432	6313	4189	7760	7686
Buenos Aires	11909	14925	Buenos Aires	7341	10268	3167	5599	7498	9130	11481	7558	5025	4919	5964	6917	6122	4591	8374	6463	5298	6867	11972	7106	1214	6929	9867	7332	11410	5650	6202
Cairo	2890	4355	11814	Cairo	3541	6340	6127	1992	7216	5064	8838	3894	2432	2358	2180	7580	7687	1803	2197	5605	1994	4688	3272	6149	1325	5137	8959	5947	5737	10268
Calcutta	7033	1664	16524	5699	Calcutta	9609	7978	4395	3758	1653	7048	5256	5727	5639	4946	8152	9494	3438	3839	7921	4883	2031	5398	9366	4486	1800	5678	3195	7805	7055
Caracas	8435	14522	5096	10203	15464	Caracas	2502	5215	11221	10166	6009	6847	4810	4044	4664	3612	2228	6175	7173	2131	4738	8947	4297	2825	5196	11407	9534	8801	2406	8154
Chicago	7084	12953	9011	9860	12839	4027	Chicago	4250	9361	7783	4247	8689	5973	3992	3949	1742	1694	4971	8005	711	4132	6588	2956	5311	4809	9369	9243	6299	435	8358
Copenhagen	357	6422	12067	3206	7072	8392	6840	Copenhagen	8017	5388	7088	5732	3436	1540	592	5594	5912	970	4167	3845	638	4475	1306	6345	951	6195	9968	5403	3892	11160
Darwin	12946	7257	14693	11612	6047	18059	15065	12903	Darwin	2654	5369	6611	8837	9391	8605	7888	9091	7053	6472	9971	8582	3735	8632	9948	8243	2081	1957	3375	9630	3309
Hong Kong	8754	4317	18478	8150	2659	16360	12526	8671	4271	Hong Kong	5543	6669	7360	6853	5980	7232	8775	4439	5453	8047	5984	1220	6015	11001	5769	1615	4582	1786	7810	5857
Honolulu	11764	12914	12164	14223	11343	9670	6836	11407	8640	8921	Honolulu	11934	10133	7821	7228	2558	3781	7036	10739	4958	7437	5070	6081	8290	8026	6721	5075	3854	4638	4669
Johannesburg	8870	6974	8088	6267	8459	11019	13984	9225	10639	10732	19206	Johannesburg	2799	5089	5637	10362	9063	5692	1818	7979	5426	7276	6797	4420	4811	5381	6860	8418	8310	7308
Lagos	5198	7612	7916	3915	9216	7741	9612	5530	14222	11845	16308	4505	Lagos	2360	3118	7713	6879	3886	2366	5268	2929	7119	4175	3750	2510	6925	9643	8376	5560	9973
Lisbon	2311	8018	9600	3794	9075	6501	6424	2478	15114	11028	12587	8191	3799	Lisbon	987	5668	5391	2427	4015	3369	903	6007	1832	4805	1157	7385	11295	6928	3565	12163
London	928	7190	11131	3508	7961	7507	6356	952	13848	9623	11632	9071	5017	1588	London	5442	5552	1552	4237	3463	212	5057	1172	5778	889	6743	10558	5942	3545	11691
Los Angeles	9311	14000	9852	12200	13120	5812	2804	9003	12695	11639	4117	16676	12414	9122	8758	Los Angeles	1549	6070	9659	2446	5645	6251	4310	6310	6331	8776	7502	5475	2170	6719
Mexico City	9732	15656	7389	12372	15280	3586	2726	9514	14631	14122	6085	14585	11071	8676	8936	2493	Mexico City	6664	9207	2090	5717	7742	4635	4780	6365	10321	8058	7024	2018	6897
Moscow	1610	5031	13477	2902	5534	9938	8000	1561	11350	7144	11323	9161	6254	3906	2498	9769	10724	Moscow	3942	4666	1545	3600	2053	7184	1477	5237	9008	4651	4637	10283
Nairobi	6370	4532	10402	3536	6179	11544	12883	6706	10415	8776	17282	2927	3807	6461	6819	15544	14818	6344	Nairobi	7358	4029	5727	5395	5548	3350	4635	7552	6996	7570	8490
New York	6385	12541	8526	9020	12747	3430	1145	6188	16047	12950	7980	12841	8477	5422	5572	3936	3364	7510	11842	New York	3626	6828	2613	4832	4280	9531	9935	6741	356	8951
Paris	876	7010	11051	3210	7858	7625	6650	1026	13812	9630	11968	8732	4714	1454	342	9085	9200	2486	6485	5836	Paris	5106	1384	5708	687	6671	10539	6038	3738	11798
Peking	7822	4757	19268	7544	3269	14399	10603	7202	6011	1963	8160	11710	11457	9668	8138	10060	12460	5794	9216	10988	8217	Peking	4897	10773	5049	2783	5561	1304	6557	6700
Reykjavik	2385	8335	11437	5266	8687	6915	4757	2103	13892	9681	9787	10938	6718	2948	1887	6936	7460	3304	8683	4206	2228	7882	Reykjavik	6135	2048	7155	10325	5469	2600	10725
Rio de Janeiro	10025	13409	1953	9896	15073	4546	8547	10211	16011	17704	13342	7113	6035	7734	9299	10155	7693	11562	8928	7777	9187	17338	9874	Rio de Janeiro	5725	9763	8389	11551	5180	7367
Rome	1180	6175	11151	2133	7219	8363	7739	1531	13265	9284	12916	7743	4039	1861	1431	10188	10243	2376	5391	6888	1105	8126	3297	9214	Rome	6229	10143	6127	4399	11523
Singapore	9944	3914	15879	8267	2897	18359	15078	9969	3349	2599	10816	8660	11145	11886	10852	14123	16610	8428	7460	15339	10737	4478	11514	15712	10025	Singapore	3915	3306	9350	5298
Sydney	16096	10160	11800	14418	9138	15343	14875	16042	3150	7374	8168	11040	15519	18178	16992	12073	12969	14497	12153	15989	16962	8949	16617	13501	16324	6300	Sydney	4861	9800	1383
Tokyo	8924	6742	18362	9571	5141	14164	10137	8696	5431	2874	6202	13547	13480	11149	9562	8811	11304	7485	11260	10849	9718	2099	8802	18589	9861	5321	7823	Tokyo	6410	5762
Toronto	6497	12488	9093	9233	12561	3873	700	6265	15498	12569	7465	13374	8948	5737	5704	3492	3247	7462	12183	574	6015	10552	4184	8336	7080	15047	15772	10316	Toronto	8820
Wellington	18140	12370	9981	16524	11354	13122	13451	17961	5325	9427	7513	11761	16050	19575	18814	10814	11100	16549	13664	14405	18987	10782	17260	11855	18545	8526	2226	9273	14194	Wellington

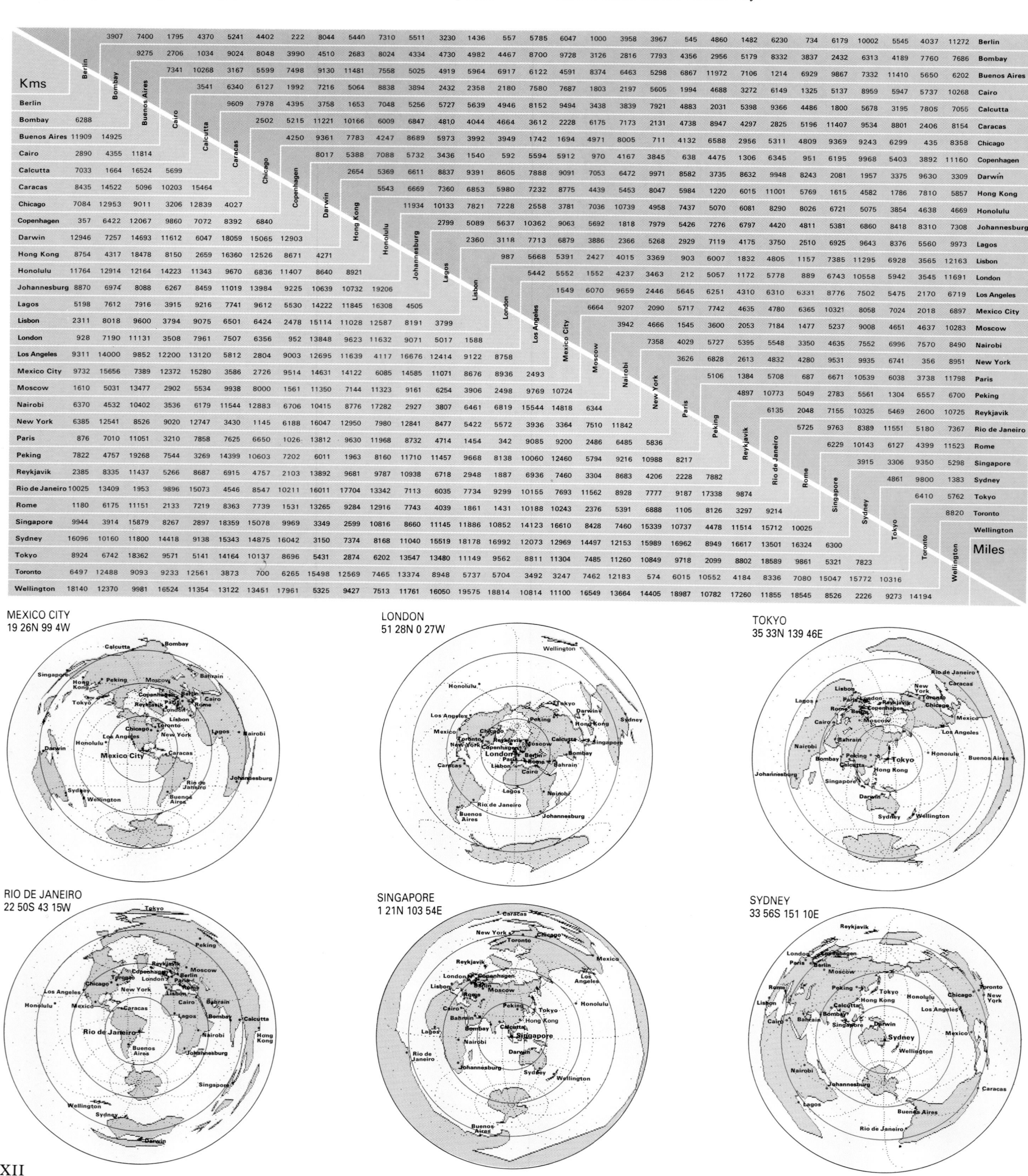

MEXICO CITY
19 26N 99 4W

LONDON
51 28N 0 27W

TOKYO
35 33N 139 46E

RIO DE JANEIRO
22 50S 43 15W

SINGAPORE
1 21N 103 54E

SYDNEY
33 56S 151 10E

WORLD STATISTICS: CLIMATE

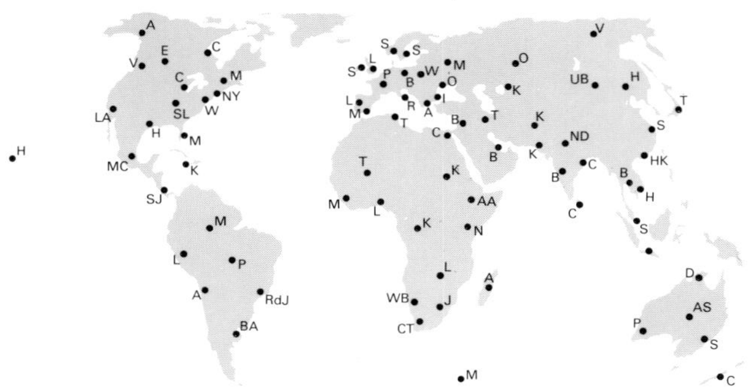

Rainfall and temperature figures are provided for more than 70 cities around the world. As climate is affected by altitude, the height of each city is shown in metres beneath its name. For each month, the figures in red show average temperature in degrees Celsius or centigrade, and in blue the total rainfall or snow in millimetres; the average annual temperature and total annual rainfall are at the end of the rows.

EUROPE	Jan.	Feb.	Mar.	Apr.	May	June	July	Aug.	Sept.	Oct.	Nov.	Dec.	Year
Athens, Greece	62	37	37	23	23	14	6	7	15	51	56	71	402
107 m	10	10	12	16	20	25	28	28	24	20	15	11	18
Berlin, Germany	46	40	33	42	49	65	73	69	48	49	46	43	603
55 m	-1	0	4	9	14	17	19	18	15	9	5	1	9
Istanbul, Turkey	109	92	72	46	38	34	34	30	58	81	103	119	816
114 m	5	6	7	11	16	20	23	23	20	16	12	8	14
Lisbon, Portugal	111	76	109	54	44	16	3	4	33	62	93	103	708
77 m	11	12	14	16	17	20	22	23	21	18	14	12	17
London, UK	54	40	37	37	46	45	57	59	49	57	64	48	593
5 m	4	5	7	9	12	16	18	17	15	11	8	5	11
Málaga, Spain	61	51	62	46	26	5	1	3	29	64	64	62	474
33 m	12	13	16	17	19	29	25	26	23	20	16	13	18
Moscow, Russia	39	38	36	37	53	58	88	71	58	45	47	54	624
156 m	-13	-10	-4	6	13	16	18	17	12	6	-1	-7	4
Odessa, Ukraine	57	62	30	21	34	34	42	37	37	13	35	71	473
64 m	-3	-1	2	9	15	20	22	22	18	12	9	1	10
Paris, France	56	46	35	42	57	54	59	64	55	50	51	50	619
75 m	3	4	8	11	15	18	20	19	17	12	7	4	12
Rome, Italy	71	62	57	51	46	37	15	21	63	99	129	93	744
17 m	8	9	11	14	18	22	25	25	22	17	13	10	16
Shannon, Irish Republic	94	67	56	53	61	57	77	79	86	86	96	117	929
2 m	5	5	7	9	12	14	16	16	14	11	8	6	10
Stockholm, Sweden	43	30	25	31	34	45	61	76	60	48	53	48	554
44 m	-3	-3	-1	5	10	15	18	17	12	7	3	0	7

ASIA	Jan.	Feb.	Mar.	Apr.	May	June	July	Aug.	Sept.	Oct.	Nov.	Dec.	Year
Bahrain	8	18	13	8	<3	0	0	0	0	0	18	18	81
5 m	17	18	21	25	29	32	33	34	31	28	24	19	26
Bangkok, Thailand	8	20	36	58	198	160	160	175	305	206	66	5	1,397
2 m	26	28	29	30	29	29	28	28	28	28	26	25	28
Beirut, Lebanon	191	158	94	53	18	3	<3	<3	5	51	132	185	892
34 m	14	14	16	18	22	24	27	28	26	24	19	16	21
Bombay, India	3	3	3	<3	18	485	617	340	264	64	13	3	1,809
11 m	24	24	26	28	30	29	27	27	27	28	27	26	27
Calcutta, India	10	31	36	43	140	297	325	328	252	114	20	5	1,600
6 m	20	22	27	30	30	30	29	29	29	28	23	19	26
Colombo, Sri Lanka	89	69	147	231	371	224	135	109	160	348	315	147	2,365
7 m	26	26	27	28	28	27	27	27	27	27	26	26	27
Harbin, China	6	5	10	23	43	94	112	104	46	33	8	5	488
160 m	-18	-15	-5	6	13	19	22	21	14	4	-6	-16	3
Ho Chi Minh, Vietnam	15	3	13	43	221	330	315	269	335	269	114	56	1,984
9 m	26	27	29	30	29	28	28	28	27	27	27	26	28
Hong Kong	33	46	74	137	292	394	381	361	257	114	43	31	2,162
33 m	16	15	18	22	26	28	28	28	27	25	21	18	23
Jakarta, Indonesia	300	300	211	147	114	97	64	43	66	112	142	203	1,798
8 m	26	26	27	27	27	27	27	27	27	27	27	26	27
Kabul, Afghanistan	31	36	94	102	20	5	3	3	<3	15	20	10	338
1,815 m	-3	-1	6	13	18	22	25	24	20	14	7	3	12
Karachi, Pakistan	13	10	8	3	3	18	81	41	13	<3	3	5	196
4 m	19	20	24	28	30	31	30	29	28	28	24	20	26
Kazalinsk, Kazakhstan	10	10	13	13	15	5	5	8	8	10	13	15	125
63 m	-12	-11	-3	6	18	23	25	23	16	8	-1	-7	7
New Delhi, India	23	18	13	8	13	74	180	172	117	10	3	10	640
218 m	14	17	23	28	33	34	31	30	29	26	20	15	25
Omsk, Russia	15	8	8	13	31	51	51	51	28	25	18	20	318
85 m	-22	-19	-12	-1	10	16	18	16	10	1	-11	-18	-1
Shanghai, China	48	58	84	94	94	180	147	142	130	71	51	36	1,135
7 m	4	5	9	14	20	24	28	28	23	19	12	7	16
Singapore	252	173	193	188	173	173	170	196	178	208	254	257	2,413
10 m	26	27	28	28	28	28	28	27	27	27	27	27	27
Tehran, Iran	46	38	46	36	13	3	3	3	3	8	20	31	246
1,220 m	2	5	9	16	21	26	30	29	25	18	12	6	17
Tokyo, Japan	48	74	107	135	147	165	142	152	234	208	97	56	1,565
6 m	3	4	7	13	17	21	25	26	23	17	11	6	14
Ulan Bator, Mongolia	<3	<3	3	5	10	28	76	51	23	5	5	3	208
1,325 m	-26	-21	-13	-1	6	14	16	14	8	-1	-13	-22	-3
Verkhoyansk, Russia	5	5	3	5	8	23	28	25	13	8	8	5	134
100 m	-50	-45	-32	-15	0	12	14	9	2	-15	-38	-48	-17

AFRICA	Jan.	Feb.	Mar.	Apr.	May	June	July	Aug.	Sept.	Oct.	Nov.	Dec.	Year
Addis Ababa, Ethiopia	<3	3	25	135	213	201	206	239	102	28	<3	0	1,151
2,450 m	19	20	20	20	19	18	18	19	21	22	21	20	20
Antananarivo, Madagas.	300	279	178	53	18	8	8	10	18	61	135	287	1,356
1,372 m	21	21	21	19	18	15	14	15	17	19	21	21	19
Cairo, Egypt	5	5	5	3	3	<3	0	0	<3	<3	3	5	28
116 m	13	15	18	21	25	28	28	28	26	24	20	15	22
Cape Town, South Africa	15	8	18	48	79	84	89	66	43	31	18	10	508
17 m	21	21	20	17	14	13	12	13	14	16	18	19	17
Johannesburg, S. Africa	114	109	89	38	25	8	8	8	23	56	107	125	709
1,665 m	20	20	18	16	13	10	11	13	16	18	19	20	16
Khartoum, Sudan	<3	<3	<3	<3	3	8	53	71	18	5	<3	0	158
390 m	24	25	28	31	33	34	32	31	32	32	28	25	29
Kinshasa, Zaïre	135	145	196	196	158	8	3	3	31	119	221	142	1,354
325 m	26	26	27	27	26	24	23	24	25	26	26	26	25
Lagos, Nigeria	28	46	102	150	269	460	279	64	140	206	69	25	1,836
3 m	27	28	29	28	28	26	26	25	26	26	28	28	27
Lusaka, Zambia	231	191	142	18	3	<3	<3	0	<3	10	91	150	836
1,277 m	21	22	21	21	19	16	16	18	22	24	23	22	21
Monrovia, Liberia	31	56	97	216	516	973	996	373	744	772	236	130	5,138
23 m	26	26	27	27	26	25	24	25	25	25	26	26	26
Nairobi, Kenya	38	64	125	211	158	46	15	23	31	53	109	86	958
1,820 m	19	19	19	19	18	16	16	16	18	19	18	18	18
Timbuktu, Mali	<3	<3	3	<3	5	23	79	81	38	3	<3	<3	231
301 m	22	24	28	32	34	35	32	30	32	31	28	23	29
Tunis, Tunisia	64	51	41	36	18	8	3	8	33	51	48	61	419
66 m	10	11	13	16	19	23	26	27	25	20	16	11	18
Walvis Bay, Namibia	<3	5	8	3	3	<3	<3	3	<3	<3	<3	<3	23
7 m	19	19	19	18	17	16	15	14	14	15	17	18	18

AUSTRALIA, NEW ZEALAND AND ANTARCTICA	Jan.	Feb.	Mar.	Apr.	May	June	July	Aug.	Sept.	Oct.	Nov.	Dec.	Year
Alice Springs, Australia	43	33	28	10	15	13	8	8	8	18	31	38	252
579 m	29	28	25	20	15	12	12	14	18	23	26	28	21
Christchurch, N. Zealand	56	43	48	48	66	66	69	48	46	43	48	56	638
10 m	16	16	14	12	9	6	6	7	9	12	14	16	11
Darwin, Australia	386	312	254	97	15	3	<3	3	13	51	119	239	1,491
30 m	29	29	29	29	28	26	25	26	28	29	30	29	28
Mawson, Antarctica	11	30	20	10	44	180	4	40	3	20	0	0	362
14 m	0	-5	-10	-14	-15	-16	-18	-18	-19	-13	-5	-1	-11
Perth, Australia	8	10	20	43	130	180	170	149	86	56	20	13	881
60 m	23	23	22	19	16	14	13	13	15	16	19	22	18
Sydney, Australia	89	102	127	135	127	117	117	76	73	71	73	73	1,181
42 m	22	22	21	18	15	13	12	13	15	18	19	21	17

NORTH AMERICA	Jan.	Feb.	Mar.	Apr.	May	June	July	Aug.	Sept.	Oct.	Nov.	Dec.	Year
Anchorage, Alaska, USA	20	18	15	10	13	18	41	66	66	56	25	23	371
40 m	-11	-8	-5	2	7	12	14	13	9	2	-5	-11	2
Chicago, Ill., USA	51	51	66	71	86	89	84	81	79	66	61	51	836
251 m	-4	-3	2	9	14	20	23	22	19	12	5	-1	10
Churchill, Man., Canada	15	13	18	23	32	44	46	58	51	43	39	21	402
13 m	-28	-26	-20	-10	-2	6	12	11	5	-2	-12	-22	-7
Edmonton, Alta., Canada	25	19	19	22	43	77	89	78	39	17	16	25	466
676 m	-15	-10	-5	4	11	15	17	16	11	6	-4	-10	3
Honolulu, Hawaii, USA	104	66	79	48	25	18	23	28	36	48	64	104	643
12 m	23	18	19	20	22	24	25	26	26	24	22	19	22
Houston, Tex., USA	89	76	84	91	119	117	99	99	104	94	89	109	1,171
12 m	12	13	17	21	24	27	28	29	26	22	16	12	21
Kingston, Jamaica	23	15	23	31	102	89	38	91	99	180	74	36	800
34 m	25	25	25	26	26	28	28	28	27	27	26	26	26
Los Angeles, Calif., USA	79	76	71	25	10	3	<3	<3	5	15	31	66	381
95 m	13	14	14	16	17	19	21	22	21	18	16	14	17
Mexico City, Mexico	13	5	10	20	53	119	170	152	130	51	18	8	747
2,309 m	12	13	16	18	19	19	17	18	18	16	14	13	16
Miami, Fla., USA	71	53	64	81	173	178	155	160	203	234	71	51	1,516
8 m	20	20	22	23	25	27	28	28	27	25	22	21	24
Montréal, Que., Canada	72	65	74	74	66	82	90	92	88	76	81	87	946
57 m	-10	-9	-3	-6	13	18	21	20	15	9	2	-7	6
New York, N.Y., USA	94	97	91	81	81	84	107	109	86	89	76	91	1,092
96 m	-1	-1	3	10	16	20	23	23	21	15	7	2	11
St Louis, Mo., USA	58	64	89	97	114	114	89	86	81	74	71	64	1,001
173 m	0	1	7	13	19	24	26	26	22	15	8	2	14
San José, Costa Rica	15	5	20	46	229	241	211	241	305	300	145	41	1,798
1,146 m	19	19	21	21	22	21	21	21	21	20	20	19	20
Vancouver, B.C., Canada	154	115	101	60	52	45	32	41	67	114	150	182	1,113
14 m	3	5	6	9	12	15	17	17	14	10	6	4	10
Washington, D.C., USA	86	76	91	84	94	99	112	109	94	74	66	79	1,064
22 m	1	2	7	12	18	23	25	24	20	14	8	3	13

SOUTH AMERICA	Jan.	Feb.	Mar.	Apr.	May	June	July	Aug.	Sept.	Oct.	Nov.	Dec.	Year
Antofagasta, Chile	0	0	0	<3	<3	3	5	3	<3	3	<3	0	13
94 m	21	21	20	18	16	15	14	14	15	16	18	19	17
Buenos Aires, Argentina	79	71	109	89	76	61	56	61	79	86	84	99	950
27 m	23	23	21	17	13	9	10	11	13	15	19	22	16
Lima, Peru	3	<3	<3	<3	5	5	8	8	8	3	3	<3	41
120 m	23	24	24	22	19	17	17	16	17	18	19	21	20
Manaus, Brazil	249	231	262	221	170	84	58	38	46	107	142	203	1,811
44 m	28	28	28	27	28	28	28	28	29	29	29	28	28
Paraná, Brazil	287	236	239	102	13	<3	3	5	28	127	231	310	1,582
260 m	23	23	23	23	23	21	21	22	24	24	24	23	23
Rio de Janeiro, Brazil	125	122	130	107	79	53	41	43	66	79	104	137	1,082
61 m	26	26	25	24	22	21	21	21	21	22	23	25	23

WORLD STATISTICS: PHYSICAL DIMENSIONS

Each topic list is divided into continents and within a continent the items are listed in order of size. The order of the continents is as in the atlas, Europe through to South America. Certain lists down to this mark > are complete; below they are selective. The world top ten are shown in square brackets; in the case of mountains this has not been done because the world top 30 are all in Asia. The figures are rounded as appropriate.

WORLD, CONTINENTS, OCEANS

	km²	miles²	%
The World	509,450,000	196,672,000	–
Land	149,450,000	57,688,000	29.3
Water	360,000,000	138,984,000	70.7
Asia	44,500,000	17,177,000	29.8
Africa	30,302,000	11,697,000	20.3
North America	24,241,000	9,357,000	16.2
South America	17,793,000	6,868,000	11.9
Antarctica	14,100,000	5,443,000	9.4
Europe	9,957,000	3,843,000	6.7
Australia & Oceania	8,557,000	3,303,000	5.7
Pacific Ocean	179,679,000	69,356,000	49.9
Atlantic Ocean	92,373,000	35,657,000	25.7
Indian Ocean	73,917,000	28,532,000	20.5
Arctic Ocean	14,090,000	5,439,000	3.9

SEAS

Pacific	km²	miles²
South China Sea	2,974,600	1,148,500
Bering Sea	2,268,000	875,000
Sea of Okhotsk	1,528,000	590,000
East China & Yellow	1,249,000	482,000
Sea of Japan	1,008,000	389,000
Gulf of California	162,000	62,500
Bass Strait	75,000	29,000

Atlantic	km²	miles²
Caribbean Sea	2,766,000	1,068,000
Mediterranean Sea	2,516,000	971,000
Gulf of Mexico	1,543,000	596,000
Hudson Bay	1,232,000	476,000
North Sea	575,000	223,000
Black Sea	462,000	178,000
Baltic Sea	422,170	163,000
Gulf of St Lawrence	238,000	92,000

Indian	km²	miles²
Red Sea	438,000	169,000
The Gulf	239,000	92,000

MOUNTAINS

Europe		m	ft
Mont Blanc	France/Italy	4,807	15,771
Monte Rosa	Italy/Switzerland	4,634	15,203
Dom	Switzerland	4,545	14,911
Weisshorn	Switzerland	4,505	14,780
Matterhorn/Cervino	Italy/Switzerland	4,478	14,691
Mt Maudit	France/Italy	4,465	14,649
Finsteraarhorn	Switzerland	4,274	14,022
Aletschhorn	Switzerland	4,182	13,720
Jungfrau	Switzerland	4,158	13,642
Barre des Ecrins	France	4,103	13,461
Schreckhorn	Switzerland	4,078	13,380
Gran Paradiso	Italy	4,061	13,323
Piz Bernina	Italy/Switzerland	4,049	13,284
Ortles	Italy	3,899	12,792
Monte Viso	Italy	3,841	12,602
Grossglockner	Austria	3,797	12,457
Wildspitze	Austria	3,774	12,382
Weisskügel	Austria/Italy	3,736	12,257
Balmhorn	Switzerland	3,709	12,169
Dammastock	Switzerland	3,630	11,909
Tödi	Switzerland	3,620	11,877
Presanella	Italy	3,556	11,667
Monte Adamello	Italy	3,554	11,660
Mulhacén	Spain	3,478	11,411
Pico de Aneto	Spain	3,404	11,168
Posets	Spain	3,375	11,073
Marmolada	Italy	3,342	10,964
> Etna	Italy	3,340	10,958
Musala	Bulgaria	2,925	9,596
Olympus	Greece	2,917	9,570
Gerlachovka	Slovak Republic	2,655	8,711
Galdhöpiggen	Norway	2,469	8,100
Pietrosul	Romania	2,305	7,562
Hvannadalshnúkur	Iceland	2,119	6,952
Narodnaya	Russia	1,894	6,214
Ben Nevis	UK	1,343	4,406

Asia		m	ft
Everest	China/Nepal	8,848	29,029
Godwin Austen (K2)	China/Kashmir	8,611	28,251
Kanchenjunga	India/Nepal	8,598	28,208
Lhotse	China/Nepal	8,516	27,939
Makalu	China/Nepal	8,481	27,824
Cho Oyu	China/Nepal	8,201	26,906
Dhaulagiri	Nepal	8,172	26,811
Manaslu	Nepal	8,156	26,758
Nanga Parbat	Kashmir	8,126	26,660
Annapurna	Nepal	8,078	26,502
Gasherbrum	China/Kashmir	8,068	26,469
Broad Peak	China/Kashmir	8,051	26,414
Gosainthan	China	8,012	26,286
Disteghil Sar	Kashmir	7,885	25,869
Nuptse	Nepal	7,879	25,849
Masherbrum	Kashmir	7,821	25,659
Nanda Devi	India	7,817	25,646
Rakaposhi	Kashmir	7,788	25,551
Kanjut Sar	India	7,760	25,459
Kamet	India	7,756	25,446
Namcha Barwa	China	7,756	25,446
Gurla Mandhata	China	7,728	25,354
Muztag	China	7,723	25,338
Kongur Shan	China	7,719	25,324
Tirich Mir	Pakistan	7,690	25,229
> Saser	Kashmir	7,672	25,170
K'ula Shan	Bhutan/China	7,543	24,747
Pik Kommunizma	Tajikistan	7,495	24,590
Aling Gangri	China	7,314	23,996
Elbrus	Russia	5,642	18,510
Demavend	Iran	5,604	18,386
Ararat	Turkey	5,165	16,945
Gunong Kinabalu	Malaysia (Borneo)	4,101	13,455
Yu Shan	Taiwan	3,997	13,113
Fuji-san	Japan	3,776	12,388
Rinjani	Indonesia	3,726	12,224
Mt Rajang	Philippines	3,364	11,037
Pidurutalagala	Sri Lanka	2,524	8,281

Africa		m	ft
Kilimanjaro	Tanzania	5,895	19,340
Mt Kenya	Kenya	5,199	17,057
Ruwenzori	Uganda/Zaïre	5,109	16,762
Ras Dashan	Ethiopia	4,620	15,157
Meru	Tanzania	4,565	14,977
Karisimbi	Rwanda/Zaïre	4,507	14,787
Mt Elgon	Kenya/Uganda	4,321	14,176
Batu	Ethiopia	4,307	14,130
Guna	Ethiopia	4,231	13,882
Toubkal	Morocco	4,165	13,665
Irhil Mgoun	Morocco	4,071	13,356
Mt Cameroon	Cameroon	4,070	13,353
Amba Ferit	Ethiopia	3,875	13,042
Teide	Spain (Tenerife)	3,718	12,198
Thabana Ntlenyana	Lesotho	3,482	11,424
> Emi Koussi	Chad	3,415	11,204
Mt aux Sources	Lesotho/S. Africa	3,282	10,768
Mt Piton	Réunion	3,069	10,069

Oceania		m	ft
Puncak Jaya	Indonesia	5,029	16,499
Puncak Trikora	Indonesia	4,750	15,584
Puncak Mandala	Indonesia	4,702	15,427
> Mt Wilhelm	Papua New Guinea	4,508	14,790
Mauna Kea	USA (Hawaii)	4,205	13,796
Mauna Loa	USA (Hawaii)	4,170	13,681
Mt Cook	New Zealand	3,753	12,313
Mt Balbi	Solomon Is.	2,439	8,002
Orohena	Tahiti	2,241	7,352
Mt Kosciusko	Australia	2,237	7,339

North America		m	ft
Mt McKinley	USA (Alaska)	6,194	20,321
Mt Logan	Canada	5,959	19,551
Citlaltepetl	Mexico	5,700	18,701
Mt St Elias	USA/Canada	5,489	18,008
Popocatepetl	Mexico	5,452	17,887
Mt Foraker	USA (Alaska)	5,304	17,401
Ixtaccihuatl	Mexico	5,286	17,342
Lucania	Canada	5,227	17,149
Mt Steele	Canada	5,073	16,644
Mt Bona	USA (Alaska)	5,005	16,420
Mt Blackburn	USA (Alaska)	4,996	16,391
Mt Sanford	USA (Alaska)	4,940	16,207
Mt Wood	Canada	4,848	15,905
Nevado de Toluca	Mexico	4,670	15,321
Mt Fairweather	USA (Alaska)	4,663	15,298
Mt Whitney	USA	4,418	14,495
Mt Elbert	USA	4,399	14,432
Mt Harvard	USA	4,395	14,419
Mt Rainier	USA	4,392	14,409
Blanca Peak	USA	4,372	14,344
Long's Peak	USA	4,345	14,255
Nevado de Colima	Mexico	4,339	14,235
Mt Shasta	USA	4,317	14,163
Tajumulco	Guatemala	4,220	13,845
> Gannett Peak	USA	4,202	13,786
Mt Waddington	Canada	3,994	13,104
Mt Robson	Canada	3,954	12,972
Chirripó Grande	Costa Rica	3,837	12,589
Pico Duarte	Dominican Rep.	3,175	10,417

South America		m	ft
Aconcagua	Argentina	6,960	22,834
Illimani	Bolivia	6,882	22,578
Bonete	Argentina	6,872	22,546
Ojos del Salado	Argentina/Chile	6,863	22,516
Tupungato	Argentina/Chile	6,800	22,309
Pissis	Argentina	6,779	22,241
Mercedario	Argentina/Chile	6,770	22,211
Huascaran	Peru	6,768	22,204
Llullaillaco	Argentina/Chile	6,723	22,057
Nudo de Cachi	Argentina	6,720	22,047
Yerupaja	Peru	6,632	21,758
N. de Tres Cruces	Argentina/Chile	6,620	21,719
Incahuasi	Argentina/Chile	6,600	21,654
Ancohuma	Bolivia	6,550	21,489
Sajama	Bolivia	6,542	21,463
Coropuna	Peru	6,425	21,079
Ausangate	Peru	6,384	20,945
Cerro del Toro	Argentina	6,380	20,932
Ampato	Peru	6,310	20,702
> Chimborasso	Ecuador	6,267	20,561
Cotopaxi	Ecuador	5,896	19,344
S. Nev. de S. Marta	Colombia	5,800	19,029
Cayambe	Ecuador	5,796	19,016
Pico Bolivar	Venezuela	5,007	16,427

Antarctica	m	ft
Vinson Massif	4,897	16,066
Mt Kirkpatrick	4,528	14,855
Mt Markham	4,349	14,268

OCEAN DEPTHS

Atlantic Ocean	m	ft	
Puerto Rico (Milwaukee) Deep	9,220	30,249	[7]
Cayman Trench	7,680	25,197	[10]
Gulf of Mexico	5,203	17,070	
Mediterranean Sea	5,121	16,801	
Black Sea	2,211	7,254	
North Sea	660	2,165	
Baltic Sea	463	1,519	
Hudson Bay	258	846	

Indian Ocean	m	ft
Java Trench	7,450	24,442
Red Sea	2,635	8,454
Persian Gulf	73	239

Pacific Ocean	m	ft	
Mariana Trench	11,022	36,161	[1]
Tonga Trench	10,882	35,702	[2]
Japan Trench	10,554	34,626	[3]
Kuril Trench	10,542	34,587	[4]
Mindanao Trench	10,497	34,439	[5]
Kermadec Trench	10,047	32,962	[6]
Peru-Chile Trench	8,050	26,410	[8]
Aleutian Trench	7,822	25,662	[9]
Middle American Trench	6,662	21,857	

Arctic Ocean	m	ft
Molloy Deep	5,608	18,399

LAND LOWS

		m	ft
Caspian Sea	Europe	−28	−92
Dead Sea	Asia	−403	−1,322
Lake Assal	Africa	−156	−512
Lake Eyre North	Oceania	−16	−52
Death Valley	N. America	−86	−282
Valdés Peninsula	S. America	−40	−131

RIVERS

Europe

		km	miles	
Volga	Caspian Sea	3,700	2,300	
Danube	Black Sea	2,850	1,770	
Ural	Caspian Sea	2,535	1,575	
Dnepr (Dnipro)	Volga	2,285	1,420	
Kama	Volga	2,030	1,260	
Don	Volga	1,990	1,240	
Petchora	Arctic Ocean	1,790	1,110	
Oka	Volga	1,480	920	
Belaya	Kama	1,420	880	
Dnestr (Dnister)	Black Sea	1,400	870	
Vyatka	Kama	1,370	850	
Rhine	North Sea	1,320	820	
N. Dvina	Arctic Ocean	1,290	800	
Desna	Dnepr	1,190	740	
Elbe	North Sea	1,145	710	
Vistula	Baltic Sea	1,090	675	
Loire	Atlantic Ocean	1,020	635	
W. Dvina	Baltic Sea	1,019	633	

Asia

		km	miles	
Yangtze	Pacific Ocean	6,380	3,960	[3]
Yenisey-Angara	Arctic Ocean	5,550	3,445	[5]
Huang He	Pacific Ocean	5,464	3,395	[6]
Ob-Irtysh	Arctic Ocean	5,410	3,360	[7]
Mekong	Pacific Ocean	4,500	2,795	[9]
Amur	Pacific Ocean	4,400	2,730	[10]
Lena	Arctic Ocean	4,400	2,730	
Irtysh	Ob	4,250	2,640	
Yenisey	Arctic Ocean	4,090	2,540	
Ob	Arctic Ocean	3,680	2,285	
Indus	Indian Ocean	3,100	1,925	
Brahmaputra	Indian Ocean	2,900	1,800	
Syrdarya	Aral Sea	2,860	1,775	
Salween	Indian Ocean	2,800	1,740	
Euphrates	Indian Ocean	2,700	1,675	
Vilyuy	Lena	2,650	1,645	
Kolyma	Arctic Ocean	2,600	1,615	
Amudarya	Aral Sea	2,540	1,575	
Ural	Caspian Sea	2,535	1,575	
Ganges	Indian Ocean	2,510	1,560	
Si Kiang	Pacific Ocean	2,100	1,305	
Irrawaddy	Indian Ocean	2,010	1,250	
Tarim-Yarkand	Lop Nor	2,000	1,240	
Tigris	Indian Ocean	1,900	1,180	
Angara	Yenisey	1,830	1,135	
Godavari	Indian Ocean	1,470	915	
Sutlej	Indian Ocean	1,450	900	
Yamuna	Indian Ocean	1,400	870	

Africa

		km	miles	
Nile	Mediterranean	6,670	4,140	[1]
Zaïre/Congo	Atlantic Ocean	4,670	2,900	[8]
Niger	Atlantic Ocean	4,180	2,595	
Zambezi	Indian Ocean	3,540	2,200	
Oubangi/Uele	Zaïre	2,250	1,400	
Kasai	Zaïre	1,950	1,210	
Shaballe	Indian Ocean	1,930	1,200	
Orange	Atlantic Ocean	1,860	1,155	
Cubango	Okavango Swamps	1,800	1,120	
Limpopo	Indian Ocean	1,600	995	
Senegal	Atlantic Ocean	1,600	995	
Volta	Atlantic Ocean	1,500	930	
Benue	Niger	1,350	840	

Australia

		km	miles
Murray-Darling	Indian Ocean	3,750	2,330
Darling	Murray	3,070	1,905
Murray	Indian Ocean	2,575	1,600
Murrumbidgee	Murray	1,690	1,050

North America

		km	miles	
Mississippi-Missouri	Gulf of Mexico	6,020	3,740	[4]
Mackenzie	Arctic Ocean	4,240	2,630	
Mississippi	Gulf of Mexico	3,780	2,350	
Missouri	Mississippi	3,780	2,350	
Yukon	Pacific Ocean	3,185	1,980	
Rio Grande	Gulf of Mexico	3,030	1,880	
Arkansas	Mississippi	2,340	1,450	
Colorado	Pacific Ocean	2,330	1,445	
Red	Mississippi	2,040	1,270	
Columbia	Pacific Ocean	1,950	1,210	
Saskatchewan	Lake Winnipeg	1,940	1,205	
Snake	Columbia	1,670	1,040	
Churchill	Hudson Bay	1,600	990	
Ohio	Mississippi	1,580	980	
Brazos	Gulf of Mexico	1,400	870	
St Lawrence	Atlantic Ocean	1,170	730	

South America

		km	miles	
Amazon	Atlantic Ocean	6,450	4,010	[2]
Paraná-Plate	Atlantic Ocean	4,500	2,800	
Purus	Amazon	3,350	2,080	
Madeira	Amazon	3,200	1,990	
São Francisco	Atlantic Ocean	2,900	1,800	
Paraná	Plate	2,800	1,740	
Tocantins	Atlantic Ocean	2,750	1,710	
Paraguay	Paraná	2,550	1,580	
Orinoco	Atlantic Ocean	2,500	1,550	
Pilcomayo	Paraná	2,500	1,550	
Araguaia	Tocantins	2,250	1,400	
Juruá	Amazon	2,000	1,240	
Xingu	Amazon	1,980	1,230	
Ucayali	Amazon	1,900	1,180	
Marañón	Amazon	1,600	990	
Uruguay	Plate	1,600	990	
Magdalena	Caribbean Sea	1,540	960	

LAKES

Europe

		km²	miles²
Lake Ladoga	Russia	17,700	6,800
Lake Onega	Russia	9,700	3,700
Saimaa system	Finland	8,000	3,100
Vänern	Sweden	5,500	2,100
Rybinsk Res.	Russia	4,700	1,800

Asia

		km²	miles²	
Caspian Sea	Asia	371,800	143,550	[1]
Aral Sea	Kazakh./Uzbek.	33,640	13,000	[6]
Lake Baykal	Russia	30,500	11,780	[9]
Tonlé Sap	Cambodia	20,000	7,700	
Lake Balkhash	Kazakhstan	18,500	7,100	
Dongting Hu	China	12,000	4,600	
Ysyk Köl	Kyrgyzstan	6,200	2,400	
Lake Urmia	Iran	5,900	2,300	
Koko Nur	China	5,700	2,200	
Poyang Hu	China	5,000	1,900	
Lake Khanka	China/Russia	4,400	1,700	
Lake Van	Turkey	3,500	1,400	
Ubsa Nur	China	3,400	1,300	

Africa

		km²	miles²	
Lake Victoria	E. Africa	68,000	26,000	[3]
Lake Tanganyika	C. Africa	33,000	13,000	[7]
Lake Malawi/Nyasa	E. Africa	29,600	11,430	[10]
Lake Chad	C. Africa	25,000	9,700	
Lake Turkana	Ethiopia/Kenya	8,500	3,300	
Lake Volta	Ghana	8,500	3,300	
Lake Bangweulu	Zambia	8,000	3,100	
Lake Rukwa	Tanzania	7,000	2,700	
Lake Mai-Ndombe	Zaïre	6,500	2,500	
Lake Kariba	Zambia/Zimbabwe	5,300	2,000	
Lake Albert	Uganda/Zaïre	5,300	2,000	
Lake Nasser	Egypt/Sudan	5,200	2,000	
Lake Mweru	Zambia/Zaïre	4,900	1,900	
Lake Cabora Bassa	Mozambique	4,500	1,700	
Lake Kyoga	Uganda	4,400	1,700	
Lake Tana	Ethiopia	3,630	1,400	
Lake Kivu	Rwanda/Zaïre	2,650	1,000	
Lake Edward	Uganda/Zaïre	2,200	850	

Australia

		km²	miles²
Lake Eyre	Australia	8,900	3,400
Lake Torrens	Australia	5,800	2,200
Lake Gairdner	Australia	4,800	1,900

North America

		km²	miles²	
Lake Superior	Canada/USA	82,350	31,800	[2]
Lake Huron	Canada/USA	59,600	23,010	[4]
Lake Michigan	USA	58,000	22,400	[5]
Great Bear Lake	Canada	31,800	12,280	[8]
Great Slave Lake	Canada	28,500	11,000	
Lake Erie	Canada/USA	25,700	9,900	
Lake Winnipeg	Canada	24,400	9,400	
Lake Ontario	Canada/USA	19,500	7,500	
Lake Nicaragua	Nicaragua	8,300	3,200	
Lake Athabasca	Canada	8,100	3,100	
Smallwood Res.	Canada	6,530	2,520	
Reindeer Lake	Canada	6,400	2,500	
Lake Winnipegosis	Canada	5,400	2,100	
Nettilling Lake	Canada	5,500	2,100	
Lake Nipigon	Canada	4,850	1,900	
Lake Manitoba	Canada	4,700	1,800	

South America

		km²	miles²
Lake Titicaca	Bolivia/Peru	8,300	3,200
Lake Poopo	Peru	2,800	1,100

ISLANDS

Europe

		km²	miles²	
Great Britain	UK	229,880	88,700	[8]
Iceland	Atlantic Ocean	103,000	39,800	
Ireland	Ireland/UK	84,400	32,600	
Novaya Zemlya (N.)	Russia	48,200	18,600	
W. Spitzbergen	Norway	39,000	15,100	
Novaya Zemlya (S.)	Russia	33,200	12,800	
Sicily	Italy	25,500	9,800	
Sardinia	Italy	24,000	9,300	
N. E. Spitzbergen	Norway	15,000	5,600	
Corsica	France	8,700	3,400	
Crete	Greece	8,350	3,200	
Zealand	Denmark	6,850	2,600	

Asia

		km²	miles²	
Borneo	S. E. Asia	744,360	287,400	[3]
Sumatra	Indonesia	473,600	182,860	[6]
Honshu	Japan	230,500	88,980	[7]
Celebes	Indonesia	189,000	73,000	
Java	Indonesia	126,700	48,900	
Luzon	Philippines	104,700	40,400	
Mindanao	Philippines	101,500	39,200	
Hokkaido	Japan	78,400	30,300	
Sakhalin	Russia	74,060	28,600	
Sri Lanka	Indian Ocean	65,600	25,300	
Taiwan	Pacific Ocean	36,000	13,900	
Kyushu	Japan	35,700	13,800	
Hainan	China	34,000	13,100	
Timor	Indonesia	33,600	13,000	
Shikoku	Japan	18,800	7,300	
Halmahera	Indonesia	18,000	6,900	
Ceram	Indonesia	17,150	6,600	
Sumbawa	Indonesia	15,450	6,000	
Flores	Indonesia	15,200	5,900	
Samar	Philippines	13,100	5,100	
Negros	Philippines	12,700	4,900	
Bangka	Indonesia	12,000	4,600	
Palawan	Philippines	12,000	4,600	
Panay	Philippines	11,500	4,400	
Sumba	Indonesia	11,100	4,300	
Mindoro	Philippines	9,750	3,800	
Buru	Indonesia	9,500	3,700	
Bali	Indonesia	5,600	2,200	
Cyprus	Mediterranean	3,570	1,400	
Wrangel Is.	Russia	2,800	1,000	

Africa

		km²	miles²	
Madagascar	Indian Ocean	587,040	226,660	[4]
Socotra	Indian Ocean	3,600	1,400	
Réunion	Indian Ocean	2,500	965	
Tenerife	Atlantic Ocean	2,350	900	
Mauritius	Indian Ocean	1,865	720	

Oceania

		km²	miles²	
New Guinea	Indon./Pap. NG	821,030	317,000	[2]
New Zealand (S.)	Pacific Ocean	150,500	58,100	
New Zealand (N.)	Pacific Ocean	114,700	44,300	
Tasmania	Australia	67,800	26,200	
New Britain	Papua NG	37,800	14,600	
New Caledonia	Pacific Ocean	19,100	7,400	
Viti Levu	Fiji	10,500	4,100	
Hawaii	Pacific Ocean	10,450	4,000	
Bougainville	Papua NG	9,600	3,700	
Guadalcanal	Solomon Is.	6,500	2,500	
Vanua Levu	Fiji	5,550	2,100	
New Ireland	Papua NG	3,200	1,200	

North America

		km²	miles²	
Greenland	Atlantic Ocean	2,175,600	839,800	[1]
Baffin Is.	Canada	508,000	196,100	[5]
Victoria Is.	Canada	212,200	81,900	[9]
Ellesmere Is.	Canada	212,000	81,800	[10]
Cuba	Caribbean Sea	110,860	42,800	
Newfoundland	Canada	110,680	42,700	
Hispaniola	Dom. Rep./Haiti	76,200	29,400	
Banks Is.	Canada	67,000	25,900	
Devon Is.	Canada	54,500	21,000	
Melville Is.	Canada	42,400	16,400	
Vancouver Is.	Canada	32,150	12,400	
Somerset Is.	Canada	24,300	9,400	
Jamaica	Caribbean Sea	11,400	4,400	
Puerto Rico	Atlantic Ocean	8,900	3,400	
Cape Breton Is.	Canada	4,000	1,500	

South America

		km²	miles²
Tierra del Fuego	Argentina/Chile	47,000	18,100
Falkland Is. (E.)	Atlantic Ocean	6,800	2,600
South Georgia	Atlantic Ocean	4,200	1,600
Galapagos (Isabela)	Pacific Ocean	2,250	870

WORLD : REGIONS IN THE NEWS

Maps show the situation in May 1995

THE BREAK UP OF YUGOSLAVIA
The former country of Yugoslavia comprised six republics. In 1991 Slovenia and Croatia declared independence. Bosnia-Herzegovina followed in 1992 and Macedonia in 1993. Yugoslavia now comprises the remaining two republics, Serbia and Montenegro.

YUGOSLAVIA
Population : 10,763,000 (Serb 62.6%, Albanian 16.5%, Montenegrin 5%, Hungarian 3.3%, Muslim 3.2%)
Serbia
Population : 5,824,211 (Serb 87.7%) excluding the former autonomous provinces of Kosovo and Vojvodina
  Kosovo
  Population : 1,956,196
  (Albanian 81.6%, Serb 9.9%)
  Vojvodina
  Population : 2,014,000
  (Serb 56.8%, Hungarian 16.9%)
Montenegro Population : 615,035
(Montenegrin 61.9%, Muslim 14.6%, Albanian 6.6%)
CROATIA
Population : 4,504,000 (Croat 78.1%, Serb 12.2%)
SLOVENIA
Population : 1,942,000 (Slovene 88%, Croat 3%, Serb 2%)
MACEDONIA (F.Y.R.O.M.)
Population : 2,142,000 (Macedonian 64%, Albanian 21.7%, Turkish 5%, Romanian 3%, Serb 2%)
BOSNIA - HERZEGOVINA
Population : 3,527,000 (Muslim 49%, Serb 31.2%, Croat 17.2%)

Civil war between Serbs and other ethnic groups continues in Bosnia-Herzegovina. The large scale map on the left shows the situation in early 1995.

BOSNIA-HERZEGOVINA
0   50   100 km

Under Croatian control
Under Serbian control
Under Muslim control

FORMER YUGOSLAVIA
0   50   100   150   200 km

- · - · -   International boundaries
- · - · -   Republic boundaries
- - - -   Province boundaries
◎   Capital cities

THE NEAR EAST
0   25   50 km

ISRAEL Population : 5,458,000 (inc. East Jerusalem and Jewish settlers in the areas under Israeli administration). (Jewish 82%, Arab Muslim 13.8%, Arab Christian 2.5%, Druze 1.7%)

West Bank Population : 973,500 (Palestinian Arabs 97% [of whom Arab Muslim 85%, Jewish 7%, Christian 8%])

Gaza Strip Population : 658,200 (Arab Muslim 98%)

JORDAN Population : 5,198,000 (Arab 99% [of whom about 50% are Palestinian Arab])

- - - - - -   1949 Armistice Line
- - - -   1974 Cease-fire Lines

Efrata ● Main Jewish settlements in the West Bank and Gaza Strip

Halhul □ Main Palestinian Arab towns in the West Bank and Gaza Strip

THE CAUCASUS
0   100   200 km

- · - · -   International boundaries
- · - · -   Republic boundaries

Georgia, Armenia and Azerbaijan achieved independence in 1991. Abkhazia, Ajaria and South Ossetia seek independence from Georgia. Chechenia has been trying to break away from Russia since 1991, but Russia has resisted with military force. Hostility also continues between Armenia and Azerbaijan over the enclave of Nagorno-Karabakh.

RUSSIA
North Ossetia
Population : 695,000 (Ossetian 53%, Russian 29%, Chechen 5.2%, Ingush 5% [expelled in 1992])
Chechenia
Population : 1,308,000 (Chechen and Ingush 70.7%, Russian 23.1%)
Neighbouring **Ingushetia** (now split from Chechenia) Population : 250,000 (mainly Ingush)
GEORGIA
Population : 5,450,000 (Georgian 70.1%, Armenian 8.1%, Russian 6.3%, Azerbaijani 5.7%, Ossetian 3%, Greek 2%, Abkhazian 2%)
Abkhazia
Population : 537,500 (Georgian 45.7%, Abkhazian 17.8%, Armenian 14.6%, Russian 14.3%)
Ajaria
Population : 382,000 (Georgian 82.8%, Russian 7.7%, Armenian 4%)
South Ossetia
Population : 99,800 (Ossetian 66.2%, Georgian 29%)
ARMENIA
Population : 3,548,000 (Armenian 93.3%, Azerbaijani 2.6%)
Nagorno-Karabakh
Population : 192,400 (Armenian 76.9%, Azerbaijani 21.5%)
AZERBAIJAN
Population : 7,472,000 (Azerbaijani 82.7%, Russian 5.6%, Armenian 5.6%, Lezgin 2.4%)
Naxçıvan
Population : 300,400 (Azerbaijani 95.9%)

MOLDOVA
0   50   100   150 km

Separatist regions

Population : 4,420,000 (Moldovan 64.5%, Ukrainian 13.9%, Russian 14%, Gagauzi 3.5%, Jewish 2%, Bulgarian 2%)

ECUADOR AND PERU
0   100   200 km

- - - -   1995 disputed border
Disputed territory allocated to Peru in 1942

INTRODUCTION TO
WORLD
GEOGRAPHY

The Universe 2,
The Solar System 4,
The Earth: Time and Motion 6, Geology 8, Oceans 10, Atmosphere 12,
Climate 14, Water and Land Use 16, Landscape 18, Environment 20,
People: Demography 22, Cities 24, The Human Family 26,
Conflict and Co-operation 28,
Production: Agriculture 30, Energy 32, Minerals 34,
Manufacturing 36, Trade 38,
Quality of Life: Wealth 40, Standards 42, Health 44, Environment 46

THE UNIVERSE

4: ORBITS OF THE
   PLANETS
   PLANETARY DATA

About 15,000 million years ago, time and space began with the most colossal explosion in cosmic history: the 'Big Bang' that initiated the universe. According to current theory, in the first millionth of a second of its existence it expanded from a dimensionless point of infinite mass and density into a fireball about 30,000 million kilometres across; and it has been expanding ever since.

It took almost a million years for the primal fireball to cool enough for atoms to form. They were mostly hydrogen, still the most abundant material in the universe. But the new matter was not evenly distributed around the young universe, and a few 1,000 million years later atoms in relatively dense regions began to cling together under the influence of gravity, forming distinct masses of gas separated by vast expanses of empty space. To begin with, these first proto-galaxies were dark places: the universe had cooled. But gravitational attraction continued, condensing matter into coherent lumps inside the galactic gas clouds. About 3,000 million years later, some of these masses had contracted so much that internal pressure produced the high temperatures necessary to bring about nuclear fusion: the first stars were born.

There were several generations of stars, each feeding on the wreckage of its extinct predecessors as well as the original galactic gas swirls. With each new generation, progressively larger atoms were forged in stellar furnaces and the galaxy's range of elements, once restricted to hydrogen, grew larger. About 10,000 million years after the Big Bang, a star formed on the outskirts of our galaxy with enough matter left over to create a retinue of planets. Nearly 5,000 million years after that, a few planetary atoms had evolved into structures of complex molecules that lived, breathed and eventually pointed telescopes at the sky.

They found that their Sun is just one of more than 100,000 million stars in the home galaxy alone. Our galaxy, in turn, forms part of a local group of 25 or so similar structures, some much larger than our own; there are at least 100 million other galaxies in the universe as a whole. The most distant ever observed, a highly energetic galactic core known only as Quasar PKS 2000–330, lies about 15,000 million light-years away.

LIFE OF A STAR

For most of its existence, a star produces energy by the nuclear fusion of hydrogen into helium at its core. The duration of this hydrogen-burning period – known as the main sequence – depends on the star's mass; the greater the mass, the higher the core temperatures and the sooner the star's supply of hydrogen is exhausted. Dim, dwarf stars consume their hydrogen slowly, eking it out over 1,000 billion years or more. The Sun, like other stars of its mass, should spend about 10,000 million years on the main sequence; since it was formed less than 5,000 million years ago, it still has half its life left.

Once all a star's core hydrogen has been fused into helium, nuclear activity moves outwards into layers of unconsumed hydrogen. For a time, energy production sharply increases: the star grows hotter and expands enormously, turning into a so-called red giant. Its energy output will increase a thousandfold, and it will swell to a hundred times its present diameter.

After a few hundred million years, helium in the core will become sufficiently compressed to initiate a new cycle of nuclear fusion: from helium to carbon. The star will contract somewhat, before beginning its last expansion, in the Sun's case engulfing the Earth and perhaps Mars. In this bloated condition, the Sun's outer layers will break off into space, leaving a tiny inner core, mainly of carbon, that shrinks progressively under the force of its own gravity: dwarf stars can attain a density more than 10,000 times that of normal matter, with crushing surface gravities to match. Gradually, the nuclear fires will die down, and the Sun will reach its terminal stage: a black dwarf, emitting insignificant amounts of energy.

However, stars more massive than the Sun may undergo another transformation. The additional mass allows gravitational collapse to continue indefinitely: eventually, all the star's remaining matter shrinks to a point, and its density approaches infinity – a state that will not permit even subatomic structures to survive.

The star has become a black hole: an anomalous 'singularity' in the fabric of space and time. Although vast coruscations of radiation will be emitted by any matter falling into its grasp, the singularity itself has an escape velocity that exceeds the speed of light, and nothing can ever be released from it. Within the boundaries of the black hole, the laws of physics are suspended, but no physicist can ever observe the extraordinary events that may occur.

THE END OF THE UNIVERSE

The likely fate of the universe is disputed. One theory (top right) dictates that the expansion begun at the time of the Big Bang will continue 'indefinitely', with ageing galaxies moving further and further apart in an immense, dark graveyard. Alternatively, gravity may overcome the expansion (bottom right). Galaxies will fall back together until everything is again concentrated at a single point, followed by a new Big Bang and a new expansion, in an endlessly repeated cycle. The first theory is supported by the amount of visible matter in the universe; the second assumes there is enough dark material to bring about the gravitational collapse.

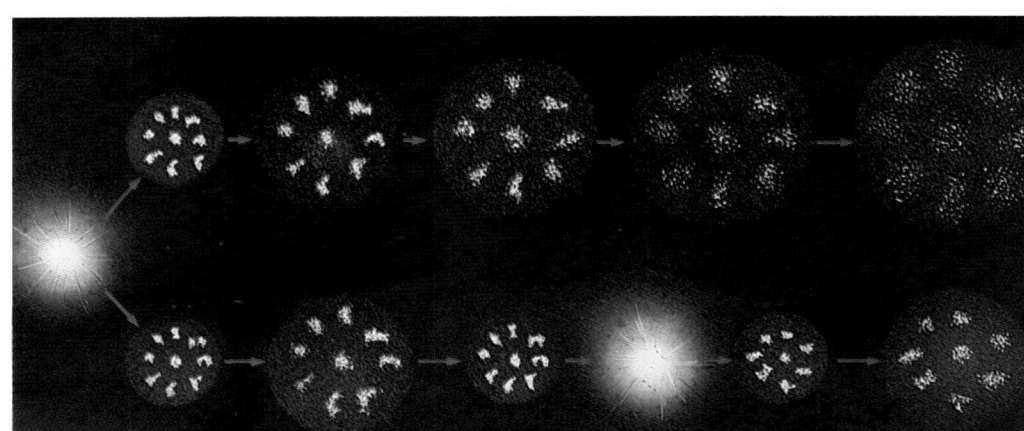

GALACTIC STRUCTURES

The universe's 100 million galaxies show clear structural patterns, originally classified by the American astronomer Edwin Hubble in 1925. Spiral galaxies like our own (top row) have a central, almost spherical bulge and a surrounding disc composed of spiral arms. Barred spirals (bottom row) have a central bar of stars across the nucleus, with spiral arms trailing from the ends of the bar. Elliptical galaxies (far left) have a uniform appearance, ranging from a flattened disc to a near sphere. So-called SO galaxies (left row, right) have a central bulge, but no spiral arms. A few have no discernible structure at all. Galaxies also vary enormously in size, from dwarfs only 2,000 light-years across to great assemblies of stars 80 or more times larger.

THE HOME GALAXY

The Sun and its planets are located in one of the spiral arms, a little less than 30,000 light-years from the galactic centre and orbiting around it in a period of more than 200 million years. The centre is invisible from the Earth, masked by vast, light-absorbing clouds of interstellar dust. The galaxy is probably around 12 billion years old and, like other spiral galaxies, has three distinct regions. The central bulge is about 30,000 light-years in diameter. The disc in which the Sun is located is not much more than 1,000 light-years thick but 100,000 light-years from end to end. Around the galaxy is the halo, a spherical zone 150,000 light-years across, studded with globular star-clusters and sprinkled with individual suns.

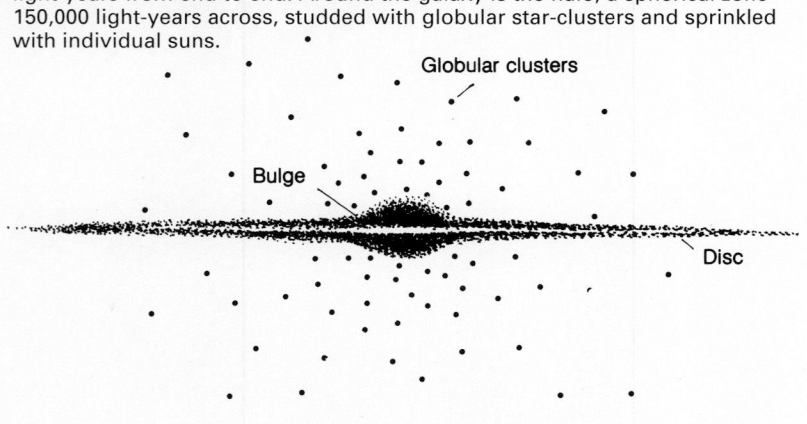

Globular clusters

Bulge

Disc

Solar System

STAR CHARTS

Star charts are drawn as projections of a vast, hollow sphere with the observer in the middle. Each circle below represents one hemisphere, centred on the north and south celestial poles respectively – projections of the Earth's poles in the heavens. At the present era, the north pole is marked by the star Polaris; the south pole has no such convenient reference point. The rectangular map shows the stars immediately above and below the celestial equator.

Astronomical co-ordinates are normally given in terms of 'Right Ascension' for longitude and 'Declination' for latitude or altitude. Since the stars appear to rotate around the Earth once every 24 hours, Right Ascension is measured eastwards – anti-clockwise – in hours and minutes. One hour is equivalent to 15 angular degrees; zero on the scale is the point at which the Sun crosses the celestial equator at the spring equinox, known to astronomers as the First Point in Aries. Unlike the Sun, stars always rise and set at the same point on the horizon. Declination measures (in degrees) a star's angular distance above or below the celestial equator.

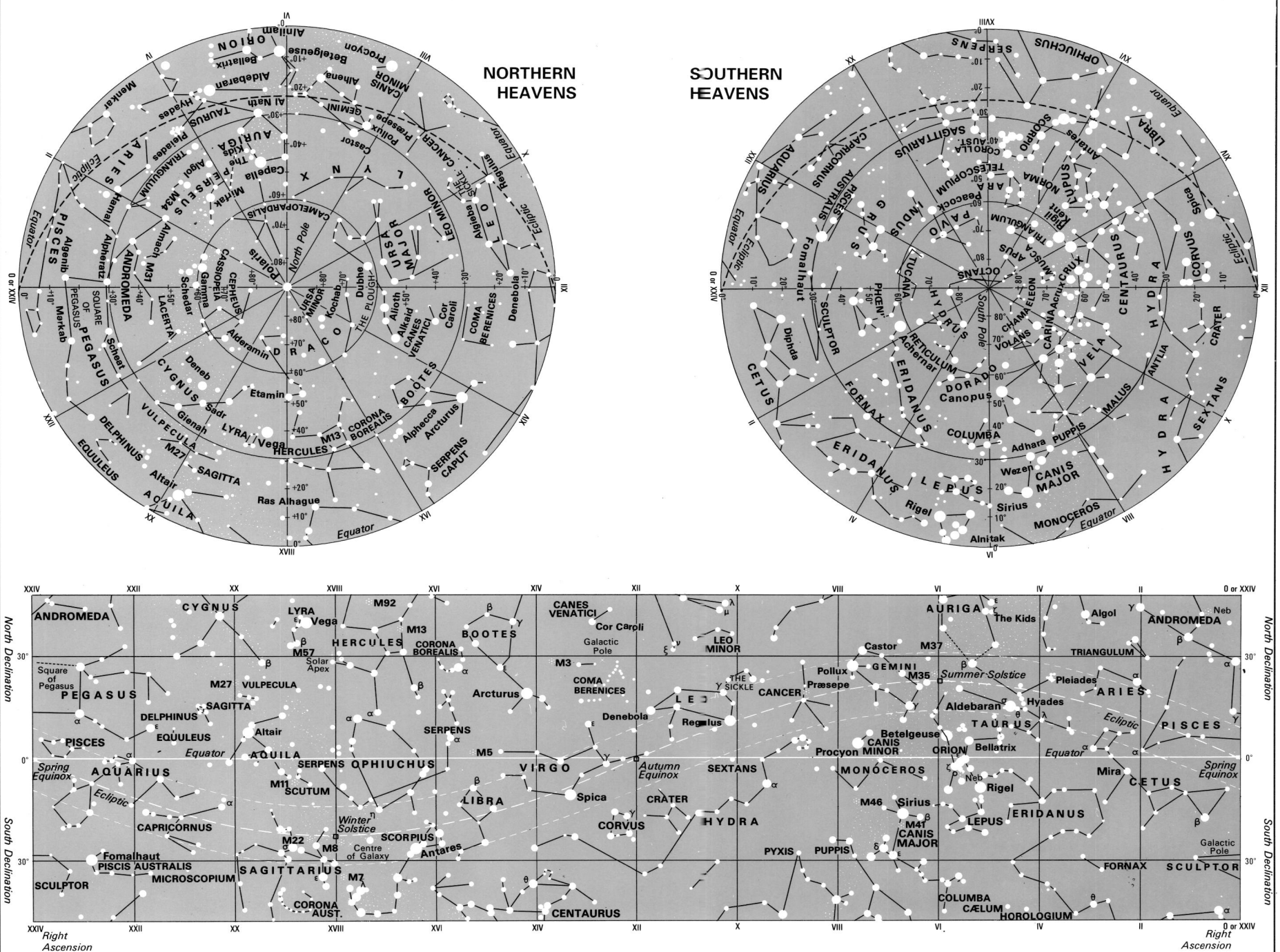

THE CONSTELLATIONS

The constellations and their English names

Andromeda	Andromeda	Circinus	Compasses
Antila	Air Pump	Columba	Dove
Apus	Bird of Paradise	Coma Berenices	Berenice's Hair
Aquarius	Water Carrier	Corona Australis	Southern Crown
Aquila	Eagle	Corona Borealis	Northern Crown
Ara	Altar	Corvus	Crow
Aries	Ram	Crater	Cup
Auriga	Charioteer	Crux	Southern Cross
Boötes	Herdsman	Cygnus	Swan
Caelum	Chisel	Delphinus	Dolphin
Camelopardalis	Giraffe	Dorado	Swordfish
Cancer	Crab	Draco	Dragon
Canes Venatici	Hunting Dogs	Equuleus	Little House
Canis Major	Great Dog	Eridanus	Eridanus
Canis Minor	Little Dog	Fornax	Furnace
Capricornus	Goat	Gemini	Twins
Carina	Keel	Grus	Crane
Cassiopeia	Cassiopeia	Hercules	Hercules
Centaurus	Centaur	Horologium	Clock
Cepheus	Cepheus	Hydra	Water Snake
Cetus	Whale	Hydrus	Sea Serpent
Chamaeleon	Chameleon	Indus	Indian

Lacerta	Lizard	Piscis Austrinus	Southern Fish
Leo	Lion	Puppis	Ship's Stern
Leo Minor	Little Lion	Pyxis	Mariner's Compass
Lepus	Hare	Reticulum	Net
Libra	Scales	Sagitta	Arrow
Lupus	Wolf	Sagittarius	Archer
Lynx	Lynx	Scorpius	Scorpion
Lyra	Harp	Sculptor	Sculptor
Mensa	Table	Scutum	Shield
Microscopium	Microscope	Serpens	Serpent
Monoceros	Unicorn	Sextans	Sextant
Musca	Fly	Taurus	Bull
Norma	Level	Telescopium	Telescope
Octans	Octant	Triangulum	Triangle
Ophiuchus	Serpent Bearer	Triangulum Australe	Southern Triangle
Orion	Orion	Tucana	Toucan
Pavo	Peacock	Ursa Major	Great Bear
Pegasus	Winged Horse	Ursa Minor	Little Bear
Perseus	Perseus	Vela	Sails
Phoenix	Phoenix	Virgo	Virgin
Pictor	Easel	Volans	Flying Fish
Pisces	Fishes	Vulpecula	Fox

THE NEAREST STARS

The 20 nearest stars, excluding the Sun, with their distance from Earth in light-years*

Proxima Centauri	4.3
Alpha Centauri A	4.3
Alpha Centauri B	4.3
Barnard's Star	6.0
Wolf 359	8.1
Lal 21185	8.2
Sirius A	8.7
Sirius B	8.7
UV Ceti A	9.0
UV Ceti B	9.0
Ross 154	9.3
Ross 248	10.3
Epsilon Eridani	10.8
L 789-6	11.1
Ross 128	11.1
61 Cygni A	11.2
61 Cygni B	11.2
Procyon A	11.3
Procyon B	11.3
Epsilon Indi	11.4

Many of the nearest stars, like Alpha Centauri A and B, are doubles, orbiting about the common centre of gravity and to all intents and purposes equidistant from Earth. Many of them are dim objects, with no name other than the designation given by the astronomers who investigated them. However, they include Sirius, the brightest star in the sky, and Procyon, the seventh brightest. Both are far larger than the Sun: of the nearest stars, only Epsilon Eridani is similar in size and luminosity.

* A light-year equals approx. 9,500,000,000,000 kilometres

THE SOLAR SYSTEM

2: THE HOME GALAXY

6: THE SEASONS
DAY AND NIGHT

7: THE MOON

Lying 27,000 light-years from the centre of one of billions of galaxies that comprise the observable universe, our Solar System contains nine planets and their moons, innumerable asteroids and comets, and a miscellany of dust and gas, all tethered by the immense gravitational field of the Sun, the middling-sized star whose thermonuclear furnaces provide them all with heat and light. The Solar System was formed about 4,600 million years ago, when a spinning cloud of gas, mostly hydrogen but seeded with other, heavier elements, condensed enough to ignite a nuclear reaction and create a star. The Sun still accounts for almost 99.9% of the system's total mass; one planet, Jupiter, contains most of the remainder.

By composition as well as distance, the planetary array divides quite neatly in two: an inner system of four small, solid planets, including the Earth, and an outer system, from Jupiter to Neptune, of four huge gas giants. Between the two groups lies a scattering of asteroids, perhaps as many as 40,000; possibly the remains of a planet destroyed by some unexplained catastrophe, they are more likely to be debris left over from the Solar System's formation, prevented by the gravity of massive Jupiter from coalescing into a larger body. The ninth planet, Pluto, seems to be a world of the inner system type: small, rocky and something of an anomaly.

By the 1990s, however, the Solar System also included some newer anomalies: several thousand spacecraft. Most were in orbit around the Earth, but some had probed far and wide around the system. The valuable information beamed back by these robotic investigators has transformed our knowledge of our celestial environment.

Much of the early history of science is the story of people trying to make sense of the errant points of light that were all they knew of the planets. Now, men have themselves stood on the Earth's Moon; probes have landed on Mars and Venus, and orbiting radars have mapped far distant landscapes with astonishing accuracy. In the 1980s, the US *Voyagers* skimmed all four major planets of the outer system, bringing new revelations with each close approach. Only Pluto, inscrutably distant in an orbit that takes it 50 times the Earth's distance from the Sun, remains unvisited by our messengers.

ORBITS OF THE PLANETS

The solar planets and their orbits, showing the relative position of each planet at the vernal equinox of 1992.

Orbits are drawn to exact scale, but with the Sun and planets greatly enlarged for clarity. The Solar System is shown from the viewpoint of an observer a few light-hours distant in the direction of the constellation Hercules. Seen from such a position, above the plane of the ecliptic, all the planets revolve about the Sun in an anti-clockwise direction. The perspective view exaggerates the elliptical form of all the planetary orbits: only Pluto and Mercury follow paths that deviate noticeably from circularity. Near perihelion – its closest approach to the Sun – Pluto actually passes inside the orbit of Neptune, an event that last occurred in 1983. Pluto will not regain its station as the Sun's outermost planet until February 1999.

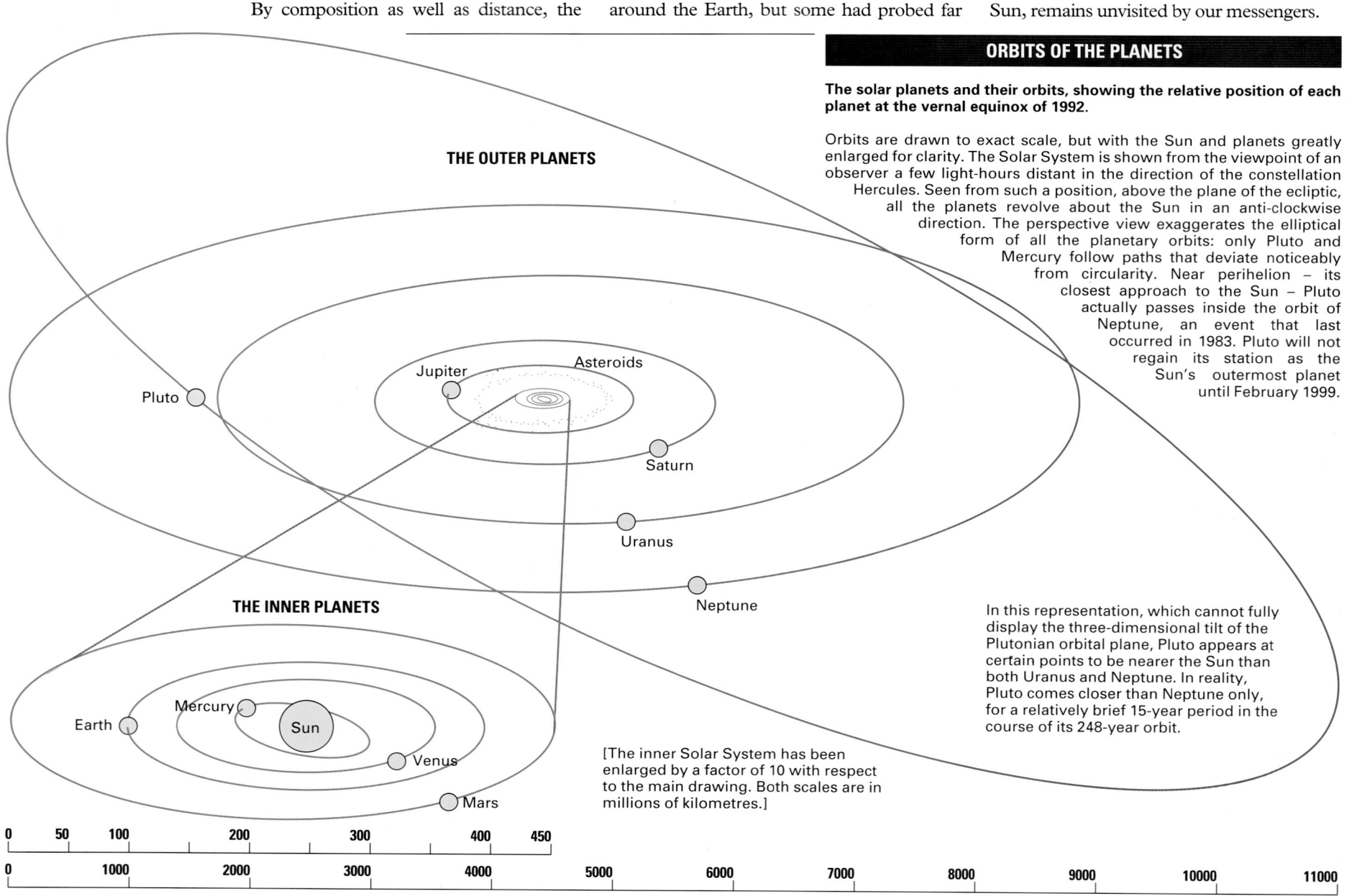

THE OUTER PLANETS

THE INNER PLANETS

Pluto / Jupiter / Asteroids / Saturn / Uranus / Neptune / Earth / Mercury / Sun / Venus / Mars

In this representation, which cannot fully display the three-dimensional tilt of the Plutonian orbital plane, Pluto appears at certain points to be nearer the Sun than both Uranus and Neptune. In reality, Pluto comes closer than Neptune only, for a relatively brief 15-year period in the course of its 248-year orbit.

[The inner Solar System has been enlarged by a factor of 10 with respect to the main drawing. Both scales are in millions of kilometres.]

PLANETARY DATA									
	Mean distance from Sun (million km)	Mass (Earth = 1)	Period of orbit (Earth years)	Period of rotation (Earth days)	Equatorial diameter (km)	Average density (water = 1)	Surface gravity (Earth = 1)	Escape velocity (km/sec)	Number of known satellites
Sun	–	*332,946*	–	*25.38*	*1,392,000*	*1.41*	*27.9*	*617.5*	–
Mercury	58.3	0.06	0.241	58.67	4,878	5.5	0.38	4.27	0
Venus	107.7	0.8	0.615	243.0	12,104	5.25	0.90	10.36	0
Earth	149.6	1.0	1.00	0.99	12,756	5.52	1.00	11.18	1
Mars	227.3	0.1	1.88	1.02	6,794	3.94	0.38	5.03	2
Jupiter	777.9	317.8	11.86	0.41	142,800	1.33	2.64	60.22	16
Saturn	1,427.1	95.2	29.63	0.42	120,000	0.706	1.16	36.25	17
Uranus	2,872.3	14.5	83.97	0.45	52,000	1.70	1.11	22.4	15
Neptune	4,502.7	17.2	164.8	0.67	48,400	1.77	1.21	23.9	8
Pluto	5,894.2	0.002	248.63	6.38	3,000	5.50	0.47	5.1	1

Planetary days are given in sidereal time – that is, with respect to the stars rather than the Sun. Most of the information in the table was confirmed by spacecraft and often obtained from photographs and other data transmitted back to the Earth. In the case of Pluto, however, only earthbound observations have been made, and no spacecraft can hope to encounter it until well into the next century. Given the planet's small size and great distance, figures for its diameter and rotation period cannot be definitive.

Since Pluto does not appear to be massive enough to account for the perturbations in the orbits of Uranus and Neptune that led to its 1930 discovery, it is quite possible that a tenth and even more distant planet may exist. Once Pluto's own 248-year orbit has been observed for long enough, further discrepancies may give a clue as to any tenth planet's whereabouts. Even so, distance alone would make it very difficult to locate, especially since telescopes powerful enough to find it are normally engaged in galactic study.

THE PLANETS

Mercury is the closest planet to the Sun and hence the fastest-moving. It has no significant atmosphere and a cratered, wrinkled surface very similar to that of Earth's moon.

Venus has much the same physical dimensions as Earth. However, its carbon dioxide atmosphere is 90 times as dense, accounting for a runaway greenhouse effect that makes the Venusian surface, at 475°C, the hottest of all the planets in the Solar System. Radar mapping shows relatively level land with volcanic regions whose sulphurous discharges explain the sulphuric acid rains reported by soft-landing space probes before they succumbed to Venus's fierce climate.

Earth seen from space is easily the most beautiful of the inner planets; it is also, and more objectively, the largest, as well the only home of known life. Living things are the main reason why the Earth is able to retain a substantial proportion of corrosive and highly reactive oxygen in its atmosphere, a state of affairs that contradicts the laws of chemical equilibrium; the oxygen in turn supports the life that constantly regenerates it.

Mars was once considered the likeliest of the other planets to share Earth's cargo of life: the seasonal expansion of dark patches strongly suggested vegetation and the planet's apparent ice-caps indicated the vital presence of water. But close inspection by spacecraft brought disappointment: chemical reactions account for the seeming vegetation, the ice-caps are mainly frozen carbon dioxide, and whatever oxygen the planet once possessed is now locked up in the iron-bearing rock that covers its cratered surface and gives it its characteristic red hue.

Jupiter masses almost three times as much as all the other planets combined; had it scooped up a little more matter during its formation, it might have evolved into a small companion star for the Sun. The planet is mostly gas, under intense pressure in the lower atmosphere above a core of fiercely compressed hydrogen and helium. The upper layers form strikingly-coloured rotating belts, the outward sign of the intense storms created by Jupiter's rapid diurnal rotation. Close approaches by spacecraft have shown an orbiting ring system and discovered several previously unknown moons: Jupiter has at least 16 moons.

Saturn is structurally similar to Jupiter, rotating fast enough to produce an obvious bulge at its equator. Ever since the invention of the telescope, however, Saturn's rings have been the feature that has attracted most observers. *Voyager* probes in 1980 and 1981 sent back detailed pictures that showed them to be composed of thousands of separate ringlets, each in turn made up of tiny icy particles, interacting in a complex dance that may serve as a model for the study of galactic and even larger structures.

Uranus was unknown to the ancients. Although it is faintly visible to the naked eye, it was not discovered until 1781. Its composition is broadly similar to Jupiter and Saturn, though its distance from the Sun ensures an even colder surface temperature. Observations in 1977 suggested the presence of a faint ring system, amply confirmed when *Voyager 2* swung past the planet in 1986.

Neptune is always more than 4,000 million kilometres from Earth, and despite its diameter of almost 50,000 km, it can only be seen by telescope. Its 1846 discovery was the result of mathematical predictions by astronomers seeking to explain irregularities in the orbit of Uranus, but until *Voyager 2* closed with the planet in 1989, little was known of it. Like Uranus, it has a ring system; *Voyager*'s photographs revealed a total of eight moons.

Pluto is the most mysterious of the solar planets, if only because even the most powerful telescopes can scarcely resolve it from a point of light to a disc. It was discovered as recently as 1930, like Neptune as the result of perturbations in the orbits of the two then outermost planets. Its small size, as well as its eccentric and highly tilted orbit, has led to suggestions that it is a former satellite of Neptune, somehow liberated from its primary. In 1978 Pluto was found to have a moon of its own, Charon, apparently half the size of Pluto itself.

Mean distance from Sun in million kilometres

Mercury	58.3
Venus	107.7
Earth	149.6
Mars	227.9
Jupiter	777.9
Saturn	1,427.1
Uranus	2,872.3
Neptune	4,502.7
Pluto	5,894.2

THE EARTH: TIME AND MOTION

The basic unit of time measurement is the day, that is, one rotation of the Earth on its axis. The subdivision of the day into hours, minutes and seconds is arbitrary and simply for our convenience. Our present calendar is based on the solar year of 365.24 days, the time taken by the Earth to orbit the Sun. As the Earth rotates from west to east, the Sun appears to rise in the east and set in the west. When the Sun is setting in Shanghai, on the opposite side of the world New York is just emerging into sunlight. Noon, when the Sun is directly overhead, is coincident at all places on the same meridian, with shadows pointing directly towards the poles.

Calendars based on the movements of the Sun and Moon have been used since ancient times. The Julian Calendar, with its leap year, introduced by Julius Caesar, fixed the average length of the year at 365.25 days, which was about 11 minutes too long (the Earth completes its orbit in 365 days, 5 hours, 48 minutes and 46 seconds of mean solar time). The cumulative error was rectified by the Gregorian Calendar, introduced by Pope Gregory XIII in 1582, when he decreed that the day following 4 October was 15 October, and that century years did not count as leap years unless divisible by 400. England did not adopt the reformed calendar until 1752, when the country found itself 11 days behind the continent.

Britain imposed the Gregorian Calendar on all its possessions, including the American colonies. All dates preceding 2 September were marked 'OS', for 'Old Style'.

4: ORBITS OF THE PLANETS

11: OCEAN CURRENTS

12: CIRCULATION OF THE AIR

EARTH DATA

Maximum distance from Sun
(Aphelion): 152,007,016 km
Minimum distance from Sun
(Perihelion): 147,000,830 km
Obliquity of the ecliptic:
23° 27' 08"
Length of year – solar tropical
(equinox to equinox):
365.24 days
Length of year – sidereal
(fixed star to fixed star):
365.26 days
Length of day – mean solar
day: 24h, 03m, 56s
Length of day – mean
sidereal day: 23h, 56m, 04s

Superficial area:
510,000,000 sq km
Land surface:
149,000,000 sq km (29.2%)
Water surface:
361,000,000 sq km (70.8%)
Equatorial circumference:
40,077 km.
Polar circumference:
40,009 km
Equatorial diameter:
12,756.8 km
Polar diameter: 12,713.8 km
Equatorial radius: 6,378.4 km
Polar radius: 6,356.9 km
Volume of the Earth:
1,083,230 x 10⁶ cu km
Mass of the Earth:
5.9 x 10²¹ tonnes

Equinox is one of the two times in the year when day and night are of equal length due to the Sun being overhead at the Equator

Solstice is one of the two times in the year when the Sun is overhead at one of the Tropics, 23½° north or south of the Equator

THE SEASONS

The Earth revolves around the Sun once a year in an 'anti-clockwise' direction, tilted at a constant angle 66½°. In June, the northern hemisphere is tilted towards the Sun: as a result, it receives more hours of sunshine in a day and therefore has its warmest season, summer. By December, the Earth has rotated halfway round the Sun so that the southern hemisphere is tilted towards the Sun and has its summer; the hemisphere that is tilted away from the Sun has winter. On 21 June the Sun is directly overhead at the Tropic of Cancer (23½° N), and this is midsummer in the northern hemisphere. Midsummer in the southern hemisphere occurs on 21 December, when the Sun is overhead at the Tropic of Capricorn (23½° S).

DAY AND NIGHT

The Sun appears to rise in the east, reach its highest point at noon, and then set in the west, to be followed by night. In reality, it is not the Sun that is moving but the Earth revolving from west to east.

At the summer solstice in the northern hemisphere (21 June), the Arctic has total daylight and the Antarctic total darkness. The opposite occurs at the winter solstice (21 December). At the Equator, the length of day and night are almost equal all year.

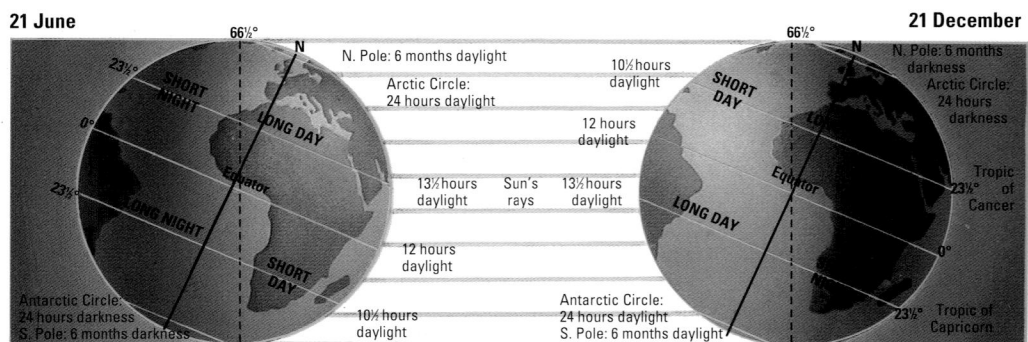

THE SUN'S PATH

The diagrams on the left illustrate the apparent path of the Sun at (A) the Equator, (B) in mid-latitude (45°), (C) at the Arctic Circle (66½°), and (D) at the North Pole, where there are six months of continuous daylight and six months of continuous night.

MEASUREMENTS OF TIME

Astronomers distinguish between solar time and sidereal time. Solar time derives from the period taken by the Earth to rotate on its axis: one rotation defines a solar day. But the speed of the Earth along its orbit around the Sun is not constant. The length of day – or 'apparent solar day', as defined by the apparent successive transits of the Sun – is irregular because the Earth must complete more than one rotation before the Sun returns to the same meridian. The constant sidereal day is defined as the interval between two successive apparent transits of a star, or the first point of Aries, across the same meridian. If the Sun is at the equinox and overhead at a meridian one day, then the next day it will be to the east by approximately 1°. Thus, the Sun will not cross the meridian until four minutes after the sidereal noon.

From the diagrams on the right it is possible to discover the time of sunrise or sunset on a given date and for latitudes between 60°N and 60°S.

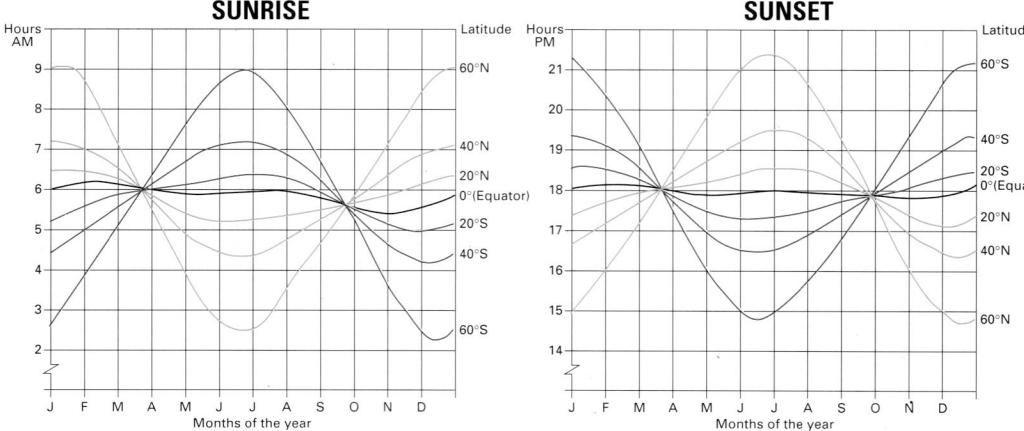

THE MOON

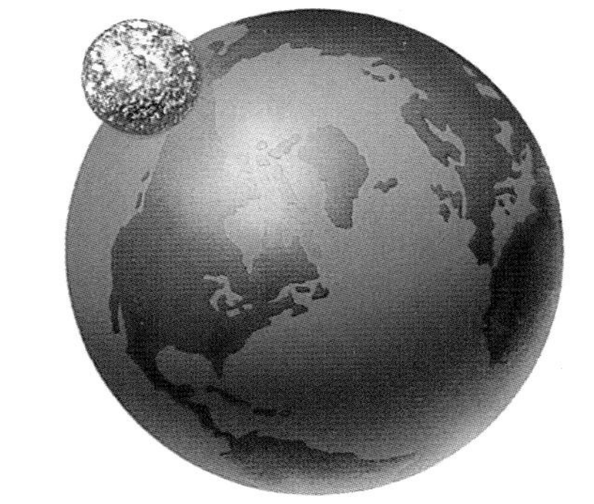

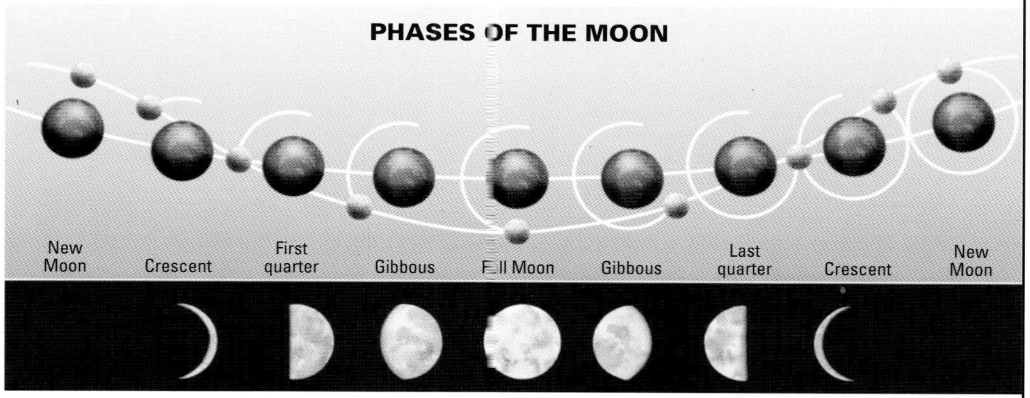

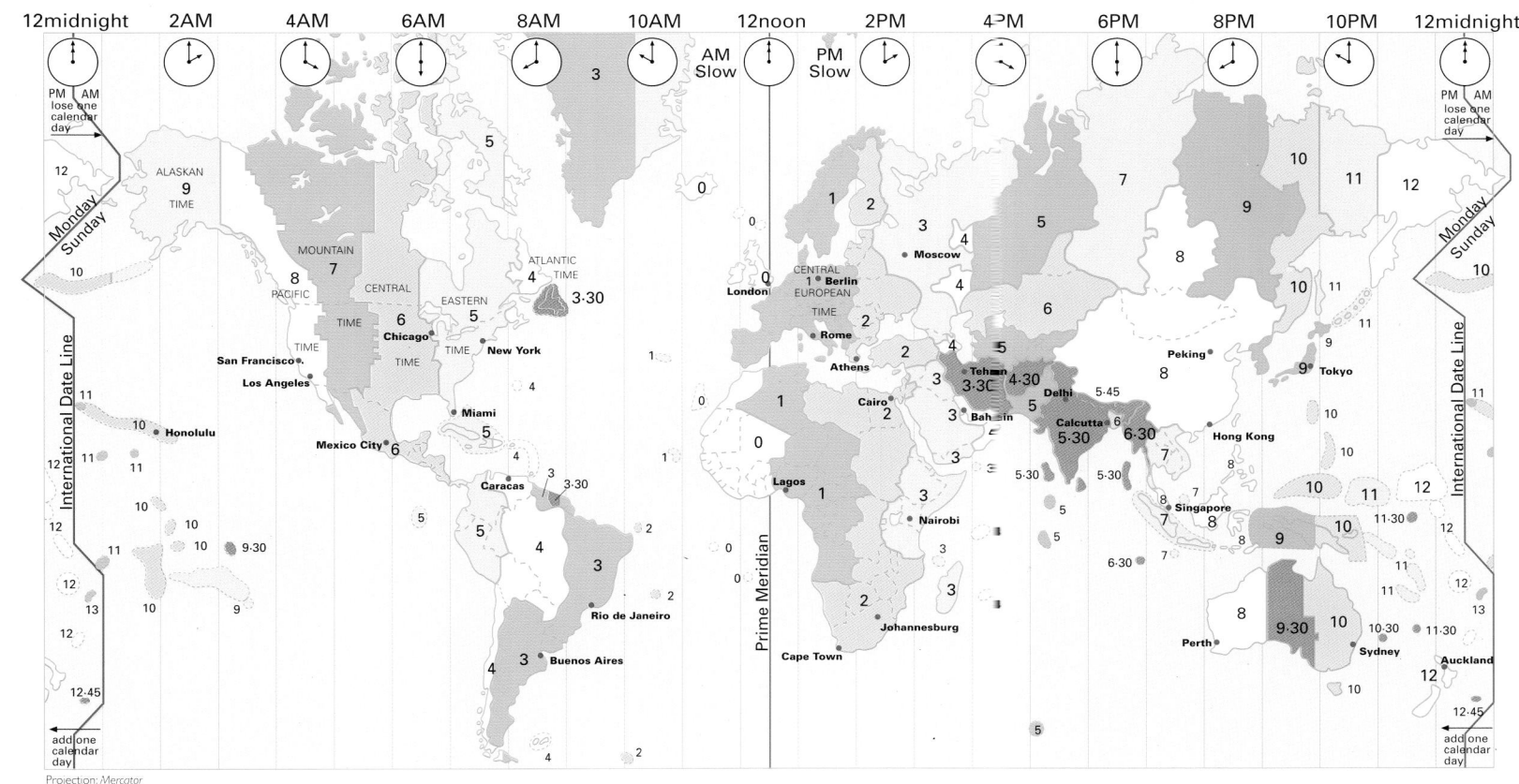

PHASES OF THE MOON

New Moon · Crescent · First quarter · Gibbous · Full Moon · Gibbous · Last quarter · Crescent · New Moon

The Moon rotates more slowly than the Earth, making one complete turn on its axis in just over 27 days. Since this corresponds to its period of revolution around the Earth, the Moon always presents the same hemisphere or face to us, and we never see 'the dark side'. The interval between one Full Moon and the next (and between New Moons) is about $29\frac{1}{2}$ days – a lunar month. The apparent changes in the shape of the Moon are caused by its changing position in relation to the Earth; like the planets, it produces no light of its own and shines only by reflecting the rays of the Sun.

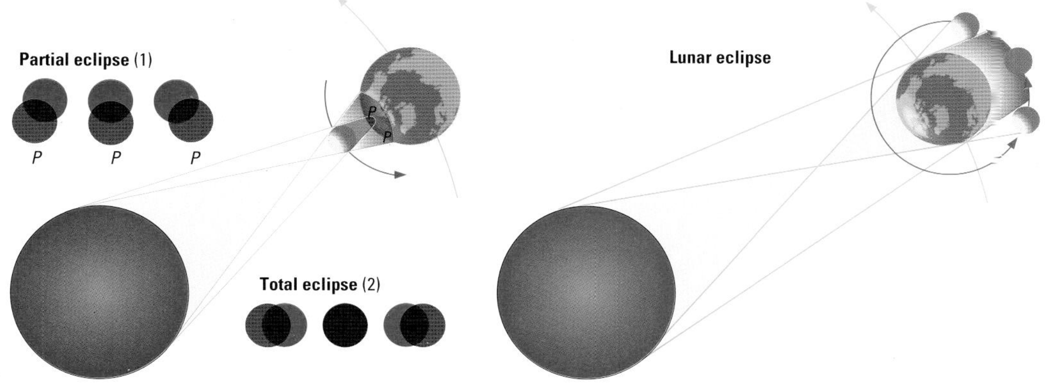

ECLIPSES

When the Moon passes between the Sun and the Earth, it causes a partial eclipse of the Sun (1) if the Earth passes through the Moon's outer shadow (P), or a total eclipse (2) if the inner cone shadow crosses the Earth's surface. In a lunar eclipse, the Earth's shadow crosses the Moon and, again, provides either a partial or total eclipse. Eclipses of the Sun and the Moon do not occur every month because of the 5° difference between the plane of the Moon's orbit and the plane in which the Earth moves. In the 1990s only 14 lunar eclipses are possible, for example, seven partial and seven total; each is visible only from certain, and variable, parts of the world. The same period witnesses 13 solar eclipses – six partial (or annular) and seven total.

Partial eclipse (1)
P   P   P

Total eclipse (2)

Lunar eclipse

TIDES

The daily rise and fall of the ocean's tides are the result of the gravitational pull of the Moon and that of the Sun, though the effect of the latter is only 46.6% as strong as that of the Moon. This effect is greatest on the hemisphere facing the Moon and causes a tidal 'bulge'. When lunar and solar forces pull together, with Sun, Earth and Moon in line (near New and Full Moons), higher 'spring tides' (and lower low tides) occur; when lunar and solar forces are least coincidental with the Sun and Moon at an angle (near the Moon's first and third quarters), 'neap tides' occur, which have a small tidal range.

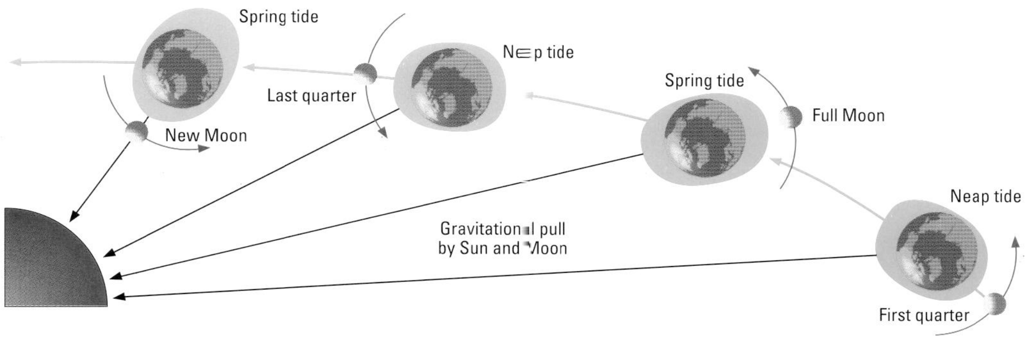

Spring tide · Neap tide · Last quarter · New Moon · Spring tide · Full Moon · Neap tide · Gravitational pull by Sun and Moon · First quarter

---

TIME ZONES

12midnight · 2AM · 4AM · 6AM · 8AM · 10AM · 12noon · 2PM · 4PM · 6PM · 8PM · 10PM · 12midnight

AM Slow · PM Slow

The Earth rotates through 360° in 24 hours, and so moves 15° every hour. The world is divided into 24 standard time zones, each centred on lines of longitude at 15° intervals. The Greenwich meridian lies at the centre of the first zone. All places to the west of Greenwich are one hour behind for every 15° of longitude; places to the east are ahead by one hour for every 15°. When it is 12 noon at the Greenwich meridian, 180° east it is midnight of the same day – while 180° west the day is just beginning. To overcome this, the International Date Line was established, approximately following the 180° meridian. Thus, if you travelled eastwards from Japan (140° East) to Samoa (170° West), you would pass from Sunday night into Sunday morning.

 Zones slow or fast of Greenwich Mean Time

 Half-hour zones

The time when it is 12 noon at Greenwich

Projection: Mercator

THE EARTH: GEOLOGY

18: THE SPREADING EARTH
TYPES OF ROCK
MOUNTAIN BUILDING

19: MOULDING THE LAND

21: THE CARBON CYLCE

34: MINERALS

The complementary, almost jigsaw-puzzle fit of the Atlantic coasts led to Alfred Wegener's proposition of continental drift in Germany (1915). His theory suggested that an ancient super-continent, which he called Pangaea, incorporating all the Earth's landmasses, gradually split up to form the continents we know today.

By 180 million years ago, Pangaea had divided into two major groups and the southern part, Gondwanaland, had itself begun to break up with India and Antarctica-Australia becoming isolated.

By 135 million years ago, the widening of the splits in the North Atlantic and Indian Oceans persisted, a South Atlantic gap had appeared, and India continued to move 'north' towards Asia.

By 65 million years ago, South America had completely split from Africa.

To form today's pattern, India 'collided' with Asia (crumpling up sediments to form the Himalayas); South America rotated and moved west to connect with North America; Australia separated from Antarctica and moved north; and the familiar gap developed between Greenland and Europe.

The origin of the Earth is still open to conjecture, although the most widely accepted theory is that it was formed from a solar cloud consisting mainly of hydrogen about 4,600 million years ago. The cloud condensed, forming the planets. The lighter elements floated to the surface of the Earth, where they cooled to form a crust; the inner material remained hot and molten. The first rocks were formed over 3,500 million years ago, but the Earth's surface has since been constantly altered.

The crust consists of a brittle, low-density material, varying from 5 kilometres to 50 kilometres thick beneath the continents, which is predominantly made up of silica and aluminium: hence its name, 'sial'. Below the sial is a basaltic layer known as 'sima', comprising mainly silica and magnesium. The crust accounts for only 1.5% of the Earth's volume.

The mantle lies immediately below the crust, with a distinct change in density and chemical properties. The rock here is rich in iron and magnesium silicates, with temperatures reaching 1,600°C. The rigid upper mantle extends down to a depth of about 1,000 kilometres, below which is a more viscous lower mantle measuring about 1,900 kilometres thick.

The outer core, measuring about 2,310 kilometres thick, consists of molten iron and nickel at temperatures ranging from 2,100°C to 5,000°C, possibly separated from the less dense mantle by an oxidized shell. About 5,000 kilometres below the planetary surface is a liquid transition zone, below which is the solid inner core, a sphere of about 2,700 kilometres diameter, where rock is three times as dense as in the crust. The temperature at the centre of the Earth is probably about 5,000°C.

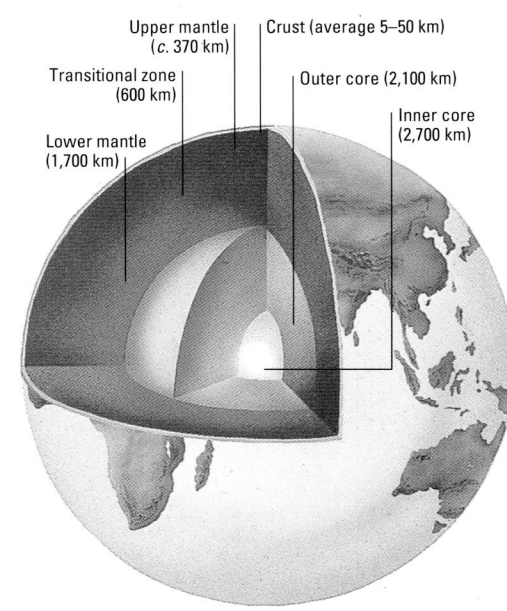

Upper mantle (c. 370 km)
Crust (average 5–50 km)
Transitional zone (600 km)
Outer core (2,100 km)
Inner core (2,700 km)
Lower mantle (1,700 km)

CONTINENTAL DRIFT

About 200 million years ago the original Pangaea landmass began to split into two continental groups, which further separated over time to produce the present-day configuration.

Laurasia

Gondwanaland

180 million years ago

135 million years ago

Present day

~~~~~ Trench
——— Rift
——— New ocean floor
——— Zones of slippage

PLATE TECTONICS

The original debate about the drift theory of Wegener and others formed a long prelude to a more radical idea: plate tectonics. The discovery that the continents are carried along on the top of slowly-moving crustal plates (which float on heavier liquid material – the lower mantle – much as icebergs do on water) provided the mechanism for the drift theories to work. The plates converge and diverge along margins marked by seismic and volcanic activity. Plates diverge from mid-ocean ridges where molten lava pushes up and forces the plates apart at a rate of up to 40 mm a year; converging plates form either a trench (where the oceanic plates sink below the lighter continental rock) or mountain ranges (where two continents collide).

The debate about plate tectonics is not over, however. In addition to abiding questions such as what force actually moves the plates (massive convection currents in the Earth's interior is the most popular explanation), and why so many volcanoes and earthquakes occur in mid-plate (such as Hawaii and central China), evidence began to emerge in the early 1990s that, with more sophisticated equipment and models, the whole theory might be in doubt.

VOLCANOES

Of some 850 volcanoes that have produced recorded eruptions, nearly three-quarters lie in the 'Ring of Fire' that surrounds the Pacific Ocean. The 1980s was a bad decade for loss of life here, with three major eruptions – Mount St Helens, USA, in 1980; El Chichon, Mexico, in 1982; and Nevado del Ruiz, Colombia, in 1985 – killing 25,000 people. This is not because the world is becoming less geologically stable: it is simply that populations are growing fast, with over 350 million people now living in areas vulnerable to seismic activity.

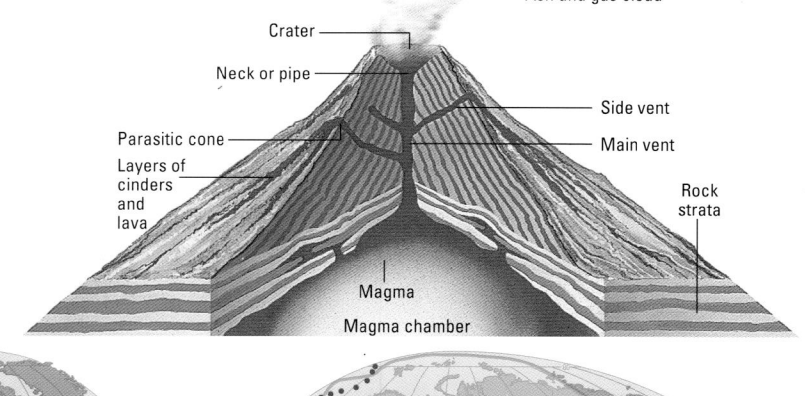

Ash and gas cloud
Crater
Neck or pipe
Side vent
Parasitic cone
Main vent
Layers of cinders and lava
Rock strata
Magma
Magma chamber

Shield cone

Hornit cone

Cinder cone

Caldera

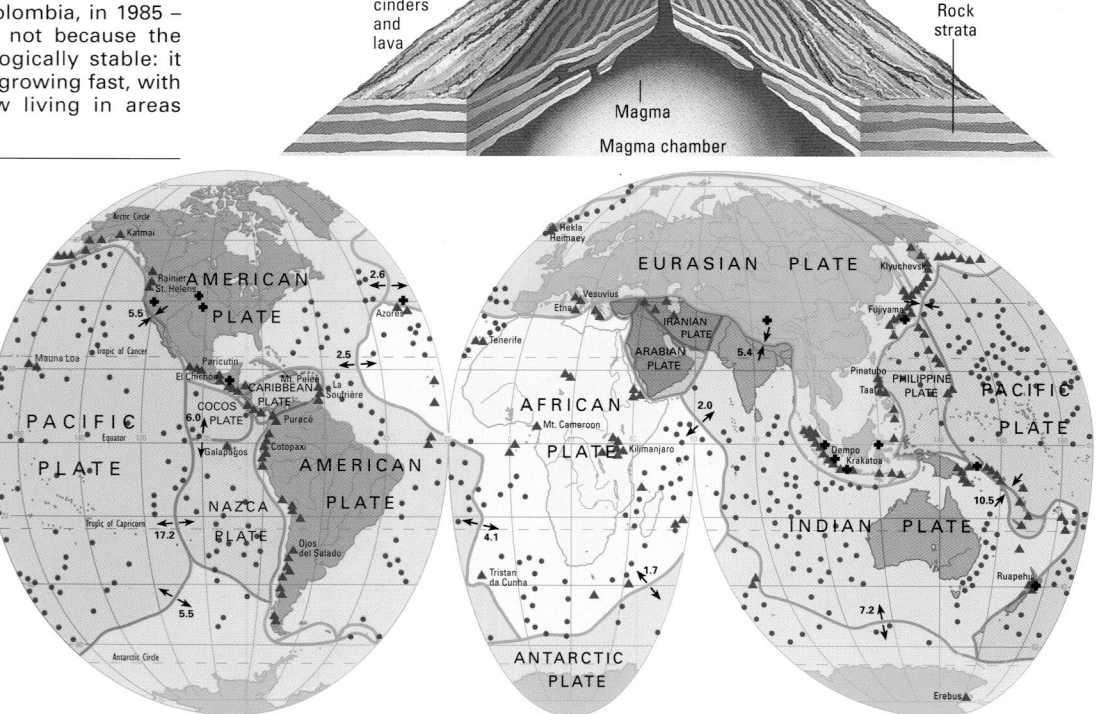

DISTRIBUTION

Land volcanoes active since 1700 ▲

Submarine volcanoes •

Geysers +

Boundaries of tectonic plates ———

Direction of movement along plate boundaries (cm/year) 7.2 ↙

Volcanoes can suddenly erupt after lying dormant for centuries: in 1991 Mount Pinatubo, Philippines, burst into life after sleeping for more than 600 years.

AMERICAN PLATE
PACIFIC PLATE
COCOS PLATE
CARIBBEAN PLATE
NAZCA PLATE
EURASIAN PLATE
IRANIAN PLATE
ARABIAN PLATE
AFRICAN PLATE
PHILIPPINE PLATE
PACIFIC PLATE
INDIAN PLATE
ANTARCTIC PLATE
~~~~~

GEOLOGICAL TIME

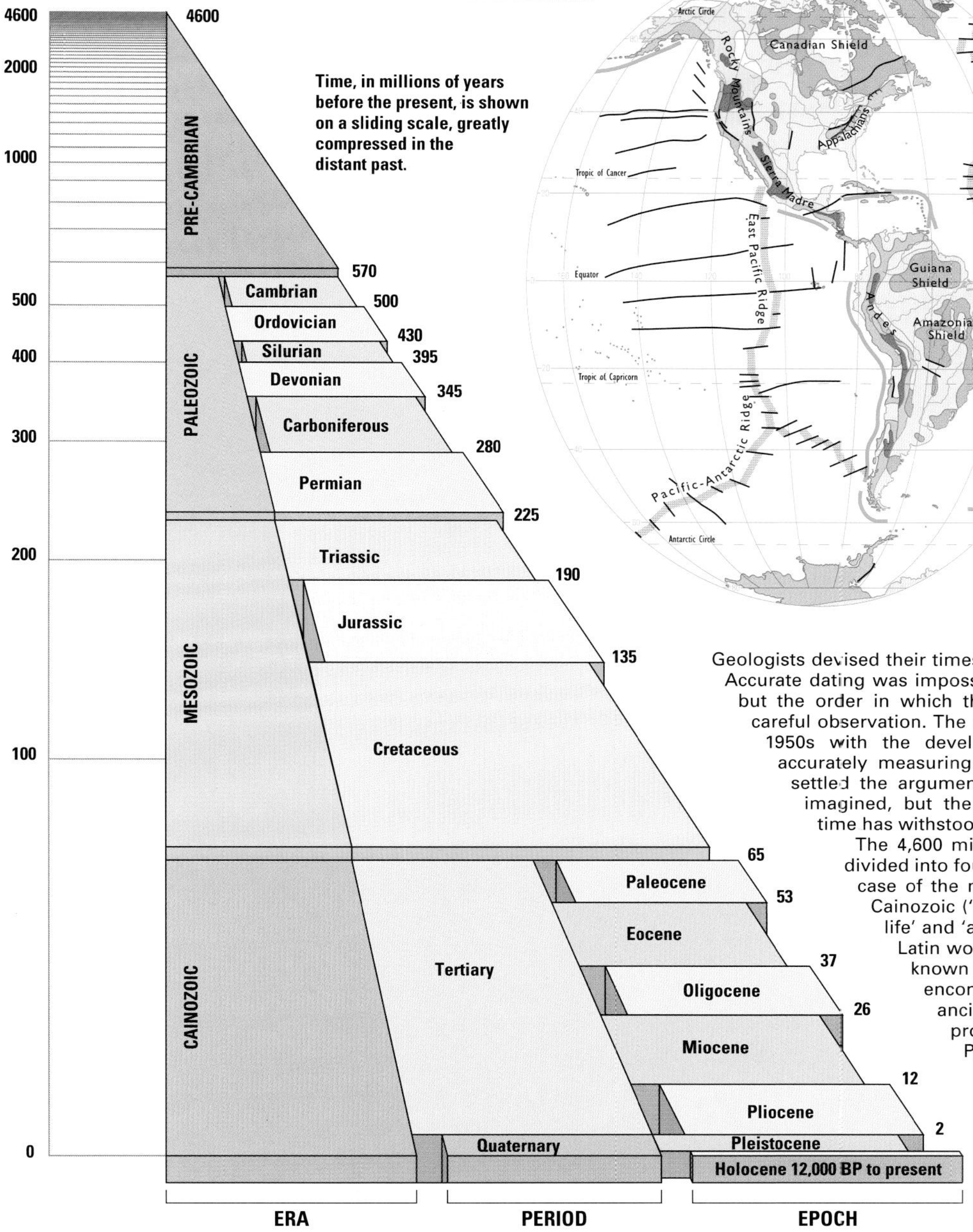

4600

Time, in millions of years before the present, is shown on a sliding scale, greatly compressed in the distant past.

ERA	PERIOD	EPOCH
PRE-CAMBRIAN (4600–570)		
PALEOZOIC	Cambrian (570–500)	
	Ordovician (500–430)	
	Silurian (430–395)	
	Devonian (395–345)	
	Carboniferous (345–280)	
	Permian (280–225)	
MESOZOIC	Triassic (225–190)	
	Jurassic (190–135)	
	Cretaceous (135–65)	
CAINOZOIC	Tertiary	Paleocene (65–53)
		Eocene (53–37)
		Oligocene (37–26)
		Miocene (26–12)
		Pliocene (12–2)
	Quaternary	Pleistocene (2–)
		Holocene 12,000 BP to present

Geologists devised their timescale on the basis of relative, not calendar, ages. Accurate dating was impossible and estimates were often bitterly disputed, but the order in which the rocks were formed could be deduced from careful observation. The advent of radioactive dating – culminating in the 1950s with the development of a mass spectrometer capable of accurately measuring tiny quantities of isotopes – appears to have settled the arguments. The Earth is far older than geologists first imagined, but their painstakingly-created structure of geological time has withstood the advent of high technology.

The 4,600 million years since the formation of the Earth are divided into four great eras, further split into periods and, in the case of the most recent era, epochs. The present era is the Cainozoic ('new life'), extending backwards through 'middle life' and 'ancient life' to the Pre-Cambrian, named after the Latin word for Wales, the location of some of the earliest known fossils. Most of the Earth's geological history is encompassed by the Pre-Cambrian: though traces of ancient life have since been found, it was largely the proliferation of fossils from the beginning of the Paleozoic era onwards, some 570 million years ago, which first allowed precise subdivisions to be made.

Like the Cambrian, most are named after regions exemplifying a period's geology. Others – such as the Carboniferous ('coal-bearing') or the Cretaceous ('chalk-bearing') – are more directly descriptive.

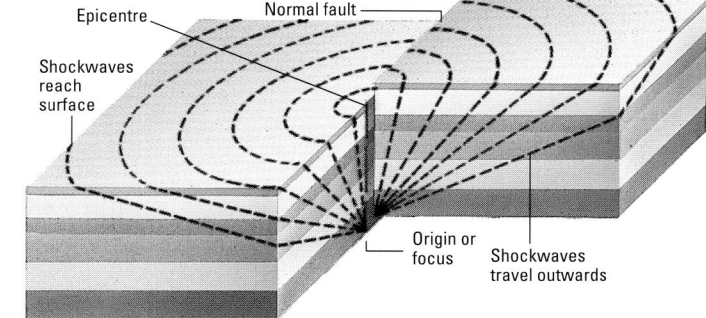

- Pre-Cambrian shields
- Sedimentary cover on Pre-Cambrian shields
- Paleozoic (Caledonian and Hercynian) folding
- Sedimentary cover on Paleozoic folding
- Mesozoic folding
- Sedimentary cover on Mesozoic folding
- Cainozoic (Alpine) folding
- Sedimentary cover on Cainozoic folding
- Intensive Mesozoic and Cainozoic vulcanism
- Principal faults
- Oceanic marginal troughs
- Mid-oceanic ridges
- Overthrust faults

EARTHQUAKES

NOTABLE EARTHQUAKES SINCE 1900

Year	Location	Mag.	Deaths
1906	San Francisco, USA	8.3	503
1906	Valparaiso, Chile	8.6	22,000
1908	Messina, Italy	7.5	83,000
1915	Avezzano, Italy	7.5	30,000
1920	Gansu (Kansu), China	8.6	180,000
1923	Yokohama, Japan	8.3	143,000
1927	Nan Shan, China	8.3	200,000
1932	Gansu (Kansu), China	7.6	70,000
1934	Bihar, India/Nepal	8.4	10,700
1935	Quetta, India*	7.5	60,000
1939	Chillan, Chile	8.3	28,000
1939	Erzincan, Turkey	7.9	30,000
1960	Agadir, Morocco	5.8	12,000
1962	Khorasan, Iran	7.1	12,230
1963	Skopje, Yugoslavia**	6.0	1,000
1964	Anchorage, Alaska	8.4	131
1968	N.E. Iran	7.4	12,000
1970	N. Peru	7.7	66,794
1972	Managua, Nicaragua	6.2	5,000
1974	N. Pakistan	6.3	5,200
1976	Guatemala	7.5	22,778
1976	Tangshan, China	8.2	650,000
1978	Tabas, Iran	7.7	25,000
1980	El Asnam, Algeria	7.3	20,000
1980	S. Italy	7.2	4,800
1985	Mexico City, Mexico	8.1	4,200
1988	N.W. Armenia	6.8	55,000
1990	N. Iran	7.7	36,000
1993	Maharashtra, India	6.4	30,000
1994	Los Angeles, USA	6.6	57
1995	Kobe, Japan	7.2	5,000

The highest magnitude recorded on the Richter scale is 8.9, in Japan on 2 March 1933 (2,990 deaths). The most devastating quake ever was at Shaanxi (Shensi) province, central China, on 24 January 1566, when an estimated 830,000 people were killed.

* now Pakistan
** now Macedonia

Earthquake magnitude is usually rated according to either the Richter or the Modified Mercalli scale, both devised by seismologists in the 1930s. The Richter scale measures absolute earthquake power with mathematical precision: each step upwards represents a ten-fold increase in shockwave amplitude. Theoretically, there is no upper limit, but the largest earthquakes measured have been rated at between 8.8 and 8.9. The 12–point Mercalli scale, based on observed effects, is often more meaningful, ranging from I (earthquakes noticed only by seismographs) to XII (total destruction); intermediate points include V (people awakened at night; unstable objects overturned), VII (collapse of ordinary buildings; chimneys and monuments fall) and IX (conspicuous cracks in ground; serious damage to reservoirs).

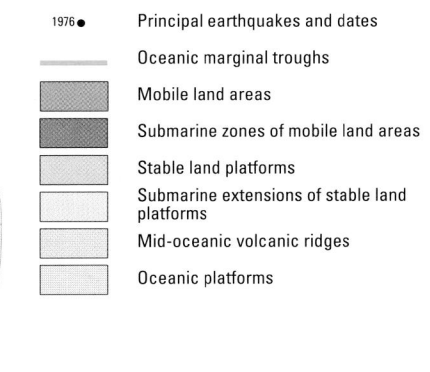

DISTRIBUTION

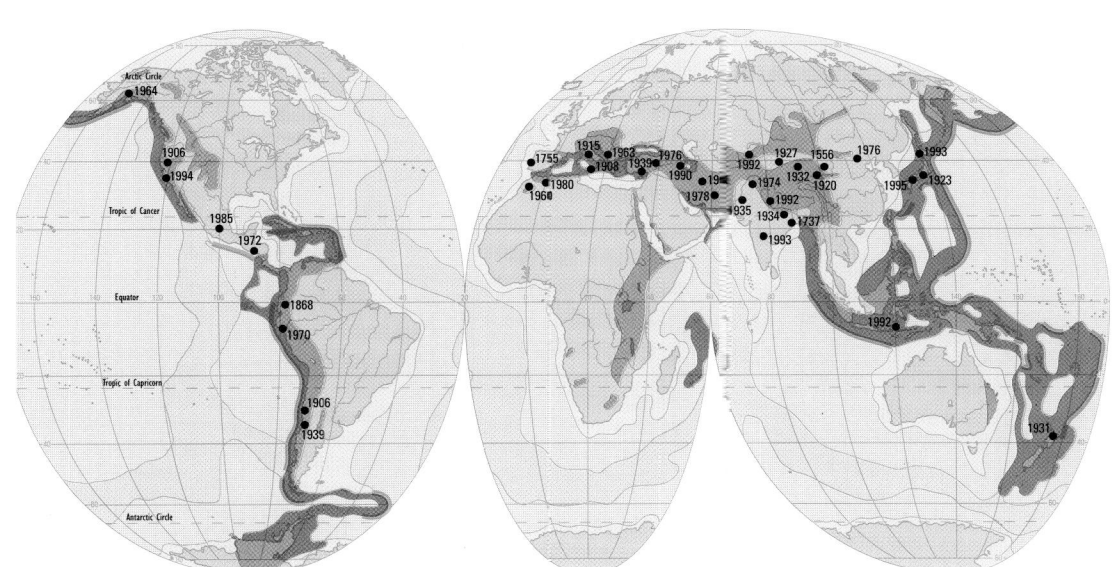

- 1976 ● Principal earthquakes and dates
- Oceanic marginal troughs
- Mobile land areas
- Submarine zones of mobile land areas
- Stable land platforms
- Submarine extensions of stable land platforms
- Mid-oceanic volcanic ridges
- Oceanic platforms

Earthquakes are a series of rapid vibrations originating from the slipping or faulting of parts of the Earth's crust when stresses within build to breaking point, and usually occur at depths between 8 and 30 kilometres.

THE EARTH: OCEANS

7:	TIDES
16:	HYDROLOGICAL CYCLE WATER DISTRIBUTION
17:	WATERSHEDS
18:	THE SPREADING EARTH
39:	SHIPPING
47:	WATER POLLUTION

The Earth is a misnamed planet: more than 70% of its total surface area – 361,740,000 square kilometres – is covered by its oceans and seas. This great cloak of liquid water gives the planet its characteristic blue appearance from space, and is one of two obvious differences between the Earth and its near-neighbours in space, Mars and Venus. The other difference is the presence of life, and the two are closely linked.

In a strict geographical sense, the Earth has only three oceans: the Atlantic, Pacific and Indian Oceans. Subdivided vertically instead of horizontally, however, there are many more. The most active is the sunlit upper layer, home of most sea life and the vital interface between air and water. In this surface zone, huge energies are exchanged between the oceans and the atmosphere above; it is also a kind of membrane through which the ocean breathes, absorbing great quantities of carbon dioxide and partially exchanging them for oxygen, largely through the phytoplankton, tiny plants that photosynthesize solar energy and provide the food base for all other marine life.

As depth increases, so light and colour gradually fade away, the longer wavelengths dying first. At 50 metres, the ocean is a world of green, blue and violet; at 100 metres, only blue remains; by 200 metres, there is only a dim twilight. The temperature falls away with the light, until just before 1,000 metres – the precise depth varies – there occurs a temperature change almost as abrupt as the transition between air and water far above. Below this thermocline, at a near-stable 3°C, the waters are forever unmoved by the winds of the upper world and are stirred only by the slow action of deep ocean currents. The pressure is crushing, reaching 1,000 atmospheres in the deepest trenches: a force of 1 tonne bearing down on every square centimetre.

Yet even here the oceans support life, and not only the handful of strange, deep-sea creatures that find a living in the near-empty abyss. The deep ocean serves as a gigantic storehouse, both for heat and for assorted atmospheric chemicals, regulating and balancing the proportions of various trace compounds and elements, and ensuring a large measure of stability for both the climate and the ecology that depend on it.

From the tidal zone at the coastline, the continental shelf, geologically still part of the continental landmass, drops gently to about 200 metres. At the end of the shelf, the seabed falls away in the steeper angle of the continental slope, exaggerated in this drawing, in which the horizontal scale has been greatly compressed. The subsequent descent to the deep ocean floor, known as the continental rise, is more gentle, with gradients between 1 in 100 and 1 in 700 until the abyssal plains, at between 2,500 and 6,000 metres below the surface. Most marine life is confined to the first 200 metres, where sunlight can still penetrate.

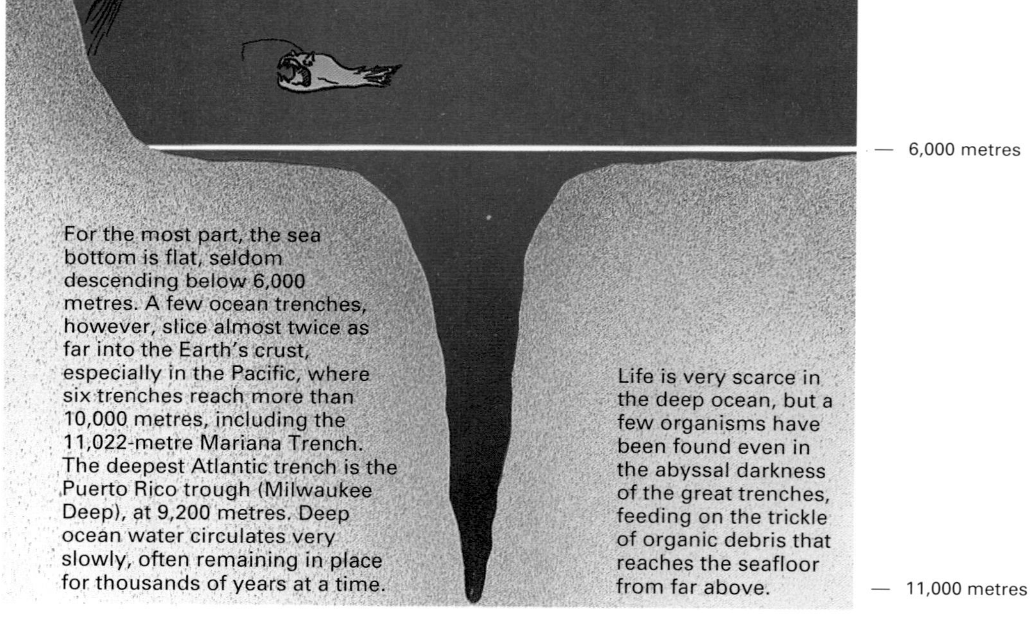

— Sea level
— 200 metres
— 500 metres
— 1,000 metres
— 1,500 metres
— 2,000 metres
— 6,000 metres
— 11,000 metres

ATOLL BUILDING

A coral atoll begins existence as a bare volcanic peak, thrusting above the ocean surface. A colony of coral – marine organisms called polyps, with skeletons of rigid calcium carbonate – forms itself in the shallow water around the peak. Its seafloor eruption over, the volcano slowly sinks, leaving the coral forming a ring around its remnant. In time, all obvious trace of the volcano vanishes, and the barrier reef of an atoll is all that remains.

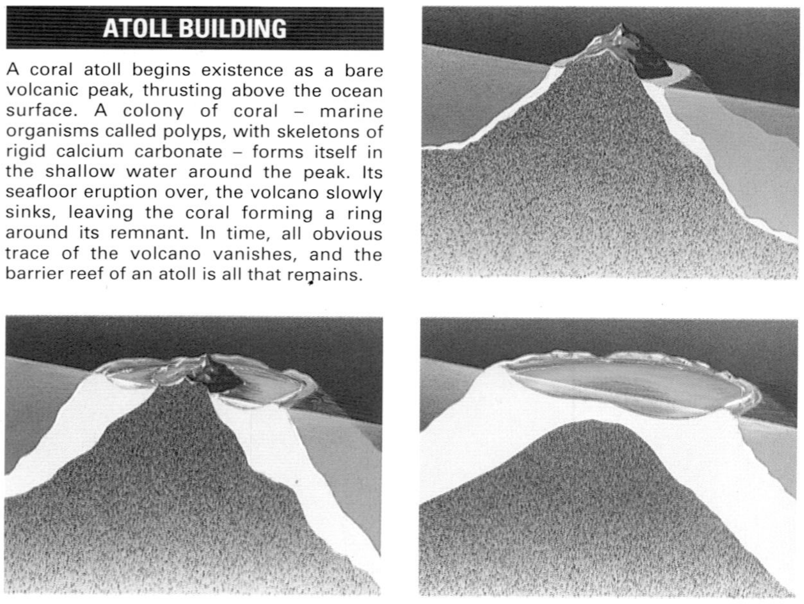

For the most part, the sea bottom is flat, seldom descending below 6,000 metres. A few ocean trenches, however, slice almost twice as far into the Earth's crust, especially in the Pacific, where six trenches reach more than 10,000 metres, including the 11,022-metre Mariana Trench. The deepest Atlantic trench is the Puerto Rico trough (Milwaukee Deep), at 9,200 metres. Deep ocean water circulates very slowly, often remaining in place for thousands of years at a time.

Life is very scarce in the deep ocean, but a few organisms have been found even in the abyssal darkness of the great trenches, feeding on the trickle of organic debris that reaches the seafloor from far above.

PROFILE OF AN OCEAN

The deep ocean floor is no more uniform than the surface of the continents, although it was not until the development of effective sonar equipment that it was possible to examine submarine contours in detail. The Atlantic (right) and the Pacific show similar patterns. Offshore comes the continental shelf, sliding downwards to the continental slope and the steeper continental rise, after which the seabed rolls onwards into the abyssal plains. In the wide Pacific, these are interrupted by gently-rising abyssal hills; in both oceans, the plains extend all the way to the mid-oceanic ridges, where the upwelling of new crustal material is constantly forcing the oceans wider. Volcanic activity is responsible for the formation of seamounts and tablemounts, or guyots, their flat-topped equivalents. In this cross-section, only the Azores are high enough to break the surface and become islands.

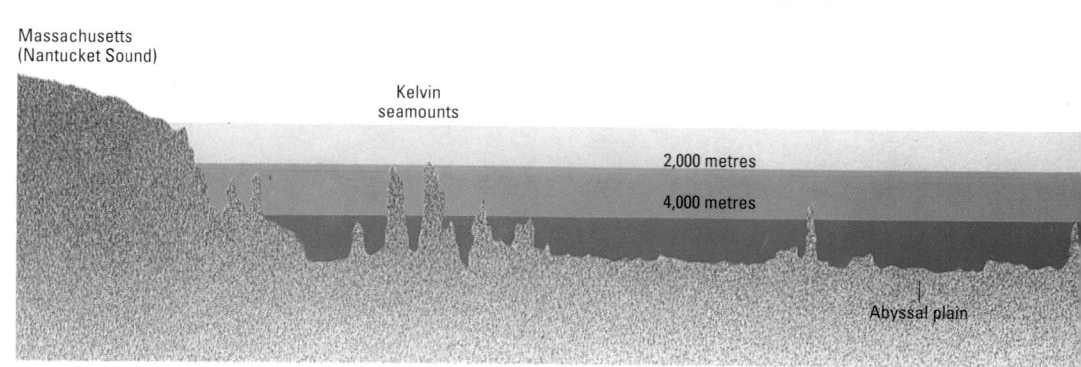

Massachusetts (Nantucket Sound)

Kelvin seamounts

2,000 metres

4,000 metres

Abyssal plain

OCEAN CURRENTS

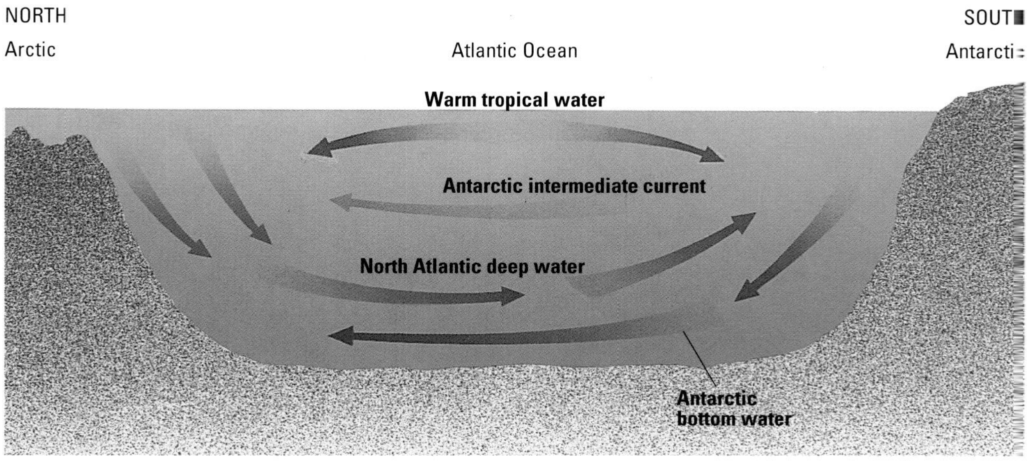

NORTH

Arctic

Atlantic Ocean

SOUTH

Antarctic

Warm tropical water

Antarctic intermediate current

North Atlantic deep water

Antarctic bottom water

Moving immense quantities of energy as well as billions of tonnes of water every hour, the ocean currents are a vital part of the great heat engine that drives the Earth's climate. They themselves are produced by a twofold mechanism. At the surface, winds push huge masses of water before them; in the deep ocean, below an abrupt temperature gradient that separates the churning surface waters from the still depths, density variations cause slow vertical movements.

The pattern of circulation of the great surface currents is determined by the displacement known as the Coriolis effect. As the Earth turns beneath a moving object – whether it is a tennis ball or a vast mass of water – it appears to be deflected to one side. The deflection is most obvious near the Equator, where the Earth's surface is spinning eastwards at 1700 km/h; currents moving polewards are curved clockwise in the northern hemisphere and anti-clockwise in the southern.

The result is a system of spinning circles known as gyres. The Coriolis effect piles up water on the left of each gyre, creating a narrow, fast-moving stream that is matched by a slower, broader returning current on the right. North and south of the Equator, the fastest currents are located in the west and in the east respectively. In each case, warm water moves from the Equator and cold water returns to it. Cold currents often bring an upwelling of nutrients with them, supporting the world's most economically important fisheries.

Depending on the prevailing winds, some currents on or near the Equator may reverse their direction in the course of the year – a seasonal variation on which Asian monsoon rains depend, and whose occasional failure can bring disaster to millions of people.

CURRENTS AND TEMPERATURES

(Northern Hemisphere: winter)

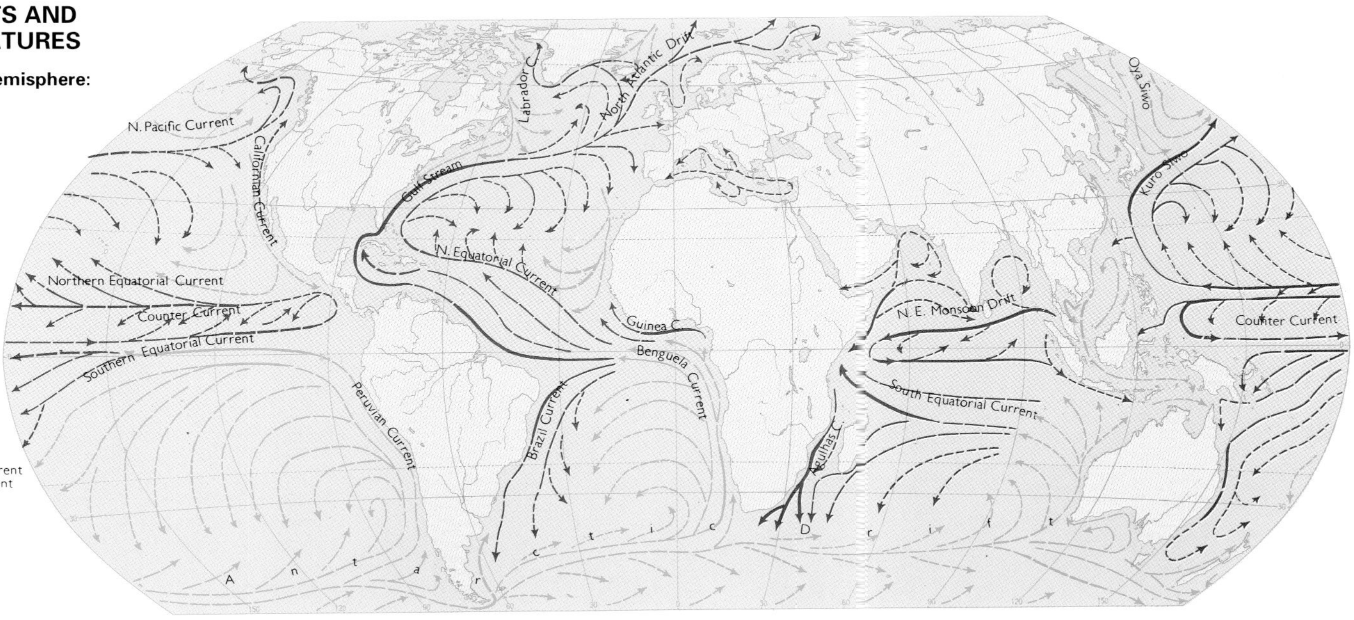

N. Pacific Current

Californian Current

Northern Equatorial Current

Counter Current

Southern Equatorial Current

Peruvian Current

Labrador

North Atlantic Drift

Gulf Stream

N. Equatorial Current

Guinea C

Benguela Current

Brazil Current

Oya Sivo

Kuro Sivo

N. E. Monsoon Drift

Counter Current

South Equatorial Current

Agulhas C.

Antarctic

← Warm Current
← Cold Current

CURRENTS AND TEMPERATURES

(Northern Hemisphere: summer)

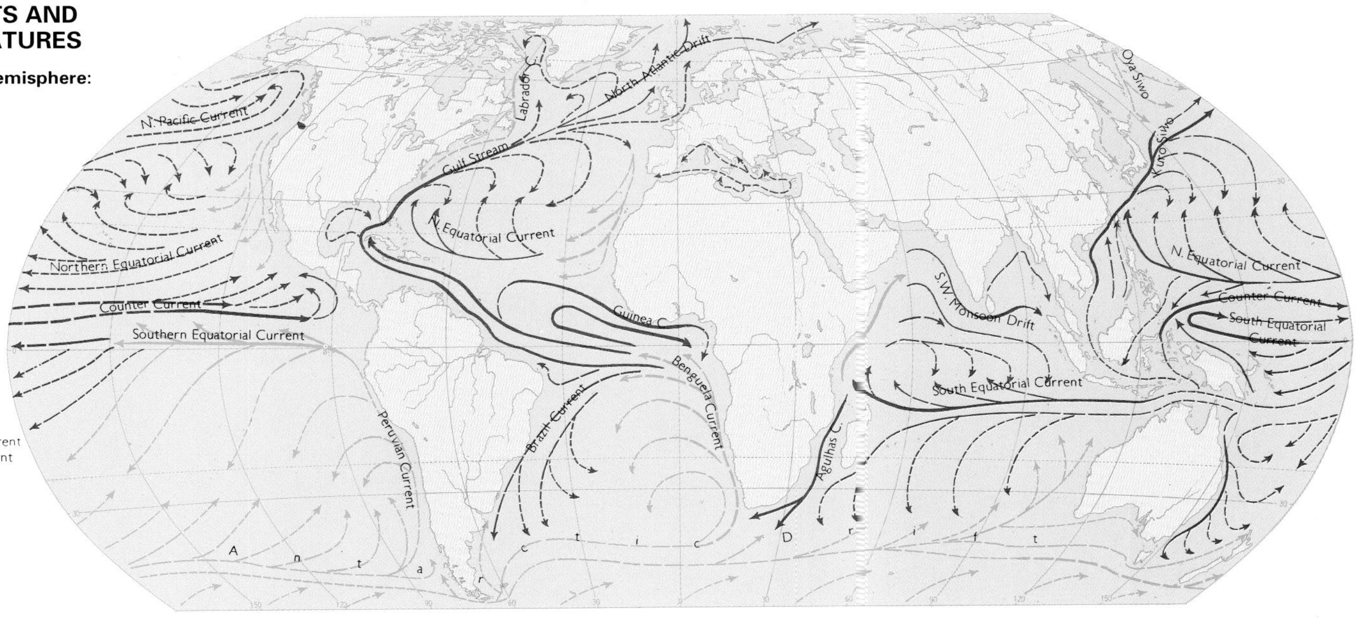

N. Pacific Current

Northern Equatorial Current

Counter Current

Southern Equatorial Current

Peruvian Current

Labrador

North Atlantic Drift

Gulf Stream

N. Equatorial Current

Guinea C

Benguela Current

Brazil Current

Agulhas C.

Oya Sivo

Kuro Sivo

N. Equatorial Current

Counter Current

South Equatorial Current

S.W. Monsoon Drift

South Equatorial Current

Antarctic

← Warm Current
← Cold Current

SEAWATER

The chemical composition of the sea, in grams per tonne of seawater, excluding the elements of water itself

Chlorine	19,400
Sodium	10,800
Magnesium	1,290
Sulphur	904
Calcium	411
Potassium	392
Bromine	67
Strontium	8.1
Boron	4.5
Fluorine	1.3
Lithium	0.17
Rubidium	0.12
Phosphorus	0.09
Iodine	0.06
Barium	0.02
Arsenic	0.003
Cesium	0.0003

Seawater also contains virtually every other element, although the quantities involved are too small for reliable measurement. In natural conditions, its composition is broadly consistent across the world's seas and oceans; but in coastal areas especially, variations, sometimes substantial, may be caused by the presence of industrial waste and sewage sludge.

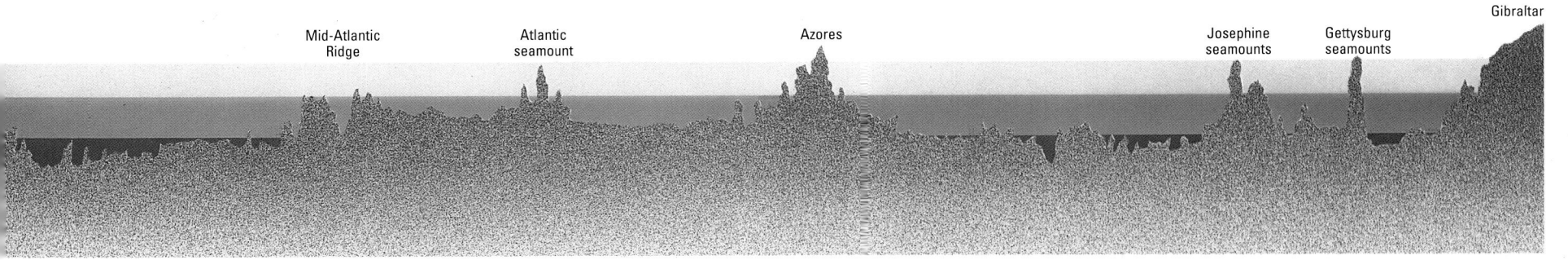

Mid-Atlantic Ridge · Atlantic seamount · Azores · Josephine seamounts · Gettysburg seamounts · Gibraltar

THE EARTH: ATMOSPHERE

11:	OCEAN CURRENTS
15:	BEAUFORT WIND SCALE
21:	SOLAR ENERGY GREENHOUSE EFFECT
46:	GREENHOUSE POWER
47:	ACID RAIN

Extending from the surface far into space, the atmosphere is a meteor shield, a radiation deflector, a thermal blanket and a source of chemical energy for the Earth's diverse inhabitants. Five-sixths of its mass is found in the first 15 kilometres, the troposphere, no thicker in relative terms than the skin of an onion. Clouds, cyclonic winds, precipitation and virtually all the phenomena we call weather occur in this narrow layer. Above, a thin layer of ozone blocks ultra-violet radiation. Beyond 100 kilometres, atmospheric density is lower than most laboratory vacuums, yet these tenuous outer reaches, composed largely of hydrogen and helium, trap cosmic debris and incoming high-energy particles alike.

CIRCULATION OF THE AIR

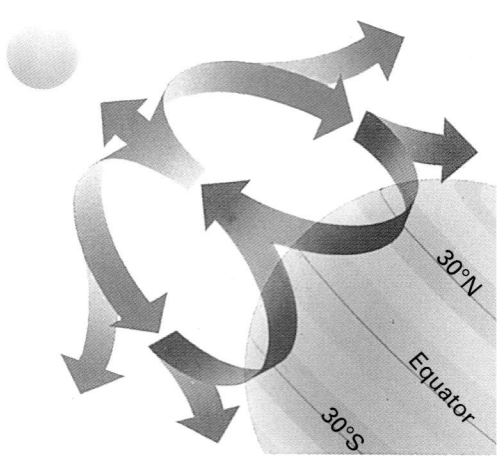

30°N

Equator

30°S

STRUCTURE OF ATMOSPHERE

1

2

F2

F1

E

D

Mesosphere
Ozone layer
Tropopause

3

4

TEMPERATURE

ca. 2,200°C

ca. 1,500°C

ca. 750°C

−58°C
−91°C
−93°C
−33°C
−8°C
−12°C
−38°C
−53°C

15°C

PRESSURE

$10^{-53}mb$

$10^{-47}mb$

$10^{-41}mb$

$10^{-35}mb$

$10^{-28}mb$

$10^{-22}mb$

$10^{-16}mb$

$10^{-10}mb$

$10^{-3}mb$

$10^{3}mb$

900 km

800 km

700 km

600 km

500 km

400 km

300 km

200 km

100 km

0

CHEMICAL STRUCTURE

Inner:
50% helium
50% hydrogen

Middle:
25% helium
75% hydrogen

Outer:
100% hydrogen

Exosphere

15% helium

15% oxygen
and atomic
oxygen

70% nitrogen

Ionosphere

1% ozone
1% argon

18% oxygen

80% nitrogen

Stratosphere

1% argon

21% oxygen

78% nitrogen

Troposphere

Exosphere
The atmosphere's upper layer has no clear outer boundary, merging imperceptibly with interplanetary space. Its lower boundary, at an altitude of approximately 600 kilometres, is almost equally vague. The exosphere is mainly composed of hydrogen and helium in changing proportions, with a small quantity of atomic oxygen up to 600 kilometres. Helium vanishes with increasing altitude, and above 2,400 kilometres the exosphere is almost entirely composed of hydrogen.

Ionosphere
Gas molecules in the ionosphere, mainly helium, oxygen and nitrogen, are electrically charged – ionized – by the Sun's radiation. Within the ionosphere's range of 50 to 600 kilometres in altitude, they group themselves into four layers, known conventionally as D, E, F1 and F2, all of which can reflect radio waves of differing frequencies. The high energy of ionospheric gas gives it a notional temperature of more than 2,000°C, although its density is negligible. The auroras – *aurora borealis* and its southern counterpart, *aurora australis* – occur in the ionosphere when charged particles from the Sun interact with the Earth's magnetic fields, at their strongest near the poles.

Stratosphere
Separated at its upper and lower limits by the distinct thresholds of the stratopause and the tropopause, the stratosphere is a remarkably stable layer between 50 kilometres and about 15 kilometres. Its temperature rises from −55°C at its lower extent to approximately 0°C near the stratopause, where a thin layer of ozone absorbs ultra-violet radiation. 'Mother-of-pearl' or nacreous cloud occurs at about 25 kilometres' altitude. Stratospheric air contains enough ozone to make it poisonous, although it is in any case far too rarified to breathe.

Troposphere
The narrowest of all the atmospheric layers, the troposphere extends up to 15 kilometres at the Equator but only 8 kilometres at the poles. Since this thin region contains about 85% of the atmosphere's total mass and almost all of its water vapour, it is also the realm of the Earth's weather. Temperatures fall steadily with increasing height by about 1°C for every 100 metres above sea level.

Heated by the relatively high surface temperatures near the Earth's Equator, air expands and rises to create a belt of low pressure. Moving northwards towards the poles, it gradually cools, sinking once more and producing high-pressure belts at about latitudes 30° North and South. Water vapour carried with the air falls as rain, releasing vast quantities of energy as well as liquid water when it condenses.

The high- and low-pressure belts are both areas of comparative calm, but between them, blowing from high-pressure to low-pressure areas, are the prevailing winds. The atmospheric circulatory system is enormously complicated by the Coriolis effect brought about by the spinning Earth: winds are deflected to the right in the northern hemisphere and to the left in the southern, giving rise to the typically cyclonic pattern of swirling clouds carried by the moving masses of air.

Although clouds appear in an almost infinite variety of shapes and sizes, there are recognizable features that form the basis of a classification first put forward by Luke Howard, a London chemist, in 1803 and later modified by the World Meteorological Organization. The system is derived from the altitude of clouds and whether they form hairlike filaments ('cirrus'), heaps or piles ('cumulus'), or layers ('stratus'). Each characteristic carries some kind of message – not always a clear one – to forecasters about the weather to come.

CLASSIFICATION OF CLOUDS

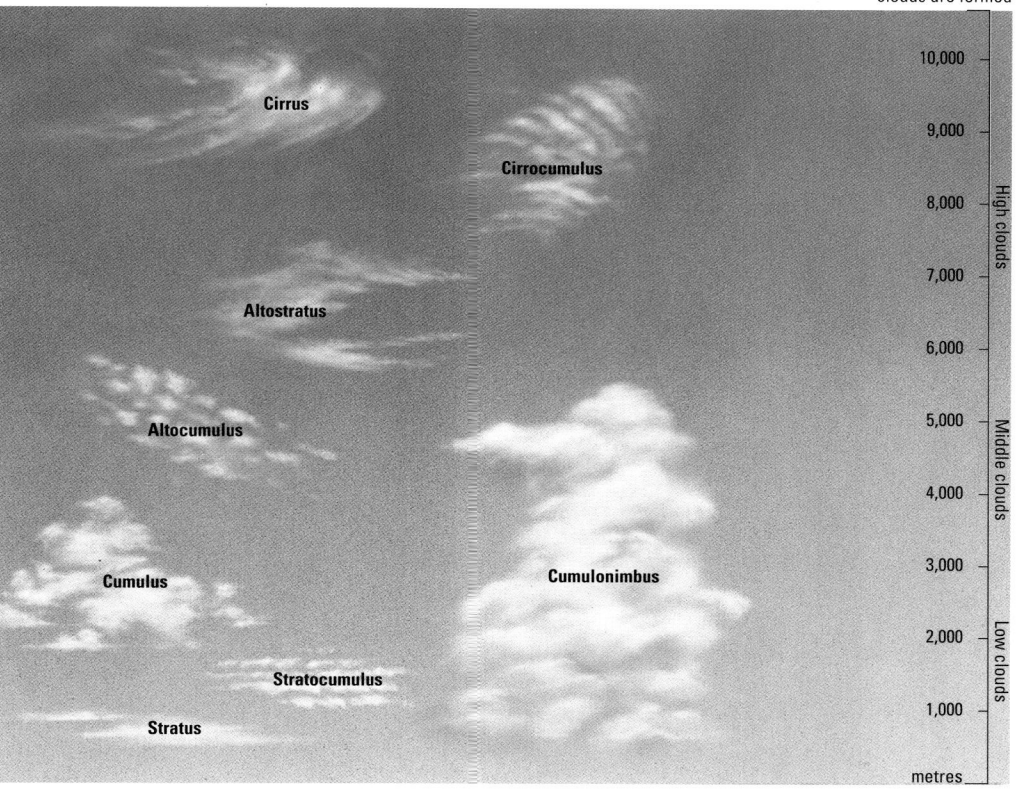

Altitude at which clouds are formed

Clouds form when damp, usually rising, air is cooled. Thus they form when a wind rises to cross hills or mountains; when a mass of air rises over, or is pushed up by, another mass of denser air; or when local heating of the ground causes convection currents.

The types of clouds are classified according to altitude as high, middle or low. The high ones, composed of ice crystals, are cirrus, cirrostratus and cirrocumulus. The middle clouds are altostratus, a grey or bluish striated, fibrous, or uniform sheet producing light drizzle, and altocumulus, a thicker and fluffier version of cirrocumulus.

The low clouds include nimbostratus, a dark grey layer that brings almost continuous rain or snow; cumulus, a detached 'heap' – brilliant white in sunlight but dark and flat at the base; and stratus, which forms dull, overcast skies at low altitudes.

Cumulonimbus, associated with storms and rains, heavy and dense with a flat base and a high, fluffy outline, can be tall enough to occupy middle as well as low altitudes.

PRESSURE AND WINDS

January

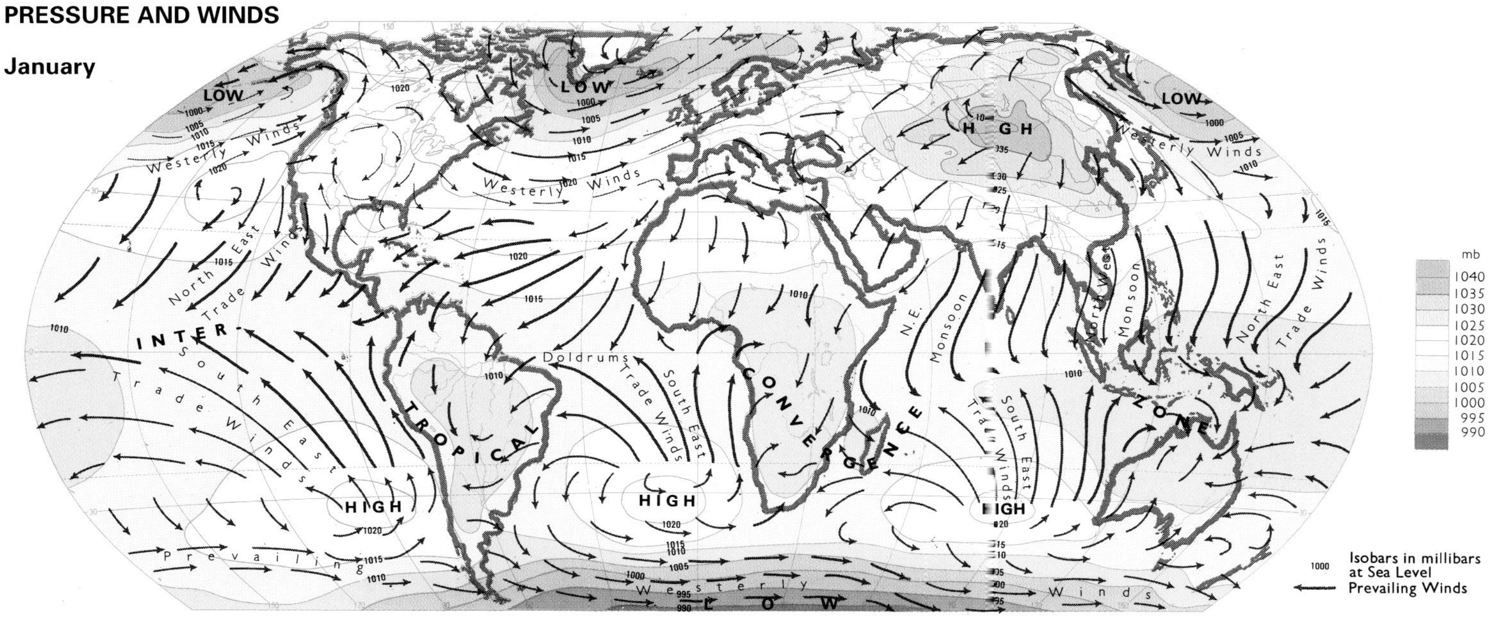

July

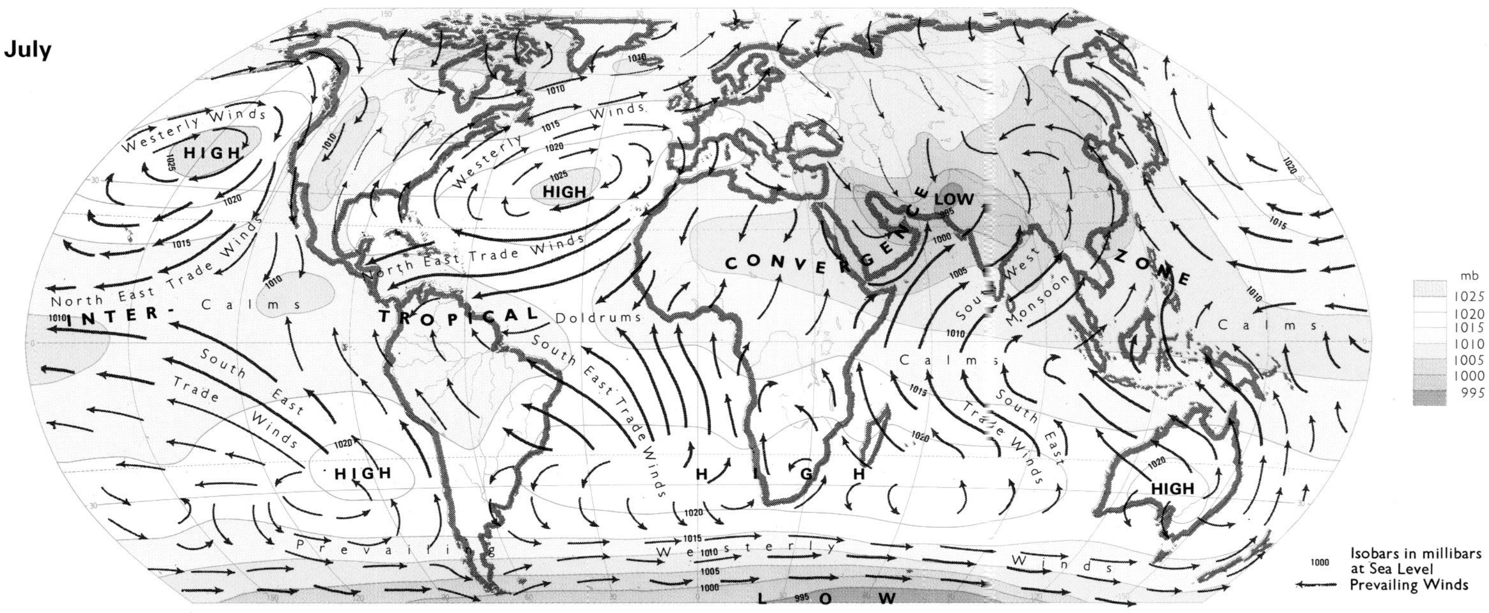

mb
1040
1035
1030
1025
1020
1015
1010
1005
1000
995
990

Isobars in millibars at Sea Level
Prevailing Winds

mb
1025
1020
1015
1010
1005
1000
995

Isobars in millibars at Sea Level
Prevailing Winds

THE EARTH: CLIMATE

11: OCEAN CURRENTS

12: CIRCULATION OF THE AIR

13: CLASSIFICATION OF CLOUDS PRESSURE AND WINDS

16: HYDROLOGICAL CYCLE

17: NATURAL VEGETATION

21: GREENHOUSE EFFECT

30: LAND USE

46: GLOBAL WARMING

Climate is weather in the long term: the seasonal pattern of hot and cold, wet and dry, averaged over time. At the simplest level, it is caused by the uneven heating of the Earth. Surplus heat at the Equator passes towards the poles, levelling out the energy differential. Its passage is marked by a ceaseless churning of the atmosphere and the oceans, further agitated by the Earth's diurnal spin and the motion it imparts to moving air and water. The heat's means of transport – by winds and ocean currents, by the continual evaporation and recondensation of water molecules – is the weather itself.

There are four basic types of climate, each of which is open to considerable subdivision: tropical, desert, temperate and polar. But although latitude is obviously a critical factor,

it is not the only determinant. The differential heating of land and sea, the funnelling and interruption of winds and ocean currents by landmasses and mountain ranges, and the transpiration of vegetation: all these factors combine to add complexity. New York, Naples and the Gobi Desert share almost the same latitude, for example, but their climates are very different. And although the sheer intricacy of the weather system often defies day-to-day prediction in these or any other places – despite the many satellites and number-crunching supercomputers with which present-day meteorologists are now equipped – their climatic patterns retain a year-on-year stability.

They are not indefinitely stable, however. The planet regularly passes through long,

cool periods lasting about 100,000 years: these are the Ice Ages, probably caused by recurring long-term oscillations in the Earth's orbital path and fluctuations in the Sun's energy output. In the present era, the Earth is nearest to the Sun in the middle of the northern hemisphere's winter; 11,000 years ago, at the end of the last Ice Age, the northern winter fell with the Sun at its most distant.

Left to its own devices, the climate even now should be drifting towards another glacial period. But global warming caused by increasing carbon dioxide levels in the atmosphere, largely the result of 20th-century fuel-burning and deforestation, may well precipitate change far faster than the great, slow cycles of the Solar System.

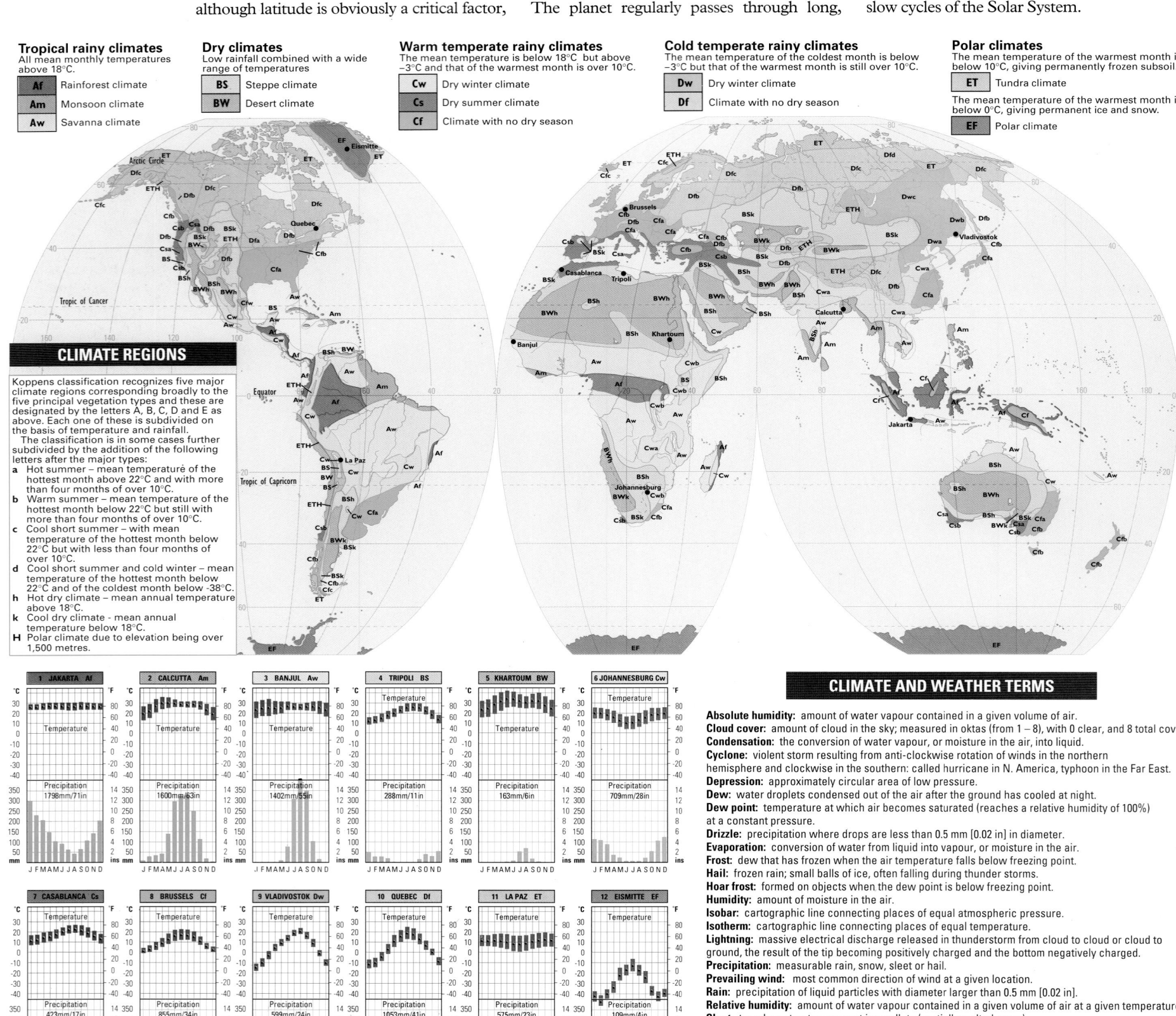

Tropical rainy climates
All mean monthly temperatures above 18°C.

Af	Rainforest climate
Am	Monsoon climate
Aw	Savanna climate

Dry climates
Low rainfall combined with a wide range of temperatures

| BS | Steppe climate |
| BW | Desert climate |

Warm temperate rainy climates
The mean temperature is below 18°C but above –3°C and that of the warmest month is over 10°C.

Cw	Dry winter climate
Cs	Dry summer climate
Cf	Climate with no dry season

Cold temperate rainy climates
The mean temperature of the coldest month is below –3°C but that of the warmest month is still over 10°C.

| Dw | Dry winter climate |
| Df | Climate with no dry season |

Polar climates
The mean temperature of the warmest month is below 10°C, giving permanently frozen subsoil.

| ET | Tundra climate |

The mean temperature of the warmest month is below 0°C, giving permanent ice and snow.

| EF | Polar climate |

CLIMATE REGIONS

Koppens classification recognizes five major climate regions corresponding broadly to the five principal vegetation types and these are designated by the letters A, B, C, D and E as above. Each one of these is subdivided on the basis of temperature and rainfall.
The classification is in some cases further subdivided by the addition of the following letters after the major types:
a Hot summer – mean temperature of the hottest month above 22°C and with more than four months of over 10°C.
b Warm summer – mean temperature of the hottest month below 22°C but still with more than four months of over 10°C.
c Cool short summer – with mean temperature of the hottest month below 22°C but with less than four months of over 10°C.
d Cool short summer and cold winter – mean temperature of the hottest month below 22°C and of the coldest month below -38°C.
h Hot dry climate – mean annual temperature above 18°C.
k Cool dry climate - mean annual temperature below 18°C.
H Polar climate due to elevation being over 1,500 metres.

CLIMATE AND WEATHER TERMS

Absolute humidity: amount of water vapour contained in a given volume of air.
Cloud cover: amount of cloud in the sky; measured in oktas (from 1 – 8), with 0 clear, and 8 total cover.
Condensation: the conversion of water vapour, or moisture in the air, into liquid.
Cyclone: violent storm resulting from anti-clockwise rotation of winds in the northern hemisphere and clockwise in the southern: called hurricane in N. America, typhoon in the Far East.
Depression: approximately circular area of low pressure.
Dew: water droplets condensed out of the air after the ground has cooled at night.
Dew point: temperature at which air becomes saturated (reaches a relative humidity of 100%) at a constant pressure.
Drizzle: precipitation where drops are less than 0.5 mm [0.02 in] in diameter.
Evaporation: conversion of water from liquid into vapour, or moisture in the air.
Frost: dew that has frozen when the air temperature falls below freezing point.
Hail: frozen rain; small balls of ice, often falling during thunder storms.
Hoar frost: formed on objects when the dew point is below freezing point.
Humidity: amount of moisture in the air.
Isobar: cartographic line connecting places of equal atmospheric pressure.
Isotherm: cartographic line connecting places of equal temperature.
Lightning: massive electrical discharge released in thunderstorm from cloud to cloud or cloud to ground, the result of the tip becoming positively charged and the bottom negatively charged.
Precipitation: measurable rain, snow, sleet or hail.
Prevailing wind: most common direction of wind at a given location.
Rain: precipitation of liquid particles with diameter larger than 0.5 mm [0.02 in].
Relative humidity: amount of water vapour contained in a given volume of air at a given temperature.
Sleet: translucent or transparent ice-pellets (partially melted snow).
Snow: formed when water vapour condenses below freezing point.
Thunder: sound produced by the rapid expansion of air heated by lightning.
Tidal wave: giant ocean wave generated by earthquakes (tsunami) or cyclonic winds.
Tornado: severe funnel-shaped storm that twists as hot air spins vertically (waterspout at sea).
Whirlwind: rapidly rotating column of air, only a few metres across, made visible by dust.

In sub-zero weather, even moderate winds significantly reduce effective temperatures. The chart below shows the windchill effect across a range of speeds. Figures in the pink zone are not dangerous to well-clad people; in the blue zone, the risk of serious frostbite is acute.

	Wind speed (km/h)				
	16	32	48	64	80
0°C	-8	-14	-17	-19	-20
-5°C	-14	-21	-25	-27	-28
-10°C	-20	-28	-33	-35	-36
-15°C	-26	-36	-40	-43	-44
-20°C	-32	-42	-48	-51	-52
-25°C	-38	-49	-56	-59	-60
-30°C	-44	-57	-63	-66	-68
-35°C	-51	-64	-72	-74	-76
-40°C	-57	-71	-78	-82	-84
-45°C	-63	-78	-86	-90	-92
-50°C	-69	-85	-94	-98	-100

BEAUFORT WIND SCALE

Named for the 19th-century British naval officer who devised it, the Beaufort Scale assesses wind speed according to its effects. It was originally designed as an aid for sailors, but has since been adapted for use on land.

Scale	Wind speed km/h	mph	Effect
0	0-1	0-1	**Calm** Smoke rises vertically
1	1-5	1-3	**Light air** Wind direction shown only by smoke drift
2	6-11	4-7	**Light breeze** Wind felt on face; leaves rustle; vanes moved by wind
3	12-19	8-12	**Gentle breeze** Leaves and small twigs in constant motion; wind extends small flag.
4	20-28	13-18	**Moderate** Raises dust and loose paper; small branches move
5	29-38	19-24	**Fresh** Small trees in leaf sway; crested wavelets on inland waters
6	39-49	25-31	**Strong** Large branches move; difficult to use umbrellas; overhead wires whistle
7	50-61	32-38	**Near gale** Whole trees in motion; difficult to walk against wind
8	62-74	39-46	**Gale** Twigs break from trees; walking very difficult
9	75-88	47-54	**Strong gale** Slight structural damage
10	89-102	55-63	**Storm** Trees uprooted; serious structural damage
11	103-117	64-72	**Violent storm** Widespread damage
12	118+	73+	**Hurricane**

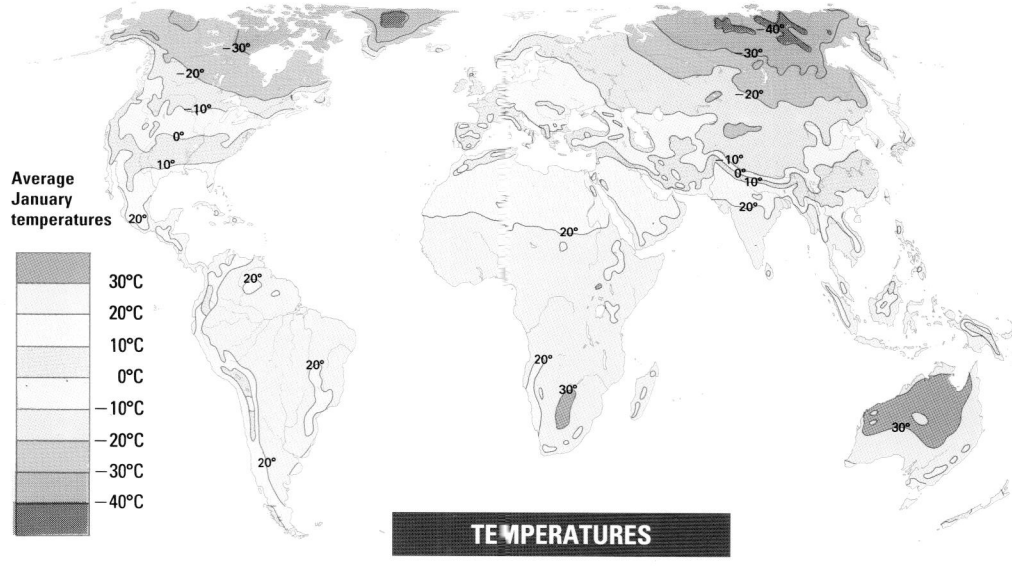

Average January temperatures

30°C
20°C
10°C
0°C
-10°C
-20°C
-30°C
-40°C

TEMPERATURES

Average July temperatures

30°C
20°C
10°C
0°C
-10°C

Average annual precipitation

3000 mm
2000 mm
1000 mm
500 mm
250 mm

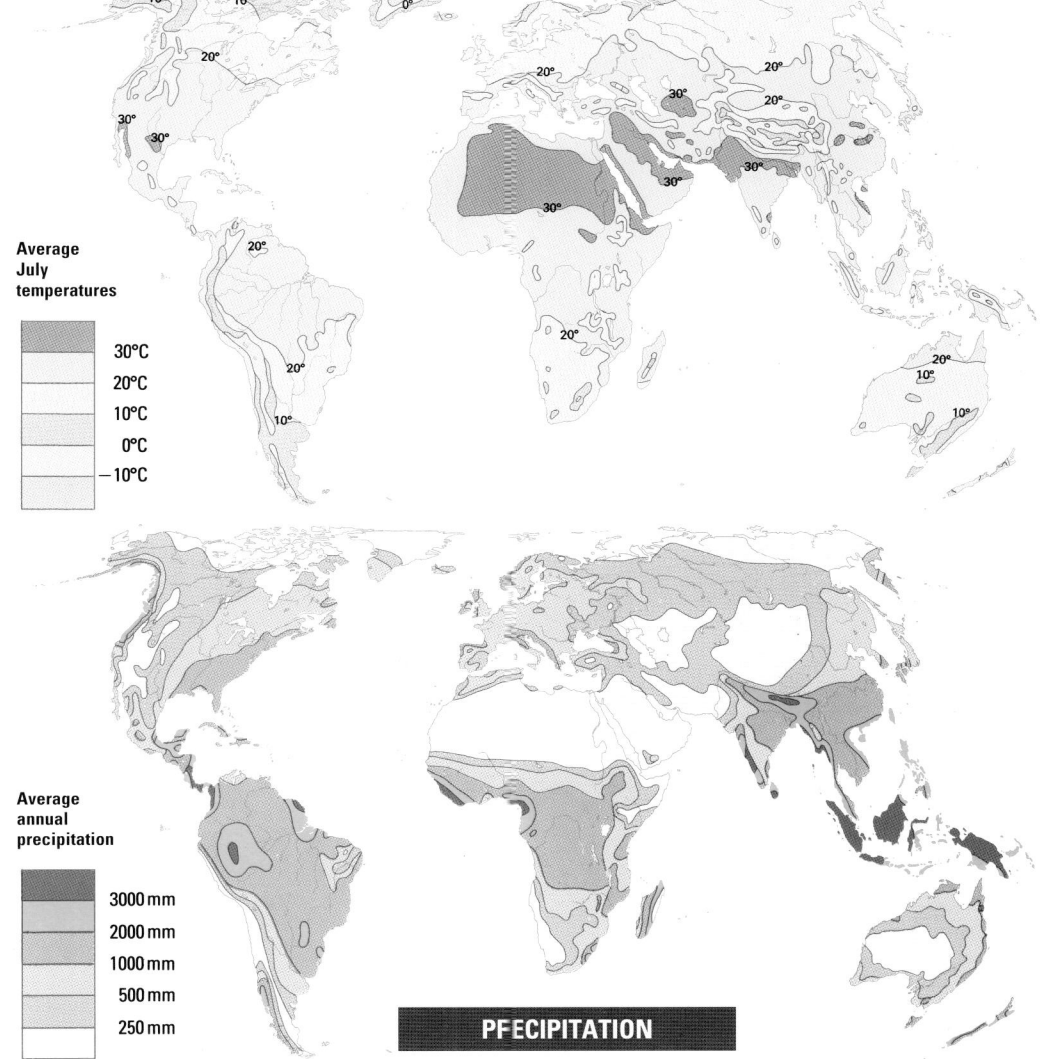

PRECIPITATION

CLIMATE RECORDS

Temperature

Highest recorded temperature: Al Aziziyah, Libya, 58°C [136.4°F], 13 September 1922.

Highest mean annual temperature: Dallol, Ethiopia, 34.4°C [94°F], 1960–66.

Longest heatwave: Marble Bar, W. Australia, 162 days over 38°C [100°F], 23 October 1923 to 7 April 1924.

Lowest recorded temperature (outside poles): Verkhoyansk, Siberia, –68°C [–90°F], 6 February 1933. Verkhoyansk also registered the greatest annual range of temperature: –70°C to 37°C [–94°F to 98°F].

Lowest mean annual temperature: Polus Nedostupnosti, Pole of Cold, Antarctica, –57.8°C [–72°F].

Precipitation

Driest place: Arica, N. Chile, 0.8mm [0.03 in] per year (60-year average).

Longest drought: Calama, N. Chile: no recorded rainfall in 400 years to 1971.

Wettest place (average): Tututendo, Colombia: mean annual rainfall 11,770 mm [463.4 in].

Wettest place (12 months): Cherrapunji, Meghalaya, N.E. India, 26,470 mm [1,040 in], August 1860 to August 1861. Cherrapunji also holds the record for rainfall in one month: 930 mm [37 in], July 1861.

Wettest place (24 hours): Cilaos, Réunion, Indian Ocean, 1,870 mm [73.6 in], 15–16 March 1952.

Heaviest hailstones: Gopalganj, Bangladesh, up to 1.02 kg [2.25 lb], 14 April 1986 (killed 92 people).

Heaviest snowfall (continuous): Bessans, Savoie, France, 1,730 mm [68 in] in 19 hours, 5–6 April 1969.

Heaviest snowfall (season/year): Paradise Ranger Station, Mt Rainier, Washington, USA, 31,102 mm [1,224.5 in], 19 February 1971 to 18 February 1972.

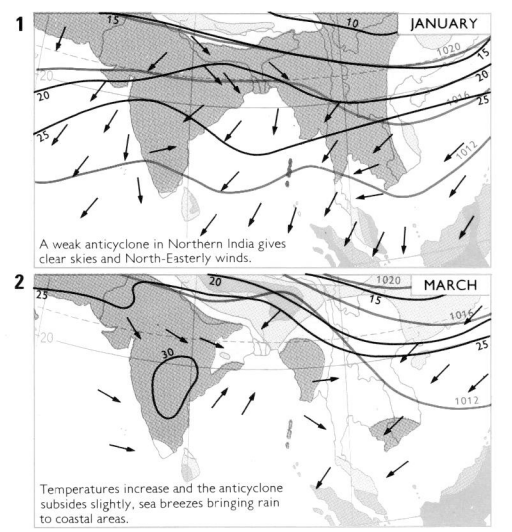

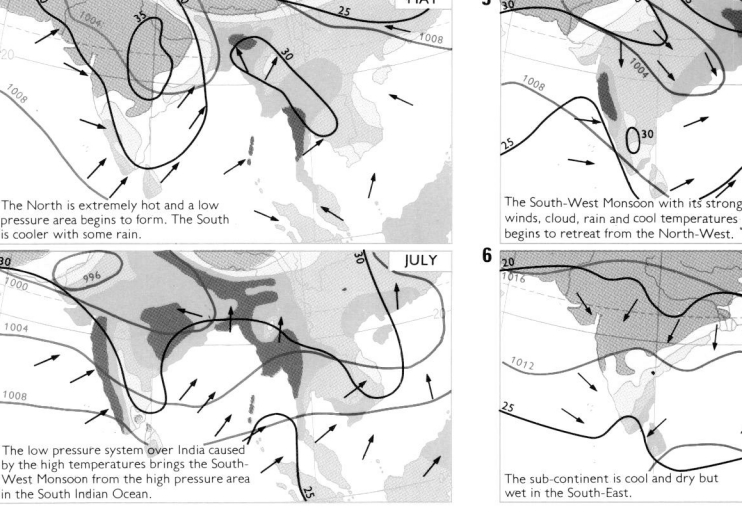

1 JANUARY
A weak anticyclone in Northern India gives clear skies and North-Easterly winds.

2 MARCH
Temperatures increase and the anticyclone subsides slightly, sea breezes bringing rain to coastal areas.

3 MAY
The North is extremely hot and a low pressure area begins to form. The South is cooler with some rain.

4 JULY
The low pressure system over India caused by the high temperatures brings the South-West Monsoon from the high pressure area in the South Indian Ocean.

5 SEPTEMBER
The South-West Monsoon with its strong winds, cloud, rain and cool temperatures begins to retreat from the North-West.

6 NOVEMBER
The sub-continent is cool and dry but wet in the South-East.

COPYRIGHT. GEORGE. PHILIP & SON. LTD.

THE MONSOON

While it is crucial to the agriculture of South Asia, the monsoon that follows the dry months is unpredictable – in duration as well as intensity. A season of very heavy rainfall, causing disastrous floods, can be succeeded by years of low precipitation, leading to serious drought.

Monthly rainfall

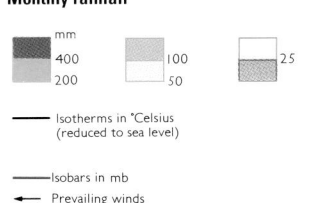

mm
400
200
100
50
25

Isotherms in °Celsius (reduced to sea level)

Isobars in mb

Prevailing winds

THE EARTH: WATER AND LAND USE

14: TYPES OF
PRECIPITATION

15: RAINFALL
THE MONSOON
CLIMATE RECORDS

19: SHAPING FORCES:
RIVERS AND GLACIERS

Fresh water is essential to all terrestrial life, from the humblest bacterium to the most advanced technological society. Yet freshwater resources form a minute fraction of the Earth's 1.41 billion cubic kilometres of water: most human needs must be met from the 2,000 cubic kilometres circulating in rivers at any one time. Agriculture accounts for huge quantities: without large-scale irrigation, most of the world's people would starve. And since fresh water is just as essential for most industrial processes – smelting a tonne of nickel, for example, requires about 4,000 tonnes of water – the growth of population and advancing industry have together put water supplies under strain.

Fortunately, water is seldom used up: the planet's hydrological cycle circulates it with benign efficiency, at least on a global scale. More locally, though, human activity can cause severe shortages: water for industry and agriculture is being withdrawn from many river basins and underground aquifers faster than natural recirculation can replace it.

THE HYDROLOGICAL CYCLE

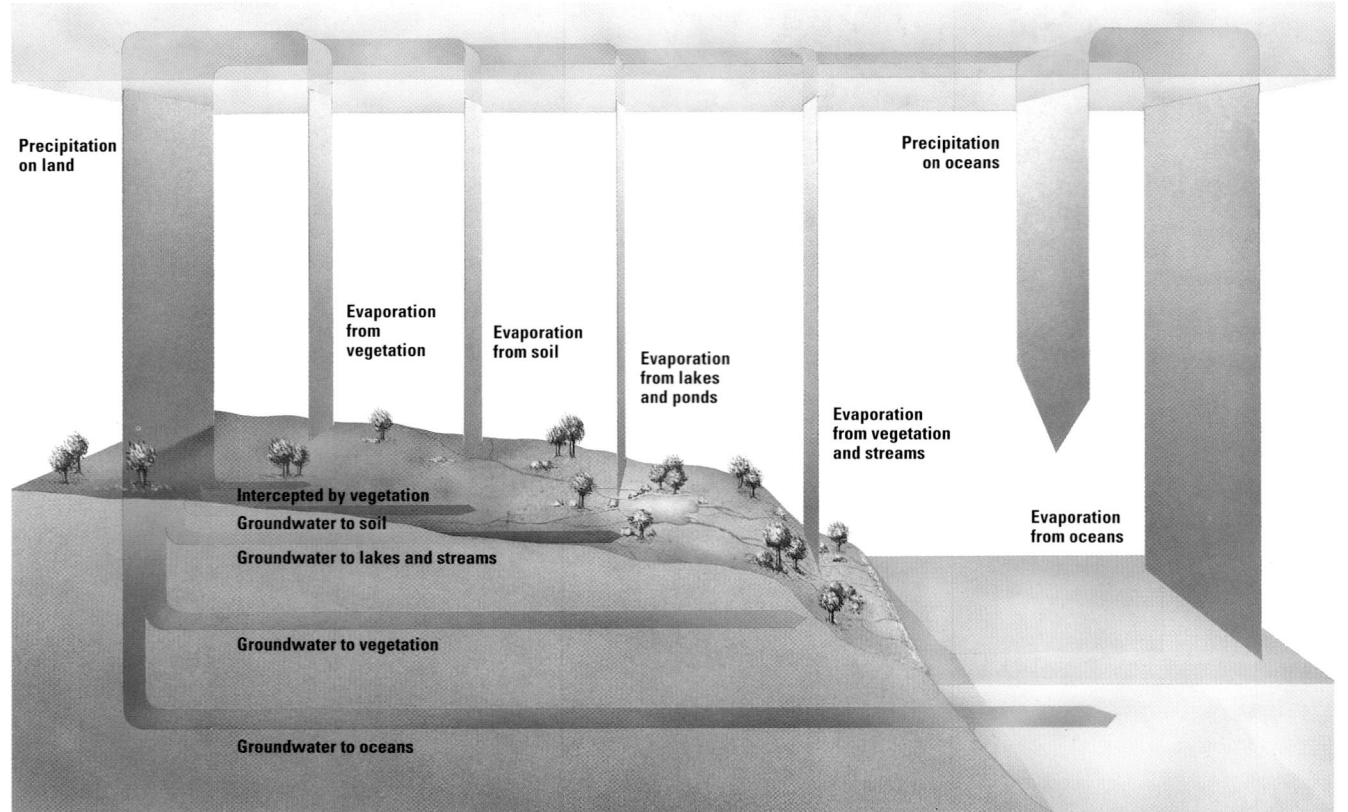

Precipitation on land
Precipitation on oceans
Evaporation from vegetation
Evaporation from soil
Evaporation from lakes and ponds
Evaporation from vegetation and streams
Evaporation from oceans
Intercepted by vegetation
Groundwater to soil
Groundwater to lakes and streams
Groundwater to vegetation
Groundwater to oceans

Water vapour is constantly drawn into the air from the Earth's rivers, lakes, seas and plant transpiration. In the atmosphere, it circulates around the planet, transporting energy as well as water itself. When the vapour cools it falls as rain or snow, and returns to the surface to evaporate once more. The whole cycle is driven by the Sun.

WATER DISTRIBUTION

The distribution of planetary water, by percentage. Oceans and ice-caps together account for more than 99% of the total; the breakdown of the remainder is estimated.

ALL WATER
97.4%
2.6%
Oceans
Fresh water

FRESH WATER
76.6%
0.5%
22.7%
Ice-caps and glaciers
Groundwater
Active water

ACTIVE WATER
52%
36%
1.4%
7.1%
3.5%
Lakes
Soil moisture
Atmosphere
Rivers
Living things

Almost all the world's water is 3,000 million years old, and all of it cycles endlessly through the hydrosphere, though at different rates. Water vapour circulates over days, even hours, deep ocean water circulates over millenia, and ice-cap water remains solid for millions of years.

WATER RUNOFF

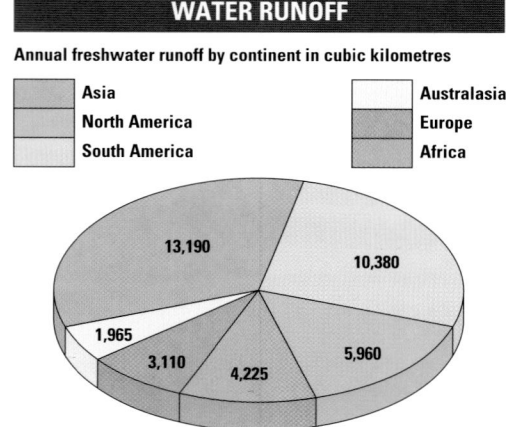

Annual freshwater runoff by continent in cubic kilometres

Asia
North America
South America
Australasia
Europe
Africa

13,190
10,380
1,965
3,110
4,225
5,960

WATER UTILIZATION

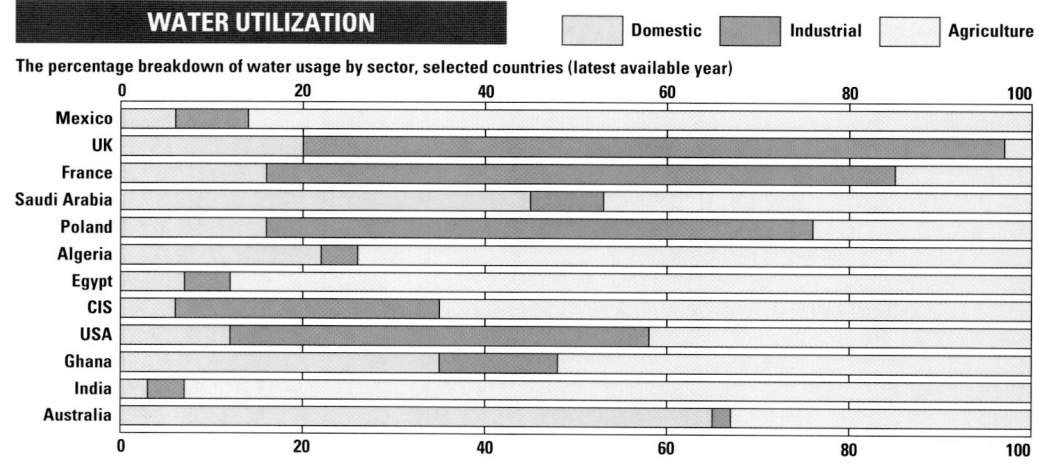

Domestic   Industrial   Agriculture

The percentage breakdown of water usage by sector, selected countries (latest available year)

Mexico
UK
France
Saudi Arabia
Poland
Algeria
Egypt
CIS
USA
Ghana
India
Australia

WATER SUPPLY

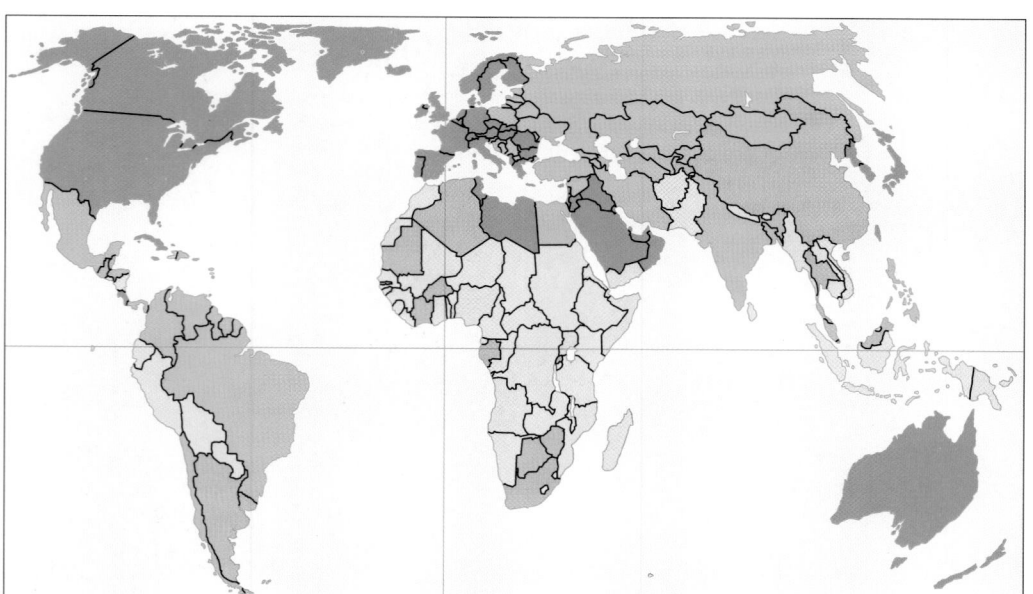

Percentage of total population with access to safe drinking water (latest available year)

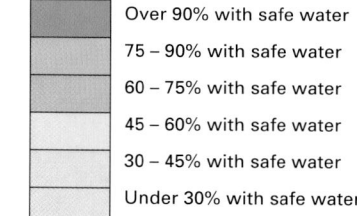

Over 90% with safe water
75 – 90% with safe water
60 – 75% with safe water
45 – 60% with safe water
30 – 45% with safe water
Under 30% with safe water

Least well-provided countries

Mozambique 22%
Madagascar 23%
Central African Rep. 24%
Vietnam 24%
Ethiopia 25%
Afghanistan 29%
Burma 32%
Papua New Guinea .. 33%
Uganda 33%
Bhutan 34%

WATERSHEDS

The world's major rivers; the world's 20 longest are shown in square brackets, led by the Nile and the Amazon.

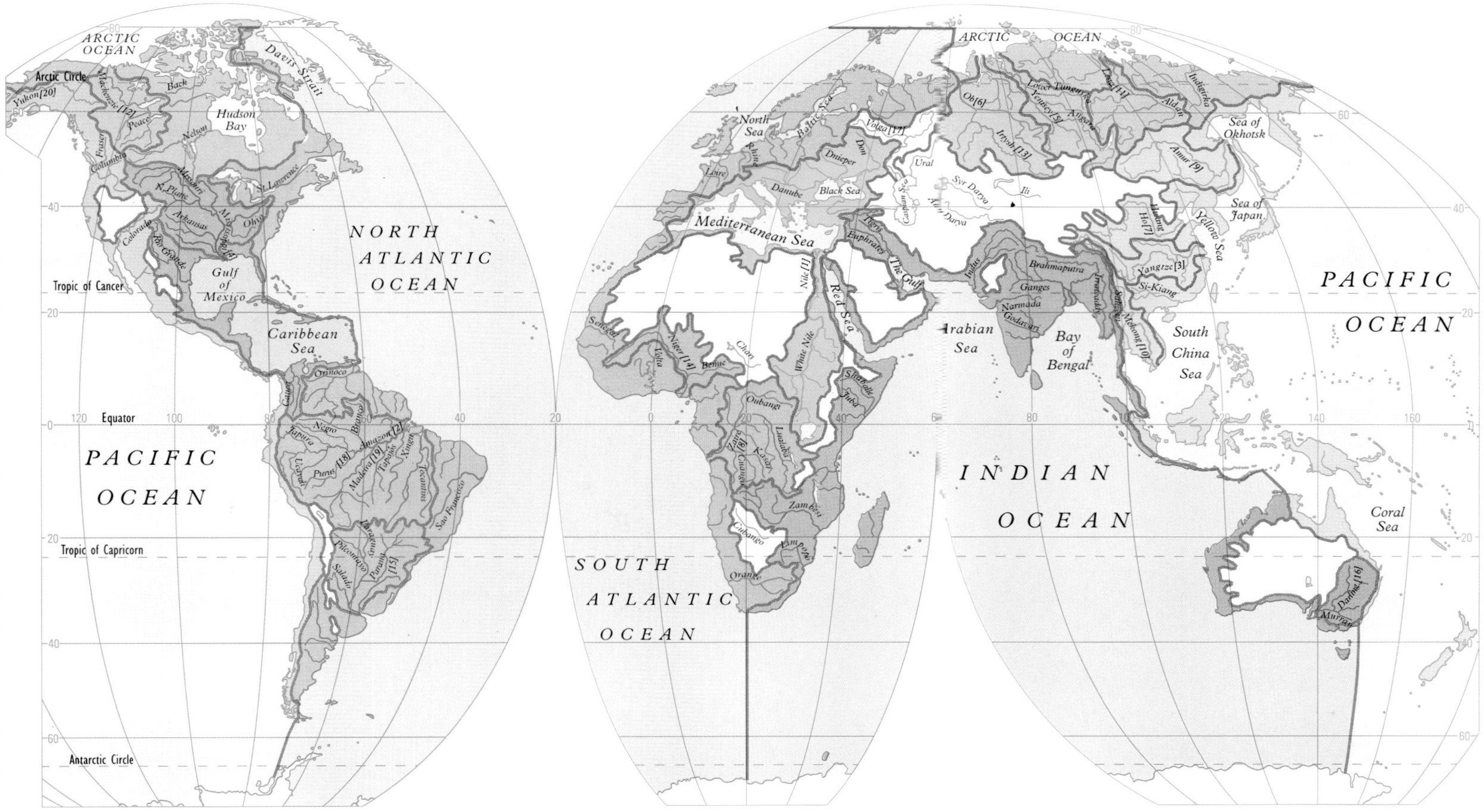

WHERE THE RIVERS RUN

- Pacific Ocean
- Indian Ocean
- Arctic Ocean
- Atlantic Ocean
- Caribbean Sea-Gulf of Mexico
- Mediterranean Sea
- Inland basins, ice-caps and deserts

The map shows the direction of freshwater flow on a continental scale; the chart opposite indicates the quantities involved. The rate of runoff varies seasonally and is affected by the surface vegetation.

LAND USE BY CONTINENT

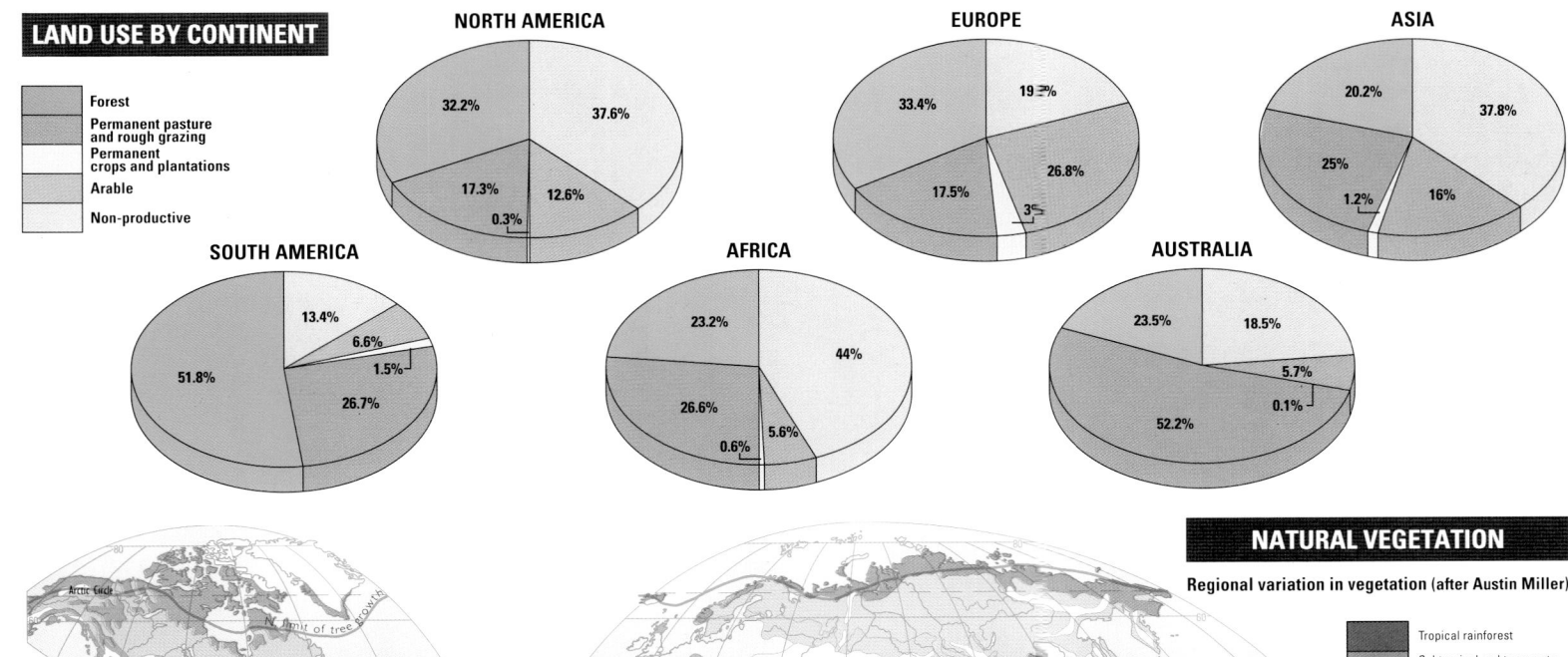

Legend:
- Forest
- Permanent pasture and rough grazing
- Permanent crops and plantations
- Arable
- Non-productive

NORTH AMERICA
37.6% / 12.6% / 0.3% / 17.3% / 32.2%

EUROPE
19.3% / 26.8% / 3% / 17.5% / 33.4%

ASIA
37.8% / 16% / 1.2% / 25% / 20.2%

SOUTH AMERICA
13.4% / 6.6% / 1.5% / 26.7% / 51.8%

AFRICA
44% / 5.6% / 0.6% / 26.6% / 23.2%

AUSTRALIA
18.5% / 5.7% / 0.1% / 52.2% / 23.5%

The proportion of productive land has reached its upper limit in Europe, and in Asia more than 80% of potential cropland is already under cultivation. Elsewhere, any increase is often matched by corresponding losses due to desertification and erosion; projections for 2025 show a decline in cropland per capita for all continents, most notably in Africa.

NATURAL VEGETATION

Regional variation in vegetation (after Austin Miller)

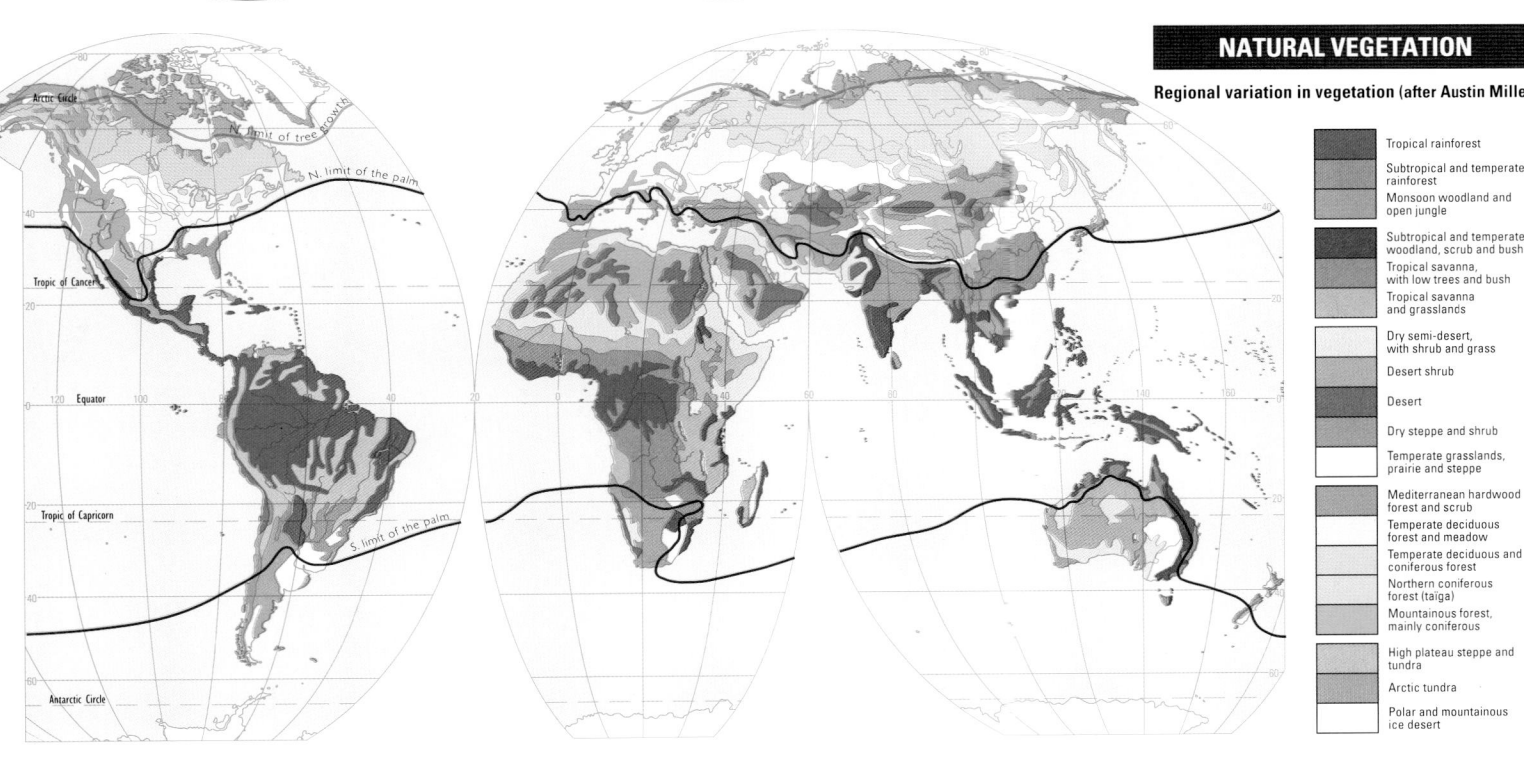

Legend:
- Tropical rainforest
- Subtropical and temperate rainforest
- Monsoon woodland and open jungle
- Subtropical and temperate woodland, scrub and bush
- Tropical savanna, with low trees and bush
- Tropical savanna and grasslands
- Dry semi-desert, with shrub and grass
- Desert shrub
- Desert
- Dry steppe and shrub
- Temperate grasslands, prairie and steppe
- Mediterranean hardwood forest and scrub
- Temperate deciduous forest and meadow
- Temperate deciduous and coniferous forest
- Northern coniferous forest (taiga)
- Mountainous forest, mainly coniferous
- High plateau steppe and tundra
- Arctic tundra
- Polar and mountainous ice desert

The map illustrates the natural 'climax vegetation' of a region, as dictated by its climate and topography. In most cases, human agricultural activity has drastically altered the vegetation pattern. Western Europe, for example, lost most of its broadleaf forest many centuries ago, while irrigation has turned some natural semi-desert into productive land.

THE EARTH: LANDSCAPE

8: THE EARTH'S
STRUCTURE
PLATE TECTONICS
VOLCANOES

9: GEOLOGICAL TIME

10: OCEANS

16: HYDROLOGICAL CYCLE

34: STRUCTURAL REGIONS

Above and below the surface of the oceans, the features of the Earth's crust are constantly changing. The phenomenal forces generated by convection currents in the molten core of our planet carry the vast segments, or 'plates', of the crust across the globe in an endless cycle of creation and destruction. New crust emerges along the central depths of the oceans, where molten magma flows from the margins of neighbouring plates to form the massive mid-ocean ridges. The sea floor spreads, and where ocean plates meet continental plates, they dip back into the Earth's core to melt once again into magma.

Less dense, the continental plates 'float' among the oceans, drifting into and apart from each other at a rate which is almost imperceptibly slow. A continent may travel little more than 25 millimetres each year – in an average lifetime, Europe will move no more than a man's height – yet in the vast span of geological time, this process throws up giant mountain ranges and opens massive rifts in the land's surface.

The world's greatest mountain ranges have been formed in this way: the Himalayas by the collision of the Indo-Australian and Eurasian plates; the Andes by the meeting of the Nazca and South American plates. The Himalayas are a classic example of 'fold mountains', formed by the crumpling of the Earth's surface where two landmasses have been driven together. The coastal range of the Andes, by contrast, was formed by the upsurge of molten volcanic rock created by the friction of the continent 'overriding' the ocean plate.

However, the destruction of the landscape begins as soon as it is formed. Wind, water, ice and sea, the main agents of erosion, mount a constant assault that even the hardest rocks cannot withstand. Mountain peaks may dwindle by as little as a few millimetres each year, but if they are not uplifted by further movements of the crust they will eventually be reduced to rubble. Water is the most powerful destroyer – it has been estimated that 100 billion tonnes of rock is washed into the oceans every year.

When water freezes, its volume increases by about 9%, and no rock is strong enough to resist this pressure. Where water has penetrated tiny fissures or seeped into softer rock, a severe freeze followed by a thaw may result in rockfalls or earthslides, creating major destruction in a few minutes. Over much longer periods, acidity in rainwater breaks down the chemical composition of porous rocks, such as limestone, eating away the rock to form deep caves and tunnels. Chemical decomposition also occurs in riverbeds and glacier valleys, hastening the process of mechanical erosion.

Rivers and glaciers, like the sea itself, generate much of their effect through abrasion – pounding the landscape with the debris they carry with them. But, as well as destroying, they also create new landscapes, many of them spectacular: vast deltas, as seen at the mouth of the Mississippi or the Nile; cliffs, rock arches and stacks, as found along the south coast of Australia; and the fjords cut by long-melted glaciers in British Columbia, Norway and New Zealand.

The vast ridges that divide the Earth's crust beneath each of the world's major oceans mark the boundaries between tectonic plates which are moving very gradually in opposite directions. As the plates shift apart, molten magma rises from the Earth's core to seal the rift and the sea floor slowly spreads towards the continental landmasses. The rate of sea floor spreading has been calculated by magnetic analysis of the rock – at about 40 mm [1.5 in] a year in the North Atlantic. Near the ocean shore, underwater volcanoes mark the line where the continental rise begins. As the plates meet, much of the denser ocean crust dips beneath the continental plate and melts back into the magma.

THE SPREADING EARTH

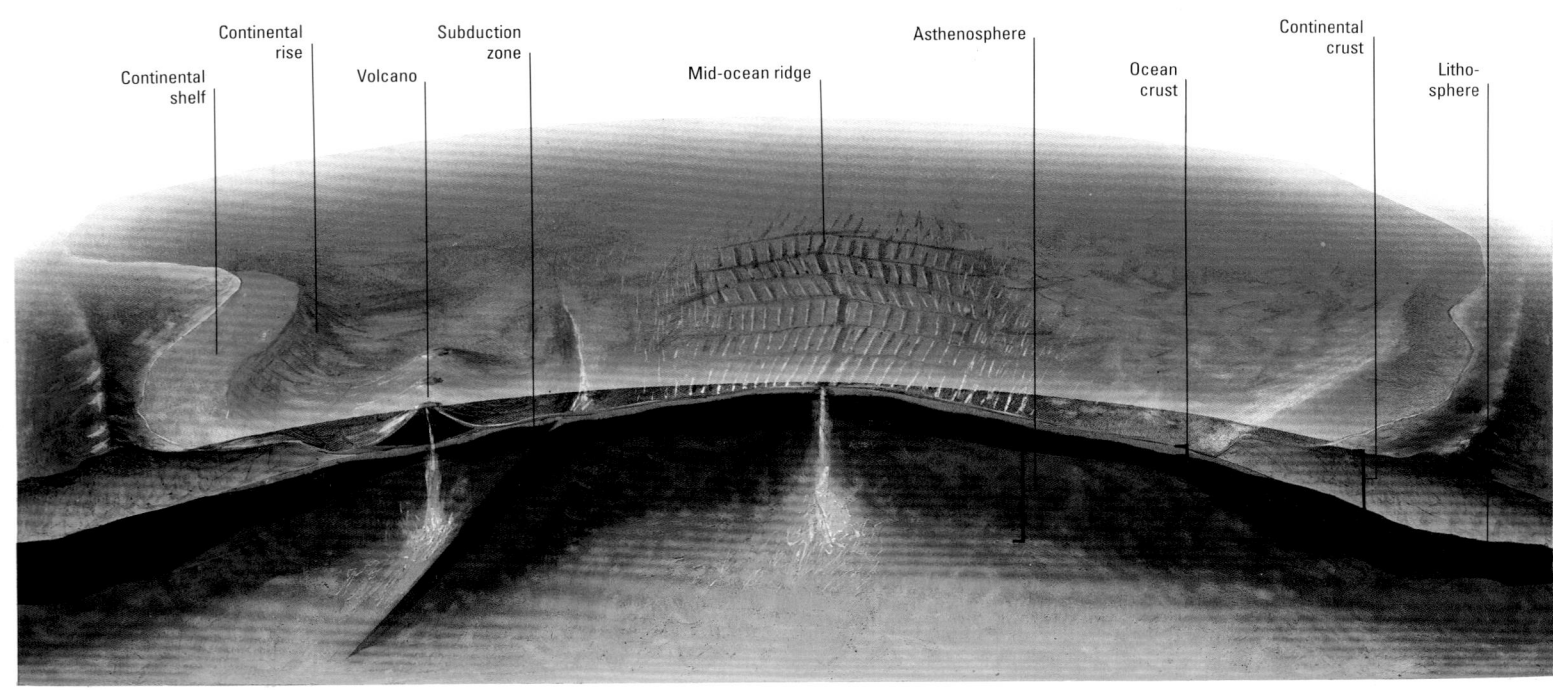

Continental shelf · Continental rise · Volcano · Subduction zone · Mid-ocean ridge · Asthenosphere · Ocean crust · Continental crust · Lithosphere

TYPES OF ROCK

Rocks are divided into three types, according to the way in which they are formed:

Igneous rocks, including granite and basalt, are formed by the cooling of magma from within the Earth's crust.

Metamorphic rocks, such as slate, marble and quartzite, are formed below the Earth's surface by the compression or baking of existing rocks.

Sedimentary rocks, like sandstone and limestone, are formed on the surface of the Earth from the remains of living organisms and eroded fragments of older rocks.

MOUNTAIN BUILDING

Mountains are formed when pressures on the Earth's crust caused by continental drift become so intense that the surface buckles or cracks. This happens most dramatically where two tectonic plates collide: the Rockies, Andes, Alps, Urals and Himalayas resulted from such impacts. These are all known as fold mountains, because they were formed by the compression of the rocks, forcing the surface to bend and fold like a crumpled rug.

The other main building process occurs when the crust fractures to create faults, allowing rock to be forced upwards in large blocks; or when the pressure of magma within the crust forces the surface to bulge into a dome, or erupts to form a volcano. Large mountain ranges may reveal a combination of those features; the Alps, for example, have been compressed so violently that the folds are fragmented by numerous faults and intrusions of molten rock.

Over millions of years, even the greatest mountain ranges can be reduced by erosion to a rugged landscape known as a peneplain.

Types of fold: Geographers give different names to the degrees of fold that result from continuing pressure on the rock strata. A simple fold may be symmetric, with even slopes on either side, but as the pressure builds up, one slope becomes steeper and the fold becomes asymmetric. Later, the ridge or 'anticline' at the top of the fold may slide over the lower ground or 'syncline' to form a recumbent fold. Eventually, the rock strata may break under the pressure to form an overthrust and finally a nappe fold.

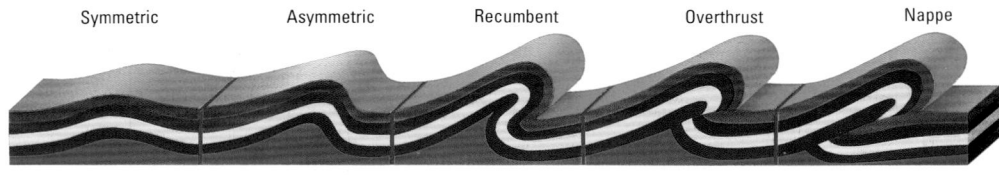

Symmetric · Asymmetric · Recumbent · Overthrust · Nappe

Types of faults: Faults are classified by the direction in which the blocks of rock have moved. A normal fault results when a vertical movement causes the surface to break apart; compression causes a reverse fault. Sideways movement causes shearing, known as a strike-slip fault. When the rock breaks in two places, the central block may be pushed up in a horst fault, or sink in a graben fault.

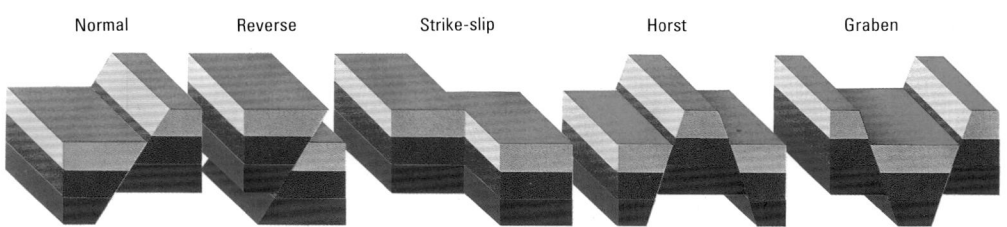

Normal · Reverse · Strike-slip · Horst · Graben

MOULDING THE LAND

While hidden forces of extraordinary power are moving the continents from below the Earth's crust, the more familiar elements of wind, water, heat and cold combine to sculpt the land surface. Erosion by weathering is seen in desert regions, where rocks degrade into sand through the effects of changing temperatures and strong winds.

The power of water is fiercer still. In severe storms, giant waves pound the shoreline with rocks and boulders, and often destroy concrete coastal defences; but even in quieter conditions, the sea steadily erodes cliffs and headlands and creates new land in the form of sand dunes, spits and salt marshes.

Rivers, too, are incessantly at work shaping the landscape on their way to join the sea. In highland regions, where the flow is rapid, they cut deep gorges and V-shaped valleys. As they reach more gentle slopes, rivers release some of the debris they have carried downstream, broadening out and raising levees along their banks by depositing mud and sand. In the lowland plains, they may drift into meanders, depositing more sediment and even building deltas when they finally approach the sea.

Ice has created some of the world's dramatic landscapes. As glaciers move slowly downhill, they scrape away rock from the mountains and valley sides, creating spectacular features.

SHAPING FORCES: THE SEA

In areas of hard rock, waves cut steep cliffs and form underwater platforms; debris is deposited as a terrace. Bays are formed when sections of soft rock are carved away between headlands of harder rock; these are then battered until the headlands are reduced to rock arches and stacks.

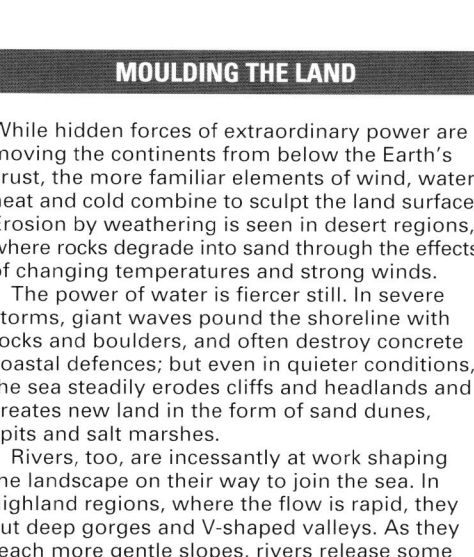

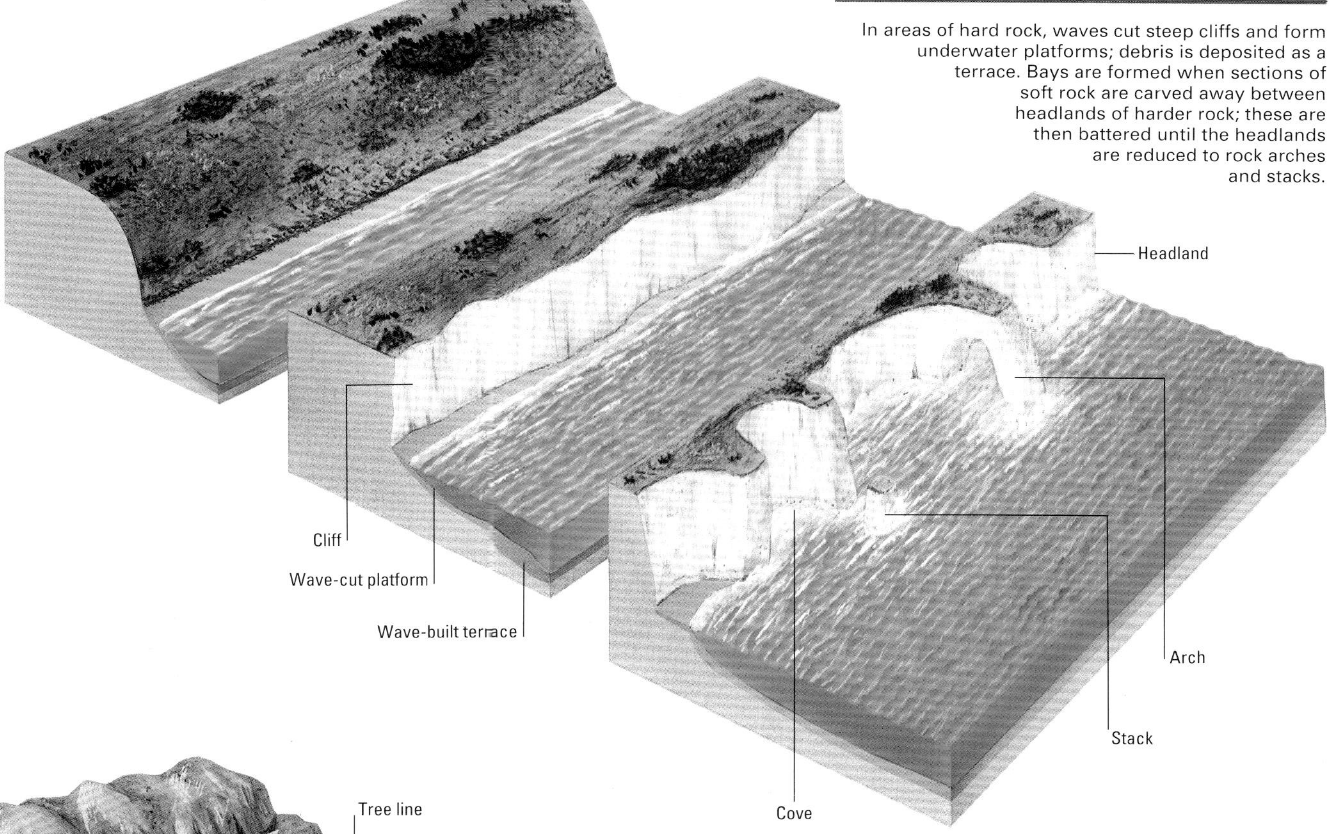

Headland

Cliff

Wave-cut platform

Wave-built terrace

Arch

Stack

Cove

SHAPING FORCES: RIVERS

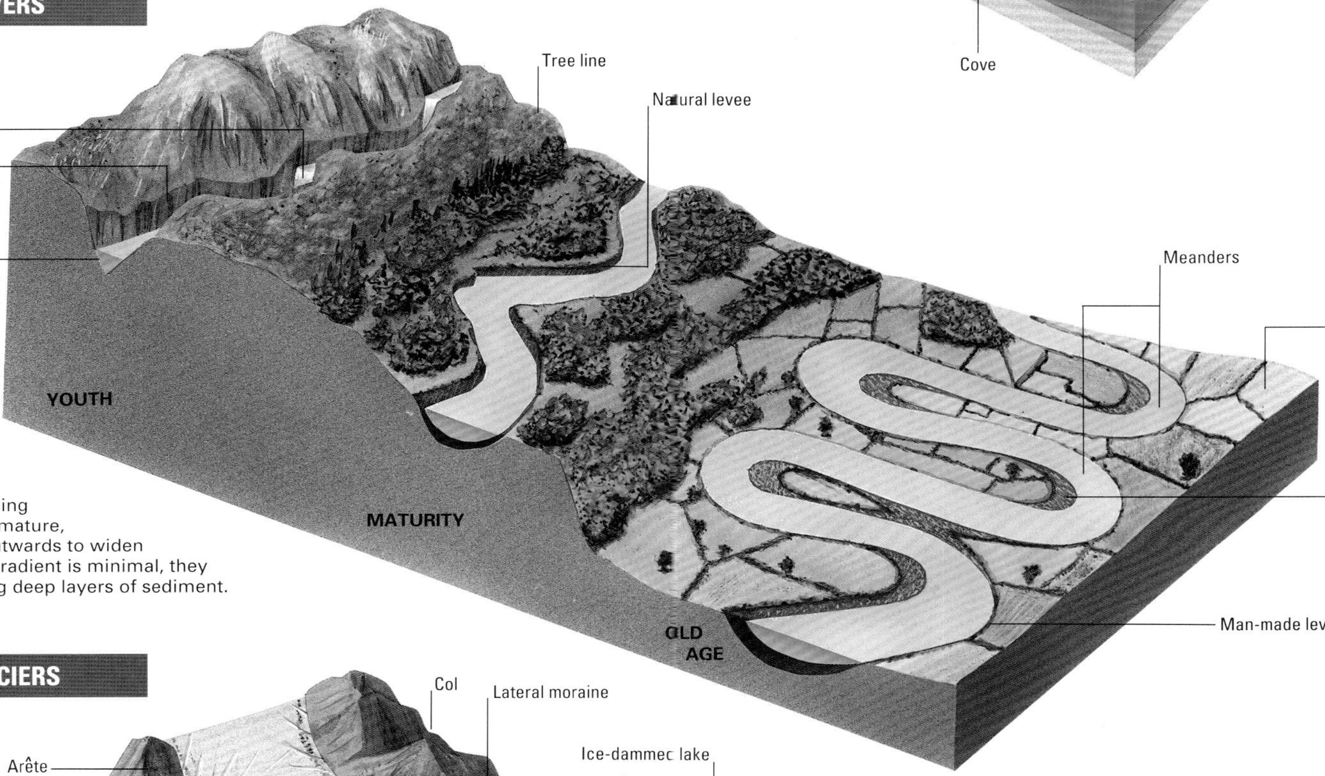

Tree line

Natural levee

Waterfall

Gorge

V-shaped valley

Meanders

Floodplain

Rivers shape the landscape according to the speed of their flow. In their youthful, upland stage they erode soft rocks quickly, cutting steep narrow valleys and tumbling in waterfalls over harder rock. As they mature, they deposit some debris and erode outwards to widen the valley. In their old age, where the gradient is minimal, they meander across wide plains, depositing deep layers of sediment.

YOUTH

MATURITY

OLD AGE

Sediment

Man-made levee

SHAPING FORCES: GLACIERS

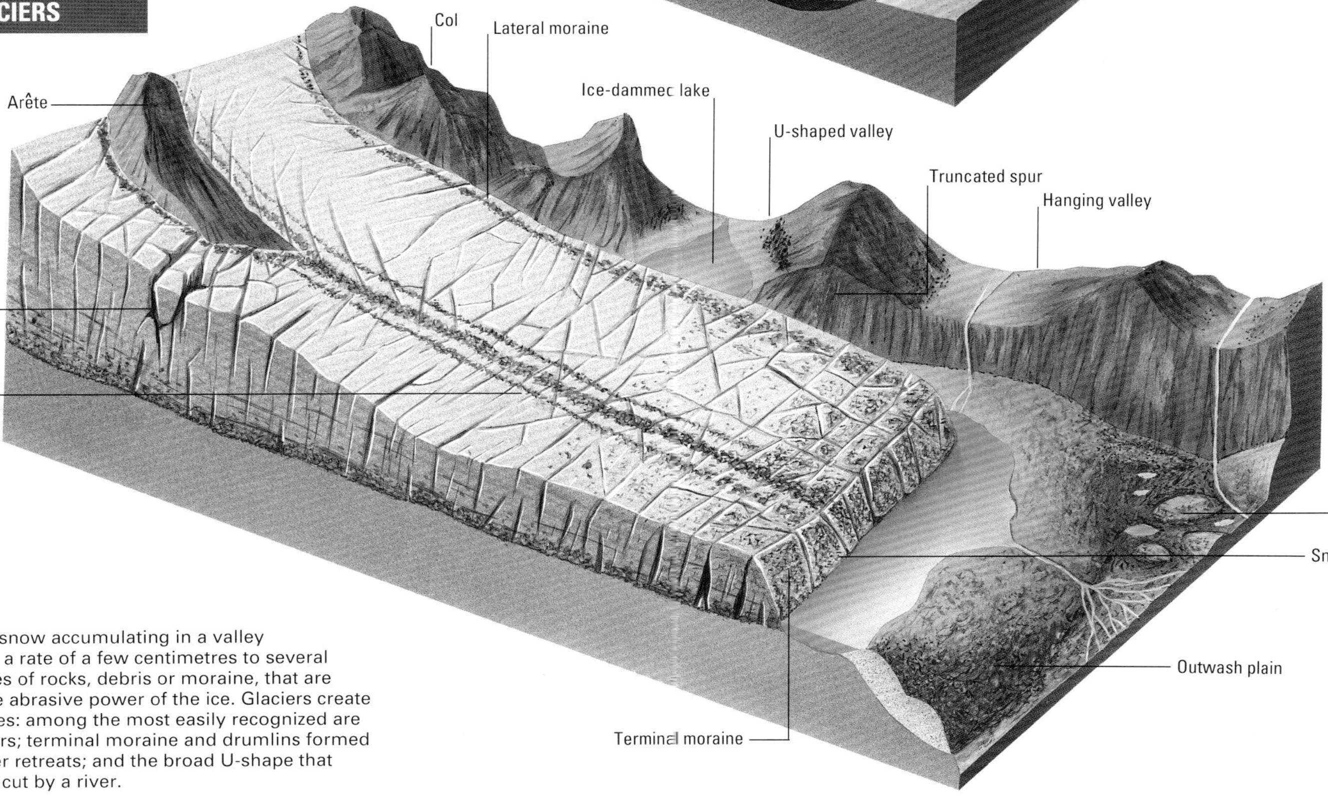

Col

Lateral moraine

Ice-dammed lake

U-shaped valley

Truncated spur

Hanging valley

Arête

Crevasse

Medial moraine

Drumlins

Snout

Outwash plain

Terminal moraine

Glaciers are formed from compressed snow accumulating in a valley head or cirque. They move downhill at a rate of a few centimetres to several metres per day, eroding large quantities of rocks, debris or moraine, that are caught up by the glacier and add to the abrasive power of the ice. Glaciers create numerous distinctive landscape features: among the most easily recognized are hanging valleys, cut by tributary glaciers; terminal moraine and drumlins formed by rock debris deposited when a glacier retreats; and the broad U-shape that distinguishes a glacial valley from one cut by a river.

THE EARTH: ENVIRONMENT

10: OCEANS

12: ATMOSPHERE

17: NATURAL VEGETATION

46: CARBON DIOXIDE
    GREENHOUSE POWER
    GLOBAL WARMING

47: ACID RAIN
    DESERTIFICATION
    DEFORESTATION
    WATER POLLUTION

Unique among the planets, the Earth has been the home of living creatures for most of its existence. Precisely how these improbable assemblies of self-replicating chemicals ever began remains a matter of conjecture, but the planet and its passengers have matured together for a very long time. Over 3,000 million years, life has not only adapted to its environment, but it has also slowly changed that environment to suit itself.

The planet and its biosphere – the entirety of its living things – function like a single organism. The British scientist James Lovelock, who first stated this 'Gaia hypothesis' in the 1970s, went further: the planet, he declared, actually was a living organism, equipped on a colossal scale with the same sort of stability-seeking mechanisms

used by lesser lifeforms like bacteria and humans to keep themselves running at optimum efficiency.

Lovelock's theory was inspired by a study of the Earth's atmosphere whose constituents he noted were very far from the state of chemical equilibrium observed elsewhere in the Solar System. The atmosphere has contained a substantial amount of free oxygen for the last 2,000 million years; yet without constant renewal, the oxygen molecules would soon be locked permanently in oxides. The nitrogen, too, would find chemical stability, probably in nitrates (accounting for some of the oxygen). Without living plants and algae to remove it, carbon dioxide would steadily increase from its present-day 0.03%; in a few million years, it

would form a thick blanket similar to the atmosphere of lifeless Venus, where surface temperatures reach 475°C.

It is not enough, however, for the biosphere simply to produce oxygen. While falling concentrations would first be uncomfortable and ultimately prove fatal for most contemporary life, at levels above the current 21% even moist vegetation is highly inflammable, and a massive conflagration becomes almost inevitable – a violent form of negative feedback to set the atmosphere on the path back to sterile equilibrium.

Fortunately, the biosphere has evolved over aeons into a subtle and complex control system, sensing changes and reacting to them quickly but gently, tending always to maintain the balance it has achieved.

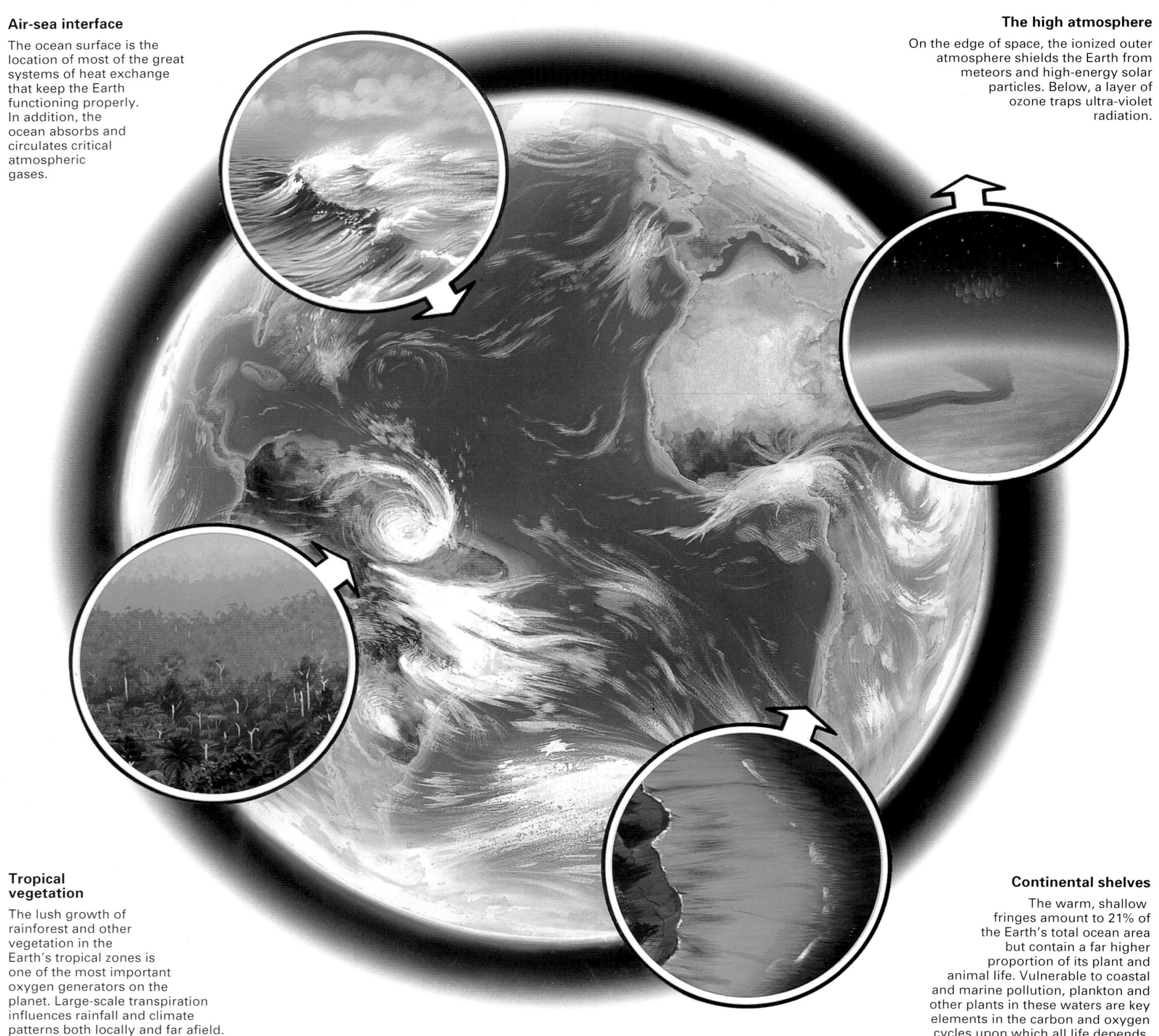

Air-sea interface
The ocean surface is the location of most of the great systems of heat exchange that keep the Earth functioning properly. In addition, the ocean absorbs and circulates critical atmospheric gases.

The high atmosphere
On the edge of space, the ionized outer atmosphere shields the Earth from meteors and high-energy solar particles. Below, a layer of ozone traps ultra-violet radiation.

Tropical vegetation
The lush growth of rainforest and other vegetation in the Earth's tropical zones is one of the most important oxygen generators on the planet. Large-scale transpiration influences rainfall and climate patterns both locally and far afield.

Continental shelves
The warm, shallow fringes amount to 21% of the Earth's total ocean area but contain a far higher proportion of its plant and animal life. Vulnerable to coastal and marine pollution, plankton and other plants in these waters are key elements in the carbon and oxygen cycles upon which all life depends.

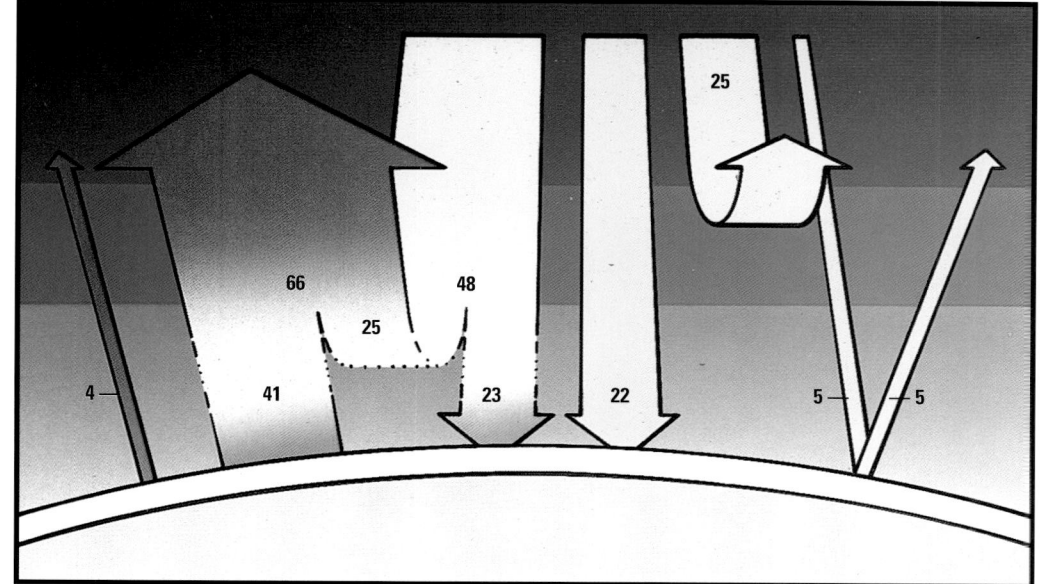

THE EARTH'S ENERGY BALANCE

Apart from a modest quantity of internal heat from its molten core, the Earth receives all of its energy from the Sun. If the planet is to remain at a constant temperature, it must reradiate exactly as much energy as it receives. Even a minute surplus would lead to a warmer Earth, a deficit to a cooler one; because the planetary energy budget is constantly audited by the laws of physics, which do not permit juggling, it must balance with absolute precision. The temperature at which thermal equilibrium is reached depends on a multitude of interconnected factors. Two of the most important are the relative brightness of the Earth – its index of reflectivity, called the 'albedo' – and the heat-trapping capacity of the atmosphere – the celebrated 'greenhouse effect'.

Because the Sun is very hot, most of its energy arrives in the form of relatively short-wave radiation: the shorter the waves, the more energy they carry. Some of the incoming energy is reflected straight back into space, exactly as it arrived; some is absorbed by the atmosphere on its way towards the surface; some is absorbed by the Earth itself. Absorbed energy heats the Earth and its atmosphere alike. But since its temperature is very much lower that that of the Sun, outgoing energy is emitted at much longer infra-red wavelengths. Some of the outgoing radiation escapes directly into outer space; some of it is reabsorbed by the atmosphere. Atmospheric energy eventually finds its way back into space, too, after a complex series of interactions. These include the air movements we call the weather and, almost incidentally, the maintenance of life on Earth.

This diagram does not attempt to illustrate the actual mechanisms of heat exchange, but gives a reasonable account (in percentages) of what happens to 100 energy 'units'. Short-wave radiation is shown in yellow, long-wave in red.

THE CARBON CYCLE

Most of the constituents of the atmosphere are kept in constant balance by complex cycles in which life plays an essential and indeed a dominant part. The control of carbon dioxide, which left to its own devices would be the dominant atmospheric gas, is possibly the most important, although since all the Earth's biological and geophysical cycles interact and interlock, it is hard to separate them even in theory and quite impossible in practice.

The Earth has a huge supply of carbon, only a small quantity of which is in the form of carbon dioxide. Of that, around 98% is dissolved in the sea; the fraction circulating in the air amounts to only 340 parts per million of the atmosphere, where its capacity as a greenhouse gas is the key regulator of the planetary temperature. In turn, life regulates the regulator, keeping carbon dioxide concentrations below danger level.

If all life were to vanish tomorrow from the Earth, the atmosphere would begin the process of change immediately, although it might take several million years to achieve a new, inorganic stability. First, the oxygen content would begin to fall away; with no more assistance than a little solar radiation, a few electrical storms and its own high chemical potential, oxygen would steadily combine with atmospheric nitrogen and volcanic outgassing. In doing so, it would yield sufficient acid to react with carbonaceous rocks such as limestone, releasing carbon dioxide. Once carbon dioxide levels exceeded about 1%, its greenhouse power would increase disproportionately. Rising temperatures – well above the boiling point of water – would speed chemical reactions; in time, the Earth's atmosphere would consist of little more than carbon dioxide and superheated water vapour.

Living things, however, circulate carbon. They do so first by simply existing: after all, the carbon atom is the basic building block of living matter. During life, plants absorb atmospheric carbon dioxide, incorporating the carbon itself into their structure – leaves and trunks in the case of land plants, shells

in the case of plankton and the tiny creatures that feed on it. The oxygen thereby freed is added to the atmosphere, at least for a time. Most plant carbon is returned to circulation when the plants die and decay, combining once more with the oxygen released during life. However, a small proportion – about one part in 1,000 – is removed almost permanently, buried beneath mud on land, or at sea sinking as dead matter to the ocean floor. In time, it is slowly compressed into sedimentary rocks such as limestone and chalk.

But in the evolution of the Earth, nothing is quite permanent. On an even longer timescale, the planet's crustal movements force new rock upwards in mid-ocean ridges. Limestone deposits are

moved, and sea levels change; ancient limestone is exposed to weathering, and a little of its carbon is released to be fixed in turn by the current generation of plants.

The carbon cycle has continued quietly for an immensely long time, and without gross disturbance there is no reason why it would not continue almost indefinitely in the future. However, human beings have found a way to release fixed carbon at a rate far faster than existing global systems can recirculate it. Oil and coal deposits represent the work of millions of years of carbon accumulation; but it has taken only a few human generations of high-energy scavenging to endanger the entire complex regulatory cycle.

Carbon cycle diagram labels

- Organic decay, animal respiration and burning
- AIR
- Plankton photosynthesis
- Absorbtion by living plants
- Plankton respiration
- Mineral washout
- LAND
- SEA
- Sea shells to sedimentary rock
- [98% of existing carbon dioxide held in solution in the sea]

THE GREENHOUSE EFFECT

Constituting barely 0.03% of the atmosphere, carbon dioxide has a hugely disproportionate effect on the Earth's climate and even its habitability. Like the glass panes in a greenhouse, it is transparent to most incoming short-wave radiation, which passes freely to heat the planet beneath. But when the warmed Earth retransmits that energy, in the form of longer-wave infra-red radiation, the carbon dioxide functions as an opaque shield, so that the planetary surface (like the interior of a greenhouse) stays relatively hot.

The recent increases in CO_2 levels are causing alarm: global warming associated with a runaway greenhouse effect could bring disaster. But a serious reduction would be just as damaging, with surface temperatures falling dramatically; during the last Ice Age, for example, the carbon dioxide concentration was around 180 parts per million, and a total absence of the gas would likely leave the planet a ball of ice, or at best frozen tundra.

The diagram shows incoming sunlight as yellow; high-energy ultra-violet (blue) is trapped by the ozone layer, while outgoing heat from the warmed Earth (red) is partially retained by carbon dioxide.

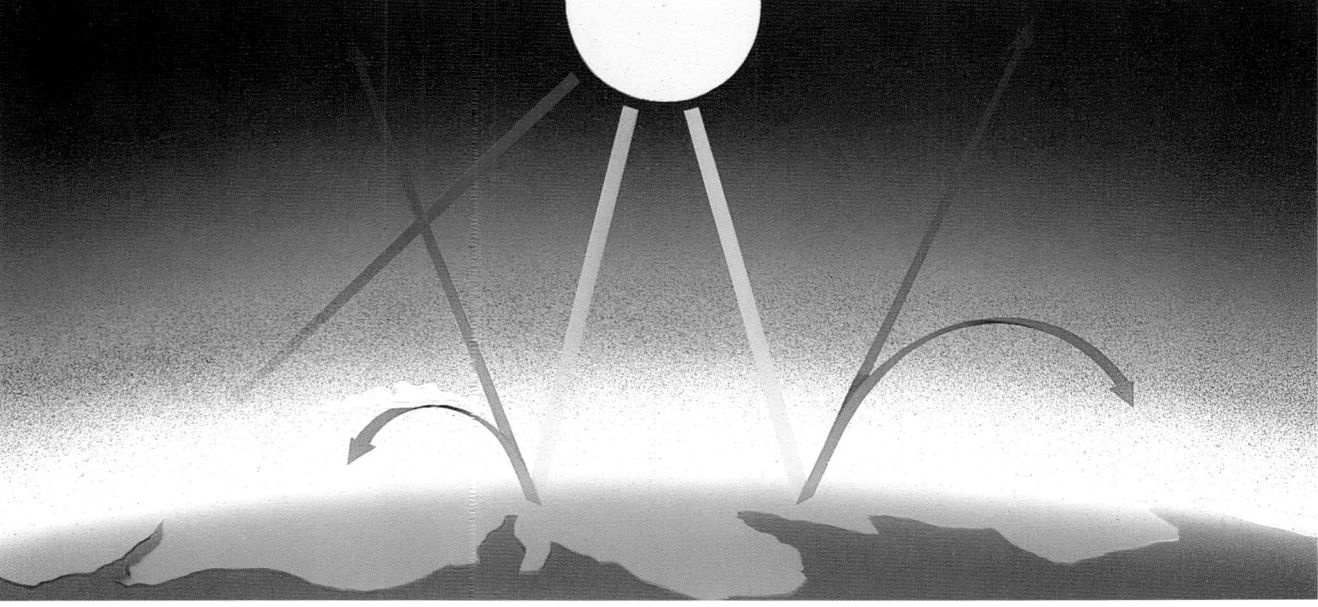

PEOPLE: DEMOGRAPHY

24: URBANIZATION OF THE EARTH URBAN POPULATION

25: LARGEST CITIES

31: FOOD AND POPULATION

40: WEALTH AND POPULATION

46: HUMAN EXPANSION

As the 20th century draws to its close, the Earth's population increases by nearly 10,000 every hour – enough to fill a new major city every week. The growth is almost entirely confined to the developing world, which accounted for 67% of total population in 1950 and is set to reach 84% by 2025. In developed countries, populations are almost static, and in some places, such as Germany, are actually falling. In fact, there is a clear correlation between wealth and low fertility: as incomes rise, reproduction rates drop.

The decline is already apparent. With the exception of Africa, the actual rates of increase are falling nearly everywhere. The population structure, however, ensures that human numbers will continue to rise even as fertility diminishes. Developed nations, like the UK, have an even spread across ages, and usually a growing proportion of elderly people: the over-75s often outnumber the under-5s, and women of child-bearing age form only a small part of the total. Developing nations fall into a pattern somewhere between that of Kenya and Brazil: the great majority of their people are in the younger age groups, about to enter their most fertile years. In time, even Kenya's population profile should resemble the developed model, but the transition will come about only after a few more generations' growth.

It remains to be seen whether the planet will tolerate the population growth that seems inevitable before stability is reached. More people consume more resources, increasing the strain on an already troubled environment. However, more people should mean a greater supply of human ingenuity – the only commodity likely to resolve the crisis.

LARGEST NATIONS

The world's most populous nations, in millions (1994)

1.	China	1,209
2.	India	919
3.	USA	261
4.	Indonesia	195
5.	Brazil	159
6.	Russia	147
7.	Pakistan	137
8.	Japan	125
9.	Bangladesh	118
10.	Mexico	92
11.	Nigeria	89
12.	Germany	81
13.	Vietnam	73
14.	Philippines	66
15.	Iran	66
16.	Egypt	62
17.	Turkey	61
18.	Thailand	58
19.	UK	58
20.	France	58
21.	Italy	57
22.	Ethiopia	53
23.	Ukraine	51
24.	Burma	46

CROWDED NATIONS

Population per square kilometre (1994), exc. nations of less than one million.

1.	Hong Kong	5,307.2
2.	Singapore	4,550.0
3.	Bangladesh	817.9
4.	Mauritius	581.1
5.	Taiwan	573.9
6.	South Korea	450.1
7.	Puerto Rico	405.1
8.	Netherlands	371.0
9.	Belgium	330.5
10.	Japan	330.2
11.	Rwanda	294.7
12.	Lebanon	280.2
13.	India	279.4
14.	Sri Lanka	276.3
15.	El Salvador	268.6
16.	Trinidad & Tobago	253.3
17.	UK	238.8
18.	Germany	224.9
19.	Jamaica	220.8
20.	Israel	202.1

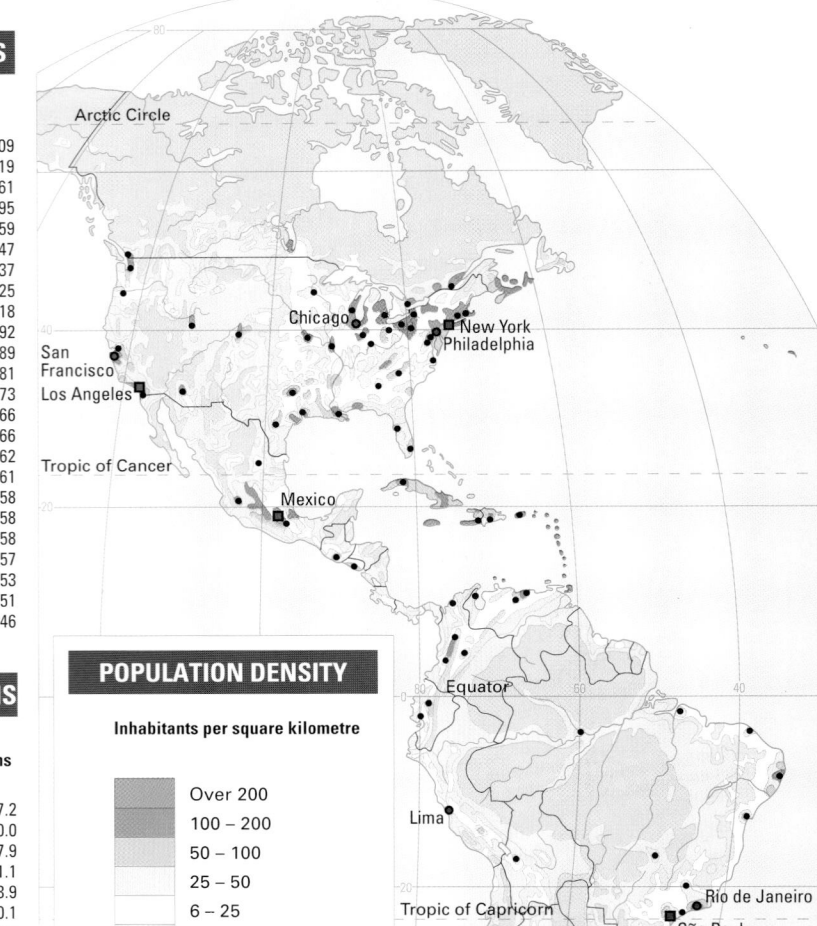

POPULATION DENSITY

Inhabitants per square kilometre

- Over 200
- 100 – 200
- 50 – 100
- 25 – 50
- 6 – 25
- 3 – 6
- 1 – 3
- Under 1

Urban population
- ■ Over 10,000,000
- ⬤ 5,000,000 – 10,000,000
- • 1,000,000 – 5,000,000

Places marked are conurbations, not city limits; San Francisco itself, for example, has an official population of less than a million.

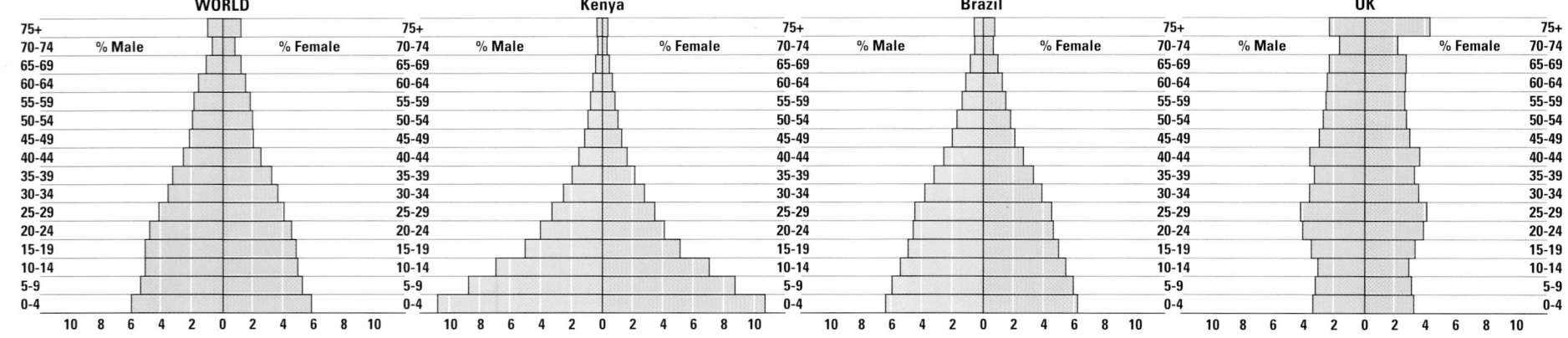

Population pyramids: WORLD, Kenya, Brazil, UK. Age groups from 0-4 to 75+; % Male and % Female scales 10 8 6 4 2 0 2 4 6 8 10.

RATES OF GROWTH

Apparently small rates of population growth lead to dramatic increases over two or three generations. The table below translates annual percentage growth into the number of years required to double a population.

% change	Doubling time
0.5	139.0
1.0	69.7
1.5	46.6
2.0	35.0
2.5	28.1
3.0	23.4
3.5	20.1
4.0	17.7

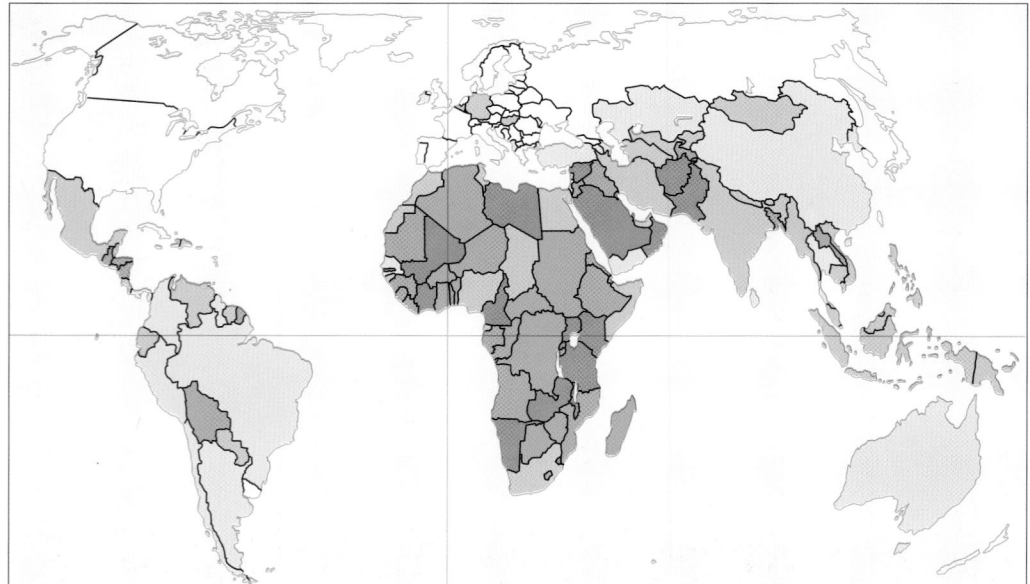

POPULATION CHANGE 1990–2000

The predicted population change for the years 1990–2000

- Over 40% population gain
- 30 – 40% population gain
- 20 – 30% population gain
- 10 – 20% population gain
- 0 – 10% population gain
- No change or population loss

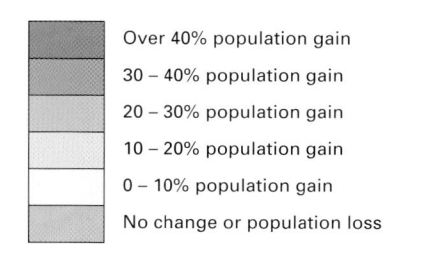

Top 5 countries		Bottom 5 countries	
Kuwait	+75.9%	Belgium	−0.1%
Namibia	+62.5%	Hungary	−0.2%
Afghanistan	+60.1%	Grenada	−2.4%
Mali	+55.5%	Germany	−3.2%
Tanzania	+54.6%	Tonga	−3.2%

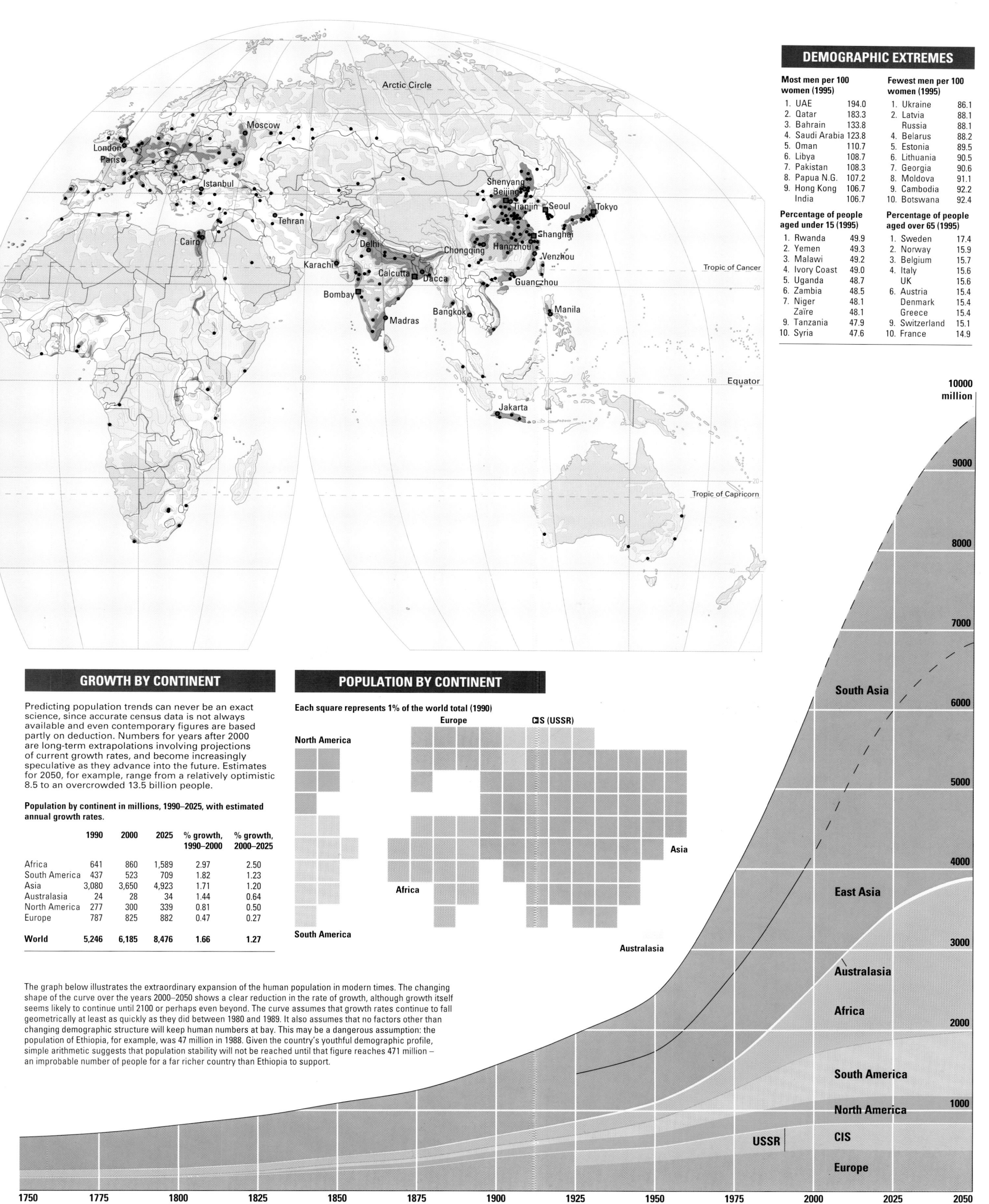

Arctic Circle

Moscow · London · Paris · Istanbul · Tehran · Cairo · Karachi · Delhi · Bombay · Calcutta · Madras · Dacca · Chongqing · Hangzhou · Shanghai · Venzhou · Shenyang · Beijing · Tianjin · Seoul · Tokyo · Guanczhou · Bangkok · Manila · Jakarta

Tropic of Cancer

Equator

Tropic of Capricorn

DEMOGRAPHIC EXTREMES

Most men per 100 women (1995)		Fewest men per 100 women (1995)	
1. UAE	194.0	1. Ukraine	86.1
2. Qatar	183.3	2. Latvia	88.1
3. Bahrain	133.8	Russia	88.1
4. Saudi Arabia	123.8	3. Belarus	88.2
5. Oman	110.7	4. Estonia	89.5
6. Libya	108.7	5. Lithuania	90.5
7. Pakistan	108.3	6. Georgia	90.6
8. Papua N.G.	107.2	7. Moldova	91.1
9. Hong Kong	106.7	8. Cambodia	92.2
India	106.7	9. Botswana	92.4

Percentage of people aged under 15 (1995)		Percentage of people aged over 65 (1995)	
1. Rwanda	49.9	1. Sweden	17.4
2. Yemen	49.3	2. Norway	15.9
3. Malawi	49.2	3. Belgium	15.7
4. Ivory Coast	49.0	4. Italy	15.6
5. Uganda	48.7	UK	15.6
6. Zambia	48.5	6. Austria	15.4
7. Niger	48.1	Denmark	15.4
Zaire	48.1	Greece	15.4
9. Tanzania	47.9	9. Switzerland	15.1
10. Syria	47.6	10. France	14.9

GROWTH BY CONTINENT

Predicting population trends can never be an exact science, since accurate census data is not always available and even contemporary figures are based partly on deduction. Numbers for years after 2000 are long-term extrapolations involving projections of current growth rates, and become increasingly speculative as they advance into the future. Estimates for 2050, for example, range from a relatively optimistic 8.5 to an overcrowded 13.5 billion people.

Population by continent in millions, 1990–2025, with estimated annual growth rates.

	1990	2000	2025	% growth, 1990–2000	% growth, 2000–2025
Africa	641	860	1,589	2.97	2.50
South America	437	523	709	1.82	1.23
Asia	3,080	3,650	4,923	1.71	1.20
Australasia	24	28	34	1.44	0.64
North America	277	300	339	0.81	0.50
Europe	787	825	882	0.47	0.27
World	**5,246**	**6,185**	**8,476**	**1.66**	**1.27**

POPULATION BY CONTINENT

Each square represents 1% of the world total (1990)

Europe · CIS (USSR) · North America · Asia · Africa · South America · Australasia

The graph below illustrates the extraordinary expansion of the human population in modern times. The changing shape of the curve over the years 2000–2050 shows a clear reduction in the rate of growth, although growth itself seems likely to continue until 2100 or perhaps even beyond. The curve assumes that growth rates continue to fall geometrically at least as quickly as they did between 1980 and 1989. It also assumes that no factors other than changing demographic structure will keep human numbers at bay. This may be a dangerous assumption: the population of Ethiopia, for example, was 47 million in 1988. Given the country's youthful demographic profile, simple arithmetic suggests that population stability will not be reached until that figure reaches 471 million – an improbable number of people for a far richer country than Ethiopia to support.

10000 million · 9000 · 8000 · 7000 · 6000 · 5000 · 4000 · 3000 · 2000 · 1000

South Asia · East Asia · Australasia · Africa · South America · North America · CIS · USSR · Europe

1750 · 1775 · 1800 · 1825 · 1850 · 1875 · 1900 · 1925 · 1950 · 1975 · 2000 · 2025 · 2050

PEOPLE: CITIES

16: WATER SUPPLY

22: POPULATION DENSITY

39: THE GREAT PORTS

In 1750, barely three humans in every hundred lived in a city; by 2000, more than half the world's population will find a home in some kind of urban area. In 1850, only London and Paris had more than a million inhabitants; by 2000, at least 24 cities will each contain over 10 million people. The increase is concentrated in the Third World, if only because levels of urbanization in most developed countries – more than 90% in the UK and Belgium, and almost 75% in the USA, despite that country's great open spaces – have already reached practical limits.

Such large-scale concentration is relatively new to the human race. Although city life has always attracted country dwellers in search of trade, employment or simply human contact, until modern times they paid a high price. Crowding and poor sanitation ensured high death rates, and until about 1850, most cities needed a steady flow of incomers simply to maintain their population levels: for example, there were 600,000 more deaths than births in 18th-century London, and some other large cities showed an even worse imbalance.

With improved public health, cities could grow from their own human resources, and large-scale urban living became common-place in the developed world. Since about 1950, the pattern has been global. Like their counterparts in 19th-century Europe and the USA, the great new cities are driven into rapid growth by a kind of push-pull mechanism. The push is generated by agricultural overcrowding: only so many people can live from a single plot of land and population pressure drives many into towns. The pull comes from the possibilities of economic improvement – an irresistible lure to the world's rural hopefuls.

Such improvement is not always obvious: the typical Third World city, with millions of people living (often illegally) in shanty towns and many thousands existing homelessly on the ill-made streets, does not present a great image of prosperity. Yet modern shanty towns are healthier than industrializing Pittsburgh or Manchester in the last century,

and these human ant-hills teem with industry as well as squalor: throughout the world, above-average rates of urbanization have gone hand-in-hand with above-average rates of economic growth. Surveys demonstrate that Third World city dwellers are generally better off than their rural counterparts, whose poverty is less concentrated but often more desperate. This only serves to increase the attraction of the city for the rural poor.

However, the sheer speed of the urbanization process threatens to overwhelm the limited abilities of city authorities to provide even rudimentary services. The 24 million people expected to live in Mexico City by 2000, for example, would swamp a more efficient local government than Mexico can provide. Improvements are often swallowed up by the relentless rise in urban population: although safe drinking water should reach 75% of Third World city dwellers by the end of the century – a considerable achievement – population growth will add 100 million to the list of those without it.

THE URBANIZATION OF THE EARTH

City-building, 1850–2000; each white spot represents a city of at least 1 million inhabitants.

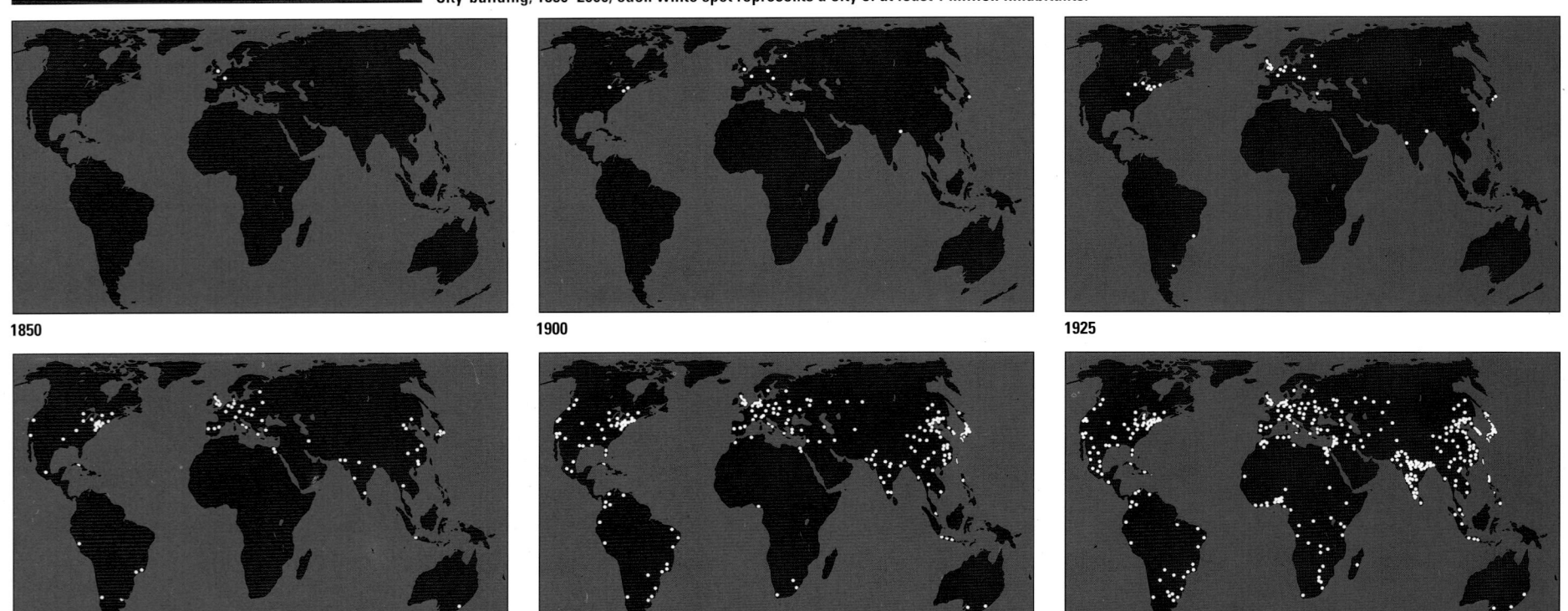

1850

1900

1925

1950

1975

2000

URBAN POPULATION

Percentage of total population living in towns and cities (1990)

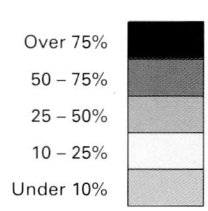

- Over 75%
- 50 – 75%
- 25 – 50%
- 10 – 25%
- Under 10%

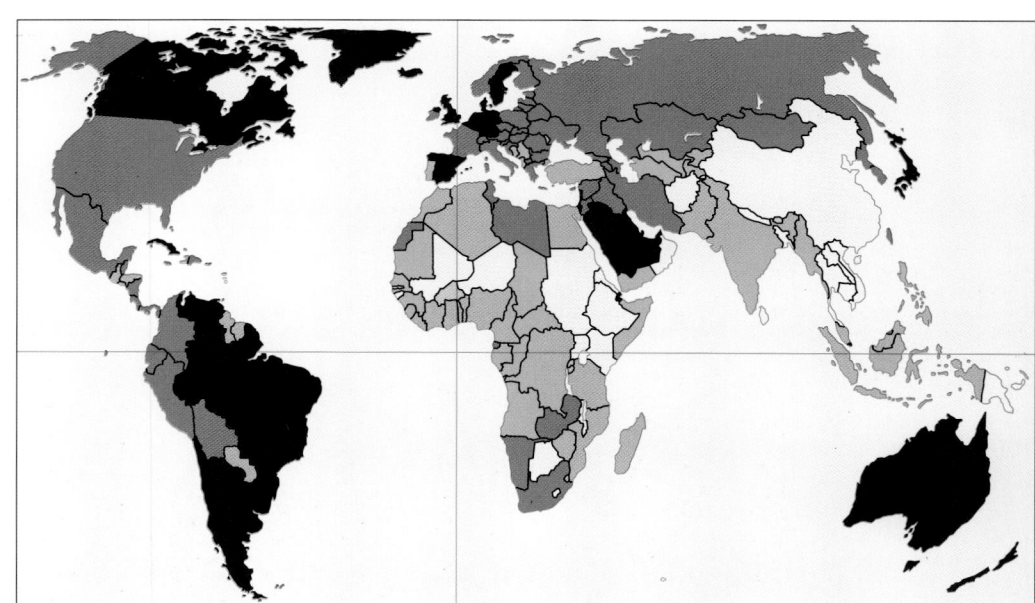

Most urbanized		Least urbanized	
Singapore	100%	Bhutan	5%
Belgium	97%	Burundi	7%
Kuwait	96%	Rwanda	8%
Hong Kong	93%	Burkina Faso	9%
UK	93%	Nepal	10%

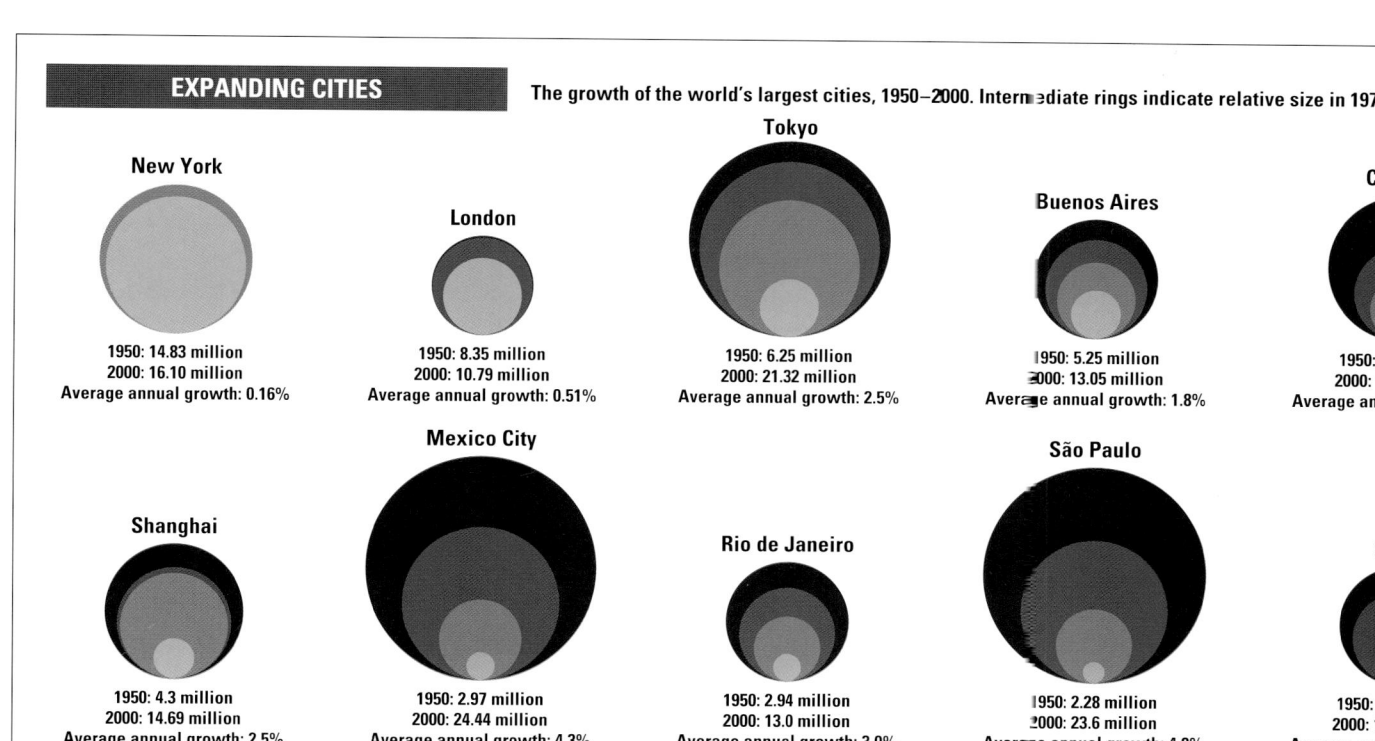

EXPANDING CITIES

The growth of the world's largest cities, 1950–2000. Intermediate rings indicate relative size in 1970 and 1985.

New York
1950: 14.83 million
2000: 16.10 million
Average annual growth: 0.16%

London
1950: 8.35 million
2000: 10.79 million
Average annual growth: 0.51%

Tokyo
1950: 6.25 million
2000: 21.32 million
Average annual growth: 2.5%

Buenos Aires
1950: 5.25 million
2000: 13.05 million
Average annual growth: 1.8%

Calcutta
1950: 4.45 million
2000: 15.94 million
Average annual growth: 2.6%

Shanghai
1950: 4.3 million
2000: 14.69 million
Average annual growth: 2.5%

Mexico City
1950: 2.97 million
2000: 24.44 million
Average annual growth: 4.3%

Rio de Janeiro
1950: 2.94 million
2000: 13.0 million
Average annual growth: 3.0%

São Paulo
1950: 2.28 million
2000: 23.6 million
Average annual growth: 4.8%

Seoul
1950: 1.45 million
2000: 12.97 million
Average annual growth: 4.5%

Each set of circles illustrates a city's size in 1950, 1970, 1985 and 2000. In most cases, expansion has been steady and, often, explosive. New York and London, however, went through patches of negative growth during the period. In New York, the world's largest city in 1950, population reached a peak around 1970. London shrank slightly between 1970 and 1985 before resuming a very modest rate of increase. In both cases, the divergence from world trends can be explained in part by counting methods: each is at the centre of a great agglomeration, and definitions of where 'city limits' lie may vary over time. But their relative decline also matches a pattern often seen in mature cities in the developed world, where urbanization, already at a very high level, has reached a plateau.

CITIES IN DANGER

As the decade of the 1980s advanced, most industrial countries, alarmed by acid rain and urban smog, took significant steps to limit air pollution. These controls, however, are expensive to install and difficult to enforce, and clean air remains a luxury most developed as well as developing cities must live without.

Those taking part in the United Nations' Global Environment Monitoring System (see right) frequently show dangerous levels of pollutants ranging from soot to sulphur dioxide and photo-chemical smog; air in the majority of cities without such sampling equipment is likely to be at least as bad.

URBAN AIR POLLUTION

The world's most polluted cities: number of days each year when sulphur dioxide levels exceeded the WHO threshold of 150 micrograms per cubic metre (averaged over 4 to 15 years, 1970s – 1980s)

Sulphur dioxide is the main pollutant associated with industrial cities. According to the World Health Organization, more than seven days in a year above 150 µg per cubic metre bring a serious risk of respiratory disease: at least 600 million people live in urban areas where SO_2 concentrations regularly reach damaging levels.

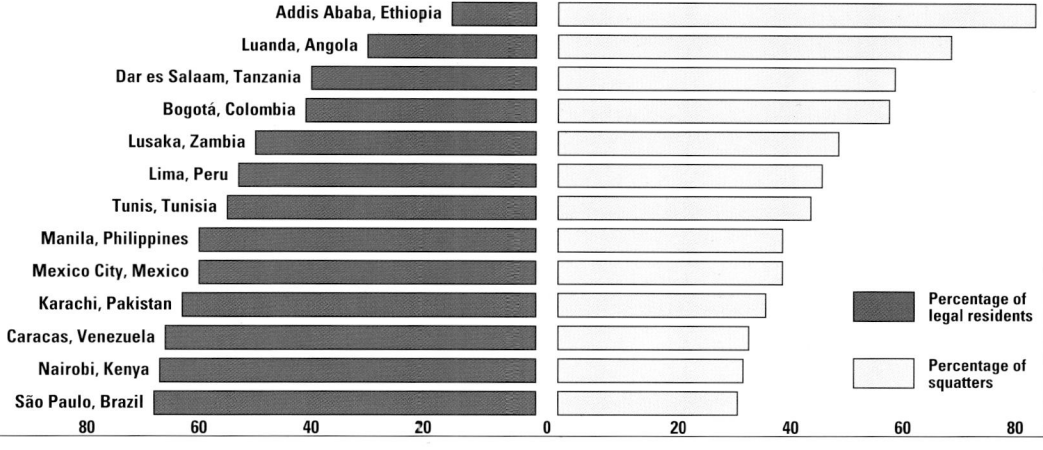

Manila, Philippines
Calcutta, India
Milan, Italy
Zagreb, Croatia
Guangzhou, China
Madrid, Spain
Peking (Beijing), China
Xian, China
Seoul, South Korea
Tehran, Iran
Shenyang, China

120   90   60   30

INFORMAL CITIZENS

Proportion of population living in squatter settlements, selected cities in the developing world (1980s)

Urbanization in most Third World countries has been coming about far faster than local governments can provide services and accommodation for the new city dwellers. Many – in some cities, most – find their homes in improvised squatter settlements, often unconnected to power, water and sanitation networks. Yet despite their ramshackle housing and marginal legality, these communities are often the most dynamic part of a city economy. They are also growing in size; and given the squatters' reluctance to be counted by tax-demanding authorities, the percentages shown here are likely to be underestimates.

Addis Ababa, Ethiopia
Luanda, Angola
Dar es Salaam, Tanzania
Bogotá, Colombia
Lusaka, Zambia
Lima, Peru
Tunis, Tunisia
Manila, Philippines
Mexico City, Mexico
Karachi, Pakistan
Caracas, Venezuela
Nairobi, Kenya
São Paulo, Brazil

80   60   40   20   0   20   40   60   80

■ Percentage of legal residents
□ Percentage of squatters

URBAN ADVANTAGES

Despite overcrowding and poor housing, living standards in the developing world's cities are almost invariably better than in the surrounding countryside. Resources – financial, material and administrative – are concentrated in the towns, which are usually also the centres of political activity and pressure. Governments – frequently unstable, and rarely established on a solid democratic base – are usually more responsive to urban discontent than rural misery.

In many countries, especially in Africa, food prices are often kept artificially low, appeasing underemployed urban masses at the expense of agricultural development. The imbalance encourages further cityward migration, helping to account for the astonishing rate of post-1950 urbanization and putting great strain on the ability of many nations to provide even modest improvements for their people.

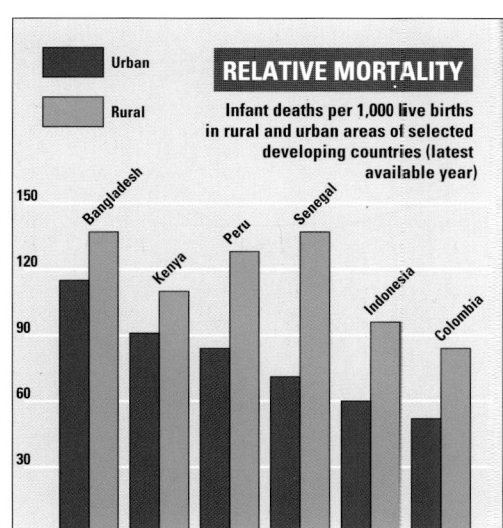

RELATIVE MORTALITY

■ Urban ■ Rural

Infant deaths per 1,000 live births in rural and urban areas of selected developing countries (latest available year)

150   120   90   60   30

Bangladesh, Kenya, Peru, Senegal, Indonesia, Colombia

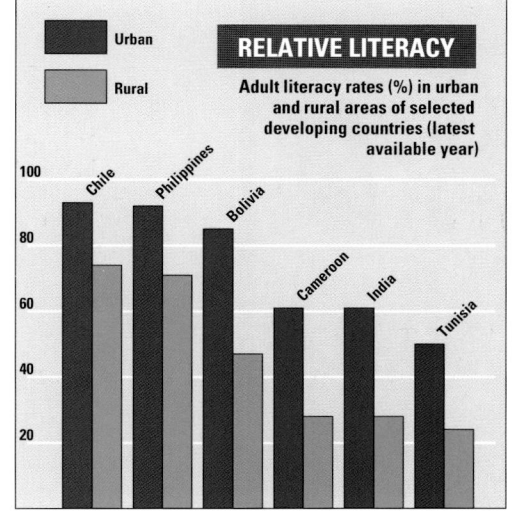

RELATIVE LITERACY

■ Urban ■ Rural

Adult literacy rates (%) in urban and rural areas of selected developing countries (latest available year)

100   80   60   40   20

Chile, Philippines, Bolivia, Cameroon, India, Tunisia

LARGEST CITIES

By early next century for the first time in history, the majority of the world's population will live in cities. Below is a list of the world's largest cities, in millions of inhabitants, based on estimates for the year 2000.*

	City	Millions
1.	Mexico City	25.6
2.	Tokyo-Yokohama	24.2
3.	São Paulo	22.1
4.	Shanghai	17.0
5.	New York	16.8
6.	Calcutta	15.7
7.	Bombay	15.4
8.	Beijing	14.0
9.	Los Angeles	13.9
10.	Jakarta	13.7
11.	Delhi	13.2
12.	Buenos Aires	12.9
	Lagos	12.9
14.	Seoul	12.7
	Tianjin	12.7
16.	Rio de Janeiro	12.5
17.	Dhaka	12.2
18.	Manila	11.8
	Cairo	11.8
20.	Karachi	11.7
21.	London	10.5
22.	Bangkok	10.3
23.	Istanbul	9.5
24.	Moscow	9.0
25.	Osaka	8.6
	Paris	8.6
27.	Tehran	8.5
28.	Bangalore	8.2
	Lima-Callao	8.2
30.	Madras	7.8
31.	Chicago	7.3
32.	Bogotá	6.4
33.	Shenyang	6.3
34.	Hong Kong	6.1
35.	Lahore	5.9
	Madrid	5.9
37.	Santiago	5.6
38.	Milan	5.4
	St Petersburg	5.4
40.	Philadelphia	4.5

[City populations are based on urban agglomerations rather than legal city limits. In some cases where two adjacent cities have merged into one concentration, such as Tokyo-Yokohama, they have been regarded as a single unit.]

* For a list of current city estimates, see page XI.

PEOPLE: THE HUMAN FAMILY

20: POPULATION DENSITY

28: THE WORLD'S REFUGEES WAR SINCE 1945

29: UNITED NATIONS INTERNATIONAL ORGANIZATIONS

46: THE HISTORY OF HUMAN EXPANSION

Strictly speaking, all human beings belong to a single race – *Homo sapiens* has no subspecies. But although all humans are interfertile, anthropologists and geneticists distinguish three main racial types: Caucasoid, Negroid and Mongoloid. Racial differences reflect not so much evolutionary origin as long periods of separation.

Racial affinities are not always obvious. The Caucasoid group stems from Europe, North Africa and India, but still includes Australian aboriginals within its broad type; Mongoloid peoples comprise American Indians and Eskimos as well as most Chinese, central Asians and Malays; Negroids are mostly of African origin, but also include the Papuan peoples of New Guinea.

Migration in modern times has mingled racial groups to an unprecedented extent, and most nations now have some degree of racially mixed population.

Language is almost the definition of a particular human culture; the world has well over 5,000, most of them with only a few hundred thousand speakers. In one important sense, all languages are equal; although different vocabularies and linguistic structures greatly influence patterns of thought, all true human languages can carry virtually unlimited information. But even if, for example, there is no theoretical difference in the communicative power of English and one of the 500 or more tribal languages of Papua New Guinea, an English speaker has access to much more of the global culture than a Papuan who knows no other tongue.

Like language, religion encourages the internal cohesion of a single human group at the expense of creating gulfs of incomprehension between different groups. All religions satisfy a deep-seated human need, assigning men and women to a comprehensible place in what most of them still consider a divinely ordered world. But religion is also a means by which a culture can assert its individuality; the startling rise of Islam in the late 20th century is partly a response by large sections of the developing world to the secular, Western-inspired world order from which many non-Western peoples feel excluded. Like uncounted millions of human beings before them, they find in their religion not only a personal faith but also a powerful group identity.

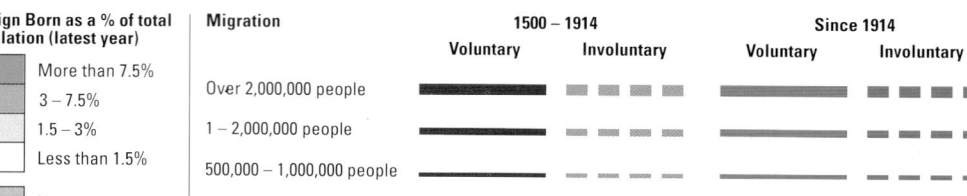

WORLD MIGRATION

The greatest voluntary migration was the colonization of North America by 30–35 million European settlers during the 19th century. The greatest forced migration involved 9–11 million Africans taken as slaves to America 1550–1860. The migrations shown on the map are mostly international as population movements within borders are not usually recorded. Many of the statistics are necessarily estimates as so many refugees and migrant workers enter countries illegally and unrecorded. Emigrants may have a variety of motives for leaving, thus making it difficult to distinguish between voluntary and involuntary migrations.

Foreign Born as a % of total population (latest year)
- More than 7.5%
- 3 – 7.5%
- 1.5 – 3%
- Less than 1.5%
- No available data

Migration
- Over 2,000,000 people
- 1 – 2,000,000 people
- 500,000 – 1,000,000 people
- Under 500,000 people

1500 – 1914: Voluntary / Involuntary
Since 1914: Voluntary / Involuntary

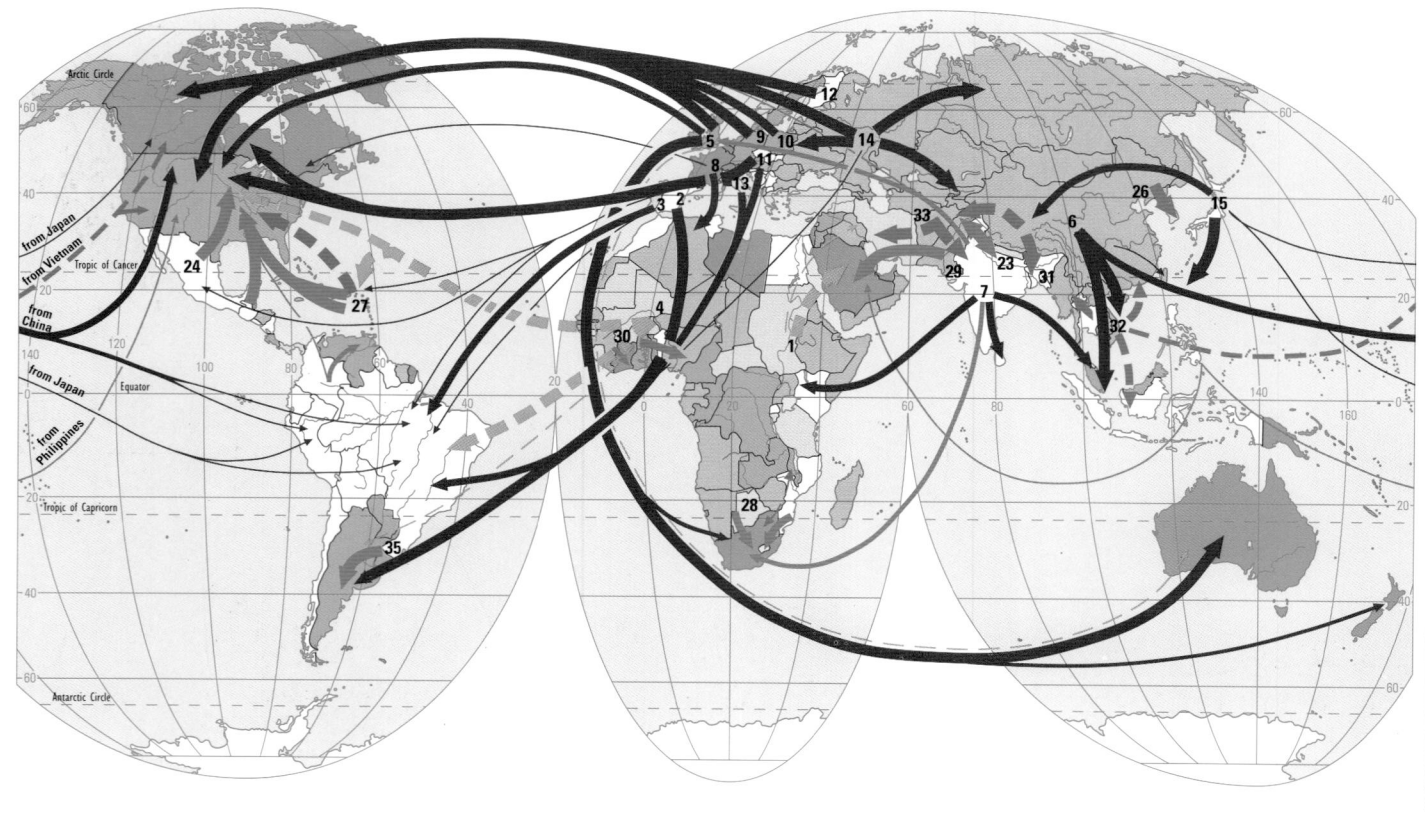

EUROPE   Migrations since 1918

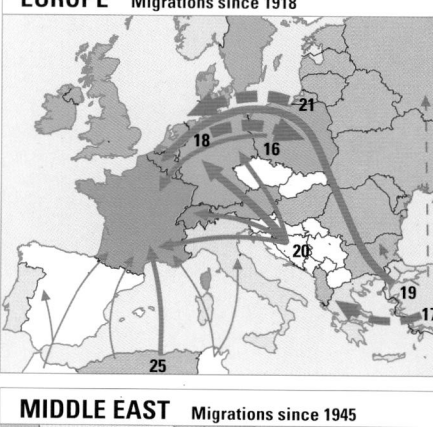

MIDDLE EAST   Migrations since 1945

BUILDING THE USA

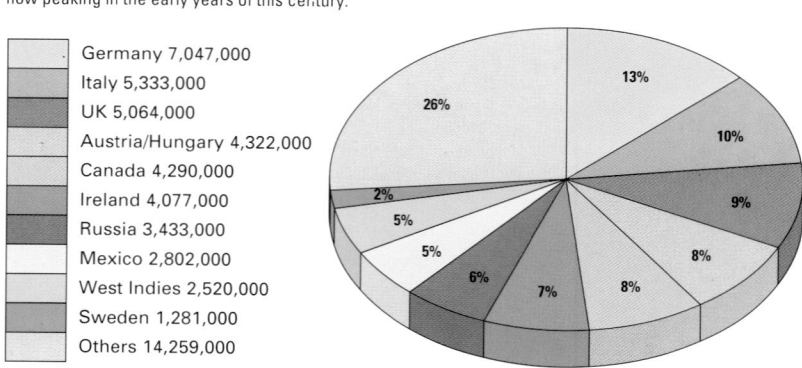

US Immigration 1820–1990

'Give me your tired, your poor/Your huddled masses yearning to breathe free....'

So starts Emma Lazarus's poem *The New Colossus*, inscribed on the Statue of Liberty. For decades the USA was the magnet that attracted millions of immigrants, notably from Central and Eastern Europe, the flow peaking in the early years of this century.

- Germany 7,047,000
- Italy 5,333,000
- UK 5,064,000
- Austria/Hungary 4,322,000
- Canada 4,290,000
- Ireland 4,077,000
- Russia 3,433,000
- Mexico 2,802,000
- West Indies 2,520,000
- Sweden 1,281,000
- Others 14,259,000

Major world migrations since 1500 (over 1,000,000 people)

1. North African and East African slaves to Arabia (4.3m) 1500–1900
2. Spanish to South and Central America (2.3m) 1530–1914
3. Portuguese to Brazil (1.4m) 1530–1914
4. West African slaves to South America (4.6m) 1550–1860
   to Caribbean (4m) 1580–1860
   to North and Central America (1m) 1650–1820
5. British and Irish to North America (13.5m) 1620–1914
   to Australasia and South Africa (3m) 1790–1914
6. Chinese to South-east Asia (22m) 1820–1914
   to North America (1m) 1880–1914
7. Indian migrant workers (3m) 1850–1914
8. French to North Africa (1.5m) 1850–1914
9. Germans to North America (5m) 1850–1914
10. Poles to North America (3.6m) 1850–1914
11. Austro-Hungarians to North America (3.2m) 1850–1914
    to Western Europe (3.4m) 1850–1914
    to South America (1.8m) 1850–1914
12. Scandinavians to North America (2.7m) 1850–1914
13. Italians to North America (5m) 1860–1914
    to South America (3.7m) 1860–1914
14. Russians to North America (2.2m) 1880–1914
    to Western Europe (2.2m) 1880–1914
    to Siberia (6m) 1880–1914
    to Central Asia (4m) 1880–1914
15. Japanese to Eastern Asia, South-east Asia and America (8m) 1900–1914
16. Poles to Western Europe (1m) 1920–1940
17. Greeks and Armenians from Turkey (1.6m) 1922–1923
18. European Jews to extermination camps (5m) 1940–1944
19. Turks to Western Europe (1.9m) 1940–
20. Yugoslavs to Western Europe (2m) 1940–
21. Germans to Western Europe (9.8m) 1945–1947
22. Palestinian refugees (2m) 1947–
23. Indian and Pakistani refugees (15m) 1947
24. Mexicans to North America (9m) 1950–
25. North Africans to Western Europe (1.1m) 1950–
26. Korean refugees (5m) 1950–1954
27. Latin Americans and West Indians to North America (4.7m) 1960–
28. Migrant workers to South Africa (1.5m) 1960–
29. Indians and Pakistanis to The Gulf (2.4m) 1970–
30. Migrant workers to Nigeria and Ivory Coast (3m) 1970–
31. Bangladeshi and Pakistani refugees (2m) 1972
32. Vietnamese and Cambodian refugees (1.5m) 1975–
33. Afghan refugees (6.1m) 1979–
34. Egyptians to The Gulf and Libya (2.9m) 1980–
35. Migrant workers to Argentina (2m) 1980–

LANGUAGE

INDO-EUROPEAN FAMILY
- 1 Balto-Slavic group (incl. Russian, Ukrainian)
- 2 Germanic group (incl. English, German)
- 3 Celtic group
- 4 Greek
- 5 Albanian
- 6 Iranian group
- 7 Armenian
- 8 Romance group (incl. Spanish, Portuguese, French, Italian)
- 9 Indo-Aryan group (incl. Hindi, Bengali, Urdu, Punjabi, Marathi)
- 10 CAUCASIAN FAMILY

AFRO-ASIATIC FAMILY
- 11 Semitic group (incl. Arabic)
- 12 Kushitic group
- 13 Berber group
- 14 KHOISAN FAMILY
- 15 NIGER-CONGO FAMILY
- 16 NILO-SAHARAN FAMILY
- 17 URALIC FAMILY

ALTAIC FAMILY
- 18 Turkic group
- 19 Mongolian group
- 20 Tungus-Manchu group
- 21 Japanese and Korean

SINO-TIBETAN FAMILY
- 22 Sinitic (Chinese) languages
- 23 Tibetic-Burmic languages
- 24 TAI FAMILY

AUSTRO-ASIATIC FAMILY
- 25 Mon-Khmer group
- 26 Munda group
- 27 Vietnamese
- 28 DRAVIDIAN FAMILY (incl. Telugu, Tamil)
- 29 AUSTRONESIAN FAMILY (incl. Malay-Indonesian)
- 30 OTHER LANGUAGES

OFFICIAL LANGUAGES

Language	Total population	World %
English	1,400m	27.0%
Chinese	1,070m	19.1%
Hindi	700m	13.5%
Spanish	280m	5.4%
Russian	270m	5.2%
French	220m	4.2%
Arabic	170m	3.3%
Portuguese	160m	3.0%
Malay	160m	3.0%
Bengali	150m	2.9%
Japanese	120m	2.3%

Languages form a kind of tree of development, splitting from a few ancient proto-tongues into branches that have grown apart and further divided with the passage of time. English and Hindi, for example, both belong to the great Indo-European family, although the relationship is only apparent after much analysis and comparison with non-Indo-European languages such as Chinese or Arabic; Hindi is part of the Indo-Aryan subgroup, whereas English is a member of Indo-European's Germanic branch; French, another Indo-European tongue, traces its descent through the Latin, or Romance, branch. A few languages – Basque is one example – have no apparent links with any other, living or dead. Most modern languages, of course, have acquired enormous quantities of vocabulary from each other.

MOTHER TONGUES

Native speakers of the major languages, in millions (1989)

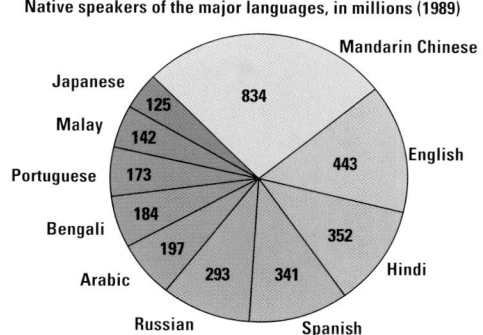

- Mandarin Chinese 834
- English 443
- Hindi 352
- Spanish 341
- Russian 293
- Arabic 197
- Bengali 184
- Portuguese 173
- Malay 142
- Japanese 125

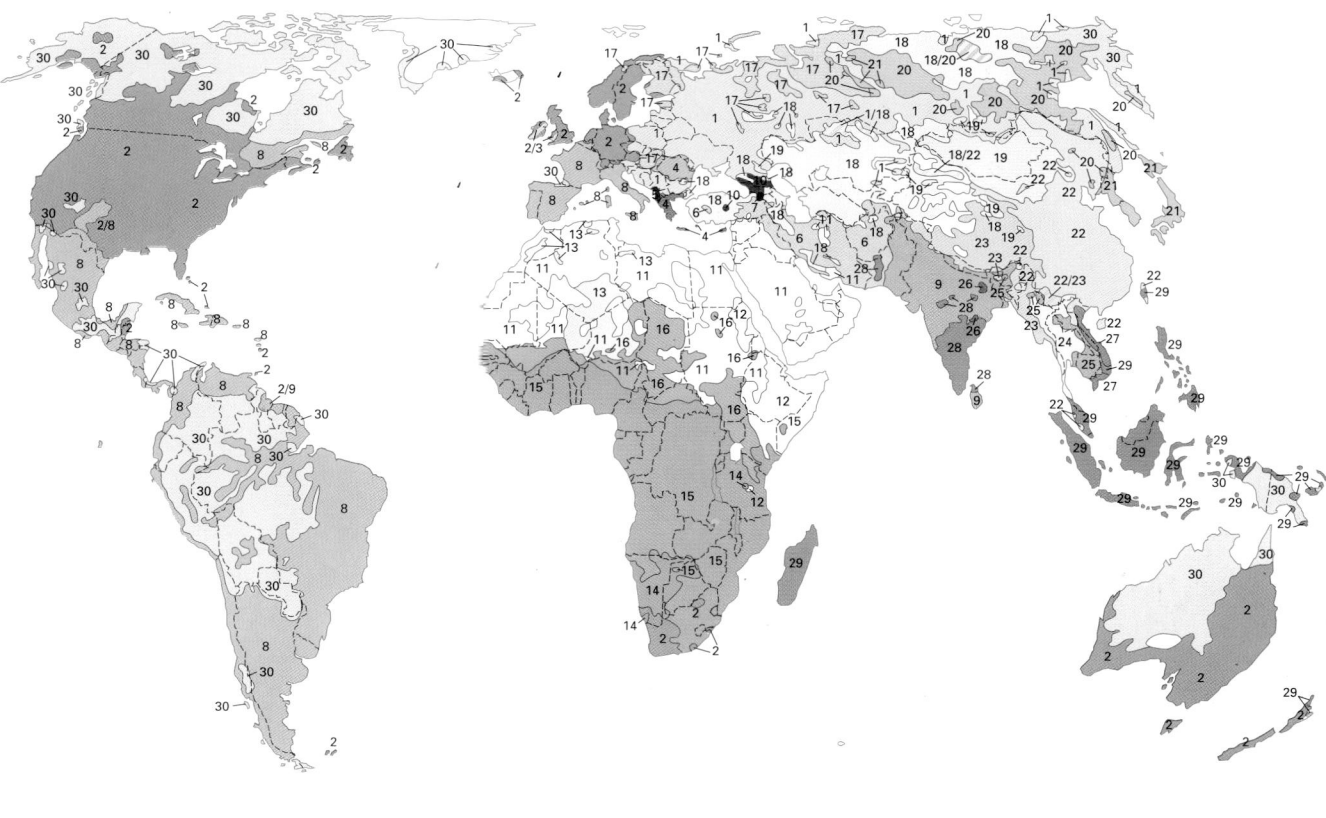

RELIGION

- ▲ Roman Catholicism
- Orthodox and other Eastern Churches
- ● Protestantism
- Sunni Islam
- Shia Islam
- Buddhism
- Hinduism
- Confucianism
- ★ Judaism
- Shintoism
- Primitive Religions

Religions are not as easily mapped as the physical contours of landscape. Divisions are often blurred and frequently overlapping: most nations include people of many different faiths – or no faith at all. Some religions, like Islam and Christianity, have proselytes worldwide; others, like Hinduism and Confucianism, are restricted to a particular area, though modern migrations have taken some Indians and Chinese very far from their cultural origins. It is also difficult to show the degree to which religion exercises control over daily life: Christian Western Europe, for example, is nowadays far less dominated by its religion than are the Islamic nations of the Middle East. Similarly, figures for the major faiths' adherents make no distinction between nominal believers enrolled at birth and those for whom religion is a vital part of existence.

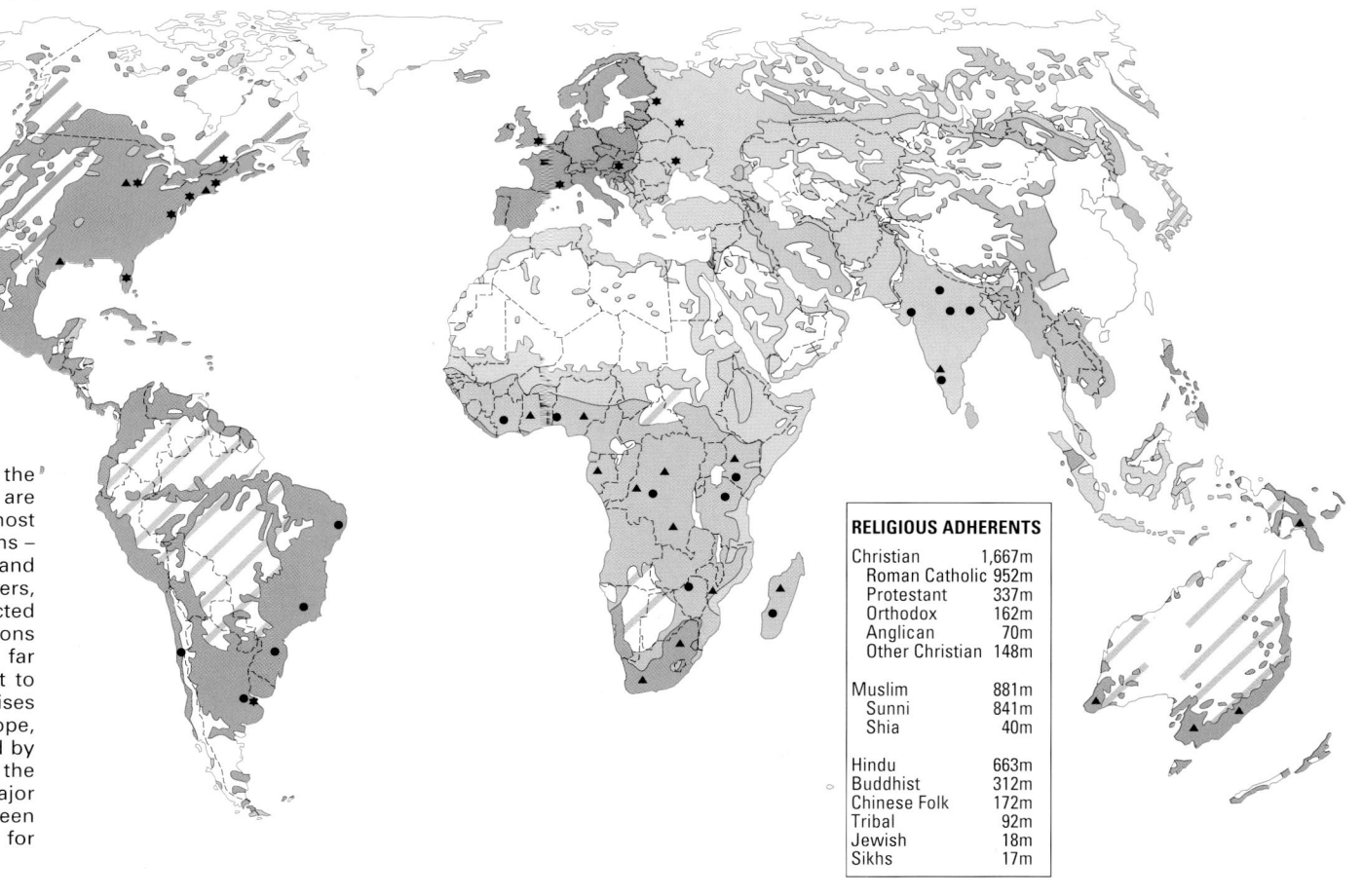

RELIGIOUS ADHERENTS

Christian	1,667m
Roman Catholic	952m
Protestant	337m
Orthodox	162m
Anglican	70m
Other Christian	148m
Muslim	881m
Sunni	841m
Shia	40m
Hindu	663m
Buddhist	312m
Chinese Folk	172m
Tribal	92m
Jewish	18m
Sikhs	17m

PEOPLE: CONFLICT & CO-OPERATION

26: MIGRATION

27: RELIGION

46: HUMAN EXPANSION

Humans are social animals, rarely functioning well except in groups. Evolution has made them so: hunter-gatherers in co-operative bands were far more effective than animals that prowled alone. Agriculture, the building of cities and industrialization are all developments that depended on human co-operative ability – and in turn increased the need for it.

Unfortunately, human groups do not always cooperate so well with other human groups, and friction between them sometimes leads to co-operatively organized violence. War is itself a very human activity, with no real equivalent in any other species. Always murderous, it is sometimes purposeful and

may even be very effective. The colonization of the Americas and Australia, for example, was in effect the waging of aggressive war by well-armed Europeans against indigenous peoples incapable of offering a serious defence.

Most often, war achieves little but death and ruin. The great 20th-century wars accomplished nothing for the nations involved in them, although the world paid a price of between 50 and 100 million dead as well as immense material damage. The relative peace in the postwar developed world is at least partly due to the nuclear weapons with which rival powers have armed themselves – weapons so powerful that their

use would leave a scarcely habitable planet with no meaningful distinction between victor and vanquished.

Yet warfare remains endemic: the second half of the 20th century was one of the bloodiest periods in history, and death by organized violence remains unhappily common. The map below attempts to show the serious conflicts that have scarred the Earth since 1945. Most are civil wars in poor countries, rather than international conflicts between rich ones; some of them are still unresolved, while others, like apparently extinct volcanoes, may erupt again at intervals, adding to the world's miserable population of refugees.

THE WORLD'S REFUGEES

Refugees and their national origin; the host nations and the relative size of their refugee populations (1991)

Refugees in millions

Refugees as a proportion of host country's population

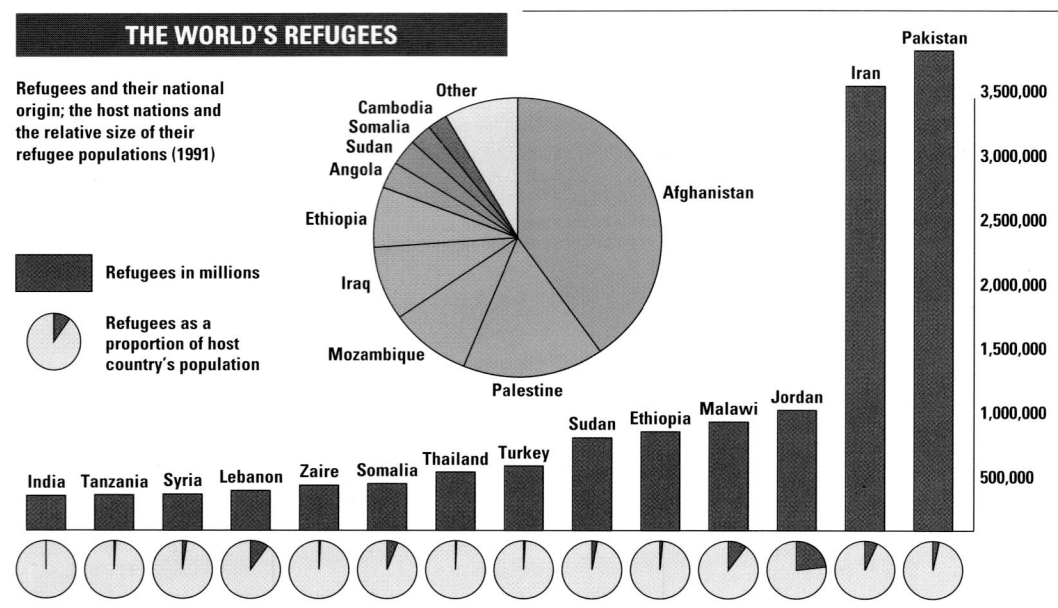

The pie-chart shows the origins of the world's refugees, while the bar-chart shows their destinations. According to the United Nations High Commissioner for Refugees, in 1990 there were almost 15 million refugees, a number that has continued to increase and is almost certain to be amplified during the decade. Some have fled from climatic change, some from economic disaster and others from political persecution; the great majority, however, are the victims of war.

All but a few who make it overseas seek asylum in neighbouring countries, which are often the least equipped to deal with them and where they are rarely welcome. Lacking any rights or power, they frequently become an embarrassment and a burden to their reluctant hosts.

Usually, the best any refugee can hope for is rudimentary food and shelter in temporary camps that all to often become semi-permanent, with little prospect of assimilation by host populations: many Palestinians, for example, have been forced to live in camps since 1948.

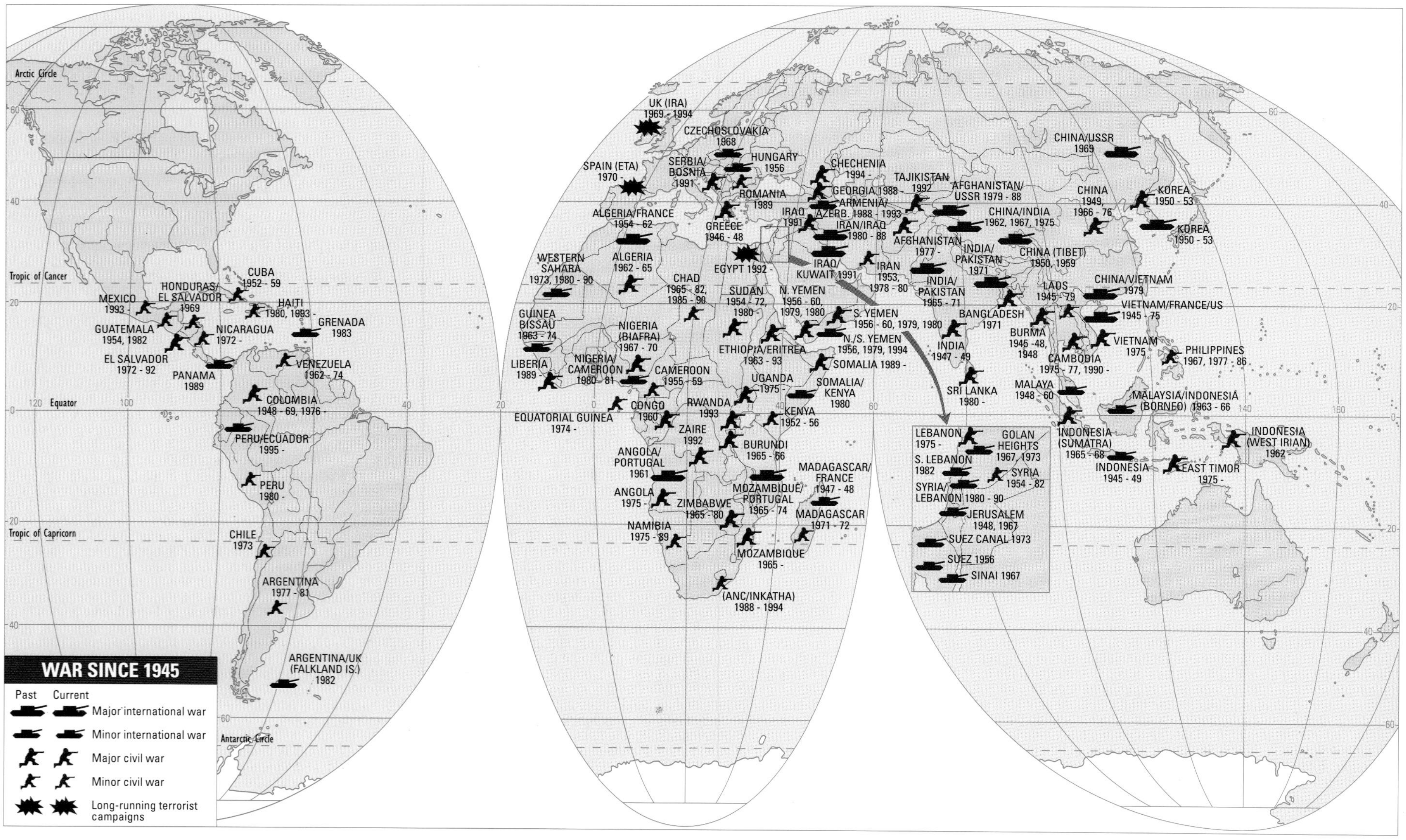

WAR SINCE 1945

Past	Current	
		Major international war
		Minor international war
		Major civil war
		Minor civil war
		Long-running terrorist campaigns

UNITED NATIONS

The United Nations Organization was born as World War II drew to its conclusion. Six years of strife had strengthened the world's desire for peace, but an effective international organization was needed to help achieve it. That body would replace the League of Nations which, since its inception in 1920, had signally failed to curb the aggression of at least some of its member nations. At the United Nations Conference on International Organization held in San Francisco, the United Nations Charter was drawn up. Ratified by the Security Council and signed by the 51 original members, it came into effect on 24 October 1945.

The Charter set out the aims of the organization: to maintain peace and security, and develop friendly relations between nations; to achieve international co-operation in solving economic, social, cultural and humanitarian problems; to promote respect for human rights and fundamental freedoms; and to harmonize the activities of nations in order to achieve these common goals.

By 1995, the UN had expanded to 185 member countries; it is the largest international political organization, employing over 25,000 people worldwide; its headquarters in New York accounts for 7,000 staff and it also has major offices in Rome, Geneva and Vienna.

The United Nations has six principal organs:

The General Assembly
The forum at which member nations discuss moral and political issues affecting world development, peace and security meets annually in September, under a newly-elected President whose tenure lasts one year. Any member can bring business to the agenda, and each member nation has one vote. Decisions are made by simple majority, save for matters of very great importance, when a two-thirds majority is required.

The Security Council
A legislative and executive body, the Security Council is the primary instrument for establishing and maintaining international peace by attempting to settle disputes between nations. It has the power to dispatch UN forces to stop aggression, and member nations undertake to make armed forces, assistance and facilities available as required. The Security Council has ten temporary members elected by the General Assembly for two-year terms, and five permanent members – China, France, Russia, UK and USA.

The Economic and Social Council
By far the largest United Nations executive, the Council operates as a conduit between the General Assembly and the many United Nations agencies it instructs to implement Assembly decisions, and whose work it co-ordinates. The Council also sets up commissions to examine economic conditions, collects data and issues studies and reports, and may make recommendations to the Assembly.

The Secretariat
This is the staff of the United Nations, and its task is to administer the policies and programmes of the UN and its organs, and assist and advise the Head of the Secretariat, the Secretary-General – a full-time, non-political, appointment made by the General Assembly.

The Trusteeship Council
The Council administers trust territories with the aim of promoting their advancement. Only one remains – the Trust Territory of the Pacific Is. (Palau).

The International Court of Justice (the World Court)
The World Court is the judicial organ of the United Nations. It deals only with United Nations disputes and all members are subject to its jurisdiction. There are 15 judges, elected for nine-year terms by the General Assembly and the Security Council. The Court sits in The Hague.

United Nations agencies and programmes, and inter-governmental agencies co-ordinated by the UN, contribute to harmonious world development. Social and humanitarian operations include:

United Nations Development Programme (UNDP) Plans and funds projects to help developing countries make better use of resources.
United Nations International Childrens' Fund (UNICEF) Created at the General Assembly's first session in 1945 to help children in the aftermath of World War II, it now provides basic health care and aid worldwide.
United Nations Fund for Population Activities (UNFPA) Promotes awareness of population issues and family planning, providing appropriate assistance.
Food and Agriculture Organization (FAO) Aims to raise living standards and nutrition levels in rural areas by improving food production and distribution.
United Nations Educational, Scientific and Cultural Organization (UNESCO) Promotes international co-operation through broader and better education.
World Health Organization (WHO) Promotes and provides for better health care, public and environmental health and medical research.

Membership There are seven independent states which are not members of the UN – Kiribati, Nauru, Switzerland, Taiwan, Tonga, Tuvalu and Vatican City. Official languages are Chinese, English, French, Russian, Spanish and Arabic.
Funding The UN budget for 1994–95 is US $2.6 billion. Contributions are assessed by the members' ability to pay, with the maximum 25% of the total, the minimum 0.01%. Contributions for 1992–94 were: USA 25%, Japan 12.45%, Germany 8.93%, Russia 6.71%, France 6%, UK 5.02%, Italy 4.29%, Canada 3.11% (others 28.49%).
Peacekeeping The UN has been involved in 33 peacekeeping operations worldwide since 1948 and there are currently 17 areas of UN patrol. In July 1993 there were 80,146 'blue berets' from 74 countries.

United Nations agencies are involved in many aspects of international trade, safety and security:

General Agreement on Tariffs and Trade (GATT) Sponsors international trade negotiations and advocates a common code of conduct.
International Maritime Organization (IMO) Promotes unity amongst merchant shipping, especially in regard to safety, marine pollution and standardization.
International Labour Organization (ILO) Seeks to improve labour conditions and promote productive employment to raise living standards.
World Meteorological Organization (WMO) Promotes co-operation in weather observation, reporting and forecasting.
World Intellectual Property Organization (WIPO) Seeks to protect intellectual property such as artistic copyright, scientific patents and trademarks.
Disarmament Commission Considers and makes recommendations to the General Assembly on disarmament issues.
International Atomic Energy Agency (IAEA) Fosters development of peaceful uses for nuclear energy, establishes safety standards and monitors the destruction of nuclear material designed for military use.

The World Bank comprises three United Nations agencies:

International Monetary Fund (IMF) Cultivates international monetary co-operation and expansion of trade.
International Bank for Reconstruction and Development (IBRD) Provides funds and technical assistance to developing countries.
International Finance Corporation (IFC) Encourages the growth of productive private enterprise in less developed countries.

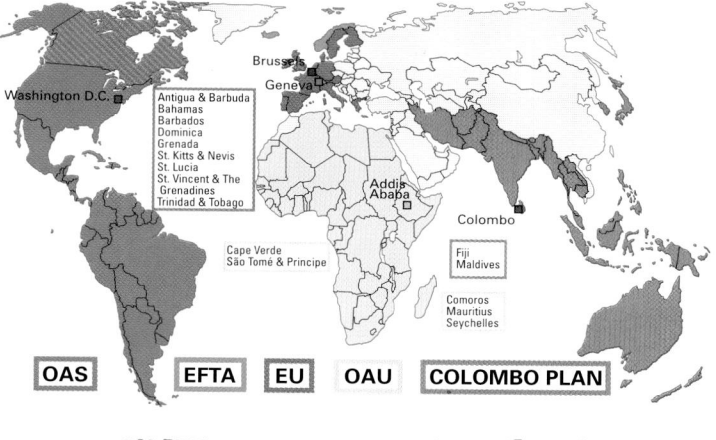

OAS   EFTA   EU   OAU   COLOMBO PLAN

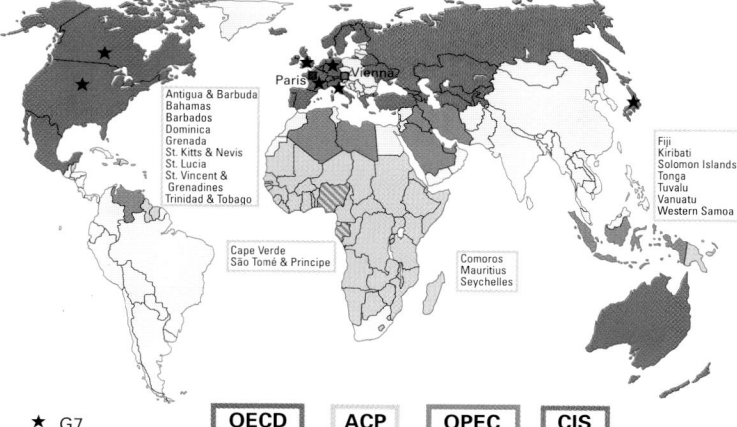

★ G7   OECD   ACP   OPEC   CIS

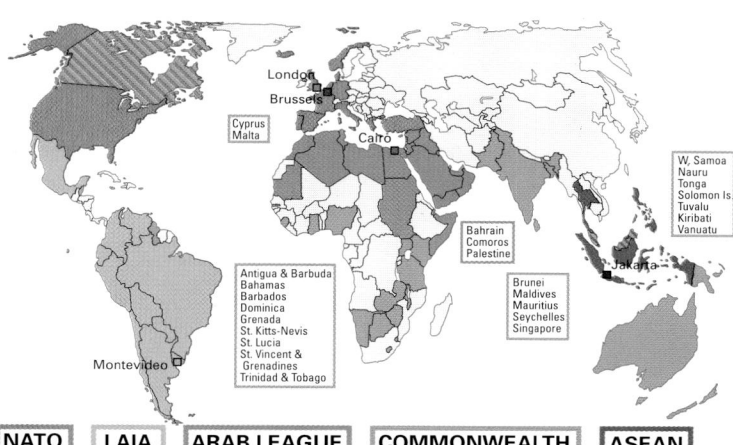

NATO   LAIA   ARAB LEAGUE   COMMONWEALTH   ASEAN

EU As from December 1993 the European Union (EU) refers to matters of foreign policy, security and justice. The European Community (EC) refers to all other matters. The 15 members – Austria, Belgium, Denmark, Finland, France, Germany, Greece, Ireland, Italy, Luxembourg, Netherlands, Portugal, Spain, Sweden and the UK – aim to integrate economies, co-ordinate social developments and bring about political union. These members of what is now the world's biggest market share agricultural and industrial policies and tariffs on trade.
EFTA European Free Trade Association (formed in 1960). Portugal left the original 'Seven' in 1989 to join the EC, followed by Austria, Finland and Sweden in 1995. There are now only four members: Norway, Iceland, Liechtenstein and Switzerland.
ACP African-Caribbean-Pacific countries associated with the EC (1963).
NATO North Atlantic Treaty Organization (formed in 1949). It continues after 1991 despite the winding up of the Warsaw Pact.
OAS Organization of American States (1948). It aims to promote social and economic co-operation between developed countries of North America and developing nations of Latin America.
ASEAN Association of South-east Asian Nations (1967).
OAU Organization of African Unity (1963). Its 53 members represent over 94% of Africa's population.
LAIA Latin American Integration Association (1980) superceded the Latin American Free Trade Association formed in 1961.
OECD Organization for Economic Co-operation and Development (1961). The 25 major Western free-market economies.* 'G7' is its 'inner group' of USA, Canada, Japan, UK, Germany, Italy and France. *Mexico joined in May 1994.
COMMONWEALTH The Commonwealth of Nations evolved from the British Empire; it comprises 19 nations recognizing the British monarch as head of state and 32 with their own heads of state.
CIS The Commonwealth of Independent States (1991) comprises the countries of the former Soviet Union except for Estonia, Latvia and Lithuania.
OPEC Organization of Petroleum Exporting Countries (1960). It controls about three-quarters of the world's oil supply. Ecuador withdrew formally on 1 January 1993.
ARAB LEAGUE (1945) The League's aim is to promote economic, social, political and military co-operation.
COLOMBO PLAN (1951) Its 26 members aim to promote economic and social development in Asia and the Pacific.

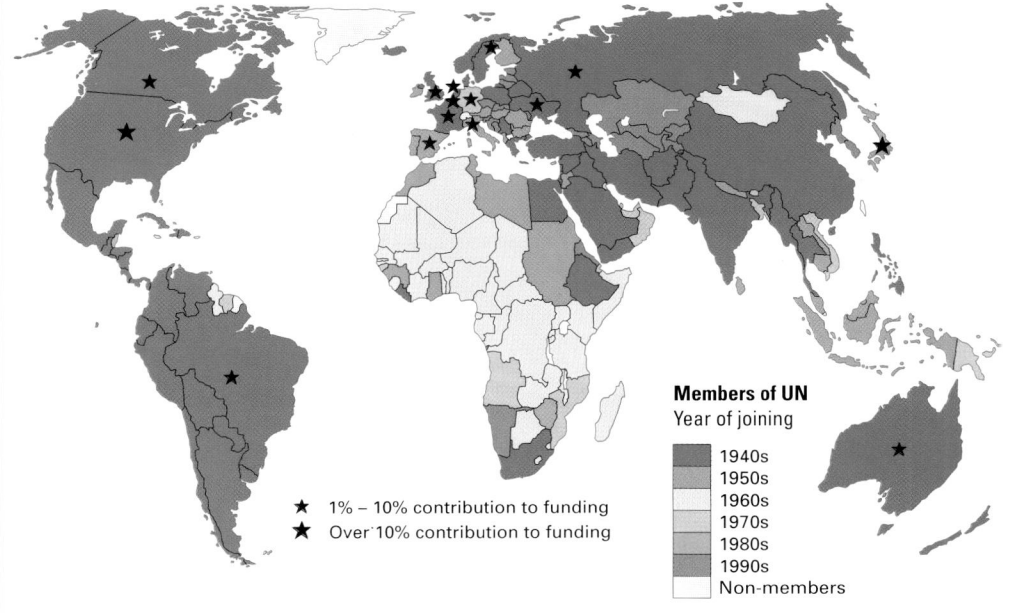

Members of UN
Year of joining

	1940s
	1950s
	1960s
	1970s
	1980s
	1990s
	Non-members

★ 1% – 10% contribution to funding
★ Over 10% contribution to funding

PRODUCTION: AGRICULTURE

14: CLIMATE REGIONS

15: TEMPERATURE AND PRECIPITATION

16: WATER UTILIZATION

17: NATURAL VEGETATION LAND USE BY CONTINENT

36: DIVISION OF EMPLOYMENT

46: HUMAN EXPANSION

The invention of agriculture transformed human existence more than any other development, though it may not have seemed much of an improvement to its first practitioners. Primitive farming required brutally hard work, and it tied men and women to a patch of land, highly vulnerable to local weather patterns and to predators, especially human predators – drawbacks still apparent in much of the world today. It is difficult to imagine early humans being interested in such an existence while there were still animals around to hunt and wild seeds and berries to gather. Probably the spur was population pressure, with consequent overhunting and scarcity.

Despite its difficulties, the new life style had a few overwhelming advantages. It supported far larger populations, eventually including substantial cities, with all the varied cultural and economic activities they allowed. Later still, it furnished the surpluses that allowed industrialization – another enormous step in the course of human development.

Machines relieved many farmers of their burden of endless toil, and made it possible for relatively small numbers to provide food for more than 5,000 million people.

Now, as in the past, the whole business of farming involves the creation of a severely simplified ecology, under the tutelage and for the benefit of the farmer. Natural plant life is divided into crops, to be protected and nurtured, and weeds, the rest, to be destroyed. From the earliest days, crops were selectively bred to increase their food yield, usually at the expense of their ability to survive, which became the farmer's responsibility; 20th-century plant geneticists have carried the technique to highly productive extremes. Due mainly to new varieties of rice and wheat, world grain production has increased by 70% since 1965, more than doubling in the developing countries, although such high yields demand equally high consumption of fertilizers and pesticides to maintain them. Mechanized farmers in North America and Europe continue to turn out huge surpluses, although not without environmental costs.

Where production is inadequate, the reasons are as likely to be political as agricultural. Africa, the only continent where food production per capita is actually falling, suffers acutely from economic mismanagement, as well as from the perennial problems of war and banditry. Dismal harvests in the USSR, despite its excellent farmland, helped bring about the collapse of the Soviet system.

There are other limits to progress too. Increasing population puts relentless pressure on farmers not only to maintain high yields but also to increase them. Most of the world's potential cropland is already under the plough. The overworking of marginal land is one of the prime causes of desertification; new farmlands burned out of former rainforests are seldom fertile for long. Human numbers may yet outrun the land's ability to feed them, as they did almost 10,000 years ago.

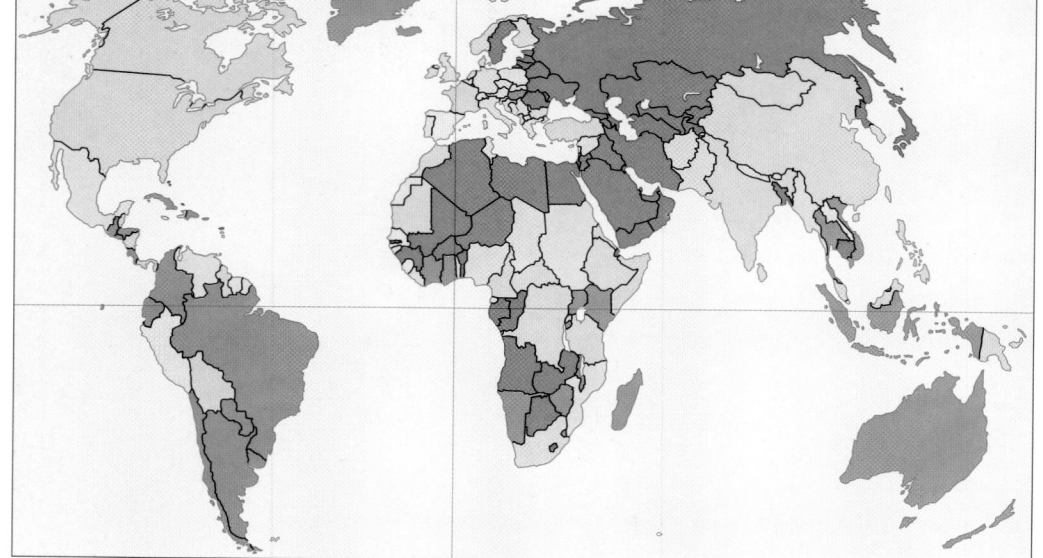

SELF-SUFFICIENCY IN FOOD

Balance of trade in food products as a percentage of total trade in food products (latest available year)

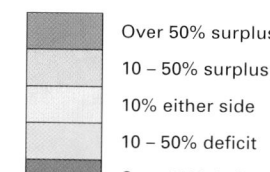

Over 50% surplus

10 – 50% surplus

10% either side

10 – 50% deficit

Over 50% deficit

Most self-sufficient		Least self-sufficient	
Argentina	95%	Algeria	−98%
Zimbabwe	87%	Djibouti	−97%
Honduras	81%	Yemen	−95%
Malawi	81%	Zambia	−95%
Costa Rica	79%	Japan	−91%
Iceland	78%	Gabon	−90%
Chile	75%	Kuwait	−75%
Uruguay	75%	Brunei	−89%
Ecuador	74%	Burkina Faso	−82%

LAND USE

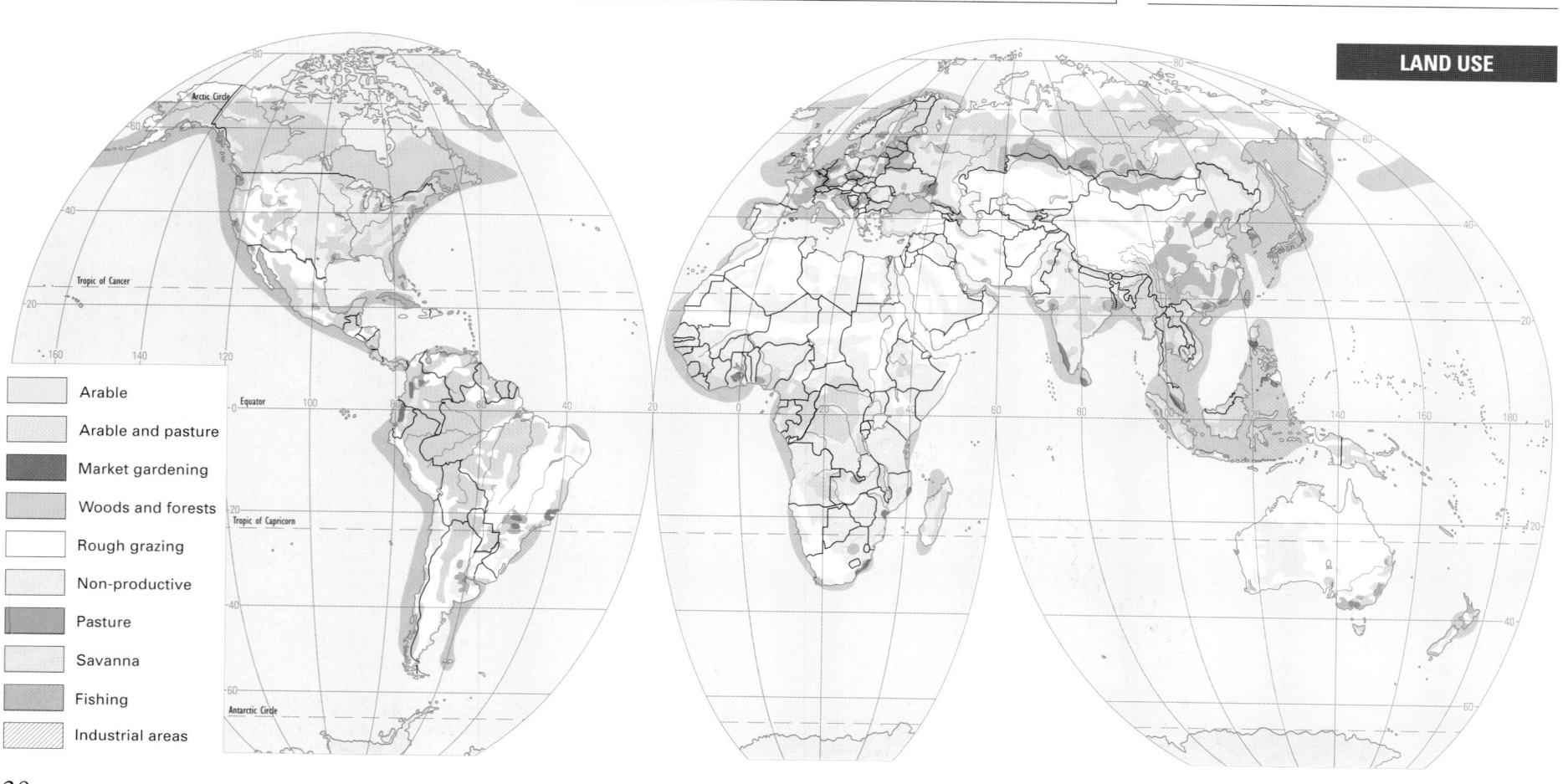

Arable

Arable and pasture

Market gardening

Woods and forests

Rough grazing

Non-productive

Pasture

Savanna

Fishing

Industrial areas

STAPLE CROPS

Wheat: Grown in a range of climates, with most varieties – including the highest-quality bread wheats – requiring temperate conditions. Mainly used in baking, it is also used for pasta and breakfast cereals.

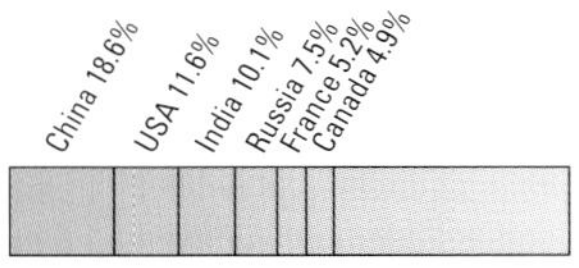
China 18.6%
USA 11.6%
India 10.1%
Russia 7.5%
France 5.2%
Canada 4.9%

World total (1993): 564,457,000 tonnes

Maize: Originating in the New World and still an important human food in Africa and Latin America, in the developed world it is processed into breakfast cereals, oil, starches and adhesives. It is also used for animal feed.

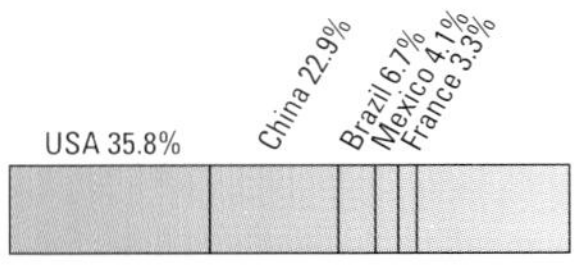
USA 35.8%
China 22.9%
Brazil 6.7%
Mexico 4.1%
France 3.3%

World total (1993): 450,570,000 tonnes

Oats: Most widely used to feed livestock, but eaten by humans as oatmeal or porridge. Oats have a beneficial effect on the cardio-vascular system, and human consumption is likely to increase.

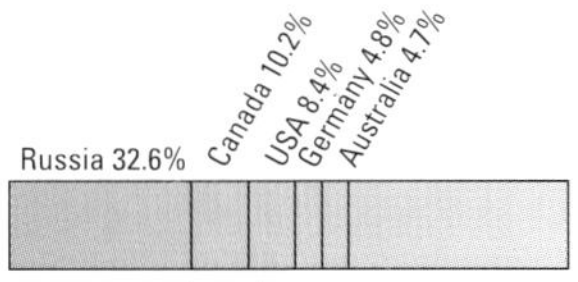
Russia 32.6%
Canada 10.2%
USA 8.4%
Germany 4.8%
Australia 4.7%

World total (1993): 35,443,000 tonnes

Millet: The name covers a number of small-grained cereals, members of the grass family with a short growing season. Used to produce flour, meal and animal feed, and fermented to make beer, especially in Africa.

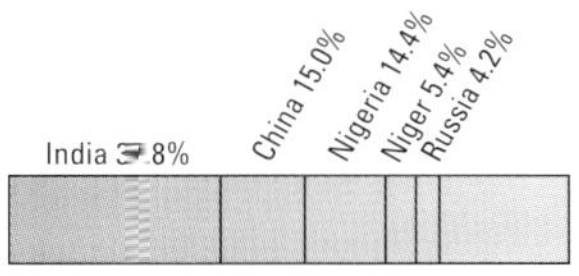
India
China 15.0%
Nigeria 14.4%
Niger 5.4%
Russia 4.2%

World total (1993): 26,442,000 tonnes

Cassava: A tropical shrub that needs high rainfall (over 1000 mm annually) and a 10–30 month growing season to produce its large, edible tubers. Used as flour by humans, as cattle feed and in industrial starches.

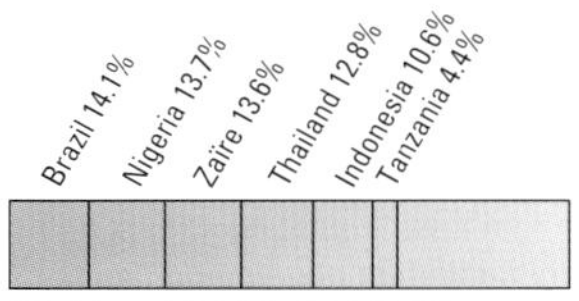
Brazil 14.1%
Nigeria 13.7%
Zaïre 13.6%
Thailand 12.8%
Indonesia 10.6%
Tanzania 4.4%

World total (1993): 153,628,000 tonnes

Rice: Thrives on the high humidity and temperatures of the Far East, where it is the traditional staple food of half the human race. Usually grown standing in water, rice responds well to continuous cultivation, with three or four crops annually.

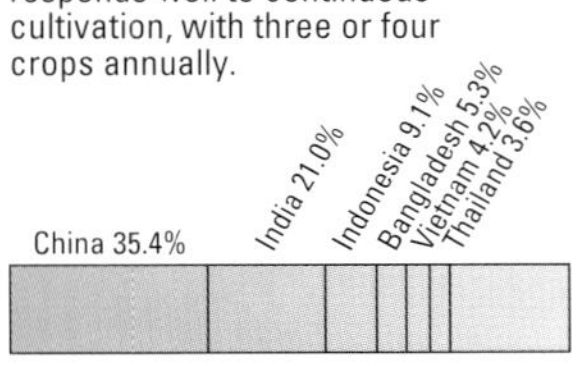
China 35.4%
India 21.0%
Indonesia 9.1%
Bangladesh 5.2%
Vietnam 4.2%
Thailand 3.6%

World total (1993): 527,413,000 tonnes

Barley: Primarily used as animal feed, but widely eaten by humans in Africa and Asia. Elsewhere, malted barley furnishes beer and spirits. Able to withstand the dry heat of subarid tropics, its growing season is only 80 days.

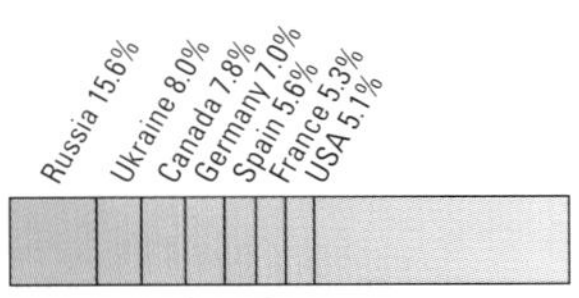
Russia 15.6%
Ukraine 8.0%
Canada 7.8%
Germany 7.0%
Spain 5.6%
France 5.3%
USA 5.1%

World total (1993): 170,364,000 tonnes

Rye: Hardy and tolerant of poor and sandy soils, it is an important foodstuff and animal feed in Central and Eastern Europe. Rye produces a dark, heavy bread as well as alcoholic drinks.

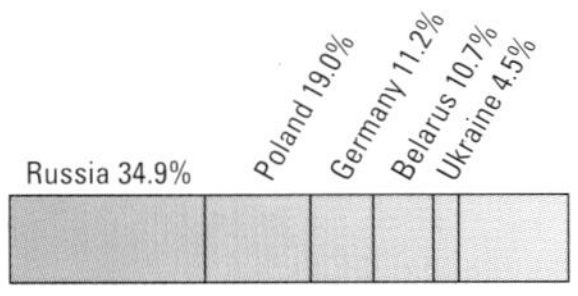
Russia 34.9%
Poland 19.0%
Germany 11.2%
Belarus 10.7%
Ukraine 4.5%

World total (1993): 26,200,000 tonnes

Potatoes: The most important of the edible tubers, potatoes grow in well-watered, temperate areas. Weight for weight less nutritious than grain, they are a human staple as well as an important animal feed.

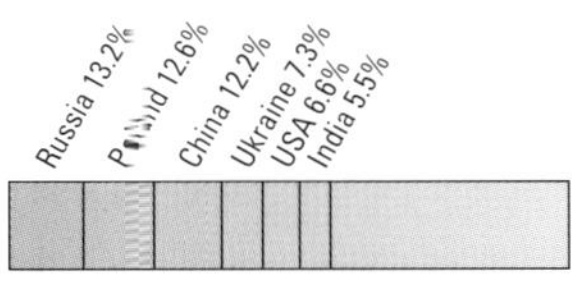
Russia 13.2%
China 12.2%
Ukraine 7.3%
USA 6.6%
India 5.5%

World total (1993): 288,183,000 tonnes

Soya: Beans from soya bushes are very high (30–40%) in protein. Most are processed into oil and proprietary protein foods. Consumption since 1950 has tripled, mainly due to the health-conscious developed world.

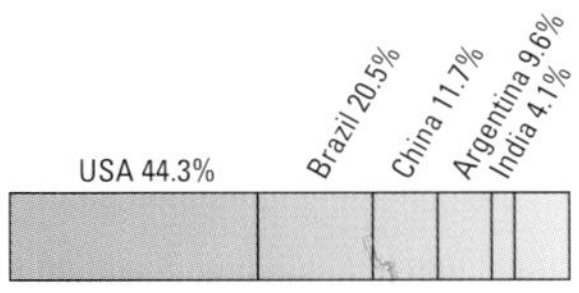
USA 44.3%
Brazil 20.5%
China 11.7%
Argentina 9.6%
India 4.1%

World total (1993): 111,011,000 tonnes

Cereals are grasses with starchy, edible seeds; every important civilization has depended on them as a source of food. The major cereal grains contain about 10% protein and 75% carbohydrate; grain is easy to store, handle and transport, and contributes more than any other group of foods to the energy and protein content of human diet. If all the cereals were consumed directly by man, there would be no shortage of food in the world, but a considerable proportion of the total output is used as animal feed.

Starchy tuber crops or root crops, represented here by potatoes and cassava, are second in importance only to cereals as staple foods; easily cultivated, they provide high yields for little effort and store well – potatoes for up to six months, cassava for up to a year in the ground. Protein content is low (2% or less), starch content high, with some minerals and vitamins present, but populations that rely heavily on these crops may suffer from malnutrition.

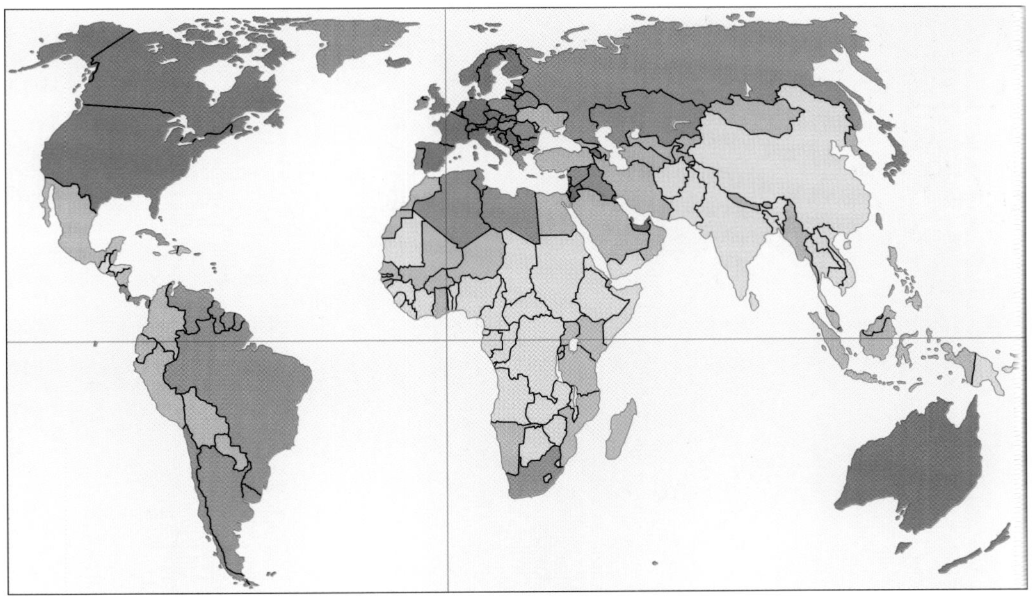

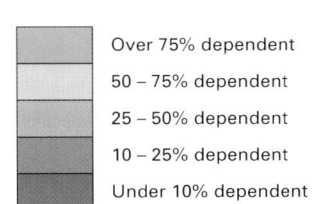

IMPORTANCE OF AGRICULTURE

Percentage of the total population dependent on agriculture (1991)

- Over 75% dependent
- 50 – 75% dependent
- 25 – 50% dependent
- 10 – 25% dependent
- Under 10% dependent

Top 5 countries		Bottom 5 countries	
Nepal	92%	Singapore	0.9%
Rwanda	91%	Hong Kong	1.2%
Burundi	91%	Bahrain	1.7%
Bhutan	91%	Belgium	1.7%
Niger	87%	UK	1.9%

FOOD & POPULATION

Comparison of food production and population by continent (latest available year). The left column indicates percentage shares of total world food production; the right shows population in proportion.

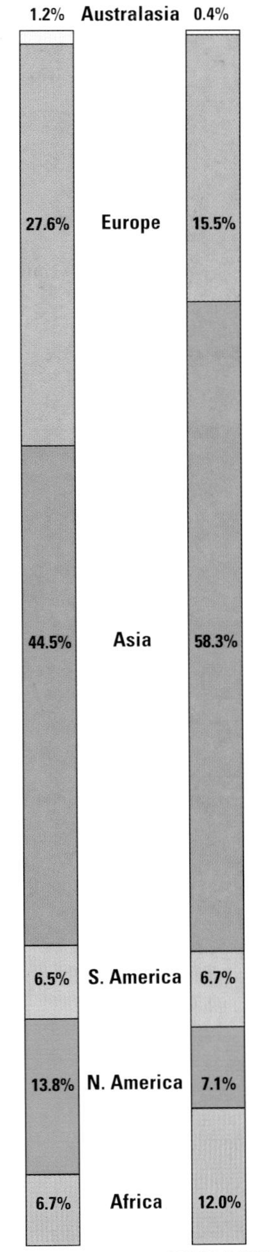
1.2% Australasia 0.4%
27.6% Europe 15.5%
44.5% Asia 58.3%
6.5% S. America 6.7%
13.8% N. America 7.1%
6.7% Africa 12.0%
FOOD
POPULATION

ANIMAL PRODUCTS

Traditionally, food animals subsisted on land unsuitable for cultivation, supporting agricultural production with their fertilizing dung. But free-ranging animals grow slowly and yield less meat than those more intensively reared; the demands of urban markets in the developed world have encouraged the growth of factory-like production methods.

A large proportion of staple crops, especially cereals, are fed to animals, an inefficient way to produce protein but one likely to continue as long as people value meat and dairy products in their diet.

Cheese: Least perishable of all dairy products, cheese is milk fermented with selected bacterial strains to produce a foodstuff with a potentially immense range of flavours and textures. The vast majority of cheeses are made from cow's milk, although sheep and goat cheeses are highly prized.

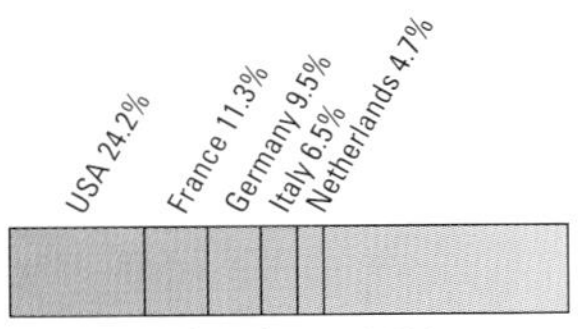
USA 24.2%
France 11.3%
Germany 9.5%
Italy 6.5%
Netherlands 4.7%

World total (1993): 13,533,000 tonnes

Lamb and Mutton: Sheep are the least demanding of domestic animals. Although unsuited to intensive rearing, they can thrive on marginal pastureland incapable of supporting beef cattle on a commercial scale. Sheep are raised as much for their valuable wool as for the meat that they provide, with Australia the world leader.

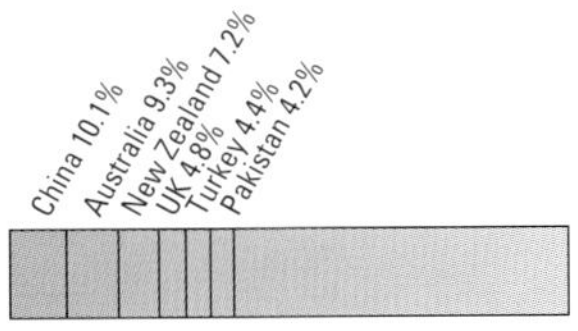
China 10.1%
Australia 9.3%
New Zealand 7.2%
UK 4.8%
Turkey 4.4%
Pakistan 4.2%

World total (1993): 6,914,000 tonnes

Beef and Veal: Most beef and veal is reared for home markets, and the top five producers are also the biggest consumers. The USA produces nearly a quarter of the world's beef and eats even more.

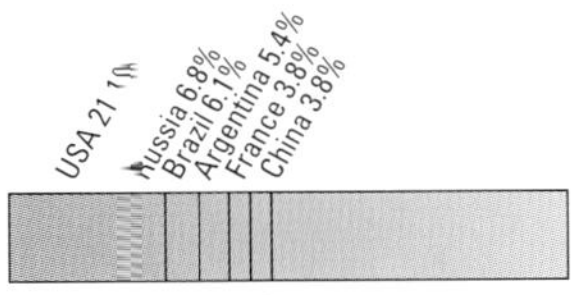
Russia 6.8%
Brazil 6.1%
Argentina 5.4%
France 3.8%
China 3.8%

World total (1993): 50,239,000 tonnes

SUGARS

Sugar cane: Confined to tropical regions, cane sugar accounts for the bulk of international trade in the commodity. Most is produced as a foodstuff, but some countries, notably Brazil and South Africa, distill sugar cane and use the resulting ethyl alcohol to make motor fuels.

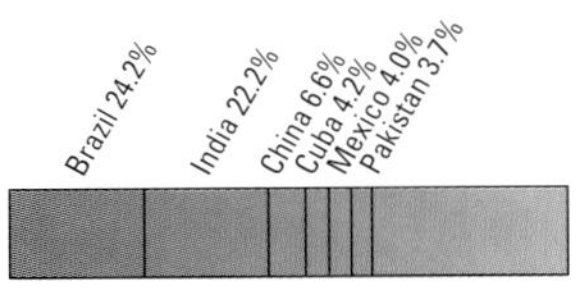
Brazil 24.2%
India 22.2%
China 6.6%
Cuba 4.2%
Mexico 4.0%
Pakistan 3.7%

World total (1993): 1,040,600,000 tonnes

Milk: Many human groups, including most Asians, find raw milk indigestible after infancy, and it is often only the starting point for other dairy products such as butter, cheese and yoghurt. Most world production comes from cows, but sheep's milk and goats' milk are also important.

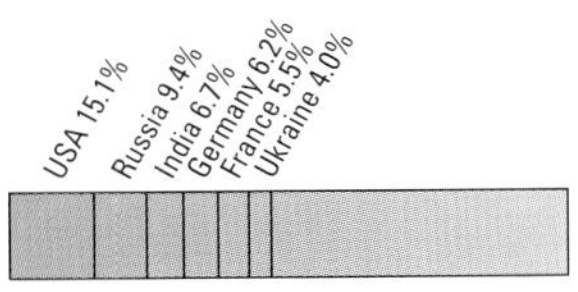
USA 15.1%
Russia 9.4%
India 6.7%
Germany 6.2%
France 5.5%
Ukraine 4.0%

World total (1993): 453,733,000 tonnes

Butter: A traditional source of vitamin A as well as calories, butter has lost much popularity in the developed world for health reasons, although it remains a valuable food. Most butter from India, the world's largest producer, is clarified into ghee, which has religious as well as nutritional importance.

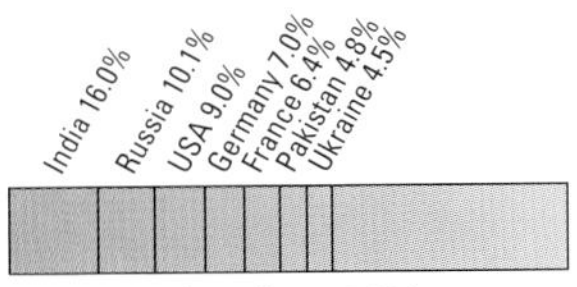
India 16.0%
Russia 10.1%
USA 9.0%
Germany 7.0%
France 6.4%
Pakistan 4.8%
Ukraine 4.5%

World total (1993): 6,956,000 tonnes

Pork: Although pork is forbidden to many millions, notably Muslims, on religious grounds, more is produced than any other meat in the world, mainly because it is the cheapest. It accounts for about 90% of China's meat output, although per capita meat consumption is relatively low.

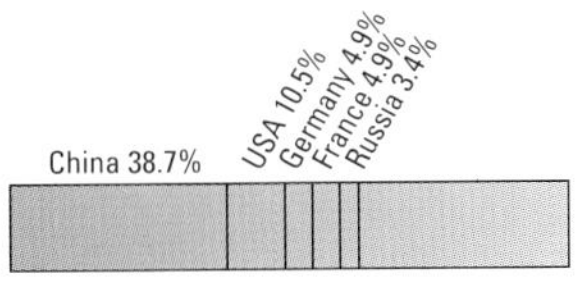
China 38.7%
USA 10.5%
Germany 4.9%
France 4.9%
Russia 3.4%

World total (1993): 73,891,000 tonnes

Fish: Commercial fishing requires large shoals of fish, often of only one species, within easy reach of markets. Although the great majority are caught wild in the sea, fish-farming of both marine and freshwater species is assuming increasing importance, especially as natural stocks become depleted.

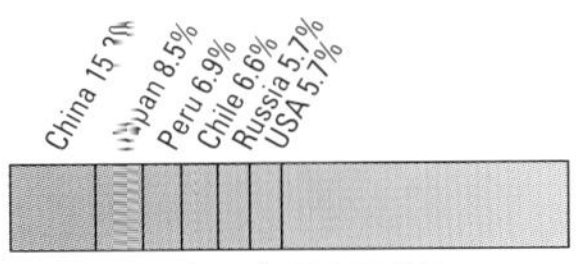
Peru 6.9%
Chile 6.6%
Russia 5.7%
USA 5.7%

World total (1993): 98,113,000 tonnes

Sugar beet: A temperate crop closely related to the humble beetroot, sugar beet's yield after processing is indistinguishable from cane sugar. Sugar beet is steadily replacing sugar cane imports in Europe, to the detriment of the developing countries that rely on it as a major cash crop.

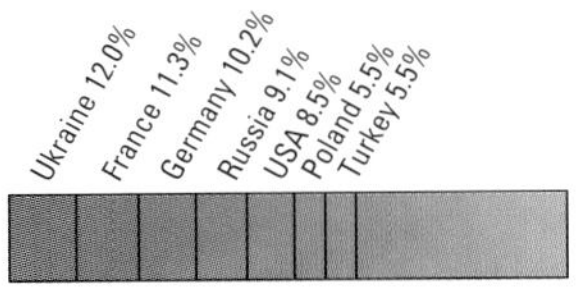
Ukraine 12.0%
France 11.3%
Germany 10.2%
Russia 9.1%
USA 8.5%
Poland 5.5%
Turkey 5.5%

World total (1993): 281,682,000 tonnes

PRODUCTION: ENERGY

39: WORLD SHIPPING

46: CARBON DIOXIDE
GREENHOUSE POWER
CO₂ PRODUCERS
GLOBAL WARMING

47: MARINE POLLUTION

We live in a high-energy civilization. While vast discrepancies exist between rich and poor – a North American consumes 13 times as much energy as a Chinese, for example – even developing nations have more power at their disposal than was imaginable a century ago. Abundant energy supplies keep us warm or cool, fuel our industries and our transport systems, and even feed us: high-intensity agriculture, with its fertilizers, pesticides and machinery, is heavily energy-dependent.

Unfortunately, most of the world's energy comes from fossil fuels: coal, oil and gas deposits laid down over many millions of years. These are the Earth's capital, not its income, and we are consuming that capital at an alarming rate. New discoveries have persistently extended the known reserves: in 1989, the reserves-to-production ratio for oil assured over 45 years' supply, an improvement of almost a decade on the 1970 situation. But despite the effort and ingenuity of prospectors, stocks are clearly limited. They are also very unequally distributed, with the Middle East accounting for most oil reserves, and the CIS, especially Russia, possessing an even higher proportion of the world's natural gas. Coal reserves are more evenly shared, and also more plentiful: coal will outlast oil and gas by a very wide margin.

It is possible to reduce energy demand by improving efficiency: most industrial nations have dramatically increased output since the 1970s without a matching rise in energy consumption. But as fossil stocks continue to diminish, renewable energy sources – solar, wave and wind power, as well as hydro-electricity – must take on greater importance.

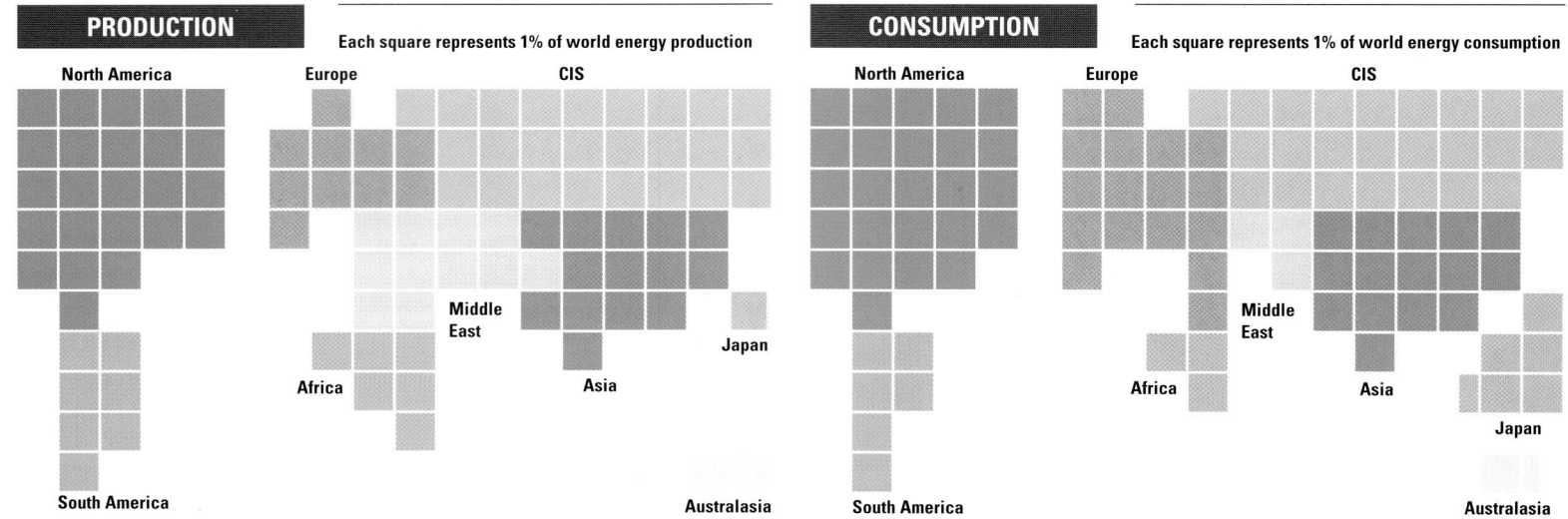

PRODUCTION

Each square represents 1% of world energy production

North America — Europe — CIS — Middle East — Japan — Africa — Asia — South America — Australasia

CONSUMPTION

Each square represents 1% of world energy consumption

North America — Europe — CIS — Middle East — Japan — Africa — Asia — South America — Australasia

CONVERSIONS

For historical reasons, oil is still traded in barrels. The weight and volume equivalents shown below are all based on average density 'Arabian light' crude oil, and should be considered approximate.

The energy equivalents given for a tonne of oil are also somewhat imprecise: oil and coal of different qualities will have varying energy contents, a fact usually reflected in their price on world markets.

1 barrel:

0.136 tonnes
159 litres
35 Imperial gallons
42 US gallons

1 tonne:

7.33 barrels
1185 litres
256 Imperial gallons
261 US gallons

1 tonne oil:

1.5 tonnes hard coal
3.0 tonnes lignite
12,000 kWh

ENERGY BALANCE

Difference between energy production and consumption in millions of tonnes of oil equivalent (1992)

Energy deficit ↑

Over 35 MtOe

1 – 35 MtOe

Approx. balance

1 – 35 MtOe

Over 35 MtOe

Energy surplus ↓

● Major oilfields

▽ Major gasfields

▲ Major coalfields

Map labels: Prudhoe Bay, Medicine Hat, California, Appalachians, Texas, Gulf of Mexico, Venezuela, Ecuador, Rio Grande/Santa Catarina, North Sea, Ruhr, Silesia, Algeria, Nigeria, Transvaal/Natal, Yamburg, Donbas, The Gulf, Oman, Bihar, Shanxi, Chongqing, Tangshan, Sumatra

WORLD ENERGY CONSUMPTION

Energy consumed by world regions, measured in million tonnes of oil equivalent in 1993. Total world consumption was 7,804 MtOe. Only energy from oil, gas, coal, nuclear and hydroelectric sources are included. Excluded are fuels such as wood, peat, animal waste, wind, solar and geothermal which, though important in some countries, are unreliably documented in terms of consumption statistics.

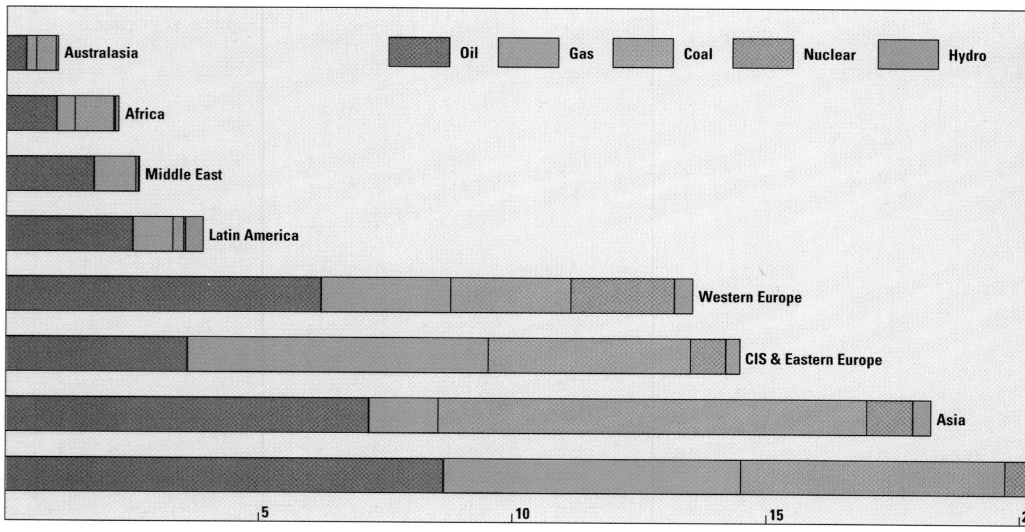

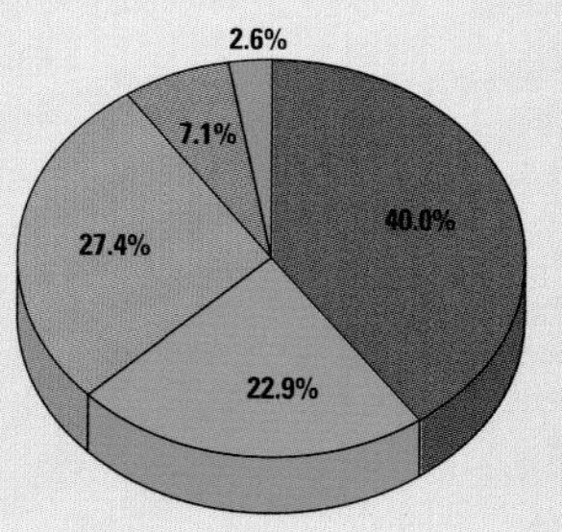

Legend: Oil — Gas — Coal — Nuclear — Hydro

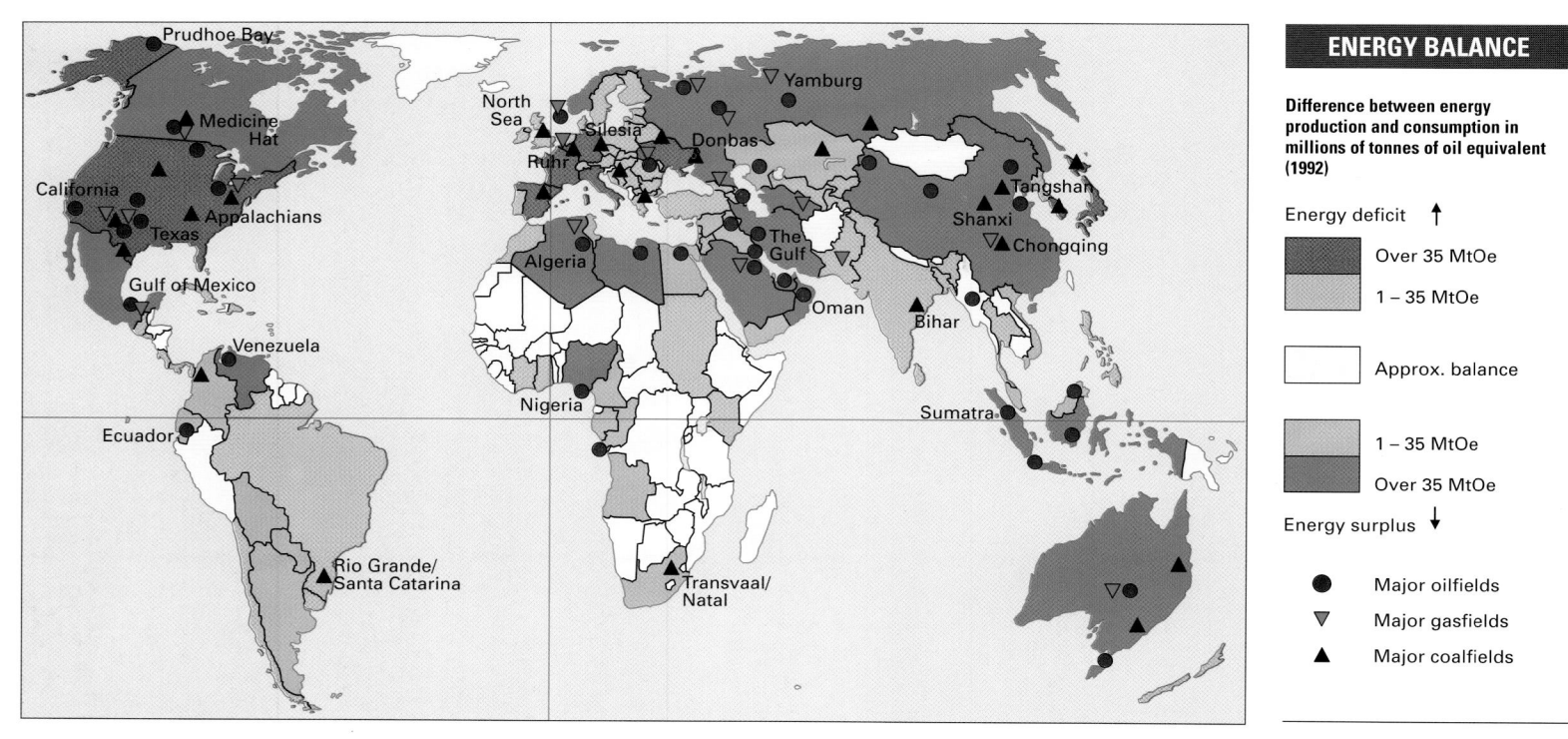

Bar chart regions: Australasia, Africa, Middle East, Latin America, Western Europe, CIS & Eastern Europe, Asia, North America

Pie chart: 40.0%, 22.9%, 27.4%, 7.1%, 2.6%

FOSSIL FUEL RESERVES

Known world reserves in years as a multiple of annual production, 1970, 1980 and 1989

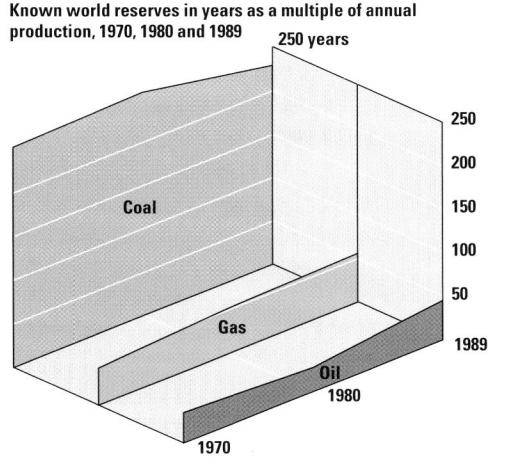

ENERGY AND OUTPUT

Tonnes of oil equivalent consumed to produce US $1,000 of GDP, four industrial nations (1973–89)

Intensity of energy use is a rough indicator of efficiency: the 1973–4 oil crisis caused a dramatic improvement in each of the countries illustrated, although the USA remains relatively profligate. Reliable figures for Russia and the other republics of the former USSR are hard to obtain, but estimates suggest that for equivalent production they use up to four times as much energy as the USA.

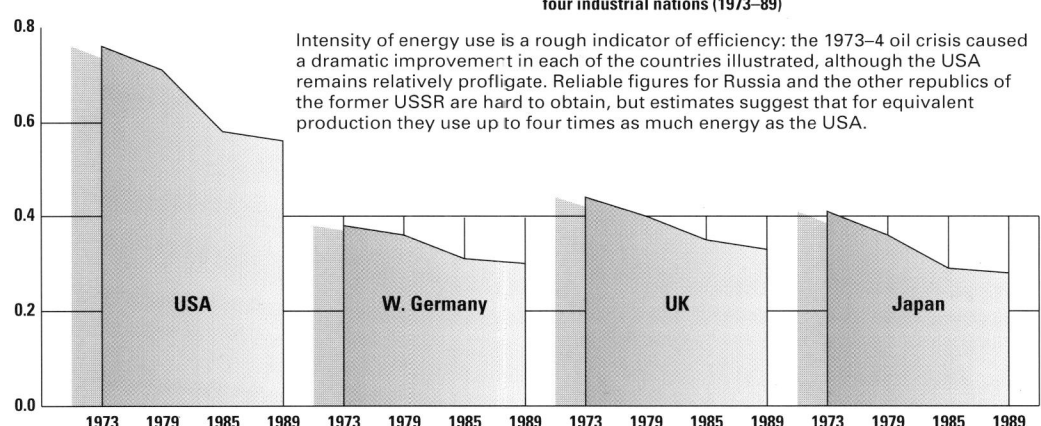

COAL RESERVES

World coal reserves by region and country, thousand million tonnes (latest available year)

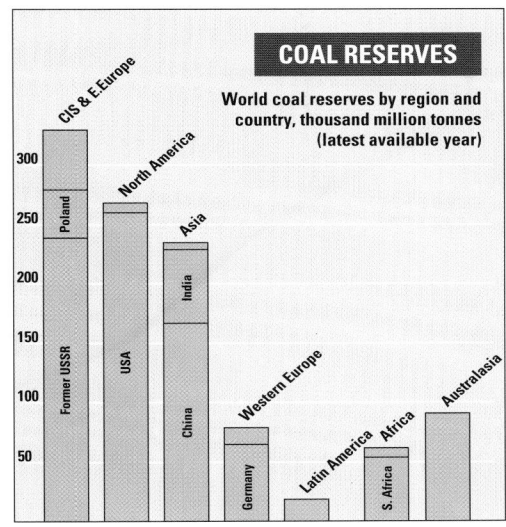

GAS RESERVES

World natural gas reserves by region and country, thousand million tonnes (latest available year)

Ca: Canada
In: Indonesia
Ma: Malaysia
AD: Abu Dhabi
SA: Saudi Arabia
Qa: Qatar
Iq: Iraq
No: Norway
Ne: Netherlands
Ve: Venezuela
Mx: Mexico
Al: Algeria
Ni: Nigeria

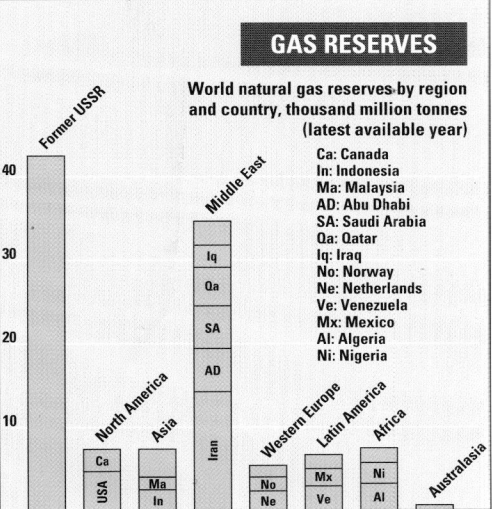

OIL RESERVES

World oil reserves by region and country, thousand million tonnes (latest available year)

A: Abu Dhabi
Ve: Venezuela
M: Mexico

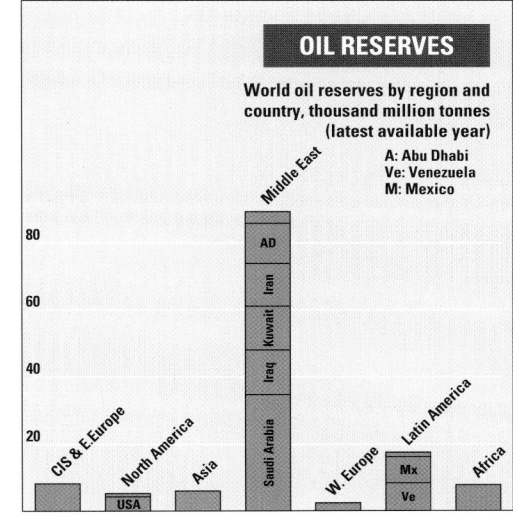

OIL MOVEMENTS

Major world movements of oil in millions of tonnes (1989)

Middle East to Western Europe	195.5
Middle East to Japan	150.0
Middle East to Asia (exc. Japan and China)	127.5
Latin America to USA	126.1
Middle East to USA	94.1
USSR to Western Europe	78.1
North Africa to Western Europe	93.5
West Africa to Western Europe	39.6
West Africa to USA	59.8
Canada to USA	45.0
South-east Asia to Japan	42.2
Latin America to Western Europe	28.7
Western Europe to USA	28.7
Middle East to Latin America	20.5

Total world movements: 1,577 million tonnes

Only inter-regional movements in excess of 20 million tonnes are shown. Other Middle Eastern oil shipments throughout the world totalled 47.4 million tonnes; miscellaneous oil exports of the then USSR amounted to 88.8 million tonnes.

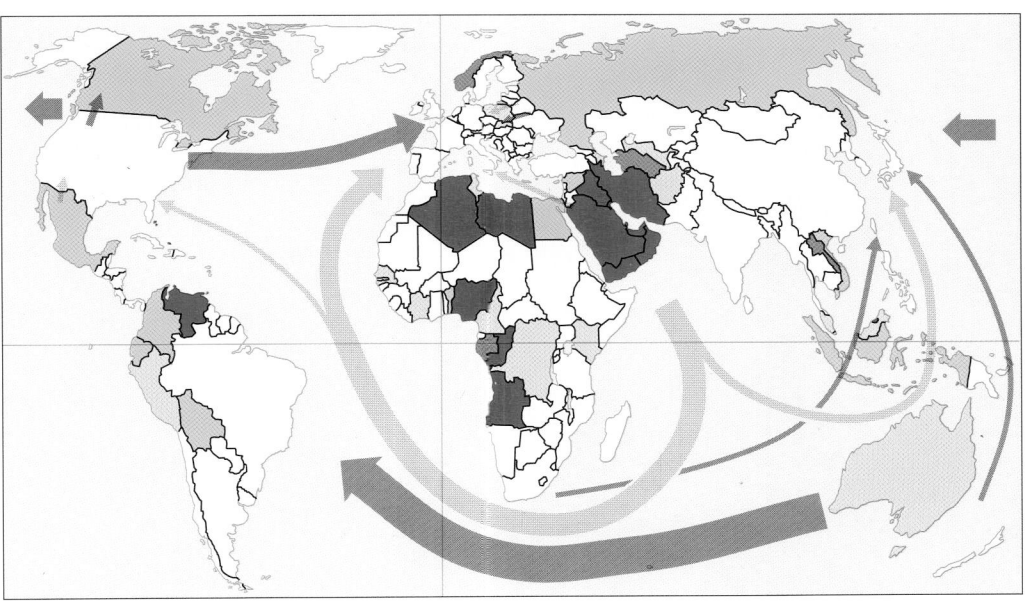

FUEL EXPORTS

Fuels as a percentage of total value of exports (latest available year)

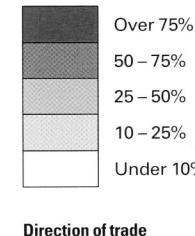

- Over 75%
- 50 – 75%
- 25 – 50%
- 10 – 25%
- Under 10%

Direction of trade

- Coal
- Oil

Arrows show the major trade direction of selected fuels, and are proportional to export value.

NUCLEAR POWER

Percentage of electricity generated by nuclear power stations, leading nations (1990)

1.	France	73%	11. Finland	34%
2.	Belgium	60%	12. Czechoslovakia..	29%
3.	Sweden	52%	13. Germany	28%
4.	Hungary	46%	14. Japan	24%
5.	South Korea	43%	15. UK	22%
6.	Switzerland	40%	16. USA	20%
7.	Taiwan	38%	17. Canada	17%
8.	Slovenia	37%	18. Argentina	14%
9.	Spain	36%	19. Russia	11%
10.	Bulgaria	34%	20. Netherlands	5%

The decade 1980–90 was a bad time for the nuclear power industry. Major projects regularly ran vastly overbudget, and fears of long-term environmental damage were heavily reinforced by the 1986 Soviet disaster at Chernobyl. Although the number of reactors in service continued to increase throughout the period, orders for new plant shrank dramatically, and most countries cut back on their nuclear programmes.

HYDROELECTRICITY

Percentage of electricity generated by hydroelectric power stations, leading nations (1990)

1.	Paraguay	99.9%	11. Zaïre	97.4%
2.	Bhutan	99.6%	12. Cameroon	97.3%
3.	Norway	99.6%	13. Nepal	97.0%
4.	Zambia	99.5%	14. Laos	95.2%
5.	Congo	99.4%	15. Costa Rica	94.2%
6.	Ghana	99.3%	16. Iceland	93.5%
7.	Uganda	99.1%	17. Brazil	92.9%
8.	Rwanda	98.9%	18. Sri Lanka	92.3%
9.	Burundi	98.5%	19. Albania	91.1%
10.	Malawi	98.1%	20. Guatemala	89.7%

Countries heavily reliant on hydroelectricity are usually small and non-industrial: a high proportion of hydroelectric power more often reflects a modest energy budget than vast hydroelectric resources. The USA, for instance, produces only 9% of power requirements from hydroelectricity; yet that 9% amounts to more than three times the hydro-power generated by all of Africa.

ALTERNATIVE ENERGY SOURCES

Solar: Each year the Sun bestows upon the Earth almost a million times as much energy as is locked up in all the planet's oil reserves, but only an insignificant fraction is trapped and used commercially. In some experimental installations, mirrors focus the Sun's rays on to boilers, whose steam generates electricity by spinning turbines. Solar cells turn the sunlight into electricity directly, and although efficiencies are still low, advancing technology offers some prospect of using the Sun as the main world electricity source by 2100.
Wind: Caused by uneven heating of the Earth, winds are themselves a form of solar energy. Windmills have been used for centuries to turn wind power into mechanical work; recent models, often arranged in banks on gust-swept high ground, usually generate electricity.
Tidal: The energy from tides is potentially enormous, although only a few installations have been built to exploit it. In theory at least, waves and currents could also provide almost unimaginable power. But work on extracting it is still in the experimental stage.
Geothermal: The Earth's temperature rises by 1°C for every 30 metres' descent, with much steeper temperature gradients in geologically active areas. El Salvador, for example, produces 39% of its electricity from geothermal power stations. More than 130 are operating worldwide.
Biomass: The oldest of human fuels ranges from animal dung, still burned in cooking fires in much of North Africa and elsewhere, to sugar cane plantations feeding high-technology distilleries to produce ethanol for motor vehicle engines. In Brazil and South Africa, plant ethanol provides up to 25% of motor fuel. Throughout the developing world, most biomass energy comes from firewood: although accurate figures are impossible to obtain, it may yield as much as 10% of the world's total energy consumption.

PRODUCTION: MINERALS

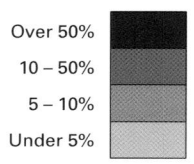

19: GEOLOGY

37: PATTERNS OF PRODUCTION

39: WORLD SHIPPING

Even during the Stone Age, when humans often settled near the outcrops of flint on which their technology depended, mineral resources have attracted human exploiters. Their descendants have learned how to make use of almost every known element. These elements can be found, in one form or another, somewhere in the Earth's bountiful crust. Iron remains the most important, but modern industrial civilization has a voracious appetite for virtually all of them.

Mineral deposits once dictated the site of new industries; today, most industrial countries are heavily dependent on imports for many of their key materials. Most mining, and much refining of raw ores, is done in developing countries, where labour is cheap.

The main map below shows the richest sources of the most important minerals at present; some reserves – lead and mercury, for example – are running very low. The map takes no account of undersea deposits, most of which are considered inaccessible. Growing shortages, though, may encourage submarine mining: plans have already been made to recover the nodules of manganese found widely scattered on ocean floors.

MINERAL EXPORTS

Minerals and metals as a percentage of total exports (latest available year)

- Over 50%
- 10 – 50%
- 5 – 10%
- Under 5%

Direction of trade

- Copper ⟶
- Iron ⟶
- Bauxite (Aluminium) ⟶

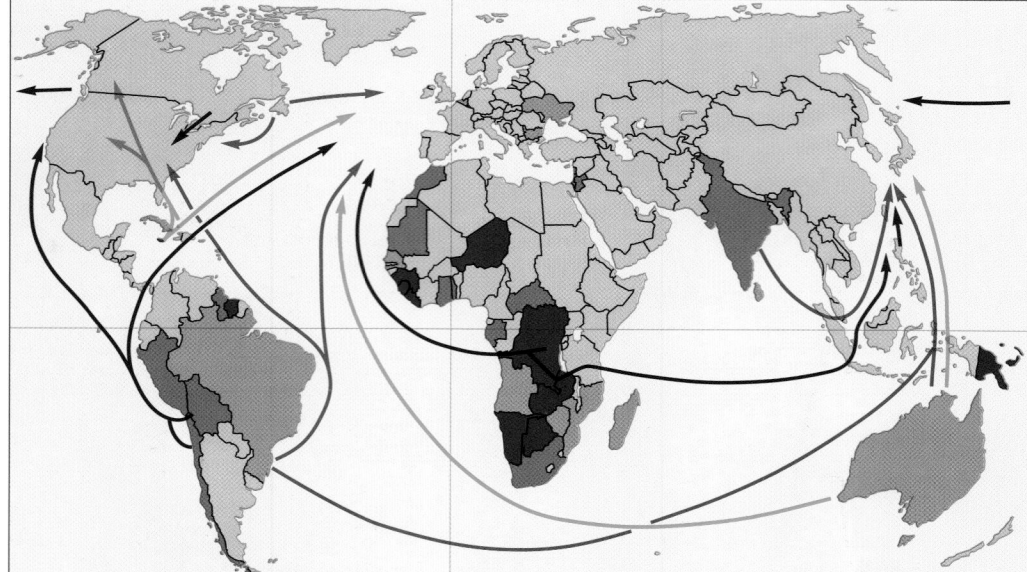

URANIUM

In its pure state, uranium is an immensely heavy, white metal; but although spent uranium is employed as projectiles in anti-missile cannons, where its mass ensures a lethal punch, its main use is as a fuel in nuclear reactors, and in nuclear weaponry. Uranium is very scarce: the main source is the rare ore pitchblende, which itself contains only 0.2% uranium oxide. Only a minute fraction of that is the radioactive U^{235} isotope, though so-called breeder reactors can transmute the more common U^{238} into highly radioactive plutonium.

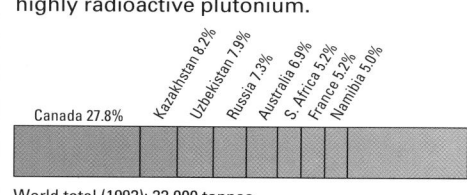

Canada 27.8% | Kazakhstan 8.2% | Uzbekistan 7.9% | Russia 7.3% | Australia 6.9% | S. Africa 5.2% | France 5.2% | Namibia 5.0%

World total (1993): 33,000 tonnes

METALS

*Figures for aluminium are for refined metal; all other figures refer to ore production

DIAMOND

Most diamond is found in kimberlite, or 'blue ground', a basic peridotite rock; erosion may wash the diamond from its kimberlite matrix and deposit it with sand or gravel on river beds. Only a small proportion of the world's diamond, the most flawless, is cut into gemstones – 'diamonds'; most is used in industry, where the material's remarkable hardness and abrasion resistance finds a use in cutting tools, drills and dies, as well as in styluses. Australia, not among the top 12 producers at the beginning of the 1980s, had by 1986 become world leader and by 1993 was the source of 40.6% of world production. The other main producers were Zaïre (16.3%), Botswana (14.6%), Russia (11.4%) and South Africa (9.7%). Between them, these five nations accounted for over 82% of the world total of 100,850,000 carats.

Aluminium: Produced mainly from its oxide, bauxite, which yields 25% of its weight in aluminium. The cost of refining and production is often too high for producer-countries to bear, so bauxite is largely exported. Lightweight and corrosion resistant, aluminium alloys are widely used in aircraft, vehicles, cans and packaging.

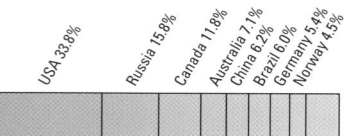

USA 33.8% | Russia 15.8% | Canada 11.8% | Australia 7.1% | China 6.2% | Brazil 6.0% | Germany 5.4% | Norway 4.5%

World total (1993): 19,609,000 tonnes *

Lead: A soft metal, obtained mainly from galena (lead sulphide), which occurs in veins associated with iron, zinc and silver sulphides. Its use in vehicle batteries accounts for the USA's prime consumer status; lead is also made into sheeting and piping. Its use as an additive to paints and petrol is decreasing.

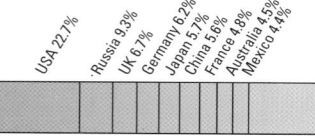

USA 22.7% | Russia 9.3% | UK 6.7% | Germany 6.2% | Japan 5.7% | China 5.6% | France 4.6% | Australia 4.5% | Mexico 4.4%

World total (1993): 5,400,000 tonnes *

Tin: Soft, pliable and non-toxic, used to coat 'tin' (tin-plated steel) cans, in the manufacture of foils and in alloys. The principal tin-bearing mineral is cassiterite (SnO_2), found in ore formed from molten rock. Producers and refiners were hit by a price collapse in 1991.

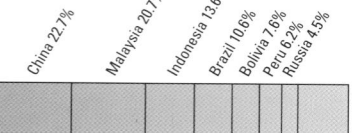

China 22.7% | Malaysia 20.7% | Indonesia 13.6% | Brazil 10.6% | Bolivia 7.6% | Peru 6.2% | Russia 4.5%

World total (1993): 220,000 tonnes *

Gold: Regarded for centuries as the most valuable metal in the world and used to make coins, gold is still recognized as the monetary standard. A soft metal, it is alloyed to make jewellery; the electronics industry values its corrosion resistance and conductivity.

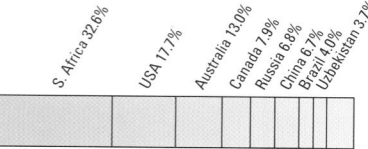

S. Africa 32.6% | USA 17.7% | Australia 13.0% | Canada 7.9% | Russia 6.8% | China 6.2% | Brazil 4.0% | Uzbekistan 3.7%

World total (1993): 1,900 tonnes *

Copper: Derived from low-yielding sulphide ores, copper is an important export for several developing countries. An excellent conductor of heat and electricity, it forms part of most electrical items, and is used in the manufacture of brass and bronze. Major importers include Japan and Germany.

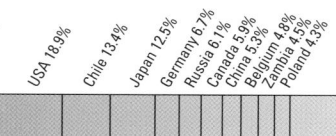

USA 18.9% | Chile 13.4% | Japan 12.5% | Germany 6.7% | Russia 6.1% | Canada 5.9% | China 5.3% | Zambia 4.5% | Belgium 4.5% | Poland 4.3%

World total (1993): 9,500,000 tonnes *

Mercury: The only metal that is liquid at normal temperatures, most is derived from its sulphide, cinnabar, found only in small quantities in volcanic areas. Apart from its value in thermometers and other instruments, most mercury production is used in anti-fungal and anti-fouling preparations, and to make detonators.

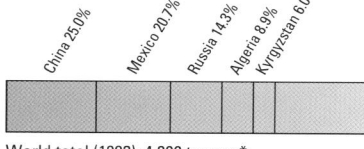

China 25.0% | Mexico 20.7% | Russia 14.3% | Algeria 8.9% | Kyrgyzstan 6.0%

World total (1993): 4,200 tonnes *

Zinc: Often found in association with lead ores, zinc is highly resistant to corrosion, and about 40% of the refined metal is used to plate sheet steel, particularly vehicle bodies – a process known as galvanizing. Zinc is also used in dry batteries, paints and dyes.

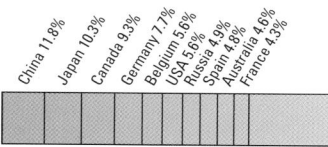

China 11.8% | Japan 10.3% | Canada 9.3% | Germany 7.7% | Belgium 5.6% | USA 5.6% | Spain 4.9% | Russia 4.8% | Australia 4.6% | France 4.3%

World total (1993): 7,127,000 tonnes *

Silver: Most silver comes from ores mined and processed for other metals (including lead and copper). Pure or alloyed with harder metals, it is used for jewellery and ornaments. Industrial use includes dentistry, electronics, photography and as a chemical catalyst.

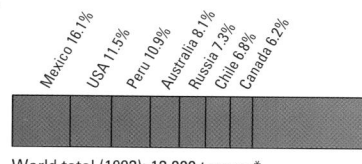

Mexico 16.1% | USA 11.5% | Peru 10.5% | Australia 8.1% | Russia 7.3% | Chile 6.8% | Canada 6.2%

World total (1993): 13,000 tonnes *

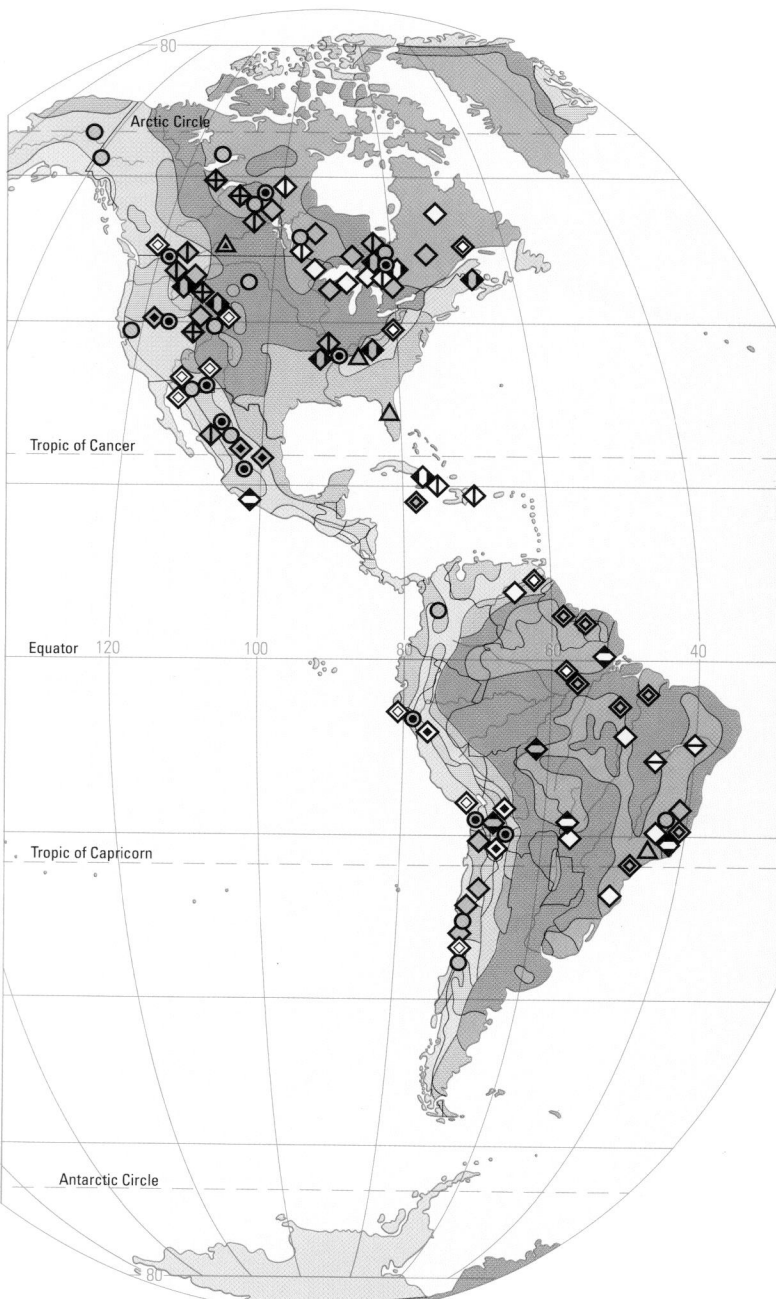

CARTOGRAPHY BY PHILIP'S. COPYRIGHT REED INTERNATIONAL BOOKS LTD

IRON AND FERRO-ALLOYS

Ever since the art of high-temperature smelting was discovered, some time in the second millennium BC, iron has been by far the most important metal known to man. The earliest iron ploughs transformed primitive agriculture and led to the first human population explosion, while iron weapons – or the lack of them – ensured the rise or fall of entire cultures.

Widely distributed around the world, iron ores usually contain 25–60% iron; blast furnaces process the raw product into pig-iron, which is then alloyed with carbon and other minerals to produce steels of various qualities. From the time of the Industrial Revolution steel has been almost literally the backbone of modern civilization, the prime structural material on which all else is built.

Iron-smelting usually developed close to sources of ore and, later, to the coalfields that fueled the furnaces. Today, most ore comes from a few richly-endowed locations where large-scale mining is possible. Iron and steel plants are generally built at coastal sites so that giant ore carriers, which account for a sizeable proportion of the world's merchant fleet, can easily discharge their cargoes.

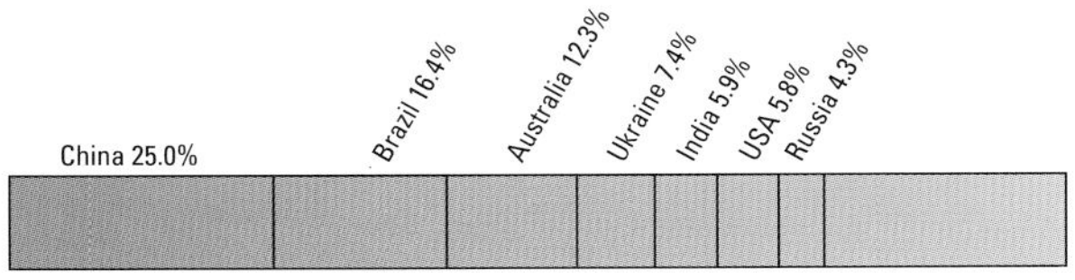

World production of pig-iron and ferro-alloys (1993). All countries with an annual output of more than one million tonnes are shown

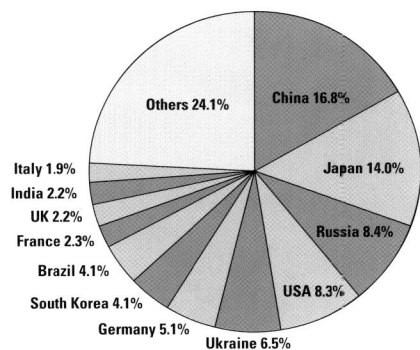

Total world production: 535 million tonnes

Development of world production of pig-iron and ferro-alloys (1945–93) in million tonnes

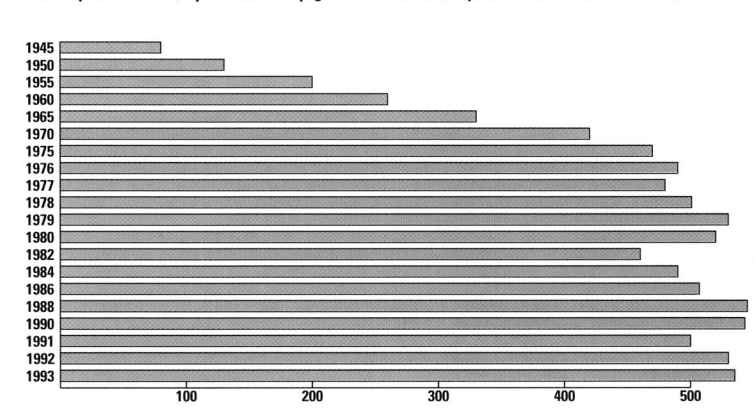

Chromium: Most of the world's chromium production is alloyed with iron and other metals to produce steels with various different properties. Combined with iron, nickel, cobalt and tungsten, chromium produces an exceptionally hard steel, resistant to heat; chrome steels are used for many household items where utility must be matched with appearance – cutlery, for example. Chromium is also used in production of refractory bricks, and its salts for tanning and dyeing leather and cloth.

Manganese: In its pure state, manganese is a hard, brittle metal. Alloyed with chrome, iron and nickel, it produces abrasion-resistant steels; manganese-aluminium alloys are light but tough. Found in batteries and inks, manganese is also used in glass production. Manganese ores are frequently found in the same location as sedimentary iron ores. Pyrolusite (MnO_2) and psilomelane are the main economically-exploitable sources.

Nickel: Combined with chrome and iron, nickel produces stainless and high-strength steels; similar alloys go to make magnets and electrical heating elements. Nickel combined with copper is widely used to make coins; cupro-nickel alloy is very resistant to corrosion. Its ores yield only modest quantities of nickel – 0.5 to 3.0% – but also contain copper, iron and small amounts of precious metals. Japan, USA, UK, Germany and France are the principal importers.

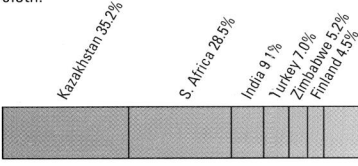

World total production of iron ore (1993): 940,000,000 tonnes

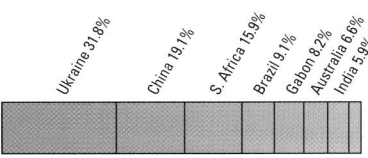

World total (1993): 9,930,000 tonnes

World total (1993): 22,000,000 tonnes

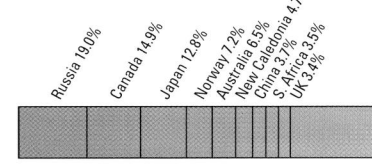

World total (1993): 790,000 tonnes

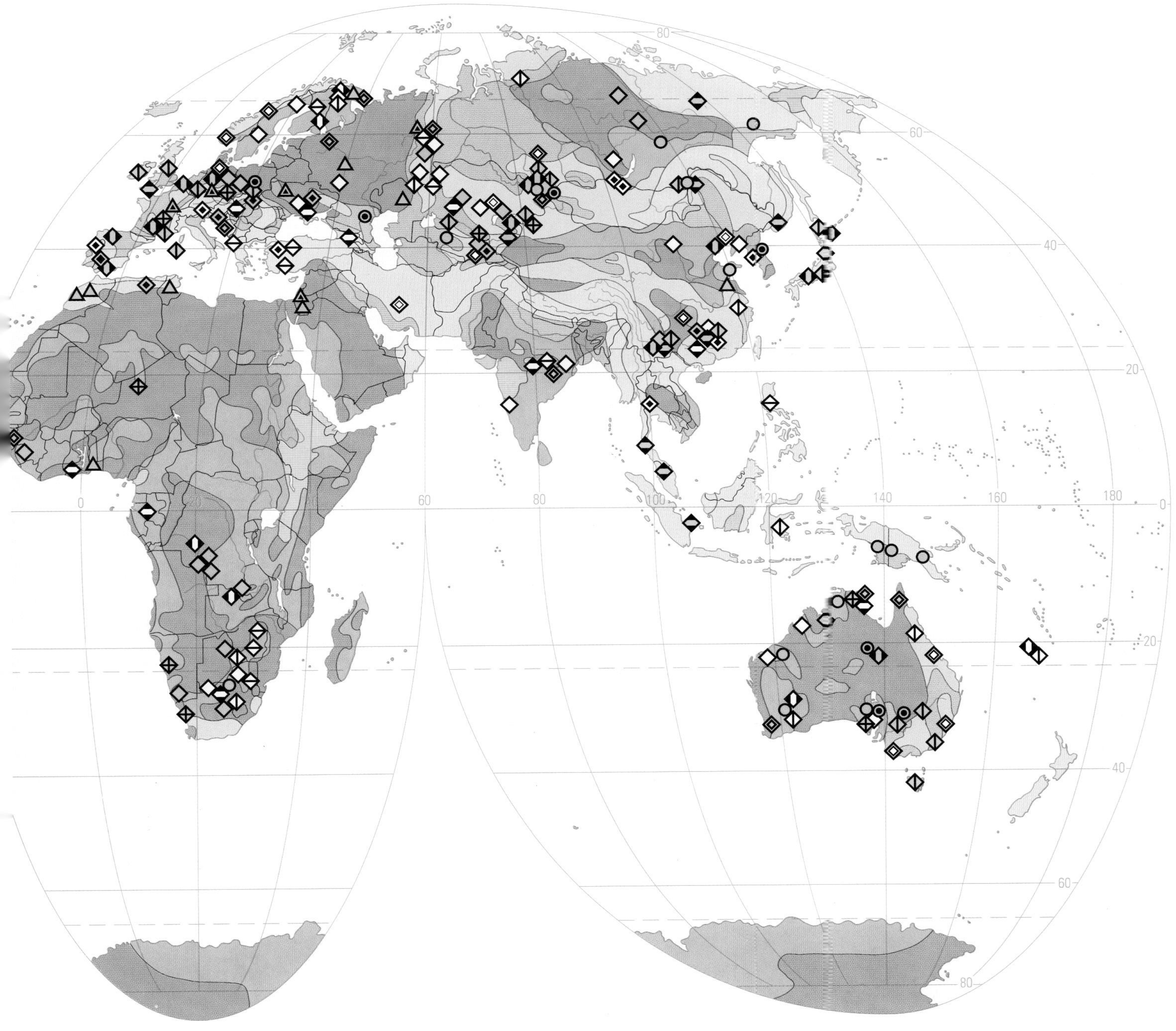

STRUCTURAL REGIONS

- Pre-Cambrian shields
- Sedimentary cover on Pre-Cambrian shields
- Paleozoic (Caledonian & Hercynian) folding
- Sedimentary cover on Paleozoic folding
- Mesozoic folding
- Sedimentary cover on Mesozoic folding
- Cainozoic (Alpine) folding
- Sedimentary cover on Cainozoic folding
- Intensive Mesozoic & Cainozoic vulcanism

DISTRIBUTION

Iron & ferro-alloys

- Chrome
- Cobalt
- Iron Ore
- Manganese
- Molybdenum
- Nickel Ore
- Tungsten

Non-ferrous metals

- Bauxite (Aluminium)
- Copper
- Lead
- Mercury
- Tin
- Zinc
- Uranium

Precious metals & stones

- Diamonds
- Gold
- Silver

Fertilizers

- Phosphates
- Potash

CARTOGRAPHY BY PHILIP'S. COPYRIGHT REED INTERNATIONAL BOOKS LTD

PRODUCTION: MANUFACTURING

16: WATER UTILIZATION

30: LAND USE AND ECONOMY

34: MINERAL PRODUCTION

35: IRON AND FERRO-ALLOYS

38: TRADING NATIONS MAJOR EXPORTS TRADED PRODUCTS

In its broadest sense, manufacturing is the application of energy, labour and skill to raw materials in order to transform them into finished goods with a higher value than the various elements used in production.

Since the early days of the Industrial Revolution, manufacturing has implied the use of an organized workforce harnessed to some form of machine. The tendency has consistently been for increasingly expensive human labour to be replaced by increasingly complex machinery, which has evolved over time from water-powered looms to fully-integrated robotic plants.

Obviously, not all the world's industries – or manufacturing countries – have reached the same level. Textiles, for example, the foundation of the early Industrial Revolution in the West, can be mass-produced with fairly modest technology; today, they are usually produced in developing countries, mostly in Asia, where the low labour costs compensate for the large workforce that the relatively simple machinery requires. Nevertheless, the trend towards high-technology production, however uneven, seems inexorable. Gains in efficiency make up for the staggering cost of the equipment itself, and the outcome is that fewer and fewer people are employed to produce more and more goods.

One paradoxical result of the increase in industrial efficiency is a relative decline in the importance of the industrial sector of a nation's economy. The economy has already passed through one transition, generations past, when workers were drawn from the land into factories. The second transition releases labour into what is called the service sector of the economy: a diffuse but vital concept that includes not only such obvious services as transport and administration, but also finance, insurance and activities as diverse as fashion design or the writing of computer software.

The process is far advanced in the mature economies of the West, with Japan not far behind. Almost two-thirds of US wealth, for example, is now generated in the service sector, and less than half of Japan's Gross National Product comes from industry. The shrinkage, though, is only relative: between them, these two industrial giants produce almost twice the amount of manufactured goods as the rest of the world put together. And it is on the solid base of production that their general prosperity is founded.

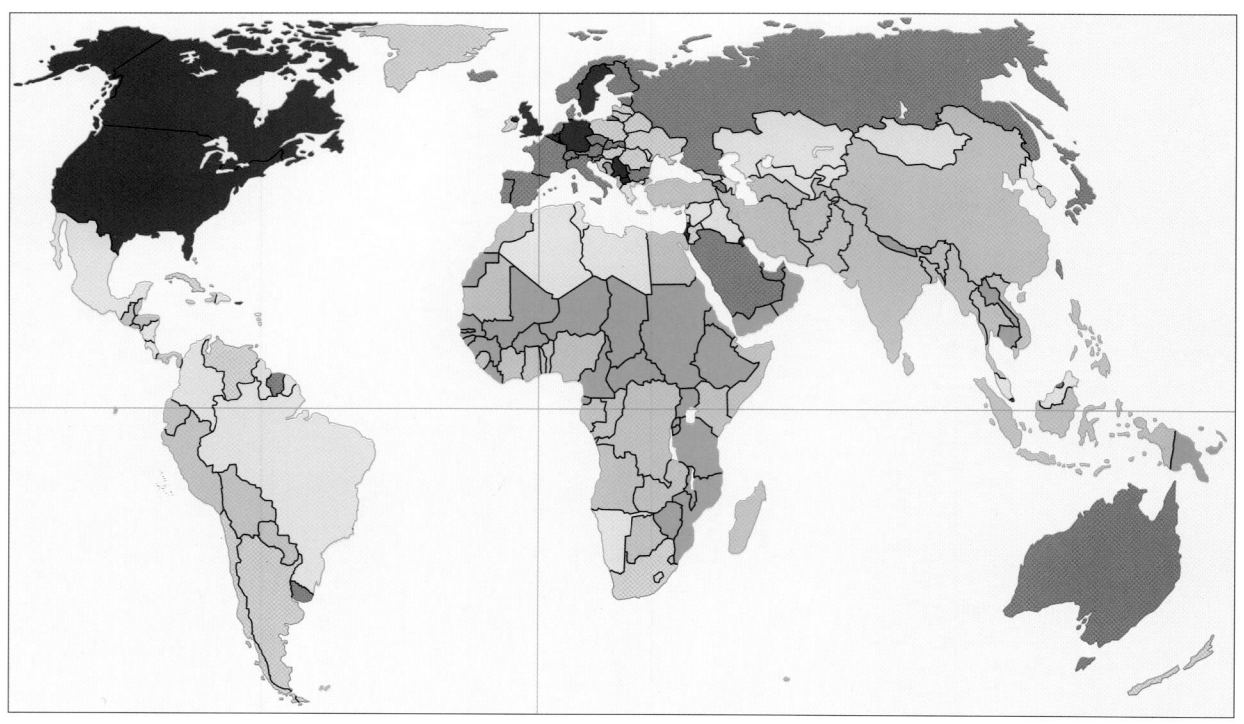

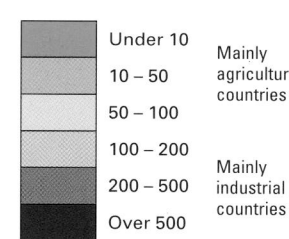

EMPLOYMENT

The number of workers employed in manufacturing for every 100 workers engaged in agriculture

Under 10	Mainly agricultural countries
10 – 50	
50 – 100	
100 – 200	Mainly industrial countries
200 – 500	
Over 500	

Selected countries (latest available year)

Singapore	8,860
Hong Kong	3,532
UK	1,270
Belgium	820
Ex-Yugoslavia	809
Germany	800
Kuwait	767
Bahrain	660
USA	657
Israel	633

DIVISION OF EMPLOYMENT

Distribution of workers between agriculture, industry and services, selected countries (latest available year)

The six countries selected illustrate the usual stages of economic development, from dependence on agriculture through industrial growth to the expansion of the services sector.

- Agriculture
- Industry
- Services

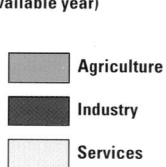 Nepal
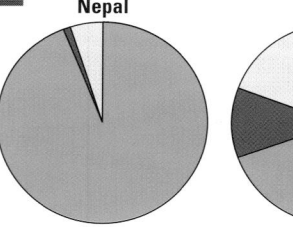 Nigeria
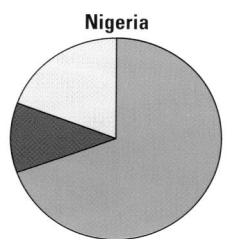 Pakistan
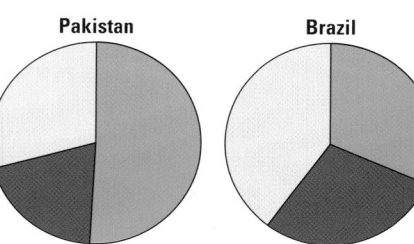 Brazil
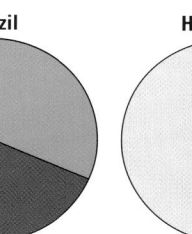 Hong Kong
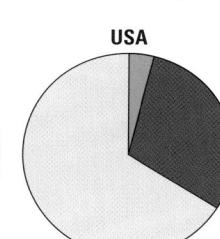 USA

THE WORKFORCE

Percentages of men and women between 15 and 64 in employment, selected countries (latest available year)

The figures include employees and self-employed, who in developing countries are often subsistence farmers. People in full-time education are excluded. Because of the population age structure in developing countries, the employed population has to support a far larger number of non-workers than its industrial equivalent. For example, more than 52% of Kenya's people are under 15, an age group that makes up less than a tenth of the UK population.

Men   Women

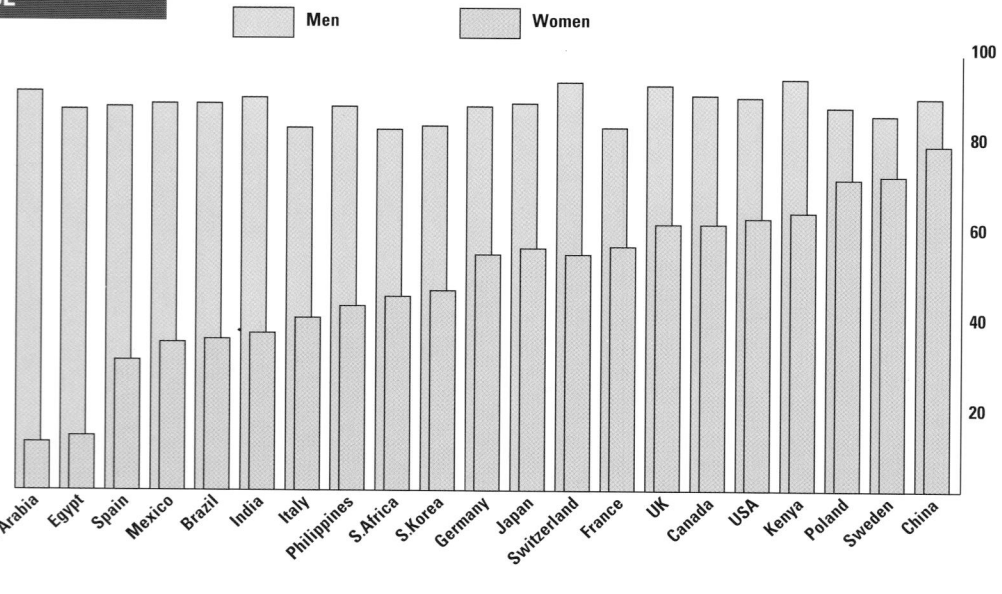

WEALTH CREATION

The Gross National Product (GNP) of the world's largest economies, US $ billion (1991)

1.	USA	5,686,038	21.	Austria	157,538
2.	Japan	3,337,191	22.	Iran	127,366
3.	Germany	1,516,785	23.	Finland	121,982
4.	France	1,167,749	24.	Denmark	121,695
5.	Italy	1,072,198	25.	Ukraine	121,458
6.	UK	963,696	26.	Indonesia	111,409
7.	Canada	568,765	27.	Saudi Arabia	105,133
8.	Spain	486,614	28.	Turkey	103,388
9.	Russia	479,546	29.	Norway	102,885
10.	Brazil	447,324	30.	Argentina	91,211
11.	China	424,012	31.	South Africa	90,953
12.	Australia	287,765	32.	Thailand	89,548
13.	India	284,668	33.	Hong Kong	77,302
14.	Netherlands	278,839	34.	Poland	70,640
15.	South Korea	274,464	35.	Greece	65,504
16.	Mexico	252,381	36.	Israel	59,128
17.	Switzerland	225,890	37.	Portugal	58,451
18.	Sweden	218,934	38.	Venezuela	52,775
19.	Belgium	192,370	39.	Algeria	52,239
20.	Taiwan	161,000	40.	Pakistan	46,725

CARTOGRAPHY BY PHILIP'S. COPYRIGHT REED INTERNATIONAL BOOKS LTD

PATTERNS OF PRODUCTION

Breakdown of industrial output by value, selected countries (latest available year)

	Food & agriculture	Textiles & clothing	Machinery & transport	Chemicals	Other
Algeria	26%	20%	11%	1%	41%
Argentina	24%	10%	16%	12%	37%
Australia	18%	7%	21%	8%	45%
Austria	17%	8%	25%	6%	43%
Belgium	19%	8%	23%	13%	36%
Brazil	15%	12%	24%	9%	40%
Burkina Faso	62%	18%	2%	1%	17%
Canada	15%	7%	25%	9%	44%
Denmark	22%	6%	23%	10%	39%
Egypt	20%	27%	13%	10%	31%
Finland	13%	6%	24%	7%	50%
France	18%	7%	33%	9%	33%
Germany	12%	5%	38%	10%	36%
Greece	20%	22%	14%	7%	38%
Hong Kong	6%	40%	20%	2%	33%
Hungary	6%	11%	37%	11%	35%
India	11%	16%	26%	15%	32%
Indonesia	23%	11%	10%	10%	47%
Iran	13%	22%	22%	7%	36%
Israel	13%	10%	28%	8%	42%
Ireland	28%	7%	20%	15%	28%
Italy	7%	13%	32%	10%	38%
Japan	10%	6%	38%	10%	37%
Kenya	35%	12%	14%	9%	29%
Malaysia	21%	5%	23%	14%	37%
Mexico	24%	12%	14%	12%	39%
Netherlands	19%	4%	28%	11%	38%
New Zealand	26%	10%	16%	6%	43%
Norway	21%	3%	26%	7%	44%
Pakistan	34%	21%	8%	12%	25%
Philippines	40%	7%	7%	10%	35%
Poland	15%	16%	30%	6%	33%
Portugal	17%	22%	16%	8%	38%
Singapore	6%	5%	46%	8%	36%
South Africa	14%	8%	17%	11%	49%
South Korea	15%	17%	24%	9%	35%
Spain	17%	9%	22%	9%	43%
Sweden	10%	2%	35%	8%	44%
Thailand	30%	17%	14%	6%	33%
Turkey	20%	14%	15%	8%	43%
UK	14%	6%	32%	11%	36%
USA	12%	5%	35%	10%	38%
Venezuela	23%	8%	9%	11%	49%

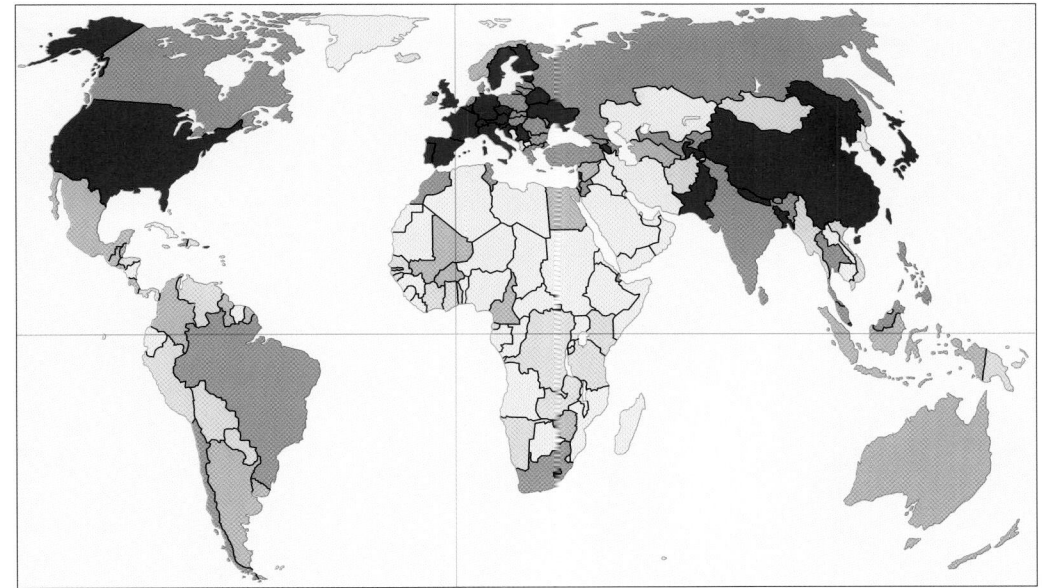

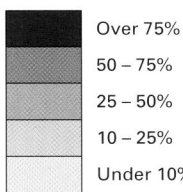

INDUSTRY AND TRADE

Manufactured goods (including machinery and transport) as a percentage of total exports (latest available year)

- Over 75%
- 50 – 75%
- 25 – 50%
- 10 – 25%
- Under 10%

The Far East and South-east Asia (Japan 98.3%, Macau 97.8%, Taiwan 92.7%, Hong Kong 93.0%, South Korea 93.4%) are most dominant, but many countries in Europe (e.g. Slovenia 92.4%) are also heavily dependent on manufactured goods.

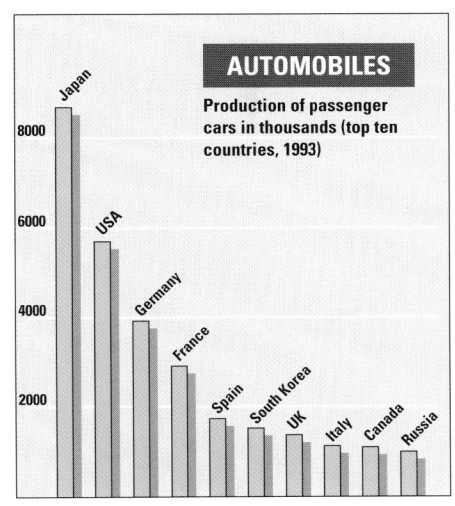

AUTOMOBILES
Production of passenger cars in thousands (top ten countries, 1993)

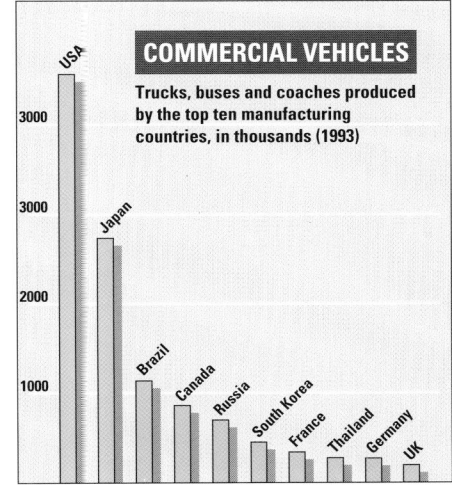

COMMERCIAL VEHICLES
Trucks, buses and coaches produced by the top ten manufacturing countries, in thousands (1993)

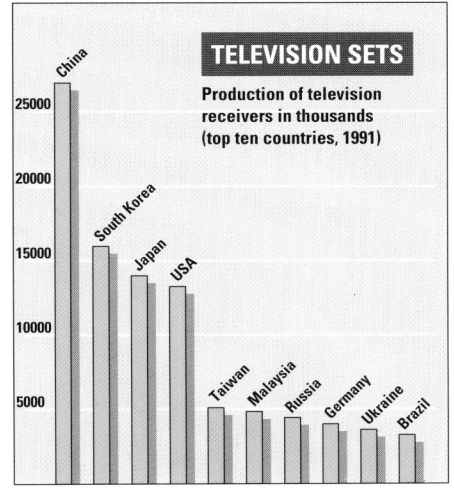

TELEVISION SETS
Production of television receivers in thousands (top ten countries, 1991)

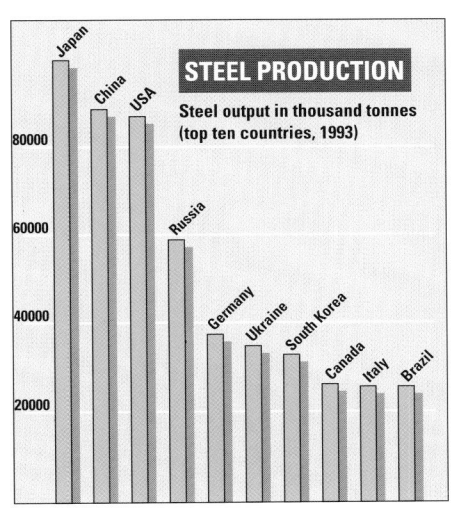

STEEL PRODUCTION
Steel output in thousand tonnes (top ten countries, 1993)

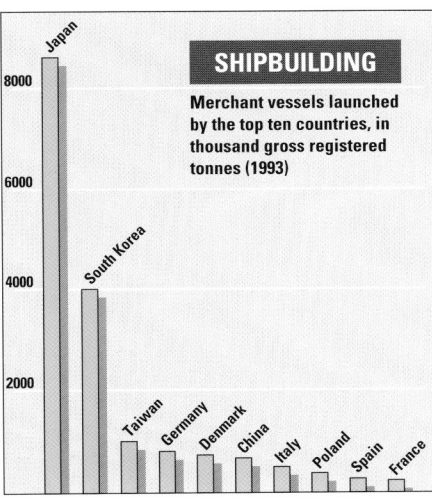

SHIPBUILDING
Merchant vessels launched by the top ten countries, in thousand gross registered tonnes (1993)

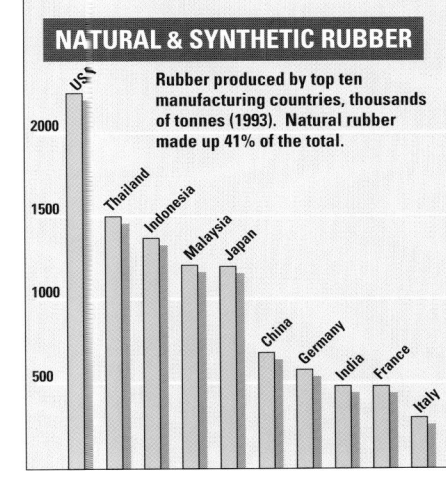

NATURAL & SYNTHETIC RUBBER
Rubber produced by top ten manufacturing countries, thousands of tonnes (1993). Natural rubber made up 41% of the total.

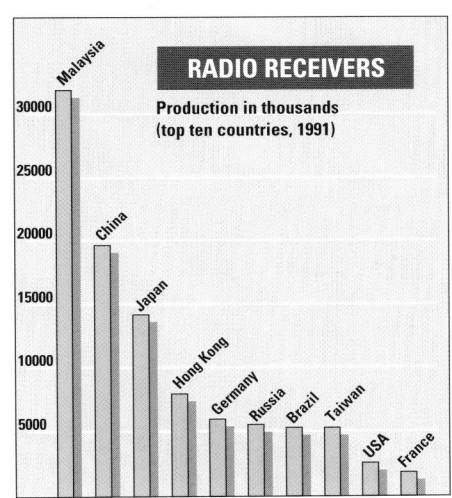

RADIO RECEIVERS
Production in thousands (top ten countries, 1991)

INDUSTRIAL POWER

Industrial output (mining, manufacturing, construction, energy and water production), top 40 nations, US $ billion (1991)

		US $ bn			US $ bn
1.	USA	1,627	21.	Saudi Arabia	56
2.	Japan	1,412	22.	Indonesia	48
3.	Germany	614	23.	Spain	47
4.	Italy	380	24.	Argentina	46
5.	France	348	25.	Poland	39
6.	UK	324	26.	Norway	38
7.	Ex-Soviet Union	250	27.	Finland	37
8.	Brazil	161	28.	Thailand	36
9.	China	155	29.	Turkey	33
10.	South Korea	127	30.	Denmark	31
11.	Canada	117	31.	Israel	23
12.	Australia	93	32.	Iran	20
	Netherlands	93	33.	Ex-Czechoslovakia	19
14.	Taiwan	86	34.	Hong Kong	17
15.	Mexico	85		Portugal (1989)	17
16.	Sweden	70	36.	Algeria	16
17.	Switzerland (1989)	61		Greece	16
18.	India	60	38.	Iraq	15
19.	Austria	59		Philippines	15
	Belgium	59		Singapore	15

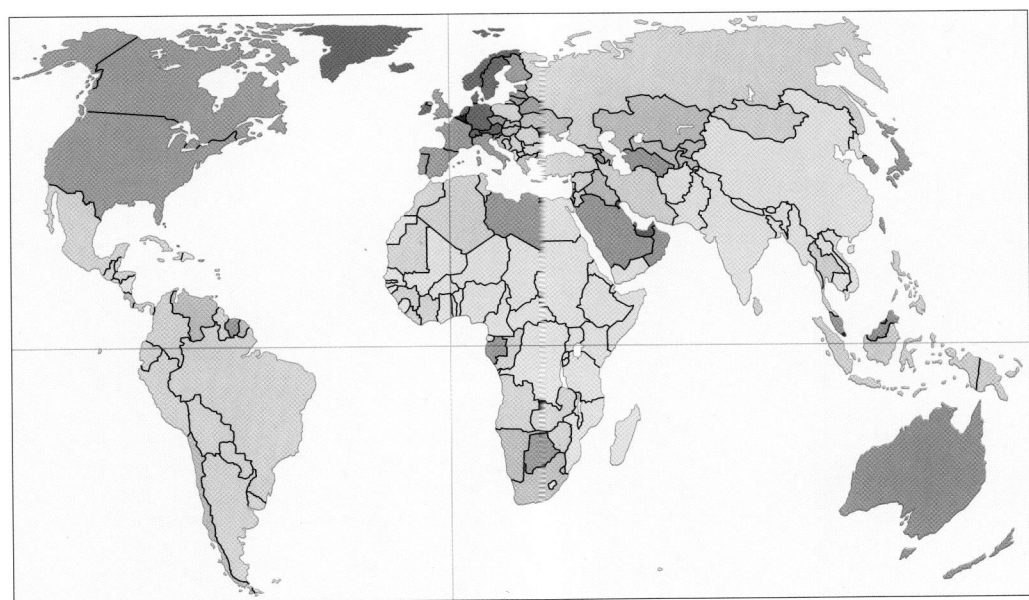

EXPORTS PER CAPITA

Value of exports in US $, divided by total population (latest available year)

- Over 10,000
- 5,000 – 10,000
- 1,000 – 5,000
- 500 – 1,000
- 100 – 500
- Under 100

[UK 3,292]

Highest per capita
Singapore	22,070
Hong Kong	20,004
Luxembourg	16,013
Belgium	12,258
Switzerland	9,428
Netherlands	9,145

PRODUCTION: TRADE

29: INTERNATIONAL ORGANIZATIONS

30: SELF-SUFFICIENCY IN FOOD

33: FUEL EXPORTS MOVEMENTS OF OIL

34: MINERAL EXPORTS

37: INDUSTRY AND TRADE EXPORTS PER CAPITA

43: TOURISM

Thriving international trade is the outward sign of a healthy world economy – the obvious indicator that some countries have goods to sell and others the wherewithal to buy them. Despite local fluctuations, trade throughout the 1980s grew consistently faster than output, increasing in value by almost 50% between 1979–89. It remains dominated by the wealthy, industrialized countries of the Organization for Economic Development:

between them, the 24 OECD members account for almost 75% of world imports and exports in most years. OECD dominance is just as marked in the trade in 'invisibles' – a column in the balance sheet that includes, among other headings, the export of services, interest payments on overseas investments, tourism, and even remittances from migrant workers abroad. In the UK, 'invisibles' account for more than half all trading income.

However, the size of these great trading

economies means that imports and exports usually comprise a fraction of their total wealth: in the case of the export-conscious Japanese, trade in goods and services amounts to less than 18% of GDP. In poorer countries, trade – often in a single commodity – may amount to 50% of GDP or more. And there are oddities: import-export figures for the entrepôt economy of Singapore, the transit point for much Asian trade, are almost double that small nation's total earnings.

WORLD TRADE

Percentage share of total world exports by value (1990)

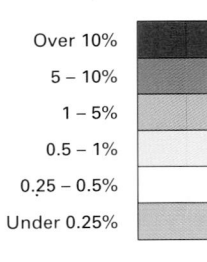

- Over 10%
- 5 – 10%
- 1 – 5%
- 0.5 – 1%
- 0.25 – 0.5%
- Under 0.25%

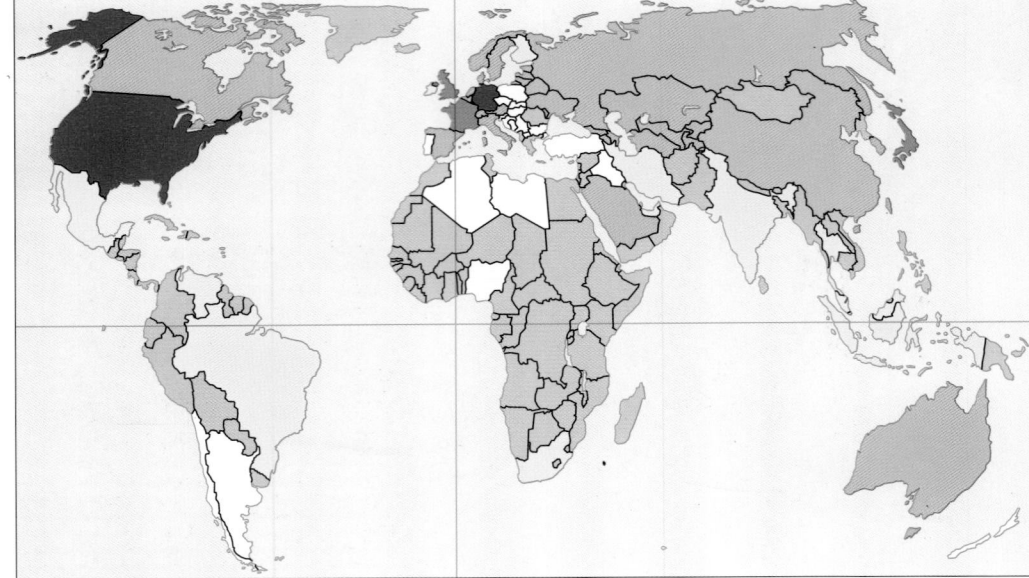

THE GREAT TRADING NATIONS

The imports and exports of the top ten trading nations as a percentage of world trade (latest available year). Each country's trade in manufactured goods is shown in orange.

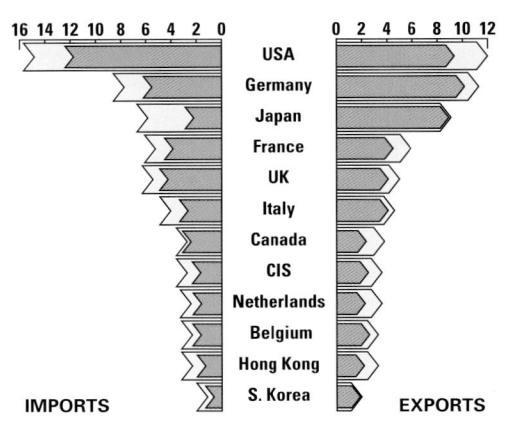

IMPORTS — 16 14 12 10 8 6 4 2 0 | 0 2 4 6 8 10 12 — EXPORTS

- USA
- Germany
- Japan
- France
- UK
- Italy
- Canada
- CIS
- Netherlands
- Belgium
- Hong Kong
- S. Korea

MAJOR EXPORTS

Leading manufactured items and their exporters, by percentage of world total in US $ (latest available year)

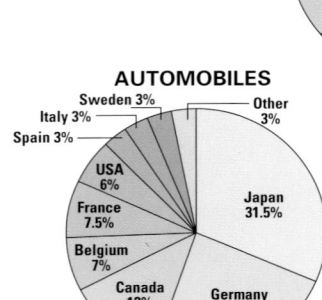

AIRCRAFT

Italy 3%, Canada 5%, Other 11%, France 8%, Germany 9%, UK 13%, USA 51%

TELECOMMUNICATIONS GEAR

Italy 3%, Canada 4%, Hong Kong 4%, Sweden 4%, UK 5%, France 5%, Germany 9%, Other 19%, Japan 33%, USA 14%

DATA PROCESSING EQUIPMENT

Singapore 4%, Italy 4%, Canada 4%, Ireland 5%, France 6%, UK 6%, Germany 11%, Other 14%, USA 24%, Japan 22%

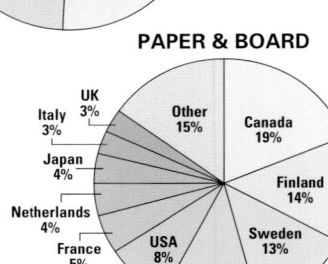

AUTOMOBILES

Sweden 3%, Italy 3%, Spain 3%, USA 6%, France 7.5%, Belgium 7%, Canada 12%, Germany 24%, Japan 31.5%, Other 3%

PAPER & BOARD

UK 3%, Italy 3%, Japan 4%, Netherlands 4%, France 5%, USA 8%, Germany 12%, Sweden 13%, Finland 14%, Canada 19%, Other 15%

ELECTRICAL MACHINERY

Belgium 4%, Switzerland 4%, Italy 4%, Netherlands 6%, France 7%, UK 8%, USA 14%, Germany 19%, Japan 22%, Other

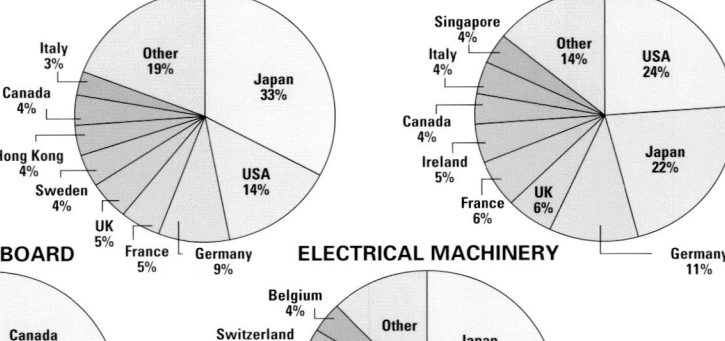

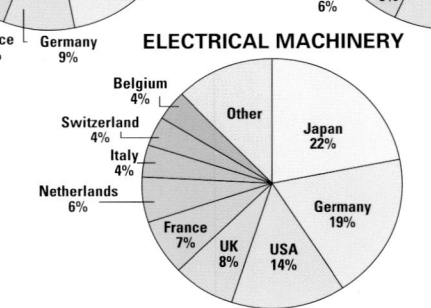

TRADED PRODUCTS

Top ten manufactures traded, by value in billions of US $ (latest available year)

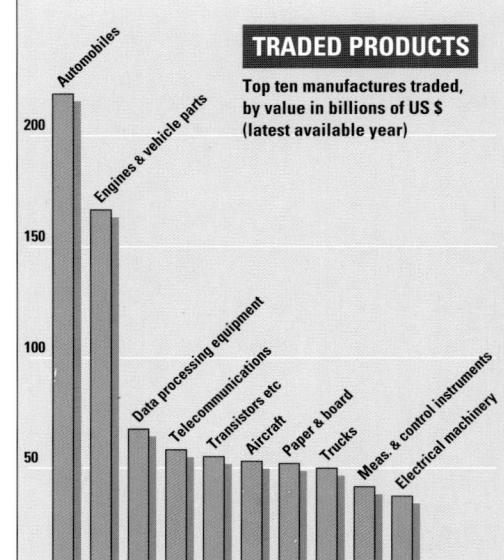

- Automobiles
- Engines & vehicle parts
- Data processing equipment
- Telecommunications
- Transistors etc
- Aircraft
- Paper & board
- Trucks
- Meas. & control instruments
- Electrical machinery

DEPENDENCE ON TRADE

Value of exports as a percentage of Gross Domestic Product (1991)

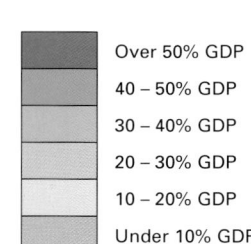

- Over 50% GDP
- 40 – 50% GDP
- 30 – 40% GDP
- 20 – 30% GDP
- 10 – 20% GDP
- Under 10% GDP

● Most dependent on industrial exports (over 75% of total exports)

● Most dependent on fuel exports (over 75% of total exports)

○ Most dependent on mineral and metal exports (over 75% of total exports)

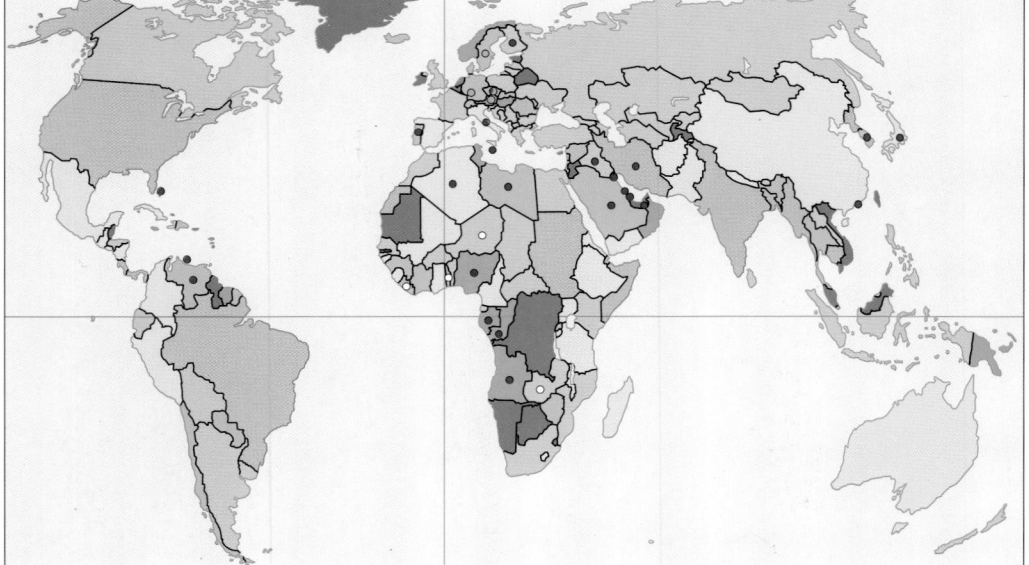

WORLD SHIPPING

While ocean passenger traffic is nowadays relatively modest, sea transport still carries most of the world's trade. Oil and bulk carriers make up the majority of the world fleet, although the general cargo category was the fastest growing in 1989, a year in which total tonnage increased by 1.5%.

Almost 30% of world shipping sails under a 'flag of convenience', whereby owners take advantage of low taxes by registering their vessels in a foreign country the ships will never see, notably Panama and Liberia.

MERCHANT FLEETS

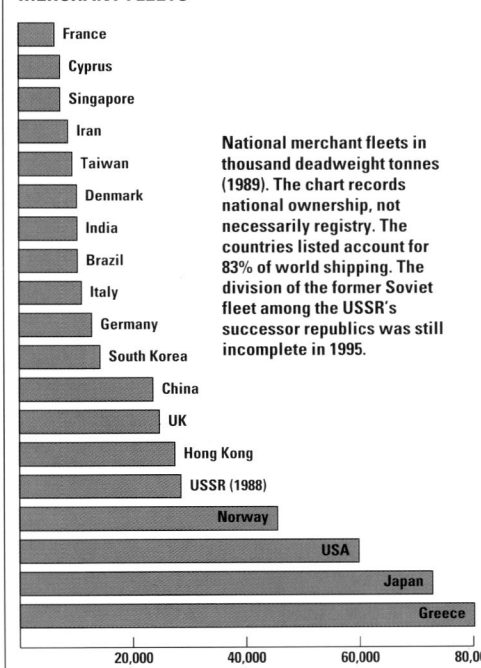

National merchant fleets in thousand deadweight tonnes (1989). The chart records national ownership, not necessarily registry. The countries listed account for 83% of world shipping. The division of the former Soviet fleet among the USSR's successor republics was still incomplete in 1995.

France
Cyprus
Singapore
Iran
Taiwan
Denmark
India
Brazil
Italy
Germany
South Korea
China
UK
Hong Kong
USSR (1988)
Norway
USA
Japan
Greece

20,000   40,000   60,000   80,000

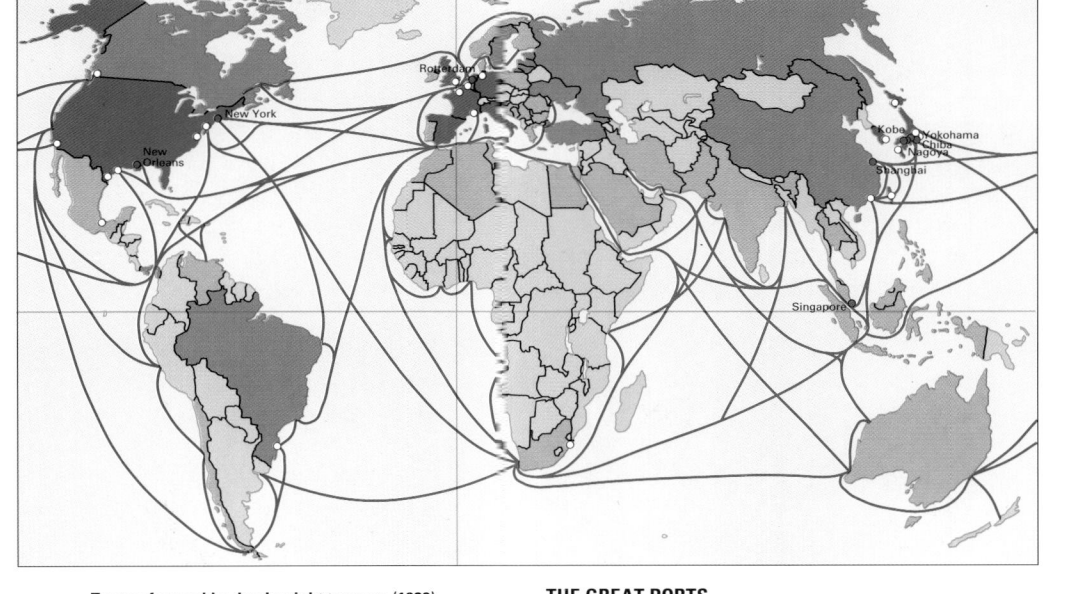

Freight unloaded in millions of tonnes (latest available year)

Over 100
50 – 100
10 – 50
5 – 10
Under 5
Landlocked countries

Major seaports

● Over 100 million tonnes per year
○ 50 – 100 million tonnes per year

Types of vessel by deadweight tonnage (1989)

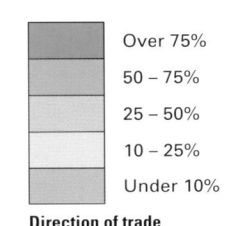

Oil tankers 38.4%
Ore & bulk carriers 29.9%
General cargo 16.1%
Others 9.7%
Ferries & passenger ships 0.5%
Liquid gas carriers 1.6%
Container ships 3.8%

THE GREAT PORTS

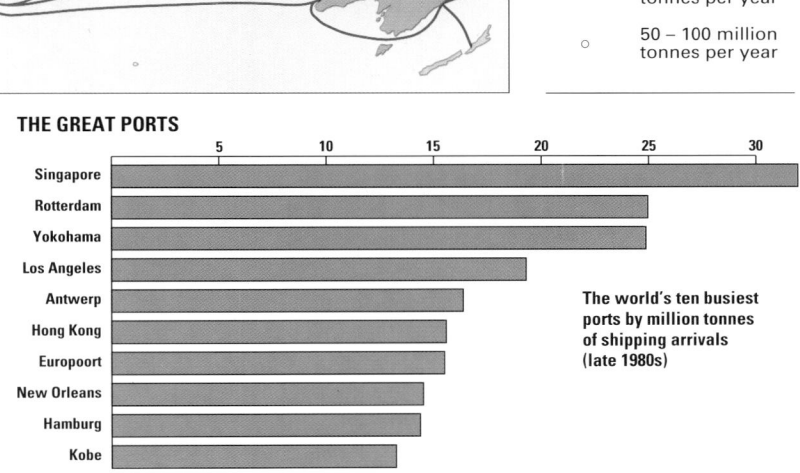

5   10   15   20   25   30

Singapore
Rotterdam
Yokohama
Los Angeles
Antwerp
Hong Kong
Europoort
New Orleans
Hamburg
Kobe

The world's ten busiest ports by million tonnes of shipping arrivals (late 1980s)

TRADE IN PRIMARY PRODUCTS

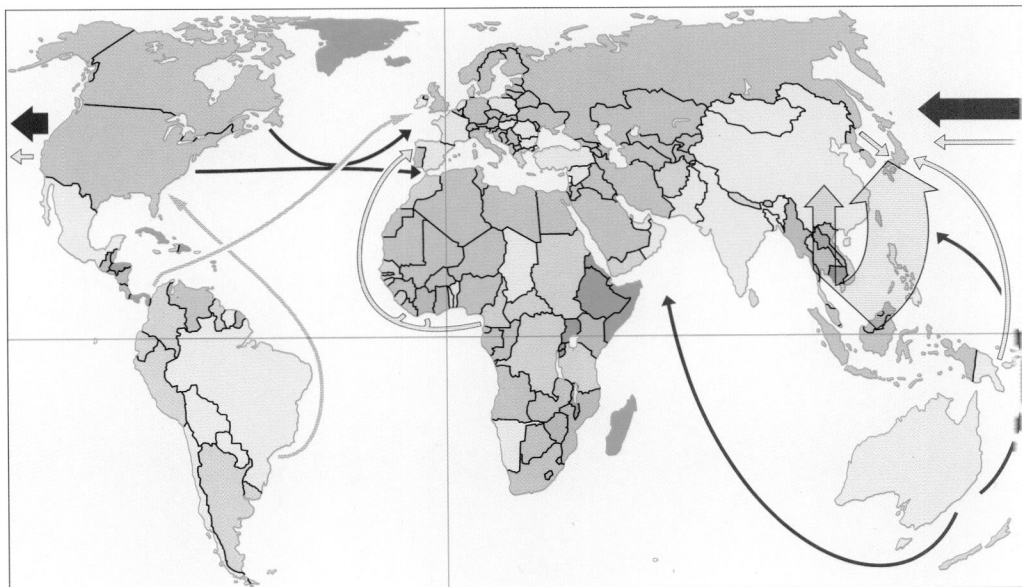

Primary products (excluding fuels, minerals and metals) as a percentage of total export value (latest available year)

Over 75%
50 – 75%
25 – 50%
10 – 25%
Under 10%

Direction of trade

→ Major movements of cereals
→ Major movements of coffee
⇒ Major movements of hardwoods

Arrows show the major trade directions of selected primary products, and are proportional to export value.

BALANCE OF TRADE

Value of exports in proportion to the value of imports (latest available year)

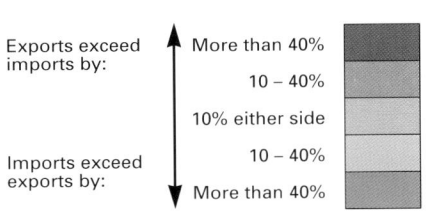

Exports exceed imports by:
More than 40%
10 – 40%
10% either side
10 – 40%
More than 40%
Imports exceed exports by:

The total world trade balance should amount to zero, since exports must equal imports on a global scale. In practice, at least $100 billion in exports go unrecorded, leaving the world with an apparent deficit and many countries in a better position than public accounting reveals. However, a favourable trade balance is not necessarily a sign of prosperity: many poorer countries must maintain a high surplus in order to service debts, and do so by restricting imports below the levels needed to sustain successful economies.

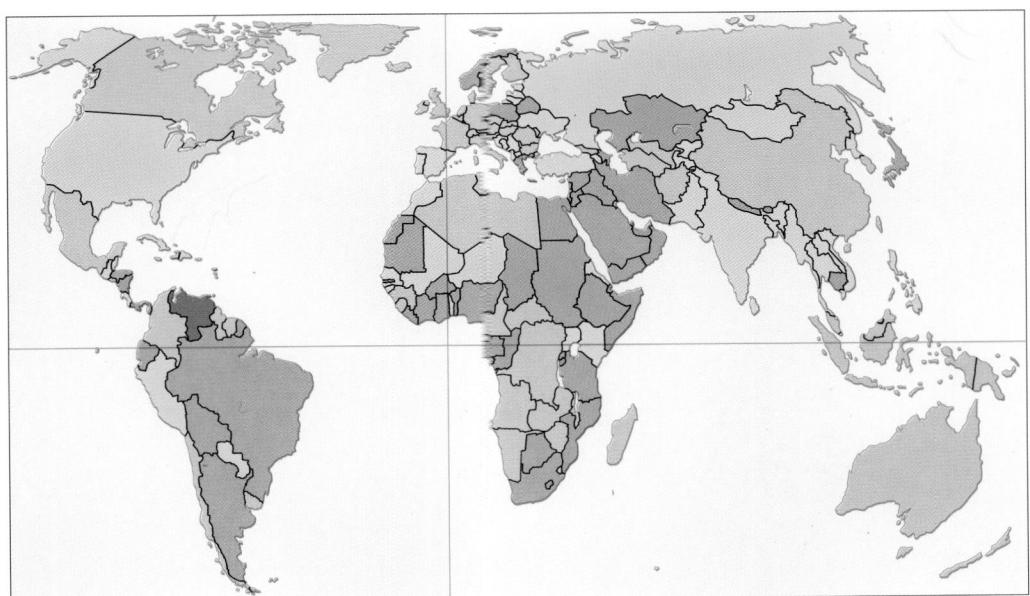

QUALITY OF LIFE: WEALTH

36: WEALTH CREATION

37: INDUSTRIAL POWER EXPORT PER CAPITA

38: WORLD TRADE MAJOR EXPORTS

39: BALANCE OF TRADE

43: DISTRIBUTION OF SPENDING DISTRIBUTION OF INCOME

Throughout the 1980s, most of the world became at least slightly richer. There were exceptions: in Africa, the poorest of the continents, many incomes actually fell, and the upheavals in Eastern Europe in 1989 left whole populations awash with political freedom but worse off financially in economies still teetering towards capitalism.

Most of the improvements, however, came to those who were already, in world terms, extremely affluent: the gap between rich and poor grew steadily wider. And in those developing countries that showed significant statistical progress, advances were often confined to a few favoured areas, while conditions in other, usually rural, districts went from bad to worse.

The pattern of world poverty varies from region to region. In most of Asia, the process of recognized development is generally under way, with production increases outpacing population growth. By 2000, less than 10% of the Chinese population should be officially rated 'poor': without the means to buy either adequate food or the basic necessities required to take a full part in everyday life. Even India's lower growth rate should be enough to reduce the burden of poverty for at least some of its people. In Latin America, average per capita production is high enough for most countries to be considered 'middle income' in world rankings. But although adequate resources exist, Latin American wealth is distributed with startling inequality. According to a 1990 World Bank report, a tax of only 2% on the richest fifth would raise enough money to pull every one of the continent's 437 million people above the poverty line.

In Africa, solutions will be much harder to find. The bane of high population growth has often been aggravated by incompetent administration, war and a succession of natural disasters. Population is the crux of the problem: numbers are growing anything up to twice as fast as the economies that try to support them. Aid from the developed world is only a partial solution; although Africa receives more aid than any other continent, much has been wasted on overambitious projects or lost in webs of inexperienced or corrupt bureaucracy. Yet without aid, Africa seems doomed to permanent crisis.

The rich countries can afford to increase their spending. The 24 members of the Organization for Economic Co-operation and Development comprise only 16% of the world's population, yet between them the nations accounted for almost 80% of total world production in 1988, a share that is likely to increase as the year 2000 approaches.

CURRENCIES

Currency units of the world's most powerful economies

1. USA: US Dollar ($, US $) = 100 cents
2. Japan: Yen (Y, ¥) = 100 sen
3. Germany: Deutsche Mark (DM) = 100 Pfennige
4. France: French Franc (Fr) = 100 centimes
5. Italy: Italian Lira (L, £, Lit) = 100 centesimi
6. UK: Pound Sterling (£) = 100 pence
7. Canada: Canadian Dollar (C$, Can$) = 100 cents
8. China: Renminbi Yuan (RMBY, $, Y) = 10 jiao = 100 fen
9. Brazil: Cruzeiro real (BRC) = 100 centavos
10. Spain: Peseta (Pta, Pa) = 100 céntimos
11. India: Indian Rupee (Re, Rs) = 100 paisa
12. Australia: Australian Dollar ($A) = 100 cents
13. Netherlands: Guilder, Florin (Gld, f) = 100 centimes
14. Switzerland: Swiss Franc (SFr, SwF) = 100 centimes
15. South Korea: Won (W) = 100 Chon
16. Sweden: Swedish Krona (SKr) = 100 ore
17. Mexico: Mexican Pesos (Mex$) = 100 centavos
18. Belgium: Belgian Franc (BFr) = 100 centimes
19. Austria: Schilling (S, Sch) = 100 groschen
20. Finland: Markka (FMk) = 100 penni
21. Denmark: Danish Krone (DKr) = 100 ore
22. Norway: Norwegian Krone (NKr) = 100 ore
23. Saudi Arabia: Riyal (SAR, SRI$) = 100 halalah
24. Indonesia: Rupiah (Rp) = 100 sen
25. South Africa: Rand (R) = 100 cents

CONTINENTAL SHARES

Shares of population and of wealth (GNP) by continent

Generalized continental figures show the startling difference between rich and poor, but mask the successes or failures of individual countries. Japan, for example, with less than 4% of Asia's population, produces almost 70% of the continent's output.

POPULATION

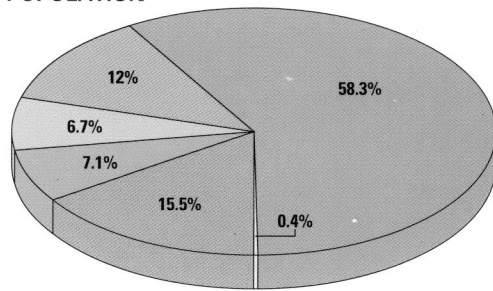

GNP

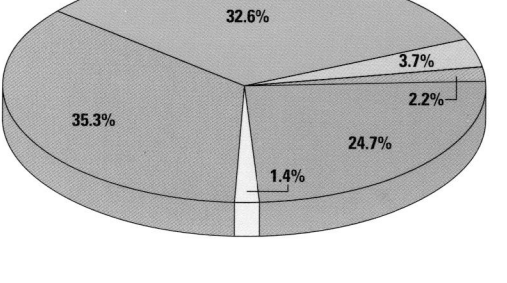

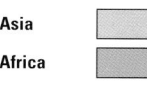

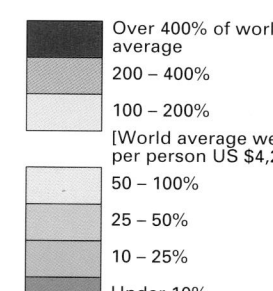

Europe	Asia	South America
Australia	Africa	North America

LEVELS OF INCOME

Gross National Product per capita: the value of total production divided by the population (1991)

- Over 400% of world average
- 200 – 400%
- 100 – 200%
- [World average wealth per person US $4,210]
- 50 – 100%
- 25 – 50%
- 10 – 25%
- Under 10%

Richest countries

Switzerland	$33,510
Luxembourg	$31,080
Japan	$26,920
Sweden	$25,490

Poorest countries

Mozambique	$70
Tanzania	$100
Ethiopia	$120
Somalia	$150

INDICATORS

The gap between the world's rich and poor is now so great that it is difficult to illustrate it on a single graph. Car ownership in the USA, for example, is almost 2,000 times as common as it is in Bangladesh. Within each income group, however, comparisons have some meaning: the affluent Japanese on their overcrowded island have far fewer cars than the Americans; the Chinese, perhaps because of propaganda value, have more television sets than people in India, whose per capita income is similar, while Nigerians prefer to spend their money on vehicles.

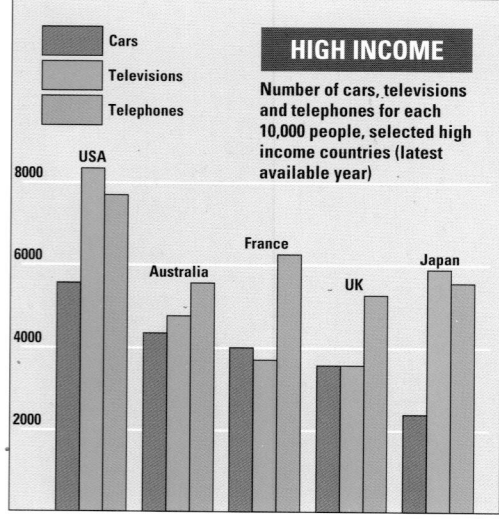

HIGH INCOME

Number of cars, televisions and telephones for each 10,000 people, selected high income countries (latest available year)

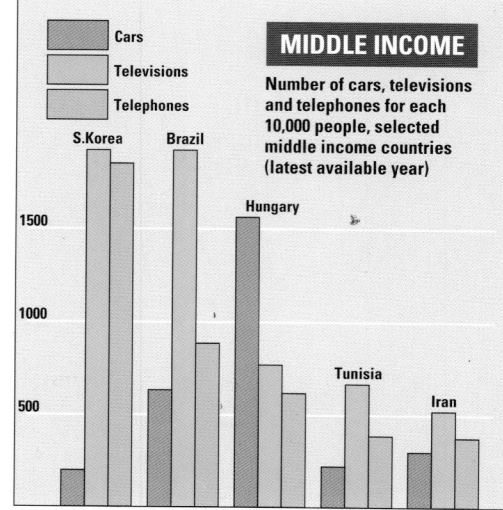

MIDDLE INCOME

Number of cars, televisions and telephones for each 10,000 people, selected middle income countries (latest available year)

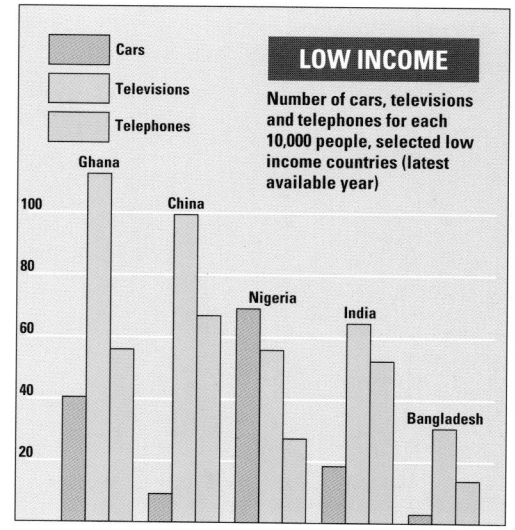

LOW INCOME

Number of cars, televisions and telephones for each 10,000 people, selected low income countries (latest available year)

DEBT AND AID

International debtors and the development aid they receive (1989)

■ Debt, $ per capita

■ Aid, $ per capita

Although aid grants make a vital contribution to many of the world's poorer countries, they are usually dwarfed by the burden of debt that developing economies are expected to repay. In the case of Mozambique, aid amounted to more than 70% of GNP. In 1990, the World Bank rated Mozambique as the world's poorest country, yet debt interest payments came to almost 75 times its entire export earnings.

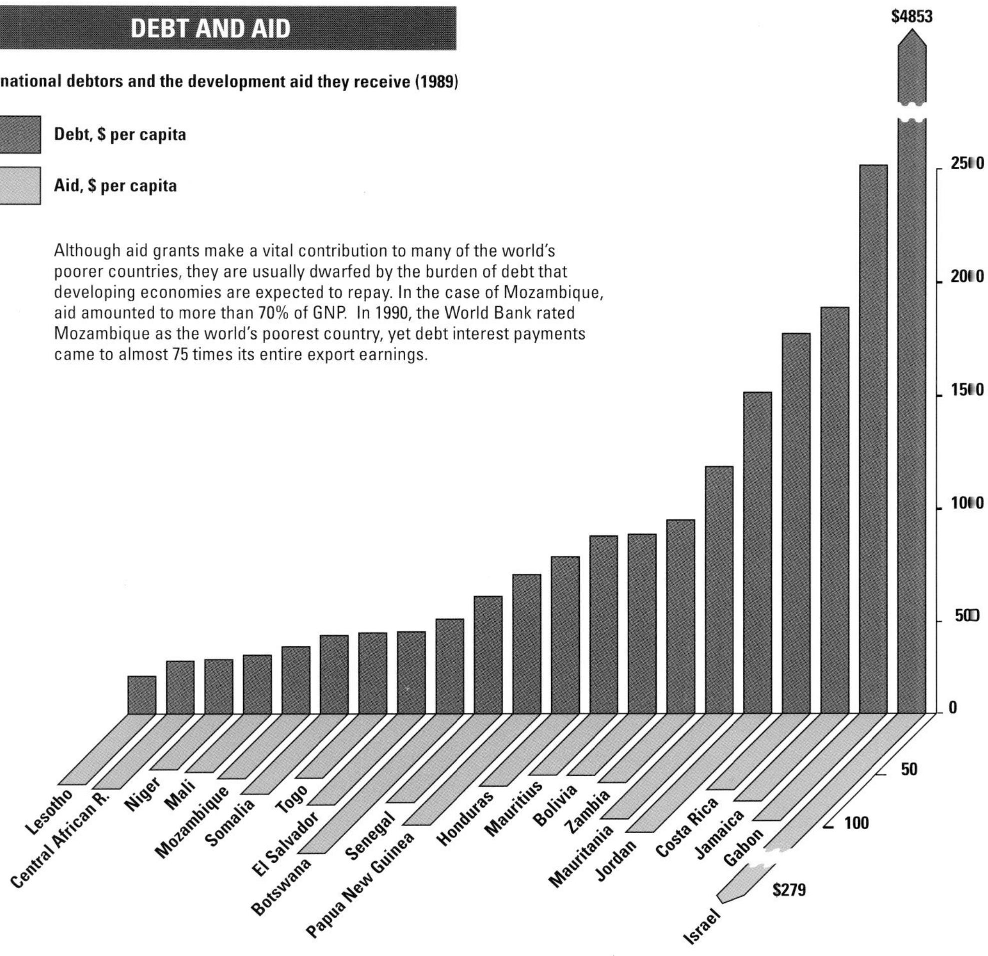

$4853

Lesotho, Central African R., Niger, Mali, Mozambique, Somalia, Togo, El Salvador, Botswana, Senegal, Papua New Guinea, Honduras, Mauritius, Bolivia, Zambia, Mauritania, Jordan, Costa Rica, Jamaica, Gabon, Israel $279

AID DONORS

Development aid by donor country, in millions of US $ and as a percentage of donor's GNP (1988)

Not all aid is given in cash grants: much is delivered in the form of cheap loans or technical assistance. Since the 1970s, OECD countries belonging to the Development Assistance Committee (DAC) have agreed in principle to give 0.7% of their GNP. Most have failed to meet their commitment. The USSR usually exceeded the DAC level, at least until 1988. After the Soviet Union's 1991 collapse, though, its impoverished heirs cut back dramatically on aid spending.

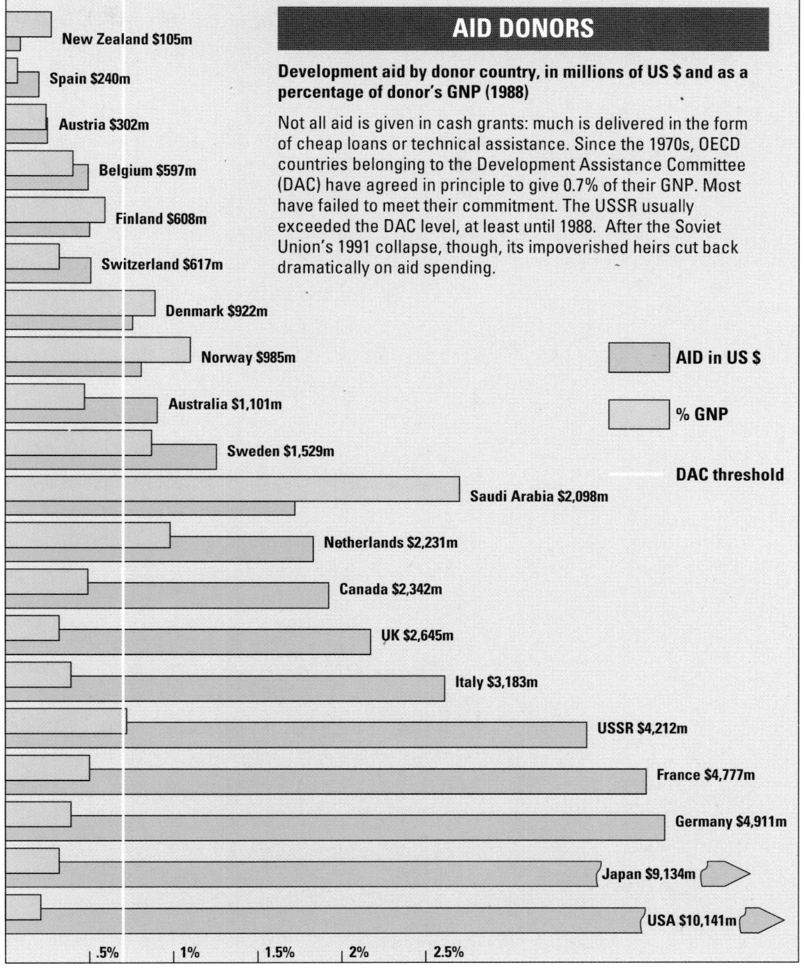

■ AID in US $

■ % GNP

DAC threshold

New Zealand $105m
Spain $240m
Austria $302m
Belgium $597m
Finland $608m
Switzerland $617m
Denmark $922m
Norway $985m
Australia $1,101m
Sweden $1,529m
Saudi Arabia $2,098m
Netherlands $2,231m
Canada $2,342m
UK $2,645m
Italy $3,183m
USSR $4,212m
France $4,777m
Germany $4,911m
Japan $9,134m
USA $10,141m

.5% 1% 1.5% 2% 2.5%

Inflation (right) is an excellent index of a country's financial stability, and usually its prosperity or at least its prospects. Inflation rates above 20% are generally matched by slow or even negative growth; above 50%, an economy is left reeling. Most advanced countries during the 1980s had to wrestle with inflation that occasionally touched or even exceeded 10%; in Japan, the growth leader, price increases averaged only 1.8% between 1980 and 1988.

Government spending (below right) is more difficult to interpret. Obviously, very low levels indicate a weak state, and high levels a strong one; but in poor countries, the 10–20% absorbed by the government may well amount to most of the liquid cash available, whereas in rich countries most of the 35–50% typically in government hands is returned in services.

GNP per capita figures (below) should also be compared with caution. They do not reveal the vast differences in living costs between different countries: the equivalent of US $100 is worth considerably more in poorer nations than it is in the USA itself.

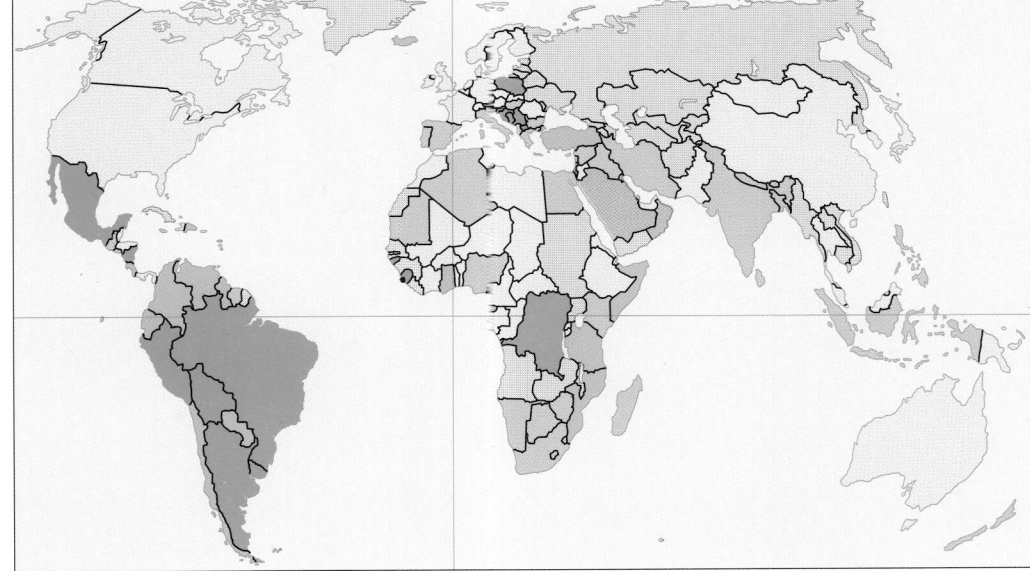

INFLATION

Average annual rate of inflation (1980–91)

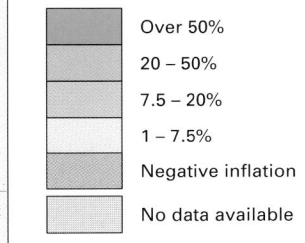

	Over 50%
	20 – 50%
	7.5 – 20%
	1 – 7.5%
	Negative inflation
	No data available

Highest average inflation
Nicaragua 584%
Argentina 417%
Brazil 328%

Lowest average inflation
Oman .... −3.1%
Kuwait .... −2.7%
Saudi Arabia .... −2.4%

THE WEALTH GAP

The world's richest and poorest countries, by Gross National Product per capita in US $ (1991)

1. Switzerland	33,510	1. Mozambique	70
2. Liechtenstein	33,000	2. Tanzania	100
3. Luxembourg	31,080	3. Ethiopia	120
4. Japan	26,920	4. Somalia	150
5. Sweden	25,490	5. Uganda	160
6. Bermuda	25,000	6. Bhutan	180
7. Finland	24,400	7. Nepal	180
8. Norway	24,160	8. Guinea-Bissau	190
9. Denmark	23,660	9. Cambodia	200
10. Germany	23,650	10. Burundi	210
11. Iceland	22,580	11. Madagascar	210
12. USA	22,560	12. Sierra Leone	210
13. Canada	21,260	13. Bangladesh	220
14. France	20,600	14. Chad	220
15. Austria	20,380	15. Zaïre	220
16. UAE	19,500	16. Laos	230
17. Belgium	19,300	17. Malawi	230
18. Italy	18,580	18. Rwanda	260
19. Netherlands	18,560	19. Mali	280
20. UK	16,750	20. Guyana	290

GNP per capita is calculated by dividing a country's Gross National Product by its population.

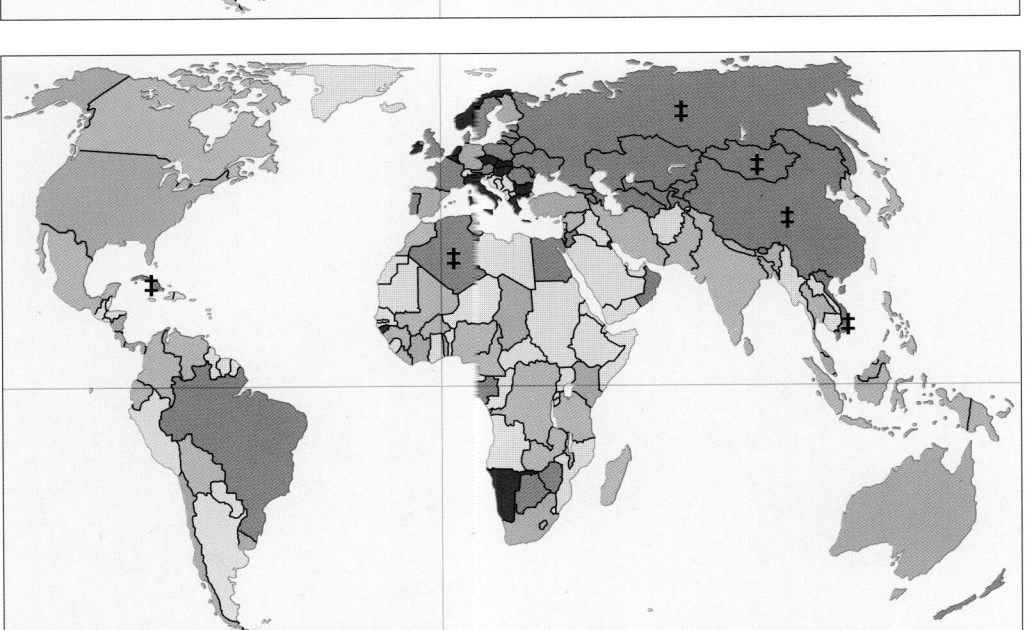

STATE SPENDING

Central government expenditure as a percentage of GNP (latest available year) [‡ estimate]

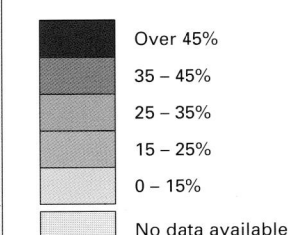

	Over 45%
	35 – 45%
	25 – 35%
	15 – 25%
	0 – 15%
	No data available

Top 5 countries
Bulgaria 77.3%
Guinea-Bissau 63.0%
Greece 60.0%
Czechoslovakia 55.6%
Hungary 54.7%

QUALITY OF LIFE: STANDARDS

16: WATER SUPPLY

22: POPULATION DENSITY

25: URBAN POLLUTION
INFORMAL CITIZENS
URBAN ADVANTAGES

28: WORLD'S REFUGEES
WAR SINCE 1945

36: EMPLOYMENT
THE WORKFORCE

40: THE WEALTH GAP

41: DEBT AND AID

45: LIFE EXPECTANCY
INFANT MORTALITY
CRIME AND
PUNISHMENT

At first sight, most international contrasts are swamped by differences in wealth. The rich not only have more money, they have more of everything, including years of life. Those with only a little money are obliged to spend most of it on food and clothing, the basic maintenance costs of existence; air travel and tourism are unlikely to feature on the lists of their expenditure. However, poverty and wealth are both relative: slum dwellers living on social security payments in an affluent industrial country have far more resources at their disposal than an average African peasant, but feel their own poverty none the less acutely. A middle-class Indian lawyer cannot command a fraction of the earnings of a counterpart in New York, London or Rome; nevertheless, he rightly sees himself as prosperous.

In 1990 the United Nations Development Programme published its first Human Development Index, an attempt to construct a comparative scale by which at least a simplified form of well-being might be measured. The index, running from 1 to 100, combined figures for life expectancy and literacy with a wealth scale that matched incomes against the official poverty lines of a group of industrialized nations. National scores ranged from a startling 98.7 for

Sweden to a miserable 11.6 for Niger, reflecting the all-too-familiar gap between rich and poor.

Comparisons between nations with similar incomes are more interesting, showing the effect of government policies. For example, Sri Lanka was awarded 78.9 against 43.9 for its only slightly poorer neighbour, India; Zimbabwe, at 57.6, had more than double the score of Senegal, despite no apparent disparities in average income. Some development indicators may be interpreted in two ways. There is a very clear correlation, for example, between the wealth of a nation and the level of education that its people enjoy. Education helps create wealth, of course; but are rich countries wealthy because they are educated, or well-educated because they are rich? Women's fertility rates appear to fall almost in direct proportion to the amount of secondary education they receive; but high levels of female education are associated with rich countries, where fertility is already low.

Not everything, though, is married to wealth. The countries cited on these pages have been chosen to give a range covering different cultures as well as different economic power, revealing disparities among rich and among poor as well as between the two obvious groups. Income distribution, for

example, shows that in Brazil (following the general pattern of Latin America) most national wealth is concentrated in a few hands; Bangladesh is much poorer, but what little wealth there is, is more evenly spread.

Among the developed countries the USA, with its poorest 20% sharing less than 5% of the national cake, has a noticeably less even distribution than Japan where, despite massive industrialization, traditional values act as a brake against poverty. Hungary, still enmeshed in Communism when these statistics were compiled, shows the most even distribution of all, which certainly matches with Socialist theory. However, the inequalities in Communist societies, a contributing factor in the demise of most of them in the late 1980s, are not easily measured in money terms. Communist élites are less often rewarded with cash than with power and privilege, commodities not easily expressed statistically.

There are other limits to statistical analysis. Even without taking account of such imponderables as personal satisfaction, it will always be more difficult to measure a reasonable standard of living than a nation's income or its productivity. Lack of money certainly brings misery, but its presence does not guarantee contentment.

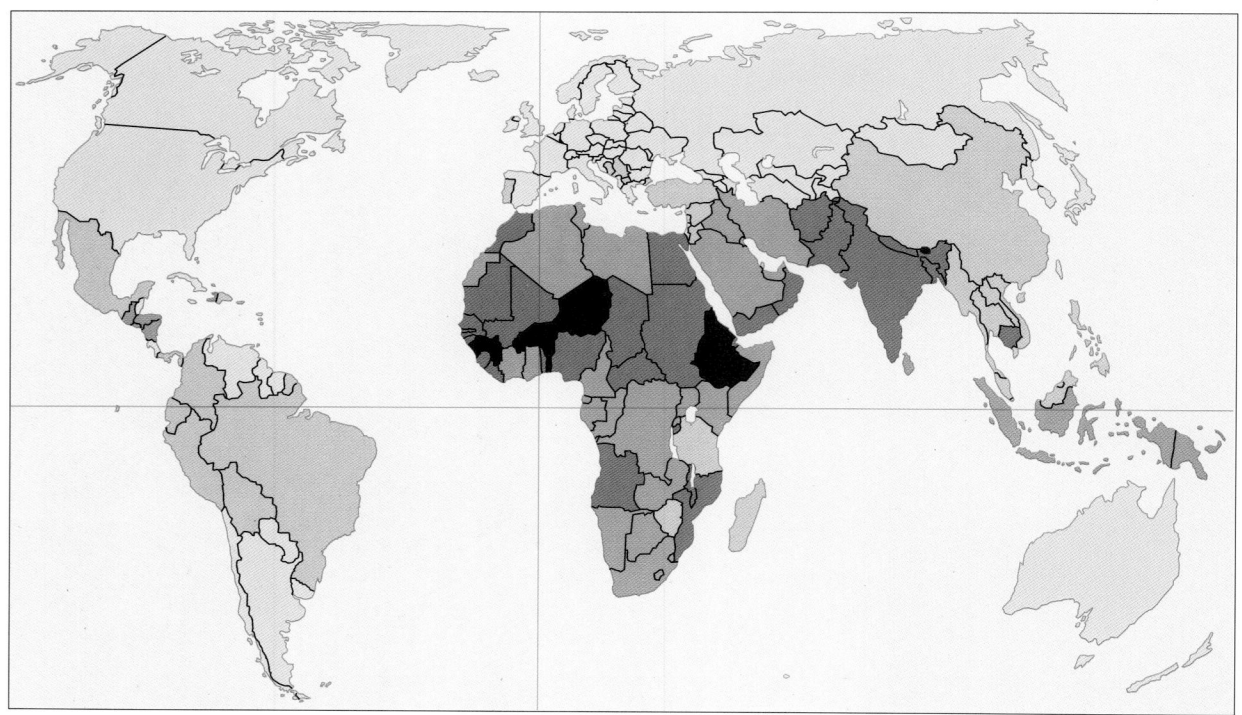

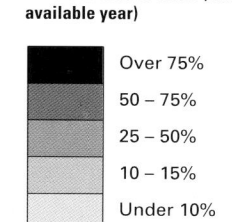

ILLITERACY

Percentage of the total population unable to read or write (latest available year)

- Over 75%
- 50 – 75%
- 25 – 50%
- 10 – 15%
- Under 10%

Educational expenditure per person (latest available year)

Top 5 countries

Sweden	$997
Qatar	$989
Canada	$983
Norway	$971
Switzerland	$796

Bottom 5 countries

Chad	$2
Bangladesh	$3
Ethiopia	$3
Nepal	$4
Somalia	$4

EDUCATION

The developing countries made great efforts in the 1970s and 1980s to bring at least a basic education to their people. Primary school enrolments rose above 60% in all but the poorest nations. Figures often include teenagers or young adults, however, and there are still an estimated 300 million children worldwide who receive no schooling at all. Secondary and higher education are expanding far more slowly, and the gap between rich and poor is probably even larger than it appears from the charts here, while the bare statistics provide no real reflection of educational quality.

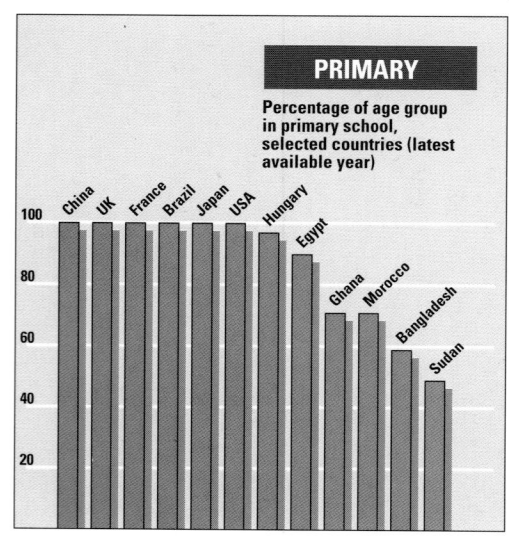

PRIMARY

Percentage of age group in primary school, selected countries (latest available year)

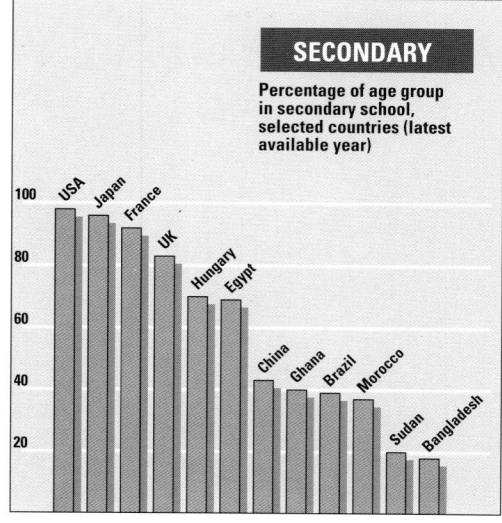

SECONDARY

Percentage of age group in secondary school, selected countries (latest available year)

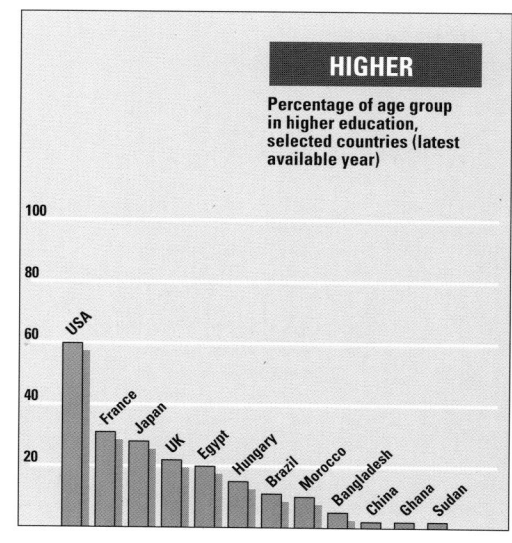

HIGHER

Percentage of age group in higher education, selected countries (latest available year)

DISTRIBUTION OF SPENDING

Percentage share of household spending (latest available year)

- Food
- Clothing
- Energy & Housing
- Medicine & Education
- Transport
- Other

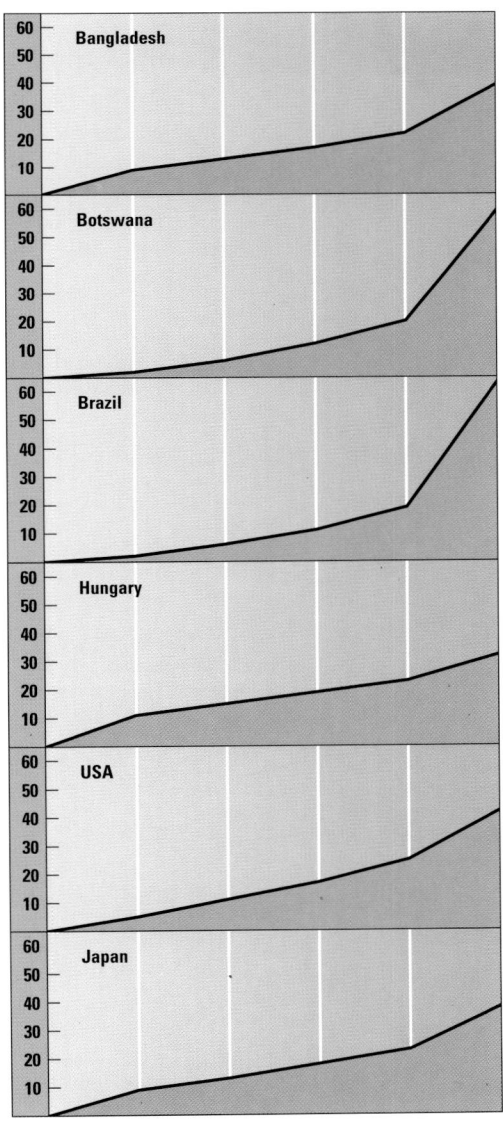

UK USA Japan Hungary Brazil Egypt Nigeria B'desh

DISTRIBUTION OF INCOME

Percentage share of household income from poorest fifth to richest fifth, selected countries (latest available year)

Bangladesh
Botswana
Brazil
Hungary
USA
Japan

FERTILITY AND EDUCATION

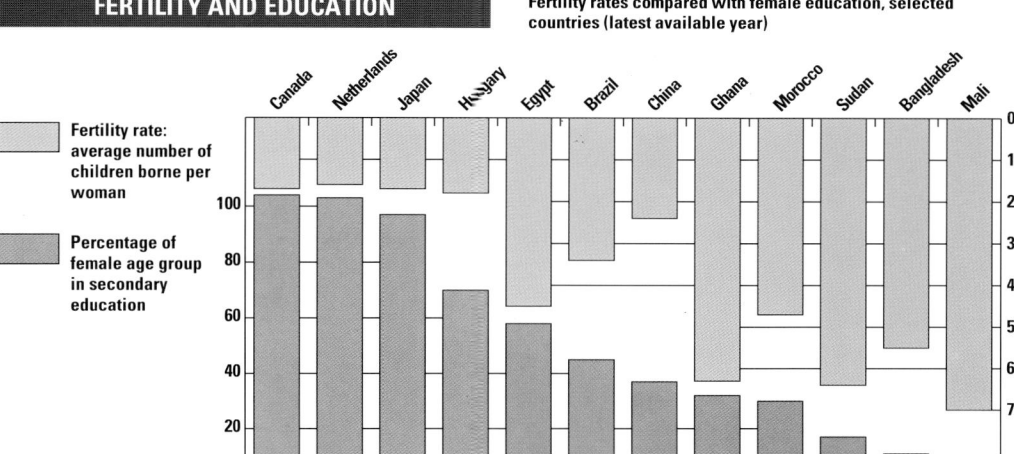

- Fertility rate: average number of children borne per woman
- Percentage of female age group in secondary education

Fertility rates compared with female education, selected countries (latest available year)

Canada Netherlands Japan Hungary Egypt Brazil China Ghana Morocco Sudan Bangladesh Mali

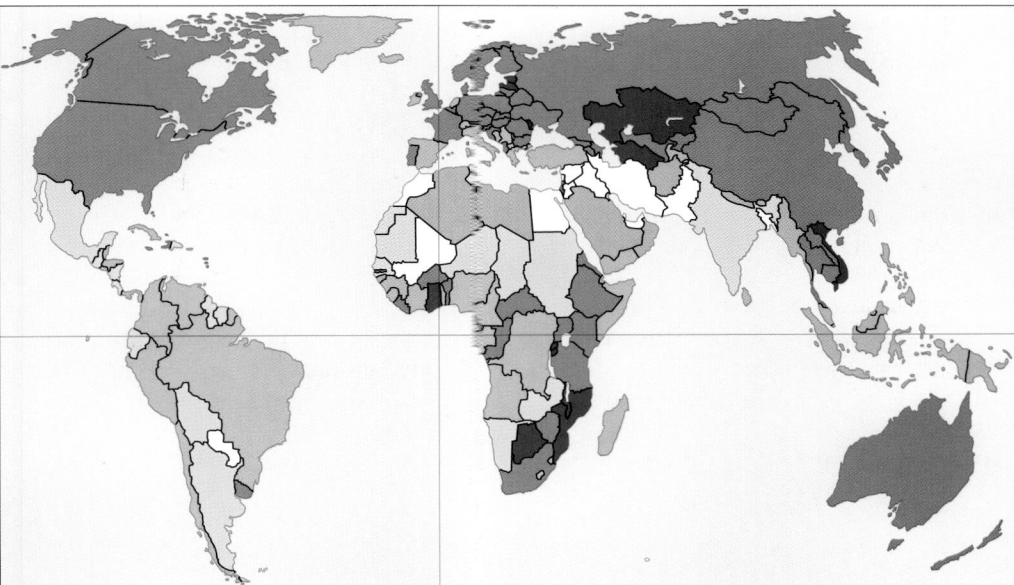

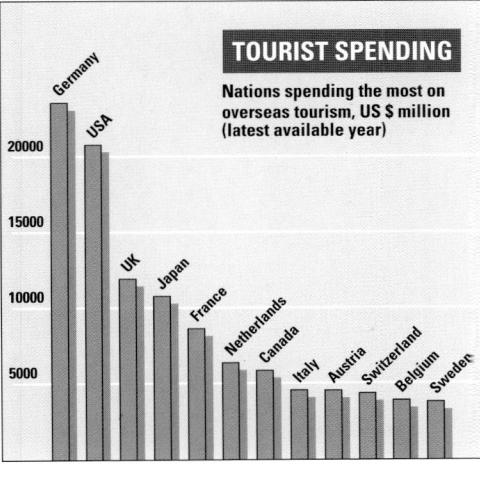

TOURIST SPENDING

Nations spending the most on overseas tourism, US $ million (latest available year)

Germany USA UK Japan France Netherlands Canada Italy Austria Switzerland Belgium Sweden

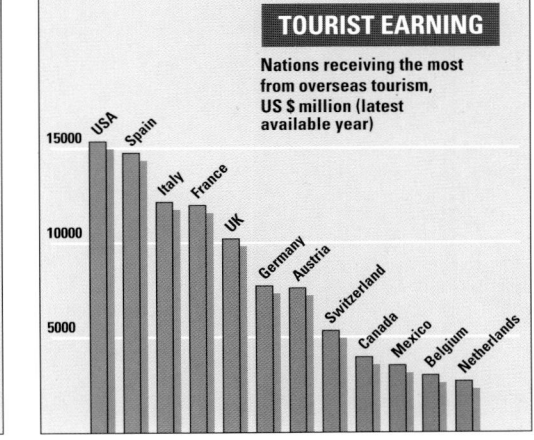

TOURIST EARNING

Nations receiving the most from overseas tourism, US $ million (latest available year)

USA Spain Italy France UK Germany Austria Switzerland Canada Mexico Belgium Netherlands

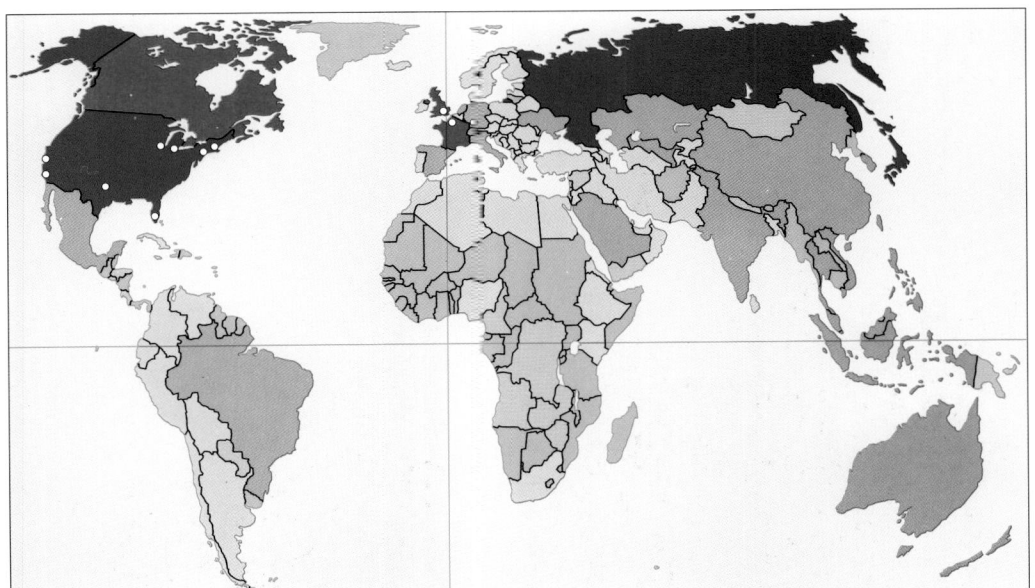

Since the age group for secondary schooling is usually defined as 12–17 years, percentages for countries with a significant number of 11- or 18-year-olds in secondary school may actually exceed 100. A high proportion of employed women may indicate either an advanced, industrial economy where female opportunities are high, or a poor country where many women's lives are dominated by agricultural toil. The lowest rates are found in Islamic nations, whose religious precepts often exclude women even from fieldwork.

WOMEN AT WORK

Women in paid employment as a percentage of the total workforce (latest available year)

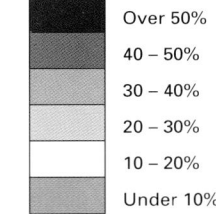

- Over 50%
- 40 – 50%
- 30 – 40%
- 20 – 30%
- 10 – 20%
- Under 10%

Most women in work

Kazakhstan 54%
Rwanda 54%
Botswana 53%

Fewest women in work

Guinea-Bissau 3%
Oman 6%
Afghanistan 8%

Small economies in attractive areas are often completely dominated by tourism: in some West Indian islands, tourist spending provides over 90% of the total income. In cash terms the USA is the world leader: its 1987 earnings exceeded $15 billion, though that sum amounted to only 0.4% of its GDP.

AIR TRAVEL

Millions of passenger km [number carried, international/domestic, multiplied by distance flown from airport of origin] (latest year)

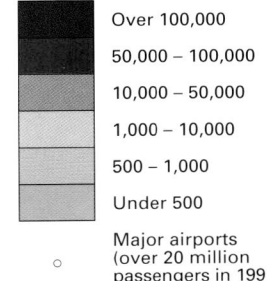

- Over 100,000
- 50,000 – 100,000
- 10,000 – 50,000
- 1,000 – 10,000
- 500 – 1,000
- Under 500
- Major airports (over 20 million passengers in 1991)

The world's busiest airport in terms of total passengers is Chicago's O'Hare; the busiest international airport is Heathrow, the largest of London's airports

QUALITY OF LIFE: HEALTH

16: WATER SUPPLY

25: URBAN POLLUTION
    INFORMAL CITIZENS
    URBAN ADVANTAGES

31: FOOD AND
    POPULATION

43: DISTRIBUTION OF
    SPENDING

According to statistics gathered in the late 1980s and early 1990s, a third of the world's population has no access to safe drinking water: malaria is on the increase; cholera, thought vanquished, is reappearing in South America; an epidemic of the AIDS virus is gathering force in Africa; and few developing countries can stretch their health care budgets beyond US $2 per person per year.

Yet human beings, by every statistical index, have never been healthier. In the richest nations, where food is plentiful, the demands of daily work are rarely onerous and medical care is both readily available and highly advanced, the average life expectancy is often more than 75 years – approaching the perceived limits for human longevity. In middle-income nations, such as Brazil and the Philippines, life expectancy usually extends at least to the mid-60s; in China, it has already reached 70 years. Even in poverty-stricken Ethiopia and Chad, lifespans are close to 50 years. Despite economic crisis, drought, famine and even war, every country in the world reported an increase between 1965 and 1990.

It was not always so, even in countries then considered rich. By comparison, in 1880 the life expectancy of an average Berliner was under 30 years and infant mortality in the United Kingdom, then the wealthiest nation, stood at 144 per thousand births – a grim toll exceeded today only by three of the poorest African countries (Mali, Sierra Leone and Guinea). Even by 1910, European death rates were almost twice as high as the world average less than 80 years later; infant mortality in Norway, Europe's healthiest country, was then higher than in present-day Indonesia. In far less than a century, human prospects have improved beyond recognition.

In global terms, the transformation is less the result of high-technology medicine – still too expensive for all but a minority, even in rich countries – than of improvements in agriculture and hence nutrition, matched by the widespread diffusion of the basic concepts of disease and public health. One obvious consequence, as death rates everywhere continue to fall, is sustained population growth. Another is the rising expectation of continued improvement felt by both rich and poor nations alike.

In some ways, the task is easier for developing countries, striving with limited resources to attain health levels to which the industrialized world has only recently become accustomed. As the tables below illustrate, infectious disease is rare among the richer nations, while ailments such as cancer, which tend to kill in advanced years, do not seriously impinge on populations with shorter lifespans.

Yet infectious disease is relatively cheap to eliminate, or at least reduce, and it is likely to be easier to raise life expectancy from 60 to 70 years than from 75 to 85 years. The ills of the developed world and its ageing population are more expensive to treat – though most poor countries would be happy to suffer from the problems of the affluent. Western nations regularly spend more money on campaigns to educate their citizens out of overeating and other bad habits than many developing countries can devote to an entire health budget – an irony that marks the dimensions of the rich-poor divide.

Indeed, wealth itself may be the most reliable indicator of longevity. Harmful habits are usually the province of the rich; yet curiously, though the dangerous effects of tobacco have been proved beyond doubt, the affluent Japanese combine very high cigarette consumption with the longest life expectancy of all the major nations. Similarly, heavy alcohol consumption seems to have no effect on longevity: the French, world leaders in 1988 and in most previous surveys, outlive the more moderate British by a year, and the abstemious Indians by almost two decades.

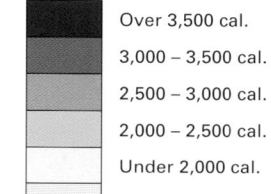

FOOD CONSUMPTION

Average daily food intake in calories per person (latest available year)

- Over 3,500 cal.
- 3,000 – 3,500 cal.
- 2,500 – 3,000 cal.
- 2,000 – 2,500 cal.
- Under 2,000 cal.
- No available data

Top 5 countries
Belgium .... 3,902 cal.
Greece .... 3,825 cal.
Ireland .... 3,778 cal.
Bulgaria .... 3,707 cal.
USA .... 3,650 cal.

Bottom 5 countries
Ethiopia....................... 1,666 cal.
Mozambique .... 1,679 cal.
Chad .... 1,742 cal.
Sierra Leone .... 1,799 cal.
Angola .... 1,806 cal.

CAUSES OF DEATH

The rich not only live longer, on average, than the poor; they also die from different causes. Infectious and parasitic diseases, all but eliminated in the developed world, remain a scourge in poorer countries. On the other hand, more than two-thirds of the populations of OECD nations eventually succumb to cancer or circulatory disease; the proportion in Latin America is only about 45%. In addition to the three major diseases shown here, respiratory infection and injury also claim more lives in developing nations, which lack the drugs and medical skills required to treat them.

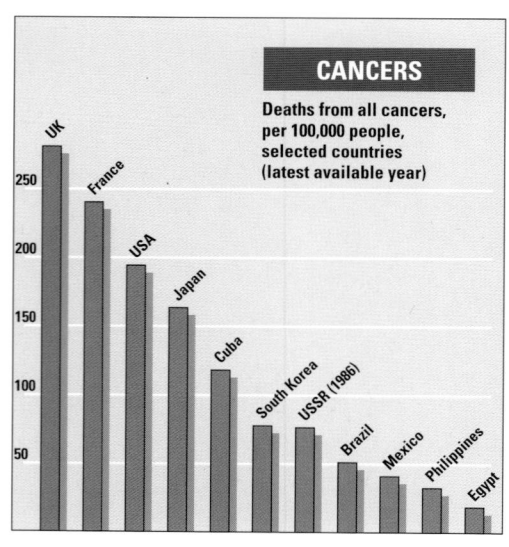

CANCERS
Deaths from all cancers, per 100,000 people, selected countries (latest available year)

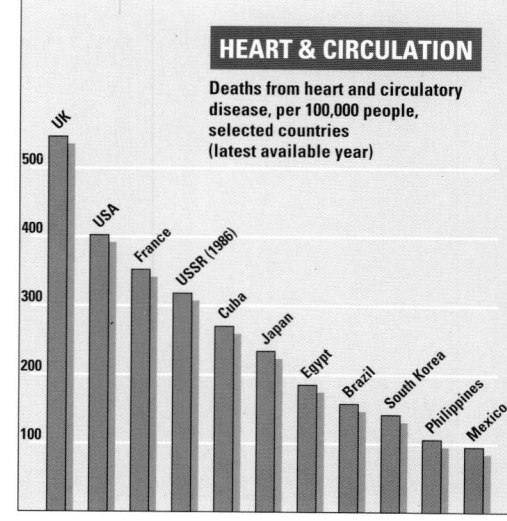

HEART & CIRCULATION
Deaths from heart and circulatory disease, per 100,000 people, selected countries (latest available year)

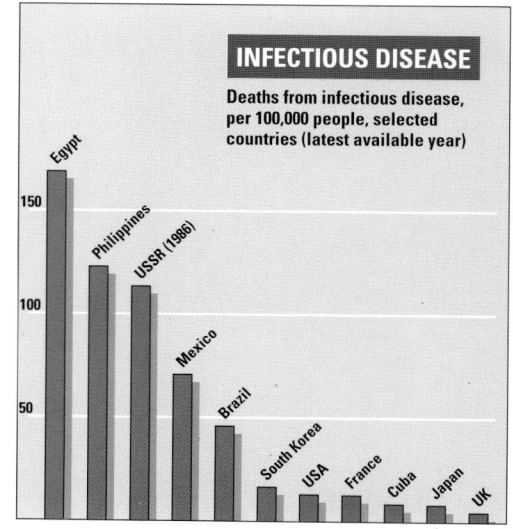

INFECTIOUS DISEASE
Deaths from infectious disease, per 100,000 people, selected countries (latest available year)

LIFE EXPECTANCY

Years of life expectancy at birth, selected countries (1990–95)

The chart shows combined data for both sexes. On average, women live longer than men worldwide, even in developing countries with high maternal mortality rates. Overall, life expectancy is steadily rising, though the difference between rich and poor nations remains dramatic.

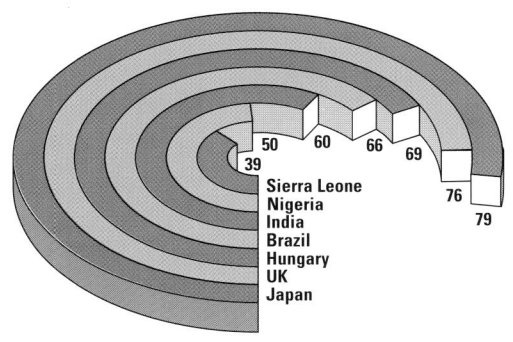

39 Sierra Leone
50 Nigeria
60 India
66 Brazil
69 Hungary
76 UK
79 Japan

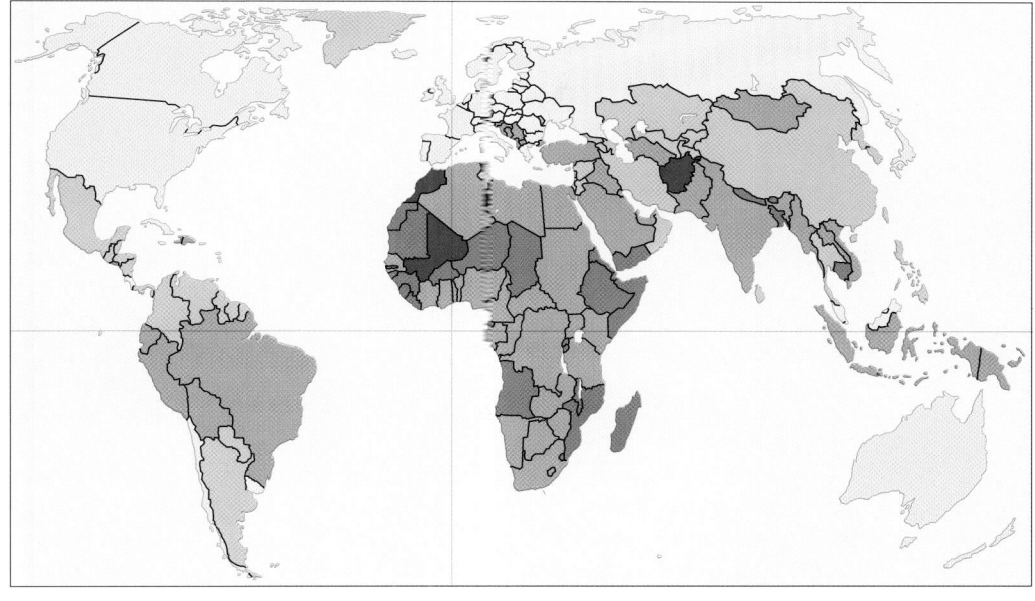

CHILD MORTALITY

Number of babies who will die under the age of one, per 1,000 births (average 1990–95)

- Over 150 deaths
- 100 – 150 deaths
- 50 – 100 deaths
- 20 – 50 deaths
- 10 – 20 deaths
- Under 10 deaths

Highest child mortality

Afghanistan...................... 162
Mali 159

Lowest child mortality

Iceland 5
Finland................................... 5

[UK 8]

HOSPITAL CAPACITY

Hospital beds available for each 1,000 people (latest available year)

Highest capacity		Lowest capacity	
Finland	14.9	Bangladesh	0.2
Sweden	13.2	Nepal	0.2
France	12.9	Ethiopia	0.3
USSR (1986)	12.8	Mauritania	0.4
Netherlands	12.0	Mali	0.5
North Korea	11.7	Burkina Faso	0.6
Switzerland	11.3	Pakistan	0.6
Austria	10.4	Niger	0.7
Czechoslovakia	10.1	Haiti	0.8
Hungary	9.1	Chad	0.8

[UK 8]

The availability of a bed can mean anything from a private room in a well-equipped Californian teaching hospital to a place in the overcrowded annexe of a rural African clinic. In the Third World especially, quality of treatment can vary enormously from place to place within the same country.

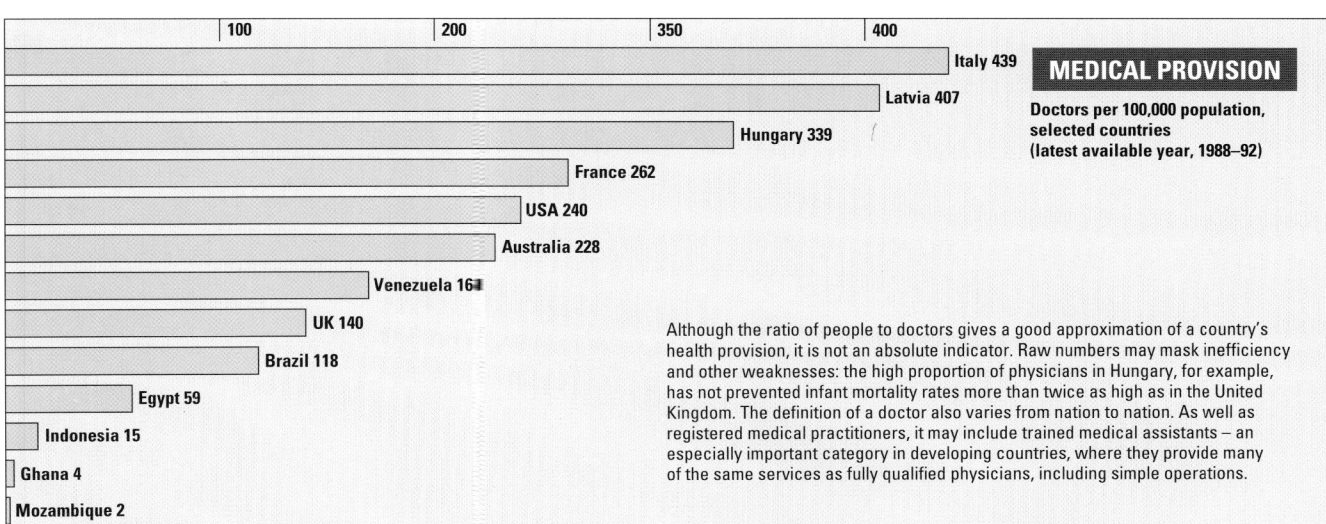

Italy 439
Latvia 407
Hungary 339
France 262
USA 240
Australia 228
Venezuela 164
UK 140
Brazil 118
Egypt 59
Indonesia 15
Ghana 4
Mozambique 2

MEDICAL PROVISION

Doctors per 100,000 population, selected countries (latest available year, 1988–92)

Although the ratio of people to doctors gives a good approximation of a country's health provision, it is not an absolute indicator. Raw numbers may mask inefficiency and other weaknesses: the high proportion of physicians in Hungary, for example, has not prevented infant mortality rates more than twice as high as in the United Kingdom. The definition of a doctor also varies from nation to nation. As well as registered medical practitioners, it may include trained medical assistants – an especially important category in developing countries, where they provide many of the same services as fully qualified physicians, including simple operations.

THE AIDS CRISIS

The Acquired Immune Deficiency Syndrome was first identified in 1981, when American doctors found otherwise healthy young men succumbing to rare infections. By 1984, the cause had been traced to the Human Immunodeficiency Virus (HIV), which can remain dormant for many years and perhaps indefinitely: only half of those known to carry the virus in 1981 had developed AIDS ten years later.

By 1991 the World Health Organization knew of more than 250,000 AIDS cases worldwide and suspected the true number to be at least four times as high. In Western countries in the early 1990s, most AIDS deaths were among male homosexuals or needle-sharing drug-users. However, the disease is spreading fastest among heterosexual men and women, which is its usual vector in the Third World, where most of its victims live. Africa is the most severely hit: a 1992 UN report estimated that 2 million African children will die of AIDS before the year 2000 – and some 10 million will be orphaned.

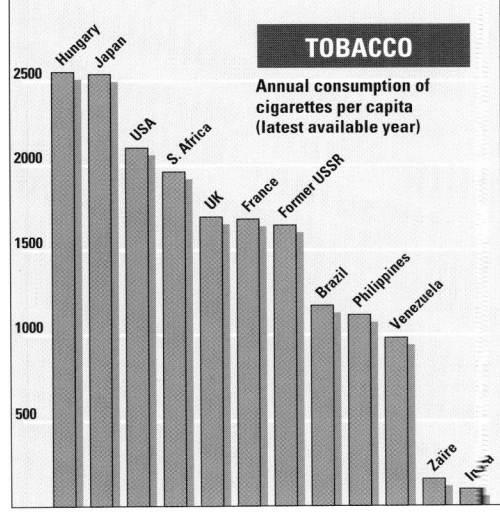

TOBACCO

Annual consumption of cigarettes per capita (latest available year)

Hungary, Japan, USA, S. Africa, UK, France, Former USSR, Brazil, Philippines, Venezuela, Zaire, India

CRIME AND PUNISHMENT

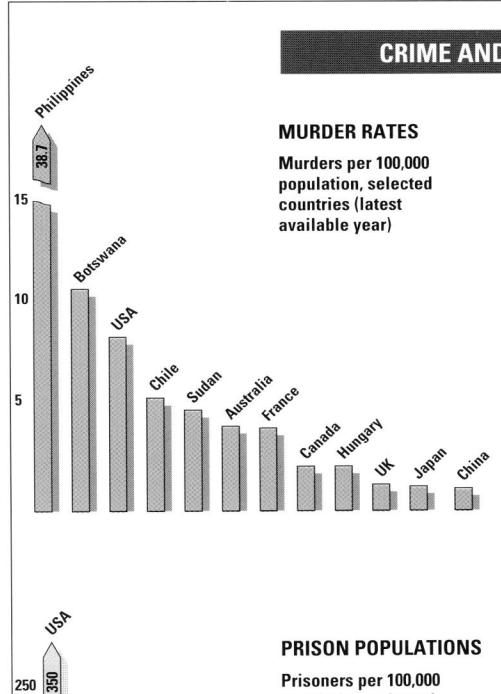

MURDER RATES

Murders per 100,000 population, selected countries (latest available year)

Philippines 38.7, Botswana, USA, Chile, Sudan, Australia, France, Canada, Hungary, UK, Japan, China

Crime rates are difficult to compare internationally. Standards of reporting and detection vary greatly, as do the definitions of many types of crime. Murder is probably the best detected as well as the most heinous, but different legal systems make different distinctions between murder and manslaughter or other forms of culpable homicide. By any reckoning, however, the USA's high murder rate stands out against otherwise similar Western countries, although it is dwarfed by the killings recorded in the very different culture of the Philippines.

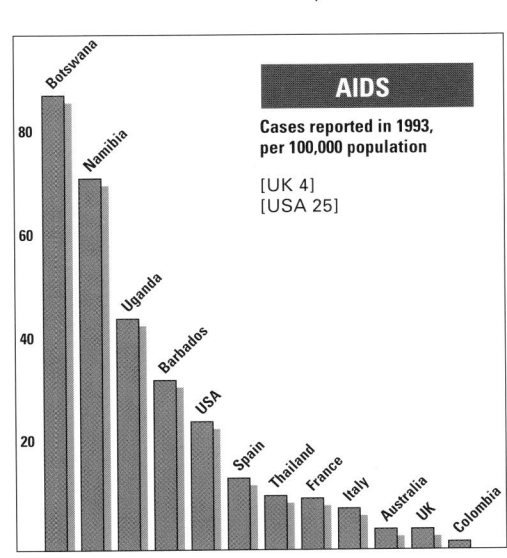

AIDS

Cases reported in 1993, per 100,000 population

[UK 4]
[USA 25]

Botswana, Namibia, Uganda, Barbados, USA, Spain, Thailand, France, Italy, Australia, UK, Colombia

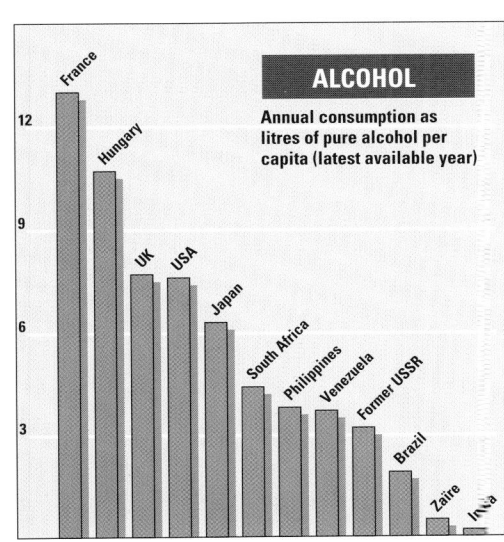

ALCOHOL

Annual consumption as litres of pure alcohol per capita (latest available year)

France, Hungary, UK, USA, Japan, South Africa, Philippines, Venezuela, Former USSR, Brazil, Zaire, India

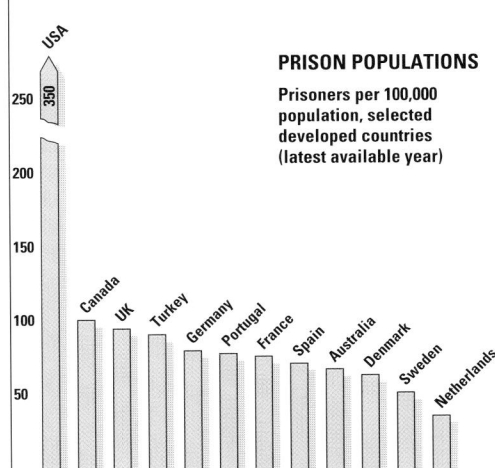

PRISON POPULATIONS

Prisoners per 100,000 population, selected developed countries (latest available year)

USA 350, Canada, UK, Turkey, Germany, Portugal, France, Spain, Australia, Denmark, Sweden, Netherlands

Differences in prison population reflect penal policies as much as the relative honesty or otherwise of different nations, and by no means all governments publish accurate figures. In more than 50 countries, people are still regularly imprisoned without trial, in 60 torture is a normal part of interrogation, and some 130 retain the death penalty, often administered for political crimes and in secret. Over 2,000 executions were recorded in 1990 by the civil rights organization Amnesty International; the real figure, as Amnesty itself maintains, was almost certainly much higher.

QUALITY OF LIFE: ENVIRONMENT

10: OCEANS

12: ATMOSPHERE

14: CLIMATE

21: GREENHOUSE EFFECT

25: URBAN POLLUTION

Humans have always had a dramatic effect on their environment, at least since the invention of agriculture almost 10,000 years ago. Generally, the Earth has accepted human interference without any obvious ill effects: the complex systems that regulate the global environment have managed to absorb substantial damage while maintaining a stable and comfortable home for the planet's trillions of lifeforms. But advancing human technology and the rapidly expanding populations it supports are now threatening to overwhelm the Earth's ability to cope.

Industrial wastes, acid rainfall, expanding deserts and large-scale deforestation all combine to create environmental change at a rate far faster than the Earth can easily accommodate. Equipped with chain-saws and flame-throwers, humans can now destroy more forest in a day than their ancestors could in a century, upsetting the balance between plant and animal, carbon dioxide and oxygen, on which all life ultimately depends. The fossil fuels that power industrial civilization have pumped enough carbon dioxide and other greenhouse gases into the atmosphere to make climatic change a near-certainty. Chlorofluorocarbons (CFCs) and other man-made chemicals are rapidly eroding the ozone layer, the planet's screen against ultra-violet radiation.

As a result, the Earth's average temperature has risen by about 0.5°C since the beginning of this century. Further rises seem inevitable, with 1990 marked as the hottest year worldwide since records began. A warmer Earth probably means a wetter Earth, with melting ice-caps raising sea levels and causing severe flooding in some of the world's most densely populated regions. Other climatic models suggest an alternative doom: rising temperatures could increase cloud cover, reflecting more solar energy back into space and causing a new Ice Age.

Either way, the consequences for humans could be disastrous – perhaps the Earth's own way of restoring the ecological balance over the next few thousand years. Fortunately, there is a far faster mechanism available. Humans have provoked the present crisis, but human ingenuity can respond to it. CFC production is already almost at a standstill, and the first faltering steps towards stabilization and the reduction of carbon dioxide have been taken, with Denmark pioneering the way by taxing emissions in 1991.

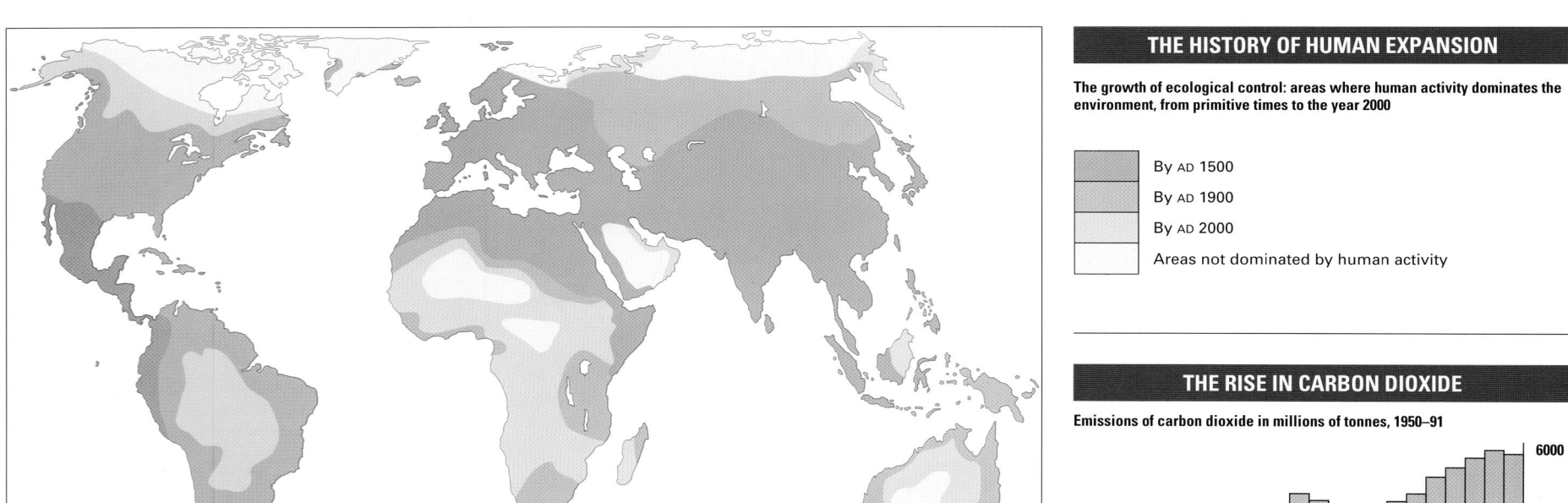

THE HISTORY OF HUMAN EXPANSION

The growth of ecological control: areas where human activity dominates the environment, from primitive times to the year 2000

- By AD 1500
- By AD 1900
- By AD 2000
- Areas not dominated by human activity

THE RISE IN CARBON DIOXIDE

Emissions of carbon dioxide in millions of tonnes, 1950–91

Since the beginning of the Industrial Revolution, human activity has pumped steadily more and more carbon dioxide into the atmosphere. Most of it was quietly absorbed by the oceans, whose immense 'sink' capacity meant that 170 years were needed for levels to increase from the pre-industrial 280 parts per million to 300 (inset graph). But the vast increase in fuel-burning since 1950 (main graph) has overwhelmed even the oceanic sink. Atmospheric concentrations are now rising almost as steeply as carbon dioxide emissions themselves.

Atmospheric concentration of carbon dioxide, parts per million, 1750–2000. Pre-1950 data were obtained from air samples trapped in Antarctic ice.

GREENHOUSE POWER

Relative contributions to the Greenhouse Effect by the major heat-absorbing gases in the atmosphere

The chart combines greenhouse potency and volume. Carbon dioxide has a greenhouse potential of only 1, but its concentration of 350 parts per million makes it predominate. CFC 12, with 25,000 times the absorption capacity of CO_2, is present only as 0.00044 ppm.

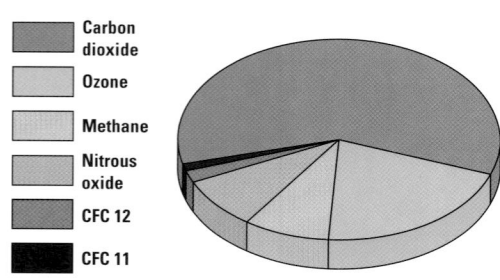

- Carbon dioxide
- Ozone
- Methane
- Nitrous oxide
- CFC 12
- CFC 11

CARBON DIOXIDE

Carbon dioxide released in millions of tonnes (1980s)

Although most of the net increase in atmospheric carbon dioxide comes from fossil fuel combustion, deforestation and changing land use also contribute.

- Fuel burning
- Deforestation

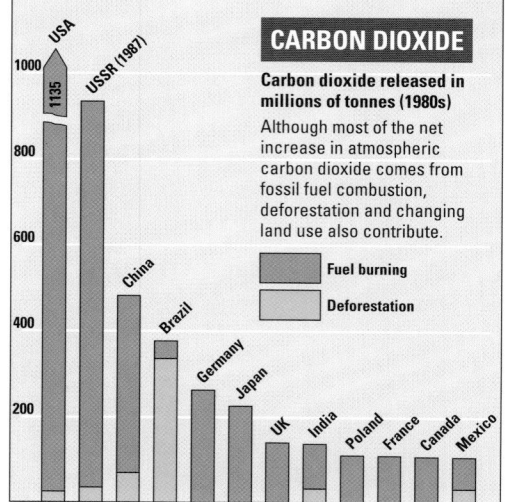

USA 1135 · USSR (1987) · China · Brazil · Germany · Japan · UK · India · Poland · France · Canada · Mexico

GLOBAL WARMING

The rise in average temperatures caused by carbon dioxide and other greenhouse gases (1960–2020)

- assumes present trends continue
- assumes drastic emissions cuts in the 1990s

Recorded change   Projected changes

ACID RAIN

Acid rainfall and sources of acidic emissions (1980s)

Acid rain is caused when sulphur and nitrogen oxides in the air combine with water vapour to form sulphuric, nitric and other acids.

Regions where sulphur and nitrogen oxides are released in high concentrations, mainly from fossil fuel combustion.

● Major cities with high levels of air pollution (including nitrogen and sulphur emissions)

Areas of heavy acid deposition

pH numbers indicate acidity, decreasing from a neutral 7. Normal rain, slightly acid from dissolved carbon dioxide, never exceeds a pH of 5.6.

pH less than 4.0 (most acidic)

pH 4.0 to 4.5

pH 4.5 to 5.0

Areas where acid rain is a potential problem

ANTARCTICA

The vast Antarctic ice-sheet, containing some 70% of the Earth's fresh water, plays a crucial role in the circulation of atmosphere and oceans and hence in determining the planetary climate. The frozen southern continent is also the last remaining wilderness – the largest area to remain free from human colonization.

Ever since Amundsen and Scott raced for the South Pole in 1911, various countries have pressed territorial claims over sections of Antarctica, spurred in recent years by its known and suspected mineral wealth: enough iron ore to supply the world at present levels for 200 years, large oil reserves and, probably, the biggest coal deposits on Earth.

However, the 1961 Antarctic Treaty set aside the area for peaceful uses only, guaranteeing freedom of scientific investigation, banning waste disposal and nuclear testing, and suspending the issue of territorial rights. By 1990, the original 12 signatories had grown to 25, with a further 15 nations granted observer status in subsequent deliberations. However, the Treaty itself was threatened by wrangles between different countries, government agencies and international pressure groups.

Finally, in July, 1991, the belated agreement of the UK and the US assured unanimity on a new accord to ban all mineral exploration for a further 50 years. The ban can only be rescinded if all the present signatories, plus a majority of any future adherents, agree. While the treaty has always lacked a formal mechanism for enforcement, it is firmly underwritten by public concern generated by the efforts of environmental pressure groups such as Greenpeace, which has been foremost in the campaign to have Antarctica declared a 'World Park'.

It now seems likely that the virtually uninhabited continent will remain untouched by tourism, staying nuclear-free and dedicated to peaceful scientific research.

DESERTIFICATION

Existing deserts

Areas with a high risk of desertification

Areas with a moderate risk of desertification

Former areas of rainforest

Existing rainforest

DEFORESTATION

5200

Thousands of hectares of forest cleared annually, tropical countries surveyed 1981–85 and 1987–90. Loss as a percentage of remaining stocks is shown in figures on each column.

3000

2000

1000

0

1987–90   1981–85

Country	1987–90	1981–85
Brazil	1.5	0.4
India	4.1	0.3
Indonesia	0.8	0.5
Burma	2.1	0.3
Thailand	2.5	2.4
Vietnam	2.0	0.?
Philippines	1.5	1.0
Costa Rica	7.6	4.0
Cameroon	0.6	0.4

WATER POLLUTION

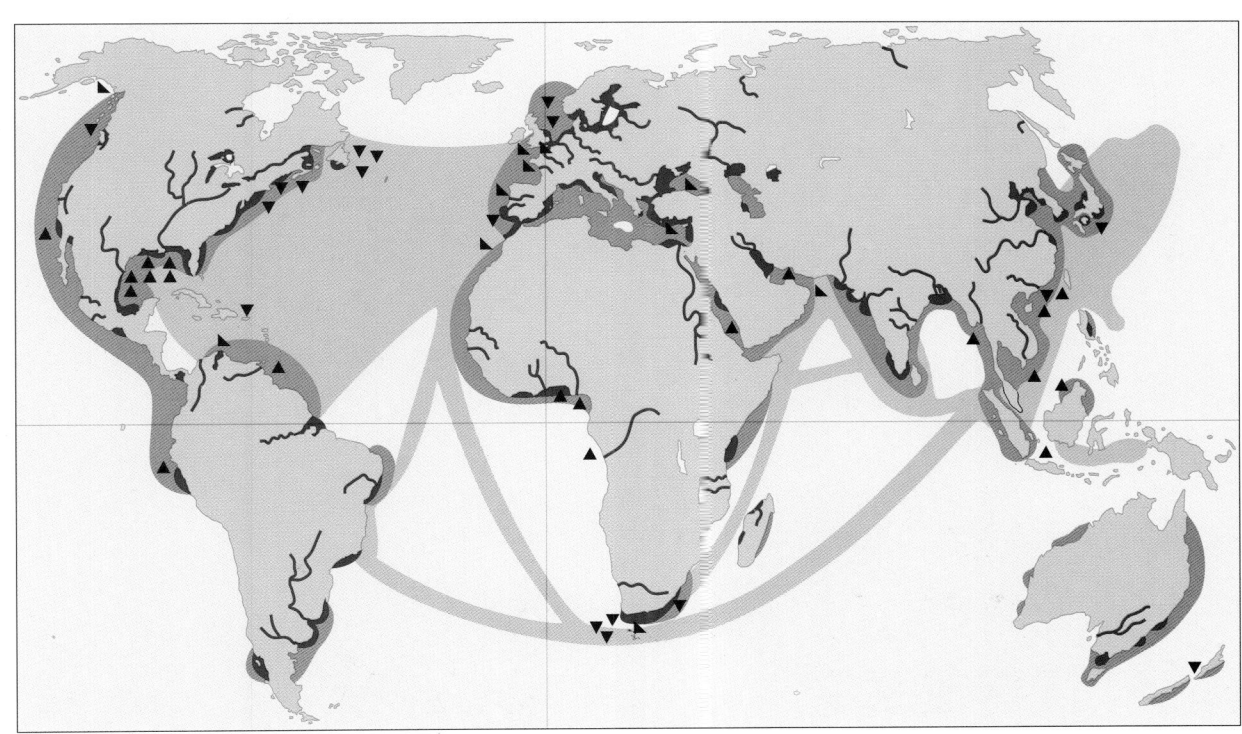

Severely polluted sea areas and lakes

Less polluted sea areas and lakes

Areas of frequent oil pollution by shipping

▶ Major oil tanker spills

▲ Major oil rig blow-outs

▼ Offshore dumpsites for industrial and municipal waste

Severely polluted rivers and estuaries

Poisoned rivers, domestic sewage and oil spillage have combined in recent years to reduce the world's oceans to a sorry state of contamination, notably near the crowded coasts of industrialized nations. Shipping routes, too, are constantly affected by tanker discharges. Oil spills of all kinds, however, declined significantly during the 1980s, from a peak of 750,000 tonnes in 1979 to under 50,000 tonnes in 1990. The most notorious tanker spill of that period – when the *Exxon Valdez* (94,999 grt) ran aground in Prince William Sound, Alaska, in March 1989 – released only 267,000 barrels, a relatively small amount compared to the results of blow-outs and war damage. Over 2,500,000 barrels were spilled during the Gulf War of 1991. The worst tanker accident in history occurred in July 1979, when the *Atlantic Empress* and the *Aegean Captain* collided off Trinidad, polluting the Caribbean with 1,890,000 barrels of crude oil.

WORLD MAPS

MAP SYMBOLS

SETTLEMENTS

⬠ PARIS   ▣ Berne   ◉ Livorno   ◉ Brugge   ◎ Algeciras   ⊙ Fréjus   ○ Oberammergau   ○ Thira

Settlement symbols and type styles vary according to the scale of each map and indicate the importance
of towns on the map rather than specific population figures

∴ Ruins or Archæological Sites   ˅ Wells in Desert

ADMINISTRATION

_____ International Boundaries

‑ ‑ ‑ International Boundaries
        (Undefined or Disputed)

⎯⎯⎯ Internal Boundaries

⬠ National Parks

Country Names

NICARAGUA

Administrative
Area Names

KENT

CALABRIA

International boundaries show the *de facto* situation where there are rival claims to territory

COMMUNICATIONS

_____ Principal Roads

⌒ Other Roads

‑∙‑∙‑ Trails and Seasonal Roads

≍ Passes

⚙ Airfields

⌒ Principal Railways

⌒∙∙∙ Railways
        Under Construction

⌒ Other Railways

⌐‑‑‑⌐ Railway Tunnels

∙∙∙∙∙∙ Principal Canals

PHYSICAL FEATURES

⌒ Perennial Streams

∙∙∙∙∙∙ Intermittent Streams

◯ Perennial Lakes

◌ Intermittent Lakes

∴ Swamps and Marshes

▭ Permanent Ice
    and Glaciers

▲ 8848 Elevations in metres

▼ 8050 Sea Depths in metres

1134 Height of Lake Surface
          Above Sea Level
          in metres

Projection: *Hammer Equal Area*

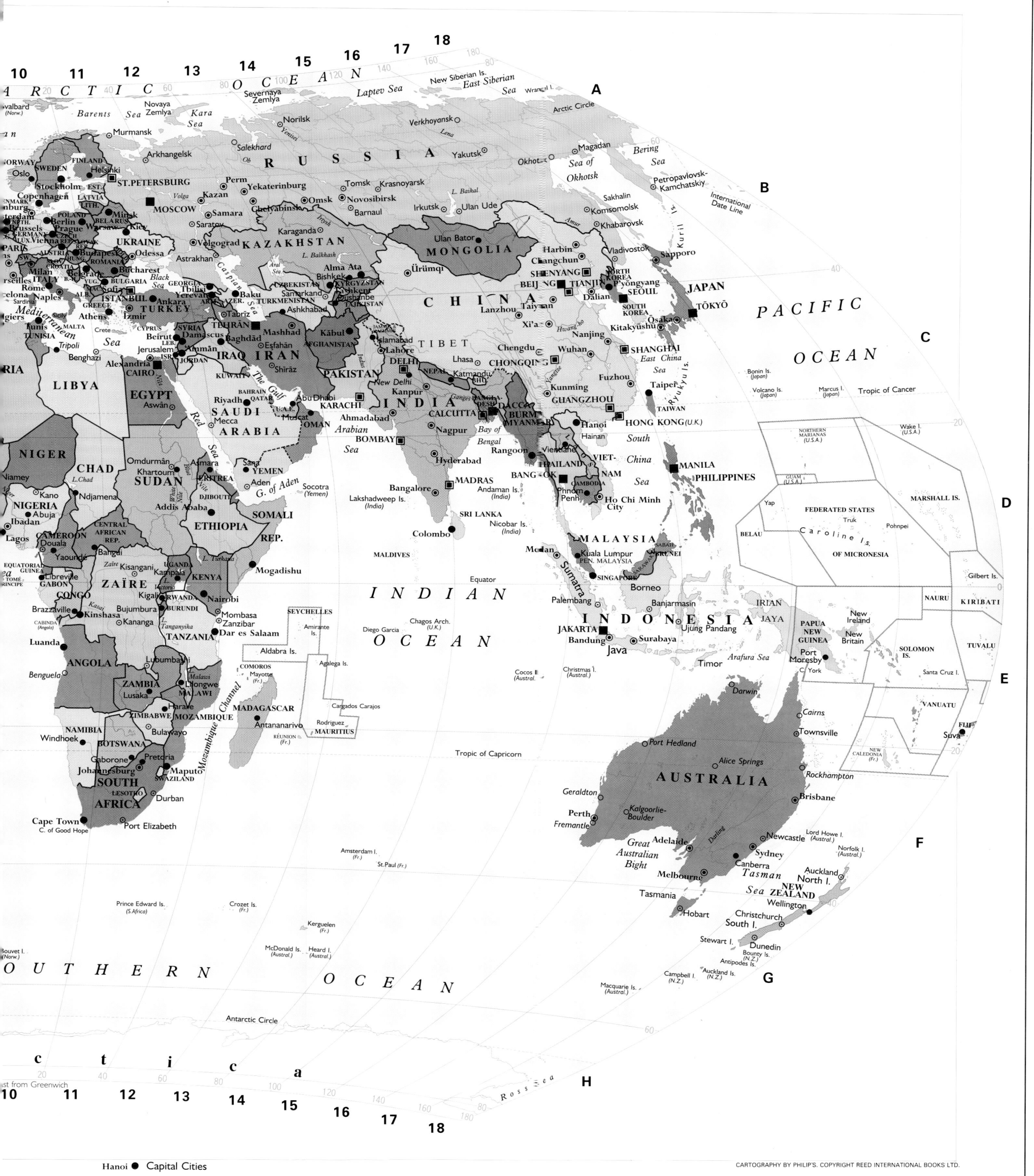

1 : 64 000 000

3

ARCTIC OCEAN

10 11 12 13 14 15 16 17 18

Svalbard (Norw.) *Barents Sea* Novaya Zemlya *Kara Sea* Severnaya Zemlya *Laptev Sea* *East Siberian Sea* New Siberian Is. Wrangel I. *Arctic Circle* **A**

Murmansk Arkhangelsk *Ob* Salekhard *Yenisey* Norilsk Verkhoyansk *Lena* Yakutsk Magadan Okhot. *Sea of Okhotsk* *Bering Sea*

NORWAY SWEDEN FINLAND Helsinki ST.PETERSBURG Perm Yekaterinburg Tomsk Krasnoyarsk R U S S I A Petropavlovsk-Kamchatskiy **B**

Oslo Stockholm *Volga* MOSCOW Kazan Omsk Novosibirsk *L. Baikal* Irkutsk Ulan Ude *International Date Line*

Copenhagen LATVIA LITH. Minsk Samara Saratov Chelyabinsk Barnaul Sakhalin Komsomolsk *Kuril Is.*

POLAND Berlin BELARUS Volgograd KAZAKHSTAN Karaganda *L. Balkhash* MONGOLIA Harbin Khabarovsk

Brussels Prague Warsaw Kiev UKRAINE Astrakhan *Aral Sea* Alma Ata Bishkek Ulan Bator Changchun Vladivostok Sapporo

PARIS Vienna Budapest ROMANIA Odessa *Caspian Sea* UZBEKISTAN KYRGYZSTAN SHENYANG NORTH KOREA JAPAN **C**

Milan CROATIA Belgrade Bucharest GEORGIA Baku Samarkand Tashkent BEIJING TIANJIN P'yŏngyang TŌKYŌ

Rome YUG. BULGARIA *Black Sea* Tbilisi Yerevan TURKMENISTAN Dushanbe C H I N A Dalian SEOUL Ōsaka PACIFIC

Naples ALB. ISTANBUL Ankara AZER. Ashkhabad TAJIKISTAN Lanzhou Xi'a SOUTH KOREA Kitakyūshū

Barcelona GREECE TURKEY Izmir Tabrīz AFGHANISTAN Kābul TIBET Nanjing SHANGHAI OCEAN

Algiers Athens CYPRUS SYRIA Damascus Mashhad Islamabad Lahore Chengdu Wuhan *East China Sea*

Tunis MALTA Beirut Baghdad I R A N Esfahān Lhasa CHONGQING Fuzhou **C**

Tripoli Jerusalem LEB. ISR. JORDAN IRAQ Shīrāz NEPAL Katmandu Kunming GUANGZHOU Taipei *Tropic of Cancer*

Benghazi *Mediterranean Sea* Alexandria KUWAIT *The Gulf* PAKISTAN DELHI BHU. Nagpur BANGLA- TAIWAN *Bonin Is. (Japan)* *Volcano Is. (Japan)* *Marcus I. (Japan)*

CAIRO Riyadh QATAR BAHRAIN Abu Dhabi New Delhi Kanpur DESH DACCA HONG KONG (U.K.) Wake I. (U.S.A.)

LIBYA EGYPT Aswān U.A.E. Muscat KARACHI I N D I A *Ganges* BURMA Hainan NORTHERN MARIANAS (U.S.A.)

Red Sea SAUDI Mecca OMAN Ahmadabad CALCUTTA MYANMAR Hanoi *South China Sea* **D**

NIGER CHAD Omdurmān ARABIA *Arabian Sea* BOMBAY Rangoon Vientiane VIET- MANILA GUAM (U.S.A.) Yap FEDERATED STATES Truk MARSHALL IS.

Niamey *L. Chad* Khartoum *Blue Nile* Sana YEMEN Hyderabad THAILAND NAM PHILIPPINES Pohnpei

Kano Ndjamena Asmara ERITREA *G. of Aden* Bangalore MADRAS Andaman Is. (India) BANGKOK CAMBODIA BELAU *Caroline Is.* OF MICRONESIA

NIGERIA Abuja SUDAN DJIBOUTI *Socotra (Yemen)* SRI LANKA Nicobar Is. (India) Phnom Penh Ho Chi Minh City

Ibadan Addis Ababa Lakshadweep Is. (India) Colombo Medan MALAYSIA SABAH *Gilbert Is.* **D**

Lagos CAMEROON CENTRAL AFRICAN REP. ETHIOPIA SOMALI REP. MALDIVES PEN. MALAYSIA BRUNEI NAURU KIRIBATI

EQUATORIAL GUINEA Douala Bangui UGANDA Kuala Lumpur *Equator* SINGAPORE Borneo IRIAN JAYA NEW

SÃO TOMÉ & PRÍNCIPE Yaounde Kisangani KENYA Mogadishu *I N D I A N* Palembang Banjarmasin New Ireland

Libreville GABON ZAÏRE Kampala Kigali Nairobi *Zaïre* *L. Turkana* SEYCHELLES Amirante Is. *Diego Garcia* *Chagos Arch. (U.K.)* I N D O N E S I A Ujung Pandang PAPUA NEW GUINEA New Britain SOLOMON IS.

CONGO Brazzaville Kinshasa RWANDA BURUNDI Bujumbura Mombasa *Tanganyika* Zanzibar JAKARTA Bandung Surabaya Port Moresby Santa Cruz I. **E**

CABINDA (Angola) Kananga TANZANIA Dar es Salaam *O C E A N* Java Timor *Arafura Sea* C. York TUVALU

Luanda Kanyama *L. Malawi* Aldabra Is. Agalega Is. (Mauritius) *Cocos I. (Austral.)* *Christmas I. (Austral.)*

ANGOLA ZAMBIA Lubumbashi COMOROS Mayotte (Fr.) Cargados Carajos Darwin VANUATU

Benguela Lusaka Lilongwe MALAWI *Mozambique Channel* MADAGASCAR Rodriguez MAURITIUS Cairns NEW CALEDONIA (Fr.) FIJI Suva

NAMIBIA ZIMBABWE MOZAMBIQUE Antananarivo RÉUNION (Fr.) *Tropic of Capricorn* Port Hedland Townsville

Windhoek Harare Bulawayo Alice Springs Rockhampton

BOTSWANA Gaborone Pretoria *Amsterdam I. (Fr.)* A U S T R A L I A Brisbane **F**

Johannesburg Maputo SWAZILAND St.Paul (Fr.) Geraldton Kalgoorlie-Boulder *Darling* Lord Howe I. (Austral.)

SOUTH AFRICA LESOTHO Durban Perth Fremantle Adelaide Newcastle Norfolk I. (Austral.)

Cape Town C. of Good Hope Port Elizabeth *Great Australian Bight* Canberra Sydney Auckland North I.

Prince Edward Is. (S.Africa) Crozet Is. (Fr.) Kerguelen (Fr.) Melbourne *Tasman Sea* NEW ZEALAND Wellington

Bouvet I. (Norw.) McDonald Is. Heard I. (Austral.) Tasmania Hobart Christchurch South I.

S O U T H E R N O C E A N Stewart I. Dunedin Bounty Is. (N.Z.) Antipodes Is. (N.Z.) **G**

Antarctic Circle Campbell I. (N.Z.) Macquarie Is. (Austral.) Auckland Is. (N.Z.)

c t i c a *Ross Sea* **H**

20 40 *East from Greenwich* 60 80 100 120 140 160 80

10 11 12 13 14 15 16 17 18

Hanoi ● Capital Cities

CARTOGRAPHY BY PHILIP'S. COPYRIGHT REED INTERNATIONAL BOOKS LTD.

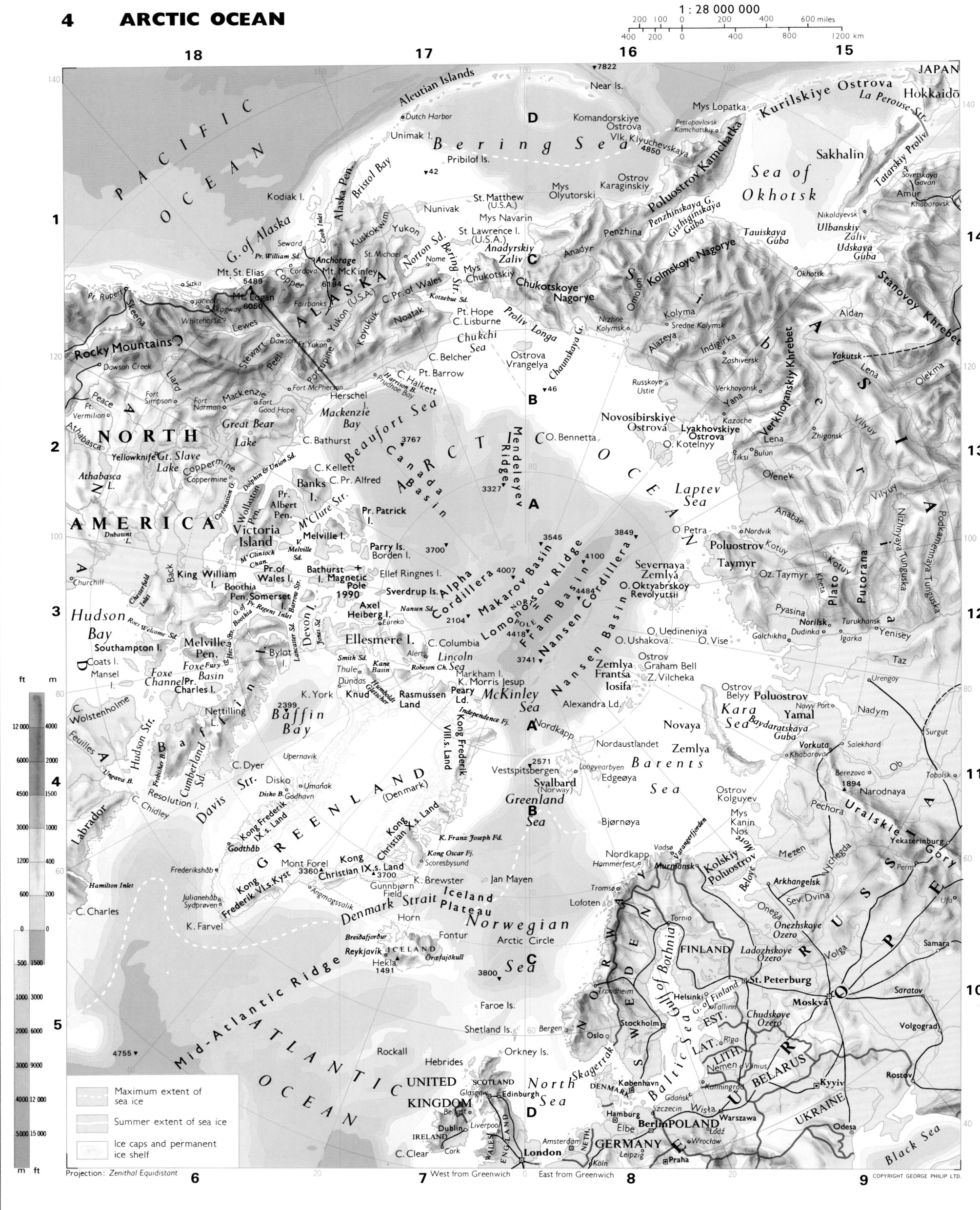

1 : 28 000 000

400 200 100 0 200 400 600 miles
400 200 0 400 800 1200 km

18 **17** **16** **15**

JAPAN

PACIFIC OCEAN

▼7822
Near Is.
Aleutian Islands
Dutch Harbor
Unimak I.
D
Bering Sea
Komandorskiye Ostrova
Mys Lopatka
Kurilskiye Ostrova
La Perouse Str.
Hokkaidō

Pribilof Is.
▼42
St. Matthew (U.S.A.)
Mys Olyutorski
Ostrov Karaginskiy
Petropavlovsk Kamchatskiy
Vlk. Klyuchevskaya 4850
Poluostrov Kamchatka
Sakhalin
Sovetskaya Gavan

1
G. of Alaska
Kodiak I.
Seward
Pr. William Sd.
Anchorage
Mt. McKinley 6194
Nunivak
St. Michael
Norton Sd.
Nome
Bering Str.
St. Lawrence I. (U.S.A.)
Anadyrskiy Zaliv
C
Anadyr
Penzhina
Penzhinskaya G.
Gizhiginskaya Guba
Tauiskaya Guba
Sea of Okhotsk
Nikolayevsk
Ulbanskiy Zaliv
Udskaya Guba
Amur
Khabarovsk
14

Sitka
Mt. St. Elias 5489
Copper
Cordova
Mt. Logan 6050
Fairbanks
Kuskokwim
Yukon
Mys Chukotskiy
Chukotskoye Nagorye
S
Nizhne Kolymsk
Omolon
Kolmskoye Nagorye
Okhotsk
Stanovoy Khrebet

Pr. Rupert
Skeena
Juneau
Skagway
Whitehorse
Lewes
ALASKA (U.S.A.)
Koyukuk
Porcupine
Pt. Hope
C. Lisburne
Proliv Longa
Srednekolymsk
Kolyma
Alazeya
Indigirka
Zashiversk
Aldan
Yakutsk
Lena
Olekma

2
Rocky Mountains
Dawson Creek
Stewart
Dawson
Ft. Yukon
Peel
Chukchi Sea
C. Belcher
Ostrova Vrangelya
Chaunskaya G.
Russkoye Ustie
Verkhoyansk
Yana
Zhigansk
Verkhoyanskiy Khrebet
Vilyuy
13

Peace
Fort Simpson
Ft. Vermilion
Liard
Fort Norman
Mackenzie
Fort Good Hope
Fort McPherson
Herschel
Mackenzie Bay
Prudhoe Bay
C. Halkett
Harrison B.
Pt. Barrow
▼46
B
A R C T I C
C O. Bennetta
Novosibirskiye Ostrova
Lyakhovskiye Ostrova
O. Kotelnyy
Lena
Tiksi
Bulun
Kazache
O C E A N

NORTH
Athabasca
Great Bear Lake
Yellowknife
Gt. Slave Lake
Coppermine
C. Bathurst
Beaufort Sea
▼3767
Canada
Mendeleyev Ridge
Laptev Sea
Olenek
Anabar

AMERICA
Athabasca L.
Dubawnt L.
Victoria Island
Coronation G.
Dolphin & Union Sd.
Banks I.
C. Kellett
C. Pr. Alfred
Wollaston Pen.
M'Clure Str.
3327
Basin
3545
Nordvik
Kotuy
O Petra
3849
Poluostrov Taymyr
Kheta
Oz. Taymyr
Putorana
Plato
Nizhnyaya Tunguska
Podkamennaya Tunguska

3
Churchill
Chesterfield
Back
King William I.
Boothia Pen.
Pr. Albert Pen.
V. Melville Sd.
M'Clintock Chan.
Melville I.
Parry Is.
Borden I.
3700▼
Ellef Ringnes I.
Alpha Cordillera 4007
Makarov Basin
Lomonosov Ridge
4100
NORTH POLE
Fram Basin
4484
Nansen Cordillera
Severnaya Zemlya
O. Oktyabrskoy Revolyutsii
Pyasina
Norilsk
Dudinka
Igarka
Turukhansk
Yenisey
12

Hudson Bay
Roes Welcome Sd.
Southampton I.
Coats I.
Mansel I.
Melville Pen.
Fury
G. of Boothia
Somerset I.
Pr. of Wales I.
Bathurst I.
Magnetic Pole 1990
Sverdrup Is.
Axel Heiberg I.
Nansen Sd.
2104
Devon I.
4418
3741
Nansen Basin
O. Uedineniya
O. Ushakova
O. Vise
Golchikha
Taz
Urengoy

4
ft m
12000 4000
Foxe Channel
Melville Pen.
Foxe Basin
Charles I.
Baffin Bay
2399
Nettilling
Ellesmere I.
Eureka
Alert
C. Columbia
Lincoln Sea
Markham I.
K. Morris Jesup
Peary Ld.
McKinley Sea
Ostrov Graham Bell
Z. Vilcheka
Zemlya Frantsa Iosifa
Alexandra Ld.
Ostrov Belyy
Poluostrov Yamal
Novyy Port
Salekhard
Baydaratskaya Guba
Nadym
11

6000 2000
C. Wolstenholme
Hudson Str.
K. York
Knud
Rasmussen Land
Kong Frederik VIII.s. Land
Independence Fj.
Kong Frederik IX.s. Land
Nordkapp
Novaya
Zemlya
Kara Sea
Poluostrov
Berezovo
Vorkuta
Khabarovo
Ob
Surgut
Tobolsk

4500 1500
Feuilles
Ungava B.
Hudson Str.
Frobisher Bay
Smith Sd.
Thule
Kane Basin
Humboldt Glacier
Dundas
Robson Ch. Sd.
Nordaustlandet
2571
Vestspitsbergen
Longyearbyen
Edgeøya
Zemlya
Ostrov Kolguyev
Mys Kanin Nos
1894 Narodnaya

11
3000 1000
Labrador
C. Dyer
Disko
Resolution I.
Davis Str.
Baffin
Upernavik
GREENLAND (Denmark)
Svalbard (Norway)
Barents Sea
Bjørnøya
Pechora
Uralskie Gory
Nadym

1200 400
Hamilton Inlet
Disko B.
Umanak
Godhavn
Greenland Sea
Nordkapp
Vadsø
Varangerfjorden
More
Mezen
Yekaterinburg
Perm

4
600 200
C. Chidley
C. Charles
Frederikshåb
Godthåb
Mont Forel
Kong Christian X.s. Land
K. Franz Joseph Fd.
Kong Oscar Fj.
Scoresbysund
Jan Mayen
Hammerfest
Tromsø
Kolskiy Poluostrov
Murmansk
Beloye
Onega
Arkhangelsk
Sev. Dvina
Ufa

0 0
Kong Frederik VI.s. Kyst
3360
Christian IX.s. Land
3700
K. Brewster
Gunnbjørn Field
Iceland
Denmark Strait Plateau
Lofoten
NORWAY
Onezhskoye Ozero
Samara

5
500 1500
Julianehåb
Sydprøven
K. Farvel
Argmagssalik
Horn
Fontur
Breiðafjorður
Reykjavík
ICELAND
Hekla 1491
Øræfajökull
Norwegian
Sea
3800▼
Arctic Circle
Trondheim
FINLAND
Ladozhskoye Ozero
St. Peterburg
Moskva
Chudskoye Ozero
Saratov

1000 3000
Mid-Atlantic Ridge
ATLANTIC OCEAN
Faroe Is.
Bergen
SWEDEN
Gulf of Bothnia
Helsinki
G. of Finland
Tallinn
EST.
Volga
Volgograd
10

2000 6000
4755▼
Rockall
Shetland Is.
Oslo
Stockholm
Baltic Sea
Riga
LAT.
LITH.
BELARUS
Kyyiv
Rostov

5
3000 9000
Hebrides
Orkney Is.
North Sea
DENMARK
København
Vilnius
Nemen
Kaliningrad
Gdańsk
UKRAINE
Odesa
Black Sea

4000 12000
Maximum extent of sea ice
SCOTLAND
Glasgow
Edinburgh
Belfast
Szczecin
Wisła
Warszawa
Łódź

5000 15000
Summer extent of sea ice
UNITED KINGDOM
Liverpool
ENGLAND
WALES
Hamburg
Elbe
Szczecin
POLAND
Wrocław

m ft
Ice caps and permanent ice shelf
IRELAND
Dublin
Cork
C. Clear
London
NETH.
Amsterdam
GERMANY
Berlin
Leipzig
Köln
Praha

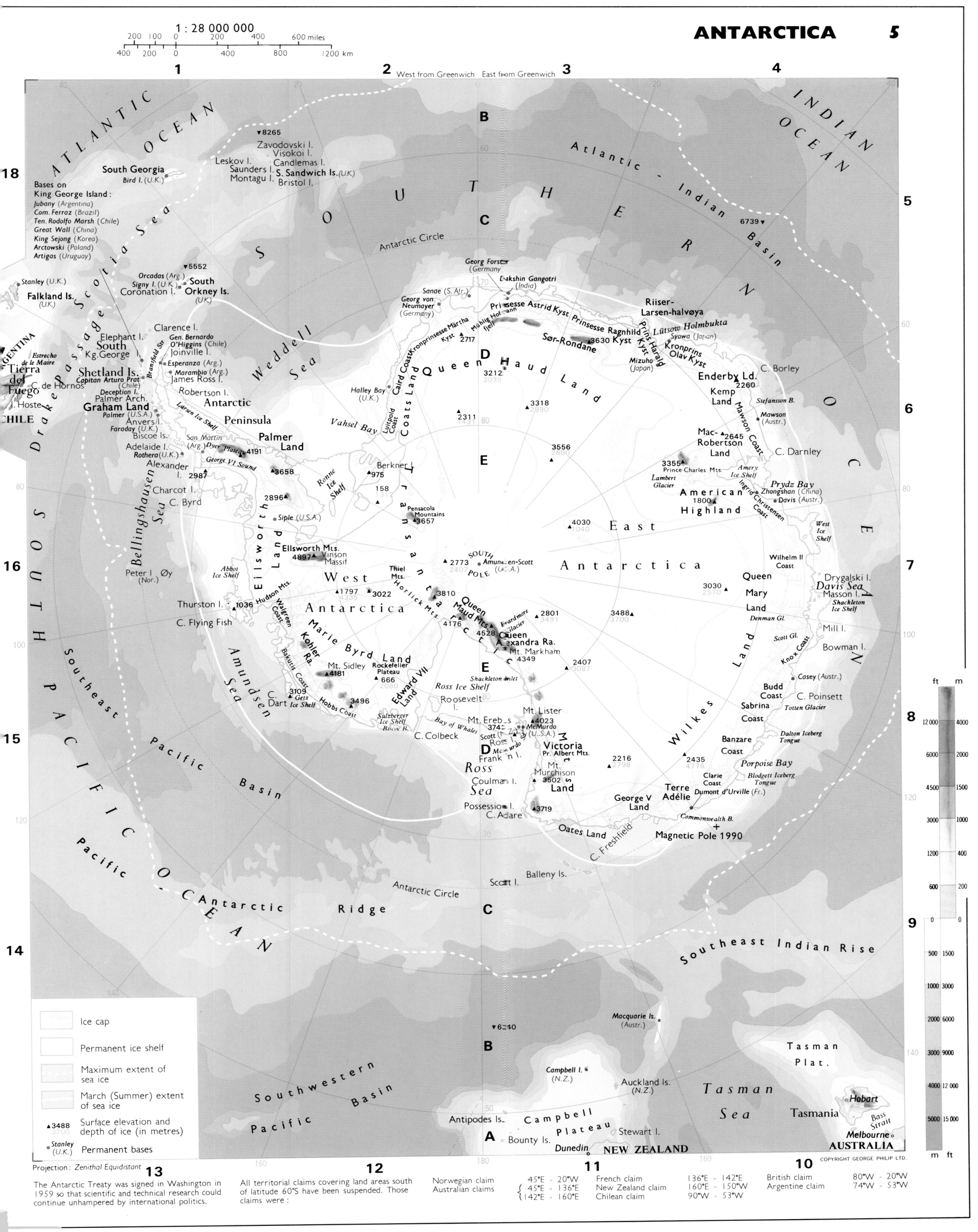

1 : 28 000 000

200 100 0   600 miles
400 200 0   400   800   1200 km

West from Greenwich   East from Greenwich

ATLANTIC   OCEAN

ATLANTIC

SOUTHERN

Atlantic - Indian Basin

INDIAN OCEAN

Antarctic Circle

▼8265
Zavodovski I.
Leskov I.   Visokoi I.
Saunders I.   Candlemas I.
Montagu I.   S. Sandwich Is.(U.K.)
Bristol I.

South Georgia
Bird I. (U.K.)

Bases on
King George Island :
Jubany (Argentina)
Com. Ferraz (Brazil)
Ten. Rodolfo Marsh (Chile)
Great Wall (China)
King Sejong (Korea)
Arctowski (Poland)
Artigas (Uruguay)

6739▼

Georg Forster (Germany)
Lakshin Gangotri (India)
Sanae (S. Afr.)
Georg von Neumayer (Germany)

Prinsesse Astrid Kyst   Prinsesse Ragnhild
Riiser-Larsen-halvøya

Orcadas (Arg.)
Signy I. (U.K.)
Coronation I.   South Orkney Is. (U.K.)

▼5552

Stanley (U.K.)
Falkland Is. (U.K.)

Kronprinsesse Märtha Kyst
2717

Mühlig Hofmann fjell
Sør-Rondane   3630 Kyst

Prins Harald Kyst
Lützow Holmbukta
Syowa (Japan)
Kronprins Olav Kyst
Mizuho (Japan)

Syowa (Japan)

Clarence I.
Elephant I.
South Shetland Is.
Kg. George I.
Gen. Bernardo O'Higgins (Chile)
Joinville I.
Esperanza (Arg.)
Marambio (Arg.)
James Ross I.
Robertson I.

Capitan Arturo Prat (Chile)
Deception I.
Palmer Arch.

ARGENTINA
Estrecho de le Maire
Tierra del Fuego
C. de Hornos
CHILE
I. Hoste

Drake Passage   Scotia Sea   Bransfield Str.

Weddell Sea

Queen   Maud Land

3212
3039

C. Borley

Enderby Ld.   2260
Kemp Land
Stefansson B.
Mawson (Austr.)

Graham Land
Palmer   Anvers I.
Faraday (U.K.)
Biscoe Is.
Adelaide I.
Rothera (U.K.)

Antarctic Peninsula

Halley Bay (U.K.)

Vahsel Bay

Coats Land

Caird Coast
Luitpold Coast

3318
2990

3556
2600

Mac-Robertson Land   2645

3355▲
Prince Charles Mts.
Lambert Glacier

Zhongshan (China)
Davis (Austr.)
Prydz Bay

Amery Ice Shelf

Ingrid Christensen Coast

Alexander I.
2987

San Martin (Arg.)
Dyer Plateau 4191
George VI Sound
3658

Charcot I.
C. Byrd

Berkner I.
Larsen Ice Shelf
Ronne Ice Shelf

975
158

4030
4040

American Highland
1800

East   Antarctica

West Ice Shelf

Peter I Øy (Nor.)

2896

Siple (U.S.A.)

Pensacola Mountains
3657

Ellsworth Mts.   4897
Vinson Massif

SOUTH POLE   2773
Amundsen-Scott (U.S.A.)   2407

3030
2570

Queen Mary Land
Davis Sea

Drygalski I.
Masson I.
Shackleton Ice Shelf

Thurston I.   1036
C. Flying Fish

Abbot Ice Shelf

Ellsworth Land

West Antarctica

Thiel Mts.
1797
3022

Horlick Mts.
4335

3810

Queen   Maud Mts.   4176
4528

Beardmore Glacier

2801
3491

3488
3700

Denman Gl.

Mill I.
Bowman I.
Scott Gl.
Knox Coast

Marie Byrd Land
Kohler Ra.
Mt. Sidley   4181

Amundsen Sea

Bakutis Coast   3105
Getz Ice Shelf
Hobbs Coast   3496

C. Dart

Rockefeller Plateau
666

Edward VII
Sulzberger Ice Shelf
Biscoe B.

Roosevelt I.

Ross Ice Shelf
Bay of Whales
C. Colbeck

Queen Alexandra Ra.
Mt. Markham   4349

2407
3087

Casey (Austr.)

Budd Coast
Sabrina Coast
Totten Glacier

Banzare Coast

Dalton Iceberg Tongue

C. Poinsett

Wilkes Land

Shackleton Inlet

Mt. Erebus
4023
McMurdo
3743
Scott (N.Z.)
McMurdo (U.S.A.)
Ross I.

Mt. Lister

Pr. Albert Mts.
Victoria Land

Franklin I.

Pacific Basin

Southeast Pacific Basin

Pacific   Ocean

Ross Sea

Coulman I.
Possession I.
C. Adare

Mt. Murchison   3502

George V Land

2216
2798

2435
4776

Porpoise Bay
Blodgett Iceberg Tongue
Clarie Coast

3719

Oates Land

Terre Adélie
Dumont d'Urville (Fr.)
Commonwealth B.
Magnetic Pole 1990

Southeast Indian Rise

Antarctic Circle

Balleny Is.
Scott I.

Antarctic Ridge

Southwestern Pacific Basin

Macquarie Is. (Austr.)

▼6240

Tasman Plat.

Campbell I. (N.Z.)

Auckland Is. (N.Z.)

Tasman Sea

Tasmania
Hobart
Bass Strait
Melbourne   AUSTRALIA

Antipodes Is.   Campbell Plateau
Bounty Is.   Stewart I.
Dunedin   NEW ZEALAND

COPYRIGHT GEORGE PHILIP LTD.

Ice cap

Permanent ice shelf

Maximum extent of sea ice

March (Summer) extent of sea ice

▲3488   Surface elevation and depth of ice (in metres)

• Stanley (U.K.)   Permanent bases

Projection: Zenithal Equidistant

The Antarctic Treaty was signed in Washington in 1959 so that scientific and technical research could continue unhampered by international politics.

All territorial claims covering land areas south of latitude 60°S have been suspended. Those claims were :

Norwegian claim   45°E - 20°W
Australian claims   { 45°E - 136°E
                    { 142°E - 160°E

French claim   136°E - 142°E
New Zealand claim   160°E - 150°W
Chilean claim   90°W - 53°W

British claim   80°W - 20°W
Argentine claim   74°W - 53°W

ft   m
12 000   4000
6000   2000
4500   1500
3000   1000
1200   400
600   200
0   0
500   1500
1000   3000
2000   6000
3000   9000
4000   12 000
5000   15 000
m   ft

1 : 16 000 000

100   0   100   200   300   400 miles

100   0 100 200 300 400 500 600 km

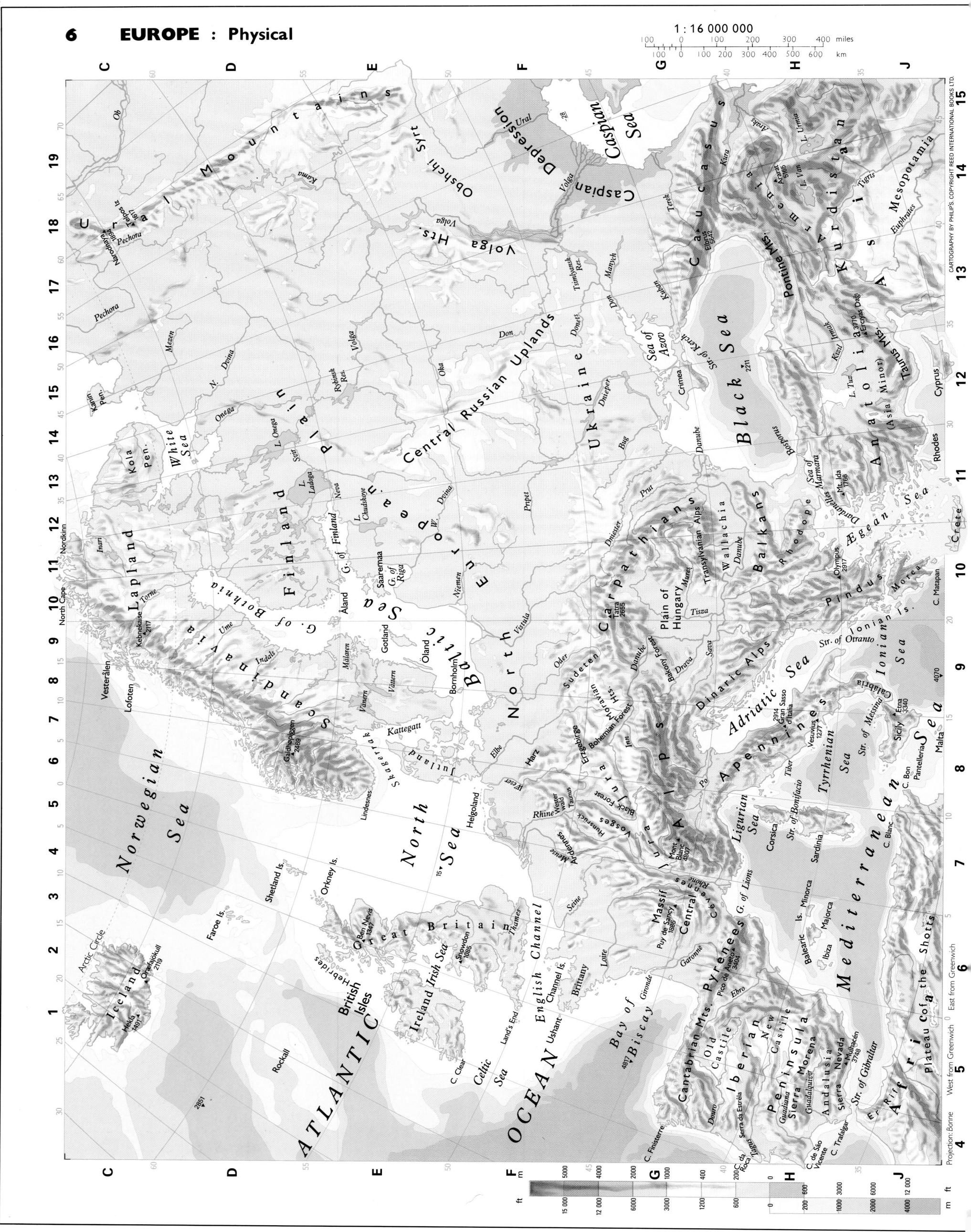

CARTOGRAPHY BY PHILIP'S. COPYRIGHT REED INTERNATIONAL BOOKS LTD.

Projection: Bonne

West from Greenwich   East from Greenwich

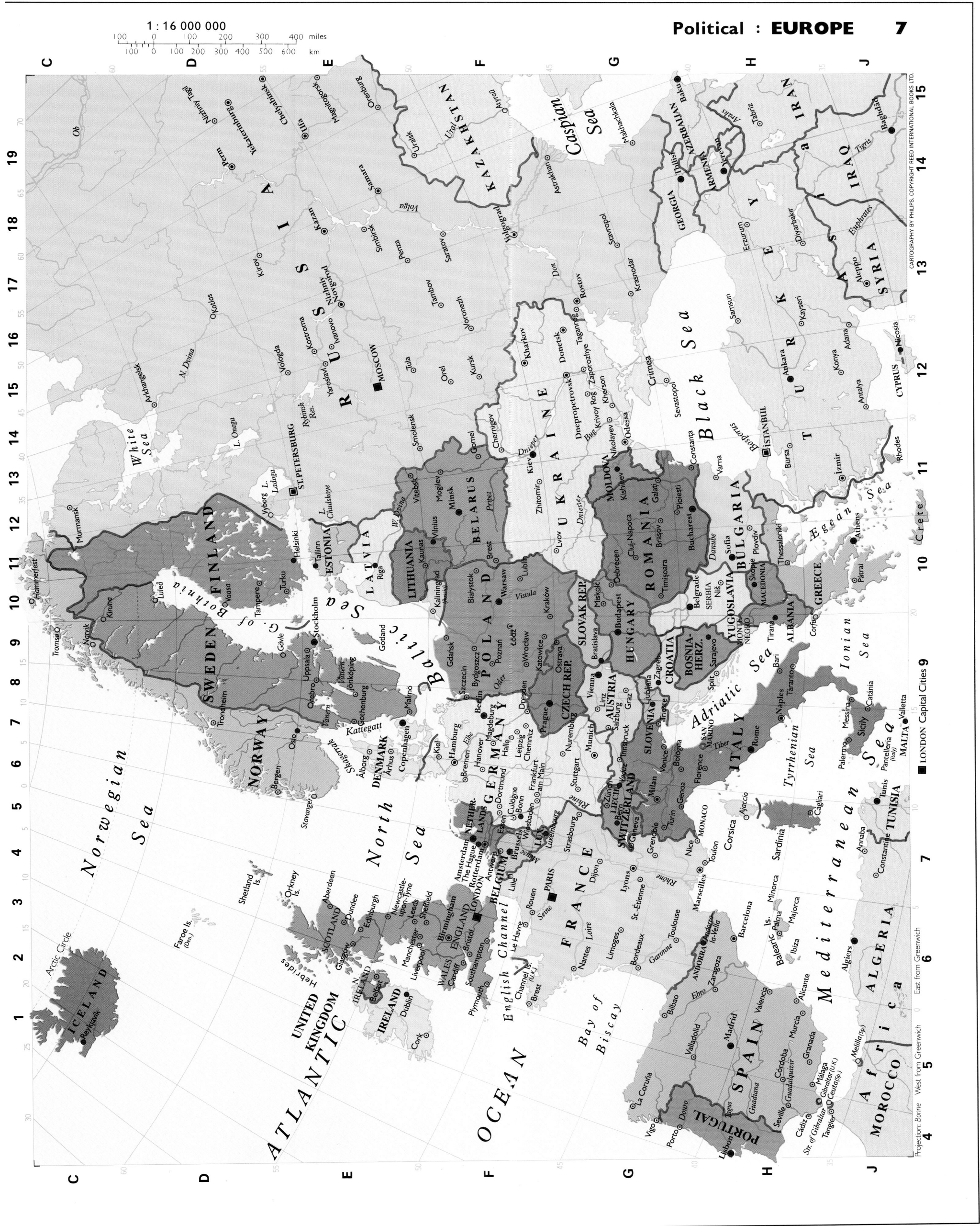

1 : 16 000 000

100   0   100   200   300   400   miles
100   0   100   200   300   400   500   600   km

CARTOGRAPHY BY PHILIP'S. COPYRIGHT REED INTERNATIONAL BOOKS LTD.

■ LONDON Capital Cities

Projection: Bonne   West from Greenwich   0   East from Greenwich

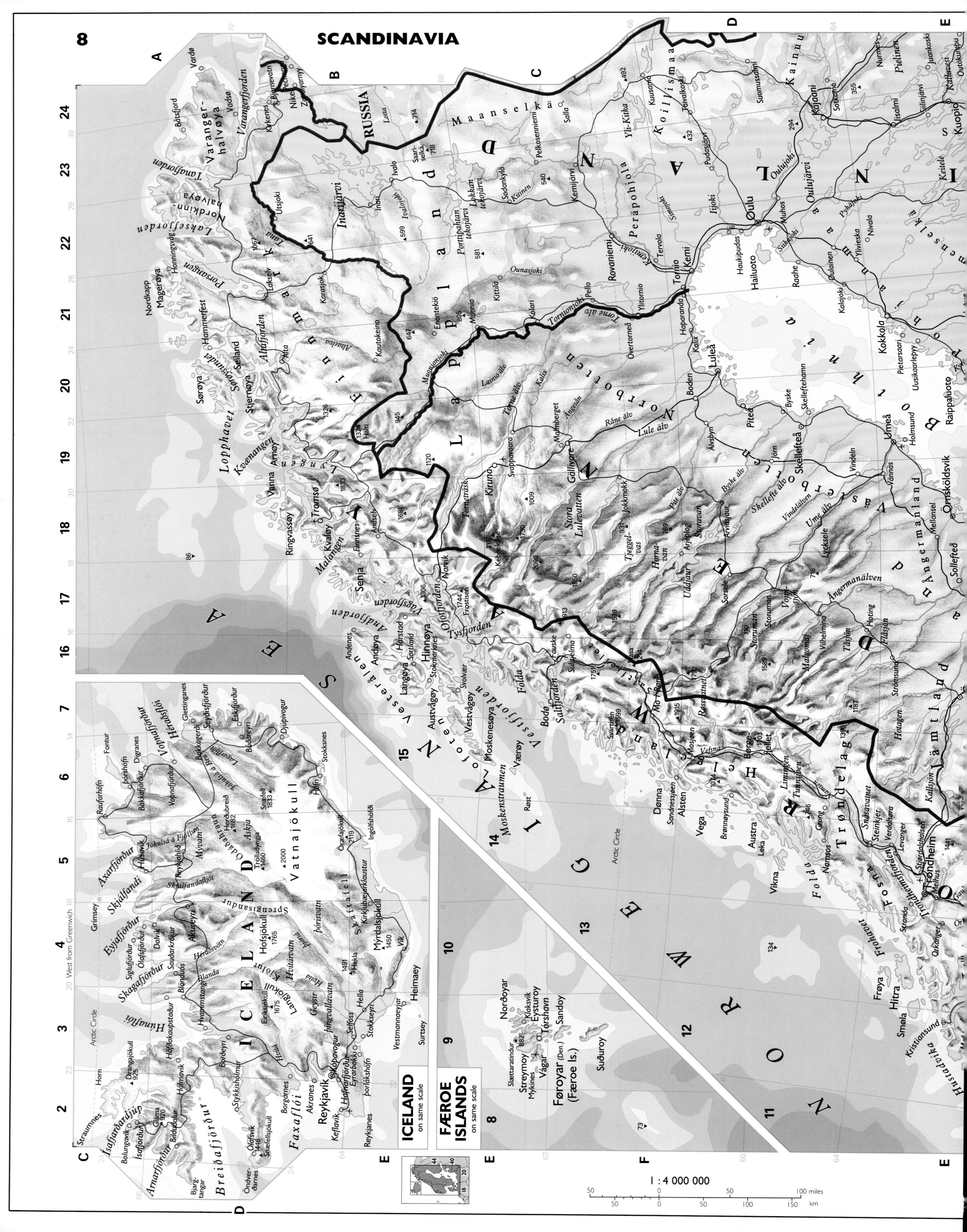

ICELAND
on same scale

FÆROE
ISLANDS
on same scale

1 : 4 000 000

Gulf of Bothnia
Trondheim
Östersund
Sundsvall
Gävle
Uppsala
Stockholm
Falun
Borlänge
Oslo
Hamar
Lillehammer
Drammen
Kongsberg
Skien
Porsgrunn
Larvik
Tønsberg
Moss
Fredrikstad
Sarpsborg
Halden
Karlstad
Örebro
Västerås
Eskilstuna
Kristiansund
Örnsköldsvik
Härnösand
Hudiksvall
Söderhamn
Mora
JÄMTLANDS LÄN
VÄSTERNORRLANDS LÄN
GÄVLEBORGS LÄN
KOPPARBERGS LÄN
VÄRMLANDS LÄN
VÄSTMANLANDS LÄN
ÖREBRO LÄN
SÖDERMANLANDS LÄN
UPPSALA LÄN
STOCKHOLMS LÄN
SØR TRØNDELAG
MØRE OG ROMSDAL FYLKE
OPPLAND FYLKE
HEDMARK FYLKE
BUSKERUD
TELEMARK FYLKE
VESTFOLD
ØSTFOLD
AKERSHUS FYLKE
Jotunheimen
Dovrefjell
Hallingskarvet
Mälaren
Hjälmaren

1 : 2 000 000

10   0   10   20   30   40   50 miles
10 0 10 20 30 40 50 60 70 80 km

Projection: Conical with two standard parallels

East from Greenwich

COPYRIGHT GEORGE PHILIP & SON, LTD.

BALTIC SEA

POLAND

GERMANY

Gotland

Öland

Bornholm

KATTEGAT

Skagerrak

Norrköping
Nyköping
Oxelösund
Linköping
Motala
Jönköping
Huskvarna
Nässjö
Värnamo
Växjö
Kalmar
Nybro
Karlskrona
Ronneby
Karlshamn
Kristianstad
Hässleholm
Helsingborg
Landskrona
Malmö
Lund
Trelleborg
Ystad
Halmstad
Falkenberg
Varberg
Göteborg
Mölndal
Kungsbacka
Trollhättan
Uddevalla
Vänersborg
Lidköping
Skara
Mariestad
Falköping
Borås
Alingsås
Skövde

KALMAR LÄN
JÖNKÖPINGS LÄN
KRONOBERGS LÄN
BLEKINGE LÄN
KRISTIANSTADS L.
MALMÖHUS
HALLANDS
ÄLVSBORGS
SKARABORGS LÄN
ÖSTERGÖTLAND
GÖTEBORGS OCH BOHUS
Västervik
Oskarshamn
Visby

Ålborg
Frederikshavn
Skagen
Sæby
Hjørring
Brønderslev
NORDJYLLANDS AMT
VIBORG AMT
Viborg
Skive
Thisted
Nykøbing
Mors
Struer
Holstebro
Herning
RINGKØBING AMT
RING KØBING
Skjern
Varde
Esbjerg
Ribe
Århus
Randers
Grenå
Silkeborg
ÅRHUS AMT
VEJLE AMT
Vejle
Kolding
Fredericia
Horsens
Skanderborg
Odder
SØNDERJYLLANDS AMT
Haderslev
Åbenrå
Sønderborg
Tønder
Flensburg
Schleswig
Rendsburg
Kiel
Husum

Odense
FYN AMT
Middelfart
Svendborg
Fåborg
Nyborg
Assens
Kerteminde

KØBENHAVN
COPENHAGEN
Helsingør
Hillerød
Frederikssund
Frederiksværk
Frederiksborg
Roskilde
SJÆLLAND
Køge
Ringsted
Sorø
Slagelse
Kalundborg
Holbæk
Næstved
Vordingborg
STORSTRØMS
LOLLAND
FALSTER
Maribo
Nakskov
Nykøbing
Gedser
MØN

Femer Bælt
Store Bælt
Lille Bælt

Holmsland Klit

m
6000
4500
3000
1200
600
200
0
ft

m
2000
1500
1000
400
200
0

NORTH SEA

IRISH SEA

SCOTLAND

SOUTHERN UPLANDS

Fife Ness
Anstruther
North Berwick
Bass Rock
Kirkcaldy
Dunfermline
Leith
Edinburgh
Musselburgh
Haddington
Dunbar
Linlithgow
Falkirk
Stirling
Alloa
Kinross
L. Leven
Ochil Hills
Helensburgh
Dumbarton
Clydebank
Glasgow
Paisley
Port Glasgow
Greenock
Rutherglen
Hamilton
Motherwell
Wishaw
Coatbridge
Airdrie
Kilmarnock
Irvine
Ayr
Saltcoats
Troon
Lanark
Carstairs
Peebles
Moorfoot Hills
Pentland Hills
Lammermuir
Galashiels
Selkirk
Hawick
Jedburgh
Kelso
Coldstream
Berwick-upon-Tweed
Eyemouth
St. Abb's Hd.
Holy I.
Flodden
The Cheviot 816
Cheviot Hills
Newton Stewart
Castle Douglas
Kirkcudbright
Dalbeattie
Dumfries
Annan
Sanquhar
Leadhills
Langholm
Gretna Green
Carlisle
Solway Firth
Silloth
Maryport
Workington
Whitehaven
St. Bee's Hd.
Seascale
Millom
Barrow
Walney I.
Furness
Cumbrian Mts.
Skiddaw 931
Derwentwater
Keswick
Helvellyn 950
Scafell Pike 978
Ullswater
Penrith
Appleby
Brough
Cross Fell 893
Alston
Hexham
Hadrian's Wall
Consett
Newcastle
Gateshead
Blaydon
Tynemouth
South Shields
Sunderland
Houghton-le-Spring
Durham
Bishop Auckland
Barnard Castle
Darlington
Stockton
Billingham
Hartlepool
Middlesbrough
Redcar
CLEVELAND (Teesside)
TYNE & WEAR
DURHAM
NORTHUMBERLAND
Morpeth
Ashington
Blyth
Alnwick
Coquet
Farne Is.
Amble
Wansbeck
Whitby
Scarborough
Filey
Flamborough Hd.
Bridlington
Pickering
Malton
N. York Moors
Northallerton
Thirsk
Ripon
Wensleydale
Richmond
NORTH YORKSHIRE
York
Selby
Harrogate
Knaresborough
Wetherby
Leeds
Bradford
Keighley
Skipton
Settle
Ingleborough
Kendal
Windermere
Ambleside
Ulverston
Morecambe
Heysham
Lancaster
Fleetwood
Cleveleys
Blackpool
Lytham St. Annes
Preston
Southport
Formby Pt.
Bootle
Wallasey
Birkenhead
Liverpool
St. Helens
Wigan
Bolton
Burnley
Nelson
Colne
Accrington
Blackburn
Chorley
LANCASTER
LANCASHIRE
Forest of Bowland
Ribble
Halifax
Huddersfield
Dewsbury
Wakefield
Barnsley
Rotherham
Sheffield
SOUTH YORKSHIRE
Doncaster
WEST YORKSHIRE
Rochdale
Oldham
MANCHESTER
Manchester
Salford
Stockport
Stalybridge
Ashton-under-Lyne
Glossop
Buxton
Macclesfield
Congleton
Crewe
Nantwich
Northwich
Winsford
Chester
Ellesmere Port
Runcorn
Widnes
MERSEYSIDE
Wirral
CHESHIRE
Newcastle-under-Lyme
Stoke-on-Trent
Leek
Uttoxeter
STAFFORD
Stafford
Market Drayton
Whitchurch
Wrexham
CLWYD
Oswestry
Llangollen
Wem
DERBY
Chesterfield
Derby
Matlock
Belper
Ilkeston
Heanor
Mansfield
Sutton in Ashfield
Worksop
Retford
Newark
Grantham
Nottingham
Beeston
Long Eaton
Loughborough
NOTT
LINCOLN
Lincoln
LINCOLN WOLD
Gainsborough
Market Rasen
Scunthorpe
Brigg
Goole
Grimsby
Cleethorpes
Immingham
Barton upon Humber
Kingston upon Hull
Hull
Beverley
Hornsea
Withernsea
Spurn Hd.
HUMBERSIDE
Holderness
Louth
Mablethorpe
Alford
Horncastle
Skegness
Boston
The Wash
Witham
Sleaford
Bourne
Spalding
Kings Lynn
Cromer
North Walsham
Hunstanton
Sandringham
Fakenham
Wells
The Broads
Great Yarmouth

WALES
GWYNEDD
GLWYD
Anglesey
Holyhead
Holy I.
Amlwch
Beaumaris
Menai Strait
Caernarfon
Bangor
Conwy
Colwyn Bay
Rhyl
Prestatyn
Flint
St. Asaph
Denbigh
Ruthin
Mold
Snowdon 1085
Ffestiniog
Porthmadog
Pwllheli
Nefyn
Bardsey I.
Harlech
Bala
L. Bala
Dolgellau
Barmouth
Tywyn
Aberystwyth

SCOTLAND
L. Katrine
Trossachs
L. Lomond
B. Lomond 974
Forth
Inveraray
Crinan
Crinan Canal
Lochgilphead
Dunoon
Jura
Sound of Jura
Gigha I.
Kintyre
Mull of Kintyre
Campbeltown
Sound of Jura
Arran
Goat Fell 874
Ailsa Craig
Girvan
Stranraer
Portpatrick
Luce Bay
Mull of Galloway
Wigtown
Whithorn
Wigtown Bay
GALLOWAY
Merrick 843
Loch Doon
Firth of Clyde
North Channel

ISLE OF MAN
Ramsey
Snaefell 620
Douglas
Castletown
Peel
Port Erin
Calf of Man
Pt. of Ayre

IRELAND
Larne
Belfast Lough
Bangor
Belfast
Newtownards
Strangford L.
Downpatrick
Ardglass
Donaghadee
Magee
Portaferry

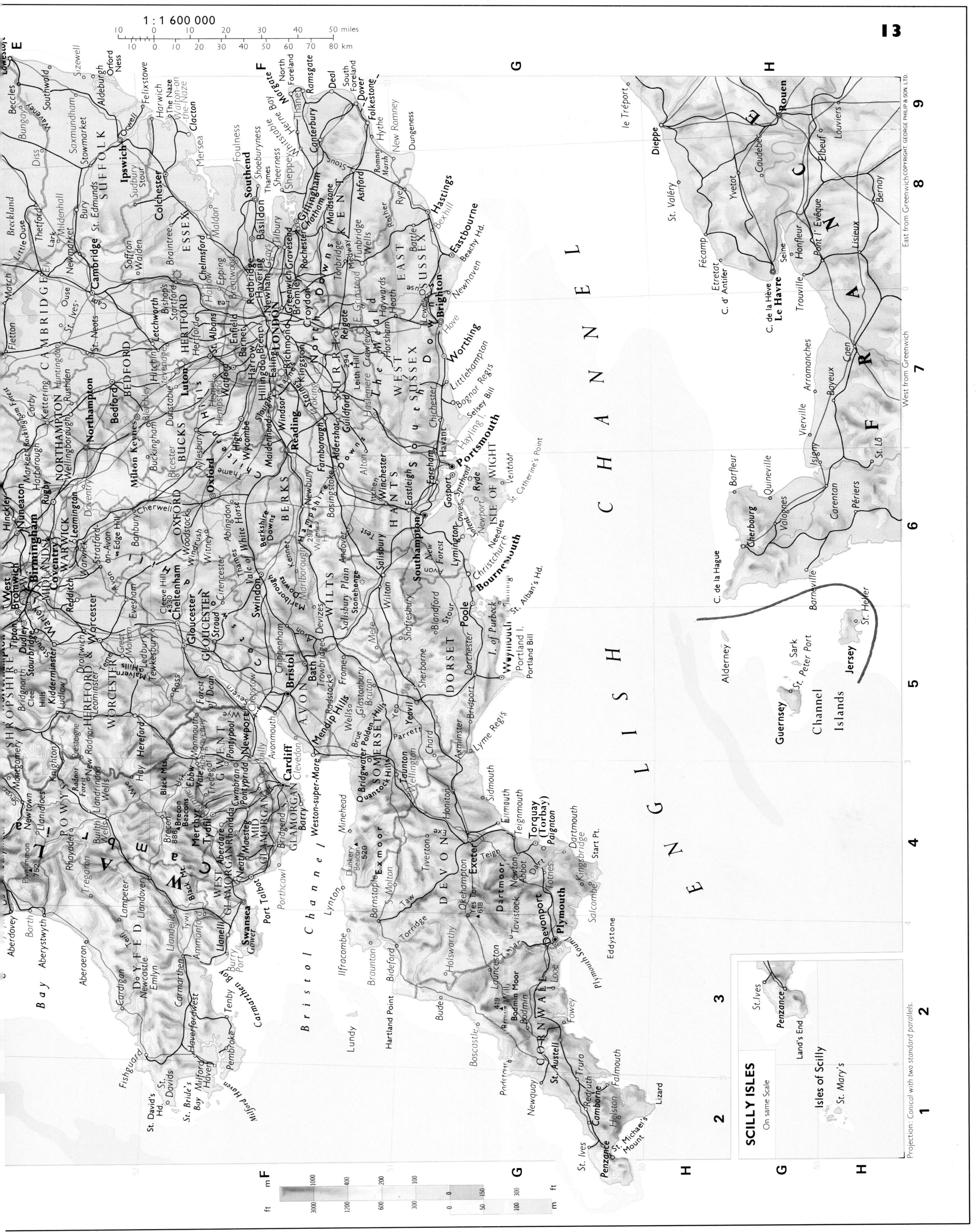

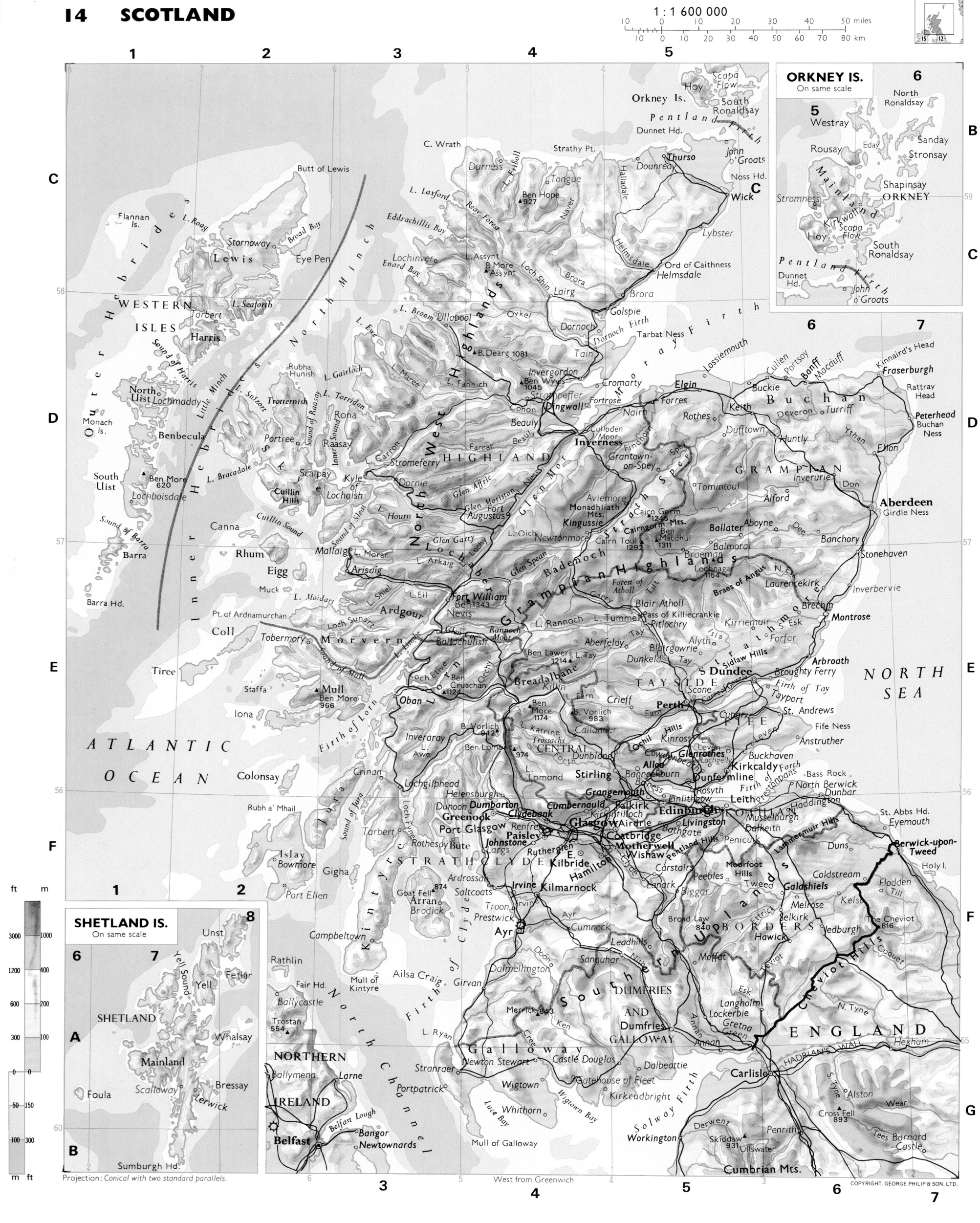

1 : 1 600 000

10   0   10   20   30   40   50 miles
10 0 10 20 30 40 50 60 70 80 km

ORKNEY IS.
On same scale

SHETLAND IS.
On same scale

Projection : Conical with two standard parallels.

West from Greenwich

COPYRIGHT. GEORGE PHILIP & SON. LTD.

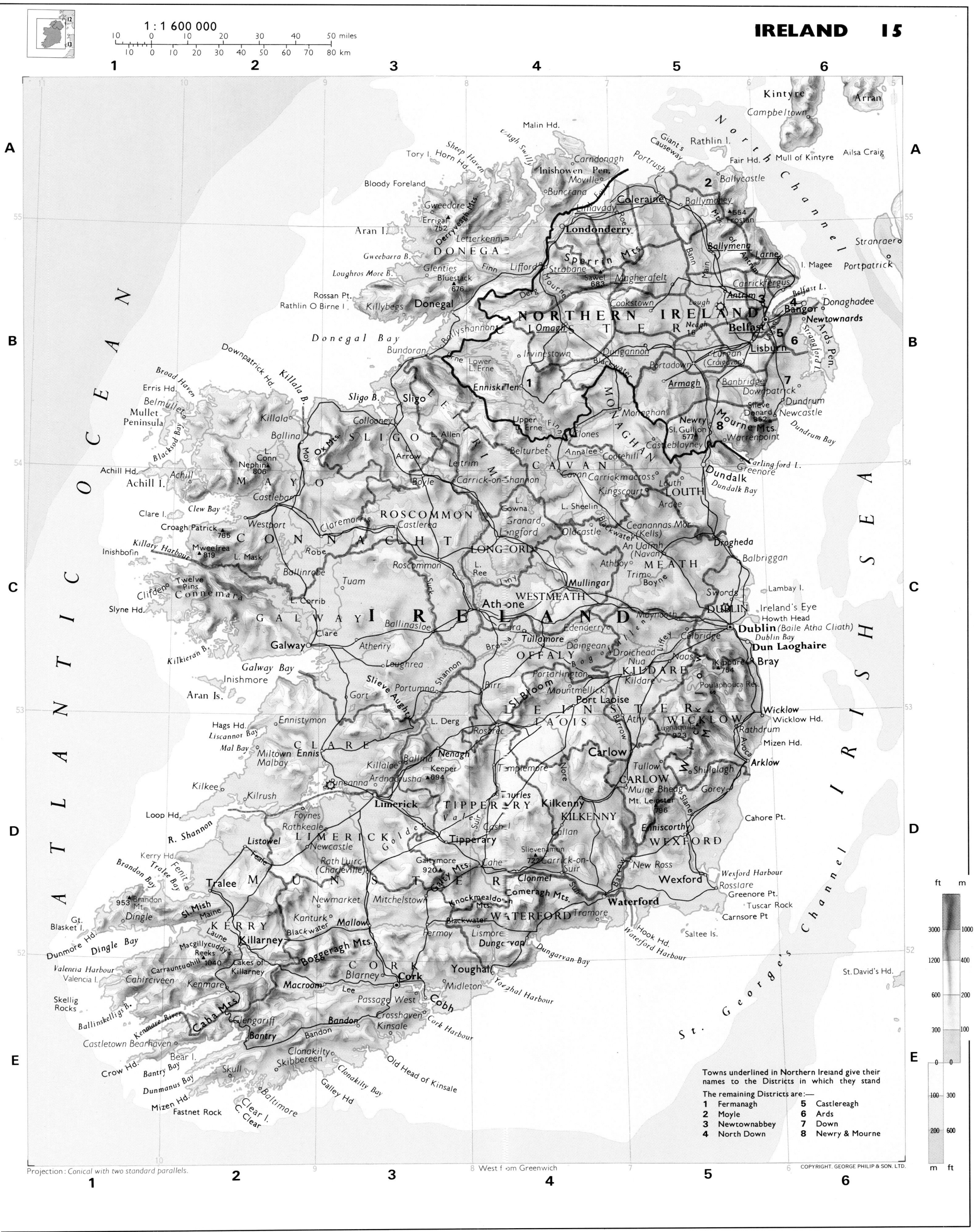

1 : 1 600 000

10   0   10   20   30   40   50 miles
10   0   10   20   30   40   50   60   70   80 km

A

North Channel

Kintyre
Campbeltown
Arran
Mull of Kintyre
Ailsa Craig

Malin Hd.
Lough Swilly
Giant's Causeway
Rathlin I.
Fair Hd.
Stranraer
Portpatrick
Portrush
Ballycastle
Sheep Haven
Horn Hd.
Tory I.
Carndonagh
Inishowen Pen.
Moville
Buncrana
Coleraine
Ballymoney
554
Trostan
I. Magee

Bloody Foreland
Gweedore
Errigal
752
Derryveagh Mts.
Letterkenny
Limavady
Ballymena
Larne
Carrickfergus

Aran I.
Londonderry
Sperrin Mts.
Antrim
Belfast L.
Bangor
Donaghadee

DONEGAL
Strabane
Sawel
683
Magherafelt
Newtownards
Ards Pen.

B
Gweebarra B.
Glenties
Bluestack
676
Lifford
Derg
Cookstown
Lough
Neagh
16
NORTHERN IRELAND
Belfast
Lisburn
Strangford L.

Loughros More B.
Finn
Mourne
Omagh
Dungannon
Portadown
Lurgan
(Craigavon)
7
Banbridge
Downpatrick

Rossan Pt.
Killybegs
Donegal
Ballyshannon
Irvinestown
Blackwater
Armagh
Dundrum

Rathlin O Birne I.
Bundoran
Lower
L. Erne
1
Enniskillen
Slieve
Donard
852
Newcastle

Donegal Bay
Upper
Erne
Finn
Clones
Newry
St. Gullion
577
8
Mourne Mts.
Dundrum Bay

Downpatrick Hd.
Killala B.
Sligo B.
Sligo
Allen
Belturbet
Monaghan
Castleblayney
Warrenpoint
Carlingford L.
Greenore

Broad Haven
Erris Hd.
Belmullet
Killala
Collooney
Arrow
CAVAN
Annalee
Coosehill
Carrickmacross
Dundalk

Mullet
Peninsula
Ballina
SLIGO
Leitrim
Cavan
Carrickmacross
Louth
Ardee
Dundalk Bay

Blacksod Bay
Nephin
806
L. Conn
Boyle
LEITRIM
Gowna
Granard
L. Sheelin
Ceanannas Mor
(Kells)
LOUTH

Achill Hd.
Achill
Clare I.
Castlebar
ROSCOMMON
Castlerea
Longford
Oldcastle
Blackwater
An Uaimh
(Navan)
Drogheda

C
Clew Bay
Croagh Patrick
765
MAYO
Robe
Roscommon
LONGFORD
L. Ree
Athboy
MEATH
Trim
Boyne
Balbriggan

Inishbofin
Killary Harbour
Mweelrea
819
L. Mask
Ballinrobe
Suck
Mullingar
Swords
Lambay I.

Slyne Hd.
Twelve
Pins
CONNACHT
Tuam
WESTMEATH
Athlone
DUBLIN
Ireland's Eye

Clifden
Connemara
L. Corrib
Clare
Cara
Maynooth
Howth Head

GALWAY
IRELAND
Ballinasloe
Brosna
Edenderry
Dublin (Baile Atha Cliath)
Dublin Bay

Slyne Hd.
Galway
Athenry
Loughrea
Shannon
OFFALY
Tullamore
Daingean
Droichead
Nua
Celbridge
Dun Laoghaire

Galway Bay
Inishmore
Aran Is.
Gort
Portumna
Slieve
Aughty
Birr
Slieve
Bloom
Mountmellick
Naas
Kilcullen
754
Poulaphouca Res.
Bray

53
Hags Hd.
Liscannor Bay
Ennistymon
L. Derg
Port Laoise
KILDARE
Kildare
WICKLOW
Lugnaquilla
923
Wicklow
Wicklow Hd.

Mal Bay
CLARE
Ennis
LAOIS
Athy
Barrow
Rathdrum
Mizen Hd.

Miltown
Malbay
Killaloe
Ballina
Nenagh
Roscrea
Nore
Tullow
Shillelagh
Arklow

D
Kilkee
Bunratty
Ardnacrusha
Keeper
894
Templemore
Muine Bheag
Mt. Leinster
796
Gorey

Loop Hd.
Foynes
Rathkeale
Limerick
Golden
Vale
Thurles
Kilkenny
CARLOW
Carlow

Kerry Hd.
Fenit
Listowel
LIMERICK
Newcastle
Suir
Cashel
KILKENNY
Callan
Enniscorthy
WEXFORD

Brandon Bay
Tralee Bay
Feale
Rath Luirc
(Charleville)
Galtymore
920
Galty Mts.
Cahir
Slievenamon
721
Carrick-on-Suir
New Ross
Wexford Harbour

Brandon
953
Brandon Mt.
Tralee
Sl. Mish
Maine
MUNSTER
Newmarket
Mitchelstown
Knockmealdown
Mts.
Clonmel
Waterford
Rosslare
Greenore Pt.

Dunmore Hd.
Dingle
KERRY
Laune
Kanturk
Blackwater
Fermoy
Lismore
Comeragh Mts.
WATERFORD
Tramore
Tuscar Rock
Carnsore Pt.

E
Valencia Harbour
Valencia I.
Macgillycuddy's
Reeks
Carrauntuohill
1040
Lakes of
Killarney
Killarney
Boggeragh Mts.
Blarney
Blackwater
Dungarvan
Dungarvan Bay
Hook Hd.
Waterford Harbour
Saltee Is.
St. David's Hd.

Skellig
Rocks
Cahirciveen
Kenmare
Lee
Cork
Midleton
Youghal
Youghal Harbour

Ballinskelligs B.
Kenmare River
Caha Mts.
Glengarriff
Macroom
CORK
Passage West
Cobh
Crosshaven
Cork Harbour

Castletown Bearhaven
Bear I.
Bantry
Bandon
Bandon
Kinsale
Old Head of Kinsale

Crow Hd.
Bantry Bay
Clonakilty
Skibbereen
Clonakilty Bay

Dunmanus Bay
Mizen Hd.
Skull
Baltimore
Clear I.
C. Clear
Galley Hd.
Fastnet Rock

Towns underlined in Northern Ireland give their
names to the Districts in which they stand

The remaining Districts are:—

1	Fermanagh	5	Castlereagh
2	Moyle	6	Ards
3	Newtownabbey	7	Down
4	North Down	8	Newry & Mourne

Projection: Conical with two standard parallels.

West from Greenwich

ft   m
3000   1000
1200   400
600   200
300   100
0   0
100   300
200   600
m   ft

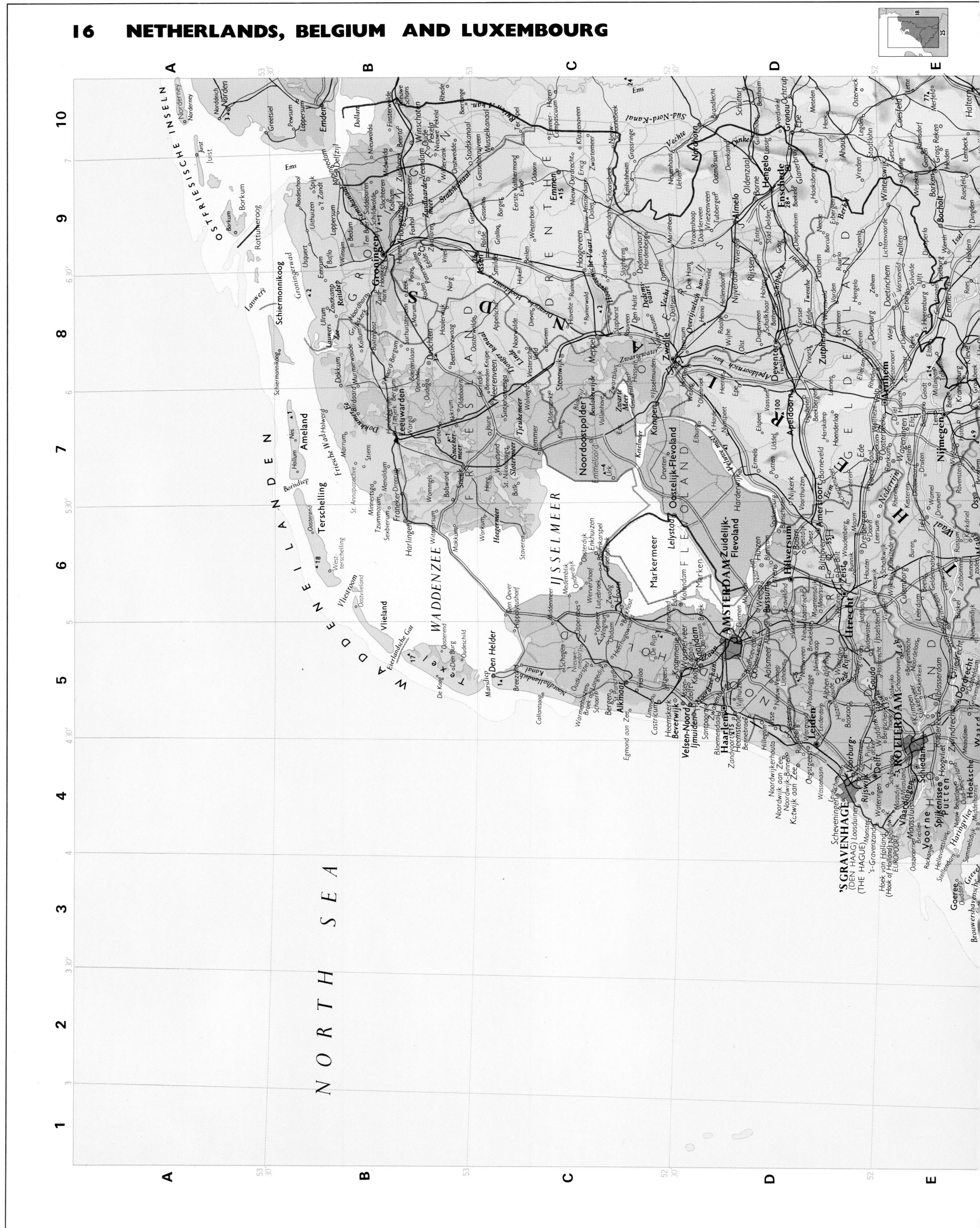

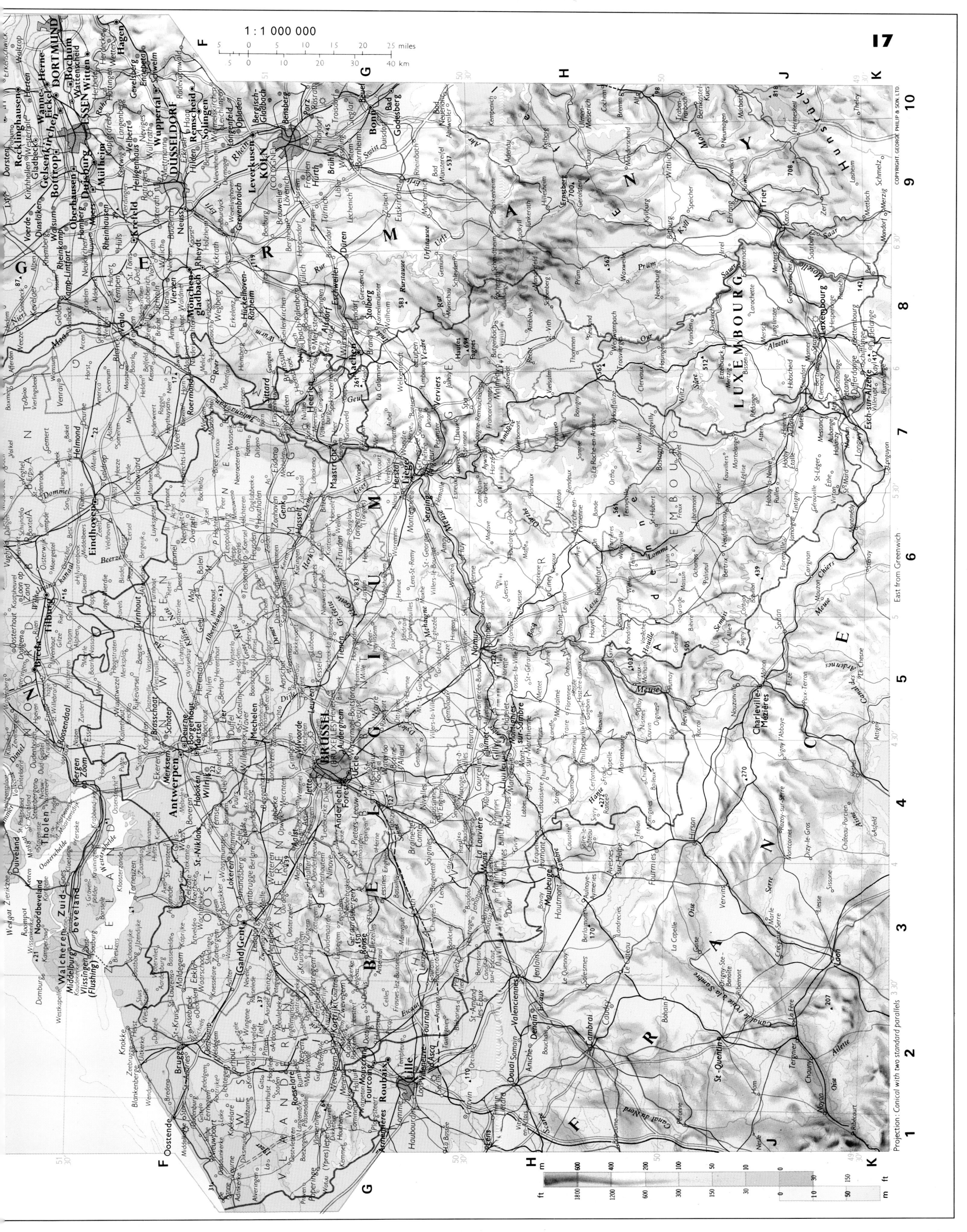

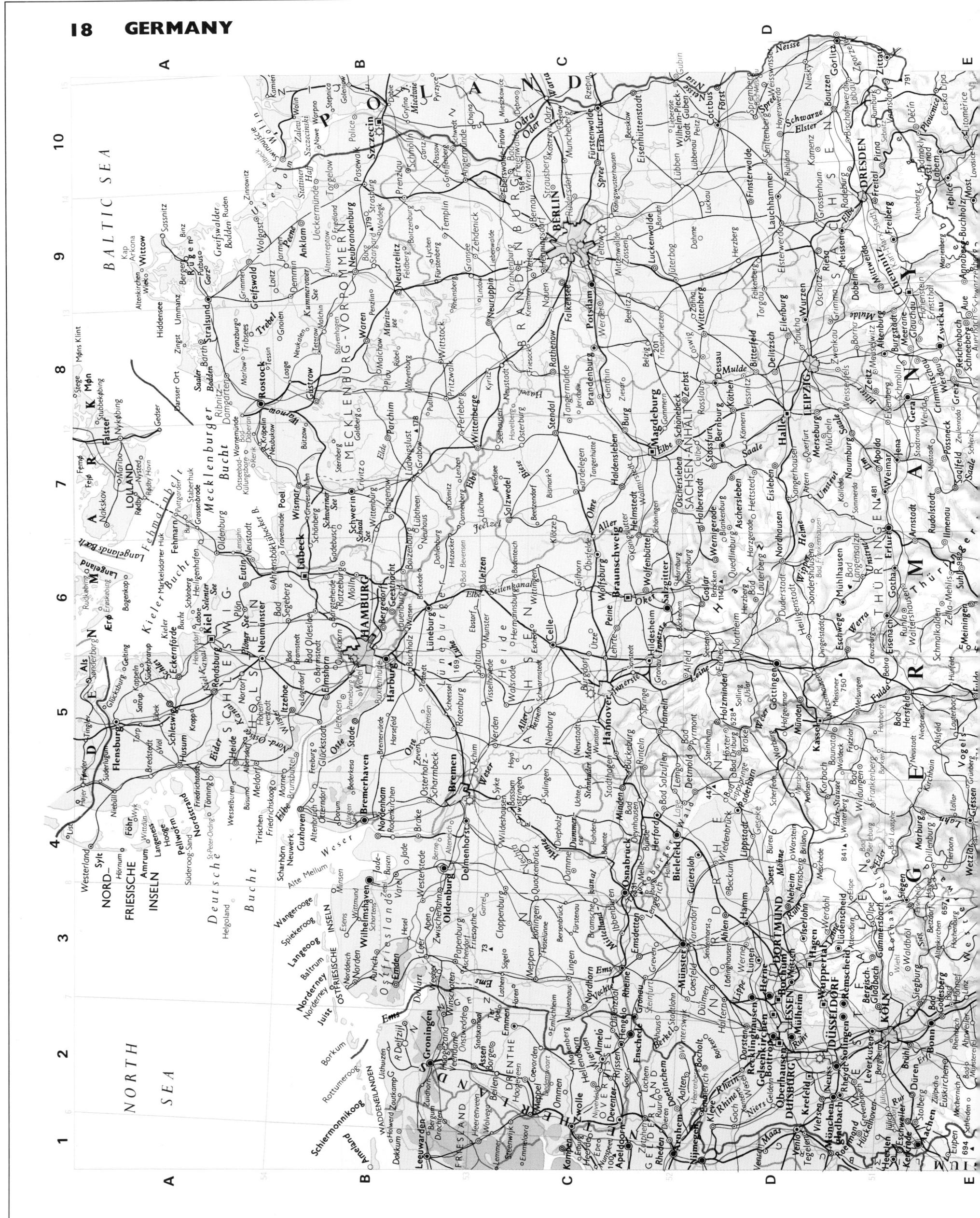

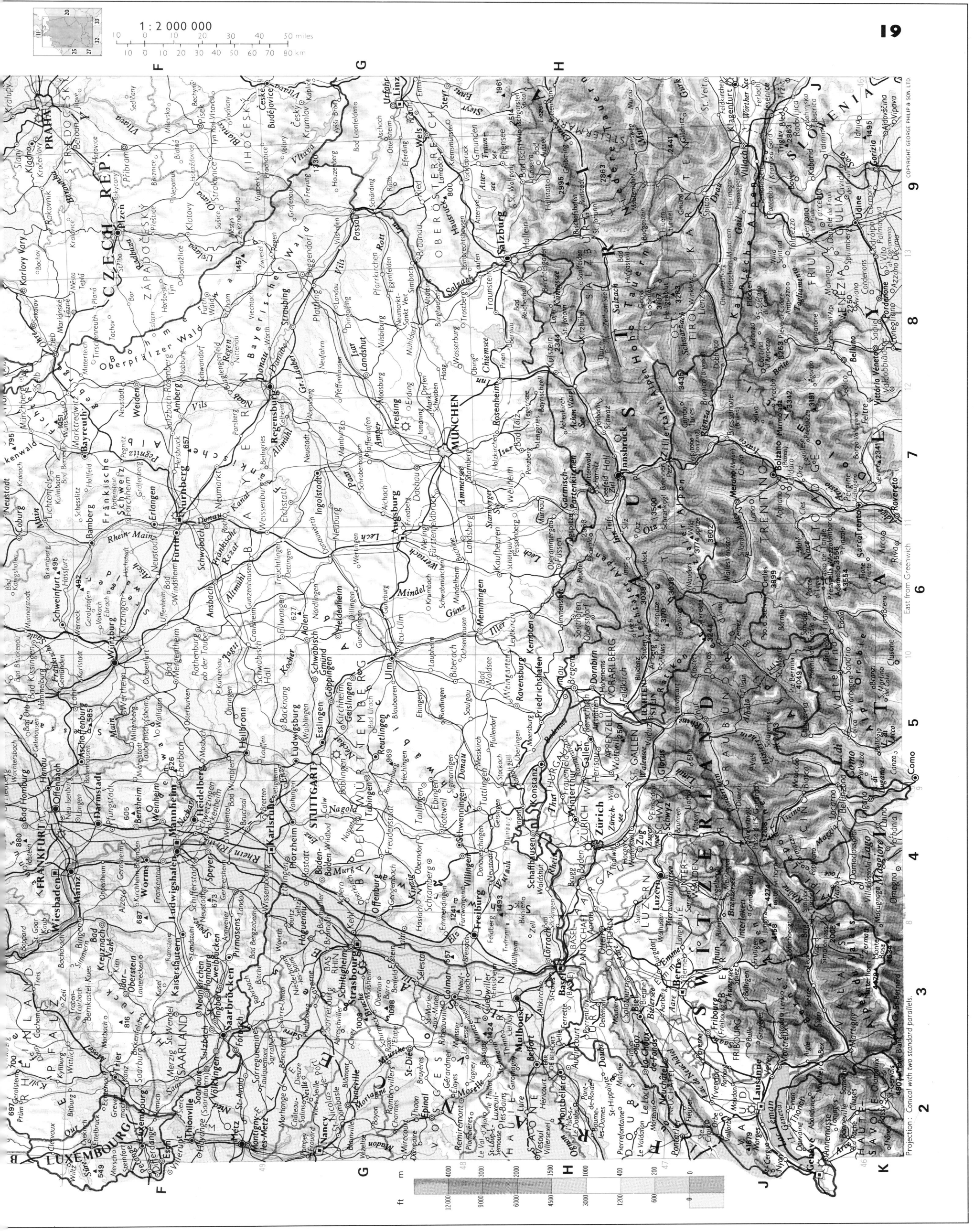

1 : 2 000 000

Projection : Conical with two standard parallels

East from Greenwich

COPYRIGHT GEORGE PHILIP & SON Ltd

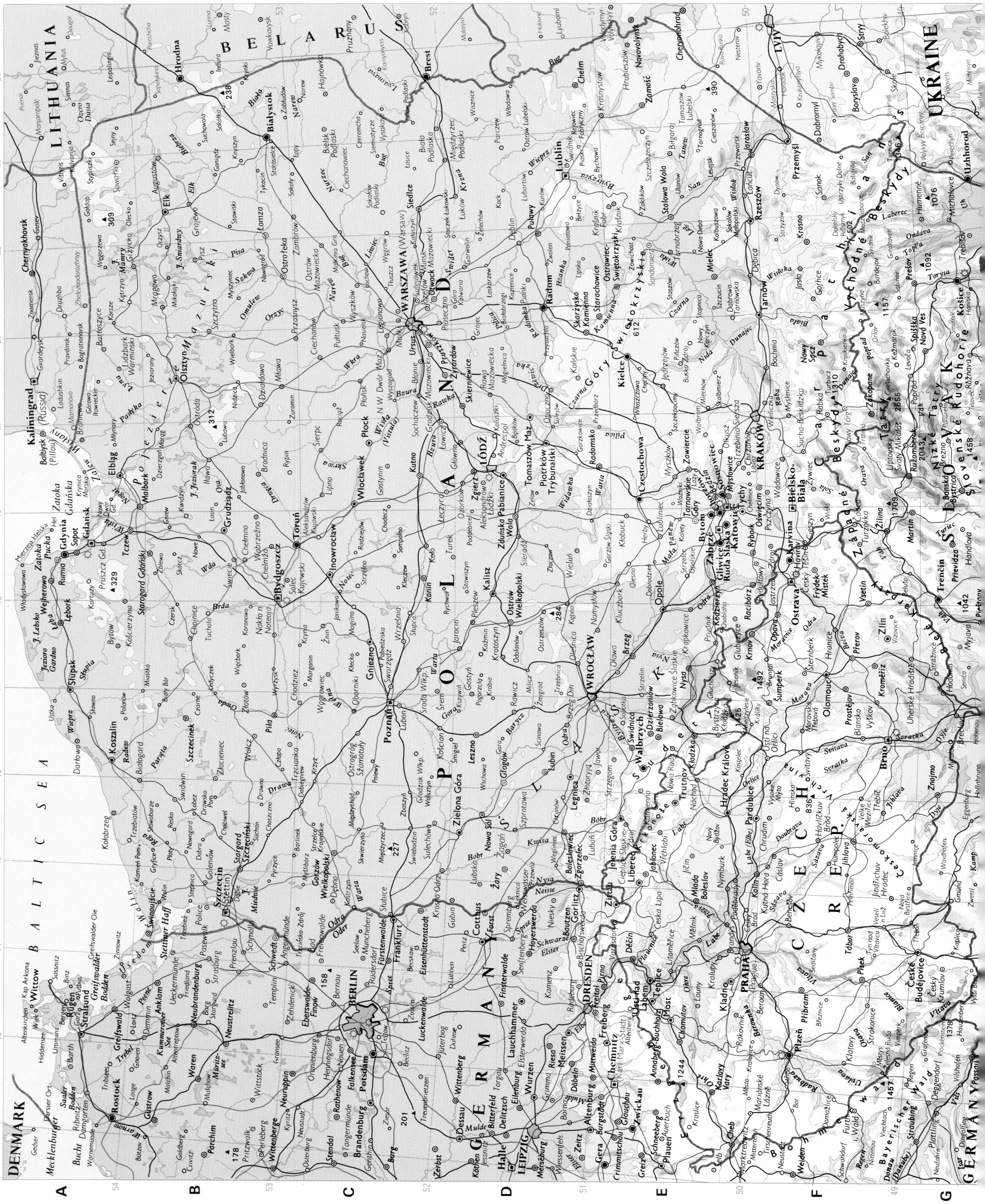

LITHUANIA

BELARUS

UKRAINE

DENMARK

GERMANY

POLAND

CZECH REP.

SLOVAK

BALTIC SEA

Kaliningrad (Russia)

WARSZAWA (Warsaw)

BERLIN

DRESDEN

LEIPZIG

PRAHA

WROCŁAW

KRAKÓW

ŁÓDŹ

Poznań

Gdańsk

Gdynia

Szczecin

Bydgoszcz

Toruń

Lublin

Radom

Białystok

Brest

Hrodna

LVIV

Przemyśl

Rzeszów

Kraków

Katowice

Ostrava

Brno

Olomouc

Zlín

Košice

Tatry

Beskydy

Sudety

1 : 2 800 000

10 0 10 20 30 40 50 100 miles
10 0 10 20 30 40 50 100 150 km

HUNGARY
ROMANIA
YUGOSLAVIA
CROATIA
BOSNIA-HERZEGOVINA
SERBIA
MONTENEGRO
ALBANIA
MACEDONIA
BULGARIA
SLOVENIA
VOJVODINA
KOSOVO
ITALY
AUSTRIA

ADRIATIC SEA

BUDAPEST
WIEN
Bratislava
Beograd (Belgrade)
SOFIYA (Sofia)
Zagreb
Sarajevo
Graz
Linz

Projection: Conical with two standard parallels
East from Greenwich
COPYRIGHT GEORGE PHILIP & SON LTD.

ft m
12,000 4000
9000 3000
6000 2000
4500 1500
3000 1000
1200 400
600 200
m ft 0

FRANCE

HAUTE-SAÔNE

Vesoul
Gray
Fayl-Billot
Jussey
Vitrey-sur-Mance
Amance
Lanterne
Faverney
Meurcourt
Luxeuil-les-Bains
St-Sauveur
Servance
Champagney
Plancher-les-Mines
Giromagny
Masevaux
Thann
Cernay
Wittelsheim
MULHOUSE
Wittenheim
Lutterbach
Brunstatt
Combeaufontaine
Port-s-Saône
Noroy-le-Bourg
Genevrières
Lavoncourt
Dampierre-sur-Salon
Vaîte
Echenoz-la-Méline
Soing
Villersexel
BELFORT
Belfort
Héricourt
Montbéliard
Audincourt
Valentigney
Mandeure
Héricourt
Porte de Bourgogne
Dannemarie
Altkirch
Illfurth
BASEL (BASLE)
Lörrach
Rheinfelden
Säckingen
Frick
HAUT-RHIN
Sundgau
SCHWARZWALD

Besançon
Marnay
Roulans
Baume-les-Dames
Pont-de-Roide
Montagnes du Lomont 839
Maîche
DOUBS
Ornans
Quingey
Dampierre
Valdahon
Le Russey
Saignelégier
Franches Montagnes
Tramelan
Tavannes
Moutier
Delémont
Porrentruy
JURA
SOLOTHURN
Balsthal
Olten
Aarau
LANDSCHAFT AARGAU
BASEL
Liestal
Dornach
Pratteln

La Chaux-de-Fonds
Le Locle
Morteau
Pontarlier
Neuchâtel
St-Blaise
Bienne (Biel)
Grenchen
Solothurn
Herzogenbuchsee
Langenthal
Burgdorf
LUZERN
Sursee
Willisau

Ste-Croix
Chasseron 1607
Grandson
Yverdon
Fleurier
Couvet
Boudry
Lac de Neuchâtel
Estavayer-le-Lac
Payerne
Avenches
Murten
Kerzers
Fribourg (Freiburg)
Schwarzenburg
BERN (BERNE)
Köniz
Worb
Münsingen
Langnau i.E.
OBWALDEN

Champagnole
Pont-du-Navoy
Mouthe
Le Sentier
Mt. Tendre 1679
Le Brassus
Vallorbe
Orbe
Moudon
Romont
Bulle
Gruyères
FRIBOURG
Gruyère
Châtel-St-Denis
Freiburger Alpen
Oberland
Thun
Steffisburg
Thunersee
Brienzersee
Interlaken
Meiringen
Grindelwald

Morez
Morbier
St-Claude
Les Rousses
LAUSANNE
Morges
Lutry
Vevey
Montreux
Villeneuve
Léman (L. Geneva)
Rolle
Nyon
Thonon-les-Bains
Évian-les-Bains
St-Gingolph
Aigle
Leysin
Les Diablerets
Gstaad
Adelboden
Wildstrubel
Blümlisalphorn 3664
Lötschbergtunnel
4158
4274

Oyonnax
Bellegarde-s.-V.
GENÈVE (GENEVA)
Vernier
Annemasse
Chêne-Bourg
HAUTE-SAVOIE
Chablais
Monthey
Bex
St-Maurice
Martigny
Sion
Sierre
Visp
Brig
Simplonpass 2005
VALAIS
Pennine Alpi

Annecy
Rumilly
Lac d'Annecy
Thônes
Tournette 2351
La Roche
Bonneville
Sallanches
Chamonix-Mont-Blanc
Col de la Forclaz 1527
Grande Dixence
Zermatt
Matterhorn 4478
Weisshorn 4506
Dom 4545
Monte Rosa
Dufourspitze

Belley
Aix-les-Bains
Lac du Bourget
Albertville
Ugine
Col du Petit St-Bernard 2188
VAL D'AOSTA
Aosta
Châtillon
PIEMONTE

Projection: Conical with two standard parallels

ft m
9000 3000
6000 2000
4500 1500
3000 1000
1200 500
600 200

1 : 800 000

5 0 5 10 15 20 25 miles
5 0 5 10 15 20 30 40 km

GERMANY

BAYERN

WÜRTTEMBERG

THURGAU

Bodensee (L. Constance)

Konstanz **Friedrichshafen** Lindau **Bregenz**

ZÜRICH **Winterthur** **St. Gallen** APPENZELL **Dornbirn**

VORARLBERG

AUSTRIA

TIROL

LIECHTENSTEIN **Vaduz** **Feldkirch** **Bludenz** Landeck

SCHWYZ **Luzern** **Zug** GLARUS **Chur**

GLARNER ALPEN

GRAUBÜNDEN

National-Park

Silvretta-Gruppe

Davos Klosters

St. Moritz Samedan Pontresina

P. Bernina 4049

TICINO

Adula Gruppe

Bellinzona **Locarno** **Lugano**

Lago Maggiore

Lago di Como

Lago di Lugano

Sóndrio Tirano

Valtellina

Alpi Orobie

Bórmio

Ortles

TRENTINO

Domodóssola **Varese** **Como** **Lecco** **BÉRGAMO**

LOMBARDIA

ITALY

Lago d'Iseo

Lago di Garda

Riva del Garda

COPYRIGHT. GEORGE PHILIP & SON. LTD.

East from Greenwich

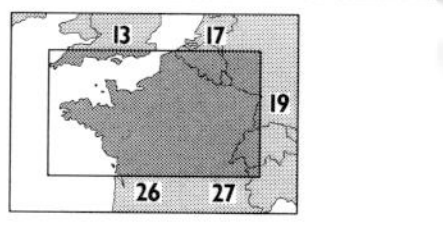

ENGLAND

English Channel

CHANNEL ISLANDS
Guernsey
St. Peter Port
Jersey
St. Helier
Alderney
Sark
Herm

Baie de la Seine

Golfe de St-Malo

Plymouth
Exeter
Dartmoor
Torquay
Paignton
Brixham
Weymouth
Bournemouth
Southampton
Portsmouth
Brighton
Eastbourne
Hastings
Newquay
Truro
St. Austell
Penzance
Land's End
Lizard Pt.
Bideford
Tiverton
Yeovil
Sherborne
Dorchester
Poole
I. of Wight
Chichester
Worthing
Le Touquet Paris
Dieppe

Le Havre
Rouen
Cherbourg
Granville
Caen
Lisieux
Bayeux
Évreux
Alençon
Le Mans
Rennes
Brest
Quimper
Lorient
Vannes
St. Nazaire
Nantes
Angers
Tours
Blois

Mer d'Iroise
Ile d'Ouessant
Ile de Sein

CÔTES-DU-NORD
MORBIHAN
Monts d'Arrée
Montagne Noire
BRETAGNE

Baie de Bourgneuf
Ile de Noirmoutier
Ile d'Yeu
La Roche-sur-Yon
Les-Sables-d'Olonne
VENDÉE

La Rochelle
Ile de Ré
Ile d'Oléron
Rochefort
Saintes
Cognac
Angoulême
AUNIS
CHARENTE-MARITIME
CHARENTE
ANGOUMOIS
POITOU
Poitiers
VIENNE
DEUX-SÈVRES
Niort
Châtellerault
Le Blanc
Cholet
MAINE-ET-LOIRE
LOIRE-ATLANTIQUE
ANJOU
TOURAINE
Samur
Chinon

Poitiers

ft   m
12 000 4000
9000   3000
6000   2000
4500   1500
3000   1000
1200   400
600   200
0   0
200   600
2000   6000
m   ft

DÉPARTEMENTS IN THE PARIS AREA
1 Ville de Paris   3 Val-de-Marne
2 Seine-St-Denis   4 Hauts-de-Seine

Projection: Conical with two standard parallels

West from Greenwich   East from Greenwich

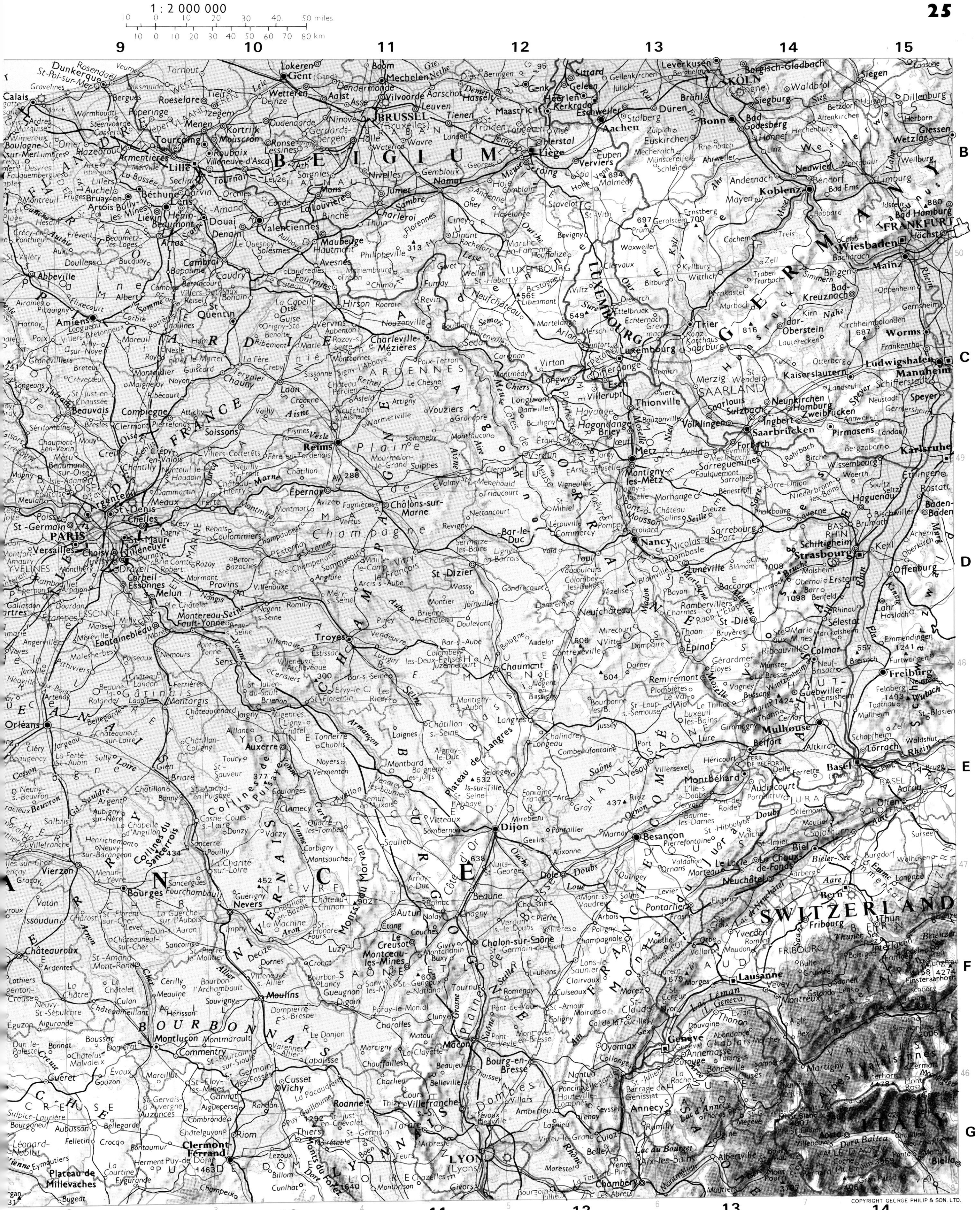

1 : 2 000 000

10   0   10   20   30   40   50 miles
10   0   10 20 30 40 50 60 70 80 km

9   10   11   12   13   14   15

BELGIUM

GERMANY

LUXEMBOURG

FRANCE

SWITZERLAND

ITALY

PARIS · FRANKFURT · KÖLN · Bonn · Koblenz · Wiesbaden · Mainz · Worms · Mannheim · Ludwigshafen · Karlsruhe · Baden-Baden · Strasbourg · Freiburg · Basel · Mulhouse · Belfort · Besançon · Dijon · Lyon · Clermont-Ferrand · Bourges · Orléans · Troyes · Reims · Amiens · Lille · Calais · Brussel · Gent · Aachen · Liège · Namur · Luxembourg · Metz · Nancy · Saarbrücken · Trier

COPYRIGHT GEORGE PHILIP & SON, LTD.

9   10   11   12   13   14

24
25
33
28
34

ATLANTIC
OCEAN
Golfe de
Gascogne
Ile de Noirmoutier
Ile d'Yeu
Ile de Ré
Ile d'Oléron
Pertuis Breton
Pertuis d'Antioche
POITOU
AUNIS
SAINTONGE
ANGOUMOIS
LIMOUSIN
MARCHE
BERRY
BOURBONNAIS
NIVERNAIS
AUVERGNE
GUYENNE
GASCOGNE
LANDES
PÉRIGORD
ROUSSILLON
PYRÉNÉES-ORIENTALES
NAVARRE
BÉARN
ANDORRA
SPAIN
NAVARRA
ARAGON
CATALUÑA
Plateau de Millevaches
Massif Central
Causse Méjean
Mts de Lacaune
Sierra de la Peña
Sierra de Guara
Sierra del Cadí
Cholet
La Roche-sur-Yon
Les Sables-d'Olonne
La Rochelle
Rochefort
Niort
Poitiers
Châtellerault
Bourges
Nevers
Châteauroux
Limoges
Angoulême
Saintes
Cognac
Périgueux
Bordeaux
Libourne
Bergerac
Agen
Montauban
Toulouse
Albi
Rodez
Millau
Cahors
Aurillac
Clermont-Ferrand
Vichy
Moulins
Montluçon
Tulle
Brive-la-Gaillarde
Mont-de-Marsan
Dax
Bayonne
Biarritz
Pau
Tarbes
Lourdes
Auch
Carcassonne
Narbonne
Béziers
Sète
Perpignan
Castres
Mazamet
Foix
Pamiers
San Sebastián
Pamplona
Huesca
Zaragoza
Lérida
Gerona
Figueras
Manresa
Golfe du Lion
Projection: Conical with two standard parallels
West from Greenwich
East from Greenwich
1 2 3 4 5 6 7
B C D E F G
ft m
12,000 4000
9000 3000
6000 2000
4500 1500
3000 1000
1200 400
600 200
0
200 600
2000 6000

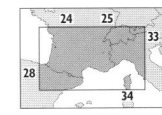

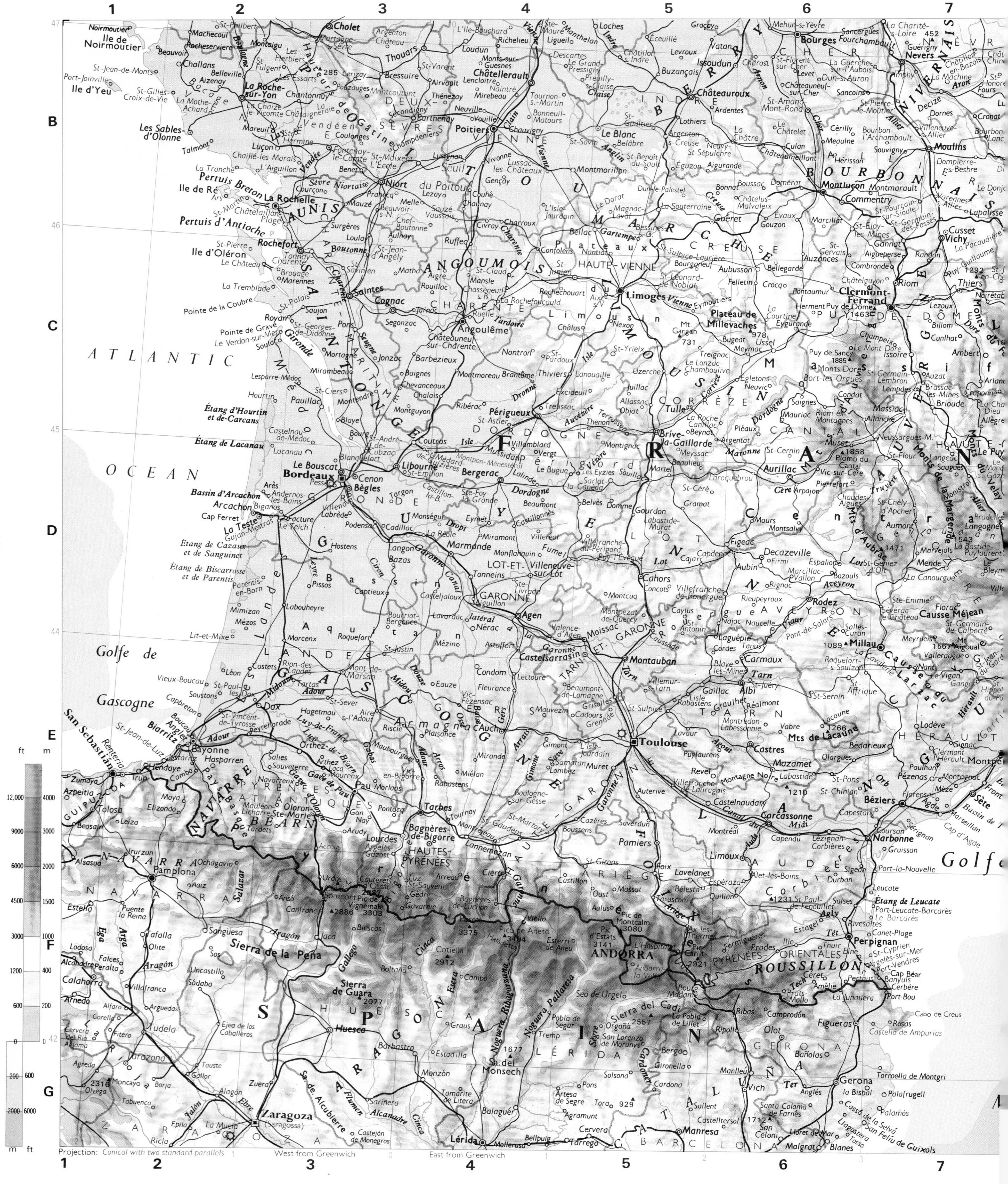

1 : 2 000 000

10 0 10 20 30 40 50 miles
10 0 10 20 30 40 50 60 70 80 km

8   9   10   11   12   13   14

SWITZERLAND

Bern · Luzern · Schwyz · FRIBOURG · Interlaken · GRAUBÜNDEN · Davos · St. Moritz · Bormio

Genève · Lausanne · Montreux · VALAIS · Zermatt · Locarno · Bellinzona · Lugano · Como · Lecco · Bergamo · Brescia

Annecy · HAUTE-SAVOIE · Mont Blanc · VALLE D'AOSTA · Aosta · Biella · Novara · MILANO (Milan) · Monza · Crema

LYON · Chambéry · SAVOIE · Torino (Turin) · Vercelli · Pavia · Lodi · Piacenza · Cremona

Vienne · Grenoble · Moncalieri · Asti · Alessandria · Tortona · Voghera · Parma

ARDÈCHE · DRÔME · Gap · Briançon · Massif du Pelvoux · Pinerolo · Cuneo · Mondovì · GENOVA (Genova) · La Spezia · Carrara · Massa

Valence · Montélimar · ALPES-DE-HAUTE-PROVENCE · PROVENCE · Savona · Finale Ligure · Albenga · Golfo di Génova

Avignon · VAUCLUSE · ALPES-MARITIMES · San Remo · Imperia · Livorno

Nîmes · Arles · Aix-en-Provence · VAR · Cannes · Nice · Antibes · Monaco · Monte-Carlo

MARSEILLE · Toulon · Hyères · ILES D'HYÈRES · Côte d'Azur

LIGURIAN SEA

Golfe du Lion

C. Corse · Capraia

MEDITERRANEAN SEA

Bastia · L'Île-Rousse · Calvi · Étang de Biguglia · Pianosa · Elba · Marciana Marina

Monte Cinto 2710 · HAUTE-CORSE · Corte · CORSE (CORSICA)

Ajaccio · G. d'Ajaccio · CORSE DU SUD · Porto-Vecchio

Bonifacio · I. de Cavallo

COPYRIGHT. GEORGE PHILIP & SON. LTD.

8   9   10   11   12   13   14

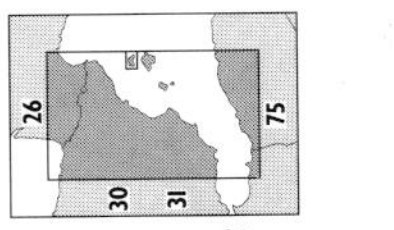

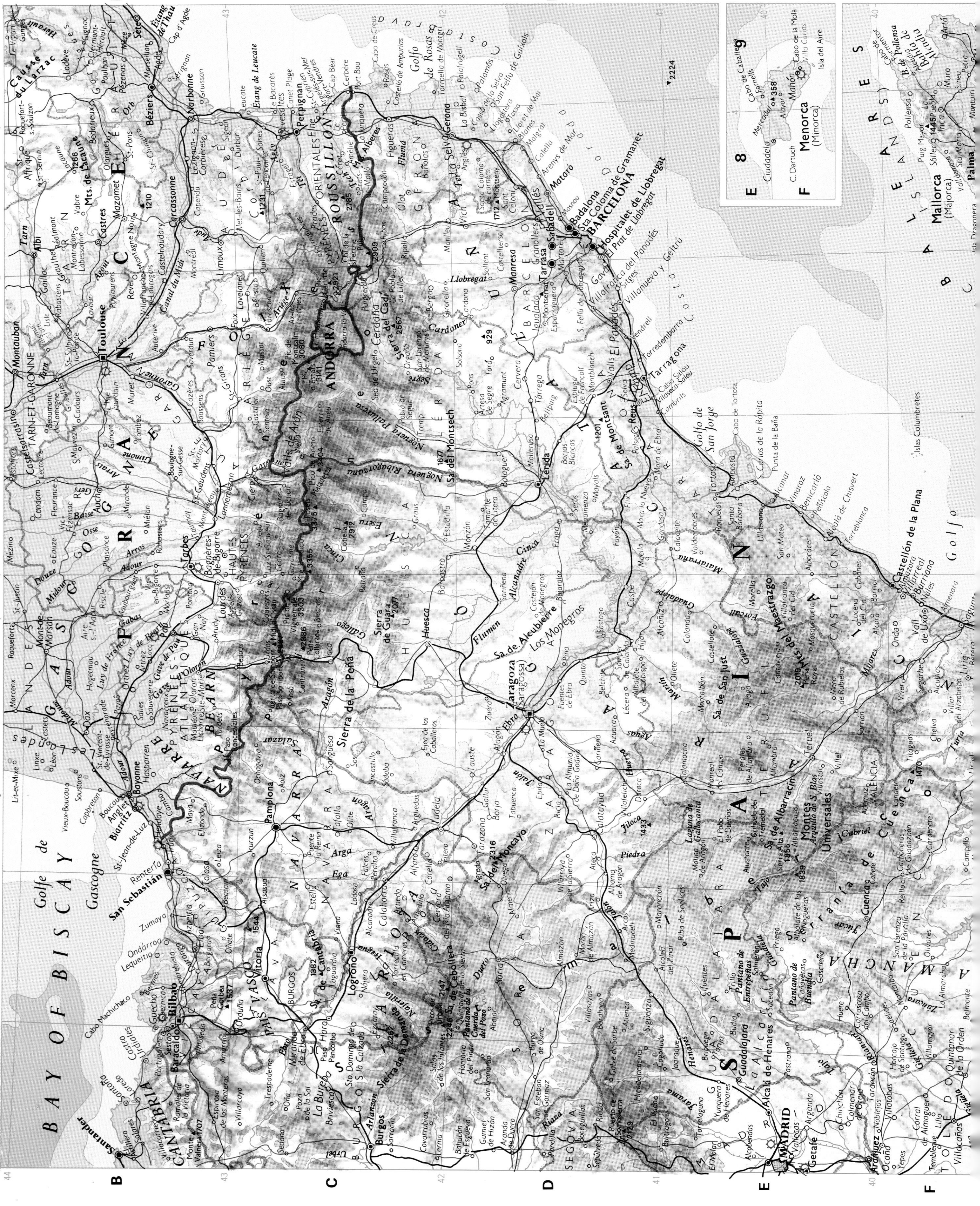

BAY OF BISCAY

Golfe de Gascogne

FRANCE

Toulouse

Montauban

Carcassonne

Narbonne

Béziers

Perpignan

PYRÉNÉES-ORIENTALES

ROUSSILLON

Costa Brava

Gerona

Figueras

BARCELONA

Badalona
Sta. Coloma de Gramanet
Sabadell
Tarrasa
Hospitalet de Llobregat

Manresa

ANDORRA

LÉRIDA

Tarragona
Reus

Zaragoza (Saragossa)

HUESCA

Huesca

Lérida

Los Monegros

NAVARRA

Pamplona

San Sebastián

Bilbao

Santander

CANTABRIA

PAÍS VASCO

Vitoria

BURGOS
Burgos

Logroño

RIOJA

SORIA

Cuenca

VALENCIA

Castellón de la Plana

Maestrazgo

Teruel

ARAGÓN

Montes Universales

Guadalajara

Alcalá de Henares

MADRID
Getafe
Aranjuez

LA MANCHA

Mallorca (Majorca)
Palma

Menorca (Minorca)
Ciudadela
Mahón

ISLAS BALEARES

Ebro

GOLFO DE SAN JORGE

Gibraltar Mediterráneo

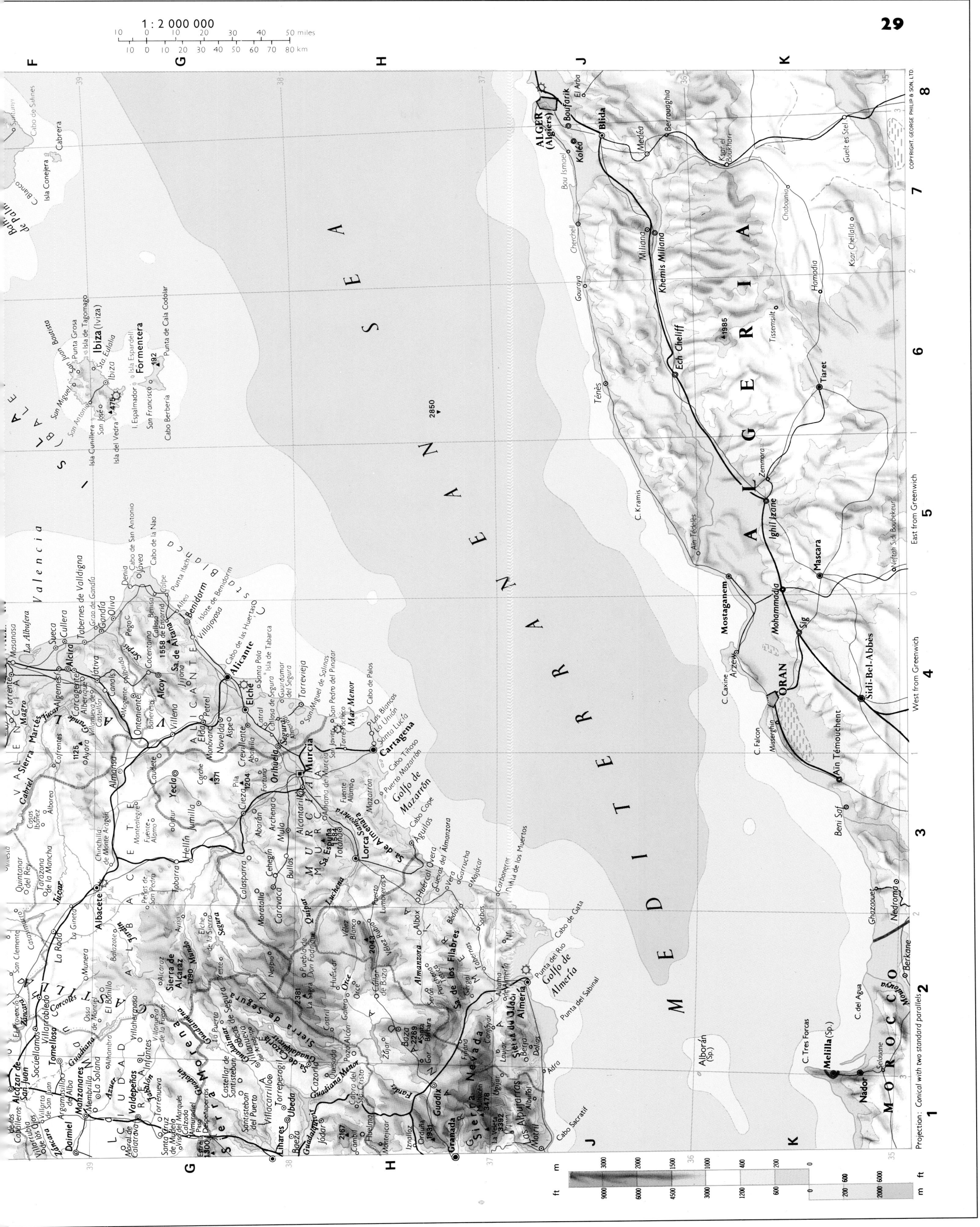

1 : 2 000 000

Projection: Conical with two standard parallels

East from Greenwich

West from Greenwich

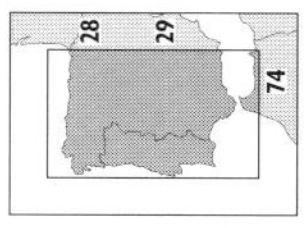

BAY OF BISCAY

ATLANTIC OCEAN

San Sebastián
Bilbao
Santander
Gijón
Oviedo
La Coruña (Coruña)
Santiago de Compostela
Pontevedra
Vigo
Orense
Lugo
León
Palencia
Valladolid
Zamora
Salamanca
Burgos
Logroño
Vitoria
MADRID
Segovia
Ávila
Guadalajara
Alcalá de Henares
Aranjuez

Porto (Oporto)
Vila Nova de Gaia
Aveiro
Coimbra
Viseu
Guarda
Braga
Vila Real
Lamego

PAÍS VASCO
CANTABRIA
ASTURIAS
GALICIA
LA RIOJA
MESETA

Duero
Douro
Ebro
Tajo
Pisuerga
Tormes
Mondego

1 : 2 000 000

10 0 10 20 30 40 50 miles

10 0 10 20 30 40 50 60 70 80 km

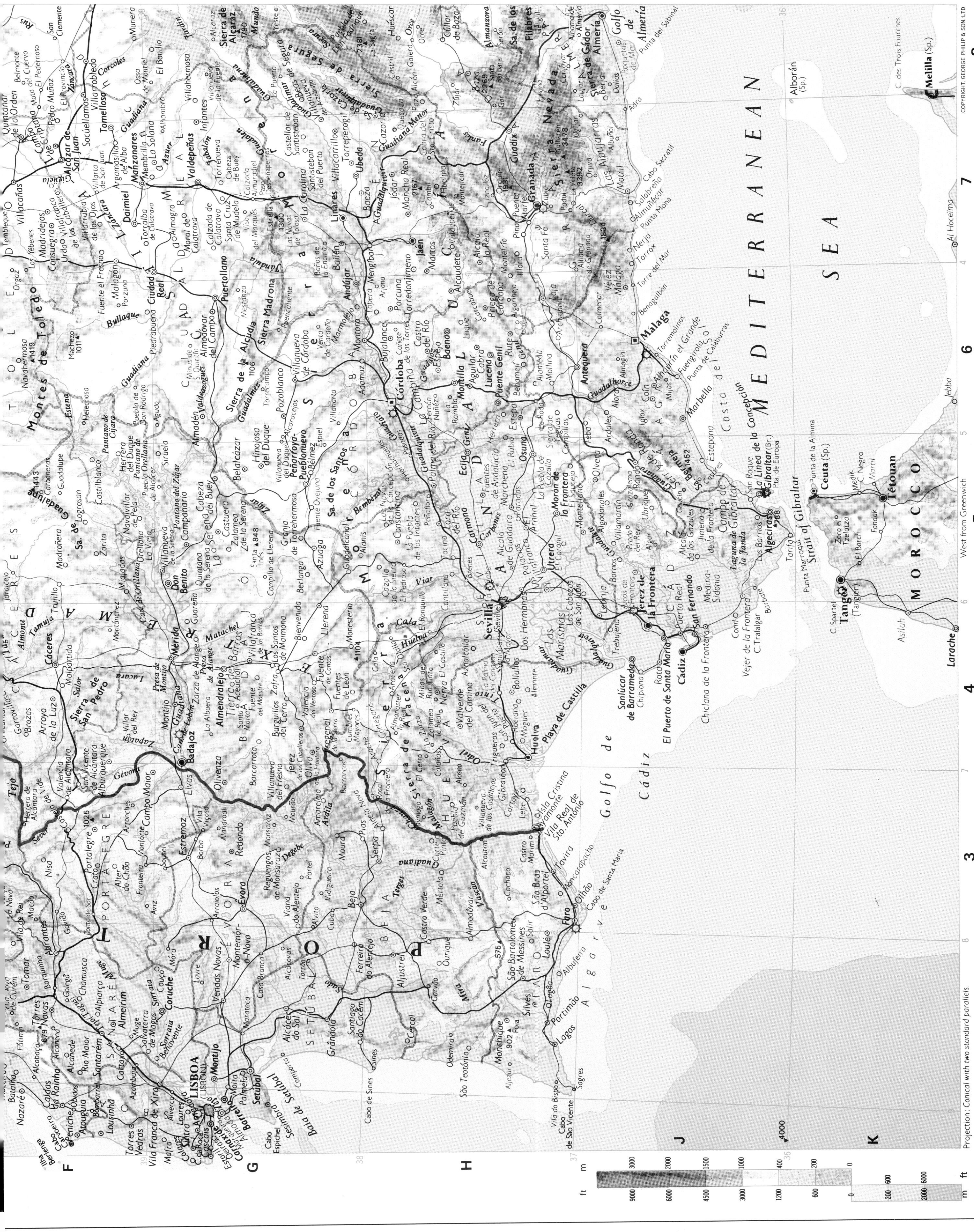

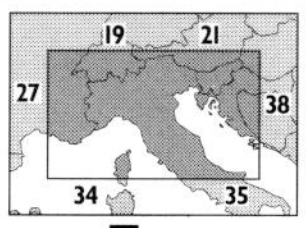

19
21
27
38
34
35

1
2
3
4
5
6
7
A
B
C
D
E
F
G
SWITZERLAND
FRANCE
LIGURIAN SEA
CORSE
(CORSICA)
Golfo di Génova
Riviera di Ponente
Riviera di Levante
ILES D'HYERES
Côte d'Azur
Arcipelago
Toscano
Lyon (Lyons)
Genève (GENEVA)
Lausanne
Bern (BERNE)
Luzern
Zürich
Grenoble
Chambéry
Annecy
Valence
Avignon
Marseille (Marseilles)
Toulon
Aix-en-Provence
Nice
Cannes
MONACO
San Remo
TORINO (Turin)
MILANO (Milan)
GENOVA (Genoa)
Novara
Vercelli
Pavia
Piacenza
Parma
Cremona
Brescia
Bergamo
Como
Lugano
Alessandria
Asti
Cúneo
Savona
La Spezia
Lucca
Pisa
Livorno (Leghorn)
Bastia
Ajaccio
Elba
Montecristo
Capraia
Gorgona
HAUTE-CORSE
CORSE-DU-SUD
Mont Blanc
4807
Matterhorn
4478
Monte Rosa
4634
Gran Paradiso
4061
Monte Viso
3841
2650
Projection: Conical with two standard parallels
East from Greenwich
ft
m
12 000
9000
6000
4500
3000
1200
600
0
200
2000
4000
3000
2000
1500
1000
400
200
0
600
6000

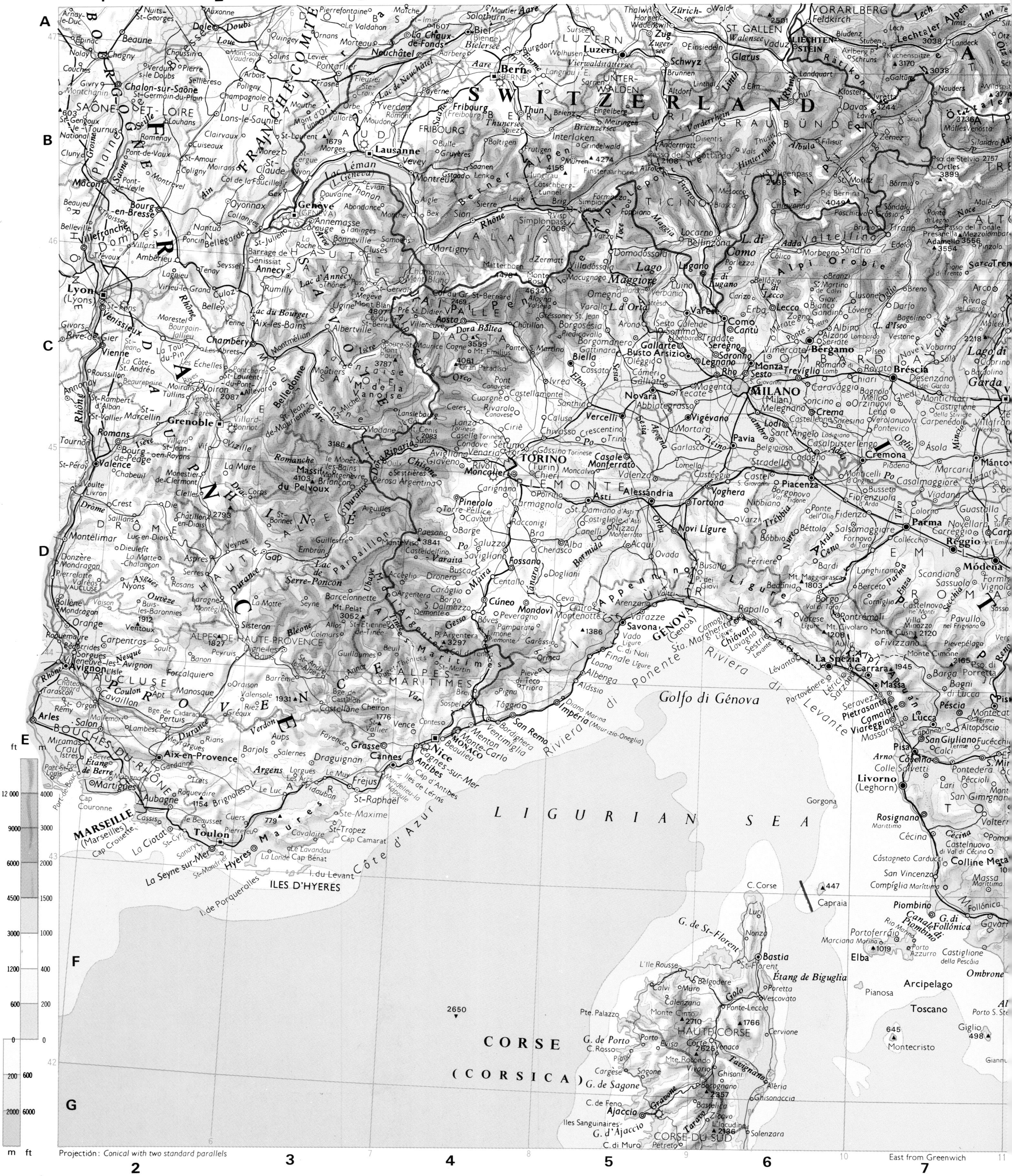

1:2 000 000

10   20   30   40   50 miles
10 0 10 20 30 40 50 60 70 80 km

8   9   10   11   12   13   14

A

B

C

D

E

F

G

HUNGARY

SLOVENIA

CROATIA

BOSNIA-HERZEGOVINA

Innsbruck

Graz

Maribor

Klagenfurt

Villach

Ljubljana

Zagreb

Trieste

Rijeka

Pula

Venézia (Venice)

Golfo di Venézia

Pádova (Padua)

Vicenza

Verona

Ferrara

Ravenna

Bologna

Firenze (Florence)

Forlì

Cesena

Rímini

SAN MARINO

Ancona

Pésaro

Fano

Senigállia

Pescara

Chieti

Vasto

Téramo

L'Aquila

ABRUZZI

MARCHE

UMBRIA

LAZIO

MOLISE

Terni

Perúgia

Assisi

Orvieto

Viterbo

ROMA (ROME)

Vatican City

Tívoli

Zadar

Split

Brač

Hvar

Vis

Korčula

Mljet

Lastovo

Banja Luka

ADRIATIC SEA

A D R I A T I C   S E A

Monte Sant'Ángelo

Vieste

Bolzano

Treviso

Udine

Gorízia

Monfalcone

Pordenone

Belluno

VENETO

FRIULI-VENEZIA GIULIA

Dinara Planina

Velebit

Svetac

Palagruža

Pianosa

Tremiti

COPYRIGHT GEORGE PHILIP & SON, LTD.

8   9   10   11   12   13

| | 1 | 2 | 3 | 4 | 5 | 6 |

A

Iles Sanguinaires
G. d'Ajaccio
C. di Muro
Petreto
Tattavo
Niccacine
Zonza
Levie
Solenzara
Favone
2136
G. de Valinco
Propriano
Porto-Vecchio
Sartène
CORSE
CORSE-DU-SUD
Iles Cerbicales
CORSICA
Bonifacio
I. de Cavallo

ROMA (Rome)
Vatican City
Tívoli
Subiaco
Trevi
Conca del Fucino
Fregene
Teano (Tiber)
Frosinone
Palestrina
Valmontone
Alatri
Véroli
Sora
Lido di Óstia (Lido di Roma)
Pomézia
Lazziano
Velletri
Angani
Isola del L.
Monte S. Giov.
Albano
Cori
Ceccano
Ceprano
Arpino
Ánzio
Aprilia
Cisterna di Latina
Sezze
Ferentino
Priverno
Pontínia
Sonnino
Poffaté
Nettuno
Latina

B

Bouches de Bonifacio
Maddalena
Santa Teresa Gallura
La Maddalena
Caprera
Punta dello Scorno
Pto. Cervo
Golfo Aranci
Asinara
Costa Smeralda
Golfo dell' Asinara
Arzachena
Líscia
G. di Ólbia
Coghinas
Ággius
Calangiánus
Ólbia
Tavolara
Pórto Tórres
Témpio Pausánia
1362
Sorso
Sénnori
M. Limbara
Sássari
Ozieri
C. dell'Argentiera
Ósilo
Óschiri
Fertília
Ittiri
L. di Coghinas
Alghero
Pattada
Posada
Villanova Monteleone
Bósa
1259
Buddusó
Siniscóla
C. Comino
Temo
Bonorva
Bitti
Orune
Macomer
Nuoro
Dorgali
Ghilarza
Oliena
Golfo di Orosei
SARDEGNA
L. del Tirso
Fonni
Bauei
C. Mannu
Sorgono
Monti del Gennargentu
1834
C. di Monte Santu
Oristano
Láconi
Cábras
M. Arci
Arbatax
Golfo di Oristano
SARDEGNA
812
Arborea
Láconi
Lanusei
Arborea
Terralba
Nurri
Ierzu
S. Gavino Monreale
Sanluri
Mándas
Gúspini
Arbus
Gonnosfanadiga
Senorbí
S. Vitao
SARDINIA
1236
M. Linas
Villacidro
Serramanna
Doliánova
Muravera
Iglésias
Assémini
Sinnai
1069
C. Ferrato
C. Pécora
Gonnesa
Siliqua
Sestu
Cíxerri
Fluminimaggiore
Villamassargia
Quartu Sant'Elena
Portoscuso
Carloforte
Carbónia
Cágliari
Serpentara
San Pietro
Sant'Antioco
1116
Santadi
Golfo di Cágliari
Sant' Antíoco
Porto Botte
Pula
C. Carbonara
G. di Palmas
Teulada
C. Spartivento

TYRRHENIAN SEA
3719
3589

ROMA area (right side):
Golfo di Gaeta
Zannone
Palmarola
Ísole Ponziane
283
Ponza
Ventotene
Terracina
Monte Circeo
541
Sabáudia
Gaeta
Fórmia
1533
Mintúrno
Garigliano
Fondi
Ísola di L.
Mondragone
Ischia
788

D
Ustica

E
Iles de la Galite
C. San Vito
Castellammare del Golfo
C. Gallo
Terrasini
Favorotta
PALERMO
Levanzo
Trápani
Érice
1110
Alcamo
Partinico
Monreale
Bagheria
Ísole Égadi
Maréttimo
Paceco
S. Giuseppe Jato
Míslmeri
Términi I.
Favignana
Calatafimi
Camporeale
Marineo
Belsito
Salemi
Corleone
1613
Marsala
Gibellina
Bisacquino
Prizzi
Lercara Friddi
Alia
Castelvetrano
Partanna
Sambuca di Sicilia
Menfi
Mazara del Vallo
Campobello di Mazara
Belice
Burgio
Mussomeli
Castelter.
San Cato
SICI
Sciacca
Caltabellotta
Platani
Racalmuto
Calt.
Campobello di Mazara
Ribera
Siculiana
Raffadali
Agrigento
Naro
Cattólica Eracléa
Porto Empédocle
Siculiana
Favara
Palma di Montechiaro
Campobello di Lica

Sicilian Channel

F
El Kala
ALGERIA
Tabarka
C. Serrat
C. Blanc
Cani
Bizerte (Binzert)
Plane
Zembra
C. Bon
Menzel-Bourguiba
Mateur
Golfe de Tunis
Téboursouk
Béja
Tébourba
Kelibia
Bou Salem
Medjerda
TUNIS
Halq el Oued
Menzel-Temime
Mejerda
TUNISIA
Soliman
Tébúrsouk
Zaghouan
Hammamet
Nabeul
Pantelleria
836
Pantelleria (It.)
1319
MEDITE

Projection: Conical with two standard parallels

ft	m
9000	3000
6000	2000
4500	1500
3000	1000
1200	400
600	200
0	0
200	600
2000	6000
4000	12,000

m ft

East from Greenwich

1 : 2 000 000

10   0   10   20   30   40   50 miles
10 0 10 20 30 40 50 60 70 80 km

7   8   9   0   11   12

ADRIATIC

SEA

Drini

Shëngjini Lezha Rrësheni
Rubiku
K. iMyzhllit
te Skënderbeut Shijaku DURRËSI
Durrësi Tirana
(Durazzo) (Tiranë)
Kalaja e Turrës Kavaja

Shkumbini Peqini Cërriku

Bishti i Pallës Lushnja A
Fieri ELBASANI
Semani Kuçova L
B E R A T I
Vjosa Berati B
Laguna e Nartës
I. Sazan Vlora (Valona) A
Gjiri i Vlorës Kanina
Kep i Gjuhës Mavrova N
Karaburuni m'e Kendervices 2130
Dukati

A

Bruzzi
Sangro Tigno Montenero
Agnone Guglionesi
Triventa Castelmauro
Casacalenda Santa Croce
Bonefro di Magliano
Molise Torremaggiore
Frosolone Biccari
Isernia Riccia Troia
Campobasso
Benevento
Caserta
Napoli
Torre del Vesuvio
Annunziata 1277 Sarno Nocera
Castellammare Salerno Campagna
Sorrento Battipaglia
Capri Sele Eboli
G. di Salerno Agropoli
Castellabate Capaccio
Punta Licosa Teggiano
Pollica Sala Consilina
Pisciotta Vallo della Lucania
C. Palinuro Camerota
G. di Policastro Maratea
Scalea Mormanno
Lao Verbicaro
Belvedere Fagnano
Marittimo Castello
Cetraro Montalto Uffugo
Páola Fuscaldo
S. Lúcido **CALABRIA**
Fiumefreddo Brúzio Cosenza
Amantea Aprigliano
Nocera Terinese Rogliano
Gizzeria Decollatura
Golfo di Nicastro
Sant'Eufémia Tiriolo
Pizzo Maida
Tropea Girifalco
Capo Vaticano Filadélfia
G. di Gióia Vibo Valéntia
Nicótera Mileto
Rosarno Laureana
Gióia Táuro di Borrello
Taurianova Polistena
Palmi Cittanova
Bagnara Oppido
Villa S. Giov. Mamertino
Messina 1956
Réggio Aspromonte
Péllaro
Palizzi

Isole Eólie o Lípari (Æolian Is.)
926 Strómboli
Filicudi Panarea
Malfa Salina
Alicudi 962 Lípari
602 Lípari
499 Vulcano
Milazzo
Sant'Ágata Barcellona
di Militello Pozzo di Gotto
San Fratello Naso
Montalbano Castroreale
1279
Santo Stefano Mi. Peloritani
di Camastro Santa Teresa
Str. di Messina
Mistretta Tortorici
Castelbuono Troina
Monti Nébrodi
Petralia 1847
Nicosia Cesaró
Leonforte Capizzi
Randazzo 3340
916 Bronte Giarre
Enna Adrano Riposto
Valguarnéra Biancavilla
Pietraperzia Centúripe Acireale
Paternó Belpasso Misterbianco
Piazza Catánia
Aidone Ramacca Golfo di
Mazzarino Palagonia Catánia
Caltagirone Scordia
Grammichele Lentini
Vizzini Carlentini
Niscemi 986 Francofonte
Chiaramonte Augusta
Vittória Cómiso Sortino
Ragusa Siracusa
Módica Noto
Scicli G. di
Pozzallo Ispica Avola
Pachino
C. Passero

Foggia L. di Lésina Sannicandro
Rodi Gargánico
Vico del Gargano Vieste
Monte Gargano
Testa del Gargano
Monte Sant'Ángelo
G. di Manfredónia
Manfredónia
Zapponeta
Margherita di Savoia
Trinitápoli
Barletta
Trani Bisceglie
Andria Molfetta
Bari Giovinazzo
Corato Terlizzi
Ruvo Bitonto
Minervino Bitetto
Murge 686 Palo del Colle
Gravina Altamura
di Púglia Grumo Appula
Casamássima Mola di Bari
Acquaviva Conversano
delle Fonti Monópoli
Castellana Grotte
Putignano Polignano a Mare
Noci Fasano
Gióia Martina Franca
Santéramo Alberobello
Locorotondo Ostuni
Cisternino Céglie Messápico
Mótola Francavilla Fontana
Massafra Mesagne
Grottáglie **Brindisi**
Táranto Oria San Vito dei Normanni
Ginosa Latiano
Palagiano Manduria
Campi Salentina
Sava Squinzano
S. Giórgio Iónico Trepuzzi
Lizzano Leverano
Maruggio **Lecce**
Copertino
Nardò Galatina
Galátone Martano
Gallípoli Máglie Otranto
Parábita C. d'Otranto
Casarano Poggiardo
Rácale Ugento Tricase
Presicce Gagliano del Capo
C. Santa Maria di Leuca

Golfo di Táranto

Erikoúsa
Othonoí Karousádhes
Kassiópi
Samothráki Korakiána
Kérkira Liapádhes Kérkira
(Corfu) Gastoúri
Áyios Matthaíos
Argyrádhes Levkími

C

IONIAN
3065 N
L'Amendolaro Trebisacce
Morano Cassano Iónio
Cálabro Crati
Roggiano Spezzano
Gravina Albanese Coriglianо
Demétrio C. Trionto
Bisignano Rossano
Acri Longobucco
Luzzi Pta. dell'Alice
S. Giovanni Marina di Cirò
in Fiore Cirò
1929 Neto Stróngoli
La Sila Petília Policastro
Croceri Crotone
Mésoraca C. de le Colonne
Sersale Cutro
Catanzaro Ísola di Capo Rizzuto
Tacina C. Rizzuto
Squillace
Golfo di Squillace
Chiaravalle Centrale
Guardavalle
Capa Stilo
Mámmola
Gioiosa Iónica
Siderno Marina
Locri
Bovalino Marina
Ardore Marina

D

SEA

Mediterranean Sea area
Mélito Bova Marina
di Porto Salvo C. Spartivento

E

4116

F

COPYRIGHT, GEORGE PHILIP & SON, LTD.

7   15   8   16   9   17   10   18   11   12

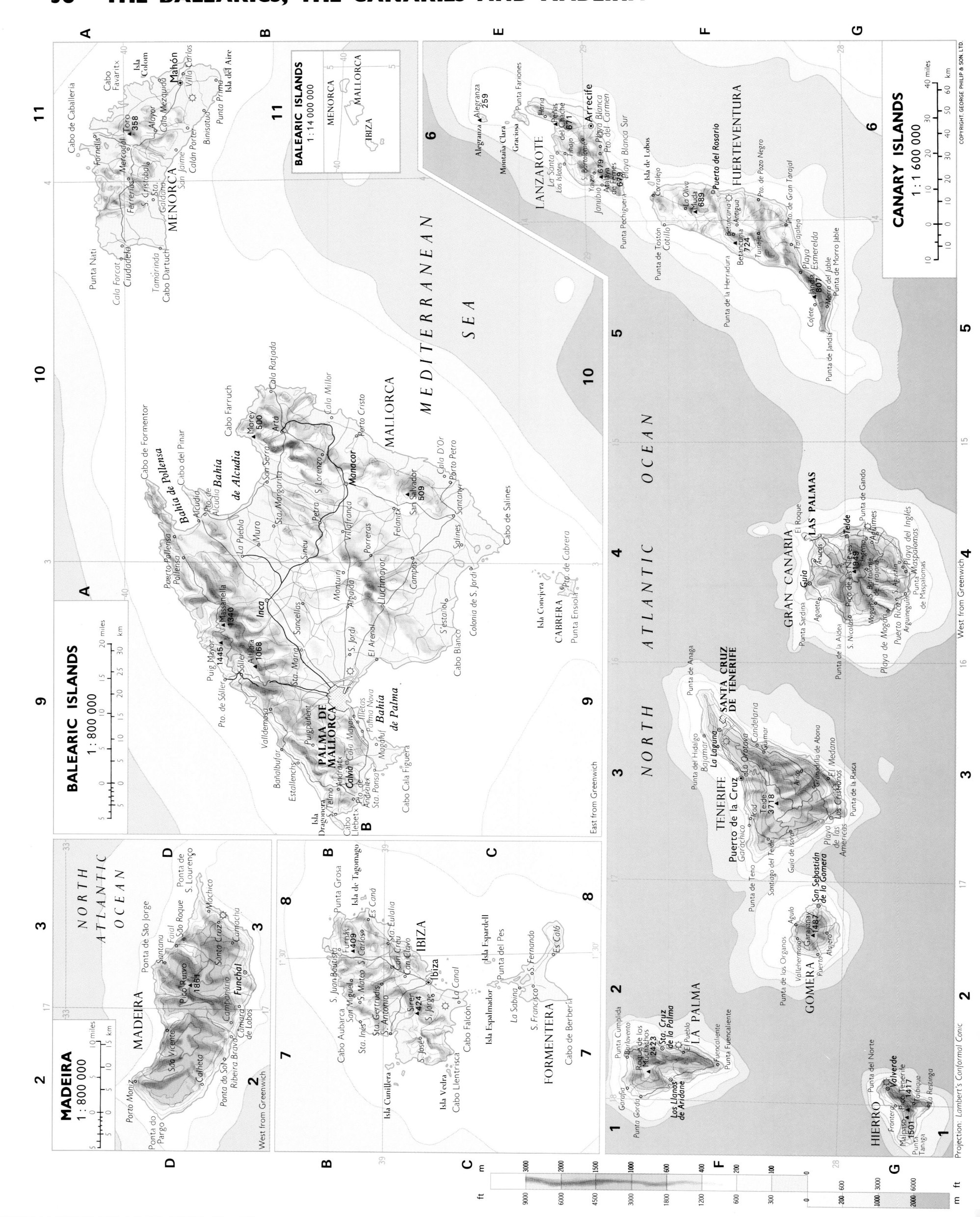

MENORCA

Cabo de Caballería · Fornells · Cabo de Favaritx · Isla Colom · Isla Carlos
Mercadal · Ferrerias · Alayor · Villa Carlos · Mahón
Punta Nati · San Jaime · Calan Porter · Punta Prima · Isla del Aire
Ciudadela · S. Cristobal · Sta. Galdana · Binisafua
Punta Forcat · Cala Forcat · Tamarinda · Cabo Dartuch · Cabo Mezquida
Toro 358

BALEARIC ISLANDS
1:14 000 000

MENORCA · MALLORCA · IBIZA

MALLORCA

Cabo de Formentor · Puerto Pollensa · Pollensa · Cabo del Pinar
Bahía de Pollensa · Bahía de Alcudia
Pto. de Sóller · Puig Mayor 1445 · Masanella 1340 · Inca · Alfabia 1068
Pto. de Alcudia · Alcudia · La Puebla · Muro · Sta. Margarita · San Serra · Cala Ratjada
Sóller · Sta. María · Sineu · Petra · S. Lorenzo · Arta · Morey 500 · Cala Millor
Pto. de Sóller · Bañalbufar · Valldemosa · Estellencs · Sta. Maria · Sancellas · Villafranca · Manacor · Porto Cristo
Puigpuñent · S. Jordi · Montuiri · Porreras · Felanitx · San Salvador 509 · Porto Petro
Andraitx · Calviá · Cala Mayor · Génova · Lluchmayor · Campos · Santany · Cala D'Or
Isla Dragonera · Cabo Llebeitx · Pto. de Andraitx · Sta. Ponsa · Paguera · Palma Nova · Illetas · Magaluf · Bahía de Palma · Salines · Colonia de S. Jordi
PALMA DE MALLORCA · El Arenal · S'estanyol · Colonia de S. Jordi · Cabo de Salines
Cabo Cala Figuera · Cabo Blanco

MEDITERRANEAN SEA

CABRERA
Isla Conejera · Pto. de Cabrera · Punta Ensiola

BALEARIC ISLANDS
1:800 000
20 miles · 30 km

IBIZA
Punta Grosa · Isla de Tagomago · Es Caná
Cabo Aubarca · S. Juan Bautista · Furnás 409 · S. Carlos
Sta. Inés · S. Miguel · S. Mateo · S. Vicente · S. Cristóbal · Sta. Eulalia
Isla Cunillera · S. Antonio · Sta. Gertrudis · San Cruz · Sirer 424 · Can Clavo
San Jorge · IBIZA
Isla Vedra · Cabo Llentrisca · Tosals · Ibiza
Cabo Falcón · Isla Espalmador · La Sabina · S. Francisco · Es Caló
Cabo de Berberih · FORMENTERA · Cabo de la Mola
Isla Espardell · Punta del Pes · S. Fernando
Isla del Pes · La Canal

MADEIRA
1:800 000
10 miles · 15 km

NORTH ATLANTIC OCEAN

MADEIRA
Porto Moniz · Ponta de Sao Jorge · Ponta de S. Lourenço · Punta de S. Lourenço
Santana · Faial · São Roque · Machico
Seixal · Sta. Cruz · Cumacha · Camacha
Pico Ruivo 1861 · Camara de Lobos · Funchal
Ponta do Sol · Ribeira Brava
Ponta do Pargo · S. Vicente · Cámara
Calheta

CANARY ISLANDS
1:1 600 000

LANZAROTE
Alegranza 259 · Montaña Clara · Graciosa · Punta Fariones
La Santa · Los Islotes · Haria · Peñas del Chache 671 · Punta Blanca
Cotillo · Yaiza · Puerto del Carmen · Arrecife · Pto. del Carmen
Janubio 619 · Atalaya 609 · Tinajo 609
Playa Blanca · Playa Blanca Sur · Isla de Lobos
Punta de Tostón

FUERTEVENTURA
La Oliva 689 · Corralejo · Puerto del Rosario
Betancuria · Antigua · Muda 724 · Tuineje
Punta de la Herradura · Pto. de Gran Tarajal
Betancuria · Pájara · Tarajalejo
Punta de Jandía · Cofete · Jandía 807 · Playa · Esmeralda · Morro del Jable · Punta de Morro Jable

GRAN CANARIA
El Roque · LAS PALMAS · Punta de Gando
Guía · Arucas · Telde · Playa del Inglés
Punta Sardina · Pico de las Nieves 1949 · Aguimes
S. Nicolás · S. Bartolomé de Tirajana · S. Agustín
Punta de la Aldea · Mogán · Puerto Rico · Punta Maspalomas · Playa de Maspalomas
Playa de Mogán · Arguineguín

TENERIFE
Punta de Anaga · SANTA CRUZ DE TENERIFE
Punta del Hidalgo · Bajamar · La Laguna · Candelaria
La Orotava · Güimar
Puerto de la Cruz · Teide 3718 · Granadilla de Abona
Garachico · Icod · El Médano
Punta de Teno · Guía de Isora · Playa de los Cristianos · Punta de la Rasca
Santiago del Teide · Playa de las Américas

LA PALMA
Punta Cumplida · Barlovento · Sta. Cruz de la Palma
Punta Gorda · Roque de los Muchachos 2423 · El Pueblo
Garafía · Puntagorda · Los Llanos de Aridane · Fuencaliente
Punta Fuencaliente

GOMERA
Agulo · Vallehermoso · San Sebastián de la Gomera
Punta de los Órganos · Garajonay 1487
Chipude · Playa de Santiago · Alajeró

HIERRO
Punta del Norte · Valverde
Frontera · Mocanal · Pico de Tenerife 1417
Malpaso 1501 · Pinar · La Restinga · Sabinosa
Punta Tanga

EAST FROM GREENWICH · WEST FROM GREENWICH · NORTH ATLANTIC OCEAN

COPYRIGHT, GEORGE PHILIP & SON, LTD.
Projection: Lambert's Conformal Conic

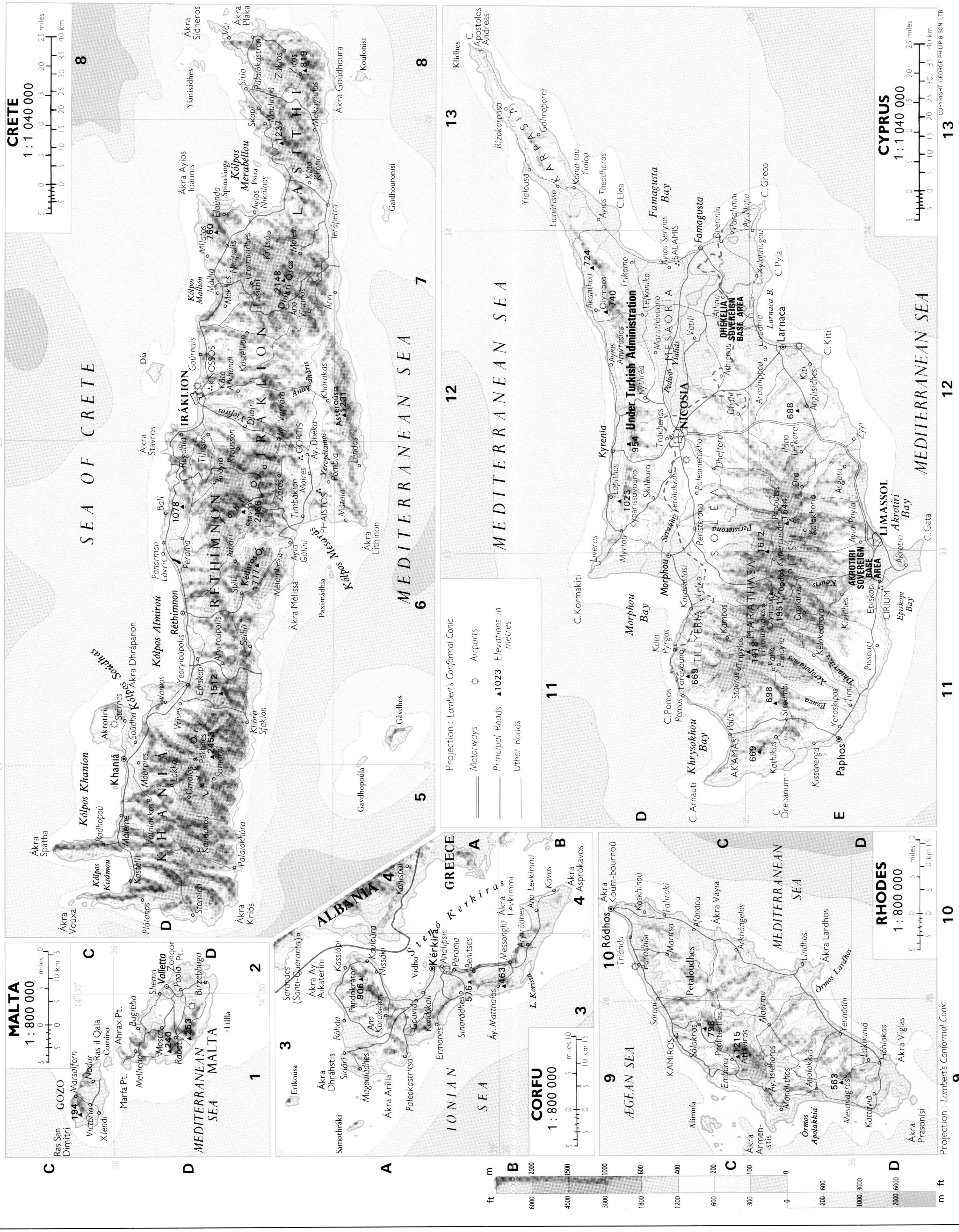

CRETE
1 : 1 040 000
SEA OF CRETE
MEDITERRANEAN SEA
KHANIÁ
RÉTHIMNON
IRÁKLION
LASÍTHI
Khaniá
Réthimnon
Iráklion
Knossós
Áy. Nikólaos
Ierápetra
Sitía
Gávdhos
Día
MALTA
1 : 800 000
GOZO
Valletta
Comino
MEDITERRANEAN SEA
CORFU
1 : 800 000
ALBANIA
GREECE
IONIAN SEA
Kérkira
RHODES
1 : 800 000
AEGEAN SEA
MEDITERRANEAN SEA
Ródhos
Líndhos
CYPRUS
1 : 1 040 000
MEDITERRANEAN SEA
NICOSIA
Under Turkish Administration
Famagusta
Famagusta Bay
Larnaca
LIMASSOL
Paphos
Kyrenia
Morphou Bay
Khrysokhou Bay
AKROTIRI SOVEREIGN BASE AREA
DHEKELIA SOVEREIGN BASE AREA
Olympus 1951
Projection : Lambert's Conformal Conic
Motorways
Principal Roads
Other Roads
Airports
1023 Elevations in metres
Projection : Lambert's Conformal Conic
COPYRIGHT, GEORGE PHILIP & SON, LTD.

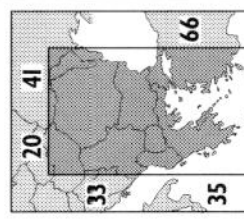

UKRAINE
MOLDOVA
ROMANIA
BULGARIA
YUGOSLAVIA
HUNGARY
BOSNIA-HERZ.
MONTENEGRO
SLOVAK REP.
BLACK SEA
TRANSILVANIA
MOLDAVIA
BESSARABIA
DOBRUJA
WALACHIA
CARPAȚII MERIDIONALI (Transylvanian Alps)
Munții Apuseni
Stara Planina
Sredna Gora
Kopaonik
KOSOVO
VOJVODINA
BUCUREȘTI (Bucharest)
BUDAPEST
BEOGRAD
SOFIYA
Chișinău
Cluj-Napoca
Timișoara
Constanța
Varna
Burgas
Debrecen
Szeged
Craiova
Iași
Galați
Brăila
Brașov
Ploiești
Novi Sad
Dunărea (Danube)
Duna (Danube)
Dunav
Tisa
Prut
Siret
Mureș
Olt
Iskar
Maritsa
Morava
A B C D E F G
1 2 3 4 5 6 7 8 9 10 11 12

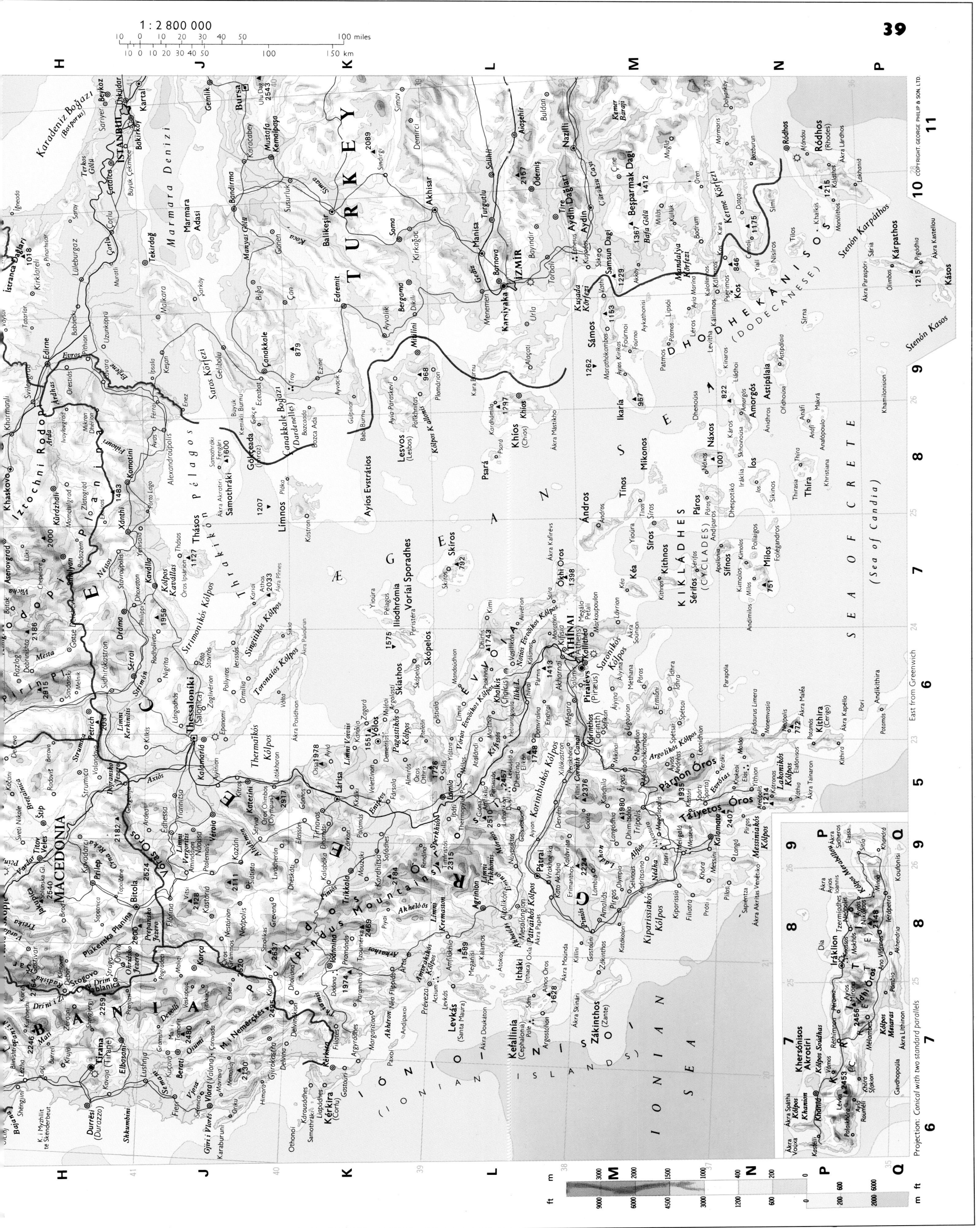

1 : 4 000 000

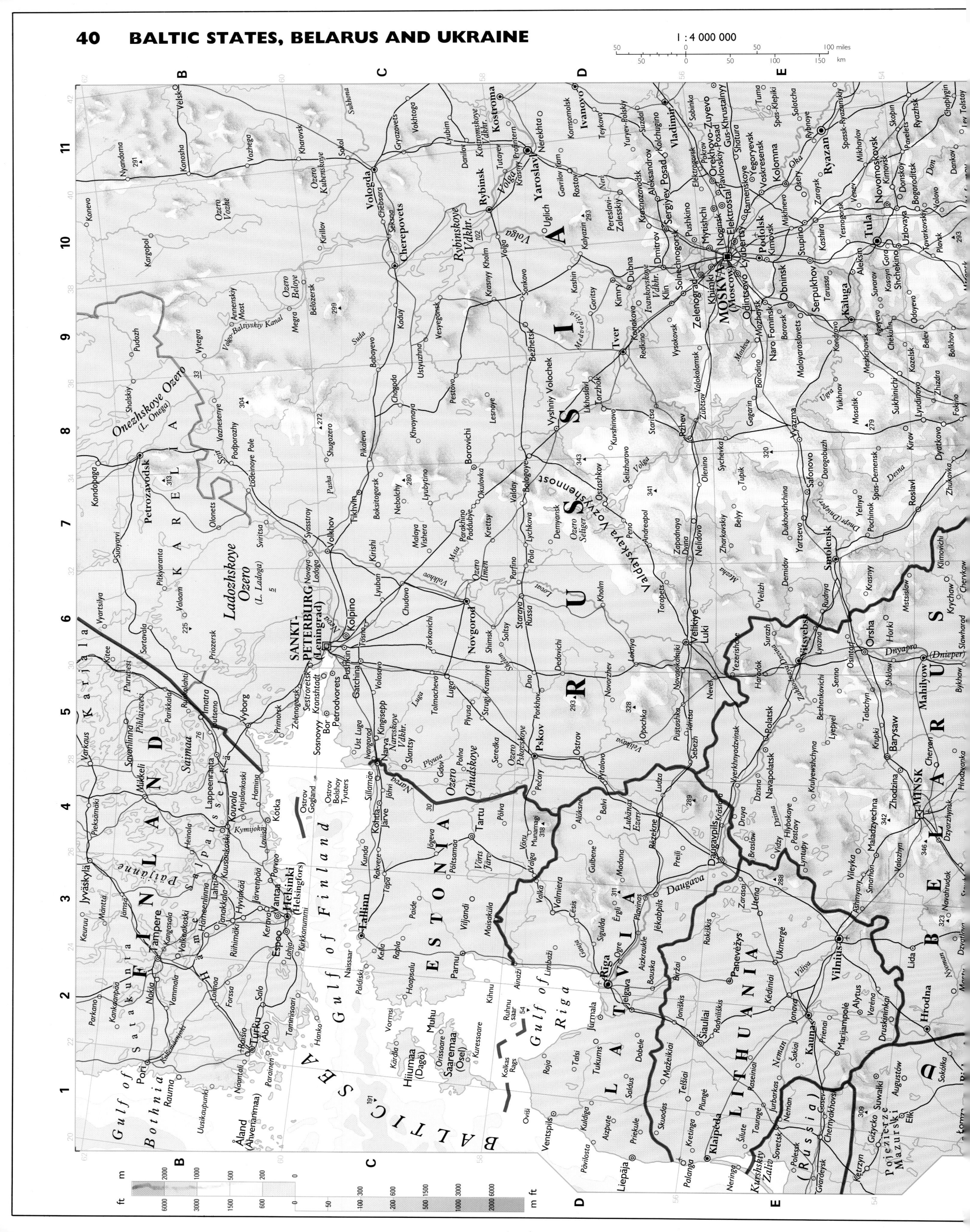

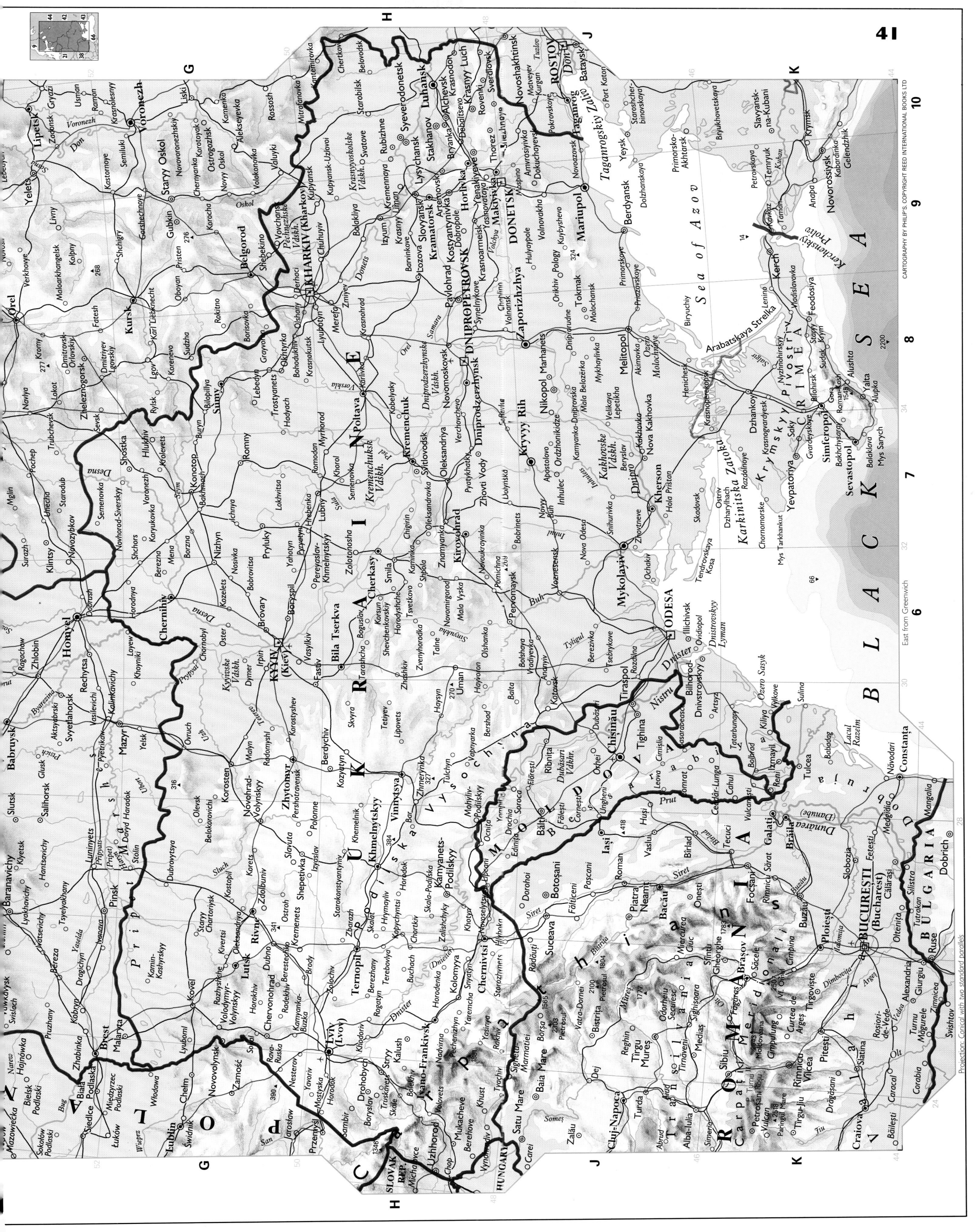

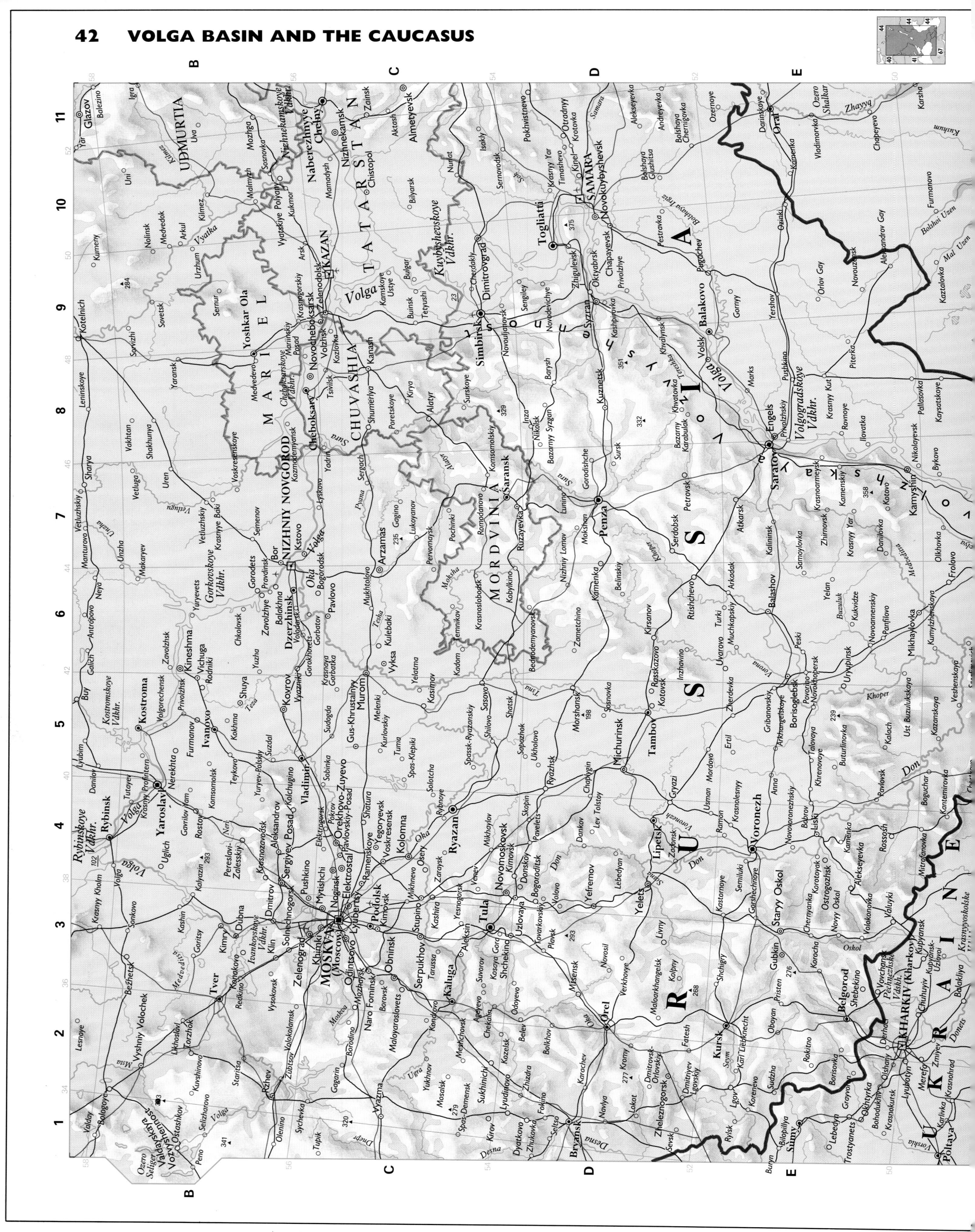

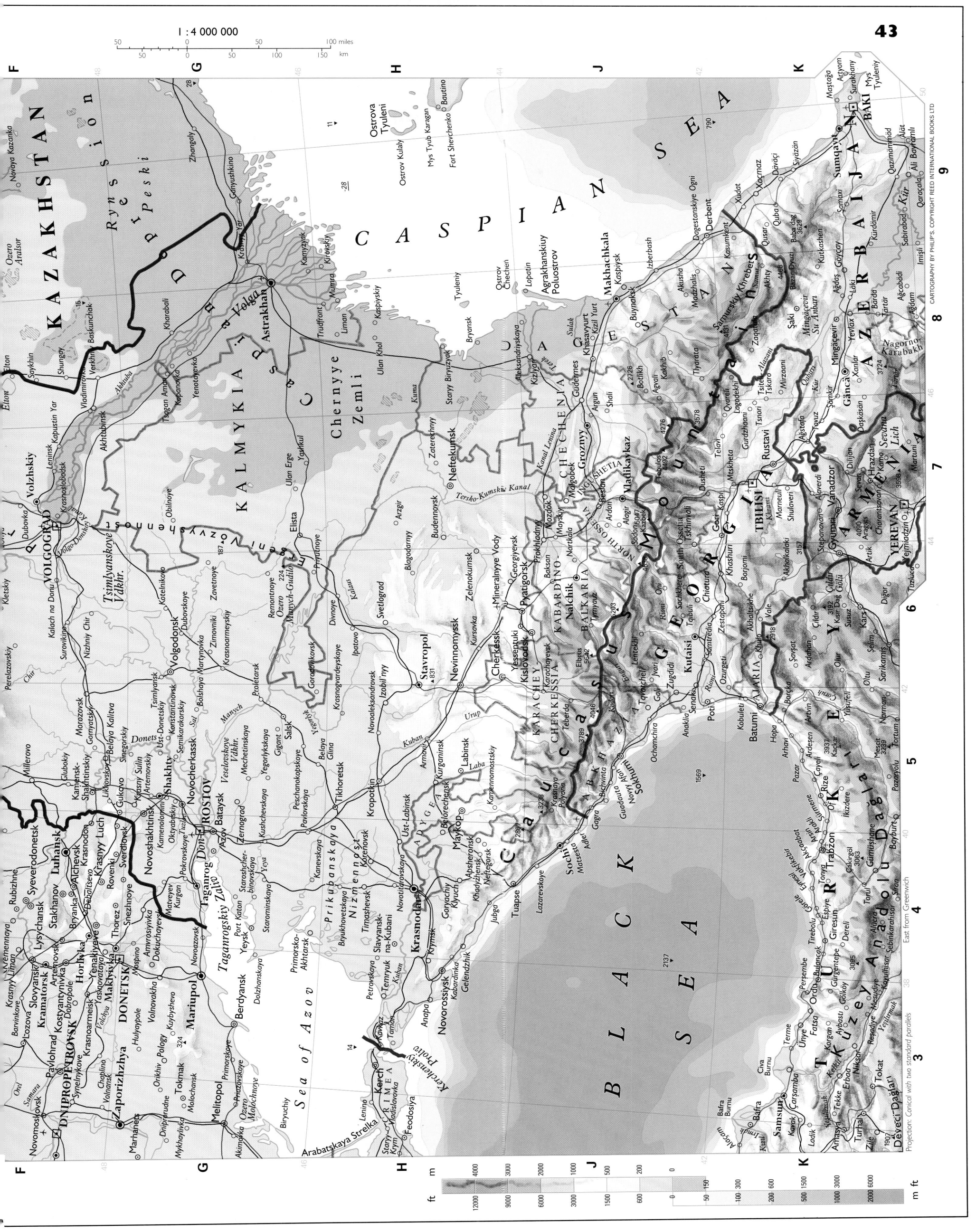

43

1 : 4 000 000

KAZAKHSTAN

CASPIAN SEA

BLACK SEA

Sea of Azov

AZERBAIJAN

ARMENIA

GEORGIA

DAGESTAN

KALMYKIA

VOLGOGRAD

ROSTOV

DONETSK

Astrakhan

Volga

BAKI

Sumqayıt

TBILISI

YEREVAN

Krasnodar

Stavropol

Grozny

Vladikavkaz

CHECHENIA

NORTH OSSETIA

KABARDINO-BALKARIA

KARACHEY-CHERKESSIA

ADYGEA

INGUSHETIA

Nagorno-Karabakh

Caucasus Mountains

Bolşoy Kavkaz

TÜRKİYE

KUZEY ANADOLU

Projection: Conic with two standard parallels

East from Greenwich

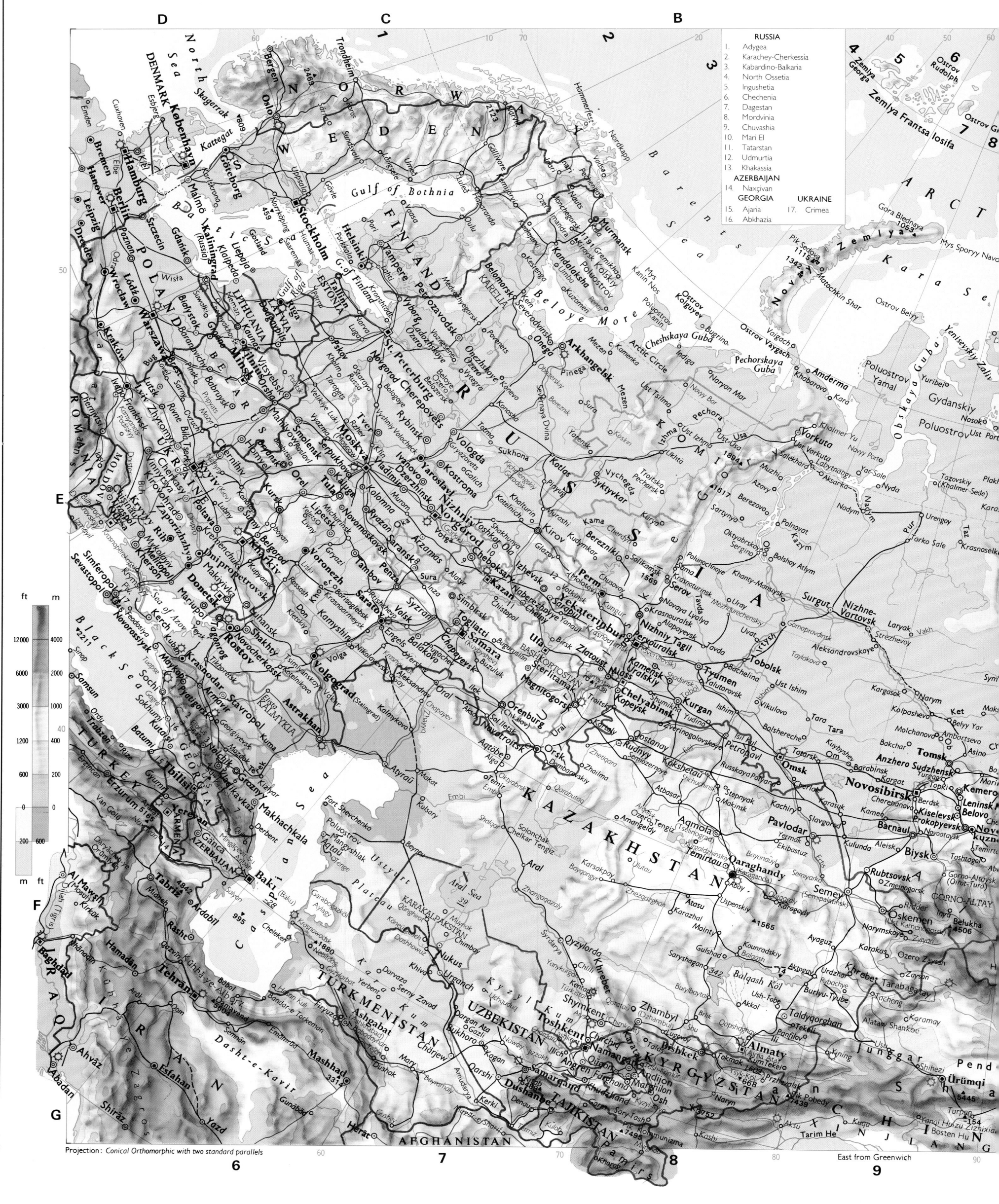

RUSSIA
1. Adygea
2. Karachey-Cherkessia
3. Kabardino-Balkaria
4. North Ossetia
5. Ingushetia
6. Chechenia
7. Dagestan
8. Mordvinia
9. Chuvashia
10. Mari El
11. Tatarstan
12. Udmurtia
13. Khakassia

AZERBAIJAN
14. Naxçivan

GEORGIA   UKRAINE
15. Ajaria   17. Crimea
16. Abkhazia

Projection: Conical Orthomorphic with two standard parallels

East from Greenwich

1 : 16 000 000

100   0   100   200   300   400 miles
100 0 100 200 300 400 500 600 km

A   B   C

D

E

F

A   B   C

9 10 11 12 13 14 15 16 17 18 19

OCEAN

Lapte v Novosibirskiye Ostrova

East Siberian Sea

Chukchi Sea

Bering Sea

Ostrov Shmidta
Mys Arkticheskiy
Ostrov Komsomolets
Ostrov Pioner
Ostrov Oktyabrskoy Revolyutsii
965
Ostrov Bolshevik
Severnaya Zemlya
Proliv Vilkitskogo

Mys Dezhneva (East C.)
Uelen
Egvekinot
Provideniya
Anadyrskiy Zaliv
St. Lawrence I. (U.S.A.)

Polu ostrov Taymyr
Goryu Byrranga
1146
Nordvik
Oz. Taymyr

Ostrov Belkovskiy
Ostrov Kotelnyy
Ostrov Stolbovoy
Lyakhovskiye Ostrova
Proliv Dmitriya Lapteva
374

Ostrova Medvezhi

Chukotskoye Nagorye
1843
Pevek
Ust-Chaun
Anadyr
2562

Norilsk
Gory Putorana
1701

Tiksi
Ust Olenek
Bulun
Tit-Ary
Nizhneyansk

Srednekolymsk
Nizhne Kolymsk
Kolyma
Pogeda 3147

Omolon
Bolshoy Anyuy
742

Gizhiga
Penzhinskaya Guba

Koryakskoye Nagorye

Arctic Circle
962

Verkhoyansk
2389
Khrebet Cherskogo
Gora Chen 2882

Magadan

Poluostrov Kamchatka
Kluchevskaya
2562
Petropavlovsk-Kamchatskiy
3456

Yakutsk
Olekminsk

Okhotsk

Sea of Okhotsk

1780

Komandorskiye Ostrova

Vilyuysk

Aldan
2246
2482

Nikolayevsk-na-Am
Okha
Sakhalin
Aleksandrovsk-Sakhalinskiy

Ostrov Paramushir
Ostrov Onekotan

Bratsk
Krasnoyarsk
Kansk
Nizhneudinsk
Tayshet

Stanovoy Khrebet
Tynda
Skovorodino

Komsomolsk
2026
Khrebet Dzhugdzur

Yuzhno-Sakhalinsk
Kurilskiye Ostrova
Ostrov Iturup
Ostrov Kunashir

Kirensk
Ust-Kut

Chita
Angarsk
Irkutsk
Ulan Ude

Yablonovyy Khrebet
Stanovoy Khrebet
Nerchinsk

Blagoveshchensk
1054
Amur

Birobidzhan
Khabarovsk
Komsomolsk
2078

Khrebet Sikhote Alin
3669

Sovetskaya Gavan
Sakhalin

Hokkaido
Sapporo
Hakodate

MONGOLIA
Ulaanbaatar (Ulan Bator)
2800
Hentiyn Nuruu
Hangayn Nuruu

Qiqihar
Harbin
Jiamusi

Ussuriysk
Vladivostok
Nakhodka

Sea of JAPAN
JAPAN
Honshū

3957
Edrengiyn Nuruu
GOBI DESERT

Changchun
Jilin
2744
Chongjin

Niigata

4 266
Hami

Baotou Hohhot
Zhangjiakou
Beijing

Shenyang
Fushun
Anshan
Dandong
Dalian

NORTH KOREA
P'yongyang
Wŏnsan

Sŏul
SOUTH KOREA
Inch'on
Taejŏn
Taegu
Pusan

Kanazawa
To-yama

Boundaries of Republics

COPYRIGHT. GEORGE PHILIP & SON. LTD.

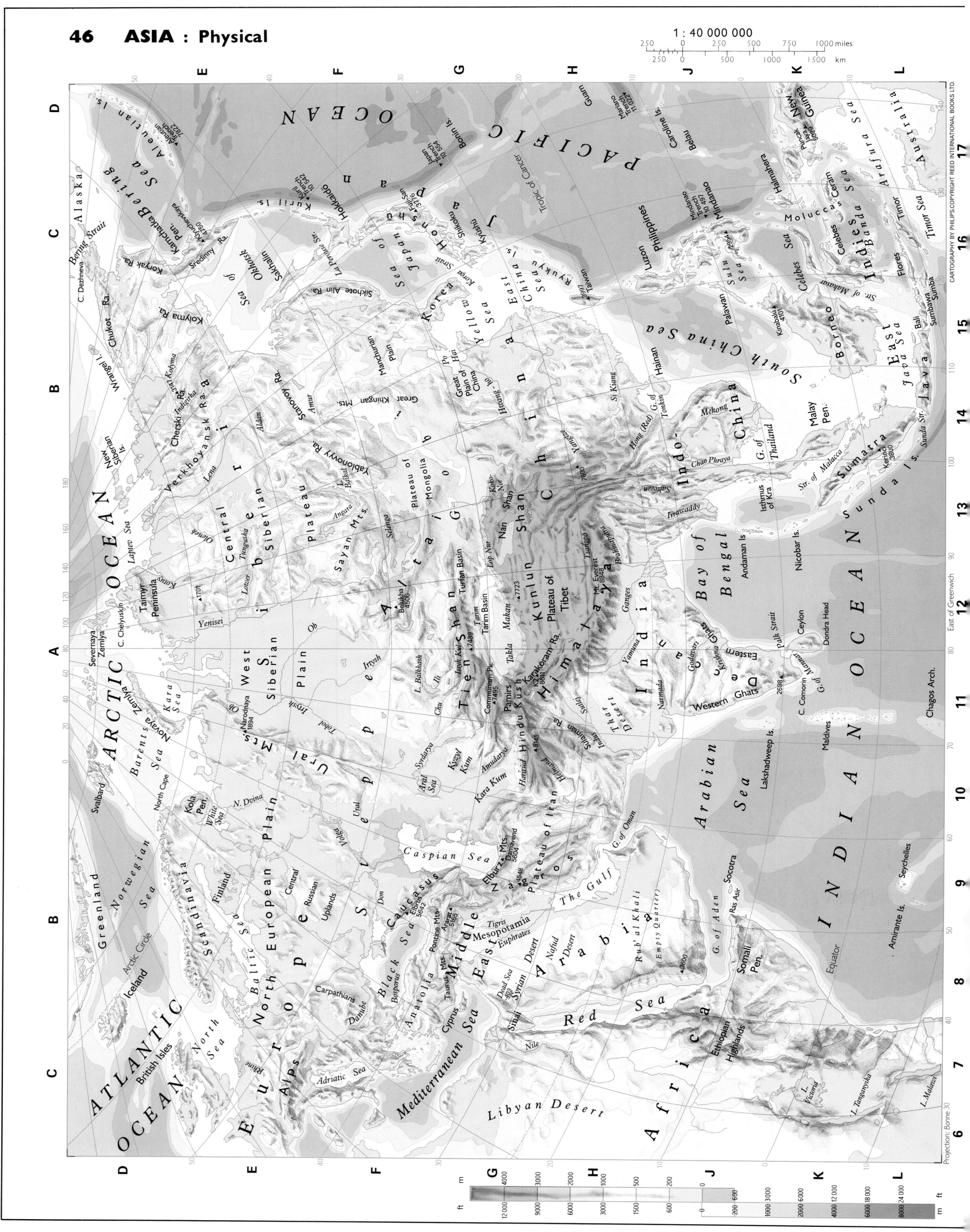

1 : 40 000 000

250   0   250   500   750   1000 miles

250   0   500   1000   1500 km

CARTOGRAPHY BY PHILIP'S.COPYRIGHT REED INTERNATIONAL BOOKS LTD.

Projection: Bonne 30

East of Greenwich

m
4000
3000
2000
1000
500
200
0
200   600
1000 3000
2000 6000
4000 12 000
6000 18 000
8000 24 000
ft

ft
12 000
9000
6000
3000
1500
600
0
m

PACIFIC OCEAN

ARCTIC OCEAN

ATLANTIC OCEAN

INDIAN OCEAN

Europe

Asia

Africa

China

India

Arabia

Himalaya

Bering Sea

Sea of Okhotsk

Sea of Japan

Yellow Sea

East China Sea

South China Sea

Bay of Bengal

Arabian Sea

Caspian Sea

Black Sea

Mediterranean Sea

Red Sea

Greenland Sea

Norwegian Sea

Baltic Sea

North Sea

Adriatic Sea

Plateau of Tibet

Plateau of Iran

Plateau of Mongolia

West Siberian Plain

Central Siberian Plateau

North European Plain

Steppe

Mesopotamia

Tarim Basin

Turfan Basin

Libyan Desert

Syrian Desert

Thar Desert

Rub' al Khali (Empty Quarter)

Nafud Desert

Kara Kum

Kizyl Kum

Takla Makan

Mt. Everest 8848

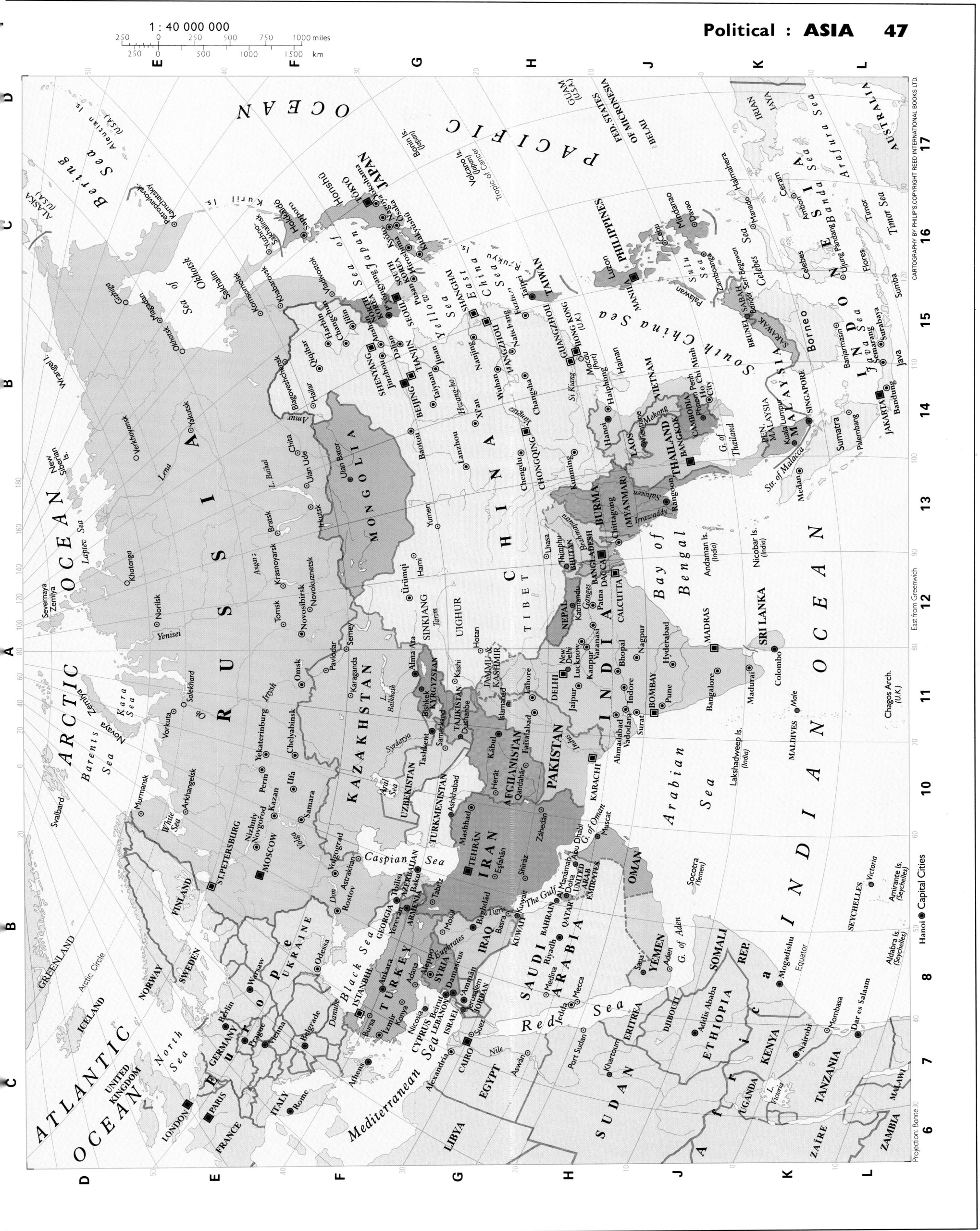

1 : 40 000 000

250   0   250   500   750   1000 miles
250   0   500   1000   1500 km

Projection: Bonne

Hanoi ● Capital Cities

East from Greenwich

PACIFIC

OCEAN

ATLANTIC

OCEAN

ARCTIC

OCEAN

INDIAN OCEAN

R U S S I A

C H I N A

MONGOLIA

KAZAKHSTAN

INDIA

IRAN

SAUDI ARABIA

PAKISTAN

AFGHANISTAN

INDONESIA

JAPAN

MALAYSIA

THAILAND

BURMA (MYANMAR)

VIETNAM

LAOS

CAMBODIA

PHILIPPINES

AUSTRALIA

TAIWAN

SRI LANKA

MALDIVES

SEYCHELLES

OMAN

YEMEN

IRAQ

SYRIA

TURKEY

UKRAINE

GERMANY

FRANCE

UNITED KINGDOM

NORWAY

SWEDEN

FINLAND

ICELAND

GREENLAND

EGYPT

SUDAN

ETHIOPIA

KENYA

TANZANIA

SOMALI REP.

ERITREA

DJIBOUTI

UGANDA

ZAIRE

ZAMBIA

MALAWI

LIBYA

UZBEKISTAN

TURKMENISTAN

KIRGYZSTAN

TAJIKISTAN

AZERBAIJAN

GEORGIA

ARMENIA

NEPAL

BHUTAN

BANGLADESH

JAMMU & KASHMIR

UNITED ARAB EMIRATES

QATAR

BAHRAIN

KUWAIT

JORDAN

ISRAEL

LEBANON

CYPRUS

BRUNEI

SABAH

SARAWAK

FED. STATES OF MICRONESIA

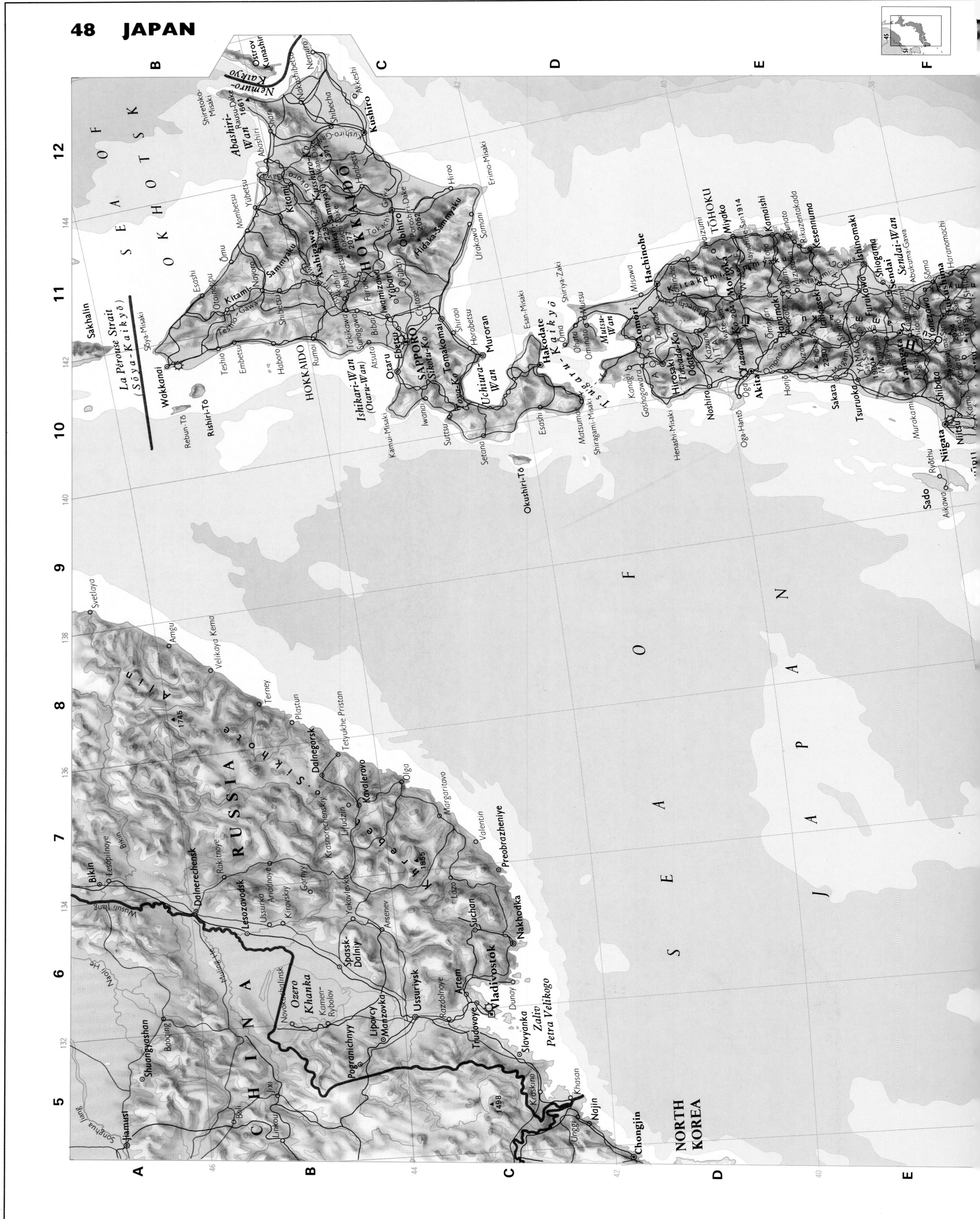

SEA OF OKHOTSK

Ostrov Kunashir
Nemuro-Kaikyō

Shiretoko-Misaki
Abashiri-Wan
Rausu-Dake 1661
Abashiri
Nokkamappu
Shari
Nemuro
Shibetsu
Akkeshi
Kushiro-Gawa
Kushiro

Sakhalin

Sōya-Misaki

La Pérouse Strait
(Sōya-Kaikyō)

Wakkanai

Rebun-Tō
Rishiri-Tō

Esashi

HOKKAIDO

Ōmu
Mombetsu
Yūbetsu
Kitami
Nayoro
Asahigawa 2290
Daisetsu-San 2291
Tokachi-Dake 2077
Kitami
Sammyaku
Teshio
Sammyaku
Asahikawa
Bihoro
Nōbori
Toyokoro
Obihiro 2052
Hidaka-Sammyaku
Poroshiri-Dake 2052
Hiroo
Erimo-Misaki

HOKKAIDO

Teshio
Embetsu
Haboro
Rumoi
Ishikari-Wan
(Otaru-Wan)
Otaru
Ebetsu
SAPPORO
Shikotu-Ko
Tomakomai
Iwamizawa
Takikawa
Sunagawa
Atsuta
Bibai
Furano
Chitose
Tokachi-
Gawa
Urakawa
Samani

Kamui-Misaki
Iwanai
Suttsu
Setana
Shiraoi
Horobetsu
Muroran
Uchiura-
Wan
Shiraoi

Okushiri-Tō

Esashi
Matsumae
Shiragami-Misaki
Matsumae-Misaki

Hakodate
Tsugaru-Kaikyō
Esan-Misaki

Ōma
Shiriya-Zaki

Mutsu-Wan
Mutsu
Ōhata
Ominato

Kanagi
Goshogawara
Hirosaki
Kuroishi
Ōdate

Shiriuchi-Ko

TŌHOKU

Misawa
Hachinohe
Iwaizumi
Miyako

Towada-Ko
Towada
Kamaishi

Noshiro
AMORI
Kitakami
Morioka
Rikuzentakada
Kesennuma

Oga-Hantō
Oga
Akita
Ōmagari
Yokote
Ichinoseki
Ishimaki

Honjō
Yazawa-Ko
Kawabe
Furukawa

Henashi-Misaki

Sakata
Tsuruoka
Yamagata
Shiogama
Sendai-Wan
Sendai
Abukuma-Gawa
Haramomachi

Murakami

Niigata
Niitsu
Shibata
Aikawa
Ryōtsu
Sado

NORTH KOREA

Chongjin
Najin
Unggi
Khasan

CHINA

Jiamusi
Shuangyashan
Boqing
Jixi
Linkou
Muling

RUSSIA

Svetlaya
Amgu
Velikaya Kema
Terney
Plastun
Tetyukhe Pristan
Dalnegorsk
Olga
Margaritovo
Valentin
Preobrazheniye

Sikhote Alin

1745
1855

Bikin
Lesopilnoye
Bikin
Dalnerechensk
Rokitnoye
Gornyi
Krasnorechenskiy
Litudzin
Kavalerovo
Lozo

Lesozavodsk
Ussurka
Kirovskiy
Ariadnoye
Arsenev
Suchan

Spassk-
Dalniy
Novostroika
Yakovlevka
Razdolnoye
Artem

Ozero
Khanka
Kamen-
Rybolov
Lipovcy
Matzovka
Ussuriysk
Trudovoye
Nakhodka

Pogranichnyy

Vladivostok
Dunay
Slavyanka
Zaliv
Petra Velikogo

Kroskino

SEA OF JAPAN

1 : 4 000 000

50   G   0   50   100 miles
50   0   50   100   150 km

H

J

K

10

RYUKYU ISLANDS
on same scale

K   L   M

4

Kikaiga-Shima
Amami-Ō-Shima   Kakeroma-Jima
Uke-Shima
KAGOSHIMA   Tokuno-Shima

Okino-erabu-Shima

Iheya-Shima   Yoron-Jima
Izena-Shima
Ii-Shima   OKINAWA   Okinawa-Jima
Naha   Koza
Kume-Shima   Kerama-
Retto
Tokashiki-Shima

East from Greenwich

3

Tori-Shima

Sōfu-Gan

PACIFIC OCEAN

Hachijō-Jima

Aoga-Shima

Niijima   Izu-Shotō

Miyake-Jima

Irō-Zaki

Nojima-Zaki

Ō-Shima

TOKYO   HKAWASAKI
YOKOHAMA   Yokosuka
Odawara   Tateyama
Atami

KANTŌ

Chōshi
Kisarazu
Chiba   HIBA

SOUTH KOREA

Tsushima

Ullung Do

Tok Do

Pohang

L

M

Senkaku-Shotō

Uotsuri-Shima
Kobi-Sho

N a n s e i

Sakishima-Guntō

Tarama-Jima   Miyako-Jima
Yonaguni-Jima   Irabu-Jima
Iriomote-   Miyako-Rettō
Jima   Kuro-Shima
Ishigaki-Shima
Yaeyama-Rettō
Hateruma-Shima

Projection: Conical with two standard parallels

2

1

124

126

128

130

Tokara-Rettō

Satsunan-Shotō

Kuchino-erabu-
Jima

Nakano-Shima
Suwanose-Shima
Akuseki-Shima

Uji-Guntō
Kuro-Shima

Koshiki-
Rettō

Ōsumi-Kaikyō
Tane-ga-
Shima

Yaku-
Shima

Miyanoura-Dake

Ōsumi-
Shotō

Nishin'omote

Take-Shima

KYŪSHŪ

FUKUOKA
KITAKYŪSHŪ
Shimonoseki

Nagasaki

Gotō-
Rettō
Fukue-Shima

KUMAMOTO
KAGOSHIMA

Miyazaki

9

8

7

6

5

4

F   G   H

MONGOLIA

ÖVÖR HANGAY
Arts Bogd Uul
▲3682

DUNDGOVĬ
Mandalgovi
Saykhan-Ovoo
Hanhongor
Ulaan Nuur
Bayandalay
▲2825
Dalandzadgad
Tsogttsetsiy
Huld
Manlay
Öndörshil
Delgerhet
Hongor
Dong Ujimqin
Dariganga

SÜHBAATAR
Ongon
Saynshand

ÖMNÖGOVĬ
Noyon
Nomgon
Hanbogd
Bayan-Ovoo
Hatanbulag
Mandah
Sayhandulaan

DORNOGOVĬ
Erdene
Dzamin Üüd
Ereenhot

Qagan Nur
Dalai Nur
Abagnar
Duolun
Xianghuang Q.
Sonid Youqi

NEI MONGGOL

Bayan Obo
Darhan Muminggan Lianheqi
Siziwang Qi
▲2174
Huade
Shangdu
Guyuan
Zhapnbei
Fengning

Lang Shan
Wuyuan
Hanggin Houqi
Linhe
Dengkou
Urad Qianqi
Shiguaigou
▲2187
Guyang
Wulanbulang
Wuchuan
Daqing Shan
Hohhot
Bikeqi
Tumd Youqi
Baotou (Paot'ou)
Horinger
Togtoh
Liangcheng
Shahukou
Youyu
Fengzhen
Yanggao
Qahar Youyi Zhongqi
Jining
Xinghe
Wanquan
Chongli
Zhangjiakou (Changchiak)
Longguan
Chicheng
Kalgan
Huailai
Yanqing

Yabrai Shan
Jartai
Jiudengkou
▲2149
Mu Us Shamo (Ordos)
Hanggin Qi
Dongsheng
Qingshuihe
Huairen
Datong
Yanggao
Tianzhen
Zhuolu
Huai'an

Alxa Zuoqi (Bayan Hot)
▲3628
3556
Helan Shan
Huinong
Pingluo
Shizuishan
Taole
Uxin Qi
Hequ
Fugu
Pingwang
Shuo Xian
Yangyuan
Yu Xian
Guangling
Lingqiu
Zhuolu
Langxiangzhen
Fengtai

BEIJING
(Peip'ing; Peking)

Mingin
Yinchuan
Hengcheng
Yongning
Guangwu
Wuzhong
Lingwu
Qingtongxia Shuiku
Yanchi
Hongliu He
Yulin
Jia Xian
Kuye He
Huang He (Yellow River)
Shenmu
Baode
Wuzhai
Kelan
Lan Xian
Jingle
Dingxiang
Wutai
▲3058
Fanshi
Fuping
Wan Xian
Quyang
Gaoyang
Baoding

THE GREAT WALL
▲4843
Yitiaoshan
Huang He
Zhongwei
Zhongning
Hui'anbu
Dingbian
Jingbian
Hengshan
Mizhi
Suide
Wubu
Zhongyang
▲2881
TAIYUAN (Yangch'u)
Yuci
Yangquan
Pingding
Shijiazhuang
Zhengding
Anping
Cangzhou

NINGXIA HUIZU ZIZHIQU (aut. reg.)
Heichengzhen
Haiyuan
Zhidan
Ansai
Yan'an
Yanchang
Yonghe
Xixian
Zhaocheng
Fenyang
Pingyao
Taigu
Qi Xian
Jiexiu
Heshun
Yushe
Zuoquan
Xingtai
Shahe
Jize

Lanzhou (Lanchow)
Hekou
Baiyin
Dingxi
Huining
Guyuan
Qingyang
Huan Xian
Heshui
Fu Xian
Ji Xian
Luochuan
Fushan
Yicheng
Qinshui
Gaoping
Changzhi
Lucheng
Hebi
Handan
Fengfeng
Feixiang
Ci Xian
Anyang

Weiyuan
Jingyuan
Tongwei
Longxi
Jingning
▲2912
Watang
Longde
Pingliang
Jingchuan
Jing He
Zhenyuan
Ning Xian
Heshui
Xifengzhen
Huangling
Huanglong
Hejin
Xinjiang
Jishan
Houma
Yuncheng
Wenxi
Jiangxian
Qinyuan
Anze
Tunliu
▲2347
Changzhi
Lingchuan
Hui Xian
Linqi
Xun Xian
Puyang

Tianshui
Gangu
Wushan
Qin'an
Long Xian
Qianyang
Fengxiang
Qishan
Bin Xian
Changwu
Lintong
Yijun
Tongchuan
Chengcheng
Xia Xian
Anyi
Yuanqu
Mianchi
Qinyang
Wen Xian
Yuanyang
Yanjin
Chengwu
Heze
Dingtao

▲3100
Li Xian
Xihe
Zhugqu
Min Xian
Lintao
Wudu
Gangu
Tianshui
Baoji
Mei Xian
Feng Xian
Xianyang
Sanyuan
Gaoling
Weinan
Hua Xian
Huayin
Tongguan
Lingbao
Sanmenxia
Luoyang
Yiyang
Xingyang
Zhengzhou (Chengchow)
Kaifeng
Qi Xian
Cao Xian
Shan Xian

Qinling Shandi
▲3767
XI'AN (Hsian; Sian)
Hu Xian
Zhouzhi
Lantian
Shangxian
Luonan
Luoning
Song Xian
Dengfeng
Baisha
Xinzheng
Weichuan
Sui Xian
Shangqiu

▲3002
Wen Xian
Mian Xian
Baocheng
Yang Xian
Ningshan
Zhen'an
Shan Xian
Shangnan
Xixia
Neixiang
Lushi
Xiping
Pingdingshan
Luohe
Shangshui
Xiangcheng
Fugou
Taikang
Zhecheng
Bo Xian

Hanzhong
Chenggu
Xixiang
Ziyang
Shiquan
Jingziguan
Xichuan
Danfeng
Shanyang
Xunyang
Bainu
Nanyang
Tanghe
Biyang
Zhumadian
Runan
Queshan
Suiping
Wuyang
Fangcheng

Ankang
Han Shui
Hanyin
Ziyang
Xunyang

Qin He
Funiu Shan
Zhongtiao Shan
Taihang Shan
Lüliang Shan

ft m
12,000 4000
9000 3000
6000 2000
4500 1500
3000 1000
1200 400
600 200
0 0
200 600
2000 6000
m ft

1 : 4 800 000

50   0   50   100   150 miles
50   0   50   100   150   200   km

9   10   11   12   13   14   15   16

HEILONGJIANG
Horqin Youyi Qianqi
HARBIN (Ha'erhpin)
Zhenlai   Bin Xian   Yanshou   Jixi
Baicheng   Zhaoyuan   Acheng   Linkou   Turiy Rog
Maoxing   Shuangcheng   Shangzhi   Ozero Khanka
Tuquan   Da'an   Wuchang   Yimianpo   Hengdaohezi   Maqiaohe
Tao'an   Fuyu   Lalin   Mudanjiang   Xiachengzi   R U S S I A
Qian Gorlos   Changchunling   Hailin   Muling   Suifenhe
Shenjingzi   Jiutai   Yushu   Shulan   Suiyang   Dongning   Pokrovka
Nong'an   Dehui   Wulaji   Jiaohe   Dunhua   Wangqing   Golenki
Changling   Jilin (Kirin)   Jingbo Hu   Yanji   Ussuriysk (Voroshilov)
Changchun   Jiaohe   Antu   Helong   Tumen   Krasnino   Razdolnoye
Huaide   Shuangyang   Panshi   Huadian   Mingyuegou   Hunchun   VLADIVOSTOK
Siping   Liaoyuan   Dongfeng   Huinan   Changbai Shan   Musan   Slavyanka
Shuangliao   Lishu   Xifeng   Tonghua   Paektu-san   Puryong   Posyet
Bamiancheng   Zhangwu   Linjiang   Hyesan   Chongjin   Najin

Tieling   Kaiyuan   Fushun   SHENYANG (Mukden)   Benxi   Anshan
LIAONING   Liaoyang   Haicheng   Dandong   Sinuiju
Jinzhou   Jinxi   Yingkou   Liaodong Wan   DALIAN (Lüda)   Lüshun
Bo Hai (Gulf of Chihli)   Korea Bay

NORTH KOREA   Hamhung   Hungnam   Wonsan   SEA OF JAPAN
P'YONGYANG   Chinnampo   Haeju   Kaesong   Panmunjom
Cease-Fire Line   INCH'ON   SEOUL   Chunchon   Kangnung

TIANJIN (Tientsin, T'ienching)   Tangshan   Qinhuangdao
Huang He   Yantai   Weihai   Shandong Bandao   QINGDAO (Ch'ingtao)
Weifang   Zibo   Linyi   Lianyungang (Hsinhailien)

SOUTH KOREA   Suwon   Chonan   Taejon   Taegu   PUSAN
Kunsan   Chonju   Kwangju   Mokpo   Chinju   Masan

HUANG HAI (Yellow Sea)

Cheju-do   Cheju   Ullung-do

JAPAN   Tsushima   Sasebo   Nagasaki   Korea Strait   Tsushima-kaikyo

COPYRIGHT. GEORGE PHILIP & SON. LTD.
East from Greenwich

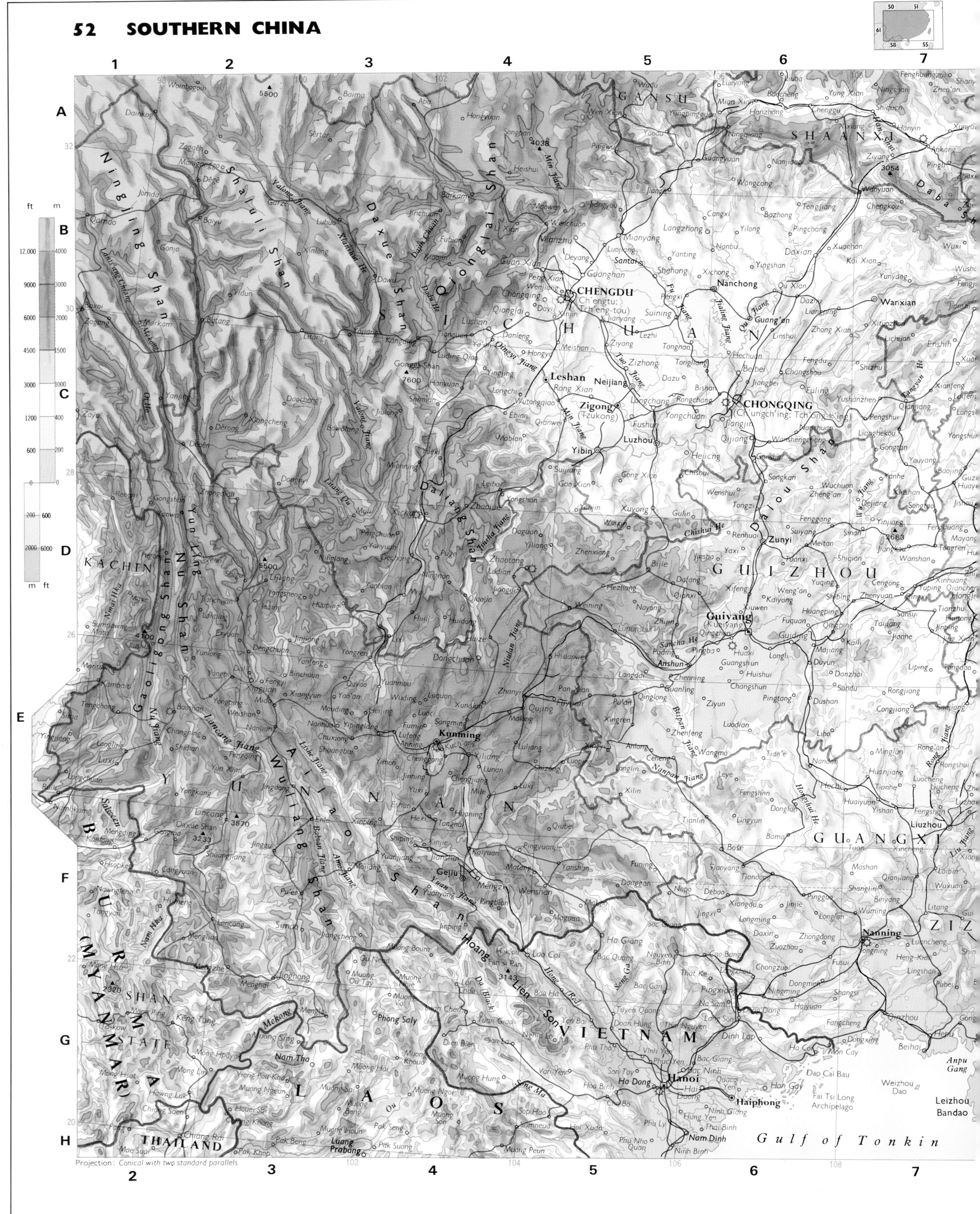

1 : 16 000 000

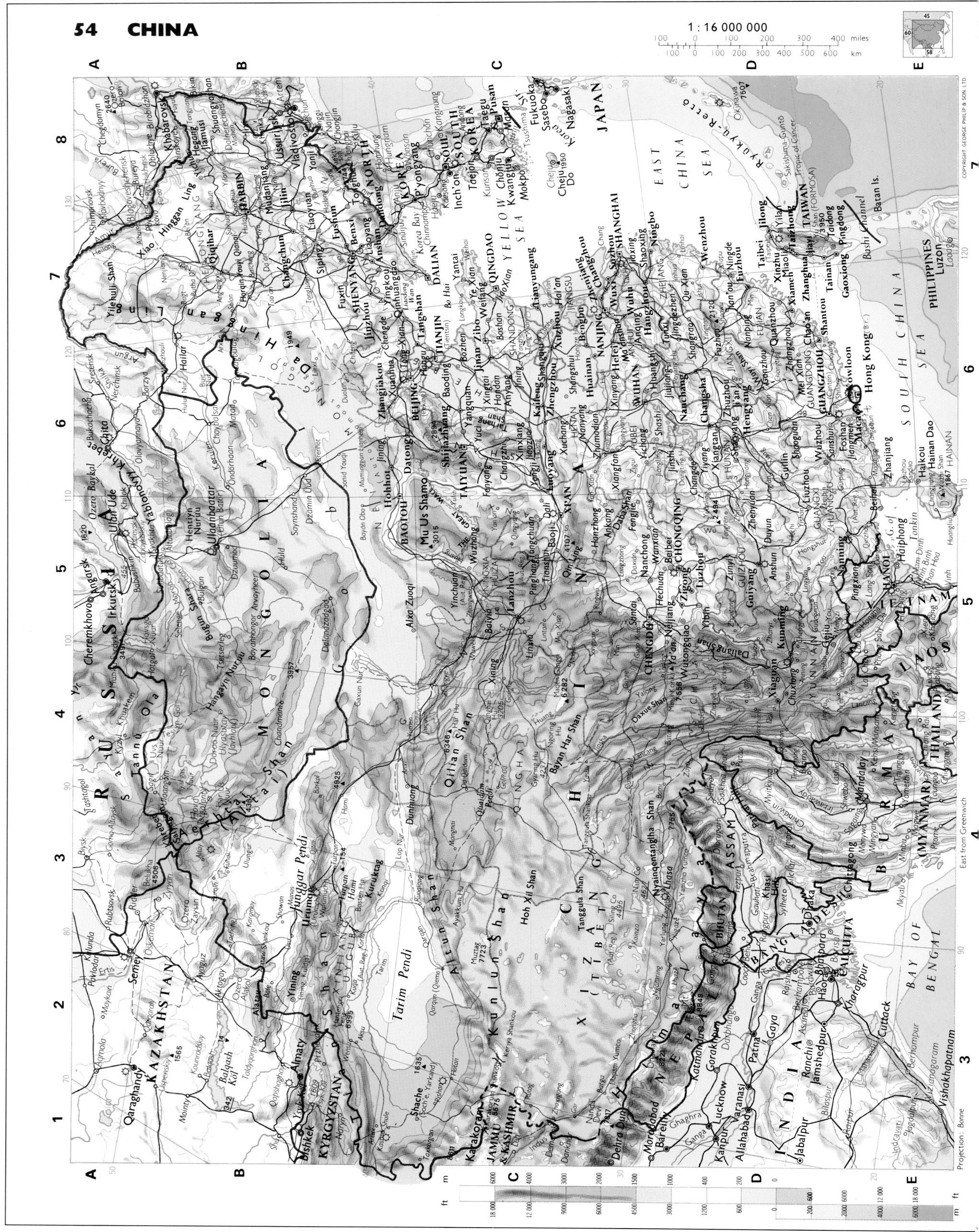

Projection: Bonne

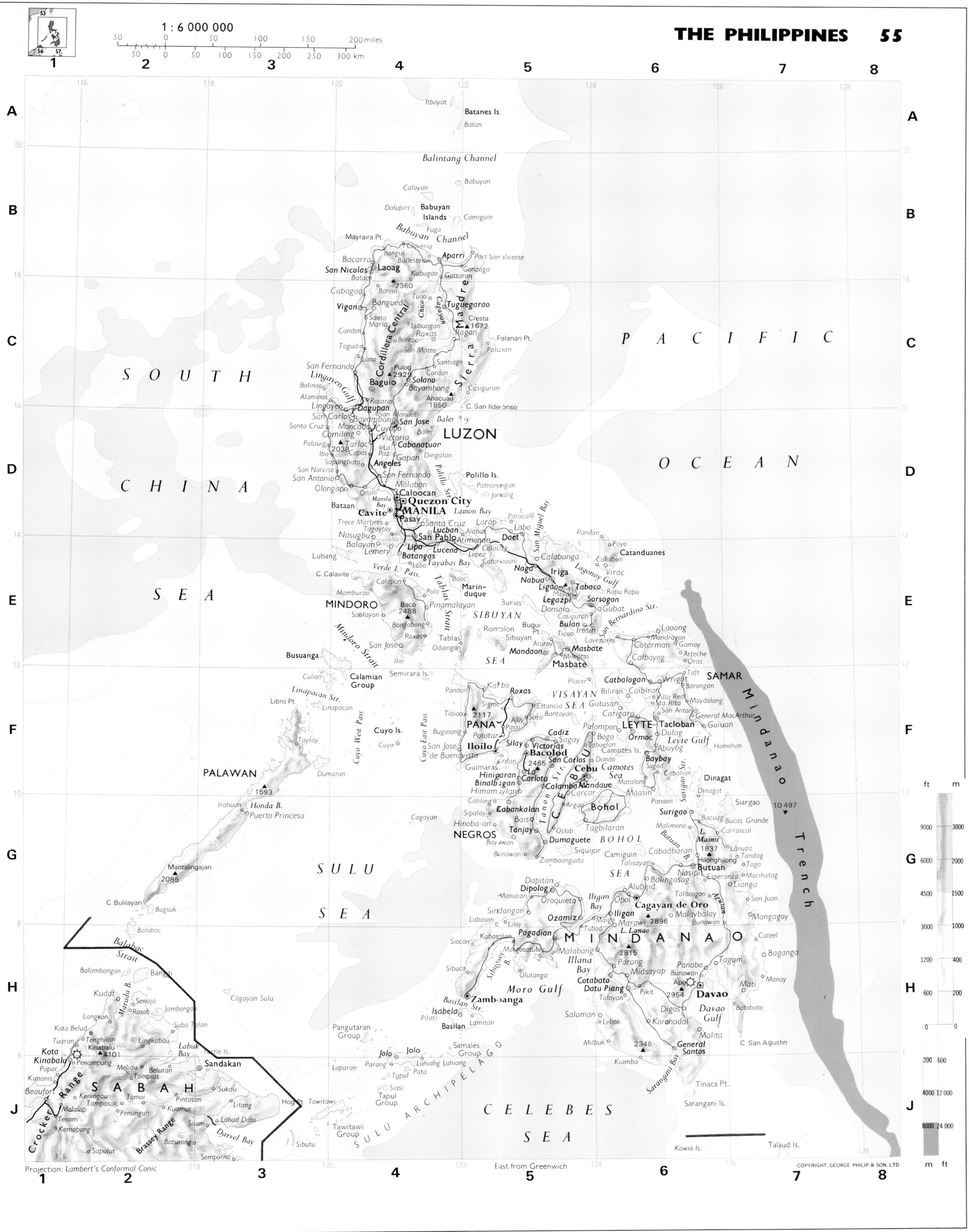

1 2 3 4 5

THAILAND

LAOS

VIET-NAM

CAMBODIA

BIRMA · MYANMAR

ANDAMAN SEA

RANGOON
G. of Martaban

Moulmein
Thaton
Letpadan
Tharrawaddy
Madauk
Insein
Yandoon
Maubin
Pyapon

Thoen
Uttaradit
Vientiane
Nong Khai
Ba Don
Dong Hoi

Tak
Phrae
Phitsanulok
Sawankhalok
Phong
Sakon Nakhon
Nakhon Phanom
Thakhek
Quang Tri
Hue
Da Nang

Bhumiphol Dam
Nakhon Sawan
Chaiyaphum
Khon Kaen
Roi Et
Dong Hene
Hoi An

2320
Phetchabun

Phra Nakhon Si Ayutthaya
Kanchanaburi
Mun
Ubon Ratchathani
Pakse
Quang Ngai
Binh Son

BANGKOK
Samut Prakan
Chon Buri
Si Racha
Phetchaburi
Chachoengsao
Samut Songkhram

Nakhon Ratchasima (Khorat)
Buriram
Surin
Sisaket
Khu Khan

Phnom Dangrek
Chéom Ksan
761
Koulen
Stung-Treng
Srepok
Pleiku
Kontum
An Nhon (Binh Dinh)
Qui Nhon
Song Cau

2598
VIET-NAM
2405

Siem Reap
Battambang
Tonle Sap
Kg. Thom
Kompong Cham
Senmonorom

Chanthaburi
Ko Chang
Trat
Pursat
1813
Chhnang
Kg. Bang
Kratie
Chhlong
Bo Duc
Da Lat

Ko Kut
Koh Kong
Phnom Penh
Prey Veng
Banam
Nha Trang

Chumphon
Kho Khot Kra
Chhung Kg. Som
Kompong Som
Takeo
Kampot
Long Xuyen
My Tho
Ba Ria
Vung Tau
Phan Rang
Mui Ca Na

GULF of THAILAND

Ranong
Phu Quoc
Rach Gia
Can Tho
Soc Trang

Ko Phangan
Ko Samui
Surat Thani
1786
Nakhon Si Thammarat
Pak Phanang
Hon Chong
Bac Lieu
Ca Mau

Phangnga
Mui Bai Bung
Con Son

Phuket
Thung Song
Trang
Phatthalung
Thale Luang
Songkhla (Singora)

Ban Kantang
Satun
Kangar
Pattani
Narathiwat
Yala
Tumpat
Kota Baharu

Langkawi
Alor Setar
Pasir Mas
Perhentian

SOUTH CHINA SEA

Pei Chiao
Hsisha
Howu Tao
Chuntao
P. Triton

4424

Flat Nanshan

Loaita I.
Itu Aba
Palawan
Sin Crowe I.

Spratly I.
Amboyna I.
Islands (Philippines)
C. Buliluyan
Balabac I.

Balabac Strait
Kudat
Kota Belud
Kota Kinabalu
Kinabalu 4101

MALAYSIA

PENINSULAR MALAYSIA

George Town
Pinang
Butterworth
Bukit Mertajam
Port Weld
Taiping
Ipoh
Teluk Anson
Kuala Kangsar
K. Kerai
Kuala Terengganu
Redang

Teluk Intan
Kuala Lipis
Jerantut
Temerloh
Kuala Dungun
Cukai

Kelang
Kuala Selangor
Pelabuhan Kelang
KUALA LUMPUR
Gemas
Kuantan

P. Dickson
Seremban
Segamat
Labis
Mersing
Tioman

Melaka
Muar
Batu Pahat
Kluang
Tg. Tinggi

Johor Baharu
SINGAPORE

SABAH
Beaufort
Victoria
Pulau Labuan
Bandar Seri Begawan
BRUNEI
Lutong
Miri
Seria
Niah
Marudi
1348

SARAWAK
Bintulu
Tubau
Mukah
Oya
Sibu
Kanowit
Kapit
Sarikei
Binatang
Simanggang
Kuching
Niut 1701
Lundu
Tg. Datu
Serian
Bau

BORNEO · KALIMANTAN · TIMUR

BARAT
Sambas
Singkawang
Mempawah
Pontianak
Sanggau
Sintang
Putussibau
2988

SUMATRA

We
Sabang (Kutaraja)
Banda Aceh (Kutaraja)
Sigli
Seulimeum
Meureudu
Bireuen
Lhokseumawe
Idi
Langsa
Pangkalansusu
Takengon
3466
Leuser

Calang
Lhoknga
Meulaboh
Pangkalanbrandan
Binjai
Belawan
Medan
Kualasimpang

Tapaktuan
Tebingtinggi
Kisaran
Tanjungbalai
Pematangsiantar
Prapat
Danau Toba

Simeulue
Sinabang
Tarutung
Sibolga
Musala

UTARA
Padangsidempuan
Rantauprapat

Lahewa
Gunungsitoli
Nias
Dumai
Rupat
Rengat

Telukdalem
Bengkalis
Sungaipakning
Batu Pahat

Kepulauan Batu
Tanahbala
Pini
Pekanbaru
RIAU
Kampar
Lingga

Siberut
Padang
Bukittinggi
Payakumbuh
B A R A T
Sawahlunto
Solok
Muaratebo
Sukadana

Sipura
Pariaman
Padangpanjang
3800
Muarabungo
Muaratembesi
Hari
JAMBI (Telanaipura)

Sungaipenuh
Kerinci
Bangko
Pangkalpinang
Bangka

Mukomuko
Sarolangun
Muntok
Selat Bangka
Tanjungpandan
Pulau Belitung (Billiton)
Manggar
Tendang

Pulau Pagai Utara
Lubuklinggau
Curup
Sekayu
Sungaigerong
PALEMBANG
Toboali

Pulau Pagai Selatan
Mentawai
Tebingtinggi
Lahat
SELATAN
Kayuagung
Prabumulih

Bengkulu
Muaraenim
Baturaja
Pagaralam

BENGKULU
Dempo 3159
Manna
Kotabumi

Menggala
Kotabumi

6073

Enggano
LAMPUNG
Tanjungkarang
Telukbetung
Kotaagung
Kalianda

INDIAN OCEAN

Selat Sunda
Pulau Rakata Besar (Krakatau)
Serang
JAKARTA
Purwakarta

Tg. Gede
Pelabuhan Ratu
Bogor
Bandung
Cirebon

Pengalengan
Tasikmalaya
Slamet 3428
Pekalongan
Kendal

Garut
Cilacap
Magelang
Semarang
Kudus

6650

Java Trench

J A V A (JAWA)

TENGAH
Surakarta
Yogyakarta
Madiun
Kediri
3265
2563

TIMUR
Surabaya
Pasuruan
Probolinggo
Situbondo
Malang
Jember
Banyuwangi

Sumenep
Bangkalan
Sampang
Pamekasan
Madura

Kepulauan Kangean

BALI
Singaraja
Denpasar
Rinjani 3726
Agung 3142

NUSA TENGGARA
Lombok
Sumbawa

INDONESIA

Kepulauan Natuna Besar
Telukbutun
Natuna Selatan
Binjai

Kemaya
Kuala
Siantan
Subi
Midai
Serasan

Kepulauan Anambas

JAVA SEA (Laut Jawa)

Greater Sunda Islands

Kepulauan Karimata
Padang
Ketapang
Kotawaringin
Pangkalanbuun
Kumai
Kualajelai
Sampit
Palangkaraya
Kualakapuas

TENGAH
Nangatayap
Buntok
Tamiang
Muarateweh
Barito

SELATAN
Kandangan
Barabai
Amuntai
1892
Martapura
Banjarmasin
Kotabaru
Pleihari
Pagatan
Pulau Laut

Tanjung
Tanahgrogot
Balikpapan
Samarinda

Projection: Mercator

East from Greenwich

ft m
12 000 · 4000
9000 · 3000
6000 · 2000
4500 · 1500
3000 · 1000
1200 · 400
600 · 200
0 · 0
-200 · 600
2000 · 6000
4000 · 12 000
6000 · 18 000
8000 · 24 000
m ft

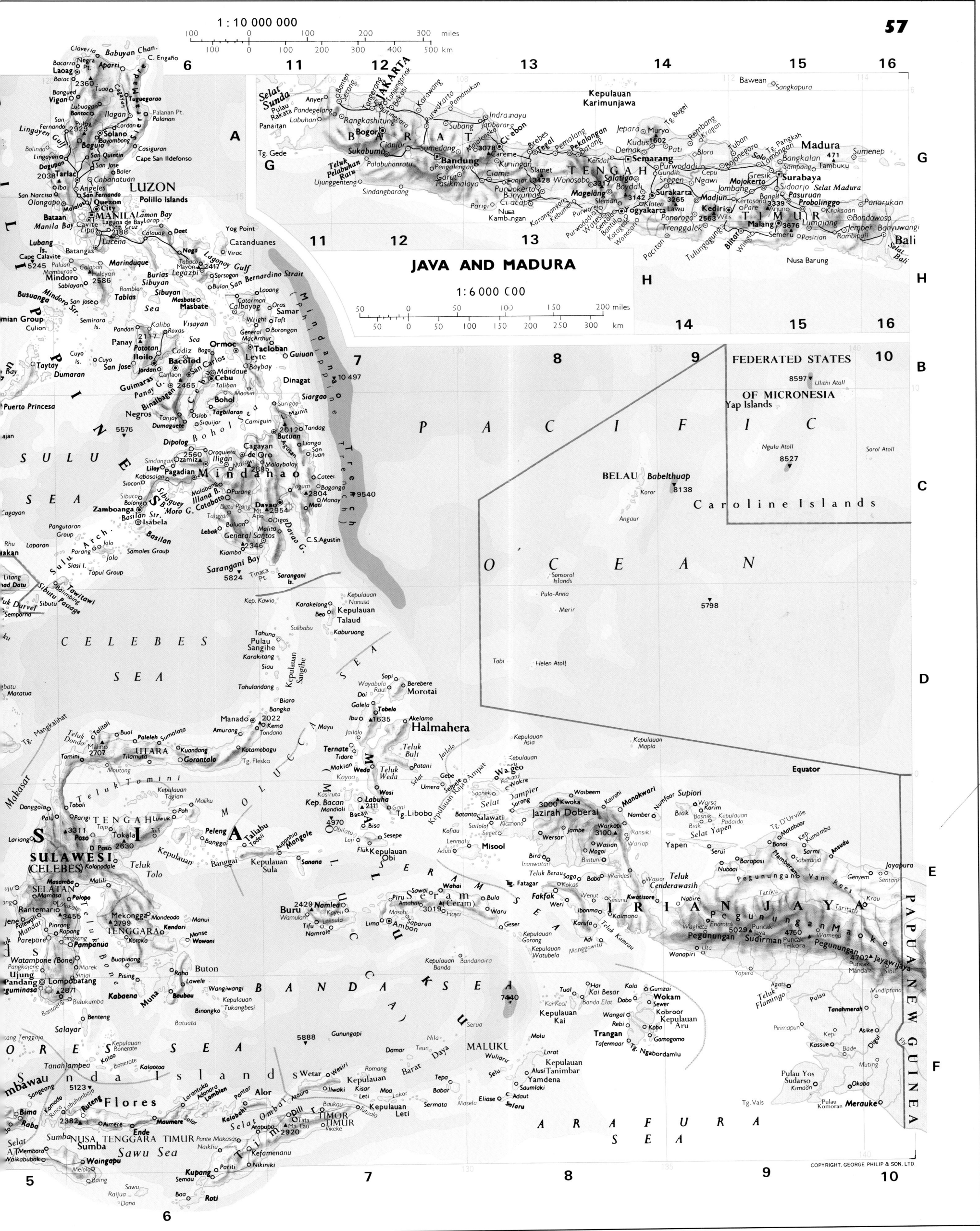

Gulf of Tonkin

HAINAN

GUANGXI ZHUANGZU ZIZHIQU AUTONOMOUS REGION

YUNNAN

BURMA (MYANMAR)

SHAN STATE

KAYAH

KAWTHULE

TENASSERIM

THAILAND

LAOS

VIETNAM

CAMBODIA

ANNAM

TONKIN

BAC BO

Red River Delta

HANOI

Haiphong

Nam Dinh

Thanh Hoa

Vinh

Ha Tinh

Dong Hoi

Hue

Da Nang

Central Highlands

Ban Me Thuot

Quy Nhon

Vientiane

Luang Prabang

Cao Nguyen Tran Ninh

Pakse

Boloven

Savanne

Phnom Dangrek

Tonle Sap (Great Lake)

Battambang

Nakhon Ratchasima (Khorat)

Khorat

Phitsanulok

Chiang Mai

Lampang

Mandalay

Rangoon

Pegu

Moulmein

Tavoy

Bangkok (Krung Thep)

Thon Buri

Gulf of Thailand

Gulf of Martaban

Dawna Range

Bilauk Taung

Mekong

Chao Phraya

Salween

Lancang Jiang

Nanning

Zhanjiang (Tsamkong)

Leizhou Bandao

Haikou

Qiongzhou Haixia (Hainan Strait)

Mergui Islands (Myeik Arch.)

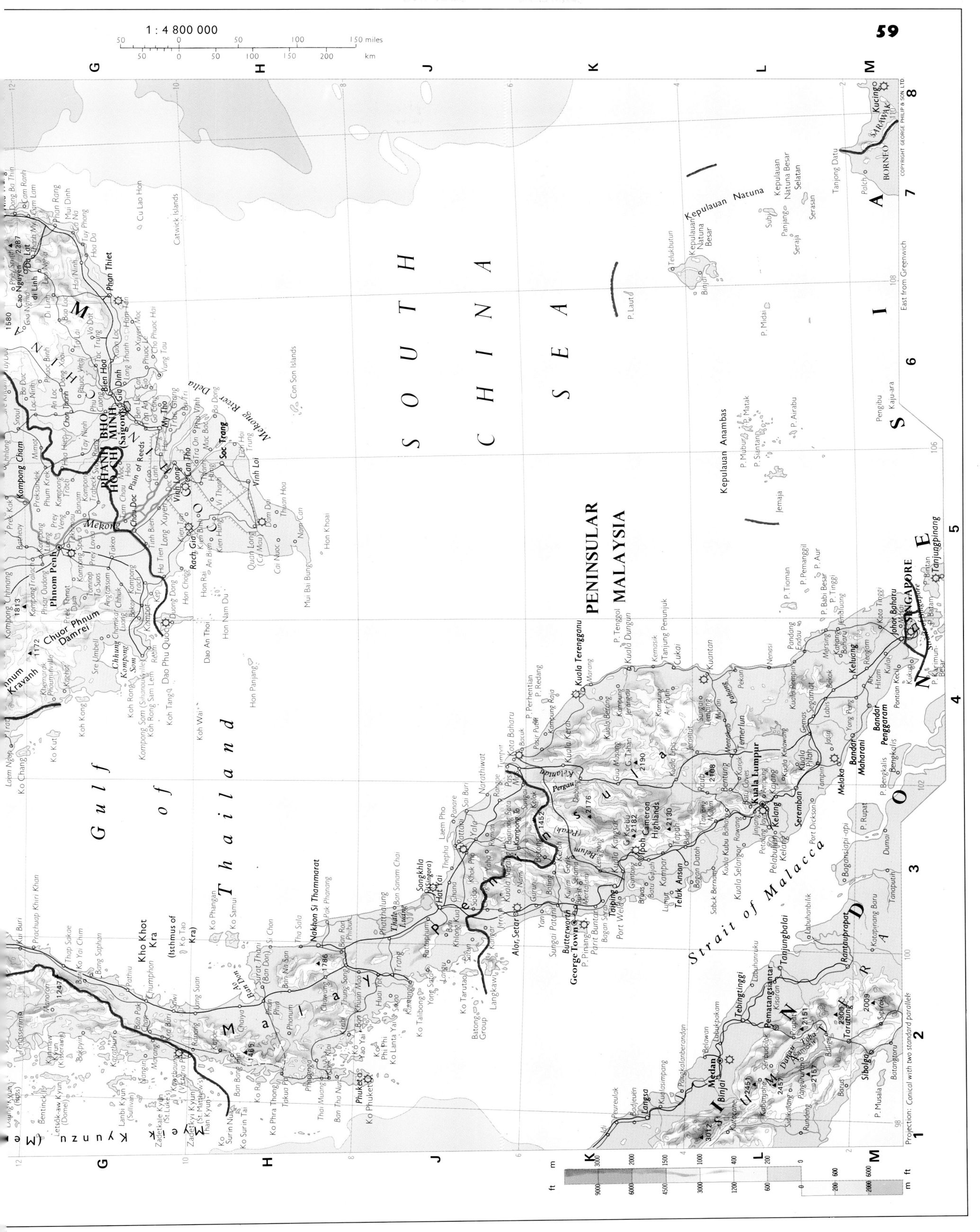

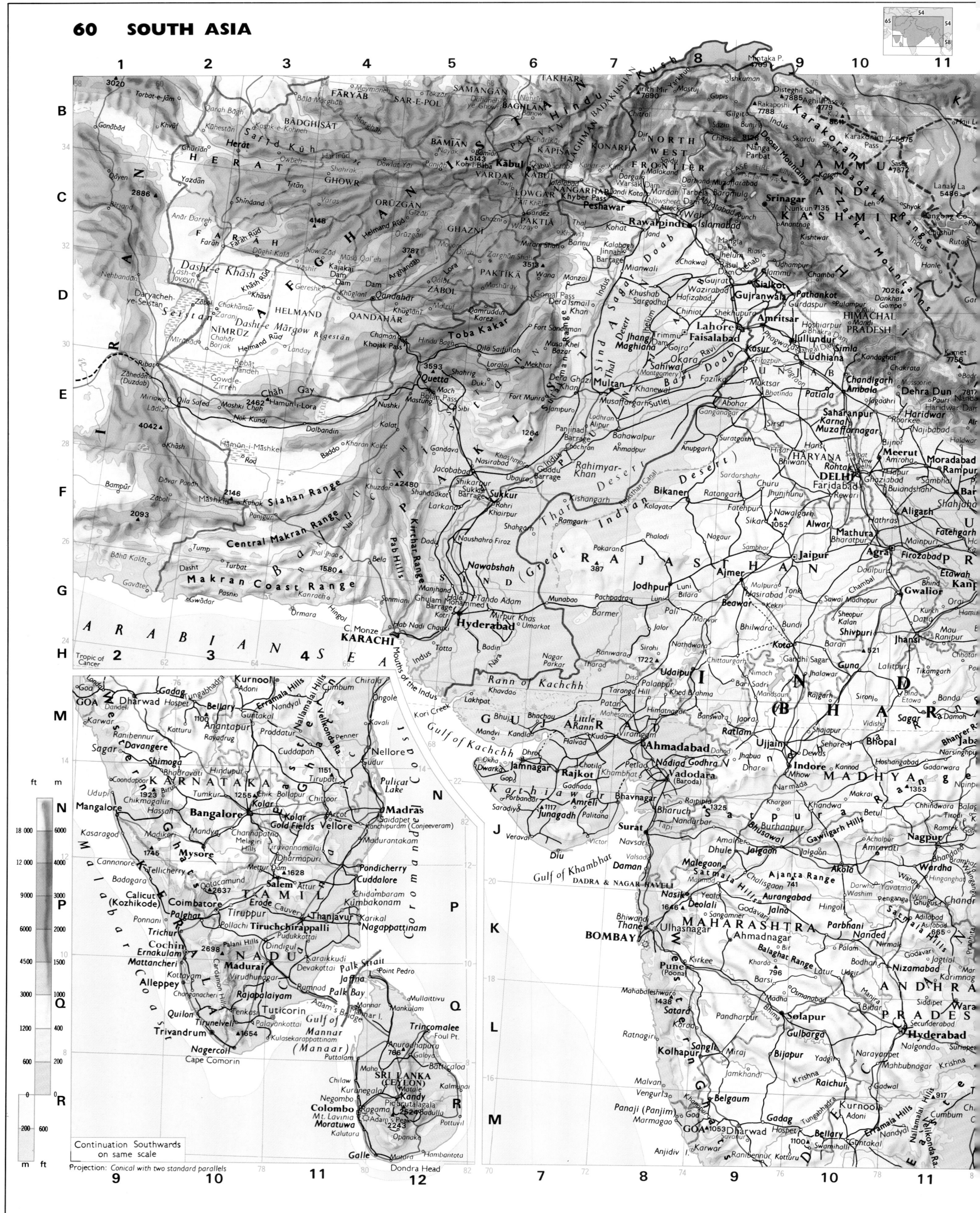

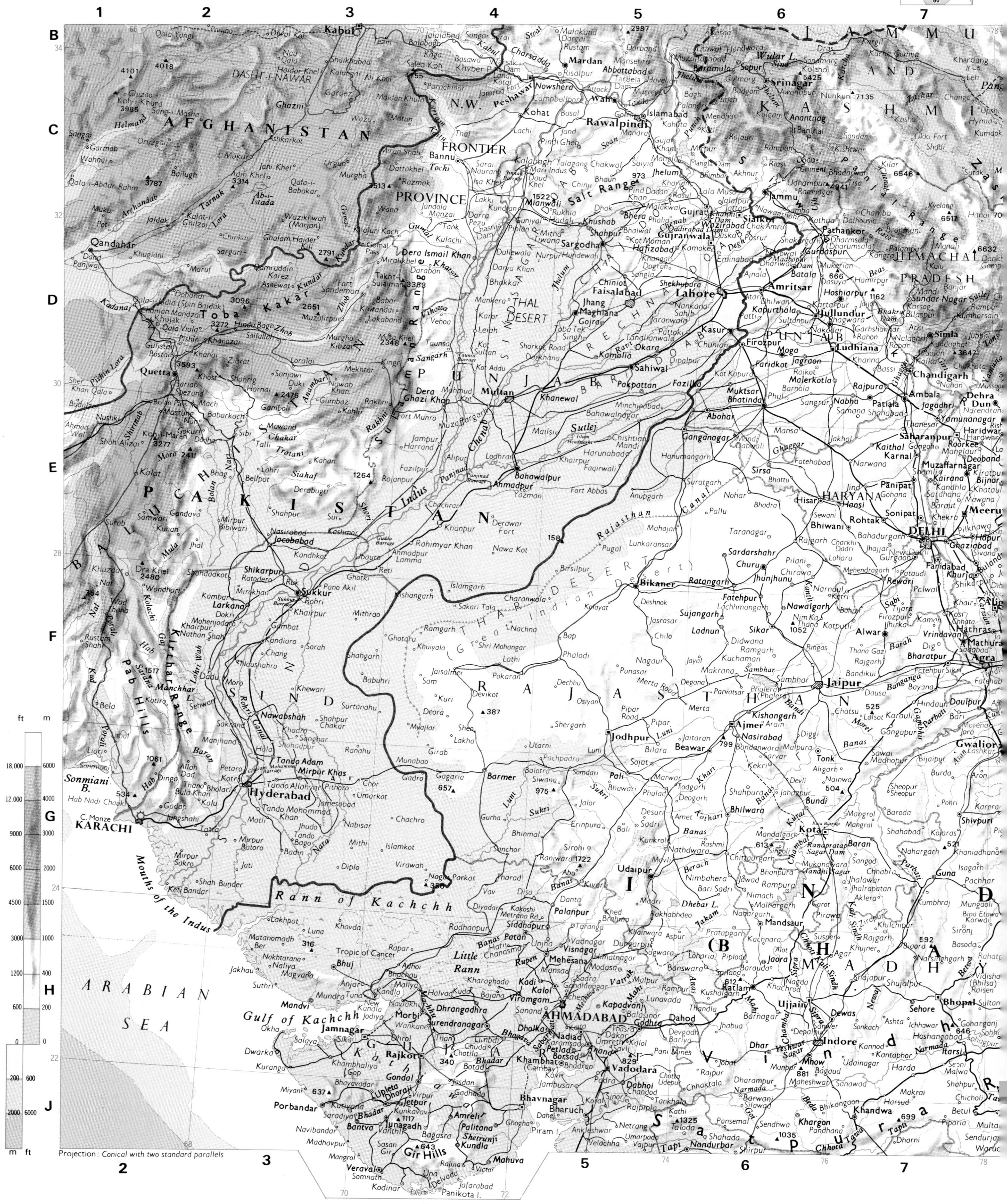

AFGHANISTAN

DASHT-I-NAWAR

N.W. FRONTIER PROVINCE

Kabul

Peshawar

Rawalpindi

Islamabad

JAMMU AND KASHMIR

Srinagar

Jammu

HIMACHAL PRADESH

Salt Range

Lahore

Amritsar

Jullundur

Ludhiana

PUNJAB

Simla

Chandigarh

Dehra Dun

THAL DESERT

Multan

DOAB

HARYANA

DELHI

Meerut

Agra

Mathura

Quetta

BALUCHISTAN

PAKISTAN

SIND

THAR DESERT (Great Indian Desert)

RAJASTHAN

Bikaner

Jaipur

Jodhpur

Ajmer

Gwalior

Sukkur

Larkana

Hyderabad

KARACHI

Mouths of the Indus

Rann of Kachchh

Little Rann

Gulf of Kachchh

ARABIAN SEA

Tropic of Cancer

KATHIAWAR

Rajkot

Jamnagar

AHMADABAD

Vadodara

Bhavnagar

Udaipur

Kota

MADHYA PRADESH

Indore

Bhopal

Ujjain

Narmada

Tapi

Gir Hills

Porbandar

Junagadh

Veraval

ft m
18,000 6000
12,000 4000
9000 3000
6000 2000
4500 1500
3000 1000
1200 400
600 200
0 0
200 600
2000 6000
m ft

Projection: Conical with two standard parallels

1 : 4 800 000

50   0   50   100 miles
50   0   50   100   150 km

JAMMU AND KASHMIR
On same scale as Main Map

East from Greenwich

COPYRIGHT. GEORGE PHILIP & SON, LTD.

43
44
66
60
76
68

T U R K E Y
ARMENIA
AZER.
NAGORNO KARABAKH
SYRIA
LEBANON
ISRAEL
JORDAN
CYPRUS
IRAQ
SAUDI ARABIA
EGYPT
KUWAIT
MEDITERRANEAN SEA
RED SEA
BĀDIYAT ASH SHĀM
AL JAZĪRAH
AN NAFŪD
AL ḤIJĀZ
MESOPOTAMIA
ES SÎNÂ
Gebel el Tîh
Toros Dağları (Taurus Mts.)
Konya
Kayseri
Sivas
Erzurum
Yerevan
Malatya
Diyarbakır
Gaziantep
Adana
Mersin
Tarsus
İskenderun
Ḥalab (Aleppo)
Ḥamāh
Ḥimṣ (Homs)
Al Lādhiqīyah (Latakia)
Nicosia
Famagusta
Limassol
Ṭarābulus (Tripoli)
Bayrūt (Beirut)
DIMASHQ (Damascus)
Tudmur (Palmyra)
Dayr az Zawr
Al Mawṣil (Mosul)
Arbīl
Kirkūk
As Sulaymānīyah
BAGHDĀD
Karbalā
An Najaf
Al Ḥillah
Al Kūt
An Nāṣirīyah
Ar Ramādī
Tabrīz
Orūmīyeh
TEL AVIV-YAFO
Jerusalem
'Ammān
Az Zarqā'
Be'er Sheva
Gaza Strip
West Bank
Elat
Al 'Aqabah
Ma'ān
Al Jawf
Sakākah
Tabūk
Ḥā'il
Buraydah
'Unayzah
Al Madīnah (Medina)
Ar Riyāḍ (Riyadh)
Ḥafar al Bāṭin
Ar Ruṭbah
Euphrates
Tigris
ft m
18 000 6000
12 000 4000
9000 3000
6000 2000
4500 1500
3000 1000
1200 400
600 200
0 0
200 600
2000 6000
m ft
1 2 3 4 5
B C D E F
Projection: Conical with two standard parallels

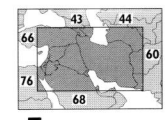

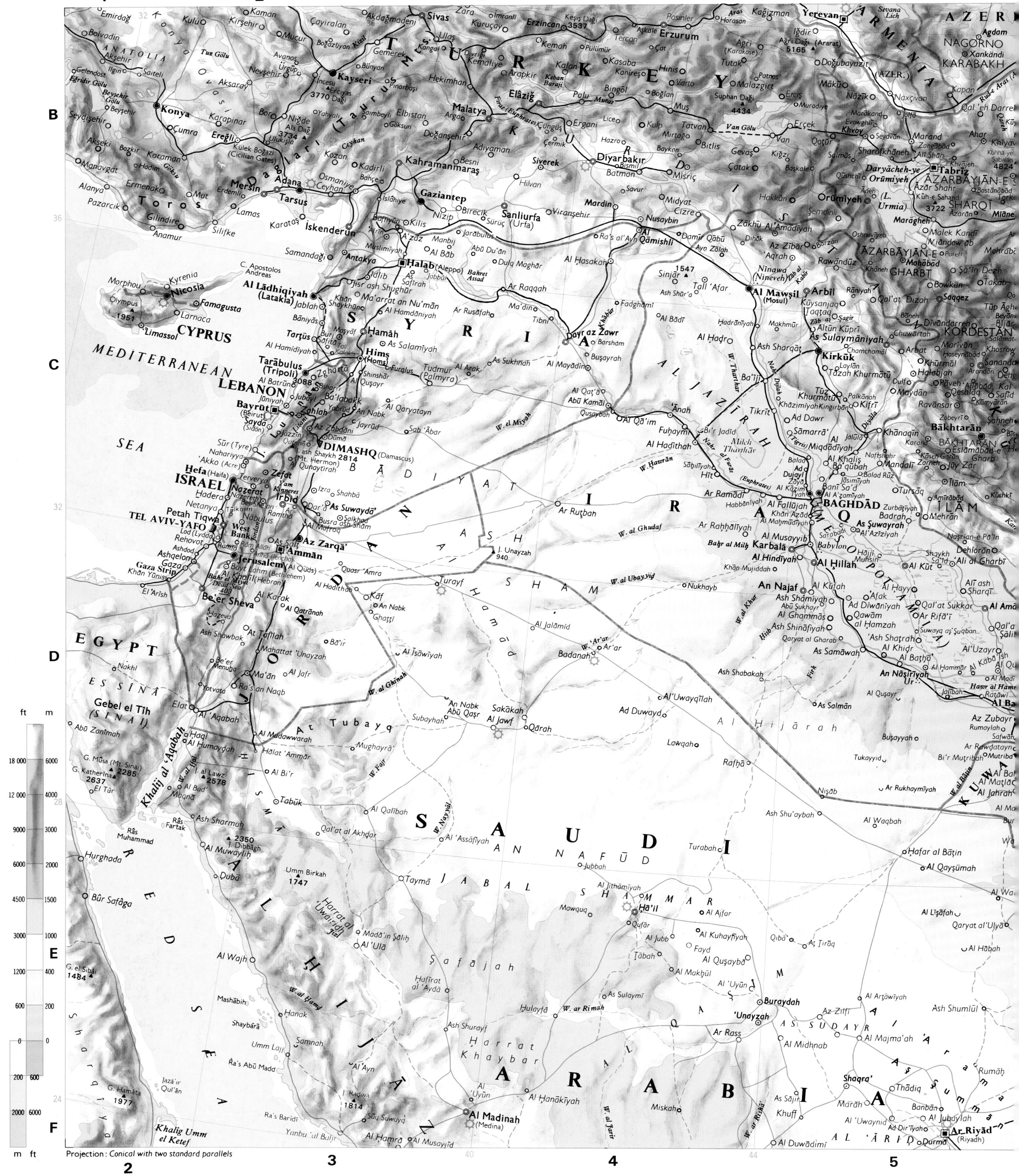

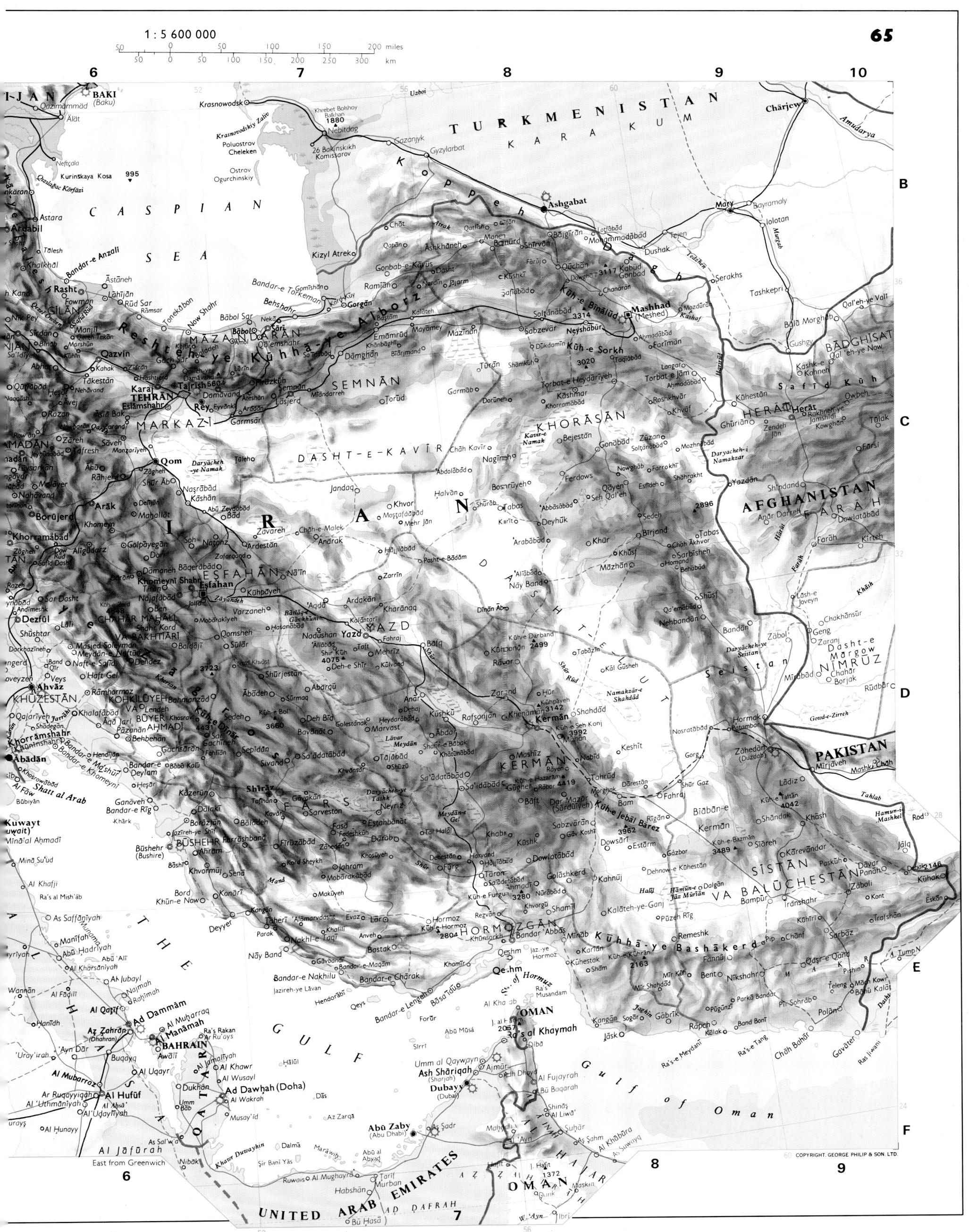

1 : 5 600 000

50 0   50   100   150   200 miles
50 0   50   100   150   200   250   300 km

6   7   8   9   10

BAKI
(Baku)

CASPIAN

SEA

TURKMENISTAN

KARAKUM

Chärjew

Ashgabat

Mary

B

Mashhad
(Meshed)

BADGHISAT

KHORĀSĀN

HERĀT   Herāt

C

DASHT-E-KAVIR

AFGHANISTAN

FARAH

I   R   A   N

Dasht-e
Margow

NIMRŪZ

D

YAZD

Esfahān

KERMĀN

PAKISTAN

Mirjāveh

E

FĀRS

HORMOZGĀN

Kuhhā-ye Bashākerd

SISTĀN

VA BALŪCHESTĀN

Bandar 'Abbās

Qeshm

Str. of Hormuz

THE

GULF

OMAN

Gulf   of   Oman

Ad Dawḥah (Doha)

BAHRAIN

QATAR

Dubayy
(Dubai)

Ash Shāriqah
(Sharjah)

OMAN

Abū Zaby
(Abu Dhabi)

East from Greenwich

6   7   8

UNITED ARAB EMIRATES

OMAN

COPYRIGHT. GEORGE PHILIP & SON. LTD.

9

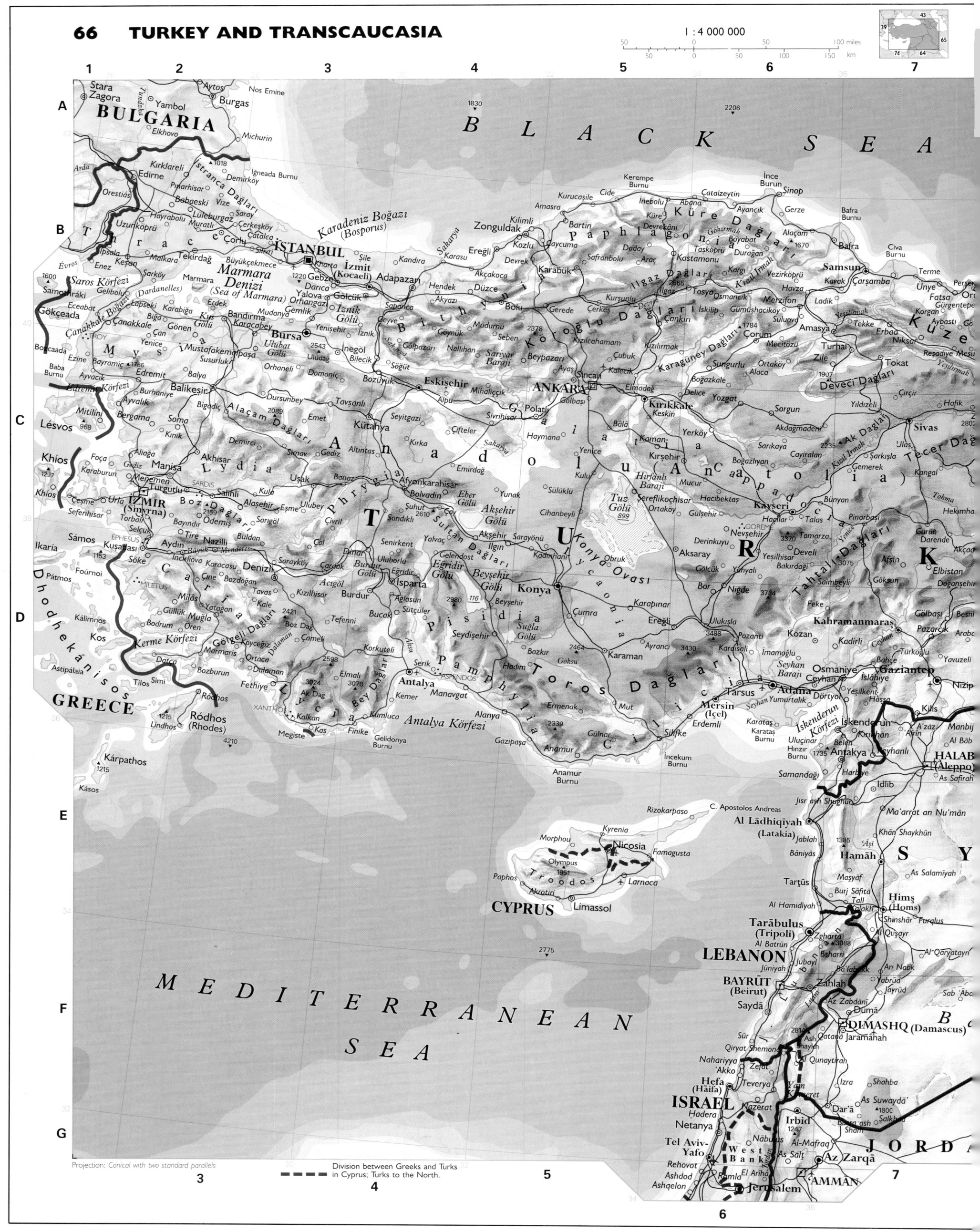

1 : 4 000 000

50   0   50   100 miles

50   0   50   100   150 km

BULGARIA

Stara Zagora
Yambol
Aytos
Nos Emine
Burgas
Michurin
Elkhovo
Arda
Kırklareli
Edirne
Demirköy
İğneada Burnu
Pınarhisar
Vize
Boğazeski
Hayrabolu
Lüleburgaz
Saray
Uzunköprü
Muratlı
Çerkesköy
Çatalca
Çorlu
Malkara
Tekirdağ
Büyükçekmece
İSTANBUL
Şile
Silivri
Enez
Keşan
Şarköy
Marmara
Gebze
İzmit (Kocaeli)
Adapazarı
Kandıra

B L A C K   S E A

Keremep Burnu
İnce Burun
Sinop
Kurucaşile
Cide
İnebolu
Abana
Çatalzeytin
Ayancık
Gerze
Bafra Burnu
Zonguldak
Kilimli
Bartın
Devrekâni
Küre
Gökırmak
Boyabat
Bafra
Civa Burnu
Samsun
Terme

T h r a c e

Évros
Samothráki
Gelibolu
Gökçeada
Eceabat
Çanakkale
Çan
Yenice
Marmara Denizi (Sea of Marmara)
Yalova
Orhangazi
İznik Gölü
İznik
Sapanca
Akyazı
Hendek
Düzce
Akçakoca
Ereğli
Karasu
Sakarya
Devrek
Bolu
Gerede
Çerkeş
Kastamonu
Taşköprü
Vezirköprü
Havza
Kavak
Çarşamba
Ünye
Fatsa

GREECE

M E D I T E R R A N E A N   S E A

CYPRUS

Kyrenia
Morphou
Nicosia
Famagusta
Olympus 1951
Larnaca
Paphos
Troodos
Akrotiri
Limassol

Division between Greeks and Turks
in Cyprus; Turks to the North.

Projection: Conical with two standard parallels

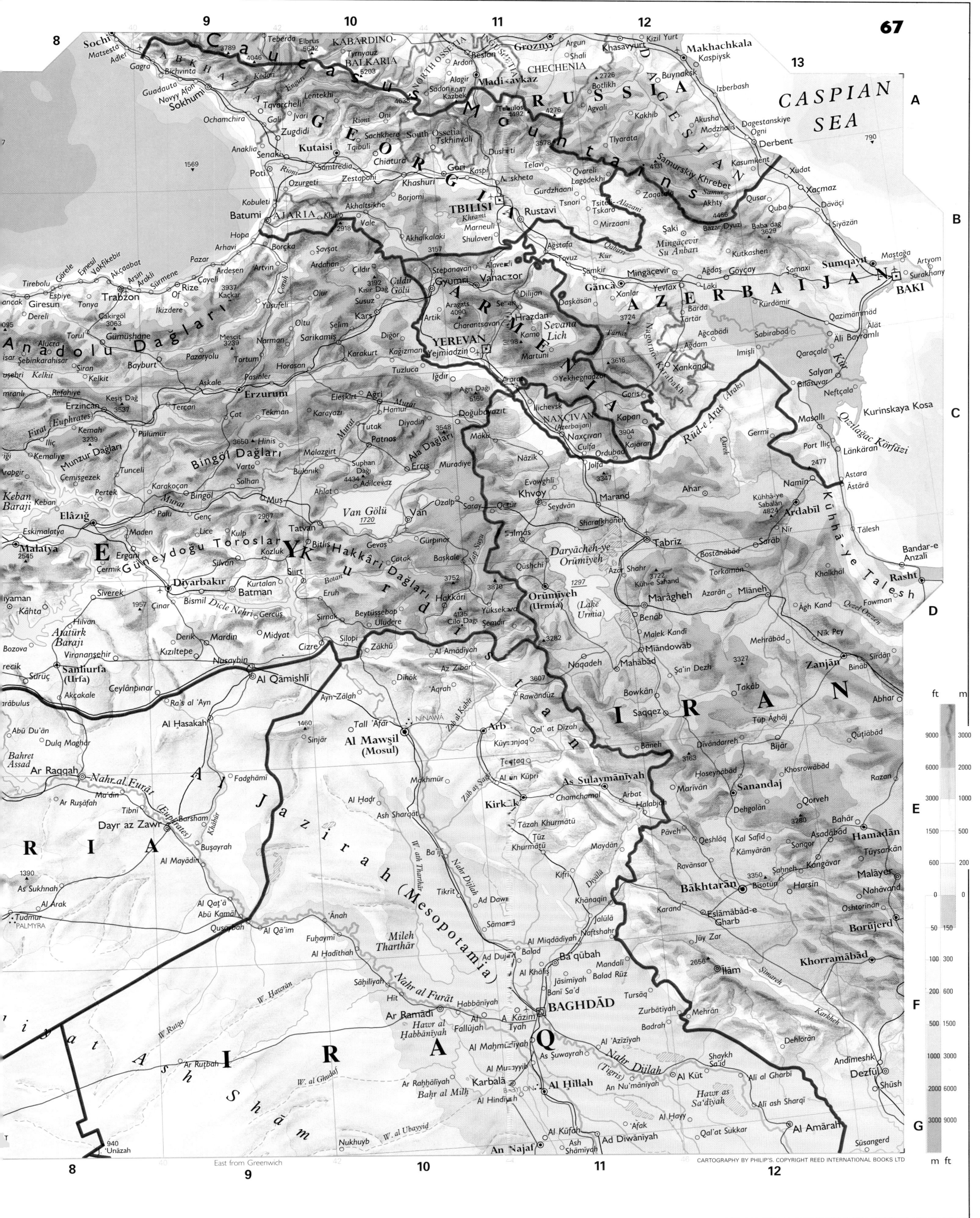

CASPIAN
SEA

CAUCASUS Mountains

ABKHAZIA
GEORGIA
KABARDINO-BALKARIA
NORTH OSSETIA
SOUTH OSSETIA
CHECHENIA
DAGESTAN
RUSSIA

AJARIA

ARMENIA

AZERBAIJAN

BAKI

NAXÇIVAN
(Azerbaijan)

Anadolu Dağları

Güneydoğu Toroslar

Bingöl Dağları

Hakkâri Dağları

Munzur Dağları

Ala Dağları

Van Gölü
1720

Daryācheh-ye
Orūmīyeh
(Lake
Urmia)

Kurdistan

IRAN

TBILISI

YEREVAN

Erzurum

Diyarbakır

Al Mawşil
(Mosul)

BAGHDAD

Al Jazirah (Mesopotamia)

SYRIA

IRAQ

Ash Shām

East from Greenwich

CARTOGRAPHY BY PHILIP'S. COPYRIGHT REED INTERNATIONAL BOOKS LTD

ft   m

9000   3000

6000   2000

3000   1000

1500   500

600   200

0   0

50   150

100   300

200   600

500   1500

1000   3000

2000   6000

3000   9000

m   ft

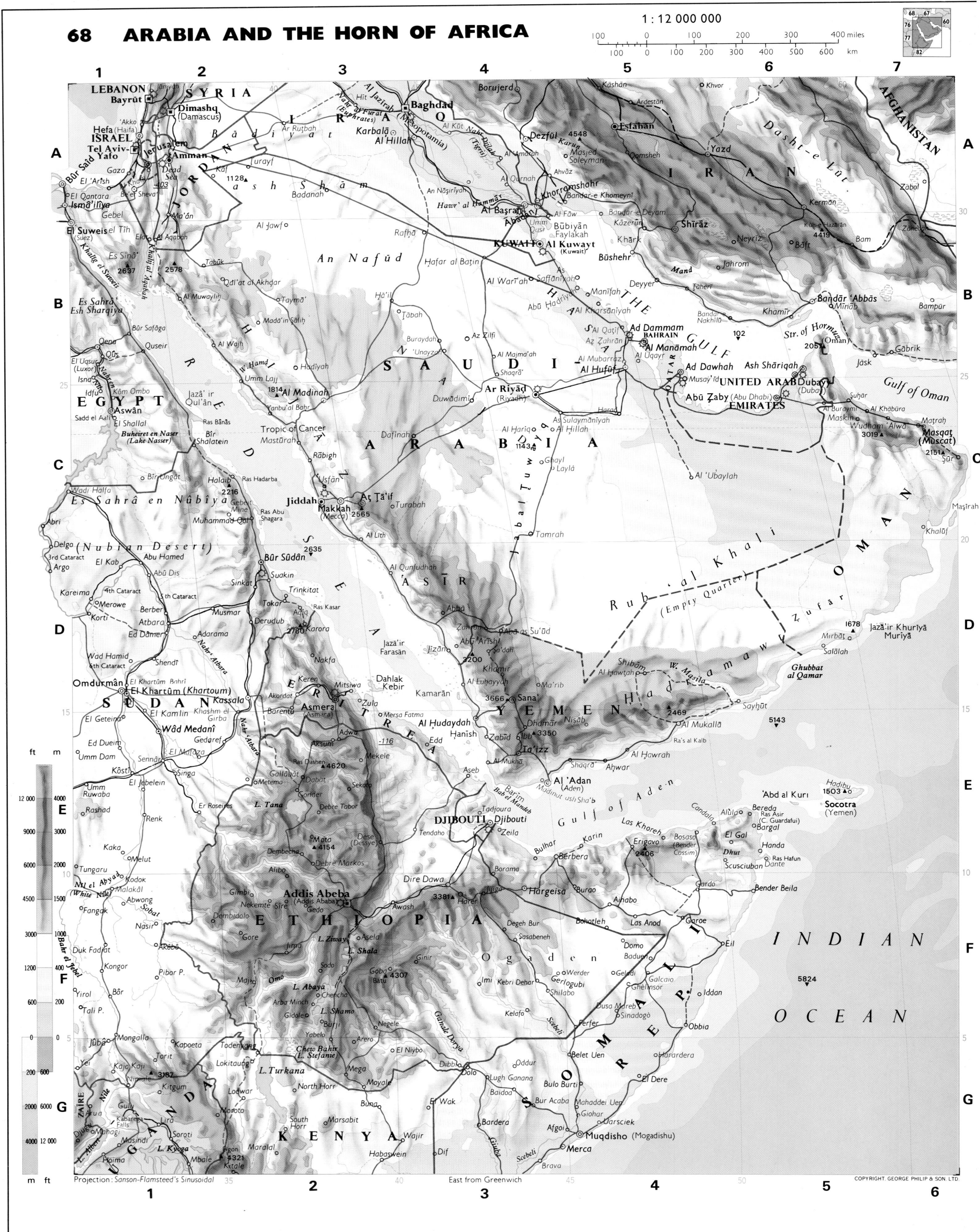

1 : 12 000 000

100   0   100   200   300   400 miles

100   0   100   200   300   400   500   600 km

1   **2**   **3**   **4**   **5**   **6**   **7**

LEBANON   SYRIA   IRAQ   Borujerd   Kāshān   Ardestān   Khvor   AFGHANISTAN
Bayrūt   Dimashq (Damascus)   Al Jazirah   Baghdad   Dasht-e Lūt
Hefa (Haifa)   Hit   Nahr al Furāt (Euphrates)   Dezfūl   4548   Eşfahān   Yazd   Zābol
Israel   Ar Ruṭbah   Karbalā   Al Kūt   Nahr-e Karkheh   Masjed Soleymān   IRAN   Kermān
Tel Aviv-Yafo   Jerusalem   Amman   Al Hillah   Al 'Amārah   Ahvāz   Oomsheh   Bām   Zāhedān

A Būr Sa'īd   El 'Arish   Gaza   Dead Sea   Al Qurnah   Khorramshahr   Shīrāz   4419   **A**
El Qantara   Beer Sheva   403   Ma'ān   Ash Shām   An Nāşirīyah   Hawr al Hammār   Al Başrah   Ābādān   Bandar-e Deylam   Bandar 'Abbās
Isma'īlīya   Gebel   Ela   Aqabah   Turayf   Al Fāw   Umm Qaşr   Būbiyān   Kāzerūn   Bāfq   Bampūr

B El Suweis (Suez)   Ela   Tabūk   Badanah   Rafhā   KUWAIT   Al Kuwayt (Kuwait)   Faylakah   Deyyer   Tāherī   Khamīr   Jāsk   Gābrīk   **B**
Es Sahrā' Esh Sharqīya   2578   Al Muwayliḥ   Hā'il   Ḥafar al Bāṭin   Būshehr   Kārk   THE GULF   Str. of Hormuz (Oman)   205   Mīnāb
Es Sīnā   2637   Qdl'at al Akhdar   Taymā   Tābah   Abū Hadrīyah   Manīfah   102   Bandar Nakhīlū
Būr Safāga   Mada'in Ṣāliḥ   Az Zilfī   Al Kharsānīyah   Ad Dammam   BAHRAIN   Ad Dawhah   Ash Shāriqah

C Qena   Quseir   Al Wajh   Burayday   'Unayzah   S Al Qaţīf   Al Manāmah   Ash Shāriqah Dubayy (Dubai)   Gulf of Oman   **C**
El Uqsur (Luxor)   Qūs   Al Madīnah   Umm Lajj   1814   Al Majma'ah   Al Mubarraz   Az Zahrān   Ad Dawhah   QATAR   UNITED ARAB   Şuḥār
Isna   Idfu   Jazā'ir Qul'ān   Yanbu' al Baḥr   Shaqrā   Al Hufūf   Al Uqayr   Musay'īd   Abū Zaby (Abu Dhabi)   EMIRATES   Al Buraymī   Al Khābūra
EGYPT   Aswān   SAUDI   Ar Riyāḍ (Riyadh)   Duwādimi   As Sulaymānīyah   As   Al Hariq   Al Hillah   Maskin   Wudhām 'Alwā   3019   Masqaţ (Muscat)

Sadd el 'Ali   El Shallal   Ras Bānās   Tropic of Cancer   Mastūrah   ARABIA   Dafīnah   Al Hariq   Jabal Tuwayq   Rub' al Khali   2151   Şūr
Buheiret en Naser (Lake Nasser)   Bīr Shalatein   Rābigh   Ghayl Layla   1143   As Su'ūd   OMAN   Maşīrah
Es Sahrâ en Nûbîya   Halaib   Ras Hadarba   Usfān   At Ţā'if   Turabah   Al 'Ubaylah   Khalūf

D Abri   Delgo   Bīr Ungāt   2216   Makkah (Mecca)   2565   ASĪR   Khamīr   W. Masila   1678   Jazā'ir Khurīyā Muriyā   **D**
(Nubian Desert)   Gebel Elba Mine   Ras Abu Shagara   Al Līth   Al Qunfudhah   Abū 'Arīsh   3200   Ma'rib   Shibām   Mirbāṭ   Salālah
3rd Cataract   El Kab   Abu Hamed   Muhammad Qol   2635   Jazā'ir Farasān   Jizān   Sa'dah   3666   Sana   Ghubbat al Qamar
Argo   4th Cataract   Abū Dis   Būr Sūdān   Suakin   Abhā   Zahrān   Abā as Su'ūd   Al Hawṭah   2469   Ghubbat al Qamar
Kareima   Merowe   6th Cataract   Sinkat   Trinkitat   Nakfa   Jīzān   Al Luhayyah   Shibām   Al Hawṭah   Sayhūt

Korti   Berber   Musmar   Tokar   Ras Kasar   2780   Karora   Kamarān   Al Luhayyah   YEMEN   Hadramawt   5143   **D**
Atbara   Adarama   Derudub   Dahlak Kebir   Al Hudaydah   Dhamār   Nisāb   Al Mukallā
Wad Hamid   Ed Dämer   Nahr Atbara   Karora   Mitsiwa   Keren   Asmera (Asmara)   Zabīd   Ibb   3350   Ta'izz
5th Cataract   Shendi   Akordat   Bārentu   Adwa   Aksum   Edd   Al Mukhā   Ahwar   'Abd al Kuri   Socotra (Yemen)
Omdurmân   El Khartūm Bahrī   Kassala   Khashm el Girba   Gedaref   Dahlak Kebir   Mersa Fatma   Al Hudaydah   Shaqrā   Ra's al Kalb   Hadibu   1503

E SUDAN   El Khartūm (Khartoum)   Zula   Adwa   -116   Al Mukhā   Al 'Adan (Aden)   Mīnat ush Sha'b   Bereda (C. Guardafui)   Bargal   **E**
El Geteina   El Kamlin   Wâd Medanî   L. Tana   4620   Mekele   Aseb   Bāb al Mandab   Ras Asir   Candala   Alūla
Ed Dueim   El Mataza   Sennār   Singa   Gonder   Debre Tabor   Tadjoura   Zeila   Gulf of Aden   Erigavo   Bosaso (Bender Cassim)   El Gal   Dhut   Handa
Umm Dam   Kôstî   Debre Markos   DJIBOUTI   Djibouti   Karin   2406   Scusciuban   Dante

F Rashad   Renk   Umm Ruwaba   Mota   4154   Dembecha   Dire Dawa   Las Khoreh   Berbera   Bender Beila   **F**
Kaka   Melut   Nîl el Abyad (White Nile)   Alibo   Awash   3381   Harer   Jijiga   Hargeisa   Burao   Ainabo   Gardo   INDIAN
Tungaru   Addis Abeba (Addis Ababa)   ETHIOPIA   Degeh Bur   Bohotleh   Las Anod   Garoe   Eil
Kodok   Nekemte   Gore   Asela   4307   Ginir   OGADEN   Sasabeneh   Domo   Badueyn   5824   OCEAN
Nasir   Dembidolo   Gimbi   Jima   L. Ziway   Gobā   Batu   Imi   Kebri Dehar   Werder   Gerlogubi   Galcaio   Domo   Obbia
Abwong   Sobat   Bahr el Jebel   L. Shala   Shilabo   Gelaat   Ghelinsor   Sinadogò

G Duk Fadiat   Fangak   Akobo   L. Abayā   Chencha   Omo   Majī   Ginir   Kelafo   Ferfer   Dusa Mareb   Iddan   **G**
Yirol   Bôr   Kongor   Pibor P.   Arba Minch   L. Shamo   Gidole   Burji   Negele   Ganale Dorya   Scebeli   Perfer   Obbia
Tali P.   Mongalla   Kapoeta   L. Stefanie   Arero   El Niybo   Dibba   Dolo   Lugh Ganana   Bulo Burti   El Dere
Jûba   Todenyang   Chew Bahr   Mega   Moyale   SOMALI REP.   Belet Uen   Harardera
ZAIRE   Kajo Kaji   Torit   Lokitaung   L. Turkana   North Horr   El Wak   Baidoa   Bur Acaba   Mahaddei Uen   Giohar   Muqdisho (Mogadishu)
UGANDA   3187   Kitgum   Loiyangalani   Loqwar   South Horr   Marsabit   Wajir   Habaswein   Bardera   Afgoi   Merca
Gulu   Nimule   4321   KENYA   Marsabit   Dif   Bur Acaba   Scebeli   Brava

Projection: Sanson-Flamsteed's Sinusoidal   East from Greenwich   COPYRIGHT. GEORGE PHILIP & SON. LTD.

1   **2**   **3**   **4**   **5**   **6**

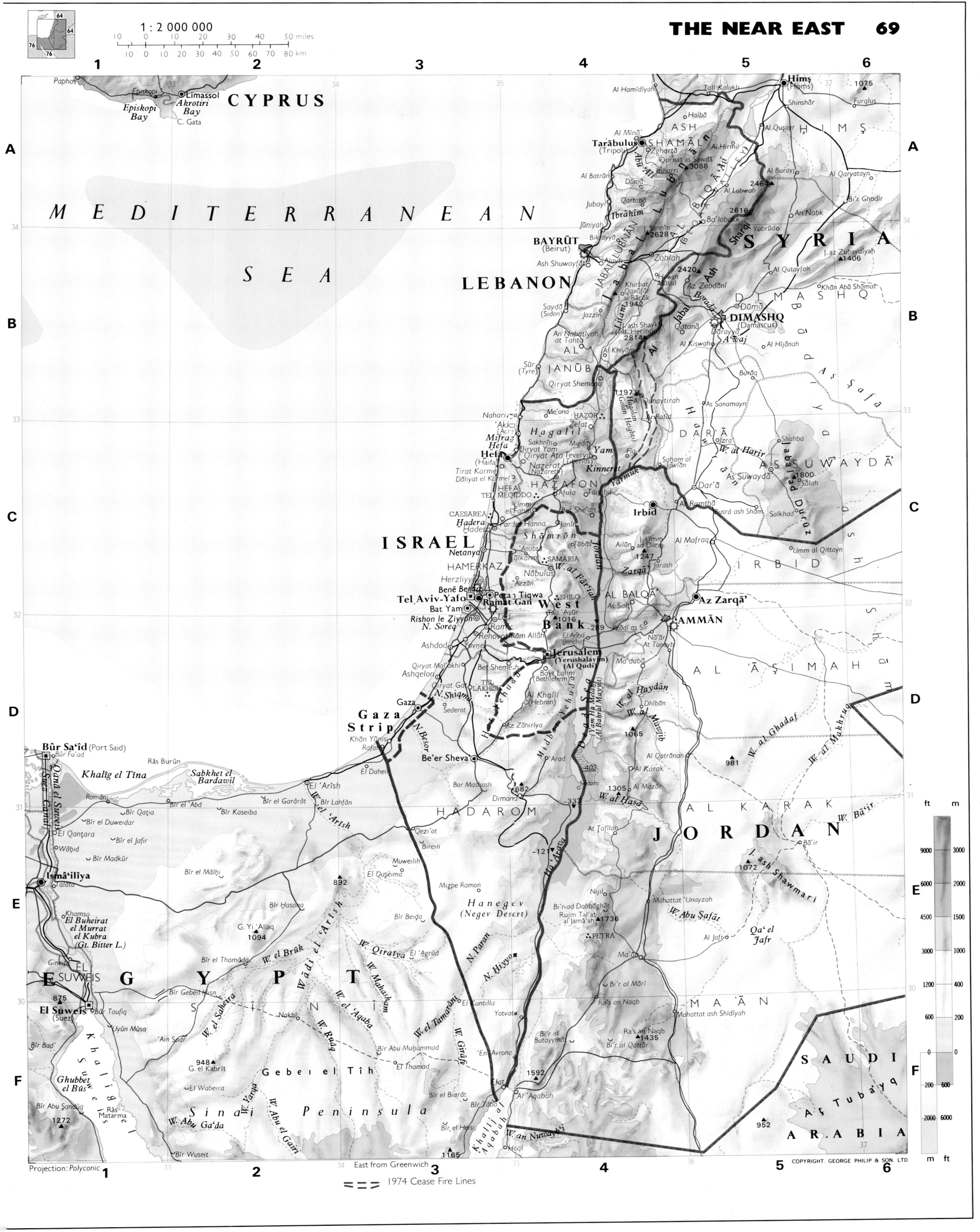

1 : 2 000 000

10   0   10   20   30   40   50 miles
10 0 10 20 30 40 50 60 70 80 km

1   2   3   4   5   6

CYPRUS
Paphos
Episkopi
Episkopi Bay
Limassol
Akrotiri Bay
C. Gata

MEDITERRANEAN

SEA

A

Al Hamidiyah
Tall Kalakh
Hims (Homs)
1075
Furqlus
Al Qusayr
Al Qaryatayn
Bi'r Ghadir
Shinshar
Halba
ASH
Tarābulus (Tripoli)
SHAMĀL
Al Hirmil
Al Buray
An Nabk
HIMS
Al Mīnā
Zgharta
Qurnat as Sawdā 3088
246▲
Al Batrūn
Dūma
Bsharri
2616
Jubayl
Qartaba
Ba'labakk
Ibrāhīm
Jūniyah
2628
Sannīn
Yabrūd
Bikfayyā
An Nabk
BAYRŪT (Beirut)
Zahlah
Jdaidet
SYRIA
Ash Shuwayfāt
Jabal Barūk
J. az Zubaydīyah 1406
Al Qutayfah

B
LEBANON
Sayda (Sidon)
Khirbat Qanafar
Al 'Ayha
2420
Az Zabdānī
Khān Abū Shāmat
Jazzīn
Litani
Ash Shaykh (Mt. Hermon) 2814
Qatanā
Darayyā
DIMASHQ (Damascus)
DIMASHQ
Al Kiswah
Al Hijānah
AL
A'waj
Sūr (Tyre)
Qiryat Shemona
Būrāq
JANŪB
1197
Hasbayya
Golan Heights
As Sanamayn
Dar'ā
Nahariyya
Me'ona
HAZOR
Zefat
Qunaytirah
Al Rafid
Shahba
As Suwaydā 1800
Sālah
'Akko (Acre)
Hagalil
Sakhnin
Migdal
Fiq
Saham al Jawlān
AS SUWAYDĀ
Hefa (Haifa)
Mifraz Hefa
Qiryat Yam
Qiryat Ata Teverya (Tiberias)
Kinneret
DAR'Ā
As Suwaydā
Jabal Druz
Salkhad
Nazerat (Nazareth)
Yarmuk
Dar'ā
Busrā ash Shām
Tirat Karmel
Dāliyat el Karmel
HAZAFON
Afula
Sāhm
Al Ramthā
Umm al Qittayn

C
HEFA
TEL MEGIDDO
Umm el Fahm
Bet She'an
Irbid
Ailūn
Al Mafraq
CAESAREA
Jenin
Umm ad Daraj
Jarash
IRBID
Hadera
Hadera
Shōmrōn
Tūbās
'Anabta
ISRAEL
Netanya
SAMARIA
1247
Zarqā
HAMERKAZ
Nābulus
W. al Fār'ah
Herzliyya
'Azzūn
Benē Beraq
Peta h Tiqwa
SHILO
AL BALQĀ'
Az Zarqā'
Tel Aviv-Yafo
Ramat Gan
Hill Asur 1016
As Salt
Bat Yam
Lod
West Bank
Wādī as Sir
AMMĀN
Rishon le Ziyyon
Ramla
289
Na'ūr
N. Soreq
Rehovot Rām Allāh
Wādī al Hasā
At Turayb
Ashdod
Yavne
Al Arīd (Jericho)

D
Qiryat Mal'akhi
Jerusalem (Yerushalayim) (Al Quds)
Ma'daba
AL 'ĀSIMAH
Ashqelon
Bet Shemesh
Bayt Lahm (Bethlehem)
Qiryat Gat
LAKHISH
TEL LAKHISH
Al Khalil (Hebron)
W. al Haydān
Dhibān
Gaza
N. Shiqma
Sederot
Az Zāhirīya
1065
W. al Mawjib
Gaza Strip
Khān Yūnis
Be'er Sheva
'Arad
Al Qatrānah
981
Rafah
N. Besor
Al Karak
Bûr Sa'îd (Port Said)
Bur Fu'ad
Bor Mashash
403
AL KARAK
Khalîg el Tîna
Rās Burūn
Sabkhet el Bardawil
El 'Arīsh
Dimona
682
1305
Al Mazār
W. al Ghadaf
Romani
Bîr el Garârât
El Daheir
333
Al Hasā
Ismâ'iliya
Qalata
Bîr el 'Abd
W. el 'Arīsh
Qezi'ot
At Tafilah
Bi'r Mari
Bîr el Duweidar
Bîr Qatia
Bîr Kaseiba
HADAROM
Birein
JORDAN
W. Bā'ir
Bîr el Jafr
Muweilih
-121
Bâ'ir
El Quseima
J. ash Shawmari 1072

E
Khamsa
El Buheirat
el Murrat el Kubra (Gt. Bitter L.)
Bîr Hasana
892
Mizpe Ramon
Nijil
Mahattat Unayzah
Al Jafr
Qa' el Jafr
EGYPT
G. Yi 'Allaq 1094
Hanegev (Negev Desert)
Bîr 'ad Dabbāghāt
Rujm Tal'at al Jamā'ah 1736
W. Abū Safāt
Bîr Beida
W. Qiratya
El 'Agrūd
N. Paran
PETRA
El Suweis
Bîr el Thamâda
W. el Brûk
W. Mahasham
N. Hiyyo
Ma'ān
Ginefa
W. Qiratya
N. Paran
Ra's an Naqb
MA'ĀN
875
Bîr Gebeil Hisn
S I N A I
W. el Mahasham
Al Kuntilla
Yotvata
Mahattat ash Shidiyah
El Suweis (Suez)
Bûr Taufiq
Nakhl
W. el 'Aqaba
Bîr Abu Muhammad
El Thamad
Ra's an Naqb 1435
'Uyūn Mūsa
Bîr Bad'
W. el Tamad
W. Giraf
Bi'r al Butayyihāt

F
Ghubbet el Bûs
Bîr Abu Sandiq
W. el Yarqa
948 G. el Kabrit
'En Avrona
SAUDI
1272
Rās Matarma
Gebeı el Tîh
El Wabeira
Bîr el Biarât
1592
1165
Aţ Tubāyq
952
ARABIA
W. Abu Ga'da
W. Abu el Gaîri
S i n a i   P e n i n s u l a
Bîr el Hoxi
Khalîg el 'Aqaba
'Aqabah
W. an Nuwaybi
Eqiat
Al 'Aqabah

34   35   East from Greenwich 36   37

ft   m
9000   3000
6000   2000
4500   1500
3000   1000
1200   400
600   200
0   0
600   2000
6000
m   ft

Projection: Polyconic

= = = 1974 Cease Fire Lines

COPYRIGHT. GEORGE PHILIP & SON. LTD.

1 : 33 600 000

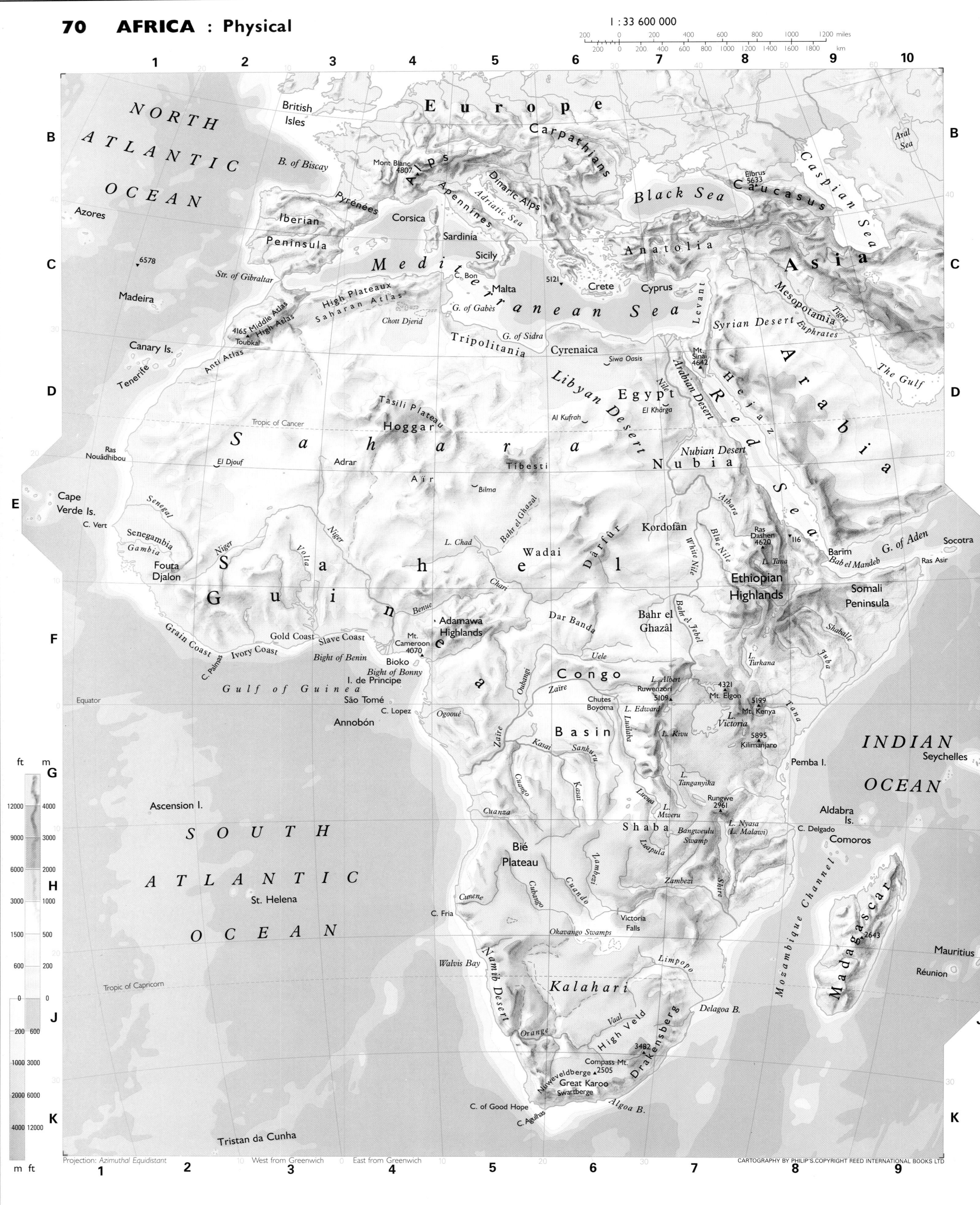

NORTH ATLANTIC OCEAN

Europe

British Isles

B. of Biscay

Mont Blanc 4807

Alps

Pyrénées

Apennines

Dinaric Alps

Adriatic Sea

Carpathians

Black Sea

Elbrus 5633

Caucasus

Caspian Sea

Aral Sea

Azores

Iberian Peninsula

Corsica

Sardinia

Sicily

Anatolia

Asia

6578

Madeira

Str. of Gibraltar

High Plateaux

Saharan Atlas

C. Bon

Malta

5121

Crete

Cyprus

Mesopotamia

Tigris

Canary Is.

4165 Middle Atlas

High Atlas

Toubkal

Chott Djerid

G. of Gabès

Mediterranean Sea

G. of Sidra

Tripolitania

Cyrenaica

Siwa Oasis

Levant

Mt. Sinai 4642

Syrian Desert

Euphrates

Arabia

The Gulf

Tenerife

Anti Atlas

Tropic of Cancer

Tasili Plateau

Libyan Desert

Egypt

El Khârga

Nile

Arabian Desert

Hejaz

Ras Nouâdhibou

S a h a r a

Hoggar

El Kufrah

Red Sea

El Djouf

Adrar

Aïr

Bilma

Tibesti

Nubia

Nubian Desert

Atbara

Ras Dashen 4620

116

Barim

Bab el Mandeb

G. of Aden

Socotra

Cape Verde Is.

C. Vert

Senegal

Niger

Niger

S a h e l

L. Chad

Bahr el Ghazal

Wadai

Dârfûr

Kordofân

White Nile

Blue Nile

L. Tana

Ras Asir

Senegambia

Gambia

Fouta Djalon

G u i n e a

Volta

Benue

Mt. Cameroon 4070

Adamawa Highlands

Chari

Dar Banda

Bahr el Ghazâl

Bahr el Jebel

Ethiopian Highlands

Somali Peninsula

Shabalie

Grain Coast

Ivory Coast

C. Palmas

Gold Coast

Slave Coast

Bight of Benin

Bioko

Bight of Bonny

I. de Principe

São Tomé

Uele

Oubangui

Uele

Congo

L. Albert

Ruwenzori 5109

4321

Mt. Elgon

5199

Mt. Kenya

L. Turkana

Juba

Gulf of Guinea

C. Lopez

Ogooué

Zaire

Chutes Boyoma

L. Edward

Tana

Equator

Annobón

Zaire

Basin

Kasai

Sankuru

Kasai

Luluaba

L. Kivu

L. Victoria

5895 Kilimanjaro

Pemba I.

INDIAN OCEAN

Seychelles

Ascension I.

SOUTH ATLANTIC OCEAN

St. Helena

Cuango

Cuanza

Cuango

Chango

Kwango

L. Tanganyika

L. Mweru

Luapula

Rungwe 2961

Lwegu

Aldabra Is.

C. Delgado

Comoros

Bié Plateau

Shaba

Bangweulu Swamp

L. Nyasa (L. Malawi)

Mozambique Channel

Madagascar

2643

Cunene

Cubango

Zambezi

Cuando

Zambezi

Shire

C. Fria

Victoria Falls

Walvis Bay

Okavango Swamps

Limpopo

Mauritius

Réunion

Tropic of Capricorn

Namib Desert

Kalahari

High Veld

Delagoa B.

Orange

Vaal

Drakensberg

3482

Compass Mt. 2505

Nuweveldberge

Great Karoo

Swartberge

Algoa B.

C. of Good Hope

C. Agulhas

Tristan da Cunha

ft m

12000 4000

9000 3000

6000 2000

3000 1000

1500 500

600 200

0 0

200 600

1000 3000

2000 6000

4000 12000

m ft

Projection: *Azimuthal Equidistant*

West from Greenwich

East from Greenwich

1 : 33 600 000

200 0 200 400 600 800 1000 1200 miles
200 0 200 400 600 800 1000 1200 1400 1600 1800 km

NORTH
ATLANTIC
OCEAN

Azores
(Port.)

Madeira
(Port.)

Canary Is.
(Sp.)

CAPE VERDE IS.

Praia

SOUTH
ATLANTIC

OCEAN

Ascension I.
(U.K.)

St. Helena
(U.K.)

Tristan da Cunha
(U.K.)

UNITED
KINGDOM
LONDON
NETH.
BELG.
PARIS
FRANCE
B. of Biscay
GERMANY POLAND
Warsaw
Prague
CZECH REP.
Vienna
SLOV. K REP.
SWITZ. AUSTRIA HUNGARY
CROATIA
BOS.-
HERZ. YUG.
ITALY
ROMANIA
Adriatic Sea
SLB.
MAC.
BULGARIA
Corsica
Rome
Sardinia
GREECE
Athens
Sicily
MALTA
Crete
CYPRUS
Mediterranean Sea

Kiev
RUSSIA
UKRAINE
Odessa
Black Sea
GEORGIA
Ankara
ARM.
AZER.
TURKEY
Aleppo
SYRIA
LEB.
Damascus
Tel Aviv
-Jaffa
ISRAEL
Jerusalem
JORDAN

Volgograd
KAZAKHSTAN
Aral
Sea
Baku
Caspian Sea
TURKMEN.
Mosul
Tigris
Baghdād
Euphrates
IRAQ
Basra
KUWAIT
TEHRĀN
Eşfahān
IRAN
The Gulf
BAHRAIN
QATAR

Madrid
SPAIN
Lisbon
PORTUGAL

Algiers
Annaba
Constantine
Tunis
TUNISIA
Sfax
Tripoli
Misrātah
Benghazi

Rabat
Tétouan
Casablanca
Fès
MOROCCO
Marrakesh
Chott Djerid

Alexandria
Port Said
CAIRO
El Faiyûm
Suez

EGYPT
Asyût

SAUDI
Medina
Riyadh
ARABIA
Jedda
Mecca

El Aaiún
WESTERN SAHARA
Dakhla
Fdérik

ALGERIA
In Salah
Tropic of Cancer

LIBYA
Marzūq
Al Jawf

Sahara

Nile
Aswān
Wadi Halfa
Port Sudan

Red Sea

YEMEN
G. of Aden
Socotra
(Yemen)

Ras
Nouâdhibou
MAURITANIA
Nouakchott

Tombouctou

NIGER
Agadès

CHAD

Atbara
Omdurmân
Khartoum
Wâd Medani
SUDAN
El Fâsher
El Obeid

ERITREA
Mesewa
Asmera

Ras Asir

St-Louis
C. Vert
Dakar
SENEGAL
GAMBIA
Banjul
GUINEA
BISSAU
Bissau

MALI
Bámako
Niger
Niamey
BURKINA
FASO
Ouagadougou
Bobo-
Dioulasso
Kano
BENIN
L. Chad
Maiduguri
Abéché
Ndjamena

L. Tana
DJIBOUTI
Djibouti
Berbera

Conakry
Freetown
SIERRA
LEONE
GUINEA
Yamoussoukro
IVORY
COAST
Bouaké
GHANA
Kumasi
TOGO
Lomé
Accra
NIGERIA
Abuja
Ibadan
Enugu
Lagos
Porto
Novo
Benue
CENTRAL
AFRICAN REP.
Wau
Malakâl
White Nile
Blue Nile
Addis Ababa
Harer
ETHIOPIA

Shabelle
SOMALI REP.
Mogadishu

Monrovia
LIBERIA
Abidjan
Sekondi-
Takoradi
Bight of Benin
CAMEROON
Douala
Yaoundé
Bangui
Chari
Bahr el Jebel

Port
Harcourt
EQUATORIAL
GUINEA
Malabo
Bight of Benin
Gulf of Guinea
SÃO TOMÉ & PRINCIPE
Equator
Libreville
CONGO
Zaïre
mbandaka
Kisangani
Ouanga
ZAÏRE
L. Albert
UGANDA
Kampala
L. Edward
RWANDA
Kigali
L. Kivu
BURUNDI
Bujumbura
L. Turkana
KENYA
Kisumu
L. Victoria
Nairobi
Kismayu
Mombasa
Juba
Tana

C. Lopez
Annobón
GABON
Kasai
Pointe Noire
Brazzaville
Kinshasa
Matadi
CABINDA
(Angola)
Kananga

Luanda
Lobito
Huambo
ANGOLA
Namibe

Lukuga
L. Tanganyika
TANZANIA
Dodoma
Dar es Salaam
Zanzibar

INDIAN
SEYCHELLES
OCEAN

Aldabra
Is.

Likasi
Lubumbashi
Ndola
ZAMBIA
Lusaka
Zambezi
L. Mweru
L. Malawi
MALAWI
Lilongwe
Blantyre
C. Delgado
COMOROS
Mayotte
(Fr.)
Antsiranana
Mahajanga

C. Fria
NAMIBIA
Windhoek
Cunene
Cubango
Livingstone
Harare
Beira
MOZAMBIQUE
Moçambique
Toamasina
MADAGASCAR
Antananarivo
MAURITIUS
Réunion
(Fr.)

BOTSWANA
Gaborone
ZIMBABWE
Bulawayo
Limpopo
Tropic of Capricorn

Orange
Vaal
Kimberley
Johannesburg
Pretoria
Maputo
Mbabane
SWAZ.
LESOTHO
Maseru
Durban

SOUTH AFRICA
Cape Town
C. of Good Hope
C. Agulhas
East
London
Port
Elizabeth

Fianarantsoa

Mozambique Channel

Projection: Azimuthal Equidistant
West from Greenwich
East from Greenwich
Dakar ● Capital Cities

1 2 3 4 5 6

NORTH ATLANTIC OCEAN

▼ 6578

Cabo de São Vicente

SPAIN
Cádiz • Málaga • Almería
Gibraltar (Br.) Sidi-Bel-Abbès Oran
Str. of Gibraltar Ceuta (Sp.) Alger (Algiers) Harrach Tizi-Ouzou Bejaia Jijel Skikda Annaba Tabarka
Tanger Tétouan Al Hoceima Melilla Mostaganem Ech Cheliff Kherrata Mil Blida Medea Setif Constantine Guelma El Kal
Larache Azrou Ksar el Boukhari Hodna Batna Khenchela Ain Beida
Ksar el Kebir Oujda Tlemcen Saïda Hauts Plateaux Bou Saâda Biskra Tebessa Gafsa
Kenitra (Port Lyautey) Ouezzane Taourirt El Aricha Mecheria Djelfa Ouled Djellal Nefta Tozeur Chott Djerid Gabes
Salé Fès Taza Jerada Chech Chergui El Bayadh Laghouat Touggourt El Oued Chott el Djerid Kebili
Rabat Meknès Ain Sefra Hassi er Rmel
Casablanca Berrechid Khemisset Bou Arfa Ghardaïa Ouargla Hassi Messaoud Sinâwa
El Jadida Settat Khouribga 2235 Figuig Beni Ounif Béchar Hassi Messaoud
Safi Ras Beddouza Beni Mellal Ar Rachidya Abadla Igli
MOROCCO Marrakech Ouarzazate Kerzaz Timimoun In Salah Ghudâmis
Essaouira Dj. Toubkal 4165 Taroudannt Dra Mengoub Beni Abbès Ft. Mac-Mahon Hassi Inifel Ft. Miribel Daro
Agadir C. Rhir Tiznit Bou Izakarn Igli Charouine Adrar In Belbel Ohanet
Ifni Anti Atlas Tindouf Plateau du Tademait Bordj Omar Driss
Islas Canarias (Sp.) Lanzarote Arrecife Zaouiet Reggane Aoulef el Arab Illizi
La Palma Fuerteventura Puerto del Rosario Bj. Fly Ste. Marie Miliana
Tenerife Gomera 3718 Sta. Cruz Gran Canaria Las Palmas C. Juby Tarfaya El Aaiún Semara Chech Arak Idelès Bj.-Tarat Sardalas Ghat
Hierro Bu Craa Ain Ben Tili Chegga Quallene Bj.-in-Eker Ahaggar Tahat 2918 Djanet
WESTERN SAHARA C. Bojador Bir Mogrein Terhazza Erg Tanezrouft Tamanrasset
Dakhla Pta. Durnford Poste Maurice Cortier (Bidon 5) Admer
C. Barbas Dérik Zouérate Taoudenni Adrar des Iforhas Tessalit
Chår S Tidjikja El Djouf Mabrouk Aïr Monts Tamgak
Nouâdhibou (Port Etienne) Ouadâne Araouane Bou Djébéha Kidal Iférouâne (Azbine) 1900
Ras Nouâdhibou La Güera Atâr Chinguetti Tichit MAURITANIA Ougeft Aguéras
C. Timiris Akjoujt Rachid Tidjikja Nioro du Sahel Tombouctou Bamba Bourem Gourma-Rharous I-n-Gall Agadez Fach
Nouakchott Boutilimit Moudjéria Togba Qualâta Néma Kabara Gao Ménaka NIGER
Mederdra Aleg Tâmchekket Kiffa Timbedgha Bâssikounou Niafouke Diré Ansongo Tahoua Tanout
St. Louis Rosso Podor Bogué Kaédi Mbout Sél-babi Yélimané Nioro du Sahel Nara Hombori Tamské Madaoua Gangara Kellé
Louga Dagana Matam Sokolo Douentza Téra Filingué Birni Nkonni Zinder Kamaguenou Nguru
Dakar Tivaouane Thiès Linguère Dahra Kayes Bafoulabé Ké-Macina Mopti Djibo Dori Kaya Tillabéri Niamey Maradi Katsina
C. Vert Kaolack Kaffrine Tiel Diafarabé MALI Bandiagara Ouahigouya Say Dosso Birni-Kebbi Gummi Zaria
SENEGAL Tambacounda Bakel Kita Banamba Ségou Sarro Dienné BURKINA FASO Ouagadougou Fada N'Gourma Diapaga Jega Gandi Katsina
GAMBIA Georgetown Kolda Satadougou Koulikoro Douna Koutiala FASO Koudougou Tenkodogo Botou Kende Anka Kano
Banjul Sedhiou Kedougou Bamako Sikasso Banfora Diébougou Léo Dédougou Pama Kaiama Funtua Kaduna
GUINEA-BISSAU Farim Tougué Siguiri Dabola Kankan Odienné Kong Bouna Nikki Parakou Jebba Minna Bauchi
Bissau Bolama Gaoual Labé Dinguiraye Kouroussa Séguéla Katiola Bondoukou Tamale Savalou Ilorin Bida Jos
Arquipélago dos Bijagós Boké Télimélé Fouta Djalon Faranah Beyla Touba Man Daloa Bouaké Kumasi Lake Volta Abomey Ogbomosho Ibadan Benin City Enugu
GUINEA Conakry Forécariah Kissidougou Macenta Guéckédou Danané Guiglo Gagnoa Dimbokro IVORY COAST Yamoussoukro GHANA TOGO BENIN Lagos Onitsha
SIERRA LEONE Freetown Makeni Magburaka Kenema Bo LIBERIA Monrovia Buchanan Greenville Tabou Sassandra San-Pédro Abidjan Grand Bassam Accra Cape Coast Sekondi-Takoradi Cotonou Porto-Novo Lomé Bight of Benin Port-Harcourt Aba Calabar CAMEROON Douala

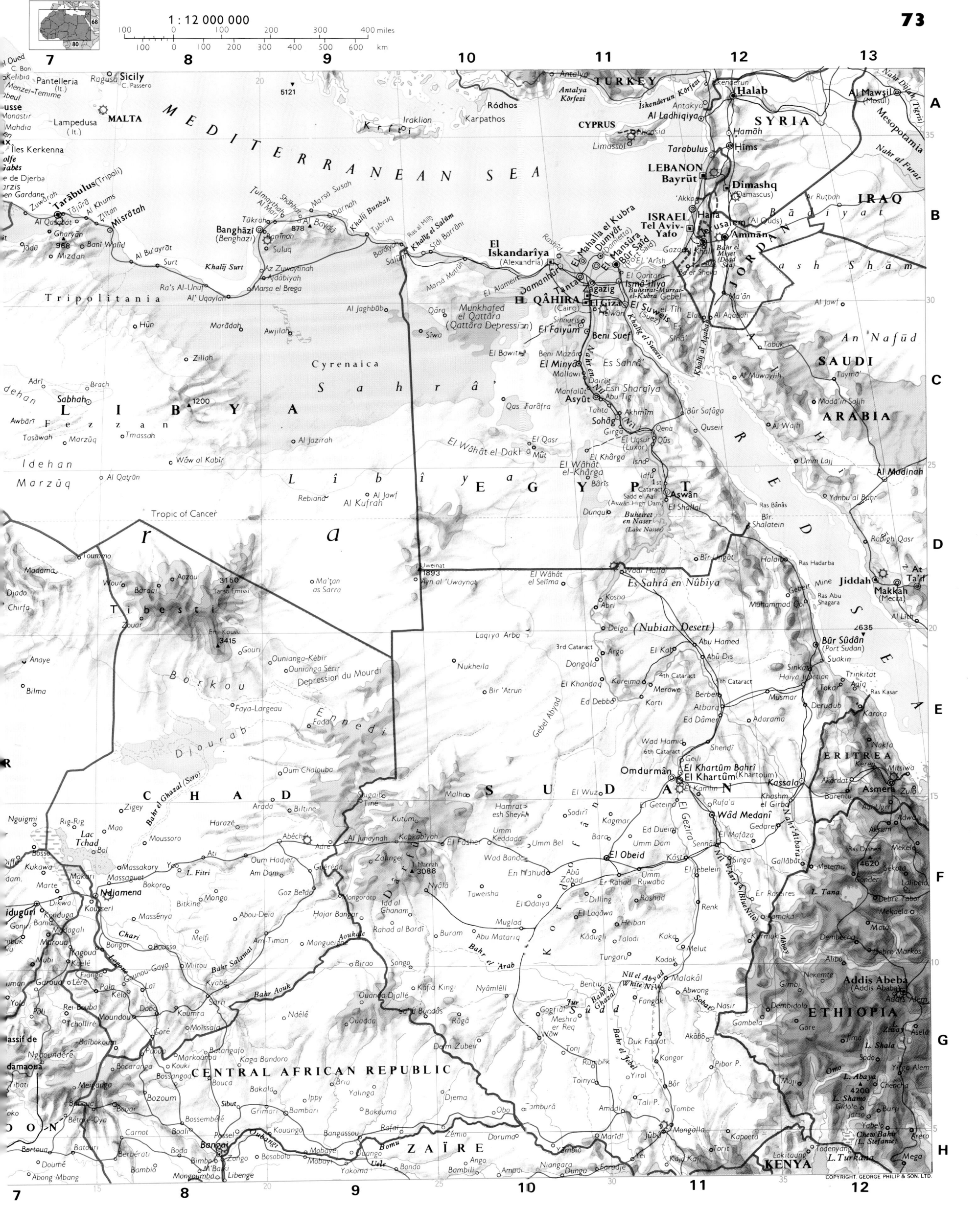

A

B

C

D

E

1   2   3

NORTH

ATLANTIC

OCEAN

Madeira (Port.)
Porto Moniz   São Vicente   I. de Porto Santo
Santana   Machico
Funchal   861
Ilhas Desertas

Ilhas Salvagens

La Palma   2423   Islas Canarias (Sp.)
Los Llanos de Aridane   Sta. Cruz de la Palma
Pta. Fuencaliente   Tenerife   Alegranza
Graciosa
La Laguna   La Orotava   Santa Cruz   Lanzarote
S. Sebastian de la G.   3718   Icod   de Tenerife   Arrecife
Gomera   Granadilla   Gula   Las   La Oliva   I. de Lobos
Valverde   de Abona   Palmas   Puerto del Rosario
Hierro   1501   Pta. de la Rasca   1949   Mogán   807
Pta. de Maspálomas   Gran Canaria   Fuerteventura

SANLÚCAR de Barramede
Cádiz   SPAIN
C. Trafalgar   Algeciras   Gibr.   1452
C. Spartel   Strait of Gibraltar
Tangier   Ras Tarf   Ceuta
Asilah   Martil   Tétouan
Larache   Chechaouen   2456
Ksar el Kebir   Oued
Souk el Arba du Rharb   Taou
Mechra-bel-Ksiri
Kenitra   Sidi Slimane   Allal-Tazi
Salé   Sidi Kacem   Sefrou
RABAT   MEKNES   Volubilis
CASABLANCA   FES
Mohammedia   Khemisset   El Hajeb
Azemmour   Ben Slimane   Rommani   Azrou
Berrechid   Benahmed   Khouribga   Khenifra
El Jadida (Mazagan)   Settat   Oued Zem
Safi   Youssoufia   Fkih ben Salah   Beni Mellal
Benguerir   O. Oum er Rbia   Kasba Tadla   3737
Essaouira   MARRAKECH   MOROCCO
C. Sim   Chichaoua   4071
C. Tafelney   Tamanar   Demnate   Azilal   Djebel Sarhro
Amizmiz   4165   Tinerhir   Boumalne   Alnif
Tamri   Taroudannt   Oj. Toubkal   Ouarzazate   Zagora   O. Draa   Rissani
Cap Rhir   O. Souss   Anti Atlas   Foum Zguid   Tarhbalt   Erfoud
Agadir   Irezgane   Tiznit   2359   Kem-Kem
Biougra   Tafraoute   Tata   Bani
Goulimine   Djebel   Mengoub   Di. Bet Tadjine
Seyad   Djebel Ouarkziz   Oum el Ksi   Zegdou
Cap Draa   Assa   Hamada Tounassine
Tan-tan   Oued Draa   Haut Plateau du Dra   Tinfouchi
O. Tigzerte   Tindouf   Khorb el Ethel   Rhemilès
Tarfaya (Villa Bens)   Messeied   Kreb r. Neggar   Tounassine
C. Juby   Ouahila   Boubout
Hagunia   Kreb es Sefia
El Aaiún   Kreb n-Naga   Kreb Chebiha
El Hasian   Smara   Gara Djebilet   Oum el Guedour   580
C. Bojador   Bu Craa   El Hadeb   Ora Djebilet   Mcherrah
Tifarati   Bir el Abbes   El Eglab
Uad Erni   Touila
Ain Ben Tili   Chegga   Chenachane
540   O. Chenachane
Amasin   Daya el Khadra   Grizim
Zemmur   Agmar   Tarhamanant
Guelta Zemmur   Bir Bel Guerdâne   Tniha
Bir Mogrein   Sebkhet Iguetti   Ayoûn el Atroûs   El Mzereb
WESTERN SAHARA   Ayoûn 'Abd el Mâlek
Pta. Elbow   Ghallamane   El Khâght   Yetti
Dakhla   Sebkhet Oumm ed Drous Telli   El Hank
Pta. Durnford   El Aargub   El Mreiti   Kreb en Naga   Terhazza
B. de Río de Oro   El Mrâyer   Aguelt el Melah
G. de Cintra   Tiris   El Beyyed   Aguerakem   Bir Chali   En Nahrat
Pta. Negra   Sidi Emhamed   MAURITANIA   Hamada Safia
C. Barbas   Imessan   Sebkhet Ijill   Hammâmi   Bir Amrâne   Taoudenni   Telig
Ezmul   Fdérik   Zouîrât   Meleizem   Mejâuda   El Guettara
C. Corbeiro   Adrar Souttuf   Kediet Ijill   915   Touîne   Dglats de Khenachiche
Uad Tenouâmir   Tichla   Zug   Maqtelr   Bir Ounane   Dhar Khenachiche
Agailos   Aguenit   Agh reijit   MALI
BK Gandús   Aghoueyyit   El Ghallaouïya   El Ksaib Dunane   Ergi
La Güera   Boû Lanoûar   Char   Guelb er Richât   Douâouīr
Ras   Nouâdhibou   Toueirma   Ouâdâne   Ouarâne   I-n-Echai
Nouâdhibou   Bîr el Gâreb   Afár   Chinguetti   Ifâfene
Dakhlet Nouâdhibou   Ahmeyim   Oujeft   Bollé
Et Tidra   Agouifa   Amsâga
Rãs Timiris   Akjoujt
Nouâmghar   Bennichchâb   Oguelleten Nmādi
Sebkhet Te-n-Dghâmcha

ft   m
12,000   4000
9000   3000
6000   2000
4500   1500
3000   1000
1200   400
600   200
0   0
200   600
2000   6000
4000   12,000
m   ft

Projection: Lambert's Equivalent Azimuthal

1   2   3   4

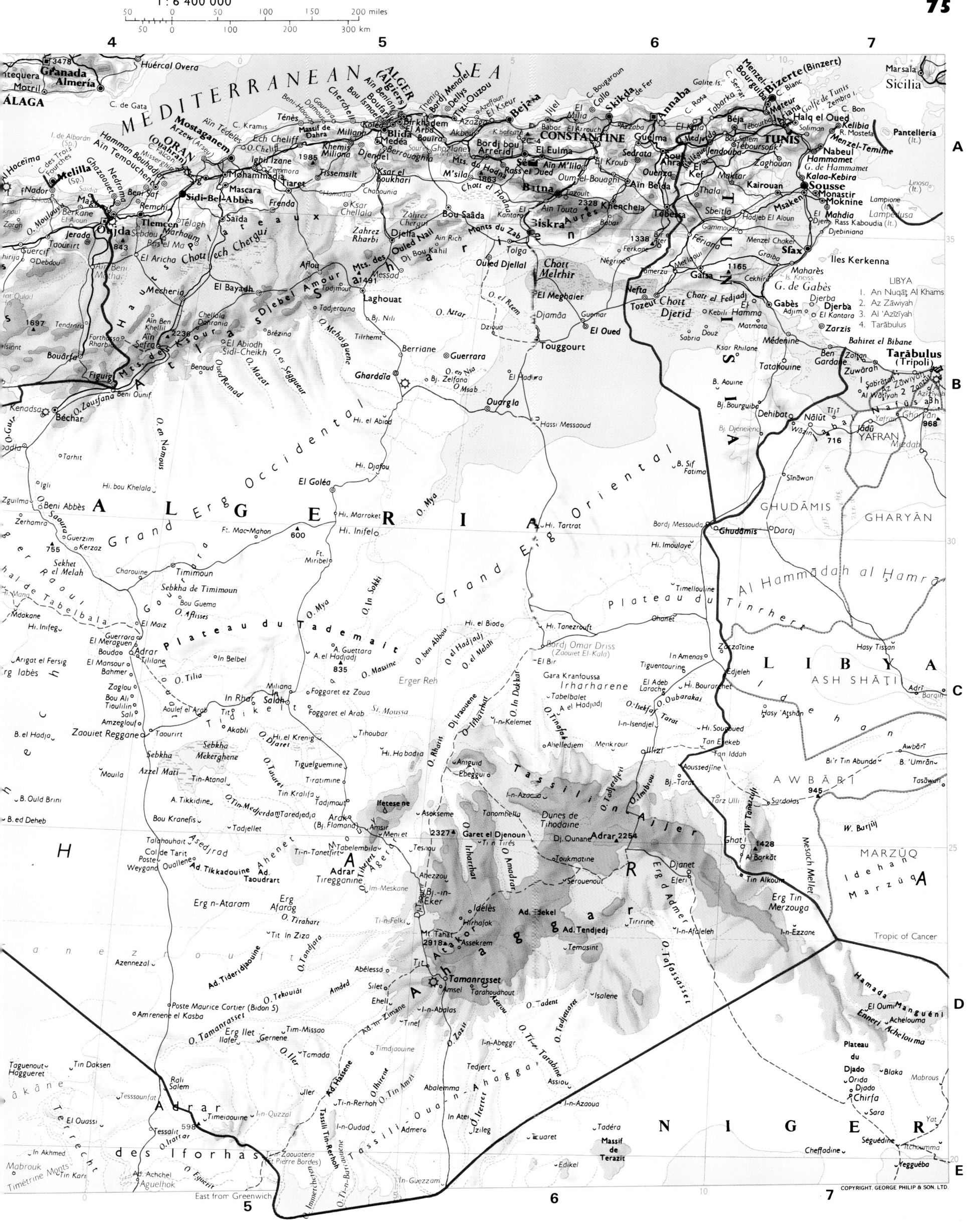

1 : 6 400 000

50   0   50   100   150   200 miles
50   0   100   200   300 km

MEDITERRANEAN SEA

ALGER (Algiers)

LIBYA
1. An Nuqāṭ Al Khams
2. Az Zāwiyah
3. Al 'Azīzīyah
4. Tarābulus

ALGERIA

TUNISIA

LIBYA

ASH SHĀṬI

GHUDĀMIS

GHARYĀN

Al Ḥammādah al Ḥamrā

Plateau du Tinrhert

Grand Erg Occidental

Grand Erg Oriental

Plateau du Tademaït

Tassili n'Ajjer

AWBĀRĪ

MARZŪQ

Idehan Marzūq

Tropic of Cancer

Hamada Manguéni

Plateau du Djado

NIGER

Adrar des Iforhas

East from Greenwich

THE NILE DELTA
1 : 3 200 000

1 : 6 400 000

50   100   150   200 miles
50   100   200   300 km

MEDITERRANEAN SEA

Nile Delta inset (1:3 200 000):

Bûr Sa'îd (Port Said)
Dumyât (Damietta)
El Manzala
El Mansûra
Fâriskûr
Shirbîn
El Simbillawein
Ismâ'îlîya
Zaqâzîq
Kafr el Sheikh
El Maḥalla el Kubra
Tanta
Benha
Qalyûb
Heliopolis
EL QÂHIRA (Cairo)
Imbâbah
El Gîza
Beni Suef
El Faiyûm
Sinnûris
Shibîn el Kôm
Minûf
Ashmûn
Damanhûr
El Mahmûdîya
El Dilingât
EL ISKANDARÎYA (Alexandria)
Rashîd (Rosetta)
Fuwa
Birket Qârûn
Wadi el Natrûn

Main map labels:

MEDITERRANEAN SEA
SAUDI ARABIA
JORDAN
ISRAEL
EGYPT
E G Y P T
ES SÎNA (Sinai)
SAHARA ESH SHARQÎYA
Western Desert (Es Saḥrâ' el Gharbîya)
Nubian Desert (Es Saḥrâ' en Nûbîya)
BAHR EL AHMAR
ESH SHAMÂLÎYA

Amman
Jerusalem (Al Quds)
Tel Aviv-Yafo
Gaza
EL ISKANDARÎYA (Alexandria)
EL QÂHIRA (Cairo)
Heliopolis
El Gîza
Beni Suef
El Faiyûm
El Minyâ
Mallawi
Asyût
Sohâg
Girga
Nag Hammâdi
Qena
Luxor (El Uqsur)
Qûs
Idfu
Kôm Ombo
Aswân
Buheiret en Nâser (Lake Nasser)
Sadd el Aali (Aswan High Dam)
Abu Simbel
Wadi Halfa
Bûr Sûdân (Port Sudan)
Berber
Atbara
Makkah (Mecca)
Al Madînah (Medina)
Jiddah
Yanbu' al Baḥr
Al Qunfudhah

Tropic of Cancer
East from Greenwich

El Wâḥât el Khârga
El Wâḥât el Dâkhla
El Wâḥât el Baḥarîya
El Wâḥât el Farâfra
Siwa
Qattâra (Munkhafad el Qattâra)
Libyan Plateau
Marsâ Maṭrûḥ
Sîdî Barrâni

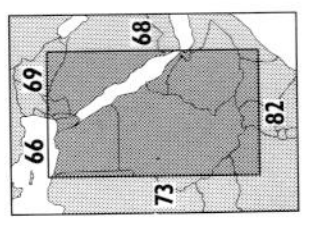

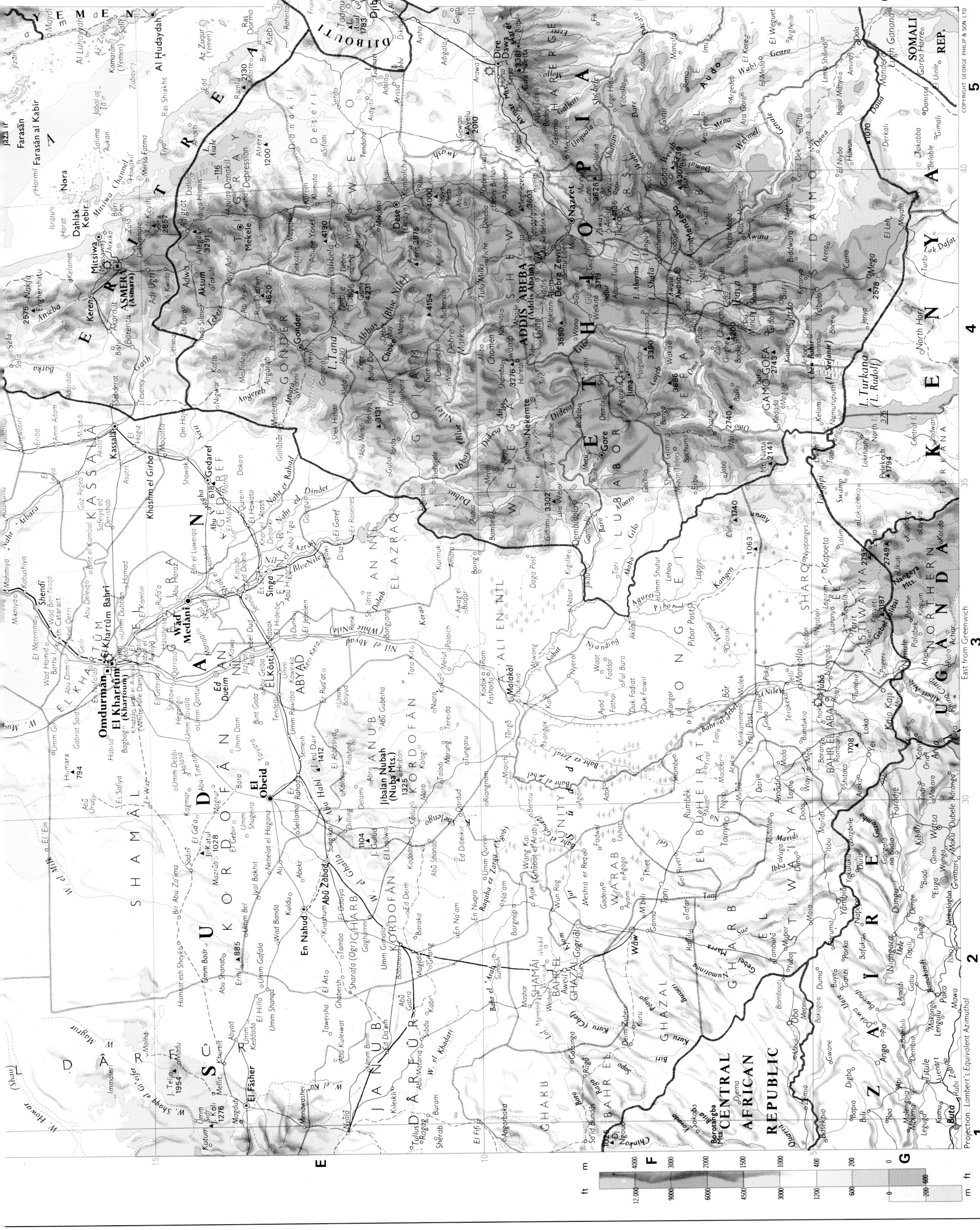

YEMEN

ERITREA

DJIBOUTI
Djibouti 1783

ETHIOPIA

Asmara (Asmära)
Mitsiwa
Keren
Mekele
Adigrat
Aksum
Adwa
Gonder
L. Tana
Dese
Debre Markos
ADDIS ABEBA (Addis Abäbä)
Debre Zeyit
Nazret
Jima

GOJAM
SHEWA
WELO
TIGRE
WELEGA
ILUBABOR
KEFA
GAMO-GOFA
SIDAMO
BALE
HARERGE
ARSI

Danakil Depression

Awash

Dire Dawa

SUDAN

KHARTUM
Omdurman
El Khartum Bahri
(Khartoum)
Wad Medani
Kassala
Gedaref
Singa
Ed Dueim
El Kosti
El Obeid
En Nahud
El Fasher

KASSALA
GEDAREF
EL KHARTUM
DARFUR
KORDOFAN
SHAMAL KORDOFAN
JANUB KORDOFAN
SHAMAL DARFUR
JANUB DARFUR
GHARB KORDOFAN
AN NIL
AN NIL EL AZRAQ
AL ABYAD
EL AZRAQ

Nuba Mts.
Jibalan Nubah 1325

White Nile (Nil el Abyad)
Blue Nile (El Azraq)

Malakal
Juba
Wau
Bor
Rumbek
Tonj

UNITY
WARAB
EL WAHDA
BAHR EL GHAZAL
GHARB BAHR EL GHAZAL
EL BUHEIRAT
JONGLEI
ALI EN NIL
SHARQ
SIWAWIYA
NORTHERN

L. Turkana (L. Rudolf)

KENYA

SOMALI REP.

UGANDA

ZAIRE

CENTRAL AFRICAN REPUBLIC

East from Greenwich

Projection: Lambert's Equivalent Azimuthal

COPYRIGHT GEORGE PHILIP & SON LTD

ft m
4000 12,000
9000 3000
6000 2000
4500 1500
3000 1000
1200 400
600 200
0 0
200–600

MAURITANIA

Nouakchott

SENEGAL

DAKAR
St. Louis

GAMBIA
Banjul

GUINEA-
BISSAU
Arquipélago dos Bijagós

Bissau

GUINEA

Conakry

SIERRA
LEONE
Freetown

LIBERIA

Monrovia

IVORY COAST

Bamako

Bobo-
Dioulasso

Bouaké

Abidjan

Projection: Lambert's Equivalent Azimuthal

West from Gree

ft	m
12 000	4000
9000	3000
6000	2000
4500	1500
3000	1000
1200	400
600	200
0	0
200	600
2000	6000
4000	12 000
6000	18 000
m	ft

1 : 6 400 000

50   0   50   100   150   200 miles
50   0   100   200   300 km

**N. E.
NIGERIA**
on same scale
as general map

ALGERIA

Adrar des Iforhas

NIGER

Aïr
(Azbine)

Agadez
(Agadès)

Talak

BURKINA FASO

Niamey

Sokoto

Kano

Zinder

Maradi

Katsina

Zaria

Kaduna

NIGERIA

Abuja

Jos

PLATEAU

ADAMAWA

GHANA

Tamale

BENIN

TOGO

Parakou

Ilorin

Ogbomosho

IBADAN

Abeokuta

LAGOS

Benin City

Makurdi

Enugu

CAMEROON

Yola

ACCRA

Lomé

Cotonou

Porto-Novo

Warri

Port-Harcourt

Calabar

Slave Coast

Bight of Benin

Niger Delta

Bight of Bonny

Bioko (Fernando Poo)

EQUATORIAL GUINEA

DOUALA

Yaoundé

East from Greenwich

OF GUINEA

COPYRIGHT GEORGE PHILIP & SON LTD.

Countries / major regions: NIGER · CHAD · SUDAN · ETHIOPIA · ERITREA · CENTRAL AFRICAN REPUBLIC · NIGERIA · CAMEROON · EQUATORIAL GUINEA · GABON · CONGO · ZAIRE · UGANDA · KENYA · TANZANIA · RWANDA · BURUNDI · ANGOLA · CABINDA

Selected cities and places: Kano · Maiduguri · Ndjamena (Fort Lamy) · El Khartûm (Khartoum) · Omdurmân · El Obeid · Wâd Medanî · Kassala · Asmera · Addis Abeba · El Fasher · Bangui · Yaoundé · Douala · Libreville · Brazzaville · Kinshasa · Matadi · Pointe Noire · Luanda · Kananga · Mbuji-Mayi · Kisangani · Bukavu · Kigali · Bujumbura · Kampala · Nairobi · Mombasa · Dar-es-Salaam · Zanzibar I. · Pemba I. · Mafia I. · Dodoma · Tabora

Lakes / water features: Lac Tchad (Lake Chad) · L. Tana · L. Abaya · L. Shala · Turkana (L. Rudolf) · L. Kyoga · Victoria · L. Albert · L. Edward · L. Kivu · Tanganyika · Rukwa · Kasai · Loango Swamp · Bahr el Ghazal · Nîl el Abyad (White Nile) · Nîl el Azraq (Blue Nile) · Congo · Ubangi · Chari

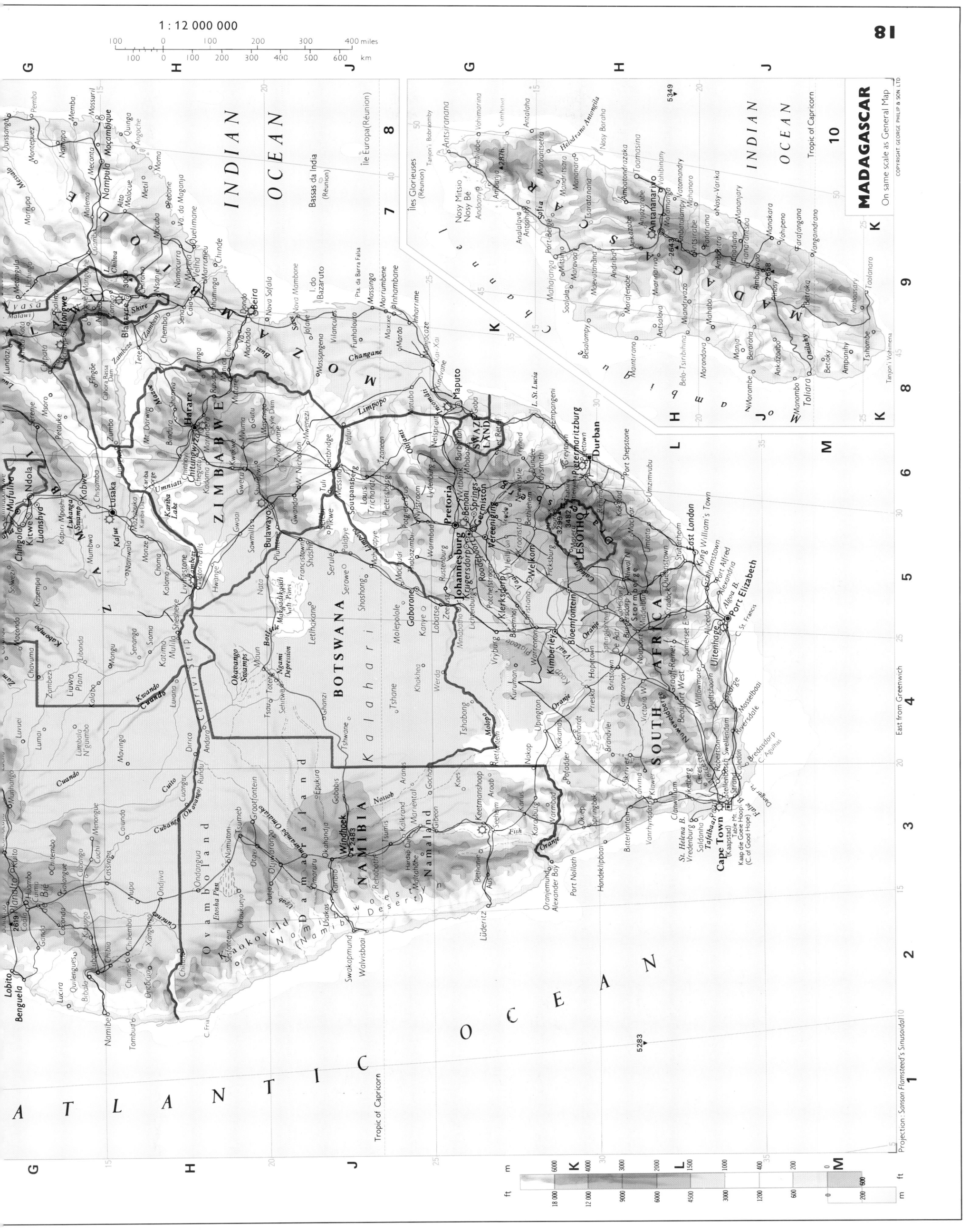

1 : 12 000 000

100   0   100   200   300   400 miles

100 0 100 200 300 400 500 600 km

MADAGASCAR
On same scale as General Map
COPYRIGHT GEORGE PHILIP & SON, LTD.

INDIAN OCEAN

ATLANTIC OCEAN

Projection: Sanson Flamsteed's Sinusoidal

East from Greenwich

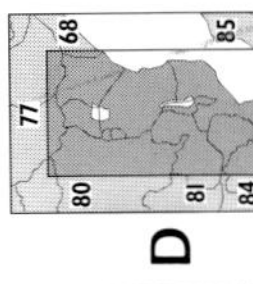

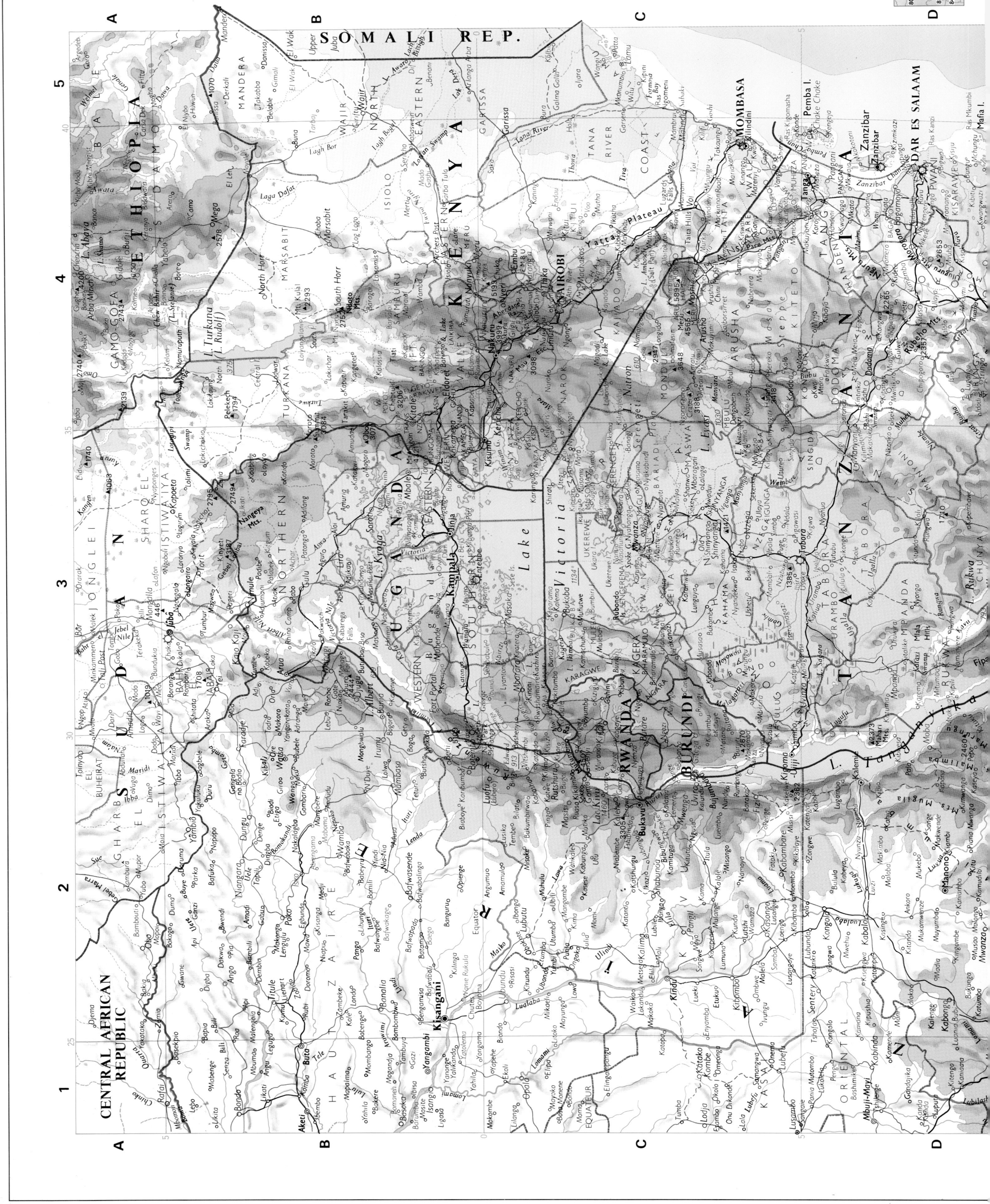

SOMALI REP.

ETHIOPIA

SUDAN

KENYA

UGANDA

TANZANIA

RWANDA

BURUNDI

CENTRAL AFRICAN REPUBLIC

ZAIRE

NAIROBI

MOMBASA

DAR ES SALAAM

Zanzibar

Pemba I.

Mafia I.

Lake Victoria

L. Tanganyika

L. Turkana (L. Rudolf)

L. Albert

L. Kyoga

L. Edward

L. Kivu

L. Natron

Kampala

Entebbe

Jinja

Kisumu

Nakuru

Eldoret

Arusha

Dodoma

Tabora

Kigoma

Ujiji

Bukavu

Kindu

Kisangani

Juba

EQUATOR

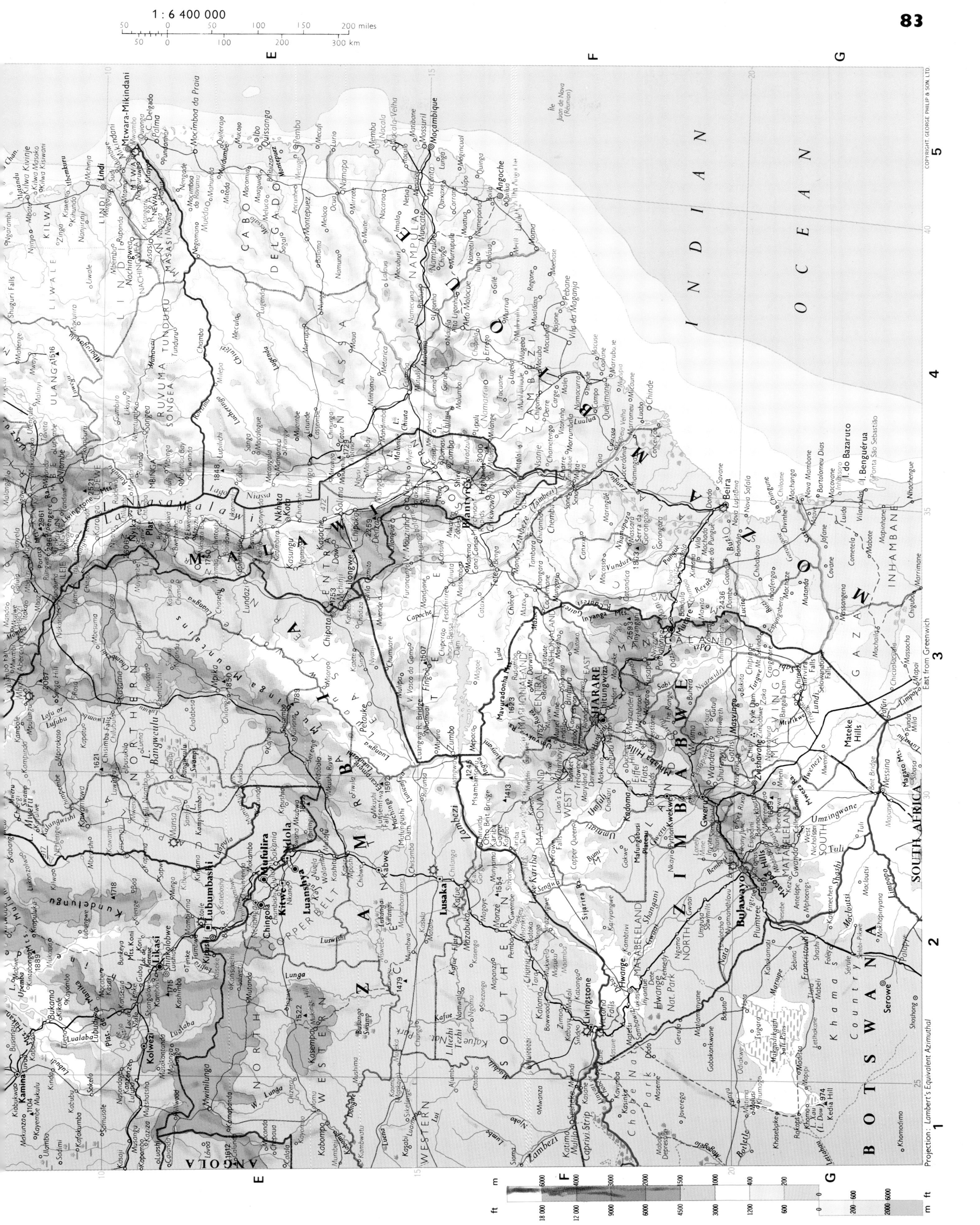

83

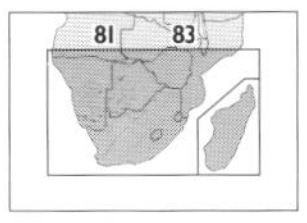

A N G O L A

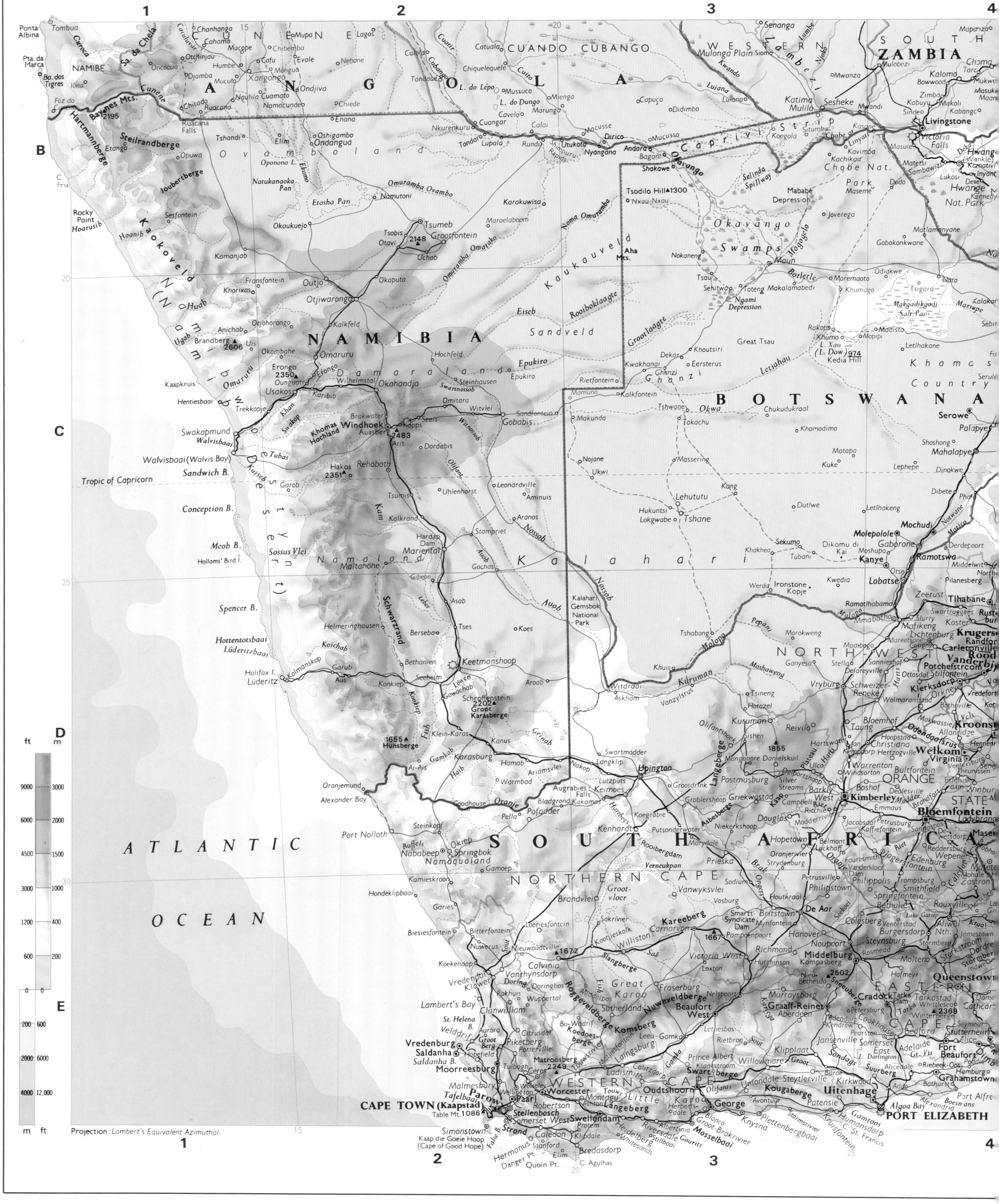

NAMIBIA

BOTSWANA

SOUTH AFRICA

ZAMBIA

ATLANTIC OCEAN

Kalahari

Namib Desert

Tropic of Capricorn

Windhoek

Walvisbaai (Walvis Bay)
Swakopmund

Lüderitz
Lüderitzbaai

Keetmanshoop

Mariental

CAPE TOWN (Kaapstad)
Table Mt. 1086

PORT ELIZABETH

Kimberley
Bloemfontein

ORANGE FREE STATE

NORTHERN CAPE

WESTERN CAPE

EASTERN CAPE

NORTH-WEST

Upington

Ovamboland
Etosha Pan
Tsumeb
Grootfontein
Otjiwarongo
Okahandja
Gobabis
Rehoboth
Maltahöhe
Bethanien
Aus
Karasburg
Oranjemund
Alexander Bay
Port Nolloth
Springbok
Namaqualand
Calvinia
Clanwilliam
Vredenburg
Saldanha
Malmesbury
Stellenbosch
Worcester
Swellendam
Mosselbaai
George
Oudtshoorn
Beaufort West
Graaff-Reinet
Cradock
Queenstown
Middelburg
De Aar
Colesberg
Hanover
Carnarvon
Victoria West
Williston
Sutherland
Great Karoo

Cape of Good Hope (Kaap die Goeie Hoop)
C. Agulhas

CUANDO CUBANGO
Caprivi Strip
Livingstone
Victoria Falls
Hwange
Okavango Swamps
Chobe Nat. Park
Maun
Ghanzi
Serowe
Gaborone
Lobatse
Kanye
Molepolole
Mochudi
Vryburg
Mafikeng
Klerksdorp
Potchefstroom
Welkom
Virginia

Projection: Lambert's Equivalent Azimuthal

MADAGASCAR

On same scale as General Map

COPYRIGHT GEORGE PHILIP & SON, LTD.

P.W.V. = Pretoria-Witwatersrand-Vereeniging

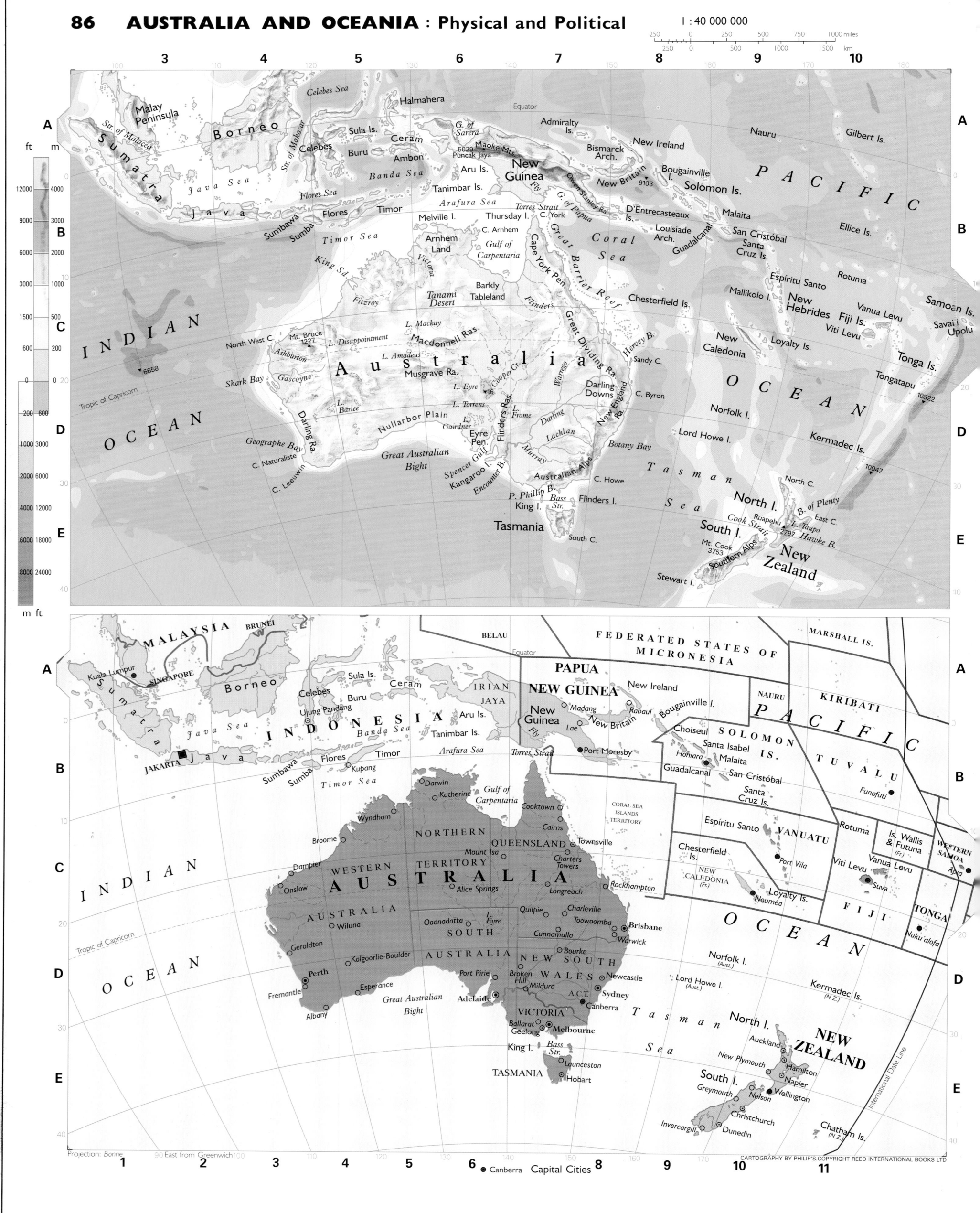

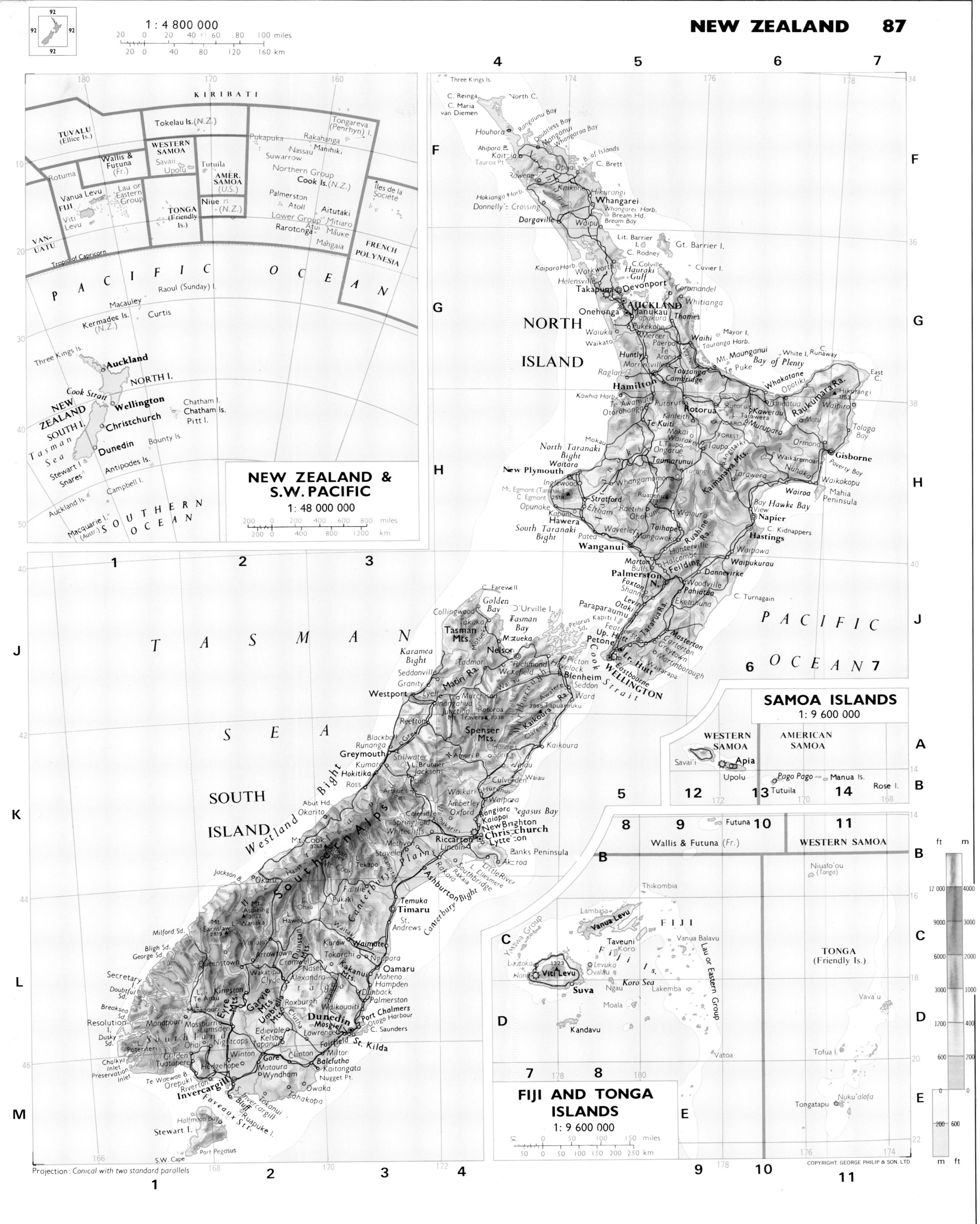

Scale 1 : 4 800 000

NEW ZEALAND & S.W. PACIFIC
1 : 48 000 000

SAMOA ISLANDS
1 : 9 600 000

FIJI AND TONGA ISLANDS
1 : 9 600 000

Projection: Conical with two standard parallels

COPYRIGHT. GEORGE PHILIP & SON, LTD.

INDONESIA

TIMOR SEA

Timor

Sumba

Sumbawa

Lombok

Semau

Roti

Sawu

Danu

Raijua

Hibernia Reef

Ashmore Reef

Cartier I.

Scott Reef

Seringapatam Reef

Lynher Reef

Mermaid Reef

Clerke Reef

Imperieuse Reef

Rowley Shoals

INDIAN OCEAN

Monte Bello Is.
Barrow I.
Pasco I.

NORTHERN TERRITORY

Tanami Desert

Great Sandy Desert

Gibson Desert

Tropic of Capricorn

C. Croker
Gran
Pt. ?
C. Don
P. Essington
C. Dundas
Dundas Str.
Van Diemen
C. Hotham
C. Gambier Pt.
Clarence Str.
C. Fawcett
Pt. Blaze
Peron Is.
Anson B.
C. Scott
C. Hay

Cobourg Pen.
Croker I.
Murgenella
Engyalgoort
Field Id.
Gulf
Oenpelli
Jabiru 480
Noogman
Rum Jungle
Adelaide River
Batchelor
Darwin
Port Darwin
Bathurst I.
Gordan B.
Melville I.

Mt. Greenwood 152
Wingate Mts.
Daly
Dolly River
Daly River
Fitzmaurice
Katherine
Pine Creek
Tindal
Maranboy
Birdum Creek
Larrimah
Birdum
Matoranka
Willeroo
Top Springs
Montejinnie

Timber Creek
Auvergne
Victoria
Cool?bah
Newcastle Ra.
Victoria River Downs
West Baines
Humbert River
Humbert Downs
Wave Hill
Hooker Creek
Winnecke Cr.
Lander
Horden Hills
Tanami
Lewis Ra.
Reynolds Ra.
Anningie
Willowra
Yuenlumu
Mt. Singleton 808
Mt. Liebig 1524
Popunya
Mt. Zeil 1510
Stuart Bluff Ra.
Hermannsburg
Missonia
James Ranges
Macdonnell Ranges
George G?
L. Neale

Joseph Bonaparte Gulf
Cambridge Gulf
Dussejour Gulf
Buckle Hd.
Cockburn
Wyndham
Ivanhoe
Kununurra
Rosewood
Ivanbe
L. Argyle
Turkey Creek
Nicholson
Gordon Downs
Sturt Creek
L. White
L. Wills
L. Hazlett
Lake Mackay
Stansmore Ra.
Kintore Ra.
L. Macdonald
Mt. Leisler 901
Bonython Ra.
Hopkins
L. Mackay

Leeuver I.
Londonderry
Kulumburu
Drysdale
Oombulgurri
Carr Boyd Ra.
Ord
Kalumburu
Pago
Auvergne
Turner
Halls Creek
Mt. Amherst
Elvire
Dunham
Daram Plains
Bedford Downs
Alice Downs
Springvale
Mount Amherst
Christmas Creek
Bohemia Downs
Billiluna
Gregory Lake
Carranya
Percival Lakes
L. Tobin
L. Auld
L. Dora
Blanche
L. George

Eclipse Is.
Vansittart B.
Sir Graham Moore Is.
Talbot
Napier Broome B.
Bigge I.
Long Reef
C. Bougainville
Admiralty Gulf
C. Voltaire
Montague Sd.
York Sd.
Prince Regent R.
Princess May Ras.
Mt. Hann 776
King Edward
Chamberlain
Black Range
Durack Range
Durack
Mt. Elizabeth
Hann
Tableland
Mornington
Margaret
Fitzroy
Margaret R.
St. George Ra.
Mt. Ord 1007
Leopold Ranges
King
Symnott Ra.
Harding Ra.
Isdell
Fitzroy Crossing
Christmas Creek
McClintock Ra.
Mueller Ra.
Albert Edward Ra.

Coronation
Brunswick B.
Camden Sd.
St. George Basin
Augustus I.
Hall Pt.
Collier B.
C. Leveque
Pender B.
Beagle Bay
Yampi Sd.
King Sound
Koolan
Cockatoo I.
Derby
Medi
Wood?s
Eagle R.
Meda
Kimberley Downs
Napier Downs
Noonkanbah
Liveringa
Myroodah
Jubilee
Geegully
Greenough
Camballin

Lacepede Is.
C. Boileau
Carnot B.
C. Latouche Treville
Broome
Roebuck B.
Thangoo
Anna Plains
Roebuck Plains
Lagrange B.
Lagrange
Frazier Downs
Wallal Downs
Eighty
Mile Beach

Adele I.
Buccaneer Archipelago
Bonaparte Archipelago

Isabella Ra.
Gregory Ra.
Shay Gap
Goldsworthy
De Grey
Warrawagine
Mt. Edgar
Nullagine
Bonney Downs
Marble Bar
Roy Hill
Newman 1053
Ethel Creek
Ophthalmia
Mt. Meharry 1251
Mt. Bruce 1235
Mt. Robinson
Robertson Ra.
Cross
Ullawarra
Trulowana
Jilgarnia
Paraburdoo
Kooline

Possonnier Pt.
C. Keraudren
Port Hedland
C. Thouin
Mallina
Pippingarra
Shaw
Esabah
Yule
Woodstock
Hillside
Chichester Ra.
Millstream
Witteroon
Wittenoom
Hamersley Range
Tom Price
Yandeearra

Legendre I.
Delambre I.
Enderby Island
Dampier
Karratha
Roebourne
Cleaverville
Dampier Archipelago
Cossack
C. Preston
Mardie
Yarraloola
Panawonica
Pyramid
Duck Cr.
Wyloo

North West C.
Exmouth
Learmonth
Exmouth Gulf
Coates
Morilla
Gadss
Onslow
Ashburton
Ashburton
Glenflorrie

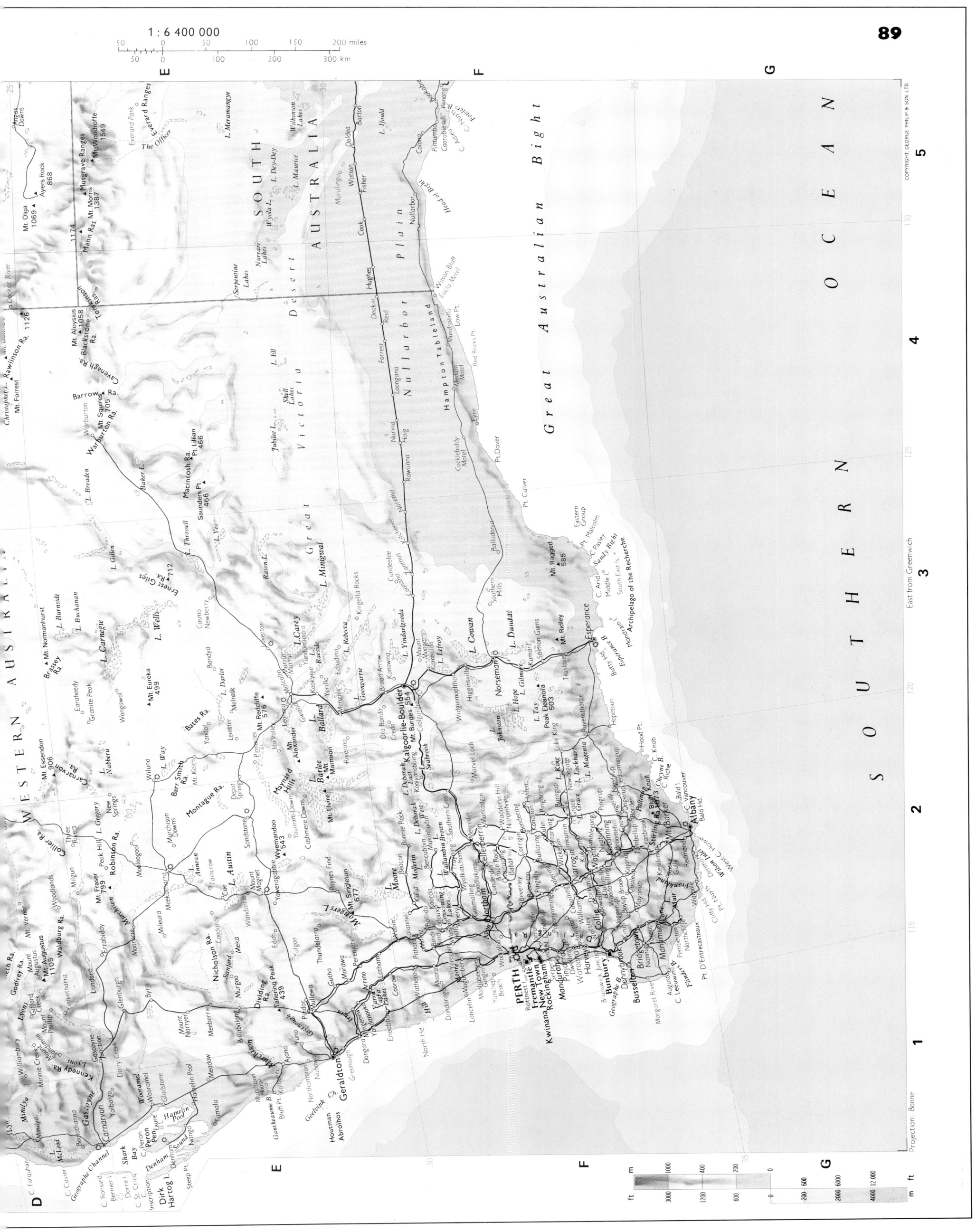

1 : 6 400 000

50   0   50   100   150   200 miles
50   0   50   100   200   300 km

COPYRIGHT GEORGE PHILIP & SON LTD

W E S T E R N   A U S T R A L I A

S O U T H   A U S T R A L I A

Great Victoria Desert

Nullarbor Plain

Hampton Tableland

Great Australian Bight

S O U T H E R N   O C E A N

Musgrave Ranges
Mt Woodroffe 1549
Mann Ras. Mt Morris 1387
Ayers Rock 868
Mt Olga 1069

Everard Ranges
The Officer
Everard Park
Ayers Downs
Docker River

PERTH
Fremantle
Rottnest I.
New
Kwinana
Rockingham
Mandurah

Geraldton
Houtman
Abrolhos

Carnarvon
Shark Bay
Dirk Hartog I.
Denham

Kalgoorlie-Boulder
Coolgardie
Norseman
Esperance
Albany
Bunbury
Busselton
Bridgetown

East from Greenwich

Projection. Bonne

ft
3000
1200
600
0

m
1000
400
200
0

ft
12 000
6000
2000
600
0

m
4000
2000
600
200
0

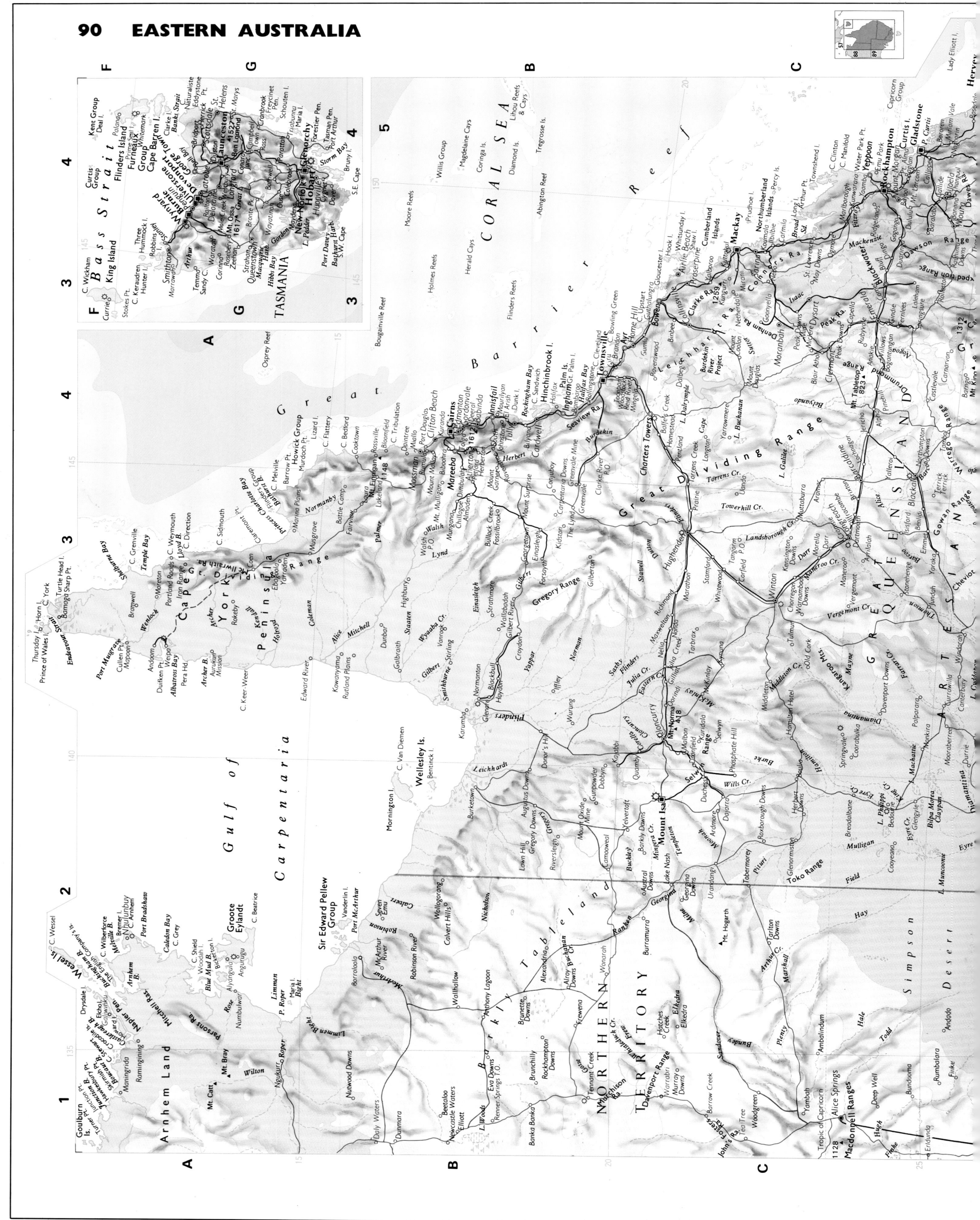

TASMANIA

Kent Group
Deal I.
C. Wickham
Curtis Group
Flinders Island
Three Hummock I.
Robbins I.
Stokes Pt.
C. Keraudren
Hunter I.
Currie
King Island
Naturaliste
St. Helens
Eddystone Pt.
Bridport
Banks Strait
Scottsdale
Herrick
Launceston
452?
Ben Lomond
Campbell Town
Schouten I.
Freycinet Pen.
Maria I.
Tasman Pen.
Port Arthur
Glenorchy
Hobart
New Norfolk
Bruny I.
S.E. Cape
Port Davey
S.W. Cape
Storm Bay
Mt. Ossa
1617
Strahan
Queenstown
Zeehan
Rosebery
Arthur
Waratah
Smithton
Stanley
Wynyard
Burnie
Devonport
Ulverstone
Latrobe
Gordon
L. Pedder
Huonville
Cygnet

Bass Strait

Coral Sea

Great Barrier Reef

Osprey Reef
Bougainville Reef
Moore Reefs
Lihou Reefs & Cays
Willis Group
Magdelaine Cays
Coringa I.
Diamond Is.
Tregrosse Is.
Abington Reef
Holmes Reefs
Herald Cays
Flinders Reefs

Cape York Peninsula

Thursday Is.
Prince of Wales
Horn I.
C. York
Turtle Head I.
Endeavour Strait
Bamaga
Sharp Pt.
Escape R.
Temple Bay
C. Grenville
Shelburne Bay
Port Musgrave
C. Weymouth
Portland Roads
C. Direction
Lloyd B.
Weipa
Andoom
Aurukun Mission
Archer R.
Archer B.
Pera Hd.
C. Keer-Weer
Duifken Pt.
Cullen Pt.
Mapoon
Coen
Port Stewart
Rokeby
Kendall
Holroyd
Edward River
Kowanyama
Rutland Plains
Mitchell
Alice
Dunbar
Staaten
Wyaaba Cr.
Vanrook
Gilbert
Stirling
Smithburne
Normanton
Karumba
Glenore
Blackbull
Haydon

Gulf of Carpentaria

C. Wessel
Wessel Is.
Elcho I.
C. Newcastle
Napier Pen.
Parsons Ra.
Mitchell Ras.
Buckingham B.
C. Wilberforce
Melville B.
C. Arnhem
Nhulunbuy
Port Bradshaw
Caledon Bay
C. Grey
C. Shield
Blue Mud B.
Woodah I.
Groote Eylandt
Angurugu
Alyangula
C. Beatrice
Maria I.
Limmen Bight
P. Roper
Sir Edward Pellew Group
Vanderlin I.
Bentinck I.
Mornington I.
C. Van Diemen
Wellesley Is.
Seven Emu
Robinson River
Calvert Hills
Wollogorang
Nicholson
Leichhardt

Arnhem Land

Goulburn Is.
Maningrida
Ramingining
Mt. Catt
Mt. Bray
Wilton
Roper
Numbulwar
Rose
McArthur River
Borroloola
Nutwood Downs

Northern Territory

Barkly Tableland
Brunette Downs
Anthony Lagoon
Alexandria
Wonarah
Alroy Downs
Burramurra
Creswell Downs
Avon Downs
Rockhampton Downs
Brunchilly
Eva Downs
Renner Springs T.O.
L. Woods
Banka Banka
Tennant Creek
Warrego
Murray Downs
Barrow Creek
Hatches Creek
Elkedra
Plenty
Hale
Todd
Ambalindum
Woodgreen
Alice Springs
Macdonnell Ranges
1128
John's Ra.
Deep Well
Finke
Erldunda
Andado
Bundooma

Queensland

Cooktown
C. Flattery
Lizard I.
C. Bedford
Bloomfield
C. Tribulation
Daintree
Port Douglas
Mossman
Cairns
Edmonton
Gordonvale
Babinda
Innisfail
Tully
Cardwell
Hinchinbrook I.
Ingham
Halifax Bay
Palm Is.
Townsville
Ayr
Home Hill
Bowen
Proserpine
Airlie Beach
Whitsunday I.
Hook I.
Cumberland Islands
Mackay
Sarina
Northumberland Islands
Broad Sd.
St. Lawrence
Marlborough
Rockhampton
Yeppoon
Curtis I.
Gladstone
Hervey
Lady Elliott I.
Capricorn Group
Mareeba
Atherton
Herberton
Ravenshoe
Mount Garnet
Mount Surprise
Croydon
Georgetown
Forsayth
Einasleigh
Kidston
Greenvale
Charters Towers
Homestead
Pentland
Hughenden
Richmond
Julia Creek
Cloncurry
Mount Isa
Mary Kathleen
Duchess
Dajarra
Boulia
Winton
Middleton
Kynuna
McKinlay
Dobbyn
Normanby
Burketown
Gregory Downs
Camooweal
Mount Oxide Mine
Barkly Downs
Lawn Hill
Augustus Downs
Donor's Hill
Iffley
Yappar
Norman
Gregory Range
Great Dividing Range
Tropic of Capricorn

57
88
89

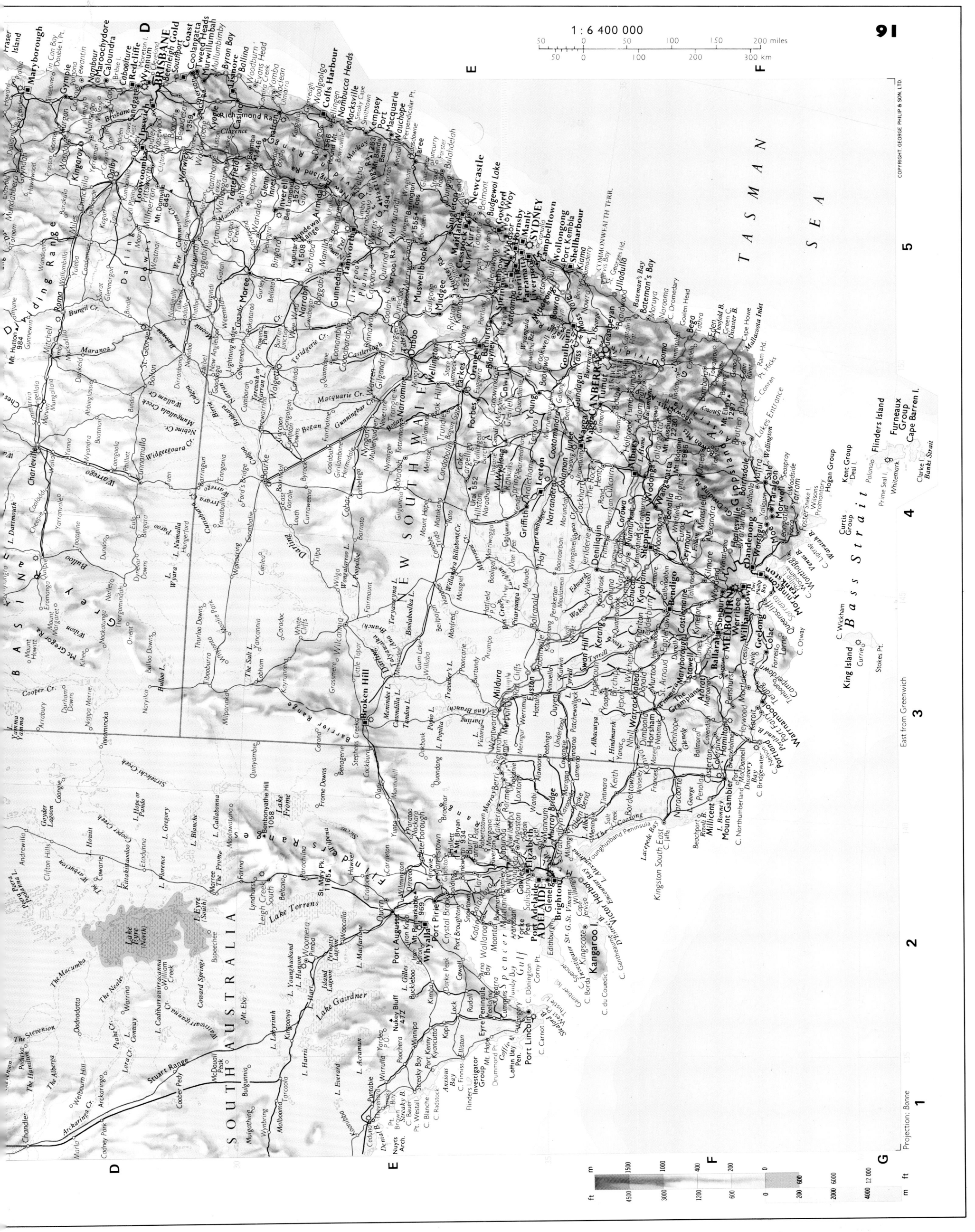

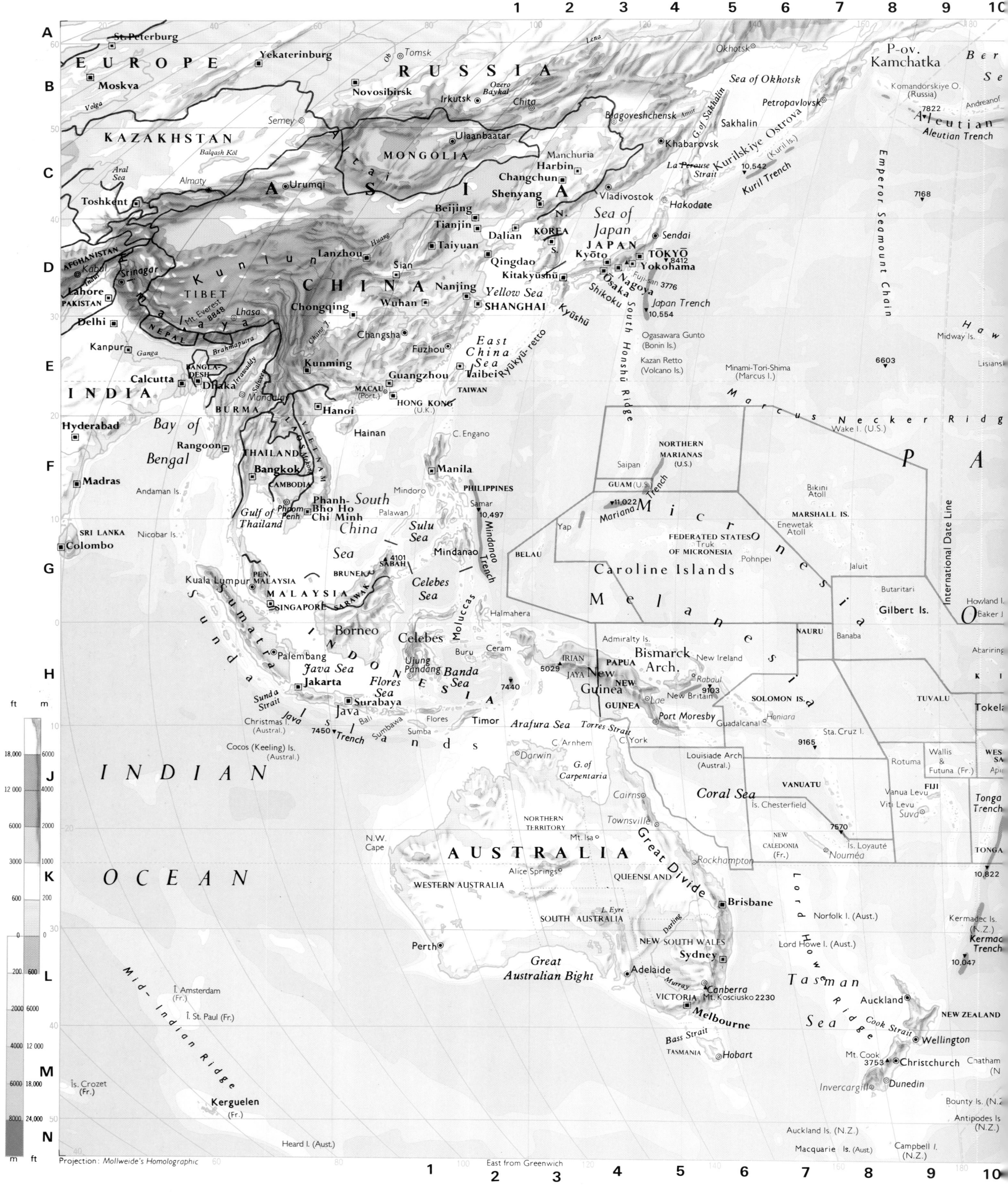

Projection: Mollweide's Homolographic

East from Greenwich

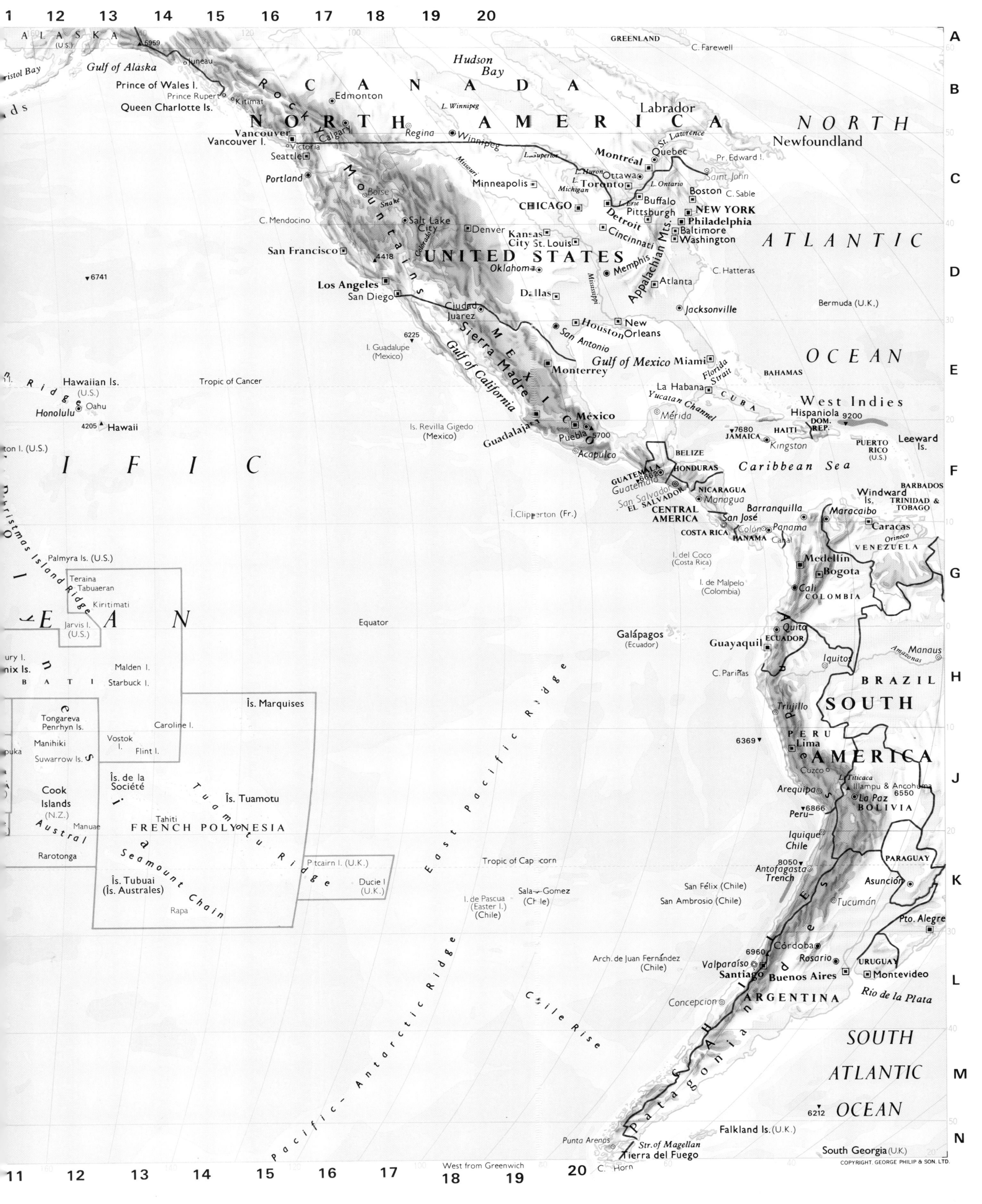

ALASKA (U.S.)

5959

Gulf of Alaska

Juneau

Prince of Wales I.

Prince Rupert

Queen Charlotte Is.

Kitimat

Edmonton

GREENLAND

C. Farewell

Hudson Bay

C A N A D A

L. Winnipeg

Labrador

NORTH AMERICA

Vancouver

Vancouver I.

Victoria

Seattle

Calgary

Regina

Winnipeg

L. Superior

St. Lawrence

Montréal

Quebec

Newfoundland

Pr. Edward I.

NORTH

Portland

Boise

Snake

Minneapolis

L. Huron

Ottawa

Toronto

L. Michigan

L. Ontario

L. Erie

Buffalo

Saint John

Boston

C. Sable

ATLANTIC

C. Mendocino

Salt Lake City

Denver

Kansas City

St. Louis

CHICAGO

Detroit

Pittsburgh

Cincinnati

NEW YORK

Philadelphia

Baltimore

Washington

San Francisco

4418

UNITED STATES

Colorado

Oklahoma

Memphis

Appalachian Mts.

C. Hatteras

Bermuda (U.K.)

6741

Los Angeles

San Diego

Ciudad Juárez

Dallas

Mississippi

Atlanta

Jacksonville

OCEAN

6225

San Antonio

Houston

New Orleans

Miami

Tropic of Cancer

I. Guadalupe (Mexico)

Sierra Madre

Gulf of Mexico

Florida Strait

BAHAMAS

Hawaiian Is. (U.S.)

Oahu

Honolulu

4205

Hawaii

Is. Revilla Gigedo (Mexico)

M E X I C O

Monterrey

Gulf of California

México

Mérida

Yucatán Channel

C U B A

La Habana

West Indies

Hispaniola

DOM. REP.

9200

Leeward Is.

P A C I F I C

Guadalajara

Puebla

5700

Acapulco

7680

JAMAICA

HAITI

Kingston

PUERTO RICO (U.S.)

BELIZE

GUATEMALA

Guatemala

4586

HONDURAS

Caribbean Sea

BARBADOS

Christmas Island Ridge

Palmyra Is. (U.S.)

Teraina

Tabuaeran

Kiritimati

San Salvador

EL SALVADOR

NICARAGUA

Managua

Barranquilla

Windward Is.

TRINIDAD & TOBAGO

CENTRAL AMERICA

San José

COSTA RICA

PANAMA

Colón

Panama Canal

Maracaibo

Caracas

Orinoco

VENEZUELA

Jarvis I. (U.S.)

Î. Clipperton (Fr.)

I. del Coco (Costa Rica)

Medellín

Bogotá

BATI

Malden I.

Starbuck I.

I. de Malpelo (Colombia)

Cali

COLOMBIA

Equator

Galápagos (Ecuador)

Quito

ECUADOR

Manaus

Amazonas

Tongareva

Penrhyn Is.

Manihiki

Suwarrow Is.

Vostok

Flint I.

Caroline I.

Îs. Marquises

Guayaquil

Iquitos

C. Pariñas

BRAZIL

SOUTH

Cook Islands (N.Z.)

Manuae

Îs. de la Société

Îs. Tuamotu

Trujillo

6369

PERU

Lima

AMERICA

Austral

Rarotonga

Tahiti

FRENCH POLYNESIA

Tuamotu Ridge

East Pacific Ridge

Cuzco

L. Titicaca

Illampu & Ancohuma

6550

Arequipa

La Paz

BOLIVIA

Peru-Chile

6866

Îs. Tubuai (Îs. Australes)

Rapa

Seamount Chain

Pitcairn I. (U.K.)

Ducie I. (U.K.)

Tropic of Capricorn

Iquique

Chile

8050

Antofagasta Trench

PARAGUAY

Asunción

I. de Pascua (Easter I.) (Chile)

Sala y Gomez (Chile)

San Félix (Chile)

San Ambrosio (Chile)

Tucumán

Pto. Alegre

Pacific - Antarctic Ridge

Chile Rise

Arch. de Juan Fernández (Chile)

6960

Córdoba

Rosario

URUGUAY

Valparaíso

Santiago

Buenos Aires

Montevideo

Rio de la Plata

Concepción

ARGENTINA

SOUTH

Patagonia

ATLANTIC

6212

OCEAN

West from Greenwich

Punta Arenas

Str. of Magellan

Tierra del Fuego

C. Horn

Falkland Is. (U.K.)

South Georgia (U.K.)

COPYRIGHT. GEORGE PHILIP & SON. LTD.

1 : 28 000 000

ARCTIC OCEAN

Greenland

Asia

Beaufort Sea

Bering Strait

Bering Sea

Brooks Ra.

Alaska Range

Mackenzie Mts.

Rocky Mountains

Great Plains

Hudson Bay

Baffin Island

Baffin Bay

Davis Strait

Coast of Labrador

Newfoundland

PACIFIC OCEAN

Great Basin

Sierra Nevada

Colorado Plateau

NORTH ATLANTIC OCEAN

Gulf of Mexico

Mississippi River Delta

Florida

Cuba

Greater Antilles

Caribbean Sea

Isthmus of Tehuantepec

Guatemala Trench

Andes

Projection: Bonne
West from Greenwich

CARTOGRAPHY BY PHILIP'S.
COPYRIGHT REED INTERNATIONAL BOOKS LTD

1 : 28 000 000

200   0   200   400   600   800 miles
400   0   200   400   800   1200 km

RUSSIA

Asia

St. Lawrence I.

Bering Strait

Bering Sea

International Date Line

ARCTIC OCEAN

Beaufort Sea

Queen Elizabeth Is.

Ellesmere I.

Victoria I.

Baffin Bay

Baffin Island

Davis Strait

Denmark Strait

ICELAND

Reykjavík

GREENLAND (Denmark)

Godthaab

Cape Farewell

ALASKA (USA)

Yukon

Porcupine

Fairbanks

Anchorage

Kodiak I.

Gulf of Alaska

YUKON TERRITORY

Whitehorse

Arctic Circle

Mackenzie

Great Bear L.

NORTHWEST TERRITORIES

Back

Hudson Strait

Juneau

Yellowknife

Great Slave L.

Liard

Dubawnt

Hudson Bay

NEWFOUNDLAND

CANADA

BRITISH COLUMBIA

Skeena

Fraser

Peace

ALBERTA

L. Athabasca

Athabasca

Churchill

Nelson

SASKATCHEWAN

Saskatchewan

MANITOBA

L. Winnipeg

Eastmain

QUÉBEC

Labrador

St. Lawrence

PRINCE EDWARD I.

Charlottetown

St-Pierre Et Miquelon (Fr.)

St. John's

Victoria

Vancouver

Edmonton

Calgary

Regina

ONTARIO

Winnipeg

NEW BRUNSWICK

Fredericton

NOVA SCOTIA

Halifax

C. Sable

WASHINGTON

Olympia

Seattle

Portland

Salem

Columbia

OREGON

MONTANA

Helena

Missouri

NORTH DAKOTA

Bismarck

SOUTH DAKOTA

MINNESOTA

Minneapolis

WISCONSIN

L. Superior

Madison

MICHIGAN

Lansing

L. Huron

Toronto

Ottawa

Montréal

Québec

MAINE

Augusta

N.H.

VER.

Concord

MASS.

Boston

Providence

Hartford

NEW YORK CITY

PHILADELPHIA

IDAHO

Boise

Snake

WYOMING

IOWA

Milwaukee

Detroit

Buffalo

L. Michigan

L. Erie

L. Ontario

NEW YORK

PA.

Cleveland

Pittsburgh

Toledo

N.J.

DE.

Baltimore

MD.

Sacramento

Carson City

Salt Lake City

Cheyenne

NEBRASKA

Lincoln

CHICAGO

ILLINOIS

INDIANA

Indianapolis

OHIO

Columbus

Cincinnati

Springfield

W.V.

Washington D.C.

Richmond

VIRGINIA

SAN FRANCISCO

San Jose

NEVADA

UTAH

UNITED STATES

Denver

COLORADO

Kansas City

Topeka

KANSAS

St. Louis

MISSOURI

KENTUCKY

Nashville

TENNESSEE

NORTH CAROLINA

Raleigh

Charlotte

Bermuda (U.K.)

LOS ANGELES

CALIFORNIA

Las Vegas

Colorado

ARIZONA

Santa Fe

Albuquerque

NEW MEXICO

OKLAHOMA

Oklahoma City

ARKANSAS

Little Rock

Memphis

Mississippi

Birmingham

GEORGIA

Atlanta

Columbia

SOUTH CAROLINA

Charleston

NORTH ATLANTIC OCEAN

San Diego

Phoenix

Tucson

El Paso

TEXAS

Dallas

Austin

Houston

MISSISSIPPI

Jackson

ALABAMA

Montgomery

Tallahassee

Jacksonville

FLORIDA

PACIFIC OCEAN

Guadalupe (Mex.)

Hermosillo

Rio Grande

Baton Rouge

LOUISIANA

New Orleans

Tampa

Miami

Florida Str.

Nassau

BAHAMAS

Turks & Caicos Is. (U.K.)

Tropic of Cancer

Culiacan

MEXICO

Monterrey

Gulf of Mexico

Havana

CUBA

Cayman Is. (U.K.)

JAMAICA

Kingston

HAITI

Port-au-Prince

DOMINICAN REP.

Santo Domingo

San Juan

PUERTO RICO (U.S.A.)

Revilla Gigedo Is. (Mex.)

Guadalajara

MÉXICO

Puebla

Acapulco

Mérida

Caribbean Sea

Belmopan

BELIZE

GUATEMALA

Guatemala

HONDURAS

Tegucigalpa

San Salvador

EL SALVADOR

NICARAGUA

Managua

L. Nicaragua

COSTA RICA

San José

PANAMA

Panamá

Maracaibo

Barranquilla

VENEZUELA

COLOMBIA

Medellín

South America

Projection: Bonne

West from Greenwich

7   ■ MÉXICO Capital Cities   8   9   10

11

12

PACIFIC OCEAN

ALASKA

YUKON TERRITORY

BRITISH COLUMBIA

ALBERTA

SASKATCHEWAN

MANITOBA

NORTH WEST TERRITORIES

INUVIK

KITIKMEOT

KEEWATIN

Amundsen Gulf
Victoria Island
Banks Island
Prince Albert Pen.
Coronation Gulf
Queen Maud Gulf
Viscount Melville Sound
Prince of Wales Island
Somerset Island
M'Clintock Channel
Bothia Pen.

Anchorage　Seward　Valdez　Cordova
Mt. St. Elias 5489　Mt. Logan 6050
Mt. Fairweather 4663
Whitehorse　Skagway　Juneau
Fairbanks　Dawson　Klondike
Yellowknife
Great Bear Lake　Gt. Bear
Great Slave L.
Lake Athabasca
Edmonton　Calgary
Red Deer　Lethbridge　Medicine Hat
Saskatoon　Regina　Moose Jaw
Prince Albert
Winnipeg　St. Boniface
Reindeer Lake
Lake Winnipeg
Queen Charlotte Is.
Vancouver Island
Vancouver　Victoria　Nanaimo
Prince Rupert

Rocky Mountains
Mackenzie Mountains

Projection: Bonne

ft　m
9000　3000
6000　2000
4500　1500
3000
1200　400
600　200
0
200　600
2000　6000
m　ft

ALASKA
1 : 24 000 000
100　0　100　200　300 miles
100　0　200　400 km

BERING SEA

PACIFIC OCEAN

GULF OF ALASKA

Brooks Range
Seward Pen.
Nome　Fairbanks　College
Mt. McKinley　Anchorage
Aleutian Is.
Kodiak I.　Alaska Peninsula
Unimak I.　Unalaska I.　Umnak I.
Pribilof Is.
St. Lawrence I. (U.S.)
Bristol Bay　Kuskokwim Bay
Bering Strait
Arctic Circle
Barrow　Prudhoe Bay
Point Barrow

Koryakskoye Nagorye
Anadyr
Providenija
Ugolnyi
Cukotskoye More (Chukchi Sea)

UNITED STATES
MONTANA
NORTH DAKOTA
SOUTH DAKOTA
WYOMING
NEBRASKA
MINNESOTA
IOWA
WASHINGTON
Seattle　Tacoma　Spokane
Missouri
Yellowstone
Minneapolis　St. Paul
Omaha　Sioux City　Des Moines
Bismarck　Fargo

West from Greenwich

1 : 12 000 000

100   0   100   200   300   400 miles

100   0   100   200   300   400   500   600 km

11   **12**   **13**   **14**   **15**   **16**

B

Devon Island

Lancaster Sound

2136

Baffin Bay

Svartenhuk Halvö

Angmagssalik

Arctic Bay

Bylot I.

Pond Inlet

Disko

Disko B.

Christianshåb

Brodeur

Milne Inlet

Pond Inlet

Scott I.

Home B.

Broughton Island

Holsteinsborg

Sondre Stromfjord

G R E E N L A N D

2850

Kong Frederik VI's Kyst

A T L A N T I C

Peninsula

C. Hewett

Clyde

B

Fury & Hecla Str.

Igloolik Island

Padloping Island

C. Dyer

Cape Dyer

Godthåb

Sukk's toppen

Frederikshåb

Fiskenæsset

Hall Lake

Prince Charles

2591

Cumberland Peninsula

Davis Strait

Vigtut

Julianehåb

Syd proven

Melville Peninsula

Foxe

Nettilling L.

Pangnirtung

Hoare B.

C. Mercy

Nanortalik

Kap Farvel

C

Rae Isthmus

Repulse Bay

Wager B.

Foxe Basin

C. Dorchester

Amadjuak L.

Cumberland Sd.

C

Southampton I.

Coral Harbour

Foxe Penin.

Cape Dorset

Amadjuak

Iqaluit

Lake Harbour

Frobisher Bay

Resolution I.

Channel

Bell Pen.

Coats I.

Digges Is.

Salluit

H u d s o n   S t r a i t

3809

Ovujivik

Ivujivik

C. Chidley

Mansel I.

Kangiqsujuaq

Quaqtaq (Notre Dame de Koartac)

Akpatok I.

Hudson

Ottawa Is.

Ungava

Arnaud Kangirsuk

Ungava Bay

1676

Kangiqsualujjuaq

Hebron

Nutok

257

Portland Promontory

P e n i n s u l a

Feuilles

Koksoak

Kuujjuaq

George

Nain

Bay

Sleeper Is.

King George Is.

Baker's Dozen Is.

L. Minto

Mélèzes

Whale

Hopedale

Rigolet

C. Harrison

Indian Harbour

King George Is.

L. à l'Eau Claire

Lac Bienville

Kaniapiskau

Schefferville

Petitsikapau

North West R.

L. Melville

Cartwright

Belcher Is.

Grand Baleine

La Grande

COAST OF LABRADOR

Church Falls

Goose Bay

Battle Harb.

Belle Isle

C. Henrietta Maria

Kuujjuarapik

Kanaaupscow

La Grande

A

Churchill

Natashquan

St-Augustin-Saguenay

Str. of Belle Isle

Notre Dame B.

Twillingate

Lewisporte

Gander

Ft. Severn

Winisk

Chisasibi

Waskaganish

La Grande

Pte. Louis-XIV

1128

G D'bon

Moisie

Romaine

Natashquan

Grand Falls

Corner Brook

Bonavista

Trinity B.

Carbonear

St. John's

Big Trout L.

D

Attawapiskat

Akimiski I.

Wemindji

Eastmain

L. Albanel

L. Mistassini

Noisie

Sept Îles

Mingan

Î. d'Anticosti

814

NEWFOUNDLAND

Harbour Grace

Placentia

Trepassey

C. Race

D

Ft. Albany

Charlton I.

Eastmain

Rupert

Péribonca

Manicouagan

Port-Cartier

Ray

Is. P. aux Basques

Albany

Moosonee

Nottaway

Harricana

Chibougamau

Baie-Comeau

Betsiamites

R. St. Lawrence

C. de Gaspé

Îs. de la Madeleine

Gulf of St. Lawrence

Cubot Str.

C. North

Cape Breton I.

ST-PIERRE et MIQUELON (Fr.)

St. Joseph

Missinaibi

Dolbeau

St-Jean

Saguenay

Matane

Rimouski

Gaspé

Cape Breton I.

Glace Bay

O

Nakina

Kenogami

Matagami

Roberval

Jonquière

Rivière-du-Loup

Newcastle

Bathurst

Northumberland Str.

Charlottetown

Summerside

PR. EDWARD I.

Sydney

C

Longlac

Hearst

Cochrane

L. Abitibi

Taschereau

Senneterre

1190

Chicoutimi

Tadoussac

Edmundston

St. Leonard

Campbellton

Chatham

PR. EDWARD I.

Port Hawkesbury

E

Nipigon

Heron Bay

Oba

Timmins

Noranda

Rouyn

Val d'Or

La Tuque

Shawinigan

NEW BRUNSWICK

Moncton

New Glasgow

Mulgrave

Thunder Bay

Michipicoten

Franz

Kirkland Lake

Rés. de Gouin

Woodstock

Fred'n

Springhill

Truro

Windsor

Dartmouth

Sable I. (Nova Scotia)

Lake Superior

Haileybury

Cobalt

Témiscamingue

Rés. de Cabonga

Trois-Rivières

Québec

Lévis

Thetford Mines

Saint John

Kentville

NOVA SCOTIA

Halifax

6309

Calumet

Keweenaw Bay

Sault Ste. Marie

Sudbury

North Bay

MONTRÉAL

Lachine

Sherbrooke

MAINE

St. Hyacinthe

Sorel

Bangor

B. of Fundy

Digby

Bridgewater

Laurium

Copper Cliff

Pembroke

Ottawa

Hull

Joliette

Augusta

Liverpool

Marquette

Sault Ste. Marie

North Chan.

Parry Sound

Arnprior

Cornwall

L. Champlain

1917

Shelburne

Ironwood

Manistique

Cheboygan

Georgian Bay

Renfrew

Belleville

Kingston

Burlington

VERMONT

NEW HAMPSHIRE

Concord

Lewiston

Portland

C. Sable

Yarmouth

Escanaba

Petoskey

Lake Huron

Orillia

Peterboro

Watertown

Manchester

Iron Mt.

Menominee

Traverse

Cadillac

Owen Sound

Oshawa

Cobourg

Utica

Worcester

MASS.

Boston

C. Cod

Antigo

Green Bay

Manitowoc

Saginaw

TORONTO

Ontario

Rochester

Syracuse

Albany

Springfield

Providence

E

Wausau

Appleton

Muskegon

Guelph

Kitchener

Brantford

Niagara Falls

NEW YORK

Binghamton

Scranton

R.I.

CONN.

New Haven

Sheboygan

Stratford

Hamilton

St. Catharines

Elmira

Waterbury

Bridgeport

Milwaukee

Racine

Grand Rapids

London

Buffalo

Jamestown

Williamsport

Reading

New York

Kenosha

Kalamazoo

Sarnia

Erie

PENNSYLVANIA

Allentown

NEW JERSEY

Jersey City

Newark

CHICAGO

Gary

Evanston

South Bend

Windsor

DETROIT

Toledo

Cleveland

Akron

Youngstown

Trenton

ILLINOIS

INDIANA

OHIO

West from Greenwich

COPYRIGHT. GEORGE PHILIP & SON. LTD.

11   **12**   **13**   **14**

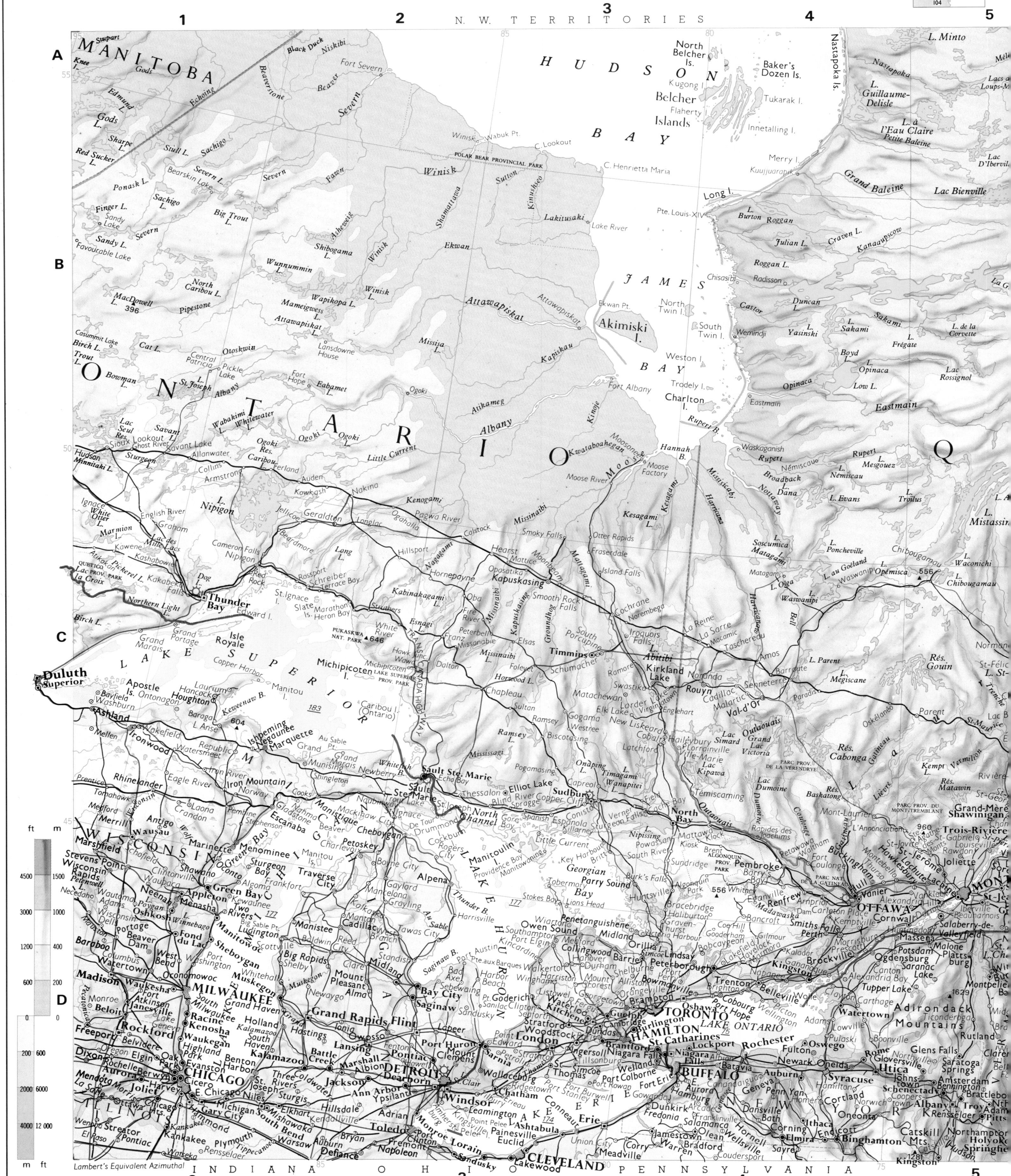

MANITOBA

N.W. TERRITORIES

HUDSON BAY

JAMES BAY

O N T A R I O

QUEBEC

Belcher Islands

Akimiski I.

Polar Bear Provincial Park

Thunder Bay

LAKE SUPERIOR

Duluth
Superior

Isle Royale

Sault Ste. Marie

Sudbury

Timmins

Kirkland Lake

Kapuskasing

Cochrane

North Bay

WISCONSIN

MICHIGAN

Green Bay

Milwaukee

MADISON

CHICAGO

ILLINOIS

INDIANA

DETROIT

Grand Rapids

Flint

Lansing

Toledo

OHIO

CLEVELAND

LAKE MICHIGAN

LAKE HURON

Georgian Bay

Parry Sound

Algonquin Prov. Park

TORONTO

HAMILTON

LAKE ONTARIO

BUFFALO

Niagara Falls

Rochester

Syracuse

NEW YORK

London

Windsor

LAKE ERIE

OTTAWA

MONTREAL

Kingston

Trois-Rivières

Shawinigan

Adirondack Mountains

PENNSYLVANIA

Lambert's Equivalent Azimuthal

1 : 5 600 000

50 0 50 100 150 200 miles
50 0 50 100 150 200 250 300 km

6 **7** **8** **9**

COAST OF LABRADOR

QUEBEC

NEWFOUNDLAND

GULF OF ST. LAWRENCE

NEW BRUNSWICK

NOVA SCOTIA

PRINCE EDWARD ISLAND

MAINE

ATLANTIC OCEAN

Cabot Strait

SAINT-PIERRE ET MIQUELON (Fr.)

Avalon Peninsula

St. John's

Halifax

BOSTON

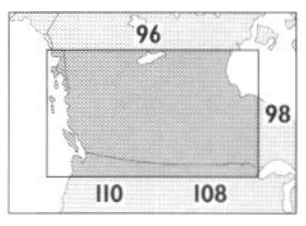

YUKON TERRITORY

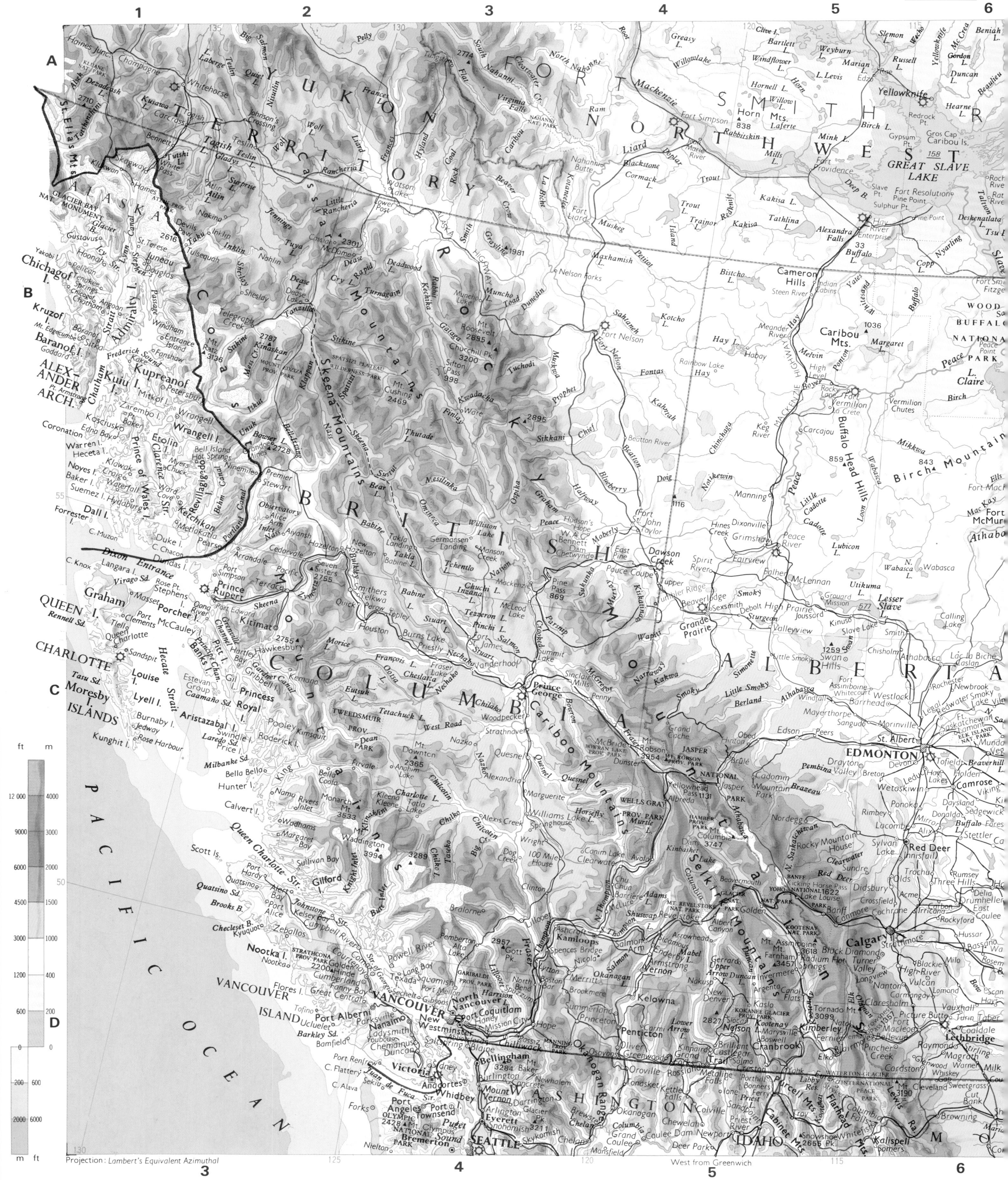

NORTH WEST TERRITORIES

FORT SMITH

ALASKA

BRITISH COLUMBIA

ALBERTA

PACIFIC OCEAN

QUEEN CHARLOTTE ISLANDS

VANCOUVER ISLAND

WASHINGTON

IDAHO

Rocky Mountains

Skeena Mountains

Coast Mountains

Cariboo Mountains

Selkirk Mountains

ALEXANDER ARCH.

GREAT SLAVE LAKE

WOOD BUFFALO NATIONAL PARK

Great Slave Lake

Whitehorse

Yellowknife

Juneau

Prince Rupert

Prince George

EDMONTON

Calgary

Red Deer

Vancouver

New Westminster

Victoria

Seattle

Kamloops

Kelowna

Penticton

Dawson Creek

Grande Prairie

Fort Nelson

Fort Simpson

Lesser Slave Lake

Williston Lake

Kitimat

Nanaimo

Port Alberni

Lethbridge

Caribou Mts.

Birch Mountains

Buffalo Head Hills

Projection: Lambert's Equivalent Azimuthal

West from Greenwich

ft m — 12 000 / 4000 / 9000 / 3000 / 6000 / 2000 / 4500 / 1500 / 3000 / 1000 / 1200 / 400 / 600 / 200 / 0 / 0

Mt. Robson 3954

Mt. Waddington 3994

St. Elias Mts.

Mackenzie R.

Peace River

Fraser R.

Columbia R.

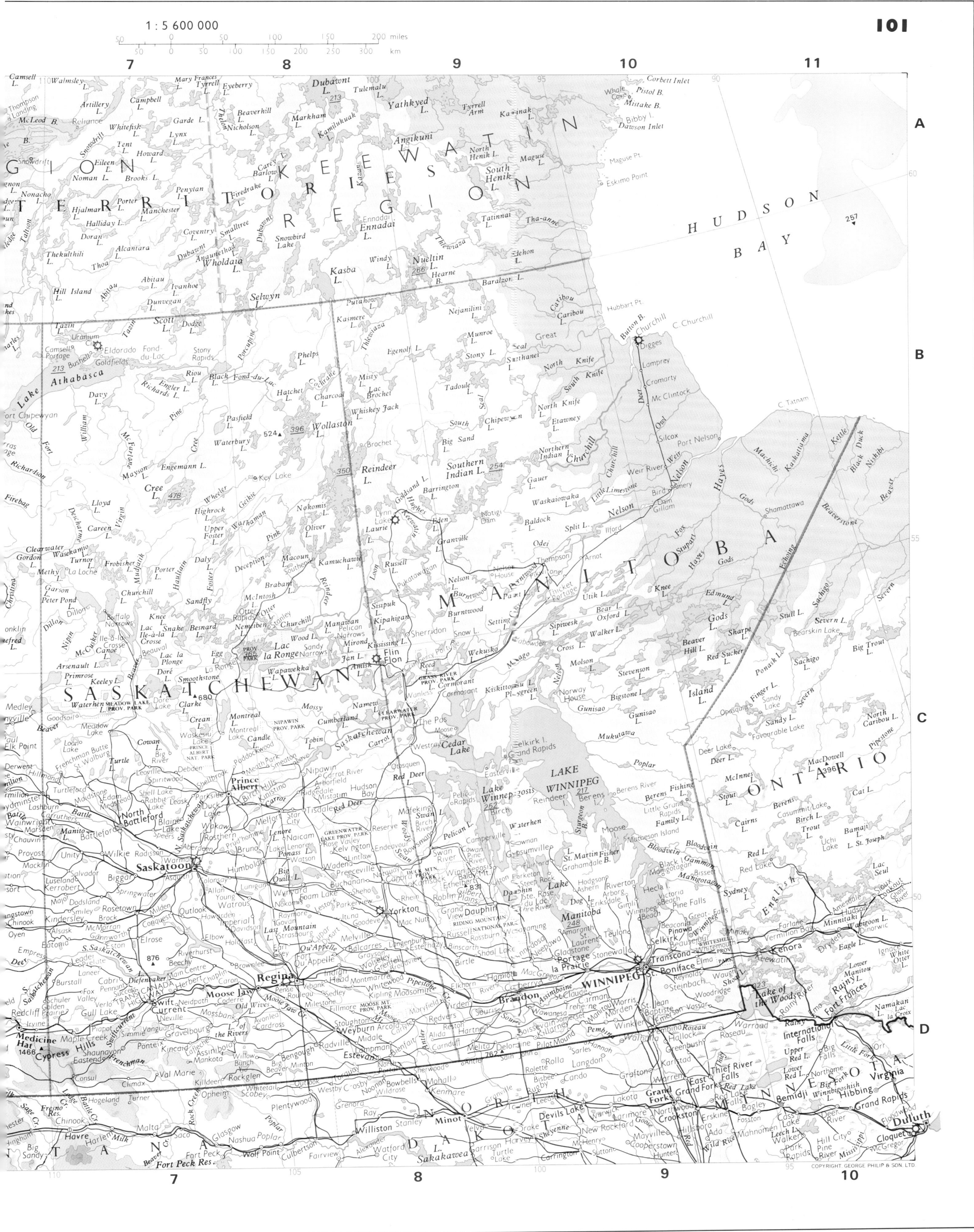

1 : 5 600 000

50   0   50   100   150   200 miles

50   0   50   100   150   200   250   300 km

COPYRIGHT GEORGE PHILIP & SON LTD.

HAWAII
1 : 8 000 000

Projection: Albers' Equal Area with two standard parallels

1 : 9 600 000

50   0   50   100 150 200 250   300 miles
50   0   50 100 150 200 250 300 350 400 450 km

8   9   10   11   12   13

A   A   N   A   D   A

Lake Winnipeg

Berens

Trout Lake   L. St. Joseph

Albany

Moosonee

Moose

St. Lawrence

Matane

Rimouski

English   L. Seul

Sioux Lookout

Nakina

Kenogami

Longlac

Missinaibi

Hearst

L. au Goéland

Rés. de Gouin

Roberval

Rivière-du-Loup

Edmundston

NEW BRUNSWICK

A

Winnipeg

Lake of the Woods

Kenora

Ignace

Seine

Nipigon

St. Ignace

Franz

White River

Oba

Timmins

L. Abitibi

Rouyn

Cabonga

Grand-Mère

Québec

La Tuque

Baie-St-Paul

Île d'Orléans

Moosehead L.

MAINE

B

Fort Frances

Thief River Falls

Red Lake

Rainy L.

Thunder Bay

Michipicoten I.

Michipicoten

Wawa

Cobalt

Temiscamingue

Res. Baskatong

Joliette

Sorel

Trois-Rivières

Nicolet

St-Hyacinthe

Sherbrooke

Farmington

Waterville

Augusta

Bangor

Bar Harbor

Grand Forks

Red Lake

Bemidji   Hibbing

Virginia

Two Harbors

Keweenaw Bay

Whitefish Bay

Sault Ste. Marie

L. Nipissing

North Bay

Mattawa

Pembroke

Ottawa

Hull

Buckingham

MONTRÉAL

St-Albans

VERMONT

1917

NEW HAMPSHIRE

Rumford

Belfast

Rockland

Penobscot Bay

MINNESOTA

Duluth   Superior

Ashland

Ironwood   Ishpeming

Bessemer

Marquette

Escanaba

Manistique

North Chan.

Manitoulin

Parry Sound

Huntsville

Gravenhurst

Perth

Smith's Falls

Brockville

Kingston

L. Champlain

Ogdensburg

Burlington

Plattsburg

Montpelier

GREEN

WHITE

Concord

Manchester

Lawrence

Lowell

Nashua

B

Moorhead

Fargo

Fergus Falls

Brainerd

St. Cloud

Rhinelander

Antigo

Iron Mt.

Menominee

Cheboygan

Traverse City

Owen Sound

Hanover

Orangeville

Peterborough

Picton

Oswego

Watertown

Rome

Utica

Glens Falls

Saratoga

Troy

Fitchburg

Worcester

Boston

Brockton

Fall River

Big Stone Lake

Minneapolis   St. Paul

Red Wing

Eau Claire

Stevens Point

Appleton

Green Bay

Manitowoc

Sheboygan

Muskegon

Ludington

Manistee

Cadillac

Midland

Bay City

Saginaw

Flint

Port Huron

Sarnia

Stratford

Kitchener

Hamilton

TORONTO

Oshawa

Rochester

Syracuse

Auburn

Binghamton

Scranton

Catskill

Poughkeepsie

Springfield

Hartford

Providence

New Bedford

Martha's Vineyard

C. Cod

Willmar

Madison

Janesville

Beloit

Rockford

Milwaukee

Racine

Kenosha

Evanston

Grand Rapids

Lansing

Battle Creek

Ann Arbor

DETROIT

Windsor

London

Brantford

Buffalo

Niagara Falls

Jamestown

Warren

Elmira

Williamsport

Wilkes Barre

Allentown

Reading

NEW YORK

Jersey City

Newark

Paterson

Bridgeport

New Haven

Waterbury

Minnesota

New Ulm

Faribault

Owatonna

Rochester

Austin

La Crosse

WISCONSIN

Wisconsin Rapids

Oshkosh

Fond du Lac

Waukegan

Elgin

Aurora

Joliet

CHICAGO

Gary

Hammond

South Bend

Toledo

Sandusky

Lorain

Lakewood

Euclid

Cleveland

Akron

Youngstown

Canton

Massillon

Erie

Oil City

Franklin

New Castle

Altoona

Johnstown

Harrisburg

York

PENNSYLVANIA

Lancaster

Chester

PHILADELPHIA

Camden

Atlantic City

C

Madison

Brookings

Albert Lea

Mason City

Cedar Falls

Dubuque

Freeport

DeKalb

Elkhart

Ft. Wayne

Lima

Findlay

Marion

Mansfield

Alliance

Steubenville

Wheeling

Pittsburgh

Connellsville

Cumberland

Hagerstown

Frederick

Wilmington

Baltimore

Annapolis

Chesapeake Bay

Delaware Bay

C. May

Cherokee

Des Moines

Fort Dodge

Ames

Marshalltown

Iowa

Newton

IOWA

Davenport

Rock Island

Moline

Clinton

Dixon

Ottawa

Kankakee

Streator

Wabash

Kokomo

Muncie

Anderson

Richmond

Piqua

Dayton

Springfield

OHIO

Columbus

Newark

Zanesville

Lancaster

Chillicothe

Parkersburg

Clarksburg

Fairmont

Elkins

WEST VIRGINIA

Staunton

Harrisonburg

Winchester

Washington

WASHINGTON D.C.

Cambridge

Salisbury

Council Bluffs

Omaha

Red Oak

Creston

Burlington

Galesburg

Peoria

Bloomington

ILLINOIS

Champaign

Urbana

Decatur

Terre Haute

INDIANA

Indianapolis

Bedford

Cincinnati

Hamilton

Middletown

Kettering

Maysville

Portsmouth

Ashland

Huntington

Charleston

Beckley

Bluefield

Roanoke

Lynchburg

Charlottesville

Richmond

Petersburg

Newport News

Norfolk

Portsmouth

C. Charles

Lincoln

Nebraska City

Beatrice

St. Joseph

Chillicothe

Quincy

Hannibal

Moberly

Mexico

St. Charles

MISSOURI

Jefferson City

St. Louis

Belleville

Centralia

Mt. Vernon

Vincennes

New Albany

Jeffersonville

Frankfort

Louisville

Lexington

Winchester

KENTUCKY

Somerset

Middlesboro

Johnson City

Kingsport

Bristol

Danville

Roanoke

Rocky Mount

Durham

Raleigh

Wilson

Goldsboro

Washington

Pamlico Sd.

C. Hatteras

D

Manhattan

Leavenworth

Kansas City

Lawrence

Ottawa

Topeka

Emporia

El Dorado

Fort Scott

Nevada

Sedalia

Rolla

MISSOURI

Lebanon

Springfield

Ozark Plateau

Cape Girardeau

Cairo

Paducah

Hopkinsville

Clarksville

Bowling Green

Green

Ohio

Henderson

Owensboro

Lebanon

Oak Ridge

Knoxville 2037

Asheville

CLINCH MTS.

GREAT SMOKY MTS.

Hendersonville

Winston Salem

Greensboro

High Pt.

Salisbury

Charlotte

Concord

Kinston

New Bern

Cape Fear

Onslow Bay

Wichita

Winfield

Arkansas City

Ponca City

Bartlesville

Joplin

Carthage

Springfield

White

Newport

Paragould

Jonesboro

Dyersburg

Union City

Mayfield

Martin

TENNESSEE

Nashville

Columbia

Lebanon

Chattanooga

Dalton

Rome

Athens

Cleveland

Greenville

Spartanburg

Gaffney

Anderson

Gainesville

NORTH CAROLINA

Columbia

SOUTH CAROLINA

Sumter

Florence

Georgetown

Long Bay

C. Fear

D

Tulsa

Cushing

Muskogee

Fayetteville

Van Buren

Fort Smith

Boston Mts.

Russellville

OKLAHOMA

Oklahoma City

Shawnee

Seminole

McAlester

Ouachita Mts.

Little Rock

Hot Springs

ARKANSAS

Stuttgart

Blytheville

Memphis

Corinth

Jackson

Florence

Huntsville

Decatur

Gadsden

Anniston

Birmingham

Bessemer

Tuscaloosa

Atlanta

East Pt.

Newnan

Griffin

La Grange

Macon

Augusta

Milledgeville

Orangeburg

Columbia

Santee

C. Royal

Charleston

Charleston Harb.

Savannah

E

Durant

Ardmore

Sherman

Paris

Texarkana

Hope

Camden

El Dorado

Pine Bluff

Cleveland

Greenwood

Greenville

Clarksdale

Columbus

MISSISSIPPI

Yazoo City

Canton

ALABAMA

Selma

Montgomery

Troy

Greenville

Dothan

GEORGIA

Columbus

Phenix City

Dublin

Cordele

Fitzgerald

Waycross

Albany

Moultrie

Bainbridge

Thomasville

Valdosta

Brunswick

Altamaha

St. Johns R.

Jacksonville

St. Augustine

E

McAlester

Denison

Sherman

Terrell

Ennis

Waxahachie

Corsicana

Hillsboro

Dallas

Tyler

Longview

Marshall

Shreveport

Minden

Monroe

Vicksburg

Jackson

Brookhaven

McComb

Hattiesburg

Laurel

Meridian

LOUISIANA

Alexandria

Natchez

Natchitoches

ALABAMA

Demopolis

Andalusia

FLORIDA

Pensacola

Mobile

Biloxi

Gulfport

Pascagoula

Panama City

Tallahassee

Apalachee B.

L. George

Palatka

Daytona Beach

Gainesville

Sanford

Orlando

C. Canaveral

Waco

Temple

Bryan

Huntsville

Trinity

Neches

Lufkin

Jasper

De Ridder

Lake Charles

Jennings

Lafayette

Baton Rouge

New Iberia

Houma

New Orleans

Morgan City

Delta of the Mississippi

Breton Sd.

Chandeleur Is.

Clearwater

Tampa

St. Petersburg

Bradenton

Sarasota

Plant City

Lakeland

Arcadia

L. Okeechobee

Ft. Pierce

West Palm Beach

Grand Bahama I.

Little Abaco

Freeport

Gt. Abaco

BAHAMAS

F

Houston

Pasadena

Galveston

Beaumont

Orange

Port Arthur

Marsh I.

Atchafalaya B.

Morgan City

Victoria

Cuero

Freeport

Brazos

Port Lavaca

Matagorda I.

Aransas Pass

Laguna Madre

Benito

Brownsville

Rio Grande

GULF OF MEXICO

Charlotte Harb.

Ft. Myers

EVERGLADES

FLORIDA

Florida Keys

Key West

Florida Bay

C. Sable

Miami

Coral Gables

Fort Lauderdale

N.W. Providence Chan.

Nassau

New Providence

N.E. Providence Channel

Eleuthera I.

Exuma Sound

Andros I.

Cat I.

Long I.

F

8   9   10   11   12

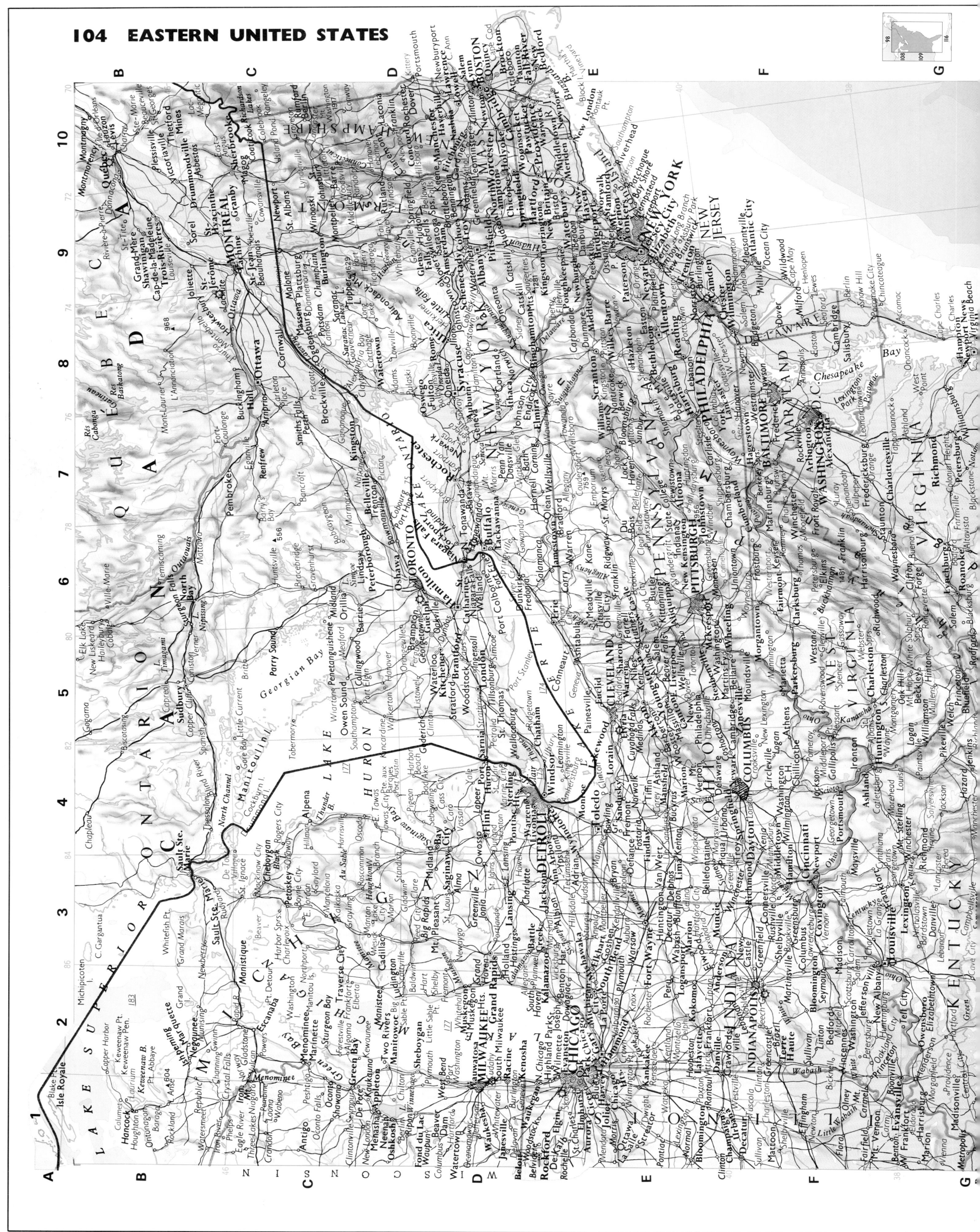

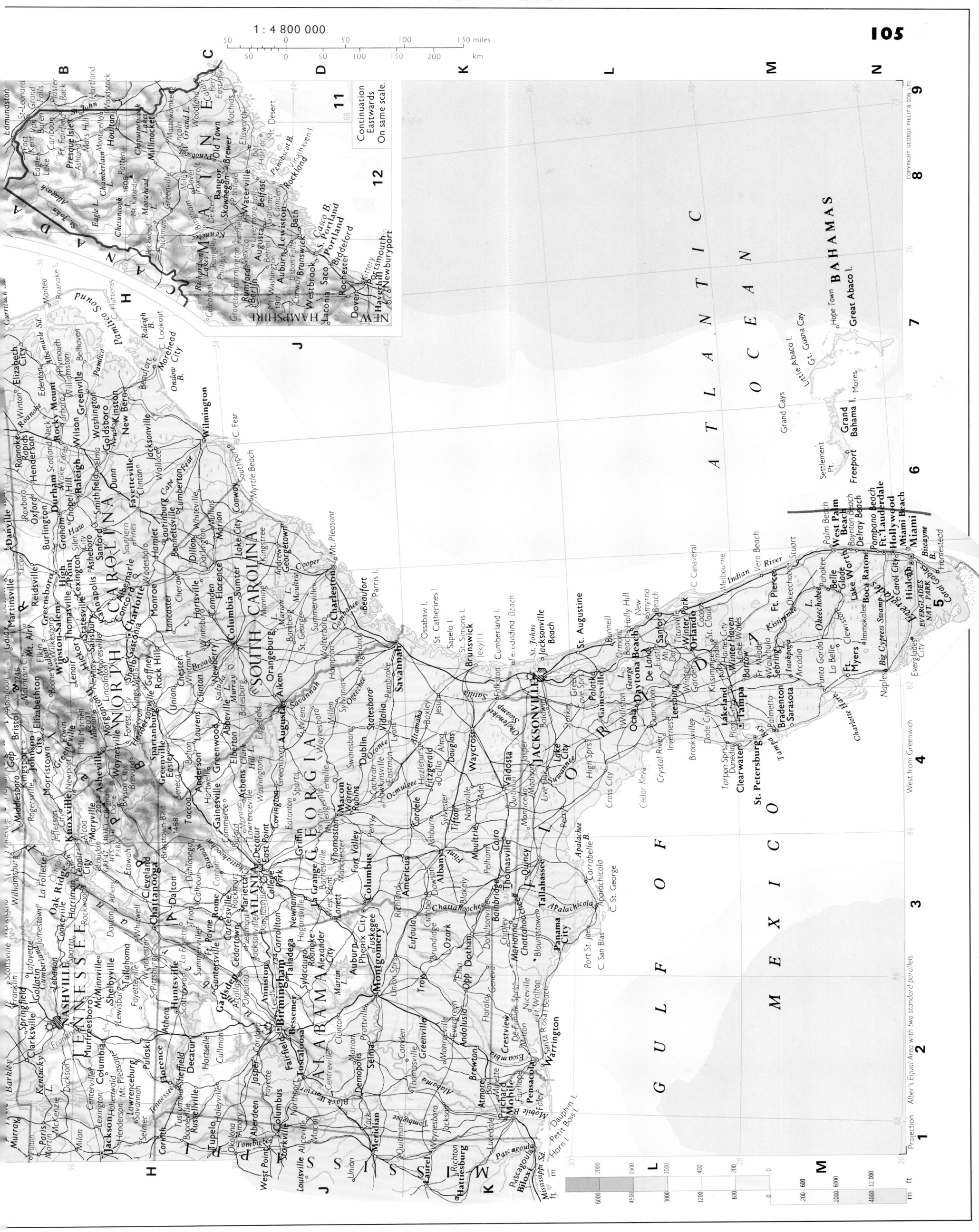

1 : 4 800 000

Continuation
Eastwards
On same scale.

CANADA

MAINE

NEW HAMPSHIRE

ATLANTIC OCEAN

BAHAMAS

Great Abaco I.
Little Abaco I.
Grand Bahama I.

NORTH CAROLINA

TENNESSEE

SOUTH CAROLINA

GEORGIA

ALABAMA

MISSISSIPPI

FLORIDA

GULF OF MEXICO

Projection: Alber's Equal Area with two standard parallels

West from Greenwich

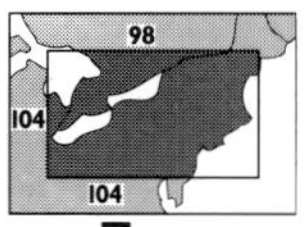

1 2 3 4 5 6 7

A

Georgian Bay

Lucas Channel
Cove I.
Tobermory
C. Hurd
Flowerpot I.
Cabot Hd.

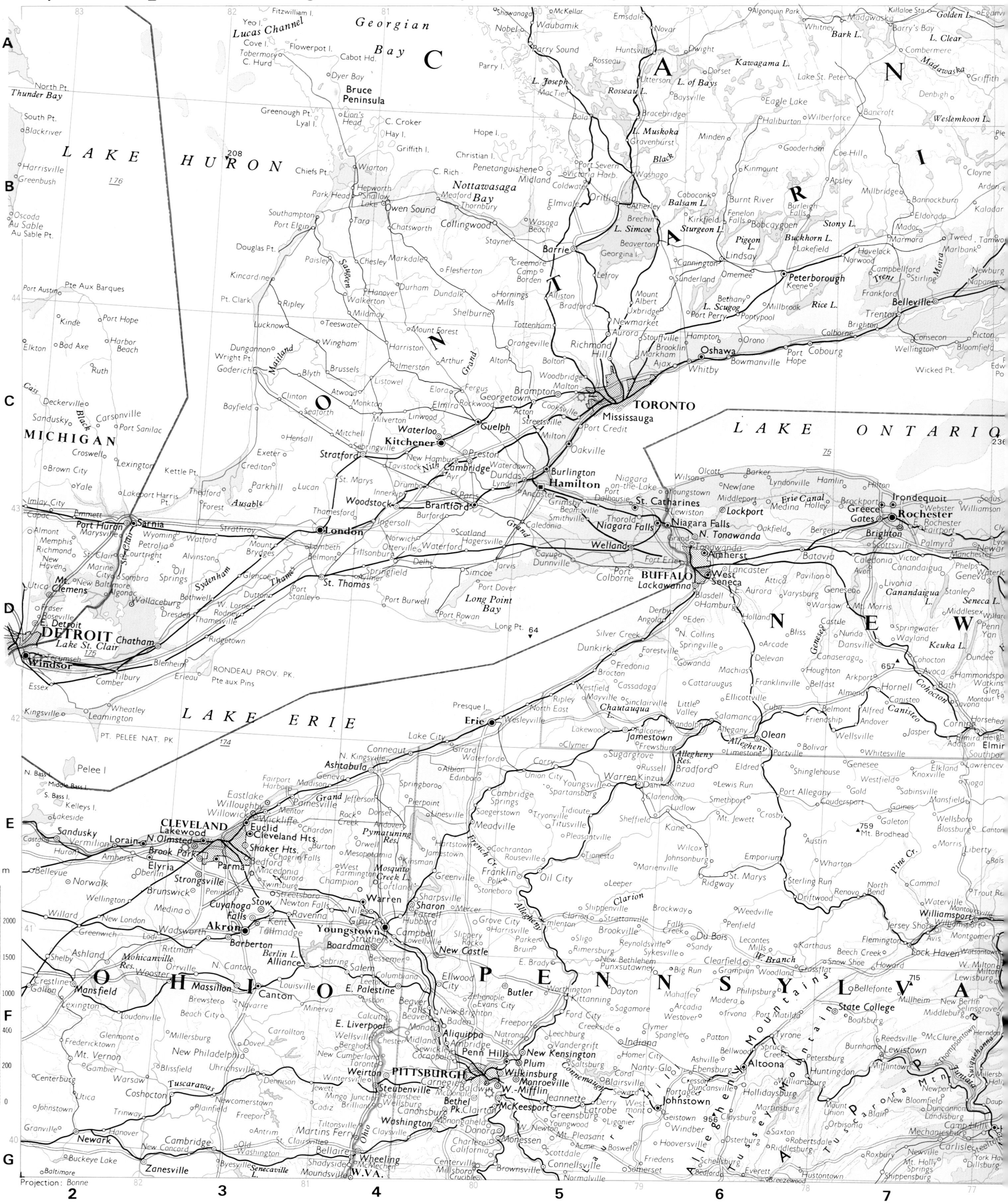

Bruce Peninsula

North Pt.
Thunder Bay

South Pt.
Blackriver

Dyer Bay
Lyal I.
Lion's Head
C. Croker
Hay I.
Griffith I.

CANADA

Shawanaga
McKellar
Nobel
Parry Sound
Parry I.

Emsdale
Novar

Algonquin Park
Whitney
Bark L.
Madawaska
Killaloe Sta.
Golden L.
Barry's Bay
L. Clear
Combermere

B

LAKE HURON
208
176

Harrisville
Greenbush

Oscoda
Au Sable
Au Sable Pt.

Greenough Pt.
Chiefs Pt.
Wiarton
Hepworth
Shallow Lake
Park Head

Owen Sound
Meaford
Thornbury

Nottawasaga Bay

Christian I.
Penetanguishene
Midland
Port Severn
Victoria Harb.
Port McNicoll
Coldwater

Huntsville
Dwight
Rosseau
L. Joseph
MacTier
L. of Bays
Dorset
Kawagama L.
Lake St. Peter
Eagle Lake
Haliburton
Wilberforce
Bancroft
Weslemkoon L.

Denbigh

Griffith

C

MICHIGAN

Cass
Deckerville
Sandusky
Port Sanilac
Carsonville

Southampton
Port Elgin
Paisley
Tara
Chatsworth

Collingwood
Wasaga Beach
Stayner
Creemore
Camp Borden

Barrie
L. Simcoe
Orillia
Brechin
Beaverton
Atherley
Balsam L.
Kirkfield
Fenelon Falls
Bobcaygeon
Burnt River
Burleigh Falls
Eldorado

Coboconk
Minden
Gooderham
Coe Hill

Cloyne
Apsley
Millbridge
Bannockburn
Kaladar
Ardant
Madoc
Tweed
Tamworth

ONTARIO

Toronto
Mississauga

LAKE ONTARIO

DETROIT

LAKE ERIE

CLEVELAND

OHIO

PENNSYLVANIA

PITTSBURGH

W.VA.

2 3 4 5 6 7

1 : 2 000 000

10   0   10   20   30   40   50 miles
10 0 10 20 30 40 50 60 70 80 km

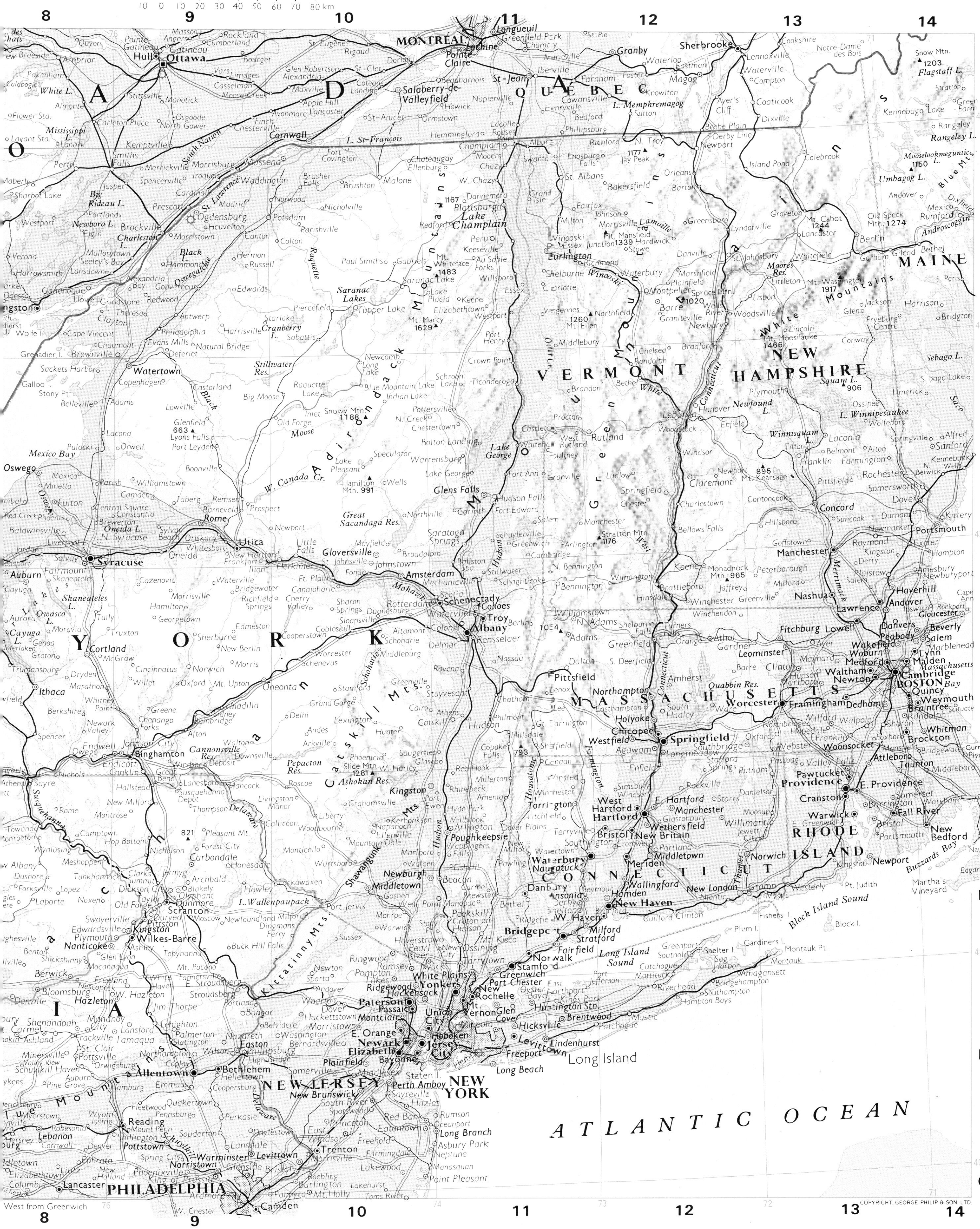

8   9   10   11   12   13   14

MONTREAL

QUEBEC

MAINE

VERMONT

NEW HAMPSHIRE

NEW YORK

MASSACHUSETTS

RHODE ISLAND

CONNECTICUT

PENNSYLVANIA

NEW JERSEY

NEW YORK

PHILADELPHIA

Long Island

ATLANTIC OCEAN

Lake Champlain

Lake George

West from Greenwich

8   9   10   11   12   13   14

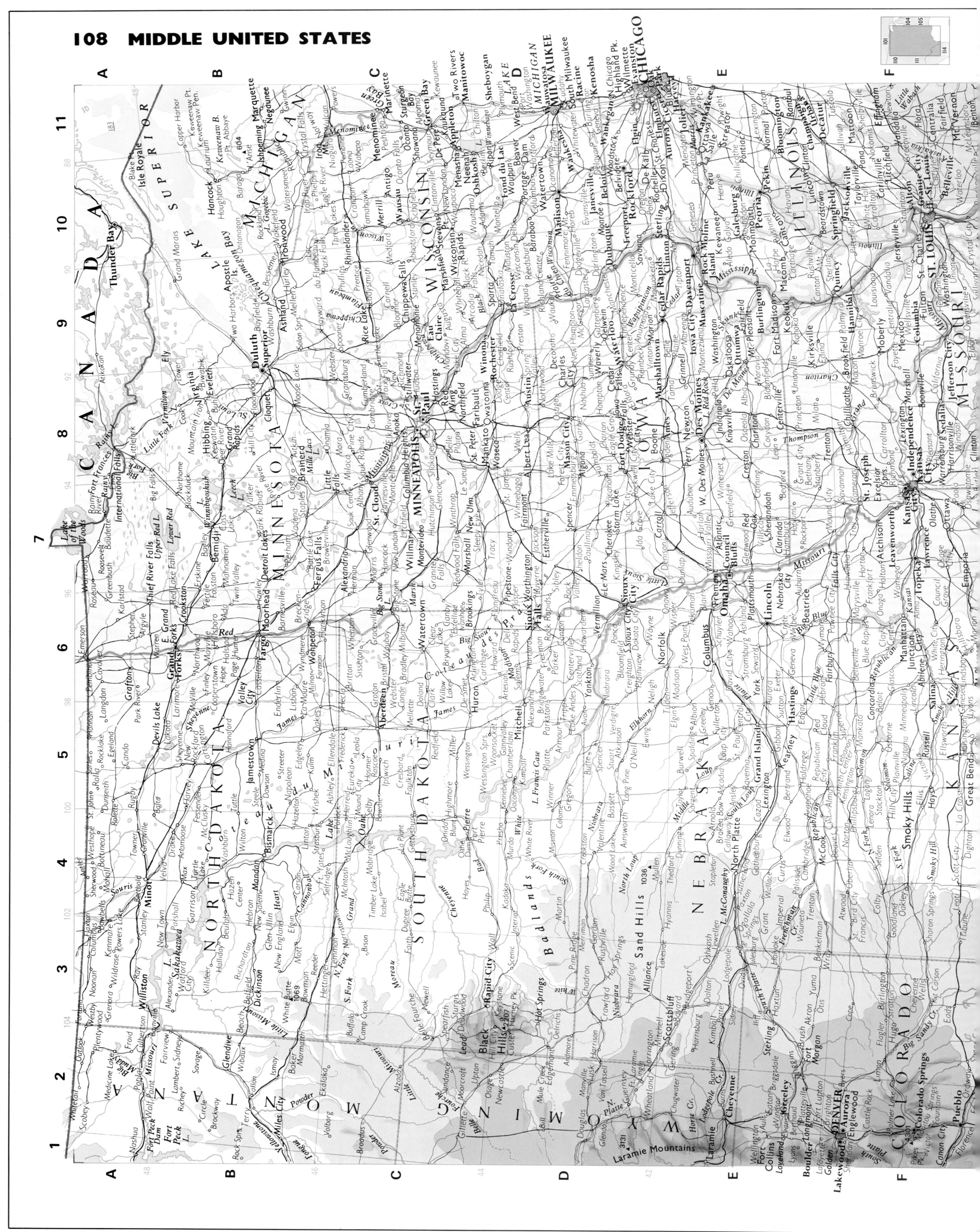

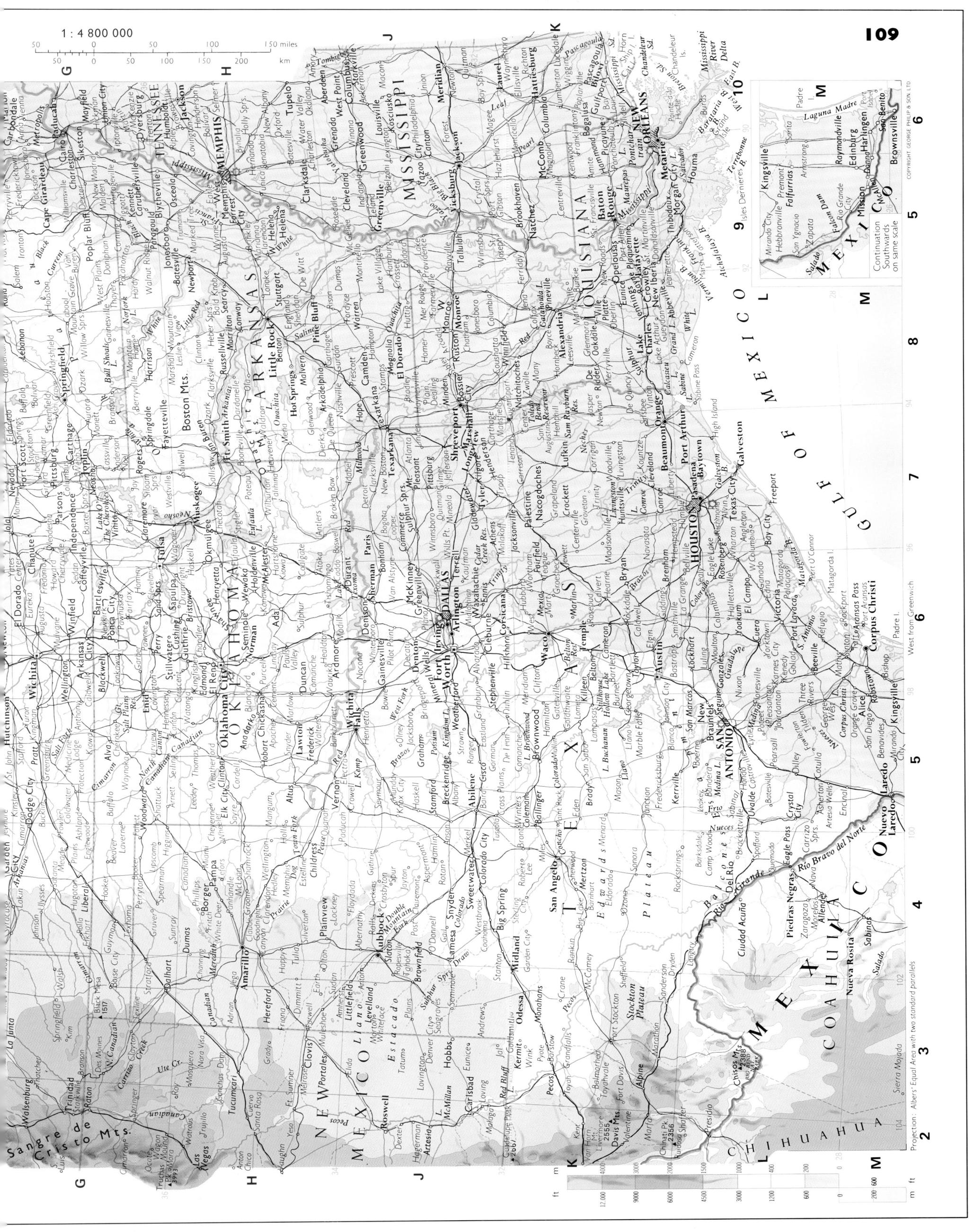

1 : 4 800 000

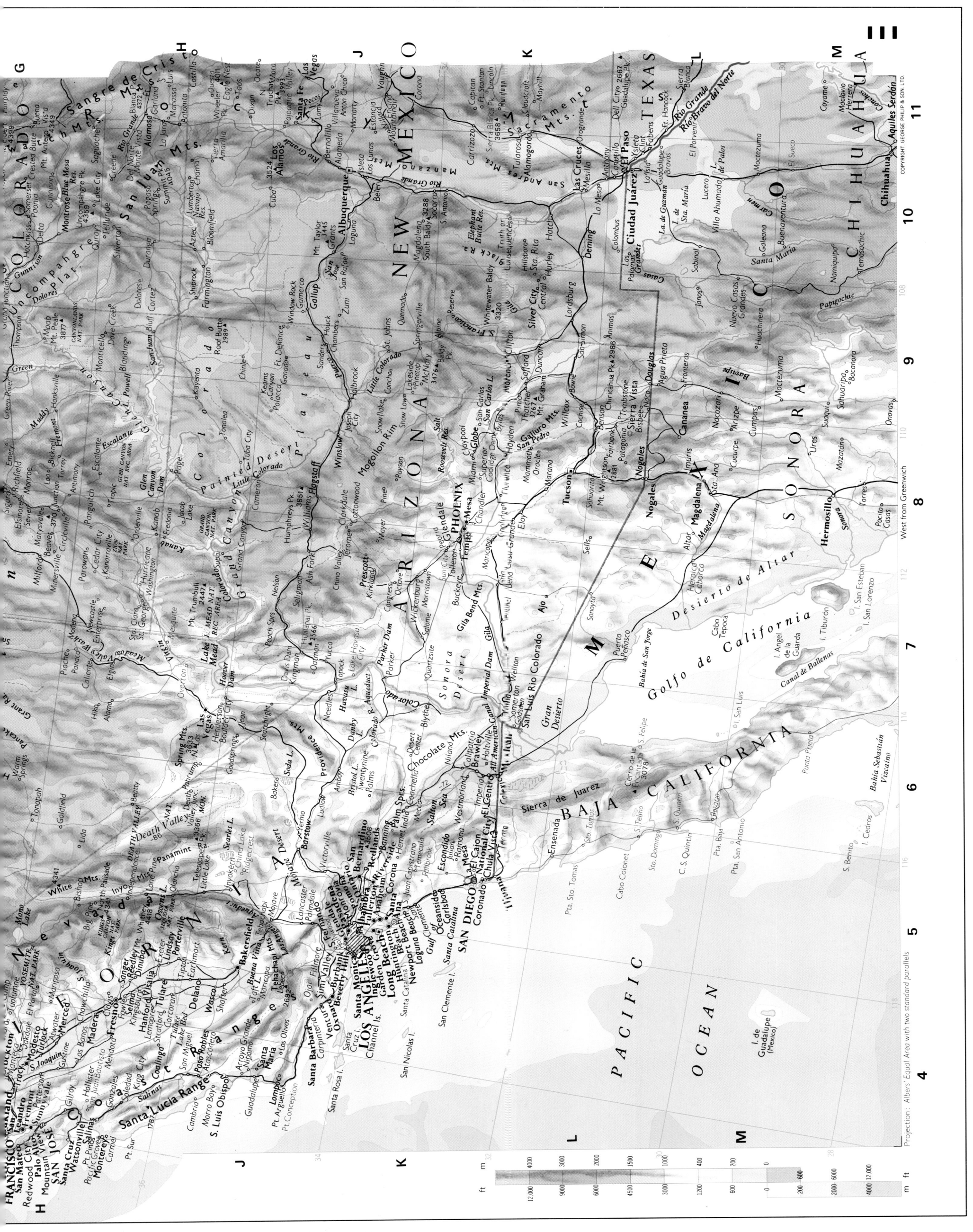

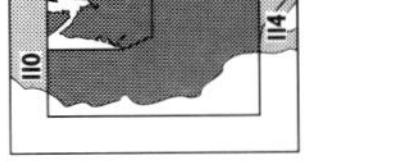

VANCOUVER

North Vancouver
Westminster
New Westminster

CANADA

Vancouver Island

Victoria

Strait of Georgia

Bellingham

Strait of Juan de Fuca

PACIFIC RIM NATIONAL PARK

Cape Flattery

Olympic Mountains
Mt Olympus 2428
OLYMPIC NATIONAL PARK

SEATTLE
Everett
Bellevue
Renton
Kent
Auburn
Tacoma
Lakewood Center
Bremerton

WASHINGTON

Olympia
Centralia
Chehalis

Longview
Columbia

MT. RAINIER NAT. PARK
Mt Rainier 4392

Mt Adams 3751

Mt St. Helens 2550

PORTLAND
Vancouver

OREGON

PACIFIC OCEAN

SEATTLE-PORTLAND REGION
On same scale

White Mts.

Owens

Inyo Mts.

Mono L.

Reno
Sparks

YOSEMITE NATIONAL PARK

KINGS CANYON NAT. PARK

SEQUOIA NAT. PARK

Pahute Mesa

SIERRA NEVADA

Honey L.

Lake Oroville
Oroville
Chico

Sacramento
North Highlands
Carmichael
Citrus Heights

Stockton

Modesto

Merced

Fresno
Clovis

Visalia
Tulare

CALIFORNIA

San Joaquin Valley

SAN FRANCISCO
Oakland
Berkeley
Richmond
San Rafael
Vallejo
Napa
Santa Rosa
Fairfield
Vacaville
Woodland
Davis
Concord
Walnut Creek
Antioch
Pittsburg
Livermore
San Leandro
Hayward
Fremont
Palo Alto
Mountain View
Sunnyvale
Santa Clara
SAN JOSE
Los Gatos
Campbell
Saratoga

Daly City
Pacifica
San Mateo
Redwood City
Menlo Park

Santa Cruz
Monterey Bay
Pacific Grove
Monterey
Carmel-by-the-Sea

Salinas

Santa Lucia Range

Watsonville
Gilroy

San Joaquin River

Tomales Bay
POINT REYES NATIONAL SEASHORE
Pt. Reyes

Russian River

Clear Lake

Diablo Range

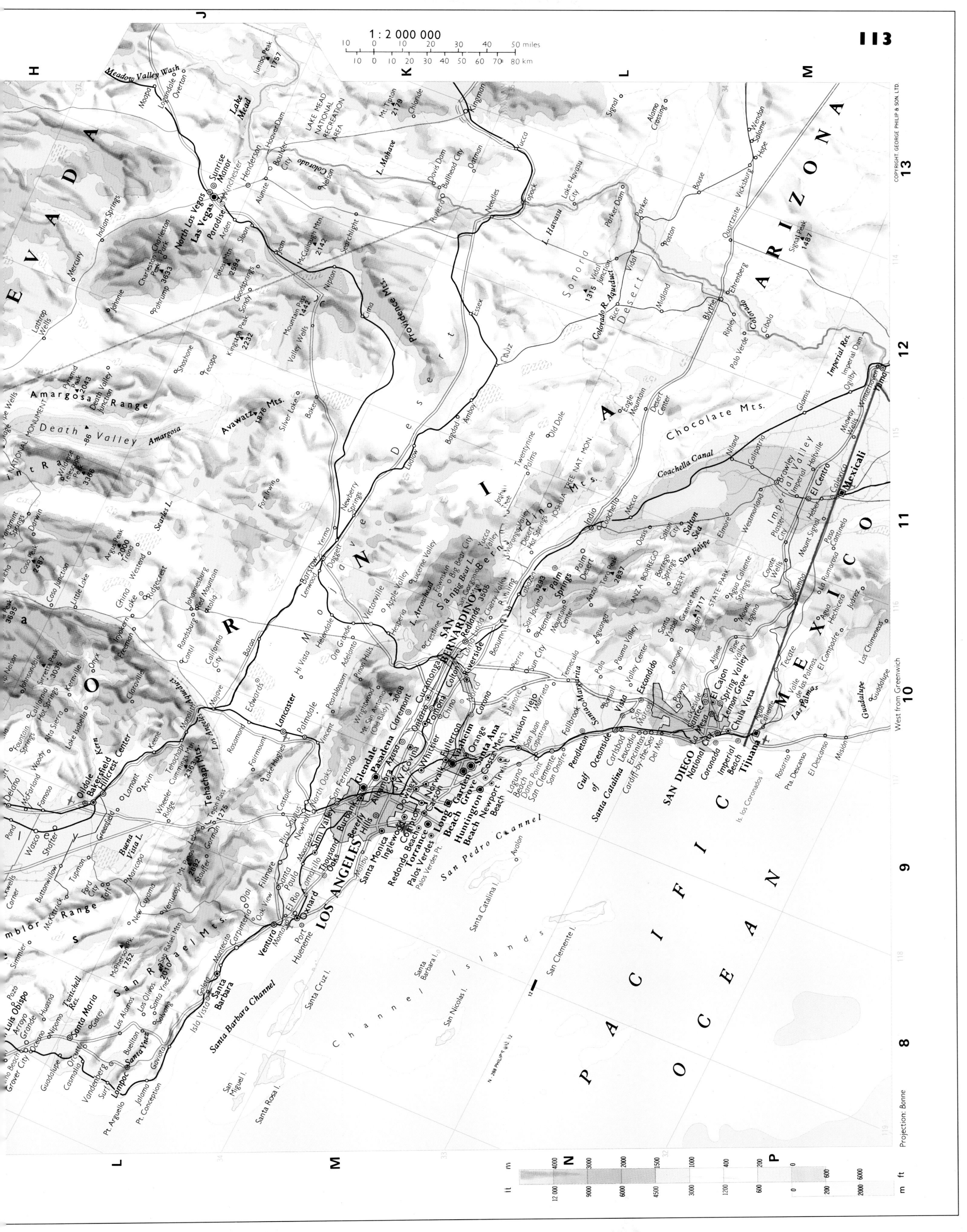

1 : 2 000 000

10   0   10   20   30   40   50 miles
10   0   10 20 30 40 50 60 70 80 km

H   J   K   L   M

N   E   V   A   D   A

A   R   I   Z   O   N   A

C   A   L   I   F   O   R   N   I   A

M   E   X   I   C   O

P   A   C   I   F   I   C   O   C   E   A   N

Meadow Valley Wash
Lake Mead
LAKE MEAD NATIONAL RECREATION AREA
Jumbo Peak 1757
Overton
Logandale
Moapa
Hoover Dam
Boulder City
Henderson
Sunrise Manor
North Las Vegas
Las Vegas
Paradise Winchester
Arden
Sloan
Mt. Tipton 2179
Chloride
Kingman
Boulder Dam
Colorado
L. Mohave
Davis Dam
Bullhead City
Oatman
Yucca
Sigsaf
Alamo Crossing
Valentine
Wendon
Indian Springs
Mercury
Charleston Peak 3633
Mt. Charleston Park
Potosi Mtn 2584
Goodsprings
McCullough Mts. 2142
Searchlight
Nelson
Nipton
Needles
Topock
Vidal
L. Havasu
Lake Havasu City
Parker Dam
Parker
Bouse
Vicksburg
Hope
Johnnie
Pahrump
Kingston Peak 2232
Cima
Mountain Pass 1442
Ibex
Essex
Bagdad
Amboy
Colorado R. Aqueduct
1315
Vidal
Rice
Midland
Ehrenberg
Blythe
Ripley
Quartzsite
Cibola
Palo Verde
Lathrop Wells
Pyramid
Salt 2043
Amargosa
Junction
Death Valley
Amargosa Range
Shoshone
Tecopa
Baker
Silver Lake
Avawatz Mts. 1916
Providence Mts.
Sonora
Desert
Signal Peak 1457
Death Valley NATIONAL MONUMENT
Telescope Peak 3366
86
Valley
Amargosa
Fort Irwin
Ludlow
Twentynine Palms
Old Dale
Eagle Mountain
Desert Center
Chocolate Mts.
Imperial Res.
Imperial Dam
Darwin
Panamint Springs
Searles L.
Valley Wells
Newberry Springs
Yermo
Daggett
Barstow
Lenwood
Ludlow
JOSHUA TREE NAT. MON.
Joshua
Coachella Canal
Glamis
Niland
Calipatria
Ogilby
Yuma
Argus Peak 2000
Trona
Ridgecrest
Randsburg
Red Mountain
Atolia
Johannesburg
Hinkley
Hodge
Helendale
Oro Grande
Adelanto
Victorville
Hesperia
Apple Valley
Lucerne Valley
Big Bear City
Big Bear L.
Yucaipa
San Bernardino Mtn 3506
Morongo Valley
Desert Hot Springs
Palm Springs
Palm Desert
Indio
Coachella
Thermal
Mecca
Salton Sea
Salton
Oasis
Westmorland
Brawley
Imperial
Holtville
El Centro
Calexico
Mexicali
Coso Peak 3695
China Lake
Little Lake
Pearsonville
Inyokern
Freeman
California City
Hi Vista
Lucerne
San Gorgonio Mtn 3506
Crestline
Redlands
Beaumont
Banning
San Jacinto 3293
Hemet
Sun City
Perris
Elsinore
Temecula
Aguanga
Anza
Hot Springs
Borrego Springs
Santa Rosa Mtn 2637
ANZA BORREGO DESERT STATE PARK
Agua Caliente
El Compadre
Los Chimeneas
Laguna
Julian 1717
Ramona
Poway
Escondido
Vista
San Marcos
Carlsbad
Oceanside
Fallbrook
San Juan Capistrano
Dana Point
San Clemente
San Onofre
Pendleton
Gulf of Santa Catalina
Santa Catalina
Bakersfield
Oildale
Hillcrest Center
Delano
McFarland
Famoso
Lamont
Arvin
Woody
Alta Sierra
Lake Isabella
Kernville
Onyx
Weldon
Fountain Springs
Ducor
Terra Bella
Sorrata Peak 3055
Tehachapi Mts. 2305
Keene
Tehachapi
Cummings Mtn 2375
Wheeler Ridge
Tejon Pass 1275
Mojave
Edwards
Rosamond
Lancaster
Palmdale
Vincent
Pearblossom
Wrightwood
Mt. San Antonio 3068
Pinon Hills
Cajon
Colton
Riverside
Corona
Norco
Moreno
Sun City
Murrieta
Valley Center
Pauma Valley
Palomar
Warner Springs
Santa Ysabel
El Cajon
La Mesa
Spring Valley
Lemon Grove
Chula Vista
National City
SAN DIEGO
Coronado
Imperial Beach
Tijuana
Tecate
Valle de las Palmas
La Puerta
Rumorosa
Agua Caliente
Hechicera
Juárez
Rosarito
El Descanso
Pta. Descanso
Mission
Misión
Guadalupe
Grover City
Arroyo Grande
Pozo
San Luis Obispo
Huasna
Nipomo
Santa Maria
Grande
Orcutt
Casmalia
Los Alamos
Buellton
Solvang
Santa Ynez
Santa Barbara
Gaviota
Goleta
Lompoc
Surf
Vandenberg
Pt. Arguello
Pt. Conception
Jalama
Los Olivos
San Rafael Mtn 1752
McPherson Peak 1752
Cuyama
Simmler
Maricopa
Taft
Tupman
Buttonwillow
Buena Vista L.
McKittrick
Temblor Range 1016
Fellows
Shafter
Wasco
Pond
Lost Hills
Corcoran
Corner
Gosford
Maricopa
Ojai
Santa Paula
Fillmore
Piru
Newhall
San Fernando
Castaic
Saugus
Solemint
Val Verde
Gorman
Mt. Pinos 2692
Frazier Mtn
Lockwood Valley
Cuddy Valley
Ventura
Oxnard
Port Hueneme
Camarillo
Thousand Oaks
Newbury Park
Simi Valley
Moorpark
Santa Susana
Chatsworth
Canoga Park
Van Nuys
North Hollywood
Burbank
Glendale
Pasadena
Altadena
Arcadia
Azusa
Glendora
Claremont
Montclair
Ontario
Cucamonga
Pomona
Covina
W. Covina
El Monte
Whittier
Norwalk
Downey
Fullerton
Anaheim
Orange
Santa Ana
Tustin
Irvine
Garden Grove
Westminster
Santa Fe Springs
LOS ANGELES
Montebello
Beverly Hills
Santa Monica
Inglewood
Hawthorne
Gardena
Torrance
Redondo Beach
Palos Verdes
Palos Verdes Pt.
San Pedro
Long Beach
Carson
Compton
Lakewood
Buena Park
Cerritos
Huntington Beach
Newport Beach
Costa Mesa
Laguna Beach
San Clemente
Oceanside
El Rio
Saticoy
Montalvo
Colonia
Carpinteria
Summerland
Malibu
San Pedro Channel
Santa Catalina I.
Avalon
San Clemente I.
San Nicolas I.
Santa Barbara I.
Santa Cruz I.
Santa Rosa I.
Santa Barbara Channel
San Miguel I.
Anacapa I.
Channel Islands
Isla Vista
 Los Coronados
La Jolla
Del Mar
Encinitas
Leucadia
Cardiff-by-the-Sea
Solana Beach

West from Greenwich

Projection: Bonne

m   ft
12 000   4000
9000   3000
6000   2000
4500   1500
3000   1000
1200   400
600   200
0   0
0   200
2000   600
6000   2000

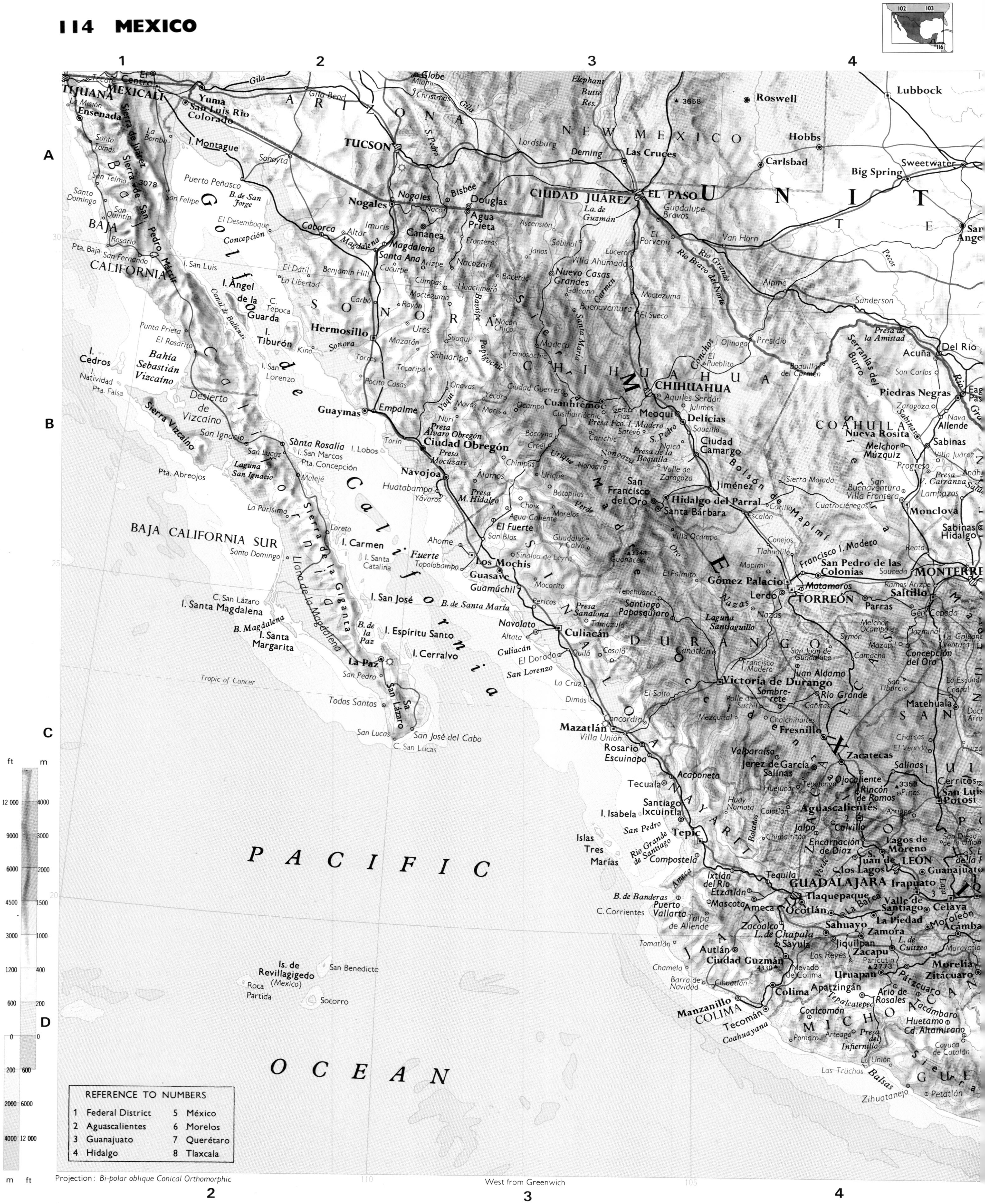

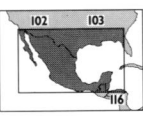

REFERENCE TO NUMBERS

1 Federal District	5 México
2 Aguascalientes	6 Morelos
3 Guanajuato	7 Querétaro
4 Hidalgo	8 Tlaxcala

Projection: Bi-polar oblique Conical Orthomorphic

West from Greenwich

PACIFIC

OCEAN

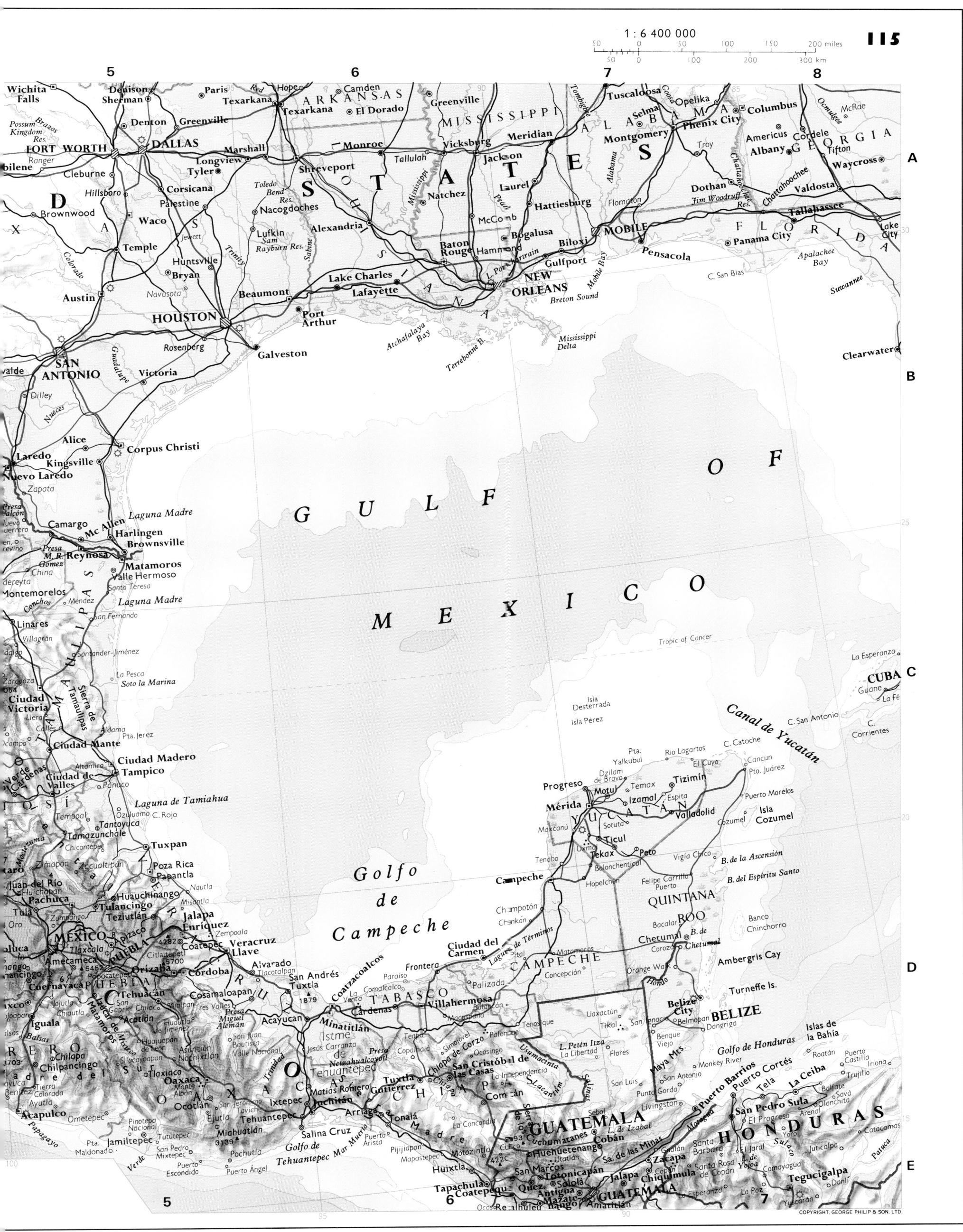

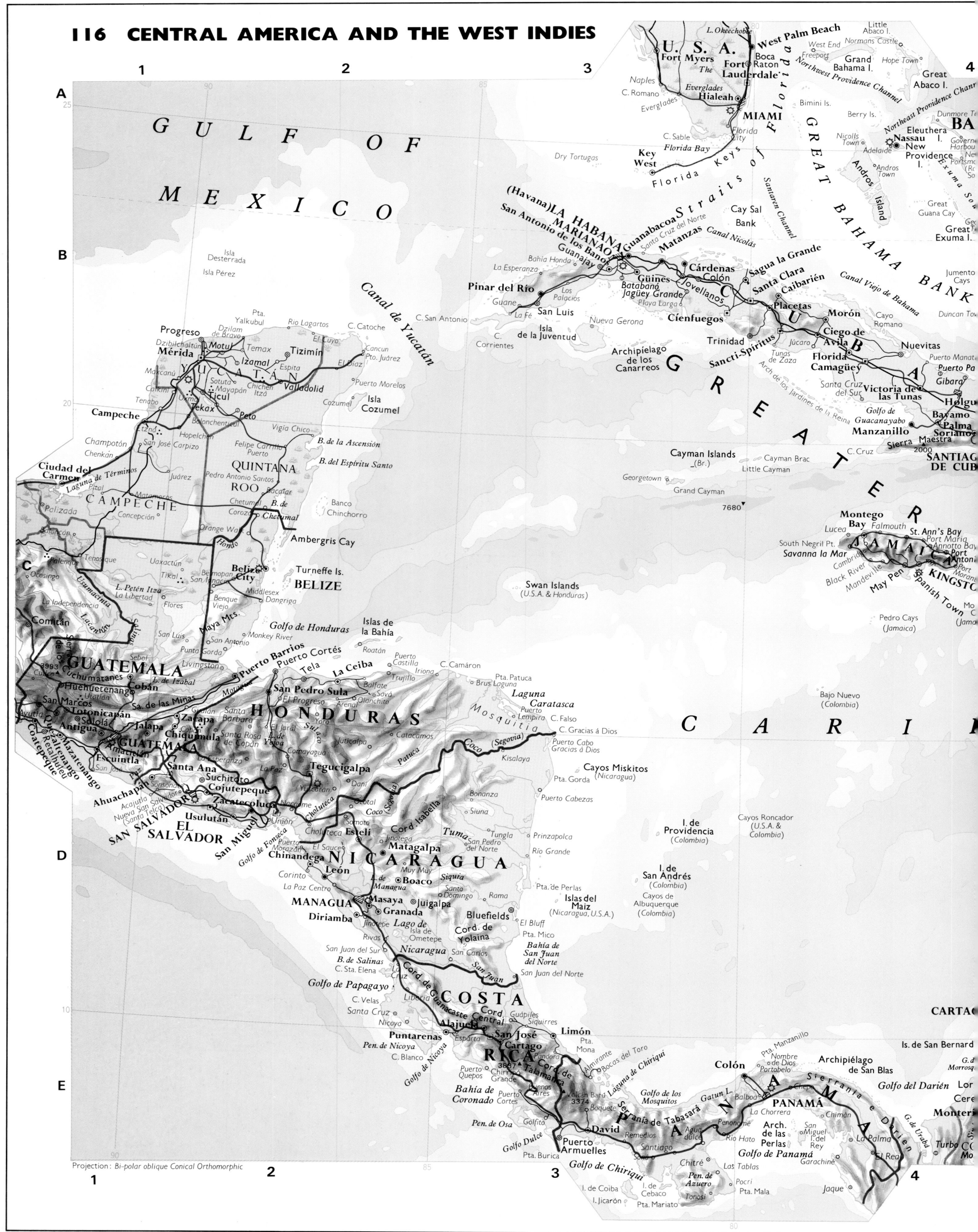

GULF OF MEXICO

U.S.A.

Fort Myers
Fort Lauderdale
West Palm Beach
Boca Raton
MIAMI
Hialeah
Naples
C. Romano
Everglades
Everglades
Key West
Dry Tortugas
C. Sable
Florida Bay
Florida City
Florida Keys

West End
Freeport
Bimini Is.
Berry Is.

Little Abaco I.
The
Grand Bahama I.
Hope Town
Normans Castle
Great Abaco I.

BA
Nassau
New Providence
Andros Town
Andros Island

Eleuthera
Governor's Harbour
New
Great Exuma I.

GREAT BAHAMA BANK

Jumento Cays

Isla Desterrada
Isla Pérez

(Havana) LA HABANA
San Antonio de los Baños
Guanajay
MARIANAO
Guanabacoa
Bahía Honda
La Esperanza
Pinar del Río
Guane
La Fé
Los Palacios
San Luis
Guines
Batabanó
Playa Larga
Jagüey Grande

Santa Cruz del Norte
Matanzas
Canal Nicolás
Cárdenas
Colón
Jovellanos
Sagua la Grande
Santa Clara
Caibarién
Placetas
Cienfuegos
Trinidad
Sancti-Spíritus
Morón
Ciego de Ávila
Júcaro
Tunas de Zaza
Camagüey
Santa Cruz del Sur
Golfo de Guacanayabo
Manzanillo
Bayamo
Palma Soriano
Sierra Maestra
SANTIAGO DE CUBA

Cay Sal Bank
Canal Viejo de Bahama
GREATER

Cayman Islands (Br.)
Cayman Brac
Little Cayman
Georgetown
Grand Cayman
7680
Swan Islands (U.S.A. & Honduras)

Nueva Gerona
Isla de la Juventud
C. Corrientes
Archipiélago de los Canarreos
Banco Chinchorro

Nuevitas
Puerto Manatí
Gibara
Holguín
Bayamo

CARIBE

Montego Bay
Lucea
Falmouth
St. Ann's Bay
Annotto
Port
Savanna la Mar
South Negril Pt.
Black River
Mandeville
May Pen
Spanish Town
KINGSTON
JAMAICA

Pedro Cays (Jamaica)

Bajo Nuevo (Colombia)

C

Progreso
Dzibilchaltún
Mérida
Izamal
Motul
Temax
Tizimín
Espita
Valladolid
Chichén Itzá
Mayapán
Peto
Ticul
Tekax
Maxcanú
Sotuta

Río Lagartos
C. Catoche
El Cuyo
Pta. Yalkubul
Dzilam de Bravo
El Díaz
Cancún
Pto. Juárez
Isla Cozumel
Puerto Morelos
Cozumel
Vigía Chico

C. San Antonio

Canal de Yucatán

Campeche
Champotón
Calkiní
Tenabo
Hecelchakán
Hopelchén
Chenkán
Bolonchenticul
Felipe Carrillo Puerto
B. de la Ascensión
B. del Espíritu Santo

CAMPECHE
Escárcega
Juárez
Concepción
QUINTANA ROO
Bacalar
Chetumal
B. de Chetumal

Ciudad del Carmen
Laguna de Términos
Palizada
Pital
Matamoros
Orange Walk
Corozal
Hondo
Ambergris Cay

Ocosingo
Tenosique
Emiliano Zapata
Uaxactún
Bermpan
Tikal
San Miguel
Belize City
Middlesex
Dangriga
BELIZE
Turneffe Is.

Comitán
La Independencia
L. Petén Itzá
La Libertad
Flores
Benque Viejo

Golfo de Honduras
Islas de la Bahía
Roatán
Monkey River

Lacandón
Usumacinta
San Luis
San Antonio
Punta Gorda
Livingston
Puerto Barrios
Puerto Cortés
Tela
La Ceiba
Balfate
Savá
Trujillo
C. Camarón
Iriona
Pta. Patuca
Brus Laguna

CARIBE

3993
GUATEMALA
Cuchumatanes
Huehuetenango
Cobán
L. de Izabal
Motagua
San Pedro Sula
El Progreso
Olanchito
Sa. de las Minas
Santa Bárbara
Zacapa
Chiquimula
Santa Rosa de Copán
El Jaral
L. de Yojoa

HONDURAS
Catacamas
Juticalpa
Laguna Caratasca
Puerto Lempira
C. Falso
C. Gracias á Dios
Puerto Cabo Gracias á Dios

San Marcos
Totonicapán
Uxtatán
Sololá
Jalapa
Antigua
Ayutla
Quezaltenango
Retalhuleu
Mazatenango
Escuintla
GUATEMALA
Comayagua
La Paz
Tegucigalpa
Danlí
Patuca
Segovia
Kisalaya
Mosquitia

Coatepeque
San José
Santa Ana
Suchitoto
Cojutepeque
Ahuachapán
Sonsonate
Nueva San Salvador (Santa Tecla)
Acajutla
SAN SALVADOR
Zacatecoluca
Usulután
Unión
San Miguel
Yoro
Choluteca
Comayagua
Nacaome
Somoto
Esteli
Jinotega
Cord. Isabella
San Pedro del Norte
Tuma
Bonanza
Siuna
Prinzapolca
Puerto Cabezas
Cayos Miskitos (Nicaragua)
Pta. Gorda

EL SALVADOR
SAN SALVADOR
Golfo de Fonseca
Chinandega
Corinto
León
La Paz Centro
MANAGUA
Diriamba
Masaya
Granada
Boaco
Juigalpa
Matagalpa
NICARAGUA
L. de Managua
Muy Muy
Siquia
Santo Domingo
Rama
Río Grande
Islas del Maíz (Nicaragua, U.S.A.)
Bluefields
El Bluff
Cord. de Yolaina
Pta. de Perlas
Cayos de Perlas
Bahía de San Juan del Norte
Pta. Mico

I. de Providencia (Colombia)
Cayos Roncador (U.S.A. & Colombia)
I. de San Andrés (Colombia)
Cayos de Albuquerque (Colombia)

Isla de Ometepe
Rivas
San Juan del Sur
B. de Salinas
C. Sta. Elena
Golfo de Papagayo
C. Velas
Santa Cruz
Nicoya
C. Blanco
Pen. de Nicoya
Nicaragua
San Carlos
San Juan
San Juan del Norte

COSTA RICA
Liberia
Cord. de Guanacaste
Cord. Central
Alajuela
SAN JOSÉ
Cartago
3837
Cord. de Talamanca
Puerto Quepos
Chirripó Grande
Golfo de Nicoya
Puntarenas
Esparta
Guápiles
Siquirres
Limón
Pta. Mona
Golfo Dulce
Pen. de Osa
Bahía de Coronado
Buenos Aires
Palmar
Volcán Barú
3374
Boquete
Puerto Armuelles
Pta. Burica
Golfo de Chiriquí
David
Remedios
Santiago
Chitré
Pocrí
Las Tablas
Pen. de Azuero
Pta. Mala
Pta. Mariato
I. de Coiba
I. de Cebaco
I. Jicarón

PANAMÁ
Colón
Gatún L.
Balboa
La Chorrera
Chimán
Penonomé
Aguadulce
Río Hato
Golfo de los Mosquitos
Nombre de Dios
Portobelo
Serranía de Tabasará
Serranía de San Blas
San Miguel
Arch. de las Perlas
I. del Rey
Golfo de Panamá
Serranía del Darién
Golfo del Darién
Golfo de Urabá
La Palma
El Real
Jaqué
Garachiné
Turbo
CARTAGO
Is. de San Bernardo
Montería
Tonosí

Projection: Bi-polar oblique Conical Orthomorphic

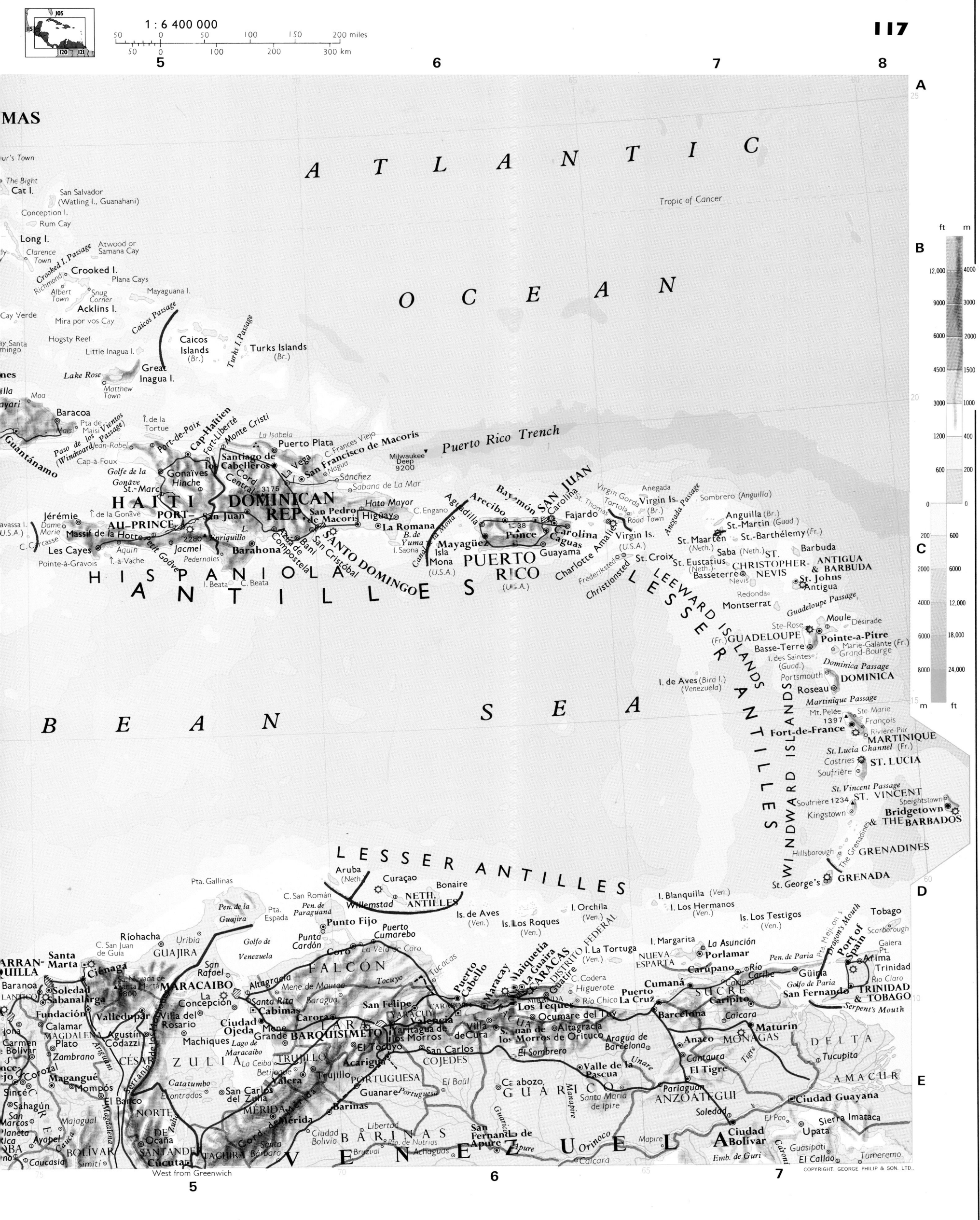

1 : 6 400 000

50   0   50   100   150   200 miles

50   0   100   200   300 km

MAS

A T L A N T I C

Tropic of Cancer

O C E A N

ur's Town

The Bight
Cat I.

San Salvador
(Watling I., Guanahani)

Conception I.

Rum Cay

Long I.

Clarence
Town

Atwood or
Samana Cay

Richmond

Plana Cays

Albert
Town

Snug
Corner

Mayaguana I.

Acklins I.

Cay Verde

Mira por vos Cay

Turks I. Passage

Caicos Passage

Hogsty Reef

Little Inagua I.

**Caicos
Islands**
(Br.)

Turks Islands
(Br.)

Lake Rose

Matthew
Town

**Great
Inagua I.**

Puerto Rico Trench

Baracoa

Pta. de
los Vientos

Î. de la
Tortue

Port-de-Paix

Cap-Haïtien

Fort-Liberté

Monte Cristi

La Isabela

Puerto Plata

C. Frances Viejo

San Francisco de Macorís

Milwaukee
Deep
9200

Paso de los
(Windward) Passage

Jean-Rabel

Santiago de
los Cabelleros

Cord.

La Vega

Nagua

Sánchez

Sabana de la Mar

Agudilla

Arecibo

Bayemón

San Juan

Carolina

St. Thomas

Virgin Gorda

Anegada

Tortola

Virgin Is.
(Br.)

Sombrero (Anguilla)

Guantánamo

Cap-à-Foux

Gonaïves

St.-Marc

Hinche

Central

3175

Hato Mayor

C. Engano

Fajardo

Road Town

Anguilla (Br.)

St.-Martin (Guad.)

St.-Barthélemy (Fr.)

Jérémie

Î. de la Gonâve

HAITI

**DOMINICAN
REP.**

San Pedro
de Macorís

Higüey

La Romana

Ponce

Carolina

Caguas

Virgin Is.
(U.S.A.)

St. Maarten
(Neth.)

Saba (Neth.)

**ST.
CHRISTOPHER-
NEVIS**

**ANTIGUA
& BARBUDA**

Dame
Marie
(U.S.A.)

**PORT-
AU-PRINCE**

San Juan

2280

L.

Enriquillo

B. de
Yuma

Mayagüez

Guayama

Charlotte Amalie

St. Eustatius

Basseterre

Nevis

Barbuda

St. Johns

C. Carcasse

Les Cayes

Aquin

Jacmel

Pedernales

Compostela

Isla
Mona
(U.S.A.)

I. Saona

**PUERTO
RICO**
(U.S.A.)

Frederiksted

St. Croix

Christiansted

Redonda

Antigua

Pointe-à-Gravois

HISPANIOLA

C. Beata

A N T I L L E S

L E S S E R

Montserrat

Guadeloupe Passage

Moule

Désirade

GUADELOUPE
(Fr.)

Ste-Rose

Pointe-a-Pitre

Basse-Terre

I. de Aves (Bird I.)
(Venezuela)

Marie-Galante (Fr.)

Grand-Bourge

I. des Saintes
(Guad.)

Portsmouth

DOMINICA

Roseau

B E A N   S E A

Dominica Passage

Martinique Passage

Mt. Pelée
1397

Ste-Marie

François

Rivière-Pilote

Fort-de-France

MARTINIQUE

St. Lucia Channel (Fr.)

Castries

ST. LUCIA

Soufrière

St. Vincent Passage

Soufrière 1234

ST. VINCENT

Speightstown

Bridgetown

& THE

BARBADOS

Kingstown

Hillsborough

The Grenadines

GRENADINES

St. George's

GRENADA

L E S S E R   A N T I L L E S

Pta. Gallinas

Aruba
(Neth.)

Curaçao

Bonaire

**NETH.
ANTILLES**

I. Blanquilla (Ven.)

I. Los Hermanos
(Ven.)

Is. Los Testigos
(Ven.)

Tobago

C. San Román

Pen. de
Paraguaná

Willemstad

Is. de Aves
(Ven.)

I. Orchila
(Ven.)

Scarborough

Pta.
Espada

Pen. de
la
Guajira

Pta.
Cardón

Punto Fijo

Puerto
Cumarebo

Is. Los Roques
(Ven.)

I. Margarita

**NUEVA
ESPARTA**

La Asunción

Porlamar

Pen. de Paria

Galera
Pt.

Arima

Río
Caribe

Dragon's Mouth

**Port
of
Spain**

Ríohacha

Uribia

Coro

La Vela de Coro

La Tortuga
(Ven.)

Carúpano

Güíria

Trinidad

Río Claro

**Santa
Marta**

Cienaga

C. San Juan
de Guia

San
Rafael

Altagracia

Tucacas

Puerto
Cabello

CARACAS

Maiquetía
La Guaira

C. Codera

Cumaná

Golfo de Paria

San Fernando

**TRINIDAD
& TOBAGO**

**ARRAN-
QUILLA**

GUAJIRA

C. San
de Guia

MARACAIBO

La
Concepción

Cabimas

Mene
Grande

Coro

FALCON

Tocuyo

Baragua

Maracay

DISTRITO FEDERAL

Higuerote

Río Chico

Puerto
La Cruz

Barcelona

Caicara

SUCRE

Caripito

Serpent's Mouth

Baranoa

Soledad

Sabanalarga

Santa Rita

San
Felipe

Villa
Valencia
Valencia

Ocumare del
del Tuy

Los Teques

Anaco

Maturín

MONAGAS

DELTA

LANTICO

Fundación

Calamar

Agustín

Codazzi

MAGDALENA

Zambrano

Ciudad
Ojeda

La Ceiba

Betijoque

Mene

Carora

Villa
del

BARQUISIMETO

El Tocuyo

San Carlos

Martagua de
los Morros

Villa
de Cura

Villa de
los Morros de Orituco

Aragua de
Barcelona

Cantaura

El Tigre

Ciudad Guayana

Tucupita

Carmen

Bolívar

Plato

Magangué

Mompós

El Banco

Valledupar

Machiques

Lago de
Maracaibo

La Grita

TRUJILLO

Trujillo

Valera

COJEDES

PORTUGUESA

San Carlos

Acarigua

El Baúl

GUARICO

abozo

Valle de la
Pascua

El Sombrero

Santa María
de Ipire

Pariaguán

Soledad

El Pao

AMACUR

Sierra Imataca

Sahagún

Sincé

San
Marcos

El Barco

NORTE

CESAR

ZULIA

San Carlos
del Zulia

Catatumbo

Barinas

MERIDA

Mérida

Libertad

BARINAS

Ciudad
Bolivia

Guanare

Barinas

ANZOATEGUI

Upata

El Callao

planeta

BOLÍVAR

Ayapel

Caucasia

Ocaña

SANTANDER

TACHIRA

Cucúta

Santa Bárbara

Bruzual

V E N E Z U E L

San
Fernando de
Apure

Achaguas

Apure

A

**Ciudad
Bolívar**

Mapire

Emb. de Guri

Guasipati

Tumeremo

West from Greenwich

COPYRIGHT. GEORGE PHILIP & SON LTD.

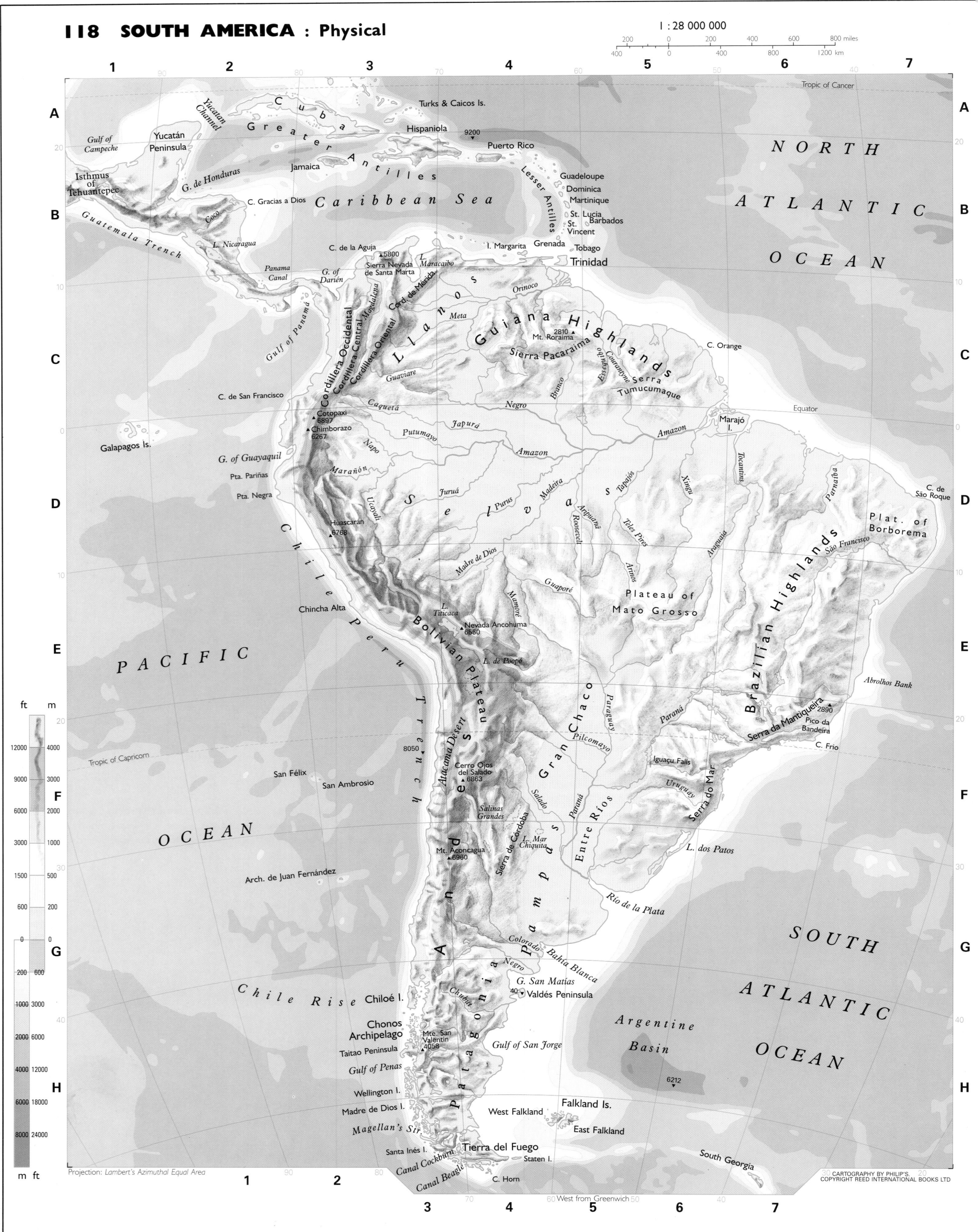

1 : 28 000 000

200   0   200   400   600   800 miles
400   0   200   400   800   1200 km

1 90 **2** 80 **3** **4** 70 60 **5** 50 **6** 40 **7**

Tropic of Cancer

A
Yucatán Channel
C u b a
Greater Antilles
Turks & Caicos Is.
Hispaniola
9200
Puerto Rico
NORTH
Gulf of Campeche
Yucatán Peninsula
G. de Honduras
Jamaica
Lesser Antilles
Guadeloupe
Dominica
Martinique
ATLANTIC

B
Isthmus of Tehuantepec
Coco
C. Gracias a Dios
Caribbean Sea
St. Lucia
Barbados
St. Vincent
OCEAN
Guatemala Trench
L. Nicaragua
C. de la Aguja
5800
I. Margarita
Grenada
Tobago
Trinidad

Panama Canal
G. of Darién
Sierra Nevada de Santa Marta
L. Maracaibo
Orinoco
C. Orange

C
Cordillera Occidental
Cordillera Central
Cordillera Oriental
Cord. de Mérida
Llanos
Meta
Guiana Highlands
2810
Mt. Roraima
Sierra Pacaraima
Serra Tumucumaque
Caroni
Essequibo
Branco

Gulf of Panamá
C. de San Francisco
Guaviare
Caquetá
Negro
Equator

0
Galapagos Is.
Cotopaxi 5897
Chimborazo 6267
Putumayo
Japurá
Amazon
Marajó I.

G. of Guayaquil
Pta. Pariñas
Pta. Negra
Napo
Marañón
Juruá
Purus
Amazon
Madeira
Tapajós
Xingu
Tocantins
Parnaíba
C. de São Roque

D
Huascaran 6768
Ucayali
S e l v a s
Madre de Dios
Aripuanã
Roosevelt
Teles Pires
Araguaia
Arinos
São Francisco
Plat. of Borborema

Chile Peru Trench
Chincha Alta
L. Titicaca
Guaporé
Mamoré
Plateau of Mato Grosso
Brazilian Highlands

E
PACIFIC
Bolivian Plateau
Nevada Ancohuma 6580
L. de Poopó
Gran Chaco
Paraguay
Paraná
Abrolhos Bank

Tropic of Capricorn
San Félix
San Ambrosio
8050
Atacama Desert
Pilcomayo
2890
Serra da Mantiqueira
Pico da Bandeira
C. Frio

F
OCEAN
A n d e s
Cerro Ojos del Salado 6863
Salinas Grandes
Salado
Iguaçu Falls
Uruguay
Serra do Mar

Arch. de Juan Fernández
Mt. Aconcagua 6960
Sierra de Córdoba
L. Mar Chiquita
Entre Ríos
L. dos Patos

G
Colorado
P a m p a s
Bahía Blanca
Rio de la Plata
SOUTH

Chile Rise
Chiloé I.
Negro
G. San Matias
40
Valdés Peninsula
Argentine Basin
ATLANTIC

H
Chonos Archipelago
Mte. San Valentin 4058
Gulf of San Jorge
OCEAN
Taitao Peninsula
Chubut
Patagonia
Wellington I.
6212
Madre de Dios I.
West Falkland
Falkland Is.
Magellan's Str.
Santa Inés I.
Tierra del Fuego
East Falkland
South Georgia
Canal Cockburn
Staten I.
Canal Beagle
C. Horn

ft   m
12000 4000
9000 3000
6000 2000
3000 1000
1500 500
600 200
0 0
200 600
1000 3000
2000 6000
4000 12000
6000 18000
8000 24000
m ft

Projection: Lambert's Azimuthal Equal Area

1 70 **2** **3** 60 West from Greenwich 50 **4** **5** **6** 40 **7**

CARTOGRAPHY BY PHILIP'S.
COPYRIGHT REED INTERNATIONAL BOOKS LTD

1 : 28 000 000

200   0   200   400   600   800 miles
400   0   400   800   1200 km

1   2   3   4   5   6   7

A

Tropic of Cancer

NORTH

Havana
CUBA   **BAHAMAS**   Turks & Caicos Is.
(U.K.)

ATLANTIC

HAITI   **DOMINICAN**   Virgin Is.
REP.   (U.K.)
Port-au-   San Juan
Prince
JAMAICA   Kingston   **PUERTO**   **ST. KITTS-**   **ANTIGUA &**
RICO   **NEVIS**   **BARBUDA**
(U.S.A.)   **ST. KITTS-**   **GUADELOUPE**
MEXICO   **NEVIS**   (Fr.)
Basse-Terre
DOMINICA
Fort-de-France   **MARTINIQUE**
GUATEMALA   **BELIZE**   Castres   (Fr.)
HONDURAS   **ST. VINCENT**   **ST. LUCIA**
Guatemala   Tegucigalpa   Kingstow   **BARBADOS**
San Salvador   **GRENADA**   Bridgetown
EL SALVADOR   **NICARAGUA**   Port o'   St. George's
Managua   Spain   **TRINIDAD &**
COSTA   San José   **TOBAGO**

OCEAN

B

Caribbean   Sea

C

Barranquilla   C. de
la Aguja
RICA   San José   Cartagena   Maracaibo   Caracas
Panamá   Barquisimeto   Valencia
PANAMA   Cúcuta
Gulf of Panamá   San Cristóbal   *Orinoco*   Ciudad Guayana
Medellín   Bucaramanga   **VENEZUELA**   Georgetown
Cali   Bogotá   **GUYANA**   Paramaribo
SURINAM   Cayenne
COLOMBIA   RORAIMA   **FRENCH**   C. Orange
GUIANA

AMAPÁ

Equator

Quito   *Japurá*   Marajó   Belém
ECUADOR   *Putumayo*   I.
Guayaquil   *Napo*   *Amazon*   Santarém   São Luís
G. of Guayaquil   Iquitos   *Marañón*   Manaus   **PARÁ**   Fortaleza
AMAZONAS   *Amazon*   **MARANHÃO**   Teresina   C. de
Chiclayo   *Juruá*   *Madeira*   *Tapajós*   *Xingu*   São Roque
Trujillo   *Purus*   **CEARÁ**   Natal
Chimbote   ACRE   Pôrto Velho   **PIAUÍ**   RIO G.
DO NORTE
PERU   RONDÔNIA   **TOCANTINS**   PARAÍBA
Madre de Dios   **B R A Z I L**   PERNAMBUCO   Campina Grande
Callao   LIMA   **MATO GROSSO**   Recife
Cuzco   *Mamoré*   ALAGOAS   Maceió
L.   SERGIPE   Aracaju
Titicaca   GOIÁS   **BAHÍA**   Salvador
Arequipa   La Paz   Cuiabá   *São Francisco*   Salvador
BOLIVIA   DIS. FED   Brasília
Cochabamba   Goiânia
Santa Cruz   **MINAS GERAIS**
Sucre   *Paraguay*   **MATO GROSSO**   Belo   ESPÍRITO
Iquique   DO SUL   Ribeirão   Horizonte   SANTO
Prêto   Juiz   Vitória
Paraná   São Paulo   de Fora   Campos
PARAGUAY   Campinas   R. DE J.
Antofagasta   *Pilcomayo*   **PARANÁ**   **SÃO**   Niterói
Salta   Asunción   **PAULO**   **RIO DE**
San Félix   Curitiba   **JANEIRO**
(Chile)   San Miguel   Resistencia   SANTA CATARINA
San Ambrosio   de Tucumán   Corrientes   *Úruguay*   Pôrto Alegre
(Chile)   *Salado*   RIO GRANDE
DO SUL
Córdoba   Santa Fe   Paraná   Pelotas
San Juan   Rosario   **URUGUAY**   Pôrto Alegre
Viña del Mar   Mendoza   Montevideo
Valparaíso   Santiago   **BUENOS AIRES**
SANTIAGO   La Plata   *Río de la Plata*
Talca   Bahía   Mar del Plata
Concepción   *Colorado*   Blanca
Valdivia   *Negro*   Viedma
Puerto Montt   *Chubut*
ARGENTINA
CHILE
Comodoro Rivadavia
Gulf of San Jorge

D

E

PACIFIC

F

Tropic of Capricorn

Arch. de Juan Fernández
(Chile)

OCEAN

G

Galapagos Is.
(Ecuador)

SOUTH

ATLANTIC

OCEAN

H

Gulf of Penas
Magellan's Str.   West Falkland   **FALKLAND IS.**
(U.K.)
Punta Arenas   Stanley
Tierra del Fuego   East Falkland

South Georgia
(U.K.)

C. Horn

West from Greenwich

1   2   3   4   5   6   7

Projection: *Lambert's Azimuthal Equal Area*

■ **LIMA**   Capital Cities

CARTOGRAPHY BY PHILIP'S.
COPYRIGHT REED INTERNATIONAL BOOKS LTD

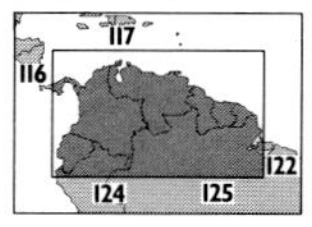

CARIBBEAN SEA

PACIFIC OCEAN

NETH. ANTILLES

PANAMA

COLOMBIA

VENEZUELA

ECUADOR

PERU

Major regions and provinces:
ATLANTICO, MAGDALENA, CESAR, ZULIA, FALCON, LARA, DISTRITO FEDERAL, ARAGUA, GUARICO, BARINAS, PORTUGUESA, COJEDES, SANTANDER, NORTE DE SANTANDER, TACHIRA, ARAUCA, ANTIOQUIA, CHOCO, CALDAS, CUNDINAMARCA, META, VICHADA, CASANARE, GUAINIA, VAUPES, GUAVIARE, CAQUETA, AMAZONAS, PUTUMAYO, NAPO, PASTAZA, MORONA-SANTIAGO, AZUAY, GUAYAS, EL ORO, MANABI, PICHINCHA, NARIÑO, CAUCA, HUILA, TOLIMA, VALLE, RISARALDA, CORDOBA, SUCRE, BOLIVAR, LA GUAJIRA, PANAMA, DARIEN, AMAZONAS (PERU), LORETO, MIRANDA, TRUJILLO, MERIDA, IMBABURA, CAÑAR, LOJA, ZAMORA

Cities and towns:
BARRANQUILLA, CARTAGENA, Santa Marta, Ciénaga, Soledad, Sabanalarga, Baranoa, Valledupar, MARACAIBO, CARACAS, Maracay, Valencia, BARQUISIMETO, BUCARAMANGA, Cúcuta, San Cristóbal, Mérida, Valera, Barinas, San Fernando de Apure, MEDELLIN, Bello, Envigado, Rionegro, Quibdó, MANIZALES, Pereira, Armenia, Ibagué, BOGOTÁ, Soacha, Fusagasugá, Girardot, Tunja, Sogamoso, CALI, Palmira, Buga, Tuluá, Buenaventura, Popayán, Neiva, Garzón, Pitalito, Florencia, PASTO, Tumaco, Ipiales, Tulcán, Ibarra, QUITO, Latacunga, Ambato, Riobamba, GUAYAQUIL, Milagro, Cuenca, Machala, Loja, Esmeraldas, Portoviejo, Manta, Quevedo, Babahoyo, Iquitos, Leticia, Mitú, Puerto Carreño, Puerto Ayacucho, Villavicencio, San José del Guaviare

Projection: Lambert's Equivalent Azimuthal

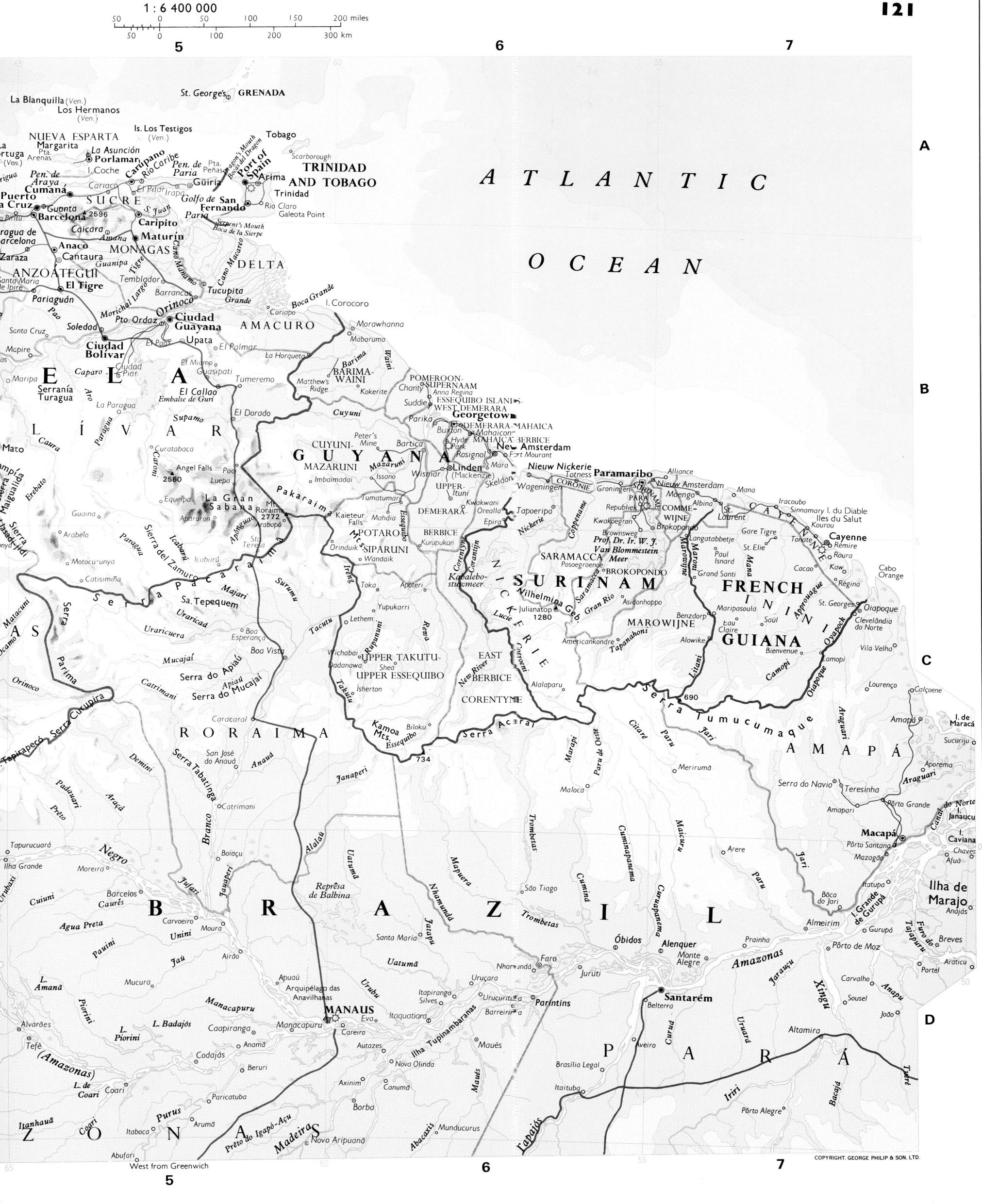

1 : 6 400 000

50   0   50   100   150   200 miles
50   0   100   200   300 km

5   6   7

St. George's GRENADA
La Blanquilla (Ven.)
Los Hermanos
(Ven.)
Is. Los Testigos
(Ven.)
Tobago
Scarborough

NUEVA ESPARTA
Margarita
La Asunción
Porlamar
I. Coche

A T L A N T I C

La
Tortuga
(Ven.)
Pta.
Arenas
Cariaco
Caripano
Rio Caribe
Irapa
Pen. de
Paria
Güiria
Port of
Spain
Arima
Trinidad

TRINIDAD
AND TOBAGO

Pen. de
Araya
Cumaná
Cariaco
El Pilar
Golfo de San
Fernando
S. Juan
Paria

O C E A N

Puerto
la Cruz
Guanta
Barcelona 2596
Caicara
Caripito
Maturín

Serpent's Mouth
Boca de la Sierpe
Rio Claro
Galeota Point

SUCRE
MONAGAS

Aragua de
Barcelona
Anaco
Cantaura
DELTA

ANZOATEGUI
El Tigre
Guanipa
Tigre
Temblador
Tucupita

Zaraza
Santa Maria
de Ipire

Pariaguán
Barrancas

Pao
Morichal Largo
Caño Manamo
Cano Macareo
AMACURO
Curiapo
Boca Grande
I. Corocoro
Morawhanna

Orinoco
Pto. Ordaz
Ciudad
Guayana
Upata
El Pao

Soledad
Mabaruma

A

B

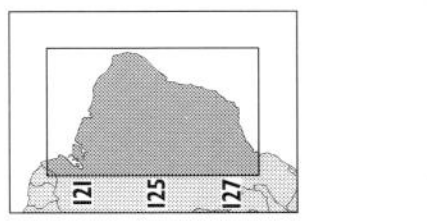

ATLANTIC OCEAN

A M A P Á

Ilha de Marajó

P A R Á

M A R A N H Ã O

P I A U Í

C E A R Á

RIO GRANDE DO NORTE

P A R A Í B A

PERNAMBUCO

A L A G O A S

S E R G I P E

B A H I A

T O C A N T I N S

BELÉM (Pará)

SÃO LUÍS (Maranhão)

FORTALEZA (Ceará)

NATAL

JOÃO PESSOA (Paraíba)

RECIFE (Pernambuco)

MACEIÓ

Teresina

Sobral

Parnaíba

Caxias

Imperatriz

Tocantinópolis

Marabá

Bragança

Capanema

Castanhal

Macapá

Amapá

Caviana

I. Mexiana

I. de Maracá

Cabo do Norte

Canal do Norte

Baía de São Marcos

Baía de São José

Pindaré Mirim

Bacabal

Vitorino Freire

Pedreiras

Codó

Timon

Floriano

Oeiras

Picos

Crateús

Crato

Juàzeiro do Norte

Iguatu

Petrolina

Juàzeiro

Senhor do Bonfim

Xique-Xique

Campo Formoso

Jacobina

Mossoró

Açu

Macau

Caicó

Patos

Campina Grande

Garanhuns

Palmeira dos Índios

Arapiraca

Propriá

Aracaju

Serra da Tabatinga

Serra Geral ou Grande

Chapada das Mangabeiras

Serra dos Gradaús

Serra dos Carajás

Serra do Estrondo

Rio São Francisco

Rio Parnaíba

Rio Tocantins

Rio Araguaia

Rio Xingu

Rio Guamá

Represa de Tucuruí

Represa de Sobradinho 1229

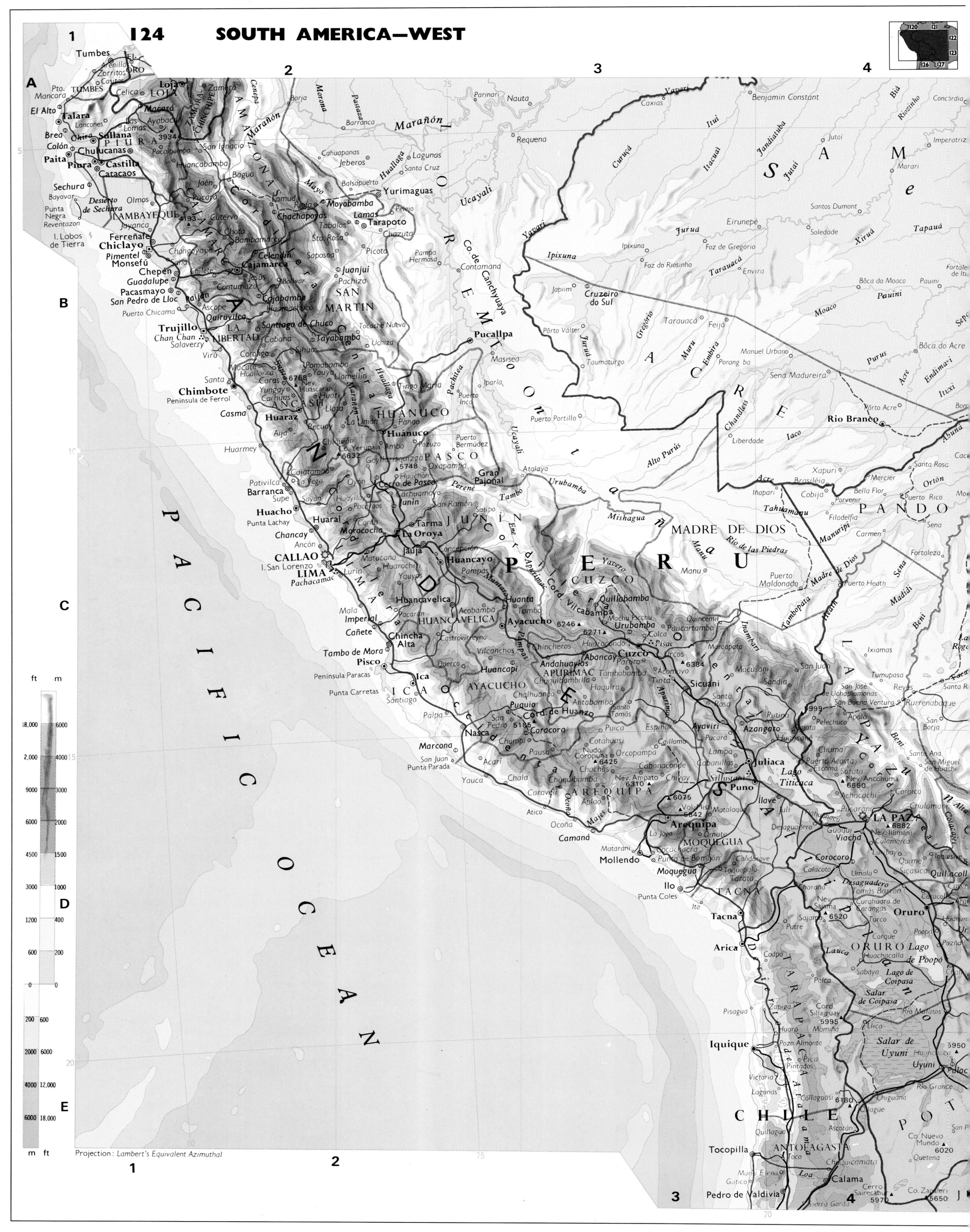

1   2   3   4

A

B

C

D

E

PACIFIC OCEAN

PERU

Tumbes
Pto. Mancora
El Alto
Talara
Bred
Colón
Paita
Piura
Castilla
Catacaos
Sechura
Bayovar
Punta Negra
Reventazon
I. Lobos de Tierra
Chiclayo
Pimentel
Monsefú
Chepen
Guadalupe
Pacasmayo
San Pedro de Lloc
Trujillo
Chan Chan
Salaverry
Viru
Chimbote
Peninsula de Ferrol
Casma
Huarmey
Barranca
Supe
Huacho
Punta Lachay
Chancay
Ancón
CALLAO
I. San Lorenzo
LIMA
Pachacamac
Mala
Imperial
Cañete
Tambo de Mora
Pisco
Peninsula Paracas
Punta Carretas
Ica
Santiago
Palpa
Nasca
Marcona
San Juan
Punta Parada
Acari
Chala
Yauca

TUMBES
Zorritos
Zarumilla
Celica
Loja
Macará
LOJA
Ayabaca
PIURA
Chulucanas
Chira
Sullana
Lancones
Lomas
Olmos
Desierto de Sechura
LAMBAYEQUE
Ferreñafe
Jayanca
Chongoyape
Cutervo
Chota
Bambamarca
Celendin
Cajamarca
Jesús
Contumaza
Cajabamba
Huamachuco
LA LIBERTAD
Santiago de Chuco
Quiruvilca
Ascope
Raijan
Cabana
Corongo
Pomabamba
Caras
Yungay
Huaras
Carhuas
Recuay
ANCASH
Huaraz
Aija
Chiquián
Cajatambo
Oyón
Huacho
Huaral
Canta
Matucana
Huarochiri
Yauyos
HUANCAVELICA
Huancavelica
Pacaran
Castrovirreyna
Vilcanchos
AYACUCHO
Huancapi
Puquio
Coracora
Chumpi
Pausa
Chuquibamba
AREQUIPA
Arequipa
Camaná
Mollendo
MOQUEGUA
Ilo
Moquegua
TACNA
Tacna
Arica

Loja
Zamora
Chinchipe
San Ignacio
Jaén
Bagua
Pucara
Cuterva
San Martin
Moyobamba
Chachapoyas
Lamas
Tarapoto
Chazuta
SAN MARTIN
Bolivar
Tayabamba
Sihuas
Llamellin
Huari
La Unión
Huánuco
HUANUCO
Pasco
Cerro de Pasco
Junin
La Oroya
Tarma
JUNIN
Huancayo
Jauja
Concepción
Acobamba
Huanta
Ayacucho
Andahuaylas
Abancay
APURIMAC
Antabamba
Santo Tomás
CUZCO
Cuzco
Sicuani
Ayaviri
Juliaca
PUNO
Puno
Lago Titicaca

Borja
Barranca
Cahuapanas
Jeberos
Balsapuerto
Yurimaguas
Santa Cruz
Lagunas
Requena

Marañón
AMAZONAS
Cenepa
Morona
Pastaza
Tigre
Ucayali
Huallaga
Yurimaguas
Pucallpa
Contamana
Masisea
Puerto Inca
Puerto Bermúdez
Atalaya
Gran Pajonal
Perené
Satipo
San Ramón
Mishagua
Urubamba
MADRE DE DIOS
Manu
Rio de las Piedras
Puerto Maldonado
Puerto Heath
Quillabamba
Machu Picchu
Urubamba
Quincemil
Marcapata
Macusani
Sandia
San Juan

Parinari
Nauta
Caxias
Yavari
Benjamin Constant
Cruzeiro do Sul
Pôrto Válter
ACRE
Feijó
Tarauacá
Sena Madureira
Manuel Urbano
Porang ba
Rio Branco
Liberdade
Iaco
Brasiléia
Cobija
Porvenir
PANDO
Filadelfia
Puerto Rico
Reyes
Rurrenabaque
LA PAZ
Sorata
LA PAZ
Viacha
Corocoro
ORURO
Oruro
Lago de Poopó
Lago de Coipasa
Salar de Coipasa
Salar de Uyuni
Uyuni
Iquique
Pisagua
TARAPACA
CHILE
Tocopilla
ANTOFAGASTA
Pedro de Valdivia
Calama

Projection: Lambert's Equivalent Azimuthal

ft   m
18,000   6000
2,000   400
9000   3000
6000   2000
4500   1500
3000   1000
1200   400
600   200
0   0
200   600
2000   6000
4000   12,000
6000   18,000
m   ft

1 : 6 400 000

50 0 50 100 150 200 miles
50 0 100 200 300 km

A

Itanhauá · Coari · L. de Coari · Coari · Paricatuba · Axinim · Canumã · Itaituba · Iriri · Bacajá
Purus · Itaboca · Arumã · Borba · Abacaxis · Mundurucus · Maués · Pôrto Alegre
Pinhuã · Abufari · Itapinima · Novo Aripuaná · Capoeira · Tapajós · Tucunaré · Entre Rios · Nazaré
Canutama · Tapauá · Manicoré · Santa Maria dos Marmeles · Sai Cinz · São Félix

B
Purus · Lábrea · Majuriã · Macuim · Humaitá · Prainha · Samaúma · Canudos · Recreia · Teles Pires · Serra do Cachimbo · Cachimbo · Xingu · Riosinho
Iuxi · Madeira · Jamari · Galama · Marmelos · Barracão do Barreto · S. Benedito · Curuás
Manoa · Abunã · Juciparaná · Caritianas · Ariquemes · Serra dos Apiacás · Alto Iriri · Iriri Novo
404 · Pôrto Velho · Tabajara · Nova Vida · Roosevelt · Peixoto de Azeredo

C
Villa Bella · Guajará-Mirim · Sa. dos Pacaás Novos · Jaru · Presidente Hermes · Serra do Norte · Serra Formosa · Manitsauá-Missu · Liberdade · Campo de Diauarum · Serra do Roncador
Guayaramerin · RONDÔNIA · Pimenta Bueno · Barão de Melgaço · Aripuanã · Serra dos Caiabis · Pôrto Cajueiro · Suiá Missu
Peralta · Puerto Siles · Lago Rogoaguado · Principe da Beira · Pedras Negras · Vilhena · 663 · Camararé · Serra do Tombador · Arinos · Pouso Alegre · Arraiãs · Xingu · Pôrto dos Meinacos
Exaltación · San Joaquin · Versalles · Mateguá · Nhambiquara · Juruena · Utiariti · Teles Pires · Ronuro · Culiseu
San Ramón · Magdalena · Guaporé · Puerto Villazón · MATO · GROSSO · Planalto · Chavantina

D
BENI · San Javier · San Martin · Perseverancia · Paraguá · Serranía de Huanchaca · Mato Grosso · Guaporé · Nortelândia · Diamantino · Cuiabá · 915 · Serra Azul · Culuene · Chavantina · Aruanã
Trinidad · Blanco · 1995 · Jauru · Tapirapuã · Arenápolis · Alto Paraguai · Mato · Grosso · do · Chapada dos Guimarães · Coronel Ponce · Barro do Garças
Negro · Santa Rosa de la Roca · Guaporé · Várzea Grande · Cuiabá · Poxoreu · Araguaiana
San Miguel · San Ignacio · Concepción · Pôrto Esperidião · Cáceres · Nossa Senhora do Livramento · Santo Antônio do Leverger · Jaciara · Tesouro · Rio das Garças · Aragarças
OLIVIA · Grande · Santa Rosa del Palmar · San Javier · Aguapeí · Poconé · Barão de Melgaço · Rondonópolis · Guiratinga · Ponte Branca · Iporaí
Chabamba · Portachuelo · Montero · Warnes · El Cerro · Laguna Concepción · San José · San Matías · Lagoa Uberaba · São Lourenço · Alto Garças · Santa Rita do Araguaia · Sa. das Divisões
SANTA CRUZ · Santa Cruz · Cotoca · Santo Corazón · Pantanal do São Lourenço · Itiquira · Alto Araguaia · Cuiapó · RIO VERDE
El Palmar · Llanos de Chiquitos · 1425 · Robore · Serra de Santiago · Santa Ana · Puerto Suárez · Corumbá · Lagoa Mandioré · Pôrto Jofre · Correntes · Baús · Serra do Mineiros · Jataí

E
Villegrande · Samaipata · Bañados de Izozog · Santa Ana · Ladário · Pantanal do Rio Negro · Rio Verde de Mato Grosso · Claro · Itarumã · Caçu
Sucre · CHUQUISACA · Gutiérrez · MATO · GROSSO · Nhecolândia · Negro · Coxim · Aporé · Cachoeira Alta
Lagunillas · Charagua · Albuquerque · DO · SUL · Corguinho · Rochedo · Jaraguari · Paraíso · Alto Sucuri · Cassilândia
Camiri · Fortin General Pando · Pôrto Esperança · Miranda · Aquidauana · Terenos · Ribas do Rio Pardo · Aparecida do Taboado · Paranaíba
Fortin Ingavi · Coimbra · CHACO · Bahia Negra · Sa. da Bodoquena · Aquidauana · Jango · Campo · Agua Clara · Pereira Barreto
Fortin Coronel Eugenio Garay · NUEVA · Boreal · Ñioaque · Sidrolândia · Grande
CHIQUISACA · Carandaiti · Chaco · Fortin Madrejón · ALTO · Bonito · Jardim · Guia Lopes da Laguna · Maracaju · Xavantina · Três Lagoas · Andradina
5614 · Villa Abecia · **PARAGUAY** · Fuerte Olimpo · Mirandópolis · Aguapeí
Tarija · TARIJA · ASUNCIÓN · PARAGUAY · Pôrto Murtinho · Anhandui · Panorama
BOQUERÓN · La Esmeralda · Tartagal · SALTA

5 6 7

West from Greenwich

Projection: Lambert's Equivalent Azimuthal

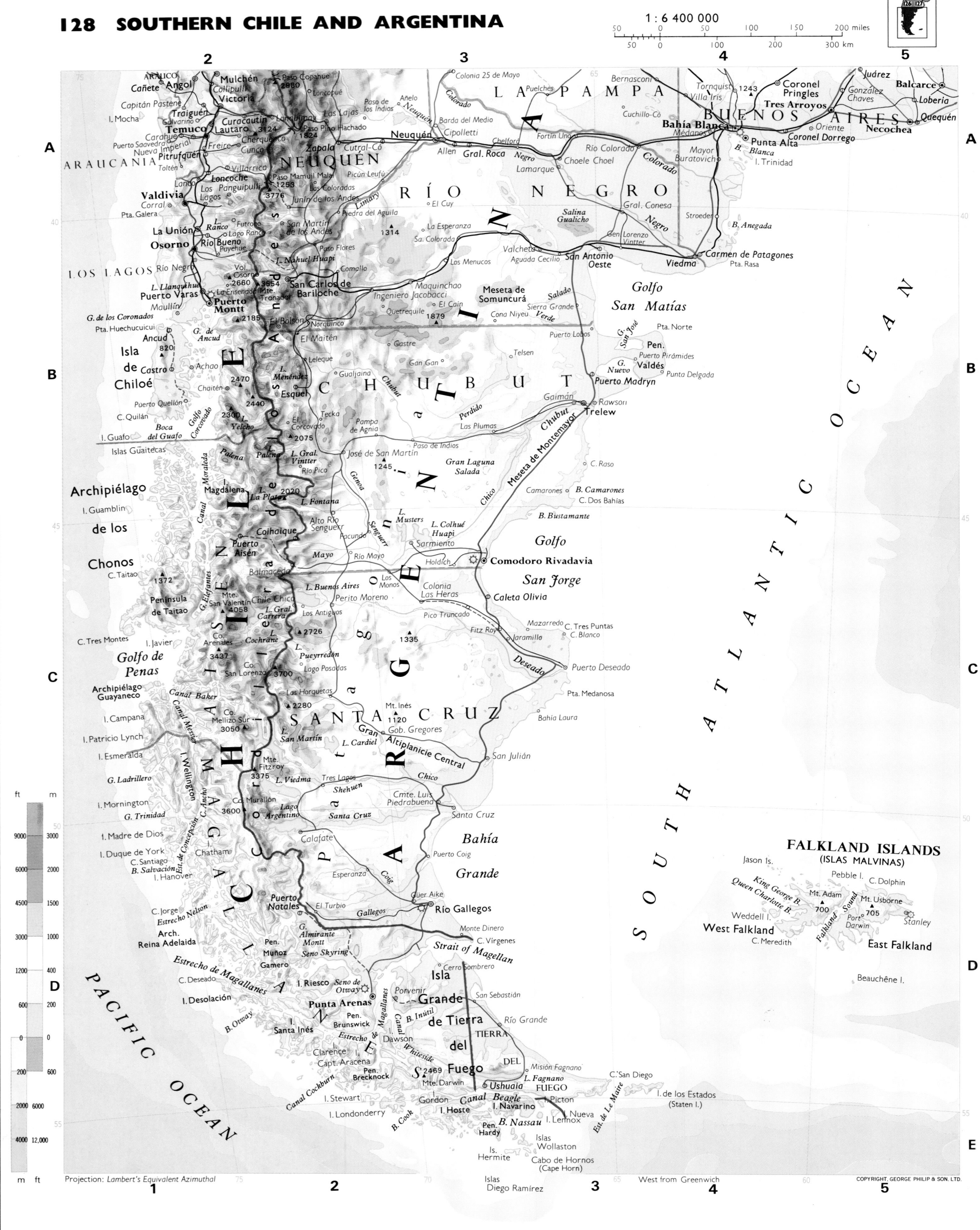

1 : 6 400 000

50   0   50   100   150   200 miles
50   0   50   100   200   300 km

Projection: Lambert's Equivalent Azimuthal

COPYRIGHT. GEORGE PHILIP & SON, LTD.

West from Greenwich

FALKLAND ISLANDS
(ISLAS MALVINAS)

Jason Is.
Pebble I.   C. Dolphin
King George B.
Queen Charlotte B.   Mt. Adam   Mt. Usborne
700   705
Weddell I.   Port
Darwin   Stanley
West Falkland
C. Meredith   East Falkland

Beauchêne I.

SOUTH ATLANTIC OCEAN

PACIFIC OCEAN

SOUTHERN OCEAN

INDEX

The index contains the names of all the principal places and features shown on the World Maps. Each name is followed by an additional entry in italics giving the country or region within which it is located. The alphabetical order of names composed of two or more words is governed primarily by the first word and then by the second. This is an example of the rule:

Mīr Kūh, *Iran*	65	**E8**
Mīr Shahdād, *Iran*	65	**E8**
Miraj, *India*	60	**L9**
Miram Shah, *Pakistan*	62	**C4**
Miramar, *Mozam.*	126	**D4**

Physical features composed of a proper name (Erie) and a description (Lake) are positioned alphabetically by the proper name. The description is positioned after the proper name and is usually abbreviated:

Erie, L., *N. Amer.*	106	**D4**

Where a description forms part of a settlement or administrative name however, it is always written in full and put in its true alphabetic position:

Mount Morris, *U.S.A.*	106	**D7**

Names beginning with M' and Mc are indexed as if they were spelt Mac. Names beginning St. are alphabetised under Saint, but Sankt, Sint, Sant', Santa and San are all spelt in full and are alphabetised accordingly. If the same place name occurs two or more times in the index and all are in the same country, each is followed by the name of the administrative subdivision in which it is located. The names are placed in the alphabetical order of the subdivisions. For example:

Jackson, *Ky., U.S.A.*	104	**G4**
Jackson, *Mich., U.S.A.*	104	**D3**
Jackson, *Minn., U.S.A.*	108	**D7**

The number in bold type which follows each name in the index refers to the number of the map page where that feature or place will be found. This is usually the largest scale at which the place or feature appears. The letter and figure which are in bold type immediately after the page number give the grid square on the map page, within which the feature is situated. The letter represents the latitude and the figure the longitude.

In some cases the feature itself may fall within the specified square, while the name is outside. This is usually the case only with features which are larger than a grid square. Rivers are indexed to their mouths or confluences, and carry the symbol → after their names. A solid square ■ follows the name of a country while an open square □ refers to a first order administrative area.

ABBREVIATIONS USED IN THE INDEX

A.C.T. — Australian Capital Territory
Afghan. — Afghanistan
Ala. — Alabama
Alta. — Alberta
Amer. — America(n)
Arch. — Archipelago
Ariz. — Arizona
Ark. — Arkansas
Atl. Oc. — Atlantic Ocean
B. — Baie, Bahía, Bay, Bucht, Bugt
B.C. — British Columbia
Bangla. — Bangladesh
Barr. — Barrage
Bos.-H. — Bosnia-Herzegovina
C. — Cabo, Cap, Cape, Coast
C.A.R. — Central African Republic
C. Prov. — Cape Province
Calif. — California
Cent. — Central
Chan. — Channel
Colo. — Colorado
Conn. — Connecticut
Cord. — Cordillera
Cr. — Creek
D.C. — District of Columbia
Del. — Delaware
Dep. — Dependency
Des. — Desert
Dist. — District
Dj. — Djebel
Domin. — Dominica
Dom. Rep. — Dominican Republic
E. — East
El Salv. — El Salvador
Eq. Guin. — Equatorial Guinea

Fla. — Florida
Falk. Is. — Falkland Is.
G. — Golfe, Golfo, Gulf, Guba, Gebel
Ga. — Georgia
Gt. — Great, Greater
Guinea-Biss. — Guinea-Bissau
H.K. — Hong Kong
H.P. — Himachal Pradesh
Hants. — Hampshire
Harb. — Harbor, Harbour
Hd. — Head
Hts. — Heights
I.(s). — Île, Ilha, Insel, Isla, Island, Isle
Ill. — Illinois
Ind. — Indiana
Ind. Oc. — Indian Ocean
Ivory C. — Ivory Coast
J. — Jabal, Jebel, Jazira
Junc. — Junction
K. — Kap, Kapp
Kans. — Kansas
Kep. — Kepulauan
Ky. — Kentucky
L. — Lac, Lacul, Lago, Lagoa, Lake, Limni, Loch, Lough
La. — Louisiana
Liech. — Liechtenstein
Lux. — Luxembourg
Mad. P. — Madhya Pradesh
Madag. — Madagascar
Man. — Manitoba
Mass. — Massachusetts
Md. — Maryland
Me. — Maine

Medit. S. — Mediterranean Sea
Mich. — Michigan
Minn. — Minnesota
Miss. — Mississippi
Mo. — Missouri
Mont. — Montana
Moza. — Mozambique
Mt.(e). — Mont, Monte, Monti, Montaña, Mountain
N. — Nord, Norte, North, Northern, Nouveau
N.B. — New Brunswick
N.C. — North Carolina
N. Cal. — New Caledonia
N. Dak. — North Dakota
N.H. — New Hampshire
N.I. — North Island
N.J. — New Jersey
N. Mex. — New Mexico
N.S. — Nova Scotia
N.S.W. — New South Wales
N.W.T. — North West Territory
N.Y. — New York
N.Z. — New Zealand
Nebr. — Nebraska
Neths. — Netherlands
Nev. — Nevada
Nfld. — Newfoundland
Nic. — Nicaragua
O. — Oued, Ouadi
Occ. — Occidentale
O.F.S. — Orange Free State
Okla. — Oklahoma
Ont. — Ontario
Or. — Orientale
Oreg. — Oregon

Os. — Ostrov
Oz. — Ozero
P. — Pass, Passo, Pasul, Pulau
P.E.I. — Prince Edward Island
Pa. — Pennsylvania
Pac. Oc. — Pacific Ocean
Papua N.G. — Papua New Guinea
Pass. — Passage
Pen. — Peninsula, Péninsule
Phil. — Philippines
Pk. — Park, Peak
Plat. — Plateau
P-ov. — Poluostrov
Prov. — Province, Provincial
Pt. — Point
Pta. — Ponta, Punta
Pte. — Pointe
Qué. — Québec
Queens. — Queensland
R. — Rio, River
R.I. — Rhode Island
Ra.(s). — Range(s)
Raj. — Rajasthan
Reg. — Region
Rep. — Republic
Res. — Reserve, Reservoir
S. — San, South, Sea
Si. Arabia — Saudi Arabia
S.C. — South Carolina
S. Dak. — South Dakota
S.I. — South Island
S. Leone — Sierra Leone
Sa. — Serra, Sierra
Sask. — Saskatchewan
Scot. — Scotland
Sd. — Sound

Sev. — Severnaya
Sib. — Siberia
Sprs. — Springs
St. — Saint, Sankt, Sint
Sta. — Santa, Station
Ste. — Sainte
Sto. — Santo
Str. — Strait, Stretto
Switz. — Switzerland
Tas. — Tasmania
Tenn. — Tennessee
Tex. — Texas
Tg. — Tanjung
Trin. & Tob. — Trinidad & Tobago
U.A.E. — United Arab Emirates
U.K. — United Kingdom
U.S.A. — United States of America
Ut. P. — Uttar Pradesh
Va. — Virginia
Vdkhr. — Vodokhranilishche
Vf. — Vîrful
Vic. — Victoria
Vol. — Volcano
Vt. — Vermont
W. — Wadi, West
W. Va. — West Virginia
Wash. — Washington
Wis. — Wisconsin
Wlkp. — Wielkopolski
Wyo. — Wyoming
Yorks. — Yorkshire
Yug. — Yugoslavia

A Coruña

A

A Coruña = La Coruña, *Spain* 30 B2
Aachen, *Germany* 18 E2
Aadorf, *Switz.* 23 B7
Aalborg = Ålborg, *Denmark* 11 G3
Aalen, *Germany* 19 G6
A'âli en Nîl □, *Sudan* 77 F3
Aalsmeer, *Neths.* 16 D5
Aalst, *Belgium* 17 G4
Aalst, *Neths.* 17 F6
Aalten, *Neths.* 16 E9
Aalter, *Belgium* 17 F2
Äänekoski, *Finland* 9 E21
Aarau, *Switz.* 22 B6
Aarberg, *Switz.* 22 B4
Aardenburg, *Belgium* 17 F2
Aare →, *Switz.* 22 A6
Aargau □, *Switz.* 22 B6
Aarhus = Århus, *Denmark* 11 H4
Aarle, *Neths.* 17 E7
Aarschot, *Belgium* 17 G5
Aarsele, *Belgium* 17 G2
Aartrijke, *Belgium* 17 F2
Aarwangen, *Switz.* 22 B5
Aba, *China* 52 A3
Aba, *Nigeria* 79 D6
Aba, *Zaïre* 82 B3
Âbâ, Jazîrat, *Sudan* 77 E3
Abacaxis →, *Brazil* 121 D6
Ābādān, *Iran* 65 D6
Abade, *Ethiopia* 77 F4
Ābādeh, *Iran* 65 D7
Abadin, *Spain* 30 B3
Abadla, *Algeria* 75 B4
Abaeté, *Brazil* 123 E2
Abaeté →, *Brazil* 123 E2
Abaetetuba, *Brazil* 122 B2
Abagnar Qi, *China* 50 C9
Abai, *Paraguay* 127 B4
Abak, *Nigeria* 79 E6
Abakaliki, *Nigeria* 79 D6
Abakan, *Russia* 45 D10
Abalemma, *Niger* 79 B6
Abana, *Turkey* 66 B6
Abancay, *Peru* 124 C3
Abanilla, *Spain* 29 G3
Abano Terme, *Italy* 33 C8
Abapó, *Bolivia* 125 D5
Abarán, *Spain* 29 G3
Abariringa, *Kiribati* 92 H10
Abarqū, *Iran* 65 D7
Abashiri, *Japan* 48 B12
Abashiri-Wan, *Japan* 48 B12
Abaújszántó, *Hungary* 21 G11
Abay, *Kazakhstan* 44 E8
Abaya, L., *Ethiopia* 77 F4
Abaza, *Russia* 44 D10
Abbadia San Salvatore, *Italy* 33 F8
'Abbāsābād, *Iran* 65 C8
Abbay = Nîl el Azraq →, *Sudan* 77 D3
Abbaye, Pt., *U.S.A.* 104 B1
Abbé, L., *Ethiopia* 77 E5
Abbeville, *France* 25 B8
Abbeville, *La., U.S.A.* 109 K8
Abbeville, *S.C., U.S.A.* 105 H4
Abbiategrasso, *Italy* 32 C5
Abbieglassie, *Australia* 91 D4
Abbot Ice Shelf, *Antarctica* 5 D16
Abbotsford, *Canada* 100 D4
Abbotsford, *U.S.A.* 108 C9
Abbottabad, *Pakistan* 62 B5
Abcoude, *Neths.* 16 D5
Abd al Kūrī, *Ind. Oc.* 68 E5
Ābdar, *Iran* 65 D7
'Abdolābād, *Iran* 65 C8
Abéché, *Chad* 73 F9
Abejar, *Spain* 28 D2
Abekr, *Sudan* 77 E2
Abêlessa, *Algeria* 75 D5
Abengourou, *Ivory C.* 78 D4
Åbenrå, *Denmark* 11 J3
Abensberg, *Germany* 19 G7
Abeokuta, *Nigeria* 79 D5
Aber, *Uganda* 82 B3
Aberaeron, *U.K.* 13 E3
Aberayron = Aberaeron, *U.K.* 13 E3
Abercorn = Mbala, *Zambia* 83 D3
Abercorn, *Australia* 91 D5
Aberdare, *U.K.* 13 F4
Aberdare Ra., *Kenya* 82 C4
Aberdeen, *Australia* 91 E5
Aberdeen, *Canada* 101 C7
Aberdeen, *S. Africa* 84 E3
Aberdeen, *U.K.* 14 D6
Aberdeen, *Ala., U.S.A.* 105 J1
Aberdeen, *Idaho, U.S.A.* 110 E7
Aberdeen, *S. Dak., U.S.A.* 108 C5
Aberdeen, *Wash., U.S.A.* 112 D3
Aberdovey = Aberdyfi, *U.K.* 13 E3
Aberdyfi, *U.K.* 13 E3
Aberfeldy, *U.K.* 14 E5
Abergaria-a-Velha, *Portugal* 30 E2
Abergavenny, *U.K.* 13 F4
Abernathy, *U.S.A.* 109 J4
Abert, L., *U.S.A.* 110 E3
Aberystwyth, *U.K.* 13 E3
Abha, *Si. Arabia* 76 D5
Abhar, *Iran* 67 D13
Abhayapuri, *India* 63 F14
Abia □, *Nigeria* 79 D6
Abidiya, *Sudan* 76 D3
Abidjan, *Ivory C.* 78 D4
Abilene, *Kans., U.S.A.* 108 F6
Abilene, *Tex., U.S.A.* 109 J5
Abingdon, *U.K.* 13 F6
Abingdon, *Ill., U.S.A.* 108 E9
Abingdon, *Va., U.S.A.* 105 G5
Abington Reef, *Australia* 90 B4
Abitau →, *Canada* 101 B7
Abitau L., *Canada* 101 A7
Abitibi L., *Canada* 98 C4
Abiy Adi, *Ethiopia* 77 E4
Abkhaz Republic = Abkhazia □, *Georgia* 43 J5
Abkhazia □, *Georgia* 43 J5
Abkit, *Russia* 45 C16
Abminga, *Australia* 91 D1
Abnûb, *Egypt* 76 B3
Åbo = Turku, *Finland* 9 F20
Abocho, *Nigeria* 79 D6
Abohar, *India* 62 D6
Aboisso, *Ivory C.* 78 D4
Abomey, *Benin* 79 D5
Abondance, *France* 27 B10
Abong-Mbang, *Cameroon* 80 D2
Abonnema, *Nigeria* 79 E6
Abony, *Hungary* 21 H10
Aboso, *Ghana* 78 D4
Abou-Deïa, *Chad* 73 F8
Aboyne, *U.K.* 14 D6
Abra Pampa, *Argentina* 126 A2
Abrantes, *Portugal* 31 F2
Abraveses, *Portugal* 30 E3
Abreojos, Pta., *Mexico* 114 B2
Abreschviller, *France* 25 D14
Abri, *Esh Shamâliya, Sudan* 76 C3
Abri, *Janub Kordofân, Sudan* 77 E3
Abrolhos, Banka, *Brazil* 123 E4
Abruzzi □, *Italy* 33 F10
Absaroka Range, *U.S.A.* 110 D9
Abū al Khaşīb, *Iraq* 65 D6
Abū 'Alī, *Si. Arabia* 65 E6
Abū 'Alī →, *Lebanon* 69 A4
Abū 'Arīsh, *Si. Arabia* 68 D3
Abû Ballas, *Egypt* 76 C2
Abu Deleiq, *Sudan* 77 D3
Abu Dhabi = Abū Ẓāby, *U.A.E.* 65 E7
Abû Dis, *Sudan* 76 D3
Abû Dom, *Sudan* 77 D3
Abū Du'ān, *Syria* 67 D8
Abu el Gairi, W. →, *Egypt* 69 F2
Abû Gabra, *Sudan* 77 E2
Abu Ga'da, W. →, *Egypt* 69 F1
Abû Gubeiha, *Sudan* 77 E3
Abu Habl, Khawr →, *Sudan* 77 E3
Abū Ḥadrīyah, *Si. Arabia* 65 E6
Abu Hamed, *Sudan* 76 D3
Abu Haraz, *An Nîl el Azraq, Sudan* 77 E3
Abû Haraz, *Esh Shamâliya, Sudan* 76 D3
Abû Higar, *Sudan* 77 E3
Abū Kamāl, *Syria* 67 E9
Abū Madd, Ra's, *Si. Arabia* 64 E3
Abu Matariq, *Sudan* 77 E2
Abu Qir, *Egypt* 76 H7
Abu Qireiya, *Egypt* 76 C4
Abu Qurqâs, *Egypt* 76 J7
Abū Şafāt, W. →, *Jordan* 69 E5
Abû Simbel, *Egypt* 76 C3
Abū Şukhayr, *Iraq* 67 G11
Abu Tig, *Egypt* 76 B3
Abu Tiga, *Sudan* 77 E3
Abû Zabad, *Sudan* 77 E2
Abū Ẓāby, *U.A.E.* 65 E7
Abū Zeydābād, *Iran* 65 C6
Abufari, *Brazil* 125 B5
Abuja, *Nigeria* 79 D6
Abukuma-Gawa →, *Japan* 48 E10
Abukuma-Sammyaku, *Japan* 48 F10
Abunã, *Brazil* 125 B4
Abunã →, *Brazil* 125 B4
Aburo, *Zaïre* 82 B3
Abut Hd., *N.Z.* 87 K3
Abwong, *Sudan* 77 F3
Åby, *Sweden* 11 F10
Aby, Lagune, *Ivory C.* 78 D4
Acacías, *Colombia* 120 C3
Acajutla, *El Salv.* 116 D2
Açailândia, *Brazil* 122 C2
Acámbaro, *Mexico* 114 C4
Acaponeta, *Mexico* 114 C3
Acapulco, *Mexico* 115 D5
Acarai, Serra, *Brazil* 121 C6
Acaraú, *Brazil* 122 B3
Acari, *Brazil* 122 C4
Acarí, *Peru* 124 D3
Acarigua, *Venezuela* 120 B4
Acatlán, *Mexico* 115 D5
Acayucan, *Mexico* 115 D6
Accéglio, *Italy* 32 D3
Accomac, *U.S.A.* 104 G8
Accous, *France* 26 E3
Accra, *Ghana* 79 D4
Accrington, *U.K.* 12 D5
Acebal, *Argentina* 126 C3
Aceh □, *Indonesia* 56 D1
Acerenza, *Italy* 35 B8
Acerra, *Italy* 35 B7
Aceuchal, *Spain* 31 G4
Achacachi, *Bolivia* 124 D4
Achaguas, *Venezuela* 120 B4
Achalpur, *India* 60 J10
Achao, *Chile* 128 B2
Achel, *Belgium* 17 F6
Acheng, *China* 51 B14
Achenkirch, *Austria* 19 H7
Achensee, *Austria* 19 H7
Acher, *India* 62 H5
Achern, *Germany* 19 G4
Achill, *Ireland* 15 C2
Achill Hd., *Ireland* 15 C1
Achill I., *Ireland* 15 C1
Achill Sd., *Ireland* 15 C2
Achim, *Germany* 18 B5
Achinsk, *Russia* 45 D10
Achol, *Sudan* 77 F3
Acıgöl, *Turkey* 66 D3
Acireale, *Italy* 35 E8
Ackerman, *U.S.A.* 109 J10
Acklins I., *Bahamas* 117 B5
Acme, *Canada* 100 C6
Acobamba, *Peru* 124 C3
Acomayo, *Peru* 124 C3
Aconcagua, Cerro, *Argentina* 126 C2
Aconquija, Mt., *Argentina* 126 B2
Acopiara, *Brazil* 122 C4
Açores, Is. dos = Azores, *Atl. Oc.* 2 C8
Acorizal, *Brazil* 125 D6
Acquapendente, *Italy* 33 F8
Acquasanta Terme, *Italy* 33 F10
Acquaviva delle Fonti, *Italy* 35 B9
Acqui Terme, *Italy* 32 D5
Acraman, L., *Australia* 91 E2
Acre = 'Akko, *Israel* 69 C4
Acre □, *Brazil* 124 B3
Acre →, *Brazil* 124 B4
Acri, *Italy* 35 C9
Acs, *Hungary* 21 H8
Acton, *Canada* 106 C4
Açu, *Brazil* 122 C4
Ad Dammām, *Si. Arabia* 65 E6
Ad Dawhah, *Qatar* 65 E6
Ad Dawr, *Iraq* 67 E10
Ad Dir'īyah, *Si. Arabia* 64 E5
Ad Dīwānīyah, *Iraq* 67 F11
Ad Dujayl, *Iraq* 67 F11
Ad Durūz, J., *Jordan* 69 C5
Ada, *Ghana* 79 D5
Ada, *Serbia, Yug.* 21 K10
Ada, *Minn., U.S.A.* 108 B6
Ada, *Okla., U.S.A.* 109 H6
Adaja →, *Spain* 30 D6
Ådalsliden, *Sweden* 10 A10
Adam, Mt., *Falk. Is.* 128 D4
Adamantina, *Brazil* 123 F1
Adamaoua, Massif de l', *Cameroon* 79 D7
Adamawa □, *Nigeria* 79 D7
Adamawa Highlands = Adamaoua, Massif de l', *Cameroon* 79 D7
Adamello, Mte., *Italy* 32 B7
Adami Tulu, *Ethiopia* 77 F4
Adaminaby, *Australia* 91 F4
Adams, *Mass., U.S.A.* 107 D11
Adams, *N.Y., U.S.A.* 107 C8
Adams, *Wis., U.S.A.* 108 D10
Adam's Bridge, *Sri Lanka* 60 Q11
Adams L., *Canada* 100 C5
Adams Mt., *U.S.A.* 112 D5
Adam's Peak, *Sri Lanka* 60 R12
Adamuz, *Spain* 31 G6
Adana, *Turkey* 66 D6
Adanero, *Spain* 30 E6
Adapazarı, *Turkey* 66 B4
Adarama, *Sudan* 77 D3
Adare, C., *Antarctica* 5 D11
Adaut, *Indonesia* 57 F8
Adavale, *Australia* 91 D3
Adda →, *Italy* 32 C6
Addis Ababa = Addis Abeba, *Ethiopia* 77 F4
Addis Abeba, *Ethiopia* 77 F4
Addis Alem, *Ethiopia* 77 F4
Addison, *U.S.A.* 106 D7
Addo, *S. Africa* 84 E4
Adebour, *Niger* 79 C7
Ādeh, *Iran* 64 B5
Adel, *U.S.A.* 105 K4
Adelaide, *Australia* 91 E2
Adelaide, *Bahamas* 116 A4
Adelaide, *S. Africa* 84 E4
Adelaide I., *Antarctica* 5 C17
Adelaide Pen., *Canada* 96 B10
Adelaide River, *Australia* 88 B5
Adelanto, *U.S.A.* 113 L9
Adelboden, *Switz.* 22 D5
Adele I., *Australia* 88 C3
Adélie, Terre, *Antarctica* 5 C10
Adélie Land = Adélie, Terre, *Antarctica* 5 C10
Ademuz, *Spain* 28 E3
Aden = Al 'Adan, *Yemen* 68 E4
Aden, G. of, *Asia* 68 E4
Adendorp, *S. Africa* 84 E3
Adh Dhayd, *U.A.E.* 65 E7
Adhoi, *India* 62 H4
Adi, *Indonesia* 57 E8
Adi Daro, *Ethiopia* 77 E4
Adi Keyih, *Eritrea* 77 E4
Adi Kwala, *Eritrea* 77 E4
Adi Ugri, *Eritrea* 77 E4
Adieu, C., *Australia* 89 F5
Adieu Pt., *Australia* 88 C3
Adigala, *Ethiopia* 77 E5
Adige →, *Italy* 33 C9
Adigrat, *Ethiopia* 77 E4
Adilabad, *India* 60 K11
Adilcevaz, *Turkey* 67 C10
Adin, *U.S.A.* 110 F3
Adin Khel, *Afghan.* 60 C6
Adinkerke, *Belgium* 17 F1
Adirondack Mts., *U.S.A.* 107 C10
Adıyaman, *Turkey* 67 D8
Adjim, *Tunisia* 75 B7
Adjohon, *Benin* 79 D5
Adjud, *Romania* 38 C10
Adjumani, *Uganda* 82 B3
Adlavik Is., *Canada* 99 B8
Adler, *Russia* 43 J4
Adliswil, *Switz.* 23 B7
Admer, *Algeria* 75 D6
Admer, Erg d', *Algeria* 75 D6
Admiralty G., *Australia* 88 B4
Admiralty I., *U.S.A.* 96 C6
Admiralty Inlet, *U.S.A.* 110 C2
Admiralty Is., *Papua N. G.* 92 H6
Ado, *Nigeria* 79 D5
Ado-Ekiti, *Nigeria* 79 D6
Adok, *Sudan* 77 F3
Adola, *Ethiopia* 77 E5
Adonara, *Indonesia* 57 F6
Adoni, *India* 60 M10
Adony, *Hungary* 21 H8
Adour →, *France* 26 E2
Adra, *India* 63 H12
Adra, *Spain* 29 J1
Adrano, *Italy* 35 E7
Adrar, *Algeria* 75 C4
Adré, *Chad* 73 F9
Adrī, *Libya* 75 C7
Ádria, *Italy* 33 C9
Adrian, *Mich., U.S.A.* 104 E3
Adrian, *Tex., U.S.A.* 109 H3
Adriatic Sea, *Medit. S.* 6 G9
Adua, *Indonesia* 57 E7
Adula, *Switz.* 23 D8
Adwa, *Ethiopia* 77 E4
Adygea □, *Russia* 43 H5
Adzhar Republic = Ajaria □, *Georgia* 43 K6
Adzopé, *Ivory C.* 78 D4
Ægean Sea, *Medit. S.* 39 L8
Æolian Is. = Eólie, Ís., *Italy* 35 D7
Aerhtai Shan, *Mongolia* 54 B4
Ærø, *Denmark* 11 K4
Ærøskøbing, *Denmark* 11 K4
Aesch, *Switz.* 22 B5
'Afak, *Iraq* 67 F11
Afándou, *Greece* 37 C10
Afarag, Erg, *Algeria* 75 D5
Afars & Issas, Terr. of = Djibouti ■, *Africa* 68 E3
Affreville = Khemis Miliana, *Algeria* 75 A5
Afghanistan ■, *Asia* 60 C4
Afgoi, *Somali Rep.* 68 G3
Afikpo, *Nigeria* 79 D6
Aflou, *Algeria* 75 B5
Afogados da Ingàzeira, *Brazil* 122 C4
Afognak I., *U.S.A.* 96 C4
Afragola, *Italy* 35 B7
Afrera, *Ethiopia* 77 E5
'Afrīn, *Syria* 66 D7
Afşin, *Turkey* 66 C7
Afton, *U.S.A.* 107 D9
Aftout, *Algeria* 74 C4
Afuá, *Brazil* 121 D7
Afula, *Israel* 69 C4
Afyonkarahisar, *Turkey* 66 C4
Aga, *Egypt* 76 H7
Agadès = Agadez, *Niger* 79 B6
Agadez, *Niger* 79 B6
Agadir, *Morocco* 74 B3
Agaete, *Canary Is.* 36 F4
Agailás, *Mauritania* 74 D2
Agapa, *Russia* 45 B9
Agar, *India* 62 H7
Agaro, *Ethiopia* 77 F4
Agartala, *India* 61 H17
Agassiz, *Canada* 100 D4
Agats, *Indonesia* 57 F9
Agbélouvé, *Togo* 79 D5
Agboville, *Ivory C.* 78 D4
Ağcabädi, *Azerbaijan* 43 K8
Ağdam, *Azerbaijan* 43 L8
Ağdaş, *Azerbaijan* 43 K8
Agde, *France* 26 E7
Agde, C. d', *France* 26 E7
Agdz, *Morocco* 74 B3
Agdzhabedi = Ağcabädi, *Azerbaijan* 43 K8
Agen, *France* 26 D4
Agersø, *Denmark* 11 J5
Ageyevo, *Russia* 42 C3
Agger, *Denmark* 11 H2
Ággius, *Italy* 34 B2
Āgh Kand, *Iran* 67 D13
Aghoueyyît, *Mauritania* 74 D1
Aginskoye, *Russia* 45 D12
Agira, *Italy* 35 E7
Ağlasun, *Turkey* 66 D4
Agly →, *France* 26 F7
Agnibilékrou, *Ivory C.* 78 D4
Agnita, *Romania* 38 D7
Agnone, *Italy* 35 A7
Agofie, *Ghana* 79 D5
Agogna →, *Italy* 32 C5
Agogo, *Sudan* 77 F2
Agon, *France* 24 C5
Agön, *Sweden* 10 C11
Ágordo, *Italy* 33 B9
Agout →, *France* 26 E5
Agra, *India* 62 F7
Agrakhanskiy Poluostrov, *Russia* 43 J8
Agramunt, *Spain* 28 D6
Agreda, *Spain* 28 D3
Ağri, *Turkey* 67 C10
Agri →, *Italy* 35 B9
Ağri Daği, *Turkey* 67 C11
Agrigento, *Italy* 34 E6
Agrinion, *Greece* 39 L4
Agrópoli, *Italy* 35 B7
Ağstafa, *Azerbaijan* 43 K7
Água Branca, *Brazil* 122 C3
Agua Caliente, *Baja Calif. Mexico* 113 N10
Agua Caliente, *Sinaloa, Mexico* 114 B3
Agua Caliente Springs, *U.S.A.* 113 N10
Água Clara, *Brazil* 125 E7
Agua Hechicero, *Mexico* 113 N10
Agua Preta →, *Brazil* 121 D5
Agua Prieta, *Mexico* 114 A3
Aguachica, *Colombia* 120 B3
Aguada Cecilio, *Argentina* 128 B3
Aguadas, *Colombia* 120 B2
Aguadilla, *Puerto Rico* 117 C6
Aguadulce, *Panama* 116 E3
Aguanga, *U.S.A.* 113 M10
Aguanish, *Canada* 99 B7
Aguanus →, *Canada* 99 B7
Aguapeí, *Brazil* 125 D6
Aguapeí →, *Brazil* 123 F1
Aguapey →, *Argentina* 126 B4
Aguaray Guazú →, *Paraguay* 126 A4
Aguarico →, *Ecuador* 120 D2
Aguas →, *Spain* 28 D4
Aguas Blancas, *Chile* 126 A2
Aguas Calientes, Sierra de, *Argentina* 126 B2
Águas Formosas, *Brazil* 123 E3
Aguascalientes, *Mexico* 114 C4
Aguascalientes □, *Mexico* 114 C4
Agudo, *Spain* 31 G6
Águeda, *Portugal* 30 E2
Águeda →, *Spain* 30 D4
Aguié, *Niger* 79 C6
Aguilafuente, *Spain* 30 D6
Aguilar, *Spain* 31 H6
Aguilar de Campóo, *Spain* 30 C6
Aguilares, *Argentina* 126 B2
Aguilas, *Spain* 29 H3
Agüimes, *Canary Is.* 36 G4
Aguja, C. de la, *Colombia* 120 A3
Agulaa, *Ethiopia* 77 E4
Agulhas, C., *S. Africa* 84 E3
Agulo, *Canary Is.* 36 F2
Agung, *Indonesia* 56 F5
Agur, *Uganda* 82 B3
Agusan →, *Phil.* 55 G6
Agustín Codazzi, *Colombia* 120 A3
Agvali, *Russia* 43 J8
Aha Mts., *Botswana* 84 B3
Ahaggar, *Algeria* 75 D6
Ahamansu, *Ghana* 79 D5
Ahar, *Iran* 67 C12
Ahaus, *Germany* 18 C3
Ahelledjem, *Algeria* 75 C6
Ahipara B., *N.Z.* 87 F4
Ahiri, *India* 60 K12
Ahlat, *Turkey* 67 C10
Ahlen, *Germany* 18 D3
Ahmad Wal, *Pakistan* 62 E1
Ahmadabad, *India* 62 H5
Aḥmadābād, *Khorāsān, Iran* 65 C9
Aḥmadābād, *Khorāsān, Iran* 65 C8
Aḥmadī, *Iran* 65 E8
Ahmadnagar, *India* 60 K9
Ahmadpur, *Pakistan* 62 E4
Ahmar, *Ethiopia* 77 F5
Ahmedabad = Ahmadabad, *India* 62 H5
Ahmednagar = Ahmadnagar, *India* 60 K9
Ahoada, *Nigeria* 79 D6
Ahome, *Mexico* 114 B3
Ahr →, *Germany* 18 E3
Ahram, *Iran* 65 D6
Ahrax Pt., *Malta* 37 D1
Ahrensbök, *Germany* 18 A6
Ahrweiler, *Germany* 18 E3
Āhū, *Iran* 65 C6
Ahuachapán, *El Salv.* 116 D2
Ahvāz, *Iran* 65 D6
Ahvenanmaa = Åland, *Finland* 9 F19
Aḥwar, *Yemen* 68 E4
Ahzar, *Mali* 79 B5
Aiari →, *Brazil* 120 C4
Aichach, *Germany* 19 G7
Aichi □, *Japan* 49 G8
Aidone, *Italy* 35 E7
Aiello Cálabro, *Italy* 35 C9
Aigle, *Switz.* 22 D3
Aignay-le-Duc, *France* 25 E11
Aigoual, Mt., *France* 26 D7
Aigre, *France* 26 C4

Aleksandrov

Aigua, *Uruguay* 127 C5
Aigueperse, *France* 26 B7
Aigues →, *France* 27 D8
Aigues-Mortes, *France* 27 E8
Aigues-Mortes, G. d', *France* 27 E8
Aiguilles, *France* 27 D10
Aiguillon, *France* 26 D4
Aigurande, *France* 26 B5
Aihui, *China* 54 A7
Aija, *Peru* 124 B2
Aikawa, *Japan* 48 E9
Aiken, *U.S.A.* 105 J5
Ailao Shan, *China* 52 F3
Aillant-sur-Tholon, *France* 25 E10
Aillik, *Canada* 99 A8
Ailly-sur-Noye, *France* 25 C9
Ailsa Craig, *U.K.* 14 F3
'Ailūn, *Jordan* 69 C4
Aim, *Russia* 45 D14
Aimere, *Indonesia* 57 F6
Aimogasta, *Argentina* 126 B2
Aimorés, *Brazil* 123 E3
Ain □, *France* 27 B9
Ain →, *France* 27 C9
Aïn Beïda, *Algeria* 75 A6
Aïn Ben Khellil, *Algeria* 75 B4
Aïn Ben Tili, *Mauritania* 74 C3
Aïn Beni Mathar, *Morocco* 75 B4
Aïn Benian, *Algeria* 75 A5
Ain Dalla, *Egypt* 76 B2
Ain el Mafki, *Egypt* 76 B2
Ain Girba, *Egypt* 76 B2
Aïn M'lila, *Algeria* 75 A6
Ain Qeiqab, *Egypt* 76 B1
Aïn-Sefra, *Algeria* 75 B4
Ain Sheikh Murzûk, *Egypt* 76 B2
'Ain Sudr, *Egypt* 69 F2
Ain Sukhna, *Egypt* 76 J8
Aïn Tédelès, *Algeria* 75 A5
Aïn-Témouchent, *Algeria* 75 A4
Aïn Touta, *Algeria* 75 A6
Ain Zeitûn, *Egypt* 76 B2
Aïn Zorah, *Morocco* 75 B4
Ainabo, *Somali Rep.* 68 F4
Ainaži, *Latvia* 9 H21
Aínos Óros, *Greece* 39 L3
Ainsworth, *U.S.A.* 108 D5
Aipe, *Colombia* 120 C2
Aiquile, *Bolivia* 125 D4
Aïr, *Niger* 79 B6
Air Hitam, *Malaysia* 59 M4
Airaines, *France* 25 C8
Airão, *Brazil* 121 D5
Airdrie, *U.K.* 14 F5
Aire →, *France* 25 C11
Aire →, *U.K.* 12 D7
Aire, I. del, *Spain* 36 B11
Aire-sur-la-Lys, *France* 25 B9
Aire-sur-l'Adour, *France* 26 E3
Airlie Beach, *Australia* 90 C4
Airolo, *Switz.* 23 C7
Airvault, *France* 24 F6
Aisch →, *Germany* 19 F7
Aisen □, *Chile* 128 C2
Aisne □, *France* 25 C10
Aisne →, *France* 25 C9
Aitana, Sierra de, *Spain* 29 G4
Aitkin, *U.S.A.* 108 B8
Aitolikón, *Greece* 39 L4
Aiuaba, *Brazil* 122 C3
Aiud, *Romania* 38 C6
Aix-en-Provence, *France* 27 E9
Aix-la-Chapelle = Aachen, *Germany* 18 E2
Aix-les-Bains, *France* 27 C9
Aixe-sur-Vienne, *France* 26 C5
Aiyansh, *Canada* 100 B3
Aíyina, *Greece* 39 M6
Aiyínion, *Greece* 39 J5
Aiyion, *Greece* 39 L5
Aizawl, *India* 61 H18
Aizenay, *France* 24 F5
Aizkraukle, *Latvia* 9 H21
Aizpute, *Latvia* 9 H19
Aizuwakamatsu, *Japan* 48 F9
Ajaccio, *France* 27 G12
Ajaccio, G. d', *France* 27 G12
Ajaju →, *Colombia* 120 C3
Ajalpan, *Mexico* 115 D5
Ajanta Ra., *India* 60 J9
Ajari Rep. = Ajaria □, *Georgia* 43 K6
Ajaria □, *Georgia* 43 K6
Ajax, *Canada* 106 C5
Ajdâbiyah, *Libya* 73 B9
Ajdovščina, *Slovenia* 33 C10
Ajibar, *Ethiopia* 77 E4
Ajka, *Hungary* 21 H7
'Ajmān, *U.A.E.* 65 E7
Ajmer, *India* 62 F6
Ajo, *U.S.A.* 111 K7
Ajoie, *Switz.* 22 B4
Ajok, *Sudan* 77 F2
Ajuy, *Phil.* 55 F5
Ak Dağ, *Turkey* 66 D3
Ak Dağlar, *Turkey* 66 C7
Akaba, *Togo* 79 D5
Akabira, *Japan* 48 C11
Akabli, *Algeria* 75 C5
Akaki Beseka, *Ethiopia* 77 F4
Akala, *Sudan* 77 D4
Akamas □, *Cyprus* 37 D11
Akanthou, *Cyprus* 37 D12
Akaroa, *N.Z.* 87 K4
Akasha, *Sudan* 76 C3
Akashi, *Japan* 49 G7
Akbou, *Algeria* 75 A5
Akçaabat, *Turkey* 67 B8
Akçadağ, *Turkey* 66 C7
Akçakale, *Turkey* 67 D8
Akçakoca, *Turkey* 66 B4
Akchâr, *Mauritania* 74 D2
Akdağmadeni, *Turkey* 66 C6
Akelamo, *Indonesia* 57 D7
Akershus fylke □, *Norway* 10 E5
Aketi, *Zaïre* 80 D4
Akhalkalaki, *Georgia* 43 K6
Akhaltsikhe, *Georgia* 43 K6
Akharnaí, *Greece* 39 L6
Akhelóös →, *Greece* 39 L4
Akhendria, *Greece* 39 Q8
Akhéron →, *Greece* 39 K3
Akhisar, *Turkey* 66 C2
Akhladhókambos, *Greece* 39 M5
Akhmîm, *Egypt* 76 B3
Akhnur, *India* 63 C6
Akhtuba →, *Russia* 43 G8
Akhtubinsk, *Russia* 43 F8
Akhty, *Russia* 43 K8
Akhtyrka = Okhtyrka, *Ukraine* 41 G8
Aki, *Japan* 49 H6
Akimiski I., *Canada* 98 B3
Akimovka, *Ukraine* 41 J8
Akita, *Japan* 48 E10
Akita □, *Japan* 48 E10
Akjoujt, *Mauritania* 78 B2
Akka, *Morocco* 74 C3
Akkeshi, *Japan* 48 C12
'Akko, *Israel* 69 C4
Akkol, *Kazakhstan* 44 E8
Akkrum, *Neths.* 16 B7
Aklampa, *Benin* 79 D5
Aklavik, *Canada* 96 B6
Akmolinsk = Aqmola, *Kazakhstan* 44 D8
Akmonte, *Spain* 31 H4
Aknoul, *Morocco* 75 B4
Akō, *Japan* 49 G7
Ako, *Nigeria* 79 C7
Akobo →, *Ethiopia* 77 F3
Akola, *India* 60 J10
Akonolinga, *Cameroon* 79 E7
Akordat, *Eritrea* 77 D4
Akosombo Dam, *Ghana* 79 D5
Akot, *Sudan* 77 F3
Akpatok I., *Canada* 97 B13
Åkrahamn, *Norway* 9 G11
Akranes, *Iceland* 8 D2
Akreïjit, *Mauritania* 78 B3
Akrítas Venétiko, Ákra, *Greece* 39 N4
Akron, *Colo., U.S.A.* 108 E3
Akron, *Ohio, U.S.A.* 106 E3
Akrotiri, *Cyprus* 66 E5
Akrotíri, Ákra, *Greece* 39 J8
Akrotiri Bay, *Cyprus* 37 E12
Aksai Chin, *India* 63 B8
Aksaray, *Turkey* 66 C6
Aksarka, *Russia* 44 C7
Aksay, *Kazakhstan* 44 D6
Akşehir, *Turkey* 66 C4
Akşehir Gölü, *Turkey* 66 C4
Aksenovo Zilovskoye, *Russia* 45 D12
Akstafa = Ağstafa, *Azerbaijan* 43 K7
Aksu, *China* 54 B3
Aksu →, *Turkey* 66 D4
Aksum, *Ethiopia* 77 E4
Aktash, *Russia* 42 C11
Aktogay, *Kazakhstan* 44 E8
Aktsyabrski, *Belarus* 41 F5
Aktyubinsk = Aqtöbe, *Kazakhstan* 44 D6
Aku, *Nigeria* 79 D6
Akure, *Nigeria* 79 D6
Akureyri, *Iceland* 8 D4
Akuseki-Shima, *Japan* 49 K4
Akusha, *Russia* 43 J8
Akwa-Ibom □, *Nigeria* 79 E6
Akyab = Sittwe, *Burma* 61 J18
Akyazı, *Turkey* 66 B4
Al 'Adan, *Yemen* 68 E4
Al Aḩsā, *Si. Arabia* 65 E6
Al Ajfar, *Si. Arabia* 64 E4
Al Amādīyah, *Iraq* 67 D10
Al Amārah, *Iraq* 67 G12
Al 'Aqabah, *Jordan* 69 F4
Al Arak, *Syria* 67 E8
Al 'Aramah, *Si. Arabia* 64 E5
Al Arṭāwīyah, *Si. Arabia* 64 E5
Al 'Āṣimah □, *Jordan* 69 D5
Al' Assāfīyah, *Si. Arabia* 64 D3
Al 'Ayn, *Oman* 65 E7
Al 'Ayn, *Si. Arabia* 64 E3
Al A'ẓamīyah, *Iraq* 64 C5
Al 'Azīzīyah, *Iraq* 67 F11
Al 'Azīzīyah, *Libya* 75 B7
Al Bāb, *Syria* 66 D7
Al Bad', *Si. Arabia* 64 D2
Al Bādī, *Iraq* 64 C4
Al Baḩrah, *Kuwait* 64 D5
Al Balqā' □, *Jordan* 69 C4
Al Barkāt, *Libya* 75 D7
Al Bārūk, J., *Lebanon* 69 B4
Al Başrah, *Iraq* 64 D5
Al Baṭḩā, *Iraq* 64 D5
Al Batrūn, *Lebanon* 69 A4
Al Bayḑā, *Libya* 73 B9
Al Biqā □, *Lebanon* 69 A5
Al Bi'r, *Si. Arabia* 64 D3
Al Bu'ayrāt al Ḩasūn, *Libya* 73 B8
Al Burayj, *Syria* 69 A5
Al Fallūjah, *Iraq* 67 F10
Al Fāw, *Iraq* 65 D6
Al Fujayrah, *U.A.E.* 65 E8
Al Ghadaf, W. →, *Jordan* 69 D5
Al Ghammās, *Iraq* 64 D5
Al Hābah, *Si. Arabia* 64 E5
Al Ḩadīthah, *Iraq* 67 E10
Al Ḩadīthah, *Si. Arabia* 64 D3
Al Ḩaḑr, *Iraq* 67 E10
Al Hājānah, *Syria* 69 B5
Al Ḩāmad, *Si. Arabia* 64 D3
Al Hamdāniyah, *Syria* 64 C3
Al Ḩamīdīyah, *Syria* 69 A4
Al Ḩammādah al Ḩamrā', *Libya* 75 C7
Al Ḩammār, *Iraq* 64 D5
Al Ḩarīr, W. →, *Syria* 69 C4
Al Ḩasā, W. →, *Jordan* 69 D4
Al Ḩasakah, *Syria* 67 D9
Al Ḩawrah, *Yemen* 68 E4
Al Ḩaydān, W. →, *Jordan* 69 D4
Al Ḩayy, *Iraq* 67 F12
Al Ḩijāz, *Si. Arabia* 68 B2
Al Ḩillah, *Iraq* 67 F11
Al Ḩillah, *Si. Arabia* 68 C4
Al Hindīyah, *Iraq* 67 F11
Al Hirmil, *Lebanon* 69 A5
Al Hoceïma, *Morocco* 74 A4
Al Ḩudaydah, *Yemen* 68 E3
Al Hufūf, *Si. Arabia* 65 E6
Al Ḩumayḑah, *Si. Arabia* 64 D2
Al Ḩunayy, *Si. Arabia* 65 E6
Al Īsāwīyah, *Si. Arabia* 64 D3
Al Ittihad = Madīnat ash Sha'b, *Yemen* 68 E3
Al Jafr, *Jordan* 69 E5
Al Jaghbūb, *Libya* 73 C9
Al Jahrah, *Kuwait* 64 D5
Al Jalāmīd, *Si. Arabia* 64 D3
Al Jamalīyah, *Qatar* 65 E6
Al Janūb □, *Lebanon* 69 B4
Al Jawf, *Libya* 73 D9
Al Jawf, *Si. Arabia* 64 D3
Al Jazirah, *Iraq* 67 E10
Al Jazirah, *Libya* 73 C9
Al Jithāmīyah, *Si. Arabia* 64 E4
Al Jubayl, *Si. Arabia* 65 E6
Al Jubaylah, *Si. Arabia* 64 E5
Al Jubb, *Si. Arabia* 64 E4
Al Junaynah, *Sudan* 73 F9
Al Kabā'ish, *Iraq* 64 D5
Al Karak, *Jordan* 69 D4
Al Karak □, *Jordan* 69 E5
Al Kāẓim Tyah, *Iraq* 67 F11
Al Khalīl, *West Bank* 69 D4
Al Khāliş, *Iraq* 67 F11
Al Khawr, *Qatar* 65 E6
Al Khiḑr, *Iraq* 64 D5
Al Khiyām, *Lebanon* 69 B4
Al Kiswah, *Syria* 69 B5
Al Kūfah, *Iraq* 67 F11
Al Kufrah, *Libya* 73 D9
Al Kuhayfiyah, *Si. Arabia* 64 E4
Al Kūt, *Iraq* 67 F11
Al Kuwayt, *Kuwait* 64 D5
Al Labwah, *Lebanon* 69 A5
Al Lādhiqīyah, *Syria* 66 E6
Al Līth, *Si. Arabia* 76 C5
Al Liwā', *Oman* 65 E8
Al Luḩayyah, *Yemen* 68 D3
Al Madīnah, *Iraq* 64 D5
Al Madīnah, *Si. Arabia* 64 E3
Al-Mafraq, *Jordan* 69 C5
Al Maḩmūdīyah, *Iraq* 67 F11
Al Majma'ah, *Si. Arabia* 64 E5
Al Makhruq, W. →, *Jordan* 69 D6
Al Makḩūl, *Si. Arabia* 64 E4
Al Manāmah, *Bahrain* 65 E6
Al Maqwa', *Kuwait* 64 D5
Al Marj, *Libya* 73 B9
Al Maṭlā, *Kuwait* 64 D5
Al Mawjib, W. →, *Jordan* 69 D4
Al Mawşil, *Iraq* 67 D10
Al Mayādin, *Syria* 67 E9
Al Mazār, *Jordan* 69 D4
Al Midhnab, *Si. Arabia* 64 E5
Al Minā', *Lebanon* 69 A4
Al Miqdādīyah, *Iraq* 67 E11
Al Mubarraz, *Si. Arabia* 65 E6
Al Mughayrā', *U.A.E.* 65 E7
Al Muḩarraq, *Bahrain* 65 E6
Al Mukallā, *Yemen* 68 E4
Al Mukhā, *Yemen* 68 E3
Al Musayjīd, *Si. Arabia* 64 E3
Al Musayyib, *Iraq* 67 F11
Al Muwaylih, *Si. Arabia* 64 E2
Al Owuho = Otukpa, *Nigeria* 79 D6
Al Qā'im, *Iraq* 67 E9
Al Qalībah, *Si. Arabia* 64 D3
Al Qāmishlī, *Syria* 67 D9
Al Qaryatayn, *Syria* 69 A6
Al Qaşabát, *Libya* 73 B7
Al Qaṭ'ā, *Syria* 67 E9
Al Qaṭīf, *Si. Arabia* 65 E6
Al Qatrānah, *Jordan* 69 D5
Al Qaṭrūn, *Libya* 73 D8
Al Qayşūmah, *Si. Arabia* 64 D5
Al Quds = Jerusalem, *Israel* 69 D4
Al Qunayţirah, *Syria* 69 C4
Al Qunfudhah, *Si. Arabia* 76 D5
Al Qurnah, *Iraq* 64 D5
Al Quşayr, *Iraq* 64 D5
Al Quşayr, *Syria* 69 A5
Al Qutayfah, *Syria* 69 B5
Al' Uḑaylīyah, *Si. Arabia* 65 E6
Al 'Ulā, *Si. Arabia* 64 E3
Al Uqaylah ash Sharqīgah, *Libya* 73 B8
Al Uqayr, *Si. Arabia* 65 E6
Al 'Uwaynid, *Si. Arabia* 64 E5
Al 'Uwayqīlah, *Si. Arabia* 64 D4
Al 'Uyūn, *Si. Arabia* 64 E4
Al 'Uyūn, *Si. Arabia* 64 E3
Al Wajh, *Si. Arabia* 64 E3
Al Wakrah, *Qatar* 65 E6
Al Wannān, *Si. Arabia* 65 E6
Al Waqbah, *Si. Arabia* 64 D5
Al Wari'āh, *Si. Arabia* 64 E5
Al Wātīyah, *Libya* 75 B7
Al Wusayl, *Qatar* 65 E6
Ala, *Italy* 32 C8
Ala Dağları, *Turkey* 67 C10
Alabama □, *U.S.A.* 105 J2
Alabama →, *U.S.A.* 105 K2
Alaca, *Turkey* 66 B6
Alaçam, *Turkey* 66 B6
Alaçam Dağları, *Turkey* 66 C3
Alaejos, *Spain* 30 D5
Alaérma, *Greece* 37 C9
Alagir, *Russia* 43 J7
Alagna Valsésia, *Italy* 32 C4
Alagoa Grande, *Brazil* 122 C4
Alagoas □, *Brazil* 122 C4
Alagoinhas, *Brazil* 123 D4
Alagón, *Spain* 28 D3
Alagón →, *Spain* 31 F4
Alajero, *Canary Is.* 36 F2
Alajuela, *Costa Rica* 116 D3
Alakamisy, *Madag.* 85 C8
Alalapura, *Surinam* 121 C6
Alalaú →, *Brazil* 121 D5
Alameda, *Spain* 31 H6
Alameda, *Calif., U.S.A.* 112 H4
Alameda, *N. Mex., U.S.A.* 111 J10
Alaminos, *Phil.* 55 C3
Alamo, *U.S.A.* 113 J11
Alamo Crossing, *U.S.A.* 113 L13
Alamogordo, *U.S.A.* 111 K11
Alamos, *Mexico* 114 B3
Alamosa, *U.S.A.* 111 H11
Åland, *Finland* 9 F19
Alandroal, *Portugal* 31 G3
Ålands hav, *Sweden* 9 F18
Alandur, *India* 60 N12
Alange, Presa de, *Spain* 31 G4
Alania = North Ossetia □, *Russia* 43 J7
Alanis, *Spain* 31 G5
Alanya, *Turkey* 66 D5
Alaotra, Farihin', *Madag.* 85 B8
Alapayevsk, *Russia* 44 D7
Alar del Rey, *Spain* 30 C6
Alaraz, *Spain* 30 E5
Alaşehir, *Turkey* 66 C3
Alaska □, *U.S.A.* 96 B5
Alaska, G. of, *Pac. Oc.* 96 C5
Alaska Highway, *Canada* 100 B3
Alaska Peninsula, *U.S.A.* 96 C4
Alaska Range, *U.S.A.* 96 B4
Alássio, *Italy* 32 D5
Älät, *Azerbaijan* 43 L9
Alataw Shankou, *China* 54 B3
Alatri, *Italy* 34 A6
Alatyr, *Russia* 42 C8
Alatyr →, *Russia* 42 C8
Alausi, *Ecuador* 120 D2
Álava □, *Spain* 28 C2
Alava, C., *U.S.A.* 110 B1
Alaverdi, *Armenia* 43 K7
Alavus, *Finland* 9 E20
Alawoona, *Australia* 91 E3
'Alayh, *Lebanon* 69 B4
Alayor, *Spain* 36 B11
Alazani →, *Azerbaijan* 43 K8
Alba, *Italy* 32 D5
Alba de Tormes, *Spain* 30 E5
Alba-Iulia, *Romania* 38 C6
Albac, *Romania* 38 C6
Albacete, *Spain* 29 G3
Albacete □, *Spain* 29 G3
Albacutya, L., *Australia* 91 F3
Ålbæk, *Denmark* 11 G4
Ålbæk Bugt, *Denmark* 11 G4
Albaida, *Spain* 29 G4
Albalate de las Nogueras, *Spain* 28 E2
Albalate del Arzobispo, *Spain* 28 D4
Albania ■, *Europe* 39 J3
Albano Laziale, *Italy* 34 A5
Albany, *Australia* 89 G2
Albany, *Ga., U.S.A.* 105 K3
Albany, *Minn., U.S.A.* 108 C7
Albany, *N.Y., U.S.A.* 107 D11
Albany, *Oreg., U.S.A.* 110 D2
Albany, *Tex., U.S.A.* 109 J5
Albany →, *Canada* 98 B3
Albardón, *Argentina* 126 C2
Albarracín, *Spain* 28 E3
Albarracín, Sierra de, *Spain* 28 E3
Albatross B., *Australia* 90 A3
Albegna →, *Italy* 33 F8
Albemarle, *U.S.A.* 105 H5
Albemarle Sd., *U.S.A.* 105 H7
Albenga, *Italy* 32 D5
Alberche →, *Spain* 30 F6
Alberdi, *Paraguay* 126 B4
Alberes, Mts., *Spain* 28 C7
Alberique, *Spain* 29 F4
Albersdorf, *Germany* 18 A5
Albert, *France* 25 B9
Albert, L., *Australia* 91 F2
Albert Canyon, *Canada* 100 C5
Albert Edward Ra., *Australia* 88 C4
Albert L., *Africa* 82 B3
Albert Lea, *U.S.A.* 108 D8
Albert Nile →, *Uganda* 82 B3
Albert Town, *Bahamas* 117 B5
Alberta □, *Canada* 100 C6
Alberti, *Argentina* 126 D3
Albertinia, *S. Africa* 84 E3
Albertkanaal →, *Belgium* 17 F4
Alberton, *Canada* 99 C7
Albertville = Kalemie, *Zaïre* 82 D2
Albertville, *France* 27 C10
Albi, *France* 26 E6
Albia, *U.S.A.* 108 E8
Albina, *Surinam* 121 B7
Albina, Ponta, *Angola* 84 B1
Albino, *Italy* 32 C6
Albion, *Idaho, U.S.A.* 110 E7
Albion, *Mich., U.S.A.* 104 D3
Albion, *Nebr., U.S.A.* 108 E5
Albion, *Pa., U.S.A.* 106 E4
Alblasserdam, *Neths.* 16 E5
Albocácer, *Spain* 28 E5
Alborán, *Medit. S.* 31 K7
Alborea, *Spain* 29 F3
Ålborg, *Denmark* 11 G3
Ålborg Bugt, *Denmark* 11 H4
Alborz, Reshteh-ye Kūhhā-ye, *Iran* 65 C7
Albox, *Spain* 29 H2
Albreda, *Canada* 100 C5
Albufeira, *Portugal* 31 H2
Albula →, *Switz.* 23 C8
Albuñol, *Spain* 29 J1
Albuquerque, *Brazil* 125 D6
Albuquerque, *U.S.A.* 111 J10
Albuquerque, Cayos de, *Caribbean* 116 D3
Alburg, *U.S.A.* 107 B11
Alburno, Mte., *Italy* 35 B8
Alburquerque, *Spain* 31 F4
Albury, *Australia* 91 F4
Alby, *Sweden* 10 B9
Alcácer do Sal, *Portugal* 31 G2
Alcaçovas, *Portugal* 31 G2
Alcalá de Chisvert, *Spain* 28 E5
Alcalá de Guadaira, *Spain* 31 H5
Alcalá de Henares, *Spain* 28 E1
Alcalá de los Gazules, *Spain* 31 J5
Alcalá la Real, *Spain* 31 H7
Alcamo, *Italy* 34 E5
Alcanadre, *Spain* 28 C2
Alcanadre →, *Spain* 28 D4
Alcanar, *Spain* 28 E5
Alcanede, *Portugal* 31 F2
Alcanena, *Portugal* 31 F2
Alcañices, *Spain* 30 D4
Alcaníz, *Spain* 28 D4
Alcântara, *Brazil* 122 B3
Alcántara, *Spain* 31 F4
Alcantara L., *Canada* 101 A7
Alcantarilla, *Spain* 29 H3
Alcaracejos, *Spain* 31 G6
Alcaraz, *Spain* 29 G2
Alcaraz, Sierra de, *Spain* 29 G2
Alcaudete, *Spain* 31 H6
Alcázar de San Juan, *Spain* 29 F1
Alchevsk, *Ukraine* 41 H10
Alcira, *Spain* 29 F4
Alcoa, *U.S.A.* 105 H4
Alcobaça, *Portugal* 31 F2
Alcobendas, *Spain* 28 E1
Alcolea del Pinar, *Spain* 28 D2
Alcora, *Spain* 28 E4
Alcorcón, *Spain* 30 E7
Alcoutim, *Portugal* 31 H3
Alcova, *U.S.A.* 110 E10
Alcoy, *Spain* 29 G4
Alcubierre, Sierra de, *Spain* 28 D4
Alcublas, *Spain* 28 F4
Alcudia, *Spain* 36 B10
Alcudia, B. de, *Spain* 36 B10
Alcudia, Sierra de la, *Spain* 31 G6
Aldabra Is., *Seychelles* 71 G8
Aldama, *Mexico* 115 C5
Aldan, *Russia* 45 D13
Aldan →, *Russia* 45 C13
Aldea, Pta. de la, *Canary Is.* 36 G4
Aldeburgh, *U.K.* 13 E9
Aldeia Nova, *Portugal* 31 H3
Alder, *U.S.A.* 110 D7
Alder Pk., *U.S.A.* 112 K5
Alderney, *U.K.* 13 H5
Aldershot, *U.K.* 13 F7
Aledo, *U.S.A.* 108 E9
Alefa, *Ethiopia* 77 E4
Aleg, *Mauritania* 78 B2
Alegranza, *Canary Is.* 36 E6
Alegranza, I., *Canary Is.* 36 E6
Alegre, *Brazil* 123 F3
Alegrete, *Brazil* 127 B4
Aleisk, *Russia* 44 D9
Aleksandriya = Oleksandriya, *Ukraine* 41 H7
Aleksandriya = Oleksandriya, *Ukraine* 41 G4
Aleksandriyskaya, *Russia* 43 J8
Aleksandrov, *Russia* 42 B4

Aleksandrov Gay

Aleksandrov Gay, Russia 42 E9
Aleksandrovac, Serbia, Yug. 21 L11
Aleksandrovka = Oleksandrovka, Ukraine 41 H7
Aleksandrovo, Bulgaria 38 F7
Aleksandrovsk-Sakhalinskiy, Russia 45 D15
Aleksandrovskiy Zavod, Russia 45 D12
Aleksandrovskoye, Russia 44 C8
Aleksandrów Kujawski, Poland 20 C8
Aleksandrów Łódźki, Poland 20 D9
Alekseyevka, Russia 42 D10
Alekseyevka, Russia 42 E4
Aleksin, Russia 42 C3
Aleksinac, Serbia, Yug. 21 M11
Além Paraíba, Brazil 123 F3
Alemania, Argentina 126 B2
Alemania, Chile 126 B2
Ålen, Norway 10 B5
Alençon, France 24 D7
Alenuihaha Channel, U.S.A. 102 H17
Aleppo = Ḥalab, Syria 66 D7
Aléria, France 27 F13
Alert Bay, Canada 100 C3
Alès, France 27 D8
Aleşd, Romania 38 B5
Alessándria, Italy 32 D5
Ålestrup, Denmark 11 H3
Ålesund, Norway 9 E12
Alet-les-Bains, France 26 F6
Aletschhorn, Switz. 22 D6
Aleutian Is., Pac. Oc. 96 C2
Aleutian Trench, Pac. Oc. 92 B10
Alexander, U.S.A. 108 B3
Alexander, Mt., Australia 89 E3
Alexander Arch., U.S.A. 100 B2
Alexander Bay, S. Africa 84 D2
Alexander City, U.S.A. 105 J3
Alexander I., Antarctica 5 C17
Alexandra, Australia 91 F4
Alexandra, N.Z. 87 L2
Alexandra Falls, Canada 100 A5
Alexandretta = Iskenderun, Turkey 66 D7
Alexandria = El Iskandarîya, Egypt 76 H6
Alexandria, Australia 90 B2
Alexandria, B.C., Canada 100 C4
Alexandria, Ont., Canada 98 C5
Alexandria, Romania 38 F8
Alexandria, S. Africa 84 E4
Alexandria, Ind., U.S.A. 104 E3
Alexandria, La., U.S.A. 109 K8
Alexandria, Minn., U.S.A. 108 C7
Alexandria, S. Dak., U.S.A. 108 D6
Alexandria, Va., U.S.A. 104 F7
Alexandria Bay, U.S.A. 107 B9
Alexandrina, L., Australia 91 F2
Alexandroúpolis, Greece 39 J8
Alexis →, Canada 99 B8
Alexis Creek, Canada 100 C4
Alfabia, Spain 36 B9
Alfambra, Spain 28 E3
Alfândega da Fé, Portugal 30 D4
Alfaro, Spain 28 C3
Alfeld, Germany 18 D5
Alfenas, Brazil 127 A6
Alfiós →, Greece 39 M4
Alfonsine, Italy 33 D9
Alford, U.K. 14 D6
Alfred, Maine, U.S.A. 107 C14
Alfred, N.Y., U.S.A. 106 D7
Alfreton, U.K. 12 D6
Alga, Kazakhstan 44 E6
Algaida, Spain 36 B9
Algar, Spain 31 J5
Algård, Norway 9 G11
Algarinejo, Spain 31 H6
Algarve, Portugal 31 J2
Algeciras, Spain 31 J5
Algemesí, Spain 29 F4
Alger, Algeria 75 A5
Algeria ■, Africa 75 C5
Alghero, Italy 34 B1
Algiers = Alger, Algeria 75 A5
Algoa B., S. Africa 84 E4
Algodonales, Spain 31 J5
Algodor →, Spain 30 F7
Algoma, U.S.A. 104 C2
Algona, U.S.A. 108 D7
Algonac, U.S.A. 106 D2
Alhama de Almería, Spain 29 J2
Alhama de Aragón, Spain 28 D3
Alhama de Granada, Spain 31 J7
Alhama de Murcia, Spain 29 H3
Alhambra, Spain 29 G1
Alhambra, U.S.A. 113 L8
Alhaurín el Grande, Spain 31 J6
Alhucemas = Al Hoceïma, Morocco 74 A4
'Alī al Gharbī, Iraq 67 F12
Alī ash Sharqī, Iraq 67 F12
Äli Bayramlı, Azerbaijan 43 L9
'Alī Khēl, Afghan. 62 C3
Ali Sahîh, Djibouti 77 E5
Alī Shāh, Iran 64 B5
Ália, Italy 34 E6
'Alīābād, Khorāsān, Iran 65 C8
'Alīābād, Kordestān, Iran 64 C5
'Alīābād, Yazd, Iran 65 D7
Aliaga, Spain 28 E4
Aliağa, Turkey 66 C2
Aliákmon →, Greece 39 J5
Alibo, Ethiopia 77 F4
Alibunar, Serbia, Yug. 21 K10
Alicante, Spain 29 G4
Alicante □, Spain 29 G4
Alice, S. Africa 84 E4
Alice, U.S.A. 109 M5
Alice →, Queens., Australia 90 C3
Alice →, Queens., Australia 90 B3
Alice, Punta dell', Italy 35 C10
Alice Arm, Canada 100 B3
Alice Downs, Australia 88 C4
Alice Springs, Australia 90 C1
Alicedale, S. Africa 84 E4
Aliceville, U.S.A. 105 J1
Alick Cr. →, Australia 90 C3
Alicudi, I., Italy 35 D7
Alida, Canada 101 D8
Aligarh, Raj., India 62 G7
Aligarh, Ut. P., India 62 F8
Alīgūdarz, Iran 65 C6
Alijó, Portugal 30 D3
Alimena, Italy 35 E7
Alimnía, Greece 37 C9
Alingsås, Sweden 11 G6
Alipur, Pakistan 62 E4
Alipur Duar, India 61 F16
Aliquippa, U.S.A. 106 F4
Aliste →, Spain 30 D5
Alitus = Alytus, Lithuania 9 J21
Alivérion, Greece 39 L7
Aliwal North, S. Africa 84 E4
Alix, Canada 100 C6
Aljezur, Portugal 31 H2
Aljustrel, Portugal 31 H2
Alkamari, Niger 79 C7
Alken, Belgium 17 G6
Alkmaar, Neths. 16 C5
All American Canal, U.S.A. 111 K6
Allada, Benin 79 D5
Allah Dad, Pakistan 62 G2
Allahabad, India 63 G9
Allakh-Yun, Russia 45 C14
Allal Tazi, Morocco 74 B3
Allan, Canada 101 C7
Allanche, France 26 C6
Allanmyo, Burma 61 K19
Allanridge, S. Africa 84 D4
Allanwater, Canada 98 B1
Allaqi, Wadi →, Egypt 76 C3
Allariz, Spain 30 C3
Allassac, France 26 C5
Alle, Belgium 17 J5
Allegan, U.S.A. 104 D3
Allegany, U.S.A. 106 D6
Allegheny →, U.S.A. 106 F5
Allegheny Plateau, U.S.A. 104 G6
Allegheny Reservoir, U.S.A. 106 E6
Allègre, France 26 C7
Allen, Argentina 128 A3
Allen, Bog of, Ireland 15 C4
Allen, L., Ireland 15 B3
Allende, Mexico 114 B4
Allentown, U.S.A. 107 F9
Alleppey, India 60 Q10
Aller →, Germany 18 C5
Alleur, Belgium 17 G7
Allevard, France 27 C10
Alliance, Surinam 121 B7
Alliance, Nebr., U.S.A. 108 D3
Alliance, Ohio, U.S.A. 106 F3
Allier □, France 26 B6
Allier →, France 25 F10
Allingåbro, Denmark 11 H4
Alliston, Canada 98 D4
Alloa, U.K. 14 E5
Allora, Australia 91 D5
Allos, France 27 D10
Alluitsup Paa = Sydprøven, Greenland 4 C5
Alma, Canada 99 C5
Alma, Ga., U.S.A. 105 K4
Alma, Kans., U.S.A. 108 F6
Alma, Mich., U.S.A. 104 D3
Alma, Nebr., U.S.A. 108 E5
Alma, Wis., U.S.A. 108 C9
Alma Ata = Almaty, Kazakhstan 44 E8
Almada, Portugal 31 G1
Almaden, Australia 90 B3
Almadén, Spain 31 G6
Almagro, Spain 31 G7
Almanor, L., U.S.A. 110 F3
Almansa, Spain 29 G3
Almanza, Spain 30 C5
Almanzor, Pico del Moro, Spain 30 E5
Almanzora →, Spain 29 H3
Almas, Brazil 123 D2
Almaty, Kazakhstan 44 E8
Almazán, Spain 28 D2
Almazora, Spain 28 F4
Almeirim, Brazil 121 D7
Almeirim, Portugal 31 F2
Almelo, Neths. 16 D9
Almenar, Spain 28 D2
Almenara, Brazil 123 E3
Almenara, Spain 28 F4
Almenara, Sierra de, Spain 29 H3
Almendralejo, Spain 31 G4
Almería, Spain 29 J2
Almería □, Spain 29 H2
Almería, G. de, Spain 29 J2
Almetyevsk, Russia 42 C11
Almirante, Panama 116 E3
Almirante Montt, G., Chile 128 D2
Almirós, Greece 39 K5
Almiroú, Kólpos, Greece 37 D6
Almodôvar, Portugal 31 H2
Almodóvar del Campo, Spain 31 G6
Almogia, Spain 31 J6
Almonaster la Real, Spain 31 H4
Almont, U.S.A. 106 D1
Almonte, Canada 107 A8
Almonte →, Spain 31 F4
Almora, India 63 E8
Almoradi, Spain 29 G4
Almorox, Spain 30 E6
Almoustarat, Mali 79 B5
Almuñécar, Spain 31 J7
Alnif, Morocco 74 B3
Alnwick, U.K. 12 B6
Aloi, Uganda 82 B3
Alon, Burma 61 H19
Alor, Indonesia 57 F6
Alor Setar, Malaysia 59 J3
Alora, Spain 31 J6
Alosno, Spain 31 H3
Alougoum, Morocco 74 B3
Aloysius, Mt., Australia 89 E4
Alpaugh, U.S.A. 112 K7
Alpedrinha, Portugal 30 E3
Alpena, U.S.A. 104 C4
Alpercatas →, Brazil 122 C3
Alpes-de-Haute-Provence □, France 27 D10
Alpes-Maritimes □, France 27 E11
Alpha, Australia 90 C4
Alphen, Neths. 17 F5
Alphen aan den Rijn, Neths. 16 D5
Alpiarça, Portugal 31 F2
Alpine, Ariz., U.S.A. 111 K9
Alpine, Calif., U.S.A. 113 N10
Alpine, Tex., U.S.A. 109 K3
Alpnach, Switz. 23 C6
Alps, Europe 6 F7
Alpu, Turkey 66 C4
Alrø, Denmark 11 J4
Alroy Downs, Australia 90 B2
Alsace, France 25 D14
Alsask, Canada 101 C7
Alsásua, Spain 28 C2
Alsdorf, Germany 18 E2
Alsen, Sweden 10 A7
Alsfeld, Germany 18 E5
Alsten, Norway 8 D15
Alta, Norway 8 B20
Alta, Sierra, Spain 28 E3
Alta Gracia, Argentina 126 C3
Alta Lake, Canada 100 C4
Alta Sierra, U.S.A. 113 K8
Altaelva →, Norway 8 B20
Altafjorden, Norway 8 A20
Altagracia, Venezuela 120 A3
Altagracia de Orituco, Venezuela 120 B4
Altai = Aerhtai Shan, Mongolia 54 B4
Altamachi →, Bolivia 124 D4
Altamaha →, U.S.A. 105 K5
Altamira, Brazil 121 D7
Altamira, Chile 126 B2
Altamira, Colombia 120 C2
Altamira, Mexico 115 C5
Altamira, Cuevas de, Spain 30 B6
Altamont, U.S.A. 107 D10
Altamura, Italy 35 B9
Altanbulag, Mongolia 54 A5
Altar, Mexico 114 A2
Altata, Mexico 114 C3
Altavista, U.S.A. 104 G6
Altay, China 54 B3
Altdorf, Switz. 23 C7
Alte Mellum, Germany 18 B4
Altea, Spain 29 G4
Altenberg, Germany 18 E9
Altenbruch, Germany 18 B4
Altenburg, Germany 18 E8
Altenkirchen, Mecklenburg-Vorpommern, Germany 18 A9
Altenkirchen, Rhld-Pfz., Germany 18 E3
Altentreptow, Germany 18 B9
Alter do Chão, Portugal 31 F3
Altıntas, Turkey 66 C4
Altiplano, Bolivia 124 D4
Altkirch, France 25 E14
Altmühl →, Germany 19 G7
Alto Adige = Trentino-Alto Adige □, Italy 32 B8
Alto Araguaia, Brazil 125 D7
Alto Cuchumatanes = Cuchumatanes, Sierra de los, Guatemala 116 C1
Alto del Inca, Chile 126 A2
Alto Garças, Brazil 125 D7
Alto Iriri →, Brazil 125 B7
Alto Ligonha, Mozam. 83 F4
Alto Molocue, Mozam. 83 F4
Alto Paraguai, Brazil 125 C6
Alto Paraguay □, Paraguay 126 A4
Alto Paraná □, Paraguay 127 B5
Alto Parnaíba, Brazil 122 C2
Alto Purús →, Peru 124 B3
Alto Río Senguerr, Argentina 128 C2
Alto Santo, Brazil 122 C4
Alto Sucuriú, Brazil 125 D7
Alto Turi, Brazil 122 B2
Alton, Canada 106 C4
Alton, U.S.A. 108 F9
Alton Downs, Australia 91 D2
Altoona, U.S.A. 106 F6
Altopáscio, Italy 32 E7
Altos, Brazil 122 C3
Altötting, Germany 19 G8
Altstätten, Switz. 23 B9
Altūn Kūprī, Iraq 67 E11
Altun Shan, China 54 C3
Alturas, U.S.A. 110 F3
Altus, U.S.A. 109 H5
Alubijid, Phil. 55 G6
Alucra, Turkey 67 B8
Alūksne, Latvia 9 H22
Alùla, Somali Rep. 68 E5
Alunite, U.S.A. 113 K12
Alupka, Ukraine 41 K8
Alushta, Ukraine 41 K8
Alusi, Indonesia 57 F8
Alustante, Spain 28 E3
Al'Uzayr, Iraq 64 D5
Alva, U.S.A. 109 G5
Alvaiázere, Portugal 30 F2
Älvängen, Sweden 11 G6
Alvarado, Mexico 115 D5
Alvarado, U.S.A. 109 J6
Alvarães, Brazil 121 D5
Alvaro Obregón, Presa, Mexico 114 B3
Alvdal, Norway 10 B4
Alvear, Argentina 126 B4
Alverca, Portugal 31 G1
Alveringen, Belgium 17 F1
Alvesta, Sweden 9 H16
Alvie, Australia 91 F3
Alvin, U.S.A. 109 L7
Alvinston, Canada 106 D3
Alvito, Portugal 31 G3
Älvkarleby, Sweden 9 F17
Älvros, Sweden 10 B8
Älvsborgs län □, Sweden 11 F6
Älvsbyn, Sweden 8 D19
Älvsered, Sweden 11 G6
Alwar, India 62 F7
Alxa Zuoqi, China 50 E3
Alyaskitovyy, Russia 45 C15
Alyata = Älät, Azerbaijan 43 L9
Alyth, U.K. 14 E5
Alytus, Lithuania 9 J21
Alzada, U.S.A. 108 C2
Alzano Lombardo, Italy 32 C6
Alzette →, Lux. 17 J8
Alzey, Germany 19 F4
Am Dam, Chad 73 F9
Am-Timan, Chad 73 F9
Amacuro □, Venezuela 121 B5
Amadeus, L., Australia 89 D5
Amâdi, Sudan 77 F3
Amadi, Zaïre 82 B2
Amadjuak, Canada 97 B12
Amadjuak L., Canada 97 B12
Amadora, Portugal 31 G1
Amagasaki, Japan 49 G7
Amager, Denmark 11 J6
Amakusa-Shotō, Japan 49 H5
Åmål, Sweden 9 G15
Amalfi, Colombia 120 B2
Amalfi, Italy 35 B7
Amaliás, Greece 39 M4
Amalner, India 60 J9
Amambaí, Brazil 127 A4
Amambaí →, Brazil 127 A5
Amambay □, Paraguay 127 A4
Amambay, Cordillera de, S. Amer. 127 A4
Amami-Guntō, Japan 49 L4
Amami-Ō-Shima, Japan 49 L4
Amana →, Venezuela 121 B5
Amaná, L., Brazil 121 D5
Amanda Park, U.S.A. 112 C3
Amándola, Italy 33 F10
Amangeldy, Kazakhstan 44 D7
Amantea, Italy 35 C9
Amapá, Brazil 121 C7
Amapá □, Brazil 121 C7
Amapari, Brazil 121 C7
Amara, Sudan 77 E3
Amarante, Brazil 122 C3
Amarante, Portugal 30 D2
Amarante do Maranhão, Brazil 122 C2
Amaranth, Canada 101 C9
Amareleja, Portugal 31 G3
Amargosa, Brazil 123 D4
Amargosa →, U.S.A. 113 J10
Amargosa Range, U.S.A. 113 J10
Amári, Greece 37 D6
Amarillo, U.S.A. 109 H4
Amaro, Mte., Italy 33 F11
Amaro Leite, Brazil 123 D2
Amarpur, India 63 G12
Amasra, Turkey 66 B5
Amassama, Nigeria 79 D6
Amasya, Turkey 66 B6
Amataurá, Brazil 120 D4
Amatikulu, S. Africa 85 D5
Amatitlán, Guatemala 116 D1
Amatrice, Italy 33 F10
Amay, Belgium 17 G6
Amazon = Amazonas →, S. Amer. 121 D7
Amazonas □, Brazil 125 B5
Amazonas □, Peru 124 B2
Amazonas □, Venezuela 120 C4
Amazonas →, S. Amer. 121 D7
Ambahakily, Madag. 85 C7
Ambala, India 62 D7
Ambalavao, Madag. 85 C8
Ambalindum, Australia 90 C2
Ambam, Cameroon 80 D2
Ambanja, Madag. 85 A8
Ambarchik, Russia 45 C17
Ambarijeby, Madag. 85 A8
Ambaro, Helodranon', Madag. 85 A8
Ambartsevo, Russia 44 D9
Ambato, Ecuador 120 D2
Ambato, Sierra de, Argentina 126 B2
Ambato Boeny, Madag. 85 B8
Ambatofinandrahana, Madag. 85 C8
Ambatolampy, Madag. 85 B8
Ambatondrazaka, Madag. 85 B8
Ambatosoratra, Madag. 85 B8
Ambenja, Madag. 85 B8
Amberg, Germany 19 F7
Ambergris Cay, Belize 115 D7
Ambérieu-en-Bugey, France 27 C9
Amberley, N.Z. 87 K4
Ambert, France 26 C7
Ambidédi, Mali 78 C2
Ambikapur, India 63 H10
Ambikol, Sudan 76 C3
Ambilobé, Madag. 85 A8
Ambinanindrano, Madag. 85 C8
Ambjörnarp, Sweden 11 G7
Ambleside, U.K. 12 C5
Amblève, Belgium 17 H8
Amblève →, Belgium 17 H7
Ambo, Ethiopia 77 E4
Ambo, Peru 124 C2
Ambodifototra, Madag. 85 B8
Ambodilazana, Madag. 85 B8
Ambohimahasoa, Madag. 85 C8
Ambohimanga, Madag. 85 C8
Ambohitra, Madag. 85 A8
Amboise, France 24 E8
Ambon, Indonesia 57 E7
Amboseli L., Kenya 82 C4
Ambositra, Madag. 85 C8
Ambovombé, Madag. 85 D8
Amboy, U.S.A. 113 L11
Amboyna I., S. China Sea 56 C4
Ambridge, U.S.A. 106 F4
Ambriz, Angola 80 F2
Amby, Australia 91 D4
Amchitka I., U.S.A. 96 C1
Amderma, Russia 44 C7
Ameca, Mexico 114 C4
Ameca →, Mexico 114 C3
Amecameca, Mexico 115 D5
Ameland, Neths. 16 B7
Amélia, Italy 33 F9
Amélie-les-Bains-Palalda, France 26 F6
Amen, Russia 45 C18
Amendolara, Italy 35 C9
America, Neths. 17 F7
American Falls, U.S.A. 110 E7
American Falls Reservoir, U.S.A. 110 E7
American Highland, Antarctica 5 D6
American Samoa ■, Pac. Oc. 87 B13
Americana, Brazil 127 A6
Americus, U.S.A. 105 J3
Amersfoort, Neths. 16 D6
Amersfoort, S. Africa 85 D4
Amery, Australia 89 F2
Amery, Canada 101 B10
Amery Ice Shelf, Antarctica 5 C6
Ames, U.S.A. 108 E8
Amesbury, U.S.A. 107 D14
Amfíklia, Greece 39 L5
Amfilokhía, Greece 39 L4
Amga, Russia 45 C14
Amga →, Russia 45 C14
Amgu, Russia 45 E14
Amgun →, Russia 45 D14
Amherst, Burma 61 L20
Amherst, Canada 99 C7
Amherst, Mass., U.S.A. 107 D12
Amherst, N.Y., U.S.A. 106 D6
Amherst, Ohio, U.S.A. 106 E2
Amherst, Tex., U.S.A. 109 H3
Amherst I., Canada 107 B8
Amherstburg, Canada 98 D3
Amiata, Mte., Italy 33 F8
Amiens, France 25 C9
Amindaion, Greece 39 J4
Amīrābād, Iran 64 C5
Amirante Is., Seychelles 3 E12
Amisk L., Canada 101 C8
Amistad, Presa de la, Mexico 114 B4
Amite, U.S.A. 109 K9
Amizmiz, Morocco 74 B3
Åmli, Norway 11 F2
Amlwch, U.K. 12 D3
Amm Adam, Sudan 77 D4
'Ammān, Jordan 69 D4
Ammanford, U.K. 13 F3
Ammassalik = Angmagssalik, Greenland 4 C6
Ammerån, Sweden 10 A10
Ammerån →, Sweden 10 A10
Ammersee, Germany 19 G7

Ammerzoden, *Neths.* 16 E6
Amnat Charoen, *Thailand* 58 E5
Amo Jiang →, *China* ... 52 F3
Amol, *Iran* 65 B7
Amorebieta, *Spain* 28 B2
Amorgós, *Greece* 39 N8
Amory, *U.S.A.* 105 J1
Amos, *Canada* 98 C4
Åmot, *Buskerud, Norway* . 10 E3
Åmot, *Telemark, Norway* . 10 E2
Åmotsdal, *Norway* 10 E2
Amour, Djebel, *Algeria* . 75 B5
Amoy = Xiamen, *China* . 53 E12
Ampang, *Malaysia* 59 L3
Ampanihy, *Madag.* 85 C7
Ampasindava,
  Helodranon', *Madag.* .. 85 A8
Ampasindava, Saikanosy,
  Madag. 85 A8
Ampato, Nevado, *Peru* .. 124 D3
Ampenan, *Indonesia* ... 56 F5
Amper →, *Nigeria* 79 D6
Amper →, *Germany* 19 G7
Ampezzo, *Italy* 33 B9
Amposta, *Spain* 28 E5
Ampotaka, *Madag.* 85 D7
Ampoza, *Madag.* 85 C7
Amqui, *Canada* 99 C6
Amravati, *India* 60 J10
Amreli, *India* 62 J4
Amrenene el Kasba,
  Algeria 75 D5
Amriswil, *Switz.* 23 A8
Amritsar, *India* 62 D6
Amroha, *India* 63 E8
Amrum, *Germany* 18 A4
Amsel, *Algeria* 75 D6
Amsterdam, *Neths.* 16 D5
Amsterdam, *U.S.A.* 107 D10
Amsterdam, I., *Ind. Oc.* .. 3 F13
Amstetten, *Austria* 21 G4
Amudarya →, *Uzbekistan* 44 E6
Amundsen Gulf, *Canada* . 96 A7
Amundsen Sea, *Antarctica* 5 D15
Amuntai, *Indonesia* 56 E5
Amur →, *Russia* 45 D15
Amurang, *Indonesia* ... 57 D6
Amuri Pass, *N.Z.* 87 K4
Amursk, *Russia* 45 D14
Amurzet, *Russia* 45 E14
Amusco, *Spain* 30 C6
Amvrakikós Kólpos, *Greece* 39 L4
Amvrosiyivka, *Ukraine* ... 41 J10
Amyderya =
  Amudarya →,
  Uzbekistan 44 E6
Amzeglouf, *Algeria* 75 C5
An Bien, *Vietnam* 59 H5
An Hoa, *Vietnam* 58 E7
An Khe, *Vietnam* 58 F7
An Nabatīyah at Tahta,
  Lebanon 69 B4
An Nabk, *Si. Arabia* ... 64 D3
An Nabk, *Syria* 69 A5
An Nabk Abū Qaşr,
  Si. Arabia 64 D3
An Nafūd, *Si. Arabia* ... 64 D4
An Najaf, *Iraq* 67 G11
An Nāşirīyah, *Iraq* 64 D5
An Nhon, *Vietnam* 58 F7
An Nīl □, *Sudan* 76 D3
An Nīl al Abyaḍ □, *Sudan* 77 E3
An Nīl al Azraq □, *Sudan* 77 E3
An Nu'ayrīyah, *Si. Arabia* 65 E6
An Nu'mānīyah, *Iraq* ... 67 F11
An Nuwayb'ī, W. →,
  Si. Arabia 69 F3
An Thoi, Dao, *Vietnam* .. 59 H4
Anabar →, *Russia* 45 B12
'Anabṭā, *West Bank* 69 C4
Anaco, *Venezuela* 121 B5
Anaconda, *U.S.A.* 110 C7
Anacortes, *U.S.A.* 112 B4
Anacuao, Mt., *Phil.* 55 C4
Anadarko, *U.S.A.* 109 H5
Anadia, *Brazil* 122 C4
Anadia, *Portugal* 30 E2
Anadolu, *Turkey* 66 C5
Anadyr, *Russia* 45 C18
Anadyr →, *Russia* 45 C18
Anadyrskiy Zaliv, *Russia* . 45 C19
Anáfi, *Greece* 39 N8
Anafópoulo, *Greece* 39 N8
Anaga, Pta. de, *Canary Is.* 36 F3
Anagni, *Italy* 34 A6
'Ānah, *Iraq* 67 E10
Anaheim, *U.S.A.* 113 M9
Anahim Lake, *Canada* .. 100 C3
Anáhuac, *Mexico* 114 B4
Anajás, *Brazil* 122 B2
Anajatuba, *Brazil* 122 B3
Anakapalle, *India* 61 L13
Anakie, *Australia* 90 C4
Anaklia, *Georgia* 43 J5
Analalava, *Madag.* 85 A8
Análipsis, *Greece* 37 A3
Anamã, *Brazil* 121 D5
Anambar →, *Pakistan* ... 62 D3
Anambas, Kepulauan,
  Indonesia 56 D3
Anambas Is. = Anambas,
  Kepulauan, *Indonesia* . 56 D3
Anambra □, *Nigeria* ... 79 D6
Anamoose, *U.S.A.* 108 B4
Anamosa, *U.S.A.* 108 D9

Anamur, *Turkey* 66 D5
Anamur Burnu, *Turkey* .. 66 D5
Anan, *Japan* 49 H7
Anand, *India* 62 H5
Anantnag, *India* 63 C6
Ananyiv, *Ukraine* 41 J5
Anapa, *Russia* 43 H3
Anápolis, *Brazil* 123 E2
Anapodháris →, *Greece* . 37 E7
Anapu →, *Brazil* 121 D7
Anār, *Iran* 65 D7
Anārak, *Iran* 65 C7
Anatolia = Anadolu,
  Turkey 66 C5
Anatone, *U.S.A.* 110 C5
Anatsogno, *Madag.* 85 C7
Añatuya, *Argentina* 126 B3
Anauá →, *Brazil* 121 C5
Anaunethad L., *Canada* . 101 A8
Anavilhanas, Arquipélago
  das, *Brazil* 121 D5
Anaye, *Niger* 73 E7
Anbyŏn, *N. Korea* 51 E14
Ancash □, *Peru* 124 B2
Ancenis, *France* 24 E5
Ancho, Canal, *Chile* 128 D2
Anchor Bay, *U.S.A.* 112 G3
Anchorage, *U.S.A.* 96 B5
Anci, *China* 50 E9
Ancohuma, Nevada,
  Bolivia 124 D4
Ancón, *Peru* 124 C2
Ancona, *Italy* 33 E10
Ancud, *Chile* 128 B2
Ancud, G. de, *Chile* 128 B2
Andacollo, *Argentina* ... 126 D1
Andacollo, *Chile* 126 C1
Andado, *Australia* 90 D2
Andahuaylas, *Peru* 124 C3
Andalgalá, *Argentina* ... 126 B2
Ándalsnes, *Norway* 10 B1
Andalucía □, *Spain* 31 H6
Andalusia, *U.S.A.* 105 K2
Andalusia = Andalucía □,
  Spain 31 H6
Andaman Is., *Ind. Oc.* .. 46 H13
Andaman Sea, *Ind. Oc.* .. 56 B1
Andara, *Namibia* 84 B3
Andaraí, *Brazil* 123 D3
Andeer, *Switz.* 23 C8
Andelfingen, *Switz.* 23 A7
Andelot, *France* 25 D12
Andenes, *Norway* 8 B17
Andenne, *Belgium* 17 H6
Andéranboukane, *Mali* . 79 B5
Anderlecht, *Belgium* ... 17 G4
Anderlues, *Belgium* 17 H4
Andermatt, *Switz.* 23 C7
Andernach, *Germany* ... 18 E3
Andernos-les-Bains, *France* 26 D2
Anderslöv, *Sweden* 11 J7
Anderson, *Calif., U.S.A.* . 110 F2
Anderson, *Ind., U.S.A.* . 104 E3
Anderson, *Mo., U.S.A.* . 109 G7
Anderson, *S.C., U.S.A.* . 105 H4
Anderson →, *Canada* ... 96 B7
Andes = Andes, Cord. de
  los, *S. Amer.* 124 C3
Andes, *S. Amer.* 124 C2
Andes, Cord. de los,
  S. Amer. 124 C3
Andfjorden, *Norway* ... 8 B17
Andhra Pradesh □, *India* 60 L11
Andijon, *Uzbekistan* ... 44 E8
Andikíthira, *Greece* 39 P6
Andímeshk, *Iran* 67 F13
Andímilos, *Greece* 39 N7
Andípaxoi, *Greece* 39 K3
Andizhan = Andijon,
  Uzbekistan 44 E8
Andoany, *Madag.* 85 A8
Andoas, *Peru* 120 D2
Andong, *S. Korea* 51 F15
Andongwei, *China* 51 G10
Andorra ■, *Europe* 28 C6
Andorra La Vella, *Andorra* 28 C6
Andover, *U.K.* 13 F6
Andover, *Mass., U.S.A.* . 107 D13
Andover, *N.Y., U.S.A.* . 106 D7
Andover, *Ohio, U.S.A.* . 106 E4
Andøya, *Norway* 8 B16
Andradina, *Brazil* 123 F1
Andrahary, Mt., *Madag.* . 85 A8
Andraitx, *Spain* 36 B9
Andramasina, *Madag.* .. 85 B8
Andranopasy, *Madag.* .. 85 C7
Andreanof Is., *U.S.A.* .. 96 C2
Andreapol, *Russia* 40 D7
Andrespol, *Poland* 20 D9
Andrewilla, *Australia* ... 91 D2
Andrews, *S.C., U.S.A.* .. 105 J6
Andrews, *Tex., U.S.A.* . 109 J3
Andreyevka, *Russia* 42 D10
Ándria, *Italy* 35 A9
Andriba, *Madag.* 85 B8
Andrijevica,
  Montenegro, Yug. 21 N9
Andrítsaina, *Greece* 39 M4
Androka, *Madag.* 85 C7
Andropov = Rybinsk,
  Russia 42 A4
Ándros, *Greece* 39 M7
Andros I., *Bahamas* 116 B4
Andros Town, *Bahamas* . 116 B4
Andselv, *Norway* 8 B18
Andújar, *Spain* 31 G6
Andulo, *Angola* 80 G3

Anegada, B., *Argentina* . 128 B4
Anegada I., *Virgin Is.* .. 117 C7
Anegada Passage,
  W. Indies 117 C7
Aného, *Togo* 79 D5
Añelo, *Argentina* 128 A3
Anergane, *Morocco* 74 B3
Aneto, Pico de, *Spain* .. 28 C5
Añez, *Bolivia* 125 D5
Anfu, *China* 53 D10
Ang Thong, *Thailand* ... 58 E3
Angamos, Punta, *Chile* . 126 A1
Ang'angxi, *China* 54 B7
Angara →, *Russia* 45 D10
Angarab, *Ethiopia* 77 E4
Angarsk, *Russia* 45 D11
Angas Downs, *Australia* . 89 E5
Angas Hills, *Australia* .. 88 D4
Angaston, *Australia* 91 E2
Ánge, *Sweden* 10 B9
Ángel, Salto = Angel Falls,
  Venezuela 121 B5
Ángel de la Guarda, I.,
  Mexico 114 B2
Angel Falls, *Venezuela* .. 121 B5
Angeles, *Phil.* 55 D4
Ängelholm, *Sweden* 11 H6
Angellala, *Australia* 91 D4
Angels Camp, *U.S.A.* .. 111 G3
Anger →, *Ethiopia* 77 F4
Angereb →, *Ethiopia* ... 77 E4
Ångermanälven →,
  Sweden 10 B12
Ångermanland, *Sweden* .. 8 E18
Angermünde, *Germany* .. 18 B10
Angers, *Canada* 107 A9
Angers, *France* 24 E6
Angerville, *France* 25 D8
Ängesån →, *Sweden* ... 8 C20
Anghiari, *Italy* 33 E9
Angical, *Brazil* 123 D3
Angikuni L., *Canada* ... 101 A9
Angkor, *Cambodia* 58 F4
Anglés, *Spain* 28 D7
Anglesey, *U.K.* 12 D3
Angleton, *U.S.A.* 109 L7
Angleur, *Belgium* 17 G7
Anglet, *France* 26 E2
Anglin →, *France* 26 B4
Anglisidhes, *Cyprus* 37 E12
Anglure, *France* 25 D10
Angmagssalik, *Greenland* 4 C6
Ango, *Zaïre* 82 B2
Angoche, *Mozam.* 83 F4
Angoche, I., *Mozam.* ... 83 F4
Angol, *Chile* 126 D1
Angola, *Ind., U.S.A.* ... 104 E3
Angola, *N.Y., U.S.A.* ... 106 D5
Angola ■, *Africa* 81 G3
Angoon, *U.S.A.* 100 B2
Angoulême, *France* 26 C4
Angoumois, *France* 26 C4
Angra dos Reis, *Brazil* .. 127 A7
Angren, *Uzbekistan* 44 E8
Angtassom, *Cambodia* .. 59 G5
Angu, *Zaïre* 82 B1
Anguang, *China* 51 B12
Anguilla ■, *W. Indies* .. 117 C7
Anguo, *China* 50 E8
Angurugu, *Australia* ... 90 A2
Angus, Braes of, *U.K.* .. 14 E5
Anhandui →, *Brazil* ... 127 A5
Anhée, *Belgium* 17 H5
Anholt, *Denmark* 11 H5
Anhua, *China* 53 C8
Anhui □, *China* 53 B11
Anhwei = Anhui □, *China* 53 B11
Anichab, *Namibia* 84 C1
Anicuns, *Brazil* 123 E2
Anidhros, *Greece* 39 N8
Anie, *Togo* 79 D5
Animas, *U.S.A.* 111 L9
Ånimskog, *Sweden* 11 F6
Anina, *Romania* 38 D4
Anivorano, *Madag.* 85 B8
Anjalankoski, *Finland* ... 9 F22
Anjar, *India* 62 H4
Anjidiv I., *India* 60 M9
Anjou, *France* 24 E6
Anjozorobe, *Madag.* ... 85 B8
Anju, *N. Korea* 51 E13
Anka, *Nigeria* 79 C6
Ankaboa, Tanjona, *Madag.* 85 C7
Ankang, *China* 50 H5
Ankara, *Turkey* 66 C5
Ankaramena, *Madag.* ... 85 C8
Ankazoabo, *Madag.* 85 C7
Ankazobe, *Madag.* 85 B8
Ankisabe, *Madag.* 85 B8
Anklam, *Germany* 18 B9
Ankober, *Ethiopia* 77 F4
Ankoro, *Zaïre* 82 D2
Anlong, *China* 52 E5
Anlu, *China* 53 B9
Anmyŏn-do, *S. Korea* .. 51 F14
Ånn, *Sweden* 10 A6
Ann, C., *U.S.A.* 107 D14
Ann Arbor, *U.S.A.* 104 D4
Anna, *Russia* 42 E5
Anna, *U.S.A.* 109 G10
Anna Plains, *Australia* .. 88 C3
Anna Regina, *Guyana* .. 121 B6
Annaba, *Algeria* 75 A6
Annaberg-Buchholz,
  Germany 18 E8
Annalee →, *Ireland* 15 B4

Annam = Trung-Phan,
  Vietnam 58 E7
Annamitique, Chaîne, *Asia* 58 D6
Annan, *U.K.* 14 G5
Annan →, *U.K.* 14 G5
Annapolis, *U.S.A.* 104 F7
Annapolis Royal, *Canada* . 99 D6
Annapurna, *Nepal* 63 E10
Annean, L., *Australia* ... 89 E2
Anneberg, *Sweden* 11 G6
Annecy, *France* 27 C10
Annecy, L. d', *France* ... 27 C10
Annemasse, *France* 27 B10
Annenskiy Most, *Russia* . 40 B9
Anning, *China* 52 E4
Anningie, *Australia* 88 D5
Anniston, *U.S.A.* 105 J3
Annobón, *Atl. Oc.* 71 G4
Annonay, *France* 27 C8
Annot, *France* 27 E10
Annotto Bay, *Jamaica* .. 116 C4
Annuello, *Australia* 91 E3
Annville, *U.S.A.* 107 F8
Annweiler, *Germany* ... 19 F3
Áno Viánnos, *Greece* ... 37 D7
Anoka, *U.S.A.* 108 C8
Anorotsangana, *Madag.* . 85 A8
Anóyia, *Greece* 37 D6
Anping, *Hebei, China* ... 50 E8
Anping, *Liaoning, China* . 51 D12
Anpu Gang, *China* 52 G7
Anqing, *China* 53 B11
Anqiu, *China* 51 F10
Anren, *China* 53 D9
Ans, *Belgium* 17 G7
Ansai, *China* 50 F5
Ansbach, *Germany* 19 F6
Anseba →, *Eritrea* 77 D4
Anserma, *Colombia* 120 B2
Anseroeul, *Belgium* 17 G3
Anshan, *China* 51 D12
Anshun, *China* 52 D5
Ansião, *Portugal* 30 F2
Ansirabe, *Madag.* 85 B8
Ansley, *U.S.A.* 108 E5
Ansó, *Spain* 28 C4
Anson, *U.S.A.* 109 J5
Anson B., *Australia* 88 B5
Ansongo, *Mali* 79 B5
Ansonia, *U.S.A.* 107 E11
Anstruther, *U.K.* 14 E6
Ansudu, *Indonesia* 57 E9
Antabamba, *Peru* 124 C3
Antakya, *Turkey* 66 D7
Antalaha, *Madag.* 85 A9
Antalya, *Turkey* 66 D4
Antalya Körfezi, *Turkey* .. 66 D4
Antananarivo, *Madag.* .. 85 B8
Antananarivo □, *Madag.* 85 B8
Antanimbaribe, *Madag.* . 85 C7
Antarctic Pen., *Antarctica* 5 C18
Antarctica 5 E3
Antelope, *Zimbabwe* ... 83 G2
Antenor Navarro, *Brazil* . 122 C4
Antequera, *Paraguay* ... 126 A4
Antequera, *Spain* 31 H6
Antero, Mt., *U.S.A.* 111 G10
Anthony, *Kans., U.S.A.* .. 109 G5
Anthony, *N. Mex., U.S.A.* 111 K10
Anthony Lagoon, *Australia* 90 B2
Anti Atlas, *Morocco* 74 C2
Anti-Lebanon = Ash
  Sharqi, Al Jabal,
  Lebanon 69 B5
Antibes, *France* 27 E11
Antibes, C. d', *France* .. 27 E11
Anticosti, I. d', *Canada* .. 99 C7
Antifer, C. d', *France* ... 24 C7
Antigo, *U.S.A.* 108 C10
Antigonish, *Canada* 99 C7
Antigua, *Canary Is.* 36 F5
Antigua, *Guatemala* 116 D1
Antigua, *W. Indies* 117 C7
Antigua & Barbuda ■,
  W. Indies 117 C7
Antilla, *Cuba* 116 B4
Antimony, *U.S.A.* 111 G8
Antioch, *U.S.A.* 112 G5
Antioche, Pertuis d',
  France 26 B2
Antioquia, *Colombia* ... 120 B2
Antioquia □, *Colombia* . 120 B2
Antipodes Is., *Pac. Oc.* .. 92 M9
Antler, *U.S.A.* 108 A4
Antler →, *Canada* 101 D8
Antlers, *U.S.A.* 109 H7
Antofagasta, *Chile* 126 A1
Antofagasta □, *Chile* ... 126 A2
Antofagasta de la Sierra,
  Argentina 126 B2
Antofalla, *Argentina* ... 126 B2
Antofalla, Salar de,
  Argentina 126 B2
Antoing, *Belgium* 17 G2
Anton, *U.S.A.* 109 J3
Anton Chico, *U.S.A.* ... 111 J11
Antongila, Helodrano,
  Madag. 85 B8
Antonibé, *Madag.* 85 B8
Antonibé, Presqu'île d',
  Madag. 85 A8
Antonina, *Brazil* 127 B6
Antônio, *Brazil* 121 C5
António Enes = Angoche,
  Mozam. 83 F4
Antrain, *France* 24 D5
Antrim, *U.K.* 15 B5
Antrim □, *U.K.* 15 B5
Antrim, Mts. of, *U.K.* ... 15 B5

Antrim Plateau, *Australia* . 88 C4
Antrodoco, *Italy* 33 F10
Antropovo, *Russia* 42 A6
Antsalova, *Madag.* 85 B7
Antsiranana, *Madag.* ... 85 A8
Antsohihy, *Madag.* 85 A8
Antsohimbondrona
  Seranana, *Madag.* 85 A8
Antu, *China* 51 C15
Antwerp = Antwerpen,
  Belgium 17 F4
Antwerp, *U.S.A.* 107 B9
Antwerpen, *Belgium* ... 17 F4
Antwerpen □, *Belgium* . 17 F5
Anupgarh, *India* 62 E5
Anuradhapura, *Sri Lanka* 60 Q12
Anveh, *Iran* 65 E7
Anvers = Antwerpen,
  Belgium 17 F4
Anvers I., *Antarctica* ... 5 C17
Anxi, *Fujian, China* 53 E12
Anxi, *Gansu, China* 54 B4
Anxiang, *China* 53 C9
Anxious B., *Australia* ... 91 E1
Anyama, *Ivory C.* 78 D4
Anyang, *China* 50 F8
Anyi, *Jiangxi, China* 53 C10
Anyi, *Shanxi, China* 50 G6
Anyuan, *China* 53 E10
Anza, *U.S.A.* 113 M10
Anze, *China* 50 F7
Anzhero-Sudzhensk, *Russia* 44 D9
Ánzio, *Italy* 34 A5
Anzoátegui □, *Venezuela* . 121 B5
Aoga-Shima, *Japan* 49 H9
Aoiz, *Spain* 28 C3
Aomori, *Japan* 48 D10
Aomori □, *Japan* 48 D10
Aonla, *India* 63 E8
Aosta, *Italy* 32 C4
Aoudéras, *Niger* 79 B6
Aouinet Torkoz, *Morocco* 74 C3
Aoukar, *Mali* 74 D4
Aouker, *Mauritania* 78 B3
Aoulef el Arab, *Algeria* .. 75 C5
Apa →, *S. Amer.* 126 A4
Apache, *U.S.A.* 109 H5
Apalachee B., *U.S.A.* ... 105 L3
Apalachicola, *U.S.A.* ... 105 L3
Apalachicola →, *U.S.A.* . 105 L3
Apapa, *Nigeria* 79 D5
Apaporis →, *Colombia* . 120 D4
Aparecida do Taboado,
  Brazil 123 F1
Aparri, *Phil.* 55 B4
Aparurén, *Venezuela* ... 121 B5
Apateu, *Romania* 38 C4
Apatin, *Serbia, Yug.* 21 K8
Apatzingán, *Mexico* 114 D4
Apeldoorn, *Neths.* 16 D7
Apeldoornsch Kanaal →,
  Neths. 16 D8
Apen, *Germany* 18 B3
Apennines = Appennini,
  Italy 32 D7
Apere →, *Bolivia* 125 C4
Apia, *W. Samoa* 87 A13
Apiacás, Serra dos, *Brazil* 125 B6
Apiaú →, *Brazil* 121 C5
Apiaú, Serra do, *Brazil* .. 121 C5
Apidiá →, *Brazil* 125 C5
Apinajé, *Brazil* 123 D2
Apizaco, *Mexico* 115 D5
Aplao, *Peru* 124 D3
Apo, Mt., *Phil.* 57 C7
Apodi, *Brazil* 122 C4
Apolakkiá, *Greece* 37 C9
Apolakkiá, Órmos, *Greece* 37 C9
Apolda, *Germany* 18 D7
Apollonia = Marsá Susah,
  Libya 73 B9
Apollonia, *Greece* 39 N7
Apolo, *Bolivia* 124 C4
Apónguao →, *Venezuela* 121 C5
Aporé, *Brazil* 125 D7
Aporé →, *Brazil* 123 E1
Aporema, *Brazil* 122 A1
Apostle Is., *U.S.A.* 108 B9
Apóstoles, *Argentina* ... 127 B4
Apostolos Andreas, C.,
  Cyprus 66 E6
Apostolovo, *Ukraine* ... 41 J7
Apoteri, *Guyana* 121 C6
Appalachian Mts., *U.S.A.* 104 G6
Appelscha, *Neths.* 16 C8
Appennini, *Italy* 32 D7
Appennino Ligure, *Italy* . 32 D5
Appenzell, *Switz.* 23 B8
Appenzell-Ausser
  Rhoden □, *Switz.* 23 B8
Appenzell-Inner
  Rhoden □, *Switz.* 23 B8
Appiano, *Italy* 33 B8
Appingedam, *Neths.* ... 16 B9
Apple Hill, *Canada* 107 A10
Apple Valley, *U.S.A.* ... 113 L9
Appleby-in-Westmorland,
  U.K. 12 C5
Appleton, *U.S.A.* 104 C1
Approuague, *Fr. Guiana* 121 C7
Approuague →,
  Fr. Guiana 121 C7
Apricena, *Italy* 35 A8
Aprigliano, *Italy* 35 C9
Aprília, *Italy* 34 A5
Apsheronsk, *Russia* 43 H4
Apt, *France* 27 E9

Apuane, Alpi

Apuane, Alpi, *Italy* 32 D7
Apuaú, *Brazil* 121 D5
Apucarana, *Brazil* 127 A5
Apulia = Púglia □, *Italy* 35 B9
Apure □, *Venezuela* 120 B4
Apure →, *Venezuela* 120 B4
Apurímac □, *Peru* 124 C3
Apurimac →, *Peru* 124 C3
Apuseni, Munţii, *Romania* 38 C5
Aqabah = Al 'Aqabah, *Jordan* 69 F4
'Aqabah, Khalīj al, *Red Sea* 64 D2
'Aqdā, *Iran* 65 C7
Aqîq, *Sudan* 76 D4
Aqîq, Khalîg, *Sudan* 76 D4
Aqmola, *Kazakhstan* 44 D8
Aqrah, *Iraq* 67 D10
Aqtöbe, *Kazakhstan* 44 D6
Aquidauana, *Brazil* 125 E6
Aquidauana →, *Brazil* 125 D6
Aquiles Serdán, *Mexico* 114 B3
Aquin, *Haiti* 117 C5
Ar Rachidiya, *Morocco* 74 B4
Ar Rafīd, *Syria* 69 C4
Ar Raḩḩālīyah, *Iraq* 67 F10
Ar Ramādī, *Iraq* 67 F10
Ar Ramthā, *Jordan* 69 C5
Ar Raqqah, *Syria* 67 E8
Ar Rass, *Si. Arabia* 64 E4
Ar Rifā'ī, *Iraq* 64 D5
Ar Riyāḑ, *Si. Arabia* 64 E5
Ar Ru'ays, *Qatar* 65 E6
Ar Rukhaymīyah, *Iraq* 64 D5
Ar Ruqayyidah, *Si. Arabia* 65 E6
Ar Ruşāfah, *Syria* 67 E8
Ar Ruţbah, *Iraq* 67 F9
Ara, *India* 63 G11
'Arab, Bahr el →, *Sudan* 77 F2
Arab, Khalîg el, *Egypt* 76 H6
'Arabābād, *Iran* 65 C8
Araban, *Turkey* 66 D7
Arabatskaya Strelka, *Ukraine* 41 K8
Arabba, *Italy* 33 B8
Arabelo, *Venezuela* 121 C5
Arabia, *Asia* 68 C4
Arabian Desert = Es Sahrâ' Esh Sharqîya, *Egypt* 76 B3
Arabian Gulf = Gulf, The, *Asia* 65 E6
Arabian Sea, *Ind. Oc.* 47 H10
Araç, *Turkey* 66 B5
Aracaju, *Brazil* 122 D4
Aracataca, *Colombia* 120 A3
Aracati, *Brazil* 122 B4
Araçatuba, *Brazil* 127 A5
Aracena, *Spain* 31 H4
Aracena, Sierra de, *Spain* 31 H4
Araçuaí, *Brazil* 123 E3
Araçuaí →, *Brazil* 123 E3
'Arad, *Israel* 69 D4
Arad, *Romania* 38 C4
Arada, *Chad* 73 F9
Aradhippou, *Cyprus* 37 E12
Arafura Sea, *E. Indies* 57 F8
Aragarças, *Brazil* 125 D7
Aragats, *Armenia* 43 K7
Aragón □, *Spain* 28 D4
Aragón →, *Spain* 28 C3
Aragona, *Italy* 34 E6
Aragua □, *Venezuela* 120 B4
Aragua de Barcelona, *Venezuela* 121 B5
Araguacema, *Brazil* 122 C2
Araguaçu, *Brazil* 123 D2
Araguaia →, *Brazil* 122 C2
Araguaiana, *Brazil* 125 D7
Araguaína, *Brazil* 122 C2
Araguari, *Brazil* 123 E2
Araguari →, *Brazil* 121 C8
Araguatins, *Brazil* 122 C2
Araioses, *Brazil* 122 B3
Arak, *Algeria* 75 C5
Arāk, *Iran* 65 C6
Arakan Coast, *Burma* 61 K19
Arakan Yoma, *Burma* 61 K19
Arakli, *Turkey* 67 B8
Araks = Aras, Rūd-e →, *Azerbaijan* 43 K9
Aral, *Kazakhstan* 44 E7
Aral Sea , *Asia* 44 E7
Aral Tengizi = Aral Sea , *Asia* 44 E7
Aralsk = Aral, *Kazakhstan* 44 E7
Aralskoye More = Aral Sea , *Asia* 44 E7
Aralsor, Ozero, *Kazakhstan* 43 F9
Aramac, *Australia* 90 C4
Arambag, *India* 63 H12
Aran I., *Ireland* 15 B3
Aran Is., *Ireland* 15 C2
Aranda de Duero, *Spain* 28 D1
Arandān, *Iran* 64 C5
Aranjuez, *Spain* 30 E7
Aranos, *Namibia* 84 C2
Aransas Pass, *U.S.A.* 109 M6
Aranzazu, *Colombia* 120 B2
Araouane, *Mali* 78 B4
Arapahoe, *U.S.A.* 108 E5
Arapari, *Brazil* 122 C2
Arapey Grande →, *Uruguay* 126 C4
Arapgir, *Turkey* 67 C8
Arapiraca, *Brazil* 122 C4
Arapongas, *Brazil* 127 A5
Ar'ar, *Si. Arabia* 64 D4
Araracuara, *Colombia* 120 D3
Araranguá, *Brazil* 127 B6
Araraquara, *Brazil* 123 F2
Ararás, Serra das, *Brazil* 127 B5
Ararat, *Armenia* 67 C11
Ararat, *Australia* 91 F3
Ararat, Mt. = Ağrı Dağı, *Turkey* 67 C11
Arari, *Brazil* 122 B3
Araria, *India* 63 F12
Araripe, Chapada do, *Brazil* 122 C3
Araripina, *Brazil* 122 C3
Araruama, L. de, *Brazil* 123 F3
Araruna, *Brazil* 122 C4
Aras, Rūd-e →, *Azerbaijan* 43 K9
Araticu, *Brazil* 122 B2
Arauca, *Colombia* 120 B3
Arauca □, *Colombia* 120 B3
Arauca →, *Venezuela* 120 B4
Arauco, *Chile* 126 D1
Arauco □, *Chile* 126 D1
Araújos, *Brazil* 123 E2
Arauquita, *Colombia* 120 B3
Araure, *Venezuela* 120 B4
Arawa, *Ethiopia* 77 F5
Araxá, *Brazil* 123 E2
Araya, Pen. de, *Venezuela* 121 A5
Arba Minch, *Ethiopia* 77 F4
Arbat, *Iraq* 67 E11
Arbatax, *Italy* 34 C2
Arbedo, *Switz.* 23 D8
Arbīl, *Iraq* 67 D11
Arbois, *France* 25 F12
Arboletes, *Colombia* 120 B2
Arbon, *Switz.* 23 A8
Arbore, *Ethiopia* 77 F4
Arboréa, *Italy* 34 C1
Arborfield, *Canada* 101 C8
Arborg, *Canada* 101 C9
Arbrå, *Sweden* 10 C10
Arbroath, *U.K.* 14 E6
Arbuckle, *U.S.A.* 112 F4
Arbus, *Italy* 34 C1
Arc, *France* 25 E12
Arc →, *France* 27 C10
Arcachon, *France* 26 D2
Arcachon, Bassin d', *France* 26 D2
Arcade, *U.S.A.* 106 D6
Arcadia, *Fla., U.S.A.* 105 M5
Arcadia, *La., U.S.A.* 109 J8
Arcadia, *Nebr., U.S.A.* 108 E5
Arcadia, *Pa., U.S.A.* 106 F6
Arcadia, *Wis., U.S.A.* 108 C9
Arcata, *U.S.A.* 110 F1
Arcévia, *Italy* 33 E9
Archangel = Arkhangelsk, *Russia* 44 C5
Archar, *Bulgaria* 38 F5
Archbald, *U.S.A.* 107 E9
Archena, *Spain* 29 G3
Archer →, *Australia* 90 A3
Archer B., *Australia* 90 A3
Archers Post, *Kenya* 82 B4
Archidona, *Spain* 31 H6
Arci, Mte., *Italy* 34 C1
Arcidosso, *Italy* 33 F8
Arcila = Asilah, *Morocco* 74 A3
Arcis-sur-Aube, *France* 25 D11
Arckaringa, *Australia* 91 D1
Arckaringa Cr. →, *Australia* 91 D2
Arco, *Italy* 32 C7
Arco, *U.S.A.* 110 E7
Arcola, *Canada* 101 D8
Arcos, *Spain* 28 D2
Arcos de la Frontera, *Spain* 31 J5
Arcos de Valdevez, *Portugal* 30 D2
Arcot, *India* 60 N11
Arcoverde, *Brazil* 122 C4
Arctic Bay, *Canada* 97 A11
Arctic Ocean, *Arctic* 4 B18
Arctic Red River, *Canada* 96 B6
Arda →, *Bulgaria* 39 H9
Arda →, *Italy* 32 D6
Ardabīl, *Iran* 67 C13
Ardahan, *Turkey* 67 B10
Ardakān = Sepīdān, *Iran* 65 D7
Ardales, *Spain* 31 J6
Årdalstangen, *Norway* 10 C1
Ardea, *Greece* 39 J5
Ardèche □, *France* 27 D8
Ardèche →, *France* 27 D8
Ardee, *Ireland* 15 C5
Arden, *Canada* 106 B8
Arden, *Denmark* 11 H3
Arden, *Calif., U.S.A.* 112 G5
Arden, *Nev., U.S.A.* 113 J11
Ardenne, *Belgium* 25 C12
Ardennes = Ardenne, *Belgium* 25 C12
Ardennes □, *France* 25 C11
Ardentes, *France* 25 F8
Ardeşen, *Turkey* 67 B9
Ardestān, *Iran* 65 C7
Ardgour, *U.K.* 14 E3
Árdhas →, *Greece* 39 H9
Ardila →, *Portugal* 31 G3
Ardlethan, *Australia* 91 E4
Ardmore, *Australia* 90 C2
Ardmore, *Okla., U.S.A.* 109 H6
Ardmore, *Pa., U.S.A.* 107 G9
Ardmore, *S. Dak., U.S.A.* 108 D3
Ardnacrusha, *Ireland* 15 D3
Ardnamurchan, Pt. of, *U.K.* 14 E2
Ardon, *Russia* 43 J7
Ardooie, *Belgium* 17 G2
Ardore, *Italy* 35 D9
Ardres, *France* 25 B8
Ardrossan, *Australia* 91 E2
Ardrossan, *U.K.* 14 F4
Ards □, *U.K.* 15 B6
Ards Pen., *U.K.* 15 B6
Ardud, *Romania* 38 B5
Åre, *Sweden* 10 A7
Arecibo, *Puerto Rico* 117 C6
Areia Branca, *Brazil* 122 B4
Arena, Pt., *U.S.A.* 112 G3
Arenales, Cerro, *Chile* 128 C2
Arenápolis, *Brazil* 125 C6
Arenas, *Spain* 30 B6
Arenas de San Pedro, *Spain* 30 E5
Arendal, *Norway* 11 F2
Arendonk, *Belgium* 17 F6
Arendsee, *Germany* 18 C7
Arenillas, *Ecuador* 120 D1
Arenys de Mar, *Spain* 28 D7
Arenzano, *Italy* 32 D5
Areópolis, *Greece* 39 N5
Arequipa, *Peru* 124 D3
Arequipa □, *Peru* 124 D3
Arere, *Brazil* 121 D7
Arero, *Ethiopia* 77 G4
Arès, *France* 26 D2
Arévalo, *Spain* 30 D6
Arezzo, *Italy* 33 E8
Arga →, *Spain* 28 C3
Argalastí, *Greece* 39 K6
Argamakmur, *Indonesia* 56 E2
Argamasilla de Alba, *Spain* 29 F1
Arganda, *Spain* 28 E1
Arganil, *Portugal* 30 E2
Argelès-Gazost, *France* 26 F3
Argelès-sur-Mer, *France* 26 F7
Argens →, *France* 27 E10
Argent-sur-Sauldre, *France* 25 E9
Argenta, *Italy* 33 D8
Argentan, *France* 24 D6
Argentário, Mte., *Italy* 33 F8
Argentat, *France* 26 C5
Argentera, *Italy* 32 D3
Argentera, Monte del, *Italy* 32 D4
Argenteuil, *France* 25 D9
Argentia, *Canada* 99 C9
Argentiera, C. dell', *Italy* 34 B1
Argentière, Aiguilles d', *Switz.* 22 E4
Argentina ■, *S. Amer.* 128 B3
Argentina Is., *Antarctica* 5 C17
Argentino, L., *Argentina* 128 D2
Argenton-Château, *France* 24 F6
Argenton-sur-Creuse, *France* 26 B5
Argeş →, *Romania* 38 E9
Arghandab →, *Afghan.* 62 D1
Argo, *Sudan* 76 D3
Argolikós Kólpos, *Greece* 39 M5
Argonne, *France* 25 C12
Árgos, *Greece* 39 M5
Argostólion, *Greece* 39 L3
Arguedas, *Spain* 28 C3
Arguello, Pt., *U.S.A.* 113 L6
Arguineguín, *Canary Is.* 36 G4
Argun, *Russia* 43 J7
Argun →, *Russia* 45 D13
Argungu, *Nigeria* 79 C5
Argus Pk., *U.S.A.* 113 K9
Argyle, *U.S.A.* 108 A6
Argyle, L., *Australia* 88 C4
Arhavi, *Turkey* 67 B9
Århus, *Denmark* 11 H4
Århus Amtskommune □, *Denmark* 11 H4
Ariadnoye, *Russia* 48 B7
Ariamsvlei, *Namibia* 84 D2
Ariana, *Tunisia* 75 A7
Ariano Irpino, *Italy* 35 A8
Ariano nel Polèsine, *Italy* 33 D9
Ariari →, *Colombia* 120 C3
Aribinda, *Burkina Faso* 79 C4
Arica, *Chile* 124 D3
Arica, *Colombia* 120 D3
Arico, *Canary Is.* 36 F3
Arid, C., *Australia* 89 F3
Arida, *Japan* 49 G7
Ariège □, *France* 26 F5
Ariège →, *France* 26 E5
Arieş →, *Romania* 38 C6
Arīḩā, *Syria* 64 C3
Arílla, Ákra, *Greece* 37 A3
Arima, *Trin. & Tob.* 117 D7
Arinos →, *Brazil* 125 C6
Ario de Rosales, *Mexico* 114 D4
Aripuanã, *Brazil* 125 B5
Aripuanã →, *Brazil* 125 B5
Ariquemes, *Brazil* 125 B5
Arisaig, *U.K.* 14 E3
Arîsh, W. el →, *Egypt* 76 H8
Arismendi, *Venezuela* 120 B4
Arissa, *Ethiopia* 77 E5
Aristazabal I., *Canada* 100 C3
Arivaca, *U.S.A.* 111 L8
Arivonimamo, *Madag.* 85 B8
Ariza, *Spain* 28 D2
Arizaro, Salar de, *Argentina* 126 A2
Arizona, *Argentina* 126 D2
Arizona □, *U.S.A.* 111 J8
Arizpe, *Mexico* 114 A2
Arjeplog, *Sweden* 8 D18
Arjona, *Colombia* 120 A2
Arjona, *Spain* 31 H6
Arjuno, *Indonesia* 57 G15
Arka, *Russia* 45 C15
Arkadak, *Russia* 42 E6
Arkadelphia, *U.S.A.* 109 H8
Arkaig, L., *U.K.* 14 E3
Arkalyk = Arqalyq, *Kazakhstan* 44 D7
Arkansas □, *U.S.A.* 109 H8
Arkansas →, *U.S.A.* 109 J9
Arkansas City, *U.S.A.* 109 G6
Árkathos →, *Greece* 39 K4
Arkhángelos, *Greece* 37 C10
Arkhangelsk, *Russia* 44 C5
Arkhangelskoye, *Russia* 42 E5
Arkiko, *Eritrea* 77 D4
Arklow, *Ireland* 15 D5
Arkona, Kap, *Germany* 18 A9
Arkösund, *Sweden* 11 F10
Arkticheskiy, Mys, *Russia* 45 A10
Arkul, *Russia* 42 B10
Arlanc, *France* 26 C7
Arlanza →, *Spain* 30 C6
Arlanzón →, *Spain* 30 C6
Arlberg P., *Austria* 19 H6
Arlee, *U.S.A.* 110 C6
Arles, *France* 27 E8
Arlesheim, *Switz.* 22 B5
Arlington, *S. Africa* 85 D4
Arlington, *Oreg., U.S.A.* 110 D3
Arlington, *S. Dak., U.S.A.* 108 C6
Arlington, *Va., U.S.A.* 104 F7
Arlington, *Wash., U.S.A.* 112 B4
Arlon, *Belgium* 17 J7
Arlöv, *Sweden* 11 J7
Arly, *Burkina Faso* 79 C5
Armagh, *U.K.* 15 B5
Armagh □, *U.K.* 15 B5
Armagnac, *France* 26 E4
Armançon →, *France* 25 E10
Armavir, *Russia* 43 H5
Armenia, *Colombia* 120 C2
Armenia ■, *Asia* 43 K7
Armenistís, Ákra, *Greece* 37 C9
Armentières, *France* 25 B9
Armidale, *Australia* 91 E5
Armour, *U.S.A.* 108 D5
Armstrong, *B.C., Canada* 100 C5
Armstrong, *Ont., Canada* 98 B2
Armstrong, *U.S.A.* 109 M6
Armstrong →, *Australia* 88 C5
Arnarfjörður, *Iceland* 8 D2
Arnaud →, *Canada* 97 B12
Arnauti, C., *Cyprus* 37 D11
Arnay-le-Duc, *France* 25 E11
Arnedillo, *Spain* 28 C2
Arnedo, *Spain* 28 C2
Arnemuiden, *Neths.* 17 F3
Årnes, *Norway* 10 D5
Arnett, *U.S.A.* 109 G5
Arnhem, *Neths.* 16 E7
Arnhem, C., *Australia* 90 A2
Arnhem B., *Australia* 90 A2
Arnhem Land, *Australia* 90 A1
Arno →, *Italy* 32 E7
Arno Bay, *Australia* 91 E2
Arnold, *Calif., U.S.A.* 112 G6
Arnold, *Nebr., U.S.A.* 108 E4
Arnoldstein, *Austria* 21 J3
Arnon →, *France* 25 E9
Arnot, *Canada* 101 B9
Arnøy, *Norway* 8 A19
Arnprior, *Canada* 98 C4
Arnsberg, *Germany* 18 D4
Arnstadt, *Germany* 18 E6
Aro →, *Venezuela* 121 B5
Aroab, *Namibia* 84 D2
Aroche, *Spain* 31 H4
Aroeiras, *Brazil* 122 C4
Arolla, *Switz.* 22 D4
Arolsen, *Germany* 18 D5
Aron →, *France* 26 B7
Arona, *Italy* 32 C5
Aroroy, *Phil.* 55 E5
Arosa, *Switz.* 23 C9
Arosa, Ria de, *Spain* 30 C2
Arpajon, *France* 25 D9
Arpajon-sur-Cère, *France* 26 D6
Arpino, *Italy* 34 A6
Arqalyq, *Kazakhstan* 44 D7
Arque, *Bolivia* 124 D4
Arrabury, *Australia* 91 D3
Arrah = Ara, *India* 63 G11
Arraias, *Brazil* 123 D2
Arraias →, *Mato Grosso, Brazil* 125 C7
Arraias →, *Pará, Brazil* 122 C2
Arraiolos, *Portugal* 31 G3
Arran, *U.K.* 14 F3
Arrandale, *Canada* 100 C3
Arras, *France* 25 B9
Arrats →, *France* 26 D4
Arreau, *France* 26 F4
Arrecife, *Canary Is.* 36 F6
Arrecifes, *Argentina* 126 C3
Arrée, Mts. d', *France* 24 D3
Arriaga, *Chiapas, Mexico* 115 D6
Arriaga, *San Luis Potosí, Mexico* 114 C4
Arrilalah P.O., *Australia* 90 C3
Arrino, *Australia* 89 E2
Arrojado →, *Brazil* 123 D3
Arromanches-les-Bains, *France* 24 C6
Arronches, *Portugal* 31 F3
Arros →, *France* 26 E3
Arrou, *France* 24 D8
Arrow, L., *Ireland* 15 B3
Arrow Rock Res., *U.S.A.* 110 E6
Arrowhead, *Canada* 100 C5
Arrowhead, L., *U.S.A.* 113 L9
Arrowtown, *N.Z.* 87 L2
Arroyo de la Luz, *Spain* 31 F4
Arroyo Grande, *U.S.A.* 113 K6
Års, *Denmark* 11 H3
Ars, *Iran* 64 B5
Ars-en-Ré, *France* 26 B2
Ars-sur-Moselle, *France* 25 C13
Arsenault L., *Canada* 101 B7
Arsenev, *Russia* 48 B6
Arsi □, *Ethiopia* 77 F4
Arsiero, *Italy* 33 C8
Arsin, *Turkey* 67 B8
Arsk, *Russia* 42 B9
Árta, *Greece* 39 K4
Artá, *Spain* 36 B10
Arteaga, *Mexico* 114 D4
Arteche, *Phil.* 55 E6
Arteijo, *Spain* 30 B2
Artem, *Russia* 48 C6
Artem, Ostrov = Artyom, *Azerbaijan* 43 K10
Artemovsk, *Russia* 45 D10
Artemovsk, *Ukraine* 41 H9
Artemovskiy, *Russia* 43 G5
Artenay, *France* 25 D8
Artern, *Germany* 18 D7
Artesa de Segre, *Spain* 28 D6
Artesia = Mosomane, *Botswana* 84 C4
Artesia, *U.S.A.* 109 J2
Artesia Wells, *U.S.A.* 109 L5
Artesian, *U.S.A.* 108 C6
Arth, *Switz.* 23 B7
Arthez-de-Béarn, *France* 26 E3
Arthington, *Liberia* 78 D2
Arthur →, *Australia* 90 G3
Arthur Cr. →, *Australia* 90 C2
Arthur Pt., *Australia* 90 C5
Arthur's Pass, *N.Z.* 87 K3
Arthur's Town, *Bahamas* 117 B4
Artigas, *Uruguay* 126 C4
Artik, *Armenia* 43 K6
Artillery L., *Canada* 101 A7
Artois, *France* 25 B9
Artsyz, *Ukraine* 41 J5
Artvin, *Turkey* 67 B9
Artyom, *Azerbaijan* 43 K10
Aru, Kepulauan, *Indonesia* 57 F8
Aru Is. = Aru, Kepulauan, *Indonesia* 57 F8
Aru Meru □, *Tanzania* 82 C4
Arua, *Uganda* 82 B3
Aruanã, *Brazil* 123 D1
Aruba ■, *W. Indies* 117 D6
Arucas, *Canary Is.* 36 F4
Arudy, *France* 26 E3
Arumã, *Brazil* 121 D5
Arumpo, *Australia* 91 E3
Arun →, *Nepal* 63 F12
Arunachal Pradesh □, *India* 61 E19
Arusha, *Tanzania* 82 C4
Arusha □, *Tanzania* 82 C4
Arusha Chini, *Tanzania* 82 C4
Aruwimi →, *Zaïre* 82 B1
Arvada, *U.S.A.* 110 D10
Arvayheer, *Mongolia* 54 B5
Arve →, *France* 27 B10
Árvi, *Greece* 37 E7
Arvida, *Canada* 99 C5
Arvidsjaur, *Sweden* 8 D18
Arvika, *Sweden* 9 G15
Arvin, *U.S.A.* 113 K8
Arxan, *China* 54 B6
Aryirádhes, *Greece* 37 B3
Aryiroúpolis, *Greece* 37 D6
Arys, *Kazakhstan* 44 E7
Arzachena, *Italy* 34 A2
Arzamas, *Russia* 42 C6
Arzew, *Algeria* 75 A4
Arzgir, *Russia* 43 H7
Arzignano, *Italy* 33 C8
As, *Belgium* 17 F7
Aş Şadr, *U.A.E.* 65 E7
Aş Şafā, *Syria* 69 B6
'As Saffānīyah, *Si. Arabia* 65 D6
As Safīrah, *Syria* 66 D7
Aş Şahm, *Oman* 65 E8
As Sājir, *Si. Arabia* 64 E5
As Salamīyah, *Syria* 66 E7
As Salţ, *Jordan* 69 C4
As Sal'w'a, *Qatar* 65 E6
As Samāwah, *Iraq* 64 D5
As Sanamayn, *Syria* 69 B5
As Sukhnah, *Syria* 67 E8
As Sulaymānīyah, *Iraq* 67 E11
As Sulaymī, *Si. Arabia* 64 E4
As Summān, *Si. Arabia* 64 E5
As Suwaydā', *Syria* 69 C5
As Suwaydā' □, *Syria* 69 C5
As Şuwayrah, *Iraq* 67 F11
Asab, *Namibia* 84 D2
Asaba, *Nigeria* 79 D6
Asadābād, *Iran* 67 E13
Asafo, *Ghana* 78 D4
Asahi-Gawa →, *Japan* 49 G6
Asahigawa, *Japan* 48 C11
Asale, L., *Ethiopia* 77 E5
Asamankese, *Ghana* 79 D4
Asansol, *India* 63 H12
Åsarna, *Sweden* 10 B8

Asbe Teferi, Ethiopia 77 F5
Asbesberge, S. Africa 84 D3
Asbestos, Canada 99 C5
Asbury Park, U.S.A. 107 F10
Ascensión, Mexico 114 A3
Ascensión, B. de la, Mexico 115 D7
Ascension I., Atl. Oc. 2 E9
Aschaffenburg, Germany . 19 F5
Aschendorf, Germany 18 B3
Aschersleben, Germany ... 18 D7
Asciano, Italy 33 E8
Áscoli Piceno, Italy 33 F10
Áscoli Satriano, Italy 35 A8
Ascona, Switz. 23 D7
Ascope, Peru 124 B2
Ascotán, Chile 126 A2
Aseb, Eritrea 68 E3
Asedjrad, Algeria 75 D5
Asela, Ethiopia 77 F4
Asenovgrad, Bulgaria 39 G7
Asfeld, France 25 C11
Asfûn el Matâ'na, Egypt .. 76 B3
Åsgårdstrand, Norway ... 10 E4
Asgata, Cyprus 37 E12
Ash Fork, U.S.A. 111 J7
Ash Grove, U.S.A. 109 G8
Ash Shamāl □, Lebanon . 69 A5
Ash Shāmīyah, Iraq 67 G11
Ash Shāriqah, U.A.E. 65 E7
Ash Sharmah, Si. Arabia . 64 D2
Ash Sharqāt, Iraq 67 E10
Ash Sharqi, Al Jabal, Lebanon 69 B5
Ash Shaṭrah, Iraq 64 D5
Ash Shawbak, Jordan 64 D2
Ash Shawmari, J., Jordan . 69 E5
Ash Shaykh, J., Lebanon . 69 B4
Ash Shināfīyah, Iraq 64 D5
Ash Shu'aybah, Si. Arabia 64 E5
Ash Shumlūl, Si. Arabia . 64 E5
Ash Shūr'a, Iraq 64 C4
Ash Shurayf, Si. Arabia . 64 D4
Ash Shuwayfāt, Lebanon . 69 B4
Ashanti □, Ghana 79 D4
Ashau, Vietnam 58 D6
Ashburn, U.S.A. 105 K4
Ashburton, N.Z. 87 K3
Ashburton →, Australia .. 88 D1
Ashburton Downs, Australia 88 D2
Ashby de la Zouch, U.K. . 12 E6
Ashcroft, Canada 100 C4
Ashdod, Israel 69 D3
Asheboro, U.S.A. 105 H6
Asherton, U.S.A. 109 L5
Asheville, U.S.A. 105 H4
Asheweig →, Canada 98 B2
Ashford, Australia 91 D5
Ashford, U.K. 13 F8
Ashford, U.S.A. 110 C2
Ashgabat, Turkmenistan . 44 F6
Ashibetsu, Japan 48 C11
Ashikaga, Japan 49 F9
Ashizuri-Zaki, Japan 49 H6
Ashkarkot, Afghan. 62 C2
Ashkhabad = Ashgabat, Turkmenistan 44 F6
Ashland, Kans., U.S.A. .. 109 G5
Ashland, Ky., U.S.A. 104 F4
Ashland, Maine, U.S.A. .. 99 C6
Ashland, Mont., U.S.A. .. 110 D10
Ashland, Nebr., U.S.A. .. 108 E6
Ashland, Ohio, U.S.A. ... 106 F2
Ashland, Oreg., U.S.A. .. 110 E2
Ashland, Pa., U.S.A. 107 F8
Ashland, Va., U.S.A. 104 G7
Ashland, Wis., U.S.A. ... 108 B9
Ashley, N. Dak., U.S.A. . 108 B5
Ashley, Pa., U.S.A. 107 E9
Ashmont, Canada 100 C6
Ashmore Reef, Australia . 88 B3
Ashmûn, Egypt 76 H7
Ashmyany, Belarus 9 J21
Ashqelon, Israel 69 D3
Ashtabula, U.S.A. 106 E4
Ashton, S. Africa 84 E3
Ashton, U.S.A. 110 D8
Ashton under Lyne, U.K. . 12 D5
Ashuanipi, L., Canada ... 99 B6
'Āṣī →, Asia 66 D6
Asia, Kepulauan, Indonesia 57 D8
Āsiā Bak, Iran 65 C6
Asiago, Italy 33 C8
Asidonhoppo, Surinam .. 121 C6
Asifabad, India 60 K11
Asike, Indonesia 57 F10
Asilah, Morocco 74 A3
Asinara, Italy 34 A1
Asinara, G. dell', Italy ... 34 B1
Asino, Russia 44 D9
Asipovichy, Belarus 40 F5
'Asīr □, Si. Arabia 68 D3
Asir, Ras, Somali Rep. ... 68 E5
Aşkale, Turkey 67 C9
Asker, Norway 10 E4
Askersund, Sweden 11 F8
Askham, S. Africa 84 D3
Askim, Norway 10 E5
Askja, Iceland 8 D5
Askøy, Norway 9 F11
Asl, Egypt 76 J8
Asmara = Asmera, Eritrea 77 D4
Asmera, Eritrea 77 D4
Asnæs, Denmark 11 J5
Åsnen, Sweden 9 H16
Asni, Morocco 74 B3

Ásola, Italy 32 C7
Asoteriba, Jebel, Sudan .. 76 C4
Asotin, U.S.A. 110 C5
Aspe, Spain 29 G4
Aspen, U.S.A. 111 G10
Aspendos, Turkey 66 D4
Aspermont, U.S.A. 109 J4
Aspiring, Mt., N.Z. 87 L2
Aspres-sur-Buëch, France . 27 D9
Asprókavos, Ákra, Greece . 37 B4
Aspromonte, Italy 35 D8
Aspur, India 62 H6
Asquith, Canada 101 C7
Assa, Morocco 74 C3
Assâba, Mauritania 78 B2
Assad, Bahret, Syria 67 D8
Assam □, India 61 F18
Assamakka, Niger 79 B6
Asse, Belgium 17 H4
Assebroek, Belgium 17 F2
Assekrem, Algeria 75 D6
Assémini, Italy 34 C2
Assen, Neths. 16 C9
Assendelft, Neths. 16 D5
Assenede, Belgium 17 F3
Assens, Århus, Denmark . 11 H4
Assens, Fyn, Denmark .. 11 J3
Assesse, Belgium 17 H6
Assini, Ivory C. 78 D4
Assiniboia, Canada 101 D7
Assiniboine →, Canada . 101 D9
Assis, Brazil 127 A5
Assisi, Italy 33 E9
Assynt, L., U.K. 14 C3
Astaffort, France 26 D4
Astara, Azerbaijan 67 C13
Āstārā, Iran 67 C13
Asten, Neths. 17 F7
Asteroúsia, Greece 37 E5
Asti, Italy 32 D5
Astipálaia, Greece 39 N9
Astorga, Spain 30 C4
Astoria, U.S.A. 112 D3
Åstorp, Sweden 11 H6
Astrakhan, Russia 43 G9
Astudillo, Spain 30 C6
Asturias □, Spain 30 B5
Asunción, Paraguay 126 B4
Asunción Nochixtlán, Mexico 115 D5
Asutri, Sudan 77 D4
Aswa →, Uganda 82 B3
Aswad, Ras al, Si. Arabia 76 C4
Aswân, Egypt 76 C3
Aswân High Dam = Sadd el Aali, Egypt 76 C3
Asyût, Egypt 76 B3
Asyûti, Wadi →, Egypt . 76 B3
Aszód, Hungary 21 H9
At Ţafīlah, Jordan 69 E4
At Tā'if, Si. Arabia 68 C3
Aţ Ţīraq, Si. Arabia 64 E5
Atacama □, Chile 126 B2
Atacama, Desierto de, Chile 126 A2
Atacama, Salar de, Chile . 126 A2
Ataco, Colombia 120 C2
Atakor, Algeria 75 D6
Atakpamé, Togo 79 D5
Atalándi, Greece 39 L5
Atalaya, Peru 124 C3
Atalaya de Femes, Canary Is. 36 F6
Ataléia, Brazil 123 E3
Atami, Japan 49 G9
Atapupu, Indonesia 57 F6
Atâr, Mauritania 74 D2
Ataram, Erg n-, Algeria . 75 D5
Atarfe, Spain 31 H7
Atascadero, U.S.A. 111 J3
Atasu, Kazakhstan 44 E8
Atatürk Barajı, Turkey . 67 D8
Atauro, Indonesia 57 F7
Atbara, Sudan 76 D3
'Atbara →, Sudan 76 D3
Atbasar, Kazakhstan ... 44 D7
Atchafalaya B., U.S.A. . 109 L9
Atchison, U.S.A. 108 F7
Atebubu, Ghana 79 D4
Ateca, Spain 28 D3
Aterno →, Italy 33 F10
Atesine, Alpi, Italy 32 B8
Atessa, Italy 33 F11
Ath, Belgium 17 G3
Athabasca, Canada 100 C6
Athabasca →, Canada . 101 B6
Athabasca, L., Canada . 101 B7
Athboy, Ireland 15 C5
Athenry, Ireland 15 C3
Athens = Athínai, Greece 39 M6
Athens, Ala., U.S.A. ... 105 H2
Athens, Ga., U.S.A. ... 105 J4
Athens, N.Y., U.S.A. .. 107 D11
Athens, Ohio, U.S.A. .. 104 F4
Athens, Pa., U.S.A. ... 107 E8
Athens, Tenn., U.S.A. . 105 H3
Athens, Tex., U.S.A. .. 109 J7
Atherley, Canada 106 B5
Atherton, Australia ... 90 B4
Athiéme, Benin 79 D5
Athienou, Cyprus 37 D12
Athínai, Greece 39 M6
Athlone, Ireland 15 C4
Athna, Cyprus 37 D12
Atholl, Forest of, U.K. . 14 E5
Atholville, Canada ... 99 C6
Áthos, Greece 39 J7

Athus, Belgium 17 J7
Athy, Ireland 15 D5
Ati, Chad 73 F8
Ati, Sudan 77 E2
Atiak, Uganda 82 B3
Atico, Peru 124 D3
Atienza, Spain 28 D2
Atikokan, Canada 98 C1
Atikonak L., Canada ... 99 B7
Atimonan, Phil. 55 E4
Atka, Russia 45 C16
Atkarsk, Russia 42 E7
Atkinson, U.S.A. 108 D5
Atlanta, Ga., U.S.A. ... 105 J3
Atlanta, Tex., U.S.A. .. 109 J7
Atlantic, U.S.A. 108 E7
Atlantic City, U.S.A. .. 104 F8
Atlantic Ocean 2 E9
Atlántico □, Colombia . 120 A2
Atlas Mts. = Haut Atlas, Morocco 74 B3
Atlin, Canada 100 B2
Atlin, L., Canada 100 B2
Atmore, U.S.A. 105 K2
Atoka, U.S.A. 109 H6
Átokos, Greece 39 L3
Atolia, U.S.A. 113 K9
Atouguia, Portugal ... 31 F1
Atoyac →, Mexico ... 115 D5
Atrak = Atrek →, Turkmenistan 65 B8
Ätran, Sweden 11 G6
Atrato →, Colombia . 120 B2
Atrauli, India 62 E8
Atrek →, Turkmenistan 65 B8
Atri, Italy 33 F10
Atsbi, Ethiopia 77 E4
Atsoum, Mts., Cameroon 79 D7
Atsuta, Japan 48 C10
Attalla, U.S.A. 105 H2
Attáviros, Greece 37 C9
Attawapiskat, Canada . 98 B3
Attawapiskat →, Canada 98 B3
Attawapiskat, L., Canada 98 B3
Attendorn, Germany .. 18 D3
Attert, Belgium 17 J7
Attica, U.S.A. 104 E2
Attichy, France 25 C10
Attigny, France 25 C11
Attikamagen L., Canada 99 A6
Attleboro, U.S.A. 107 E13
Attock, Pakistan 62 C5
Attopeu, Laos 58 E6
Attur, India 60 P11
Atuel →, Argentina .. 126 D2
Åtvidaberg, Sweden .. 11 F10
Atwater, U.S.A. 111 H3
Atwood, Canada 106 C3
Atwood, U.S.A. 108 F4
Atyraū, Kazakhstan .. 44 E6
Au Sable →, U.S.A. . 104 C4
Au Sable Pt., U.S.A. . 98 C2
Aubagne, France 27 E9
Aubange, Belgium ... 17 J7
Aubarca, C., Spain .. 36 B7
Aube □, France 25 D11
Aube →, France 25 D10
Aubel, Belgium 17 G7
Aubenas, France 27 D8
Aubenton, France ... 25 C11
Auberry, U.S.A. 112 H7
Aubigny-sur-Nère, France 25 E9
Aubin, France 26 D6
Aubrac, Mts. d', France 26 D7
Auburn, Ala., U.S.A. . 105 J3
Auburn, Calif., U.S.A. . 112 G5
Auburn, Ind., U.S.A. . 104 E3
Auburn, N.Y., U.S.A. . 107 D8
Auburn, Nebr., U.S.A. . 108 E7
Auburn, Wash., U.S.A. 112 C4
Auburn Ra., Australia . 91 D5
Auburndale, U.S.A. .. 105 L5
Aubusson, France ... 26 C6
Auch, France 26 E4
Auchel, France 25 B9
Auchi, Nigeria 79 D6
Auckland, N.Z. 87 G5
Auckland Is., Pac. Oc. . 92 N8
Aude □, France 26 E6
Aude →, France ... 26 E7
Auden, Canada 98 B2
Auderghem, Belgium . 17 G4
Auderville, France ... 24 C5
Audierne, France ... 24 D2
Audincourt, France .. 25 E13
Audo, Ethiopia 77 F5
Audubon, U.S.A. ... 108 E7
Aue, Germany 18 E8
Auerbach, Germany . 18 E8
Aueti Paraná →, Brazil 120 D4
Aufist, W. Sahara ... 74 C2
Augathella, Australia . 91 D4
Augrabies Falls, S. Africa 84 D3
Augsburg, Germany . 19 G6
Augusta, Australia ... 89 F2
Augusta, Italy 35 E8
Augusta, Ark., U.S.A. . 109 H9
Augusta, Kans., U.S.A. 109 G6
Augusta, Maine, U.S.A. 99 D6
Augusta, Mont., U.S.A. 110 C7
Augusta, Wis., U.S.A. . 108 C9
Augustów, Poland ... 20 B12
Augustus, Mt., Australia 88 D2
Augustus Downs, Australia 90 B2
Augustus I., Australia . 88 C3

Aukan, Eritrea 77 D5
Aukum, U.S.A. 112 G6
Auld, L., Australia 88 D3
Aulla, Italy 32 D6
Aulnay, France 26 B3
Aulne →, France 24 D2
Aulnoye-Aymeries, France 25 B10
Ault, France 24 B8
Ault, U.S.A. 108 E2
Aulus-les-Bains, France . 26 F5
Aumale, France 25 C8
Aumont-Aubrac, France . 26 D7
Auna, Nigeria 79 C5
Aunis, France 26 B3
Auponhia, Indonesia . 57 E7
Aur, P., Malaysia 59 L5
Auraiya, India 63 F8
Aurangabad, Bihar, India 63 G11
Aurangabad, Maharashtra, India 60 K9
Auray, France 24 E4
Aurès, Algeria 75 A6
Aurich, Germany ... 18 B3
Aurilândia, Brazil ... 123 E1
Aurillac, France 26 D6
Auronzo di Cadore, Italy 33 B9
Aurora, Canada 106 C5
Aurora, S. Africa ... 84 E2
Aurora, Colo., U.S.A. . 108 F2
Aurora, Ill., U.S.A. . 104 E1
Aurora, Mo., U.S.A. . 109 G8
Aurora, Nebr., U.S.A. 108 E6
Aurora, Ohio, U.S.A. . 106 E3
Aursmoen, Norway .. 10 E5
Aurukun Mission, Australia 90 A3
Aus, Namibia 84 D2
Auschwitz = Oświęcim, Poland 20 E9
Austin, Minn., U.S.A. . 108 D8
Austin, Nev., U.S.A. . 110 G5
Austin, Pa., U.S.A. .. 106 E6
Austin, Tex., U.S.A. . 109 K6
Austin, L., Australia . 89 E2
Austra, Norway 8 D14
Austral Downs, Australia 90 C2
Austral Is. = Tubuai Is., Pac. Oc. 93 K12
Austral Seamount Chain, Pac. Oc. 93 K13
Australia ■, Oceania .. 92 K5
Australian Alps, Australia 91 F4
Australian Capital Territory □, Australia . 91 F4
Austria ■, Europe ... 21 H4
Austvågøy, Norway .. 8 B16
Autazes, Brazil 121 D6
Autelbas, Belgium .. 17 J7
Auterive, France 26 E5
Authie →, France .. 25 B8
Authon-du-Perche, France 24 D7
Autlán, Mexico 114 D4
Autun, France 25 F11
Auvergne, Australia . 88 C5
Auvergne, France ... 26 C7
Auvergne, Mts. d', France 26 C6
Auvézère →, France . 26 C4
Auxerre, France 25 E10
Auxi-le-Château, France 25 B9
Auxonne, France 25 E12
Auzances, France ... 26 B6
Auzat-sur-Allier, France 26 C7
Avallon, France 25 E10
Avalon, U.S.A. 113 M8
Avalon Pen., Canada . 99 C9
Avaré, Brazil 127 A6
Avawatz Mts., U.S.A. 113 K10
Aveiro, Brazil 121 D6
Aveiro, Portugal ... 30 E2
Aveiro □, Portugal . 30 E2
Āvej, Iran 65 C6
Avelgem, Belgium .. 17 G2
Avellaneda, Argentina 126 C4
Avellino, Italy 35 B7
Avenal, U.S.A. 112 K6
Avenches, Switz. ... 22 C4
Averøya, Norway ... 10 A1
Aversa, Italy 35 B7
Avery, U.S.A. 110 C6
Aves, I. de, W. Indies . 117 C7
Aves, Is. de, Venezuela . 117 D6
Avesnes-sur-Helpe, France 25 B10
Avesta, Sweden 9 F17
Aveyron □, France . 26 D6
Aveyron →, France . 26 D5
Avezzano, Italy 33 F10
Aviá Terai, Argentina 126 B3
Aviano, Italy 33 B9
Avigliana, Italy 32 C4
Avigliano, Italy 35 B8
Avignon, France ... 27 E8
Ávila, Spain 30 E6
Ávila □, Spain 30 E6
Ávila, Sierra de, Spain . 30 E6
Avila Beach, U.S.A. . 113 K6
Avilés, Spain 30 B5
Avío, Italy 33 B8
Aviz, Portugal 31 F3
Avize, France 25 D11
Avoca, Ireland 15 D5
Avoca, U.S.A. 106 D7
Avoca →, Australia . 91 F3
Avola, Canada 100 C5
Avola, Italy 35 F8
Avon, N.Y., U.S.A. . 106 D7

Avon, S. Dak., U.S.A. ... 108 D5
Avon □, U.K. 13 F5
Avon →, Australia 89 F2
Avon →, Avon, U.K. .. 13 F5
Avon →, Hants., U.K. . 13 G6
Avon →, Warks., U.K. . 13 F5
Avondale, Zimbabwe .. 83 F3
Avonlea, Canada 101 D7
Avonmore, Canada ... 107 A10
Avonmouth, U.K. 13 F5
Avranches, France ... 24 D5
Avre →, France 24 D8
Awag el Baqar, Sudan . 77 E3
A'waj →, Syria 69 B5
Awaji-Shima, Japan .. 49 G7
'Awālī, Bahrain 65 E6
Awantipur, India 63 C6
Awasa, L., Ethiopia .. 77 F4
Awash, Ethiopia 68 F3
Awash →, Ethiopia .. 77 E5
Awaso, Ghana 78 D4
Awatere →, N.Z. 87 J5
Awbārī, Libya 75 C7
Awbārī □, Libya 75 C7
Awe, L., U.K. 14 E3
Aweil, Sudan 77 F2
Awgu, Nigeria 79 D6
Awjilah, Libya 73 C9
Ax-les-Thermes, France 26 F5
Axarfjörður, Iceland . 8 C5
Axel, Neths. 17 F3
Axel Heiberg I., Canada 4 B3
Axim, Ghana 78 E4
Axinim, Brazil 121 D6
Axintele, Romania .. 38 E9
Axioma, Brazil 125 B5
Axiós →, Greece ... 39 J5
Axminster, U.K. 13 G4
Aÿ, France 25 C11
Ayabaca, Peru 124 A2
Ayabe, Japan 49 G7
Ayacucho, Argentina . 126 D4
Ayacucho, Peru 124 C3
Ayaguz, Kazakhstan . 44 E9
Ayamonte, Spain ... 31 H3
Ayan, Russia 45 D14
Ayancık, Turkey ... 66 B6
Ayapel, Colombia .. 120 B2
Ayas, Turkey 66 B5
Ayaviri, Peru 124 C3
Aybastı, Turkey 66 B7
Aydın, Turkey 66 D2
Aye, Belgium 17 H6
Ayenngré, Togo 79 D5
Ayer's Cliff, Canada . 107 A12
Ayers Rock, Australia 89 E5
Ayiá, Greece 39 K5
Ayia Aikateríni, Ákra, Greece 37 A3
Ayia Dhéka, Greece . 37 D6
Ayía Gálini, Greece . 37 D6
Ayía Marína, Greece . 39 M9
Ayia Napa, Cyprus .. 37 E13
Ayía Paraskeví, Greece 39 K9
Ayía Phyla, Cyprus . 37 E12
Ayía Rouméli, Greece 39 P6
Ayía Varvára, Greece 37 D6
Áyios Amvrósios, Cyprus 37 D12
Áyios Andréas, Greece 39 M5
Áyios Evstrátios, Greece 39 K7
Áyios Ioánnis, Ákra, Greece 37 D7
Áyios Isídhoros, Greece 37 C9
Áyios Kiríkos, Greece 39 M9
Áyios Matthaíos, Greece 37 B3
Áyios Mírono, Greece 39 P8
Áyios Nikólaos, Greece 37 D7
Áyios Seryios, Cyprus 37 D12
Ayios Theodhoros, Cyprus 37 D13
Ayíos Yeóryios, Greece 39 M9
Aylesbury, U.K. 13 F7
Aylmer, Canada 106 D4
Aylmer, L., Canada . 96 B8
Ayn Zālah, Iraq 67 D10
Ayna, Spain 29 G2
Ayolas, Paraguay ... 126 B4
Ayom, Sudan 77 F2
Ayon, Ostrov, Russia 45 C17
Ayora, Spain 29 F3
Ayr, Australia 90 B4
Ayr, U.K. 14 F4
Ayr →, U.K. 14 F4
Ayre, Pt. of, U.K. .. 12 C3
Aysha, Ethiopia ... 77 E5
Aytos, Bulgaria 38 G10
Ayu, Kepulauan, Indonesia 57 D8
Ayutla, Guatemala . 116 D1
Ayutla, Mexico 115 D5
Ayvacık, Turkey ... 66 C2
Ayvalık, Turkey ... 66 C2
Aywaille, Belgium . 17 H7
Az Zabdānī, Syria . 69 B5
Az Zāhirīyah, West Bank 69 D3
Az Zarqā, Jordan .. 69 C5
Az Zāwiyah, Libya . 75 B7
Az Zībār, Iraq 67 D11
Az-Zilfī, Si. Arabia 64 E5
Az Zubayr, Iraq ... 64 D5
Az Zuwaytīnah, Libya 73 B9
Azambuja, Portugal 31 F2
Azamgarh, India .. 63 F10
Azángaro, Peru ... 124 C3
Azaouak, Vallée de l', Mali 79 B5
Āzār Shahr, Iran .. 67 D11

Azarān, Iran 67 D12
Azärbayjan = Azerbaijan ■, Asia 43 K9
Azärbāyjān-e Gharbī □, Iran 64 B5
Azärbāyjān-e Sharqī □, Iran 64 B5
Azare, Nigeria 79 C7
Azay-le-Rideau, France 24 E7
A'zāz, Syria 66 D7
Azazga, Algeria 75 A5
Azbine = Aïr, Niger 79 B6
Azefal, Mauritania 74 D2
Azeffoun, Algeria 75 A5
Azemmour, Morocco 74 B3
Azerbaijan ■, Asia 43 K9
Azerbaijchan = Azerbaijan ■, Asia 43 K9
Azezo, Ethiopia 77 E4
Azimganj, India 63 G13
Aznalcóllar, Spain 31 H4
Azogues, Ecuador 120 D2
Azores, Atl. Oc. 2 C8
Azov, Russia 43 G4
Azov, Sea of, Europe 43 H3
Azovskoye More = Azov, Sea of, Europe 43 H3
Azovy, Russia 44 C7
Azpeitia, Spain 28 B2
Azrou, Morocco 74 B3
Aztec, U.S.A. 111 H10
Azúa, Dom. Rep. 117 C5
Azuaga, Spain 31 G5
Azuara, Spain 28 D4
Azuay □, Ecuador 120 D2
Azuer →, Spain 31 F7
Azuero, Pen. de, Panama 116 E3
Azul, Argentina 126 D4
Azul, Serra, Brazil 125 C7
Azurduy, Bolivia 125 D5
Azusa, U.S.A. 113 L9
Azzaba, Algeria 75 A6
Azzano Décimo, Italy 33 C9
'Azzūn, West Bank 69 C4

B

Ba Don, Vietnam 58 D6
Ba Dong, Vietnam 59 H6
Ba Ngoi = Cam Lam, Vietnam 59 G7
Ba Ria, Vietnam 59 G6
Ba Tri, Vietnam 59 G6
Ba Xian, China 50 E9
Baa, Indonesia 57 F6
Baamonde, Spain 30 B3
Baar, Switz. 23 B7
Baarle Nassau, Belgium 17 F5
Baarlo, Neths. 17 F8
Baarn, Neths. 16 D6
Bab el Mandeb, Red Sea 68 E3
Baba Burnu, Turkey 66 C2,
Baba dag, Azerbaijan 43 K9
Bābā Kalū, Iran 65 D6
Babaçulândia, Brazil 122 C2
Babadag, Romania 38 E11
Babadayhan, Turkmenistan 44 F7
Babaeski, Turkey 66 B2
Babahoyo, Ecuador 120 D2
Babakin, Australia 89 F2
Babana, Nigeria 79 C5
Babar, Algeria 75 A6
Babar, Indonesia 57 F7
Babar, Pakistan 62 D3
Babarkach, Pakistan 62 E2
Babayevo, Russia 40 C8
Babb, U.S.A. 110 B7
Babenhausen, Germany 19 F4
Babi Besar, P., Malaysia 59 L4
Babian Jiang →, China 52 F3
Babile, Ethiopia 77 F5
Babinda, Australia 90 B4
Babine, Canada 100 B3
Babine →, Canada 100 B3
Babine L., Canada 100 C3
Babo, Indonesia 57 E8
Bābol, Iran 65 B7
Bābol Sar, Iran 65 B7
Baboua, C.A.R. 80 C2
Babruysk, Belarus 41 F5
Babura, Nigeria 79 C6
Babusar Pass, Pakistan 63 B5
Babušnica, Serbia, Yug. 21 M12
Babuyan Chan., Phil. 55 B4
Babuyan Is., Phil. 55 B4
Babylon, Iraq 67 F11
Bac Can, Vietnam 58 A5
Bac Giang, Vietnam 58 B6
Bac Ninh, Vietnam 58 B6
Bac Phan, Vietnam 58 B5
Bac Quang, Vietnam 58 A5
Bacabal, Brazil 122 B3
Bacajá →, Brazil 121 D7
Bacalar, Mexico 115 D7
Bacan, Kepulauan, Indonesia 57 E7
Bacan, Pulau, Indonesia 57 E7
Bacarra, Phil. 55 B4
Bacău, Romania 38 C9
Baccarat, France 25 D13
Bacerac, Mexico 114 A3
Băceşti, Romania 38 C10
Bach Long Vi, Dao, Vietnam 58 B6

Bachaquero, Venezuela 120 B3
Bacharach, Germany 19 E3
Bachelina, Russia 44 D7
Bachuma, Ethiopia 77 F4
Back →, Canada 96 B9
Bačka Palanka, Serbia, Yug. 21 K9
Bačka Topola, Serbia, Yug. 21 K9
Bäckefors, Sweden 11 F6
Backnang, Germany 19 G5
Backstairs Passage, Australia 91 F2
Baco, Mt., Phil. 55 E4
Bacolod, Phil. 55 F5
Bacqueville-en-Caux, France 24 C8
Bácsalmás, Hungary 21 J9
Bacuag, Phil. 55 G6
Bacuk, Malaysia 59 J4
Bād, Iran 65 C7
Bad →, U.S.A. 108 C4
Bad Axe, U.S.A. 106 C2
Bad Bergzabern, Germany 19 F4
Bad Berleburg, Germany 18 D4
Bad Bevensen, Germany 18 B6
Bad Bramstedt, Germany 18 B5
Bad Brückenau, Germany 19 E5
Bad Doberan, Germany 18 A7
Bad Driburg, Germany 18 D5
Bad Ems, Germany 19 E3
Bad Frankenhausen, Germany 18 D7
Bad Freienwalde, Germany 18 C10
Bad Godesberg, Germany 18 E3
Bad Hersfeld, Germany 18 E5
Bad Hofgastein, Austria 21 H3
Bad Homburg, Germany 19 E4
Bad Honnef, Germany 18 E3
Bad Ischl, Austria 21 H3
Bad Kissingen, Germany 19 E6
Bad Königshofen, Germany 19 E6
Bad Kreuznach, Germany 19 F3
Bad Laasphe, Germany 18 E4
Bad Lands, U.S.A. 108 D3
Bad Langensalza, Germany 18 D6
Bad Lauterberg, Germany 18 D6
Bad Lippspringe, Germany 18 D4
Bad Mergentheim, Germany 19 F5
Bad Münstereifel, Germany 18 E2
Bad Muskau, Germany 18 D10
Bad Nauheim, Germany 19 E4
Bad Oeynhausen, Germany 18 C4
Bad Oldesloe, Germany 18 B6
Bad Orb, Germany 19 E5
Bad Pyrmont, Germany 18 D5
Bad Ragaz, Switz. 23 B9
Bad Reichenhall, Germany 19 H8
Bad Säckingen, Germany 19 H3
Bad Salzuflen, Germany 18 C4
Bad Salzungen, Germany 18 E6
Bad Segeberg, Germany 18 B6
Bad Tölz, Germany 19 H7
Bad Urach, Germany 19 G5
Bad Waldsee, Germany 19 H5
Bad Wildungen, Germany 18 D5
Bad Wimpfen, Germany 19 F5
Bad Windsheim, Germany 19 F6
Badagara, India 60 P9
Badagri, Nigeria 79 D5
Badajós, L., Brazil 121 D5
Badajoz, Spain 31 G4
Badajoz □, Spain 31 G4
Badalona, Spain 28 D7
Badalzai, Afghan. 62 E1
Badampahar, India 61 H15
Badanah, Si. Arabia 64 D4
Badarinath, India 63 D8
Badas, Brunei 56 D4
Badas, Kepulauan, Indonesia 56 D3
Baddo →, Pakistan 60 F4
Bade, Indonesia 57 F9
Baden, Austria 21 G6
Baden, Switz. 23 B6
Baden-Baden, Germany 19 G4
Baden-Württemberg □, Germany 19 G5
Badenoch, U.K. 14 E4
Badger, Canada 99 C8
Badger, U.S.A. 112 J7
Bādghīsāt □, Afghan. 60 B3
Badgom, India 63 B6
Badhoevedorp, Neths. 16 D5
Badia Polésine, Italy 33 C8
Badin, Pakistan 62 G3
Badogo, Mali 78 C3
Badong, China 53 B8
Badrah, Iraq 67 F11
Baduen, Somali Rep. 68 F4
Badulla, Sri Lanka 60 R12
Baena, Spain 31 H6
Baexem, Neths. 17 F7
Baeza, Ecuador 120 D2
Baeza, Spain 29 H1
Bafang, Cameroon 79 D7
Bafatá, Guinea-Biss. 78 C2
Baffin B., Canada 4 B4
Baffin I., Canada 97 B12
Bafia, Cameroon 79 D7
Bafilo, Togo 79 D5
Bafing →, Mali 78 C2
Bafliyūn, Syria 64 B3
Baflo, Neths. 16 B9
Bafoulabé, Mali 78 C2
Bafoussam, Cameroon 79 D7
Bāfq, Iran 65 D7

Bafra, Turkey 66 B6
Bafra Burnu, Turkey 66 B7
Bāft, Iran 65 D8
Bafut, Cameroon 79 D7
Bafwasende, Zaïre 82 B2
Bagamoyo, Tanzania 82 D4
Bagamoyo □, Tanzania 82 D4
Bagan Datoh, Malaysia 59 L3
Bagan Serai, Malaysia 59 K3
Baganga, Phil. 55 H7
Bagani, Namibia 84 B3
Bagansiapiapi, Indonesia 56 D2
Bagasra, India 62 J4
Bagawi, Sudan 77 E3
Bagdad, U.S.A. 113 L11
Bagdarin, Russia 45 D12
Bagé, Brazil 127 C5
Bagenalstown = Muine Bheag, Ireland 15 D5
Baggs, U.S.A. 110 F10
Bagh, Pakistan 63 C5
Baghdād, Iraq 67 F11
Bagheria, Italy 34 D5
Baghlān, Afghan. 60 A6
Bagley, U.S.A. 108 B7
Bagnacavallo, Italy 33 D8
Bagnara Cálabra, Italy 35 D8
Bagnères-de-Bigorre, France 26 E4
Bagnères-de-Luchon, France 26 F4
Bagni di Lucca, Italy 32 D7
Bagno di Romagna, Italy 33 E8
Bagnoles-de-l'Orne, France 24 D6
Bagnoli di Sopra, Italy 33 C8
Bagnolo Mella, Italy 32 C7
Bagnols-sur-Cèze, France 27 D8
Bagnorégio, Italy 33 F9
Bagolino, Italy 32 C7
Bagotville, Canada 99 C5
Bagrationovsk, Russia 9 J19
Bagua, Peru 124 B2
Baguio, Phil. 55 C4
Bahábón de Esgueva, Spain 28 D1
Bahadurgarh, India 62 E7
Bahama, Canal Viejo de, W. Indies 116 B4
Bahamas ■, N. Amer. 117 B5
Bahār, Iran 67 E6
Baharampur, India 63 G13
Baharîya, El Wâhât al, Egypt 76 J6
Bahau, Malaysia 59 L4
Bahawalnagar, Pakistan 62 D5
Bahawalpur, Pakistan 62 E4
Bahçe, Turkey 66 D7
Baheri, India 63 E8
Bahi, Tanzania 82 D4
Bahi Swamp, Tanzania 82 D4
Bahía = Salvador, Brazil 123 D4
Bahía □, Brazil 123 D3
Bahía, Is. de la, Honduras 116 C2
Bahía Blanca, Argentina 126 D3
Bahía de Caráquez, Ecuador 120 D1
Bahía Honda, Cuba 116 B3
Bahía Laura, Argentina 128 C3
Bahía Negra, Paraguay 125 E6
Bahir Dar, Ethiopia 77 E4
Bahmanzād, Iran 65 D6
Bahmer, Algeria 75 C4
Bahönye, Hungary 21 J7
Bahr Aouk →, C.A.R. 80 C3
Bahr el Ahmar □, Sudan 76 C3
Bahr el Ghazâl □, Sudan 77 F2
Bahr Salamat →, Chad 73 G8
Bahr Yûsef →, Egypt 76 J7
Bahra el Burullus, Egypt 76 H7
Bahraich, India 63 F9
Bahrain ■, Asia 65 E6
Bahror, India 62 F7
Bāhū Kalāt, Iran 65 E9
Bai, Mali 78 C4
Bai Bung, Mui, Vietnam 59 H5
Bai Duc, Vietnam 58 C5
Bai Thuong, Vietnam 58 C5
Baia Mare, Romania 38 B6
Baia-Sprie, Romania 38 B6
Baião, Brazil 122 B2
Baïbokoum, Chad 73 G8
Baicheng, China 51 B12
Baidoa, Somali Rep. 68 G3
Baie Comeau, Canada 99 C6
Baie-St-Paul, Canada 99 C5
Baie Trinité, Canada 99 C6
Baie Verte, Canada 99 C8
Baignes-Ste.-Radegonde, France 26 C3
Baigneux-les-Juifs, France 25 E11
Baihe, China 50 H6
Baihe, Taiwan 53 F13
Ba'ijī, Iraq 67 E10
Baikal, L. = Baykal, Oz., Russia 45 D11
Baile Atha Cliath = Dublin, Ireland 15 C5
Bailei, Ethiopia 77 F5
Bailén, Spain 31 G7
Băileşti, Romania 38 E6
Baileux, Belgium 17 H4
Bailique, Ilha, Brazil 122 A2
Bailleul, France 25 B9
Bailundo, Angola 81 G3
Baima, China 52 A3
Bain-de-Bretagne, France 24 E5
Bainbridge, Ga., U.S.A. 105 K3
Bainbridge, N.Y., U.S.A. 107 D9

Baing, Indonesia 57 F6
Bainiu, China 50 H7
Bainville, U.S.A. 108 A2
Bā'ir, Jordan 69 E5
Baird, U.S.A. 109 J5
Baird Mts., U.S.A. 96 B3
Bairin Youqi, China 51 C10
Bairin Zuoqi, China 51 C10
Bairnsdale, Australia 91 F4
Bais, Phil. 55 G5
Baisha, China 50 G7
Baïsole →, France 26 E4
Baissa, Nigeria 79 D7
Baitadi, Nepal 63 E9
Baixa Grande, Brazil 123 D3
Baiyin, China 50 F3
Baiyü, China 52 B2
Baiyu Shan, China 50 F4
Baiyuda, Sudan 76 D3
Baj Baj, India 63 H13
Baja, Hungary 21 J8
Baja, Pta., Mexico 114 B1
Baja California, Mexico 114 A1
Baja California □, Mexico 114 B2
Baja California Sur □, Mexico 114 B2
Bajamar, Canary Is. 36 F3
Bajana, India 62 H4
Bājgīrān, Iran 65 B8
Bajimba, Mt., Australia 91 D5
Bajo Nuevo, Caribbean 116 C4
Bajoga, Nigeria 79 C7
Bajool, Australia 90 C5
Bakala, C.A.R. 73 G9
Bakar, Croatia 33 C11
Bakchar, Russia 44 D9
Bakel, Neths. 17 E7
Bakel, Senegal 78 C2
Baker, Calif., U.S.A. 113 K10
Baker, Mont., U.S.A. 108 B2
Baker, Oreg., U.S.A. 110 D5
Baker, Canal, Chile 128 C2
Baker, L., Canada 96 B10
Baker I., Pac. Oc. 92 G10
Baker L., Australia 89 E4
Baker Lake, Canada 96 B10
Baker Mt., U.S.A. 110 B3
Bakers Creek, Australia 90 C4
Baker's Dozen Is., Canada 98 A4
Bakersfield, Calif., U.S.A. 113 K7
Bakersfield, Vt., U.S.A. 107 B12
Bakhchysaray, Ukraine 41 K7
Bakhmach, Ukraine 41 G7
Bākhtarān, Iran 67 E12
Bākhtarān □, Iran 64 C5
Bakı, Azerbaijan 43 K9
Bakırdaği, Turkey 66 C6
Bakırköy, Turkey 39 H11
Bakkafjörður, Iceland 8 C6
Bakkagerði, Iceland 8 D7
Bakony →, Hungary 21 H7
Bakony Forest = Bakony Hegyseg, Hungary 21 H7
Bakony Hegyseg, Hungary 21 H7
Bakori, Nigeria 79 C6
Bakouma, C.A.R. 73 G9
Baksan, Russia 43 J6
Baku = Bakı, Azerbaijan 43 K9
Bakutis Coast, Antarctica 5 D15
Baky = Bakı, Azerbaijan 43 K9
Bala, Canada 106 A5
Bâlâ, Turkey 66 C5
Bala, L., U.K. 12 E4
Balabac I., Phil. 55 H2
Balabac Str., E. Indies 56 C5
Balabagh, Afghan. 62 B4
Ba'labakk, Lebanon 69 A5
Balabalangan, Kepulauan, Indonesia 56 E5
Balad, Iraq 67 F11
Balad Rūz, Iraq 67 F11
Bālādeh, Fārs, Iran 65 D6
Bālādeh, Māzandaran, Iran 65 B6
Balaghat, India 60 J12
Balaghat Ra., India 60 K10
Balaguer, Spain 28 D5
Balakhna, Russia 42 B6
Balaklava, Australia 91 E2
Balaklava, Ukraine 41 K7
Balakliya, Ukraine 41 H9
Balakovo, Russia 42 D8
Balancán, Mexico 115 D6
Balashov, Russia 42 E6
Balasinor, India 62 H5
Balasore = Baleshwar, India 61 J15
Balassagyarmat, Hungary 21 G9
Balât, Egypt 76 B2
Balaton, Hungary 21 J7
Balayan, Phil. 55 E4
Balazote, Spain 29 G2
Balbina, Reprêsa de, Brazil 121 D6
Balboa, Panama 116 E4
Balbriggan, Ireland 15 C5

Bale, Croatia 33 C10
Bale □, Ethiopia 77 F5
Baleares □, Spain 28 F7
Baleares, Is., Spain 36 B10
Balearic Is. = Baleares, Is., Spain 36 B10
Baleia, Pta. da, Brazil 123 E4
Balen, Belgium 17 F6
Baler, Phil. 55 D4
Baler Bay, Phil. 55 D4
Balerna, Switz. 23 D8
Baleshwar, India 61 J15
Balezino, Russia 42 B11
Balfate, Honduras 116 C2
Balfe's Creek, Australia 90 C4
Bali, Cameroon 79 D6
Balí, Greece 37 D6
Bali, Indonesia 56 F5
Bali □, Indonesia 56 F5
Bali, Selat, Indonesia 57 H16
Baligród, Poland 20 F12
Balikeşir, Turkey 66 C2
Balikpapan, Indonesia 56 E5
Balimbing, Phil. 57 C5
Baling, Malaysia 59 K3
Balintang Channel, Phil. 55 B4
Balipara, India 61 F18
Baliza, Brazil 125 D7
Balk, Neths. 16 C7
Balkan Mts. = Stara Planina, Bulgaria 38 F6
Balkhash = Balqash, Kazakhstan 44 E8
Balkhash, Ozero = Balqash Köl, Kazakhstan 44 E8
Balla, Bangla. 61 G17
Ballachulish, U.K. 14 E3
Balladonia, Australia 89 F3
Ballarat, Australia 91 F3
Ballard, L., Australia 89 E3
Ballater, U.K. 14 D5
Ballenas, Canal de, Mexico 114 B2
Balleny Is., Antarctica 5 C11
Ballesteros, Phil. 55 B4
Ballia, India 63 G11
Ballidu, Australia 89 F2
Ballina, Australia 91 D5
Ballina, Mayo, Ireland 15 B2
Ballina, Tipp., Ireland 15 D3
Ballinasloe, Ireland 15 C3
Ballinger, U.S.A. 109 K5
Ballinrobe, Ireland 15 C2
Ballinskelligs B., Ireland 15 E1
Ballon, France 24 D7
Ballycastle, U.K. 15 A5
Ballymena, U.K. 15 B5
Ballymena □, U.K. 15 B5
Ballymoney, U.K. 15 A5
Ballymoney □, U.K. 15 A5
Ballyshannon, Ireland 15 B3
Balmaceda, Chile 128 C2
Balmazújváros, Hungary 21 H11
Balmhorn, Switz. 22 D5
Balmoral, Australia 91 F3
Balmoral, U.K. 14 D5
Balmorhea, U.S.A. 109 K3
Balonne →, Australia 91 D4
Balqash, Kazakhstan 44 E8
Balqash Köl, Kazakhstan 44 E8
Balrampur, India 63 F10
Balranald, Australia 91 E3
Balş, Romania 38 E7
Balsapuerto, Peru 124 B2
Balsas, Mexico 115 D5
Balsas →, Maranhão, Brazil 122 C3
Balsas →, Tocantins, Brazil 122 C2
Balsas →, Mexico 114 D4
Bålsta, Sweden 10 E11
Balsthal, Switz. 22 B5
Balston Spa, U.S.A. 107 D11
Balta, Romania 38 E5
Balta, Ukraine 41 H5
Balta, U.S.A. 108 A4
Baltanás, Spain 30 D6
Bălți, Moldova 41 J4
Baltic Sea, Europe 9 H18
Baltîm, Egypt 76 H7
Baltimore, Ireland 15 E2
Baltimore, U.S.A. 104 F7
Baltit, Pakistan 63 A6
Baltiysk, Russia 9 J18
Baltrum, Germany 18 B3
Baluchistan □, Pakistan 60 F4
Balurghat, India 63 G13
Balvi, Latvia 9 H22
Balya, Turkey 66 C2
Balygychan, Russia 45 C16
Balzar, Ecuador 120 D2
Bam, Iran 65 D8
Bama, China 52 E6
Bama, Nigeria 79 C7
Bamako, Mali 78 C3
Bamba, Mali 79 B4
Bambamarca, Peru 124 B2
Bambari, C.A.R. 73 G9
Bambaroo, Australia 90 B4
Bamberg, Germany 19 F6
Bamberg, U.S.A. 105 J5
Bambesi, Ethiopia 77 F3
Bambey, Senegal 78 C1
Bambili, Zaïre 82 B2
Bambuí, Brazil 123 H3
Bamenda, Cameroon 79 D7
Bamfield, Canada 100 D3
Bāmīān □, Afghan. 60 B5

Bamiancheng, *China* 51 C13
Bamkin, *Cameroon* 79 D7
Bampūr, *Iran* 65 E9
Ban Aranyaprathet,
  Thailand 58 F4
Ban Ban, *Laos* 58 C4
Ban Bang Hin, *Thailand* .. 59 H2
Ban Chiang Klang,
  Thailand 58 C3
Ban Chik, *Laos* 58 D4
Ban Choho, *Thailand* ... 58 E4
Ban Dan Lan Hoi,
  Thailand 58 D2
Ban Don = Surat Thani,
  Thailand 59 H2
Ban Don, *Vietnam* 58 F6
Ban Don, Ao, *Thailand* .. 59 H2
Ban Dong, *Thailand* 58 C3
Ban Hong, *Thailand* 58 C2
Ban Kaeng, *Thailand* ... 58 D3
Ban Keun, *Laos* 58 C4
Ban Khai, *Thailand* 58 F3
Ban Kheun, *Laos* 58 B3
Ban Khlong Kua, *Thailand* 59 J3
Ban Khuan Mao, *Thailand* 59 J2
Ban Khun Yuam, *Thailand* 58 C1
Ban Ko Yai Chim,
  Thailand 59 G2
Ban Kok, *Thailand* 58 D4
Ban Laem, *Thailand* 58 F2
Ban Lao Ngam, *Laos* 58 E6
Ban Le Kathe, *Thailand* . 58 E2
Ban Mae Chedi, *Thailand* 58 C2
Ban Mae Laeng, *Thailand* 58 B2
Ban Mae Sariang, *Thailand* 58 C1
Ban Mê Thuôt = Buon Me
  Thuot, *Vietnam* 58 F7
Ban Mi, *Thailand* 58 E3
Ban Muong Mo, *Laos* ... 58 C4
Ban Na Mo, *Laos* 58 D5
Ban Na San, *Thailand* ... 59 H2
Ban Na Tong, *Laos* 58 B3
Ban Nam Bac, *Laos* 58 B4
Ban Nam Ma, *Laos* 58 A3
Ban Ngang, *Laos* 58 E6
Ban Nong Bok, *Laos* 58 D5
Ban Nong Boua, *Laos* ... 58 E6
Ban Nong Pling, *Thailand* 58 E3
Pak Chan, *Thailand* .. 59 G2
Ban Phai, *Thailand* 58 D4
Ban Pong, *Thailand* 58 F2
Ban Ron Phibun, *Thailand* 59 H2
Ban Sanam Chai, *Thailand* 59 J3
Ban Sangkha, *Thailand* . 58 E4
Ban Tak, *Thailand* 58 D2
Ban Tako, *Thailand* 58 E4
Ban Tha Dua, *Thailand* .. 58 D2
Ban Tha Li, *Thailand* ... 58 D3
Ban Tha Nun, *Thailand* . 59 H2
Ban Thahine, *Laos* 58 E5
Ban Xien Kok, *Laos* 58 B3
Ban Yen Nhan, *Vietnam* . 58 B6
Baña, Punta de la, *Spain* . 28 E5
Banaba, *Kiribati* 92 H8
Bañalbufar, *Spain* 36 B9
Banalia, *Zaïre* 82 B2
Banam, *Cambodia* 59 G5
Banamba, *Mali* 78 C3
Banana, *Australia* 90 C5
Bananal, I. do, *Brazil* ... 123 D1
Banaras = Varanasi, *India* 63 G10
Banas →, *Gujarat, India* . 62 H4
Banas →, *Mad. P., India* . 63 G9
Bânâs, Ras, *Egypt* 76 C4
Banaz, *Turkey* 66 C3
Banbān, *Si. Arabia* 64 E5
Banbridge, *U.K.* 15 B5
Banbridge □, *U.K.* 15 B5
Banbury, *U.K.* 13 E6
Banchory, *U.K.* 14 D6
Bancroft, *Canada* 98 C4
Band Bonī, *Iran* 65 E8
Band Qīr, *Iran* 65 D6
Banda, *India* 63 G9
Banda, Kepulauan,
  Indonesia 57 E7
Banda Aceh, *Indonesia* ... 56 C1
Banda Banda, Mt.,
  Australia 91 E5
Banda Elat, *Indonesia* ... 57 F8
Banda Is. = Banda,
  Kepulauan, *Indonesia* . 57 E7
Banda Sea, *Indonesia* ... 57 F7
Bandai-San, *Japan* 48 F10
Bandama →, *Ivory C.* ... 78 D3
Bandān, *Iran* 65 D9
Bandanaira, *Indonesia* ... 57 E7
Bandanwara, *India* 62 F6
Bandar = Machilipatnam,
  India 61 L12
Bandār 'Abbās, *Iran* 65 E8
Bandar-e Anzalī, *Iran* ... 67 D13
Bandar-e Büshehr =
  Büshehr, *Iran* 65 D6
Bandar-e Chārak, *Iran* ... 65 E7
Bandar-e Deylam, *Iran* .. 65 D6
Bandar-e Khomeynī, *Iran* . 65 D6
Bandar-e Lengeh, *Iran* ... 65 E7
Bandar-e Maqām, *Iran* .. 65 E7
Bandar-e Ma'shur, *Iran* .. 65 D6
Bandar-e Nakhīlū, *Iran* .. 65 E7
Bandar-e Rīg, *Iran* 65 D6
Bandar-e Torkeman, *Iran* . 65 B7
Bandar Maharani = Muar,
  Malaysia 59 L4
Bandar Penggaram = Batu
  Pahat, *Malaysia* 59 M4

Bandar Seri Begawan,
  Brunei 56 C4
Bandawe, *Malawi* 83 E3
Bande, *Belgium* 17 H6
Bande, *Spain* 30 C3
Bandeira, Pico da, *Brazil* . 123 F3
Bandeirante, *Brazil* 123 D1
Bandera, *Argentina* 126 B3
Bandera, *U.S.A.* 109 L5
Banderas, B. de, *Mexico* . 114 C3
Bandiagara, *Mali* 78 C4
Bandırma, *Turkey* 66 B3
Bandon, *Ireland* 15 E3
Bandon →, *Ireland* 15 E3
Bandula, *Mozam.* 83 F3
Bandundu, *Zaïre* 80 E3
Bandung, *Indonesia* 57 G12
Bandya, *Australia* 89 E3
Bāneh, *Iran* 67 E11
Bañeres, *Spain* 29 G4
Banes, *Cuba* 117 B4
Banff, *Canada* 100 C5
Banff, *U.K.* 14 D6
Banff Nat. Park, *Canada* . 100 C5
Banfora, *Burkina Faso* ... 78 C4
Bang Fai →, *Laos* 58 D5
Bang Hieng →, *Laos* 58 D5
Bang Krathum, *Thailand* . 58 D3
Bang Lamung, *Thailand* . 58 F3
Bang Mun Nak, *Thailand* . 58 D3
Bang Pa In, *Thailand* ... 58 E3
Bang Rakam, *Thailand* .. 58 D3
Bang Saphan, *Thailand* .. 59 G2
Bangala Dam, *Zimbabwe* 83 G3
Bangalore, *India* 60 N10
Bangante, *Cameroon* 79 D7
Bangaon, *India* 63 H13
Bangassou, *C.A.R.* 80 D4
Banggai, Kepulauan,
  Indonesia 57 E6
Banggi, P., *Malaysia* 56 C5
Banghāzī, *Libya* 73 B9
Bangil, *Indonesia* 57 G15
Bangjang, *Sudan* 77 E3
Bangka, P., Sulawesi,
  Indonesia 57 D7
Bangka, P., Sumatera,
  Indonesia 56 E3
Bangka, Selat, *Indonesia* . 56 E3
Bangkalan, *Indonesia* ... 57 G15
Bangkinang, *Indonesia* .. 56 D2
Bangko, *Indonesia* 56 E2
Bangkok, *Thailand* 58 F3
Bangladesh ■, *Asia* 61 H17
Bangolo, *Ivory C.* 78 D3
Bangong Co, *India* 63 B8
Bangor, *Down, U.K.* 15 B6
Bangor, *Gwynedd, U.K.* . 12 D3
Bangor, *Maine, U.S.A.* .. 99 D6
Bangor, *Pa., U.S.A.* 107 F9
Bangued, *Phil.* 55 C4
Bangui, *C.A.R.* 80 D3
Bangui, *Phil.* 55 B4
Banguru, *Zaïre* 82 B2
Bangweulu, L., *Zambia* .. 83 E3
Bangweulu Swamp, *Zambia* 83 E3
Bani, *Dom. Rep.* 117 C5
Bani →, *Mali* 78 C4
Bani, Djebel, *Morocco* .. 74 C3
Bani Bangou, *Niger* 79 B5
Banī Sa'd, *Iraq* 67 F11
Banī Walīd, *Libya* 73 B7
Bania, *Ivory C.* 78 D4
Banihal Pass, *India* 63 C6
Banīnah, *Libya* 73 B9
Bāniyās, *Syria* 66 E6
Banja Luka, *Bos.-H.* 21 L7
Banjar, *Indonesia* 57 G13
Banjarmasin, *Indonesia* .. 56 E4
Banjarnegara, *Indonesia* . 57 G13
Banjul, *Gambia* 78 C1
Banka Banka, *Australia* .. 90 B1
Banket, *Zimbabwe* 83 F3
Bankilaré, *Niger* 79 C5
Bankipore, *India* 63 G11
Banks I., *B.C., Canada* .. 100 C3
Banks I., *N.W.T., Canada* 96 A7
Banks Pen., *N.Z.* 87 K4
Banks Str., *Australia* 90 G4
Bankura, *India* 63 H12
Bann →, *L'derry., U.K.* . 15 A5
Bann →, *Tyrone, U.K.* .. 15 B5
Banna, *Phil.* 55 C4
Bannalec, *France* 24 E3
Bannang Sata, *Thailand* . 59 J3
Banning, *U.S.A.* 113 M10
Banningville = Bandundu,
  Zaïre 80 E3
Bannockburn, *Canada* ... 106 B7
Bannockburn, *U.K.* 14 E5
Bannockburn, *Zimbabwe* . 83 G2
Bannu, *Pakistan* 60 C7
Bañolas, *Spain* 28 C7
Banon, *France* 27 D9
Baños de la Encina, *Spain* 31 G7
Baños de Molgas, *Spain* . 30 C3
Banská Bystrica,
  Slovak Rep. 20 G9
Banská Štiavnica,
  Slovak Rep. 21 G8
Banswara, *India* 62 H6
Bantayan, *Phil.* 55 F5
Banten, *Indonesia* 57 G12
Bantry, *Ireland* 15 E2
Bantry B., *Ireland* 15 E2
Bantul, *Indonesia* 57 G14
Bantva, *India* 62 J4

Banu, *Afghan.* 60 B6
Banyak, Kepulauan,
  Indonesia 56 D1
Banyo, *Cameroon* 79 D7
Banyuls-sur-Mer, *France* . 26 F7
Banyumas, *Indonesia* ... 57 G13
Banyuwangi, *Indonesia* .. 57 H16
Banzare Coast, *Antarctica* 5 C9
Banzyville = Mobayi, *Zaïre* 80 D4
Bao Ha, *Vietnam* 58 A5
Bao Lac, *Vietnam* 58 A5
Bao Loc, *Vietnam* 59 G6
Bao'an = Shenzhen, *China* 53 F10
Baocheng, *China* 50 H4
Baode, *China* 50 E6
Baodi, *China* 51 E9
Baoding, *China* 50 E8
Baoji, *China* 50 G4
Baojing, *China* 52 C7
Baokang, *China* 53 B8
Baoshan, *Shanghai, China* 53 B13
Baoshan, *Yunnan, China* 52 E2
Baotou, *China* 50 D6
Baoying, *China* 51 H10
Bap, *India* 62 F5
Bapatla, *India* 61 M12
Bapaume, *France* 25 B9
Bāqerābād, *Iran* 65 C6
Ba'qūbah, *Iraq* 67 F11
Barisal, *Bangla.* 61 H17
Barisan, Bukit, *Indonesia* . 56 E2
Barito →, *Indonesia* 56 E4
Barjac, *France* 27 D8
Barjols, *France* 27 E10
Barjūj, Wadi →, *Libya* .. 75 C7
Bark L., *Canada* 106 A7
Barka = Baraka →, *Sudan* 76 D4
Barkam, *China* 52 B4
Barker, *U.S.A.* 106 C6
Barkley Sound, *Canada* .. 100 D3
Barkly Downs, *Australia* . 90 C2
Barkly East, *S. Africa* ... 84 E4
Barkly Tableland, *Australia* 90 B2
Barkly West, *S. Africa* ... 84 D3
Barkol, Wadi →, *Sudan* . 76 D3
Barksdale, *U.S.A.* 109 L4
Barlee, L., *Australia* 89 E2
Barlee, Mt., *Australia* 89 D4
Barletta, *Italy* 35 A9
Barlinek, *Poland* 20 C5
Barlovento, *Canary Is.* ... 36 F2
Barlow L., *Canada* 101 A8
Barmedman, *Australia* ... 91 E4
Barmer, *India* 62 G4
Barmera, *Australia* 91 E3
Barmouth, *U.K.* 12 E3
Barmstedt, *Germany* 18 B6
Barnagar, *India* 62 H6
Barnard Castle, *U.K.* 12 C6
Barnato, *Australia* 91 E3
Barnaul, *Russia* 44 D9
Barnesville, *U.S.A.* 105 J3
Barnet, *U.K.* 13 F7
Barneveld, *Neths.* 16 D7
Barneveld, *U.S.A.* 107 C9
Barneville-Cartevert,
  France 24 C5
Barngo, *Australia* 90 D4
Barnhart, *U.S.A.* 109 K4
Barnsley, *U.K.* 12 D6
Barnstaple, *U.K.* 13 F3
Barnsville, *U.S.A.* 108 B6
Baro, *Nigeria* 79 D6
Baro →, *Ethiopia* 77 F3
Baroda = Vadodara, *India* 62 H5
Baroda, *India* 62 G7
Baroe, *S. Africa* 84 E3
Baron Ra., *Australia* 88 D4
Barpeta, *India* 61 F17
Barques, Pt. Aux, *U.S.A.* 104 C4
Barquinha, *Portugal* 31 F2
Barquísimeto, *Venezuela* . 120 A4
Barr, *France* 25 D14
Barra, *Brazil* 122 D3
Barra, *U.K.* 14 E1
Barra, Sd. of, *U.K.* 14 D1
Barra da Estiva, *Brazil* ... 123 D3
Barra de Navidad, *Mexico* 114 D4
Barra do Corda, *Brazil* ... 122 C2
Barra do Mendes, *Brazil* . 123 D3
Barra do Piraí, *Brazil* ... 123 F3
Barra Falsa, Pta. da,
  Mozam. 85 C6
Barra Hd., *U.K.* 14 E1
Barra Mansa, *Brazil* 123 F3
Barraba, *Australia* 91 E5
Barração do Barreto, *Brazil* 125 B6
Barrackpur = Barakpur,
  India 63 H13
Barrafranca, *Italy* 35 E7
Barraigh = Barra, *U.K.* . 14 E1
Barranca, *Lima, Peru* ... 124 C2
Barranca, *Loreto, Peru* .. 120 D2
Barrancabermeja, *Colombia* 120 B3
Barrancas, *Colombia* 120 A3
Barrancas, *Venezuela* ... 121 B5
Barrancos, *Portugal* 31 G4
Barranqueras, *Argentina* . 126 B4
Barranquilla, *Colombia* ... 120 A3
Barras, *Brazil* 122 B3
Barras, *Colombia* 120 D3
Barraute, *Canada* 98 C4
Barre, *Mass., U.S.A.* 107 D12
Barre, *Vt., U.S.A.* 107 B12
Barre do Bugres, *Brazil* .. 125 C6
Barreal, *Argentina* 126 C2
Barreiras, *Brazil* 123 D3
Barreirinha, *Brazil* 121 D6

Barreirinhas, *Brazil* 122 B3
Barreiro, *Portugal* 31 G1
Barreiros, *Brazil* 122 C4
Barrême, *France* 27 E10
Barren, Nosy, *Madag.* ... 85 B7
Barretos, *Brazil* 123 F2
Barrhead, *Canada* 100 C6
Barrie, *Canada* 98 D4
Barrier Ra., *Australia* 91 E3
Barrière, *Canada* 100 C4
Barrington, *U.S.A.* 107 E13
Barrington L., *Canada* ... 101 B8
Barrington Tops, *Australia* 91 E5
Barringun, *Australia* 91 D4
Barro do Garças, *Brazil* . 125 D7
Barrow, *U.S.A.* 96 A4
Barrow →, *Ireland* 15 D4
Barrow Creek, *Australia* . 90 C1
Barrow I., *Australia* 88 D2
Barrow-in-Furness, *U.K.* . 12 C4
Barrow Pt., *Australia* 90 A3
Barrow Ra., *Australia* ... 89 E4
Barrow Str., *Canada* 4 B3
Barruecopardo, *Spain* ... 30 D4
Barruelo, *Spain* 30 C6
Barry, *U.K.* 13 F4
Barry's Bay, *Canada* 98 C4
Barsalogho, *Burkina Faso* 79 C4
Barsat, *Pakistan* 63 A5
Barsham, *Syria* 67 E9
Barsi, *India* 60 K9
Barsø, *Denmark* 11 J3
Barsoi, *India* 61 G15
Barstow, *Calif., U.S.A.* .. 113 L9
Barstow, *Tex., U.S.A.* .. 109 K3
Barth, *Germany* 18 A8
Barthélemy, Col, *Vietnam* 58 C5
Bartica, *Guyana* 121 B6
Bartin, *Turkey* 66 B5
Bartlesville, *U.S.A.* 109 G7
Bartlett, *Calif., U.S.A.* ... 112 J8
Bartlett, *Tex., U.S.A.* ... 109 K6
Bartlett, L., *Canada* 100 A5
Bartolomeu Dias, *Mozam.* 83 G4
Barton, *Australia* 89 F5
Barton upon Humber, *U.K.* 12 D7
Bartoszyce, *Poland* 20 A10
Bartow, *U.S.A.* 105 M5
Barú, I. de, *Colombia* ... 120 A2
Barú, Volcan, *Panama* .. 116 E3
Barumba, *Zaïre* 82 B1
Baruth, *Germany* 18 C9
Barvaux, *Belgium* 17 H6
Barvinkove, *Ukraine* 41 H9
Barwani, *India* 62 H6
Barysaw, *Belarus* 40 E5
Barysh, *Russia* 42 D8
Barzān, *Iraq* 64 B5
Bas-Rhin □, *France* 25 D14
Bašaid, *Serbia, Yug.* 21 K10
Bāsa'idū, *Iran* 65 E7
Basal, *Pakistan* 62 C5
Basankusa, *Zaïre* 80 D3
Basarabeasca, *Moldova* .. 41 J5
Basawa, *Afghan.* 62 B4
Bascharage, *Lux.* 17 J7
Bascuñán, C., *Chile* 126 B1
Basècles, *Belgium* 17 G3
Basel, *Switz.* 22 A5
Basel-Stadt □, *Switz.* ... 22 A5
Baselland □, *Switz.* 22 B5
Basento →, *Italy* 35 B9
Bāshī, *Iran* 65 D6
Bashi Channel, *Phil.* 54 D7
Bashkir Republic =
  Bashkortostan □, *Russia* 44 D6
Bashkortostan □, *Russia* . 44 D6
Basilan, *Phil.* 55 H5
Basilan Str., *Phil.* 55 H5
Basildon, *U.K.* 13 F8
Basilicata □, *Italy* 35 B9
Basim = Washim, *India* . 60 J10
Basin, *U.S.A.* 110 D9
Basingstoke, *U.K.* 13 F6
Baška, *Croatia* 33 D11
Başkale, *Turkey* 67 C10
Baskatong, Rés., *Canada* . 98 C4
Basle = Basel, *Switz.* ... 22 A5
Basoda, *India* 62 H7
Basodino, *Switz.* 23 D6
Basoka, *Zaïre* 82 B1
Basongo, *Zaïre* 80 E4
Basque, Pays, *France* ... 26 E2
Basque Provinces = País
  Vasco □, *Spain* 28 C2
Basra = Al Başrah, *Iraq* . 64 D5
Bass Rock, *U.K.* 14 E6
Bass Str., *Australia* 90 F4
Bassano, *Canada* 100 C6
Bassano del Grappa, *Italy* 33 C8
Bassar, *Togo* 79 D5
Bassas da India, *Ind. Oc.* 81 J7
Basse Santa-Su, *Gambia* . 78 C2
Basse-Terre, *Guadeloupe* . 117 C7
Bassecourt, *Switz.* 22 B4
Bassein, *Burma* 61 L19
Basseterre,
  St. Christopher-Nevis . 117 C7
Bassett, *Nebr., U.S.A.* .. 108 D5
Bassett, *Va., U.S.A.* 105 G6
Basseveld, *Belgium* 17 F3
Bassi, *India* 62 D7
Bassigny, *France* 25 E12
Bassikounou, *Mauritania* . 78 B3
Bassilly, *Belgium* 17 G3
Bassum, *Germany* 18 C4
Båstad, *Sweden* 11 H6

Bastak, *Iran* 65 E7
Baştām, *Iran* 65 B7
Bastar, *India* 61 K12
Bastelica, *France* 27 F13
Basti, *India* 63 F10
Bastia, *France* 27 F13
Bastia Umbra, *Italy* 33 E9
Bastogne, *Belgium* 17 H7
Bastrop, *U.S.A.* 109 K6
Bat Yam, *Israel* 69 C3
Bata, *Eq. Guin.* 80 D1
Bata, *Romania* 38 C5
Bataan, *Phil.* 55 D4
Batabanó, *Cuba* 116 B3
Batabanó, G. de, *Cuba* ... 116 B3
Batac, *Phil.* 55 B4
Batagoy, *Russia* 45 C14
Batak, *Bulgaria* 39 H7
Batalha, *Portugal* 31 F2
Batama, *Zaïre* 82 B2
Batamay, *Russia* 45 C13
Batan I., *Phil.* 55 A4
Batanes Is., *Phil.* 55 A4
Batang, *China* 52 B2
Batang, *Indonesia* 57 G13
Batangafo, *C.A.R.* 73 G8
Batangas, *Phil.* 55 E4
Batanta, *Indonesia* 57 E8
Batatais, *Brazil* 127 A6
Batavia, *U.S.A.* 106 D6
Bataysk, *Russia* 43 G4
Batchelor, *Australia* 88 B5
Bateman's B., *Australia* .. 91 F5
Batemans Bay, *Australia* .. 91 F5
Bates Ra., *Australia* 89 E3
Batesburg, *U.S.A.* 105 J5
Batesville, *Ark., U.S.A.* .. 109 H9
Batesville, *Miss., U.S.A.* . 109 H10
Batesville, *Tex., U.S.A.* .. 109 L5
Bath, *U.K.* 13 F5
Bath, *Maine, U.S.A.* 99 D6
Bath, *N.Y., U.S.A.* 106 D7
Batheay, *Cambodia* 59 G5
Bathgate, *U.K.* 14 F5
Bathmen, *Neths.* 16 D8
Bathurst = Banjul, *Gambia* 78 C1
Bathurst, *Australia* 91 E4
Bathurst, *Canada* 99 C6
Bathurst, *S. Africa* 84 E4
Bathurst, C., *Canada* 96 A7
Bathurst B., *Australia* 90 A3
Bathurst Harb., *Australia* . 90 G4
Bathurst I., *Australia* 88 B5
Bathurst I., *Canada* 4 B2
Bathurst Inlet, *Canada* ... 96 B9
Batie, *Burkina Faso* 78 D4
Batlow, *Australia* 91 F4
Batman, *Turkey* 67 D9
Batna, *Algeria* 75 A6
Batobato, *Phil.* 55 H7
Batoka, *Zambia* 83 F2
Baton Rouge, *U.S.A.* 109 K9
Batong, Ko, *Thailand* 59 J2
Batopilas, *Mexico* 114 B3
Batouri, *Cameroon* 80 D2
Båtsfjord, *Norway* 8 A23
Battambang, *Cambodia* ... 58 F4
Batticaloa, *Sri Lanka* 60 R12
Battice, *Belgium* 17 G7
Battipáglia, *Italy* 35 B7
Battle, *U.K.* 13 G8
Battle →, *Canada* 101 C7
Battle Camp, *Australia* ... 90 B3
Battle Creek, *U.S.A.* 104 D3
Battle Ground, *U.S.A.* 112 E4
Battle Harbour, *Canada* .. 99 B8
Battle Lake, *U.S.A.* 108 B7
Battle Mountain, *U.S.A.* .. 110 F5
Battlefields, *Zimbabwe* ... 83 F2
Battleford, *Canada* 101 C7
Battonya, *Hungary* 21 J11
Batu, *Ethiopia* 68 F2
Batu, Kepulauan, *Indonesia* 56 E1
Batu Caves, *Malaysia* 59 L3
Batu Gajah, *Malaysia* 59 K3
Batu Is. = Batu,
  Kepulauan, *Indonesia* .. 56 E1
Batu Pahat, *Malaysia* 59 M4
Batuata, *Indonesia* 57 F6
Batumi, *Georgia* 43 K5
Baturaja, *Indonesia* 56 E2
Baturité, *Brazil* 122 B4
Bau, *Malaysia* 56 D4
Baubau, *Indonesia* 57 F6
Bauchi, *Nigeria* 79 C6
Bauchi □, *Nigeria* 79 C6
Baud, *France* 24 E3
Baudette, *U.S.A.* 108 A7
Baudour, *Belgium* 17 H3
Bauer, C., *Australia* 91 E1
Baugé, *France* 24 E6
Bauhinia Downs, *Australia* 90 C4
Baukau, *Indonesia* 57 F7
Bauma, *Switz.* 23 B7
Baume-les-Dames, *France* 25 E13
Baunatal, *Germany* 18 D5
Baunei, *Italy* 34 B2
Baures, *Bolivia* 125 C5
Bauru, *Brazil* 127 A6
Baús, *Brazil* 125 D7
Bauska, *Latvia* 9 H21
Bautino, *Kazakhstan* 43 H10
Bautzen, *Germany* 18 D10
Bavānāt, *Iran* 65 D7
Bavaria = Bayern □,
  Germany 19 F7
Båven, *Sweden* 10 F10

Bavi Sadri, *India* 62 G6
Bavispe →, *Mexico* 114 B3
Bawdwin, *Burma* 61 H20
Bawean, *Indonesia* 56 F4
Bawku, *Ghana* 79 C4
Bawlake, *Burma* 61 K20
Bawolung, *China* 52 C3
Baxley, *U.S.A.* 105 K4
Baxoi, *China* 52 B1
Baxter Springs, *U.S.A.* ... 109 G7
Bay, L. de, *Phil.* 57 B6
Bay Bulls, *Canada* 99 C9
Bay City, *Mich., U.S.A.* .. 104 D4
Bay City, *Oreg., U.S.A.* .. 110 D2
Bay City, *Tex., U.S.A.* ... 109 L7
Bay de Verde, *Canada* ... 99 C9
Bay Minette, *U.S.A.* 105 K2
Bay St. Louis, *U.S.A.* 109 K10
Bay Springs, *U.S.A.* 109 K10
Bay View, *N.Z.* 87 H6
Baya, *Zaïre* 83 E2
Bayamo, *Cuba* 116 B4
Bayamón, *Puerto Rico* ... 117 C6
Bayan Har Shan, *China* .. 54 C4
Bayan Hot = Alxa Zuoqi,
  China 50 E3
Bayan Obo, *China* 50 D5
Bayan-Ovoo, *Mongolia* ... 50 C4
Bayana, *India* 62 F7
Bayanaūyl, *Kazakhstan* ... 44 D8
Bayandalay, *Mongolia* 50 C2
Bayanhongor, *Mongolia* .. 54 B5
Bayard, *U.S.A.* 108 E3
Bayawan, *Phil.* 55 G5
Baybay, *Phil.* 55 F6
Bayburt, *Turkey* 67 B9
Bayerischer Wald,
  Germany 19 F8
Bayern □, *Germany* 19 F7
Bayeux, *France* 24 C6
Bayfield, *Canada* 106 C3
Bayfield, *U.S.A.* 108 B9
Bayındır, *Turkey* 66 C2
Baykal, Oz., *Russia* 45 D11
Baykit, *Russia* 45 C10
Baykonur = Bayqongyr,
  Kazakhstan 44 E7
Baynes Mts., *Namibia* 84 B1
Bayombong, *Phil.* 55 C4
Bayon, *France* 25 D13
Bayona, *Spain* 30 C2
Bayonne, *France* 26 E2
Bayonne, *U.S.A.* 107 F10
Bayovar, *Peru* 124 B1
Bayqongyr, *Kazakhstan* .. 44 E7
Bayram-Ali = Bayramaly,
  Turkmenistan 44 F7
Bayramaly, *Turkmenistan* . 44 F7
Bayramiç, *Turkey* 66 C2
Bayreuth, *Germany* 19 F7
Bayrischzell, *Germany* ... 19 H8
Bayrūt, *Lebanon* 69 B4
Bayt Lahm, *West Bank* ... 69 D4
Baytown, *U.S.A.* 109 L7
Bayzo, *Niger* 79 C5
Baza, *Spain* 29 H2
Bazar Dyuzi, *Russia* 43 K8
Bazardüzü = Bazar Dyuzi,
  Russia 43 K8
Bazarny Karabulak, *Russia* 42 D8
Bazarnyy Syzgan, *Russia* . 42 D8
Bazaruto, I. do, *Mozam.* . 85 C6
Bazas, *France* 26 D3
Bazhong, *China* 52 B6
Bazmān, Kūh-e, *Iran* 65 D9
Beach, *U.S.A.* 108 B3
Beach City, *U.S.A.* 106 F3
Beachport, *Australia* 91 F2
Beachy Hd., *U.K.* 13 G8
Beacon, *Australia* 89 F2
Beacon, *U.S.A.* 107 E11
Beaconia, *Canada* 101 C9
Beagle, Canal, *S. Amer.* . 128 E3
Beagle Bay, *Australia* 88 C3
Bealanana, *Madag.* 85 A8
Beamsville, *Canada* 106 C5
Bear →, *U.S.A.* 112 G5
Béar, C., *France* 26 F7
Bear I., *Ireland* 15 E2
Bear L., *B.C., Canada* ... 100 B3
Bear L., *Man., Canada* ... 101 B9
Bear L., *U.S.A.* 110 E8
Bearcreek, *U.S.A.* 110 D9
Beardmore, *Canada* 98 C2
Beardmore Glacier,
  Antarctica 5 E11
Beardstown, *U.S.A.* 108 F9
Béarn, *France* 26 E3
Bearpaw Mts., *U.S.A.* ... 110 B9
Bearskin Lake, *Canada* ... 98 B1
Beas de Segura, *Spain* ... 29 G2
Beasain, *Spain* 28 B2
Beata, C., *Dom. Rep.* 117 C5
Beata, I., *Dom. Rep.* 117 C5
Beatrice, *U.S.A.* 108 E6
Beatrice, *Zimbabwe* 83 F3
Beatrice, C., *Australia* ... 90 A2
Beatton →, *Canada* 100 B4
Beatton River, *Canada* ... 100 B4
Beatty, *U.S.A.* 111 H5
Beaucaire, *France* 27 E8
Beauce, Plaine de la,
  France 25 D8
Beauceville, *Canada* 99 C5
Beauchêne, I., *Falk. Is.* . 128 D5
Beaudesert, *Australia* 91 D5
Beaufort, *Malaysia* 56 C5

Beaufort, *N.C., U.S.A.* ... 105 H7
Beaufort, *S.C., U.S.A.* ... 105 J5
Beaufort Sea, *Arctic* 4 B1
Beaufort West, *S. Africa* . 84 E3
Beaugency, *France* 25 E8
Beauharnois, *Canada* 98 C5
Beaujeu, *France* 27 B8
Beaulieu →, *Canada* 100 A6
Beaulieu-sur-Dordogne,
  France 26 D5
Beaulieu-sur-Mer, *France* . 27 E11
Beauly, *U.K.* 14 D4
Beauly →, *U.K.* 14 D4
Beaumaris, *U.K.* 12 D3
Beaumetz-lès-Loges, *France* 25 B9
Beaumont, *Belgium* 17 H4
Beaumont, *France* 26 D4
Beaumont, *Calif., U.S.A.* . 113 M10
Beaumont, *Tex., U.S.A.* .. 109 K7
Beaumont-de-Lomagne,
  France 26 E4
Beaumont-le-Roger, *France* 24 C7
Beaumont-sur-Oise, *France* 25 C9
Beaumont-sur-Sarthe,
  France 24 D7
Beaune, *France* 25 E11
Beaune-la-Rolande, *France* 25 D9
Beaupréau, *France* 24 E6
Beauraing, *Belgium* 17 H5
Beauséjour, *Canada* 101 C9
Beauvais, *France* 25 C9
Beauval, *Canada* 101 B7
Beauvoir-sur-Mer, *France* . 24 F4
Beauvoir-sur-Niort, *France* 26 B3
Beaver, *Alaska, U.S.A.* ... 96 B5
Beaver, *Okla., U.S.A.* 109 G4
Beaver, *Pa., U.S.A.* 106 F4
Beaver, *Utah, U.S.A.* 111 G7
Beaver →, *B.C., Canada* . 100 B4
Beaver →, *Ont., Canada* . 98 A2
Beaver →, *Sask., Canada* 101 B7
Beaver City, *U.S.A.* 108 E5
Beaver Dam, *U.S.A.* 108 D10
Beaver Falls, *U.S.A.* 106 F4
Beaver Hill L., *Canada* ... 101 C10
Beaver I., *U.S.A.* 104 C3
Beaverhill L., *Alta.,
  Canada* 100 C6
Beaverhill L., *N.W.T.,
  Canada* 101 A8
Beaverlodge, *Canada* 100 B5
Beavermouth, *Canada* 100 C5
Beaverstone →, *Canada* . 98 B2
Beaverton, *Canada* 106 B5
Beaverton, *U.S.A.* 112 E4
Beawar, *India* 62 F6
Bebedouro, *Brazil* 127 A6
Beboa, *Madag.* 85 B7
Bebra, *Germany* 18 E5
Beccles, *U.K.* 13 E9
Bečej, *Serbia, Yug.* 21 K10
Becerreá, *Spain* 30 C3
Béchar, *Algeria* 75 B4
Beckley, *U.S.A.* 104 G5
Beckum, *Germany* 18 D4
Bečva →, *Czech.* 20 F7
Bédar, *Spain* 29 H3
Bédarieux, *France* 26 E7
Bédarrides, *France* 27 D8
Beddouza, Ras, *Morocco* . 74 B3
Bedele, *Ethiopia* 77 F4
Bederkesa, *Germany* 18 B4
Bedeso, *Ethiopia* 77 F5
Bedford, *Canada* 98 C5
Bedford, *S. Africa* 84 E4
Bedford, *U.K.* 13 E7
Bedford, *Ind., U.S.A.* 104 F2
Bedford, *Iowa, U.S.A.* ... 108 E7
Bedford, *Ohio, U.S.A.* ... 106 E3
Bedford, *Pa., U.S.A.* 106 F6
Bedford, *Va., U.S.A.* 104 G6
Bedford, C., *Australia* ... 90 B4
Bedford Downs, *Australia* . 88 C4
Bedfordshire □, *U.K.* 13 E7
Będków, *Poland* 20 D9
Bednja →, *Croatia* 33 B13
Bednodemyanovsk, *Russia* 42 D6
Bedónia, *Italy* 32 D6
Bedourie, *Australia* 90 C2
Bedretto, *Switz.* 23 C7
Bedum, *Neths.* 16 B9
Będzin, *Poland* 20 E9
Beech Grove, *U.S.A.* 104 F2
Beechy, *Canada* 101 C7
Beek, *Gelderland, Neths.* . 16 E8
Beek, *Limburg, Neths.* ... 17 G7
Beek, *Noord-Brabant,
  Neths.* 16 E7
Beekbergen, *Neths.* 16 D7
Beelitz, *Germany* 18 C8
Beenleigh, *Australia* 91 D5
Be'er Menuḥa, *Israel* 64 D2
Be'er Sheva, *Israel* 69 D3
Beersheba = Be'er Sheva,
  Israel 69 D3
Beerta, *Neths.* 16 B10
Beerze →, *Neths.* 16 E6
Beesd, *Neths.* 16 E6
Beeskow, *Germany* 18 C10
Beeston, *U.K.* 12 E6
Beetaloo, *Australia* 90 B1
Beetsterzwaag, *Neths.* ... 16 B8
Beetzendorf, *Germany* ... 18 C7
Beeville, *U.S.A.* 109 L6
Befale, *Zaïre* 80 D4
Befandriana, *Madag.* 85 C7
Befotaka, *Madag.* 85 C8

Bega, *Australia* 91 F4
Bega, Canalul, *Romania* .. 38 D3
Bégard, *France* 24 D3
Bègles, *France* 26 D3
Begna →, *Norway* 10 D4
Begonte, *Spain* 30 B3
Begusarai, *India* 63 G12
Behbehān, *Iran* 65 D6
Behara, *Madag.* 85 C8
Behshahr, *Iran* 65 B7
Bei Jiang →, *China* 53 F9
Bei'an, *China* 54 B7
Beibei, *China* 54 D5
Beigang, *Taiwan* 53 F13
Beihai, *China* 52 G7
Beijing, *China* 50 E9
Beijing □, *China* 50 E9
Beilen, *Neths.* 16 C8
Beiliu, *China* 53 F8
Beilngries, *Germany* 19 F7
Beilpajah, *Australia* 91 E3
Beilul, *Eritrea* 77 E5
Beinn na Faoghla =
  Benbecula, *U.K.* 14 D1
Beipiao, *China* 51 D11
Beira, *Mozam.* 83 F3
Beirut = Bayrūt, *Lebanon* 69 B4
Beitaolaizhao, *China* 51 B13
Beitbridge, *Zimbabwe* ... 83 G3
Beiuş, *Romania* 38 C5
Beizhen, *Liaoning, China* . 51 D11
Beizhen, *Shandong, China* 51 F10
Beizhengzhen, *China* 51 B12
Beja, *Portugal* 31 G3
Béja, *Tunisia* 75 A6
Beja □, *Portugal* 31 H3
Bejaia, *Algeria* 75 A6
Béjar, *Spain* 30 E5
Bejestān, *Iran* 65 C8
Bekaa Valley = Al Biqā □,
  Lebanon 69 A5
Bekasi, *Indonesia* 57 G12
Békés, *Hungary* 21 J11
Békéscsaba, *Hungary* 21 J11
Bekily, *Madag.* 85 C8
Bekoji, *Ethiopia* 77 F4
Bekok, *Malaysia* 59 L4
Bekwai, *Ghana* 79 D4
Bela, *India* 63 G9
Bela, *Pakistan* 62 F2
Bela Crkva, *Serbia, Yug.* . 21 L11
Bela Palanka, *Serbia, Yug.* 21 M12
Bela Vista, *Brazil* 126 A4
Bela Vista, *Mozam.* 85 D5
Belalcázar, *Spain* 31 G5
Belarus ■, *Europe* 40 F4
Belau ■, *Pac. Oc.* 92 G5
Belavenona, *Madag.* 85 C8
Belawan, *Indonesia* 56 D1
Belaya, *Ethiopia* 77 E4
Belaya →, *Russia* 34 A10
Belaya Glina, *Russia* 43 G5
Belaya Kalitva, *Russia* ... 43 F5
Belaya Tserkov = Bila
  Tserkva, *Ukraine* 41 H6
Belcher Is., *Canada* 97 C12
Belchite, *Spain* 28 D4
Belden, *U.S.A.* 112 E5
Belém, *Brazil* 122 B2
Belém de São Francisco,
  Brazil 122 C4
Belén, *Argentina* 126 B2
Belén, *Colombia* 120 C2
Belén, *Paraguay* 126 A4
Belen, *U.S.A.* 111 J10
Beleni, *Turkey* 66 D7
Bélesta, *France* 26 F5
Belet Uen, *Somali Rep.* .. 68 G4
Belev, *Russia* 42 D3
Belfair, *U.S.A.* 112 C4
Belfast, *S. Africa* 85 D5
Belfast, *U.K.* 15 B6
Belfast, *Maine, U.S.A.* ... 99 D6
Belfast, *N.Y., U.S.A.* 106 D6
Belfast □, *U.K.* 15 B6
Belfast L., *U.K.* 15 B6
Belfeld, *Neths.* 17 F8
Belfield, *U.S.A.* 108 B3
Belfort, *France* 25 E13
Belfort, Territoire de □,
  France 25 E13
Belfry, *U.S.A.* 110 D9
Belgaum, *India* 60 M9
Belgioioso, *Italy* 32 C6
Belgium ■, *Europe* 17 G5
Belgorod, *Russia* 42 E3
Belgorod-Dnestrovskiy =
  Bilhorod-Dnivstrovskyy,
  Ukraine 41 J6
Belgrade = Beograd,
  Serbia, Yug. 21 L10
Belgrade, *U.S.A.* 110 D8
Belhaven, *U.S.A.* 105 H7
Beli Drim →, *Europe* 21 N10
Beli Manastir, *Croatia* ... 21 K8
Belice →, *Italy* 34 E5
Belin-Béliet, *France* 26 D3
Belinga, *Gabon* 80 D2
Belinskiy, *Russia* 42 D6
Belinyu, *Indonesia* 56 E3
Beliton Is. = Belitung,
  Indonesia 56 E3
Belitung, *Indonesia* 56 E3
Beliu, *Romania* 38 C5
Belize ■, *Cent. Amer.* ... 115 D7

Belize City, *Belize* 115 D7
Beljanica, *Serbia, Yug.* .. 21 L11
Belkovskiy, Ostrov, *Russia* 45 B14
Bell →, *Canada* 98 C4
Bell Bay, *Australia* 90 G4
Bell I., *Canada* 99 B8
Bell-Irving →, *Canada* ... 100 B3
Bell Peninsula, *Canada* .. 97 B11
Bell Ville, *Argentina* 126 C3
Bella Bella, *Canada* 100 C3
Bella Coola, *Canada* 100 C3
Bella Flor, *Bolivia* 124 C4
Bella Unión, *Uruguay* ... 126 C4
Bella Vista, *Corrientes,
  Argentina* 126 B4
Bella Vista, *Tucuman,
  Argentina* 126 B2
Bellac, *France* 26 B5
Bellágio, *Italy* 32 C6
Bellaire, *U.S.A.* 106 F4
Bellary, *India* 60 M10
Bellata, *Australia* 91 D4
Belle Fourche, *U.S.A.* ... 108 C3
Belle Fourche →, *U.S.A.* 108 C3
Belle Glade, *U.S.A.* 105 M5
Belle-Ile, *France* 24 E3
Belle Isle, *Canada* 99 B8
Belle Isle, Str. of, *Canada* 99 B8
Belle-Isle-en-Terre, *France* 24 D3
Belle Plaine, *Iowa, U.S.A.* 108 E8
Belle Plaine, *Minn., U.S.A.* 108 C8
Belle Yella, *Liberia* 78 D3
Belledonne, Chaîne de,
  France 27 C10
Belledune, *Canada* 99 C6
Bellefontaine, *U.S.A.* 104 E4
Bellefonte, *U.S.A.* 106 F7
Bellegarde, *France* 25 E9
Bellegarde-en-Marche,
  France 26 C6
Bellegarde-sur-Valserine,
  France 27 B9
Bellême, *France* 24 D7
Belleoram, *Canada* 99 C8
Belleville, *Canada* 98 D4
Belleville, *France* 27 B8
Belleville, *Ill., U.S.A.* ... 108 F10
Belleville, *Kans., U.S.A.* . 108 F6
Belleville, *N.Y., U.S.A.* .. 107 C8
Belleville-sur-Vie, *France* . 24 F5
Bellevue, *Canada* 100 D6
Bellevue, *Idaho, U.S.A.* .. 110 E6
Bellevue, *Ohio, U.S.A.* .. 106 E2
Bellevue, *Wash., U.S.A.* . 112 C4
Belley, *France* 27 C9
Bellin = Kangirsuk,
  Canada 97 B13
Bellingen, *Australia* 91 E5
Bellingham, *U.S.A.* 112 B4
Bellingshausen Sea,
  Antarctica 5 C17
Bellinzona, *Switz.* 23 D8
Bello, *Colombia* 120 B2
Bellows Falls, *U.S.A.* 107 C12
Bellpat, *Pakistan* 62 E3
Bellpuig, *Spain* 28 D6
Belluno, *Italy* 33 B9
Bellville, *U.S.A.* 109 L6
Bellwood, *U.S.A.* 106 F6
Bélmez, *Spain* 31 G5
Belmont, *Australia* 91 E5
Belmont, *Canada* 106 D3
Belmont, *S. Africa* 84 D3
Belmont, *U.S.A.* 106 D6
Belmonte, *Brazil* 123 E4
Belmonte, *Portugal* 30 E3
Belmonte, *Spain* 28 F2
Belmopan, *Belize* 115 D7
Belmullet, *Ireland* 15 B2
Belo Horizonte, *Brazil* ... 123 E3
Belo Jardim, *Brazil* 122 C4
Belo-sur-Mer, *Madag.* ... 85 C7
Belo-Tsiribihina, *Madag.* . 85 B7
Belogorsk = Bilohirsk,
  Ukraine 41 K8
Belogorsk, *Russia* 45 D13
Belogradchik, *Bulgaria* ... 38 F5
Beloha, *Madag.* 85 D8
Beloit, *Kans., U.S.A.* 108 F5
Beloit, *Wis., U.S.A.* 108 D10
Belokorovichi, *Ukraine* ... 41 G5
Belomorsk, *Russia* 44 C4
Belonia, *India* 61 H17
Belopolye = Bilopillya,
  Ukraine 41 G8
Belorechensk, *Russia* 43 H4
Belorussia = Belarus ■,
  Europe 40 F4
Belovo, *Russia* 44 D9
Belovodsk, *Ukraine* 41 H10
Beloye, Ozero, *Russia* ... 40 B9
Beloye More, *Russia* 44 C4
Belozersk, *Russia* 40 B9
Belpasso, *Italy* 35 E7
Belsele, *Belgium* 17 F4
Belsito, *Italy* 34 E6
Beltana, *Australia* 91 E2
Belterra, *Brazil* 121 D7
Belton, *S.C., U.S.A.* 105 H4
Belton, *Tex., U.S.A.* 109 K6
Belton Res., *U.S.A.* 109 K6
Beltsy = Bălți, *Moldova* . 41 J4
Belturbet, *Ireland* 15 B4
Belukha, *Russia* 44 E9
Beluran, *Malaysia* 56 C5
Belvedere Maríttimo, *Italy* 35 C8

Belvès, France 26 D5
Belvidere, Ill., U.S.A. .. 108 D10
Belvidere, N.J., U.S.A. .. 107 F9
Belvis de la Jara, Spain ... 31 F6
Belyando →, Australia ... 90 C4
Belyy, Russia 40 E7
Belyy, Ostrov, Russia ... 44 B8
Belyy Yar, Russia 44 D9
Belzig, Germany 18 C8
Belzoni, U.S.A. 109 J9
Bemaraha, Lembalemban'i, Madag. 85 B7
Bemarivo, Madag. 85 C7
Bemarivo →, Madag. 85 B8
Bemavo, Madag. 85 C8
Bembéréke, Benin 79 C5
Bembesi, Zimbabwe 83 F2
Bembesi →, Zimbabwe .. 83 F2
Bembézar →, Spain 31 H5
Bemidji, U.S.A. 108 B7
Bemmel, Neths. 16 E7
Ben, Iran 65 C6
Ben Cruachan, U.K. 14 E3
Ben Dearg, U.K. 14 D4
Ben Gardane, Tunisia ... 75 B7
Ben Hope, U.K. 14 C4
Ben Lawers, U.K. 14 E4
Ben Lomond, N.S.W., Australia 91 E5
Ben Lomond, Tas., Australia 90 G4
Ben Lomond, U.K. 14 E4
Ben Luc, Vietnam 59 G6
Ben Macdhui, U.K. 14 D5
Ben Mhor, U.K. 14 D1
Ben More, Central, U.K. . 14 E4
Ben More, Strath., U.K. . 14 E2
Ben More Assynt, U.K. .. 14 C4
Ben Nevis, U.K. 14 E4
Ben Quang, Vietnam 58 D6
Ben Slimane, Morocco .. 74 B3
Ben Tre, Vietnam 59 G6
Ben Vorlich, U.K. 14 E4
Ben Wyvis, U.K. 14 D4
Bena, Nigeria 79 C6
Bena Dibele, Zaïre 80 E4
Benāb, Iran 67 D12
Benagalbón, Spain 31 J6
Benagerie, Australia 91 E3
Benahmed, Morocco 74 B3
Benalla, Australia 91 F4
Benambra, Mt., Australia . 91 F4
Benamejí, Spain 31 H6
Benares = Varanasi, India 63 G10
Bénat, C., France 27 E10
Benavente, Portugal 31 G2
Benavente, Spain 30 C5
Benavides, Spain 30 C5
Benavides, U.S.A. 109 M5
Benbecula, U.K. 14 D1
Benbonyathe, Australia .. 91 E2
Bencubbin, Australia 89 F2
Bend, U.S.A. 110 D3
Bender Beila, Somali Rep. 68 F5
Bendering, Australia 89 F2
Bendery = Tighina, Moldova 41 J5
Bendigo, Australia 91 F3
Bendorf, Germany 18 E3
Benē Beraq, Israel 69 C3
Beneden Knijpe, Neths. .. 16 C7
Benedictinos, Brazil 122 C3
Benedito Leite, Brazil ... 122 C3
Bénéna, Mali 78 C4
Benenitra, Madag. 85 C8
Benešov, Czech. 20 F4
Bénestroff, France 25 D13
Benet, France 26 B3
Benevento, Italy 35 A7
Benfeld, France 25 D14
Benga, Mozam. 83 F3
Bengal, Bay of, Ind. Oc. . 61 K16
Bengbu, China 51 H9
Benghazi = Banghāzī, Libya 73 B9
Bengkalis, Indonesia ... 56 D2
Bengkulu, Indonesia ... 56 E2
Bengkulu □, Indonesia ... 56 E2
Bengough, Canada 101 D7
Benguela, Angola 81 G2
Benguerir, Morocco 74 B3
Benguérua, I., Mozam. .. 85 C6
Benha, Egypt 76 H7
Beni, Zaïre 82 B2
Beni □, Bolivia 125 C4
Beni →, Bolivia 125 C4
Beni-Abbès, Algeria 75 B4
Beni-Haoua, Algeria 75 A5
Beni Mazâr, Egypt 76 J7
Beni Mellal, Morocco ... 74 B3
Beni Ounif, Algeria 75 B4
Beni Saf, Algeria 75 A4
Beni Suef, Egypt 76 J7
Beniah L., Canada 100 A6
Benicarló, Spain 28 E5
Benicia, U.S.A. 112 G4
Benidorm, Spain 29 G4
Benidorm, Islote de, Spain 29 G4
Benin ■, Africa 79 D5
Benin, Bight of, W. Afr. .. 79 D5
Benin City, Nigeria 79 D6
Benisa, Spain 29 G5
Benitses, Greece 37 A3
Benjamin Aceval, Paraguay 126 A4
Benjamin Constant, Brazil 120 D3
Benjamin Hill, Mexico .. 114 A2
Benkelman, U.S.A. 108 E4

Benkovac, Croatia 33 D12
Benlidi, Australia 90 C3
Bennebroek, Neths. 16 D5
Bennekom, Neths. 16 D7
Bennett, Canada 100 B2
Bennett, L., Australia ... 88 D5
Bennett, Ostrov, Russia .. 45 B15
Bennettsville, U.S.A. ... 105 H6
Bennington, U.S.A. 107 D11
Bénodet, France 24 E2
Benoni, S. Africa 85 D4
Benoud, Algeria 75 B5
Benque Viejo, Belize ... 115 D7
Bensheim, Germany 19 F4
Benson, U.S.A. 111 L8
Bent, Iran 65 E8
Benteng, Indonesia 57 F6
Bentinck I., Australia ... 90 B2
Bentiu, Sudan 77 F2
Bento Gonçalves, Brazil . 127 B5
Benton, Ark., U.S.A. 109 H8
Benton, Calif., U.S.A. ... 112 H8
Benton, Ill., U.S.A. 108 F10
Benton Harbor, U.S.A. .. 104 D2
Bentu Liben, Ethiopia ... 77 F4
Bentung, Malaysia 59 L3
Benue □, Nigeria 79 D6
Benue →, Nigeria 79 D6
Benxi, China 51 D12
Benzdorp, Surinam 121 C7
Beo, Indonesia 57 D7
Beograd, Serbia, Yug. ... 21 L10
Beowawe, U.S.A. 110 F5
Bepan Jiang →, China ... 52 E6
Beppu, Japan 49 H5
Beqaa Valley = Al Biqā □, Lebanon 69 A5
Berati, Albania 39 J2
Berau, Teluk, Indonesia . 57 E8
Berber, Sudan 76 D3
Berbera, Somali Rep. ... 68 E4
Berbérati, C.A.R. 80 D3
Berberia, C. del, Spain .. 36 C7
Berbice →, Guyana 121 B6
Berceto, Italy 32 D7
Berchtesgaden, Germany . 19 H8
Berck-Plage, France 25 B8
Berdichev = Berdychiv, Ukraine 41 H5
Berdsk, Russia 44 D9
Berdyansk, Ukraine 41 J9
Berdychiv, Ukraine 41 H5
Berea, U.S.A. 104 G3
Berebere, Indonesia 57 D7
Bereda, Somali Rep. 68 E5
Berehove, Ukraine 41 H2
Berekum, Ghana 78 D4
Berenice, Egypt 76 C4
Berens →, Canada 101 C9
Berens I., Canada 101 C9
Berens River, Canada 101 C9
Berestechko, Ukraine ... 41 G3
Berești, Romania 38 C10
Beretău →, Romania ... 38 B4
Berettyo →, Hungary ... 21 J11
Berettyóújfalu, Hungary . 21 H11
Berevo, Mahajanga, Madag. 85 B7
Berevo, Toliara, Madag. .. 85 B7
Bereza, Belarus 41 F3
Berezhany, Ukraine 41 H3
Berezina = Byarezina →, Belarus 41 F6
Berezivka, Ukraine 41 J6
Berezna, Ukraine 41 G6
Berezniki, Russia 44 D6
Berezovo, Russia 44 C7
Berga, Spain 28 C6
Bergama, Turkey 66 C2
Bergambacht, Neths. ... 16 E5
Bérgamo, Italy 32 C6
Bergantiños, Spain 30 B2
Bergara, Spain 28 B2
Bergdorf, Germany 18 B6
Bergeijk, Neths. 17 F6
Bergen, Germany 18 A9
Bergen, Neths. 16 C5
Bergen, Norway 9 F11
Bergen, U.S.A. 106 C7
Bergen-op-Zoom, Neths. . 17 F4
Bergerac, France 26 D4
Bergheim, Germany 18 E2
Berghem, Neths. 16 E7
Bergisch Gladbach, Germany 18 E3
Bergschenhoek, Neths. .. 16 E5
Bergsjö, Sweden 10 C11
Bergues, France 25 B9
Bergum, Neths. 16 B7
Bergville, S. Africa 85 D4
Berhala, Selat, Indonesia . 56 E2
Berhampore = Baharampur, India ... 63 G13
Berhampur, India 61 K14
Berheci →, Romania ... 38 C10
Bering Sea, Pac. Oc. 96 C1
Bering Strait, U.S.A. 96 B3
Beringen, Belgium 17 F6
Beringen, Switz. 23 A7
Beringovskiy, Russia ... 45 C18
Berisso, Argentina 126 C4
Berja, Spain 29 J2
Berkane, Morocco 75 B4
Berkel →, Neths. 16 D8
Berkeley, U.K. 13 F5
Berkeley, U.S.A. 112 H4
Berkeley Springs, U.S.A. . 104 F6

Berkhout, Neths. 16 C5
Berkner I., Antarctica ... 5 D18
Berkovitsa, Bulgaria ... 38 F6
Berkshire □, U.K. 13 F6
Berlaar, Belgium 17 F5
Berlare, Belgium 17 F4
Berland →, Canada 100 C5
Berlanga, Spain 31 G5
Berlenga, I., Portugal ... 31 F1
Berlin, Germany 18 C9
Berlin, Md., U.S.A. 104 F8
Berlin, N.H., U.S.A. 107 B13
Berlin, Wis., U.S.A. 104 D1
Bermeja, Sierra, Spain .. 31 J5
Bermejo →, Formosa, Argentina 126 B4
Bermejo →, San Juan, Argentina 126 C2
Bermeo, Spain 28 B2
Bermillo de Sayago, Spain 30 D4
Bermuda ■, Atl. Oc. ... 2 C6
Bern, Switz. 22 C4
Bern □, Switz. 22 C5
Bernado, U.S.A. 111 J10
Bernalda, Italy 35 B9
Bernalillo, U.S.A. 111 J10
Bernardo de Irigoyen, Argentina 127 B5
Bernardo O'Higgins □, Chile 126 C1
Bernasconi, Argentina ... 126 D3
Bernau, Bayern, Germany . 19 H8
Bernau, Brandenburg, Germany 18 C9
Bernay, France 24 C7
Bernburg, Germany 18 D7
Berne = Bern, Switz. ... 22 C4
Berne = Bern □, Switz. . 22 C5
Berner Alpen, Switz. ... 22 D5
Bernese Oberland = Oberland, Switz. 22 C5
Bernier I., Australia 89 D1
Bernina, Piz, Switz. 23 D9
Bernina, Pizzo, Switz. .. 23 D9
Bernkastel-Kues, Germany 19 F3
Beroroha, Madag. 85 C8
Béroubouay, Benin 79 C5
Beroun, Czech. 20 F4
Berounka →, Czech. ... 20 F4
Berovo, Macedonia 39 H5
Berrahal, Algeria 75 A6
Berre, Étang de, France .. 27 E9
Berrechid, Morocco 74 B3
Berri, Australia 91 E3
Berriane, Algeria 75 B5
Berrouaghia, Algeria ... 75 A5
Berry, Australia 91 E5
Berry, France 25 F8
Berry Is., Bahamas 116 A4
Berryessa L., U.S.A. 112 G4
Berryville, U.S.A. 109 G8
Bersenbrück, Germany .. 18 C3
Bershad, Ukraine 41 H5
Berthold, U.S.A. 108 A4
Berthoud, U.S.A. 108 E2
Bertincourt, France 25 B9
Bertoua, Cameroon 80 D2
Bertrand, U.S.A. 108 E5
Bertrange, Lux. 17 J8
Bertrix, Belgium 17 J6
Beruri, Brazil 121 D5
Berwick, U.S.A. 107 E8
Berwick-upon-Tweed, U.K. 12 B5
Berwyn Mts., U.K. 12 E4
Beryslav, Ukraine 41 J7
Berzasca, Romania 38 E4
Besal, Pakistan 63 B5
Besalampy, Madag. 85 B7
Besançon, France 25 E13
Besar, Indonesia 56 E5
Beshenkovichi, Belarus . 40 E5
Besnard L., Canada 101 B7
Besni, Turkey 66 D7
Besor, N. →, Egypt 69 D3
Bessarabiya, Moldova ... 41 J5
Bessarabka = Basarabeasca, Moldova . 41 J5
Bessèges, France 27 D8
Bessemer, Ala., U.S.A. .. 105 J2
Bessemer, Mich., U.S.A. . 108 B9
Bessin, France 24 C5
Bessines-sur-Gartempe, France 26 B5
Best, Neths. 17 E6
Bet She'an, Israel 69 C4
Bet Shemesh, Israel 69 D3
Bet Tadjine, Djebel, Algeria 74 C4
Betafo, Madag. 85 B8
Betancuria, Canary Is. .. 36 F5
Betanzos, Bolivia 125 D4
Betanzos, Spain 30 B2
Bétaré Oya, Cameroon .. 80 C2
Bétera, Spain 28 F4
Bethal, S. Africa 85 D4
Bethanien, Namibia 84 D2
Bethany, U.S.A. 108 E7
Bethel, Alaska, U.S.A. .. 96 B3
Bethel, Vt., U.S.A. 107 C12
Bethel Park, U.S.A. 106 F4
Bethlehem = Bayt Laḥm, West Bank 69 D4
Bethlehem, S. Africa ... 85 D4
Bethlehem, U.S.A. 107 F9
Bethulie, S. Africa 84 E4

Béthune, France 25 B9
Béthune →, France 24 C8
Bethungra, Australia ... 91 E4
Betijoque, Venezuela ... 120 B3
Betim, Brazil 123 E3
Betioky, Madag. 85 C7
Beton-Bazoches, France . 25 D10
Betong, Thailand 59 K3
Betoota, Australia 90 D3
Betroka, Madag. 85 C8
Betsiamites, Canada ... 99 C6
Betsiamites →, Canada . 99 C6
Betsiboka →, Madag. .. 85 B8
Bettembourg, Lux. 17 J8
Bettiah, India 63 F11
Béttola, Italy 32 D6
Betul, India 60 J10
Betung, Malaysia 56 D4
Betzdorf, Germany 18 E3
Beuca, Romania 38 E7
Beulah, U.S.A. 108 B4
Beuvron →, France 24 E8
Beveren, Belgium 17 F4
Beverley, Australia 89 F2
Beverley, U.K. 12 D7
Beverlo, Belgium 17 F6
Beverly, Mass., U.S.A. .. 107 D14
Beverly, Wash., U.S.A. .. 110 C4
Beverly Hills, U.S.A. ... 113 L8
Beverwijk, Neths. 16 D5
Bex, Switz. 22 D4
Bey Dağları, Turkey 66 D4
Beya, Russia 45 D10
Beyānlū, Iran 64 C5
Beyin, Ghana 78 D4
Beyla, Guinea 78 D3
Beynat, France 26 C5
Beyneu, Kazakhstan ... 44 E6
Beypazarı, Turkey 66 C4
Beyşehir, Turkey 66 D4
Beyşehir Gölü, Turkey .. 66 D4
Beytüşşebap, Turkey ... 67 D10
Bezhetsk, Russia 42 B3
Bezhitsa, Russia 44 D4
Béziers, France 26 E7
Bezwada = Vijayawada, India 61 L12
Bhachau, India 60 H7
Bhadarwah, India 63 C6
Bhadra, India 60 N9
Bhadrakh, India 61 J15
Bhadravati, India 60 N9
Bhagalpur, India 63 G12
Bhakkar, Pakistan 62 D4
Bhakra Dam, India 62 D7
Bhamo, Burma 61 G20
Bhandara, India 60 J11
Bhanrer Ra., India 62 H8
Bharat = India ■, Asia . 60 K11
Bharatpur, India 62 F7
Bhatinda, India 62 D6
Bhatpara, India 63 H13
Bhaun, Pakistan 62 C5
Bhaunagar = Bhavnagar, India 62 J5
Bhavnagar, India 62 J5
Bhawanipatna, India ... 61 K12
Bhera, Pakistan 62 C5
Bhilsa = Vidisha, India . 62 H7
Bhilwara, India 62 G6
Bhima →, India 60 L10
Bhimavaram, India 61 L12
Bhimbar, Pakistan 63 C6
Bhind, India 63 F8
Bhiwandi, India 60 K8
Bhiwani, India 62 E7
Bhola, Bangla. 61 H17
Bhopal, India 62 H7
Bhubaneshwar, India ... 61 J14
Bhuj, India 62 H3
Bhumiphol Dam = Phumiphon, Khuan, Thailand 58 D2
Bhusaval, India 60 J9
Bhutan ■, Asia 61 F17
Biá →, Brazil 120 D4
Biafra, B. of = Bonny, Bight of, Africa 79 E6
Biak, Indonesia 57 E9
Biała →, Poland 20 E10
Biała Podlaska, Poland .. 20 C13
Białogard, Poland 20 A5
Białystok, Poland 20 B13
Biancavilla, Italy 35 E7
Biaro, Indonesia 57 D7
Biarritz, France 26 E2
Biasca, Switz. 23 D7
Biba, Egypt 76 J7
Bibai, Japan 48 C10
Bibala, Angola 81 G2
Bibane, Bahiret el, Tunisia 75 B7
Bibbiena, Italy 33 E8
Bibby I., Canada 101 A10
Biberach, Germany 19 G5
Biberist, Switz. 22 B5
Bibey →, Spain 30 C3
Bibiani, Ghana 78 D4
Biboohra, Australia 90 B4
Bibungwa, Zaïre 82 C2
Bic, Canada 99 C6
Bicaz, Romania 38 C9
Biccari, Italy 35 A8
Bichena, Ethiopia 77 E4
Bichvinta, Georgia 43 J5
Bickerton I., Australia .. 90 A2
Bicknell, Ind., U.S.A. .. 104 F2

Bicknell, Utah, U.S.A. ... 111 G8
Bida, Nigeria 79 D6
Bidar, India 60 L10
Biddeford, U.S.A. 99 D5
Biddwara, Ethiopia 77 F4
Bideford, U.K. 13 F3
Bidon 5 = Poste Maurice Cortier, Algeria 75 D5
Bidor, Malaysia 59 K3
Bié, Planalto de, Angola . 81 G3
Bieber, U.S.A. 110 F3
Biel, Switz. 22 B4
Bielawa, Poland 20 E6
Bielé Karpaty, Europe .. 20 F7
Bielefeld, Germany 18 C4
Bielersee, Switz. 22 B4
Biella, Italy 32 C5
Bielsk Podlaski, Poland . 20 C13
Bielsko-Biała, Poland .. 20 F9
Bien Hoa, Vietnam 59 G6
Bienfait, Canada 101 D8
Bienne = Biel, Switz. ... 22 B4
Bienvenida, Spain 31 G4
Bienvenue, Fr. Guiana .. 121 C7
Bienville, L., Canada ... 98 A5
Biescas, Spain 28 C4
Biese →, Germany 18 C7
Biesiesfontein, S. Africa . 84 E2
Bietigheim, Germany ... 19 G5
Bièvre, Belgium 17 J6
Biferno →, Italy 35 A8
Big →, Canada 99 B8
Big B., Canada 99 A7
Big Bear City, U.S.A. ... 113 L10
Big Bear Lake, U.S.A. .. 113 L10
Big Beaver, Canada 101 D7
Big Belt Mts., U.S.A. ... 110 C8
Big Bend, Swaziland ... 85 D5
Big Bend National Park, U.S.A. 109 L3
Big Black →, U.S.A. ... 109 J9
Big Blue →, U.S.A. 108 F6
Big Cr. →, Canada 100 C4
Big Creek, U.S.A. 112 H7
Big Cypress Swamp, U.S.A. 105 M5
Big Falls, U.S.A. 108 A8
Big Fork →, U.S.A. 108 A8
Big Horn Mts. = Bighorn Mts., U.S.A. 110 D10
Big Lake, U.S.A. 109 K4
Big Moose, U.S.A. 107 C10
Big Muddy Cr. →, U.S.A. 108 A2
Big Pine, U.S.A. 111 H4
Big Piney, U.S.A. 110 E8
Big Quill L., Canada ... 101 C8
Big Rapids, U.S.A. 104 D3
Big River, Canada 101 C7
Big Run, U.S.A. 106 F6
Big Sable Pt., U.S.A. ... 104 C2
Big Sand L., Canada ... 101 B9
Big Sandy, U.S.A. 110 B8
Big Sandy Cr. →, U.S.A. 108 F3
Big Sioux →, U.S.A. ... 108 D6
Big Spring, U.S.A. 109 J4
Big Springs, U.S.A. 108 E3
Big Stone City, U.S.A. .. 108 C6
Big Stone Gap, U.S.A. .. 105 G4
Big Stone L., U.S.A. ... 108 C6
Big Sur, U.S.A. 112 J5
Big Timber, U.S.A. 110 D9
Big Trout L., Canada ... 98 B1
Biğa, Turkey 66 B2
Bigadiç, Turkey 66 C3
Biganos, France 26 D3
Bigfork, U.S.A. 110 B6
Biggar, Canada 101 C7
Biggar, U.K. 14 F5
Bigge I., Australia 88 B4
Biggenden, Australia ... 91 D5
Biggs, U.S.A. 112 F5
Bighorn, U.S.A. 110 C10
Bighorn →, U.S.A. 110 C10
Bighorn Mts., U.S.A. ... 110 D10
Bignona, Senegal 78 C1
Bigorre, France 26 E4
Bigstone L., Canada 101 C9
Biguglia, Étang de, France 27 F13
Bigwa, Tanzania 82 D4
Bihać, Bos.-H. 33 D12
Bihar, India 63 G11
Bihar □, India 63 G11
Biharamulo, Tanzania .. 82 C3
Biharamulo □, Tanzania . 82 C3
Bihor, Munții, Romania . 38 C5
Bijagós, Arquipélago dos, Guinea-Biss. 78 C1
Bijaipur, India 62 F7
Bijapur, Karnataka, India 60 L9
Bijapur, Mad. P., India . 61 K12
Bijār, Iran 67 E12
Bijeljina, Bos.-H. 21 L9
Bijelo Polje, Montenegro, Yug. ... 21 M9
Bijie, China 52 D5
Bijnor, India 62 E8
Bikaner, India 62 E5
Bikapur, India 63 F10
Bikeqi, China 50 D6
Bikfayyā, Lebanon 69 B4
Bikin, Russia 45 E14
Bikini Atoll, Pac. Oc. ... 92 F8
Bikoué, Cameroon 79 E7
Bila Tserkva, Ukraine .. 41 H6
Bilara, India 62 F5
Bilaspur, Mad. P., India . 63 H10

Bilaspur, *Punjab, India* ... 62 D7
Biläsuvar, *Azerbaijan* 67 C13
Bilauk Taungdan, *Thailand* 58 F2
Bilbao, *Spain* 28 B2
Bilbeis, *Egypt* 76 H7
Bilbo = Bilbao, *Spain* ... 28 B2
Bilbor, *Romania* 38 B8
Bíldudalur, *Iceland* 8 D2
Bileća, *Bos.-H.* 21 N8
Bilecik, *Turkey* 66 B4
Bilgoraj, *Poland* 20 E12
Bilhorod-Dnivstrovskyy,
  Ukraine 41 J6
Bilibino, *Russia* 45 C17
Bilibiza, *Mozam.* 83 E5
Bilir, *Russia* 45 C14
Biliran I., *Phil.* 55 F6
Bill, *U.S.A.* 108 D2
Billabalong, *Australia* 89 E2
Billiluna, *Australia* 88 C4
Billingham, *U.K.* 12 C6
Billings, *U.S.A.* 110 D9
Billiton Is. = Belitung,
  Indonesia 56 E3
Billom, *France* 26 C7
Bilma, *Niger* 73 E7
Bilo Gora, *Croatia* 21 K7
Biloela, *Australia* 90 C5
Bilohirsk, *Ukraine* 41 K8
Biloku, *Guyana* 121 C6
Bilopillya, *Ukraine* 41 G8
Biloxi, *U.S.A.* 109 K10
Bilpa Morea Claypan,
  Australia 90 D2
Bilthoven, *Neths.* 16 D6
Biltine, *Chad* 73 F9
Bilyana, *Australia* 90 B4
Bilyarsk, *Russia* 42 C10
Bilzen, *Belgium* 17 G7
Bima, *Indonesia* 57 F5
Bimban, *Egypt* 76 C3
Bimbila, *Ghana* 79 D5
Bimbo, *C.A.R.* 80 D3
Bimini Is., *Bahamas* 116 A4
Bin Xian, *Heilongjiang,
  China* 51 B14
Bin Xian, *Shaanxi, China* . 50 G5
Bina-Etawah, *India* 62 G8
Bināb, *Iran* 67 D13
Binalbagan, *Phil.* 55 F5
Binalong, *Australia* 91 E4
Bīnālūd, Kūh-e, *Iran* 65 B8
Binatang, *Malaysia* 56 D4
Binbee, *Australia* 90 C4
Binche, *Belgium* 17 H4
Binchuan, *China* 52 E3
Binda, *Australia* 91 D4
Bindle, *Australia* 91 D4
Bindura, *Zimbabwe* 83 F3
Bingara, *N.S.W., Australia* 91 D5
Bingara, *Queens., Australia* 91 D3
Bingen, *Germany* 19 F3
Bingerville, *Ivory C.* 78 D4
Bingham, *U.S.A.* 99 C6
Bingham Canyon, *U.S.A.* . 110 F7
Binghamton, *U.S.A.* 107 D9
Bingöl, *Turkey* 67 C9
Bingöl Dağları, *Turkey* ... 67 C9
Binh Dinh = An Nhon,
  Vietnam 58 F7
Binh Khe, *Vietnam* 58 F7
Binh Son, *Vietnam* 58 E7
Binhai, *China* 51 G10
Binisatua, *Spain* 36 B11
Binjai, *Indonesia* 56 D1
Binnaway, *Australia* 91 E4
Binongko, *Indonesia* 57 F6
Binscarth, *Canada* 101 C8
Bintan, *Indonesia* 56 D2
Bintulu, *Malaysia* 56 D4
Bintuni, *Indonesia* 57 E8
Binyang, *China* 52 F7
Binz, *Germany* 18 A9
Binzert = Bizerte, *Tunisia* 75 A6
Bío Bío □, *Chile* 126 D1
Biograd, *Croatia* 33 E12
Bioko, *Eq. Guin.* 79 E6
Biougra, *Morocco* 74 B3
Bir, *India* 60 K9
Bir, Ras, *Djibouti* 77 E5
Bîr Abu Hashim, *Egypt* ... 76 C3
Bîr Abu M'nqar, *Egypt* ... 76 B2
Bîr Abu Muḥammad, *Egypt* 69 F3
Bîr Adal Deib, *Sudan* 76 C4
Bi'r al Butayyihât, *Jordan* . 69 F4
Bi'r al Mārī, *Jordan* 69 E4
Bi'r al Qattār, *Jordan* 69 F4
Bir Aouine, *Tunisia* 75 B6
Bîr 'Asal, *Egypt* 76 B3
Bir Autrun, *Sudan* 76 D2
Bîr Beiḍa, *Egypt* 69 E3
Bîr Diqnash, *Egypt* 76 A2
Bîr el Abbes, *Algeria* 74 C3
Bîr el 'Abd, *Egypt* 69 D2
Bîr el Ater, *Algeria* 75 B6
Bîr el Basur, *Egypt* 76 B2
Bîr el Biarât, *Egypt* 69 F3
Bîr el Duweidar, *Egypt* ... 69 E1
Bîr el Garârât, *Egypt* 69 D2
Bîr el Gellaz, *Egypt* 76 A2
Bîr el Heisi, *Egypt* 69 F3
Bîr el Jafir, *Egypt* 69 E1
Bîr el Mâlḥi, *Egypt* 69 E2
Bîr el Shaqqa, *Egypt* 76 A2
Bîr el Thamâda, *Egypt* ... 69 E2
Bîr Fuad, *Egypt* 76 A2

Bîr Gebeil Ḥişn, *Egypt* ... 69 E2
Bi'r Ghadīr, *Syria* 69 A6
Bîr Haimur, *Egypt* 76 C3
Bi'r Jadīd, *Iraq* 64 C4
Bîr Kanayis, *Egypt* 76 C3
Bîr Kaseiba, *Egypt* 69 E2
Bîr Kerawein, *Egypt* 76 B2
Bîr Lahfân, *Egypt* 69 E2
Bir Lahrache, *Algeria* 75 B6
Bîr Madkûr, *Egypt* 69 E1
Bîr Maql, *Egypt* 76 C3
Bîr Misaha, *Egypt* 76 C2
Bir Mogrein, *Mauritania* .. 74 C2
Bîr Murr, *Egypt* 76 C3
Bi'r Muṭribah, *Kuwait* 64 D5
Bîr Nakheila, *Egypt* 76 C3
Bîr Qaṭia, *Egypt* 69 E1
Bîr Qatrani, *Egypt* 76 A2
Bîr Ranga, *Egypt* 76 C4
Bîr Sahara, *Egypt* 76 C2
Bîr Seiyâla, *Egypt* 76 B3
Bir Semguine, *Morocco* .. 74 B3
Bîr Shalatein, *Egypt* 76 C4
Bîr Shebb, *Egypt* 76 C2
Bîr Shût, *Egypt* 76 C4
Bîr Terfawi, *Egypt* 76 C2
Bîr Umm Qubûr, *Egypt* .. 76 C3
Bîr Ungât, *Egypt* 76 C3
Bîr Za'farâna, *Egypt* 76 J8
Bîr Zeidûn, *Egypt* 76 B3
Bira, *Indonesia* 57 E8
Bîra, *Romania* 38 B10
Biramféro, *Guinea* 78 C3
Birao, *C.A.R.* 73 F9
Birawa, *Zaïre* 82 C2
Bîrca, *Romania* 38 F6
Birch Hills, *Canada* 101 C7
Birch I., *Canada* 101 C9
Birch L., *N.W.T., Canada* . 100 A5
Birch L., *Ont., Canada* ... 98 B1
Birch L., *U.S.A.* 98 C1
Birch Mts., *Canada* 100 B6
Birch River, *Canada* 101 C8
Birchip, *Australia* 91 F3
Bird, *Canada* 101 B10
Bird City, *U.S.A.* 108 F4
Bird I. = Aves, I. de,
  W. Indies 117 C7
Birdaard, *Neths.* 16 B7
Birdlip, *U.K.* 13 F5
Birdsville, *Australia* 90 D2
Birdum, *Australia* 88 C5
Birecik, *Turkey* 67 D8
Birein, *Israel* 69 E3
Bireuen, *Indonesia* 56 C1
Birifo, *Gambia* 78 C2
Birigui, *Brazil* 127 A5
Birkenfeld, *Germany* 19 F3
Birkenhead, *U.K.* 12 D4
Birket Qârûn, *Egypt* 76 J7
Birkhadem, *Algeria* 75 A5
Bîrlad, *Romania* 38 C10
Birmingham, *U.K.* 13 E6
Birmingham, *U.S.A.* 105 J2
Birmitrapur, *India* 61 H14
Birni Ngaouré, *Niger* 79 C5
Birni Nkonni, *Niger* 79 C6
Birnin Gwari, *Nigeria* 79 C6
Birnin Kebbi, *Nigeria* 79 C5
Birnin Kudu, *Nigeria* 79 C6
Birobidzhan, *Russia* 45 E14
Birr, *Ireland* 15 C4
Birrie →, *Australia* 91 D4
Birs →, *Switz.* 22 B5
Birsilpur, *India* 62 E5
Birsk, *Russia* 44 D6
Birtin, *Romania* 38 C5
Birtle, *Canada* 101 C8
Birur, *India* 60 N9
Biryuchiy, *Ukraine* 41 J8
Biržai, *Lithuania* 9 H21
Bîrzava, *Romania* 38 C4
Birzebugga, *Malta* 37 D2
Bisa, *Indonesia* 57 E7
Bisáccia, *Italy* 35 A8
Bisacquino, *Italy* 34 E6
Bisalpur, *India* 63 E8
Bisbee, *U.S.A.* 111 L9
Biscarrosse et de Parentis,
  Étang de, *France* 26 D2
Biscay, B. of, *Atl. Oc.* 6 F5
Biscayne B., *U.S.A.* 105 N5
Biscéglie, *Italy* 35 A9
Bischofshofen, *Austria* ... 21 H3
Bischofswerda, *Germany* . 18 D10
Bischofszell, *Switz.* 23 B8
Bischwiller, *France* 25 D14
Biscoe Bay, *Antarctica* ... 5 D13
Biscoe Is., *Antarctica* 5 C17
Biscostasing, *Canada* 98 C3
Biscucuy, *Venezuela* 120 B4
Biševo, *Croatia* 33 F13
Bisha, *Eritrea* 77 D4
Bishah, W. →, *Si. Arabia* . 76 C5
Bishan, *China* 52 C6
Bishkek, *Kyrgyzstan* 44 E8
Bishnupur, *India* 63 H12
Bisho, *S. Africa* 85 E4
Bishop, *Calif., U.S.A.* 111 H4
Bishop, *Tex., U.S.A.* 109 M6
Bishop Auckland, *U.K.* ... 12 C6
Bishop's Falls, *Canada* ... 99 C8
Bishop's Stortford, *U.K.* .. 13 F8
Bisignano, *Italy* 35 C9
Bisina, L., *Uganda* 82 B3

Biskra, *Algeria* 75 B6
Bislig, *Phil.* 57 C7
Bismarck, *U.S.A.* 108 B4
Bismarck Arch.,
  Papua N. G. 92 H6
Bismark, *Germany* 18 C7
Bismil, *Turkey* 67 D9
Biso, *Uganda* 82 B3
Bison, *U.S.A.* 108 C3
Bīsotūn, *Iran* 67 E12
Bispgården, *Sweden* 10 A10
Bissagos = Bijagós,
  Arquipélago dos,
  Guinea-Biss. 78 C1
Bissau, *Guinea-Biss.* 78 C1
Bissett, *Canada* 101 C9
Bissikrima, *Guinea* 78 C2
Bistcho L., *Canada* 100 B5
Bistreţu, *Romania* 38 F6
Bistrica = Ilirska-Bistrica,
  Slovenia 33 C11
Bistriţa, *Romania* 38 B7
Bistriţa →, *Romania* 38 C9
Bistriţei, Munţii, *Romania* 38 B8
Biswan, *India* 63 F9
Bitam, *Gabon* 80 D2
Bitburg, *Germany* 19 F2
Bitche, *France* 25 C14
Bithynia, *Turkey* 66 B4
Bitkine, *Chad* 73 F8
Bitlis, *Turkey* 67 C10
Bitola, *Macedonia* 39 H4
Bitolj = Bitola, *Macedonia* 39 H4
Bitonto, *Italy* 35 A9
Bitter Creek, *U.S.A.* 110 F9
Bitter L. = Buheirat-
  Murrat-el-Kubra, *Egypt* 76 H8
Bitterfeld, *Germany* 18 D8
Bitterfontein, *S. Africa* ... 84 E2
Bitterroot →, *U.S.A.* 110 C6
Bitterroot Range, *U.S.A.* . 110 D6
Bitterwater, *U.S.A.* 112 J6
Bitti, *Italy* 34 B2
Bittou, *Burkina Faso* 79 C4
Biu, *Nigeria* 79 C7
Bivolari, *Romania* 38 B10
Biwa-Ko, *Japan* 49 G8
Biwabik, *U.S.A.* 108 B8
Bixad, *Romania* 38 B6
Biyang, *China* 50 H7
Biysk, *Russia* 44 D9
Bizana, *S. Africa* 85 E4
Bizen, *Japan* 49 G7
Bizerte, *Tunisia* 75 A6
Bjargtangar, *Iceland* 8 D1
Bjelasica,
  Montenegro, Yug. 21 N9
Bjelovar, *Croatia* 21 K6
Bjerringbro, *Denmark* 11 H3
Bjervamoen, *Norway* 10 E3
Bjørnevatn, *Norway* 8 B23
Bjørnøya, *Arctic* 4 B8
Bjuv, *Sweden* 11 H6
Blace, *Serbia, Yug.* 21 M11
Black = Da →, *Vietnam* .. 58 B5
Black →, *Canada* 106 B5
Black →, *Ark., U.S.A.* 109 H9
Black →, *N.Y., U.S.A.* ... 107 C8
Black →, *Wis., U.S.A.* ... 108 D9
Black Diamond, *Canada* .. 100 C6
Black Forest =
  Schwarzwald, *Germany* . 19 H4
Black Hills, *U.S.A.* 108 C3
Black I., *Canada* 101 C9
Black L., *Canada* 101 B7
Black L., *U.S.A.* 104 C3
Black Mesa, *U.S.A.* 109 G3
Black Mt. = Mynydd Du,
  U.K. 13 F4
Black Mts., *U.K.* 13 F4
Black Range, *U.S.A.* 111 K10
Black River, *Jamaica* 116 C4
Black River Falls, *U.S.A.* . 108 C9
Black Sea, *Eurasia* 46 E7
Black Volta →, *Africa* 78 D4
Black Warrior →, *U.S.A.* . 105 J2
Blackall, *Australia* 90 C4
Blackball, *N.Z.* 87 K3
Blackbull, *Australia* 90 B3
Blackburn, *U.K.* 12 D5
Blackduck, *U.S.A.* 108 B7
Blackfoot, *U.S.A.* 110 E7
Blackfoot →, *U.S.A.* 110 C7
Blackfoot River Reservoir,
  U.S.A. 110 E8
Blackie, *Canada* 100 C6
Blackpool, *U.K.* 12 D4
Blackriver, *U.S.A.* 106 B1
Blacks Harbour, *Canada* . 99 C6
Blacksburg, *U.S.A.* 104 G5
Blacksod B., *Ireland* 15 B1
Blackstone, *U.S.A.* 104 G6
Blackstone →, *Canada* ... 100 A4
Blackstone Ra., *Australia* . 89 E4
Blackville, *Canada* 99 C6
Blackwater, *Australia* 90 C4
Blackwater →, *Ireland* ... 15 E4
Blackwater →, *U.K.* 15 B5
Blackwater Cr. →,
  Australia 91 D3
Blackwell, *U.S.A.* 109 G6
Blackwells Corner, *U.S.A.* 113 K7
Bladel, *Neths.* 17 F6
Blaenau Ffestiniog, *U.K.* . 12 E4
Blagodarnoye =
  Blagodarnyy, *Russia* .. 43 H6
Blagodarnyy, *Russia* 43 H6

Blagoevgrad, *Bulgaria* 39 G6
Blagoveshchensk, *Russia* . 45 D13
Blain, *France* 24 E5
Blaine, *U.S.A.* 112 B4
Blaine Lake, *Canada* 101 C7
Blair, *U.S.A.* 108 E6
Blair Athol, *Australia* 90 C4
Blair Atholl, *U.K.* 14 E5
Blairgowrie, *U.K.* 14 E5
Blairmore, *Canada* 100 D6
Blairsden, *U.S.A.* 112 F6
Blairsville, *U.S.A.* 106 F5
Blaj, *Romania* 38 C6
Blake Pt., *U.S.A.* 108 A10
Blakely, *U.S.A.* 105 K3
Blâmont, *France* 25 D13
Blanc, C., *Tunisia* 75 A6
Blanc, Mont, *Alps* 27 C10
Blanca, B., *Argentina* 128 A4
Blanca Peak, *U.S.A.* 111 H11
Blanchard, *U.S.A.* 109 H6
Blanche, C., *Australia* 91 E1
Blanche, L., *S. Austral.,
  Australia* 91 D2
Blanche, L., *W. Austral.,
  Australia* 88 D3
Blanco, *S. Africa* 84 E3
Blanco, *U.S.A.* 109 K5
Blanco →, *Argentina* 126 C2
Blanco, C., *Costa Rica* ... 116 E2
Blanco, C., *Spain* 36 B9
Blanco, C., *U.S.A.* 110 E1
Blanda →, *Iceland* 8 D3
Blandford Forum, *U.K.* .. 13 G5
Blanding, *U.S.A.* 111 H9
Blanes, *Spain* 28 D7
Blangy-sur-Bresle, *France* . 25 C8
Blankenberge, *Belgium* ... 17 F2
Blankenburg, *Germany* ... 18 D6
Blanquefort, *France* 26 D3
Blanquillo, *Uruguay* 127 C4
Blansko, *Czech.* 20 F6
Blantyre, *Malawi* 83 F4
Blaricum, *Neths.* 16 D6
Blarney, *Ireland* 15 E3
Blato, *Croatia* 33 F13
Blatten, *Switz.* 22 D5
Blaubeuren, *Germany* 19 G5
Blauvands Huk, *Denmark* . 9 J13
Blaydon, *U.K.* 12 C6
Blaye, *France* 26 C3
Blaye-les-Mines, *France* .. 26 D6
Blayney, *Australia* 91 E4
Blaze, Pt., *Australia* 88 B5
Bleckede, *Germany* 18 B6
Bled, *Slovenia* 33 B11
Blednaya, Gora, *Russia* ... 44 B7
Bléharis, *Belgium* 17 G2
Blejeşti, *Romania* 38 E8
Blekinge, *Sweden* 9 H16
Blenheim, *Canada* 106 D2
Blenheim, *N.Z.* 87 J4
Bléone →, *France* 27 D10
Blerick, *Neths.* 17 F8
Bletchley, *U.K.* 13 F7
Blida, *Algeria* 75 A5
Blidet Amor, *Algeria* 75 B6
Blidö, *Sweden* 10 E12
Bligh Sound, *N.Z.* 87 L1
Blind River, *Canada* 98 C3
Blinnenhorn, *Switz.* 23 D6
Blitar, *Indonesia* 57 H15
Blitta, *Togo* 79 D5
Block I., *U.S.A.* 107 E13
Block Island Sd., *U.S.A.* . 107 E13
Blodgett Iceberg Tongue,
  Antarctica 5 C9
Bloemendaal, *Neths.* 16 D5
Bloemfontein, *S. Africa* ... 84 D4
Bloemhof, *S. Africa* 84 D4
Blois, *France* 24 E8
Blokziji, *Neths.* 16 C7
Blönduós, *Iceland* 8 D3
Bloody Foreland, *Ireland* . 15 A3
Bloomer, *U.S.A.* 108 C9
Bloomfield, *Australia* 90 B4
Bloomfield, *Canada* 106 C7
Bloomfield, *Iowa, U.S.A.* . 108 E8
Bloomfield, *N. Mex.,
  U.S.A.* 111 H10
Bloomfield, *Nebr., U.S.A.* 108 D6
Bloomington, *Ill., U.S.A.* . 108 E10
Bloomington, *Ind., U.S.A.* 104 F2
Bloomsburg, *U.S.A.* 107 F8
Blora, *Indonesia* 57 G14
Blossburg, *U.S.A.* 106 E7
Blouberg, *S. Africa* 85 C4
Blountstown, *U.S.A.* 105 K3
Bludenz, *Austria* 19 H5
Blue Island, *U.S.A.* 104 E2
Blue Lake, *U.S.A.* 110 F2
Blue Mesa Reservoir,
  U.S.A. 111 G10
Blue Mts., *Oreg., U.S.A.* . 110 D4
Blue Mts., *Pa., U.S.A.* ... 107 F8
Blue Mud B., *Australia* ... 90 A2
Blue Nile = Nîl el
  Azraq →, *Sudan* 77 D3
Blue Rapids, *U.S.A.* 108 F6
Blue Ridge Mts., *U.S.A.* . 105 G5
Blue Stack Mts., *Ireland* . 15 B3
Blueberry →, *Canada* 100 B4
Bluefield, *U.S.A.* 104 G5
Bluefields, *Nic.* 116 D3

Bluff, *Australia* 90 C4
Bluff, *N.Z.* 87 M2
Bluff, *U.S.A.* 111 H9
Bluff Knoll, *Australia* 89 F2
Bluff Pt., *Australia* 89 E1
Bluffton, *U.S.A.* 104 E3
Blumenau, *Brazil* 127 B6
Blümisalphorn, *Switz.* 22 D5
Blunt, *U.S.A.* 108 C4
Bly, *U.S.A.* 110 E3
Blyth, *Canada* 106 C3
Blyth, *U.K.* 12 B6
Blyth Bridge, *U.K.* 12 E5
Blythe, *U.S.A.* 113 M12
Bø, *Norway* 10 E3
Bo, *S. Leone* 78 D2
Bo Duc, *Vietnam* 59 G6
Bo Hai, *China* 51 E10
Bo Xian, *China* 50 H8
Boa Esperança, *Brazil* 123 F3
Boa Esperança, Reprêsa,
  Brazil 122 C3
Boa Nova, *Brazil* 123 D3
Boa Viagem, *Brazil* 122 C4
Boa Vista, *Brazil* 121 C5
Boac, *Phil.* 55 E4
Boaco, *Nic.* 116 D2
Bo'ai, *China* 50 G7
Boal, *Spain* 30 B4
Boardman, *U.S.A.* 106 E4
Boatman, *Australia* 91 D4
Bobadah, *Australia* 91 E4
Bobai, *China* 52 F7
Bobbili, *India* 61 K13
Bóbbio, *Italy* 32 D6
Bobcaygeon, *Canada* 98 D4
Böblingen, *Germany* 19 G5
Bobo-Dioulasso,
  Burkina Faso 78 C4
Boboc, *Romania* 38 D9
Bobonaza →, *Ecuador* ... 120 D2
Bobov Dol, *Bulgaria* 38 G5
Bóbr →, *Poland* 20 C5
Bobraomby, Tanjon' i,
  Madag. 85 A8
Bobrinets, *Ukraine* 41 H7
Bobrov, *Russia* 42 E5
Bobrovitsa, *Ukraine* 41 G6
Bobruysk = Babruysk,
  Belarus 41 F5
Bobures, *Venezuela* 120 B3
Boca de Drago, *Venezuela* 121 A5
Bôca do Acre, *Brazil* 124 B4
Bôca do Jari, *Brazil* 121 D7
Bôca do Moaco, *Brazil* ... 124 B4
Boca Grande, *Venezuela* . 121 B5
Boca Raton, *U.S.A.* 105 M5
Bocaiúva, *Brazil* 123 E3
Bocanda, *Ivory C.* 78 D4
Bocaranga, *C.A.R.* 73 G8
Bocas del Toro, *Panama* . 116 E3
Boceguillas, *Spain* 28 D1
Bochnia, *Poland* 20 F11
Bocholt, *Belgium* 17 F7
Bocholt, *Germany* 18 D2
Bochum, *Germany* 18 D3
Bockenem, *Germany* 18 C6
Bocognano, *France* 27 F13
Boconó, *Venezuela* 120 B3
Boconó →, *Venezuela* ... 120 B3
Bocoyna, *Mexico* 114 B3
Bocq →, *Belgium* 17 H5
Boda, *C.A.R.* 80 D3
Bodaybo, *Russia* 45 D12
Boddington, *Australia* 89 F2
Bodega Bay, *U.S.A.* 112 G3
Bodegraven, *Neths.* 16 D5
Boden, *Sweden* 8 D19
Bodensee, *Europe* 23 A8
Bodenteich, *Germany* 18 C6
Bodhan, *India* 60 K10
Bodinga, *Nigeria* 79 C6
Bodio, *Switz.* 23 D7
Bodmin, *U.K.* 13 G3
Bodmin Moor, *U.K.* 13 G3
Bodø, *Norway* 8 C16
Bodoquena, Serra da,
  Brazil 125 E6
Bodrog →, *Hungary* 21 G11
Bodrum, *Turkey* 66 D2
Boechout, *Belgium* 17 F5
Boekelo, *Neths.* 16 D9
Boelenslaan, *Neths.* 16 B8
Boën, *France* 27 C8
Boende, *Zaïre* 80 E4
Boerne, *U.S.A.* 109 L5
Boertange, *Neths.* 16 B10
Boezinge, *Belgium* 17 G1
Boffa, *Guinea* 78 C2
Bogalusa, *U.S.A.* 109 K10
Bogan Gate, *Australia* ... 91 E4
Bogantungan, *Australia* .. 90 C4
Bogata, *U.S.A.* 109 J7
Bogatić, *Serbia, Yug.* 21 L9
Boğazkale, *Turkey* 66 B6
Boğazlıyan, *Turkey* 66 C6
Bogense, *Denmark* 11 J4
Boggabilla, *Australia* 91 D5
Boggabri, *Australia* 91 E5
Boggeragh Mts., *Ireland* . 15 D3
Bognor Regis, *U.K.* 13 G7
Bogø, *Denmark* 11 K6
Bogo, *Phil.* 55 F6
Bogodukhov =
  Bohodukhiv, *Ukraine* .. 41 G8
Bogong, Mt., *Australia* ... 91 F4
Bogor, *Indonesia* 57 G12

Bogoroditsk, *Russia* 42 D4
Bogorodsk, *Russia* 42 B6
Bogorodskoye, *Russia* ... 45 D15
Bogoso, *Ghana* 78 D4
Bogotá, *Colombia* 120 C3
Bogotol, *Russia* 44 D9
Bogra, *Bangla.* 61 G16
Boguchany, *Russia* 45 D10
Boguchar, *Russia* 42 F5
Bogué, *Mauritania* 78 B2
Boguslav, *Ukraine* 41 H6
Bohain-en-Vermandois, *France* 25 C10
Bohemia Downs, *Australia* 88 C4
Bohemian Forest = Böhmerwald, *Germany* . 19 F8
Bohena Cr., *Australia* .. 91 E4
Bohinjska Bistrica, *Slovenia* 33 B11
Böhmerwald, *Germany* ... 19 F8
Bohmte, *Germany* 18 C4
Bohodukhiv, *Ukraine* ... 41 G8
Bohol, *Phil.* 55 G6
Bohol Sea, *Phil.* 57 C6
Bohotleh, *Somali Rep.* .. 68 F4
Bohuslän, *Sweden* 9 G14
Boi, *Nigeria* 79 D6
Boi, Pta. de, *Brazil* 127 A6
Boiaçu, *Brazil* 121 D5
Boiano, *Italy* 35 A7
Boileau, C., *Australia* ... 88 C3
Boipeba, I. de, *Brazil* .. 123 D4
Bois →, *Brazil* 123 E1
Boischot, *Belgium* 17 F5
Boise, *U.S.A.* 110 E5
Boise City, *U.S.A.* 109 G3
Boissevain, *Canada* 101 D8
Boite →, *Italy* 33 B9
Boitzenburg, *Germany* ... 18 B9
Boizenburg, *Germany* ... 18 B6
Bojador C., *W. Sahara* .. 74 C2
Bojnūrd, *Iran* 65 B8
Bojonegoro, *Indonesia* .. 57 G14
Boju, *Nigeria* 79 D6
Boka Kotorska, *Montenegro, Yug.* 21 N8
Bokala, *Ivory C.* 78 D4
Boké, *Guinea* 78 C2
Bokhara →, *Australia* .. 91 D4
Bokkos, *Nigeria* 79 D6
Boknafjorden, *Norway* .. 9 G11
Bokoro, *Chad* 73 F8
Bokote, *Zaïre* 80 E4
Boksitogorsk, *Russia* ... 40 C7
Bokungu, *Zaïre* 80 E4
Bol, *Chad* 73 F7
Bol, *Croatia* 33 E13
Bolama, *Guinea-Biss.* ... 78 C1
Bolan Pass, *Pakistan* ... 60 E5
Bolaños →, *Mexico* 114 C4
Bolbec, *France* 24 C7
Boldājī, *Iran* 65 D6
Boldeşti, *Romania* 38 D9
Bole, *China* 54 B3
Bole, *Ethiopia* 77 F4
Bolekhiv, *Ukraine* 41 H2
Bolekhov = Bolekhiv, *Ukraine* 41 H2
Bolesławiec, *Poland* 20 D5
Bolgatanga, *Ghana* 79 C4
Bolgrad = Bolhrad, *Ukraine* 41 K5
Bolhrad, *Ukraine* 41 K5
Boli, *Sudan* 77 F2
Bolinao, *Phil.* 55 C3
Bolinao C., *Phil.* 57 A5
Bolívar, *Argentina* 126 D3
Bolívar, *Antioquía, Colombia* 120 B2
Bolívar, *Cauca, Colombia* 120 C2
Bolívar, *Peru* 124 B2
Bolivar, *Mo., U.S.A.* ... 109 G8
Bolivar, *Tenn., U.S.A.* . 109 H10
Bolívar □, *Colombia* ... 120 B3
Bolívar □, *Ecuador* 120 D2
Bolívar □, *Venezuela* ... 121 B5
Bolivia ■, *S. Amer.* ... 125 D5
Bolivian Plateau, *S. Amer.* 118 E4
Bolkhov, *Russia* 42 D3
Bollène, *France* 27 D8
Bollnäs, *Sweden* 10 C10
Bollon, *Australia* 91 D4
Bollstabruk, *Sweden* 10 A11
Bollullos, *Spain* 31 H4
Bolmen, *Sweden* 9 H15
Bolobo, *Zaïre* 80 E3
Bologna, *Italy* 33 D8
Bologne, *France* 25 D12
Bologoye, *Russia* 42 B2
Bolomba, *Zaïre* 80 D3
Bolonchenticul, *Mexico* . 115 D7
Bolong, *Phil.* 57 C6
Boloven, Cao Nguyen, *Laos* 58 E6
Bolpur, *India* 63 H12
Bolsena, *Italy* 33 F8
Bolsena, L. di, *Italy* 33 F8
Bolshaya Chernigovka, *Russia* 42 D10
Bolshaya Glushitsa, *Russia* 42 D10
Bolshaya Martynovka, *Russia* 43 G5
Bolshaya Vradiyevka, *Ukraine* 41 J6
Bolshereche, *Russia* 44 D8
Bolshevik, Ostrov, *Russia* . 45 B11
Bolshoi Kavkas = Caucasus Mountains, *Eurasia* ... 43 J7

Bolshoy Anyuy →, *Russia* 45 C17
Bolshoy Atlym, *Russia* .. 44 C7
Bolshoy Begichev, Ostrov, *Russia* 45 B12
Bolshoy Lyakhovskiy, Ostrov, *Russia* 45 B15
Bolshoy Tokmak = Tokmak, *Ukraine* 41 J8
Bolshoy Tyuters, Ostrov, *Russia* 9 G22
Bolsward, *Neths.* 16 B7
Boltaña, *Spain* 28 C5
Boltigen, *Switz.* 22 C4
Bolton, *Canada* 106 C5
Bolton, *U.K.* 12 D5
Bolu, *Turkey* 66 B4
Bolungavík, *Iceland* 8 C2
Boluo, *China* 53 F10
Bolvadin, *Turkey* 66 C4
Bolzano, *Italy* 33 B8
Bom Comércio, *Brazil* .. 125 B4
Bom Conselho, *Brazil* .. 122 C4
Bom Despacho, *Brazil* .. 123 E2
Bom Jesus, *Brazil* 122 C3
Bom Jesus da Gurguéia, Serra, *Brazil* 122 C3
Bom Jesus da Lapa, *Brazil* 123 D3
Boma, *Zaïre* 80 F2
Bomaderry, *Australia* ... 91 E5
Bombala, *Australia* 91 F4
Bombarral, *Portugal* 31 F1
Bombay, *India* 60 K8
Bomboma, *Zaïre* 80 D3
Bombomba, *Zaïre* 82 B2
Bomi Hills, *Liberia* 78 D2
Bomili, *Zaïre* 82 B2
Bømlo, *Norway* 9 G11
Bommel, *Neths.* 16 E4
Bomokandi →, *Zaïre* ... 82 B2
Bomongo, *Zaïre* 80 D3
Bomu →, *C.A.R.* 80 D4
Bon, C., *Tunisia* 75 A7
Bon Sar Pa, *Vietnam* ... 58 F6
Bonaduz, *Switz.* 23 C8
Bonaire, *Neth. Ant.* 117 D6
Bonang, *Australia* 91 F4
Bonanza, *Nic.* 116 D3
Boñar, *Spain* 30 C5
Bonaparte Arch., *Australia* 88 B3
Bonaventure, *Canada* ... 99 C6
Bonavista, *Canada* 99 C9
Bonavista, C., *Canada* .. 99 C9
Bonawan, *Phil.* 55 G5
Bondeno, *Italy* 33 D8
Bondo, *Zaïre* 82 B1
Bondoukou, *Ivory C.* ... 78 D4
Bondowoso, *Indonesia* .. 57 G15
Bone, Teluk, *Indonesia* .. 57 E6
Bonefro, *Italy* 35 A7
Bonerate, *Indonesia* 57 F6
Bonerate, Kepulauan, *Indonesia* 57 F6
Bo'ness, *U.K.* 14 E5
Bonete, Cerro, *Argentina* 126 B2
Bong Son = Hoai Nhon, *Vietnam* 58 E7
Bongabong, *Phil.* 55 E4
Bongandanga, *Zaïre* 80 D4
Bongor, *Chad* 73 F8
Bongouanou, *Ivory C.* .. 78 D4
Bonham, *U.S.A.* 109 J6
Bonheiden, *Belgium* 17 F5
Bonifacio, *France* 27 G13
Bonifacio, Bouches de, *Medit. S.* 34 A2
Bonin Is. = Ogasawara Gunto, *Pac. Oc.* 92 E6
Bonke, *Ethiopia* 77 F4
Bonn, *Germany* 18 E3
Bonnat, *France* 26 B5
Bonne Terre, *U.S.A.* ... 109 G9
Bonners Ferry, *U.S.A.* .. 110 B5
Bonnétable, *France* 24 D7
Bonneuil-Matours, *France* 24 F7
Bonneval, *France* 24 D8
Bonneville, *France* 27 B10
Bonney, L., *Australia* ... 91 F3
Bonnie Downs, *Australia* 90 C3
Bonnie Rock, *Australia* . 89 F2
Bonny, *Nigeria* 79 E6
Bonny →, *Nigeria* 79 E6
Bonny, Bight of, *Africa* . 79 E6
Bonny-sur-Loire, *France* . 25 E9
Bonnyville, *Canada* 101 C6
Bonoi, *Indonesia* 57 E9
Bonorva, *Italy* 34 B1
Bonsall, *U.S.A.* 113 M9
Bontang, *Indonesia* 56 D5
Bonthain, *Indonesia* 57 F5
Bonthe, S. *Leone* 78 D2
Bontoc, *Phil.* 55 C4
Bonyeri, *Ghana* 78 D4
Bonython Ra., *Australia* . 88 D4
Bookabie, *Australia* 89 F5
Booker, *U.S.A.* 109 G4
Boolaboolka L., *Australia* 91 E3
Booligal, *Australia* 91 E3
Boom, *Belgium* 17 F4
Boonah, *Australia* 91 D5
Boone, *Iowa, U.S.A.* ... 108 D8
Boone, *N.C., U.S.A.* ... 105 G5
Booneville, *Ark., U.S.A.* 109 H8
Booneville, *Miss., U.S.A.* 105 H1
Boonville, *Calif., U.S.A.* 112 F3
Boonville, *Ind., U.S.A.* . 104 F2
Boonville, *Mo., U.S.A.* . 108 F8
Boonville, *N.Y., U.S.A.* 107 C9

Boorindal, *Australia* 91 E4
Boorowa, *Australia* 91 E4
Boothia, Gulf of, *Canada* 97 A11
Boothia Pen., *Canada* ... 96 A10
Bootle, *U.K.* 12 D4
Booué, *Gabon* 80 E2
Boppard, *Germany* 19 E3
Boquerón □, *Paraguay* .. 125 E5
Boquete, *Panama* 116 E3
Boquilla, Presa de la, *Mexico* 114 B3
Boquillas del Carmen, *Mexico* 114 B4
Bor, *Czech.* 20 F2
Bor, *Russia* 42 B7
Bor, *Serbia, Yug.* 21 L12
Bôr, *Sudan* 77 F3
Bor, *Turkey* 66 D6
Bor Mashash, *Israel* 69 D3
Boradā →, *Syria* 69 B5
Borah Peak, *U.S.A.* 110 D7
Borama, *Somali Rep.* ... 68 F3
Borang, *Sudan* 77 G3
Borås, *Sweden* 11 G6
Borāzjān, *Iran* 65 D6
Borba, *Brazil* 121 D6
Borba, *Portugal* 31 G3
Borborema, Planalto da, *Brazil* 122 C4
Borçka, *Turkey* 67 B9
Borculo, *Neths.* 16 D9
Bord Khūn-e Now, *Iran* . 55 D6
Borda, C., *Australia* 91 F2
Bordeaux, *France* 26 D3
Borden, *Australia* 89 F2
Borden, *Canada* 99 C7
Borden I., *Canada* 4 B2
Borders □, *U.K.* 14 F6
Bordertown, *Australia* .. 91 F3
Borðeyri, *Iceland* 8 D3
Bordighera, *Italy* 32 E4
Bordj bou Arreridj, *Algeria* 75 A5
Bordj Bourguiba, *Tunisia* . 75 B7
Bordj Fly Ste. Marie, *Algeria* 74 C4
Bordj-in-Eker, *Algeria* ... 75 D6
Bordj Menaiel, *Algeria* .. 75 A5
Bordj Messouda, *Algeria* . 75 B6
Bordj Nili, *Algeria* 75 B5
Bordj Omar Driss, *Algeria* 75 C6
Bordj Sif Fatima, *Algeria* . 75 B6
Bordj-Tarat, *Algeria* 75 C6
Bordj Zelfana, *Algeria* ... 75 B5
Borebgsberg, *Sweden* 11 F9
Borga = Porvoo, *Finland* . 9 F21
Borgarnes, *Iceland* 8 D3
Børgefjellet, *Norway* 8 D15
Borger, *Neths.* 16 C9
Borger, *U.S.A.* 109 H4
Borgerhout, *Belgium* 17 F4
Borghamn, *Sweden* 11 F8
Borgholm, *Sweden* 9 H17
Borgo San Dalmazzo, *Italy* 32 D4
Borgo San Lorenzo, *Italy* . 33 E8
Borgo Valsugano, *Italy* .. 33 B8
Borgomanero, *Italy* 32 C5
Borgonovo Val Tidone, *Italy* 32 C6
Borgorose, *Italy* 33 F10
Borgosésia, *Italy* 32 C5
Borgvattnet, *Sweden* 10 A9
Borikhane, *Laos* 58 C4
Borisoglebsk, *Russia* 42 E6
Borisov = Barysaw, *Belarus* 40 E5
Borisovka, *Russia* 42 E3
Borja, *Peru* 120 D2
Borja, *Spain* 28 D3
Borjas Blancas, *Spain* ... 28 D5
Borjomi, *Georgia* 43 K6
Borken, *Germany* 18 D2
Borkou, *Chad* 73 E8
Borkum, *Germany* 18 B2
Borlänge, *Sweden* 9 F16
Borley, C., *Antarctica* ... 5 C5
Bórmida →, *Italy* 32 D5
Bórmio, *Italy* 32 B7
Born, *Neths.* 17 F7
Borna, *Germany* 18 D8
Borndiep, *Neths.* 16 B7
Borne, *Neths.* 16 D9
Bornem, *Belgium* 17 F4
Borneo, E. *Indies* 56 D5
Bornholm, *Denmark* ... 9 J16
Borno □, *Nigeria* 79 C7
Bornos, *Spain* 31 J5
Bornu Yassa, *Nigeria* ... 79 C7
Borobudur, *Indonesia* ... 57 G14
Borodino, *Russia* 42 C2
Borogontsy, *Russia* 45 C14
Boromo, *Burkina Faso* .. 78 C4
Boron, *U.S.A.* 113 L9
Borongan, *Phil.* 55 F6
Bororen, *Australia* 90 C5
Borotangba Mts., *C.A.R.* . 77 F1
Borovan, *Bulgaria* 38 F6
Borovichi, *Russia* 40 C7
Borovsk, *Russia* 42 C3
Borrego Springs, *U.S.A.* . 113 M10
Borriol, *Spain* 28 E4
Borroloola, *Australia* 90 B2
Borşa, *Romania* 38 B7
Borssele, *Neths.* 17 F3
Bort-les-Orgues, *France* . 26 C6
Borth, *U.K.* 13 E3

Borūjerd, *Iran* 67 F13
Boryslav, *Ukraine* 41 H2
Boryspil, *Ukraine* 41 G6
Borzhomi = Borjomi, *Georgia* 43 K6
Borzna, *Ukraine* 41 G7
Borzya, *Russia* 45 D12
Bosa, *Italy* 34 B1
Bosanska Dubica, *Bos.-H.* 33 C13
Bosanska Gradiška, *Bos.-H.* 21 K7
Bosanska Kostajnica, *Bos.-H.* 33 C13
Bosanska Krupa, *Bos.-H.* . 33 D13
Bosanski Novi, *Bos.-H.* .. 33 C13
Bosanski Šamac, *Bos.-H.* . 21 K8
Bosansko Grahovo, *Bos.-H.* 33 D13
Bosansko Petrovac, *Bos.-H.* 33 D13
Bosaso, *Somali Rep.* 68 E4
Boscastle, *U.K.* 13 G3
Boscotrecase, *Italy* 35 B7
Bose, *China* 52 F6
Boshan, *China* 51 F9
Boshof, *S. Africa* 84 D4
Boshrūyeh, *Iran* 65 C8
Bosilegrad, *Serbia, Yug.* .. 21 N12
Boskoop, *Neths.* 16 D5
Bosna →, *Bos.-H.* 21 K8
Bosna i Hercegovina = Bosnia-Herzegovina ■, *Europe* 21 L7
Bosnia-Herzegovina ■, *Europe* 21 L7
Bosnik, *Indonesia* 57 E9
Bosobolo, *Zaïre* 80 D3
Bosporus = Karadeniz Boğazı, *Turkey* 66 B3
Bossangoa, *C.A.R.* 73 G8
Bossembélé, *C.A.R.* 73 G8
Bossier City, *U.S.A.* 109 J8
Bosso, *Niger* 79 C7
Bostānābād, *Iran* 67 D12
Bosten Hu, *China* 54 B3
Boston, *U.K.* 12 E7
Boston, *U.S.A.* 107 D14
Boston Bar, *Canada* 100 D4
Bosut →, *Croatia* 21 K8
Boswell, *Canada* 100 D5
Boswell, *Okla., U.S.A.* .. 109 H7
Boswell, *Pa., U.S.A.* ... 106 F5
Botad, *India* 62 H4
Botan →, *Turkey* 67 D10
Botany B., *Australia* 91 E5
Botene, *Laos* 58 D3
Botevgrad, *Bulgaria* 38 G6
Bothaville, *S. Africa* 84 D4
Bothnia, G. of, *Europe* .. 8 E19
Bothwell, *Australia* 90 G4
Bothwell, *Canada* 106 D3
Boticas, *Portugal* 30 D3
Botletle →, *Botswana* .. 84 C3
Botlikh, *Russia* 43 J8
Botoşani, *Romania* 38 B9
Botro, *Ivory C.* 78 D3
Botswana ■, *Africa* 84 C3
Bottineau, *U.S.A.* 108 A4
Bottrop, *Germany* 17 E9
Botucatu, *Brazil* 127 A6
Botwood, *Canada* 99 C8
Bou Alam, *Algeria* 75 B5
Bou Ali, *Algeria* 75 C4
Bou Djébéha, *Mali* 78 B4
Bou Guema, *Algeria* 75 C5
Bou Ismael, *Algeria* 75 A5
Bou Izakarn, *Morocco* .. 74 C3
Boû Lanouâr, *Mauritania* . 74 D1
Bou Saâda, *Algeria* 75 A5
Bou Salem, *Tunisia* 75 A6
Bouaké, *Ivory C.* 78 D3
Bouar, *C.A.R.* 80 C3
Bouârfa, *Morocco* 75 B4
Bouca, *C.A.R.* 73 G8
Boucau, *France* 26 E2
Boucaut B., *Australia* ... 90 A1
Bouches-du-Rhône □, *France* 27 E9
Bouda, *Algeria* 75 C4
Boudenib, *Morocco* 74 B4
Boudry, *Switz.* 22 C3
Boufarik, *Algeria* 75 A5
Bougainville, C., *Australia* 88 B4
Bougainville Reef, *Australia* 90 B4
Bougaroun, C., *Algeria* .. 75 A6
Bougie = Bejaia, *Algeria* . 75 A6
Bougouni, *Mali* 78 C3
Bouillon, *Belgium* 17 J6
Bouïra, *Algeria* 75 A5
Boulder, *Colo., U.S.A.* .. 108 E2
Boulder, *Mont., U.S.A.* . 110 C7
Boulder City, *U.S.A.* ... 113 K12
Boulder Creek, *U.S.A.* .. 112 H4
Boulder Dam = Hoover Dam, *U.S.A.* 113 K12
Bouli, *Mauritania* 78 B2
Boulia, *Australia* 90 C2
Bouligny, *France* 25 C12
Boulogne →, *France* ... 24 E5
Boulogne-sur-Gesse, *France* 26 E4
Boulogne-sur-Mer, *France* 25 B8
Bouloire, *France* 24 E7
Boulsa, *Burkina Faso* ... 79 C4
Boultoum, *Niger* 79 C7
Boumalne, *Morocco* 74 B3
Boun Neua, *Laos* 58 B3

Boun Tai, *Laos* 58 B3
Bouna, *Ivory C.* 78 D4
Boundary Peak, *U.S.A.* . 112 H8
Boundiali, *Ivory C.* 78 D3
Bountiful, *U.S.A.* 110 F8
Bounty Is., *Pac. Oc.* 92 M9
Bourbon-Lancy, *France* .. 26 B7
Bourbon-l'Archambault, *France* 26 B7
Bourbonnais, *France* 26 B7
Bourbonne-les-Bains, *France* 25 E12
Bourem, *Mali* 79 B4
Bourg, *France* 26 C3
Bourg-Argental, *France* .. 27 C8
Bourg-de-Péage, *France* .. 27 C9
Bourg-en-Bresse, *France* . 27 B9
Bourg-St.-Andéol, *France* . 27 D8
Bourg-St.-Maurice, *France* 27 C10
Bourg-St.-Pierre, *Switz.* . 22 E4
Bourganeuf, *France* 26 C5
Bourges, *France* 25 E9
Bourget, *Canada* 107 A9
Bourget, L. du, *France* .. 27 C9
Bourgneuf, B. de, *France* . 24 E4
Bourgneuf-en-Retz, *France* 24 E5
Bourgogne, *France* 25 F11
Bourgoin-Jallieu, *France* . 27 C9
Bourgueil, *France* 24 E7
Bourke, *Australia* 91 E4
Bournemouth, *U.K.* 13 G6
Bourriot-Bergonce, *France* 26 D3
Bouse, *U.S.A.* 113 M13
Boussac, *France* 26 B6
Boussens, *France* 26 E4
Bousso, *Chad* 73 F8
Boussu, *Belgium* 17 H3
Boutilimit, *Mauritania* .. 78 B2
Boutonne →, *France* ... 26 C3
Bouvet I. = Bouvetøya, *Antarctica* 3 G10
Bouvetøya, *Antarctica* ... 3 G10
Bouznika, *Morocco* 74 B3
Bouzonville, *France* 25 C13
Bova Marina, *Italy* 35 E8
Bovalino Marina, *Italy* .. 35 D9
Bovec, *Slovenia* 33 B10
Bovenkarspel, *Neths.* 16 C6
Bovigny, *Belgium* 17 H7
Bovill, *U.S.A.* 110 C5
Bovino, *Italy* 35 A8
Bow Island, *Canada* 100 D6
Bowbells, *U.S.A.* 108 A3
Bowdle, *U.S.A.* 108 C5
Bowelling, *Australia* 89 F2
Bowen, *Australia* 90 C4
Bowen Mts., *Australia* .. 91 F4
Bowie, *Ariz., U.S.A.* ... 111 K9
Bowie, *Tex., U.S.A.* 109 J6
Bowkān, *Iran* 67 D12
Bowland, Forest of, *U.K.* . 12 D5
Bowling Green, *Ky., U.S.A.* 104 G2
Bowling Green, *Ohio, U.S.A.* 104 E4
Bowling Green, C., *Australia* 90 B4
Bowman, *U.S.A.* 108 B3
Bowman I., *Antarctica* .. 5 C8
Bowmans, *Australia* 91 E2
Bowmanville, *Canada* ... 98 D4
Bowmore, *U.K.* 14 F2
Bowral, *Australia* 91 E5
Bowraville, *Australia* 91 E5
Bowron →, *Canada* 100 C4
Bowser L., *Canada* 100 B3
Bowsman, *Canada* 101 C8
Bowwood, *Zambia* 83 F2
Boxholm, *Sweden* 11 F9
Boxmeer, *Neths.* 17 E7
Boxtel, *Neths.* 17 E6
Boyabat, *Turkey* 66 B6
Boyaca = Casanare □, *Colombia* 120 B3
Boyce, *U.S.A.* 109 K8
Boyer →, *Canada* 100 B5
Boyle, *Ireland* 15 C3
Boyne →, *Ireland* 15 C5
Boyne City, *U.S.A.* 104 C3
Boynton Beach, *U.S.A.* . 105 M5
Boyoma, Chutes, *Zaïre* .. 82 B2
Boyup Brook, *Australia* . 89 F2
Boz Dağ, *Turkey* 66 D3
Boz Dağları, *Turkey* 66 C3
Bozburun, *Turkey* 66 D3
Bozcaada, *Turkey* 66 B2
Bozdoğan, *Turkey* 66 D3
Bozeman, *U.S.A.* 110 D8
Bozen = Bolzano, *Italy* .. 33 B8
Bozkır, *Turkey* 66 D5
Bozouls, *France* 26 D6
Bozoum, *C.A.R.* 73 G8
Bozovici, *Romania* 38 E5
Bozüyük, *Turkey* 66 C4
Bra, *Italy* 32 D4
Brabant □, *Belgium* 17 G5
Brabant L., *Canada* 101 B8
Brabrand, *Denmark* 11 H4
Brač, *Croatia* 33 E13
Bracadale, L., *U.K.* 14 D2
Bracciano, *Italy* 33 F9
Bracciano, L. di, *Italy* ... 33 F9
Bracebridge, *Canada* 98 C4
Brach, *Libya* 73 C7
Bracieux, *France* 25 E8
Bräcke, *Sweden* 10 B9

Brackettville

Brackettville, U.S.A. 109 L4
Bački Kanal, Croatia 33 E13
Brad, Romania 38 C5
Brádano →, Italy 35 B9
Bradenton, U.S.A. 105 M4
Bradford, Canada 106 B5
Bradford, U.K. 12 D6
Bradford, Pa., U.S.A. 106 E6
Bradford, Vt., U.S.A. 107 C12
Brădiceni, Romania 38 D6
Bradley, Ark., U.S.A. 109 J8
Bradley, Calif., U.S.A. 112 K6
Bradley, S. Dak., U.S.A. 108 C6
Bradley Institute, Zimbabwe 83 F3
Bradore Bay, Canada 99 B8
Bradshaw, Australia 88 C5
Brady, U.S.A. 109 K5
Brædstrup, Denmark 11 J3
Braemar, Australia 91 E2
Braeside, Canada 107 A8
Braga, Portugal 30 D2
Braga □, Portugal 30 D2
Bragado, Argentina 126 D3
Bragança, Brazil 122 B2
Bragança, Portugal 30 D4
Bragança □, Portugal 30 D4
Bragança Paulista, Brazil 127 A6
Brahmanbaria, Bangla. 61 H17
Brahmani →, India 61 J15
Brahmaputra →, India 63 G13
Braich-y-pwll, U.K. 12 E3
Braidwood, Australia 91 F4
Brăila, Romania 38 D10
Braine-l'Alleud, Belgium 17 G4
Braine-le-Comte, Belgium 17 G4
Brainerd, U.S.A. 108 B7
Braintree, U.K. 13 F8
Braintree, U.S.A. 107 D14
Brak →, S. Africa 84 D3
Brake, Germany 18 B4
Brakel, Germany 18 D5
Brakel, Neths. 16 E6
Brakwater, Namibia 84 C2
Brålanda, Sweden 11 F6
Bralorne, Canada 100 C4
Bramberg, Germany 19 E6
Bramminge, Denmark 11 J2
Brämön, Sweden 10 B11
Brampton, Canada 98 D4
Bramsche, Germany 18 C3
Bramwell, Australia 90 A3
Branco →, Brazil 121 D5
Branco, C., Brazil 122 C5
Brande, Denmark 11 J3
Brandenburg = Neubrandenburg, Germany 18 B9
Brandenburg, Germany 18 C8
Brandenburg □, Germany 18 C9
Brandfort, S. Africa 84 D4
Brandon, Canada 101 D9
Brandon, U.S.A. 107 C11
Brandon B., Ireland 15 D1
Brandon Mt., Ireland 15 D1
Brandsen, Argentina 126 D4
Brandval, Norway 10 D6
Brandvlei, S. Africa 84 E3
Brandýs, Czech. 20 E4
Branford, U.S.A. 107 E12
Braniewo, Poland 20 A9
Bransfield Str., Antarctica 5 C18
Branson, Colo., U.S.A. 109 G3
Branson, Mo., U.S.A. 109 G8
Brantford, Canada 98 D3
Brantôme, France 26 C4
Branxholme, Australia 91 F3
Branzi, Italy 32 B6
Bras d'Or, L., Canada 99 C7
Brasiléia, Brazil 124 C4
Brasília, Brazil 123 E2
Brasília Legal, Brazil 121 D6
Braslaw, Belarus 9 J22
Braslovce, Slovenia 33 B12
Braşov, Romania 38 D8
Brass, Nigeria 79 E6
Brass →, Nigeria 79 E6
Brassac-les-Mines, France 26 C7
Brasschaat, Belgium 17 F4
Brassey, Banjaran, Malaysia 56 D5
Brassey Ra., Australia 89 E3
Brasstown Bald, U.S.A. 105 H4
Brastad, Sweden 9 G14
Bratislava, Slovak Rep. 21 G7
Bratsk, Russia 45 D11
Brattleboro, U.S.A. 107 D12
Braunau, Austria 21 G3
Braunschweig, Germany 18 C6
Braunton, U.K. 13 F3
Brava, Somali Rep. 68 G3
Bråviken, Sweden 10 F10
Bravo del Norte →, Mexico 114 B5
Bravo del Norte, R. = Grande, Rio →, U.S.A. 109 N6
Brawley, U.S.A. 113 N11
Bray, Ireland 15 C5
Bray, Mt., Australia 90 A1
Bray, Pays de, France 25 C8
Bray-sur-Seine, France 25 D10
Brazeau →, Canada 100 C5
Brazil, U.S.A. 104 F2
Brazil ■, S. Amer. 123 D2
Brazo Sur →, S. Amer. 126 B4
Brazos →, U.S.A. 109 L7
Brazzaville, Congo 80 E3
Brčko, Bos.-H. 21 L8
Brea, Peru 124 A1
Breadalbane, Australia 90 C2
Breadalbane, U.K. 14 E4
Breaden, L., Australia 89 E4
Breaksea Sd., N.Z. 87 L1
Bream B., N.Z. 87 F5
Bream Hd., N.Z. 87 F5
Breas, Chile 126 B1
Brebes, Indonesia 57 G13
Brechin, Canada 106 B5
Brechin, U.K. 14 E6
Brecht, Belgium 17 F5
Breckenridge, Colo., U.S.A. 110 G10
Breckenridge, Minn., U.S.A. 108 B6
Breckenridge, Tex., U.S.A. 109 J5
Breckland, U.K. 13 E8
Brecknock, Pen., Chile 128 D2
Břeclav, Czech. 20 G6
Brecon, U.K. 13 F4
Brecon Beacons, U.K. 13 F4
Breda, Neths. 17 E5
Bredasdorp, S. Africa 84 E3
Bredbo, Australia 91 F4
Bredene, Belgium 17 F1
Bredstedt, Germany 18 A4
Bree, Belgium 17 F7
Breezand, Neths. 16 C5
Bregalnica →, Macedonia 39 H5
Bregenz, Austria 19 H5
Bréhal, France 24 D5
Bréhat, I. de, France 24 D4
Breiðafjörður, Iceland 8 D2
Breil-sur-Roya, France 27 E11
Breisach, Germany 19 G3
Brejinho de Nazaré, Brazil 122 D2
Brejo, Brazil 122 B3
Bremen, Germany 18 B4
Bremen □, Germany 18 B4
Bremer I., Australia 90 A2
Bremerhaven, Germany 18 B4
Bremerton, U.S.A. 112 C4
Bremervörde, Germany 18 B5
Bremsnes, Norway 10 A1
Brenes, Spain 31 H5
Brenham, U.S.A. 109 K6
Brenner P., Austria 19 H7
Breno, Italy 32 C7
Brent, Canada 98 C4
Brent, U.K. 13 F7
Brenta →, Italy 33 C9
Brentwood, U.K. 13 F8
Brentwood, U.S.A. 107 F11
Bréscia, Italy 32 C7
Breskens, Neths. 17 F3
Breslau = Wrocław, Poland 20 D7
Bresle →, France 24 B8
Bresles, France 25 C9
Bressanone, Italy 33 B8
Bressay, U.K. 14 A7
Bresse, France 25 F12
Bressuire, France 24 F6
Brest, Belarus 41 F2
Brest, France 24 D2
Brest-Litovsk = Brest, Belarus 41 F2
Bretagne, France 24 D4
Bretçu, Romania 38 C9
Breteuil, Eure, France 24 D7
Breteuil, Oise, France 25 C9
Breton, Canada 100 C6
Breton, Pertuis, France 26 B2
Breton Sd., U.S.A. 109 L10
Brett, C., N.Z. 87 F5
Bretten, Germany 19 F4
Breukelen, Neths. 16 D6
Brevard, U.S.A. 105 H4
Breves, Brazil 122 B1
Brevik, Norway 10 E3
Brewarrina, Australia 91 D4
Brewer, U.S.A. 99 D6
Brewer, Mt., U.S.A. 112 J8
Brewster, N.Y., U.S.A. 107 E11
Brewster, Wash., U.S.A. 110 B4
Brewster, Kap, Greenland 4 B6
Brewton, U.S.A. 105 K2
Breyten, S. Africa 85 D4
Brezhnev = Naberezhnyye Chelny, Russia 42 C11
Brežice, Slovenia 33 C12
Brézina, Algeria 75 B5
Březnice, Czech. 20 F3
Breznik, Bulgaria 38 G5
Brezno, Slovak Rep. 20 G9
Bria, C.A.R. 73 G9
Briançon, France 27 D10
Briare, France 25 E9
Bribie I., Australia 91 D5
Bricquebec, France 24 C5
Bridgehampton, U.S.A. 107 F12
Bridgend, U.K. 13 F4
Bridgeport, Calif., U.S.A. 111 G4
Bridgeport, Conn., U.S.A. 107 E11
Bridgeport, Nebr., U.S.A. 108 E3
Bridgeport, Tex., U.S.A. 109 J6
Bridger, U.S.A. 110 D9
Bridgeton, U.S.A. 104 F8
Bridgetown, Australia 89 F2
Bridgetown, Barbados 117 D8
Bridgetown, Canada 99 D6
Bridgewater, Canada 99 D7
Bridgewater, Mass., U.S.A. 107 E14
Bridgewater, S. Dak., U.S.A. 108 D6
Bridgewater, C., Australia 91 F3
Bridgnorth, U.K. 13 E5
Bridgton, U.S.A. 107 B14
Bridgwater, U.K. 13 F4
Bridlington, U.K. 12 C7
Bridport, Australia 90 G4
Bridport, U.K. 13 G5
Brie, Plaine de la, France 25 D10
Brie-Comte-Robert, France 25 D9
Briec, France 24 D2
Brielle, Neths. 16 E4
Brienne-le-Château, France 25 D11
Brienon-sur-Armançon, France 25 E10
Brienz, Switz. 22 C6
Brienzersee, Switz. 22 C5
Brig, Switz. 22 D5
Brigg, U.K. 12 D7
Briggsdale, U.S.A. 108 E2
Brigham City, U.S.A. 110 F7
Bright, Australia 91 F4
Brighton, Australia 91 F2
Brighton, Canada 98 D4
Brighton, U.K. 13 G7
Brighton, U.S.A. 108 F2
Brignogan-Plage, France 24 D2
Brignoles, France 27 E10
Brihuega, Spain 28 E2
Brikama, Gambia 78 C1
Brilliant, Canada 100 D5
Brilliant, U.S.A. 106 F4
Brilon, Germany 18 D4
Bríndisi, Italy 35 B10
Brinje, Croatia 33 D12
Brinkley, U.S.A. 109 H9
Brinkworth, Australia 91 E2
Brinnon, U.S.A. 112 C4
Brion, I., Canada 99 C7
Brionne, France 24 C7
Brionski, Croatia 33 D10
Brioude, France 26 C7
Briouze, France 24 D6
Brisbane, Australia 91 D5
Brisbane →, Australia 91 D5
Brisighella, Italy 33 D8
Bristol, U.K. 13 F5
Bristol, Conn., U.S.A. 107 E12
Bristol, Pa., U.S.A. 107 F10
Bristol, R.I., U.S.A. 107 E13
Bristol, S. Dak., U.S.A. 108 C6
Bristol, Tenn., U.S.A. 105 G4
Bristol B., U.S.A. 96 C4
Bristol Channel, U.K. 13 F3
Bristol I., Antarctica 5 B1
Bristol L., U.S.A. 111 J5
Bristow, U.S.A. 109 H6
British Columbia □, Canada 100 C3
British Isles, Europe 6 E5
Brits, S. Africa 85 D4
Britstown, S. Africa 84 E3
Britt, Canada 98 C3
Brittany = Bretagne, France 24 D4
Britton, U.S.A. 108 C6
Brive-la-Gaillarde, France 26 C5
Briviesca, Spain 28 C1
Brixen = Bressanone, Italy 33 B8
Brixton, Australia 90 C3
Brlik, Kazakhstan 44 E8
Brno, Czech. 20 F6
Bro, Sweden 10 E11
Broad →, U.S.A. 105 J5
Broad Arrow, Australia 89 F3
Broad B., U.K. 14 C2
Broad Haven, Ireland 15 B2
Broad Law, U.K. 14 F5
Broad Sd., Australia 90 C4
Broadhurst Ra., Australia 88 D3
Broads, The, U.K. 12 E9
Broadus, U.S.A. 108 C2
Broadview, Canada 101 C8
Broager, Denmark 11 K3
Broaryd, Sweden 11 G7
Brochet, Canada 101 B8
Brochet, L., Canada 101 B8
Brock, Canada 101 C7
Brocken, Germany 18 D6
Brockport, U.S.A. 106 C7
Brockton, U.S.A. 107 D13
Brockville, Canada 98 D4
Brockway, Mont., U.S.A. 108 B2
Brockway, Pa., U.S.A. 106 E6
Brocton, U.S.A. 106 D5
Brod, Macedonia 39 H4
Brodarevo, Serbia, Yug. 21 M9
Brodeur Pen., Canada 97 A11
Brodick, U.K. 14 F3
Brodnica, Poland 20 B9
Brody, Ukraine 41 G3
Broechem, Belgium 17 F5
Broek, Neths. 16 D6
Broek op Langedijk, Neths. 16 C5
Brogan, U.S.A. 110 D5
Broglie, France 24 C7
Broken Bow, Nebr., U.S.A. 108 E5
Broken Bow, Okla., U.S.A. 109 H7
Broken Hill = Kabwe, Zambia 83 E2
Broken Hill, Australia 91 E3
Brokind, Sweden 11 F9
Brokopondo, Surinam 121 B7
Brokopondo □, Surinam 121 C6
Bromfield, U.K. 13 E5
Bromley, U.K. 13 F8
Brønderslev, Denmark 11 G3
Brong-Ahafo □, Ghana 78 D4
Bronkhorstspruit, S. Africa 85 D4
Brønnøysund, Norway 8 D15
Bronte, Italy 35 E7
Bronte, U.S.A. 109 K4
Bronte Park, Australia 90 G4
Brook Park, U.S.A. 106 E4
Brookfield, U.S.A. 108 F8
Brookhaven, U.S.A. 109 K9
Brookings, Oreg., U.S.A. 110 E1
Brookings, S. Dak., U.S.A. 108 C6
Brooklin, Canada 106 C6
Brookmere, Canada 100 D4
Brooks, Canada 100 C6
Brooks B., Canada 100 C3
Brooks L., Canada 101 A7
Brooks Ra., U.S.A. 96 B5
Brooksville, U.S.A. 105 L4
Brookville, U.S.A. 104 F3
Brooloo, Australia 91 D5
Broom, L., U.K. 14 D3
Broome, Australia 88 C3
Broomehill, Australia 89 F2
Broons, France 24 D4
Brora, U.K. 14 C5
Brora →, U.K. 14 C5
Brosna →, Ireland 15 C4
Broşteni, Romania 38 B8
Brotas de Macaúbas, Brazil 123 D3
Brothers, U.S.A. 110 E3
Brøttum, Norway 10 C4
Brou, France 24 D8
Brouage, Ramparts de, France 26 C2
Brough, U.K. 12 C5
Broughton Island, Canada 97 B13
Broughty Ferry, U.K. 14 E6
Brouwershaven, Neths. 16 E3
Brouwershavensche Gat, Neths. 16 E3
Brovary, Ukraine 41 G6
Brovst, Denmark 11 G3
Browerville, U.S.A. 108 B7
Brown, Pt., Australia 91 E1
Brown Willy, U.K. 13 G3
Brownfield, U.S.A. 109 J3
Browning, U.S.A. 110 B7
Brownlee, Canada 101 C7
Brownsville, Oreg., U.S.A. 110 D2
Brownsville, Tenn., U.S.A. 109 H10
Brownsville, Tex., U.S.A. 109 N6
Brownsweg, Surinam 121 B6
Brownwood, U.S.A. 109 K5
Brownwood, L., U.S.A. 109 K5
Browse I., Australia 88 B3
Broye →, Switz. 22 C3
Brozas, Spain 31 F4
Bruas, Malaysia 59 K3
Bruay-en-Artois, France 25 B9
Bruce, Mt., Australia 88 D2
Bruce Pen., Canada 106 A3
Bruce Rock, Australia 89 F2
Bruche →, France 25 D14
Bruchsal, Germany 19 F4
Bruck an der Leitha, Austria 21 G6
Bruck an der Mur, Austria 21 H5
Brue →, U.K. 13 F5
Brugelette, Belgium 17 G3
Bruges = Brugge, Belgium 17 F2
Brugg, Switz. 22 B6
Brugge, Belgium 17 F2
Brühl, Germany 18 E2
Bruinisse, Neths. 17 E4
Brûlé, Canada 100 C5
Brûlon, France 24 E6
Brûly, Belgium 17 J5
Brumado, Brazil 123 D3
Brumado →, Brazil 123 D3
Brumath, France 25 D14
Brummen, Neths. 16 D8
Brumunddal, Norway 10 D4
Brunchilly, Australia 90 B1
Brundidge, U.S.A. 105 K3
Bruneau, U.S.A. 110 E6
Bruneau →, U.S.A. 110 E6
Bruneck = Brunico, Italy 33 B8
Brunei = Bandar Seri Begawan, Brunei 56 C4
Brunei ■, Asia 56 D4
Brunette Downs, Australia 90 B2
Brunflo, Sweden 10 A8
Brunico, Italy 33 B8
Brünig, P., Switz. 22 C6
Brunkeberg, Norway 10 E2
Brunna, Sweden 10 E11
Brunnen, Switz. 23 C7
Brunner, L., N.Z. 87 K3
Bruno, Canada 101 C7
Brunsbüttel, Germany 18 B5
Brunssum, Neths. 17 G7
Brunswick = Braunschweig, Germany 18 C6
Brunswick, Ga., U.S.A. 105 K5
Brunswick, Maine, U.S.A. 99 D6
Brunswick, Md., U.S.A. 104 F7
Brunswick, Mo., U.S.A. 108 F8
Brunswick, Ohio, U.S.A. 106 E3
Brunswick, Pen. de, Chile 128 D2
Brunswick B., Australia 88 C3
Brunswick Junction, Australia 89 F2
Bruntál, Czech. 20 F7
Bruny I., Australia 90 G4
Brus Laguna, Honduras 116 C3
Brusartsi, Bulgaria 38 F6
Brush, U.S.A. 108 E3
Brushton, U.S.A. 107 B10
Brusio, Switz. 23 D10
Brusque, Brazil 127 B6
Brussel, Belgium 17 G4
Brussels = Brussel, Belgium 17 G4
Brussels, Canada 106 C3
Brustem, Belgium 17 G6
Bruthen, Australia 91 F4
Bruxelles = Brussel, Belgium 17 G4
Bruyères, France 25 D13
Bryan, Ohio, U.S.A. 104 E3
Bryan, Tex., U.S.A. 109 K6
Bryan, Mt., Australia 91 E2
Bryanka, Ukraine 41 H10
Bryansk, Russia 42 D2
Bryansk, Russia 43 H8
Bryanskoye = Bryansk, Russia 43 H8
Bryant, U.S.A. 108 C6
Bryne, Norway 9 G11
Bryson City, U.S.A. 105 H4
Bryukhovetskaya, Russia 43 H4
Brza Palanka, Serbia, Yug. 21 L12
Brzava →, Serbia, Yug. 21 K10
Brzeg, Poland 20 E7
Brzeg Din, Poland 20 D6
Bsharri, Lebanon 69 A5
Bū Baqarah, U.A.E. 65 E8
Bu Craa, W. Sahara 74 C2
Bū Ḩasā, U.A.E. 65 F7
Bua Yai, Thailand 58 E4
Buapinang, Indonesia 57 E6
Buayan, Phil. 57 C7
Buba, Guinea-Biss. 78 C2
Bubanza, Burundi 82 C2
Būbiyān, Kuwait 65 D6
Bucak, Turkey 66 D4
Bucaramanga, Colombia 120 B3
Bucas Grande I., Phil. 55 G6
Buccaneer Arch., Australia 88 C3
Bucchiánico, Italy 33 F11
Bucecea, Romania 38 B9
Buchach, Ukraine 41 H3
Buchan, U.K. 14 D6
Buchan Ness, U.K. 14 D7
Buchanan, Canada 101 C8
Buchanan, Liberia 78 D2
Buchanan, L., Queens., Australia 90 C4
Buchanan, L., W. Austral., Australia 89 E3
Buchanan, L., U.S.A. 109 K5
Buchanan Cr. →, Australia 90 B2
Buchans, Canada 99 C8
Bucharest = Bucureşti, Romania 38 E9
Buchholz, Germany 18 B5
Buchloe, Germany 19 G6
Buchon, Pt., U.S.A. 112 K6
Buchs, Switz. 23 B8
Bückeburg, Germany 18 C5
Buckeye, U.S.A. 111 K7
Buckhannon, U.S.A. 104 F5
Buckhaven, U.K. 14 E5
Buckie, U.K. 14 D6
Buckingham, Canada 98 C4
Buckingham, U.K. 13 F7
Buckingham B., Australia 90 A2
Buckinghamshire □, U.K. 13 F7
Buckle Hd., Australia 88 B4
Buckleboo, Australia 91 E2
Buckley, U.S.A. 110 C2
Buckley →, Australia 90 C2
Bucklin, U.S.A. 109 G5
Bucks L., U.S.A. 112 F5
Bucquoy, France 25 B9
Buctouche, Canada 99 C7
Bucureşti, Romania 38 E9
Bucyrus, U.S.A. 104 E4
Budafok, Hungary 21 H9
Budalin, Burma 61 H19
Budapest, Hungary 21 H9
Budaun, India 63 E8
Budd Coast, Antarctica 5 C8
Buddusò, Italy 34 B2
Bude, U.K. 13 G3
Budel, Neths. 17 F7
Budennovsk, Russia 43 H7
Budeşti, Romania 38 E9
Budge Budge = Baj Baj, India 63 H13
Budgewoi, Australia 91 E5
Búðareyri, Iceland 8 D6
Budia, Spain 28 E2
Budjala, Zaïre 80 D3
Búdrio, Italy 33 D8
Buea, Cameroon 79 E6
Buellton, U.S.A. 113 L6
Buena Vista, Bolivia 125 D5
Buena Vista, Colo., U.S.A. 111 G10
Buena Vista, Va., U.S.A. 104 G6
Buena Vista L., U.S.A. 113 K7
Buenaventura, Colombia 120 C2
Buenaventura, Mexico 114 B3
Buenaventura, B. de, Colombia 120 C2
Buendía, Pantano de, Spain 28 E2
Buenópolis, Brazil 123 E3
Buenos Aires, Argentina 126 C4
Buenos Aires, Colombia 120 C3
Buenos Aires, Costa Rica 116 E3
Buenos Aires □, Argentina 126 D4
Buenos Aires, L., Chile 128 C2
Buesaco, Colombia 120 C2
Buffalo, Mo., U.S.A. 109 G8

Buffalo, N.Y., U.S.A. 106 D6
Buffalo, Okla., U.S.A. 109 G5
Buffalo, S. Dak., U.S.A. .. 108 C3
Buffalo, Wyo., U.S.A. 110 D10
Buffalo →, Canada 100 A5
Buffalo Head Hills, Canada 100 B5
Buffalo L., Canada 100 C6
Buffalo Narrows, Canada . 101 B7
Buffels →, S. Africa 84 D2
Buford, U.S.A. 105 H4
Bug = Buh →, Ukraine .. 41 J6
Bug →, Poland 20 C11
Buga, Colombia 120 C2
Buganda, Uganda 82 C3
Buganga, Uganda 82 C3
Bugasong, Phil. 55 F5
Bugeat, France 26 C5
Bugel, Tanjung, Indonesia 56 F4
Buggenhout, Belgium 17 F4
Bugibba, Malta 37 D1
Bugsuk, Phil. 55 G2
Buguma, Nigeria 79 E6
Bugun Shara, Mongolia .. 54 B5
Buguruslan, Russia 44 D6
Buh →, Ukraine 41 J6
Buhăeşti, Romania 38 C10
Buheirat-Murrat-el-Kubra,
  Egypt 76 H8
Buhl, Idaho, U.S.A. 110 E6
Buhl, Minn., U.S.A. 108 B8
Buick, U.S.A. 109 G9
Builth Wells, U.K. 13 E4
Buinsk, Russia 42 C9
Buíque, Brazil 122 C4
Buir Nur, Mongolia 54 B6
Buis-les-Baronnies, France 27 D9
Buitenpost, Neths. 16 B8
Buitrago, Spain 30 E7
Bujalance, Spain 31 H6
Buján, Spain 30 C2
Bujaraloz, Spain 28 D4
Buje, Croatia 33 C10
Bujumbura, Burundi 82 C2
Bukachacha, Russia 45 D12
Bukama, Zaïre 83 D2
Bukavu, Zaïre 82 C2
Bukene, Tanzania 82 C3
Bukhara = Bukhoro,
  Uzbekistan 44 F7
Bukhoro, Uzbekistan 44 F7
Bukima, Tanzania 82 C3
Bukit Mertajam, Malaysia 59 K3
Bukittinggi, Indonesia ... 56 E2
Bukoba, Tanzania 82 C3
Bukoba □, Tanzania 82 C3
Bukuru, Nigeria 79 D6
Bukuya, Uganda 82 B3
Bula, Guinea-Biss. 78 C1
Bula, Indonesia 57 E8
Bülach, Switz. 23 A7
Bulahdelah, Australia 91 E5
Bulancak, Turkey 67 B8
Bulandshahr, India 62 E7
Bulanık, Turkey 67 C10
Bûlâq, Egypt 76 B3
Bulan, Phil. 55 E5
Bulgan, Mongolia 54 B5
Bulgar, Russia 42 C9
Bulgaria ■, Europe 38 G8
Bulgroo, Australia 91 D3
Bulgunnia, Australia 91 E1
Bulhar, Somali Rep. 68 E3
Buli, Teluk, Indonesia ... 57 D7
Buliluyan, C., Phil. 55 G2
Bulki, Ethiopia 77 F4
Bulkley →, Canada 100 B3
Bull Shoals L., U.S.A. .. 109 G8
Bullange, Belgium 17 H8
Bullaque →, Spain 31 G6
Bullara, Australia 88 D1
Bullaring, Australia 89 F2
Bullas, Spain 29 G3
Bulle, Switz. 22 C4
Bulli, Australia 91 E5
Bullock Creek, Australia . 90 B3
Bulloo →, Australia 91 D3
Bulloo Downs, Queens.,
  Australia 91 D3
Bulloo Downs, W. Austral.,
  Australia 88 D2
Bulloo L., Australia 91 D3
Bulls, N.Z. 87 J5
Bully-les-Mines, France ... 25 B9
Bulnes, Chile 126 D1
Bulo Burti, Somali Rep. . 68 G4
Bulsar = Valsad, India .. 60 J8
Bultfontein, S. Africa .. 84 D4
Bulu Karakelong, Indonesia 57 D7
Bulukumba, Indonesia ... 57 F6
Bulun, Russia 45 B13
Bulus, Russia 45 C13
Bumba, Zaïre 80 D4
Bumbiri I., Tanzania 82 C3
Bumhpa Bum, Burma .. 61 F20
Bumi →, Zimbabwe 83 F2
Buna, Kenya 82 B4
Bunawan, Agusan del S.,
  Phil. 55 G6
Bunawan, Davao del S.,
  Phil. 55 H6
Bunazi, Tanzania 82 C3
Bunbah, Khalīj, Libya .. 73 B9
Bunbury, Australia 89 F2
Buncrana, Ireland 15 A4
Bundaberg, Australia 91 C5

Bünde, Germany 18 C4
Bundey →, Australia 90 C2
Bundi, India 62 G6
Bundooma, Australia 90 C1
Bundoran, Ireland 15 B3
Bundukia, Sudan 77 F3
Bung Kan, Thailand 58 C4
Bungatakada, Japan 49 H5
Bungil Cr. →, Australia 90 D4
Bungo-Suidō, Japan 49 H6
Bungoma, Kenya 82 B3
Bungu, Tanzania 82 D4
Bunia, Zaïre 82 B3
Bunji, Pakistan 63 B6
Bunkie, U.S.A. 109 K8
Bunnell, U.S.A. 105 L5
Bunnik, Neths. 16 D6
Buñol, Spain 29 F4
Bunsbeek, Belgium 17 G5
Bunschoten, Neths. 16 D6
Buntok, Indonesia 56 E4
Bununu, Nigeria 79 D6
Bununu Dass, Nigeria .. 79 C6
Bünyan, Turkey 66 C6
Bunyu, Indonesia 56 D5
Buol, Indonesia 57 D6
Buon Brieng, Vietnam .. 58 F7
Buon Me Thuot, Vietnam . 58 F7
Buong Long, Cambodia .. 58 F6
Buorkhaya, Mys, Russia .. 45 B14
Buqayq, Si. Arabia 65 E6
Buqbuq, Egypt 76 A2
Bur Acaba, Somali Rep. . 68 G3
Bûr Fuad, Egypt 76 H8
Bûr Safâga, Egypt 76 B3
Bûr Sa'îd, Egypt 76 H8
Bûr Sûdân, Sudan 76 D4
Bûr Taufiq, Egypt 76 J8
Bura, Kenya 82 C4
Burao, Somali Rep. 68 F4
Burāq, Syria 69 B5
Buras, U.S.A. 109 L10
Buraydah, Si. Arabia .. 64 E5
Burbank, U.S.A. 113 L8
Burcher, Australia 91 E4
Burdekin →, Australia .. 90 B4
Burdett, Canada 100 D6
Burdur, Turkey 66 D4
Burdur Gölü, Turkey 66 D4
Burdwan = Barddhaman,
  India 63 H12
Bure, Ethiopia 77 E4
Bure →, U.K. 12 E9
Büren, Germany 18 D4
Buren, Neths. 16 E6
Bureya →, Russia 45 E13
Burford, Canada 106 C4
Burg, Germany 18 C7
Burg auf Fehmarn,
  Germany 18 A7
Burg el Arab, Egypt 76 H6
Burg et Tuyur, Sudan 76 C2
Burg Stargard, Germany . 18 B9
Burgas, Bulgaria 38 G10
Burgdorf, Germany 18 C5
Burgdorf, Switz. 22 B5
Burgeo, Canada 99 C8
Burgersdorp, S. Africa .. 84 E4
Burges, Mt., Australia .. 89 F3
Burghausen, Germany .. 19 G8
Búrgio, Italy 34 E6
Bürglen, Switz. 23 C7
Burglengenfeld, Germany . 19 F8
Burgo de Osma, Spain .. 28 D1
Burgohondo, Spain 30 E6
Burgos, Spain 28 C1
Burgos □, Spain 28 C1
Burgstädt, Germany 18 E8
Burgsvik, Sweden 9 H18
Burguillos del Cerro, Spain 31 G4
Burgundy = Bourgogne,
  France 25 F11
Burhaniye, Turkey 66 C2
Burhanpur, India 60 J10
Burhou, U.K. 24 C4
Buri Pen., Eritrea 77 D4
Burias, Phil. 55 E5
Burica, Pta., Costa Rica . 116 E3
Buriti Alegre, Brazil 123 E2
Buriti Bravo, Brazil 122 C3
Buriti dos Lopes, Brazil . 122 B3
Burj Sāfitā, Syria 66 E7
Burji, Ethiopia 77 F4
Burkburnett, U.S.A. 109 H5
Burke, U.S.A. 110 C6
Burke →, Australia 90 C2
Burketown, Australia 90 B2
Burkina Faso ■, Africa . 78 C4
Burk's Falls, Canada .. 98 C4
Burley, U.S.A. 110 E7
Burlingame, U.S.A. 112 H4
Burlington, Canada 106 C5
Burlington, Colo., U.S.A. 108 F3
Burlington, Iowa, U.S.A. 108 E9
Burlington, Kans., U.S.A. 108 F7
Burlington, N.C., U.S.A. 105 G6
Burlington, N.J., U.S.A. . 107 F10
Burlington, Vt., U.S.A. .. 107 B11
Burlington, Wash., U.S.A. 112 B4
Burlington, Wis., U.S.A. . 104 D1
Burlyu-Tyube, Kazakhstan 44 E8
Burma ■, Asia 61 J20
Burnaby I., Canada 100 C2

Burnet, U.S.A. 109 K5
Burney, U.S.A. 110 F3
Burngup, Australia 89 F2
Burnham, U.S.A. 106 F7
Burnie, Australia 90 G4
Burnley, U.K. 12 D5
Burns, Oreg., U.S.A. .. 110 E4
Burns, Wyo., U.S.A. .. 108 E2
Burns Lake, Canada 100 C3
Burnside →, Canada .. 96 B9
Burnside, L., Australia .. 89 E3
Burnt River, Canada .. 106 B6
Burntwood →, Canada . 101 B9
Burntwood L., Canada .. 101 B8
Burqān, Kuwait 64 D5
Burqin, China 54 B3
Burra, Australia 91 E2
Burramurra, Australia .. 90 C2
Burreli, Albania 39 H3
Burren Junction, Australia 91 E4
Burrendong Dam, Australia 91 E4
Burriana, Spain 28 F4
Burrinjuck Res., Australia 91 F4
Burro, Serranías del,
  Mexico 114 B4
Burruyacú, Argentina 126 B3
Burry Port, U.K. 13 F3
Bursa, Turkey 66 B3
Burseryd, Sweden 11 G7
Burstall, Canada 101 C7
Burton L., Canada 98 B4
Burton upon Trent, U.K. . 12 E6
Burtundy, Australia 91 E3
Buru, Indonesia 57 E7
Burullus, Bahra el, Egypt 76 H7
Burûn, Râs, Egypt 69 D2
Burundi ■, Africa 82 C3
Bururi, Burundi 82 C2
Burutu, Nigeria 79 D6
Burwell, U.S.A. 108 E5
Bury, U.K. 12 D5
Bury St. Edmunds, U.K. . 13 E8
Buryatia □, Russia 45 D11
Buryn, Ukraine 41 G7
Busalla, Italy 32 D5
Busango Swamp, Zambia . 83 E2
Buşayrah, Syria 67 E9
Buşayyah, Iraq 64 D5
Busca, Italy 32 D4
Büshehr, Iran 65 D6
Büshehr □, Iran 65 D6
Bushell, Canada 101 B7
Bushenyi, Uganda 82 C3
Bushire = Büshehr, Iran . 65 D6
Bushnell, Ill., U.S.A. .. 108 E9
Bushnell, Nebr., U.S.A. . 108 E3
Busia □, Kenya 82 B3
Busie, Ghana 78 C4
Businga, Zaïre 80 D4
Buskerud fylke □, Norway 10 D3
Busko Zdrój, Poland .. 20 E10
Busovača, Bos.-H. 21 L7
Busra ash Shām, Syria .. 69 C5
Bussang, France 25 E13
Busselton, Australia 89 F2
Busseto, Italy 32 D7
Bussigny, Switz. 22 C3
Bussum, Neths. 16 D6
Bustamante, B., Argentina 128 C3
Busto, C., Spain 30 B4
Busto Arsízio, Italy 32 C5
Busu-Djanoa, Zaïre 80 D4
Busuanga, Phil. 55 E3
Büsum, Germany 18 A4
Buta, Zaïre 82 B1
Butare, Rwanda 82 C2
Butaritari, Kiribati 92 G9
Bute, U.K. 14 F3
Bute Inlet, Canada 100 C4
Butemba, Uganda 82 B3
Butembo, Zaïre 82 B2
Butera, Italy 35 E7
Bütgenbach, Belgium .. 17 H8
Butha Qi, China 54 B7
Butiaba, Uganda 82 B3
Butler, Mo., U.S.A. 108 F7
Butler, Pa., U.S.A. 106 F5
Buton, Indonesia 57 E6
Bütschwil, Switz. 23 B8
Butte, Mont., U.S.A. .. 110 C7
Butte, Nebr., U.S.A. .. 108 D5
Butte Creek →, U.S.A. . 112 F5
Butterworth = Gcuwa,
  S. Africa 85 E4
Butterworth, Malaysia ... 59 K3
Buttfield, Mt., Australia . 89 E4
Button B., Canada 101 B10
Buttonwillow, U.S.A. .. 113 K7
Butty Hd., Australia 89 F3
Butuan, Phil. 55 G6
Butuku-Luba, Eq. Guin. . 79 E6
Butung = Buton, Indonesia 57 E6
Buturlinovka, Russia 42 E5
Butzbach, Germany 18 E4
Bützow, Germany 18 B7
Buxar, India 63 G10
Buxton, Guyana 121 B6
Buxton, U.K. 12 D6
Buxy, France 25 F11
Buy, Russia 42 A5
Buynaksk, Russia 43 J8
Büyük Menderes →,
  Turkey 66 D2
Büyükçekmece, Turkey .. 66 B3
Buzançais, France 24 F8
Buzău, Romania 38 D9
Buzău →, Romania 38 D10

Buzău, Pasul, Romania .. 38 D9
Buzen, Japan 49 H5
Buzet, Croatia 33 C10
Buzi →, Mozam. 83 F3
Buziaş, Romania 38 D4
Buzuluk, Russia 44 D6
Buzuluk →, Russia 42 E6
Buzzards Bay, U.S.A. .. 107 E14
Bwana Mkubwe, Zaïre ... 83 E2
Byala, Bulgaria 38 F8
Byala Slatina, Bulgaria .. 38 F6
Byarezina →, Belarus .. 41 F6
Byaroza, Belarus 41 F3
Bychawa, Poland 20 D12
Bydgoszcz, Poland 20 B8
Byelarus = Belarus ■,
  Europe 40 F4
Byelorussia = Belarus ■,
  Europe 40 F4
Byers, U.S.A. 108 F2
Byesville, U.S.A. 106 G3
Byhalia, U.S.A. 109 H10
Bykhaw, Belarus 40 F6
Bykhov = Bykhaw, Belarus 40 F6
Bykovo, Russia 42 F7
Bylas, U.S.A. 111 K8
Bylderup, Denmark 11 K3
Bylot I., Canada 97 A12
Byrd, C., Antarctica 5 C17
Byro, Australia 89 E2
Byrock, Australia 91 E4
Byron Bay, Australia 91 D5
Byrranga, Gory, Russia .. 45 B11
Byrranga Mts. = Byrranga,
  Gory, Russia 45 B11
Byrum, Denmark 11 G5
Byske, Sweden 8 D19
Byske älv →, Sweden .. 8 D19
Bystrzyca Kłodzka, Poland 20 E6
Bytom, Poland 20 E8
Bytów, Poland 20 A7
Byumba, Rwanda 82 C3

C

Ca →, Vietnam 58 C5
Ca Mau = Quan Long,
  Vietnam 59 H5
Ca Mau, Mui = Bai Bung,
  Mui, Vietnam 59 H5
Ca Na, Vietnam 59 G7
Caacupé, Paraguay 126 B4
Caála, Angola 81 G3
Caamano Sd., Canada .. 100 C3
Caapiranga, Brazil 121 D5
Caazapá, Paraguay 126 B4
Caazapá □, Paraguay .. 127 B4
Cabadbaran, Phil. 55 G6
Cabalian, Phil. 55 F6
Caballeria, C. de, Spain . 36 A11
Cabana, Peru 124 B2
Cabanaconde, Peru 124 D3
Cabañaquinta, Spain .. 30 B5
Cabanatuan, Phil. 55 D4
Cabanes, Spain 28 E5
Cabanillas, Peru 124 D3
Cabano, Canada 99 C6
Čabar, Croatia 33 C11
Cabazon, U.S.A. 113 M10
Cabedelo, Brazil 122 C5
Cabeza del Buey, Spain . 31 G5
Cabildo, Chile 126 C1
Cabimas, Venezuela .. 120 A3
Cabinda, Angola 80 F2
Cabinda □, Angola 80 F2
Cabinet Mts., U.S.A. .. 110 C6
Cabo Blanco, Argentina . 128 C3
Cabo Frio, Brazil 123 F3
Cabo Pantoja, Peru 120 D2
Cabo Raso, Argentina .. 128 B3
Cabonga, Réservoir,
  Canada 98 C4
Cabool, U.S.A. 109 G8
Caboolture, Australia .. 91 D5
Cabora Bassa Dam =
  Cahora Bassa Dam,
  Mozam. 83 F3
Caborca, Mexico 114 A2
Cabot, Mt., U.S.A. 107 B13
Cabot Str., Canada 99 C8
Cabra, Spain 31 H6
Cabra del Santo Cristo,
  Spain 29 H1
Cábras, Italy 34 C1
Cabrera, Spain 36 B9
Cabrera, Sierra, Spain .. 30 C4
Cabri, Canada 101 C7
Cabriel →, Spain 29 F3
Cabruta, Venezuela .. 120 B4
Cabugao, Phil. 55 C4
Cabuyaro, Colombia .. 120 C3
Čačak, Serbia, Yug. .. 21 M10
Cacao, Fr. Guiana 121 C7
Cáceres, Brazil 125 D6
Cáceres, Colombia .. 120 B2
Cáceres, Spain 31 F4
Cáceres □, Spain 31 F4
Cache Bay, Canada 98 C4
Cache Cr. →, U.S.A. .. 112 G5
Cachepo, Portugal 31 H3
Cachéu, Guinea-Biss. .. 78 C1
Cachi, Argentina 126 B2
Cachimbo, Brazil 125 B7
Cachimbo, Serra do, Brazil 125 B6

Cachoeira, Brazil 123 D4
Cachoeira Alta, Brazil .. 123 E1
Cachoeira de Itapemirim,
  Brazil 123 F3
Cachoeira do Sul, Brazil . 127 C5
Cachoeiro do Arari, Brazil 122 B2
Cachopo, Portugal 31 H3
Cachuela Esperanza,
  Bolivia 125 C4
Cacólo, Angola 80 G3
Caconda, Angola 81 G3
Cacongo, Angola 80 F2
Caçu, Brazil 123 E1
Caculé, Brazil 123 D3
Cadarache, France 27 E9
Čadca, Slovak Rep. 20 F8
Caddo, U.S.A. 109 H6
Cadell Cr. →, Australia . 90 C3
Cadenazzo, Switz. 23 D7
Cader Idris, U.K. 12 E4
Cadí, Sierra del, Spain .. 28 C6
Cadibarrawirracanna, L.,
  Australia 91 D2
Cadillac, Canada 98 C4
Cadillac, France 26 D3
Cadillac, U.S.A. 104 C3
Cadiz, Phil. 55 F5
Cádiz, Spain 31 J4
Cadiz, U.S.A. 106 F4
Cádiz □, Spain 31 J5
Cádiz, G. de, Spain 31 J4
Cadney Park, Australia . 91 D1
Cadomin, Canada 100 C5
Cadotte →, Canada .. 100 B5
Cadours, France 26 E5
Cadoux, Australia 89 F2
Caen, France 24 C6
Caernarfon, U.K. 12 D3
Caernarfon B., U.K. .. 12 D3
Caernarvon = Caernarfon,
  U.K. 12 D3
Caerphilly, U.K. 13 F4
Caesarea, Israel 69 C3
Caeté, Brazil 123 E3
Caetité, Brazil 123 D3
Cafayate, Argentina .. 126 B2
Cafifi, Colombia 120 B3
Cafu, Angola 84 B2
Cagayan →, Phil. 55 B4
Cagayan de Oro, Phil. . 55 G6
Cagayan Is., Phil. 55 G4
Cagayan Sulu I., Phil. . 55 H3
Cagli, Italy 33 E9
Cágliari, Italy 34 C2
Cágliari, G. di, Italy .. 34 C2
Cagnano Varano, Italy .. 35 A8
Cagnes-sur-Mer, France . 27 E11
Caguán →, Colombia 120 D3
Caguas, Puerto Rico .. 117 C6
Caha Mts., Ireland 15 E2
Cahama, Angola 84 B1
Caher, Ireland 15 D4
Cahersiveen, Ireland .. 15 E1
Cahora Bassa Dam,
  Mozam. 83 F3
Cahore Pt., Ireland 15 D5
Cahors, France 26 D5
Cahuapanas, Peru 124 B2
Cahuinari →, Colombia . 120 D3
Cahul, Moldova 41 K5
Cai Bau, Dao, Vietnam .. 58 B6
Cai Nuoc, Vietnam 59 H5
Caia, Mozam. 83 F4
Caiabis, Serra dos, Brazil . 125 C6
Caianda, Angola 83 E1
Caiapó, Serra do, Brazil . 125 D7
Caiapônia, Brazil 125 D7
Caibarién, Cuba 116 B4
Caibiran, Phil. 55 F6
Caicara, Bolívar, Venezuela 120 B4
Caicara, Monagas,
  Venezuela 121 B5
Caicó, Brazil 122 C4
Caicos Is., W. Indies .. 117 B5
Caicos Passage, W. Indies . 117 B5
Cailloma, Peru 124 D3
Caine →, Bolivia 125 D4
Caird Coast, Antarctica . 5 D1
Cairn Gorm, U.K. 14 D5
Cairn Toul, U.K. 14 D5
Cairngorm Mts., U.K. .. 14 D5
Cairns, Australia 90 B4
Cairo = El Qâhira, Egypt 76 H7
Cairo, Ga., U.S.A. 105 K3
Cairo, Ill., U.S.A. 109 G10
Cairo Montenotte, Italy . 32 D5
Caithness, Ord of, U.K. . 14 C5
Caiundo, Angola 81 H3
Caiza, Bolivia 125 E4
Cajabamba, Peru 124 B2
Cajamarca, Peru 124 B2
Cajamarca □, Peru 124 B2
Cajapió, Brazil 122 B3
Cajarc, France 26 D5
Cajatambo, Peru 124 C2
Cajàzeiras, Brazil 122 C4
Čajetina, Serbia, Yug. .. 21 M9
Çakirgol, Turkey 67 B8
Čakovec, Croatia 33 B13
Çal, Turkey 66 C3
Cala, Spain 31 H4
Cala →, Spain 31 H4
Cala Cadolar, Punta de,
  Spain 29 G6
Cala d'Or, Spain 36 B10
Cala Figuera, C., Spain . 36 B9
Cala Forcat, Spain 36 A10

143

Cala Mayor

Cala Mayor, *Spain* 36 B9
Cala Mezquida, *Spain* 36 B11
Cala Millor, *Spain* 36 B10
Cala Ratjada, *Spain* 36 B10
Calabanga, *Phil.* 55 E5
Calabar, *Nigeria* 79 E6
Calabozo, *Venezuela* 120 B4
Calábria □, *Italy* 35 C9
Calaburras, Pta. de, *Spain* 31 J6
Calaceite, *Spain* 28 D5
Calacota, *Bolivia* 124 D4
Calafate, *Argentina* 128 D2
Calahorra, *Spain* 28 C3
Calais, *France* 25 B8
Calais, *U.S.A.* 99 C6
Calais, Pas de, *France* 25 B8
Calalaste, Cord. de, *Argentina* 126 B2
Calama, *Brazil* 125 B5
Calama, *Chile* 126 A2
Calamar, *Bolívar, Colombia* 120 A3
Calamar, *Vaupés, Colombia* 120 C3
Calamarca, *Bolivia* 124 D4
Calamba, *Phil.* 55 F5
Calamian Group, *Phil.* 55 F3
Calamocha, *Spain* 28 E3
Calán Porter, *Spain* 36 B11
Calañas, *Spain* 31 H4
Calanda, *Spain* 28 E4
Calang, *Indonesia* 56 D1
Calangiánus, *Italy* 34 B2
Calapan, *Phil.* 55 E4
Călăraşi, *Romania* 38 E10
Calasparra, *Spain* 29 G3
Calatafimi, *Italy* 34 E5
Calatayud, *Spain* 28 D3
Calato = Kálathos, *Greece* 39 N11
Calauag, *Phil.* 55 E5
Calavà, C., *Italy* 35 D7
Calavite, C., *Phil.* 55 E4
Calayan, *Phil.* 55 B4
Calbayog, *Phil.* 55 E6
Calbe, *Germany* 18 D7
Calca, *Peru* 124 C3
Calcasieu L., *U.S.A.* 109 L8
Calci, *Italy* 32 E7
Calcutta, *India* 63 H13
Caldaro, *Italy* 33 B8
Caldas □, *Colombia* 120 B2
Caldas da Rainha, *Portugal* 31 F1
Caldas de Reyes, *Spain* 30 C2
Caldas Novas, *Brazil* 123 E2
Calder →, *U.K.* 12 D6
Caldera, *Chile* 126 B1
Caldwell, *Idaho, U.S.A.* 110 E5
Caldwell, *Kans., U.S.A.* 109 G6
Caldwell, *Tex., U.S.A.* 109 K6
Caledon, *S. Africa* 84 E2
Caledon →, *S. Africa* 84 E4
Caledon B., *Australia* 90 A2
Caledonia, *Canada* 106 C5
Caledonia, *U.S.A.* 106 D7
Calella, *Spain* 28 D7
Calemba, *Angola* 84 B2
Calenzana, *France* 27 F12
Caleta Olivia, *Argentina* 128 C3
Calexico, *U.S.A.* 113 N11
Calf of Man, *U.K.* 12 C3
Calgary, *Canada* 100 C6
Calheta, *Madeira* 36 D2
Calhoun, *U.S.A.* 105 H3
Cali, *Colombia* 120 C2
Calicut, *India* 60 P9
Caliente, *U.S.A.* 111 H6
California, *Mo., U.S.A.* 108 F8
California, *Pa., U.S.A.* 106 F5
California □, *U.S.A.* 111 H4
California, Baja, *Mexico* 114 A1
California, Baja, T.N. = Baja California □, *Mexico* 114 B2
California, Baja, T.S. = Baja California Sur □, *Mexico* 114 B2
California, G. de, *Mexico* 114 B2
California City, *U.S.A.* 113 K9
California Hot Springs, *U.S.A.* 113 K8
Călimăneşti, *Romania* 38 D7
Călimani, Munţii, *Romania* 38 B8
Călineşti, *Romania* 38 D7
Calingasta, *Argentina* 126 C2
Calipatria, *U.S.A.* 113 M11
Calistoga, *U.S.A.* 112 G4
Calitri, *Italy* 35 B8
Calitzdorp, *S. Africa* 84 E3
Callabonna, L., *Australia* 91 D3
Callac, *France* 24 D3
Callan, *Ireland* 15 D4
Callander, *U.K.* 14 E4
Callantsoog, *Neths.* 16 C5
Callao, *Peru* 124 C2
Callaway, *U.S.A.* 108 E5
Calles, *Mexico* 115 C5
Callide, *Australia* 90 C5
Calling Lake, *Canada* 100 B6
Calliope, *Australia* 90 C5
Callosa de Ensarriá, *Spain* 29 G4
Callosa de Segura, *Spain* 29 G4
Calola, *Angola* 84 B2
Calolbon, *Phil.* 55 E6
Caloocan, *Phil.* 55 D4
Calore →, *Italy* 35 A7
Caloundra, *Australia* 91 D5
Calpe, *Spain* 29 G5
Calpella, *U.S.A.* 112 F3
Calpine, *U.S.A.* 112 F6
Calstock, *Canada* 98 C3
Caltabellotta, *Italy* 34 E6
Caltagirone, *Italy* 35 E7
Caltanissetta, *Italy* 35 E7
Calulo, *Angola* 80 G2
Calumet, *U.S.A.* 104 B1
Calunda, *Angola* 81 G4
Caluso, *Italy* 32 C4
Calvados □, *France* 24 C6
Calvert, *U.S.A.* 109 K6
Calvert →, *Australia* 90 B2
Calvert Hills, *Australia* 90 B2
Calvert I., *Canada* 100 C3
Calvert Ra., *Australia* 88 D3
Calvi, *France* 27 F12
Calvillo, *Mexico* 114 C4
Calvinia, *S. Africa* 84 E2
Calw, *Germany* 19 G4
Calwa, *U.S.A.* 112 J7
Calzada Almuradiel, *Spain* 29 G1
Calzada de Calatrava, *Spain* 31 G7
Cam →, *U.K.* 13 E8
Cam Lam, *Vietnam* 59 G7
Cam Pha, *Vietnam* 58 B6
Cam Ranh, *Vietnam* 59 G7
Cam Xuyen, *Vietnam* 58 C6
Camabatela, *Angola* 80 F3
Camacã, *Brazil* 123 E4
Camaçari, *Brazil* 123 D4
Camacha, *Madeira* 36 D3
Camacho, *Mexico* 114 C4
Camacupa, *Angola* 81 G3
Camaguán, *Venezuela* 120 B4
Camagüey, *Cuba* 116 B4
Camaiore, *Italy* 32 E7
Camamu, *Brazil* 123 D4
Camaná, *Peru* 124 D3
Camanche Reservoir, *U.S.A.* 112 G6
Camaquã →, *Brazil* 127 C5
Câmara de Lobos, *Madeira* 36 D3
Camararé →, *Brazil* 125 C6
Camarat, C., *France* 27 E10
Camaret, *France* 24 D2
Camargo, *Bolivia* 125 E4
Camargue, *France* 27 E8
Camarillo, *U.S.A.* 113 L7
Camariñas, *Spain* 30 B1
Camarón, C., *Honduras* 116 C2
Camarones, *Argentina* 128 B3
Camarones, B., *Argentina* 128 B3
Camas, *U.S.A.* 112 E4
Camas Valley, *U.S.A.* 110 E2
Cambados, *Spain* 30 C2
Cambará, *Brazil* 127 A5
Cambay = Khambhat, *India* 62 H5
Cambay, G. of = Khambat, G. of, *India* 62 J5
Cambil, *Spain* 29 H1
Cambo-les-Bains, *France* 26 E2
Cambodia ■, *Asia* 58 F5
Camborne, *U.K.* 13 G2
Cambrai, *France* 25 B10
Cambria, *U.S.A.* 111 J3
Cambrian Mts., *U.K.* 13 E4
Cambridge, *Canada* 98 D3
Cambridge, *Jamaica* 116 C4
Cambridge, *N.Z.* 87 G5
Cambridge, *U.K.* 13 E8
Cambridge, *Idaho, U.S.A.* 110 D5
Cambridge, *Mass., U.S.A.* 107 D13
Cambridge, *Md., U.S.A.* 104 F7
Cambridge, *Minn., U.S.A.* 108 C8
Cambridge, *N.Y., U.S.A.* 107 C11
Cambridge, *Nebr., U.S.A.* 108 E4
Cambridge, *Ohio, U.S.A.* 106 F3
Cambridge Bay, *Canada* 96 B9
Cambridge G., *Australia* 88 B4
Cambridge Springs, *U.S.A.* 106 E4
Cambridgeshire □, *U.K.* 13 E8
Cambrils, *Spain* 28 D6
Cambuci, *Brazil* 123 F3
Cambundi-Catembo, *Angola* 80 G3
Camden, *Ala., U.S.A.* 105 K2
Camden, *Ark., U.S.A.* 109 J8
Camden, *Maine, U.S.A.* 99 D6
Camden, *N.J., U.S.A.* 107 G9
Camden, *S.C., U.S.A.* 105 H5
Camden Sd., *Australia* 88 C3
Camdenton, *U.S.A.* 109 F8
Çameli, *Turkey* 66 D3
Camembert, *France* 24 D7
Cámeri, *Italy* 32 C5
Camerino, *Italy* 33 E10
Cameron, *Ariz., U.S.A.* 111 J8
Cameron, *La., U.S.A.* 109 L8
Cameron, *Mo., U.S.A.* 108 F7
Cameron, *Tex., U.S.A.* 109 K6
Cameron Falls, *Canada* 98 C2
Cameron Highlands, *Malaysia* 59 K3
Cameron Hills, *Canada* 100 B5
Cameroon ■, *Africa* 73 G7
Camerota, *Italy* 35 B8
Cameroun →, *Cameroon* 79 E6
Cameroun, Mt., *Cameroon* 79 E6
Cametá, *Brazil* 122 B2
Camiguin □, *Phil.* 55 G6
Camiguin I., *Phil.* 55 B4
Camiling, *Phil.* 55 D4
Caminha, *Portugal* 30 D2
Camino, *U.S.A.* 112 G6
Camira Creek, *Australia* 91 D5
Camiranga, *Brazil* 122 B2
Camiri, *Bolivia* 125 E5
Camissombo, *Angola* 80 F4
Cammal, *U.S.A.* 106 E7
Camocim, *Brazil* 122 B3
Camogli, *Italy* 32 D6
Camooweal, *Australia* 90 B2
Camopi, *Fr. Guiana* 121 C7
Camopi →, *Fr. Guiana* 121 C7
Camotes Is., *Phil.* 55 F6
Camotes Sea, *Phil.* 55 F6
Camp Crook, *U.S.A.* 108 C3
Camp Nelson, *U.S.A.* 113 J8
Camp Wood, *U.S.A.* 109 L4
Campagna, *Italy* 35 B8
Campana, *Argentina* 126 C4
Campana, I., *Chile* 128 C1
Campanário, *Madeira* 36 D2
Campanario, *Spain* 31 G5
Campánia □, *Italy* 35 B7
Campbell, *S. Africa* 84 D3
Campbell, *Calif., U.S.A.* 112 H5
Campbell, *Ohio, U.S.A.* 106 E4
Campbell I., *Pac. Oc.* 92 N8
Campbell L., *Canada* 101 A7
Campbell River, *Canada* 100 C3
Campbell Town, *Australia* 90 G4
Campbellford, *Canada* 106 B7
Campbellpur, *Pakistan* 62 C5
Campbellsville, *U.S.A.* 104 G3
Campbellton, *Canada* 99 C6
Campbelltown, *Australia* 91 E5
Campbeltown, *U.K.* 14 F3
Campeche, *Mexico* 115 D6
Campeche □, *Mexico* 115 D6
Campeche, B. de, *Mexico* 115 D6
Camperdown, *Australia* 91 F3
Camperville, *Canada* 101 C8
Campi Salentina, *Italy* 35 B11
Campidano, *Italy* 34 C1
Campíglia Maríttima, *Italy* 32 E7
Campillo de Altobuey, *Spain* 28 F3
Campillo de Llerena, *Spain* 31 G5
Campillos, *Spain* 31 H6
Campina Grande, *Brazil* 122 C4
Campina Verde, *Brazil* 123 E2
Campinas, *Brazil* 127 A6
Campine, *Belgium* 17 F6
Campli, *Italy* 33 F10
Campo, *Cameroon* 80 D1
Campo, *Spain* 28 C5
Campo Belo, *Brazil* 123 F2
Campo de Criptana, *Spain* 29 F1
Campo de Diauarum, *Brazil* 125 C7
Campo de Gibraltar, *Spain* 31 J5
Campo Flórido, *Brazil* 123 E2
Campo Formoso, *Brazil* 122 D3
Campo Grande, *Brazil* 125 E7
Campo Maíor, *Brazil* 122 B3
Campo Maior, *Portugal* 31 G3
Campo Mourão, *Brazil* 127 A5
Campo Tencia, *Switz.* 23 D7
Campo Túres, *Italy* 33 B8
Campoalegre, *Colombia* 120 C2
Campobasso, *Italy* 35 A7
Campobello di Licata, *Italy* 34 E6
Campobello di Mazara, *Italy* 34 E5
Campofelice di Roccella, *Italy* 34 E6
Camporeale, *Italy* 34 E6
Campos, *Brazil* 123 F3
Campos Altos, *Brazil* 123 E2
Campos Belos, *Brazil* 123 D2
Campos del Puerto, *Spain* 36 B10
Campos Novos, *Brazil* 127 B5
Campos Sales, *Brazil* 122 C3
Camprodón, *Spain* 28 C7
Camptonville, *U.S.A.* 112 F5
Campuya →, *Peru* 120 D3
Camrose, *Canada* 100 C6
Camsell Portage, *Canada* 101 B7
Çan, *Turkey* 66 B2
Can Clavo, *Spain* 36 C7
Can Creu, *Spain* 36 C7
Can Gio, *Vietnam* 59 G6
Can Tho, *Vietnam* 59 G5
Canaan, *U.S.A.* 107 D11
Canada ■, *N. Amer.* 96 C10
Cañada de Gómez, *Argentina* 126 C3
Canadian, *U.S.A.* 109 H4
Canadian →, *U.S.A.* 109 H7
Canadian Shield, *Canada* 97 C10
Çanakkale, *Turkey* 66 B2
Çanakkale Boğazı, *Turkey* 66 B2
Canal Flats, *Canada* 100 C5
Canalejas, *Argentina* 126 D2
Canals, *Argentina* 126 C3
Canals, *Spain* 29 G4
Canandaigua, *U.S.A.* 106 D7
Cananea, *Mexico* 114 A2
Cañar, *Ecuador* 120 D2
Cañar □, *Ecuador* 120 D2
Canarias, Is., *Atl. Oc.* 36 F4
Canarreos, Arch. de los, *Cuba* 116 B3
Canary Is. = Canarias, Is., *Atl. Oc.* 36 F4
Canastra, Serra da, *Brazil* 123 F2
Canatlán, *Mexico* 114 C4
Canaveral, C., *U.S.A.* 105 L5
Cañaveras, *Spain* 28 E2
Canavieiras, *Brazil* 123 E4
Canbelego, *Australia* 91 E4
Canberra, *Australia* 91 F4
Canby, *Calif., U.S.A.* 110 F3
Canby, *Minn., U.S.A.* 108 C6
Canby, *Oreg., U.S.A.* 112 E4
Cancale, *France* 24 D5
Canche →, *France* 25 B8
Canchyuaya, Cordillera de, *Peru* 124 B3
Cancún, *Mexico* 115 C7
Candala, *Somali Rep.* 68 E4
Candarave, *Peru* 124 D3
Candas, *Spain* 30 B5
Candé, *France* 24 E5
Candeias →, *Brazil* 125 B5
Candela, *Italy* 35 A8
Candelaria, *Argentina* 127 B4
Candelaria, *Canary Is.* 36 F3
Candelaria, Pta. de la, *Spain* 30 B2
Candeleda, *Spain* 30 E5
Candelo, *Australia* 91 F4
Candia = Iráklion, *Greece* 37 D7
Candia, Sea of = Crete, Sea of, *Greece* 39 N8
Cândido de Abreu, *Brazil* 123 F1
Cândido Mendes, *Brazil* 122 B2
Candle L., *Canada* 101 C7
Candlemas I., *Antarctica* 5 B1
Cando, *U.S.A.* 108 A5
Candon, *Phil.* 55 C4
Canea = Khaniá, *Greece* 37 D6
Canela, *Brazil* 122 D2
Canelli, *Italy* 32 D5
Canelones, *Uruguay* 127 C4
Canet-Plage, *France* 26 F7
Cañete, *Chile* 126 D1
Cañete, *Peru* 124 C2
Cañete, *Spain* 28 E3
Cañete de las Torres, *Spain* 31 H6
Canfranc, *Spain* 28 C4
Cangas, *Spain* 30 C2
Cangas de Narcea, *Spain* 30 B4
Cangas de Onís, *Spain* 30 B5
Canguaretama, *Brazil* 122 C4
Canguçu, *Brazil* 127 C5
Cangxi, *China* 52 B5
Cangyuan, *China* 52 F2
Cangzhou, *China* 50 E9
Canicattì, *Italy* 34 E6
Canicattini Bagni, *Italy* 35 E8
Canim Lake, *Canada* 100 C4
Canindé, *Brazil* 122 B4
Canindé →, *Brazil* 122 C3
Canindeyu □, *Paraguay* 127 A4
Canipaan, *Phil.* 56 C5
Canisteo, *U.S.A.* 106 D7
Canisteo →, *U.S.A.* 106 D7
Cañitas, *Mexico* 114 C4
Cañizal, *Spain* 30 D5
Canjáyar, *Spain* 29 H2
Çankırı, *Turkey* 66 B5
Cankuzo, *Burundi* 82 C3
Canmore, *Canada* 100 C5
Cann River, *Australia* 91 F4
Canna, *U.K.* 14 D2
Cannanore, *India* 60 P9
Cannes, *France* 27 E11
Canning Town = Port Canning, *India* 63 H13
Cannington, *Canada* 106 B5
Cannock, *U.K.* 12 E5
Cannon Ball →, *U.S.A.* 108 B4
Cannondale Mt., *Australia* 90 D4
Caño Colorado, *Colombia* 120 C4
Canoas, *Brazil* 127 B5
Canoe L., *Canada* 101 B7
Canon City, *U.S.A.* 108 F2
Canora, *Canada* 101 C8
Canosa di Púglia, *Italy* 35 A9
Canowindra, *Australia* 91 E4
Canso, *Canada* 99 C7
Canta, *Peru* 124 C2
Cantabria □, *Spain* 30 B6
Cantabria, Sierra de, *Spain* 28 C2
Cantabrian Mts. = Cantábrica, Cordillera, *Spain* 30 C5
Cantábrica, Cordillera, *Spain* 30 C5
Cantal □, *France* 26 C6
Cantal, Plomb du, *France* 26 C6
Cantanhede, *Portugal* 30 E2
Cantaura, *Venezuela* 121 B5
Cantavieja, *Spain* 28 E4
Canterbury, *Australia* 90 D3
Canterbury, *U.K.* 13 F9
Canterbury □, *N.Z.* 87 K3
Canterbury Bight, *N.Z.* 87 L3
Canterbury Plains, *N.Z.* 87 K3
Cantil, *U.S.A.* 113 K9
Cantillana, *Spain* 31 H5
Canto do Buriti, *Brazil* 122 C3
Canton = Guangzhou, *China* 53 F9
Canton, *Ga., U.S.A.* 105 H3
Canton, *Ill., U.S.A.* 108 E9
Canton, *Miss., U.S.A.* 109 J9
Canton, *Mo., U.S.A.* 108 E9
Canton, *N.Y., U.S.A.* 107 B9
Canton, *Ohio, U.S.A.* 106 F3
Canton, *Okla., U.S.A.* 109 G5
Canton, *S. Dak., U.S.A.* 108 D6
Canton L., *U.S.A.* 109 G5
Cantù, *Italy* 32 C6
Canudos, *Brazil* 125 B6
Canumã, *Amazonas, Brazil* 121 D6
Canumã, *Amazonas, Brazil* 125 B5
Canumã →, *Brazil* 125 A6
Canutama, *Brazil* 125 B5
Canutillo, *U.S.A.* 111 L10
Canyon, *Tex., U.S.A.* 109 H4
Canyon, *Wyo., U.S.A.* 110 D8
Canyonlands National Park, *U.S.A.* 111 G9
Canyonville, *U.S.A.* 110 E2
Canzo, *Italy* 32 C6
Cao Bang, *Vietnam* 58 A6
Cao He →, *China* 51 D13
Cao Lanh, *Vietnam* 59 G5
Cao Xian, *China* 50 G8
Cáorle, *Italy* 33 C9
Cap-aux-Meules, *Canada* 99 C7
Cap-Chat, *Canada* 99 C6
Cap-de-la-Madeleine, *Canada* 98 C5
Cap-Haïtien, *Haiti* 117 C5
Cap St.-Jacques = Vung Tau, *Vietnam* 59 G6
Capa, *Vietnam* 58 A4
Capa Stilo, *Italy* 35 D9
Capáccio, *Italy* 35 B8
Capaia, *Angola* 80 F4
Capanaparo →, *Venezuela* 120 B4
Capanema, *Brazil* 122 B2
Caparo →, *Barinas, Venezuela* 120 B3
Caparo →, *Bolívar, Venezuela* 121 B5
Capatárida, *Venezuela* 120 A3
Capbreton, *France* 26 E2
Capdenac, *France* 26 D6
Cape →, *Australia* 90 C4
Cape Barren I., *Australia* 90 G4
Cape Breton Highlands Nat. Park, *Canada* 99 C7
Cape Breton I., *Canada* 99 C7
Cape Charles, *U.S.A.* 104 G8
Cape Coast, *Ghana* 79 D4
Cape Dorset, *Canada* 97 B12
Cape Dyer, *Canada* 97 B13
Cape Fear →, *U.S.A.* 105 H6
Cape Girardeau, *U.S.A.* 109 G10
Cape Jervis, *Australia* 91 F2
Cape May, *U.S.A.* 104 F8
Cape May Point, *U.S.A.* 103 C12
Cape Palmas, *Liberia* 78 E3
Cape Tormentine, *Canada* 99 C7
Cape Town, *S. Africa* 84 E2
Cape Verde Is. ■, *Atl. Oc.* 2 D8
Cape Vincent, *U.S.A.* 107 B8
Cape York Peninsula, *Australia* 90 A3
Capela, *Brazil* 122 D4
Capela de Campo, *Brazil* 122 B3
Capelinha, *Brazil* 123 E3
Capella, *Australia* 90 C4
Capendu, *France* 26 E6
Capestang, *France* 26 E7
Capim, *Brazil* 122 B2
Capim →, *Brazil* 122 B2
Capinópolis, *Brazil* 123 E2
Capinota, *Bolivia* 124 D4
Capitan, *U.S.A.* 111 K11
Capitán Aracena, I., *Chile* 128 D2
Capitán Pastene, *Chile* 128 A2
Capitola, *U.S.A.* 112 J5
Capivara, Serra da, *Brazil* 123 D3
Capizzi, *Italy* 35 E7
Čapljina, *Bos.-H.* 21 M7
Capoche →, *Mozam.* 83 F3
Capoeira, *Brazil* 125 B6
Cappadocia, *Turkey* 66 C6
Capraia, *Italy* 32 E6
Caprarola, *Italy* 33 F9
Capreol, *Canada* 98 C3
Caprera, *Italy* 34 A2
Capri, *Italy* 35 B7
Capricorn Group, *Australia* 90 C5
Capricorn Ra., *Australia* 88 D2
Caprino Veronese, *Italy* 32 C7
Caprivi Strip, *Namibia* 84 B3
Captainganj, *India* 63 F10
Captain's Flat, *Australia* 91 F4
Captieux, *France* 26 D3
Cápua, *Italy* 35 A7
Caquetá □, *Colombia* 120 C3
Caquetá →, *Colombia* 120 D4
Carabobo, *Venezuela* 120 A4
Carabobo □, *Venezuela* 120 A4
Caracal, *Romania* 38 E7
Caracaraí, *Brazil* 121 C5
Caracas, *Venezuela* 120 A4
Caracol, *Brazil* 122 C3
Caracollo, *Bolivia* 124 D4
Caradoc, *Australia* 91 E3
Caráglio, *Italy* 32 D4
Carahue, *Chile* 128 A2
Caraí, *Brazil* 123 E3
Carajás, Serra dos, *Brazil* 122 C1
Caranapatuba, *Brazil* 125 B5
Carandaiti, *Bolivia* 125 E5
Carangola, *Brazil* 123 F3
Carani, *Australia* 89 F2
Caransebeş, *Romania* 38 D5
Carantec, *France* 24 D3
Caraparaná →, *Colombia* 120 D3
Carapelle →, *Italy* 35 A8
Caras, *Peru* 124 B2
Caratasca, L., *Honduras* 116 C3
Caratinga, *Brazil* 123 E3
Caraúbas, *Brazil* 122 C4
Caravaca, *Spain* 29 G3
Caravággio, *Italy* 32 C6
Caravelas, *Brazil* 123 E4

Cedar

Caraveli, *Peru* 124 D3
Caràzinho, *Brazil* 127 B5
Carballino, *Spain* 30 C2
Carballo, *Spain* 30 B2
Carberry, *Canada* 101 D9
Carbia, *Spain* 30 C2
Carbó, *Mexico* 114 B2
Carbon, *Canada* 100 C6
Carbonara, C., *Italy* 34 C2
Carbondale, *Colo., U.S.A.* 110 G10
Carbondale, *Ill., U.S.A.* 109 G10
Carbondale, *Pa., U.S.A.* 107 E9
Carbonear, *Canada* 99 C9
Carboneras, *Spain* 29 J3
Carboneras de Guadazaón, *Spain* 28 F3
Carbonia, *Italy* 34 C1
Carcabuey, *Spain* 31 H6
Carcagente, *Spain* 29 F4
Carcajou, *Canada* 100 B5
Carcar, *Phil.* 55 F5
Carcasse, C., *Haiti* 117 C5
Carcassonne, *France* 26 E6
Carche, *Spain* 29 G3
Carchi □, *Ecuador* 120 C2
Carcross, *Canada* 96 B6
Cardabia, *Australia* 88 D1
Çardak, *Turkey* 66 D3
Cardamon Hills, *India* 60 Q10
Cárdenas, *Cuba* 116 B3
Cárdenas, *San Luis Potosí, Mexico* 115 C5
Cárdenas, *Tabasco, Mexico* 115 D6
Cardenete, *Spain* 28 F3
Cardiel, L., *Argentina* 128 C2
Cardiff, *U.K.* 13 F4
Cardiff-by-the-Sea, *U.S.A.* 113 M9
Cardigan, *U.K.* 13 E3
Cardigan B., *U.K.* 13 E3
Cardinal, *Canada* 107 B9
Cardón, Punta, *Venezuela* 120 A3
Cardona, *Spain* 28 D6
Cardona, *Uruguay* 126 C4
Cardoner →, *Spain* 28 D6
Cardross, *Canada* 101 D7
Cardston, *Canada* 100 D6
Cardwell, *Australia* 90 B4
Careen L., *Canada* 101 B7
Carei, *Romania* 38 B5
Careiro, *Brazil* 121 D6
Careme, *Indonesia* 57 G13
Carentan, *France* 24 C5
Carey, *Idaho, U.S.A.* 110 E7
Carey, *Ohio, U.S.A.* 104 E4
Carey, L., *Australia* 89 E3
Carey L., *Canada* 101 A8
Careysburg, *Liberia* 78 D2
Cargèse, *France* 27 F12
Carhaix-Plouguer, *France* 24 D3
Carhuamayo, *Peru* 124 C2
Carhuas, *Peru* 124 B2
Carhué, *Argentina* 126 D3
Caria, *Turkey* 66 D3
Cariacica, *Brazil* 123 F3
Caribbean Sea, *W. Indies* 117 C5
Cariboo Mts., *Canada* 100 C4
Caribou, *U.S.A.* 99 C6
Caribou →, *Man., Canada* 101 B10
Caribou →, *N.W.T., Canada* 100 A3
Caribou I., *Canada* 98 C2
Caribou Is., *Canada* 100 A6
Caribou L., *Man., Canada* 101 B9
Caribou L., *Ont., Canada* 98 B2
Caribou Mts., *Canada* 100 B5
Carichic, *Mexico* 114 B3
Carigara, *Phil.* 55 F6
Carignan, *France* 25 C12
Carignano, *Italy* 32 D4
Carillo, *Mexico* 114 B4
Carinda, *Australia* 91 E4
Cariñena, *Spain* 28 D3
Carinhanha, *Brazil* 123 D3
Carinhanha →, *Brazil* 123 D3
Carini, *Italy* 34 D6
Carinola, *Italy* 34 A6
Caripito, *Venezuela* 121 A5
Caritianas, *Brazil* 125 B5
Carlbrod = Dimitrovgrad, *Serbia, Yug.* 21 M12
Carlentini, *Italy* 35 E8
Carleton Place, *Canada* 98 C4
Carletonville, *S. Africa* 84 D4
Carlin, *U.S.A.* 110 F5
Carlingford L., *U.K.* 15 B5
Carlinville, *U.S.A.* 108 F10
Carlisle, *U.K.* 12 C5
Carlisle, *U.S.A.* 106 F7
Carlit, Pic, *France* 26 F5
Carloforte, *Italy* 34 C1
Carlos Casares, *Argentina* 126 D3
Carlos Chagas, *Brazil* 123 E3
Carlos Tejedor, *Argentina* 126 D3
Carlow, *Ireland* 15 D5
Carlow □, *Ireland* 15 D5
Carlsbad, *Calif., U.S.A.* 113 M9
Carlsbad, *N. Mex., U.S.A.* 109 J2
Carlyle, *Canada* 101 D8
Carlyle, *U.S.A.* 108 F10
Carmacks, *Canada* 96 B6
Carmagnola, *Italy* 32 D4
Carman, *Canada* 101 D9
Carmangay, *Canada* 100 C6
Carmanville, *Canada* 99 C9
Carmarthen, *U.K.* 13 F3
Carmarthen B., *U.K.* 13 F3
Carmaux, *France* 26 D6
Carmel, *U.S.A.* 107 E11
Carmel-by-the-Sea, *U.S.A.* 111 H3
Carmel Valley, *U.S.A.* 112 J5
Carmelo, *Uruguay* 126 C4
Carmen, *Bolivia* 124 C4
Carmen, *Colombia* 120 B2
Carmen, *Paraguay* 127 B4
Carmen →, *Mexico* 114 A3
Carmen, I., *Mexico* 114 B2
Carmen de Patagones, *Argentina* 128 B4
Cármenes, *Spain* 30 C5
Carmensa, *Argentina* 126 D2
Carmi, *U.S.A.* 104 F1
Carmichael, *U.S.A.* 112 G5
Carmila, *Australia* 90 C4
Carmona, *Spain* 31 H5
Carnac, *France* 24 E3
Carnarvon, *Queens., Australia* 90 C4
Carnarvon, *W. Austral., Australia* 89 D1
Carnarvon, *S. Africa* 84 E3
Carnarvon Ra., *Queens., Australia* 90 D4
Carnarvon Ra., *W. Austral., Australia* 89 E3
Carnation, *U.S.A.* 112 C5
Carnaxide, *Portugal* 31 G1
Carndonagh, *Ireland* 15 A4
Carnduff, *Canada* 101 D8
Carnegie, *U.S.A.* 106 F4
Carnegie, L., *Australia* 89 E3
Carnic Alps = Karnische Alpen, *Europe* 21 J3
Carniche Alpi = Karnische Alpen, *Europe* 21 J3
Carnot, *C.A.R.* 80 D3
Carnot, C., *Australia* 91 E2
Carnot B., *Australia* 88 C3
Carnsore Pt., *Ireland* 15 D5
Caro, *U.S.A.* 104 D4
Carol City, *U.S.A.* 105 N5
Carolina, *Brazil* 122 C2
Carolina, *Puerto Rico* 117 C6
Carolina, *S. Africa* 85 D5
Caroline I., *Kiribati* 93 H12
Caroline Is., *Pac. Oc.* 92 G6
Caron, *Canada* 101 C7
Caroni →, *Venezuela* 121 B5
Caronie = Nébrodi, Monti, *Italy* 35 E7
Caroona, *Australia* 91 E5
Carora, *Venezuela* 120 A3
Carovigno, *Italy* 35 B10
Carpathians, *Europe* 20 F11
Carpaţii Meridionali, *Romania* 38 D8
Carpenédolo, *Italy* 32 C7
Carpentaria, G. of, *Australia* 90 A2
Carpentaria Downs, *Australia* 90 B3
Carpentras, *France* 27 D9
Carpi, *Italy* 32 D7
Carpina, *Brazil* 122 C4
Carpino, *Italy* 35 A8
Carpinteria, *U.S.A.* 113 L7
Carpio, *Spain* 30 D5
Carpolac = Morea, *Australia* 91 F3
Carr Boyd Ra., *Australia* 88 C4
Carrabelle, *U.S.A.* 105 L3
Carranya, *Australia* 88 C4
Carrara, *Italy* 32 D7
Carrascal, *Phil.* 55 G6
Carrascosa del Campo, *Spain* 28 E2
Carrauntoohill, *Ireland* 15 E2
Carretas, Punta, *Peru* 124 C2
Carrick-on-Shannon, *Ireland* 15 C3
Carrick-on-Suir, *Ireland* 15 D4
Carrickfergus, *U.K.* 15 B6
Carrickfergus □, *U.K.* 15 B6
Carrickmacross, *Ireland* 15 C5
Carrieton, *Australia* 91 E2
Carrington, *U.S.A.* 108 B5
Carrión →, *Spain* 30 D6
Carrión de los Condes, *Spain* 30 C6
Carrizal Bajo, *Chile* 126 B1
Carrizalillo, *Chile* 126 B1
Carrizo Cr. →, *U.S.A.* 109 G3
Carrizo Springs, *U.S.A.* 109 L5
Carrizozo, *U.S.A.* 111 K11
Carroll, *U.S.A.* 108 D7
Carrollton, *Ga., U.S.A.* 105 J3
Carrollton, *Ill., U.S.A.* 108 F9
Carrollton, *Ky., U.S.A.* 104 F3
Carrollton, *Mo., U.S.A.* 108 F8
Carrollton, *Ohio, U.S.A.* 106 F3
Carron →, *U.K.* 14 D3
Carron, L., *U.K.* 14 D3
Carrot →, *Canada* 101 C8
Carrot River, *Canada* 101 C8
Carrouges, *France* 24 D6
Carruthers, *Canada* 101 C7
Çarşamba, *Turkey* 66 B7
Carse of Gowrie, *U.K.* 14 E5
Carsóli, *Italy* 33 F10
Carson, *Calif., U.S.A.* 113 M8
Carson, *N. Dak., U.S.A.* 108 B4
Carson →, *U.S.A.* 112 F8
Carson City, *U.S.A.* 112 F7
Carson Sink, *U.S.A.* 110 G4
Carstairs, *U.K.* 14 F5
Cartagena, *Colombia* 120 A2
Cartagena, *Spain* 29 H4
Cartago, *Colombia* 120 C2
Cartago, *Costa Rica* 116 E3
Cartaxo, *Portugal* 31 F2
Cartaya, *Spain* 31 H3
Carteret, *France* 24 C5
Cartersville, *U.S.A.* 105 H3
Carterton, *N.Z.* 87 J5
Carthage, *Ark., U.S.A.* 109 H8
Carthage, *Ill., U.S.A.* 108 E9
Carthage, *Mo., U.S.A.* 109 G7
Carthage, *S. Dak., U.S.A.* 108 C6
Carthage, *Tex., U.S.A.* 109 J7
Cartier I., *Australia* 88 B3
Cartwright, *Canada* 99 B8
Caruaru, *Brazil* 122 C4
Carúpano, *Venezuela* 121 A5
Carutapera, *Brazil* 122 B2
Caruthersville, *U.S.A.* 109 G10
Carvalho, *Brazil* 121 D7
Carvin, *France* 25 B9
Carvoeiro, *Brazil* 121 D5
Carvoeiro, C., *Portugal* 31 F1
Casa Branca, *Brazil* 123 F2
Casa Branca, *Portugal* 31 G2
Casa Grande, *U.S.A.* 111 K8
Casablanca, *Chile* 126 C1
Casablanca, *Morocco* 74 B3
Casacalenda, *Italy* 35 A7
Casal di Principe, *Italy* 35 B7
Casalbordino, *Italy* 33 F11
Casale Monferrato, *Italy* 32 C5
Casalmaggiore, *Italy* 32 D7
Casalpusterlengo, *Italy* 32 C6
Casamance →, *Senegal* 78 C1
Casamássima, *Italy* 35 B9
Casanare □, *Colombia* 120 B3
Casanare →, *Colombia* 120 B4
Casarano, *Italy* 35 B11
Casares, *Spain* 31 J5
Casas Grandes, *Mexico* 114 A3
Casas Ibañez, *Spain* 29 F3
Casasimarro, *Spain* 29 F2
Casatejada, *Spain* 30 F5
Casavieja, *Spain* 30 E6
Cascade, *Idaho, U.S.A.* 110 D5
Cascade, *Mont., U.S.A.* 110 C8
Cascade Locks, *U.S.A.* 112 E5
Cascade Ra., *U.S.A.* 112 D5
Cascais, *Portugal* 31 G1
Cascavel, *Brazil* 127 A5
Cáscina, *Italy* 32 E7
Caselle Torinese, *Italy* 32 C4
Caserta, *Italy* 35 A7
Cashel, *Ireland* 15 D4
Cashmere, *U.S.A.* 110 C3
Cashmere Downs, *Australia* 89 E2
Casibare →, *Colombia* 120 C3
Casiguran, *Phil.* 55 C5
Casilda, *Argentina* 126 C3
Casino, *Australia* 91 D5
Casiquiare →, *Venezuela* 120 C4
Casitas, *Peru* 124 A1
Caslan, *Canada* 100 C6
Čáslav, *Czech.* 20 F5
Casma, *Peru* 124 B2
Casmalia, *U.S.A.* 113 L6
Casola Valsenio, *Italy* 33 D8
Cásoli, *Italy* 33 F11
Caspe, *Spain* 28 D4
Casper, *U.S.A.* 110 E10
Caspian Depression, *Eurasia* 43 G9
Caspian Sea, *Eurasia* 44 E6
Casquets, *U.K.* 24 C4
Cass City, *U.S.A.* 104 D4
Cass Lake, *U.S.A.* 108 B7
Cassá de la Selva, *Spain* 28 D7
Cassano Iónio, *Italy* 35 C9
Cassel, *France* 25 B9
Casselman, *Canada* 107 A9
Casselton, *U.S.A.* 108 B6
Cassiar, *Canada* 100 B3
Cassiar Mts., *Canada* 100 B2
Cassilândia, *Brazil* 125 D7
Cassinga, *Angola* 81 H3
Cassino, *Italy* 34 A6
Cassis, *France* 27 E9
Cassville, *U.S.A.* 109 G8
Cástagneto Carducci, *Italy* 32 E7
Castaic, *U.S.A.* 113 L8
Castanhal, *Brazil* 122 B2
Casteau, *Belgium* 17 G4
Castéggio, *Italy* 32 C6
Castejón de Monegros, *Spain* 28 D4
Castel di Sangro, *Italy* 33 G11
Castel San Giovanni, *Italy* 32 C6
Castel San Pietro Terme, *Italy* 33 D8
Castelbuono, *Italy* 35 E7
Casteldelfino, *Italy* 32 D4
Castelfiorentino, *Italy* 32 E7
Castelfranco Emília, *Italy* 32 D8
Castelfranco Véneto, *Italy* 33 C8
Casteljaloux, *France* 26 D4
Castellabate, *Italy* 35 B7
Castellammare, G. di, *Italy* 34 D5
Castellammare del Golfo, *Italy* 34 D5
Castellammare di Stábia, *Italy* 35 B7
Castellamonte, *Italy* 32 C4
Castellana Grotte, *Italy* 35 B10
Castellane, *France* 27 E10
Castellaneta, *Italy* 35 B9
Castellar de Santisteban, *Spain* 29 G1
Castelleone, *Italy* 32 C6
Castelli, *Argentina* 126 D4
Castelló de Ampurias, *Spain* 28 C8
Castellón □, *Spain* 28 E4
Castellón de la Plana, *Spain* 28 F4
Castellote, *Spain* 28 E4
Castelltersol, *Spain* 28 D7
Castelmáuro, *Italy* 35 A7
Castelnau-de-Médoc, *France* 26 C3
Castelnaudary, *France* 26 E5
Castelnovo ne' Monti, *Italy* 32 D7
Castelnuovo di Val di Cécina, *Italy* 32 E7
Castelo, *Brazil* 123 F3
Castelo Branco, *Portugal* 30 F3
Castelo Branco □, *Portugal* 30 F3
Castelo de Paiva, *Portugal* 30 D2
Castelo de Vide, *Portugal* 31 F3
Castelo do Piauí, *Brazil* 122 C3
Castelsarrasin, *France* 26 D5
Casteltérmini, *Italy* 34 E6
Castelvetrano, *Italy* 34 E5
Casterton, *Australia* 91 F3
Castets, *France* 26 E2
Castiglione del Lago, *Italy* 33 E9
Castiglione della Pescáia, *Italy* 32 F7
Castiglione delle Stiviere, *Italy* 32 C7
Castiglione Fiorentino, *Italy* 33 E8
Castilblanco, *Spain* 31 F5
Castilla, *Peru* 124 B1
Castilla, Playa de, *Spain* 31 H4
Castilla La Mancha □, *Spain* 31 F7
Castilla y Leon □, *Spain* 30 D6
Castillon, Barr. de, *France* 27 E10
Castillon-en-Couserans, *France* 26 F5
Castillon-la-Bataille, *France* 26 D3
Castillonès, *France* 26 D4
Castillos, *Uruguay* 127 C5
Castle Dale, *U.S.A.* 110 G8
Castle Douglas, *U.K.* 14 G5
Castle Rock, *Colo., U.S.A.* 108 F2
Castle Rock, *Wash., U.S.A.* 112 D4
Castlebar, *Ireland* 15 C2
Castleblaney, *Ireland* 15 B5
Castlegar, *Canada* 100 D5
Castlemaine, *Australia* 91 F3
Castlerea, *Ireland* 15 C3
Castlereagh □, *U.K.* 15 B6
Castlereagh →, *Australia* 91 E4
Castlereagh B., *Australia* 90 A2
Castletown, *U.K.* 12 C3
Castletown Bearhaven, *Ireland* 15 E2
Castlevale, *Australia* 90 C4
Castor, *Canada* 100 C6
Castres, *France* 26 E6
Castricum, *Neths.* 16 C5
Castries, *St. Lucia* 117 D7
Castril, *Spain* 29 H2
Castro, *Brazil* 127 A5
Castro, *Chile* 128 B2
Castro Alves, *Brazil* 123 D4
Castro del Río, *Spain* 31 H6
Castro Marim, *Portugal* 31 H3
Castro Urdiales, *Spain* 28 B1
Castro Verde, *Portugal* 31 H2
Castrojeriz, *Spain* 30 C6
Castropol, *Spain* 30 B3
Castroreale, *Italy* 35 D8
Castrovillari, *Italy* 35 C9
Castroville, *Calif., U.S.A.* 112 J5
Castroville, *Tex., U.S.A.* 109 L5
Castrovirreyna, *Peru* 124 C2
Castuera, *Spain* 31 G5
Casummit Lake, *Canada* 98 B1
Çat, *Turkey* 67 C9
Cat Ba, Dao, *Vietnam* 58 B6
Cat I., *Bahamas* 117 B4
Cat I., *U.S.A.* 109 K10
Cat L., *Canada* 98 B1
Catacamas, *Honduras* 116 D2
Catacáos, *Peru* 124 B1
Cataguases, *Brazil* 123 F3
Catahoula L., *U.S.A.* 109 K8
Çatak, *Turkey* 67 C10
Catalão, *Brazil* 123 E2
Çatalca, *Turkey* 66 B3
Catalina, *Canada* 99 C9
Catalonia = Cataluña □, *Spain* 28 D6
Cataluña □, *Spain* 28 D6
Çatalzeytin, *Turkey* 66 B6
Catamarca, *Argentina* 126 B2
Catamarca □, *Argentina* 126 B2
Catanauan, *Phil.* 55 E5
Catanduanes, *Phil.* 55 E6
Catanduva, *Brazil* 127 A6
Catánia, *Italy* 35 E8
Catánia, G. di, *Italy* 35 E8
Catanzaro, *Italy* 35 D9
Catarman, *Phil.* 55 E6
Catbalogan, *Phil.* 55 F6
Cateel, *Phil.* 55 H7
Catende, *Brazil* 122 C4
Cathcart, *S. Africa* 84 E4
Cathlamet, *U.S.A.* 112 D3
Catio, *Guinea-Biss.* 78 C1
Catismiña, *Venezuela* 121 C5
Catita, *Brazil* 122 C3
Catlettsburg, *U.S.A.* 104 F4
Catoche, C., *Mexico* 115 C7
Catolé do Rocha, *Brazil* 122 C4
Catral, *Spain* 29 G4
Catria, Mt., *Italy* 33 E9
Catrimani, *Brazil* 121 C5
Catrimani →, *Brazil* 121 C5
Catskill, *U.S.A.* 107 D11
Catskill Mts., *U.S.A.* 107 D10
Catt, Mt., *Australia* 90 A1
Cattaraugus, *U.S.A.* 106 D6
Cattólica, *Italy* 33 E9
Cattólica Eraclea, *Italy* 34 E6
Catu, *Brazil* 123 D4
Catuala, *Angola* 84 B2
Catur, *Mozam.* 83 E4
Catwick Is., *Vietnam* 59 G7
Cauca □, *Colombia* 120 C2
Cauca →, *Colombia* 120 B3
Caucaia, *Brazil* 122 B4
Caucasia, *Colombia* 120 B2
Caucasus Mountains, *Eurasia* 43 J7
Caudebec-en-Caux, *France* 24 C7
Caudebec-lès-Elbeuf, *France* 24 C8
Caudete, *Spain* 29 G3
Caudry, *France* 25 B10
Caulnes, *France* 24 D4
Caulónia, *Italy* 35 D9
Caúngula, *Angola* 80 F3
Cauquenes, *Chile* 126 D1
Caura →, *Venezuela* 121 B5
Caurés →, *Brazil* 121 D5
Cauresi →, *Mozam.* 83 F3
Causapscal, *Canada* 99 C6
Caussade, *France* 26 D5
Causse-Méjean, *France* 26 D7
Cauterets, *France* 26 F3
Cautín □, *Chile* 128 A2
Cauvery →, *India* 60 P11
Caux, Pays de, *France* 24 C7
Cava dei Tirreni, *Italy* 35 B7
Cávado →, *Portugal* 30 D2
Cavaillon, *France* 27 E9
Cavalaire-sur-Mer, *France* 27 E10
Cavalcante, *Brazil* 123 D2
Cavalese, *Italy* 33 B8
Cavalier, *U.S.A.* 108 A6
Cavalla = Cavally →, *Africa* 78 E3
Cavallo, I. de, *France* 27 G13
Cavally →, *Africa* 78 E3
Cavan, *Ireland* 15 C4
Cavan □, *Ireland* 15 C4
Cavárzere, *Italy* 33 C9
Cave City, *U.S.A.* 104 G3
Cavenagh Ra., *Australia* 89 E4
Cavendish, *Australia* 91 F3
Caviana, I., *Brazil* 121 C7
Cavite, *Phil.* 55 D4
Cavour, *Italy* 32 D4
Cavtat, *Croatia* 21 N8
Cawndilla L., *Australia* 91 E3
Cawnpore = Kanpur, *India* 63 F9
Caxias, *Brazil* 122 B3
Caxias do Sul, *Brazil* 127 B5
Caxito, *Angola* 80 F2
Çay, *Turkey* 66 C4
Cay Sal Bank, *Bahamas* 116 B3
Cayambe, *Napo, Ecuador* 120 C2
Cayambe, *Quito, Ecuador* 120 C2
Çaycuma, *Turkey* 66 B5
Çayeli, *Turkey* 67 B9
Cayenne, *Fr. Guiana* 121 B7
Cayenne □, *Fr. Guiana* 121 C7
Cayeux-sur-Mer, *France* 25 B8
Cayiralan, *Turkey* 66 C6
Caylus, *France* 26 D5
Cayman Brac, *Cayman Is.* 116 C4
Cayman Is. ■, *W. Indies* 116 C3
Cayo Romano, *Cuba* 117 B4
Cayuga, *Canada* 106 D5
Cayuga, *U.S.A.* 107 D8
Cayuga L., *U.S.A.* 107 D8
Cazalla de la Sierra, *Spain* 31 H5
Căzăneşti, *Romania* 38 E10
Cazaux et de Sanguinet, Étang de, *France* 26 D2
Cazères, *France* 26 E5
Cazin, *Bos.-H.* 33 D12
Čazma, *Croatia* 33 C13
Čazma →, *Croatia* 33 C13
Cazombo, *Angola* 81 G4
Cazorla, *Spain* 29 H1
Cazorla, *Venezuela* 120 B4
Cazorla, Sierra de, *Spain* 29 G2
Cea →, *Spain* 30 C5
Ceadâr-Lunga, *Moldova* 41 J5
Ceanannus Mor, *Ireland* 15 C5
Ceará = Fortaleza, *Brazil* 122 B4
Ceará □, *Brazil* 122 C4
Ceará Mirim, *Brazil* 122 C4
Cebaco, I. de, *Panama* 116 E3
Cebollar, *Argentina* 126 B2
Cebollera, Sierra de, *Spain* 28 D2
Cebreros, *Spain* 30 E6
Cebu, *Phil.* 55 F5
Ceccano, *Italy* 34 A6
Cechi, *Ivory C.* 78 D4
Čechy, *Czech.* 19 F9
Cecil Plains, *Australia* 91 D5
Cécina, *Italy* 32 E7
Cécina →, *Italy* 32 E7
Ceclavin, *Spain* 30 F4
Cedar →, *U.S.A.* 108 E9

Cedar City

Cedar City, U.S.A. 111 H7
Cedar Creek Reservoir, U.S.A. 109 J6
Cedar Falls, Iowa, U.S.A. 108 D8
Cedar Falls, Wash., U.S.A. 112 C5
Cedar Key, U.S.A. 105 L4
Cedar L., Canada 101 C8
Cedar Rapids, U.S.A. 108 E9
Cedartown, U.S.A. 105 H3
Cedarvale, Canada 100 B3
Cedarville, S. Africa 85 E4
Cedarville, U.S.A. 110 F3
Cedeira, Spain 30 B2
Cedral, Mexico 114 C4
Cedrino →, Italy 34 B2
Cedro, Brazil 122 C4
Cedros, I. de, Mexico 114 B1
Ceduna, Australia 91 E1
Cefalù, Italy 35 D7
Cega →, Spain 30 D6
Cegléd, Hungary 21 H9
Céglie Messápico, Italy 35 B10
Cehegín, Spain 29 G3
Ceheng, China 52 E5
Cehu-Silvaniei, Romania 38 B6
Ceira →, Portugal 30 E2
Cekhira, Tunisia 75 B7
Celano, Italy 33 F10
Celanova, Spain 30 C3
Celaya, Mexico 114 C4
Celbridge, Ireland 15 C5
Celebes = Sulawesi □, Indonesia 57 E6
Celebes Sea, Indonesia 57 D6
Celendín, Peru 124 B2
Čelić, Bos.-H. 21 L8
Celica, Ecuador 120 D2
Celina, U.S.A. 104 E3
Celje, Slovenia 33 B12
Celle, Germany 18 C6
Celles, Belgium 17 G2
Celorico da Beira, Portugal 30 E3
Cement, U.S.A. 109 H5
Çemişgezek, Turkey 67 C8
Cenepa →, Peru 120 D2
Cengong, China 52 D7
Ceno →, Italy 32 D7
Cenon, France 26 D3
Centallo, Italy 32 D4
Centenário do Sul, Brazil 123 F1
Center, N. Dak., U.S.A. 108 B4
Center, Tex., U.S.A. 109 K7
Centerfield, U.S.A. 111 G8
Centerville, Calif., U.S.A. 112 J7
Centerville, Iowa, U.S.A. 108 E8
Centerville, Pa., U.S.A. 106 F5
Centerville, S. Dak., U.S.A. 108 D6
Centerville, Tenn., U.S.A. 105 H2
Centerville, Tex., U.S.A. 109 K7
Cento, Italy 33 D8
Central, Brazil 122 D3
Central, U.S.A. 111 K9
Central □, Kenya 82 C4
Central □, Malawi 83 E3
Central □, U.K. 14 E4
Central □, Zambia 83 E2
Central, Cordillera, Bolivia 125 D5
Central, Cordillera, Colombia 120 C2
Central, Cordillera, Costa Rica 116 D3
Central, Cordillera, Dom. Rep. 117 C5
Central, Cordillera, Peru 124 B2
Central, Cordillera, Phil. 55 C4
Central, Sistema, Spain 30 E5
Central African Rep. ■, Africa 73 G9
Central City, Ky., U.S.A. 104 G2
Central City, Nebr., U.S.A. 108 E5
Central I., Kenya 82 B4
Central Makran Range, Pakistan 60 F4
Central Patricia, Canada 98 B1
Central Russian Uplands, Europe 6 E13
Central Siberian Plateau, Russia 46 C14
Centralia, Ill., U.S.A. 108 F10
Centralia, Mo., U.S.A. 108 F8
Centralia, Wash., U.S.A. 112 D4
Centreville, Ala., U.S.A. 105 J2
Centreville, Miss., U.S.A. 109 K9
Centúripe, Italy 35 E7
Cephalonia = Kefallinía, Greece 39 L3
Ceprano, Italy 34 A6
Cepu, Indonesia 57 G14
Ceram = Seram, Indonesia 57 E7
Ceram Sea = Seram Sea, Indonesia 57 E7
Cerbère, France 26 F7
Cerbicales, Is., France 27 G13
Cercal, Portugal 31 H2
Cercemaggiore, Italy 35 A7
Cerdaña, Spain 28 C6
Cerdedo, Spain 30 C2
Cère →, France 26 D5
Cerea, Italy 33 C8
Ceres, Argentina 126 B3
Ceres, Brazil 123 E2
Ceres, Italy 32 C4
Ceres, S. Africa 84 E2
Ceres, U.S.A. 112 H6
Céret, France 26 F6
Cereté, Colombia 120 B2
Cerfontaine, Belgium 17 H4
Cerignola, Italy 35 A8
Cerigo = Kíthira, Greece 39 N7
Cérilly, France 26 B6
Cerisiers, France 25 D10
Cerizay, France 24 F6
Çerkeş, Turkey 66 B5
Çerkeşköy, Turkey 66 B2
Cerknica, Slovenia 33 C11
Çermik, Turkey 67 C8
Cerna →, Romania 38 E7
Cernavodă, Romania 38 E11
Cernay, France 25 E14
Cernik, Croatia 21 K7
Cerralvo, I., Mexico 114 C3
Cerreto Sannita, Italy 35 A7
Cerritos, Mexico 114 C4
Cerro Sombrero, Chile 128 D3
Certaldo, Italy 32 E8
Cervaro →, Italy 35 A8
Cervera, Spain 28 D6
Cervera de Pisuerga, Spain 30 C6
Cervera del Río Alhama, Spain 28 C3
Cérvia, Italy 33 D9
Cervignano del Friuli, Italy 33 C10
Cervinara, Italy 35 A7
Cervione, France 27 F13
Cervo, Spain 30 B3
César □, Colombia 120 B3
Cesaro, Italy 35 E7
Cesena, Italy 33 D9
Cesenático, Italy 33 D9
Cēsis, Latvia 9 H21
Česká Lípa, Czech. 20 E4
Česka Republika = Czech Rep. ■, Europe 20 F4
České Budějovice, Czech. 20 G4
Ceskomoravská Vrchovina, Czech. 20 F5
Český Brod, Czech. 20 E4
Český Krumlov, Czech. 20 G4
Český Těšin, Czech. 20 F8
Çeşme, Turkey 66 C2
Cessnock, Australia 91 E5
Cestos →, Liberia 78 D3
Cétin Grad, Croatia 33 C12
Cetina →, Croatia 33 E13
Cetraro, Italy 35 C8
Ceuta, N. Afr. 74 A3
Ceva, Italy 32 D5
Cévennes, France 26 D7
Ceyhan, Turkey 66 D6
Ceyhan →, Turkey 66 D6
Ceylânpınar, Turkey 67 D9
Ceylon = Sri Lanka ■, Asia 60 R12
Cèze →, France 27 D8
Cha-am, Thailand 58 F2
Chaam, Neths. 17 E5
Chabeuil, France 27 D9
Chablais, France 27 B10
Chablis, France 25 E10
Chabounia, Algeria 75 A5
Chacabuco, Argentina 126 C3
Chachapoyas, Peru 124 B2
Chachasp, Peru 124 D3
Chachoengsao, Thailand 58 F3
Chachran, Pakistan 60 E7
Chachro, Pakistan 62 G4
Chaco □, Argentina 126 B3
Chaco □, Paraguay 126 B3
Chad ■, Africa 73 E8
Chad, L. = Tchad, L., Chad 73 F7
Chadan, Russia 45 D10
Chadileuvú →, Argentina 126 D2
Chadiza, Zambia 83 E3
Chadron, U.S.A. 108 D3
Chadyr-Lunga = Ceadâr-Lunga, Moldova 41 J5
Chae Hom, Thailand 58 C2
Chaem →, Thailand 58 C2
Chaeryŏng, N. Korea 51 E13
Chagai Hills, Afghan. 60 E3
Chagda, Russia 45 D14
Chagny, France 25 F11
Chagoda, Russia 40 C8
Chagos Arch., Ind. Oc. 46 K11
Chāh Ākhvor, Iran 65 C8
Chāh Bahār, Iran 65 E9
Chāh-e-Malek, Iran 65 D8
Chāh Kavīr, Iran 65 D7
Chahar Burjak, Afghan. 60 D3
Chaibasa, India 61 H14
Chaillé-les-Marais, France 26 B2
Chainat, Thailand 58 E3
Chaitén, Chile 128 B2
Chaiya, Thailand 59 H2
Chaj Doab, Pakistan 62 C5
Chajari, Argentina 126 C4
Chake Chake, Tanzania 82 D4
Chakhānsūr, Afghan. 60 D3
Chakonipau, L., Canada 99 A6
Chakradharpur, India 63 H11
Chakwal, Pakistan 62 C5
Chala, Peru 124 D3
Chalais, France 26 C4
Chalchihuites, Mexico 114 C4
Chalcis = Khalkís, Greece 39 L6
Chaleur B., Canada 99 C6
Chalfant, U.S.A. 112 H8
Chalhuanca, Peru 124 C3
Chalindrey, France 25 E12
Chaling, China 53 D9
Chalisgaon, India 60 J9
Chalky Inlet, N.Z. 87 M1
Challans, France 24 F5
Challapata, Bolivia 124 D4
Challis, U.S.A. 110 D6
Chalna, India 63 H13
Chalon-sur-Saône, France 25 F11
Chalonnes-sur-Loire, France 24 E6
Châlons-sur-Marne, France 25 D11
Châlus, France 26 C4
Chalyaphum, Thailand 58 E4
Cham, Germany 19 F8
Cham, Switz. 23 B6
Cham, Cu Lao, Vietnam 58 E7
Chama, U.S.A. 111 H10
Chaman, Pakistan 60 D5
Chamba, India 62 C7
Chamba, Tanzania 83 E4
Chambal →, India 63 F8
Chamberlain, U.S.A. 108 D5
Chamberlain →, Australia 88 C4
Chambers, U.S.A. 111 J9
Chambersburg, U.S.A. 104 F7
Chambéry, France 27 C9
Chambly, Canada 107 A11
Chambord, Canada 99 C5
Chamchamal, Iraq 67 E11
Chamela, Mexico 114 D3
Chamical, Argentina 126 C2
Chamkar Luong, Cambodia 59 G4
Chamonix-Mont Blanc, France 27 C10
Champa, India 63 H10
Champagne, Canada 100 A1
Champagne, France 25 D11
Champagne, Plaine de, France 25 D11
Champagnole, France 25 F12
Champaign, U.S.A. 104 E1
Champassak, Laos 58 E5
Champaubert, France 25 D10
Champdeniers, France 26 B3
Champeix, France 26 C7
Champlain, Canada 104 B9
Champlain, U.S.A. 107 B11
Champlain, L., U.S.A. 107 B11
Champotón, Mexico 115 D6
Chamusca, Portugal 31 F2
Chan Chan, Peru 124 B2
Chana, Thailand 59 J3
Chañaral, Chile 126 B1
Chanārān, Iran 65 B8
Chanasma, India 62 H5
Chancay, Peru 124 C2
Chancy, Switz. 22 D1
Chandannagar, India 63 H13
Chandausi, India 63 E8
Chandeleur Is., U.S.A. 109 L10
Chandeleur Sd., U.S.A. 109 L10
Chandigarh, India 62 D7
Chandler, Australia 91 D1
Chandler, Canada 99 C7
Chandler, Ariz., U.S.A. 111 K8
Chandler, Okla., U.S.A. 109 H6
Chandless →, Brazil 124 B4
Chandmani, Mongolia 54 B4
Chandpur, Bangla. 61 H17
Chandpur, India 62 E8
Chandrapur, India 60 K11
Chānf, Iran 65 E9
Chang, Pakistan 62 F3
Chang, Ko, Thailand 59 F4
Ch'ang Chiang = Chang Jiang →, China 53 B13
Chang Jiang →, China 53 B13
Changa, India 63 C7
Changanacheri, India 60 Q10
Changane →, Mozam. 85 C5
Changbai, China 51 D15
Changbai Shan, China 51 C15
Changchiak'ou = Zhangjiakou, China 50 D8
Ch'angchou = Changzhou, China 53 B12
Changchun, China 51 C13
Changchunling, China 51 B13
Changde, China 53 C8
Changdo-ri, N. Korea 51 E14
Changfeng, China 53 A11
Changhai = Shanghai, China 53 B13
Changhua, China 53 B12
Changhŭng, S. Korea 51 G14
Changhŭngni, N. Korea 51 D15
Changjiang, China 54 E5
Changjin, N. Korea 51 D14
Changjin-chŏsuji, N. Korea 51 D14
Changle, China 53 E12
Changli, China 51 E10
Changling, China 51 B12
Changlun, Malaysia 59 J3
Changning, Hunan, China 53 D9
Changning, Yunnan, China 52 E2
Changping, China 50 D9
Changsha, China 53 C9
Changshan, China 53 C12
Changshou, China 52 C6
Changshu, China 53 B13
Changshun, China 52 D6
Changtai, China 53 E11
Changting, China 53 E11
Changwu, China 50 G4
Changxing, China 53 B12
Changyang, China 53 B8
Changyi, China 51 F10
Changyŏn, N. Korea 51 E13
Changyuan, China 50 G8
Changzhi, China 50 F7
Changzhou, China 53 B12
Chanhanga, Angola 84 B1
Chanlar = Xanlar, Azerbaijan 43 K8
Channapatna, India 60 N10
Channel Is., U.K. 13 H5
Channel Is., U.S.A. 113 M7
Channel-Port aux Basques, Canada 99 C8
Channing, Mich., U.S.A. 104 B1
Channing, Tex., U.S.A. 109 H3
Chantada, Spain 30 C3
Chanthaburi, Thailand 58 F4
Chantilly, France 25 C9
Chantonnay, France 24 F5
Chantrey Inlet, Canada 96 B10
Chanute, U.S.A. 109 G7
Chanza →, Spain 31 H3
Chao Hu, China 53 B11
Chao Phraya →, Thailand 58 F3
Chao Phraya Lowlands, Thailand 58 E3
Chao Xian, China 53 B11
Chao'an, China 53 F11
Chaocheng, China 50 F8
Chaoyang, Guangdong, China 53 F11
Chaoyang, Liaoning, China 51 D11
Chapada dos Guimarães, Brazil 125 D6
Chapala, Mozam. 83 F4
Chapala, L. de, Mexico 114 C4
Chaparé →, Bolivia 125 D5
Chaparral, Colombia 120 C2
Chapayev, Kazakhstan 42 E10
Chapayevsk, Russia 42 D9
Chapecó, Brazil 127 B5
Chapel Hill, U.S.A. 105 H6
Chapleau, Canada 98 C3
Chaplin, Canada 101 C7
Chaplino, Ukraine 41 H9
Chaplygin, Russia 42 D5
Chapra = Chhapra, India 63 G11
Châr, Mauritania 74 D2
Chara, Russia 45 D12
Charadai, Argentina 126 B4
Charagua, Bolivia 125 D5
Charalá, Colombia 120 B3
Charambirá, Punta, Colombia 120 C2
Charaña, Bolivia 124 D4
Charantsavan, Armenia 43 K7
Charapita, Colombia 120 D3
Charata, Argentina 126 B3
Charcas, Mexico 114 C4
Charcoal L., Canada 101 B8
Chard, U.K. 13 G5
Chardara, Kazakhstan 44 E7
Chardon, U.S.A. 106 E3
Chardzhou = Chärjew, Turkmenistan 44 F7
Charente □, France 26 C4
Charente →, France 26 C2
Charente-Maritime □, France 26 C3
Chari →, Chad 73 F7
Chārīkār, Afghan. 60 B6
Chariton →, U.S.A. 108 F8
Charity, Guyana 121 B6
Chärjew, Turkmenistan 44 F7
Charkhari, India 63 G8
Charkhi Dadri, India 62 E7
Charleroi, Belgium 17 H4
Charleroi, U.S.A. 106 F5
Charles, C., U.S.A. 104 G8
Charles City, U.S.A. 108 D8
Charles L., Canada 101 B6
Charles Town, U.S.A. 104 F7
Charleston, Ill., U.S.A. 104 F1
Charleston, Miss., U.S.A. 109 H9
Charleston, Mo., U.S.A. 109 G10
Charleston, S.C., U.S.A. 105 J6
Charleston, W. Va., U.S.A. 104 F5
Charleston Peak, U.S.A. 113 J11
Charlestown, S. Africa 85 D4
Charlestown, U.S.A. 104 F3
Charlesville, Zaïre 80 F4
Charleville = Rath Luirc, Ireland 15 D3
Charleville, Australia 91 D4
Charleville-Mézières, France 25 C11
Charlevoix, U.S.A. 104 C3
Charlieu, France 27 B8
Charlotte, Mich., U.S.A. 104 D3
Charlotte, N.C., U.S.A. 105 H5
Charlotte Amalie, Virgin Is. 117 C7
Charlotte Harbor, U.S.A. 105 M4
Charlottesville, U.S.A. 104 F6
Charlottetown, Canada 99 C7
Charlton, Australia 91 F3
Charlton, U.S.A. 108 E8
Charlton I., Canada 98 B4
Charmes, France 25 D13
Charny, Canada 99 C5
Charolles, France 27 B8
Chârost, France 25 F9
Charouine, Algeria 75 C4
Charre, Mozam. 83 F4
Charroux, France 26 B4
Charsadda, Pakistan 62 B4
Charters Towers, Australia 90 C4
Chartres, France 24 D8
Chascomús, Argentina 126 D4
Chasefu, Zambia 83 E3
Chasovnya-Uchurskaya, Russia 45 D14
Chasseneuil-sur-Bonnieure, France 26 C4
Chāt, Iran 65 B7
Chatal Balkan = Udvoy Balkan, Bulgaria 38 G9
Château-Arnoux, France 27 D10
Château-Chinon, France 25 E10
Château d'Oex, Switz. 22 D4
Château-du-Loir, France 24 E7
Château-Gontier, France 24 E6
Château-la-Vallière, France 24 E7
Château-Landon, France 25 D9
Château-Porcien, France 25 C11
Château-Renault, France 24 E7
Château-Salins, France 25 D13
Château-Thierry, France 25 C10
Châteaubourg, France 24 D5
Châteaubriant, France 24 E5
Châteaudun, France 24 D8
Châteaugiron, France 24 D5
Châteaulin, France 24 D2
Châteaumeillant, France 26 B6
Châteauneuf-du-Faou, France 24 D3
Châteauneuf-en-Thymerais, France 24 D8
Châteauneuf-sur-Charente, France 26 C3
Châteauneuf-sur-Cher, France 25 F9
Châteauneuf-sur-Loire, France 25 E9
Châteaurenard, Bouches-du-Rhône, France 27 E8
Châteaurenard, Loiret, France 25 E9
Châteauroux, France 25 F8
Châtel-St.-Denis, Switz. 22 C3
Châtelaillon-Plage, France 26 B2
Châtelaudren, France 24 D4
Chatelet, Belgium 17 H5
Châtelguyon, France 26 C7
Châtellerault, France 24 F7
Châtelus-Malvaleix, France 26 B6
Chatfield, U.S.A. 108 D9
Chatham, N.B., Canada 99 C6
Chatham, Ont., Canada 98 D3
Chatham, U.K. 13 F8
Chatham, La., U.S.A. 109 J8
Chatham, N.Y., U.S.A. 107 D11
Chatham, I., Chile 128 D2
Chatham Is., Pac. Oc. 92 M10
Chatham Str., U.S.A. 100 B2
Châtillon, Italy 32 C4
Châtillon-Coligny, France 25 E9
Châtillon-en-Bazois, France 25 E10
Châtillon-en-Diois, France 27 D9
Châtillon-sur-Indre, France 24 F8
Châtillon-sur-Loire, France 25 E9
Châtillon-sur-Marne, France 25 C10
Châtillon-sur-Seine, France 25 E11
Chatmohar, Bangla. 63 G13
Chatra, India 63 G11
Chatrapur, India 61 K14
Chats, L. des, Canada 107 A8
Chatsworth, Canada 106 B4
Chatsworth, Zimbabwe 83 F3
Chattahoochee →, U.S.A. 105 K3
Chattanooga, U.S.A. 105 H3
Chaturat, Thailand 58 E3
Chau Doc, Vietnam 59 G5
Chaudanne, Barr. de, France 27 E10
Chaudes-Aigues, France 26 D7
Chauffailles, France 27 B8
Chauk, Burma 61 J19
Chaukan La, Burma 61 F20
Chaulnes, France 25 C9
Chaumont, France 25 D12
Chaumont, U.S.A. 107 B8
Chaumont-en-Vexin, France 25 C8
Chaumont-sur-Loire, France 24 E8
Chaunay, France 26 B4
Chauny, France 25 C10
Chausey, Is., France 24 D5
Chaussin, France 25 F12
Chautauqua L., U.S.A. 106 D5
Chauvigny, France 24 F7
Chauvin, Canada 101 C6
Chavantina, Brazil 125 C7
Chaves, Brazil 122 B2
Chaves, Portugal 30 D3
Chavuma, Zambia 81 G4
Chawang, Thailand 59 H2
Chazelles-sur-Lyon, France 27 C8
Chazuta, Peru 124 B2
Chazy, U.S.A. 107 B11
Cheb, Czech. 20 E2
Cheboksarskoye Vdkhr., Russia 42 B8
Cheboksary, Russia 42 B8
Cheboygan, U.S.A. 104 C3
Chebsara, Russia 40 C10
Chech, Erg, Africa 74 D4
Chechaouen, Morocco 74 A3
Chechen, Ostrov, Russia 43 H8
Chechenia □, Russia 43 J7
Checheno-Ingush Republic = Chechenia □, Russia 43 J7

Chuquibamba

Chechnya = Chechenia □, Russia 43 J7
Chechon, S. Korea 51 F15
Chęciny, Poland 20 E10
Checleset B., Canada 100 C3
Checotah, U.S.A. 109 H7
Chedabucto B., Canada 99 C7
Cheduba I., Burma 61 K18
Cheepie, Australia 91 D4
Chef-Boutonne, France 26 B3
Chegdomyn, Russia 45 D14
Chegga, Mauritania 74 C3
Chegutu, Zimbabwe 83 F3
Chehalis, U.S.A. 112 D4
Cheiron, Mt., France 27 E10
Cheju Do, S. Korea 51 H14
Chekalin, Russia 42 C3
Chekiang = Zhejiang □, China 53 C13
Chel = Kuru, Bahr el →, Sudan 77 F2
Chela, Sa. da, Angola 84 B1
Chelan, U.S.A. 110 C4
Chelan, L., U.S.A. 110 C3
Cheleken, Turkmenistan 44 F6
Chelforó, Argentina 128 A3
Chéliff, O. →, Algeria 75 A5
Chelkar = Shalqar, Kazakhstan 44 E6
Chelkar Tengiz, Solonchak, Kazakhstan 44 E7
Chellala Dahrania, Algeria 75 B5
Chelles, France 25 D9
Chełm, Poland 20 D13
Chełmek, Poland 20 E9
Chełmno, Poland 20 B8
Chelmsford, U.K. 13 F8
Chełmża, Poland 20 B8
Chelsea, Okla., U.S.A. 109 G7
Chelsea, Vt., U.S.A. 107 C12
Cheltenham, U.K. 13 F5
Chelva, Spain 28 F4
Chelyabinsk, Russia 44 D7
Chelyuskin, C., Russia 46 B14
Chemainus, Canada 100 D4
Chembar = Belinskiy, Russia 42 D6
Chemillé, France 24 E6
Chemnitz, Germany 18 E8
Chemult, U.S.A. 110 E3
Chen, Gora, Russia 45 C15
Chen Xian, China 53 E9
Chenab →, Pakistan 62 D4
Chenachane, O. →, Algeria 74 C4
Chenango Forks, U.S.A. 107 D9
Chencha, Ethiopia 77 F4
Chenchiang = Zhenjiang, China 53 A12
Chênée, Belgium 17 G7
Cheney, U.S.A. 110 C5
Cheng Xian, China 50 H3
Chengbu, China 53 D8
Chengcheng, China 50 G5
Chengchou = Zhengzhou, China 50 G7
Chengde, China 51 D9
Chengdong Hu, China 53 A11
Chengdu, China 52 B5
Chenggong, China 52 E4
Chenggu, China 50 H4
Chengjiang, China 52 E4
Chengkou, China 52 B7
Ch'engtu = Chengdu, China 52 B5
Chengwu, China 50 G8
Chengxi Hu, China 53 A11
Chengyang, China 51 F11
Chenjiagang, China 51 G10
Chenkán, Mexico 115 D6
Chenxi, China 53 C8
Cheo Reo, Vietnam 58 F7
Cheom Ksan, Cambodia 58 E5
Chepelare, Bulgaria 39 H7
Chepén, Peru 124 B2
Chepes, Argentina 126 C2
Chepo, Panama 116 E4
Cheptulil, Mt., Kenya 82 B4
Chequamegon B., U.S.A. 108 B9
Cher □, France 25 E9
Cher →, France 24 E7
Cherasco, Italy 32 D4
Cheratte, Belgium 17 G7
Cheraw, U.S.A. 105 H6
Cherbourg, France 24 C5
Cherchell, Algeria 75 A5
Cherdakly, Russia 42 C9
Cherdyn, Russia 44 C6
Cheremkhovo, Russia 45 D11
Cherepanovo, Russia 44 D9
Cherepovets, Russia 40 C9
Chergui, Chott ech, Algeria 75 B5
Cherikov = Cherykaw, Belarus 40 F6
Cherkasy, Ukraine 41 H7
Cherkessk, Russia 43 H6
Cherlak, Russia 44 D8
Chernaya, Russia 45 B9
Cherni, Bulgaria 38 G6
Chernigov = Chernihiv, Ukraine 41 G6
Chernihiv, Ukraine 41 G6
Chernivtsi, Ukraine 41 H3
Chernobyl = Chornobyl, Ukraine 41 G6
Chernogorsk, Russia 45 D10
Chernomorskoye = Chornomorske, Ukraine 41 K7
Chernovtsy = Chernivtsi, Ukraine 41 H3
Chernyakhovsk, Russia 9 J19
Chernyanka, Russia 42 E3
Chernyshovskiy, Russia 45 C12
Chernyye Zemli, Russia 43 H8
Cherokee, Iowa, U.S.A. 108 D7
Cherokee, Okla., U.S.A. 109 G5
Cherokees, Lake O' The, U.S.A. 109 G7
Cherquenco, Chile 128 A2
Cherrapunji, India 61 G17
Cherry Creek, U.S.A. 110 G6
Cherry Valley, U.S.A. 113 M10
Cherryvale, U.S.A. 109 G7
Cherskiy, Russia 45 C17
Cherskogo Khrebet, Russia 45 C15
Chertkovo, Russia 42 F5
Cherven, Belarus 40 F5
Cherven-Bryag, Bulgaria 38 F7
Chervonohrad, Ukraine 41 G3
Cherwell →, U.K. 13 F6
Cherykaw, Belarus 40 F6
Chesapeake, U.S.A. 104 G7
Chesapeake B., U.S.A. 104 F7
Cheshire □, U.K. 12 D5
Cheshskaya Guba, Russia 44 C5
Cheslatta L., Canada 100 C3
Chesley, Canada 106 B3
Cheste, Spain 29 F4
Chester, U.K. 12 D5
Chester, Calif., U.S.A. 110 F3
Chester, Ill., U.S.A. 109 G10
Chester, Mont., U.S.A. 110 B8
Chester, Pa., U.S.A. 104 F8
Chester, S.C., U.S.A. 105 H5
Chesterfield, U.K. 12 D6
Chesterfield, Is., N. Cal. 92 J7
Chesterfield Inlet, Canada 96 B10
Chesterton Ra., Australia 91 D4
Chesterville, Canada 107 A9
Chesuncook L., U.S.A. 99 C6
Chéticamp, Canada 99 C7
Chetumal, B. de, Mexico 115 D7
Chetwynd, Canada 100 B4
Chevanceaux, France 26 C3
Cheviot, The, U.K. 12 B5
Cheviot Hills, U.K. 12 B5
Cheviot Ra., Australia 90 D3
Chew Bahir, Ethiopia 77 G4
Chewelah, U.S.A. 110 B5
Cheyenne, Okla., U.S.A. 109 H5
Cheyenne, Wyo., U.S.A. 108 E2
Cheyenne →, U.S.A. 108 C4
Cheyenne Wells, U.S.A. 108 F3
Cheyne B., Australia 89 F2
Chhabra, India 62 G7
Chhapra, India 63 G11
Chhata, India 62 F7
Chhatarpur, India 63 G8
Chhep, Cambodia 58 F5
Chhindwara, India 63 H8
Chhlong, Cambodia 59 F5
Chhuk, Cambodia 59 G5
Chi →, Thailand 58 E5
Chiamis, Indonesia 57 G13
Chiamussu = Jiamusi, China 54 B8
Chiang Dao, Thailand 58 C2
Chiang Kham, Thailand 58 C3
Chiang Khan, Thailand 58 D3
Chiang Khong, Thailand 58 B3
Chiang Mai, Thailand 58 C2
Chiang Saen, Thailand 58 B3
Chiange, Angola 81 H2
Chiapa →, Mexico 115 D6
Chiapa de Corzo, Mexico 115 D6
Chiapas □, Mexico 115 D6
Chiaramonte Gulfi, Italy 35 E7
Chiaravalle, Italy 33 E10
Chiaravalle Centrale, Italy 35 D9
Chiari, Italy 32 C6
Chiasso, Switz. 23 E8
Chiatura, Georgia 43 J6
Chiautla, Mexico 115 D5
Chiávari, Italy 32 D6
Chiavenna, Italy 32 B6
Chiba, Japan 49 G10
Chibabava, Mozam. 85 C5
Chibatu, Indonesia 57 G12
Chibemba, Cunene, Angola 81 H2
Chibemba, Huila, Angola 84 B2
Chibia, Angola 81 H2
Chibougamau, Canada 98 C5
Chibougamau L., Canada 98 C5
Chibuk, Nigeria 79 C7
Chic-Chocs, Mts., Canada 99 C6
Chicacole = Srikakulam, India 61 K13
Chicago, U.S.A. 104 E2
Chicago Heights, U.S.A. 104 E2
Chichagof I., U.S.A. 100 B1
Chichaoua, Morocco 74 B3
Chicheng, China 50 D8
Chichester, U.K. 13 G7
Chichibu, Japan 49 F9
Ch'ich'ihaerh = Qiqihar, China 45 E13
Chickasha, U.S.A. 109 H5
Chiclana de la Frontera, Spain 31 J4
Chiclayo, Peru 124 B2
Chico, U.S.A. 112 F5
Chico →, Chubut, Argentina 128 B3
Chico →, Santa Cruz, Argentina 128 C3
Chicomo, Mozam. 85 C5
Chicontepec, Mexico 115 C5
Chicopee, U.S.A. 107 D12
Chicoutimi, Canada 99 C5
Chicualacuala, Mozam. 85 C5
Chidambaram, India 60 P11
Chidenguele, Mozam. 85 C5
Chidley, C., Canada 97 B13
Chiede, Angola 84 B2
Chiefs Pt., Canada 106 B3
Chiem Hoa, Vietnam 58 A5
Chiemsee, Germany 19 H8
Chiengi, Zambia 83 D2
Chiengmai = Chiang Mai, Thailand 58 C2
Chienti →, Italy 33 E10
Chieri, Italy 32 D4
Chiers →, France 25 C11
Chiese →, Italy 32 C7
Chieti, Italy 33 F11
Chièvres, Belgium 17 G3
Chifeng, China 51 C10
Chigirin, Ukraine 41 H7
Chignecto B., Canada 99 C7
Chigorodó, Colombia 120 B2
Chiguana, Bolivia 126 A2
Chiha-ri, N. Korea 51 E14
Chihli, G. of = Bo Hai, China 51 E10
Chihuahua, Mexico 114 B3
Chihuahua □, Mexico 114 B3
Chiili, Kazakhstan 44 E7
Chik Bollapur, India 60 N10
Chikmagalur, India 60 N9
Chikwawa, Malawi 83 F3
Chilac, Mexico 115 D5
Chilako →, Canada 100 C4
Chilam Chavki, Pakistan 63 B6
Chilanga, Zambia 83 F2
Chilapa, Mexico 115 D5
Chilas, Pakistan 63 B6
Chilaw, Sri Lanka 60 R11
Chilcotin →, Canada 100 C4
Childers, Australia 91 D5
Childress, U.S.A. 109 H4
Chile ■, S. Amer. 128 B2
Chile Chico, Chile 128 C2
Chile Rise, Pac. Oc. 93 L18
Chilecito, Argentina 126 B2
Chilete, Peru 124 B2
Chilia, Bratul →, Romania 38 D12
Chililabombwe, Zambia 83 E2
Chilin = Jilin, China 51 C14
Chilka L., India 61 K14
Chilko →, Canada 100 C4
Chilko, L., Canada 100 C4
Chillagoe, Australia 90 B3
Chillán, Chile 126 D1
Chillicothe, Ill., U.S.A. 108 E10
Chillicothe, Mo., U.S.A. 108 F8
Chillicothe, Ohio, U.S.A. 104 F4
Chilliwack, Canada 100 D4
Chilo, India 62 F5
Chiloane, I., Mozam. 85 C5
Chiloé □, Chile 128 B2
Chiloé, I. de, Chile 128 B2
Chilpancingo, Mexico 115 D5
Chiltern Hills, U.K. 13 F7
Chilton, U.S.A. 104 C1
Chiluage, Angola 80 F4
Chilubi, Zambia 83 E2
Chilubula, Zambia 83 E3
Chilumba, Malawi 83 E3
Chilwa, L., Malawi 83 F4
Chimaltitán, Mexico 114 C4
Chimán, Panama 116 E4
Chimay, Belgium 17 H4
Chimbay, Uzbekistan 44 E6
Chimborazo, Ecuador 120 D2
Chimborazo □, Ecuador 120 D2
Chimbote, Peru 124 B2
Chimkent = Shymkent, Kazakhstan 44 E7
Chimoio, Mozam. 83 F3
Chimpembe, Zambia 83 D2
Chin □, Burma 61 J18
Chin Ling Shan = Qinling Shandi, China 50 H5
China, Mexico 115 B5
China ■, Asia 50 E3
China Lake, U.S.A. 113 K9
Chinacota, Colombia 120 B3
Chinan = Jinan, China 50 F9
Chinandega, Nic. 116 D2
Chinati Peak, U.S.A. 109 K2
Chincha Alta, Peru 124 C2
Chinchilla, Australia 91 D5
Chinchilla de Monte Aragón, Spain 29 G3
Chinchón, Spain 28 E1
Chinchorro, Banco, Mexico 115 D7
Chinchou = Jinzhou, China 51 D11
Chincoteague, U.S.A. 104 G8
Chinde, Mozam. 83 F4
Chindo, S. Korea 51 G14
Chindwin →, Burma 61 J19
Chineni, India 63 C6
Chinga, Mozam. 83 F4
Chingola, Zambia 83 E2
Chingole, Malawi 83 E3
Ch'ingtao = Qingdao, China 51 F11
Chinguetti, Mauritania 74 D2
Chingune, Mozam. 85 C5
Chinhae, S. Korea 51 G15
Chinhanguanine, Mozam. 85 D5
Chinhoyi, Zimbabwe 83 F3
Chiniot, Pakistan 62 D5
Chínipas, Mexico 114 B3
Chinju, S. Korea 51 G15
Chinle, U.S.A. 111 H9
Chinnampo, N. Korea 51 E13
Chino, Japan 49 G9
Chino, U.S.A. 113 L9
Chino Valley, U.S.A. 111 J7
Chinon, France 24 E7
Chinook, Canada 101 C6
Chinook, U.S.A. 110 B9
Chinsali, Zambia 83 E3
Chióggia, Italy 33 C9
Chíos = Khíos, Greece 39 L9
Chipata, Zambia 83 E3
Chipewyan L., Canada 101 B9
Chipinge, Zimbabwe 83 G3
Chipiona, Spain 31 J4
Chipley, U.S.A. 105 K3
Chipman, Canada 99 C6
Chipoka, Malawi 83 E3
Chippenham, U.K. 13 F5
Chippewa →, U.S.A. 108 C8
Chippewa Falls, U.S.A. 108 C9
Chiquián, Peru 124 C2
Chiquimula, Guatemala 116 D2
Chiquinquira, Colombia 120 B3
Chiquitos, Llanos de, Bolivia 125 D5
Chir →, Russia 43 F6
Chirala, India 60 M12
Chiramba, Mozam. 83 F3
Chirawa, India 62 E6
Chirchiq, Uzbekistan 44 E7
Chirgua →, Venezuela 120 B4
Chiricahua Peak, U.S.A. 111 L9
Chiriquí, G. de, Panama 116 E3
Chiriquí, L. de, Panama 116 E3
Chirivira Falls, Zimbabwe 83 G3
Chirmiri, India 61 H13
Chiromo, Malawi 81 H7
Chirpan, Bulgaria 38 G8
Chirripó Grande, Cerro, Costa Rica 116 E3
Chisamba, Zambia 83 E2
Chisapani Garhi, Nepal 61 F14
Chisasibi, Canada 98 B4
Chisholm, Canada 100 C6
Chishtian Mandi, Pakistan 62 E5
Chishui, China 52 C5
Chishui He →, China 52 C5
Chisimba Falls, Zambia 83 E3
Chişinău, Moldova 41 J5
Chisone →, Italy 32 D4
Chisos Mts., U.S.A. 109 L3
Chistopol, Russia 42 C10
Chita, Colombia 120 B3
Chita, Russia 45 D12
Chitado, Angola 81 H2
Chitembo, Angola 81 G3
Chitipa, Malawi 83 D3
Chitose, Japan 48 C10
Chitral, Pakistan 60 B7
Chitré, Panama 116 E3
Chittagong, Bangla. 61 H17
Chittagong □, Bangla. 61 G17
Chittaurgarh, India 62 G6
Chittoor, India 60 N11
Chitungwiza, Zimbabwe 83 F3
Chiusa, Italy 33 B8
Chiusi, Italy 33 E8
Chiva, Spain 29 F4
Chivacoa, Venezuela 120 A4
Chivasso, Italy 32 C4
Chivay, Peru 124 D3
Chivhu, Zimbabwe 83 F3
Chivilcoy, Argentina 126 C4
Chiwanda, Tanzania 83 E3
Chixi, China 53 G9
Chizera, Zambia 83 E1
Chkalov = Orenburg, Russia 44 D6
Chkolovsk, Russia 42 B6
Chloride, U.S.A. 113 K12
Cho Bo, Vietnam 58 B5
Cho-do, N. Korea 51 E13
Cho Phuoc Hai, Vietnam 59 G6
Choba, Kenya 82 B4
Chobe National Park, Botswana 84 B3
Chochiwŏn, S. Korea 51 F14
Chociwel, Poland 20 B5
Chocó □, Colombia 120 B2
Chocontá, Colombia 120 B3
Choctawhatchee B., U.S.A. 103 D9
Chodecz, Poland 20 C9
Chodziez, Poland 20 C6
Choele Choel, Argentina 128 A3
Choisy-le-Roi, France 25 D9
Choix, Mexico 114 B3
Chojnice, Poland 20 B7
Chojnów, Poland 20 D5
Chōkai-San, Japan 48 E10
Choke, Ethiopia 77 E4
Chokurdakh, Russia 45 B15
Cholame, U.S.A. 112 K6
Cholet, France 24 E6
Choluteca, Honduras 116 D2
Choluteca →, Honduras 116 D2
Chom Bung, Thailand 58 F2
Chom Thong, Thailand 58 C2
Choma, Zambia 83 F2
Chomen Swamp, Ethiopia 77 F4
Chomun, India 62 F6
Chomutov, Czech. 20 E3
Chon Buri, Thailand 58 F3
Chon Thanh, Vietnam 59 G6
Chonan, S. Korea 51 F14
Chone, Ecuador 120 D2
Chong Kai, Cambodia 58 F4
Chong Mek, Thailand 58 E5
Chong'an, China 53 D12
Chongde, China 53 B13
Chŏngdo, S. Korea 51 G15
Chŏngha, S. Korea 51 F15
Chŏngjin, N. Korea 51 D15
Chŏngju, N. Korea 51 E13
Chŏngju, S. Korea 51 F14
Chongli, China 50 D8
Chongming, China 53 B13
Chongming Dao, China 53 B13
Chongoyape, Peru 124 B2
Chongqing, Sichuan, China 52 C6
Chongqing, Sichuan, China 52 B4
Chongren, China 53 D11
Chŏngŭp, S. Korea 51 G14
Chongzuo, China 52 F6
Chŏnju, S. Korea 51 G14
Chonos, Arch. de los, Chile 128 C2
Chop, Ukraine 41 H2
Chopim →, Brazil 127 B5
Chorbat La, India 63 B7
Chorley, U.K. 12 D5
Chornobyl, Ukraine 41 G6
Chornomorske, Ukraine 41 K7
Chorolque, Cerro, Bolivia 126 A2
Chorregon, Australia 90 C3
Chortkiv, Ukraine 41 H3
Chŏrwŏn, S. Korea 51 E14
Chorzów, Poland 20 E8
Chos-Malal, Argentina 126 D1
Chosan, N. Korea 51 D13
Choszczno, Poland 20 B5
Chota, Peru 124 B2
Choteau, U.S.A. 110 C7
Chotila, India 62 H4
Chowchilla, U.S.A. 111 H3
Choybalsan, Mongolia 54 B6
Christchurch, N.Z. 87 K4
Christchurch, U.K. 13 G6
Christian I., Canada 106 B4
Christiana, S. Africa 84 D4
Christiansfeld, Denmark 11 J3
Christiansted, Virgin Is. 117 C7
Christie B., Canada 101 A6
Christina →, Canada 101 B6
Christmas Cr. →, Australia 88 C4
Christmas Creek, Australia 88 C4
Christmas I. = Kiritimati, Kiribati 93 G12
Christmas I., Ind. Oc. 92 J2
Christopher L., Australia 89 D4
Chrudim, Czech. 20 F5
Chrzanów, Poland 20 E9
Chtimba, Malawi 83 E3
Chu = Shu, Kazakhstan 44 E8
Chu →, Vietnam 58 C5
Chu Chua, Canada 100 C4
Chu Lai, Vietnam 58 E7
Chu Xian, China 53 A12
Ch'uanchou = Quanzhou, China 53 E12
Chuankou, China 50 G6
Chūbu □, Japan 49 F8
Chubut □, Argentina 128 B3
Chubut →, Argentina 128 B3
Chuchi L., Canada 100 B4
Chudovo, Russia 40 C6
Chudskoye, Oz., Russia 9 G22
Chūgoku □, Japan 49 G6
Chūgoku-Sanchi, Japan 49 G6
Chuguyev = Chuhuyiv, Ukraine 41 H9
Chugwater, U.S.A. 108 E2
Chuhuyiv, Ukraine 41 H9
Chukchi Sea, Russia 45 C19
Chukotskoye Nagorye, Russia 45 C18
Chula Vista, U.S.A. 113 N9
Chulman, Russia 45 D13
Chulucanas, Peru 124 B1
Chulumani, Bolivia 124 D4
Chulym →, Russia 44 D9
Chum Phae, Thailand 58 D4
Chum Saeng, Thailand 58 E3
Chuma, Bolivia 124 D4
Chumar, India 63 C8
Chumbicha, Argentina 126 B2
Chumerna, Bulgaria 38 G8
Chumikan, Russia 45 D14
Chumphon, Thailand 59 G2
Chumpi, Peru 124 D3
Chumuare, Mozam. 83 E3
Chumunjin, S. Korea 51 F15
Chuna →, Russia 45 D10
Chun'an, China 53 C12
Chunchŏn, S. Korea 51 F14
Chunchura, India 63 H13
Chunga, Zambia 83 F2
Chunggang-ŭp, N. Korea 51 D14
Chunghwa, N. Korea 51 E13
Chungju, S. Korea 51 F14
Chungking = Chongqing, China 52 C6
Chungmu, S. Korea 51 G15
Chungt'iaoshan = Zhongtiao Shan, China 50 G6
Chunian, Pakistan 62 D6
Chunya, Tanzania 83 D3
Chunya □, Tanzania 82 D3
Chunyang, China 51 C15
Chuquibamba, Peru 124 D3

Chuquibambilla, *Peru* 124 C3
Chuquicamata, *Chile* 126 A2
Chuquisaca □, *Bolivia* 125 E5
Chur, *Switz.* 23 C9
Churachandpur, *India* ... 61 G18
Churchill, *Canada* 101 B10
Churchill →, *Man.,*
  Canada 101 B10
Churchill →, *Nfld.,*
  Canada 99 B7
Churchill, C., *Canada* ... 101 B10
Churchill Falls, *Canada* ... 99 B7
Churchill L., *Canada* 101 B7
Churchill Pk., *Canada* ... 100 B3
Churfisten, *Switz.* 23 B8
Churu, *India* 62 E6
Churún Merú = Angel
  Falls, *Venezuela* 121 B5
Churwalden, *Switz.* 23 C9
Chushal, *India* 63 C8
Chusovoy, *Russia* 44 D6
Chuuronjang, *N. Korea* ... 51 D15
Chuvash Republic =
  Chuvashia □, *Russia* ... 42 C8
Chuvashia □, *Russia* 42 C8
Chuwārtah, *Iraq* 64 C5
Chuxiong, *China* 52 E3
Ci Xian, *China* 50 F8
Ciacova, *Romania* 38 D4
Cianjur, *Indonesia* 57 G12
Cibadok, *Indonesia* 57 G12
Cibatu, *Indonesia* 57 G12
Cibola, *U.S.A.* 113 M12
Cicero, *U.S.A.* 104 E2
Cícero Dantas, *Brazil* ... 122 D4
Cidacos →, *Spain* 28 C3
Cide, *Turkey* 66 B5
Ciechanów, *Poland* 20 C10
Ciego de Avila, *Cuba* 116 B4
Ciénaga, *Colombia* 120 A3
Ciénaga de Oro, *Colombia* 120 B2
Cienfuegos, *Cuba* 116 B3
Cieplice Śląskie Zdrój,
  Poland 20 E5
Cierp, *France* 26 F4
Cieszyn, *Poland* 20 F8
Cieza, *Spain* 29 G3
Çifteler, *Turkey* 66 C4
Cifuentes, *Spain* 28 E2
Cihanbeyli, *Turkey* 66 C5
Cihuatlán, *Mexico* 114 D4
Cijara, Pantano de, *Spain* 31 F6
Cijulang, *Indonesia* 57 G13
Cikajang, *Indonesia* 57 G12
Cikampek, *Indonesia* 57 G12
Cilacap, *Indonesia* 57 G13
Çıldır, *Turkey* 67 B10
Çıldır Gölü, *Turkey* 67 B10
Cili, *China* 53 C8
Cilicia, *Turkey* 66 D5
Cill Chainnigh = Kilkenny,
  Ireland 15 D4
Cilo Dağı, *Turkey* 67 D10
Cima, *U.S.A.* 113 K11
Cimahi, *Indonesia* 57 G12
Cimarron, *Kans., U.S.A.* . 109 G4
Cimarron, *N. Mex., U.S.A.* 109 G2
Cimarron →, *U.S.A.* 109 G6
Cimişlia, *Moldova* 41 J5
Cimone, Mte., *Italy* 32 D7
Cîmpina, *Romania* 38 D8
Cîmpulung, *Argeş,*
  Romania 38 D8
Cîmpulung, *Suceava,*
  Romania 38 B8
Çınar, *Turkey* 67 D9
Cinca →, *Spain* 28 D5
Cincinnati, *U.S.A.* 104 F3
Cîndeşti, *Romania* 38 D9
Çine, *Turkey* 66 D3
Ciney, *Belgium* 17 H6
Cíngoli, *Italy* 33 E10
Cinigiano, *Italy* 33 F8
Cinto, Mte., *France* 27 F12
Ciorani, *Romania* 38 E9
Ćiovo, *Croatia* 33 E13
Cipó, *Brazil* 122 D4
Circeo, Mte., *Italy* 34 A6
Çırçır, *Turkey* 66 C7
Circle, *Alaska, U.S.A.* ... 96 B5
Circle, *Mont., U.S.A.* 108 B2
Circleville, *Ohio, U.S.A.* . 104 F4
Circleville, *Utah, U.S.A.* . 111 G7
Cirebon, *Indonesia* 57 G13
Cirencester, *U.K.* 13 F6
Cirey-sur-Vezouze, *France* 25 D13
Ciriè, *Italy* 32 C4
Cirium, *Cyprus* 37 E11
Cirò, *Italy* 35 C10
Ciron →, *France* 26 D3
Cisco, *U.S.A.* 109 J5
Cislău, *Romania* 38 D9
Cisneros, *Colombia* 120 B2
Cisterna di Latina, *Italy* .. 34 A5
Cisternino, *Italy* 35 B10
Citaré →, *Brazil* 121 C7
Citeli-Ckaro = Tsiteli-
  Tskaro, *Georgia* 43 K8
Citlaltépetl, *Mexico* 115 D5
Citrus Heights, *U.S.A.* ... 112 G5
Citrusdal, *S. Africa* 84 E2
Città della Pieve, *Italy* ... 33 F9
Città di Castello, *Italy* ... 33 E9
Città Sant' Angelo, *Italy* . 33 F11
Cittadella, *Italy* 33 C8
Cittaducale, *Italy* 33 F9

Cittanova, *Italy* 35 D9
Ciucaş, *Romania* 38 D8
Ciudad Altamirano, *Mexico* 114 D4
Ciudad Bolívar, *Venezuela* 121 B5
Ciudad Camargo, *Mexico* . 114 B3
Ciudad Chetumal, *Mexico* 115 D7
Ciudad de Valles, *Mexico* . 115 C5
Ciudad del Carmen, *Mexico* 115 D6
Ciudad del Este, *Paraguay* 127 B5
Ciudad Delicias = Delicias,
  Mexico 114 B3
Ciudad Guayana,
  Venezuela 121 B5
Ciudad Guerrero, *Mexico* . 114 B3
Ciudad Guzmán, *Mexico* . 114 D4
Ciudad Juárez, *Mexico* ... 114 A3
Ciudad Madero, *Mexico* .. 115 C5
Ciudad Mante, *Mexico* ... 115 C5
Ciudad Obregón, *Mexico* . 114 B3
Ciudad Ojeda, *Venezuela* . 120 A3
Ciudad Real, *Spain* 31 G7
Ciudad Real □, *Spain* 31 G7
Ciudad Rodrigo, *Spain* ... 30 E4
Ciudad Trujillo = Santo
  Domingo, *Dom. Rep.* .. 117 C6
Ciudad Victoria, *Mexico* .. 115 C5
Ciudadela, *Spain* 36 B10
Ciulniţa, *Romania* 38 E10
Civa Burnu, *Turkey* 66 B7
Cividale del Friuli, *Italy* .. 33 B10
Cívita Castellana, *Italy* ... 33 F9
Civitanova Marche, *Italy* . 33 E10
Civitavécchia, *Italy* 33 F8
Civitella del Tronto, *Italy* . 33 F10
Civray, *France* 26 B4
Çivril, *Turkey* 66 C3
Cixerri →, *Italy* 34 C1
Cizre, *Turkey* 67 D10
Clacton-on-Sea, *U.K.* 13 F9
Clain →, *France* 24 F7
Claire, L., *Canada* 100 B6
Clairemont, *U.S.A.* 109 J4
Clairton, *U.S.A.* 106 F5
Clairvaux-les-Lacs, *France* 27 B9
Clallam Bay, *U.S.A.* 112 B2
Clamecy, *France* 25 E10
Clanton, *U.S.A.* 105 J2
Clanwilliam, *S. Africa* ... 84 E2
Clara, *Ireland* 15 C4
Clara →, *Australia* 90 B3
Clare, *Australia* 91 E2
Clare, *U.S.A.* 104 D3
Clare □, *Ireland* 15 D3
Clare →, *Ireland* 15 C2
Clare I., *Ireland* 15 C1
Claremont, *Calif., U.S.A.* . 113 L9
Claremont, *N.H., U.S.A.* . 107 C12
Claremont Pt., *Australia* . 90 A3
Claremore, *U.S.A.* 109 G7
Claremorris, *Ireland* 15 C3
Clarence →, *Australia* ... 91 D5
Clarence →, *N.Z.* 87 K4
Clarence, I., *Chile* 128 D2
Clarence I., *Antarctica* ... 5 C18
Clarence Str., *Australia* .. 88 B5
Clarence Str., *U.S.A.* 100 B2
Clarence Town, *Bahamas* . 117 B5
Clarendon, *Ark., U.S.A.* .. 109 H9
Clarendon, *Tex., U.S.A.* .. 109 H4
Clarenville, *Canada* 99 C9
Claresholm, *Canada* 100 C6
Clarie Coast, *Antarctica* .. 5 C9
Clarinda, *U.S.A.* 108 E7
Clarion, *Iowa, U.S.A.* 108 D8
Clarion, *Pa., U.S.A.* 106 E5
Clarion →, *U.S.A.* 106 E5
Clark, *U.S.A.* 108 C6
Clark, Pt., *Canada* 106 B3
Clark Fork, *U.S.A.* 110 B5
Clark Fork →, *U.S.A.* 110 B5
Clark Hill Res., *U.S.A.* ... 105 J4
Clarkdale, *U.S.A.* 111 J7
Clarke City, *Canada* 99 B6
Clarke I., *Australia* 90 G4
Clarke L., *Canada* 101 C7
Clarke Ra., *Australia* 90 C4
Clark's Fork →, *U.S.A.* ... 110 D9
Clark's Harbour, *Canada* . 99 D6
Clarks Summit, *U.S.A.* ... 107 E9
Clarksburg, *U.S.A.* 104 F5
Clarksdale, *U.S.A.* 109 H9
Clarkston, *U.S.A.* 110 C5
Clarksville, *Ark., U.S.A.* .. 109 H8
Clarksville, *Tenn., U.S.A.* . 105 G2
Clarksville, *Tex., U.S.A.* .. 109 J7
Claro →, *Brazil* 123 E1
Clatskanie, *U.S.A.* 112 D3
Claude, *U.S.A.* 109 H4
Claveria, *Phil.* 55 B4
Clay, *U.S.A.* 112 G5
Clay Center, *U.S.A.* 108 F6
Claypool, *U.S.A.* 111 K8
Claysville, *U.S.A.* 106 F4
Clayton, *Idaho, U.S.A.* ... 110 D6
Clayton, *N. Mex., U.S.A.* . 109 G3
Cle Elum, *U.S.A.* 110 C3
Clear, C., *Ireland* 15 E2
Clear I., *Ireland* 15 E2
Clear L., *U.S.A.* 112 F4
Clear Lake, *S. Dak.,*
  U.S.A. 108 C6
Clear Lake, *Wash., U.S.A.* 110 B2
Clear Lake Reservoir,
  U.S.A. 110 F3
Clearfield, *Pa., U.S.A.* ... 104 E6
Clearfield, *Utah, U.S.A.* .. 110 F7

Clearlake Highlands,
  U.S.A. 112 G4
Clearmont, *U.S.A.* 110 D10
Clearwater, *Canada* 100 C4
Clearwater, *U.S.A.* 105 M4
Clearwater →, *Alta.,*
  Canada 100 C6
Clearwater →, *Alta.,*
  Canada 101 B6
Clearwater Cr. →, *Canada* 100 A3
Clearwater Mts., *U.S.A.* .. 110 C6
Clearwater Prov. Park,
  Canada 101 C8
Cleburne, *U.S.A.* 109 J6
Cleethorpes, *U.K.* 12 D7
Cleeve Hill, *U.K.* 13 F6
Clelles, *France* 27 D9
Clemency, *Lux.* 17 J7
Clerke Reef, *Australia* 88 C2
Clermont, *Australia* 90 C4
Clermont, *France* 25 C9
Clermont-en-Argonne,
  France 25 C12
Clermont-Ferrand, *France* 26 C7
Clermont-l'Hérault, *France* 26 E7
Clerval, *France* 25 E13
Clervaux, *Lux.* 17 H8
Cléry-St.-André, *France* ... 25 E8
Cles, *Italy* 32 B8
Cleveland, *Australia* 91 D5
Cleveland, *Miss., U.S.A.* .. 109 J9
Cleveland, *Ohio, U.S.A.* .. 106 E3
Cleveland, *Okla., U.S.A.* .. 109 G6
Cleveland, *Tenn., U.S.A.* . 105 H3
Cleveland, *Tex., U.S.A.* ... 109 K7
Cleveland □, *U.K.* 12 C9
Cleveland, C., *Australia* .. 90 B4
Cleveland Heights, *U.S.A.* 106 E3
Clevelândia, *Brazil* 127 B5
Clevelândia do Norte,
  Brazil 121 C7
Clew B., *Ireland* 15 C2
Clewiston, *U.S.A.* 105 M5
Clifden, *Ireland* 15 C1
Clifden, *N.Z.* 87 M1
Cliffdell, *U.S.A.* 112 D5
Clifton, *Australia* 91 D5
Clifton, *Ariz., U.S.A.* 111 K9
Clifton, *Tex., U.S.A.* 109 K6
Clifton Beach, *Australia* .. 90 B4
Clifton Forge, *U.S.A.* 104 G6
Clifton Hills, *Australia* ... 91 D2
Climax, *Canada* 101 D7
Clinch →, *U.S.A.* 105 H3
Clingmans Dome, *U.S.A.* . 105 H4
Clint, *U.S.A.* 111 L10
Clinton, *B.C., Canada* 100 C4
Clinton, *Ont., Canada* ... 98 D3
Clinton, *N.Z.* 87 M2
Clinton, *Ark., U.S.A.* 109 H8
Clinton, *Ill., U.S.A.* 108 E10
Clinton, *Ind., U.S.A.* 104 F2
Clinton, *Iowa, U.S.A.* 108 E9
Clinton, *Mass., U.S.A.* ... 107 D13
Clinton, *Mo., U.S.A.* 108 F8
Clinton, *N.C., U.S.A.* 105 H6
Clinton, *Okla., U.S.A.* ... 109 H5
Clinton, *S.C., U.S.A.* 105 H5
Clinton, *Tenn., U.S.A.* ... 105 G3
Clinton, *Wash., U.S.A.* ... 112 C4
Clinton C., *Australia* 90 C5
Clinton Colden L., *Canada* 96 B9
Clintonville, *U.S.A.* 108 C10
Clipperton, I., *Pac. Oc.* .. 93 F17
Clisson, *France* 24 E5
Cliza, *Bolivia* 125 D4
Cloates, Pt., *Australia* 88 D1
Clocolan, *S. Africa* 85 D4
Clodomira, *Argentina* 126 B3
Clonakilty, *Ireland* 15 E3
Clonakilty B., *Ireland* 15 E3
Cloncurry, *Australia* 90 C3
Cloncurry →, *Australia* ... 90 B3
Clones, *Ireland* 15 B4
Clonmel, *Ireland* 15 D4
Cloppenburg, *Germany* ... 18 C4
Cloquet, *U.S.A.* 108 B8
Clorinda, *Argentina* 126 B4
Cloud Peak, *U.S.A.* 110 D10
Cloudcroft, *U.S.A.* 111 K11
Cloverdale, *U.S.A.* 112 G4
Clovis, *Calif., U.S.A.* 111 H4
Clovis, *N. Mex., U.S.A.* .. 109 H3
Cloyes-sur-le-Loir, *France* 24 E8
Cluj-Napoca, *Romania* ... 38 C6
Clunes, *Australia* 91 F3
Cluny, *France* 27 B8
Cluses, *France* 27 B10
Clusone, *Italy* 32 C6
Clutha →, *N.Z.* 87 M2
Clwyd □, *U.K.* 12 D4
Clwyd →, *U.K.* 12 D4
Clyde, *N.Z.* 87 L2
Clyde, *U.S.A.* 106 C8
Clyde →, *U.K.* 14 F4
Clyde, Firth of, *U.K.* 14 F4
Clyde River, *Canada* 97 A13
Clydebank, *U.K.* 14 F4
Clymer, *U.S.A.* 106 D5
Cõa →, *Portugal* 30 D3
Coachella, *U.S.A.* 113 M10
Coachella Canal, *U.S.A.* .. 113 N12
Coahoma, *U.S.A.* 109 J4
Coahuayana →, *Mexico* .. 114 D4
Coahuayutla, *Mexico* 114 D4
Coahuila □, *Mexico* 114 B4

Coal →, *Canada* 100 B3
Coalane, *Mozam.* 83 F4
Coalcomán, *Mexico* 114 D4
Coaldale, *Canada* 100 D6
Coalgate, *U.S.A.* 109 H6
Coalinga, *U.S.A.* 111 H3
Coalville, *U.K.* 12 E6
Coalville, *U.S.A.* 110 F8
Coaraci, *Brazil* 123 D4
Coari, *Brazil* 121 D5
Coari →, *Brazil* 121 D5
Coari, L. de, *Brazil* 121 D5
Coast □, *Kenya* 82 C4
Coast Mts., *Canada* 100 C3
Coast Ranges, *U.S.A.* 112 G4
Coatbridge, *U.K.* 14 F4
Coatepec, *Mexico* 115 D5
Coatepeque, *Guatemala* .. 116 D1
Coatesville, *U.S.A.* 104 F8
Coaticook, *Canada* 99 C5
Coats I., *Canada* 97 B11
Coats Land, *Antarctica* ... 5 D1
Coatzacoalcos, *Mexico* ... 115 D6
Cobalt, *Canada* 98 C4
Cobán, *Guatemala* 116 C1
Cobar, *Australia* 91 E4
Cóbh, *Ireland* 15 E3
Cobham, *Australia* 91 E3
Cobija, *Bolivia* 124 C4
Cobleskill, *U.S.A.* 107 D10
Coboconk, *Canada* 106 B6
Cobourg, *Canada* 98 D4
Cobourg Pen., *Australia* .. 88 B5
Cobram, *Australia* 91 F4
Cobre, *U.S.A.* 110 F6
Cóbué, *Mozam.* 83 E3
Coburg, *Germany* 19 E6
Coca, *Spain* 30 D6
Coca →, *Ecuador* 120 D2
Cocachacra, *Peru* 124 D3
Cocal, *Brazil* 122 B3
Cocanada = Kakinada,
  India 61 L13
Cocentaina, *Spain* 29 G4
Cochabamba, *Bolivia* 125 D4
Coche, I., *Venezuela* 121 A5
Cochem, *Germany* 19 E3
Cochemane, *Mozam.* 83 F3
Cochin, *India* 60 Q10
Cochin China = Nam-
  Phan, *Vietnam* 59 G6
Cochise, *U.S.A.* 111 K9
Cochran, *U.S.A.* 105 J4
Cochrane, *Alta., Canada* . 100 C6
Cochrane, *Ont., Canada* .. 98 C3
Cochrane →, *Canada* 101 B8
Cochrane, L., *Chile* 128 C2
Cockburn, *Australia* 91 E3
Cockburn, Canal, *Chile* .. 128 D2
Cockburn I., *Canada* 98 C3
Cockburn Ra., *Australia* .. 88 C4
Cocklebiddy Motel,
  Australia 89 F4
Coco →, *Cent. Amer.* 116 D3
Coco, Pta., *Colombia* 120 C2
Cocoa, *U.S.A.* 105 L5
Cocobeach, *Gabon* 80 D1
Côcos, *Brazil* 123 D3
Côcos →, *Brazil* 123 D3
Cocos, I. del, *Pac. Oc.* ... 93 G19
Cocos, Is., *Ind. Oc.* 92 J1
Cod, C., *U.S.A.* 103 B13
Codajás, *Brazil* 121 D5
Codera, C., *Venezuela* ... 120 A4
Coderre, *Canada* 101 C7
Codigoro, *Italy* 33 D9
Codó, *Brazil* 122 B3
Codogno, *Italy* 32 C6
Codpa, *Chile* 124 D4
Codroipo, *Italy* 33 C10
Cody, *U.S.A.* 110 D9
Coe Hill, *Canada* 98 D4
Coelemu, *Chile* 126 D1
Coelho Neto, *Brazil* 122 B3
Coen, *Australia* 90 A3
Coeroeni →, *Surinam* 121 C6
Coesfeld, *Germany* 18 D3
Cœur d'Alene, *U.S.A.* 110 C5
Cœur d'Alene L., *U.S.A.* . 110 C5
Coevorden, *Neths.* 16 C9
Cofete, *Canary Is.* 36 F5
Coffeyville, *U.S.A.* 109 G7
Coffin B., *Australia* 91 E2
Coffin Bay Peninsula,
  Australia 91 E2
Coffs Harbour, *Australia* . 91 E5
Cofrentes, *Spain* 29 F3
Cogealac, *Romania* 38 E11
Coghinas →, *Italy* 34 B1
Coghinas, L. di, *Italy* 34 B2
Cognac, *France* 26 C3
Cogne, *Italy* 32 C4
Cogolludo, *Spain* 28 E1
Cohagen, *U.S.A.* 110 C10
Cohoes, *U.S.A.* 107 D11
Cohuna, *Australia* 91 F3
Coiba, I., *Panama* 116 E3
Coig →, *Argentina* 128 D3
Coihaique, *Chile* 128 C2
Coimbatore, *India* 60 P10
Coimbra, *Brazil* 125 D6
Coimbra, *Portugal* 30 E2
Coimbra □, *Portugal* 30 E2
Coín, *Spain* 31 J6
Coipasa, L. de, *Bolivia* ... 124 D4
Coipasa, Salar de, *Bolivia* 124 D4
Cojata, *Peru* 124 D4

Cojedes □, *Venezuela* 120 B4
Cojedes →, *Venezuela* ... 120 B4
Cojimies, *Ecuador* 120 C1
Cojocna, *Romania* 38 C6
Cojutepequé, *El Salv.* 116 D2
Cokeville, *U.S.A.* 110 E8
Colac, *Australia* 91 F3
Colares, *Portugal* 31 G1
Colatina, *Brazil* 123 E3
Colbeck, C., *Antarctica* ... 5 D13
Colbinabbin, *Australia* ... 91 F3
Colborne, *Canada* 106 B7
Colby, *U.S.A.* 108 F4
Colchagua □, *Chile* 126 C1
Colchester, *U.K.* 13 F8
Coldstream, *U.K.* 14 F6
Coldwater, *Canada* 106 B5
Coldwater, *U.S.A.* 109 G5
Colebrook, *Australia* 90 G4
Colebrook, *U.S.A.* 107 B13
Coleman, *Canada* 100 D6
Coleman, *U.S.A.* 109 K5
Coleman →, *Australia* 90 B3
Colenso, *S. Africa* 85 D4
Coleraine, *Australia* 91 F3
Coleraine, *U.K.* 15 A5
Coleraine □, *U.K.* 15 A5
Coleridge, L., *N.Z.* 87 K3
Colesberg, *S. Africa* 84 E4
Coleville, *U.S.A.* 112 G7
Colfax, *Calif., U.S.A.* 112 F6
Colfax, *La., U.S.A.* 109 K8
Colfax, *Wash., U.S.A.* ... 110 C5
Colhué Huapi, L.,
  Argentina 128 C3
Cólico, *Italy* 32 B6
Coligny, *France* 27 B9
Coligny, *S. Africa* 85 D4
Colima, *Mexico* 114 D4
Colima □, *Mexico* 114 D4
Colima, Nevado de, *Mexico* 114 D4
Colina, *Chile* 126 C1
Colina do Norte,
  Guinea-Biss. 78 C2
Colinas, *Goiás, Brazil* ... 123 D2
Colinas, *Maranhão, Brazil* 122 C3
Coll, *U.K.* 14 E2
Collaguasi, *Chile* 126 A2
Collarada, Peña, *Spain* ... 28 C4
Collarenebri, *Australia* ... 91 D4
Collbran, *U.S.A.* 111 G10
Colle di Val d'Elsa, *Italy* .. 33 E8
Colle Salvetti, *Italy* 32 E7
Colle Sannita, *Italy* 35 A7
Collécchio, *Italy* 32 D7
Colleen Bawn, *Zimbabwe* . 83 G2
College Park, *U.S.A.* 105 J3
Collette, *Canada* 99 C6
Collie, *Australia* 89 F2
Collier B., *Australia* 88 C3
Collier Ra., *Australia* 88 D2
Colline Metallifere, *Italy* .. 32 E7
Collingwood, *Canada* 98 D3
Collingwood, *N.Z.* 87 J4
Collins, *Canada* 98 B2
Collinsville, *Australia* 90 C4
Collipulli, *Chile* 126 D1
Collo, *Algeria* 75 A6
Collonges, *France* 27 B9
Collooney, *Ireland* 15 B3
Colmar, *France* 25 D14
Colmars, *France* 27 D10
Colmenar, *Spain* 31 J6
Colmenar de Oreja, *Spain* 28 E1
Colmenar Viejo, *Spain* ... 30 E7
Colne, *U.K.* 12 D5
Colo →, *Australia* 91 E5
Cologna Véneta, *Italy* 33 C8
Cologne = Köln, *Germany* 18 E2
Colom, I., *Spain* 36 B11
Colomb-Béchar = Béchar,
  Algeria 75 B4
Colombey-les-Belles,
  France 25 D12
Colombey-les-Deux-Églises,
  France 25 D11
Colômbia, *Brazil* 123 F2
Colombia ■, *S. Amer.* ... 120 C3
Colombier, *Switz.* 22 C3
Colombo, *Sri Lanka* 60 R11
Colome, *U.S.A.* 108 D5
Colón, *Argentina* 126 C4
Colón, *Cuba* 116 B3
Colón, *Panama* 116 E4
Colón, *Peru* 124 A1
Colona, *Australia* 89 F5
Colonella, *Italy* 33 F10
Colonia, *Uruguay* 126 C4
Colonia de San Jordi, *Spain* 36 B9
Colonia Dora, *Argentina* . 126 B3
Colonial Heights, *U.S.A.* . 104 G7
Colonne, C. delle, *Italy* .. 35 C10
Colonsay, *Canada* 101 C7
Colonsay, *U.K.* 14 E2
Colorado □, *U.S.A.* 111 G10
Colorado →, *Argentina* .. 128 A4
Colorado →, *N. Amer.* ... 111 L6
Colorado →, *U.S.A.* 109 L7
Colorado City, *U.S.A.* ... 109 J4
Colorado Desert, *U.S.A.* . 102 D3
Colorado Plateau, *U.S.A.* . 111 H8
Colorado River Aqueduct,
  U.S.A. 113 L12
Colorado Springs, *U.S.A.* 108 F2
Colorno, *Italy* 32 D7
Colotlán, *Mexico* 114 C4

Colquechaca, *Bolivia* 125 D4
Colton, *Calif., U.S.A.* 113 L9
Colton, *N.Y., U.S.A.* 107 B10
Colton, *Wash., U.S.A.* 110 C5
Columbia, *La., U.S.A.* 109 J8
Columbia, *Miss., U.S.A.* . 109 K10
Columbia, *Mo., U.S.A.* ... 108 F8
Columbia, *Pa., U.S.A.* ... 107 F8
Columbia, *S.C., U.S.A.* ... 105 H5
Columbia, *Tenn., U.S.A.* . 105 H2
Columbia →, *U.S.A.* 110 C1
Columbia, C., *Canada* ... 4 A4
Columbia, District of □,
U.S.A. 104 F7
Columbia, Mt., *Canada* .. 100 C5
Columbia Basin, *U.S.A.* .. 110 C4
Columbia Falls, *U.S.A.* ... 110 B6
Columbia Heights, *U.S.A.* 108 C8
Columbiana, *U.S.A.* 106 F4
Columbretes, Is., *Spain* .. 28 F5
Columbus, *Ga., U.S.A.* ... 105 J3
Columbus, *Ind., U.S.A.* .. 104 F3
Columbus, *Kans., U.S.A.* . 109 G7
Columbus, *Miss., U.S.A.* . 105 J1
Columbus, *Mont., U.S.A.* 110 D9
Columbus, *N. Dak.,*
U.S.A. 108 A3
Columbus, *N. Mex.,*
U.S.A. 111 L10
Columbus, *Nebr., U.S.A.* . 108 E6
Columbus, *Ohio, U.S.A.* .. 104 F4
Columbus, *Tex., U.S.A.* .. 109 L6
Columbus, *Wis., U.S.A.* .. 108 D10
Colunga, *Spain* 30 B5
Colusa, *U.S.A.* 112 F4
Colville, *U.S.A.* 110 B5
Colville →, *U.S.A.* 96 A4
Colville, C., *N.Z.* 87 G5
Colwyn Bay, *U.K.* 12 D4
Coma, *Ethiopia* 77 F4
Comácchio, *Italy* 33 D9
Comalcalco, *Mexico* 115 D6
Comallo, *Argentina* 128 B2
Comanche, *Okla., U.S.A.* 109 H6
Comanche, *Tex., U.S.A.* . 109 K5
Comandante Luis
Piedrabuena, *Argentina* . 128 C3
Comăneşti, *Romania* 38 C9
Comarapa, *Bolivia* 125 D5
Comayagua, *Honduras* ... 116 D2
Combahee →, *U.S.A.* 105 J5
Combeaufontaine, *France* . 25 E12
Comber, *Canada* 106 D2
Comblain-au-Pont, *Belgium* 17 H7
Combles, *France* 25 B9
Combourg, *France* 24 D5
Combronde, *France* 26 C7
Comeragh Mts., *Ireland* . 15 D4
Comet, *Australia* 90 C4
Comilla, *Bangla.* 61 H17
Comines, *Belgium* 17 G1
Comino, *Malta* 37 C1
Comino, C., *Italy* 34 B2
Cómiso, *Italy* 35 F7
Comitán, *Mexico* 115 D6
Commentry, *France* 26 B6
Commerce, *Ga., U.S.A.* .. 105 H4
Commerce, *Tex., U.S.A.* . 109 J7
Commercy, *France* 25 D12
Commewijne □, *Surinam* . 121 B7
Committee B., *Canada* ... 97 B11
Commonwealth B.,
Antarctica 5 C10
Commoron Cr. →,
Australia 91 D5
Communism Pk. =
Kommunizma, Pik,
Tajikistan 44 F8
Como, *Italy* 32 C6
Como, L. di, *Italy* 32 B6
Comodoro Rivadavia,
Argentina 128 C3
Comorin, C., *India* 60 Q10
Comoro Is. = Comoros ■,
Ind. Oc. 71 H8
Comoros ■, *Ind. Oc.* 71 H8
Comox, *Canada* 100 D4
Compiègne, *France* 25 C9
Comporta, *Portugal* 31 G2
Compostela, *Mexico* 114 C4
Comprida, I., *Brazil* 127 A6
Compton, *U.S.A.* 113 M8
Compton Downs, *Australia* 91 E4
Comrat, *Moldova* 41 J5
Con Cuong, *Vietnam* 58 C5
Con Son, *Vietnam* 59 H6
Cona Niyeu, *Argentina* .. 128 B3
Conakry, *Guinea* 78 D2
Conara Junction, *Australia* 90 G4
Concarneau, *France* 24 E3
Conceição, *Brazil* 122 C4
Conceição, *Mozam.* 83 F4
Conceição da Barra, *Brazil* 123 E4
Conceição do Araguaia,
Brazil 122 C2
Conceição do Canindé,
Brazil 122 C3
Concepción, *Argentina* .. 126 B2
Concepción, *Bolivia* 125 D5
Concepción, *Chile* 126 D1
Concepción, *Mexico* 115 D6
Concepción, *Paraguay* ... 126 A4
Concepción, *Peru* 124 C2
Concepción □, *Chile* 126 D1
Concepción →, *Mexico* .. 114 A2
Concepción, Est. de, *Chile* 128 D2
Concepción, L., *Bolivia* .. 125 D5

Concepción, Punta, *Mexico* 114 B2
Concepción del Oro,
Mexico 114 C4
Concepción del Uruguay,
Argentina 126 C4
Conception B., *Namibia* .. 84 C1
Conception I., *Bahamas* .. 117 B4
Concession, *Zimbabwe* ... 83 F3
Conchas Dam, *U.S.A.* ... 109 H2
Conche, *Canada* 99 B8
Conches-en-Ouche, *France* 24 D7
Concho, *U.S.A.* 111 J9
Concho →, *U.S.A.* 109 K5
Conchos →, *Chihuahua,*
Mexico 114 B4
Conchos →, *Tamaulipas,*
Mexico 115 B5
Concord, *Calif., U.S.A.* .. 112 H4
Concord, *N.C., U.S.A.* .. 105 H5
Concord, *N.H., U.S.A.* .. 107 C13
Concordia, *Argentina* ... 126 C4
Concórdia, *Brazil* 120 D4
Concordia, *Mexico* 114 C3
Concordia, *U.S.A.* 108 F6
Concots, *France* 26 D5
Concrete, *U.S.A.* 110 B3
Condamine, *Australia* ... 91 D5
Condat, *France* 26 C6
Conde, *Brazil* 123 D4
Conde, *U.S.A.* 108 C5
Condé-sur-l'Escaut, *France* 25 B10
Condé-sur-Noireau, *France* 24 D6
Condeúba, *Brazil* 123 D3
Condobolin, *Australia* ... 91 E4
Condom, *France* 26 E4
Condon, *U.S.A.* 110 D3
Condove, *Italy* 32 C4
Conegliano, *Italy* 33 C9
Conejera, I., *Spain* 36 B9
Conejos, *Mexico* 114 B4
Conflans-en-Jarnisy, *France* 25 C12
Confolens, *France* 26 B4
Confuso →, *Paraguay* ... 126 B4
Congjiang, *China* 52 E7
Congleton, *U.K.* 12 D5
Congo = Zaïre →, *Africa* 80 F2
Congo, *Brazil* 122 C4
Congo (Kinshasa) =
Zaïre ■, *Africa* 80 E4
Congo ■, *Africa* 80 E3
Congo Basin, *Africa* 70 G6
Congonhas, *Brazil* 123 F3
Congress, *U.S.A.* 111 J7
Conil, *Spain* 31 J4
Coniston, *Canada* 98 C3
Conjeeveram =
Kanchipuram, *India* ... 60 N11
Conjuboy, *Australia* 90 B3
Conklin, *Canada* 101 B6
Conlea, *Australia* 91 E3
Conn, L., *Ireland* 15 B2
Connacht □, *Ireland* 15 C3
Conneaut, *U.S.A.* 106 E4
Connecticut □, *U.S.A.* .. 107 E12
Connecticut →, *U.S.A.* .. 107 E12
Connell, *U.S.A.* 110 C4
Connellsville, *U.S.A.* 106 F5
Connemara, *Ireland* 15 C2
Connemaugh →, *U.S.A.* . 106 F5
Connerré, *France* 24 D7
Connersville, *U.S.A.* 104 F3
Connors Ra., *Australia* .. 90 C4
Conoble, *Australia* 91 E3
Cononaco →, *Ecuador* .. 120 D2
Cononbridge, *U.K.* 14 D4
Conquest, *Canada* 101 C7
Conrad, *U.S.A.* 110 B8
Conran, C., *Australia* ... 91 F4
Conroe, *U.S.A.* 109 K7
Conselheiro Lafaiete,
Brazil 123 F3
Conselheiro Pena, *Brazil* . 123 E3
Consort, *Canada* 101 C6
Constance = Konstanz,
Germany 19 H5
Constance, L. = Bodensee,
Europe 23 A8
Constanţa, *Romania* 38 E11
Constantina, *Spain* 31 H5
Constantine, *Algeria* 75 A6
Constitución, *Chile* 126 D1
Constitución, *Uruguay* .. 126 C4
Consuegra, *Spain* 31 F7
Consul, *Canada* 101 D7
Contact, *U.S.A.* 110 F6
Contai, *India* 63 J12
Contamana, *Peru* 124 B3
Contarina, *Italy* 33 C9
Contas →, *Brazil* 123 D4
Contes, *France* 27 E11
Conthey, *Switz.* 22 D4
Contoocook, *U.S.A.* 107 C13
Contra Costa, *Mozam.* .. 85 D5
Contres, *France* 24 E8
Contrexéville, *France* 25 D12
Contumazá, *Peru* 124 B2
Convención, *Colombia* ... 120 B3
Conversano, *Italy* 35 B10
Conway = Conwy, *U.K.* . 12 D4
Conway → = Conwy →,
U.K. 12 D4
Conway, *Ark., U.S.A.* ... 109 H8
Conway, *N.H., U.S.A.* .. 107 C13
Conway, *S.C., U.S.A.* ... 105 J6
Conway, L., *Australia* ... 91 D2
Conwy, *U.K.* 12 D4

Conwy →, *U.K.* 12 D4
Coober Pedy, *Australia* .. 91 D1
Cooch Behar = Koch
Bihar, *India* 61 F16
Coodardy, *Australia* 89 E2
Cook, *Australia* 89 F5
Cook, *U.S.A.* 108 B8
Cook, B., *Chile* 128 E2
Cook Inlet, *U.S.A.* 96 C4
Cook Is., *Pac. Oc.* 93 J11
Cook Strait, *N.Z.* 87 J5
Cookeville, *U.S.A.* 105 G3
Cookhouse, *S. Africa* 84 E4
Cookshire, *Canada* 107 A13
Cookstown, *U.K.* 15 B5
Cookstown □, *U.K.* 15 B5
Cooksville, *Canada* 106 C5
Cooktown, *Australia* 90 B4
Coolabah, *Australia* 91 E4
Cooladdi, *Australia* 91 D4
Coolah, *Australia* 91 E4
Coolamon, *Australia* 91 E4
Coolangatta, *Australia* ... 91 D5
Coolgardie, *Australia* 89 F3
Coolibah, *Australia* 88 C5
Coolidge, *U.S.A.* 111 K8
Coolidge Dam, *U.S.A.* .. 111 K8
Cooma, *Australia* 91 F4
Coonabarabran, *Australia* . 91 E4
Coonamble, *Australia* 91 E4
Coonana, *Australia* 89 F3
Coondapoor, *India* 60 N9
Coongie, *Australia* 91 D3
Coongoola, *Australia* 91 D4
Cooninie, L., *Australia* .. 91 D2
Cooper, *U.S.A.* 109 J7
Cooper →, *U.S.A.* 105 J6
Cooper Cr. →, *Australia* 91 D2
Cooperstown, *N. Dak.,*
U.S.A. 108 B5
Cooperstown, *N.Y., U.S.A.* 107 D10
Coorabie, *Australia* 89 F5
Coorabulka, *Australia* ... 90 C3
Coorow, *Australia* 89 E2
Cooroy, *Australia* 91 D5
Coos Bay, *U.S.A.* 110 E1
Cootamundra, *Australia* .. 91 E4
Cootehill, *Ireland* 15 B4
Cooyar, *Australia* 91 D5
Cooyeana, *Australia* 90 C2
Copahue Paso, *Argentina* . 126 D1
Copainalá, *Mexico* 115 D6
Copán, *Honduras* 116 D2
Copatana, *Brazil* 120 D4
Cope, *U.S.A.* 108 F3
Cope, C., *Spain* 29 H3
Copenhagen = København,
Denmark 11 J6
Copertino, *Italy* 35 B11
Copiapó, *Chile* 126 B1
Copiapó →, *Chile* 126 B1
Copley, *Australia* 91 E2
Copp L., *Canada* 100 A6
Copparo, *Italy* 33 D8
Coppename →, *Surinam* . 121 B6
Copper Center, *U.S.A.* .. 96 B5
Copper Cliff, *Canada* 98 C3
Copper Harbor, *U.S.A.* . 104 B2
Copper Queen, *Zimbabwe* 83 F2
Copperbelt □, *Zambia* ... 83 E2
Coppermine, *Canada* 96 B8
Coppermine →, *Canada* . 96 B8
Copperopolis, *U.S.A.* 112 H6
Coquet →, *U.K.* 12 B6
Coquilhatville =
Mbandaka, *Zaïre* 80 D3
Coquille, *U.S.A.* 110 E1
Coquimbo, *Chile* 126 C1
Coquimbo □, *Chile* 126 C1
Corabia, *Romania* 38 F7
Coração de Jesus, *Brazil* . 123 E3
Coracora, *Peru* 124 D3
Coraki, *Australia* 91 D5
Coral Gables, *U.S.A.* 105 N5
Coral Harbour, *Canada* .. 97 B11
Coral Sea, *Pac. Oc.* 92 J7
Corantijn →, *Surinam* .. 121 B6
Coraopolis, *U.S.A.* 106 F4
Corato, *Italy* 35 A9
Corbeil-Essonnes, *France* . 25 D9
Corbie, *France* 25 C9
Corbières, *France* 26 F6
Corbigny, *France* 25 E10
Corbin, *U.S.A.* 104 G3
Corbion, *Belgium* 17 J6
Corbones →, *Spain* 31 H5
Corby, *U.K.* 13 E7
Corby Glen, *U.K.* 13 E7
Corcaigh = Cork, *Ireland* . 15 E3
Corcoles →, *Spain* 29 F1
Corcoran, *U.S.A.* 111 H4
Corcubión, *Spain* 30 C1
Cordele, *U.S.A.* 105 K4
Cordell, *U.S.A.* 109 H5
Cordenons, *Italy* 33 C9
Cordes, *France* 26 D5
Cordisburgo, *Brazil* 123 E3
Córdoba, *Argentina* 126 C3
Córdoba, *Mexico* 115 D5
Córdoba, *Spain* 31 H6
Córdoba □, *Argentina* ... 126 C3
Córdoba □, *Colombia* ... 120 B2
Córdoba □, *Spain* 31 G6
Córdoba, Sierra de,
Argentina 126 C3
Cordon, *Phil.* 55 C4

Cordova, *Ala., U.S.A.* ... 105 J2
Cordova, *Alaska, U.S.A.* . 96 B5
Corella, *Spain* 28 C3
Corella →, *Australia* 90 B3
Coremas, *Brazil* 122 C4
Corentyne →, *Guyana* .. 121 B6
Corfield, *Australia* 90 C3
Corfu = Kérkira, *Greece* . 37 A3
Corfu, Str of, *Greece* 37 A4
Corgo, *Spain* 30 C3
Corguinho, *Brazil* 125 D7
Cori, *Italy* 34 A5
Coria, *Spain* 30 F4
Corigliano Cálabro, *Italy* . 35 C9
Coringa Is., *Australia* 90 B4
Corinna, *Australia* 90 G4
Corinth = Kórinthos,
Greece 39 M5
Corinth, *Miss., U.S.A.* .. 105 H1
Corinth, *N.Y., U.S.A.* .. 107 C11
Corinth, G. of =
Korinthiakós Kólpos,
Greece 39 L5
Corinth Canal, *Greece* ... 39 M6
Corinto, *Brazil* 123 E3
Corinto, *Nic.* 116 D2
Cork, *Ireland* 15 E3
Cork □, *Ireland* 15 E3
Cork Harbour, *Ireland* ... 15 E3
Corlay, *France* 24 D3
Corleone, *Italy* 34 E6
Corleto Perticara, *Italy* .. 35 B9
Çorlu, *Turkey* 66 B2
Cormack L., *Canada* 100 A4
Cormòns, *Italy* 33 C10
Cormorant, *Canada* 101 C8
Cormorant L., *Canada* ... 101 C8
Corn Is. = Maíz, Is. del,
Nic. 116 D3
Cornélio Procópio, *Brazil* . 127 A5
Cornell, *U.S.A.* 108 C9
Corner Brook, *Canada* ... 99 C8
Corniglio, *Italy* 32 D7
Corning, *Ark., U.S.A.* ... 109 G9
Corning, *Calif., U.S.A.* .. 110 G2
Corning, *Iowa, U.S.A.* .. 108 E7
Corning, *N.Y., U.S.A.* .. 106 D7
Corno, Monte, *Italy* 33 F10
Cornwall, *Canada* 98 C5
Cornwall □, *U.K.* 13 G3
Corny Pt., *Australia* 91 E2
Coro, *Venezuela* 120 A4
Coroaci, *Brazil* 123 E3
Coroatá, *Brazil* 122 B3
Corocoro, *Bolivia* 124 D4
Corocoro, I., *Venezuela* .. 121 B5
Coroico, *Bolivia* 124 D4
Coromandel, *Brazil* 123 E2
Coromandel, *N.Z.* 87 G5
Coromandel Coast, *India* . 60 N12
Corona, *Australia* 91 E3
Corona, *Calif., U.S.A.* ... 113 M9
Corona, *N. Mex., U.S.A.* 111 J11
Coronado, *U.S.A.* 113 N9
Coronado, B. de,
Costa Rica 116 E3
Coronados, G. de los, *Chile* 128 B2
Coronados, Is. los, *U.S.A.* 113 N9
Coronation, *Canada* 100 C6
Coronation Gulf, *Canada* . 96 B8
Coronation I., *Antarctica* . 5 C18
Coronation I., *U.S.A.* ... 100 B2
Coronation Is., *Australia* . 88 B3
Coronda, *Argentina* 126 C3
Coronel, *Chile* 126 D1
Coronel Bogado, *Paraguay* 126 B4
Coronel Dorrego,
Argentina 126 D3
Coronel Fabriciano, *Brazil* 123 E3
Coronel Murta, *Brazil* ... 123 E3
Coronel Oviedo, *Paraguay* 126 B4
Coronel Ponce, *Brazil* ... 125 D6
Coronel Pringles, *Argentina* 126 D3
Coronel Suárez, *Argentina* 126 D3
Coronel Vidal, *Argentina* . 126 D4
Corongo, *Peru* 124 B2
Coronie □, *Surinam* 121 B6
Coropuna, Nevado, *Peru* . 124 D3
Çorovoda, *Albania* 39 J3
Corowa, *Australia* 91 F4
Corozal, *Belize* 115 D7
Corozal, *Colombia* 120 B2
Corps, *France* 27 D9
Corpus, *Argentina* 127 B4
Corpus Christi, *U.S.A.* ... 109 M6
Corpus Christi, L., *U.S.A.* 109 L6
Corque, *Bolivia* 124 D4
Corral, *Chile* 128 A2
Corral de Almaguer, *Spain* 28 F1
Corralejo, *Canary Is.* 36 F6
Corrente, *Brazil* 122 D2
Corrente →, *Brazil* 123 D3
Correntes, *Brazil* 125 D6
Correntes, C. das, *Mozam.* 85 C6
Correntina, *Brazil* 123 D3
Corrèze □, *France* 26 C5
Corrèze →, *France* 26 C5
Corrib, L., *Ireland* 15 C2
Corrientes, *Argentina* ... 126 B4
Corrientes □, *Argentina* . 126 C4
Corrientes →, *Argentina* . 126 C4
Corrientes →, *Peru* 120 D3
Corrientes, C., *Colombia* . 120 B2
Corrientes, C., *Cuba* 116 B3
Corrientes, C., *Mexico* ... 114 C3

Corrigan, *U.S.A.* 109 K7
Corrigin, *Australia* 89 F2
Corry, *U.S.A.* 106 E5
Corse, *France* 27 F13
Corse, C., *France* 27 E13
Corse-du-Sud □, *France* . 27 G13
Corsica = Corse, *France* . 27 F13
Corsicana, *U.S.A.* 109 J6
Corte, *France* 27 F13
Corte do Pinto, *Portugal* . 31 H3
Cortegana, *Spain* 31 H4
Cortez, *U.S.A.* 111 H9
Cortina d'Ampezzo, *Italy* . 33 B9
Cortland, *U.S.A.* 107 D8
Cortona, *Italy* 33 E8
Coruche, *Portugal* 31 G2
Çoruh →, *Turkey* 43 K5
Çorum, *Turkey* 66 B5
Corumbá, *Brazil* 125 D6
Corumbá →, *Brazil* 123 E2
Corumbá de Goiás, *Brazil* 123 E2
Corumbaíba, *Brazil* 123 E2
Corunna = La Coruña,
Spain 30 B2
Corvallis, *U.S.A.* 110 D2
Corvette, L. de la, *Canada* 98 B5
Corydon, *U.S.A.* 108 E8
Cosalá, *Mexico* 114 C3
Cosamaloapan, *Mexico* .. 115 D5
Cosenza, *Italy* 35 C9
Coshocton, *U.S.A.* 106 F3
Cosmo Newberry, *Australia* 89 E3
Cosne-sur-Loire, *France* .. 25 E9
Coso Junction, *U.S.A.* ... 113 J9
Coso Pk., *U.S.A.* 113 J9
Cospeito, *Spain* 30 B3
Cosquín, *Argentina* 126 C3
Cossato, *Italy* 32 C5
Cossé-le-Vivien, *France* ... 24 E6
Cosson →, *France* 24 E8
Costa Blanca, *Spain* 29 G4
Costa Brava, *Spain* 28 D8
Costa del Sol, *Spain* 31 J6
Costa Dorada, *Spain* 28 E6
Costa Mesa, *U.S.A.* 113 M9
Costa Rica ■, *Cent. Amer.* 116 D3
Costa Smeralda, *Italy* 34 A2
Costigliole d'Asti, *Italy* ... 32 D5
Costilla, *U.S.A.* 111 H11
Cosumnes →, *U.S.A.* ... 112 G5
Coswig, *Germany* 18 D8
Cotabato, *Phil.* 55 H6
Cotacajes →, *Bolivia* ... 124 D4
Cotagaita, *Bolivia* 126 A2
Cotahuasi, *Peru* 124 D3
Côte d'Azur, *France* 27 E11
Côte-d'Ivoire = Ivory
Coast ■, *Africa* 78 D3
Côte d'Or, *France* 25 E11
Côte-d'Or □, *France* 25 E11
Coteau des Prairies, *U.S.A.* 108 C6
Coteau du Missouri, *U.S.A.* 108 B4
Coteau Landing, *Canada* . 107 A10
Cotegipe, *Brazil* 123 D3
Cotentin, *France* 24 C5
Côtes-d'Armor □, *France* . 24 D4
Côtes de Meuse, *France* .. 25 C12
Côtes-du-Nord = Côtes-
d'Armor □, *France* 24 D4
Cotiella, *Spain* 28 C5
Cotillo, *Canary Is.* 36 F5
Cotina →, *Bos.-H.* 21 M8
Cotoca, *Bolivia* 125 D5
Cotonou, *Benin* 79 D5
Cotopaxi, *Ecuador* 120 D2
Cotopaxi □, *Ecuador* 120 D2
Cotronei, *Italy* 35 C9
Cotswold Hills, *U.K.* 13 F5
Cottage Grove, *U.S.A.* ... 110 E2
Cottbus, *Germany* 18 D10
Cottingham, *U.K.* 12 C5
Cottonwood, *U.S.A.* 111 J7
Cotulla, *U.S.A.* 109 L5
Coubre, Pte. de la, *France* 26 C2
Couches, *France* 25 F11
Couço, *Portugal* 31 G2
Coudersport, *U.S.A.* 106 E6
Couedic, C. du, *Australia* . 91 F2
Couëron, *France* 24 E5
Couesnon →, *France* 24 D5
Couhé, *France* 26 B4
Coulanges-sur-Yonne,
France 25 E10
Coulee City, *U.S.A.* 110 C4
Coulman I., *Antarctica* ... 5 D11
Coulommiers, *France* 25 D10
Coulon →, *France* 27 E9
Coulonge →, *Canada* ... 98 C4
Coulonges-sur-l'Autize,
France 26 B3
Coulterville, *U.S.A.* 112 H6
Council, *Alaska, U.S.A.* .. 96 B3
Council, *Idaho, U.S.A.* .. 110 D5
Council Bluffs, *U.S.A.* ... 108 E7
Council Grove, *U.S.A.* ... 108 F6
Coupeville, *U.S.A.* 112 B4
Courantyne →, *S. Amer.* 121 B6
Courcelles, *Belgium* 17 H4
Courçon, *France* 26 B3
Couronne, C., *France* 27 E9
Cours-la-Ville, *France* 27 B8
Coursan, *France* 26 E7
Courseulles-sur-Mer,
France 24 C6
Court-St.-Etienne, *Belgium* 17 G5
Courtenay, *Canada* 100 D3
Courtland, *U.S.A.* 112 G5

Courtrai

Courtrai = Kortrijk, *Belgium* 17 G2
Courtright, *Canada* 106 D2
Courville-sur-Eure, *France* 24 D8
Coushatta, *U.S.A.* 109 J8
Coutances, *France* 24 C5
Couterne, *France* 24 D6
Coutras, *France* 26 C3
Coutts, *Canada* 100 D6
Couvet, *Switz.* 22 C3
Couvin, *Belgium* 17 H4
Covarrubias, *Spain* 28 C1
Coveñas, *Colombia* 120 B2
Coventry, *U.K.* 13 E6
Coventry L., *Canada* 101 A7
Covilhã, *Portugal* 30 E3
Covington, *Ga., U.S.A.* 105 J4
Covington, *Ky., U.S.A.* 104 F3
Covington, *Okla., U.S.A.* 109 G6
Covington, *Tenn., U.S.A.* 109 H10
Cowal, L., *Australia* 91 E4
Cowan, *Canada* 101 C8
Cowan, L., *Australia* 89 F3
Cowan L., *Canada* 101 C7
Cowangie, *Australia* 91 F3
Cowansville, *Canada* 107 A12
Cowarie, *Australia* 91 D2
Cowcowing Lakes, *Australia* 89 F2
Cowdenbeath, *U.K.* 14 E5
Cowell, *Australia* 91 E2
Cowes, *U.K.* 13 G6
Cowlitz →, *U.S.A.* 112 D4
Cowra, *Australia* 91 E4
Coxilha Grande, *Brazil* 127 B5
Coxim, *Brazil* 125 D7
Coxim →, *Brazil* 125 D7
Cox's Bazar, *Bangla.* 61 J17
Cox's Cove, *Canada* 99 C8
Coyame, *Mexico* 114 B3
Coyote Wells, *U.S.A.* 113 N11
Coyuca de Benítez, *Mexico* 115 D4
Coyuca de Catalan, *Mexico* 114 D4
Cozad, *U.S.A.* 108 E5
Cozumel, *Mexico* 115 C7
Cozumel, I. de, *Mexico* 115 C7
Craboon, *Australia* 91 E4
Cracow = Kraków, *Poland* 20 E9
Cracow, *Australia* 91 D5
Cradock, *S. Africa* 84 E4
Craig, *Alaska, U.S.A.* 100 B2
Craig, *Colo., U.S.A.* 110 F10
Craigavon, *U.K.* 15 B5
Craigmore, *Zimbabwe* 83 G3
Crailsheim, *Germany* 19 F6
Craiova, *Romania* 38 E6
Cramsie, *Australia* 90 C3
Cranberry Portage, *Canada* 101 C8
Cranbrook, *Tas., Australia* 90 G4
Cranbrook, *W. Austral., Australia* 89 F2
Cranbrook, *Canada* 100 D5
Crandon, *U.S.A.* 108 C10
Crane, *Oreg., U.S.A.* 110 E4
Crane, *Tex., U.S.A.* 109 K3
Cranston, *U.S.A.* 107 E13
Craon, *France* 24 E6
Craonne, *France* 25 C10
Craponne-sur-Arzon, *France* 26 C7
Crasna, *Romania* 38 C10
Crater L., *U.S.A.* 110 E2
Crateús, *Brazil* 122 C3
Crati →, *Italy* 35 C9
Crato, *Brazil* 122 C4
Crato, *Portugal* 31 F3
Cravo Norte, *Colombia* 120 B3
Cravo Norte →, *Colombia* 120 B3
Crawford, *U.S.A.* 108 D3
Crawfordsville, *U.S.A.* 104 E2
Crawley, *U.K.* 13 F7
Crazy Mts., *U.S.A.* 110 C8
Crean L., *Canada* 101 C7
Crécy-en-Brie, *France* 25 D9
Crécy-en-Ponthieu, *France* 25 B8
Crediton, *Canada* 106 C3
Credo, *Australia* 89 F3
Cree →, *Canada* 101 B7
Cree →, *U.K.* 14 G4
Cree L., *Canada* 101 B7
Creede, *U.S.A.* 111 H10
Creel, *Mexico* 114 B3
Creighton, *U.S.A.* 108 D6
Creil, *France* 25 C9
Crema, *Italy* 32 C6
Cremona, *Italy* 32 C7
Crepori →, *Brazil* 125 B6
Crépy, *France* 25 C10
Crépy-en-Valois, *France* 25 C9
Cres, *Croatia* 33 D11
Cresbard, *U.S.A.* 108 C5
Crescent, *Okla., U.S.A.* 109 H6
Crescent, *Oreg., U.S.A.* 110 E3
Crescent City, *U.S.A.* 110 F1
Crescentino, *Italy* 32 C5
Crespino, *Italy* 33 D8
Crespo, *Argentina* 126 C3
Cressy, *Australia* 91 F3
Crest, *France* 27 D9
Cresta, Mt., *Phil.* 55 C5
Crested Butte, *U.S.A.* 111 G10
Crestline, *Calif., U.S.A.* 113 L9
Crestline, *Ohio, U.S.A.* 106 F2
Creston, *Canada* 100 D5
Creston, *Calif., U.S.A.* 112 K6
Creston, *Iowa, U.S.A.* 108 E7
Creston, *Wash., U.S.A.* 110 C4
Crestview, *Calif., U.S.A.* 112 H8
Crestview, *Fla., U.S.A.* 105 K2
Crete = Kríti, *Greece* 37 D7
Crete, *U.S.A.* 108 E6
Crete, Sea of, *Greece* 39 N8
Creus, C. de, *Spain* 28 C8
Creuse □, *France* 26 B6
Creuse →, *France* 26 B4
Creuzburg, *Germany* 18 D6
Crevalcore, *Italy* 33 D8
Crèvecœur-le-Grand, *France* 25 C9
Crevillente, *Spain* 29 G4
Crewe, *U.K.* 12 D5
Criciúma, *Brazil* 127 B6
Crieff, *U.K.* 14 E5
Crikvenica, *Croatia* 33 C11
Crimea □, *Ukraine* 41 K8
Crimean Pen. = Krymskyy Pivostriv, *Ukraine* 41 K8
Crimmitschau, *Germany* 18 E8
Cristalândia, *Brazil* 122 D2
Cristino Castro, *Brazil* 122 C3
Crişul Alb →, *Romania* 38 C4
Crişul Negru →, *Romania* 38 C4
Crişul Repede →, *Romania* 38 C3
Crivitz, *Germany* 18 B7
Crixás, *Brazil* 123 D2
Crna Gora = Montenegro □, *Yugoslavia* 21 N9
Crni Drim →, *Macedonia* 39 H3
Črnomelj, *Slovenia* 33 C12
Croagh Patrick, *Ireland* 15 C2
Croatia ■, *Europe* 33 C13
Crocker, Banjaran, *Malaysia* 56 C5
Crockett, *U.S.A.* 109 K7
Crocodile = Krokodil →, *Mozam.* 85 D5
Crocodile Is., *Australia* 90 A1
Crocq, *France* 26 C6
Croisette, C., *France* 27 E9
Croisic, Pte. du, *France* 24 E4
Croix, L. La, *Canada* 98 C1
Croker, C., *Australia* 88 B5
Croker I., *Australia* 88 B5
Cromarty, *Canada* 101 B10
Cromarty, *U.K.* 14 D4
Cromer, *U.K.* 12 E9
Cromwell, *N.Z.* 87 L2
Cronat, *France* 25 F10
Cronulla, *Australia* 91 E5
Crooked →, *Canada* 100 C4
Crooked →, *U.S.A.* 110 D3
Crooked I., *Bahamas* 117 B5
Crooked Island Passage, *Bahamas* 117 B5
Crookston, *Minn., U.S.A.* 108 B6
Crookston, *Nebr., U.S.A.* 108 D4
Crooksville, *U.S.A.* 104 F4
Crookwell, *Australia* 91 E4
Crosby, *Minn., U.S.A.* 108 B8
Crosby, *N. Dak., U.S.A.* 108 D8
Crosby, *Pa., U.S.A.* 106 E6
Crosbyton, *U.S.A.* 109 J4
Cross →, *Nigeria* 79 E6
Cross City, *U.S.A.* 105 L4
Cross Fell, *U.K.* 12 C5
Cross L., *Canada* 101 C9
Cross Plains, *U.S.A.* 109 J5
Cross River □, *Nigeria* 79 D6
Cross Sound, *U.S.A.* 96 C6
Crossett, *U.S.A.* 109 J9
Crossfield, *Canada* 100 C6
Crosshaven, *Ireland* 15 E3
Croton-on-Hudson, *U.S.A.* 107 E11
Crotone, *Italy* 35 C10
Crow →, *Canada* 100 B4
Crow Agency, *U.S.A.* 110 D10
Crow Hd., *Ireland* 15 E1
Crowell, *U.S.A.* 109 J5
Crowley, *U.S.A.* 109 K8
Crowley, L., *U.S.A.* 112 H8
Crown Point, *U.S.A.* 104 E2
Crows Landing, *U.S.A.* 112 H5
Crows Nest, *Australia* 91 D5
Crowsnest Pass, *Canada* 100 D6
Croydon, *Australia* 90 B3
Croydon, *U.K.* 13 F7
Crozet Is., *Ind. Oc.* 3 G12
Crozon, *France* 24 D2
Cruz, C., *Cuba* 116 C4
Cruz Alta, *Brazil* 127 B5
Cruz das Almas, *Brazil* 123 D4
Cruz de Malta, *Brazil* 122 C3
Cruz del Eje, *Argentina* 126 C3
Cruzeiro, *Brazil* 123 F2
Cruzeiro do Oeste, *Brazil* 127 A5
Cruzeiro do Sul, *Brazil* 124 B3
Cry L., *Canada* 100 B3
Crystal Bay, *U.S.A.* 112 F7
Crystal Brook, *Australia* 91 E2
Crystal City, *Mo., U.S.A.* 108 F9
Crystal City, *Tex., U.S.A.* 109 L5
Crystal Falls, *U.S.A.* 104 B1
Crystal River, *U.S.A.* 105 L4
Crystal Springs, *U.S.A.* 109 K9
Csongrád, *Hungary* 21 J10
Csorna, *Hungary* 21 H7
Csurgo, *Hungary* 21 J7
Cu Lao Hon, *Vietnam* 59 G7
Cua Rao, *Vietnam* 58 C5
Cuácua →, *Mozam.* 83 F4
Cuamato, *Angola* 84 B2
Cuamba, *Mozam.* 83 E4
Cuando →, *Angola* 81 H4
Cuando Cubango □, *Angola* 84 B3
Cuangar, *Angola* 84 B2
Cuanza →, *Angola* 70 G5
Cuarto →, *Argentina* 126 C3
Cuatrociénegas, *Mexico* 114 B4
Cuauhtémoc, *Mexico* 114 B3
Cuba, *Portugal* 31 G3
Cuba, *N. Mex., U.S.A.* 111 J10
Cuba, *N.Y., U.S.A.* 106 D6
Cuba ■, *W. Indies* 116 B4
Cuballing, *Australia* 89 F2
Cubango →, *Africa* 84 B3
Çubuk, *Turkey* 66 B5
Cucamonga, *U.S.A.* 113 L9
Cuchi, *Angola* 81 G3
Cuchillo-Có, *Argentina* 128 A4
Cuchivero →, *Venezuela* 120 B4
Cuchumatanes, Sierra de los, *Guatemala* 116 C1
Cucuí, *Brazil* 120 C4
Cucurpe, *Mexico* 114 A2
Cucurrupí, *Colombia* 120 C2
Cúcuta, *Colombia* 120 B3
Cudahy, *U.S.A.* 104 D2
Cudalbi, *Romania* 38 D10
Cuddalore, *India* 60 P11
Cuddapah, *India* 60 M11
Cuddapan, L., *Australia* 90 D3
Cudgewa, *Australia* 91 F4
Cudillero, *Spain* 30 B4
Cue, *Australia* 89 E2
Cuéllar, *Spain* 30 D6
Cuenca, *Ecuador* 120 D2
Cuenca, *Spain* 28 E2
Cuenca □, *Spain* 28 F2
Cuenca, Serranía de, *Spain* 28 F3
Cuerdo del Pozo, Pantano de la, *Spain* 28 D2
Cuernavaca, *Mexico* 115 D5
Cuero, *U.S.A.* 109 L6
Cuers, *France* 27 E10
Cuervo, *U.S.A.* 109 H2
Cuesmes, *Belgium* 17 H3
Cuevas, Cerro, *Bolivia* 125 E4
Cuevas del Almanzora, *Spain* 29 H3
Cuevo, *Bolivia* 125 E5
Cuiabá, *Brazil* 125 D6
Cuiabá →, *Brazil* 125 D6
Cuilco, *Guatemala* 116 C1
Cuillin Hills, *U.K.* 14 D2
Cuillin Sd., *U.K.* 14 D2
Cuima, *Angola* 81 G3
Cuiseaux, *France* 27 B9
Cuité, *Brazil* 122 C4
Cuito →, *Angola* 84 B3
Cuitzeo, L. de, *Mexico* 114 D4
Cuiuni →, *Brazil* 121 D5
Cukai, *Malaysia* 59 K4
Culan, *France* 26 B6
Culbertson, *U.S.A.* 108 A2
Culcairn, *Australia* 91 F4
Culebra, Sierra de la, *Spain* 30 D4
Culemborg, *Neths.* 16 E6
Culfa, *Azerbaijan* 67 C11
Culgoa →, *Australia* 91 D4
Culiacán, *Mexico* 114 C3
Culiacán →, *Mexico* 114 C3
Culion, *Phil.* 55 F4
Culiseu →, *Brazil* 125 C7
Cúllar de Baza, *Spain* 29 H2
Cullarin Ra., *Australia* 91 E4
Cullen, *U.K.* 14 D6
Cullen Pt., *Australia* 90 A3
Cullera, *Spain* 29 F4
Cullman, *U.S.A.* 105 H2
Culloden, *U.K.* 14 D4
Culoz, *France* 27 C9
Culpeper, *U.S.A.* 104 F7
Culuene →, *Brazil* 125 C7
Culver, Pt., *Australia* 89 F3
Culverden, *N.Z.* 87 K4
Cumaná, *Venezuela* 121 A5
Cumare, *Colombia* 120 C3
Cumari, *Brazil* 123 E2
Cumberland, *Canada* 100 D3
Cumberland, *Md., U.S.A.* 104 F6
Cumberland, *Wis., U.S.A.* 108 C8
Cumberland →, *U.S.A.* 105 G2
Cumberland I., *U.S.A.* 105 K5
Cumberland Is., *Australia* 90 C4
Cumberland L., *Canada* 101 C8
Cumberland Pen., *Canada* 97 B13
Cumberland Plateau, *U.S.A.* 105 H3
Cumberland Sd., *Canada* 97 B13
Cumborah, *Australia* 91 D4
Cumbres Mayores, *Spain* 31 G4
Cumbria □, *U.K.* 12 C5
Cumbrian Mts., *U.K.* 12 C4
Cumbum, *India* 60 M11
Cuminá →, *Brazil* 121 D6
Cuminapanema →, *Brazil* 121 D7
Cummings Mt., *U.S.A.* 113 K8
Cummins, *Australia* 91 E2
Cumnock, *Australia* 91 E4
Cumnock, *U.K.* 14 F4
Cumpas, *Mexico* 114 A3
Cumplida, Pta., *Canary Is.* 36 F2
Çumra, *Turkey* 66 D5
Cuncumén, *Chile* 126 C1
Cundeelee, *Australia* 89 F3
Cunderdin, *Australia* 89 F2
Cundinamarca □, *Colombia* 120 C3
Cunene →, *Angola* 84 B1
Cúneo, *Italy* 32 D4
Cunillera, I., *Spain* 36 C7
Cunlhat, *France* 26 C7
Cunnamulla, *Australia* 91 D4
Cuorgnè, *Italy* 32 C4
Cupar, *Canada* 101 C8
Cupar, *U.K.* 14 E5
Cupica, G. de, *Colombia* 120 B2
Ćuprija, *Serbia, Yug.* 21 M11
Curaçá, *Brazil* 122 C4
Curaçao, *Neth. Ant.* 117 D6
Curacautín, *Chile* 128 A2
Curahuara de Carangas, *Bolivia* 124 D4
Curanilahue, *Chile* 126 D1
Curaray →, *Peru* 120 D3
Curatabaca, *Venezuela* 121 B5
Cure →, *France* 25 E10
Curepto, *Chile* 126 D1
Curiapo, *Venezuela* 121 B5
Curicó, *Chile* 126 C1
Curicó □, *Chile* 126 C1
Curicuriari →, *Brazil* 120 D4
Curimatá, *Brazil* 122 D3
Curiplaya, *Colombia* 120 C3
Curitiba, *Brazil* 127 B6
Currabubula, *Australia* 91 E5
Currais Novos, *Brazil* 122 C4
Curralinho, *Brazil* 122 B2
Currant, *U.S.A.* 110 G6
Curraweena, *Australia* 91 E4
Currawilla, *Australia* 90 D3
Current →, *U.S.A.* 109 G9
Currie, *Australia* 90 F3
Currie, *U.S.A.* 110 F6
Currituck Sd., *U.S.A.* 105 G8
Curtea de Argeş, *Romania* 38 D7
Curtis, *Spain* 30 B2
Curtis, *U.S.A.* 108 E4
Curtis Group, *Australia* 90 F4
Curtis I., *Australia* 90 C5
Curuá →, *Pará, Brazil* 121 D7
Curuá →, *Pará, Brazil* 125 B7
Curuá, I., *Brazil* 122 A1
Curuaés →, *Brazil* 125 B7
Curuápanema →, *Brazil* 121 D6
Curuçá, *Brazil* 122 B2
Curuguaty, *Paraguay* 127 A4
Curup, *Indonesia* 56 E2
Curupira, Serra, *S. Amer.* 121 C5
Cururu →, *Brazil* 125 B6
Cururupu, *Brazil* 122 B3
Curuzú Cuatiá, *Argentina* 126 B4
Curvelo, *Brazil* 123 E3
Cushing, *U.S.A.* 109 H6
Cushing, Mt., *Canada* 100 B3
Cusihuiriáchic, *Mexico* 114 B3
Cusna, Mte., *Italy* 32 D7
Cusset, *France* 26 B7
Custer, *U.S.A.* 108 D3
Cut Bank, *U.S.A.* 110 B7
Cutervo, *Peru* 124 B2
Cuthbert, *U.S.A.* 105 K3
Cutler, *U.S.A.* 112 J7
Cutral-Có, *Argentina* 128 A3
Cutro, *Italy* 35 C9
Cuttaburra →, *Australia* 91 D3
Cuttack, *India* 61 J14
Cuvier, C., *Australia* 89 D1
Cuvier I., *N.Z.* 87 G5
Cuxhaven, *Germany* 18 B4
Cuyabeno, *Ecuador* 120 D2
Cuyahoga Falls, *U.S.A.* 106 E3
Cuyapo, *Phil.* 55 D4
Cuyo, *Phil.* 55 F4
Cuyo East Pass, *Phil.* 55 F4
Cuyo West Pass, *Phil.* 55 F4
Cuyuni →, *Guyana* 121 B6
Cuzco, *Bolivia* 124 E4
Cuzco, *Peru* 124 C3
Cuzco □, *Peru* 124 C3
Cwmbran, *U.K.* 13 F4
Cyangugu, *Rwanda* 82 C2
Cyclades = Kikládhes, *Greece* 39 M7
Cygnet, *Australia* 90 G4
Cynthiana, *U.S.A.* 104 F3
Cypress Hills, *Canada* 101 D7
Cyprus ■, *Asia* 66 E5
Cyrenaica, *Libya* 73 C9
Cyrene = Shaḥḥāt, *Libya* 73 B9
Czar, *Canada* 101 C6
Czarne, *Poland* 20 B6
Czech Rep. ■, *Europe* 20 F4
Czersk, *Poland* 20 B7
Częstochowa, *Poland* 20 E9

D

Da →, *Vietnam* 58 B5
Da Hinggan Ling, *China* 54 B7
Da Lat, *Vietnam* 59 G7
Da Nang, *Vietnam* 58 D7
Da Qaidam, *China* 54 C4
Da Yunhe →, *China* 51 G11
Da'an, *China* 51 B13
Daarlerveen, *Neths.* 16 D9
Dab'a, Râs el, *Egypt* 76 H6
Daba Shan, *China* 52 B7
Dabai, *Nigeria* 79 C6
Dabajuro, *Venezuela* 120 A3
Dabakala, *Ivory C.* 78 D4
Dabeiba, *Colombia* 120 B2
Dabhoi, *India* 62 H5
Dąbie, *Poland* 20 B4
Dabie Shan, *China* 53 B10
Dabo, *Indonesia* 56 E2
Dabola, *Guinea* 78 C2
Dabou, *Ivory C.* 78 D4
Daboya, *Ghana* 79 D4
Dabrowa Tarnówska, *Poland* 20 E10
Dabu, *China* 53 E11
Dabung, *Malaysia* 59 K4
Dabus →, *Ethiopia* 77 E4
Dacato →, *Ethiopia* 77 F5
Dacca = Dhaka, *Bangla.* 63 H14
Dacca = Dhaka □, *Bangla.* 63 G14
Dachau, *Germany* 19 G7
Dadanawa, *Guyana* 121 C6
Daday, *Turkey* 66 B5
Dade City, *U.S.A.* 105 L4
Dades, Oued →, *Morocco* 74 B3
Dadiya, *Nigeria* 79 D7
Dadra and Nagar Haveli □, *India* 60 J8
Dadri = Charkhi Dadri, *India* 62 E7
Dadu, *Pakistan* 62 F2
Dadu He →, *China* 52 C4
Dăeni, *Romania* 38 E11
Daet, *Phil.* 55 D5
Dafang, *China* 52 D5
Dagana, *Senegal* 78 B1
Dagash, *Sudan* 76 D3
Dagestan □, *Russia* 43 J8
Dagestanskiye Ogni, *Russia* 43 J9
Daggett, *U.S.A.* 113 L10
Daghestan Republic = Dagestan □, *Russia* 43 J8
Daghfeli, *Sudan* 76 D3
Dağlıq Qarabağ = Nagorno-Karabakh, *Azerbaijan* 67 C12
Dagö = Hiiumaa, *Estonia* 9 G20
Dagu, *China* 51 E9
Daguan, *China* 52 D4
Dagupan, *Phil.* 55 C4
Dahab, *Egypt* 76 B3
Dahlak Kebir, *Eritrea* 68 D3
Dahlenburg, *Germany* 18 B6
Dahlonega, *U.S.A.* 105 H4
Dahme, *Germany* 18 D9
Dahod, *India* 62 H6
Dahomey = Benin ■, *Africa* 79 D5
Dahong Shan, *China* 53 B9
Dahra, *Senegal* 78 B1
Dahra, Massif de, *Algeria* 75 A5
Dai Hao, *Vietnam* 58 C6
Dai-Sen, *Japan* 49 G6
Dai Shan, *China* 53 B14
Dai Xian, *China* 50 E7
Daicheng, *China* 50 E9
Daimiel, *Spain* 29 F1
Daingean, *Ireland* 15 C4
Dainkog, *China* 52 A1
Daintree, *Australia* 90 B4
Daiō-Misaki, *Japan* 49 G8
Dairût, *Egypt* 76 B3
Daisetsu-Zan, *Japan* 48 C11
Dajarra, *Australia* 90 C2
Dajia, *Taiwan* 53 E13
Dajin Chuan →, *China* 52 B3
Dak Dam, *Cambodia* 58 F6
Dak Nhe, *Vietnam* 58 E6
Dak Pek, *Vietnam* 58 E6
Dak Song, *Vietnam* 59 F6
Dak Sui, *Vietnam* 58 E6
Dakar, *Senegal* 78 C1
Dakhla, *W. Sahara* 74 D1
Dakhla, El Wâhât el-, *Egypt* 76 B2
Dakingari, *Nigeria* 79 C5
Dakor, *India* 62 H5
Dakoro, *Niger* 79 C6
Dakota City, *U.S.A.* 108 D6
Đakovica, *Serbia, Yug.* 21 N10
Đakovo, *Croatia* 21 K8
Dalaba, *Guinea* 78 C2
Dalachi, *China* 50 F3
Dalai Nur, *China* 50 C9
Dālakī, *Iran* 65 D6
Dalälven, *Sweden* 9 F17
Dalaman, *Turkey* 66 D3
Dalaman →, *Turkey* 66 D3
Dalandzadgad, *Mongolia* 50 C3
Dalarna, *Sweden* 9 F16
Dālbandīn, *Pakistan* 60 E4
Dalbeattie, *U.K.* 14 G5
Dalbosjön, *Sweden* 11 F6
Dalby, *Australia* 91 D5
Dalby, *Sweden* 11 J7
Dalen, *Neths.* 16 C9
Dalen, *Norway* 10 E2
Dalfsen, *Neths.* 16 C8
Dalga, *Egypt* 76 B3
Dalgān, *Iran* 65 E8
Dalhart, *U.S.A.* 109 G3
Dalhousie, *Canada* 99 C6
Dalhousie, *India* 62 C6
Dali, *Shaanxi, China* 50 G5
Dali, *Yunnan, China* 52 E3
Dalian, *China* 51 E11
Daliang Shan, *China* 52 D4
Dalias, *Spain* 29 J2
Daling He →, *China* 51 D11
Dāliyat el Karmel, *Israel* 69 C4
Dalkeith, *U.K.* 14 F5
Dall I., *U.S.A.* 100 C2
Dallarnil, *Australia* 91 D5

Dergaon

Dallas, *Oreg., U.S.A.* 110 D2
Dallas, *Tex., U.S.A.* 109 J6
Dallol, *Ethiopia* 77 E5
Dalmacija, *Croatia* 21 M7
Dalmatia = Dalmacija, *Croatia* 21 M7
Dalmellington, *U.K.* 14 F4
Dalnegorsk, *Russia* 45 E14
Dalnerechensk, *Russia* 45 E14
Daloa, *Ivory C.* 78 D3
Dalou Shan, *China* 52 C6
Dalsjöfors, *Sweden* 11 G7
Dalskog, *Sweden* 11 F6
Dalsland, *Sweden* 9 G14
Daltenganj, *India* 63 G11
Dalton, *Canada* 98 C3
Dalton, *Ga., U.S.A.* 105 H3
Dalton, *Mass., U.S.A.* 107 D11
Dalton, *Nebr., U.S.A.* 108 E3
Dalton Iceberg Tongue, *Antarctica* 5 C9
Dalupiri I., *Phil.* 55 B4
Dalvík, *Iceland* 8 D4
Daly →, *Australia* 88 B5
Daly City, *U.S.A.* 112 H4
Daly L., *Canada* 101 B7
Daly Waters, *Australia* 90 B1
Dam Doi, *Vietnam* 59 H5
Dam Ha, *Vietnam* 58 B6
Daman, *India* 60 J8
Dāmaneh, *Iran* 65 C6
Damanhûr, *Egypt* 76 H7
Damanzhuang, *China* 50 E9
Damar, *Indonesia* 57 F7
Damaraland, *Namibia* 84 C2
Damascus = Dimashq, *Syria* 69 B5
Damaturu, *Nigeria* 79 C7
Damāvand, *Iran* 65 C7
Damāvand, Qolleh-ye, *Iran* 65 C7
Damba, *Angola* 80 F3
Dame Marie, *Haiti* 117 C5
Dāmghān, *Iran* 65 B7
Dămienesti, *Romania* 38 C10
Damietta = Dumyât, *Egypt* 76 H7
Daming, *China* 50 F8
Damīr Qābū, *Syria* 64 B4
Dammam = Ad Dammām, *Si. Arabia* 65 E6
Dammarie, *France* 24 D8
Dammartin-en-Goële, *France* 25 C9
Dammastock, *Switz.* 23 C6
Damme, *Germany* 18 C4
Damodar →, *India* 63 H12
Damoh, *India* 63 H8
Damous, *Algeria* 75 A5
Dampier, *Australia* 88 D2
Dampier, Selat, *Indonesia* 57 E8
Dampier Arch., *Australia* 88 D2
Damrei, Chuor Phnum, *Cambodia* 59 G4
Damville, *France* 24 D8
Damvillers, *France* 25 C12
Dan-Gulbi, *Nigeria* 79 C6
Dana, *Indonesia* 57 F6
Dana, L., *Canada* 98 B4
Dana, Mt., *U.S.A.* 112 H7
Danakil Depression, *Ethiopia* 77 E5
Danao, *Phil.* 55 F6
Danbury, *U.S.A.* 107 E11
Danby L., *U.S.A.* 111 J6
Dand, *Afghan.* 62 D1
Dandaragan, *Australia* 89 F2
Dandeldhura, *Nepal* 63 E9
Dandeli, *India* 60 M9
Dandenong, *Australia* 91 F4
Dandong, *China* 51 D13
Danfeng, *China* 50 H6
Danforth, *U.S.A.* 99 C6
Dangan Liedao, *China* 53 F10
Danger Is. = Pukapuka, *Cook Is.* 93 J11
Danger Pt., *S. Africa* 84 E2
Dangla, *Ethiopia* 77 E4
Dangora, *Nigeria* 79 C6
Dangrek, Phnom, *Thailand* 58 E5
Dangriga, *Belize* 115 D7
Dangshan, *China* 50 G9
Dangtu, *China* 53 B12
Dangyang, *China* 53 B8
Daniel, *U.S.A.* 110 E8
Daniel's Harbour, *Canada* 99 B8
Danielskuil, *S. Africa* 84 D3
Danielson, *U.S.A.* 107 E13
Danilov, *Russia* 42 A5
Danilovka, *Russia* 42 E7
Daning, *China* 50 F6
Danissa, *Kenya* 82 B5
Danja, *Nigeria* 79 C6
Dankalwa, *Nigeria* 79 C7
Dankama, *Nigeria* 79 C6
Dankhar Gompa, *India* 60 C11
Dankov, *Russia* 42 D4
Danleng, *China* 52 B4
Danlí, *Honduras* 116 D2
Dannemora, *U.S.A.* 107 B11
Dannenberg, *Germany* 18 B7
Dannevirke, *N.Z.* 87 J6
Dannhauser, *S. Africa* 85 D5
Danshui, *Taiwan* 53 E13
Dansville, *U.S.A.* 106 D7
Dantan, *India* 63 J12
Dante, *Somali Rep.* 68 E5
Danube = Dunărea →, *Europe* 41 K5
Danvers, *U.S.A.* 107 D14
Danville, *Ill., U.S.A.* 104 E2
Danville, *Ky., U.S.A.* 104 G3
Danville, *Va., U.S.A.* 105 G6
Danyang, *China* 53 B12
Danzhai, *China* 52 D6
Danzig = Gdańsk, *Poland* 20 A8
Dao, *Phil.* 57 B6
Dão →, *Portugal* 30 E2
Dao Xian, *China* 53 E8
Daocheng, *China* 52 C3
Daora, *W. Sahara* 74 C2
Daoud = Aïn Beïda, *Algeria* 75 A6
Daoulas, *France* 24 D2
Dapitan, *Phil.* 55 G5
Dapong, *Togo* 79 C5
Daqing Shan, *China* 50 D6
Daqu Shan, *China* 53 B14
Dar el Beida = Casablanca, *Morocco* 74 B3
Dar es Salaam, *Tanzania* 82 D4
Dar Mazār, *Iran* 65 D8
Dar'ā, *Syria* 69 C5
Dar'ā □, *Syria* 69 C5
Dārāb, *Iran* 65 D7
Daraj, *Libya* 75 B7
Dārān, *Iran* 65 C6
Daravica, *Serbia, Yug.* 21 N10
Daraw, *Egypt* 76 C3
Dārayyā, *Syria* 69 B5
Darazo, *Nigeria* 79 C7
Darband, *Pakistan* 62 B5
Darband, Kūh-e, *Iran* 65 D8
Darbhanga, *India* 63 F11
Darby, *U.S.A.* 110 C6
Dardanelle, *Ark., U.S.A.* 109 H8
Dardanelle, *Calif., U.S.A.* 112 G7
Dardanelles = Çanakkale Boğazı, *Turkey* 66 B2
Darende, *Turkey* 66 C7
Dārestān, *Iran* 65 D8
Darfo, *Italy* 32 C7
Dârfûr, *Sudan* 73 F9
Dargai, *Pakistan* 62 B4
Dargan Ata, *Uzbekistan* 44 E7
Dargaville, *N.Z.* 87 F4
Darhan Muminggan Lianheqi, *China* 50 D6
Dari, *Sudan* 77 F3
Darıca, *Turkey* 66 B3
Darién, G. del, *Colombia* 120 B2
Darién, Serranía del, *Colombia* 120 B2
Dariganga, *Mongolia* 50 B7
Darinskoye, *Kazakhstan* 42 E10
Darjeeling = Darjiling, *India* 63 F13
Darjiling, *India* 63 F13
Dark Cove, *Canada* 99 C9
Darkan, *Australia* 89 F2
Darkhazīneh, *Iran* 65 D6
Darkot Pass, *Pakistan* 63 A5
Darling →, *Australia* 91 E3
Darling Downs, *Australia* 91 D5
Darling Ra., *Australia* 89 F2
Darlington, *U.K.* 12 C6
Darlington, *S.C., U.S.A.* 105 H6
Darlington, *Wis., U.S.A.* 108 D9
Darlington, L., *S. Africa* 84 E4
Darlot, L., *Australia* 89 E3
Darłowo, *Poland* 20 A6
Darmstadt, *Germany* 19 F4
Darnah, *Libya* 73 B9
Darnall, *S. Africa* 85 D5
Darnétal, *France* 24 C8
Darney, *France* 25 D13
Darnley, C., *Antarctica* 5 C6
Darnley B., *Canada* 96 B7
Daroca, *Spain* 28 D3
Darr, *Australia* 90 C3
Darr →, *Australia* 90 C3
Darrington, *U.S.A.* 110 B3
Darsser Ort, *Germany* 18 A8
Dart →, *U.K.* 13 G4
Dart, C., *Antarctica* 5 D14
Dartmoor, *U.K.* 13 G4
Dartmouth, *Australia* 90 C3
Dartmouth, *Canada* 99 D7
Dartmouth, *U.K.* 13 G4
Dartmouth, L., *Australia* 91 D4
Dartuch, C., *Spain* 36 B10
Darvaza, *Turkmenistan* 44 E6
Darvel, Teluk, *Malaysia* 57 D5
Darwha, *India* 60 J10
Darwin, *Australia* 88 B5
Darwin, *U.S.A.* 113 J9
Darwin, Mt., *Chile* 128 D3
Darwin River, *Australia* 88 B5
Daryoi Amu = Amudarya →, *Uzbekistan* 44 E6
Dās, *U.A.E.* 65 E7
Dashetai, *China* 50 D5
Dashhowuz, *Turkmenistan* 44 E6
Dashkesan = Daşkäsän, *Azerbaijan* 43 K7
Dasht, *Iran* 65 B8
Dasht →, *Pakistan* 60 G2
Dasht-e Mārgow, *Afghan.* 60 D3
Dasht-i-Nawar, *Afghan.* 62 C3
Daska, *Pakistan* 62 C6
Daşkäsän, *Azerbaijan* 43 K7
Dassa-Zoume, *Benin* 79 D5
Datça, *Turkey* 66 D2
Datia, *India* 63 G8
Datian, *China* 53 E11
Datong, *Anhui, China* 53 B11
Datong, *Shanxi, China* 50 D7
Datu, Tanjung, *Indonesia* 56 D3
Datu Piang, *Phil.* 55 H6
Daugava →, *Latvia* 9 H21
Daugavpils, *Latvia* 9 J22
Daule, *Ecuador* 120 D2
Daule →, *Ecuador* 120 D2
Daulpur, *India* 62 F7
Daun, *Germany* 19 E2
Dauphin, *Canada* 101 C8
Dauphin I., *U.S.A.* 105 K1
Dauphin L., *Canada* 101 C9
Dauphiné, *France* 27 C9
Daura, *Borno, Nigeria* 79 C7
Daura, *Kaduna, Nigeria* 79 C6
Dausa, *India* 62 F7
Däväçi, *Azerbaijan* 43 K9
Davangere, *India* 60 M9
Davao, *Phil.* 55 H6
Davao, G. of, *Phil.* 55 H6
Dāvar Panāh, *Iran* 65 E9
Davenport, *Calif., U.S.A.* 112 H4
Davenport, *Iowa, U.S.A.* 108 E9
Davenport, *Wash., U.S.A.* 110 C4
Davenport Downs, *Australia* 90 C3
Davenport Ra., *Australia* 90 C1
David, *Panama* 116 E3
David City, *U.S.A.* 108 E6
David Gorodok = Davyd Haradok, *Belarus* 41 F4
Davidson, *Canada* 101 C7
Davis, *U.S.A.* 112 G5
Davis Dam, *U.S.A.* 113 K12
Davis Inlet, *Canada* 99 A7
Davis Mts., *U.S.A.* 109 K2
Davis Sea, *Antarctica* 5 C7
Davis Str., *N. Amer.* 97 B14
Davos, *Switz.* 23 C9
Davy L., *Canada* 101 B7
Davyd Haradok, *Belarus* 41 F4
Dawa →, *Ethiopia* 77 G5
Dawaki, *Bauchi, Nigeria* 79 D6
Dawaki, *Kano, Nigeria* 79 C6
Dawes Ra., *Australia* 90 C5
Dawson, *Canada* 96 B6
Dawson, *Ga., U.S.A.* 105 K3
Dawson, *N. Dak., U.S.A.* 108 B5
Dawson, I., *Chile* 128 D2
Dawson Creek, *Canada* 100 B4
Dawson Inlet, *Canada* 101 A10
Dawson Ra., *Australia* 90 C4
Dawu, *China* 52 B3
Dax, *France* 26 E2
Daxi, *Taiwan* 53 E13
Daxian, *China* 52 B6
Daxin, *China* 52 F6
Daxindian, *China* 51 F11
Daxinggou, *China* 51 C15
Daxue Shan, *Sichuan, China* 52 B3
Daxue Shan, *Yunnan, China* 52 F2
Dayao, *China* 52 E3
Daye, *China* 53 B10
Dayi, *China* 52 B4
Daylesford, *Australia* 91 F3
Dayong, *China* 53 C8
Dayr az Zawr, *Syria* 67 E9
Daysland, *Canada* 100 C6
Dayton, *Nev., U.S.A.* 112 F7
Dayton, *Ohio, U.S.A.* 104 F3
Dayton, *Pa., U.S.A.* 106 F5
Dayton, *Tenn., U.S.A.* 105 H3
Dayton, *Wash., U.S.A.* 110 C4
Daytona Beach, *U.S.A.* 105 L5
Dayu, *China* 53 E10
Dayville, *U.S.A.* 110 D4
Dazhu, *China* 52 B6
Dazu, *China* 52 C5
De Aar, *S. Africa* 84 E3
De Bilt, *Neths.* 16 D6
De Funiak Springs, *U.S.A.* 105 K2
De Grey, *Australia* 88 D2
De Grey →, *Australia* 88 D2
De Kalb, *U.S.A.* 108 E10
De Koog, *Neths.* 16 B5
De Land, *U.S.A.* 105 L5
De Leon, *U.S.A.* 109 J5
De Panne, *Belgium* 17 F1
De Pere, *U.S.A.* 104 C1
De Queen, *U.S.A.* 109 H7
De Quincy, *U.S.A.* 109 K8
De Ridder, *U.S.A.* 109 K8
De Rijp, *Neths.* 16 C5
De Smet, *U.S.A.* 108 C6
De Soto, *U.S.A.* 108 F9
De Tour Village, *U.S.A.* 104 C4
De Witt, *U.S.A.* 109 H9
Dead Sea, *Asia* 69 D4
Deadwood, *U.S.A.* 108 C3
Deadwood L., *Canada* 100 B3
Deakin, *Australia* 89 F4
Deal, *U.K.* 13 F9
Deal I., *Australia* 90 F4
Dealesville, *S. Africa* 84 D4
De'an, *China* 53 C10
Dean, Forest of, *U.K.* 13 F5
Deán Funes, *Argentina* 126 C3
Dearborn, *U.S.A.* 98 D3
Dease →, *Canada* 100 B3
Dease L., *Canada* 100 B2
Dease Lake, *Canada* 100 B2
Death Valley, *U.S.A.* 113 J10
Death Valley Junction, *U.S.A.* 113 J10
Death Valley National Monument, *U.S.A.* 113 J10
Deauville, *France* 24 C7
Deba Habe, *Nigeria* 79 C7
Debaltsevo, *Ukraine* 41 H10
Debao, *China* 52 F6
Debar, *Macedonia* 39 H3
Debden, *Canada* 101 C7
Debdou, *Morocco* 75 B4
Dębica, *Poland* 20 E11
Dęblin, *Poland* 20 D11
Débo, L., *Mali* 78 B4
Debolt, *Canada* 100 B5
Deborah East, L., *Australia* 89 F2
Deborah West, L., *Australia* 89 F2
Debre Birhan, *Ethiopia* 77 F4
Debre Markos, *Ethiopia* 77 E4
Debre May, *Ethiopia* 77 E4
Debre Sina, *Ethiopia* 77 F4
Debre Tabor, *Ethiopia* 77 E4
Debre Zebit, *Ethiopia* 77 E4
Debrecen, *Hungary* 21 H11
Dečani, *Serbia, Yug.* 21 N10
Decatur, *Ala., U.S.A.* 105 H2
Decatur, *Ga., U.S.A.* 105 J3
Decatur, *Ill., U.S.A.* 108 F10
Decatur, *Ind., U.S.A.* 104 E3
Decatur, *Tex., U.S.A.* 109 J6
Decazeville, *France* 26 D6
Deccan, *India* 60 M10
Deception L., *Canada* 101 B8
Dechang, *China* 52 D4
Děčín, *Czech.* 20 E4
Decize, *France* 25 F10
Deckerville, *U.S.A.* 106 C2
Decollatura, *Italy* 35 C9
Decorah, *U.S.A.* 108 D9
Dedéagach = Alexandroúpolis, *Greece* 39 J8
Dedemsvaart, *Neths.* 16 C8
Dedham, *U.S.A.* 107 D13
Dédougou, *Burkina Faso* 78 C4
Dedovichi, *Russia* 40 D5
Dedza, *Malawi* 83 E3
Dee →, *Clwyd, U.K.* 12 D4
Dee →, *Gramp., U.K.* 14 D6
Deep B., *Canada* 100 A5
Deep Well, *Australia* 90 C1
Deepwater, *Australia* 91 D5
Deer →, *Canada* 101 B10
Deer Lake, *Nfld., Canada* 99 C8
Deer Lake, *Ont., Canada* 101 C10
Deer Lodge, *U.S.A.* 110 C7
Deer Park, *U.S.A.* 110 C5
Deer River, *U.S.A.* 108 B8
Deeral, *Australia* 90 B4
Deerdepoort, *S. Africa* 84 C4
Deerlijk, *Belgium* 17 G2
Deferiet, *U.S.A.* 107 B9
Defiance, *U.S.A.* 104 E3
Dêgê, *China* 52 B2
Degebe →, *Portugal* 31 G3
Degeh Bur, *Ethiopia* 68 F3
Degema, *Nigeria* 79 E6
Degersheim, *Switz.* 23 B8
Deggendorf, *Germany* 19 G8
Deh Bīd, *Iran* 65 D7
Deh-e Shīr, *Iran* 65 D7
Dehaj, *Iran* 65 D7
Dehdez, *Iran* 65 D6
Dehestān, *Iran* 65 D7
Dehgolān, *Iran* 67 E12
Dehi Titan, *Afghan.* 60 C3
Dehibat, *Tunisia* 75 B7
Dehlorān, *Iran* 67 F12
Dehnow-e Kūhestān, *Iran* 65 E8
Dehra Dun, *India* 62 D8
Dehri, *India* 63 G11
Dehua, *China* 53 E12
Dehui, *China* 51 B13
Deinze, *Belgium* 17 G3
Dej, *Romania* 38 B6
Dejiang, *China* 52 C7
Dekemhare, *Eritrea* 77 D4
Dekese, *Zaïre* 80 E4
Del Mar, *U.S.A.* 113 N9
Del Norte, *U.S.A.* 111 H10
Del Rio, *U.S.A.* 109 L4
Delai, *Sudan* 76 D4
Delano, *U.S.A.* 113 K7
Delareyville, *S. Africa* 84 D4
Delavan, *U.S.A.* 108 D10
Delaware, *U.S.A.* 104 E4
Delaware □, *U.S.A.* 104 F8
Delaware →, *U.S.A.* 104 F8
Delaware B., *U.S.A.* 103 C12
Delegate, *Australia* 91 F4
Delémont, *Switz.* 22 B4
Delft, *Neths.* 16 D4
Delfzijl, *Neths.* 16 B9
Delgado, C., *Mozam.* 83 E5
Delgerhet, *Mongolia* 50 B6
Delgo, *Sudan* 76 C3
Delhi, *Canada* 106 D4
Delhi, *India* 62 E7
Delhi, *U.S.A.* 107 D10
Delia, *Canada* 100 C6
Delice, *Turkey* 66 C6
Delicias, *Mexico* 114 B3
Delījān, *Iran* 65 C6
Delitzsch, *Germany* 18 D8
Dell City, *U.S.A.* 111 L11
Dell Rapids, *U.S.A.* 108 D6
Delle, *France* 25 E14
Dellys, *Algeria* 75 A5
Delmar, *U.S.A.* 107 D11
Delmenhorst, *Germany* 18 B4
Delmiro Gouveia, *Brazil* 122 C4
Delnice, *Croatia* 33 C11
Delong, Ostrova, *Russia* 45 B15
Deloraine, *Australia* 90 G4
Deloraine, *Canada* 101 D8
Delphi, *U.S.A.* 104 E2
Delphos, *U.S.A.* 104 E3
Delportshoop, *S. Africa* 84 D3
Delray Beach, *U.S.A.* 105 M5
Delsbo, *Sweden* 10 C10
Delta, *Colo., U.S.A.* 111 G9
Delta, *Utah, U.S.A.* 110 G7
Delta □, *Nigeria* 79 D6
Delta Amacuro □, *Venezuela* 121 B5
Delungra, *Australia* 91 D5
Delvinákion, *Greece* 39 K3
Delvinë, *Albania* 39 K3
Demanda, Sierra de la, *Spain* 28 C1
Demavand = Damāvand, *Iran* 65 C7
Demba, *Zaïre* 80 F4
Dembecha, *Ethiopia* 77 E4
Dembi, *Ethiopia* 77 F4
Dembia, *Zaïre* 82 B2
Dembidolo, *Ethiopia* 77 F3
Demer →, *Belgium* 17 G5
Demidov, *Russia* 40 E6
Deming, *N. Mex., U.S.A.* 111 K10
Deming, *Wash., U.S.A.* 112 B4
Demini →, *Brazil* 121 D5
Demirci, *Turkey* 66 C3
Demirköy, *Turkey* 66 B2
Demmin, *Germany* 18 B9
Demnate, *Morocco* 74 B3
Demonte, *Italy* 32 D4
Demopolis, *U.S.A.* 105 J2
Dempo, *Indonesia* 56 E2
Demyansk, *Russia* 40 D7
Den Burg, *Neths.* 16 B5
Den Chai, *Thailand* 58 D3
Den Dungen, *Neths.* 17 E6
Den Haag = 's-Gravenhage, *Neths.* 16 D4
Den Ham, *Neths.* 16 D8
Den Helder, *Neths.* 16 C5
Den Hulst, *Neths.* 16 C8
Den Oever, *Neths.* 16 C6
Denain, *France* 25 B10
Denair, *U.S.A.* 112 H6
Denau, *Uzbekistan* 44 F7
Denbigh, *U.K.* 12 D4
Dendang, *Indonesia* 56 E3
Dender →, *Belgium* 17 F4
Denderhoutem, *Belgium* 17 G4
Denderleeuw, *Belgium* 17 G4
Dendermonde, *Belgium* 17 F4
Deneba, *Ethiopia* 77 F4
Denekamp, *Neths.* 16 D10
Deng Xian, *China* 53 A9
Dengchuan, *China* 52 E3
Denge, *Nigeria* 79 C6
Dengfeng, *China* 50 G7
Dengi, *Nigeria* 79 D6
Dengkou, *China* 50 D4
Denham, *Australia* 89 E1
Denham Ra., *Australia* 90 C4
Denham Sd., *Australia* 89 E1
Denia, *Spain* 29 G5
Denial B., *Australia* 91 E1
Deniliquin, *Australia* 91 F3
Denison, *Iowa, U.S.A.* 108 D7
Denison, *Tex., U.S.A.* 109 J6
Denison Plains, *Australia* 88 C4
Denizli, *Turkey* 66 D3
Denman Glacier, *Antarctica* 5 C7
Denmark, *Australia* 89 F2
Denmark ■, *Europe* 11 J3
Denmark Str., *Atl. Oc.* 4 C6
Dennison, *U.S.A.* 106 F3
Denpasar, *Indonesia* 56 F5
Denton, *Mont., U.S.A.* 110 C9
Denton, *Tex., U.S.A.* 109 J6
D'Entrecasteaux, Pt., *Australia* 89 F2
Dents du Midi, *Switz.* 22 D3
Denu, *Ghana* 79 D5
Denver, *U.S.A.* 108 F2
Denver City, *U.S.A.* 109 J3
Deoband, *India* 62 E7
Deoghar, *India* 63 G12
Deolali, *India* 60 K8
Deoli = Devli, *India* 62 G6
Deoria, *India* 63 F10
Deosai Mts., *Pakistan* 63 B6
Deping, *China* 51 F9
Deposit, *U.S.A.* 107 D9
Depot Springs, *Australia* 89 E3
Deputatskiy, *Russia* 45 C14
Dêqên, *China* 52 C2
Deqing, *China* 53 F8
Dera Ghazi Khan, *Pakistan* 62 D4
Dera Ismail Khan, *Pakistan* 62 D4
Derbent, *Russia* 43 J9
Derby, *Australia* 88 C3
Derby, *U.K.* 12 E6
Derby, *Conn., U.S.A.* 107 E11
Derby, *N.Y., U.S.A.* 106 D6
Derbyshire □, *U.K.* 12 E6
Dereli, *Turkey* 67 B8
Derg →, *U.K.* 15 B4
Derg, L., *Ireland* 15 D3
Dergachi = Derhaci, *Ukraine* 41 G9
Dergaon, *India* 61 F19

Derhaci, *Ukraine* 41 G9
Derik, *Turkey* 67 D9
Derinkuyu, *Turkey* 66 C6
Dêrong, *China* 52 C2
Derry = Londonderry,
  U.K. 15 B4
Derryveagh Mts., *Ireland* . 15 B3
Derudub, *Sudan* 76 D4
Derval, *France* 24 E5
Dervéni, *Greece* 39 L5
Derwent, *Canada* 101 C6
Derwent →, *Derby, U.K.* . 12 E6
Derwent →, *N. Yorks.,*
  U.K. 12 D7
Derwent Water, *U.K.* 12 C4
Des Moines, *Iowa, U.S.A.* 108 E8
Des Moines, *N. Mex.,*
  U.S.A. 109 G3
Des Moines →, *U.S.A.* .. 108 E9
Desaguadero →, *Argentina* 126 C2
Desaguadero →, *Bolivia* . 124 D4
Descanso, Pta., *Mexico* ... 113 N9
Descartes, *France* 26 A4
Deschaillons, *Canada* ... 99 C5
Descharme →, *Canada* .. 101 B7
Deschutes →, *U.S.A.* 110 D3
Dese, *Ethiopia* 68 E2
Deseado, C., *Chile* 128 D2
Desenzano del Garda, *Italy* 32 C7
Desert Center, *U.S.A.* .. 113 M11
Desert Hot Springs, *U.S.A.* 113 M10
Deskenatlata L., *Canada* . 100 A6
Desna →, *Ukraine* 41 G6
Desnățui →, *Romania* ... 38 E6
Desolación, I., *Chile* 128 D2
Despeñaperros, Paso, *Spain* 29 G1
Despotovac, *Serbia, Yug.* . 21 L11
Dessau, *Germany* 18 D8
Dessel, *Belgium* 17 F6
Dessye = Dese, *Ethiopia* . 68 E2
D'Estrees B., *Australia* .. 91 F2
Desuri, *India* 62 G5
Desvres, *France* 25 B8
Det Udom, *Thailand* 58 E5
Dete, *Zimbabwe* 83 F2
Detinja →, *Serbia, Yug.* . 21 M9
Detmold, *Germany* 18 D4
Detour, Pt., *U.S.A.* 104 C2
Detroit, *Mich., U.S.A.* ... 98 D3
Detroit, *Tex., U.S.A.* 109 J7
Detroit Lakes, *U.S.A.* ... 108 B7
Deurne, *Belgium* 17 F4
Deurne, *Neths.* 17 F7
Deutsche Bucht, *Germany* 18 A4
Deutschlandsberg, *Austria* 21 J5
Deux-Sèvres □, *France* .. 24 F6
Deva, *Romania* 38 D5
Devakottai, *India* 60 Q11
Devaprayag, *India* 63 D8
Dévaványa, *Hungary* ... 21 H10
Deveci Dağları, *Turkey* .. 66 B7
Develi, *Turkey* 66 C6
Deventer, *Neths.* 16 D8
Deveron →, *U.K.* 14 D6
Devgadh Bariya, *India* .. 62 H5
Devils Den, *U.S.A.* 112 K7
Devils Lake, *U.S.A.* 108 A5
Devils Paw, *Canada* 100 B2
Devizes, *U.K.* 13 F6
Devli, *India* 62 G6
Devnya, *Bulgaria* 38 F10
Devolii →, *Albania* 39 J3
Devon, *Canada* 100 C6
Devon □, *U.K.* 13 G4
Devon I., *Canada* 4 B3
Devonport, *Australia* ... 90 G4
Devonport, *N.Z.* 87 G5
Devonport, *U.K.* 13 G3
Devrek, *Turkey* 66 B4
Devrekâni, *Turkey* 66 B5
Devrez →, *Turkey* 66 B6
Dewas, *India* 62 H7
Dewetsdorp, *S. Africa* ... 84 D4
Dewsbury, *U.K.* 12 D6
Dexing, *China* 53 C11
Dexter, *Mo., U.S.A.* 109 G9
Dexter, *N. Mex., U.S.A.* . 109 J2
Dey-Dey, L., *Australia* .. 89 E5
Deyang, *China* 52 B5
Deyhūk, *Iran* 65 C8
Deyyer, *Iran* 65 E6
Dezadeash L., *Canada* .. 100 A1
Dezfūl, *Iran* 67 F13
Dezhneva, Mys, *Russia* .. 45 C19
Dezhou, *China* 50 F9
Dháfni, *Greece* 37 D7
Dhahaban, *Si. Arabia* ... 76 C4
Dhahiriya = Az̧ Z̧āhirīyah,
  West Bank 69 D3
Dhahran = Az̧ Z̧ahrān,
  Si. Arabia 65 E6
Dhaka, *Bangla.* 63 H14
Dhaka □, *Bangla.* 63 G14
Dhali, *Cyprus* 37 D12
Dhamar, *Yemen* 68 E3
Dhamási, *Greece* 39 K5
Dhampur, *India* 63 E8
Dhamtari, *India* 61 J12
Dhanbad, *India* 63 H12
Dhangarhi, *Nepal* 61 E12
Dhankuta, *Nepal* 63 F12
Dhar, *India* 62 H6
Dharampur, *India* 62 H6
Dharamsala = Dharmsala,
  India 62 C7

Dharmapuri, *India* 60 N11
Dharmsala, *India* 62 C7
Dharwad, *India* 60 M9
Dhaulagiri, *Nepal* 63 E10
Dhebar, L., *India* 62 G6
Dhenkanal, *India* 61 J14
Dhenoúsa, *Greece* 39 M8
Dheftera, *Cyprus* 37 D12
Dherinia, *Cyprus* 37 D12
Dheskáti, *Greece* 39 K4
Dhespotikó, *Greece* 39 N7
Dhestina, *Greece* 39 L5
Dhiarrizos →, *Cyprus* ... 37 E11
Dhíkti Óros, *Greece* 37 D7
Dhimitsána, *Greece* 39 M5
Dhírfis, *Greece* 39 L6
Dhodhekánisos, *Greece* . 39 N10
Dholiana, *Greece* 39 K3
Dholka, *India* 62 H5
Dhoraji, *India* 62 J4
Dhoxáton, *Greece* 39 H7
Dhrángadhra, *India* 62 H4
Dhráhstis, Ákra, *Greece* . 37 A3
Dhrápanon, Ákra, *Greece* 37 D6
Dhrol, *India* 62 H4
Dhuburi, *India* 61 F16
Dhule, *India* 60 J9
Dhut →, *Somali Rep.* ... 68 E5
Di Linh, *Vietnam* 59 G7
Di Linh, Cao Nguyen,
  Vietnam 59 G7
Día, *Greece* 37 D7
Diablo, Mt., *U.S.A.* 112 H5
Diablo Range, *U.S.A.* ... 112 J5
Diafarabé, *Mali* 78 C4
Diala, *Mali* 78 C3
Dialakoro, *Mali* 78 C3
Diallassagou, *Mali* 78 C4
Diamante, *Argentina* ... 126 C3
Diamante →, *Argentina* . 126 C2
Diamantina, *Brazil* 123 E3
Diamantina →, *Australia* 91 D2
Diamantino, *Brazil* 125 C6
Diamond Harbour, *India* . 63 H13
Diamond Is., *Australia* .. 90 B5
Diamond Mts., *U.S.A.* ... 110 G6
Diamond Springs, *U.S.A.* 112 G6
Diamondville, *U.S.A.* ... 110 F8
Dianbai, *China* 53 G8
Diancheng, *China* 53 G8
Diano Marina, *Italy* 32 E5
Dianópolis, *Brazil* 123 D2
Dianra, *Ivory C.* 78 D3
Diapaga, *Burkina Faso* .. 79 C5
Diapangou, *Burkina Faso* 79 C5
Diariguila, *Guinea* 78 C2
Dībā, *Oman* 65 E8
Dibaya, *Zaïre* 80 F4
Dibaya-Lubue, *Zaïre* ... 80 E3
Dibbi, *Ethiopia* 68 G3
Dibete, *Botswana* 84 C4
Dibrugarh, *India* 61 F19
Dickinson, *U.S.A.* 108 B3
Dickson, *Russia* 44 B9
Dickson, *U.S.A.* 105 G2
Dickson City, *U.S.A.* ... 107 E9
Dicle Nehri →, *Turkey* .. 67 D9
Dicomano, *Italy* 33 E8
Didam, *Neths.* 16 E8
Didesa, W. →, *Ethiopia* . 77 F4
Didiéni, *Mali* 78 C3
Didsbury, *Canada* 100 C6
Didwana, *India* 62 F6
Die, *France* 27 D9
Diébougou, *Burkina Faso* 78 C4
Diefenbaker L., *Canada* . 101 C7
Diego Garcia, *Ind. Oc.* .. 3 E13
Diekirch, *Lux.* 17 J8
Diélette, *France* 24 C5
Diéma, *Mali* 78 C3
Diémbéring, *Senegal* ... 78 C1
Diemen, *Neths.* 16 D5
Dien Ban, *Vietnam* 58 E7
Dien Bien, *Vietnam* 58 B4
Dien Khanh, *Vietnam* ... 59 F7
Diepenbeek, *Belgium* ... 17 G6
Diepenheim, *Neths.* 16 D9
Diepenveen, *Neths.* 16 D8
Diepholz, *Germany* 18 C4
Diepoldsau, *Switz.* 23 B9
Dieppe, *France* 24 C8
Dieren, *Neths.* 16 D8
Dierks, *U.S.A.* 109 H7
Diessen, *Neths.* 17 F6
Diessenhofen, *Switz.* ... 23 A7
Diest, *Belgium* 17 G6
Dietikon, *Switz.* 23 B6
Dieulefit, *France* 27 D9
Dieuze, *France* 25 D13
Diever, *Neths.* 16 C8
Differdange, *Lux.* 17 J7
Dig, *India* 62 F7
Digba, *Zaïre* 82 B2
Digby, *Canada* 99 D6
Digges, *Canada* 101 B10
Digges Is., *Canada* 97 B12
Dighinala, *Bangla.* 61 H18
Dighton, *U.S.A.* 108 F4
Digne-les-Bains, *France* . 27 D10
Digoin, *France* 26 B7
Digor, *Turkey* 67 B10
Digos, *Phil.* 55 H6
Digranes, *Iceland* 8 C6
Digul →, *Indonesia* 57 F9
Dihang →, *India* 61 F19
Dihōk, *Iraq* 67 D10

Dijlah, Nahr →, *Asia* ... 64 D5
Dijle →, *Belgium* 17 G5
Dijon, *France* 25 E12
Dikala, *Sudan* 77 G3
Dikimdya, *Russia* 45 D13
Dikkil, *Djibouti* 77 E5
Dikomu di Kai, *Botswana* 84 C3
Dikson = Dickson, *Russia* 44 B9
Dikwa, *Nigeria* 79 C7
Dila, *Ethiopia* 77 F4
Dilbeek, *Belgium* 17 G4
Dili, *Indonesia* 57 F7
Dilijan, *Armenia* 43 K7
Dilizhan = Dilijan,
  Armenia 43 K7
Dillenburg, *Germany* ... 18 E4
Dilley, *U.S.A.* 109 L5
Dilling, *Sudan* 77 E2
Dillingen, *Germany* 19 G6
Dillingham, *U.S.A.* 96 C4
Dillon, *Canada* 101 B7
Dillon, *Mont., U.S.A.* ... 110 D7
Dillon, *S.C., U.S.A.* 105 H6
Dillon →, *Canada* 101 B7
Dilolo, *Zaïre* 80 G4
Dilsen, *Belgium* 17 F7
Dilston, *Australia* 90 G4
Dimas, *Mexico* 114 C3
Dimashq, *Syria* 69 B5
Dimashq □, *Syria* 69 B5
Dimbaza, S. *Africa* 85 E4
Dimbokro, *Ivory C.* 78 D4
Dimboola, *Australia* 91 F3
Dîmbovița →, *Romania* . 38 E9
Dîmbovnic →, *Romania* . 38 E8
Dimbulah, *Australia* 90 B4
Dimitrovgrad, *Bulgaria* . 39 G8
Dimitrovgrad, *Russia* ... 42 C9
Dimitrovgrad, *Serbia, Yug.* 21 M12
Dimitrovo = Pernik,
  Bulgaria 38 G6
Dimmitt, *U.S.A.* 109 H3
Dimo, *Sudan* 77 F2
Dimona, *Israel* 69 D4
Dimovo, *Bulgaria* 38 F5
Dinagat, *Phil.* 55 F6
Dinajpur, *Bangla.* 61 G16
Dinan, *France* 24 D4
Dīnān Āb, *Iran* 65 C8
Dinant, *Belgium* 17 H5
Dinapur, *India* 63 G11
Dinar, *Turkey* 66 C4
Dīnār, Kūh-e, *Iran* 65 D6
Dinara Planina, *Croatia* . 33 E13
Dinard, *France* 24 D4
Dinaric Alps = Dinara
  Planina, *Croatia* 33 E13
Dinder, Nahr ed →, *Sudan* 77 E3
Dindigul, *India* 60 P11
Ding Xian, *China* 50 E8
Dingalan, *Phil.* 55 D4
Dingbian, *China* 50 F4
Dingelstädt, *Germany* .. 18 D6
Dingle, *Ireland* 15 D1
Dingle B., *Ireland* 15 D1
Dingmans Ferry, *U.S.A.* . 107 E10
Dingnan, *China* 53 E10
Dingo, *Australia* 90 C4
Dingolfing, *Germany* ... 19 G8
Dingtao, *China* 50 G8
Dinguiraye, *Guinea* 78 C2
Dingwall, *U.K.* 14 D4
Dingxi, *China* 50 G3
Dingxiang, *China* 50 E7
Dingyuan, *China* 53 A11
Dinh, *Vietnam* 59 G7
Dinh Lap, *Vietnam* 58 B6
Dinkel →, *Neths.* 16 D9
Dinokwe, *Botswana* 84 C4
Dinosaur National
  Monument, *U.S.A.* .. 110 F9
Dinslaken, *Germany* ... 17 E9
Dintel →, *Neths.* 17 E4
Dinteloord, *Neths.* 17 E4
Dinuba, *U.S.A.* 111 H4
Dinxperlo, *Neths.* 16 E9
Diósgyör, *Hungary* 21 G10
Diourbel, *Senegal* 78 C1
Diplo, *Pakistan* 62 G3
Dipolog, *Phil.* 55 G5
Dipșa, *Romania* 38 C7
Dir, *Pakistan* 60 B7
Diré, *Mali* 78 B4
Dire Dawa, *Ethiopia* ... 68 F3
Diriamba, *Nic.* 116 D2
Dirico, *Angola* 81 H4
Dirk Hartog I., *Australia* 89 E1
Dirranbandi, *Australia* .. 91 D4
Disa, *India* 62 G5
Disa, *Sudan* 77 E3
Disappointment, C.,
  U.S.A. 110 C1
Disappointment, L.,
  Australia 88 D3
Disaster B., *Australia* ... 91 F4
Discovery B., *Australia* . 91 F3
Disentis, *Switz.* 23 C7
Dishna, *Egypt* 76 B3
Disina, *Nigeria* 79 C6
Disko, *Greenland* 4 C5
Disko Bugt, *Greenland* . 4 C5
Disna = Dzisna →,
  Belarus 40 E5
Dison, *Belgium* 17 G7
Disteghil Sar, *Pakistan* . 63 A6

Distrito Federal □, *Brazil* 123 E2
Distrito Federal □,
  Venezuela 120 A4
Disûq, *Egypt* 76 H7
Diu, *India* 62 J4
Dīvāndarreh, *Iran* 67 E12
Dives →, *France* 24 C6
Dives-sur-Mer, *France* .. 24 C6
Divichi = Dāvәçi,
  Azerbaijan 43 K9
Divide, *U.S.A.* 110 D7
Dividing Ra., *Australia* .. 89 E2
Divinópolis, *Brazil* 123 F3
Divisões, Serra dos, *Brazil* 123 E1
Divnoye, *Russia* 43 H6
Divo, *Ivory C.* 78 D3
Divriği, *Turkey* 67 C8
Dīwāl Kol, *Afghan.* 62 B2
Dixie Mt., *U.S.A.* 112 F6
Dixon, *Calif., U.S.A.* ... 112 G5
Dixon, *Ill., U.S.A.* 108 E10
Dixon, *Mont., U.S.A.* ... 110 C6
Dixon, *N. Mex., U.S.A.* . 111 H11
Dixon Entrance, *U.S.A.* . 100 C2
Dixonville, *Canada* 100 B5
Diyadin, *Turkey* 67 C10
Diyālā →, *Iraq* 67 F11
Diyarbakır, *Turkey* 67 D9
Djado, *Niger* 73 D7
Djakarta = Jakarta,
  Indonesia 57 G12
Djamâa, *Algeria* 75 B6
Djamba, *Angola* 84 B1
Djambala, *Congo* 80 E2
Djanet, *Algeria* 75 D6
Djawa = Jawa, *Indonesia* 57 G14
Djebiniana, *Tunisia* 75 A7
Djelfa, *Algeria* 75 B5
Djema, *C.A.R.* 82 A2
Djendel, *Algeria* 75 A5
Djeneïene, *Tunisia* 75 B7
Djenné, *Mali* 78 C4
Djerba, *Tunisia* 75 B7
Djerba, I. de, *Tunisia* ... 73 B7
Djerid, Chott, *Tunisia* .. 75 B6
Djibo, *Burkina Faso* 79 C4
Djibouti, *Djibouti* 68 E3
Djibouti ■, *Africa* 68 E3
Djolu, *Zaïre* 80 D4
Djougou, *Benin* 79 D5
Djoum, *Cameroon* 80 D2
Djourab, *Chad* 73 E8
Djugu, *Zaïre* 82 B3
Djúpivogur, *Iceland* ... 8 D6
Djursholm, *Sweden* ... 10 E12
Djursland, *Denmark* ... 11 H4
Dmitriya Lapteva, Proliv,
  Russia 45 B15
Dmitriyev Lgovskiy, *Russia* 42 D2
Dmitrov, *Russia* 42 B3
Dmitrovsk-Orlovskiy,
  Russia 42 D2
Dnepr = Dnipro →,
  Ukraine 41 J7
Dneprodzerzhinsk =
  Dniprodzerzhynsk,
  Ukraine 41 H8
Dneprodzerzhinskoye
  Vdkhr. =
  Dniprodzerzhynske
  Vdskh., *Ukraine* 41 H8
Dnepropetrovsk =
  Dnipropetrovsk, *Ukraine* 41 H8
Dneprorudnoye =
  Dniprorudne, *Ukraine* . 41 J8
Dnestr = Dnister →,
  Europe 41 J6
Dnestrovski = Belgorod,
  Russia 42 E3
Dnieper = Dnipro →,
  Ukraine 41 J7
Dniester = Dnister →,
  Europe 41 J6
Dnipro →, *Ukraine* 41 J7
Dniprodzerzhynsk, *Ukraine* 41 H8
Dniprodzerzhynske Vdskh.,
  Ukraine 41 H8
Dnipropetrovsk, *Ukraine* . 41 H8
Dniprorudne, *Ukraine* ... 41 J8
Dnister →, *Europe* 41 J6
Dnistrovskyy Lyman,
  Ukraine 41 J6
Dno, *Russia* 40 D5
Dnyapro = Dnipro →,
  Ukraine 41 J7
Doan Hung, *Vietnam* ... 58 B5
Doba, *Chad* 73 G8
Dobbiaco, *Italy* 33 B9
Dobbyn, *Australia* 90 B3
Dobele, *Latvia* 9 H20
Doberai, Jazirah, *Indonesia* 57 E8
Dobiegniew, *Poland* 20 C5
Doblas, *Argentina* 126 D3
Dobo, *Indonesia* 57 F8
Doboj, *Bos.-H.* 21 L8
Dobra, *Dîmbovita,*
  Romania 38 E8
Dobra, *Hunedoara,*
  Romania 38 D5
Dobreta-Turnu-Severin,
  Romania 38 E6
Dobrich, *Bulgaria* 38 F10
Dobrinishta, *Bulgaria* .. 39 H6
Dobrodzień, *Poland* 20 E8
Dobropole, *Ukraine* 41 H9

Dobruja, *Romania* 38 E11
Dobrush, *Belarus* 41 F6
Dobtong, *Sudan* 77 F3
Doc, Mui, *Vietnam* 58 D6
Doce →, *Brazil* 123 E4
Doda, *India* 63 C6
Dodecanese =
  Dhodhekánisos, *Greece* . 39 N10
Dodewaard, *Neths.* 16 E7
Dodge Center, *U.S.A.* .. 108 C8
Dodge City, *U.S.A.* 109 G5
Dodge L., *Canada* 101 B7
Dodgeville, *U.S.A.* 108 D9
Dodo, *Sudan* 77 F2
Dodola, *Ethiopia* 77 F4
Dodoma, *Tanzania* 82 D4
Dodoma □, *Tanzania* .. 82 D4
Dodsland, *Canada* 101 C7
Dodson, *U.S.A.* 110 B9
Doesburg, *Neths.* 16 D8
Doetinchem, *Neths.* ... 16 E8
Dog Creek, *Canada* 100 C4
Dog L., *Man., Canada* . 101 C9
Dog L., *Ont., Canada* .. 98 C2
Doğanşehir, *Turkey* 66 C7
Dogi, *Afghan.* 60 C3
Dogliani, *Italy* 32 D4
Dogondoutchi, *Niger* ... 79 C5
Dogran, *Pakistan* 62 D5
Doğubayazıt, *Turkey* ... 67 C11
Doguéraoua, *Niger* 79 C6
Doha = Ad Dawhah, *Qatar* 65 E6
Dohazari, *Bangla.* 61 H18
Doi, *Indonesia* 57 D7
Doi Luang, *Thailand* ... 58 C3
Doi Saket, *Thailand* 58 C2
Doig →, *Canada* 100 B4
Dois Irmãos, Sa., *Brazil* . 122 C3
Dokka →, *Norway* 10 D4
Dokkum, *Neths.* 16 B7
Dokkumer Ee →, *Neths.* 16 B7
Dokri, *Pakistan* 62 F3
Dokuchayevsk, *Ukraine* . 41 J9
Dol-de-Bretagne, *France* . 24 D5
Doland, *U.S.A.* 108 C5
Dolbeau, *Canada* 99 C5
Dole, *France* 25 E12
Doleib, Wadi →, *Sudan* . 77 E3
Dolgellau, *U.K.* 12 E4
Dolgelley = Dolgellau,
  U.K. 12 E4
Dolianova, *Italy* 34 C2
Dolinskaya = Dolynska,
  Ukraine 41 H7
Dollart, *Neths.* 16 B10
Dolna Banya, *Bulgaria* .. 38 G6
Dolni Dŭbnik, *Bulgaria* . 38 F7
Dolo, *Ethiopia* 77 G5
Dolo, *Italy* 33 C9
Dolomites = Dolomiti,
  Italy 33 B8
Dolomiti, *Italy* 33 B8
Dolores, *Argentina* 126 D4
Dolores, *Uruguay* 126 C4
Dolores, *U.S.A.* 111 H9
Dolores →, *U.S.A.* 111 G9
Dolphin, C., *Falk. Is.* ... 128 D5
Dolphin and Union Str.,
  Canada 96 B8
Dolynska, *Ukraine* 41 H7
Dolzhanskaya, *Russia* .. 43 G3
Dom, *Switz.* 22 D5
Dom Joaquim, *Brazil* .. 123 E3
Dom Pedrito, *Brazil* ... 127 C5
Dom Pedro, *Brazil* 122 B3
Doma, *Nigeria* 79 D6
Domaniç, *Turkey* 66 C3
Domasi, *Malawi* 83 F4
Domat Ems, *Switz.* 23 C8
Domazlice, *Czech.* 20 F2
Dombarovskiy, *Russia* .. 44 D6
Dombås, *Norway* 9 E13
Dombasle-sur-Meurthe,
  France 25 D13
Dombes, *France* 27 B8
Dombóvár, *Hungary* ... 21 J8
Domburg, *Neths.* 17 E3
Domérat, *France* 26 B6
Domeyko, *Chile* 126 B1
Domeyko, Cordillera, *Chile* 126 A2
Domfront, *France* 24 D6
Dominador, *Chile* 126 A2
Dominica ■, *W. Indies* . 117 C7
Dominica Passage,
  W. Indies 117 C7
Dominican Rep. ■,
  W. Indies 117 C5
Dömitz, *Germany* 18 B7
Domme, *France* 26 D5
Dommel →, *Neths.* ... 17 E6
Domo, *Ethiopia* 68 F4
Domodóssola, *Italy* 32 B5
Dompaire, *France* 25 D13
Dompierre-sur-Besbre,
  France 26 B7
Dompim, *Ghana* 78 D4
Domrémy-la-Pucelle,
  France 25 D12
Domsjö, *Sweden* 10 A12
Domville, Mt., *Australia* . 91 D5
Domvraína, *Greece* 39 L5
Domžale, *Slovenia* 33 B11
Don →, *Russia* 43 G4
Don →, *Gramp., U.K.* .. 14 D7
Don →, *Humber., U.K.* . 12 D7
Don, C., *Australia* 88 B5
Don Benito, *Spain* 31 G5

Don Duong, Vietnam 59 G7
Don Martín, Presa de, Mexico 114 B4
Dona Ana = Nhamaabué, Mozam. 83 F4
Donaghadee, U.K. 15 B6
Donald, Australia 91 F3
Donalda, Canada 100 C6
Donaldsonville, U.S.A. .. 109 K9
Donalsonville, U.S.A. .. 105 K3
Donau = Dunărea →, Europe 41 K5
Donau →, Austria 21 G7
Donaueschingen, Germany 19 H4
Donauwörth, Germany .. 19 G6
Doncaster, U.K. 12 D6
Dondo, Angola 80 F2
Dondo, Mozam. 83 F3
Dondo, Teluk, Indonesia 57 D6
Dondra Head, Sri Lanka . 60 S12
Donegal, Ireland 15 B3
Donegal □, Ireland 15 B4
Donegal B., Ireland 15 B3
Donets →, Russia 43 G5
Donetsk, Ukraine 41 J9
Dong Ba Thin, Vietnam .. 59 F7
Dong Dang, Vietnam 58 B5
Dong Giam, Vietnam 58 C5
Dong Ha, Vietnam 58 D6
Dong Hene, Laos 58 D5
Dong Hoi, Vietnam 58 D6
Dong Jiang →, China 53 F10
Dong Khe, Vietnam 58 A6
Dong Ujimqin Qi, China .. 50 B9
Dong Van, Vietnam 58 A5
Dong Xoai, Vietnam 59 G6
Donga, Nigeria 79 D7
Dong'an, China 53 D8
Dongara, Australia 89 E1
Dongbei, China 51 D13
Dongchuan, China 52 D4
Dongen, Neths. 17 E5
Donges, France 24 E4
Dongfang, China 58 C7
Dongfeng, China 51 C13
Donggala, Indonesia 57 E5
Donggan, China 52 F5
Donggou, China 51 E13
Dongguan, China 53 F9
Dongguang, China 50 F9
Donghai Dao, China 53 G8
Dongjingcheng, China ... 51 B15
Donglan, China 52 E6
Dongliu, China 53 B11
Dongmen, China 52 F6
Dongning, China 51 B16
Dongnyi, China 52 C3
Dongola, Sudan 76 D3
Dongou, Congo 80 D3
Dongping, China 50 G9
Dongshan, China 53 F11
Dongsheng, China 50 E6
Dongshi, Taiwan 53 E13
Dongtai, China 51 H11
Dongting Hu, China 53 C9
Dongxiang, China 53 C11
Dongxing, China 52 G7
Dongyang, China 53 C13
Dongzhi, China 53 B11
Donington, C., Australia . 91 E2
Doniphan, U.S.A. 109 G9
Donja Stubica, Croatia .. 33 C13
Donji Dušnik, Serbia, Yug. 21 M12
Donji Miholjac, Croatia .. 21 K8
Donji Milanovac, Serbia, Yug. 21 L12
Donji Vakuf, Bos.-H. 21 L7
Dønna, Norway 8 C15
Donna, U.S.A. 109 M5
Donnaconna, Canada ... 99 C5
Donnelly's Crossing, N.Z. 87 F4
Donnybrook, Australia .. 89 F2
Donnybrook, S. Africa .. 85 D4
Donora, U.S.A. 106 F5
Donor's Hill, Australia ... 90 B3
Donostia = San Sebastián, Spain 28 B3
Donskoy, Russia 42 D4
Donsol, Phil. 55 E5
Donya Lendava, Slovenia . 33 B13
Donzère, France 27 D8
Donzère-Mondragon, Barr. de, France 27 D8
Donzy, France 25 E10
Doon →, U.K. 14 F4
Doorn, Neths. 16 D6
Dora, L., Australia 88 D3
Dora Báltea →, Italy 32 C5
Dora Ripária →, Italy 32 C4
Doran L., Canada 101 A7
Dorchester, U.K. 13 G5
Dorchester, C., Canada .. 97 B12
Dordogne □, France 26 C4
Dordogne →, France 26 C3
Dordrecht, Neths. 16 E5
Dordrecht, S. Africa 84 E4
Dore →, France 26 C7
Dore, Mts., France 26 C6
Doré L., Canada 101 B7
Doré Lake, Canada 101 C7
Dores do Indaiá, Brazil . 123 E2
Dorfen, Germany 19 G8
Dorgali, Italy 34 B2
Dori, Burkina Faso 79 C4
Doring →, S. Africa 84 E2
Doringbos, S. Africa 84 E2
Dorion, Canada 98 C5

Dormaa-Ahenkro, Ghana . 78 D4
Dormo, Ras, Eritrea 77 E5
Dornach, Switz. 22 B5
Dornberg, Slovenia 33 C10
Dornbirn, Austria 19 H5
Dornes, France 25 F10
Dornoch, U.K. 14 D4
Dornoch Firth, U.K. 14 D4
Dornogovĭ □, Mongolia . 50 B6
Doro, Mali 79 B4
Dorogobuzh, Russia 40 E7
Dorohoi, Romania 38 B9
Doröö Nuur, Mongolia .. 54 B4
Dorr, Iran 65 C6
Dorre I., Australia 89 E1
Dorrigo, Australia 91 E5
Dorris, U.S.A. 110 F3
Dorset, Canada 106 A6
Dorset, U.S.A. 106 E4
Dorset □, U.K. 13 G5
Dorsten, Germany 18 D2
Dortmund, Germany 18 D3
Dörtyol, Turkey 66 D7
Dorum, Germany 18 B4
Doruma, Zaïre 82 B2
Dorūneh, Iran 65 C8
Dos Bahías, C., Argentina 128 B3
Dos Hermanas, Spain ... 31 H5
Dos Palos, U.S.A. 112 J6
Dosso, Niger 79 C5
Dothan, U.S.A. 105 K3
Dottignies, Belgium 17 G2
Doty, U.S.A. 112 D3
Douai, France 25 B10
Douala, Cameroon 79 E6
Douarnenez, France 24 D2
Double Island Pt., Australia 91 D5
Doubrava →, Czech. 20 F5
Doubs □, France 25 E13
Doubs →, France 25 F12
Doubtful Sd., N.Z. 87 L1
Doubtless B., N.Z. 87 F4
Doudeville, France 24 C7
Doué-la-Fontaine, France . 24 E6
Douentza, Mali 78 C4
Douglas, S. Africa 84 D3
Douglas, U.K. 12 C3
Douglas, Alaska, U.S.A. . 100 B2
Douglas, Ariz., U.S.A. .. 111 L9
Douglas, Ga., U.S.A. ... 105 K4
Douglas, Wyo., U.S.A. .. 108 D2
Douglastown, Canada ... 99 C7
Douglasville, U.S.A. 105 J3
Douirat, Morocco 74 B4
Doukáton, Ákra, Greece . 39 L3
Doulevant-le-Château, France 25 D11
Doullens, France 25 B9
Doumé, Cameroon 80 D2
Douna, Mali 78 C3
Dounan, Taiwan 53 F13
Dounreay, U.K. 14 C5
Dour, Belgium 17 H3
Dourada, Serra, Brazil .. 123 D2
Dourados, Brazil 127 A5
Dourados →, Brazil 127 A5
Dourdan, France 25 D9
Douro →, Europe 30 D2
Douvaine, France 27 B10
Douz, Tunisia 75 B6
Douze →, France 26 E3
Dove →, U.K. 12 E6
Dove Creek, U.S.A. 111 H9
Dover, Australia 90 G4
Dover, U.K. 13 F9
Dover, Del., U.S.A. 104 F8
Dover, N.H., U.S.A. 107 C14
Dover, N.J., U.S.A. 107 F10
Dover, Ohio, U.S.A. 106 F3
Dover, Pt., Australia 89 F4
Dover, Str. of, Europe ... 24 B8
Dover-Foxcroft, U.S.A. .. 99 C6
Dover Plains, U.S.A. 107 E11
Dovey = Dyfi →, U.K. .. 13 E4
Dovrefjell, Norway 10 B3
Dow Rūd, Iran 65 C6
Dowa, Malawi 83 E3
Dowagiac, U.S.A. 104 E2
Dowgha'i, Iran 65 B8
Dowlatābād, Iran 65 D8
Down □, U.K. 15 B6
Downey, Calif., U.S.A. .. 113 M8
Downey, Idaho, U.S.A. .. 110 E7
Downham Market, U.K. . 13 E8
Downieville, U.S.A. 112 F6
Downpatrick, U.K. 15 B6
Downpatrick Hd., Ireland 15 B2
Dowsārī, Iran 65 D8
Doyle, U.S.A. 112 E6
Doylestown, U.S.A. 107 F9
Draa, C., Morocco 74 C2
Draa, Oued →, Morocco . 74 C2
Drac →, France 27 C9
Drachten, Neths. 16 B8
Drăgănești, Romania 38 E8
Drăgănești-Viașca, Romania 38 E8
Dragaš, Serbia, Yug. 21 N10
Drăgășani, Romania 38 E7
Dragichyn, Belarus 41 F3
Dragonera, I., Spain 36 B9
Draguignan, France 27 E10
Drain, U.S.A. 110 E2
Drake, Australia 91 D5
Drake, U.S.A. 108 B4
Drake Passage, S. Ocean . 5 B17
Drakensberg, S. Africa ... 85 E4

Dráma, Greece 39 H7
Drammen, Norway 10 E4
Drangajökull, Iceland ... 8 C2
Drangedal, Norway 10 E3
Dranov, Ostrov, Romania 38 E12
Dras, India 63 B6
Drau = Drava →, Croatia 21 K8
Drava →, Croatia 21 K8
Draveil, France 25 D9
Dravograd, Slovenia 33 B12
Drawa →, Poland 20 C5
Drawno, Poland 20 B5
Drayton Valley, Canada .. 100 C6
Dreibergen, Neths. 16 D6
Drenthe □, Neths. 16 C9
Drentsche Hoofdvaart, Neths. 16 C8
Drepanum, C., Cyprus .. 37 E11
Dresden, Canada 106 D2
Dresden, Germany 18 D9
Dreux, France 24 D8
Driel, Neths. 16 E7
Driffield, U.K. 12 C7
Driftwood, U.S.A. 106 E6
Driggs, U.S.A. 110 E8
Drin i zi →, Albania 39 H3
Drina →, Bos.-H. 21 L9
Drincea →, Romania 38 E5
Drini →, Albania 38 G3
Drinjača →, Bos.-H. 21 L9
Drissa = Vyerkhnyadzvinsk, Belarus 40 E4
Drivstua, Norway 10 B3
Drniš, Croatia 33 E13
Drøbak, Norway 10 E4
Drochia, Moldova 41 H4
Drogheda, Ireland 15 C5
Drogichin = Dragichyn, Belarus 41 F3
Drogobych = Drohobych, Ukraine 41 H2
Drohobych, Ukraine 41 H2
Droichead Atha = Drogheda, Ireland ... 15 C5
Droichead Nua, Ireland . 15 C5
Droitwich, U.K. 13 E5
Drôme □, France 27 D9
Drôme →, France 27 D8
Dromedary, C., Australia . 91 F5
Dronero, Italy 32 D4
Dronfield, Australia 90 C3
Dronne →, France 26 C3
Dronninglund, Denmark .. 11 G4
Dronrijp, Neths. 16 B7
Dropt →, France 26 D3
Drumbo, Canada 106 C4
Drumheller, Canada 100 C6
Drummond, U.S.A. 110 C7
Drummond I., U.S.A. ... 98 C3
Drummond Pt., Australia 91 E2
Drummond Ra., Australia 90 C4
Drummondville, Canada . 98 C5
Drumright, U.S.A. 109 H6
Drunen, Neths. 17 E6
Druskininkai, Lithuania . 9 J20
Drut →, Belarus 41 F6
Druten, Neths. 16 E7
Druya, Belarus 40 E4
Druzhina, Russia 45 C15
Drvar, Bos.-H. 33 D13
Drvenik, Croatia 33 E13
Dry Tortugas, U.S.A. 116 B3
Dryanovo, Bulgaria 38 G8
Dryden, Canada 101 D10
Dryden, U.S.A. 109 K3
Drygalski I., Antarctica .. 5 C7
Drysdale →, Australia .. 88 B4
Drysdale I., Australia ... 90 A2
Dschang, Cameroon 79 D7
Du Bois, U.S.A. 106 E6
Du Quoin, U.S.A. 108 G10
Duanesburg, U.S.A. 107 D10
Duaringa, Australia 90 C4
Dūbā, Si. Arabia 64 E2
Dubai = Dubayy, U.A.E. 65 E7
Dubăsari, Moldova 41 J5
Dubăsari Vdkhr., Moldova 41 J5
Dubawnt →, Canada ... 101 A8
Dubawnt, L., Canada ... 101 A8
Dubayy, U.A.E. 65 E7
Dubbeldam, Neths. 16 E5
Dubbo, Australia 91 E4
Dubele, Zaïre 82 B2
Dübendorf, Switz. 23 B7
Dubica, Croatia 33 C13
Dublin, Ireland 15 C5
Dublin, Ga., U.S.A. 105 J4
Dublin, Tex., U.S.A. 109 J5
Dublin □, Ireland 15 C5
Dublin B., Ireland 15 C5
Dubna, Russia 42 B3
Dubno, Ukraine 41 G3
Dubois, U.S.A. 110 D7
Dubossary = Dubăsari, Moldova 41 J5
Dubossary Vdkhr. = Dubăsari Vdkhr., Moldova 41 J5
Dubovka, Russia 43 F7
Dubovskoye, Russia 43 G6
Dubrajpur, India 63 H12
Dubréka, Guinea 78 D2
Dubrovitsa = Dubrovytsya, Ukraine 41 G4
Dubrovnik, Croatia 21 N8
Dubrovskoye, Russia 45 D12

Dubrovytsya, Ukraine 41 G4
Dubuque, U.S.A. 108 D9
Duchang, China 53 C11
Duchesne, U.S.A. 110 F8
Duchess, Australia 90 C2
Ducie I., Pac. Oc. 93 K15
Duck Cr. →, Australia .. 88 D2
Duck Lake, Canada 101 C7
Duck Mountain Prov. Park, Canada 101 C8
Duckwall, Mt., U.S.A. .. 112 H6
Düdelange, Lux. 17 K8
Duderstadt, Germany ... 18 D6
Dudhi, India 61 G13
Dudinka, Russia 45 C9
Dudley, U.K. 13 E5
Dueñas, Spain 30 D6
Dueré, Brazil 123 D2
Duero = Douro →, Europe 30 D2
Duffel, Belgium 17 F5
Dufftown, U.K. 14 D5
Dufourspitz, Switz. 22 E5
Dugi Otok, Croatia 33 E12
Dugo Selo, Croatia 33 C13
Duifken Pt., Australia ... 90 A3
Duisburg, Germany 18 D2
Duitama, Colombia 120 B3
Duiveland, Neths. 17 E4
Duiwelskloof, S. Africa .. 85 C5
Duke I., U.S.A. 100 C2
Dukhān, Qatar 65 E6
Dukhovshchina, Russia .. 40 E7
Duki, Pakistan 60 D6
Duku, Bauchi, Nigeria .. 79 C7
Duku, Sokoto, Nigeria .. 79 C5
Dulag, Phil. 55 F6
Dulce →, Argentina 126 C3
Dulce, G., Costa Rica ... 116 E3
Dulf, Iraq 64 C5
Dŭlgopol, Bulgaria 38 F10
Dulit, Banjaran, Malaysia . 56 D4
Duliu, China 50 E9
Dullewala, Pakistan 62 D4
Dülmen, Germany 18 D3
Dulovo, Bulgaria 38 F10
Dululu, Australia 90 C5
Duluth, U.S.A. 108 B8
Dum Dum, India 63 H13
Dum Duma, India 61 F19
Dum Hadjer, Chad 73 F8
Dūmā, Lebanon 69 A4
Dūmā, Syria 69 B5
Dumaguete, Phil. 55 G5
Dumai, Indonesia 56 D2
Dumaran, Phil. 55 F3
Dumas, Ark., U.S.A. ... 109 J9
Dumas, Tex., U.S.A. ... 109 H4
Dumbarton, U.K. 14 F4
Dumbleyung, Australia . 89 F2
Dumfries, U.K. 14 F5
Dumfries & Galloway □, U.K. 14 F5
Dumka, India 63 G12
Dümmer See, Germany .. 18 C4
Dumoine →, Canada ... 98 C4
Dumoine L., Canada ... 98 C4
Dumraon, India 63 G11
Dumyât, Egypt 76 H7
Dumyât, Masabb, Egypt . 76 H7
Dún Dealgan = Dundalk, Ireland 15 B5
Dun Laoghaire, Ireland .. 15 C5
Dun-le-Palestel, France .. 26 B5
Dun-sur-Auron, France .. 25 F9
Duna = Dunărea →, Europe 41 K5
Duna →, Hungary 21 K8
Dunaföldvár, Hungary ... 21 J8
Dunaj = Dunărea →, Europe 41 K5
Dunaj →, Slovak Rep. .. 21 H9
Dunajec →, Poland 20 E10
Dunajska Streda, Slovak Rep. 21 H7
Dunapatai, Hungary ... 21 J9
Dunărea →, Europe ... 41 K5
Dunaújváros, Hungary .. 21 J8
Dunav = Dunărea →, Europe 41 K5
Dunav →, Serbia, Yug. .. 21 L11
Dunay, Russia 48 C6
Dunback, N.Z. 87 L3
Dunbar, Australia 90 B3
Dunbar, U.K. 14 E6
Dunblane, U.K. 14 E5
Duncan, Canada 100 D4
Duncan, Ariz., U.S.A. .. 111 K9
Duncan, Okla., U.S.A. .. 109 H6
Duncan, L., Canada 98 B4
Duncan L., Canada 100 A6
Duncan Town, Bahamas . 116 B4
Duncannon, U.S.A. 106 F7
Dundalk, Canada 106 B4
Dundalk, Ireland 15 B5
Dundalk Bay, Ireland ... 15 C5
Dundas, Canada 98 D4
Dundas, L., Australia ... 89 F3
Dundas I., Canada 100 C2
Dundas Str., Australia .. 88 B5
Dundee, S. Africa 85 D5
Dundee, U.K. 14 E6
Dundgovĭ □, Mongolia .. 50 B4
Dundoo, Australia 91 D3

Dundrum, U.K. 15 B6
Dundrum B., U.K. 15 B6
Dundwara, India 63 F8
Dunedin, N.Z. 87 L3
Dunedin, U.S.A. 105 L4
Dunfermline, U.K. 14 E5
Dungannon, Canada 106 C3
Dungannon, U.K. 15 B5
Dungannon □, U.K. 15 B5
Dungarpur, India 62 H5
Dungarvan, Ireland 15 D4
Dungarvan Harbour, Ireland 15 D4
Dungeness, U.K. 13 G8
Dungo, L. do, Angola ... 84 B2
Dungog, Australia 91 E5
Dungu, Zaïre 82 B2
Dungunâb, Sudan 76 C4
Dungunâb, Khalij, Sudan 76 C4
Dunhua, China 51 C15
Dunhuang, China 54 B4
Dunières, France 27 C8
Dunk I., Australia 90 B4
Dunkeld, U.K. 14 E5
Dunkerque, France 25 A9
Dunkery Beacon, U.K. .. 13 F4
Dunkirk = Dunkerque, France 25 A9
Dunkirk, U.S.A. 106 D5
Dunkuj, Sudan 77 E3
Dunkwa, Central, Ghana . 78 D4
Dunkwa, Central, Ghana . 79 D4
Dunlap, U.S.A. 108 E7
Dúnleary = Dun Laoghaire, Ireland 15 C5
Dunmanus B., Ireland ... 15 E2
Dunmara, Australia 90 B1
Dunmore, U.S.A. 107 E9
Dunmore Hd., Ireland ... 15 D1
Dunmore Town, Bahamas 116 A4
Dunn, U.S.A. 105 H6
Dunnellon, U.S.A. 105 L4
Dunnet Hd., U.K. 14 C5
Dunning, U.S.A. 108 E4
Dunnville, Canada 106 D5
Dunolly, Australia 91 F3
Dunoon, U.K. 14 F4
Dunqul, Egypt 76 C3
Duns, U.K. 14 F6
Dunseith, U.S.A. 108 A4
Dunsmuir, U.S.A. 110 F2
Dunstable, U.K. 13 F7
Dunstan Mts., N.Z. 87 L2
Dunster, Canada 100 C5
Dunvegan L., Canada ... 101 A7
Duolun, China 50 C9
Duong Dong, Vietnam ... 59 G4
Dupree, U.S.A. 108 C4
Dupuyer, U.S.A. 110 B7
Duque de Caxias, Brazil . 123 F3
Duque de York, I., Chile . 128 D1
Durack →, Australia 88 C4
Durack Ra., Australia ... 88 C4
Durağan, Turkey 66 B6
Durance →, France 27 E8
Durand, U.S.A. 104 D4
Durango = Victoria de Durango, Mexico ... 114 C4
Durango, Spain 28 B2
Durango, U.S.A. 111 H10
Durango □, Mexico 114 C4
Duranillin, Australia 89 F2
Durant, U.S.A. 109 J6
Duratón →, Spain 30 D6
Durazno, Uruguay 126 C4
Durazzo = Durrësi, Albania 39 H2
Durban, France 26 F6
Durban, S. Africa 85 D5
Dúrcal, Spain 31 J7
Düren, Germany 18 E2
Durg, India 61 J12
Durgapur, India 63 H12
Durham, Canada 98 D3
Durham, U.K. 12 C6
Durham, Calif., U.S.A. .. 112 F5
Durham, N.C., U.S.A. .. 105 G6
Durham □, U.K. 12 C6
Durham Downs, Australia 91 D4
Durmitor, Montenegro, Yug. 21 M9
Durness, U.K. 14 C4
Durrësi, Albania 39 H2
Durrie, Australia 90 D3
Dursunbey, Turkey 66 C3
Durtal, France 24 E6
Duru, Zaïre 82 B2
D'Urville, Tanjung, Indonesia 57 E9
D'Urville I., N.Z. 87 J4
Duryea, U.S.A. 107 E9
Dusa Mareb, Somali Rep. 68 F4
Dûsh, Egypt 76 C3
Dushak, Turkmenistan .. 44 F7
Dushan, China 52 E6
Dushanbe, Tajikistan ... 44 F7
Dusheti, Georgia 43 J7
Dusky Sd., N.Z. 87 L1
Dussejour, C., Australia . 88 B4
Düsseldorf, Germany ... 18 D2
Dussen, Neths. 16 E5
Dutch Harbor, U.S.A. ... 96 C3
Dutlwe, Botswana 84 C3
Dutsan Wai, Nigeria 79 C6
Dutton, Canada 106 D3
Dutton →, Australia 90 C3

Name	Page	Ref
Duved, *Sweden*	10	A6
Duvno, *Bos.-H.*	21	M7
Duyun, *China*	52	D6
Düzce, *Turkey*	66	B4
Duzdab = Zāhedān, *Iran*	65	D9
Dvina, Severnaya →, *Russia*	44	C5
Dvinsk = Daugavpils, *Latvia*	9	J22
Dvor, *Croatia*	33	C13
Dwarka, *India*	62	H3
Dwellingup, *Australia*	89	F2
Dwight, *Canada*	106	A5
Dwight, *U.S.A.*	104	E1
Dyatkovo, *Russia*	42	D2
Dyatlovo = Dzyatlava, *Belarus*	40	F3
Dyer, C., *Canada*	97	B13
Dyer Plateau, *Antarctica*	5	D17
Dyersburg, *U.S.A.*	109	G10
Dyfed □, *U.K.*	13	E3
Dyfi →, *U.K.*	13	E4
Dyje →, *Czech.*	20	G6
Dyle →, *Belgium*	17	G5
Dymer, *Ukraine*	41	G6
Dynevor Downs, *Australia*	91	D3
Dynów, *Poland*	20	F12
Dysart, *Canada*	101	C8
Dzamin Üüd, *Mongolia*	50	C6
Dzerzhinsk, *Russia*	42	B6
Dzhalinda, *Russia*	45	D13
Dzhambul = Zhambyl, *Kazakhstan*	44	E8
Dzhankoy, *Ukraine*	41	K8
Dzhanybek, *Kazakhstan*	42	F8
Dzhardzhan, *Russia*	45	C13
Dzharylhach, Ostriv, *Ukraine*	41	J7
Dzhetygara = Zhetiqara, *Kazakhstan*	44	D7
Dzhezkazgan = Zhezqazghan, *Kazakhstan*	44	E7
Dzhizak = Jizzakh, *Uzbekistan*	44	E7
Dzhugdzur, Khrebet, *Russia*	45	D14
Dzhvari = Jvari, *Georgia*	43	J6
Działdowa, *Poland*	20	B10
Działoszyn, *Poland*	20	D8
Dzierzgoń, *Poland*	20	B9
Dzierzoniów, *Poland*	20	E6
Dzilam de Bravo, *Mexico*	115	C7
Dzioua, *Algeria*	75	B6
Dzisna, *Belarus*	40	E5
Dzisna →, *Belarus*	40	E5
Dzungaria = Junggar Pendi, *China*	54	B3
Dzungarian Gate = Alataw Shankou, *China*	54	B3
Dzuumod, *Mongolia*	54	B5
Dzyarzhynsk, *Belarus*	40	F4
Dzyatlava, *Belarus*	40	F3

E

Name	Page	Ref
Eabamet, L., *Canada*	98	B2
Eads, *U.S.A.*	108	F3
Eagle, *U.S.A.*	110	G10
Eagle →, *Canada*	99	B8
Eagle Butte, *U.S.A.*	108	C4
Eagle Grove, *U.S.A.*	108	D8
Eagle L., *Calif., U.S.A.*	110	F3
Eagle L., *Maine, U.S.A.*	99	C6
Eagle Lake, *U.S.A.*	109	L6
Eagle Mountain, *U.S.A.*	113	M11
Eagle Nest, *U.S.A.*	111	H11
Eagle Pass, *U.S.A.*	109	L4
Eagle Pk., *U.S.A.*	112	G7
Eagle Pt., *Australia*	88	C3
Eagle River, *U.S.A.*	108	C10
Ealing, *U.K.*	13	F7
Earaheedy, *Australia*	89	E3
Earl Grey, *Canada*	101	C8
Earle, *U.S.A.*	109	H9
Earlimart, *U.S.A.*	113	K7
Earn →, *U.K.*	14	E5
Earn, L., *U.K.*	14	E4
Earnslaw, Mt., *N.Z.*	87	L2
Earth, *U.S.A.*	109	H3
Easley, *U.S.A.*	105	H4
East Angus, *Canada*	99	C5
East Aurora, *U.S.A.*	106	D6
East B., *U.S.A.*	109	L10
East Bengal, *Bangla.*	61	G17
East Beskids = Vychodné Beskydy, *Europe*	41	H2
East Brady, *U.S.A.*	106	F5
East C., *N.Z.*	87	G7
East Chicago, *U.S.A.*	104	E2
East China Sea, *Asia*	54	C7
East Coulee, *Canada*	100	C6
East Falkland, *Falk. Is.*	128	D5
East Grand Forks, *U.S.A.*	108	B6
East Greenwich, *U.S.A.*	107	E13
East Hartford, *U.S.A.*	107	E12
East Helena, *U.S.A.*	110	C8
East Indies, *Asia*	57	E6
East Jordan, *U.S.A.*	104	C3
East Lansing, *U.S.A.*	104	D3
East Liverpool, *U.S.A.*	106	F4
East London, *S. Africa*	85	E4
East Main = Eastmain, *Canada*	98	B4
East Orange, *U.S.A.*	107	F10
East Pacific Ridge, *Pac. Oc.*	93	J17
East Pakistan = Bangladesh ■, *Asia*	61	H17
East Palestine, *U.S.A.*	106	F4
East Pine, *Canada*	100	B4
East Point, *U.S.A.*	105	J3
East Providence, *U.S.A.*	107	E13
East Pt., *Canada*	99	C7
East Retford = Retford, *U.K.*	12	D7
East St. Louis, *U.S.A.*	108	F9
East Schelde →= Oosterschelde, *Neths.*	17	E4
East Siberian Sea, *Russia*	45	B17
East Stroudsburg, *U.S.A.*	107	E9
East Sussex □, *U.K.*	13	G8
East Tawas, *U.S.A.*	104	C4
East Toorale, *Australia*	91	E4
East Walker →, *U.S.A.*	112	G7
Eastbourne, *N.Z.*	87	J5
Eastbourne, *U.K.*	13	G8
Eastend, *Canada*	101	D7
Easter Islands = Pascua, I. de, *Pac. Oc.*	93	K17
Eastern □, *Kenya*	82	B4
Eastern □, *Uganda*	82	B3
Eastern Cape, *S. Africa*	84	E4
Eastern Cr. →, *Australia*	90	C3
Eastern Ghats, *India*	60	N11
Eastern Group = Lau Group, *Fiji*	87	C9
Eastern Group, *Australia*	89	F3
Eastern Province □, *S. Leone*	78	D2
Eastern Transvaal □, *S. Africa*	85	B5
Easterville, *Canada*	101	C9
Easthampton, *U.S.A.*	107	D12
Eastland, *U.S.A.*	109	J5
Eastmain, *Canada*	98	B4
Eastmain →, *Canada*	98	B4
Eastman, *Canada*	107	A12
Eastman, *U.S.A.*	105	J4
Easton, *Md., U.S.A.*	104	F7
Easton, *Pa., U.S.A.*	107	F9
Easton, *Wash., U.S.A.*	112	C5
Eastport, *U.S.A.*	99	D6
Eastsound, *U.S.A.*	112	B4
Eaton, *U.S.A.*	108	E2
Eatonia, *Canada*	101	C7
Eatonton, *U.S.A.*	105	J4
Eatontown, *U.S.A.*	107	F10
Eatonville, *U.S.A.*	112	D4
Eau Claire, *Fr. Guiana*	121	C7
Eau Claire, *U.S.A.*	108	C9
Eauze, *France*	26	E4
Ebagoola, *Australia*	90	A3
Eban, *Nigeria*	79	D5
Ebbw Vale, *U.K.*	13	F4
Ebeggui, *Algeria*	75	C6
Ebeltoft, *Denmark*	9	H14
Ebensburg, *U.S.A.*	106	F6
Ebensee, *Austria*	21	H3
Eber Gölü, *Turkey*	66	C4
Eberbach, *Germany*	19	F4
Eberswalde-Finow, *Germany*	18	C9
Ebetsu, *Japan*	48	C10
Ebian, *China*	52	C4
Ebikon, *Switz.*	23	B6
Ebingen, *Germany*	19	G5
Ebnat-Kappel, *Switz.*	23	B8
Eboli, *Italy*	35	B8
Ebolowa, *Cameroon*	79	E7
Ebrach, *Germany*	19	F6
Ébrié, Lagune, *Ivory C.*	78	D4
Ebro →, *Spain*	28	E5
Ebro, Pantano del, *Spain*	30	B7
Ebstorf, *Germany*	18	B6
Ecaussines-d' Enghien, *Belgium*	17	G4
Eceabat, *Turkey*	66	B2
Ech Cheliff, *Algeria*	75	A5
Echallens, *Switz.*	22	C3
Echeng, *China*	53	B10
Echigo-Sammyaku, *Japan*	49	F9
Echizen-Misaki, *Japan*	49	G7
Echmiadzin = Yejmiadzin, *Armenia*	43	K7
Echo Bay, *N.W.T., Canada*	96	B8
Echo Bay, *Ont., Canada*	98	C3
Echoing →, *Canada*	101	B10
Echt, *Neths.*	17	F7
Echternach, *Lux.*	17	J8
Echuca, *Australia*	91	F3
Ecija, *Spain*	31	H5
Eckernförde, *Germany*	18	A5
Eclipse Is., *Australia*	88	B4
Écommoy, *France*	24	E7
Ecoporanga, *Brazil*	123	E3
Écos, *France*	25	C8
Écouché, *France*	24	D6
Ecuador ■, *S. Amer.*	120	D2
Écueillé, *France*	24	E8
Ed, *Sweden*	11	F5
Ed Dabbura, *Sudan*	76	D3
Ed Dâmer, *Sudan*	76	D3
Ed Debba, *Sudan*	76	D3
Ed-Déffa, *Egypt*	76	A2
Ed Deim, *Sudan*	77	E2
Ed Dueim, *Sudan*	77	E3
Edah, *Australia*	89	E2
Edam, *Canada*	101	C7
Edam, *Neths.*	16	C6
Eday, *U.K.*	14	B6
Edd, *Eritrea*	68	E3
Eddrachillis B., *U.K.*	14	C3
Eddystone, *U.K.*	13	G3
Eddystone Pt., *Australia*	90	G4
Ede, *Neths.*	16	D7
Ede, *Nigeria*	79	D5
Édea, *Cameroon*	79	E7
Edegem, *Belgium*	17	F4
Edehon L., *Canada*	101	A9
Edekel, Adrar, *Algeria*	75	D6
Eden, *Australia*	91	F4
Eden, *N.C., U.S.A.*	105	G6
Eden, *N.Y., U.S.A.*	106	D6
Eden, *Tex., U.S.A.*	109	K5
Eden, *Wyo., U.S.A.*	110	E9
Eden →, *U.K.*	12	C4
Eden L., *Canada*	101	B8
Edenburg, *S. Africa*	84	D4
Edendale, *S. Africa*	85	D5
Edenderry, *Ireland*	15	C4
Edenton, *U.S.A.*	105	G7
Edenville, *S. Africa*	85	D4
Eder →, *Germany*	18	D5
Eder-Stausee, *Germany*	18	D5
Edgar, *U.S.A.*	108	E5
Edgartown, *U.S.A.*	107	E14
Edge Hill, *U.K.*	13	E6
Edgefield, *U.S.A.*	105	J5
Edgeley, *U.S.A.*	108	B5
Edgemont, *U.S.A.*	108	D3
Edgeøya, *Svalbard*	4	B9
Édhessa, *Greece*	39	J5
Ediévale, *N.Z.*	87	L2
Edina, *Liberia*	78	D2
Edina, *U.S.A.*	108	E8
Edinburg, *U.S.A.*	109	M5
Edinburgh, *U.K.*	14	F5
Ediniţa, *Moldova*	41	H4
Edirne, *Turkey*	66	B2
Edison, *U.S.A.*	112	B4
Edithburgh, *Australia*	91	F2
Edjeleh, *Algeria*	75	C6
Edjudina, *Australia*	89	E3
Edmeston, *U.S.A.*	107	D9
Edmond, *U.S.A.*	109	H6
Edmonds, *U.S.A.*	112	C4
Edmonton, *Australia*	90	B4
Edmonton, *Canada*	100	C6
Edmund L., *Canada*	101	C10
Edmundston, *Canada*	99	C6
Edna, *U.S.A.*	109	L6
Edna Bay, *U.S.A.*	100	B2
Edo □, *Nigeria*	79	D6
Edolo, *Italy*	32	B7
Edremit, *Turkey*	66	C2
Edremit Körfezi, *Turkey*	66	C2
Edsbyn, *Sweden*	10	C9
Edsele, *Sweden*	10	A10
Edson, *Canada*	100	C5
Eduardo Castex, *Argentina*	126	D3
Edward →, *Australia*	91	F3
Edward, L., *Africa*	82	C2
Edward I., *Canada*	98	C2
Edward River, *Australia*	90	A3
Edward VII Land, *Antarctica*	5	E13
Edwards, *U.S.A.*	113	L9
Edwards Plateau, *U.S.A.*	109	K4
Edwardsville, *U.S.A.*	107	E9
Edzo, *Canada*	100	A5
Eefde, *Neths.*	16	D8
Eekloo, *Belgium*	17	F3
Eelde, *Neths.*	16	B9
Eem →, *Neths.*	16	D6
Eems →, *Neths.*	16	B9
Eems Kanaal, *Neths.*	16	B9
Eenrum, *Neths.*	16	B8
Eerste Valthermond, *Neths.*	16	C9
Eersel, *Belgium*	17	F2
Eernegem, *Belgium*	17	F2
Eferi, *Algeria*	75	D6
Effingham, *U.S.A.*	104	F1
Effretikon, *Switz.*	23	B7
Eforie Sud, *Romania*	38	E11
Ega →, *Spain*	28	C3
Égadi, Ísole, *Italy*	34	E5
Eganville, *Canada*	98	C4
Egeland, *U.S.A.*	108	A5
Egenolf L., *Canada*	101	B9
Eger = Cheb, *Czech.*	20	E2
Eger, *Hungary*	21	H10
Eger →, *Hungary*	21	H10
Egersund, *Norway*	9	G12
Egg L., *Canada*	101	B7
Eggenburg, *Austria*	20	G5
Eggenfelden, *Germany*	19	G8
Eggiwil, *Switz.*	22	C5
Éghezée, *Belgium*	17	G5
Eginbah, *Australia*	88	D2
Égletons, *France*	26	C6
Eglisau, *Switz.*	23	A7
Egmond-aan-Zee, *Neths.*	16	C5
Egmont, C., *N.Z.*	87	H4
Egmont, Mt., *N.Z.*	87	H5
Eğridir, *Turkey*	66	D4
Eğridir Gölü, *Turkey*	66	D4
Egtved, *Denmark*	11	J3
Éguas →, *Brazil*	123	D3
Egume, *Nigeria*	79	D6
Éguzon, *France*	26	B5
Egvekinot, *Russia*	45	C19
Egypt ■, *Africa*	76	J7
Eha Amufu, *Nigeria*	79	D6
Ehime □, *Japan*	49	H6
Ehingen, *Germany*	19	G5
Ehrenberg, *U.S.A.*	113	M12
Ehrwald, *Austria*	19	H6
Eibar, *Spain*	28	B2
Eibergen, *Neths.*	16	D9
Eichstätt, *Germany*	19	G7
Eider →, *Germany*	18	A4
Eidsvold, *Australia*	91	D5
Eidsvoll, *Norway*	9	F14
Eifel, *Germany*	19	E2
Eiffel Flats, *Zimbabwe*	83	F3
Eigg, *U.K.*	14	E2
Eighty Mile Beach, *Australia*	88	C3
Eil, *Somali Rep.*	68	F4
Eil, L., *U.K.*	14	E3
Eildon, L., *Australia*	91	F4
Eileen L., *Canada*	101	A7
Eilenburg, *Germany*	18	D8
Ein el Luweiqa, *Sudan*	77	E3
Einasleigh, *Australia*	90	B3
Einasleigh →, *Australia*	90	B3
Einbeck, *Germany*	18	D5
Eindhoven, *Neths.*	17	F6
Einsiedeln, *Switz.*	23	B7
Eire = Ireland ■, *Europe*	15	D4
Eiríksjökull, *Iceland*	8	D3
Eirlandsche Gat, *Neths.*	16	B5
Eirunepé, *Brazil*	124	B4
Eisden, *Belgium*	17	G7
Eisenach, *Germany*	18	E6
Eisenberg, *Germany*	18	E7
Eisenerz, *Austria*	21	H4
Eisenhüttenstadt, *Germany*	18	C10
Eisenstadt, *Austria*	21	H6
Eiserfeld, *Germany*	18	E3
Eisfeld, *Germany*	18	E6
Eisleben, *Germany*	18	D7
Eivissa = Ibiza, *Spain*	36	C7
Ejby, *Denmark*	11	J3
Eje, Sierra del, *Spain*	30	C4
Ejea de los Caballeros, *Spain*	28	C3
Ejutla, *Mexico*	115	D5
Ekalaka, *U.S.A.*	108	C2
Ekeren, *Belgium*	17	F4
Eket, *Nigeria*	79	E6
Eketahuna, *N.Z.*	87	J5
Ekhínos, *Greece*	39	H8
Ekibastuz, *Kazakhstan*	44	D8
Ekimchan, *Russia*	45	D14
Ekoli, *Zaïre*	82	C1
Eksel, *Belgium*	17	F6
Eksjö, *Sweden*	9	H16
Ekwan →, *Canada*	98	B3
Ekwan Pt., *Canada*	98	B3
El Aaiún, *W. Sahara*	74	C2
El Aargub, *Mauritania*	74	D1
El Abiodh-Sidi-Cheikh, *Algeria*	75	B5
El 'Agrûd, *Egypt*	69	E3
El Aïoun, *Morocco*	75	B4
El 'Aiyat, *Egypt*	76	J7
El Alamein, *Egypt*	76	H6
El 'Aqaba, W. →, *Egypt*	69	E2
El 'Arag, *Egypt*	76	B2
El Arahal, *Spain*	31	H5
El Arenal, *Spain*	36	B9
El Aricha, *Algeria*	75	B4
El Arīhā, *West Bank*	69	D4
El Arish, *Australia*	90	B4
El 'Arîsh, *Egypt*	69	D2
El 'Arîsh, W. →, *Egypt*	69	D2
El Arrouch, *Algeria*	75	A6
El Asnam = Ech Cheliff, *Algeria*	75	A5
El Astillero, *Spain*	30	B7
El Badâri, *Egypt*	76	B3
El Bahrein, *Egypt*	76	B2
El Ballâs, *Egypt*	76	B3
El Balyana, *Egypt*	76	B3
El Banco, *Colombia*	120	B3
El Baqeir, *Sudan*	76	D3
El Barco de Ávila, *Spain*	30	E5
El Barco de Valdeorras, *Spain*	30	C4
El Bauga, *Sudan*	76	D3
El Baúl, *Venezuela*	120	B4
El Bawiti, *Egypt*	76	J6
El Bayadh, *Algeria*	75	B5
El Bierzo, *Spain*	30	C4
El Bluff, *Nic.*	116	D3
El Bolsón, *Argentina*	128	B2
El Bonillo, *Spain*	29	G2
El Brûk, W. →, *Egypt*	69	E2
El Buheirat □, *Sudan*	77	F2
El Caín, *Argentina*	128	B3
El Cajon, *U.S.A.*	113	N10
El Callao, *Venezuela*	121	B5
El Camp, *Spain*	28	D6
El Campo, *U.S.A.*	109	L6
El Carmen, *Bolivia*	125	C5
El Carmen, *Venezuela*	120	C4
El Castillo, *Spain*	31	H4
El Centro, *U.S.A.*	113	N11
El Cerro, *Bolivia*	125	D5
El Cerro, *Spain*	31	H4
El Cocuy, *Colombia*	120	B3
El Compadre, *Mexico*	113	N10
El Corcovado, *Argentina*	128	B2
El Coronil, *Spain*	31	H5
El Cuy, *Argentina*	128	A3
El Cuyo, *Mexico*	115	C7
El Dab'a, *Egypt*	76	H6
El Daheir, *Egypt*	69	D3
El Deir, *Egypt*	76	B3
El Dere, *Somali Rep.*	68	G4
El Descanso, *Mexico*	113	N10
El Desemboque, *Mexico*	114	A2
El Dilingat, *Egypt*	76	H7
El Diviso, *Colombia*	120	C2
El Djem, *Tunisia*	75	A7
El Djouf, *Mauritania*	72	E3
El Dorado, *Ark., U.S.A.*	109	J8
El Dorado, *Kans., U.S.A.*	109	G6
El Dorado, *Venezuela*	121	B5
El Eglab, *Algeria*	74	C4
El Escorial, *Spain*	30	E6
El Eulma, *Algeria*	75	A6
El Faiyûm, *Egypt*	76	J7
El Fâsher, *Sudan*	77	E2
El Fashn, *Egypt*	76	J7
El Ferrol, *Spain*	30	B2
El Fîfi, *Sudan*	77	E1
El Fuerte, *Mexico*	114	B3
El Gal, *Somali Rep.*	68	E5
El Gebir, *Sudan*	77	E2
El Gedida, *Egypt*	76	B2
El Geteina, *Sudan*	77	E3
El Gezira □, *Sudan*	77	E3
El Gîza, *Egypt*	76	H7
El Goléa, *Algeria*	75	B5
El Hadeb, *W. Sahara*	74	C2
El Hadjira, *Algeria*	75	B6
El Hagiz, *Sudan*	77	D4
El Hajeb, *Morocco*	74	B3
El Hammam, *Egypt*	76	H6
El Hammâmi, *Mauritania*	74	D2
El Hank, *Mauritania*	74	D3
El Hasian, *W. Sahara*	74	C2
El Hawata, *Sudan*	77	E3
El Heiz, *Egypt*	76	B2
El 'Idisât, *Egypt*	76	B3
El Iskandarîya, *Egypt*	76	H6
El Jadida, *Morocco*	74	B3
El Jebelein, *Sudan*	77	E3
El Kab, *Sudan*	76	D3
El Kabrît, G., *Egypt*	69	F2
El Kala, *Algeria*	75	A6
El Kalâa, *Morocco*	74	B3
El Kamlin, *Sudan*	77	D3
El Kantara, *Algeria*	75	A6
El Kantara, *Tunisia*	75	B7
El Karaba, *Sudan*	76	D3
El Kef, *Tunisia*	75	A6
El Khandaq, *Sudan*	76	D3
El Khârga, *Egypt*	76	B3
El Khartûm, *Sudan*	77	D3
El Khartûm □, *Sudan*	77	D3
El Khartûm Bahrî, *Sudan*	77	D3
El Khroub, *Algeria*	75	A6
El Kseur, *Algeria*	75	A6
El Ksiba, *Morocco*	74	B3
El Kuntilla, *Egypt*	69	E3
El Laqâwa, *Sudan*	77	E2
El Laqeita, *Egypt*	76	B3
El Leiya, *Sudan*	77	D4
El Mafâza, *Sudan*	77	E3
El Mahalla el Kubra, *Egypt*	76	H7
El Mahârîq, *Egypt*	76	B3
El Mahmûdîya, *Egypt*	76	H7
El Maitén, *Argentina*	128	B2
El Maiz, *Algeria*	75	C4
El-Maks el-Bahari, *Egypt*	76	C3
El Manshâh, *Egypt*	76	B3
El Mansour, *Algeria*	75	C4
El Mansûra, *Egypt*	76	H7
El Mantico, *Venezuela*	121	B5
El Manzala, *Egypt*	76	H7
El Marâgha, *Egypt*	76	B3
El Masid, *Sudan*	77	D3
El Matariya, *Egypt*	76	H8
El Medano, *Canary Is.*	36	F3
El Meghaier, *Algeria*	75	B6
El Meraguen, *Algeria*	75	C4
El Metemma, *Sudan*	77	D3
El Miamo, *Venezuela*	121	B5
El Milagro, *Argentina*	126	C2
El Milia, *Algeria*	75	A6
El Minyâ, *Egypt*	76	J7
El Molar, *Spain*	28	E1
El Mreyye, *Mauritania*	78	B3
El Obeid, *Sudan*	77	E3
El Odaiya, *Sudan*	77	E2
El Oro, *Mexico*	115	D4
El Oro □, *Ecuador*	120	D2
El Oued, *Algeria*	75	B6
El Palmar, *Bolivia*	125	D5
El Palmar, *Venezuela*	121	B5
El Palmito, Presa, *Mexico*	114	B3
El Panadés, *Spain*	28	D6
El Pardo, *Spain*	30	E7
El Paso, *U.S.A.*	111	L10
El Paso Robles, *U.S.A.*	112	K6
El Pedernoso, *Spain*	29	F2
El Pedroso, *Spain*	31	H5
El Pobo de Dueñas, *Spain*	28	E3
El Portal, *U.S.A.*	111	H4
El Prat de Llobregat, *Spain*	28	D7
El Progreso, *Honduras*	116	C2
El Provencio, *Spain*	29	F2
El Pueblito, *Mexico*	114	B3
El Pueblo, *Canary Is.*	36	F2
El Puerto de Santa María, *Spain*	31	J4
El Qâhira, *Egypt*	76	H7
El Qantara, *Egypt*	69	E1
El Qasr, *Egypt*	76	B2
El Quseima, *Egypt*	69	E3
El Qusîya, *Egypt*	76	B3
El Râshda, *Egypt*	76	B2
El Reno, *U.S.A.*	109	H6
El Ribero, *Spain*	30	C2
El Rîdisiya, *Egypt*	76	C3
El Rio, *U.S.A.*	113	L7

El Ronquillo, *Spain*	31	H4
El Roque, Pta., *Canary Is.*	36	F4
El Rosarito, *Mexico*	114	B2
El Rubio, *Spain*	31	H5
El Saff, *Egypt*	76	J7
El Saheira, W. →, *Egypt*	69	E2
El Salto, *Mexico*	114	C3
El Salvador ■, *Cent. Amer.*	116	D2
El Sancejo, *Spain*	31	H5
El Sauce, *Nic.*	116	D2
El Shallal, *Egypt*	76	C3
El Simbillawein, *Egypt*	76	H7
El Sombrero, *Venezuela*	120	B4
El Suweis, *Egypt*	76	J8
El Tamarâni, W. →, *Egypt*	69	F3
El Thamad, *Egypt*	69	F3
El Tigre, *Venezuela*	121	B5
El Tîh, G., *Egypt*	69	F2
El Tina, Khalîg, *Egypt*	69	D1
El Tocuyo, *Venezuela*	120	B4
El Tofo, *Chile*	126	B1
El Tránsito, *Chile*	126	B1
El Turbio, *Argentina*	128	D2
El Uqsur, *Egypt*	76	B3
El Vado, *Spain*	28	D1
El Vallés, *Spain*	28	D7
El Venado, *Mexico*	114	C4
El Vigía, *Venezuela*	120	B3
El Wabeira, *Egypt*	69	F2
El Wak, *Kenya*	82	B5
El Waqf, *Egypt*	76	B3
El Wâsta, *Egypt*	76	J7
El Weguet, *Ethiopia*	77	F5
El Wuz, *Sudan*	77	D3
Elafónisos, *Greece*	39	N5
Élassa, *Greece*	39	P9
Elassón, *Greece*	39	K5
Elat, *Israel*	69	F3
Elâzığ, *Turkey*	67	C8
Elba, *Italy*	32	F7
Elba, *U.S.A.*	105	K2
Elbasani, *Albania*	39	H3
Elbe, *U.S.A.*	112	D4
Elbe →, *Europe*	18	B4
Elbe-Seiten Kanal, *Germany*	18	C6
Elbert, Mt., *U.S.A.*	111	G10
Elberta, *U.S.A.*	104	C2
Elberton, *U.S.A.*	105	H4
Elbeuf, *France*	24	C8
Elbing = Elbląg, *Poland*	20	A9
Elbistan, *Turkey*	66	C7
Elbląg, *Poland*	20	A9
Elbow, *Canada*	101	C7
Elbrus, *Asia*	43	J6
Elburg, *Neths.*	16	D7
Elburz Mts. = Alborz, Reshteh-ye Kühhä-ye, *Iran*	65	C7
Elche, *Spain*	29	G4
Elche de la Sierra, *Spain*	29	G2
Elcho I., *Australia*	90	A2
Elda, *Spain*	29	G4
Eldon, *Mo., U.S.A.*	108	F8
Eldon, *Wash., U.S.A.*	112	C3
Eldora, *U.S.A.*	108	D8
Eldorado, *Argentina*	127	B5
Eldorado, *Canada*	101	B7
Eldorado, *Mexico*	114	C3
Eldorado, *Ill., U.S.A.*	104	G1
Eldorado, *Tex., U.S.A.*	109	K4
Eldorado Springs, *U.S.A.*	109	G8
Eldoret, *Kenya*	82	B4
Eldred, *U.S.A.*	106	E6
Elea, C., *Cyprus*	37	D13
Electra, *U.S.A.*	109	H5
Elefantes →, *Mozam.*	85	C5
Elefantes, G., *Chile*	128	C2
Elektrogorsk, *Russia*	42	C4
Elektrostal, *Russia*	42	C4
Elele, *Nigeria*	79	D6
Elephant Butte Reservoir, *U.S.A.*	111	K10
Elephant I., *Antarctica*	5	C18
Elesbão Veloso, *Brazil*	122	C3
Eleşkirt, *Turkey*	67	C10
Eleuthera, *Bahamas*	116	A4
Elgepiggen, *Norway*	10	B5
Elgeyo-Marakwet □, *Kenya*	82	B4
Elgg, *Switz.*	23	B7
Elgin, *N.B., Canada*	99	C6
Elgin, *Ont., Canada*	107	B8
Elgin, *U.K.*	14	D5
Elgin, *Ill., U.S.A.*	104	D1
Elgin, *N. Dak., U.S.A.*	108	B4
Elgin, *Nebr., U.S.A.*	108	E5
Elgin, *Nev., U.S.A.*	111	H6
Elgin, *Oreg., U.S.A.*	110	D5
Elgin, *Tex., U.S.A.*	109	K6
Elgon, Mt., *Africa*	82	B3
Eliase, *Indonesia*	57	F8
Elida, *U.S.A.*	109	J3
Elikón, *Greece*	39	L5
Elim, *S. Africa*	84	E2
Elisabethville = Lubumbashi, *Zaïre*	83	E2
Eliseu Martins, *Brazil*	122	C3
Elista, *Russia*	43	G7
Elizabeth, *Australia*	91	E2
Elizabeth, *U.S.A.*	107	F10
Elizabeth City, *U.S.A.*	105	G7
Elizabethton, *U.S.A.*	105	G4
Elizabethtown, *Ky., U.S.A.*	104	G3
Elizabethtown, *N.Y., U.S.A.*	107	B11
Elizabethtown, *Pa., U.S.A.*	107	F8

Elizondo, *Spain*	28	B3
Ełk, *Poland*	20	B12
Elk City, *U.S.A.*	109	H5
Elk Creek, *U.S.A.*	112	F4
Elk Grove, *U.S.A.*	112	G5
Elk Island Nat. Park, *Canada*	100	C6
Elk Lake, *Canada*	98	C3
Elk Point, *Canada*	101	C6
Elk River, *Idaho, U.S.A.*	110	C5
Elk River, *Minn., U.S.A.*	108	C8
Elkedra, *Australia*	90	C2
Elkedra →, *Australia*	90	C2
Elkhart, *Ind., U.S.A.*	104	E3
Elkhart, *Kans., U.S.A.*	109	G4
Elkhorn, *Canada*	101	D8
Elkhorn →, *U.S.A.*	108	E6
Elkhovo, *Bulgaria*	38	G9
Elkin, *U.S.A.*	105	G5
Elkins, *U.S.A.*	104	F6
Elko, *Canada*	100	D5
Elko, *U.S.A.*	110	F6
Ell, L., *Australia*	89	E4
Ellecom, *Neths.*	16	D8
Ellef Ringnes I., *Canada*	4	B2
Ellendale, *Australia*	88	C3
Ellendale, *U.S.A.*	108	B5
Ellensburg, *U.S.A.*	110	C3
Ellenville, *U.S.A.*	107	E10
Ellery, Mt., *Australia*	91	F4
Ellesmere, L., *N.Z.*	87	M4
Ellesmere I., *Canada*	4	B4
Ellesmere Port, *U.K.*	12	D5
Ellezelles, *Belgium* ■	17	G3
Ellice Is. = Tuvalu ■, *Pac. Oc.*	92	H9
Ellinwood, *U.S.A.*	108	F5
Elliot, *Australia*	90	B1
Elliot, *S. Africa*	85	E4
Elliotdale = Xhora, *S. Africa*	85	E4
Ellis, *U.S.A.*	108	F5
Elliston, *Australia*	91	E1
Ellisville, *U.S.A.*	109	K10
Ellon, *U.K.*	14	D6
Ells →, *Canada*	100	B6
Ellsworth, *U.S.A.*	108	F5
Ellsworth Land, *Antarctica*	5	D16
Ellsworth Mts., *Antarctica*	5	D16
Ellwangen, *Germany*	19	G6
Ellwood City, *U.S.A.*	106	F4
Elm, *Switz.*	23	C8
Elma, *Canada*	101	D9
Elma, *U.S.A.*	112	D3
Elmadağ, *Turkey*	66	C5
Elmalı, *Turkey*	66	D3
Elmhurst, *U.S.A.*	104	E2
Elmina, *Ghana*	79	D4
Elmira, *Canada*	106	C4
Elmira, *U.S.A.*	106	D8
Elmore, *Australia*	91	F3
Elmore, *U.S.A.*	113	M11
Elmshorn, *Germany*	18	B5
Elmvale, *Canada*	106	B5
Elne, *France*	26	F6
Elora, *Canada*	106	C4
Elorza, *Venezuela*	120	B4
Eloúnda, *Greece*	37	D7
Eloy, *U.S.A.*	111	K8
Éloyes, *France*	25	D13
Elrose, *Canada*	101	C7
Elsas, *Canada*	98	C3
Elsie, *Canada*	112	E3
Elsinore = Helsingør, *Denmark*	11	H6
Elsinore, *U.S.A.*	111	G7
Elspe, *Germany*	18	D4
Elspeet, *Neths.*	16	D7
Elst, *Neths.*	16	E7
Elster →, *Germany*	18	D7
Elsterwerda, *Germany*	18	D9
Elten, *Neths.*	16	E8
Eltham, *N.Z.*	87	H5
Elton, *Russia*	43	F8
Elton, Ozero, *Russia*	43	F8
Eluanbi, *Taiwan*	53	G13
Eluru, *India*	61	L12
Elvas, *Portugal*	31	G3
Elven, *France*	24	E4
Elverum, *Norway*	10	D5
Elvire →, *Australia*	88	C4
Elvo →, *Italy*	32	C5
Elvran, *Norway*	10	A5
Elwood, *Ind., U.S.A.*	104	E3
Elwood, *Nebr., U.S.A.*	108	E5
Elx = Elche, *Spain*	29	G4
Ely, *U.K.*	13	E8
Ely, *Minn., U.S.A.*	108	B9
Ely, *Nev., U.S.A.*	110	G6
Elyria, *U.S.A.*	106	E2
Elz →, *Germany*	19	G3
Emāmrūd, *Iran*	65	B7
Emba = Embi, *Kazakhstan*	44	E6
Emba = Embi →, *Kazakhstan*	44	E6
Embarcación, *Argentina*	126	A3
Embarras Portage, *Canada*	101	B6
Embetsu, *Japan*	48	B10
Embi, *Kazakhstan*	44	E6
Embi →, *Kazakhstan*	44	E6
Embira →, *Brazil*	124	B3
Embóna, *Greece*	37	C9
Embrach, *Switz.*	23	A7
Embrun, *France*	27	D10
Embu, *Kenya*	82	C4

Embu □, *Kenya*	82	C4
Emden, *Germany*	18	B3
Emerald, *Australia*	90	C4
Emerson, *Canada*	101	D9
Emery, *U.S.A.*	111	G8
Emet, *Turkey*	66	C3
Emi Koussi, *Chad*	73	E8
Emília-Romagna □, *Italy*	32	D7
Emílius, Mte., *Italy*	32	C4
Eminabad, *Pakistan*	62	C6
Emirdağ, *Turkey*	66	C4
Emlembe, *Swazi.*	85	D5
Emlenton, *U.S.A.*	106	E5
Emlichheim, *Germany*	18	C2
Emme →, *Switz.*	22	B5
Emmeloord, *Neths.*	16	C7
Emmen, *Neths.*	16	C9
Emmendingen, *Germany*	19	G3
Emmental, *Switz.*	22	C4
Emmer-Compascuum, *Neths.*	16	C10
Emmerich, *Germany*	18	D2
Emmet, *Australia*	90	C3
Emmetsburg, *U.S.A.*	108	D7
Emmett, *U.S.A.*	110	E5
Empalme, *Mexico*	114	B2
Empangeni, *S. Africa*	85	D5
Empedrado, *Argentina*	126	B4
Emperor Seamount Chain, *Pac. Oc.*	92	D9
Empoli, *Italy*	32	E7
Emporia, *Kans., U.S.A.*	108	F6
Emporia, *Va., U.S.A.*	105	G7
Emporium, *U.S.A.*	106	E6
Empress, *Canada*	101	C6
Emptinne, *Belgium*	17	H6
Empty Quarter = Rub' al Khali, *Si. Arabia*	68	D4
Ems →, *Germany*	18	B3
Emsdale, *Canada*	106	A5
Emsdetten, *Germany*	18	C3
Emu, *China*	51	C15
Emu Park, *Australia*	90	C5
'En 'Avrona, *Israel*	69	F3
En Nahud, *Sudan*	77	E2
Ena, *Japan*	49	G8
Enafors, *Sweden*	10	A6
Enambú, *Colombia*	120	C3
Enana, *Namibia*	84	B2
Enånger, *Sweden*	10	C11
Enaratoli, *Indonesia*	57	E9
Enard B., *U.K.*	14	C3
Enare = Inarijärvi, *Finland*	8	B22
Encantadas, Serra, *Brazil*	127	C5
Encanto, C., *Phil.*	57	A6
Encarnación, *Paraguay*	127	B4
Encarnación de Diaz, *Mexico*	114	C4
Enchi, *Ghana*	78	D4
Encinal, *U.S.A.*	109	L5
Encinitas, *U.S.A.*	113	M9
Encino, *U.S.A.*	111	J11
Encontrados, *Venezuela*	120	B3
Encounter B., *Australia*	91	F2
Encruzilhada, *Brazil*	123	E3
Ende, *Indonesia*	57	F6
Endeavour, *Canada*	101	C8
Endeavour Str., *Australia*	90	A3
Endelave, *Denmark*	11	J4
Enderbury I., *Kiribati*	92	H10
Enderby, *Canada*	100	C5
Enderby I., *Australia*	88	D2
Enderby Land, *Antarctica*	5	C5
Enderlin, *U.S.A.*	108	B6
Endicott, *N.Y., U.S.A.*	107	D8
Endicott, *Wash., U.S.A.*	110	C5
Endimari →, *Brazil*	124	B4
Endyalgout I., *Australia*	88	B5
Ene →, *Peru*	124	C3
Enewetak Atoll, *Pac. Oc.*	92	F8
Enez, *Turkey*	66	B2
Enfield, *U.K.*	13	F7
Engadin, *Switz.*	19	J6
Engaño, C., *Dom. Rep.*	117	C6
Engaño, C., *Phil.*	57	A6
Engcobo, *S. Africa*	85	E4
Engelberg, *Switz.*	23	C6
Engels, *Russia*	42	E8
Engemann L., *Canada*	101	B7
Enger, *Norway*	10	D4
Enggano, *Indonesia*	56	F2
Enghien, *Belgium*	17	G4
Engil, *Morocco*	74	B4
Engkilili, *Malaysia*	56	D4
England □, *U.K.*	109	H9
England □, *U.K.*	7	E5
Englee, *Canada*	99	B8
Englehart, *Canada*	98	C4
Engler L., *Canada*	101	B7
Englewood, *Colo., U.S.A.*	108	F2
Englewood, *Kans., U.S.A.*	109	G5
English →, *Canada*	101	C10
English Bazar = Ingraj Bazar, *India*	63	G13
English Channel, *Europe*	13	G6
English River, *Canada*	98	C1
Enguri →, *Georgia*	43	J5
Enid, *U.S.A.*	109	G6
Enipévs →, *Greece*	39	K5
Enkhuizen, *Neths.*	16	C6
Enköping, *Sweden*	10	E11
Enle, *China*	52	E3
Enna, *Italy*	35	E7
Ennadai, *Canada*	101	A8
Ennadai L., *Canada*	101	A8
Ennedi, *Chad*	73	E9
Enngonia, *Australia*	91	D4
Ennis, *Ireland*	15	D3

Ennis, *Mont., U.S.A.*	110	D8
Ennis, *Tex., U.S.A.*	109	J6
Enniscorthy, *Ireland*	15	D5
Enniskillen, *U.K.*	15	B4
Ennistimon, *Ireland*	15	D2
Enns →, *Austria*	21	G4
Enontekiö, *Finland*	8	B20
Enping, *China*	53	F9
Enriquillo, L., *Dom. Rep.*	117	C5
Ens, *Neths.*	16	C7
Enschede, *Neths.*	16	D9
Ensenada, *Argentina*	126	C4
Ensenada, *Mexico*	114	A1
Enshi, *China*	52	B7
Ensiola, Pta., *Spain*	36	B9
Ensisheim, *France*	25	E14
Entebbe, *Uganda*	82	B3
Enter, *Neths.*	16	D9
Enterprise, *Canada*	100	A5
Enterprise, *Oreg., U.S.A.*	110	D5
Enterprise, *Utah, U.S.A.*	111	H7
Entlebuch, *Switz.*	22	C6
Entre Ríos, *Bolivia*	126	A3
Entre Rios, *Bahia, Brazil*	123	D4
Entre Ríos, *Pará, Brazil*	125	D7
Entre Ríos □, *Argentina*	126	C4
Entrepeñas, Pantano de, *Spain*	28	E2
Enugu, *Nigeria*	79	D6
Enugu □, *Nigeria*	79	D6
Enugu Ezike, *Nigeria*	79	D6
Enumclaw, *U.S.A.*	112	C5
Envermeu, *France*	24	C8
Envigado, *Colombia*	120	B2
Envira, *Brazil*	124	B3
Enz →, *Germany*	19	F5
Enza →, *Italy*	32	D7
Eólie, Ís., *Italy*	35	D7
Epanomí, *Greece*	39	J5
Epe, *Neths.*	16	D7
Epe, *Nigeria*	79	D5
Épernay, *France*	25	C10
Épernon, *France*	25	D8
Ephesus, *Turkey*	66	D2
Ephraim, *U.S.A.*	110	G8
Ephrata, *U.S.A.*	110	C4
Épila, *Spain*	28	D3
Épinac-les-Mines, *France*	25	F11
Épinal, *France*	25	D13
Epira, *Guyana*	121	B6
Episkopi, *Cyprus*	37	E11
Episkopí, *Greece*	37	D6
Episkopi Bay, *Cyprus*	37	E11
Eppan = Appiano, *Italy*	33	B8
Epping, *U.K.*	13	F8
Epukiro, *Namibia*	84	C2
Equatorial Guinea ■, *Africa*	80	D1
Equeipa, *Venezuela*	121	B5
Er Rahad, *Sudan*	77	E3
Er Rif, *Morocco*	75	A4
Er Roseires, *Sudan*	77	E3
Erāwadī Myit = Irrawaddy →, *Burma*	61	M19
Erba, *Italy*	32	C6
Erba, *Sudan*	76	D4
Erbaa, *Turkey*	66	B7
Erbil = Arbīl, *Iraq*	67	D11
Erçiş, *Turkey*	67	C10
Erdao Jiang →, *China*	51	C14
Erdek, *Turkey*	66	B2
Erdemli, *Turkey*	66	D6
Erdene, *Mongolia*	50	B6
Erding, *Germany*	19	G7
Erdre →, *France*	24	E5
Erebato →, *Venezuela*	121	B5
Erebus, Mt., *Antarctica*	5	D11
Erechim, *Brazil*	127	B5
Ereğli, *Konya, Turkey*	66	D6
Ereğli, *Zonguldak, Turkey*	66	B4
Erei, Monti, *Italy*	35	E7
Erembodegem, *Belgium*	17	G4
Erenhot, *China*	50	C7
Eresma →, *Spain*	30	D6
Erewadi Myitwanya, *Burma*	61	M19
Erfenisdam, *S. Africa*	84	D4
Erft →, *Germany*	18	D2
Erfoud, *Morocco*	74	B4
Erft →, *Germany*	18	D2
Erfurt, *Germany*	18	E7
Ergani, *Turkey*	67	C8
Ergeni Vozvyshennost, *Russia*	43	G7
Ērgli, *Latvia*	9	H21
Eria →, *Spain*	30	C5
Eriba, *Sudan*	77	D4
Eriboll, L., *U.K.*	14	C4
Erica, *Neths.*	16	C9
Érice, *Italy*	34	D5
Erie, *U.S.A.*	106	D4
Erie, L., *N. Amer.*	106	D3
Erie Canal, *U.S.A.*	106	C6
Erieau, *Canada*	106	D3
Erigavo, *Somali Rep.*	68	E4
Erikoúsa, *Greece*	37	A3
Eriksdale, *Canada*	101	C9
Erikslund, *Sweden*	10	B9
Erímanthos, *Greece*	39	M4
Erimo-misaki, *Japan*	48	D11
Eriswil, *Switz.*	22	B5
Erithraí, *Greece*	39	L6
Eritrea ■, *Africa*	77	E4
Erjas →, *Portugal*	31	F3
Erlangen, *Germany*	19	F7
Erldunda, *Australia*	90	D1
Erlin, *Taiwan*	53	F13
Ermelo, *Neths.*	16	D7
Ermelo, *S. Africa*	85	D4

Ermenak, *Turkey*	66	D5
Ermióni, *Greece*	39	M6
Ermones, *Greece*	37	A3
Ermoúpolis = Síros, *Greece*	39	M7
Ernakulam = Cochin, *India*	60	Q10
Erne →, *Ireland*	15	B3
Erne, Lower L., *U.K.*	15	B4
Erne, Upper L., *U.K.*	15	B4
Ernée, *France*	24	D6
Ernest Giles Ra., *Australia*	89	E3
Ernstberg, *Germany*	19	E2
Erode, *India*	60	P10
Eromanga, *Australia*	91	D3
Erongo, *Namibia*	84	C2
Erp, *Neths.*	17	E7
Erquelinnes, *Belgium*	17	H4
Erquy, *France*	24	D4
Erquy, C. d', *France*	24	D4
Err, Piz d', *Switz.*	23	C9
Errabiddy, *Australia*	89	E2
Erramala Hills, *India*	60	M11
Errer →, *Ethiopia*	77	F5
Errigal, *Ireland*	15	A3
Erris Hd., *Ireland*	15	B1
Erseka, *Albania*	39	J3
Erskine, *U.S.A.*	108	B7
Erstein, *France*	25	D14
Erstfeld, *Switz.*	23	C7
Ertil, *Russia*	42	E5
Ertis = Irtysh →, *Russia*	44	C7
Ertvelde, *Belgium*	17	F3
Eruh, *Turkey*	67	D10
Eruwa, *Nigeria*	79	D5
Ervy-le-Châtel, *France*	25	D10
Erwin, *U.S.A.*	105	G4
Eryuan, *China*	52	D2
Erzgebirge, *Germany*	18	E9
Erzin, *Russia*	45	D10
Erzincan, *Turkey*	67	C8
Erzurum, *Turkey*	67	C9
Es Caló, *Spain*	36	C8
Es Caná, *Spain*	36	B8
Es Sahrâ' Esh Sharqîya, *Egypt*	76	B3
Es Sînâ', *Egypt*	76	J8
Es Sûkî, *Sudan*	77	E3
Esambo, *Zaïre*	82	C1
Esan-Misaki, *Japan*	48	D10
Esashi, *Hokkaidō, Japan*	48	B11
Esashi, *Hokkaidō, Japan*	48	D10
Esbjerg, *Denmark*	11	J2
Escada, *Brazil*	122	C4
Escalante, *U.S.A.*	111	H8
Escalante →, *U.S.A.*	111	H8
Escalón, *Mexico*	114	B4
Escalona, *Spain*	30	E6
Escambia →, *U.S.A.*	105	K2
Escanaba, *U.S.A.*	104	C2
Escaut →, *Belgium*	17	F3
Esch-sur-Alzette, *Lux.*	17	J7
Eschede, *Germany*	18	C6
Escholzmatt, *Switz.*	22	C5
Eschwege, *Germany*	18	D6
Eschweiler, *Germany*	18	E2
Escocia, *Bolivia*	124	E4
Escondido, *U.S.A.*	113	M9
Escuinapa, *Mexico*	114	C3
Escuintla, *Guatemala*	116	D1
Eséka, *Cameroon*	79	E7
Esens, *Germany*	18	B3
Esera →, *Spain*	28	C5
Eşfahān, *Iran*	65	C6
Eşfahān □, *Iran*	65	C6
Esfīdeh, *Iran*	65	C8
Esgueva →, *Spain*	30	D6
Esh Sham = Dimashq, *Syria*	69	B5
Esh Shamâlîya □, *Sudan*	76	D2
Eshan, *China*	52	E4
Eshowe, *S. Africa*	85	D5
Esiama, *Ghana*	78	E4
Esil = Ishim →, *Russia*	44	D8
Esino →, *Italy*	33	E10
Esk →, *Cumb., U.K.*	14	G5
Esk →, *N. Yorks., U.K.*	12	C7
Eskifjörður, *Iceland*	8	D7
Eskilstuna, *Sweden*	10	E10
Eskimalatya, *Turkey*	67	C8
Eskimo Pt., *Canada*	101	A10
Eskişehir, *Turkey*	66	C4
Esla →, *Spain*	30	D4
Esla, Pantano del, *Spain*	30	D4
Eslāmābād-e Gharb, *Iran*	67	E12
Eslöv, *Sweden*	11	J7
Eşme, *Turkey*	66	C3
Esmeralda, I., *Chile*	128	C1
Esmeraldas, *Ecuador*	120	C2
Esmeraldas □, *Ecuador*	120	C2
Esneux, *Belgium*	17	G7
Espada, Pta., *Colombia*	120	A3
Espalion, *France*	26	D6
Espalmador, I., *Spain*	36	C7
Espanola, *Canada*	98	C3
Espardell, I. del, *Spain*	36	C7
Esparraguera, *Spain*	28	D6
Esparta, *Costa Rica*	116	E3
Espejo, *Spain*	31	H6
Esperança, *Brazil*	122	C4
Esperance, *Australia*	89	F3
Esperance B., *Australia*	89	F3
Esperantinópolis, *Brazil*	122	B3
Esperanza, Santa Cruz, *Argentina*	128	D2
Esperanza, Santa Fe, *Argentina*	126	C3
Esperanza, *Phil.*	55	G6
Espéraza, *France*	26	F6

Espichel, C., *Portugal* ... 31 G1
Espiel, *Spain* ... 31 G5
Espigão, Serra do, *Brazil* 127 B5
Espinal, *Colombia* ... 120 C3
Espinar, *Peru* ... 124 C3
Espinazo, Sierra del = Espinhaço, Serra do, *Brazil* 123 E3
Espinhaço, Serra do, *Brazil* 123 E3
Espinho, *Portugal* ... 30 D2
Espinilho, Serra do, *Brazil* 127 B5
Espino, *Venezuela* ... 120 B4
Espinosa de los Monteros, *Spain* ... 30 B7
Espírito Santo □, *Brazil* 123 F3
Espíritu Santo, B. del, *Mexico* ... 115 D7
Espíritu Santo, I., *Mexico* 114 C2
Espita, *Mexico* ... 115 C7
Espiye, *Turkey* ... 67 B8
Esplanada, *Brazil* ... 123 D4
Espluga de Francolí, *Spain* 28 D6
Espoo, *Finland* ... 9 F21
Espuña, Sierra, *Spain* ... 29 H3
Espungabera, *Mozam.* ... 85 C5
Esquel, *Argentina* ... 128 B2
Esquina, *Argentina* ... 126 B4
Essaouira, *Morocco* ... 74 B3
Essebie, *Zaïre* ... 82 B3
Essen, *Belgium* ... 17 F4
Essen, *Germany* ... 18 D2
Essendon, Mt., *Australia* 89 E3
Essequibo →, *Guyana* ... 121 B6
Essex, *Canada* ... 106 D2
Essex, *Calif., U.S.A.* ... 113 L11
Essex, *N.Y., U.S.A.* ... 107 B11
Essex □, *U.K.* ... 13 F8
Esslingen, *Germany* ... 19 G5
Essvik, *Sweden* ... 10 B11
Estaca, Pta. del, *Spain* ... 30 B3
Estadilla, *Spain* ... 28 C5
Estados, I. de Los, *Argentina* ... 128 D4
Estagel, *France* ... 26 F6
Eştahbānāt, *Iran* ... 65 D7
Estallenchs, *Spain* ... 36 B9
Estância, *Brazil* ... 122 D4
Estancia, *U.S.A.* ... 111 J10
Estārm, *Iran* ... 65 D8
Estarreja, *Portugal* ... 30 E2
Estats, Pic d', *Spain* ... 28 C6
Estavayer-le-Lac, *Switz.* ... 22 C3
Estcourt, *S. Africa* ... 85 D4
Este, *Italy* ... 33 C8
Esteban, *Spain* ... 30 B4
Estelí, *Nic.* ... 116 D2
Estella, *Spain* ... 28 C2
Estelline, *S. Dak., U.S.A.* 108 C6
Estelline, *Tex., U.S.A.* ... 109 H4
Estena →, *Spain* ... 31 F6
Estepa, *Spain* ... 31 H6
Estepona, *Spain* ... 31 J5
Esterhazy, *Canada* ... 101 C8
Esternay, *France* ... 25 D10
Esterri de Aneu, *Spain* ... 28 C6
Estevan, *Canada* ... 101 D8
Estevan Group, *Canada* ... 100 C3
Estherville, *U.S.A.* ... 108 D7
Estissac, *France* ... 25 D10
Eston, *Canada* ... 101 C7
Estonia ■, *Europe* ... 9 G21
Estoril, *Portugal* ... 31 G1
Estouk, *Mali* ... 79 B5
Estrêla, Serra da, *Portugal* 30 E3
Estrella, *Spain* ... 29 G1
Estremoz, *Portugal* ... 31 G3
Estrondo, Serra do, *Brazil* 122 C2
Esztergom, *Hungary* ... 21 H8
Et Tîdra, *Mauritania* ... 78 B1
Et Tîra, *India* ... 63 F8
Étain, *France* ... 25 C12
Étalle, *Belgium* ... 17 J7
Etamamu, *Canada* ... 99 B8
Étampes, *France* ... 25 D9
Étang-sur-Arroux, *France* 27 B8
Etanga, *Namibia* ... 84 B1
Étaples, *France* ... 25 B8
Etawah, *India* ... 63 F8
Etawah →, *U.S.A.* ... 105 H3
Etawney L., *Canada* ... 101 B9
Ete, *Nigeria* ... 79 D6
Éthe, *Belgium* ... 17 J7
Ethel, *U.S.A.* ... 112 D4
Ethel, Oued el →, *Algeria* 74 C4
Ethel Creek, *Australia* ... 88 D3
Ethelbert, *Canada* ... 101 C8
Ethiopia ■, *Africa* ... 68 F3
Ethiopian Highlands, *Ethiopia* ... 70 E7
Etive, L., *U.K.* ... 14 E3
Etna, *Italy* ... 35 E8
Etoile, *Zaïre* ... 83 E2
Etolin I., *U.S.A.* ... 100 B2
Etosha Pan, *Namibia* ... 84 B2
Étowah, *U.S.A.* ... 105 H3
Étrépagny, *France* ... 25 C8
Étretat, *France* ... 24 C7
Ettelbruck, *Lux.* ... 17 J8
Etten, *Neths.* ... 17 E5
Ettlingen, *Germany* ... 19 G4
Ettrick Water →, *U.K.* ... 14 F6
Etuku, *Zaïre* ... 82 C2
Etzatlán, *Mexico* ... 114 C4
Eu, *France* ... 24 B8

Euboea = Évvoia, *Greece* 39 L7
Eucla Motel, *Australia* ... 89 F4
Euclid, *U.S.A.* ... 106 E3
Euclides da Cunha, *Brazil* 122 D4
Eucumbene, L., *Australia* 91 F4
Eudora, *U.S.A.* ... 109 J9
Eufaula, *Ala., U.S.A.* ... 105 K3
Eufaula, *Okla., U.S.A.* ... 109 H7
Eufaula L., *U.S.A.* ... 109 H7
Eugene, *U.S.A.* ... 110 E2
Eugowra, *Australia* ... 91 E4
Eulo, *Australia* ... 91 D4
Eunice, *La., U.S.A.* ... 109 K8
Eunice, *N. Mex., U.S.A.* 109 J3
Eupen, *Belgium* ... 17 G8
Euphrates = Furāt, Nahr al →, *Asia* ... 64 D5
Eure □, *France* ... 24 C8
Eure →, *France* ... 24 C8
Eure-et-Loir □, *France* ... 24 D8
Eureka, *Canada* ... 4 B3
Eureka, *Calif., U.S.A.* ... 110 F1
Eureka, *Kans., U.S.A.* ... 109 G6
Eureka, *Mont., U.S.A.* ... 110 B6
Eureka, *Nev., U.S.A.* ... 110 G5
Eureka, *S. Dak., U.S.A.* 108 C5
Eureka, *Utah, U.S.A.* ... 110 G7
Eureka, Mt., *Australia* ... 89 E3
Euroa, *Australia* ... 91 F4
Europa, I., *Ind. Oc.* ... 81 J8
Europa, Picos de, *Spain* ... 30 B6
Europa, Pta. de, *Gib.* ... 31 J5
Europa Pt. = Europa, Pta. de, *Gib.* ... 31 J5
Europoort, *Neths.* ... 16 E4
Euskirchen, *Germany* ... 18 E2
Eustis, *U.S.A.* ... 105 L5
Eutin, *Germany* ... 18 A6
Eutsuk L., *Canada* ... 100 C3
Eva, *Brazil* ... 121 D6
Eva Downs, *Australia* ... 90 B1
Evale, *Angola* ... 84 B2
Evans, *U.S.A.* ... 108 E2
Evans Head, *Australia* ... 91 D5
Evans, L., *Canada* ... 98 B4
Evans Mills, *U.S.A.* ... 107 B9
Evanston, *Ill., U.S.A.* ... 104 D2
Evanston, *Wyo., U.S.A.* 110 F8
Evansville, *Ind., U.S.A.* ... 104 F2
Evansville, *Wis., U.S.A.* 108 D10
Évaux-les-Bains, *France* ... 26 B6
Evaz, *Iran* ... 65 E7
Eveleth, *U.S.A.* ... 108 B8
Evensk, *Russia* ... 45 C16
Evenstad, *Norway* ... 10 C5
Everard, L., *Australia* ... 91 E1
Everard Park, *Australia* ... 89 E5
Everard Ras., *Australia* ... 89 E5
Evere, *Belgium* ... 17 G4
Everest, Mt., *Nepal* ... 63 E12
Everett, *Pa., U.S.A.* ... 106 F6
Everett, *Wash., U.S.A.* ... 112 C4
Evergem, *Belgium* ... 17 F3
Everglades, The, *U.S.A.* 105 N5
Everglades City, *U.S.A.* 105 N5
Everglades National Park, *U.S.A.* ... 105 N5
Evergreen, *U.S.A.* ... 105 K2
Everson, *U.S.A.* ... 110 B2
Evesham, *U.K.* ... 13 E6
Évian-les-Bains, *France* ... 27 B10
Evinayong, *Eq. Guin.* ... 80 D2
Évinos →, *Greece* ... 39 L4
Évisa, *France* ... 27 F12
Evje, *Norway* ... 9 G12
Evora, *Portugal* ... 31 G3
Évora, *Portugal* ... 31 G3
Évora □, *Portugal* ... 31 G3
Evowghlī, *Iran* ... 67 C11
Évreux, *France* ... 24 C8
Évron, *France* ... 24 D6
Évros →, *Bulgaria* ... 66 B2
Évrótas →, *Greece* ... 39 N5
Évvoia, *Greece* ... 39 L7
Évvoia □, *Greece* ... 39 L6
Ewe, L., *U.K.* ... 14 D3
Ewing, *U.S.A.* ... 108 D5
Ewo, *Congo* ... 80 E2
Exaltación, *Bolivia* ... 125 C4
Excelsior Springs, *U.S.A.* 108 F7
Excideuil, *France* ... 26 C5
Exe →, *U.K.* ... 13 G4
Exeter, *Canada* ... 106 C3
Exeter, *U.K.* ... 13 G4
Exeter, *Calif., U.S.A.* ... 111 H4
Exeter, *N.H., U.S.A.* ... 107 D14
Exeter, *Nebr., U.S.A.* ... 108 E6
Exloo, *Neths.* ... 16 C9
Exmes, *France* ... 24 D7
Exmoor, *U.K.* ... 13 F4
Exmouth, *Australia* ... 88 D1
Exmouth, *U.K.* ... 13 G4
Exmouth G., *Australia* ... 88 D1
Expedition Ra., *Australia* 90 C4
Exuma Sound, *Bahamas* 116 B4
Eyasi, L., *Tanzania* ... 82 C4
Eyeberry L., *Canada* ... 101 A8
Eyemouth, *U.K.* ... 14 F6
Eygurande, *France* ... 26 C6
Eyjafjörður, *Iceland* ... 8 C4
Eymet, *France* ... 26 D4
Eymoutiers, *France* ... 26 C5
Eynsil, *Turkey* ... 67 B8
Eyre, *Australia* ... 89 F4
Eyre (North), L., *Australia* 91 D2
Eyre (South), L., *Australia* 91 D2
Eyre Cr. →, *Australia* ... 91 D2

Eyre Mts., *N.Z.* ... 87 L2
Eyre Pen., *Australia* ... 91 E2
Eysturoy, *Færoe Is.* ... 8 E9
Eyvānkī, *Iran* ... 65 C6
Ez Zeidab, *Sudan* ... 76 D3
Ezcaray, *Spain* ... 28 C2
Ezine, *Turkey* ... 66 C2
Ezmul, *Mauritania* ... 74 D1
Ezouza →, *Cyprus* ... 37 E11

F

F.Y.R.O.M. = Macedonia ■, *Europe* .. 39 H4
Fabens, *U.S.A.* ... 111 L10
Fåborg, *Denmark* ... 11 J4
Fabriano, *Italy* ... 33 E9
Făcăeni, *Romania* ... 38 E10
Facatativá, *Colombia* ... 120 C3
Fachi, *Niger* ... 72 E7
Facture, *France* ... 26 D3
Fada, *Chad* ... 73 E9
Fada-n-Gourma, *Burkina Faso* ... 79 C5
Faddeyevskiy, Ostrov, *Russia* ... 45 B15
Fadghāmī, *Syria* ... 67 E9
Fadlab, *Sudan* ... 76 D3
Faenza, *Italy* ... 33 D8
Færoe Is. = Føroyar, *Atl. Oc.* ... 8 F9
Fafa, *Mali* ... 79 B5
Fafe, *Portugal* ... 30 D2
Fagam, *Nigeria* ... 79 C7
Făgăras, *Romania* ... 38 D7
Făgăras, Munţii, *Romania* 38 D7
Fågelsjö, *Sweden* ... 10 C8
Fagersta, *Sweden* ... 9 F16
Făget, *Romania* ... 38 D6
Fagnano, L., *Argentina* ... 128 D3
Fagnano Castello, *Italy* ... 35 C9
Fagnières, *France* ... 25 D11
Fahlīān, *Iran* ... 65 D6
Fahraj, *Kermān, Iran* ... 65 D8
Fahraj, *Yazd, Iran* ... 65 D7
Faial, *Madeira* ... 36 D3
Faido, *Switz.* ... 23 D7
Fair Hd., *U.K.* ... 15 A5
Fair Oaks, *U.S.A.* ... 112 G5
Fairbank, *U.S.A.* ... 111 L8
Fairbanks, *U.S.A.* ... 96 B5
Fairbury, *U.S.A.* ... 108 E6
Fairfax, *U.S.A.* ... 109 G6
Fairfield, *Ala., U.S.A.* ... 105 J2
Fairfield, *Calif., U.S.A.* 112 G4
Fairfield, *Conn., U.S.A.* 107 E11
Fairfield, *Idaho, U.S.A.* ... 110 E6
Fairfield, *Ill., U.S.A.* ... 104 F1
Fairfield, *Iowa, U.S.A.* ... 108 E9
Fairfield, *Mont., U.S.A.* 110 C8
Fairfield, *Tex., U.S.A.* ... 109 K7
Fairford, *Canada* ... 101 C9
Fairhope, *U.S.A.* ... 105 K2
Fairlie, *N.Z.* ... 87 L3
Fairmead, *U.S.A.* ... 112 H6
Fairmont, *Minn., U.S.A.* 108 D7
Fairmont, *W. Va., U.S.A.* 104 F5
Fairmount, *U.S.A.* ... 113 L8
Fairplay, *U.S.A.* ... 111 G11
Fairport, *U.S.A.* ... 106 C7
Fairport Harbor, *U.S.A.* 106 E3
Fairview, *Australia* ... 90 B3
Fairview, *Canada* ... 100 B5
Fairview, *Mont., U.S.A.* 108 B2
Fairview, *Okla., U.S.A.* 109 G5
Fairview, *Utah, U.S.A.* ... 110 G8
Fairweather, Mt., *U.S.A.* 96 C6
Faisalabad, *Pakistan* ... 62 D5
Faith, *U.S.A.* ... 108 C3
Faizabad, *India* ... 63 F10
Fajardo, *Puerto Rico* ... 117 C6
Fakfak, *Indonesia* ... 57 E8
Fakobli, *Ivory C.* ... 78 D3
Fakse, *Denmark* ... 11 J6
Fakse B., *Denmark* ... 11 J6
Fakse Ladeplads, *Denmark* 11 J6
Faku, *China* ... 51 C12
Falaise, *France* ... 24 D6
Falaise, Mui, *Vietnam* ... 58 C5
Falam, *Burma* ... 61 H18
Falces, *Spain* ... 28 C3
Fălciu, *Romania* ... 38 C11
Falcón □, *Venezuela* ... 120 A4
Falcon, C., *Algeria* ... 75 A4
Falcón, C., *Spain* ... 36 C7
Falcon Dam, *U.S.A.* ... 109 M5
Falconara Maríttima, *Italy* 33 E10
Falconer, *U.S.A.* ... 106 D5
Faléa, *Mali* ... 78 C2
Faleshty = Fălesti, *Moldova* ... 41 J4
Fălesti, *Moldova* ... 41 J4
Falfurrias, *U.S.A.* ... 109 M5
Falher, *Canada* ... 100 B5
Falirakí, *Greece* ... 37 C10
Falkenberg, *Germany* ... 18 D9
Falkenberg, *Sweden* ... 11 H6
Falkensee, *Germany* ... 18 C9
Falkenstein, *Germany* ... 18 E8
Falkirk, *U.K.* ... 14 F5
Falkland, East, I., *Falk. Is.* 128 D5
Falkland, West, I., *Falk. Is.* 128 D4
Falkland Is. □, *Atl. Oc.* 128 D5
Falkland Sd., *Falk. Is.* ... 128 D5

Falköping, *Sweden* ... 11 F7
Fall River, *U.S.A.* ... 107 E13
Fall River Mills, *U.S.A.* 110 F3
Fallbrook, *U.S.A.* ... 111 K5
Fallbrook, *Calif., U.S.A.* 113 M9
Fallon, *Mont., U.S.A.* ... 108 B2
Fallon, *Nev., U.S.A.* ... 110 G4
Falls City, *Nebr., U.S.A.* 108 E7
Falls City, *Oreg., U.S.A.* 110 D2
Falls Creek, *U.S.A.* ... 106 E6
Falmouth, *Jamaica* ... 116 C4
Falmouth, *U.K.* ... 13 G2
Falmouth, *U.S.A.* ... 104 F3
False B., *S. Africa* ... 84 E2
Falset, *Spain* ... 28 D5
Falso, C., *Honduras* ... 116 C3
Falster, *Denmark* ... 11 K5
Falsterbo, *Sweden* ... 11 J6
Fălticeni, *Romania* ... 38 B9
Falun, *Sweden* ... 9 F16
Famagusta, *Cyprus* ... 66 E5
Famagusta Bay, *Cyprus* 37 D13
Famatina, Sierra de, *Argentina* ... 126 B2
Family L., *Canada* ... 101 C9
Famoso, *U.S.A.* ... 113 K7
Fan Xian, *China* ... 50 G8
Fana, *Mali* ... 78 C3
Fandriana, *Madag.* ... 85 C8
Fang, *Thailand* ... 58 C2
Fang Xian, *China* ... 53 A8
Fangchang, *China* ... 53 B12
Fangcheng, *Guangxi Zhuangzu, China* ... 52 G7
Fangcheng, *Henan, China* 50 H7
Fangliao, *Taiwan* ... 53 F13
Fangshan, *China* ... 50 E6
Fangzi, *China* ... 51 F10
Fanjiatun, *China* ... 51 C13
Fannich, L., *U.K.* ... 14 D4
Fannūj, *Iran* ... 65 E8
Fanny Bay, *Canada* ... 100 D4
Fanø, *Denmark* ... 11 J2
Fano, *Italy* ... 33 E10
Fanshaw, *U.S.A.* ... 100 B2
Fanshi, *China* ... 50 E7
Fao = Al Fāw, *Iraq* ... 65 D6
Faqirwali, *Pakistan* ... 62 E5
Fara in Sabina, *Italy* ... 33 F9
Faradje, *Zaïre* ... 82 B2
Farafangana, *Madag.* ... 85 C8
Farāfra, El Wâhât el-, *Egypt* ... 76 B2
Farāh, *Afghan.* ... 60 C3
Farāh □, *Afghan.* ... 60 C3
Farahalana, *Madag.* ... 85 A9
Faraid, Gebel, *Egypt* ... 76 C4
Faramana, *Burkina Faso* 78 C4
Faranah, *Guinea* ... 78 C2
Farasān, Jazā'ir, *Si. Arabia* 68 D3
Farasān Is. = Farasān, Jazā'ir, *Si. Arabia* ... 68 D3
Faratsiho, *Madag.* ... 85 B8
Fardes →, *Spain* ... 29 H1
Fareham, *U.K.* ... 13 G6
Farewell, C., *N.Z.* ... 87 J4
Farewell C. = Farvel, Kap, *Greenland* ... 4 D5
Farghona, *Uzbekistan* ... 44 E8
Fargo, *U.S.A.* ... 108 B6
Fār'iah, W. al →, *West Bank* ... 69 C4
Faribault, *U.S.A.* ... 108 C8
Faridkot, *India* ... 62 D6
Faridpur, *Bangla.* ... 63 H13
Farim, *Guinea-Biss.* ... 78 C1
Farīmān, *Iran* ... 65 C8
Farina, *Australia* ... 91 E2
Farinha →, *Brazil* ... 122 C2
Fariones, Pta., *Canary Is.* 36 E6
Fâriskûr, *Egypt* ... 76 H7
Farmerville, *U.S.A.* ... 109 J8
Farmington, *Calif., U.S.A.* 112 H6
Farmington, *N.H., U.S.A.* 107 C13
Farmington, *N. Mex., U.S.A.* ... 111 H9
Farmington, *Utah, U.S.A.* 110 F8
Farmington →, *U.S.A.* 107 E12
Farmville, *U.S.A.* ... 104 G6
Farnborough, *U.K.* ... 13 F7
Farne Is., *U.K.* ... 12 B6
Farnham, *Canada* ... 107 A12
Faro, *Brazil* ... 121 D6
Faro, *Portugal* ... 31 H3
Fårö, *Sweden* ... 9 H18
Faro □, *Portugal* ... 31 H2
Farquhar, C., *Australia* ... 89 D1
Farrars Cr. →, *Australia* 90 D3
Farrāshband, *Iran* ... 65 D7
Farrell, *U.S.A.* ... 106 E4
Farrell Flat, *Australia* ... 91 E2
Farrokhī, *Iran* ... 65 C8
Farruch, C., *Spain* ... 36 B10
Farrukhabad-cum-Fatehgarh, *India* ... 63 F8
Fārs □, *Iran* ... 65 D7
Fársala, *Greece* ... 39 K5
Farsø, *Denmark* ... 11 H3
Farsund, *Norway* ... 9 G12
Fartak, Râs, *Si. Arabia* ... 64 D2
Fartura, Serra da, *Brazil* 127 B5
Faru, *Nigeria* ... 79 C6
Fārūj, *Iran* ... 65 B8
Farum, *Denmark* ... 11 J6

Farvel, Kap, *Greenland* ... 4 D5
Farwell, *U.S.A.* ... 109 H3
Fasā, *Iran* ... 65 D7
Fasano, *Italy* ... 35 B10
Fashoda, *Sudan* ... 77 F3
Fastiv, *Ukraine* ... 41 G5
Fastnet Rock, *Ireland* ... 15 E2
Fastov = Fastiv, *Ukraine* 41 G5
Fatagar, Tanjung, *Indonesia* 57 E8
Fatehgarh, *India* ... 63 F8
Fatehpur, *Raj., India* ... 62 F6
Fatehpur, *Ut. P., India* ... 63 G9
Fatesh, *Russia* ... 42 D2
Fatick, *Senegal* ... 78 C1
Fatima, *Canada* ... 99 C7
Fátima, *Portugal* ... 31 F2
Fatoya, *Guinea* ... 78 C3
Fatsa, *Turkey* ... 66 B7
Faucille, Col de la, *France* 27 B10
Faulkton, *U.S.A.* ... 108 C5
Faulquemont, *France* ... 25 C13
Fauquembergues, *France* 25 B9
Faure I., *Australia* ... 89 E1
Făurei, *Romania* ... 38 D10
Fauresmith, *S. Africa* ... 84 D4
Fauske, *Norway* ... 8 C16
Fauvillers, *Belgium* ... 17 J7
Favara, *Italy* ... 34 E6
Favaritx, C., *Spain* ... 36 A11
Favignana, *Italy* ... 34 E5
Favignana, I., *Italy* ... 34 E5
Favourable Lake, *Canada* 98 B1
Fawn →, *Canada* ... 98 A2
Fawnskin, *U.S.A.* ... 113 L10
Faxaflói, *Iceland* ... 8 D2
Faya-Largeau, *Chad* ... 73 E8
Fayd, *Si. Arabia* ... 64 E4
Fayence, *France* ... 27 E10
Fayette, *Ala., U.S.A.* ... 105 J2
Fayette, *Mo., U.S.A.* ... 108 F8
Fayetteville, *Ark., U.S.A.* 109 G7
Fayetteville, *N.C., U.S.A.* 105 H6
Fayetteville, *Tenn., U.S.A.* 105 H2
Fayón, *Spain* ... 28 D5
Fazenda Nova, *Brazil* ... 123 E1
Fazilka, *India* ... 62 D6
Fazilpur, *Pakistan* ... 62 E4
Fdérik, *Mauritania* ... 74 D2
Feale →, *Ireland* ... 15 D2
Fear, C., *U.S.A.* ... 105 J7
Feather →, *U.S.A.* ... 110 G3
Feather Falls, *U.S.A.* ... 112 F5
Featherston, *N.Z.* ... 87 J5
Featherstone, *Zimbabwe* 83 F3
Fécamp, *France* ... 24 C7
Fedala = Mohammedia, *Morocco* ... 74 B3
Federación, *Argentina* ... 126 C4
Fedeshkûh, *Iran* ... 65 D7
Fedjadj, Chott el, *Tunisia* 75 B6
Fehmarn, *Germany* ... 18 A7
Fehmarn Bælt, *Denmark* 9 J14
Fei Xian, *China* ... 51 G9
Feijó, *Brazil* ... 124 B3
Feilding, *N.Z.* ... 87 J5
Feira de Santana, *Brazil* 123 D4
Feixiang, *China* ... 50 F8
Fejø, *Denmark* ... 11 K5
Feke, *Turkey* ... 66 D6
Felanitx, *Spain* ... 36 B10
Feldberg, *Baden-W., Germany* ... 19 H3
Feldberg, *Mecklenburg-Vorpommern, Germany* ... 18 B9
Feldkirch, *Austria* ... 19 H5
Felipe Carrillo Puerto, *Mexico* ... 115 D7
Felixlândia, *Brazil* ... 123 E3
Felixstowe, *U.K.* ... 13 F9
Felletin, *France* ... 26 C6
Felton, *U.K.* ... 12 B6
Felton, *U.S.A.* ... 112 H4
Feltre, *Italy* ... 33 B8
Femø, *Denmark* ... 11 K5
Femunden, *Norway* ... 10 B5
Fen He →, *China* ... 50 G6
Fenelon Falls, *Canada* ... 106 B6
Feneroa, *Ethiopia* ... 77 E4
Feng Xian, *Jiangsu, China* 50 G9
Feng Xian, *Shaanxi, China* 50 H4
Fengari, *Greece* ... 39 J8
Fengcheng, *Jiangxi, China* 53 C10
Fengcheng, *Liaoning, China* ... 51 D13
Fengdu, *China* ... 52 C6
Fengfeng, *China* ... 50 F8
Fenggang, *China* ... 52 D6
Fenghua, *China* ... 53 C13
Fenghuang, *China* ... 52 D7
Fenghuangzui, *China* ... 52 A7
Fengjie, *China* ... 52 B7
Fengkai, *China* ... 53 F8
Fengle, *China* ... 53 B9
Fengning, *China* ... 50 D9
Fengqiu, *China* ... 50 G8
Fengqing, *China* ... 52 E2
Fengqiu, *China* ... 51 E10
Fengshan, *Guangxi Zhuangzu, China* ... 52 E7
Fengshan, *Guangxi Zhuangzu, China* ... 52 E6
Fengtai, *Anhui, China* ... 53 A11
Fengtai, *Beijing, China* ... 50 E9
Fengxian, *China* ... 53 B13

Fengxiang, *China* 50 G4
Fengxin, *China* 53 C10
Fengyang, *China* 51 H9
Fengzhen, *China* 50 D7
Fengyi, *China* 52 E3
Fenit, *Ireland* 15 D2
Fennimore, *U.S.A.* 108 D9
Feno, C. de, *France* 27 G12
Fenoarivo Afovoany,
Madag. 85 B8
Fenoarivo Atsinanana,
Madag. 85 B8
Fens, The, *U.K.* 12 E8
Fenton, *U.S.A.* 104 D4
Fenxi, *China* 50 F6
Fenyang, *China* 50 F6
Fenyi, *China* 53 D10
Feodosiya, *Ukraine* 41 K8
Fer, C. de, *Algeria* 75 A6
Ferdows, *Iran* 65 C8
Fère-Champenoise, *France* 25 D10
Fère-en-Tardenois, *France* 25 C10
Ferentino, *Italy* 34 A6
Ferfer, *Somali Rep.* 68 F4
Fergana = Farghona,
Uzbekistan 44 E8
Fergus, *Canada* 98 D3
Fergus Falls, *U.S.A.* ... 108 B6
Fériana, *Tunisia* 75 B6
Feričanci, *Croatia* 21 K8
Ferkane, *Algeria* 75 B6
Ferkéssédougou, *Ivory C.* 78 D3
Ferlach, *Austria* 21 J4
Ferland, *Canada* 98 B2
Ferlo, Vallée du, *Senegal* 78 B2
Fermanagh □, *U.K.* 15 B4
Fermo, *Italy* 33 E10
Fermoselle, *Spain* 30 D4
Fermoy, *Ireland* 15 D3
Fernán Nuñéz, *Spain* 31 H6
Fernández, *Argentina* ... 126 B3
Fernandina Beach, *U.S.A.* 105 K5
Fernando de Noronha,
Brazil 122 B5
Fernando Póo = Bioko,
Eq. Guin. 79 E6
Fernandópolis, *Brazil* .. 123 F7
Ferndale, *Calif., U.S.A.* 110 F1
Ferndale, *Wash., U.S.A.* 112 B4
Fernie, *Canada* 100 D5
Fernlees, *Australia* 90 C4
Fernley, *U.S.A.* 110 G4
Ferozepore = Firozpur,
India 62 D6
Férrai, *Greece* 39 J9
Ferrandina, *Italy* 35 B9
Ferrara, *Italy* 33 D8
Ferrato, C., *Italy* 34 C2
Ferreira do Alentejo,
Portugal 31 G2
Ferreñafe, *Peru* 124 B2
Ferrerías, *Spain* 36 B11
Ferret, C., *France* 26 D2
Ferrette, *France* 25 E14
Ferriday, *U.S.A.* 109 K9
Ferrières, *France* 25 D9
Ferriete, *Italy* 32 D6
Ferrol = El Ferrol, *Spain* 30 B2
Ferrol, Pen. de, *Peru* .. 124 B2
Ferron, *U.S.A.* 111 G8
Ferros, *Brazil* 123 E3
Ferryland, *Canada* 99 C9
Fertile, *U.S.A.* 108 B6
Fertília, *Italy* 34 B1
Fès, *Morocco* 74 B4
Feschaux, *Belgium* 17 H5
Feshi, *Zaïre* 80 F3
Fessenden, *U.S.A.* 108 B5
Feteşti, *Romania* 38 E10
Fethiye, *Turkey* 66 D3
Fetlar, *U.K.* 14 A8
Feuerthalen, *Switz.* 23 A7
Feuilles →, *Canada* 97 C12
Feurs, *France* 27 C8
Fezzan, *Libya* 73 C8
Ffestiniog, *U.K.* 12 E4
Fiambalá, *Argentina* 126 B2
Fianarantsoa, *Madag.* ... 85 C8
Fianarantsoa □, *Madag.* . 85 B8
Fianga, *Cameroon* 73 G8
Fichtelgebirge, *Germany* 19 E7
Ficksburg, *S. Africa* ... 85 D4
Fidenza, *Italy* 32 D7
Fiditi, *Nigeria* 79 D5
Field, *Canada* 98 C3
Field →, *Australia* 90 C2
Field I., *Australia* 88 B5
Fieri, *Albania* 39 J3
Fiesch, *Switz.* 22 D6
Fife □, *U.K.* 14 E5
Fife Ness, *U.K.* 14 E6
Fifth Cataract, *Sudan* .. 76 D3
Figeac, *France* 26 D6
Figline Valdarno, *Italy* 33 E8
Figtree, *Zimbabwe* 83 G2
Figueira Castelo Rodrigo,
Portugal 30 E4
Figueira da Foz, *Portugal* . 30 E2
Figueiró dos Vinhos,
Portugal 30 F2
Figueras, *Spain* 28 C7
Figuig, *Morocco* 75 B4
Fihaonana, *Madag.* 85 B8
Fiherenana, *Madag.* 85 C7
Fiherenana →, *Madag.* ... 85 C7
Fiji ■, *Pac. Oc.* 87 C8
Fika, *Nigeria* 79 C7

Filabres, Sierra de los,
Spain 29 H2
Filadelfia, *Bolivia* 124 C4
Filadélfia, *Brazil* 122 C2
Filadélfia, *Italy* 35 D9
Filer, *U.S.A.* 110 E6
Filey, *U.K.* 12 C7
Filfla, *Malta* 37 D1
Filiaşi, *Romania* 38 E6
Filiátes, *Greece* 39 K3
Filiatrá, *Greece* 39 M4
Filicudi, *Italy* 35 D7
Filiourí →, *Greece* 39 H8
Filipstad, *Sweden* 9 G16
Filisur, *Switz.* 23 C9
Fillmore, *Canada* 101 D8
Fillmore, *Calif., U.S.A.* 113 L8
Fillmore, *Utah, U.S.A.* . 111 G7
Filottrano, *Italy* 33 E10
Finale Lígure, *Italy* ... 32 D5
Finale nell' Emília, *Italy* 33 D8
Fiñana, *Spain* 29 H2
Finch, *Canada* 107 A9
Findhorn →, *U.K.* 14 D5
Findlay, *U.S.A.* 104 E4
Finger L., *Canada* 101 C10
Fíngöe, *Mozam.* 83 E3
Finike, *Turkey* 66 D4
Finistère □, *France* 24 D2
Finisterre, *Spain* 30 C1
Finisterre, C., *Spain* .. 30 C1
Finke, *Australia* 90 D1
Finke →, *Australia* 91 D2
Finland ■, *Europe* 8 E22
Finland, G. of, *Europe* . 9 G21
Finlay →, *Canada* 100 B3
Finley, *Australia* 91 F4
Finley, *U.S.A.* 108 B6
Finn →, *Ireland* 15 B4
Finnigan, Mt., *Australia* 90 B4
Finniss, C., *Australia* . 91 E1
Finnmark, *Norway* 8 B20
Finnsnes, *Norway* 8 B18
Finspång, *Sweden* 9 G16
Finsteraarhorn, *Switz.* . 22 C6
Finsterwalde, *Germany* .. 18 D9
Finsterwolde, *Neths.* ... 16 B10
Fiora →, *Italy* 33 F8
Fiorenzuola d'Arda, *Italy* 32 D6
Fíq, *Syria* 69 C4
Firat = Furāt, Nahr al →,
Asia 64 D5
Fire River, *Canada* 98 C3
Firebag →, *Canada* 101 B6
Firebaugh, *U.S.A.* 112 J6
Firedrake L., *Canada* ... 101 A8
Firenze, *Italy* 33 E8
Firk →, *Iraq* 64 D5
Firmi, *France* 26 D6
Firminy, *France* 27 C8
Firozabad, *India* 63 F8
Firozpur, *India* 62 D6
Firūzābād, *Iran* 65 D7
Firūzkūh, *Iran* 65 C7
Firvale, *Canada* 100 C3
Fish →, *Namibia* 84 D2
Fish →, *S. Africa* 84 E3
Fisher, *Australia* 89 F5
Fisher B., *Canada* 101 C9
Fishguard, *U.K.* 13 F3
Fishing L., *Canada* 101 C9
Fismes, *France* 25 C10
Fitchburg, *U.S.A.* 107 D13
Fitero, *Spain* 28 C3
Fitri, L., *Chad* 73 F8
Fitz Roy, *Argentina* 128 C3
Fitzgerald, *Canada* 100 B6
Fitzgerald, *U.S.A.* 105 K4
Fitzmaurice →, *Australia* 88 B5
Fitzroy →, *Queens.,
Australia* 90 C5
Fitzroy →, *W. Austral.,
Australia* 88 C3
Fitzroy Crossing, *Australia* 88 C4
Fitzwilliam I., *Canada* . 106 A3
Fiume = Rijeka, *Croatia* 33 C11
Fiumefreddo Brúzio, *Italy* 35 C9
Five Points, *U.S.A.* 112 J6
Fivizzano, *Italy* 32 D7
Fizi, *Zaïre* 82 C2
Fjellerup, *Denmark* 11 H4
Fjerritslev, *Denmark* ... 11 G3
Fkih ben Salah, *Morocco* 74 B3
Flå, *Norway* 10 A4
Flagler, *U.S.A.* 108 F3
Flagstaff, *U.S.A.* 111 J8
Flaherty I., *Canada* 98 A4
Flåm, *Norway* 9 F12
Flambeau →, *U.S.A.* 108 C9
Flamborough Hd., *U.K.* .. 12 C7
Flaming Gorge Dam,
U.S.A. 110 F9
Flaming Gorge Reservoir,
U.S.A. 110 F9
Flamingo, Teluk, *Indonesia* 57 F9
Flanders = West-
Vlaanderen □, *Belgium* 17 G2
Flandre Occidentale =
West-Vlaanderen □,
Belgium 17 G2
Flandre Orientale = Oost-
Vlaanderen □, *Belgium* 17 F3
Flandreau, *U.S.A.* 108 C6
Flanigan, *U.S.A.* 112 E7
Flannan Is., *U.K.* 14 C1
Flåsjön, *Sweden* 8 D16
Flat →, *Canada* 100 A3

Flat River, *U.S.A.* 109 G9
Flathead L., *U.S.A.* 110 C6
Flattery, C., *Australia* 90 A4
Flattery, C., *U.S.A.* ... 112 B2
Flavy-le-Martel, *France* 25 C10
Flawil, *Switz.* 23 B8
Flaxton, *U.S.A.* 108 A3
Fleetwood, *U.K.* 12 D4
Flekkefjord, *Norway* 9 G12
Flémalle, *Belgium* 17 G6
Flemington, *U.S.A.* 106 E7
Flensburg, *Germany* 18 A5
Flensburger Förde,
Germany 11 K3
Flers, *France* 24 D6
Flesherton, *Canada* 106 B4
Flesko, Tanjung, *Indonesia* 57 D6
Fleurance, *France* 26 E4
Fleurier, *Switz.* 22 C3
Fleurus, *Belgium* 17 H5
Flevoland □, *Neths.* 16 C7
Flims, *Switz.* 23 C8
Flin Flon, *Canada* 101 C8
Flinders →, *Australia* .. 90 B3
Flinders B., *Australia* . 89 F2
Flinders Group, *Australia* 90 A3
Flinders I., *Australia* . 90 F4
Flinders Ras., *Australia* 91 E2
Flinders Reefs, *Australia* 90 B4
Flint, *U.K.* 12 D4
Flint, *U.S.A.* 104 D4
Flint →, *U.S.A.* 105 K3
Flint I., *Kiribati* 93 J12
Flinton, *Australia* 91 D4
Flix, *Spain* 28 D5
Flixecourt, *France* 25 B9
Flobecq, *Belgium* 17 G3
Flodden, *U.K.* 12 B5
Floodwood, *U.S.A.* 108 B8
Flora, *Norway* 10 A5
Flora, *U.S.A.* 104 F1
Florac, *France* 26 D7
Florala, *U.S.A.* 105 K2
Florânia, *Brazil* 122 C4
Floreffe, *Belgium* 17 H5
Florence = Firenze, *Italy* 33 E8
Florence, *Ala., U.S.A.* . 105 H2
Florence, *Ariz., U.S.A.* 111 K8
Florence, *Colo., U.S.A.* 108 F2
Florence, *Oreg., U.S.A.* 110 E1
Florence, *S.C., U.S.A.* . 105 H6
Florence, L., *Australia* 91 D2
Florennes, *Belgium* 17 H5
Florensac, *France* 26 E7
Florenville, *Belgium* ... 17 J6
Flores, *Brazil* 122 C4
Flores, *Guatemala* 116 C2
Flores, *Indonesia* 57 F6
Flores I., *Canada* 100 D3
Flores Sea, *Indonesia* .. 57 F6
Floresta, *Brazil* 122 C4
Floresti, *Moldova* 41 J5
Floresville, *U.S.A.* 109 L5
Floriano, *Brazil* 122 C3
Florianópolis, *Brazil* .. 127 B6
Fórmia, *Italy* 34 A6
Florida, *Cuba* 116 B4
Florida, *Uruguay* 127 C4
Florida □, *U.S.A.* 105 L5
Florida, Straits of, *U.S.A.* 116 B3
Florida B., *U.S.A.* 116 A3
Florida Keys, *U.S.A.* ... 103 F10
Florídia, *Italy* 35 E8
Floridsdorf, *Austria* ... 21 G6
Flórina, *Greece* 39 J4
Florø, *Norway* 9 F11
Flower Station, *Canada* . 107 A8
Flower's Cove, *Canada* .. 99 B8
Floydada, *U.S.A.* 109 J4
Fluk, *Indonesia* 57 E7
Flumen →, *Spain* 28 D4
Flumendosa →, *Italy* 34 C2
Fluminimaggiore, *Italy* . 34 C1
Flushing = Vlissingen,
Neths. 17 F3
Fluviá →, *Spain* 28 C8
Fly →, *Papua N. G.* 92 E3
Flying Fish, C., *Antarctica* 5 D15
Foam Lake, *Canada* 101 C8
Foča, *Bos.-H.* 21 M8
Foça, *Turkey* 66 C2
Focşani, *Romania* 38 D10
Fochabers = Fuzhou, *China* 53 D12
Fogang, *China* 53 F9
Foggaret el Arab, *Algeria* 75 C5
Foggaret ez Zoua, *Algeria* 75 C5
Fóggia, *Italy* 35 A8
Foglia →, *Italy* 33 E9
Fogo, *Canada* 99 C9
Fogo I., *Canada* 99 C9
Fohnsdorf, *Austria* 21 H4
Föhr, *Germany* 18 A4
Foia, *Portugal* 31 H2
Foix, *France* 26 F5
Fokino, *Russia* 42 D2
Folda, Nord-Trøndelag,
Norway 8 D14
Folda, Nordland, *Norway* 8 C16
Foleyet, *Canada* 98 C3
Folgefonni, *Norway* 9 F12
Foligno, *Italy* 33 F9
Folkestone, *U.K.* 13 F9
Folkston, *U.S.A.* 105 K5
Follett, *U.S.A.* 109 G4
Follónica, *Italy* 32 F7
Follónica, G. di, *Italy* 32 F7
Folsom Res., *U.S.A.* 112 G5
Fond-du-Lac, *Canada* 101 B7
Fond du Lac, *U.S.A.* 108 D10

Fond-du-Lac →, *Canada* . 101 B7
Fonda, *U.S.A.* 107 D10
Fondi, *Italy* 34 A6
Fonfría, *Spain* 30 D4
Fongen, *Norway* 10 A5
Fonni, *Italy* 34 B2
Fonsagrada, *Spain* 30 B3
Fonseca, G. de,
Cent. Amer. 116 D2
Fontaine-Française, *France* 25 E12
Fontainebleau, *France* .. 25 D9
Fontana, *U.S.A.* 113 L9
Fontana, L., *Argentina* . 128 B2
Fontas →, *Canada* 100 B4
Fonte Boa, *Brazil* 120 D4
Fontem, *Cameroon* 79 D6
Fontenay-le-Comte, *France* 26 B3
Fontur, *Iceland* 8 C6
Fonyód, *Hungary* 21 J7
Foochow = Fuzhou, *China* 53 D12
Foping, *China* 50 H4
Foppiano, *Italy* 32 B5
Forbach, *France* 25 C13
Forbes, *Australia* 91 E4
Forbesganj, *India* 63 F12
Forcados, *Nigeria* 79 D6
Forcados →, *Nigeria* 79 D6
Forcall →, *Spain* 28 E4
Forcalquier, *France* 27 E9
Forchheim, *Germany* 19 F7
Forclaz, Col de la, *Switz.* 22 D4
Ford City, *Calif., U.S.A.* 113 K7
Ford City, *Pa., U.S.A.* . 106 F5
Ford's Bridge, *Australia* 91 D4
Fordyce, *U.S.A.* 109 J8
Forécariah, *Guinea* 78 D2
Forel, Mt., *Greenland* .. 4 C6
Foremost, *Canada* 100 D6
Forenza, *Italy* 35 B8
Forest, *Belgium* 17 G4
Forest, *Canada* 106 C3
Forest, *U.S.A.* 109 J10
Forest City, *Iowa, U.S.A.* 108 D8
Forest City, *N.C., U.S.A.* 105 H5
Forest City, *Pa., U.S.A.* 107 E9
Forest Grove, *U.S.A.* ... 112 E3
Forestburg, *Canada* 100 C6
Foresthill, *U.S.A.* 112 F6
Forestier Pen., *Australia* 90 G4
Forestville, *Canada* 99 C6
Forestville, *Calif., U.S.A.* 112 G4
Forestville, *Wis., U.S.A.* 104 C2
Forez, Mts. du, *France* . 26 C7
Forfar, *U.K.* 14 E6
Forges-les-Eaux, *France* 25 C8
Forks, *U.S.A.* 112 C2
Forlì, *Italy* 33 D9
Forman, *U.S.A.* 108 B6
Formazza, *Italy* 32 B5
Formby Pt., *U.K.* 12 D4
Formentera, *Spain* 36 C7
Formentor, C. de, *Spain* 36 B10
Former Yugoslav Republic
of Macedonia =
Macedonia ■, *Europe* . 39 H4
Fórmia, *Italy* 34 A6
Formiga, *Brazil* 123 F2
Formigine, *Italy* 32 D7
Formiguères, *France* 26 F6
Formosa = Taiwan ■, *Asia* 53 F13
Formosa, *Argentina* 126 B4
Formosa, *Brazil* 123 E2
Formosa □, *Argentina* ... 126 B3
Formosa, Serra, *Brazil* . 125 C6
Formoso →, *Brazil* 123 D2
Formosa Bay, *Kenya* 82 C5
Formosa Strait, *Asia* ... 53 E12
Fornells, *Spain* 36 A11
Fornos de Algodres,
Portugal 30 E3
Fornovo di Taro, *Italy* . 32 D7
Føroyar, *Atl. Oc.* 8 F9
Forres, *U.K.* 14 D5
Forrest, *Vic., Australia* 91 F3
Forrest, *W. Austral.,
Australia* 89 F4
Forrest, Mt., *Australia* 89 D4
Forrest City, *U.S.A.* ... 109 H9
Forrières, *Belgium* 17 H6
Forsa, *Sweden* 10 C10
Forsayth, *Australia* 90 B3
Forsmo, *Sweden* 10 A11
Forssa, *Finland* 9 F20
Forst, *Germany* 18 D10
Forster, *Australia* 91 E5
Forsyth, *Ga., U.S.A.* ... 105 J4
Forsyth, *Mont., U.S.A.* . 110 C10
Fort Albany, *Canada* 98 B3
Fort Apache, *U.S.A.* 111 K9
Fort Assiniboine, *Canada* 100 C6
Fort Augustus, *U.K.* 14 D4
Fort Beaufort, *S. Africa* 84 E4
Fort Benton, *U.S.A.* 110 C8
Fort Bragg, *U.S.A.* 110 G2
Fort Bridger, *U.S.A.* ... 110 F8
Fort Chipewyan, *Canada* . 101 B6
Fort Collins, *U.S.A.* ... 108 E2
Fort-Coulonge, *Canada* .. 98 C4
Fort Davis, *U.S.A.* 109 K3
Fort-de-France, *Martinique* 117 D7
Fort de Possel = Possel,
C.A.R. 80 C3
Fort Defiance, *U.S.A.* .. 111 J9
Fort Dodge, *U.S.A.* 108 D7
Fort Edward, *U.S.A.* 107 C11
Fort Frances, *Canada* ... 101 D10
Fort Franklin, *Canada* .. 96 B7

Fort Garland, *U.S.A.* ... 111 H11
Fort George = Chisasibi,
Canada 98 B4
Fort Good-Hope, *Canada* . 96 B7
Fort Hancock, *U.S.A.* ... 111 L11
Fort Hertz = Putao, *Burma* 61 F20
Fort Hope, *Canada* 98 B2
Fort Irwin, *U.S.A.* 113 K10
Fort Jameson = Chipata,
Zambia 83 E3
Fort Kent, *U.S.A.* 99 C6
Fort Klamath, *U.S.A.* ... 110 E3
Fort-Lamy = Ndjamena,
Chad 73 F7
Fort Laramie, *U.S.A.* ... 108 D2
Fort Lauderdale, *U.S.A.* 105 M5
Fort Liard, *Canada* 100 A4
Fort Liberté, *Haiti* 117 C5
Fort Lupton, *U.S.A.* 108 E2
Fort Mackay, *Canada* 100 B6
Fort McKenzie, *Canada* .. 99 A6
Fort Macleod, *Canada* ... 100 D6
Fort MacMahon, *Algeria* . 75 C5
Fort McMurray, *Canada* .. 100 B6
Fort McPherson, *Canada* . 96 B6
Fort Madison, *U.S.A.* ... 108 E9
Fort Meade, *U.S.A.* 105 M5
Fort Miribel, *Algeria* .. 75 C5
Fort Morgan, *U.S.A.* 108 E3
Fort Myers, *U.S.A.* 105 M5
Fort Nelson, *Canada* 100 B4
Fort Nelson →, *Canada* .. 100 B4
Fort Norman, *Canada* 96 B7
Fort Payne, *U.S.A.* 105 H3
Fort Peck, *U.S.A.* 110 B10
Fort Peck Dam, *U.S.A.* .. 110 C10
Fort Peck L., *U.S.A.* ... 110 C10
Fort Pierce, *U.S.A.* 105 M5
Fort Pierre, *U.S.A.* 108 C4
Fort Pierre Bordes = Ti-n-
Zaouâtene, *Algeria* ... 75 E5
Fort Plain, *U.S.A.* 107 D10
Fort Portal, *Uganda* 82 B3
Fort Providence, *Canada* 100 A5
Fort Qu'Appelle, *Canada* 101 C8
Fort Resolution, *Canada* 100 A6
Fort Rixon, *Zimbabwe* ... 83 G2
Fort Rosebery = Mansa,
Zambia 83 E2
Fort Ross, *U.S.A.* 112 G3
Fort Rupert =
Waskaganish, *Canada* . 98 B4
Fort St. James, *Canada* 100 C4
Fort St. John, *Canada* .. 100 B4
Fort Sandeman, *Pakistan* 62 D3
Fort Saskatchewan, *Canada* 100 C6
Fort Scott, *U.S.A.* 109 G7
Fort Severn, *Canada* 98 A2
Fort Shevchenko,
Kazakhstan 43 H10
Fort Simpson, *Canada* ... 100 A4
Fort Smith, *Canada* 100 B6
Fort Smith, *U.S.A.* 109 H7
Fort Stanton, *U.S.A.* ... 111 K11
Fort Stockton, *U.S.A.* .. 109 K3
Fort Sumner, *U.S.A.* 109 H2
Fort Trinquet = Bir
Mogreïn, *Mauritania* . 74 C2
Fort Valley, *U.S.A.* 105 J4
Fort Vermilion, *Canada* . 100 B5
Fort Walton Beach, *U.S.A.* 105 K2
Fort Wayne, *U.S.A.* 104 E3
Fort William, *U.K.* 14 E3
Fort Worth, *U.S.A.* 109 J6
Fort Yates, *U.S.A.* 108 B4
Fort Yukon, *U.S.A.* 96 B5
Fortaleza, *Bolivia* 124 C4
Fortaleza, *Brazil* 122 B4
Forteau, *Canada* 99 B8
Forth →, *U.K.* 14 E5
Forth, Firth of, *U.K.* .. 14 E6
Forthassa Rharbia, *Algeria* 75 B4
Fortín Coronel Eugenio
Garay, *Paraguay* 125 E5
Fortín Garrapatal,
Paraguay 125 E5
Fortín General Pando,
Paraguay 125 D6
Fortín Madrejón, *Paraguay* 125 E6
Fortín Uno, *Argentina* .. 128 A3
Fortore →, *Italy* 33 G12
Fortrose, *U.K.* 14 D4
Fortuna, *Spain* 29 G3
Fortuna, *Calif., U.S.A.* 110 F1
Fortuna, *N. Dak., U.S.A.* 108 A3
Fortune B., *Canada* 99 C8
Fos-sur-Mer, *France* 27 E8
Foshan, *China* 53 F9
Fosna, *Norway* 8 E14
Fosnavåg, *Norway* 9 E11
Fossacésia, *Italy* 33 F11
Fossano, *Italy* 32 D4
Fosses-la-Ville, *Belgium* 17 H5
Fossil, *U.S.A.* 110 D3
Fossilbrook, *Australia* . 90 B3
Fossombrone, *Italy* 33 E9
Fosston, *U.S.A.* 108 B7
Foster →, *Canada* 107 A12
Foster →, *Canada* 101 B7
Fosters Ra., *Australia* . 90 C1
Fostoria, *U.S.A.* 104 E4
Fougamou, *Gabon* 80 E2
Fougères, *France* 24 D5
Foul Pt., *Sri Lanka* 60 Q12
Foula, *U.K.* 14 A6
Foulness I., *U.K.* 13 F8
Foulpointe, *Madag.* 85 B8

Foum Assaka

Foum Assaka, *Morocco* 74 C2
Foum Zguid, *Morocco* 74 B3
Foumban, *Cameroon* 79 D7
Foundiougne, *Senegal* 78 C1
Fountain, *Colo., U.S.A.* 108 F2
Fountain, *Utah, U.S.A.* 110 G8
Fountain Springs, *U.S.A.* 113 K8
Fourchambault, *France* 25 E10
Fourchu, *Canada* 99 C7
Fouriesburg, *S. Africa* 84 D4
Fourmies, *France* 25 B11
Foúrnoi, *Greece* 39 M9
Fours, *France* 25 F10
Fouta Djalon, *Guinea* 78 C2
Foux, Cap-à-, *Haiti* 117 C5
Foveaux Str., *N.Z.* 87 M2
Fowey, *U.K.* 13 G3
Fowler, *Calif., U.S.A.* 111 H4
Fowler, *Colo., U.S.A.* 108 F2
Fowler, *Kans., U.S.A.* 109 G4
Fowlers B., *Australia* 89 F5
Fowlerton, *U.S.A.* 109 L5
Fowman, *Iran* 67 D13
Fox →, *Canada* 101 B10
Fox Valley, *Canada* 101 C7
Foxe Basin, *Canada* 97 B12
Foxe Chan., *Canada* 97 B11
Foxe Pen., *Canada* 97 B12
Foxhol, *Neths.* 16 B9
Foxpark, *U.S.A.* 110 F10
Foxton, *N.Z.* 87 J5
Foyle, Lough, *U.K.* 15 A4
Foynes, *Ireland* 15 D2
Foz, *Spain* 30 B3
Fóz do Cunene, *Angola* 84 B1
Foz do Gregório, *Brazil* 124 B3
Foz do Iguaçu, *Brazil* 127 B5
Foz do Riosinho, *Brazil* 124 B3
Frackville, *U.S.A.* 107 F8
Fraga, *Spain* 28 D5
Fraire, *Belgium* 17 H5
Frameries, *Belgium* 17 H3
Framingham, *U.S.A.* 107 D13
Franca, *Brazil* 123 F2
Francavilla al Mare, *Italy* 33 F11
Francavilla Fontana, *Italy* 35 B10
France ■, *Europe* 7 F6
Frances, *Australia* 91 F3
Frances →, *Canada* 100 A3
Frances L., *Canada* 100 A3
Francés Viejo, C., *Dom. Rep.* 117 C6
Franceville, *Gabon* 80 E2
Franche-Comté, *France* 25 F12
Franches Montagnes, *Switz.* 22 B4
Francisco de Orellana, *Ecuador* 120 D2
Francisco I. Madero, *Coahuila, Mexico* 114 B4
Francisco I. Madero, *Durango, Mexico* 114 C4
Francisco Sá, *Brazil* 123 E3
Francistown, *Botswana* 85 C4
Francofonte, *Italy* 35 E7
François, *Canada* 99 C8
François L., *Canada* 100 C3
Francorchamps, *Belgium* 17 H7
Franeker, *Neths.* 16 B7
Frankado, *Djibouti* 77 E5
Frankenberg, *Germany* 18 D4
Frankenthal, *Germany* 19 F4
Frankenwald, *Germany* 19 E7
Frankfort, *S. Africa* 85 D4
Frankfort, *Ind., U.S.A.* 104 E2
Frankfort, *Kans., U.S.A.* 108 F6
Frankfort, *Ky., U.S.A.* 104 F3
Frankfort, *Mich., U.S.A.* 104 C2
Frankfurt, *Brandenburg, Germany* 18 C10
Frankfurt, *Hessen, Germany* 19 E4
Fränkische Alb, *Germany* 19 F7
Fränkische Rezal →, *Germany* 19 F7
Fränkische Saale →, *Germany* 19 E5
Fränkische Schweiz, *Germany* 19 F7
Frankland →, *Australia* 89 G2
Franklin, *Ky., U.S.A.* 105 G2
Franklin, *La., U.S.A.* 109 L9
Franklin, *Mass., U.S.A.* 107 D13
Franklin, *N.H., U.S.A.* 107 C13
Franklin, *Nebr., U.S.A.* 108 E5
Franklin, *Pa., U.S.A.* 106 E5
Franklin, *Tenn., U.S.A.* 105 H2
Franklin, *Va., U.S.A.* 105 G7
Franklin, *W. Va., U.S.A.* 104 F6
Franklin B., *Canada* 96 B7
Franklin D. Roosevelt L., *U.S.A.* 110 B4
Franklin I., *Antarctica* 5 D11
Franklin L., *U.S.A.* 110 F6
Franklin Mts., *Canada* 96 B7
Franklin Str., *Canada* 96 A10
Franklinton, *U.S.A.* 109 K9
Franklinville, *U.S.A.* 106 D6
Franks Pk., *U.S.A.* 110 E9
Frankston, *Australia* 91 F4
Fränsta, *Sweden* 10 B10
Frantsa Iosifa, Zemlya, *Russia* 44 A6
Franz, *Canada* 98 C3
Franz Josef Land = Frantsa Iosifa, Zemlya, *Russia* 44 A6
Franzburg, *Germany* 18 A8
Frascati, *Italy* 34 A5
Fraser →, *B.C., Canada* 100 D4
Fraser →, *Nfld., Canada* 99 A7
Fraser, Mt., *Australia* 89 E2
Fraser I., *Australia* 91 D5
Fraser Lake, *Canada* 100 C4
Fraserburg, *S. Africa* 84 E3
Fraserburgh, *U.K.* 14 D6
Fraserdale, *Canada* 98 C3
Frasne, *France* 25 F13
Frauenfeld, *Switz.* 23 A7
Fray Bentos, *Uruguay* 126 C4
Frazier Downs, *Australia* 88 C3
Frechilla, *Spain* 30 C6
Fredericia, *Denmark* 11 J3
Frederick, *Md., U.S.A.* 104 F7
Frederick, *Okla., U.S.A.* 109 H5
Frederick, *S. Dak., U.S.A.* 108 C5
Frederick Sd., *U.S.A.* 100 B2
Fredericksburg, *Tex., U.S.A.* 109 K5
Fredericksburg, *Va., U.S.A.* 104 F7
Fredericktown, *U.S.A.* 109 G9
Frederico I. Madero, Presa, *Mexico* 114 B3
Fredericton, *Canada* 99 C6
Fredericton Junc., *Canada* 99 C6
Frederikshåb, *Greenland* 4 C5
Frederikshavn, *Denmark* 11 G4
Frederikssund, *Denmark* 11 J6
Frederiksted, *Virgin Is.* 117 C7
Fredonia, *Ariz., U.S.A.* 111 H7
Fredonia, *Kans., U.S.A.* 109 G7
Fredonia, *N.Y., U.S.A.* 106 D5
Fredrikstad, *Norway* 10 E4
Freehold, *U.S.A.* 107 F10
Freel Peak, *U.S.A.* 112 G7
Freeland, *U.S.A.* 107 E9
Freels, C., *Canada* 99 C9
Freeman, *Calif., U.S.A.* 113 K9
Freeman, *S. Dak., U.S.A.* 108 D6
Freeport, *Bahamas* 116 A4
Freeport, *Canada* 99 D6
Freeport, *Ill., U.S.A.* 108 D10
Freeport, *N.Y., U.S.A.* 107 F11
Freeport, *Tex., U.S.A.* 109 L7
Freetown, *S. Leone* 78 D2
Frégate, L., *Canada* 98 B5
Fregenal de la Sierra, *Spain* 31 G4
Fregene, *Italy* 34 A5
Fréhel, C., *France* 24 D4
Freiberg, *Germany* 18 E9
Freibourg = Fribourg, *Switz.* 22 C4
Freiburg, *Baden-W., Germany* 19 H3
Freiburg, *Niedersachsen, Germany* 18 B5
Freiburger Alpen, *Switz.* 22 C4
Freire, *Chile* 128 A2
Freirina, *Chile* 126 B1
Freising, *Germany* 19 G7
Freistadt, *Austria* 20 G4
Freital, *Germany* 18 E9
Fréjus, *France* 27 E10
Fremantle, *Australia* 89 F2
Fremont, *Calif., U.S.A.* 111 H2
Fremont, *Mich., U.S.A.* 104 D3
Fremont, *Nebr., U.S.A.* 108 E6
Fremont, *Ohio, U.S.A.* 104 E4
Fremont →, *U.S.A.* 111 G8
Fremont L., *U.S.A.* 110 E9
French Camp, *U.S.A.* 112 H5
French Creek →, *U.S.A.* 106 E5
French Guiana ■, *S. Amer.* 121 C7
French Pass, *N.Z.* 87 J4
French Polynesia ■, *Pac. Oc.* 93 J13
French Terr. of Afars & Issas = Djibouti ■, *Africa* 68 E3
Frenchglen, *U.S.A.* 110 E4
Frenchman Butte, *Canada* 101 C7
Frenchman Cr. →, *Mont., U.S.A.* 110 B10
Frenchman Cr. →, *Nebr., U.S.A.* 108 E4
Frenda, *Algeria* 75 A5
Fresco →, *Brazil* 125 B7
Freshfield, C., *Antarctica* 5 C10
Fresnay-sur-Sarthe, *France* 24 D7
Fresnillo, *Mexico* 114 C4
Fresno, *U.S.A.* 111 H4
Fresno Alhandiga, *Spain* 30 E5
Fresno Reservoir, *U.S.A.* 110 B9
Freudenstadt, *Germany* 19 G4
Freux, *Belgium* 17 J6
Frévent, *France* 25 B9
Frew →, *Australia* 90 C2
Frewena, *Australia* 90 B2
Freycinet Pen., *Australia* 90 G4
Freyming-Merlebach, *France* 25 C13
Freyung, *Germany* 19 G9
Fria, *Guinea* 78 C2
Fria, C., *Namibia* 84 B1
Friant, *U.S.A.* 112 J7
Frías, *Argentina* 126 B2
Fribourg, *Switz.* 22 C4
Fribourg □, *Switz.* 22 C4
Frick, *Switz.* 22 A6
Friday Harbor, *U.S.A.* 112 B3
Friedberg, *Bayern, Germany* 19 G6
Friedberg, *Hessen, Germany* 19 E4
Friedland, *Germany* 18 B9
Friedrichshafen, *Germany* 19 H5
Friedrichskoog, *Germany* 18 A4
Friedrichstadt, *Germany* 18 A5
Friendly Is. = Tonga ■, *Pac. Oc.* 87 D11
Friesack, *Germany* 18 C8
Friesche Wad, *Neths.* 16 B7
Friesland □, *Neths.* 16 B7
Friesoythe, *Germany* 18 B3
Frillesås, *Sweden* 11 G6
Frio →, *U.S.A.* 109 L5
Friona, *U.S.A.* 109 H3
Frisian Is., *Europe* 18 B2
Fristad, *Sweden* 11 G7
Fritch, *U.S.A.* 109 H4
Fritsla, *Sweden* 11 G6
Fritzlar, *Germany* 18 D5
Friuli-Venézia Giulia □, *Italy* 33 B10
Frobisher B., *Canada* 97 B13
Frobisher Bay = Iqaluit, *Canada* 97 B13
Frobisher L., *Canada* 101 B7
Frohavet, *Norway* 8 E13
Froid, *U.S.A.* 108 A2
Froid-Chapelle, *Belgium* 17 H4
Frolovo, *Russia* 42 F6
Fromberg, *U.S.A.* 110 D9
Frome, *U.K.* 13 F5
Frome, L., *Australia* 91 E2
Frome Downs, *Australia* 91 E2
Frómista, *Spain* 30 C6
Front Range, *U.S.A.* 110 G11
Front Royal, *U.S.A.* 104 F6
Fronteira, *Portugal* 31 F3
Fronteiras, *Brazil* 122 C3
Frontera, *Canary Is.* 36 G2
Frontera, *Mexico* 115 D6
Frontignan, *France* 26 E7
Frosinone, *Italy* 34 A6
Frosolone, *Italy* 35 A7
Frostburg, *U.S.A.* 104 F6
Frostisen, *Norway* 8 B17
Frouard, *France* 25 D13
Frøya, *Norway* 8 E13
Fruges, *France* 25 B9
Frumoasa, *Romania* 38 C8
Frunze = Bishkek, *Kyrgyzstan* 44 E8
Frutal, *Brazil* 123 F2
Frutigen, *Switz.* 22 C5
Frýdek-Místek, *Czech.* 20 F8
Frýdlant, *Czech.* 20 E5
Fu Jiang →, *China* 52 C6
Fu Xian, *Liaoning, China* 51 E11
Fu Xian, *Shaanxi, China* 50 F5
Fu'an, *China* 53 D12
Fubian, *China* 52 B4
Fucécchio, *Italy* 32 E7
Fucheng, *China* 50 F9
Fuchou = Fuzhou, *China* 53 D12
Fuchū, *Japan* 49 G6
Fuchuan, *China* 53 E8
Fuchun Jiang →, *China* 53 B13
Fúcino, Conca del, *Italy* 33 F10
Fuding, *China* 53 D13
Fuencaliente, *Canary Is.* 36 F2
Fuencaliente, *Spain* 31 G6
Fuencaliente, Pta., *Canary Is.* 36 F2
Fuengirola, *Spain* 31 J6
Fuente Alamo, *Albacete, Spain* 29 G3
Fuente Álamo, *Murcia, Spain* 29 H3
Fuente de Cantos, *Spain* 31 G4
Fuente del Maestre, *Spain* 31 G4
Fuente el Fresno, *Spain* 31 F7
Fuente Ovejuna, *Spain* 31 G5
Fuentes de Andalucía, *Spain* 31 H5
Fuentes de Ebro, *Spain* 28 D4
Fuentes de León, *Spain* 31 G4
Fuentes de Oñoro, *Spain* 30 E4
Fuentesaúco, *Spain* 30 D5
Fuerte →, *Mexico* 114 B3
Fuerte Olimpo, *Paraguay* 126 A4
Fuerteventura, *Canary Is.* 36 F6
Fufeng, *China* 50 G4
Fuga I., *Phil.* 55 B4
Fugong, *China* 52 D2
Fugou, *China* 50 G8
Fugu, *China* 50 E6
Fuhai, *China* 54 B3
Fuḩaymī, *Iraq* 67 E10
Fuji, *Japan* 49 G9
Fuji-San, *Japan* 49 G9
Fuji-yoshida, *Japan* 49 G9
Fujian □, *China* 53 E12
Fujinomiya, *Japan* 49 G9
Fujisawa, *Japan* 49 G9
Fukien = Fujian □, *China* 53 E12
Fukuchiyama, *Japan* 49 G7
Fukue-Shima, *Japan* 49 H4
Fukui, *Japan* 49 F8
Fukui □, *Japan* 49 G8
Fukuoka, *Japan* 49 H5
Fukuoka □, *Japan* 49 H5
Fukushima, *Japan* 48 F10
Fukushima □, *Japan* 48 F10
Fukuyama, *Japan* 49 G6
Fulda, *Germany* 18 E5
Fulda →, *Germany* 18 D5
Fuling, *China* 52 C6
Fullerton, *Calif., U.S.A.* 113 M9
Fullerton, *Nebr., U.S.A.* 108 E5
Fulongquan, *China* 51 B13
Fulton, *Mo., U.S.A.* 108 F9
Fulton, *N.Y., U.S.A.* 107 C8
Fulton, *Tenn., U.S.A.* 105 G1
Fuluälven →, *Sweden* 10 C7
Fulufjället, *Sweden* 10 C6
Fumay, *France* 25 C11
Fumel, *France* 26 D4
Fumin, *China* 52 E4
Funabashi, *Japan* 49 G10
Funchal, *Madeira* 36 D3
Fundación, *Colombia* 120 A3
Fundão, *Brazil* 123 E3
Fundão, *Portugal* 30 E3
Fundy, B. of, *Canada* 99 D6
Funing, *Hebei, China* 51 E10
Funing, *Jiangsu, China* 51 H10
Funing, *Yunnan, China* 52 F5
Funiu Shan, *China* 50 H7
Funsi, *Ghana* 78 C4
Funtua, *Nigeria* 79 C6
Fuping, *Hebei, China* 50 E8
Fuping, *Shaanxi, China* 50 G5
Fuqing, *China* 53 E12
Fuquan, *China* 52 D6
Fur, *Denmark* 11 H3
Furano, *Japan* 48 C11
Furāt, Nahr al →, *Asia* 64 D5
Fūrg, *Iran* 65 D7
Furkapass, *Switz.* 23 C7
Furmanov, *Russia* 42 B5
Furmanovo, *Kazakhstan* 42 F9
Furnás, *Spain* 36 B8
Furnas, Reprêsa de, *Brazil* 123 F2
Furneaux Group, *Australia* 90 G4
Furness, *U.K.* 12 C4
Furqlus, *Syria* 69 A6
Fürstenau, *Germany* 18 C3
Fürstenberg, *Germany* 18 B9
Fürstenfeld, *Austria* 21 H6
Fürstenfeldbruck, *Germany* 19 G7
Fürstenwalde, *Germany* 18 C10
Fürth, *Germany* 19 F6
Furth im Wald, *Germany* 19 F8
Furtwangen, *Germany* 19 G4
Furukawa, *Japan* 48 E10
Furusund, *Sweden* 10 E12
Fury and Hecla Str., *Canada* 97 B11
Fusagasuga, *Colombia* 120 C3
Fuscaldo, *Italy* 35 C9
Fushan, *Shandong, China* 51 F11
Fushan, *Shanxi, China* 50 G6
Fushun, *Liaoning, China* 51 D12
Fushun, *Sichuan, China* 52 C5
Fusio, *Switz.* 23 D7
Fusong, *China* 51 C14
Füssen, *Germany* 19 H6
Fusui, *China* 52 F6
Futrono, *Chile* 128 B2
Futuna, *Wall. & F. Is.* 87 B8
Fuwa, *Egypt* 76 H7
Fuxin, *China* 51 C11
Fuyang, *Anhui, China* 50 H8
Fuyang, *Zhejiang, China* 53 B12
Fuyang He →, *China* 50 E9
Fuying Dao, *China* 53 D13
Fuyu, *China* 51 B13
Fuyuan, *Heilongjiang, China* 54 B8
Fuyuan, *Yunnan, China* 52 E5
Fuzhou, *China* 53 D12
Fylde, *U.K.* 12 D5
Fyn, *Denmark* 11 J4
Fyne, L., *U.K.* 14 F3
Fyns Amtskommune □, *Denmark* 11 J4
Fyresvatn, *Norway* 10 E2

G

Gaanda, *Nigeria* 79 C7
Gabarin, *Nigeria* 79 C7
Gabas →, *France* 26 E3
Gabela, *Angola* 80 G2
Gabès, *Tunisia* 75 B7
Gabès, G. de, *Tunisia* 75 B7
Gabgaba, W. →, *Egypt* 76 C3
Gabon ■, *Africa* 80 E2
Gaborone, *Botswana* 84 C4
Gabriels, *U.S.A.* 107 B10
Gābrīk, *Iran* 65 E8
Gabrovo, *Bulgaria* 38 G8
Gacé, *France* 24 D7
Gāch Sār, *Iran* 65 B6
Gachsārān, *Iran* 65 D6
Gacko, *Bos.-H.* 21 M8
Gadag, *India* 60 M9
Gadamai, *Sudan* 77 D4
Gadap, *Pakistan* 62 G2
Gadarwara, *India* 63 H8
Gadebusch, *Germany* 18 B7
Gadein, *Sudan* 77 F2
Gadhada, *India* 62 J4
Gadmen, *Switz.* 23 C6
Gádor, Sierra de, *Spain* 29 J2
Gadsden, *Ala., U.S.A.* 105 H2
Gadsden, *Ariz., U.S.A.* 111 K6
Gadwal, *India* 60 L10
Gadyach = Hadyach, *Ukraine* 41 G8
Găeşti, *Romania* 38 E8
Gaeta, *Italy* 34 A6
Gaeta, G. di, *Italy* 34 A6
Gaffney, *U.S.A.* 105 H5
Gafsa, *Tunisia* 75 B6
Gagarin, *Russia* 42 C2
Gagetown, *Canada* 99 C6
Gagino, *Russia* 42 C7
Gagliano del Capo, *Italy* 35 C11
Gagnoa, *Ivory C.* 78 D3
Gagnon, *Canada* 99 B6
Gagnon, L., *Canada* 101 A6
Gagra, *Georgia* 43 J5
Gahini, *Rwanda* 82 C3
Gahmar, *India* 63 G10
Gai Xian, *China* 51 D12
Gaïdhouronísi, *Greece* 37 E7
Gail, *U.S.A.* 109 J4
Gail →, *Austria* 21 J3
Gaillac, *France* 26 E5
Gaillimh = Galway, *Ireland* 15 C2
Gaillon, *France* 24 C8
Gaimán, *Argentina* 128 B3
Gaines, *U.S.A.* 106 E7
Gainesville, *Fla., U.S.A.* 105 L4
Gainesville, *Ga., U.S.A.* 105 H4
Gainesville, *Mo., U.S.A.* 109 G8
Gainesville, *Tex., U.S.A.* 109 J6
Gainsborough, *U.K.* 12 D7
Gairdner, L., *Australia* 91 E2
Gairloch, L., *U.K.* 14 D3
Gais, *Switz.* 23 B8
Gakuch, *Pakistan* 63 A5
Galán, Cerro, *Argentina* 126 B2
Galana →, *Kenya* 82 C5
Galangue, *Angola* 81 G3
Galápagos, *Pac. Oc.* 93 H18
Galashiels, *U.K.* 14 F6
Galaţi, *Romania* 38 D11
Galatia, *Turkey* 66 C5
Galatina, *Italy* 35 B11
Galátone, *Italy* 35 B11
Galax, *U.S.A.* 105 G5
Galaxídhion, *Greece* 39 L5
Galbraith, *Australia* 90 B3
Galcaio, *Somali Rep.* 68 F4
Galdhøpiggen, *Norway* 10 C2
Galeana, *Mexico* 114 C4
Galela, *Indonesia* 57 D7
Galera, *Spain* 29 H2
Galera, Pta., *Chile* 128 A2
Galera Point, *Trin. & Tob.* 117 D7
Galesburg, *U.S.A.* 108 E9
Galeton, *U.S.A.* 106 E7
Galheirão →, *Brazil* 123 D2
Galheiros, *Brazil* 123 D2
Gali, *Georgia* 43 J5
Galich, *Russia* 42 A6
Galiche, *Bulgaria* 38 F6
Galicia □, *Spain* 30 C3
Galilee = Hagalil, *Israel* 69 C4
Galilee, L., *Australia* 90 C4
Galilee, Sea of = Yam Kinneret, *Israel* 69 C4
Galinoporni, *Cyprus* 37 D13
Galion, *U.S.A.* 106 F2
Galite, Is. de la, *Tunisia* 75 A6
Galiuro Mts., *U.S.A.* 111 K8
Gallabat, *Sudan* 77 E4
Gallardon, *France* 25 D8
Gallarte, *Italy* 32 C5
Gallatin, *U.S.A.* 105 G2
Galle, *Sri Lanka* 60 R12
Gállego →, *Spain* 28 D4
Gallegos →, *Argentina* 128 D3
Galley Hd., *Ireland* 15 E3
Galliate, *Italy* 32 C5
Gallinas, Pta., *Colombia* 120 A3
Gallipoli = Gelibolu, *Turkey* 66 B2
Gallípoli, *Italy* 35 B11
Gallipolis, *U.S.A.* 104 F4
Gällivare, *Sweden* 8 C19
Gallo, C., *Italy* 34 D6
Gallocanta, L. de, *Spain* 28 E3
Galloway, *U.K.* 14 G4
Galloway, Mull of, *U.K.* 14 G4
Gallup, *U.S.A.* 111 J9
Gallur, *Spain* 28 D3
Galong, *Australia* 91 E4
Galoya, *Sri Lanka* 60 Q12
Galt, *U.S.A.* 112 G5
Galtström, *Sweden* 10 B11
Galtür, *Austria* 19 J6
Galty Mts., *Ireland* 15 D3
Galtymore, *Ireland* 15 D3
Galva, *U.S.A.* 108 E9
Galvarino, *Chile* 128 A2
Galve de Sorbe, *Spain* 28 D1
Galveston, *U.S.A.* 109 L7
Galveston B., *U.S.A.* 109 L7
Gálvez, *Argentina* 126 C3
Gálvez, *Spain* 31 F6
Galway, *Ireland* 15 C2
Galway □, *Ireland* 15 C2
Galway B., *Ireland* 15 C2
Gam →, *Vietnam* 58 B5
Gamagori, *Japan* 49 G8
Gamari, L., *Ethiopia* 77 E5
Gamawa, *Nigeria* 79 C7
Gamay, *Phil.* 55 E6
Gambaga, *Ghana* 79 C4
Gambat, *Pakistan* 62 F3
Gambela, *Ethiopia* 77 F3
Gambia ■, *W. Afr.* 78 C1
Gambia →, *W. Afr.* 78 C1
Gambier, C., *Australia* 88 B5
Gambier Is., *Australia* 91 F2
Gamboli, *Pakistan* 62 E3
Gamboma, *Congo* 80 E3
Gamerco, *U.S.A.* 111 J9

Gamlakarleby = Kokkola, Finland ... 8 E20
Gammon →, Canada ... 101 C9
Gammouda, Tunisia ... 75 A6
Gamu-Gofa □, Ethiopia ... 77 F4
Gan, France ... 26 E3
Gan Gan, Argentina ... 128 B3
Gan Goriama, Mts., Cameroon ... 79 D7
Gan Jiang →, China ... 53 C10
Ganado, Ariz., U.S.A. ... 111 J9
Ganado, Tex., U.S.A. ... 109 L6
Gananoque, Canada ... 98 D4
Ganāveh, Iran ... 65 D6
Gäncä, Azerbaijan ... 43 K8
Gand = Gent, Belgium ... 17 F3
Ganda, Angola ... 81 G2
Gandak →, India ... 63 G11
Gandava, Pakistan ... 62 E2
Gander, Canada ... 99 C9
Gander L., Canada ... 99 C9
Ganderowe Falls, Zimbabwe ... 83 F2
Gandesa, Spain ... 28 D5
Gandhi Sagar, India ... 62 G6
Gandi, Nigeria ... 79 C6
Gandía, Spain ... 29 G4
Gandino, Italy ... 32 C6
Gando, Pta., Canary Is. ... 36 G4
Gandole, Nigeria ... 79 D7
Gandu, Brazil ... 123 D4
Ganedidalem = Gani, Indonesia ... 57 E7
Ganetti, Sudan ... 76 D3
Ganga →, India ... 63 H14
Ganga, Mouths of the, India ... 63 J13
Ganganagar, India ... 62 E5
Gangapur, India ... 62 F7
Gangara, Niger ... 79 C6
Gangaw, Burma ... 61 H19
Gangdisê Shan, China ... 61 D12
Ganges = Ganga →, India ... 63 H14
Ganges, France ... 26 E7
Gangoh, India ... 62 E7
Gangtok, India ... 61 F16
Gangu, China ... 50 G3
Gangyao, China ... 51 B14
Gani, Indonesia ... 57 E7
Ganj, India ... 63 F8
Gannat, France ... 26 B7
Gannett Peak, U.S.A. ... 110 E9
Gannvalley, U.S.A. ... 108 C5
Ganquan, China ... 50 F5
Gänserdorf, Austria ... 21 G6
Ganshui, China ... 52 C6
Gansu □, China ... 50 G3
Ganta, Liberia ... 78 D3
Gantheaume, C., Australia ... 91 F2
Gantheaume B., Australia ... 89 E1
Gantsevichi = Hantsavichy, Belarus ... 41 F4
Ganyem, Indonesia ... 57 E10
Ganyu, China ... 51 G10
Ganyushkino, Kazakhstan ... 43 G9
Ganzhou, China ... 53 E10
Gao, Mali ... 79 B5
Gao Xian, China ... 52 C5
Gao'an, China ... 53 C10
Gaohe, China ... 53 F9
Gaohebu, China ... 53 B11
Gaokeng, China ... 53 D9
Gaolan Dao, China ... 53 G9
Gaoligong Shan, China ... 52 E2
Gaomi, China ... 51 F10
Gaoping, China ... 50 G7
Gaotang, China ... 50 F9
Gaoua, Burkina Faso ... 78 C4
Gaoual, Guinea ... 78 C2
Gaoxiong, Taiwan ... 53 F13
Gaoyang, China ... 50 E8
Gaoyou, China ... 53 A12
Gaoyou Hu, China ... 51 H10
Gaoyuan, China ... 51 F9
Gaozhou, China ... 53 G8
Gap, France ... 27 D10
Gapan, Phil. ... 55 D4
Gar, China ... 54 C2
Garabogazköl Aylagy, Turkmenistan ... 44 E6
Garachico, Canary Is. ... 36 F3
Garachiné, Panama ... 116 E4
Garafia, Canary Is. ... 36 F2
Garajonay, Canary Is. ... 36 F2
Garanhuns, Brazil ... 122 C4
Garawe, Liberia ... 78 E3
Garba Tula, Kenya ... 82 B4
Garber, U.S.A. ... 109 G6
Garberville, U.S.A. ... 110 F2
Garça, Brazil ... 123 F2
Garças →, Mato Grosso, Brazil ... 125 D7
Garças →, Pernambuco, Brazil ... 122 C4
Garcias, Brazil ... 125 E7
Gard, Somali Rep. ... 68 F4
Gard □, France ... 27 D8
Gard →, France ... 27 E8
Garda, L. di, Italy ... 32 C7
Gardanne, France ... 27 E9
Garde L., Canada ... 101 A7
Gardelegen, Germany ... 18 C7
Garden City, Kans., U.S.A. ... 109 G4
Garden City, Tex., U.S.A. ... 109 K4
Garden Grove, U.S.A. ... 113 M9
Gardēz, Afghan. ... 62 C3
Gardiner, U.S.A. ... 110 D8

Gardiners I., U.S.A. ... 107 E12
Gardner, U.S.A. ... 107 D13
Gardner Canal, Canada ... 100 C3
Gardnerville, U.S.A. ... 112 G7
Gare Tigre, Fr. Guiana ... 121 C7
Garéssio, Italy ... 32 D5
Garey, U.S.A. ... 113 L6
Garfield, U.S.A. ... 110 C5
Gargan, Mt., France ... 26 C5
Gargano, Mte., Italy ... 35 A8
Gargouna, Mali ... 79 B5
Garhshankar, India ... 62 D7
Garibaldi Prov. Park, Canada ... 100 D4
Garies, S. Africa ... 84 E2
Garigliano →, Italy ... 34 A6
Garissa, Kenya ... 82 C4
Garissa □, Kenya ... 82 C5
Garkida, Nigeria ... 79 C7
Garko, Nigeria ... 79 C6
Garland, U.S.A. ... 110 F7
Garlasco, Italy ... 32 C5
Garm, Tajikistan ... 44 F8
Garmāb, Iran ... 65 C8
Garmisch-Partenkirchen, Germany ... 19 H7
Garmsār, Iran ... 65 C7
Garner, U.S.A. ... 108 D8
Garnett, U.S.A. ... 108 F7
Garo Hills, India ... 63 G14
Garoe, Somali Rep. ... 68 F4
Garonne →, France ... 26 C3
Garonne, Canal Latéral à la →, France ... 26 D4
Garoua, Cameroon ... 79 D7
Garrel, Germany ... 18 C3
Garrigue, France ... 26 E7
Garrison, Mont., U.S.A. ... 110 C7
Garrison, N. Dak., U.S.A. ... 108 B4
Garrison, Tex., U.S.A. ... 109 K7
Garrison Res. = Sakakawea, L., U.S.A. ... 108 B3
Garrovillas, Spain ... 31 F4
Garrucha, Spain ... 29 H3
Garry →, U.K. ... 14 E5
Garry, L., Canada ... 96 B9
Garsen, Kenya ... 82 C5
Garson L., Canada ... 101 B6
Gartempe →, France ... 26 B4
Gartz, Germany ... 18 B10
Garu, Ghana ... 79 C4
Garub, Namibia ... 84 D2
Garut, Indonesia ... 57 G12
Garvão, Portugal ... 31 H2
Garvie Mts., N.Z. ... 87 L2
Garwa = Garoua, Cameroon ... 79 D7
Garwa, India ... 63 G10
Garwolin, Poland ... 20 D11
Gary, U.S.A. ... 104 E2
Garz, Germany ... 18 A9
Garzê, China ... 52 B3
Garzón, Colombia ... 120 C2
Gas-San, Japan ... 48 E10
Gasan Kuli = Hasan Kuli, Turkmenistan ... 44 F6
Gascogne, France ... 26 E4
Gascogne, G. de, Europe ... 28 B2
Gascony = Gascogne, France ... 26 E4
Gascoyne →, Australia ... 89 D1
Gascoyne Junc. T.O., Australia ... 89 E2
Gascueña, Spain ... 28 E2
Gash, Wadi →, Ethiopia ... 77 D4
Gashaka, Nigeria ... 79 D7
Gasherbrum, Pakistan ... 63 B7
Gashua, Nigeria ... 79 C7
Gaspé, Canada ... 99 C7
Gaspé, C. de, Canada ... 99 C7
Gaspé, Pén. de, Canada ... 99 C6
Gaspésie, Parc Prov. de la, Canada ... 99 C6
Gassaway, U.S.A. ... 104 F5
Gasselte, Neths. ... 16 C9
Gasselternijveen, Neths. ... 16 C9
Gássino Torinese, Italy ... 32 C4
Gassol, Nigeria ... 79 D7
Gasteiz = Vitoria, Spain ... 28 C2
Gastonia, U.S.A. ... 105 H5
Gastoúni, Greece ... 39 M4
Gastoúri, Greece ... 39 K3
Gastre, Argentina ... 128 B3
Gata, C., Cyprus ... 37 E12
Gata, C. de, Spain ... 29 J2
Gata, Sierra de, Spain ... 30 E4
Gataga →, Canada ... 100 B3
Gătaia, Romania ... 38 D4
Gatchina, Russia ... 40 C6
Gates, U.S.A. ... 106 C7
Gateshead, U.K. ... 12 C6
Gatesville, U.S.A. ... 109 K6
Gaths, Zimbabwe ... 83 G3
Gatico, Chile ... 126 A1
Gâtinais, France ... 25 D9
Gâtine, Hauteurs de, France ... 26 B3
Gatineau →, Canada ... 98 C4
Gatineau, Parc de la, Canada ... 98 C4
Gattaran, Phil. ... 55 B4
Gattinara, Italy ... 32 C5
Gatun, L., Panama ... 116 E4
Gatyana, S. Africa ... 85 E4
Gau, Fiji ... 87 D8
Gaucín, Spain ... 31 J5
Gauer L., Canada ... 101 B9

Gauhati, India ... 63 F14
Gauja →, Latvia ... 9 H21
Gaula →, Norway ... 8 E14
Gaurain-Ramecroix, Belgium ... 17 G3
Gausta, Norway ... 10 E2
Gauteng = P.W.V. □, S. Africa ... 85 D4
Gāv Koshī, Iran ... 65 D8
Gavá, Spain ... 28 D6
Gāvakān, Iran ... 65 D7
Gavarnie, France ... 26 F3
Gāvāter, Iran ... 65 E9
Gāvbandī, Iran ... 65 E7
Gavdhopoúla, Greece ... 37 E6
Gávdhos, Greece ... 37 E6
Gavere, Belgium ... 17 G3
Gavião, Portugal ... 31 F3
Gaviota, U.S.A. ... 113 L6
Gävle, Sweden ... 9 F17
Gävleborgs län □, Sweden ... 10 C10
Gavorrano, Italy ... 32 F7
Gavray, France ... 24 D5
Gavrilov Yam, Russia ... 42 B4
Gawachab, Namibia ... 84 D2
Gawilgarh Hills, India ... 60 J10
Gawler, Australia ... 91 E2
Gaxun Nur, China ... 54 B5
Gaya, India ... 63 G11
Gaya, Niger ... 79 C5
Gaya, Nigeria ... 79 C6
Gaylord, U.S.A. ... 104 C3
Gayndah, Australia ... 91 D5
Gaysin = Haysyn, Ukraine ... 41 H5
Gayvoron = Hayvoron, Ukraine ... 41 H5
Gaza, Gaza Strip ... 69 D3
Gaza □, Mozam. ... 85 C5
Gaza Strip = Asia ... 69 D3
Gazaoua, Niger ... 79 C6
Gāzbor, Iran ... 65 D8
Gazi, Zaïre ... 82 B1
Gaziantep, Turkey ... 66 D7
Gazipaşa, Turkey ... 66 D5
Gazli, Uzbekistan ... 44 E7
Gbarnga, Liberia ... 78 D3
Gbekebo, Nigeria ... 79 D5
Gboko, Nigeria ... 79 D6
Gbongan, Nigeria ... 79 D5
Gcuwa, S. Africa ... 85 E4
Gdańsk, Poland ... 20 A8
Gdańska, Zatoka, Poland ... 20 A9
Gdov, Russia ... 9 G22
Gdynia, Poland ... 20 A8
Gebe, Indonesia ... 57 D7
Gebeit Mine, Sudan ... 76 C4
Gebel Mûsa, Egypt ... 76 J8
Gebze, Turkey ... 66 B3
Gecha, Ethiopia ... 77 F4
Gedaref, Sudan ... 77 E4
Gede, Tanjung, Indonesia ... 56 F3
Gedinne, Belgium ... 17 J5
Gediz, Turkey ... 66 C3
Gediz →, Turkey ... 66 C2
Gedo, Ethiopia ... 77 F4
Gedser, Denmark ... 11 K5
Gedser Odde, Denmark ... 11 K5
Geegully Cr. →, Australia ... 88 C3
Geel, Belgium ... 17 F5
Geelong, Australia ... 91 F3
Geelvink Chan., Australia ... 89 E1
Geer →, Belgium ... 17 G7
Geesthacht, Germany ... 18 B6
Geffen, Neths. ... 16 E6
Geidam, Nigeria ... 79 C7
Geikie →, Canada ... 101 B8
Geili, Sudan ... 77 D3
Geilo, Norway ... 10 D2
Geisingen, Germany ... 19 H4
Geislingen, Germany ... 19 G5
Geita, Tanzania ... 82 C3
Geita □, Tanzania ... 82 C3
Gejiu, China ... 52 F4
Gel →, Sudan ... 77 F2
Gel River, Sudan ... 77 F2
Gela, Italy ... 35 E7
Gela, G. di, Italy ... 35 F7
Geladi, Ethiopia ... 68 F4
Gelderland □, Neths. ... 16 D8
Geldermalsen, Neths. ... 16 E6
Geldern, Germany ... 18 D2
Geldrop, Neths. ... 17 F7
Geleen, Neths. ... 17 G7
Gelehun, S. Leone ... 78 D2
Gelendost, Turkey ... 66 C4
Gelendzhik, Russia ... 43 H4
Gelibolu, Turkey ... 66 D2
Gelidonya Burnu, Turkey ... 66 D4
Gelnhausen, Germany ... 19 E5
Gelsenkirchen, Germany ... 18 D3
Gelting, Germany ... 18 A5
Gemas, Malaysia ... 59 L4
Gembloux, Belgium ... 17 G5
Gemena, Zaïre ... 80 D3
Gemerek, Turkey ... 66 C7
Gemert, Neths. ... 17 E7
Gemlik, Turkey ... 66 B3
Gemona del Friuli, Italy ... 33 B10
Gemsa, Egypt ... 76 B3
Gemünden, Germany ... 19 E5
Genale, Ethiopia ... 77 F4
Genappe, Belgium ... 17 G4
Genç, Turkey ... 67 C9
Gençay, France ... 26 B4
Gendringen, Neths. ... 16 E8
Gendt, Neths. ... 16 E7

Geneina, Gebel, Egypt ... 76 J8
Genemuiden, Neths. ... 16 C8
General Acha, Argentina ... 126 D3
General Alvear, Buenos Aires, Argentina ... 126 D3
General Alvear, Mendoza, Argentina ... 126 D2
General Artigas, Paraguay ... 126 B4
General Belgrano, Argentina ... 126 D4
General Cabrera, Argentina ... 126 C3
General Carrera, L., Chile ... 128 C2
General Cepeda, Mexico ... 114 B4
General Conesa, Argentina ... 128 B4
General Guido, Argentina ... 126 D4
General Juan Madariaga, Argentina ... 126 D4
General La Madrid, Argentina ... 126 D3
General Lorenzo Vintter, Argentina ... 128 B4
General MacArthur, Phil. ... 55 F6
General Martin Miguel de Güemes, Argentina ... 126 A3
General Paz, Argentina ... 126 B4
General Pico, Argentina ... 126 D3
General Pinedo, Argentina ... 126 B3
General Pinto, Argentina ... 126 C3
General Sampaio, Brazil ... 122 B4
General Santos, Phil. ... 55 H6
General Toshevo, Bulgaria ... 38 F11
General Trevino, Mexico ... 115 B5
General Trías, Mexico ... 114 B3
General Viamonte, Argentina ... 126 D3
General Villegas, Argentina ... 126 D3
General Vintter, L., Argentina ... 128 B2
Generoso, Mte., Switz. ... 23 E8
Genesee, Idaho, U.S.A. ... 110 C5
Genesee, Pa., U.S.A. ... 106 E7
Genesee →, U.S.A. ... 106 C7
Geneseo, Ill., U.S.A. ... 108 E9
Geneseo, Kans., U.S.A. ... 108 F5
Geneseo, N.Y., U.S.A. ... 106 D7
Geneva = Genève, Switz. ... 22 D2
Geneva, Ala., U.S.A. ... 105 K3
Geneva, N.Y., U.S.A. ... 106 D7
Geneva, Nebr., U.S.A. ... 108 E6
Geneva, Ohio, U.S.A. ... 106 E4
Geneva, L. = Léman, L., Europe ... 22 D3
Geneva, L., U.S.A. ... 104 D1
Genève, Switz. ... 22 D2
Genève □, Switz. ... 22 D2
Genichesk = Henichesk, Ukraine ... 41 J8
Genil →, Spain ... 31 H5
Génissiat, Barr. de, France ... 27 B9
Genk, Belgium ... 17 G7
Genlis, France ... 25 E12
Gennargentu, Mti. del, Italy ... 34 C2
Gennep, Neths. ... 17 E7
Gennes, France ... 24 E6
Genoa = Génova, Italy ... 32 D5
Genoa, Australia ... 91 F4
Genoa, N.Y., U.S.A. ... 107 D8
Genoa, Nebr., U.S.A. ... 108 E6
Genoa, Nev., U.S.A. ... 112 F7
Genoa →, Argentina ... 128 B2
Génova, Italy ... 32 D5
Génova, G. di, Italy ... 32 E6
Gent, Belgium ... 17 F3
Gentbrugge, Belgium ... 17 F3
Genthin, Germany ... 18 C8
Gentio do Ouro, Brazil ... 122 D3
Geographe B., Australia ... 89 F2
Geographe Chan., Australia ... 89 D1
Geokchay = Göyçay, Azerbaijan ... 43 K8
Georga, Zemlya, Russia ... 44 A5
George, S. Africa ... 84 E3
George →, Canada ... 99 A6
George, L., N.S.W., Australia ... 91 F4
George, L., S. Austral., Australia ... 91 F3
George, L., W. Austral., Australia ... 88 D3
George, L., Uganda ... 82 B3
George, L., Fla., U.S.A. ... 105 L5
George, L., N.Y., U.S.A. ... 107 C11
George Gill Ra., Australia ... 88 D5
George River = Kangiqsualujjuaq, Canada ... 97 C13
George Sound, N.Z. ... 87 L1
George Town, Bahamas ... 116 B4
George Town, Malaysia ... 59 K3
George V Land, Antarctica ... 5 C10
George VI Sound, Antarctica ... 5 D17
George West, U.S.A. ... 109 L5
Georgetown, Australia ... 90 B3
Georgetown, Ont., Canada ... 98 D4
Georgetown, P.E.I., Canada ... 99 C7
Georgetown, Cayman Is. ... 116 C3
Georgetown, Gambia ... 78 C2
Georgetown, Guyana ... 121 B6
Georgetown, Calif., U.S.A. ... 112 G6
Georgetown, Colo., U.S.A. ... 110 G11
Georgetown, Ky., U.S.A. ... 104 F3
Georgetown, S.C., U.S.A. ... 105 J6

Georgetown, Tex., U.S.A. ... 109 K6
Georgia □, U.S.A. ... 105 J4
Georgia ■, Asia ... 43 J6
Georgia, Str. of, Canada ... 100 D4
Georgian B., Canada ... 98 C3
Georgina →, Australia ... 90 C2
Georgina Downs, Australia ... 90 C2
Georgiu-Dezh = Liski, Russia ... 42 E4
Georgiyevsk, Russia ... 43 H6
Gera, Germany ... 18 E8
Geraardsbergen, Belgium ... 17 G3
Geral, Serra, Bahia, Brazil ... 123 D3
Geral, Serra, Goiás, Brazil ... 122 D2
Geral, Serra, Sta. Catarina, Brazil ... 127 B6
Geral de Goiás, Serra, Brazil ... 123 D2
Geral do Paraná Serra, Brazil ... 123 E2
Geraldine, U.S.A. ... 110 C8
Geraldton, Australia ... 89 E1
Geraldton, Canada ... 98 C2
Gérardmer, France ... 25 D13
Gerçüş, Turkey ... 67 D9
Gerede, Turkey ... 66 B5
Gereshk, Afghan. ... 60 D4
Gérgal, Spain ... 29 H2
Gerik, Malaysia ... 59 K3
Gering, U.S.A. ... 108 E3
Gerlach, U.S.A. ... 110 F4
Gerlachovka, Slovak Rep. ... 20 F10
Germansen Landing, Canada ... 100 B4
Germany ■, Europe ... 18 E6
Germersheim, Germany ... 19 F4
Germī, Iran ... 67 C13
Germiston, S. Africa ... 85 D4
Gernsheim, Germany ... 19 F4
Gero, Japan ... 49 G8
Gerolstein, Germany ... 19 E2
Gerolzhofen, Germany ... 19 F6
Gerona, Spain ... 28 D7
Gerona □, Spain ... 28 C7
Gérouville, Belgium ... 17 J6
Gerrard, Canada ... 100 C5
Gers □, France ... 26 E4
Gers →, France ... 26 D4
Gersfeld, Germany ... 18 E5
Gerze, Turkey ... 66 B6
Geseke, Germany ... 18 D4
Geser, Indonesia ... 57 E8
Gesso →, Italy ... 32 D4
Gestro, Wabi →, Ethiopia ... 77 G5
Gesves, Belgium ... 17 H6
Getafe, Spain ... 30 E7
Gethsémani, Canada ... 99 B7
Gettysburg, Pa., U.S.A. ... 104 F7
Gettysburg, S. Dak., U.S.A. ... 108 C5
Getz Ice Shelf, Antarctica ... 5 D14
Geul →, Neths. ... 17 G7
Gevaş, Turkey ... 67 C10
Gévaudan, France ... 26 D7
Gevgelija, Macedonia ... 39 H5
Gévora →, Spain ... 31 G4
Gex, France ... 27 B10
Geyser, U.S.A. ... 110 C8
Geyserville, U.S.A. ... 112 G4
Geyve, Turkey ... 66 B4
Ghâbat el Arab = Wang Kai, Sudan ... 77 F2
Ghaghara →, India ... 63 G11
Ghalla, Wadi el →, Sudan ... 77 E2
Ghallamane, Mauritania ... 74 D3
Ghana ■, W. Afr. ... 79 D4
Ghansor, India ... 63 H9
Ghanzi, Botswana ... 84 C3
Ghanzi □, Botswana ... 84 C3
Gharb el Istiwa'iya □, Sudan ... 77 F2
Gharbîya, Es Sahrâ el, Egypt ... 76 B2
Ghard Abû Muharik, Egypt ... 76 B2
Ghardaïa, Algeria ... 75 B5
Ghârib, G., Egypt ... 76 J8
Gharyān, Libya ... 75 B7
Gharyān □, Libya ... 75 B7
Ghat, Libya ... 75 D7
Ghatal, India ... 63 H12
Ghatampur, India ... 63 F9
Ghatti, Si. Arabia ... 64 D3
Ghawdex = Gozo, Malta ... 37 C1
Ghazal, Bahr el →, Chad ... 73 F8
Ghazâl, Bahr el →, Sudan ... 77 F3
Ghazaouet, Algeria ... 75 A4
Ghaziabad, India ... 62 E7
Ghazipur, India ... 63 G10
Ghaznī, Afghan. ... 62 C3
Ghaznī □, Afghan. ... 60 C6
Ghedi, Italy ... 32 C7
Ghèlinsor, Somali Rep. ... 68 F4
Ghent = Gent, Belgium ... 17 F3
Gheorghe Gheorghiu-Dej = Oneşti, Romania ... 38 C9
Gheorgheni, Romania ... 38 C8
Ghergani, Romania ... 38 E8
Gherla, Romania ... 38 B6
Ghilarza, Italy ... 34 B1
Ghisonaccia, France ... 27 F13
Ghisoni, France ... 27 F13
Ghizao, Afghan. ... 62 C1
Ghizar →, Pakistan ... 63 A5
Ghogha, India ... 62 J5
Ghot Ogrein, Egypt ... 76 A2
Ghotaru, India ... 62 F4

Ghotki

Ghotki, *Pakistan*	62	E3
Ghowr □, *Afghan.*	60	C4
Ghudaf, W. al →, *Iraq*	67	F10
Ghudāmis, *Libya*	75	B6
Ghughri, *India*	63	H9
Ghugus, *India*	60	K11
Ghulam Mohammad Barrage, *Pakistan*	62	G3
Ghūriān, *Afghan.*	60	B2
Gia Dinh, *Vietnam*	59	G6
Gia Lai = Pleiku, *Vietnam*	58	F7
Gia Nghia, *Vietnam*	59	G6
Gia Ngoc, *Vietnam*	58	E7
Gia Vuc, *Vietnam*	58	E7
Gian, *Phil.*	57	C7
Giannutri, *Italy*	32	F8
Giant Forest, *U.S.A.*	112	J8
Giant Mts. = Krkonoše, *Czech.*	20	E5
Giants Causeway, *U.K.*	15	A5
Giarabub = Al Jaghbūb, *Libya*	73	C9
Giarre, *Italy*	35	E8
Giaveno, *Italy*	32	C4
Gibara, *Cuba*	116	B4
Gibb River, *Australia*	88	C4
Gibbon, *U.S.A.*	108	E5
Gibe →, *Ethiopia*	77	F4
Gibellina, *Italy*	34	E6
Gibraléon, *Spain*	31	H4
Gibraltar ■, *Europe*	31	J5
Gibraltar, Str. of, *Medit. S.*	31	K5
Gibson Desert, *Australia*	88	D4
Gibsons, *Canada*	100	D4
Gibsonville, *U.S.A.*	112	F6
Giddings, *U.S.A.*	109	K6
Gidole, *Ethiopia*	77	F4
Giessen, *Germany*	18	E4
Gieten, *Neths.*	16	B9
Gīfān, *Iran*	65	B8
Gifatin, Geziret, *Egypt*	76	B3
Gifford Creek, *Australia*	88	D2
Gifhorn, *Germany*	18	C6
Gifu, *Japan*	49	G8
Gifu □, *Japan*	49	G8
Gigant, *Russia*	43	G5
Giganta, Sa. de la, *Mexico*	114	B2
Gigen, *Bulgaria*	38	F7
Gigha, *U.K.*	14	F3
Giglio, *Italy*	32	F7
Gignac, *France*	26	E7
Gigüela →, *Spain*	29	F1
Gijón, *Spain*	30	B5
Gil I., *Canada*	100	C3
Gila →, *U.S.A.*	111	K6
Gila Bend, *U.S.A.*	111	K7
Gila Bend Mts., *U.S.A.*	111	K7
Gīlān □, *Iran*	65	B6
Gilbert →, *Australia*	90	B3
Gilbert Is., *Kiribati*	92	G9
Gilbert Plains, *Canada*	101	C8
Gilbert River, *Australia*	90	B3
Gilberton, *Australia*	90	B3
Gilbués, *Brazil*	122	C2
Gilf el Kebîr, Hadabat el, *Egypt*	76	C2
Gilford I., *Canada*	100	C3
Gilgandra, *Australia*	91	E4
Gilgil, *Kenya*	82	C4
Gilgit, *India*	63	B6
Gilgit →, *Pakistan*	63	B6
Giljeva Planina, *Serbia, Yug.*	21	M10
Gillam, *Canada*	101	B10
Gilleleje, *Denmark*	11	H6
Gillen, L., *Australia*	89	E3
Gilles, L., *Australia*	91	E2
Gillette, *U.S.A.*	108	C2
Gilliat, *Australia*	90	C3
Gillingham, *U.K.*	13	F8
Gilly, *Belgium*	17	H4
Gilmer, *U.S.A.*	109	J7
Gilmore, *Australia*	91	F4
Gilmore, L., *Australia*	89	F3
Gilmour, *Canada*	98	D4
Gilo →, *Ethiopia*	77	F3
Gilort →, *Romania*	38	E6
Gilroy, *U.S.A.*	111	H3
Gilze, *Neths.*	17	E5
Gimbi, *Ethiopia*	77	F4
Gimigliano, *Italy*	35	D9
Gimli, *Canada*	101	C9
Gimone →, *France*	26	E5
Gimont, *France*	26	E4
Gin Gin, *Australia*	91	D5
Gināh, *Egypt*	76	B3
Gindie, *Australia*	90	C4
Gingin, *Australia*	89	F2
Gîngiova, *Romania*	38	F6
Ginir, *Ethiopia*	68	F3
Ginosa, *Italy*	35	B9
Ginzo de Limia, *Spain*	30	C3
Giohar, *Somali Rep.*	68	G4
Gióia, G. di, *Italy*	35	D8
Gióia del Colle, *Italy*	35	B9
Gióia Táuro, *Italy*	35	D8
Gioiosa Iónica, *Italy*	35	D9
Gióna, Óros, *Greece*	39	L5
Giovi, Passo dei, *Italy*	32	D5
Giovinazzo, *Italy*	35	A9
Gir Hills, *India*	62	J4
Girab, *India*	62	F4
Girâfi, W. →, *Egypt*	69	F3
Giraltovce, *Slovak Rep.*	20	F11
Girard, Kans., *U.S.A.*	109	G7
Girard, Ohio, *U.S.A.*	106	E4
Girard, Pa., *U.S.A.*	106	D4
Girardot, *Colombia*	120	C3
Girdle Ness, *U.K.*	14	D6
Giresun, *Turkey*	67	B8
Girga, *Egypt*	76	B3
Giridih, *India*	63	G12
Girifalco, *Italy*	35	D9
Girilambone, *Australia*	91	E4
Girne = Kyrenia, *Cyprus*	66	E5
Giro, *Nigeria*	79	C5
Giromagny, *France*	25	E13
Girona = Gerona, *Spain*	28	D7
Gironde □, *France*	26	D3
Gironde →, *France*	26	C2
Gironella, *Spain*	28	C6
Giru, *Australia*	90	B4
Girvan, *U.K.*	14	F4
Gisborne, *N.Z.*	87	H7
Gisenyi, *Rwanda*	82	C2
Gislaved, *Sweden*	9	H15
Gisors, *France*	25	C8
Gistel, *Belgium*	17	F1
Giswil, *Switz.*	22	C6
Gitega, *Burundi*	82	C2
Gits, *Belgium*	17	F2
Giugliano in Campania, *Italy*	35	B7
Giulianova, *Italy*	33	F10
Giurgeni, *Romania*	38	E10
Giurgiu, *Romania*	38	F8
Give, *Denmark*	11	J3
Givet, *France*	25	B11
Givors, *France*	27	C8
Givry, *Belgium*	17	H4
Givry, *France*	25	F11
Giyon, *Ethiopia*	77	F4
Giza = El Gîza, *Egypt*	76	H7
Gizhiga, *Russia*	45	C17
Gizhiginskaya Guba, *Russia*	45	C16
Giżycko, *Poland*	20	A11
Gizzeria, *Italy*	35	D9
Gjegjan, *Albania*	39	H3
Gjerstad, *Norway*	10	F3
Gjirokastra, *Albania*	39	J3
Gjoa Haven, *Canada*	96	B10
Gjøl, *Denmark*	11	G3
Gjøvik, *Norway*	10	D4
Glace Bay, *Canada*	99	C8
Glacier Bay, *U.S.A.*	100	B1
Glacier Nat. Park, *Canada*	100	C6
Glacier Park, *U.S.A.*	110	B7
Glacier Peak, *U.S.A.*	110	B3
Gladewater, *U.S.A.*	109	J7
Gladstone, Queens., *Australia*	90	C5
Gladstone, S. Austral., *Australia*	91	E2
Gladstone, W. Austral., *Australia*	89	E1
Gladstone, *Canada*	101	C9
Gladstone, *U.S.A.*	104	C2
Gladwin, *U.S.A.*	104	D3
Gladys L., *Canada*	100	B2
Glåma = Glomma →, *Norway*	10	E4
Gláma, *Iceland*	8	D2
Glamis, *U.S.A.*	113	N11
Glamoč, *Bos.-H.*	33	D13
Glan, *Sweden*	11	F10
Glanerbrug, *Neths.*	16	D9
Glarner Alpen, *Switz.*	23	C8
Glärnisch, *Switz.*	23	C7
Glarus, *Switz.*	23	B8
Glarus □, *Switz.*	23	C8
Glasco, Kans., *U.S.A.*	108	F6
Glasco, N.Y., *U.S.A.*	107	D11
Glasgow, *U.K.*	14	F4
Glasgow, Ky., *U.S.A.*	104	G3
Glasgow, Mont., *U.S.A.*	110	B10
Glastonbury, *U.K.*	13	F5
Glastonbury, *U.S.A.*	107	E12
Glatt →, *Switz.*	23	B7
Glattfelden, *Switz.*	23	A7
Glauchau, *Germany*	18	E8
Glazov, *Russia*	42	A11
Gleiwitz = Gliwice, *Poland*	20	E8
Glen, *U.S.A.*	107	B13
Glen Affric, *U.K.*	14	D4
Glen Canyon Dam, *U.S.A.*	111	H8
Glen Canyon National Recreation Area, *U.S.A.*	111	H8
Glen Coe, *U.K.*	14	E4
Glen Cove, *U.S.A.*	107	F11
Glen Garry, *U.K.*	14	D4
Glen Innes, *Australia*	91	D5
Glen Lyon, *U.S.A.*	107	E8
Glen Mor, *U.K.*	14	D4
Glen Moriston, *U.K.*	14	D4
Glen Orchy, *U.K.*	14	E4
Glen Spean, *U.K.*	14	E4
Glen Ullin, *U.S.A.*	108	B4
Glénan, Is. de, *France*	24	E2
Glenburgh, *Australia*	89	E2
Glencoe, *Canada*	106	D3
Glencoe, *S. Africa*	85	D5
Glencoe, *U.S.A.*	108	C7
Glendale, Ariz., *U.S.A.*	111	K7
Glendale, Calif., *U.S.A.*	113	L8
Glendale, Oreg., *U.S.A.*	110	E2
Glendale, *Zimbabwe*	83	F3
Glendive, *U.S.A.*	108	B2
Glendo, *U.S.A.*	108	D2
Glenelg, *Australia*	91	E2
Glenelg →, *Australia*	91	B3
Glengarriff, *Ireland*	15	E2
Glengyle, *Australia*	90	C2
Glenmora, *U.S.A.*	109	K8
Glenmorgan, *Australia*	91	D4
Glenn, *U.S.A.*	112	F4
Glenns Ferry, *U.S.A.*	110	E6
Glenorchy, *Australia*	90	G4
Glenore, *Australia*	90	B3
Glenormiston, *Australia*	90	C2
Glenreagh, *Australia*	91	E5
Glenrock, *U.S.A.*	110	E11
Glenrothes, *U.K.*	14	E5
Glens Falls, *U.S.A.*	107	C11
Glenties, *Ireland*	15	B3
Glenville, *U.S.A.*	104	F5
Glenwood, Alta., *Canada*	100	D6
Glenwood, Nfld., *Canada*	99	C9
Glenwood, Ark., *U.S.A.*	109	H8
Glenwood, Hawaii, *U.S.A.*	102	J17
Glenwood, Iowa, *U.S.A.*	108	E7
Glenwood, Minn., *U.S.A.*	108	C7
Glenwood, Wash., *U.S.A.*	112	D5
Glenwood Springs, *U.S.A.*	110	G10
Gletsch, *Switz.*	23	C6
Glettinganes, *Iceland*	8	D7
Glina, *Croatia*	33	C13
Glittertind, *Norway*	10	C2
Gliwice, *Poland*	20	E8
Globe, *U.S.A.*	111	K8
Glödnitz, *Austria*	21	J4
Głogów, *Poland*	20	D6
Glomma →, *Norway*	10	E4
Glorieuses, Is., *Ind. Oc.*	85	A8
Glossop, *U.K.*	12	D6
Gloucester, *Australia*	91	E5
Gloucester, *U.K.*	13	F5
Gloucester, *U.S.A.*	107	D14
Gloucester I., *Australia*	90	B4
Gloucestershire □, *U.K.*	13	F5
Gloversville, *U.S.A.*	107	C10
Glovertown, *Canada*	99	C9
Głowno, *Poland*	20	D9
Głubczyce, *Poland*	20	E7
Glubokiy, *Russia*	43	F5
Glubokoye = Hlybokaye, *Belarus*	40	E4
Głuchołazy, *Poland*	20	E7
Glücksburg, *Germany*	18	A5
Glückstadt, *Germany*	18	B5
Glukhov = Hlukhiv, *Ukraine*	41	G7
Glusk, *Belarus*	41	F5
Glyngøre, *Denmark*	11	H2
Gmünd, Kärnten, *Austria*	21	J3
Gmünd, Niederösterreich, *Austria*	20	G5
Gnarp, *Sweden*	10	B11
Gnesta, *Sweden*	10	E11
Gniew, *Poland*	20	B8
Gniezno, *Poland*	20	C7
Gnoien, *Germany*	18	B8
Gnowangerup, *Australia*	89	F2
Go Cong, *Vietnam*	59	G6
Gō-no-ura, *Japan*	49	H4
Go Quao, *Vietnam*	59	H5
Goa, *India*	60	M8
Goa □, *India*	60	M8
Goalen Hd., *Australia*	91	F5
Goalpara, *India*	61	F17
Goalundo Ghat, *Bangla.*	63	H13
Goaso, *Ghana*	78	D4
Goat Fell, *U.K.*	14	F3
Goba, *Ethiopia*	68	F2
Goba, *Mozam.*	85	D5
Gobabis, *Namibia*	84	C2
Gobernador Gregores, *Argentina*	128	C2
Gobi, *Asia*	50	C5
Gobō, *Japan*	49	H7
Gobo, *Sudan*	77	F3
Goch, *Germany*	18	D2
Gochas, *Namibia*	84	C2
Godavari →, *India*	61	L13
Godavari Point, *India*	61	L13
Godbout, *Canada*	99	C6
Godda, *India*	63	G12
Godegård, *Sweden*	11	F9
Goderich, *Canada*	98	D3
Goderville, *France*	24	C7
Godhavn, *Greenland*	4	C5
Godhra, *India*	62	H5
Gödöllő, *Hungary*	21	H9
Godoy Cruz, *Argentina*	126	C2
Gods →, *Canada*	101	B10
Gods L., *Canada*	101	C10
Godthåb, *Greenland*	97	B14
Godwin Austen = K2, Mt., *Pakistan*	63	B7
Goeie Hoop, Kaap die = Good Hope, C. of, *S. Africa*	84	E2
Goéland, L. au, *Canada*	98	C4
Goeree, *Neths.*	16	E4
Goes, *Neths.*	17	F3
Gogama, *Canada*	98	C3
Gogango, *Australia*	90	C5
Gogebic, L., *U.S.A.*	108	B10
Gogland, Ostrov, *Russia*	9	F22
Gogra = Ghaghara →, *India*	63	G11
Gogriâl, *Sudan*	77	F2
Goiana, *Brazil*	122	C5
Goianésia, *Brazil*	123	E2
Goiânia, *Brazil*	123	E2
Goiás, *Brazil*	123	E1
Goiás □, *Brazil*	122	D2
Goiatuba, *Brazil*	123	E2
Goio-Ere, *Brazil*	127	A5
Goirle, *Neths.*	17	E6
Góis, *Portugal*	30	E2
Gojam □, *Ethiopia*	77	E4
Gojeb, Wabi →, *Ethiopia*	77	F4
Gojō, *Japan*	49	G7
Gojra, *Pakistan*	62	D5
Gokarannath, *India*	63	F9
Gökçeada, *Turkey*	66	B1
Gökirmak →, *Turkey*	66	B6
Göksu →, *Turkey*	66	D6
Göksun, *Turkey*	66	C7
Gokteik, *Burma*	61	H20
Gokurt, *Pakistan*	62	E2
Gola, *India*	63	E9
Golakganj, *India*	63	F13
Golan Heights = Hagolan, *Syria*	69	B4
Golāshkerd, *Iran*	65	E8
Golaya Pristen = Hola Pristan, *Ukraine*	41	J7
Gölbaşı, Adiyaman, *Turkey*	66	D7
Gölbaşı, Ankara, *Turkey*	66	C5
Golchikha, *Russia*	4	B12
Golconda, *U.S.A.*	110	F5
Gölcük, Kocaeli, *Turkey*	66	B3
Gölcük, Niğde, *Turkey*	66	C6
Gold Beach, *U.S.A.*	110	E1
Gold Coast, *Australia*	91	D5
Gold Coast, *W. Afr.*	79	E4
Gold Hill, *U.S.A.*	110	E2
Goldach, *Switz.*	23	B8
Goldau, *Switz.*	23	B7
Goldberg, *Germany*	18	B8
Golden, *Canada*	100	C5
Golden, *U.S.A.*	108	F2
Golden B., *N.Z.*	87	J4
Golden Gate, *U.S.A.*	110	H2
Golden Hinde, *Canada*	100	D3
Golden Lake, *Canada*	106	A7
Golden Prairie, *Canada*	101	C7
Golden Vale, *Ireland*	15	D3
Goldendale, *U.S.A.*	110	D3
Goldfield, *U.S.A.*	111	H5
Goldsand L., *Canada*	101	B8
Goldsboro, *U.S.A.*	105	H7
Goldsmith, *U.S.A.*	109	K3
Goldsworthy, *Australia*	88	D2
Goldthwaite, *U.S.A.*	109	K5
Golegã, *Portugal*	31	F2
Goleniów, *Poland*	20	B4
Golestānak, *Iran*	65	D7
Goleta, *U.S.A.*	113	L7
Golfito, *Costa Rica*	116	E3
Golfo Aranci, *Italy*	34	B2
Gölgeli Dağları, *Turkey*	66	D3
Goliad, *U.S.A.*	109	L6
Golija, *Serbia, Yug.*	21	M10
Gölköy, *Turkey*	66	B7
Golo →, *France*	27	F13
Golpāyegān, *Iran*	65	C6
Gölpazarı, *Turkey*	66	B4
Golra, *Pakistan*	62	C5
Golspie, *U.K.*	14	D5
Golyama Kamchiya →, *Bulgaria*	38	F10
Goma, *Rwanda*	82	C2
Goma, *Zaïre*	82	C2
Gomati →, *India*	63	G10
Gombari, *Zaïre*	82	B2
Gombe, *Nigeria*	79	C7
Gombe →, *Tanzania*	82	C3
Gombi, *Nigeria*	79	C7
Gomel = Homyel, *Belarus*	41	F6
Gomera, *Canary Is.*	36	F2
Gómez Palacio, *Mexico*	114	B4
Gomīshān, *Iran*	65	B7
Gommern, *Germany*	18	C7
Gomogomo, *Indonesia*	57	F8
Gomoh, *India*	61	H15
Gompa = Ganta, *Liberia*	78	D3
Goms, *Switz.*	22	D6
Gonābād, *Iran*	65	C8
Gonaïves, *Haiti*	117	C5
Gonâve, G. de la, *Haiti*	117	C5
Gonâve, I. de la, *Haiti*	117	C5
Gonbab-e Kāvūs, *Iran*	65	B7
Gonda, *India*	63	F9
Gondal, *India*	62	J4
Gonder, *Ethiopia*	77	E4
Gonder □, *Ethiopia*	77	E4
Gondia, *India*	60	J12
Gondola, *Mozam.*	83	F3
Gondomar, *Portugal*	30	D2
Gondomar, *Spain*	30	C2
Gondrecourt-le-Château, *France*	25	D12
Gönen, *Turkey*	66	B2
Gong Xian, *China*	52	C5
Gong'an, *China*	53	B9
Gongcheng, *China*	53	E8
Gongga Shan, *China*	52	C3
Gongguan, *China*	52	G7
Gonghe, *China*	54	C5
Gongolgon, *Australia*	91	E4
Gongshan, *China*	52	D2
Gongtan, *China*	52	C7
Goniadz, *Poland*	20	B12
Goniri, *Nigeria*	79	C7
Gonjo, *China*	52	B2
Gonnesa, *Italy*	34	C1
Gónnos, *Greece*	39	K5
Gonnosfanádiga, *Italy*	34	C1
Gonzaga, *Phil.*	55	B5
Gonzales, Calif., *U.S.A.*	111	H3
Gonzales, Tex., *U.S.A.*	109	L6
González Chaves, *Argentina*	126	D3
Good Hope, C. of, *S. Africa*	84	E2
Gooderham, *Canada*	98	D4
Goodeve, *Canada*	101	C8
Gooding, *U.S.A.*	110	E6
Goodland, *U.S.A.*	108	F4
Goodnight, *U.S.A.*	109	H4
Goodooga, *Australia*	91	D4
Goodsoil, *Canada*	101	C7
Goodsprings, *U.S.A.*	111	J6
Goole, *U.K.*	12	D7
Goolgowi, *Australia*	91	E4
Goomalling, *Australia*	89	F2
Goombalie, *Australia*	91	D4
Goonda, *Mozam.*	83	F3
Goondiwindi, *Australia*	91	D5
Goongarrie, L., *Australia*	89	F3
Goonyella, *Australia*	90	C4
Goor, *Neths.*	16	D9
Gooray, *Australia*	91	D5
Goose →, *Canada*	99	B7
Goose L., *U.S.A.*	110	F3
Gop, *India*	60	H6
Gopalganj, *India*	63	F11
Goppenstein, *Switz.*	22	D5
Göppingen, *Germany*	19	G5
Gor, *Spain*	29	H2
Góra, *Poland*	20	D6
Gorakhpur, *India*	63	F10
Gorbatov, *Russia*	42	B6
Gorbea, Peña, *Spain*	28	B2
Gorda, *U.S.A.*	112	K5
Gorda, Pta., *Canary Is.*	36	F2
Gorda, Pta., *Nic.*	116	D3
Gordan B., *Australia*	88	B5
Gordon, *U.S.A.*	108	D3
Gordon →, *Australia*	90	G4
Gordon, I., *Chile*	128	D3
Gordon Downs, *Australia*	88	C4
Gordon L., Alta., *Canada*	101	B6
Gordon L., N.W.T., *Canada*	100	A6
Gordonvale, *Australia*	90	B4
Gore, *Australia*	91	D5
Goré, *Chad*	73	G8
Gore, *Ethiopia*	77	F4
Gore, *N.Z.*	87	M2
Gore Bay, *Canada*	98	C3
Görele, *Turkey*	67	B8
Goreme, *Turkey*	66	C6
Gorey, *Ireland*	15	D5
Gorg, *Iran*	65	D8
Gorgān, *Iran*	65	B7
Gorgona, isola, *Italy*	32	E6
Gorgora, *Ethiopia*	77	E4
Gorham, *U.S.A.*	107	B13
Gori, *Georgia*	43	J7
Gorinchem, *Neths.*	16	E5
Gorinhatã, *Brazil*	123	E2
Goris, *Armenia*	67	C12
Goritsy, *Russia*	42	B3
Gorízia, *Italy*	33	C10
Gorki = Horki, *Belarus*	40	E6
Gorki = Nizhniy Novgorod, *Russia*	42	B7
Gorkiy = Nizhniy Novgorod, *Russia*	42	B7
Gorkovskoye Vdkhr., *Russia*	42	B6
Gørlev, *Denmark*	11	J5
Gorlice, *Poland*	20	F11
Görlitz, *Germany*	18	D10
Gorlovka = Horlivka, *Ukraine*	41	H10
Gorman, Calif., *U.S.A.*	113	L8
Gorman, Tex., *U.S.A.*	109	J5
Gorna Dzhumayo = Blagoevgrad, *Bulgaria*	39	G6
Gorna Oryahovitsa, *Bulgaria*	38	F8
Gornja Radgona, *Slovenia*	33	B13
Gornja Tuzla, *Bos.-H.*	21	L8
Gornji Grad, *Slovenia*	33	B11
Gornji Milanovac, *Serbia, Yug.*	21	M10
Gornji Vakuf, *Bos.-H.*	21	M7
Gorno-Altay □, *Russia*	44	D9
Gorno-Altaysk, *Russia*	44	D9
Gorno Slinkino = Gornopravdinsk, *Russia*	44	C8
Gornopravdinsk, *Russia*	44	C8
Gornyatskiy, *Russia*	43	F5
Gornyi, *Russia*	48	B6
Gornyy, *Russia*	42	E9
Gorodenka = Horodenka, *Ukraine*	41	H3
Gorodets, *Russia*	42	B6
Gorodishche = Horodyshche, *Ukraine*	41	H6
Gorodishche, *Russia*	42	D7
Gorodnya = Horodnya, *Ukraine*	41	G6
Gorodok = Haradok, *Belarus*	40	E6
Gorodok = Horodok, *Ukraine*	41	H2
Gorodovikovsk, *Russia*	43	G5
Gorokhov = Horokhiv, *Ukraine*	41	G3
Gorokhovets, *Russia*	42	B6
Gorom Gorom, *Burkina Faso*	79	C4
Goromonzi, *Zimbabwe*	83	F3
Gorongose →, *Mozam.*	85	C5

Gorongoza, *Mozam.* 83 F3
Gorongoza, Sa. da,
  Mozam. 83 F3
Goronyo, *Nigeria* 79 C6
Gorredijk, *Neths.* 16 C8
Gorron, *France* 24 D6
Gorshechnoye, *Russia* 42 E4
Gorssel, *Neths.* 16 D8
Gort, *Ireland* 15 C3
Gortis, *Greece* 37 D6
Goryachiy Klyuch, *Russia* . 43 H4
Gorzkowice, *Poland* 20 D9
Gorzów Śląski, *Poland* ... 20 D8
Gorzów Wielkopolski,
  Poland 20 C5
Göschenen, *Switz.* 23 C7
Gosford, *Australia* 91 E5
Goshen, *Calif., U.S.A.* .. 112 J7
Goshen, *Ind., U.S.A.* ... 104 E3
Goshen, *N.Y., U.S.A.* ... 107 E10
Goshogawara, *Japan* 48 D10
Goslar, *Germany* 18 D6
Gospič, *Croatia* 33 D12
Gosport, *U.K.* 13 G6
Gossau, *Switz.* 23 B8
Gosse →, *Australia* 90 B1
Gostivar, *Macedonia* 39 H3
Gostyń, *Poland* 20 D7
Gostynin, *Poland* 20 C9
Göta älv →, *Sweden* 11 G5
Göta kanal, *Sweden* 9 G16
Götaland, *Sweden* 9 G15
Göteborg, *Sweden* 11 G5
Götene, *Sweden* 11 F7
Gotha, *Germany* 18 E6
Gothenburg = Göteborg,
  Sweden 11 G5
Gothenburg, *U.S.A.* 108 E4
Gotland, *Sweden* 9 H18
Gotse Delchev, *Bulgaria* . 39 H6
Gotska Sandön, *Sweden* .. 9 G18
Gōtsu, *Japan* 49 G6
Göttingen, *Germany* 18 D5
Gottwald = Zmiyev,
  Ukraine 41 H9
Gottwaldov = Zlin, *Czech.* 20 F7
Goubangzi, *China* 51 D11
Gouda, *Neths.* 16 D5
Goúdhoura, Ákra, *Greece* . 37 E8
Goudiry, *Senegal* 78 C2
Gough I., *Atl. Oc.* 2 G9
Gouin, Rés., *Canada* 98 C5
Gouitafla, *Ivory C.* 78 D3
Goulburn, *Australia* 91 E4
Goulburn Is., *Australia* . 90 A1
Goulia, *Ivory C.* 78 C3
Goulimine, *Morocco* 74 C3
Goulmina, *Morocco* 74 B4
Gounou-Gaya, *Chad* 73 G8
Goúra, *Greece* 39 M5
Gouraya, *Algeria* 75 A5
Gourdon, *France* 26 D5
Gouré, *Niger* 79 C7
Gouri, *Chad* 73 E8
Gourits →, *S. Africa* ... 84 E3
Gourma Rharous, *Mali* ... 79 B4
Goúrnais, *Greece* 37 D7
Gournay-en-Bray, *France* . 25 C8
Gourock Ra., *Australia* . 91 F4
Goursi, *Burkina Faso* ... 78 C4
Gouvêa, *Brazil* 123 E3
Gouverneur, *U.S.A.* 107 B9
Gouviá, *Greece* 37 A3
Gouzon, *France* 26 B6
Govan, *Canada* 101 C8
Governador Valadares,
  Brazil 123 E3
Governor's Harbour,
  Bahamas 116 A4
Gowan Ra., *Australia* ... 90 C4
Gowanda, *U.S.A.* 106 D6
Gowd-e Zirreh, *Afghan.* . 60 E3
Gower, *U.K.* 13 F3
Gowna, L., *Ireland* 15 C4
Goya, *Argentina* 126 B4
Göyçay, *Azerbaijan* 43 K8
Goyder Lagoon, *Australia* 91 D2
Goyllarisquisga, *Peru* .. 124 C2
Göynük, *Turkey* 66 B4
Goz Beïda, *Chad* 73 F9
Goz Regeb, *Sudan* 77 D4
Gozo, *Malta* 37 C1
Graaff-Reinet, *S. Africa* . 84 E3
Grabow, *Germany* 18 B7
Grabs, *Switz.* 23 B8
Gračac, *Croatia* 33 D12
Gračanica, *Bos.-H.* 21 L8
Graçay, *France* 25 E4
Grace, *U.S.A.* 110 E8
Graceville, *U.S.A.* 108 C6
Gracias a Dios, C.,
  Honduras 116 C3
Graciosa, I., *Canary Is.* . 36 E6
Gradaús, *Brazil* 122 C1
Gradaús, Serra dos, *Brazil* 122 C1
Gradets, *Bulgaria* 38 G9
Grado, *Italy* 33 C10
Grado, *Spain* 30 B4
Gradule, *Australia* 91 D4
Grady, *U.S.A.* 109 H3
Graeca, Lacul, *Romania* . 38 E9
Grafenau, *Germany* 19 G9
Gräfenberg, *Germany* 19 F7
Grafton, *Australia* 91 D5
Grafton, *U.S.A.* 108 A6
Gragnano, *Italy* 35 B7

Graham, *Canada* 98 C1
Graham, *N.C., U.S.A.* ... 105 G6
Graham, *Tex., U.S.A.* ... 109 J5
Graham →, *Canada* 100 B4
Graham, Mt., *U.S.A.* 111 K9
Graham Bell, Os., *Russia* . 44 A7
Graham I., *Canada* 100 C2
Graham Land, *Antarctica* . 5 C17
Grahamdale, *Canada* 101 C9
Grahamstown, *S. Africa* . 84 E4
Graíba, *Tunisia* 75 B7
Graide, *Belgium* 17 J6
Graie, Alpi, *Europe* 32 C4
Grain Coast, *W. Afr.* ... 78 E3
Grajaú, *Brazil* 122 C2
Grajaú →, *Brazil* 122 B3
Grajewo, *Poland* 20 B12
Gramada, *Bulgaria* 38 F5
Gramat, *France* 26 D5
Grammichele, *Italy* 35 E7
Grampian □, *U.K.* 14 D6
Grampian Highlands =
  Grampian Mts., *U.K.* .. 14 E5
Grampian Mts., *U.K.* 14 E5
Gran →, *Surinam* 121 C6
Gran Altiplanicie Central,
  Argentina 128 C3
Gran Canaria, *Canary Is.* . 36 F4
Gran Chaco, *S. Amer.* ... 126 B3
Gran Paradiso, *Italy* ... 32 C4
Gran Sasso d'Italia, *Italy* . 33 F10
Granada, *Nic.* 116 D2
Granada, *Spain* 29 H1
Granada, *U.S.A.* 109 F3
Granada □, *Spain* 31 H7
Granadilla de Abona,
  Canary Is. 36 F3
Granard, *Ireland* 15 C4
Granbury, *U.S.A.* 109 J6
Granby, *Canada* 98 C5
Grand →, *Mo., U.S.A.* ... 108 F8
Grand →, *S. Dak., U.S.A.* 108 C4
Grand Bahama, *Bahamas* .. 116 A4
Grand Bank, *Canada* 99 C8
Grand Bassam, *Ivory C.* . 78 D4
Grand Béréby, *Ivory C.* . 78 E3
Grand-Bourg, *Guadeloupe* . 117 C7
Grand Canal = Yun
  Ho →, *China* 51 E9
Grand Canyon, *U.S.A.* ... 111 H7
Grand Canyon National
  Park, *U.S.A.* 111 H7
Grand Cayman, *Cayman Is.* 116 C3
Grand Cess, *Liberia* 78 E3
Grand Coulee, *U.S.A.* ... 110 C4
Grand Coulee Dam,
  U.S.A. 110 C4
Grand Erg Occidental,
  Algeria 75 B5
Grand Erg Oriental,
  Algeria 75 C6
Grand Falls, *Canada* 99 C8
Grand Forks, *Canada* 100 D5
Grand Forks, *U.S.A.* 108 B6
Grand-Fougeray, *France* . 24 E5
Grand Haven, *U.S.A.* 104 D2
Grand I., *U.S.A.* 104 B2
Grand Island, *U.S.A.* ... 108 E5
Grand Isle, *U.S.A.* 109 L10
Grand Junction, *U.S.A.* . 111 G9
Grand L., *N.B., Canada* . 99 C6
Grand L., *Nfld., Canada* . 99 C8
Grand L., *Nfld., Canada* . 99 B7
Grand L., *U.S.A.* 109 L8
Grand Lac Victoria,
  Canada 98 C4
Grand Lahou, *Ivory C.* .. 78 D3
Grand Lake, *U.S.A.* 110 F11
Grand-Leez, *Belgium* 17 G5
Grand-Lieu, L. de, *France* 24 E5
Grand Manan I., *Canada* . 99 D6
Grand Marais, *Canada* ... 108 B9
Grand Marais, *U.S.A.* ... 104 B3
Grand-Mère, *Canada* 98 C5
Grand Popo, *Benin* 79 D5
Grand Portage, *U.S.A.* .. 98 C2
Grand Rapids, *Canada* ... 101 C9
Grand Rapids, *Mich.,
  U.S.A.* 104 D2
Grand Rapids, *Minn.,
  U.S.A.* 108 B8
Grand St.-Bernard, Col du,
  Europe 22 E4
Grand Santi, *Fr. Guiana* . 121 C7
Grand Teton, *U.S.A.* 110 E8
Grand Valley, *U.S.A.* ... 110 G9
Grand View, *Canada* 101 C8
Grandas de Salime, *Spain* . 30 B4
Grande →, *Jujuy,
  Argentina* 126 A2
Grande →, *Mendoza,
  Argentina* 126 D2
Grande →, *Bolivia* 125 D5
Grande →, *Bahia, Brazil* . 122 D3
Grande →, *Minas Gerais,
  Brazil* 123 F1
Grande →, *Spain* 29 F4
Grande →, *Venezuela* 121 B5
Grande, B., *Argentina* .. 128 D3
Grande, I., *Argentina* .. 123 F3
Grande, Rio →, *U.S.A.* .. 109 N6
Grande, Serra, *Piauí,
  Brazil* 122 C2
Grande, Serra, *Tocantins,
  Brazil* 122 D2
Grande Baie, *Canada* 99 C5

Grande Baleine, R. de
  la →, *Canada* 98 A4
Grande Cache, *Canada* ... 100 C5
Grande de Santiago →,
  Mexico 114 C3
Grande Dixence, Barr. de
  la, *Switz.* 22 D4
Grande-Entrée, *Canada* .. 99 C7
Grande Prairie, *Canada* . 100 B5
Grande-Rivière, *Canada* . 99 C7
Grande Sauldre →, *France* 25 E9
Grande-Vallée, *Canada* .. 99 C6
Grandes-Bergeronnes,
  Canada 99 C5
Grandfalls, *U.S.A.* 109 K3
Grandoe Mines, *Canada* .. 100 B3
Grândola, *Portugal* 31 G2
Grandpré, *France* 25 C11
Grandson, *Switz.* 22 C3
Grandview, *U.S.A.* 110 C4
Grandvilliers, *France* .. 25 C8
Graneros, *Chile* 126 C1
Grangemouth, *U.K.* 14 E5
Granger, *Wash., U.S.A.* . 110 C3
Granger, *Wyo., U.S.A.* .. 110 F9
Grangeville, *U.S.A.* 110 D5
Granite City, *U.S.A.* ... 108 F9
Granite Falls, *U.S.A.* .. 108 C7
Granite Mt., *U.S.A.* 113 M10
Granite Peak, *Australia* . 89 E3
Granite Peak, *U.S.A.* ... 110 D9
Granity, *N.Z.* 87 J3
Granja, *Brazil* 122 B3
Granja de Moreruela, *Spain* 30 D5
Granja de Torrehermosa,
  Spain 31 G5
Granollers, *Spain* 28 D7
Gransee, *Germany* 18 B9
Grant, *U.S.A.* 108 E4
Grant, Mt., *U.S.A.* 110 G4
Grant City, *U.S.A.* 108 E7
Grant I., *Australia* 88 B5
Grant Range, *U.S.A.* 111 G6
Grantham, *U.K.* 12 E7
Grantown-on-Spey, *U.K.* . 14 D5
Grants, *U.S.A.* 111 J10
Grants Pass, *U.S.A.* 110 E2
Grantsburg, *U.S.A.* 108 C8
Grantsville, *U.S.A.* 110 F7
Granville, *France* 24 D5
Granville, *N. Dak., U.S.A.* 108 A4
Granville, *N.Y., U.S.A.* . 104 D9
Granville L., *Canada* ... 101 B8
Grao de Gandía, *Spain* .. 29 F4
Grapeland, *U.S.A.* 109 K7
Gras, L. de, *Canada* 96 B8
Graskop, *S. Africa* 85 C5
Grass →, *Canada* 101 B9
Grass Range, *U.S.A.* 110 C9
Grass River Prov. Park,
  Canada 101 C8
Grass Valley, *Calif.,
  U.S.A.* 112 F6
Grass Valley, *Oreg.,
  U.S.A.* 110 D3
Grassano, *Italy* 35 B9
Grasse, *France* 27 E10
Grassmere, *Australia* ... 91 E3
Graubünden □, *Switz.* ... 23 C9
Graulhet, *France* 26 E5
Graus, *Spain* 28 C5
Gravatá, *Brazil* 122 C4
Grave, *Neths.* 16 E7
Grave, Pte. de, *France* . 26 C2
Gravelbourg, *Canada* 101 D7
Gravelines, *France* 25 B9
's-Graveland, *Neths.* ... 16 D6
Gravelotte, *S. Africa* .. 85 C5
Gravenhurst, *Canada* 106 B5
's-Gravendeel, *Neths.* .. 16 E5
's-Gravenhage, *Neths.* .. 16 D4
Gravesend, *Australia* ... 91 D5
Gravesend, *U.K.* 13 F8
Gravina di Púglia, *Italy* . 35 B9
Gravois, Pointe-à-, *Haiti* 117 C5
Gravone →, *France* 27 G12
Gray, *France* 25 E12
Grayling, *U.S.A.* 104 C3
Grayling →, *Canada* 100 B3
Grays Harbor, *U.S.A.* ... 110 C1
Grays L., *U.S.A.* 110 E8
Grays River, *U.S.A.* 112 D3
Grayson, *Canada* 101 C8
Grayvoron, *Russia* 42 E2
Graz, *Austria* 21 H5
Grazalema, *Spain* 31 J5
Greasy L., *Canada* 100 A4
Great Abaco I., *Bahamas* . 116 A4
Great Artesian Basin,
  Australia 90 C3
Great Australian Bight,
  Australia 89 F5
Great Bahama Bank,
  Bahamas 116 B4
Great Barrier I., *N.Z.* . 87 G5
Great Barrier Reef,
  Australia 90 B4
Great Barrington, *U.S.A.* . 107 D11
Great Basin, *U.S.A.* 110 G5
Great Bear →, *Canada* ... 96 B7
Great Bear L., *Canada* .. 96 B7
Great Belt = Store Bælt,
  Denmark 11 J5
Great Bend, *Kans., U.S.A.* 108 F5
Great Bend, *Pa., U.S.A.* . 107 E9
Great Blasket I., *Ireland* . 15 D1

Great Britain, *Europe* .. 6 E5
Great Central, *Canada* .. 100 D3
Great Dividing Ra.,
  Australia 90 C4
Great Driffield = Driffield,
  U.K. 12 C7
Great Exuma I., *Bahamas* . 116 B4
Great Falls, *Canada* 101 C9
Great Falls, *U.S.A.* 110 C8
Great Fish = Groot
  Vis →, *S. Africa* 84 E4
Great Guana Cay,
  Bahamas 116 B4
Great Harbour Deep,
  Canada 99 B8
Great I., *Canada* 101 B9
Great Inagua I., *Bahamas* 117 B5
Great Indian Desert =
  Thar Desert, *India* ... 62 F4
Great Karoo, *S. Africa* . 84 E3
Great Lake, *Australia* .. 90 G4
Great Malvern, *U.K.* 13 E5
Great Ormes Head, *U.K.* . 12 D4
Great Ouse →, *U.K.* 12 E8
Great Palm I., *Australia* 90 B4
Great Plains, *N. Amer.* . 102 A6
Great Ruaha →, *Tanzania* 82 D4
Great Saint Bernard P. =
  Grand St.-Bernard, Col
  du, *Europe* 22 E4
Great Salt L., *U.S.A.* .. 110 F7
Great Salt Lake Desert,
  U.S.A. 110 F7
Great Salt Plains L.,
  U.S.A. 109 G5
Great Sandy Desert,
  Australia 88 D3
Great Sangi = Sangihe, P.,
  Indonesia 57 D7
Great Scarcies →,
  S. Leone 78 D2
Great Slave L., *Canada* . 100 A5
Great Smoky Mts. Nat.
  Pk., *U.S.A.* 105 H4
Great Stour = Stour →,
  U.K. 13 F9
Great Victoria Desert,
  Australia 89 E4
Great Wall, *China* 50 E5
Great Whernside, *U.K.* .. 12 C6
Great Yarmouth, *U.K.* ... 12 E9
Greater Antilles, *W. Indies* 117 C5
Greater London □, *U.K.* . 13 F7
Greater Manchester □,
  U.K. 12 D5
Greater Sunda Is.,
  Indonesia 56 F4
Grebbestad, *Sweden* 11 F5
Grebenka = Hrebenka,
  Ukraine 41 G7
Greco, C., *Cyprus* 37 E13
Greco, Mte., *Italy* 34 A6
Gredos, Sierra de, *Spain* . 30 E5
Greece, *U.S.A.* 106 C7
Greece ■, *Europe* 39 K6
Greeley, *Colo., U.S.A.* . 108 E2
Greeley, *Nebr., U.S.A.* . 108 E5
Green →, *Ky., U.S.A.* ... 104 G2
Green →, *Utah, U.S.A.* .. 111 G9
Green B., *U.S.A.* 104 C2
Green Bay, *U.S.A.* 104 C2
Green C., *Australia* 91 F5
Green Cove Springs,
  U.S.A. 105 L5
Green River, *U.S.A.* 111 G8
Greenbank, *U.S.A.* 112 B4
Greenbush, *Mich., U.S.A.* 106 B1
Greenbush, *Minn., U.S.A.* 108 A6
Greencastle, *U.S.A.* 104 F2
Greene, *U.S.A.* 107 D9
Greenfield, *Calif., U.S.A.* 112 J5
Greenfield, *Calif., U.S.A.* 113 K8
Greenfield, *Ind., U.S.A.* 104 F3
Greenfield, *Iowa, U.S.A.* 108 E7
Greenfield, *Mass., U.S.A.* 107 D12
Greenfield, *Mo., U.S.A.* . 109 G8
Greenfield Park, *Canada* . 107 A11
Greenland ■, *N. Amer.* .. 4 C5
Greenland Sea, *Arctic* .. 4 B7
Greenock, *U.K.* 14 F4
Greenore, *Ireland* 15 B5
Greenore Pt., *Ireland* .. 15 D5
Greenough →, *Australia* . 89 E1
Greenport, *U.S.A.* 107 E12
Greensboro, *Ga., U.S.A.* . 105 J4
Greensboro, *N.C., U.S.A.* 105 G6
Greensburg, *Ind., U.S.A.* 104 F3
Greensburg, *Kans., U.S.A.* 109 G5
Greensburg, *Pa., U.S.A.* . 106 F5
Greenville, *Liberia* 78 D3
Greenville, *Ala., U.S.A.* 105 K2
Greenville, *Calif., U.S.A.* 112 E6
Greenville, *Ill., U.S.A.* 108 F10
Greenville, *Maine, U.S.A.* 99 C6
Greenville, *Mich., U.S.A.* 104 D3
Greenville, *Miss., U.S.A.* 109 J9
Greenville, *N.C., U.S.A.* 105 H7
Greenville, *Ohio, U.S.A.* 104 E3
Greenville, *Pa., U.S.A.* . 106 E4
Greenville, *S.C., U.S.A.* 105 H4
Greenville, *Tenn., U.S.A.* 105 G4
Greenville, *Tex., U.S.A.* 109 J6
Greenwater Lake Prov.
  Park, *Canada* 101 C8
Greenwich, *U.K.* 13 F8
Greenwich, *Conn., U.S.A.* 107 E11
Greenwich, *N.Y., U.S.A.* . 107 C11

Greenwich, *Ohio, U.S.A.* . 106 E2
Greenwood, *Canada* 100 D5
Greenwood, *Miss., U.S.A.* 109 J9
Greenwood, *S.C., U.S.A.* . 105 H4
Greenwood, Mt., *Australia* 88 B5
Gregório →, *Brazil* 124 B3
Gregory, *U.S.A.* 108 D5
Gregory →, *Australia* ... 90 B2
Gregory, L., *S. Austral.,
  Australia* 91 D2
Gregory, L., *W. Austral.,
  Australia* 89 E2
Gregory Downs, *Australia* 90 B2
Gregory L., *Australia* .. 88 D4
Gregory Ra., *Queens.,
  Australia* 90 B3
Gregory Ra., *W. Austral.,
  Australia* 88 D3
Greiffenberg, *Germany* .. 18 B9
Greifswald, *Germany* 18 A9
Greifswalder Bodden,
  Germany 18 A9
Grein, *Austria* 21 G4
Greiz, *Germany* 18 E8
Gremikha, *Russia* 44 C4
Grenå, *Denmark* 11 H4
Grenada, *U.S.A.* 109 J10
Grenada ■, *W. Indies* ... 117 D7
Grenade, *France* 26 E5
Grenadines, *W. Indies* .. 117 D7
Grenchen, *Switz.* 22 B4
Grenen, *Denmark* 11 G4
Grenfell, *Australia* 91 E4
Grenfell, *Canada* 101 C8
Grenoble, *France* 27 C9
Grenora, *U.S.A.* 108 A3
Grenville, C., *Australia* 90 A3
Grenville Chan., *Canada* . 100 C3
Gréoux-les-Bains, *France* 27 E9
Gresham, *U.S.A.* 112 E4
Gresik, *Indonesia* 57 G15
Grëssoney St. Jean, *Italy* 32 C4
Gretna Green, *U.K.* 14 F5
Grevelingen Krammer,
  Neths. 16 E4
Greven, *Germany* 18 C3
Grevená, *Greece* 39 J4
Grevenbroich, *Germany* .. 18 D2
Grevenmacher, *Lux.* 17 J8
Grevesmühlen, *Germany* .. 18 B7
Grevie, *Sweden* 11 H6
Grey →, *N.Z.* 87 K3
Grey, C., *Australia* 90 A2
Grey Ra., *Australia* 91 D3
Grey Res., *Canada* 99 C8
Greybull, *U.S.A.* 110 D9
Greymouth, *N.Z.* 87 K3
Greytown, *N.Z.* 87 J5
Greytown, *S. Africa* 85 D5
Gribanovskiy, *Russia* ... 42 E5
Gribbell I., *Canada* 100 C3
Gridley, *U.S.A.* 112 F5
Griekwastad, *S. Africa* . 84 D3
Griffin, *U.S.A.* 105 J3
Griffith, *Australia* 91 E4
Grijpskerk, *Neths.* 16 B8
Grillby, *Sweden* 10 E11
Grimari, *C.A.R.* 73 G9
Grimaylov = Hrymayliv,
  Ukraine 41 H4
Grimbergen, *Belgium* 17 G4
Grimes, *U.S.A.* 112 F5
Grimma, *Germany* 18 D8
Grimmen, *Germany* 18 A9
Grimsby, *Canada* 106 C5
Grimsby, *U.K.* 12 D7
Grimselpass, *Switz.* 23 C6
Grímsey, *Iceland* 8 C5
Grimshaw, *Canada* 100 B5
Grimstad, *Norway* 11 F2
Grindelwald, *Switz.* 22 C6
Grindsted, *Denmark* 11 J2
Grindu, *Romania* 38 E9
Grinnell, *U.S.A.* 108 E8
Griñón, *Spain* 30 E7
Grintavec, *Slovenia* 33 B11
Grip, *Norway* 10 A1
Gris-Nez, C., *France* ... 25 B8
Grisolles, *France* 26 E5
Grisons = Graubünden □,
  Switz. 23 C9
Grivegnée, *Belgium* 17 G7
Grmeč Planina, *Bos.-H.* . 33 D13
Groais I., *Canada* 99 B8
Groblersdal, *S. Africa* . 85 D4
Grobming, *Austria* 21 H3
Grodno = Hrodna, *Belarus* 40 F2
Grodzisk Mázowiecki,
  Poland 20 C10
Grodzisk Wielkopolski,
  Poland 20 C6
Grodzyanka =
  Hrodzyanka, *Belarus* .. 40 F5
Groenlo, *Neths.* 16 D9
Groesbeck, *U.S.A.* 109 K6
Groesbeek, *Neths.* 16 E7
Groix, *France* 24 E3
Groix, I. de, *France* ... 24 E3
Grójec, *Poland* 20 D10
Grolloo, *Neths.* 16 C9
Gronau, *Niedersachsen,
  Germany* 18 C5
Gronau,
  *Nordrhein-Westfalen,
  Germany* 18 C3
Grong, *Norway* 8 D15
Groningen, *Neths.* 16 B9

Groningen, *Surinam* 121 B6
Groningen □, *Neths.* 16 B9
Groninger Wad, *Neths.* ... 16 B9
Gronsveld, *Neths.* 17 G7
Groom, *U.S.A.* 109 H4
Groot →, *S. Africa* 84 E3
Groot Berg →, *S. Africa* .. 84 E2
Groot-Brakrivier, *S. Africa* 84 E3
Groot-Kei →, *S. Africa* ... 85 E4
Groot Vis →, *S. Africa* ... 84 E4
Groote Eylandt, *Australia* . 90 A2
Grootebroek, *Neths.* 16 C6
Grootfontein, *Namibia* ... 84 B2
Grootlaagte →, *Africa* ... 84 C3
Grootvloer, *S. Africa* 84 E3
Gros C., *Canada* 100 A6
Grosa, Pta., *Spain* 36 B8
Grósio, *Italy* 32 B7
Grosne →, *France* 27 B8
Gross Glockner, *Austria* .. 21 H2
Grossenbrode, *Germany* .. 18 A7
Grossenhain, *Germany* ... 18 D9
Grosseto, *Italy* 32 F8
Groswater B., *Canada* 99 B8
Grote Gette →, *Neths.* ... 17 G6
Grote Nete →, *Belgium* ... 17 F5
Groton, *Conn., U.S.A.* ... 107 E12
Groton, *S. Dak., U.S.A.* .. 108 C5
Grottáglie, *Italy* 35 B10
Grottaminarda, *Italy* 35 A8
Grottammare, *Italy* 33 F10
Grouard Mission, *Canada* . 100 B5
Grouin, Pte. du, *France* .. 24 D5
Groundhog →, *Canada* ... 98 C3
Grouse Creek, *U.S.A.* 110 F7
Grouw, *Neths.* 16 B7
Grove City, *U.S.A.* 106 E4
Groveland, *U.S.A.* 112 H6
Grover City, *U.S.A.* 113 K6
Groveton, *N.H., U.S.A.* .. 107 B13
Groveton, *Tex., U.S.A.* .. 109 K7
Grožnjan, *Croatia* 33 C10
Groznyy, *Russia* 43 J7
Grubbenvorst, *Neths.* 17 F8
Grudziądz, *Poland* 20 B8
Gruissan, *France* 26 E7
Grumo Áppula, *Italy* 35 A9
Grünberg, *Germany* 18 E4
Grundy Center, *U.S.A.* ... 108 D8
Gruver, *U.S.A.* 109 G4
Gruyères, *Switz.* 22 C4
Gryazi, *Russia* 42 D4
Gryazovets, *Russia* 40 C11
Gstaad, *Switz.* 22 D4
Gua, *India* 61 H14
Gua Musang, *Malaysia* ... 59 K3
Guacanayabo, G. de, *Cuba* 116 B4
Guacara, *Venezuela* 120 A4
Guachípas, *Argentina* ... 126 B2
Guachiría →, *Colombia* .. 120 B3
Guadajoz →, *Spain* 31 H6
Guadalajara, *Mexico* 114 C4
Guadalajara, *Spain* 28 E1
Guadalajara □, *Spain* ... 28 E2
Guadalcanal, *Solomon Is.* . 92 H8
Guadalcanal, *Spain* 31 G5
Guadalén →, *Spain* 31 G7
Guadales, *Argentina* 126 C2
Guadalete →, *Spain* 31 J4
Guadalhorce →, *Spain* ... 31 J6
Guadalimar →, *Spain* ... 29 G1
Guadalmena →, *Spain* ... 29 G2
Guadalmez →, *Spain* 31 G5
Guadalope →, *Spain* 28 D4
Guadalquivir →, *Spain* .. 31 J4
Guadalupe =
Guadeloupe ■, *W. Indies* 117 C7
Guadalupe, *Brazil* 122 C3
Guadalupe, *Mexico* 113 N10
Guadalupe, *Spain* 31 F5
Guadalupe, *U.S.A.* 113 L6
Guadalupe □, *Mexico* ... 113 N10
Guadalupe →, *U.S.A.* ... 109 L6
Guadalupe, Sierra de,
    Spain 31 F5
Guadalupe Bravos, *Mexico* 114 A3
Guadalupe Peak, *U.S.A.* . 111 L11
Guadalupe y Calvo, *Mexico* 114 B3
Guadarrama, Sierra de,
    Spain 30 E6
Guadauta, *Georgia* 43 J5
Guadeloupe ■, *W. Indies* . 117 C7
Guadeloupe Passage,
    W. Indies 117 C7
Guadiamar →, *Spain* 31 J4
Guadiana →, *Portugal* ... 31 H3
Guadiana Menor →, *Spain* 29 H1
Guadiaro →, *Spain* 31 J5
Guadiato →, *Spain* 31 H5
Guadiela →, *Spain* 28 E2
Guadix, *Spain* 29 H1
Guafo, Boca del, *Chile* ... 128 B2
Guafo, I., *Chile* 128 B2
Guainía □, *Colombia* 120 C4
Guainía →, *Colombia* 120 C4
Guaíra, *Brazil* 127 A5
Guaitecas, Is., *Chile* 128 B2
Guajará-Mirim, *Brazil* ... 125 C4
Guajira □, *Colombia* 120 A3
Guajira, Pen. de la,
    Colombia 120 A3
Gualaceo, *Ecuador* 120 D2
Gualán, *Guatemala* 116 C2
Gualeguay, *Argentina* ... 126 C4
Gualeguaychú, *Argentina* 126 C4
Gualicho, Salina, *Argentina* 128 B3

Gualjaina, *Argentina* 128 B2
Guam ■, *Pac. Oc.* 92 F6
Guamá, *Brazil* 122 B2
Guamá →, *Brazil* 122 B2
Guamblin, I., *Chile* 128 B1
Guaminí, *Argentina* 126 D3
Guamote, *Ecuador* 120 D2
Guampí, Sierra de,
    Venezuela 121 B4
Guamúchil, *Mexico* 114 B3
Guan Xian, *China* 52 B4
Guanabacoa, *Cuba* 116 B3
Guanacaste, Cordillera del,
    Costa Rica 116 D2
Guanaceví, *Mexico* 114 B3
Guanahani = San Salvador,
    Bahamas 117 B5
Guanajay, *Cuba* 116 B3
Guanajuato, *Mexico* 114 C4
Guanajuato □, *Mexico* ... 114 C4
Guanambi, *Brazil* 123 D3
Guanare, *Venezuela* 120 B4
Guanare →, *Venezuela* ... 120 B4
Guandacol, *Argentina* ... 126 B2
Guane, *Cuba* 116 B3
Guang'an, *China* 52 B6
Guangchang, *China* 53 D11
Guangde, *China* 53 B12
Guangdong □, *China* 53 F9
Guangfeng, *China* 53 C12
Guanghan, *China* 52 B5
Guanghua, *China* 53 A8
Guangji, *China* 53 C10
Guangling, *China* 50 E8
Guangning, *China* 53 F9
Guangrao, *China* 51 F10
Guangshun, *China* 52 D6
Guangwu, *China* 50 F3
Guangxi Zhuangzu
    Zizhiqu □, *China* ... 52 E7
Guangyuan, *China* 52 A5
Guangze, *China* 53 D11
Guangzhou, *China* 53 F9
Guanhães, *Brazil* 123 E3
Guanipa →, *Venezuela* ... 121 B5
Guanling, *China* 52 E5
Guannan, *China* 51 G10
Guanta, *Venezuela* 121 A5
Guantánamo, *Cuba* 117 B4
Guantao, *China* 50 F8
Guanyang, *China* 53 E8
Guanyun, *China* 51 G10
Guapí, *Colombia* 120 C2
Guápiles, *Costa Rica* 116 D3
Guaporé →, *Brazil* 125 C4
Guaqui, *Bolivia* 124 D4
Guara, Sierra de, *Spain* .. 28 C4
Guarabira, *Brazil* 122 C4
Guaranda, *Ecuador* 120 D2
Guarapari, *Brazil* 123 F3
Guarapuava, *Brazil* 123 G1
Guaratinguetá, *Brazil* ... 127 A6
Guaratuba, *Brazil* 127 B6
Guarda, *Portugal* 30 E3
Guarda □, *Portugal* 30 E3
Guardafui, C. = Asir, Ras,
    Somali Rep. 68 E5
Guardamar del Segura,
    Spain 29 G4
Guardavalle, *Italy* 35 D9
Guardiagrele, *Italy* 33 F11
Guardo, *Spain* 30 C6
Guareña, *Spain* 31 G4
Guareña →, *Spain* 30 D5
Guaria □, *Paraguay* 126 B4
Guárico □, *Venezuela* ... 120 B4
Guarrojo →, *Colombia* ... 120 C3
Guarujá, *Brazil* 127 A6
Guarus, *Brazil* 123 F3
Guasave, *Mexico* 114 B3
Guascama, Pta., *Colombia* 120 C2
Guasdualito, *Venezuela* .. 120 B3
Guasipati, *Venezuela* 121 B5
Guastalla, *Italy* 32 D7
Guatemala, *Guatemala* .. 116 D1
Guatemala ■, *Cent. Amer.* 116 C1
Guatire, *Venezuela* 120 A4
Guaviare □, *Colombia* ... 120 C3
Guaviare →, *Colombia* ... 120 C4
Guaxupé, *Brazil* 127 A6
Guayabero →, *Colombia* . 120 C3
Guayama, *Puerto Rico* ... 117 C6
Guayaneco, Arch., *Chile* . 128 C1
Guayaquil, *Ecuador* 120 D2
Guayaquil, G. de, *Ecuador* 120 D1
Guayaramerín, *Bolivia* ... 125 C4
Guayas →, *Ecuador* 120 D2
Guaymas, *Mexico* 114 B2
Guazhou, *China* 53 A12
Guba, *Zaïre* 83 E2
Gûbâl, Madîq, *Egypt* 76 B3
Gubat, *Phil.* 55 E6
Gúbbio, *Italy* 33 E9
Gubin, *Nigeria* 79 C7
Gubkin, *Russia* 42 E3
Gudata = Guadauta,
    Georgia 43 J5
Gudbrandsdalen, *Norway* . 9 F14
Guddu Barrage, *Pakistan* 60 E6
Gudenå, *Denmark* 11 H3
Gudermes, *Russia* 43 J8
Gudivada, *India* 61 L12
Gudur, *India* 60 M11
Guebwiller, *France* 25 E14
Guecho, *Spain* 28 B2
Guékédou, *Guinea* 78 D2
Guelma, *Algeria* 75 A6

Guelph, *Canada* 98 D3
Guemar, *Algeria* 75 B6
Guéméné-Penfao, *France* . 24 E5
Guéméné-sur-Scorff, *France* 24 D3
Guéné, *Benin* 79 C5
Güepi, *Peru* 120 D2
Guer, *France* 24 E4
Güer Aike, *Argentina* 128 D3
Guérande, *France* 24 E4
Guercif, *Morocco* 75 B4
Guéréda, *Chad* 73 F9
Guéret, *France* 26 B5
Guérigny, *France* 25 E10
Guerneville, *U.S.A.* 112 G4
Guernica, *Spain* 28 B2
Guernsey, *U.K.* 13 H5
Guernsey, *U.S.A.* 108 D2
Guerrara, Oasis, *Algeria* . 75 B5
Guerrara, Saoura, *Algeria* 75 C4
Guerrero □, *Mexico* 115 D5
Guerzim, *Algeria* 75 C4
Gueugnon, *France* 27 B8
Gueydan, *U.S.A.* 109 K8
Gügher, *Iran* 65 D8
Guglionesi, *Italy* 35 A7
Gui Jiang →, *China* 53 F8
Gui Xian, *China* 52 F7
Guia, *Canary Is.* 36 F4
Guia de Isora, *Canary Is.* . 36 F3
Guia Lopes da Laguna,
    Brazil 127 A4
Guichi, *China* 53 B11
Guider, *Cameroon* 79 D7
Guidimouni, *Niger* 79 C6
Guiding, *China* 52 D6
Guidong, *China* 53 D9
Guiglo, *Ivory C.* 78 D3
Guiji, *China* 53 B11
Guijá, *Mozam.* 85 C5
Guijo de Coria, *Spain* ... 30 E4
Guildford, *U.K.* 13 F7
Guilford, *U.S.A.* 99 C6
Guilin, *China* 53 E8
Guillaumes, *France* 27 D10
Guillestre, *France* 27 D10
Guilvinec, *France* 24 E2
Güimar, *Canary Is.* 36 F3
Guimarães, *Brazil* 122 B3
Guimarães, *Portugal* 30 D2
Guimaras, *Phil.* 55 F5
Guinda, *U.S.A.* 112 G4
Guinea ■, *W. Afr.* 78 C2
Guinea, Gulf of, *Atl. Oc.* . 79 E5
Guinea-Bissau ■, *Africa* . 78 C2
Güines, *Cuba* 116 B3
Guingamp, *France* 24 D3
Guipavas, *France* 24 D2
Guiping, *China* 53 F8
Guipúzcoa □, *Spain* 28 B2
Guir, O. →, *Algeria* 75 B4
Guiratinga, *Brazil* 125 D7
Güiria, *Venezuela* 121 A5
Guiscard, *France* 25 C10
Guise, *France* 25 C10
Guitiriz, *Spain* 30 B3
Guiuan, *Phil.* 55 F6
Guixi, *China* 53 C11
Guiyang, *Guizhou, China* 52 D6
Guiyang, *Hunan, China* . 53 E9
Guizhou □, *China* 52 D6
Gujan-Mestras, *France* .. 26 D2
Gujarat □, *India* 62 H4
Gujiang, *China* 53 D10
Gujranwala, *Pakistan* ... 62 C6
Gujrat, *Pakistan* 62 C6
Gukovo, *Russia* 43 F5
Gulbarga, *India* 60 L10
Gulbene, *Latvia* 9 H22
Gulf, The, *Asia* 65 E6
Gulfport, *U.S.A.* 109 K10
Gulgong, *Australia* 91 E4
Gulin, *China* 52 C5
Gulistan, *Pakistan* 62 D2
Gull Lake, *Canada* 101 C7
Gullegem, *Belgium* 17 G2
Güllük, *Turkey* 66 D2
Gulma, *Nigeria* 79 C5
Gulmarg, *India* 63 B6
Gülnar, *Turkey* 66 D5
Gulpen, *Neths.* 17 G7
Gülşehir, *Turkey* 66 C6
Gulshad, *Kazakhstan* ... 44 E8
Gulsvik, *Norway* 10 D3
Gulu, *Uganda* 82 B3
Gulwe, *Tanzania* 82 D4
Gulyaypole = Hulyaypole,
    Ukraine 41 J9
Gum Lake, *Australia* 91 E3
Gumal →, *Pakistan* 62 D4
Gumbaz, *Pakistan* 62 D3
Gumel, *Nigeria* 79 C6
Gumiel de Hizán, *Spain* . 28 D1
Gumlu, *Australia* 90 B4
Gumma □, *Japan* 49 F9
Gummersbach, *Germany* . 18 D3
Gummi, *Nigeria* 79 C6
Gümüşhacıköy, *Turkey* .. 66 B6
Gümüşhane, *Turkey* 67 B8
Gumzai, *Indonesia* 57 F8
Guna, *Ethiopia* 77 E4
Guna, *India* 62 G7
Gundagai, *Australia* 91 F4
Gundelfingen, *Germany* . 19 G6
Gundih, *Indonesia* 57 G14
Güneydoğu Toroslar,
    Turkey 67 C9
Gungu, *Zaïre* 80 F3
Gunisao →, *Canada* 101 C9

Gunisao L., *Canada* 101 C9
Gunnbjørn Fjeld,
    Greenland 4 C6
Gunnedah, *Australia* 91 E5
Gunningbar Cr. →,
    Australia 91 E4
Gunnison, *Colo., U.S.A.* . 111 G10
Gunnison, *Utah, U.S.A.* . 110 G8
Gunnison →, *U.S.A.* 111 G9
Gunpowder, *Australia* ... 90 B2
Guntakal, *India* 60 M10
Guntersville, *U.S.A.* 105 H2
Guntong, *Malaysia* 59 K3
Guntur, *India* 61 L12
Gunungapi, *Indonesia* ... 57 F7
Gunungsitoli, *Indonesia* . 56 D1
Günz →, *Germany* 19 G6
Günzburg, *Germany* 19 G6
Gunzenhausen, *Germany* 19 F6
Guo He →, *China* 51 H9
Guoyang, *China* 50 H9
Gupis, *Pakistan* 63 A5
Gura Humorului, *Romania* 38 B8
Gurag, *Ethiopia* 77 F4
Gurdaspur, *India* 62 C6
Gurdon, *U.S.A.* 109 J8
Gurdzhaani, *Georgia* 43 K7
Gurgaon, *India* 62 E7
Gurgueia →, *Brazil* 122 C3
Gurha, *India* 62 G4
Guri, Embalse de,
    Venezuela 121 B5
Gurk →, *Austria* 21 J4
Gurkha, *Nepal* 63 E11
Gurley, *Australia* 91 D4
Gürpınar, *Turkey* 67 C10
Gurué, *Mozam.* 83 F4
Gurun, *Malaysia* 59 K3
Gurupá, *Brazil* 121 D7
Gurupá, I. Grande de,
    Brazil 121 D7
Gurupi, *Brazil* 123 D2
Gurupi →, *Brazil* 122 B2
Gurupi, Serra do, *Brazil* . 122 C2
Guryev = Atyraū,
    Kazakhstan 44 E6
Gus-Khrustalnyy, *Russia* . 42 C5
Gusau, *Nigeria* 79 C6
Gusev, *Russia* 9 J20
Gushan, *China* 51 E12
Gushgy, *Turkmenistan* .. 44 F7
Gushi, *China* 53 A10
Gushiago, *Ghana* 79 D4
Gusinje, *Montenegro, Yug.* 21 N9
Gusinoozersk, *Russia* ... 45 D11
Güspini, *Italy* 34 C1
Gustanj, *Slovenia* 33 B11
Gustine, *U.S.A.* 111 H3
Güstrow, *Germany* 18 B8
Gusum, *Sweden* 11 F10
Guta = Kalárovo,
    Slovak Rep. 21 H7
Gütersloh, *Germany* 18 D4
Gutha, *Australia* 89 E2
Guthalongra, *Australia* .. 90 B4
Guthrie, *U.S.A.* 109 H6
Gutian, *China* 53 D12
Gutiérrez, *Bolivia* 125 D5
Guttannen, *Switz.* 23 C6
Guttenberg, *U.S.A.* 108 D9
Guyana ■, *S. Amer.* 121 B6
Guyane française = French
    Guiana ■, *S. Amer.* . 121 C7
Guyang, *China* 50 D6
Guyenne, *France* 26 D4
Guymon, *U.S.A.* 109 G4
Guyra, *Australia* 91 E5
Guyuan, *Hebei, China* .. 50 D8
Guyuan, *Ningxia Huizu,
    China* 50 F4
Guzhang, *China* 52 C7
Guzhen, *China* 51 H9
Guzmán, L. de, *Mexico* .. 114 A3
Gvardeysk, *Russia* 9 J19
Gvardeyskoye, *Ukraine* .. 41 K8
Gwa, *Burma* 61 L19
Gwaai, *Zimbabwe* 83 F2
Gwabegar, *Australia* 91 E4
Gwadabawa, *Nigeria* 79 C6
Gwādar, *Pakistan* 60 G3
Gwagwada, *Nigeria* 79 C6
Gwalia, *Australia* 89 E3
Gwalior, *India* 62 F8
Gwanda, *Zimbabwe* 83 G2
Gwandu, *Nigeria* 79 C5
Gwane, *Zaïre* 82 B2
Gwaram, *Nigeria* 79 C7
Gwarzo, *Nigeria* 79 C6
Gweebarra B., *Ireland* ... 15 B3
Gweedore, *Ireland* 15 A3
Gwent □, *U.K.* 13 F5
Gweru, *Zimbabwe* 83 F2
Gwi, *Nigeria* 79 D6
Gwinn, *U.S.A.* 104 B2
Gwio Kura, *Nigeria* 79 C7
Gwol, *Ghana* 78 C4
Gwoza, *Nigeria* 79 C7
Gwydir →, *Australia* 91 D4
Gwynedd □, *U.K.* 12 E4
Gyandzha = Gäncä,
    Azerbaijan 43 K8
Gyaring Hu, *China* 54 C4
Gydanskiy P-ov., *Russia* . 44 C8
Gympie, *Australia* 91 D5

Gyoma, *Hungary* 21 J10
Gyöngyös, *Hungary* 21 H9
Győr, *Hungary* 21 H7
Gypsum Pt., *Canada* 100 A6
Gypsumville, *Canada* ... 101 C9
Gyula, *Hungary* 21 J11
Gyumri, *Armenia* 43 K6
Gyzylarbat, *Turkmenistan* 44 F6
Gzhatsk = Gagarin, *Russia* 42 C2

H

Ha 'Arava →, *Israel* 69 E4
Ha Coi, *Vietnam* 58 B6
Ha Dong, *Vietnam* 58 B5
Ha Giang, *Vietnam* 58 A5
Ha Tien, *Vietnam* 59 G5
Ha Tinh, *Vietnam* 58 C5
Ha Trung, *Vietnam* 58 C5
Haacht, *Belgium* 17 G5
Haag, *Germany* 19 G8
Haaksbergen, *Neths.* 16 D9
Haaltert, *Belgium* 17 G4
Haamstede, *Neths.* 17 E3
Haapsalu, *Estonia* 9 G20
Haarlem, *Neths.* 16 D5
Haast →, *N.Z.* 87 K2
Haast Bluff, *Australia* ... 88 D5
Haastrecht, *Neths.* 16 E5
Hab Nadi Chauki, *Pakistan* 62 G2
Habaswein, *Kenya* 82 B4
Habay, *Canada* 100 B5
Habay-la-Neuve, *Belgium* 17 J7
Ḥabbānīyah, *Iraq* 67 F10
Ḥabbānīyah, Hawr al, *Iraq* 67 F10
Haboro, *Japan* 48 B10
Haccourt, *Belgium* 17 G7
Hachenburg, *Germany* .. 18 E3
Hachijō-Jima, *Japan* 49 H9
Hachinohe, *Japan* 48 D10
Hachiōji, *Japan* 49 G9
Hachŏn, *N. Korea* 51 D15
Hachy, *Belgium* 17 J7
Hacıbektaş, *Turkey* 66 C6
Hacılar, *Turkey* 66 C6
Hackensack, *U.S.A.* 107 F10
Hadali, *Pakistan* 62 C5
Hadarba, Ras, *Sudan* 76 C4
Hadarom □, *Israel* 69 E3
Haddington, *U.K.* 14 F6
Hadejia, *Nigeria* 79 C7
Hadejia →, *Nigeria* 79 C7
Haden, *Australia* 91 D5
Hadera, *Israel* 69 C3
Hadera, N. →, *Israel* ... 69 C3
Haderslev, *Denmark* 11 J3
Hadhramaut =
    Ḥaḍramawt, *Yemen* . 68 D4
Hadım, *Turkey* 66 D5
Hadjeb El Aïoun, *Tunisia* 75 A6
Hadong, S. Korea 51 G14
Ḥaḍramawt, *Yemen* 68 D4
Ḥaḍrānīyah, *Iraq* 64 C4
Hadsten, *Denmark* 11 H4
Hadsund, *Denmark* 11 H4
Hadyach, *Ukraine* 41 G8
Haeju, *N. Korea* 51 E13
Haenam, *S. Korea* 51 G14
Haerhpin = Harbin, *China* 51 B14
Hafar al Bāṭin, *Si. Arabia* 64 D5
Hafik, *Turkey* 66 C7
Ḥafīrat al 'Aydā, *Si. Arabia* 64 E3
Hafizabad, *Pakistan* 62 C5
Haflong, *India* 61 G18
Hafnarfjörður, *Iceland* ... 8 D3
Hafun, Ras, *Somali Rep.* . 68 E5
Hagalil, *Israel* 69 C4
Hagen, *Germany* 18 D3
Hagenow, *Germany* 18 B7
Hagerman, *U.S.A.* 109 J2
Hagerstown, *U.S.A.* 104 F7
Hagetmau, *France* 26 E3
Hagfors, *Sweden* 9 F15
Häggenås, *Sweden* 10 A8
Hagi, *Japan* 49 G5
Hagolan, *Syria* 69 B4
Hagondange-Briey, *France* 25 C13
Hags Hd., *Ireland* 15 D2
Hague, C. de la, *France* .. 24 C5
Hague, The = 's-
    Gravenhage, *Neths.* . 16 D4
Haguenau, *France* 25 D14
Hai □, *Tanzania* 82 C4
Hai Duong, *Vietnam* 58 B6
Hai'an, *Guangdong, China* 53 G8
Hai'an, *Jiangsu, China* ... 53 A13
Haicheng, *Fujian, China* . 53 E11
Haicheng, *Liaoning, China* 51 D12
Haidar Khel, *Afghan.* ... 62 C3
Haifa = Hefa, *Israel* 69 C3
Haifeng, *China* 53 F10
Haig, *Australia* 89 F4
Haiger, *Germany* 18 E4
Haikang, *China* 53 G8
Haikou, *China* 54 D6
Ḥā'il, *Si. Arabia* 64 E4
Hailar, *China* 54 B6
Hailey, *U.S.A.* 110 E6
Haileybury, *Canada* 98 C4
Hailin, *China* 51 B15
Hailing Dao, *China* 53 G8
Hailong, *China* 51 C13
Hailun, *China* 54 B7

Hailuoto, *Finland* 8 D21
Haimen, *Guangdong, China* 53 F11
Haimen, *Jiangsu, China* . 53 B13
Haimen, *Zhejiang, China* . 53 C13
Hainan □, *China* 54 E5
Hainaut □, *Belgium* 17 H4
Haines, *U.S.A.* 110 D5
Haines City, *U.S.A.* 105 L5
Haines Junction, *Canada* . 100 A1
Haining, *China* 53 B13
Haiphong, *Vietnam* 54 D5
Haiti ■, *W. Indies* 117 C5
Haiya Junction, *Sudan* .. 76 D4
Haiyan, *China* 53 B13
Haiyang, *China* 51 F11
Haiyuan, *Guangxi Zhuangzu, China* 52 F6
Haiyuan, *Ningxia Huizu, China* 50 F3
Haizhou, *China* 51 G10
Haizhou Wan, *China* 51 G10
Hajar Bangar, *Sudan* ... 73 F9
Hajdúböszörmény, *Hungary* 21 H11
Hajdúszoboszló, *Hungary* . 21 H11
Hajipur, *India* 63 G11
Hājjī Muhsin, *Iraq* 64 C5
Hājjīābād, *Esfahan, Iran* . 65 C7
Hājjīābād, *Hormozgān, Iran* 65 D7
Hakansson, Mts., *Zaïre* . 83 D2
Håkantorp, *Sweden* 11 F6
Hakkâri, *Turkey* 67 D10
Hakkâri Dağları, *Turkey* . 67 C10
Hakken-Zan, *Japan* 49 G7
Hakodate, *Japan* 48 D10
Hakui, *Japan* 49 F8
Haku-San, *Japan* 49 F8
Hala, *Pakistan* 60 G6
Halab, *Syria* 66 D7
Halabjah, *Iraq* 67 E11
Halaib, *Sudan* 76 C4
Halanzy, *Belgium* 17 J7
Hālat 'Ammār, *Si. Arabia* 64 D3
Halbā, *Lebanon* 69 A5
Halberstadt, *Germany* ... 18 D7
Halcombe, *N.Z.* 87 J5
Halcon, Mt., *Phil.* 57 B6
Halden, *Norway* 10 E5
Haldensleben, *Germany* .. 18 C7
Haldia, *India* 61 H16
Haldwani, *India* 63 E8
Hale →, *Australia* 90 C2
Haleakala Crater, *U.S.A.* . 102 H16
Halen, *Belgium* 17 G6
Haleyville, *U.S.A.* 105 H2
Half Assini, *Ghana* 78 D4
Halfway →, *Canada* 100 B4
Haliburton, *Canada* 98 C4
Halifax, *Australia* 90 B4
Halifax, *Canada* 99 D7
Halifax, *U.K.* 12 D6
Halifax B., *Australia* ... 90 B4
Halifax I., *Namibia* 84 D2
Halīl →, *Iran* 65 E8
Hall, *Austria* 19 H7
Hall Beach, *Canada* 97 B11
Hall Pt., *Australia* 88 C3
Halland, *Sweden* 9 H15
Hallands län □, *Sweden* . 11 H6
Hallands Väderö, *Sweden* . 11 H6
Hallandsås, *Sweden* 11 H7
Halle, *Belgium* 17 G4
Halle, *Nordrhein-Westfalen, Germany* 18 C4
Halle, *Sachsen-Anhalt, Germany* 18 D7
Hällefors, *Sweden* 9 G16
Hallein, *Austria* 21 H3
Hällekis, *Sweden* 11 F7
Hallett, *Australia* 91 E2
Hallettsville, *U.S.A.* ... 109 L6
Hällevadsholm, *Sweden* . 11 F5
Halliday, *U.S.A.* 108 B3
Halliday L., *Canada* 101 A7
Hallim, *S. Korea* 51 H14
Hallingdalselva →, *Norway* 9 F13
Hallock, *U.S.A.* 101 D9
Halls Creek, *Australia* ... 88 C4
Hallsberg, *Sweden* 9 G16
Hallstahammar, *Sweden* . 10 E10
Hallstead, *U.S.A.* 107 E9
Halmahera, *Indonesia* ... 57 D7
Halmeu, *Romania* 38 B6
Halmstad, *Sweden* 11 H6
Halq el Oued, *Tunisia* ... 75 A7
Hals, *Denmark* 11 H4
Halsafjorden, *Norway* ... 10 A2
Hälsingborg = Helsingborg, *Sweden* 11 H6
Hälsingland, *Sweden* 9 F16
Halstad, *U.S.A.* 108 B6
Haltdalen, *Norway* 10 B5
Haltern, *Germany* 18 D3
Halti, *Finland* 8 B19
Halul, *Qatar* 65 E7
Halvān, *Iran* 65 C8
Ham, *France* 25 C10
Ham Tan, *Vietnam* 59 G6
Ham Yen, *Vietnam* 58 A5
Hamab, *Namibia* 84 D2
Hamad, *Sudan* 77 D3
Hamada, *Japan* 49 G6
Hamadān, *Iran* 67 E13
Hamadān □, *Iran* 65 C6
Hamada, *Algeria* 75 A5

Hamāh, *Syria* 66 E7
Hamamatsu, *Japan* 49 G8
Hamar, *Norway* 10 D5
Hamâta, Gebel, *Egypt* ... 76 C3
Hambantota, *Sri Lanka* . 60 R12
Hamber Prov. Park, *Canada* 100 C5
Hamburg, *Germany* 18 B5
Hamburg, *Ark., U.S.A.* . 109 J9
Hamburg, *Iowa, U.S.A.* . 108 E7
Hamburg, *N.Y., U.S.A.* . 106 D6
Hamburg, *Pa., U.S.A.* .. 107 F9
Hamburg □, *Germany* ... 18 B6
Hamd, W. al →, *Si. Arabia* 64 E3
Hamden, *U.S.A.* 107 E12
Häme, *Finland* 9 F20
Hämeenlinna, *Finland* ... 9 F21
Hamélé, *Ghana* 78 C4
Hamelin Pool, *Australia* . 89 E1
Hameln, *Germany* 18 C5
Hamer Koke, *Ethiopia* .. 77 F4
Hamerkaz □, *Israel* 69 C3
Hamersley Ra., *Australia* . 88 D2
Hamhung, *N. Korea* 51 E14
Hami, *China* 54 B4
Hamilton, *Australia* 91 F3
Hamilton, *Canada* 98 D4
Hamilton, *N.Z.* 87 G5
Hamilton, *U.K.* 14 F4
Hamilton, *Mo., U.S.A.* . 108 F8
Hamilton, *Mont., U.S.A.* 110 C6
Hamilton, *N.Y., U.S.A.* . 107 D9
Hamilton, *Ohio, U.S.A.* . 104 F3
Hamilton, *Tex., U.S.A.* . 109 K5
Hamilton →, *Australia* .. 90 C2
Hamilton City, *U.S.A.* .. 112 F4
Hamilton Hotel, *Australia* 90 C3
Hamilton Inlet, *Canada* . 99 B8
Hamina, *Finland* 9 F22
Hamiota, *Canada* 101 C8
Hamlet, *U.S.A.* 105 H6
Hamley Bridge, *Australia* . 91 E2
Hamlin = Hameln, *Germany* 18 C5
Hamlin, *N.Y., U.S.A.* .. 106 C7
Hamlin, *Tex., U.S.A.* .. 109 J4
Hamm, *Germany* 18 D3
Hammam Bouhadjar, *Algeria* 75 A4
Hammamet, *Tunisia* 75 A7
Hammamet, G. de, *Tunisia* 75 A7
Hammarstrand, *Sweden* . 10 A10
Hamme, *Belgium* 17 F4
Hamme-Mille, *Belgium* .. 17 G5
Hammel, *Denmark* 11 H3
Hammelburg, *Germany* .. 19 E5
Hammerfest, *Norway* ... 8 A20
Hammond, *Ind., U.S.A.* . 104 E2
Hammond, *La., U.S.A.* . 109 K9
Hammonton, *U.S.A.* 104 F8
Hamoir, *Belgium* 17 H7
Hamont, *Belgium* 17 F7
Hamoyet, Jebel, *Sudan* .. 76 D4
Hampden, *N.Z.* 87 L3
Hampshire □, *U.K.* 13 F6
Hampshire Downs, *U.K.* . 13 F6
Hampton, *Ark., U.S.A.* . 109 J8
Hampton, *Iowa, U.S.A.* . 108 D8
Hampton, *N.H., U.S.A.* . 107 D14
Hampton, *S.C., U.S.A.* . 105 J5
Hampton, *Va., U.S.A.* .. 104 G7
Hampton Tableland, *Australia* 89 F4
Hamrat esh Sheykh, *Sudan* 77 E2
Hamur, *Turkey* 67 C10
Hamyang, *S. Korea* 51 G14
Han Jiang →, *China* 53 F11
Han Shui →, *China* 53 B10
Hana, *U.S.A.* 102 H17
Hanak, *Si. Arabia* 64 E3
Hanamaki, *Japan* 48 E10
Hanang, *Tanzania* 82 C4
Hanau, *Germany* 19 E4
Hanbogd, *Mongolia* 50 C4
Hancheng, *China* 50 G6
Hanchuan, *China* 53 B9
Hancock, *Mich., U.S.A.* . 108 B10
Hancock, *Minn., U.S.A.* . 108 C7
Hancock, *N.Y., U.S.A.* . 107 E9
Handa, *Japan* 49 G8
Handa, *Somali Rep.* 68 E5
Handan, *China* 50 F8
Handen, *Sweden* 10 E12
Handeni, *Tanzania* 82 D4
Handeni □, *Tanzania* ... 82 D4
Handub, *Sudan* 76 D4
Handwara, *India* 63 B6
Handzame, *Belgium* 17 F2
Hanegev, *Israel* 69 E3
Haney, *Canada* 100 D4
Hanford, *U.S.A.* 111 H4
Hang Chat, *Thailand* ... 58 C2
Hang Dong, *Thailand* ... 58 C2
Hangang →, *S. Korea* ... 51 F14
Hangayn Nuruu, *Mongolia* 54 B4
Hangchou = Hangzhou, *China* 53 B13
Hanggin Houqi, *China* .. 50 D4
Hanggin Qi, *China* 50 E5
Hangu, *China* 51 E9
Hangzhou, *China* 53 B13
Hangzhou Wan, *China* .. 53 B13
Hanhongor, *Mongolia* ... 50 C3
Hanīdh, *Si. Arabia* 65 E6
Hanīsh, *Yemen* 68 E3
Hanjiang, *China* 53 E12

Hankinson, *U.S.A.* 108 B6
Hanko, *Finland* 9 G20
Hankou, *China* 53 B10
Hanksville, *U.S.A.* 111 G8
Hanle, *India* 63 C8
Hanmer Springs, *N.Z.* .. 87 K4
Hann →, *Australia* 88 C4
Hann, Mt., *Australia* ... 88 C4
Hanna, *Canada* 100 C6
Hannaford, *U.S.A.* 108 B5
Hannah, *U.S.A.* 108 A5
Hannah B., *Canada* 98 B4
Hannibal, *U.S.A.* 108 F9
Hannik, *Sudan* 76 D3
Hannover, *Germany* 18 C5
Hannut, *Belgium* 17 G6
Hanoi, *Vietnam* 54 D5
Hanover = Hannover, *Germany* 18 C5
Hanover, *Canada* 106 B3
Hanover, *S. Africa* 84 E3
Hanover, *N.H., U.S.A.* . 107 C12
Hanover, *Ohio, U.S.A.* . 106 F2
Hanover, *Pa., U.S.A.* .. 104 F7
Hanover, I., *Chile* 128 D2
Hanshou, *China* 53 C8
Hansi, *India* 62 E6
Hanson, L., *Australia* ... 91 E2
Hantsavichy, *Belarus* ... 41 F4
Hanyang, *China* 53 B10
Hanyin, *China* 52 A7
Hanyuan, *China* 52 C4
Hanzhong, *China* 50 H4
Hanzhuang, *China* 51 G9
Haora, *India* 63 H13
Haoxue, *China* 53 B9
Haparanda, *Sweden* 8 D21
Hapert, *Neths.* 17 F6
Happy, *U.S.A.* 109 H4
Happy Camp, *U.S.A.* ... 110 F2
Happy Valley-Goose Bay, *Canada* 99 B7
Hapsu, *N. Korea* 51 D15
Hapur, *India* 62 E7
Haql, *Si. Arabia* 69 F3
Haquira, *Peru* 124 C3
Har, *Indonesia* 57 F8
Har-Ayrag, *Mongolia* ... 50 B5
Har Hu, *China* 54 C4
Har Us Nuur, *Mongolia* . 54 B4
Har Yehuda, *Israel* 69 D3
Harad, *Si. Arabia* 68 C4
Haradok, *Belarus* 40 E6
Haranomachi, *Japan* 48 F10
Harardera, *Somali Rep.* . 68 G4
Harare, *Zimbabwe* 83 F3
Harat, *Eritrea* 77 D4
Harazé, *Chad* 73 F8
Harbin, *China* 51 B14
Harbiye, *Turkey* 66 D7
Harboør, *Denmark* 11 H2
Harbor Beach, *U.S.A.* .. 104 D4
Harbor Springs, *U.S.A.* . 104 C3
Harbour Breton, *Canada* . 99 C8
Harbour Grace, *Canada* . 99 C9
Harburg, *Germany* 18 B5
Hårby, *Denmark* 11 J4
Harda, *India* 62 H7
Hardangerfjorden, *Norway* 9 F12
Hardangervidda, *Norway* . 9 F12
Hardap Dam, *Namibia* .. 84 C2
Hardegarijp, *Neths.* 16 B7
Hardenberg, *Neths.* 16 C9
Harderwijk, *Neths.* 16 D7
Hardey →, *Australia* 88 D2
Hardin, *U.S.A.* 110 D10
Harding, *S. Africa* 85 E4
Harding Ra., *Australia* .. 88 C3
Hardisty, *Canada* 100 C6
Hardman, *U.S.A.* 110 D4
Hardoi, *India* 63 F9
Hardwar = Haridwar, *India* 62 E8
Hardwick, *U.S.A.* 107 B12
Hardy, *U.S.A.* 109 G9
Hardy, Pen., *Chile* 128 E3
Hare B., *Canada* 99 B8
Hareid, *Norway* 9 E12
Harelbeke, *Belgium* 17 G2
Haren, *Germany* 18 C3
Haren, *Neths.* 16 B9
Harer, *Ethiopia* 68 F3
Harerge □, *Ethiopia* ... 77 F5
Hareto, *Ethiopia* 77 F4
Harfleur, *France* 24 C7
Hargeisa, *Somali Rep.* .. 68 F3
Hari →, *Indonesia* 56 E2
Haria, *Canary Is.* 36 E6
Haricha, Hamada el, *Mali* 74 D4
Haridwar, *India* 62 E8
Haringhata →, *Bangla.* . 61 J16
Haringvliet, *Neths.* 16 E4
Harīrūd →, *Asia* 60 A2
Härjedalen, *Sweden* 9 E15
Harlan, *Iowa, U.S.A.* ... 108 E7
Harlan, *Ky., U.S.A.* 105 G4
Harlech, *U.K.* 12 E3
Harlem, *U.S.A.* 110 B9
Harlingen, *Neths.* 16 B6
Harlingen, *U.S.A.* 109 M6
Harlowton, *U.S.A.* 110 C9
Harmånger, *Sweden* 10 C11
Harmil, *Eritrea* 77 D5
Harney Basin, *U.S.A.* .. 110 E4
Harney L., *U.S.A.* 110 E4
Harney Peak, *U.S.A.* ... 108 D3
Härnön, *Sweden* 10 B12
Härnösand, *Sweden* 10 B11

Haro, *Spain* 28 C2
Harp L., *Canada* 99 A7
Harper, *Liberia* 78 E3
Harplinge, *Sweden* 11 H6
Harrand, *Pakistan* 62 E4
Harriman, *U.S.A.* 105 H3
Harrington Harbour, *Canada* 99 B8
Harris, *U.K.* 14 D2
Harris, Sd. of, *U.K.* ... 14 D1
Harris L., *Australia* 91 E2
Harrisburg, *Ill., U.S.A.* . 109 G10
Harrisburg, *Nebr., U.S.A.* 108 E3
Harrisburg, *Oreg., U.S.A.* 110 D2
Harrisburg, *Pa., U.S.A.* . 106 F8
Harrismith, *S. Africa* ... 85 D4
Harrison, *Ark., U.S.A.* . 109 G8
Harrison, *Nebr., U.S.A.* . 108 D3
Harrison, C., *Canada* ... 99 B8
Harrison Bay, *U.S.A.* .. 96 A4
Harrison L., *Canada* 100 D4
Harrisonburg, *U.S.A.* ... 104 F6
Harrisonville, *U.S.A.* ... 108 F7
Harriston, *Canada* 98 D3
Harrisville, *U.S.A.* 106 B1
Harrogate, *U.K.* 12 D6
Harrow, *U.K.* 13 F7
Harsefeld, *Germany* 18 B5
Harsīn, *Iran* 67 E12
Harskamp, *Neths.* 16 D7
Harstad, *Norway* 8 B17
Hart, *U.S.A.* 104 D2
Hart, L., *Australia* 91 E2
Hartbees →, *S. Africa* .. 84 D3
Hartberg, *Austria* 21 H5
Hartford, *Conn., U.S.A.* . 107 E12
Hartford, *Ky., U.S.A.* .. 104 G2
Hartford, *S. Dak., U.S.A.* 108 D6
Hartford, *Wis., U.S.A.* . 108 D10
Hartford City, *U.S.A.* .. 104 E3
Hartland, *Canada* 99 C6
Hartland Pt., *U.K.* 13 F3
Hartlepool, *U.K.* 12 C6
Hartley Bay, *Canada* ... 100 C3
Hartmannberge, *Namibia* . 84 B1
Hartney, *Canada* 101 D8
Harts →, *S. Africa* 84 D3
Hartselle, *U.S.A.* 105 H2
Hartshorne, *U.S.A.* 109 H7
Hartsville, *U.S.A.* 105 H5
Hartwell, *U.S.A.* 105 H4
Harunabad, *Pakistan* ... 62 E5
Harvand, *Iran* 65 D7
Harvey, *Australia* 89 F2
Harvey, *Ill., U.S.A.* 104 E2
Harvey, *N. Dak., U.S.A.* 108 B5
Harwich, *U.K.* 13 F9
Haryana □, *India* 62 E7
Haryn →, *Belarus* 41 F4
Harz, *Germany* 18 D6
Harzé, *Belgium* 17 H7
Harzgerode, *Germany* ... 18 D7
Hasaheisa, *Sudan* 77 E3
Hasan Kīādeh, *Iran* 65 B6
Hasan Kuli, *Turkmenistan* 44 F6
Hasanābād, *Iran* 65 C7
Hasanpur, *India* 62 E8
Haselünne, *Germany* ... 18 C3
Hashimoto, *Japan* 49 G7
Hashtjerd, *Iran* 65 C6
Håsjö, *Sweden* 10 A10
Haskell, *Okla., U.S.A.* .. 109 H7
Haskell, *Tex., U.S.A.* .. 109 J5
Haslach, *Germany* 19 G4
Haslev, *Denmark* 11 J5
Hasparren, *France* 26 E2
Hassa, *Turkey* 66 D7
Hasselt, *Belgium* 17 G6
Hasselt, *Neths.* 16 C8
Hassene, Adrar, *Algeria* . 75 D5
Hassfurt, *Germany* 19 E6
Hassi bou Khelala, *Algeria* 75 B5
Hassi Djafou, *Algeria* ... 75 B5
Hassi el Abiod, *Algeria* .. 75 B5
Hassi el Biod, *Algeria* ... 75 C6
Hassi el Hadjar, *Algeria* . 75 B5
Hassi Imoulaye, *Algeria* . 75 C6
Hassi Inifel, *Algeria* 75 C5
Hassi Messaoud, *Algeria* . 75 B6
Hassi Tartrat, *Algeria* ... 75 B6
Hassi Zerzour, *Morocco* . 74 B4
Hässleholm, *Sweden* 11 H7
Hastière-Lavaux, *Belgium* 17 H5
Hastings, *N.Z.* 87 H6
Hastings, *U.K.* 13 G8
Hastings, *Mich., U.S.A.* . 104 D3
Hastings, *Minn., U.S.A.* . 108 C8
Hastings, *Nebr., U.S.A.* . 108 E5
Hastings Ra., *Australia* .. 91 E5
Hat Yai, *Thailand* 59 J3
Hatanbulag, *Mongolia* ... 50 C5
Hatay = Antalya, *Turkey* . 66 E4
Hatch, *U.S.A.* 111 K10
Hatches Creek, *Australia* . 90 C2
Hatchet L., *Canada* 101 B8
Hateg, *Romania* 38 D5
Hateg, Mții., *Romania* .. 38 D6
Hatert, *Neths.* 16 E7
Hateruma-Shima, *Japan* . 49 M1
Hatfield P.O., *Australia* . 91 E3
Hatgal, *Mongolia* 54 A5
Hathras, *India* 62 F8
Hatia, *Bangla.* 61 H17
Hato de Corozal, *Colombia* 120 B3
Hato Mayor, *Dom. Rep.* . 117 C6
Hattah, *Australia* 91 E3

Hattem, *Neths.* 16 D8
Hatteras, C., *U.S.A.* ... 105 H8
Hattiesburg, *U.S.A.* 109 K10
Hatvan, *Hungary* 21 H9
Hau Bon = Cheo Reo, *Vietnam* 58 F7
Hau Duc, *Vietnam* 58 E7
Haug, *Norway* 10 D4
Haugastøl, *Norway* 10 D1
Haugesund, *Norway* 9 G11
Haukipudas, *Finland* ... 8 D21
Haulerwijk, *Neths.* 16 B8
Haultain →, *Canada* 101 B7
Hauraki G., *N.Z.* 87 G5
Haut Atlas, *Morocco* 74 B3
Haut-Rhin □, *France* ... 25 E14
Haut Zaïre □, *Zaïre* 82 B2
Haute-Corse □, *France* .. 27 F13
Haute-Garonne □, *France* 26 E5
Haute-Loire □, *France* .. 26 C7
Haute-Marne □, *France* . 25 D12
Haute-Saône □, *France* . 25 E13
Haute-Savoie □, *France* . 27 C10
Haute-Vienne □, *France* . 26 C5
Hauterive, *Canada* 99 C6
Hautes-Alpes □, *France* . 27 D10
Hautes Fagnes = Hohe Venn, *Belgium* 17 H8
Hautes-Pyrénées □, *France* 26 F4
Hauteville-Lompnès, *France* 27 C9
Hautmont, *France* 25 B10
Hautrage, *Belgium* 17 H3
Hauts-de-Seine □, *France* . 25 D9
Hauts Plateaux, *Algeria* . 75 B4
Hauzenberg, *Germany* ... 19 G9
Havana = La Habana, *Cuba* 116 B3
Havana, *U.S.A.* 108 E9
Havant, *U.K.* 13 G7
Havasu, L., *U.S.A.* 113 L12
Havel →, *Germany* 18 C8
Havelange, *Belgium* 17 H6
Havelian, *Pakistan* 62 B5
Havelock, *N.B., Canada* . 99 C6
Havelock, *Ont., Canada* . 98 D4
Havelock, *N.Z.* 87 J4
Havelte, *Neths.* 16 C8
Haverfordwest, *U.K.* 13 F3
Haverhill, *U.S.A.* 107 D13
Havering, *U.K.* 13 F8
Haverstraw, *U.S.A.* 107 E11
Håverud, *Sweden* 11 F6
Havlíčkův Brod, *Czech.* . 20 F5
Havneby, *Denmark* 11 J2
Havre, *U.S.A.* 110 B9
Havre-Aubert, *Canada* .. 99 C7
Havre-St.-Pierre, *Canada* . 99 B7
Havza, *Turkey* 66 B6
Haw →, *U.S.A.* 105 H6
Hawaii □, *U.S.A.* 102 H16
Hawaii I., *Pac. Oc.* 102 J17
Hawaiian Is., *Pac. Oc.* . 102 H17
Hawaiian Ridge, *Pac. Oc.* 93 E11
Hawarden, *Canada* 101 C7
Hawarden, *U.S.A.* 108 D6
Hawea, L., *N.Z.* 87 L2
Hawera, *N.Z.* 87 H5
Hawick, *U.K.* 14 F6
Hawk Junction, *Canada* . 98 C3
Hawke B., *N.Z.* 87 H6
Hawker, *Australia* 91 E2
Hawkesbury, *Canada* ... 98 C5
Hawkesbury I., *Canada* . 100 C3
Hawkesbury Pt., *Australia* 90 A1
Hawkinsville, *U.S.A.* ... 105 J4
Hawkwood, *Australia* ... 91 D5
Hawley, *U.S.A.* 108 B6
Hawrān, *Syria* 69 C5
Hawrān, W. →, *Iraq* ... 67 F10
Hawsh Mūssá, *Lebanon* . 69 B4
Hawthorne, *U.S.A.* 110 G4
Hawzen, *Ethiopia* 77 E4
Haxtun, *U.S.A.* 108 E3
Hay, *Australia* 91 E3
Hay →, *Australia* 90 C2
Hay →, *Canada* 100 A5
Hay, C., *Australia* 88 B4
Hay L., *Canada* 100 B5
Hay Lakes, *Canada* 100 C6
Hay-on-Wye, *U.K.* 13 E4
Hay River, *Canada* 100 A5
Hay Springs, *U.S.A.* 108 D3
Haya, *Indonesia* 57 E7
Hayachine-San, *Japan* .. 48 E10
Hayange, *France* 25 C13
Hayden, *Ariz., U.S.A.* .. 111 K8
Hayden, *Colo., U.S.A.* .. 110 F10
Haydon, *Australia* 90 B3
Hayes, *U.S.A.* 108 C4
Hayes →, *Canada* 101 B10
Haymana, *Turkey* 66 C5
Haynesville, *U.S.A.* 109 J8
Hayrabolu, *Turkey* 66 B2
Hays, *Canada* 100 C6
Hays, *U.S.A.* 108 F5
Haysyn, *Ukraine* 41 H5
Hayvoron, *Ukraine* 41 H5
Hayward, *Calif., U.S.A.* . 112 H4
Hayward, *Wis., U.S.A.* . 108 B9
Haywards Heath, *U.K.* .. 13 G7
Hazafon □, *Israel* 69 C4
Hazarām, Kūh-e, *Iran* .. 65 D8
Hazard, *U.S.A.* 104 G4
Hazaribag, *India* 63 H11
Hazaribag Road, *India* .. 63 G11
Hazebrouck, *France* 25 B9

Hazelton, Canada 100 B3
Hazelton, U.S.A. 108 B4
Hazen, N. Dak., U.S.A. 108 B4
Hazen, Nev., U.S.A. 110 G4
Hazerswoude, Neths. 16 D5
Hazlehurst, Ga., U.S.A. 105 K4
Hazlehurst, Miss., U.S.A. 109 K9
Hazleton, U.S.A. 107 F9
Hazlett, L., Australia 88 D4
Ḥazor, Israel 69 B4
He Xian, Anhui, China 53 B12
He Xian, Guangxi Zhuangzu, China 53 E8
Head of Bight, Australia 89 F5
Headlands, Zimbabwe 83 F3
Healdsburg, U.S.A. 112 G4
Healdton, U.S.A. 109 H6
Healesville, Australia 91 F4
Heanor, U.K. 12 D6
Heard I., Ind. Oc. 3 G13
Hearne, U.S.A. 109 K6
Hearne B., Canada 101 A9
Hearne L., Canada 100 A6
Hearst, Canada 98 C3
Heart →, U.S.A. 108 B4
Heart's Content, Canada 99 C9
Heath →, Bolivia 124 C4
Heath Pt., Canada 99 C7
Heath Steele, Canada 99 C6
Heavener, U.S.A. 109 H7
Hebbronville, U.S.A. 109 M5
Hebei □, China 50 E9
Hebel, Australia 91 D4
Heber, U.S.A. 113 N11
Heber Springs, U.S.A. 109 H9
Hebert, Canada 101 C7
Hebgen L., U.S.A. 110 D8
Hebi, China 50 G8
Hebrides, U.K. 14 D1
Hebron = Al Khalīl, West Bank 69 D4
Hebron, Canada 97 C13
Hebron, N. Dak., U.S.A. 108 B3
Hebron, Nebr., U.S.A. 108 E6
Hecate Str., Canada 100 C2
Hechi, China 52 E7
Hechingen, Germany 19 G4
Hechtel, Belgium 17 F6
Hechuan, China 52 B6
Hecla, U.S.A. 108 C5
Hecla I., Canada 101 C9
Heddal, Norway 10 E3
Hédé, France 24 D5
Hede, Sweden 10 B7
Hedemora, Sweden 9 F16
Hedley, U.S.A. 109 H4
Hedmark fylke □, Norway 10 C5
Hedrum, Norway 10 E4
Heeg, Neths. 16 C7
Heegermeer, Neths. 16 C7
Heemskerk, Neths. 16 C5
Heemstede, Neths. 16 D5
Heer, Neths. 17 G7
Heerde, Neths. 16 D8
's Heerenberg, Neths. 16 E8
Heerenveen, Neths. 16 C7
Heerhugowaard, Neths. 16 C5
Heerlen, Neths. 17 G7
Heers, Belgium 17 G6
Heesch, Neths. 16 E7
Heestert, Belgium 17 G2
Heeze, Neths. 17 F7
Hefa, Israel 69 C3
Hefa □, Israel 69 C4
Hefei, China 53 B11
Hegang, China 54 B8
Hegyalja, Hungary 21 G11
Heichengzhen, China 50 F4
Heide, Germany 18 A5
Heidelberg, Germany 19 F4
Heidelberg, S. Africa 84 E3
Heidenheim, Germany 19 G6
Heijing, China 52 E3
Heilbron, S. Africa 85 D4
Heilbronn, Germany 19 F5
Heiligenblut, Austria 21 H2
Heiligenhafen, Germany 18 A6
Heiligenstadt, Germany 18 D6
Heilongjiang □, China 51 B14
Heilunkiang = Heilongjiang □, China 51 B14
Heimaey, Iceland 8 E3
Heino, Neths. 16 D8
Heinola, Finland 9 F22
Heinsch, Belgium 17 J7
Heinze Is., Burma 61 M20
Heishan, China 51 D12
Heishui, Liaoning, China 51 C10
Heishui, Sichuan, China 52 A4
Heist, Belgium 17 F2
Heist-op-den-Berg, Belgium 17 F5
Hejaz = Al Ḥijāz, Si. Arabia 68 B2
Hejian, China 50 E9
Hejiang, China 52 C5
Hejin, China 50 G6
Hekelgem, Belgium 17 G4
Hekimhan, Turkey 66 C7
Hekla, Iceland 8 E4
Hekou, Gansu, China 50 F2
Hekou, Guangdong, China 53 F9
Hekou, Yunnan, China 54 D5
Helagsfjället, Sweden 10 B6
Helan Shan, China 50 E3
Helchteren, Belgium 17 F6
Helden, Neths. 17 F7

Helechosa, Spain 31 F6
Helena, Ark., U.S.A. 109 H9
Helena, Mont., U.S.A. 110 C7
Helendale, U.S.A. 113 L9
Helensburgh, U.K. 14 E4
Helensville, N.Z. 87 G5
Helgeland, Norway 8 C15
Helgeroa, Norway 10 F3
Helgoland, Germany 18 A3
Heligoland = Helgoland, Germany 18 A3
Heligoland B. = Deutsche Bucht, Germany 18 A4
Heliopolis, Egypt 76 H7
Hella, Iceland 8 E3
Hellebæk, Denmark 11 H6
Hellendoorn, Neths. 16 D8
Hellevoetsluis, Neths. 16 E4
Hellín, Spain 29 G3
Helmand □, Afghan. 60 D4
Helmand →, Afghan. 60 D2
Helme →, Germany 18 D7
Helmond, Neths. 17 F7
Helmsdale, U.K. 14 C5
Helmstedt, Germany 18 C7
Helnæs, Denmark 11 J4
Helong, China 51 C15
Helper, U.S.A. 110 G8
Helsingborg, Sweden 11 H6
Helsinge, Denmark 11 H6
Helsingfors = Helsinki, Finland 9 F21
Helsingør, Denmark 11 H6
Helsinki, Finland 9 F21
Helston, U.K. 13 G2
Helvellyn, U.K. 12 C4
Helvoirt, Neths. 17 E6
Helwân, Egypt 76 J7
Hemet, U.S.A. 113 M10
Hemingford, U.S.A. 108 D3
Hemphill, U.S.A. 109 K8
Hempstead, U.S.A. 109 K6
Hemse, Sweden 9 H18
Hemsö, Sweden 10 B12
Henan □, China 50 G8
Henares →, Spain 28 E1
Henashi-Misaki, Japan 48 D9
Hendaye, France 26 E2
Hendek, Turkey 66 B4
Henderson, Argentina 126 D3
Henderson, Ky., U.S.A. 104 G2
Henderson, N.C., U.S.A. 105 G6
Henderson, Nev., U.S.A. 113 J12
Henderson, Tenn., U.S.A. 105 H1
Henderson, Tex., U.S.A. 109 J7
Hendersonville, U.S.A. 105 H4
Hendījān, Iran 65 D6
Hendon, Australia 91 D5
Heng Xian, China 52 F7
Hengcheng, China 50 E4
Hengdaohezi, China 51 B15
Hengelo, Gelderland, Neths. 16 D8
Hengelo, Overijssel, Neths. 16 D9
Hengfeng, China 53 C10
Hengshan, Hunan, China 53 D9
Hengshan, Shaanxi, China 50 F5
Hengshui, China 50 F8
Hengyang, Hunan, China 53 D9
Hengyang, Hunan, China 53 D9
Henichesk, Ukraine 41 J8
Hénin-Beaumont, France 25 B9
Hennan, Sweden 10 B9
Hennebont, France 24 E3
Hennenman, S. Africa 84 D4
Hennessey, U.S.A. 109 G6
Hennigsdorf, Germany 18 C9
Henrichemont, France 25 E9
Henrietta, U.S.A. 109 J5
Henrietta, Ostrov, Russia 45 B16
Henrietta Maria, C., Canada 98 A3
Henry, U.S.A. 108 E10
Henryetta, U.S.A. 109 H6
Hensall, Canada 106 C3
Hentiyn Nuruu, Mongolia 54 B5
Henty, Australia 91 F4
Henzada, Burma 61 L19
Heping, China 53 E10
Hepo, China 53 F11
Heppner, U.S.A. 110 D4
Hepu, China 52 G7
Hepworth, Canada 106 B3
Heqing, China 52 D3
Hequ, China 50 E6
Héraðsflói, Iceland 8 D6
Héraðsvötn →, Iceland 8 D4
Herald Cays, Australia 90 B4
Hérault □, France 26 E7
Hérault →, France 26 E7
Herbault, France 24 E8
Herbert →, Australia 90 B4
Herbert Downs, Australia 90 C2
Herberton, Australia 90 B4
Herbignac, France 24 E4
Herborn, Germany 18 E4
Herby, Poland 20 E8
Hercegnovi, Montenegro, Yug. 21 N8
Herðubreið, Iceland 8 D5
Hereford, U.K. 13 E5
Hereford, U.S.A. 109 H3
Hereford and Worcester □, U.K. 13 E5
Herefoss, Norway 11 F2

Herent, Belgium 17 G5
Herentals, Belgium 17 F5
Herenthout, Belgium 17 F5
Herfølge, Denmark 11 J6
Herford, Germany 18 C4
Héricourt, France 25 E13
Herington, U.S.A. 108 F6
Herisau, Switz. 23 B8
Hérisson, France 26 B6
Herk →, Belgium 17 G6
Herkenbosch, Neths. 17 F8
Herkimer, U.S.A. 107 D10
Herlong, U.S.A. 112 E6
Herm, U.K. 24 C4
Hermagor-Pressegger See, Austria 21 J3
Herman, U.S.A. 108 C6
Hermann, U.S.A. 108 F9
Hermannsburg, Germany 18 C6
Hermannsburg Mission, Australia 88 D5
Hermanus, S. Africa 84 E2
Herment, France 26 C6
Hermidale, Australia 91 E4
Hermiston, U.S.A. 110 D4
Hermitage, N.Z. 87 K3
Hermite, I., Chile 128 E3
Hermon, Mt. = Ash Shaykh, J., Lebanon 69 B4
Hermosillo, Mexico 114 B2
Hernád →, Hungary 21 H11
Hernandarias, Paraguay 127 B5
Hernandez, U.S.A. 112 J6
Hernando, Argentina 126 C3
Hernando, U.S.A. 109 H10
Herne, Belgium 17 G4
Herne, Germany 17 E10
Herne Bay, U.K. 13 F9
Herning, Denmark 11 H2
Heroica = Caborca, Mexico 114 A2
Heroica Nogales = Nogales, Mexico 114 A2
Heron Bay, Canada 98 C2
Herradura, Pta. de la, Canary Is. 36 F5
Herreid, U.S.A. 108 C4
Herrera, Spain 31 H6
Herrera de Alcántar, Spain 31 F3
Herrera de Pisuerga, Spain 30 C6
Herrera del Duque, Spain 31 F5
Herrick, Australia 90 G4
Herrin, U.S.A. 109 G10
Herrljunga, Sweden 11 F7
Hersbruck, Germany 19 F7
Herseaux, Belgium 17 G2
Herselt, Belgium 17 F5
Hersonissos, Greece 37 D7
Herstal, Belgium 17 G7
Hertford, U.K. 13 F7
Hertfordshire □, U.K. 13 F7
's-Hertogenbosch, Neths. 17 E6
Hertzogville, S. Africa 84 D4
Hervás, Spain 30 E5
Herve, Belgium 17 G7
Herwijnen, Neths. 16 E6
Herzberg, Brandenburg, Germany 18 D9
Herzberg, Niedersachsen, Germany 18 D6
Herzele, Belgium 17 G3
Herzliyya, Israel 69 C3
Herzogenbuchsee, Switz. 22 B5
Heşar, Fārs, Iran 65 D6
Heşar, Markazī, Iran 65 C6
Hesdin, France 25 B9
Hesel, Germany 18 B3
Heshui, China 50 G5
Heshun, China 50 F7
Hesperange, Lux. 17 J8
Hesperia, U.S.A. 113 L9
Hesse = Hessen □, Germany 18 E5
Hessen □, Germany 18 E5
Hetch Hetchy Aqueduct, U.S.A. 112 H5
Hettinger, U.S.A. 108 C3
Hettstedt, Germany 18 D7
Heugem, Neths. 17 G7
Heule, Belgium 17 G2
Heusden, Belgium 17 F6
Heusden, Neths. 16 E6
Hève, C. de la, France 24 C7
Heverlee, Belgium 17 G5
Hewett, C., Canada 97 A13
Hexham, U.K. 12 C5
Hexi, Yunnan, China 52 E4
Hexi, Zhejiang, China 53 D12
Hexigten Qi, China 51 C9
Heydarābād, Iran 65 D7
Heyfield, Australia 91 F4
Heysham, U.K. 12 C5
Heythuysen, Neths. 17 F7
Heyuan, China 53 F10
Heywood, Australia 91 F3
Heze, China 50 G8
Hezhang, China 52 D5
Hi Vista, U.S.A. 113 L9
Hialeah, U.S.A. 105 N5
Hiawatha, Kans., U.S.A. 108 F7
Hiawatha, Utah, U.S.A. 110 G8
Hibbing, U.S.A. 108 B8
Hibbs B., Australia 90 G4
Hibernia Reef, Australia 88 B3
Hickory, U.S.A. 105 H5
Hicks, Pt., Australia 91 F4
Hicksville, U.S.A. 107 F11
Hida, Romania 38 B6

Hida-Gawa →, Japan 49 G8
Hida-Sammyaku, Japan 49 F8
Hidaka-Sammyaku, Japan 48 C11
Hidalgo, Mexico 115 C5
Hidalgo □, Mexico 115 C5
Hidalgo, Presa M., Mexico 114 B3
Hidalgo, Pta. del, Canary Is. 36 F3
Hidalgo del Parral, Mexico 114 B3
Hiddensee, Germany 18 A9
Hidrolândia, Brazil 123 E2
Hieflau, Austria 21 H4
Hiendelaencina, Spain 28 D1
Hierro, Canary Is. 36 G1
Higashiajima-San, Japan 48 F10
Higashiōsaka, Japan 49 G7
Higgins, U.S.A. 109 G4
Higgins Corner, U.S.A. 112 F5
Higginsville, Australia 89 F3
High Atlas = Haut Atlas, Morocco 74 B3
High I., Canada 99 A13
High Island, U.S.A. 109 L7
High Level, Canada 100 B5
High Point, U.S.A. 105 H6
High Prairie, Canada 100 B5
High River, Canada 100 C6
High Springs, U.S.A. 105 L4
High Tatra = Tatry, Slovak Rep. 20 F9
High Wycombe, U.K. 13 F7
Highbury, Australia 90 B3
Highland □, U.K. 14 D4
Highland Park, U.S.A. 104 D2
Highmore, U.S.A. 108 C5
Highrock L., Canada 101 B7
Higüay, Dom. Rep. 117 C6
Hihya, Egypt 76 H7
Hiiumaa, Estonia 9 G20
Híjar, Spain 28 D4
Ḥijāz □, Si. Arabia 68 C2
Hijken, Neths. 16 C8
Hijo = Tagum, Phil. 55 H6
Hikari, Japan 49 H5
Hiko, U.S.A. 111 H6
Hikone, Japan 49 G8
Hikurangi, N.Z. 87 F5
Hikurangi, Mt., N.Z. 87 H6
Hildburghausen, Germany 19 E6
Hildesheim, Germany 18 C5
Hill →, Australia 89 F2
Hill City, Idaho, U.S.A. 110 E6
Hill City, Kans., U.S.A. 108 F5
Hill City, Minn., U.S.A. 108 B8
Hill City, S. Dak., U.S.A. 108 D3
Hill Island L., Canada 101 A7
Hillared, Sweden 11 G7
Hillcrest Center, U.S.A. 113 K8
Hillegom, Neths. 16 D5
Hillerød, Denmark 11 J6
Hillingdon, U.K. 13 F7
Hillman, U.S.A. 104 C4
Hillmond, Canada 101 C7
Hillsboro, Kans., U.S.A. 108 F6
Hillsboro, N. Dak., U.S.A. 108 B6
Hillsboro, N.H., U.S.A. 107 C13
Hillsboro, N. Mex., U.S.A. 111 K10
Hillsboro, Oreg., U.S.A. 112 E4
Hillsboro, Tex., U.S.A. 109 J6
Hillsborough, Grenada 117 D7
Hillsdale, Mich., U.S.A. 104 E3
Hillsdale, N.Y., U.S.A. 107 D11
Hillside, Australia 88 D2
Hillsport, Canada 98 C2
Hillston, Australia 91 E4
Hilo, U.S.A. 102 J17
Hilton, U.S.A. 106 C7
Hilvan, Turkey 67 D8
Hilvarenbeek, Neths. 17 F6
Hilversum, Neths. 16 D6
Himachal Pradesh □, India 62 D7
Himalaya, Asia 63 E11
Himamaylan, Phil. 55 F5
Himara, Albania 39 J2
Himatnagar, India 60 H8
Himeji, Japan 49 G7
Himi, Japan 49 F8
Himmerland, Denmark 11 H3
Ḥimş, Syria 69 A5
Ḥimş □, Syria 69 A5
Hinche, Haiti 117 C5
Hinchinbrook I., Australia 90 B4
Hinckley, U.K. 13 E6
Hinckley, U.S.A. 110 G7
Hindås, Sweden 11 G6
Hindaun, India 62 F7
Hindmarsh, L., Australia 91 F3
Hindsholm, Denmark 11 J4
Hindu Bagh, Pakistan 62 D2
Hindu Kush, Asia 60 B7
Hindubagh, Pakistan 60 D5
Hindupur, India 60 N10
Hines Creek, Canada 100 B5
Hinganghat, India 60 J11
Hingeon, Belgium 17 G5
Hingham, U.S.A. 110 B8
Hingoli, India 60 K10
Hinigaran, Phil. 55 F5
Hinis, Turkey 67 C9
Hinna = Imi, Ethiopia 68 F3
Hinna, Nigeria 79 C7
Hinnøya, Norway 8 B16
Hinojosa del Duque, Spain 31 G5
Hinsdale, U.S.A. 110 B10
Hinterrhein →, Switz. 23 C8
Hinton, Canada 100 C5

Hinton, U.S.A. 104 G5
Hinwil, Switz. 23 B7
Hınzır Burnu, Turkey 66 D6
Hippolytushoef, Neths. 16 C5
Hirado, Japan 49 H4
Hirakud Dam, India 61 J13
Hiratsuka, Japan 49 G9
Hirfanlı Baraji, Turkey 66 C5
Hirhafok, Algeria 75 D6
Hîrlău, Romania 38 B9
Hiroo, Japan 48 C11
Hirosaki, Japan 48 D10
Hiroshima, Japan 49 G6
Hiroshima □, Japan 49 G6
Hirsholmene, Denmark 11 G4
Hirson, France 25 C11
Hîrşova, Romania 38 E10
Hirtshals, Denmark 11 G3
Hisar, India 62 E6
Hisb →, Iraq 64 D5
Ḥismá, Si. Arabia 64 D3
Hispaniola, W. Indies 117 C5
Ḥīt, Iraq 67 F10
Hita, Japan 49 H5
Hitachi, Japan 49 F10
Hitchin, U.K. 13 F7
Hitoyoshi, Japan 49 H5
Hitra, Norway 8 E13
Hitzacker, Germany 18 B7
Ḥiyyon, N. →, Israel 69 E4
Hjalmar L., Canada 101 A7
Hjälmare kanal, Sweden 10 E9
Hjälmaren, Sweden 10 E9
Hjartdal, Norway 10 E2
Hjerkinn, Norway 10 B3
Hjørring, Denmark 11 G3
Hjortkvarn, Sweden 11 F9
Hlinsko, Czech. 20 F5
Hluhluwe, S. Africa 85 D5
Hlukhiv, Ukraine 41 G7
Hlyboka, Ukraine 41 H3
Hlybokaye, Belarus 40 E4
Ho, Ghana 79 D5
Ho Chi Minh City = Phanh Bho Ho Chi Minh, Vietnam 59 G6
Ho Thuong, Vietnam 58 C5
Hoa Binh, Vietnam 58 B5
Hoa Da, Vietnam 59 G7
Hoa Hiep, Vietnam 59 G5
Hoai Nhon, Vietnam 58 E7
Hoang Lien Son, Vietnam 58 A4
Hoare B., Canada 97 B13
Hobart, Australia 90 G4
Hobart, U.S.A. 109 H5
Hobbs, U.S.A. 109 J3
Hobbs Coast, Antarctica 5 D14
Hobo, Colombia 120 C2
Hoboken, Belgium 17 F4
Hoboken, U.S.A. 107 F10
Hobro, Denmark 11 H3
Hobscheid, Lux. 17 J7
Hoburgen, Sweden 9 H18
Hochdorf, Switz. 23 B6
Hochschwab, Austria 21 H5
Höchstadt, Germany 19 F6
Hockenheim, Germany 19 F4
Hodaka-Dake, Japan 49 F8
Hodgson, Canada 101 C9
Hódmezővásárhely, Hungary 21 J10
Hodna, Chott el, Algeria 75 A5
Hodna, Monts du, Algeria 75 A5
Hodonín, Czech. 20 G7
Hoeamdong, N. Korea 51 C16
Hœdic, I. de, France 24 E4
Hoegaarden, Belgium 17 G5
Hoek van Holland, Neths. 16 E4
Hoeksche Waard, Neths. 16 E4
Hoenderloo, Neths. 16 D7
Hoengsŏng, S. Korea 51 F14
Hoensbroek, Neths. 17 G7
Hoeryong, N. Korea 51 C15
Hoeselt, Belgium 17 G6
Hoeven, Neths. 17 F5
Hoeyang, N. Korea 51 E14
Hof, Germany 19 E7
Höfðakaupstaður, Iceland 8 D3
Hofgeismar, Germany 18 D5
Hofmeyr, S. Africa 84 E4
Höfn, Iceland 8 D6
Hofors, Sweden 9 F17
Hofsjökull, Iceland 8 D4
Hōfu, Japan 49 G5
Hogan Group, Australia 90 F4
Hogansville, U.S.A. 105 J3
Hogeland, U.S.A. 110 B9
Hoggar = Ahaggar, Algeria 75 D6
Högsäter, Sweden 11 F6
Hogsty Reef, Bahamas 117 B5
Hoh →, U.S.A. 112 C2
Hoh Xil Shan, China 54 C3
Hohe Rhön, Germany 19 E5
Hohe Tauern, Austria 21 H2
Hohe Venn, Belgium 17 H8
Hohenau, Austria 20 G6
Hohenems, Austria 19 H5
Hohenstein-Ernstthal, Germany 18 E8
Hohenwald, U.S.A. 105 H2
Hohenwestedt, Germany 18 A5
Hohhot, China 50 D6
Hóhlakas, Greece 37 D9
Hohoe, Ghana 79 D5
Hoi An, Vietnam 58 E7
Hoi Xuan, Vietnam 58 B5

Humptulips

Hoisington, *U.S.A.* 108 F5
Højer, *Denmark* 11 K2
Hōjō, *Japan* 49 H6
Hökerum, *Sweden* 11 G7
Hokianga Harbour, *N.Z.* 87 F4
Hokitika, *N.Z.* 87 K3
Hokkaidō □, *Japan* 48 C11
Hokksund, *Norway* 10 E3
Hol-Hol, *Djibouti* 77 E5
Hola Pristan, *Ukraine* 41 J7
Holbæk, *Denmark* 11 J5
Holbrook, *Australia* 91 F4
Holbrook, *U.S.A.* 111 J8
Holden, *Canada* 100 C6
Holden, *U.S.A.* 110 G7
Holdenville, *U.S.A.* 109 H6
Holderness, *U.K.* 12 D7
Holdfast, *Canada* 101 C7
Holdich, *Argentina* 128 C3
Holdrege, *U.S.A.* 108 E5
Holguín, *Cuba* 116 B4
Hollabrunn, *Austria* 20 G6
Hollams Bird I., *Namibia* 84 C1
Holland, *U.S.A.* 104 D2
Hollandia = Jayapura, *Indonesia* 57 E10
Hollandsch Diep, *Neths.* 17 E5
Hollandsch IJssel →, *Neths.* 16 E5
Hollfeld, *Germany* 19 F7
Hollidaysburg, *U.S.A.* 106 F6
Hollis, *U.S.A.* 109 H5
Hollister, *Calif., U.S.A.* 111 H3
Hollister, *Idaho, U.S.A.* 110 E6
Hollum, *Neths.* 16 B7
Holly, *U.S.A.* 108 F3
Holly Hill, *U.S.A.* 105 L5
Holly Springs, *U.S.A.* 109 H10
Hollywood, *Calif., U.S.A.* 111 J4
Hollywood, *Fla., U.S.A.* 105 N5
Holm, *Sweden* 10 B10
Holman Island, *Canada* 96 A8
Hólmavík, *Iceland* 8 D3
Holmes Reefs, *Australia* 90 B4
Holmestrand, *Norway* 10 E4
Holmsbu, *Norway* 10 E4
Holmsjön, *Sweden* 10 B9
Holmsland Klit, *Denmark* 11 J2
Holmsund, *Sweden* 8 E19
Holroyd →, *Australia* 90 A3
Holstebro, *Denmark* 11 H2
Holsworthy, *U.K.* 13 G3
Holte, *Denmark* 11 J6
Holten, *Neths.* 16 D8
Holton, *Canada* 99 B8
Holton, *U.S.A.* 108 F7
Holtville, *U.S.A.* 113 N11
Holwerd, *Neths.* 16 B7
Holy Cross, *U.S.A.* 96 B4
Holy I., *Gwynedd, U.K.* 12 D3
Holy I., *Northumb., U.K.* 12 B6
Holyhead, *U.K.* 12 D3
Holyoke, *Colo., U.S.A.* 108 E3
Holyoke, *Mass., U.S.A.* 107 D12
Holyrood, *Canada* 99 C9
Holzkirchen, *Germany* 19 H7
Holzminden, *Germany* 18 D5
Homa Bay, *Kenya* 82 C3
Homa Bay □, *Kenya* 82 C3
Homalin, *Burma* 61 G19
Homand, *Iran* 65 C8
Homberg, *Germany* 18 D5
Hombori, *Mali* 79 B4
Homburg, *Germany* 19 F3
Home B., *Canada* 97 B13
Home Hill, *Australia* 90 B4
Homedale, *U.S.A.* 110 E5
Homer, *Alaska, U.S.A.* 96 C4
Homer, *La., U.S.A.* 109 J8
Homestead, *Australia* 90 C4
Homestead, *Fla., U.S.A.* 105 N5
Homestead, *Oreg., U.S.A.* 110 D5
Homewood, *U.S.A.* 112 F6
Hominy, *U.S.A.* 109 G6
Homoine, *Mozam.* 85 C6
Homoljske Planina, *Serbia, Yug.* 21 L11
Homorod, *Romania* 38 C8
Homs = Ḥimṣ, *Syria* 69 A5
Homyel, *Belarus* 41 F6
Hon Chong, *Vietnam* 59 G5
Hon Me, *Vietnam* 58 C5
Hon Quan, *Vietnam* 59 G6
Honan = Henan □, *China* 50 G8
Honbetsu, *Japan* 48 C11
Honcut, *U.S.A.* 112 F5
Honda, *Colombia* 120 B3
Honda Bay, *Phil.* 55 G3
Hondeklipbaai, *S. Africa* 84 E2
Hondo, *Japan* 49 H5
Hondo, *U.S.A.* 109 L5
Hondo →, *Belize* 115 D7
Honduras ■, *Cent. Amer.* 116 D2
Honduras, G. de, *Caribbean* 116 C2
Hønefoss, *Norway* 9 F14
Honesdale, *U.S.A.* 107 E9
Honey L., *U.S.A.* 112 E6
Honfleur, *France* 24 C7
Hong Gai, *Vietnam* 58 B6
Hong He →, *China* 50 H8
Hong Kong ■, *Asia* 53 F10
Hong'an, *China* 53 B10
Hongchŏn, *S. Korea* 51 F14
Honghai Wan, *China* 53 F10
Honghu, *China* 53 C9
Hongjiang, *China* 52 D7
Hongliu He →, *China* 50 F5
Hongor, *Mongolia* 50 B7
Hongsa, *Laos* 58 C3
Hongshui He →, *China* 52 F7
Hongsŏng, *S. Korea* 51 F14
Hongtong, *China* 50 F6
Honguedo, Détroit d', *Canada* 99 C7
Hongwon, *N. Korea* 51 E14
Hongya, *China* 52 C4
Hongyuan, *China* 52 A4
Hongze Hu, *China* 51 H10
Honiara, *Solomon Is.* 92 H7
Honiton, *U.K.* 13 G4
Honjō, *Japan* 48 E10
Honkorâb, Ras, *Egypt* 76 C4
Honningsvåg, *Norway* 8 A21
Honolulu, *U.S.A.* 102 H16
Honshū, *Japan* 49 G9
Hontoria del Pinar, *Spain* 28 D1
Hood, Mt., *U.S.A.* 110 D3
Hood, Pt., *Australia* 89 F2
Hood River, *U.S.A.* 110 D3
Hoodsport, *U.S.A.* 112 C3
Hooge, *Germany* 18 A4
Hoogerheide, *Neths.* 17 F4
Hoogeveen, *Neths.* 16 C8
Hoogeveensche Vaart, *Neths.* 16 C8
Hoogezand, *Neths.* 16 B9
Hooghly = Hughli →, *India* 63 J13
Hooghly-Chinsura = Chunchura, *India* 63 H13
Hoogkerk, *Neths.* 16 B9
Hooglede, *Belgium* 17 G2
Hoogstraten, *Belgium* 17 F5
Hoogvliet, *Neths.* 16 E4
Hook Hd., *Ireland* 15 D5
Hook I., *Australia* 90 C4
Hook of Holland = Hoek van Holland, *Neths.* 16 E4
Hooker, *U.S.A.* 109 G4
Hooker Creek, *Australia* 88 C5
Hoopeston, *U.S.A.* 104 E2
Hoopstad, *S. Africa* 84 D4
Hoorn, *Neths.* 16 C6
Hoover Dam, *U.S.A.* 113 K12
Hooversville, *U.S.A.* 106 F6
Hop Bottom, *U.S.A.* 107 E9
Hopa, *Turkey* 67 B9
Hope, *Canada* 100 D4
Hope, *Ariz., U.S.A.* 113 M13
Hope, *Ark., U.S.A.* 109 J8
Hope, *N. Dak., U.S.A.* 108 B6
Hope, L., *Australia* 91 D2
Hope, Pt., *U.S.A.* 96 B3
Hope Town, *Bahamas* 116 A4
Hopedale, *Canada* 99 A7
Hopefield, *S. Africa* 84 E2
Hopei = Hebei □, *China* 50 E9
Hopelchén, *Mexico* 115 D7
Hopetoun, *Vic., Australia* 91 F3
Hopetoun, *W. Austral., Australia* 89 F3
Hopetown, *S. Africa* 84 D3
Hopkins, *U.S.A.* 108 E7
Hopkins, L., *Australia* 88 D4
Hopkinsville, *U.S.A.* 105 G2
Hopland, *U.S.A.* 112 G3
Hoptrup, *Denmark* 11 J3
Hoquiam, *U.S.A.* 112 D3
Horasan, *Turkey* 67 B10
Horcajo de Santiago, *Spain* 28 F1
Horden Hills, *Australia* 88 D5
Horezu, *Romania* 38 D6
Horgen, *Switz.* 23 B7
Horinger, *China* 50 D6
Horki, *Belarus* 40 E6
Horlick Mts., *Antarctica* 5 E15
Horlivka, *Ukraine* 41 H10
Hormoz, *Iran* 65 E7
Hormoz, Jaz. ye, *Iran* 65 E8
Hormuz, Str. of, *The Gulf* 65 E8
Horn, *Iceland* 8 C2
Horn, *Neths.* 17 F7
Horn →, *Canada* 100 A5
Horn, Cape = Hornos, C. de, *Chile* 128 E3
Horn Head, *Ireland* 15 A3
Horn I., *Australia* 90 A3
Horn I., *U.S.A.* 105 K1
Horn Mts., *Canada* 100 A5
Hornachuelos, *Spain* 31 H5
Hornavan, *Sweden* 8 C17
Hornbæk, *Denmark* 11 H6
Hornbeck, *U.S.A.* 109 K8
Hornbrook, *U.S.A.* 110 F2
Hornburg, *Germany* 18 C6
Horncastle, *U.K.* 12 D7
Hornell, *U.S.A.* 106 D7
Hornell L., *Canada* 100 A5
Hornepayne, *Canada* 98 C3
Hornitos, *U.S.A.* 112 H6
Hornos, C. de, *Chile* 128 E3
Hornoy, *France* 25 C8
Hornsby, *Australia* 91 E5
Hornsea, *U.K.* 12 D7
Hornslandet, *Sweden* 10 C11
Hornslet, *Denmark* 11 H4
Hornu, *Belgium* 17 H3
Hörnum, *Germany* 18 A4
Horobetsu, *Japan* 48 C10
Horodenka, *Ukraine* 41 H3
Horodnya, *Ukraine* 41 G6
Horodok, *Khmelnytskyy, Ukraine* 41 H4
Horodok, *Lviv, Ukraine* 41 H2
Horodyshche, *Ukraine* 41 H6
Horokhiv, *Ukraine* 41 G3
Horqin Youyi Qianqi, *China* 51 A12
Horqueta, *Paraguay* 126 A4
Horred, *Sweden* 11 G6
Horse Creek, *U.S.A.* 108 E3
Horse Is., *Canada* 99 B8
Horsefly L., *Canada* 100 C4
Horsens, *Denmark* 11 J3
Horsens Fjord, *Denmark* 11 J4
Horsham, *Australia* 91 F3
Horsham, *U.K.* 13 F7
Horst, *Neths.* 17 F8
Horten, *Norway* 10 E4
Hortobágy →, *Hungary* 21 H11
Horton, *U.S.A.* 108 F7
Horton →, *Canada* 96 B7
Horw, *Switz.* 23 B6
Horwood, L., *Canada* 98 C3
Hosaina, *Ethiopia* 77 F4
Hose, Gunung-Gunung, *Malaysia* 56 D4
Ḥoseynābād, *Khuzestān, Iran* 65 C6
Ḥoseynābād, *Kordestān, Iran* 67 E12
Hoshangabad, *India* 62 H7
Hoshiarpur, *India* 62 D6
Hosingen, *Lux.* 17 H8
Hosmer, *U.S.A.* 108 C5
Hospental, *Switz.* 23 C7
Hospet, *India* 60 M10
Hospitalet de Llobregat, *Spain* 28 D7
Hoste, I., *Chile* 128 E3
Hostens, *France* 26 D3
Hot, *Thailand* 58 C2
Hot Creek Range, *U.S.A.* 110 G5
Hot Springs, *Ark., U.S.A.* 109 H8
Hot Springs, *S. Dak., U.S.A.* 108 D3
Hotagen, *Sweden* 8 E16
Hotan, *China* 54 C2
Hotazel, *S. Africa* 84 D3
Hotchkiss, *U.S.A.* 111 G10
Hotham, C., *Australia* 88 B5
Hoting, *Sweden* 8 D17
Hotte, Massif de la, *Haiti* 117 C5
Hottentotsbaai, *Namibia* 84 D1
Hotton, *Belgium* 17 H6
Houat, I. de, *France* 24 E4
Houck, *U.S.A.* 111 J9
Houdan, *France* 25 D8
Houdeng-Goegnies, *Belgium* 17 H4
Houei Sai, *Laos* 58 B3
Houffalize, *Belgium* 17 H7
Houghton, *U.S.A.* 108 B10
Houghton L., *U.S.A.* 104 C3
Houghton-le-Spring, *U.K.* 12 C6
Houhora Heads, *N.Z.* 87 F4
Houille →, *Belgium* 17 H5
Houlton, *U.S.A.* 99 C6
Houma, *U.S.A.* 109 L9
Houndé, *Burkina Faso* 78 C4
Hourtin, *France* 26 C2
Hourtin-Carcans, Étang d', *France* 26 C2
Houston, *Canada* 100 C3
Houston, *Mo., U.S.A.* 109 G9
Houston, *Tex., U.S.A.* 109 L7
Houten, *Neths.* 16 D6
Houthalen, *Belgium* 17 F6
Houthem, *Belgium* 17 G1
Houthulst, *Belgium* 17 G2
Houtman Abrolhos, *Australia* 89 E1
Houyet, *Belgium* 17 H6
Hov, *Denmark* 11 J4
Hova, *Sweden* 11 F8
Høvåg, *Norway* 11 F2
Hovd, *Mongolia* 54 B4
Hove, *U.K.* 13 G7
Hoveyzeh, *Iran* 65 D6
Hövsgöl, *Mongolia* 50 C5
Hövsgöl Nuur, *Mongolia* 54 A5
Howakil, *Eritrea* 77 D5
Howar, Wadi →, *Sudan* 77 D2
Howard, *Australia* 91 D5
Howard, *Kans., U.S.A.* 109 G6
Howard, *Pa., U.S.A.* 106 E7
Howard, *S. Dak., U.S.A.* 108 C6
Howard I., *Australia* 90 A2
Howard L., *Canada* 101 A7
Howe, *U.S.A.* 110 E7
Howe, C., *Australia* 91 F5
Howell, *U.S.A.* 104 D4
Howick, *Canada* 107 A11
Howick, *S. Africa* 85 D5
Howick Group, *Australia* 90 A4
Howitt, L., *Australia* 91 D2
Howland I., *Pac. Oc.* 92 G10
Howley, *Canada* 99 C8
Howrah = Haora, *India* 63 H13
Howth Hd., *Ireland* 15 C5
Höxter, *Germany* 18 D5
Hoy, *U.K.* 14 C5
Hoya, *Germany* 18 C5
Høyanger, *Norway* 9 F12
Hoyerswerda, *Germany* 18 D10
Hoyos, *Spain* 30 E4
Hpungan Pass, *Burma* 61 F20
Hradec Králové, *Czech.* 20 E5
Hranice, *Czech.* 20 F7
Hrazdan, *Armenia* 43 K7
Hrebenka, *Ukraine* 41 G7
Hrodna, *Belarus* 40 F2
Hrodzyanka, *Belarus* 40 F5
Hron →, *Slovak Rep.* 21 H8
Hrubieszów, *Poland* 20 E13
Hrvatska = Croatia ■, *Europe* 33 C13
Hrymayliv, *Ukraine* 41 H4
Hsenwi, *Burma* 61 H20
Hsiamen = Xiamen, *China* 53 E12
Hsian = Xi'an, *China* 50 G5
Hsinhailien = Lianyungang, *China* 51 G10
Hsisha Chuntao, *Pac. Oc.* 56 A4
Hsüchou = Xuzhou, *China* 51 G9
Hu Xian, *China* 50 G5
Hua Hin, *Thailand* 58 F2
Hua Xian, *Henan, China* 50 G8
Hua Xian, *Shaanxi, China* 50 G5
Hua'an, *China* 53 E11
Huacaya, *Bolivia* 125 E5
Huacheng, *China* 53 E10
Huachinera, *Mexico* 114 A3
Huacho, *Peru* 124 C2
Huachón, *Peru* 124 C2
Huade, *China* 50 D7
Huadian, *China* 51 C14
Huai He →, *China* 53 A12
Huai Yot, *Thailand* 59 J2
Huai'an, *Hebei, China* 50 D8
Huai'an, *Jiangsu, China* 51 H10
Huaibei, *China* 50 G9
Huaide, *China* 51 C13
Huaidezhen, *China* 51 C13
Huaihua, *China* 52 D7
Huaiji, *China* 53 F9
Huainan, *China* 53 A11
Huaining, *China* 53 B11
Huairen, *China* 50 E7
Huairou, *China* 50 D9
Huaiyang, *China* 50 H8
Huaiyuan, *Anhui, China* 51 H9
Huaiyuan, *Guangxi Zhuangzu, China* 52 E7
Huajianzi, *China* 51 D13
Huajuapan de Leon, *Mexico* 115 D5
Hualapai Peak, *U.S.A.* 111 J7
Hualian, *Taiwan* 53 F13
Huallaga →, *Peru* 124 B2
Huallanca, *Peru* 124 B2
Huamachuco, *Peru* 124 B2
Huambo, *Angola* 81 G3
Huan Jiang →, *China* 50 G5
Huan Xian, *China* 50 F4
Huancabamba, *Peru* 124 B2
Huancane, *Peru* 124 D4
Huancapi, *Peru* 124 C3
Huancavelica, *Peru* 124 C2
Huancavelica □, *Peru* 124 C3
Huancayo, *Peru* 124 C2
Huanchaca, *Bolivia* 124 E4
Huanchaca, Serranía de, *Bolivia* 125 C5
Huang Hai = Yellow Sea, *China* 51 G12
Huang He →, *China* 51 F10
Huang Xian, *China* 51 F11
Huangchuan, *China* 53 A10
Huanggang, *China* 53 B10
Huangling, *China* 50 G5
Huangliu, *China* 54 E5
Huanglong, *China* 50 G5
Huanglongtan, *China* 53 A8
Huangmei, *China* 53 B10
Huangpi, *China* 53 B10
Huangping, *China* 52 D6
Huangshi, *China* 53 B10
Huangsongdian, *China* 51 C14
Huangyan, *China* 53 C13
Huangyangsi, *China* 53 D8
Huaning, *China* 52 E4
Huanjiang, *China* 52 E7
Huanta, *Peru* 124 C3
Huantai, *China* 51 F9
Huánuco, *Peru* 124 B2
Huánuco □, *Peru* 124 B2
Huanuni, *Bolivia* 124 D4
Huanzo, Cordillera de, *Peru* 124 C3
Huaping, *China* 52 D3
Huaral, *Peru* 124 C2
Huaraz, *Peru* 124 B2
Huari, *Peru* 124 B2
Huarmey, *Peru* 124 C2
Huarochiri, *Peru* 124 C2
Huarocondo, *Peru* 124 C3
Huarong, *China* 53 C9
Huascarán, *Peru* 124 B2
Huascarán, Nevado, *Peru* 124 B2
Huasco, *Chile* 126 B1
Huasco →, *Chile* 126 B1
Huasna, *U.S.A.* 113 K6
Huatabampo, *Mexico* 114 B3
Huauchinango, *Mexico* 115 C5
Huautla de Jiménez, *Mexico* 115 D5
Huaxi, *China* 52 D6
Huay Namota, *Mexico* 114 C4
Huayin, *China* 50 G6
Huayllay, *Peru* 124 C2
Huayuan, *China* 52 C7
Huazhou, *China* 53 G8
Hubbard, *U.S.A.* 109 K6
Hubbart Pt., *Canada* 101 B10
Hubei □, *China* 53 B9
Hubli-Dharwad = Dharwad, *India* 60 M9
Huchang, *N. Korea* 51 D14
Hückelhoven, *Germany* 18 D2
Huddersfield, *U.K.* 12 D6
Hudi, *Sudan* 76 D3
Hudiksvall, *Sweden* 10 C11
Hudson, *Canada* 101 C10
Hudson, *Mass., U.S.A.* 107 D13
Hudson, *Mich., U.S.A.* 104 E3
Hudson, *N.Y., U.S.A.* 107 D11
Hudson, *Wis., U.S.A.* 108 C8
Hudson, *Wyo., U.S.A.* 110 E9
Hudson →, *U.S.A.* 107 F10
Hudson Bay, *N.W.T., Canada* 97 C11
Hudson Bay, *Sask., Canada* 101 C8
Hudson Falls, *U.S.A.* 107 C11
Hudson Mts., *Antarctica* 5 D16
Hudson Str., *Canada* 97 B13
Hudson's Hope, *Canada* 100 B4
Hue, *Vietnam* 58 D6
Huebra →, *Spain* 30 D4
Huechucuicui, Pta., *Chile* 128 B2
Huedin, *Romania* 38 C6
Huehuetenango, *Guatemala* 116 C1
Huejúcar, *Mexico* 114 C4
Huelgoat, *France* 24 D3
Huelma, *Spain* 29 H1
Huelva, *Spain* 31 H4
Huelva □, *Spain* 31 H4
Huelva →, *Spain* 31 H5
Huentelauquén, *Chile* 126 C1
Huércal Overa, *Spain* 29 H3
Huerta, Sa. de la, *Argentina* 126 C2
Huertas, C. de las, *Spain* 29 G4
Huerva →, *Spain* 28 D4
Huesca, *Spain* 28 C4
Huesca □, *Spain* 28 C5
Huéscar, *Spain* 29 H2
Huetamo, *Mexico* 114 D4
Huete, *Spain* 28 E2
Hugh →, *Australia* 90 D1
Hughenden, *Australia* 90 C3
Hughes, *Australia* 89 F4
Hughli →, *India* 63 J13
Hugo, *U.S.A.* 108 F3
Hugoton, *U.S.A.* 109 G4
Hui Xian, *Gansu, China* 50 H4
Hui Xian, *Henan, China* 50 G7
Hui'an, *China* 53 E12
Hui'anbu, *China* 50 F4
Huichang, *China* 53 E10
Huichapán, *Mexico* 115 C5
Huidong, *China* 52 D4
Huifa He →, *China* 51 C14
Huila □, *Colombia* 120 C2
Huila, Nevado del, *Colombia* 120 C2
Huilai, *China* 53 F11
Huili, *China* 52 D4
Huimin, *China* 51 F9
Huinan, *China* 51 C14
Huinca Renancó, *Argentina* 126 C3
Huining, *China* 50 G3
Huinong, *China* 50 E4
Huise, *Belgium* 17 G3
Huishui, *China* 52 D6
Huisne →, *France* 24 E7
Huissen, *Neths.* 16 E7
Huiting, *China* 50 G9
Huitong, *China* 52 D7
Huixtla, *Mexico* 115 D6
Huize, *China* 52 D4
Huizen, *Neths.* 16 D6
Huizhou, *China* 53 F10
Hukawng Valley, *Burma* 61 F20
Hukou, *China* 53 C11
Hukuntsi, *Botswana* 84 C3
Hula, *Ethiopia* 77 F4
Hulan, *China* 54 B7
Ḥulayfā', *Si. Arabia* 64 E4
Huld, *Mongolia* 50 B3
Hulin He →, *China* 51 B12
Hull = Kingston upon Hull, *U.K.* 12 D7
Hull, *Canada* 98 C4
Hull →, *U.K.* 12 D7
Hulst, *Neths.* 17 F4
Hulun Nur, *China* 54 B6
Hulyaypole, *Ukraine* 41 J9
Humahuaca, *Argentina* 126 A2
Humaitá, *Brazil* 125 B5
Humaitá, *Paraguay* 126 B4
Humansdorp, *S. Africa* 84 E3
Humbe, *Angola* 84 B1
Humber →, *U.K.* 12 D7
Humberside □, *U.K.* 12 D7
Humbert River, *Australia* 88 C5
Humble, *U.S.A.* 109 L8
Humboldt, *Canada* 101 C7
Humboldt, *Iowa, U.S.A.* 108 D7
Humboldt, *Tenn., U.S.A.* 109 H10
Humboldt →, *U.S.A.* 110 F4
Humboldt Gletscher, *Greenland* 4 B4
Hume, *U.S.A.* 112 J8
Hume, L., *Australia* 91 F4
Humenné, *Slovak Rep.* 20 G11
Humphreys, Mt., *U.S.A.* 112 H8
Humphreys Peak, *U.S.A.* 111 J8
Humpolec, *Czech.* 20 F5
Humptulips, *U.S.A.* 112 C3

Hūn, *Libya* 73 C8
Hun Jiang →, *China* 51 D13
Húnaflói, *Iceland* 8 D3
Hunan □, *China* 53 D9
Hunchun, *China* 51 C16
Hundested, *Denmark* 11 J5
Hundred Mile House,
  Canada 100 C4
Hunedoara, *Romania* 38 D5
Hünfeld, *Germany* 18 E5
Hung Yen, *Vietnam* 58 B6
Hungary ■, *Europe* 21 H9
Hungary, Plain of, *Europe* 6 F9
Hungerford, *Australia* .. 91 D3
Hŭngnam, *N. Korea* 51 E14
Hunsberge, *Namibia* 84 D2
Hunsrück, *Germany* 19 F3
Hunstanton, *U.K.* 12 E8
Hunte →, *Germany* 18 C4
Hunter, *N. Dak., U.S.A.* 108 B6
Hunter, *N.Y., U.S.A.* .. 107 D10
Hunter I., *Australia* 90 G3
Hunter I., *Canada* 100 C3
Hunter Ra., *Australia* .. 91 E5
Hunters Road, *Zimbabwe* 83 F2
Hunterville, *N.Z.* 87 H5
Huntingburg, *U.S.A.* ... 104 F2
Huntingdon, *Canada* ... 98 C5
Huntingdon, *U.K.* 13 E7
Huntingdon, *U.S.A.* ... 106 F6
Huntington, *Ind., U.S.A.* 104 E3
Huntington, *N.Y., U.S.A.* 107 F11
Huntington, *Oreg., U.S.A.* 110 D5
Huntington, *Utah, U.S.A.* 110 G8
Huntington, *W. Va.,*
  U.S.A. 104 F4
Huntington Beach, *U.S.A.* 113 M8
Huntington Park, *U.S.A.* 111 K4
Huntly, *N.Z.* 87 G5
Huntly, *U.K.* 14 D6
Huntsville, *Canada* 98 C4
Huntsville, *Ala., U.S.A.* 105 H2
Huntsville, *Tex., U.S.A.* 109 K7
Hunyani →, *Zimbabwe* . 83 F3
Hunyuan, *China* 50 E7
Hunza →, *India* 63 B6
Huoqiu, *China* 53 C9
Huoshan, *Anhui, China* . 53 A12
Huoshan, *Shanxi, China* . 53 B11
Huoshao Dao, *Taiwan* .. 53 F13
Hupeh = Hubei □, *China* 53 B9
Hūr, *Iran* 65 D8
Hure Qi, *China* 51 C11
Hurezani, *Romania* 38 E6
Hurghada, *Egypt* 76 B3
Hurley, *N. Mex., U.S.A.* 111 K9
Hurley, *Wis., U.S.A.* ... 108 B9
Huron, *Calif., U.S.A.* .. 112 J6
Huron, *Ohio, U.S.A.* ... 106 E2
Huron, *S. Dak., U.S.A.* 108 C5
Huron, L., *U.S.A.* 106 B2
Hurricane, *U.S.A.* 111 H7
Hurso, *Ethiopia* 77 F5
Hurum, *Norway* 10 C2
Hurunui →, *N.Z.* 87 K4
Hurup, *Denmark* 11 H2
Húsavík, *Iceland* 8 C5
Huşi, *Romania* 38 C11
Huskvarna, *Sweden* 9 H16
Hussar, *Canada* 100 C6
Hustadvika, *Norway* 8 E12
Husum, *Germany* 18 A5
Husum, *Sweden* 10 A13
Hutchinson, *Kans., U.S.A.* 109 F6
Hutchinson, *Minn., U.S.A.* 108 C7
Huttig, *U.S.A.* 109 J8
Hutton, Mt., *Australia* . 91 D4
Huttwil, *Switz.* 22 B5
Huwun, *Ethiopia* 77 G5
Huy, *Belgium* 17 G6
Hvammstangi, *Iceland* .. 8 D3
Hvar, *Croatia* 33 E13
Hvarski Kanal, *Croatia* . 33 E13
Hvítá →, *Iceland* 8 D3
Hwachon-chosuji, *S. Korea* 51 E14
Hwang Ho = Huang
  He →, *China* 51 F10
Hwange, *Zimbabwe* 83 F2
Hwange Nat. Park,
  Zimbabwe 84 B4
Hyannis, *U.S.A.* 108 E4
Hyargas Nuur, *Mongolia* 54 B4
Hybo, *Sweden* 10 C10
Hyde Park, *Guyana* ... 121 B6
Hyden, *Australia* 89 F2
Hyderabad, *India* 60 L11
Hyderabad, *Pakistan* .. 62 G3
Hyères, *France* 27 E10
Hyères, Is. d', *France* .. 27 F10
Hyesan, *N. Korea* 51 D15
Hyland →, *Canada* 100 B3
Hyltebruk, *Sweden* 11 H7
Hymia, *India* 63 C8
Hyndman Peak, *U.S.A.* 110 E6
Hyōgo □, *Japan* 49 G7
Hyrum, *U.S.A.* 110 F8
Hysham, *U.S.A.* 110 C10
Hythe, *U.K.* 13 F9
Hyūga, *Japan* 49 H5
Hyvinge = Hyvinkää,
  Finland 9 F21
Hyvinkää, *Finland* 9 F21

I

I-n-Échaï, *Mali* 74 D4
I-n-Gall, *Niger* 79 B6
Iabès, Erg, *Algeria* 75 C4
Iaco →, *Brazil* 124 B4
Iaçu, *Brazil* 123 D3
Iakora, *Madag.* 85 C8
Iaşi, *Romania* 38 B10
Iauaretê, *Colombia* ... 120 C4
Iba, *Phil.* 55 D3
Ibadan, *Nigeria* 79 D5
Ibagué, *Colombia* 120 C2
Ibaiti, *Brazil* 123 F1
Iballja, *Albania* 38 G3
Ibănești, *Romania* 38 C7
Ibar →, *Serbia, Yug.* .. 21 M10
Ibaraki □, *Japan* 49 F10
Ibarra, *Ecuador* 120 C2
Ibba, *Sudan* →, ... 77 G2
Ibba, Bahr el →, *Sudan* 77 F2
Ibbenbüren, *Germany* .. 18 C3
Ibembo, *Zaïre* 82 B1
Ibera, L., *Argentina* ... 126 B4
Iberian Peninsula, *Europe* 6 G5
Iberico, Sistema, *Spain* . 28 E2
Iberville, *Canada* 98 C5
Iberville, Lac d', *Canada* 98 A5
Ibi, *Nigeria* 79 D6
Ibiá, *Brazil* 123 E2
Ibicaraí, *Brazil* 123 D4
Ibicuí, *Brazil* 123 D4
Ibicuy, *Argentina* 126 C4
Ibioapaba, Sa. da, *Brazil* 122 B3
Ibipetuba, *Brazil* 122 D3
Ibitiara, *Brazil* 123 D3
Ibiza, *Spain* 36 C7
Íblei, Monti, *Italy* 35 E7
Ibo, *Mozam.* 83 E5
Ibonma, *Indonesia* 57 E8
Ibotirama, *Brazil* 123 D3
Ibrāhīm →, *Lebanon* .. 69 A4
Ibshawâi, *Egypt* 76 J7
Ibu, *Indonesia* 57 D7
Iburg, *Germany* 18 C4
Ibusuki, *Japan* 49 J5
Icá, *Peru* 124 C2
Ica □, *Peru* 124 C2
Içá →, *Brazil* 124 A4
Icabarú, *Venezuela* 121 C5
Icabarú →, *Venezuela* . 121 C5
Içana, *Brazil* 120 C4
Içana →, *Brazil* 120 C4
Icatu, *Brazil* 122 B3
İçel = Mersin, *Turkey* . 66 D6
Iceland ■, *Europe* 8 D4
Icha, *Russia* 45 D16
Ich'ang = Yichang, *China* 53 B8
Ichchapuram, *India* ... 61 K14
Ichihara, *Japan* 49 G10
Ichikawa, *Japan* 49 G9
Ichilo →, *Bolivia* 125 D5
Ichinohe, *Japan* 48 D10
Ichinomiya, *Japan* 49 G8
Ichinoseki, *Japan* 48 E10
Ichnya, *Ukraine* 41 G7
Ichŏn, *S. Korea* 51 F14
Icht, *Morocco* 74 C3
Ichtegem, *Belgium* 17 F2
Icó, *Brazil* 122 C4
Icod, *Canary Is.* 36 F3
Icoraci, *Brazil* 122 B2
Icy Str., *U.S.A.* 100 B1
Ida Grove, *U.S.A.* 108 D7
Ida Valley, *Australia* .. 89 E3
Idabel, *U.S.A.* 109 J7
Idaga Hamus, *Ethiopia* 77 E4
Idah, *Nigeria* 79 D6
Idaho □, *U.S.A.* 110 D6
Idaho City, *U.S.A.* 110 E6
Idaho Falls, *U.S.A.* ... 110 E7
Idaho Springs, *U.S.A.* . 110 G11
Idanha-a-Nova, *Portugal* 30 F3
Idar-Oberstein, *Germany* 19 F3
Idd el Ghanam, *Sudan* . 73 F9
Idehan, *Libya* 75 C7
Idehan Marzūq, *Libya* . 73 D7
Idelès, *Algeria* 75 D6
Idfû, *Egypt* 76 C3
Ídhi Óros, *Greece* 37 D6
Ídhra, *Greece* 39 M6
Idi, *Indonesia* 56 C1
Idiofa, *Zaïre* 80 E3
Idku, Bahra el, *Egypt* . 76 H7
Idlib, *Syria* 66 E7
Idria, *U.S.A.* 112 J6
Idrija, *Slovenia* 33 B11
Idritsa, *Russia* 40 D5
Idstein, *Germany* 19 E4
Idutywa, *S. Africa* 85 E4
Ieper, *Belgium* 17 G1
Ierápetra, *Greece* 37 E7
Ierissós, *Greece* 39 J6
Ierzu, *Italy* 34 C2
Iesi, *Italy* 33 E10
Ifach, Punta, *Spain* ... 29 G5
Ifanadiana, *Madag.* ... 85 C8
Ife, *Nigeria* 79 D5
Iférouâne, *Niger* 79 B6
Iffley, *Australia* 90 B3
Ifni, *Morocco* 74 C2
Ifon, *Nigeria* 79 D6
Iforas, Adrar des, *Mali* 79 B5
Ifould, L., *Australia* ... 89 F5

Ifrane, *Morocco* 74 B3
Iganga, *Uganda* 82 B3
Igara Paraná →, *Colombia* 120 D3
Igarapava, *Brazil* 123 F2
Igarapé Açu, *Brazil* ... 122 B2
Igarapé-Mirim, *Brazil* . 122 B2
Igarka, *Russia* 44 C9
Igatimi, *Paraguay* 127 A4
Igbetti, *Nigeria* 79 D5
Igbo-Ora, *Nigeria* 79 D5
Igboho, *Nigeria* 79 D5
Iğdır, *Turkey* 67 C11
Iggesund, *Sweden* 10 C11
Ighil Izane, *Algeria* ... 75 A5
Iglésias, *Italy* 34 C1
Igli, *Algeria* 75 B4
Igloolik, *Canada* 97 B11
Igma, Gebel el, *Egypt* . 76 J8
Ignace, *Canada* 98 C1
İğneada Burnu, *Turkey* 66 B3
Igra, *Russia* 42 B11
Iguaçu →, *Brazil* 127 B5
Iguaçu, Cat. del, *Brazil* 127 B5
Iguaçu Falls = Iguaçu, Cat.
  del, *Brazil* 127 B5
Iguala, *Mexico* 115 D5
Igualada, *Spain* 28 D6
Iguape, *Brazil* 123 F2
Iguassu = Iguaçu →,
  Brazil 127 B5
Iguatu, *Brazil* 122 C4
Iguéla, *Gabon* 80 E1
Igunga, *Tanzania* 82 C3
Iheya-Shima, *Japan* ... 49 L3
Ihiala, *Nigeria* 79 D6
Ihosy, *Madag.* 85 C8
Ihotry, L., *Madag.* 85 C7
Ii, *Finland* 8 D21
Ii-Shima, *Japan* 49 L3
Iida, *Japan* 49 G8
Iijoki →, *Finland* 8 D21
Iisalmi, *Finland* 8 E22
Iiyama, *Japan* 49 F9
Iizuka, *Japan* 49 H5
Ijâfene, *Mauritania* ... 74 D3
Ijebu-Igbo, *Nigeria* ... 79 D5
Ijebu-Ode, *Nigeria* ... 79 D5
IJmuiden, *Neths.* 16 D5
IJssel →, *Neths.* 16 C7
IJsselmeer, *Neths.* 16 C6
IJsselmuiden, *Neths.* .. 16 C7
IJsselstein, *Neths.* 16 D6
Ijuí →, *Brazil* 127 B4
IJzendijke, *Neths.* 17 F3
IJzer →, *Belgium* 17 F1
Ikale, *Nigeria* 79 D6
Ikare, *Nigeria* 79 D6
Ikaría, *Greece* 39 M9
Ikast, *Denmark* 11 H3
Ikeda, *Japan* 49 G6
Ikeja, *Nigeria* 79 D5
Ikela, *Zaïre* 80 E4
Ikerre-Ekiti, *Nigeria* .. 79 D6
Ikhtiman, *Bulgaria* ... 38 G6
Iki, *Japan* 49 H4
Ikimba L., *Tanzania* ... 82 C3
Ikire, *Nigeria* 79 D5
Ikizdere, *Turkey* 67 B9
Ikom, *Nigeria* 79 D6
Ikopa →, *Madag.* 85 B8
Ikot Ekpene, *Nigeria* .. 79 D6
Ikungu, *Tanzania* 82 C3
Ikurun, *Nigeria* 79 D5
Ila, *Nigeria* 79 D5
Ilagan, *Phil.* 55 C4
Ílām, *Iran* 67 F12
Ilam, *Nepal* 63 F12
Ilanskiy, *Russia* 45 D10
Ilanz, *Switz.* 23 C8
Ilaro, *Nigeria* 79 D5
Iława, *Poland* 20 B9
Ilbilbie, *Australia* 90 C4
Ile-à-la-Crosse, *Canada* . 101 B7
Ile-à-la-Crosse, Lac,
  Canada 101 B7
Île-de-France, *France* .. 25 D9
Ilebo, *Zaïre* 80 E4
Ileje □, *Tanzania* 83 D3
Ilek, *Russia* 44 D6
Ilek →, *Russia* 44 D6
Ilero, *Nigeria* 79 D5
Ilesha, *Kwara, Nigeria* 79 D5
Ilesha, *Oyo, Nigeria* .. 79 D5
Ilford, *Canada* 101 B10
Ilfracombe, *Australia* .. 90 C3
Ilfracombe, *U.K.* 13 F3
Ilgaz, *Turkey* 66 B5
Ilgaz Dağları, *Turkey* . 66 B5
Ilgın, *Turkey* 66 C4
Ilha Grande, *Brazil* ... 121 D4
Ilha Grande, B. da, *Brazil* 123 F3
Ílhavo, *Portugal* 30 E2
Ilhéus, *Brazil* 123 D4
Ili →, *Kazakhstan* 44 E8
Iliç, *Turkey* 67 C8
Ilich, *Kazakhstan* 44 E7
Ilichevsk, *Azerbaijan* . 67 C11
Iliff, *U.S.A.* 108 E3
Iligan, *Phil.* 55 G6
Iligan Bay, *Phil.* 55 G6
Iliki, L., *Greece* 39 L6
Ilin I., *Phil.* 55 E4
Iliodhrómia, *Greece* ... 39 K6
Ilion, *U.S.A.* 107 D9
Ilirska-Bistrica, *Slovenia* 33 C11
Ilkeston, *U.K.* 12 E6

Illampu = Ancohuma,
  Nevada, Bolivia 124 D4
Illana B., *Phil.* 55 H5
Illapel, *Chile* 126 C1
Ille-et-Vilaine □, *France* 24 D5
Ille-sur-Têt, *France* ... 26 F6
Iller →, *Germany* 19 G5
Illescas, *Spain* 30 E7
Illetas, *Spain* 36 B9
Illichivsk, *Ukraine* 41 J6
Illiers-Combray, *France* 24 D8
Illimani, *Bolivia* 124 D4
Illinois □, *U.S.A.* 103 C9
Illinois →, *U.S.A.* 103 C8
Illium = Troy, *Turkey* 66 C2
Illizi, *Algeria* 75 C6
Illora, *Spain* 31 H7
Ilm →, *Germany* 18 D7
Ilmajoki, *Finland* 9 E20
Ilmen, Ozero, *Russia* .. 40 C6
Ilmenau, *Germany* 18 E6
Ilo, *Peru* 124 D3
Ilobu, *Nigeria* 79 D5
Iloilo, *Phil.* 55 F5
Ilora, *Nigeria* 79 D5
Ilorin, *Nigeria* 79 D5
Ilovatka, *Russia* 42 E7
Ilovlya, *Russia* 43 F7
Ilovlya →, *Russia* 43 F7
Ilubabor □, *Ethiopia* .. 77 F3
Ilulissat, *Greenland* ... 4 C5
Ilva Mică, *Romania* ... 38 B7
Ilwaco, *U.S.A.* 112 D2
Ilwaki, *Indonesia* 57 F7
Ilyichevsk = Illichivsk,
  Ukraine 41 J6
Imabari, *Japan* 49 G6
Imaloto →, *Madag.* ... 85 C8
Imamoğlu, *Turkey* 66 D6
Imandra, Ozero, *Russia* 44 C4
Imari, *Japan* 49 H4
Imasa, *Sudan* 76 D4
Imatra, *Finland* 40 B5
Imbâbah, *Egypt* 76 H7
Imbabura □, *Ecuador* . 120 C2
Imbaimadai, *Guyana* .. 121 B5
Imbler, *U.S.A.* 110 D5
Imdahane, *Morocco* ... 74 B3
imeni 26 Bakinskikh
  Komissarov = Neftçala,
  Azerbaijan 67 C13
Imeni Poliny Osipenko,
  Russia 45 D14
Imeri, Serra, *Brazil* ... 120 C4
Imerimandroso, *Madag.* 85 B8
Imesan, *Mauritania* ... 74 D1
Imi, *Ethiopia* 68 F3
Imishly = Imişli,
  Azerbaijan 43 L9
Imişli, *Azerbaijan* 43 L9
Imitek, *Morocco* 74 C3
Imlay, *U.S.A.* 110 F4
Imlay City, *U.S.A.* 106 C1
Immenstadt, *Germany* . 19 H6
Immingham, *U.K.* 12 D7
Immokalee, *U.S.A.* ... 105 M5
Imo □, *Nigeria* 79 D6
Imola, *Italy* 33 D8
Imotski, *Croatia* 21 M7
Imperatriz, *Amazonas,*
  Brazil 124 B4
Imperatriz, *Maranhão,*
  Brazil 122 C2
Impéria, *Italy* 32 E5
Imperial, *Canada* 101 C7
Imperial, *Peru* 124 C2
Imperial, *Calif., U.S.A.* 113 N11
Imperial, *Nebr., U.S.A.* 108 E4
Imperial Beach, *U.S.A.* 113 N9
Imperial Dam, *U.S.A.* . 113 N12
Imperial Reservoir, *U.S.A.* 113 N12
Imperial Valley, *U.S.A.* 113 N11
Imperieuse Reef, *Australia* 88 C2
Impfondo, *Congo* 80 D3
Imphal, *India* 61 G18
Imphy, *France* 26 B7
Imranlı, *Turkey* 67 C8
Imroz = Gökçeada, *Turkey* 66 B1
Imst, *Austria* 19 H6
Imuruan B., *Phil.* 57 B5
In Belbel, *Algeria* 75 C5
In Delimane, *Mali* 79 B5
In Rhar, *Algeria* 75 C5
In Salah, *Algeria* 75 C5
In Tallak, *Mali* 79 B5
Ina, *Japan* 49 G8
Inajá, *Brazil* 122 C4
Inangahua Junction, *N.Z.* 87 J3
Inanwatan, *Indonesia* . 57 E8
Iñapari, *Peru* 124 C4
Inari, *Finland* 8 B22
Inarijärvi, *Finland* 8 B22
Inawashiro-Ko, *Japan* . 48 F10
Inca, *Spain* 36 B9
Incaguasi, *Chile* 126 B1
Ince-Burnu, *Turkey* ... 66 A6
İnce Burun, *Turkey* ... 66 D5
Inch'on, *S. Korea* 51 F14
Incio, *Spain* 30 C3
Incirliova, *Turkey* 66 D2
Incomáti →, *Mozam.* .. 85 D5
Inda Silase, *Ethiopia* .. 77 E4
Indalsälven →, *Sweden* 10 B11
Indaw, *Burma* 61 G20
Indbir, *Ethiopia* 77 F4
Independence, *Calif.,*
  U.S.A. 111 H4

Independence, *Iowa,*
  U.S.A. 108 D9
Independence, *Kans.,*
  U.S.A. 109 G7
Independence, *Mo., U.S.A.* 108 F7
Independence, *Oreg.,*
  U.S.A. 110 D2
Independence Fjord,
  Greenland 4 A6
Independence Mts., *U.S.A.* 110 F5
Independência, *Brazil* . 122 C4
Independenţa, *Romania* 38 D10
Index, *U.S.A.* 112 C5
India ■, *Asia* 60 K11
Indian →, *U.S.A.* 105 M5
Indian Cabins, *Canada* 100 B5
Indian Harbour, *Canada* 99 B8
Indian Head, *Canada* .. 101 C8
Indian Ocean 46 J10
Indian Springs, *U.S.A.* 113 J11
Indiana, *U.S.A.* 106 F5
Indiana □, *U.S.A.* 104 E3
Indianapolis, *U.S.A.* .. 104 F2
Indianola, *Iowa, U.S.A.* 108 E8
Indianola, *Miss., U.S.A.* 109 J9
Indiapora, *Brazil* 123 E1
Indiga, *Russia* 44 C5
Indigirka →, *Russia* ... 45 B15
Indija, *Serbia, Yug.* ... 21 K10
Indio, *U.S.A.* 113 M10
Indonesia ■, *Asia* 56 F5
Indore, *India* 62 H6
Indramayu, *Indonesia* . 57 G13
Indravati →, *India* 61 K12
Indre □, *France* 25 F8
Indre →, *France* 24 E7
Indre-et-Loire □, *France* 24 E7
Indus →, *Pakistan* 62 G2
Indus, Mouth of the,
  Pakistan 62 H2
İnebolu, *Turkey* 66 B5
İnegöl, *Turkey* 66 B3
Inés, Mt., *Argentina* .. 128 C3
Ineu, *Romania* 38 C4
Inezgane, *Morocco* 74 B3
Infantes, *Spain* 29 G1
Infiernillo, Presa del,
  Mexico 114 D4
Infiesto, *Spain* 30 B5
Ingapirca, *Ecuador* ... 120 C2
Ingelmunster, *Belgium* 17 G2
Ingende, *Zaïre* 80 E3
Ingeniero Jacobacci,
  Argentina 128 B3
Ingenio, *Canary Is.* ... 36 G4
Ingenio Santa Ana,
  Argentina 126 B2
Ingersoll, *Canada* 106 C4
Ingham, *Australia* 90 B4
Ingleborough, *U.K.* ... 12 C5
Inglewood, *Queens.,*
  Australia 91 D5
Inglewood, *Vic., Australia* 91 F3
Inglewood, *N.Z.* 87 H5
Inglewood, *U.S.A.* ... 113 M8
Ingólfshöfði, *Iceland* .. 8 E5
Ingolstadt, *Germany* .. 19 G7
Ingomar, *U.S.A.* 110 C10
Ingonish, *Canada* 99 C7
Ingore, *Guinea-Biss.* .. 78 C1
Ingraj Bazar, *India* ... 63 G13
Ingrid Christensen Coast,
  Antarctica 5 C6
Ingul = Inhul →, *Ukraine* 41 J7
Ingulec = Inhulets →,
  Ukraine 41 J7
Inguri = Enguri →,
  Georgia 43 J5
Ingushetia □, *Russia* . 43 J7
Ingwavuma, *S. Africa* . 85 D5
Inhaca, I., *Mozam.* ... 85 D5
Inhafenga, *Mozam.* ... 85 C5
Inhambane, *Mozam.* .. 85 C6
Inhambane □, *Mozam.* 85 C5
Inhambupe, *Brazil* 123 D4
Inhaminga, *Mozam.* ... 83 F3
Inharrime, *Mozam.* ... 85 C6
Inharrime →, *Mozam.* 85 C6
Inhul →, *Ukraine* 41 J7
Inhulec, *Ukraine* 41 J7
Inhulets →, *Ukraine* .. 41 J7
Inhuma, *Brazil* 122 C3
Inhumas, *Brazil* 123 E2
Iniesta, *Spain* 29 F3
Ining = Yining, *China* . 44 E9
Inini □, *Fr. Guiana* ... 121 C7
Inírida →, *Colombia* .. 120 C4
Inishbofin, *Ireland* 15 C1
Inishmore, *Ireland* 15 C2
Inishowen Pen., *Ireland* 15 A4
Injune, *Australia* 91 D4
Inklin, *Canada* 100 B2
Inklin →, *Canada* 100 B2
Inkom, *U.S.A.* 110 E7
Inle L., *Burma* 61 J20
Inn →, *Austria* 19 G9
Innamincka, *Australia* . 91 D3
Inner Hebrides, *U.K.* .. 14 D2
Inner Mongolia = Nei
  Monggol Zizhiqu □,
  China 50 C6
Inner Sound, *U.K.* 14 D3
Innerkip, *Canada* 106 C4
Innerkirchen, *Switz.* .. 22 C6
Innerste →, *Germany* . 18 C5
Innetalling I., *Canada* . 98 A4

Innisfail, *Australia* 90 B4
Innisfail, *Canada* 100 C6
In'no-shima, *Japan* 49 G6
Innsbruck, *Austria* 19 H7
Inny →, *Ireland* 15 C4
Inocência, *Brazil* 123 E1
Inongo, *Zaïre* 80 E3
Inoucdjouac = Inukjuak,
  Canada 97 C12
Inowrocław, *Poland* 20 C8
Inpundong, *N. Korea* 51 D14
Inquisivi, *Bolivia* 124 D4
Ins, *Switz.* 22 B4
Inscription, C., *Australia* 89 E1
Insein, *Burma* 61 L20
Însurăţei, *Romania* 38 E10
Intendente Alvear,
  Argentina 126 D3
Interior, *U.S.A.* 108 D4
Interlaken, *Switz.* 25 C7
International Falls, *U.S.A.* 108 A8
Intiyaco, *Argentina* 126 B3
Intragna, *Switz.* 23 D7
Intutu, *Peru* 120 D3
Inukjuak, *Canada* 97 C12
Inútil, B., *Chile* 128 D2
Inuvik, *Canada* 96 B6
Inveraray, *U.K.* 14 E3
Inverbervie, *U.K.* 14 E6
Invercargill, *N.Z.* 87 M2
Inverell, *Australia* 91 D5
Invergordon, *U.K.* 14 D4
Invermere, *Canada* 100 C5
Inverness, *Canada* 99 C7
Inverness, *U.K.* 14 D4
Inverness, *U.S.A.* 105 L4
Inverurie, *U.K.* 14 D6
Inverway, *Australia* 88 C4
Investigator Group,
  Australia 91 E1
Investigator Str., *Australia* 91 F2
Inya, *Russia* 44 D9
Inyanga, *Zimbabwe* 83 F3
Inyangani, *Zimbabwe* 83 F3
Inyantue, *Zimbabwe* 83 F2
Inyo Mts., *U.S.A.* 111 H5
Inyokern, *U.S.A.* 113 K9
Inza, *Russia* 42 D8
Inzhavino, *Russia* 42 D6
Iō-Jima, *Japan* 49 J5
Ioánnina, *Greece* 39 K3
Iola, *U.S.A.* 109 G7
Ion Corvin, *Romania* 38 E10
Iona, *U.K.* 14 E2
Ione, *Calif., U.S.A.* 112 G6
Ione, *Wash., U.S.A.* 110 B5
Ionia, *U.S.A.* 104 D3
Ionian Is. = Iónioi Nísoi,
  Greece 39 L3
Ionian Sea, *Medit. S.* 6 H9
Iónioi Nísoi, *Greece* 39 L3
Íos, *Greece* 39 N8
Iowa □, *U.S.A.* 108 D8
Iowa City, *U.S.A.* 108 E9
Iowa Falls, *U.S.A.* 108 D8
Ipala, *Tanzania* 82 C3
Ipameri, *Brazil* 123 E2
Iparía, *Peru* 124 B3
Ipáti, *Greece* 39 L5
Ipatinga, *Brazil* 123 E3
Ipatovo, *Russia* 43 H6
Ipel →, *Europe* 21 G9
Ipiales, *Colombia* 120 C2
Ipiaú, *Brazil* 123 D4
Ipin = Yibin, *China* 52 C5
Ipirá, *Brazil* 123 D4
Ipiranga, *Brazil* 120 D4
Ipixuna, *Brazil* 124 B3
Ipixuna →, *Amazonas,
  Brazil* 124 B3
Ipixuna →, *Amazonas,
  Brazil* 125 B5
Ipoh, *Malaysia* 59 K3
Iporá, *Brazil* 123 D1
Ippy, *C.A.R.* 73 G9
Ipsala, *Turkey* 66 B2
Ipsárion Óros, *Greece* 39 J7
Ipswich, *Australia* 91 D5
Ipswich, *U.K.* 13 E9
Ipswich, *Mass., U.S.A.* 107 D14
Ipswich, *S. Dak., U.S.A.* 108 C5
Ipu, *Brazil* 122 B3
Ipueiras, *Brazil* 122 B3
Ipupiara, *Brazil* 123 D3
Iqaluit, *Canada* 97 B13
Iquique, *Chile* 124 E3
Iquitos, *Peru* 120 D3
Irabu-Jima, *Japan* 49 M2
Iracoubo, *Fr. Guiana* 121 B7
Irafshān, *Iran* 65 E9
Irahuan, *Phil.* 55 G3
Iráklia, *Greece* 39 N8
Iráklion, *Greece* 37 D7
Iráklion □, *Greece* 37 D7
Irala, *Paraguay* 127 B5
Iramba □, *Tanzania* 82 C3
Iran ■, *Asia* 65 C7
Iran, Gunung-Gunung,
  Malaysia 56 D4
Iran Ra. = Iran, Gunung-
  Gunung, *Malaysia* 56 D4
Īrānshahr, *Iran* 65 E9
Irapa, *Venezuela* 121 A5
Irapuato, *Mexico* 114 C4
Iraq ■, *Asia* 67 F10
Irarrar, O. →, *Mali* 75 D5
Irati, *Brazil* 127 B5

Irbid, *Jordan* 69 C4
Irbid □, *Jordan* 69 C5
Irebu, *Zaïre* 80 E3
Irecê, *Brazil* 122 D3
Iregua →, *Spain* 28 C7
Ireland ■, *Europe* 15 D4
Ireland's Eye, *Ireland* 15 C5
Irele, *Nigeria* 79 D6
Ireng →, *Brazil* 121 C6
Iret, *Russia* 45 C16
Irgiz, Bolshaya →, *Russia* 42 D9
Irhârharene, *Algeria* 75 C6
Irharrhar, O. →, *Algeria* 75 C6
Irherm, *Morocco* 74 B3
Irhil Mgoun, *Morocco* 74 B3
Irhyangdong, *N. Korea* 51 D15
Iri, *S. Korea* 51 G14
Irian Jaya □, *Indonesia* 57 E9
Irié, *Guinea* 78 D3
Iriga, *Phil.* 55 E5
Iringa, *Tanzania* 82 D4
Iringa □, *Tanzania* 82 D4
Iriomote-Jima, *Japan* 49 M1
Iriona, *Honduras* 116 C2
Iriri →, *Brazil* 121 D7
Iriri Novo →, *Brazil* 125 B7
Irish Republic ■, *Europe* 15 D4
Irish Sea, *U.K.* 12 D3
Irkineyeva, *Russia* 45 D10
Irkutsk, *Russia* 45 D11
Irma, *Canada* 101 C6
Irō-Zaki, *Japan* 49 G9
Iroise, Mer d', *France* 24 D2
Iron Baron, *Australia* 91 E2
Iron Gate = Portile de
  Fier, *Europe* 38 E5
Iron Knob, *Australia* 91 E2
Iron Mountain, *U.S.A.* 104 C1
Iron Ra., *Australia* 90 A3
Iron River, *U.S.A.* 108 B10
Ironbridge, *U.K.* 13 E5
Irondequoit, *U.S.A.* 106 C7
Ironstone Kopje, *Botswana* 84 D3
Ironton, *Mo., U.S.A.* 109 G9
Ironton, *Ohio, U.S.A.* 104 F4
Ironwood, *U.S.A.* 108 B9
Iroquois Falls, *Canada* 98 C3
Irosin, *Phil.* 55 E6
Irpin, *Ukraine* 41 G6
Irrara Cr. →, *Australia* 91 D4
Irrawaddy □, *Burma* 61 L19
Irrawaddy →, *Burma* 61 M19
Irsina, *Italy* 35 B9
Irtysh →, *Russia* 44 C7
Irumu, *Zaïre* 82 B2
Irún, *Spain* 28 B3
Irunea = Pamplona, *Spain* 28 C3
Irurzun, *Spain* 28 C3
Irvine, *Canada* 101 D6
Irvine, *U.K.* 14 F4
Irvine, *Calif., U.S.A.* 113 M9
Irvine, *Ky., U.S.A.* 104 G4
Irvinestown, *U.K.* 15 B4
Irving, *U.S.A.* 109 J6
Irvona, *U.S.A.* 106 F6
Irwin →, *Australia* 89 E1
Irymple, *Australia* 91 E3
Is-sur-Tille, *France* 25 E12
Isa, *Nigeria* 79 C6
Isaac →, *Australia* 90 C4
Isabel, *U.S.A.* 108 C4
Isabela, I., *Mexico* 114 C3
Isabela, *Phil.* 55 H5
Isabella, Cord., *Nic.* 116 D2
Isabella Ra., *Australia* 88 D3
Ísafjarðardjúp, *Iceland* 8 C2
Ísafjörður, *Iceland* 8 C2
Isagarh, *India* 62 G7
Isahaya, *Japan* 49 H5
Isaka, *Tanzania* 82 C3
Isakly, *Russia* 42 C10
Isana = Içana →, *Brazil* 120 C4
Isangi, *Zaïre* 80 D4
Isar →, *Germany* 19 G8
Isarco →, *Italy* 33 B8
Ísari, *Greece* 39 M5
Isbergues, *France* 25 B9
Íschia, *Italy* 34 B6
Iscuandé, *Colombia* 120 C2
Isdell →, *Australia* 88 C3
Ise, *Japan* 49 G8
Ise-Wan, *Japan* 49 G8
Isefjord, *Denmark* 11 J5
Iseltwald, *Switz.* 23 C7
Isenthal, *Switz.* 23 C7
Iseo, *Italy* 32 C7
Iseo, L. d', *Italy* 32 C7
Iseramagazi, *Tanzania* 82 C3
Isère □, *France* 27 C9
Isère →, *France* 27 D8
Iserlohn, *Germany* 18 D3
Isérnia, *Italy* 35 A7
Iseyin, *Nigeria* 79 D5
Isherton, *Guyana* 121 C6
Ishigaki-Shima, *Japan* 49 M2
Ishikari-Gawa →, *Japan* 48 C10
Ishikari-Sammyaku, *Japan* 48 C11
Ishikari-Wan, *Japan* 48 C10
Ishikawa □, *Japan* 49 F8
Ishim, *Russia* 44 D7
Ishim →, *Russia* 44 D8
Ishinomaki, *Japan* 48 E10
Ishioka, *Japan* 49 F10
Ishkuman, *Pakistan* 63 A5
Ishpeming, *U.S.A.* 104 B2

Isigny-sur-Mer, *France* 24 C5
Isil Kul, *Russia* 44 D8
Isiolo, *Kenya* 82 B4
Isiolo □, *Kenya* 82 B4
Isiro, *Zaïre* 82 B2
Isisford, *Australia* 90 C3
Iskenderun, *Turkey* 66 D7
Iskenderun Körfezi, *Turkey* 66 D6
Iskilip, *Turkey* 66 B6
Iskŭr →, *Bulgaria* 38 F7
Iskut →, *Canada* 100 B2
Isla →, *U.K.* 14 E5
Isla Cristina, *Spain* 31 H3
Isla Vista, *U.S.A.* 113 L7
Islâhiye, *Turkey* 66 D7
Islamabad, *Pakistan* 62 C5
Islamkot, *Pakistan* 62 G6
Island →, *Canada* 100 A4
Island Falls, *Canada* 98 C3
Island Falls, *U.S.A.* 99 C6
Island L., *Canada* 101 C10
Island Lagoon, *Australia* 91 E2
Island Pond, *U.S.A.* 107 B13
Islands, B. of, *Canada* 99 C8
Islay, *U.K.* 14 F2
Isle →, *France* 26 D3
Isle aux Morts, *Canada* 99 C8
Isle of Wight □, *U.K.* 13 G6
Isle Royale, *U.S.A.* 108 A10
Isleta, *U.S.A.* 111 J10
Isleton, *U.S.A.* 112 G5
Ismail = Izmayil, *Ukraine* 41 K5
Ismā'ilîya, *Egypt* 76 H8
Ismaning, *Germany* 19 G7
Ismay, *U.S.A.* 108 B2
Isna, *Egypt* 76 B3
Isogstalo, *India* 63 B8
Isola del Gran Sasso
  d'Italia, *Italy* 33 F10
Ísola del Liri, *Italy* 34 A6
Ísola della Scala, *Italy* 32 C8
Ísola di Capo Rizzuto, *Italy* 35 D10
Isparta, *Turkey* 66 D4
Isperikh, *Bulgaria* 38 F9
Íspica, *Italy* 35 F7
Israel ■, *Asia* 69 D3
Issano, *Guyana* 121 B6
Issia, *Ivory C.* 78 D3
Issoire, *France* 26 C7
Issoudun, *France* 25 F8
Issyk-Kul, Ozero = Ysyk-
  Köl, Ozero, *Kyrgyzstan* 44 E8
Ist, *Croatia* 33 D11
Istaihah, *U.A.E.* 65 F7
Istanbul, *Turkey* 66 B3
Istiaía, *Greece* 39 L5
Istok, *Serbia, Yug.* 21 N10
Istokpoga, L., *U.S.A.* 105 M5
Istra, *Croatia* 33 C11
Istranca Dağları, *Turkey* 66 B2
Istres, *France* 27 E8
Istria = Istra, *Croatia* 33 C11
Itá, *Paraguay* 126 B4
Itabaiana, *Paraíba, Brazil* 122 C4
Itabaiana, *Sergipe, Brazil* 122 D4
Itabaianinha, *Brazil* 122 D4
Itaberaba, *Brazil* 123 D3
Itaberaí, *Brazil* 123 E2
Itabira, *Brazil* 123 E3
Itabirito, *Brazil* 123 F3
Itaboca, *Brazil* 121 D5
Itabuna, *Brazil* 123 D4
Itacajá, *Brazil* 122 D2
Itacaunas →, *Brazil* 122 C2
Itacoatiara, *Brazil* 121 D6
Itacuaí →, *Brazil* 124 A3
Itaguaçu, *Brazil* 123 E3
Itaguari →, *Brazil* 123 D3
Itaguatins, *Brazil* 122 C2
Itaim →, *Brazil* 122 C3
Itainópolis, *Brazil* 122 C3
Itaipu, Reprêsa de, *Brazil* 127 B5
Itaituba, *Brazil* 121 D6
Itajaí, *Brazil* 127 B6
Itajubá, *Brazil* 123 F2
Itajuípe, *Brazil* 123 D4
Itaka, *Tanzania* 83 D3
Italy ■, *Europe* 7 G8
Itamataré, *Brazil* 122 B2
Itambacuri, *Brazil* 123 E3
Itambé, *Brazil* 123 E3
Itampolo, *Madag.* 85 C7
Itanhauã →, *Brazil* 121 D5
Itanhém, *Brazil* 123 E3
Itapaci, *Brazil* 123 D2
Itapagé, *Brazil* 122 B4
Itaparica, I. de, *Brazil* 123 D4
Itapebi, *Brazil* 123 E4
Itapecuru-Mirim, *Brazil* 122 B3
Itaperuna, *Brazil* 123 F3
Itapetinga, *Brazil* 123 E3
Itapetininga, *Brazil* 127 A6
Itapeva, *Brazil* 127 A6
Itapicuru →, *Bahia, Brazil* 122 D4
Itapicuru →, *Maranhão,
  Brazil* 122 B3
Itapinima, *Brazil* 125 B5
Itapipoca, *Brazil* 122 B4
Itapiranga, *Brazil* 121 D6
Itapiúna, *Brazil* 122 B4
Itaporanga, *Brazil* 122 C4
Itapuá □, *Paraguay* 127 B4
Itapuranga, *Brazil* 123 E2
Itaquari, *Brazil* 123 D6
Itaquatiara, *Brazil* 121 D6
Itaquí, *Brazil* 126 B4

Itararé, *Brazil* 127 A6
Itarsi, *India* 62 H7
Itarumã, *Brazil* 123 E1
Itatí, *Argentina* 126 B4
Itatira, *Brazil* 122 B4
Itatuba, *Brazil* 125 B5
Itatupa, *Brazil* 121 D7
Itaueira, *Brazil* 122 C3
Itaueira →, *Brazil* 122 C3
Itaúna, *Brazil* 123 F3
Itbayat, *Phil.* 55 A4
Itchen →, *U.K.* 13 G6
Ite, *Peru* 124 D3
Itezhi Tezhi, L., *Zambia* 83 F2
Ithaca = Itháki, *Greece* 39 L3
Ithaca, *U.S.A.* 107 D8
Itháki, *Greece* 39 L3
Itinga, *Brazil* 123 E3
Itiquira, *Brazil* 125 D7
Itiquira →, *Brazil* 125 D6
Itiruçu, *Brazil* 123 D3
Itiúba, *Brazil* 122 D4
Ito, *Japan* 49 G9
Itoigawa, *Japan* 49 F8
Iton →, *France* 24 C8
Itonamas →, *Bolivia* 125 C5
Itsa, *Egypt* 76 J7
Íttiri, *Italy* 34 B1
Ittoqqortoormiit =
  Scoresbysund, *Greenland* 4 B6
Itu, *Brazil* 127 A6
Itu, *Nigeria* 79 D6
Ituaçu, *Brazil* 123 D3
Ituango, *Colombia* 120 B2
Ituiutaba, *Brazil* 123 E2
Itumbiara, *Brazil* 123 E2
Ituna, *Canada* 101 C8
Itunge Port, *Tanzania* 83 D3
Ituni, *Guyana* 121 B6
Itupiranga, *Brazil* 122 C2
Iturama, *Brazil* 123 E1
Iturbe, *Argentina* 126 A2
Ituri →, *Zaïre* 82 B2
Iturup, Ostrov, *Russia* 45 E15
Ituverava, *Brazil* 123 F2
Ituxi →, *Brazil* 125 B5
Ituyuro →, *Argentina* 126 A3
Itzehoe, *Germany* 18 B5
Ivaí →, *Brazil* 127 A5
Ivalo, *Finland* 8 B22
Ivalojoki →, *Finland* 8 B22
Ivanava, *Belarus* 41 F3
Ivanhoe, *N.S.W., Australia* 91 E3
Ivanhoe, *W. Austral.,
  Australia* 88 C4
Ivanhoe, *U.S.A.* 112 J7
Ivanhoe L., *Canada* 101 A7
Ivanić Grad, *Croatia* 33 C13
Ivanjica, *Serbia, Yug.* 21 M10
Ivanjšcice, *Croatia* 33 B13
Ivankoyskoye Vdkhr.,
  Russia 42 B3
Ivano-Frankivsk, *Ukraine* 41 H3
Ivano-Frankovsk = Ivano-
  Frankivsk, *Ukraine* 41 H3
Ivanovo = Ivanava, *Belarus* 41 F3
Ivanovo, *Russia* 42 B5
Ivato, *Madag.* 85 C8
Ivatsevichy, *Belarus* 41 F3
Ivaylovgrad, *Bulgaria* 39 H9
Ivinheima →, *Brazil* 127 A5
Iviza = Ibiza, *Spain* 36 C7
Ivohibe, *Madag.* 85 C8
Ivolândia, *Brazil* 123 E1
Ivory Coast ■, *Africa* 78 D3
Ivrea, *Italy* 32 C4
Ivujivik, *Canada* 97 B12
Iwahig, *Phil.* 56 C5
Iwaizumi, *Japan* 48 E10
Iwaki, *Japan* 49 F10
Iwakuni, *Japan* 49 G6
Iwamizawa, *Japan* 48 C10
Iwanai, *Japan* 48 C10
Iwata, *Japan* 49 G8
Iwate □, *Japan* 48 E10
Iwate-San, *Japan* 48 E10
Iwo, *Nigeria* 79 D5
Ixiamas, *Bolivia* 124 C4
Ixopo, *S. Africa* 85 E5
Ixtepec, *Mexico* 115 D5
Ixtlán del Río, *Mexico* 114 C4
Iyo, *Japan* 49 H6
Izabal, L. de, *Guatemala* 116 C2
Izamal, *Mexico* 115 C7
Izberbash, *Russia* 43 J8
Izegem, *Belgium* 17 G2
Izena-Shima, *Japan* 49 L3
Izhevsk, *Russia* 44 D6
Izmayil, *Ukraine* 41 K5
Izmir, *Turkey* 66 C2
Izmit, *Turkey* 66 B3
Iznajar, *Spain* 31 H6
Iznalloz, *Spain* 29 H1
Iznik, *Turkey* 66 B3
Iznik Gölü, *Turkey* 66 B3
Izobil'nyy, *Russia* 43 H5
Izola, *Slovenia* 33 C10
Izozog, Bañados de, *Bolivia* 125 D5
Izra, *Syria* 69 C5
Iztochni Rodopi, *Bulgaria* 39 H8
Izu-Shotō, *Japan* 49 G10
Izu-sano, *Japan* 49 G7
Izumo, *Japan* 49 G6
Izyaslav, *Ukraine* 41 G4
Izyum, *Ukraine* 41 H9

J

J.F. Rodrigues, *Brazil* 122 B1
Jaba, *Ethiopia* 77 F4
Jabal el Awlîya, *Sudan* 77 D3
Jabal Lubnān, *Lebanon* 69 B4
Jabalón →, *Spain* 31 G6
Jabalpur, *India* 63 H8
Jabbūl, *Syria* 64 B3
Jablah, *Syria* 66 E6
Jablanac, *Croatia* 33 D11
Jablonec, *Czech.* 20 E5
Jabłonowo, *Poland* 20 B9
Jaboatão, *Brazil* 122 C4
Jaboticabal, *Brazil* 127 A6
Jaburu, *Brazil* 125 B5
Jaca, *Spain* 28 C4
Jacaré →, *Brazil* 122 D3
Jacareí, *Brazil* 127 A6
Jacarèzinho, *Brazil* 127 A6
Jaciara, *Brazil* 125 D7
Jacinto, *Brazil* 123 E3
Jaciparaná, *Brazil* 125 B5
Jackman, *U.S.A.* 99 C5
Jacksboro, *U.S.A.* 109 J5
Jackson, *Australia* 91 D4
Jackson, *Ala., U.S.A.* 105 K2
Jackson, *Calif., U.S.A.* 112 G6
Jackson, *Ky., U.S.A.* 104 G4
Jackson, *Mich., U.S.A.* 104 D3
Jackson, *Minn., U.S.A.* 108 D7
Jackson, *Miss., U.S.A.* 109 J9
Jackson, *Mo., U.S.A.* 109 G10
Jackson, *Ohio, U.S.A.* 104 F4
Jackson, *Tenn., U.S.A.* 105 H1
Jackson, *Wyo., U.S.A.* 110 E8
Jackson B., *N.Z.* 87 K2
Jackson L., *U.S.A.* 110 E8
Jacksons, *N.Z.* 87 K3
Jacksonville, *Ala., U.S.A.* 105 J3
Jacksonville, *Calif., U.S.A.* 112 H6
Jacksonville, *Fla., U.S.A.* 105 K5
Jacksonville, *Ill., U.S.A.* 108 F9
Jacksonville, *N.C., U.S.A.* 105 H7
Jacksonville, *Oreg., U.S.A.* 110 E2
Jacksonville, *Tex., U.S.A.* 109 K7
Jacksonville Beach, *U.S.A.* 105 K5
Jacmel, *Haiti* 117 C5
Jacob Lake, *U.S.A.* 111 H7
Jacobabad, *Pakistan* 62 E3
Jacobina, *Brazil* 122 D3
Jacques-Cartier, Mt.,
  Canada 99 C6
Jacqueville, *Ivory C.* 78 D4
Jacuí →, *Brazil* 127 C5
Jacumba, *U.S.A.* 113 N10
Jacundá →, *Brazil* 122 B1
Jade, *Germany* 18 B4
Jadebusen, *Germany* 18 B4
Jadoigne, *Belgium* 17 G5
Jadotville = Likasi, *Zaïre* 83 E2
Jadraque, *Spain* 28 E2
Jādū, *Libya* 75 B7
Jaén, *Peru* 124 B2
Jaén, *Spain* 31 H7
Jaén □, *Spain* 31 H7
Jafène, *Africa* 74 D3
Jaffa = Tel Aviv-Yafo,
  Israel 69 C3
Jaffa, C., *Australia* 91 F2
Jaffna, *Sri Lanka* 60 Q12
Jagadhri, *India* 62 D7
Jagadishpur, *India* 63 G11
Jagdalpur, *India* 61 K12
Jagersfontein, *S. Africa* 84 D4
Jagraon, *India* 60 D9
Jagst →, *Germany* 19 F5
Jagtial, *India* 60 K11
Jaguariaíva, *Brazil* 127 A6
Jaguaribe, *Brazil* 122 C4
Jaguaribe →, *Brazil* 122 B4
Jaguaruana, *Brazil* 122 B4
Jagüey Grande, *Cuba* 116 B3
Jahangirabad, *India* 62 E8
Jahrom, *Iran* 65 D7
Jaicós, *Brazil* 122 C3
Jailolo, *Indonesia* 57 D7
Jailolo, Selat, *Indonesia* 57 D7
Jaipur, *India* 62 F6
Jājarm, *Iran* 65 B8
Jajce, *Bos.-H.* 21 L7
Jakarta, *Indonesia* 57 G12
Jakobstad = Pietarsaari,
  Finland 8 E20
Jakupica, *Macedonia* 39 H4
Jal, *U.S.A.* 109 J3
Jalalabad, *Afghan.* 62 B4
Jalalabad, *India* 63 F8
Jalalpur Jattan, *Pakistan* 62 C6
Jalama, *U.S.A.* 113 L6
Jalapa, *Guatemala* 116 D2
Jalapa Enríquez, *Mexico* 115 D5
Jalasjärvi, *Finland* 9 E20
Jalaun, *India* 63 F8
Jales, *Brazil* 123 F1
Jaleswar, *Nepal* 63 F11
Jalgaon, *Maharashtra, India* 60 J10
Jalgaon, *Maharashtra, India* 60 J9
Jalhay, *Belgium* 17 G7
Jalībah, *Iraq* 64 D5
Jalingo, *Nigeria* 79 D7
Jalisco □, *Mexico* 114 C4
Jalkot, *Pakistan* 63 B5
Jallas →, *Spain* 30 C1
Jalna, *India* 60 K9

Jalón →, Spain 28 D3
Jalpa, Mexico 114 C4
Jalpaiguri, India 61 F16
Jaluit I., Pac. Oc. 92 G8
Jalūlā, Iraq 67 E11
Jamaari, Nigeria 79 C6
Jamaica ■, W. Indies ... 116 C4
Jamalpur, Bangla. 61 G16
Jamalpur, India 63 G12
Jamalpurganj, India 63 H13
Jamanxim →, Brazil 125 A6
Jamari, Brazil 125 B5
Jamari →, Brazil 125 B5
Jambe, Indonesia 57 E8
Jambes, Belgium 17 H5
Jambi, Indonesia 56 E2
Jambi □, Indonesia 56 E2
Jambusar, India 62 H5
James →, U.S.A. 108 D6
James B., Canada 97 C11
James Ras., Australia ... 88 D5
James Ross I., Antarctica . 5 C18
Jamestown, Australia ... 91 E2
Jamestown, S. Africa ... 84 E4
Jamestown, Ky., U.S.A. . 104 G3
Jamestown, N. Dak.,
  U.S.A. 108 B5
Jamestown, N.Y., U.S.A. . 106 D5
Jamestown, Pa., U.S.A. .. 106 E4
Jamestown, Tenn., U.S.A. . 105 G3
Jamīlābād, Iran 65 C6
Jamiltepec, Mexico 115 D5
Jamkhandi, India 60 L9
Jammerbugt, Denmark .. 11 G3
Jammu, India 62 C6
Jammu & Kashmir □, India 63 B7
Jamnagar, India 62 H4
Jamoigne, Belgium 17 J6
Jampur, Pakistan 62 E4
Jamrud, Pakistan 62 C4
Jämsä, Finland 9 F21
Jamshedpur, India 63 H12
Jamtara, India 63 H12
Jämtland, Sweden 8 E15
Jämtlands län □, Sweden . 10 B7
Jan L., Canada 101 C8
Jan Mayen, Arctic 4 B7
Janakkala, Finland 9 F21
Janaúba, Brazil 123 E3
Janaucu, I., Brazil 122 A1
Jand, Pakistan 62 C5
Janda, L. de la, Spain .. 31 J5
Jandaia, Brazil 123 E1
Jandaq, Iran 65 C7
Jandia, Canary Is. 36 F5
Jandia, Pta. de, Canary Is. 36 F5
Jandiatuba →, Brazil .. 120 D4
Jandola, Pakistan 62 C4
Jandowae, Australia ... 91 D5
Jandrain-Jandrenouilles,
  Belgium 17 G5
Jándula →, Spain 31 G6
Janesville, U.S.A. 108 D10
Janga, Ghana 79 C4
Jango, Brazil 125 E6
Janin, West Bank 69 C4
Janjina, Croatia 21 N7
Janos, Mexico 114 A3
Jánosháza, Hungary ... 21 H7
Janów Podlaski, Poland .. 20 C13
Januária, Brazil 123 E3
Janub Dârfûr □, Sudan . 77 E2
Janub Kordofân □, Sudan . 77 E3
Janubio, Canary Is. 36 F6
Janville, France 25 D8
Janzé, France 24 E5
Jaora, India 62 H6
Japan ■, Asia 49 G8
Japan, Sea of, Asia 48 E7
Japan Trench, Pac. Oc. .. 92 D6
Japen = Yapen, Indonesia 57 E9
Japurá →, Brazil 120 D4
Jaque, Panama 120 B2
Jarābulus, Syria 67 D8
Jaraguá, Brazil 123 E2
Jaraguari, Brazil 125 E7
Jaraicejo, Spain 31 F5
Jaraiz, Spain 30 E5
Jarama →, Spain 28 E1
Jaramānah, Syria 66 F7
Jaramillo, Argentina ... 128 C3
Jarandilla, Spain 30 E5
Jaranwala, Pakistan ... 62 D5
Jarash, Jordan 69 C4
Jarauçu →, Brazil 121 D7
Jardim, Brazil 126 A4
Jardín →, Spain 29 G2
Jardines de la Reina, Is.,
  Cuba 116 B4
Jargalang, China 51 C12
Jargalant = Hovd,
  Mongolia 54 B4
Jargeau, France 25 E9
Jari →, Brazil 121 D7
Jarīr, W. al →, Si. Arabia 64 E4
Jarmen, Germany 18 B9
Jarnac, France 26 C3
Jarny, France 25 C12
Jarocin, Poland 20 D7
Jarosław, Poland 20 E12
Järpås, Sweden 11 F6
Järpen, Sweden 10 A7
Jarrahdale, Australia .. 89 F2
Jarres, Plaine des, Laos . 58 C4
Jarso, Ethiopia 77 F4
Jartai, China 50 E3
Jaru, Brazil 125 C5

Jaru →, Brazil 125 C5
Jarud Qi, China 51 B11
Järvenpää, Finland ... 9 F21
Jarvis, Canada 106 D4
Jarvis I., Pac. Oc. 93 H12
Jarwa, India 63 F10
Jaša Tomić, Serbia, Yug. . 21 K10
Jāsimīyah, Iraq 67 F11
Jasin, Malaysia 59 L4
Jāsk, Iran 65 E8
Jasło, Poland 20 F11
Jason, Is., Falk. Is. ... 128 D4
Jasper, Alta., Canada .. 100 C5
Jasper, Ont., Canada .. 107 B9
Jasper, Ala., U.S.A. ... 93 J2
Jasper, Fla., U.S.A. ... 105 K4
Jasper, Minn., U.S.A. .. 108 D6
Jasper, Tex., U.S.A. ... 109 K8
Jasper Nat. Park, Canada . 100 C5
Jassy = Iaşi, Romania . 38 B10
Jastrebarsko, Croatia .. 33 C12
Jastrzębie Zdrój, Poland . 20 F8
Jászárokszállás, Hungary . 21 H10
Jászberény, Hungary ... 21 H9
Jászladány, Hungary .. 21 H10
Jataí, Brazil 123 E1
Jatapu →, Brazil 121 D6
Jati, Pakistan 62 G3
Jatibarang, Indonesia .. 57 G13
Jatinegara, Indonesia .. 57 G12
Jatobal, Brazil 122 B2
Jaú, Brazil 127 A6
Jaú →, Brazil 121 D5
Jauaperí →, Brazil ... 121 D5
Jauche, Belgium 17 G5
Jauja, Peru 124 C2
Jaunpur, India 63 G10
Jauru →, Brazil 125 D6
Java = Jawa, Indonesia . 57 G14
Java Sea, Indonesia ... 56 E3
Java Trench, Ind. Oc. .. 92 H2
Jávea, Spain 29 G5
Javhlant = Ulyasutay,
  Mongolia 54 B4
Javier, I., Chile 128 C2
Javron, France 24 D6
Jawa, Indonesia 57 G14
Jawor, Poland 20 D6
Jaworzno, Poland 20 E9
Jay, U.S.A. 109 G7
Jaya, Puncak, Indonesia . 57 E9
Jayanca, Peru 124 B2
Jayanti, India 61 F16
Jayapura, Indonesia .. 57 E10
Jayawijaya, Pegunungan,
  Indonesia 57 E9
Jaynagar, India 61 F15
Jayrūd, Syria 66 F7
Jayton, U.S.A. 109 J4
Jazīreh-ye Shīf, Iran .. 65 D6
Jazminal, Mexico 114 C4
Jazzīn, Lebanon 69 B4
Jean, U.S.A. 113 K11
Jean Marie River, Canada 100 A4
Jean Rabel, Haiti 117 C5
Jeanerette, U.S.A. ... 109 L9
Jeanette, Ostrov, Russia . 45 B16
Jeannette, U.S.A. 106 F5
Jebba, Morocco 74 A4
Jebba, Nigeria 79 D5
Jebel, Bahr el →, Sudan . 77 F3
Jebel Qerri, Sudan ... 77 D3
Jeberos, Peru 124 B2
Jedburgh, U.K. 14 F6
Jedda = Jiddah, Si. Arabia 68 C2
Jędrzejów, Poland ... 20 E10
Jedway, Canada 100 C2
Jeetzel →, Germany .. 18 B7
Jefferson, Iowa, U.S.A. . 108 D7
Jefferson, Ohio, U.S.A. . 106 E4
Jefferson, Tex., U.S.A. . 109 J7
Jefferson, Wis., U.S.A. . 108 D10
Jefferson, Mt., Nev.,
  U.S.A. 110 G5
Jefferson, Mt., Oreg.,
  U.S.A. 110 D3
Jefferson City, Mo., U.S.A. 108 F8
Jefferson City, Tenn.,
  U.S.A. 105 G4
Jeffersonville, U.S.A. . 104 F3
Jega, Nigeria 79 C5
Jēkabpils, Latvia 9 H21
Jelenia Góra, Poland .. 20 E5
Jelgava, Latvia 9 H20
Jelli, Sudan 77 F3
Jellicoe, Canada 98 C2
Jemaja, Indonesia ... 56 D3
Jemaluang, Malaysia .. 59 L4
Jemappes, Belgium ... 17 H3
Jember, Indonesia ... 57 H15
Jembongan, Malaysia .. 56 C5
Jemeppe, Belgium ... 17 G7
Jemnice, Czech. 20 F5
Jena, Germany 18 E7
Jena, U.S.A. 109 K8
Jendouba, Tunisia ... 75 A6
Jenkins, U.S.A. 104 G4
Jenner, U.S.A. 112 G3
Jennings, U.S.A. 109 K8
Jennings →, Canada .. 100 B2
Jeparit, Australia 91 F3
Jequié, Brazil 123 D3
Jequitaí →, Brazil ... 123 E3
Jequitinhonha, Brazil .. 123 E3
Jequitinhonha →, Brazil . 123 E4
Jerada, Morocco 75 B4

Jerantut, Malaysia ... 59 L4
Jérémie, Haiti 117 C5
Jeremoabo, Brazil ... 122 D4
Jerez, Punta, Mexico .. 115 C5
Jerez de García Salinas,
  Mexico 114 C4
Jerez de la Frontera, Spain 31 J4
Jerez de los Caballeros,
  Spain 31 G4
Jericho = Arīḥā, Syria . 64 C3
Jericho = El Arīḥā,
  West Bank 69 D4
Jericho, Australia 90 C4
Jerichow, Germany ... 18 C8
Jerilderie, Australia .. 91 F4
Jermyn, U.S.A. 107 E9
Jerome, U.S.A. 111 J8
Jersey, U.K. 13 H5
Jersey City, U.S.A. ... 107 F10
Jersey Shore, U.S.A. .. 106 E7
Jerseyville, U.S.A. ... 108 F9
Jerusalem, Israel 69 D4
Jervis B., Australia ... 91 F5
Jesenice, Slovenia ... 33 B11
Jesenké, Slovak Rep. .. 21 G10
Jesselton = Kota Kinabalu,
  Malaysia 56 C5
Jessnitz, Germany ... 18 D8
Jessore, Bangla. 61 H16
Jesup, U.S.A. 105 K5
Jesús, Peru 124 B2
Jesús Carranza, Mexico . 115 D5
Jesús María, Argentina . 126 C3
Jetmore, U.S.A. 109 F5
Jetpur, India 62 J4
Jette, Belgium 17 G4
Jevnaker, Norway ... 10 D4
Jewett, Ohio, U.S.A. .. 106 F3
Jewett, Tex., U.S.A. .. 109 K6
Jewett City, U.S.A. ... 107 E13
Jeyḥūnābād, Iran 65 C6
Jeypore, India 61 K13
Jeziorany, Poland ... 20 B10
Jhajjar, India 62 E7
Jhal Jhao, Pakistan .. 60 F4
Jhalawar, India 62 G7
Jhang Maghiana, Pakistan 62 D5
Jhansi, India 63 G8
Jharia, India 63 H12
Jharsaguda, India ... 61 J14
Jhelum, Pakistan ... 62 C5
Jhelum →, Pakistan .. 62 D5
Jhunjhunu, India ... 62 E6
Ji Xian, Hebei, China . 50 F8
Ji Xian, Henan, China . 50 G8
Ji Xian, Shanxi, China . 50 F6
Jia Xian, Henan, China . 50 H7
Jia Xian, Shaanxi, China . 50 E6
Jiading, China 53 B13
Jiahe, China 53 E9
Jiali, Taiwan 53 F13
Jialing Jiang →, China . 52 C6
Jiamusi, China 54 B8
Ji'an, Jiangxi, China .. 53 D10
Ji'an, Jilin, China 51 D14
Jianchang, China 51 D11
Jianchangying, China . 51 D10
Jianchuan, China 52 D2
Jiande, China 53 C12
Jiangbei, China 52 C6
Jiangcheng, China ... 52 F3
Jiangdi, China 52 D4
Jiange, China 52 A5
Jiangjin, China 52 C6
Jiangkou, China 52 D7
Jiangle, China 53 D11
Jiangling, China 53 B9
Jiangmen, China 53 F9
Jiangshan, China 53 C12
Jiangsu □, China 51 H10
Jiangxi □, China 53 D10
Jiangyin, China 53 B13
Jiangyong, China 53 E8
Jiangyou, China 52 B5
Jianhe, China 52 D7
Jianli, China 53 C9
Jianning, China 53 D11
Jian'ou, China 53 D12
Jianshi, China 52 B7
Jianshui, China 52 F4
Jianyang, Fujian, China . 53 D12
Jianyang, Sichuan, China . 52 B5
Jiao Xian, China 51 F11
Jiaohe, Hebei, China .. 50 E9
Jiaohe, Jilin, China .. 51 C14
Jiaoling, China 53 E11
Jiaozhou Wan, China . 51 F11
Jiaozuo, China 50 G7
Jiashan, China 53 A11
Jiawang, China 51 G9
Jiaxiang, China 50 G9
Jiaxing, China 53 B13
Jiayi, Taiwan 53 F13
Jiayu, China 53 C9
Jibão, Serra do, Brazil . 123 D3
Jibiya, Nigeria 79 C6
Jibou, Romania 38 B6
Jibuti = Djibouti ■, Africa 68 E3
Jicarón, I., Panama .. 116 E3
Jičín, Czech. 20 E5
Jiddah, Si. Arabia ... 68 C2
Jido, India 61 E19
Jieshou, China 50 H8
Jiexiu, China 50 F6
Jieyang, China 53 F11
Jigawa □, Nigeria ... 79 C6
Jiggalong, Australia .. 88 D3

Jihlava, Czech. 20 F5
Jijel, Algeria 75 A6
Jijiga, Ethiopia 68 F3
Jijona, Spain 29 G4
Jikamshi, Nigeria ... 79 C6
Jilin, China 51 C14
Jilin □, China 51 C13
Jiloca →, Spain 28 D3
Jilong, Taiwan 53 E13
Jima, Ethiopia 77 F4
Jimbolia, Romania ... 38 D3
Jimena de la Frontera,
  Spain 31 J5
Jiménez, Mexico 114 B4
Jimo, China 51 F11
Jin Jiang →, China .. 53 C10
Jin Xian, Hebei, China . 50 E8
Jin Xian, Liaoning, China 51 E11
Jinan, China 50 F9
Jincheng, China 50 G7
Jinchuan, China 52 B4
Jind, India 62 E7
Jindabyne, Australia . 91 F4
Jindrichuv Hradeç, Czech. 20 F5
Jing He →, China ... 50 G5
Jing Shan, China 53 B8
Jing Xian, Anhui, China . 53 B12
Jing Xian, Hunan, China . 52 D7
Jing'an, China 53 C10
Jingbian, China 50 F5
Jingchuan, China 50 G4
Jingde, China 53 B12
Jingdezhen, China ... 53 C11
Jingdong, China 52 E3
Jinggu, China 52 F3
Jinghai, China 50 E9
Jinghong, China 52 F3
Jingjiang, China 53 A13
Jingle, China 50 E6
Jingmen, China 53 B9
Jingning, China 50 G3
Jingpo Hu, China 51 C15
Jingshan, China 53 B9
Jingtai, China 50 F3
Jingxi, China 52 F6
Jingxing, China 50 E8
Jingyang, China 50 G5
Jingyu, China 51 C14
Jingyuan, China 50 F3
Jingziguan, China ... 50 H6
Jinhua, China 53 C12
Jining,
  Nei Mongol Zizhiqu,
  China 50 D7
Jining, Shandong, China . 50 G9
Jinja, Uganda 82 B3
Jinjang, Malaysia ... 59 L3
Jinji, China 50 F4
Jinjiang, Fujian, China . 53 E12
Jinjiang, Yunnan, China . 52 D3
Jinjie, China 52 F6
Jinjini, Ghana 78 D4
Jinkou, China 53 B10
Jinmen Dao, China .. 53 E12
Jinnah Barrage, Pakistan . 60 C7
Jinning, China 52 E4
Jinotega, Nic. 116 D2
Jinotepe, Nic. 116 D2
Jinping, Guizhou, China . 52 D7
Jinping, Yunnan, China . 52 F4
Jinsha, China 52 D6
Jinsha Jiang →, China . 52 C5
Jinshan, China 53 B13
Jinshi, China 53 C8
Jintan, China 53 B12
Jinxi, Jiangxi, China .. 53 D11
Jinxi, Liaoning, China . 51 D11
Jinxian, China 53 C11
Jinxiang, China 50 G9
Jinyun, China 53 C13
Jinzhai, China 53 B10
Jinzhou, China 51 D11
Jiparaná →, Brazil .. 125 B5
Jipijapa, Ecuador ... 120 D1
Jiquilpan, Mexico ... 114 D4
Jishan, China 50 G6
Jishou, China 52 C7
Jishui, China 53 D10
Jisr ash Shughūr, Syria . 66 E7
Jitarning, Australia .. 89 F2
Jitra, Malaysia 59 J3
Jiu →, Romania 38 F6
Jiudengkou, China ... 50 E4
Jiujiang, Guangdong, China 53 F9
Jiujiang, Jiangxi, China . 53 C10
Jiuling Shan, China .. 53 C10
Jiulong, China 52 C3
Jiuquan, China 54 C4
Jiutai, China 51 B13
Jiuxiangcheng, China . 50 H8
Jiuxincheng, China .. 50 E8
Jiuyuhang, China ... 53 B12
Jixi, Anhui, China ... 53 B12
Jixi, Heilongjiang, China . 51 B16
Jiyang, China 51 F9
Jīzān, Si. Arabia 68 D3
Jize, China 50 F8
Jizera →, Czech. 20 E4
Jizō-Zaki, Japan 49 G6
Jizzakh, Uzbekistan .. 44 E7
Joaçaba, Brazil 127 B5
Joaíma, Brazil 123 E3
João, Brazil 122 B1
João Amaro, Brazil .. 123 D3
João Câmara, Brazil .. 122 C4
João Pessoa, Brazil .. 122 C4
João Pinheiro, Brazil .. 123 E2

Joaquim Távora, Brazil ... 123 F2
Joaquín V. González,
  Argentina 126 B3
Jobourg, Nez de, France .. 24 C5
Jódar, Spain 29 H1
Jodhpur, India 62 F5
Jœuf, France 25 C13
Jofane, Mozam. 85 C5
Jõgeva, Estonia 9 G22
Joggins, Canada 99 C7
Jogjakarta = Yogyakarta,
  Indonesia 57 G14
Johannesburg, S. Africa . 85 D4
Johannesburg, U.S.A. .. 113 K9
John Day, U.S.A. 110 D4
John Day →, U.S.A. .. 110 D3
John H. Kerr Reservoir,
  U.S.A. 105 G6
John o' Groats, U.K. ... 14 C5
Johnnie, U.S.A. 113 J10
John's Ra., Australia .. 90 C1
Johnson, U.S.A. 109 G4
Johnson City, N.Y., U.S.A. 107 D9
Johnson City, Tenn.,
  U.S.A. 105 G4
Johnson City, Tex., U.S.A. 109 K5
Johnsonburg, U.S.A. .. 106 E6
Johnsondale, U.S.A. .. 113 K8
Johnson's Crossing, Canada 100 A2
Johnston, L., Australia . 89 F3
Johnston Falls =
  Mambilima Falls, Zambia 83 E2
Johnston I., Pac. Oc. .. 93 F11
Johnstone Str., Canada . 100 C3
Johnstown, N.Y., U.S.A. . 107 C10
Johnstown, Pa., U.S.A. . 106 F6
Johor Baharu, Malaysia . 59 M4
Jõhvi, Estonia 9 G22
Joigny, France 25 E10
Joinville, Brazil 127 B6
Joinville, France 25 D12
Joinville I., Antarctica . 5 C18
Jojutla, Mexico 115 D5
Jokkmokk, Sweden .. 8 C18
Jökulsá á Bru →, Iceland 8 D6
Jökulsá á Fjöllum →,
  Iceland 8 C5
Jolfā, Āzarbājān-e Sharqī,
  Iran 67 C11
Jolfā, Esfahan, Iran .. 65 C6
Joliet, U.S.A. 104 E1
Joliette, Canada 98 C5
Jolo, Phil. 55 J4
Jolon, U.S.A. 112 K5
Jomalig, Phil. 55 D5
Jombang, Indonesia .. 57 G15
Jomda, China 52 B2
Jome, Indonesia 57 E7
Jomfruland, Norway .. 11 F3
Jönåker, Sweden 11 F10
Jonava, Lithuania ... 9 J21
Jones Sound, Canada . 4 B3
Jonesboro, Ark., U.S.A. . 109 H9
Jonesboro, Ill., U.S.A. . 109 G10
Jonesboro, La., U.S.A. . 109 J8
Jonesport, U.S.A. ... 99 D6
Jonglei, Sudan 77 F3
Jonglei □, Sudan 77 F3
Joniškis, Lithuania .. 9 H20
Jönköping, Sweden .. 9 H16
Jonquière, Canada ... 99 C5
Jonsberg, Sweden ... 11 F10
Jonsered, Sweden ... 11 G6
Jonzac, France 26 C3
Joplin, U.S.A. 109 G7
Jordan, U.S.A. 110 C10
Jordan ■, Asia 69 E5
Jordan →, Asia 69 D4
Jordan Valley, U.S.A. . 110 E5
Jordânia, Brazil 123 E3
Jorge, C., Chile 128 D1
Jorhat, India 61 F19
Jörn, Sweden 8 D19
Jorong, Indonesia ... 56 E4
Jørpeland, Norway .. 9 G11
Jorquera →, Chile ... 126 B2
Jos, Nigeria 79 D6
José Batlle y Ordóñez,
  Uruguay 127 C4
José de San Martín,
  Argentina 128 B2
Joseph, U.S.A. 110 D5
Joseph, L., Nfld., Canada 99 B6
Joseph, L., Ont., Canada . 106 A5
Joseph Bonaparte G.,
  Australia 88 B4
Joseph City, U.S.A. .. 111 J8
Joshua Tree, U.S.A. .. 113 L10
Joshua Tree National
  Monument, U.S.A. .. 113 M10
Josselin, France 24 E4
Jostedalsbreen, Norway . 9 F12
Jotunheimen, Norway . 10 D4
Jourdanton, U.S.A. .. 109 L5
Joure, Neths. 16 C2
Joussard, Canada ... 100 B5
Joutseno, Finland ... 40 B5
Joyeuse, France 27 D8
Józefów, Poland 20 C11
Ju Xian, China 51 F10
Juan Aldama, Mexico . 114 C4
Juan Bautista Alberdi,
  Argentina 126 C3
Juan de Fuca Str., Canada 112 B2
Juan de Nova, Ind. Oc. .. 85 B7

Juan Fernández, Arch. de, *Pac. Oc.* 93 L20
Juan José Castelli, *Argentina* 126 B3
Juan L. Lacaze, *Uruguay* . 126 C4
Juanjuí, *Peru* 124 B2
Juankoski, *Finland* 8 E23
Juárez, *Argentina* 126 D4
Juárez, *Mexico* 113 N11
Juárez, Sierra de, *Mexico* . 114 A1
Juatinga, Ponta de, *Brazil* 123 F3
Jubàzeiro, *Brazil* 122 C3
Juàzeiro do Norte, *Brazil* . 122 C4
Jubayl, *Lebanon* 69 A4
Jubbah, *Si. Arabia* 64 D4
Jubbulpore = Jabalpur, *India* 63 H8
Jübek, *Germany* 18 A5
Jubga, *Russia* 43 H4
Jubilee L., *Australia* 89 E4
Juby, C., *Morocco* 74 C2
Júcar →, *Spain* 29 F4
Júcaro, *Cuba* 116 B4
Juchitán, *Mexico* 115 D5
Judaea = Har Yehuda, *Israel* 69 D3
Judenburg, *Austria* 21 H4
Judith →, *U.S.A.* 110 C9
Judith, Pt., *U.S.A.* 107 E13
Judith Gap, *U.S.A.* 110 C9
Jufari →, *Brazil* 121 D5
Jugoslavia = Yugoslavia ■, *Europe* 21 M10
Juigalpa, *Nic.* 116 D2
Juillac, *France* 26 C5
Juist, *Germany* 18 B2
Juiz de Fora, *Brazil* 123 F3
Jujuy □, *Argentina* 126 A2
Julesburg, *U.S.A.* 108 E3
Juli, *Peru* 124 D4
Julia Cr. →, *Australia* . . . 90 C3
Julia Creek, *Australia* . . . 90 C3
Juliaca, *Peru* 124 D3
Julian, *U.S.A.* 113 M10
Julian Alps = Julijske Alpe →, *Slovenia* 33 B11
Julianakanaal, *Neths.* . . . 17 F7
Julianatop, *Surinam* 121 C6
Julianeháb, *Greenland* . . . 4 C5
Jülich, *Germany* 18 E2
Julierpass, *Switz.* 23 D9
Julijske Alpe, *Slovenia* . . . 33 B11
Julimes, *Mexico* 114 B3
Jullundur, *India* 62 D6
Julu, *China* 50 F8
Jumbo, *Zimbabwe* 83 F3
Jumbo Pk., *U.S.A.* 113 J12
Jumentos Cays, *Bahamas* . 117 B4
Jumet, *Belgium* 17 H4
Jumilla, *Spain* 29 G3
Jumla, *Nepal* 63 E10
Jumna = Yamuna →, *India* 63 G9
Junagadh, *India* 62 J4
Junction, Tex., *U.S.A.* . . . 109 K5
Junction, Utah, *U.S.A.* . . . 111 G7
Junction B., *Australia* . . . 90 A1
Junction City, Kans., *U.S.A.* 108 F6
Junction City, Oreg., *U.S.A.* 110 D2
Junction Pt., *Australia* . . . 90 A1
Jundah, *Australia* 90 C3
Jundiaí, *Brazil* 127 A6
Juneau, *U.S.A.* 96 C6
Junee, *Australia* 91 E4
Jungfrau, *Switz.* 22 C5
Junggar Pendi, *China* 54 B3
Junglinster, *Lux.* 17 J8
Jungshahi, *Pakistan* 62 G2
Juniata →, *U.S.A.* 106 F7
Junín, *Argentina* 126 C3
Junín, *Peru* 124 C2
Junín □, *Peru* 124 C3
Junín de los Andes, *Argentina* 128 A2
Jūniyah, *Lebanon* 69 B4
Juntura, *U.S.A.* 110 E4
Juparanã, L., *Brazil* 123 E3
Jupiter →, *Canada* 99 C7
Juquiá, *Brazil* 123 F2
Jur, Nahr el →, *Sudan* . . . 77 F2
Jura = Jura, Mts. du, *Europe* 27 B10
Jura = Schwäbische Alb, *Germany* 19 G5
Jura, *Europe* 25 F13
Jura, *U.K.* 14 F3
Jura □, *France* 25 F12
Jura, Mts. du, *Europe* . . . 27 B10
Jura, Sd. of, *U.K.* 14 F3
Jura Suisse, *Switz.* 22 B3
Jurado, *Colombia* 120 B2
Jurbarkas, *Lithuania* 9 J20
Jurilovca, *Romania* 38 E11
Jūrmala, *Latvia* 9 H20
Jurong, *China* 53 B12
Juruá →, *Brazil* 120 D4
Juruena, *Brazil* 125 C6
Juruena →, *Brazil* 125 B6
Juruti, *Brazil* 121 D6
Jussey, *France* 25 E12
Justo Daract, *Argentina* . . 126 C2
Jutaí, *Brazil* 124 B4
Jutaí →, *Brazil* 120 D4
Jüterbog, *Germany* 18 D9
Juticalpa, *Honduras* 116 D2

Jutland = Jylland, *Denmark* 11 H3
Jutphaas, *Neths.* 16 D6
Juventud, I. de la, *Cuba* . . 116 B3
Juvigny-sous-Andaine, *France* 24 D6
Juvisy-sur-Orge, *France* . . 25 D9
Juwain, *Afghan.* 60 D2
Jūy Zar, *Iran* 67 F12
Juye, *China* 50 G9
Jvari, *Georgia* 43 J6
Jylland, *Denmark* 11 H3
Jyväskylä, *Finland* 9 E21

K

K2, Mt., *Pakistan* 63 B7
Kaap Plateau, *S. Africa* . . 84 D3
Kaapkruis, *Namibia* 84 C1
Kaapstad = Cape Town, *S. Africa* 84 E2
Kaatsheuvel, *Neths.* 17 E6
Kabaena, *Indonesia* 57 F6
Kabala, *S. Leone* 78 D2
Kabale, *Uganda* 82 C3
Kabalo, *Zaïre* 82 D2
Kabambare, *Zaïre* 82 C2
Kabango, *Zaïre* 83 D2
Kabanjahe, *Indonesia* 56 D1
Kabankalan, *Phil.* 55 G5
Kabara, *Mali* 78 B4
Kabardinka, *Russia* 43 H4
Kabardino-Balkar Republic = Kabardino Balkaria □, *Russia* . . . 43 J6
Kabardino Balkaria □, *Russia* 43 J6
Kabare, *Indonesia* 57 E8
Kabarega Falls, *Uganda* . . 82 B3
Kabasalan, *Phil.* 55 H5
Kabba, *Nigeria* 79 D6
Kabin Buri, *Thailand* 58 F3
Kabinakagami L., *Canada* . 98 C3
Kabīr, Zab al →, *Iraq* 67 D10
Kabkabīyah, *Sudan* 73 F9
Kabna, *Sudan* 76 D3
Kabompo, *Zambia* 83 E1
Kabompo →, *Zambia* 81 G4
Kabondo, *Zaïre* 83 D2
Kabongo, *Zaïre* 82 D2
Kabou, *Togo* 79 D5
Kaboudia, Rass, *Tunisia* . . 75 A7
Kabra, *Australia* 90 C5
Kabūd Gonbad, *Iran* 65 B8
Kabugao, *Phil.* 55 B4
Kābul, *Afghan.* 62 B3
Kābul □, *Afghan.* 60 B6
Kabul →, *Pakistan* 62 C5
Kabunga, *Zaïre* 82 C2
Kaburuang, *Indonesia* . . . 57 D7
Kabushiya, *Sudan* 77 D3
Kabwe, *Zambia* 83 E2
Kačanik, *Serbia, Yug.* . . . 21 N11
Kachchh, Gulf of, *India* . . 62 H3
Kachchh, Rann of, *India* . . 62 G4
Kachebera, *Zambia* 83 E3
Kachin □, *Burma* 61 F20
Kachira, L., *Uganda* 82 C3
Kachiry, *Kazakhstan* 44 D8
Kachisi, *Ethiopia* 77 F4
Kachot, *Cambodia* 59 G4
Kaçkar, *Turkey* 67 B9
Kadan Kyun, *Burma* 56 B1
Kadanai →, *Afghan.* 62 D1
Kadarkút, *Hungary* 21 J7
Kade, *Ghana* 79 D4
Kadi, *India* 62 H5
Kadina, *Australia* 91 E2
Kadınhanı, *Turkey* 66 C5
Kadirli, *Turkey* 66 D7
Kadiyevka = Stakhanov, *Ukraine* 41 H10
Kadoka, *U.S.A.* 108 D4
Kadom, *Russia* 42 C6
Kadoma, *Zimbabwe* 83 F2
Kâdugli, *Sudan* 77 E2
Kaduna, *Nigeria* 79 C6
Kaduna □, *Nigeria* 79 C6
Kaduy, *Russia* 40 C9
Kaédi, *Mauritania* 78 B2
Kaélé, *Cameroon* 79 C7
Kaeng Khoï, *Thailand* . . . 58 E3
Kaesŏng, N. Korea 51 F14
Kāf, *Si. Arabia* 64 D3
Kafakumba, *Zaïre* 80 F4
Kafan = Kapan, *Armenia* . 67 C12
Kafanchan, *Nigeria* 79 D6
Kafareti, *Nigeria* 79 C7
Kaffrine, *Senegal* 78 C1
Kafia Kingi, *Sudan* 73 G9
Kafinda, *Zambia* 83 E3
Kafirévs, Ákra, *Greece* . . . 39 L7
Kafr el Dauwâr, *Egypt* . . . 76 H7
Kafr el Sheikh, *Egypt* . . . 76 H7
Kafue, *Zambia* 81 H5
Kafue →, *Zambia* 83 F2
Kafue Flats, *Zambia* 83 F2
Kafue Nat. Park, *Zambia* . 83 F2
Kafulwe, *Zambia* 83 D2
Kaga, *Afghan.* 62 B4
Kaga Bandoro, *C.A.R.* . . . 73 G8
Kagan, *Uzbekistan* 44 F7
Kagawa □, *Japan* 49 G6

Kagera □, *Tanzania* 82 C3
Kagera →, *Uganda* 82 C3
Kağizman, *Turkey* 67 B10
Kagoshima, *Japan* 49 J5
Kagoshima □, *Japan* 49 J5
Kagul = Cahul, *Moldova* . . 41 K5
Kahak, *Iran* 65 B6
Kahama, *Tanzania* 82 C3
Kahama □, *Tanzania* 82 C3
Kahang, *Malaysia* 59 L4
Kahayan →, *Indonesia* . . . 56 E4
Kahe, *Tanzania* 82 C4
Kahemba, *Zaïre* 80 F3
Kahil, Djebel bou, *Algeria* . 75 B5
Kahniah →, *Canada* 100 B4
Kahnūj, *Iran* 65 E8
Kahoka, *U.S.A.* 108 E9
Kahoolawe, *U.S.A.* 102 H16
Kahramanmaraş, *Turkey* . . 66 D7
Kâhta, *Turkey* 67 D8
Kahuta, *Pakistan* 62 C5
Kai, Kepulauan, *Indonesia* . 57 F8
Kai Besar, *Indonesia* 57 F8
Kai Is. = Kai, Kepulauan, *Indonesia* 57 F8
Kai Kecil, *Indonesia* 57 F8
Kai Xian, *China* 52 B7
Kaiama, *Nigeria* 79 D5
Kaiapoi, *N.Z.* 87 K4
Kaieteur Falls, *Guyana* . . . 121 B6
Kaifeng, *China* 50 G8
Kaihua, *China* 53 C12
Kaikohe, *N.Z.* 87 F4
Kaikoura, *N.Z.* 87 K4
Kaikoura Ra., *N.Z.* 87 J4
Kailahun, *S. Leone* 78 D2
Kaili, *China* 52 D6
Kailu, *China* 51 C11
Kailua Kona, *U.S.A.* 102 J17
Kaimana, *Indonesia* 57 E8
Kaimanawa Mts., *N.Z.* . . . 87 H5
Kaimganj, *India* 63 F8
Kaimur Hills, *India* 63 G9
Kaingaroa Forest, *N.Z.* . . . 87 H6
Kainji Res., *Nigeria* 79 C5
Kainuu, *Finland* 8 D23
Kaipara Harbour, *N.Z.* . . . 87 G5
Kaiping, *China* 53 F9
Kaipokok B., *Canada* 99 B8
Kairana, *India* 62 E7
Kairoi, *Indonesia* 57 E8
Kairouan, *Tunisia* 75 A7
Kaiserslautern, *Germany* . . 19 F3
Kaitaia, *N.Z.* 87 F4
Kaitangata, *N.Z.* 87 M2
Kaithal, *India* 62 E7
Kaitu →, *Pakistan* 62 C4
Kaiwi Channel, *U.S.A.* . . . 102 H16
Kaiyang, *China* 52 D6
Kaiyuan, Liaoning, *China* . 51 C13
Kaiyuan, Yunnan, *China* . . 52 F4
Kajaani, *Finland* 8 D22
Kajabbi, *Australia* 90 B3
Kajana = Kajaani, *Finland* . 8 D22
Kajang, *Malaysia* 59 L3
Kajaran, *Armenia* 67 C12
Kajiado, *Kenya* 82 C4
Kajiado □, *Kenya* 82 C4
Kajo Kaji, *Sudan* 77 G3
Kaka, *Sudan* 77 E3
Kakabeka Falls, *Canada* . . 98 C2
Kakamas, *S. Africa* 84 D3
Kakamega, *Kenya* 82 B3
Kakamega □, *Kenya* 82 B3
Kakanj, *Bos.-H.* 21 L8
Kakanui Mts., *N.Z.* 87 L3
Kake, *Japan* 49 G6
Kakegawa, *Japan* 49 G9
Kakeroma-Jima, *Japan* . . . 49 K4
Kakhib, *Russia* 43 J8
Kakhovka, *Ukraine* 41 J7
Kakhovske Vdskh., *Ukraine* 41 J7
Kakinada, *India* 61 L13
Kakisa →, *Canada* 100 A5
Kakisa L., *Canada* 100 A5
Kakogawa, *Japan* 49 G7
Kakwa →, *Canada* 100 C5
Kāl Gūsheh, *Iran* 65 D8
Kal Safīd, *Iran* 67 E12
Kala, *Nigeria* 79 C7
Kalaa-Kebira, *Tunisia* . . . 75 A7
Kalabagh, *Pakistan* 62 C4
Kalabahi, *Indonesia* 57 F6
Kalábaka, *Greece* 39 K4
Kalabo, *Zambia* 81 G4
Kalach, *Russia* 42 E5
Kalach na Donu, *Russia* . . 43 F6
Kaladan →, *Burma* 61 J18
Kaladar, *Canada* 106 B7
Kalahari, *Africa* 84 C3
Kalahari Gemsbok Nat. Park, *S. Africa* 84 D3
Kalajoki, *Finland* 8 D20
Kālak, *Iran* 65 E8
Kalakamati, *Botswana* . . . 85 C4
Kalakan, *Russia* 45 D12
Kalakh, *Syria* 64 C3
K'alak'unlun Shank'ou, *Pakistan* 63 B7
Kalam, *Pakistan* 63 B5
Kalama, *U.S.A.* 112 D4
Kalama, *Zaïre* 82 C2
Kalambo Falls, *Tanzania* . . 83 D3
Kálamos, *Greece* 39 L3
Kalannie, *Australia* 89 F2
Kalāntarī, *Iran* 65 C7
Kalao, *Indonesia* 57 F6
Kalaotoa, *Indonesia* 57 F6
Kälarne, *Sweden* 10 B10
Kalárovo, *Slovak Rep.* . . . 21 H7
Kalasin, *Thailand* 58 D4
Kalat, *Pakistan* 60 E5
Kalāteh, *Iran* 65 B7
Kalāteh-ye-Ganj, *Iran* . . . 65 E8
Kálathos, *Greece* 39 N11
Kalaus →, *Russia* 43 H7
Kalávrita, *Greece* 39 L5
Kalbarri, *Australia* 89 E1
Kale, *Turkey* 66 D3
Kalecik, *Turkey* 66 B5
Kalegauk Kyun, *Burma* . . . 61 M20
Kalehe, *Zaïre* 82 C2
Kalema, *Tanzania* 82 C3
Kalemie, *Zaïre* 82 D2
Kalety, *Poland* 20 E8
Kalewa, *Burma* 61 H19
Kalgan = Zhangjiakou, *China* 50 D8
Kalgoorlie-Boulder, *Australia* 89 F3
Kaliakra, Nos, *Bulgaria* . . . 38 F11
Kalianda, *Indonesia* 56 F3
Kalibo, *Phil.* 55 F5
Kaliganj, *Bangla.* 63 H13
Kalima, *Zaïre* 82 C2
Kalimantan, *Indonesia* . . . 56 E4
Kalimantan Barat □, *Indonesia* 56 E4
Kalimantan Selatan □, *Indonesia* 56 E5
Kalimantan Tengah □, *Indonesia* 56 E4
Kalimantan Timur □, *Indonesia* 56 D5
Kálimnos, *Greece* 39 N10
Kalimpong, *India* 63 F13
Kalinin = Tver, *Russia* . . . 42 B2
Kaliningrad, *Russia* 9 J19
Kalininsk, *Russia* 42 E7
Kalinkavichy, *Belarus* . . . 41 F5
Kalinkovichi = Kalinkavichy, *Belarus* . . 41 F5
Kalinovik, *Bos.-H.* 21 M8
Kalipetrovo, *Bulgaria* 38 E10
Kaliro, *Uganda* 82 B3
Kalispell, *U.S.A.* 110 B6
Kalisz, *Poland* 20 D8
Kaliua, *Tanzania* 82 D3
Kalix, *Sweden* 8 D20
Kalix →, *Sweden* 8 D20
Kalka, *India* 62 D7
Kalkan, *Turkey* 66 D3
Kalkaska, *U.S.A.* 104 C3
Kalkfeld, *Namibia* 84 C2
Kalkfontein, *Botswana* . . . 84 C3
Kalkrand, *Namibia* 84 C2
Kållandsö, *Sweden* 11 F7
Kallavesi, *Finland* 8 E22
Kallithéa, *Greece* 39 M6
Kallonís, Kólpos, *Greece* . . 39 K9
Kallsjön, *Sweden* 8 E15
Kalmalo, *Nigeria* 79 C6
Kalmar, *Sweden* 9 H17
Kalmthout, *Belgium* 17 F4
Kalmyk Republic = Kalmykia □, *Russia* . . 43 G8
Kalmykia □, *Russia* 43 G8
Kalmykovo, *Kazakhstan* . . 44 E6
Kalna, *India* 63 H13
Kalocsa, *Hungary* 21 J9
Kalokhorio, *Cyprus* 37 E12
Kaloko, *Zaïre* 82 D2
Kalol, Gujarat, *India* 62 H5
Kalol, Gujarat, *India* 62 H5
Kalolímnos, *Greece* 39 M10
Kalomo, *Zambia* 83 F2
Kalpi, *India* 63 F8
Kaltbrunn, *Switz.* 23 B8
Kaltern = Caldaro, *Italy* . . 33 B8
Kaltungo, *Nigeria* 79 D7
Kalu, *Pakistan* 62 G2
Kaluga, *Russia* 42 C3
Kalulushi, *Zambia* 83 E2
Kalundborg, *Denmark* . . . 11 J5
Kalush, *Ukraine* 41 H3
Kałuszyn, *Poland* 20 C11
Kalutara, *Sri Lanka* 60 R11
Kalyazin, *Russia* 42 B3
Kama, *Zaïre* 82 C2
Kama →, *Russia* 44 D6
Kamachumu, *Tanzania* . . . 82 C3
Kamaishi, *Japan* 48 E10
Kamalia, *Pakistan* 62 D5
Kaman, *Turkey* 66 C5
Kamapanda, *Zambia* 83 E1
Kamaran, *Yemen* 68 D3
Kamativi, *Zimbabwe* 83 F2
Kamba, *Nigeria* 79 C5
Kambalda, *Australia* 89 F3
Kambia, *S. Leone* 78 D2
Kambolé, *Zambia* 83 D3
Kambos, *Cyprus* 37 D11
Kambove, *Zaïre* 83 E2
Kamchatka, P-ov., *Russia* . 45 D16
Kamchatka Pen. = Kamchatka, P-ov., *Russia* 45 D16

Kamen, *Russia* 44 D9
Kamen-Rybolov, *Russia* . . 48 B6
Kamenjak, Rt., *Croatia* . . . 33 D10
Kamenka = Kaminka, *Ukraine* 41 H7
Kamenka, *Kazakhstan* . . . 42 E10
Kamenka, *Russia* 42 D6
Kamenka, *Russia* 42 E4
Kamenka Bugskaya = Kamyanka-Buzka, *Ukraine* 41 G3
Kamenka Dneprovskaya = Kamyanka-Dniprovska, *Ukraine* 41 J8
Kamennomostskiy, *Russia* . 43 H5
Kamenolomni, *Russia* 43 G5
Kamensk-Shakhtinskiy, *Russia* 43 F5
Kamensk Uralskiy, *Russia* . 44 D7
Kamenskiy, *Russia* 42 E7
Kamenskoye, *Russia* 45 C17
Kamenyak, *Bulgaria* 38 F9
Kamenz, *Germany* 18 D10
Kameoka, *Japan* 49 G7
Kamiah, *U.S.A.* 110 C5
Kamień Pomorski, *Poland* . 20 B4
Kamieskroon, *S. Africa* . . . 84 E2
Kamilukuak, L., *Canada* . . 101 A8
Kamin-Kashyrskyy, *Ukraine* 41 G3
Kamina, *Zaïre* 83 D1
Kaminak L., *Canada* 101 A9
Kaminka, *Ukraine* 41 H7
Kaminoyama, *Japan* 48 E10
Kamiros, *Greece* 37 C9
Kamituga, *Zaïre* 82 C2
Kamloops, *Canada* 100 C4
Kamnik, *Slovenia* 33 B11
Kamo, *Armenia* 43 K7
Kamo, *Japan* 48 F9
Kamoa Mts., *Guyana* 121 C6
Kamoke, *Pakistan* 62 C6
Kamp →, *Austria* 21 G5
Kampala, *Uganda* 82 B3
Kampar, *Malaysia* 59 K3
Kampar →, *Indonesia* . . . 56 D2
Kampen, *Neths.* 16 C7
Kamperland, *Neths.* 17 E3
Kamphaeng Phet, *Thailand* 58 D2
Kampolombo, L., *Zambia* . . 83 E2
Kampong To, *Thailand* . . . 59 J3
Kampot, *Cambodia* 59 G5
Kampti, *Burkina Faso* . . . 78 C4
Kampuchea = Cambodia ■, *Asia* 58 F5
Kampung →, *Indonesia* . . 57 F9
Kampung Air Putih, *Malaysia* 59 K4
Kampung Jerangau, *Malaysia* 59 K4
Kampung Raja, *Malaysia* . 59 K4
Kampungbaru = Tolitoli, *Indonesia* 57 D6
Kamrau, Teluk, *Indonesia* . 57 E8
Kamsack, *Canada* 101 C8
Kamskoye Ustye, *Russia* . . 42 C9
Kamuchawie L., *Canada* . . 101 B8
Kamui-Misaki, *Japan* 48 C10
Kamyanets-Podilskyy, *Ukraine* 41 H4
Kamyanka-Buzka, *Ukraine* 41 G3
Kamyanka-Dniprovska, *Ukraine* 41 J8
Kāmyārān, *Iran* 67 E12
Kamyshin, *Russia* 42 E7
Kamyzyak, *Russia* 43 G9
Kanaaupscow, *Canada* . . . 98 B4
Kanab, *U.S.A.* 111 H7
Kanab →, *U.S.A.* 111 H7
Kanagi, *Japan* 48 D10
Kanairiktok →, *Canada* . . 99 A7
Kanália, *Greece* 39 K5
Kananga, *Zaïre* 80 F4
Kanarraville, *U.S.A.* 111 H7
Kanash, *Russia* 42 C8
Kanaskat, *U.S.A.* 112 C5
Kanawha →, *U.S.A.* 104 F4
Kanazawa, *Japan* 49 F8
Kanchanaburi, *Thailand* . . 58 E2
Kanchenjunga, *Nepal* 63 F13
Kanchipuram, *India* 60 N11
Kanda Kanda, *Zaïre* 80 F4
Kandahar = Qandahār, *Afghan.* 60 D4
Kandalaksha, *Russia* 44 C4
Kandalu, *Afghan.* 60 E3
Kandangan, *Indonesia* . . . 56 E5
Kandanos, *Greece* 37 D5
Kander →, *Switz.* 22 C5
Kandersteg, *Switz.* 22 D5
Kandhíla, *Greece* 39 M5
Kandhkot, *Pakistan* 62 E3
Kandhla, *India* 62 E7
Kandi, *Benin* 79 C5
Kandi, *India* 63 H13
Kandra, *Turkey* 66 B4
Kandla, *India* 62 H4
Kandos, *Australia* 91 E4
Kandy, *Sri Lanka* 60 R12
Kane, *U.S.A.* 106 E6
Kane Basin, *Greenland* . . . 4 B4
Kanevskaya, *Russia* 43 G4
Kanfanar, *Croatia* 33 C10
Kangaba, *Mali* 78 C3
Kangal, *Turkey* 66 C7
Kangān, Fārs, *Iran* 65 E7
Kangān, Hormozgān, *Iran* . 65 E8
Kangar, *Malaysia* 59 J3

Kangaroo I., *Australia* 91 F2
Kangasala, *Finland* 9 F21
Kangāvar, *Iran* 67 E12
Kangding, *China* 52 B3
Kăngdong, *N. Korea* 51 E14
Kangean, Kepulauan,
  Indonesia 56 F5
Kangean Is. = Kangean,
  Kepulauan, *Indonesia* .. 56 F5
Kanggye, *N. Korea* 51 D14
Kanggyŏng, *S. Korea* 51 F14
Kanghwa, *S. Korea* 51 F14
Kangiqsualujjuaq, *Canada* 97 C13
Kangiqsujuaq, *Canada* ... 97 B12
Kangirsuk, *Canada* 97 B13
Kangnŭng, *S. Korea* 51 F15
Kango, *Gabon* 80 D2
Kangping, *China* 51 C12
Kangto, *India* 61 F18
Kani, *Ivory C.* 78 D3
Kaniama, *Zaïre* 82 D1
Kaniapiskau →, *Canada* . 99 A6
Kaniapiskau L., *Canada* . 99 B6
Kanin, Poluostrov, *Russia* 44 C5
Kanin Nos, Mys, *Russia* .. 44 C5
Kanin Pen. = Kanin,
  Poluostrov, *Russia* 44 C5
Kaniva, *Australia* 91 F3
Kanjiža, *Serbia, Yug.* 21 J10
Kanjut Sar, *Pakistan* 63 A6
Kankaanpää, *Finland* ... 9 F20
Kankakee, *U.S.A.* 104 E2
Kankakee →, *U.S.A.* 104 E1
Kankan, *Guinea* 78 C3
Kankendy = Xankändi,
  Azerbaijan 67 C12
Kanker, *India* 61 J12
Kankunskiy, *Russia* 45 D13
Kannapolis, *U.S.A.* 105 H5
Kannauj, *India* 63 F8
Kannod, *India* 60 H10
Kano, *Nigeria* 79 C6
Kano □, *Nigeria* 79 C6
Kan'onji, *Japan* 49 G6
Kanoroba, *Ivory C.* 78 D3
Kanowit, *Malaysia* 56 D4
Kanowna, *Australia* 89 F3
Kanoya, *Japan* 49 J5
Kanpetlet, *Burma* 61 J18
Kanpur, *India* 63 F9
Kansas □, *U.S.A.* 108 F6
Kansas →, *U.S.A.* 108 F7
Kansas City, *Kans., U.S.A.* 108 F7
Kansas City, *Mo., U.S.A.* 108 F7
Kansenia, *Zaïre* 83 E2
Kansk, *Russia* 45 D10
Kansŏng, *S. Korea* 51 E15
Kansu = Gansu □, *China* 50 G3
Kantang, *Thailand* 59 J2
Kantché, *Niger* 79 C6
Kanté, *Togo* 79 D5
Kantemirovka, *Russia* ... 42 F4
Kantharalak, *Thailand* .. 58 E5
Kantō □, *Japan* 49 F9
Kantō-Sanchi, *Japan* 49 G9
Kanturk, *Ireland* 15 D3
Kanuma, *Japan* 49 F9
Kanus, *Namibia* 84 D2
Kanye, *Botswana* 84 C4
Kanzenze, *Zaïre* 83 E2
Kanzi, Ras, *Tanzania* 82 D4
Kaohsiung = Gaoxiong,
  Taiwan 53 F13
Kaokoveld, *Namibia* 84 B1
Kaolack, *Senegal* 78 C1
Kaoshan, *China* 51 B13
Kapadvanj, *India* 62 H5
Kapan, *Armenia* 67 C12
Kapanga, *Zaïre* 80 F4
Kapchagai = Qapshaghay,
  Kazakhstan 44 E8
Kapellen, *Belgium* 17 F4
Kapéllo, Ákra, *Greece* ... 39 N6
Kapema, *Zaïre* 83 E2
Kapfenberg, *Austria* 21 H5
Kapiri Mposhi, *Zambia* .. 83 E2
Kapiskau →, *Canada* ... 98 B3
Kapit, *Malaysia* 56 D4
Kapiti I., *N.Z.* 87 J5
Kaplice, *Czech.* 20 G4
Kapoe, *Thailand* 59 H2
Kapoeta, *Sudan* 77 G3
Kapos →, *Hungary* 21 J8
Kaposvár, *Hungary* 21 J7
Kapowsin, *U.S.A.* 112 D4
Kappeln, *Germany* 18 A5
Kapps, *Namibia* 84 C2
Kaprije, *Croatia* 33 E12
Kaprijke, *Belgium* 17 F3
Kapsan, *N. Korea* 51 D15
Kapsukas = Marijampolė,
  Lithuania 9 J20
Kapuas →, *Indonesia* .. 56 E3
Kapuas Hulu, Pegunungan,
  Malaysia 56 D4
Kapuas Hulu Ra. =
  Kapuas Hulu,
  Pegunungan, *Malaysia* . 56 D4
Kapulo, *Zaïre* 83 D2
Kapunda, *Australia* 91 E2
Kapuni, *N.Z.* 87 H5
Kapurthala, *India* 62 D6
Kapuskasing, *Canada* ... 98 C3
Kapuskasing →, *Canada* 98 C3
Kapustin Yar, *Russia* ... 43 F7
Kaputar, *Australia* 91 E5
Kaputir, *Kenya* 82 B4

Kapuvár, *Hungary* 21 H7
Kara, *Russia* 44 C7
Kara Bogaz Gol, Zaliv =
  Garabogazköl Aylagy,
  Turkmenistan 44 E6
Kara Kalpak Republic =
  Karakalpakstan □,
  Uzbekistan 44 E6
Kara Kum, *Turkmenistan* . 44 F6
Kara Sea, *Russia* 44 B7
Karabiğa, *Turkey* 66 B2
Karabük, *Turkey* 66 B5
Karaburun, *Turkey* 66 C2
Karaburuni, *Albania* 39 J2
Karabutak = Qarabutaq,
  Kazakhstan 44 E7
Karacabey, *Turkey* 66 B3
Karacasu, *Turkey* 66 D3
Karachala = Qaraçala,
  Azerbaijan 43 L9
Karachayevsk, *Russia* ... 43 J5
Karachev, *Russia* 42 D2
Karachey-Cherkessia □,
  Russia 43 J5
Karachi, *Pakistan* 62 G2
Karad, *India* 60 L9
Karadeniz Boğazı, *Turkey* 66 B3
Karaga, *Ghana* 79 D4
Karaganda = Qaraghandy,
  Kazakhstan 44 E8
Karagayly, *Kazakhstan* .. 44 E8
Karaginskiy, Ostrov, *Russia* 45 D17
Karagüney Dağları, *Turkey* 66 B6
Karagwe □, *Tanzania* ... 82 C3
Karaikal, *India* 60 P11
Karaikkudi, *India* 60 P11
Karaisali, *Turkey* 66 D6
Karaj, *Iran* 65 C6
Karak, *Malaysia* 59 L4
Karakalpakstan □,
  Uzbekistan 44 E6
Karakas, *Kazakhstan* 44 E9
Karakitang, *Indonesia* .. 57 D7
Karaklis = Vanadzor,
  Armenia 43 K7
Karakoçan, *Turkey* 67 C9
Karakoram Pass, *Pakistan* 63 B7
Karakoram Ra., *Pakistan* . 63 B7
Karakurt, *Turkey* 67 B10
Karalon, *Russia* 45 D12
Karaman, *Turkey* 66 D5
Karamay, *China* 54 B3
Karambu, *Indonesia* 56 E5
Karamea Bight, *N.Z.* 87 J3
Karamsad, *India* 62 H5
Karand, *Iran* 67 E12
Karanganyar, *Indonesia* . 57 G13
Karapınar, *Turkey* 66 D5
Karasburg, *Namibia* 84 D2
Karasino, *Russia* 44 C9
Karasjok, *Norway* 8 B21
Karasu, *Turkey* 66 B4
Karasuk, *Russia* 44 D8
Karasuyama, *Japan* 49 F10
Karataş, *Turkey* 66 D6
Karataş Burnu, *Turkey* .. 66 D6
Karatau = Qarataū,
  Kazakhstan 44 E8
Karatau, Khrebet,
  Kazakhstan 44 E7
Karauli, *India* 62 F7
Karavostasi, *Cyprus* 37 D11
Karawang, *Indonesia* ... 57 G12
Karawanken, *Europe* 21 J4
Karayazı, *Turkey* 67 C10
Karazhal, *Kazakhstan* ... 44 E8
Karbalā, *Iraq* 67 F11
Kårböle, *Sweden* 10 C9
Karcag, *Hungary* 21 H10
Karcha →, *Pakistan* 63 B7
Karda, *Russia* 45 D11
Kardhámila, *Greece* 39 L9
Kardhítsa, *Greece* 39 K4
Kärdla, *Estonia* 9 G20
Kareeberge, *S. Africa* .. 84 E3
Kareima, *Sudan* 76 D3
Karelia □, *Russia* 44 C4
Karelian Republic =
  Karelia □, *Russia* 44 C4
Kārevāndar, *Iran* 65 E9
Kargasok, *Russia* 44 D9
Kargat, *Russia* 44 D9
Kargı, *Turkey* 66 B6
Kargil, *India* 63 B7
Kargopol, *Russia* 40 B10
Kargueri, *Niger* 79 C7
Karia ba Mohammed,
  Morocco 74 B3
Kariān, *Iran* 65 E8
Kariba, *Zimbabwe* 83 F2
Kariba, L., *Zimbabwe* ... 83 F2
Kariba Dam, *Zimbabwe* . 83 F2
Kariba Gorge, *Zambia* .. 83 F2
Karibib, *Namibia* 84 C2
Karimata, Kepulauan,
  Indonesia 56 E3
Karimata, Selat, *Indonesia* 56 E3
Karimata Is. = Karimata,
  Kepulauan, *Indonesia* . 56 E3
Karimnagar, *India* 60 K11
Karimunjawa, Kepulauan,
  Indonesia 56 F4
Karin, *Somali Rep.* 68 E4
Karīt, *Iran* 65 C8
Kariya, *Japan* 49 G8
Karjala, *Finland* 40 A5

Karkaralinsk = Qarqaraly,
  Kazakhstan 44 E8
Karkinitska Zatoka,
  Ukraine 41 K7
Karkinitskiy Zaliv =
  Karkinitska Zatoka,
  Ukraine 41 K7
Karkur Tohl, *Egypt* 76 C2
Karl Liebknecht, *Russia* .. 42 E2
Karl-Marx-Stadt =
  Chemnitz, *Germany* ... 18 E8
Karla, L. = Voiviïs Límni,
  Greece 39 K5
Karlivka, *Ukraine* 41 H8
Karlobag, *Croatia* 33 D12
Karlovac, *Croatia* 33 C12
Karlovka = Karlivka,
  Ukraine 41 H8
Karlovo, *Bulgaria* 38 G7
Karlovy Vary, *Czech.* ... 20 E2
Karlsbad = Karlovy Vary,
  Czech. 20 E2
Karlsborg, *Sweden* 11 F8
Karlshamn, *Sweden* 9 H16
Karlskoga, *Sweden* 9 G16
Karlskrona, *Sweden* 9 H16
Karlsruhe, *Germany* 19 F4
Karlstad, *Sweden* 9 G15
Karlstad, *U.S.A.* 108 A6
Karlstadt, *Germany* 19 F5
Karnal, *India* 62 E7
Karnali →, *Nepal* 63 E9
Karnaphuli Res., *Bangla.* . 61 H18
Karnataka □, *India* 60 N10
Karnes City, *U.S.A.* 109 L6
Karnische Alpen, *Europe* . 21 J3
Karo, *Mali* 78 C4
Karoi, *Zimbabwe* 83 F2
Karonga, *Malawi* 83 D3
Karoonda, *Australia* 91 F2
Karora, *Sudan* 76 D4
Káros, *Greece* 39 N8
Karousádhes, *Greece* ... 39 K2
Karpasia □, *Cyprus* 37 D13
Kárpathos, *Greece* 39 P10
Kárpathos, Stenón, *Greece* 39 P10
Karpuz Burnu = Apostolos
  Andreas, C., *Cyprus* ... 66 E6
Karrebæk, *Denmark* 11 J5
Kars, *Turkey* 67 B10
Karsakpay, *Kazakhstan* .. 44 E7
Karsha, *Kazakhstan* 42 F10
Karshi = Qarshi,
  Uzbekistan 44 F7
Karsiyang, *India* 63 F13
Kartaly, *Russia* 44 D7
Kartapur, *India* 62 D6
Karthaus, *U.S.A.* 106 E6
Kartuzy, *Poland* 20 A8
Karufa, *Indonesia* 57 E8
Karumba, *Australia* 90 B3
Karumo, *Tanzania* 82 C3
Karumwa, *Tanzania* 82 C3
Karungu, *Kenya* 82 C3
Karup, *Denmark* 11 H3
Karviná, *Czech.* 20 F8
Karwar, *India* 60 M9
Karwi, *India* 63 G9
Kaş, *Turkey* 66 D3
Kasache, *Malawi* 83 E3
Kasai →, *Zaïre* 80 E3
Kasai Oriental □, *Zaïre* . 82 C1
Kasaji, *Zaïre* 83 E1
Kasama, *Zambia* 83 E3
Kasan-dong, *N. Korea* .. 51 D14
Kasane, *Namibia* 84 B3
Kasanga, *Tanzania* 83 D3
Kasangulu, *Zaïre* 80 E3
Kasaragod, *India* 60 N9
Kasba L., *Canada* 101 A8
Kasba Tadla, *Morocco* .. 74 B3
Kāseh Garān, *Iran* 64 C5
Kasempa, *Zambia* 83 E2
Kasenga, *Zaïre* 83 E2
Kasese, *Uganda* 82 B3
Kasewa, *Zambia* 83 E2
Kasganj, *India* 63 F8
Kashabowie, *Canada* ... 98 C1
Kāshān, *Iran* 65 C6
Kashi, *China* 54 C2
Kashimbo, *Zaïre* 83 E2
Kashin, *Russia* 42 B3
Kashipur, *India* 63 E8
Kashira, *Russia* 42 C4
Kashiwazaki, *Japan* 49 F9
Kashk-e Kohneh, *Afghan.* 60 B3
Kāshmar, *Iran* 65 C8
Kashmir, *Asia* 63 C7
Kashmor, *Pakistan* 62 E3
Kashpirovka, *Russia* 42 D9
Kashun Noerh = Gaxun
  Nur, *China* 54 B5
Kasimov, *Russia* 42 C5
Kasinge, *Zaïre* 82 D2
Kasiruta, *Indonesia* 57 E7
Kaskaskia →, *U.S.A.* ... 108 G10
Kaskattama →, *Canada* 101 B10
Kaskinen, *Finland* 9 E19
Kaslo, *Canada* 100 D5
Kasmere L., *Canada* 101 B8
Kasongo, *Zaïre* 82 C2
Kasongo Lunda, *Zaïre* .. 80 F3
Kásos, *Greece* 39 P9
Kásos, Stenón, *Greece* .. 39 P9
Kaspi, *Georgia* 43 K7
Kaspiysk, *Russia* 43 J8

Kaspiyskiy, *Russia* 43 H8
Kassab ed Doleib, *Sudan* . 77 E3
Kassala, *Egypt* 76 C2
Kassalā, *Sudan* 77 D4
Kassalā □, *Sudan* 77 D4
Kassel, *Germany* 18 D5
Kassinger, *Sudan* 76 D3
Kassiópi, *Greece* 37 A3
Kassue, *Indonesia* 57 F9
Kastamonu, *Turkey* 66 B5
Kastav, *Croatia* 33 C11
Kastélli, *Greece* 37 D5
Kastéllion, *Greece* 37 D7
Kastellou, Ákra, *Greece* . 39 P10
Kasterlee, *Belgium* 17 F5
Kastóri, *Greece* 39 M5
Kastoría, *Greece* 39 J4
Kastornoye, *Russia* 42 E4
Kástron, *Greece* 39 K8
Kastsyukovichy, *Belarus* . 40 F7
Kasulu, *Tanzania* 82 C3
Kasulu □, *Tanzania* 82 C3
Kasumi, *Japan* 49 G7
Kasumkent, *Russia* 43 K9
Kasungu, *Malawi* 83 E3
Kasur, *Pakistan* 62 D6
Kata, *Russia* 45 D11
Kataba, *Zambia* 83 F2
Katako Kombe, *Zaïre* ... 82 C1
Katákolon, *Greece* 39 M4
Katale, *Tanzania* 82 C3
Katamatite, *Australia* ... 91 F4
Katanda, *Kivu, Zaïre* ... 82 C2
Katanda, *Shaba, Zaïre* .. 82 D1
Katanga = Shaba □, *Zaïre* 82 D2
Katangi, *India* 60 J11
Katangli, *Russia* 45 D15
Katavi Swamp, *Tanzania* . 82 D3
Kateríni, *Greece* 39 J5
Katha, *Burma* 61 G20
Katherîna, Gebel, *Egypt* . 76 J8
Katherine, *Australia* 88 B5
Kathiawar, *India* 62 H4
Kathikas, *Cyprus* 37 E11
Kati, *Mali* 78 C3
Katihar, *India* 63 G12
Katima Mulilo, *Zambia* . 84 B3
Katimbira, *Malawi* 83 E3
Katingan = Mendawai →,
  Indonesia 56 E4
Katiola, *Ivory C.* 78 D3
Káto Akhaïa, *Greece* ... 39 L4
Káto Arkhánai, *Greece* .. 37 D7
Káto Khorió, *Greece* 37 D7
Kato Pyrgos, *Cyprus* 37 D11
Káto Stavros, *Greece* ... 39 J6
Katompe, *Zaïre* 82 D2
Katonga →, *Uganda* ... 82 B3
Katoomba, *Australia* ... 91 E5
Katowice, *Poland* 20 E9
Katrine, L., *U.K.* 14 E4
Katrineholm, *Sweden* .. 10 E10
Katsepe, *Madag.* 85 B8
Katsina, *Nigeria* 79 C6
Katsina □, *Nigeria* 79 C6
Katsina Ala →, *Nigeria* . 79 D6
Katsumoto, *Japan* 49 H4
Katsuura, *Japan* 49 G10
Katsuyama, *Japan* 49 F8
Kattaviá, *Greece* 37 D9
Kattegat, *Denmark* 11 H5
Katumba, *Zaïre* 82 D2
Katungu, *Kenya* 82 C5
Katwa, *India* 63 H13
Katwijk-aan-Zee, *Neths.* . 16 D4
Kauai, *U.S.A.* 102 H15
Kauai Channel, *U.S.A.* .. 102 H15
Kaub, *Germany* 19 E3
Kaufbeuren, *Germany* .. 19 H6
Kaufman, *U.S.A.* 109 J6
Kauhajoki, *Finland* 9 E20
Kaukauna, *U.S.A.* 104 C1
Kaukauveld, *Namibia* ... 84 C3
Kaunas, *Lithuania* 9 J20
Kaura Namoda, *Nigeria* . 79 C6
Kautokeino, *Norway* 8 B20
Kavacha, *Russia* 45 C17
Kavadarci, *Macedonia* .. 39 H5
Kavaja, *Albania* 39 H2
Kavak, *Turkey* 66 B7
Kavalerovo, *Russia* 48 B7
Kavali, *India* 60 M12
Kaválla, *Greece* 39 J7
Kavār, *Iran* 65 D7
Kavarna, *Bulgaria* 38 F11
Kavkaz, *Russia* 43 H3
Kavos, *Greece* 37 B4
Kaw, *Fr. Guiana* 121 C7
Kawa, *Sudan* 77 E3
Kawagama L., *Canada* .. 106 A6
Kawagoe, *Japan* 49 G9
Kawaguchi, *Japan* 49 G9
Kawaihae, *U.S.A.* 102 H17
Kawambwa, *Zambia* ... 83 D2
Kawanoe, *Japan* 49 G6
Kawardha, *India* 63 J9
Kawasaki, *Japan* 49 G9
Kawene, *Canada* 98 C1
Kawerau, *N.Z.* 87 H6
Kawhia Harbour, *N.Z.* .. 87 H5
Kawio, Kepulauan,
  Indonesia 57 D7
Kawnro, *Burma* 61 H21
Kawthoolei = Kawthule □,
  Burma 61 L20
Kawthule □, *Burma* 61 L20

Kaya, *Burkina Faso* 79 C4
Kayah □, *Burma* 61 K20
Kayan →, *Indonesia* ... 56 D5
Kaycee, *U.S.A.* 110 E10
Kayeli, *Indonesia* 57 E7
Kayenta, *U.S.A.* 111 H8
Kayes, *Mali* 78 C2
Kayima, *S. Leone* 78 D2
Kayl, *Lux.* 17 K8
Kayoa, *Indonesia* 57 E7
Kayomba, *Zambia* 83 E1
Kayoro, *Ghana* 79 C4
Kayrunnera, *Australia* .. 91 E3
Kaysatskoye, *Russia* 42 F8
Kayseri, *Turkey* 66 C6
Kaysville, *U.S.A.* 110 F8
Kayuagung, *Indonesia* .. 56 E2
Kazachye, *Russia* 45 B14
Kazakhstan ■, *Asia* 44 E7
Kazan, *Russia* 42 C9
Kazan-Rettō, *Pac. Oc.* .. 92 E6
Kazanlŭk, *Bulgaria* 38 G8
Kazanskaya, *Russia* 42 F5
Kazatin = Kozyatyn,
  Ukraine 41 H5
Kazbek, *Russia* 43 J7
Kăzerūn, *Iran* 65 D6
Kazi Magomed =
  Qazimämmäd,
  Azerbaijan 43 K9
Kazincbarcika, *Hungary* . 21 G10
Kaztalovka, *Kazakhstan* . 42 F9
Kazumba, *Zaïre* 80 F4
Kazuno, *Japan* 48 D10
Kazym →, *Russia* 44 C7
Kcynia, *Poland* 20 C7
Ké-Macina, *Mali* 78 C3
Kéa, *Greece* 39 M7
Keams Canyon, *U.S.A.* .. 111 J8
Kearney, *U.S.A.* 108 E5
Keban, *Turkey* 67 C8
Keban Baraji, *Turkey* ... 67 C8
Kebbi □, *Nigeria* 79 C6
Kébi, *Ivory C.* 78 D3
Kebili, *Tunisia* 75 B6
Kebnekaise, *Sweden* 8 C18
Kebri Dehar, *Ethiopia* .. 68 F3
Kebumen, *Indonesia* ... 57 G13
Kecel, *Hungary* 21 J9
Kechika →, *Canada* 100 B3
Kecskemét, *Hungary* ... 21 J9
Kedada, *Ethiopia* 77 F4
Kedgwick, *Canada* 99 C6
Kédhros Óros, *Greece* .. 37 D6
Kedia Hill, *Botswana* ... 84 C3
Kediniai, *Lithuania* 9 J21
Kediri, *Indonesia* 57 G15
Kédougou, *Senegal* 78 C2
Kedzierzyn, *Poland* 20 E8
Keeler, *U.S.A.* 112 J9
Keeley L., *Canada* 101 C7
Keeling Is. = Cocos Is.,
  Ind. Oc. 92 J1
Keene, *Calif., U.S.A.* ... 113 K8
Keene, *N.H., U.S.A.* 107 D12
Keeper Hill, *Ireland* 15 D3
Keer-Weer, C., *Australia* . 90 A3
Keerbergen, *Belgium* ... 17 F5
Keeseville, *U.S.A.* 107 B11
Keeten Mastgat, *Neths.* . 17 E4
Keetmanshoop, *Namibia* . 84 D2
Keewatin, *U.S.A.* 108 B8
Keewatin □, *Canada* ... 101 A9
Keewatin →, *Canada* .. 101 B8
Kefa □, *Ethiopia* 77 F4
Kefallinía, *Greece* 39 L3
Kefamenanu, *Indonesia* . 57 F6
Keffi, *Nigeria* 79 D6
Keflavík, *Iceland* 8 D2
Keg River, *Canada* 100 B5
Kegaska, *Canada* 99 B7
Kehl, *Germany* 19 G3
Keighley, *U.K.* 12 D6
Keila, *Estonia* 9 G21
Keimoes, *S. Africa* 84 D3
Keita, *Niger* 79 C6
Keitele, *Finland* 8 E22
Keith, *Australia* 91 F3
Keith, *U.K.* 14 D6
Keith Arm, *Canada* 96 B7
Kejser Franz Joseph
  Fjord = Kong Franz
  Joseph Fd., *Greenland* . 4 B6
Kekri, *India* 62 G6
Kël, *Russia* 45 C13
Kelamet, *Eritrea* 77 D4
Kelan, *China* 50 E6
Kelang, *Malaysia* 59 L3
Kelantan →, *Malaysia* .. 59 J4
Kelheim, *Germany* 19 G7
Kelibia, *Tunisia* 75 A7
Kelkit, *Turkey* 67 B8
Kelkit →, *Turkey* 66 B7
Kellé, *Congo* 80 E2
Keller, *U.S.A.* 110 B4
Kellerberrin, *Australia* .. 89 F2
Kellett, C., *Canada* 4 B1
Kelleys I., *U.S.A.* 106 E2
Kellogg, *U.S.A.* 110 C5
Kells = Ceanannus Mor,
  Ireland 15 C5
Kélo, *Chad* 73 G8
Kelokedhara, *Cyprus* ... 37 E11
Kelowna, *Canada* 100 D5
Kelsey Bay, *Canada* 100 C3
Kelseyville, *U.S.A.* 112 G4
Kelso, *N.Z.* 87 L2

Kelso, *U.K.* 14 F6
Kelso, *U.S.A.* 112 D4
Keluang, *Malaysia* 59 L4
Kelvington, *Canada* 101 C8
Kem, *Russia* 44 C4
Kem-Kem, *Morocco* 74 B4
Kema, *Indonesia* 57 D7
Kemah, *Turkey* 67 C8
Kemaliye, *Turkey* 67 C8
Kemano, *Canada* 100 C3
Kemasik, *Malaysia* 59 K4
Kembolcha, *Ethiopia* 77 E4
Kemer, *Turkey* 66 D4
Kemerovo, *Russia* 44 D9
Kemi, *Finland* 8 D21
Kemi älv = Kemijoki →,
   Finland 8 D21
Kemijärvi, *Finland* 8 C22
Kemijoki →, *Finland* 8 D21
Kemmel, *Belgium* 17 G8
Kemmerer, *U.S.A.* 110 F8
Kemmuna = Comino,
   Malta 37 C1
Kemp, L., *U.S.A.* 109 J5
Kemp Land, *Antarctica* .. 5 C5
Kempsey, *Australia* 91 E5
Kempt, L., *Canada* 98 C5
Kempten, *Germany* 19 H6
Kemptville, *Canada* 98 C4
Kenadsa, *Algeria* 75 B4
Kendal, *Indonesia* 56 F4
Kendal, *U.K.* 12 C5
Kendall, *Australia* 91 E5
Kendall →, *Australia* 90 A3
Kendallville, *U.S.A.* 104 E3
Kendari, *Indonesia* 57 E6
Kendawangan, *Indonesia* . 56 E4
Kende, *Nigeria* 79 C5
Kendenup, *Australia* 89 F2
Kendrapara, *India* 61 J15
Kendrew, *S. Africa* 84 E3
Kendrick, *U.S.A.* 110 C5
Kene Thao, *Laos* 58 D3
Kenedy, *U.S.A.* 109 L6
Kenema, *S. Leone* 78 D2
Keng Kok, *Laos* 58 D5
Keng Tawng, *Burma* 61 J21
Keng Tung, *Burma* 61 J21
Kenge, *Zaïre* 80 E3
Kengeja, *Tanzania* 82 D4
Kenhardt, *S. Africa* 84 D3
Kenitra, *Morocco* 74 B3
Kenli, *China* 51 F10
Kenmare, *Ireland* 15 E2
Kenmare, *U.S.A.* 108 A3
Kenmare →, *Ireland* 15 E2
Kennebec, *U.S.A.* 108 D5
Kennedy, *Zimbabwe* 83 F2
Kennedy Ra., *Australia* .. 89 D2
Kennedy Taungdeik,
   Burma 61 H18
Kennet →, *U.K.* 13 F7
Kenneth Ra., *Australia* .. 88 D2
Kennett, *U.S.A.* 109 G9
Kennewick, *U.S.A.* 110 C4
Kénogami, *Canada* 99 C5
Kenogami →, *Canada* 98 B3
Kenora, *Canada* 101 D10
Kenosha, *U.S.A.* 104 D2
Kensington, *Canada* 99 C7
Kensington, *U.S.A.* 108 F5
Kensington Downs,
   Australia 90 C3
Kent, *Ohio, U.S.A.* 106 E3
Kent, *Oreg., U.S.A.* 110 D3
Kent, *Tex., U.S.A.* 109 K2
Kent, *Wash., U.S.A.* 112 C4
Kent □, *U.K.* 13 F8
Kent Group, *Australia* ... 90 F4
Kent Pen., *Canada* 96 B9
Kentau, *Kazakhstan* 44 E7
Kentland, *U.S.A.* 104 E2
Kenton, *U.S.A.* 104 E4
Kentucky □, *U.S.A.* 104 G3
Kentucky →, *U.S.A.* 104 F3
Kentucky L., *U.S.A.* 105 G2
Kentville, *Canada* 99 C7
Kentwood, *U.S.A.* 109 K9
Kenya ■, *Africa* 82 B4
Kenya, Mt., *Kenya* 82 C4
Keo Neua, Deo, *Vietnam* . 58 C5
Keokuk, *U.S.A.* 108 E9
Kep, *Cambodia* 59 G5
Kep, *Vietnam* 58 B6
Kepi, *Indonesia* 57 F9
Kępno, *Poland* 20 D7
Kerala □, *India* 60 P10
Kerama-Rettō, *Japan* 49 L3
Keran, *Pakistan* 63 B5
Kerang, *Australia* 91 F3
Keraudren, C., *Australia* . 88 C2
Kerava, *Finland* 9 F21
Kerch, *Ukraine* 41 K9
Kerchenskiy Proliv,
   Black Sea 41 K9
Kerchoual, *Mali* 79 B5
Kerempe Burnu, *Turkey* .. 66 A5
Keren, *Eritrea* 77 D4
Kerewan, *Gambia* 78 C1
Kerguelen, *Ind. Oc.* 3 G13
Keri Kera, *Sudan* 77 E3
Kericho, *Kenya* 82 C4
Kericho □, *Kenya* 82 C4
Kerinci, *Indonesia* 56 E2
Kerkdriel, *Neths.* 16 E6
Kerkenna, Is., *Tunisia* .. 75 B7
Kerki, *Turkmenistan* 44 F7

Kérkira, *Greece* 37 A3
Kerkrade, *Neths.* 17 G8
Kerma, *Sudan* 76 D3
Kermadec Is., *Pac. Oc.* . 92 K10
Kermadec Trench, *Pac. Oc.* 92 L10
Kermān, *Iran* 65 D8
Kerman, *U.S.A.* 112 J6
Kermān □, *Iran* 65 D8
Kermānshāh = Bākhtarān,
   Iran 67 E12
Kerme Körfezi, *Turkey* .. 66 D2
Kermit, *U.S.A.* 109 K3
Kerrville, *U.S.A.* 109 K5
Kerry □, *Ireland* 15 D2
Kerry Hd., *Ireland* 15 D2
Kersa, *Ethiopia* 77 F5
Kerteminde, *Denmark* 11 J4
Kertosono, *Indonesia* ... 57 G15
Kerulen →, *Asia* 54 B6
Kerzaz, *Algeria* 75 C4
Kerzers, *Switz.* 22 C4
Kesagami →, *Canada* 98 B4
Kesagami L., *Canada* 98 B3
Keşan, *Turkey* 66 B2
Kesch, Piz, *Switz.* 23 C9
Kesennuma, *Japan* 48 E10
Keshit, *Iran* 65 D8
Keşiş Dağ, *Turkey* 67 C8
Keskin, *Turkey* 66 C5
Kessel, *Belgium* 17 F5
Kessel, *Neths.* 17 F8
Kessel-Lo, *Belgium* 17 G5
Kestell, *S. Africa* 85 D4
Kestenga, *Russia* 44 C4
Kesteren, *Neths.* 16 E7
Keswick, *U.K.* 12 C4
Keszthely, *Hungary* 21 J7
Ket →, *Russia* 44 D9
Keta, *Ghana* 79 D5
Ketapang, *Indonesia* 56 E4
Ketchikan, *U.S.A.* 96 C6
Ketchum, *U.S.A.* 110 E6
Kete Krachi, *Ghana* 79 D4
Ketef, Khalîg Umm el,
   Egypt 76 C4
Ketelmeer, *Neths.* 16 C7
Keti Bandar, *Pakistan* .. 62 G2
Ketri, *India* 62 E6
Kętrzyn, *Poland* 20 A11
Kettering, *U.K.* 13 E7
Kettle →, *Canada* 101 B11
Kettle Falls, *U.S.A.* ... 110 B4
Kettleman City, *U.S.A.* . 112 J7
Keuruu, *Finland* 9 E21
Kevin, *U.S.A.* 110 B8
Kewanee, *U.S.A.* 108 E10
Kewaunee, *U.S.A.* 104 C2
Keweenaw B., *U.S.A.* 104 B1
Keweenaw Pen., *U.S.A.* .. 104 B2
Keweenaw Pt., *U.S.A.* ... 104 B2
Key Harbour, *Canada* 98 C3
Key West, *U.S.A.* 103 F10
Keyser, *U.S.A.* 104 F6
Keystone, *U.S.A.* 108 D3
Kezhma, *Russia* 45 D11
Kežmarok, *Slovak Rep.* .. 20 F10
Khabarovo, *Russia* 44 C7
Khabarovsk, *Russia* 45 E14
Khabr, *Iran* 65 D8
Khābūr →, *Syria* 67 E9
Khachmas = Xaçmaz,
   Azerbaijan 43 K9
Khachrod, *India* 62 H6
Khadari, W. el →, *Sudan* . 77 E2
Khadro, *Pakistan* 62 F3
Khadyzhensk, *Russia* 43 H4
Khadzhilyangar, *India* .. 63 B8
Khagaria, *India* 63 G12
Khaipur, *Bahawalpur,
   Pakistan* 62 E5
Khaipur, *Hyderabad,
   Pakistan* 62 F3
Khair, *India* 62 F7
Khairabad, *India* 63 F9
Khairagarh, *India* 63 J9
Khairpur, *Pakistan* 60 F6
Khakassia □, *Russia* 44 D9
Khakhea, *Botswana* 84 C3
Khalafābād, *Iran* 65 D6
Khalfallah, *Algeria* 75 B5
Khalilabad, *India* 63 F10
Khalīlī, *Iran* 65 E7
Khalkhāl, *Iran* 67 D13
Khálki, *Greece* 39 K5
Khalkís, *Greece* 39 L6
Khalmer-Sede = Tazovskiy,
   Russia 44 C8
Khalmer Yu, *Russia* 44 C7
Khalturin, *Russia* 44 D5
Khalūf, *Oman* 68 C6
Kham Keut, *Laos* 58 C5
Khamas Country, *Botswana* 84 C4
Khambat, G. of, *India* .. 62 J5
Khambhaliya, *India* 62 H3
Khambhat, *India* 62 H5
Khamilonísion, *Greece* .. 39 P9
Khamir, *Iran* 65 E7
Khamir, *Yemen* 68 D3
Khamsa, *Egypt* 69 E1
Khān Abū Shāmat, *Syria* . 69 B5
Khān Azād, *Iraq* 67 C5
Khān Mujiddah, *Iraq* 64 C4

Khān Shaykhūn, *Syria* ... 66 E7
Khān Yūnis, *Gaza Strip* . 69 D3
Khānaqīn, *Iraq* 67 E11
Khānbāghī, *Iran* 65 B7
Khandrá, *Greece* 39 P9
Khandwa, *India* 60 J10
Khandyga, *Russia* 45 C14
Khāneh, *Iran* 64 B5
Khanewal, *Pakistan* 62 D4
Khanh Duong, *Vietnam* ... 58 F7
Khaniá, *Greece* 37 D6
Khaniá □, *Greece* 37 D6
Khaníon, Kólpos, *Greece* . 37 D5
Khanka, Ozero, *Asia* 45 E14
Khankendy = Xankändi,
   Azerbaijan 67 C12
Khanna, *India* 62 D7
Khanpur, *Pakistan* 62 E4
Khanty-Mansiysk, *Russia* . 44 C7
Khapalu, *Pakistan* 63 B7
Khapcheranga, *Russia* ... 45 E12
Kharabali, *Russia* 43 G8
Kharagpur, *India* 63 H12
Kharan Kalat, *Pakistan* . 60 E4
Kharānaq, *Iran* 65 C7
Kharda, *India* 60 K9
Khardung La, *India* 63 B7
Khârga, El Wâhât el, *Egypt* 76 B3
Khargon, *India* 60 J9
Kharit, Wadi el →, *Egypt* 76 C3
Khārk, Jazireh, *Iran* ... 65 D6
Kharkiv, *Ukraine* 41 H9
Kharkov = Kharkiv,
   Ukraine 41 H9
Kharmanli, *Bulgaria* 39 H8
Kharovsk, *Russia* 40 C11
Kharta, *Turkey* 66 B3
Khartoum = El Khartûm,
   Sudan 77 D3
Khasan, *Russia* 48 C5
Khasavyurt, *Russia* 43 J8
Khāsh, *Iran* 60 E2
Khashm el Girba, *Sudan* . 77 E4
Khashuri, *Georgia* 43 J6
Khaskovo, *Bulgaria* 39 H8
Khatanga, *Russia* 45 B11
Khatanga →, *Russia* 45 B11
Khatauli, *India* 62 E7
Khātūnābād, *Iran* 65 D7
Khatyrka, *Russia* 45 C18
Khaybar, Harrat,
   Si. Arabia 64 E4
Khāzimiyah, *Iraq* 64 C4
Khazzân Jabal el Awliyâ,
   Sudan 77 D3
Khe Bo, *Vietnam* 58 C5
Khe Long, *Vietnam* 58 B5
Khed Brahma, *India* 60 G8
Khekra, *India* 62 E7
Khemarak Phouminville,
   Cambodia 59 G4
Khemelnik, *Ukraine* 41 H4
Khemis Miliana, *Algeria* . 75 A5
Khemissèt, *Morocco* 74 B3
Khemmarat, *Thailand* 58 D5
Khenāman, *Iran* 65 D8
Khenchela, *Algeria* 75 A6
Khenifra, *Morocco* 74 B3
Kherrata, *Algeria* 75 A6
Kherson, *Ukraine* 41 J7
Khersónisos Akrotíri,
   Greece 37 D6
Kheta →, *Russia* 45 B11
Khilok, *Russia* 45 D12
Khimki, *Russia* 42 C3
Khíos, *Greece* 39 L9
Khirbat Qanāfar, *Lebanon* 69 B4
Khiuma = Hiiumaa,
   Estonia 9 G20
Khiva, *Uzbekistan* 44 E7
Khīyāv, *Iran* 64 B5
Khlong Khlung, *Thailand* . 58 D2
Khmelnitskiy =
   Khmelnytskyy, *Ukraine* 41 H4
Khmelnytskyy, *Ukraine* .. 41 H4
Khmer Rep. =
   Cambodia ■, *Asia* 58 F5
Khoai, Hon, *Vietnam* 59 H5
Khodoriv, *Ukraine* 41 H3
Khodzent = Khudzhand,
   Tajikistan 44 E7
Khojak P., *Afghan.* 60 D5
Khok Kloi, *Thailand* 59 H2
Khok Pho, *Thailand* 59 J3
Kholm, *Russia* 40 D6
Kholmsk, *Russia* 45 E15
Khomas Hochland,
   Namibia 84 C2
Khomeyn, *Iran* 65 C6
Khon Kaen, *Thailand* 58 D4
Khong, *Laos* 58 E5
Khong Sedone, *Laos* 58 E5
Khonuu, *Russia* 45 C15
Khoper →, *Russia* 42 F6
Khor el 'Atash, *Sudan* .. 77 E3
Khóra, *Greece* 39 M4
Khóra Sfakíon, *Greece* .. 37 D6
Khorāsān □, *Iran* 65 C8
Khorat = Nakhon
   Ratchasima, *Thailand* . 58 E4
Khorat, Cao Nguyen,
   Thailand 58 E4
Khorb el Ethel, *Algeria* . 74 C3
Khorixas, *Namibia* 84 C1
Khorol, *Ukraine* 41 H7

Khorrāmābād, *Khorāsān,
   Iran* 65 C8
Khorrāmābād, *Lorestān,
   Iran* 67 F13
Khorrāmshahr, *Iran* 65 D6
Khorugh, *Tajikistan* 44 F8
Khosravī, *Iran* 65 D6
Khosrowābād, *Khuzestān,
   Iran* 65 D6
Khosrowābād, *Kordestān,
   Iran* 67 E12
Khosūyeh, *Iran* 65 D7
Khotyn, *Ukraine* 41 H4
Khouribga, *Morocco* 74 B3
Khowai, *Bangla.* 61 G17
Khoyniki, *Belarus* 41 G5
Khrami →, *Georgia* 43 K7
Khrenovoye, *Russia* 42 E5
Khristianá, *Greece* 39 N8
Khrysokhou B., *Cyprus* .. 37 D11
Khu Khan, *Thailand* 58 E5
Khudzhand, *Tajikistan* .. 44 E7
Khuff, *Si. Arabia* 64 E5
Khūgīānī, *Afghan.* 62 D1
Khulna, *Bangla.* 61 H16
Khulna □, *Bangla.* 61 H16
Khulo, *Georgia* 43 K6
Khumago, *Botswana* 84 C3
Khūnsorkh, *Iran* 65 E8
Khūr, *Iran* 65 C8
Khurai, *India* 62 G8
Khurays, *Si. Arabia* 65 E6
Khūrīyā Mūrīyā, Jazā 'ir,
   Oman 68 D6
Khurja, *India* 62 E7
Khūsf, *Iran* 65 C8
Khush, *Afghan.* 60 C3
Khushab, *Pakistan* 62 C5
Khust, *Ukraine* 41 H2
Khuzdar, *Pakistan* 62 F2
Khūzestān □, *Iran* 65 D6
Khvājeh, *Iran* 64 B5
Khvānsār, *Iran* 65 D7
Khvatovka, *Russia* 42 D8
Khvor, *Iran* 65 C7
Khvorgū, *Iran* 65 E8
Khvormūj, *Iran* 65 D6
Khvoy, *Iran* 67 C11
Khvoynaya, *Russia* 40 C8
Khyber Pass, *Afghan.* ... 62 B4
Kiabukwa, *Zaïre* 83 D1
Kiama, *Australia* 91 E5
Kiamba, *Phil.* 55 H6
Kiambi, *Zaïre* 82 D2
Kiambu, *Kenya* 82 C4
Kiangsi = Jiangxi □, *China* 53 D10
Kiangsu = Jiangsu □,
   China 51 H10
Kibæk, *Denmark* 11 H2
Kibangou, *Congo* 80 E2
Kibara, *Tanzania* 82 C3
Kibare, Mts., *Zaïre* 82 D2
Kibombo, *Zaïre* 82 C2
Kibondo, *Tanzania* 82 C3
Kibondo □, *Tanzania* 82 C3
Kibumbu, *Burundi* 82 C2
Kibungu, *Rwanda* 82 C3
Kibuye, *Burundi* 82 C2
Kibuye, *Rwanda* 82 C2
Kibwesa, *Tanzania* 82 D2
Kibwezi, *Kenya* 82 C4
Kichiga, *Russia* 45 D17
Kicking Horse Pass,
   Canada 100 C5
Kidal, *Mali* 79 B5
Kidderminster, *U.K.* 13 E5
Kidete, *Tanzania* 82 D4
Kidira, *Senegal* 78 C2
Kidnappers, C., *N.Z.* ... 87 H6
Kidston, *Australia* 90 B3
Kidugallo, *Tanzania* 82 D4
Kiel, *Germany* 18 A6
Kiel Kanal = Nord-Ostsee-
   Kanal →, *Germany* 18 A5
Kielce, *Poland* 20 E10
Kieldrecht, *Belgium* 17 F4
Kieler Bucht, *Germany* .. 18 A6
Kien Binh, *Vietnam* 59 H5
Kien Tan, *Vietnam* 59 H5
Kienge, *Zaïre* 83 E2
Kiessé, *Niger* 79 C5
Kiev = Kyyiv, *Ukraine* .. 41 G6
Kiffa, *Mauritania* 78 B2
Kifisiá, *Greece* 39 L6
Kifisós →, *Greece* 39 L6
Kifrī, *Iraq* 67 E11
Kigali, *Rwanda* 82 C3
Kigarama, *Tanzania* 82 C3
Kigoma □, *Tanzania* 82 D2
Kigoma-Ujiji, *Tanzania* . 82 C2
Kigomasha, Ras, *Tanzania* 82 C4
Kihee, *Australia* 91 D3
Kihnu, *Estonia* 9 G21
Kii-Sanchi, *Japan* 49 G7
Kii-Suidō, *Japan* 49 H7
Kikaiga-Shima, *Japan* ... 49 K4
Kikinda, *Serbia, Yug.* .. 21 K10
Kikládhes, *Greece* 39 M7
Kikwit, *Zaïre* 80 E3
Kílalki, *Greece* 39 N10
Kilauea Crater, *U.S.A.* . 102 J17
Kilchberg, *Switz.* 23 B7
Kilcoy, *Australia* 91 D5
Kildare, *Ireland* 15 C5
Kildare □, *Ireland* 15 C5

Kilgore, *U.S.A.* 109 J7
Kilifi, *Kenya* 82 C4
Kilifi □, *Kenya* 82 C4
Kilimanjaro, *Tanzania* .. 82 C4
Kilimanjaro □, *Tanzania* . 82 C4
Kilimli, *Turkey* 66 B4
Kilindini, *Kenya* 82 C4
Kilis, *Turkey* 66 D7
Kiliya, *Ukraine* 41 K5
Kilju, *N. Korea* 51 D15
Kilkee, *Ireland* 15 D2
Kilkenny, *Ireland* 15 D4
Kilkenny □, *Ireland* 15 D4
Kilkieran B., *Ireland* .. 15 C2
Kilkís, *Greece* 39 J5
Killala, *Ireland* 15 B2
Killala B., *Ireland* 15 B2
Killaloe, *Ireland* 15 D3
Killaloe Sta., *Canada* .. 106 A7
Killam, *Canada* 100 C6
Killarney, *Australia* ... 91 D5
Killarney, *Canada* 98 C3
Killarney, *Ireland* 15 D2
Killarney, Lakes of, *Ireland* 15 E2
Killary Harbour, *Ireland* 15 C2
Killdeer, *Canada* 101 D7
Killdeer, *U.S.A.* 108 B3
Killeen, *U.S.A.* 109 K6
Killiecrankie, Pass of, *U.K.* 14 E5
Killin, *U.K.* 14 E4
Killíni, Ilía, *Greece* .. 39 M4
Killíni, Korinthía, *Greece* 39 M5
Killybegs, *Ireland* 15 B3
Kilmarnock, *U.K.* 14 F4
Kilmez, *Russia* 42 B10
Kilmez →, *Russia* 42 B10
Kilmore, *Australia* 91 F3
Kilondo, *Tanzania* 83 D3
Kilosa, *Tanzania* 82 D4
Kilosa □, *Tanzania* 82 D4
Kilrush, *Ireland* 15 D2
Kilwa □, *Tanzania* 83 D4
Kilwa Kisiwani, *Tanzania* 83 D4
Kilwa Kivinje, *Tanzania* . 83 D4
Kilwa Masoko, *Tanzania* . 83 D4
Kim, *U.S.A.* 109 G3
Kimaam, *Indonesia* 57 F9
Kimamba, *Tanzania* 82 D4
Kimba, *Australia* 91 E2
Kimball, *Nebr., U.S.A.* . 108 E3
Kimball, *S. Dak., U.S.A.* 108 D5
Kimberley, *Canada* 100 D5
Kimberley, *S. Africa* ... 84 D3
Kimberley Downs,
   Australia 88 C3
Kimberly, *U.S.A.* 110 E6
Kimchaek, *N. Korea* 51 D15
Kimchŏn, *S. Korea* 51 F15
Kími, *Greece* 39 L7
Kimje, *S. Korea* 51 G14
Kímolos, *Greece* 39 N7
Kimovsk, *Russia* 42 C3
Kimparana, *Mali* 78 C4
Kimry, *Russia* 42 B3
Kimsquit, *Canada* 100 C3
Kimstad, *Sweden* 11 F9
Kinabalu, Gunong,
   Malaysia 56 C5
Kínaros, *Greece* 39 N9
Kinaskan L., *Canada* 100 B2
Kinbasket L., *Canada* ... 100 C5
Kincaid, *Canada* 101 D7
Kincardine, *Canada* 98 D3
Kinda, *Zaïre* 83 D2
Kinder Scout, *U.K.* 12 D6
Kindersley, *Canada* 101 C7
Kindia, *Guinea* 78 C2
Kindu, *Zaïre* 82 C2
Kinel, *Russia* 42 D10
Kineshma, *Russia* 42 B6
Kinesi, *Tanzania* 82 C3
King, L., *Australia* 89 F2
King, Mt., *Australia* ... 90 D4
King City, *U.S.A.* 111 H3
King Cr. →, *Australia* .. 90 C2
King Edward →, *Australia* 88 B4
King Frederick VI Land =
   Kong Frederik VI.s Kyst,
   Greenland 4 C5
King George B., *Falk. Is.* 128 D4
King George I., *Antarctica* 5 C18
King George Is., *Canada* . 97 C11
King I. = Kadan Kyun,
   Burma 56 B1
King I., *Australia* 90 F3
King I., *Canada* 100 C3
King Leopold Ras.,
   Australia 88 C4
King Sd., *Australia* 88 C3
King William I., *Canada* . 96 B10
King William's Town,
   S. Africa 84 E4
Kingaroy, *Australia* 91 D5
Kingfisher, *U.S.A.* 109 H6
Kingirbān, *Iraq* 64 C5
Kingisepp = Kuressaare,
   Estonia 9 G20
Kingisepp = Kuressaare,
   Russia 40 C5
Kingman, *Ariz., U.S.A.* . 113 K12
Kingman, *Kans., U.S.A.* . 109 G5
Kings →, *U.S.A.* 111 H4
Kings Canyon National
   Park, *U.S.A.* 111 H4
King's Lynn, *U.K.* 12 E8
Kings Mountain, *U.S.A.* . 105 H5

171

King's Peak, *U.S.A.* 110 F8
Kingsbridge, *U.K.* 13 G4
Kingsburg, *U.S.A.* 111 H4
Kingscote, *Australia* 91 F2
Kingscourt, *Ireland* 15 C5
Kingsley, *U.S.A.* 108 D7
Kingsport, *U.S.A.* 105 G4
Kingston, *Canada* 98 D4
Kingston, *Jamaica* 116 C4
Kingston, *N.Z.* 87 L2
Kingston, *N.Y., U.S.A.* 107 E10
Kingston, *Pa., U.S.A.* 107 E9
Kingston, *R.I., U.S.A.* 107 E13
Kingston Pk., *U.S.A.* 113 K11
Kingston South East, *Australia* 91 F2
Kingston upon Hull, *U.K.* 12 D7
Kingston-upon-Thames, *U.K.* 13 F7
Kingstown, *St. Vincent* 117 D7
Kingstree, *U.S.A.* 105 J6
Kingsville, *Canada* 98 D3
Kingsville, *U.S.A.* 109 M6
Kingussie, *U.K.* 14 D4
Kınık, *Turkey* 66 C2
Kinistino, *Canada* 101 C7
Kinkala, *Congo* 80 E2
Kinki □, *Japan* 49 H8
Kinleith, *N.Z.* 87 H5
Kinmount, *Canada* 106 B6
Kinna, *Sweden* 11 G6
Kinnaird, *Canada* 100 D5
Kinnairds Hd., *U.K.* 14 D7
Kinnared, *Sweden* 11 G7
Kinnarodden, *Norway* 6 A11
Kino, *Mexico* 114 B2
Kinoje →, *Canada* 98 B3
Kinomoto, *Japan* 49 G8
Kinoni, *Uganda* 82 C3
Kinrooi, *Belgium* 17 F7
Kinross, *U.K.* 14 E5
Kinsale, *Ireland* 15 E3
Kinsale, Old Hd. of, *Ireland* 15 E3
Kinsha = Chang Jiang →, *China* 53 B13
Kinshasa, *Zaïre* 80 E3
Kinsley, *U.S.A.* 109 G5
Kinston, *U.S.A.* 105 H7
Kintampo, *Ghana* 79 D4
Kintap, *Indonesia* 56 E5
Kintore Ra., *Australia* 88 D4
Kintyre, *U.K.* 14 F3
Kintyre, Mull of, *U.K.* 14 F3
Kinushseo →, *Canada* 98 A3
Kinuso, *Canada* 100 B5
Kinyangiri, *Tanzania* 82 C3
Kinzig →, *Germany* 19 G3
Kinzua, *U.S.A.* 106 E6
Kinzua Dam, *U.S.A.* 106 E6
Kiosk, *Canada* 98 C4
Kiowa, *Kans., U.S.A.* 109 G5
Kiowa, *Okla., U.S.A.* 109 H7
Kipahigan L., *Canada* 101 B8
Kipanga, *Tanzania* 82 D4
Kiparissía, *Greece* 39 M4
Kiparissiakós Kólpos, *Greece* 39 M4
Kipembawe, *Tanzania* 82 D3
Kipengere Ra., *Tanzania* 83 D3
Kipili, *Tanzania* 82 D3
Kipini, *Kenya* 82 C5
Kipling, *Canada* 101 C8
Kippure, *Ireland* 15 C5
Kipushi, *Zaïre* 83 E2
Kiratpur, *India* 62 E8
Kirchberg, *Switz.* 22 B5
Kirchhain, *Germany* 18 E4
Kirchheim, *Germany* 19 G5
Kirchheim-Bolanden, *Germany* 19 F4
Kirensk, *Russia* 45 D11
Kirgella Rocks, *Australia* 89 F3
Kirghizia = Kyrgyzstan ■, *Asia* 44 E8
Kirghizstan = Kyrgyzstan ■, *Asia* 44 E8
Kiri, *Zaïre* 80 E3
Kiribati ■, *Pac. Oc.* 92 H10
Kırıkhan, *Turkey* 66 D7
Kırıkkale, *Turkey* 66 C5
Kirillov, *Russia* 40 C10
Kirin = Jilin, *China* 51 C14
Kirin = Jilin □, *China* 51 C13
Kirishi, *Russia* 40 C7
Kiritimati, *Kiribati* 93 G12
Kırka, *Turkey* 66 C4
Kirkcaldy, *U.K.* 14 E5
Kirkcudbright, *U.K.* 14 G4
Kirkee, *India* 60 K8
Kirkenær, *Norway* 10 D6
Kirkenes, *Norway* 8 B23
Kirkintilloch, *U.K.* 14 F4
Kirkjubæjarklaustur, *Iceland* 8 E4
Kirkkonummi, *Finland* 9 F21
Kirkland, *U.S.A.* 111 J7
Kirkland Lake, *Canada* 98 C3
Kırklareli, *Turkey* 66 B2
Kirksville, *U.S.A.* 108 E8
Kirkūk, *Iraq* 67 E11
Kirkwall, *U.K.* 14 C6
Kirkwood, *S. Africa* 84 E4
Kirn, *Germany* 19 F3
Kirov, *Russia* 42 C2
Kirov, *Russia* 44 D5

Kirovabad = Gäncä, *Azerbaijan* 43 K8
Kirovakan = Vanadzor, *Armenia* 43 K7
Kirovograd = Kirovohrad, *Ukraine* 41 H7
Kirovohrad, *Ukraine* 41 H7
Kirovsk = Babadayhan, *Turkmenistan* 44 F7
Kirovsk, *Russia* 44 C4
Kirovskiy, *Russia* 43 H9
Kirovskiy, *Kamchatka, Russia* 45 D16
Kirovskiy, *Primorsk, Russia* 48 B6
Kirriemuir, *U.K.* 14 E6
Kirsanov, *Russia* 42 D6
Kırşehir, *Turkey* 66 C6
Kirtachi, *Niger* 79 C5
Kirthar Range, *Pakistan* 62 F2
Kiruna, *Sweden* 8 C19
Kirundu, *Zaïre* 82 C2
Kirup, *Australia* 89 F2
Kirya, *Russia* 42 C8
Kiryū, *Japan* 49 F9
Kisaga, *Tanzania* 82 C3
Kisalaya, *Nic.* 116 D3
Kisámou, Kólpos, *Greece* 37 D5
Kisanga, *Zaïre* 82 B2
Kisangani, *Zaïre* 82 B2
Kisar, *Indonesia* 57 F7
Kisaran, *Indonesia* 56 D1
Kisarawe, *Tanzania* 82 D4
Kisarawe □, *Tanzania* 82 D4
Kisarazu, *Japan* 49 G9
Kisbér, *Hungary* 21 H8
Kiselevsk, *Russia* 44 D9
Kishanganga →, *Pakistan* 63 B5
Kishanganj, *India* 63 F13
Kishangarh, *India* 62 F4
Kishi, *Nigeria* 79 D5
Kishinev = Chișinău, *Moldova* 41 J5
Kishiwada, *Japan* 49 G7
Kishtwar, *India* 63 C6
Kisii, *Kenya* 82 C3
Kisii □, *Kenya* 82 C3
Kisiju, *Tanzania* 82 D4
Kisir, *Turkey* 67 B10
Kisizi, *Uganda* 82 C2
Kiska I., *U.S.A.* 96 C1
Kiskatinaw →, *Canada* 100 B4
Kiskittogisu L., *Canada* 101 C9
Kiskörös, *Hungary* 21 J9
Kiskundorozsma, *Hungary* 21 J10
Kiskunfélegyháza, *Hungary* 21 J9
Kiskunhalas, *Hungary* 21 J9
Kiskunmajsa, *Hungary* 21 J9
Kislovodsk, *Russia* 43 J6
Kiso-Gawa →, *Japan* 49 G8
Kiso-Sammyaku, *Japan* 49 G8
Kisofukushima, *Japan* 49 G8
Kisoro, *Uganda* 82 C2
Kispest, *Hungary* 21 H9
Kissidougou, *Guinea* 78 D2
Kissimmee, *U.S.A.* 105 L5
Kissimmee →, *U.S.A.* 105 M5
Kississing L., *Canada* 101 B8
Kissónerga, *Cyprus* 37 E11
Kistanje, *Croatia* 33 E12
Kisújszállás, *Hungary* 21 H10
Kisumu, *Kenya* 82 C3
Kisvárda, *Hungary* 21 G12
Kiswani, *Tanzania* 82 C4
Kiswere, *Tanzania* 83 D4
Kit Carson, *U.S.A.* 108 F3
Kita, *Mali* 78 C3
Kitab, *Uzbekistan* 44 F7
Kitaibaraki, *Japan* 49 F10
Kitakami, *Japan* 48 E10
Kitakami-Gawa →, *Japan* 48 E10
Kitakami-Sammyaku, *Japan* 48 E10
Kitakata, *Japan* 48 F9
Kitakyūshū, *Japan* 49 H5
Kitami, *Japan* 48 C11
Kitami-Sammyaku, *Japan* 48 B11
Kitangiri, L., *Tanzania* 82 C3
Kitaya, *Tanzania* 83 E5
Kitchener, *Australia* 89 F3
Kitchener, *Canada* 98 D3
Kitee, *Finland* 40 A6
Kitega = Gitega, *Burundi* 82 C2
Kitengo, *Zaïre* 82 D1
Kiteto □, *Tanzania* 82 C4
Kitgum, *Uganda* 82 B3
Kíthira, *Greece* 39 N7
Kíthnos, *Greece* 39 M7
Kiti, *Cyprus* 37 E12
Kiti, C., *Cyprus* 37 E12
Kitikmeot □, *Canada* 96 A9
Kitimat, *Canada* 100 C3
Kitinen →, *Finland* 8 C22
Kitiyab, *Sudan* 77 D3
Kítros, *Greece* 39 J5
Kitsuki, *Japan* 49 H5
Kittakittaooloo, L., *Australia* 91 D2
Kittanning, *U.S.A.* 106 F5
Kittatinny Mts., *U.S.A.* 107 E10
Kittery, *U.S.A.* 105 D10
Kittilä, *Finland* 8 C21
Kitui, *Kenya* 82 C4
Kitui □, *Kenya* 82 C4
Kitwe, *Zambia* 83 E2
Kitzbühel, *Austria* 19 H8
Kitzingen, *Germany* 19 F6
Kivarli, *India* 62 G5

Kivertsi, *Ukraine* 41 G3
Kividhes, *Cyprus* 37 E11
Kivu □, *Zaïre* 82 C2
Kivu, L., *Zaïre* 82 C2
Kiyev = Kyyiv, *Ukraine* 41 G6
Kiyevskoye Vdkhr. = Kyyivske Vdskh., *Ukraine* 41 G6
Kiziguru, *Rwanda* 82 C3
Kızıl Irmak →, *Turkey* 66 B6
Kizil Jilga, *India* 63 B8
Kizil Yurt, *Russia* 43 J8
Kızılcahamam, *Turkey* 66 B5
Kızılhisar, *Turkey* 66 D3
Kızılırmak, *Turkey* 66 B5
Kızıltepe, *Turkey* 67 D9
Kizimkazi, *Tanzania* 82 D4
Kizlyar, *Russia* 43 J8
Kizyl-Arvat = Gyzylarbat, *Turkmenistan* 44 F6
Kjellerup, *Denmark* 11 H3
Kjölur, *Iceland* 8 D4
Kladanj, *Bos.-H.* 21 L8
Kladno, *Czech.* 20 E4
Kladovo, *Serbia, Yug.* 21 L12
Klaeng, *Thailand* 58 F3
Klagenfurt, *Austria* 21 J4
Klagshamn, *Sweden* 11 J6
Klagstorp, *Sweden* 11 J7
Klaipėda, *Lithuania* 9 J19
Klaksvík, *Færoe Is.* 8 E9
Klamath →, *U.S.A.* 110 F1
Klamath Falls, *U.S.A.* 110 E3
Klamath Mts., *U.S.A.* 110 F2
Klanjec, *Croatia* 33 B12
Klappan →, *Canada* 100 B3
Klarälven →, *Sweden* 9 G15
Klaten, *Indonesia* 57 G14
Klatovy, *Czech.* 20 F3
Klausen = Chiusa, *Italy* 33 B8
Klawer, *S. Africa* 84 E2
Klawock, *U.S.A.* 100 B2
Klazienaveen, *Neths.* 16 C10
Kleczew, *Poland* 20 C8
Kleena Kleene, *Canada* 100 C4
Klein, *U.S.A.* 110 C9
Klein-Karas, *Namibia* 84 D2
Kleine Gette →, *Belgium* 17 G6
Kleine Nete →, *Belgium* 17 F5
Klekovača, *Bos.-H.* 33 D13
Klenovec, *Macedonia* 39 H3
Klenovec, *Slovak Rep.* 20 G9
Klerksdorp, *S. Africa* 84 D4
Kletnya, *Russia* 40 F7
Kletsk = Klyetsk, *Belarus* 41 F4
Kletskiy, *Russia* 43 F6
Kleve, *Germany* 18 D2
Klickitat, *U.S.A.* 110 D3
Klickitat →, *U.S.A.* 112 E5
Klidhes, *Cyprus* 37 D13
Klimovichi, *Belarus* 40 F6
Klin, *Russia* 42 B3
Klinaklini →, *Canada* 100 C3
Klintsy, *Russia* 41 F7
Klipdale, *S. Africa* 84 E2
Klipplaat, *S. Africa* 84 E3
Klitmøller, *Denmark* 11 G2
Kljajićevo, *Serbia, Yug.* 21 K9
Ključ, *Bos.-H.* 33 D13
Kłobuck, *Poland* 20 E8
Kłodzko, *Poland* 20 E6
Kloetinge, *Neths.* 17 F3
Klondike, *Canada* 96 B6
Kloosterzande, *Neths.* 17 F4
Klosterneuburg, *Austria* 21 G6
Klosters, *Switz.* 23 C9
Kloten, *Switz.* 23 B7
Klötze, *Germany* 18 C7
Klouto, *Togo* 79 D5
Kluane L., *Canada* 96 B6
Kluczbork, *Poland* 20 E8
Klundert, *Neths.* 17 E5
Klyetsk, *Belarus* 41 F4
Klyuchevskaya, Gora, *Russia* 45 D17
Knaresborough, *U.K.* 12 C6
Knee L., *Man., Canada* 101 B10
Knee L., *Sask., Canada* 101 B7
Kneïss, Is., *Tunisia* 75 B7
Knesselare, *Belgium* 17 F2
Knezha, *Bulgaria* 38 F7
Knić, *Serbia, Yug.* 21 M10
Knight Inlet, *Canada* 100 C3
Knighton, *U.K.* 13 E4
Knights Ferry, *U.S.A.* 112 H6
Knights Landing, *U.S.A.* 112 G5
Knin, *Croatia* 33 D13
Knittelfeld, *Austria* 21 H4
Knjaževac, *Serbia, Yug.* 21 M12
Knob, C., *Australia* 89 F2
Knockmealdown Mts., *Ireland* 15 D4
Knokke, *Belgium* 17 F2
Knossós, *Greece* 37 D7
Knox, *U.S.A.* 104 E2
Knox, C., *Canada* 100 C2
Knox City, *U.S.A.* 109 J5
Knox Coast, *Antarctica* 5 C8
Knoxville, *Iowa, U.S.A.* 108 E8
Knoxville, *Tenn., U.S.A.* 105 H4
Knutshø, *Norway* 10 B3
Knysna, *S. Africa* 84 E3
Knyszyn, *Poland* 20 B12
Ko Kha, *Thailand* 58 C2
Ko Tao, *Thailand* 59 G2
Koartac = Quaqtaq, *Canada* 97 B13

Koba, *Aru, Indonesia* 57 F8
Koba, *Bangka, Indonesia* 56 E3
Kobarid, *Slovenia* 33 B10
Kobayashi, *Japan* 49 J5
Kobdo = Hovd, *Mongolia* 54 B4
Kōbe, *Japan* 49 G7
Kobelyaky, *Ukraine* 41 H8
København, *Denmark* 11 J6
Kōbi-Sho, *Japan* 49 M1
Koblenz, *Germany* 19 E3
Koblenz, *Switz.* 22 A6
Kobo, *Ethiopia* 77 E4
Kobroor, Kepulauan, *Indonesia* 57 F8
Kobryn, *Belarus* 41 F3
Kobuleti, *Georgia* 43 K5
Kobyłka, *Poland* 20 C11
Kobylkino, *Russia* 42 C6
Kocaeli = İzmit, *Turkey* 66 B3
Kočani, *Macedonia* 39 H5
Koceljevo, *Serbia, Yug.* 21 L9
Kočevje, *Slovenia* 33 C11
Koch Bihar, *India* 61 F16
Kochang, *S. Korea* 51 G14
Kochas, *India* 63 G10
Kocher →, *Germany* 19 F5
Kocheya, *Russia* 45 D13
Kōchi, *Japan* 49 H6
Kōchi □, *Japan* 49 H6
Kochiu = Gejiu, *China* 52 F4
Kodaira, *Japan* 49 G9
Kodiak, *U.S.A.* 96 C4
Kodiak I., *U.S.A.* 96 C4
Kodinar, *India* 62 J4
Kodori →, *Georgia* 43 J5
Koekelare, *Belgium* 17 F1
Koersel, *Belgium* 17 F6
Koes, *Namibia* 84 D2
Koffiefontein, *S. Africa* 84 D4
Kofiau, *Indonesia* 57 E7
Koforidua, *Ghana* 79 D4
Kōfu, *Japan* 49 G9
Koga, *Japan* 49 F9
Kogaluk →, *Canada* 99 A7
Kogan, *Australia* 91 D5
Køge, *Denmark* 9 J15
Kogi □, *Nigeria* 79 D6
Kogin Baba, *Nigeria* 79 D7
Koh-i-Bābā, *Afghan.* 60 B5
Koh-i-Khurd, *Afghan.* 62 C1
Kohat, *Pakistan* 62 C4
Kohima, *India* 61 G19
Kohkīlūyeh va Būyer Aḥmadi □, *Iran* 65 D6
Kohler Ra., *Antarctica* 5 D15
Kohtla-Järve, *Estonia* 9 G22
Koillismaa, *Finland* 8 D23
Koin-dong, *N. Korea* 51 D14
Kojō, *N. Korea* 51 E14
Kojonup, *Australia* 89 F2
Kojūr, *Iran* 65 B6
Koka, *Sudan* 76 C3
Kokand = Qŭqon, *Uzbekistan* 44 E8
Kokanee Glacier Prov. Park, *Canada* 100 D5
Kokas, *Indonesia* 57 E8
Kokchetav = Kökshetaū, *Kazakhstan* 44 D7
Kokemäenjoki →, *Finland* 9 F19
Kokerite, *Guyana* 121 B6
Kokhma, *Russia* 42 B5
Kokkola, *Finland* 8 E20
Koko, *Nigeria* 79 C5
Koko Kyunzu, *Burma* 61 M18
Kokolopozo, *Ivory C.* 78 D3
Kokomo, *U.S.A.* 104 E2
Kokonau, *Indonesia* 57 E9
Kokoro, *Niger* 79 C5
Koksan, *N. Korea* 51 E14
Kökshetaū, *Kazakhstan* 44 D7
Koksoak →, *Canada* 97 C13
Kokstad, *S. Africa* 85 E4
Kokubu, *Japan* 49 J5
Kokuora, *Russia* 45 B15
Kola, *Indonesia* 57 F8
Kola, *Russia* 44 C4
Kola Pen. = Kolskiy Poluostrov, *Russia* 44 C4
Kolahoi, *India* 63 B6
Kolahun, *Liberia* 78 D2
Kolaka, *Indonesia* 57 E6
Kolar, *India* 60 N11
Kolar Gold Fields, *India* 60 N11
Kolari, *Finland* 8 C20
Kolayat, *India* 60 F8
Kolby Kås, *Denmark* 11 J4
Kolchugino = Leninsk-Kuznetskiy, *Russia* 44 D9
Kolchugino, *Russia* 42 B4
Kolda, *Senegal* 78 C2
Kolding, *Denmark* 11 J3
Kole, *Zaïre* 80 E4
Koléa, *Algeria* 75 A5
Kolepom = Yos Sudarso, Pulau, *Indonesia* 57 F9
Kolguyev, Ostrov, *Russia* 44 A8
Kolham, *Neths.* 16 B9
Kolhapur, *India* 60 L9
Kolia, *Ivory C.* 78 D3
Kolín, *Czech.* 20 E5
Kolkas Rags, *Latvia* 9 H20
Kölleda, *Germany* 18 D7
Kollum, *Neths.* 16 B8
Kolmanskop, *Namibia* 84 D2
Köln, *Germany* 18 E2
Koło, *Poland* 20 C8

Kołobrzeg, *Poland* 20 A5
Kolokani, *Mali* 78 C3
Kolomna, *Russia* 42 C4
Kolomyya, *Ukraine* 41 H3
Kolondiéba, *Mali* 78 C3
Kolonodale, *Indonesia* 57 E6
Kolosib, *India* 61 G18
Kolpashevo, *Russia* 44 D9
Kolpino, *Russia* 40 C6
Kolpny, *Russia* 42 D3
Kolskiy Poluostrov, *Russia* 44 C4
Kolubara →, *Serbia, Yug.* 21 L10
Koluszki, *Poland* 20 D9
Kolwezi, *Zaïre* 83 E2
Kolyma →, *Russia* 45 C17
Kolymskoye Nagorye, *Russia* 45 C16
Kôm Ombo, *Egypt* 76 C3
Komandorskiye Is. = Komandorskiye Ostrova, *Russia* 45 D17
Komandorskiye Ostrova, *Russia* 45 D17
Komárno, *Slovak Rep.* 21 H8
Komárom, *Hungary* 21 H8
Komatipoort, *S. Africa* 85 D5
Komatou Yialou, *Cyprus* 37 D13
Komatsu, *Japan* 49 F8
Komatsujima, *Japan* 49 H7
Kombissiri, *Burkina Faso* 79 C4
Kombori, *Burkina Faso* 78 C4
Komen, *Slovenia* 33 C10
Komenda, *Ghana* 79 D4
Komi □, *Russia* 44 C6
Komiža, *Croatia* 33 E13
Komló, *Hungary* 21 J8
Kommunarsk = Alchevsk, *Ukraine* 41 H10
Kommunizma, Pik, *Tajikistan* 44 F8
Komodo, *Indonesia* 57 F5
Komoé →, *Ivory C.* 78 D4
Komono, *Congo* 80 E2
Komoran, Pulau, *Indonesia* 57 F9
Komoro, *Japan* 49 F9
Komotini, *Greece* 39 H8
Kompasberg, *S. Africa* 84 E3
Kompong Bang, *Cambodia* 59 F5
Kompong Cham, *Cambodia* 59 F5
Kompong Chhnang, *Cambodia* 59 F5
Kompong Chikreng, *Cambodia* 58 F5
Kompong Kleang, *Cambodia* 58 F5
Kompong Luong, *Cambodia* 59 G5
Kompong Pranak, *Cambodia* 58 F5
Kompong Som, *Cambodia* 59 G4
Kompong Som, Chhung, *Cambodia* 59 G4
Kompong Speu, *Cambodia* 59 G5
Kompong Sralao, *Cambodia* 58 E5
Kompong Thom, *Cambodia* 58 F5
Kompong Trabeck, *Cambodia* 58 F5
Kompong Trabeck, *Cambodia* 59 G5
Kompong Trach, *Cambodia* 59 G5
Kompong Tralach, *Cambodia* 59 G5
Komrat = Comrat, *Moldova* 41 J5
Komsberg, *S. Africa* 84 E3
Komsomolets, Ostrov, *Russia* 45 A10
Komsomolsk, *Russia* 42 B5
Komsomolsk, *Russia* 45 D14
Komsomolskiy, *Russia* 42 C7
Konakovo, *Russia* 42 B3
Konarhá □, *Afghan.* 60 B7
Konārī, *Iran* 65 D6
Konawa, *U.S.A.* 109 H6
Konch, *India* 63 G8
Kondakovo, *Russia* 45 C16
Konde, *Tanzania* 82 C4
Kondinin, *Australia* 89 F2
Kondoa, *Tanzania* 82 C4
Kondoa □, *Tanzania* 82 C4
Kondókali, *Greece* 37 A3
Kondopaga, *Russia* 40 A9
Kondratyevo, *Russia* 45 D10
Kondrovo, *Russia* 42 C2
Konduga, *Nigeria* 79 C7
Köneürgench, *Turkmenistan* 44 E6
Konevo, *Russia* 40 A10
Kong, *Ivory C.* 78 D4
Kong →, *Cambodia* 58 F5
Kong, Koh, *Cambodia* 59 G4
Kong Christian IX.s Land, *Greenland* 4 C6
Kong Christian X.s Land, *Greenland* 4 B6
Kong Franz Joseph Fd., *Greenland* 4 B6
Kong Frederik IX.s Land, *Greenland* 4 C5
Kong Frederik VI.s Kyst, *Greenland* 4 C5
Kong Frederik VIII.s Land, *Greenland* 4 B6
Kong Oscar Fjord, *Greenland* 4 B6
Kongeå →, *Denmark* 11 J3

Kulyab

Kongju, *S. Korea* 51 F14
Konglu, *Burma* 61 F20
Kongolo, *Kasai Or., Zaïre* 82 D1
Kongolo, *Shaba, Zaïre* 82 D2
Kongor, *Sudan* 77 F3
Kongoussi, *Burkina Faso* 79 C4
Kongsberg, *Norway* 10 E3
Kongsvinger, *Norway* 10 D6
Kongwa, *Tanzania* 82 D4
Koni, *Zaïre* 83 E2
Koni, Mts., *Zaïre* 83 E2
Königsberg = Kaliningrad, *Russia* 9 J19
Königslutter, *Germany* 18 C6
Königswusterhausen, *Germany* 18 C9
Konin, *Poland* 20 C8
Kónitsa, *Greece* 39 J3
Köniz, *Switz.* 22 C4
Konjice, *Slovenia* 33 B12
Konkiep, *Namibia* 84 D2
Konkouré →, *Guinea* 78 D2
Könnern, *Germany* 18 D7
Kono, *S. Leone* 78 D2
Konolfingen, *Switz.* 22 C5
Konongo, *Ghana* 79 D4
Konosha, *Russia* 40 B11
Kōnosu, *Japan* 49 F9
Konotop, *Ukraine* 41 G7
Konqi He →, *China* 54 B4
Końskie, *Poland* 20 D10
Konstantinovka = Kostyantynivka, *Ukraine* 41 H9
Konstantinovsk, *Russia* 43 G5
Konstanz, *Germany* 19 H5
Kont, *Iran* 65 E9
Kontagora, *Nigeria* 79 C6
Kontich, *Belgium* 17 F4
Kontum, *Vietnam* 58 E7
Kontum, Plateau du, *Vietnam* 58 E7
Konya, *Turkey* 66 D5
Konya Ovası, *Turkey* 66 C5
Konz, *Germany* 19 F2
Konza, *Kenya* 82 C4
Kookynie, *Australia* 89 E3
Kooline, *Australia* 88 D2
Kooloonong, *Australia* 91 E3
Koolyanobbing, *Australia* 89 F2
Koondrook, *Australia* 91 F3
Koonibba, *Australia* 91 E1
Koorawatha, *Australia* 91 E4
Koorda, *Australia* 89 F2
Kooskia, *U.S.A.* 110 C6
Kootenai →, *Canada* 110 B5
Kootenay L., *Canada* 100 D5
Kootenay Nat. Park, *Canada* 100 C5
Kootjieskolk, *S. Africa* 84 E3
Kopanovka, *Russia* 43 G8
Kopaonik, *Serbia, Yug.* 21 M11
Kópavogur, *Iceland* 8 D3
Koper, *Slovenia* 33 C10
Kopervik, *Norway* 9 G11
Kopeysk, *Russia* 44 D7
Kopi, *Australia* 91 E2
Köping, *Sweden* 10 E10
Kopiste, *Croatia* 33 F13
Köpmanholmen, *Sweden* 10 A12
Koppang, *Norway* 10 C5
Kopperå, *Norway* 10 A5
Koppies, *S. Africa* 85 D4
Koprivnica, *Croatia* 33 B13
Kopychyntsi, *Ukraine* 41 H3
Korab, *Macedonia* 39 H3
Korakiána, *Greece* 37 A3
Korba, *India* 63 H10
Korbach, *Germany* 18 D4
Korbu, G., *Malaysia* 59 K3
Korça, *Albania* 39 J3
Korce = Korça, *Albania* 39 J3
Korčula, *Croatia* 33 F14
Korčulanski Kanal, *Croatia* 33 E13
Kord Kūy, *Iran* 65 B7
Kord Sheykh, *Iran* 65 D7
Kordestān □, *Iran* 64 C5
Kordofân, *Sudan* 73 F10
Korea, North ■, *Asia* 51 E14
Korea, South ■, *Asia* 51 F15
Korea Bay, *Korea* 51 E13
Korea Strait, *Asia* 51 G15
Korenevo, *Russia* 42 E2
Korenovsk, *Russia* 43 H4
Korets, *Ukraine* 41 G4
Korgan, *Turkey* 66 B7
Korgus, *Sudan* 76 D3
Korhogo, *Ivory C.* 78 D3
Koribundu, *S. Leone* 78 D2
Korim, *Indonesia* 57 E9
Korinthiakós Kólpos, *Greece* 39 L5
Kórinthos, *Greece* 39 M5
Korioumé, *Mali* 78 B4
Koríssa, Límni, *Greece* 37 B3
Kōriyama, *Japan* 48 F10
Korkuteli, *Turkey* 66 D4
Kormakiti, C., *Cyprus* 37 D11
Körmend, *Hungary* 21 H6
Kornat, *Croatia* 33 E12
Korneshty = Cornești, *Moldova* 41 J5
Kornsjø, *Norway* 10 F5
Kornstad, *Norway* 10 B1
Koro, *Fiji* 87 C8
Koro, *Ivory C.* 78 D3
Koro, *Mali* 78 C4
Koro Sea, *Fiji* 87 C9
Korocha, *Russia* 42 E3
Köroğlu Dağları, *Turkey* 66 B5
Korogwe, *Tanzania* 82 D4
Korogwe □, *Tanzania* 82 D4
Koroit, *Australia* 91 F3
Koronadal, *Phil.* 55 H6
Koronowo, *Poland* 20 B7
Koror, *Pac. Oc.* 57 C8
Körös →, *Hungary* 21 J10
Korosten, *Ukraine* 41 G5
Korostyshev, *Ukraine* 41 G5
Korotoyak, *Russia* 42 E4
Korraraika, Helodranon' i, *Madag.* 85 B7
Korsakov, *Russia* 45 E15
Korshunovo, *Russia* 45 D12
Korsør, *Denmark* 9 J14
Korsun Shevchenkovskiy, *Ukraine* 41 H6
Korsze, *Poland* 20 A11
Kortemark, *Belgium* 17 F2
Kortessem, *Belgium* 17 G6
Korti, *Sudan* 76 D3
Kortrijk, *Belgium* 17 G2
Korwai, *India* 62 G8
Koryakskoye Nagorye, *Russia* 45 C18
Koryŏng, *S. Korea* 51 G15
Koryukovka, *Ukraine* 41 G7
Kos, *Greece* 39 N10
Kosa, *Ethiopia* 77 F4
Kosaya Gora, *Russia* 42 C3
Kościan, *Poland* 20 C6
Kościerzyna, *Poland* 20 A7
Kosciusko, *U.S.A.* 109 J10
Kosciusko, Mt., *Australia* 91 F4
Kosciusko I., *U.S.A.* 100 B2
Kösély →, *Hungary* 21 H11
Kosha, *Sudan* 76 C3
K'oshih = Kashi, *China* 54 C2
Koshiki-Rettō, *Japan* 49 J4
Kosi, *India* 62 F7
Košice, *Slovak Rep.* 20 G11
Kosjerić, *Serbia, Yug.* 21 M9
Koskhinoú, *Greece* 37 C10
Kosŏng, *N. Korea* 51 E15
Kosovska-Mitrovica = Titova-Mitrovica, *Serbia, Yug.* 21 N10
Kostajnica, *Croatia* 33 C13
Kostanjevica, *Slovenia* 33 C12
Kostelec, *Czech.* 20 E6
Koster, *S. Africa* 84 D4
Kôstî, *Sudan* 77 E3
Kostopil, *Ukraine* 41 G4
Kostroma, *Russia* 42 B5
Kostromskoye Vdkhr., *Russia* 42 B5
Kostyantynivka, *Ukraine* 41 H9
Kostyukovichi = Kastsyukovichy, *Belarus* 40 F7
Koszalin, *Poland* 20 A6
Kőszeg, *Hungary* 21 H6
Kot Addu, *Pakistan* 62 D4
Kot Moman, *Pakistan* 62 C5
Kota, *India* 62 G6
Kota Baharu, *Malaysia* 59 J4
Kota Belud, *Malaysia* 56 C5
Kota Kinabalu, *Malaysia* 56 C5
Kota Tinggi, *Malaysia* 59 M4
Kotaagung, *Indonesia* 56 F2
Kotabaru, *Indonesia* 56 E5
Kotabumi, *Indonesia* 56 E2
Kotagede, *Indonesia* 57 G14
Kotamobagu, *Indonesia* 57 D6
Kotaneelee →, *Canada* 100 A4
Kotawaringin, *Indonesia* 56 E4
Kotcho L., *Canada* 100 B4
Kotelnich, *Russia* 42 A9
Kotelnikovo, *Russia* 43 G6
Kotelnyy, Ostrov, *Russia* 45 B14
Köthen, *Germany* 18 D7
Kothi, *India* 63 G9
Kotiro, *Pakistan* 62 F2
Kotka, *Finland* 9 F22
Kotlas, *Russia* 44 C5
Kotli, *Pakistan* 62 C5
Kotmul, *Pakistan* 63 B6
Kotonkoro, *Nigeria* 79 C6
Kotor, *Montenegro, Yug.* 21 N8
Kotoriba, *Croatia* 33 B13
Kotovo, *Russia* 42 E7
Kotovsk, *Russia* 42 D5
Kotovsk, *Ukraine* 41 J5
Kotputli, *India* 62 F7
Kotri, *Pakistan* 62 G3
Kótronas, *Greece* 39 N5
Kottayam, *India* 60 Q10
Kotturu, *India* 60 M10
Kotuy →, *Russia* 45 B11
Kotzebue, *U.S.A.* 96 B3
Kouango, *C.A.R.* 80 C4
Koudekerke, *Neths.* 17 F3
Koudougou, *Burkina Faso* 78 C4
Koufonísi, *Greece* 37 E8
Kougaberge, *S. Africa* 84 E3
Kouibli, *Ivory C.* 78 D3
Kouilou →, *Congo* 80 E2
Kouki, *C.A.R.* 80 C3
Koula Moutou, *Gabon* 80 E2
Koulen, *Cambodia* 58 F5
Koulikoro, *Mali* 78 C3
Kouloúra, *Greece* 37 A3
Koúm-bournoú, Ákra, *Greece* 37 C10
Koumala, *Australia* 90 C4
Koumankou, *Mali* 78 C3
Koumbia, *Burkina Faso* 78 C4
Koumbia, *Guinea* 78 C2
Koumboum, *Guinea* 78 C2
Koumpenntoum, *Senegal* 78 C2
Koumra, *Chad* 73 G8
Koundara, *Guinea* 78 C2
Kounradskiy, *Kazakhstan* 44 E8
Kountze, *U.S.A.* 109 K7
Koupéla, *Burkina Faso* 79 C4
Kouris →, *Cyprus* 37 E11
Kourou, *Fr. Guiana* 121 B7
Kouroussa, *Guinea* 78 C3
Koussané, *Mali* 78 C2
Kousseri, *Cameroon* 73 F7
Koutiala, *Mali* 78 C3
Kouto, *Ivory C.* 78 D3
Kouvé, *Togo* 79 D5
Kouvola, *Finland* 9 F22
Kovačica, *Serbia, Yug.* 21 K10
Kovel, *Ukraine* 41 G3
Kovin, *Serbia, Yug.* 21 L10
Kovrov, *Russia* 42 B5
Kowanyama, *Australia* 90 B3
Kowkash, *Canada* 98 B2
Kowloon, *H.K.* 53 F10
Kowŏn, *N. Korea* 51 E14
Köyceğiz, *Turkey* 66 D3
Koyuk, *U.S.A.* 96 B3
Koyukuk →, *U.S.A.* 96 B4
Koyulhisar, *Turkey* 66 B7
Koza, *Japan* 49 L3
Kozan, *Turkey* 66 D6
Kozáni, *Greece* 39 J4
Kozara, *Bos.-H.* 33 D14
Kozarac, *Bos.-H.* 33 D13
Kozelets, *Ukraine* 41 G6
Kozelsk, *Russia* 42 C2
Kozhikode = Calicut, *India* 60 P9
Kozje, *Slovenia* 33 B12
Kozlovets, *Bulgaria* 38 F8
Kozlovka, *Russia* 42 C9
Kozlu, *Turkey* 66 B4
Kozluk, *Turkey* 67 C9
Koźmin, *Poland* 20 D7
Kozmodemyansk, *Russia* 42 B8
Kozyatyn, *Ukraine* 41 H5
Kpabia, *Ghana* 79 D4
Kpalimé, *Togo* 79 D5
Kpandae, *Ghana* 79 D4
Kpessi, *Togo* 79 D5
Kra, Isthmus of = Kra, Kho Khot, *Thailand* 59 G2
Kra, Kho Khot, *Thailand* 59 G2
Kra Buri, *Thailand* 59 G2
Krabbendijke, *Neths.* 17 F4
Krabi, *Thailand* 59 H2
Kragan, *Indonesia* 57 G14
Kragerø, *Norway* 10 F3
Kragujevac, *Serbia, Yug.* 21 L10
Krajina, *Bos.-H.* 33 D13
Krakatau = Rakata, Pulau, *Indonesia* 56 F3
Krakor, *Cambodia* 58 F5
Kraków, *Poland* 20 E9
Kraksaan, *Indonesia* 57 G15
Kråkstad, *Norway* 10 E4
Kralanh, *Cambodia* 58 F4
Králiky, *Czech.* 20 E6
Kraljevo, *Serbia, Yug.* 21 M10
Kralovice, *Czech.* 20 F3
Kralupy, *Czech.* 20 E4
Kramatorsk, *Ukraine* 41 H9
Kramfors, *Sweden* 10 B11
Kramis, C., *Algeria* 75 A5
Krångede, *Sweden* 10 A10
Kranj, *Slovenia* 33 B11
Kranjska Gora, *Slovenia* 33 B10
Krankskop, *S. Africa* 85 D5
Krapina, *Croatia* 33 B12
Krapina →, *Croatia* 33 C12
Krapkowice, *Poland* 20 E7
Kraskino, *Russia* 45 E14
Krāslava, *Latvia* 40 E4
Kraslice, *Czech.* 20 E2
Krasnaya Gorbatka, *Russia* 42 C5
Krasnaya Polyana, *Russia* 43 J5
Kraśnik, *Poland* 20 E12
Kraśnik Fabryczny, *Poland* 20 E12
Krasnoarmeisk, *Ukraine* 41 H9
Krasnoarmeysk, *Russia* 42 E7
Krasnoarmeyskiy, *Russia* 43 G6
Krasnodar, *Russia* 43 H4
Krasnodon, *Ukraine* 41 H10
Krasnogorskiy, *Russia* 42 B9
Krasnograd = Krasnohrad, *Ukraine* 41 H8
Krasnogvardeyskoye, *Russia* 43 H5
Krasnogvardyesk, *Ukraine* 41 K8
Krasnohrad, *Ukraine* 41 H8
Krasnokutsk, *Ukraine* 41 G8
Krasnolesnyy, *Russia* 42 E4
Krasnoperekopsk, *Ukraine* 41 J7
Krasnorechenskiy, *Russia* 45 B7
Krasnoselkupsk, *Russia* 44 C9
Krasnoslobodsk, *Russia* 42 C6
Krasnoslobodsk, *Russia* 43 F7
Krasnoturinsk, *Russia* 44 D7
Krasnoufimsk, *Russia* 44 D6
Krasnouralsk, *Russia* 44 D7
Krasnovodsk = Krasnowodsk, *Turkmenistan* 44 E6
Krasnowodsk, *Turkmenistan* 44 E6
Krasnoyarsk, *Russia* 45 D10
Krasnoye = Krasnyy, *Russia* 40 E6
Krasnozavodsk, *Russia* 42 B4
Krasny Sulin, *Russia* 43 G5
Krasnystaw, *Poland* 20 E13
Krasnyy, *Russia* 40 E6
Krasnyy Kholm, *Russia* 42 A3
Krasnyy Kut, *Russia* 42 E8
Krasnyy Liman, *Ukraine* 41 H9
Krasnyy Luch, *Ukraine* 41 H10
Krasnyy Profintern, *Russia* 42 B5
Krasnyy Yar, *Russia* 42 D10
Krasnyy Yar, *Russia* 42 E7
Krasnyy Yar, *Russia* 43 G9
Krasnyye Baki, *Russia* 42 B7
Krasnyyoskolske Vdskh., *Ukraine* 41 H9
Kraszna →, *Hungary* 21 G12
Kratie, *Cambodia* 58 F6
Krau, *Indonesia* 57 E10
Kravanh, Chuor Phnum, *Cambodia* 59 G4
Krefeld, *Germany* 18 D2
Krémaston, Límni, *Greece* 39 L4
Kremenchug = Kremenchuk, *Ukraine* 41 H7
Kremenchuk, *Ukraine* 41 H7
Kremenchuksk Vdskh., *Ukraine* 41 H7
Kremenets, *Ukraine* 41 G3
Kremennaya, *Ukraine* 41 H10
Kremges = Svitlovodsk, *Ukraine* 41 H7
Kremikovtsi, *Bulgaria* 38 G6
Kremmen, *Germany* 18 C9
Kremmling, *U.S.A.* 110 F10
Krems, *Austria* 21 G5
Kremsmünster, *Austria* 21 G4
Kretinga, *Lithuania* 9 J19
Krettamia, *Algeria* 74 C4
Krettsy, *Russia* 40 C7
Kreuzberg, *Germany* 19 E5
Kreuzlingen, *Switz.* 23 A8
Kribi, *Cameroon* 79 E6
Krichem, *Bulgaria* 38 G7
Krichev = Krychaw, *Belarus* 40 F6
Krim, *Slovenia* 33 C11
Krimpen, *Neths.* 16 E5
Kriós, Ákra, *Greece* 37 D5
Krishna →, *India* 61 M12
Krishnanagar, *India* 63 H13
Kristiansand, *Norway* 9 G13
Kristianstad, *Sweden* 9 H16
Kristiansund, *Norway* 10 A1
Kristiinankaupunki, *Finland* 9 E19
Kristinehamn, *Sweden* 9 G16
Kristinestad = Kristiinankaupunki, *Finland* 9 E19
Kríti, *Greece* 37 D7
Kritsá, *Greece* 37 D7
Kriva →, *Macedonia* 38 G4
Kriva Palanka, *Macedonia* 38 G5
Krivaja →, *Bos.-H.* 21 L8
Krivoy Rog = Kryvyy Rih, *Ukraine* 41 J7
Križevci, *Croatia* 33 B13
Krk, *Croatia* 33 C11
Krka →, *Slovenia* 33 C12
Krkonoše, *Czech.* 20 E5
Krnov, *Czech.* 20 E7
Krobia, *Poland* 20 D6
Krokeaí, *Greece* 39 N5
Krokodil →, *Mozam.* 85 D5
Krokom, *Sweden* 10 A8
Krolevets, *Ukraine* 41 G7
Kroměříz, *Czech.* 20 F7
Krommenie, *Neths.* 16 D5
Kromy, *Russia* 42 D2
Kronach, *Germany* 19 E7
Kronprins Olav Kyst, *Antarctica* 5 C5
Kronshtadt, *Russia* 40 C5
Kroonstad, *S. Africa* 84 D4
Kröpelin, *Germany* 18 A7
Kropotkin, *Irkutsk, Russia* 45 D12
Kropotkin, *Krasnodar, Russia* 43 H5
Kropp, *Germany* 18 A5
Krościenko, *Poland* 20 F10
Krosno, *Poland* 20 F11
Krosno Odrzańskie, *Poland* 20 C5
Krotoszyn, *Poland* 20 D7
Krotovka, *Russia* 42 D10
Kroussón, *Greece* 37 D6
Krško, *Slovenia* 33 C12
Kruger Nat. Park, *S. Africa* 85 C5
Krugersdorp, *S. Africa* 85 D4
Kruiningen, *Neths.* 17 F4
Kruisfontein, *S. Africa* 84 E3
Kruishoutem, *Belgium* 17 G3
Kruisland, *Neths.* 17 E4
Kruja, *Albania* 39 H2
Krulevshchina = Krulyewshchyna, *Belarus* 40 E4
Krulyewshchyna, *Belarus* 40 E4
Kruma, *Albania* 38 G3
Krumbach, *Germany* 19 G6
Krung Thep = Bangkok, *Thailand* 58 F3
Krupanj, *Serbia, Yug.* 21 L9
Krupinica →, *Slovak Rep.* 21 G8
Krupki, *Belarus* 40 E5
Kruševac, *Serbia, Yug.* 21 M11
Kruzof I., *U.S.A.* 100 B1
Krychaw, *Belarus* 40 F6
Krymsk, *Russia* 43 H4
Krymskiy Poluostrov = Krymskyy Pivostriv, *Ukraine* 41 K8
Krymskyy Pivostriv, *Ukraine* 41 K8
Krynica Morska, *Poland* 20 A9
Krynki, *Poland* 20 B13
Kryvyy Rih, *Ukraine* 41 J7
Krzywiń, *Poland* 20 D6
Krzyz, *Poland* 20 C6
Ksabi, *Morocco* 74 B4
Ksar Chellala, *Algeria* 75 A5
Ksar el Boukhari, *Algeria* 75 A5
Ksar el Kebir, *Morocco* 74 B3
Ksar es Souk = Ar Rachidiya, *Morocco* 74 B4
Ksar Rhilane, *Tunisia* 75 B6
Ksour, Mts. des, *Algeria* 75 B4
Kstovo, *Russia* 42 B7
Kuala, *Indonesia* 56 D3
Kuala Berang, *Malaysia* 59 K4
Kuala Dungun, *Malaysia* 59 K4
Kuala Kangsar, *Malaysia* 59 K3
Kuala Kelawang, *Malaysia* 59 L4
Kuala Kerai, *Malaysia* 59 K4
Kuala Kubu Baharu, *Malaysia* 59 L3
Kuala Lipis, *Malaysia* 59 K4
Kuala Lumpur, *Malaysia* 59 L3
Kuala Nerang, *Malaysia* 59 J3
Kuala Pilah, *Malaysia* 59 L4
Kuala Rompin, *Malaysia* 59 L4
Kuala Selangor, *Malaysia* 59 L3
Kuala Terengganu, *Malaysia* 59 K4
Kualajelai, *Indonesia* 56 E4
Kualakapuas, *Indonesia* 56 E4
Kualakurun, *Indonesia* 56 E4
Kualapembuang, *Indonesia* 56 E4
Kualasimpang, *Indonesia* 56 D1
Kuancheng, *China* 51 D10
Kuandang, *Indonesia* 57 D6
Kuandian, *China* 51 D13
Kuangchou = Guangzhou, *China* 53 F9
Kuantan, *Malaysia* 59 L4
Kuba = Quba, *Azerbaijan* 43 K9
Kuban →, *Russia* 43 H3
Kubenskoye, Ozero, *Russia* 40 C10
Kubokawa, *Japan* 49 H6
Kubrat, *Bulgaria* 38 F9
Kučevo, *Serbia, Yug.* 21 L11
Kucha Gompa, *India* 63 B7
Kuchaman, *India* 62 F6
Kuchino-eruba-Jima, *Japan* 49 J5
Kuchino-Shima, *Japan* 49 K4
Kuchinotsu, *Japan* 49 H5
Kucing, *Malaysia* 56 D4
Kuçova, *Albania* 39 J2
Kud →, *Pakistan* 62 F2
Kuda, *India* 60 H7
Kudat, *Malaysia* 56 C5
Kudus, *Indonesia* 57 G14
Kudymkar, *Russia* 44 D6
Kueiyang = Guiyang, *China* 52 D6
Kufstein, *Austria* 19 H8
Kugong I., *Canada* 98 A4
Kūh-e-Hazārām, *Iran* 65 D8
Kūhak, *Iran* 60 F3
Kūhbonān, *Iran* 65 D8
Kūhestak, *Iran* 65 E8
Kūhīn, *Iran* 65 C6
Kūhīrī, *Iran* 65 E9
Kuhnsdorf, *Austria* 21 J4
Kūhpāyeh, *Eşfahan, Iran* 65 C7
Kūhpāyeh, *Kermān, Iran* 65 D8
Kui Buri, *Thailand* 59 F2
Kuinre, *Neths.* 16 C7
Kuito, *Angola* 81 G3
Kujang, *N. Korea* 51 E14
Kuji, *Japan* 48 D10
Kujū-San, *Japan* 49 H5
Kukawa, *Nigeria* 79 C7
Kukerin, *Australia* 89 F2
Kukmor, *Russia* 42 B10
Kukup, *Malaysia* 59 M4
Kukvidze, *Russia* 42 E6
Kula, *Serbia, Yug.* 21 K9
Kula, *Turkey* 66 C3
Kulai, *Malaysia* 59 M4
Kulal, Mt., *Kenya* 82 B4
Kulaly, Ostrov, *Kazakhstan* 43 H10
Kulasekarappattinam, *India* 60 Q11
Kuldiga, *Latvia* 9 H19
Kuldja = Yining, *China* 44 E9
Kuldu, *Sudan* 77 E2
Kulebaki, *Russia* 42 C6
Kulen Vakuf, *Bos.-H.* 33 D13
Kulgam, *India* 63 C6
Kulim, *Malaysia* 59 K3
Kulin, *Australia* 89 F2
Kulja, *Australia* 89 F2
Kulm, *U.S.A.* 108 B5
Kulmbach, *Germany* 19 E7
Kŭlob, *Tajikistan* 44 F7
Kulp, *Turkey* 67 C9
Kulsary, *Kazakhstan* 44 E6
Kulti, *India* 63 H12
Kulu, *Turkey* 66 C5
Kulumbura, *Australia* 88 B4
Kulunda, *Russia* 44 D8
Kulungar, *Afghan.* 62 C3
Kūlvand, *Iran* 65 D7
Kulwin, *Australia* 91 F3
Kulyab = Kŭlob, *Tajikistan* 44 F7

Kum Tekei

Kum Tekei, *Kazakhstan* 44 E8
Kuma →, *Russia* 43 H8
Kumaganum, *Nigeria* 79 C7
Kumagaya, *Japan* 49 F9
Kumai, *Indonesia* 56 E4
Kumamba, Kepulauan, *Indonesia* 57 E9
Kumamoto, *Japan* 49 H5
Kumamoto □, *Japan* 49 H5
Kumanovo, *Macedonia* 38 G4
Kumara, *N.Z.* 87 K3
Kumarl, *Australia* 89 F3
Kumasi, *Ghana* 78 D4
Kumayri = Gyumri, *Armenia* 43 K6
Kumba, *Cameroon* 79 E6
Kumbakonam, *India* 60 P11
Kumbarilla, *Australia* 91 D5
Kumbo, *Cameroon* 79 D7
Kŭmchŏn, *N. Korea* 51 E14
Kumdok, *India* 63 C8
Kume-Shima, *Japan* 49 L3
Kumeny, *Russia* 42 A9
Kŭmhwa, *S. Korea* 51 E14
Kumi, *Uganda* 82 B3
Kumla, *Sweden* 9 G16
Kumluca, *Turkey* 66 D4
Kummerower See, *Germany* 18 B8
Kumo, *Nigeria* 79 C7
Kumon Bum, *Burma* 61 F20
Kumylzhenskaya, *Russia* 42 F6
Kunama, *Australia* 91 F4
Kunashir, Ostrov, *Russia* 45 E15
Kunda, *Estonia* 9 G22
Kundla, *India* 62 J4
Kungala, *Australia* 91 D5
Kungälv, *Sweden* 11 G5
Kunghit I., *Canada* 100 C2
Kungrad = Qŭnghirot, *Uzbekistan* 44 E6
Kungsbacka, *Sweden* 11 G6
Kungur, *Russia* 44 D6
Kungurri, *Australia* 90 C4
Kunhar →, *Pakistan* 63 B5
Kunhegyes, *Hungary* 21 H10
Kuningan, *Indonesia* 57 G13
Kunlong, *Burma* 61 H21
Kunlun Shan, *Asia* 54 C3
Kunming, *China* 52 E4
Kunrade, *Neths.* 17 G7
Kunsan, *S. Korea* 51 G14
Kunshan, *China* 53 B13
Kununurra, *Australia* 88 C4
Kunwarara, *Australia* 90 C5
Kunya-Urgench = Köneürgench, *Turkmenistan* 44 E6
Künzelsau, *Germany* 19 F5
Kuopio, *Finland* 8 E22
Kupa →, *Croatia* 33 C13
Kupang, *Indonesia* 57 F6
Kupres, *Bos.-H.* 21 L7
Kupyansk, *Ukraine* 41 H9
Kupyansk-Uzlovoi, *Ukraine* 41 H9
Kuqa, *China* 54 B3
Kür →, *Azerbaijan* 67 C13
Kura = Kür →, *Azerbaijan* 67 C13
Kuranda, *Australia* 90 B4
Kurashiki, *Japan* 49 G6
Kurayoshi, *Japan* 49 G6
Kürdämir, *Azerbaijan* 43 K9
Kurdistan, *Asia* 67 D10
Kŭrdzhali, *Bulgaria* 39 H8
Kure, *Japan* 49 G6
Küre, *Turkey* 66 B5
Küre Dağları, *Turkey* 66 B6
Kuressaare, *Estonia* 9 G20
Kuressaare, *Russia* 40 C5
Kurgaldzhinskiy, *Kazakhstan* 44 D8
Kurgan, *Russia* 44 D7
Kurganinsk, *Russia* 43 H5
Kurgannaya = Kurganinsk, *Russia* 43 H5
Kuria Maria Is. = Khūrīyā Mūrīyā, Jazā 'ir, *Oman* 68 D6
Kuridala, *Australia* 90 C3
Kurigram, *Bangla.* 61 G16
Kurikka, *Finland* 9 E20
Kuril Is. = Kurilskiye Ostrova, *Russia* 45 E15
Kuril Trench, *Pac. Oc.* 92 C7
Kurilsk, *Russia* 45 E15
Kurilskiye Ostrova, *Russia* 45 E15
Kuringen, *Belgium* 17 G6
Kurino, *Japan* 49 J5
Kurinskaya Kosa, *Azerbaijan* 67 C13
Kurkur, *Egypt* 76 C3
Kurlovskiy, *Russia* 42 C5
Kurmuk, *Sudan* 77 E3
Kurnool, *India* 60 M10
Kuro-Shima, *Kagoshima, Japan* 49 J4
Kuro-Shima, *Okinawa, Japan* 49 M2
Kurow, *N.Z.* 87 L3
Kurrajong, *Australia* 91 E5
Kurram →, *Pakistan* 62 C4
Kurri Kurri, *Australia* 91 E5
Kursavka, *Russia* 43 H6
Kurshskiy Zaliv, *Russia* 9 J19
Kursk, *Russia* 42 E3
Kuršumlija, *Serbia, Yug.* 21 M11
Kurşunlu, *Turkey* 66 B5
Kurtalan, *Turkey* 67 D9
Kuru, Bahr el →, *Sudan* 77 F2
Kurucaşile, *Turkey* 66 B5
Kuruktag, *China* 54 B3
Kuruman, *S. Africa* 84 D3
Kuruman →, *S. Africa* 84 D3
Kurume, *Japan* 49 H5
Kurunegala, *Sri Lanka* 60 R12
Kurupukari, *Guyana* 121 C6
Kurya, *Russia* 45 C11
Kus Gölü, *Turkey* 66 B2
Kuşadası, *Turkey* 66 D2
Kusatsu, *Japan* 49 F9
Kusawa L., *Canada* 100 A1
Kusel, *Germany* 19 F3
Kushchevskaya, *Russia* 43 G4
Kushikino, *Japan* 49 J5
Kushima, *Japan* 49 J5
Kushimoto, *Japan* 49 H7
Kushiro, *Japan* 48 C12
Kushiro →, *Japan* 48 C12
Kūshk, *Iran* 65 D8
Kushka = Gushgy, *Turkmenistan* 44 F7
Kūshkī, *Īlām, Iran* 64 C5
Kūshkī, *Khorāsān, Iran* 65 B8
Kūshkū, *Iran* 65 E7
Kushol, *India* 63 C7
Kushtia, *Bangla.* 61 H16
Kushum →, *Kazakhstan* 42 F10
Kuskokwim →, *U.S.A.* 96 B3
Kuskokwim B., *U.S.A.* 96 C3
Küsnacht, *Switz.* 23 B7
Kussharo-Ko, *Japan* 48 C12
Küssnacht, *Switz.* 23 B6
Kustanay = Qostanay, *Kazakhstan* 44 D7
Kut, Ko, *Thailand* 59 G4
Kütahya, *Turkey* 66 C4
Kutaisi, *Georgia* 43 J6
Kutaraja = Banda Aceh, *Indonesia* 56 C1
Kutch, Gulf of = Kachchh, Gulf of, *India* 62 H3
Kutch, Rann of = Kachchh, Rann of, *India* 62 G4
Kutina, *Croatia* 33 C13
Kutiyana, *India* 62 J4
Kutkashen, *Azerbaijan* 43 K8
Kutná Hora, *Czech.* 20 F5
Kutno, *Poland* 20 C9
Kuttabul, *Australia* 90 C4
Kutu, *Zaïre* 80 E3
Kutum, *Sudan* 77 E1
Kuujjuaq, *Canada* 97 C13
Kuŭp-tong, *N. Korea* 51 D14
Kuurne, *Belgium* 17 G2
Kuusamo, *Finland* 8 D23
Kuusankoski, *Finland* 9 F22
Kuvshinovo, *Russia* 42 B2
Kuwait = Al Kuwayt, *Kuwait* 64 D5
Kuwait ■, *Asia* 64 D5
Kuwana, *Japan* 49 G8
Kuybyshev = Samara, *Russia* 42 D10
Kuybyshev, *Russia* 44 D8
Kuybyshevo, *Ukraine* 41 J9
Kuybyshevskoye Vdkhr., *Russia* 42 C9
Kuye He →, *China* 50 E6
Kūyeh, *Iran* 64 B5
Kūysanjaq, *Iraq* 67 D11
Kuyumba, *Russia* 45 C10
Kuzey Anadolu Dağları, *Turkey* 66 B7
Kuznetsk, *Russia* 42 D8
Kvænangen, *Norway* 8 A19
Kvaløy, *Norway* 8 B18
Kvam, *Norway* 10 C3
Kvareli = Qvareli, *Georgia* 43 K7
Kvarner, *Croatia* 33 D11
Kvarnerič, *Croatia* 33 D11
Kviteseid, *Norway* 10 E2
Kwabhaca, *S. Africa* 85 E4
Kwadacha →, *Canada* 100 B3
Kwakhanai, *Botswana* 84 C3
Kwakoegron, *Surinam* 121 B6
Kwale, *Kenya* 82 C4
Kwale, *Nigeria* 79 D6
Kwale □, *Kenya* 82 C4
KwaMashu, *S. Africa* 85 D5
Kwamouth, *Zaïre* 80 E3
Kwando →, *Africa* 84 B3
Kwangdaeri, *N. Korea* 51 D14
Kwangju, *S. Korea* 51 G14
Kwangsi-Chuang = Guangxi Zhuangzu Zizhiqu □, *China* 52 E7
Kwangtung = Guangdong □, *China* 53 F9
Kwara □, *Nigeria* 79 D5
Kwataboahegan →, *Canada* 98 B3
Kwatisore, *Indonesia* 57 E8
KwaZulu Natal □, *S. Africa* 85 D5
Kweichow = Guizhou □, *China* 52 D6
Kwekwe, *Zimbabwe* 83 F2
Kwimba □, *Tanzania* 82 C3
Kwinana New Town, *Australia* 89 F2
Kwoka, *Indonesia* 57 E8
Kyabé, *Chad* 73 G8
Kyabra Cr. →, *Australia* 91 D3
Kyabram, *Australia* 91 F4
Kyaikto, *Burma* 58 D1
Kyakhta, *Russia* 45 D11
Kyancutta, *Australia* 91 E2
Kyangin, *Burma* 61 K19
Kyaukpadaung, *Burma* 61 J19
Kyaukpyu, *Burma* 61 K18
Kyaukse, *Burma* 61 J20
Kyburz, *U.S.A.* 112 G6
Kyenjojo, *Uganda* 82 B3
Kyle Dam, *Zimbabwe* 83 G3
Kyle of Lochalsh, *U.K.* 14 D3
Kyll →, *Germany* 19 F2
Kyllburg, *Germany* 19 E2
Kymijoki →, *Finland* 9 F22
Kyneton, *Australia* 91 F3
Kynuna, *Australia* 90 C3
Kyō-ga-Saki, *Japan* 49 G7
Kyoga, L., *Uganda* 82 B3
Kyogle, *Australia* 91 D5
Kyongju, *S. Korea* 51 G15
Kyongpyaw, *Burma* 61 L19
Kyŏngsŏng, *N. Korea* 51 D15
Kyōto, *Japan* 49 G7
Kyōto □, *Japan* 49 G7
Kyparissovouno, *Cyprus* 37 D12
Kyperounda, *Cyprus* 37 E11
Kyren, *Russia* 45 D11
Kyrenia, *Cyprus* 66 E5
Kyrgyzstan ■, *Asia* 44 E8
Kyritz, *Germany* 18 C8
Kyrönjoki →, *Finland* 8 E19
Kystatyam, *Russia* 45 C13
Kytal Ktakh, *Russia* 45 C13
Kythréa, *Cyprus* 37 D12
Kyulyunken, *Russia* 45 C14
Kyunhla, *Burma* 61 H19
Kyuquot, *Canada* 100 C3
Kyurdamir = Kürdämir, *Azerbaijan* 43 K9
Kyūshū, *Japan* 49 H5
Kyūshū □, *Japan* 49 H5
Kyūshū-Sanchi, *Japan* 49 H5
Kyustendil, *Bulgaria* 38 G5
Kyusyur, *Russia* 45 B13
Kywong, *Australia* 91 E4
Kyyiv, *Ukraine* 41 G6
Kyyivske Vdskh., *Ukraine* 41 G6
Kyzyl, *Russia* 45 D10
Kyzyl Kum, *Uzbekistan* 44 E7
Kyzyl-Kyya, *Kyrgyzstan* 44 E8
Kzyl-Orda = Qyzylorda, *Kazakhstan* 44 E7

L

La Albuera, *Spain* 31 G4
La Albufera, *Spain* 29 F4
La Alcarria, *Spain* 28 E2
La Algaba, *Spain* 31 H4
La Almarcha, *Spain* 28 F2
La Almunia de Doña Godina, *Spain* 28 D3
La Asunción, *Venezuela* 121 A5
La Banda, *Argentina* 126 B3
La Bañeza, *Spain* 30 C5
La Barca, *Mexico* 114 C4
La Barge, *U.S.A.* 110 E8
La Bassée, *France* 25 B9
La Bastide-Puylaurent, *France* 26 D7
La Baule, *France* 24 E4
La Belle, *U.S.A.* 105 M5
La Biche →, *Canada* 100 B4
La Bisbal, *Spain* 28 D8
La Blanquilla, *Venezuela* 121 A5
La Bomba, *Mexico* 114 A1
La Bresse, *France* 25 D13
La Bureba, *Spain* 28 C1
La Cal →, *Bolivia* 125 D6
La Calera, *Chile* 126 C1
La Campiña, *Spain* 31 H6
La Canal, *Spain* 36 C7
La Cañiza, *Spain* 30 C2
La Capelle, *France* 25 C10
La Carlota, *Argentina* 126 C3
La Carlota, *Phil.* 55 F5
La Carolina, *Spain* 31 G7
La Cavalerie, *France* 26 D7
La Ceiba, *Honduras* 116 C2
La Chaise-Dieu, *France* 26 C7
La Chaize-le-Vicomte, *France* 24 F5
La Chapelle d'Angillon, *France* 25 E9
La Chapelle-Glain, *France* 24 E5
La Charité-sur-Loire, *France* 25 E10
La Chartre-sur-le-Loir, *France* 24 E7
La Châtaigneraie, *France* 26 B3
La Châtre, *France* 26 B5
La Chaux de Fonds, *Switz.* 22 B3
La Chorrera, *Colombia* 120 D3
La Ciotat, *France* 27 E9
La Clayette, *France* 27 B8
La Cocha, *Argentina* 126 B2
La Concepción = Ri-Aba, *Eq. Guin.* 79 E6
La Concepción, *Venezuela* 120 A3
La Concordia, *Mexico* 115 D6
La Conner, *U.S.A.* 110 B2
La Coruña, *Spain* 30 B2
La Coruña □, *Spain* 30 B2
La Côte, *Switz.* 22 D2
La Côte-St.-André, *France* 27 C9
La Courtine-le-Trucq, *France* 26 C6
La Crau, *France* 27 E8
La Crete, *Canada* 100 B5
La Crosse, *Kans., U.S.A.* 108 F5
La Crosse, *Wis., U.S.A.* 108 D9
La Cruz, *Costa Rica* 116 D2
La Cruz, *Mexico* 114 C3
La Dorada, *Colombia* 120 B3
La Ensenada, *Chile* 128 B2
La Escondida, *Mexico* 114 C5
La Esmeralda, *Paraguay* 126 A3
La Esperanza, *Argentina* 128 B3
La Esperanza, *Cuba* 116 B3
La Esperanza, *Honduras* 116 D2
La Estrada, *Spain* 30 C2
La Fayette, *U.S.A.* 105 H3
La Fé, *Cuba* 116 B3
La Fère, *France* 25 C10
La Ferté-Bernard, *France* 24 D7
La Ferté-Macé, *France* 24 D6
La Ferté-St.-Aubin, *France* 25 E8
La Ferté-sous-Jouarre, *France* 25 D10
La Ferté-Vidame, *France* 24 D7
La Flèche, *France* 24 E6
La Follette, *U.S.A.* 105 G3
La Fregeneda, *Spain* 30 E4
La Fría, *Venezuela* 120 B3
La Fuente de San Esteban, *Spain* 30 E4
La Gineta, *Spain* 29 F2
La Gloria, *Colombia* 120 B3
La Gran Sabana, *Venezuela* 121 B5
La Grand-Combe, *France* 27 D8
La Grande, *U.S.A.* 110 D4
La Grande-Motte, *France* 27 E8
La Grange, *Calif., U.S.A.* 112 H6
La Grange, *Ga., U.S.A.* 105 J3
La Grange, *Ky., U.S.A.* 104 F3
La Grange, *Tex., U.S.A.* 109 L6
La Grita, *Venezuela* 120 B3
La Guaira, *Venezuela* 120 A4
La Guardia, *Spain* 30 D2
La Gudiña, *Spain* 30 C3
La Güera, *Mauritania* 74 D1
La Guerche-de-Bretagne, *France* 24 E5
La Guerche-sur-l'Aubois, *France* 25 F9
La Habana, *Cuba* 116 B3
La Harpe, *U.S.A.* 108 E9
La Haye-du-Puits, *France* 24 C5
La Horqueta, *Venezuela* 121 B5
La Horra, *Spain* 30 D7
La Independencia, *Mexico* 115 D6
La Isabela, *Dom. Rep.* 117 C5
La Jara, *U.S.A.* 111 H11
La Joya, *Peru* 124 D3
La Junquera, *Spain* 28 C7
La Junta, *U.S.A.* 109 F3
La Laguna, *Canary Is.* 36 F3
La Libertad, *Guatemala* 116 C1
La Libertad, *Mexico* 114 B2
La Libertad □, *Peru* 124 B2
La Ligua, *Chile* 126 C1
La Línea de la Concepción, *Spain* 31 J5
La Loche, *Canada* 101 B7
La Londe-les-Maures, *France* 27 E10
La Lora, *Spain* 30 C7
La Loupe, *France* 24 D8
La Louvière, *Belgium* 17 H4
La Machine, *France* 25 F10
La Maddalena, *Italy* 34 A2
La Malbaie, *Canada* 99 C5
La Mancha, *Spain* 29 F2
La Mariña, *Spain* 30 B3
La Mesa, *Calif., U.S.A.* 113 N9
La Mesa, *N. Mex., U.S.A.* 111 K10
La Misión, *Mexico* 114 A1
La Mothe-Achard, *France* 24 F5
La Motte, *France* 27 D10
La Motte-Chalançon, *France* 27 D9
La Moure, *U.S.A.* 108 B5
La Muela, *Spain* 28 D3
La Mure, *France* 27 D9
La Negra, *Chile* 126 A1
La Neuveville, *Switz.* 22 B4
La Oliva, *Canary Is.* 36 F6
La Oraya, *Peru* 124 C2
La Orotava, *Canary Is.* 36 F3
La Pacaudière, *France* 26 B7
La Palma, *Canary Is.* 36 F2
La Palma, *Panama* 116 E4
La Palma del Condado, *Spain* 31 H4
La Paloma, *Chile* 126 C1
La Pampa □, *Argentina* 126 D2
La Paragua, *Venezuela* 121 B5
La Paz, *Entre Ríos, Argentina* 126 C4
La Paz, *San Luis, Argentina* 126 C2
La Paz, *Bolivia* 124 D4
La Paz, *Honduras* 116 D2
La Paz, *Mexico* 114 C2
La Paz, *Phil.* 55 D4
La Paz □, *Bolivia* 124 D4
La Paz Centro, *Nic.* 116 D2
La Pedrera, *Colombia* 120 D4
La Perouse Str., *Asia* 48 B11
La Pesca, *Mexico* 115 C5
La Piedad, *Mexico* 114 C4
La Pine, *U.S.A.* 110 E3
La Plant, *U.S.A.* 108 C4
La Plata, *Argentina* 126 D4
La Plata, *Colombia* 120 C2
La Plata, L., *Argentina* 128 B2
La Pobla de Lillet, *Spain* 28 C6
La Pola de Gordón, *Spain* 30 C5
La Porte, *U.S.A.* 104 E2
La Puebla, *Spain* 28 F8
La Puebla de Cazalla, *Spain* 31 H5
La Puebla de los Infantes, *Spain* 31 H5
La Puebla de Montalbán, *Spain* 30 F6
La Puerta, *Spain* 29 G2
La Punt, *Switz.* 23 C9
La Purísima, *Mexico* 114 B2
La Push, *U.S.A.* 112 C2
La Quiaca, *Argentina* 126 A2
La Rambla, *Spain* 31 H6
La Reine, *Canada* 98 C4
La Réole, *France* 26 D3
La Restinga, *Canary Is.* 36 G2
La Rioja, *Argentina* 126 B2
La Rioja □, *Argentina* 126 B2
La Rioja □, *Spain* 28 C2
La Robla, *Spain* 30 C5
La Roche, *Switz.* 22 C4
La Roche-Bernard, *France* 24 E4
La Roche-Canillac, *France* 26 C5
La Roche-en-Ardenne, *Belgium* 17 H7
La Roche-sur-Yon, *France* 24 F5
La Rochefoucauld, *France* 26 C4
La Rochelle, *France* 26 B2
La Roda, *Albacete, Spain* 29 F2
La Roda, *Sevilla, Spain* 31 H6
La Romana, *Dom. Rep.* 117 C6
La Ronge, *Canada* 101 B7
La Rumorosa, *Mexico* 113 N10
La Sabina, *Spain* 36 C7
La Sagra, *Spain* 29 H2
La Salle, *U.S.A.* 108 E10
La Sanabria, *Spain* 30 C4
La Santa, *Canary Is.* 36 E6
La Sarraz, *Switz.* 22 C3
La Sarre, *Canada* 98 C4
La Scie, *Canada* 99 C8
La Selva, *Spain* 28 D7
La Selva Beach, *U.S.A.* 112 J5
La Serena, *Chile* 126 B1
La Serena, *Spain* 31 G5
La Seyne-sur-Mer, *France* 27 E9
La Sila, *Italy* 35 C9
La Solana, *Spain* 29 G1
La Souterraine, *France* 26 B5
La Spézia, *Italy* 32 D6
La Suze-sur-Sarthe, *France* 24 E7
La Tagua, *Colombia* 120 C3
La Teste, *France* 26 D2
La Tortuga, *Venezuela* 117 D6
La Tour-du-Pin, *France* 27 C9
La Tranche-sur-Mer, *France* 24 F5
La Tremblade, *France* 26 C2
La Tuque, *Canada* 98 C5
La Unión, *Chile* 128 B2
La Unión, *Colombia* 120 C2
La Unión, *El Salv.* 116 D2
La Unión, *Mexico* 114 D4
La Unión, *Peru* 124 B2
La Unión, *Spain* 29 H4
La Urbana, *Venezuela* 120 B4
La Vecilla, *Spain* 30 C5
La Vega, *Dom. Rep.* 117 C5
La Vega, *Peru* 124 C2
La Vela, *Venezuela* 120 A4
La Veleta, *Spain* 31 H7
La Venta, *Mexico* 115 D6
La Ventura, *Mexico* 114 C4
La Venturosa, *Colombia* 120 B4
La Victoria, *Venezuela* 120 A4
La Voulte-sur-Rhône, *France* 27 D8
La Zarza, *Spain* 31 H4
Laaber →, *Germany* 19 G8
Laage, *Germany* 18 B8
Laba →, *Russia* 43 H4
Labason, *Phil.* 55 G5
Labastide-Murat, *France* 26 D5
Labastide-Rouairoux, *France* 26 E6
Labbézenga, *Mali* 79 B5
Labe = Elbe →, *Europe* 18 B4
Labé, *Guinea* 78 C2
Laberec →, *Slovak Rep.* 20 G11
Laberge, L., *Canada* 100 A1
Labin, *Croatia* 33 C11
Labinsk, *Russia* 43 H5
Labis, *Malaysia* 59 L4
Labo, *Phil.* 55 D5
Laboe, *Germany* 18 A6
Labouheyre, *France* 26 D3
Laboulaye, *Argentina* 126 C3
Labra, Peña, *Spain* 30 B6
Labrador, Coast of □, *Canada* 99 B7
Labrador City, *Canada* 99 B6
Lábrea, *Brazil* 125 B5
Labrède, *France* 26 D3
Labuan, Pulau, *Malaysia* 56 C5
Labuha, *Indonesia* 57 E7
Labuhan, *Indonesia* 57 G11
Labuhanbajo, *Indonesia* 57 F6
Labuissière, *Belgium* 17 H4
Labuk, Telok, *Malaysia* 56 C5

Labyrinth, L., *Australia* .. 91 E2
Labytnangi, *Russia* 44 C7
Lac Allard, *Canada* 99 B7
Lac Bouchette, *Canada* ... 99 C5
Lac du Flambeau, *U.S.A.* . 108 B10
Lac Édouard, *Canada* 98 C5
Lac La Biche, *Canada* 100 C6
Lac la Martre, *Canada* ... 96 B8
Lac-Mégantic, *Canada* ... 99 C5
Lac Seul, Res., *Canada* ... 98 B1
Lac Thien, *Vietnam* 58 F7
Lacanau, *France* 26 D2
Lacanau, Étang de, *France* . 26 D2
Lacantúm →, *Mexico* 115 D6
Lacara →, *Spain* 31 G4
Lacaune, *France* 26 E6
Lacaune, Mts. de, *France* . 26 E6
Laccadive Is. =
  Lakshadweep Is.,
  Ind. Oc. 46 H11
Lacepede B., *Australia* ... 91 F2
Lacepede Is., *Australia* ... 88 C3
Lacerdónia, *Mozam.* 83 F4
Lacey, *U.S.A.* 112 C4
Lachay, Pta., *Peru* 124 C2
Lachen, *Switz.* 23 B7
Lachhmangarh, *India* 62 F6
Lachi, *Pakistan* 62 C4
Lachine, *Canada* 98 C5
Lachlan →, *Australia* 91 E3
Lachute, *Canada* 98 C5
Lackawanna, *U.S.A.* 106 D6
Lacolle, *Canada* 107 A11
Lacombe, *Canada* 100 C6
Lacona, *U.S.A.* 107 C8
Láconi, *Italy* 34 C2
Laconia, *U.S.A.* 107 C13
Lacq, *France* 26 E3
Lacrosse, *U.S.A.* 110 C5
Ladakh Ra., *India* 63 B8
Ladário, *Brazil* 125 D6
Ládhon →, *Greece* 39 M4
Ladik, *Turkey* 66 B6
Ladismith, *S. Africa* 84 E3
Lādīz, *Iran* 65 D9
Ladnun, *India* 62 F6
Ladoga, L. = Ladozhskoye
  Ozero, *Russia* 40 B6
Ladon, *France* 25 D9
Ladozhskoye Ozero, *Russia* 40 B6
Ladrillero, G., *Chile* 128 C1
Lady Grey, *S. Africa* 84 E4
Ladybrand, *S. Africa* 84 D4
Ladysmith, *Canada* 100 D4
Ladysmith, *S. Africa* 85 D4
Ladysmith, *U.S.A.* 108 C9
Lae, *Papua N. G.* 92 H6
Laem Ngop, *Thailand* ... 59 F4
Laem Pho, *Thailand* ... 59 J3
Læsø, *Denmark* 11 G4
Læsø Rende, *Denmark* .. 11 G4
Lafayette, Colo., *U.S.A.* . 108 F2
Lafayette, Ind., *U.S.A.* .. 104 E2
Lafayette, La., *U.S.A.* ... 109 K9
Lafayette, Tenn., *U.S.A.* . 105 G3
Laferte →, *Canada* 100 A5
Lafia, *Nigeria* 79 D6
Lafiagi, *Nigeria* 79 D6
Lafleche, *Canada* 101 D7
Lafon, *Sudan* 77 F3
Laforsen, *Sweden* 10 C9
Lagan →, *Sweden* 11 H7
Lagan →, *U.K.* 15 B6
Lagarfljót →, *Iceland* .. 8 D6
Lagarto, *Brazil* 122 D4
Lage, *Germany* 18 D4
Lage, *Spain* 30 B2
Lage-Mierde, *Neths.* ... 17 F6
Lågen →, Oppland,
  Norway 9 F14
Lågen →, Vestfold,
  Norway 9 G14
Lägerdorf, *Germany* ... 18 B5
Laghouat, *Algeria* 75 B5
Lagnieu, *France* 27 C9
Lagny, *France* 25 D9
Lago, *Italy* 35 C9
Lago Posadas, *Argentina* . 128 C2
Lago Ranco, *Chile* 128 B2
Lagôa, *Portugal* 31 H2
Lagoaça, *Portugal* 30 D4
Lagodekhi, *Georgia* ... 43 K8
Lagonégro, *Italy* 35 B8
Lagonoy Gulf, *Phil.* ... 55 E5
Lagos, *Nigeria* 79 D5
Lagos, *Portugal* 31 H2
Lagos de Moreno, *Mexico* 114 C4
Lagrange, *Australia* ... 88 C3
Lagrange B., *Australia* . 88 C3
Laguardia, *Spain* 28 C2
Laguépie, *France* 26 D5
Laguna, *Brazil* 127 B6
Laguna, *U.S.A.* 111 J10
Laguna Beach, *U.S.A.* .. 113 M9
Laguna de la Janda, *Spain* 31 J5
Laguna Limpia, *Argentina* 126 B4
Laguna Madre, *U.S.A.* .. 115 B5
Lagunas, *Chile* 126 A2
Lagunas, *Peru* 124 B2
Lagunillas, *Bolivia* 125 D5
Lahad Datu, *Malaysia* .. 57 C5
Lahan Sai, *Thailand* ... 58 E4
Lahanam, *Laos* 58 D5
Laharpur, *India* 63 F9
Lahat, *Indonesia* 56 E2
Lahewa, *Indonesia* 56 D1

Lāhījān, *Iran* 65 B6
Lahn →, *Germany* 19 E3
Laholm, *Sweden* 11 H7
Laholmsbukten, *Sweden* . 11 H6
Lahontan Reservoir,
  U.S.A. 110 G4
Lahore, *Pakistan* 62 D6
Lahr, *Germany* 19 G3
Lahti, *Finland* 9 F21
Lahtis = Lahti, *Finland* . 9 F21
Laï, *Chad* 73 G8
Lai Chau, *Vietnam* 58 A4
Lai'an, *China* 53 A12
Laibin, *China* 52 F7
Laidley, *Australia* 91 D5
L'Aigle, *France* 24 D7
Laignes, *France* 25 E11
L'Aiguillon-sur-Mer, *France* 26 B2
Laikipia □, *Kenya* 82 B4
Laingsburg, *S. Africa* .. 84 E3
Lainio älv →, *Sweden* . 8 C20
Lairg, *U.K.* 14 C4
Laishui, *China* 50 E8
Laiwu, *China* 51 F9
Laixi, *China* 51 F11
Laiyang, *China* 51 F11
Laiyuan, *China* 50 E8
Laizhou Wan, *China* .. 51 F10
Laja →, *Mexico* 114 C4
Lajere, *Nigeria* 79 C7
Lajes, Rio Grande do N.,
  Brazil 122 C4
Lajes, Sta. Catarina, *Brazil* 127 B5
Lajinha, *Brazil* 123 F3
Lajkovac, *Serbia, Yug.* .. 21 L10
Lajosmizse, *Hungary* .. 21 H9
Lak Sao, *Laos* 58 C5
Lakaband, *Pakistan* ... 62 D3
Lake Alpine, *U.S.A.* ... 112 G7
Lake Andes, *U.S.A.* ... 108 D5
Lake Anse, *U.S.A.* 104 B1
Lake Arthur, *U.S.A.* ... 109 K8
Lake Cargelligo, *Australia* 91 E4
Lake Charles, *U.S.A.* .. 109 K8
Lake City, Colo., *U.S.A.* . 111 G10
Lake City, Fla., *U.S.A.* .. 105 K4
Lake City, Iowa, *U.S.A.* . 108 D7
Lake City, Mich., *U.S.A.* . 104 C3
Lake City, Minn., *U.S.A.* . 108 C8
Lake City, Pa., *U.S.A.* .. 106 D4
Lake City, S.C., *U.S.A.* .. 105 J6
Lake George, *U.S.A.* ... 107 C11
Lake Grace, *Australia* .. 89 F2
Lake Harbour, *Canada* . 97 B13
Lake Havasu City, *U.S.A.* 113 L12
Lake Hughes, *U.S.A.* ... 113 L8
Lake Isabella, *U.S.A.* .. 113 K8
Lake King, *Australia* ... 89 F2
Lake Lenore, *Canada* .. 101 C8
Lake Louise, *Canada* .. 100 C5
Lake Mead National
  Recreation Area, *U.S.A.* 113 K12
Lake Mills, *U.S.A.* 108 D8
Lake Nash, *Australia* .. 90 C2
Lake Providence, *U.S.A.* 109 J9
Lake River, *Canada* ... 98 B3
Lake Superior Prov. Park,
  Canada 98 C3
Lake Village, *U.S.A.* ... 109 J9
Lake Wales, *U.S.A.* ... 105 M5
Lake Worth, *U.S.A.* ... 105 M5
Lakefield, *Canada* 98 D4
Lakeland, *Australia* ... 90 B3
Lakeland, *U.S.A.* 105 L5
Lakemba, *Fiji* 87 D9
Lakeport, *U.S.A.* 112 F4
Lakes Entrance, *Australia* 91 F4
Lakeside, Ariz., *U.S.A.* . 111 J9
Lakeside, Calif., *U.S.A.* . 113 N10
Lakeside, Nebr., *U.S.A.* . 108 D3
Lakeview, *U.S.A.* 110 E3
Lakewood, Colo., *U.S.A.* 108 F2
Lakewood, N.J., *U.S.A.* . 107 F10
Lakewood, Ohio, *U.S.A.* 106 E3
Lakewood Center, *U.S.A.* 112 C4
Lakhaniá, *Greece* 37 D9
Lakhonpheng, *Laos* ... 58 E5
Lakhpat, *India* 62 H3
Laki, *Azerbaijan* 43 K8
Lakin, *U.S.A.* 109 G4
Lakitusaki →, *Canada* . 98 B3
Lákkoi, *Greece* 37 D5
Lakonikós Kólpos, *Greece* 39 N5
Lakor, *Indonesia* 57 F7
Lakota, *Ivory C.* 78 D3
Lakota, *U.S.A.* 108 A5
Laksefjorden, *Norway* . 8 A22
Lakselv, *Norway* 8 A21
Lakshadweep Is., *Ind. Oc.* 46 H11
Lakshmikantapur, *India* 63 H13
Lala Ghat, *India* 61 G18
Lala Musa, *Pakistan* .. 62 C5
Lalago, *Tanzania* 82 C3
Lalapanzi, *Zimbabwe* .. 83 F3
Lalganj, *India* 63 G11
Lalibela, *Ethiopia* 77 E4
Lalín, *Spain* 30 C2
Lalin He →, *China* 51 B13
Lalinde, *France* 26 D4
Lalitapur = Patan, *Nepal* 61 F14
Lalitpur, *India* 63 G8
Lam, *Vietnam* 58 B6
Lam Pao Res., *Thailand* 58 D4
Lama Kara, *Togo* 79 D5
Lamaing, *Burma* 61 M20

Lamar, Colo., *U.S.A.* ... 108 F3
Lamar, Mo., *U.S.A.* ... 109 G7
Lamarque, *Argentina* .. 128 A3
Lamastre, *France* 27 D8
Lamballe, *France* 24 D4
Lambaréné, *Gabon* ... 80 E2
Lambasa, *Fiji* 87 C8
Lambay I., *Ireland* 15 C5
Lambayeque □, *Peru* .. 124 B2
Lambert, *U.S.A.* 108 B2
Lambert Glacier, *Antarctica* 5 D6
Lamberts Bay, *S. Africa* . 84 E2
Lambesc, *France* 27 E9
Lámbia, *Greece* 39 M4
Lambro →, *Italy* 32 C6
Lame, *Nigeria* 79 C6
Lame Deer, *U.S.A.* 110 D10
Lamego, *Portugal* 30 D3
Lamèque, *Canada* 99 C7
Lameroo, *Australia* ... 91 F3
Lamesa, *U.S.A.* 109 J4
Lamía, *Greece* 39 L5
Lamitan, *Phil.* 55 H5
Lammermuir Hills, *U.K.* . 14 F6
Lamon Bay, *Phil.* 55 D5
Lamont, *Canada* 100 C6
Lamont, *U.S.A.* 113 K8
Lampa, *Peru* 124 D3
Lampang, *Thailand* ... 58 C2
Lampasas, *U.S.A.* 109 K5
Lampazos de Naranjo,
  Mexico 114 B4
Lampeter, *U.K.* 13 E3
Lampione, *Medit. S.* .. 75 A7
Lampman, *Canada* 101 D8
Lamprey, *Canada* 101 B10
Lampung □, *Indonesia* . 56 F2
Lamu, *Kenya* 82 C5
Lamu □, *Kenya* 82 C5
Lamud, *Peru* 124 B2
Lamy, *U.S.A.* 111 J11
Lan Xian, *China* 50 E6
Lan Yu, *Taiwan* 53 F13
Lanai I., *U.S.A.* 102 H16
Lanak La, *India* 63 B8
Lanak'o Shank'ou = Lanak
  La, *India* 63 B8
Lanao, L., *Phil.* 55 H6
Lanark, *Canada* 107 A8
Lanark, *U.K.* 14 F5
Lancang, *China* 52 F2
Lancang Jiang →, *China* 52 G3
Lancashire □, *U.K.* ... 12 D5
Lancaster, *Canada* 107 A10
Lancaster, *U.K.* 12 C5
Lancaster, Calif., *U.S.A.* . 113 L8
Lancaster, Ky., *U.S.A.* . 104 G3
Lancaster, N.H., *U.S.A.* . 107 B13
Lancaster, N.Y., *U.S.A.* . 106 D6
Lancaster, Pa., *U.S.A.* . 107 F8
Lancaster, S.C., *U.S.A.* . 105 H5
Lancaster, Wis., *U.S.A.* . 108 D9
Lancaster Sd., *Canada* . 97 A11
Lancer, *Canada* 101 C7
Lanchow = Lanzhou,
  China 50 F2
Lanciano, *Italy* 33 F11
Lanco, *Chile* 128 A2
Lancones, *Peru* 124 A1
Lancun, *China* 51 F11
Lancut, *Poland* 20 E12
Lancy, *Switz.* 22 D2
Landau, Bayern, *Germany* 19 G8
Landau, Rhld-Pfz.,
  Germany 19 F4
Landeck, *Austria* 19 H6
Landen, *Belgium* 17 G6
Lander →, *Australia* .. 88 D5
Landerneau, *France* .. 24 D2
Landeryd, *Sweden* ... 11 G7
Landes, *France* 25 D3
Landes □, *France* 26 E3
Landete, *Spain* 28 F3
Landi Kotal, *Pakistan* . 62 B4
Landivisiau, *France* .. 24 D2
Landor, *Australia* 89 E2
Landquart, *Switz.* 23 C9
Landquart →, *Switz.* .. 23 C9
Landrecies, *France* ... 25 B10
Land's End, *U.K.* 13 G2
Landsberg, *Germany* .. 19 G6
Landsborough Cr. →,
  Australia 90 C3
Landshut, *Germany* ... 19 G7
Landskrona, *Sweden* .. 11 J6
Landstuhl, *Germany* .. 19 F3
Landvetter, *Sweden* .. 11 G6
Laneffe, *Belgium* 17 H5
Lanesboro, *U.S.A.* 107 E9
Lanett, *U.S.A.* 105 J3
Lang Bay, *Canada* 100 D4
Lang Qua, *Vietnam* ... 58 A5
Lang Shan, *China* 50 D4
Lang Son, *Vietnam* ... 58 B6
Lang Suan, *Thailand* .. 59 H2
La'nga Co, *China* 61 D12
Langadhás, *Greece* ... 39 J6
Langádhia, *Greece* ... 39 M5
Långan →, *Sweden* ... 10 A8
Langar, *Iran* 65 C9
Langara I., *U.S.A.* 100 C2
Langatabbetje, *Surinam* . 121 C7
Langdai, *China* 52 D5

Langdon, *U.S.A.* 108 A5
Langeac, *France* 26 C7
Langeais, *France* 24 E7
Langeb Baraka →, *Sudan* 76 D4
Langeberg, *S. Africa* .. 84 E3
Langeberge, *S. Africa* . 84 D3
Langeland, *Denmark* .. 11 K4
Langemark, *Belgium* .. 17 G1
Langen, *Germany* 19 F4
Langenburg, *Canada* .. 101 C8
Langeneß, *Germany* .. 18 A4
Langenthal, *Switz.* ... 22 B5
Langeoog, *Germany* .. 18 B3
Langesund, *Norway* .. 10 F3
Länghem, *Sweden* ... 11 G7
Langhirano, *Italy* 32 D7
Langholm, *U.K.* 14 F6
Langhus, *Norway* 10 E4
Langjökull, *Iceland* ... 8 D3
Langkawi, P., *Malaysia* . 59 J2
Langklip, *S. Africa* ... 84 D3
Langkon, *Malaysia* ... 56 C5
Langlade, *St- P. & M.* . 99 C8
Langlois, *U.S.A.* 110 E1
Langnau, *Switz.* 22 C5
Langogne, *France* 26 D7
Langon, *France* 26 D3
Langøya, *Norway* 8 B16
Langres, *France* 25 E12
Langres, Plateau de, *France* 25 E12
Langsa, *Indonesia* ... 56 D1
Långsele, *Sweden* ... 10 A11
Langtry, *U.S.A.* 109 L4
Langu, *Thailand* 59 J2
Languedoc, *France* .. 26 E7
Langwies, *Switz.* 23 C9
Langxi, *China* 53 B12
Langxiangzhen, *China* 50 E9
Langzhong, *China* ... 52 B5
Lanigan, *Canada* 101 C7
Lankao, *China* 50 G8
Länkäran, *Azerbaijan* . 67 C13
Lannemezan, *France* . 26 E4
Lannilis, *France* 24 D2
Lannion, *France* 24 D3
L'Annonciation, *Canada* 98 C5
Lanouaille, *France* ... 26 C5
Lanping, *China* 52 D2
Lansdale, *U.S.A.* 107 F9
Lansdowne, *Australia* . 91 E5
Lansdowne, *Canada* .. 107 B8
Lansdowne House, *Canada* 98 B2
L'Anse, *U.S.A.* 98 C2
L'Anse au Loup, *Canada* 99 B8
Lansford, *U.S.A.* 107 F9
Lanshan, *China* 53 E9
Lansing, *U.S.A.* 104 D3
Lanslebourg-Mont-Cenis,
  France 27 C10
Lanta Yai, Ko, *Thailand* . 59 J2
Lantian, *China* 50 G5
Lanus, *Argentina* 126 C4
Lanusei, *Italy* 34 C2
Lanuza, *Phil.* 55 G7
Lanxi, *China* 53 C12
Lanzarote, *Canary Is.* .. 36 E6
Lanzhou, *China* 50 F2
Lanzo Torinese, *Italy* . 32 C4
Lao →, *Italy* 35 C8
Lao Bao, *Laos* 58 D6
Lao Cai, *Vietnam* 58 A4
Laoag, *Phil.* 55 B4
Laoang, *Phil.* 55 E6
Laoha He →, *China* .. 51 C11
Laois □, *Ireland* 15 D4
Laon, *France* 25 C10
Laona, *U.S.A.* 104 C1
Laos ■, *Asia* 58 D5
Lapa, *Brazil* 127 B6
Lapalisse, *France* 26 B7
Laparan, *Phil.* 57 C6
Lapeer, *U.S.A.* 104 D4
Lapithos, *Cyprus* 37 D12
Laporte, *U.S.A.* 107 E8
Lapovo, *Serbia, Yug.* . 21 L11
Lappeenranta, *Finland* . 9 F23
Lappland, *Europe* 8 B21
Laprida, *Argentina* ... 126 D3
Lapseki, *Turkey* 66 B2
Laptev Sea, *Russia* ... 45 B13
Lapua, *Finland* 8 E20
Lāpusul →, *Romania* . 38 B6
L'Aquila, *Italy* 33 F10
Lār, Āzarbāijān-e Sharqī,
  Iran 64 B5
Lār, Fārs, *Iran* 65 E7
Lara □, *Venezuela* ... 120 A4
Larabanga, *Ghana* ... 78 D4
Laracha, *Spain* 30 B2
Larache, *Morocco* ... 74 A3
Laragne-Montéglin, *France* 27 D9
Laramie, *U.S.A.* 108 E2
Laramie Mts., *U.S.A.* . 108 E2
Laranjeiras, *Brazil* ... 122 D4
Laranjeiras do Sul, *Brazil* 127 B5
Larantuka, *Indonesia* . 57 F6
Larap, *Phil.* 55 D5
Larat, *Indonesia* 57 F8
L'Arbresle, *France* ... 27 C8
Larde, *Mozam.* 83 F4
Larder Lake, *Canada* . 98 C4
Lardhos, Ákra, *Greece* 37 C10
Lardhos, Órmos, *Greece* 37 C10

Laredo, *Spain* 28 B1
Laredo, *U.S.A.* 109 M5
Laredo Sd., *Canada* ... 100 C3
Laren, *Neths.* 16 D6
Largentière, *France* .. 27 D8
L'Argentière-la-Bessée,
  France 27 D10
Largs, *U.K.* 14 F4
Lari, *Italy* 32 E7
Lariang, *Indonesia* ... 57 E5
Larimore, *U.S.A.* 108 B6
Lārīn, *Iran* 65 C7
Larino, *Italy* 35 A7
Lárisa, *Greece* 39 K5
Larkana, *Pakistan* ... 62 F3
Larnaca, *Cyprus* 66 E5
Larnaca Bay, *Cyprus* .. 37 E12
Larne, *U.K.* 15 B6
Larned, *U.S.A.* 108 F5
Larochette, *Belgium* .. 17 J8
Laroquebrou, *France* . 26 D6
Larrimah, *Australia* .. 88 C5
Larsen Ice Shelf, *Antarctica* 5 C17
Larvik, *Norway* 10 E4
Laryak, *Russia* 44 C8
Larzac, Causse du, *France* 26 E7
Las Alpujarras, *Spain* . 29 J1
Las Animas, *U.S.A.* ... 108 F3
Las Anod, *Somali Rep.* . 68 F4
Las Blancos, *Spain* ... 29 H4
Las Brenãs, *Argentina* . 126 B3
Las Cabezas de San Juan,
  Spain 31 J5
Las Chimeneas, *Mexico* 113 N10
Las Coloradas, *Argentina* 128 A2
Las Cruces, *U.S.A.* ... 111 K10
Las Flores, *Argentina* . 126 D4
Las Heras, *Argentina* . 126 C2
Las Horquetas, *Argentina* 128 C2
Las Khoreh, *Somali Rep.* 68 E4
Las Lajas, *Argentina* .. 128 A2
Las Lomas, *Peru* 124 A1
Las Lomitas, *Argentina* 126 A3
Las Marismas, *Spain* .. 31 H4
Las Mercedes, *Venezuela* 120 B4
Las Navas de la
  Concepción, *Spain* .. 31 H5
Las Navas de Tolosa, *Spain* 31 G7
Las Navas del Marqués,
  Spain 30 E6
Las Palmas, *Argentina* . 126 B4
Las Palmas, *Canary Is.* . 36 F4
Las Palmas →, *Mexico* . 113 N10
Las Piedras, *Uruguay* . 127 C4
Las Pipinas, *Argentina* . 126 D4
Las Plumas, *Argentina* . 128 B3
Las Rosas, *Argentina* . 126 C3
Las Tablas, *Panama* ... 116 E3
Las Termas, *Argentina* . 126 B3
Las Truchas, *Mexico* .. 114 D4
Las Varillas, *Argentina* . 126 C3
Las Vegas, N. Mex.,
  U.S.A. 111 J11
Las Vegas, Nev., *U.S.A.* . 113 J11
Lascano, *Uruguay* 127 C5
Lashburn, *Canada* 101 C7
Lashio, *Burma* 61 H20
Lashkar, *India* 62 F8
Łasin, *Poland* 20 B9
Lasíthi, *Greece* 37 D7
Lasíthi □, *Greece* 37 D7
Laško, *Slovenia* 33 B12
Lassance, *Brazil* 123 E3
Lassay, *France* 24 D6
Lassen Pk., *U.S.A.* ... 110 F3
Last Mountain L., *Canada* 101 C7
Lastchance Cr. →, *U.S.A.* 112 E5
Lastoursville, *Gabon* . 80 E2
Lastovo, *Croatia* 33 F13
Lastovski Kanal, *Croatia* 33 F13
Lat Yao, *Thailand* 58 E2
Latacunga, *Ecuador* .. 120 D2
Latakia = Al Lādhiqīyah,
  Syria 66 E6
Latchford, *Canada* ... 98 C4
Laterza, *Italy* 35 B9
Latham, *Australia* 89 E2
Lathen, *Germany* 18 C3
Lathrop Wells, *U.S.A.* . 113 J10
Latiano, *Italy* 35 B10
Latina, *Italy* 34 A5
Latisana, *Italy* 33 C10
Latium = Lazio □, *Italy* . 33 F9
Laton, *U.S.A.* 112 J7
Latorica →, *Slovak Rep.* 21 G11
Latouche Treville, C.,
  Australia 88 C3
Latrobe, *Australia* ... 90 G4
Latrobe, *U.S.A.* 106 F5
Latrónico, *Italy* 35 B9
Latvia ■, *Europe* 9 H20
Lau Group, *Fiji* 87 C9
Lauca →, *Bolivia* 124 D4
Lauchhammer, *Germany* 18 D9
Lauenburg, *Germany* . 18 B6
Läufelfingen, *Switz.* .. 22 B5
Laufen, *Switz.* 22 B5
Lauffen, *Germany* ... 19 F5
Laujar, *Spain* 29 J2
Laukaa, *Finland* 9 E21
Launceston, *Australia* . 90 G4
Launceston, *U.K.* 13 G3
Laune →, *Ireland* 15 D2
Laupheim, *Germany* . 19 G5
Laura, *Australia* 90 B3
Laureana di Borrello, *Italy* 35 D9
Laurel, Miss., *U.S.A.* .. 109 K10

Laurel, Mont., U.S.A. 110 D9
Laurencekirk, U.K. 14 E6
Laurens, U.S.A. 105 H4
Laurentian Plateau, Canada 99 B6
Laurentides, Parc Prov.
　des, Canada 99 C5
Lauria, Italy 35 B8
Laurie L., Canada 101 B8
Laurinburg, U.S.A. 105 H6
Laurium, U.S.A. 104 B1
Lausanne, Switz. 22 C3
Laut, Indonesia 56 D3
Laut Kecil, Kepulauan,
　Indonesia 56 E5
Lautaro, Chile 128 A2
Lauterbach, Germany 18 E5
Lauterbrunnen, Switz. 22 C5
Lauterecken, Germany ... 19 F3
Lautoka, Fiji 87 C7
Lauwe, Belgium 17 G2
Lauwers, Neths. 16 A8
Lauwers Zee, Neths. 16 B8
Lauzon, Canada 99 C5
Lava Hot Springs, U.S.A. 110 E7
Lavadores, Spain 30 C2
Lavagna, Italy 32 D6
Laval, France 24 D6
Lavalle, Argentina 126 B2
Lávara, Greece 39 H9
Lavardac, France 26 D4
Lavaur, France 26 E5
Lavaux, Switz. 22 D3
Lavelanet, France 26 F5
Lavello, Italy 35 A8
Laverne, U.S.A. 109 G5
Laverton, Australia 89 E3
Lavos, Portugal 30 E2
Lavras, Brazil 123 F3
Lavre, Portugal 31 G2
Lavrentiya, Russia 45 C19
Lávrion, Greece 39 M7
Lávris, Greece 37 D6
Lavumisa, Swaziland 85 D5
Lawas, Malaysia 56 D5
Lawele, Indonesia 57 F6
Lawn Hill, Australia 90 B2
Lawng Pit, Burma 61 G20
Lawqah, Si. Arabia 64 D4
Lawra, Ghana 78 C4
Lawrence, N.Z. 87 L2
Lawrence, Kans., U.S.A. . 108 F7
Lawrence, Mass., U.S.A. . 107 D13
Lawrenceburg, Ind.,
　U.S.A. 104 F3
Lawrenceburg, Tenn.,
　U.S.A. 105 H2
Lawrenceville, U.S.A. 105 J4
Laws, U.S.A. 112 H8
Lawton, U.S.A. 109 H5
Lawu, Indonesia 57 G14
Laxford, L., U.K. 14 C3
Lay →, France 26 B2
Laylān, Iraq 64 C5
Layon →, France 24 E6
Laysan I., Pac. Oc. 93 E11
Laytonville, U.S.A. 110 G4
Lazarevskoye, Russia 43 J4
Lazio □, Italy 33 F9
Lazo, Russia 48 C6
Le Barcarès, France 26 F7
Le Beausset, France 27 E9
Le Blanc, France 26 B5
Le Bleymard, France 26 D7
Le Bourgneuf-la-Fôret,
　France 24 D6
Le Bouscat, France 26 D3
Le Brassus, Switz. 22 C2
Le Bugue, France 26 D4
Le Canourgue, France ... 26 D7
Le Cateau, France 25 B10
Le Chambon-Feugerolles,
　France 27 C8
Le Château-d'Oléron,
　France 26 C2
Le Châtelard, Switz. 22 D3
Le Châtelet, France 26 B6
Le Châtelet-en-Brie, France 25 D9
Le Chesne, France 25 C11
Le Cheylard, France 27 D8
Le Conquet, France 24 D2
Le Creusot, France 25 F11
Le Croisic, France 24 E4
Le Donjon, France 26 B7
Le Dorat, France 26 B5
Le François, Martinique .. 117 D7
Le Grand-Lucé, France .. 24 E7
Le Grand-Pressigny, France 24 F7
Le Havre, France 24 C7
Le Lavandou, France 27 E10
Le Lion-d'Angers, France . 24 E6
Le Locle, Switz. 22 B3
Le Louroux-Béconnais,
　France 24 E6
Le Luc, France 27 E10
Le Madonie, Italy 34 E6
Le Maire, Estr. de,
　Argentina 128 D4
Le Mans, France 24 D7
Le Mars, U.S.A. 108 D6
Le Mêle-sur-Sarthe, France 24 D7
Le Merlerault, France ... 24 D7
Le Monastier-sur-Gazeille,
　France 27 D7
Le Monêtier-les-Bains,
　France 27 D10
Le Mont d'Or, France ... 25 F13
Le Mont-Dore, France ... 26 C6

Le Mont-St.-Michel, France 24 D5
Le Moule, Guadeloupe ... 117 C7
Le Muy, France 27 E10
Le Palais, France 24 E3
Le Perthus, France 26 F6
Le Pont, Switz. 22 C2
Le Pouldu, France 24 E3
Le Puy-en-Velay, France . 26 C7
Le Quesnoy, France 25 B10
Le Roy, U.S.A. 109 F7
Le Sentier, Switz. 22 C2
Le Sueur, U.S.A. 108 C8
Le Teil, France 27 D8
Le Teilleul, France 24 D6
Le Theil, France 24 D7
Le Thillot, France 25 E13
Le Thuy, Vietnam 58 D6
Le Touquet-Paris-Plage,
　France 25 B8
Le Tréport, France 24 B8
Le Val-d'Ajol, France 25 E13
Le Verdon-sur-Mer, France 26 C2
Le Vigan, France 26 E7
Lea →, U.K. 13 F7
Leach, Cambodia 59 F4
Lead, U.S.A. 108 C3
Leader, Canada 101 C7
Leadhills, U.K. 14 F5
Leadville, U.S.A. 111 G10
Leaf →, U.S.A. 109 K10
Leakey, U.S.A. 109 L5
Leamington, Canada 98 D3
Leamington, U.S.A. 110 G7
Leamington Spa = Royal
　Leamington Spa, U.K. . 13 E6
Le'an, China 53 D10
Leandro Norte Alem,
　Argentina 127 B4
Learmonth, Australia 88 D1
Leask, Canada 101 C7
Leavenworth, Kans.,
　U.S.A. 108 F7
Leavenworth, Wash.,
　U.S.A. 110 C3
Łeba, Poland 20 A7
Lebak, Phil. 55 H6
Lebam, U.S.A. 112 D3
Lebanon, Ind., U.S.A. ... 104 E2
Lebanon, Kans., U.S.A. .. 108 F5
Lebanon, Ky., U.S.A. 104 G3
Lebanon, Mo., U.S.A. ... 109 G8
Lebanon, Oreg., U.S.A. .. 110 D2
Lebanon, Pa., U.S.A. 107 F8
Lebanon, Tenn., U.S.A. .. 105 G2
Lebanon ■, Asia 69 B4
Lebbeke, Belgium 17 G4
Lebec, U.S.A. 113 L8
Lebedyan, Russia 42 D4
Lebedyn, Ukraine 41 G8
Lebomboberge, S. Africa . 85 C5
Lębork, Poland 20 A7
Lebrija, Spain 31 J4
Lebu, Chile 126 D1
Lecce, Italy 35 B11
Lecco, Italy 32 C6
Lecco, L. di, Italy 32 C6
Lécera, Spain 28 D4
Lech, Austria 19 H6
Lech →, Germany 19 G6
Lechang, China 53 E9
Lechtaler Alpen, Austria . 19 H6
Lectoure, France 26 E4
Łęczyca, Poland 20 C9
Ledbury, U.K. 13 E5
Lede, Belgium 17 G3
Ledeberg, Belgium 17 F3
Ledesma, Spain 30 D5
Leduc, Canada 100 C6
Ledyczek, Poland 20 B6
Lee →, Ireland 107 D11
Lee →, Ireland 15 E3
Lee Vining, U.S.A. 112 H7
Leech L., U.S.A. 108 B7
Leedey, U.S.A. 109 H5
Leeds, U.K. 12 D6
Leeds, U.S.A. 105 J2
Leek, Neths. 16 B8
Leek, U.K. 12 D5
Leende, Neths. 17 F7
Leer, Germany 18 B3
Leerdam, Neths. 16 E6
Leersum, Neths. 16 E6
Leesburg, U.S.A. 105 L5
Leesville, U.S.A. 109 K8
Leeton, Australia 91 E4
Leetonia, U.S.A. 106 F4
Leeu Gamka, S. Africa .. 84 E3
Leeuwarden, Neths. 16 B7
Leeuwin, C., Australia ... 89 F2
Leeward Is., Atl. Oc. 117 C7
Lefka, Cyprus 37 D11
Lefkoniko, Cyprus 37 D12
Lefors, U.S.A. 109 H4
Lefroy, L., Australia 89 F3
Legal, Canada 100 C6
Leganés, Spain 30 E7
Legazpi, Phil. 55 E5
Legendre I., Australia ... 88 D2
Leghorn = Livorno, Italy . 32 E7
Legionowo, Poland 20 C10
Léglise, Belgium 17 J7
Legnago, Italy 33 C8
Legnano, Italy 32 C5
Legnica, Poland 20 D6
Legrad, Croatia 33 B13
Legume, Australia 91 D5

Leh, India 63 B7
Lehi, U.S.A. 110 F8
Lehighton, U.S.A. 107 F9
Lehrte, Germany 18 C5
Lehututu, Botswana 84 C3
Lei Shui →, China 53 D9
Leiah, Pakistan 62 D4
Leibnitz, Austria 21 J5
Leibo, China 52 C4
Leicester, U.K. 13 E6
Leicestershire □, U.K. ... 13 E6
Leichhardt →, Australia . 90 B2
Leichhardt Ra., Australia . 90 C4
Leiden, Neths. 16 D5
Leiderdorp, Neths. 16 D5
Leidschendam, Neths. .. 16 D4
Leie →, Belgium 25 A10
Leignon, Belgium 17 H6
Leine →, Germany 18 C5
Leinster, Australia 89 E3
Leinster □, Ireland 15 C4
Leinster, Mt., Ireland ... 15 D5
Leipzig, Germany 18 D8
Leiria, Portugal 31 F2
Leiria □, Portugal 31 F2
Leirvik, Norway 9 G11
Leisler, Mt., Australia ... 88 D4
Leith, U.K. 14 F5
Leith Hill, U.K. 13 F7
Leitha →, Europe 21 H7
Leitrim, Ireland 15 B3
Leitrim □, Ireland 15 B3
Leiyang, China 53 D9
Leiza, Spain 28 B3
Leizhou Bandao, China .. 54 D6
Leizhou Wan, China 53 G8
Lek →, Neths. 16 E5
Leka, Norway 8 D14
Leke, Belgium 17 F1
Lekkerkerk, Neths. 16 E5
Leksula, Indonesia 57 E7
Lékva Ori, Greece 37 D6
Leland, U.S.A. 109 J9
Leland Lakes, Canada ... 101 A6
Leleque, Argentina 128 B2
Lelystad, Neths. 16 D6
Lema, Nigeria 79 C5
Léman, L., Europe 22 D3
Lemelerveld, Neths. 16 D8
Lemera, Zaïre 82 C2
Lemery, Phil. 55 E4
Lemgo, Germany 18 C4
Lemhi Ra., U.S.A. 110 D7
Lemmer, Neths. 16 C7
Lemmon, U.S.A. 108 C3
Lemon Grove, U.S.A. ... 113 N9
Lemoore, U.S.A. 111 H4
Lempdes, France 26 C7
Lemsid, W. Sahara 74 C2
Lemvig, Denmark 11 H2
Lena →, Russia 45 B13
Lencloître, France 24 F7
Lençóis, Brazil 123 D3
Léndas, Greece 37 E6
Lendeh, Iran 65 D6
Lendelede, Belgium 17 G2
Lendinara, Italy 33 C8
Lengerich, Germany 18 C3
Lenggong, Malaysia 59 K3
Lenggries, Germany 19 H7
Lengua de Vaca, Pta.,
　Chile 126 C1
Lenina, Kanal →, Russia . 43 J7
Leninabad = Khudzhand,
　Tajikistan 44 E7
Leninakan = Gyumri,
　Armenia 43 K6
Leningrad = Sankt-
　Peterburg, Russia 40 C6
Lenino, Ukraine 41 K8
Leninogorsk = Ridder,
　Kazakhstan 44 D9
Leninsk, Russia 43 F7
Leninsk-Kuznetskiy, Russia 44 D9
Leninskoye, Russia 42 A8
Leninskoye, Russia 45 E14
Lenk, Switz. 22 D4
Lenkoran = Länkäran,
　Azerbaijan 67 C13
Lenmalu, Indonesia 57 E8
Lenne →, Germany 18 D3
Lennox, I., Chile 128 E3
Lennoxville, Canada 107 A13
Leno, Italy 32 C7
Lenoir, U.S.A. 105 H5
Lenoir City, U.S.A. 105 H3
Lenora, U.S.A. 108 F4
Lenore L., Canada 101 C8
Lenox, U.S.A. 107 D11
Lens, Belgium 17 G3
Lens, France 25 B9
Lens St. Remy, Belgium . 17 G6
Lensk, Russia 45 C12
Lent, Neths. 16 E7
Lentekhi, Georgia 43 J6
Lentini, Italy 35 E8
Lenwood, U.S.A. 113 L9
Lenzburg, Switz. 22 B6
Lenzen, Germany 18 B7
Leo, Burkina Faso 78 C4
Leoben, Austria 21 H5
Leodhas = Lewis, U.K. .. 14 C2
Leola, U.S.A. 108 C5
Leominster, U.K. 13 E5
Leominster, U.S.A. 107 D13
Léon, France 26 E2

León, Mexico 114 C4
León, Nic. 116 D2
León, Spain 30 C5
León □, Spain 30 C5
León, Montañas de, Spain 30 C4
Leonardtown, U.S.A. ... 104 F7
Leone, Mte., Switz. 22 D6
Leonforte, Italy 35 E7
Leongatha, Australia ... 91 F4
Leonídhion, Greece 39 M5
Leonora, Australia 89 E3
Léopold II, Lac = Mai-
　Ndombe, L., Zaïre 80 E3
Leopoldina, Brazil 123 F3
Leopoldo Bulhões, Brazil . 123 E2
Leopoldsburg, Belgium . 17 F6
Léopoldville = Kinshasa,
　Zaïre 80 E3
Leoti, U.S.A. 108 F4
Leova, Moldova 41 J5
Leoville, Canada 101 C7
Lépa, L. do, Angola 84 B2
Lepe, Spain 31 H3
Lepel = Lyepyel, Belarus . 40 E5
Lepikha, Russia 45 C13
Leping, China 53 C11
Lepontine, Alpi, Italy ... 23 D6
Leppävirta, Finland 9 E22
Lequeitio, Spain 28 B2
Lercara Friddi, Italy 34 E6
Lerdo, Mexico 114 B4
Léré, Chad 73 G7
Lere, Nigeria 79 D6
Leribe, Lesotho 85 D4
Lérici, Italy 32 D6
Lérida, Spain 28 D5
Lérida □, Spain 28 C6
Lerma, Spain 30 C7
Léros, Greece 39 M9
Lérouville, France 25 D12
Lerwick, U.K. 14 A7
Les Abrets, France 27 C9
Les Andelys, France 24 C8
Les Arcs, France 27 E10
Les Baux-de-Provence,
　France 27 E8
Les Bois, Switz. 22 B3
Les Cayes, Haiti 117 C5
Les Diablerets, Switz. ... 22 D4
Les Échelles, France 27 C9
Les Essarts, France 24 F5
Les Étroits, Canada 99 C6
Les Eyzies-de-Tayac-
　Sireuil, France 26 D5
Les Herbiers, France ... 24 F5
Les Minquiers, Chan. Is. . 24 D4
Les Ponts-de-Cé, France . 24 E6
Les Riceys, France 25 E11
Les Sables-d'Olonne,
　France 26 B2
Les Vans, France 27 D8
Les Verrières, Switz. ... 22 C2
Lesbos = Lésvos, Greece . 39 K9
Leshan, China 52 C4
Lésina, L. di, Italy 33 G12
Lesja, Norway 10 B2
Lesjaverk, Norway 10 B2
Leskov I., Antarctica 5 B1
Leskovac, Serbia, Yug. .. 21 M11
Leslie, U.S.A. 109 H8
Lesneven, France 24 D2
Lešnica, Serbia, Yug. ... 21 L9
Lesnoye, Russia 42 A2
Lesopilnoye, Russia 48 A7
Lesotho ■, Africa 85 D4
Lesozavodsk, Russia 45 E14
Lesparre-Médoc, France . 26 C3
Lessay, France 24 C5
Lesse →, Belgium 17 H5
Lesser Antilles, W. Indies . 117 C7
Lesser Slave L., Canada . 100 B5
Lesser Sunda Is., Indonesia 57 F6
Lessines, Belgium 17 G3
Lester, U.S.A. 112 C5
Lestock, Canada 101 C8
Lesuer I., Australia 88 B4
Lésvos, Greece 39 K9
Leszno, Poland 20 D6
Letchworth, U.K. 13 F7
Letea, Ostrov, Romania . 38 D12
Lethbridge, Canada 100 D6
Lethem, Guyana 121 C6
Leti, Kepulauan, Indonesia 57 F7
Leti Is. = Leti, Kepulauan,
　Indonesia 57 F7
Letiahau →, Botswana .. 84 C3
Leticia, Colombia 120 D4
Leting, China 51 E10
Letjiesbos, S. Africa 84 E3
Letlhakeng, Botswana .. 84 C3
Letpadan, Burma 61 L19
Letpan, Burma 61 K19
Letterkenny, Ireland 15 B4
Leu, Romania 38 E7
Leucadia, U.S.A. 113 M9
Leucate, France 26 F7
Leucate, Étang de, France 26 F7
Leuk, Switz. 22 D5
Leukerbad, Switz. 22 D5
Leupegem, Belgium ... 17 G3
Leuser, G., Indonesia .. 56 D1
Leutkirch, Germany ... 19 H6
Leuven, Belgium 17 G5
Leuze, Hainaut, Belgium 17 G3
Leuze, Namur, Belgium . 17 G5

Lev Tolstoy, Russia 42 D4
Levádhia, Greece 39 L5
Levan, U.S.A. 110 G8
Levanger, Norway 8 E14
Levant, I. du, France ... 27 E10
Lévanto, Italy 32 D6
Levanzo, Italy 34 E5
Levelland, U.S.A. 109 J3
Leven, U.K. 14 E6
Leven, L., U.K. 14 E5
Leven, Toraka, Madag. .. 85 A8
Levens, Canada 27 E11
Leveque C., Australia ... 88 C3
Leverano, Italy 35 B10
Leverkusen, Germany .. 18 D2
Levet, France 25 F9
Levice, Slovak Rep. 21 G8
Levico, Italy 33 C8
Levie, France 27 G13
Levier, France 25 F13
Levin, N.Z. 87 J5
Lévis, Canada 99 C5
Levis, L., Canada 100 A5
Levítha, Greece 39 M9
Levittown, N.Y., U.S.A. . 107 F11
Levittown, Pa., U.S.A. .. 107 F10
Levkás, Greece 39 L3
Levkímmi, Greece 37 B4
Levkími, Ákra, Greece .. 37 B4
Levkôsia = Nicosia, Cyprus 66 E5
Levoča, Slovak Rep. 20 F10
Levroux, France 25 F8
Levski, Bulgaria 38 F8
Levskigrad = Karlovo,
　Bulgaria 38 G7
Lewellen, U.S.A. 108 E3
Lewes, U.K. 13 G8
Lewes, U.S.A. 104 F8
Lewis, U.K. 14 C2
Lewis →, U.S.A. 112 E4
Lewis, Butt of, U.K. 14 C2
Lewis Ra., Australia 88 D4
Lewis Range, U.S.A. 110 C7
Lewisburg, Pa., U.S.A. .. 106 F8
Lewisburg, Tenn., U.S.A. 105 H2
Lewisporte, Canada 99 C8
Lewiston, Idaho, U.S.A. . 110 C5
Lewiston, Maine, U.S.A. . 105 C11
Lewistown, Mont., U.S.A. 110 C9
Lewistown, Pa., U.S.A. .. 106 F7
Lexington, Ill., U.S.A. ... 108 E10
Lexington, Ky., U.S.A. .. 104 F3
Lexington, Miss., U.S.A. . 109 J9
Lexington, Mo., U.S.A. .. 108 F8
Lexington, N.C., U.S.A. . 105 H5
Lexington, Nebr., U.S.A. 108 E5
Lexington, Ohio, U.S.A. . 106 F2
Lexington, Oreg., U.S.A. 110 D4
Lexington, Tenn., U.S.A. 105 H1
Lexington Park, U.S.A. .. 104 F7
Leye, China 52 E6
Leyre →, France 26 D2
Leysin, Switz. 22 D4
Leyte, Phil. 55 F6
Leyte Gulf, Phil. 55 F6
Lezay, France 26 B4
Lezha, Albania 39 H2
Lezhi, China 52 B5
Lézignan-Corbières, France 26 E6
Lezoux, France 26 C7
Lgov, Russia 42 E2
Lhasa, China 54 D4
Lhazê, China 54 D3
Lhokkruet, Indonesia ... 56 D1
Lhokseumawe, Indonesia 56 C1
Lhuntsi Dzong, India ... 61 F17
Li, Thailand 58 D2
Li Shui →, China 53 C9
Li Xian, Gansu, China .. 50 G3
Li Xian, Hebei, China ... 50 E8
Li Xian, Hunan, China .. 53 C8
Li Xian, Sichuan, China . 52 B4
Liádhoi, Greece 39 N9
Lian Xian, China 53 E9
Liancheng, China 53 E11
Lianga, Phil. 55 G7
Liangcheng,
　Nei Mongol Zizhiqu,
　China 50 D7
Liangcheng, Shandong,
　China 51 G10
Liangdang, China 50 H4
Lianghekou, China 52 C7
Liangping, China 52 B6
Lianhua, China 53 D9
Lianjiang, Fujian, China . 53 D12
Lianjiang, Guangdong,
　China 53 G8
Lianping, China 53 E10
Lianshan, China 53 E9
Lianshanguan, China ... 51 D12
Lianshui, China 51 H10
Lianyuan, China 53 D8
Lianyungang, China 51 G10
Liao He →, China 51 D11
Liaocheng, China 50 F8
Liaodong Bandao, China 51 E12
Liaodong Wan, China .. 51 D11
Liaoning □, China 51 D12
Liaoyang, China 51 D12
Liaoyuan, China 51 C13
Liaozhong, China 51 D12
Liapádhes, Greece 39 K2
Liard →, Canada 100 A4
Liari, Pakistan 62 G2
Líbano, Colombia 120 C2
Libau = Liepāja, Latvia .. 9 H19

Libby, *U.S.A.* 110 B6
Libenge, *Zaïre* 80 D3
Liberal, *Kans., U.S.A.* .. 109 G4
Liberal, *Mo., U.S.A.* 109 G7
Liberdade, *Brazil* 124 C3
Liberdade →, *Brazil* 125 B7
Liberec, *Czech.* 20 E5
Liberia, *Costa Rica* 116 D2
Liberia ■, *W. Afr.* 78 D3
Libertad, *Venezuela* 120 B4
Liberty, *Mo., U.S.A.* 108 F7
Liberty, *Tex., U.S.A.* ... 109 K7
Libin, *Belgium* 17 J6
Lîbîya, Sahrâ', *Africa* .. 73 C9
Libo, *China* 52 E6
Libobo, Tanjung, *Indonesia* 57 E7
Libode, *S. Africa* 85 E4
Libonda, *Zambia* 81 G4
Libourne, *France* 26 D3
Libramont, *Belgium* 17 J6
Libreville, *Gabon* 80 D1
Libya ■, *N. Afr.* 73 C8
Libyan Desert = Lîbîya,
  Sahrâ', *Africa* 73 C9
Libyan Plateau = Ed-
  Déffa, *Egypt* 76 A2
Licantén, *Chile* 126 D1
Licata, *Italy* 34 E6
Lice, *Turkey* 67 C9
Licheng, *China* 50 F7
Lichfield, *U.K.* 12 E6
Lichinga, *Mozam.* 83 E4
Lichtaart, *Belgium* 17 F5
Lichtenburg, *S. Africa* .. 84 D4
Lichtenfels, *Germany* .. 19 E7
Lichtenvoorde, *Neths.* .. 16 E9
Lichtervelde, *Belgium* .. 17 F2
Lichuan, *Hubei, China* .. 52 B7
Lichuan, *Jiangxi, China* . 53 D11
Licosa, Punta, *Italy* 35 B7
Lida, *Belarus* 9 K21
Lida, *U.S.A.* 111 H5
Lidingö, *Sweden* 10 E12
Lidköping, *Sweden* 11 F7
Lido, *Italy* 33 C9
Lido, *Niger* 79 C5
Lido di Roma = Óstia,
  Lido di, *Italy* 34 A5
Lidzbark Warmiński,
  Poland 20 A10
Liebenwalde, *Germany* .. 18 C9
Lieberose, *Germany* 18 D10
Liebig, Mt., *Australia* .. 88 D5
Liechtenstein ■, *Europe* . 23 B9
Liederkerke, *Belgium* ... 17 G4
Liège, *Belgium* 17 G7
Liège □, *Belgium* 17 G7
Liegnitz = Legnica, *Poland* 20 D6
Liempde, *Neths.* 17 E6
Lienart, *Zaïre* 82 B2
Lienyünchiangshih =
  Lianyungang, *China* . 51 G10
Lienz, *Austria* 21 J2
Liepāja, *Latvia* 9 H19
Lier, *Belgium* 17 F5
Lierneux, *Belgium* 17 H7
Lieshout, *Neths.* 17 E7
Liestal, *Switz.* 22 B5
Liévin, *France* 25 B9
Lièvre →, *Canada* 98 C4
Liezen, *Austria* 21 H4
Liffey →, *Ireland* 15 C5
Lifford, *Ireland* 15 B4
Liffré, *France* 24 D5
Lifjell, *Norway* 10 E2
Lifudzin, *Russia* 48 B7
Ligao, *Phil.* 55 E5
Lightning Ridge, *Australia* 91 D4
Lignano Sabbiadoro, *Italy* 33 C10
Ligny-en-Barrois, *France* . 25 D12
Ligny-le-Châtel, *France* . 25 E10
Ligourion, *Greece* 39 M6
Ligueil, *France* 24 E7
Liguria □, *Italy* 32 D6
Ligurian Sea, *Medit. S.* . 32 E5
Lihou Reefs and Cays,
  Australia 90 B4
Lihue, *U.S.A.* 102 H15
Lijiang, *China* 52 D3
Likasi, *Zaïre* 83 E2
Likati, *Zaïre* 80 D4
Likhoslavl, *Russia* 42 B3
Likhovskoy, *Russia* 43 F5
Likoma I., *Malawi* 83 E3
Likumburu, *Tanzania* .. 83 D4
L'Île-Bouchard, *France* . 24 E7
L'Île-Rousse, *France* ... 27 F12
Liling, *China* 53 D9
Lille, *Belgium* 17 F5
Lille, *France* 25 B10
Lille Bælt, *Denmark* 11 J3
Lillebonne, *France* 24 C7
Lillehammer, *Norway* .. 10 C4
Lillers, *France* 25 B9
Lillesand, *Norway* 11 F2
Lilleshall, *U.K.* 13 E5
Lillestrøm, *Norway* 10 E4
Lillian Point, Mt., *Australia* 89 E4
Lillo, *Spain* 28 F1
Lillooet →, *Canada* 100 D4
Lilongwe, *Malawi* 83 E3
Liloy, *Phil.* 57 C6
Lim →, *Bos.-H.* 21 M9
Lima, *Indonesia* 57 E7
Lima, *Peru* 124 C2
Lima, *Mont., U.S.A.* 110 D7
Lima, *Ohio, U.S.A.* 104 E3

Lima □, *Peru* 124 C2
Lima →, *Portugal* 30 D2
Limages, *Canada* 107 A9
Liman, *Russia* 43 H8
Limassol, *Cyprus* 66 E5
Limavady, *U.K.* 15 A5
Limavady □, *U.K.* 15 B5
Limay →, *Argentina* 128 A3
Limay Mahuida, *Argentina* 126 D2
Limbang, *Brunei* 56 D5
Limbara, Mte., *Italy* 34 B2
Limbaži, *Latvia* 9 H21
Limbdi, *India* 62 H4
Limbe, *Cameroon* 79 E6
Limbri, *Australia* 91 E5
Limbunya, *Australia* 88 C4
Limburg, *Germany* 19 E4
Limburg □, *Belgium* 17 F6
Limburg □, *Neths.* 17 F7
Limeira, *Brazil* 127 A6
Limerick, *Ireland* 15 D3
Limerick □, *Ireland* 15 D3
Limestone, *U.S.A.* 106 D6
Limestone →, *Canada* .. 101 B10
Limfjorden, *Denmark* .. 11 H3
Limia = Lima →, *Portugal* 30 D2
Limingen, *Norway* 8 D15
Limmared, *Sweden* 11 G7
Limmat →, *Switz.* 23 B6
Limmen, *Neths.* 16 C5
Limmen Bight, *Australia* . 90 A2
Limmen Bight →,
  Australia 90 B2
Límni, *Greece* 39 L6
Límnos, *Greece* 39 K8
Limoeiro, *Brazil* 122 C4
Limoeiro do Norte, *Brazil* 122 C4
Limoges, *France* 26 C5
Limón, *Costa Rica* 116 D3
Limon, *U.S.A.* 108 F3
Limone Piemonte, *Italy* . 32 D4
Limousin, *France* 26 C5
Limousin, Plateaux du,
  France 26 C5
Limoux, *France* 26 E6
Limpopo →, *Africa* 85 D5
Limuru, *Kenya* 82 C4
Lin Xian, *China* 50 F6
Lin'an, *China* 53 B12
Linapacan I., *Phil.* 55 F3
Linapacan Str., *Phil.* .. 55 F3
Linares, *Chile* 126 D1
Linares, *Colombia* 120 C2
Linares, *Mexico* 115 C5
Linares, *Spain* 29 G1
Linares □, *Chile* 126 D1
Línas Mte., *Italy* 34 C1
Lincang, *China* 52 F3
Lincheng, *China* 50 F8
Linchuan, *China* 53 D11
Lincoln, *Argentina* 126 C3
Lincoln, *N.Z.* 87 K4
Lincoln, *U.K.* 12 D7
Lincoln, *Calif., U.S.A.* . 112 G5
Lincoln, *Ill., U.S.A.* 108 E10
Lincoln, *Kans., U.S.A.* .. 108 F5
Lincoln, *Maine, U.S.A.* . 99 C6
Lincoln, *N.H., U.S.A.* .. 107 B13
Lincoln, *N. Mex., U.S.A.* 111 K11
Lincoln, *Nebr., U.S.A.* .. 108 E6
Lincoln Hav = Lincoln
  Sea, *Arctic* 4 A5
Lincoln Sea, *Arctic* 4 A5
Lincolnshire □, *U.K.* .. 12 D7
Lincolnshire Wolds, *U.K.* 12 D7
Lincolnton, *U.S.A.* 105 H5
L'Incudine, *France* 27 G13
Lind, *U.S.A.* 110 C4
Linda, *U.S.A.* 112 F5
Lindau, *Germany* 19 H5
Linde →, *Neths.* 16 C7
Linden, *Guyana* 121 B6
Linden, *Calif., U.S.A.* .. 112 G5
Linden, *Tex., U.S.A.* 109 J7
Lindenheuvel, *Neths.* .. 17 G7
Lindenhurst, *U.S.A.* 107 F11
Linderöd, *Sweden* 11 J7
Linderödsåsen, *Sweden* . 11 J7
Lindesnes, *Norway* 9 H12
Líndhos, *Greece* 66 D3
Lindi, *Tanzania* 83 D4
Lindi □, *Tanzania* 83 D4
Lindi →, *Zaïre* 82 B2
Lindoso, *Portugal* 30 D2
Lindow, *Germany* 18 C8
Lindsay, *Canada* 98 D4
Lindsay, *Calif., U.S.A.* . 111 H4
Lindsay, *Okla., U.S.A.* . 109 H6
Lindsborg, *U.S.A.* 108 F6
Linfen, *China* 50 F6
Ling Xian, *Hunan, China* 53 D9
Ling Xian, *Shandong,
  China* 50 F9
Lingao, *China* 58 C7
Lingayen, *Phil.* 57 A6
Lingayen G., *Phil.* 55 C5
Lingbi, *China* 51 H9
Lingchuan,
  *Guangxi Zhuangzu,
  China* 53 E8
Lingchuan, *Shanxi, China* . 50 G7
Lingen, *Germany* 18 C3
Lingga, *Indonesia* 56 E2
Lingga, Kepulauan,
  Indonesia 56 E2

Lingga Arch. = Lingga,
  Kepulauan, *Indonesia* .. 56 E2
Lingle, *U.S.A.* 108 D2
Lingling, *China* 53 D8
Lingqiu, *China* 50 E8
Lingshan, *China* 52 F7
Lingshi, *China* 50 F6
Lingshou, *China* 50 E8
Lingshui, *China* 58 C8
Lingtai, *China* 50 G4
Linguéré, *Senegal* 78 B1
Lingwu, *China* 50 E4
Lingyuan, *China* 51 D10
Lingyun, *China* 52 E6
Linh Cam, *Vietnam* 58 C5
Linhai, *China* 53 C13
Linhares, *Brazil* 123 E3
Linhe, *China* 50 D4
Linjiang, *China* 51 D14
Linköping, *Sweden* 11 F9
Linkou, *China* 51 B16
Linli, *China* 53 C8
Linlithgow, *U.K.* 14 F5
Linnhe, L., *U.K.* 14 E3
Linosa, I., *Medit. S.* 75 A7
Linqi, *China* 50 G7
Linqing, *China* 50 F8
Linqu, *China* 51 F10
Linru, *China* 50 G7
Lins, *Brazil* 127 A6
Linshui, *China* 52 B6
Lintao, *China* 50 G2
Linth →, *Switz.* 19 H5
Linthal, *Switz.* 23 C8
Lintlaw, *Canada* 101 C8
Linton, *Ind., U.S.A.* 104 F2
Linton, *N. Dak., U.S.A.* . 108 B4
Lintong, *China* 50 G5
Linville, *Australia* 91 D5
Linwood, *Canada* 106 C4
Linwu, *China* 53 E9
Linxi, *China* 51 C10
Linxia, *China* 54 C5
Linxiang, *China* 53 C9
Linyanti →, *Africa* 84 B4
Linyi, *China* 51 G10
Linz, *Austria* 21 G4
Linz, *Germany* 18 E3
Linzhenzhen, *China* 50 F5
Linzi, *China* 51 F10
Lion, G. du, *France* 27 E8
Lionárisso, *Cyprus* 37 D13
Lioni, *Italy* 35 B8
Lions, G. of = Lion, G.
  du, *France* 27 E8
Lion's Den, *Zimbabwe* .. 83 F3
Lion's Head, *Canada* .. 98 D3
Liozno = Lyozna, *Belarus* 43 E6
Lipa, *Phil.* 55 E4
Lipali, *Mozam.* 83 E4
Lípari, *Italy* 35 D7
Lípari, Is. = Eólie, Ís.,
  Italy 35 D7
Lipcani, *Moldova* 41 H4
Lipetsk, *Russia* 42 D4
Liping, *China* 52 D7
Lipkany = Lipcani,
  Moldova 41 H4
Lipljan, *Serbia, Yug.* .. 21 N11
Lipno, *Poland* 20 C9
Lipova, *Romania* 38 C4
Lipovcy Manzovka, *Russia* 48 B6
Lipovets, *Ukraine* 41 H5
Lippe →, *Germany* 18 D2
Lippstadt, *Germany* 18 D4
Lipscomb, *U.S.A.* 109 G4
Lipsko, *Poland* 20 D11
Lipsói, *Greece* 39 M9
Liptovský Svatý Mikuláš,
  Slovak Rep. 20 F9
Liptrap C., *Australia* .. 91 F4
Lipu, *China* 53 E8
Lira, *Uganda* 82 B3
Liri →, *Italy* 34 A6
Liria, *Spain* 29 F4
Lisala, *Zaïre* 80 D4
Lisboa, *Portugal* 31 G1
Lisboa □, *Portugal* 31 G1
Lisbon = Lisboa, *Portugal* 31 G1
Lisbon, *N. Dak., U.S.A.* . 108 B6
Lisbon, *N.H., U.S.A.* .. 107 B13
Lisbon, *Ohio, U.S.A.* .. 106 F4
Lisburn, *U.K.* 15 B5
Lisburne, C., *U.S.A.* .. 96 B3
Liscannor, B., *Ireland* .. 15 D2
Liscia →, *Italy* 34 A2
Lishe Jiang →, *China* .. 52 E3
Lishi, *China* 50 F6
Lishu, *China* 51 C13
Lishui, *Jiangsu, China* .. 53 B12
Lishui, *Zhejiang, China* . 53 C12
Lisianski I., *Pac. Oc.* .. 92 E10
Lisichansk = Lysychansk,
  Ukraine 41 H10
Lisieux, *France* 24 C7
Liski, *Russia* 42 E4
L'Isle-Adam, *France* 25 C9
L'Isle-Jourdain, Gers,
  France 26 E5
L'Isle-Jourdain, Vienne,
  France 26 B4
L'Isle-sur-le-Doubs, *France* 25 E13
Lisle-sur-Tarn, *France* .. 26 E5
Lismore, *Australia* 91 D5
Lismore, *Ireland* 15 D4
Lisse, *Neths.* 16 D5

List, *Germany* 18 A4
Lista, *Norway* 9 G12
Lister, Mt., *Antarctica* .. 5 D11
Liston, *Australia* 91 D5
Listowel, *Canada* 98 D3
Listowel, *Ireland* 15 D2
Lit-et-Mixe, *France* 26 D2
Litang, *Guangxi Zhuangzu,
  China* 52 F7
Litang, *Sichuan, China* . 52 B3
Litang, *Malaysia* 57 C5
Litang Qu →, *China* 52 C3
Litani →, *Lebanon* 69 B4
Litchfield, *Calif., U.S.A.* . 112 E6
Litchfield, *Conn., U.S.A.* 107 E11
Litchfield, *Ill., U.S.A.* .. 108 F10
Litchfield, *Minn., U.S.A.* 108 C7
Lithgow, *Australia* 91 E5
Líthinon, Ákra, *Greece* . 37 E6
Lithuania ■, *Europe* 9 J20
Litija, *Slovenia* 33 B11
Litókhoron, *Greece* 39 J5
Litoměřice, *Czech.* 20 E4
Little Abaco I., *Bahamas* . 112 E6
Little Barrier I., *N.Z.* .. 87 G5
Little Blue →, *U.S.A.* .. 108 F6
Little Cadotte →, *Canada* 100 B5
Little Cayman I.,
  Cayman Is. 116 C3
Little Churchill →, *Canada* 101 B10
Little Colorado →, *U.S.A.* 111 H8
Little Current, *Canada* .. 98 C3
Little Current →, *Canada* 98 B3
Little Falls, *Minn., U.S.A.* 108 C7
Little Falls, *N.Y., U.S.A.* 107 C10
Little Fork →, *U.S.A.* .. 108 A8
Little Grand Rapids,
  Canada 101 C9
Little Humboldt →,
  U.S.A. 110 F5
Little Inagua I., *Bahamas* . 117 B5
Little Karoo, *S. Africa* .. 84 E3
Little Lake, *U.S.A.* 113 K9
Little Laut Is. = Laut
  Kecil, Kepulauan,
  Indonesia 56 E5
Little Minch, *U.K.* 14 D2
Little Missouri →, *U.S.A.* 108 B3
Little Ouse →, *U.K.* 13 E8
Little Rann, *India* 62 H4
Little Red →, *U.S.A.* .. 109 H9
Little River, *N.Z.* 87 K4
Little Rock, *U.S.A.* 109 H8
Little Ruaha →, *Tanzania* 82 D4
Little Sable Pt., *U.S.A.* . 104 D2
Little Sioux →, *U.S.A.* . 108 E6
Little Smoky →, *Canada* . 100 C5
Little Snake →, *U.S.A.* . 110 F9
Little Valley, *U.S.A.* 106 D6
Little Wabash →, *U.S.A.* 104 G1
Littlefield, *U.S.A.* 109 J3
Littlefork, *U.S.A.* 108 A8
Littlehampton, *U.K.* 13 G7
Littleton, *U.S.A.* 107 B13
Liu He →, *China* 51 D11
Liu Jiang →, *China* 52 F7
Liuba, *China* 50 H4
Liucheng, *China* 52 E7
Liugou, *China* 51 D10
Liuhe, *China* 51 C13
Liuheng Dao, *China* 53 C14
Liukang Tenggaja,
  Indonesia 57 F5
Liuli, *Tanzania* 83 E3
Liuwa Plain, *Zambia* .. 81 G4
Liuyang, *China* 53 C9
Liuzhou, *China* 52 E7
Liuzhuang, *China* 51 H11
Livadherón, *Greece* 39 J4
Livadhia, *Cyprus* 37 E12
Livarot, *France* 24 D7
Live Oak, *Calif., U.S.A.* . 112 F5
Live Oak, *Fla., U.S.A.* .. 105 K4
Liveras, *Cyprus* 37 D11
Liveringa, *Australia* 88 C3
Livermore, *U.S.A.* 112 H5
Livermore, Mt., *U.S.A.* . 109 K2
Liverpool, *Australia* 91 E5
Liverpool, *Canada* 99 D7
Liverpool, *U.K.* 12 D5
Liverpool Plains, *Australia* 91 E5
Liverpool Ra., *Australia* . 91 E5
Livingston, *Guatemala* .. 116 C2
Livingston, *Calif., U.S.A.* 112 H6
Livingston, *Mont., U.S.A.* 110 D8
Livingston, *Tex., U.S.A.* 109 K7
Livingstone, *Zambia* 83 F2
Livingstone Mts., *Tanzania* 83 D3
Livingstonia, *Malawi* .. 83 E3
Livny, *Russia* 42 D3
Livonia, *U.S.A.* 104 D4
Livorno, *Italy* 32 E7
Livramento, *Brazil* 127 C4
Livramento do Brumado,
  Brazil 123 D3
Livron-sur-Drôme, *France* 27 D8
Liwale, *Tanzania* 83 D4
Liwale □, *Tanzania* 83 D4
Lixi, *China* 52 D3
Liyang, *China* 53 B12
Lizard I., *Australia* 90 A4
Lizard Pt., *U.K.* 13 H2
Lizarda, *Brazil* 122 C2
Lizzano, *Italy* 35 B10

Ljubno, *Slovenia* 33 B11
Ljubuški, *Bos.-H.* 21 M7
Ljung, *Sweden* 11 F7
Ljungan →, *Sweden* 10 B11
Ljungaverk, *Sweden* 10 B10
Ljungby, *Sweden* 9 H15
Ljusdal, *Sweden* 10 C10
Ljusnan →, *Sweden* 9 F17
Ljusne, *Sweden* 9 F17
Ljutomer, *Slovenia* 33 B13
Llagostera, *Spain* 28 D7
Llamellín, *Peru* 124 B2
Llancanelo, Salina,
  Argentina 126 D2
Llandeilo, *U.K.* 13 F3
Llandovery, *U.K.* 13 F4
Llandrindod Wells, *U.K.* . 13 E4
Llandudno, *U.K.* 12 D4
Llanelli, *U.K.* 13 F3
Llanes, *Spain* 30 B6
Llangollen, *U.K.* 12 E4
Llanidloes, *U.K.* 13 E4
Llano, *U.S.A.* 109 K5
Llano →, *U.S.A.* 109 K5
Llano Estacado, *U.S.A.* . 109 J3
Llanos, *S. Amer.* 118 C3
Llanquihue □, *Chile* 128 B2
Llanquihue, L., *Chile* .. 128 B1
Llebetx, C., *Spain* 36 B9
Lleida = Lérida, *Spain* .. 28 D5
Llentrisca, C., *Spain* .. 36 C7
Llera, *Mexico* 115 C5
Llerena, *Spain* 31 G4
Llica, *Bolivia* 124 D4
Llico, *Chile* 126 C1
Llobregat →, *Spain* 28 D7
Lloret de Mar, *Spain* .. 28 D7
Lloyd B., *Australia* 90 A3
Lloyd L., *Canada* 101 B7
Lloydminster, *Canada* .. 101 C6
Lluchmayor, *Spain* 36 B9
Llullaillaco, Volcán,
  S. Amer. 126 A2
Lo, *Belgium* 17 G1
Lo →, *Vietnam* 58 B5
Loa, *U.S.A.* 111 G8
Loa →, *Chile* 126 A1
Loano, *Italy* 32 D5
Lobatse, *Botswana* 84 D4
Löbau, *Germany* 18 D10
Lobbes, *Belgium* 17 H4
Lobenstein, *Germany* .. 18 E7
Lobería, *Argentina* 126 D4
Lobito, *Angola* 81 G2
Lobón, Canal de, *Spain* . 31 G4
Lobos, *Argentina* 126 D4
Lobos, I., *Mexico* 114 B2
Lobos, I. de, *Canary Is.* . 36 F6
Lobos de Tierra, I., *Peru* 124 B1
Loc Binh, *Vietnam* 58 B6
Loc Ninh, *Vietnam* 59 G6
Locarno, *Switz.* 23 D7
Loch Garman = Wexford,
  Ireland 15 D5
Lochaber, *U.K.* 14 E4
Lochcarron, *U.K.* 14 D3
Lochem, *Neths.* 16 D8
Loches, *France* 24 E8
Lochgelly, *U.K.* 14 E5
Lochgilphead, *U.K.* 14 E3
Lochinver, *U.K.* 14 C3
Lochnagar, *Australia* .. 90 C4
Lochnagar, *U.K.* 14 E5
Łochów, *Poland* 20 C11
Lochy →, *U.K.* 14 E3
Lock, *Australia* 91 E2
Lock Haven, *U.S.A.* 106 E7
Lockeford, *U.S.A.* 112 G5
Lockeport, *Canada* 99 D6
Lockerbie, *U.K.* 14 F5
Lockhart, *U.S.A.* 109 L6
Lockhart, L., *Australia* .. 89 F2
Lockney, *U.S.A.* 109 H4
Lockport, *U.S.A.* 106 C6
Locminé, *France* 24 E4
Locri, *Italy* 35 D9
Locronan, *France* 24 D2
Loctudy, *France* 24 E2
Lod, *Israel* 69 D3
Lodeinoye Pole, *Russia* . 40 B7
Lodève, *France* 26 E7
Lodge Grass, *U.S.A.* .. 110 D10
Lodgepole, *U.S.A.* 108 E2
Lodgepole Cr. →, *U.S.A.* 108 E2
Lodhran, *Pakistan* 62 E4
Lodi, *Italy* 32 C6
Lodi, *U.S.A.* 112 G5
Lodja, *Zaïre* 82 C1
Lodosa, *Spain* 28 C2
Lödöse, *Sweden* 11 F6
Lodwar, *Kenya* 82 B4
Łódź, *Poland* 20 D9
Loei, *Thailand* 58 D3
Loenen, *Neths.* 16 D8
Loengo, *Zaïre* 82 C2
Loeriesfontein, *S. Africa* . 84 E2
Lofoten, *Norway* 8 B16
Lofsdalen, *Sweden* 10 B7
Lofsen →, *Sweden* 10 B7
Logan, *Kans., U.S.A.* .. 108 F5
Logan, *Ohio, U.S.A.* 104 F4
Logan, *Utah, U.S.A.* 110 F8
Logan, *W. Va., U.S.A.* . 104 G5
Logan, Mt., *Canada* 96 B5
Logan Pass, *U.S.A.* 100 D6
Logandale, *U.S.A.* 113 J12
Logansport, *Ind., U.S.A.* 104 E2

Logansport

Logansport, La., U.S.A. 109 K8
Logo, Sudan 77 F3
Logone →, Chad 73 F8
Logroño, Spain 28 C2
Logrosán, Spain 31 F5
Løgstør, Denmark 11 H3
Lohardaga, India 63 H11
Lohja, Finland 9 F21
Lohr, Germany 19 F5
Loi-kaw, Burma 61 K20
Loimaa, Finland 9 F20
Loir →, France 24 E6
Loir-et-Cher □, France 24 E8
Loire □, France 27 C8
Loire →, France 24 E4
Loire-Atlantique □, France 24 E5
Loiret □, France 25 E9
Loitz, Germany 18 B9
Loja, Ecuador 124 A2
Loja, Spain 31 H6
Loja □, Ecuador 120 D2
Loji, Indonesia 57 E7
Loka, Sudan 77 G3
Lokandu, Zaïre 82 C2
Løken, Norway 10 E5
Lokeren, Belgium 17 F3
Lokhvitsa, Ukraine 41 G7
Lokichokio, Kenya 82 B3
Lokitaung, Kenya 82 B4
Lokkan tekojärvi, Finland 8 C22
Løkken, Denmark 11 G3
Løkken, Norway 10 A3
Loknya, Russia 40 D6
Lokoja, Nigeria 79 D6
Lokolama, Zaïre 80 E3
Lokot, Russia 42 D2
Lol →, Sudan 77 F2
Lola, Guinea 78 D3
Lola, Mt., U.S.A. 112 F6
Lolibai, Gebel, Sudan 77 G3
Lolimi, Sudan 77 G3
Loliondo, Tanzania 82 C4
Lolland, Denmark 11 K5
Lollar, Germany 18 E4
Lolo, U.S.A. 110 C6
Lolodorf, Cameroon 79 E7
Lom, Bulgaria 38 F6
Lom →, Bulgaria 38 F6
Lom Kao, Thailand 58 D3
Lom Sak, Thailand 58 D3
Loma, U.S.A. 110 C8
Loma Linda, U.S.A. 113 L9
Lomami →, Zaïre 82 B1
Lomas de Zamóra, Argentina 126 C4
Lombadina, Australia 88 C3
Lombárdia □, Italy 32 C6
Lombardy = Lombárdia □, Italy 32 C6
Lombez, France 26 E4
Lomblen, Indonesia 57 F6
Lombok, Indonesia 56 F5
Lomé, Togo 79 D5
Lomela, Zaïre 80 E4
Lomela →, Zaïre 80 E4
Lomello, Italy 32 C5
Lometa, U.S.A. 109 K5
Lomié, Cameroon 80 D2
Lomma, Sweden 11 J7
Lomme →, Belgium 17 H6
Lommel, Belgium 17 F6
Lomond, Canada 100 C6
Lomond, L., U.K. 14 E4
Lomphat, Cambodia 58 F6
Lompobatang, Indonesia 57 F5
Lompoc, U.S.A. 113 L6
Lomsegga, Norway 10 C2
Łomza, Poland 20 B12
Loncoche, Chile 128 A2
Loncopuè, Argentina 128 A2
Londa, India 60 M9
Londerzeel, Belgium 17 G4
Londiani, Kenya 82 C4
Londinières, France 24 C8
London, Canada 98 D3
London, U.K. 13 F7
London, Ky., U.S.A. 104 G3
London, Ohio, U.S.A. 104 F4
London, Greater □, U.K. 13 F7
Londonderry, U.K. 15 B4
Londonderry □, U.K. 15 B4
Londonderry, C., Australia 88 B4
Londonderry, I., Chile 128 E2
Londrina, Brazil 127 A5
Lone Pine, U.S.A. 111 H4
Long Beach, Calif., U.S.A. 113 M8
Long Beach, N.Y., U.S.A. 107 F11
Long Beach, Wash., U.S.A. 112 D2
Long Branch, U.S.A. 107 F11
Long Creek, U.S.A. 110 D4
Long Eaton, U.K. 12 E6
Long I., Australia 90 C4
Long I., Bahamas 117 B4
Long I., U.S.A. 107 F11
Long Island Sd., U.S.A. 107 E12
Long L., Canada 98 C2
Long Lake, U.S.A. 107 C10
Long Pine, U.S.A. 108 D5
Long Point B., Canada 106 D4
Long Pt., Nfld., Canada 99 C8
Long Pt., Ont., Canada 106 D4
Long Range Mts., Canada 99 C8
Long Reef, Australia 88 B4
Long Str. = Longa, Proliv, Russia 4 C16
Long Thanh, Vietnam 59 G6
Long Xian, China 50 G4
Long Xuyen, Vietnam 59 G5
Longá, Greece 39 N4
Longa, Proliv, Russia 4 C16
Long'an, China 52 F6
Longarone, Italy 33 B9
Longchang, China 52 C5
Longchi, China 52 C4
Longchuan, Guangdong, China 53 E10
Longchuan, Yunnan, China 52 E1
Longde, China 50 G4
Longeau, France 25 E12
Longford, Australia 90 G4
Longford, Ireland 15 C4
Longford □, Ireland 15 C4
Longguan, China 50 D8
Longhua, China 51 D9
Longhui, China 53 D8
Longido, Tanzania 82 C4
Longiram, Indonesia 56 E5
Longkou, Jiangxi, China 53 D10
Longkou, Shandong, China 51 F11
Longlac, Canada 98 C2
Longli, China 52 D6
Longlier, Belgium 17 J6
Longlin, China 52 E5
Longling, China 52 E2
Longmen, China 53 F10
Longming, China 52 F6
Longmont, U.S.A. 108 E2
Longnan, China 53 E10
Longnawan, Indonesia 56 D4
Longobucco, Italy 35 C9
Longquan, China 53 C12
Longreach, Australia 90 C3
Longshan, China 52 C7
Longsheng, China 53 E8
Longton, Australia 90 C4
Longtown, U.K. 13 F5
Longué-Jumelles, France 24 E6
Longueau, France 25 C9
Longueuil, Canada 107 A11
Longuyon, France 25 C12
Longview, Canada 100 C6
Longview, Tex., U.S.A. 109 J7
Longview, Wash., U.S.A. 112 D4
Longvilly, Belgium 17 H7
Longwy, France 25 C12
Longxi, China 50 G3
Longyou, China 53 C12
Longzhou, China 52 F6
Lonigo, Italy 33 C8
Löningen, Germany 18 C3
Lonja →, Croatia 33 C13
Lonoke, U.S.A. 109 H9
Lonquimay, Chile 128 A2
Lons-le-Saunier, France 25 F12
Lønstrup, Denmark 11 G3
Lookout, C., Canada 98 A3
Lookout, C., U.S.A. 105 H7
Loolmalasin, Tanzania 82 C4
Loon →, Alta., Canada 100 B5
Loon →, Man., Canada 101 B8
Loon Lake, Canada 101 C7
Loon-op-Zand, Neths. 17 E6
Loongana, Australia 89 F4
Loop Hd., Ireland 15 D2
Loosduinen, Neths. 16 D4
Lop Buri, Thailand 58 E3
Lop Nor = Lop Nur, China 54 B4
Lop Nur, China 54 B4
Lopare, Bos.-H. 21 L8
Lopatin, Russia 43 J8
Lopatina, G., Russia 45 D15
Lopaye, Sudan 77 F3
Lopera, Spain 31 H6
Lopez, Phil. 55 E5
Lopez, C., Gabon 80 E1
Loppersum, Neths. 16 B9
Lopphavet, Norway 8 A19
Lora →, Afghan. 60 D4
Lora, Hamun-i-, Pakistan 60 E4
Lora Cr. →, Australia 91 D2
Lora del Río, Spain 31 H5
Lorain, U.S.A. 106 E2
Loralai, Pakistan 62 D3
Lorca, Spain 29 H3
Lord Howe I., Pac. Oc. 92 L7
Lord Howe Ridge, Pac. Oc. 92 L8
Lordsburg, U.S.A. 111 K9
Loreto, Bolivia 125 D5
Loreto, Brazil 122 C2
Loreto, Italy 33 E10
Loreto, Mexico 114 B2
Loreto □, Peru 120 D3
Loreto Aprutino, Italy 33 F10
Lorgues, France 27 E10
Lorica, Colombia 120 B2
Lorient, France 24 E3
Lorn, U.K. 14 E3
Lorn, Firth of, U.K. 14 E3
Lorne, Australia 91 F3
Lorovouno, Cyprus 37 D11
Lörrach, Germany 19 H3
Lorraine, France 25 D12
Lorrainville, Canada 98 C4
Los, Îles de, Guinea 78 D2
Los Alamos, Calif., U.S.A. 113 L6
Los Alamos, N. Mex., U.S.A. 111 J10
Los Altos, U.S.A. 112 H4
Los Andes, Chile 126 C1
Los Angeles, Chile 126 D1
Los Angeles, U.S.A. 113 L8
Los Angeles Aqueduct, U.S.A. 113 K9
Los Antiguos, Argentina 128 C2
Los Banos, U.S.A. 111 H3
Los Barrios, Spain 31 J5
Los Blancos, Argentina 126 A3
Los Cristianos, Canary Is. 36 F3
Los Gatos, U.S.A. 112 H5
Los Hermanos, Venezuela 117 D7
Los Islotes, Canary Is. 36 E6
Los Lagos, Chile 128 A2
Los Llanos de Aridane, Canary Is. 36 F2
Los Lomas, Peru 124 A1
Los Lunas, U.S.A. 111 J10
Los Menucos, Argentina 128 B3
Los Mochis, Mexico 114 B3
Los Monegros, Spain 28 D4
Los Monos, Argentina 128 C3
Los Olivos, U.S.A. 113 L6
Los Palacios, Cuba 116 B3
Los Palacios y Villafranca, Spain 31 H5
Los Reyes, Mexico 114 D4
Los Ríos □, Ecuador 120 D2
Los Roques, Venezuela 120 A4
Los Santos de Maimona, Spain 31 G4
Los Teques, Venezuela 120 A4
Los Testigos, Venezuela 121 A5
Los Vilos, Chile 126 C1
Los Yébenes, Spain 31 F7
Losada →, Colombia 120 C3
Loshkalakh, Russia 45 C15
Lošinj, Croatia 33 D11
Losser, Neths. 16 D10
Lossiemouth, U.K. 14 D5
Lot □, France 26 D5
Lot →, France 26 D4
Lot-et-Garonne □, France 26 D4
Lota, Chile 126 D1
Løten, Norway 10 D5
Loṭfābād, Iran 65 B8
Lothair, S. Africa 85 D5
Lothian □, U.K. 14 F5
Lothiers, France 25 F8
Lötschbergtunnel, Switz. 22 D5
Lottefors, Sweden 10 C10
Lotzwil, Switz. 22 B5
Loubomo, Congo 80 E2
Loudéac, France 24 D4
Loudi, China 53 D8
Loudon, U.S.A. 105 H3
Loudonville, U.S.A. 106 F2
Loudun, France 24 E7
Loué, France 24 E6
Loue →, France 25 E12
Louga, Senegal 78 B1
Loughborough, U.K. 12 E6
Loughrea, Ireland 15 C3
Loughros More B., Ireland 15 B3
Louhans, France 27 B9
Louis Trichardt, S. Africa 85 C4
Louis XIV, Pte., Canada 98 B4
Louisa, U.S.A. 104 F4
Louisbourg, Canada 99 C8
Louise I., Canada 100 C2
Louiseville, Canada 98 C5
Louisiade Arch., Papua N. G. 92 J7
Louisiana, U.S.A. 108 F9
Louisiana □, U.S.A. 109 K9
Louisville, Ky., U.S.A. 104 F3
Louisville, Miss., U.S.A. 109 J10
Loulay, France 26 B3
Loulé, Portugal 31 H2
Louny, Czech. 20 E3
Loup City, U.S.A. 108 E5
Lourdes, France 26 E3
Lourdes-du-Blanc-Sablon, Canada 99 B8
Lourenço, Brazil 121 C7
Lourenço-Marques = Maputo, Mozam. 85 D5
Loures, Portugal 31 G1
Lourinhã, Portugal 31 F1
Lousã, Portugal 30 E2
Louth, Australia 91 E4
Louth, Ireland 15 C5
Louth, U.K. 12 D7
Louth □, Ireland 15 C5
Louvain = Leuven, Belgium 17 G5
Louveigné, Belgium 17 G7
Louviers, France 24 C8
Louwsburg, S. Africa 85 D5
Lovat →, Russia 40 C6
Love, Canada 101 C8
Lovech, Bulgaria 38 F7
Loveland, U.S.A. 108 E2
Lovell, U.S.A. 110 D9
Lovelock, U.S.A. 110 F4
Lóvere, Italy 32 C7
Loviisa, Finland 9 F22
Loving, U.S.A. 109 J2
Lovington, U.S.A. 109 J3
Lovios, Spain 30 D2
Lovisa = Loviisa, Finland 9 F22
Lovran, Croatia 33 C11
Low Pt., Australia 89 F4
Low Tatra = Nízké Tatry, Slovak Rep. 20 G9
Lowa, Zaïre 82 C2
Lowa →, Zaïre 82 C2
Lowell, U.S.A. 107 D13
Lower Arrow L., Canada 100 D5
Lower California = Baja California, Mexico 114 A1
Lower Hutt, N.Z. 87 J5
Lower L., U.S.A. 110 F3
Lower Lake, U.S.A. 112 G4
Lower Post, Canada 100 B3
Lower Red L., U.S.A. 108 B7
Lower Saxony = Niedersachsen □, Germany 18 C5
Lower Tunguska = Tunguska, Nizhnyaya →, Russia 45 C9
Lowestoft, U.K. 13 E9
Łowicz, Poland 20 C9
Lowville, U.S.A. 107 C9
Loxton, Australia 91 E3
Loxton, S. Africa 84 E3
Loyalton, U.S.A. 112 F6
Loyalty Is. = Loyauté, Is., N. Cal. 92 K8
Loyang = Luoyang, China 50 G7
Loyauté, Is., N. Cal. 92 K8
Loyev = Loyew, Belarus 41 G6
Loyew, Belarus 41 G6
Loyoro, Uganda 82 B3
Lož, Slovenia 33 C11
Lozère □, France 26 D7
Loznica, Serbia, Yug. 21 L9
Lozova, Ukraine 41 H9
Luachimo, Angola 80 F4
Luacono, Angola 80 G4
Lualaba →, Zaïre 82 B5
Luampa, Zambia 83 F1
Lu'an, China 53 B11
Luan Chau, Vietnam 58 B4
Luan He →, China 51 E10
Luan Xian, China 51 E10
Luancheng, Guangxi Zhuangzu, China 52 F7
Luancheng, Hebei, China 50 F8
Luanda, Angola 80 F2
Luang Prabang, Laos 58 C4
Luang Thale, Thailand 59 J3
Luangwa, Zambia 83 F3
Luangwa →, Zambia 83 E3
Luangwa Valley, Zambia 83 E3
Luanne, China 51 D9
Luanping, China 51 D9
Luanshya, Zambia 83 E2
Luapula □, Zambia 83 E2
Luapula →, Africa 83 D2
Luarca, Spain 30 B4
Luashi, Zaïre 83 E1
Luau, Angola 80 G4
Lubalo, Angola 80 F3
Lubań, Poland 20 D5
Lubana, Ozero = Lubānas Ezers, Latvia 9 H22
Lubānas Ezers, Latvia 9 H22
Lubang, Phil. 55 E4
Lubang Is., Phil. 57 B6
Lubartów, Poland 20 D12
Lubawa, Poland 20 B9
Lubbeek, Belgium 17 G5
Lübben, Germany 18 D9
Lübbenau, Germany 18 D9
Lubbock, U.S.A. 109 J4
Lübeck, Germany 18 B6
Lübecker Bucht, Germany 18 A7
Lubefu, Zaïre 82 C1
Lubefu →, Zaïre 82 C1
Lubero = Luofu, Zaïre 82 C2
Lubicon L., Canada 100 B5
Lublin, Poland 20 D12
Lubliniec, Poland 20 E8
Lubnān, J., Lebanon 69 B4
Lubny, Ukraine 41 G7
Lubon, Poland 20 C6
Lubongola, Zaïre 82 C2
Lubsko, Poland 20 D4
Lübtheen, Germany 18 B7
Lubuagan, Phil. 55 C4
Lubudi →, Zaïre 83 D2
Lubuk Antu, Malaysia 56 D4
Lubuklinggau, Indonesia 56 E2
Lubuksikaping, Indonesia 56 D2
Lubumbashi, Zaïre 83 E2
Lubunda, Zaïre 82 D2
Lubungu, Zambia 83 E2
Lubutu, Zaïre 82 C2
Luc An Chau, Vietnam 58 A5
Luc-en-Diois, France 27 D9
Lucan, Canada 106 C3
Lucban, Phil. 55 D4
Lucca, Italy 32 E7
Luce Bay, U.K. 14 G4
Lucea, Jamaica 116 C4
Lucedale, U.S.A. 105 K1
Lucena, Phil. 55 E4
Lucena, Spain 31 H6
Lucena del Cid, Spain 28 E4
Lučenec, Slovak Rep. 21 G9
Lucens, Switz. 22 C3
Lucera, Italy 35 A8
Lucerne = Luzern, Switz. 23 B6
Lucerne, U.S.A. 112 F4
Lucerne Valley, U.S.A. 113 L10
Lucero, Mexico 114 A3
Luchena →, Spain 29 H3
Lucheng, China 50 F7
Lucheringo →, Mozam. 83 E4
Lüchow, Germany 18 C7
Luchuan, China 53 F8
Lucie →, Surinam 121 C6
Lucira, Angola 81 G2
Luckau, Germany 18 D9
Luckenwalde, Germany 18 C9
Lucknow, India 63 F9
Luçon, France 26 B2
Lüda = Dalian, China 51 E11
Luda Kamchiya →, Bulgaria 38 F10
Ludbreg, Croatia 33 B13
Lüdenscheid, Germany 18 D3
Lüderitz, Namibia 84 D2
Ludewe □, Tanzania 83 D3
Ludhiana, India 62 D6
Ludian, China 52 D4
Luding Qiao, China 52 C4
Lüdinghausen, Germany 18 D3
Ludington, U.S.A. 104 D2
Ludlow, U.K. 13 E5
Ludlow, Calif., U.S.A. 113 L10
Ludlow, Vt., U.S.A. 107 C12
Ludus, Romania 38 C7
Ludvika, Sweden 9 F16
Ludwigsburg, Germany 19 G5
Ludwigshafen, Germany 19 F4
Ludwigslust, Germany 18 B7
Ludza, Latvia 40 D4
Luebo, Zaïre 80 F4
Lueki, Zaïre 82 C2
Luena, Zaïre 83 D2
Luena, Zambia 83 E3
Luepa, Venezuela 121 B5
Lüeyang, China 50 H4
Lufeng, Guangdong, China 53 F10
Lufeng, Yunnan, China 52 E4
Lufira →, Zaïre 83 D2
Lufkin, U.S.A. 109 K7
Lufupa, Zaïre 83 E1
Luga, Russia 40 C5
Luga →, Russia 40 C5
Lugang, Taiwan 53 E13
Lugano, Switz. 23 D7
Lugano, L. di, Switz. 23 E8
Lugansk = Luhansk, Ukraine 41 H10
Lugard's Falls, Kenya 82 C4
Lugela, Mozam. 83 F4
Lugenda →, Mozam. 83 E4
Lugh Ganana, Somali Rep. 68 G3
Lugnaquilla, Ireland 15 D5
Lugnvik, Sweden 10 B11
Lugo, Italy 33 D8
Lugo, Spain 30 B3
Lugo □, Spain 30 C3
Lugoj, Romania 38 D4
Lugones, Spain 30 B5
Lugovoy, Kazakhstan 44 E8
Luhansk, Ukraine 41 H10
Luhe, China 53 A12
Luhe →, Germany 18 B6
Luhuo, China 52 B3
Luiana, Angola 84 B3
Luimneach = Limerick, Ireland 15 D3
Luino, Italy 32 C5
Luís Correia, Brazil 122 B3
Luís Gonçalves, Brazil 122 C1
Luitpold Coast, Antarctica 5 D1
Luiza, Zaïre 80 F4
Luizi, Zaïre 82 D2
Luján, Argentina 126 C4
Lujiang, China 53 B11
Lukanga Swamp, Zambia 83 E2
Lukenie →, Zaïre 80 E3
Lukhisaral, India 63 G12
Lŭki, Bulgaria 39 H7
Lukolela, Equateur, Zaïre 80 E3
Lukolela, Kasai Or., Zaïre 82 D1
Lukosi, Zimbabwe 83 F2
Lukovit, Bulgaria 38 F7
Łuków, Poland 20 D12
Lukoyanov, Russia 42 C7
Lule älv →, Sweden 8 D19
Luleå, Sweden 8 D20
Lüleburgaz, Turkey 66 B2
Luliang, China 52 E4
Luling, U.S.A. 109 L6
Lulong, China 51 E10
Lulonga →, Zaïre 80 D3
Lulua →, Zaïre 80 E4
Luluabourg = Kananga, Zaïre 80 F4
Lumai, Angola 81 G4
Lumajang, Indonesia 57 H15
Lumbala N'guimbo, Angola 81 G4
Lumberton, Miss., U.S.A. 109 K10
Lumberton, N.C., U.S.A. 105 H6
Lumberton, N. Mex., U.S.A. 111 H10
Lumbres, France 25 B9
Lumbwa, Kenya 82 C4
Lummen, Belgium 17 G6
Lumsden, N.Z. 87 L2
Lumut, Malaysia 59 K3
Lumut, Tg., Indonesia 56 E3
Luna, Phil. 55 C4
Lunan, China 52 E4
Lunavada, India 62 H5
Lunca, Romania 38 B8
Lund, Sweden 11 J7
Lund, U.S.A. 110 G6
Lundazi, Zambia 83 E3
Lunderskov, Denmark 11 J3
Lundi →, Zimbabwe 83 G3
Lundu, Malaysia 56 D3
Lundy, U.K. 13 F3
Lune →, U.K. 12 C5
Lüneburg, Germany 18 B6
Lüneburg Heath = Lüneburger Heide, Germany 18 C6

Lüneburger Heide, Germany 18 C6
Lunel, France 27 E8
Lünen, Germany 18 D3
Lunenburg, Canada 99 D7
Lunéville, France 25 D13
Lunga →, Zambia 83 E2
Lungern, Switz. 22 C6
Lunglei, India 61 H18
Luni, India 62 F5
Luni →, India 62 G4
Luninets = Luninyets, Belarus 41 F4
Luning, U.S.A. 110 G4
Lunino, Russia 42 D7
Luninyets, Belarus 41 F4
Lunner, Norway 10 D4
Lunsemfwa →, Zambia 83 E3
Lunsemfwa Falls, Zambia 83 E2
Lunteren, Neths. 16 D7
Luo He →, China 50 G6
Luocheng, China 52 E7
Luochuan, China 50 G5
Luoci, China 52 E4
Luodian, China 52 E6
Luoding, China 53 F8
Luodong, Taiwan 53 E13
Luofu, Zaïre 82 C2
Luohe, China 50 H8
Luojiang, China 52 B5
Luonan, China 50 G6
Luoning, China 50 G6
Luoshan, China 53 A10
Luotian, China 53 B10
Luoyang, China 50 G7
Luoyuan, China 53 D12
Luozi, Zaïre 80 E2
Luozigou, China 51 C16
Lupanshui, China 52 D5
Lupeni, Romania 38 D6
Lupilichi, Mozam. 83 E4
Lupoing, China 52 E5
Luquan, China 52 E4
Luque, Paraguay 126 B4
Luque, Spain 31 H6
Luray, U.S.A. 104 F6
Lure, France 25 E13
Luremo, Angola 80 F3
Lurgan, U.K. 15 B5
Luri, France 27 F13
Luribay, Bolivia 124 D4
Lurin, Peru 124 C2
Lusaka, Zambia 83 F2
Lusambo, Zaïre 82 C1
Lusangaye, Zaïre 82 C2
Luseland, Canada 101 C7
Lushan, Henan, China 50 H7
Lushan, Sichuan, China 52 B4
Lushi, China 50 G6
Lushnja, Albania 39 J2
Lushoto, Tanzania 82 C4
Lushoto □, Tanzania 82 C4
Lushui, China 52 E2
Lüshun, China 51 E11
Lusignan, France 26 B4
Lusigny-sur-Barse, France 25 D11
Lusk, U.S.A. 108 D2
Lussac-les-Châteaux, France 26 B4
Lussanvira, Brazil 123 F1
Luta = Dalian, China 51 E11
Luton, U.K. 13 F7
Lutong, Malaysia 56 D4
Lutry, Switz. 22 C3
Lutsk, Ukraine 41 G3
Lützow Holmbukta, Antarctica 5 C4
Lutzputs, S. Africa 84 D3
Luverne, U.S.A. 108 D6
Luvua, Zaïre 83 D2
Luvua →, Zaïre 82 D2
Luwegu →, Tanzania 83 D4
Luwuk, Indonesia 57 E6
Luxembourg, Lux. 17 J8
Luxembourg □, Belgium 17 J7
Luxembourg ■, Europe 17 J8
Luxeuil-les-Bains, France 25 E13
Luxi, Hunan, China 53 C8
Luxi, Yunnan, China 52 E4
Luxi, Yunnan, China 52 E2
Luxor = El Uqsur, Egypt 76 B3
Luy →, France 26 E2
Luy-de-Béarn →, France 26 E3
Luy-de-France →, France 26 E3
Luyi, China 50 H8
Luyksgestel, Neths. 17 F6
Luz-St.-Sauveur, France 26 F4
Luzern, Switz. 23 B6
Luzern □, Switz. 22 B5
Luzhai, China 52 E7
Luzhou, China 52 C5
Luziânia, Brazil 123 E2
Luzilândia, Brazil 122 B3
Luzon, Phil. 55 D4
Luzy, France 25 F10
Luzzi, Italy 35 C9
Lviv, Ukraine 41 H3
Lvov = Lviv, Ukraine 41 H3
Lyakhavichy, Belarus 41 F4
Lyakhovskiye, Ostrova, Russia 45 B15
Lyaki = Läki, Azerbaijan 43 K8
Lyallpur = Faisalabad, Pakistan 62 D5
Lycaonia, Turkey 66 D5
Lychen, Germany 18 B9

Lychkova, Russia 40 D7
Lycia, Turkey 66 D3
Lycksele, Sweden 8 D18
Lydda = Lod, Israel 69 D3
Lydenburg, S. Africa 85 D5
Lydia, Turkey 66 C3
Lyell, N.Z. 87 J4
Lyell I., Canada 100 C2
Lyepyel, Belarus 40 E5
Lygnern, Sweden 11 G6
Lyman, U.S.A. 110 F8
Lyme Regis, U.K. 13 G5
Lymington, U.K. 13 G6
Łyna →, Poland 9 J19
Lynchburg, U.S.A. 104 G6
Lynd →, Australia 90 B3
Lynd Ra., Australia 91 D4
Lynden, Canada 106 C4
Lynden, U.S.A. 112 B4
Lyndhurst, Queens., Australia 90 B3
Lyndhurst, S. Austral., Australia 91 E2
Lyndon →, Australia 89 D1
Lyndonville, N.Y., U.S.A. 106 C6
Lyndonville, Vt., U.S.A. 107 B12
Lyngdal, Norway 10 E3
Lyngen, Norway 8 B19
Lynher Reef, Australia 88 C3
Lynn, U.S.A. 107 D14
Lynn Canal, U.S.A. 100 B1
Lynn Lake, Canada 101 B8
Lynnwood, U.S.A. 112 C4
Lynton, U.K. 13 F4
Lyntupy, Belarus 9 J22
Lynx L., Canada 101 A7
Lyø, Denmark 11 J4
Lyon, France 27 C8
Lyonnais, France 27 C8
Lyons = Lyon, France 27 C8
Lyons, Colo., U.S.A. 108 E2
Lyons, Ga., U.S.A. 105 J4
Lyons, Kans., U.S.A. 108 F5
Lyons, N.Y., U.S.A. 106 C8
Lyozna, Belarus 40 E6
Lyrestad, Sweden 11 F8
Lys = Leie →, Belgium 25 A10
Lysekil, Sweden 11 F5
Lyskovo, Russia 42 B7
Lyss, Switz. 22 B4
Lysychansk, Ukraine 41 H10
Lytle, U.S.A. 109 L5
Lyttelton, N.Z. 87 K4
Lytton, Canada 100 C4
Lyuban, Russia 40 C6
Lyubertsy, Russia 42 C3
Lyubim, Russia 42 A5
Lyuboml, Ukraine 41 G3
Lyubotyn, Ukraine 41 H8
Lyubytino, Russia 40 C7
Lyudinovo, Russia 42 D2

M

Ma →, Vietnam 58 C5
Ma'adaba, Jordan 69 E4
Maamba, Zambia 84 B4
Ma'ān, Jordan 69 E4
Ma'ān □, Jordan 69 F5
Maanselkä, Finland 8 C23
Ma'anshan, China 53 B12
Maarheeze, Neths. 17 F7
Maarianhamina, Finland 9 F18
Maarn, Neths. 16 D6
Ma'arrat an Nu'mān, Syria 66 E7
Maarssen, Neths. 16 D6
Maartensdijk, Neths. 16 D6
Maas →, Neths. 16 E5
Maasbracht, Belgium 17 F7
Maasbree, Neths. 17 F8
Maasdam, Neths. 16 E5
Maasdijk, Neths. 16 E4
Maaseik, Belgium 17 F7
Maasland, Neths. 16 E4
Maasniel, Neths. 17 F8
Maassluis, Neths. 16 E4
Maastricht, Neths. 17 G7
Maave, Mozam. 85 C5
Mabaruma, Guyana 121 B6
Mabel L., Canada 100 C5
Mabenge, Zaïre 82 B1
Mabian, China 52 C4
Maboma, Zaïre 82 B2
Mabrouk, Mali 79 B4
Mabton, U.S.A. 110 C3
Mac Bac, Vietnam 59 H6
Macachín, Argentina 126 D3
Macaé, Brazil 123 F3
Macaíba, Brazil 122 C4
Macajuba, Brazil 123 D3
McAlester, U.S.A. 109 H7
McAllen, U.S.A. 109 M5
Macamic, Canada 98 C4
Macao = Macau ■, China 53 F9
Macão, Portugal 31 F3
Macapá, Brazil 121 C7
Macará, Ecuador 120 D2
Macarani, Brazil 123 E3
Macarena, Serranía de la, Colombia 120 C3
McArthur →, Australia 90 B2
McArthur, Port, Australia 90 B2
McArthur River, Australia 90 B2

Macas, Ecuador 120 D2
Macate, Peru 124 C2
Macau, Brazil 122 C4
Macau ■, China 53 F9
Macaúbas, Brazil 123 D3
Macaya →, Colombia 120 C3
McBride, Canada 100 C4
McCall, U.S.A. 110 D5
McCamey, U.S.A. 109 K3
McCammon, U.S.A. 110 E7
McCauley I., Canada 100 C2
McCleary, U.S.A. 112 C3
Macclesfield, U.K. 12 D5
McClintock, Canada 101 B10
M'Clintock Chan., Canada 96 A9
McClintock Ra., Australia 88 C4
McCloud, U.S.A. 110 F2
M'Cluer I., Canada 98 B5
McClure, U.S.A. 106 F7
McClure, L., U.S.A. 112 H6
M'Clure Str., Canada 4 B2
McClusky, U.S.A. 108 B4
McComb, U.S.A. 109 K9
McConaughy, L., U.S.A. 108 E4
McCook, U.S.A. 108 E4
McCullough Mt., U.S.A. 113 K11
McCusker →, Canada 101 B7
McDame, Canada 100 B3
McDermitt, U.S.A. 110 F5
Macdonald, L., Australia 88 D4
Macdonnell Ras., Australia 88 D5
McDouall Peak, Australia 91 D1
Macdougall L., Canada 96 B10
MacDowell L., Canada 98 B1
Maceda, Spain 30 C3
Macedonia ■, Europe 39 H4
Maceió, Brazil 122 C4
Maceira, Portugal 31 F2
Macenta, Guinea 78 D3
Macerata, Italy 33 E10
McFarland, U.S.A. 113 K7
McFarlane →, Canada 101 B7
Macfarlane, L., Australia 91 E2
McGehee, U.S.A. 109 J9
McGill, U.S.A. 110 G6
Macgillycuddy's Reeks, Ireland 15 D2
MacGregor, Canada 101 D9
McGregor, U.S.A. 108 D9
McGregor →, Canada 100 B4
McGregor Ra., Australia 91 D3
Mach, Pakistan 60 E5
Māch Kowr, Iran 65 E9
Machacalis, Brazil 123 E3
Machado = Jiparaná →, Brazil 125 B5
Machagai, Argentina 126 B3
Machakos, Kenya 82 C4
Machakos □, Kenya 82 C4
Machala, Ecuador 120 D2
Machanga, Mozam. 85 C6
Machattie, L., Australia 90 C2
Machava, Mozam. 85 D5
Machece, Mozam. 83 F4
Machecoul, France 24 F5
Machelen, Belgium 17 G4
Macheng, China 53 B10
Machevna, Russia 45 C18
Machezo, Spain 31 F6
Machias, U.S.A. 99 D6
Machichaco, C., Spain 28 B2
Machico, Madeira 36 D3
Machilipatnam, India 61 L12
Machiques, Venezuela 120 A3
Machupicchu, Peru 124 C3
Machynlleth, U.K. 13 E4
McIlwraith Ra., Australia 90 A3
Măcin, Romania 38 D11
Macina, Mali 78 C4
McIntosh, U.S.A. 108 C4
McIntosh L., Canada 101 B8
Macintosh Ra., Australia 89 E4
McIntyre →, Australia 91 D5
Macizo Galaico, Spain 30 C3
Mackay, Australia 90 C4
Mackay, U.S.A. 110 E7
MacKay →, Canada 100 B6
Mackay, L., Australia 88 D4
McKay Ra., Australia 88 D3
McKeesport, U.S.A. 106 F5
McKenna, U.S.A. 112 D4
Mackenzie, Canada 100 B4
McKenzie, U.S.A. 105 G1
Mackenzie →, Australia 90 C4
Mackenzie →, Canada 96 B6
McKenzie →, U.S.A. 110 D2
Mackenzie Bay, Canada 4 B1
Mackenzie City = Linden, Guyana 121 B6
Mackenzie Highway, Canada 100 B5
Mackenzie Mts., Canada 96 B6
Mackinaw City, U.S.A. 104 C3
McKinlay, Australia 90 C3
McKinlay →, Australia 90 C3
McKinley, Mt., U.S.A. 96 B4
McKinley Sea, Arctic 4 A7
McKinney, U.S.A. 109 J6
Mackinnon Road, Kenya 82 C4
Macksville, Australia 91 E5
McLaughlin, U.S.A. 108 C4
Maclean, Australia 91 D5
McLean, U.S.A. 109 H4

McLeansboro, U.S.A. 108 F10
Maclear, S. Africa 85 E4
Macleay →, Australia 91 E5
McLennan, Canada 100 B5
MacLeod, B., Canada 101 A7
McLeod Lake, Canada 100 C4
McLoughlin, Mt., U.S.A. 110 E2
McLure, Canada 100 C4
McMechen, U.S.A. 106 G4
McMillan, L., U.S.A. 109 J2
McMinnville, Oreg., U.S.A. 110 D2
McMinnville, Tenn., U.S.A. 105 H3
McMorran, Canada 101 C7
McMurdo Sd., Antarctica 5 D11
McMurray = Fort McMurray, Canada 100 B6
McMurray, U.S.A. 112 B4
McNary, U.S.A. 111 J9
MacNutt, Canada 101 C8
Macodoene, Mozam. 85 C6
Macomb, U.S.A. 108 E9
Macomer, Italy 34 B1
Mâcon, France 27 B8
Macon, Ga., U.S.A. 105 J4
Macon, Miss., U.S.A. 105 J1
Macon, Mo., U.S.A. 108 F8
Macondo, Angola 81 G4
Macossa, Mozam. 83 F3
Macoun L., Canada 101 B8
Macovane, Mozam. 85 C6
McPherson, U.S.A. 108 F6
McPherson Pk., U.S.A. 113 L7
McPherson Ra., Australia 91 D5
Macquarie Harbour, Australia 90 G4
Macquarie Is., Pac. Oc. 92 N7
MacRobertson Land, Antarctica 5 D6
Macroom, Ireland 15 E3
Macroy, Australia 88 D2
MacTier, Canada 106 A5
Macubela, Mozam. 83 F4
Macugnaga, Italy 32 C4
Macuiza, Mozam. 83 F3
Macujer, Colombia 120 C3
Macusani, Peru 124 C3
Macuse, Mozam. 83 F4
Macusse, Angola 84 B3
McVille, U.S.A. 108 B5
Madadeni, S. Africa 85 D5
Madagali, Nigeria 79 C7
Madagascar ■, Africa 85 C8
Madā'in Sālih, Si. Arabia 64 E3
Madama, Niger 73 D7
Madame I., Canada 99 C7
Madaoua, Niger 79 C6
Madara, Niger 79 C7
Madaripur, Bangla. 61 H17
Madauk, Burma 61 L20
Madawaska, Canada 106 A7
Madawaska →, Canada 98 C4
Madaya, Burma 61 H20
Madbar, Sudan 77 F3
Maddaloni, Italy 35 A7
Made, Neths. 17 E5
Madeira, Atl. Oc. 36 D3
Madeira →, Brazil 121 D6
Madeleine, Is. de la, Canada 99 C7
Maden, Turkey 67 C8
Madera, U.S.A. 111 H3
Madha, India 60 L9
Madhubani, India 63 F12
Madhya Pradesh □, India 62 J7
Madian, China 53 A11
Madidi →, Bolivia 124 C4
Madikeri, India 60 N9
Madill, U.S.A. 109 H6
Madimba, Zaïre 80 E3
Ma'din, Syria 67 E8
Madīnat ash Sha'b, Yemen 68 E3
Madingo, Congo 80 E2
Madirovalo, Madag. 85 B8
Madison, Calif., U.S.A. 112 G5
Madison, Fla., U.S.A. 105 K4
Madison, Ind., U.S.A. 104 F3
Madison, Nebr., U.S.A. 108 E6
Madison, Ohio, U.S.A. 106 E3
Madison, S. Dak., U.S.A. 108 D6
Madison, Wis., U.S.A. 108 D10
Madison →, U.S.A. 110 D8
Madisonville, Ky., U.S.A. 104 G2
Madisonville, Tex., U.S.A. 109 K7
Madista, Botswana 84 C4
Madiun, Indonesia 57 G14
Madley, U.K. 13 E5
Madol, Sudan 77 F2
Madon →, France 25 D13
Madona, Latvia 9 H22
Madras = Tamil Nadu □, India 60 P10
Madras, India 60 N12
Madras, U.S.A. 110 D3
Madre, L., Mexico 115 B5
Madre, Laguna, U.S.A. 109 M6
Madre, Sierra, Phil. 55 C5
Madre de Dios □, Peru 124 C3
Madre de Dios →, Bolivia 124 C4
Madre de Dios, I., Chile 128 D1
Madre del Sur, Sierra, Mexico 115 D5
Madre Occidental, Sierra, Mexico 114 B3

Madre Oriental, Sierra, Mexico 114 C4
Madri, India 62 G5
Madrid, Spain 30 E7
Madrid □, Spain 30 E7
Madridejos, Spain 31 F7
Madrigal de las Altas Torres, Spain 30 D6
Madrona, Sierra, Spain 31 G6
Madroñera, Spain 31 F5
Madu, Sudan 77 E2
Madura, Indonesia 57 G15
Madura Motel, Australia 89 F4
Madurai, India 60 Q11
Madurantakam, India 60 N11
Madzhalis, Russia 43 J8
Mae Chan, Thailand 58 B2
Mae Hong Son, Thailand 58 C2
Mae Khlong →, Thailand 58 F3
Mae Phrik, Thailand 58 D2
Mae Ramat, Thailand 58 D2
Mae Rim, Thailand 58 C2
Mae Sot, Thailand 58 D2
Mae Suai, Thailand 58 C2
Mae Tha, Thailand 58 C2
Maebashi, Japan 49 F9
Maella, Spain 28 D5
Măeruş, Romania 38 D8
Maesteg, U.K. 13 F4
Maestra, Sierra, Cuba 116 B4
Maestrazgo, Mts. del, Spain 28 E4
Maevatanana, Madag. 85 B8
Mafeking = Mafikeng, S. Africa 84 D4
Mafeking, Canada 101 C8
Maféré, Ivory C. 78 D4
Mafeteng, Lesotho 84 D4
Maffra, Australia 91 F4
Maffe, Belgium 17 H6
Mafia I., Tanzania 82 D4
Mafikeng, S. Africa 84 D4
Mafra, Brazil 127 B6
Mafra, Portugal 31 G1
Mafungabusi Plateau, Zimbabwe 83 F2
Magadan, Russia 45 D16
Magadi, Kenya 82 C4
Magadi, L., Kenya 82 C4
Magaliesburg, S. Africa 85 D4
Magallanes □, Chile 128 D2
Magallanes, Estrecho de, Chile 128 D2
Magangué, Colombia 120 B3
Magaria, Niger 79 C6
Magburaka, S. Leone 78 D2
Magdalen Is. = Madeleine, Is. de la, Canada 99 C7
Magdalena, Argentina 126 D4
Magdalena, Bolivia 125 C5
Magdalena, Malaysia 56 D5
Magdalena, Mexico 114 A2
Magdalena, U.S.A. 111 J10
Magdalena □, Colombia 120 A3
Magdalena →, Colombia 120 A3
Magdalena →, Mexico 114 A2
Magdalena, B., Mexico 114 C2
Magdalena, I., Chile 128 B2
Magdalena, Llano de la, Mexico 114 C2
Magdeburg, Germany 18 C7
Magdelaine Cays, Australia 90 B5
Magdub, Sudan 77 E2
Magee, U.S.A. 109 K10
Magee, I., U.K. 15 B6
Magelang, Indonesia 57 G14
Magellan's Str. = Magallanes, Estrecho de, Chile 128 D2
Magenta, Italy 32 C5
Magenta, L., Australia 89 F2
Magerøya, Norway 8 A21
Maggia, Switz. 23 D7
Maggia →, Switz. 23 D7
Maggiorasca, Mte., Italy 32 D6
Maggiore, L., Italy 32 C5
Maghama, Mauritania 78 B2
Magherafelt, U.K. 15 B5
Maghnia, Algeria 75 B4
Magione, Italy 33 E9
Magistralnyy, Russia 45 D11
Magliano in Toscana, Italy 33 F8
Máglie, Italy 35 B11
Magnac-Laval, France 26 B5
Magnetic Pole (North) = North Magnetic Pole, Canada 4 B2
Magnetic Pole (South) = South Magnetic Pole, Antarctica 5 C9
Magnitogorsk, Russia 44 D6
Magnolia, Ark., U.S.A. 109 J8
Magnolia, Miss., U.S.A. 109 K9
Magnor, Norway 10 E6
Magny-en-Vexin, France 25 C8
Magog, Canada 99 C5
Magoro, Uganda 82 B3
Magosa = Famagusta, Cyprus 66 E5
Magouládhes, Greece 37 A3
Magoye, Zambia 83 F2
Magpie L., Canada 99 B7
Magrath, Canada 100 D6
Magro →, Spain 29 F4
Magrur, Wadi →, Sudan 77 D2
Magu □, Tanzania 82 C3
Maguan, China 52 F5
Maguarinho, C., Brazil 122 B2

Mağusa = Famagusta,
Cyprus 66 E5
Maguse L., Canada 101 A9
Maguse Pt., Canada 101 A10
Magwe, Burma 61 J19
Maha Sarakham, Thailand 58 D4
Mahābād, Iran 67 D11
Mahabharat Lekh, Nepal . 63 E9
Mahabo, Madag. 85 C7
Mahadeo Hills, India .. 62 H8
Mahagi, Zaïre 82 B3
Mahaicony, Guyana 121 B6
Mahajamba →, Madag. .. 85 B8
Mahajamba, Helodranon' i,
Madag. 85 B8
Mahajan, India 62 E5
Mahajanga, Madag. 85 B8
Mahajanga □, Madag. .. 85 B8
Mahajilo →, Madag. 85 B8
Mahakam →, Indonesia . 56 E5
Mahalapye, Botswana .. 84 C4
Maḥallāt, Iran 65 C6
Māhān, Iran 65 D8
Mahanadi →, India 61 J15
Mahanoro, Madag. 85 B8
Mahanoy City, U.S.A. .. 107 F8
Maharashtra □, India .. 60 J9
Maharès, Tunisia 75 B7
Mahari Mts., Tanzania .. 82 D2
Mahasham, W. →, Egypt 69 E3
Mahasolo, Madag. 85 B8
Mahattat ash Shīdīyah,
Jordan 69 F4
Mahattat 'Unayzah, Jordan 69 E4
Mahaxay, Laos 58 D5
Mahbes, W. Sahara ... 74 C3
Mahbubnagar, India ... 60 L10
Maḥḍah, Oman 65 E7
Mahdia, Guyana 121 B6
Mahdia, Tunisia 75 A7
Mahe, India 63 C8
Mahenge, Tanzania ... 83 D4
Maheno, N.Z. 87 L3
Mahesana, India 62 H5
Mahia Pen., N.Z. 87 H6
Mahilyow, Belarus 40 F6
Mahirija, Morocco 75 B4
Mahmiya, Sudan 77 D3
Mahmud Kot, Pakistan . 62 D4
Mahmudia, Romania ... 38 D12
Mahnomen, U.S.A. 108 B7
Mahoba, India 63 G8
Mahón, Spain 36 B11
Mahone Bay, Canada .. 99 D7
Mahuta, Nigeria 79 C5
Mai-Ndombe, L., Zaïre . 80 E3
Mai-Sai, Thailand 58 B2
Maicao, Colombia 120 A3
Maîche, France 25 E13
Maici →, Brazil 125 B5
Maicurú →, Brazil 121 D7
Máida, Italy 35 D9
Maidan Khula, Afghan. . 62 C3
Maidenhead, U.K. 13 F7
Maidi, Yemen 77 D5
Maidstone, Canada ... 101 C7
Maidstone, U.K. 13 F8
Maiduguri, Nigeria ... 79 C7
Maignelay, France ... 25 C9
Maigo, Phil. 55 G5
Maigualida, Sierra,
Venezuela 121 B4
Maigudo, Ethiopia ... 77 F4
Maijdi, Bangla. 61 H17
Maikala Ra., India ... 61 J12
Mailly-le-Camp, France 25 D11
Mailsi, Pakistan 62 E5
Main →, Germany 19 F4
Main →, U.K. 15 B5
Main Centre, Canada .. 101 C7
Mainburg, Germany .. 19 G7
Maine, France 24 E6
Maine □, U.S.A. 99 C6
Maine →, Ireland 15 D2
Maine-et-Loire □, France 24 E6
Maïne-Soroa, Niger .. 79 C7
Maingkwan, Burma .. 61 F20
Mainit, L., Phil. 55 G6
Mainland, Orkney, U.K. 14 C5
Mainland, Shet., U.K. .. 14 A7
Mainpuri, India 63 F8
Maintenon, France ... 25 D8
Maintirano, Madag. .. 85 B7
Mainvault, Belgium .. 17 G3
Mainz, Germany 19 F4
Maipú, Argentina ... 126 D4
Maiquetía, Venezuela . 120 A4
Maira →, Italy 32 D4
Mairabari, India 61 F18
Mairipotaba, Brazil . 123 E2
Maisí, Cuba 117 B5
Maisí, Pta. de, Cuba .. 117 B5
Maisse, France 25 D9
Maissin, Belgium ... 17 J6
Maitland, N.S.W., Australia 91 E5
Maitland, S. Austral.,
Australia 91 E2
Maitland →, Canada .. 106 C3
Maiyema, Nigeria ... 79 C5
Maiyuan, China 53 E11
Maíz, Is. del, Nic. ... 116 D3
Maizuru, Japan 49 G7
Majagual, Colombia .. 120 B3
Majalengka, Indonesia . 57 G13
Majari →, Brazil ... 121 C5
Majene, Indonesia .. 57 E5
Majes →, Peru 124 D3

Maji, Ethiopia 77 F4
Majiang, China 52 D6
Major, Canada 101 C7
Majorca = Mallorca, Spain 36 B10
Majuriã, Brazil 125 B5
Maka, Senegal 78 C2
Makak, Cameroon 79 E7
Makale, Indonesia 57 E5
Makamba, Burundi 82 C2
Makari, Cameroon 80 B2
Makarikari =
Makgadikgadi Salt Pans,
Botswana 84 C4
Makarovo, Russia 45 D11
Makarska, Croatia 21 M7
Makaryev, Russia 42 B6
Makasar = Ujung Pandang,
Indonesia 57 F5
Makasar, Selat, Indonesia . 57 E5
Makasar, Str. of =
Makasar, Selat, Indonesia 57 E5
Makat, Kazakhstan 44 E6
Makedonija =
Macedonia ■, Europe . 39 H4
Makena, U.S.A. 102 H16
Makeni, S. Leone 78 D2
Makeyevka = Makiyivka,
Ukraine 41 H9
Makgadikgadi Salt Pans,
Botswana 84 C4
Makhachkala, Russia ... 43 J8
Makharadze = Ozurgeti,
Georgia 43 K5
Makhmūr, Iraq 67 E10
Makian, Indonesia 57 D7
Makindu, Kenya 82 C4
Makinsk, Kazakhstan .. 44 D8
Makiyivka, Ukraine ... 41 H9
Makkah, Si. Arabia ... 68 C2
Makkovik, Canada 99 A8
Makkum, Neths. 16 B6
Makó, Hungary 21 J10
Makokou, Gabon 80 D2
Makongo, Zaïre 82 B2
Makoro, Zaïre 82 B2
Makoua, Congo 80 E3
Makrá, Greece 39 N8
Makrai, India 60 H10
Makran Coast Range,
Pakistan 60 G4
Makrana, India 62 F6
Makriyialos, Greece .. 37 D7
Maktar, Tunisia 75 A6
Mākū, Iran 67 C11
Makumbi, Zaïre 80 F4
Makunda, Botswana . 84 C3
Makurazaki, Japan .. 49 J5
Makurdi, Nigeria ... 79 D6
Makūyeh, Iran 65 D7
Makwassie, S. Africa . 84 D4
Makwiro, Zimbabwe . 83 F3
Mal B., Ireland 15 D2
Mal i Nemërçkës, Albania 39 J3
Mala, Peru 124 C2
Mala, Pta., Panama .. 116 E3
Mala Belozёrka, Ukraine . 41 J8
Mala Kapela, Croatia .. 33 D12
Mala Vyska, Ukraine .. 41 H6
Malabang, Phil. 55 H6
Malabar Coast, India .. 60 P9
Malabo = Rey Malabo,
Eq. Guin. 79 E6
Malabon, Phil. 55 D4
Malacca, Str. of, Indonesia 59 L3
Malacky, Slovak Rep. .. 21 G7
Malad City, U.S.A. ... 110 E7
Maladzyechna, Belarus . 40 E4
Málaga, Colombia ... 120 B3
Málaga, Spain 31 J6
Malaga, U.S.A. 109 J2
Málaga □, Spain 31 J6
Malagarasi, Tanzania .. 82 D3
Malagarasi →, Tanzania . 82 D2
Malagón, Spain 31 F7
Malagón →, Spain ... 31 H3
Malaimbandy, Madag. . 85 C8
Malakâl, Sudan 77 F3
Malakand, Pakistan .. 62 B4
Malakoff, U.S.A. 109 J7
Malamyzh, Russia ... 45 E14
Malang, Indonesia ... 57 G15
Malangen, Norway .. 8 B18
Malanje, Angola 80 F3
Mälaren, Sweden ... 10 E11
Malargüe, Argentina . 126 D2
Malartic, Canada ... 98 C4
Malaryta, Belarus ... 41 G3
Malatya, Turkey 67 C8
Malawi ■, Africa ... 83 E3
Malawi, L., Africa ... 83 E3
Malay Pen., Asia 59 J3
Malaya Belozёrka = Mala
Belozёrka, Ukraine .. 41 J8
Malaya Vishera, Russia . 40 C7
Malaya Viska = Mala
Vyska, Ukraine 41 H6
Malaybalay, Phil. 55 G6
Malāyer, Iran 67 E13
Malaysia ■, Asia 56 D4
Malazgirt, Turkey ... 67 C10
Malbon, Australia ... 90 C3
Malbooma, Australia . 91 E1
Malbork, Poland 20 A9
Malcésine, Italy 32 C7
Malchin, Germany .. 18 B8
Malchow, Germany . 18 B8
Malcolm, Australia .. 89 E3

Malcolm, Pt., Australia .. 89 F3
Maldegem, Belgium 17 F2
Malden, Mass., U.S.A. .. 107 D13
Malden, Mo., U.S.A. ... 109 G10
Malden I., Kiribati 93 H12
Maldives ■, Ind. Oc. .. 47 J11
Maldonado, Uruguay ... 127 C5
Maldonado, Punta, Mexico 115 D5
Malè, Italy 32 B7
Maléa, Ákra, Greece ... 39 N6
Malegaon, India 60 J9
Malei, Mozam. 83 F4
Malek Kandī, Iran 67 D12
Malela, Zaïre 82 C2
Malema, Mozam. 83 E4
Máleme, Greece 37 D5
Malerkotla, India 62 D6
Males, Greece 37 D7
Malesherbes, France .. 25 D9
Malestroit, France ... 24 E4
Malfa, Italy 35 D7
Malgobek, Russia 43 J7
Malgomaj, Sweden ... 8 D17
Malgrat, Spain 28 D7
Malha, Sudan 77 D2
Malheur →, U.S.A. ... 110 D5
Malheur L., U.S.A. ... 110 E4
Mali, Guinea 78 C2
Mali ■, Africa 78 B4
Mali →, Burma 61 G20
Mali Kanal, Serbia, Yug. . 21 K9
Malibu, U.S.A. 113 L8
Malik, Indonesia 57 E6
Malili, Indonesia 57 E6
Malimba, Mts., Zaïre .. 82 D2
Malin Hd., Ireland ... 15 A4
Malindi, Kenya 82 C5
Malines = Mechelen,
Belgium 17 F4
Malino, Indonesia ... 57 D6
Malinyi, Tanzania ... 83 D4
Malipo, China 52 F5
Maliqi, Albania 39 J3
Malita, Phil. 57 C7
Malkara, Turkey 66 B2
Małkinia Górna, Poland . 20 C12
Malko Tŭrnovo, Bulgaria . 39 H10
Mallacoota, Australia . 91 F4
Mallacoota Inlet, Australia 91 F4
Mallaig, U.K. 14 E3
Mallawan, India 63 F9
Mallawi, Egypt 76 B3
Malleco □, Chile 128 A2
Mallemort, France ... 27 E9
Málles Venosta, Italy .. 32 B7
Mállia, Greece 37 D7
Mallión, Kólpos, Greece . 37 D7
Mallorca, Spain 36 B10
Mallorytown, Canada . 107 B9
Mallow, Ireland 15 D3
Malmberget, Sweden . 8 C19
Malmédy, Belgium .. 17 H8
Malmesbury, S. Africa . 84 E2
Malmö, Sweden 11 J6
Malmöhus län □, Sweden 11 J7
Malmslätt, Sweden .. 11 F9
Malmyzh, Russia ... 42 B10
Maloarkhangelsk, Russia . 42 D3
Maloca, Brazil 121 C6
Maloja, Switz. 23 D9
Maloja, P., Switz. ... 23 D9
Malolos, Phil. 57 B6
Malombe L., Malawi .. 83 E4
Malone, U.S.A. 107 B10
Malong, China 52 E4
Måløy, Norway 9 F11
Maloyaroslovets, Russia . 42 C3
Malpartida, Spain ... 31 F4
Malpaso, Canary Is. .. 36 G1
Malpica, Spain 30 B2
Mals = Málles Venosta,
Italy 32 B7
Malta, Brazil 122 C4
Malta, Idaho, U.S.A. .. 110 E7
Malta, Mont., U.S.A. .. 110 B10
Malta ■, Europe 37 D1
Malta Channel, Medit. S. 34 F6
Maltahöhe, Namibia .. 84 C2
Malters, Switz. 22 B6
Malton, Canada 106 C5
Malton, U.K. 12 C7
Maluku, Indonesia .. 57 E7
Maluku □, Indonesia . 57 E7
Maluku Sea = Molucca
Sea, Indonesia 57 E6
Malumfashi, Nigeria . 79 C6
Malvan, India 60 L8
Malvern, U.S.A. 109 H8
Malvern Hills, U.K. .. 13 E5
Malvik, Norway 10 A4
Malvinas, Is. = Falkland
Is. □, Atl. Oc. 128 D5
Malya, Tanzania ... 82 C3
Malyn, Ukraine 41 G5
Malyy Lyakhovskiy,
Ostrov, Russia 45 B15
Malyy Nimnyr, Russia . 45 D13
Mama, Russia 45 D12
Mamadysh, Russia .. 42 C10
Mamanguape, Brazil . 122 C4
Mamasa, Indonesia .. 57 E5
Mambasa, Zaïre 82 B2
Mamberamo →, Indonesia 57 E9
Mambilima Falls, Zambia 83 E2
Mambirima, Zaïre ... 83 E2
Mambo, Tanzania ... 82 C4
Mambrui, Kenya ... 82 C5

Mamburao, Phil. 55 E4
Mameigwess L., Canada . 98 B2
Mamer, Lux. 17 J8
Mamers, France 24 D7
Mamfe, Cameroon ... 79 D6
Mamiña, Chile 124 E4
Mámmola, Italy 35 D9
Mammoth, U.S.A. ... 111 K8
Mamoré →, Bolivia .. 125 C4
Mamou, Guinea 78 C2
Mampatá, Guinea-Biss. . 78 C2
Mampong, Ghana ... 79 D4
Mamuil Malal, Paso,
S. Amer. 128 A2
Mamuju, Indonesia .. 57 E5
Man, Ivory C. 78 D3
Man, I. of, U.K. ... 12 C3
Man Na, Burma 61 H20
Mana, Fr. Guiana ... 121 B7
Mana →, Fr. Guiana . 121 B7
Måna →, Norway ... 10 E2
Manaar, G. of = Mannar,
G. of, Asia 60 Q11
Manabí □, Ecuador .. 120 D1
Manacacías →, Colombia 120 C3
Manacapuru, Brazil .. 121 D5
Manacapuru →, Brazil . 121 D5
Manacor, Spain 36 B10
Manado, Indonesia .. 57 D6
Managua, Nic. 116 D2
Managua, L., Nic. ... 116 D2
Manakara, Madag. .. 85 C8
Manama = Al Manāmah,
Bahrain 65 E6
Manambao →, Madag. . 85 B7
Manambato, Madag. .. 85 A8
Manambolo →, Madag. . 85 B7
Manambolosy, Madag. . 85 B8
Mananara, Madag. .. 85 B8
Mananara →, Madag. . 85 C8
Mananjary, Madag. .. 85 C8
Manantenina, Madag. . 85 C8
Manaos = Manaus, Brazil 121 D6
Manapire →, Venezuela . 120 B4
Manapouri, N.Z. 87 L1
Manapouri, L., N.Z. . 87 L1
Manas, China 54 B3
Manas →, India 61 F17
Manaslu, Nepal 63 E11
Manasquan, U.S.A. .. 107 F10
Manassa, U.S.A. ... 111 H11
Manaung, Burma ... 61 K18
Manaus, Brazil 121 D6
Manavgat, Turkey .. 66 D4
Manawan L., Canada . 101 B8
Manay, Phil. 55 H7
Manbij, Syria 66 D7
Mancelona, U.S.A. .. 104 C3
Mancha Real, Spain .. 31 H7
Manche □, France .. 24 C5
Manchester, U.K. ... 12 D5
Manchester, Calif., U.S.A. 112 G3
Manchester, Conn., U.S.A. 107 E12
Manchester, Ga., U.S.A. 105 J3
Manchester, Iowa, U.S.A. 108 D9
Manchester, Ky., U.S.A. 104 G4
Manchester, N.H., U.S.A. 107 D13
Manchester, N.Y., U.S.A. 106 D7
Manchester, Vt., U.S.A. 107 C11
Manchester L., Canada . 101 A7
Manchuria = Dongbei,
China 51 D13
Manciano, Italy 33 F8
Mancifa, Ethiopia ... 77 F5
Mancora, Pta., Peru .. 124 A1
Mand →, Iran 65 D7
Manda, Chunya, Tanzania 82 D3
Manda, Ludewe, Tanzania 83 E3
Mandabé, Madag. ... 85 C7
Mandaguari, Brazil .. 127 A5
Mandah, Mongolia .. 50 B5
Mandal, Norway 9 G12
Mandalay, Burma ... 61 J20
Mandale = Mandalay,
Burma 61 J20
Mandalgovi, Mongolia . 50 B4
Mandalī, Iraq 67 F11
Mandan, U.S.A. 108 B4
Mandaon, Phil. 55 E5
Mandar, Teluk, Indonesia 57 E5
Mandas, Italy 34 C2
Mandasor = Mandsaur,
India 62 G6
Mandaue, Phil. 55 F5
Mandelieu-la-Napoule,
France 27 E10
Mandera, Kenya ... 82 B5
Mandera □, Kenya .. 82 B5
Manderfeld, Belgium . 17 H8
Mandi, India 62 D7
Mandimba, Mozam. .. 83 E4
Mandioli, Indonesia .. 57 E7
Mandioré, L., S. Amer. . 125 D6
Mandla, India 63 H9
Mandø, Denmark .. 11 J2
Mandoto, Madag. .. 85 B8
Mandoúdhion, Greece . 39 L6
Mandra, Pakistan .. 62 C5
Mandrare →, Madag. . 85 D8
Mandritsara, Madag. . 85 B8
Mandsaur, India ... 62 G6
Mandurah, Australia . 89 F2
Mandúria, Italy 35 B10
Mandvi, India 62 H3
Mandya, India 60 N10
Mandzai, Pakistan .. 62 D2

Mané, Burkina Faso 79 C4
Maneh, Iran 65 B8
Manengouba, Mts.,
Cameroon 79 D6
Maneroo, Australia .. 90 C3
Maneroo Cr. →, Australia 90 C3
Manfalût, Egypt ... 76 B3
Manfred, Australia .. 91 E3
Manfredónia, Italy .. 35 A8
Manfredónia, G. di, Italy . 35 A9
Manga, Brazil 123 D3
Manga, Burkina Faso . 79 C4
Manga, Niger 79 C7
Mangabeiras, Chapada das,
Brazil 122 D2
Mangalia, Romania .. 38 F11
Mangalore, India ... 60 N9
Manganeses, Spain .. 30 D5
Mangaweka, N.Z. ... 87 H5
Manggar, Indonesia .. 56 E3
Manggawitu, Indonesia . 57 E8
Mangkalihat, Tanjung,
Indonesia 57 D5
Mangla Dam, Pakistan . 63 C5
Manglares, C., Colombia . 120 C2
Manglaur, India ... 62 E7
Mangnai, China 54 C4
Mango, Togo 79 C5
Mangoche, Malawi .. 83 E4
Mangoky →, Madag. . 85 C7
Mangole, Indonesia .. 57 E7
Mangombe, Zaïre ... 82 C2
Mangonui, N.Z. 87 F4
Mangualde, Portugal . 30 E3
Mangueira, L. da, Brazil . 127 C5
Manguéni, Hamada, Niger 75 D7
Mangum, U.S.A. ... 109 H5
Mangyshlak Poluostrov,
Kazakhstan 44 E6
Manhattan, U.S.A. .. 108 F6
Manhiça, Mozam. ... 85 D5
Manhuaçu, Brazil ... 123 F3
Manhumirim, Brazil . 123 F3
Maní, Colombia 120 C3
Mania →, Madag. .. 85 B8
Maniago, Italy 33 B9
Manica, Mozam. ... 85 B5
Manica e Sofala □,
Mozam. 85 B5
Manicaland □, Zimbabwe 83 F3
Manicoré, Brazil ... 125 B5
Manicoré →, Brazil . 125 B5
Manicouagan →, Canada 99 C6
Maniema □, Zaïre .. 82 C2
Manīfah, Si. Arabia . 65 E6
Manifold, Australia .. 90 C5
Manifold, C., Australia . 90 C5
Maniganggo, China .. 52 B2
Manigotagan, Canada . 101 C9
Manihiki, Cook Is. .. 93 J11
Manika, Plateau de la,
Zaïre 83 E2
Manila, Phil. 55 D4
Manila, U.S.A. 110 F9
Manila B., Phil. 55 D4
Manilla, Australia .. 91 E5
Manimpé, Mali 78 C3
Maningrida, Australia . 90 A1
Manipur □, India .. 61 G18
Manipur →, Burma .. 61 H19
Manisa, Turkey 66 C2
Manistee, U.S.A. .. 104 C2
Manistee →, U.S.A. . 104 C2
Manistique, U.S.A. . 104 C2
Manito L., Canada .. 101 C7
Manitoba □, Canada . 101 B9
Manitoba, L., Canada . 101 C9
Manitou, Canada ... 101 D9
Manitou I., U.S.A. .. 98 C2
Manitou Is., U.S.A. . 104 C2
Manitou L., Canada .. 99 B6
Manitou Springs, U.S.A. 108 F2
Manitoulin I., Canada . 98 C3
Manitowaning, Canada . 98 C3
Manitowoc, U.S.A. .. 104 C2
Manitsauá-Missu →, Brazil 125 C7
Manizales, Colombia . 120 B2
Manja, Madag. 85 C7
Manjacaze, Mozam. .. 85 C5
Manjakandriana, Madag. . 85 B8
Manjhand, Pakistan . 62 G3
Manjil, Iran 65 B6
Manjimup, Australia . 89 F2
Manjra →, India ... 60 K10
Mankato, Kans., U.S.A. 108 F5
Mankato, Minn., U.S.A. 108 C8
Mankayane, Swaziland . 85 D5
Mankono, Ivory C. .. 78 D3
Mankota, Canada ... 101 D7
Manlay, Mongolia .. 50 B4
Manlleu, Spain 28 C7
Manly, Australia ... 91 E5
Manmad, India 60 J9
Mann Ras., Australia . 89 E5
Manna, Indonesia .. 56 E2
Mannahill, Australia . 91 E3
Mannar, Sri Lanka .. 60 Q11
Mannar, G. of, Asia .. 60 Q11
Mannar I., Sri Lanka . 60 Q11
Männedorf, Switz. .. 23 B7
Mannheim, Germany . 19 F4
Manning, Canada ... 100 B5
Manning, Oreg., U.S.A. 112 E3
Manning, S.C., U.S.A. 105 J5
Manning Prov. Park,
Canada 100 D4
Mannington, U.S.A. . 104 F5

Mannu →, *Italy* 34 C2
Mannu, C., *Italy* 34 B1
Mannum, *Australia* 91 E2
Mano, *S. Leone* 78 D2
Manoa, *Bolivia* 125 D4
Manokwari, *Indonesia* .. 57 E8
Manombo, *Madag.* 85 C7
Manono, *Zaïre* 82 D2
Manosque, *France* 27 E9
Manouane, L., *Canada* .. 99 B5
Manpojin, *N. Korea* 51 D14
Manresa, *Spain* 28 D6
Mansa, *Gujarat, India* .. 62 H5
Mansa, *Punjab, India* .. 62 E6
Mansa, *Zambia* 83 E2
Mansehra, *Pakistan* 62 B5
Mansel I., *Canada* 97 B11
Mansfield, *Australia* 91 F4
Mansfield, *U.K.* 12 D6
Mansfield, *La., U.S.A.* .. 109 J8
Mansfield, *Mass., U.S.A.* . 107 D13
Mansfield, *Ohio, U.S.A.* . 106 F2
Mansfield, *Pa., U.S.A.* .. 106 E7
Mansfield, *Wash., U.S.A.* . 110 C4
Mansidão, *Brazil* 122 D3
Mansilla de las Mulas,
  Spain 30 C5
Mansle, *France* 26 C4
Manso →, *Brazil* 123 D2
Mansoa, *Guinea-Biss.* .. 78 C1
Manson Creek, *Canada* . 100 B4
Mansoura, *Algeria* 75 A5
Manta, *Ecuador* 120 D1
Manta, B. de, *Ecuador* .. 120 D1
Mantalingajan, Mt., *Phil.* . 55 G2
Mantare, *Tanzania* 82 C3
Manteca, *U.S.A.* 111 H3
Mantecal, *Venezuela* ... 120 B4
Mantena, *Brazil* 123 E3
Manteo, *U.S.A.* 105 H8
Mantes-la-Jolie, *France* . 25 D8
Manthani, *India* 60 K11
Manthelan, *France* 24 E7
Manti, *U.S.A.* 110 G8
Mantiqueira, Serra da,
  Brazil 123 F3
Manton, *U.S.A.* 104 C3
Mantorp, *Sweden* 11 F9
Mántova, *Italy* 32 C7
Mänttä, *Finland* 9 E21
Mantua = Mántova, *Italy* . 32 C7
Manturovo, *Russia* 42 A7
Manu, *Peru* 124 C3
Manú →, *Peru* 124 C3
Manua Is., *Amer. Samoa* . 87 B14
Manuae, *Cook Is.* 93 J12
Manuel Alves →, *Brazil* . 123 D2
Manuel Alves Grande →,
  Brazil 122 C2
Manuel Urbano, *Brazil* .. 124 B4
Manui, *Indonesia* 57 E6
Manuripi →, *Bolivia* ... 124 C4
Manville, *U.S.A.* 108 D2
Many, *U.S.A.* 109 K8
Manyara, L., *Tanzania* .. 82 C4
Manych →, *Russia* 43 G5
Manych-Gudilo, Ozero,
  Russia 43 G6
Manyonga →, *Tanzania* . . 82 C3
Manyoni, *Tanzania* 82 D3
Manyoni □, *Tanzania* ... 82 D3
Manzai, *Pakistan* 62 C4
Manzala, Bahra el, *Egypt* . 76 H7
Manzanares, *Spain* 29 F1
Manzaneda, Cabeza de,
  Spain 30 C3
Manzanillo, *Cuba* 116 B4
Manzanillo, *Mexico* 114 D4
Manzanillo, Pta., *Panama* . 116 E4
Manzano Mts., *U.S.A.* .. 111 J10
Manẓarīyeh, *Iran* 65 C6
Manzhouli, *China* 54 B6
Manzini, *Swaziland* 85 D5
Mao, *Chad* 73 F8
Maoke, Pegunungan,
  Indonesia 57 E9
Maolin, *China* 51 C12
Maoming, *China* 53 G8
Maowen, *China* 52 B4
Maoxing, *China* 51 B13
Mapam Yumco, *China* .. 54 C3
Mapastepec, *Mexico* 115 D6
Mapia, Kepulauan,
  Indonesia 57 D8
Mapimí, *Mexico* 114 B4
Mapimí, Bolsón de, *Mexico* 114 B4
Maping, *China* 53 B9
Mapinga, *Tanzania* 82 D4
Mapinhane, *Mozam.* 85 C6
Mapire, *Venezuela* 121 B5
Maple Creek, *Canada* ... 101 D7
Maple Valley, *U.S.A.* ... 112 C4
Mapleton, *U.S.A.* 110 D2
Mapuera →, *Brazil* 121 D6
Maputo, *Mozam.* 85 D5
Maputo, B. de, *Mozam.* . 85 D5
Maqiaohe, *China* 51 B16
Maqnā, *Si. Arabia* 64 D2
Maqteïr, *Mauritania* 74 D2
Maquela do Zombo,
  Angola 80 F3
Maquinchao, *Argentina* . 128 B3
Maquoketa, *U.S.A.* 108 D9
Mar, Serra do, *Brazil* ... 127 B6
Mar Chiquita, L.,
  Argentina 126 C3
Mar del Plata, *Argentina* . 126 D4

Mar Menor, *Spain* 29 H4
Mara, *Guyana* 121 B6
Mara, *Tanzania* 82 C3
Mara □, *Tanzania* 82 C3
Maraã, *Brazil* 120 D4
Marabá, *Brazil* 122 C2
Maracá, I. de, *Brazil* ... 121 C7
Maracaibo, *Venezuela* .. 120 A3
Maracaibo, L. de,
  Venezuela 120 B3
Maracaju, *Brazil* 127 A4
Maracajú, Serra de, *Brazil* 125 E6
Maracanã, *Brazil* 122 B2
Maracás, *Brazil* 123 D3
Maracay, *Venezuela* 120 A4
Marādah, *Libya* 73 C8
Maradi, *Niger* 79 C6
Maradun, *Nigeria* 79 C6
Marāgheh, *Iran* 67 D12
Maragogipe, *Brazil* 123 D4
Marajó, B. de, *Brazil* ... 122 B2
Marajó, I. de, *Brazil* 122 B2
Marākand, *Iran* 64 B5
Maralal, *Kenya* 82 B4
Maralinga, *Australia* 89 F5
Marama, *Australia* 91 F3
Marampa, *S. Leone* 78 D2
Maran, *Malaysia* 59 L4
Marana, *U.S.A.* 111 K8
Maranboy, *Australia* 88 B5
Maranchón, *Spain* 28 D2
Marand, *Iran* 67 C11
Marang, *Malaysia* 59 K4
Maranguape, *Brazil* 122 B4
Maranhão = São Luís,
  Brazil 122 B3
Maranhão □, *Brazil* 122 B2
Marano, L. di, *Italy* 33 C10
Maranoa →, *Australia* .. 91 D4
Marañón →, *Peru* 124 A3
Marão, *Mozam.* 85 C5
Marapi →, *Brazil* 121 C6
Marari, *Brazil* 124 B4
Maraş = Kahramanmaraş,
  Turkey 66 D7
Mărăşeşti, *Romania* 38 D10
Maratea, *Italy* 35 C8
Marateca, *Portugal* 31 G2
Marathasa □, *Cyprus* ... 37 E11
Marathókambos, *Greece* . 39 M9
Marathon, *Australia* 90 C3
Marathon, *Canada* 98 C2
Marathón, *Greece* 39 L6
Marathon, *N.Y., U.S.A.* . 107 D8
Marathon, *Tex., U.S.A.* . 109 K3
Marathóvouno, *Cyprus* . 37 D12
Maratua, *Indonesia* 57 D5
Maraú, *Brazil* 123 D4
Maravatío, *Mexico* 114 D4
Marawi City, *Phil.* 55 G6
Marāwih, *U.A.E.* 65 E7
Marbella, *Spain* 31 J6
Marble Bar, *Australia* ... 88 D2
Marble Falls, *U.S.A.* 109 K5
Marblehead, *U.S.A.* 107 D14
Marburg, *Germany* 18 E4
Marby, *Sweden* 10 A8
Marcal →, *Hungary* 21 H7
Marcapata, *Peru* 124 C3
Marcaria, *Italy* 32 C7
March, *U.K.* 13 E8
Marchand = Rommani,
  Morocco 74 B3
Marche, *France* 26 B5
Marche □, *Italy* 33 E10
Marche-en-Famenne,
  Belgium 17 H6
Marchena, *Spain* 31 H5
Marches = Marche □, *Italy* 33 E10
Marciana Marina, *Italy* .. 32 F7
Marcianise, *Italy* 35 A7
Marcigny, *France* 27 B8
Marcillat-en-Combraille,
  France 26 B6
Marcinelle, *Belgium* 17 H4
Marckolsheim, *France* .. 25 D14
Marcona, *Peru* 124 D2
Marcos Juárez, *Argentina* . 126 C3
Marcus I. = Minami-Tori-
  Shima, *Pac. Oc.* 92 E7
Marcus Necker Ridge,
  Pac. Oc. 92 F9
Marcy, Mt., *U.S.A.* 107 B11
Mardan, *Pakistan* 62 B5
Mardie, *Australia* 88 D2
Mardin, *Turkey* 67 D9
Marechal Deodoro, *Brazil* 122 C4
Maree, L., *U.K.* 14 D3
Mareeba, *Australia* 90 B4
Marek = Stanke Dimitrov,
  Bulgaria 38 G6
Marek, *Indonesia* 57 E6
Maremma, *Italy* 32 F8
Maréna, *Mali* 78 C3
Marenberg, *Slovenia* ... 33 B12
Marengo, *U.S.A.* 108 E8
Marennes, *France* 26 C3
Marenyi, *Kenya* 82 C4
Marerano, *Madag.* 85 C7
Maréttimo, *Italy* 34 E5
Mareuil-sur-Lay, *France* . 26 B3
Marfa, *U.S.A.* 109 K2
Marfa Pt., *Malta* 37 D1
Marganets = Marhanets,
  Ukraine 41 J8

Margaret →, *Australia* .. 88 C4
Margaret Bay, *Canada* .. 100 C3
Margaret L., *Canada* 100 B5
Margaret River, *Australia* . 88 C4
Margarita, I. de, *Venezuela* 121 A5
Margarítion, *Greece* 39 K3
Margaritovo, *Russia* 48 C7
Margate, *S. Africa* 85 E5
Margate, *U.K.* 13 F9
Margelan = Marghilon,
  Uzbekistan 44 E8
Margeride, Mts. de la,
  France 26 D7
Margherita di Savóia, *Italy* 35 A9
Marghilon, *Uzbekistan* .. 44 E8
Margosatubig, *Phil.* 55 H5
Marguerite, *Canada* 100 C4
Marhanets, *Ukraine* 41 J8
Marhoum, *Algeria* 75 B4
Mari El □, *Russia* 42 B8
Mari Republic = Mari
  El □, *Russia* 42 B8
María Elena, *Chile* 126 A2
María Grande, *Argentina* . 126 C4
Maria I., *N. Terr.,
  Australia* 90 A2
Maria I., *Tas., Australia* . 90 G4
Maria van Diemen, C.,
  N.Z. 87 F4
Mariager, *Denmark* 11 H4
Mariager Fjord, *Denmark* . 11 H4
Mariakani, *Kenya* 82 C4
Marian L., *Canada* 100 A5
Mariana Trench, *Pac. Oc.* . 92 F6
Marianao, *Cuba* 116 B3
Marianna, *Ark., U.S.A.* . 109 H9
Marianna, *Fla., U.S.A.* . 105 K3
Mariánské Lázně, *Czech.* . 20 F2
Marias →, *U.S.A.* 110 C8
Mariato, Punta, *Panama* . 116 E3
Mariazell, *Austria* 21 H5
Ma'rib, *Yemen* 68 D4
Maribo, *Denmark* 11 K5
Maribor, *Slovenia* 33 B12
Marico →, *Africa* 84 C4
Maricopa, *Ariz., U.S.A.* . 111 K7
Maricopa, *Calif., U.S.A.* . 113 K7
Marîdî, *Sudan* 77 G2
Maridi, Wadi →, *Sudan* . 77 F2
Marié →, *Brazil* 120 D4
Marie Byrd Land,
  Antarctica 5 D14
Marie-Galante, *Guadeloupe* 117 C7
Mariecourt =
  Kangiqsujuaq, *Canada* . 97 B12
Mariefred, *Sweden* 10 E11
Marienbad = Mariánské
  Lázně, *Czech.* 20 F2
Marienberg, *Germany* ... 18 E9
Marienberg, *Neths.* 16 D9
Marienbourg, *Belgium* .. 17 H5
Mariental, *Namibia* 84 C2
Marienville, *U.S.A.* 106 E5
Mariestad, *Sweden* 11 F7
Marietta, *Ga., U.S.A.* ... 105 J3
Marietta, *Ohio, U.S.A.* . 104 F5
Marieville, *Canada* 107 A11
Marignane, *France* 27 E9
Marihatag, *Phil.* 55 G7
Mariinsk, *Russia* 44 D9
Mariinskiy Posad, *Russia* . 42 B8
Marijampolė, *Lithuania* . 9 J20
Marília, *Brazil* 127 A5
Marillana, *Australia* 88 D2
Marín, *Spain* 30 C2
Marina, *U.S.A.* 112 J5
Marina di Cirò, *Italy* ... 35 C10
Marina Plains, *Australia* . 90 A3
Marinduque, *Phil.* 55 E5
Marine City, *U.S.A.* 104 D4
Marineo, *Italy* 34 E6
Marinette, *U.S.A.* 104 C2
Maringá, *Brazil* 127 A5
Marinha Grande, *Portugal* 31 F2
Marion, *Ala., U.S.A.* ... 105 J2
Marion, *Ill., U.S.A.* 109 G10
Marion, *Ind., U.S.A.* ... 104 E3
Marion, *Iowa, U.S.A.* .. 108 D9
Marion, *Kans., U.S.A.* . 108 F6
Marion, *Mich., U.S.A.* . 104 C3
Marion, *N.C., U.S.A.* .. 105 H4
Marion, *Ohio, U.S.A.* .. 104 E4
Marion, *S.C., U.S.A.* ... 105 H6
Marion, *Va., U.S.A.* ... 105 G5
Marion, L., *U.S.A.* 105 J5
Maripa, *Venezuela* 121 B4
Maripasoula, *Fr. Guiana* . 121 C7
Mariposa, *U.S.A.* 111 H4
Mariscal Estigarribia,
  Paraguay 126 A3
Maritime Alps =
  Maritimes, Alpes,
  Europe 27 D11
Maritimes, Alpes, *Europe* 27 D11
Maritsa = Évros →,
  Bulgaria 66 B2
Maritsa, *Greece* 37 C10
Mariupol, *Ukraine* 41 J9
Marīvān, *Iran* 67 E12
Markam, *China* 52 C2
Markazī □, *Iran* 65 C6
Markdale, *Canada* 106 B4
Marke, *Belgium* 17 G2
Marked Tree, *U.S.A.* ... 109 H9
Markelsdorfer Huk,
  Germany 18 A6

Marken, *Neths.* 16 D6
Markermeer, *Neths.* 16 C6
Market Drayton, *U.K.* .. 12 E5
Market Harborough, *U.K.* . 13 E7
Markham, *Canada* 106 C5
Markham, Mt., *Antarctica* 5 E11
Markham, L., *Canada* ... 101 A8
Marki, *Poland* 20 C11
Markleeville, *U.S.A.* 112 G7
Markoupoulon, *Greece* . 39 M6
Markovo, *Russia* 45 C17
Marks, *Russia* 42 E8
Marksville, *U.S.A.* 109 K8
Markt Schwaben, *Germany* 19 G7
Marktredwitz, *Germany* . 19 E8
Marla, *Australia* 91 D1
Marlboro, *U.S.A.* 107 D13
Marlborough, *Australia* . 90 C4
Marlborough Downs, *U.K.* 13 F6
Marle, *France* 25 C10
Marlin, *U.S.A.* 109 K6
Marlow, *Germany* 18 A8
Marlow, *U.S.A.* 109 H6
Marmagao, *India* 60 M8
Marmande, *France* 26 D4
Marmara, *Turkey* 66 B2
Marmara, Sea of =
  Marmara Denizi, *Turkey* 66 B3
Marmara Denizi, *Turkey* . 66 B3
Marmaris, *Turkey* 66 D3
Marmarth, *U.S.A.* 108 B3
Marmelos →, *Brazil* 125 B5
Marmion, Mt., *Australia* . 89 E2
Marmion L., *Canada* 98 C1
Marmolada, Mte., *Italy* . 33 B8
Marmolejo, *Spain* 31 G6
Marmora, *Canada* 98 D4
Marnay, *France* 25 E12
Marne, *Germany* 18 B5
Marne □, *France* 25 D11
Marne →, *France* 25 D9
Marneuli, *Georgia* 43 K7
Maroa, *Venezuela* 120 C4
Maroala, *Madag.* 85 B8
Maroantsetra, *Madag.* .. 85 B8
Maromandia, *Madag.* ... 85 A8
Maromme, *France* 24 C8
Marondera, *Zimbabwe* .. 83 F3
Maroni →, *Fr. Guiana* .. 121 B7
Maronne →, *France* 26 C5
Maroochydore, *Australia* . 91 D5
Maroona, *Australia* 91 F3
Maros →, *Hungary* 21 J10
Marosakoa, *Madag.* 85 B8
Marostica, *Italy* 33 C8
Marotandrano, *Madag.* . 85 B8
Marovoay, *Madag.* 85 B8
Marowijne □, *Surinam* .. 121 C7
Marowijne →, *Surinam* . 121 B7
Marquard, *S. Africa* 84 D4
Marqueira, *Portugal* 31 G1
Marquesas Is. = Marquises,
  Is., *Pac. Oc.* 93 H14
Marquette, *U.S.A.* 104 B2
Marquise, *France* 25 B8
Marquises, Is., *Pac. Oc.* . 93 H14
Marra, Gebel, *Sudan* ... 77 F2
Marracuene, *Mozam.* ... 85 D5
Marradi, *Italy* 33 D8
Marrakech, *Morocco* ... 74 B3
Marrawah, *Australia* 90 G3
Marrecas, Serra das, *Brazil* 122 C3
Marree, *Australia* 91 D2
Marrilla, *Australia* 88 D1
Marrimane, *Mozam.* 85 C5
Marromeu, *Mozam.* 85 B6
Marroquí, Punta, *Spain* . 31 K5
Marrowie Cr. →, *Australia* 91 E4
Marrubane, *Mozam.* 83 F4
Marrum, *Neths.* 16 B7
Marrupa, *Mozam.* 83 E4
Marsá Matrûh, *Egypt* ... 76 A2
Marsá Susah, *Libya* 73 B9
Marsabit, *Kenya* 82 B4
Marsabit □, *Kenya* 82 B4
Marsala, *Italy* 34 E5
Marsalforn, *Malta* 37 C1
Marsberg, *Germany* 18 D4
Marsciano, *Italy* 33 F9
Marsden, *Australia* 91 E4
Marsdiep, *Neths.* 16 C5
Marseillan, *France* 26 E7
Marseille, *France* 27 E9
Marseilles = Marseille,
  France 27 E9
Marsh I., *U.S.A.* 109 L9
Marsh L., *U.S.A.* 108 C6
Marshall, *Liberia* 78 D2
Marshall, *Ark., U.S.A.* . 109 H8
Marshall, *Mich., U.S.A.* . 104 D3
Marshall, *Minn., U.S.A.* . 108 C7
Marshall, *Mo., U.S.A.* .. 108 F8
Marshall, *Tex., U.S.A.* . 109 J7
Marshall →, *Australia* .. 90 C2
Marshall Is. ■, *Pac. Oc.* . 92 G9
Marshalltown, *U.S.A.* ... 108 D8
Marshfield, *Mo., U.S.A.* . 109 G8
Marshfield, *Wis., U.S.A.* . 108 C9
Märsta, *Sweden* 10 E11
Marstal, *Denmark* 11 K4
Marstrand, *Sweden* 11 G5
Mart, *U.S.A.* 109 K6
Marta →, *Italy* 33 F8
Martaban, *Burma* 61 L20

Martaban, G. of, *Burma* . 61 L20
Martano, *Italy* 35 B11
Martapura, *Kalimantan,
  Indonesia* 56 E4
Martapura, *Sumatera,
  Indonesia* 56 E2
Marte, *Nigeria* 79 C7
Martel, *France* 26 D5
Martelange, *Belgium* ... 17 J7
Martés, Sierra, *Spain* ... 29 F4
Martha's Vineyard, *U.S.A.* 107 E14
Martigné-Ferchaud, *France* 24 E5
Martigny, *Switz.* 22 D4
Martigues, *France* 27 E9
Martil, *Morocco* 74 A3
Martin, *Slovak Rep.* 20 F8
Martin, *S. Dak., U.S.A.* . 108 D4
Martin, *Tenn., U.S.A.* .. 109 G10
Martín →, *Spain* 28 D4
Martin L., *U.S.A.* 105 J3
Martina, *Switz.* 23 C10
Martina Franca, *Italy* ... 35 B10
Martinborough, *N.Z.* ... 87 J5
Martinez, *U.S.A.* 112 G4
Martinho Campos, *Brazil* . 123 E2
Martinique ■, *W. Indies* . 117 D7
Martinique Passage,
  W. Indies 117 C7
Martínon, *Greece* 39 L6
Martinópolis, *Brazil* 127 A5
Martins Ferry, *U.S.A.* .. 106 F4
Martinsburg, *Pa., U.S.A.* . 106 F6
Martinsburg, *W. Va.,
  U.S.A.* 104 F7
Martinsville, *Ind., U.S.A.* . 104 F2
Martinsville, *Va., U.S.A.* . 105 G6
Marton, *N.Z.* 87 J5
Martorell, *Spain* 28 D6
Martos, *Spain* 31 H7
Martuni, *Armenia* 43 K7
Maru, *Nigeria* 79 C6
Marudi, *Malaysia* 56 D4
Ma'ruf, *Afghan.* 60 D5
Marugame, *Japan* 49 G6
Marúggio, *Italy* 35 B10
Maruim, *Brazil* 122 D4
Marulan, *Australia* 91 E5
Marum, *Neths.* 16 B8
Marunga, *Angola* 84 B3
Marungu, Mts., *Zaïre* ... 82 D2
Marvast, *Iran* 65 D7
Marvejols, *France* 26 D7
Marwar, *India* 62 G5
Mary, *Turkmenistan* 44 F7
Mary Frances L., *Canada* . 101 A7
Mary Kathleen, *Australia* . 90 C2
Maryborough = Port
  Laoise, *Ireland* 15 C4
Maryborough, *Queens.,
  Australia* 91 D5
Maryborough, *Vic.,
  Australia* 91 F3
Maryfield, *Canada* 101 D8
Maryland □, *U.S.A.* 104 F7
Maryland Junction,
  Zimbabwe 83 F3
Maryport, *U.K.* 12 C4
Mary's Harbour, *Canada* . 99 B8
Marystown, *Canada* 99 C8
Marysvale, *U.S.A.* 111 G7
Marysville, *Canada* 100 D5
Marysville, *Calif., U.S.A.* . 112 F5
Marysville, *Kans., U.S.A.* . 108 F6
Marysville, *Mich., U.S.A.* . 106 D2
Marysville, *Ohio, U.S.A.* . 104 E4
Marysville, *Wash., U.S.A.* . 112 B4
Maryvale, *Australia* 91 D5
Maryville, *U.S.A.* 105 H4
Marzo, Punta, *Colombia* . 120 B2
Marzūq, *Libya* 73 C7
Masahunga, *Tanzania* ... 82 C3
Masai, *Malaysia* 59 M4
Masai Steppe, *Tanzania* . 82 C4
Masaka, *Uganda* 82 C3
Masalembo, Kepulauan,
  Indonesia 56 F4
Masalima, Kepulauan,
  Indonesia 56 F5
Masallı, *Azerbaijan* 67 C13
Masamba, *Indonesia* ... 57 E6
Masan, *S. Korea* 51 G15
Masanasa, *Spain* 29 F4
Masasi, *Tanzania* 83 E4
Masasi □, *Tanzania* 83 E4
Masaya, *Nic.* 116 D2
Masba, *Nigeria* 79 C7
Mascara, *Algeria* 75 A5
Mascota, *Mexico* 114 C4
Masela, *Indonesia* 57 F7
Maseru, *Lesotho* 84 D4
Mashaba, *Zimbabwe* ... 83 G3
Mashābih, *Si. Arabia* ... 64 E3
Mashan, *China* 52 F7
Masherbrum, *Pakistan* .. 63 B7
Mashhad, *Iran* 65 B8
Mashi, *Nigeria* 79 C6
Mashīz, *Iran* 65 D8
Mashkel, Hamun-i-,
  Pakistan 60 E3
Mashki Chāh, *Pakistan* .. 60 E3
Mashonaland Central □,
  Zimbabwe 85 B5
Mashonaland East □,
  Zimbabwe 85 B5
Mashonaland West □,
  Zimbabwe 85 B4

Mashtaga = Maştağa,
Azerbaijan 43 K10
Masi Manimba, *Zaïre* 80 E3
Masindi, *Uganda* 82 B3
Masindi Port, *Uganda* 82 B3
Masisea, *Peru* 124 B3
Masisi, *Zaïre* 82 C2
Masjed Soleyman, *Iran* .. 65 D6
Mask, L., *Ireland* 15 C2
Maslinica, *Croatia* 33 E13
Masnou, *Spain* 28 D7
Masoala, Tanjon' i, *Madag.* 85 B9
Masoarivo, *Madag.* 85 B7
Masohi, *Indonesia* 57 E7
Masomeloka, *Madag.* 85 C8
Mason, *Nev., U.S.A.* 112 G7
Mason, *Tex., U.S.A.* 109 K5
Mason City, *U.S.A.* 108 D8
Maspalomas, *Canary Is.* . 36 G4
Maspalomas, Pta.,
Canary Is. 36 G4
Masqat, *Oman* 68 C6
Massa, *Italy* 32 D7
Massa, O. →, *Morocco* ... 74 B3
Massa Maríttima, *Italy* . 32 E7
Massachusetts □, *U.S.A.* . 107 D12
Massachusetts B., *U.S.A.* 107 D14
Massafra, *Italy* 35 B10
Massaguet, *Chad* 73 F8
Massakory, *Chad* 73 F8
Massanella, *Spain* 36 B9
Massangena, *Mozam.* 85 C5
Massapê, *Brazil* 122 B3
Massarosa, *Italy* 32 E7
Massat, *France* 26 F5
Massawa = Mitsiwa,
Eritrea 77 D4
Massena, *U.S.A.* 107 B10
Massénya, *Chad* 73 F8
Masset, *Canada* 100 C2
Massiac, *France* 26 C7
Massif Central, *France* . 26 D7
Massillon, *U.S.A.* 106 F3
Massinga, *Mozam.* 85 C6
Masson, *Canada* 107 A9
Masson I., *Antarctica* .. 5 C7
Maştağa, *Azerbaijan* 43 K10
Mastanli = Momchilgrad,
Bulgaria 39 H8
Masterton, *N.Z.* 87 J5
Mástikho, Ákra, *Greece* . 39 L9
Mastuj, *Pakistan* 63 A5
Mastung, *Pakistan* 60 E5
Mastūrah, *Si. Arabia* ... 76 C4
Masty, *Belarus* 40 F3
Masuda, *Japan* 49 G5
Masvingo, *Zimbabwe* 83 G3
Masvingo □, *Zimbabwe* ... 83 G3
Maswa □, *Tanzania* 82 C3
Maşyāf, *Syria* 66 E7
Mata de São João, *Brazil* 123 D4
Matabeleland North □,
Zimbabwe 83 F2
Matabeleland South □,
Zimbabwe 83 G2
Mataboor, *Indonesia* 57 E9
Matachel →, *Spain* 31 G4
Matachewan, *Canada* 98 C3
Matacuni →, *Venezuela* .. 121 C4
Matad, *Mongolia* 54 B6
Matadi, *Zaïre* 80 F2
Matagalpa, *Nic.* 116 D2
Matagami, *Canada* 98 C4
Matagami, L., *Canada* ... 98 C4
Matagorda, *U.S.A.* 109 L7
Matagorda B., *U.S.A.* ... 109 L6
Matagorda I., *U.S.A.* ... 109 L6
Matak, P., *Indonesia* ... 59 L6
Matakana, *Australia* 91 E4
Mátala, *Greece* 37 E6
Matalaque, *Peru* 124 D3
Matam, *Senegal* 78 B2
Matameye, *Niger* 79 C6
Matamoros, Campeche,
Mexico 115 D6
Matamoros, Coahuila,
Mexico 114 B4
Matamoros, Puebla, *Mexico* 115 D5
Matamoros, Tamaulipas,
Mexico 115 B5
Ma'ţan as Sarra, *Libya* . 73 D9
Matandu →, *Tanzania* ... 83 D3
Matane, *Canada* 99 C6
Matang, *China* 52 F5
Matankari, *Niger* 79 C5
Matanzas, *Cuba* 116 B3
Matapan, C. = Taínaron,
Ákra, *Greece* 39 N5
Matapédia, *Canada* 99 C6
Matara, *Sri Lanka* 60 S12
Mataram, *Indonesia* 56 F5
Matarani, *Peru* 124 D3
Mataranka, *Australia* ... 88 B5
Mátarma, Râs, *Egypt* 69 E1
Mataró, *Spain* 28 D7
Matarraña →, *Spain* 28 D5
Matatiele, *S. Africa* ... 85 E4
Mataura, *N.Z.* 87 M2
Mategua, *Bolivia* 125 C5
Matehuala, *Mexico* 114 C4
Mateira, *Brazil* 123 E1
Mateke Hills, *Zimbabwe* . 83 G3
Matélica, *Italy* 33 E10
Matera, *Italy* 35 B9
Mátészalka, *Hungary* 21 H12
Matetsi, *Zimbabwe* 83 F2
Mateur, *Tunisia* 75 A6

Matfors, *Sweden* 10 B11
Matha, *France* 26 C3
Matheson Island, *Canada* 101 C9
Mathis, *U.S.A.* 109 L6
Mathura, *India* 62 F7
Mati, *Phil.* 55 H7
Mati →, *Albania* 39 H2
Matías Romero, *Mexico* .. 115 D5
Matibane, *Mozam.* 83 E5
Matima, *Botswana* 84 C3
Matiri Ra., *N.Z.* 87 J4
Matlock, *U.K.* 12 D6
Matmata, *Tunisia* 75 B6
Matna, *Sudan* 77 E4
Mato →, *Venezuela* 121 B4
Mato, Serrania de,
Venezuela 120 B4
Mato Grosso □, *Brazil* .. 125 C6
Mato Grosso, Planalto do,
Brazil 125 C7
Mato Grosso do Sul □,
Brazil 125 D7
Matochkin Shar, *Russia* . 44 B6
Matopo Hills, *Zimbabwe* . 83 G2
Matopos, *Zimbabwe* 83 G2
Matosinhos, *Portugal* ... 30 D2
Matour, *France* 27 B8
Matsena, *Nigeria* 79 C7
Matsesta, *Russia* 43 J4
Matsue, *Japan* 49 G6
Matsumae, *Japan* 48 D10
Matsumoto, *Japan* 49 F9
Matsusaka, *Japan* 49 G8
Matsuura, *Japan* 49 H4
Matsuyama, *Japan* 49 H6
Mattagami →, *Canada* ... 98 B3
Mattancheri, *India* 60 Q10
Mattawa, *Canada* 98 C4
Mattawamkeag, *U.S.A.* ... 99 C6
Matterhorn, *Switz.* 22 E5
Matthew Town, *Bahamas* . 117 B5
Matthew's Ridge, *Guyana* 121 B5
Mattice, *Canada* 98 C3
Mattituck, *U.S.A.* 107 F12
Mattmar, *Sweden* 10 A7
Matuba, *Mozam.* 85 C5
Matucana, *Peru* 124 C2
Matun, *Afghan.* 62 C3
Maturín, *Venezuela* 121 B5
Matveyev Kurgan, *Russia* 43 G4
Mau, *India* 63 G10
Mau Escarpment, *Kenya* . 82 C4
Mau Ranipur, *India* 63 G8
Maubeuge, *France* 25 B10
Maubourguet, *France* 26 E4
Maud, Pt., *Australia* ... 88 D1
Maude, *Australia* 91 E3
Maudin Sun, *Burma* 61 M19
Maués, *Brazil* 121 D6
Mauganj, *India* 61 G12
Maui, *U.S.A.* 102 H16
Maulamyaing = Moulmein,
Burma 61 L20
Maule □, *Chile* 126 D1
Mauléon-Licharre, *France* 26 E3
Maullín, *Chile* 128 E2
Maumee, *U.S.A.* 104 E4
Maumee →, *U.S.A.* 104 E4
Maumere, *Indonesia* 57 F6
Maun, *Botswana* 84 B3
Mauna Kea, *U.S.A.* 102 J17
Mauna Loa, *U.S.A.* 102 J17
Maungmagan Kyunzu,
Burma 61 M20
Maupin, *U.S.A.* 110 D3
Maure-de-Bretagne, *France* 24 E5
Maurepas, L., *U.S.A.* ... 109 K9
Maures, *France* 27 E10
Mauriac, *France* 26 C6
Maurice, L., *Australia* . 89 E5
Maurienne, *France* 27 C10
Mauritania ■, *Africa* ... 74 D3
Mauritius ■, *Ind. Oc.* .. 71 J9
Mauron, *France* 24 D4
Maurs, *France* 26 D6
Mauston, *U.S.A.* 108 D9
Mauterndorf, *Austria* ... 21 H3
Mauvezin, *France* 26 E4
Mauzé-sur-le-Mignon,
France 26 B3
Mavaca →, *Venezuela* 121 C4
Mavinga, *Angola* 81 H4
Mavli, *India* 62 G5
Mavrova, *Albania* 39 J2
Mavuradonha Mts.,
Zimbabwe 83 F3
Mawa, *Zaïre* 82 B2
Mawana, *India* 62 E7
Mawand, *Pakistan* 62 E3
Mawk Mai, *Burma* 61 J20
Mawlaik, *Burma* 61 H19
Mawquq, *Si. Arabia* 64 E4
Mawson Coast, *Antarctica* 5 C6
Max, *U.S.A.* 108 B4
Maxcanú, *Mexico* 115 C6
Maxesibeni, *S. Africa* .. 85 E4
Maxhamish L., *Canada* ... 100 B4
Maxixe, *Mozam.* 85 C6
Maxville, *Canada* 107 A10
Maxwell, *U.S.A.* 112 F4
Maxwelton, *Australia* ... 90 C3
May Downs, *Australia* ... 90 C4
May Pen, *Jamaica* 116 C4
Maya, *Spain* 28 B3
Maya →, *Russia* 45 D14
Maya Mts., *Belize* 115 D7
Mayaguana, *Bahamas* 117 B5

Mayagüez, *Puerto Rico* .. 117 C6
Mayahi, *Niger* 79 C6
Mayals, *Spain* 28 D5
Mayang, *China* 52 D7
Mayāmey, *Iran* 65 B7
Mayang, *China* 52 D7
Mayarí, *Cuba* 117 B4
Maybell, *U.S.A.* 110 F9
Maychew, *Ethiopia* 77 E4
Maydān, *Iraq* 67 E11
Maydena, *Australia* 90 G4
Mayen, *Germany* 19 E3
Mayenne, *France* 24 D6
Mayenne □, *France* 24 D6
Mayenne →, *France* 24 E6
Mayer, *U.S.A.* 111 J7
Mayerthorpe, *Canada* 100 C5
Mayfield, *U.S.A.* 105 G1
Mayhill, *U.S.A.* 111 K11
Maykop, *Russia* 43 H5
Maymyo, *Burma* 58 A1
Maynard, *U.S.A.* 112 C4
Maynard Hills, *Australia* 89 E2
Mayne →, *Australia* 90 C3
Maynooth, *Ireland* 15 C5
Mayo, *Canada* 96 B6
Mayo □, *Ireland* 15 C2
Mayo →, *Argentina* 128 C3
Mayo →, *Peru* 124 B2
Mayo L., *Canada* 96 B6
Mayon Volcano, *Phil.* ... 55 E5
Mayor I., *N.Z.* 87 G6
Mayorga, *Spain* 30 C5
Mayraira Pt., *Phil.* 55 B4
Mayskiy, *Russia* 43 J7
Mayson L., *Canada* 101 B7
Maysville, *U.S.A.* 104 F4
Mayu, *Indonesia* 57 D7
Mayville, *N. Dak., U.S.A.* 108 B6
Mayville, *N.Y., U.S.A.* . 106 D5
Mayya, *Russia* 45 C14
Mazabuka, *Zambia* 83 F2
Mazagān = El Jadida,
Morocco 74 B3
Mazagão, *Brazil* 121 D7
Mazamet, *France* 26 E6
Mazán, *Peru* 120 D3
Māzandarān □, *Iran* 65 B7
Mazapil, *Mexico* 114 C4
Mazar, O. →, *Algeria* ... 75 B5
Mazar del Vallo, *Italy* . 34 E5
Mazarredo, *Argentina* ... 128 C3
Mazarrón, *Spain* 29 H3
Mazarrón, G. de, *Spain* . 29 H3
Mazaruni →, *Guyana* 121 B6
Mazatán, *Mexico* 114 B2
Mazatenango, *Guatemala* 116 D1
Mazatlán, *Mexico* 114 C3
Mažeikiai, *Lithuania* ... 9 H20
Māzhān, *Iran* 65 C8
Mazīnān, *Iran* 65 B8
Mazoe, *Mozam.* 83 F3
Mazoe →, *Mozam.* 83 F3
Mazowe, *Zimbabwe* 83 F3
Mazrûb, *Sudan* 77 E2
Mazu Dao, *China* 53 D12
Mazurian Lakes =
Mazurski, Pojezierze,
Poland 20 B10
Mazurski, Pojezierze,
Poland 20 B10
Mazyr, *Belarus* 41 F5
Mazzarino, *Italy* 35 E7
Mbaba, *Senegal* 78 C1
Mbabane, *Swaziland* 85 D5
Mbagne, *Mauritania* 78 B2
M'bahiakro, *Ivory C.* ... 78 D4
Mbaïki, *C.A.R.* 80 D3
Mbala, *Zambia* 83 D3
Mbale, *Uganda* 82 B3
Mbalmayo, *Cameroon* 79 E7
Mbamba Bay, *Tanzania* ... 83 E3
Mbandaka, *Zaïre* 80 D3
Mbanga, *Cameroon* 79 E6
Mbanza Congo, *Angola* ... 80 F2
Mbanza Ngungu, *Zaïre* ... 80 F2
Mbarara, *Uganda* 82 C3
Mbashe →, *S. Africa* 85 E4
Mbatto, *Ivory C.* 78 D4
Mbenkuru →, *Tanzania* ... 83 D4
Mberengwa, *Zimbabwe* 83 G2
Mberengwa, Mt.,
Zimbabwe 83 G2
Mberubu, *Nigeria* 79 D6
Mbesuma, *Zambia* 83 D3
Mbeya, *Tanzania* 83 D3
Mbeya □, *Tanzania* 82 D3
Mbinga, *Tanzania* 83 E4
Mbinga □, *Tanzania* 83 E3
Mbini □, *Eq. Guin.* 80 D2
Mboki, *C.A.R.* 77 F2
Mboro, *Senegal* 78 B1
Mboune, *Senegal* 78 C2
Mbour, *Senegal* 78 C1
Mbout, *Mauritania* 78 B2
Mbozi □, *Tanzania* 83 D3
Mbuji-Mayi, *Zaïre* 82 D1
Mbulu, *Tanzania* 82 C4
Mbulu □, *Tanzania* 82 C4
Mburucuyá, *Argentina* ... 126 B4
Mchinja, *Tanzania* 83 D4
Mchinji, *Malawi* 83 E3
Mdennah, *Mauritania* 74 D3
Mead, L., *U.S.A.* 113 J12
Meade, *U.S.A.* 109 G4
Meadow, *Australia* 89 E1
Meadow Lake, *Canada* ... 101 C7

Meadow Lake Prov. Park,
Canada 101 C7
Meadow Valley Wash →,
U.S.A. 113 J12
Meadville, *U.S.A.* 106 E4
Meaford, *Canada* 98 D3
Mealhada, *Portugal* 30 E2
Mealy Mts., *Canada* 99 B8
Meander River, *Canada* . 100 B5
Meares, C., *U.S.A.* 110 D2
Mearim →, *Brazil* 122 B3
Meath □, *Ireland* 15 C5
Meath Park, *Canada* 101 C7
Meaulne, *France* 26 B6
Meaux, *France* 25 D9
Mebechi-Gawa →, *Japan* . 48 D10
Mecanhelas, *Mozam.* 83 F4
Mecca = Makkah,
Si. Arabia 68 C2
Mecca, *U.S.A.* 113 M10
Mechanicsburg, *U.S.A.* .. 106 F8
Mechanicville, *U.S.A.* .. 107 D11
Mechara, *Ethiopia* 77 F5
Mechelen, *Antwerpen,
Belgium* 17 F4
Mechelen, *Limburg,
Belgium* 17 G7
Mecheria, *Algeria* 75 B4
Mechernich, *Germany* 18 E2
Mechetinskaya, *Russia* .. 43 G5
Mechra Benâbbou,
Morocco 74 B3
Mecitözü, *Turkey* 66 B6
Mecklenburg-
Vorpommern □,
Germany 18 B8
Mecklenburger Bucht,
Germany 18 A7
Meconta, *Mozam.* 83 E4
Meda, *Australia* 88 C3
Meda, *Portugal* 30 E3
Medan, *Indonesia* 56 D1
Médanos, *Argentina* 128 A4
Medanosa, Pta., *Argentina* 128 C3
Medawachchiya, ... *(?)*
Medeiros Neto, *Brazil* .. 123 E3
Medel, Pic, *Switz.* 23 C7
Medellín, *Colombia* 120 B2
Medelpad, *Sweden* 9 E17
Medemblik, *Neths.* 16 C6
Médenine, *Tunisia* 75 B7
Mederdra, *Mauritania* ... 78 B1
Medford, *Mass., U.S.A.* . 107 D13
Medford, *Oreg., U.S.A.* . 110 E2
Medford, *Wis., U.S.A.* .. 108 C9
Medgidia, *Romania* 38 E11
Medi, *Sudan* 77 F3
Media Agua, *Argentina* .. 126 C2
Media Luna, *Argentina* .. 126 C2
Mediaş, *Romania* 38 C7
Medical Lake, *U.S.A.* ... 110 C5
Medicina, *Italy* 33 D8
Medicine Bow, *U.S.A.* ... 110 F10
Medicine Bow Pk., *U.S.A.* 110 F10
Medicine Bow Ra., *U.S.A.* 110 F10
Medicine Hat, *Canada* ... 101 D6
Medicine Lake, *U.S.A.* .. 108 A2
Medicine Lodge, *U.S.A.* . 109 G5
Medina = Al Madīnah,
Si. Arabia 64 E3
Medina, *Brazil* 123 E3
Medina, *Colombia* 120 C3
Medina, *N. Dak., U.S.A.* 108 B5
Medina, *N.Y., U.S.A.* ... 106 C6
Medina, *Ohio, U.S.A.* ... 106 E3
Medina →, *U.S.A.* 109 L5
Medina de Ríoseco, *Spain* 30 D5
Medina del Campo, *Spain* 30 D6
Medina-Sidonia, *Spain* .. 31 J5
Medinaceli, *Spain* 28 D2
Medinipur, *India* 63 H12
Mediterranean Sea, *Europe* 70 C5
Medjerda, O. →, *Tunisia* 75 A7
Medley, *Canada* 101 C6
Médoc, *France* 26 C3
Medstead, *Canada* 101 C7
Medulin, *Croatia* 33 D10
Medveda, *Serbia, Yug.* .. 21 N11
Medvedevo, *Russia* 42 B8
Medveditsa →, *Russia* ... 42 F6
Medveditsa →, *Russia* ... 42 F6
Medvedok, *Russia* 42 B10
Medvezhi, Ostrava, *Russia* 45 B17
Medvezhyegorsk, *Russia* . 44 C4
Medway →, *U.K.* 13 F8
Medzilaborce, *Slovak Rep.* 20 F11
Meekatharra, *Australia* . 89 E2
Meeker, *U.S.A.* 110 F10
Meer, *Belgium* 17 F5
Meerane, *Germany* 18 E8
Meerbeke, *Belgium* 17 G4
Meerhout, *Belgium* 17 F6
Meerle, *Belgium* 17 F5
Meersburg, *Germany* 19 H5
Meerssen, *Neths.* 17 G7
Meerut, *India* 62 E7
Meeteetse, *U.S.A.* 110 D9
Meeuwen, *Belgium* 17 F7
Mega, *Ethiopia* 77 G4
Megálo Petalí, *Greece* .. 39 M7
Megalópolis, *Greece* 39 M5
Meganísi, *Greece* 39 L3
Mégara, *Greece* 39 M6
Megève, *France* 27 C10

Meghalaya □, *India* 61 G17
Meghezez, *Ethiopia* 77 F4
Mégiscane, L., *Canada* .. 98 C4
Megra, *Russia* 40 B9
Mehadia, *Romania* 38 E5
Mehaigne →, *Belgium* 17 G6
Mehaïguene, O. →,
Algeria 75 B5
Meheisa, *Sudan* 76 D3
Mehndawal, *India* 63 F10
Mehr Jān, *Iran* 65 C7
Mehrābād, *Iran* 67 D12
Mehrān, *Iran* 67 F12
Mehrīz, *Iran* 65 D7
Mehun-sur-Yèvre, *France* 25 E9
Mei Jiang →, *China* 53 E11
Mei Xian, *Guangdong,
China* 53 E11
Mei Xian, *Shaanxi, China* 50 G4
Meia Ponte →, *Brazil* ... 123 E2
Meicheng, *China* 53 C12
Meichengzhen, *China* 53 C8
Meichuan, *China* 53 B10
Meiganga, *Cameroon* 80 C2
Meijel, *Neths.* 17 F7
Meiktila, *Burma* 61 J19
Meilen, *Switz.* 23 B7
Meiningen, *Germany* 18 E6
Meio →, *Brazil* 123 D3
Meira, Sierra de, *Spain* 30 B3
Meiringen, *Switz.* 22 C6
Meishan, *China* 52 B4
Meissen, *Germany* 18 D9
Meissner, *Germany* 18 D5
Meitan, *China* 52 D6
Mejillones, *Chile* 126 A1
Meka, *Australia* 89 E2
Mékambo, *Gabon* 80 D2
Mekdela, *Ethiopia* 77 E4
Mekele, *Ethiopia* 77 E4
Mekhtar, *Pakistan* 60 D6
Meknès, *Morocco* 74 B3
Meko, *Nigeria* 79 D5
Mekong →, *Asia* 59 H6
Mekongga, *Indonesia* 57 E6
Mekvari = Kür →,
Azerbaijan 67 C13
Melagiri Hills, *India* .. 60 N10
Melah, Sebkhet el, *Algeria* 75 C4
Melaka, *Malaysia* 59 L4
Melalap, *Malaysia* 56 C5
Mélambes, *Greece* 37 D6
Melanesia, *Pac. Oc.* 92 H7
Melbourne, *Australia* ... 91 F3
Melbourne, *U.S.A.* 105 L5
Melchor Múzquiz, *Mexico* 114 B4
Melchor Ocampo, *Mexico* 114 C4
Méldola, *Italy* 33 D9
Meldorf, *Germany* 18 A5
Melegnano, *Italy* 32 C6
Melenci, *Serbia, Yug.* .. 21 K10
Melenki, *Russia* 42 C5
Mélèzes →, *Canada* 97 C12
Melfi, *Chad* 73 F8
Melfi, *Italy* 35 B8
Melfort, *Canada* 101 C8
Melfort, *Zimbabwe* 83 F3
Melgaço, *Madeira* 30 C2
Melgar de Fernamental,
Spain 30 C6
Melhus, *Norway* 10 A4
Melick, *Neths.* 17 F8
Melide, *Switz.* 23 E7
Meligalá, *Greece* 39 M4
Melilla, *N. Afr.* 75 A4
Melipilla, *Chile* 126 C1
Mélissa, Ákra, *Greece* .. 37 D6
Melita, *Canada* 101 D8
Mélito di Porto Salvo, *Italy* 35 E8
Melitopol, *Ukraine* 41 J8
Melk, *Austria* 21 G5
Mellansel, *Sweden* 8 E18
Melle, *Belgium* 17 G3
Melle, *France* 26 B3
Melle, *Germany* 18 C4
Mellégue, O. →, *Tunisia* 75 A6
Mellen, *U.S.A.* 108 B9
Mellerud, *Sweden* 11 F6
Mellette, *U.S.A.* 108 C5
Mellid, *Spain* 30 C2
Mellieha, *Malta* 37 D1
Mellit, *Sudan* 77 E2
Mellizo Sur, Cerro, *Chile* 128 C2
Mellrichstadt, *Germany* . 19 E6
Melnik, *Bulgaria* 39 H6
Mělník, *Czech.* 20 E4
Melo, *Uruguay* 127 C5
Melolo, *Indonesia* 57 F6
Melouprey, *Cambodia* 58 F5
Melrhir, Chott, *Algeria* 75 B6
Melrose, *N.S.W., Australia* 91 E4
Melrose, *W. Austral.,
Australia* 89 E3
Melrose, *U.K.* 14 F6
Melrose, *U.S.A.* 109 H3
Mels, *Switz.* 23 B8
Melsele, *Belgium* 17 F4
Melstone, *U.S.A.* 110 C10
Melsungen, *Germany* 18 D5
Melton Mowbray, *U.K.* ... 12 E7
Melun, *France* 25 D9
Melut, *Sudan* 77 E3
Melville, *Canada* 101 C8
Melville, C., *Australia* 90 A3
Melville, L., *Canada* ... 99 B8
Melville B., *Australia* . 90 A2
Melville I., *Australia* . 88 B5

Melville I., *Canada* 4 B2
Melville Pen., *Canada* .. 97 B11
Melvin →, *Canada* 100 B5
Memaliaj, *Albania* 39 J2
Memba, *Mozam.* 83 E5
Memboro, *Indonesia* 57 F5
Membrilla, *Spain* 29 G1
Memel = Klaipėda,
  Lithuania 9 J19
Memel, *S. Africa* 85 D4
Memmingen, *Germany* ... 19 H6
Mempawah, *Indonesia* ... 56 D3
Memphis, *Tenn., U.S.A.* 109 H10
Memphis, *Tex., U.S.A.* .. 109 H4
Mena, *Ukraine* 41 G7
Mena, *U.S.A.* 109 H7
Mena →, *Ethiopia* 77 F5
Menai Strait, *U.K.* 12 D3
Ménaka, *Mali* 79 B5
Menaldum, *Neths.* 16 B7
Menan = Chao Phraya →,
  Thailand 58 F3
Menarandra →, *Madag.* .. 85 D7
Menard, *U.S.A.* 109 K5
Menasha, *U.S.A.* 104 C1
Menate, *Indonesia* 56 E4
Mendawai →, *Indonesia* . 56 E4
Mende, *France* 26 D7
Mendebo, *Ethiopia* 77 F4
Mendez, *Mexico* 115 B5
Mendhar, *India* 63 C6
Mendi, *Ethiopia* 77 F4
Mendip Hills, *U.K.* 13 F5
Mendocino, *U.S.A.* 110 G2
Mendocino, C., *U.S.A.* .. 110 F1
Mendota, *Calif., U.S.A.* 111 H3
Mendota, *Ill., U.S.A.* ... 108 E10
Mendoza, *Argentina* 126 C2
Mendoza □, *Argentina* .. 126 C2
Mendrisio, *Switz.* 23 E7
Mene Grande, *Venezuela* 120 B3
Menemen, *Turkey* 66 C2
Menen, *Belgium* 17 G2
Menéndez, L., *Argentina* 128 B2
Menfi, *Italy* 34 E5
Mengcheng, *China* 53 A11
Mengdingjie, *China* 52 F2
Mengeš, *Slovenia* 33 B11
Menggala, *Indonesia* 56 E3
Menghai, *China* 52 G3
Mengíbar, *Spain* 31 H7
Mengjin, *China* 50 G7
Mengla, *China* 52 G3
Menglian, *China* 52 F2
Mengoub, *Algeria* 74 C3
Mengshan, *China* 53 E8
Mengyin, *China* 51 G9
Mengzhe, *China* 52 F3
Mengzi, *China* 52 F4
Menihek L., *Canada* 99 B6
Menin = Menen, *Belgium* 17 G2
Menindee, *Australia* 91 E3
Menindee L., *Australia* .. 91 E3
Meningie, *Australia* 91 F2
Menlo Park, *U.S.A.* 112 H4
Menominee, *U.S.A.* 104 C2
Menominee →, *U.S.A.* ... 104 C2
Menomonie, *U.S.A.* 108 C9
Menongue, *Angola* 81 G3
Menorca, *Spain* 36 B11
Mentakab, *Malaysia* 59 L4
Mentawai, Kepulauan,
  Indonesia 56 E1
Menton, *France* 27 E11
Mentor, *U.S.A.* 106 E3
Menzel-Bourguiba, *Tunisia* 75 A6
Menzel Chaker, *Tunisia* . 75 B7
Menzel-Temime, *Tunisia* . 75 A7
Menzies, *Australia* 89 E3
Me'ona, *Israel* 69 B4
Meoqui, *Mexico* 114 B3
Mepaco, *Mozam.* 83 F3
Meppel, *Neths.* 16 C8
Meppen, *Germany* 18 C3
Mequinenza, *Spain* 28 D5
Mer, *France* 24 E8
Mer Rouge, *U.S.A.* 109 J9
Merabéllou, Kólpos, *Greece* 37 D7
Meramangye, L., *Australia* 89 E5
Meran = Merano, *Italy* .. 33 B8
Merano, *Italy* 33 B8
Merate, *Italy* 32 C6
Merauke, *Indonesia* 57 F10
Merbabu, *Indonesia* 57 G14
Merbein, *Australia* 91 E3
Merca, *Somali Rep.* 68 G3
Mercadal, *Spain* 36 B11
Mercato Saraceno, *Italy* . 33 E9
Merced, *U.S.A.* 111 H3
Merced Pk., *U.S.A.* 112 H7
Mercedes, *Buenos Aires,*
  Argentina 126 C4
Mercedes, *Corrientes,*
  Argentina 126 B4
Mercedes, *San Luis,*
  Argentina 126 C2
Mercedes, *Uruguay* 126 C4
Merceditas, *Chile* 126 B1
Mercer, *N.Z.* 87 G5
Mercer, *U.S.A.* 106 E4
Merchtem, *Belgium* 17 G4
Mercury, *U.S.A.* 113 J11
Mercy C., *Canada* 97 B13
Merdrignac, *France* 24 D4
Mere, *Belgium* 17 G3
Meredith, C., *Falk. Is.* .. 128 D4

Meredith, L., *U.S.A.* 109 H4
Merefa, *Ukraine* 41 H9
Merelbeke, *Belgium* 17 G3
Méréville, *France* 25 D9
Merga = Nukheila, *Sudan* 76 D2
Mergui Arch. = Myeik
  Kyunzu, *Burma* 59 G1
Mérida, *Mexico* 115 C7
Mérida, *Spain* 31 G4
Mérida, *Venezuela* 120 B3
Mérida □, *Venezuela* ... 120 B3
Mérida, Cord. de,
  Venezuela 120 B3
Meriden, *U.S.A.* 107 E12
Meridian, *Calif., U.S.A.* 112 F5
Meridian, *Idaho, U.S.A.* 110 E5
Meridian, *Miss., U.S.A.* 105 J1
Meridian, *Tex., U.S.A.* . 109 K6
Mering, *Germany* 19 G7
Meriruma, *Brazil* 121 C7
Merkel, *U.S.A.* 109 J4
Merksem, *Belgium* 17 F4
Merksplas, *Belgium* 17 F5
Mermaid Reef, *Australia* 88 C2
Mern, *Denmark* 11 J6
Merowe, *Sudan* 76 D3
Merredin, *Australia* 89 F2
Merrick, *U.K.* 14 F4
Merrickville, *Canada* 107 B9
Merrill, *Oreg., U.S.A.* .. 110 E3
Merrill, *Wis., U.S.A.* ... 108 C10
Merriman, *U.S.A.* 108 D4
Merritt, *Canada* 100 C4
Merriwa, *Australia* 91 E5
Merriwagga, *Australia* ... 91 E4
Merry I., *Canada* 98 A4
Merrygoen, *Australia* 91 E4
Merryville, *U.S.A.* 109 K8
Mersa Fatma, *Eritrea* ... 68 E3
Mersch, *Lux.* 17 J8
Merseburg, *Germany* 18 D7
Mersey →, *U.K.* 12 D5
Merseyside □, *U.K.* 12 D5
Mersin, *Turkey* 66 D6
Mersing, *Malaysia* 59 L4
Merta, *India* 62 F6
Mertert, *Lux.* 17 J8
Merthyr Tydfil, *U.K.* 13 F4
Mértola, *Portugal* 31 H3
Mertzig, *Lux.* 17 J8
Mertzon, *U.S.A.* 109 K4
Méru, *France* 25 C9
Meru, *Kenya* 82 B4
Meru, *Tanzania* 82 C4
Meru □, *Kenya* 82 B4
Merville, *France* 25 B9
Méry-sur-Seine, *France* . 25 D10
Merzifon, *Turkey* 66 B6
Merzig, *Germany* 19 F2
Merzouga, Erg Tin, *Algeria* 75 D7
Mesa, *U.S.A.* 111 K8
Mesach Mellet, *Libya* ... 75 D7
Mesagne, *Italy* 35 B10
Mesanagrós, *Greece* 37 C9
Mesaoría □, *Cyprus* 37 D12
Mesarás, Kólpos, *Greece* . 37 D6
Meschede, *Germany* 18 D4
Mescit, *Turkey* 67 B9
Mesfinto, *Ethiopia* 77 E4
Mesgouez, L., *Canada* ... 98 B4
Meshchovsk, *Russia* 42 C2
Meshed = Mashhad, *Iran* . 65 B8
Meshoppen, *U.S.A.* 107 E8
Meshra er Req, *Sudan* ... 77 F2
Mesick, *U.S.A.* 104 C3
Mesilinka →, *Canada* 100 B4
Mesilla, *U.S.A.* 111 K10
Meslay-du-Maine, *France* . 24 E6
Mesocco, *Switz.* 23 D8
Mesolóngion, *Greece* 39 L4
Mesopotamia = Al Jazirah,
  Iraq 67 E10
Mesoraca, *Italy* 35 C9
Mesquite, *U.S.A.* 111 H6
Mess Cr. →, *Canada* 100 B2
Messac, *France* 24 E5
Messad, *Algeria* 75 B5
Messalo →, *Mozam.* 83 E4
Messaména, *Cameroon* .. 79 E7
Messancy, *Belgium* 17 J7
Messier, Canal, *Chile* ... 128 C2
Messina, *Italy* 35 D8
Messina, *S. Africa* 85 C5
Messina, Str. di, *Italy* .. 35 D8
Messíni, *Greece* 39 M5
Messiniakós Kólpos, *Greece* 39 N5
Messkirch, *Germany* 19 H5
Messonghi, *Greece* 37 B3
Mesta →, *Bulgaria* 39 H7
Mestanza, *Spain* 31 G6
Mestre, *Italy* 33 C9
Mestre, Espigão, *Brazil* . 123 D2
Městys Zelezná Ruda,
  Czech. 20 F3
Mesudiye, *Turkey* 66 B7
Meta □, *Colombia* 120 C3
Meta →, *S. Amer.* 120 B4
Metairie, *U.S.A.* 109 L9
Metaline Falls, *U.S.A.* .. 110 B5
Metán, *Argentina* 126 B3
Metangula, *Mozam.* 83 E3
Metáuro →, *Italy* 33 E10
Metema, *Ethiopia* 77 E4
Metengobalame, *Mozam.* . 83 E3
Methana, *Greece* 39 M6
Methven, *N.Z.* 87 K3
Methy L., *Canada* 101 B7

Metil, *Mozam.* 83 F4
Metlakatla, *U.S.A.* 100 B2
Metlaoui, *Tunisia* 75 B6
Metlika, *Slovenia* 33 C12
Metropolis, *U.S.A.* 109 G10
Mettet, *Belgium* 17 H5
Mettur Dam, *India* 60 P10
Metz, *France* 25 C13
Meulaboh, *Indonesia* 56 D1
Meulan, *France* 25 C8
Meung-sur-Loire, *France* . 25 E8
Meureudu, *Indonesia* 56 C1
Meurthe →, *France* 25 D13
Meurthe-et-Moselle □,
  France 25 D13
Meuse □, *France* 25 C12
Meuse →, *Europe* 17 G7
Meuselwitz, *Germany* ... 18 D8
Mexborough, *U.K.* 12 D6
Mexia, *U.S.A.* 109 K6
Mexiana, I., *Brazil* 122 A2
Mexicali, *Mexico* 114 A1
Mexico, *Maine, U.S.A.* .. 107 B14
Mexico, *Mo., U.S.A.* 108 F9
México □, *Mexico* 114 D5
Mexico ■, *Cent. Amer.* .. 114 C4
Mexico, G. of, *Cent. Amer.* 115 C7
Meyenburg, *Germany* 18 B8
Meymac, *France* 26 C6
Meymaneh, *Afghan.* 60 B4
Meyrargues, *France* 27 E9
Meyrueis, *France* 26 D7
Meyssac, *France* 26 C5
Mezdra, *Bulgaria* 38 F6
Mèze, *France* 26 E7
Mezen, *Russia* 44 C5
Mezen →, *Russia* 44 C5
Mézenc, *France* 27 D8
Mezha →, *Russia* 40 E6
Mézidon, *France* 24 C6
Mézilhac, *France* 27 D8
Mézin, *France* 26 D4
Mezőberény, *Hungary* ... 21 J11
Mezőkovácsháza, *Hungary* 21 J10
Mezőkövesd, *Hungary* ... 21 H10
Mézos, *France* 26 D2
Mezőtúr, *Hungary* 21 J10
Mezquital, *Mexico* 114 C4
Mezzolombardo, *Italy* ... 32 B8
Mgeta, *Tanzania* 83 D4
Mglin, *Russia* 41 F7
Mhlaba Hills, *Zimbabwe* . 83 F3
Mhow, *India* 62 H6
Miahuatlán, *Mexico* 115 D5
Miajadas, *Spain* 31 F5
Miallo, *Australia* 90 B4
Miami, *Ariz., U.S.A.* 111 K8
Miami, *Fla., U.S.A.* 105 N5
Miami, *Tex., U.S.A.* 109 H4
Miami →, *U.S.A.* 104 F3
Miami Beach, *U.S.A.* 105 N5
Miamisburg, *U.S.A.* 104 F3
Mian Xian, *China* 50 H4
Mianchi, *China* 50 G6
Mianduab, *Iran* 67 D12
Miandrivazo, *Madag.* 85 B8
Mianeh, *Iran* 67 D12
Mianning, *China* 52 C4
Mianwali, *Pakistan* 62 C4
Mianyang, *Hubei, China* . 53 B9
Mianyang, *Sichuan, China* 52 B5
Mianzhu, *China* 52 B5
Miaoli, *Taiwan* 53 E13
Miarinarivo, *Madag.* 85 B8
Miass, *Russia* 44 D7
Miastko, *Poland* 20 A6
Michalovce, *Slovak Rep.* . 21 G11
Michelstadt, *Germany* ... 19 F5
Michigan □, *U.S.A.* 104 C3
Michigan, L., *U.S.A.* 104 C2
Michigan City, *U.S.A.* ... 104 E2
Michikamau L., *Canada* . 99 B7
Michipicoten, *Canada* ... 98 C3
Michipicoten I., *Canada* . 98 C2
Michoacan □, *Mexico* ... 114 D4
Michurin, *Bulgaria* 38 G10
Michurinsk, *Russia* 42 D5
Miclere, *Australia* 90 C4
Mico, Pta., *Nic.* 116 D3
Micronesia, Federated
  States of ■, *Pac. Oc.* . 92 G7
Mid Glamorgan □, *U.K.* . 13 F4
Midai, P., *Indonesia* 59 L6
Midale, *Canada* 101 D8
Middagsfjället, *Sweden* .. 10 A6
Middelbeers, *Neths.* 17 F6
Middelburg, *Neths.* 17 F3
Middelburg, *Eastern Cape,*
  S. Africa 84 E3
Middelburg,
  Eastern Trans., S. Africa 85 D4
Middelfart, *Denmark* 11 J3
Middelharnis, *Neths.* 16 E4
Middelkerke, *Belgium* ... 17 F1
Middenmeer, *Neths.* 16 C5
Middelwit, *S. Africa* 84 C4
Middle Alkali L., *U.S.A.* . 110 F3
Middle Fork Feather →,
  U.S.A. 112 F5
Middle I., *Australia* 89 F4
Middle Loup →, *U.S.A.* . 108 E5
Middleboro, *U.S.A.* 107 E14
Middleburg, *N.Y., U.S.A.* 107 D10
Middleburg, *Pa., U.S.A.* . 106 F7
Middleburg, *U.S.A.* 107 B11
Middleport, *U.S.A.* 104 F4
Middlesboro, *Ky., U.S.A.* 105 G10

Middlesboro, *Ky., U.S.A.* 105 G4
Middlesbrough, *U.K.* 12 C6
Middlesex, *Belize* 116 C2
Middlesex, *U.S.A.* 107 F10
Middleton, *Australia* 90 C3
Middleton, *Canada* 99 D6
Middletown, *Calif., U.S.A.* 112 G4
Middletown, *Conn., U.S.A.* 107 E12
Middletown, *N.Y., U.S.A.* 107 E10
Middletown, *Ohio, U.S.A.* 104 F3
Middletown, *Pa., U.S.A.* . 107 F8
Midelt, *Morocco* 74 B4
Midi, Canal du →, *France* 26 E5
Midi d'Ossau, Pic du,
  France 26 F3
Midland, *Canada* 98 D4
Midland, *Calif., U.S.A.* . 113 M12
Midland, *Mich., U.S.A.* . 104 D3
Midland, *Pa., U.S.A.* 106 F4
Midland, *Tex., U.S.A.* ... 109 K3
Midlands □, *Zimbabwe* .. 83 F2
Midleton, *Ireland* 15 E3
Midlothian, *U.S.A.* 109 J6
Midongy, Tangorombohitr'
  i, *Madag.* 85 C8
Midongy Atsimo, *Madag.* . 85 C8
Midou →, *France* 26 E3
Midouze →, *France* 26 E3
Midsayap, *Phil.* 55 H6
Midu, *China* 52 E3
Midway Is., *Pac. Oc.* 92 E10
Midway Wells, *U.S.A.* ... 113 N11
Midwest, *U.S.A.* 103 B9
Midwest, *Wyo., U.S.A.* .. 110 E10
Midwolda, *Neths.* 16 B9
Midyat, *Turkey* 67 D9
Mie □, *Japan* 49 G8
Miechów, *Poland* 20 E10
Międzychód, *Poland* 20 C5
Międzyrzec Podlaski,
  Poland 20 D12
Międzyrzecz, *Poland* 20 C5
Miélan, *France* 26 E4
Mielec, *Poland* 20 E11
Mienga, *Angola* 84 B2
Miercurea Ciuc, *Romania* . 38 C8
Mieres, *Spain* 30 B5
Mierlo, *Neths.* 17 F7
Mieso, *Ethiopia* 77 F5
Mifflintown, *U.S.A.* 106 F7
Mifraz Ḥefa, *Israel* 69 C4
Migdāl, *Israel* 69 C4
Migennes, *France* 25 E10
Migliarino, *Italy* 33 D8
Miguel Alemán, Presa,
  Mexico 115 D5
Miguel Alves, *Brazil* 122 B3
Miguel Calmon, *Brazil* .. 122 D3
Mihaliçcik, *Turkey* 66 C4
Mihara, *Japan* 49 G6
Mijares →, *Spain* 28 F4
Mijas, *Spain* 31 J6
Mikese, *Tanzania* 82 D4
Mikha-Tskhakaya =
  Senaki, *Georgia* 43 J6
Mikhailovka =
  Mykhaylivka, *Ukraine* . 41 J8
Mikhaylov, *Russia* 42 C4
Mikhaylovgrad, *Bulgaria* . 38 F6
Mikhaylovka, *Russia* 42 E6
Mikhnevo, *Russia* 42 C4
Míkinai, *Greece* 39 M5
Mikkeli, *Finland* 9 F22
Mikkwa →, *Canada* 100 B6
Mikniya, *Sudan* 77 D3
Mikolajki, *Poland* 20 B11
Míkonos, *Greece* 39 M8
Mikrón Dhérion, *Greece* . 39 H9
Mikulov, *Czech.* 20 G6
Mikumi, *Tanzania* 82 D4
Milaca, *U.S.A.* 108 C8
Milagro, *Ecuador* 120 D2
Milagros, *Phil.* 55 E5
Milan = Milano, *Italy* ... 32 C6
Milan, *Mo., U.S.A.* 108 E8
Milan, *Tenn., U.S.A.* 105 H1
Milang, *Australia* 91 E2
Milange, *Mozam.* 83 F4
Milano, *Italy* 32 C6
Milâs, *Turkey* 66 D2
Mílatos, *Greece* 37 D7
Milazzo, *Italy* 35 D8
Milbank, *U.S.A.* 108 C6
Milden, *Canada* 101 C7
Mildmay, *Canada* 106 B3
Mildura, *Australia* 91 E3
Mile, *China* 52 E4
Miléai, *Greece* 39 K6
Miles, *Australia* 91 D5
Miles, *U.S.A.* 109 K4
Miles City, *U.S.A.* 108 B2
Mileto, *Italy* 35 D9
Miletto, Mte., *Italy* 35 A7
Miletus, *Turkey* 66 D2
Mileura, *Australia* 89 E2
Milford, *Calif., U.S.A.* .. 112 E6
Milford, *Conn., U.S.A.* .. 107 E11
Milford, *Del., U.S.A.* 104 F8
Milford, *Mass., U.S.A.* .. 107 D13
Milford, *Pa., U.S.A.* 107 E10
Milford, *Utah, U.S.A.* ... 111 G7
Milford Haven, *U.K.* 13 F2
Milford Sd., *N.Z.* 87 L1
Milgun, *Australia* 89 D2
Milh, Baḥr al, *Iraq* 67 F10
Miliana, Aïn Salah, *Algeria* 75 C5

Miliana, *Médéa, Algeria* .. 75 A5
Miling, *Australia* 89 F2
Militello in Val di Catánia,
  Italy 35 E7
Milk →, *U.S.A.* 110 B10
Milk, Wadi el →, *Sudan* . 76 D3
Milk River, *Canada* 100 D6
Mill, *Neths.* 17 E7
Mill City, *U.S.A.* 110 D2
Mill I., *Antarctica* 5 C8
Mill Valley, *U.S.A.* 112 H4
Millau, *France* 26 D7
Millbridge, *Canada* 106 B7
Millbrook, *Canada* 106 B6
Mille Lacs, L. des, *Canada* 98 C1
Mille Lacs L., *U.S.A.* 108 B8
Milledgeville, *U.S.A.* 105 J4
Millen, *U.S.A.* 105 J5
Miller, *U.S.A.* 108 C5
Millerovo, *Russia* 43 F5
Millersburg, *Ohio, U.S.A.* 106 F3
Millersburg, *Pa., U.S.A.* . 106 F8
Millerton, *U.S.A.* 107 E11
Millerton L., *U.S.A.* 112 J7
Millevaches, Plateau de,
  France 26 C6
Millicent, *Australia* 91 F3
Millingen, *Neths.* 16 E8
Millinocket, *U.S.A.* 99 C6
Millmerran, *Australia* ... 91 D5
Mills L., *Canada* 100 A5
Millsboro, *U.S.A.* 106 G4
Milltown Malbay, *Ireland* 15 D2
Millville, *U.S.A.* 104 F8
Millwood L., *U.S.A.* 109 J8
Milly-la-Forêt, *France* ... 25 D9
Milna, *Croatia* 33 E13
Milne →, *Australia* 90 C2
Milne Inlet, *Canada* 97 A11
Milnor, *U.S.A.* 108 B6
Milo, *Canada* 100 C6
Mílos, *Greece* 39 N7
Miloševo, *Serbia, Yug.* .. 21 K10
Milparinka P.O., *Australia* 91 D3
Miltenberg, *Germany* 19 F5
Milton, *Canada* 106 C5
Milton, *N.Z.* 87 M2
Milton, *U.K.* 14 D4
Milton, *Calif., U.S.A.* ... 112 G6
Milton, *Fla., U.S.A.* 105 K2
Milton, *Pa., U.S.A.* 106 F8
Milton-Freewater, *U.S.A.* 110 D4
Milton Keynes, *U.K.* 13 E7
Miltou, *Chad* 73 F8
Milverton, *Canada* 106 C4
Milwaukee, *U.S.A.* 104 D2
Milwaukee Deep, *Atl. Oc.* 117 C6
Milwaukie, *U.S.A.* 112 E4
Mim, *Ghana* 78 D4
Mimizan, *France* 26 D2
Mimoso, *Brazil* 123 E2
Min Chiang →, *China* ... 53 E12
Min Jiang →, *China* 52 C5
Min Xian, *China* 50 G3
Mina, *U.S.A.* 111 G4
Mina Pirquitas, *Argentina* 126 A2
Mīnā Su'ud, *Si. Arabia* .. 65 D6
Mīnā'al Aḥmadī, *Kuwait* . 65 D6
Mīnāb, *Iran* 65 E8
Minago →, *Canada* 101 C9
Minaki, *Canada* 101 D10
Minamata, *Japan* 49 H5
Minami-Tori-Shima,
  Pac. Oc. 92 E7
Minas, *Uruguay* 127 C4
Minas, Sierra de las,
  Guatemala 116 C2
Minas Basin, *Canada* 99 C7
Minas de Rio Tinto, *Spain* 31 H4
Minas de San Quintín,
  Spain 31 G6
Minas Gerais □, *Brazil* .. 123 E2
Minas Novas, *Brazil* 123 E3
Minatitlán, *Mexico* 115 D6
Minbu, *Burma* 61 J19
Mincio →, *Italy* 32 C7
Mindanao, *Phil.* 55 H6
Mindanao Sea = Bohol
  Sea, *Phil.* 57 C6
Mindanao Trench, *Pac. Oc.* 55 F7
Mindel →, *Germany* 19 G6
Mindelheim, *Germany* ... 19 G6
Minden, *Canada* 106 B6
Minden, *Germany* 18 C4
Minden, *La., U.S.A.* 109 J8
Minden, *Nev., U.S.A.* ... 112 G7
Mindiptana, *Indonesia* ... 57 F10
Mindoro, *Phil.* 55 E4
Mindoro Str., *Phil.* 55 E4
Mindouli, *Congo* 80 E2
Mine, *Japan* 49 G5
Minehead, *U.K.* 13 F4
Mineiros, *Brazil* 125 D7
Mineola, *U.S.A.* 109 J7
Mineral King, *U.S.A.* 112 J8
Mineral Wells, *U.S.A.* ... 109 J5
Mineralnyye Vody, *Russia* 43 H6
Minersville, *U.S.A.* 107 F8
Minersville, *Utah, U.S.A.* 111 G7
Minerva, *U.S.A.* 106 F3
Minervino Murge, *Italy* .. 35 A9
Minetto, *U.S.A.* 107 C8
Mingäçevir, *Azerbaijan* .. 43 K8
Mingäçevir Su Anbarı,
  Azerbaijan 43 K8
Mingan, *Canada* 99 B7

Mingechaur = Mingäçevir, Azerbaijan 43 K8
Mingechaurskoye Vdkhr. = Mingäçevir Su Anbarı, Azerbaijan 43 K8
Mingela, Australia 90 B4
Mingenew, Australia 89 E2
Mingera Cr. →, Australia . 90 C2
Minggang, China 53 A10
Mingin, Burma 61 H19
Minglanilla, Spain 28 F3
Minglun, China 52 E7
Mingorria, Spain 30 E6
Mingt'iehkaitafan = Mintaka Pass, Pakistan . 63 A6
Mingxi, China 53 D11
Mingyuegue, China 51 C15
Minho = Miño →, Spain . 30 D2
Minhou, China 53 E12
Minićevo, Serbia, Yug. . . 21 M12
Minidoka, U.S.A. 110 E7
Minigwal, L., Australia . . . 89 E3
Minilya, Australia 89 D1
Minilya →, Australia 89 D1
Minipi, L., Canada 99 B7
Mink L., Canada 100 A5
Minna, Nigeria 79 D6
Minneapolis, Kans., U.S.A. 108 F6
Minneapolis, Minn., U.S.A. 108 C8
Minnedosa, Canada 101 C9
Minnesota □, U.S.A. 108 B8
Minnesund, Norway 10 D5
Minnie Creek, Australia . . 89 D2
Minnipa, Australia 91 E2
Minnitaki L., Canada 98 C1
Mino, Japan 49 G8
Miño →, Spain 30 D2
Minorca = Menorca, Spain 36 B11
Minore, Australia 91 E4
Minot, U.S.A. 108 A4
Minqin, China 50 E2
Minqing, China 53 D12
Minsen, Germany 18 B3
Minsk, Belarus 40 F4
Mińsk Mazowiecki, Poland 20 C11
Mintaka Pass, Pakistan . . 63 A6
Minto, Canada 96 B5
Minton, Canada 101 D8
Minturn, U.S.A. 110 G10
Minturno, Italy 34 A6
Minûf, Egypt 76 H7
Minusinsk, Russia 45 D10
Minutang, India 61 E20
Minvoul, Gabon 80 D2
Minya el Qamh, Egypt . . . 76 H7
Mionica, Serbia, Yug. . . . 21 L10
Mir, Niger 79 C7
Mīr Kūh, Iran 65 E8
Mīr Shahdād, Iran 65 E8
Mira, Italy 33 C9
Mira, Portugal 30 E2
Mira →, Colombia 120 C2
Mira →, Portugal 31 H2
Mira por vos Cay, Bahamas 117 B5
Mirabella Eclano, Italy . . 35 A7
Miracema do Norte, Brazil 122 C2
Mirador, Brazil 122 C3
Miraflores, Colombia . . . 120 C3
Miraj, India 60 L9
Miram Shah, Pakistan . . . 62 C4
Miramar, Argentina 126 D4
Miramar, Mozam. 85 C6
Miramas, France 27 E8
Mirambeau, France 26 C3
Miramichi B., Canada . . . 99 C7
Miramont-de-Guyenne, France 26 D4
Miranda, Brazil 125 E6
Miranda □, Venezuela . . 120 A4
Miranda →, Brazil 125 D6
Miranda de Ebro, Spain . . 28 C2
Miranda do Corvo, Spain . 30 E2
Miranda do Douro, Portugal 30 D4
Mirande, France 26 E4
Mirandela, Portugal 30 D3
Mirando City, U.S.A. . . . 109 M5
Mirándola, Italy 32 D8
Mirandópolis, Brazil 127 A5
Mirango, Malawi 83 E3
Mirani, Australia 90 C4
Mirano, Italy 33 C9
Mirassol, Brazil 127 A6
Mirbāţ, Oman 68 D5
Mirear, Egypt 76 C4
Mirebeau, Côte-d'Or, France 25 E12
Mirebeau, Vienne, France . 24 F7
Mirecourt, France 25 D13
Mirgorod = Myrhorod, Ukraine 41 H7
Miri, Malaysia 56 D4
Miriam Vale, Australia . . . 90 C5
Mirim, L., S. Amer. 127 C5
Mirimire, Venezuela 120 A4
Miriti, Brazil 125 B6
Mirnyy, Russia 45 C12
Mirond L., Canada 101 B8
Mirpur, Pakistan 63 C5
Mirpur Bibiwari, Pakistan . 62 E2
Mirpur Khas, Pakistan . . . 62 G3
Mirpur Sakro, Pakistan . . 62 G2
Mirria, Niger 79 C6
Mirror, Canada 100 C6
Mîrşani, Romania 38 E7
Miryang, S. Korea 51 G15
Mirzaani, Georgia 43 K8

Mirzapur, India 63 G10
Mirzapur-cum-Vindhyachal = Mirzapur, India 63 G10
Misantla, Mexico 115 D5
Misawa, Japan 48 D10
Miscou I., Canada 99 C7
Mish'āb, Ra's al, Si. Arabia 65 D6
Mishagua →, Peru 124 C3
Mishan, China 54 B8
Mishawaka, U.S.A. 104 E2
Mishbih, Gebel, Egypt . . . 76 C3
Mishima, Japan 49 G9
Misilmeri, Italy 34 D6
Misión, Mexico 113 N10
Misión Fagnano, Argentina 128 D3
Misiones □, Argentina . . 127 B5
Misiones □, Paraguay . . 126 B4
Miskah, Si. Arabia 64 E4
Miskitos, Cayos, Nic. . . . 116 D3
Miskolc, Hungary 21 G10
Misoke, Zaïre 82 C2
Misool, Indonesia 57 E8
Misrātah, Libya 73 B8
Misrātah, Sudan 77 D4
Missanabie, Canada 98 C3
Missão Velha, Brazil . . . 122 C4
Missinaibi →, Canada . . . 98 B3
Missinaibi L., Canada . . . 98 C3
Mission, S. Dak., U.S.A. . 108 D4
Mission, Tex., U.S.A. . . . 109 M5
Mission City, Canada . . . 100 D4
Mission Viejo, U.S.A. . . . 113 M9
Missisa L., Canada 98 B2
Mississagi →, Canada . . . 98 C3
Mississippi □, U.S.A. . . . 109 J10
Mississippi →, U.S.A. . . . 109 L10
Mississippi L., Canada . . 107 A8
Mississippi River Delta, U.S.A. 109 L9
Mississippi Sd., U.S.A. . . 109 K10
Missoula, U.S.A. 110 C6
Missour, Morocco 74 B4
Missouri □, U.S.A. 108 F8
Missouri →, U.S.A. 108 F9
Missouri Valley, U.S.A. . . 108 E7
Mist, U.S.A. 112 E3
Mistake B., Canada 101 A10
Mistassini →, Canada . . . 99 C5
Mistassini L., Canada . . . 98 B5
Mistastin L., Canada 99 A7
Mistatim, Canada 101 C8
Mistelbach, Austria 20 G6
Misterbianco, Italy 35 E8
Mistretta, Italy 35 E7
Misty L., Canada 101 B8
Misurata = Misrātah, Libya 73 B8
Mît Ghamr, Egypt 76 H7
Mitatib, Sudan 77 D4
Mitchell, Australia 91 D4
Mitchell, Canada 106 C3
Mitchell, Ind., U.S.A. . . . 104 F2
Mitchell, Nebr., U.S.A. . . 108 E3
Mitchell, Oreg., U.S.A. . . 110 D3
Mitchell, S. Dak., U.S.A. . 108 D5
Mitchell →, Australia 90 B3
Mitchell, Mt., U.S.A. 105 H4
Mitchell Ras., Australia . . 90 A2
Mitchelstown, Ireland . . . 15 D3
Mitha Tiwana, Pakistan . . 62 C5
Mitilíni, Greece 39 K9
Mito, Japan 49 F10
Mitrofanovka, Russia 42 F4
Mitrovica = Titova-Mitrovica, Serbia, Yug. . 21 N10
Mitsinjo, Madag. 85 B8
Mitsiwa, Eritrea 77 D4
Mitsiwa Channel, Eritrea . 77 D5
Mitsukaidō, Japan 49 F9
Mittagong, Australia 91 E5
Mittelland, Switz. 22 C4
Mittellandkanal →, Germany 18 C3
Mittenwalde, Germany . . . 18 C9
Mitterteich, Germany 19 F8
Mittweida, Germany 18 E8
Mitú, Colombia 120 C3
Mituas, Colombia 120 C4
Mitumba, Tanzania 82 D3
Mitumba, Chaîne des, Zaïre 82 D2
Mitumba Mts. = Mitumba, Chaîne des, Zaïre . . . 82 D2
Mitwaba, Zaïre 83 D2
Mityana, Uganda 82 B3
Mitzic, Gabon 80 D2
Mixteco →, Mexico 115 D5
Miyagi □, Japan 48 E10
Miyâh, W. el →, Egypt . . 76 B3
Miyah, W. el →, Syria . . . 64 C3
Miyako, Japan 48 E10
Miyako-Jima, Japan 49 M2
Miyako-Rettō, Japan 49 M2
Miyakonojō, Japan 49 J5
Miyazaki, Japan 49 J5
Miyazaki □, Japan 49 H5
Miyazu, Japan 49 G7
Miyet, Bahr el = Dead Sea, Asia 69 D4
Miyi, China 52 D4
Miyoshi, Japan 49 G6
Miyun, China 50 D9
Miyun Shuiku, China 51 D9
Mizamis = Ozamiz, Phil. . 55 G5
Mizdah, Libya 75 B7

Mizen Hd., Cork, Ireland . 15 E2
Mizen Hd., Wick., Ireland . 15 D5
Mizhi, China 50 F6
Mizil, Romania 38 E9
Mizoram □, India 61 H18
Mizpe Ramon, Israel 69 E3
Mizusawa, Japan 48 E10
Mjöbäck, Sweden 11 G6
Mjölby, Sweden 11 F9
Mjörn, Sweden 11 G6
Mjøsa, Norway 10 D5
Mkata, Tanzania 82 D4
Mkokotoni, Tanzania 82 D4
Mkomazi, Tanzania 82 C4
Mkomazi →, S. Africa . . . 85 E5
Mkulwe, Tanzania 83 D3
Mkumbi, Ras, Tanzania . . 82 D4
Mkushi, Zambia 83 E2
Mkushi River, Zambia . . . 83 E2
Mkuze, S. Africa 85 D5
Mladá Boleslav, Czech. . . 20 E4
Mladenovac, Serbia, Yug. . 21 L10
Mlala Hills, Tanzania 82 D3
Mlange, Malawi 83 F4
Mlava →, Serbia, Yug. . . 21 L11
Mława, Poland 20 B10
Mljet, Croatia 21 N7
Młynąry, Poland 20 A9
Mmabatho, S. Africa 84 D4
Mme, Cameroon 79 D7
Mo i Rana, Norway 8 C16
Moa, Indonesia 57 F7
Moa →, S. Leone 78 D2
Moab, U.S.A. 111 G9
Moabi, Gabon 80 E2
Moaco →, Brazil 124 B4
Moala, Fiji 87 D8
Moalie Park, Australia . . . 91 D3
Moaña, Spain 30 C2
Moba, Zaïre 82 D2
Mobārakābād, Iran 65 D7
Mobārakīyeh, Iran 65 C6
Mobaye, C.A.R. 80 D4
Mobayi, Zaïre 80 D4
Moberly, U.S.A. 108 F8
Moberly →, Canada 100 B4
Mobile, U.S.A. 105 K1
Mobile B., U.S.A. 105 K2
Mobridge, U.S.A. 108 C4
Mobutu Sese Seko, L. = Albert L., Africa 82 B3
Moc Chau, Vietnam 58 B5
Moc Hoa, Vietnam 59 G5
Mocabe Kasari, Zaïre 83 D2
Mocajuba, Brazil 122 B2
Moçambique, Mozam. . . . 83 F5
Moçâmedes = Namibe, Angola 81 H2
Mocapra →, Venezuela . . 120 B4
Mocha, I., Chile 128 A2
Mococa, Brazil 127 A6
Mocorito, Mexico 114 B3
Moctezuma, Mexico 114 B3
Moctezuma →, Mexico . . 115 C5
Mocuba, Mozam. 83 F4
Mocúzari, Presa, Mexico . 114 B3
Modane, France 27 C10
Modasa, India 62 H5
Modave, Belgium 17 H6
Modder →, S. Africa 84 D3
Modderrivier, S. Africa . . 84 D3
Módena, Italy 32 D7
Modena, U.S.A. 111 H7
Modesto, U.S.A. 111 H3
Módica, Italy 35 F7
Modigliana, Italy 33 D8
Modo, Sudan 77 F3
Modra, Slovak Rep. 21 G7
Moe, Australia 91 F4
Moebase, Mozam. 83 F4
Moëlan-sur-Mer, France . . 24 E3
Moengo, Surinam 121 B7
Moergestel, Neths. 17 E6
Moers, Germany 17 F9
Moësa →, Switz. 23 D8
Moffat, U.K. 14 F5
Moga, India 62 D6
Mogadishu = Muqdisho, Somali Rep. 68 G4
Mogador = Essaouira, Morocco 74 B3
Mogadouro, Portugal . . . 30 D4
Mogalakwena →, S. Africa 85 C4
Mogami →, Japan 48 E10
Mogán, Canary Is. 36 G4
Mogaung, Burma 61 G20
Møgeltønder, Denmark . . 11 K2
Mogente, Spain 29 G4
Mogho, Ethiopia 77 G5
Mogi das Cruzes, Brazil . 127 A6
Mogi-Guaçu →, Brazil . . 127 A6
Mogi-Mirim, Brazil 127 A6
Mogielnica, Poland 20 D10
Mogilev = Mahilyow, Belarus 40 F6
Mogilev-Podolskiy = Mohyliv-Podilskyy, Ukraine 41 H4
Mogilno, Poland 20 C7
Mogincual, Mozam. 83 F5

Mogocha, Russia 45 D12
Mogoi, Indonesia 57 E8
Mogok, Burma 61 H20
Moguer, Spain 31 H4
Mogumber, Australia 89 F2
Mohács, Hungary 21 K8
Mohales Hoek, Lesotho . . 84 E4
Mohall, U.S.A. 108 A4
Moḩammadābād, Iran . . . 65 B8
Mohammadia, Algeria . . . 75 A5
Mohammedia, Morocco . . 74 B3
Mohave, L., U.S.A. 113 K12
Mohawk →, U.S.A. 107 D11
Möhne →, Germany 18 D3
Moholm, Sweden 11 F8
Mohoro, Tanzania 82 D4
Mohyliv-Podilskyy, Ukraine 41 H4
Moia, Sudan 77 F2
Moidart, L., U.K. 14 E3
Moineşti, Romania 38 C9
Mointy, Kazakhstan 44 E8
Moirans, France 27 C9
Moirans-en-Montagne, France 27 B9
Moíres, Greece 37 D6
Moisaküla, Estonia 9 G21
Moisie, Canada 99 B6
Moisie →, Canada 99 B6
Moissac, France 26 D5
Moïssala, Chad 73 G8
Moita, Portugal 31 G2
Mojácar, Spain 29 H3
Mojados, Spain 30 D6
Mojave, U.S.A. 113 K8
Mojave Desert, U.S.A. . . 113 L10
Mojiang, China 52 F3
Mojo, Bolivia 126 A2
Mojo, Ethiopia 77 F4
Mojokerto, Indonesia 57 G15
Mojos, Llanos de, Bolivia 125 D5
Moju →, Brazil 122 B2
Mokai, N.Z. 87 H5
Mokambo, Zaïre 83 E2
Mokameh, India 63 G11
Mokelumne →, U.S.A. . . 112 G5
Mokelumne Hill, U.S.A. . . 112 G6
Mokhós, Greece 37 D7
Mokhotlong, Lesotho . . . 85 D4
Moknine, Tunisia 75 A7
Mokokchung, India 61 F19
Mokra Gora, Serbia, Yug. 21 N10
Mokronog, Slovenia 33 C12
Moksha →, Russia 42 C6
Mokshan, Russia 42 D7
Mol, Belgium 17 F6
Mola, C. de la, Spain 28 F9
Mola di Bari, Italy 35 A10
Moláoi, Greece 39 N5
Molat, Croatia 33 D11
Molchanovo, Russia 44 D9
Mold, U.K. 12 D4
Moldavia, Romania 38 C10
Moldavia = Moldova ■, Europe 41 J5
Molde, Norway 8 E12
Moldova ■, Europe 41 J5
Moldova Nouă, Romania . 38 E4
Moldoveana, Romania . . . 38 D7
Molepolole, Botswana . . . 84 C4
Moléson, Switz. 22 C4
Molfetta, Italy 35 A9
Molina de Aragón, Spain . 28 E3
Moline, U.S.A. 108 E9
Molinella, Italy 33 D8
Molinos, Argentina 126 B2
Moliro, Zaïre 82 D3
Molise □, Italy 33 G11
Moliterno, Italy 35 B8
Mollahat, Bangla. 63 H13
Mölle, Sweden 11 H6
Molledo, Spain 30 B6
Mollendo, Peru 124 D3
Mollerin, L., Australia . . . 89 F2
Mollerusa, Spain 28 D5
Mollina, Spain 31 H6
Mölln, Germany 18 B6
Mölltorp, Sweden 11 F8
Mölndal, Sweden 11 G6
Molochansk, Ukraine 41 J8
Molochnoye, Ozero, Ukraine 41 J8
Molodechno = Maladzyechna, Belarus . 40 E4
Molokai, U.S.A. 102 H16
Molong, Australia 91 E4
Molopo →, Africa 84 D3
Mólos, Greece 39 L5
Molotov = Perm, Russia . . 44 D6
Moloundou, Cameroon . . 80 D3
Molsheim, France 25 D14
Molson L., Canada 101 C9
Molteno, S. Africa 84 E4
Molu, Indonesia 57 F8
Molucca Sea, Indonesia . . 57 E6
Moluccas = Maluku, Indonesia 57 E7
Moma, Mozam. 83 F4
Moma, Zaïre 82 C1
Mombaça, Brazil 122 C4
Mombasa, Kenya 82 C4
Mombetsu, Japan 48 B11
Mombuey, Spain 30 C4
Momchilgrad, Bulgaria . . 39 H8
Momi, Zaïre 82 C2
Momignies, Belgium 17 H4
Mompós, Colombia 120 B3
Møn, Denmark 11 K6

Mon →, Burma 61 J19
Mona, Canal de la, W. Indies 117 C6
Mona, Isla, Puerto Rico . 117 C6
Mona, Pta., Costa Rica . . 116 E3
Mona, Pta., Spain 31 J7
Monach Is., U.K. 14 D1
Monaco ■, Europe 27 E11
Monadhliath Mts., U.K. . . 14 D4
Monagas □, Venezuela . . 121 B5
Monaghan, Ireland 15 B5
Monaghan □, Ireland . . . 15 B5
Monahans, U.S.A. 109 K3
Monapo, Mozam. 83 E5
Monarch Mt., Canada . . . 100 C3
Monastir = Bitola, Macedonia 39 H4
Monastir, Tunisia 75 A7
Moncada, Phil. 55 D4
Moncada, Spain 28 F4
Moncalieri, Italy 32 D4
Moncalvo, Italy 32 C5
Monção, Portugal 30 C2
Moncarapacho, Portugal . 31 H3
Moncayo, Sierra del, Spain 28 D3
Mönchengladbach, Germany 18 D2
Monchique, Portugal 31 H2
Monclova, Mexico 114 B4
Moncontour, France 24 D4
Moncoutant, France 26 B3
Moncton, Canada 99 C7
Mondego →, Portugal . . . 30 E2
Mondego, C., Portugal . . 30 E2
Mondeodo, Indonesia . . . 57 E6
Mondolfo, Italy 33 E10
Mondoñedo, Spain 30 B3
Mondovì, Italy 32 D4
Mondovi, U.S.A. 108 C9
Mondragon, France 27 D8
Mondragone, Italy 34 A6
Mondrain I., Australia . . . 89 F3
Monduli, Tanzania 82 C4
Monemvasía, Greece 39 N6
Monessen, U.S.A. 106 F5
Monesterio, Spain 31 G4
Monestier-de-Clermont, France 27 D9
Monett, U.S.A. 109 G8
Monfalcone, Italy 33 C10
Monflanquin, France 26 D4
Monforte, Portugal 31 F3
Monforte de Lemos, Spain 30 C3
Mong Hsu, Burma 61 J21
Mong Kung, Burma 61 J20
Mong Nai, Burma 61 J20
Mong Pawk, Burma 61 H21
Mong Ton, Burma 61 J21
Mong Wa, Burma 61 J22
Mong Yai, Burma 61 H21
Mongalla, Sudan 77 F3
Mongers, L., Australia . . . 89 E2
Monghyr = Munger, India 63 G12
Mongibello = Etna, Italy . 35 E8
Mongo, Chad 73 F8
Mongolia ■, Asia 45 B10
Mongororo, Chad 73 F9
Mongu, Zambia 81 H4
Môngua, Angola 84 B2
Monistrol-d'Allier, France 26 D7
Monistrol-sur-Loire, France 27 C8
Monkey Bay, Malawi 83 E4
Monkey River, Belize . . . 115 D7
Monkira, Australia 90 C3
Monkoto, Zaïre 80 E4
Monmouth, U.K. 13 F5
Monmouth, U.S.A. 108 E9
Mono L., U.S.A. 111 H4
Monolith, U.S.A. 113 K8
Monólithos, Greece 37 C9
Monongahela, U.S.A. . . . 106 F5
Monópoli, Italy 35 B10
Monor, Hungary 21 H9
Monóvar, Spain 29 G4
Monqoumba, C.A.R. 80 D3
Monreal del Campo, Spain 28 E3
Monreale, Italy 34 D6
Monroe, Ga., U.S.A. 105 J4
Monroe, La., U.S.A. 109 J8
Monroe, Mich., U.S.A. . . 104 E4
Monroe, N.C., U.S.A. . . . 105 H5
Monroe, N.Y., U.S.A. . . . 107 E10
Monroe, Utah, U.S.A. . . . 111 G7
Monroe, Wash., U.S.A. . . 112 C5
Monroe, Wis., U.S.A. . . . 108 D10
Monroe City, U.S.A. 108 F9
Monroeville, Ala., U.S.A. . 105 K2
Monroeville, Pa., U.S.A. . 106 F5
Monrovia, Liberia 78 D2
Monrovia, U.S.A. 111 J4
Mons, Belgium 17 H3
Monsaraz, Portugal 31 G3
Monse, Indonesia 57 E6
Monsefú, Peru 124 B2
Monségur, France 26 D4
Monsélice, Italy 33 C8
Monster, Neths. 16 D4
Mont Cenis, Col du, France 27 C10
Mont-de-Marsan, France . 26 E3
Mont-Joli, Canada 99 C6
Mont-Laurier, Canada . . . 98 C4
Mont-St.-Michel, Le = Mont-St.-Michel, France 24 D5
Mont-sous-Vaudrey, France 25 F12

Mount Desert I.

Mont-sur-Marchienne, Belgium 17 H4
Mont Tremblant Prov. Park, Canada 98 C5
Montabaur, Germany 18 E3
Montagnac, France 26 E7
Montagnana, Italy 33 C8
Montagu, S. Africa 84 E3
Montagu I., Antarctica 5 B1
Montague, Canada 99 C7
Montague, U.S.A. 110 F2
Montague, I., Mexico 114 A2
Montague Ra., Australia 89 E2
Montague Sd., Australia 88 B4
Montaigu, France 24 F5
Montalbán, Spain 28 E4
Montalbano di Elicona, Italy 35 D8
Montalbano Iónico, Italy 35 B9
Montalbo, Spain 28 F2
Montalcino, Italy 33 E8
Montalegre, Portugal 30 D3
Montalto di Castro, Italy 33 F8
Montalto Uffugo, Italy 35 C9
Montalvo, U.S.A. 113 L7
Montamarta, Spain 30 D5
Montaña, Peru 124 B3
Montana, Switz. 22 D4
Montana □, U.S.A. 110 C9
Montaña Clara, I., Canary Is. 36 E6
Montánchez, Spain 31 F4
Montañita, Colombia 120 C2
Montargis, France 25 E9
Montauban, France 26 D5
Montauk, U.S.A. 107 E13
Montauk Pt., U.S.A. 107 E13
Montbard, France 25 E11
Montbéliard, France 25 E13
Montblanch, Spain 28 D6
Montbrison, France 27 C8
Montcalm, Pic de, France 26 F5
Montceau-les-Mines, France 25 F11
Montchanin, France 27 B8
Montclair, U.S.A. 107 F10
Montcornet, France 25 C11
Montcuq, France 26 D5
Montdidier, France 25 C9
Monte Albán, Mexico 115 D5
Monte Alegre, Brazil 121 D7
Monte Alegre de Goiás, Brazil 123 D2
Monte Alegre de Minas, Brazil 123 E2
Monte Azul, Brazil 123 E3
Monte Bello Is., Australia 88 D2
Monte-Carlo, Monaco 27 E11
Monte Carmelo, Brazil 123 E2
Monte Caseros, Argentina 126 C4
Monte Comán, Argentina 126 C2
Monte Cristi, Dom. Rep. 117 C5
Monte Dinero, Argentina 128 D3
Monte Lindo →, Paraguay 126 A4
Monte Quemado, Argentina 126 B3
Monte Redondo, Portugal 30 F2
Monte Rio, U.S.A. 112 G4
Monte San Giovanni Campano, Italy 34 A6
Monte San Savino, Italy 33 E8
Monte Sant' Ángelo, Italy 35 A8
Monte Santu, C. di, Italy 34 B2
Monte Vista, U.S.A. 111 H10
Monteagudo, Argentina 127 B5
Monteagudo, Bolivia 125 D5
Montealegre, Spain 29 G3
Montebello, Canada 98 C5
Montebelluna, Italy 33 C9
Montebourg, France 24 C5
Montecastrilli, Italy 33 F9
Montecatini Terme, Italy 32 E7
Montecito, U.S.A. 113 L7
Montecristi, Ecuador 120 D1
Montecristo, Italy 32 F7
Montefalco, Italy 33 F9
Montefiascone, Italy 33 F9
Montefrío, Spain 31 H6
Montegnée, Belgium 17 G7
Montego Bay, Jamaica 116 C4
Montegranaro, Italy 33 E10
Monteiro, Brazil 122 C4
Montejicar, Spain 29 H1
Montejinnie, Australia 88 C5
Montelíbano, Colombia 120 B2
Montélimar, France 27 D8
Montella, Italy 35 B8
Montellano, Spain 31 J5
Montello, U.S.A. 108 D10
Montelupo Fiorentino, Italy 32 E8
Montemor-o-Novo, Portugal 31 G2
Montemor-o-Velho, Portugal 30 E2
Montemorelos, Mexico 115 B5
Montendre, France 26 C3
Montenegro, Brazil 127 B5
Montenegro □, Yugoslavia 21 N9
Montenero di Bisáccia, Italy 33 G11
Montepuez, Mozam. 83 E4
Montepuez →, Mozam. 83 E5
Montepulciano, Italy 33 E8
Montereale, Italy 33 F10
Montereau-Fault-Yonne, France 25 D9
Monterey, U.S.A. 111 H3
Monterey B., U.S.A. 112 J5
Montería, Colombia 120 B2
Montero, Bolivia 125 D5
Monteros, Argentina 126 B2
Monterotondo, Italy 33 F9
Monterrey, Mexico 114 B4
Montes Altos, Brazil 122 C2
Montes Claros, Brazil 123 E3
Montesano, U.S.A. 112 D3
Montesárchio, Italy 35 A7
Montescaglioso, Italy 35 B9
Montesilvano Marina, Italy 33 F11
Montevarchi, Italy 33 E8
Montevideo, Uruguay 127 C4
Montevideo, U.S.A. 108 C7
Montezuma, U.S.A. 108 E8
Montfaucon, France 25 C12
Montfaucon-en-Velay, France 27 C8
Montfort, France 24 D5
Montfort, Neths. 17 F7
Montfort-l'Amaury, France 25 D8
Montgenèvre, France 27 D10
Montgomery = Sahiwal, Pakistan 62 D5
Montgomery, U.K. 13 E4
Montgomery, Ala., U.S.A. 105 J2
Montgomery, W. Va., U.S.A. 104 F5
Montguyon, France 26 C3
Monthey, Switz. 22 D3
Monticelli d'Ongina, Italy 32 C6
Monticello, Ark., U.S.A. 109 J9
Monticello, Fla., U.S.A. 105 K4
Monticello, Ind., U.S.A. 104 E2
Monticello, Iowa, U.S.A. 108 D9
Monticello, Ky., U.S.A. 105 G3
Monticello, Minn., U.S.A. 108 C8
Monticello, Miss., U.S.A. 109 K9
Monticello, N.Y., U.S.A. 107 E10
Monticello, Utah, U.S.A. 111 H9
Montichiari, Italy 32 C7
Montier-en-Der, France 25 D11
Montignac, France 26 C5
Montignies-sur-Sambre, Belgium 17 H4
Montigny, France 25 C13
Montigny-sur-Aube, France 25 E11
Montijo, Spain 31 G4
Montijo, Presa de, Spain 31 G4
Montilla, Spain 31 H6
Montlhéry, France 25 D9
Montluçon, France 26 B6
Montmagny, Canada 99 C5
Montmarault, France 26 B6
Montmartre, Canada 101 C8
Montmédy, France 25 C12
Montmélian, France 27 C10
Montmirail, France 25 D10
Montmoreau-St.-Cybard, France 26 C4
Montmorency, Canada 99 C5
Montmorillon, France 26 B4
Montmort, France 25 D10
Monto, Australia 90 C5
Montoir-sur-le-Loir, France 24 E7
Montório al Vomano, Italy 33 F10
Montoro, Spain 31 G6
Montour Falls, U.S.A. 106 D8
Montpelier, Idaho, U.S.A. 110 E8
Montpelier, Ohio, U.S.A. 104 E3
Montpelier, Vt., U.S.A. 107 B12
Montpellier, France 26 E7
Montpezat-de-Quercy, France 26 D5
Montpon-Ménestérol, France 26 D4
Montréal, Canada 98 C5
Montréal, France 26 E6
Montreal L., Canada 101 C7
Montreal Lake, Canada 101 C7
Montredon-Labessonnié, France 26 E6
Montréjeau, France 26 E4
Montrésor, France 24 E8
Montreuil, France 25 B8
Montreuil-Bellay, France 24 E6
Montreux, Switz. 22 D3
Montrevault, France 24 E5
Montrevel-en-Bresse, France 27 B9
Montrichard, France 24 E8
Montrose, U.K. 14 E6
Montrose, Colo., U.S.A. 111 G10
Montrose, Pa., U.S.A. 107 E9
Monts, Pte. des, Canada 99 C6
Monts-sur-Guesnes, France 24 F7
Montsalvy, France 26 D6
Montsant, Sierra de, Spain 28 D5
Montsauche, France 25 E11
Montsech, Sierra del, Spain 28 C5
Montseny, Spain 28 D2
Montserrat, Spain 28 D6
Montserrat ■, W. Indies 117 C7
Montuenga, Spain 30 D6
Montuiri, Spain 36 B9
Monveda, Zaïre 80 D4
Monywa, Burma 61 H19
Monza, Italy 32 C6
Monze, Zambia 83 F2
Monze, C., Pakistan 62 G2
Monzón, Spain 28 D5
Mooi River, S. Africa 85 D4
Mook, Neths. 16 E7
Moolawatana, Australia 91 D2
Mooliabeenee, Australia 89 F2
Mooloogool, Australia 89 E2
Moomin Cr. →, Australia 91 D4
Moonah →, Australia 90 C2
Moonbeam, Canada 98 C3
Moonda, L., Australia 90 D3
Moonie, Australia 91 D5
Moonie →, Australia 91 D4
Moonta, Australia 91 E2
Moora, Australia 89 F2
Mooraberree, Australia 90 D3
Moorarie, Australia 89 E2
Moorcroft, U.S.A. 108 C2
Moore →, Australia 89 F2
Moore, L., Australia 89 E2
Moore Reefs, Australia 90 B4
Moorefield, U.S.A. 104 F6
Moores Res., U.S.A. 107 B13
Mooresville, U.S.A. 105 H5
Moorfoot Hills, U.K. 14 F5
Moorhead, U.S.A. 108 B6
Mooroopna, Australia 91 F4
Moorpark, U.S.A. 113 L8
Moorreesburg, S. Africa 84 E2
Moorslede, Belgium 17 G2
Moosburg, Germany 19 G7
Moose →, Canada 98 B3
Moose Factory, Canada 98 B3
Moose I., Canada 101 C9
Moose Jaw, Canada 101 C7
Moose Jaw →, Canada 101 C7
Moose Lake, Canada 101 C8
Moose Lake, U.S.A. 108 B8
Moose Mountain Cr. →, Canada 101 D8
Moose Mountain Prov. Park, Canada 101 D8
Moose River, Canada 98 B3
Moosehead L., U.S.A. 99 C6
Moosomin, Canada 101 C8
Moosonee, Canada 98 B3
Moosup, U.S.A. 107 E13
Mopeia Velha, Mozam. 83 F4
Mopipi, Botswana 84 C3
Mopoi, C.A.R. 82 A2
Mopti, Mali 78 C4
Moqatta, Sudan 77 E4
Moquegua, Peru 124 D3
Moquegua □, Peru 124 D3
Mór, Hungary 21 H8
Móra, Portugal 31 G2
Mora, Sweden 9 F16
Mora, Minn., U.S.A. 108 C8
Mora, N. Mex., U.S.A. 111 J11
Mora de Ebro, Spain 28 D5
Mora de Rubielos, Spain 28 E4
Mora la Nueva, Spain 28 D5
Morača →, Montenegro, Yug. 21 N9
Morada Nova, Brazil 122 C4
Morada Nova de Minas, Brazil 123 E2
Moradabad, India 63 E8
Morafenobe, Madag. 85 B7
Morąg, Poland 20 B9
Moral de Calatrava, Spain 29 G1
Moraleja, Spain 30 E4
Morales, Colombia 120 C2
Moramanga, Madag. 85 B8
Moran, Kans., U.S.A. 109 G7
Moran, Wyo., U.S.A. 110 E8
Moranbah, Australia 90 C4
Morano Cálabro, Italy 35 C9
Morant Cays, Jamaica 116 C4
Morant Pt., Jamaica 116 C4
Morar, L., U.K. 14 E3
Moratalla, Spain 29 G3
Moratuwa, Sri Lanka 60 R11
Morava →, Slovak Rep. 20 G6
Moravia, U.S.A. 108 E8
Moravian Hts. = Ceskomoravská Vrchovina, Czech. 20 F5
Moravica →, Serbia, Yug. 21 M10
Moravice →, Czech. 20 F7
Moraviţa, Romania 21 K11
Moravská Třebová, Czech. 20 F6
Morawa, Australia 89 E2
Morawhanna, Guyana 121 B6
Moray Firth, U.K. 14 D5
Morbach, Germany 19 F3
Morbegno, Italy 32 B6
Morbi, India 62 H4
Morbihan □, France 24 E4
Morcenx, France 26 D3
Mordelles, France 24 D5
Morden, Canada 101 D9
Mordovian Republic = Mordvinia □, Russia 42 C7
Mordovo, Russia 42 D5
Mordvinia □, Russia 42 C7
Møre og Romsdal fylke □, Norway 10 B2
Morea, Australia 91 F3
Morea, Greece 6 H10
Moreau →, U.S.A. 108 C4
Morecambe, U.K. 12 C5
Morecambe B., U.K. 12 C5
Moree, Australia 91 D4
Morehead, U.S.A. 104 F4
Morehead City, U.S.A. 105 H7
Morelia, Mexico 114 D4
Morella, Australia 90 C3
Morella, Spain 28 E4
Morelos, Mexico 114 B3
Morelos □, Mexico 115 D5
Morena, Sierra, Spain 31 G7
Morenci, U.S.A. 111 K9
Moreni, Romania 38 E8
Morero, Bolivia 125 C4
Moreru →, Brazil 125 C6
Moresby I., Canada 100 C2
Morestel, France 27 C9
Moret-sur-Loing, France 25 D9
Moreton, Australia 90 A3
Moreton I., Australia 91 D5
Moreuil, France 25 C9
Morey, Spain 36 B10
Morez, France 27 B10
Morgan, Australia 91 E2
Morgan, U.S.A. 110 F8
Morgan City, U.S.A. 109 L9
Morgan Hill, U.S.A. 112 H5
Morganfield, U.S.A. 104 G2
Morganton, U.S.A. 105 H5
Morgantown, U.S.A. 104 F6
Morgat, France 24 D2
Morgenzon, S. Africa 85 D4
Morges, Switz. 22 C2
Morghak, Iran 65 D8
Morhange, France 25 D13
Mori, Italy 32 C7
Morialmée, Belgium 17 H5
Morice L., Canada 100 C3
Morichal, Colombia 120 C3
Morichal Largo →, Venezuela 121 B5
Moriki, Nigeria 79 C6
Morinville, Canada 100 C6
Morioka, Japan 48 E10
Moris, Mexico 114 B3
Morlaàs, France 26 E3
Morlaix, France 24 D3
Morlanwelz, Belgium 17 H4
Mormanno, Italy 35 C8
Mormant, France 25 D9
Mornington, Vic., Australia 91 F4
Mornington, W. Austral., Australia 88 C4
Mornington, I., Chile 128 C1
Mornington I., Australia 90 B2
Mórnos →, Greece 39 L4
Moro, Sudan 77 E3
Moro G., Phil. 55 H5
Morocco ■, N. Afr. 74 B3
Morococha, Peru 124 C2
Morogoro, Tanzania 82 D4
Morogoro □, Tanzania 82 D4
Moroleón, Mexico 114 C4
Morombe, Madag. 85 C7
Moron, Argentina 126 C4
Morón, Cuba 116 B4
Mörön →, Mongolia 54 B6
Morón de Almazán, Spain 28 D2
Morón de la Frontera, Spain 31 H5
Morona →, Peru 120 D2
Morona-Santiago □, Ecuador 120 D2
Morondava, Madag. 85 C7
Morondo, Ivory C. 78 D3
Morongo Valley, U.S.A. 113 L10
Moronou, Ivory C. 78 D4
Morotai, Indonesia 57 D7
Moroto, Uganda 82 B3
Moroto Summit, Kenya 82 B3
Morozovsk, Russia 43 F5
Morpeth, U.K. 12 B6
Morphou, Cyprus 66 E5
Morphou Bay, Cyprus 37 D11
Morrilton, U.S.A. 109 H8
Morrinhos, Ceara, Brazil 122 B3
Morrinhos, Minas Gerais, Brazil 123 E2
Morrinsville, N.Z. 87 G5
Morris, Canada 101 D9
Morris, Ill., U.S.A. 104 E1
Morris, Minn., U.S.A. 108 C7
Morris, Mt., Australia 89 E5
Morrisburg, Canada 98 D4
Morrison, U.S.A. 108 E10
Morristown, Ariz., U.S.A. 111 K7
Morristown, N.J., U.S.A. 107 F10
Morristown, S. Dak., U.S.A. 108 C4
Morristown, Tenn., U.S.A. 105 G4
Morro, Pta., Chile 126 B1
Morro Bay, U.S.A. 111 J3
Morro del Jable, Canary Is. 36 F5
Morro do Chapéu, Brazil 123 D3
Morro Jable, Pta. de, Canary Is. 36 F5
Morros, Brazil 122 B3
Morrosquillo, G. de, Colombia 116 E4
Morrumbene, Mozam. 85 C6
Mors Nykøbing, Denmark 11 H2
Morshansk, Russia 42 D5
Mörsil, Sweden 10 A7
Mortagne →, France 25 D13
Mortagne-au-Perche, France 24 D7
Mortagne-sur-Gironde, France 26 C3
Mortagne-sur-Sèvre, France 24 F6
Mortain, France 24 D6
Mortara, Italy 32 C5
Morteau, France 25 E13
Morteros, Argentina 126 C3
Mortes, R. das →, Brazil 123 D1
Mortlake, Australia 91 F3
Morton, Tex., U.S.A. 109 J3
Morton, Wash., U.S.A. 112 D4
Mortsel, Belgium 17 F4
Morundah, Australia 91 E4
Moruya, Australia 91 F5
Morvan, France 25 E11
Morven, Australia 91 D4
Morvern, U.K. 14 E3
Morwell, Australia 91 F4
Mosalsk, Russia 42 C2
Mosbach, Germany 19 F5
Mošćenice, Croatia 33 C11
Mosciano Sant' Ángelo, Italy 33 F10
Moscos Is., Burma 58 E1
Moscow = Moskva, Russia 42 C3
Moscow, U.S.A. 110 C5
Mosel →, Europe 19 E3
Moselle = Mosel →, Europe 19 E3
Moselle □, France 25 D13
Moses Lake, U.S.A. 110 C4
Mosgiel, N.Z. 87 L3
Moshi, Tanzania 82 C4
Moshi □, Tanzania 82 C4
Moshupa, Botswana 84 C4
Mosjøen, Norway 8 D15
Moskenesøya, Norway 8 C15
Moskenstraumen, Norway 8 C15
Moskva, Russia 42 C3
Moskva →, Russia 42 C4
Moslavačka Gora, Croatia 33 C13
Mosomane, Botswana 84 C4
Moson-magyaróvar, Hungary 21 H7
Mospino, Ukraine 41 J9
Mosquera, Colombia 120 C2
Mosquero, U.S.A. 109 H3
Mosqueruela, Spain 28 E4
Mosquitia, Honduras 116 C3
Mosquitos, G. de los, Panama 116 E3
Moss, Norway 10 E4
Moss Vale, Australia 91 E5
Mossaka, Congo 80 E3
Mossâmedes, Brazil 123 E1
Mossbank, Canada 101 D7
Mossburn, N.Z. 87 L2
Mosselbaai, S. Africa 84 E3
Mossendjo, Congo 80 E2
Mosses, Col des, Switz. 22 D4
Mossgiel, Australia 91 E3
Mossman, Australia 90 B4
Mossoró, Brazil 122 C4
Mossuril, Mozam. 83 E5
Mossy →, Canada 101 C8
Most, Czech. 20 E3
Mosta, Malta 37 D1
Moşţafāābād, Iran 65 C7
Mostaganem, Algeria 75 A5
Mostar, Bos.-H. 21 M7
Mostardas, Brazil 127 C5
Mostefa, Rass, Tunisia 75 A7
Mostiska = Mostyska, Ukraine 41 H2
Móstoles, Spain 30 E7
Mosty = Masty, Belarus 40 F3
Mostyska, Ukraine 41 H2
Mosul = Al Mawşil, Iraq 67 D10
Mosulpo, S. Korea 51 H14
Mota del Cuervo, Spain 28 F2
Mota del Marqués, Spain 30 D5
Motagua →, Guatemala 116 C2
Motala, Sweden 11 F9
Motherwell, U.K. 14 F5
Motihari, India 63 F11
Motilla del Palancar, Spain 28 F3
Motnik, Slovenia 33 B11
Motocurunya, Venezuela 121 C5
Motovun, Croatia 33 C10
Motozintla de Mendoza, Mexico 115 D6
Motril, Spain 29 J1
Motru →, Romania 38 E6
Mott, U.S.A. 108 B3
Móttola, Italy 35 B10
Motueka, N.Z. 87 J4
Motueka →, N.Z. 87 J4
Motul, Mexico 115 C7
Mouanda, Gabon 80 E2
Mouchalagane →, Canada 99 B6
Mouding, China 52 E3
Moudjeria, Mauritania 78 B2
Moudon, Switz. 22 C3
Mouila, Gabon 80 E2
Moulamein, Australia 91 F3
Moulianá, Greece 37 D7
Moulins, France 26 B7
Moulmein, Burma 61 L20
Moulouya, O. →, Morocco 75 A4
Moulton, U.S.A. 109 L6
Moultrie, U.S.A. 105 K4
Moultrie, L., U.S.A. 105 J5
Mound City, Mo., U.S.A. 108 E7
Mound City, S. Dak., U.S.A. 108 C4
Moúnda, Ákra, Greece 39 L3
Moundou, Chad 73 G8
Moundsville, U.S.A. 106 G4
Moung, Cambodia 58 F4
Mount Airy, U.S.A. 105 G5
Mount Albert, Canada 106 B5
Mount Amherst, Australia 88 C4
Mount Angel, U.S.A. 110 D2
Mount Augustus, Australia 88 D2
Mount Barker, S. Austral., Australia 91 F2
Mount Barker, W. Austral., Australia 89 F2
Mount Carmel, U.S.A. 104 F2
Mount Clemens, U.S.A. 98 D3
Mount Coolon, Australia 90 C4
Mount Darwin, Zimbabwe 83 F3
Mount Desert I., U.S.A. 99 D6

Mount Dora, *U.S.A.* 105 L5
Mount Douglas, *Australia* . 90 C4
Mount Eba, *Australia* 91 E2
Mount Edgecumbe, *U.S.A.* 100 B1
Mount Elizabeth, *Australia* 88 C4
Mount Fletcher, *S. Africa* . 85 E4
Mount Forest, *Canada* 98 D3
Mount Gambier, *Australia* . 91 F3
Mount Garnet, *Australia* .. 90 B4
Mount Hope, *N.S.W.,*
   Australia 91 E4
Mount Hope, *S. Austral.,*
   Australia 91 E2
Mount Hope, *U.S.A.* 104 G5
Mount Horeb, *U.S.A.* 108 D10
Mount Howitt, *Australia* .. 91 D3
Mount Isa, *Australia* 90 C2
Mount Keith, *Australia* ... 89 E3
Mount Laguna, *U.S.A.* ... 113 N10
Mount Larcom, *Australia* .. 90 C5
Mount Lofty Ra., *Australia* 91 E2
Mount McKinley National
   Park, *U.S.A.* 96 B5
Mount Magnet, *Australia* . 89 E2
Mount Margaret, *Australia* 91 D3
Mount Maunganui, *N.Z.* .. 87 G6
Mount Molloy, *Australia* .. 90 B4
Mount Monger, *Australia* . 89 F3
Mount Morgan, *Australia* . 90 C5
Mount Morris, *Australia* .. 106 D7
Mount Mulligan, *Australia* 90 B3
Mount Narryer, *Australia* . 89 E2
Mount Olympus = Uludağ,
   Turkey 66 B3
Mount Oxide Mine,
   Australia 90 B2
Mount Pearl, *Canada* 99 C9
Mount Perry, *Australia* ... 91 D5
Mount Phillips, *Australia* . 88 D2
Mount Pleasant, *Iowa,*
   U.S.A. 108 E9
Mount Pleasant, *Mich.,*
   U.S.A. 104 D3
Mount Pleasant, *Pa.,*
   U.S.A. 106 F5
Mount Pleasant, *S.C.,*
   U.S.A. 105 J6
Mount Pleasant, *Tenn.,*
   U.S.A. 105 H2
Mount Pleasant, *Tex.,*
   U.S.A. 109 J7
Mount Pleasant, *Utah,*
   U.S.A. 110 G8
Mount Pocono, *U.S.A.* ... 107 E9
Mount Rainier National
   Park, *U.S.A.* 112 D5
Mount Revelstoke Nat.
   Park, *Canada* 100 C5
Mount Robson Prov. Park,
   Canada 100 C5
Mount Sandiman, *Australia* 89 D2
Mount Shasta, *U.S.A.* 110 F2
Mount Signal, *U.S.A.* 113 N11
Mount Sterling, *Ill., U.S.A.* 108 F9
Mount Sterling, *Ky.,*
   U.S.A. 104 F4
Mount Surprise, *Australia* . 90 B3
Mount Union, *U.S.A.* 106 F7
Mount Vernon, *Australia* . 88 D2
Mount Vernon, *Ind.,*
   U.S.A. 108 F10
Mount Vernon, *N.Y.,*
   U.S.A. 107 F11
Mount Vernon, *Ohio,*
   U.S.A. 106 F2
Mount Vernon, *Wash.,*
   U.S.A. 112 B4
Mountain Center, *U.S.A.* . 113 M10
Mountain City, *Nev.,*
   U.S.A. 110 F6
Mountain City, *Tenn.,*
   U.S.A. 105 G5
Mountain Grove, *U.S.A.* . 109 G8
Mountain Home, *Ark.,*
   U.S.A. 109 G8
Mountain Home, *Idaho,*
   U.S.A. 110 E6
Mountain Iron, *U.S.A.* ... 108 B8
Mountain Park, *Canada* .. 100 C5
Mountain Pass, *U.S.A.* ... 113 K11
Mountain View, *Ark.,*
   U.S.A. 109 H8
Mountain View, *Calif.,*
   U.S.A. 111 H2
Mountainair, *U.S.A.* 111 J10
Mountmellick, *Ireland* ... 15 C4
Moura, *Australia* 90 C4
Moura, *Brazil* 121 D5
Moura, *Portugal* 31 G3
Mourão, *Portugal* 31 G3
Mourdi, Dépression du,
   Chad 73 E9
Mourdiah, *Mali* 78 C3
Mourenx-Ville-Nouvelle,
   France 26 E3
Mouri, *Ghana* 79 D4
Mourilyan, *Australia* 90 B4
Mourmelon-le-Grand,
   France 25 C11
Mourne →, *U.K.* 15 B4
Mourne Mts., *U.K.* 15 B5
Mournies, *Greece* 37 D6
Mouscron, *Belgium* 17 G2
Moussoro, *Chad* 73 F8
Mouthe, *France* 25 F13
Moutier, *Switz.* 22 B4
Moûtiers, *France* 27 C10

Moutohara, *N.Z.* 87 H6
Moutong, *Indonesia* 57 D6
Mouy, *France* 25 C9
Mouzáki, *Greece* 39 K4
Movas, *Mexico* 114 B3
Moville, *Ireland* 15 A4
Moxhe, *Belgium* 17 G6
Moxotó →, *Brazil* 122 C4
Moy →, *Ireland* 15 B3
Moyale, *Kenya* 68 G2
Moyamba, *S. Leone* 78 D2
Moyen Atlas, *Morocco* .. 74 B3
Moyle □, *U.K.* 15 A5
Moyo, *Indonesia* 56 F5
Moyobamba, *Peru* 124 B2
Moyyero →, *Russia* 45 C11
Mozambique =
   Moçambique, *Mozam.* . 83 F5
Mozambique ■, *Africa* .. 83 F4
Mozambique Chan., *Africa* 83 B7
Mozdok, *Russia* 43 J7
Mozdūrān, *Iran* 65 B9
Mozhaysk, *Russia* 42 C3
Mozhga, *Russia* 42 B11
Mozhnābād, *Iran* 65 C9
Mozirje, *Slovenia* 33 B11
Mozyr = Mazyr, *Belarus* 41 F5
Mpanda, *Tanzania* 82 D3
Mpanda □, *Tanzania* ... 82 D3
Mpésoba, *Mali* 78 C3
Mpika, *Zambia* 83 E3
Mpulungu, *Zambia* 83 D3
Mpumalanga, *S. Africa* . 85 D5
Mpwapwa, *Tanzania* 82 D4
Mpwapwa □, *Tanzania* . 82 D4
Mqinvartsveri = Kazbek,
   Russia 43 J7
Mrągowo, *Poland* 20 B11
Mramor, *Serbia, Yug.* .. 21 M11
Mrimina, *Morocco* 74 C3
Mrkonjić Grad, *Bos.-H.* . 21 L7
Mrkopalj, *Croatia* 33 C11
Msab, Oued en →, *Algeria* 75 B6
Msaken, *Tunisia* 75 A7
Msambansovu, *Zimbabwe* 83 F3
M'sila, *Algeria* 75 A5
Msoro, *Zambia* 83 E3
Msta →, *Russia* 40 C6
Mstislavl = Mstsislaw,
   Belarus 40 E6
Mstsislaw, *Belarus* 40 E6
Mtama, *Tanzania* 83 E4
Mtilikwe →, *Zimbabwe* . 83 G3
Mtsensk, *Russia* 42 D3
Mtskheta, *Georgia* 43 K7
Mtubatuba, *S. Africa* ... 85 D5
Mtwara-Mikindani,
   Tanzania 83 E5
Mu Gia, Deo, *Vietnam* .. 58 D5
Mu Us Shamo, *China* ... 50 E5
Muaná, *Brazil* 122 B2
Muang Chiang Rai,
   Thailand 58 C2
Muang Lamphun, *Thailand* 58 C2
Muang Pak Beng, *Laos* .. 58 C3
Muar, *Malaysia* 59 L4
Muarabungo, *Indonesia* . 56 E2
Muaraenim, *Indonesia* .. 56 E2
Muarajuloi, *Indonesia* ... 56 E4
Muarakaman, *Indonesia* . 56 E5
Muaratebo, *Indonesia* ... 56 E2
Muaratembesi, *Indonesia* 56 E2
Muaratewe, *Indonesia* ... 56 E4
Mubarakpur, *India* 63 F10
Mubarraz = Al Mubarraz,
   Si. Arabia 65 E6
Mubende, *Uganda* 82 B3
Mubi, *Nigeria* 79 C7
Mubur, P., *Indonesia* ... 59 L6
Mucajaí →, *Brazil* 121 C5
Mucajaí, Serra do, *Brazil* 121 C5
Muchachos, Roque de los,
   Canary Is. 36 F2
Mücheln, *Germany* 18 D7
Muchinga Mts., *Zambia* . 83 E3
Muchkapskiy, *Russia* ... 42 E6
Muck, *U.K.* 14 E2
Muckadilla, *Australia* ... 91 D4
Muco →, *Colombia* 120 C3
Muconda, *Angola* 80 G4
Mucuim →, *Brazil* 125 B5
Mucur, *Turkey* 66 C6
Mucura, *Brazil* 121 D5
Mucuri, *Brazil* 123 E4
Mucurici, *Brazil* 123 E3
Mucusso, *Angola* 84 B3
Muda, *Canary Is.* 36 F6
Mudan Jiang →, *China* . 51 A15
Mudanjiang, *China* 51 B15
Mudanya, *Turkey* 66 B3
Muddy Cr. →, *U.S.A.* .. 111 H8
Mudgee, *Australia* 91 E4
Mudjatik →, *Canada* 101 B7
Mudurnu, *Turkey* 66 B4
Muecate, *Mozam.* 83 E4
Muêda, *Mozam.* 83 E4
Mueller Ra., *Australia* .. 88 C4
Muende, *Mozam.* 83 E3
Muerto, Mar, *Mexico* ... 115 D6
Muertos, Punta de los,
   Spain 29 J3
Mufindi □, *Tanzania* 83 D4
Mufu Shan, *China* 53 C10
Mufulira, *Zambia* 83 E2
Mufumbiro Range, *Africa* 82 C2
Mugardos, *Spain* 30 B2
Muge, *Portugal* 31 F2

Muge →, *Portugal* 31 F2
Múggia, *Italy* 33 C10
Mughayrā', *Si. Arabia* .. 64 D3
Mugi, *Japan* 49 H7
Mugia, *Spain* 30 B1
Mugila, Mts., *Zaïre* 82 D2
Mugu, *Nepal* 63 E10
Muhammad, Râs, *Egypt* . 76 B3
Muhammad Qol, *Sudan* . 76 C4
Muhammadabad, *India* .. 63 F10
Muhesi →, *Tanzania* 82 D4
Muheza □, *Tanzania* 82 C4
Mühldorf, *Germany* 19 G8
Mühlhausen, *Germany* .. 18 D6
Mühlig Hofmann fjella,
   Antarctica 5 D3
Muhos, *Finland* 8 D22
Muhu, *Estonia* 9 G20
Muhutwe, *Tanzania* 82 C3
Muiden, *Neths.* 16 D6
Muikamachi, *Japan* 49 F9
Muine Bheag, *Ireland* ... 15 D5
Muiños, *Spain* 30 D3
Muir, L., *Australia* 89 F2
Mukacheve, *Ukraine* 41 H2
Mukachevo = Mukacheve,
   Ukraine 41 H2
Mukah, *Malaysia* 56 D4
Mukawwa, Geziret, *Egypt* 76 C4
Mukdahan, *Thailand* 58 D5
Mukden = Shenyang,
   China 51 D12
Mukhtolovo, *Russia* 42 C6
Mukhtuya = Lensk, *Russia* 45 C12
Mukinbudin, *Australia* .. 89 F2
Mukishi, *Zaïre* 83 D1
Mukomuko, *Indonesia* .. 56 E2
Mukomwenze, *Zaïre* 82 D2
Muktsar, *India* 62 D6
Mukur, *Afghan.* 62 C2
Mukutawa →, *Canada* .. 101 C9
Mukwela, *Zambia* 83 F2
Mula, *Spain* 29 G3
Mulange, *Zaïre* 82 C2
Mulchén, *Chile* 126 D1
Mulde →, *Germany* 18 D8
Mule Creek, *U.S.A.* 108 D2
Muleba, *Tanzania* 82 C3
Muleba □, *Tanzania* 82 C3
Mulegns, *Switz.* 23 C9
Muleshoe, *U.S.A.* 109 H3
Mulgathing, *Australia* ... 91 E1
Mulgrave, *Canada* 99 C7
Mulhacén, *Spain* 29 H1
Mülheim, *Germany* 18 D2
Mulhouse, *France* 25 E14
Muli, *China* 52 D3
Muling, *China* 51 B16
Mull, *U.K.* 14 E3
Mullaittvu, *Sri Lanka* ... 60 Q12
Mullen, *U.S.A.* 108 D4
Mullengudgery, *Australia* 91 E4
Mullens, *U.S.A.* 104 G5
Muller, Pegunungan,
   Indonesia 56 D4
Mullet Pen., *Ireland* 15 B1
Mullewa, *Australia* 89 E2
Müllheim, *Germany* 19 H3
Mulligan →, *Australia* .. 90 C2
Mullin, *U.S.A.* 109 K5
Mullingar, *Ireland* 15 C4
Mullins, *U.S.A.* 105 H6
Mullumbimby, *Australia* . 91 D5
Mulobezi, *Zambia* 83 F2
Multan, *Pakistan* 62 D4
Multrå, *Sweden* 10 A11
Mulumbe, Mts., *Zaïre* .. 83 D2
Mulungushi Dam, *Zambia* 83 E2
Mulvane, *U.S.A.* 109 G6
Mulwad, *Sudan* 76 D3
Mulwala, *Australia* 91 F4
Mumbaī = Bombay, *India* 60 K8
Mumbwa, *Zambia* 83 E2
Mumra, *Russia* 43 H8
Mun →, *Thailand* 58 E5
Muna, *Indonesia* 57 F6
Munamagi, *Estonia* 9 H22
Münchberg, *Germany* ... 19 E7
Müncheberg, *Germany* .. 18 C10
München, *Germany* 19 G7
Munchen-Gladbach =
   Mönchengladbach,
   Germany 18 D2
Muncho Lake, *Canada* .. 100 B3
Munchŏn, *N. Korea* 51 E14
Münchwilen, *Switz.* 23 B7
Muncie, *U.S.A.* 104 E3
Muncoonie, L., *Australia* . 90 D2
Mundala, *Indonesia* 57 E10
Mundare, *Canada* 100 C6
Munday, *U.S.A.* 109 J5
Münden, *Germany* 18 D5
Mundiwindi, *Australia* .. 88 D3
Mundo →, *Spain* 29 G2
Mundo Novo, *Brazil* 123 D3
Mundra, *India* 62 H3
Mundrabilla, *Australia* .. 89 F4
Munducurus, *Brazil* 121 D6
Munera, *Spain* 29 F2
Mungallala, *Australia* ... 91 D4
Mungallala Cr. →,
   Australia 91 D4
Mungana, *Australia* 90 B3
Mungaoli, *India* 62 G8
Mungari, *Mozam.* 83 F3

Mungbere, *Zaïre* 82 B2
Munger, *India* 63 G12
Mungindi, *Australia* 91 D4
Munhango, *Angola* 81 G3
Munich = München,
   Germany 19 G7
Munising, *U.S.A.* 104 B2
Munka-Ljungby, *Sweden* 11 H6
Munkedal, *Sweden* 11 F5
Munku-Sardyk, *Russia* .. 45 D11
Münnerstadt, *Germany* . 19 E6
Muñoz Gamero, Pen.,
   Chile 128 D2
Munroe L., *Canada* 101 B9
Munsan, *S. Korea* 51 F14
Münsingen, *Switz.* 22 C5
Munster, *France* 25 D14
Munster, *Niedersachsen,*
   Germany 18 C6
Münster,
   Nordrhein-Westfalen,
   Germany 18 D3
Münster, *Switz.* 23 D6
Munster □, *Ireland* 15 D3
Muntadgin, *Australia* ... 89 F2
Muntele Mare, *Romania* . 38 C6
Muntok, *Indonesia* 56 E3
Munyama, *Zambia* 83 F2
Muong Beng, *Laos* 58 B3
Muong Boum, *Vietnam* . 58 A4
Muong Et, *Laos* 58 B5
Muong Hai, *Laos* 58 B3
Muong Hiem, *Laos* 58 B4
Muong Houn, *Laos* 58 B3
Muong Hung, *Vietnam* . 58 B4
Muong Kau, *Laos* 58 E5
Muong Khao, *Laos* 58 C4
Muong Khoua, *Laos* 58 B4
Muong Liep, *Laos* 58 C3
Muong May, *Laos* 58 E6
Muong Ngeun, *Laos* 58 B3
Muong Ngoi, *Laos* 58 B4
Muong Nhie, *Vietnam* .. 58 A4
Muong Nong, *Laos* 58 D6
Muong Ou Tay, *Laos* ... 58 A3
Muong Oua, *Laos* 58 C3
Muong Peun, *Laos* 58 B4
Muong Phalane, *Laos* ... 58 D5
Muong Phieng, *Laos* 58 C3
Muong Phine, *Laos* 58 D6
Muong Sai, *Laos* 58 B3
Muong Saiapoun, *Laos* . 58 C3
Muong Sen, *Vietnam* ... 58 C5
Muong Sing, *Laos* 58 B3
Muong Son, *Laos* 58 B4
Muong Soui, *Laos* 58 C4
Muong Va, *Laos* 58 B4
Muong Xia, *Vietnam* ... 58 B5
Muonio, *Finland* 8 C20
Muonionjoki →, *Finland* 8 C20
Muotathal, *Switz.* 23 C7
Mupa, *Angola* 81 H3
Muping, *China* 51 F11
Muqaddam, Wadi →,
   Sudan 76 D3
Muqdisho, *Somali Rep.* . 68 G4
Mur-de-Bretagne, *France* 24 D4
Mura →, *Slovenia* 33 B13
Muradiye, *Turkey* 67 C10
Murakami, *Japan* 48 E9
Murallón, Cuerro, *Chile* . 128 C2
Muralto, *Switz.* 23 D7
Muranda, *Rwanda* 82 C2
Murang'a, *Kenya* 82 C4
Murashi, *Russia* 44 D5
Murat, *France* 26 C6
Murat →, *Turkey* 67 C9
Muratlı, *Turkey* 66 B2
Muravera, *Italy* 34 C2
Murayama, *Japan* 48 E10
Murban, *U.A.E.* 65 F7
Murça, *Portugal* 30 D3
Murchison →, *Australia* . 89 E1
Murchison, Mt., *Antarctica* 5 D11
Murchison Falls =
   Kabarega Falls, *Uganda* 82 B3
Murchison House, *Australia* 89 E1
Murchison Ra., *Australia* . 90 C1
Murchison Rapids, *Malawi* 83 F3
Murcia, *Spain* 29 G3
Murcia □, *Spain* 29 H3
Murdo, *U.S.A.* 108 D4
Murdoch Pt., *Australia* .. 90 A3
Mureş →, *Romania* 38 C3
Mureşul = Mureş →,
   Romania 38 C3
Muret, *France* 26 E5
Murfatlar, *Romania* 38 E11
Murfreesboro, *U.S.A.* ... 105 H2
Murg, *Switz.* 23 B8
Murg →, *Germany* 19 G4
Murgab = Murghob,
   Tajikistan 44 F8
Murgenthal, *Switz.* 22 B5
Murghob, *Tajikistan* 44 F8
Murgon, *Australia* 91 D5
Murgoo, *Australia* 89 E2
Muri, *Switz.* 23 B6
Muria, *Indonesia* 57 G14
Muriaé, *Brazil* 123 F3
Murias de Paredes, *Spain* . 30 C4
Murici, *Brazil* 122 C4
Muriel Mine, *Zimbabwe* . 83 F3
Müritz-see, *Germany* 18 B8

Murmerwoude, *Neths.* ... 16 B8
Murnau, *Germany* 19 H7
Muro, *France* 27 F12
Muro, *Spain* 36 B10
Muro, C. de, *France* 27 G12
Muro Lucano, *Italy* 35 B8
Murom, *Russia* 42 C6
Muroran, *Japan* 48 C10
Muros, *Spain* 30 C1
Muros y de Noya, Ría de,
   Spain 30 C2
Muroto, *Japan* 49 H7
Muroto-Misaki, *Japan* ... 49 H7
Murphy, *U.S.A.* 110 E5
Murphys, *U.S.A.* 112 G6
Murphysboro, *U.S.A.* ... 109 G10
Murrat, *Sudan* 76 D2
Murray, *Ky., U.S.A.* 105 G1
Murray, *Utah, U.S.A.* ... 110 F8
Murray →, *Australia* 91 F2
Murray →, *Canada* 100 B4
Murray, L., *U.S.A.* 105 H5
Murray Bridge, *Australia* 91 F2
Murray Downs, *Australia* 90 C1
Murray Harbour, *Canada* 99 C7
Murraysburg, *S. Africa* .. 84 E3
Murree, *Pakistan* 62 C5
Murrieta, *U.S.A.* 113 M9
Murrin Murrin, *Australia* . 89 E3
Murrumbidgee →,
   Australia 91 E3
Murrumburrah, *Australia* 91 E4
Murrurundi, *Australia* ... 91 E5
Murshid, *Sudan* 76 C3
Murshidabad, *India* 63 G13
Murska Sobota, *Slovenia* 33 B13
Murten, *Switz.* 22 C4
Murtensee, *Switz.* 22 C4
Murtle L., *Canada* 100 C5
Murtoa, *Australia* 91 F3
Murtosa, *Portugal* 30 E2
Muru →, *Brazil* 124 B3
Murungu, *Tanzania* 82 C3
Murwara, *India* 63 H9
Murwillumbah, *Australia* 91 D5
Mürz →, *Austria* 21 H5
Mürzzuschlag, *Austria* .. 21 H5
Muş, *Turkey* 67 C9
Mûsa, G., *Egypt* 76 J8
Musa Khel, *Pakistan* 62 C4
Mūsa Qal'eh, *Afghan.* ... 60 C4
Musaffargarh, *Pakistan* .. 60 D7
Musala, *Bulgaria* 38 G4
Musala, *Indonesia* 56 D1
Musan, *N. Korea* 51 C15
Musangu, *Zaïre* 83 E1
Musasa, *Tanzania* 82 C3
Musay'īd, *Qatar* 65 E6
Muscat = Masqat, *Oman* 68 C6
Muscat & Oman =
   Oman ■, *Asia* 68 C6
Muscatine, *U.S.A.* 108 E9
Musel, *Spain* 30 B4
Musgrave, *Australia* 90 A3
Musgrave Ras., *Australia* . 89 E5
Mushie, *Zaïre* 80 E3
Mushin, *Nigeria* 79 D5
Musi →, *Indonesia* 56 E2
Muskeg →, *Canada* 100 A4
Muskegon, *U.S.A.* 104 D2
Muskegon →, *U.S.A.* ... 104 D2
Muskegon Heights, *U.S.A.* 104 D2
Muskogee, *U.S.A.* 109 H7
Muskwa →, *Canada* 100 B4
Muslīmiyah, *Syria* 64 B3
Musmar, *Sudan* 76 D4
Musofu, *Zambia* 83 E2
Musoma, *Tanzania* 82 C3
Musoma □, *Tanzania* ... 82 C3
Musquaro, L., *Canada* ... 99 B7
Musquodoboit Harbour,
   Canada 99 D7
Musselburgh, *U.K.* 14 F5
Musselkanaal, *Neths.* ... 16 C10
Musselshell →, *U.S.A.* .. 110 C10
Mussidan, *France* 26 C4
Mussomeli, *Italy* 34 E6
Musson, *Belgium* 17 J7
Mussoorie, *India* 62 D8
Mussuco, *Angola* 84 B2
Mustafakemalpaşa, *Turkey* 66 B3
Mustang, *Nepal* 63 E10
Musters, L., *Argentina* .. 128 C3
Musudan, *N. Korea* 51 D15
Muswellbrook, *Australia* . 91 E5
Mût, *Egypt* 76 B2
Mut, *Turkey* 66 D5
Mutanda, *Mozam.* 85 C5
Mutanda, *Zambia* 83 E2
Mutare, *Zimbabwe* 83 F3
Muting, *Indonesia* 57 F10
Mutoray, *Russia* 45 C11
Mutshatsha, *Zaïre* 83 E1
Mutsu, *Japan* 48 D10
Mutsu-Wan, *Japan* 48 D10
Muttaburra, *Australia* ... 90 C3
Muttama Cr. →,
   Australia 91 E4
Mutoray, *Russia* 45 C11
Mutshatsha, *Zaïre* 83 E1
Muweilih, *Egypt* 69 E3
Muxima, *Angola* 80 F2
Muy Muy, *Nic.* 116 D2
Muyinga, *Burundi* 82 C3
Muynak, *Uzbekistan* 44 E6
Muzaffarabad, *Pakistan* . 63 B5
Muzaffargarh, *Pakistan* . 62 D4
Muzaffarnagar, *India* ... 62 E7
Muzaffarpur, *India* 63 F11

Muzhi, *Russia* ... 44 C7
Muzillac, *France* ... 24 E4
Muzon, C., *U.S.A.* ... 100 C2
Muztag, *China* ... 54 C3
Mvôlô, *Sudan* ... 77 F2
Mvuma, *Zimbabwe* ... 83 F3
Mvurwi, *Zimbabwe* ... 83 F3
Mwadui, *Tanzania* ... 82 C3
Mwambo, *Tanzania* ... 83 E5
Mwandi, *Zambia* ... 83 F1
Mwanza, *Tanzania* ... 82 C3
Mwanza, *Zaïre* ... 82 D2
Mwanza, *Zambia* ... 83 F1
Mwanza □, *Tanzania* ... 82 C3
Mwaya, *Tanzania* ... 83 D3
Mweelrea, *Ireland* ... 15 C2
Mweka, *Zaïre* ... 80 E4
Mwenezi, *Zimbabwe* ... 83 G3
Mwenezi →, *Mozam.* ... 83 G3
Mwenga, *Zaïre* ... 82 C2
Mweru, L., *Zambia* ... 83 D2
Mweza Range, *Zimbabwe* ... 83 G3
Mwilambwe, *Zaïre* ... 82 D5
Mwimbi, *Tanzania* ... 83 D3
Mwinilunga, *Zambia* ... 83 E1
My Tho, *Vietnam* ... 59 G6
Mya, O. →, *Algeria* ... 75 B5
Myajlar, *India* ... 62 F4
Myanaung, *Burma* ... 61 K19
Myanmar = Burma ■, *Asia* ... 61 J20
Myaungmya, *Burma* ... 61 L19
Myeik Kyunzu, *Burma* ... 59 G1
Myerstown, *U.S.A.* ... 107 F8
Myingyan, *Burma* ... 61 J19
Myitkyina, *Burma* ... 61 G20
Myjava, *Slovak Rep.* ... 20 G7
Mykhaylivka, *Ukraine* ... 41 J8
Mykines, *Færoe Is.* ... 8 E9
Mykolayiv, *Ukraine* ... 41 J7
Mymensingh, *Bangla.* ... 61 G17
Mynydd Du, *U.K.* ... 13 F4
Mýrdalsjökull, *Iceland* ... 8 E4
Myrhorod, *Ukraine* ... 41 H7
Myroodah, *Australia* ... 88 C3
Myrtle Beach, *U.S.A.* ... 105 J6
Myrtle Creek, *U.S.A.* ... 110 E2
Myrtle Point, *U.S.A.* ... 110 E1
Myrtou, *Cyprus* ... 37 D12
Mysen, *Norway* ... 10 E5
Mysia, *Turkey* ... 66 C2
Myslenice, *Poland* ... 20 F9
Myślibórz, *Poland* ... 20 C4
Mysłowice, *Poland* ... 20 E9
Mysore = Karnataka □, *India* ... 60 N10
Mysore, *India* ... 60 N10
Mystic, *U.S.A.* ... 107 E13
Myszków, *Poland* ... 20 E9
Mythen, *Switz.* ... 23 B7
Mytishchi, *Russia* ... 42 C3
Myton, *U.S.A.* ... 110 F8
Mývatn, *Iceland* ... 8 D5
Mzimba, *Malawi* ... 83 E3
Mzimkulu →, *S. Africa* ... 85 E5
Mzimvubu →, *S. Africa* ... 85 E4
Mzuzu, *Malawi* ... 83 E3

N

N' Dioum, *Senegal* ... 78 B2
Na Hearadh = Harris, *U.K.* ... 14 D2
Na Noi, *Thailand* ... 58 C3
Na Phao, *Laos* ... 58 D5
Na Sam, *Vietnam* ... 58 A6
Na San, *Vietnam* ... 58 B5
Naab →, *Germany* ... 19 F8
Naaldwijk, *Neths.* ... 16 E4
Na'am, *Sudan* ... 77 F2
Naantali, *Finland* ... 9 F19
Naarden, *Neths.* ... 16 D6
Naas, *Ireland* ... 15 C5
Nababiep, *S. Africa* ... 84 D2
Nabadwip = Navadwip, *India* ... 63 H13
Nabari, *Japan* ... 49 G8
Nabawa, *Australia* ... 89 E1
Nabberu, L., *Australia* ... 89 E3
Nabburg, *Germany* ... 19 F8
Naberezhnye Chelny, *Russia* ... 42 C11
Nabeul, *Tunisia* ... 75 A7
Nabha, *India* ... 62 D7
Nabīd, *Iran* ... 65 D8
Nabire, *Indonesia* ... 57 E9
Nabisar, *Pakistan* ... 62 G3
Nabisipi →, *Canada* ... 99 B7
Nabiswera, *Uganda* ... 82 B3
Nablus = Nābulus, *West Bank* ... 69 C4
Naboomspruit, *S. Africa* ... 85 C4
Nabua, *Phil.* ... 55 E5
Nābulus, *West Bank* ... 69 C4
Nacala, *Mozam.* ... 83 E5
Nacala-Velha, *Mozam.* ... 83 E5
Nacaome, *Honduras* ... 116 D2
Nacaroa, *Mozam.* ... 83 E4
Naches, *U.S.A.* ... 110 C3
Naches →, *U.S.A.* ... 112 D6
Nachingwea, *Tanzania* ... 83 E4
Nachingwea □, *Tanzania* ... 83 E4
Nachna, *India* ... 62 F4
Náchod, *Czech.* ... 20 E6

Nacimiento Reservoir, *U.S.A.* ... 112 K6
Nacka, *Sweden* ... 10 E12
Nackara, *Australia* ... 91 E2
Naco, *Mexico* ... 114 A3
Naco, *U.S.A.* ... 111 L9
Nacogdoches, *U.S.A.* ... 109 K7
Nácori Chico, *Mexico* ... 114 B3
Nacozari, *Mexico* ... 114 A3
Nadi, *Sudan* ... 76 D3
Nadiad, *India* ... 62 H5
Nădlac, *Romania* ... 38 C3
Nador, *Morocco* ... 75 A4
Nadur, *Malta* ... 37 C1
Nadūshan, *Iran* ... 65 C7
Nadvirna, *Ukraine* ... 41 H3
Nadvornaya = Nadvirna, *Ukraine* ... 41 H3
Nadym, *Russia* ... 44 C8
Nadym →, *Russia* ... 44 C8
Nærbø, *Norway* ... 9 G11
Næstved, *Denmark* ... 11 J5
Nafada, *Nigeria* ... 79 C7
Näfels, *Switz.* ... 23 B8
Naftshahr, *Iran* ... 67 E11
Nafud Desert = An Nafūd, *Si. Arabia* ... 64 D4
Nafūsah, Jabal, *Libya* ... 75 B7
Nag Hammâdi, *Egypt* ... 76 B3
Naga, *Phil.* ... 55 E5
Naga, Kreb en, *Africa* ... 74 D3
Nagagami →, *Canada* ... 98 C3
Nagahama, *Japan* ... 49 G8
Nagai, *Japan* ... 48 E10
Nagaland □, *India* ... 61 F19
Nagano, *Japan* ... 49 F9
Nagano □, *Japan* ... 49 F9
Nagaoka, *Japan* ... 49 F9
Nagappattinam, *India* ... 60 P11
Nagar Parkar, *Pakistan* ... 62 G4
Nagasaki, *Japan* ... 49 H4
Nagasaki □, *Japan* ... 49 H4
Nagato, *Japan* ... 49 G5
Nagaur, *India* ... 62 F5
Nagercoil, *India* ... 60 Q10
Nagina, *India* ... 63 E8
Nagineh, *Iran* ... 65 C8
Nagir, *Pakistan* ... 63 A6
Nagold, *Germany* ... 19 G4
Nagold →, *Germany* ... 19 G4
Nagoorin, *Australia* ... 90 C5
Nagorno-Karabakh, *Azerbaijan* ... 67 C12
Nagornyy, *Russia* ... 45 D13
Nagoya, *Japan* ... 49 G8
Nagpur, *India* ... 60 J11
Nagua, *Dom. Rep.* ... 117 C6
Nagykanizsa, *Hungary* ... 21 J7
Nagykőrös, *Hungary* ... 21 H9
Nagyléta, *Hungary* ... 21 H11
Naha, *Japan* ... 49 L3
Nahanni Butte, *Canada* ... 100 A4
Nahanni Nat. Park, *Canada* ... 100 A3
Nahariyya, *Israel* ... 66 F6
Nahāvand, *Iran* ... 67 E13
Nahe →, *Germany* ... 19 F3
Nahīya, W. →, *Egypt* ... 76 J7
Nahlin, *Canada* ... 100 B2
Nahuel Huapi, L., *Argentina* ... 128 B2
Naicá, *Mexico* ... 114 B3
Naicam, *Canada* ... 101 C8
Nā'ifah, *Si. Arabia* ... 68 D5
Naila, *Germany* ... 19 E7
Nā'īn, *Iran* ... 65 C7
Naini Tal, *India* ... 63 E8
Nainpur, *India* ... 60 H12
Naintré, *France* ... 24 F7
Naipu, *Romania* ... 38 E8
Naira, *Indonesia* ... 57 E7
Nairn, *U.K.* ... 14 D5
Nairobi, *Kenya* ... 82 C4
Naissaar, *Estonia* ... 9 G21
Naivasha, *Kenya* ... 82 C4
Naivasha, L., *Kenya* ... 82 C4
Najac, *France* ... 26 D5
Najafābād, *Iran* ... 65 C6
Nájera, *Spain* ... 28 C2
Najerilla →, *Spain* ... 28 C2
Najibabad, *India* ... 62 E8
Najin, *N. Korea* ... 51 C16
Najmah, *Si. Arabia* ... 65 E6
Naju, *S. Korea* ... 51 G14
Nakadōri-Shima, *Japan* ... 49 H4
Nakalagba, *Zaïre* ... 82 B2
Nakaminato, *Japan* ... 49 F10
Nakamura, *Japan* ... 49 H6
Nakano, *Japan* ... 49 F9
Nakano-Shima, *Japan* ... 49 K4
Nakashibetsu, *Japan* ... 48 C12
Nakfa, *Eritrea* ... 77 D4
Nakhichevan = Naxçivan, *Azerbaijan* ... 67 C11
Nakhichevan Republic = Naxçivan □, *Azerbaijan* ... 67 C11
Nakhl, *Egypt* ... 69 F2
Nakhl-e Taqī, *Iran* ... 65 E7
Nakhodka, *Russia* ... 45 E14
Nakhon Nayok, *Thailand* ... 58 E3
Nakhon Pathom, *Thailand* ... 58 F3
Nakhon Phanom, *Thailand* ... 58 D5
Nakhon Ratchasima, *Thailand* ... 58 E4
Nakhon Sawan, *Thailand* ... 58 E3
Nakhon Si Thammarat, *Thailand* ... 59 H3

Nakhon Thai, *Thailand* ... 58 D3
Nakina, B.C., *Canada* ... 100 B2
Nakina, Ont., *Canada* ... 98 B2
Nakło nad Notecią, *Poland* ... 20 B7
Nakodar, *India* ... 62 D6
Nakskov, *Denmark* ... 11 K5
Naktong →, *S. Korea* ... 51 G15
Nakuru, *Kenya* ... 82 C4
Nakuru □, *Kenya* ... 82 C4
Nakuru, L., *Kenya* ... 82 C4
Nakusp, *Canada* ... 100 C5
Nal →, *Pakistan* ... 62 G1
Nalchik, *Russia* ... 43 J6
Nälden, *Sweden* ... 10 A8
Näldsjön, *Sweden* ... 10 A8
Nalerigu, *Ghana* ... 79 C4
Nalgonda, *India* ... 60 L11
Nalhati, *India* ... 63 G12
Nallamalai Hills, *India* ... 60 M11
Nallhan, *Turkey* ... 66 B4
Nalón →, *Spain* ... 30 B4
Nālūt, *Libya* ... 75 B7
Nam Can, *Vietnam* ... 59 H5
Nam Dinh, *Vietnam* ... 58 B6
Nam Du, Hon, *Vietnam* ... 59 H5
Nam Ngum Dam, *Laos* ... 58 C4
Nam-Phan, *Vietnam* ... 59 G6
Nam Phong, *Thailand* ... 58 D4
Nam Tha, *Laos* ... 58 B3
Nam Tok, *Thailand* ... 58 E2
Namacunde, *Angola* ... 84 B2
Namacurra, *Mozam.* ... 85 B6
Namak, Daryācheh-ye, *Iran* ... 65 C7
Namak, Kavir-e, *Iran* ... 65 C8
Namaland, *Namibia* ... 84 C2
Namangan, *Uzbekistan* ... 44 E8
Namapa, *Mozam.* ... 83 E4
Namaqualand, *S. Africa* ... 84 D2
Namasagali, *Uganda* ... 82 B3
Namber, *Indonesia* ... 57 E8
Nambour, *Australia* ... 91 D5
Nambucca Heads, *Australia* ... 91 E5
Namche Bazar, *Nepal* ... 63 F12
Namchonjŏm, *N. Korea* ... 51 E14
Namêche, *Belgium* ... 17 H6
Namecunda, *Mozam.* ... 83 E4
Nameh, *Indonesia* ... 56 D5
Nameponda, *Mozam.* ... 83 F4
Nametil, *Mozam.* ... 83 F4
Namew L., *Canada* ... 101 C8
Namib Desert = Namibwoestyn, *Namibia* ... 84 C2
Namibe, *Angola* ... 81 H2
Namibe □, *Angola* ... 84 B1
Namibia ■, *Africa* ... 84 C2
Namibwoestyn, *Namibia* ... 84 C2
Namīn, *Iran* ... 67 C13
Namlea, *Indonesia* ... 57 E7
Namoi →, *Australia* ... 91 E4
Namous, O. en →, *Algeria* ... 75 B4
Nampa, *U.S.A.* ... 110 E5
Nampō-Shotō, *Japan* ... 49 J10
Nampula, *Mozam.* ... 83 F4
Namrole, *Indonesia* ... 57 E7
Namse Shankou, *China* ... 61 E13
Namsen →, *Norway* ... 8 D14
Namsos, *Norway* ... 8 D14
Namtsy, *Russia* ... 45 C13
Namtu, *Burma* ... 61 H20
Namtumbo, *Tanzania* ... 83 E4
Namu, *Canada* ... 100 C3
Namur, *Belgium* ... 17 H5
Namur □, *Belgium* ... 17 H5
Namutoni, *Namibia* ... 84 B2
Namwala, *Zambia* ... 83 F2
Namwŏn, *S. Korea* ... 51 G14
Namysłów, *Poland* ... 20 D7
Nan, *Thailand* ... 58 C3
Nan →, *Thailand* ... 58 E3
Nan Xian, *China* ... 53 C9
Nanaimo, *Canada* ... 100 D4
Nanam, *N. Korea* ... 51 D15
Nanan, *China* ... 53 E12
Nanango, *Australia* ... 91 D5
Nanao, *Japan* ... 49 F8
Nanbu, *China* ... 52 B6
Nanchang, *China* ... 53 C10
Nancheng, *China* ... 53 D11
Nanchong, *China* ... 52 B6
Nanching = Nanjing, *China* ... 53 A12
Nanchuan, *China* ... 52 C6
Nancy, *France* ... 25 D13
Nanda Devi, *India* ... 63 D8
Nandan, *China* ... 52 E6
Nandan, *Japan* ... 49 G7
Nanded, *India* ... 60 K10
Nandewar Ra., *Australia* ... 91 E5
Nandi, *Fiji* ... 87 C7
Nandi □, *Kenya* ... 82 B4
Nandurbar, *India* ... 60 J9
Nandyal, *India* ... 60 M11
Nanfeng, Guangdong, *China* ... 53 F8
Nanfeng, Jiangxi, *China* ... 53 D11
Nanga, *Australia* ... 89 E1
Nanga-Eboko, *Cameroon* ... 79 E7
Nangade, *Mozam.* ... 83 E4
Nangapinoh, *Indonesia* ... 56 E4
Nangarhár □, *Afghan.* ... 60 B7
Nangatayap, *Indonesia* ... 56 E4
Nangeya Mts., *Uganda* ... 82 B3
Nangis, *France* ... 25 D10

Nangong, *China* ... 50 F8
Nanhua, *China* ... 52 E3
Nanhuang, *China* ... 51 F11
Nanhui, *China* ... 53 B13
Nanjeko, *Zambia* ... 83 F1
Nanji Shan, *China* ... 53 D13
Nanjian, *China* ... 52 E3
Nanjiang, *China* ... 52 A6
Nanjing, Fujian, *China* ... 53 E11
Nanjing, Jiangsu, *China* ... 53 A12
Nanjirinji, *Tanzania* ... 83 D4
Nankana Sahib, *Pakistan* ... 62 D5
Nankang, *China* ... 53 E10
Nanking = Nanjing, *China* ... 53 A12
Nankoku, *Japan* ... 49 H6
Nanling, *China* ... 53 B12
Nanning, *China* ... 52 F7
Nannup, *Australia* ... 89 F2
Nanpan Jiang →, *China* ... 52 E6
Nanpara, *India* ... 63 F9
Nanpi, *China* ... 50 E9
Nanping, Fujian, *China* ... 53 D12
Nanping, Henan, *China* ... 53 C9
Nanri Dao, *China* ... 53 E12
Nanripe, *Mozam.* ... 83 E4
Nansei-Shotō = Ryūkyū-rettō, *Japan* ... 49 M2
Nansen Sd., *Canada* ... 4 A3
Nansio, *Tanzania* ... 82 C3
Nant, *France* ... 26 D7
Nantes, *France* ... 24 E5
Nanteuil-le-Haudouin, *France* ... 25 C9
Nantiat, *France* ... 26 B5
Nanticoke, *U.S.A.* ... 107 E8
Nanton, *Canada* ... 100 C6
Nantong, *China* ... 53 A13
Nantua, *France* ... 27 B9
Nantucket I., *U.S.A.* ... 94 E12
Nanuque, *Brazil* ... 123 E3
Nanutarra, *Australia* ... 88 D2
Nanxiong, *China* ... 53 E10
Nanyang, *China* ... 50 H7
Nanyi Hu, *China* ... 53 B12
Nanyuan, *China* ... 50 E9
Nanyuki, *Kenya* ... 82 B4
Nanzhang, *China* ... 53 B8
Nao, C. de la, *Spain* ... 29 G5
Naococane L., *Canada* ... 99 B5
Naoetsu, *Japan* ... 49 F9
Náousa, *Greece* ... 39 J5
Naozhou Dao, *China* ... 53 G8
Napa, *U.S.A.* ... 112 G4
Napa →, *U.S.A.* ... 112 G4
Napanee, *Canada* ... 98 D4
Napanoch, *U.S.A.* ... 107 E10
Nape, *Laos* ... 58 C5
Nape Pass = Keo Neua, Deo, *Vietnam* ... 58 C5
Napf, *Switz.* ... 22 B5
Napier, *N.Z.* ... 87 H6
Napier Broome B., *Australia* ... 88 B4
Napier Downs, *Australia* ... 88 C3
Napier Pen., *Australia* ... 90 A2
Naples = Nápoli, *Italy* ... 35 B7
Naples, *U.S.A.* ... 105 M5
Napo, *China* ... 52 F5
Napo □, *Ecuador* ... 120 D2
Napo →, *Peru* ... 120 D3
Napoleon, N. Dak., *U.S.A.* ... 108 B5
Napoleon, Ohio, *U.S.A.* ... 104 E3
Nápoli, *Italy* ... 35 B7
Nápoli, G. di, *Italy* ... 35 B7
Napopo, *Zaïre* ... 82 B2
Nappa Merrie, *Australia* ... 91 D3
Naqâda, *Egypt* ... 76 B3
Naqadeh, *Iran* ... 67 D11
Naqqâsh, *Iran* ... 65 C6
Nara, *Japan* ... 49 G7
Nara, *Mali* ... 78 B3
Nara □, *Japan* ... 49 G8
Nara Canal, *Pakistan* ... 62 G3
Nara Visa, *U.S.A.* ... 109 H3
Naracoorte, *Australia* ... 91 F3
Naradhan, *Australia* ... 91 E4
Narasapur, *India* ... 61 L12
Narathiwat, *Thailand* ... 59 J3
Narayanganj, *Bangla.* ... 61 H17
Narayanpet, *India* ... 60 L10
Narbonne, *France* ... 26 E7
Narcea →, *Spain* ... 30 B4
Nardīn, *Iran* ... 65 B7
Nardò, *Italy* ... 35 B11
Narembeen, *Australia* ... 89 F2
Nares Str., *Arctic* ... 94 B13
Naretha, *Australia* ... 89 F3
Narew →, *Poland* ... 20 C10
Nari →, *Pakistan* ... 62 E2
Narin, *Afghan.* ... 60 A6
Narindra, Helodranon' i, *Madag.* ... 85 A8
Narino □, *Colombia* ... 120 C2
Narita, *Japan* ... 49 G10
Narmada →, *India* ... 62 J5
Narman, *Turkey* ... 67 B9
Narmland, *Sweden* ... 9 F15
Narnaul, *India* ... 62 E7
Narni, *Italy* ... 33 F9
Naro, *Ghana* ... 78 C4
Naro, *Italy* ... 34 E6
Naro Fominsk, *Russia* ... 42 C3
Narodnaya, *Russia* ... 6 D11
Narok, *Kenya* ... 82 C4
Narok □, *Kenya* ... 82 C4
Narón, *Spain* ... 30 B2
Narooma, *Australia* ... 91 F5

Narowal, *Pakistan* ... 62 C6
Narrabri, *Australia* ... 91 E4
Narran →, *Australia* ... 91 D4
Narrandera, *Australia* ... 91 E4
Narraway →, *Canada* ... 100 B5
Narrogin, *Australia* ... 89 F2
Narromine, *Australia* ... 91 E4
Narsimhapur, *India* ... 63 H8
Naruto, *Japan* ... 49 G7
Narva, *Estonia* ... 40 C5
Narva →, *Russia* ... 9 G22
Narvik, *Norway* ... 8 B17
Narvskoye Vdkhr., *Russia* ... 40 C5
Narwana, *India* ... 62 E7
Naryan-Mar, *Russia* ... 44 C6
Naryilco, *Australia* ... 91 D3
Narym, *Russia* ... 44 D9
Narymskoye, *Kazakhstan* ... 44 E9
Naryn, *Kyrgyzstan* ... 44 E8
Nasa, *Norway* ... 8 C16
Nasarawa, *Nigeria* ... 79 D6
Năsăud, *Romania* ... 38 B7
Naseby, *N.Z.* ... 87 L3
Naselle, *U.S.A.* ... 112 D3
Naser, Buheirat en, *Egypt* ... 76 C3
Nashua, Iowa, *U.S.A.* ... 108 D8
Nashua, Mont., *U.S.A.* ... 110 B10
Nashua, N.H., *U.S.A.* ... 107 D13
Nashville, Ark., *U.S.A.* ... 109 J8
Nashville, Ga., *U.S.A.* ... 105 K4
Nashville, Tenn., *U.S.A.* ... 105 G2
Našice, *Croatia* ... 21 K8
Nasielsk, *Poland* ... 20 C10
Nasik, *India* ... 60 K8
Nasipit, *Phil.* ... 55 G6
Nasirabad, *India* ... 62 F6
Naskaupi →, *Canada* ... 99 B7
Naso, *Italy* ... 35 D7
Naṣrīān-e Pā'īn, *Iran* ... 64 C5
Nass →, *Canada* ... 100 B3
Nassau, *Bahamas* ... 116 A4
Nassau, *U.S.A.* ... 107 D11
Nassau, B., *Chile* ... 128 E3
Nasser, L. = Naser, Buheirat en, *Egypt* ... 76 C3
Nasser City = Kôm Ombo, *Egypt* ... 76 C3
Nassian, *Ivory C.* ... 78 D4
Nässjö, *Sweden* ... 9 H16
Nasugbu, *Phil.* ... 55 D4
Näsviken, *Sweden* ... 10 C10
Nat Kyizin, *Burma* ... 61 M20
Nata, *Botswana* ... 84 C4
Natagaima, *Colombia* ... 120 C2
Natal, *Brazil* ... 122 C4
Natal, *Canada* ... 100 D6
Natal, *Indonesia* ... 56 D1
Natalinci, Serbia, *Yug.* ... 21 L10
Natanz, *Iran* ... 65 C6
Natashquan, *Canada* ... 99 B7
Natashquan →, *Canada* ... 99 B7
Natchez, *U.S.A.* ... 109 K9
Natchitoches, *U.S.A.* ... 109 K8
Naters, *Switz.* ... 22 D5
Nathalia, *Australia* ... 91 F4
Nathdwara, *India* ... 62 G5
Nati, Pta., *Spain* ... 36 A10
Natimuk, *Australia* ... 91 F3
Nation →, *Canada* ... 100 B4
National City, *U.S.A.* ... 113 N9
Natitingou, *Benin* ... 79 C5
Natividad, I., *Mexico* ... 114 B1
Natoma, *U.S.A.* ... 108 F5
Natron, L., *Tanzania* ... 82 C4
Natrona Heights, *U.S.A.* ... 106 F5
Natrûn, W. el →, *Egypt* ... 76 H7
Natuna Besar, Kepulauan, *Indonesia* ... 59 L7
Natuna Is. = Natuna Besar, Kepulauan, *Indonesia* ... 59 L7
Natuna Selatan, Kepulauan, *Indonesia* ... 59 L7
Natural Bridge, *U.S.A.* ... 107 B9
Naturaliste, C., *Australia* ... 90 G4
Nau Qala, *Afghan.* ... 62 B3
Naubinway, *U.S.A.* ... 98 C2
Naucelle, *France* ... 26 D6
Nauders, *Austria* ... 19 J6
Nauen, *Germany* ... 18 C8
Naugatuck, *U.S.A.* ... 107 E11
Naumburg, *Germany* ... 18 D7
Nā'ūr at Tunayb, *Jordan* ... 69 D4
Nauru ■, *Pac. Oc.* ... 92 H8
Naushahra = Nowshera, *Pakistan* ... 60 B8
Nauta, *Peru* ... 120 D3
Nautanwa, *India* ... 61 F13
Nautla, *Mexico* ... 115 C5
Nava, *Mexico* ... 114 B4
Nava del Rey, *Spain* ... 30 D5
Navacerrada, Puerto de, *Spain* ... 30 E7
Navadwip, *India* ... 63 H13
Navahermosa, *Spain* ... 31 F6
Navahrudak, *Belarus* ... 40 F3
Navajo Reservoir, *U.S.A.* ... 111 H10
Navalcarnero, *Spain* ... 30 E6
Navalmoral de la Mata, *Spain* ... 30 F5
Navalvillar de Pela, *Spain* ... 31 F5
Navan = An Uaimh, *Ireland* ... 15 C5
Navapolatsk, *Belarus* ... 40 E5
Navarino, I., *Chile* ... 128 E3
Navarra □, *Spain* ... 28 C3

Navarre, *U.S.A.* 106 F3
Navarrenx, *France* 26 E3
Navarro →, *U.S.A.* 112 F3
Navasota, *U.S.A.* 109 K6
Navassa, *W. Indies* 117 C4
Nave, *Italy* 32 C7
Naver →, *U.K.* 14 C4
Navia, *Spain* 30 B4
Navia →, *Spain* 30 B4
Navia de Suarna, *Spain* ... 30 C4
Navidad, *Chile* 126 C1
Navlya, *Russia* 42 D2
Navoi = Nawoiy,
  Uzbekistan 44 E7
Navojoa, *Mexico* 114 B3
Navolato, *Mexico* 114 C3
Návpaktos, *Greece* 39 L4
Návplion, *Greece* 39 M5
Navrongo, *Ghana* 79 C4
Navsari, *India* 60 J8
Nawa Kot, *Pakistan* 62 E4
Nawabganj, *Ut. P., India* . 63 F9
Nawabganj, *Ut. P., India* . 63 E8
Nawabshah, *Pakistan* 62 F3
Nawada, *India* 63 G11
Nawakot, *Nepal* 63 F11
Nawalgarh, *India* 62 F6
Nawanshahr, *India* 63 C6
Nawi, *Sudan* 76 D3
Nawoiy, *Uzbekistan* 44 E7
Naxçıvan, *Azerbaijan* ... 67 C11
Naxçıvan □, *Azerbaijan* .. 67 C11
Náxos, *Greece* 39 M8
Nay, *France* 26 E3
Nāy Band, *Iran* 65 E7
Naya →, *Colombia* 120 C2
Nayakhan, *Russia* 45 C16
Nayarit □, *Mexico* 114 C4
Nayé, *Senegal* 78 C2
Nayong, *China* 52 D5
Nayoro, *Japan* 48 B11
Nayyāl, W. →, *Si. Arabia* . 64 D3
Nazaré, *Bahia, Brazil* ... 123 D4
Nazaré, *Pará, Brazil* 125 B7
Nazaré, *Tocantins, Brazil* . 122 C2
Nazaré, *Portugal* 31 F1
Nazareth = Nazerat, *Israel* 69 C4
Nazas, *Mexico* 114 B4
Nazas →, *Mexico* 114 B4
Naze, The, *U.K.* 13 F9
Nazerat, *Israel* 69 C4
Nāzik, *Iran* 67 C11
Nazilli, *Turkey* 66 D3
Nazir Hat, *Bangla.* 61 H17
Nazko, *Canada* 100 C4
Nazko →, *Canada* 100 C4
Nazret, *Ethiopia* 77 F4
Nchanga, *Zambia* 83 E2
Ncheu, *Malawi* 83 E3
Ndala, *Tanzania* 82 C3
Ndalatando, *Angola* 80 F2
Ndali, *Benin* 79 D5
Ndareda, *Tanzania* 82 C4
Ndélé, *C.A.R.* 73 G9
Ndendé, *Gabon* 80 E2
Ndjamena, *Chad* 73 F7
Ndjolé, *Gabon* 80 E2
Ndola, *Zambia* 83 E2
Ndoto Mts., *Kenya* 82 B4
Nduguti, *Tanzania* 82 C3
Nea →, *Norway* 10 A5
Néa Flippiás, *Greece* ... 39 K3
Neagh, Lough, *U.K.* 15 B5
Neah Bay, *U.S.A.* 112 B2
Neale, L., *Australia* ... 88 D5
Neápolis, *Kozan, Greece* . 39 J4
Neápolis, *Kríti, Greece* . 37 D7
Neápolis, *Lakonia, Greece* 39 N6
Near Is., *U.S.A.* 96 C1
Neath, *U.K.* 13 F4
Nebbou, *Burkina Faso* ... 79 C4
Nebine Cr. →, *Australia* . 91 D4
Nebitdag, *Turkmenistan* .. 44 F6
Nebolchy, *Russia* 40 C7
Nebraska □, *U.S.A.* 108 E5
Nebraska City, *U.S.A.* .. 108 E7
Nébrodi, Monti, *Italy* ... 35 E7
Necedah, *U.S.A.* 108 C9
Nechako →, *Canada* 100 C4
Neches →, *U.S.A.* 109 L8
Neckar →, *Germany* 19 F4
Necochea, *Argentina* 126 D4
Nedelišće, *Croatia* 33 B13
Neder Rijn →, *Neths.* ... 16 E8
Nederbrakel, *Belgium* ... 17 G3
Nederweert, *Neths.* 17 F7
Nédha →, *Greece* 39 M4
Nedroma, *Algeria* 75 A4
Neede, *Neths.* 16 D9
Needles, *U.S.A.* 113 L12
Needles, The, *U.K.* 13 G6
Ñeembucú □, *Paraguay* ... 126 B4
Neemuch = Nimach, *India* . 62 G6
Neenah, *U.S.A.* 104 C1
Neepawa, *Canada* 101 C9
Neer, *Neths.* 17 F7
Neerpelt, *Belgium* 17 F6
Nefta, *Tunisia* 75 B6
Neftah Sidi Boubekeur,
  Algeria 75 A5
Neftçala, *Azerbaijan* ... 67 C13
Neftegorsk, *Russia* 43 H4
Neftekumsk, *Russia* 43 H7
Neftenbach, *Switz.* 23 A7
Negapatam =
  Nagappattinam, *India* . 60 P11
Negaunee, *U.S.A.* 104 B2

Negele, *Ethiopia* 68 F2
Negev Desert = Hanegev,
  Israel 69 E3
Negombo, *Sri Lanka* 60 R11
Negotin, *Serbia, Yug.* ... 21 L12
Negra, Peña, *Spain* 30 C4
Negra, Pta., *Mauritania* . 74 D1
Negra, Pta., *Peru* 124 B1
Negra Pt., *Phil.* 57 A6
Negrais, C. = Maudin Sun,
  Burma 61 M19
Negreira, *Spain* 30 C2
Négrine, *Algeria* 75 B6
Negro →, *Argentina* 128 B4
Negro →, *Bolivia* 125 C5
Negro →, *Brazil* 121 D6
Negro →, *Uruguay* 127 C4
Negros, *Phil.* 55 G5
Nehalem →, *U.S.A.* 112 E3
Nehāvand, *Iran* 65 C6
Nehbandān, *Iran* 65 D9
Neheim, *Germany* 18 D3
Nehoiaşu, *Romania* 38 D9
Nei Monggol Zizhiqu □,
  China 50 C6
Neidpath, *Canada* 101 C7
Neihart, *U.S.A.* 110 C8
Neijiang, *China* 52 C5
Neilton, *U.S.A.* 110 C2
Neiqiu, *China* 50 F8
Neira de Jusá, *Spain* ... 30 C3
Neiva, *Colombia* 120 C2
Neixiang, *China* 50 H6
Nejanilini L., *Canada* .. 101 B9
Nejo, *Ethiopia* 77 F4
Nekā, *Iran* 65 B7
Nekemte, *Ethiopia* 77 F4
Nêkheb, *Egypt* 76 B3
Neksø, *Denmark* 9 J16
Nelas, *Portugal* 30 E3
Nelia, *Australia* 90 C3
Nelidovo, *Russia* 40 D7
Neligh, *U.S.A.* 108 D5
Nelkan, *Russia* 45 D14
Nellore, *India* 60 M11
Nelma, *Russia* 45 E14
Nelson, *Canada* 100 D5
Nelson, *N.Z.* 87 J4
Nelson, *U.K.* 12 D5
Nelson, *U.S.A.* 111 J7
Nelson →, *Canada* 101 C9
Nelson, C., *Australia* .. 91 F3
Nelson, Estrecho, *Chile* . 128 D2
Nelson Forks, *Canada* ... 100 B4
Nelson House, *Canada* ... 101 B9
Nelson L., *Canada* 101 B8
Nelspoort, *S. Africa* ... 84 E3
Nelspruit, *S. Africa* ... 85 D5
Néma, *Mauritania* 78 B3
Neman →, *Lithuania* 9 J19
Nemeiben L., *Canada* 101 B7
Nemira, *Romania* 38 C9
Nemours, *France* 25 D9
Nemunas = Neman →,
  Lithuania 9 J19
Nemuro, *Japan* 48 C12
Nemuro-Kaikyō, *Japan* ... 48 C12
Nemuy, *Russia* 45 D14
Nen Jiang →, *China* 51 B13
Nenagh, *Ireland* 15 D3
Nenana, *U.S.A.* 96 B5
Nenasi, *Malaysia* 59 L4
Nene →, *U.K.* 12 E8
Nenjiang, *China* 54 B7
Neno, *Malawi* 83 F3
Nenusa, Kepulauan,
  Indonesia 57 D7
Neodesha, *U.S.A.* 109 G7
Neópolis, *Brazil* 122 D4
Neosho, *U.S.A.* 109 G7
Neosho →, *U.S.A.* 109 H7
Nepal ■, *Asia* 63 F11
Nepalganj, *Nepal* 63 E9
Nephi, *U.S.A.* 110 G8
Nephin, *Ireland* 15 B2
Neptune, *U.S.A.* 107 F10
Néra →, *Romania* 38 E4
Nérac, *France* 26 D4
Nerchinsk, *Russia* 45 D12
Nerchinskiy Zavod, *Russia* 45 D12
Nereju, *Romania* 38 D9
Nerekhta, *Russia* 42 B5
Néret L., *Canada* 99 B5
Neringa, *Lithuania* 9 J19
Nerja, *Spain* 31 J7
Nerl →, *Russia* 42 B5
Nerpio, *Spain* 29 G2
Nerva, *Spain* 31 H4
Nes, *Neths.* 16 B7
Nesbyen, *Norway* 10 D3
Nesebŭr, *Bulgaria* 38 G10
Nesland, *Norway* 10 E1
Neslandsvatn, *Norway* ... 10 F3
Nesle, *France* 25 C9
Nesodden, *Norway* 10 E4
Nesque →, *France* 27 E8
Ness, L., *U.K.* 14 D4
Nesslau, *Switz.* 23 B8
Nesterov, *Ukraine* 41 G2
Néstos →, *Greece* 39 H7
Nesvizh = Nyasvizh,
  Belarus 41 F4
Netanya, *Israel* 69 C3
Nète →, *Belgium* 17 F4
Netherdale, *Australia* .. 90 C4
Netherlands ■, *Europe* .. 16 E6

Netherlands Antilles ■,
  W. Indies 120 A4
Neto →, *Italy* 35 C10
Nettancourt, *France* 25 D11
Nettilling L., *Canada* .. 97 B12
Nettuno, *Italy* 34 A5
Netzahualcoyotl, Presa,
  Mexico 115 D6
Neu-Isenburg, *Germany* .. 19 E4
Neu-Ulm, *Germany* 19 G6
Neubrandenburg, *Germany* 18 B9
Neubukow, *Germany* 18 A7
Neuburg, *Germany* 19 G7
Neuchâtel, *Switz.* 22 C3
Neuchâtel □, *Switz.* 22 C3
Neuchâtel, Lac de, *Switz.* 22 C3
Neudau, *Austria* 21 H6
Neuenegg, *Switz.* 22 C4
Neuenhaus, *Germany* 18 C2
Neuf-Brisach, *France* ... 25 D14
Neufahrn, *Germany* 19 G8
Neufchâteau, *Belgium* ... 17 J6
Neufchâteau, *France* 25 D12
Neufchâtel-en-Bray, *France* 24 C8
Neufchâtel-sur-Aisne,
  France 25 C11
Neuhaus, *Germany* 18 B6
Neuhausen, *Switz.* 23 A7
Neuillé-Pont-Pierre, *France* 24 E7
Neuilly-St.-Front, *France* . 25 C10
Neukalen, *Germany* 18 B8
Neumarkt, *Germany* 19 F7
Neumarkt-Sankt Veit,
  Germany 19 G8
Neumünster, *Germany* 18 A5
Neung-sur-Beuvron, *France* 25 E8
Neunkirchen, *Austria* ... 21 H6
Neunkirchen, *Germany* ... 19 F3
Neuquén, *Argentina* 128 A3
Neuquén □, *Argentina* ... 126 D2
Neuquén →, *Argentina* ... 128 A3
Neuruppin, *Germany* 18 C8
Neuse →, *U.S.A.* 105 H7
Neusiedler See, *Austria* . 21 H6
Neuss, *Germany* 17 F9
Neussargues-Moissac,
  France 26 C7
Neustadt, *Baden-W.,*
  Germany 19 H4
Neustadt, *Bayern, Germany* 19 F8
Neustadt, *Bayern, Germany* 19 G7
Neustadt, *Bayern, Germany* 19 F6
Neustadt, *Bayern, Germany* 19 E7
Neustadt, *Brandenburg,*
  Germany 18 C8
Neustadt, *Hessen, Germany* 18 E5
Neustadt, *Niedersachsen,*
  Germany 18 C5
Neustadt, *Rhld.-Pfz.,*
  Germany 19 F4
Neustadt,
  Schleswig-Holstein,
  Germany 18 A6
Neustadt, *Thüringen,*
  Germany 18 E7
Neustrelitz, *Germany* ... 18 B9
Neuvic, *France* 26 C6
Neuville, *Belgium* 17 H5
Neuville-aux-Bois, *France* . 25 D9
Neuville-de-Poitou, *France* 26 B4
Neuville-sur-Saône, *France* 27 C8
Neuvy-le-Roi, *France* ... 24 E7
Neuvy-St.-Sépulchre,
  France 26 B5
Neuvy-sur-Barangeon,
  France 25 E9
Neuwerk, *Germany* 18 B4
Neuwied, *Germany* 18 E3
Neva →, *Russia* 40 C6
Nevada, *U.S.A.* 109 G7
Nevada □, *U.S.A.* 110 G5
Nevada, Sierra, *Spain* .. 29 H1
Nevada, Sierra, *U.S.A.* . 110 G3
Nevada City, *U.S.A.* 112 F6
Nevado, Cerro, *Argentina* 126 D2
Nevanka, *Russia* 45 D10
Nevel, *Russia* 40 D5
Nevele, *Belgium* 17 F3
Nevers, *France* 25 F10
Nevertire, *Australia* ... 91 E4
Neville, *Canada* 101 D7
Nevinnomyssk, *Russia* ... 43 H6
Nevis, *W. Indies* 117 C7
Nevrokop = Gotse
  Delchev, *Bulgaria* 39 H6
Nevşehir, *Turkey* 66 C6
New →, *Guyana* 121 C6
New Albany, *Ind., U.S.A.* 104 F3
New Albany, *Miss., U.S.A.* 109 H10
New Albany, *Pa., U.S.A.* . 107 E8
New Amsterdam, *Guyana* .. 121 B6
New Angledool, *Australia* 91 D4
New Bedford, *U.S.A.* 107 E14
New Bern, *U.S.A.* 105 H7
New Bethlehem, *U.S.A.* .. 106 E5
New Bloomfield, *U.S.A.* . 106 F7
New Boston, *U.S.A.* 109 J7
New Braunfels, *U.S.A.* .. 109 L5
New Brighton, *N.Z.* 87 K4
New Brighton, *U.S.A.* ... 106 F4
New Britain, *Papua N. G.* 92 H7
New Britain, *U.S.A.* 107 E12
New Brunswick, *U.S.A.* .. 107 F10
New Brunswick □, *Canada* 99 C6
New Bussa, *Nigeria* 79 D5
New Caledonia ■, *Pac. Oc.* 92 K8
New Castle, *Ind., U.S.A.* 104 F3

New Castle, *Pa., U.S.A.* . 106 E4
New City, *U.S.A.* 107 E11
New Cumberland, *U.S.A.* . 106 F4
New Cuyama, *U.S.A.* 113 L7
New Delhi, *India* 62 E7
New Denver, *Canada* 100 D5
New Don Pedro Reservoir,
  U.S.A. 112 H6
New England, *U.S.A.* 108 B3
New England Ra.,
  Australia 91 E5
New Forest, *U.K.* 13 G6
New Glasgow, *Canada* 99 C7
New Guinea, *Oceania* 92 H5
New Hamburg, *Canada* 106 C4
New Hampshire □, *U.S.A.* 107 C13
New Hampton, *U.S.A.* 108 D8
New Hanover, *S. Africa* . 85 D5
New Haven, *Conn., U.S.A.* 107 E12
New Haven, *Mich., U.S.A.* 106 D4
New Hazelton, *Canada* ... 100 B3
New Hebrides =
  Vanuatu ■, *Pac. Oc.* .. 92 J8
New Iberia, *U.S.A.* 109 K9
New Ireland, *Papua N. G.* 92 H7
New Jersey □, *U.S.A.* ... 107 F10
New Kensington, *U.S.A.* . 106 F5
New Lexington, *U.S.A.* .. 104 F4
New Liskeard, *Canada* ... 98 C4
New London, *Conn.,*
  U.S.A. 107 E12
New London, *Minn.,*
  U.S.A. 108 C7
New London, *Ohio, U.S.A.* 106 E2
New London, *Wis., U.S.A.* 108 C10
New Madrid, *U.S.A.* 109 G10
New Meadows, *U.S.A.* 110 D5
New Melones L., *U.S.A.* . 112 H6
New Mexico □, *U.S.A.* ... 111 J10
New Milford, *Conn.,*
  U.S.A. 107 E11
New Milford, *Pa., U.S.A.* 107 E9
New Norcia, *Australia* .. 89 F2
New Norfolk, *Australia* . 90 G4
New Orleans, *U.S.A.* 109 K9
New Philadelphia, *U.S.A.* 106 F3
New Plymouth, *N.Z.* 87 H5
New Plymouth, *U.S.A.* ... 110 E5
New Providence, *Bahamas* 116 A4
New Radnor, *U.K.* 13 E4
New Richmond, *U.S.A.* ... 108 C8
New Roads, *U.S.A.* 109 K9
New Rochelle, *U.S.A.* ... 107 F11
New Rockford, *U.S.A.* ... 108 B5
New Ross, *Ireland* 15 D5
New Salem, *U.S.A.* 108 B4
New Scone, *U.K.* 14 E5
New Siberian Is. =
  Novosibirskiye Ostrova,
  Russia 45 B15
New Smyrna Beach, *U.S.A.* 105 L5
New South Wales □,
  Australia 91 E4
New Springs, *Australia* . 89 E3
New Town, *U.S.A.* 108 A3
New Ulm, *U.S.A.* 108 C7
New Waterford, *Canada* .. 99 C7
New Westminster, *Canada* 100 D4
New York □, *U.S.A.* 107 D9
New York City, *U.S.A.* .. 107 F11
New Zealand ■, *Oceania* . 87 J5
Newala, *Tanzania* 83 E4
Newala □, *Tanzania* 83 E4
Newark, *Del., U.S.A.* ... 104 F8
Newark, *N.J., U.S.A.* ... 107 F10
Newark, *N.Y., U.S.A.* ... 106 C7
Newark, *Ohio, U.S.A.* ... 106 F2
Newark-on-Trent, *U.K.* .. 12 D7
Newaygo, *U.S.A.* 104 D3
Newberg, *U.S.A.* 110 D2
Newberry, *Mich., U.S.A.* 104 B3
Newberry, *S.C., U.S.A.* . 105 H5
Newberry Springs, *U.S.A.* 113 L10
Newbridge = Droichead
  Nua, *Ireland* 15 C5
Newbrook, *Canada* 100 C6
Newburgh, *U.S.A.* 107 E10
Newbury, *U.K.* 13 F6
Newbury, *U.S.A.* 107 B12
Newburyport, *U.S.A.* 107 D14
Newcastle, *Australia* ... 91 E5
Newcastle, *Canada* 99 C6
Newcastle, *S. Africa* ... 85 D4
Newcastle, *U.K.* 15 B6
Newcastle, *Calif., U.S.A.* 112 G5
Newcastle, *Wyo., U.S.A.* 108 D2
Newcastle Emlyn, *U.K.* .. 13 E3
Newcastle Ra., *Australia* 88 C5
Newcastle-under-Lyme,
  U.K. 12 D5
Newcastle-upon-Tyne, *U.K.* 12 C6
Newcastle Waters, *Australia* 90 B1
Newdegate, *Australia* ... 89 F2
Newell, *U.S.A.* 108 C3
Newfoundland □, *Canada* . 99 B8
Newhalem, *U.S.A.* 100 D4
Newhall, *U.S.A.* 113 L8
Newham, *U.K.* 13 F8
Newhaven, *U.K.* 13 G8
Newkirk, *U.S.A.* 109 G6
Newman, *Australia* 88 D2
Newman, *U.S.A.* 112 H5
Newmarket, *Canada* 106 B5
Newmarket, *Ireland* 15 D3
Newmarket, *U.K.* 13 E8
Newmarket, *U.S.A.* 107 C14
Newnan, *U.S.A.* 105 J3

Newport, *Gwent, U.K.* ... 13 F5
Newport, *I. of W., U.K.* . 13 G6
Newport, *Ark., U.S.A.* .. 109 H9
Newport, *Ky., U.S.A.* ... 104 F3
Newport, *N.H., U.S.A.* .. 107 C12
Newport, *Oreg., U.S.A.* . 110 D1
Newport, *Pa., U.S.A.* ... 106 F7
Newport, *R.I., U.S.A.* .. 107 E13
Newport, *Tenn., U.S.A.* . 105 H4
Newport, *Vt., U.S.A.* ... 107 B12
Newport, *Wash., U.S.A.* . 110 B5
Newport Beach, *U.S.A.* .. 113 M9
Newport News, *U.S.A.* ... 104 G7
Newquay, *U.K.* 13 G2
Newry, *U.K.* 15 B5
Newry & Mourne □, *U.K.* . 15 B5
Newton, *Iowa, U.S.A.* ... 108 E8
Newton, *Mass., U.S.A.* .. 107 D13
Newton, *Miss., U.S.A.* .. 109 J10
Newton, *N.C., U.S.A.* ... 105 H5
Newton, *N.J., U.S.A.* ... 107 E10
Newton, *Tex., U.S.A.* ... 109 K8
Newton Abbot, *U.K.* 13 G4
Newton Boyd, *Australia* . 91 D5
Newton Stewart, *U.K.* ... 14 G4
Newtonmore, *U.K.* 14 D4
Newtown, *U.K.* 13 E4
Newtownabbey □, *U.K.* ... 15 B6
Newtownards, *U.K.* 15 B6
Newville, *U.S.A.* 106 F7
Nexon, *France* 26 C5
Neya, *Russia* 42 A6
Neyrīz, *Iran* 65 D7
Neyshābūr, *Iran* 65 B8
Nezhin = Nizhyn, *Ukraine* 41 G6
Nezperce, *U.S.A.* 110 C5
Ngabang, *Indonesia* 56 D3
Ngabordamlu, Tanjung,
  Indonesia 57 F8
Ngambé, *Cameroon* 79 D7
Ngami Depression,
  Botswana 84 C3
Ngamo, *Zimbabwe* 83 F2
Nganglong Kangri, *China* 61 C12
Nganjuk, *Indonesia* 57 G14
Ngao, *Thailand* 58 C2
Ngaoundéré, *Cameroon* ... 80 C2
Ngapara, *N.Z.* 87 L3
Ngara, *Tanzania* 82 C3
Ngara □, *Tanzania* 82 C3
Ngawi, *Indonesia* 57 G14
Nghia Lo, *Vietnam* 58 B5
Ngoma, *Malawi* 83 E3
Ngomahura, *Zimbabwe* 83 G3
Ngomba, *Tanzania* 83 D3
Ngop, *Sudan* 77 F3
Ngoring Hu, *China* 54 C4
Ngorkou, *Mali* 78 B4
Ngorongoro, *Tanzania* ... 82 C4
Ngozi, *Burundi* 82 C2
Ngudu, *Tanzania* 82 C3
Nguigmi, *Niger* 73 F7
Ngukurr, *Australia* 90 A1
Ngunga, *Tanzania* 82 C3
Nguru, *Nigeria* 79 C7
Nguru Mts., *Tanzania* ... 82 D4
Nguyen Binh, *Vietnam* ... 58 A5
Nha Trang, *Vietnam* 59 F7
Nhacoongo, *Mozam.* 85 C6
Nhamaabué, *Mozam.* 83 F4
Nhambiquara, *Brazil* 125 C6
Nhamundá, *Brazil* 121 D6
Nhamundá →, *Brazil* 121 D6
Nhangutazi, L., *Mozam.* . 85 C5
Nhecolândia, *Brazil* 125 D6
Nhill, *Australia* 91 F3
Nho Quan, *Vietnam* 58 B5
Nhulunbuy, *Australia* ... 90 A2
Nia-nia, *Zaïre* 82 B2
Niafounké, *Mali* 78 B4
Niagara, *U.S.A.* 104 C1
Niagara Falls, *Canada* .. 98 D4
Niagara Falls, *U.S.A.* .. 106 C6
Niagara-on-the-Lake,
  Canada 106 C5
Niah, *Malaysia* 56 D4
Niamey, *Niger* 79 C5
Nianforando, *Guinea* 78 D2
Nianfors, *Sweden* 10 C10
Niangara, *Zaïre* 82 B2
Nias, *Indonesia* 56 D1
Niassa □, *Mozam.* 83 E4
Nibbiano, *Italy* 32 D6
Nibe, *Denmark* 11 H3
Nicaragua ■, *Cent. Amer.* 116 D2
Nicaragua, L. de, *Nic.* . 116 D2
Nicastro, *Italy* 35 D9
Nice, *France* 27 E11
Niceville, *U.S.A.* 105 K2
Nichinan, *Japan* 49 J5
Nicholás, Canal, *W. Indies* 116 B3
Nicholasville, *U.S.A.* .. 104 G3
Nichols, *U.S.A.* 107 D8
Nicholson, *Australia* ... 88 C4
Nicholson, *U.S.A.* 107 E9
Nicholson →, *Australia* . 90 B2
Nicholson Ra., *Australia* 89 E2
Nickerie □, *Surinam* 121 C6
Nickerie →, *Surinam* 121 B6
Nicobar Is., *Ind. Oc.* .. 46 J13
Nicoclí, *Colombia* 120 B2
Nicola, *Canada* 100 C4
Nicolet, *Canada* 98 C5
Nicolls Town, *Bahamas* .. 116 A4
Nicosia, *Cyprus* 66 E5
Nicosia, *Italy* 35 E7
Nicótera, *Italy* 35 D8

Nicoya, Costa Rica 116 D2
Nicoya, G. de, Costa Rica 116 E2
Nicoya, Pen. de, Costa Rica 116 E2
Nidau, Switz. 22 B4
Nidd →, U.K. 12 C6
Nidda, Germany 18 E5
Nidda →, Germany 19 E4
Nidwalden □, Switz. 23 C6
Nidzica, Poland 20 B10
Niebüll, Germany 18 A4
Nied →, Germany 25 C13
Niederaula, Germany ... 18 E5
Niederbipp, Switz. 22 B5
Niederbronn-les-Bains, France 25 D14
Niedere Tauern, Austria .. 21 H4
Niedersachsen □, Germany 18 C5
Niekerkshoop, S. Africa .. 84 D3
Niel, Belgium 17 F4
Niellé, Ivory C. 78 C3
Niemba, Zaïre 82 D2
Niemen = Neman →, Lithuania 9 J19
Nienburg, Germany 18 C5
Niers →, Germany 18 D2
Niesen, Switz. 22 C5
Niesky, Germany 18 D10
Nieu Bethesda, S. Africa . 84 E3
Nieuw-Amsterdam, Neths. 16 C9
Nieuw Amsterdam, Surinam 121 B6
Nieuw Beijerland, Neths. . 16 E4
Nieuw-Dordrecht, Neths. . 16 C9
Nieuw Loosdrecht, Neths. . 16 D6
Nieuw Nickerie, Surinam . 121 B6
Nieuw-Schoonebeek, Neths. 16 C10
Nieuw-Vennep, Neths. ... 16 D5
Nieuwe-Vossemeer, Neths. . 17 E4
Nieuwe-Niedorp, Neths. .. 16 C5
Nieuwe-Pekela, Neths. ... 16 B9
Nieuwe-Schans, Neths. ... 16 B10
Nieuwendijk, Neths. 16 E5
Nieuwerkerken, Belgium .. 17 G6
Nieuwkoop, Neths. 16 D5
Nieuwleusen, Neths. 16 C8
Nieuwnamen, Neths. 17 F4
Nieuwolda, Neths. 16 B9
Nieuwoudtville, S. Africa . 84 E2
Nieuwpoort, Belgium 17 F1
Nieuwveen, Neths. 16 D5
Nieves, Spain 30 C2
Nieves, Pico de las, Canary Is. 36 G4
Nièvre □, France 25 E10
Niğde, Turkey 66 D6
Nigel, S. Africa 85 D4
Niger □, Nigeria 79 C6
Niger ■, W. Afr. 79 B6
Niger →, W. Afr. 79 D6
Nigeria ■, W. Afr. 79 D6
Nightcaps, N.Z. 87 L2
Nigríta, Greece 39 J6
Nihtaur, India 63 E8
Nii-Jima, Japan 49 G9
Niigata, Japan 48 F9
Niigata □, Japan 49 F9
Niihama, Japan 49 H6
Niihau, U.S.A. 102 H14
Niimi, Japan 49 G6
Niitsu, Japan 48 F9
Níjar, Spain 29 J2
Nijil, Jordan 69 E4
Nijkerk, Neths. 16 D7
Nijlen, Belgium 17 F5
Nijmegen, Neths. 16 E7
Nijverdal, Neths. 16 D8
Nīk Pey, Iran 67 D13
Nike, Nigeria 79 D6
Nikiniki, Indonesia ... 57 F6
Nikki, Benin 79 D5
Nikkō, Japan 49 F9
Nikolayev = Mykolayiv, Ukraine 41 J7
Nikolayevsk, Russia ... 42 E7
Nikolayevsk-na-Amur, Russia 45 D15
Nikolsk, Russia 42 D8
Nikolskoye, Russia 45 D17
Nikopol, Bulgaria 38 F7
Nikopol, Ukraine 41 J8
Niksar, Turkey 66 B7
Nīkshahr, Iran 65 E9
Nikšić, Montenegro, Yug. . 21 N8
Nîl, Nahr en →, Africa . 76 H7
Nîl el Abyad →, Sudan . 77 D3
Nîl el Azraq →, Sudan . 77 D3
Niland, U.S.A. 113 M11
Nile = Nîl, Nahr en →, Africa 76 H7
Nile Delta, Egypt 76 H7
Niles, U.S.A. 106 E4
Nilo Peçanha, Brazil ... 123 D4
Nimach, India 62 G6
Nimbahera, India 62 G6
Nîmes, France 27 E8
Nimfaíon = Pínnes, Ákra, Greece 39 J7
Nimmitabel, Australia .. 91 F4
Nimule, Sudan 77 G3
Nin, Croatia 33 D12
Nīnawá, Iraq 67 D10
Nindigully, Australia ... 91 D4
Ninemile, U.S.A. 100 B2
Nineveh = Nīnawá, Iraq . 67 D10
Ning Xian, China 50 G4
Ningaloo, Australia ... 88 D1
Ning'an, China 51 B15

Ningbo, China 53 C13
Ningcheng, China 51 D10
Ningde, China 53 D12
Ningdu, China 53 D10
Ninggang, China 53 D9
Ningguo, China 53 B12
Ninghai, China 53 C13
Ninghua, China 53 D11
Ningjin, China 50 F8
Ningjing Shan, China .. 52 B2
Ninglang, China 52 D3
Ningling, China 50 G8
Ningming, China 52 F6
Ningnan, China 52 D4
Ningpo = Ningbo, China . 53 C13
Ningqiang, China 50 H4
Ningshan, China 50 H5
Ningsia Hui A.R. = Ningxia Huizu Zizhiqu □, China 50 E3
Ningwu, China 50 E7
Ningxia Huizu Zizhiqu □, China 50 E3
Ningxiang, China 53 C9
Ningyang, China 50 G9
Ningyuan, China 53 E8
Ninh Binh, Vietnam .. 58 B5
Ninh Giang, Vietnam . 58 B6
Ninh Hoa, Vietnam .. 58 F7
Ninh Ma, Vietnam ... 58 F7
Ninove, Belgium 17 G4
Nioaque, Brazil 127 A4
Niobrara, U.S.A. 108 D6
Niobrara →, U.S.A. .. 108 D6
Niono, Mali 78 C3
Nioro du Rip, Senegal .. 78 C1
Nioro du Sahel, Mali .. 78 B3
Niort, France 26 B3
Nipawin, Canada 101 C8
Nipawin Prov. Park, Canada 101 C8
Nipigon, Canada 98 C2
Nipigon, L., Canada .. 98 C2
Nipin →, Canada 101 B7
Nipishish L., Canada . 99 B7
Nipissing L., Canada . 98 C4
Nipomo, U.S.A. 113 K6
Nipton, U.S.A. 113 K11
Niquelândia, Brazil .. 123 D2
Nīr, Iran 67 C12
Nirasaki, Japan 49 G9
Nirmal, India 60 K11
Nirmali, India 63 F12
Niš, Serbia, Yug. ... 21 M11
Nisa, Portugal 31 F3
Nişāb, Si. Arabia ... 64 D5
Nişāb, Yemen 68 E4
Nišava →, Serbia, Yug. . 21 M11
Niscemi, Italy 35 E7
Nishinomiya, Japan .. 49 G7
Nishin'omote, Japan . 49 J5
Nishiwaki, Japan ... 49 G7
Nísíros, Greece 39 N10
Niskibi →, Canada .. 98 A2
Nispen, Neths. 17 F4
Nissáki, Greece 37 A3
Nissan →, Sweden .. 11 H6
Nissedal, Norway ... 10 E2
Nisser, Norway 10 E2
Nissum Bredning, Denmark 9 H13
Nissum Fjord, Denmark . 11 H2
Nistelrode, Neths. .. 17 E7
Nistru = Dnister →, Europe 41 J6
Nisutlin →, Canada .. 100 A2
Nitchequon, Canada .. 99 B5
Niterói, Brazil 123 F3
Nith →, U.K. 14 F5
Nitra, Slovak Rep. .. 21 G8
Nitra →, Slovak Rep. . 21 H8
Nittedal, Norway ... 10 D4
Nittenau, Germany .. 19 F8
Niuafo'ou, Tonga ... 87 B11
Niue, Cook Is. 93 J11
Niulan Jiang →, China . 52 D4
Niut, Indonesia 56 D4
Niutou Shan, China . 53 C13
Niuzhuang, China .. 51 D12
Nivala, Finland 8 E21
Nivelles, Belgium .. 17 G4
Nivernais, France .. 25 E10
Nixon, U.S.A. 109 L6
Nizamabad, India .. 60 K11
Nizamghat, India .. 61 E19
Nizhne Kolymsk, Russia . 45 C17
Nizhne-Vartovsk, Russia . 44 C8
Nizhneangarsk, Russia . 45 D11
Nizhnegorskiy = Nyzhnohirskyy, Ukraine 41 K8
Nizhnekamsk, Russia ... 42 C10
Nizhneudinsk, Russia .. 45 D10
Nizhneyansk, Russia .. 45 B14
Nizhniy Chir, Russia .. 43 F6
Nizhniy Lomov, Russia . 42 D6
Nizhniy Novgorod, Russia 42 B7
Nizhniy Tagil, Russia . 44 D6
Nizhyn, Ukraine 41 G6
Nizip, Turkey 66 D7
Nízké Tatry, Slovak Rep. . 20 G9
Nizza Monferrato, Italy . 32 D5
Njakwa, Malawi 83 E3
Njanji, Zambia 83 E3
Njinjo, Tanzania ... 83 D4
Njombe, Tanzania .. 83 D3
Njombe □, Tanzania . 83 D3
Njombe →, Tanzania . 82 D4
Nkambe, Cameroon .. 79 D7

Nkana, Zambia 83 E2
Nkawkaw, Ghana 79 D4
Nkayi, Zimbabwe 83 F2
Nkhata Bay, Malawi ... 80 G6
Nkhota Kota, Malawi .. 83 E3
Nkongsamba, Cameroon . 79 E6
Nkurenkuru, Namibia .. 84 B2
Nkwanta, Ghana 78 D4
Nmai →, Burma 61 G20
Noakhali = Maijdi, Bangla. 61 H17
Noatak, U.S.A. 96 B3
Nobel, Canada 106 A4
Nobeoka, Japan 49 H5
Noblejas, Spain 28 F1
Noblesville, U.S.A. ... 104 E3
Noce →, Italy 32 B8
Nocera Inferiore, Italy . 35 B7
Nocera Terinese, Italy . 35 C9
Nocera Umbra, Italy .. 33 E9
Noci, Italy 35 B10
Nockatunga, Australia . 91 D3
Nocona, U.S.A. 109 J6
Noda, Japan 49 G9
Noel, U.S.A. 109 G7
Nogales, Mexico 114 A2
Nogales, U.S.A. 111 L8
Nogent-en-Bassigny, France 25 D12
Nogent-le-Rotrou, France . 24 D7
Nogent-sur-Seine, France . 25 D10
Noggerup, Australia .. 89 F2
Noginsk, Moskva, Russia . 42 C4
Noginsk, Sib., Russia .. 45 C10
Nogoa →, Australia .. 90 C4
Nogoyá, Argentina .. 126 C4
Nogueira de Ramuin, Spain 30 C3
Noguera Pallaresa →, Spain 28 D5
Noguera Ribagorzana →, Spain 28 D5
Nohar, India 62 E6
Noire, Montagne, France . 26 E6
Noire, Mt., France .. 24 D3
Noirétable, France .. 26 C7
Noirmoutier, I. de, France 24 F4
Noirmoutier-en-l'Ile, France 24 F4
Nojane, Botswana .. 84 C3
Nojima-Zaki, Japan . 49 G9
Nok Kundi, Pakistan . 60 E3
Nokaneng, Botswana . 84 B3
Nokhtuysk, Russia .. 45 C12
Nokia, Finland 9 F20
Nokomis, Canada ... 101 C8
Nokomis L., Canada . 101 B8
Nol, Sweden 11 G6
Nola, C.A.R. 80 D3
Nola, Italy 35 B7
Nolay, France 25 F11
Noli, C. di, Italy ... 32 D5
Nolinsk, Russia 42 B9
Noma Omuramba →, Namibia 84 B3
Noman L., Canada .. 101 A7
Nombre de Dios, Panama 116 E4
Nome, U.S.A. 96 B3
Nomo-Zaki, Japan .. 49 H4
Nonacho L., Canada . 101 A7
Nonancourt, France . 24 D8
Nonant-le-Pin, France . 24 D7
Nonda, Australia ... 90 C3
Nong Chang, Thailand . 58 E2
Nong Het, Laos 58 C4
Nong Khai, Thailand . 58 D4
Nong'an, China 51 B13
Nongoma, S. Africa .. 85 D5
Nonthaburi, Thailand . 58 F3
Nontron, France ... 26 C4
Nonza, France 27 F13
Noonamah, Australia . 88 B5
Noonan, U.S.A. 108 A3
Noondoo, Australia . 91 D4
Noonkanbah, Australia . 88 C3
Noord-Bergum, Neths. . 16 B8
Noord Brabant □, Neths. . 17 E6
Noord Holland □, Neths. . 16 D5
Noordbeveland, Neths. . 17 E3
Noordeloos, Neths. .. 16 E5
Noordhollandsch Kanaal, Neths. 16 C5
Noordhorn, Neths. .. 16 B8
Noordoostpolder, Neths. . 16 C7
Noordwijk aan Zee, Neths. 16 D4
Noordwijk-Binnen, Neths. 16 D4
Noordwijkerhout, Neths. . 16 D5
Noordzee Kanaal, Neths. . 16 D5
Noorwolde, Neths. .. 16 C8
Nootka, Canada 100 D3
Nootka I., Canada .. 100 D3
Nóqui, Angola 80 F2
Nora, Eritrea 77 D5
Noranda, Canada ... 98 C4
Nórcia, Italy 33 F10
Norco, U.S.A. 113 M9
Nord □, France 25 B10
Nord-Ostsee-Kanal →, Germany 18 A5
Nordagutu, Norway . 10 E3
Nordaustlandet, Svalbard . 4 B9
Nordborg, Denmark .. 11 J3
Nordby, Århus, Denmark . 11 J4
Nordby, Ribe, Denmark . 11 J2
Norddeich, Germany . 18 B3
Nordegg, Canada ... 100 C5
Norden, Germany ... 18 B3
Nordenham, Germany . 18 B4
Norderhov, Norway . 10 D4

Norderney, Germany ... 18 B3
Nordfjord, Norway 9 F11
Nordfriesische Inseln, Germany 18 A4
Nordhausen, Germany . 18 D6
Nordhorn, Germany .. 18 C3
Norðoyar, Færoe Is. .. 8 E9
Nordjylland Amtskommune □, Denmark 11 H4
Nordkapp, Norway ... 8 A21
Nordkapp, Svalbard .. 4 A9
Nordkinn = Kinnarodden, Norway 6 A11
Nordkinn-halvøya, Norway 8 A22
Nördlingen, Germany . 19 G6
Nordrhein-Westfalen □, Germany 18 D3
Nordstrand, Germany . 18 A4
Nordvik, Russia 45 B12
Nore, Norway 10 D3
Norefjell, Norway ... 10 D3
Norembega, Canada .. 98 C3
Noresund, Norway .. 10 D3
Norfolk, Nebr., U.S.A. . 108 D6
Norfolk, Va., U.S.A. . 104 G7
Norfolk □, U.K. 12 E9
Norfolk Broads, U.K. . 12 E9
Norfolk I., Pac. Oc. .. 92 K8
Norfork Res., U.S.A. . 109 G8
Norg, Neths. 16 B8
Norilsk, Russia 45 C9
Norley, Australia ... 91 D3
Norma, Mt., Australia . 90 C3
Normal, U.S.A. 108 E10
Norman, U.S.A. 109 H6
Norman →, Australia . 90 B3
Norman Wells, Canada . 96 B7
Normanby →, Australia . 90 A3
Normandie, France .. 24 D7
Normandie, Collines de, France 24 D6
Normandin, Canada .. 98 C5
Normandy = Normandie, France 24 D7
Normanhurst, Mt., Australia 89 E3
Normanton, Australia . 90 B3
Norquay, Canada ... 101 C8
Norquinco, Argentina . 128 B2
Norrbotten □, Sweden . 8 C19
Nørre Åby, Denmark . 11 J3
Nørre Nebel, Denmark . 11 J2
Nørresundby, Denmark . 11 G3
Norris, U.S.A. 110 D8
Norristown, U.S.A. .. 107 F9
Norrköping, Sweden . 11 F10
Norrland, Sweden ... 9 E16
Norrtälje, Sweden .. 10 E12
Norseman, Australia . 89 F3
Norsholm, Sweden .. 11 F9
Norsk, Russia 45 D14
Norte, Pta., Argentina . 128 B4
Norte, Pte. del, Canary Is. 36 G2
Norte de Santander □, Colombia 120 B3
Nortelândia, Brazil .. 125 C6
North Adams, U.S.A. . 107 D11
North Battleford, Canada . 101 C7
North Bay, Canada .. 98 C4
North Belcher Is., Canada 98 A4
North Bend, Canada . 100 D4
North Bend, Oreg., U.S.A. 110 E1
North Bend, Pa., U.S.A. 106 E7
North Bend, Wash., U.S.A. 112 C5
North Berwick, U.K. . 14 E6
North Berwick, U.S.A. . 107 C14
North C., Canada ... 99 C7
North C., N.Z. 87 F4
North Canadian →, U.S.A. 109 H7
North Cape = Nordkapp, Norway 8 A21
North Cape = Nordkapp, Svalbard 4 A9
North Caribou L., Canada 98 B1
North Carolina □, U.S.A. 105 H5
North Channel, Canada . 98 C3
North Channel, U.K. . 14 G3
North Chicago, U.S.A. . 104 D2
North Dakota □, U.S.A. . 108 B5
North Dandalup, Australia 89 F2
North Down □, U.K. . 15 B6
North Downs, U.K. .. 13 F8
North East, U.S.A. .. 106 D5
North East Frontier Agency = Arunachal Pradesh □, India .. 61 E19
North East Providence Chan., W. Indies ... 116 A4
North Eastern □, Kenya . 82 B5
North Esk →, U.K. .. 14 E6
North European Plain, Europe 6 D11
North Foreland, U.K. . 13 F9
North Fork, U.S.A. .. 112 H7
North Fork American →, U.S.A. 112 G5
North Fork Feather →, U.S.A. 112 F5
North Frisian Is. = Nordfriesische Inseln, Germany 18 A4
North Henik L., Canada . 101 A9
North Highlands, U.S.A. . 112 G5
North Horr, Kenya .. 82 B4
North I., Kenya 82 B4

North I., N.Z. 87 H5
North Kingsville, U.S.A. . 106 E4
North Knife →, Canada . 101 B10
North Koel →, India .. 63 G10
North Korea ■, Asia .. 51 E14
North Lakhimpur, India . 61 F19
North Las Vegas, U.S.A. . 113 J11
North Loup →, U.S.A. . 108 E5
North Magnetic Pole, Canada 4 B2
North Minch, U.K. ... 14 C3
North Nahanni →, Canada 100 A4
North Olmsted, U.S.A. . 106 E3
North Ossetia □, Russia . 43 J7
North Pagai, I. = Pagai Utara, Indonesia ... 56 E2
North Palisade, U.S.A. . 111 H4
North Platte, U.S.A. .. 108 E4
North Platte →, U.S.A. . 108 E4
North Pole, Arctic ... 4 A
North Portal, Canada . 101 D8
North Powder, U.S.A. . 110 D5
North Pt., Canada ... 99 C7
North Rhine Westphalia = Nordrhein-Westfalen □, Germany 18 D3
North Ronaldsay, U.K. . 14 B6
North Saskatchewan →, Canada 101 C7
North Sea, Europe ... 6 D6
North Sporades = Voríai Sporádhes, Greece .. 39 K6
North Sydney, Canada . 99 C7
North Taranaki Bight, N.Z. 87 H5
North Thompson →, Canada 100 C4
North Tonawanda, U.S.A. 106 C6
North Troy, U.S.A. .. 107 B12
North Truchas Pk., U.S.A. 111 J11
North Twin I., Canada . 98 B3
North Tyne →, U.K. .. 12 C5
North Uist, U.K. 14 D1
North Vancouver, Canada 100 D4
North Vernon, U.S.A. . 104 F3
North Wabasca L., Canada 100 B6
North Walsham, U.K. . 12 E9
North-West □, S. Africa . 84 D4
North West C., Australia . 88 D1
North West Christmas I. Ridge, Pac. Oc. ... 93 G11
North West Frontier □, Pakistan 62 C4
North West Highlands, U.K. 14 D3
North West Providence Channel, W. Indies ... 116 A4
North West River, Canada 99 B7
North West Territories □, Canada 96 B9
North Western □, Zambia 83 E2
North York Moors, U.K. . 12 C7
North Yorkshire □, U.K. . 12 C6
Northallerton, U.K. .. 12 C6
Northam, S. Africa .. 84 C4
Northam, Australia .. 89 E1
Northampton, Australia . 89 E1
Northampton, U.K. .. 13 E7
Northampton, Mass., U.S.A. 107 D12
Northampton, Pa., U.S.A. 107 F9
Northampton Downs, Australia 90 C4
Northamptonshire □, U.K. 13 E7
Northbridge, U.S.A. . 107 D13
Northcliffe, Australia . 89 F2
Northeim, Germany . 18 D6
Northern □, Malawi .. 83 E3
Northern □, Uganda . 82 B3
Northern □, Zambia .. 83 E3
Northern Cape □, S. Africa 84 D3
Northern Circars, India . 61 L13
Northern Indian L., Canada 101 B9
Northern Ireland □, U.K. 15 B5
Northern Light, L., Canada 98 C1
Northern Marianas ■, Pac. Oc. 92 F6
Northern Province □, S. Leone 78 D2
Northern Territory □, Australia 88 D5
Northern Transvaal □, S. Africa 85 C4
Northfield, U.S.A. .. 108 C8
Northland □, N.Z. .. 87 F4
Northome, U.S.A. ... 108 B7
Northport, Ala., U.S.A. . 105 J2
Northport, Mich., U.S.A. 104 C3
Northport, Wash., U.S.A. 110 B5
Northumberland □, U.K. 12 B5
Northumberland, C., Australia 91 F3
Northumberland Is., Australia 90 C4
Northumberland Str., Canada 99 C7
Northwich, U.K. 12 D5
Northwood, Iowa, U.S.A. 108 D8
Northwood, N. Dak., U.S.A. 108 B6
Norton, U.S.A. 108 F5
Norton, Zimbabwe .. 83 F3
Norton Sd., U.S.A. .. 96 B3
Nortorf, Germany ... 18 A5
Norwalk, Calif., U.S.A. . 113 M8
Norwalk, Conn., U.S.A. . 107 E11
Norwalk, Ohio, U.S.A. . 106 E2
Norway, U.S.A. 104 C2

Norway ■, *Europe* 8 E14
Norway House, *Canada* . . 101 C9
Norwegian Sea, *Atl. Oc.* . . 4 C8
Norwich, *Canada* 106 D4
Norwich, *U.K.* 12 E9
Norwich, *Conn., U.S.A.* . . 107 E12
Norwich, *N.Y., U.S.A.* . . . 107 D9
Norwood, *Canada* 106 B7
Noshiro, *Japan* 48 D10
Nosivka, *Ukraine* 41 G6
Nosok, *Russia* 44 B9
Nosovka = Nosivka,
   Ukraine 41 G6
Noss Hd., *U.K.* 14 C5
Nossa Senhora da Glória,
   Brazil 122 D4
Nossa Senhora das Dores,
   Brazil 122 D4
Nossa Senhora do
   Livramento, *Brazil* . . 125 D6
Nossebro, *Sweden* 11 F6
Nossob →, *S. Africa* . . . 84 D3
Nosy Bé, *Madag.* 81 G9
Nosy Boraha, *Madag.* 85 B8
Nosy Mitsio, *Madag.* 81 G9
Nosy Varika, *Madag.* 85 C8
Noteć →, *Poland* 20 C5
Notigi Dam, *Canada* 101 B9
Notikewin →, *Canada* . . . 100 B5
Notios Evvoïkos Kólpos,
   Greece 39 L7
Noto, *Italy* 35 F8
Noto, G. di, *Italy* 35 F8
Notodden, *Norway* 10 E3
Notre-Dame, *Canada* 99 C7
Notre Dame B., *Canada* . . 99 C8
Notre Dame de Koartac =
   Quaqtaq, *Canada* . . . 97 B13
Notre Dame d'Ivugivic =
   Ivujivik, *Canada* 97 B12
Notsé, *Togo* 79 D5
Nottaway →, *Canada* 98 B4
Nøtterøy, *Norway* 10 E4
Nottingham, *U.K.* 12 E6
Nottinghamshire □, *U.K.* . 12 D7
Nottoway →, *U.S.A.* 104 G7
Notwane →, *Botswana* . . . 84 C4
Nouâdhibou, *Mauritania* . . 74 D1
Nouâdhibou, Ras,
   Mauritania 74 D1
Nouakchott, *Mauritania* . . 78 B1
Nouméa, *N. Cal.* 92 K8
Noupoort, *S. Africa* 84 E3
Nouveau Comptoir =
   Wemindji, *Canada* 98 B4
Nouvelle-Calédonie = New
   Caledonia ■, *Pac. Oc.* . 92 K8
Nouzonville, *France* 25 C11
Nová Baňa, *Slovak Rep.* . . 21 G8
Nová Bystřice, *Czech.* . . . 20 F5
Nova Casa Nova, *Brazil* . . 122 C3
Nova Cruz, *Brazil* 122 C4
Nova Era, *Brazil* 123 E3
Nova Esperança, *Brazil* . . 127 A5
Nova Friburgo, *Brazil* . . . 123 F3
Nova Gaia = Cambundi-
   Catembo, *Angola* 80 G3
Nova Gradiška, *Croatia* . . 21 K7
Nova Granada, *Brazil* . . . 123 F2
Nova Iguaçu, *Brazil* 123 F3
Nova Iorque, *Brazil* 122 C3
Nova Kakhovka, *Ukraine* . . 41 J7
Nova Lamego, *Guinea-Biss.* 78 C2
Nova Lima, *Brazil* 127 A7
Nova Lisboa = Huambo,
   Angola 81 G3
Nova Lusitânia, *Mozam.* . . 83 F3
Nova Mambone, *Mozam.* . . 85 C6
Nova Odesa, *Ukraine* . . . 41 J6
Nova Ponte, *Brazil* 123 E2
Nova Scotia □, *Canada* . . 99 C7
Nova Sofala, *Mozam.* . . . 85 C5
Nova Venécia, *Brazil* . . . 123 E3
Nova Vida, *Brazil* 125 C5
Nova Zagora, *Bulgaria* . . . 38 G8
Novaleksandrovskaya =
   Novoaleksandrovsk,
   Russia 43 H5
Novannenskiy =
   Novoannenskiy, *Russia* . 42 E6
Novara, *Italy* 32 C5
Novato, *U.S.A.* 112 G4
Novaya Kakhovka = Nova
   Kakhovka, *Ukraine* . . . 41 J7
Novaya Kazanka,
   Kazakhstan 43 F9
Novaya Ladoga, *Russia* . . 40 B7
Novaya Lyalya, *Russia* . . 44 D7
Novaya Zemlya, *Russia* . . 44 B6
Novelda, *Spain* 29 G4
Novellara, *Italy* 32 D7
Noventa Vicentina, *Italy* . 33 C8
Novgorod, *Russia* 40 C6
Novgorod-Severskiy =
   Novhorod-Siverskyy,
   Ukraine 41 G7
Novhorod-Siverskyy,
   Ukraine 41 G7
Novi Bečej, *Serbia, Yug.* . 21 K10
Novi Grad, *Croatia* 33 C10
Novi Krichim, *Bulgaria* . . 38 G7
Novi Lígure, *Italy* 32 D5
Novi Pazar, *Bulgaria* 38 F10
Novi Pazar, *Serbia, Yug.* . 21 M10
Novi Sad, *Serbia, Yug.* . . 21 K9
Novi Vinodolski, *Croatia* . 33 C11
Novigrad, *Croatia* 33 D12

Noville, *Belgium* 17 H7
Novo Acôrdo, *Brazil* 122 D2
Novo Aripuanã, *Brazil* . . . 121 E5
Nôvo Cruzeiro, *Brazil* . . . 123 E3
Nôvo Hamburgo, *Brazil* . . 127 B5
Novo Horizonte, *Brazil* . . 123 F2
Novo Mesto, *Slovenia* . . . 33 C12
Novo Remanso, *Brazil* . . . 122 C3
Novoaleksandrovsk, *Russia* 43 H5
Novoannenskiy, *Russia* . . 42 E6
Novoataysk, *Russia* 44 D9
Novoazovsk, *Ukraine* . . . 41 J10
Novocheboksarsk, *Russia* . 42 B8
Novocherkassk, *Russia* . . 43 G5
Novodevichye, *Russia* . . . 42 D9
Novogrudok =
   Navahrudak, *Belarus* . . 40 F3
Novohrad-Volynskyy,
   Ukraine 41 G4
Novokachalinsk, *Russia* . . 48 B6
Novokazalinsk =
   Zhangaqazaly,
   Kazakhstan 44 E7
Novokhopersk, *Russia* . . . 42 E5
Novokuybyshevsk, *Russia* . 42 D9
Novokuznetsk, *Russia* . . . 44 D9
Novomirgorod, *Ukraine* . . 41 H6
Novomoskovsk, *Russia* . . 42 C4
Novomoskovsk, *Ukraine* . . 41 H8
Novopolotsk =
   Navapolatsk, *Belarus* . . 40 E5
Novorossiysk, *Russia* . . . 43 H3
Novorybnoye, *Russia* . . . 45 B11
Novorzhev, *Russia* 40 D5
Novoselytsya, *Ukraine* . . 41 H4
Novoshakhtinsk, *Russia* . . 43 G4
Novosibirsk, *Russia* 44 D9
Novosibirskiye Ostrova,
   Russia 45 B15
Novosil, *Russia* 42 D3
Novosokolniki, *Russia* . . . 40 D6
Novotitarovskaya, *Russia* . 43 H4
Novotroitsk, *Russia* 44 D6
Novoukrayinka, *Ukraine* . . 41 H6
Novouljanovsk, *Russia* . . 42 C9
Novouzensk, *Russia* 42 E9
Novovolynsk, *Ukraine* . . . 41 G3
Novovoronezhskiy, *Russia* . 42 E4
Novozybkov, *Russia* 41 F6
Novska, *Croatia* 21 K6
Novy Bug = Novyy Buh,
   Ukraine 41 J7
Nový Bydzov, *Czech.* . . . 20 E5
Novy Dwór Mazowiecki,
   Poland 20 C10
Novyy Afon, *Georgia* . . . 43 J5
Novyy Buh, *Ukraine* 41 J7
Novyy Oskol, *Russia* . . . 42 E3
Novyy Port, *Russia* 44 C8
Now Shahr, *Iran* 65 B6
Nowa Deba, *Poland* 20 E11
Nowa Ruda, *Poland* 20 E6
Nowa Sól, *Poland* 20 D5
Nowbarān, *Iran* 65 C6
Nowe, *Poland* 20 B8
Nowghāb, *Iran* 65 C8
Nowgong, *India* 61 F18
Nowogard, *Poland* 20 B5
Nowogród, *Poland* 20 B11
Nowra, *Australia* 91 E5
Nowshera, *Pakistan* 60 B8
Nowy Korczyn, *Poland* . . . 20 E10
Nowy Sącz, *Poland* 20 F10
Noxen, *U.S.A.* 107 E8
Noxon, *U.S.A.* 110 C6
Noya, *Spain* 30 C2
Noyant, *France* 24 E7
Noyers, *France* 25 E10
Noyes I., *U.S.A.* 100 B2
Noyon, *France* 25 C9
Noyon, *Mongolia* 50 C2
Nozay, *France* 24 E5
Nsa, O. en →, *Algeria* . . 75 B6
Nsanje, *Malawi* 83 F4
Nsawam, *Ghana* 79 D4
Nsomba, *Zambia* 83 E2
Nsukka, *Nigeria* 79 D6
Nu Jiang →, *China* 52 C1
Nu Shan, *China* 52 D2
Nuba Mts. = Nubah,
   Jibalan, *Sudan* 77 E3
Nubah, Jibalan, *Sudan* . . 77 E3
Nubian Desert = Nûbîya,
   Es Sahrâ En, *Sudan* . . 76 C3
Nûbîya, Es Sahrâ En,
   Sudan 76 C3
Ñuble □, *Chile* 126 D1
Nuboai, *Indonesia* 57 E9
Nubra →, *India* 63 B7
Nueces →, *U.S.A.* 109 M6
Nueltin L., *Canada* 101 A9
Nuenen, *Neths.* 17 F7
Nueva, I., *Chile* 128 E3
Nueva Antioquia,
   Colombia 120 B4
Nueva Asunción □,
   Paraguay 126 A3
Nueva Esparta □,
   Venezuela 121 A5
Nueva Gerona, *Cuba* . . . 116 B3
Nueva Imperial, *Chile* . . . 128 A2
Nueva Palmira, *Uruguay* . 126 C4
Nueva Rosita, *Mexico* . . . 114 B4
Nueva San Salvador,
   El Salv. 116 D2
Nueve de Julio, *Argentina* 126 D3
Nuevitas, *Cuba* 116 B4

Nuevo, G., *Argentina* . . . 128 B4
Nuevo Guerrero, *Mexico* . 115 B5
Nuevo Laredo, *Mexico* . . . 115 B5
Nuevo León □, *Mexico* . . 114 C4
Nuevo Mundo, Cerro,
   Bolivia 124 E4
Nuevo Rocafuerte, *Ecuador* 120 D2
Nugget Pt., *N.Z.* 87 M2
Nugrus, Gebel, *Egypt* . . . 76 C3
Nuhaka, *N.Z.* 87 H6
Nuits-St.-Georges, *France* 25 E11
Nukey Bluff, *Australia* . . . 91 E2
Nukheila, *Sudan* 76 D2
Nukhuyb, *Iraq* 67 F10
Nuku'alofa, *Tonga* 87 E11
Nukus, *Uzbekistan* 44 E6
Nuland, *Neths.* 16 E6
Nulato, *U.S.A.* 96 B4
Nules, *Spain* 28 F4
Nullagine →, *Australia* . . 88 D3
Nullarbor, *Australia* 89 F5
Nullarbor Plain, *Australia* . 89 F4
Numalla, L., *Australia* . . . 91 D3
Numan, *Nigeria* 79 D7
Numansdorp, *Neths.* 16 E4
Numata, *Japan* 49 F9
Numatinna →, *Sudan* . . . 77 F2
Numazu, *Japan* 49 G9
Numbulwar, *Australia* . . . 90 A2
Numfoor, *Indonesia* 57 E8
Numurkah, *Australia* 91 F4
Nunaksaluk I., *Canada* . . 99 A7
Nuneaton, *U.K.* 13 E6
Nungo, *Mozam.* 83 E4
Nungwe, *Tanzania* 82 C3
Nunivak I., *U.S.A.* 96 C3
Nunkun, *India* 63 C7
Nunspeet, *Neths.* 16 D7
Núoro, *Italy* 34 B2
Nuquí, *Colombia* 120 B2
Nūrābād, *Iran* 65 E8
Nure →, *Italy* 32 C6
Nuremburg = Nürnberg,
   Germany 19 F7
Nuri, *Mexico* 114 B3
Nurina, *Australia* 89 F4
Nuriootpa, *Australia* 91 E2
Nurlat, *Russia* 42 C10
Nurmes, *Finland* 8 E23
Nürnberg, *Germany* 19 F7
Nurran, L. = Terewah, L.,
   Australia 91 D4
Nurrari Lakes, *Australia* . . 89 E5
Nurri, *Italy* 34 C2
Nusa Barung, *Indonesia* . . 57 H15
Nusa Kambangan,
   Indonesia 57 G13
Nusa Tenggara Barat □,
   Indonesia 56 F5
Nusa Tenggara Timur □,
   Indonesia 57 F6
Nusaybin, *Turkey* 67 D9
Nushki, *Pakistan* 62 E2
Nutak, *Canada* 97 C13
Nuth, *Neths.* 17 G7
Nutwood Downs, *Australia* 90 B1
Nuuk = Godthåb,
   Greenland 97 B14
Nuwakot, *Nepal* 63 E10
Nuweiba', *Egypt* 76 B3
Nuweveldberge, *S. Africa* . 84 E3
Nuyts, C., *Australia* 89 F5
Nuyts Arch., *Australia* . . . 91 E1
Nxau-Nxau, *Botswana* . . . 84 B3
Nyaake, *Liberia* 78 E3
Nyack, *U.S.A.* 107 E11
Nyadal, *Sweden* 10 B11
Nyah West, *Australia* . . . 91 F3
Nyahanga, *Tanzania* 82 C3
Nyahua, *Tanzania* 82 D3
Nyahururu, *Kenya* 82 B4
Nyainqentanglha Shan,
   China 54 C4
Nyakanazi, *Tanzania* . . . 82 C3
Nyakrom, *Ghana* 79 D4
Nyâlâ, *Sudan* 77 E1
Nyamandhlovu, *Zimbabwe* . 83 F2
Nyambiti, *Tanzania* 82 C3
Nyamwaga, *Tanzania* . . . 82 C3
Nyandekwa, *Tanzania* . . . 82 C3
Nyanding →, *Sudan* 77 F3
Nyandoma, *Russia* 40 B11
Nyangana, *Namibia* 84 B3
Nyanguge, *Tanzania* 82 C3
Nyankpala, *Ghana* 79 D4
Nyanza, *Burundi* 82 C2
Nyanza, *Rwanda* 82 C2
Nyanza □, *Kenya* 82 C3
Nyarling →, *Canada* 100 A6
Nyasa, L. = Malawi, L.,
   Africa 83 E3
Nyasvizh, *Belarus* 41 F4
Nyazura, *Zimbabwe* 83 F3
Nyazwidzi →, *Zimbabwe* . 83 F3
Nyborg, *Denmark* 11 J4
Nybro, *Sweden* 9 H16
Nyda, *Russia* 44 C8
Nyeri, *Kenya* 82 C4
Nyerol, *Sudan* 77 F3
Nyhem, *Sweden* 10 B9
Nyiel, *Sudan* 77 F3
Nyinahin, *Ghana* 78 D4
Nyírbátor, *Hungary* 21 H12
Nyíregyháza, *Hungary* . . 21 H11
Nykøbing, Sjælland,
   Denmark 11 J5

Nykøbing, Storstrøm,
   Denmark 11 K5
Nykøbing, Viborg,
   Denmark 11 H2
Nyköping, *Sweden* 11 F11
Nykvarn, *Sweden* 10 E11
Nyland, *Sweden* 10 A11
Nylstroom, *S. Africa* 85 C4
Nymagee, *Australia* 91 E4
Nymburk, *Czech.* 20 E5
Nynäshamn, *Sweden* . . . 10 F11
Nyngan, *Australia* 91 E4
Nyoman = Neman →,
   Lithuania 9 J19
Nyon, *Switz.* 22 D2
Nyong →, *Cameroon* . . . 79 E6
Nyons, *France* 27 D9
Nyord, *Denmark* 11 J6
Nyou, *Burkina Faso* 79 C4
Nysa, *Poland* 20 E7
Nysa →, *Europe* 18 C10
Nyssa, *U.S.A.* 110 E5
Nysted, *Denmark* 11 K5
Nyunzu, *Zaïre* 82 D2
Nyurbe, *Russia* 45 C12
Nyzhnohirskyy, *Ukraine* . . 41 K8
Nzega, *Tanzania* 82 C3
Nzega □, *Tanzania* 82 C3
N'Zérékoré, *Guinea* 78 D3
Nzeto, *Angola* 80 F2
Nzilo, Chutes de, *Zaïre* . . 83 E2
Nzubuka, *Tanzania* 82 C3

O

Ō-Shima, *Nagasaki, Japan* . 49 G4
Ō-Shima, *Shizuoka, Japan* . 49 G9
Oacoma, *U.S.A.* 108 D5
Oahe, L., *U.S.A.* 108 C4
Oahe Dam, *U.S.A.* 108 C4
Oahu, *U.S.A.* 102 H16
Oak Creek, *U.S.A.* 110 F10
Oak Harbor, *U.S.A.* 112 B4
Oak Hill, *U.S.A.* 104 G5
Oak Park, *U.S.A.* 104 E2
Oak Ridge, *U.S.A.* 105 G3
Oak View, *U.S.A.* 113 L7
Oakan-Dake, *Japan* 48 C12
Oakbank, *Australia* 91 E3
Oakdale, *Calif., U.S.A.* . . 111 H3
Oakdale, *La., U.S.A.* 109 K8
Oakengates, *U.K.* 12 E5
Oakes, *U.S.A.* 108 B5
Oakesdale, *U.S.A.* 110 C5
Oakey, *Australia* 91 D5
Oakham, *U.K.* 12 E7
Oakhurst, *U.S.A.* 112 H7
Oakland, *Calif., U.S.A.* . . 111 H2
Oakland, *Oreg., U.S.A.* . . 110 E2
Oakland City, *U.S.A.* . . . 104 F2
Oakley, *Idaho, U.S.A.* . . . 110 E7
Oakley, *Kans., U.S.A.* . . . 108 F4
Oakover →, *Australia* . . . 88 D3
Oakridge, *U.S.A.* 110 E2
Oakville, *U.S.A.* 112 D3
Oamaru, *N.Z.* 87 L3
Oasis, *Calif., U.S.A.* 113 M10
Oasis, *Nev., U.S.A.* 112 H9
Oates Land, *Antarctica* . . 5 C11
Oatman, *U.S.A.* 113 K12
Oaxaca, *Mexico* 115 D5
Oaxaca □, *Mexico* 115 D5
Ob →, *Russia* 44 C7
Oba, *Canada* 98 C3
Obala, *Cameroon* 79 E7
Obama, *Japan* 49 G7
Oban, *U.K.* 14 E3
Obbia, *Somali Rep.* 68 F4
Obdam, *Neths.* 16 C5
Obed, *Canada* 100 C5
Ober-Aagau, *Switz.* 22 B5
Obera, *Argentina* 127 B4
Oberalppass, *Switz.* 23 C7
Oberalpstock, *Switz.* 23 C7
Oberammergau, *Germany* . 19 H7
Oberdrauburg, *Austria* . . 21 J2
Oberengadin, *Switz.* 23 C9
Oberentfelden, *Switz.* . . . 22 B6
Oberhausen, *Germany* . . 18 D2
Oberkirch, *Germany* 19 G4
Oberland, *Switz.* 22 C5
Oberlin, *Kans., U.S.A.* . . . 108 F4
Oberlin, *La., U.S.A.* 109 K8
Oberlin, *Ohio, U.S.A.* . . . 106 E2
Obernai, *France* 25 D14
Oberndorf, *Germany* 19 G4
Oberon, *Australia* 91 E4
Oberpfälzer Wald,
   Germany 19 F8
Obersiggenthal, *Switz.* . . . 23 B6
Oberstdorf, *Germany* . . . 19 H6
Oberwil, *Switz.* 22 A5
Obi, Kepulauan, *Indonesia* 57 E7
Obi Is. = Obi, Kepulauan,
   Indonesia 57 E7
Obiaruku, *Nigeria* 79 D6
Óbidos, *Brazil* 121 D6
Óbidos, *Portugal* 31 F1
Obihiro, *Japan* 48 C11
Obilatu, *Indonesia* 57 E7
Obilnoye, *Russia* 43 G7
Obing, *Germany* 19 H8
Öbisfelde, *Germany* 18 C6
Objat, *France* 26 C5

Obluchye, *Russia* 45 E14
Obninsk, *Russia* 42 C3
Obo, *C.A.R.* 82 A2
Obo, *Ethiopia* 77 G4
Oboa, Mt., *Uganda* 82 B3
Obock, *Djibouti* 77 E5
Oborniki, *Poland* 20 C6
Oboyan, *Russia* 42 E3
Obozerskaya =
   Obozerskiy, *Russia* . . . 44 C5
Obozerskiy, *Russia* 44 C5
Obrovac, *Croatia* 33 D12
Obruk, *Turkey* 66 C5
Observatory Inlet, *Canada* 100 B3
Obshchi Syrt, *Russia* . . . 6 D16
Obskaya Guba, *Russia* . . . 44 C8
Obuasi, *Ghana* 79 D4
Obubra, *Nigeria* 79 D6
Obwalden □, *Switz.* 22 C6
Obzor, *Bulgaria* 38 G10
Ocala, *U.S.A.* 105 L4
Ocamo →, *Venezuela* . . . 121 C4
Ocampo, *Mexico* 114 B3
Ocaña, *Colombia* 120 B3
Ocaña, *Spain* 28 F1
Ocanomowoc, *U.S.A.* . . . 108 D10
Ocate, *U.S.A.* 109 G2
Occidental, Cordillera,
   Colombia 120 C3
Occidental, Cordillera,
   Peru 124 C3
Ocean City, *N.J., U.S.A.* . 104 F8
Ocean City, *Wash., U.S.A.* 112 C2
Ocean I. = Banaba,
   Kiribati 92 H8
Ocean Park, *U.S.A.* 112 D2
Oceano, *U.S.A.* 113 K6
Oceanport, *U.S.A.* 107 F10
Oceanside, *U.S.A.* 113 M9
Ochagavia, *Spain* 28 C3
Ochakiv, *Ukraine* 41 J6
Ochamchira, *Georgia* . . . 43 J5
Ochamps, *Belgium* 17 J6
Ochil Hills, *U.K.* 14 E5
Ochre River, *Canada* . . . 101 C9
Ochsenfurt, *Germany* . . . 19 F6
Ochsenhausen, *Germany* . 19 G5
Ocilla, *U.S.A.* 105 K4
Ocmulgee →, *U.S.A.* . . . 105 K4
Ocna Sibiului, *Romania* . . 38 D7
Ocniţa, *Moldova* 41 H4
Ocoña, *Peru* 124 D3
Ocoña →, *Peru* 124 D3
Oconee →, *U.S.A.* 105 K4
Oconto, *U.S.A.* 104 C2
Oconto Falls, *U.S.A.* 104 C1
Ocosingo, *Mexico* 115 D6
Ocotal, *Nic.* 116 D2
Ocotlán, *Mexico* 114 C4
Ocquier, *Belgium* 17 H6
Ocreza →, *Portugal* 31 F3
Octave, *U.S.A.* 111 J7
Octeville, *France* 24 C5
Ocumare del Tuy,
   Venezuela 120 A4
Ocuri, *Bolivia* 125 D4
Oda, *Ghana* 79 D4
Ōda, *Japan* 49 G6
Oda, J., *Sudan* 76 C4
Óðáðahraun, *Iceland* 8 D5
Öðåkra, *Sweden* 11 H6
Odate, *Japan* 48 D10
Odawara, *Japan* 49 G9
Odda, *Norway* 9 F12
Odder, *Denmark* 11 J4
Oddur, *Somali Rep.* 68 G3
Ödeborg, *Sweden* 11 F5
Odei →, *Canada* 101 B9
Odemira, *Portugal* 31 H2
Ödemiş, *Turkey* 66 C3
Odendaalsrus, *S. Africa* . . 84 D4
Odense, *Denmark* 11 J4
Odenwald, *Germany* 19 F5
Oder →, *Germany* 18 B10
Oderzo, *Italy* 33 C9
Odesa, *Ukraine* 41 J6
Odessa = Odesa, *Ukraine* 41 J6
Odessa, *Canada* 107 B8
Odessa, *Tex., U.S.A.* . . . 109 K3
Odessa, *Wash., U.S.A.* . . 110 C4
Odiakwe, *Botswana* 84 C4
Odiel →, *Spain* 31 H4
Odienné, *Ivory C.* 78 D3
Odintsovo, *Russia* 42 C3
Odiongan, *Phil.* 55 E4
Odobeşti, *Romania* 38 D10
O'Donnell, *U.S.A.* 109 J4
Odoorn, *Neths.* 16 C9
Odorheiu Secuiesc,
   Romania 38 C8
Odoyevo, *Russia* 42 D3
Odra = Oder →, *Germany* 18 B10
Odra →, *Poland* 20 B4
Odra →, *Spain* 30 C6
Odžaci, *Serbia, Yug.* . . . 21 K9
Odzi, *Zimbabwe* 85 B5
Oedelem, *Belgium* 17 F2
Oegstgeest, *Neths.* 16 D4
Oeiras, *Brazil* 122 C3
Oeiras, *Portugal* 31 G1
Oelrichs, *U.S.A.* 108 D3
Oelsnitz, *Germany* 18 E8
Oelwein, *U.S.A.* 108 D9
Oenpelli, *Australia* 88 B5
Of, *Turkey* 67 B9
Ofanto →, *Italy* 35 A9
Offa, *Nigeria* 79 D5

Offaly □, Ireland 15 C4
Offenbach, Germany ... 19 E4
Offenburg, Germany ... 19 G3
Offerdal, Sweden 10 A8
Offida, Italy 33 F10
Offranville, France ... 24 C8
Ofidhousa, Greece 39 N9
Ofotfjorden, Norway 8 B17
Ōfunato, Japan 48 E10
Oga, Japan 48 E9
Oga-Hantō, Japan 48 E9
Ogahalla, Canada 98 B2
Ōgaki, Japan 49 G8
Ogallala, U.S.A. 108 E4
Ogasawara Gunto,
  Pac. Oc. 92 E6
Ogbomosho, Nigeria ... 79 D5
Ogden, Iowa, U.S.A. ... 108 D8
Ogden, Utah, U.S.A. 110 F7
Ogdensburg, U.S.A. 107 B9
Ogeechee →, U.S.A. ... 105 K5
Ogilby, U.S.A. 113 N12
Oglio →, Italy 32 C7
Ogmore, Australia 90 C4
Ognon →, France 25 E12
Ogoja, Nigeria 79 D6
Ogoki →, Canada 98 B2
Ogoki L., Canada 98 B2
Ogoki Res., Canada 98 B2
Ogooué →, Gabon 80 E1
Ogosta →, Bulgaria .. 38 F6
Ogowe = Ogooué →,
  Gabon 80 E1
Ogr = Sharafa, Sudan .. 77 E2
Ogre, Latvia 9 H21
Ogrein, Sudan 76 D3
Ogulin, Croatia 33 C12
Ogun □, Nigeria 79 D5
Oguta, Nigeria 79 D6
Ogwashi-Uku, Nigeria .. 79 D6
Ogwe, Nigeria 79 E6
Ohai, N.Z. 87 L2
Ohakune, N.Z. 87 H5
Ohanet, Algeria 75 C6
Ohata, Japan 48 D10
Ohau, L., N.Z. 87 L2
Ohey, Belgium 17 H6
Ohio □, U.S.A. 104 E3
Ohio →, U.S.A. 104 G1
Ohre →, Czech. 20 E4
Ohře →, Germany 18 C7
Ohrid, Macedonia 39 H3
Ohridsko Jezero,
  Macedonia 39 H3
Ohrigstad, S. Africa ... 85 C5
Öhringen, Germany 19 F5
Oiapoque →, Brazil ... 121 C7
Oikou, China 51 E9
Oil City, U.S.A. 106 E5
Oildale, U.S.A. 113 K7
Oirschot, Neths. 17 E6
Oise □, France 25 C9
Oise →, France 25 D9
Oisterwijk, Neths. 17 E6
Ōita, Japan 49 H5
Ōita □, Japan 49 H5
Oiticica, Brazil 122 C3
Ojai, U.S.A. 113 L7
Ojinaga, Mexico 114 B4
Ojiya, Japan 49 F9
Ojos del Salado, Cerro,
  Argentina 126 B2
Oka →, Russia 42 B7
Okaba, Indonesia 57 F9
Okahandja, Namibia ... 84 C2
Okahukura, N.Z. 87 H5
Okanagan L., Canada .. 100 C5
Okandja, Gabon 80 E2
Okanogan, U.S.A. 110 B4
Okanogan →, U.S.A. .. 110 B4
Okaputa, Namibia 84 C2
Okara, Pakistan 62 D5
Okarito, N.Z. 87 K3
Okaukuejo, Namibia ... 84 B2
Okavango Swamps,
  Botswana 84 B3
Okaya, Japan 49 F9
Okayama, Japan 49 G6
Okayama □, Japan 49 G6
Okazaki, Japan 49 G8
Oke-Iho, Nigeria 79 D5
Okeechobee, U.S.A. ... 105 M5
Okeechobee, L., U.S.A. .. 105 M5
Okefenokee Swamp,
  U.S.A. 105 K4
Okehampton, U.K. 13 G3
Okene, Nigeria 79 D6
Oker →, Germany 18 C6
Okha, Russia 45 D15
Ōkhi Óros, Greece 39 L7
Okhotsk, Russia 45 D15
Okhotsk, Sea of, Asia .. 45 D15
Okhotskiy Perevoz, Russia 45 C14
Okhtyrka, Ukraine 41 G8
Oki-Shotō, Japan 49 F6
Okiep, S. Africa 84 D2
Okigwi, Nigeria 79 D6
Okija, Nigeria 79 D6
Okinawa □, Japan 49 L3
Okinawa-Guntō, Japan .. 49 L3
Okinawa-Jima, Japan .. 49 L4
Okino-erabu-Shima, Japan 49 L4
Okitipupa, Nigeria 79 D5
Oklahoma □, U.S.A. ... 109 H6
Oklahoma City, U.S.A. .. 109 H6
Okmulgee, U.S.A. 109 H7
Oknitsa = Ocniţa, Moldova 41 H4

Okolo, Uganda 82 B3
Okolona, U.S.A. 109 H10
Okrika, Nigeria 79 E6
Oktabrsk = Oktyabrsk,
  Kazakhstan 44 E6
Oktyabrsk, Kazakhstan ... 44 E6
Oktyabrsk, Russia 42 D9
Oktyabrskiy = Aktsyabrski,
  Belarus 41 F5
Oktyabrskiy, Russia ... 43 G5
Oktyabrskoy Revolyutsii,
  Os., Russia 45 B10
Oktyabrskoye =
  Zhovtneve, Ukraine ... 41 J7
Oktyabrskoye, Russia .. 44 C7
Okulovka, Russia 40 C7
Okuru, N.Z. 87 K2
Okushiri-Tō, Japan 48 C9
Okuta, Nigeria 79 D5
Okwa →, Botswana ... 84 C3
Ola, U.S.A. 109 H8
Ólafsfjörður, Iceland ... 8 C4
Ólafsvík, Iceland 8 D2
Olancha, U.S.A. 113 J8
Olancha Pk., U.S.A. ... 113 J8
Olanchito, Honduras ... 116 C2
Öland, Sweden 9 H17
Olargues, France 26 E6
Olary, Australia 91 E3
Olascoaga, Argentina .. 126 D3
Olathe, U.S.A. 108 F7
Olavarría, Argentina .. 126 D3
Oława, Poland 20 E7
Ólbia, Italy 34 B2
Ólbia, G. di, Italy 34 B2
Old Bahama Chan. =
  Bahama, Canal Viejo de,
  W. Indies 116 B4
Old Baldy Pk. = San
  Antonio, Mt., U.S.A. .. 113 L9
Old Cork, Australia ... 90 C3
Old Crow, Canada 96 B6
Old Dale, U.S.A. 113 L11
Old Dongola, Sudan ... 76 D3
Old Fletton, U.K. 13 E7
Old Forge, N.Y., U.S.A. . 107 C10
Old Forge, Pa., U.S.A. .. 107 E9
Old Fort →, Canada .. 101 B6
Old Shinyanga, Tanzania 82 C3
Old Speck Mt., U.S.A. .. 107 B14
Old Town, U.S.A. 99 D6
Old Wives L., Canada .. 101 C7
Oldbury, U.K. 13 F5
Oldcastle, Ireland 15 C4
Oldeani, Tanzania 82 C4
Oldenburg, Niedersachsen,
  Germany 18 B4
Oldenburg,
  Schleswig-Holstein,
  Germany 18 A6
Oldenzaal, Neths. 16 D9
Oldham, U.K. 12 D5
Oldman →, Canada ... 100 D6
Olds, Canada 100 C6
Olean, U.S.A. 106 D6
Oléggio, Italy 32 C5
Oleiros, Portugal 30 F3
Olekma →, Russia 45 C13
Olekminsk, Russia 45 C13
Oleksandriya, Ukraine .. 41 H7
Oleksandriya, Ukraine .. 41 G4
Oleksandrovka, Ukraine .. 41 H7
Olema, U.S.A. 112 G4
Olen, Belgium 17 F5
Olenek, Russia 45 C12
Olenek →, Russia 45 B13
Olenino, Russia 42 B1
Olevsk, Ukraine 41 G4
Olga, Russia 45 E14
Olga, L., Canada 98 C4
Olga, Mt., Australia ... 89 E5
Ølgod, Denmark 11 J2
Olhão, Portugal 31 H3
Olib, Croatia 33 D11
Oliena, Italy 34 B2
Oliete, Spain 28 D4
Olifants →, Africa 85 C5
Olifantshoek, S. Africa .. 84 D3
Ólimbos, Greece 39 P10
Ólimbos, Óros, Greece .. 39 J5
Olímpia, Brazil 127 A6
Olinda, Brazil 122 C5
Olindiná, Brazil 122 D4
Olite, Spain 28 C3
Oliva, Argentina 126 C3
Oliva, Spain 29 G4
Oliva, Punta del, Spain .. 30 B5
Oliva de la Frontera, Spain 31 G4
Olivares, Spain 28 F2
Olivehurst, U.S.A. 112 F5
Oliveira, Brazil 123 F3
Oliveira de Azemeis,
  Portugal 30 E2
Oliveira dos Brejinhos,
  Brazil 123 D3
Olivenza, Spain 31 G3
Oliver, Canada 100 D5
Oliver L., Canada 101 B8
Olivone, Switz. 23 C7
Olkhovka, Russia 42 F7
Olkusz, Poland 20 E9
Ollagüe, Chile 126 A2
Olloy, Belgium 17 H5
Olmedo, Spain 30 D6

Olmos, Peru 124 B2
Olney, Ill., U.S.A. 104 F1
Olney, Tex., U.S.A. ... 109 J5
Oloma, Cameroon 79 E7
Olomane →, Canada .. 99 B7
Olomouc, Czech. 20 F7
Olonets, Russia 40 B7
Olongapo, Phil. 55 D4
Oloron, Gave d' →,
  France 26 E2
Oloron-Ste.-Marie, France 26 E3
Olot, Spain 28 C7
Olovo, Bos.-H. 21 L8
Olovyannaya, Russia .. 45 D12
Oloy →, Russia 45 C16
Olpe, Germany 18 D3
Olshanka, Ukraine 41 H6
Olshany, Ukraine 41 G8
Olst, Neths. 16 D8
Olsztyn, Poland 20 B10
Olt □, Romania 38 F7
Olt →, Romania 38 F7
Olten, Switz. 22 B5
Olteniţa, Romania 38 E9
Olton, U.S.A. 109 H3
Oltu, Turkey 67 B9
Olur, Turkey 67 B10
Olutanga, Phil. 55 H5
Olvega, Spain 28 D3
Olvera, Spain 31 J5
Olymbos, Cyprus 37 D12
Olympia, Greece 39 M4
Olympia, U.S.A. 112 D4
Olympic Mts., U.S.A. .. 112 C3
Olympic Nat. Park, U.S.A. 112 C3
Olympus, Cyprus 66 E5
Olympus, Mt. = Ólimbos,
  Óros, Greece 39 J5
Olympus, Mt., U.S.A. .. 112 C3
Olyphant, U.S.A. 107 E9
Om →, Russia 44 D8
Om Hajer, Eritrea ... 77 E4
Om Koi, Thailand 58 D2
Ōma, Japan 48 D10
Ōmachi, Japan 49 F8
Omae-Zaki, Japan 49 G9
Ōmagari, Japan 48 E10
Omagh, U.K. 15 B4
Omagh □, U.K. 15 B4
Omaha, U.S.A. 108 E7
Omak, U.S.A. 110 B4
Omalos, Greece 37 D5
Oman ■, Asia 68 C6
Oman, G. of, Asia 65 E8
Omaruru, Namibia ... 84 C2
Omaruru →, Namibia .. 84 C1
Omate, Peru 124 D3
Ombai, Selat, Indonesia .. 57 F6
Omboué, Gabon 80 E1
Ombrone →, Italy ... 32 F8
Omdurmân, Sudan ... 77 D3
Omega, Italy 32 C5
Omeonga, Zaïre 82 C1
Ometepe, I. de, Nic. ... 116 D2
Ometepec, Mexico ... 115 D5
Ominato, Japan 48 D10
Omineca →, Canada .. 100 B4
Omiš, Croatia 33 E13
Omišalj, Croatia 33 C11
Omitara, Namibia 84 C2
Ōmiya, Japan 49 G9
Ommen, Neths. 16 C8
Omme Å →, Denmark .. 11 J2
Ōmnōgovĭ □, Mongolia .. 50 C3
Omo →, Ethiopia 77 F4
Omodhos, Cyprus 37 E11
Omolon →, Russia ... 45 C16
Omono-Gawa →, Japan .. 48 E10
Omsk, Russia 44 D8
Omsukchan, Russia ... 45 C16
Ōmu, Japan 48 B11
Omul, Vf., Romania ... 38 D8
Ōmura, Japan 49 H4
Omuramba Omatako →,
  Namibia 81 H4
Ōmurtag, Bulgaria ... 38 F9
Ōmuta, Japan 49 H5
On, Belgium 17 H6
Ōnaga, U.S.A. 108 F6
Onalaska, U.S.A. 108 D9
Onamia, U.S.A. 108 B8
Onancock, U.S.A. 104 G8
Onang, Indonesia 57 E5
Onaping L., Canada ... 98 C3
Oñate, Spain 28 B2
Onavas, Mexico 114 B3
Onawa, U.S.A. 108 D6
Onaway, U.S.A. 104 C3
Oncócua, Angola 84 B1
Onda, Spain 28 F4
Ondangua, Namibia .. 84 B2
Ondárroa, Spain 28 B2
Ondas →, Brazil 123 D3
Ondava →, Slovak Rep. .. 20 G11
Onderdijk, Neths. 16 C6
Ondjiva, Angola 84 B2
Ondo, Nigeria 79 D5
Ondo □, Nigeria 79 D6
Öndörhaan, Mongolia .. 54 B6
Öndörshil, Mongolia .. 50 B5
Öndverðarnes, Iceland .. 8 D1
Onega, Russia 44 C4
Onega →, Russia 6 C13
Onega, G. of =
  Onezhskaya Guba,
  Russia 44 C4

Onega, L. = Onezhskoye
  Ozero, Russia 40 B8
Onehunga, N.Z. 87 G5
Oneida, U.S.A. 107 C9
Oneida L., U.S.A. 107 C9
O'Neill, U.S.A. 108 D5
Onekotan, Ostrov, Russia .. 45 E16
Onema, Zaïre 82 C1
Oneonta, Ala., U.S.A. .. 105 J2
Oneonta, N.Y., U.S.A. .. 107 D9
Oneşti, Romania 38 C9
Onezhskaya Guba, Russia .. 44 C4
Onezhskoye Ozero, Russia .. 40 B8
Ongarue, N.Z. 87 H5
Ongerup, Australia ... 89 F2
Ongjin, N. Korea 51 F13
Ongkharak, Thailand .. 58 E3
Ongniud Qi, China ... 51 C10
Ongoka, Zaïre 82 C2
Ongole, India 60 M12
Ongon, Mongolia 50 B7
Onguren, Russia 45 D11
Onhaye, Belgium 17 H5
Oni, Georgia 43 J6
Onida, U.S.A. 108 C4
Onilahy →, Madag. .. 85 C7
Onitsha, Nigeria 79 D6
Onoda, Japan 49 G5
Onpyŏng-ni, S. Korea .. 51 H14
Ons, Is. d', Spain 30 C2
Onsala, Sweden 11 G6
Onslow, Australia 88 D2
Onslow B., U.S.A. 105 H7
Onstwedde, Neths. ... 16 B10
Ontake-San, Japan ... 49 G8
Ontaneda, Spain 30 B7
Ontario, Calif., U.S.A. .. 113 L9
Ontario, Oreg., U.S.A. .. 110 D5
Ontario □, Canada ... 98 B2
Ontario, L., N. Amer. .. 98 D4
Onteniente, Spain ... 29 G4
Ontonagon, U.S.A. ... 108 B10
Ontur, Spain 29 G3
Onyx, U.S.A. 113 K8
Oodnadatta, Australia .. 91 D2
Ooldea, Australia 89 F5
Ooltgensplaat, Neths. .. 17 E4
Oona River, Canada .. 100 C2
Oorindi, Australia ... 90 C3
Oost-Vlaanderen □,
  Belgium 17 F3
Oost-Vlieland, Neths. .. 16 B6
Oostakker, Belgium ... 17 F3
Oostburg, Neths. 17 F3
Oostduinkerke, Belgium .. 17 F1
Oostende, Belgium ... 17 F1
Oosterbeek, Neths. ... 16 E7
Oosterdijk, Neths. ... 16 C6
Oosterend, Friesland,
  Neths. 16 B6
Oosterend, Noord-Holland,
  Neths. 16 B5
Oosterhout, Neths. ... 17 E5
Oosterschelde, Neths. .. 17 E4
Oosterwolde, Neths. .. 16 B8
Oosterzele, Belgium .. 17 G3
Oostkamp, Belgium ... 17 F2
Oostmalle, Belgium .. 17 F5
Oostrozebeke, Belgium .. 17 G2
Oostvleteven, Belgium .. 17 G1
Oostvoorne, Neths. ... 16 E4
Oostzaan, Neths. 16 D5
Ootacamund, India ... 60 P10
Ootmarsum, Neths. .. 16 D9
Ootsa L., Canada 100 C3
Opala, Russia 45 D16
Opala, Zaïre 82 C1
Opanake, Sri Lanka ... 60 R12
Opasatika, Canada ... 98 C3
Opasquia, Canada 101 C10
Opatija, Croatia 33 C11
Opava, Czech. 20 F7
Opeinde, Neths. 16 B8
Opelousas, U.S.A. 109 K8
Opémisca, L., Canada .. 98 C5
Opglabbeek, Belgium .. 17 F7
Opheim, U.S.A. 110 B10
Ophthalmia Ra., Australia .. 88 D2
Opi, Nigeria 79 D6
Opinaca →, Canada .. 98 B4
Opinaca L., Canada ... 98 B4
Opiskotish, L., Canada .. 99 B6
Ploo, Neths. 17 E7
Opmeer, Neths. 16 C5
Opobo, Nigeria 79 E6
Opochka, Russia 40 D5
Opoczno, Poland 20 D10
Opol, Phil. 55 G6
Opole, Poland 20 E7
Oporto = Porto, Portugal .. 30 D2
Opotiki, N.Z. 87 H6
Opp, U.S.A. 105 K2
Oppdal, Norway 9 E13
Oppenheim, Germany .. 19 F4
Opperdoes, Neths. ... 16 C6
Óppido Mamertina, Italy .. 35 D8
Oppland fylke □, Norway .. 10 C3
Oppstad, Norway 10 D5
Oprtalj, Croatia 33 C10
Opua, N.Z. 87 F5
Opunake, N.Z. 87 H4
Opuzen, Croatia 21 M7
Ora, Cyprus 37 E12
Ora, Italy 33 B8

Ora Banda, Australia .. 89 F3
Oracle, U.S.A. 111 K8
Oradea, Romania 38 B4
Öræfajökull, Iceland .. 8 D5
Orahovac, Serbia, Yug. .. 21 N10
Orai, India 63 G8
Oraison, France 27 E9
Oral = Zhayyq →,
  Kazakhstan 44 E6
Oral, Kazakhstan 42 E10
Oran, Algeria 75 A4
Oran, Argentina 126 A3
Orange = Oranje →,
  S. Africa 84 D2
Orange, Australia 91 E4
Orange, France 27 D8
Orange, Calif., U.S.A. .. 113 M9
Orange, Mass., U.S.A. .. 107 D12
Orange, Tex., U.S.A. .. 109 K8
Orange, Va., U.S.A. .. 104 F6
Orange, C., Brazil ... 121 C7
Orange Cove, U.S.A. .. 112 J7
Orange Free State □,
  S. Africa 84 D4
Orange Grove, U.S.A. .. 109 M6
Orange Walk, Belize ... 115 D7
Orangeburg, U.S.A. ... 105 J5
Orangeville, Canada .. 98 D3
Orani, Phil. 55 D4
Oranienburg, Germany .. 18 C9
Oranje →, S. Africa .. 84 D2
Oranje Vrystaat = Orange
  Free State □, S. Africa .. 84 D4
Oranjemund, Namibia .. 84 D2
Oranjerivier, S. Africa .. 84 D3
Oras, Phil. 55 E6
Orăştie, Romania 38 D6
Orava →, Slovak Rep. .. 20 F9
Oravita, Romania 38 D4
Orb →, France 26 E7
Orba →, Italy 32 D5
Ørbæk, Denmark 11 J4
Orbe, Switz. 22 C3
Orbec, France 24 C7
Orbetello, Italy 33 F8
Órbigo →, Spain 30 C5
Orbost, Australia 91 F4
Orce, Spain 29 H2
Orce →, Spain 29 H2
Orchies, France 25 B10
Orchila, I., Venezuela .. 120 A4
Orco →, Italy 32 C4
Orcopampa, Peru 124 D3
Orcutt, U.S.A. 113 L6
Ord →, Australia 88 C4
Ord, Mt., Australia ... 88 C4
Ordenes, Spain 30 B2
Orderville, U.S.A. 111 H7
Ording = St-Peter-Ording,
  Germany 18 A4
Ordos = Mu Us Shamo,
  China 50 E5
Ordu, Turkey 66 B7
Ordubad, Azerbaijan .. 67 C12
Orduña, Álava, Spain .. 28 C7
Orduña, Granada, Spain .. 29 H1
Ordway, U.S.A. 108 F3
Ordzhonikidze =
  Vladikavkaz, Russia .. 43 J7
Ordzhonikidze, Ukraine .. 41 J8
Ore, Zaïre 82 B2
Ore Mts. = Erzgebirge,
  Germany 18 E9
Orealla, Guyana 121 B6
Orebić, Croatia 21 M7
Örebro, Sweden 9 G16
Oregon, U.S.A. 108 D10
Oregon □, U.S.A. 110 E3
Oregon City, U.S.A. .. 112 E4
Orekhov = Orikhiv,
  Ukraine 41 J8
Orekhovo-Zuyevo, Russia .. 42 C4
Orel, Russia 42 D3
Orel →, Ukraine 41 H8
Orellana, Canal de, Spain .. 31 F5
Orellana, Pantano de,
  Spain 31 F5
Orellana la Vieja, Spain .. 31 F5
Orem, U.S.A. 110 F8
Ören, Turkey 66 D2
Orenburg, Russia 44 D6
Orense, Spain 30 C3
Orense □, Spain 30 C3
Orepuki, N.Z. 87 M1
Orestiás, Greece 39 H9
Øresund, Europe 11 J6
Orford Ness, U.K. 13 E9
Organá, Spain 28 C6
Organos, Pta. de los,
  Canary Is. 36 F2
Orgaz, Spain 31 F7
Orgeyev = Orhei, Moldova 41 J5
Orgon, France 27 E9
Orhaneli, Turkey 66 C3
Orhangazi, Turkey ... 66 B3
Orhei, Moldova 41 J5
Orhon Gol →, Mongolia .. 54 A5
Ória, Italy 35 B10
Orient, Australia 91 D3
Oriental, Cordillera,
  Bolivia 125 D4
Oriental, Cordillera,
  Colombia 120 B3
Oriente, Argentina ... 126 D3
Origny-Ste.-Benoîte, France 25 C10

Orihuela, *Spain*	29	G4
Orihuela del Tremedal, *Spain*	28	E3
Orikhiv, *Ukraine*	41	J8
Oriku, *Albania*	39	J2
Orinduik, *Guyana*	121	C5
Orinoco →, *Venezuela*	121	B5
Orissa □, *India*	61	K14
Orissaare, *Estonia*	9	G20
Oristano, *Italy*	34	C1
Oristano, G. di, *Italy*	34	C1
Orituco →, *Venezuela*	120	B4
Orizaba, *Mexico*	115	D5
Orizona, *Brazil*	123	E2
Orjen, *Bos.-H.*	21	N8
Orjiva, *Spain*	29	J1
Orkanger, *Norway*	10	A3
Örkelljunga, *Sweden*	11	H7
Örkény, *Hungary*	21	H9
Orkla →, *Norway*	10	A3
Orkney, *S. Africa*	84	D4
Orkney □, *U.K.*	14	C6
Orkney Is., *U.K.*	14	C6
Orland, *U.S.A.*	112	F4
Orlando, *U.S.A.*	105	L5
Orlando, C. d', *Italy*	35	D7
Orléanais, *France*	25	E9
Orléans, *France*	25	E8
Orleans, *U.S.A.*	107	B12
Orléans, I. d', *Canada*	99	C5
Orlice →, *Czech.*	20	E6
Orlov, *Slovak Rep.*	20	F10
Orlov Gay, *Russia*	42	E9
Ormara, *Pakistan*	60	G4
Ormea, *Italy*	32	D4
Ormília, *Greece*	39	J6
Ormoc, *Phil.*	55	F6
Ormond, *N.Z.*	87	H6
Ormond Beach, *U.S.A.*	105	L5
Ormož, *Slovenia*	33	B13
Ormstown, *Canada*	107	A11
Ornans, *France*	25	E13
Orne □, *France*	24	D7
Orne →, *France*	24	C6
Ørnhøj, *Denmark*	11	H2
Örnö, *Sweden*	10	E12
Örnsköldsvik, *Sweden*	10	A12
Oro, *N. Korea*	51	D14
Oro →, *Mexico*	114	B3
Oro Grande, *U.S.A.*	113	L9
Orobie, Alpi, *Italy*	32	B6
Orocué, *Colombia*	120	C3
Orodo, *Nigeria*	79	D6
Orogrande, *U.S.A.*	111	K10
Orol, *Spain*	30	B3
Orol Dengizi = Aral Sea , *Asia*	44	E7
Oromocto, *Canada*	99	C6
Oron, *Nigeria*	79	E6
Oron, *Switz.*	22	C3
Orono, *Canada*	106	C6
Oropesa, *Spain*	30	F5
Oroquieta, *Phil.*	55	G5
Orós, *Brazil*	122	C4
Orosei, G. di, *Italy*	34	B2
Orosháza, *Hungary*	21	J10
Orotukan, *Russia*	45	C16
Oroville, *Calif., U.S.A.*	112	F5
Oroville, *Wash., U.S.A.*	110	B4
Oroville, L., *U.S.A.*	112	F5
Orroroo, *Australia*	91	E2
Orrville, *U.S.A.*	106	F3
Orsara di Púglia, *Italy*	35	A8
Orsha, *Belarus*	40	E6
Orsières, *Switz.*	22	D4
Orsk, *Russia*	44	D6
Ørslev, *Denmark*	11	J5
Orsogna, *Italy*	33	F11
Orşova, *Romania*	38	E4
Ørsted, *Denmark*	11	H4
Orta, L. d', *Italy*	32	C5
Orta Nova, *Italy*	35	A8
Ortaca, *Turkey*	66	D3
Ortaköy, *Çorum, Turkey*	66	B6
Ortaköy, *Niğde, Turkey*	66	C6
Orte, *Italy*	33	F9
Ortegal, C., *Spain*	30	B3
Orteguaza →, *Colombia*	120	C2
Orthez, *France*	26	E3
Ortho, *Belgium*	17	H7
Ortigueira, *Spain*	30	B3
Orting, *U.S.A.*	112	C4
Ortles, *Italy*	32	B7
Ortón →, *Bolivia*	124	C4
Ortona, *Italy*	33	F11
Orūmīyeh, *Iran*	67	D11
Orūmīyeh, Daryācheh-ye, *Iran*	67	D11
Orune, *Italy*	34	B2
Oruro, *Bolivia*	124	D4
Oruro □, *Bolivia*	124	D4
Orust, *Sweden*	11	F5
Oruzgān □, *Afghan.*	60	C5
Orvault, *France*	24	E5
Orvieto, *Italy*	33	F9
Orwell, *U.S.A.*	106	E4
Orwell →, *U.K.*	13	E9
Oryakhovo, *Bulgaria*	38	F6
Orzinuovi, *Italy*	32	C6
Orzysz, *Poland*	20	B11
Osa, Pen. de, *Costa Rica*	116	E3
Osage, *Iowa, U.S.A.*	108	D8
Osage, *Wyo., U.S.A.*	108	D2
Osage →, *U.S.A.*	108	F9
Osage City, *U.S.A.*	108	F7
Ōsaka, *Japan*	49	G7
Osan, *S. Korea*	51	F14
Osawatomie, *U.S.A.*	108	F7
Osborne, *U.S.A.*	108	F5
Osceola, *Ark., U.S.A.*	109	H10
Osceola, *Iowa, U.S.A.*	108	E8
Oschatz, *Germany*	18	D9
Oschersleben, *Germany*	18	C7
Oschiri, *Italy*	34	B2
Oscoda, *U.S.A.*	106	B1
Ösel = Saaremaa, *Estonia*	9	G20
Osery, *Russia*	42	C4
Osh, *Kyrgyzstan*	44	E8
Oshawa, *Canada*	98	D4
Oshkosh, *Nebr., U.S.A.*	108	E3
Oshkosh, *Wis., U.S.A.*	108	C10
Oshmyany = Ashmyany, *Belarus*	9	J21
Oshnovīyeh, *Iran*	64	B5
Oshogbo, *Nigeria*	79	D5
Oshtorīnān, *Iran*	67	E13
Oshwe, *Zaïre*	80	E3
Osijek, *Croatia*	21	K8
Ósilo, *Italy*	34	B1
Ósimo, *Italy*	33	E10
Osintorf, *Belarus*	40	E6
Osipenko = Berdyansk, *Ukraine*	41	J9
Osipovichi = Asipovichy, *Belarus*	40	F5
Osizweni, *S. Africa*	85	D5
Oskaloosa, *U.S.A.*	108	E8
Oskarshamn, *Sweden*	9	H17
Oskélanéo, *Canada*	98	C4
Öskemen, *Kazakhstan*	44	E9
Oskol →, *Ukraine*	41	H9
Oslo, *Norway*	10	E4
Oslob, *Phil.*	55	G5
Oslofjorden, *Norway*	10	E4
Osmanabad, *India*	60	K10
Osmancık, *Turkey*	66	B6
Osmaniye, *Turkey*	66	D7
Ösmo, *Sweden*	10	F11
Osnabrück, *Germany*	18	C4
Osor, *Italy*	33	D11
Osório, *Brazil*	127	B5
Osorno, *Chile*	128	B2
Osorno, *Spain*	30	C6
Osorno □, *Chile*	128	B2
Osorno, Vol., *Chile*	128	B2
Osoyoos, *Canada*	100	D5
Osøyri, *Norway*	9	F11
Ospika →, *Canada*	100	B4
Osprey Reef, *Australia*	90	A4
Oss, *Neths.*	16	E7
Ossa, Mt., *Australia*	90	G4
Óssa, Oros, *Greece*	39	K5
Ossa de Montiel, *Spain*	29	G2
Ossabaw I., *U.S.A.*	105	K5
Osse →, *France*	26	D4
Ossendrecht, *Neths.*	17	F4
Ossining, *U.S.A.*	107	E11
Ossipee, *U.S.A.*	107	C13
Ossokmanuan L., *Canada*	99	B7
Ossora, *Russia*	45	D17
Ostashkov, *Russia*	42	B11
Oste →, *Germany*	18	B5
Ostend = Oostende, *Belgium*	17	F1
Oster, *Ukraine*	41	G6
Osterburg, *Germany*	18	C7
Osterburken, *Germany*	19	F5
Österdalälven, *Sweden*	9	F16
Østerdalen, *Norway*	9	F14
Östergötlands län □, *Sweden*	11	F9
Osterholz-Scharmbeck, *Germany*	18	B4
Østerild, *Denmark*	11	G2
Ostermundigen, *Switz.*	22	C4
Östersund, *Sweden*	10	A8
Østfold fylke □, *Norway*	10	E5
Ostfriesische Inseln, *Germany*	18	B3
Ostfriesland, *Germany*	18	B3
Óstia, Lido di, *Italy*	34	A5
Ostíglia, *Italy*	33	C8
Ostra, *Italy*	33	E10
Ostrava, *Czech.*	20	F8
Ostróda, *Poland*	20	B9
Ostrogozhsk, *Russia*	42	E4
Ostrogróg Szamotuly, *Poland*	20	C6
Ostroh, *Ukraine*	41	G4
Ostrołęka, *Poland*	20	B11
Ostrov, *Bulgaria*	38	F7
Ostrov, *Romania*	38	E10
Ostrov, *Russia*	40	D5
Ostrów Mazowiecka, *Poland*	20	C11
Ostrów Wielkopolski, *Poland*	20	D7
Ostrowiec-Świętokrzyski, *Poland*	20	E11
Ostrzeszów, *Poland*	20	D7
Ostseebad Kühlungsborn, *Germany*	18	A7
Osttirol □, *Austria*	19	J8
Ostuni, *Italy*	35	B10
Osum →, *Bulgaria*	38	F7
Osumi →, *Albania*	39	J3
Ōsumi-Kaikyō, *Japan*	49	J5
Ōsumi-Shotō, *Japan*	49	J5
Osun □, *Nigeria*	79	D5
Osuna, *Spain*	31	H5
Oswego, *U.S.A.*	107	C8
Oswestry, *U.K.*	12	E4
Oświęcim, *Poland*	20	E9
Otago □, *N.Z.*	87	L2
Otago Harbour, *N.Z.*	87	L3
Ōtake, *Japan*	49	G6
Otaki, *N.Z.*	87	J5
Otaru, *Japan*	48	C10
Otaru-Wan = Ishikari-Wan, *Japan*	48	C10
Otava →, *Czech.*	20	F4
Otavalo, *Ecuador*	120	C2
Otavi, *Namibia*	84	B2
Otchinjau, *Angola*	84	B1
Otelec, *Romania*	38	D3
Otero de Rey, *Spain*	30	B3
Othello, *U.S.A.*	110	C4
Othonoí, *Greece*	39	K2
Óthris, Óros, *Greece*	39	K5
Otira Gorge, *N.Z.*	87	K3
Otis, *U.S.A.*	108	E3
Otjiwarongo, *Namibia*	84	C2
Otočac, *Croatia*	33	D12
Otoineppu, *Japan*	48	B11
Otorohanga, *N.Z.*	87	H5
Otoskwin →, *Canada*	98	B2
Otosquen, *Canada*	101	C8
Otra →, *Norway*	9	G13
Otradnyy, *Russia*	42	D10
Otranto, *Italy*	35	B11
Otranto, C. d', *Italy*	35	B11
Otranto, Str. of, *Italy*	35	B11
Otse, *S. Africa*	84	D4
Ōtsu, *Japan*	49	G7
Ōtsuki, *Japan*	49	G9
Otta, *Norway*	10	C3
Ottawa = Outaouais →, *Canada*	98	C5
Ottawa, *Canada*	98	C4
Ottawa, *Ill., U.S.A.*	108	E10
Ottawa, *Kans., U.S.A.*	108	F7
Ottawa Is., *Canada*	97	C11
Ottélé, *Cameroon*	79	E7
Otter L., *Canada*	101	B8
Otter Rapids, *Ont., Canada*	98	B3
Otter Rapids, *Sask., Canada*	101	B8
Otterndorf, *Germany*	18	B4
Otterup, *Denmark*	11	J4
Otterville, *Canada*	106	D4
Ottignies, *Belgium*	17	G5
Otto Beit Bridge, *Zimbabwe*	83	F2
Ottosdal, *S. Africa*	84	D4
Ottsjön, *Sweden*	10	A7
Ottumwa, *U.S.A.*	108	E8
Otu, *Nigeria*	79	D5
Otukpa, *Nigeria*	79	D6
Oturkpo, *Nigeria*	79	D6
Otway, B., *Chile*	128	D2
Otway, C., *Australia*	91	F3
Otwock, *Poland*	20	C11
Ötz, *Austria*	19	H6
Ötz →, *Austria*	19	H6
Ötztaler Alpen, *Austria*	19	J7
Ou →, *Laos*	58	B4
Ou Neua, *Laos*	58	A3
Ou-Sammyaku, *Japan*	48	E10
Ouachita →, *U.S.A.*	109	K9
Ouachita, L., *U.S.A.*	109	H8
Ouachita Mts., *U.S.A.*	109	H7
Ouadâne, *Mauritania*	74	D2
Ouadda, *C.A.R.*	73	G9
Ouagadougou, *Burkina Faso*	79	C4
Ouahigouya, *Burkina Faso*	78	C4
Ouahila, *Algeria*	74	C3
Ouahran = Oran, *Algeria*	75	A4
Oualâta, *Mauritania*	78	B3
Ouallene, *Algeria*	75	D5
Ouanda Djallé, *C.A.R.*	73	G9
Ouango, *C.A.R.*	80	D4
Ouarâne, *Mauritania*	74	D2
Ouargla, *Algeria*	75	B6
Ouarkziz, Djebel, *Algeria*	74	C3
Ouarzazate, *Morocco*	74	B3
Ouatagouna, *Mali*	79	B5
Oubangi →, *Zaïre*	80	E3
Oubarakai, O. →, *Algeria*	75	C6
Ouche →, *France*	25	E12
Oud-Beijerland, *Neths.*	16	E5
Oud-Gastel, *Neths.*	17	E4
Oud Turnhout, *Belgium*	17	F6
Ouddorp, *Neths.*	16	E3
Oude-Pekela, *Neths.*	16	B10
Oude Rijn →, *Neths.*	16	D4
Oudega, *Neths.*	16	B8
Oudenaarde, *Belgium*	17	G3
Oudenbosch, *Neths.*	17	E5
Oudenburg, *Belgium*	17	F2
Ouderkerk, *Utrecht, Neths.*	16	D5
Ouderkerk, *Zuid-Holland, Neths.*	16	E5
Oudeschild, *Neths.*	16	B5
Oudewater, *Neths.*	16	D5
Oudkarspel, *Neths.*	16	C5
Oudon →, *France*	24	E5
Oudon →, *France*	24	E6
Oudtshoorn, *S. Africa*	84	E3
Oued Zem, *Morocco*	74	B3
Ouellé, *Ivory C.*	78	D4
Ouenza, *Algeria*	75	A6
Ouessa, *Burkina Faso*	78	C4
Ouessant, I. d', *France*	24	D1
Ouesso, *Congo*	80	D3
Ouest, Pte., *Canada*	99	C7
Ouezzane, *Morocco*	74	B3
Ouffet, *Belgium*	17	H6
Ouidah, *Benin*	79	D5
Ouistreham, *France*	24	C6
Oujda, *Morocco*	75	B4
Oujeft, *Mauritania*	74	D2
Oulainen, *Finland*	8	D21
Ould Yenjé, *Mauritania*	78	B2
Ouled Djellal, *Algeria*	75	B6
Ouled Naïl, Mts. des, *Algeria*	75	B5
Oulmès, *Morocco*	74	B3
Oulu, *Finland*	8	D21
Oulujärvi, *Finland*	8	D22
Oulujoki →, *Finland*	8	D21
Oulx, *Italy*	32	C3
Oum Chalouba, *Chad*	73	E9
Oum-el-Bouaghi, *Algeria*	75	A6
Oum el Ksi, *Algeria*	74	C3
Oum-er-Rbia, O. →, *Morocco*	74	B3
Oumè, *Ivory C.*	78	D3
Ounane, Dj., *Algeria*	75	C6
Ounasjoki →, *Finland*	8	C21
Ounguati, *Namibia*	84	C2
Ounianga-Kébir, *Chad*	73	E9
Ounianga Sérir, *Chad*	73	E9
Our →, *Lux.*	17	J8
Ouray, *U.S.A.*	111	G10
Ourcq →, *France*	25	C10
Ourém, *Brazil*	122	B2
Ourense = Orense, *Spain*	30	C3
Ouricuri, *Brazil*	122	C3
Ourinhos, *Brazil*	127	A6
Ourique, *Portugal*	31	H2
Ouro Fino, *Brazil*	127	A6
Ouro Prêto, *Brazil*	123	F3
Ouro Sogui, *Senegal*	78	B2
Oursi, *Burkina Faso*	79	C4
Ourthe →, *Belgium*	17	H7
Ouse, *Australia*	90	G4
Ouse →, *E. Susx., U.K.*	13	G8
Ouse →, *N. Yorks., U.K.*	12	C8
Oust, *France*	26	F5
Oust →, *France*	24	E4
Outaouais →, *Canada*	98	C5
Outardes →, *Canada*	99	C6
Outat Oulad el Haj, *Morocco*	75	B4
Outer Hebrides, *U.K.*	14	D1
Outer I., *Canada*	99	B8
Outes, *Spain*	30	C2
Outjo, *Namibia*	84	C2
Outlook, *Canada*	101	C7
Outlook, *U.S.A.*	108	A2
Outokumpu, *Finland*	8	E23
Outreau, *France*	25	B8
Ouvèze →, *France*	27	E8
Ouyen, *Australia*	91	F3
Ouzouer-le-Marché, *France*	25	E8
Ovada, *Italy*	32	D5
Ovalau, *Fiji*	87	C8
Ovalle, *Chile*	126	C1
Ovamboland, *Namibia*	84	B2
Ovar, *Portugal*	30	E2
Ovejas, *Colombia*	120	B2
Overdinkel, *Neths.*	16	D10
Overflakkee, *Neths.*	16	E4
Overijse, *Belgium*	17	G5
Overijssel □, *Neths.*	16	D9
Overijsselsch Kanaal →, *Neths.*	16	C8
Overpelt, *Belgium*	17	F6
Overton, *U.S.A.*	113	J12
Övertorneå, *Sweden*	8	C20
Ovid, *U.S.A.*	108	E3
Ovidiopol, *Ukraine*	41	J6
Oviedo, *Spain*	30	B5
Oviedo □, *Spain*	30	B5
Oviken, *Sweden*	10	A8
Oviksfjällen, *Sweden*	10	B7
Oviši, *Latvia*	9	H19
Övör Hangay □, *Mongolia*	50	B2
Ovoro, *Nigeria*	79	D6
Øvre Årdal, *Norway*	9	F12
Ovruch, *Ukraine*	41	G5
Owaka, *N.Z.*	87	M2
Owase, *Japan*	49	G8
Owatonna, *U.S.A.*	108	C8
Owbeh, *Afghan.*	60	B3
Owego, *U.S.A.*	107	D8
Owen Falls Dam, *Uganda*	82	B3
Owen Sound, *Canada*	98	D3
Owendo, *Gabon*	80	D1
Owens →, *U.S.A.*	112	J9
Owens L., *U.S.A.*	113	J9
Owensboro, *U.S.A.*	104	G2
Owensville, *U.S.A.*	108	F9
Owerri, *Nigeria*	79	D6
Owl →, *Canada*	101	B10
Owo, *Nigeria*	79	D6
Owosso, *U.S.A.*	104	D3
Owyhee, *U.S.A.*	110	F5
Owyhee →, *U.S.A.*	110	E5
Owyhee, L., *U.S.A.*	110	E5
Oxapampa, *Peru*	124	C2
Oxelösund, *Sweden*	11	F11
Oxford, *N.Z.*	87	K4
Oxford, *U.K.*	13	F6
Oxford, *Miss., U.S.A.*	109	H10
Oxford, *N.C., U.S.A.*	105	G6
Oxford, *Ohio, U.S.A.*	104	F3
Oxford L., *Canada*	101	C9
Oxfordshire □, *U.K.*	13	F6
Oxley, *Australia*	91	E3
Oxnard, *U.S.A.*	113	L7
Oxus = Amudarya →, *Uzbekistan*	44	E6
Oya, *Malaysia*	56	D4
Oyama, *Japan*	49	F9
Oyapock →, *Fr. Guiana*	121	C7
Oyem, *Gabon*	80	D2
Oyen, *Canada*	101	C6
Øyeren, *Norway*	10	E5
Oykel →, *U.K.*	14	D4
Oymyakon, *Russia*	45	C15
Oyo, *Nigeria*	79	D5
Oyo □, *Nigeria*	79	D5
Oyón, *Peru*	124	C2
Oyonnax, *France*	27	B9
Oyster Bay, *U.S.A.*	107	F11
Ōyūbari, *Japan*	48	C11
Ozalp, *Turkey*	67	C10
Ozamiz, *Phil.*	55	G5
Ozark, *Ala., U.S.A.*	105	K3
Ozark, *Ark., U.S.A.*	109	H8
Ozark, *Mo., U.S.A.*	109	G8
Ozark Plateau, *U.S.A.*	109	G9
Ozarks, L. of the, *U.S.A.*	108	F8
Ózd, *Hungary*	21	G10
Ozernoye, *Russia*	42	E10
Ozette L., *U.S.A.*	112	B2
Ozieri, *Italy*	34	B2
Ozinki, *Russia*	42	E9
Ozona, *U.S.A.*	109	K4
Ozorków, *Poland*	20	D9
Ozuluama, *Mexico*	115	C5
Ozurgeti, *Georgia*	43	K5

P

P.W.V. □, *S. Africa*	85	D4
Pa, *Burkina Faso*	78	C4
Pa-an, *Burma*	61	L20
Pa Mong Dam, *Thailand*	58	D4
Paal, *Belgium*	17	F6
Paamiut = Frederikshåb, *Greenland*	4	C5
Paar →, *Germany*	19	G6
Paarl, *S. Africa*	84	E2
Paauilo, *U.S.A.*	102	H17
Pab Hills, *Pakistan*	62	F2
Pabianice, *Poland*	20	D9
Pabna, *Bangla.*	61	G16
Pabo, *Uganda*	82	B3
Pacaás Novos, Serra dos, *Brazil*	125	C5
Pacaipampa, *Peru*	124	B2
Pacaja →, *Brazil*	122	B1
Pacajus, *Brazil*	122	B4
Pacaraima, Sierra, *Venezuela*	121	C5
Pacarán, *Peru*	124	C2
Pacaraos, *Peru*	124	C2
Pacasmayo, *Peru*	124	B2
Paceco, *Italy*	34	E5
Pachacamac, *Peru*	124	C2
Pachhar, *India*	62	G7
Pachino, *Italy*	35	F8
Pachitea →, *Peru*	124	B3
Pachiza, *Peru*	124	B2
Pacho, *Colombia*	120	B3
Pachpadra, *India*	60	G8
Pachuca, *Mexico*	115	C5
Pacific, *Canada*	100	C3
Pacific-Antarctic Ridge, *Pac. Oc.*	93	M16
Pacific Grove, *U.S.A.*	111	H3
Pacific Ocean, *Pac. Oc.*	93	G14
Pacifica, *U.S.A.*	112	H4
Pacitan, *Indonesia*	57	H14
Packwood, *U.S.A.*	112	D5
Pacuí →, *Brazil*	123	E2
Pacy-sur-Eure, *France*	24	C8
Padaido, Kepulauan, *Indonesia*	57	E9
Padang, *Indonesia*	56	E2
Padangpanjang, *Indonesia*	56	E2
Padangsidempuan, *Indonesia*	56	D1
Padauari →, *Brazil*	121	D5
Padborg, *Denmark*	11	K3
Padcaya, *Bolivia*	125	E5
Paddockwood, *Canada*	101	C7
Paderborn, *Germany*	18	D4
Padilla, *Bolivia*	125	D5
Padloping Island, *Canada*	97	B13
Pádova, *Italy*	33	C8
Padra, *India*	62	H5
Padrauna, *India*	63	F10
Padre I., *U.S.A.*	109	M6
Padro, Mte., *France*	27	F12
Padrón, *Spain*	30	C2
Padstow, *U.K.*	13	G3
Padua = Pádova, *Italy*	33	C8
Paducah, *Ky., U.S.A.*	104	G1
Paducah, *Tex., U.S.A.*	109	H4
Padul, *Spain*	31	H7
Padula, *Italy*	35	B8
Paengnyong-do, *S. Korea*	51	F13
Paeroa, *N.Z.*	87	G5
Paesana, *Italy*	32	D4
Pafúri, *Mozam.*	85	C5
Pag, *Croatia*	33	D11
Paga, *Ghana*	79	C4
Pagadian, *Phil.*	55	H5
Pagai Selatan, P., *Indonesia*	56	E2
Pagai Utara, *Indonesia*	56	E2
Pagalu = Annobón, *Atl. Oc.*	71	G4
Pagastikós Kólpos, *Greece*	39	K6
Pagatan, *Indonesia*	56	E5
Page, *Ariz., U.S.A.*	111	H8
Page, *N. Dak., U.S.A.*	108	B6

Pataudi

Paglieta, *Italy* 33 F11
Pagny-sur-Moselle, *France* 25 D13
Pago Pago, *Amer. Samoa* 87 B13
Pagosa Springs, *U.S.A.* 111 H10
Pagwa River, *Canada* 98 B2
Pahala, *U.S.A.* 102 J17
Pahang →, *Malaysia* 59 L4
Pahiatua, *N.Z.* 87 J5
Pahokee, *U.S.A.* 105 M5
Pahrump, *U.S.A.* 113 J11
Pahute Mesa, *U.S.A.* 112 H10
Pai, *Thailand* 58 C2
Paia, *U.S.A.* 102 H16
Paicines, *U.S.A.* 112 J5
Paide, *Estonia* 9 G21
Paignton, *U.K.* 13 G4
Paiján, *Peru* 124 B2
Päijänne, *Finland* 9 F21
Paimbœuf, *France* 24 E4
Paimpol, *France* 24 D3
Painan, *Indonesia* 56 E2
Painesville, *U.S.A.* 106 E3
Paint Hills = Wemindji, *Canada* 98 B4
Paint L., *Canada* 101 B9
Paint Rock, *U.S.A.* 109 K5
Painted Desert, *U.S.A.* 111 J8
Paintsville, *U.S.A.* 104 G4
País Vasco □, *Spain* 28 C2
Paisley, *Canada* 106 B3
Paisley, *U.K.* 14 F4
Paisley, *U.S.A.* 110 E3
Paita, *Peru* 124 B1
Paiva →, *Portugal* 30 D2
Paizhou, *China* 53 B9
Pajares, *Spain* 30 B5
Pajares, Puerto de, *Spain* 30 C5
Pak Lay, *Laos* 58 C3
Pak Phanang, *Thailand* 59 H3
Pak Sane, *Laos* 58 C4
Pak Song, *Laos* 58 E6
Pak Suong, *Laos* 58 C4
Pakaraima Mts., *Guyana* 121 B5
Pákhnes, *Greece* 37 D6
Pakistan ■, *Asia* 62 E3
Pakistan, East = Bangladesh ■, *Asia* 61 H17
Pakkading, *Laos* 58 C4
Pakokku, *Burma* 61 J19
Pakpattan, *Pakistan* 62 D5
Pakrac, *Croatia* 21 K7
Paks, *Hungary* 21 J8
Pakse, *Laos* 58 E5
Paktīā □, *Afghan.* 60 C6
Pakwach, *Uganda* 82 B3
Pala, *Chad* 73 G8
Pala, *U.S.A.* 113 M9
Pala, *Zaïre* 82 D2
Palabek, *Uganda* 82 B3
Palacios, *U.S.A.* 109 L6
Palafrugell, *Spain* 28 D8
Palagiano, *Italy* 35 B10
Palagonía, *Italy* 35 E7
Palagruža, *Croatia* 33 F13
Palaiókastron, *Greece* 37 D8
Palaiokhóra, *Greece* 37 D5
Palam, *India* 60 K10
Palamás, *Greece* 39 K5
Palamós, *Spain* 28 D8
Palampur, *India* 62 C7
Palana, *Australia* 90 F4
Palana, *Russia* 45 D16
Palanan, *Phil.* 55 C5
Palanan Pt., *Phil.* 55 C5
Palandri, *Pakistan* 63 C5
Palanga, *Lithuania* 9 J19
Palangkaraya, *Indonesia* 56 E4
Palani Hills, *India* 60 P10
Palanpur, *India* 62 G5
Palanro, *Indonesia* 57 E5
Palapye, *Botswana* 84 C4
Palas, *Pakistan* 63 B5
Palatka, *Russia* 45 C16
Palatka, *U.S.A.* 105 L5
Palau = Belau ■, *Pac. Oc.* 92 G5
Palawan, *Phil.* 55 G3
Palayankottai, *India* 60 Q10
Palazzo, Pte., *France* 27 F12
Palazzo San Gervásio, *Italy* 35 B8
Palazzolo Acréide, *Italy* 35 E7
Palca, *Chile* 124 D4
Paldiski, *Estonia* 9 G21
Paleleh, *Indonesia* 57 D6
Palembang, *Indonesia* 56 E2
Palena →, *Chile* 128 B2
Palena, L., *Chile* 128 B2
Palencia, *Spain* 30 C6
Palencia □, *Spain* 30 C6
Paleokastrítsa, *Greece* 37 A3
Paleometokho, *Cyprus* 37 D12
Palermo, *Colombia* 120 C2
Palermo, *Italy* 34 D6
Palermo, *U.S.A.* 110 G3
Palestine, *Asia* 69 D4
Palestine, *U.S.A.* 109 K7
Palestrina, *Italy* 34 A5
Paletwa, *Burma* 61 J18
Palghat, *India* 60 P10
Palgrave, Mt., *Australia* 88 D2
Pali, *India* 62 G5
Palinuro, C., *Italy* 35 B8
Palisade, *U.S.A.* 108 E4
Paliseul, *Belgium* 17 J6
Palitana, *India* 62 J4
Palizada, *Mexico* 115 D6
Palizzi Marina, *Italy* 35 E8
Palk Bay, *Asia* 60 Q11
Palk Strait, *Asia* 60 Q11
Palkānah, *Iraq* 64 C5
Palla Road = Dinokwe, *Botswana* 84 C4
Pallanza = Verbánia, *Italy* 32 C5
Pallasovka, *Russia* 42 E8
Pallisa, *Uganda* 82 B3
Pallu, *India* 62 E6
Palm Beach, *U.S.A.* 105 M6
Palm Desert, *U.S.A.* 113 M10
Palm Is., *Australia* 90 B4
Palm Springs, *U.S.A.* 113 M10
Palma, *Mozam.* 83 E5
Palma →, *Brazil* 123 D2
Palma, B. de, *Spain* 36 B9
Palma de Mallorca, *Spain* 36 B9
Palma del Río, *Spain* 31 H5
Palma di Montechiaro, *Italy* 34 E6
Palma Soriano, *Cuba* 116 B4
Palmanova, *Italy* 33 C10
Palmares, *Brazil* 122 C4
Palmarito, *Venezuela* 120 B3
Palmarola, *Italy* 34 B5
Palmas, *Brazil* 127 B5
Palmas, C., *Liberia* 78 E3
Pálmas, G. di, *Italy* 34 C1
Palmas de Monte Alto, *Brazil* 123 D3
Palmdale, *U.S.A.* 113 L8
Palmeira, *Brazil* 123 G2
Palmeira dos Índios, *Brazil* 122 C4
Palmeirais, *Brazil* 122 C3
Palmeiras →, *Brazil* 123 D2
Palmeirinhas, Pta. das, *Angola* 80 F2
Palmela, *Portugal* 31 G2
Palmelo, *Brazil* 123 E2
Palmer, *U.S.A.* 96 B5
Palmer →, *Australia* 90 B3
Palmer Arch., *Antarctica* 5 C17
Palmer Lake, *U.S.A.* 108 F2
Palmer Land, *Antarctica* 5 D18
Palmerston, *Canada* 106 C4
Palmerston, *N.Z.* 87 L3
Palmerston North, *N.Z.* 87 J5
Palmerton, *U.S.A.* 107 F9
Palmetto, *U.S.A.* 105 M4
Palmi, *Italy* 35 D8
Palmira, *Argentina* 126 C2
Palmira, *Colombia* 120 C2
Palmyra = Tudmur, *Syria* 67 E8
Palmyra, *Mo., U.S.A.* 108 F9
Palmyra, *N.Y., U.S.A.* 106 C7
Palmyra Is., *Pac. Oc.* 93 G11
Palo Alto, *U.S.A.* 111 H2
Palo del Colle, *Italy* 35 A9
Palo Verde, *U.S.A.* 113 M12
Palombara Sabina, *Italy* 33 F9
Palompon, *Phil.* 55 F6
Palopo, *Indonesia* 57 E6
Palos, C. de, *Spain* 29 H4
Palos Verdes, *U.S.A.* 113 M8
Palos Verdes, Pt., *U.S.A.* 113 M8
Palouse, *U.S.A.* 110 C5
Palpa, *Peru* 124 C2
Palparara, *Australia* 90 C3
Pålsboda, *Sweden* 10 E9
Palu, *Indonesia* 57 E5
Palu, *Turkey* 67 C9
Paluan, *Phil.* 57 B6
Palwal, *India* 62 E7
Pama, *Burkina Faso* 79 C5
Pamanukan, *Indonesia* 57 G12
Pamekasan, *Indonesia* 57 G15
Pamiers, *France* 26 E5
Pamirs, *Tajikistan* 44 F8
Pamlico →, *U.S.A.* 105 H7
Pamlico Sd., *U.S.A.* 105 H8
Pampa, *U.S.A.* 109 H4
Pampa de Agma, *Argentina* 128 B3
Pampa de las Salinas, *Argentina* 126 C2
Pampa Grande, *Bolivia* 125 D5
Pampa Hermosa, *Peru* 124 B2
Pampanua, *Indonesia* 57 E6
Pamparato, *Italy* 32 D4
Pampas, *Argentina* 126 D3
Pampas, *Peru* 124 C3
Pampas →, *Peru* 124 C3
Pamphylia, *Turkey* 66 D4
Pamplona, *Colombia* 120 B3
Pamplona, *Spain* 28 C3
Pampoenpoort, *S. Africa* 84 E3
Pan Xian, *China* 52 E5
Pana, *U.S.A.* 108 F10
Panabo, *Phil.* 55 H6
Panaca, *U.S.A.* 111 H6
Panagyurishte, *Bulgaria* 38 G7
Panaitan, *Indonesia* 57 G11
Panaji, *India* 60 M8
Panamá, *Panama* 116 E4
Panama ■, *Cent. Amer.* 116 E4
Panamá, G. de, *Panama* 116 E4
Panama Canal, *Panama* 116 E4
Panama City, *U.S.A.* 105 K3
Panamint Range, *U.S.A.* 113 J9
Panamint Springs, *U.S.A.* 113 J9
Panão, *Peru* 124 B2
Panaon I., *Phil.* 55 F6
Panare, *Thailand* 59 J3
Panarea, *Italy* 35 D8
Panaro →, *Italy* 32 D8
Panarukan, *Indonesia* 57 G15
Panay, *Phil.* 55 F5
Panay, G., *Phil.* 57 B6
Pancake Range, *U.S.A.* 111 G6
Pančevo, *Serbia, Yug.* 21 L10
Pancorbo, Paso, *Spain* 28 C1
Pandan, *Antique, Phil.* 55 F5
Pandan, *Catanduanes, Phil.* 55 D6
Pandegelang, *Indonesia* 57 G12
Pandharpur, *India* 60 L9
Pandilla, *Spain* 28 D1
Pando, *Uruguay* 127 C4
Pando □, *Bolivia* 124 C4
Pando, L. = Hope, L., *Australia* 91 D2
Pandokrátor, *Greece* 37 A3
Pandora, *Costa Rica* 116 E3
Panevėžys, *Lithuania* 9 J21
Panfilov, *Kazakhstan* 44 E8
Panfilovo, *Russia* 42 E6
Pang-Long, *Burma* 61 H21
Pang-Yang, *Burma* 61 H21
Panga, *Zaïre* 82 B2
Pangalanes, Canal des, *Madag.* 85 C8
Pangani, *Tanzania* 82 D4
Pangani □, *Tanzania* 82 D4
Pangani →, *Tanzania* 82 D4
Pangfou = Bengbu, *China* 51 H9
Pangil, *Zaïre* 82 C2
Pangkah, Tanjung, *Indonesia* 57 G15
Pangkajene, *Indonesia* 57 E5
Pangkalanbrandan, *Indonesia* 56 D1
Pangkalanbuun, *Indonesia* 56 E4
Pangkalansusu, *Indonesia* 56 D1
Pangkalpinang, *Indonesia* 56 E3
Pangkoh, *Indonesia* 56 E4
Pangnirtung, *Canada* 97 B13
Pangrango, *Indonesia* 57 G12
Panguipulli, *Chile* 128 A2
Panguitch, *U.S.A.* 111 H7
Pangutaran Group, *Phil.* 55 H4
Panhandle, *U.S.A.* 109 H4
Pani Mines, *India* 62 H5
Pania-Mutombo, *Zaïre* 82 D1
Panipat, *India* 62 E7
Panjal Range, *India* 62 C7
Panjgur, *Pakistan* 60 F4
Panjim = Panaji, *India* 60 M8
Panjinad Barrage, *Pakistan* 60 E7
Panjwai, *Afghan.* 62 D1
Pankshin, *Nigeria* 79 D6
Panmunjŏm, *N. Korea* 51 F14
Panna, *India* 63 G9
Panna Hills, *India* 63 G9
Pano Lefkara, *Cyprus* 37 E12
Pano Panayia, *Cyprus* 37 E11
Panorama, *Brazil* 127 A5
Pánormon, *Greece* 37 D6
Panshan, *China* 51 D12
Panshi, *China* 51 C14
Pantar, *Indonesia* 57 F6
Pante Macassar, *Indonesia* 57 F6
Pantelleria, *Italy* 34 F5
Pantón, *Spain* 30 C3
Pánuco, *Mexico* 115 C5
Panyam, *Nigeria* 79 D6
Panyu, *China* 53 F9
Pao →, *Anzoátegui, Venezuela* 121 B5
Pao →, *Apure, Venezuela* 120 B4
Páola, *Italy* 35 C9
Paola, *Malta* 37 D2
Paola, *U.S.A.* 108 F7
Paonia, *U.S.A.* 111 G10
Paoting = Baoding, *China* 50 E8
Paot'ou = Baotou, *China* 50 D6
Paoua, *C.A.R.* 73 G8
Pápa, *Hungary* 21 H7
Papagayo →, *Mexico* 115 D5
Papagayo, G. de, *Costa Rica* 116 D2
Papakura, *N.Z.* 87 G5
Papantla, *Mexico* 115 C5
Papar, *Malaysia* 55 C5
Pápas, Ákra, *Greece* 39 L4
Papenburg, *Germany* 18 B3
Paphlagonia, *Turkey* 66 B5
Paphos, *Cyprus* 66 E5
Papien Chiang = Da →, *Vietnam* 58 B5
Papigochic →, *Mexico* 114 B3
Paposo, *Chile* 126 B1
Papoutsa, *Cyprus* 37 E12
Papua New Guinea ■, *Oceania* 92 H6
Papuča, *Croatia* 33 D12
Papudo, *Chile* 126 C1
Papuk, *Croatia* 21 K7
Papun, *Burma* 61 K20
Papunya, *Australia* 88 D5
Pará = Belém, *Brazil* 122 B2
Pará □, *Brazil* 125 A7
Pará □, *Surinam* 121 B6
Parábita, *Italy* 35 B11
Paraburdoo, *Australia* 88 D2
Paracale, *Phil.* 55 D5
Paracas, Pen., *Peru* 124 C2
Paracatu, *Brazil* 123 E2
Paracatu →, *Brazil* 123 E2
Paracel Is. = Hsisha Chuntao, *Pac. Oc.* 56 A4
Parachilna, *Australia* 91 E2
Parachinar, *Pakistan* 62 C4
Paraćin, *Serbia, Yug.* 21 M11
Paracuru, *Brazil* 122 B4
Parada, Punta, *Peru* 124 D2
Paradas, *Spain* 31 H5
Paradela, *Spain* 30 C3
Paradhísi, *Greece* 37 C10
Paradip, *India* 61 J15
Paradise, *Calif., U.S.A.* 112 F5
Paradise, *Mont., U.S.A.* 110 C6
Paradise, *Nev., U.S.A.* 113 J11
Paradise →, *Canada* 99 B8
Paradise Valley, *U.S.A.* 110 F5
Parado, *Indonesia* 57 F5
Paragould, *U.S.A.* 109 G9
Paraguá →, *Bolivia* 125 C5
Paragua →, *Venezuela* 121 B5
Paraguaçu →, *Brazil* 123 D4
Paraguaçu Paulista, *Brazil* 127 A5
Paraguaipoa, *Venezuela* 120 A3
Paraguaná, Pen. de, *Venezuela* 120 A3
Paraguarí, *Paraguay* 126 B4
Paraguarí □, *Paraguay* 126 B4
Paraguay ■, *S. Amer.* 126 A4
Paraguay →, *Paraguay* 126 B4
Paraíba = João Pessoa, *Brazil* 122 C5
Paraíba □, *Brazil* 122 C4
Paraíba do Sul →, *Brazil* 123 F3
Parainen, *Finland* 9 F20
Paraiso, *Mexico* 115 D6
Parak, *Iran* 65 E7
Parakhino Paddubye, *Russia* 40 C7
Parakou, *Benin* 79 D5
Paralimni, *Cyprus* 37 D12
Paramaribo, *Surinam* 121 B6
Parambu, *Brazil* 122 C3
Paramillo, Nudo del, *Colombia* 120 B2
Paramirim, *Brazil* 123 D3
Paramirim →, *Brazil* 123 D3
Paramithiá, *Greece* 39 K3
Paramushir, Ostrov, *Russia* 45 D16
Paran →, *Israel* 69 E4
Paraná, *Argentina* 126 C3
Paranã, *Brazil* 123 D2
Paraná □, *Brazil* 127 A5
Paraná →, *Argentina* 126 C4
Paranaguá, *Brazil* 127 B6
Paranaíba →, *Brazil* 123 F1
Paranapanema →, *Brazil* 127 A5
Paranapiacaba, Serra do, *Brazil* 127 A6
Paranavaí, *Brazil* 127 A5
Parang, *Jolo, Phil.* 55 J4
Parang, *Mindanao, Phil.* 57 C6
Parangaba, *Brazil* 122 B4
Parapóla, *Greece* 39 N6
Paraspóri, Ákra, *Greece* 39 P10
Paratinga, *Brazil* 123 D3
Paratoo, *Australia* 91 E2
Parattah, *Australia* 90 G4
Paraúna, *Brazil* 123 E1
Paray-le-Monial, *France* 27 B8
Parbati →, *India* 62 G7
Parbhani, *India* 60 K10
Parchim, *Germany* 18 B7
Parczew, *Poland* 20 D12
Pardes Hanna, *Israel* 69 C3
Pardilla, *Spain* 30 D7
Pardo →, *Bahia, Brazil* 123 E4
Pardo →, *Mato Grosso, Brazil* 127 A5
Pardo →, *Minas Gerais, Brazil* 123 E3
Pardo →, *São Paulo, Brazil* 123 F2
Pardubice, *Czech.* 20 E5
Pare, *Indonesia* 57 G15
Pare □, *Tanzania* 82 C4
Pare Mts., *Tanzania* 82 C4
Parecis, Serra dos, *Brazil* 125 C6
Paredes de Nava, *Spain* 30 C6
Pareh, *Iran* 64 B5
Parelhas, *Brazil* 122 C4
Paren, *Russia* 45 C17
Parent, *Canada* 98 C5
Parent, L., *Canada* 98 C4
Parentis-en-Born, *France* 26 D2
Parepare, *Indonesia* 57 E5
Parfino, *Russia* 40 D6
Pargo, Pta. do, *Madeira* 36 D2
Paria, G. de, *Venezuela* 121 A5
Paria, Pen. de, *Venezuela* 121 A5
Pariaguán, *Venezuela* 121 B5
Pariaman, *Indonesia* 56 E2
Paricatuba, *Brazil* 121 D5
Paricutín, Cerro, *Mexico* 114 D4
Parigi, *Java, Indonesia* 57 G13
Parigi, *Sulawesi, Indonesia* 57 E6
Parika, *Guyana* 121 B6
Parikkala, *Finland* 40 B5
Parima, Serra, *Brazil* 121 C5
Parinari, *Peru* 124 A3
Parîngul Mare, *Romania* 38 D6
Parintins, *Brazil* 121 D6
Pariparit Kyun, *Burma* 61 M18
Paris, *Canada* 98 D3
Paris, *France* 25 D9
Paris, *Idaho, U.S.A.* 110 E8
Paris, *Ky., U.S.A.* 104 F3
Paris, *Tenn., U.S.A.* 105 G1
Paris, *Tex., U.S.A.* 109 J7
Paris, Ville de □, *France* 25 D9
Parish, *U.S.A.* 107 C8
Pariti, *Indonesia* 57 F6
Park, *U.S.A.* 112 B4
Park City, *U.S.A.* 110 F8
Park Falls, *U.S.A.* 108 C9
Park Range, *U.S.A.* 110 G10
Park Rapids, *U.S.A.* 108 B7
Park River, *U.S.A.* 108 A6
Park Rynie, *S. Africa* 85 E5
Parkā Bandar, *Iran* 65 E8
Parkano, *Finland* 9 E20
Parker, *Ariz., U.S.A.* 113 L12
Parker, *S. Dak., U.S.A.* 108 D6
Parker Dam, *U.S.A.* 113 L12
Parkersburg, *U.S.A.* 104 F5
Parkerview, *Canada* 101 C8
Parkes, *Australia* 91 E4
Parkfield, *U.S.A.* 112 K6
Parkland, *U.S.A.* 112 C4
Parkside, *Canada* 101 C7
Parkston, *U.S.A.* 108 D5
Parksville, *Canada* 100 D4
Parma, *Italy* 32 D7
Parma, *Idaho, U.S.A.* 110 E5
Parma, *Ohio, U.S.A.* 106 E3
Parma →, *Italy* 32 D7
Parnaguá, *Brazil* 122 D3
Parnaíba, *Piauí, Brazil* 122 B3
Parnaíba, *São Paulo, Brazil* 125 D7
Parnaíba →, *Brazil* 122 B3
Parnamirim, *Brazil* 122 C4
Parnarama, *Brazil* 122 C3
Parnassós, *Greece* 39 L5
Párnis, *Greece* 39 L6
Párnon Óros, *Greece* 39 M5
Parnu, *Estonia* 9 G21
Paroo →, *Australia* 91 E3
Páros, *Greece* 39 M8
Parowan, *U.S.A.* 111 H7
Parpaillon, *France* 27 D10
Parral, *Chile* 126 D1
Parramatta, *Australia* 91 E5
Parras, *Mexico* 114 B4
Parrett →, *U.K.* 13 F5
Parris I., *U.S.A.* 105 J5
Parrsboro, *Canada* 99 C7
Parry Is., *Canada* 4 B2
Parry Sound, *Canada* 98 C3
Parsberg, *Germany* 19 F7
Parshall, *U.S.A.* 108 B3
Parsnip →, *Canada* 100 B4
Parsons, *U.S.A.* 109 G7
Parsons Ra., *Australia* 90 A2
Partanna, *Italy* 34 E5
Parthenay, *France* 24 F6
Partinico, *Italy* 34 D6
Paru →, *Brazil* 121 D7
Parú →, *Venezuela* 120 C4
Paru de Oeste →, *Brazil* 121 C6
Parucito →, *Venezuela* 120 B4
Paruro, *Peru* 124 C3
Parvān □, *Afghan.* 60 B6
Parvatipuram, *India* 61 K13
Parys, *S. Africa* 84 D4
Pas-de-Calais □, *France* 25 B9
Pasadena, *Calif., U.S.A.* 113 L8
Pasadena, *Tex., U.S.A.* 109 L7
Pasaje, *Ecuador* 120 D2
Pasaje →, *Argentina* 126 B3
Pasay, *Phil.* 55 D4
Pascagoula, *U.S.A.* 109 K10
Pascagoula →, *U.S.A.* 109 K10
Paşcani, *Romania* 38 B9
Pasco, *U.S.A.* 110 C4
Pasco □, *Peru* 124 C2
Pasco, Cerro de, *Peru* 124 C2
Pascua, I. de, *Pac. Oc.* 93 K17
Pasewalk, *Germany* 18 B10
Pasfield L., *Canada* 101 B7
Pasha →, *Russia* 40 B7
Pashiwari, *Pakistan* 63 B6
Pashmakli = Smolyan, *Bulgaria* 39 H7
Pasinler, *Turkey* 67 C9
Pasirian, *Indonesia* 57 H15
Paskūh, *Iran* 65 E9
Pasley, C., *Australia* 89 F3
Pašman, *Croatia* 33 E12
Pasni, *Pakistan* 60 G3
Paso Cantinela, *Mexico* 113 N11
Paso de Indios, *Argentina* 128 B3
Paso de los Libres, *Argentina* 126 B4
Paso de los Toros, *Uruguay* 126 C4
Paso Flores, *Argentina* 128 B2
Paso Robles, *U.S.A.* 111 J3
Pasorapa, *Bolivia* 125 D5
Paspébiac, *Canada* 99 C6
Pasrur, *Pakistan* 62 C6
Passage West, *Ireland* 15 E3
Passaic, *U.S.A.* 107 F10
Passau, *Germany* 19 G9
Passendale, *Belgium* 17 G2
Passero, C., *Italy* 35 F8
Passo Fundo, *Brazil* 127 B5
Passos, *Brazil* 123 F2
Passow, *Germany* 18 B10
Passwang, *Switz.* 22 B5
Passy, *France* 27 C10
Pastavy, *Belarus* 9 J22
Pastaza □, *Ecuador* 120 D2
Pastaza →, *Peru* 120 D2
Pastęk, *Poland* 20 A9
Pasto, *Colombia* 120 C2
Pastos Bons, *Brazil* 122 C3
Pastrana, *Spain* 28 E2
Pasuruan, *Indonesia* 57 G15
Patagonia, *Argentina* 128 C2
Patagonia, *U.S.A.* 111 L8
Patambar, *Iran* 65 D9
Patan, *India* 60 H8
Patan, *Maharashtra, India* 62 H5
Patan, *Nepal* 61 F14
Patani, *Indonesia* 57 D7
Pataudi, *India* 62 E7

Patay, France 25 D8
Patchewollock, Australia .. 91 F3
Patchogue, U.S.A. 107 F11
Patea, N.Z. 87 H5
Pategi, Nigeria 79 D6
Patensie, S. Africa 84 E3
Paternò, Italy 35 E7
Pateros, U.S.A. 110 B4
Paterson, U.S.A. 107 F10
Paterson Ra., Australia ... 88 D3
Paterswolde, Neths. 16 B9
Pathankot, India 62 C6
Pathfinder Reservoir,
   U.S.A. 110 E10
Pathiu, Thailand 59 G2
Pathum Thani, Thailand .. 58 E3
Pati, Indonesia 57 G14
Patía, Colombia 120 C2
Patía →, Colombia 120 C2
Patiala, India 62 D7
Patine Kouka, Senegal ... 78 C2
Pativilca, Peru 124 C2
Patkai Bum, India 61 F19
Pátmos, Greece 39 M9
Patna, India 63 G11
Patnos, Turkey 67 C10
Patonga, Uganda 82 B3
Patos, Brazil 122 C4
Patos, L. dos, Brazil 127 C5
Patos de Minas, Brazil ... 123 E2
Patquía, Argentina 126 C2
Pátrai, Greece 39 L4
Pátraikós Kólpos, Greece . 39 L4
Patras = Pátrai, Greece .. 39 L4
Patricio Lynch, I., Chile .. 128 C1
Patrocínio, Brazil 123 E2
Patta, Kenya 82 C5
Pattada, Italy 34 B2
Pattani, Thailand 59 J3
Patten, U.S.A. 99 C6
Patterson, Calif., U.S.A. . 111 H3
Patterson, La., U.S.A. ... 109 L9
Patterson, Mt., U.S.A. ... 112 G7
Patti, India 62 D6
Patti, Italy 35 D7
Pattoki, Pakistan 62 D5
Patton, U.S.A. 106 F6
Patu, Brazil 122 C4
Patuakhali, Bangla. 61 H17
Patuca →, Honduras 116 C3
Patuca, Punta, Honduras . 116 C3
Pâturages, Belgium 17 H4
Pátzcuaro, Mexico 114 D4
Pau, France 26 E3
Pau, Gave de →, France . 26 E2
Pau d' Arco, Brazil 122 C2
Pau dos Ferros, Brazil ... 122 C4
Paucartambo, Peru 124 C3
Pauillac, France 26 C3
Pauini, Brazil 124 B4
Pauini →, Brazil 121 D5
Pauk, Burma 61 J19
Paul I., Canada 99 A7
Paul Isnard, Fr. Guiana . 121 C7
Paulhan, France 26 E7
Paulis = Isiro, Zaïre 82 B2
Paulista, Brazil 122 C5
Paulistana, Brazil 122 C3
Paullina, U.S.A. 108 D7
Paulo Afonso, Brazil 122 C4
Paulo de Faria, Brazil ... 123 F2
Paulpietersburg, S. Africa . 85 D5
Pauls Valley, U.S.A. 109 H6
Pauma Valley, U.S.A. ... 113 M10
Pausa, Peru 124 D3
Pauto →, Colombia 120 B3
Pāveh, Iran 67 E12
Pavelets, Russia 42 D4
Pavia, Italy 32 C6
Pāvilosta, Latvia 9 H19
Pavlikeni, Bulgaria 38 F8
Pavlodar, Kazakhstan ... 44 D8
Pavlograd = Pavlohrad,
   Ukraine 41 H8
Pavlohrad, Ukraine 41 H8
Pavlovo, Russia 42 C6
Pavlovo, Russia 45 C12
Pavlovsk, Russia 42 E5
Pavlovskaya, Russia 43 G4
Pavlovskiy-Posad, Russia . 42 C4
Pavullo nel Frignano, Italy 32 D7
Pawhuska, U.S.A. 109 G6
Pawling, U.S.A. 107 E11
Pawnee, U.S.A. 109 G6
Pawnee City, U.S.A. 108 E6
Pawtucket, U.S.A. 107 E13
Paximádhia, Greece 37 D6
Paxoí, Greece 39 K3
Paxton, Ill., U.S.A. 104 E1
Paxton, Nebr., U.S.A. ... 108 E4
Payakumbuh, Indonesia .. 56 E2
Payerne, Switz. 22 C3
Payette, U.S.A. 110 D5
Paymogo, Spain 31 H3
Payne Bay = Kangirsuk,
   Canada 97 B13
Paynes Find, Australia ... 89 E2
Paynesville, Liberia 78 D2
Paynesville, U.S.A. 108 C7
Paysandú, Uruguay 126 C4
Payson, Ariz., U.S.A. ... 111 J8
Payson, Utah, U.S.A. ... 110 F8
Paz →, Guatemala 116 D1
Paz, B. la, Mexico 114 C2
Pāzanān, Iran 65 D6
Pazar, Turkey 67 B9
Pazarcık, Turkey 66 D7

Pazardzhik, Bulgaria 38 G7
Pazaryolu, Turkey 67 B9
Pazin, Croatia 33 C10
Pazña, Bolivia 124 D4
Pčinja →, Macedonia ... 39 H4
Pe Ell, U.S.A. 112 D3
Peabody, U.S.A. 107 D14
Peace →, Canada 100 B6
Peace Point, Canada 100 B6
Peace River, Canada 100 B5
Peach Springs, U.S.A. ... 111 J7
Peak, The = Kinder Scout,
   U.K. 12 D6
Peak Downs, Australia ... 90 C4
Peak Downs Mine,
   Australia 90 C4
Peak Hill, N.S.W.,
   Australia 91 E4
Peak Hill, W. Austral.,
   Australia 89 E2
Peak Ra., Australia 90 C4
Peake, Australia 91 F2
Peake Cr. →, Australia . 91 D2
Peale, Mt., U.S.A. 111 G9
Pearblossom, U.S.A. 113 L9
Pearl →, U.S.A. 109 K10
Pearl City, U.S.A. 102 H16
Pearsall, U.S.A. 109 L5
Pearse I., Canada 100 C2
Peary Land, Greenland .. 4 A6
Pease →, U.S.A. 109 H5
Pebane, Mozam. 83 F4
Pebas, Peru 120 D3
Pebble, I., Falk. Is. 128 D5
Pebble Beach, U.S.A. ... 112 J5
Peć, Serbia, Yug. 21 N10
Peçanha, Brazil 123 E3
Péccioli, Italy 32 E7
Pechea, Romania 38 D10
Pechenga, Russia 44 C4
Pechenizhyn, Ukraine ... 41 H3
Pechiguera, Pta.,
   Canary Is. 36 F6
Pechnezhskoye Vdkhr.,
   Ukraine 41 G9
Pechora →, Russia 44 C6
Pechorskaya Guba, Russia 44 C6
Pecica, Romania 38 C5
Pečka, Serbia, Yug. 21 L9
Pécora, C., Italy 34 C1
Pečory, Russia 9 H22
Pecos, U.S.A. 109 K3
Pecos →, U.S.A. 109 L3
Pécs, Hungary 21 J8
Pedder, L., Australia 90 G4
Peddie, S. Africa 85 E4
Pédernales, Dom. Rep. .. 117 C5
Pedirka, Australia 91 D2
Pedra Azul, Brazil 123 E3
Pedra Grande, Recifes de,
   Brazil 123 E4
Pedras Negras, Brazil ... 125 C5
Pedreiras, Brazil 122 B3
Pedro Afonso, Brazil 122 C2
Pedro Cays, Jamaica 116 C4
Pedro Chico, Colombia .. 120 C3
Pedro de Valdivia, Chile . 126 A2
Pedro Juan Caballero,
   Paraguay 127 A4
Pedro Muñoz, Spain 29 F2
Pedrógão Grande, Portugal 30 F2
Peebinga, Australia 91 E3
Peebles, U.K. 14 F5
Peekskill, U.S.A. 107 E11
Peel, U.K. 12 C3
Peel →, Australia 91 E5
Peel →, Canada 96 B6
Peene →, Germany 18 A9
Peera Peera Poolanna L.,
   Australia 91 D2
Peers, Canada 100 C5
Pegasus Bay, N.Z. 87 K4
Pegnitz, Germany 19 F7
Pegnitz →, Germany ... 19 F6
Pego, Spain 29 G4
Pegu, Burma 61 L20
Pegu Yoma, Burma 61 K19
Pehuajó, Argentina 126 D3
Pei Xian, China 50 G9
Peine, Chile 126 A2
Peine, Germany 18 C6
Peip'ing = Beijing, China . 50 E9
Peipus, L. = Chudskoye,
   Oz., Russia 9 G22
Peissenberg, Germany ... 19 H7
Peitz, Germany 18 D10
Peixe, Brazil 123 D2
Peixe →, Brazil 123 F1
Peixoto de Azeredo →,
   Brazil 125 C6
Peize, Neths. 16 B8
Pek →, Serbia, Yug. ... 21 L11
Pekalongan, Indonesia ... 57 G13
Pekan, Malaysia 59 L4
Pekanbaru, Indonesia ... 56 D2
Pekin, U.S.A. 108 E10
Peking = Beijing, China .. 50 E9
Pelabuhan Kelang,
   Malaysia 59 L3
Pelabuhan Ratu, Teluk,
   Indonesia 57 G12
Pelabuhanratu, Indonesia . 57 G12
Pélagos, Greece 39 K7
Pelaihari, Indonesia 56 E4
Pelat, Mt., France 27 D10
Peleaga, Vf., Romania .. 38 D5

Pelechuco, Bolivia 124 C4
Pelée, Mt., Martinique .. 117 D7
Pelee I., Canada 98 D3
Pelee, Pt., Canada 98 D3
Pelejo, Peru 124 B2
Pelekech, Kenya 82 B4
Peleng, Indonesia 57 E6
Pelham, U.S.A. 105 K3
Pelican L., Canada 101 C8
Pelican Narrows, Canada 101 B8
Pelican Rapids, Canada . 101 C8
Pelkosenniemi, Finland ... 8 C22
Pella, S. Africa 84 D2
Pella, U.S.A. 108 E8
Péllaro, Italy 35 D8
Pello, Finland 8 C21
Pellworm, Germany 18 A4
Pelly →, Canada 96 B6
Pelly Bay, Canada 97 B11
Pelly L., Canada 96 B9
Peloponnese =
   Pelopónnisos □, Greece 39 M5
Pelopónnisos □, Greece .. 39 M5
Peloritani, Monti, Italy .. 35 D8
Peloro, C., Italy 35 D8
Pelorus Sd., N.Z. 87 J4
Pelotas, Brazil 127 C5
Pelvoux, Massif du, France 27 D10
Pemalang, Indonesia 57 G13
Pemba, Mozam. 83 E5
Pemba, Zambia 83 F2
Pemba Channel, Tanzania 82 D4
Pemba I., Tanzania 82 D4
Pemberton, Australia ... 89 F2
Pemberton, Canada 100 C4
Pembina, U.S.A. 108 A6
Pembina →, U.S.A. 101 D9
Pembine, U.S.A. 104 C2
Pembroke, Canada 98 C4
Pembroke, U.K. 13 F3
Pembroke, U.S.A. 105 J5
Pen-y-Ghent, U.K. 12 C5
Peña de Francia, Sierra de,
   Spain 30 E4
Peñafiel, Portugal 30 D2
Peñafiel, Spain 30 D6
Peñaflor, Spain 31 H5
Peñalara, Pico, Spain ... 30 E7
Penalva, Brazil 122 B2
Penamacôr, Portugal 30 E3
Penang = Pinang, Malaysia 59 K3
Penápolis, Brazil 127 A6
Peñaranda de Bracamonte,
   Spain 30 E5
Peñarroya-Pueblonuevo,
   Spain 31 G5
Peñas, C. de, Spain 30 B5
Penas, G. de, Chile 128 C2
Peñas, Pta., Venezuela .. 121 A5
Peñas de San Pedro, Spain 29 G2
Peñas del Chache,
   Canary Is. 36 E6
Peñausende, Spain 30 D5
Pench'i = Benxi, China .. 51 D12
Pend Oreille →, U.S.A. . 110 B5
Pend Oreille L., U.S.A. .. 110 C5
Pendembu, S. Leone 78 D2
Pendências, Brazil 122 C4
Pender B., Australia 88 C3
Pendleton, Calif., U.S.A. 113 M9
Pendleton, Oreg., U.S.A. 110 D4
Penedo, Brazil 122 D4
Penetanguishene, Canada 98 D4
Peng Xian, China 52 B4
Penge, Kasai Or., Zaïre . 82 D1
Penge, Kivu, Zaïre 82 C2
Penglai, China 51 F11
Pengshui, China 52 C7
Penguin, Australia 90 G4
Pengxi, China 52 B5
Pengze, China 53 C11
Penhalonga, Zimbabwe .. 83 F3
Peniche, Portugal 31 F1
Penicuik, U.K. 14 F5
Penida, Indonesia 56 F5
Peninsular Malaysia □,
   Malaysia 59 L4
Peñíscola, Spain 28 E5
Penitente, Serra dos, Brazil 122 C2
Penmarch, France 24 E2
Penmarch, Pte. de, France 24 E2
Penn Hills, U.S.A. 106 F5
Penn Yan, U.S.A. 106 D7
Pennabilli, Italy 33 E9
Pennant, Canada 101 C7
Penne, Italy 33 F10
Penner →, India 60 M12
Pennine, Alpi, Alps 32 B4
Pennines, U.K. 12 C5
Pennington, U.S.A. 112 F5
Pennino, Mte., Italy 33 E9
Pennsylvania □, U.S.A. . 104 E6
Penny, Canada 100 C4
Peno, Russia 42 B1
Penola, Australia 91 F3
Penong, Australia 89 F5
Penonomé, Panama 116 E3
Penrith, Australia 91 E5
Penrith, U.K. 12 C5
Pensacola, U.S.A. 105 K2
Pensacola Mts., Antarctica 5 E1
Pense, Canada 101 C8
Penshurst, Australia 91 F3

Pentecoste, Brazil 122 B4
Penticton, Canada 100 D5
Pentland, Australia 90 C4
Pentland Firth, U.K. 14 C5
Pentland Hills, U.K. 14 F5
Penylan L., Canada 101 A7
Penza, Russia 42 D7
Penzance, U.K. 13 G2
Penzberg, Germany 19 H7
Penzhino, Russia 45 C17
Penzhinskaya Guba, Russia 45 C17
Penzlin, Germany 18 B9
Peoria, Ariz., U.S.A. ... 111 K7
Peoria, Ill., U.S.A. 108 E10
Pepingen, Belgium 17 G4
Pepinster, Belgium 17 G7
Pera Hd., Australia 90 A3
Perabumulih, Indonesia .. 56 E2
Perakhóra, Greece 39 L5
Perales de Alfambra, Spain 28 E4
Perales del Puerto, Spain . 30 E4
Peralta, Spain 28 C3
Perché, Canada 99 C7
Perche, France 24 D8
Perche, Collines du, France 24 D7
Percival Lakes, Australia . 88 D4
Percy, France 24 D5
Percy Is., Australia 90 C5
Perdido, Mte., Spain ... 28 C6
Perdido, Mte., Spain ... 26 F4
Perdu, Mt. = Perdido,
   Mte., Spain 26 F4
Pereira, Colombia 120 C2
Pereira Barreto, Brazil ... 123 F1
Perekerten, Australia ... 91 E3
Perelazovskiy, Russia ... 43 F6
Perené →, Peru 124 C3
Perenjori, Australia 89 E2
Pereslavl-Zalesskiy, Russia 42 B4
Pereyaslav-Khmelnytskyy,
   Ukraine 41 G6
Pérez, I., Mexico 115 C7
Pergamino, Argentina ... 126 C3
Pergau →, Malaysia ... 59 K3
Pérgine Valsugana, Italy . 33 B8
Pérgola, Italy 33 E9
Perham, U.S.A. 108 B7
Perhentian, Kepulauan,
   Malaysia 59 K4
Periam, Romania 38 C3
Péribonca →, Canada .. 99 C5
Péribonca, L., Canada .. 99 B5
Perico, Argentina 126 A2
Pericos, Mexico 114 B3
Périers, France 24 C5
Périgord, France 26 D4
Périgueux, France 26 C4
Perijá, Sierra de, Colombia 120 B3
Peristéra, Greece 39 K6
Peristerona →, Cyprus . 37 D12
Perito Moreno, Argentina 128 C2
Peritoró, Brazil 122 B3
Perković, Croatia 33 E13
Perlas, Arch. de las,
   Panama 116 E4
Perlas, Punta de, Nic. ... 116 D3
Perleberg, Germany 18 B7
Perm, Russia 44 D6
Pernambuco = Recife,
   Brazil 122 C5
Pernambuco □, Brazil ... 122 C3
Pernatty Lagoon, Australia 91 E2
Pernik, Bulgaria 38 G6
Peron, C., Australia 89 E1
Peron Is., Australia 88 B5
Peron Pen., Australia ... 89 E1
Péronne, France 25 C9
Péronnes, Belgium 17 H4
Perosa Argentina, Italy .. 32 D4
Perow, Canada 100 C3
Perpendicular Pt., Australia 91 E5
Perpignan, France 26 F6
Perris, U.S.A. 113 M9
Perros-Guirec, France ... 24 D3
Perry, Fla., U.S.A. 105 K4
Perry, Ga., U.S.A. 105 J4
Perry, Iowa, U.S.A. 108 E7
Perry, Maine, U.S.A. ... 105 C12
Perry, Okla., U.S.A. ... 109 G6
Perryton, U.S.A. 109 G4
Perryville, U.S.A. 109 G10
Persembe, Turkey 66 B7
Perseverancia, Bolivia ... 125 C5
Pershotravensk, Ukraine . 41 G4
Persia = Iran ■, Asia ... 65 C7
Persian Gulf = Gulf, The,
   Asia 65 E6
Perstorp, Sweden 11 H7
Pertek, Turkey 67 C8
Perth, Australia 89 F2
Perth, Canada 98 D4
Perth, U.K. 14 E5
Perth Amboy, U.S.A. ... 107 F10
Pertuis, France 27 E9
Pertusato, France 27 G13
Peru, Ill., U.S.A. 108 E10
Peru, Ind., U.S.A. 104 E2
Peru ■, S. Amer. 120 D2
Peru-Chile Trench,
   Pac. Oc. 93 K20
Perúgia, Italy 33 E9
Perušić, Croatia 33 D12
Péruwelz, Belgium 17 G3
Pervomaysk, Russia 42 C6
Pervomaysk, Ukraine ... 41 H6

Pervouralsk, Russia 44 D6
Perwez, Belgium 17 G5
Pes, Pta. del, Spain 36 C7
Pésaro, Italy 33 E9
Pescara, Italy 33 F11
Pescara →, Italy 33 F11
Peschanokopskoye, Russia 43 G5
Péscia, Italy 32 E7
Pescina, Italy 33 G10
Peseux, Switz. 22 C3
Peshawar, Pakistan 62 B4
Peshtigo, U.S.A. 104 C2
Peski, Russia 42 E6
Pêso da Régua, Portugal . 30 D3
Pesqueira, Brazil 122 C4
Pessac, France 26 D3
Pessoux, Belgium 17 H6
Pestovo, Russia 40 C8
Pestravka, Russia 42 D9
Petah Tiqwa, Israel 69 C3
Petaling Jaya, Malaysia . 59 L3
Petaloudhes, Greece 37 C10
Petaluma, U.S.A. 112 G4
Petange, Lux. 17 J7
Petatlán, Mexico 114 D4
Petauke, Zambia 83 E3
Petawawa, Canada 98 C4
Petegem, Belgium 17 G3
Petén Itzá, L., Guatemala 116 C2
Peter I.s Øy, Antarctica . 5 C16
Peter Pond L., Canada .. 101 B7
Peterbell, Canada 98 C3
Peterborough, Australia . 91 E2
Peterborough, Canada .. 97 D12
Peterborough, U.K. 13 E7
Peterborough, U.S.A. ... 107 D13
Peterhead, U.K. 14 D7
Petermann Bjerg,
   Greenland 94 B17
Peter's Mine, Guyana ... 121 B6
Petersburg, Alaska, U.S.A. 100 B2
Petersburg, Ind., U.S.A. 104 F2
Petersburg, Va., U.S.A. . 104 G7
Petersburg, W. Va., U.S.A. 104 F6
Petford, Australia 90 B3
Petília Policastro, Italy .. 35 C9
Petit Bois I., U.S.A. 105 K1
Petit-Cap, Canada 99 C7
Petit Goâve, Haiti 117 C5
Petit Lac Manicouagan,
   Canada 99 B6
Petit Saint Bernard, Col
   du, Italy 32 C3
Petitcodiac, Canada 99 C6
Petite Baleine →, Canada 98 A4
Petite Saguenay, Canada . 99 C5
Petitsikapau, L., Canada . 99 B6
Petlad, India 62 H5
Peto, Mexico 115 C7
Petone, N.Z. 87 J5
Petoskey, U.S.A. 104 C3
Petra, Jordan 69 E4
Petra, Spain 36 B10
Petra, Ostrova, Russia ... 4 B13
Petra Velikogo, Zaliv,
   Russia 48 C5
Petralia Sottana, Italy ... 35 E7
Petrel, Australia 29 G4
Petreto-Bicchisano, France 27 G12
Petrich, Bulgaria 39 H6
Petrijanec, Croatia 33 B13
Petrikov = Pyetrikaw,
   Belarus 41 F5
Petrinja, Croatia 33 C13
Petrodvorets, Russia 40 C5
Petrograd = Sankt-
   Peterburg, Russia 40 C6
Petrolândia, Brazil 122 C4
Petrolia, Canada 98 D3
Petrolina, Brazil 122 C3
Petropavl, Kazakhstan .. 44 D7
Petropavlovsk = Petropavl,
   Kazakhstan 44 D7
Petropavlovsk-
   Kamchatskiy, Russia .. 45 D16
Petropavlovskiy =
   Akhtubinsk, Russia 43 F8
Petrópolis, Brazil 123 F3
Petrosani, Romania 38 D6
Petrova Gora, Croatia .. 33 C12
Petrovac, Montenegro, Yug. 21 N8
Petrovsk, Russia 42 D8
Petrovsk-Zabaykalskiy,
   Russia 45 D11
Petrovskaya, Russia 43 H3
Petrovskoye = Svetlograd,
   Russia 43 H6
Petrozavodsk, Russia ... 40 B8
Petrus Steyn, S. Africa .. 85 D4
Petrusburg, S. Africa ... 84 D4
Peumo, Chile 126 C1
Peureulak, Indonesia ... 56 D1
Pevek, Russia 45 C18
Peveragno, Italy 32 D4
Peyrehorade, France 26 E2
Peyruis, France 27 D9
Pézenas, France 26 E7
Pfaffenhofen, Germany .. 19 G7
Pfäffikon, Switz. 23 B7
Pfarrkirchen, Germany .. 19 G8
Pfeffenhausen, Germany . 19 G7
Pforzheim, Germany 19 G4
Pfullendorf, Germany ... 19 H5
Pfungstadt, Germany ... 19 F4
Phagwara, India 60 D9
Phaistós, Greece 37 D6
Phala, Botswana 84 C4

Phalera = Phulera, India . 62 F6
Phalodi, India 62 F5
Phalsbourg, France 25 D14
Phan, Thailand 58 C2
Phan Rang, Vietnam 59 G7
Phan Ri = Hoa Da,
  Vietnam 59 G7
Phan Thiet, Vietnam 59 G7
Phanat Nikhom, Thailand . 58 F3
Phangan, Ko, Thailand . . 59 H3
Phangnga, Thailand 59 H2
Phanh Bho Ho Chi Minh,
  Vietnam 59 G6
Phanom Sarakham,
  Thailand 58 F3
Pharenda, India 63 F10
Phatthalung, Thailand . . . 59 J3
Phayao, Thailand 58 C2
Phelps, N.Y., U.S.A. 106 D7
Phelps, Wis., U.S.A. 108 B10
Phelps L., Canada 101 B8
Phenix City, U.S.A. 105 J3
Phet Buri, Thailand 58 F2
Phetchabun, Thailand . . . 58 D3
Phetchabun, Thiu Khao,
  Thailand 58 E3
Phetchaburi = Phet Buri,
  Thailand 58 F2
Phi Phi, Ko, Thailand . . . 59 J2
Phiafay, Laos 58 E6
Phibun Mangsahan,
  Thailand 58 E5
Phichai, Thailand 58 D3
Phichit, Thailand 58 D3
Philadelphia, Miss., U.S.A. 109 J10
Philadelphia, N.Y., U.S.A. 107 B9
Philadelphia, Pa., U.S.A. . 107 F9
Philip, U.S.A. 108 C4
Philippeville, Belgium . . . 17 H5
Philippi L., Australia 90 C2
Philippines ■, Asia 55 F5
Philippolis, S. Africa 84 E4
Philippopolis = Plovdiv,
  Bulgaria 38 G7
Philipsburg, Mont., U.S.A. 110 C7
Philipsburg, Pa., U.S.A. . . 106 F6
Philipstown = Daingean,
  Ireland 15 C4
Philipstown, S. Africa . . . 84 E3
Phillip I., Australia 91 F4
Phillips, Tex., U.S.A. 109 H4
Phillips, Wis., U.S.A. 108 C9
Phillipsburg, Kans., U.S.A. 108 F5
Phillipsburg, N.J., U.S.A. . 107 F9
Phillott, Australia 91 D4
Philmont, U.S.A. 107 D11
Philomath, U.S.A. 110 D2
Phimai, Thailand 58 E4
Phitsanulok, Thailand . . . 58 D3
Phnom Dangrek, Thailand 58 E5
Phnom Penh, Cambodia . . 59 G5
Phoenix, Ariz., U.S.A. . . . 111 K7
Phoenix, N.Y., U.S.A. . . . 107 C8
Phoenix Is., Kiribati 92 H10
Phoenixville, U.S.A. 107 F9
Phon, Thailand 58 E4
Phon Tiou, Laos 58 D5
Phong →, Thailand 58 D4
Phong Saly, Laos 58 B4
Phong Tho, Vietnam 58 A4
Phonhong, Laos 58 C4
Phonum, Thailand 59 H2
Phosphate Hill, Australia . 90 C2
Photharam, Thailand 58 F2
Phra Chedi Sam Ong,
  Thailand 58 E2
Phra Nakhon Si Ayutthaya,
  Thailand 58 E3
Phra Thong, Ko, Thailand 59 H2
Phrae, Thailand 58 C3
Phrom Phiram, Thailand . . 58 D3
Phrygia, Turkey 66 C4
Phu Dien, Vietnam 58 C5
Phu Loi, Laos 58 B4
Phu Ly, Vietnam 58 B5
Phu Tho, Vietnam 58 B5
Phuc Yen, Vietnam 58 B5
Phuket, Thailand 59 J2
Phuket, Ko, Thailand . . . 59 J2
Phulera, India 62 F6
Phumiphon, Khuan,
  Thailand 58 D2
Phun Phin, Thailand 59 H2
Piacá, Brazil 122 C2
Piacenza, Italy 32 C6
Piaçubaçu, Brazil 122 C4
Piádena, Italy 32 C7
Pialba, Australia 91 D5
Pian Cr. →, Australia . . . 91 E4
Piana, France 27 F12
Pianella, Italy 33 F11
Pianoro, Italy 33 D8
Pianosa, Puglia, Italy . . . 33 F12
Pianosa, Toscana, Italy . . 32 F7
Piapot, Canada 101 D7
Piare →, Italy 33 C9
Pias, Portugal 31 G3
Piaseczno, Poland 20 C11
Piatã, Brazil 123 D3
Piatra, Romania 38 F8
Piatra Neamţ, Romania . . 38 C8
Piauí □, Brazil 122 C3
Piauí →, Brazil 122 C3
Piave →, Italy 33 C9
Piazza Armerina, Italy . . 35 E7
Pibor →, Sudan 77 F3
Pibor Post, Sudan 77 F3

Pica, Chile 124 E4
Picardie, France 25 C9
Picardie, Plaine de, France 25 C9
Picardy = Picardie, France 25 C9
Picayune, U.S.A. 109 K10
Picerno, Italy 35 B8
Pichilemu, Chile 126 C1
Pichincha, □, Ecuador . . 120 D2
Pickerel L., Canada 98 C1
Pickle Lake, Canada 98 B1
Pico Truncado, Argentina . 128 C3
Picos, Brazil 122 C3
Picos Ancares, Sierra de,
  Spain 30 C4
Picota, Peru 124 B2
Picquigny, France 25 C9
Picton, Australia 91 E5
Picton, Canada 98 D4
Picton, N.Z. 87 J5
Picton, I., Chile 128 E3
Pictou, Canada 99 C7
Picture Butte, Canada . . . 100 D6
Picuí, Brazil 122 C4
Picún Leufú, Argentina . . 128 A3
Pidurutalagala, Sri Lanka . 60 R12
Piedecuesta, Colombia . . 120 B3
Piedicavallo, Italy 32 C4
Piedmont = Piemonte □,
  Italy 32 D4
Piedmont, U.S.A. 105 J3
Piedmont Plateau, U.S.A. . 105 J5
Piedmonte d'Alife, Italy . . 35 A7
Piedra →, Spain 28 D3
Piedra del Anguila,
  Argentina 128 B2
Piedra Lais, Venezuela . . 120 C4
Piedrabuena, Spain 31 F6
Piedrahita, Spain 30 E5
Piedras, R. de las →, Peru 124 C4
Piedras Negras, Mexico . . 114 B4
Pieksämäki, Finland 9 E22
Piemonte □, Italy 32 D4
Pierce, U.S.A. 110 C6
Piercefield, U.S.A. 107 B10
Pierre, U.S.A. 108 C4
Pierre Bénite, Barrage de
  la, France 27 C8
Pierre-de-Bresse, France . . 27 B9
Pierrefeu-du-Var, France . 27 E10
Pierrefonds, France 25 C9
Pierrefontaine-les-Varans,
  France 25 E13
Pierrefort, France 26 D6
Pierrelatte, France 27 D8
Pieštany, Slovak Rep. . . . 20 G7
Piesting →, Austria 21 G6
Piet Retief, S. Africa 85 D5
Pietarsaari, Finland 8 E20
Pietermaritzburg, S. Africa 85 D5
Pietersburg, S. Africa . . . 85 C4
Pietraperzía, Italy 35 E7
Pietrasanta, Italy 32 E7
Pietrosul, Romania 38 B8
Pietrosul, Romania 38 B7
Pieve di Cadore, Italy . . . 33 B9
Pieve di Teco, Italy 32 D4
Pievepélago, Italy 32 D7
Pigádhia, Greece 39 P10
Pigeon, U.S.A. 104 D4
Piggott, U.S.A. 109 G9
Pigna, Italy 32 E4
Pigüe, Argentina 126 D3
Pihani, India 63 F9
Pihlajavesi, Finland 9 F23
Pijnacker, Neths. 16 D4
Pikalevo, Russia 40 C8
Pikes Peak, U.S.A. 108 F2
Piketberg, S. Africa 84 E2
Pikeville, U.S.A. 104 G4
Pikou, China 51 E12
Pikwitonei, Canada 101 B9
Piła, Poland 20 B6
Pila, Spain 29 G3
Pilani, India 62 E6
Pilar, Brazil 122 C4
Pilar, Paraguay 126 B4
Pilas Group, Phil. 57 C6
Pilaya →, Bolivia 125 E5
Pilcomayo →, Paraguay . . 126 B4
Pilibhit, India 63 E8
Pilica →, Poland 20 D11
Pilkhawa, India 62 E7
Pillaro, Ecuador 120 D2
Pílos, Greece 39 N4
Pilot Mound, Canada . . . 101 D9
Pilot Point, U.S.A. 109 J6
Pilot Rock, U.S.A. 110 D4
Pilsen = Plzeň, Czech. . . 20 D4
Pilštanj, Slovenia 33 B12
Pima, U.S.A. 111 K9
Pimba, Australia 91 E2
Pimenta Bueno, Brazil . . 125 C5
Pimentel, Peru 124 B2
Pina, Spain 28 D4
Pinamalayan, Phil. 55 E4
Pinang, Malaysia 59 K3
Pinar, C. del, Spain 36 B10
Pinar del Río, Cuba 116 B3
Pınarbaşı, Turkey 66 C7
Pınarhisar, Turkey 66 B2
Pinchang, China 52 B6
Pincher Creek, Canada . . 100 D6
Pinchi L., Canada 100 C4
Pinckneyville, U.S.A. . . . 108 F10
Pincota, Romania 38 C4
Pind Dadan Khan, Pakistan 62 C5
Pindar, Australia 89 E2

Pindaré →, Brazil 122 B3
Pindaré Mirim, Brazil . . . 122 B2
Pindi Gheb, Pakistan . . . 62 C5
Pindiga, Nigeria 79 D7
Pindobal, Brazil 122 B2
Pindos Óros, Greece 39 K4
Pindus Mts. = Pindos
  Óros, Greece 39 K4
Pine, U.S.A. 111 J8
Pine →, Canada 101 B7
Pine, C., Canada 99 C9
Pine Bluff, U.S.A. 109 H8
Pine City, U.S.A. 108 C8
Pine Falls, Canada 101 C9
Pine Flat L., U.S.A. 112 J7
Pine Pass, Canada 100 B4
Pine Point, Canada 100 A6
Pine Ridge, U.S.A. 108 D3
Pine River, Canada 101 C8
Pine River, U.S.A. 108 B7
Pine Valley, U.S.A. 113 N10
Pinecrest, U.S.A. 112 G6
Pinedale, U.S.A. 112 J7
Pinega →, Russia 44 C5
Pinehill, Australia 90 C4
Pinerolo, Italy 32 D4
Pineto, Italy 33 F11
Pinetop, U.S.A. 111 J9
Pinetown, S. Africa 85 D5
Pinetree, U.S.A. 110 E11
Pineville, Ky., U.S.A. . . . 105 G4
Pineville, La., U.S.A. . . . 109 K8
Piney, France 25 D11
Ping →, Thailand 58 E3
Pingaring, Australia 89 F2
Pingba, China 52 D6
Pingchuan, China 52 D3
Pingding, China 50 F7
Pingdingshan, China 50 H7
Pingdong, Taiwan 53 F13
Pingdu, China 51 F10
Pingelly, Australia 89 F2
Pingguo, China 52 F6
Pinghe, China 53 E11
Pinghu, China 53 B13
Pingjiang, China 53 C9
Pingle, China 53 E8
Pingli, China 52 A7
Pingliang, China 50 G4
Pinglu, China 50 E7
Pingluo, China 50 E4
Pingnan, Fujian, China . . 53 D12
Pingnan,
  Guangxi Zhuangzu,
  China 53 F8
Pingquan, China 51 D10
Pingrup, Australia 89 F2
Pingtan, China 53 E12
Pingtang, China 52 E6
Pingwu, China 50 H3
Pingxiang,
  Guangxi Zhuangzu,
  China 52 F6
Pingxiang, Jiangxi, China . 53 D9
Pingyao, China 50 F7
Pingyi, China 51 G9
Pingyin, China 50 F9
Pingyuan, Guangdong,
  China 53 E10
Pingyuan, Shandong, China 50 F9
Pingyuanjie, China 52 F4
Pinhal, Brazil 127 A6
Pinheiro, Brazil 122 B2
Pinhel, Portugal 30 E3
Pinhuá →, Brazil 125 B4
Pini, Indonesia 56 D1
Piniós →, Ília, Greece . . . 39 M4
Piniós →, Trikkala, Greece 39 K5
Pinjarra, Australia 89 F2
Pink →, Canada 101 B8
Pinnacles, Australia 89 E3
Pinnacles, U.S.A. 112 J5
Pinnaroo, Australia 91 F3
Pinneberg, Germany 18 B5
Pínnes, Ákra, Greece . . . 39 J7
Pino Hachado, Paso,
  S. Amer. 128 A2
Pinon Hills, U.S.A. 113 L9
Pinos, Mexico 114 C4
Pinos, Mt., U.S.A. 113 L7
Pinos Pt., U.S.A. 111 H3
Pinos Puente, Spain 31 H7
Pinotepa Nacional, Mexico 115 D5
Pinrang, Indonesia 57 E5
Pinsk, Belarus 41 F4
Pintados, Chile 124 E4
Pintumba, Australia 89 F5
Pinyang, China 53 D13
Pinyug, Russia 44 C5
Pinzolo, Italy 32 B7
Pio XII, Brazil 122 B2
Pioche, U.S.A. 111 H6
Piombino, Italy 32 F7
Piombino, Canale di, Italy 32 F7
Pioner, Os., Russia 45 B10
Pionki, Poland 20 D11
Piorini →, Brazil 121 D5
Piorini, L., Brazil 121 D5
Piotrków Trybunalski,
  Poland 20 D9
Piove di Sacco, Italy 33 C9
Pip, Iran 65 E9
Pipar, India 62 F5
Piparia, India 62 H8
Pipestone, U.S.A. 108 D6
Pipestone →, Canada . . . 98 B2
Pipestone Cr. →, Canada 101 D8

Pipmuacan, Rés., Canada . 99 C5
Pippingarra, Australia . . . 88 D2
Pipriac, France 24 E5
Piqua, U.S.A. 104 E3
Piquet Carneiro, Brazil . . 122 C4
Piquiri →, Brazil 127 A5
Pīr Sohrāb, Iran 65 E9
Piracanjuba, Brazil 123 E2
Piracicaba, Brazil 127 A6
Piracuruca, Brazil 122 B3
Piræus = Piraiévs, Greece 39 M6
Piraiévs, Greece 39 M6
Piráino, Italy 35 D7
Pirajuí, Brazil 127 A6
Piran, Slovenia 33 C10
Pirané, Argentina 126 B4
Piranhas, Brazil 122 C4
Pirano = Piran, Slovenia . 33 C10
Pirapemas, Brazil 122 B3
Pirapora, Brazil 123 E3
Piray →, Bolivia 125 D5
Pires do Rio, Brazil 123 E2
Pírgos, Ilía, Greece 39 M4
Pírgos, Messinia, Greece . 39 N5
Pirgovo, Bulgaria 38 F8
Piribebuy, Paraguay 126 B4
Pirin Planina, Bulgaria . . 39 H6
Pirineos, Spain 28 C5
Piripiri, Brazil 122 B3
Piritu, Venezuela 120 B4
Pirmasens, Germany 19 F3
Pirna, Germany 18 E9
Pirot, Serbia, Yug. 21 M12
Piru, Indonesia 57 E7
Piru, U.S.A. 113 L8
Piryatin = Pyryatyn,
  Ukraine 41 G7
Pisa, Italy 32 E7
Pisac, Peru 124 C3
Pisagua, Chile 124 D3
Pisarovina, Croatia 33 C12
Pisciotta, Italy 35 B8
Pisco, Peru 124 C2
Písek, Czech. 20 F4
Pishan, China 54 C2
Pishin Lora →, Pakistan . 62 E1
Pisidia, Turkey 66 D4
Pising, Indonesia 57 F6
Pismo Beach, U.S.A. 113 K6
Pissis, Cerro, Argentina . 126 B2
Pissos, France 26 D3
Pissouri, Cyprus 37 E11
Pisticci, Italy 35 B9
Pistóia, Italy 32 E7
Pistol B., Canada 101 A10
Pisuerga →, Spain 30 D6
Pisz, Poland 20 B11
Pitalito, Colombia 120 C2
Pitanga, Brazil 123 F1
Pitangui, Brazil 123 E3
Pitarpunga, L., Australia . 91 E3
Pitcairn I., Pac. Oc. 93 K14
Pite älv →, Sweden 8 D19
Piteå, Sweden 8 D19
Piterka, Russia 42 E8
Piteşti, Romania 38 E7
Pithapuram, India 61 L13
Pithara, Australia 89 F2
Píthion, Greece 39 H9
Pithiviers, France 25 D9
Pitigliano, Italy 33 F8
Pitkyaranta, Russia 40 B5
Pitlochry, U.K. 14 E5
Pitrufquén, Chile 128 A2
Pitsilia □, Cyprus 37 E12
Pitt I., Canada 100 C3
Pittem, Belgium 17 F2
Pittsburg, Kans., U.S.A. . 109 G7
Pittsburg, Tex., U.S.A. . . 109 J7
Pittsburg, U.S.A. 106 F5
Pittsfield, Ill., U.S.A. . . . 108 F9
Pittsfield, Mass., U.S.A. . 107 D11
Pittsfield, N.H., U.S.A. . . 107 C13
Pittston, U.S.A. 107 E9
Pittsworth, Australia 91 D5
Pituri →, Australia 90 C2
Piuí, Brazil 123 F2
Pium, Brazil 122 D2
Piura, Peru 124 B1
Piura □, Peru 124 A2
Pivijay, Colombia 120 A3
Pixley, U.S.A. 113 K7
Piyai, Greece 39 K4
Pizarro, Colombia 120 C2
Pizol, Switz. 23 C8
Pizzo, Italy 35 D9
Placentia, Canada 99 C9
Placentia B., Canada . . . 99 C9
Placer, Phil. 55 F5
Placerville, U.S.A. 112 G6
Placetas, Cuba 116 B4
Plaffeien, Switz. 22 C4
Plain Dealing, U.S.A. . . . 109 J8
Plainfield, U.S.A. 107 F10
Plains, Mont., U.S.A. . . . 110 C6
Plains, Tex., U.S.A. 109 J3
Plainview, Nebr., U.S.A. . 108 D6
Plainview, Tex., U.S.A. . . 109 H4
Plainville, U.S.A. 108 F5
Plainwell, U.S.A. 104 D3
Plaisance, France 26 E4
Pláka, Greece 39 J8
Pláka, Ákra, Greece 37 D8
Plakhino, Russia 44 C9
Plana Cays, Bahamas . . . 117 B5

Planada, U.S.A. 112 H6
Plancoët, France 24 D4
Plandište, Serbia, Yug. . . 21 K11
Planeta Rica, Colombia . . 120 B2
Planina, Slovenia 33 B12
Planina, Slovenia 33 C11
Plankinton, U.S.A. 108 D5
Plano, U.S.A. 109 J6
Plant City, U.S.A. 105 L4
Plaquemine, U.S.A. 109 K9
Plasencia, Spain 30 E4
Plaški, Croatia 33 C12
Plaster City, U.S.A. 113 N11
Plaster Rock, Canada . . . 99 C6
Plastun, Russia 48 B8
Plata, Río de la, S. Amer. 126 C4
Platani →, Italy 34 E6
Plátanos, Greece 37 D5
Plateau □, Nigeria 79 D6
Plateau du Coteau du
  Missouri, U.S.A. 108 B4
Plato, Colombia 120 B3
Platta, Piz, Switz. 23 D9
Platte, U.S.A. 108 D5
Platte →, U.S.A. 108 F7
Platteville, U.S.A. 108 E2
Plattling, Germany 19 G8
Plattsburgh, U.S.A. 107 B11
Plattsmouth, U.S.A. 108 E7
Plau, Germany 18 B8
Plauen, Germany 18 E8
Plavinas, Latvia 9 H21
Plavnica, Montenegro, Yug. 21 N9
Plavsk, Russia 42 D3
Playa Blanca, Canary Is. . 36 F6
Playa Blanca Sur,
  Canary Is. 36 F6
Playa de las Americas,
  Canary Is. 36 F3
Playa de Mogán, Canary Is. 36 G4
Playa del Inglés, Canary Is. 36 G4
Playa Esmerelda,
  Canary Is. 36 F5
Playgreen L., Canada . . . 101 C9
Pleasant Bay, Canada . . . 99 C7
Pleasant Hill, Calif.,
  U.S.A. 112 H4
Pleasant Hill, Mo., U.S.A. 108 F7
Pleasanton, U.S.A. 109 L5
Pleasantville, U.S.A. 104 F8
Pléaux, France 26 C6
Pleiku, Vietnam 58 F7
Plélan-le-Grand, France . . 24 D4
Plémet-la-Pierre, France . . 24 D4
Pléneuf-Val-André, France 24 D4
Pleniţa, Romania 38 E6
Plenty →, Australia 90 C2
Plenty, B. of, N.Z. 87 G6
Plentywood, U.S.A. 108 A2
Plessisville, Canada 99 C5
Plestin-les-Grèves, France . 24 D3
Pleszew, Poland 20 D7
Pleternica, Croatia 21 K7
Pletipi L., Canada 99 B5
Pleven, Bulgaria 38 F7
Plevlja, Montenegro, Yug. 21 M9
Płock, Poland 20 C9
Plöcken Passo, Italy 33 B9
Ploegsteert, Belgium . . . 17 G1
Ploemeur, France 24 E3
Ploërmel, France 24 E4
Ploieşti, Romania 38 E9
Plombières-les-Bains,
  France 25 E13
Plomin, Croatia 33 C11
Plön, Germany 18 A6
Plöner See, Germany . . . 18 A6
Plonge, Lac la, Canada . . 101 B7
Płońsk, Poland 20 C10
Płoty, Poland 20 B5
Plouaret, France 24 D3
Plouay, France 24 E3
Ploudalmézeau, France . . 24 D2
Plougasnou, France 24 D3
Plouha, France 24 D4
Plouhinec, France 24 E2
Plovdiv, Bulgaria 38 G7
Plum, U.S.A. 106 F5
Plum I., U.S.A. 107 E12
Plumas, U.S.A. 112 F7
Plummer, U.S.A. 110 C5
Plumtree, Zimbabwe . . . 83 G2
Plunge, Lithuania 9 J19
Pluvigner, France 24 E3
Plymouth, U.K. 13 G3
Plymouth, Calif., U.S.A. . 112 G6
Plymouth, Ind., U.S.A. . . 104 E2
Plymouth, Mass., U.S.A. . 107 E14
Plymouth, N.C., U.S.A. . . 105 H7
Plymouth, N.H., U.S.A. . . 107 C13
Plymouth, Pa., U.S.A. . . . 107 E9
Plymouth, Wis., U.S.A. . . 104 D2
Plynlimon = Pumlumon
  Fawr, U.K. 13 E4
Plyusa, Russia 40 C5
Plyusa →, Russia 40 C5
Plyussa = Plyusa, Russia . 40 C5
Plyussa = Plyusa →,
  Russia 40 C5
Plzeň, Czech. 20 F3
Pniewy, Poland 20 C6
Pô, Burkina Faso 79 C4
Po →, Italy 33 D9
Po, Foci del, Italy 33 D9
Po Hai = Bo Hai, China . 51 E10
Pobé, Benin 79 D5
Pobeda, Russia 45 C15

Pobedino

Pobedino, *Russia* 45 E15
Pobedy Pik, *Kyrgyzstan* . . 44 E8
Pobiedziska, *Poland* 20 C7
Pobla de Segur, *Spain* . . . 28 C5
Pobladura de Valle, *Spain* . 30 C5
Pocahontas, *Ark., U.S.A.* . 109 G9
Pocahontas, *Iowa, U.S.A.* . 108 D7
Pocatello, *U.S.A.* 110 E7
Pochep, *Russia* 41 F7
Pochinki, *Russia* 42 C7
Pochinok, *Russia* 40 E7
Pochutla, *Mexico* 115 D5
Poci, *Venezuela* 121 B5
Pocinhos, *Brazil* 122 C4
Pocito Casas, *Mexico* 114 B2
Poções, *Brazil* 123 D3
Pocomoke City, *U.S.A.* . . . 104 F8
Poconé, *Brazil* 125 D6
Poços de Caldas, *Brazil* . . 127 A6
Poddebice, *Poland* 20 D8
Poděbrady, *Czech.* 20 E5
Podensac, *France* 26 D3
Podgorica,
  Montenegro, Yug. 21 N9
Podilska Vysochyna,
  Ukraine 41 H4
Podkamennaya
  Tunguska →, *Russia* . . . 45 C10
Podlapac, *Croatia* 33 D12
Podolsk, *Russia* 42 C3
Podor, *Senegal* 78 B1
Podporozhy, *Russia* 40 B8
Podravska Slatina, *Croatia* 21 K7
Podujevo, *Serbia, Yug.* . . . 21 N11
Poel, *Germany* 18 B7
Pofadder, *S. Africa* 84 D2
Pogamasing, *Canada* 98 C3
Poggiardo, *Italy* 35 B11
Poggibonsi, *Italy* 33 E8
Pogoanele, *Romania* 38 E9
Pogradeci, *Albania* 39 J3
Pogranitšnyi, *Russia* 48 B5
Poh, *Indonesia* 57 E6
Pohang, *S. Korea* 51 F15
Pohjanmaa, *Finland* 8 E20
Pohnpei, *Pac. Oc.* 92 G7
Pohorelá, *Slovak Rep.* . . . 20 G10
Pohorje, *Slovenia* 33 B12
Poiana Mare, *Romania* . . 38 F6
Poinsett, C., *Antarctica* . . 5 C8
Point Edward, *Canada* . . . 98 D3
Point Pedro, *Sri Lanka* . . 60 Q12
Point Pleasant, *N.J.,*
  U.S.A. 107 F10
Point Pleasant, *W. Va.,*
  U.S.A. 104 F4
Pointe-à-la Hache, *U.S.A.* 109 L10
Pointe-à-Pitre, *Guadeloupe* 117 C7
Pointe Noire, *Congo* 80 E2
Poirino, *Italy* 32 D4
Poisonbush Ra., *Australia* 88 D3
Poissy, *France* 25 D9
Poitiers, *France* 24 F7
Poitou, *France* 26 B3
Poitou, Seuil du, *France* . . 26 B4
Poix de Picardie, *France* . . 25 C8
Poix-Terron, *France* 25 C11
Pojoaque Valley, *U.S.A.* . . 111 J11
Pokaran, *India* 60 F7
Pokataroo, *Australia* 91 D4
Pokhvistnevo, *Russia* 42 D11
Poko, *Sudan* 77 F3
Poko, *Zaïre* 82 B2
Pokrov, *Russia* 42 C4
Pokrovsk = Engels, *Russia* 42 E8
Pokrovsk, *Russia* 45 C13
Pokrovskoye, *Russia* 43 G4
Pol, *Spain* 30 B3
Pola = Pula, *Croatia* 33 D10
Pola, *Russia* 40 D7
Pola de Allande, *Spain* . . . 30 B4
Pola de Lena, *Spain* 30 B5
Pola de Siero, *Spain* 30 B5
Pola de Somiedo, *Spain* . . 30 B4
Polacca, *U.S.A.* 111 J8
Polan, *Iran* 65 E9
Poland ■, *Europe* 20 C9
Polanów, *Poland* 20 A6
Polatlı, *Turkey* 66 C5
Polatsk, *Belarus* 40 E5
Polcura, *Chile* 126 D1
Polden Hills, *U.K.* 13 F5
Polessk, *Russia* 9 J19
Polesye = Pripet Marshes,
  Europe 41 F5
Polgar, *Hungary* 21 H11
Pŏlgyo-ri, *S. Korea* 51 G14
Poli, *Cameroon* 80 C2
Políaigos, *Greece* 39 N7
Policastro, G. di, *Italy* . . . 35 C8
Police, *Poland* 20 B4
Polignano a Mare, *Italy* . . 35 B10
Poligny, *France* 25 F12
Políkhnitas, *Greece* 39 K9
Polillo Is., *Phil.* 55 D4
Polillo Strait, *Phil.* 55 D4
Polis, *Cyprus* 37 D11
Polístena, *Italy* 35 D9
Políyiros, *Greece* 39 J6
Polk, *U.S.A.* 106 E5
Polla, *Italy* 35 B8
Pollachi, *India* 60 P10
Pollensa, *Spain* 36 B10
Pollensa, B. de, *Spain* . . . 36 B10
Póllica, *Italy* 35 B8
Pollino, Mte., *Italy* 35 C9
Pollock, *U.S.A.* 108 C4

Polna, *Russia* 40 C5
Polnovat, *Russia* 44 C7
Polo, *U.S.A.* 108 E10
Pology, *Ukraine* 41 J9
Polonne, *Ukraine* 41 G4
Polonnoye = Polonne,
  Ukraine 41 G4
Polson, *U.S.A.* 110 C6
Poltava, *Ukraine* 41 H8
Põltsamaa, *Estonia* 9 G21
Polunochnoye, *Russia* . . . 44 C7
Põlva, *Estonia* 9 G22
Polynesia, *Pac. Oc.* 93 H11
Polynésie française =
  French Polynesia ■,
  Pac. Oc. 93 J13
Pomarance, *Italy* 32 E7
Pomárico, *Italy* 35 B9
Pomaro, *Mexico* 114 D4
Pombal, *Brazil* 122 C4
Pombal, *Portugal* 30 F2
Pómbia, *Greece* 37 D6
Pomeroy, *Ohio, U.S.A.* . . 104 F4
Pomeroy, *Wash., U.S.A.* . 110 C5
Pomichna, *Ukraine* 41 H6
Pomona, *U.S.A.* 113 L9
Pomorie, *Bulgaria* 38 G10
Pomos, *Cyprus* 37 D11
Pomos, C., *Cyprus* 37 D11
Pompano Beach, *U.S.A.* . . 105 M5
Pompei, *Italy* 35 B7
Pompey, *France* 25 D13
Pompeys Pillar, *U.S.A.* . . 110 D10
Ponape = Pohnpei,
  Pac. Oc. 92 G7
Ponask, L., *Canada* 98 B1
Ponass L., *Canada* 101 C8
Ponca, *U.S.A.* 108 D6
Ponca City, *U.S.A.* 109 G6
Ponce, *Puerto Rico* 117 C6
Ponchatoula, *U.S.A.* 109 K9
Ponchevi!le, L., *Canada* . . 98 B4
Poncin, *France* 27 B9
Pond, *U.S.A.* 113 K7
Pond Inlet, *Canada* 97 A12
Pondicherry, *India* 60 P11
Pondrôme, *Belgium* 17 H6
Ponds, I. of, *Canada* 99 B8
Ponferrada, *Spain* 30 C4
Pongo, Wadi →, *Sudan* . . 77 F2
Poniatowa, *Poland* 20 D12
Ponikva, *Slovenia* 33 B12
Ponnani, *India* 60 P9
Ponnyadaung, *Burma* . . . 61 J19
Ponoka, *Canada* 100 C6
Ponorogo, *Indonesia* 57 G14
Ponoy →, *Russia* 44 C5
Pons, *France* 26 C3
Pons, *Spain* 28 D6
Ponsul →, *Portugal* 31 F3
Pont-à-Celles, *Belgium* . . 17 G4
Pont-à-Mousson, *France* . 25 D13
Pont-Audemer, *France* . . . 24 C7
Pont-Aven, *France* 24 E3
Pont Canavese, *Italy* 32 C4
Pont-de-Roide, *France* . . . 25 E13
Pont-de-Salars, *France* . . 26 D6
Pont-de-Vaux, *France* . . . 25 F11
Pont-de-Veyle, *France* . . . 27 B8
Pont-l'Abbé, *France* 24 E2
Pont-l'Évêque, *France* . . . 24 C7
Pont-St.-Esprit, *France* . . 27 D8
Pont-Saint-Martin, *Italy* . . 32 C4
Pont-sur-Yonne, *France* . . 25 D10
Ponta de Pedras, *Brazil* . . 122 B2
Ponta do Sol, *Madeira* . . 36 D2
Ponta Grossa, *Brazil* 127 B5
Ponta Porã, *Brazil* 127 A4
Pontacq, *France* 26 E3
Pontailler-sur-Saône,
  France 25 E12
Pontal →, *Brazil* 122 C3
Pontalina, *Brazil* 123 E2
Pontarlier, *France* 25 F13
Pontassieve, *Italy* 33 E8
Pontaubault, *France* 24 D5
Pontaumur, *France* 26 C6
Pontcharra, *France* 27 C10
Pontchartrain L., *U.S.A.* . 109 K9
Pontchâteau, *France* 24 E4
Ponte Alta, Serra do,
  Brazil 123 E2
Ponte Alta do Norte, *Brazil* 122 D2
Ponte Branca, *Brazil* 125 D7
Ponte da Barca, *Portugal* . 30 D2
Ponte de Sor, *Portugal* . . . 31 F3
Ponte dell'Ólio, *Italy* 32 D6
Ponte di Legno, *Italy* 32 B7
Ponte do Lima, *Portugal* . 30 D2
Ponte do Pungué, *Mozam.* 83 F3
Ponte-Leccia, *France* 27 F13
Ponte Nova, *Brazil* 123 F3
Ponte nelle Alpi, *Italy* . . . 33 B9
Ponte San Pietro, *Italy* . . 32 C6
Pontebba, *Italy* 33 B10
Pontecorvo, *Italy* 34 A6
Pontedera, *Italy* 32 E7
Pontefract, *U.K.* 12 D6
Ponteix, *Canada* 101 D7
Pontelandolfo, *Italy* 35 A7
Pontevedra, *Spain* 30 C2
Pontevedra □, *Spain* 30 C2
Pontevedra, R. de →,
  Spain 30 C2
Pontevico, *Italy* 32 C7
Pontiac, *Ill., U.S.A.* 108 E10
Pontiac, *Mich., U.S.A.* . . 104 D4

Pontian Kecil, *Malaysia* . . 59 M4
Pontianak, *Indonesia* 56 E3
Pontic Mts. = Kuzey
  Anadolu Dağları, *Turkey* 66 B7
Pontine Is. = Ponziane,
  Ísole, *Italy* 34 B5
Pontine Mts. = Kuzey
  Anadolu Dağları, *Turkey* 66 B7
Pontínia, *Italy* 34 A6
Pontivy, *France* 24 D4
Pontoise, *France* 25 C9
Ponton →, *Canada* 100 B5
Pontorson, *France* 24 D5
Pontrémoli, *Italy* 32 D6
Pontresina, *Switz.* 23 D9
Pontrieux, *France* 24 D3
Pontypool, *Canada* 106 B6
Pontypool, *U.K.* 13 F4
Pontypridd, *U.K.* 13 F4
Ponza, *Italy* 34 B5
Ponziane, Ísole, *Italy* 34 B5
Poochera, *Australia* 91 E1
Poole, *U.K.* 13 G6
Pooley I., *Canada* 100 C3
Poona = Pune, *India* 60 K8
Pooncarie, *Australia* 91 E3
Poopelloe L., *Australia* . . 91 E3
Poopó, *Bolivia* 124 D4
Poopó, L. de, *Bolivia* 124 D4
Popanyinning, *Australia* . . 89 F2
Popayán, *Colombia* 120 C2
Poperinge, *Belgium* 17 G1
Popigay, *Russia* 45 B12
Popilta, L., *Australia* 91 E3
Popio L., *Australia* 91 E3
Poplar, *U.S.A.* 108 A2
Poplar →, *Man., Canada* . 101 C9
Poplar →, *N.W.T.,*
  Canada 100 A4
Poplar Bluff, *U.S.A.* 109 G9
Poplarville, *U.S.A.* 109 K10
Popocatépetl, Volcán,
  Mexico 115 D5
Popokabaka, *Zaïre* 80 F3
Pópoli, *Italy* 33 F10
Popovača, *Croatia* 33 C13
Popovo, *Bulgaria* 38 F9
Poppel, *Belgium* 17 F6
Poprád, *Slovak Rep.* 20 F10
Poprád →, *Slovak Rep.* . . 20 F10
Porali →, *Pakistan* 62 G2
Porangaba, *Brazil* 124 B3
Porangatu, *Brazil* 123 D2
Porbandar, *India* 62 J3
Porce →, *Colombia* 120 B3
Porcher I., *Canada* 100 C2
Porco, *Bolivia* 125 D4
Porcos →, *Brazil* 123 D2
Porcuna, *Spain* 31 H6
Porcupine →, *Canada* . . . 101 B8
Porcupine →, *U.S.A.* 96 B5
Pordenone, *Italy* 33 C9
Poreč, *Croatia* 33 C10
Porecatu, *Brazil* 123 F1
Poretskoye, *Russia* 42 C8
Pori, *Finland* 9 F19
Porkhov, *Russia* 40 D5
Porlamar, *Venezuela* 121 A5
Porlezza, *Italy* 32 B6
Porma →, *Spain* 30 C5
Pornic, *France* 24 E4
Poronaysk, *Russia* 45 E15
Póros, *Greece* 39 M6
Poroshiri-Dake, *Japan* . . . 48 C11
Poroto Mts., *Tanzania* . . . 83 D3
Porpoise B., *Antarctica* . . 5 C9
Porquerolles, I. de, *France* 27 F10
Porrentruy, *Switz.* 22 B4
Porreras, *Spain* 36 B10
Porretta, Passo di, *Italy* . . 32 D7
Porsangen, *Norway* 8 A21
Porsgrunn, *Norway* 10 E3
Port Adelaide, *Australia* . . 91 E2
Port Alberni, *Canada* 100 D4
Port Alfred, *Canada* 99 C5
Port Alfred, *S. Africa* 84 E4
Port Alice, *Canada* 100 C3
Port Allegany, *U.S.A.* . . . 106 E6
Port Allen, *U.S.A.* 109 K9
Port Alma, *Australia* 90 C5
Port Angeles, *U.S.A.* 112 B3
Port Antonio, *Jamaica* . . . 116 C4
Port Aransas, *U.S.A.* 109 M6
Port Arthur = Lüshun,
  China 51 E11
Port Arthur, *Australia* . . . 90 G4
Port Arthur, *U.S.A.* 109 L8
Port au Port B., *Canada* . . 99 C8
Port-au-Prince, *Haiti* 117 C5
Port Augusta, *Australia* . . 91 E2
Port Augusta West,
  Australia 91 E2
Port Austin, *U.S.A.* 98 D3
Port Bell, *Uganda* 82 B3
Port Bergé Vaovao,
  Madag. 85 B8
Port Blandford, *Canada* . . 99 C9
Port Bou, *Spain* 28 C8
Port Bouët, *Ivory C.* 78 D4
Port Bradshaw, *Australia* . 90 A2
Port Broughton, *Australia* 91 E2
Port Burwell, *Canada* . . . 98 D3
Port Canning, *India* 63 H13
Port-Cartier, *Canada* 99 B6
Port Chalmers, *N.Z.* 87 L3
Port Chester, *U.S.A.* 107 F11
Port Clements, *Canada* . . 100 C2

Port Clinton, *U.S.A.* 104 E4
Port Colborne, *Canada* . . 98 D4
Port Coquitlam, *Canada* . . 100 D4
Port Credit, *Canada* 106 C5
Port Curtis, *Australia* 90 C5
Port Dalhousie, *Canada* . . 106 C5
Port Darwin, *Australia* . . . 88 B5
Port Darwin, *Falk. Is.* . . . 128 D5
Port Davey, *Australia* 90 G4
Port-de-Bouc, *France* 27 E8
Port-de-Paix, *Haiti* 117 C5
Port Dickson, *Malaysia* . . 59 L3
Port Douglas, *Australia* . . 90 B4
Port Dover, *Canada* 106 D4
Port Edward, *Canada* 100 C2
Port Elgin, *Canada* 98 D3
Port Elizabeth, *S. Africa* . 84 E4
Port Ellen, *U.K.* 14 F2
Port Erin, *U.K.* 12 C3
Port Essington, *Australia* . 88 B5
Port Etienne =
  Nouâdhibou, *Mauritania* 74 D1
Port Fairy, *Australia* 91 F3
Port Fouâd = Bûr Fuad,
  Egypt 76 H8
Port Gamble, *U.S.A.* 112 C4
Port-Gentil, *Gabon* 80 E1
Port Gibson, *U.S.A.* 109 K9
Port Glasgow, *U.K.* 14 F4
Port Harcourt, *Nigeria* . . . 79 E6
Port Hardy, *Canada* 100 C3
Port Harrison = Inukjuak,
  Canada 97 C12
Port Hawkesbury, *Canada* 99 C7
Port Hedland, *Australia* . . 88 D2
Port Henry, *U.S.A.* 107 B11
Port Hood, *Canada* 99 C7
Port Hope, *Canada* 98 D4
Port Hueneme, *U.S.A.* . . . 113 L7
Port Huron, *U.S.A.* 104 D4
Port Iliç, *Azerbaijan* 67 C13
Port Isabel, *U.S.A.* 109 M6
Port Jefferson, *U.S.A.* . . . 107 F11
Port Jervis, *U.S.A.* 107 E10
Port-Joinville, *France* 24 F4
Port Katon, *Russia* 43 G4
Port Kelang = Pelabuhan
  Kelang, *Malaysia* 59 L3
Port Kembla, *Australia* . . . 91 E5
Port Kenny, *Australia* . . . 91 E1
Port-la-Nouvelle, *France* . . 26 E7
Port Lairge = Waterford,
  Ireland 15 D4
Port Laoise, *Ireland* 15 C4
Port Lavaca, *U.S.A.* 109 L6
Port-Leucate, *France* 26 F7
Port Lincoln, *Australia* . . . 91 E2
Port Loko, *S. Leone* 78 D2
Port Louis, *France* 24 E3
Port Lyautey = Kenitra,
  Morocco 74 B3
Port MacDonnell, *Australia* 91 F3
Port Macquarie, *Australia* . 91 E5
Port Maria, *Jamaica* 116 C4
Port Mellon, *Canada* 100 D4
Port-Menier, *Canada* 99 C7
Port Morant, *Jamaica* 116 C4
Port Moresby, *Papua N. G.* 92 H6
Port Mourant, *Guyana* . . . 121 B6
Port Mouton, *Canada* 99 D7
Port Musgrave, *Australia* . 90 A3
Port-Navalo, *France* 24 E4
Port Nelson, *Canada* 101 B10
Port Nolloth, *S. Africa* . . . 84 D2
Port Nouveau-Québec =
  Kangiqsualujjuaq,
  Canada 97 C13
Port O'Connor, *U.S.A.* . . 109 L6
Port of Spain, *Trin. & Tob.* 117 D7
Port Orchard, *U.S.A.* 112 C4
Port Orford, *U.S.A.* 110 E1
Port Pegasus, *N.Z.* 87 M1
Port Perry, *Canada* 98 D4
Port Phillip B., *Australia* . 91 F3
Port Pirie, *Australia* 91 E2
Port Radium = Echo Bay,
  Canada 96 B8
Port Renfrew, *Canada* . . . 100 D4
Port Roper, *Australia* 90 A2
Port Rowan, *Canada* 98 D3
Port Safaga = Bûr Safâga,
  Egypt 76 B3
Port Said = Bûr Sa'îd,
  Egypt 76 H8
Port St. Joe, *U.S.A.* 105 L3
Port St. Johns, *S. Africa* . 85 E4
Port-St.-Louis-du-Rhône,
  France 27 E8
Port San Vicente, *Phil.* . . . 55 B5
Port Sanilac, *U.S.A.* 98 D3
Port Saunders, *Canada* . . 99 B8
Port Severn, *Canada* 106 B5
Port Shepstone, *S. Africa* . 85 E5
Port Simpson, *Canada* . . . 100 C2
Port Stanley = Stanley,
  Falk. Is. 128 D5
Port Stanley, *Canada* 98 D3
Port Sudan = Bûr Sûdân,
  Sudan 76 D4
Port-sur-Saône, *France* . . 25 E13
Port Talbot, *U.K.* 13 F4
Port Taufiq = Bûr Taufiq,
  Egypt 76 J8
Port Townsend, *U.S.A.* . . 112 B4
Port-Vendres, *France* 26 F7
Port Wakefield, *Australia* . 91 E2

Port Washington, *U.S.A.* . 104 D2
Port Weld, *Malaysia* 59 K3
Portachuelo, *Bolivia* 125 D5
Portadown, *U.K.* 15 B5
Portage, *U.S.A.* 108 D10
Portage La Prairie, *Canada* 101 D9
Portageville, *U.S.A.* 109 G10
Portalegre, *Portugal* 31 F3
Portalegre □, *Portugal* . . . 31 F3
Portales, *U.S.A.* 109 H3
Portarlington, *Ireland* 15 C4
Porteirinha, *Brazil* 123 E3
Portel, *Brazil* 122 B1
Portel, *Portugal* 31 G3
Porter L., *N.W.T., Canada* 101 A7
Porter L., *Sask., Canada* . 101 B7
Porterville, *S. Africa* 84 E2
Porterville, *U.S.A.* 111 H4
Porthcawl, *U.K.* 13 F4
Porthill, *U.S.A.* 110 B5
Portile de Fier, *Europe* . . . 38 E5
Portimão, *Portugal* 31 H2
Portland, *N.S.W., Australia* 91 E4
Portland, *Vic., Australia* . . 91 F3
Portland, *Canada* 107 B8
Portland, *Conn., U.S.A.* . . 107 E12
Portland, *Maine, U.S.A.* . . 99 D5
Portland, *Mich., U.S.A.* . . 104 D3
Portland, *Oreg., U.S.A.* . . 112 E4
Portland, I. of, *U.K.* 13 G5
Portland B., *Australia* 91 F3
Portland Bill, *U.K.* 13 G5
Portland Prom., *Canada* . . 97 C12
Portlands Roads, *Australia* 90 A3
Portneuf, *Canada* 99 C5
Pôrto, *Brazil* 122 B3
Porto, *France* 27 F12
Porto, *Portugal* 30 D2
Porto □, *Portugal* 30 D2
Porto, G. de, *France* 27 F12
Pôrto Acre, *Brazil* 124 B4
Pôrto Alegre, *Pará, Brazil* 121 D7
Pôrto Alegre,
  Rio Grande do S., Brazil 127 C5
Porto Amboim = Gunza,
  Angola 80 G2
Porto Argentera, *Italy* . . . 32 C4
Porto Azzurro, *Italy* 32 F7
Porto Botte, *Italy* 34 C1
Pôrto Cajueiro, *Brazil* . . . 125 C6
Porto Civitanova, *Italy* . . . 33 E10
Porto Cristo, *Spain* 36 B10
Pôrto da Fôlha, *Brazil* . . . 122 C4
Pôrto de Móz, *Brazil* 121 D7
Pôrto de Pedras, *Brazil* . . 122 C4
Pôrto des Meinacos, *Brazil* 125 C7
Porto Empédocle, *Italy* . . . 34 E6
Pôrto Esperança, *Brazil* . . 125 D6
Pôrto Esperidão, *Brazil* . . 125 D6
Pôrto Franco, *Brazil* 122 C2
Porto Garibaldi, *Italy* 33 D9
Pôrto Grande, *Brazil* 121 C7
Pôrto Jofre, *Brazil* 125 D6
Pórto Lágo, *Greece* 39 J8
Pôrto Mendes, *Brazil* 127 A5
Porto Moniz, *Madeira* . . . 36 D2
Pôrto Murtinho, *Brazil* . . . 125 E6
Pôrto Nacional, *Brazil* . . . 122 D2
Pôrto Novo, *Benin* 79 D5
Porto Novo, *India* 60 P11
Pôrto Petro, *Spain* 36 B10
Porto Recanati, *Italy* 33 E10
Porto San Giórgio, *Italy* . . 33 E10
Pôrto Santana, *Brazil* 121 D7
Porto Santo, *Madeira* 72 B1
Porto Santo Stéfano, *Italy* 32 F8
Pôrto São José, *Brazil* . . . 127 A5
Pôrto Seguro, *Brazil* 123 E4
Porto Tolle, *Italy* 33 D9
Pôrto Tôrres, *Italy* 34 B1
Pôrto União, *Brazil* 127 B5
Pôrto Válter, *Brazil* 124 B3
Porto-Vecchio, *France* . . . 27 G13
Pôrto Velho, *Brazil* 125 B5
Portobelo, *Panama* 116 E4
Portoferráio, *Italy* 32 F7
Portogruaro, *Italy* 33 C9
Portola, *U.S.A.* 112 F6
Portomaggiore, *Italy* 33 D8
Portoscuso, *Italy* 34 C1
Portovénere, *Italy* 32 D6
Portovíejo, *Ecuador* 120 D1
Portpatrick, *U.K.* 14 G3
Portree, *U.K.* 14 D2
Portrush, *U.K.* 15 A5
Portsall, *France* 24 D2
Portsmouth, *Domin.* 117 C7
Portsmouth, *U.K.* 13 G6
Portsmouth, *N.H., U.S.A.* 107 C14
Portsmouth, *Ohio, U.S.A.* 104 F4
Portsmouth, *R.I., U.S.A.* . 107 E13
Portsmouth, *Va., U.S.A.* . 104 G7
Portsoy, *U.K.* 14 D6
Porttipahtan tekojärvi,
  Finland 8 B22
Portugal ■, *Europe* 30 F3
Portugalete, *Spain* 28 B1
Portuguesa □, *Venezuela* . 120 B4
Portumna, *Ireland* 15 C3
Portville, *U.S.A.* 106 D6
Porvenir, *Bolivia* 124 C4
Porvenir, *Chile* 128 D2
Porvoo, *Finland* 9 F21
Porzuna, *Spain* 31 F6
Posada →, *Italy* 34 B2
Posadas, *Argentina* 127 B4
Posadas, *Spain* 31 H5
Poschiavo, *Switz.* 23 D10

Punasar

Posets, *Spain* 28 C5
Poshan = Boshan, *China* 51 F9
Posht-e-Badam, *Iran* 65 C7
Posídhion, Ákra, *Greece* 39 K6
Poso, *Indonesia* 57 E6
Posoegroenoe, *Surinam* 121 C6
Posong, *S. Korea* 51 G14
Posse, *Brazil* 123 D2
Possel, *C.A.R.* 80 C3
Possession I., *Antarctica* 5 D11
Pössneck, *Germany* 18 E7
Post, *U.S.A.* 109 J4
Post Falls, *U.S.A.* 110 C5
Postavy = Pastavy, *Belarus* 9 J22
Poste Maurice Cortier, *Algeria* 75 D5
Postmasburg, *S. Africa* 84 D3
Postojna, *Slovenia* 33 C11
Poston, *U.S.A.* 113 M12
Potchefstroom, *S. Africa* 84 D4
Poté, *Brazil* 123 E3
Poteau, *U.S.A.* 109 H7
Poteet, *U.S.A.* 109 L5
Potelu, Lacul, *Romania* 38 F7
Potenza, *Italy* 35 B8
Potenza –►, *Italy* 33 E10
Potenza Picena, *Italy* 33 E10
Poteriteri, L., *N.Z.* 87 M1
Potes, *Spain* 30 B6
Potgietersrus, *S. Africa* 85 C4
Poti, *Georgia* 43 J5
Potiraguá, *Brazil* 123 E4
Potiskum, *Nigeria* 79 C7
Potomac –►, *U.S.A.* 104 F7
Potosí, *Bolivia* 125 D4
Potosí □, *Bolivia* 124 E4
Potosi Mt., *U.S.A.* 113 K11
Pototan, *Phil.* 55 F5
Potrerillos, *Chile* 126 B2
Potsdam, *Germany* 18 C9
Potsdam, *U.S.A.* 107 B10
Pottenstein, *Germany* 19 F7
Potter, *U.S.A.* 108 E3
Pottery Hill = Abû Ballas, *Egypt* 76 C2
Pottstown, *U.S.A.* 107 F9
Pottsville, *U.S.A.* 107 F8
Pottuvil, *Sri Lanka* 60 R12
Pouancé, *France* 24 E5
Pouce Coupé, *Canada* 100 B4
Poughkeepsie, *U.S.A.* 107 E11
Pouilly-sur-Loire, *France* 25 E9
Poulaphouca Res., *Ireland* 15 C5
Poulsbo, *U.S.A.* 112 C4
Pourri, Mt., *France* 27 C10
Pouso Alegre, *Mato Grosso, Brazil* 125 C6
Pouso Alegre, *Minas Gerais, Brazil* 127 A6
Pouzauges, *France* 24 F6
Povenets, *Russia* 44 C4
Poverty B., *N.Z.* 87 H7
Póvoa de Lanhosa, *Portugal* 30 D2
Póvoa de Varzim, *Portugal* 30 D2
Povorino, *Russia* 42 E6
Powassan, *Canada* 98 C4
Poway, *U.S.A.* 113 N9
Powder –►, *U.S.A.* 108 B2
Powder River, *U.S.A.* 110 E10
Powell, *U.S.A.* 110 D9
Powell L., *U.S.A.* 111 H8
Powell River, *Canada* 100 D4
Powers, *Mich., U.S.A.* 104 C2
Powers, *Oreg., U.S.A.* 110 E1
Powers Lake, *U.S.A.* 108 A3
Powys □, *U.K.* 13 E4
Poxoreu, *Brazil* 125 D7
Poyang Hu, *China* 53 C11
Poyarkovo, *Russia* 45 E13
Poza de la Sal, *Spain* 28 C1
Poza Rica, *Mexico* 115 C5
Pozanti, *Turkey* 66 D6
Požarevac, *Serbia, Yug.* 21 L11
Pozi, *Taiwan* 53 F13
Poznań, *Poland* 20 C6
Pozo, *U.S.A.* 113 K6
Pozo Alcón, *Spain* 29 H2
Pozo Almonte, *Chile* 124 E4
Pozo Colorado, *Paraguay* 126 A4
Pozo del Dátil, *Mexico* 114 B2
Pozoblanco, *Spain* 31 G6
Pozuzo, *Peru* 124 C2
Pozzallo, *Italy* 35 F7
Pozzuoli, *Italy* 35 B7
Pra –►, *Ghana* 79 D4
Prachin Buri, *Thailand* 58 E3
Prachuap Khiri Khan, *Thailand* 59 G2
Pradelles, *France* 26 D7
Pradera, *Colombia* 120 C2
Prades, *France* 26 F6
Prado, *Brazil* 123 E4
Prado del Rey, *Spain* 31 J5
Præstø, *Denmark* 11 J6
Pragersko, *Slovenia* 33 B12
Prague = Praha, *Czech.* 20 E4
Praha, *Czech.* 20 E4
Prahecq, *France* 26 B3
Prahova –►, *Romania* 38 E8
Prahovo, *Serbia, Yug.* 21 L12
Praid, *Romania* 38 C8
Prainha, *Amazonas, Brazil* 125 B5
Prainha, *Pará, Brazil* 121 D7
Prairie, *Australia* 90 C3
Prairie –►, *U.S.A.* 109 H5
Prairie City, *U.S.A.* 110 D4
Prairie du Chien, *U.S.A.* 108 D9
Prairies, *Canada* 96 C9
Pramánda, *Greece* 39 K4
Pran Buri, *Thailand* 58 F2
Prang, *Ghana* 79 D4
Prapat, *Indonesia* 56 D1
Prasonísi, Ákra, *Greece* 37 D9
Prata, *Brazil* 123 E2
Pratapgarh, *India* 62 G6
Prática di Mare, *Italy* 34 A5
Prätigau, *Switz.* 23 C9
Prato, *Italy* 32 E8
Prátola Peligna, *Italy* 33 F10
Pratovécchio, *Italy* 33 E8
Prats-de-Mollo-la-Preste, *France* 26 F6
Pratt, *U.S.A.* 109 G5
Pratteln, *Switz.* 22 A5
Prattville, *U.S.A.* 105 J2
Pravdinsk, *Russia* 42 B6
Pravia, *Spain* 30 B4
Praya, *Indonesia* 56 F5
Pré-en-Pail, *France* 24 D6
Pré-Saint-Didier, *Italy* 32 C4
Precordillera, *Argentina* 126 C2
Predáppio, *Italy* 33 D8
Predazzo, *Italy* 33 B8
Predejane, *Serbia, Yug.* 21 N12
Preeceville, *Canada* 101 C8
Préfailles, *France* 24 E4
Pregonero, *Venezuela* 120 B3
Pregrada, *Croatia* 33 B12
Preiļi, *Latvia* 9 H22
Preko, *Croatia* 33 D12
Prelate, *Canada* 101 C7
Prelog, *Croatia* 33 B13
Premier, *Canada* 100 B3
Premont, *U.S.A.* 109 M5
Premuda, *Croatia* 33 D11
Prenjasi, *Albania* 39 H3
Prentice, *U.S.A.* 108 C9
Prenzlau, *Germany* 18 B9
Preobrazheniye, *Russia* 48 C6
Preparis North Channel, *Ind. Oc.* 61 M18
Preparis South Channel, *Ind. Oc.* 61 M18
Přerov, *Czech.* 20 F7
Presanella, *Italy* 32 B7
Prescott, *Canada* 98 D4
Prescott, *Ariz., U.S.A.* 111 J7
Prescott, *Ark., U.S.A.* 109 J8
Preservation Inlet, *N.Z.* 87 M1
Preševo, *Serbia, Yug.* 21 N11
Presho, *U.S.A.* 108 D4
Presicce, *Italy* 35 C11
Presidencia de la Plaza, *Argentina* 126 B4
Presidencia Roque Saenz Peña, *Argentina* 126 B3
Presidente Epitácio, *Brazil* 123 F1
Presidente Hayes □, *Paraguay* 126 A4
Presidente Hermes, *Brazil* 125 C5
Presidente Prudente, *Brazil* 127 A5
Presidio, *Mexico* 114 B4
Presidio, *U.S.A.* 109 L2
Preslav, *Bulgaria* 38 F9
Prešov, *Slovak Rep.* 20 F11
Prespa, L. = Prespansko Jezero, *Macedonia* 39 J4
Prespansko Jezero, *Macedonia* 39 J4
Presque Isle, *U.S.A.* 99 C6
Prestbury, *U.K.* 13 F5
Prestea, *Ghana* 78 D4
Presteigne, *U.K.* 13 E5
Presto, *Bolivia* 125 D5
Preston, *Canada* 106 C4
Preston, *U.K.* 12 D5
Preston, *Idaho, U.S.A.* 110 E8
Preston, *Minn., U.S.A.* 108 D8
Preston, *Nev., U.S.A.* 110 G6
Preston, C., *Australia* 88 D2
Prestonpans, *U.K.* 14 F6
Prestwick, *U.K.* 14 F4
Prêto –►, *Amazonas, Brazil* 121 D5
Prêto –►, *Bahia, Brazil* 122 D3
Prêto do Igapó-Açu –►, *Brazil* 121 D6
Pretoria, *S. Africa* 85 D4
Preuilly-sur-Claise, *France* 24 F7
Préveza, *Greece* 39 L3
Priazovskoye, *Ukraine* 41 J8
Pribilof Is., *Bering S.* 4 D17
Priboj, *Serbia, Yug.* 21 M9
Příbram, *Czech.* 20 F4
Price, *U.S.A.* 110 G8
Price I., *Canada* 100 C3
Prichard, *U.S.A.* 105 K1
Priego, *Spain* 28 E2
Priego de Córdoba, *Spain* 31 H6
Priekule, *Latvia* 9 H19
Prien, *Germany* 19 H8
Prienai, *Lithuania* 9 J20
Prieska, *S. Africa* 84 D3
Priest –►, *U.S.A.* 110 B5
Priest L., *U.S.A.* 110 B5
Priest Valley, *U.S.A.* 112 J6
Priestly, *Canada* 100 C3
Prievidza, *Slovak Rep.* 20 G8
Prijedor, *Bos.-H.* 33 D13
Prikaspiyskaya Nizmennost = Caspian Depression, *Eurasia* 43 G9
Prikubanskaya Nizmennost, *Russia* 43 H4
Prilep, *Macedonia* 39 H4
Priluki = Pryluky, *Ukraine* 41 G7
Prime Seal I., *Australia* 90 G4
Primeira Cruz, *Brazil* 122 B3
Primorsk, *Russia* 40 B5
Primorsko-Akhtarsk, *Russia* 43 G4
Primorskoye, *Ukraine* 41 J9
Primrose L., *Canada* 101 C7
Prince Albert, *Canada* 101 C7
Prince Albert, *S. Africa* 84 E3
Prince Albert Mts., *Antarctica* 5 D11
Prince Albert Nat. Park, *Canada* 101 C7
Prince Albert Pen., *Canada* 96 A8
Prince Albert Sd., *Canada* 96 A8
Prince Alfred, C., *Canada* 4 B1
Prince Charles I., *Canada* 97 B12
Prince Charles Mts., *Antarctica* 5 D6
Prince Edward I. □, *Canada* 99 C7
Prince Edward Is., *Ind. Oc.* 3 G11
Prince George, *Canada* 100 C4
Prince of Wales, C., *U.S.A.* 94 C3
Prince of Wales I., *Australia* 90 A3
Prince of Wales I., *Canada* 96 A10
Prince of Wales I., *U.S.A.* 100 B2
Prince Patrick I., *Canada* 4 B2
Prince Regent Inlet, *Canada* 4 B3
Prince Rupert, *Canada* 100 C2
Princenhage, *Neths.* 17 F5
Princesa Isabel, *Brazil* 122 C4
Princess Charlotte B., *Australia* 90 A3
Princess May Ras., *Australia* 88 C4
Princess Royal I., *Canada* 100 C3
Princeton, *Canada* 100 D4
Princeton, *Calif., U.S.A.* 112 F4
Princeton, *Ill., U.S.A.* 108 E10
Princeton, *Ind., U.S.A.* 104 F2
Princeton, *Ky., U.S.A.* 104 G2
Princeton, *Mo., U.S.A.* 108 E8
Princeton, *N.J., U.S.A.* 107 F10
Princeton, *W. Va., U.S.A.* 104 G5
Principe, I. de, *Atl. Oc.* 70 F4
Principe Chan., *Canada* 100 C2
Principe da Beira, *Brazil* 125 C5
Prineville, *U.S.A.* 110 D3
Prins Harald Kyst, *Antarctica* 5 D4
Prinsesse Astrid Kyst, *Antarctica* 5 D3
Prinsesse Ragnhild Kyst, *Antarctica* 5 D4
Prinzapolca, *Nic.* 116 D3
Prior, C., *Spain* 30 B2
Priozersk, *Russia* 40 B6
Pripet = Prypyat –►, *Europe* 41 G6
Pripet Marshes, *Europe* 41 F5
Pripyat Marshes = Pripet Marshes, *Europe* 41 F5
Pripyats = Prypyat –►, *Europe* 41 G6
Prislop, Pasul, *Romania* 38 B8
Pristen, *Russia* 42 E3
Priština, *Serbia, Yug.* 21 N11
Pritzwalk, *Germany* 18 B8
Privas, *France* 27 D8
Priverno, *Italy* 34 A6
Privolzhsk, *Russia* 42 B5
Privolzhskaya Vozvyshennost, *Russia* 42 E7
Privolzhskiy, *Russia* 42 E8
Privolzhye, *Russia* 42 D9
Priyutnoye, *Russia* 43 G6
Prizren, *Serbia, Yug.* 21 N10
Prizzi, *Italy* 34 E6
Prnjavor, *Bos.-H.* 21 L7
Probolinggo, *Indonesia* 57 G15
Procida, *Italy* 35 B7
Proddatur, *India* 60 M11
Prodhromos, *Cyprus* 37 E11
Proença-a-Nova, *Portugal* 31 F3
Prof. Van Blommestein Meer, *Surinam* 121 C6
Profítis Ilías, *Greece* 37 C9
Profondeville, *Belgium* 17 H5
Progreso, *Mexico* 115 C7
Prokhladnyy, *Russia* 43 J7
Prokletije, *Albania* 38 G2
Prokopyevsk, *Russia* 44 D9
Prokuplje, *Serbia, Yug.* 21 M11
Proletarsk, *Russia* 43 G5
Proletarskaya = Proletarsk, *Russia* 43 G5
Prome = Pyè, *Burma* 61 K19
Prophet –►, *Canada* 100 B4
Propriá, *Brazil* 122 D4
Propriano, *France* 27 G12
Proserpine, *Australia* 90 C4
Prosser, *U.S.A.* 110 C4
Prostějov, *Czech.* 20 F7
Proston, *Australia* 91 D5
Protection, *U.S.A.* 109 G5
Próti, *Greece* 39 M4
Provadiya, *Bulgaria* 38 F10
Proven, *Belgium* 17 G1
Provence, *France* 27 E9
Providence, *Ky., U.S.A.* 104 G2
Providence, *R.I., U.S.A.* 107 E13
Providence Bay, *Canada* 98 C3
Providence Mts., *U.S.A.* 111 J6
Providencia, *Ecuador* 120 D2
Providencia, I. de, *Colombia* 116 D3
Provideniya, *Russia* 45 C19
Provins, *France* 25 D10
Provo, *U.S.A.* 110 F8
Provost, *Canada* 101 C6
Prozor, *Bos.-H.* 21 M7
Prudentópolis, *Brazil* 123 G1
Prud'homme, *Canada* 101 C7
Prudnik, *Poland* 20 E7
Prüm, *Germany* 19 E2
Pruszcz Gdański, *Poland* 20 A8
Pruszków, *Poland* 20 C10
Prut –►, *Romania* 38 D11
Pruzhany, *Belarus* 41 F3
Prvič, *Croatia* 33 D11
Prydz B., *Antarctica* 5 C6
Pryluky, *Ukraine* 41 G7
Pryor, *U.S.A.* 109 G7
Prypyat –►, *Europe* 41 G6
Przasnysz, *Poland* 20 B10
Przedbórz, *Poland* 20 D9
Przemyśl, *Poland* 20 F12
Przeworsk, *Poland* 20 E12
Przewóz, *Poland* 20 D4
Przhevalsk, *Kyrgyzstan* 44 E8
Przysuchla, *Poland* 20 D10
Psakhná, *Greece* 39 L6
Psará, *Greece* 39 L8
Psel –►, *Ukraine* 41 H7
Pserimos, *Greece* 39 N10
Psíra, *Greece* 37 D7
Pskov, *Russia* 40 D5
Pskovskoye, Ozero, *Russia* 9 H22
Psunj, *Croatia* 21 K7
Pszczyna, *Poland* 20 F8
Pteleón, *Greece* 39 K5
Ptich = Ptsich –►, *Belarus* 41 F5
Ptolemaís, *Greece* 39 J4
Ptsich –►, *Belarus* 41 F5
Ptuj, *Slovenia* 33 B12
Ptujska Gora, *Slovenia* 33 B12
Pu Xian, *China* 50 F6
Pua, *Thailand* 58 C3
Puán, *Argentina* 126 D3
Pu'an, *China* 52 E5
Puan, *S. Korea* 51 G14
Pubei, *China* 52 F7
Pucacuro –►, *Peru* 120 D3
Pucallpa, *Peru* 124 B3
Pucará, *Bolivia* 125 D5
Pucará, *Peru* 124 D3
Pucarani, *Bolivia* 124 D4
Pucheng, *China* 53 D12
Pučišće, *Croatia* 33 E13
Pucka, Zatoka, *Poland* 20 A8
Pudasjärvi, *Finland* 8 D22
Puding, *China* 52 D5
Pudozh, *Russia* 40 B9
Pudukkottai, *India* 60 P11
Puebla, *Mexico* 115 D5
Puebla □, *Mexico* 115 D5
Puebla de Alcocer, *Spain* 31 G5
Puebla de Don Fadrique, *Spain* 29 H2
Puebla de Don Rodrigo, *Spain* 31 F6
Puebla de Guzmán, *Spain* 31 H3
Puebla de Sanabria, *Spain* 30 C4
Puebla de Trives, *Spain* 30 C3
Puebla del Caramiñal, *Spain* 30 C2
Pueblo, *U.S.A.* 108 F2
Pueblo Hundido, *Chile* 126 B1
Pueblo Nuevo, *Venezuela* 120 B3
Puelches, *Argentina* 126 D2
Puelén, *Argentina* 126 D2
Puente Alto, *Chile* 126 C1
Puente del Arzobispo, *Spain* 30 F5
Puente-Genil, *Spain* 31 H6
Puente la Reina, *Spain* 28 C3
Puenteareas, *Spain* 30 C2
Puentedeume, *Spain* 30 B2
Puentes de Garcia Rodriguez, *Spain* 30 B3
Pu'er, *China* 52 F3
Puerco –►, *U.S.A.* 111 J10
Puerto, *Canary Is.* 36 F2
Puerto Acosta, *Bolivia* 124 D4
Puerto Aisén, *Chile* 128 C2
Puerto Ángel, *Mexico* 115 D5
Puerto Arista, *Mexico* 115 D6
Puerto Armuelles, *Panama* 116 E3
Puerto Ayacucho, *Venezuela* 120 B4
Puerto Barrios, *Guatemala* 116 C2
Puerto Bermejo, *Argentina* 126 B4
Puerto Bermúdez, *Peru* 124 C3
Puerto Bolívar, *Ecuador* 120 D2
Puerto Cabello, *Venezuela* 120 A4
Puerto Cabezas, *Nic.* 116 D3
Puerto Cabo Gracias á Dios, *Nic.* 116 D3
Puerto Capaz = Jebba, *Morocco* 74 A4
Puerto Carreño, *Colombia* 120 B4
Puerto Castilla, *Honduras* 116 C2
Puerto Chicama, *Peru* 124 B2
Puerto Coig, *Argentina* 128 D3
Puerto Cortes, *Costa Rica* 116 E3
Puerto Cortés, *Honduras* 116 C2
Puerto Cumarebo, *Venezuela* 120 A4
Puerto de Alcudia, *Spain* 36 B10
Puerto de Andraitx, *Spain* 36 B9
Puerto de Cabrera, *Spain* 36 B9
Puerto de Gran Tarajal, *Canary Is.* 36 F5
Puerto de la Cruz, *Canary Is.* 36 F3
Puerto de Pozo Negro, *Canary Is.* 36 F6
Puerto de Sóller, *Spain* 36 B9
Puerto del Carmen, *Canary Is.* 36 F6
Puerto del Rosario, *Canary Is.* 36 F6
Puerto Deseado, *Argentina* 128 C3
Puerto Guaraní, *Paraguay* 125 E6
Puerto Heath, *Bolivia* 124 C4
Puerto Huitoto, *Colombia* 120 C3
Puerto Inca, *Peru* 124 B3
Puerto Juárez, *Mexico* 115 C7
Puerto La Cruz, *Venezuela* 121 A5
Puerto Leguízamo, *Colombia* 120 D3
Puerto Limón, *Colombia* 120 C3
Puerto Lobos, *Argentina* 128 B3
Puerto López, *Colombia* 120 C3
Puerto Lumbreras, *Spain* 29 H3
Puerto Madryn, *Argentina* 128 B3
Puerto Maldonado, *Peru* 124 C4
Puerto Manotí, *Cuba* 116 B4
Puerto Mazarrón, *Spain* 29 H3
Puerto Mercedes, *Colombia* 120 C3
Puerto Miraña, *Colombia* 120 D3
Puerto Montt, *Chile* 128 B2
Puerto Morelos, *Mexico* 115 C7
Puerto Nariño, *Colombia* 120 C4
Puerto Natales, *Chile* 128 D2
Puerto Nuevo, *Colombia* 120 B4
Puerto Nutrias, *Venezuela* 120 B4
Puerto Ordaz, *Venezuela* 121 B5
Puerto Padre, *Cuba* 116 B4
Puerto Páez, *Venezuela* 120 B4
Puerto Peñasco, *Mexico* 114 A2
Puerto Pinasco, *Paraguay* 126 A4
Puerto Pirámides, *Argentina* 128 B4
Puerto Plata, *Dom. Rep.* 117 C5
Puerto Pollensa, *Spain* 36 B10
Puerto Portillo, *Peru* 124 B3
Puerto Princesa, *Phil.* 55 G3
Puerto Quellón, *Chile* 128 B2
Puerto Quepos, *Costa Rica* 116 E3
Puerto Real, *Spain* 31 J4
Puerto Rico, *Bolivia* 124 C4
Puerto Rico, *Canary Is.* 36 G4
Puerto Rico ■, *W. Indies* 117 C6
Puerto Rico Trench, *Atl. Oc.* 117 C6
Puerto Saavedra, *Chile* 128 A2
Puerto Sastre, *Paraguay* 126 A4
Puerto Siles, *Bolivia* 125 C4
Puerto Suárez, *Bolivia* 125 D6
Puerto Tejada, *Colombia* 120 C2
Puerto Umbría, *Colombia* 120 C2
Puerto Vallarta, *Mexico* 114 C3
Puerto Varas, *Chile* 128 B2
Puerto Villazón, *Bolivia* 125 C5
Puerto Wilches, *Colombia* 120 B3
Puertollano, *Spain* 31 G6
Puertomarin, *Spain* 30 C3
Puesto Cunambo, *Peru* 120 D2
Pueyrredón, L., *Argentina* 128 C2
Pugachev, *Russia* 42 D9
Puge, *China* 52 D4
Puge, *Tanzania* 82 C3
Puget Sound, *U.S.A.* 110 C2
Puget-Théniers, *France* 27 E10
Púglia □, *Italy* 35 B9
Pugŏdong, *N. Korea* 51 C16
Pugu, *Tanzania* 82 D4
Pūgūnzī, *Iran* 65 E8
Pui, *Romania* 38 D6
Puica, *Peru* 124 C3
Puig Mayor, *Spain* 36 B9
Puigcerdá, *Spain* 28 C6
Puigmal, *Spain* 28 C7
Puigpuñent, *Spain* 36 B9
Puisaye, Collines de la, *France* 25 E10
Puiseaux, *France* 25 D9
Pujilí, *Ecuador* 120 D2
Pujon-chosuji, *N. Korea* 51 D14
Puka, *Albania* 38 G2
Pukaki L., *N.Z.* 87 L3
Pukapuka, *Cook Is.* 93 J11
Pukatawagan, *Canada* 101 B8
Pukchin, *N. Korea* 51 D13
Pukchŏng, *N. Korea* 51 D15
Pukekohe, *N.Z.* 87 G5
Pukou, *China* 53 A12
Pula, *Croatia* 33 D10
Pula, *Italy* 34 D2
Pulacayo, *Bolivia* 124 E4
Pulaski, *N.Y., U.S.A.* 107 C8
Pulaski, *Tenn., U.S.A.* 105 H2
Pulaski, *Va., U.S.A.* 104 G5
Puławy, *Poland* 20 D11
Pulga, *U.S.A.* 112 F5
Pulicat, L., *India* 60 N12
Pullman, *U.S.A.* 110 C5
Pulog, *Phil.* 55 C4
Pułtusk, *Poland* 20 C11
Pülümür, *Turkey* 67 C8
Pumlumon Fawr, *U.K.* 13 E4
Puna, *Bolivia* 125 D4
Puná, I., *Ecuador* 120 D1
Punakha, *Bhutan* 61 F16
Punasar, *India* 62 F5

Punata, *Bolivia* 125 D4
Punch, *India* 63 C6
Pune, *India* 60 K8
Pungsan, *N. Korea* 51 D15
Pungue, Ponte de, *Mozam.* 83 F3
Puning, *China* 53 F11
Punjab □, *India* 62 D6
Punjab □, *Pakistan* 62 E6
Puno, *Peru* 124 D3
Punta Alta, *Argentina* ... 128 A4
Punta Arenas, *Chile* 128 D2
Punta Cardón, *Venezuela* 120 A3
Punta Coles, *Peru* 124 D3
Punta de Bombón, *Peru* 124 D3
Punta de Díaz, *Chile* 126 B1
Punta Delgado, *Argentina* 128 B4
Punta Gorda, *Belize* 115 D7
Punta Gorda, *U.S.A.* 105 M5
Punta Prieta, *Mexico* 114 B2
Punta Prima, *Spain* 36 B11
Puntabie, *Australia* 91 E1
Puntarenas, *Costa Rica* .. 116 E3
Punto Fijo, *Venezuela* ... 120 A3
Punxsatawney, *U.S.A.* ... 106 F5
Puqi, *China* 53 C9
Puquio, *Peru* 124 C3
Pur →, *Russia* 44 C8
Purace, Vol., *Colombia* .. 120 C2
Puralia = Puruliya, *India* 63 H12
Purbeck, Isle of, *U.K.* .. 13 G5
Purcell, *U.S.A.* 109 H6
Purchena Tetica, *Spain* .. 29 H2
Puri, *India* 61 K14
Purificación, *Colombia* .. 120 C3
Purmerend, *Neths.* 16 C5
Purnia, *India* 63 G12
Purukcahu, *Indonesia* ... 56 E4
Puruliya, *India* 63 H12
Purus →, *Brazil* 121 D5
Puruvesi, *Finland* 40 B5
Pŭrvomay, *Bulgaria* 38 G8
Purwakarta, *Indonesia* .. 57 G12
Purwodadi, *Jawa, Indonesia* 57 G14
Purwodadi, *Jawa, Indonesia* 57 G13
Purwokerto, *Indonesia* .. 57 G13
Purworejo, *Indonesia* ... 57 G14
Puryŏng, *N. Korea* 51 C15
Pusan, *S. Korea* 51 G15
Pushchino, *Russia* 45 D16
Pushkin, *Russia* 40 C6
Pushkino, *Russia* 42 E8
Pushkino, *Russia* 42 B3
Püspökladány, *Hungary* . 21 H11
Pustoshka, *Russia* 40 D5
Putahow L., *Canada* 101 B8
Putao, *Burma* 61 F20
Putaruru, *N.Z.* 87 H5
Putbus, *Germany* 18 A9
Puthein Myit →, *Burma* 61 M19
Putian, *China* 53 E12
Putignano, *Italy* 35 B10
Putina, *Peru* 124 C4
Puting, Tanjung, *Indonesia* 56 E4
Putlitz, *Germany* 18 B8
Putna →, *Romania* 38 D10
Putnam, *U.S.A.* 107 E13
Putorana, Gory, *Russia* . 45 C10
Putre, *Chile* 124 D4
Puttalam, *Sri Lanka* 60 Q11
Putte, *Neths.* 17 F4
Putten, *Neths.* 16 D7
Puttgarden, *Germany* ... 18 A7
Putumayo →, *S. Amer.* 120 D4
Putuo, *China* 53 C14
Putussibau, *Indonesia* .. 56 D4
Puurs, *Belgium* 17 F4
Puy-de-Dôme, *France* .. 26 C6
Puy-de-Dôme □, *France* 26 C7
Puy-Guillaume, *France* . 26 C7
Puy-l'Évêque, *France* ... 26 D5
Puyallup, *U.S.A.* 112 C4
Puyang, *China* 50 G8
Puyehue, *Chile* 128 B2
Puylaurens, *France* 26 E6
Puyo, *Ecuador* 120 D2
Pŭzeh Rīg, *Iran* 65 E8
Pwani □, *Tanzania* 82 D4
Pweto, *Zaïre* 83 D2
Pwllheli, *U.K.* 12 E3
Pyana →, *Russia* 42 C8
Pyapon, *Burma* 61 L19
Pyasina →, *Russia* 45 B9
Pyatigorsk, *Russia* 43 H6
Pyatykhatky, *Ukraine* ... 41 H7
Pyè, *Burma* 61 K19
Pyetrikaw, *Belarus* 41 F5
Pyhäjoki, *Finland* 8 D21
Pyinmana, *Burma* 61 K20
Pyla, C., *Cyprus* 37 E12
Pyŏktong, *N. Korea* 51 D13
Pyŏnggang, *N. Korea* .. 51 E14
Pyŏngtaek, *S. Korea* ... 51 F14
P'yŏngyang, *N. Korea* .. 51 E13
Pyote, *U.S.A.* 109 K3
Pyramid L., *U.S.A.* 110 G4
Pyramid Pk., *U.S.A.* 113 J10
Pyramids, *Egypt* 76 J7
Pyrénées, *Europe* 26 F4
Pyrénées-Atlantiques □,
  France 26 E3
Pyrénées-Orientales □,
  France 26 F6
Pyryatyn, *Ukraine* 41 G7
Pyrzyce, *Poland* 20 B4
Pytalovo, *Russia* 40 D4
Pyttegga, *Norway* 10 B1
Pyu, *Burma* 61 K20

Q

Qaanaaq = Thule,
  Greenland 4 B4
Qabirri →, *Azerbaijan* .. 43 K8
Qachasnek, *S. Africa* 85 E4
Qādib, *Yemen* 68 E5
Qa'el Jafr, *Jordan* 69 E5
Qa'emābād, *Iran* 65 D9
Qā'emshahr, *Iran* 65 B7
Qagan Nur, *China* 50 C8
Qahar Youyi Zhongqi,
  China 50 D7
Qahremānshahr =
  Bākhtarān, *Iran* 67 E12
Qaidam Pendi, *China* ... 54 C4
Qajarīyeh, *Iran* 65 D6
Qala, Ras il, *Malta* 37 C1
Qala-i-Jadid, *Afghan.* ... 62 D2
Qala Yangi, *Afghan.* 62 B2
Qal'at al Akhḍar,
  Si. Arabia 64 E3
Qal'at Dīzah, *Iraq* 67 D11
Qal'at Sukkar, *Iraq* 67 G12
Qal'eh Darreh, *Iran* 64 B5
Qal'eh Shaharak, *Afghan.* 60 B4
Qalyûb, *Egypt* 76 H7
Qamar, Ghubbat al, *Yemen* 68 D5
Qamdo, *China* 52 B1
Qamruddin Karez, *Pakistan* 62 D3
Qandahār, *Afghan.* 60 D4
Qandahār □, *Afghan.* ... 60 D4
Qapān, *Iran* 65 B7
Qapshaghay, *Kazakhstan* 44 E8
Qaqortoq = Julianehåb,
  Greenland 4 C5
Qâra, *Egypt* 76 B2
Qara Qash →, *India* ... 63 B8
Qarabutaq, *Kazakhstan* . 44 E7
Qaraçala, *Azerbaijan* ... 43 L9
Qaraghandy, *Kazakhstan* 44 E8
Qārah, *Si. Arabia* 64 D4
Qarataū, *Kazakhstan* ... 44 E8
Qardud, *Sudan* 77 E2
Qareh →, *Iran* 67 C12
Qareh Tekān, *Iran* 65 B6
Qarqan, *China* 54 C3
Qarqan He →, *China* .. 54 C3
Qarqaraly, *Kazakhstan* . 44 E8
Qarrasa, *Sudan* 77 E3
Qarshi, *Uzbekistan* 44 F7
Qartabā, *Lebanon* 69 A4
Qaryat al Gharab, *Iraq* .. 64 D5
Qaryat al 'Ulyā, *Si. Arabia* 64 E5
Qasr 'Amra, *Jordan* 64 D3
Qaṣr-e Qand, *Iran* 65 E9
Qasr Farâfra, *Egypt* 76 B2
Qatanā, *Syria* 69 B5
Qatar ■, *Asia* 65 E6
Qaţlīsh, *Iran* 65 B8
Qattâra, *Egypt* 76 A2
Qattâra, Munkhafed el,
  Egypt 76 B2
Qattâra Depression =
  Qattâra, Munkhafed el,
  Egypt 76 B2
Qawām al Ḥamzah, *Iraq* . 64 D5
Qāyen, *Iran* 65 C8
Qazaqstan =
  Kazakhstan ■, *Asia* .. 44 E7
Qazimämmäd, *Azerbaijan* 43 K9
Qazvin, *Iran* 65 B6
Qena, *Egypt* 76 B3
Qena, W. →, *Egypt* ... 76 B3
Qeqertarsuaq = Disko,
  Greenland 4 C5
Qeqertarsuaq = Godhavn,
  Greenland 4 C5
Qeshlāq, *Iran* 67 E12
Qeshm, *Iran* 65 E8
Qezi'ot, *Israel* 69 E3
Qi Xian, *China* 50 G8
Qian Gorlos, *China* 51 B13
Qian Xian, *China* 50 G5
Qiancheng, *China* 52 D7
Qianjiang,
  Guangxi Zhuangzu,
  China 52 F7
Qianjiang, *Hubei, China* . 53 B9
Qianjiang, *Sichuan, China* 52 C7
Qianshan, *China* 53 B11
Qianwei, *China* 52 C4
Qianxi, *China* 52 D6
Qianyang, *Hunan, China* . 53 D8
Qianyang, *Shaanxi, China* 50 G4
Qianyang, *Zhejiang, China* 53 B12
Qiaojia, *China* 52 D4
Qiba', *Si. Arabia* 64 E5
Qichun, *China* 53 B10
Qidong, *Hunan, China* .. 53 D9
Qidong, *Jiangsu, China* . 53 B13
Qijiang, *China* 52 C6
Qila Safed, *Pakistan* 60 E2
Qila Saifullāh, *Pakistan* . 62 D3
Qilian Shan, *China* 54 C4
Qimen, *China* 53 C11
Qin He →, *China* 50 G7
Qin Jiang →, *China* 53 D10
Qin Ling = Qinling Shandi,
  China 50 H5
Qin'an, *China* 50 G3
Qing Xian, *China* 50 E9
Qingcheng, *China* 51 F9
Qingdao, *China* 51 F11
Qingfeng, *China* 50 G8
Qinghai □, *China* 54 C4

Qinghai Hu, *China* 54 C5
Qinghecheng, *China* ... 51 D13
Qinghemen, *China* 51 D11
Qingjian, *China* 50 F6
Qingjiang, *Jiangsu, China* 51 H10
Qingjiang, *Jiangxi, China* 53 C10
Qingliu, *China* 53 D11
Qinglong, *China* 52 E5
Qingping, *China* 52 D6
Qingpu, *China* 53 B13
Qingshui, *China* 50 G4
Qingshuihe, *China* 50 E6
Qingtian, *China* 53 C13
Qingtongxia Shuiku, *China* 50 F3
Qingxi, *China* 52 D7
Qingxu, *China* 50 F7
Qingyang, *Anhui, China* . 53 B11
Qingyang, *Gansu, China* . 50 F4
Qingyi Jiang →, *China* .. 52 C4
Qingyuan, *Guangdong,*
  China 53 F9
Qingyuan, *Liaoning, China* 51 C13
Qingyuan, *Zhejiang, China* 53 D12
Qingyuan, *China* 51 F9
Qingzhen, *China* 52 D6
Qinhuangdao, *China* ... 51 E10
Qinling Shandi, *China* ... 50 H5
Qinshui, *China* 50 G7
Qinyang, *China* 50 G7
Qinyuan, *China* 50 F7
Qinzhou, *China* 52 G7
Qionghai, *China* 58 C8
Qionglai, *China* 52 B4
Qionglai Shan, *China* ... 52 B4
Qiongshan, *China* 58 C8
Qiongzhou Haixia, *China* 58 B8
Qiqihar, *China* 45 E13
Qiraîya, W. →, *Egypt* .. 69 E3
Qiryat Ata, *Israel* 69 C4
Qiryat Gat, *Israel* 69 D3
Qiryat Mal'akhi, *Israel* .. 69 D3
Qiryat Shemona, *Israel* . 69 B4
Qiryat Yam, *Israel* 69 C4
Qishan, *China* 50 G4
Qishan, *Taiwan* 53 F13
Qitai, *China* 54 B3
Qiubei, *China* 52 E5
Qixia, *China* 51 F11
Qiyang, *China* 53 D8
Qīzlağac Körfäzi,
  Azerbaijan 67 C13
Qojūr, *Iran* 64 B5
Qom, *Iran* 65 C6
Qomsheh, *Iran* 65 D6
Qorveh, *Iran* 67 E12
Qostanay, *Kazakhstan* .. 44 D7
Qotūr, *Iran* 67 C11
Qu Jiang →, *China* 52 B6
Qu Xian, *Sichuan, China* . 52 B6
Qu Xian, *Zhejiang, China* 53 C12
Quairading, *Australia* ... 89 F2
Quakenbrück, *Germany* . 18 C3
Quakertown, *U.S.A.* 107 F9
Qualeup, *Australia* 89 F2
Quambatook, *Australia* . 91 F3
Quambone, *Australia* ... 91 E4
Quamby, *Australia* 90 C3
Quan Long, *Vietnam* ... 59 H5
Quanah, *U.S.A.* 109 H5
Quandialla, *Australia* ... 91 E4
Quang Ngai, *Vietnam* .. 58 E7
Quang Yen, *Vietnam* ... 58 B6
Quannan, *China* 53 E10
Quantock Hills, *U.K.* 13 F4
Quanzhou, *Fujian, China* 53 E12
Quanzhou,
  Guangxi Zhuangzu,
  China 53 E8
Quaqtaq, *Canada* 97 B13
Quaraí, *Brazil* 126 C4
Quarré-les-Tombes, *France* 25 E10
Quartu Sant'Elena, *Italy* . 34 C2
Quartzsite, *U.S.A.* 113 M12
Quatsino, *Canada* 100 C3
Quatsino Sd., *Canada* ... 100 C3
Quba, *Azerbaijan* 43 K9
Qūchān, *Iran* 65 B8
Queanbeyan, *Australia* . 91 F4
Québec, *Canada* 99 C5
Québec □, *Canada* 99 B6
Quedlinburg, *Germany* . 18 D7
Queen Alexandra Ra.,
  Antarctica 5 E11
Queen Charlotte, *Canada* 100 C2
Queen Charlotte Bay,
  Falk. Is. 128 D4
Queen Charlotte Is.,
  Canada 100 C2
Queen Charlotte Str.,
  Canada 100 C3
Queen Elizabeth Is.,
  Canada 94 B10
Queen Elizabeth Nat. Park,
  Uganda 82 C3
Queen Mary Land,
  Antarctica 5 D7
Queen Maud G., *Canada* . 96 B9
Queen Maud Land,
  Antarctica 5 D3
Queen Maud Mts.,
  Antarctica 5 E13
Queens Chan., *Australia* . 88 C4
Queenscliff, *Australia* ... 91 F3
Queensland □, *Australia* 90 C3
Queenstown, *Australia* . 90 G4
Queenstown, *N.Z.* 87 L2
Queenstown, *S. Africa* .. 84 E4

Queets, *U.S.A.* 112 C2
Queguay Grande →,
  Uruguay 126 C4
Queimadas, *Brazil* 122 D4
Quela, *Angola* 80 F3
Quelimane, *Mozam.* ... 83 F4
Quelpart = Cheju Do,
  S. Korea 51 H14
Quemado, *N. Mex., U.S.A.* 111 J9
Quemado, *Tex., U.S.A.* . 109 L4
Quemú-Quemú, *Argentina* 126 D3
Quequén, *Argentina* 126 D4
Querco, *Peru* 124 C3
Querétaro, *Mexico* 114 C4
Querétaro □, *Mexico* ... 114 C5
Querfurt, *Germany* 18 D7
Quesada, *Spain* 29 H1
Queshan, *China* 50 H8
Quesnel, *Canada* 100 C4
Quesnel →, *Canada* ... 100 C4
Quesnel L., *Canada* 100 C4
Questa, *U.S.A.* 111 H11
Questembert, *France* ... 24 E4
Quetena, *Bolivia* 124 E4
Quetico Prov. Park,
  Canada 98 C1
Quetrequile, *Argentina* . 128 B3
Quetta, *Pakistan* 62 D2
Quevedo, *Ecuador* 120 D2
Quezaltenango, *Guatemala* 116 D1
Quezon City, *Phil.* 55 D4
Qufār, *Si. Arabia* 64 E4
Qui Nhon, *Vietnam* 58 F7
Quibaxe, *Angola* 80 F2
Quibdo, *Colombia* 120 B2
Quiberon, *France* 24 E3
Quibor, *Venezuela* 120 B4
Quick, *Canada* 100 C3
Quickborn, *Germany* ... 18 B5
Quiet L., *Canada* 100 A2
Quiévrain, *Belgium* 17 H3
Quiindy, *Paraguay* 126 B4
Quila, *Mexico* 114 C3
Quilán, C., *Chile* 128 B2
Quilcene, *U.S.A.* 112 C4
Quilengues, *Angola* 81 G2
Quilimarí, *Chile* 126 C1
Quilino, *Argentina* 126 C3
Quillabamba, *Peru* 124 C3
Quillacollo, *Bolivia* 124 D4
Quillagua, *Chile* 126 A2
Quillaicillo, *Chile* 126 C1
Quillan, *France* 26 F6
Quillebeuf-sur-Seine,
  France 24 C7
Quillota, *Chile* 126 C1
Quilmes, *Argentina* 126 C4
Quilon, *India* 60 Q10
Quilpie, *Australia* 91 D3
Quilpué, *Chile* 126 C1
Quilua, *Mozam.* 83 F4
Quime, *Bolivia* 124 D4
Quimilí, *Argentina* 126 B3
Quimper, *France* 24 D2
Quimperlé, *France* 24 E3
Quinault →, *U.S.A.* 112 C2
Quincemil, *Peru* 124 C3
Quincy, *Calif., U.S.A.* ... 112 F6
Quincy, *Fla., U.S.A.* 105 K3
Quincy, *Ill., U.S.A.* 108 F9
Quincy, *Mass., U.S.A.* .. 107 D14
Quincy, *Wash., U.S.A.* .. 110 C4
Quines, *Argentina* 126 C2
Quinga, *Mozam.* 83 F5
Quingey, *France* 25 E12
Quintana de la Serena,
  Spain 31 G5
Quintana Roo □, *Mexico* 115 D7
Quintanar de la Orden,
  Spain 28 F1
Quintanar de la Sierra,
  Spain 28 D2
Quintanar del Rey, *Spain* 29 F3
Quintero, *Chile* 126 C1
Quintin, *France* 24 D4
Quinto, *Spain* 28 D4
Quinyambie, *Australia* .. 91 E3
Quípar →, *Spain* 29 G3
Quipungo, *Angola* 81 G2
Quirihue, *Chile* 126 D1
Quirindi, *Australia* 91 E5
Quiroga, *Spain* 30 C3
Quiruvilca, *Peru* 124 B2
Quissac, *France* 27 E8
Quissanga, *Mozam.* 83 E5
Quitilipi, *Argentina* 126 B3
Quitman, *Ga., U.S.A.* ... 105 K4
Quitman, *Miss., U.S.A.* . 105 J1
Quitman, *Tex., U.S.A.* .. 109 J7
Quito, *Ecuador* 120 D2
Quixadá, *Brazil* 122 B4
Quixaxe, *Mozam.* 83 F5
Quixeramobim, *Brazil* .. 122 C4
Qujing, *China* 52 E4
Qul'ân, Jazâ'ir, *Egypt* ... 76 C4
Qumbu, *S. Africa* 85 E4
Quneitra, *Syria* 69 B4
Qŭnghirot, *Uzbekistan* .. 44 E6
Quoin I., *Australia* 88 B4
Quoin Pt., *S. Africa* 84 E2
Quondong, *Australia* ... 91 E3
Quorn, *Australia* 91 E2
Qŭqon, *Uzbekistan* 44 E8
Qurein, *Sudan* 77 E3
Qurnat as Sawdā', *Lebanon* 69 A5
Qûs, *Egypt* 76 B3
Qusar, *Azerbaijan* 43 K9

Qusaybah, *Iraq* 67 E9
Quseir, *Egypt* 76 B3
Qūshchī, *Iran* 67 D11
Quthing, *Lesotho* 85 E4
Qūṭīābād, *Iran* 67 E13
Quwo, *China* 50 G6
Quyang, *China* 50 E8
Quynh Nhai, *Vietnam* .. 58 B4
Quzi, *China* 50 F4

R

Ra, Ko, *Thailand* 59 H2
Råå, *Sweden* 11 J6
Raahe, *Finland* 8 D21
Raalte, *Neths.* 16 D8
Raamsdonksveer, *Neths.* 17 E5
Raasay, *U.K.* 14 D2
Raasay, Sd. of, *U.K.* ... 14 D2
Rab, *Croatia* 33 D11
Raba, *Indonesia* 57 F5
Rába →, *Hungary* 21 H7
Rabaçal →, *Portugal* ... 30 D3
Rabah, *Nigeria* 79 C6
Rabai, *Kenya* 82 C4
Rabastens, *France* 26 E5
Rabastens-de-Bigorre,
  France 26 E4
Rabat, *Malta* 37 D1
Rabat, *Morocco* 74 B3
Rabaul, *Papua N. G.* ... 92 H7
Rabbit →, *Canada* 100 B3
Rabbit Lake, *Canada* ... 101 C7
Rabbitskin →, *Canada* . 100 A4
Rabka, *Poland* 20 F9
Rābor, *Iran* 65 D8
Rácale, *Italy* 35 C11
Racalmuto, *Italy* 34 E6
Racconigi, *Italy* 32 D4
Race, C., *Canada* 99 C9
Rach Gia, *Vietnam* 59 G5
Raciąż, *Poland* 20 C10
Racibórz, *Poland* 20 E8
Racine, *U.S.A.* 104 D2
Rackerby, *U.S.A.* 112 F5
Radama, Nosy, *Madag.* . 85 A8
Radama, Saikanosy,
  Madag. 85 A8
Rădăuţi, *Romania* 38 B8
Radbuza →, *Czech.* 20 F3
Radeberg, *Germany* 18 D9
Radeče, *Slovenia* 33 B12
Radekhiv, *Ukraine* 41 G3
Radekhov = Radekhiv,
  Ukraine 41 G3
Radford, *U.S.A.* 104 G5
Radhanpur, *India* 62 H4
Radiska →, *Macedonia* . 39 H3
Radisson, *Canada* 101 C7
Radium Hot Springs,
  Canada 100 C5
Radna, *Romania* 38 C4
Radnor Forest, *U.K.* 13 E4
Radolfzell, *Germany* 19 H4
Radom, *Poland* 20 D11
Radomir, *Bulgaria* 38 G6
Radomsko, *Poland* 20 D9
Radomyshl, *Ukraine* ... 41 G5
Radoviš, *Macedonia* ... 39 H5
Radovljica, *Slovenia* 33 B11
Radstock, *U.K.* 13 F5
Radstock, C., *Australia* . 91 E1
Răducăneni, *Romania* .. 38 C10
Radviliškis, *Lithuania* ... 9 J20
Radville, *Canada* 101 D8
Rae, *Canada* 100 A5
Rae Bareli, *India* 63 F9
Rae Isthmus, *Canada* .. 97 B11
Raeren, *Belgium* 17 G8
Raeside, L., *Australia* ... 89 E3
Raetihi, *N.Z.* 87 H5
Rafaela, *Argentina* 126 C3
Rafah, *Gaza Strip* 69 D3
Rafai, *C.A.R.* 82 B1
Raffadali, *Italy* 34 E6
Rafḥā, *Si. Arabia* 64 D4
Rafsanjān, *Iran* 65 D8
Raft Pt., *Australia* 88 C3
Ragachov, *Belarus* 41 F6
Ragag, *Sudan* 77 E1
Ragama, *Sri Lanka* 60 R11
Ragged, Mt., *Australia* . 89 F3
Raglan, *Australia* 90 C5
Raglan, *N.Z.* 87 G5
Ragunda, *Sweden* 10 A10
Ragusa, *Italy* 35 F7
Raha, *Indonesia* 57 E6
Rahad, Nahr ed →, *Sudan* 77 E3
Rahad al Bardī, *Sudan* .. 77 E1
Rahaeng = Tak, *Thailand* 58 D2
Rahden, *Germany* 18 C4
Raheita, *Eritrea* 77 E5
Raḥīmah, *Si. Arabia* 65 E6
Rahimyar Khan, *Pakistan* . 62 E4
Rāhjerd, *Iran* 65 C6
Raichur, *India* 60 L10
Raiganj, *India* 63 G13
Raigarh, *India* 61 J13
Raijua, *Indonesia* 57 F6
Railton, *Australia* 90 G4

Rainbow Lake, Canada	...	100	B5
Rainier, U.S.A.	...	112	D4
Rainier, Mt., U.S.A.	...	112	D5
Rainy L., Canada	...	101	D10
Rainy River, Canada	...	101	D10
Raippaluoto, Finland	...	8	E19
Raipur, India	...	61	J12
Raisio, Finland	...	9	F20
Raj Nandgaon, India	...	61	J12
Raja, Ujung, Indonesia	...	56	D1
Raja Ampat, Kepulauan, Indonesia	...	57	E7
Rajahmundry, India	...	61	L12
Rajang →, Malaysia	...	56	D4
Rajapalaiyam, India	...	60	Q10
Rajasthan □, India	...	62	F5
Rajasthan Canal, India	...	62	E5
Rajauri, India	...	63	C6
Rajgarh, Mad. P., India	...	62	G7
Rajgarh, Raj., India	...	62	E6
Rajhenburg, Slovenia	...	33	B12
Rajkot, India	...	62	H4
Rajmahal Hills, India	...	63	G12
Rajpipla, India	...	60	J8
Rajpura, India	...	62	D7
Rajshahi, Bangla.	...	61	G16
Rajshahi □, Bangla.	...	63	G13
Rakaia, N.Z.	...	87	K4
Rakaia →, N.Z.	...	87	K4
Rakan, Ra's, Qatar	...	65	E6
Rakaposhi, Pakistan	...	63	A6
Rakata, Pulau, Indonesia	...	56	F3
Rakhiv, Ukraine	...	41	H3
Rakhni, Pakistan	...	62	D3
Rakitnoye, Russia	...	48	B7
Rakkestad, Norway	...	10	E5
Rakops, Botswana	...	84	C3
Rákospalota, Hungary	...	21	H9
Rakovica, Croatia	...	33	D12
Rakovník, Czech.	...	20	E3
Rakovski, Bulgaria	...	38	G7
Rakvere, Estonia	...	9	G22
Raleigh, U.S.A.	...	105	H6
Raleigh B., U.S.A.	...	105	H7
Ralja, Serbia, Yug.	...	21	L10
Ralls, U.S.A.	...	109	J4
Ram →, Canada	...	100	A4
Rām Allāh, West Bank	...	69	D4
Ram Hd., Australia	...	91	F4
Rama, Nic.	...	116	D3
Ramacca, Italy	...	35	E7
Ramales de la Victoria, Spain	...	28	B1
Ramalho, Serra do, Brazil		123	D3
Raman, Thailand	...	59	J3
Ramanathapuram, India	...	60	Q11
Ramanetaka, B. de, Madag.	...	85	A8
Ramat Gan, Israel	...	69	C3
Ramatlhabama, S. Africa	...	84	D4
Ramban, India	...	63	C6
Rambervillers, France	...	25	D13
Rambipuji, Indonesia	...	57	H15
Rambouillet, France	...	25	D8
Ramea, Canada	...	99	C8
Ramechhap, Nepal	...	63	F12
Ramelau, Indonesia	...	57	F7
Ramenskoye, Russia	...	42	C4
Ramgarh, Bihar, India	...	63	H11
Ramgarh, Raj., India	...	62	F6
Ramgarh, Raj., India	...	62	F4
Rāmhormoz, Iran	...	65	D6
Ramīān, Iran	...	65	B7
Ramingining, Australia	...	90	A2
Ramla, Israel	...	69	D3
Ramlu, Eritrea	...	77	E5
Ramme, Denmark	...	11	H2
Ramnad = Ramanathapuram, India		60	Q11
Ramnagar, India	...	63	C6
Ramnäs, Sweden	...	10	E10
Ramon, Russia	...	42	E4
Ramona, U.S.A.	...	113	M10
Ramore, Canada	...	98	C3
Ramotswa, Botswana	...	84	C4
Rampur, H.P., India	...	62	D7
Rampur, Mad. P., India	...	62	H5
Rampur, Ut. P., India	...	63	E8
Rampur Hat, India	...	63	G12
Rampura, India	...	62	G6
Ramree I. = Ramree Kyun, Burma		61	K18
Ramree Kyun, Burma	...	61	K18
Rāmsar, Iran	...	65	B6
Ramsel, Belgium	...	17	F5
Ramsey, Canada	...	98	C3
Ramsey, U.K.	...	12	C3
Ramsgate, U.K.	...	13	F9
Ramsjö, Sweden	...	10	B9
Ramtek, India	...	60	J11
Ramvik, Sweden	...	10	B11
Ranaghat, India	...	63	H13
Ranahu, Pakistan	...	62	G3
Ranau, Malaysia	...	56	C5
Rancagua, Chile	...	126	C1
Rance, Belgium	...	17	H4
Rance →, France	...	24	D5
Rance, Barrage de la, France	...	24	D4
Rancharia, Brazil	...	123	F1
Rancheria →, Canada	...	100	A3
Ranchester, U.S.A.	...	110	D10
Ranchi, India	...	63	H11
Ranco, L., Chile	...	128	B2
Randan, France	...	26	B7
Randazzo, Italy	...	35	E7
Randers, Denmark	...	11	H4
Randers Fjord, Denmark	.	11	H4
Randfontein, S. Africa	...	85	D4
Randle, U.S.A.	...	112	D5
Randolph, Mass., U.S.A.	.	107	D13
Randolph, N.Y., U.S.A.	...	106	D6
Randolph, Utah, U.S.A.	...	110	F8
Randolph, Vt., U.S.A.	...	107	C12
Randsfjorden, Norway	...	10	D4
Råne älv →, Sweden	...	8	D20
Rangae, Thailand	...	59	J3
Rangaunu B., N.Z.	...	87	F4
Rångedala, Sweden	...	11	G7
Rangeley, U.S.A.	...	107	B14
Rangely, U.S.A.	...	110	F9
Ranger, U.S.A.	...	109	J5
Rangia, India	...	61	F17
Rangiora, N.Z.	...	87	K4
Rangitaiki →, N.Z.	...	87	G6
Rangitata →, N.Z.	...	87	K3
Rangkasbitung, Indonesia	.	57	G12
Rangon →, Burma	...	61	L20
Rangoon, Burma	...	61	L20
Rangpur, Bangla.	...	61	G16
Rangsit, Thailand	...	58	F3
Ranibennur, India	...	60	M9
Raniganj, India	...	63	H12
Raniwara, India	...	60	G8
Rānīyah, Iraq	...	64	B5
Ranken →, Australia	...	90	C2
Rankin, U.S.A.	...	109	K4
Rankin Inlet, Canada	...	96	B10
Rankins Springs, Australia		91	E4
Rannoch, L., U.K.	...	14	E4
Rannoch Moor, U.K.	...	14	E4
Ranobe, Helodranon' i, Madag.	...	85	C7
Ranohira, Madag.	...	85	C8
Ranomafana, Toamasina, Madag.	...	85	B8
Ranomafana, Toliara, Madag.	...	85	C8
Ranong, Thailand	...	59	H2
Ränsa, Iran	...	65	C6
Ransiki, Indonesia	...	57	E8
Rantau, Indonesia	...	56	E5
Rantauprapat, Indonesia	..	56	D1
Rantemario, Indonesia	...	57	E5
Rantoul, U.S.A.	...	104	E1
Ranum, Denmark	...	11	H3
Raon l'Étape, France	...	25	D13
Raoui, Erg er, Algeria	...	75	C4
Raoyang, China	...	50	E8
Rapa, Pac. Oc.	...	93	K13
Rapallo, Italy	...	32	D6
Rāpch, Iran	...	65	E8
Rapid →, Canada	...	100	B3
Rapid City, U.S.A.	...	108	D3
Rapid River, U.S.A.	...	104	C2
Rapides des Joachims, Canada	...	98	C4
Rapla, Estonia	...	9	G21
Rapperswil, Switz.	...	23	B7
Rapu Rapu I., Phil.	...	55	E6
Rarotonga, Cook Is.	...	93	K12
Ra's al 'Ayn, Syria	...	67	D9
Ra's al Khaymah, U.A.E.	.	65	E8
Ra's al-Unuf, Libya	...	73	B8
Ra's an Naqb, Jordan	...	69	F4
Ras Bânâs, Egypt	...	76	C4
Ras Dashen, Ethiopia	...	77	E4
Ras el Ma, Algeria	...	75	B4
Râs Ghârib, Egypt	...	76	J8
Ras Mallap, Egypt	...	76	J8
Râs Timirist, Mauritania	.	78	B1
Rasa, Punta, Argentina	...	128	B4
Rasca, Pta. de la, Canary Is.	...	36	G3
Raseiniai, Lithuania	...	9	J20
Rashad, Sudan	...	77	E3
Rashîd, Egypt	...	76	H7
Rashîd, Masabb, Egypt	..	76	H7
Rasht, Iran	...	67	D13
Rasi Salai, Thailand	...	58	E5
Raška, Serbia, Yug.	...	21	M10
Rason L., Australia	...	89	E3
Rașova, Romania	...	38	E10
Rasra, India	...	63	G10
Rass el Oued, Algeria	...	75	A6
Rasskazovo, Russia	...	42	D5
Rastatt, Germany	...	19	G4
Rat Buri, Thailand	...	58	F2
Rat Islands, U.S.A.	...	96	C1
Rat River, Canada	...	100	A6
Ratangarh, India	...	62	E6
Raṭāwī, Iraq	...	64	D5
Rath, India	...	63	G8
Rath Luirc, Ireland	...	15	D3
Rathdrum, Ireland	...	15	D5
Rathenow, Germany	...	18	C8
Rathkeale, Ireland	...	15	D3
Rathlin, U.K.	...	15	A5
Rathlin O'Birne I., Ireland		15	B3
Ratibor = Racibórz, Poland	...	20	E8
Ratlam, India	...	62	H6
Ratnagiri, India	...	60	L8
Raton, U.S.A.	...	109	G2
Rattaphum, Thailand	...	59	J3
Rattray Hd., U.K.	...	14	D7
Ratz, Mt., Canada	...	100	B2
Ratzeburg, Germany	...	18	B6
Raub, Malaysia	...	59	L3
Rauch, Argentina	...	126	D4
Raufarhöfn, Iceland	...	8	C6
Raufoss, Norway	...	10	D4
Raukumara Ra., N.Z.	...	87	H6
Raul Soares, Brazil	...	123	F3
Rauland, Norway	...	10	E2
Rauma, Finland	...	9	F19
Rauma →, Norway	...	10	B1
Raurkela, India	...	63	H11
Rausu-Dake, Japan	...	48	B12
Rava-Ruska, Ukraine	...	41	G2
Rava Russkaya = Rava-Ruska, Ukraine	...	41	G2
Ravānsar, Iran	...	67	E12
Ravanusa, Italy	...	34	E6
Rāvar, Iran	...	65	D8
Ravels, Belgium	...	17	F6
Ravena, U.S.A.	...	107	D11
Ravenna, Italy	...	33	D9
Ravenna, Nebr., U.S.A.	..	108	E5
Ravenna, Ohio, U.S.A.	..	106	E3
Ravensburg, Germany	...	19	H5
Ravenshoe, Australia	...	90	B4
Ravenstein, Neths.	...	16	E7
Ravensthorpe, Australia	..	89	F3
Ravenswood, Australia	...	90	C4
Ravenswood, U.S.A.	...	104	F5
Ravi →, Pakistan	...	62	D4
Ravna Gora, Croatia	...	33	C11
Rawa Mazowiecka, Poland		20	D10
Rawalpindi, Pakistan	...	62	C5
Rawāndūz, Iraq	...	67	D11
Rawang, Malaysia	...	59	L3
Rawdon, Canada	...	98	C5
Rawene, N.Z.	...	87	F4
Rawicz, Poland	...	20	D6
Rawlinna, Australia	...	89	F4
Rawlins, U.S.A.	...	110	F10
Rawlinson Ra., Australia	.	89	D4
Rawson, Argentina	...	128	B3
Ray, U.S.A.	...	108	A3
Ray, C., Canada	...	99	C8
Rayadurg, India	...	60	M10
Rayagada, India	...	61	K13
Rāyen, Iran	...	65	D8
Raymond, Canada	...	100	D6
Raymond, Calif., U.S.A.	.	112	H7
Raymond, Wash., U.S.A.	.	112	D3
Raymondville, U.S.A.	...	109	M6
Raymore, Canada	...	101	C8
Rayne, U.S.A.	...	109	K8
Rayón, Mexico	...	114	B2
Rayong, Thailand	...	58	F3
Rayville, U.S.A.	...	109	J9
Raz, Pte. du, France	...	24	D2
Razan, Iran	...	67	E13
Ražana, Serbia, Yug.	...	21	L9
Ražanj, Serbia, Yug.	...	21	M11
Razdel'naya = Rozdilna, Ukraine	...	41	J6
Razdolnoye, Russia	...	48	C5
Razdolnoye, Ukraine	...	41	K7
Razeh, Iran	...	65	C6
Razelm, Lacul, Romania	.	38	E12
Razgrad, Bulgaria	...	38	F9
Razmak, Pakistan	...	62	C3
Ré, I. de, France	...	26	B2
Reading, U.K.	...	13	F7
Reading, U.S.A.	...	107	F9
Real, Cordillera, Bolivia	.	124	D4
Realicó, Argentina	...	126	D3
Réalmont, France	...	26	E6
Reata, Mexico	...	114	B4
Rebais, France	...	25	D10
Rebecca, L., Australia	...	89	F3
Rebi, Indonesia	...	57	F8
Rebiana, Libya	...	73	D9
Rebun-Tō, Japan	...	48	B10
Recanati, Italy	...	33	E10
Recaș, Romania	...	38	D4
Recherche, Arch. of the, Australia	...	89	F3
Recht, Belgium	...	17	H8
Rechytsa, Belarus	...	41	F6
Recife, Brazil	...	122	C5
Recklinghausen, Germany		17	E10
Reconquista, Argentina	..	126	B4
Recreio, Brazil	...	125	B6
Recreo, Argentina	...	126	B2
Recuay, Peru	...	124	B2
Red →, La., U.S.A.	...	109	K9
Red →, N. Dak., U.S.A.	.	108	A6
Red Bank, U.S.A.	...	107	F10
Red Bay, Canada	...	99	B8
Red Bluff, U.S.A.	...	110	F2
Red Bluff L., U.S.A.	...	109	K3
Red Cliffs, Australia	...	91	E3
Red Cloud, U.S.A.	...	108	E5
Red Deer, Canada	...	100	C6
Red Deer →, Alta., Canada	...	101	C6
Red Deer →, Man., Canada	...	101	C8
Red Deer L., Canada	...	101	C8
Red Indian L., Canada	...	99	C8
Red Lake, Canada	...	101	C10
Red Lake Falls, U.S.A.	..	108	B6
Red Lodge, U.S.A.	...	110	D9
Red Oak, U.S.A.	...	108	E7
Red Rock, Canada	...	98	C2
Red Rock, L., U.S.A.	...	108	E8
Red Rocks Pt., Australia	.	89	F4
Red Sea, Asia	...	68	C2
Red Slate Mt., U.S.A.	...	112	H8
Red Sucker L., Canada	..	101	C10
Red Tower Pass = Turnu Roșu, P., Romania	...	38	D7
Red Wing, U.S.A.	...	108	C8
Redange, Lux.	...	17	J7
Redbridge, U.K.	...	13	F8
Redcar, U.K.	...	12	C6
Redcliff, Canada	...	101	C6
Redcliffe, Australia	...	91	D5
Redcliffe, Mt., Australia	.	89	E3
Reddersburg, S. Africa	..	84	D4
Redding, U.S.A.	...	110	F2
Redditch, U.K.	...	13	E6
Redenção, Brazil	...	122	B4
Redfield, U.S.A.	...	108	C5
Redkino, Russia	...	42	B3
Redknife →, Canada	...	100	A5
Redlands, U.S.A.	...	113	M9
Redmond, Australia	...	89	F2
Redmond, Oreg., U.S.A.	.	110	D3
Redmond, Wash., U.S.A.	.	112	C4
Redon, France	...	24	E4
Redonda, Antigua	...	117	C7
Redondela, Spain	...	30	C2
Redondo, Portugal	...	31	G3
Redondo Beach, U.S.A.	..	113	M8
Redrock Pt., Canada	...	100	A5
Redruth, U.K.	...	13	G2
Redvers, Canada	...	101	D8
Redwater, Canada	...	100	C6
Redwood, U.S.A.	...	107	B9
Redwood City, U.S.A.	...	111	H2
Redwood Falls, U.S.A.	..	108	C7
Ree, L., Ireland	...	15	C4
Reed, L., Canada	...	101	C8
Reed City, U.S.A.	...	104	D3
Reeder, U.S.A.	...	108	B3
Reedley, U.S.A.	...	111	H4
Reedsburg, U.S.A.	...	108	D9
Reedsport, U.S.A.	...	110	E1
Reefton, N.Z.	...	87	K3
Refahiye, Turkey	...	67	C8
Refugio, U.S.A.	...	109	L6
Rega →, Poland	...	20	A5
Regalbuto, Italy	...	35	E7
Regen, Germany	...	19	G9
Regen →, Germany	...	19	F8
Regeneração, Brazil	...	122	C3
Regensburg, Germany	...	19	F8
Regenstauf, Germany	...	23	B6
Réggio di Calábria, Italy	.	35	D8
Réggio nell'Emília, Italy	.	32	D7
Regina, Canada	...	101	C8
Régina, Fr. Guiana	...	121	C7
Registro, Brazil	...	127	A6
Reguengos de Monsaraz, Portugal	...	31	G3
Rehar →, India	...	63	H10
Rehoboth, Namibia	...	84	C2
Rehovot, Israel	...	69	D3
Rei-Bouba, Cameroon	...	73	G7
Reichenbach, Germany	...	18	E8
Reichenbach, Switz.	...	22	C5
Reid, Australia	...	89	F4
Reid River, Australia	...	90	B4
Reiden, Switz.	...	22	B5
Reidsville, U.S.A.	...	105	G6
Reigate, U.K.	...	13	F7
Reims, France	...	25	C11
Reina Adelaida, Arch., Chile	...	128	D2
Reinach, Aargau, Switz.	..	22	B6
Reinach, Basel, Switz.	...	22	B5
Reinbeck, U.S.A.	...	108	D8
Reindeer →, Canada	...	101	B8
Reindeer I., Canada	...	101	C9
Reindeer L., Canada	...	101	B8
Reinga, C., N.Z.	...	87	F4
Reinosa, Spain	...	30	B6
Reinosa, Paso, Spain	...	30	C6
Reitdiep, Neths.	...	16	B9
Reitz, S. Africa	...	85	D4
Reivilo, S. Africa	...	84	D3
Rejmyre, Sweden	...	11	F9
Reka →, Slovenia	...	33	C11
Rekinniki, Russia	...	45	C17
Reliance, Canada	...	101	A7
Remad, Oued →, Algeria		75	B4
Rémalard, France	...	24	D7
Remarkable, Mt., Australia		91	E2
Rembang, Indonesia	...	57	G14
Remchi, Algeria	...	75	A4
Remedios, Colombia	...	120	B3
Remedios, Panama	...	116	E3
Remeshk, Iran	...	65	E8
Remich, Lux.	...	17	J8
Rémire, Fr. Guiana	...	121	C7
Remiremont, France	...	25	D13
Remo, Ethiopia	...	77	F5
Remontnoye, Russia	...	43	G6
Remoulins, France	...	27	E8
Remscheid, Germany	...	18	D3
Ren Xian, China	...	50	F8
Renascença, Brazil	...	120	D4
Rende, Italy	...	35	C9
Rendeux, Belgium	...	17	H7
Rendína, Greece	...	39	K4
Rendsburg, Germany	...	18	A5
Rene, Russia	...	45	C19
Renfrew, Canada	...	98	C4
Renfrew, U.K.	...	14	F4
Rengat, Indonesia	...	56	E2
Rengo, Chile	...	126	C1
Renhua, China	...	53	E9
Renhuai, China	...	52	D6
Reni, Ukraine	...	41	K5
Renk, Sudan	...	77	E3
Renkum, Neths.	...	16	E7
Renmark, Australia	...	91	E3
Rennell Sd., Canada	...	100	C2
Renner Springs T.O., Australia	...	90	B1
Rennes, France	...	24	D5
Rennes, Bassin de, France		24	E5
Reno, U.S.A.	...	112	F7
Reno →, Italy	...	33	D9
Renovo, U.S.A.	...	106	E7
Renqiu, China	...	50	E9
Rensselaer, Ind., U.S.A.	.	104	E2
Rensselaer, N.Y., U.S.A.	.	107	D11
Rentería, Spain	...	28	B3
Renton, U.S.A.	...	112	C4
Réo, Burkina Faso	...	78	C4
Reotipur, India	...	63	G10
Republic, Mich., U.S.A.	.	104	B2
Republic, Wash., U.S.A.	.	110	B4
Republican →, U.S.A.	...	108	F6
Republican City, U.S.A.	.	108	E5
Republiek, Surinam	...	121	B6
Repulse Bay, Canada	...	97	B11
Requena, Peru	...	124	B3
Requena, Spain	...	29	F3
Resadiye = Datça, Turkey		66	D2
Reşadiye, Turkey	...	66	B7
Resele, Sweden	...	10	A11
Reserve, Canada	...	101	C8
Reserve, U.S.A.	...	111	K9
Resht = Rasht, Iran	...	67	D13
Resistencia, Argentina	...	126	B4
Resolution I., Canada	...	97	B13
Resolution I., N.Z.	...	87	L1
Resplandes, Brazil	...	122	C2
Resplendor, Brazil	...	123	E3
Ressano Garcia, Mozam.	.	85	D5
Reston, Canada	...	101	D8
Retalhuleu, Guatemala	...	116	D1
Reteag, Romania	...	38	B7
Retenue, L. de, Zaïre	...	83	E2
Retford, U.K.	...	12	D7
Rethel, France	...	25	C11
Rethem, Germany	...	18	C5
Réthímnon, Greece	...	37	D6
Réthímnon □, Greece	...	37	D6
Retiche, Alpi, Switz.	...	23	D10
Retie, Belgium	...	17	F6
Retiers, France	...	24	E5
Retortillo, Spain	...	30	E4
Reuland, Belgium	...	17	H8
Réunion ■, Ind. Oc.	...	71	J9
Reus, Spain	...	28	D6
Reusel, Neths.	...	17	F6
Reuss →, Switz.	...	23	B6
Reutlingen, Germany	...	19	G5
Reutte, Austria	...	19	H6
Reuver, Neths.	...	17	F8
Reval = Tallinn, Estonia	.	9	G21
Revel, France	...	26	E6
Revelganj, India	...	63	G11
Revelstoke, Canada	...	100	C5
Reventazón, Peru	...	124	B1
Revigny-sur-Ornain, France		25	D11
Revilla Gigedo, Is., Pac. Oc.	...	93	F16
Revillagigedo I., U.S.A.	..	100	B2
Revin, France	...	25	C11
Revuè →, Mozam.	...	83	F3
Rewa, India	...	63	G9
Rewa →, Guyana	...	121	C6
Rewari, India	...	62	E7
Rexburg, U.S.A.	...	110	E8
Rey, Iran	...	65	C6
Rey, Rio del →, Nigeria	.	79	E6
Rey Malabo, Eq. Guin.	..	79	E6
Reyes, Bolivia	...	124	C4
Reyes, Pt., U.S.A.	...	112	H3
Reyhanlı, Turkey	...	66	D7
Reykjahlíð, Iceland	...	8	D5
Reykjanes, Iceland	...	8	E2
Reykjavík, Iceland	...	8	D3
Reynolds, Canada	...	101	D9
Reynolds Ra., Australia	..	88	D5
Reynoldsville, U.S.A.	...	106	E6
Reynosa, Mexico	...	115	B5
Rēzekne, Latvia	...	9	H22
Rezvān, Iran	...	65	E8
Rharis, O. →, Algeria	...	75	C6
Rhayader, U.K.	...	13	E4
Rheden, Neths.	...	16	D8
Rhein, Canada	...	101	C8
Rhein →, Europe	...	16	E8
Rhein-Main-Donau-Kanal, Germany	...	19	F7
Rheinbach, Germany	...	18	E2
Rheine, Germany	...	18	C3
Rheineck, Switz.	...	23	B9
Rheinfelden, Switz.	...	22	A5
Rheinland-Pfalz □, Germany	...	19	E2
Rheinsberg, Germany	...	18	B8
Rheinwaldhorn, Switz.	...	23	D8
Rhenen, Neths.	...	16	E7
Rheriss, Oued →, Morocco	...	74	B4
Rheydt, Germany	...	18	D2
Rhin = Rhein →, Europe		16	E8
Rhinau, France	...	25	D14
Rhine = Rhein →, Europe		16	E8
Rhineland-Palatinate = Rheinland-Pfalz □, Germany	...	19	E2
Rhinelander, U.S.A.	...	108	C10
Rhino Camp, Uganda	...	82	B3
Rhir, Cap, Morocco	...	74	B3
Rhisnes, Belgium	...	17	G5
Rho, Italy	...	32	C6
Rhode Island □, U.S.A.	.	107	E13
Rhodes = Ródhos, Greece		37	C10

Rhodesia = Zimbabwe ■, Africa 83 F2
Rhodope Mts. = Rhodopi Planina, Bulgaria 39 H7
Rhodopi Planina, Bulgaria 39 H7
Rhön = Hohe Rhön, Germany 19 E5
Rhondda, U.K. 13 F4
Rhône □, France 27 C8
Rhône →, France 27 E8
Rhum, U.K. 14 E2
Rhyl, U.K. 12 D4
Rhymney, U.K. 13 F4
Ri-Aba, Eq. Guin. 79 E6
Riachão, Brazil 122 C2
Riacho de Santana, Brazil 123 D3
Rialma, Brazil 123 E2
Riaño, Spain 30 C5
Rians, France 27 E9
Riansares →, Spain 28 F1
Riasi, India 63 C6
Riau □, Indonesia 56 D2
Riau, Kepulauan, Indonesia 56 D2
Riau Arch. = Riau, Kepulauan, Indonesia .. 56 D2
Riaza, Spain 28 D1
Riaza →, Spain 28 D1
Riba de Saelices, Spain . 28 E2
Ribadavia, Spain 30 C2
Ribadeo, Spain 30 B3
Ribadesella, Spain 30 B5
Ribamar, Brazil 122 B3
Ribas, Spain 28 C7
Ribas do Rio Pardo, Brazil 125 D7
Ribble →, U.K. 12 C5
Ribe, Denmark 11 J2
Ribeauvillé, France 25 D14
Ribécourt, France 25 C9
Ribeira, Spain 30 C2
Ribeira Brava, Madeira . 36 D2
Ribeira do Pombal, Brazil 122 D4
Ribeirão Prêto, Brazil .. 127 A6
Ribeiro Gonçalves, Brazil 122 C2
Ribémont, France 25 C10
Ribera, Italy 34 E6
Ribérac, France 26 C4
Riberalta, Bolivia 125 C4
Ribnica, Slovenia 33 C11
Ribnița, Moldova 41 J5
Ribnitz-Damgarten, Germany 18 A8
Riccarton, N.Z. 87 K4
Riccia, Italy 35 A7
Riccione, Italy 33 D9
Rice, U.S.A. 113 L12
Rice L., Canada 106 B6
Rice Lake, U.S.A. 108 C9
Rich, Morocco 74 B4
Rich Hill, U.S.A. 109 F7
Richards Bay, S. Africa . 85 D5
Richards L., Canada ... 101 B7
Richardson →, Canada . 101 B6
Richardson →, U.S.A. . 108 B3
Richardson Springs, U.S.A. 112 F5
Richibucto, Canada ... 99 C7
Richland, U.S.A. 105 J3
Richland, Oreg., U.S.A. 110 D5
Richland, Wash., U.S.A. 110 C4
Richland Center, U.S.A. 108 D9
Richlands, U.S.A. 104 G5
Richmond, N.S.W., Australia 91 E5
Richmond, Queens., Australia 90 C3
Richmond, N.Z. 87 J4
Richmond, U.K. 12 C6
Richmond, Calif., U.S.A. 112 H4
Richmond, Ind., U.S.A. 104 F3
Richmond, Ky., U.S.A. 104 G3
Richmond, Mich., U.S.A. 106 D2
Richmond, Mo., U.S.A. 108 F8
Richmond, Tex., U.S.A. 109 L7
Richmond, Utah, U.S.A. 110 F8
Richmond, Va., U.S.A. 104 G7
Richmond Ra., Australia 91 D5
Richmond-upon-Thames, U.K. 13 F7
Richterswil, Switz. 23 B7
Richton, U.S.A. 105 K1
Richwood, U.S.A. 104 F5
Ricla, Spain 28 D3
Ridder, Kazakhstan ... 44 D9
Ridderkerk, Neths. 16 E5
Riddes, Switz. 22 D4
Ridgecrest, U.S.A. 113 K9
Ridgedale, Canada 101 C8
Ridgefield, U.S.A. 112 E4
Ridgeland, U.S.A. 105 J5
Ridgelands, Australia .. 90 C5
Ridgetown, Canada ... 98 D3
Ridgewood, U.S.A. ... 107 F10
Ridgway, U.S.A. 106 E6
Riding Mountain Nat. Park, Canada 101 C8
Ridley, Mt., Australia .. 89 F3
Ried, Austria 21 G3
Riedlingen, Germany .. 19 G5
Riel, Neths. 17 E6
Rienza →, Italy 33 B8
Riesa, Germany 18 D9
Riesco, I., Chile 128 D2

Riesi, Italy 35 E7
Riet →, S. Africa 84 D3
Rieti, Italy 33 F9
Rieupeyroux, France .. 26 D6
Riez, France 27 E10
Riffe L., U.S.A. 112 D4
Rifle, U.S.A. 110 G10
Rift Valley □, Kenya .. 82 B4
Rig Rig, Chad 73 F7
Riga, Latvia 9 H21
Riga, G. of, Latvia ... 9 H20
Rīgān, Iran 65 D8
Rīgas Jūras Līcis = Riga, G. of, Latvia 9 H20
Rigaud, Canada 107 A10
Rigby, U.S.A. 110 E8
Rīgestān □, Afghan. .. 60 D4
Riggins, U.S.A. 110 D5
Rignac, France 26 D6
Rigolet, Canada 99 B8
Riihimäki, Finland 9 F21
Riiser-Larsen-halvøya, Antarctica 5 C4
Rijau, Nigeria 79 C6
Rijeka, Croatia 33 C11
Rijen, Neths. 17 E5
Rijkevorsel, Belgium .. 17 F5
Rijn →, Neths. 16 D4
Rijnsberg, Neths. 16 D4
Rijsbergen, Neths. 17 E5
Rijssen, Neths. 16 D9
Rijswijk, Neths. 16 D4
Rike, Ethiopia 77 E4
Rikuzentakada, Japan . 48 E10
Rila Planina, Bulgaria . 38 G6
Riley, U.S.A. 110 E4
Rima →, Nigeria 79 C6
Rimah, Wadi ar →, Si. Arabia 64 E4
Rimavská Sobota, Slovak Rep. 21 G10
Rimbey, Canada 100 C6
Rimbo, Sweden 10 E12
Rimi, Nigeria 79 C6
Rímini, Italy 33 D9
Rîmnicu Sărat, Romania . 38 D10
Rîmnicu Vîlcea, Romania . 38 D7
Rimouski, Canada 99 C6
Rimrock, U.S.A. 112 D5
Rinca, Indonesia 57 F5
Rincón de Romos, Mexico 114 C4
Rinconada, Argentina . 126 A2
Ringarum, Sweden ... 11 F10
Ringe, Denmark 11 J4
Ringim, Nigeria 79 C6
Ringkøbing, Denmark . 11 H2
Ringling, U.S.A. 110 C8
Ringsaker, Norway ... 10 D4
Ringsted, Denmark ... 11 J5
Ringvassøy, Norway .. 8 B18
Rinjani, Indonesia 56 F5
Rinteln, Germany 18 C5
Río, Punta del, Spain . 29 J2
Rio Branco, Brazil 124 B4
Rio Branco, Uruguay . 127 C5
Rio Brilhante, Brazil .. 127 A5
Río Bueno, Chile 128 B2
Rio Chico, Venezuela . 120 A4
Rio Claro, Brazil 127 A6
Río Claro, Chile 126 D1
Rio Claro, Trin. & Tob. 117 D7
Río Colorado, Argentina 128 A4
Río Cuarto, Argentina 126 C3
Rio das Pedras, Mozam. 85 C6
Rio de Contas, Brazil . 123 D3
Rio de Janeiro, Brazil . 123 F3
Rio de Janeiro □, Brazil 123 F3
Rio do Prado, Brazil .. 123 E3
Rio do Sul, Brazil 127 B6
Río Gallegos, Argentina 128 D3
Río Grande, Argentina 128 D3
Río Grande, Bolivia .. 124 G4
Rio Grande, Brazil ... 127 C5
Río Grande, Mexico .. 114 C4
Río Grande, Nic. 116 D3
Río Grande →, U.S.A. 109 N6
Río Grande City, U.S.A. 109 M5
Río Grande del Norte →, N. Amer. 103 E7
Rio Grande do Norte □, Brazil 122 C4
Rio Grande do Sul □, Brazil 127 C5
Río Hato, Panama 116 E3
Rio Lagartos, Mexico . 115 C7
Rio Largo, Brazil 122 C4
Rio Maior, Portugal .. 31 F2
Rio Marina, Italy 32 F7
Río Mayo, Argentina . 128 C2
Río Mulatos, Bolivia . 124 D4
Río Muni = Mbini □, Eq. Guin. 80 D2
Rio Negro, Brazil 127 B6
Rio Negro, Chile 128 B2
Rio Negro, Pantanal do, Brazil 125 D6
Rio Pardo, Brazil 127 C5
Río Pico, Argentina .. 128 B2
Rio Real, Brazil 123 D4
Río Segundo, Argentina 126 C3
Río Tercero, Argentina 126 C3
Rio Tinto, Brazil 122 C4
Rio Tinto, Portugal ... 30 D2
Río Verde, Brazil 123 E1
Río Verde, Mexico 115 C5
Rio Verde de Mato Grosso, Brazil 125 D7
Rio Vista, U.S.A. 112 G5

Ríobamba, Ecuador ... 120 D2
Ríohacha, Colombia .. 120 A3
Rioja, Peru 124 B2
Riom, France 26 C7
Riom-ès-Montagnes, France 26 C6
Rion-des-Landes, France 26 E3
Rionegro, Colombia .. 120 B2
Rionero in Vúlture, Italy 35 B8
Rioni →, Georgia 43 J5
Rios, Spain 30 D3
Ríosucio, Caldas, Colombia 120 B2
Ríosucio, Choco, Colombia 120 B2
Riou L., Canada 101 B7
Rioz, France 25 E13
Riozinho →, Brazil ... 120 D4
Riparia, Dora →, Italy 32 C4
Ripatransone, Italy ... 33 F10
Ripley, Canada 106 B3
Ripley, Calif., U.S.A. . 113 M12
Ripley, N.Y., U.S.A. . 106 D5
Ripley, Tenn., U.S.A. . 109 H10
Ripoll, Spain 28 C7
Ripon, U.K. 12 C6
Ripon, Calif., U.S.A. . 112 H5
Ripon, Wis., U.S.A. .. 104 D1
Riposto, Italy 35 E8
Risalpur, Pakistan 62 B4
Risan, Montenegro, Yug. 21 N8
Rishā', W. ar →, Si. Arabia 64 E5
Rishiri-Tō, Japan 48 B10
Rishon le Ziyyon, Israel 69 D3
Risle →, France 24 C7
Rison, U.S.A. 109 J8
Risør, Norway 11 F3
Rissani, Morocco 74 B4
Riti, Nigeria 79 D6
Rittman, U.S.A. 106 F3
Ritzville, U.S.A. 110 C4
Riva Bella, France 24 C6
Riva del Garda, Italy .. 32 C7
Rivadavia, Buenos Aires, Argentina 126 D3
Rivadavia, Mendoza, Argentina 126 C2
Rivadavia, Salta, Argentina 126 A3
Rivadavia, Chile 126 B1
Rivarolo Canavese, Italy 32 C4
Rivas, Nic. 116 D2
Rive-de-Gier, France .. 27 C8
River Cess, Liberia ... 78 D3
Rivera, Uruguay 127 C4
Riverdale, U.S.A. 112 J7
Riverhead, U.S.A. 107 F12
Riverhurst, Canada ... 101 C7
Riverina, Australia ... 89 E3
Rivers, Canada 101 C8
Rivers □, Nigeria 79 E6
Rivers, L. of the, Canada 101 D7
Rivers Inlet, Canada .. 100 C3
Riversdale, S. Africa .. 84 E3
Riverside, Calif., U.S.A. 113 M9
Riverside, Wyo., U.S.A. 110 F10
Riversleigh, Australia . 90 B2
Riverton, Australia ... 91 E2
Riverton, Canada 101 C9
Riverton, N.Z. 87 M1
Riverton, U.S.A. 110 E9
Riverton Heights, U.S.A. 112 C4
Rives, France 27 C9
Rivesaltes, France 26 F6
Riviera, Europe 32 E5
Riviera di Levante, Italy 32 D6
Riviera di Ponente, Italy 32 D5
Rivière-à-Pierre, Canada 99 C5
Rivière-au-Renard, Canada 99 C7
Rivière-du-Loup, Canada 99 C6
Rivière-Pentecôte, Canada 99 C6
Rivière-Pilote, Martinique 117 D7
Rivne, Ukraine 41 G4
Rívoli, Italy 32 C4
Rivoli B., Australia ... 91 F3
Rixensart, Belgium ... 17 G5
Riyadh = Ar Riyāḍ, Si. Arabia 64 E5
Rize, Turkey 67 B9
Rizhao, China 51 G10
Rizokarpaso, Cyprus . 66 E6
Rizzuto, C., Italy 35 D10
Rjukan, Norway 10 E2
Roa, Norway 10 D4
Roa, Spain 30 D7
Road Town, Virgin Is. . 117 C7
Roag, L., U.K. 14 C2
Roanne, France 27 B8
Roanoke, Ala., U.S.A. 105 J3
Roanoke, Va., U.S.A. 104 G6
Roanoke →, U.S.A. .. 105 H7
Roanoke I., U.S.A. ... 105 H8
Roanoke Rapids, U.S.A. 105 G7
Roatán, Honduras 116 C2
Robbins I., Australia .. 90 G4
Robe →, Australia ... 88 D2
Robe →, Ireland 15 C2
Röbel, Germany 18 B8
Robert Lee, U.S.A. ... 109 K4
Roberts, U.S.A. 110 E7
Robertsganj, India ... 63 G10
Robertson, S. Africa .. 84 E2
Robertson I., Antarctica 5 C18
Robertson Ra., Australia 88 D3
Robertsport, Liberia .. 78 D2
Robertstown, Australia 91 E2
Roberval, Canada 99 C5
Robeson Chan., Greenland 4 A4

Robinson →, Australia 90 B2
Robinson Ra., Australia 89 E2
Robinson River, Australia 90 B2
Robinvale, Australia .. 91 E3
Roblin, Canada 101 C8
Roboré, Bolivia 125 D6
Robson, Mt., Canada . 100 C5
Robstown, U.S.A. 109 M6
Roca, C. da, Portugal . 6 H4
Roca Partida, I., Mexico 114 D2
Rocas, I., Brazil 122 B5
Rocca d'Aspidé, Italy . 35 B8
Rocca San Casciano, Italy 33 D8
Roccalbegna, Italy ... 33 F8
Roccastrada, Italy 33 F8
Roccella Iónica, Italy . 35 D9
Rocha, Uruguay 127 C5
Rochdale, U.K. 12 D5
Rochechouart, France 26 C4
Rochedo, Brazil 125 D7
Rochefort, Belgium ... 17 H6
Rochefort, France 26 C3
Rochefort-en-Terre, France 24 E4
Rochelle, U.S.A. 108 E10
Rocher River, Canada . 100 A6
Rocherath, Belgium .. 17 H8
Rocheservière, France 24 F5
Rochester, Canada ... 100 C6
Rochester, U.K. 13 F8
Rochester, Ind., U.S.A. 104 E2
Rochester, Minn., U.S.A. 108 C8
Rochester, N.H., U.S.A. 107 C14
Rochester, N.Y., U.S.A. 106 C7
Rociana, Spain 31 H4
Rociu, Romania 38 E8
Rock →, Canada 100 A3
Rock Hill, U.S.A. 105 H5
Rock Island, U.S.A. .. 108 E9
Rock Rapids, U.S.A. . 108 D6
Rock River, U.S.A. ... 110 F11
Rock Sound, Bahamas 116 B4
Rock Springs, Mont., U.S.A. 110 C10
Rock Springs, Wyo., U.S.A. 110 F9
Rock Valley, U.S.A. .. 108 D6
Rockall, Atl. Oc. 6 D3
Rockanje, Neths. 16 E4
Rockdale, Tex., U.S.A. 109 K6
Rockdale, Wash., U.S.A. 112 C5
Rockefeller Plateau, Antarctica 5 E14
Rockford, U.S.A. 108 D10
Rockglen, Canada 101 D7
Rockhampton, Australia 90 C5
Rockhampton Downs, Australia 90 B2
Rockingham, Australia 89 F2
Rockingham B., Australia 90 B4
Rockingham Forest, U.K. 13 E7
Rocklake, U.S.A. 108 A5
Rockland, Canada 107 A9
Rockland, Idaho, U.S.A. 110 E7
Rockland, Maine, U.S.A. 99 D6
Rockland, Mich., U.S.A. 108 B10
Rocklin, U.S.A. 112 G5
Rockmart, U.S.A. 105 H3
Rockport, Mo., U.S.A. 108 E7
Rockport, Tex., U.S.A. 109 L6
Rocksprings, U.S.A. .. 109 K4
Rockville, Conn., U.S.A. 97 E12
Rockville, Md., U.S.A. 104 F7
Rockwall, U.S.A. 109 J6
Rockwell City, U.S.A. 108 D7
Rockwood, U.S.A. 105 H3
Rocky Ford, U.S.A. .. 108 F3
Rocky Gully, Australia 89 F2
Rocky Lane, Canada .. 100 B5
Rocky Mount, U.S.A. 105 H7
Rocky Mountain House, Canada 100 C6
Rocky Mts., N. Amer. 100 C4
Rockyford, Canada ... 100 C6
Rocroi, France 25 C11
Rod, Pakistan 60 E3
Rødberg, Norway 10 D2
Rødby, Denmark 11 K5
Rødbyhavn, Denmark 11 K5
Roddickton, Canada .. 99 B8
Rødding, Denmark ... 11 J3
Rødekro, Denmark ... 11 J3
Roden, Neths. 16 B8
Rodenkirchen, Germany 18 B4
Roderick I., Canada .. 100 C3
Rodez, France 26 D6
Rodholívas, Greece ... 39 J6
Rodhopoú, Greece ... 37 D5
Ródhos, Greece 37 C10
Rodi Gargánico, Italy . 35 A8
Rodna, Romania 38 B7
Rodney, Canada 106 D3
Rodney, C., N.Z. 87 G5
Rodniki, Russia 42 B5
Rodríguez, Ind. Oc. .. 3 E13
Roe →, U.K. 15 A5
Roebling, U.S.A. 107 F10
Roebourne, Australia . 88 D2
Roebuck B., Australia . 88 C3
Roebuck Plains, Australia 88 C3
Roer →, Neths. 17 F7
Roermond, Neths. ... 17 F7
Roes Welcome Sd., Canada 97 B11
Roeselare, Belgium ... 17 G2
Rœulx, Belgium 17 G4
Rogachev = Ragachow, Belarus 41 F6

Rogagua, L., Bolivia .. 124 C4
Rogaška Slatina, Slovenia . 33 B12
Rogatec, Slovenia 33 B12
Rogatyn, Ukraine 41 H3
Rogdhia, Greece 37 D7
Rogers, U.S.A. 109 G7
Rogers City, U.S.A. .. 104 C4
Rogerson, U.S.A. 110 E6
Rogersville, U.S.A. ... 105 G4
Roggan River, Canada 98 B4
Roggel, Neths. 17 F7
Roggeveldberge, S. Africa 84 E3
Roggiano Gravina, Italy 35 C9
Rogliano, France 27 F13
Rogliano, Italy 35 C9
Rogoaguado, L., Bolivia 125 C4
Rogue →, U.S.A. 110 E1
Rohan, France 24 D4
Róhda, Greece 37 A3
Rohnert Park, U.S.A. . 112 G4
Rohrbach-lès-Bitche, France 25 C14
Rohri, Pakistan 62 F3
Rohri Canal, Pakistan . 62 F3
Rohtak, India 62 E7
Roi Et, Thailand 58 D4
Roisel, France 25 C10
Roja, Latvia 9 H20
Rojas, Argentina 126 C3
Rojo, C., Mexico 115 C5
Rokan →, Indonesia . 56 D2
Rokeby, Australia 90 A3
Rokiškis, Lithuania ... 9 J21
Rokitno, Russia 42 E2
Rolândia, Brazil 127 A5
Rolde, Neths. 16 C9
Rolette, U.S.A. 108 A5
Rolla, Kans., U.S.A. .. 109 G4
Rolla, Mo., U.S.A. ... 109 G9
Rolla, N. Dak., U.S.A. 108 A5
Rollag, Norway 10 D3
Rolle, Switz. 22 D2
Rolleston, Australia .. 90 C4
Rollingstone, Australia 90 B4
Rom, Sudan 77 F3
Roma, Australia 91 D4
Roma, Italy 34 A5
Roma, Sweden 9 H18
Roman, Romania 38 C9
Roman, Russia 45 C12
Roman-Kosh, Gora, Ukraine 41 K8
Romanche →, France 27 C9
Romang, Indonesia ... 57 F7
Români, Egypt 69 E1
Romania ■, Europe .. 38 D8
Romano, Cayo, Cuba . 116 B4
Romano di Lombárdia, Italy 32 C6
Romanovka = Basarabeasca, Moldova 41 J5
Romans-sur-Isère, France 27 C9
Romanshorn, Switz. . 23 A8
Romblon, Phil. 55 E5
Rombo □, Tanzania .. 82 C4
Rome = Roma, Italy . 34 A5
Rome, Ga., U.S.A. ... 105 H3
Rome, N.Y., U.S.A. .. 107 C9
Romeleåsen, Sweden . 11 J7
Romenay, France 27 B9
Romerike, Norway ... 10 D5
Romilly-sur-Seine, France 25 D10
Romîni, Romania 38 E7
Rommani, Morocco .. 74 B3
Romney, U.S.A. 104 F6
Romney Marsh, U.K. . 13 F8
Romny, Ukraine 41 G7
Rømø, Denmark 11 J2
Romodan, Ukraine ... 41 G7
Romodanovo, Russia . 42 C7
Romont, Switz. 22 C3
Romorantin-Lanthenay, France 25 E8
Romsdalen, Norway . 10 B2
Ron, Vietnam 58 D6
Rona, U.K. 14 D3
Ronan, U.S.A. 110 C6
Roncador, Cayos, Caribbean 116 D3
Roncador, Serra do, Brazil 123 D1
Roncesvalles, Paso, Spain 28 B3
Ronceverte, U.S.A. ... 104 G5
Roncíglione, Italy 33 F9
Ronco →, Italy 33 D9
Ronda, Spain 31 J5
Ronda, Serranía de, Spain 31 J5
Rondane, Norway 10 C3
Rondón, Colombia ... 120 B3
Rondônia, Brazil 125 C5
Rondônia □, Brazil ... 125 C5
Rondonópolis, Brazil . 125 D7
Rong Jiang →, China . 52 E7
Rong Xian, Guangxi Zhuangzu, China ... 53 F8
Rong Xian, Sichuan, China 52 C5
Rong'an, China 52 E7
Rongchang, China ... 52 C5
Ronge, L. la, Canada . 101 B7
Rongjiang, China 52 E7
Rongshui, China 52 E7
Rønne, Denmark 9 J16
Ronne Ice Shelf, Antarctica 5 D18
Ronsard, C., Australia 89 D1
Ronse, Belgium 17 G3
Ronuro →, Brazil 125 D7
Roodepoort, S. Africa . 85 D4

Sahara

Roodeschool, *Neths.* 16 B9
Roof Butte, *U.S.A.* 111 H9
Roompot, *Neths.* 17 E3
Roorkee, *India* 62 E7
Roosendaal, *Neths.* 17 E4
Roosevelt, *Minn., U.S.A.* 108 A7
Roosevelt, *Utah, U.S.A.* 110 F8
Roosevelt →, *Brazil* 125 B5
Roosevelt, Mt., *Canada* 100 B3
Roosevelt I., *Antarctica* 5 D12
Roosevelt Res., *U.S.A.* 111 K8
Roper →, *Australia* 90 A2
Ropesville, *U.S.A.* 109 J3
Roque Pérez, *Argentina* 126 D4
Roquefort, *France* 26 D3
Roquemaure, *France* 27 D8
Roquetas, *Spain* 28 E5
Roquevaire, *France* 27 E9
Roraima □, *Brazil* 121 C5
Roraima, Mt., *Venezuela* 121 B5
Rorketon, *Canada* 101 C9
Røros, *Norway* 10 B5
Rorschach, *Switz.* 23 B8
Rosa, *Zambia* 83 D3
Rosa, C., *Algeria* 75 A6
Rosa, Monte, *Europe* 22 E5
Rosal, *Spain* 30 D2
Rosal de la Frontera, *Spain* 31 H3
Rosalia, *U.S.A.* 110 C5
Rosamond, *U.S.A.* 113 L8
Rosans, *France* 27 D9
Rosario, *Argentina* 126 C3
Rosário, *Brazil* 122 B3
Rosario, *Baja Calif. Mexico* 114 A1
Rosario, *Sinaloa, Mexico* 114 C3
Rosario, *Paraguay* 126 A4
Rosario, Villa del, *Venezuela* 120 A3
Rosario de la Frontera, *Argentina* 126 B3
Rosario de Lerma, *Argentina* 126 A2
Rosario del Tala, *Argentina* 126 C4
Rosário do Sul, *Brazil* 127 C5
Rosário Oeste, *Brazil* 125 C6
Rosarito, *Mexico* 113 N9
Rosarno, *Italy* 35 D8
Rosas, *Spain* 28 C8
Rosas, G. de, *Spain* 28 C8
Roscoe, *U.S.A.* 108 C5
Roscoff, *France* 24 D3
Roscommon, *Ireland* 15 C3
Roscommon, *U.S.A.* 104 C3
Roscommon □, *Ireland* 15 C3
Roscrea, *Ireland* 15 D4
Rose →, *Australia* 90 A2
Rose Blanche, *Canada* 99 C8
Rose Harbour, *Canada* 100 C2
Rose Pt., *Canada* 100 C2
Rose Valley, *Canada* 101 C8
Roseau, *Domin.* 117 C7
Roseau, *U.S.A.* 108 A7
Rosebery, *Australia* 90 G4
Rosebud, *U.S.A.* 109 K6
Roseburg, *U.S.A.* 110 E2
Rosedale, *Australia* 90 C5
Rosedale, *U.S.A.* 109 J9
Rosée, *Belgium* 17 H5
Roseland, *U.S.A.* 112 G4
Rosemary, *Canada* 100 C6
Rosenberg, *U.S.A.* 109 L7
Rosendaël, *France* 25 A9
Rosenheim, *Germany* 19 H8
Roseto degli Abruzzi, *Italy* 33 F11
Rosetown, *Canada* 101 C7
Rosetta = Rashîd, *Egypt* 76 H7
Roseville, *U.S.A.* 112 G5
Rosewood, *N. Terr., Australia* 88 C4
Rosewood, *Queens., Australia* 91 D5
Roshkhvār, *Iran* 65 C8
Rosières-en-Santerre, *France* 25 C9
Rosignano Maríttimo, *Italy* 32 E7
Rosignol, *Guyana* 121 B6
Roşiori de Vede, *Romania* 38 E8
Rositsa, *Bulgaria* 38 F10
Rositsa →, *Bulgaria* 38 F8
Roskilde, *Denmark* 11 J6
Roskilde Amtskommune □, *Denmark* 11 J6
Roskilde Fjord, *Denmark* 11 J6
Roslavl, *Russia* 40 F7
Roslyn, *Australia* 91 E4
Rosmaninhal, *Portugal* 31 F3
Rosmead, *S. Africa* 84 E4
Røsnæs, *Denmark* 11 J4
Rosolini, *Italy* 35 F7
Rosporden, *France* 24 E3
Ross, *Australia* 90 G4
Ross, *N.Z.* 87 K3
Ross I., *Antarctica* 5 D11
Ross Ice Shelf, *Antarctica* 5 E12
Ross L., *U.S.A.* 110 B3
Ross-on-Wye, *U.K.* 13 F5
Ross Sea, *Antarctica* 5 D11
Rossa, *Switz.* 23 D8
Rossan Pt., *Ireland* 15 B3
Rossano Cálabro, *Italy* 35 C9
Rossburn, *Canada* 101 C8
Rosseau, *Canada* 106 A5
Rossignol, L., *Canada* 98 B5
Rossignol Res., *Canada* 99 D6
Rossland, *Canada* 100 D5
Rosslare, *Ireland* 15 D5
Rosslau, *Germany* 18 D8
Rosso, *Mauritania* 78 B1
Rosso, C., *France* 27 F12
Rossosh, *Russia* 42 E4
Rossport, *Canada* 98 C2
Rossum, *Neths.* 16 E6
Røssvatnet, *Norway* 8 D16
Rossville, *Australia* 90 B4
Røst, *Norway* 8 C15
Rosthern, *Canada* 101 C7
Rostock, *Germany* 18 A8
Rostov, *Don, Russia* 43 G4
Rostov, *Yarosl., Russia* 42 B4
Rostrenen, *France* 24 D3
Roswell, *U.S.A.* 109 J2
Rosyth, *U.K.* 14 E5
Rota, *Spain* 31 J4
Rotälven →, *Sweden* 10 C8
Rotan, *U.S.A.* 109 J4
Rotem, *Belgium* 17 F7
Rotenburg, *Germany* 18 B5
Roth, *Germany* 19 F7
Rothaargebirge, *Germany* 18 E4
Rothenburg, *Switz.* 23 B6
Rothenburg ob der Tauber, *Germany* 19 F6
Rother →, *U.K.* 13 G8
Rotherham, *U.K.* 12 D6
Rothes, *U.K.* 14 D5
Rothesay, *Canada* 99 C6
Rothesay, *U.K.* 14 F3
Rothrist, *Switz.* 22 B5
Roti, *Indonesia* 57 F6
Roto, *Australia* 91 E4
Rotondella, *Italy* 35 B9
Rotoroa, L., *N.Z.* 87 J4
Rotorua, *N.Z.* 87 H6
Rotorua, L., *N.Z.* 87 H6
Rotselaar, *Belgium* 17 G5
Rott →, *Germany* 19 G9
Rotten →, *Switz.* 22 D5
Rottenburg, *Germany* 19 G4
Rotterdam, *Neths.* 16 E5
Rottnest I., *Australia* 89 F2
Rottumeroog, *Neths.* 16 A9
Rottweil, *Germany* 19 G4
Rotuma, *Fiji* 92 J9
Roubaix, *France* 25 B10
Rouen, *France* 24 C8
Rouergue, *France* 26 D5
Rouillac, *France* 26 C3
Rouleau, *Canada* 101 C8
Round Mountain, *U.S.A.* 110 G5
Round Mt., *Australia* 91 E5
Roundup, *U.S.A.* 110 C9
Roura, *Fr. Guiana* 121 C7
Rousay, *U.K.* 14 B5
Rouses Point, *U.S.A.* 107 B11
Roussillon, *Isère, France* 27 C8
Roussillon, *Pyrénées-Or., France* 26 F6
Rouveen, *Neths.* 16 C8
Rouxville, *S. Africa* 84 E4
Rouyn, *Canada* 98 C4
Rovaniemi, *Finland* 8 C21
Rovato, *Italy* 32 C7
Rovenki, *Ukraine* 41 H10
Rovereto, *Italy* 32 C8
Rovigo, *Italy* 33 C8
Rovinari, *Romania* 38 E6
Rovinj, *Croatia* 33 C10
Rovira, *Colombia* 120 C2
Rovno = Rivne, *Ukraine* 41 G4
Rovnoye, *Russia* 42 E8
Rovuma →, *Tanzania* 83 E5
Row'ān, *Iran* 65 C6
Rowena, *Australia* 91 D4
Rowley Shoals, *Australia* 88 C2
Roxa, *Guinea-Biss.* 78 C1
Roxas, *Capiz, Phil.* 55 F5
Roxas, *Isabela, Phil.* 55 C4
Roxas, *Mindoro, Phil.* 55 E4
Roxboro, *U.S.A.* 105 G6
Roxborough Downs, *Australia* 90 C2
Roxburgh, *N.Z.* 87 L2
Roxen, *Sweden* 11 F9
Roy, *Mont., U.S.A.* 110 C9
Roy, *N. Mex., U.S.A.* 109 H2
Roy Hill, *Australia* 88 D2
Roya, Peña, *Spain* 28 E4
Royal Leamington Spa, *U.K.* 13 E6
Royal Tunbridge Wells, *U.K.* 13 F8
Royan, *France* 26 C2
Roye, *France* 25 C9
Røyken, *Norway* 10 E4
Rožaj, *Montenegro, Yug.* 21 N10
Rozay-en-Brie, *France* 25 D9
Rozdilna, *Ukraine* 41 J6
Rozhyshche, *Ukraine* 41 G3
Rožňava, *Slovak Rep.* 20 G10
Rozoy-sur-Serre, *France* 25 C11
Rtishchevo, *Russia* 42 D6
Rúa, *Spain* 30 C3
Ruacaná, *Angola* 84 B1
Ruahine Ra., *N.Z.* 87 H6
Ruapehu, *N.Z.* 87 H5
Ruapuke I., *N.Z.* 87 M2
Ruâq, W. →, *Egypt* 69 F2
Rub' al Khali, *Si. Arabia* 68 D4
Rubeho Mts., *Tanzania* 82 D4
Rubezhnoye = Rubizhne, *Ukraine* 41 H10
Rubh a' Mhail, *U.K.* 14 F2
Rubha Hunish, *U.K.* 14 D2
Rubha Robhanais = Lewis, Butt of, *U.K.* 14 C2
Rubiataba, *Brazil* 123 E2
Rubicon →, *U.S.A.* 112 G5
Rubicone →, *Italy* 33 D9
Rubinéia, *Brazil* 123 F1
Rubino, *Ivory C.* 78 D4
Rubio, *Venezuela* 120 B3
Rubizhne, *Ukraine* 41 H10
Rubtsovsk, *Russia* 44 D9
Ruby L., *U.S.A.* 110 F6
Ruby Mts., *U.S.A.* 110 F6
Rucheng, *China* 53 E9
Rud, *Norway* 10 D4
Rūd Sar, *Iran* 65 B6
Ruda Śląska, *Poland* 20 E8
Rudall, *Australia* 91 E2
Rudall →, *Australia* 88 D3
Ruden, *Germany* 18 A9
Rüdersdorf, *Germany* 18 C9
Rudewa, *Tanzania* 83 E3
Rudkøbing, *Denmark* 11 K4
Rudnik, *Serbia, Yug.* 21 L10
Rudnogorsk, *Russia* 45 D11
Rudnya, *Russia* 40 E6
Rudnyy, *Kazakhstan* 44 D7
Rudolf, Ostrov, *Russia* 44 A6
Rudolstadt, *Germany* 18 E7
Rudong, *China* 53 A13
Rudozem, *Bulgaria* 39 H7
Rudyard, *U.S.A.* 104 B3
Rue, *France* 25 B8
Ruelle, *France* 26 C4
Rufa'a, *Sudan* 77 E3
Ruffec, *France* 26 B4
Rufiji □, *Tanzania* 82 D4
Rufiji →, *Tanzania* 82 D4
Rufino, *Argentina* 126 C3
Rufisque, *Senegal* 78 C1
Rufunsa, *Zambia* 83 F2
Rugao, *China* 53 A13
Rugby, *U.K.* 13 E6
Rugby, *U.S.A.* 108 A5
Rügen, *Germany* 18 A9
Rugles, *France* 24 D7
Ruhengeri, *Rwanda* 82 C2
Ruhla, *Germany* 18 E6
Ruhland, *Germany* 18 D9
Ruhnu saar, *Estonia* 9 H20
Ruhr →, *Germany* 18 D2
Ruhuhu →, *Tanzania* 83 E3
Rui Barbosa, *Brazil* 123 D3
Rui'an, *China* 53 D13
Ruichang, *China* 53 C10
Ruidosa, *U.S.A.* 109 L2
Ruidoso, *U.S.A.* 111 K11
Ruili, *China* 52 E1
Ruinen, *Neths.* 16 C8
Ruinerwold, *Neths.* 16 C8
Ruiten A Kanaal →, *Neths.* 16 C10
Ruivo, Pico, *Madeira* 36 D3
Rujm Tal'at al Jamā'ah, *Jordan* 69 E4
Ruk, *Pakistan* 62 F3
Rukwa □, *Tanzania* 82 D3
Rukwa L., *Tanzania* 82 D3
Rulhieres, C., *Australia* 88 B4
Rulles, *Belgium* 17 J7
Rum Cay, *Bahamas* 117 B5
Rum Jungle, *Australia* 88 B5
Ruma, *Serbia, Yug.* 21 K9
Rumāḥ, *Si. Arabia* 64 E5
Rumania = Romania ■, *Europe* 38 D8
Rumaylah, *Iraq* 64 D5
Rumbalara, *Australia* 90 D1
Rumbêk, *Sudan* 77 F2
Rumbeke, *Belgium* 17 G2
Rumelange, *Lux.* 17 K8
Rumford, *U.S.A.* 107 B14
Rumilly, *France* 27 C9
Rumoi, *Japan* 48 C10
Rumonge, *Burundi* 82 C2
Rumsey, *Canada* 100 C6
Rumula, *Australia* 90 B4
Rumuruti, *Kenya* 82 B4
Runan, *China* 50 H8
Runanga, *N.Z.* 87 K3
Runaway, C., *N.Z.* 87 G6
Runcorn, *U.K.* 12 D5
Rungwa, *Tanzania* 82 D3
Rungwa →, *Tanzania* 82 D3
Rungwe, *Tanzania* 83 D3
Rungwe □, *Tanzania* 83 D3
Runka, *Nigeria* 79 C6
Runton Ra., *Australia* 88 D3
Ruokolahti, *Finland* 40 B5
Ruoqiang, *China* 54 C3
Rupa, *India* 61 F18
Rupar, *India* 62 D7
Rupat, *Indonesia* 56 D2
Rupert →, *Canada* 98 B4
Rupert House = Waskaganish, *Canada* 98 B4
Rupununi →, *Guyana* 121 C6
Rur →, *Germany* 18 E2
Rurrenabaque, *Bolivia* 124 C4
Rus →, *Spain* 29 F2
Rusambo, *Zimbabwe* 83 F3
Rusape, *Zimbabwe* 83 F3
Ruschuk = Ruse, *Bulgaria* 38 F8
Ruse, *Bulgaria* 38 F8
Ruşeţu, *Romania* 38 E10
Rushan, *China* 51 F11
Rushden, *U.K.* 13 E7
Rushford, *U.S.A.* 108 D9
Rushville, *Ill., U.S.A.* 108 E9
Rushville, *Ind., U.S.A.* 104 F3
Rushville, *Nebr., U.S.A.* 108 D3
Rushworth, *Australia* 91 F4
Russas, *Brazil* 122 B4
Russell, *Canada* 101 C8
Russell, *U.S.A.* 108 F5
Russell L., *Man., Canada* 101 B8
Russell L., *N.W.T., Canada* 100 A5
Russellkonda, *India* 61 K14
Russellville, *Ala., U.S.A.* 105 H2
Russellville, *Ark., U.S.A.* 109 H8
Russellville, *Ky., U.S.A.* 105 G2
Russi, *Italy* 33 D9
Russia ■, *Eurasia* 45 C11
Russian →, *U.S.A.* 112 G3
Russkaya Polyana, *Kazakhstan* 44 D8
Russkoye Ustie, *Russia* 4 B15
Rustam, *Pakistan* 62 B5
Rustam Shahr, *Pakistan* 62 F2
Rustavi, *Georgia* 43 K7
Rustenburg, *S. Africa* 84 D4
Ruston, *U.S.A.* 109 J8
Ruswil, *Switz.* 22 B6
Rutana, *Burundi* 82 C2
Rute, *Spain* 31 H6
Ruteng, *Indonesia* 57 F6
Ruth, *Mich., U.S.A.* 106 C2
Ruth, *Nev., U.S.A.* 110 G6
Rutherford, *U.S.A.* 112 G4
Rutherglen, *U.K.* 14 F4
Rüti, *Switz.* 23 B7
Rutigliano, *Italy* 35 A10
Rutland Plains, *Australia* 90 B3
Rutledge →, *Canada* 101 A6
Rutledge L., *Canada* 101 A6
Rutqa, W. →, *Syria* 67 E9
Rutshuru, *Zaïre* 82 C2
Ruurlo, *Neths.* 16 D8
Ruvo di Púglia, *Italy* 35 A9
Ruvu, *Tanzania* 82 D4
Ruvu →, *Tanzania* 82 D4
Ruvuma □, *Tanzania* 83 E4
Ruwais, *U.A.E.* 65 E7
Ruwenzori, *Africa* 82 B2
Ruyigi, *Burundi* 82 C3
Ruyuan, *China* 53 E9
Ruzayevka, *Russia* 42 C7
Ružomberok, *Slovak Rep.* 20 F9
Rwanda ■, *Africa* 82 C3
Ry, *Denmark* 11 H3
Ryakhovo, *Bulgaria* 38 F9
Ryan, L., *U.K.* 14 G3
Ryazan, *Russia* 42 C4
Ryazhsk, *Russia* 42 D5
Rybache = Rybachye, *Kazakhstan* 44 E9
Rybachye, *Kazakhstan* 44 E9
Rybinsk, *Russia* 42 A4
Rybinskoye Vdkhr., *Russia* 40 C10
Rybnik, *Poland* 20 E8
Rybnitsa = Rîbniţa, *Moldova* 41 J5
Rybnoye, *Russia* 42 C4
Rychwał, *Poland* 20 C8
Ryde, *U.K.* 13 G6
Ryderwood, *U.S.A.* 112 D3
Rydöbruk, *Sweden* 11 H7
Rydułtowy, *Poland* 20 E8
Rye, *U.K.* 13 G8
Rye →, *U.K.* 12 C7
Rye Patch Reservoir, *U.S.A.* 110 F4
Ryegate, *U.S.A.* 110 C9
Rylsk, *Russia* 42 E2
Rylstone, *Australia* 91 E4
Ryn Peski, *Kazakhstan* 43 G9
Ryōthu, *Japan* 48 E9
Rypin, *Poland* 20 B9
Ryūgasaki, *Japan* 49 G10
Ryūkyū Is. = Ryūkyū-rettō, *Japan* 49 M2
Ryūkyū-rettō, *Japan* 49 M2
Rzeszów, *Poland* 20 E11
Rzhev, *Russia* 42 B2

S

Sa, *Thailand* 58 C3
Sa Dec, *Vietnam* 59 G5
Sa'ādatābād, *Fārs, Iran* 65 D7
Sa'ādatābād, *Kermān, Iran* 65 D7
Saale →, *Germany* 18 D7
Saaler Bodden, *Germany* 18 A8
Saalfeld, *Germany* 18 E7
Saane →, *Switz.* 22 B4
Saar →, *Europe* 25 C13
Saarbrücken, *Germany* 19 F2
Saarburg, *Germany* 19 F2
Saaremaa, *Estonia* 9 G20
Saarijärvi, *Finland* 9 E21
Saariselkä, *Finland* 8 B23
Saarland □, *Germany* 25 C13
Saarlouis, *Germany* 19 F2
Saas Fee, *Switz.* 22 D5
Sab 'Ābar, *Syria* 66 F7
Saba, *W. Indies* 117 C7
Šabac, *Serbia, Yug.* 21 L9
Sabadell, *Spain* 28 D7
Sabah □, *Malaysia* 56 C5
Sabak Bernam, *Malaysia* 59 L3
Sabalān, Kūhhā-ye, *Iran* 67 C12
Sábana de la Mar, *Dom. Rep.* 117 C6
Sábanalarga, *Colombia* 120 A3
Sabang, *Indonesia* 56 C1
Sabará, *Brazil* 123 E3
Sabattis, *U.S.A.* 107 B10
Sabáudia, *Italy* 34 A6
Sabaya, *Bolivia* 124 D4
Saberania, *Indonesia* 57 E9
Sabhah, *Libya* 73 C7
Sabie, *S. Africa* 85 D5
Sabinal, *Mexico* 114 A3
Sabinal, *U.S.A.* 109 L5
Sabinal, Punta del, *Spain* 29 J2
Sabinas, *Mexico* 114 B4
Sabinas →, *Mexico* 114 B4
Sabinas Hidalgo, *Mexico* 114 B4
Sabine →, *U.S.A.* 109 L8
Sabine L., *U.S.A.* 109 L8
Sabine Pass, *U.S.A.* 109 L8
Sabinópolis, *Brazil* 123 E3
Sabinov, *Slovak Rep.* 20 F11
Sabirabad, *Azerbaijan* 43 K9
Sabkhet el Bardawîl, *Egypt* 69 D2
Sablayan, *Phil.* 55 E4
Sable, C., *Canada* 99 D6
Sable, C., *U.S.A.* 103 E10
Sable I., *Canada* 99 D8
Sablé-sur-Sarthe, *France* 24 E6
Saboeiro, *Brazil* 122 C4
Sabor →, *Portugal* 30 D3
Sabou, *Burkina Faso* 78 C4
Sabrātah, *Libya* 75 B7
Sabria, *Tunisia* 75 B6
Sabrina Coast, *Antarctica* 5 C9
Sabugal, *Portugal* 30 E3
Sabulubek, *Indonesia* 56 E1
Sabzevār, *Iran* 65 B8
Sabzvārān, *Iran* 65 D8
Sac City, *U.S.A.* 108 D7
Sacedón, *Spain* 28 E2
Sachigo →, *Canada* 98 A2
Sachigo, L., *Canada* 98 B1
Sachkhere, *Georgia* 43 J6
Sachseln, *Switz.* 23 C6
Sachsen □, *Germany* 18 E9
Sachsen-Anhalt □, *Germany* 18 D8
Sacile, *Italy* 33 C9
Sackets Harbor, *U.S.A.* 107 C8
Saco, *Maine, U.S.A.* 105 D10
Saco, *Mont., U.S.A.* 110 B10
Sacramento, *Brazil* 123 E2
Sacramento, *U.S.A.* 112 G5
Sacramento →, *U.S.A.* 112 G5
Sacramento Mts., *U.S.A.* 111 K11
Sacramento Valley, *U.S.A.* 112 G5
Sacratif, C., *Spain* 29 J1
Săcueni, *Romania* 38 B5
Sada, *Spain* 30 B2
Sádaba, *Spain* 28 C3
Sadani, *Tanzania* 82 D4
Sadao, *Thailand* 59 J3
Sadd el Aali, *Egypt* 76 C3
Saddle Mt., *U.S.A.* 112 E3
Sade, *Nigeria* 79 C7
Sadimi, *Zaïre* 83 D1
Sa'dīyah, Hawr as, *Iraq* 67 F12
Sado, *Japan* 48 E9
Sado →, *Portugal* 31 G2
Sadon, *Burma* 61 G20
Sadon, *Russia* 43 J6
Sæby, *Denmark* 11 G4
Saegerstown, *U.S.A.* 106 E4
Saelices, *Spain* 28 F2
Safaga, *Egypt* 76 B3
Şafājah, *Si. Arabia* 64 E3
Säffle, *Sweden* 9 G15
Safford, *U.S.A.* 111 K9
Saffron Walden, *U.K.* 13 E8
Safi, *Morocco* 74 B3
Şafīābād, *Iran* 65 B8
Safīd Dasht, *Iran* 65 C6
Safīd Kūh, *Afghan.* 60 B3
Safonovo, *Russia* 40 E7
Safranbolu, *Turkey* 66 B5
Safwān, *Iraq* 64 D5
Sag Harbor, *U.S.A.* 107 F12
Saga, *Indonesia* 57 E8
Saga, *Japan* 49 H5
Saga □, *Japan* 49 H5
Sagae, *Japan* 48 E10
Sagala, *Mali* 78 C3
Sagar, *India* 60 M9
Sagara, L., *Tanzania* 82 D3
Sagay, *Phil.* 55 F5
Sagil, *Mongolia* 54 A4
Saginaw, *U.S.A.* 104 D4
Saginaw B., *U.S.A.* 104 D4
Şagīr, Zāb aş →, *Iraq* 67 E10
Sagleipie, *Liberia* 78 D3
Saglouc = Salluit, *Canada* 97 B12
Sagŏ-ri, *S. Korea* 51 G14
Sagone, *France* 27 F12
Sagone, G. de, *France* 27 F12
Sagres, *Portugal* 31 J2
Sagua la Grande, *Cuba* 116 B3
Saguache, *U.S.A.* 111 G10
Saguenay →, *Canada* 99 C5
Sagunto, *Spain* 28 F4
Sahaba, *Sudan* 76 D3
Sahagún, *Colombia* 120 B2
Sahagún, *Spain* 30 C5
Saḩam al Jawlān, *Syria* 69 C4
Sahand, Kūh-e, *Iran* 67 D12
Sahara, *Africa* 72 D5

Saharan Atlas = Saharien,
 Atlas, *Algeria* 75 B5
Saharanpur, *India* 62 E7
Saharien, Atlas, *Algeria* .. 75 B5
Sahasinaka, *Madag.* 85 C8
Sahaswan, *India* 63 E8
Sahel, Canal du, *Mali* 78 C3
Sahibganj, *India* 63 G12
Sāḥilīyah, *Iraq* 67 F10
Sahiwal, *Pakistan* 62 D5
Şahneh, *Iran* 67 E12
Sahtaneh →, *Canada* 100 B4
Sahuaripa, *Mexico* 114 B3
Sahuarita, *U.S.A.* 111 L8
Sahuayo, *Mexico* 114 C4
Sahy, *Slovak Rep.* 21 G8
Sai Buri, *Thailand* 59 J3
Sai-Cinza, *Brazil* 125 B6
Sa'id Bundas, *Sudan* 73 G9
Saïda, *Algeria* 75 B5
Sa'īdābād, *Kermān, Iran* .. 65 D7
Sa'īdābād, *Semnān, Iran* .. 65 B7
Saïdia, *Morocco* 75 A4
Sa'īdīyeh, *Iran* 65 B6
Saidpur, *Bangla.* 61 G16
Saidu, *Pakistan* 63 B5
Saignelégier, *Switz.* 22 B3
Saignes, *France* 26 C6
Saigon = Phanh Bho Ho
 Chi Minh, *Vietnam* 59 G6
Saijō, *Japan* 49 H6
Saiki, *Japan* 49 H5
Saillans, *France* 27 D9
Sailolof, *Indonesia* 57 E8
Saimaa, *Finland* 9 F23
Saimbeyli, *Turkey* 66 D7
Şa'in Dezh, *Iran* 67 D12
St. Abb's Head, *U.K.* 14 F6
St. Aegyd, *Austria* 21 H5
St.-Affrique, *France* 26 E6
St.-Agrève, *France* 27 C8
St.-Aignan, *France* 24 E8
St. Alban's, *Canada* 99 C8
St. Albans, *U.K.* 13 F7
St. Albans, *Vt., U.S.A.* .. 107 B11
St. Albans, *W. Va., U.S.A.* 104 F5
St. Alban's Head, *U.K.* ... 13 G5
St. Albert, *Canada* 100 C6
St.-Amand-en-Puisaye,
 France 25 E10
St.-Amand-les-Eaux,
 France 25 B10
St.-Amand-Mont-Rond,
 France 26 B6
St.-Amarin, *France* 25 E14
St.-Amour, *France* 27 B9
St.-André-de-Cubzac,
 France 26 D3
St.-André-de-l'Eure, *France* 24 D8
St.-André-les-Alpes, *France* 27 E10
St. Andrew's, *Canada* 99 C8
St. Andrews, *U.K.* 14 E6
St-Anicet, *Canada* 107 A10
St. Ann B., *Canada* 99 C7
St. Anne, *U.K.* 24 C4
St. Ann's Bay, *Jamaica* .. 116 C4
St. Anthony, *Canada* 99 B8
St. Anthony, *U.S.A.* 110 E8
St.-Antonin-Noble-Val,
 France 26 D5
St. Arnaud, *Australia* ... 91 F3
St. Arthur, *Canada* 99 C6
St. Asaph, *U.K.* 12 D4
St.-Astier, *France* 26 C4
St.-Aubin, *Switz.* 22 C3
St.-Aubin-du-Cormier,
 France 24 D5
St-Augustin-Saguenay,
 Canada 99 B8
St. Augustine, *U.S.A.* ... 105 L5
St. Austell, *U.K.* 13 G3
St.-Avold, *France* 25 C13
St.-Barthélemy, I.,
 W. Indies 117 C7
St. Bee's Hd., *U.K.* 12 C4
St.-Benoît-du-Sault, *France* 26 B5
St.-Bernard, Col du Grand,
 Europe 22 E4
St.-Bernard, Col du Petit,
 France 27 C10
St.-Blaise, *Switz.* 22 B3
St. Boniface, *Canada* ... 101 D9
St.-Bonnet, *France* 27 D10
St.-Brévin-les-Pins, *France* 24 E4
St. Bride's, *Canada* 99 C9
St. Brides B., *U.K.* 13 F2
St.-Brieuc, *France* 24 D4
St.-Calais, *France* 24 E7
St.-Cast-le-Guildo, *France* 24 D4
St. Catharines, *Canada* .. 98 D4
St. Catherines I., *U.S.A.* . 105 K5
St. Catherine's Pt., *U.K.* . 13 G6
St.-Céré, *France* 26 D5
St.-Cergue, *Switz.* 22 D2
St.-Cernin, *France* 26 C6
St.-Chamond, *France* 27 C8
St. Charles, *Ill., U.S.A.* . 104 E1
St. Charles, *Mo., U.S.A.* . 108 F9
St.-Chély-d'Apcher, *France* 26 D7
St.-Chinian, *France* 26 E6
St. Christopher = St. Kitts,
 W. Indies 117 C7
St. Christopher-Nevis ■,
 W. Indies 117 C7

St.-Ciers-sur-Gironde,
 France 26 C3
St. Clair, *Mich., U.S.A.* . 106 D2
St. Clair, *Pa., U.S.A.* ... 107 F8
St. Clair, L., *Canada* 98 D3
St. Clairsville, *U.S.A.* ... 106 F4
St.-Claud, *France* 26 C4
St. Claude, *Canada* 101 D9
St.-Claude, *France* 27 B9
St. Cloud, *Fla., U.S.A.* .. 105 L5
St. Cloud, *Minn., U.S.A.* 108 C7
St-Coeur de Marie, *Canada* 99 C5
St. Cricq, C., *Australia* .. 89 E1
St. Croix, *Virgin Is.* ... 117 C7
St. Croix →, *U.S.A.* 108 C8
St. Croix Falls, *U.S.A.* .. 108 C8
St.-Cyr-sur-Mer, *France* . 27 E9
St. David's, *Canada* 99 C8
St. David's, *U.K.* 13 F2
St. David's Head, *U.K.* .. 13 F2
St.-Denis, *France* 25 D9
St.-Denis-d'Orques, *France* 24 D6
St.-Dié, *France* 25 D13
St.-Dizier, *France* 25 D11
St.-Égrève, *France* 27 C9
St. Elias, Mt., *U.S.A.* ... 96 B5
St. Elias Mts., *Canada* .. 100 A1
St.-Élie, *Fr. Guiana* ... 121 C7
St.-Éloy-les-Mines, *France* 26 B6
St.-Émilion, *France* 26 D3
St.-Étienne, *France* 27 C8
St.-Étienne-de-Tinée,
 France 27 D10
St. Eugène, *Canada* 107 A10
St. Eustatius, *W. Indies* .. 117 C7
St-Félicien, *Canada* 98 C5
St.-Florent, *France* 27 F13
St.-Florent, G. de, *France* 27 F13
St.-Florent-sur-Cher,
 France 25 F9
St.-Florentin, *France* 25 D10
St.-Flour, *France* 26 C7
St.-Fons, *France* 27 C8
St. Francis, *U.S.A.* 108 F4
St. Francis →, *U.S.A.* .. 109 H9
St. Francis, C., *S. Africa* 84 E3
St. Francisville, *U.S.A.* .. 109 K9
St.-François, L., *Canada* . 107 A10
St.-Fulgent, *France* 24 F5
St-Gabriel-de-Brandon,
 Canada 98 C5
St. Gallen = Sankt Gallen,
 Switz. 23 B8
St.-Gaudens, *France* 26 E4
St.-Gengoux-le-National,
 France 27 B8
St.-Geniez-d'Olt, *France* . 26 D6
St. George, *Australia* 91 D4
St. George, *Canada* 99 C6
St. George, *S.C., U.S.A.* . 105 J5
St. George, *Utah, U.S.A.* . 111 H7
St. George, C., *Canada* .. 99 C8
St. George, C., *U.S.A.* ... 105 L3
St. George Ra., *Australia* 88 C4
St-Georges, *Belgium* 17 G6
St. George's, *Canada* 99 C8
St-Georges, *Canada* 99 C5
St.-Georges, *Fr. Guiana* . 121 C7
St.-Georges, *Grenada* ... 117 D7
St. George's B., *Canada* . 99 C8
St. Georges Basin,
 Australia 88 C4
St. George's Channel,
 Europe 15 E6
St.-Georges-de-Didonne,
 France 26 C3
St. Georges Hd., *Australia* 91 F5
St.-Gérard, *Belgium* 17 H5
St.-Germain-de-Calberte,
 France 26 D7
St.-Germain-des-Fossés,
 France 26 B7
St.-Germain-du-Plain,
 France 25 F11
St.-Germain-en-Laye,
 France 25 D9
St.-Germain-Laval, *France* 27 C8
St.-Germain-Lembron,
 France 26 C7
St.-Gervais-d'Auvergne,
 France 26 B6
St.-Gervais-les-Bains,
 France 27 C10
St.-Gildas, Pte. de, *France* 24 E4
St.-Gilles, *France* 27 E8
St.-Gilles-Croix-de-Vie,
 France 26 B2
St.-Gingolph, *Switz.* 22 D3
St.-Girons, *France* 26 F5
St. Gotthard P. = San
 Gottardo, P. del, *Switz.* 23 C7
St.-Gualtier, *France* 24 F8
St.-Guénolé, *France* 24 E2
St. Helena, *U.S.A.* 110 G2
St. Helena ■, *Atl. Oc.* ... 2 G9
St. Helena, Mt., *U.S.A.* .. 112 G4
St. Helena B., *S. Africa* . 84 E2
St. Helens, *Australia* 90 G4
St. Helens, *U.K.* 12 D5
St. Helens, *U.S.A.* 112 E4
St. Helens, Mt., *U.S.A.* .. 112 D4
St. Helier, *U.K.* 13 H5
St.-Hilaire-du-Harcouët,
 France 24 D5
St.-Hippolyte, *France* ... 25 E13
St.-Hippolyte-du-Fort,
 France 26 E7

St.-Honoré-les-Bains,
 France 25 F10
St-Hubert, *Belgium* 17 H6
St-Hyacinthe, *Canada* ... 98 C5
St. Ignace, *U.S.A.* 104 C3
St. Ignace I., *Canada* ... 98 C2
St. Ignatius, *U.S.A.* 110 C6
St-Imier, *Switz.* 22 B3
St. Ives, *Cambs., U.K.* .. 13 E7
St. Ives, *Corn., U.K.* ... 13 G2
St.-James, *France* 24 D5
St. James, *U.S.A.* 108 D7
St-Jean, *Canada* 98 C5
St-Jean →, *Canada* 99 B7
St-Jean, L., *Canada* 99 C5
St. Jean Baptiste, *Canada* . 101 D9
St.-Jean-d'Angély, *France* . 26 C3
St-Jean-de-Bournay,
 France 27 C9
St.-Jean-de-Luz, *France* . 26 E2
St.-Jean-de-Maurienne,
 France 27 C10
St.-Jean-de-Monts, *France* 24 F4
St.-Jean-du-Gard, *France* . 26 D7
St-Jean-en-Royans, *France* 27 C9
St-Jean-Port-Joli, *Canada* . 99 C5
St-Jérôme, *Qué., Canada* . 98 C5
St-Jérôme, *Qué., Canada* . 99 C5
St. John, *Canada* 99 C6
St. John, *Kans., U.S.A.* .. 109 G5
St. John, *N. Dak., U.S.A.* 108 A5
St. John →, *U.S.A.* 99 C6
St. John, C., *Canada* 99 B8
St. John's, *Antigua* 117 C7
St. John's, *Canada* 99 C9
St. Johns, *Ariz., U.S.A.* . 111 J9
St. Johns, *Mich., U.S.A.* 104 D3
St. Johns →, *U.S.A.* ... 105 K5
St. Johnsbury, *U.S.A.* .. 107 B12
St. Johnsville, *U.S.A.* .. 107 C10
St. Joseph, *La., U.S.A.* .. 109 K9
St. Joseph, *Mich., U.S.A.* 104 D2
St. Joseph, *Mo., U.S.A.* . 108 F7
St. Joseph →, *U.S.A.* .. 104 D2
St. Joseph, I., *Canada* ... 98 C3
St. Joseph, L., *Canada* .. 98 B1
St-Jovite, *Canada* 98 C5
St.-Juéry, *France* 26 E6
St-Julien-Chapteuil, *France* 27 C8
St.-Julien-du-Sault, *France* 25 D10
St-Julien-en-Genevois,
 France 27 B10
St.-Junien, *France* 26 C4
St.-Just-en-Chaussée,
 France 25 C9
St.-Just-en-Chevalet, *France* 26 C7
St.-Justin, *France* 26 E3
St. Kilda, *N.Z.* 87 L3
St. Kitts, *W. Indies* 117 C7
St. Kitts-Nevis = St.
 Christopher-Nevis ■,
 W. Indies 117 C7
St.-Laurent, *Canada* ... 101 C9
St.-Laurent, *Fr. Guiana* . 121 B7
St.-Laurent-du-Pont, *France* 27 C9
St.-Laurent-en-Grandvaux,
 France 27 B9
St.-Lawrence, *Australia* .. 90 C4
St.-Lawrence, *Canada* ... 99 C8
St. Lawrence →, *Canada* . 99 C6
St. Lawrence, Gulf of,
 Canada 99 C7
St. Lawrence I., *U.S.A.* . 96 B3
St.-Léger, *Belgium* 17 J7
St. Leonard, *Canada* ... 99 C6
St.-Léonard-de-Noblat,
 France 26 C5
St. Lewis →, *Canada* ... 99 B8
St.-Lô, *France* 24 C5
St-Louis, *Senegal* 78 B1
St. Louis, *Mich., U.S.A.* . 104 D3
St. Louis, *Mo., U.S.A.* .. 108 F9
St. Louis →, *U.S.A.* ... 108 B8
St.-Loup-sur-Semouse,
 France 25 E13
St. Lucia ■, *W. Indies* .. 117 D7
St. Lucia, L., *S. Africa* . 85 D5
St. Lucia Channel,
 W. Indies 117 D7
St. Lunaire-Griquet,
 Canada 99 B8
St. Maarten, *W. Indies* .. 117 C7
St.-Maixent-l'École, *France* 26 B3
St.-Malo, *France* 24 D4
St.-Malo, G. de, *France* . 24 D4
St.-Mandrier-sur-Mer,
 France 27 E9
St-Marc, *Haiti* 117 C5
St.-Marcellin, *France* ... 27 C9
St.-Marcouf, Is., *France* . 24 C5
St. Maries, *U.S.A.* 110 C5
St-Martin, *W. Indies* ... 117 C7
St. Martin, L., *Canada* .. 101 C9
St.-Martin-de-Ré, *France* 26 B2
St.-Martin-Vésubie, *France* 27 D11
St. Martins, *Canada* 99 C6
St. Martinville, *U.S.A.* .. 109 K9
St.-Martory, *France* 26 E4
St. Mary Pk., *Australia* .. 91 E2
St. Marys, *Australia* 90 G4
St. Marys, *Canada* 106 C3
St. Mary's, *U.K.* 13 H1
St. Marys, *U.S.A.* 106 E6
St. Mary's, C., *Canada* .. 99 C9
St. Mary's B., *Canada* .. 99 C9
St. Marys Bay, *Canada* .. 99 D6
St.-Mathieu, Pte., *France* . 24 D2

St. Matthews, I. =
 Zadetkyi Kyun, *Burma* . 59 H2
St.-Maur-des-Fossés, *France* 25 D9
St. Maurice, *Switz.* 22 D4
St-Maurice →, *Canada* .. 98 C5
St.-Médard-de-Guizières,
 France 26 C3
St.-Méen-le-Grand, *France* 24 D4
St. Michael's Mount, *U.K.* 13 G2
St.-Michel-de-Maurienne,
 France 27 C10
St.-Mihiel, *France* 25 D12
St.-Nazaire, *France* 24 E4
St. Neots, *U.K.* 13 E7
St.-Nicolas-de-Port, *France* 25 D13
St. Niklaas = Sint Niklaas,
 Belgium 17 F4
St. Niklaus, *Switz.* 22 D5
St.-Omer, *France* 25 B9
St-Pacome, *Canada* 99 C6
St.-Palais-sur-Mer, *France* 26 C2
St-Pamphile, *Canada* ... 99 C6
St.-Pardoux-la-Rivière,
 France 26 C4
St. Pascal, *Canada* 99 C6
St. Paul, *Canada* 100 C6
St. Paul, *Minn., U.S.A.* .. 108 C8
St. Paul, *Nebr., U.S.A.* .. 108 E5
St. Paul, I., *Ind. Oc.* ... 3 F13
St.-Paul-de-Fenouillet,
 France 26 F6
St. Paul I., *Canada* 99 C7
St.-Paul-lès-Dax, *France* . 26 E2
St.-Péray, *France* 27 D8
St.-Père-en-Retz, *France* . 24 E4
St. Peter, *U.S.A.* 108 C8
St-Peter-Ording, *Germany* 18 A4
St. Peter Port, *U.K.* 13 H5
St. Peters, *N.S., Canada* . 99 C7
St. Peters, *P.E.I., Canada* 99 C7
St. Petersburg = Sankt-
 Peterburg, *Russia* 40 C6
St. Petersburg, *U.S.A.* .. 105 M4
St.-Philbert-de-Grand-Lieu,
 France 24 E5
St.-Pierre, *St- P. & M.* .. 99 C8
St.-Pierre, L., *Canada* .. 98 C5
St.-Pierre-d'Oléron, *France* 26 C2
St.-Pierre-Église, *France* . 24 C5
St.-Pierre-en-Port, *France* . 24 C7
St.-Pierre et Miquelon □,
 St- P. & M. 99 C8
St.-Pierre-le-Moûtier,
 France 25 F10
St.-Pierre-sur-Dives, *France* 24 C6
St.-Pieters Leew, *Belgium* 17 G4
St.-Pol-de-Léon, *France* . 24 D2
St.-Pol-sur-Mer, *France* . 25 A9
St.-Pol-sur-Ternoise, *France* 25 B9
St.-Pons, *France* 26 E6
St.-Pourçain-sur-Sioule,
 France 26 B7
St.-Quay-Portrieux, *France* 24 D4
St.-Quentin, *France* 25 C10
St.-Rambert-d'Albon,
 France 27 C8
St.-Raphaël, *France* 27 E10
St. Regis, *U.S.A.* 110 C6
St.-Rémy-de-Provence,
 France 27 E8
St.-Renan, *France* 24 D2
St.-Saëns, *France* 24 C8
St.-Sauveur-en-Puisaye,
 France 25 E10
St.-Sauveur-le-Vicomte,
 France 24 C5
St.-Savin, *France* 26 B4
St.-Savinien, *France* 26 C3
St. Sebastien, Tanjon' i,
 Madag. 85 A8
St.-Seine-l'Abbaye, *France* 25 E11
St.-Sernin-sur-Rance,
 France 26 E6
St.-Servan-sur-Mer, *France* 24 D4
St.-Sever, *France* 26 E3
St.-Sever-Calvados, *France* 24 D5
St-Siméon, *Canada* 99 C6
St. Stephen, *Canada* 99 C6
St.-Sulpice, *France* 26 E5
St.-Sulpice-Laurière, *France* 26 B5
St.-Sulpice-le-Verdon,
 France 26 F7
St.-Thégonnec, *France* .. 24 D3
St. Thomas, *Canada* 98 D3
St. Thomas I., *Virgin Is.* . 117 C7
St-Tite, *Canada* 98 C5
St.-Tropez, *France* 27 E10
St. Troud = Sint Truiden,
 Belgium 17 G6
St.-Vaast-la-Hougue,
 France 24 C5
St.-Valéry-en-Caux, *France* 24 C7
St.-Valéry-sur-Somme,
 France 25 B8
St.-Vallier, *France* 27 C8
St.-Vallier-de-Thiey, *France* 27 E10
St.-Varent, *France* 24 F6
St. Vincent, *W. Indies* ... 117 D7
St. Vincent, G., *Australia* 91 F2
St. Vincent & the
 Grenadines ■, *W. Indies* 117 D7
St.-Vincent-de-Tyrosse,
 France 26 E2
St. Vincent Passage,
 W. Indies 117 D7
St-Vith, *Belgium* 17 H8
St.-Yrieix-la-Perche, *France* 26 C5
Ste.-Adresse, *France* 24 C7

Ste-Agathe-des-Monts,
 Canada 98 C5
Ste-Anne de Beaupré,
 Canada 99 C5
Ste-Anne-des-Monts,
 Canada 99 C6
Ste-Croix, *Switz.* 22 C3
Ste.-Enimie, *France* 26 D7
Ste.-Foy-la-Grande, *France* 26 D4
Ste. Genevieve, *U.S.A.* .. 108 G9
Ste.-Hermine, *France* ... 26 B2
Ste.-Livrade-sur-Lot,
 France 26 D4
Ste-Marguerite →, *Canada* 99 B6
Ste.-Marie, *Martinique* ... 117 D7
Ste.-Marie-aux-Mines,
 France 25 D14
Ste-Marie de la Madeleine,
 Canada 99 C5
Ste.-Maure-de-Touraine,
 France 24 E7
Ste.-Maxime, *France* 27 E10
Ste.-Menehould, *France* . 25 C11
Ste.-Mère-Église, *France* . 24 C5
Ste.-Rose, *Guadeloupe* .. 117 C7
Ste. Rose du Lac, *Canada* 101 C9
Saintes, *France* 26 C3
Saintes, I. des, *Guadeloupe* 117 C7
Stes.-Maries-de-la-Mer,
 France 27 E8
Saintonge, *France* 26 C3
Saipan, *Pac. Oc.* 92 F6
Sairang, *India* 61 H18
Saitama □, *Japan* 49 F9
Sajama, *Bolivia* 124 D4
Sajum, *India* 63 C8
Sak →, *S. Africa* 84 E3
Sakai, *Japan* 49 G7
Sakaide, *Japan* 49 G6
Sakaiminato, *Japan* 49 G6
Sakākah, *Si. Arabia* 64 D4
Sakakawea, L., *U.S.A.* ... 108 B3
Sakami, L., *Canada* 98 B4
Sâkâne, 'Erg i-n, *Mali* .. 74 D4
Sakania, *Zaïre* 83 E2
Sakarya = Adapazarı,
 Turkey 66 B4
Sakarya →, *Turkey* 66 B4
Sakashima-Guntō, *Japan* . 49 M2
Sakata, *Japan* 48 E9
Sakchu, *N. Korea* 51 D13
Sakeny →, *Madag.* 85 C8
Sakété, *Benin* 79 D5
Sakha □, *Russia* 45 C13
Sakhalin, *Russia* 45 D15
Sakhalinskiy Zaliv, *Russia* 45 D15
Şaki, *Azerbaijan* 43 K8
Šakiai, *Lithuania* 9 J20
Sakon Nakhon, *Thailand* . 58 D5
Sakrand, *Pakistan* 62 F3
Sakrivier, *S. Africa* 84 E3
Sakskøbing, *Denmark* ... 11 K5
Sakuma, *Japan* 49 G8
Sakurai, *Japan* 49 G7
Saky, *Ukraine* 41 K7
Sal →, *Russia* 43 G5
Sala, *Sweden* 9 G17
Sala Consilina, *Italy* ... 35 B8
Sala-y-Gómez, *Pac. Oc.* . 93 K17
Salaberry-de-Valleyfield,
 Canada 98 C5
Saladas, *Argentina* 126 B4
Saladillo, *Argentina* ... 126 D4
Salado →, *Buenos Aires,
 Argentina* 126 D4
Salado →, *La Pampa,
 Argentina* 128 A3
Salado →, *Río Negro,
 Argentina* 128 B3
Salado →, *Santa Fe,
 Argentina* 126 C3
Salado →, *Mexico* 114 B5
Salaga, *Ghana* 79 D4
Sālah, *Syria* 69 C5
Sálakhos, *Greece* 37 C9
Salala, *Liberia* 78 D2
Salala, *Sudan* 76 C4
Salālah, *Oman* 68 D5
Salamanca, *Chile* 126 C1
Salamanca, *Spain* 30 E5
Salamanca, *U.S.A.* 106 D6
Salamanca □, *Spain* ... 30 E5
Salāmatābād, *Iran* 64 C5
Salamina, *Colombia* ... 120 B2
Salamis, *Cyprus* 37 D12
Salamís, *Greece* 39 M6
Salar de Atacama, *Chile* . 126 A2
Salar de Uyuni, *Bolivia* . 124 E4
Sălard, *Romania* 38 B3
Salas, *Spain* 30 B4
Salas de los Infantes, *Spain* 28 C1
Salatiga, *Indonesia* 57 G14
Salaverry, *Peru* 124 B2
Salawati, *Indonesia* 57 E8
Salayar, *Indonesia* 57 F6
Salazar →, *Spain* 28 C3
Salbris, *France* 25 E9
Salcombe, *U.K.* 13 G4
Saldaña, *Spain* 30 C6
Saldanha, *S. Africa* 84 E2
Saldanha B., *S. Africa* .. 84 E2
Saldus, *Latvia* 9 H20
Sale, Australia 91 F4
Salé, *Morocco* 74 B3
Sale, *U.K.* 12 D5
Salekhard, *Russia* 44 C7

San Matías

Salem, India 60 P11
Salem, Ind., U.S.A. 104 F2
Salem, Mass., U.S.A. 107 D14
Salem, Mo., U.S.A. 109 G9
Salem, N.J., U.S.A. 104 F8
Salem, Ohio, U.S.A. 106 F4
Salem, Oreg., U.S.A. 110 D2
Salem, S. Dak., U.S.A. 108 D6
Salem, Va., U.S.A. 104 G5
Salemi, Italy 34 E5
Salernes, France 27 E10
Salerno, Italy 35 B7
Salerno, G. di, Italy 35 B7
Salford, U.K. 12 D5
Salgir →, Ukraine 41 K8
Salgótarján, Hungary 21 G9
Salgueiro, Brazil 122 C4
Salida, U.S.A. 102 C5
Salies-de-Béarn, France 26 E3
Salihli, Turkey 66 C3
Salihorsk, Belarus 41 F4
Salima, Malawi 81 G6
Salina, Italy 35 D7
Salina, U.S.A. 108 F6
Salina Cruz, Mexico 115 D5
Salinas, Brazil 123 E3
Salinas, Chile 126 A2
Salinas, Ecuador 120 D1
Salinas, U.S.A. 111 H3
Salinas →, Guatemala 115 D6
Salinas →, U.S.A. 111 H3
Salinas, B. de, Nic. 116 D2
Salinas, C. de, Spain 36 B10
Salinas, Pampa de las, Argentina 126 C2
Salinas Ambargasta, Argentina 126 B3
Salinas de Hidalgo, Mexico 114 C4
Salinas Grandes, Argentina 126 B2
Saline →, Ark., U.S.A. 109 J8
Saline →, Kans., U.S.A. 108 F6
Salines, Spain 36 B10
Salinópolis, Brazil 122 B2
Salins-les-Bains, France 25 F12
Salir, Portugal 31 H2
Salisbury = Harare, Zimbabwe 83 F3
Salisbury, Australia 91 E2
Salisbury, U.K. 13 F6
Salisbury, Md., U.S.A. 104 F8
Salisbury, N.C., U.S.A. 105 H5
Salisbury Plain, U.K. 13 F6
Săliște, Romania 38 D6
Salitre →, Brazil 122 C3
Salka, Nigeria 79 C5
Şalkhad, Syria 69 C5
Salla, Finland 8 C23
Sallent, Spain 28 D6
Salles-Curan, France 26 D6
Salling, Denmark 11 H2
Sallisaw, U.S.A. 109 H7
Sallom Junction, Sudan 76 D4
Salluit, Canada 97 B12
Salmās, Iran 67 C11
Salmerón, Spain 28 E2
Salmo, Canada 100 D5
Salmon, U.S.A. 110 D7
Salmon →, Canada 100 C4
Salmon →, U.S.A. 110 D5
Salmon Arm, Canada 100 C5
Salmon Falls, U.S.A. 110 E6
Salmon Gums, Australia 89 F3
Salmon Res., Canada 99 C8
Salmon River Mts., U.S.A. 110 D6
Salo, Finland 9 F20
Salò, Italy 32 C7
Salobreña, Spain 31 J7
Salome, U.S.A. 113 M13
Salon-de-Provence, France 27 E9
Salonica = Thessaloníki, Greece 39 J5
Salonta, Romania 38 C4
Salor →, Spain 31 F3
Salou, C., Spain 28 D6
Salpausselkä, Finland 9 F22
Salsacate, Argentina 126 C2
Salses, France 26 F6
Salsk, Russia 43 G5
Salso →, Italy 34 E6
Salsomaggiore Terme, Italy 32 D6
Salt →, Canada 100 B6
Salt →, U.S.A. 111 K7
Salt Creek, Australia 91 F2
Salt Fork Arkansas →, U.S.A. 109 G6
Salt Lake City, U.S.A. 110 F8
Salt Range, Pakistan 62 C5
Salta, Argentina 126 A2
Salta □, Argentina 126 A2
Saltcoats, U.K. 14 F4
Saltee Is., Ireland 15 D5
Saltfjellet, Norway 8 C16
Saltfjorden, Norway 8 C16
Saltholm, Denmark 11 J6
Saltillo, Mexico 114 B4
Salto, Argentina 126 C3
Salto, Uruguay 126 C4
Salto da Divisa, Brazil 123 E4
Salton City, U.S.A. 113 M11
Salton Sea, U.S.A. 113 M11
Saltpond, Ghana 79 D4
Saltsjöbaden, Sweden 10 E12
Saltville, U.S.A. 104 G5
Saluda →, U.S.A. 105 H5
Salûm, Egypt 76 A2
Salûm, Khâlig el, Egypt 76 A2
Salur, India 61 K13
Salut, Is. du, Fr. Guiana 121 B7
Saluzzo, Italy 32 D4
Salvación, B., Chile 128 D1
Salvador, Brazil 123 D4
Salvador, Canada 101 C7
Salvador, L., U.S.A. 109 L9
Salvaterra, Brazil 122 B2
Salvaterra de Magos, Portugal 31 F2
Sálvora, I., Spain 30 C2
Salween →, Burma 61 L20
Salyan, Azerbaijan 67 C13
Salyersville, U.S.A. 104 G4
Salza →, Austria 21 H4
Salzach →, Austria 21 G2
Salzburg, Austria 21 H3
Salzgitter, Germany 18 C6
Salzwedel, Germany 18 C7
Sam Neua, Laos 58 B5
Sam Ngao, Thailand 58 D2
Sam Rayburn Reservoir, U.S.A. 109 K7
Sam Son, Vietnam 58 C5
Sam Teu, Laos 58 C5
Sama, Russia 44 C7
Sama de Langreo, Spain 30 B5
Samagaltay, Russia 45 D10
Samaipata, Bolivia 125 D5
Samales Group, Phil. 55 J4
Samâlût, Egypt 76 J7
Samana, India 62 D7
Samana Cay, Bahamas 117 B5
Samandağı, Turkey 66 D6
Samanga, Tanzania 83 D4
Samangwa, Zaïre 82 C1
Samani, Japan 48 C11
Samar, Phil. 55 F6
Samara, Russia 42 D10
Samara →, Russia 42 D10
Samara →, Ukraine 41 H8
Samaria = Shōmrōn, West Bank 69 C4
Samariá, Greece 37 D5
Samarinda, Indonesia 56 E5
Samarkand = Samarqand, Uzbekistan 44 F7
Samarqand, Uzbekistan 44 F7
Sāmarrā, Iraq 67 E10
Samastipur, India 63 G11
Samatan, France 26 E4
Samaúma, Brazil 125 B5
Şamaxi, Azerbaijan 43 K9
Samba, India 63 C6
Samba, Zaïre 82 C2
Sambaíba, Brazil 122 C2
Sambalpur, India 61 J14
Sambar, Tanjung, Indonesia 56 E4
Sambas, Indonesia 56 D3
Sambava, Madag. 85 A9
Sambawizi, Zimbabwe 83 F2
Sambhal, India 63 E8
Sambhar, India 62 F6
Sambiase, Italy 35 D9
Sambir, Ukraine 41 H2
Sambonifacio, Italy 32 C8
Sambor, Cambodia 58 F6
Sambre →, Europe 17 H5
Sambuca di Sicília, Italy 34 E6
Samburu □, Kenya 82 B4
Samchŏk, S. Korea 51 F15
Samchonpo, S. Korea 51 G15
Same, Tanzania 82 C4
Samedan, Switz. 23 C9
Samer, France 25 B8
Samfya, Zambia 83 E2
Sámi, Greece 39 L3
Şämkir, Azerbaijan 43 K8
Samnah, Si. Arabia 64 E3
Samnaun, Switz. 23 C10
Samo Alto, Chile 126 C1
Samobor, Croatia 33 C12
Samoëns, France 27 B10
Samokov, Bulgaria 38 G6
Samoorombón, B., Argentina 126 D4
Samorogouan, Burkina Faso 78 C4
Sámos, Greece 39 M9
Samoš, Serbia, Yug. 21 K10
Samos, Spain 30 C3
Samothráki, Évros, Greece 39 J8
Samothráki, Kérkira, Greece 37 A3
Samoylovka, Russia 42 E6
Sampa, Ghana 78 D4
Sampacho, Argentina 126 C3
Sampang, Indonesia 57 G15
Samper de Calanda, Spain 28 D4
Sampit, Indonesia 56 E4
Sampit, Teluk, Indonesia 56 E4
Samrée, Belgium 17 H7
Samrong, Cambodia 58 E4
Samrong, Thailand 58 E3
Samsø, Denmark 11 J4
Samsø Bælt, Denmark 11 J4
Samsun, Turkey 66 B7
Samtredia, Georgia 43 J6
Samui, Ko, Thailand 59 H3
Samur →, Russia 43 K9
Samurskiy Khrebet, Russia 43 K8
Samusole, Zaïre 83 E1
Samut Prakan, Thailand 58 F3
Samut Sakhon, Thailand 58 F3
Samut Songkhram →, Thailand 58 F3
Samwari, Pakistan 62 E2
San, Mali 78 C4
San →, Cambodia 58 F5
San →, Poland 20 E11
San Adrián, C. de, Spain 30 B2
San Agustín, Colombia 120 C2
San Agustin, C., Phil. 55 H7
San Agustín de Valle Fértil, Argentina 126 C2
San Ambrosio, Pac. Oc. 93 K20
San Andreas, U.S.A. 112 G6
San Andrés, I. de, Caribbean 116 D3
San Andres Mts., U.S.A. 111 K10
San Andrés Tuxtla, Mexico 115 D5
San Angelo, U.S.A. 109 K4
San Anselmo, U.S.A. 112 H4
San Antonio, Belize 115 D7
San Antonio, Chile 126 C1
San Antonio, Phil. 55 D4
San Antonio, Spain 36 C7
San Antonio, N. Mex., U.S.A. 111 K10
San Antonio, Tex., U.S.A. 109 L5
San Antonio, Venezuela 120 C4
San Antonio →, U.S.A. 109 L6
San Antonio, C., Argentina 126 D4
San Antonio, C., Cuba 116 B3
San Antonio, C. de, Spain 29 G5
San Antonio, Mt., U.S.A. 113 L9
San Antonio de los Baños, Cuba 116 B3
San Antonio de los Cobres, Argentina 126 A2
San Antonio Oeste, Argentina 128 B4
San Arcángelo, Italy 35 B9
San Ardo, U.S.A. 112 J6
San Augustín, Canary Is. 36 G4
San Augustine, U.S.A. 109 K7
San Bartolomé, Canary Is. 36 F6
San Bartolomé de Tirajana, Canary Is. 36 G4
San Bartolomeo in Galdo, Italy 35 A8
San Benedetto del Tronto, Italy 33 F10
San Benedetto Po, Italy 32 C7
San Benedicto, I., Mexico 114 D2
San Benito, U.S.A. 109 M6
San Benito →, U.S.A. 112 J5
San Benito Mt., U.S.A. 112 J6
San Bernardino, U.S.A. 113 L9
San Bernardino, Paso del, Switz. 23 D8
San Bernardino Mts., U.S.A. 113 L10
San Bernardino Str., Phil. 55 E6
San Bernardo, Chile 126 C1
San Bernardo, I. de, Colombia 120 B2
San Blas, Mexico 114 B3
San Blas, Arch. de, Panama 116 E4
San Blas, C., U.S.A. 105 L3
San Borja, Bolivia 124 C4
San Buenaventura, Bolivia 124 C4
San Buenaventura, Mexico 114 B4
San Carlos = Butuku-Luba, Eq. Guin. 79 E6
San Carlos, Argentina 126 C2
San Carlos, Bolivia 125 D5
San Carlos, Chile 126 D1
San Carlos, Mexico 114 B4
San Carlos, Nic. 116 D3
San Carlos, Negros, Phil. 55 F5
San Carlos, Pangasinan, Phil. 55 D4
San Carlos, Spain 36 B8
San Carlos, Uruguay 127 C5
San Carlos, U.S.A. 111 K8
San Carlos, Amazonas, Venezuela 120 C4
San Carlos, Cojedes, Venezuela 120 B4
San Carlos de Bariloche, Argentina 128 B2
San Carlos de la Rápita, Spain 28 E5
San Carlos del Zulia, Venezuela 120 B3
San Carlos L., U.S.A. 111 K8
San Cataldo, Italy 34 E6
San Celoni, Spain 28 D7
San Clemente, Chile 126 D1
San Clemente, Spain 29 F2
San Clemente, U.S.A. 113 M9
San Clemente I., U.S.A. 113 N8
San Costanzo, Italy 33 E10
San Cristóbal, Argentina 126 C3
San Cristóbal, Colombia 120 D3
San Cristóbal, Dom. Rep. 117 C5
San Cristóbal, Mexico 115 D6
San Cristóbal, Spain 36 B11
San Cristóbal, Venezuela 120 B3
San Damiano d'Asti, Italy 32 D5
San Daniele del Friuli, Italy 33 B10
San Demétrio Corone, Italy 35 C9
San Diego, Calif., U.S.A. 113 N9
San Diego, Tex., U.S.A. 109 M5
San Diego, C., Argentina 128 D3
San Diego de la Unión, Mexico 114 C4
San Dimitri, Ras, Malta 37 C1
San Doná di Piave, Italy 33 C9
San Elpídio a Mare, Italy 33 E10
San Estanislao, Paraguay 126 A4
San Esteban de Gormaz, Spain 28 D1
San Felice sul Panaro, Italy 32 D8
San Felipe, Chile 126 C1
San Felipe, Colombia 120 C4
San Felipe, Mexico 114 A2
San Felipe, Venezuela 120 A4
San Felipe →, U.S.A. 113 M11
San Felíu de Guíxols, Spain 28 D8
San Felíu de Llobregat, Spain 28 D7
San Félix, Pac. Oc. 93 K20
San Fernando, Chile 126 C1
San Fernando, Mexico 114 B1
San Fernando, La Union, Phil. 55 C4
San Fernando, Pampanga, Phil. 55 D4
San Fernando, Baleares, Spain 36 C7
San Fernando, Cádiz, Spain 31 J4
San Fernando, Trin. & Tob. 117 D7
San Fernando, U.S.A. 113 L8
San Fernando →, Mexico 114 C5
San Fernando de Apure, Venezuela 120 B4
San Fernando de Atabapo, Venezuela 120 C4
San Fernando di Púglia, Italy 35 A9
San Francisco, Argentina 126 C3
San Francisco, Bolivia 125 D4
San Francisco, U.S.A. 111 H2
San Francisco →, U.S.A. 111 K9
San Francisco, Paso de, S. Amer. 126 B2
San Francisco de Macorîs, Dom. Rep. 117 C5
San Francisco del Monte de Oro, Argentina 126 C2
San Francisco del Oro, Mexico 114 B3
San Francisco Javier, Spain 36 C7
San Francisco Solano, Pta., Colombia 120 B2
San Fratello, Italy 35 D7
San Gabriel, Ecuador 120 C2
San Gavino Monreale, Italy 34 C1
San Gil, Colombia 120 B3
San Gimignano, Italy 32 E8
San Giórgio di Nogaro, Italy 33 C10
San Giórgio Iónico, Italy 35 B10
San Giovanni Bianco, Italy 32 C6
San Giovanni in Fiore, Italy 35 C9
San Giovanni in Persiceto, Italy 33 D8
San Giovanni Rotondo, Italy 35 A8
San Giovanni Valdarno, Italy 33 E8
San Giuliano Terme, Italy 32 E7
San Gorgonio Mt., U.S.A. 113 L10
San Gottardo, P. del, Switz. 23 C7
San Gregorio, Uruguay 127 C4
San Gregorio, U.S.A. 112 H4
San Guiseppe Iato, Italy 34 E6
San Ignacio, Belize 115 D7
San Ignacio, Bolivia 125 D5
San Ignacio, Mexico 114 B2
San Ignacio, Paraguay 126 B4
San Ignacio, L., Mexico 114 B2
San Ildefonso, C., Phil. 55 C5
San Isidro, Argentina 126 C4
San Jacinto, Colombia 120 B2
San Jacinto, U.S.A. 113 M10
San Jaime, Spain 36 B11
San Javier, Misiones, Argentina 127 B4
San Javier, Santa Fe, Argentina 126 C4
San Javier, Beni, Bolivia 125 C5
San Javier, Santa Cruz, Bolivia 125 D5
San Javier, Chile 126 D1
San Javier, Spain 29 H4
San Jerónimo, Sa. de, Colombia 120 B2
San Jeronimo Taviche, Mexico 115 D5
San Joaquín, Bolivia 125 C5
San Joaquin, U.S.A. 112 J6
San Joaquín, Venezuela 120 A4
San Joaquín →, Bolivia 125 C5
San Joaquin →, U.S.A. 111 G3
San Joaquin Valley, U.S.A. 112 J6
San Jordi, Spain 36 B9
San Jorge, Argentina 126 C3
San Jorge, Spain 36 C7
San Jorge, B. de, Mexico 114 A2
San Jorge, G., Argentina 128 C3
San Jorge, G. de, Spain 28 E4
San José, Bolivia 125 D5
San José, Costa Rica 116 E3
San José, Guatemala 116 D1
San José, Mexico 114 C2
San Jose, Phil. 55 D4
San José, Spain 36 C7
San Jose, U.S.A. 111 H3
San Jose →, U.S.A. 111 J10
San Jose de Buenovista, Phil. 55 E4
San José de Feliciano, Argentina 126 C4
San José de Jáchal, Argentina 126 C2
San José de Mayo, Uruguay 126 C4
San José de Ocune, Colombia 120 C3
San José de Uchapiamonas, Bolivia 124 C4
San José del Cabo, Mexico 114 C3
San José del Guaviare, Colombia 120 C3
San José do Anauá, Brazil 121 C5
San Juan, Argentina 126 C2
San Juan, Colombia 120 B2
San Juan, Mexico 114 C4
San Juan, Ica, Peru 124 D2
San Juan, Puno, Peru 124 C4
San Juan, Phil. 55 G7
San Juan, Puerto Rico 117 C6
San Juan □, Argentina 126 C2
San Juan →, Argentina 126 C2
San Juan →, Bolivia 125 E4
San Juan →, Colombia 120 C2
San Juan →, Nic. 116 D3
San Juan →, U.S.A. 111 H8
San Juan →, Venezuela 121 A5
San Juan, C., Eq. Guin. 80 D1
San Juan Bautista, Paraguay 126 B4
San Juan Bautista, Spain 36 B8
San Juan Bautista, U.S.A. 111 H3
San Juan Bautista Valle Nacional, Mexico 115 D5
San Juan Capistrano, U.S.A. 113 M9
San Juan Cr. →, U.S.A. 112 J5
San Juan de Guadalupe, Mexico 114 C4
San Juan de los Morros, Venezuela 120 B4
San Juan del César, Colombia 120 A3
San Juan del Norte, Nic. 116 D3
San Juan del Norte, B. de, Nic. 116 D3
San Juan del Puerto, Spain 31 H4
San Juan del Río, Mexico 115 C5
San Juan del Sur, Nic. 116 D2
San Juan I., U.S.A. 112 B3
San Juan Mts., U.S.A. 111 H10
San Julián, Argentina 128 C3
San Just, Sierra de, Spain 28 E4
San Justo, Argentina 126 C3
San Kamphaeng, Thailand 58 C2
San Lázaro, C., Mexico 114 C2
San Lázaro, Sa., Mexico 114 C3
San Leandro, U.S.A. 111 H2
San Leonardo, Spain 28 D1
San Lorenzo, Argentina 126 C3
San Lorenzo, Beni, Bolivia 125 D4
San Lorenzo, Tarija, Bolivia 125 E5
San Lorenzo, Ecuador 120 C2
San Lorenzo, Paraguay 126 B4
San Lorenzo, Spain 36 B10
San Lorenzo, Venezuela 120 B3
San Lorenzo →, Mexico 114 C3
San Lorenzo, I., Mexico 114 B2
San Lorenzo, I., Peru 124 C2
San Lorenzo, Mt., Argentina 128 C2
San Lorenzo de la Parrilla, Spain 28 F2
San Lorenzo de Morunys, Spain 28 C6
San Lucas, Bolivia 125 E4
San Lucas, Baja Calif. S., Mexico 114 C3
San Lucas, Baja Calif. S., Mexico 114 B2
San Lucas, U.S.A. 112 J5
San Lucas, C., Mexico 114 C3
San Lúcido, Italy 35 C9
San Luis, Argentina 126 C2
San Luis, Cuba 116 B3
San Luis, Guatemala 116 C2
San Luis, U.S.A. 111 H11
San Luis □, Argentina 126 C2
San Luis, I., Mexico 114 B2
San Luis, L. de, Bolivia 125 C5
San Luis, Sierra de, Argentina 126 C2
San Luis de la Paz, Mexico 114 C4
San Luis Obispo, U.S.A. 113 K6
San Luis Potosí, Mexico 114 C4
San Luis Potosí □, Mexico 114 C4
San Luis Reservoir, U.S.A. 112 H5
San Luis Río Colorado, Mexico 114 A2
San Marco Argentano, Italy 35 C9
San Marco dei Cavoti, Italy 35 A7
San Marco in Lámis, Italy 35 A8
San Marcos, Colombia 120 B2
San Marcos, Guatemala 116 D1
San Marcos, Mexico 114 B2
San Marcos, U.S.A. 109 L6
San Marino ■, Europe 33 E9
San Martín, Argentina 126 C2
San Martín, Colombia 120 C3
San Martín →, Bolivia 125 C5
San Martín, L., Argentina 128 C2
San Martín de los Andes, Argentina 128 B2
San Martín de Valdeiglesias, Spain 30 E6
San Martino de Calvi, Italy 32 C6
San Mateo, Phil. 55 C4
San Mateo, Baleares, Spain 36 B7
San Mateo, Valencia, Spain 28 E5
San Mateo, U.S.A. 111 H2
San Matías, Bolivia 125 D6

San Matías, G., *Argentina* **128** B4
San Miguel, *El Salv.* **116** D2
San Miguel, *Panama* **116** E4
San Miguel, *Spain* **36** B7
San Miguel, *U.S.A.* **111** J3
San Miguel, *Venezuela* **120** B4
San Miguel →, *Bolivia* **125** C5
San Miguel →, *S. Amer.* ... **120** C2
San Miguel de Huachi,
 Bolivia **124** D4
San Miguel de Salinas,
 Spain **29** H4
San Miguel de Tucumán,
 Argentina **126** B2
San Miguel del Monte,
 Argentina **126** D4
San Miguel I., *U.S.A.* **113** L6
San Miniato, *Italy* **32** E7
San Narciso, *Phil.* **55** D4
San Nicolás, *Canary Is.* ... **36** G4
San Nicolas, *Phil.* **55** B4
San Nicolás de los Arroyas,
 Argentina **126** C3
San Nicolas I., *U.S.A.* **113** M7
San Onofre, *Colombia* **120** B2
San Onofre, *U.S.A.* **113** M9
San Pablo, *Bolivia* **126** A2
San Pablo, *Phil.* **55** D4
San Páolo di Civitate, *Italy* **35** A8
San Pedro, *Buenos Aires,*
 Argentina **127** B5
San Pedro, *Jujuy, Argentina* **126** A3
San Pedro, *Colombia* **120** C3
San-Pédro, *Ivory C.* **78** E3
San Pedro, *Mexico* **114** C2
San Pedro, *Peru* **124** C3
San Pedro □, *Paraguay* ... **126** A4
San Pedro →, *Chihuahua,*
 Mexico **114** B3
San Pedro →, *Michoacan,*
 Mexico **114** D4
San Pedro →, *Nayarit,*
 Mexico **114** C3
San Pedro →, *U.S.A.* **111** K8
San Pedro, Pta., *Chile* **126** B1
San Pedro, Sierra de, *Spain* **31** F4
San Pedro Channel, *U.S.A.* **113** M8
San Pedro de Arimena,
 Colombia **120** C3
San Pedro de Atacama,
 Chile **126** A2
San Pedro de Jujuy,
 Argentina **126** A3
San Pedro de las Colonias,
 Mexico **114** B4
San Pedro de Lloc, *Peru* .. **124** B2
San Pedro de Macorís,
 Dom. Rep. **117** C6
San Pedro del Norte, *Nic.* . **116** D3
San Pedro del Paraná,
 Paraguay **126** B4
San Pedro del Pinatar,
 Spain **29** H4
San Pedro Mártir, Sierra,
 Mexico **114** A1
San Pedro Mixtepec,
 Mexico **115** D5
San Pedro Ocampo =
 Melchor Ocampo,
 Mexico **114** C4
San Pedro Sula, *Honduras* **116** C2
San Pieto, *Italy* **34** C1
San Pietro Vernótico, *Italy* **35** B11
San Quintín, *Mexico* **114** A1
San Rafael, *Argentina* **126** C2
San Rafael, *Calif., U.S.A.* . **112** H4
San Rafael, *N. Mex.,*
 U.S.A. **111** J10
San Rafael, *Venezuela* **120** A3
San Rafael Mt., *U.S.A.* ... **113** L7
San Rafael Mts., *U.S.A.* .. **113** L7
San Ramón, *Bolivia* **125** C5
San Ramón, *Peru* **124** C2
San Ramón de la Nueva
 Orán, *Argentina* **126** A3
San Remo, *Italy* **32** E4
San Román, C., *Venezuela* **120** A3
San Roque, *Argentina* **126** B4
San Roque, *Spain* **31** J5
San Rosendo, *Chile* **126** D1
San Saba, *U.S.A.* **109** K5
San Salvador, *Bahamas* ... **117** B5
San Salvador, *El Salv.* **116** D2
San Salvador, *Spain* **36** B10
San Salvador de Jujuy,
 Argentina **126** A3
San Salvador I., *Bahamas* . **117** B5
San Sebastián, *Argentina* . **128** D3
San Sebastián, *Spain* **28** B3
San Sebastián, *Venezuela* . **120** B4
San Sebastian de la
 Gomera, *Canary Is.* ... **36** F2
San Serra, *Spain* **36** B10
San Serverino Marche, *Italy* **33** E10
San Simeon, *U.S.A.* **112** K5
San Simon, *U.S.A.* **111** K9
San Stéfano di Cadore,
 Italy **33** B9
San Telmo, *Mexico* **114** A1
San Telmo, *Spain* **36** B9
San Tiburcio, *Mexico* **114** C4
San Valentin, Mte., *Chile* . **128** C2
San Vicente de Alcántara,
 Spain **31** F3
San Vicente de la
 Barquera, *Spain* **30** B6

San Vicente del Caguán,
 Colombia **120** C3
San Vincenzo, *Italy* **32** E7
San Vito, *Italy* **34** C2
San Vito, C., *Italy* **34** D5
San Vito al Tagliamento,
 Italy **33** C9
San Vito Chietino, *Italy* .. **33** F11
San Vito dei Normanni,
 Italy **35** B10
San Yanaro, *Colombia* ... **120** C4
San Ygnacio, *U.S.A.* **109** M5
Saña, *Peru* **124** B2
Sana', *Yemen* **68** D3
Sana →, *Bos.-H.* **33** C13
Sanaba, *Burkina Faso* **78** C4
Şanâfir, *Si. Arabia* **76** B3
Sanaga →, *Cameroon* **79** E6
Sanaloa, Presa, *Mexico* ... **114** C3
Sanana, *Indonesia* **57** E7
Sanand, *India* **62** H5
Sanandaj, *Iran* **67** E12
Sanandita, *Bolivia* **126** A3
Sanary-sur-Mer, *France* ... **27** E9
Sanawad, *India* **62** H7
Sancellas, *Spain* **36** B9
Sancergues, *France* **25** E9
Sancerre, *France* **25** E9
Sancerrois, Collines du,
 France **25** E9
Sancha He →, *China* **52** D6
Sanchahe, *China* **51** B14
Sánchez, *Dom. Rep.* **117** C6
Sanchor, *India* **62** G4
Sanco Pt., *Phil.* **57** C7
Sancoins, *France* **25** F9
Sancti-Spíritus, *Cuba* **116** B4
Sancy, Puy de, *France* **26** C6
Sand →, *S. Africa* **85** C5
Sand Springs, *U.S.A.* **109** G6
Sanda, *Japan* **49** G7
Sandakan, *Malaysia* **56** C5
Sandan = Sambor,
 Cambodia **58** F6
Sandanski, *Bulgaria* **39** H6
Sandaré, *Mali* **78** C2
Sanday, *U.K.* **14** B6
Sandefjord, *Norway* **10** E4
Sanders, *U.S.A.* **111** J9
Sanderson, *U.S.A.* **109** K3
Sandfly L., *Canada* **101** B7
Sandgate, *Australia* **91** D5
Sandía, *Peru* **124** C4
Sandıklı, *Turkey* **66** C4
Sandnes, *Norway* **9** G11
Sandness, *U.K.* **14** A7
Sandnessjøen, *Norway* ... **8** C15
Sandoa, *Zaïre* **80** F4
Sandomierz, *Poland* **20** C11
Sandona, *Colombia* **120** C2
Sandover →, *Australia* ... **90** C2
Sandoway, *Burma* **61** K19
Sandoy, *Færoe Is.* **8** F9
Sandpoint, *U.S.A.* **110** B5
Sandringham, *U.K.* **12** E8
Sandslân, *Sweden* **10** A11
Sandspit, *Canada* **100** C2
Sandstone, *Australia* **89** E2
Sandu, *China* **52** E6
Sandusky, *Mich., U.S.A.* . **98** D3
Sandusky, *Ohio, U.S.A.* .. **106** E2
Sandvig, *Sweden* **11** J8
Sandviken, *Sweden* **9** F17
Sandwich, C., *Australia* .. **90** B4
Sandwich B., *Canada* **99** B8
Sandwich B., *Namibia* ... **84** C1
Sandwip Chan., *Bangla.* .. **61** H17
Sandy, *Nev., U.S.A.* **113** K11
Sandy, *Oreg., U.S.A.* **112** E4
Sandy Bight, *Australia* ... **89** F3
Sandy C., *Queens.,*
 Australia **90** C5
Sandy C., *Tas., Australia* . **90** G3
Sandy Cay, *Bahamas* **117** B4
Sandy Cr. →, *U.S.A.* ... **110** F9
Sandy L., *Canada* **98** B1
Sandy Lake, *Canada* **98** B1
Sandy Narrows, *Canada* .. **101** B8
Sanford, *Fla., U.S.A.* **105** L5
Sanford, *Maine, U.S.A.* .. **107** C14
Sanford, *N.C., U.S.A.* ... **105** H6
Sanford →, *Australia* **89** E2
Sanford, Mt., *U.S.A.* **96** B5
Sang-i-Masha, *Afghan.* ... **62** C2
Sanga, *Mozam.* **83** E4
Sanga →, *Congo* **80** E3
Sanga-Tolon, *Russia* **45** C15
Sangamner, *India* **60** K9
Sangar, *Afghan.* **62** C1
Sangar, *Russia* **45** C13
Sangar Sarai, *Afghan.* ... **62** B4
Sangasangadalam,
 Indonesia **56** E5
Sangatte, *France* **25** B8
Sangay, *Ecuador* **120** D2
Sange, *Zaïre* **82** D2
Sangeang, *Indonesia* **57** F5
Sanger, *U.S.A.* **111** H4
Sangerhausen, *Germany* .. **18** D7
Sanggan He →, *China* ... **50** E9
Sanggau, *Indonesia* **56** D4
Sangihe, Kepulauan,
 Indonesia **57** D7
Sangihe, P., *Indonesia* ... **57** D7
Sangju, *S. Korea* **51** F15
Sangkapura, *Indonesia* ... **56** F4
Sangkhla, *Thailand* **58** E2
Sangli, *India* **60** L9

Sangmélina, *Cameroon* ... **79** E7
Sangonera →, *Spain* **29** H3
Sangre de Cristo Mts.,
 U.S.A. **109** G2
Sangro →, *Italy* **33** F11
Sangudo, *Canada* **100** C6
Sangue →, *Brazil* **125** C6
Sangüesa, *Spain* **28** C3
Sanguinaires, Is., *France* . **27** G12
Sangzhi, *China* **53** C8
Sanhala, *Ivory C.* **78** C3
Sanje, *Uganda* **82** C3
Sanjiang, *China* **52** E7
Sanjo, *Japan* **48** F9
Sankhala, *Ivory C.* **78** C3
Sankt Antönien, *Switz.* ... **23** C9
Sankt Blasien, *Germany* .. **19** H4
Sankt Gallen, *Switz.* **23** B8
Sankt Gallen □, *Switz.* .. **23** B8
Sankt Goar, *Germany* **19** E3
Sankt Ingbert, *Germany* .. **19** F3
Sankt Margrethen, *Switz.* . **23** B9
Sankt Moritz, *Switz.* **23** D9
Sankt-Peterburg, *Russia* .. **40** C6
Sankt Pölten, *Austria* **21** G5
Sankt Valentin, *Austria* .. **21** G4
Sankt Veit, *Austria* **21** J4
Sankt Wendel, *Germany* .. **19** F3
Sankuru →, *Zaïre* **80** E4
Sanlıurfa, *Turkey* **67** D8
Sanlúcar de Barrameda,
 Spain **31** J4
Sanlúcar la Mayor, *Spain* . **31** H4
Sanluri, *Italy* **34** C1
Sanmenxia, *China* **50** G6
Sanming, *China* **53** D11
Sannaspos, *S. Africa* **84** D4
Sannicandro Gargánico,
 Italy **35** A8
Sannidal, *Norway* **10** F3
Sannieshof, *S. Africa* **84** D4
Sannîn, J., *Lebanon* **69** B4
Sanok, *Poland* **20** F12
Sanquhar, *U.K.* **14** F5
Sansanding Dam, *Mali* ... **78** C3
Sansepolcro, *Italy* **33** E9
Sansha, *China* **53** D13
Sanshui, *China* **53** F9
Sanski Most, *Bos.-H.* **33** D13
Sansui, *China* **52** D7
Santa, *Peru* **124** B2
Sant' Ágata de Goti, *Italy* . **35** A7
Sant' Ágata di Militello,
 Italy **35** D7
Santa Ana, *Beni, Bolivia* . **125** C4
Santa Ana, *Santa Cruz,*
 Bolivia **125** D6
Santa Ana, *Santa Cruz,*
 Bolivia **125** D5
Santa Ana, *Ecuador* **120** D1
Santa Ana, *El Salv.* **116** D2
Santa Ana, *Mexico* **114** A2
Santa Ana, *U.S.A.* **113** M9
Santa Ana →, *Venezuela* . **120** B3
Sant' Ángelo Lodigiano,
 Italy **32** C6
Sant' Antíoco, *Italy* **34** C1
Sant' Arcángelo di
 Romagna, *Italy* **33** D9
Santa Bárbara, *Colombia* . **120** B2
Santa Bárbara, *Honduras* . **116** D2
Santa Bárbara, *Mexico* ... **114** B3
Santa Bárbara, *Spain* **28** E5
Santa Bárbara, *U.S.A.* ... **113** L7
Santa Bárbara, *Venezuela* **120** B3
Santa Bárbara, Mt., *Spain* **29** H2
Santa Barbara Channel,
 U.S.A. **113** L7
Santa Barbara I., *U.S.A.* . **113** M7
Santa Catalina, *Colombia* . **120** A2
Santa Catalina, *Mexico* ... **114** B2
Santa Catalina, Gulf of,
 U.S.A. **113** N9
Santa Catalina I., *U.S.A.* . **113** M8
Santa Catarina □, *Brazil* . **127** B6
Santa Catarina, I. de,
 Brazil **127** B6
Santa Caterina Villarmosa,
 Italy **35** E7
Santa Cecília, *Brazil* **127** B5
Santa Clara, *Cuba* **116** B4
Santa Clara, *Calif., U.S.A.* **111** H3
Santa Clara, *Utah, U.S.A.* **111** H7
Santa Clara de Olimar,
 Uruguay **127** C5
Santa Clotilde, *Peru* **120** D3
Santa Coloma de Farners,
 Spain **28** D7
Santa Coloma de
 Gramanet, *Spain* **28** D7
Santa Comba, *Spain* **30** B2
Santa Croce Camerina,
 Italy **35** F7
Santa Croce di Magliano,
 Italy **35** A7
Santa Cruz, *Argentina* ... **128** D3
Santa Cruz, *Bolivia* **125** D5
Santa Cruz, *Brazil* **122** C4
Santa Cruz, *Chile* **126** C1
Santa Cruz, *Costa Rica* .. **116** D2
Santa Cruz, *Madeira* **36** D3
Santa Cruz, *Peru* **124** B2
Santa Cruz, *Phil.* **55** D4
Santa Cruz, *U.S.A.* **111** H2
Santa Cruz, *Venezuela* ... **121** B5
Santa Cruz □, *Argentina* . **128** C3
Santa Cruz □, *Bolivia* ... **125** D5
Santa Cruz →, *Argentina* **128** D3

Santa Cruz Cabrália, *Brazil* **123** E4
Santa Cruz de la Palma,
 Canary Is. **36** F2
Santa Cruz de Mudela,
 Spain **29** G1
Santa Cruz de Tenerife,
 Canary Is. **36** F3
Santa Cruz del Norte, *Cuba* **116** B3
Santa Cruz del Retamar,
 Spain **30** E6
Santa Cruz del Sur, *Cuba* . **116** B4
Santa Cruz do Rio Pardo,
 Brazil **127** A6
Santa Cruz do Sul, *Brazil* . **127** B5
Santa Cruz I., *Solomon Is.* **92** J8
Santa Cruz I., *U.S.A.* **113** M7
Santa Domingo, Cay,
 Bahamas **116** B4
Santa Elena, *Argentina* ... **126** C4
Santa Elena, *Ecuador* **120** D1
Santa Elena, C., *Costa Rica* **116** D2
Sant' Eufémia, G. di, *Italy* . **35** D9
Santa Eugenia, Pta.,
 Mexico **114** B1
Santa Eulalia, *Spain* **36** C8
Santa Fe, *Argentina* **126** C3
Santa Fe, *Spain* **31** H7
Santa Fe, *U.S.A.* **111** J11
Santa Fé □, *Argentina* ... **126** C3
Santa Filomena, *Brazil* ... **122** C2
Santa Galdana, *Spain* **36** B10
Santa Gertrudis, *Spain* ... **36** B7
Santa Helena, *Brazil* **122** B2
Santa Helena de Goiás,
 Brazil **123** E1
Santa Inês, *Brazil* **123** D4
Santa Inés, *Baleares, Spain* **36** B7
Santa Inés, *Extremadura,*
 Spain **31** G5
Santa Inés, I., *Chile* **128** D2
Santa Isabel = Rey
 Malabo, *Eq. Guin.* **79** E6
Santa Isabel, *Argentina* .. **126** D2
Santa Isabel, *Brazil* **123** D1
Santa Isabel, Pico,
 Eq. Guin. **79** E6
Santa Isabel do Araguaia,
 Brazil **122** C2
Santa Isabel do Morro,
 Brazil **123** D1
Santa Lúcia, *Corrientes,*
 Argentina **126** B4
Santa Lúcia, *San Juan,*
 Argentina **126** C2
Santa Lúcia, *Spain* **29** H4
Santa Lucía, *Uruguay* **126** C4
Santa Lucia Range, *U.S.A.* **111** J3
Santa Magdalena, I.,
 Mexico **114** C2
Santa Margarita, *Argentina* **126** D3
Santa Margarita, *Mexico* . **114** C2
Santa Margarita, *Spain* ... **36** B10
Santa Margarita, *U.S.A.* .. **112** K6
Santa Margarita →,
 U.S.A. **113** M9
Santa Margherita, *Italy* ... **32** D6
Santa María, *Argentina* ... **126** B2
Santa Maria, *Brazil* **127** B5
Santa María, *Phil.* **55** D4
Santa María, *Spain* **36** B9
Santa Maria, *Switz.* **23** C10
Santa Maria, *U.S.A.* **113** L6
Santa María →, *Mexico* .. **114** A3
Santa María, B. de, *Mexico* **114** B2
Santa Maria, C. de,
 Portugal **31** J3
Santa Maria Cápua Vétere,
 Italy **35** A7
Santa Maria da Vitória,
 Brazil **123** D3
Santa María de Ipire,
 Venezuela **121** B4
Santa Maria di Leuca, C.,
 Italy **35** C11
Santa Maria do Suaçuí,
 Brazil **123** E3
Santa Maria dos Marmelos,
 Brazil **125** B5
Santa María la Real de
 Nieva, *Spain* **30** D6
Santa Marta, *Colombia* ... **120** A3
Santa Marta, *Spain* **31** G4
Santa Marta, Ría de, *Spain* **30** B2
Santa Marta, Sierra Nevada
 de, *Colombia* **120** A3
Santa Marta Grande, C.,
 Brazil **127** B6
Santa Maura = Levkás,
 Greece **39** L3
Santa Monica, *U.S.A.* **113** M8
Santa Olalla, *Huelva, Spain* **31** H4
Santa Olalla, *Toledo, Spain* **30** E6
Sant' Onofrio, *Italy* **35** D9
Santa Pola, *Spain* **29** G4
Santa Ponsa, *Spain* **36** B9
Santa Quitéria, *Brazil* **122** B3
Santa Rita, *U.S.A.* **111** K10
Santa Rita, *Guarico,*
 Venezuela **120** B4
Santa Rita, *Zulia,*
 Venezuela **120** A3
Santa Rita do Araquaia,
 Brazil **125** D7
Santa Rosa, *La Pampa,*
 Argentina **126** D3
Santa Rosa, *San Luis,*
 Argentina **126** C2

Santa Rosa, *Bolivia* **124** C4
Santa Rosa, *Brazil* **127** B5
Santa Rosa, *Colombia* **120** C4
Santa Rosa, *Ecuador* **120** D2
Santa Rosa, *Peru* **124** C3
Santa Rosa, *Calif., U.S.A.* **112** G4
Santa Rosa, *N. Mex.,*
 U.S.A. **109** H2
Santa Rosa, *Venezuela* ... **120** C4
Santa Rosa de Cabal,
 Colombia **120** C2
Santa Rosa de Copán,
 Honduras **116** D2
Santa Rosa de Osos,
 Colombia **120** B2
Santa Rosa de Río
 Primero, *Argentina* ... **126** C3
Santa Rosa de Viterbo,
 Colombia **120** B3
Santa Rosa del Palmar,
 Bolivia **125** D5
Santa Rosa I., *Calif.,*
 U.S.A. **113** M6
Santa Rosa I., *Fla., U.S.A.* **105** K2
Santa Rosa Range, *U.S.A.* **110** F5
Santa Rosalía, *Mexico* **114** B2
Santa Sofia, *Italy* **33** E8
Santa Sylvina, *Argentina* . **126** B3
Santa Tecla = Nueva San
 Salvador, *El Salv.* **116** D2
Santa Teresa, *Argentina* .. **126** C3
Santa Teresa, *Brazil* **123** E3
Santa Teresa, *Mexico* **115** B5
Santa Teresa, *Venezuela* .. **121** C5
Santa Teresa di Riva, *Italy* **35** E8
Santa Teresa Gallura, *Italy* **34** A2
Santa Vitória do Palmar,
 Brazil **127** C5
Santa Ynez →, *U.S.A.* ... **113** L6
Santa Ynez Mts., *U.S.A.* . **113** L6
Santa Ysabel, *U.S.A.* **113** M10
Santadi, *Italy* **34** C1
Santai, *China* **52** B5
Santaluz, *Brazil* **122** D4
Santana, *Brazil* **123** D3
Santana, *Madeira* **36** D3
Santana, Coxilha de, *Brazil* **127** C4
Santana do Ipanema, *Brazil* **122** C4
Santana do Livramento,
 Brazil **127** C4
Santanyí, *Spain* **36** B10
Santander, *Colombia* **120** C2
Santander, *Spain* **30** B7
Santander Jiménez, *Mexico* **115** C5
Santaquin, *U.S.A.* **110** G8
Santarém, *Brazil* **121** D7
Santarém, *Portugal* **31** F2
Santarém □, *Portugal* **31** F2
Santaren Channel,
 W. Indies **116** B4
Santee, *U.S.A.* **113** N10
Santéramo in Colle, *Italy* . **35** B9
Santerno →, *Italy* **33** D8
Santhià, *Italy* **32** C5
Santiago, *Bolivia* **125** D6
Santiago, *Brazil* **127** B5
Santiago, *Chile* **126** C1
Santiago, *Panama* **116** E3
Santiago, *Peru* **124** C3
Santiago, *Phil.* **55** C4
Santiago □, *Chile* **126** C1
Santiago →, *Peru* **120** D2
Santiago, C., *Chile* **128** D1
Santiago, Punta de,
 Eq. Guin. **79** E6
Santiago, Serranía de,
 Bolivia **125** D6
Santiago de Chuco, *Peru* . **124** C3
Santiago de Compostela,
 Spain **30** C2
Santiago de Cuba, *Cuba* . **116** C4
Santiago de los Cabelleros,
 Dom. Rep. **117** C5
Santiago del Estero,
 Argentina **126** B3
Santiago del Estero □,
 Argentina **126** B3
Santiago del Teide,
 Canary Is. **36** F3
Santiago do Cacém,
 Portugal **31** G2
Santiago Ixcuintla, *Mexico* **114** C3
Santiago Papasquiaro,
 Mexico **114** B3
Santiaguillo, L. de, *Mexico* **114** C4
Santillana del Mar, *Spain* . **30** B6
Säntis, *Switz.* **23** B8
Santisteban del Puerto,
 Spain **29** G1
Santo →, *Peru* **124** B2
Santo Amaro, *Brazil* **123** D4
Santo Anastácio, *Brazil* .. **127** A5
Santo André, *Brazil* **127** B5
Santo Ângelo, *Brazil* **127** B5
Santo Antônio, *Brazil* **125** D6
Santo Antônio de Jesus,
 Brazil **123** D4
Santo Antônio do Içá,
 Brazil **120** D4
Santo Antônio do
 Leverger, *Brazil* **125** D6
Santo Corazón, *Bolivia* .. **125** D6
Santo Domingo,
 Dom. Rep. **117** C6
Santo Domingo, *Baja Calif.*
 Mexico **114** A1

Santo Domingo, Baja Calif. S., Mexico .. 114 B2
Santo Domingo, Nic. 116 D3
Santo Domingo de la Calzada, Spain 28 C2
Santo Domingo de los Colorados, Ecuador 120 D2
Santo Stéfano di Camastro, Italy 35 D7
Santo Stino di Livenza, Italy 33 C9
Santo Tirso, Portugal ... 30 D2
Santo Tomás, Mexico ... 114 A1
Santo Tomás, Peru 124 C3
Santo Tomé, Argentina .. 127 B4
Santo Tomé de Guayana = Ciudad Guayana, Venezuela 121 B5
Santoña, Spain 30 B7
Santoríni = Thíra, Greece 39 N8
Santos, Brazil 127 A6
Santos, Sierra de los, Spain 31 G5
Santos Dumont, Brazil ... 123 F3
Santpoort, Neths. 16 D5
Sanvignes-les-Mines, France 25 F11
Sanyuan, China 50 G5
Sanza Pombo, Angola .. 80 F3
São Anastácio, Brazil ... 127 A5
São Bartolomeu de Messines, Portugal .. 31 H2
São Benedito, Brazil 122 B3
São Bento, Brazil 127 B4
São Bento do Norte, Brazil 122 C4
São Bernado de Campo, Brazil 123 F2
São Borja, Brazil 127 B4
São Bras d'Alportel, Portugal 31 H3
São Caitano, Brazil 122 C4
São Carlos, Brazil 127 A6
São Cristóvão, Brazil ... 122 D4
São Domingos, Brazil ... 123 D2
São Domingos do Maranhão, Brazil 122 C3
São Félix, Brazil 123 D1
São Francisco, Brazil ... 123 E3
São Francisco →, Brazil . 122 D4
São Francisco do Maranhão, Brazil 122 C3
São Francisco do Sul, Brazil 127 B6
São Gabriel, Brazil 127 C5
São Gabriel da Palha, Brazil 123 E3
São Gonçalo, Brazil 123 F3
São Gotardo, Brazil 123 E2
Sao Hill, Tanzania 83 D4
São João da Boa Vista, Brazil 127 A6
São João da Pesqueira, Portugal 30 D3
São João da Ponte, Brazil 123 E3
São João del Rei, Brazil .. 123 F3
São João do Araguaia, Brazil 122 C2
São João do Paraíso, Brazil 123 E3
São João do Piauí, Brazil 122 C3
São João dos Patos, Brazil 122 C3
São Joaquim da Barra, Brazil 123 F2
São Jorge, Pta. de, Madeira 36 D3
São José, B. de, Brazil .. 122 B3
São José da Laje, Brazil . 122 C4
São José de Mipibu, Brazil 122 C4
São José do Peixe, Brazil . 122 C3
São José do Rio Prêto, Brazil 127 A6
São José dos Campos, Brazil 127 A6
São Leopoldo, Brazil 127 B5
São Lourenço, Brazil 123 F2
São Lourenço →, Brazil . 125 D6
São Lourenço, Pantanal do, Brazil 125 D6
São Lourenço, Pta. de, Madeira 36 D3
São Luís, Brazil 122 B3
São Luís de Curu, Brazil . 122 B4
São Luís Gonzaga, Brazil . 127 B5
São Marcos →, Brazil ... 123 E2
São Marcos, B. de, Brazil 122 B3
São Martinho, Portugal .. 30 E2
São Mateus, Brazil 123 E4
São Mateus →, Brazil ... 123 E4
São Miguel do Araguaia, Brazil 123 D1
São Miguel dos Campos, Brazil 122 C4
São Nicolau →, Brazil ... 122 C3
São Paulo, Brazil 127 A6
São Paulo □, Brazil 127 A6
São Paulo, I., Atl. Oc. ... 2 D8
São Paulo de Olivença, Brazil 120 D4
São Pedro do Sul, Portugal 30 E2
São Rafael, Brazil 122 C4
São Raimundo das Mangabeiras, Brazil .. 122 C2
São Raimundo Nonato, Brazil 122 C3
São Romão, Brazil 123 E2
São Roque, Madeira 36 D3
São Roque, C. de, Brazil . 122 C4
São Sebastião, I. de, Brazil 127 A6
São Sebastião do Paraíso, Brazil 127 A6
São Simão, Brazil 123 E1

São Teotónio, Portugal ... 31 H2
São Tomé, Atl. Oc. 70 F4
São Tomé, Brazil 122 C4
São Tomé, C. de, Brazil .. 123 F3
São Tomé & Príncipe ■, Africa 71 F4
São Vicente, Brazil 127 A6
São Vicente, Madeira 36 D2
São Vicente, C. de, Portugal 31 H2
Saona, I., Dom. Rep. 117 C6
Saône →, France 27 C8
Saône-et-Loire □, France . 25 F11
Saonek, Indonesia 57 E8
Saoura, O. →, Algeria ... 75 C4
Sapanca, Turkey 66 B4
Sapão →, Brazil 122 D2
Saparua, Indonesia 57 E7
Sapé, Brazil 122 C4
Sapele, Nigeria 79 D6
Sapelo I., U.S.A. 105 K5
Sapiéntza, Greece 39 N4
Sapone, Burkina Faso ... 79 C4
Saposoa, Peru 124 B2
Sapozhok, Russia 42 D5
Sappemeer, Neths. 16 B9
Sappho, U.S.A. 112 B2
Sapporo, Japan 48 C10
Sapri, Italy 35 B8
Sapudi, Indonesia 57 G16
Sapulpa, U.S.A. 109 G7
Saqqez, Iran 67 D12
Sar Dasht, Iran 65 C6
Sar Gachīneh, Iran 65 D6
Sar Planina, Macedonia . 38 G4
Sara, Burkina Faso 78 C4
Sara, Phil. 55 F5
Sara Buri, Thailand 58 E3
Sarāb, Iran 67 D12
Sarabadi, Iraq 64 C5
Sarada →, India 61 F12
Saragossa = Zaragoza, Spain 28 D4
Saraguro, Ecuador 120 D2
Sarajevo, Bos.-H. 21 M8
Saramacca □, Surinam .. 121 C6
Saramacca →, Surinam .. 121 B6
Saran, G., Indonesia 56 E4
Saranac Lake, U.S.A. ... 107 B10
Saranda, Tanzania 82 D3
Sarandí del Yi, Uruguay . 127 C4
Sarandí Grande, Uruguay 126 C4
Sarangani B., Phil. 55 J6
Sarangani Is., Phil. 55 J6
Sarangarh, India 61 J13
Saransk, Russia 42 C7
Sarapul, Russia 44 D6
Sarasota, U.S.A. 105 M4
Saratoga, Calif., U.S.A. . 111 H4
Saratoga, Wyo., U.S.A. .. 110 F10
Saratoga Springs, U.S.A. . 107 C11
Saratov, Russia 42 E7
Saravane, Laos 58 E6
Sarawak □, Malaysia 56 D4
Saray, Tekirdağ, Turkey . 66 B2
Saray, Van, Turkey 67 C11
Saraya, Senegal 78 C2
Sarayköy, Turkey 66 D3
Sarayönü, Turkey 66 C5
Sarbāz, Iran 65 E9
Sarbīsheh, Iran 65 C8
Sarca →, Italy 32 C7
Sarda = Sarada →, India 61 F12
Sardalas, Libya 75 C7
Sardarshahr, India 62 E6
Sardegna □, Italy 34 B2
Sardhana, India 62 E7
Sardina, Pta., Canary Is. . 36 F4
Sardinata, Colombia 120 B3
Sardinia = Sardegna □, Italy 34 B2
Sardis, Turkey 66 C2
Sārdūīyeh = Dar Mazār, Iran 65 D8
Saréyamou, Mali 78 B4
Sargent, U.S.A. 108 E5
Sargodha, Pakistan 62 C5
Sarh, Chad 73 G8
Sarhro, Djebel, Morocco . 74 B3
Sārī, Iran 65 B7
Sária, Greece 39 P10
Sarıgöl, Turkey 66 C3
Sarikamış, Turkey 67 B10
Sarıkaya, Turkey 66 C6
Sarikei, Malaysia 56 D4
Sarina, Australia 90 C4
Sariñena, Spain 28 D4
Sarita, U.S.A. 109 M6
Sariwon, N. Korea 51 E13
Sariyar Baraji, Turkey ... 66 B4
Sark, U.K. 13 H5
Sarkad, Hungary 21 J11
Şarkışla, Turkey 66 C7
Şarköy, Turkey 66 B2
Sarlat-la-Canéda, France . 26 D5
Sarles, U.S.A. 108 A5
Sărmaşu, Romania 38 C7
Sarmi, Indonesia 57 E9
Sarmiento, Argentina ... 128 C3
Särna, Sweden 10 C7
Sarnano, Italy 33 E10
Sarnen, Switz. 22 C6
Sarnia, Canada 98 D3
Sarno, Italy 35 B7
Sarny, Ukraine 44 D3
Särö, Sweden 11 G5
Sarolangun, Indonesia .. 56 E2

Saronikós Kólpos, Greece . 39 M6
Saronno, Italy 32 C6
Saros Körfezi, Turkey ... 66 B2
Sárospatak, Hungary 21 G11
Sarpsborg, Norway 10 E5
Sarracín, Spain 28 C1
Sarralbe, France 25 D14
Sarre = Saar →, Europe . 25 C13
Sarre-Union, France 25 D14
Sarrebourg, France 25 D14
Sarreguemines, France .. 25 C14
Sarriá, Spain 30 C3
Sarrión, Spain 28 E4
Sarro, Mali 78 C3
Sarstedt, Germany 18 C5
Sartène, France 27 G12
Sarthe □, France 24 E7
Sarthe →, France 24 E6
Sartilly, France 24 D5
Sartynya, Russia 44 C7
Sárvár, Hungary 21 H6
Sarvestān, Iran 65 D7
Särvfjället, Sweden 10 B7
Sárviz →, Hungary 21 J8
Sary-Tash, Kyrgyzstan .. 44 F8
Sarych, Mys, Ukraine ... 41 K7
Saryshagan, Kazakhstan 44 E8
Sarzana, Italy 32 D6
Sarzeau, France 24 E4
Sas van Gent, Neths. ... 17 F3
Sasabeneh, Ethiopia 68 F3
Sasaram, India 63 G11
Sasebo, Japan 49 H4
Saser, India 63 B7
Saskatchewan □, Canada 101 C7
Saskatchewan →, Canada 101 C8
Saskatoon, Canada 101 C7
Saskylakh, Russia 45 B12
Sasolburg, S. Africa 85 D4
Sasovo, Russia 42 C5
Sassandra, Ivory C. 78 E3
Sassandra →, Ivory C. .. 78 E3
Sássari, Italy 34 B1
Sassenheim, Neths. 16 D5
Sassnitz, Germany 18 A9
Sasso Marconi, Italy 33 D8
Sassocorvaro, Italy 33 E9
Sassoferrato, Italy 33 E9
Sassuolo, Italy 32 D7
Sástago, Spain 28 D4
Sastown, Liberia 78 E3
Sasumua Dam, Kenya ... 82 C4
Sasyk, Ozero, Ukraine .. 41 K5
Sata-Misaki, Japan 49 J5
Satadougou, Mali 78 C2
Satakunta, Finland 9 F20
Satanta, U.S.A. 109 G4
Satara, India 60 L8
Satilla →, U.S.A. 105 K5
Satipo, Peru 124 C3
Satka, Russia 44 D6
Satmala Hills, India 60 J9
Satna, India 63 G9
Šator, Bos.-H. 33 D13
Sátoraljaújhely, Hungary . 21 G11
Satpura Ra., India 62 J7
Satrup, Germany 18 A5
Satsuna-Shotō, Japan ... 49 K5
Sattahip, Thailand 58 F3
Satu Mare, Romania 38 B5
Satui, Indonesia 56 E5
Satun, Thailand 59 J3
Saturnina →, Brazil 125 C6
Sauce, Argentina 126 C4
Sauceda, Mexico 114 B4
Saucillo, Mexico 114 B3
Sauda, Norway 9 G12
Saúde, Brazil 122 D3
Sauðarkrókur, Iceland .. 8 D4
Saudi Arabia ■, Asia ... 68 B3
Sauer →, Germany 17 J9
Saugeen →, Canada 106 B3
Saugerties, U.S.A. 107 D11
Saugues, France 26 D7
Sauk Centre, U.S.A. 108 C7
Sauk Rapids, U.S.A. 108 C7
Saül, Fr. Guiana 121 C7
Saulgau, Germany 19 G5
Saulieu, France 25 E11
Sault, France 27 D9
Sault Ste. Marie, Canada . 98 C3
Sault Ste. Marie, U.S.A. . 104 B3
Saumlaki, Indonesia 57 F8
Saumur, France 24 E6
Saunders C., N.Z. 87 L3
Saunders I., Antarctica .. 5 B1
Saunders Point, Australia 89 E4
Sauri, Nigeria 79 C6
Saurimo, Angola 80 F4
Sausalito, U.S.A. 112 H4
Sautatá, Colombia 120 B2
Sauveterre-de-Béarn, France 26 E3
Sauzé-Vaussais, France .. 26 B4
Savá, Honduras 116 C2
Sava →, Serbia, Yug. ... 21 L10
Savage, U.S.A. 108 B2
Savage I. = Niue, Cook Is. 93 J11
Savai'i, W. Samoa 87 A13
Savalou, Benin 79 D5
Savane, Mozam. 83 F4
Savanna, U.S.A. 108 D9
Savanna la Mar, Jamaica . 116 C4
Savannah, Ga., U.S.A. .. 105 J5
Savannah, Mo., U.S.A. .. 108 F7
Savannah, Tenn., U.S.A. . 105 H1

Savannah →, U.S.A. 105 J5
Savannakhet, Laos 58 D5
Savant L., Canada 98 B1
Savant Lake, Canada ... 98 B1
Savanur, India 60 M9
Savé, Benin 79 D5
Save →, Mozam. 85 C5
Sāveh, Iran 65 C6
Savelugu, Ghana 79 D4
Savenay, France 24 E5
Saverdun, France 26 E5
Saverne, France 25 D14
Savigliano, Italy 32 D4
Savigny-sur-Braye, France 24 E7
Saviñao, Spain 30 C3
Savo, Finland 8 E22
Savoie □, France 27 C10
Savona, Italy 32 D5
Savonlinna, Finland 40 B5
Savoy = Savoie □, France 27 C10
Savşat, Turkey 67 B10
Sawahlunto, Indonesia .. 56 E2
Sawai, Indonesia 57 E7
Sawai Madhopur, India . 62 F7
Sawang Daen Din, Thailand 58 D4
Sawankhalok, Thailand . 58 D2
Sawara, Japan 49 G10
Sawatch Mts., U.S.A. ... 111 G10
Sawel Mt., U.K. 15 B4
Sawi, Thailand 59 G2
Sawmills, Zimbabwe ... 83 F2
Sawu, Indonesia 57 F6
Sawu Sea, Indonesia ... 57 F6
Saxby →, Australia 90 B3
Saxon, Switz. 22 D4
Saxony, Lower = Niedersachsen □, Germany 18 C5
Saxton, U.S.A. 106 F6
Say, Niger 79 C5
Saya, Nigeria 79 D5
Sayabec, Canada 99 C6
Sayaboury, Laos 58 C3
Sayán, Peru 124 C2
Sayan, Vostochnyy, Russia 45 D10
Sayan, Zapadnyy, Russia 45 D10
Saydā, Lebanon 69 B4
Sayhan-Ovoo, Mongolia . 50 B2
Sayhandulaan, Mongolia 50 B5
Sayhut, Yemen 68 D5
Saykhin, Kazakhstan ... 43 F8
Saynshand, Mongolia ... 50 B6
Sayre, Okla., U.S.A. 109 H5
Sayre, Pa., U.S.A. 107 E8
Sayula, Mexico 114 D4
Sazin, Pakistan 63 B5
Sazlika →, Bulgaria 39 H8
Sbeïtla, Tunisia 75 A6
Scaër, France 24 D3
Scafell Pike, U.K. 12 C4
Scalea, Italy 35 C8
Scalpay, U.K. 14 D2
Scandia, Canada 100 C6
Scandiano, Italy 32 D7
Scandinavia, Europe 6 C8
Scansano, Italy 33 F8
Scapa Flow, U.K. 14 C5
Scappoose, U.S.A. 112 E4
Scarborough, Trin. & Tob. 117 D7
Scarborough, U.K. 12 C7
Scebeli, Wabi →, Somali Rep. 68 G3
Scenic, U.S.A. 108 D3
Schaalsee, Germany 18 B6
Schaan, Liech. 23 B9
Schaesberg, Neths. 17 G8
Schaffen, Belgium 17 G6
Schaffhausen, Switz. ... 23 A7
Schaffhausen □, Switz. . 23 A7
Schagen, Neths. 16 C5
Schaijk, Neths. 16 E7
Schalkhaar, Neths. 16 D8
Schalkwijk, Neths. 16 E6
Schangnau, Switz. 22 C5
Schänis, Switz. 23 B8
Schärding, Austria 20 G3
Scharhörn, Germany ... 18 B4
Scharnitz, Austria 19 H7
Scheessel, Germany 18 B5
Schefferville, Canada ... 99 B6
Schelde →, Belgium 17 F4
Schell Creek Ra., U.S.A. . 110 G6
Schenectady, U.S.A. ... 107 D11
Scherfede, Germany 18 D5
Scherpenheuvel, Belgium 17 G5
Scherpenisse, Neths. ... 17 E4
Scherpenzeel, Neths. ... 16 D7
Schesaplana, Switz. 23 B9
Schesslitz, Germany 19 F7
Scheveningen, Neths. .. 16 D4
Schiedam, Neths. 16 E4
Schiermonnikoog, Neths. 16 B8
Schiers, Switz. 23 C9
Schifferstadt, Germany . 19 F4
Schifflange, Lux. 17 K8
Schijndel, Neths. 17 E6
Schiltigheim, France ... 25 D14
Schio, Italy 33 C8
Schipbeek, Neths. 16 D8
Schipluiden, Neths. 16 E4
Schirmeck, France 25 D14
Schlanders = Silandro, Italy 32 B7

Schlei →, Germany 18 A5
Schleiden, Germany 18 E2
Schleiz, Germany 18 E7
Schleswig, Germany 18 A5
Schleswig-Holstein □, Germany 18 A5
Schlieren, Switz. 23 B6
Schlüchtern, Germany .. 19 E5
Schmalkalden, Germany . 18 E6
Schmölln, Brandenburg, Germany 18 B10
Schmölln, Thüringen, Germany 18 E8
Schneeberg, Austria 21 H5
Schneeberg, Germany .. 18 E8
Schoenberg, Belgium ... 17 H8
Schofield, U.S.A. 108 C10
Scholls, U.S.A. 112 E4
Schönberg, Mecklenburg-Vorpommern, Germany 18 B6
Schönberg, Schleswig-Holstein, Germany 18 A6
Schönebeck, Germany .. 18 C7
Schönenwerd, Switz. ... 22 B5
Schongau, Germany 19 H6
Schöningen, Germany .. 18 C6
Schoondijke, Neths. 17 F3
Schoonebeek, Neths. ... 16 C9
Schoonhoven, Neths. .. 16 E5
Schoorl, Neths. 16 C5
Schortens, Germany ... 18 B3
Schoten, Belgium 17 F5
Schouten I., Australia .. 90 G4
Schouten Is. = Supiori, Indonesia 57 E9
Schouwen, Neths. 17 E3
Schramberg, Germany .. 19 G4
Schrankogl, Austria 19 H7
Schreckhorn, Switz. ... 22 C6
Schreiber, Canada 98 C2
Schrobenhausen, Germany 19 G7
Schruns, Austria 19 H5
Schuler, Canada 101 C6
Schuls, Switz. 23 C10
Schumacher, Canada ... 98 C3
Schüpfen, Switz. 22 B4
Schüpfheim, Switz. 22 C6
Schurz, U.S.A. 110 G4
Schuyler, U.S.A. 108 E6
Schuylkill Haven, U.S.A. . 107 F8
Schwabach, Germany .. 19 F7
Schwäbisch Gmünd, Germany 19 G5
Schwäbisch Hall, Germany 19 F5
Schwäbische Alb, Germany 19 G5
Schwabmünchen, Germany 19 G6
Schwanden, Switz. 23 C8
Schwandorf, Germany .. 19 F8
Schwaner, Pegunungan, Indonesia 56 E4
Schwarmstedt, Germany 18 C5
Schwärze, Germany 18 C9
Schwarze Elster →, Germany 18 D8
Schwarzenberg, Germany 18 E8
Schwarzenburg, Switz. . 22 C4
Schwarzwald, Germany . 19 H4
Schwaz, Austria 19 H7
Schwedt, Germany 18 B10
Schweinfurt, Germany .. 19 E6
Schweizer Mittelland, Switz. 22 C4
Schweizer-Reneke, S. Africa 84 D4
Schwenningen = Villingen-Schwenningen, Germany 19 G4
Schwerin, Germany 18 B7
Schweriner See, Germany 18 B7
Schwetzingen, Germany . 19 F4
Schwyz, Switz. 23 B7
Schwyz □, Switz. 23 B7
Sciacca, Italy 34 E6
Scicli, Italy 35 F7
Scilla, Italy 35 D8
Scilly, Isles of, U.K. 13 H1
Ścinawa, Poland 20 D6
Scioto →, U.S.A. 104 F4
Scobey, U.S.A. 108 A2
Scone, Australia 91 E5
Scórdia, Italy 35 E7
Scoresbysund, Greenland 4 B6
Scorno, Punta dello, Italy 34 A1
Scotia, Calif., U.S.A. ... 110 F1
Scotia, N.Y., U.S.A. 107 D11
Scotia Sea, Antarctica ... 5 B18
Scotland, U.S.A. 108 D6
Scotland □, U.K. 14 E5
Scotland Neck, U.S.A. .. 105 G7
Scott, C., Australia 88 B4
Scott City, U.S.A. 108 F4
Scott Glacier, Antarctica . 5 C8
Scott I., Antarctica 5 C11
Scott Inlet, Canada 97 A12
Scott Is., Canada 100 C3
Scott L., Canada 101 B7
Scott Reef, Australia ... 88 B3
Scottburgh, S. Africa ... 85 E5
Scottdale, U.S.A. 106 F5
Scottsbluff, U.S.A. 108 E3
Scottsboro, U.S.A. 105 H2
Scottsburg, U.S.A. 104 F3
Scottsdale, Australia ... 90 G4
Scottsville, Ky., U.S.A. .. 105 G2
Scottsville, N.Y., U.S.A. . 106 C7
Scottville, U.S.A. 104 D2

Scranton, *U.S.A.* 107 E9
Scugog, L., *Canada* 106 B6
Scunthorpe, *U.K.* 12 D7
Scuol, *Switz.* 23 C10
Scusciuban, *Somali Rep.* . . 68 E5
Seabra, *Brazil* 123 D3
Seabrook, L., *Australia* . . . 89 F2
Seaford, *U.S.A.* 104 F8
Seaforth, *Canada* 98 D3
Seagraves, *U.S.A.* 109 J3
Seal →, *Canada* 101 B10
Seal Cove, *Canada* 99 C8
Seal L., *Canada* 99 B7
Sealy, *U.S.A.* 109 L6
Searchlight, *U.S.A.* 113 K12
Searcy, *U.S.A.* 109 H9
Searles L., *U.S.A.* 113 K9
Seaside, *Calif., U.S.A.* . . . 112 J5
Seaside, *Oreg., U.S.A.* . . . 112 E3
Seaspray, *Australia* 91 F4
Seattle, *U.S.A.* 112 C4
Seaview Ra., *Australia* 90 B4
Sebastián Vizcaíno, B.,
  Mexico 114 B2
Sebastopol = Sevastopol,
  Ukraine 41 K7
Sebastopol, *U.S.A.* 112 G4
Sebderat, *Eritrea* 77 D4
Sebdou, *Algeria* 75 B4
Seben, *Turkey* 66 B4
Sebewaing, *U.S.A.* 104 D4
Sebezh, *Russia* 40 D5
Sebha = Sabhah, *Libya* . . 73 C7
Sébi, *Mali* 78 B4
Şebinkarahisar, *Turkey* . . . 67 B8
Sebiş, *Romania* 38 C5
Sebkhet Te-n-Dghâmcha,
  Mauritania 78 B1
Sebkra Azzel Mati, *Algeria* 75 C5
Sebkra Mekerghene,
  Algeria 75 C5
Sebnitz, *Germany* 18 E10
Sebou, Oued →, *Morocco* 74 B3
Sebring, *Fla., U.S.A.* 105 M5
Sebring, *Ohio, U.S.A.* . . . 106 F3
Sebringville, *Canada* 106 C3
Sebta = Ceuta, *N. Afr.* . . 74 A3
Sebuku, *Indonesia* 56 E5
Sebuku, Teluk, *Malaysia* . . 56 D5
Secchia →, *Italy* 32 C8
Sechelt, *Canada* 100 D4
Sechura, *Peru* 124 B1
Sechura, Desierto de, *Peru* 124 B1
Seclin, *France* 25 B10
Secondigny, *France* 24 F6
Secretary I., *N.Z.* 87 L1
Secunderabad, *India* 60 L11
Sécure →, *Bolivia* 125 D5
Sedalia, *U.S.A.* 108 F8
Sedan, *Australia* 91 E2
Sedan, *France* 25 C11
Sedan, *U.S.A.* 109 G6
Sedano, *Spain* 28 C1
Seddon, *N.Z.* 87 J5
Seddonville, *N.Z.* 87 J4
Sedeh, *Fārs, Iran* 65 D7
Sedeh, *Khorāsān, Iran* . . . 65 C8
Sederot, *Israel* 69 D3
Sedgewick, *Canada* 100 C6
Sedhiou, *Senegal* 78 C1
Sedičany, *Czech.* 20 F4
Sedico, *Italy* 33 B9
Sedley, *Canada* 101 C8
Sedova, Pik, *Russia* 44 B6
Sedrata, *Algeria* 75 A6
Sedro-Woolley, *U.S.A.* . . . 112 B4
Sedrun, *Switz.* 23 C7
Seebad Ahlbeck, *Germany* 18 B10
Seehausen, *Germany* 18 C7
Seeheim, *Namibia* 84 D2
Seekoei →, *S. Africa* . . . 84 E4
Seelow, *Germany* 18 C10
Sées, *France* 24 D7
Seesen, *Germany* 18 D6
Sefadu, *S. Leone* 78 D2
Seferihisar, *Turkey* 66 C2
Séfeto, *Mali* 78 C3
Sefrou, *Morocco* 74 B4
Sefwi Bekwai, *Ghana* 78 D4
Segamat, *Malaysia* 59 L4
Segbwema, *S. Leone* 78 D2
Seget, *Indonesia* 57 E8
Seggueur, O. →, *Algeria* 75 B5
Segonzac, *France* 26 C3
Segorbe, *Spain* 28 F4
Segou, *Mali* 78 C3
Segovia = Coco →,
  Cent. Amer. 116 D3
Segovia, *Colombia* 120 B3
Segovia, *Spain* 30 E6
Segovia □, *Spain* 30 E6
Segré, *France* 24 E6
Segre →, *Spain* 28 D5
Séguéla, *Ivory C.* 78 D3
Seguin, *U.S.A.* 109 L6
Segundo →, *Argentina* . . 126 C3
Segura →, *Spain* 29 G4
Segura, Sierra de, *Spain* . . 29 G2
Seh Qal'eh, *Iran* 65 C8
Sehitwa, *Botswana* 84 C3
Sehore, *India* 62 H7
Sehwan, *Pakistan* 62 F2
Şeica Mare, *Romania* 38 C7
Seiland, *Norway* 8 A20
Seiling, *U.S.A.* 109 G5

Seille →, *Moselle, France* 25 C13
Seille →, *Saône-et-Loire,*
  France 27 B8
Seilles, *Belgium* 17 G6
Sein, I. de, *France* 24 D2
Seine →, *France* 24 C7
Seine, B. de la, *France* . . . 24 C6
Seine-et-Marne □, *France* 25 D9
Seine-Maritime □, *France* 24 C7
Seine-St.-Denis □, *France* 25 D9
Seistan, *Iran* 65 D9
Sejerø, *Denmark* 11 J5
Sejerø Bugt, *Denmark* . . . 11 J5
Seka, *Ethiopia* 77 F4
Sekayu, *Indonesia* 56 E2
Seke, *Tanzania* 82 C3
Sekenke, *Tanzania* 82 C3
Sekondi-Takoradi, *Ghana* . 78 E4
Seksna, *Russia* 40 C10
Selah, *U.S.A.* 110 C3
Selama, *Malaysia* 59 K3
Selárgius, *Italy* 34 C2
Selaru, *Indonesia* 57 F8
Selb, *Germany* 19 E8
Selby, *U.K.* 12 D6
Selby, *U.S.A.* 108 C4
Selca, *Croatia* 33 E13
Selçuk, *Turkey* 66 D2
Selden, *U.S.A.* 108 F4
Sele →, *Italy* 35 B7
Selemdzha →, *Russia* . . 45 D13
Selenga = Selenge
  Mörön →, *Asia* 54 A5
Selenge Mörön →, *Asia* . . 54 A5
Selenica, *Albania* 39 J2
Selenter See, *Germany* . . . 18 A6
Sélestat, *France* 25 D14
Seletan, Tg., *Indonesia* . . . 56 E4
Selfridge, *U.S.A.* 108 B4
Sélibabi, *Mauritania* 78 B2
Seliger, Ozero, *Russia* 42 B1
Seligman, *U.S.A.* 111 J7
Şelim, *Turkey* 67 B10
Selîma, El Wâhât el, *Sudan* 76 C2
Selinda Spillway, *Botswana* 84 B3
Selinoús, *Greece* 39 M4
Selizharovo, *Russia* 42 B1
Seljord, *Norway* 10 E2
Selkirk, *Canada* 101 C9
Selkirk, *U.K.* 14 F6
Selkirk I., *Canada* 101 C9
Selkirk Mts., *Canada* 100 C5
Selles-sur-Cher, *France* . . . 25 E8
Selliá, *Greece* 37 D6
Sellières, *France* 25 F12
Sells, *U.S.A.* 111 L8
Sellye, *Hungary* 21 K7
Selma, *Ala., U.S.A.* 105 J2
Selma, *Calif., U.S.A.* 111 H4
Selma, *N.C., U.S.A.* 105 H6
Selmer, *U.S.A.* 105 H1
Selongey, *France* 25 E12
Selowandoma Falls,
  Zimbabwe 83 G3
Selpele, *Indonesia* 57 E8
Selsey Bill, *U.K.* 13 G7
Seltso, *Russia* 42 D2
Seltz, *France* 25 D15
Selu, *Indonesia* 57 F8
Sélune →, *France* 24 D5
Selva, *Argentina* 126 B3
Selva, *Italy* 33 B8
Selva, *Spain* 28 D6
Selvas, *Brazil* 124 B4
Selwyn, *Australia* 90 C3
Selwyn L., *Canada* 101 A8
Selwyn Ra., *Australia* 90 C3
Selyatyn, *Ukraine* 38 B8
Semani →, *Albania* 39 J2
Semara, *W. Sahara* 74 C2
Semarang, *Indonesia* 57 G14
Semau, *Indonesia* 57 F6
Sembabule, *Uganda* 82 C3
Semeih, *Sudan* 77 E3
Semenov, *Russia* 42 B7
Semenovka, *Ukraine* 41 H7
Semenovka, *Ukraine* 41 F7
Semeru, *Indonesia* 57 H15
Semey, *Kazakhstan* 44 D9
Semikarakorskiy, *Russia* . . 43 G5
Semiluki, *Russia* 42 E4
Semiozernoye, *Kazakhstan* 44 D7
Semipalatinsk = Semey,
  Kazakhstan 44 D9
Semirara Is., *Phil.* 55 F4
Semisopochnoi I., *U.S.A.* . . 96 C2
Semitau, *Indonesia* 56 D4
Semiyarka, *Kazakhstan* . . . 44 D8
Semiyarskoye = Semiyarka,
  Kazakhstan 44 D8
Semmering, P., *Austria* . . . 21 H5
Semnān, *Iran* 65 C7
Semnān □, *Iran* 65 C7
Semois →, *Europe* 17 J5
Semporna, *Malaysia* 57 D5
Semuda, *Indonesia* 56 E4
Semur-en-Auxois, *France* . 25 E11
Sena, *Bolivia* 124 C4
Senã, *Iran* 65 D6
Sena, *Mozam.* 83 F3

Sena →, *Bolivia* 124 C4
Sena Madureira, *Brazil* . . . 124 B4
Senador Pompeu, *Brazil* . . 122 C4
Senaja, *Malaysia* 56 C5
Senaki, *Georgia* 43 D7
Senanga, *Zambia* 84 B3
Senatobia, *U.S.A.* 109 H10
Sendafa, *Ethiopia* 77 F4
Sendai, *Kagoshima, Japan* 49 J5
Sendai, *Miyagi, Japan* . . . 48 E10
Sendai-Wan, *Japan* 48 E10
Sendenhorst, *Germany* . . . 18 D3
Seneca, *Oreg., U.S.A.* . . . 110 D4
Seneca, *S.C., U.S.A.* 105 H4
Seneca Falls, *U.S.A.* 107 D8
Seneca L., *U.S.A.* 106 D8
Seneffe, *Belgium* 17 G4
Senegal ■, *W. Afr.* 78 C2
Senegal →, *W. Afr.* 78 B1
Senegambia, *Africa* 70 E2
Senekal, *S. Africa* 85 D4
Senftenberg, *Germany* . . . 18 D10
Senga Hill, *Zambia* 83 D3
Senge Khambab =
  Indus →, *Pakistan* 62 G2
Sengerema □, *Tanzania* . . 82 C3
Sengiley, *Russia* 42 D9
Sengkang, *Indonesia* 57 E6
Sengua →, *Zimbabwe* . . . 83 F2
Senguerr →, *Argentina* . . 128 C3
Senhor-do-Bonfim, *Brazil* . 122 D3
Senica, *Slovak Rep.* 20 G7
Senigállia, *Italy* 33 E10
Senio →, *Italy* 33 D9
Senirkent, *Turkey* 66 C4
Senise, *Italy* 35 B9
Senj, *Croatia* 33 D11
Senja, *Norway* 8 B17
Senlis, *France* 25 C9
Senmonorom, *Cambodia* . . 58 F6
Sennâr, *Sudan* 77 E3
Senne →, *Belgium* 17 G4
Senneterre, *Canada* 98 C4
Senniquelle, *Liberia* 78 D3
Senno, *Belarus* 40 E5
Sennori, *Italy* 34 B1
Seno, *Laos* 58 D5
Senonches, *France* 24 D8
Senorbí, *Italy* 34 C2
Senožeče, *Slovenia* 33 C11
Sens, *France* 25 D10
Senta, *Serbia, Yug.* 21 K10
Sentani, *Indonesia* 57 E10
Sentery, *Zaïre* 82 D2
Sentinel, *U.S.A.* 111 K7
Sentolo, *Indonesia* 57 G14
Senya Beraku, *Ghana* 79 D4
Seo de Urgel, *Spain* 28 C6
Seohara, *India* 63 E8
Seoni, *India* 63 H8
Seoul = Sŏul, *S. Korea* . . . 51 F14
Separation Point, *Canada* . 99 B8
Sepīdān, *Iran* 65 D7
Sepo-ri, *N. Korea* 51 E14
Sepone, *Laos* 58 D6
Sept-Îles, *Canada* 99 B6
Septemvri, *Bulgaria* 38 G7
Sepúlveda, *Spain* 30 D7
Sequeros, *Spain* 30 E4
Sequim, *U.S.A.* 112 B3
Sequoia National Park,
  U.S.A. 111 H4
Serafimovich, *Russia* 42 F6
Seraing, *Belgium* 17 G7
Seraja, *Indonesia* 59 L7
Serakhis →, *Cyprus* 37 D11
Seram, *Indonesia* 57 E7
Seram Laut, Kepulauan,
  Indonesia 57 E8
Seram Sea, *Indonesia* 57 E7
Serang, *Indonesia* 57 G12
Serasan, *Indonesia* 59 L7
Seravezza, *Italy* 32 E7
Serbia □, *Yugoslavia* 21 M11
Serdo, *Ethiopia* 77 E5
Serdobsk, *Russia* 42 D7
Seredka, *Russia* 40 C5
Şereflikoçhisar, *Turkey* . . . 66 C5
Seregno, *Italy* 32 C6
Seremban, *Malaysia* 59 L3
Serengeti □, *Tanzania* . . . 82 C3
Serengeti Plain, *Tanzania* . 82 C3
Serenje, *Zambia* 83 E3
Sereth = Siret →,
  Romania 38 D11
Sergach, *Russia* 42 C7
Serge →, *Spain* 28 D5
Sergino, *Russia* 44 C7
Sergipe □, *Brazil* 122 D4
Sergiyev Posad, *Russia* . . . 42 B4
Seria, *Brunei* 56 D4
Serian, *Malaysia* 56 D4
Seriate, *Italy* 32 C6
Seribu, Kepulauan,
  Indonesia 56 F3
Sérifontaine, *France* 25 C8
Sérifos, *Greece* 39 M7
Sérignan, *France* 26 E7
Serik, *Turkey* 66 D4
Seringapatam Reef,
  Australia 88 B3
Sermaize-les-Bains, *France* 25 D11
Sermata, *Indonesia* 57 F7
Sérmide, *Italy* 33 C8
Sernovodsk, *Russia* 42 D10
Sernur, *Russia* 42 B9
Serny Zavod, *Turkmenistan* 44 F6

Serón, *Spain* 29 H2
Serós, *Spain* 28 D5
Serov, *Russia* 44 D7
Serowe, *Botswana* 84 C4
Serpa, *Portugal* 31 H3
Serpeddi, Punta, *Italy* 34 C2
Serpentara, Isola, *Italy* . . . 34 C2
Serpentine, *Australia* 89 F2
Serpentine Lakes, *Australia* 89 E4
Serpis →, *Spain* 29 G4
Serpukhov, *Russia* 42 C3
Serra do Navio, *Brazil* . . . 121 C7
Serra San Bruno, *Italy* . . . 35 D9
Serra Talhada, *Brazil* 122 C4
Serracapriola, *Italy* 35 A8
Serradilla, *Spain* 30 F4
Sérrai, *Greece* 39 H6
Serramanna, *Italy* 34 C1
Serrat, C., *Tunisia* 75 A6
Serre-Ponçon, L. de,
  France 27 D10
Serres, *France* 27 D9
Serrezuela, *Argentina* . . . 126 C2
Serrinha, *Brazil* 123 D4
Serrita, *Brazil* 122 C4
Sersale, *Italy* 35 C9
Sertã, *Portugal* 30 F2
Sertânia, *Brazil* 122 C4
Sertanópolis, *Brazil* 127 A5
Sêrtar, *China* 52 A3
Serua, *Indonesia* 57 F8
Serui, *Indonesia* 57 E9
Serule, *Botswana* 84 C4
Sérvia, *Greece* 39 J4
Sese Is., *Uganda* 82 C3
Sesepe, *Indonesia* 57 E7
Sesfontein, *Namibia* 84 B1
Sesheke, *Zambia* 84 B3
Sesia →, *Italy* 32 C5
Sesimbra, *Portugal* 31 G1
Sessa Aurunca, *Italy* 34 A6
S'estanyol, *Spain* 36 B9
Sesto San Giovanni, *Italy* . 32 C6
Sestri Levante, *Italy* 32 D6
Sestriere, *Italy* 32 D3
Sestroretsk, *Russia* 40 B6
Sestrunj, *Croatia* 33 D12
Sestu, *Italy* 34 C2
Sesvenna, *Switz.* 23 C10
Setana, *Japan* 48 C9
Sète, *France* 26 E7
Sete Lagôas, *Brazil* 123 E3
Sétif, *Algeria* 75 A6
Seto, *Japan* 49 G8
Setonaikai, *Japan* 49 G6
Setté-Cama, *Gabon* 80 E1
Séttimo Tor, *Italy* 32 C4
Setting L., *Canada* 101 B9
Settle, *U.K.* 12 C5
Settlement Pt., *Bahamas* . . 105 M6
Setúbal, *Portugal* 31 G2
Setúbal □, *Portugal* 31 G2
Setúbal, B. de, *Portugal* . . 31 G2
Seugne →, *France* 26 C3
Seulimeum, *Indonesia* 56 C1
Seuzach, *Switz.* 23 A7
Sevan, *Armenia* 43 K7
Sevan, Ozero = Sevana
  Lich, *Armenia* 43 K7
Sevana Lich, *Armenia* 43 K7
Sevastopol, *Ukraine* 41 K7
Sevelen, *Switz.* 23 B8
Seven Emu, *Australia* 90 B2
Seven Sisters, *Canada* . . . 100 C3
Sevenum, *Neths.* 17 F8
Sever →, *Spain* 31 F3
Sévérac-le-Château, *France* 26 D7
Severn →, *Canada* 98 A2
Severn →, *U.K.* 13 F5
Severn L., *Canada* 98 B1
Severnaya Zemlya, *Russia* . 45 B10
Severo-Kurilsk, *Russia* . . . 45 D16
Severo-Yenisegskiy, *Russia* 45 C10
Severodonetsk =
  Syeverodonetsk, *Ukraine* 41 H10
Severodvinsk, *Russia* 44 C4
Sevier, *U.S.A.* 111 G7
Sevier →, *U.S.A.* 111 G7
Sevier L., *U.S.A.* 110 G7
Sevilla, *Colombia* 120 C2
Sevilla, *Spain* 31 H5
Sevilla □, *Spain* 31 H5
Seville = Sevilla, *Spain* . . . 31 H5
Sevnica, *Slovenia* 33 B12
Sèvre-Nantaise →, *France* 24 E5
Sèvre-Niortaise →, *France* 26 B3
Sevsk, *Russia* 42 D2
Seward, *Alaska, U.S.A.* . . . 96 B5
Seward, *Nebr., U.S.A.* . . . 108 E6
Seward Pen., *U.S.A.* 96 B3
Sewell, *Chile* 126 C1
Sewer, *Indonesia* 57 F8
Sewickley, *U.S.A.* 106 F4
Sexbierum, *Neths.* 16 B6
Sexsmith, *Canada* 100 B5
Seychelles ■, *Ind. Oc.* . . . 47 K9
Seyðisfjörður, *Iceland* 8 D6
Seydişehir, *Turkey* 66 D4
Seydvān, *Iran* 67 C11
Seyhan Barajı, *Turkey* 66 D6
Seyitgazi, *Turkey* 66 C4
Seym →, *Ukraine* 41 G7
Seymchan, *Russia* 45 C16
Seymour, *Australia* 91 F4

Seymour, *S. Africa* 85 E4
Seymour, *Conn., U.S.A.* . . 107 E11
Seymour, *Ind., U.S.A.* . . . 104 F3
Seymour, *Tex., U.S.A.* . . . 109 J5
Seymour, *Wis., U.S.A.* . . . 104 C1
Seyne, *France* 27 D10
Seyssel, *France* 27 C9
Sežana, *Slovenia* 33 C10
Sézanne, *France* 25 D10
Sezze, *Italy* 34 A6
Sfax, *Tunisia* 75 B7
Sfîntu Gheorghe, *Romania* 38 D8
Sfîntu Gheorghe,
  Bratul →, *Romania* 38 E12
Sha Xi →, *China* 53 D12
Sha Xian, *China* 53 D11
Shaanxi □, *China* 50 G5
Shaba □, *Zaïre* 82 D2
Shabunda, *Zaïre* 82 C2
Shache, *China* 54 C2
Shackleton Ice Shelf,
  Antarctica 5 C8
Shackleton Inlet, *Antarctica* 5 E11
Shādegān, *Iran* 65 D6
Shadi, *China* 53 D10
Shadi, *India* 63 C7
Shadrinsk, *Russia* 44 D7
Shaffa, *Nigeria* 79 C7
Shafter, *Calif., U.S.A.* 113 K7
Shafter, *Tex., U.S.A.* 109 L2
Shaftesbury, *U.K.* 13 F5
Shagamu, *Nigeria* 79 D5
Shagram, *Pakistan* 63 A5
Shah Bunder, *Pakistan* . . . 62 G2
Shahabad, *Punjab, India* . . 62 D7
Shahabad, *Raj., India* 62 G7
Shahabad, *Ut. P., India* . . . 63 F8
Shahadpur, *Pakistan* 62 G3
Shahba, *Syria* 69 C5
Shahdād, *Iran* 65 D8
Shahdadkot, *Pakistan* 62 F2
Shahe, *China* 50 F8
Shahganj, *India* 63 F10
Shahgarh, *India* 60 F6
Shaḩḩāt, *Libya* 73 B9
Shahjahanpur, *India* 63 F8
Shahpur, *India* 62 H7
Shahpur, *Pakistan* 62 E3
Shahpura, *India* 63 H9
Shahr Kord, *Iran* 65 C6
Shāhrakht, *Iran* 65 C9
Shahrig, *Pakistan* 62 D2
Shahukou, *China* 50 D7
Shaikhabad, *Afghan.* 62 B3
Shajapur, *India* 62 H7
Shakargarh, *Pakistan* 62 C6
Shakawe, *Botswana* 84 B3
Shaker Heights, *U.S.A.* . . . 106 E3
Shakhty, *Russia* 43 G5
Shakhunya, *Russia* 42 B8
Shaki, *Nigeria* 79 D5
Shakopee, *U.S.A.* 108 C8
Shala, L., *Ethiopia* 77 F4
Shali, *Russia* 43 J7
Shallow Lake, *Canada* . . . 106 B3
Shalqar, *Kazakhstan* 44 E6
Shaluli Shan, *China* 52 B2
Shām, *Iran* 65 E8
Shamāl Dârfûr □, *Sudan* . 77 D2
Shamāl Kordofân □, *Sudan* 77 D2
Shamanovo, *Russia* 45 C15
Shamattawa, *Canada* 101 B10
Shamattawa →, *Canada* . . 98 A2
Shambe, *Sudan* 77 F3
Shambu, *Ethiopia* 77 F4
Shamīl, *Iran* 65 E8
Shamkhor = Şämkir,
  Azerbaijan 43 K8
Shāmkūh, *Iran* 65 C8
Shamli, *India* 62 E7
Shamo = Gobi, *Asia* 50 C5
Shamo, L., *Ethiopia* 77 F4
Shamokin, *U.S.A.* 107 F8
Shamrock, *U.S.A.* 109 H4
Shamva, *Zimbabwe* 83 F3
Shan □, *Burma* 61 J21
Shan Xian, *China* 50 G9
Shanan →, *Ethiopia* 77 F5
Shanchengzhen, *China* . . . 51 C13
Shāndak, *Iran* 65 D9
Shandon, *U.S.A.* 112 K6
Shandong □, *China* 51 F10
Shandong Bandao, *China* . 51 F11
Shang Xian, *China* 50 H5
Shangalowe, *Zaïre* 83 E2
Shangani →, *Zimbabwe* . . 83 F2
Shangbancheng, *China* . . . 51 D10
Shangcai, *China* 53 A10
Shangcheng, *China* 53 B10
Shangchuan Dao, *China* . . 53 G9
Shangdu, *China* 50 D7
Shanggao, *China* 53 C10
Shanghai, *China* 53 B13
Shanghang, *China* 53 E11
Shanghe, *China* 51 F9
Shangjin, *China* 53 A8
Shanglin, *China* 52 F7
Shangnan, *China* 50 H6
Shangqiu, *China* 50 G8
Shangrao, *China* 53 C11
Shangshui, *China* 50 H8
Shangsi, *China* 52 F6
Shangyou, *China* 53 E10
Shangzhi, *China* 51 B14
Shanhetun, *China* 51 B14
Shani, *Nigeria* 79 C7

Shaniko, U.S.A.	110	D3
Shannon, N.Z.	87	J5
Shannon →, Ireland	15	D2
Shansi = Shanxi □, China	50	F7
Shantar, Ostrov Bolshoy, Russia	45	D14
Shantipur, India	63	H13
Shantou, China	53	F11
Shantung = Shandong □, China	51	F10
Shanxi □, China	50	F7
Shanyang, China	50	H5
Shaowu, China	53	D11
Shaoxing, China	53	C13
Shaoyang, Hunan, China	53	D8
Shaoyang, Hunan, China	53	D8
Shapinsay, U.K.	14	B6
Shaqra', Si. Arabia	64	E5
Shaqra', Yemen	68	E4
Sharafa, Sudan	77	E2
Sharafkhāneh, Iran	67	C11
Sharbot Lake, Canada	107	B8
Shari, Japan	48	C12
Sharjah = Ash Shāriqah, U.A.E.	65	E7
Shark B., Australia	89	E1
Sharm el Sheikh, Egypt	76	B3
Sharon, Mass., U.S.A.	107	D13
Sharon, Pa., U.S.A.	106	E4
Sharon Springs, U.S.A.	108	F4
Sharp Pt., Australia	90	A3
Sharpe L., Canada	101	C10
Sharpsville, U.S.A.	106	E4
Sharq el Istiwa'iya □, Sudan	77	F3
Sharya, Russia	42	A7
Shasha, Ethiopia	77	F4
Shashemene, Ethiopia	77	F4
Shashi, Botswana	85	C4
Shashi, China	53	B9
Shashi →, Africa	83	G2
Shasta, Mt., U.S.A.	110	F2
Shasta L., U.S.A.	110	F2
Shatsk, Russia	42	C5
Shatt al'Arab →, Iraq	65	D6
Shattuck, U.S.A.	109	G5
Shatura, Russia	42	C4
Shaumyani = Shulaveri, Georgia	43	K7
Shaunavon, Canada	101	D7
Shaver L., U.S.A.	112	H7
Shaw →, Australia	88	D2
Shaw I., Australia	90	C4
Shawan, China	54	B3
Shawanaga, Canada	106	A4
Shawano, U.S.A.	104	C1
Shawinigan, Canada	98	C5
Shawnee, U.S.A.	109	H6
Shaybārā, Si. Arabia	64	E3
Shayib el Banat, Gebel, Egypt	76	B3
Shaykh Sa'īd, Iraq	67	F12
Shchekino, Russia	42	C3
Shcherbakov = Rybinsk, Russia	42	A4
Shchigry, Russia	42	E3
Shchors, Ukraine	41	G6
Shchuchinsk, Kazakhstan	44	D8
She Xian, Anhui, China	53	C12
She Xian, Hebei, China	50	F7
Shea, Guyana	121	C6
Shebekino, Russia	42	E3
Shebele = Scebeli, Wabi →, Somali Rep.	68	G3
Sheboygan, U.S.A.	104	D2
Shediac, Canada	99	C7
Sheelin, L., Ireland	15	C4
Sheep Haven, Ireland	15	A4
Sheerness, U.K.	13	F8
Sheet Harbour, Canada	99	D7
Sheffield, U.K.	12	D6
Sheffield, Ala., U.S.A.	105	H2
Sheffield, Mass., U.S.A.	107	D11
Sheffield, Pa., U.S.A.	106	E5
Sheffield, Tex., U.S.A.	109	K4
Sheho, Canada	101	C8
Shehojele, Ethiopia	77	E4
Shehong, China	52	B5
Sheikhpura, India	63	G11
Shek Hasan, Ethiopia	77	E4
Shekhupura, Pakistan	62	D5
Sheki = Şaki, Azerbaijan	43	K8
Shelburne, N.S., Canada	99	D6
Shelburne, Ont., Canada	98	D3
Shelburne, U.S.A.	107	B11
Shelburne B., Australia	90	A3
Shelburne Falls, U.S.A.	107	D12
Shelby, Mich., U.S.A.	104	D2
Shelby, Mont., U.S.A.	110	B8
Shelby, N.C., U.S.A.	105	H5
Shelby, Ohio, U.S.A.	106	F2
Shelbyville, Ill., U.S.A.	108	F10
Shelbyville, Ind., U.S.A.	104	F3
Shelbyville, Tenn., U.S.A.	105	H2
Sheldon, U.S.A.	108	D7
Sheldrake, Canada	99	B7
Shelikhova, Zaliv, Russia	45	D16
Shell Lake, Canada	101	C7
Shell Lakes, Australia	89	E4
Shellbrook, Canada	101	C7
Shellharbour, Australia	91	E5
Shelling Rocks, Ireland	15	E1
Shelon →, Russia	40	C6
Shelton, Conn., U.S.A.	107	E11
Shelton, Wash., U.S.A.	112	C3
Shemakha = Şamaxi, Azerbaijan	43	K9
Shen Xian, China	50	F8
Shenandoah, Iowa, U.S.A.	108	E7
Shenandoah, Pa., U.S.A.	107	F8
Shenandoah, Va., U.S.A.	104	F6
Shenandoah →, U.S.A.	104	F7
Shenchi, China	50	E7
Shendam, Nigeria	79	D6
Shendī, Sudan	77	D3
Sheng Xian, China	53	C13
Shengfang, China	50	E9
Shēngjergji, Albania	39	H3
Shēngjini, Albania	39	H2
Shenjingzi, China	51	B13
Shenmu, China	50	E6
Shennongjia, China	53	B8
Shenqiu, China	50	H8
Shenqiucheng, China	50	H8
Shensi = Shaanxi □, China	50	G5
Shenyang, China	51	D12
Shenzhen, China	53	F10
Sheopur Kalan, India	60	G10
Shepetivka, Ukraine	41	G4
Shepetovka = Shepetivka, Ukraine	41	G4
Shepparton, Australia	91	F4
Sheqi, China	50	H7
Sher Qila, Pakistan	63	A6
Sherborne, U.K.	13	G5
Sherbro I., S. Leone	78	D2
Sherbrooke, Canada	99	C5
Shereik, Sudan	76	D3
Sheridan, Ark., U.S.A.	109	H8
Sheridan, Wyo., U.S.A.	110	D10
Sherkot, India	63	E8
Sherman, U.S.A.	109	J6
Sherridon, Canada	101	B8
Sherwood, N. Dak., U.S.A.	108	A4
Sherwood, Tex., U.S.A.	109	K4
Sherwood Forest, U.K.	12	D6
Sheslay, Canada	100	B2
Sheslay →, Canada	100	B2
Shethanei L., Canada	101	B9
Shetland □, U.K.	14	A7
Shetland Is., U.K.	14	A7
Shewa □, Ethiopia	77	F4
Shewa Gimira, Ethiopia	77	F4
Sheyenne, U.S.A.	108	B5
Sheyenne →, U.S.A.	108	B6
Shibām, Yemen	68	D4
Shibata, Japan	48	F9
Shibecha, Japan	48	C12
Shibetsu, Japan	48	B11
Shibīn el Kôm, Egypt	76	H7
Shibīn el Qanâtir, Egypt	76	H7
Shibing, China	52	D7
Shibogama L., Canada	98	B2
Shibushi, Japan	49	J5
Shicheng, China	53	D11
Shickshock Mts. = Chic-Chocs, Mts., Canada	99	C6
Shidao, China	51	F12
Shidian, China	52	E2
Shido, Japan	49	G7
Shiel, L., U.K.	14	E3
Shiga □, Japan	49	G8
Shigaib, Sudan	73	E9
Shigu, China	52	D2
Shiguaigou, China	50	D6
Shihchiachuangi = Shijiazhuang, China	50	E8
Shijiazhuang, China	50	E8
Shijiu Hu, China	53	B12
Shikarpur, India	62	E8
Shikarpur, Pakistan	62	F3
Shikoku □, Japan	49	H6
Shikoku-Sanchi, Japan	49	H6
Shilabo, Ethiopia	68	F3
Shiliguri, India	61	F16
Shilka, Russia	45	D12
Shilka →, Russia	45	D13
Shillelagh, Ireland	15	D5
Shillong, India	61	G17
Shilo, West Bank	69	C4
Shilong, China	53	F9
Shilou, China	50	F6
Shilovo, Russia	42	C5
Shimabara, Japan	49	H5
Shimada, Japan	49	G9
Shimane □, Japan	49	G6
Shimanovsk, Russia	45	D13
Shimen, China	53	C8
Shimenjie, China	53	C11
Shimian, China	52	C4
Shimizu, Japan	49	G9
Shimodate, Japan	49	F9
Shimoga, India	60	N9
Shimoni, Kenya	82	C4
Shimonoseki, Japan	49	H5
Shimpuru Rapids, Angola	84	B2
Shimsk, Russia	40	C6
Shin, L., U.K.	14	C4
Shin-Tone →, Japan	49	G10
Shinan, China	52	F7
Shinano →, Japan	49	F9
Shīndand, Afghan.	60	C3
Shingleton, U.S.A.	98	C2
Shingū, Japan	49	H7
Shinjō, Japan	48	E10
Shinkafe, Nigeria	79	C6
Shinshār, Syria	69	A5
Shinyanga, Tanzania	82	C3
Shinyanga □, Tanzania	82	C3
Shiogama, Japan	48	E10
Shiojiri, Japan	49	F8
Ship I., U.S.A.	109	K10
Shipchenski Prokhod, Bulgaria	38	G8
Shiping, China	52	F4
Shipki La, India	60	D11
Shippegan, Canada	99	C7
Shippensburg, U.S.A.	106	F7
Shiprock, U.S.A.	111	H9
Shiqian, China	52	D7
Shiqma, N. →, Israel	69	D3
Shiquan, China	50	H5
Shīr Kūh, Iran	65	D7
Shiragami-Misaki, Japan	48	D10
Shirakawa, Fukushima, Japan	49	F10
Shirakawa, Gifu, Japan	49	F8
Shirane-San, Gumma, Japan	49	F9
Shirane-San, Yamanashi, Japan	49	G9
Shiraoi, Japan	48	C10
Shīrāz, Iran	65	D7
Shirbin, Egypt	76	H7
Shire →, Africa	83	F4
Shiretoko-Misaki, Japan	48	B12
Shirinab →, Pakistan	62	D2
Shiriya-Zaki, Japan	48	D10
Shiroishi, Japan	48	E10
Shīrvān, Iran	65	B8
Shirwa, L. = Chilwa, L., Malawi	83	F4
Shishou, China	53	C9
Shitai, China	53	B11
Shivpuri, India	62	G7
Shixian, China	51	C15
Shixing, China	53	E10
Shiyan, China	53	A8
Shiyata, Egypt	76	B2
Shizhu, China	52	C7
Shizong, China	52	E5
Shizuishan, China	50	E4
Shizuoka, Japan	49	G9
Shizuoka □, Japan	49	G9
Shklov = Shklow, Belarus	40	E6
Shklow, Belarus	40	E6
Shkoder = Shkodra, Albania	38	G2
Shkodra, Albania	38	G2
Shkumbini →, Albania	39	H2
Shmidta, O., Russia	45	A10
Shō-Gawa →, Japan	49	F8
Shoal Lake, Canada	101	C8
Shōdo-Shima, Japan	49	G7
Shoeburyness, U.K.	13	F8
Sholapur = Solapur, India	60	L9
Shologontsy, Russia	45	C12
Shōmrōn, West Bank	69	C4
Shoshone, Calif., U.S.A.	113	K10
Shoshone, Idaho, U.S.A.	110	E6
Shoshone L., U.S.A.	110	D8
Shoshone Mts., U.S.A.	110	G5
Shoshong, Botswana	84	C4
Shoshoni, U.S.A.	110	E9
Shostka, Ukraine	41	G7
Shou Xian, China	53	A11
Shouchang, China	53	C12
Shouguang, China	51	F10
Shouning, China	53	D12
Shouyang, China	50	F7
Show Low, U.S.A.	111	J9
Shpola, Ukraine	41	H6
Shreveport, U.S.A.	109	J8
Shrewsbury, U.K.	12	E5
Shrirampur, India	63	H13
Shropshire □, U.K.	13	E5
Shu, Kazakhstan	44	E8
Shu →, Kazakhstan	44	E8
Shuangbai, China	52	E3
Shuangcheng, China	51	B14
Shuangfeng, China	53	D9
Shuanggou, China	51	G9
Shuangjiang, China	52	F2
Shuangliao, China	51	C12
Shuangshanzi, China	51	D10
Shuangyang, China	51	C13
Shuangyashan, China	54	B8
Shucheng, China	53	B11
Shugozero, Russia	40	C8
Shuguri Falls, Tanzania	83	D4
Shuiji, China	53	D12
Shuiye, China	50	F8
Shujalpur, India	62	H7
Shukpa Kunzang, India	63	B8
Shulan, China	51	B14
Shulaveri, Georgia	43	K7
Shule, China	54	C2
Shumagin Is., U.S.A.	96	C4
Shumerlya, Russia	42	C8
Shumikha, Russia	44	D7
Shunchang, China	53	D11
Shunde, China	53	F9
Shungay, Kazakhstan	43	F8
Shungnak, U.S.A.	96	B4
Shuo Xian, China	50	E7
Shūr →, Iran	65	D7
Shūr Āb, Iran	65	C6
Shūr Gaz, Iran	65	D8
Shūrāb, Iran	65	C8
Shūrjestān, Iran	65	D7
Shūsf, Iran	65	D9
Shūsh, Iran	67	F13
Shūshtar, Iran	65	D6
Shuswap L., Canada	100	C5
Shuya, Russia	42	B5
Shuyang, China	51	G10
Shūzū, Iran	65	D7
Shwebo, Burma	61	H19
Shwegu, Burma	61	G20
Shweli →, Burma	61	H20
Shymkent, Kazakhstan	44	E7
Shyok, India	63	B8
Shyok →, Pakistan	63	B6
Si Chon, Thailand	59	H2
Si Kiang = Xi Jiang →, China	53	F9
Si-ngan = Xi'an, China	50	G5
Si Prachan, Thailand	58	E3
Si Racha, Thailand	58	F3
Si Xian, China	51	H9
Siahan Range, Pakistan	60	F4
Siaksriindrapura, Indonesia	56	D2
Sialkot, Pakistan	62	C6
Siam = Thailand ■, Asia	58	E4
Siantan, P., Indonesia	59	L6
Siāpo →, Venezuela	120	C4
Siāreh, Iran	65	D9
Siargao, Phil.	55	G7
Siari, Pakistan	63	B7
Siasi, Phil.	57	C6
Siasi I., Phil.	55	J4
Siátista, Greece	39	J4
Siau, Indonesia	57	D7
Siauliai, Lithuania	9	J20
Siaya □, Kenya	82	B3
Siazan = Siyäzän, Azerbaijan	43	K9
Sibâi, Gebel el, Egypt	76	B3
Sibari, Italy	35	C9
Sibay, Russia	44	D6
Sibayi, L., S. Africa	85	D5
Šibenik, Croatia	33	E12
Siberia, Russia	4	D13
Siberut, Indonesia	56	E1
Sibi, Pakistan	62	E2
Sibil, Indonesia	57	E10
Sibiti, Congo	80	E2
Sibiu, Romania	38	D7
Sibley, Iowa, U.S.A.	108	D7
Sibley, La., U.S.A.	109	J8
Sibolga, Indonesia	56	D1
Sibret, Belgium	17	J7
Sibsagar, India	61	F19
Sibu, Malaysia	56	D4
Sibuco, Phil.	55	H5
Sibuguey B., Phil.	55	H5
Sibut, C.A.R.	73	G8
Sibutu, Phil.	57	D5
Sibutu Group, Phil.	55	J3
Sibutu Passage, E. Indies	57	D5
Sibuyan, Phil.	55	E5
Sibuyan Sea, Phil.	55	E5
Sicamous, Canada	100	C5
Sichuan □, China	52	B5
Sicilia, Italy	35	E7
Sicilia □, Italy	35	E7
Sicilia, Canale di, Italy	34	E5
Sicilian Channel = Sicilia, Canale di, Italy	34	E5
Sicily = Sicilia, Italy	35	E7
Sicuani, Peru	124	C3
Siculiana, Italy	34	E6
Sidamo □, Ethiopia	77	G4
Sidaouet, Niger	79	B6
Sidári, Greece	37	A3
Siddeburen, Neths.	16	B9
Siddhapur, India	62	H5
Siddipet, India	60	K11
Sidéradougou, Burkina Faso	78	C4
Siderno, Italy	35	D9
Sídheros, Ákra, Greece	37	D8
Sidhirókastron, Greece	39	H6
Sîdi Abd el Rahmân, Egypt	76	H6
Sîdi Barrâni, Egypt	76	A2
Sidi-bel-Abbès, Algeria	75	A4
Sidi Bennour, Morocco	74	B3
Sidi Haneish, Egypt	76	A2
Sidi Kacem, Morocco	74	B3
Sidi Omar, Egypt	76	A1
Sidi Slimane, Morocco	74	B3
Sidi Smaïl, Morocco	74	B3
Sidlaw Hills, U.K.	14	E5
Sidley, Mt., Antarctica	5	D14
Sidmouth, U.K.	13	G4
Sidmouth, C., Australia	90	A3
Sidney, Canada	100	D4
Sidney, Mont., U.S.A.	108	B2
Sidney, N.Y., U.S.A.	107	D9
Sidney, Nebr., U.S.A.	108	E3
Sidney, Ohio, U.S.A.	104	E3
Sidoarjo, Indonesia	57	G15
Sidon = Saydā, Lebanon	69	B4
Sidra, G. of = Surt, Khalīj, Libya	73	B8
Siedlce, Poland	20	C12
Sieg →, Germany	18	E3
Siegburg, Germany	18	E3
Siegen, Germany	18	E4
Siem Pang, Cambodia	58	E6
Siem Reap, Cambodia	58	F4
Siena, Italy	33	E8
Sieradz, Poland	20	D8
Sierck-les-Bains, France	25	C13
Sierpc, Poland	20	C9
Sierpe, Bocas de la, Venezuela	121	B5
Sierra Blanca, U.S.A.	111	L11
Sierra Blanca Peak, U.S.A.	111	K11
Sierra City, U.S.A.	112	F6
Sierra Colorada, Argentina	128	E3
Sierra de Yeguas, Spain	31	H6
Sierra Gorda, Chile	126	A2
Sierra Grande, Argentina	128	E3
Sierra Leone ■, W. Afr.	78	D2
Sierra Madre, Mexico	115	D6
Sierra Mojada, Mexico	114	B4
Sierraville, U.S.A.	112	F6
Sierre, Switz.	22	D5
Sifnos, Greece	39	N7
Sifton, Canada	101	C8
Sifton Pass, Canada	100	B3
Sig, Algeria	75	A4
Sigdal, Norway	10	D3
Sigean, France	26	E6
Sighetu-Marmatiei, Romania	38	B5
Sighişoara, Romania	38	C7
Sigli, Indonesia	56	C1
Siglufjörður, Iceland	8	C4
Sigmaringen, Germany	19	G5
Signakhi = Tsnori, Georgia	43	K7
Signal, U.S.A.	113	L13
Signal Pk., U.S.A.	113	M12
Signau, Switz.	22	C5
Signy-l'Abbaye, France	25	C11
Sigsig, Ecuador	120	D2
Sigtuna, Sweden	10	E11
Sigüenza, Spain	28	D2
Siguiri, Guinea	78	C3
Sigulda, Latvia	9	H21
Sigurd, U.S.A.	111	G8
Sihanoukville = Kompong Som, Cambodia	59	G4
Sihaus, Peru	124	B2
Sihui, China	53	F9
Siikajoki →, Finland	8	D21
Siilinjärvi, Finland	8	E22
Siirt, Turkey	67	D9
Sijarira Ra., Zimbabwe	83	F2
Sikao, Thailand	59	J2
Sikar, India	62	F6
Sikasso, Mali	78	C3
Sikeston, U.S.A.	109	G10
Sikhote Alin, Khrebet, Russia	45	E14
Sikhote Alin Ra. = Sikhote Alin, Khrebet, Russia	45	E14
Sikiá, Greece	39	J6
Síkinos, Greece	39	N8
Sikkani Chief →, Canada	100	B4
Sikkim □, India	61	F16
Sikotu-Ko, Japan	48	C10
Sil →, Spain	30	C3
Silacayoapan, Mexico	115	D5
Silandro, Italy	32	B7
Silay, Phil.	55	F5
Silba, Croatia	33	D11
Silchar, India	61	G18
Silcox, Canada	101	B10
Şile, Turkey	66	B3
Silenrieux, Belgium	17	H4
Siler City, U.S.A.	105	H6
Silesia = Śląsk, Poland	20	E6
Silet, Algeria	75	D5
Silgarhi Doti, Nepal	63	E9
Silghat, India	61	F18
Silifke, Turkey	66	D5
Siliguri = Shiliguri, India	61	F16
Siling Co, China	54	C3
Silíqua, Italy	34	C1
Silistra, Bulgaria	38	E10
Silivri, Turkey	66	B3
Siljan, Sweden	9	F16
Silkeborg, Denmark	11	H3
Sillajhuay, Cordillera, Chile	124	D4
Sillamäe, Estonia	9	G22
Sillustani, Peru	124	D3
Sillé-le-Guillaume, France	24	D6
Silopi, Turkey	67	D10
Silsbee, U.S.A.	109	K7
Šilute, Lithuania	9	J19
Silva Porto = Kuito, Angola	81	G3
Silvan, Turkey	67	C9
Silvaplana, Switz.	23	D9
Silver City, N. Mex., U.S.A.	111	K9
Silver City, Nev., U.S.A.	110	G4
Silver Cr. →, U.S.A.	110	E4
Silver Creek, U.S.A.	106	D5
Silver L., Calif., U.S.A.	112	G6
Silver L., Calif., U.S.A.	113	K10
Silver Lake, U.S.A.	110	E3
Silver Streams, S. Africa	84	D3
Silverton, Colo., U.S.A.	111	H10
Silverton, Tex., U.S.A.	109	H4
Silves, Portugal	31	H2
Silvi Marina, Italy	33	F11
Silvia, Colombia	120	C2
Silvies →, U.S.A.	110	E4
Silvolde, Neths.	16	E8
Silvretta-Gruppe, Switz.	23	C10
Silwa Bahari, Egypt	76	C3
Silz, Austria	19	H6
Sim, C., Morocco	74	B3
Simanggang, Malaysia	56	D4
Simao, China	52	F3
Simão Dias, Brazil	122	D4
Simard, L., Canada	98	C4
Şimareh →, Iran	67	F12
Simav, Turkey	66	C3
Simba, Tanzania	82	C4
Simbach, Germany	19	G9
Simbirsk, Russia	42	C9
Simbo, Tanzania	82	C2
Simcoe, Canada	98	D3
Simcoe, L., Canada	98	D4
Simenga, Russia	45	C11
Simeto →, Italy	35	E8
Simeulue, Indonesia	56	D1

Simferopol, *Ukraine* 41 K8
Símí, *Greece* 66 D2
Simi Valley, *U.S.A.* 113 L8
Simikot, *Nepal* 63 E9
Simití, *Colombia* 120 B3
Simla, *India* 62 D7
Şimleu-Silvaniei, *Romania* . 38 B5
Simme →, *Switz.* 22 C4
Simmern, *Germany* 19 F3
Simmie, *Canada* 101 D7
Simmler, *U.S.A.* 113 K7
Simões, *Brazil* 122 C3
Simojoki →, *Finland* 8 D21
Simojovel, *Mexico* 115 D6
Simonette →, *Canada* 100 B5
Simonstown, *S. Africa* 84 E2
Simplício Mendes, *Brazil* . 122 C3
Simplon, *Switz.* 22 D6
Simplon P., *Switz.* 22 D6
Simplon Pass = Simplon
 P., *Switz.* 22 D6
Simplon Tunnel, *Switz.* ... 22 D6
Simpson Desert, *Australia* . 90 D2
Simpungdong, *N. Korea* .. 51 D15
Simrishamn, *Sweden* 9 J16
Simunjan, *Malaysia* 56 D4
Simushir, Ostrov, *Russia* .. 45 E16
Sinabang, *Indonesia* 56 D1
Sinadogo, *Somali Rep.* ... 68 F4
Sinai = Es Sînâ', *Egypt* ... 76 J8
Sinai,Mt. = Gebel Mûsa,
 Egypt 76 J8
Sinai, Mt. = Mûsa, G.,
 Egypt 76 J8
Sinai Peninsula, *Egypt* ... 69 F2
Sinaia, *Romania* 38 D8
Sinaloa □, *Mexico* 114 C3
Sinaloa de Levya, *Mexico* . 114 B3
Sinalunga, *Italy* 33 E8
Sinan, *China* 52 D7
Sinarádhes, *Greece* 37 A3
Sināwan, *Libya* 75 B7
Sincan, *Turkey* 66 B5
Sincé, *Colombia* 120 B2
Sincelejo, *Colombia* 120 B2
Sinchang, *N. Korea* 51 D15
Sinchang-ni, *N. Korea* ... 51 E14
Sinclair, *U.S.A.* 110 F10
Sinclair Mills, *Canada* ... 100 C4
Sincorá, Serra do, *Brazil* . 123 D3
Sind, *Pakistan* 62 G3
Sind □, *Pakistan* 62 F3
Sind →, *India* 63 B6
Sind Sagar Doab, *Pakistan* 62 D4
Sindal, *Denmark* 11 G4
Sindangan, *Phil.* 55 G5
Sindangbarang, *Indonesia* . 57 G12
Sinde, *Zambia* 83 F2
Sinegorskiy, *Russia* 43 G5
Sinelnikovo =
 Synelnykove, *Ukraine* .. 41 H8
Sines, *Portugal* 31 H2
Sines, C. de, *Portugal* 31 H2
Sineu, *Spain* 36 B10
Sinfra, *Ivory C.* 78 D3
Sing Buri, *Thailand* 58 E3
Singa, *Sudan* 77 E3
Singapore ■, *Asia* 59 M4
Singapore, Straits of, *Asia* . 59 M5
Singaraja, *Indonesia* 56 F5
Singen, *Germany* 19 H4
Singida, *Tanzania* 82 C3
Singida □, *Tanzania* 82 D3
Singitikós Kólpos, *Greece* . 39 J6
Singkaling Hkamti, *Burma* . 61 G19
Singkawang, *Indonesia* ... 56 D3
Singleton, *Australia* 91 E5
Singleton, Mt., *N. Terr.,*
 Australia 88 D5
Singleton, Mt., *W. Austral.,*
 Australia 89 E2
Singoli, *India* 62 G6
Singora = Songkhla,
 Thailand 59 J3
Singosan, *N. Korea* 51 E14
Sinhung, *N. Korea* 51 D14
Sîni □, *Egypt* 69 F2
Siniscóla, *Italy* 34 B2
Sinj, *Croatia* 33 E13
Sinjai, *Indonesia* 57 F6
Sinjār, *Iraq* 67 D9
Sinkat, *Sudan* 76 D4
Sinkiang Uighur = Xinjiang
 Uygur Zizhiqu □, *China* 54 B3
Sinmak, *N. Korea* 51 E14
Sínnai, *Italy* 34 C2
Sinni →, *Italy* 35 B9
Sinnuris, *Egypt* 76 J7
Sinoe, L., *Romania* 38 E11
Sinop, *Turkey* 66 A6
Sinpo, *N. Korea* 51 E15
Sins, *Switz.* 23 B6
Sinsk, *Russia* 45 C13
Sint-Amandsberg, *Belgium* 17 F3
Sint Annaland, *Neths.* ... 17 E4
Sint Annaparoch, *Neths.* .. 16 B7
Sint-Denijs, *Belgium* 17 G2
Sint Eustatius, I.,
 Neth. Ant. 117 C7
Sint-Genesius-Rode,
 Belgium 17 G4
Sint-Gillis-Waas, *Belgium* . 17 F4
Sint-Huibrechts-Lille,
 Belgium 17 F6
Sint-Katelijne-Waver,
 Belgium 17 F5
Sint-Kruis, *Belgium* 17 F2

Sint-Laureins, *Belgium* ... 17 F3
Sint Maarten, I., *W. Indies* 117 C7
Sint-Michiels, *Belgium* ... 17 F2
Sint Nicolaasga, *Neths.* ... 16 C7
Sint Niklaas, *Belgium* ... 17 F4
Sint Oedenrode, *Neths.* ... 17 E6
Sint Pancras, *Neths.* 16 C5
Sint Philipsland, *Neths.* .. 17 E4
Sint Truiden, *Belgium* ... 17 G6
Sint Willebrord, *Neths.* ... 17 E5
Sîntana, *Romania* 38 C4
Sintang, *Indonesia* 56 D4
Sintjohannesga, *Neths.* ... 16 C7
Sinton, *U.S.A.* 109 L6
Sintra, *Portugal* 31 G1
Sinüiju, *N. Korea* 51 D13
Sinyukha →, *Ukraine* ... 41 H6
Siocon, *Phil.* 55 H5
Siófok, *Hungary* 21 J8
Sioma, *Zambia* 84 B3
Sion, *Switz.* 22 D4
Sioux City, *U.S.A.* 108 D6
Sioux Falls, *U.S.A.* 108 D6
Sioux Lookout, *Canada* .. 98 B1
Sipalay, *Phil.* 55 G5
Siping, *China* 51 C13
Sipiwesk L., *Canada* ... 101 B9
Sipura, *Indonesia* 56 E1
Siquia →, *Nic.* 116 D3
Siquijor, *Phil.* 55 G5
Siquirres, *Costa Rica* 116 D3
Siquisique, *Venezuela* ... 120 A4
Sir Edward Pellew Group,
 Australia 90 B2
Sir Graham Moore Is.,
 Australia 88 B4
Sira →, *Norway* 9 G12
Siracusa, *Italy* 35 E8
Sirajganj, *Bangla.* 63 G13
Sirakoro, *Mali* 78 C3
Şiran, *Turkey* 67 B8
Sirasso, *Ivory C.* 78 D3
Sīrdān, *Iran* 67 D13
Sirdaryo = Syrdarya →,
 Kazakhstan 44 E7
Sirer, *Spain* 36 C7
Siret, *Romania* 38 B9
Siret →, *Romania* 38 D11
Şiria, *Romania* 38 C4
Sirino, Mte., *Italy* 35 B8
Sírna, *Greece* 39 N9
Sirnach, *Switz.* 23 B7
Şırnak, *Turkey* 67 D10
Sirohi, *India* 62 G5
Sironj, *India* 62 G7
Síros, *Greece* 39 M7
Sirretta Pk., *U.S.A.* 113 K8
Sirsa, *India* 62 E6
Siruela, *Spain* 31 G5
Sisak, *Croatia* 33 C13
Sisaket, *Thailand* 58 E5
Sisante, *Spain* 29 F2
Sisargas, Is., *Spain* 30 B2
Sishen, *S. Africa* 84 D3
Sishui, *Henan, China* ... 50 G7
Sishui, *Shandong, China* . 51 G9
Sisipuk L., *Canada* 101 B8
Sisophon, *Cambodia* 58 F4
Sissach, *Switz.* 22 B5
Sisseton, *U.S.A.* 108 C6
Sissonne, *France* 25 C10
Sīstān va Balūchestān □,
 Iran 65 E9
Sisteron, *France* 27 D9
Sisters, *U.S.A.* 110 D3
Sitamarhi, *India* 63 F11
Sitapur, *India* 63 F9
Siteki, *Swaziland* 85 D5
Sitges, *Spain* 28 D6
Sitía, *Greece* 37 D8
Sítio da Abadia, *Brazil* .. 123 D2
Sitka, *U.S.A.* 96 C6
Sitoti, *Botswana* 84 C3
Sitra, *Egypt* 76 B2
Sittang Myit →, *Burma* .. 61 L20
Sittard, *Neths.* 17 G7
Sittensen, *Germany* 18 B5
Sittona, *Eritrea* 77 E4
Sittwe, *Burma* 61 J18
Siuna, *Nic.* 116 D3
Siuri, *India* 63 H12
Sivana, *India* 62 E8
Sīvand, *Iran* 65 D7
Sivas, *Turkey* 66 C7
Siverek, *Turkey* 67 D8
Sivrihisar, *Turkey* 66 C4
Sivry, *Belgium* 17 H4
Sîwa, *Egypt* 76 B2
Sīwa, El Wâhât es, *Egypt* . 76 B2
Siwalik Range, *Nepal* ... 63 F10
Siwan, *India* 63 F11
Siyâl, Jazâ'ir, *Egypt* 76 C4
Siyäzän, *Azerbaijan* 43 K9
Sizewell, *U.K.* 13 E9
Siziwang Qi, *China* 50 D6
Sjælland, *Denmark* 11 J5
Sjællands Odde, *Denmark* 11 J5
Sjælevad, *Sweden* 10 A12
Sjenica, *Serbia, Yug.* ... 21 M10
Sjoa, *Norway* 10 C3
Sjöbo, *Sweden* 11 J7
Sjösa, *Sweden* 11 F11
Sjumen = Šumen, *Bulgaria* 38 F9
Skadovsk, *Ukraine* 41 J7
Skaftafell, *Iceland* 8 D5
Skagafjörður, *Iceland* ... 8 D4
Skagastølstindane, *Norway* 9 F12

Skagen, *Denmark* 11 G4
Skagerrak, *Denmark* 11 G3
Skagit →, *U.S.A.* 112 B4
Skagway, *U.S.A.* 100 B1
Skala-Podilska, *Ukraine* . 41 H4
Skala Podolskaya = Skala-
 Podilska, *Ukraine* 41 H4
Skalat, *Ukraine* 41 H3
Skalni Dol = Kamenyak,
 Bulgaria 38 F9
Skals, *Denmark* 11 H3
Skanderborg, *Denmark* .. 11 H3
Skåne, *Sweden* 9 J15
Skanör, *Sweden* 11 J6
Skara, *Sweden* 9 G15
Skardu, *Pakistan* 63 B6
Skärrild, *Denmark* 11 J2
Skarzysko-Kamienna,
 Poland 20 D10
Skebokvarn, *Sweden* ... 10 E10
Skeena →, *Canada* ... 100 C2
Skeena Mts., *Canada* ... 100 B3
Skegness, *U.K.* 12 D8
Skeldon, *Guyana* 121 B6
Skellefte älv →, *Sweden* . 8 D19
Skellefteå, *Sweden* 8 D19
Skelleftehamn, *Sweden* .. 8 D19
Skender Vakuf, *Bos.-H.* . 21 L7
Skene, *Sweden* 11 G6
Skerries, The, *U.K.* 12 D3
Skhoinoúsa, *Greece* 39 N8
Ski, *Norway* 10 E4
Skíathos, *Greece* 39 K6
Skibbereen, *Ireland* ... 15 E2
Skiddaw, *U.K.* 12 C4
Skien, *Norway* 10 E3
Skierniewice, *Poland* ... 20 D10
Skikda, *Algeria* 75 A6
Skilloura, *Cyprus* 37 D12
Skinári, Ákra, *Greece* .. 39 M3
Skipton, *Australia* 91 F3
Skipton, *U.K.* 12 D5
Skíros, *Greece* 39 L7
Skive, *Denmark* 11 H3
Skjálfandafljót →, *Iceland* 8 D5
Skjálfandi, *Iceland* 8 C5
Skjeberg, *Norway* 10 E5
Skjern, *Denmark* 11 J2
Škofja Loka, *Slovenia* .. 33 B11
Skoghall, *Sweden* 9 G15
Skole, *Ukraine* 41 H2
Skópelos, *Greece* 39 K6
Skopí, *Greece* 37 D8
Skopin, *Russia* 42 D4
Skopje, *Macedonia* 39 G4
Skórcz, *Poland* 20 B8
Skövde, *Sweden* 9 G15
Skovorodino, *Russia* ... 45 D13
Skowhegan, *U.S.A.* ... 99 D6
Skownan, *Canada* 101 C9
Skradin, *Croatia* 33 E12
Skreanäs, *Sweden* 11 H6
Skull, *Ireland* 15 E2
Skultorp, *Sweden* 11 F7
Skunk →, *U.S.A.* 108 E9
Skuodas, *Lithuania* ... 9 H19
Skurup, *Sweden* 11 J7
Skutskär, *Sweden* 10 D11
Skvyra, *Ukraine* 41 H5
Skwierzyna, *Poland* ... 20 C5
Skye, *U.K.* 14 D2
Skykomish, *U.S.A.* ... 110 C3
Skyros = Skíros, *Greece* . 39 L7
Slættaratindur, *Færoe Is.* . 8 E9
Slagelse, *Denmark* 11 J5
Slagharen, *Neths.* 16 C9
Slamet, *Indonesia* 56 F3
Slaney →, *Ireland* 15 D5
Slangerup, *Denmark* ... 11 J6
Slano, *Croatia* 21 N7
Slantsy, *Russia* 40 C5
Ślask, *Poland* 20 E6
Slate Is., *Canada* 98 C2
Slatina, *Romania* 38 E7
Slaton, *U.S.A.* 109 J4
Slave →, *Canada* 100 A6
Slave Coast, *W. Afr.* ... 79 D5
Slave Lake, *Canada* ... 100 B6
Slave Pt., *Canada* 100 A5
Slavgorod, *Russia* 44 D8
Slavonska Požega, *Croatia* 21 K7
Slavonski Brod, *Croatia* . 21 K8
Slavuta, *Ukraine* 41 G4
Slavyanka, *Russia* 48 C5
Slavyansk = Slovyansk,
 Ukraine 41 H9
Slavyansk-na-Kubani,
 Russia 43 H4
Slawharad, *Belarus* ... 40 F6
Sławno, *Poland* 20 A6
Sławoborze, *Poland* ... 20 B5
Sleaford, *U.K.* 12 E7
Sleaford B., *Australia* .. 91 E2
Sleat, Sd. of, *U.K.* 14 D3
Sleeper Is., *Canada* ... 97 C11
Sleepy Eye, *U.S.A.* ... 108 C7
Sleidinge, *Belgium* ... 17 F3
Sleman, *Indonesia* 57 G14
Slemon L., *Canada* ... 100 A5
Slidell, *U.S.A.* 109 K10
Sliedrecht, *Neths.* 16 E5
Sliema, *Malta* 37 D2
Slieve Aughty, *Ireland* . 15 C3
Slieve Bloom, *Ireland* .. 15 C4
Slieve Donard, *U.K.* ... 15 B6

Slieve Gullion, *U.K.* 15 B5
Slieve Mish, *Ireland* ... 15 D2
Slievenamon, *Ireland* .. 15 D4
Sligeach = Sligo, *Ireland* . 15 B3
Sligo, *Ireland* 15 B3
Sligo □, *Ireland* 15 B3
Sligo B., *Ireland* 15 B3
Slijpe, *Belgium* 17 F1
Slikkerveer, *Neths.* ... 16 E5
Slite, *Sweden* 9 H18
Sliven, *Bulgaria* 38 G9
Slivnitsa, *Bulgaria* ... 38 G6
Sljeme, *Croatia* 33 C12
Sloan, *U.S.A.* 113 K11
Sloansville, *U.S.A.* ... 107 D10
Slobozia, *Romania* ... 38 E10
Slocan, *Canada* 100 D5
Slochteren, *Neths.* ... 16 B9
Slöinge, *Sweden* 11 H6
Slonim, *Belarus* 41 F3
Slotermeer, *Neths.* ... 16 C7
Slough, *U.K.* 13 F7
Sloughhouse, *U.S.A.* . 112 G5
Slovak Rep. ■, *Europe* . 20 G9
Slovakia = Slovak Rep. ■,
 Europe 20 G9
Slovakian Ore Mts. =
 Slovenské Rudohorie,
 Slovak Rep. 20 G9
Slovenia ■, *Europe* ... 33 C11
Slovenija = Slovenia ■,
 Europe 33 C11
Slovenj Gradec, *Slovenia* . 33 B12
Slovenska Bistrica, *Slovenia* 33 B12
Slovenská Republika =
 Slovak Rep. ■, *Europe* . 20 G9
Slovenské Rudohorie,
 Slovak Rep. 20 G9
Slovyansk, *Ukraine* ... 41 H9
Słubice, *Poland* 20 C4
Sluch →, *Ukraine* ... 41 G4
Sluis, *Neths.* 17 F2
Slunj, *Croatia* 33 C12
Słupca, *Poland* 20 C7
Słupsk, *Poland* 20 A7
Slurry, *S. Africa* 84 D4
Slutsk, *Belarus* 41 F4
Slyne Hd., *Ireland* ... 15 C1
Slyudyanka, *Russia* .. 45 D11
Småland, *Sweden* ... 9 H16
Smålandsfarvandet,
 Denmark 11 J5
Smålandsstenar, *Sweden* . 11 G7
Smalltree L., *Canada* .. 101 A7
Smara, *Morocco* 72 B3
Smarhon, *Belarus* ... 40 E4
Smarje, *Slovenia* 33 B12
Smartt Syndicate Dam,
 S. Africa 84 E3
Smartville, *U.S.A.* ... 112 F5
Smeaton, *Canada* ... 101 C8
Smederevo, *Serbia, Yug.* . 21 L10
Smederevska Palanka,
 Serbia, Yug. 21 L10
Smela = Smila, *Ukraine* . 41 H6
Smethport, *U.S.A.* ... 106 E6
Smidovich, *Russia* ... 45 E14
Smila, *Ukraine* 41 H6
Smilde, *Neths.* 16 C8
Smiley, *Canada* 101 C7
Smith, *Canada* 100 B6
Smith →, *Canada* ... 100 B3
Smith Arm, *Canada* .. 96 B7
Smith Center, *U.S.A.* . 108 F5
Smith Sund, *Greenland* . 4 B4
Smithburne →, *Australia* 90 B3
Smithers, *Canada* ... 100 C3
Smithfield, *S. Africa* .. 85 E4
Smithfield, *N.C., U.S.A.* 105 H6
Smithfield, *Utah, U.S.A.* 110 F8
Smiths Falls, *Canada* .. 98 D4
Smithton, *Australia* .. 90 G4
Smithtown, *Australia* . 91 E5
Smithville, *Canada* ... 106 C5
Smithville, *U.S.A.* ... 109 K6
Smoky →, *Canada* ... 100 B5
Smoky Bay, *Australia* . 91 E1
Smoky Falls, *Canada* .. 98 B3
Smoky Hill →, *U.S.A.* 108 F6
Smoky Lake, *Canada* .. 100 C6
Smøla, *Norway* 10 A2
Smolensk, *Russia* ... 40 E7
Smolikas, Óros, *Greece* . 39 J3
Smolník, *Slovak Rep.* .. 20 G10
Smolyan, *Bulgaria* ... 39 H7
Smooth Rock Falls, *Canada* 98 C3
Smoothstone L., *Canada* . 101 C7
Smorgon = Smarhon,
 Belarus 40 E4
Smyadovo, *Bulgaria* .. 38 F10
Smyrna = İzmir, *Turkey* . 66 C2
Snæfell, *Iceland* 8 D6
Snaefell, *U.K.* 12 C3
Snæfellsjökull, *Iceland* . 8 D2
Snake →, *U.S.A.* ... 110 C4
Snake I., *Australia* ... 91 F4
Snake L., *Canada* 101 B7
Snake Range, *U.S.A.* .. 110 G6
Snake River Plain, *U.S.A.* 110 E7
Snarum, *Norway* 10 D3
Snåsavatnet, *Norway* .. 8 D14
Snedsted, *Denmark* ... 11 H2
Sneek, *Neths.* 16 B7
Sneeker-meer, *Neths.* .. 16 B7
Sneeuberge, *S. Africa* .. 84 E3
Snejbjerg, *Denmark* .. 11 H2
Snelling, *U.S.A.* 112 H6

Snezhnoye, *Ukraine* 41 J10
Snežnik, *Slovenia* 33 C11
Snigirevka = Snihurivka,
 Ukraine 41 J7
Snihurivka, *Ukraine* ... 41 J7
Snizort, L., *U.K.* 14 D2
Snøhetta, *Norway* 10 B3
Snohomish, *U.S.A.* ... 112 C4
Snoul, *Cambodia* 59 F6
Snow Hill, *U.S.A.* ... 104 F8
Snow Lake, *Canada* ... 101 C8
Snow Mt., *U.S.A.* 112 F4
Snowbird L., *Canada* .. 101 A8
Snowdon, *U.K.* 12 D3
Snowdrift, *Canada* ... 101 A6
Snowdrift →, *Canada* . 101 A6
Snowflake, *U.S.A.* ... 111 J8
Snowshoe Pk., *U.S.A.* . 110 B6
Snowtown, *Australia* .. 91 E2
Snowville, *U.S.A.* 110 F7
Snowy →, *Australia* .. 91 F4
Snowy Mts., *Australia* . 91 F4
Snug Corner, *Bahamas* . 117 B5
Snyatyn, *Ukraine* 41 H3
Snyder, *Okla., U.S.A.* . 109 H5
Snyder, *Tex., U.S.A.* .. 109 J4
Soacha, *Colombia* 120 C3
Soahanina, *Madag.* ... 85 B7
Soalala, *Madag.* 85 B8
Soan →, *Pakistan* ... 62 C4
Soanierana-Ivongo, *Madag.* 85 B8
Soap Lake, *U.S.A.* ... 110 C4
Sobat, Nahr →, *Sudan* ... 77 F3
Sobhapur, *India* 62 H8
Sobinka, *Russia* 42 C5
Sobolevo, *Russia* 45 D16
Sobótka, *Poland* 20 E6
Sobradinho, Reprêsa de,
 Brazil 122 C3
Sobrado, *Spain* 30 B2
Sobral, *Brazil* 122 B3
Sobreira Formosa, *Portugal* 31 F3
Soc Giang, *Vietnam* ... 58 A6
Soc Trang, *Vietnam* ... 59 H5
Soča →, *Europe* 33 B10
Sochaczew, *Poland* ... 20 C10
Soch'e = Shache, *China* . 54 C2
Sochi, *Russia* 43 J4
Société, Is. de la, *Pac. Oc.* 93 J12
Society Is. = Société, Is. de
 la, *Pac. Oc.* 93 J12
Socompa, Portezuelo de,
 Chile 126 A2
Socorro, *Colombia* ... 120 B3
Socorro, *U.S.A.* 111 J10
Socorro, I., *Mexico* .. 114 D2
Socotra, *Ind. Oc.* ... 68 E5
Socuéllmos, *Spain* ... 29 F2
Soda L., *U.S.A.* 111 J5
Soda Plains, *India* ... 63 B8
Soda Springs, *U.S.A.* . 110 E8
Sodankylä, *Finland* .. 8 C22
Söderhamn, *Sweden* .. 9 F17
Söderköping, *Sweden* . 9 G17
Södermanland, *Sweden* . 9 G17
Södermanlands län □,
 Sweden 10 E10
Sodiri, *Sudan* 77 E2
Sodo, *Ethiopia* 77 F4
Sodražica, *Slovenia* .. 33 C11
Sodus, *U.S.A.* 106 C7
Soekmekaar, *S. Africa* .. 85 C4
Soest, *Germany* 18 D4
Soest, *Neths.* 16 D6
Soestdijk, *Neths.* ... 16 D6
Sofádhes, *Greece* ... 39 K5
Sofara, *Mali* 78 C4
Sofia = Sofiya, *Bulgaria* . 38 G6
Sofia →, *Madag.* ... 85 B8
Sofievka, *Ukraine* ... 41 H7
Sofikón, *Greece* 39 M6
Sofiya, *Bulgaria* 38 G6
Sofiysk, *Russia* 45 D14
Sôfu-Gan, *Japan* 49 K10
Sogakofe, *Ghana* ... 79 D5
Sogamoso, *Colombia* . 120 B3
Sogār, *Iran* 65 E8
Sögel, *Germany* 18 C3
Sogndalsfjøra, *Norway* . 9 F12
Søgne, *Norway* 9 G12
Sognefjorden, *Norway* . 9 F11
Söğüt, *Turkey* 66 B4
Sögwi-po, *S. Korea* .. 51 H14
Soh, *Iran* 65 C6
Sohâg, *Egypt* 76 B3
Sohano, *P.N.G.* 88 H7
Sŏhori, *N. Korea* ... 51 D15
Soignies, *Belgium* ... 17 G4
Soira, *Eritrea* 77 E4
Soissons, *France* ... 25 C10
Sôja, *Japan* 49 G6
Sojat, *India* 62 G5
Sok →, *Russia* 42 D10
Sokal, *Ukraine* 41 G3
Söke, *Turkey* 66 D2
Sokelo, *Zaïre* 83 D1
Sokhumi, *Georgia* .. 43 J5
Sokki, Oued In →, *Algeria* 75 C5
Sokna, *Norway* 10 D4
Soknedal, *Norway* .. 10 B4
Soko Banja, *Serbia, Yug.* . 21 M11
Sokodé, *Togo* 79 D5
Sokol, *Russia* 40 C11
Sokółka, *Poland* ... 20 B13
Sokolo, *Mali* 78 C3
Sokołów Małopolski, *Poland* 20 E12
Sokołów Podlaski, *Poland* 20 C12

Staffordshire

Sokoto, *Nigeria* 79 C6
Sokoto □, *Nigeria* 79 C6
Sokoto →, *Nigeria* 79 C5
Sol Iletsk, *Russia* 44 D6
Solai, *Kenya* 82 B4
Solano, *Phil.* 55 C4
Solapur, *India* 60 L9
Solares, *Spain* 30 B7
Soléa □, *Cyprus* 37 D12
Solec Kujawski, *Poland* 20 B8
Soledad, *Colombia* 120 A3
Soledad, *U.S.A.* 111 H3
Soledad, *Venezuela* 121 B5
Solent, The, *U.K.* 13 G6
Solenzara, *France* 27 G13
Solesmes, *France* 25 B10
Solfonn, *Norway* 9 F12
Solhan, *Turkey* 67 C9
Soligorsk = Salihorsk, *Belarus* 41 F4
Solikamsk, *Russia* 44 D6
Solila, *Madag.* 85 C8
Solimões = Amazonas →, *S. Amer.* 121 D7
Solingen, *Germany* 17 F10
Sollebrunn, *Sweden* 11 F6
Sollefteå, *Sweden* 10 A11
Sollentuna, *Sweden* 10 E11
Sóller, *Spain* 36 B9
Solling, *Germany* 18 D5
Solna, *Sweden* 10 E12
Solnechnogorsk, *Russia* 42 B3
Sologne, *France* 25 E8
Solok, *Indonesia* 56 E2
Sololá, *Guatemala* 116 D1
Solomon, N. Fork →, *U.S.A.* 108 F5
Solomon, S. Fork →, *U.S.A.* 108 F5
Solomon Is. ■, *Pac. Oc.* 92 H7
Solon, *China* 54 B7
Solon Springs, *U.S.A.* 108 B9
Solonópole, *Brazil* 122 C4
Solor, *Indonesia* 57 F6
Solotcha, *Russia* 42 C4
Solothurn, *Switz.* 22 B5
Solothurn □, *Switz.* 22 B5
Solsona, *Spain* 28 D6
Šolta, *Croatia* 33 E13
Solṭānābād, *Khorāsān, Iran* 65 C8
Solṭānābād, *Khorāsān, Iran* 65 B8
Solṭānābād, *Markazī, Iran* 65 C6
Soltau, *Germany* 18 C5
Soltsy, *Russia* 40 C6
Solunska Glava, *Macedonia* 39 H4
Solvang, *U.S.A.* 113 L6
Solvay, *U.S.A.* 107 C8
Sölvesborg, *Sweden* 9 H16
Solway Firth, *U.K.* 12 C4
Solwezi, *Zambia* 83 E2
Sōma, *Japan* 48 F10
Soma, *Turkey* 66 C2
Somali Rep. ■, *Africa* 68 F4
Somalia = Somali Rep. ■, *Africa* 68 F4
Sombernon, *France* 25 E11
Sombor, *Serbia, Yug.* 21 K9
Sombra, *Canada* 106 D2
Sombrerete, *Mexico* 114 C4
Sombrero, *Anguilla* 117 C7
Someren, *Neths.* 17 F7
Somers, *U.S.A.* 110 B6
Somerset, *Canada* 101 D9
Somerset, *Colo., U.S.A.* 111 G10
Somerset, *Ky., U.S.A.* 104 G3
Somerset, *Mass., U.S.A.* 107 E13
Somerset, *Pa., U.S.A.* 106 F5
Somerset □, *U.K.* 13 F5
Somerset East, *S. Africa* 84 E4
Somerset I., *Canada* 96 A10
Somerset West, *S. Africa* 84 E2
Somerton, *U.S.A.* 111 K6
Somerville, *U.S.A.* 107 F10
Someş →, *Romania* 38 B5
Someşul Mare →, *Romania* 38 B7
Somma Lombardo, *Italy* 32 C5
Somma Vesuviana, *Italy* 35 B7
Sommariva, *Australia* 91 D4
Sommatino, *Italy* 34 E6
Somme □, *France* 25 C9
Somme →, *France* 25 B8
Somme, B. de la, *France* 24 B8
Sommelsdijk, *Neths.* 16 E4
Sommepy-Tahure, *France* 25 C11
Sömmerda, *Germany* 18 D7
Sommesous, *France* 25 D11
Sommières, *France* 27 E8
Somoto, *Nic.* 116 D2
Sompolno, *Poland* 20 C8
Somport, Paso, *Spain* 28 C4
Somport, Puerto de, *Spain* 28 C4
Somuncurá, Meseta de, *Argentina* 128 B3
Son, *Neths.* 17 E6
Son, *Norway* 10 E4
Son, *Spain* 30 C2
Son Ha, *Vietnam* 58 E7
Son Hoa, *Vietnam* 58 F7
Son La, *Vietnam* 58 B4
Son Tay, *Vietnam* 58 B5
Soná, *Panama* 116 E3
Sonamarg, *India* 63 B6
Sonamukhi, *India* 63 H12
Sŏnchŏn, *N. Korea* 51 E13
Soncino, *Italy* 32 C6
Sondags →, *S. Africa* 84 E4
Sóndalo, *Italy* 32 B7
Sondar, *India* 63 C6
Sønder Omme, *Denmark* 11 J2
Sønder Tornby, *Denmark* 11 G3
Sønderborg, *Denmark* 11 K3
Sønderjyllands Amtskommune □, *Denmark* 11 J3
Sondershausen, *Germany* 18 D6
Søndre Strømfjord, *Greenland* 97 B14
Sóndrio, *Italy* 32 B6
Sone, *Mozam.* 83 F3
Sonepur, *India* 61 J13
Song, *Thailand* 58 C3
Song Cau, *Vietnam* 58 F7
Song Xian, *China* 50 G7
Songchŏn, *N. Korea* 51 E14
Songea, *Tanzania* 83 E4
Songea □, *Tanzania* 83 E4
Songeons, *France* 25 C8
Songhua Hu, *China* 51 C14
Songhua Jiang →, *China* 54 B8
Songjiang, *China* 53 B13
Songjin, *N. Korea* 51 D15
Songjŏng-ni, *S. Korea* 51 G14
Songkan, *China* 52 C6
Songkhla, *Thailand* 59 J3
Songming, *China* 52 E4
Songnim, *N. Korea* 51 E13
Songpan, *China* 52 A4
Songtao, *China* 52 C7
Songwe, *Zaïre* 82 C2
Songwe →, *Africa* 83 D3
Songxi, *China* 53 D12
Songzi, *China* 53 B8
Sonid Youqi, *China* 50 C7
Sonipat, *India* 62 E7
Sonkovo, *Russia* 42 B3
Sonmiani, *Pakistan* 62 G2
Sonnino, *Italy* 34 A6
Sono →, *Minas Gerais, Brazil* 123 E2
Sono →, *Tocantins, Brazil* 122 C2
Sonogno, *Switz.* 23 D7
Sonora, *Calif., U.S.A.* 111 H3
Sonora, *Tex., U.S.A.* 109 K4
Sonora □, *Mexico* 114 B2
Sonora →, *Mexico* 114 B2
Sonora Desert, *U.S.A.* 113 L12
Sonoyta, *Mexico* 114 A2
Sonqor, *Iran* 67 E12
Sŏnsan, *S. Korea* 51 F15
Sonsonate, *El Salv.* 116 D2
Sonthofen, *Germany* 19 H6
Soochow = Suzhou, *China* 53 B13
Sop Hao, *Laos* 58 B5
Sop Prap, *Thailand* 58 D2
Sopachuy, *Bolivia* 125 D5
Sopi, *Indonesia* 57 D7
Sopo, Nahr →, *Sudan* 77 F2
Sopot, *Poland* 20 A8
Sopotnica, *Macedonia* 39 H4
Sopron, *Hungary* 21 H6
Sop's Arm, *Canada* 99 C8
Sopur, *India* 63 B6
Sør-Rondane, *Antarctica* 5 D4
Sør-Trøndelag fylke □, *Norway* 10 B3
Sora, *Italy* 34 A6
Sorah, *Pakistan* 62 F3
Söråker, *Sweden* 10 B11
Sorano, *Italy* 33 F8
Sorata, *Bolivia* 124 D4
Sorbas, *Spain* 29 H2
Sorel, *Canada* 98 C5
Sörenberg, *Switz.* 22 C6
Soreq, N. →, *Israel* 69 D3
Soresina, *Italy* 32 C6
Sorgono, *Italy* 34 B2
Sorgues, *France* 27 D8
Sorgun, *Turkey* 66 C6
Soria, *Spain* 28 D2
Soria □, *Spain* 28 D2
Soriano, *Uruguay* 126 C4
Soriano nel Cimino, *Italy* 33 F9
Sorkh, Kuh-e, *Iran* 65 C8
Sorø, *Denmark* 11 J5
Soro, *Guinea* 78 C3
Soroca, *Moldova* 41 H5
Sorocaba, *Brazil* 127 A6
Soroki = Soroca, *Moldova* 41 H5
Soron, *India* 63 F8
Sorong, *Indonesia* 57 E8
Soroní, *Greece* 37 C10
Soroti, *Uganda* 82 B3
Sørøya, *Norway* 8 A20
Sørøysundet, *Norway* 8 A20
Sorraia →, *Portugal* 31 G2
Sorrento, *Australia* 91 F3
Sorrento, *Italy* 35 B7
Sorsele, *Sweden* 8 D17
Sorso, *Italy* 34 B1
Sorsogon, *Phil.* 55 E6
Sortavala, *Russia* 40 B6
Sortino, *Italy* 35 E8
Sortland, *Norway* 8 B16
Sorvizhi, *Russia* 42 B9
Sos, *Spain* 28 C3
Sŏsan, *S. Korea* 51 F14
Soscumica, L., *Canada* 98 B4
Sosna →, *Russia* 42 D4
Sosnovka, *Russia* 42 B10
Sosnovka, *Russia* 42 D5
Sosnovka, *Russia* 45 D11
Sosnovyy Bor, *Russia* 40 C5
Sosnowiec, *Poland* 20 E9
Sospel, *France* 27 E11
Sostanj, *Slovenia* 33 B12
Sŏsura, *N. Korea* 51 C16
Sotkamo, *Finland* 8 D23
Soto la Marina →, *Mexico* 115 C5
Soto y Amío, *Spain* 30 C5
Sotteville-lès-Rouen, *France* 24 C8
Sotuta, *Mexico* 115 C7
Souanké, *Congo* 80 D2
Soúdha, *Greece* 37 D6
Soúdhas, Kólpos, *Greece* 37 D6
Sougne-Remouchamps, *Belgium* 17 H7
Souillac, *France* 26 D5
Souk-Ahras, *Algeria* 75 A6
Souk el Arba du Rharb, *Morocco* 74 B3
Soukhouma, *Laos* 58 E5
Sŏul, *S. Korea* 51 F14
Soulac-sur-Mer, *France* 26 C2
Soultz-sous-Forêts, *France* 25 D14
Soumagne, *Belgium* 17 G7
Sound, The = Øresund, *Europe* 11 J6
Sound, The, *U.K.* 13 G3
Soúnion, Ákra, *Greece* 39 M7
Sour el Ghozlane, *Algeria* 75 A5
Sources, Mt. aux, *Lesotho* 85 D4
Sourdeval, *France* 24 D6
Soure, *Brazil* 122 B2
Soure, *Portugal* 30 E2
Souris, *Man., Canada* 101 D8
Souris, *P.E.I., Canada* 99 C7
Souris →, *Canada* 108 A5
Sousa, *Brazil* 122 C4
Sousel, *Brazil* 122 B1
Sousel, *Portugal* 31 G3
Souss, O. →, *Morocco* 74 B3
Sousse, *Tunisia* 75 A7
Soustons, *France* 26 E2
South Africa ■, *Africa* 84 E3
South Aulatsivik I., *Canada* 99 A7
South Australia □, *Australia* 91 E2
South Baldy, *U.S.A.* 111 J10
South Bend, *Ind., U.S.A.* 104 E2
South Bend, *Wash., U.S.A.* 112 D3
South Boston, *U.S.A.* 105 G6
South Branch, *Canada* 99 C8
South Brook, *Canada* 99 C8
South Carolina □, *U.S.A.* 105 J5
South Charleston, *U.S.A.* 104 F5
South China Sea, *Asia* 56 C4
South Dakota □, *U.S.A.* 108 C5
South Downs, *U.K.* 13 G7
South East C., *Australia* 90 G4
South East Is., *Australia* 89 F3
South Esk →, *U.K.* 14 E5
South Foreland, *U.K.* 13 F9
South Fork →, *U.S.A.* 110 C7
South Fork, American →, *U.S.A.* 112 G5
South Fork, Feather →, *U.S.A.* 112 F5
South Georgia, *Antarctica* 5 B1
South Glamorgan □, *U.K.* 13 F4
South Haven, *U.S.A.* 104 D2
South Henik, L., *Canada* 101 A9
South Honshu Ridge, *Pac. Oc.* 92 E6
South Horr, *Kenya* 82 B4
South I., *Kenya* 82 B4
South I., *N.Z.* 87 L3
South Invercargill, *N.Z.* 87 M2
South Knife →, *Canada* 101 B10
South Korea ■, *Asia* 51 F15
South Lake Tahoe, *U.S.A.* 112 G6
South Loup →, *U.S.A.* 108 E5
South Magnetic Pole, *Antarctica* 5 C9
South Milwaukee, *U.S.A.* 104 D2
South Molton, *U.K.* 13 F4
South Nahanni →, *Canada* 100 A4
South Natuna Is. = Natuna Selatan, Kepulauan, *Indonesia* 59 L7
South Negril Pt., *Jamaica* 116 C4
South Orkney Is., *Antarctica* 5 C18
South Ossetia □, *Georgia* 43 J7
South Pagai, I. = Pagai Selatan, P., *Indonesia* 56 E2
South Pass, *U.S.A.* 110 E9
South Pittsburg, *U.S.A.* 105 H3
South Platte →, *U.S.A.* 108 E4
South Pole, *Antarctica* 5 E
South Porcupine, *Canada* 98 C3
South River, *Canada* 98 C4
South River, *U.S.A.* 107 F10
South Ronaldsay, *U.K.* 14 C6
South Sandwich Is., *Antarctica* 5 B1
South Saskatchewan →, *Canada* 101 C7
South Seal →, *Canada* 101 B9
South Shetland Is., *Antarctica* 5 C18
South Shields, *U.K.* 12 C6
South Sioux City, *U.S.A.* 108 D6
South Taranaki Bight, *N.Z.* 87 H5
South Thompson →, *Canada* 100 C4
South Twin I., *Canada* 98 B4
South Tyne →, *U.K.* 12 C5
South Uist, *U.K.* 14 D1
South West Africa = Namibia ■, *Africa* 84 C2
South West C., *Australia* 90 G4
South Yorkshire □, *U.K.* 12 D6
Southampton, *Canada* 98 D3
Southampton, *U.K.* 13 G6
Southampton, *U.S.A.* 107 F12
Southampton I., *Canada* 97 B11
Southbridge, *N.Z.* 87 K4
Southbridge, *U.S.A.* 107 D12
Southend, *Canada* 101 B8
Southend-on-Sea, *U.K.* 13 F8
Southern □, *Malawi* 83 F4
Southern □, *S. Leone* 78 D2
Southern □, *Uganda* 82 C3
Southern □, *Zambia* 83 F2
Southern Alps, *N.Z.* 87 K3
Southern Cross, *Australia* 89 F2
Southern Hills, *Australia* 89 F3
Southern Indian L., *Canada* 101 B9
Southern Ocean, *Antarctica* 5 C6
Southern Pines, *U.S.A.* 105 H6
Southern Uplands, *U.K.* 14 F5
Southington, *U.S.A.* 107 E12
Southold, *U.S.A.* 107 E12
Southport, *Australia* 91 D5
Southport, *U.K.* 12 D4
Southport, *U.S.A.* 105 J6
Southwest C., *N.Z.* 87 M1
Southwold, *U.K.* 13 E9
Soutpansberg, *S. Africa* 85 C4
Souvigny, *France* 26 B7
Sovetsk, *Kaliningd., Russia* 9 J19
Sovetsk, *Kirov, Russia* 42 B9
Sovetskaya Gavan, *Russia* 45 E15
Sovicille, *Italy* 33 E8
Sovra, *Croatia* 21 N7
Soweto, *S. Africa* 85 D4
Sōya-Kaikyō = La Perouse Str., *Asia* 48 B11
Sōya-Misaki, *Japan* 48 B10
Soyo, *Angola* 80 F2
Sozh →, *Belarus* 41 F6
Sozopol, *Bulgaria* 38 G10
Spa, *Belgium* 17 H7
Spain ■, *Europe* 7 H5
Spakenburg, *Neths.* 16 D6
Spalding, *Australia* 91 E2
Spalding, *U.K.* 12 E7
Spalding, *U.S.A.* 108 E5
Spangler, *U.S.A.* 106 F6
Spaniard's Bay, *Canada* 99 C9
Spanish, *Canada* 98 C3
Spanish Fork, *U.S.A.* 110 F8
Spanish Town, *Jamaica* 116 C4
Sparks, *U.S.A.* 112 F7
Sparta = Spárti, *Greece* 39 M5
Sparta, *Ga., U.S.A.* 105 J4
Sparta, *Wis., U.S.A.* 108 D9
Spartanburg, *U.S.A.* 105 H4
Spartansburg, *U.S.A.* 106 E5
Spartel, C., *Morocco* 74 A3
Spárti, *Greece* 39 M5
Spartivento, C., *Calabria, Italy* 35 E9
Spartivento, C., *Sard., Italy* 34 D1
Spas-Demensk, *Russia* 42 C2
Spas-Klepiki, *Russia* 42 C5
Spassk Dalniy, *Russia* 45 E14
Spassk-Ryazanskiy, *Russia* 42 C5
Spátha, Ákra, *Greece* 37 D5
Spatsizi →, *Canada* 100 B3
Spearfish, *U.S.A.* 108 C3
Spearman, *U.S.A.* 109 G4
Speer, *Switz.* 23 B8
Speers, *Canada* 101 C7
Speightstown, *Barbados* 117 D8
Speke Gulf, *Tanzania* 82 C3
Spekholzerheide, *Neths.* 17 G8
Spence Bay, *Canada* 96 B10
Spencer, *Idaho, U.S.A.* 110 D7
Spencer, *Iowa, U.S.A.* 108 D7
Spencer, *N.Y., U.S.A.* 107 D8
Spencer, *Nebr., U.S.A.* 108 D5
Spencer, *W. Va., U.S.A.* 104 F5
Spencer, C., *Australia* 91 F2
Spencer B., *Namibia* 84 D1
Spencer G., *Australia* 91 E2
Spencerville, *Canada* 107 B9
Spences Bridge, *Canada* 100 C4
Spenser Mts., *N.Z.* 87 K4
Sperkhiós →, *Greece* 39 L5
Sperrin Mts., *U.K.* 15 B5
Spessart, *Germany* 19 E5
Spétsai, *Greece* 39 M6
Spey →, *U.K.* 14 D5
Speyer, *Germany* 19 F4
Speyer →, *Germany* 19 F4
Spezzano Albanese, *Italy* 35 C9
Spiekeroog, *Germany* 18 B3
Spielfeld, *Austria* 33 B12
Spiez, *Switz.* 22 C5
Spijk, *Neths.* 16 B9
Spijkenisse, *Neths.* 16 E4
Spíli, *Greece* 37 D6
Spilimbergo, *Italy* 33 B9
Spin Baldak = Qala-i-Jadid, *Afghan.* 62 D2
Spinalónga, *Greece* 37 D7
Spinazzola, *Italy* 35 B9
Spirit Lake, *Idaho, U.S.A.* 110 C5
Spirit Lake, *Wash., U.S.A.* 112 D4
Spirit River, *Canada* 100 B5
Spiritwood, *Canada* 101 C7
Spišská Nová Ves, *Slovak Rep.* 20 G10
Spithead, *U.K.* 13 G6
Spittal, *Austria* 21 J3
Spitzbergen = Svalbard, *Arctic* 4 B8
Spjelkavik, *Norway* 9 E12
Split, *Croatia* 33 E13
Split L., *Canada* 101 B9
Splitski Kanal, *Croatia* 33 E13
Splügen, *Switz.* 23 C8
Splügenpass, *Switz.* 23 C8
Spofford, *U.S.A.* 109 L4
Spokane, *U.S.A.* 110 C5
Spoleto, *Italy* 33 F9
Spooner, *U.S.A.* 108 C9
Sporyy Navolok, Mys, *Russia* 44 B7
Spragge, *Canada* 98 C3
Sprague, *U.S.A.* 110 C5
Sprague River, *U.S.A.* 110 E3
Spratly I., *S. China Sea* 56 C4
Spray, *U.S.A.* 110 D4
Spree →, *Germany* 18 C9
Spremberg, *Germany* 18 D10
Sprengisandur, *Iceland* 8 D5
Sprimont, *Belgium* 17 G7
Spring City, *U.S.A.* 110 G8
Spring Garden, *U.S.A.* 112 F6
Spring Mts., *U.S.A.* 111 H6
Spring Valley, *Calif., U.S.A.* 113 N10
Spring Valley, *Minn., U.S.A.* 108 D8
Springbok, *S. Africa* 84 D2
Springdale, *Canada* 99 C8
Springdale, *Ark., U.S.A.* 109 G7
Springdale, *Wash., U.S.A.* 110 B5
Springe, *Germany* 18 C5
Springer, *U.S.A.* 109 G2
Springerville, *U.S.A.* 111 J9
Springfield, *Canada* 106 D4
Springfield, *N.Z.* 87 K3
Springfield, *Colo., U.S.A.* 109 G3
Springfield, *Ill., U.S.A.* 108 F10
Springfield, *Mass., U.S.A.* 107 D12
Springfield, *Mo., U.S.A.* 109 G8
Springfield, *Ohio, U.S.A.* 104 F4
Springfield, *Oreg., U.S.A.* 110 D2
Springfield, *Tenn., U.S.A.* 105 G2
Springfield, *Vt., U.S.A.* 107 C12
Springfontein, *S. Africa* 84 E4
Springhill, *Canada* 99 C7
Springhouse, *Canada* 100 C4
Springhurst, *Australia* 91 F4
Springs, *S. Africa* 85 D4
Springsure, *Australia* 90 C4
Springvale, *Queens., Australia* 90 C3
Springvale, *W. Austral., Australia* 88 C4
Springvale, *U.S.A.* 107 C14
Springville, *Calif., U.S.A.* 112 J8
Springville, *N.Y., U.S.A.* 106 D6
Springville, *Utah, U.S.A.* 110 F8
Springwater, *Canada* 101 C7
Spruce-Creek, *U.S.A.* 106 F6
Spur, *U.S.A.* 109 J4
Spurn Hd., *U.K.* 12 D8
Spuž, *Montenegro, Yug.* 21 N9
Spuzzum, *Canada* 100 D4
Squam L., *U.S.A.* 107 C13
Squamish, *Canada* 100 D4
Square Islands, *Canada* 99 B8
Squillace, G. di, *Italy* 35 D9
Squinzano, *Italy* 35 B11
Squires, Mt., *Australia* 89 E4
Sragen, *Indonesia* 57 G14
Srbac, *Bos.-H.* 21 K7
Srbija = Serbia □, *Yugoslavia* 21 M11
Srbobran, *Serbia, Yug.* 21 K9
Sre Khtum, *Cambodia* 59 F6
Sre Umbell, *Cambodia* 59 G4
Srebrnica, *Bos.-H.* 21 L9
Sredinny Ra. = Sredinnyy Khrebet, *Russia* 45 D16
Sredinnyy Khrebet, *Russia* 45 D16
Središče, *Slovenia* 33 B13
Sredna Gora, *Bulgaria* 38 G7
Sredne Tambovskoye, *Russia* 45 D14
Srednekolymsk, *Russia* 45 C16
Srednevilyuysk, *Russia* 45 C13
Śrem, *Poland* 20 C7
Sremska Mitrovica, *Serbia, Yug.* 21 L9
Srepok →, *Cambodia* 58 F6
Sretensk, *Russia* 45 D12
Sri Lanka ■, *Asia* 60 R12
Srikakulam, *India* 61 K13
Srinagar, *India* 63 B6
Środa Wielkopolski, *Poland* 20 C7
Srpska Itabej, *Serbia, Yug.* 21 K10
Staaten →, *Australia* 90 B3
Staberhuk, *Germany* 18 A7
Stabroek, *Belgium* 17 F4
Stad Delden, *Neths.* 16 D9
Stade, *Germany* 18 B5
Staden, *Belgium* 17 G2
Städjan, *Sweden* 10 C6
Stadskanaal, *Neths.* 16 B9
Stadthagen, *Germany* 18 C5
Stadtlohn, *Germany* 18 D2
Stadtroda, *Germany* 18 E7
Stäfa, *Switz.* 23 B7
Staffa, *U.K.* 14 E2
Stafford, *U.K.* 12 E5
Stafford, *U.S.A.* 109 G5
Stafford Springs, *U.S.A.* 107 E12
Staffordshire □, *U.K.* 12 E5

Name	Region	Page	Grid
Stagnone, Isole dello,	*Italy*	34	E5
Staines,	*U.K.*	13	F7
Stakhanov,	*Ukraine*	41	H10
Stalden,	*Switz.*	22	D5
Stalingrad = Volgograd,	*Russia*	43	F7
Staliniri = Tskhinvali,	*Georgia*	43	J7
Stalino = Donetsk,	*Ukraine*	41	J9
Stalinogorsk = Novomoskovsk,	*Russia*	42	C4
Stalis,	*Greece*	37	D7
Stalowa Wola,	*Poland*	20	E12
Stalybridge,	*U.K.*	12	D5
Stamford,	*Australia*	90	C3
Stamford,	*U.K.*	13	E7
Stamford, Conn.,	*U.S.A.*	107	E11
Stamford, Tex.,	*U.S.A.*	109	J5
Stamps,	*U.S.A.*	109	J8
Stanberry,	*U.S.A.*	108	E7
Stančevo = Kalipetrovo,	*Bulgaria*	38	E10
Standerton,	*S. Africa*	85	D4
Standish,	*U.S.A.*	104	D4
Stanford,	*U.S.A.*	110	C8
Stange,	*Norway*	10	D5
Stanger,	*S. Africa*	85	D5
Stanislaus →,	*U.S.A.*	112	H5
Stanislav = Ivano-Frankivsk,	*Ukraine*	41	H3
Stanke Dimitrov,	*Bulgaria*	38	G6
Stanley,	*Australia*	90	G4
Stanley, N.B.,	*Canada*	99	C6
Stanley, Sask.,	*Canada*	101	B8
Stanley,	*Falk. Is.*	128	D5
Stanley, Idaho,	*U.S.A.*	110	D6
Stanley, N. Dak.,	*U.S.A.*	108	A3
Stanley, N.Y.,	*U.S.A.*	106	D7
Stanley, Wis.,	*U.S.A.*	108	C9
Stanovoy Khrebet,	*Russia*	45	D13
Stanovoy Ra. = Stanovoy Khrebet,	*Russia*	45	D13
Stans,	*Switz.*	23	C6
Stansmore Ra.,	*Australia*	88	D4
Stanthorpe,	*Australia*	91	D5
Stanton,	*U.S.A.*	109	J4
Stanwood,	*U.S.A.*	112	B4
Staphorst,	*Neths.*	16	C8
Staples,	*U.S.A.*	108	B7
Stapleton,	*U.S.A.*	108	E4
Star City,	*Canada*	101	C8
Stara Moravica,	*Serbia, Yug.*	21	K9
Stara Planina,	*Bulgaria*	38	F6
Stara Zagora,	*Bulgaria*	38	G8
Starachowice,	*Poland*	20	D11
Staraya Russa,	*Russia*	40	D6
Starbuck I.,	*Kiribati*	93	H12
Stargard Szczeciński,	*Poland*	20	B5
Stari Trg,	*Slovenia*	33	C12
Staritsa,	*Russia*	42	B2
Starke,	*U.S.A.*	105	K4
Starkville, Colo.,	*U.S.A.*	109	G2
Starkville, Miss.,	*U.S.A.*	105	J1
Starnberg,	*Germany*	19	G7
Starnberger See,	*Germany*	19	H7
Starobilsk,	*Ukraine*	41	H10
Starodub,	*Russia*	41	F7
Starogard Gdański,	*Poland*	20	B8
Starokonstantinov = Starokonstyantyniv,	*Ukraine*	41	H4
Starokonstyantyniv,	*Ukraine*	41	H4
Starominskaya,	*Russia*	43	G4
Staroshcherbinovskaya,	*Russia*	43	G4
Start Pt.,	*U.K.*	13	G4
Staryy Biryuzyak,	*Russia*	43	H8
Staryy Chartoriysk,	*Ukraine*	41	G3
Staryy Kheydzhan,	*Russia*	45	C15
Staryy Krym,	*Ukraine*	41	K8
Staryy Oskol,	*Russia*	42	E3
Stassfurt,	*Germany*	18	D7
State College,	*U.S.A.*	106	F7
Stateline,	*U.S.A.*	112	G7
Staten, I. = Estados, I. de Los,	*Argentina*	128	D4
Staten I.,	*U.S.A.*	107	F10
Statesboro,	*U.S.A.*	105	J5
Statesville,	*U.S.A.*	105	H5
Stauffer,	*U.S.A.*	113	L7
Staunton, Ill.,	*U.S.A.*	108	F10
Staunton, Va.,	*U.S.A.*	104	F6
Stavanger,	*Norway*	9	G11
Staveley,	*N.Z.*	87	K3
Stavelot,	*Belgium*	17	H7
Stavenhagen,	*Germany*	18	B8
Stavenisse,	*Neths.*	17	E4
Staveren,	*Neths.*	16	C6
Stavern,	*Norway*	10	F4
Stavre,	*Sweden*	10	B9
Stavropol,	*Russia*	43	H6
Stavros,	*Cyprus*	37	D11
Stavrós,	*Greece*	37	D6
Stavros, Ákra,	*Greece*	37	D6
Stavroúpolis,	*Greece*	39	H7
Stawell,	*Australia*	91	F3
Stawell →,	*Australia*	90	C3
Stawiszyn,	*Poland*	20	D8
Stayner,	*Canada*	106	B4
Steamboat Springs,	*U.S.A.*	110	F10
Steckborn,	*Switz.*	23	A7
Steele,	*U.S.A.*	108	B5
Steelton,	*U.S.A.*	106	F8
Steelville,	*U.S.A.*	109	G9
Steen River,	*Canada*	100	B5
Steenbergen,	*Neths.*	17	E4
Steenkool = Bintuni,	*Indonesia*	57	E8
Steenvoorde,	*France*	25	B9
Steenwijk,	*Neths.*	16	C8
Steep Pt.,	*Australia*	89	E1
Steep Rock,	*Canada*	101	C9
Ştefănești,	*Romania*	38	B10
Stefanie L. = Chew Bahir,	*Ethiopia*	77	G4
Stefansson Bay,	*Antarctica*	5	C5
Steffisburg,	*Switz.*	22	C5
Stege,	*Denmark*	11	K6
Steiermark □,	*Austria*	21	H5
Steigerwald,	*Germany*	19	F6
Steilacoom,	*U.S.A.*	112	C4
Stein,	*Neths.*	17	G7
Steinbach,	*Canada*	101	D9
Steinfort,	*Lux.*	17	J7
Steinfurt,	*Germany*	18	C3
Steinheim,	*Germany*	18	D5
Steinhuder Meer,	*Germany*	18	C5
Steinkjer,	*Norway*	8	D14
Steinkopf,	*S. Africa*	84	D2
Stekene,	*Belgium*	17	F4
Stellarton,	*Canada*	99	C7
Stellenbosch,	*S. Africa*	84	E2
Stellendam,	*Neths.*	16	E4
Stelvio, Paso dello,	*Italy*	32	B7
Stemshaug,	*Norway*	10	A2
Stendal,	*Germany*	18	C7
Stene,	*Belgium*	17	F1
Stenstorp,	*Sweden*	11	F7
Steornabhaigh = Stornoway,	*U.K.*	14	C2
Stepanakert = Xankändi,	*Azerbaijan*	67	C12
Stepanavan,	*Armenia*	43	K7
Stephen,	*U.S.A.*	108	A6
Stephens Creek,	*Australia*	91	E3
Stephens I.,	*Canada*	100	C2
Stephenville,	*Canada*	99	C8
Stephenville,	*U.S.A.*	109	J5
Stepnica,	*Poland*	20	B4
Stepnoi = Elista,	*Russia*	43	G7
Stepnyak,	*Kazakhstan*	44	D8
Steppe,	*Asia*	46	E7
Sterkstroom,	*S. Africa*	84	E4
Sterling, Colo.,	*U.S.A.*	108	E3
Sterling, Ill.,	*U.S.A.*	108	E10
Sterling, Kans.,	*U.S.A.*	108	F5
Sterling City,	*U.S.A.*	109	K4
Sterling Run,	*U.S.A.*	106	E6
Sterlitamak,	*Russia*	44	D6
Sternberg,	*Germany*	18	B7
Šternberk,	*Czech.*	20	F7
Stérnes,	*Greece*	37	D6
Sterzing = Vipiteno,	*Italy*	33	B8
Stettin = Szczecin,	*Poland*	20	B4
Stettiner Haff,	*Germany*	18	B10
Stettler,	*Canada*	100	C6
Steubenville,	*U.S.A.*	106	F4
Stevens Point,	*U.S.A.*	108	C10
Stevenson,	*U.S.A.*	112	E5
Stevenson L.,	*Canada*	101	C9
Stevns Klint,	*Denmark*	11	J6
Stewart, B.C.,	*Canada*	100	B3
Stewart, N.W.T.,	*Canada*	96	B6
Stewart →,	*Canada*	112	F7
Stewart, C.,	*Australia*	90	A1
Stewart, I.,	*Chile*	128	D2
Stewart I.,	*N.Z.*	87	M1
Stewarts Point,	*U.S.A.*	112	G3
Stewiacke,	*Canada*	99	C7
Steynsburg,	*S. Africa*	84	E4
Steyr,	*Austria*	21	G4
Steytlerville,	*S. Africa*	84	E3
Stia,	*Italy*	33	E8
Stiens,	*Neths.*	16	B7
Stigler,	*U.S.A.*	109	H7
Stigliano,	*Italy*	35	B9
Stigsnæs,	*Denmark*	11	J5
Stigtomta,	*Sweden*	11	F10
Stikine →,	*Canada*	100	B2
Stilfontein,	*S. Africa*	84	D4
Stilís,	*Greece*	39	L5
Stillwater,	*N.Z.*	87	K3
Stillwater, Minn.,	*U.S.A.*	108	C8
Stillwater, N.Y.,	*U.S.A.*	107	D11
Stillwater, Okla.,	*U.S.A.*	109	G6
Stillwater Range,	*U.S.A.*	110	G4
Stilwell,	*U.S.A.*	109	H7
Štip,	*Macedonia*	39	H5
Stira,	*Greece*	39	L7
Stirling,	*Australia*	90	B3
Stirling,	*Canada*	100	D6
Stirling,	*U.K.*	14	E5
Stirling Ra.,	*Australia*	89	F2
Stittsville,	*Canada*	107	A9
Stjernøya,	*Norway*	8	A20
Stjørdalshalsen,	*Norway*	8	E14
Stockach,	*Germany*	19	H5
Stockerau,	*Austria*	21	G6
Stockett,	*U.S.A.*	110	C8
Stockholm,	*Sweden*	10	E12
Stockholms län □,	*Sweden*	10	E12
Stockhorn,	*Switz.*	22	C5
Stockport,	*U.K.*	12	D5
Stockton, Calif.,	*U.S.A.*	111	H3
Stockton, Kans.,	*U.S.A.*	108	F5
Stockton, Mo.,	*U.S.A.*	109	G8
Stockton-on-Tees,	*U.K.*	12	C6
Stockvik,	*Sweden*	10	B11
Stöde,	*Sweden*	10	B10
Stogovo,	*Macedonia*	39	H3
Stoke on Trent,	*U.K.*	12	D5
Stokes Bay,	*Canada*	98	C3
Stokes Pt.,	*Australia*	90	G3
Stokes Ra.,	*Australia*	88	C5
Stokksnes,	*Iceland*	8	D6
Stokmarknes,	*Norway*	8	B16
Stolac,	*Bos.-H.*	21	M7
Stolberg,	*Germany*	18	E2
Stolbovaya,	*Russia*	45	C16
Stolbovoy, Ostrov,	*Russia*	45	D17
Stolbtsy = Stowbtsy,	*Belarus*	40	F4
Stolin,	*Belarus*	41	G4
Stolwijk,	*Neths.*	16	E5
Stomíon,	*Greece*	37	D5
Ston,	*Croatia*	21	N7
Stonehaven,	*U.K.*	14	E6
Stonehenge,	*Australia*	90	C3
Stonewall,	*Canada*	101	C9
Stony L., Man.,	*Canada*	101	B9
Stony L., Ont.,	*Canada*	106	B6
Stony Rapids,	*Canada*	101	B7
Stony Tunguska = Podkamennaya Tunguska →,	*Russia*	45	C10
Stonyford,	*U.S.A.*	112	F4
Stopnica,	*Poland*	20	E10
Stora Lulevatten,	*Sweden*	8	C18
Storavan,	*Sweden*	8	D18
Stord,	*Norway*	9	G11
Store Bælt,	*Denmark*	11	J5
Store Creek,	*Australia*	91	E4
Store Heddinge,	*Denmark*	11	J6
Støren,	*Norway*	10	A4
Storm B.,	*Australia*	90	G4
Storm Lake,	*U.S.A.*	108	D7
Stormberge,	*S. Africa*	84	E4
Stormsrivier,	*S. Africa*	84	E3
Stornoway,	*U.K.*	14	C2
Storozhinets = Storozhynets,	*Ukraine*	41	H3
Storozhynets,	*Ukraine*	41	H3
Storsjö,	*Sweden*	10	B7
Storsjøen, Hedmark,	*Norway*	10	D5
Storsjøen, Hedmark,	*Norway*	10	C5
Storsjön,	*Sweden*	10	B7
Storstrøms Amt. □,	*Denmark*	11	K5
Storuman,	*Sweden*	8	D17
Storuman, sjö,	*Sweden*	8	D17
Stoughton,	*Canada*	101	D8
Stour →, Dorset,	*U.K.*	13	G5
Stour →, Here. & Worcs.,	*U.K.*	13	E5
Stour →, Kent,	*U.K.*	13	F9
Stour →, Suffolk,	*U.K.*	13	F9
Stourbridge,	*U.K.*	13	E5
Stout, L.,	*Canada*	101	C10
Stove Pipe Wells Village,	*U.S.A.*	113	J9
Stowbtsy,	*Belarus*	40	F4
Stowmarket,	*U.K.*	13	E9
Strabane,	*U.K.*	15	B4
Strabane □,	*U.K.*	15	B4
Stracin,	*Macedonia*	38	G5
Stradella,	*Italy*	32	C6
Strahan,	*Australia*	90	G4
Strakonice,	*Czech.*	20	F3
Straldzha,	*Bulgaria*	38	G9
Stralsund,	*Germany*	18	A9
Strand,	*S. Africa*	84	E2
Stranda, Møre og Romsdal,	*Norway*	9	E12
Stranda, Nord-Trøndelag,	*Norway*	8	E14
Strangford L.,	*U.K.*	15	B6
Strängnäs,	*Sweden*	10	E11
Stranraer,	*U.K.*	14	G3
Strasbourg,	*Canada*	101	C8
Strasbourg,	*France*	25	D14
Strasburg,	*Germany*	18	B9
Strasburg,	*U.S.A.*	108	B4
Strassen,	*Lux.*	17	J8
Stratford,	*Canada*	98	D3
Stratford,	*N.Z.*	87	H5
Stratford, Calif.,	*U.S.A.*	111	H4
Stratford, Conn.,	*U.S.A.*	107	E11
Stratford, Tex.,	*U.S.A.*	109	G3
Stratford-upon-Avon,	*U.K.*	13	E6
Strath Spey,	*U.K.*	14	D5
Strathalbyn,	*Australia*	91	F2
Strathclyde □,	*U.K.*	14	F4
Strathcona Prov. Park,	*Canada*	100	D3
Strathmore,	*Australia*	90	B3
Strathmore,	*Canada*	100	C6
Strathmore,	*U.K.*	14	E5
Strathmore,	*U.S.A.*	112	J7
Strathnaver,	*Canada*	100	C4
Strathpeffer,	*U.K.*	14	D4
Strathroy,	*Canada*	98	D3
Strathy Pt.,	*U.K.*	14	C4
Stratton,	*U.S.A.*	108	F3
Straubing,	*Germany*	19	G8
Straumnes,	*Iceland*	8	C2
Strausberg,	*Germany*	18	C9
Strawberry Reservoir,	*U.S.A.*	110	F8
Strawn,	*U.S.A.*	109	J5
Strážnice,	*Czech.*	20	G7
Streaky B.,	*Australia*	91	E1
Streaky Bay,	*Australia*	91	E1
Streator,	*U.S.A.*	108	E10
Streé,	*Belgium*	17	H4
Street,	*U.K.*	13	F5
Streetsville,	*Canada*	106	C5
Strehaia,	*Romania*	38	E6
Strelcha,	*Bulgaria*	38	G7
Strelka,	*Russia*	45	D10
Streng →,	*Cambodia*	58	F4
Strésa,	*Italy*	32	C5
Streymoy,	*Færoe Is.*	8	E9
Strezhevoy,	*Russia*	44	C8
Stříbro,	*Czech.*	20	F3
Strijen,	*Neths.*	16	E5
Strimón →,	*Greece*	39	J6
Strimonikós Kólpos,	*Greece*	39	J6
Stroeder,	*Argentina*	128	B4
Strofádhes,	*Greece*	39	M4
Strömbacka,	*Sweden*	10	C10
Strómboli,	*Italy*	35	D8
Stromeferry,	*U.K.*	14	D3
Stromness,	*U.K.*	14	C5
Stromsburg,	*U.S.A.*	108	E6
Strömstad,	*Sweden*	9	G14
Strömsund,	*Sweden*	8	E16
Stróngoli,	*Italy*	35	C10
Stronsay,	*U.K.*	14	B6
Stroud,	*U.K.*	13	F5
Stroud Road,	*Australia*	91	E5
Stroudsburg,	*U.S.A.*	107	F9
Stroumbi,	*Cyprus*	37	E11
Struer,	*Denmark*	11	H2
Struga,	*Macedonia*	39	H3
Strugi Krasnyye,	*Russia*	40	C5
Struma →,	*Europe*	39	H6
Strumica,	*Macedonia*	39	H5
Strumica →,	*Europe*	39	H6
Struthers,	*Canada*	98	C2
Struthers,	*U.S.A.*	106	E4
Stryker,	*U.S.A.*	110	B6
Stryy,	*Ukraine*	41	H2
Strzegom,	*Poland*	20	E6
Strzelce Krajeńskie,	*Poland*	20	C5
Strzelecki Cr. →,	*Australia*	91	D2
Strzelin,	*Poland*	20	E7
Strzelno,	*Poland*	20	C8
Strzyżów,	*Poland*	20	F11
Stuart, Fla.,	*U.S.A.*	105	M5
Stuart, Nebr.,	*U.S.A.*	108	D5
Stuart →,	*Canada*	100	C4
Stuart Bluff Ra.,	*Australia*	88	D5
Stuart L.,	*Canada*	100	C4
Stuart Ra.,	*Australia*	91	D1
Stubbekøbing,	*Denmark*	11	K6
Stugun,	*Sweden*	10	A9
Stull, L.,	*Canada*	98	B1
Stung Treng,	*Cambodia*	58	F5
Stupart →,	*Canada*	101	B10
Stupino,	*Russia*	42	C4
Sturgeon B.,	*Canada*	101	C9
Sturgeon Bay,	*U.S.A.*	104	C2
Sturgeon Falls,	*Canada*	98	C4
Sturgeon L., Alta.,	*Canada*	100	B5
Sturgeon L., Ont.,	*Canada*	106	B6
Sturgeon L., Ont.,	*Canada*	98	B1
Sturgis, Mich.,	*U.S.A.*	104	E3
Sturgis, S. Dak.,	*U.S.A.*	108	C3
Sturt Cr. →,	*Australia*	88	C4
Sturt Creek,	*Australia*	88	C4
Stutterheim,	*S. Africa*	84	E4
Stuttgart,	*Germany*	19	G5
Stuttgart,	*U.S.A.*	109	H9
Stuyvesant,	*U.S.A.*	107	D11
Stykkishólmur,	*Iceland*	8	D2
Styria = Steiermark □,	*Austria*	21	H5
Su Xian,	*China*	50	H9
Suakin,	*Sudan*	76	D4
Suapure →,	*Venezuela*	120	B4
Suaqui,	*Mexico*	114	B3
Suatá →,	*Venezuela*	121	B4
Subang,	*Indonesia*	57	G12
Subansiri →,	*India*	61	F18
Subayhah,	*Si. Arabia*	64	D3
Subi,	*Indonesia*	59	L7
Subiaco,	*Italy*	33	G10
Subotica,	*Serbia, Yug.*	21	J9
Success,	*Canada*	101	C7
Suceava,	*Romania*	38	B9
Suceava →,	*Romania*	38	B9
Sucha-Beskidzka,	*Poland*	20	F9
Suchan,	*Poland*	20	B5
Suchan,	*Russia*	48	C6
Suchitoto,	*El Salv.*	116	D2
Suchou = Suzhou,	*China*	53	B13
Süchow = Xuzhou,	*China*	51	G9
Suchowola,	*Poland*	20	B13
Sucio →,	*Colombia*	120	B2
Suck →,	*Ireland*	15	C3
Sucre,	*Bolivia*	125	D4
Sucre,	*Colombia*	120	B3
Sucre □,	*Colombia*	120	B2
Sucre □,	*Venezuela*	121	A5
Sucuaro,	*Colombia*	120	C4
Sucuriú →,	*Brazil*	122	A2
Sucuriú →,	*Brazil*	125	E7
Sud, Pte.,	*Canada*	99	C7
Sud-Ouest, Pte. du,	*Canada*	99	C7
Suda →,	*Russia*	40	C9
Sudak,	*Ukraine*	41	K8
Sudan,	*U.S.A.*	109	H3
Sudan ■,	*Africa*	77	E3
Sudbury,	*Canada*	98	C3
Sudbury,	*U.K.*	13	E8
Sûdd,	*Sudan*	77	F2
Suddie,	*Guyana*	121	B6
Süderbrarup,	*Germany*	18	A5
Süderlügum,	*Germany*	18	A4
Süderoogsand,	*Germany*	18	A4
Sudeten Mts. = Sudety,	*Europe*	20	E6
Sudety,	*Europe*	20	E6
Suðuroy,	*Færoe Is.*	8	F9
Sudi,	*Tanzania*	83	E4
Sudirman, Pegunungan,	*Indonesia*	57	E9
Sudogda,	*Russia*	42	C5
Sudr,	*Egypt*	76	J8
Sudzha,	*Russia*	42	E2
Sueca,	*Spain*	29	F4
Suedala,	*Sweden*	11	J7
Suez = El Suweis,	*Egypt*	76	J8
Suez, G. of = Suweis, Khalîg el,	*Egypt*	76	J8
Suez Canal = Suweis, Qanâ es,	*Egypt*	76	H8
Suffield,	*Canada*	101	C6
Suffolk,	*U.S.A.*	104	G7
Suffolk □,	*U.K.*	13	E9
Sugar City,	*U.S.A.*	108	F3
Suğla Gölü,	*Turkey*	66	D5
Sugluk = Salluit,	*Canada*	97	B12
Sugny,	*Belgium*	17	J5
Suhaia, L.,	*Romania*	38	F8
Suhār,	*Oman*	65	E8
Suhbaatar,	*Mongolia*	54	A5
Sühbaatar □,	*Mongolia*	50	B8
Suhl,	*Germany*	18	E6
Suhr,	*Switz.*	22	B6
Sui Xian, Henan,	*China*	50	G8
Sui Xian, Henan,	*China*	53	B9
Suiá Missu →,	*Brazil*	125	C7
Suichang,	*China*	53	C12
Suichuan,	*China*	53	D10
Suide,	*China*	50	F6
Suifenhe,	*China*	51	B16
Suihua,	*China*	54	B7
Suijiang,	*China*	52	C4
Suining, Hunan,	*China*	53	D8
Suining, Jiangsu,	*China*	51	H9
Suining, Sichuan,	*China*	52	B5
Suiping,	*China*	50	H7
Suippes,	*France*	25	C11
Suir →,	*Ireland*	15	D4
Suixi,	*China*	53	G8
Suiyang, Guizhou,	*China*	52	D6
Suiyang, Heilongjiang,	*China*	51	B16
Suizhong,	*China*	51	D11
Sujangarh,	*India*	62	F6
Sukabumi,	*Indonesia*	57	G12
Sukadana, Kalimantan,	*Indonesia*	56	E3
Sukadana, Sumatera,	*Indonesia*	56	F3
Sukagawa,	*Japan*	49	F10
Sukaraja,	*Indonesia*	56	E4
Sukarnapura = Jayapura,	*Indonesia*	57	E10
Sukchŏn,	*N. Korea*	51	E13
Sukhinichi,	*Russia*	42	C2
Sukhona →,	*Russia*	44	D4
Sukhothai,	*Thailand*	58	D2
Sukhumi = Sokhumi,	*Georgia*	43	J5
Sukkur,	*Pakistan*	62	F3
Sukkur Barrage,	*Pakistan*	62	F3
Sukumo,	*Japan*	49	H6
Sukunka →,	*Canada*	100	B4
Sul, Canal do,	*Brazil*	122	B2
Sula →,	*Ukraine*	41	H7
Sula, Kepulauan,	*Indonesia*	57	E7
Sulaco →,	*Honduras*	116	C2
Sulaiman Range,	*Pakistan*	62	D3
Sulak →,	*Russia*	43	J8
Sūlār,	*Iran*	65	D6
Sulawesi □,	*Indonesia*	57	E6
Sulawesi Sea = Celebes Sea,	*Indonesia*	57	D6
Sulechów,	*Poland*	20	C5
Sulejów,	*Poland*	20	D9
Sulgen,	*Switz.*	23	A8
Sulima,	*S. Leone*	78	D2
Sulina,	*Romania*	38	D12
Sulina, Brațul →,	*Romania*	38	D12
Sulingen,	*Germany*	18	C4
Sulitjelma,	*Norway*	8	C17
Sullana,	*Peru*	124	A1
Sullivan, Ill.,	*U.S.A.*	108	F10
Sullivan, Ind.,	*U.S.A.*	104	F2
Sullivan, Mo.,	*U.S.A.*	108	F9
Sullivan Bay,	*Canada*	100	C3
Sully-sur-Loire,	*France*	25	E9
Sulmona,	*Italy*	33	F10
Sulphur, La.,	*U.S.A.*	109	K8
Sulphur, Okla.,	*U.S.A.*	109	H6
Sulphur Pt.,	*Canada*	100	A6
Sulphur Springs,	*U.S.A.*	109	J7
Sulphur Springs Draw →,	*U.S.A.*	109	J4
Sultan,	*Canada*	98	C3
Sultan,	*U.S.A.*	112	C5
Sultan Dağları,	*Turkey*	66	C4
Sultanpur,	*India*	63	F10
Sulu Arch.,	*Phil.*	55	J4
Sulu Sea,	*E. Indies*	55	J4
Sülüklü,	*Turkey*	66	C5
Sululta,	*Ethiopia*	77	F4
Suluova,	*Turkey*	66	B6
Suluq,	*Libya*	73	B9
Sulzbach,	*Germany*	19	F3
Sulzbach-Rosenberg,	*Germany*	19	F7
Sulzberger Ice Shelf,	*Antarctica*	5	D10

Sumalata, *Indonesia*	57	D6
Sumampa, *Argentina*	126	B3
Sumatera □, *Indonesia*	56	D2
Sumatra = Sumatera □, *Indonesia*	56	D2
Sumatra, *U.S.A.*	110	C10
Sumba, *Indonesia*	57	F5
Sumba, Selat, *Indonesia*	57	F5
Sumbawa, *Indonesia*	56	F5
Sumbawa Besar, *Indonesia*	56	F5
Sumbawanga □, *Tanzania*	82	D3
Sumbe, *Angola*	80	G2
Sumburgh Hd., *U.K.*	14	B7
Sumdo, *India*	63	B8
Sumé, *Brazil*	122	C4
Sumedang, *Indonesia*	57	G12
Šumen, *Bulgaria*	38	F9
Sumenep, *Indonesia*	57	G15
Sumgait = Sumqayıt, *Azerbaijan*	43	K9
Sumiswald, *Switz.*	22	B5
Summer L., *U.S.A.*	110	E3
Summerland, *Canada*	100	D5
Summerside, *Canada*	99	C7
Summerville, *Ga., U.S.A.*	105	H3
Summerville, *S.C., U.S.A.*	105	J5
Summit Lake, *Canada*	100	C4
Summit Peak, *U.S.A.*	111	H10
Sumner, *Iowa, U.S.A.*	108	D8
Sumner, *Wash., U.S.A.*	112	C4
Sumoto, *Japan*	49	G7
Sumqayıt, *Azerbaijan*	43	K9
Sumter, *U.S.A.*	105	J5
Sumy, *Ukraine*	41	G8
Sun City, *Ariz., U.S.A.*	111	K7
Sun City, *Calif., U.S.A.*	113	M9
Sunagawa, *Japan*	48	C10
Sunan, *N. Korea*	51	E13
Sunart, L., *U.K.*	14	E3
Sunburst, *U.S.A.*	110	B8
Sunbury, *Australia*	91	F3
Sunbury, *U.S.A.*	107	F8
Sunchales, *Argentina*	126	C3
Suncho Corral, *Argentina*	126	B3
Sunchon, *S. Korea*	51	G14
Suncook, *U.S.A.*	107	C13
Sunda, Selat, *Indonesia*	56	F3
Sunda Is., *Indonesia*	46	K13
Sunda Str. = Sunda, Selat, *Indonesia*	56	F3
Sundance, *U.S.A.*	108	C2
Sundarbans, The, *Asia*	61	J16
Sundargarh, *India*	61	H14
Sundays = Sondags →, *S. Africa*	84	E4
Sundbyberg, *Sweden*	10	E11
Sunderland, *Canada*	106	B5
Sunderland, *U.K.*	12	C6
Sundre, *Canada*	100	C6
Sundridge, *Canada*	98	C4
Sunds, *Denmark*	11	H3
Sundsjö, *Sweden*	10	B9
Sundsvall, *Sweden*	10	B11
Sung Hei, *Vietnam*	59	G6
Sungai Kolok, *Thailand*	59	J3
Sungai Lembing, *Malaysia*	59	L4
Sungai Patani, *Malaysia*	59	K3
Sungaigerong, *Indonesia*	56	E2
Sungailiat, *Indonesia*	56	E3
Sungaipakning, *Indonesia*	56	D2
Sungaipenuh, *Indonesia*	56	E2
Sungaitiram, *Indonesia*	56	E5
Sungari = Songhua Jiang →, *China*	54	B8
Sungguminasa, *Indonesia*	57	F5
Sunghua Chiang = Songhua Jiang →, *China*	54	B8
Sungikai, *Sudan*	77	E2
Sungurlu, *Turkey*	66	B6
Sunja, *Croatia*	33	C13
Sunndalsøra, *Norway*	9	E13
Sunnyside, *Utah, U.S.A.*	110	G8
Sunnyside, *Wash., U.S.A.*	110	C3
Sunnyvale, *U.S.A.*	111	H2
Sunray, *U.S.A.*	109	G4
Suntar, *Russia*	45	C12
Sunyani, *Ghana*	78	D4
Suomenselkä, *Finland*	8	E21
Suomussalmi, *Finland*	8	D23
Suoyarvi, *Russia*	40	A7
Supai, *U.S.A.*	111	H7
Supamo →, *Venezuela*	121	B5
Supaul, *India*	63	F12
Supe, *Peru*	124	C2
Superior, *Ariz., U.S.A.*	111	K8
Superior, *Mont., U.S.A.*	110	C6
Superior, *Nebr., U.S.A.*	108	E5
Superior, *Wis., U.S.A.*	108	B8
Superior, L., *U.S.A.*	98	C2
Supetar, *Croatia*	33	E13
Suphan Buri, *Thailand*	58	E3
Suphan Dağı, *Turkey*	67	C10
Supiori, *Indonesia*	57	E9
Supung Sk., *China*	51	D13
Sūq Suwayq, *Si. Arabia*	64	E3
Suqian, *China*	51	H10
Sūr, *Lebanon*	69	B4
Sur, Pt., *U.S.A.*	111	H3
Sura →, *Russia*	42	C8
Surab, *Pakistan*	62	E2
Surabaia = Surabaya, *Indonesia*	57	G15
Surabaya, *Indonesia*	57	G15
Suraia, *Romania*	38	D10
Surakarta, *Indonesia*	57	G14
Surakhany, *Azerbaijan*	43	K10
Surat, *Australia*	91	D4
Surat, *India*	60	J8
Surat Thani, *Thailand*	59	H2
Suratgarh, *India*	62	E5
Surazh, *Belarus*	40	E6
Surazh, *Russia*	41	F7
Surduc Pasul, *Romania*	38	D6
Surdulica, *Serbia, Yug.*	21	N12
Sûre = Sauer →, *Germany*	17	J9
Surendranagar, *India*	62	H4
Surf, *U.S.A.*	113	L6
Surgères, *France*	26	B3
Surgut, *Russia*	44	C8
Surhuisterveen, *Neths.*	16	B8
Suriapet, *India*	60	L11
Surigao, *Phil.*	55	G6
Surigao Strait, *Phil.*	55	F6
Surin, *Thailand*	58	E4
Surin Nua, Ko, *Thailand*	59	H1
Surinam ■, *S. Amer.*	121	C6
Suriname = Surinam ■, *S. Amer.*	121	C6
Suriname →, *Surinam*	121	B6
Sūrmaq, *Iran*	65	D7
Sürmene, *Turkey*	67	B9
Surovikino, *Russia*	43	F6
Surprise L., *Canada*	100	B2
Surrey □, *U.K.*	13	F7
Sursee, *Switz.*	22	B6
Sursk, *Russia*	42	D7
Surskoye, *Russia*	42	C8
Surt, *Libya*	73	B8
Surt, Khalīj, *Libya*	73	B8
Surtsey, *Iceland*	8	E3
Surubim, *Brazil*	122	C4
Sürüç, *Turkey*	67	D8
Suruga-Wan, *Japan*	49	G9
Surumu →, *Brazil*	121	C5
Susa, *Italy*	32	C4
Suså →, *Denmark*	11	J5
Sušac, *Croatia*	33	F13
Susak, *Croatia*	33	D11
Susaki, *Japan*	49	H6
Süsangerd, *Iran*	67	G13
Susanino, *Russia*	45	D15
Susanville, *U.S.A.*	110	F3
Susch, *Switz.*	23	C10
Suşehri, *Turkey*	67	B8
Susong, *China*	53	B11
Susquehanna →, *U.S.A.*	107	G8
Susquehanna Depot, *U.S.A.*	107	E9
Susques, *Argentina*	126	A2
Sussex, *Canada*	99	C6
Sussex, *U.S.A.*	107	E10
Sussex, E. □, *U.K.*	13	G8
Sussex, W. □, *U.K.*	13	G7
Susteren, *Neths.*	17	F7
Sustut →, *Canada*	100	B3
Susuman, *Russia*	45	C15
Susunu, *Indonesia*	57	E8
Susurluk, *Turkey*	66	C3
Susuz, *Turkey*	67	B10
Sütçüler, *Turkey*	66	D4
Sutherland, *S. Africa*	84	E3
Sutherland, *U.S.A.*	108	E4
Sutherland Falls, *N.Z.*	87	L1
Sutherlin, *U.S.A.*	110	E2
Sutivan, *Croatia*	33	E13
Sutlej →, *Pakistan*	62	E4
Sutter, *U.S.A.*	112	F5
Sutter Creek, *U.S.A.*	112	G6
Sutton, *Canada*	107	A12
Sutton, *U.S.A.*	108	E6
Sutton →, *Canada*	98	A3
Sutton →, *Australia*	90	C4
Sutton in Ashfield, *U.K.*	12	D6
Suttsu, *Japan*	48	C10
Suva, *Fiji*	87	D8
Suva Reka, *Serbia, Yug.*	21	N10
Suvo Rudište, *Serbia, Yug.*	21	M10
Suvorov, *Russia*	42	C3
Suvorov Is. = Suwarrow Is., *Cook Is.*	93	J11
Suwałki, *Poland*	20	A12
Suwannaphum, *Thailand*	58	E4
Suwannee →, *U.S.A.*	105	L4
Suwanose-Jima, *Japan*	49	K4
Suwarrow Is., *Cook Is.*	93	J11
Suwayq aş Şuqban, *Iraq*	64	D5
Suweis, Khalîg el, *Egypt*	76	J8
Suweis, Qanâ es, *Egypt*	76	H8
Suwŏn, *S. Korea*	51	F14
Suzdal, *Russia*	42	B5
Suzhou, *China*	53	B13
Suzu, *Japan*	49	F8
Suzu-Misaki, *Japan*	49	F8
Suzuka, *Japan*	49	G8
Suzzara, *Italy*	32	C7
Svalbard, *Arctic*	4	B8
Svalöv, *Sweden*	11	J7
Svappavaara, *Sweden*	8	C19
Svarstad, *Norway*	10	E3
Svartisen, *Norway*	8	C15
Svartvik, *Sweden*	10	B11
Svatove, *Ukraine*	41	H10
Svatovo = Svatove, *Ukraine*	41	H10
Svay Chek, *Cambodia*	58	F4
Svay Rieng, *Cambodia*	59	G5
Svealand □, *Sweden*	9	G16
Sveg, *Sweden*	9	E16
Svendborg, *Denmark*	11	J4
Svene, *Norway*	10	E3
Svenljunga, *Sweden*	11	G7
Svenstrup, *Denmark*	11	H3
Sverdlovsk = Yekaterinburg, *Russia*	44	D7
Sverdlovsk, *Ukraine*	41	H10
Sverdrup Is., *Canada*	4	B3
Svetac, *Croatia*	33	E12
Sveti Ivan Zelina, *Croatia*	33	C13
Sveti Jurij, *Slovenia*	33	B12
Sveti Lenart, *Slovenia*	33	B12
Sveti Nikole, *Macedonia*	39	H4
Sveti Trojica, *Slovenia*	33	B12
Svetlogorsk = Svyetlahorsk, *Belarus*	41	F5
Svetlograd, *Russia*	43	H6
Svetlovodsk = Svitlovodsk, *Ukraine*	41	H7
Svetozarevo, *Serbia, Yug.*	21	L11
Svilach, *Belarus*	41	F3
Svishtov, *Bulgaria*	38	F8
Svislach, *Belarus*	41	F3
Svitava →, *Czech.*	20	F6
Svitavy, *Czech.*	20	F6
Svitlovodsk, *Ukraine*	41	H7
Svobodnyy, *Russia*	45	D13
Svolvær, *Norway*	8	B16
Svratka →, *Czech.*	20	F6
Svrljig, *Serbia, Yug.*	21	M12
Svyetlahorsk, *Belarus*	41	F5
Swabian Alps = Schwäbische Alb, *Germany*	19	G5
Swainsboro, *U.S.A.*	105	J4
Swakopmund, *Namibia*	84	C1
Swale →, *U.K.*	12	C6
Swalmen, *Neths.*	17	F8
Swan Hill, *Australia*	91	F3
Swan Hills, *Canada*	100	C5
Swan Is., *W. Indies*	116	C3
Swan L., *Canada*	101	C8
Swan River, *Canada*	101	C8
Swanage, *U.K.*	13	G6
Swansea, *Australia*	91	E5
Swansea, *U.K.*	13	F4
Swar →, *Pakistan*	63	B5
Swartberge, *S. Africa*	84	E3
Swartmodder, *S. Africa*	84	D3
Swartruggens, *S. Africa*	84	D4
Swarzędz, *Poland*	20	C7
Swastika, *Canada*	98	C3
Swatow = Shantou, *China*	53	F11
Swaziland ■, *Africa*	85	D5
Sweden ■, *Europe*	9	G16
Swedru, *Ghana*	79	D4
Sweet Home, *U.S.A.*	110	D2
Sweetwater, *Nev., U.S.A.*	112	G7
Sweetwater, *Tex., U.S.A.*	109	J4
Sweetwater →, *U.S.A.*	110	E10
Swellendam, *S. Africa*	84	E3
Świdnica, *Poland*	20	E6
Świdnik, *Poland*	20	D12
Świdwin, *Poland*	20	B5
Świebodzin, *Poland*	20	D5
Świecie, *Poland*	20	B8
Świętokrzyskie, Góry, *Poland*	20	E10
Swift Current, *Canada*	101	C7
Swiftcurrent →, *Canada*	101	C7
Swilly, L., *Ireland*	15	A4
Swindle, I., *Canada*	100	C3
Swindon, *U.K.*	13	F6
Swinemünde = Świnoujście, *Poland*	20	B4
Świnoujście, *Poland*	20	B4
Switzerland ■, *Europe*	22	D6
Swords, *Ireland*	15	C5
Syasstroy, *Russia*	40	B7
Sychevka, *Russia*	42	C2
Sydney, *Australia*	91	E5
Sydney, *Canada*	99	C7
Sydney Mines, *Canada*	99	C7
Sydprøven, *Greenland*	4	C5
Sydra, G. of = Surt, Khalīj, *Libya*	73	B8
Syeverodonetsk, *Ukraine*	41	H10
Syke, *Germany*	18	C4
Syktyvkar, *Russia*	44	C2
Sylacauga, *U.S.A.*	105	J2
Sylarna, *Sweden*	8	E15
Sylhet, *Bangla.*	61	G17
Sylt, *Germany*	18	A4
Sylvan Lake, *Canada*	100	C6
Sylvania, *U.S.A.*	105	J5
Sylvester, *U.S.A.*	105	K4
Sym, *Russia*	44	C9
Symón, *Mexico*	114	C4
Synelnykove, *Ukraine*	41	H8
Synnott Ra., *Australia*	88	C4
Syracuse, *Kans., U.S.A.*	109	F4
Syracuse, *N.Y., U.S.A.*	107	C8
Syrdarya →, *Kazakhstan*	44	E7
Syria ■, *Asia*	64	C3
Syul'dzhyukyor, *Russia*	45	C12
Syzran, *Russia*	42	D9
Szabadka = Subotica, *Serbia, Yug.*	—	—
Szarvas, *Hungary*	21	J10
Szczebrzeszyn, *Poland*	20	E12
Szczecin, *Poland*	20	B4
Szczecinek, *Poland*	20	B6
Szczytno, *Poland*	20	B11
Szechwan = Sichuan □, *China*	52	B5
Szeged, *Hungary*	21	J10
Szeghalom, *Hungary*	21	H11
Székesfehérvár, *Hungary*	21	H8
Szekszárd, *Hungary*	21	J8
Szendrö, *Hungary*	21	G10
Szentendre, *Hungary*	21	H9
Szentes, *Hungary*	21	J10
Szentgotthárd, *Hungary*	21	J6
Szentlőrinc, *Hungary*	21	J8
Szigetvár, *Hungary*	21	J7
Szolnok, *Hungary*	21	H10
Szombathely, *Hungary*	21	H6
Szprotawa, *Poland*	20	D5
Szydłowiec, *Poland*	20	D10
Szypliszki, *Poland*	20	A13

T

't Harde, *Neths.*	16	D7
't Zandt, *Neths.*	16	B9
Ta Khli Khok, *Thailand*	58	E3
Ta Lai, *Vietnam*	59	G6
Tabacal, *Argentina*	126	A3
Tabaco, *Phil.*	55	E6
Tabagné, *Ivory C.*	78	D4
Tabalos, *Peru*	124	B2
Tabarca, I. de, *Spain*	29	G4
Tabarka, *Tunisia*	75	A6
Tabas, *Khorāsān, Iran*	65	C9
Tabas, *Khorāsān, Iran*	65	C8
Tabasará, Serranía de, *Panama*	116	E3
Tabasco □, *Mexico*	115	D6
Tabatinga, Serra da, *Brazil*	122	D3
Tabāzīn, *Iran*	65	D8
Tabelbala, Kahal de, *Algeria*	75	C4
Taber, *Canada*	100	D6
Tabernas, *Spain*	29	H2
Tabernes de Valldigna, *Spain*	29	F4
Tabira, *Brazil*	122	C4
Tablas, *Phil.*	55	E5
Tablas Strait, *Phil.*	55	E4
Table B. = Tafelbaai, *S. Africa*	84	E2
Table Mt., *S. Africa*	84	E2
Tableland, *Australia*	88	C4
Tabletop, Mt., *Australia*	90	C4
Tábor, *Czech.*	20	F4
Tabora, *Tanzania*	82	D3
Tabora □, *Tanzania*	82	D3
Tabou, *Ivory C.*	78	E3
Tabrīz, *Iran*	67	C12
Tabuaeran, *Pac. Oc.*	93	G12
Tabuelan, *Phil.*	55	F5
Tabuenca, *Spain*	28	D3
Tabūk, *Si. Arabia*	64	D3
Tacámbaro de Codallos, *Mexico*	114	D4
Tacheng, *China*	54	B3
Tach'ing Shan = Daqing Shan, *China*	50	D6
Táchira □, *Venezuela*	120	B3
Tácina →, *Italy*	35	D9
Tacloban, *Phil.*	55	F6
Tacna, *Peru*	124	D3
Tacna □, *Peru*	124	D3
Tacoma, *U.S.A.*	112	C4
Tacuarembó, *Uruguay*	127	C4
Tacutu →, *Brazil*	121	C5
Tademaït, Plateau du, *Algeria*	75	C5
Tadent, O. →, *Algeria*	75	D6
Tadjerdjeri, O. →, *Algeria*	75	D5
Tadjerouna, *Algeria*	75	B5
Tadjettaret, O. →, *Algeria*	75	D6
Tadjmout, *Oasis, Algeria*	75	B5
Tadjmout, *Saoura, Algeria*	75	C5
Tadjoura, *Djibouti*	68	E3
Tadjoura, Golfe de, *Djibouti*	77	E5
Tadmor, *N.Z.*	87	J4
Tadoule, L., *Canada*	101	B9
Tadoussac, *Canada*	99	C6
Tadzhikistan = Tajikistan ■, *Asia*	44	F8
Taechŏn-ni, *S. Korea*	51	F14
Taegu, *S. Korea*	51	G15
Taegwan, *N. Korea*	51	D13
Taejŏn, *S. Korea*	51	F14
Tafalla, *Spain*	28	C3
Tafar, *Sudan*	77	F2
Tafassasset, O. →, *Algeria*	75	D6
Tafelbaai, *S. Africa*	84	E2
Tafelney, C., *Morocco*	74	B3
Tafermaar, *Indonesia*	57	F8
Taffermit, *Morocco*	74	C3
Tafí Viejo, *Argentina*	126	B2
Tafīhān, *Iran*	65	D7
Tafiré, *Ivory C.*	78	D3
Tafnidilt, *Morocco*	74	C2
Tafraoute, *Morocco*	74	C2
Taft, *Iran*	65	D7
Taft, *Phil.*	55	F6
Taft, *Calif., U.S.A.*	113	K7
Taft, *Tex., U.S.A.*	109	M6
Taga Dzong, *Bhutan*	61	F16
Taganrog, *Russia*	43	G4
Taganrogskiy Zaliv, *Russia*	43	G4
Tagatay, *Phil.*	55	D4
Tagbilaran, *Phil.*	55	G5
Tággia, *Italy*	32	E4
Taghzout, *Morocco*	74	B4
Tagish, *Canada*	100	A2
Tagish L., *Canada*	100	A2
Tagliacozzo, *Italy*	33	F10
Tagliamento →, *Italy*	33	C10
Táglio di Po, *Italy*	33	D9
Tagna, *Colombia*	120	D3
Tago, *Phil.*	55	G7
Tagomago, I. de, *Spain*	36	B8
Taguatinga, *Brazil*	123	D3
Tagudin, *Phil.*	55	C4
Tagum, *Phil.*	55	H6
Tagus = Tejo →, *Europe*	31	G1
Tahakopa, *N.Z.*	87	M2
Tahala, *Morocco*	74	B4
Tahan, Gunong, *Malaysia*	59	K4
Tahat, *Algeria*	75	D6
Tāherī, *Iran*	65	E7
Tahiti, *Pac. Oc.*	93	J13
Tahoe, L., *U.S.A.*	112	G6
Tahoe City, *U.S.A.*	112	F6
Taholah, *U.S.A.*	112	C2
Tahoua, *Niger*	79	C6
Tahta, *Egypt*	76	B3
Tahtalı Dağları, *Turkey*	66	C7
Tahuamanu →, *Bolivia*	124	C4
Tahulandang, *Indonesia*	57	D7
Tahuna, *Indonesia*	57	D7
Taï, *Ivory C.*	78	D3
Tai Hu, *China*	54	C7
Tai Shan, *China*	51	F9
Tai Xian, *China*	53	A13
Tai'an, *China*	51	F9
Taibei, *Taiwan*	53	E13
Taibique, *Canary Is.*	36	G2
Taibus Qi, *China*	50	D8
T'aichung = Taizhong, *Taiwan*	53	E13
Taidong, *Taiwan*	53	F13
Taieri →, *N.Z.*	87	M3
Taigu, *China*	50	F7
Taihang Shan, *China*	50	G7
Taihape, *N.Z.*	87	H5
Taihe, *Anhui, China*	50	H8
Taihe, *Jiangxi, China*	53	D10
Taihu, *China*	53	B11
Taijiang, *China*	52	D7
Taikang, *China*	50	G8
Tailem Bend, *Australia*	91	F2
Tailfingen, *Germany*	19	G5
Taimyr Peninsula = Taymyr, Poluostrov, *Russia*	45	B11
Tain, *U.K.*	14	D4
Tainan, *Taiwan*	53	F13
Taínaron, Ákra, *Greece*	39	N5
Taining, *China*	53	D11
Taintignies, *Belgium*	17	G2
Taiobeiras, *Brazil*	123	E3
T'aipei = Taibei, *Taiwan*	53	E13
Taiping, *China*	53	B12
Taiping, *Malaysia*	59	K3
Taipingzhen, *China*	50	H6
Taipu, *Brazil*	122	C4
Tairbeart = Tarbert, *U.K.*	14	D2
Taishan, *China*	53	F9
Taishun, *China*	53	D12
Taita □, *Kenya*	82	C4
Taita Hills, *Kenya*	82	C4
Taitao, C., *Chile*	128	C1
Taitao, Pen. de, *Chile*	128	C2
Taivalkoski, *Finland*	8	D23
Taiwan ■, *Asia*	53	F13
Taiwan Shan, *Taiwan*	53	F13
Taixing, *China*	53	A13
Taíyetos Óros, *Greece*	39	N5
Taiyiba, *Israel*	69	C4
Taiyuan, *China*	50	F7
Taizhong, *Taiwan*	53	E13
Taizhou, *China*	53	A12
Taizhou Liedao, *China*	53	C13
Ta'izz, *Yemen*	68	E3
Tājābād, *Iran*	65	D7
Tajapuru, Furo do, *Brazil*	122	B1
Tajikistan ■, *Asia*	44	F8
Tajima, *Japan*	49	F9
Tajo = Tejo →, *Europe*	31	G1
Tajrīsh, *Iran*	65	C6
Tājūrā, *Libya*	73	B7
Tak, *Thailand*	58	D2
Takāb, *Iran*	67	D12
Takachiho, *Japan*	49	H5
Takada, *Japan*	49	F9
Takahagi, *Japan*	49	F10
Takaka, *N.Z.*	87	J4
Takamatsu, *Japan*	49	G7
Takaoka, *Japan*	49	F8
Takapuna, *N.Z.*	87	G5
Takasaki, *Japan*	49	F9
Takatsuki, *Japan*	49	G7
Takaungu, *Kenya*	82	C4
Takayama, *Japan*	49	F8
Take-Shima, *Japan*	49	J5
Takefu, *Japan*	49	G8
Takengon, *Indonesia*	56	D1
Takeo, *Cambodia*	59	G5
Takeo, *Japan*	49	H5
Taketa, *Japan*	49	H5
Takh, *India*	63	C7
Takhman, *Cambodia*	59	G5
Takikawa, *Japan*	48	C10
Takla L., *Canada*	100	B3
Takla Landing, *Canada*	100	B3

Takla Makan = Taklamakan Shamo, China 46 F12
Taklamakan Shamo, China 46 F12
Taku →, Canada 100 B2
Takum, Nigeria 79 D6
Takutu →, Guyana 121 C5
Tal Halāl, Iran 65 D7
Tala, Uruguay 127 C4
Talachyn, Belarus 40 E5
Talacogan, Phil. 55 G6
Talagante, Chile 126 C1
Talaïnt, Morocco 74 C3
Talak, Niger 79 B6
Talamanca, Cordillera de, Cent. Amer. 116 E3
Talara, Peru 124 A1
Talas, Kyrgyzstan 44 E8
Talas, Turkey 66 C6
Talāta, Egypt 69 E1
Talata Mafara, Nigeria 79 C6
Talaud, Kepulauan, Indonesia 57 D7
Talaud Is. = Talaud, Kepulauan, Indonesia 57 D7
Talavera de la Reina, Spain 30 F6
Talawana, Australia 88 D3
Talayan, Phil. 55 H6
Talbert, Sillon de, France 24 D3
Talbot, C., Australia 88 B4
Talbragar →, Australia 91 E4
Talca, Chile 126 D1
Talca □, Chile 126 D1
Talcahuano, Chile 126 D1
Talcher, India 61 J14
Talcho, Niger 79 C5
Taldy Kurgan = Taldyqorghan, Kazakhstan 44 E8
Taldyqorghan, Kazakhstan 44 E8
Tālesh, Iran 67 D13
Tālesh, Kūhhā-ye, Iran 67 D13
Talguharai, Sudan 76 D4
Tali Post, Sudan 77 F3
Talibon, Phil. 57 B6
Talibong, Ko, Thailand 59 J2
Talihina, U.S.A. 109 H7
Talisayan, Phil. 55 G6
Taliwang, Indonesia 56 F5
Tall 'Afar, Iraq 67 D10
Tall 'Asūr, West Bank 69 D4
Tall Kalakh, Syria 69 A5
Talla, Egypt 76 J7
Talladega, U.S.A. 105 J2
Tallahassee, U.S.A. 105 K3
Tallangatta, Australia 91 F4
Tallarook, Australia 91 F4
Tallering Pk., Australia 89 E2
Tallinn, Estonia 9 G21
Tallulah, U.S.A. 109 J9
Talmest, Morocco 74 B3
Talmont, France 26 B2
Talne, Ukraine 41 H6
Talnoye = Talne, Ukraine 41 H6
Talodi, Sudan 77 E3
Talovaya, Russia 42 E5
Talpa de Allende, Mexico 114 C4
Talsi, Latvia 9 H20
Talsinnt, Morocco 75 B4
Taltal, Chile 126 B1
Taltson →, Canada 100 A6
Talwood, Australia 91 D4
Talyawalka Cr. →, Australia 91 E3
Tam Chau, Vietnam 59 G5
Tam Ky, Vietnam 58 E7
Tam Quan, Vietnam 58 E7
Tama, U.S.A. 108 E8
Tamala, Australia 89 E1
Tamalameque, Colombia 120 B3
Tamale, Ghana 79 D4
Taman, Russia 43 H3
Tamanar, Morocco 74 B3
Tamano, Japan 49 G6
Tamanrasset, Algeria 75 D6
Tamanrasset, O. →, Algeria 75 D5
Tamaqua, U.S.A. 107 F9
Tamar →, U.K. 13 G3
Támara, Colombia 120 B3
Tamarang, Australia 91 E5
Tamarinda, Spain 36 B10
Tamarite de Litera, Spain 28 D5
Tamashima, Japan 49 G6
Tamaské, Niger 79 C6
Tamaulipas □, Mexico 115 C5
Tamaulipas, Sierra de, Mexico 115 C5
Tamazula, Mexico 114 C3
Tamazunchale, Mexico 115 C5
Tamba-Dabatou, Guinea 78 C2
Tambacounda, Senegal 78 C2
Tambelan, Kepulauan, Indonesia 56 D3
Tambellup, Australia 89 F2
Tambo, Australia 90 C4
Tambo, Peru 124 C3
Tambo →, Peru 124 C3
Tambo de Mora, Peru 124 C2
Tambobamba, Peru 124 C3
Tambohorano, Madag. 85 B7
Tambopata →, Peru 124 C4
Tambora, Indonesia 56 F5
Tambov, Russia 42 D5
Tambre →, Spain 30 C2
Tambuku, Indonesia 57 G15
Tamburâ, Sudan 77 F2

Tâmchekket, Mauritania 78 B2
Tame, Colombia 120 B3
Tamega →, Portugal 30 D2
Tamelelt, Morocco 74 B3
Tamenglong, India 61 G18
Tamerza, Tunisia 75 B6
Tamgak, Mts., Niger 72 E6
Tamiahua, L. de, Mexico 115 C5
Tamil Nadu □, India 60 P10
Tamines, Belgium 17 H5
Tamis →, Serbia, Yug. 38 E3
Tamluk, India 63 H12
Tammerfors = Tampere, Finland 9 F20
Tammisaari = Tampere, Finland 9 F20
Tamo Abu, Pegunungan, Malaysia 56 D5
Tampa, U.S.A. 105 M4
Tampa B., U.S.A. 105 M4
Tampere, Finland 9 F20
Tampico, Mexico 115 C5
Tampin, Malaysia 59 L4
Tamri, Morocco 74 B3
Tamrida = Qādib, Yemen 68 E5
Tamsagbulag, Mongolia 54 B6
Tamu, Burma 61 G19
Tamuja →, Spain 31 F4
Tamworth, Australia 91 E5
Tamworth, U.K. 13 E6
Tamyang, S. Korea 51 G14
Tan An, Vietnam 59 G6
Tan-tan, Morocco 74 C2
Tana →, Kenya 82 C5
Tana →, Norway 8 A23
Tana, L., Ethiopia 77 E4
Tana River, Kenya 82 C4
Tanabe, Japan 49 H7
Tanabi, Brazil 123 F2
Tanafjorden, Norway 8 A23
Tanaga, Pta., Canary Is. 36 G1
Tanagro →, Italy 35 B8
Tanahbala, Indonesia 56 E1
Tanahgrogot, Indonesia 56 E5
Tanahjampea, Indonesia 57 F6
Tanahmasa, Indonesia 56 E1
Tanahmerah, Indonesia 57 F10
Tanakura, Japan 49 F10
Tanami, Australia 88 C4
Tanami Desert, Australia 88 C5
Tanana, U.S.A. 96 B4
Tanana →, U.S.A. 96 B4
Tananarive = Antananarivo, Madag. 85 B8
Tanannt, Morocco 74 B3
Tánaro →, Italy 32 C5
Tanaunella, Italy 34 B2
Tanbar, Australia 90 D3
Tancarville, France 24 C7
Tancheng, China 51 G10
Tanchön, N. Korea 51 D15
Tanda, Ut. P., India 63 F10
Tanda, Ut. P., India 63 E8
Tanda, Ivory C. 78 D4
Tandag, Phil. 55 G7
Tandaia, Tanzania 83 D3
Tăndărei, Romania 38 E10
Tandaué, Angola 84 B2
Tandil, Argentina 126 D4
Tandil, Sa. del, Argentina 126 D4
Tandlianwala, Pakistan 62 D5
Tando Adam, Pakistan 62 G3
Tandou L., Australia 91 E3
Tandsbyn, Sweden 10 A8
Tane-ga-Shima, Japan 49 J5
Taneatua, N.Z. 87 H6
Tanen Tong Dan, Burma 58 D2
Tanezrouft, Algeria 75 D5
Tang, Koh, Cambodia 59 G4
Tang Krasang, Cambodia 58 F5
Tanga, Tanzania 82 D4
Tanga □, Tanzania 82 D4
Tanganyika, L., Africa 82 D2
Tanger, Morocco 74 A3
Tangerang, Indonesia 57 G12
Tangerhütte, Germany 18 C7
Tangermünde, Germany 18 C7
Tanggu, China 51 E9
Tanggula Shan, China 54 C4
Tanghe, China 50 H7
Tangier = Tanger, Morocco 74 A3
Tangorin P.O., Australia 90 C3
Tangshan, China 51 E10
Tangtou, China 51 G10
Tanguiéta, Benin 79 C5
Tangxi, China 53 C12
Tangyan He →, China 52 C7
Tanimbar, Kepulauan, Indonesia 57 F8
Tanimbar Is. = Tanimbar, Kepulauan, Indonesia 57 F8
Taninges, France 27 B10
Tanjay, Phil. 55 G6
Tanjong Malim, Malaysia 59 L3
Tanjore = Thanjavur, India 60 P11
Tanjung, Indonesia 56 E5
Tanjungbalai, Indonesia 56 D1
Tanjungbatu, Indonesia 56 D5
Tanjungkarang Telukbetung, Indonesia 56 F3
Tanjungpandan, Indonesia 56 E3
Tanjungpinang, Indonesia 56 D2
Tanjungpriok, Indonesia 57 G12
Tanjungredeb, Indonesia 56 D5
Tanjungselor, Indonesia 56 D5
Tank, Pakistan 62 C4
Tänndalen, Sweden 10 B6

Tannis Bugt, Denmark 11 G4
Tannu-Ola, Russia 45 D10
Tano →, Ghana 78 D4
Tanon Str., Phil. 55 F5
Tanout, Niger 79 C6
Tanquinho, Brazil 123 D4
Tanta, Egypt 76 H7
Tantoyuca, Mexico 115 C5
Tantung = Dandong, China 51 D13
Tanumshede, Sweden 11 F5
Tanunda, Australia 91 E2
Tanus, France 26 D6
Tanzania ■, Africa 82 D3
Tanzilla →, Canada 100 B2
Tao Ko, Thailand 59 G2
Tao'an, China 51 B12
Tao'er He →, China 51 B13
Taohua Dao, China 53 C14
Taolanaro, Madag. 85 D8
Taole, China 50 E4
Taormina, Italy 35 E8
Taos, U.S.A. 111 H11
Taoudenni, Mali 74 D4
Taoudrart, Adrar, Algeria 75 D5
Taounate, Morocco 74 B4
Taourirt, Algeria 75 C5
Taourirt, Morocco 75 B4
Taouz, Morocco 74 B4
Taoyuan, China 53 C8
Taoyuan, Taiwan 53 E13
Tapa, Estonia 9 G21
Tapa Shan = Daba Shan, China 52 B7
Tapachula, Mexico 115 D6
Tapah, Malaysia 59 K3
Tapajós →, Brazil 121 D7
Tapaktuan, Indonesia 56 D1
Tapanui, N.Z. 87 L2
Tapauá, Brazil 125 B5
Tapauá →, Brazil 125 B5
Tapeta, Liberia 78 D3
Taphan Hin, Thailand 58 D3
Tapi →, India 60 J8
Tapia, Spain 30 B4
Tápiószele, Hungary 21 H9
Tapirai, Brazil 123 E2
Tapirapé →, Brazil 122 D1
Tapirapecó, Serra, Venezuela 121 C5
Tapirapuã, Brazil 125 C6
Tapoeripa, Surinam 121 B6
Tapolca, Hungary 21 J7
Tappahannock, U.S.A. 104 G7
Tapuaenuku, Mt., N.Z. 87 J4
Tapul Group, Phil. 55 J4
Tapurucuará, Brazil 121 D4
Taqīābād, Iran 65 C8
Taqtaq, Iraq 67 E11
Taquara, Brazil 127 B5
Taquari →, Brazil 125 D6
Taquaritinga, Brazil 123 F2
Tara, Australia 91 D5
Tara, Canada 106 B3
Tara, Russia 44 D8
Tara, Zambia 83 F2
Tara →, Russia 44 D8
Taraba □, Nigeria 79 D7
Tarabagatay, Khrebet, Kazakhstan 44 E9
Tarabuco, Bolivia 125 D5
Tarābulus, Lebanon 69 A4
Tarābulus, Libya 75 B7
Tarahouahout, Algeria 75 D6
Tarajalejo, Canary Is. 36 F5
Tarakan, Indonesia 56 D5
Tarakit, Mt., Kenya 82 B4
Taralga, Australia 91 E4
Tarama-Jima, Japan 49 M2
Taran, Mys, Russia 9 J18
Taranagar, India 62 E6
Taranaki □, N.Z. 87 H5
Tarancón, Spain 28 E1
Taranga, India 62 H5
Taranga Hill, India 62 H5
Táranto, Italy 35 B10
Táranto, G. di, Italy 35 B10
Tarapacá, Colombia 120 D4
Tarapacá □, Chile 126 A2
Tarapoto, Peru 124 B2
Taraquá, Brazil 120 C4
Tarare, France 27 C8
Tararua Ra., N.Z. 87 J5
Tarascon, France 27 E8
Tarascon-sur-Ariège, France 26 F5
Tarashcha, Ukraine 41 H6
Tarata, Peru 124 D3
Tarauacá, Brazil 124 B3
Tarauacá →, Brazil 124 B4
Taravo →, France 27 G12
Tarawa, N.Z. 87 H6
Tarawera, N.Z. 87 H6
Tarawera L., N.Z. 87 H6
Tarazona, Spain 28 D3
Tarazona de la Mancha, Spain 29 F3
Tarbat Ness, U.K. 14 D5
Tarbela Dam, Pakistan 62 B5
Tarbert, Strath., U.K. 14 F3
Tarbert, W. Isles, U.K. 14 D2
Tarbes, France 26 E4
Tarboro, U.S.A. 105 H7
Tarbrax, Australia 90 C3
Tarcento, Italy 33 B10
Tarcoola, Australia 91 E1
Tarcoon, Australia 91 E4
Tardets-Sorholus, France 26 E3

Tardoire →, France 26 C4
Taree, Australia 91 E5
Tarentaise, France 27 C10
Tarf, Ras, Morocco 74 A3
Tarfa, W. el →, Egypt 76 J7
Tarfaya, Morocco 74 C2
Targon, France 26 D3
Targuist, Morocco 74 B4
Tarhit, Algeria 75 B4
Táriba, Venezuela 120 B3
Tarifa, Spain 31 J5
Tarija, Bolivia 126 A3
Tarija □, Bolivia 126 A3
Tariku →, Indonesia 57 E9
Tarim Basin = Tarim Pendi, China 54 C3
Tarim He →, China 54 C3
Tarim Pendi, China 54 C3
Tarime □, Tanzania 82 C3
Taritatu →, Indonesia 57 E9
Tarka →, S. Africa 84 E4
Tarkastad, S. Africa 84 E4
Tarkhankut, Mys, Ukraine 41 K7
Tarko Sale, Russia 44 C8
Tarkwa, Ghana 78 D4
Tarlac, Phil. 55 D4
Tarlton Downs, Australia 90 C2
Tarm, Denmark 11 J2
Tarma, Peru 124 C2
Tarn □, France 26 E6
Tarn →, France 26 D5
Tarn-et-Garonne □, France 26 D5
Tarna →, Hungary 21 H9
Tárnobrzeg, Poland 20 E11
Tarnów, Poland 20 F11
Táro →, Italy 32 D7
Taroom, Australia 91 D4
Taroudannt, Morocco 74 B3
Tarp, Germany 18 A5
Tarpon Springs, U.S.A. 105 L4
Tarquínia, Italy 33 F8
Tarragona, Spain 28 D6
Tarragona □, Spain 28 D6
Tarrasa, Spain 28 D7
Tárrega, Spain 28 D6
Tarrytown, U.S.A. 107 E11
Tarshiha = Me'ona, Israel 69 B4
Tarso Emissi, Chad 73 D8
Tarsus, Turkey 66 D6
Tartagal, Argentina 126 A3
Tärtär, Azerbaijan 43 K8
Tärtär →, Azerbaijan 43 K8
Tartas, France 26 E3
Tartu, Estonia 9 G22
Tarțūs, Syria 66 E6
Tarumirim, Brazil 123 E3
Tarumizu, Japan 49 J5
Tarussa, Russia 42 C3
Tarutao, Ko, Thailand 59 J2
Tarutung, Indonesia 56 D1
Tarvísio, Italy 33 B10
Tarz Ulli, Libya 75 C7
Tasāwah, Libya 73 C7
Taschereau, Canada 98 C4
Taseko →, Canada 100 C4
Tash-Kömür, Kyrgyzstan 44 E8
Tash-Kumyr = Tash-Kömür, Kyrgyzstan 44 E8
Tashauz = Dashhowuz, Turkmenistan 44 E6
Tashi Chho Dzong = Thimphu, Bhutan 61 F16
Tashkent = Toshkent, Uzbekistan 44 E7
Tashtagol, Russia 44 D9
Tasikmalaya, Indonesia 57 G13
Tåsjön, Sweden 8 D16
Taskan, Russia 45 C16
Taşköprü, Turkey 66 B6
Tasman B., N.Z. 87 J4
Tasman Mts., N.Z. 87 J4
Tasman Pen., Australia 90 G4
Tasman Sea, Pac. Oc. 92 L8
Tasmania □, Australia 90 G4
Tăşnad, Romania 38 B5
Tassil Tin-Rerhoh, Algeria 75 D5
Tassili n-Ajjer, Algeria 75 C6
Tassili-Oua-n-Ahaggar, Algeria 75 D6
Tasu Sd., Canada 100 C2
Tata, Morocco 74 C3
Tatabánya, Hungary 21 H8
Tatahouine, Tunisia 75 B7
Tatar Republic = Tatarstan □, Russia 42 C10
Tatarbunary, Ukraine 41 K5
Tatarsk, Russia 44 D8
Tatarstan □, Russia 42 C10
Tateyama, Japan 49 G9
Tathlina L., Canada 100 A5
Tathra, Australia 91 F4
Tatinnai L., Canada 101 A9
Tatnam, C., Canada 101 B10
Tatra = Tatry, Slovak Rep. 20 F9
Tatry, Slovak Rep. 20 F9
Tatsuno, Japan 49 G7
Tatta, Pakistan 62 G2
Tatuī, Brazil 127 A6
Tatum, U.S.A. 109 J3
Tauberbischofsheim, Germany 19 F5

Taucha, Germany 18 D8
Taufikia, Sudan 77 F3
Taumarunui, N.Z. 87 H5
Taumaturgo, Brazil 124 B3
Taung, S. Africa 84 D3
Taungdwingyi, Burma 61 J19
Taunggyi, Burma 61 J20
Taungup, Burma 61 K19
Taungup Pass, Burma 61 K19
Taungup Taunggya, Burma 61 K18
Taunsa Barrage, Pakistan 62 D4
Taunton, U.K. 13 F4
Taunton, U.S.A. 107 E13
Taunus, Germany 19 E4
Taupo, N.Z. 87 H6
Taupo, L., N.Z. 87 H5
Tauragė, Lithuania 9 J20
Tauranga, N.Z. 87 G6
Tauranga Harb., N.Z. 87 G6
Taurianova, Italy 35 D9
Taurus Mts. = Toros Dağları, Turkey 66 C5
Tauste, Spain 28 D3
Tauz = Tovuz, Azerbaijan 43 K7
Tavannes, Switz. 22 B4
Tavas, Turkey 66 D3
Tavda, Russia 44 D7
Tavda →, Russia 44 D7
Taverny, France 25 C9
Taveta, Tanzania 82 C4
Taveuni, Fiji 87 C9
Tavignano →, France 27 F13
Tavira, Portugal 31 H3
Tavistock, Canada 106 C4
Tavistock, U.K. 13 G3
Tavolara, Italy 34 B2
Távora →, Portugal 30 D3
Tavoy, Burma 58 E2
Tavşanlı, Turkey 66 C3
Taw →, U.K. 13 F3
Tawas City, U.S.A. 104 C4
Tawau, Malaysia 56 D5
Tawitawi, Phil. 55 J4
Taxila, Pakistan 62 C5
Tay →, U.K. 14 E5
Tay, Firth of, U.K. 14 E5
Tay, L., Australia 89 F3
Tay, L., U.K. 14 E4
Tay Ninh, Vietnam 59 G6
Tayabamba, Peru 124 B2
Tayabas Bay, Phil. 55 E4
Taylakova, Russia 44 D8
Taylakovy = Taylakova, Russia 44 D8
Taylor, Canada 100 B4
Taylor, Nebr., U.S.A. 108 E5
Taylor, Pa., U.S.A. 107 E9
Taylor, Tex., U.S.A. 109 K6
Taylor, Mt., U.S.A. 111 J10
Taylorville, U.S.A. 108 F10
Taymā, Si. Arabia 64 E3
Taymyr, Oz., Russia 45 B11
Taymyr, Poluostrov, Russia 45 B11
Tayport, U.K. 14 E6
Tayshet, Russia 45 D10
Tayside □, U.K. 14 E5
Taytay, Phil. 55 F3
Taz →, Russia 44 C8
Taza, Morocco 74 B4
Tazah Khurmātū, Iraq 67 E11
Tazawa-Ko, Japan 48 E10
Tazenakht, Morocco 74 B3
Tazin L., Canada 101 B7
Tazoult, Algeria 75 A6
Tazovskiy, Russia 44 C8
Tbilisi, Georgia 43 K7
Tchad = Chad ■, Africa 73 E8
Tchad, L., Chad 73 F7
Tchaourou, Benin 79 D5
Tch'eng-tou = Chengdu, China 52 B5
Tchentlo L., Canada 100 B4
Tchibanga, Gabon 80 E2
Tchien, Liberia 78 D3
Tchin Tabaraden, Niger 79 B6
Tch'ong-k'ing = Chongqing, China 52 C6
Tczew, Poland 20 A8
Te Anau, L., N.Z. 87 L1
Te Aroha, N.Z. 87 G5
Te Awamutu, N.Z. 87 H5
Te Kuiti, N.Z. 87 H5
Te Puke, N.Z. 87 G6
Te Waewae B., N.Z. 87 M1
Tea →, Brazil 120 D4
Tea Tree, Australia 90 C1
Teague, U.S.A. 109 K6
Teano, Italy 35 A7
Teapa, Mexico 115 D6
Teba, Spain 31 J6
Tebakang, Malaysia 56 D4
Teberda, Russia 43 J5
Tébessa, Algeria 75 A6
Tebicuary →, Paraguay 126 B4
Tebingtinggi, Indonesia 56 D1
Tébourba, Tunisia 75 A6
Téboursouk, Tunisia 75 A6
Tebulos, Georgia 43 J7
Tecate, Mexico 113 N10
Tech →, France 26 F7
Techiman, Ghana 78 D4
Tecka, Argentina 128 B2
Tecomán, Mexico 114 D4
Tecopa, U.S.A. 113 K10
Tecoripa, Mexico 114 B3
Tecuala, Mexico 114 C3

Tecuci, *Romania*	38	D10
Tecumseh, *U.S.A.*	104	D4
Tedzhen = Tejen, *Turkmenistan*	44	F7
Tees →, *U.K.*	12	C6
Teesside, *U.K.*	12	C6
Teeswater, *Canada*	106	C3
Tefé, *Brazil*	121	D5
Tefé →, *Brazil*	121	D5
Tefenni, *Turkey*	66	D3
Tegal, *Indonesia*	57	G13
Tegelen, *Neths.*	17	F8
Tegernsee, *Germany*	19	H7
Teggiano, *Italy*	35	B8
Teghra, *India*	63	G11
Tegid, L. = Bala, L., *U.K.*	12	E4
Tegina, *Nigeria*	79	C6
Tegucigalpa, *Honduras*	116	D2
Tehachapi, *U.S.A.*	113	K8
Tehachapi Mts., *U.S.A.*	113	L8
Tehamiyam, *Sudan*	76	D4
Tehilla, *Sudan*	76	D4
Téhini, *Ivory C.*	78	D4
Tehrān, *Iran*	65	C6
Tehuacán, *Mexico*	115	D5
Tehuantepec, *Mexico*	115	D5
Tehuantepec, G. de, *Mexico*	115	D5
Tehuantepec, Istmo de, *Mexico*	115	D6
Teide, *Canary Is.*	36	F3
Teifi →, *U.K.*	13	E3
Teign →, *U.K.*	13	G4
Teignmouth, *U.K.*	13	G4
Teixeira, *Brazil*	122	C4
Teixeira Pinto, *Guinea-Biss.*	78	C1
Tejen, *Turkmenistan*	44	F7
Tejo →, *Europe*	31	G1
Tejon Pass, *U.S.A.*	113	L8
Tekamah, *U.S.A.*	108	E6
Tekapo, L., *N.Z.*	87	K3
Tekax, *Mexico*	115	C7
Tekeli, *Kazakhstan*	44	E8
Tekeze →, *Ethiopia*	77	E4
Tekija, *Serbia, Yug.*	21	L12
Tekirdağ, *Turkey*	66	B2
Tekkali, *India*	61	K14
Tekke, *Turkey*	66	B7
Tekman, *Turkey*	67	C9
Tekoa, *U.S.A.*	110	C5
Tekouïât, O. →, *Algeria*	75	D5
Tel Aviv-Yafo, *Israel*	69	C3
Tel Lakhish, *Israel*	69	D3
Tel Megiddo, *Israel*	69	C4
Tela, *Honduras*	116	C2
Télagh, *Algeria*	75	B4
Telanaipura = Jambi, *Indonesia*	56	E2
Telavi, *Georgia*	43	J7
Telde, *Canary Is.*	36	G4
Telegraph Creek, *Canada*	100	B2
Telekhany = Tsyelyakhany, *Belarus*	41	F3
Telemark, *Norway*	9	G12
Telemark fylke □, *Norway*	10	E2
Telén, *Argentina*	126	D2
Teleng, *Iran*	65	E9
Teleño, *Spain*	30	C4
Teleorman →, *Romania*	38	E8
Teles Pires →, *Brazil*	125	B6
Telescope Pk., *U.S.A.*	113	J9
Teletaye, *Mali*	79	B5
Telford, *U.K.*	12	E5
Telfs, *Austria*	19	H7
Télimélé, *Guinea*	78	C2
Telkwa, *Canada*	100	C3
Tell City, *U.S.A.*	104	G2
Tellicherry, *India*	60	P9
Tellin, *Belgium*	17	H6
Telluride, *U.S.A.*	111	H10
Teloloapán, *Mexico*	115	D5
Telpos Iz, *Russia*	6	C17
Telsen, *Argentina*	128	B3
Telšiai, *Lithuania*	9	H20
Teltow, *Germany*	18	C9
Teluk Anson, *Malaysia*	59	K3
Teluk Betung = Tanjungkarang Telukbetung, *Indonesia*	56	F3
Teluk Intan = Teluk Anson, *Malaysia*	59	K3
Telukbutun, *Indonesia*	59	K7
Telukdalem, *Indonesia*	56	D1
Tema, *Ghana*	79	D5
Temanggung, *Indonesia*	57	G14
Temapache, *Mexico*	115	C5
Temax, *Mexico*	115	C7
Temba, *S. Africa*	85	D4
Tembe, *Zaïre*	82	C2
Temblador, *Venezuela*	121	B5
Tembleque, *Spain*	28	F1
Temblor Range, *U.S.A.*	113	K7
Teme →, *U.K.*	13	E5
Temecula, *U.S.A.*	113	M9
Temerloh, *Malaysia*	59	L4
Temir, *Kazakhstan*	44	E6
Temirtau, *Kazakhstan*	44	D8
Temirtau, *Russia*	44	D9
Témiscaming, *Canada*	98	C4
Temma, *Australia*	90	G3
Temnikov, *Russia*	42	C6
Temo →, *Italy*	34	B1
Temora, *Australia*	91	E4
Temosachic, *Mexico*	114	B3
Tempe, *U.S.A.*	111	K8
Tempe Downs, *Australia*	88	D5
Témpio Pausánia, *Italy*	34	B2
Tempiute, *U.S.A.*	112	H11
Temple, *U.S.A.*	109	K6
Temple B., *Australia*	90	A3
Templemore, *Ireland*	15	D4
Templeton, *U.S.A.*	112	K6
Templeton →, *Australia*	90	C2
Templeuve, *Belgium*	17	G2
Templin, *Germany*	18	B9
Tempoal, *Mexico*	115	C5
Temryuk, *Russia*	43	H3
Temse, *Belgium*	17	F4
Temska →, *Serbia, Yug.*	21	M12
Temuco, *Chile*	128	A2
Temuka, *N.Z.*	87	L3
Ten Boer, *Neths.*	16	B9
Tena, *Ecuador*	120	D2
Tenabo, *Mexico*	115	C6
Tenaha, *U.S.A.*	109	K7
Tenali, *India*	60	L12
Tenancingo, *Mexico*	115	D5
Tenango, *Mexico*	115	D5
Tenasserim, *Burma*	59	F2
Tenasserim □, *Burma*	58	F2
Tenay, *France*	27	C9
Tenby, *U.K.*	13	F3
Tenda, Col di, *France*	27	D11
Tendaho, *Ethiopia*	68	E3
Tende, *France*	27	D11
Tendelti, *Sudan*	77	E3
Tendrara, *Morocco*	75	B4
Tendre, Mt., *Switz.*	22	C2
Tendrovskaya Kosa, *Ukraine*	41	J6
Teneida, *Egypt*	76	B2
Tenente Marques →, *Brazil*	125	C6
Ténéré, *Niger*	79	B7
Tenerife, *Canary Is.*	36	F3
Tenerife, Pico, *Canary Is.*	36	G1
Ténès, *Algeria*	75	A5
Teng Xian, *Guangxi Zhuangzu, China*	53	F8
Teng Xian, *Shandong, China*	51	G9
Tengah □, *Indonesia*	57	E6
Tengah Kepulauan, *Indonesia*	56	F5
Tengchong, *China*	52	E2
Tengchowfu = Penglai, *China*	51	F11
Tenggara □, *Indonesia*	57	E6
Tenggarong, *Indonesia*	56	E5
Tenggol, P., *Malaysia*	59	K4
Tengiz, Ozero, *Kazakhstan*	44	D7
Tenigerbad, *Switz.*	23	C7
Tenino, *U.S.A.*	112	D4
Tenkasi, *India*	60	Q10
Tenke, Shaba, *Zaïre*	83	E2
Tenke, Shaba, *Zaïre*	83	E2
Tenkodogo, *Burkina Faso*	79	C4
Tenna →, *Italy*	33	E10
Tennant Creek, *Australia*	90	B1
Tennessee □, *U.S.A.*	105	H2
Tennessee →, *U.S.A.*	104	G1
Tenneville, *Belgium*	17	H7
Tennille, *U.S.A.*	105	J4
Tennsift, Oued →, *Morocco*	74	B3
Teno, Pta. de, *Canary Is.*	36	F3
Tenom, *Malaysia*	56	C5
Tenosique, *Mexico*	115	D6
Tenryū-Gawa →, *Japan*	49	G8
Tent L., *Canada*	101	A7
Tenterfield, *Australia*	91	D5
Teófilo Otoni, *Brazil*	123	E3
Teotihuacán, *Mexico*	115	D5
Tepa, *Indonesia*	57	F7
Tepalcatepec →, *Mexico*	114	D4
Tepehuanes, *Mexico*	114	B3
Tepequem, Serra, *Brazil*	121	C5
Tepetongo, *Mexico*	114	C4
Tepic, *Mexico*	114	C4
Tepoca, C., *Mexico*	114	A2
Tequila, *Mexico*	114	C4
Ter →, *Spain*	28	C8
Ter Apel, *Neths.*	16	C10
Téra, *Niger*	79	C5
Tera →, *Spain*	30	D5
Teraina, *Kiribati*	93	G11
Téramo, *Italy*	33	F10
Terang, *Australia*	91	F3
Terborg, *Neths.*	16	E8
Tercan, *Turkey*	67	C9
Tercero →, *Argentina*	126	C3
Terebovlya, *Ukraine*	41	H3
Terek →, *Russia*	43	J8
Terenos, *Brazil*	125	E7
Tereshka →, *Russia*	42	E8
Teresina, *Brazil*	122	C3
Teresina, *Brazil*	121	C7
Terewah, L., *Australia*	91	D4
Terges →, *Portugal*	31	H3
Tergnier, *France*	25	C10
Terhazza, *Mali*	74	D3
Terheijden, *Neths.*	17	E5
Teridgerie Cr. →, *Australia*	91	E4
Terlizzi, *Italy*	35	A9
Terme, *Turkey*	66	B7
Termez = Termiz, *Uzbekistan*	44	F7
Términi Imerese, *Italy*	34	E6
Términos, L. de, *Mexico*	115	D6
Termiz, *Uzbekistan*	44	F7
Térmoli, *Italy*	33	F12
Ternate, *Indonesia*	57	D7
Terneuzen, *Neths.*	17	F3
Terney, *Russia*	45	E14
Terni, *Italy*	33	F9
Ternitz, *Austria*	21	H6
Ternopil, *Ukraine*	41	H3
Ternopol = Ternopil, *Ukraine*	41	H3
Terowie, *N.S.W., Australia*	91	E4
Terowie, *S. Austral., Australia*	91	E2
Terra Bella, *U.S.A.*	113	K7
Terrace, *Canada*	100	C3
Terrace Bay, *Canada*	98	C2
Terracina, *Italy*	34	A6
Terralba, *Italy*	34	C1
Terranova = Ólbia, *Italy*	34	B2
Terranuova Bracciolini, *Italy*	33	E8
Terrasini Favarotta, *Italy*	34	D6
Terrassa = Tarrasa, *Spain*	28	D7
Terrasson-la-Villedieu, *France*	26	C5
Terre Haute, *U.S.A.*	104	F2
Terrebonne B., *U.S.A.*	109	L9
Terrecht, *Mali*	75	D4
Terrell, *U.S.A.*	109	J6
Terrenceville, *Canada*	99	C9
Terrick Terrick, *Australia*	90	C4
Terry, *U.S.A.*	108	B2
Terschelling, *Neths.*	16	B6
Tersko-Kumskiy Kanal →, *Russia*	43	H7
Terter = Tärtär →, *Azerbaijan*	43	K8
Teruel, *Spain*	28	E3
Teruel □, *Spain*	28	E4
Tervel, *Bulgaria*	38	F10
Tervola, *Finland*	8	C21
Teryaweyna L., *Australia*	91	E3
Tešanj, *Bos.-H.*	21	L7
Teseney, *Eritrea*	77	D4
Tesha →, *Russia*	42	C6
Teshio, *Japan*	48	B10
Teshio-Gawa →, *Japan*	48	B10
Tesiyn Gol →, *Mongolia*	54	A4
Teslin, *Canada*	100	A2
Teslin →, *Canada*	100	A2
Teslin L., *Canada*	100	A2
Tesouro, *Brazil*	125	D7
Tessalit, *Mali*	79	A5
Tessaoua, *Niger*	79	C6
Tessenderlo, *Belgium*	17	F6
Tessin, *Germany*	18	A8
Tessit, *Mali*	79	B5
Test →, *U.K.*	13	F6
Testa del Gargano, *Italy*	35	A9
Têt →, *France*	26	F7
Tetachuck L., *Canada*	100	C3
Tetas, Pta., *Chile*	126	A1
Tete, *Mozam.*	83	F3
Tete □, *Mozam.*	83	F3
Teterev →, *Ukraine*	41	G6
Teteringen, *Neths.*	17	E5
Teterow, *Germany*	18	B8
Teteven, *Bulgaria*	38	G7
Tethul →, *Canada*	100	A6
Tetiyev, *Ukraine*	41	H5
Teton →, *U.S.A.*	110	C8
Tétouan, *Morocco*	74	A3
Tetovo, *Macedonia*	38	G4
Tetuán = Tétouan, *Morocco*	74	A3
Tetyukhe Pristan, *Russia*	48	B7
Tetyushi, *Russia*	42	C9
Teuco →, *Argentina*	126	B3
Teufen, *Switz.*	23	B8
Teulada, *Italy*	34	D1
Teulon, *Canada*	101	C9
Teun, *Indonesia*	57	F7
Teutoburger Wald, *Germany*	18	C4
Tévere →, *Italy*	33	G9
Teverya, *Israel*	69	C4
Tewantin, *Australia*	91	D5
Tewkesbury, *U.K.*	13	F5
Texada I., *Canada*	100	D4
Texarkana, *Ark., U.S.A.*	109	J8
Texarkana, *Tex., U.S.A.*	109	J7
Texas, *Australia*	91	D5
Texas □, *U.S.A.*	109	K5
Texas City, *U.S.A.*	109	L7
Texel, *Neths.*	16	B5
Texhoma, *U.S.A.*	109	G4
Texline, *U.S.A.*	109	G3
Texoma, L., *U.S.A.*	109	J6
Teykovo, *Russia*	42	B5
Teza →, *Russia*	42	B5
Tezin, *Afghan.*	62	B3
Teziutlán, *Mexico*	115	D5
Tezpur, *India*	61	F18
Tezzeron L., *Canada*	100	C4
Tha-anne →, *Canada*	101	A10
Tha Deua, *Laos*	58	D4
Tha Deua, *Laos*	58	C3
Tha Pla, *Thailand*	58	D3
Tha Rua, *Thailand*	58	E3
Tha Sala, *Thailand*	59	H2
Tha Song Yang, *Thailand*	58	D1
Thaba Putsoa, *Lesotho*	85	D4
Thabana Ntlenyana, *Lesotho*	85	D4
Thabazimbi, *S. Africa*	85	C4
Thai Binh, *Vietnam*	58	B6
Thai Hoa, *Vietnam*	58	C5
Thai Muang, *Thailand*	59	H2
Thai Nguyen, *Vietnam*	58	B5
Thailand ■, *Asia*	58	E4
Thailand, G. of, *Asia*	59	G3
Thakhek, *Laos*	58	D5
Thal, *Pakistan*	62	C4
Thal Desert, *Pakistan*	62	D4
Thala, *Tunisia*	75	A6
Thala La, *Burma*	61	E20
Thalabarivat, *Cambodia*	58	F5
Thallon, *Australia*	91	D4
Thalwil, *Switz.*	23	B7
Thame →, *U.K.*	13	F6
Thames, *N.Z.*	87	G5
Thames →, *Canada*	98	D3
Thames →, *U.K.*	13	F8
Thames →, *U.S.A.*	107	E12
Thamesford, *Canada*	106	C3
Thamesville, *Canada*	106	D3
Than Uyen, *Vietnam*	58	B4
Thane, *India*	60	K8
Thanesar, *India*	62	D7
Thanet, I. of, *U.K.*	13	F9
Thangoo, *Australia*	88	C3
Thangool, *Australia*	90	C5
Thanh Hoa, *Vietnam*	58	C5
Thanh Hung, *Vietnam*	59	H5
Thanh Pho Ho Chi Minh = Phanh Bho Ho Chi Minh, *Vietnam*	59	G6
Thanh Thuy, *Vietnam*	58	A5
Thanjavur, *India*	60	P11
Thann, *France*	25	E14
Thaon-les-Vosges, *France*	25	D13
Thap Sakae, *Thailand*	59	G2
Thap Than, *Thailand*	58	E2
Thar Desert, *India*	62	F4
Tharad, *India*	62	G4
Tharrawaddy, *Burma*	61	L19
Tharthar, Mileh, *Iraq*	67	E10
Tharthār, W. ath →, *Iraq*	67	E10
Thásos, *Greece*	39	J7
That Khe, *Vietnam*	58	A6
Thatcher, *Ariz., U.S.A.*	111	K9
Thatcher, *Colo., U.S.A.*	109	G2
Thaton, *Burma*	61	L20
Thau, Bassin de, *France*	26	E7
Thaungdut, *Burma*	61	G19
Thayer, *U.S.A.*	109	G9
Thayetmyo, *Burma*	61	K19
Thazi, *Burma*	61	J20
The Alberga →, *Australia*	91	D2
The Bight, *Bahamas*	117	B4
The Coorong, *Australia*	91	F2
The Dalles, *U.S.A.*	110	D3
The English Company's Is., *Australia*	90	A2
The Frome →, *Australia*	91	D2
The Grampians, *Australia*	91	F3
The Great Divide = Great Dividing Ra., *Australia*	90	C4
The Hague = 's-Gravenhage, *Neths.*	16	D4
The Hamilton →, *Australia*	91	D2
The Macumba →, *Australia*	91	D2
The Neales →, *Australia*	91	D2
The Officer →, *Australia*	89	E5
The Pas, *Canada*	101	C8
The Range, *Zimbabwe*	83	F3
The Rock, *Australia*	91	F4
The Salt L., *Australia*	91	E3
The Stevenson →, *Australia*	91	D2
The Warburton →, *Australia*	91	D2
Thebes = Thívai, *Greece*	39	L6
Thebes, *Egypt*	76	B3
Thedford, *Canada*	106	C3
Thedford, *U.S.A.*	108	E4
Theebine, *Australia*	91	D5
Thekulthili L., *Canada*	101	A7
Thelon →, *Canada*	101	A8
Thénezay, *France*	24	F6
Thenia, *Algeria*	75	A5
Thenon, *France*	26	C5
Theodore, *Australia*	90	C5
Thepha, *Thailand*	59	J3
Thérain →, *France*	25	C9
Theresa, *U.S.A.*	107	B9
Thermaïkós Kólpos, *Greece*	39	J5
Thermopolis, *U.S.A.*	110	E9
Thermopylae P., *Greece*	39	L5
Thessalía □, *Greece*	39	L4
Thessalon, *Canada*	98	C3
Thessaloníki, *Greece*	39	J5
Thessaloníki, Gulf of = Thermaïkós Kólpos, *Greece*	39	J5
Thessaly = Thessalía □, *Greece*	39	L4
Thetford, *U.K.*	13	E8
Thetford Mines, *Canada*	99	C5
Theun →, *Laos*	58	C5
Theunissen, *S. Africa*	84	D4
Theux, *Belgium*	17	G7
Thevenard, *Australia*	91	E1
Thiámis →, *Greece*	39	K3
Thiberville, *France*	24	C7
Thibodaux, *U.S.A.*	109	L9
Thicket Portage, *Canada*	101	B9
Thief River Falls, *U.S.A.*	108	A6
Thiel Mts., *Antarctica*	5	E16
Thiene, *Italy*	33	C8
Thiérache, *France*	25	C10
Thiers, *France*	26	C7
Thies, *Senegal*	78	C1
Thiet, *Sudan*	77	F2
Thika, *Kenya*	82	C4
Thikombia, *Fiji*	87	B9
Thille-Boubacar, *Senegal*	78	B1
Thimphu, *Bhutan*	61	F16
þingvallavatn, *Iceland*	8	D3
Thionville, *France*	25	C13
Thíra, *Greece*	39	N8
Thirasía, *Greece*	39	N8
Thirsk, *U.K.*	12	C6
Thisted, *Denmark*	9	H13
Thistle I., *Australia*	91	F2
Thívai, *Greece*	39	L6
Thiviers, *France*	26	C4
Thizy, *France*	27	B8
þjórsá →, *Iceland*	8	E3
Thlewiaza →, *Man., Canada*	101	B8
Thlewiaza →, *N.W.T., Canada*	101	A10
Thmar Puok, *Cambodia*	58	F4
Tho Vinh, *Vietnam*	58	C5
Thoa →, *Canada*	101	A7
Thoen, *Thailand*	58	D2
Thoeng, *Thailand*	58	C3
Thoissey, *France*	27	B8
Tholdi, *Pakistan*	63	B7
Tholen, *Neths.*	17	E4
Thomas, *Okla., U.S.A.*	109	H5
Thomas, *W. Va., U.S.A.*	104	F6
Thomas, L., *Australia*	91	D2
Thomaston, *U.S.A.*	105	J3
Thomasville, *Ala., U.S.A.*	105	K2
Thomasville, *Ga., U.S.A.*	105	K3
Thomasville, *N.C., U.S.A.*	105	H5
Thommen, *Belgium*	17	H8
Thompson, *Canada*	101	B9
Thompson, *U.S.A.*	111	G9
Thompson →, *Canada*	100	C4
Thompson →, *U.S.A.*	108	F8
Thompson Falls, *U.S.A.*	110	C6
Thompson Landing, *Canada*	101	A6
Thompson Pk., *U.S.A.*	110	F2
Thomson's Falls = Nyahururu, *Kenya*	82	B4
Thon Buri, *Thailand*	59	F3
Thônes, *France*	27	C10
Thonon-les-Bains, *France*	27	B10
Thorez, *Ukraine*	41	H10
þórisvatn, *Iceland*	8	D4
Thornaby on Tees, *U.K.*	12	C6
Thornbury, *Canada*	106	B4
Thorold, *Canada*	106	C5
þórshöfn, *Iceland*	8	C6
Thouarcé, *France*	24	E6
Thouars, *France*	24	F6
Thouet →, *France*	24	E6
Thouin, C., *Australia*	88	D2
Thousand Oaks, *U.S.A.*	113	L8
Thrace, *Turkey*	66	D2
Three Forks, *U.S.A.*	110	D8
Three Hills, *Canada*	100	C6
Three Hummock I., *Australia*	90	G3
Three Lakes, *U.S.A.*	108	C10
Three Points, C., *Ghana*	78	E4
Three Rivers, *Australia*	89	E2
Three Rivers, *Calif., U.S.A.*	112	J8
Three Rivers, *Tex., U.S.A.*	109	L5
Three Sisters, *U.S.A.*	110	D3
Throssell, L., *Australia*	89	E3
Throssell Ra., *Australia*	88	D3
Thuan Hoa, *Vietnam*	59	H5
Thubun Lakes, *Canada*	101	A6
Thueyts, *France*	27	D8
Thuillies, *Belgium*	17	H4
Thuin, *Belgium*	17	H4
Thuir, *France*	26	F6
Thule, *Greenland*	4	B4
Thun, *Switz.*	22	C5
Thundelarra, *Australia*	89	E2
Thunder B., *U.S.A.*	106	B1
Thunder Bay, *Canada*	98	C2
Thunersee, *Switz.*	22	C5
Thung Song, *Thailand*	59	H2
Thunkar, *Bhutan*	61	F17
Thuong Tra, *Vietnam*	58	D6
Thur →, *Switz.*	23	A8
Thurgau □, *Switz.*	23	A8
Thüringen □, *Germany*	18	E7
Thüringer Wald, *Germany*	18	E7
Thurles, *Ireland*	15	D4
Thurloo Downs, *Australia*	91	D3
Thurn P., *Austria*	19	H8
Thursday I., *Australia*	90	A3
Thurso, *Canada*	98	C4
Thurso, *U.K.*	14	C5
Thurston I., *Antárctica*	5	D16
Thury-Harcourt, *France*	24	D6
Thusis, *Switz.*	23	C8
Thutade L., *Canada*	100	B3
Thyborøn, *Denmark*	11	H2
Thylungra, *Australia*	91	D3
Thyolo, *Malawi*	83	F4
Thysville = Mbanza Ngungu, *Zaïre*	80	F2
Ti-n-Barraouene, O. →, *Africa*	79	B5
Ti-n-Medjerdam, O. →, *Algeria*	75	C5

Ti-n-Tarabine, O.

Ti-n-Tarabine, O. →, *Algeria* 75 D6
Ti-n-Zaouaténe, *Algeria* 75 E5
Tia, *Australia* 91 E5
Tiahuanacu, *Bolivia* 124 D4
Tian Shan, *China* 54 B3
Tianchang, *China* 53 A12
Tiandong, *China* 52 F6
Tian'e, *China* 52 E6
Tianguá, *Brazil* 122 B3
Tianhe, *China* 52 E7
Tianjin, *China* 51 E9
Tiankoura, *Burkina Faso* 78 C4
Tianlin, *China* 52 E6
Tianmen, *China* 53 B9
Tianquan, *China* 52 B4
Tianshui, *China* 50 G3
Tiantai, *China* 53 C13
Tianyang, *China* 52 F6
Tianzhen, *China* 50 D8
Tianzhu, *China* 52 D7
Tianzhuangtai, *China* 51 D12
Tiaret, *Algeria* 75 A5
Tiassalé, *Ivory C.* 78 D4
Tibagi, *Brazil* 127 A5
Tibagi →, *Brazil* 127 A5
Tibati, *Cameroon* 79 D7
Tiber = Tévere →, *Italy* 33 G9
Tiber Reservoir, *U.S.A.* 110 B8
Tiberias = Teverya, *Israel* 69 C4
Tiberias, L. = Yam Kinneret, *Israel* 69 C4
Tibesti, *Chad* 73 D8
Tibet = Xizang □, *China* 54 C3
Tibiao, *Phil.* 55 F5
Tibiri, *Niger* 79 C6
Ţibleş, *Romania* 38 B7
Tibnī, *Syria* 67 E8
Tibooburra, *Australia* 91 D3
Tibro, *Sweden* 11 F8
Tibugá, G. de, *Colombia* 120 B2
Tiburón, *Mexico* 114 B2
Ticao I., *Phil.* 55 E5
Tîchît, *Mauritania* 78 B3
Tichla, *Mauritania* 74 D2
Ticho, *Ethiopia* 77 F4
Ticino □, *Switz.* 23 D7
Ticino →, *Italy* 32 C6
Ticonderoga, *U.S.A.* 107 C11
Ticul, *Mexico* 115 C7
Tidaholm, *Sweden* 11 F7
Tiddim, *Burma* 61 H18
Tideridjaouine, Adrar, *Algeria* 75 D5
Tidikelt, *Algeria* 75 C5
Tidjikja, *Mauritania* 78 B2
Tidore, *Indonesia* 57 D7
Tiébissou, *Ivory C.* 78 D3
Tiefencastel, *Switz.* 23 C9
Tiel, *Neths.* 16 E6
Tiel, *Senegal* 78 C1
Tieling, *China* 51 C12
Tielt, *Belgium* 17 F2
Tien Shan, *Asia* 46 E11
Tien-tsin = Tianjin, *China* 51 E9
Tien Yen, *Vietnam* 58 B6
T'ienching = Tianjin, *China* 51 E9
Tienen, *Belgium* 17 G5
Tiénigbé, *Ivory C.* 78 D3
Tientsin = Tianjin, *China* 51 E9
Tierra Amarilla, *Chile* 126 B1
Tierra Amarilla, *U.S.A.* 111 H10
Tierra Colorada, *Mexico* 115 D5
Tierra de Barros, *Spain* 31 G4
Tierra de Campos, *Spain* 30 C6
Tierra del Fuego □, *Argentina* 128 D3
Tierra del Fuego, I. Gr. de, *Argentina* 128 D3
Tierralta, *Colombia* 120 B2
Tiétar →, *Spain* 30 F4
Tieté →, *Brazil* 127 A5
Tieyon, *Australia* 91 D1
Tifarati, *W. Sahara* 74 C2
Tiffin, *U.S.A.* 104 E4
Tiflèt, *Morocco* 74 B3
Tiflis = Tbilisi, *Georgia* 43 K7
Tifton, *U.S.A.* 105 K4
Tifu, *Indonesia* 57 E7
Tighina, *Moldova* 41 J5
Tigil, *Russia* 45 D16
Tignish, *Canada* 99 C7
Tigray □, *Ethiopia* 77 E4
Tigre →, *Peru* 120 D3
Tigre →, *Venezuela* 121 B5
Tigris = Dijlah, Nahr →, *Asia* 64 D5
Tiguentourine, *Algeria* 75 C6
Tigyaing, *Burma* 61 H20
Tigzerte, O. →, *Morocco* 74 C3
Tîh, Gebel el, *Egypt* 76 J8
Tihodaine, Dunes de, *Algeria* 75 C6
Tijesno, *Croatia* 33 E12
Tījī, *Libya* 75 B7
Tijuana, *Mexico* 113 N9
Tikal, *Guatemala* 116 C2
Tikamgarh, *India* 63 G8
Tikhoretsk, *Russia* 43 H5
Tikhvin, *Russia* 40 C7
Tikkadouine, Adrar, *Algeria* 75 D5
Tiko, *Cameroon* 79 E6
Tikrīt, *Iraq* 67 E10
Tiksi, *Russia* 45 B13
Tilamuta, *Indonesia* 57 D6
Tilburg, *Neths.* 17 E6
Tilbury, *Canada* 98 D3
Tilbury, *U.K.* 13 F8
Tilcara, *Argentina* 126 A2
Tilden, *Nebr., U.S.A.* 108 D6
Tilden, *Tex., U.S.A.* 109 L5
Tilemses, *Niger* 79 B5
Tilemsi, Vallée du, *Mali* 79 B5
Tilhar, *India* 63 F8
Tilia, O. →, *Algeria* 75 C5
Tilichiki, *Russia* 45 C17
Tililane, *Algeria* 75 C4
Tílissos, *Greece* 37 D7
Till →, *U.K.* 12 B5
Tillabéri, *Niger* 79 C5
Tillamook, *U.S.A.* 110 D2
Tillberga, *Sweden* 10 E10
Tillia, *Niger* 79 B5
Tillsonburg, *Canada* 98 D3
Tillyeria □, *Cyprus* 37 D11
Tílos, *Greece* 39 N10
Tilpa, *Australia* 91 E3
Tilrhemt, *Algeria* 75 B5
Tilsit = Sovetsk, *Russia* 9 J19
Tilt →, *U.K.* 14 E5
Tilton, *U.S.A.* 107 C13
Timagami L., *Canada* 98 C3
Timaru, *N.Z.* 87 L3
Timashevo, *Russia* 42 D10
Timashevsk, *Russia* 43 H4
Timau, *Italy* 33 B10
Timau, *Kenya* 82 B4
Timbákion, *Greece* 37 D6
Timbaúba, *Brazil* 122 C4
Timbedgha, *Mauritania* 78 B3
Timber Lake, *U.S.A.* 108 C4
Timber Mt., *U.S.A.* 112 H10
Timbío, *Colombia* 120 C2
Timbiquí, *Colombia* 120 C2
Timboon, *Australia* 91 F3
Timbuktu = Tombouctou, *Mali* 78 B4
Timellouline, *Algeria* 75 C6
Timétrine Montagnes, *Mali* 79 B4
Timfristós, Óros, *Greece* 39 L4
Timhadit, *Morocco* 74 B3
Timi, *Cyprus* 37 E11
Tîmia, *Niger* 79 B6
Timimoun, *Algeria* 75 C5
Timiş = Tamis →, *Serbia, Yug.* 38 E3
Timişoara, *Romania* 38 D4
Timmins, *Canada* 98 C3
Timok →, *Serbia, Yug.* 21 L12
Timon, *Brazil* 122 C3
Timor, *Indonesia* 57 F7
Timor □, *Indonesia* 57 F7
Timor Sea, *Ind. Oc.* 88 B4
Tin Alkoum, *Algeria* 75 D7
Tin Gornai, *Mali* 79 B4
Tin Mt., *U.S.A.* 112 J9
Tîna, Khalîg el, *Egypt* 76 H8
Tinaca Pt., *Phil.* 55 J6
Tinaco, *Venezuela* 120 B4
Tinafak, O. →, *Algeria* 75 C6
Tinajo, *Canary Is.* 36 E6
Tinaquillo, *Venezuela* 120 B4
Tinca, *Romania* 38 C4
Tinchebray, *France* 24 D6
Tindouf, *Algeria* 74 C3
Tinée →, *France* 27 E11
Tineo, *Spain* 30 B4
Tinerhir, *Morocco* 74 B3
Tinfouchi, *Algeria* 74 C3
Ting Jiang →, *China* 53 E11
Tinggi, Pulau, *Malaysia* 59 L5
Tinglev, *Denmark* 11 K3
Tingo Maria, *Peru* 124 B2
Tinh Bien, *Vietnam* 59 G5
Tinharé, I. de, *Brazil* 123 D4
Tinjoub, *Algeria* 72 C3
Tinkurrin, *Australia* 89 F2
Tinnevelly = Tirunelveli, *India* 60 Q10
Tinnoset, *Norway* 10 E3
Tinnsjø, *Norway* 10 E2
Tinogasta, *Argentina* 126 B2
Tínos, *Greece* 39 M8
Tiñoso, C., *Spain* 29 H3
Tinta, *Peru* 124 C3
Tintigny, *Belgium* 17 J7
Tintina, *Argentina* 126 B3
Tintinara, *Australia* 91 F3
Tinto →, *Spain* 31 H4
Tioga, *U.S.A.* 106 E7
Tioman, Pulau, *Malaysia* 59 L5
Tione di Trento, *Italy* 32 B7
Tionesta, *U.S.A.* 106 E5
Tior, *Sudan* 77 F3
Tioulilin, *Algeria* 75 C4
Tipongpani, *India* 61 F19
Tipperary, *Ireland* 15 D3
Tipperary □, *Ireland* 15 D4
Tipton, *U.K.* 13 E5
Tipton, *Calif., U.S.A.* 111 H4
Tipton, *Ind., U.S.A.* 104 E2
Tipton, *Iowa, U.S.A.* 108 E9
Tipton Mt., *U.S.A.* 113 K12
Tiptonville, *U.S.A.* 109 G10
Tiquié →, *Brazil* 120 C4
Tiracambu, Serra do, *Brazil* 122 B2
Tīrān, *Iran* 65 C6
Tīrân, *Si. Arabia* 76 B3
Tirana, *Albania* 39 H2
Tiranë = Tirana, *Albania* 39 H2
Tirano, *Italy* 32 B7
Tiraspol, *Moldova* 41 J5
Tirat Karmel, *Israel* 69 C3
Tiratimine, *Algeria* 75 C5
Tirdout, *Mali* 79 B4
Tire, *Turkey* 66 C2
Tirebolu, *Turkey* 67 B8
Tiree, *U.K.* 14 E2
Tîrgovişte, *Romania* 38 E8
Tîrgu Frumos, *Romania* 38 B10
Tîrgu-Jiu, *Romania* 38 D6
Tîrgu Mureş, *Romania* 38 C7
Tîrgu Neamţ, *Romania* 38 B9
Tîrgu Ocna, *Romania* 38 C9
Tîrgu Secuiesc, *Romania* 38 D9
Tirich Mir, *Pakistan* 60 A7
Tiriolo, *Italy* 35 D9
Tiririca, Serra da, *Brazil* 123 E2
Tiris, *W. Sahara* 74 D2
Tîrnava Mare →, *Romania* 38 C7
Tîrnava Mică →, *Romania* 38 C7
Tîrnăveni, *Romania* 38 C7
Tírnavos, *Greece* 39 K5
Tirodi, *India* 60 J11
Tiros, *Brazil* 123 E2
Tirschenreuth, *Germany* 19 F8
Tirso →, *Italy* 34 C1
Tirso, L. del, *Italy* 34 B1
Tiruchchirappalli, *India* 60 P11
Tirunelveli, *India* 60 Q10
Tirupati, *India* 60 N11
Tiruppur, *India* 60 P10
Tiruvannamalai, *India* 60 N11
Tisa →, *Serbia, Yug.* 21 J10
Tisdale, *Canada* 101 C8
Tishomingo, *U.S.A.* 109 H6
Tisnaren, *Sweden* 10 F9
Tisovec, *Slovak Rep.* 20 G9
Tissemsilt, *Algeria* 75 A5
Tissint, *Morocco* 74 C3
Tissø, *Denmark* 11 J5
Tisza = Tisa →, *Serbia, Yug.* 21 J10
Tiszafüred, *Hungary* 21 H10
Tiszavasvári, *Hungary* 21 H11
Tit, *Ahaggar, Algeria* 75 D6
Tit, *Tademait, Algeria* 75 C5
Tit-Ary, *Russia* 45 B13
Titaguas, *Spain* 28 F3
Titel, *Serbia, Yug.* 21 K10
Tithwal, *Pakistan* 63 B5
Titicaca, L., *S. Amer.* 124 D4
Titiwa, *Nigeria* 79 C7
Titlis, *Switz.* 23 C6
Titograd = Podgorica, *Montenegro, Yug.* 21 N9
Titov Veles, *Macedonia* 39 H4
Titova Korenica, *Croatia* 33 D12
Titova-Mitrovica, *Serbia, Yug.* 21 N10
Titovo Užice, *Serbia, Yug.* 21 M9
Titule, *Zaïre* 82 B2
Titumate, *Colombia* 120 B2
Titusville, *Fla., U.S.A.* 105 L5
Titusville, *Pa., U.S.A.* 106 E5
Tivaouane, *Senegal* 78 C1
Tiveden, *Sweden* 11 F8
Tiverton, *U.K.* 13 G4
Tívoli, *Italy* 33 G9
Tiyo, *Eritrea* 77 E5
Tizga, *Morocco* 74 B3
Ti'zi N'Isli, *Morocco* 74 B3
Tizi-Ouzou, *Algeria* 75 A5
Tizimín, *Mexico* 115 C7
Tiznados →, *Venezuela* 120 B4
Tiznit, *Morocco* 74 C3
Tjeggelvas, *Sweden* 8 C17
Tjeukemeer, *Neths.* 16 C7
Tjirebon = Cirebon, *Indonesia* 57 G13
Tjøme, *Norway* 10 E4
Tjonger Kanaal, *Neths.* 16 C7
Tjörn, *Sweden* 11 G5
Tkibuli = Tqibuli, *Georgia* 43 J6
Tkvarcheli = Tqvarcheli, *Georgia* 43 J5
Tlacotalpan, *Mexico* 115 D5
Tlahualilo, *Mexico* 114 B4
Tlaquepaque, *Mexico* 114 C4
Tlaxcala, *Mexico* 115 D5
Tlaxcala □, *Mexico* 115 D5
Tlaxiaco, *Mexico* 115 D5
Tlell, *Canada* 100 C2
Tlemcen, *Algeria* 75 B4
Tleta Sidi Bouguedra, *Morocco* 74 B3
Tlyarata, *Russia* 43 J8
Tmassah, *Libya* 73 C8
Tnine d'Anglou, *Morocco* 74 C3
To Bong, *Vietnam* 58 F7
Toad →, *Canada* 100 B4
Toamasina, *Madag.* 85 B8
Toamasina □, *Madag.* 85 B8
Toay, *Argentina* 126 D3
Toba, *Japan* 49 G8
Toba Kakar, *Pakistan* 62 D3
Toba Tek Singh, *Pakistan* 62 D5
Tobago, *W. Indies* 117 D7
Tobarra, *Spain* 29 G3
Tobelo, *Indonesia* 57 D7
Tobermorey, *Australia* 90 C2
Tobermory, *Canada* 98 C3
Tobermory, *U.K.* 14 E2
Tobin, *U.S.A.* 112 F5
Tobin, L., *Australia* 88 D4
Tobin L., *Canada* 101 C8
Toblach = Dobbiaco, *Italy* 33 B9
Toboali, *Indonesia* 56 E3
Tobol, *Kazakhstan* 44 D7
Tobol →, *Russia* 44 D7
Toboli, *Indonesia* 57 E6
Tobolsk, *Russia* 44 D7
Tobruk = Tubruq, *Libya* 73 B9
Tobyhanna, *U.S.A.* 107 E9
Tobyl = Tobol →, *Russia* 44 D7
Tocache Nuevo, *Peru* 124 B2
Tocantínia, *Brazil* 122 C2
Tocantinópolis, *Brazil* 122 C2
Tocantins □, *Brazil* 122 D2
Tocantins →, *Brazil* 122 B2
Toccoa, *U.S.A.* 105 H4
Toce →, *Italy* 32 C5
Tochigi, *Japan* 49 F9
Tochigi □, *Japan* 49 F9
Tocina, *Spain* 31 H5
Tocopilla, *Chile* 126 A1
Tocumwal, *Australia* 91 F4
Tocuyo →, *Venezuela* 120 A4
Tocuyo de la Costa, *Venezuela* 120 A4
Todd →, *Australia* 90 C2
Todeli, *Indonesia* 57 E6
Todenyang, *Kenya* 82 B4
Todi, *Italy* 33 F9
Tödi, *Switz.* 23 C7
Todos os Santos, B. de, *Brazil* 123 D4
Todos Santos, *Mexico* 114 C2
Todtnau, *Germany* 19 H3
Toecé, *Burkina Faso* 79 C4
Tofield, *Canada* 100 C6
Tofino, *Canada* 100 D3
Töfsingdalens nationalpark, *Sweden* 10 B6
Toftlund, *Denmark* 11 J3
Tofua, *Tonga* 87 D11
Tōgane, *Japan* 49 G10
Togba, *Mauritania* 78 B2
Toggenburg, *Switz.* 23 B8
Togian, Kepulauan, *Indonesia* 57 E6
Togliatti, *Russia* 42 D9
Togo ■, *W. Afr.* 79 D5
Togtoh, *China* 50 D6
Tohma →, *Turkey* 66 C7
Tōhoku □, *Japan* 48 E10
Toinya, *Sudan* 77 F2
Tojikiston = Tajikistan ■, *Asia* 44 F8
Tojo, *Indonesia* 57 E6
Tōjō, *Japan* 49 G6
Toka, *Guyana* 121 C6
Tokachi-Dake, *Japan* 48 C11
Tokachi-Gawa →, *Japan* 48 C11
Tokaj, *Hungary* 21 G11
Tokala, *Indonesia* 57 E6
Tōkamachi, *Japan* 49 F9
Tokanui, *N.Z.* 87 M2
Tokar, *Sudan* 76 D4
Tokara-Rettō, *Japan* 49 K4
Tokarahi, *N.Z.* 87 L3
Tokashiki-Shima, *Japan* 49 L3
Tokat, *Turkey* 66 B7
Tŏkchŏn, *N. Korea* 51 E14
Tokeland, *U.S.A.* 112 D3
Tokelau Is., *Pac. Oc.* 92 H10
Tokmak, *Kyrgyzstan* 44 E8
Tokmak, *Ukraine* 41 J8
Toko Ra., *Australia* 90 C2
Tokoro-Gawa →, *Japan* 48 B12
Tokuno-Shima, *Japan* 49 L4
Tokushima, *Japan* 49 G7
Tokushima □, *Japan* 49 H7
Tokuyama, *Japan* 49 G5
Tōkyō, *Japan* 49 G9
Tolaga Bay, *N.Z.* 87 H7
Tolbukhin = Dobrich, *Bulgaria* 38 F10
Toledo, *Spain* 30 F6
Toledo, *Ohio, U.S.A.* 104 E4
Toledo, *Oreg., U.S.A.* 110 D2
Toledo, *Wash., U.S.A.* 110 C2
Toledo, Montes de, *Spain* 31 F6
Tolentino, *Italy* 33 E10
Tolga, *Algeria* 75 B6
Tolga, *Norway* 10 B5
Toliara, *Madag.* 85 C7
Toliara □, *Madag.* 85 C8
Tolima, *Colombia* 120 C2
Tolima □, *Colombia* 120 C2
Tolitoli, *Indonesia* 57 D6
Tolkamer, *Neths.* 16 E8
Tolleson, *U.S.A.* 111 K7
Tollhouse, *U.S.A.* 112 H7
Tolmachevo, *Russia* 40 C5
Tolmezzo, *Italy* 33 B10
Tolmin, *Slovenia* 33 B10
Tolo, *Zaïre* 80 E3
Tolo, Teluk, *Indonesia* 57 E6
Tolochin = Talachyn, *Belarus* 40 E5
Tolosa, *Spain* 28 B2
Tolox, *Spain* 31 J6
Toltén, *Chile* 128 A2
Toluca, *Mexico* 115 D5
Tom Burke, *S. Africa* 85 C4
Tom Price, *Australia* 88 D2
Tomah, *U.S.A.* 108 D9
Tomahawk, *U.S.A.* 108 C10
Tomakomai, *Japan* 48 C10
Tomales, *U.S.A.* 112 G4
Tomales B., *U.S.A.* 112 G3
Tomar, *Portugal* 31 F2
Tomarza, *Turkey* 66 C6
Tomás Barrón, *Bolivia* 124 D4
Tomaszów Mazowiecki, *Poland* 20 D9
Tomatlán, *Mexico* 114 D3
Tombador, Serra do, *Brazil* 125 C6
Tombé, *Sudan* 77 F3
Tombigbee →, *U.S.A.* 105 K2
Tombouctou, *Mali* 78 B4
Tombstone, *U.S.A.* 111 L8
Tombua, *Angola* 84 B1
Tomé, *Chile* 126 D1
Tomé-Açu, *Brazil* 122 B2
Tomelilla, *Sweden* 11 J7
Tomelloso, *Spain* 29 F1
Tomingley, *Australia* 91 E4
Tomini, *Indonesia* 57 D6
Tomini, Teluk, *Indonesia* 57 E6
Tominian, *Mali* 78 C4
Tomiño, *Spain* 30 D2
Tomkinson Ras., *Australia* 89 E4
Tommot, *Russia* 45 D13
Tomnavoulin, *U.K.* 14 D5
Tomnop Ta Suos, *Cambodia* 59 G5
Tomo, *Colombia* 120 C4
Tomo →, *Colombia* 120 B4
Tomorit, *Albania* 39 J3
Toms Place, *U.S.A.* 112 H8
Toms River, *U.S.A.* 107 G10
Tomsk, *Russia* 44 D9
Tonalá, *Mexico* 115 D6
Tonale, Passo del, *Italy* 32 B7
Tonalea, *U.S.A.* 111 H8
Tonantins, *Brazil* 120 D4
Tonasket, *U.S.A.* 110 B4
Tonate, *Fr. Guiana* 121 C7
Tonawanda, *U.S.A.* 106 D6
Tonbridge, *U.K.* 13 F8
Tondano, *Indonesia* 57 D6
Tondela, *Portugal* 30 E2
Tønder, *Denmark* 11 K2
Tondi Kiwindi, *Niger* 79 C5
Tondibi, *Mali* 79 B4
Tonekābon, *Iran* 65 B6
Tong Xian, *China* 50 E9
Tonga ■, *Pac. Oc.* 87 D11
Tonga Trench, *Pac. Oc.* 92 J10
Tongaat, *S. Africa* 85 D5
Tong'an, *China* 53 E12
Tongareva, *Cook Is.* 93 H12
Tongatapu, *Tonga* 87 E11
Tongbai, *China* 53 A9
Tongcheng, *Anhui, China* 53 B11
Tongcheng, *Hubei, China* 53 C9
Tongchŏn-ni, *N. Korea* 51 E14
Tongchuan, *China* 50 G5
Tongdao, *China* 52 D7
Tongeren, *Belgium* 17 G6
Tonggu, *China* 53 C10
Tongguan, *China* 50 G6
Tonghai, *China* 52 E4
Tonghua, *China* 51 D13
Tongjiang, *Heilongjiang, China* 54 B8
Tongjiang, *Sichuan, China* 52 B6
Tongjosŏn Man, *N. Korea* 51 E14
Tongking, G. of = Tonkin, G. of, *Asia* 58 B7
Tongliang, *China* 52 C6
Tongliao, *China* 51 C12
Tongling, *China* 53 B11
Tonglu, *China* 53 C12
Tongnae, *S. Korea* 51 G15
Tongnan, *China* 52 B5
Tongobory, *Madag.* 85 C7
Tongoy, *Chile* 126 C1
Tongren, *China* 52 D7
Tongres = Tongeren, *Belgium* 17 G6
Tongsa Dzong, *Bhutan* 61 F17
Tongue, *U.K.* 14 C4
Tongue →, *U.S.A.* 108 B2
Tongwei, *China* 50 G3
Tongxin, *China* 50 F3
Tongyang, *N. Korea* 51 E14
Tongyu, *China* 51 B12
Tongzi, *China* 52 C6
Tonj, *Sudan* 77 F2
Tonk, *India* 62 F6
Tonkawa, *U.S.A.* 109 G6
Tonkin = Bac Phan, *Vietnam* 58 B5
Tonkin, G. of, *Asia* 58 B7
Tonlé Sap, *Cambodia* 58 F4
Tonnay-Charente, *France* 26 C3
Tonneins, *France* 26 D4
Tonnerre, *France* 25 E10
Tönning, *Germany* 18 A4
Tono, *Japan* 48 E10
Tonopah, *U.S.A.* 111 G5
Tonosí, *Panama* 116 E3
Tønsberg, *Norway* 10 E4
Tonya, *Turkey* 67 B8
Tooele, *U.S.A.* 110 F7
Toompine, *Australia* 91 D3
Toonpan, *Australia* 90 B4
Toora, *Australia* 91 F4
Toora-Khem, *Russia* 45 D10
Toowoomba, *Australia* 91 D5
Topalu, *Romania* 38 E11
Topaz, *U.S.A.* 112 G7
Topeka, *U.S.A.* 108 F7
Topki, *Russia* 44 D9
Topl'a →, *Slovak Rep.* 20 G11
Topley, *Canada* 100 C3
Toplica →, *Serbia, Yug.* 21 M11
Toplița, *Romania* 38 C8
Topocalma, Pta., *Chile* 126 C1
Topock, *U.S.A.* 113 L12
Topola, *Serbia, Yug.* 21 L10

Topol'čany, Slovak Rep. .. 20 G8
Topolnitsa →, Bulgaria .. 38 G7
Topolobampo, Mexico .. 114 B3
Topolovgrad, Bulgaria .. 38 G9
Toppenish, U.S.A. 110 C3
Topusko, Croatia 33 C12
Toquepala, Peru 124 D3
Torá, Spain 28 D6
Tora Kit, Sudan 77 E3
Toraka Vestale, Madag. . 85 B7
Torata, Peru 124 D3
Torbalı, Turkey 66 C2
Torbay, Canada 99 C9
Torbay, U.K. 13 G4
Tørdal, Norway 10 E2
Tordesillas, Spain 30 D6
Tordoya, Spain 30 B2
Töreboda, Sweden 11 F8
Torgau, Germany 18 D8
Torgelow, Germany 18 B9
Torhout, Belgium 17 F2
Tori, Ethiopia 77 F3
Tori-Shima, Japan 49 J10
Torigni-sur-Vire, France . 24 C6
Torija, Spain 28 E1
Torin, Mexico 114 B2
Toriñana, C., Spain 30 B1
Torino, Italy 32 C4
Torit, Sudan 77 G3
Torkamān, Iran 67 D12
Torkovichi, Russia 40 C6
Tormes →, Spain 30 D4
Tornado Mt., Canada .. 100 D6
Torne älv →, Sweden .. 8 D21
Torneå = Tornio, Finland 8 D21
Torneträsk, Sweden ... 8 B18
Tornio, Finland 8 D21
Tornionjoki →, Finland . 8 D21
Tornquist, Argentina .. 126 D3
Toro, Baleares, Spain .. 36 B11
Toro, Zamora, Spain ... 30 D5
Torö, Sweden 11 F11
Toro, Cerro del, Chile .. 126 B2
Toro Pk., U.S.A. 113 M10
Törökszentmiklós, Hungary 21 H10
Toroníios Kólpos, Greece . 39 J6
Toronto, Australia 91 E5
Toronto, Canada 98 D4
Toronto, U.S.A. 106 F4
Toropets, Russia 40 D6
Tororo, Uganda 82 B3
Toros Dağları, Turkey .. 66 D5
Torotoro, Bolivia 125 D4
Torpshammar, Sweden .. 10 B10
Torquay, Canada 101 D8
Torquay, U.K. 13 G4
Torquemada, Spain 30 C6
Torralba de Calatrava,
  Spain 31 F7
Torrance, U.S.A. 113 M8
Torrão, Portugal 31 G2
Torre Annunziata, Italy . 35 B7
Tôrre de Moncorvo,
  Portugal 30 D3
Torre del Greco, Italy ... 35 B7
Torre del Mar, Spain ... 31 J6
Torre-Pacheco, Spain ... 29 H4
Torre Péllice, Italy 32 D4
Torreblanca, Spain 28 E5
Torrecampo, Spain 31 G6
Torrecilla en Cameros,
  Spain 28 C2
Torredembarra, Spain .. 28 D6
Torredonjimeno, Spain .. 31 H7
Torrejoncillo, Spain ... 30 F4
Torrelaguna, Spain 28 E1
Torrelavega, Spain 30 B6
Torremaggiore, Italy ... 35 A8
Torremolinos, Spain ... 31 J6
Torrens, L., Australia .. 91 E2
Torrens Cr. →, Australia 90 C4
Torrens Creek, Australia . 90 C4
Torrente, Spain 29 F4
Torrenueva, Spain 29 G1
Torreón, Mexico 114 B4
Torreperogil, Spain ... 29 G1
Torres, Mexico 114 B2
Torres Novas, Portugal . 31 F2
Torres Strait, Australia . 92 H6
Torres Vedras, Portugal . 31 F1
Torrevieja, Spain 29 H4
Torrey, U.S.A. 111 G8
Torridge →, U.K. 13 G3
Torridon, L., U.K. 14 D3
Torrijos, Spain 30 F6
Torrington, Conn., U.S.A. 107 E11
Torrington, Wyo., U.S.A. 108 D2
Torroella de Montgri, Spain 28 C8
Torrox, Spain 31 J7
Tórshavn, Færoe Is. ... 8 E9
Torsö, Sweden 11 F7
Tortola, Virgin Is. 117 C7
Tórtoles de Esgueva, Spain 30 D6
Tortona, Italy 32 D5
Tortoreto, Italy 33 F10
Tortorici, Italy 35 D7
Tortosa, Spain 28 E5
Tortosa, C. de, Spain ... 28 E5
Tortosendo, Portugal .. 30 E3
Tortue, I. de la, Haiti .. 117 B5
Tortum, Turkey 67 B9
Ţorūd, Iran 65 C7
Torul, Turkey 67 B8
Toruń, Poland 20 B8
Torup, Denmark 11 G3
Torup, Sweden 11 H7
Tory I., Ireland 15 A3

Torysa →, Slovak Rep. .. 20 G11
Torzhok, Russia 42 B2
Tosa, Japan 49 H6
Tosa-Shimizu, Japan ... 49 H6
Tosa-Wan, Japan 49 H6
Toscana □, Italy 32 E8
Toscano, Arcipelago, Italy 32 F7
Toshkent, Uzbekistan .. 44 E7
Tosno, Russia 40 C6
Tossa, Spain 28 D7
Tostado, Argentina 126 B3
Tostedt, Germany 18 B5
Tostón, Pta. de, Canary Is. 36 F5
Tosu, Japan 49 H5
Tosya, Turkey 66 B6
Totana, Spain 29 H3
Tôtes, France 24 C8
Tótkomlós, Hungary ... 21 J10
Totma, Russia 44 C5
Totnes, U.K. 13 G4
Totness, Surinam 121 B6
Totonicapán, Guatemala . 116 D1
Totora, Bolivia 125 D4
Totten Glacier, Antarctica 5 C8
Tottenham, Australia .. 91 E4
Tottenham, Canada ... 106 B5
Tottori, Japan 49 G7
Tottori □, Japan 49 G7
Touat, Algeria 75 C5
Touba, Ivory C. 78 D3
Toubkal, Djebel, Morocco 74 B3
Toucy, France 25 E10
Tougan, Burkina Faso .. 78 C4
Touggourt, Algeria ... 75 B6
Tougué, Guinea 78 C2
Toukmatine, Algeria ... 75 D6
Toul, France 25 D12
Toulepleu, Ivory C. ... 78 D3
Toulon, France 27 E9
Toulouse, France 26 E5
Toummo, Niger 73 D7
Toumodi, Ivory C. 78 D3
Tounassine, Hamada,
  Algeria 74 C3
Toungoo, Burma 61 K20
Touques →, France .. 24 C7
Touraine, France 24 E7
Tourane = Da Nang,
  Vietnam 58 D7
Tourcoing, France 25 B10
Tourine, Mauritania .. 74 D2
Tournai, Belgium 17 G2
Tournan-en-Brie, France . 25 D9
Tournay, France 26 E4
Tournon, France 27 C8
Tournon-St.-Martin, France 24 F7
Tournus, France 27 B8
Touros, Brazil 122 C4
Tours, France 24 E7
Touwsrivier, S. Africa .. 84 E3
Tovar, Venezuela 120 B3
Tovarkovskiy, Russia .. 42 D4
Tovdal, Norway 11 F2
Tovdalselva →, Norway . 11 F2
Tovuz, Azerbaijan 43 K7
Towada, Japan 48 D10
Towada-Ko, Japan ... 48 D10
Towamba, Australia .. 91 F4
Towanda, U.S.A. 107 E8
Towang, India 61 F17
Tower, U.S.A. 108 B8
Towerhill Cr. →, Australia 90 C3
Towner, U.S.A. 108 A4
Townsend, U.S.A. 110 C8
Townshend I., Australia . 90 C5
Townsville, Australia .. 90 B4
Towson, U.S.A. 104 F7
Toya-Ko, Japan 48 C10
Toyah, U.S.A. 109 K3
Toyahvale, U.S.A. 109 K3
Toyama, Japan 49 F8
Toyama □, Japan 49 F8
Toyama-Wan, Japan .. 49 F8
Toyohashi, Japan 49 G8
Toyokawa, Japan 49 G8
Toyonaka, Japan 49 G7
Toyooka, Japan 49 G7
Toyota, Japan 49 G8
Tozeur, Tunisia 75 B6
Tqibuli, Georgia 43 J6
Tqvarcheli, Georgia .. 43 J5
Trá Li = Tralee, Ireland . 15 D2
Tra On, Vietnam 59 H5
Trabancos →, Spain .. 30 D5
Traben-Trarbach, Germany 19 F3
Trabzon, Turkey 67 B8
Tracadie, Canada 99 C7
Tracy, Calif., U.S.A. .. 111 H3
Tracy, Minn., U.S.A. .. 108 C7
Tradate, Italy 32 C5
Trafalgar, C., Spain ... 31 J4
Traiguén, Chile 128 A2
Trail, Canada 100 D5
Trainor L., Canada ... 100 A4
Traíra →, Brazil 120 D4
Tralee, Ireland 15 D2
Tralee B., Ireland 15 D2
Tramelan, Switz. 22 B4
Tramore, Ireland 15 D4
Tran Ninh, Cao Nguyen,
  Laos 58 C4
Tranås, Sweden 9 G16
Trancas, Argentina .. 126 B2
Trancoso, Portugal .. 30 E3

Tranebjerg, Denmark 11 J4
Tranemo, Sweden 11 G7
Trang, Thailand 59 J2
Trangahy, Madag. 85 B7
Trangan, Indonesia ... 57 F8
Trangie, Australia 91 E4
Trångsviken, Sweden .. 10 A8
Trani, Italy 35 A9
Tranoroa, Madag. 85 C8
Tranqueras, Uruguay .. 127 C4
Trans Nzoia □, Kenya .. 82 B3
Transantarctic Mts.,
  Antarctica 5 E12
Transcona, Canada ... 101 D9
Transilvania, Romania . 38 D8
Transilvanian Alps =
  Carpaţii Meridionali,
  Romania 38 D8
Transylvania =
  Transilvania, Romania .. 38 D8
Transylvanian Alps =
  Carpaţii Meridionali,
  Romania 6 F10
Trápani, Italy 34 D5
Trapper Pk., U.S.A. .. 110 D6
Traralgon, Australia .. 91 F4
Trarza, Mauritania ... 78 B2
Trasacco, Italy 33 G10
Trăscău, Munţii, Romania 38 C6
Trasimeno, L., Italy ... 33 E9
Trat, Thailand 59 F4
Traun, Austria 21 G4
Traunstein, Germany .. 19 H8
Travers, Mt., N.Z. 87 K4
Traverse City, U.S.A. .. 104 C3
Traveller's L., Australia . 91 E3
Travemünde, Germany . 18 B6
Travnik, Bos.-H. 21 L7
Trayning, Australia .. 89 F2
Trazo, Spain 30 B2
Trbovlje, Slovenia ... 33 B12
Trébbia →, Italy 32 C6
Trebel →, Germany .. 18 B9
Trébeurden, France .. 24 D3
Trebinje, Bos.-H. 21 N8
Trebisacce, Italy 35 C9
Trebišnica →, Bos.-H. .. 21 N8
Trebišov, Slovak Rep. .. 20 G11
Trebižat →, Bos.-H. .. 21 M7
Trebnje, Slovenia 33 C12
Třeboň, Czech. 20 G4
Trebujena, Spain 31 J4
Trecate, Italy 32 C5
Trece Martires, Phil. .. 55 D4
Tredegar, U.K. 13 F4
Tregaron, U.K. 13 E4
Trégastel-Plage, France . 24 D3
Tregnago, Italy 33 C8
Tregrosse Is., Australia . 90 B5
Tréguier, France 24 D3
Trégunc, France 24 E3
Treherne, Canada ... 101 D9
Tréia, Italy 33 E10
Treignac, France 26 C5
Treinta y Tres, Uruguay . 127 C5
Treis, Germany 19 E3
Trelde Næs, Denmark . 11 J3
Trelew, Argentina ... 128 B3
Trélissac, France 26 C4
Trelleborg, Sweden ... 11 J7
Trélon, France 25 B11
Tremiti, Italy 33 F12
Tremonton, U.S.A. ... 110 F7
Tremp, Spain 28 C5
Trenche →, Canada .. 98 C5
Trenčín, Slovak Rep. .. 20 G8
Trenggalek, Indonesia . 57 H14
Trenque Lauquen,
  Argentina 126 D3
Trent →, U.K. 12 D7
Trentino-Alto Adige □,
  Italy 32 B8
Trento, Italy 32 B8
Trenton, Canada 98 D4
Trenton, Mo., U.S.A. .. 108 E8
Trenton, N.J., U.S.A. .. 107 F10
Trenton, Nebr., U.S.A. . 108 E4
Trenton, Tenn., U.S.A. . 109 H10
Trepassey, Canada ... 99 C9
Trepuzzi, Italy 35 B11
Tres Arroyos, Argentina . 126 D3
Três Corações, Brazil .. 123 F2
Três Lagoas, Brazil ... 123 F1
Tres Lagos →, Argentina 128 C2
Tres Marías, Mexico .. 114 C3
Três Marias, Reprêsa,
  Brazil 123 E2
Tres Montes, C., Chile . 128 C1
Tres Pinos, U.S.A. 112 J5
Três Pontas, Brazil ... 123 F2
Tres Puentes, Chile ... 126 B1
Tres Puntas, C., Argentina 128 C3
Três Rios, Brazil 123 F3
Tres Valles, Mexico .. 115 D5
Treska →, Macedonia . 39 H4
Trespaderne, Spain .. 28 C1
Trets, France 27 E9
Treuchtlingen, Germany . 19 G6
Treuenbrietzen, Germany 18 C8
Treviglio, Italy 32 C6
Treviño, Peña, Spain .. 30 C4
Treviso, Italy 33 C9
Trévoux, France 27 C8
Treysa, Germany 18 E5
Trgovište, Serbia, Yug. . 21 N12
Triabunna, Australia .. 90 G4
Triánda, Greece 37 C10
Triang, Malaysia 59 L4

Triaucourt-en-Argonne,
  France 25 D12
Tribsees, Germany ... 18 A8
Tribulation, C., Australia . 90 B4
Tribune, U.S.A. 108 F4
Tricárico, Italy 35 B9
Tricase, Italy 35 C11
Trichinopoly =
  Tiruchchirappalli, India . 60 P11
Trichur, India 60 P10
Trida, Australia 91 E4
Trier, Germany 19 F2
Trieste, Italy 33 C10
Trieste, G. di, Italy ... 33 C10
Trieux →, France 24 D3
Triggiano, Italy 35 A9
Triglav, Slovenia 33 B10
Trigno →, Italy 33 F11
Trigueros, Spain 31 H4
Trikhonis, Límni, Greece . 39 L4
Tríkkala, Greece 39 K4
Trikomo, Cyprus 37 D12
Trikora, Puncak, Indonesia 57 E9
Trilj, Croatia 33 E13
Trillo, Spain 28 E2
Trim, Ireland 15 C5
Trincomalee, Sri Lanka . 60 Q12
Trindade, Brazil 123 E2
Trindade, I., Atl. Oc. .. 2 F8
Trinidad, Bolivia 125 C5
Trinidad, Colombia ... 120 B3
Trinidad, Cuba 116 B3
Trinidad, Uruguay ... 126 C4
Trinidad, U.S.A. 109 G2
Trinidad, W. Indies ... 117 D7
Trinidad →, Mexico .. 115 D5
Trinidad, G., Chile ... 128 C1
Trinidad, I., Argentina . 128 A4
Trinidad & Tobago ■,
  W. Indies 117 D7
Trinitápoli, Italy 35 A9
Trinity, Canada 99 C9
Trinity, U.S.A. 109 K7
Trinity →, Calif., U.S.A. 110 F2
Trinity →, Tex., U.S.A. . 109 L7
Trinity B., Canada ... 99 C9
Trinity Range, U.S.A. .. 110 F4
Trinkitat, Sudan 76 D4
Trino, Italy 32 C5
Trion, U.S.A. 105 H3
Trionto, C., Italy 35 C9
Triora, Italy 32 E4
Tripoli = Tarābulus,
  Lebanon 69 A4
Tripoli = Tarābulus, Libya 75 B7
Tripp, U.S.A. 108 D6
Tripura □, India 61 H17
Tripylos, Cyprus 37 E11
Trischen, Germany ... 18 A4
Tristan da Cunha, Atl. Oc. 2 F9
Trivandrum, India ... 60 Q10
Trivento, Italy 35 A7
Trnava, Slovak Rep. .. 21 G7
Trochu, Canada 100 C6
Trodely I., Canada ... 98 B4
Trogir, Croatia 33 E13
Troglav, Croatia 33 E13
Trøgstad, Norway ... 10 E5
Tróia, Italy 35 A8
Troilus, L., Canada .. 98 B5
Troina, Italy 35 E7
Trois Fourches, Cap des,
  Morocco 75 A4
Trois-Pistoles, Canada . 99 C6
Trois-Rivières, Canada . 98 C5
Troisvierges, Belgium . 17 H8
Troitsk, Russia 44 D7
Troitsko Pechorsk, Russia 44 C6
Tröllaskagi, Iceland .. 8 D5
Trollhättan, Sweden .. 11 F6
Trollheimen, Norway . 10 B3
Trombetas →, Brazil . 121 D6
Tromsø, Norway 8 B18
Trona, U.S.A. 113 K9
Tronador, Argentina .. 128 B2
Trøndelag, Norway .. 8 D14
Trondheim, Norway .. 10 A4
Trondheimsfjorden,
  Norway 8 E14
Trönninge, Sweden .. 11 H6
Trönö, Sweden 10 C10
Tronto →, Italy 33 F10
Troon, U.K. 14 F4
Troodos, Cyprus 66 E5
Tropea, Italy 35 D8
Tropic, U.S.A. 111 H7
Tropoja, Albania 38 G3
Trossachs, The, U.K. .. 14 E4
Trostan, U.K. 15 A5
Trostberg, Germany .. 19 G8
Trostyanets, Ukraine . 41 G8
Trotternish, U.K. ... 14 D2
Troup, U.S.A. 109 J7
Trout →, Canada ... 100 A5
Trout L., N.W.T., Canada 100 A4
Trout L., Ont., Canada . 101 C10
Trout Lake, Mich., U.S.A. 98 C2
Trout Lake, Wash., U.S.A. 112 E5
Trout River, Canada .. 99 C8
Trouville-sur-Mer, France 24 C7
Trowbridge, U.K. 13 F5
Troy, Turkey 66 C2
Troy, Ala., U.S.A. ... 105 K3
Troy, Idaho, U.S.A. .. 110 C5
Troy, Kans., U.S.A. .. 108 F7
Troy, Mo., U.S.A. ... 108 F9
Troy, Mont., U.S.A. .. 110 B6

Troy, N.Y., U.S.A. 107 D11
Troy, Ohio, U.S.A. 104 E3
Troyan, Bulgaria 38 G7
Troyes, France 25 D11
Trpanj, Croatia 21 M7
Trstena, Slovak Rep. ... 20 F9
Trstenik, Serbia, Yug. .. 21 M10
Trubchevsk, Russia ... 41 F7
Trucial States = United
  Arab Emirates ■, Asia . 65 F7
Truckee, U.S.A. 112 F6
Trudfront, Russia 43 H8
Trudovoye, Russia 48 C6
Trujillo, Colombia 120 C2
Trujillo, Honduras 116 C2
Trujillo, Peru 124 B2
Trujillo, Spain 31 F5
Trujillo, U.S.A. 109 H2
Trujillo, Venezuela ... 120 B3
Trujillo □, Venezuela .. 120 B3
Truk, Pac. Oc. 92 G7
Trumann, U.S.A. 109 H9
Trumbull, Mt., U.S.A. . 111 H7
Trun, France 24 D7
Trun, Switz. 23 C7
Trundle, Australia 91 E4
Trung-Phan, Vietnam .. 58 E7
Truro, Canada 99 C7
Truro, U.K. 13 G2
Truskavets, Ukraine ... 41 H2
Truslove, Australia ... 89 F3
Trustrup, Denmark ... 11 H4
Truth or Consequences,
  U.S.A. 111 K10
Trutnov, Czech. 20 E5
Truyère →, France ... 26 D6
Tryavna, Bulgaria 38 G8
Tryon, U.S.A. 105 H4
Tryonville, U.S.A. 106 E5
Trzcianka, Poland 20 B6
Trzebiatów, Poland ... 20 A5
Trzebiez, Poland 20 B4
Trzebinia-Siersza, Poland . 20 E9
Trzebnica, Poland 20 D7
Tržič, Slovenia 33 B11
Tsagan Aman, Russia .. 43 G8
Tsaratanana, Madag. ... 85 B8
Tsaratanana, Mt. de,
  Madag. 85 A8
Tsarevo = Michurin,
  Bulgaria 38 G10
Tsau, Botswana 84 C3
Tsebrykove, Ukraine .. 41 J6
Tselinograd = Aqmola,
  Kazakhstan 44 D8
Tsetserleg, Mongolia .. 54 B5
Tshabong, Botswana ... 84 D3
Tshane, Botswana 84 C3
Tshela, Zaïre 80 E2
Tshesebe, Botswana ... 85 C2
Tshibeke, Zaïre 82 C2
Tshibinda, Zaïre 82 C2
Tshikapa, Zaïre 80 F4
Tshilenge, Zaïre 82 D1
Tshinsenda, Zaïre 83 E2
Tshofa, Zaïre 82 D2
Tshwane, Botswana ... 84 C3
Tsigara, Botswana 84 C4
Tsihombe, Madag. 85 D8
Tsimlyansk, Russia ... 43 G6
Tsimlyansk Res. =
  Tsimlyanskoye Vdkhr.,
  Russia 43 F6
Tsimlyanskoye Vdkhr.,
  Russia 43 F6
Tsinan = Jinan, China .. 50 F9
Tsineng, S. Africa 84 D3
Tsinghai = Qinghai □,
  China 54 C4
Tsingtao = Qingdao, China 51 F11
Tsinjomitondraka, Madag. 85 B8
Tsiroanomandidy, Madag. 85 B8
Tsiteli-Tskaro, Georgia . 43 K8
Tsivilsk, Russia 42 C8
Tsivory, Madag. 85 C8
Tskhinvali, Georgia ... 43 J7
Tsna →, Russia 42 D5
Tsnori, Georgia 43 K7
Tso Moriri, L., India ... 63 C8
Tsodilo Hill, Botswana . 84 B3
Tsogttsetsiy, Mongolia . 50 C3
Tsolo, S. Africa 85 E4
Tsomo, S. Africa 85 E4
Tsu, Japan 49 G8
Tsu L., Canada 100 A6
Tsuchiura, Japan 49 F10
Tsugaru-Kaikyō, Japan . 48 D10
Tsumeb, Namibia 84 B2
Tsumis, Namibia 84 C2
Tsuruga, Japan 49 G8
Tsurugi-San, Japan ... 49 H7
Tsuruoka, Japan 48 E9
Tsushima, Gifu, Japan . 49 G8
Tsushima, Nagasaki, Japan 49 G4
Tsvetkovo, Ukraine ... 41 H6
Tsyelyakhany, Belarus . 41 F3
Tua →, Portugal 30 D3
Tual, Indonesia 57 F8
Tuam, Ireland 15 C3
Tuamotu Arch. = Tuamotu
  Is., Pac. Oc. 93 J13
Tuamotu Is., Pac. Oc. . 93 J13
Tuamotu Ridge, Pac. Oc. 93 K14
Tuanfeng, China 53 B10
Tuanxi, China 52 D6
Tuao, Phil. 55 C4
Tuapse, Russia 43 H4
Tuatapere, N.Z. 87 M1

Tuba City, U.S.A. 111 H8
Tuban, Indonesia 57 G15
Tubarão, Brazil 127 B6
Tûbâs, West Bank 69 C4
Tubau, Malaysia 56 D4
Tubbergen, Neths. 16 D9
Tübingen, Germany 19 G5
Tubize, Belgium 17 G4
Tubruq, Libya 73 B9
Tubuai Is., Pac. Oc. 93 K12
Tuc Trung, Vietnam 59 G6
Tucacas, Venezuela 120 A4
Tucano, Brazil 122 D4
Tuchang, Taiwan 53 E13
Tuchodi →, Canada 100 B4
Tuchola, Poland 20 B7
Tucson, U.S.A. 111 K8
Tucumán □, Argentina 126 B2
Tucumcari, U.S.A. 109 H3
Tucunaré, Brazil 125 B6
Tucupido, Venezuela 120 B4
Tucupita, Venezuela 121 B5
Tucuruí, Brazil 122 B2
Tucuruí, Reprêsa de, Brazil 122 B2
Tudela, Spain 28 C3
Tudela de Duero, Spain 30 D6
Tudmur, Syria 67 E8
Tudor, L., Canada 99 A6
Tudora, Romania 38 B9
Tuella →, Portugal 30 D3
Tuen, Australia 91 D4
Tueré →, Brazil 122 B1
Tugela →, S. Africa 85 D5
Tuguegarao, Phil. 55 C4
Tugur, Russia 45 D14
Tuineje, Canary Is. 36 F5
Tukangbesi, Kepulauan,
  Indonesia 57 F6
Tukarak I., Canada 98 A4
Tukayyid, Iraq 64 D5
Tûkh, Egypt 76 H7
Tukobo, Ghana 78 D4
Tükrah, Libya 73 B9
Tuktoyaktuk, Canada 96 B6
Tukums, Latvia 9 H20
Tukuyu, Tanzania 83 D3
Tula, Hidalgo, Mexico 115 C5
Tula, Tamaulipas, Mexico . . 115 C5
Tula, Nigeria 79 D7
Tula, Russia 42 C3
Tulancingo, Mexico 115 C5
Tulare, U.S.A. 111 H4
Tulare Lake Bed, U.S.A. . . . 111 J4
Tularosa, U.S.A. 111 K10
Tulbagh, S. Africa 84 E2
Tulcán, Ecuador 120 C2
Tulcea, Romania 38 D11
Tulchyn, Ukraine 41 H5
Tūleh, Iran 65 C7
Tulemalu L., Canada 101 A9
Tuli, Indonesia 57 E6
Tuli, Zimbabwe 83 G2
Tulia, U.S.A. 109 H4
Tūlkarm, West Bank 69 C4
Tullahoma, U.S.A. 105 H2
Tullamore, Australia 91 E4
Tullamore, Ireland 15 C4
Tulle, France 26 C5
Tullibigeal, Australia 91 E4
Tullins, France 27 C9
Tulln, Austria 21 G6
Tullow, Ireland 15 D4
Tullus, Sudan 77 E1
Tully, Australia 90 B4
Tulmaythah, Libya 73 B9
Tulmur, Australia 90 C3
Tulnici, Romania 38 D9
Tulovo, Bulgaria 38 G8
Tulsa, U.S.A. 109 G7
Tulsequah, Canada 100 B2
Tulu Milki, Ethiopia 77 F4
Tulu Welel, Ethiopia 77 F3
Tulua, Colombia 120 C2
Tulun, Russia 45 D11
Tulungagung, Indonesia 56 F4
Tum, Indonesia 57 E8
Tuma →, Nic. 116 D3
Tuma, Russia 42 C5
Tumaco, Colombia 120 C2
Tumaco, Ensenada,
  Colombia 120 C2
Tumatumari, Guyana 121 B6
Tumba, Sweden 10 E11
Tumba, L., Zaïre 80 E3
Tumbarumba, Australia 91 F4
Tumbaya, Argentina 126 A2
Túmbes, Peru 124 A1
Tumbes □, Peru 124 A1
Tumbwe, Zaïre 83 E2
Tumby Bay, Australia 91 E2
Tumd Youqi, China 50 D6
Tumen, China 51 C15
Tumen Jiang →, China 51 C16
Tumeremo, Venezuela 121 B5
Tumiritinga, Brazil 123 E3
Tumkur, India 60 N10
Tummel, L., U.K. 14 E5
Tump, Pakistan 60 F3
Tumpat, Malaysia 59 J4
Tumu, Ghana 78 C4
Tumucumaque, Serra,
  Brazil 121 C7
Tumupasa, Bolivia 124 C4
Tumut, Australia 91 F4
Tumwater, U.S.A. 110 C2
Tunas de Zaza, Cuba 116 B4
Tunbridge Wells = Royal
  Tunbridge Wells, U.K. . . 13 F8

Tunceli, Turkey 67 C8
Tuncurry, Australia 91 E5
Tunduru, Tanzania 83 E4
Tunduru □, Tanzania 83 E4
Tundzha →, Bulgaria 39 H9
Tunga Pass, India 61 E19
Tungabhadra →, India 60 M11
Tungaru, Sudan 77 E3
Tungla, Nic. 116 D3
Tungsten, Canada 100 A3
Tungurahua □, Ecuador . . . 120 D2
Tunguska, Nizhnyaya →,
  Russia 45 C9
Tunia, Colombia 120 C2
Tunica, U.S.A. 109 H9
Tunis, Tunisia 75 A7
Tunis, Golfe de, Tunisia . . . 75 A7
Tunisia ■, Africa 75 B6
Tunja, Colombia 120 B3
Tunkhannock, U.S.A. 107 E9
Tunliu, China 50 F7
Tunnsjøen, Norway 8 D15
Tunungayualok I., Canada . . 99 A7
Tunuyán, Argentina 126 C2
Tunuyán →, Argentina 126 C2
Tunxi, China 53 C12
Tuo Jiang →, China 52 C5
Tuolumne, U.S.A. 111 H3
Tuolumne →, U.S.A. 112 H5
Tuoy-Khaya, Russia 45 C12
Tūp Āghāj, Iran 67 D12
Tupã, Brazil 127 A5
Tupaciguara, Brazil 123 E2
Tupelo, U.S.A. 105 H1
Tupik, Russia 42 C1
Tupik, Russia 45 D12
Tupinambaranas, Brazil . . . 121 D6
Tupirama, Brazil 122 C2
Tupiratins, Brazil 122 C2
Tupiza, Bolivia 126 A2
Tupman, U.S.A. 113 K7
Tupper, Canada 100 B4
Tupper Lake, U.S.A. 107 B10
Tupungato, Cerro,
  S. Amer. 126 C2
Tuquan, China 51 B11
Túquerres, Colombia 120 C2
Tura, Russia 45 C11
Turabah, Si. Arabia 64 D4
Turagua, Serranía,
  Venezuela 121 B5
Tūrān, Iran 65 C8
Turan, Russia 45 D10
Turayf, Si. Arabia 64 D3
Turbenthal, Switz. 23 B7
Turégano, Spain 30 D6
Turek, Poland 20 C8
Turen, Venezuela 120 B4
Turfan = Turpan, China . . . 54 B3
Turfan Depression =
  Turpan Hami, China . . . 54 B3
Tŭrgovishte, Bulgaria 38 F9
Turgutlu, Turkey 66 C2
Turhal, Turkey 66 B7
Turia →, Spain 29 F4
Turiaçu, Brazil 122 B2
Turiaçu →, Brazil 122 B2
Turin = Torino, Italy 32 C4
Turin, Canada 100 D6
Turkana □, Kenya 82 B4
Turkana, L., Africa 82 B4
Turkestan = Türkistan,
  Kazakhstan 44 E7
Túrkeve, Hungary 21 H10
Turkey ■, Eurasia 66 C7
Turkey Creek, Australia . . . 88 C4
Turki, Russia 42 D6
Türkistan, Kazakhstan 44 E7
Turkmenistan ■, Asia 44 F6
Türkoğlu, Turkey 66 D7
Turks & Caicos Is. ■,
  W. Indies 117 B5
Turks Island Passage,
  W. Indies 117 B5
Turku, Finland 9 F20
Turkwe →, Kenya 82 B4
Turlock, U.S.A. 111 H3
Turnagain →, Canada 100 B3
Turnagain, C., N.Z. 87 J6
Turneffe Is., Belize 115 D7
Turner, Australia 88 C4
Turner, U.S.A. 110 B9
Turner Pt., Australia 90 A1
Turner Valley, Canada 100 C6
Turners Falls, U.S.A. 107 D12
Turnhout, Belgium 17 F5
Turnor L., Canada 101 B7
Tŭrnovo = Veliko
  Tŭrnovo, Bulgaria 38 F8
Turnu Măgurele, Romania . . 38 F7
Turnu Roşu, P., Romania . . 38 D7
Turon, U.S.A. 109 G5
Turpan, China 54 B3
Turpan Hami, China 54 B3
Turriff, U.K. 14 D6
Tursāq, Iraq 67 F11
Tursi, Italy 35 B9
Turtle Head I., Australia . . . 90 A3
Turtle L., Canada 101 C7
Turtle Lake, N. Dak.,
  U.S.A. 108 B4
Turtle Lake, Wis., U.S.A. . . 108 C8
Turtleford, Canada 101 C7
Turukhansk, Russia 45 C9
Turzovka, Slovak Rep. 20 F8
Tuscaloosa, U.S.A. 105 J2
Tuscánia, Italy 33 F8

Tuscany = Toscana □, Italy 32 E8
Tuscola, Ill., U.S.A. 104 F1
Tuscola, Tex., U.S.A. 109 J5
Tuscumbia, U.S.A. 105 H2
Tuskar Rock, Ireland 15 D5
Tuskegee, U.S.A. 105 J3
Tustna, Norway 10 A2
Tutak, Turkey 67 C10
Tutayev, Russia 42 B4
Tuticorin, India 60 Q11
Tutin, Serbia, Yug. 21 N10
Tutóia, Brazil 122 B3
Tutong, Brunei 56 D4
Tutova →, Romania 38 C10
Tutrakan, Bulgaria 38 E9
Tutshi L., Canada 100 B2
Tuttle, U.S.A. 108 B5
Tuttlingen, Germany 19 H4
Tutuala, Indonesia 57 F7
Tutuila, Amer. Samoa 87 B13
Tututepec, Mexico 115 D5
Tuva □, Russia 45 D10
Tuvalu ■, Pac. Oc. 92 H9
Tuxpan, Mexico 115 C5
Tuxtla Gutiérrez, Mexico . . 115 D6
Tuy, Spain 30 C2
Tuy An, Vietnam 58 F7
Tuy Duc, Vietnam 59 F6
Tuy Hoa, Vietnam 58 F7
Tuy Phong, Vietnam 59 G7
Tuya L., Canada 100 B2
Tuyen Hoa, Vietnam 58 D6
Tuyen Quang, Vietnam 58 B5
Tūysarkān, Iran 67 E13
Tuz Gölü, Turkey 66 C5
Tūz Khurmātū, Iraq 67 E11
Tuzla, Bos.-H. 21 L8
Tuzlov →, Russia 43 G4
Tuzluca, Turkey 67 B10
Tvååker, Sweden 11 G6
Tvedestrand, Norway 11 F2
Tver, Russia 42 B2
Tvŭrditsa, Bulgaria 38 G8
Twain, U.S.A. 112 E5
Twain Harte, U.S.A. 112 G6
Tweed, Canada 106 B7
Tweed →, U.K. 14 F7
Tweed Heads, Australia . . . 91 D5
Tweedsmuir Prov. Park,
  Canada 100 C3
Twello, Neths. 16 D8
Twentynine Palms, U.S.A. . . 113 L10
Twillingate, Canada 99 C9
Twin Bridges, U.S.A. 110 D7
Twin Falls, U.S.A. 110 E6
Twin Valley, U.S.A. 108 B6
Twisp, U.S.A. 110 B3
Twistringen, Germany 18 C4
Two Harbors, U.S.A. 108 B9
Two Hills, Canada 100 C6
Two Rivers, U.S.A. 104 C2
Twofold B., Australia 91 F4
Tychiv, Ukraine 41 H2
Tychy, Poland 20 E8
Tykocin, Poland 20 B12
Tyler, U.S.A. 103 D7
Tyler, Minn., U.S.A. 108 C6
Tyler, Tex., U.S.A. 109 J7
Tyligul →, Ukraine 41 J6
Tylldal, Norway 10 B4
Týn nad Vltavou, Czech. . . . 20 F4
Tynda, Russia 45 D13
Tyne →, U.K. 12 C6
Tyne & Wear □, U.K. 12 C6
Tynemouth, U.K. 12 B6
Tynset, Norway 10 B4
Tyre = Sūr, Lebanon 69 B4
Tyrifjorden, Norway 10 D4
Tyringe, Sweden 11 H7
Tyristrand, Norway 10 D4
Tyrnyauz, Russia 43 J6
Tyrone, U.S.A. 106 F6
Tyrrell →, Australia 91 F3
Tyrrell, L., Australia 91 F3
Tyrrell Arm, Canada 101 A9
Tyrrell L., Canada 101 A7
Tyrrhenian Sea, Medit. S. . . 34 B5
Tysfjorden, Norway 8 B17
Tystberga, Sweden 11 F11
Tyub Karagan, Mys,
  Kazakhstan 43 H10
Tyuleni, Ostrova,
  Kazakhstan 43 H10
Tyuleniy, Russia 43 H8
Tyuleniy, Mys, Azerbaijan . 43 K10
Tyumen, Russia 44 D7
Tywi →, U.K. 13 F3
Tywyn, U.K. 13 E3
Tzaneen, S. Africa 85 C5
Tzermiádhes, Greece 37 D7
Tzermiádhes Neápolis,
  Greece 39 P8
Tzoumérka, Óros, Greece . 39 K4
Tzukong = Zigong, China . . 52 C5
Tzummarum, Neths. 16 B7

U

U Taphao, Thailand 58 F3
U.S.A. = United States of
  America ■, N. Amer. . . . 102 C7
Uachadi, Sierra, Venezuela . 121 C4
Uainambi, Colombia 120 C4
Uanda, Australia 90 C3

Uarsciek, Somali Rep. 68 G4
Uasin □, Kenya 82 B4
Uato-Udo, Indonesia 57 F7
Uatumã →, Brazil 121 D6
Uauá, Brazil 122 C4
Uaupés, Brazil 120 D4
Uaupés →, Brazil 120 C4
Ubá, Brazil 123 F3
Ubaitaba, Brazil 123 D4
Ubangi = Oubangi →,
  Zaïre 80 E3
Ubaté, Colombia 120 B3
Ubauro, Pakistan 62 E3
Ubaye →, France 27 D10
Ubayyiḍ, W. al →, Iraq . . . 67 F10
Ube, Japan 49 H5
Ubeda, Spain 29 G1
Uberaba, Brazil 123 E2
Uberaba, L., Brazil 125 D6
Uberlândia, Brazil 123 E2
Überlingen, Germany 19 H5
Ubiaja, Nigeria 79 D6
Ubolratna Res., Thailand . . 58 D4
Ubombo, S. Africa 85 D5
Ubon Ratchathani,
  Thailand 58 E5
Ubondo, Zaïre 82 C2
Ubort →, Belarus 41 F5
Ubrique, Spain 31 J5
Ubundu, Zaïre 82 C2
Ucayali →, Peru 124 A3
Uccle, Belgium 17 G4
Uchi Lake, Canada 101 C10
Uchiura-Wan, Japan 48 C10
Uchiza, Peru 124 B2
Uchte, Germany 18 C4
Uchur →, Russia 45 D14
Uckfield, U.K. 13 G8
Ucluelet, Canada 100 D3
Ucuriş, Romania 38 C4
Uda →, Russia 45 D14
Udaipur, India 62 G5
Udaipur Garhi, Nepal 63 F12
Udbina, Croatia 33 D12
Uddel, Neths. 16 D7
Uddevalla, Sweden 11 F5
Uddjaur, Sweden 8 D17
Uden, Neths. 17 E7
Udgir, India 60 K10
Udhampur, India 63 C6
Udi, Nigeria 79 D6
Údine, Italy 33 B10
Udmurtia □, Russia 44 D6
Udon Thani, Thailand 58 D4
Udupi, India 60 N9
Udvoy Balkan, Bulgaria . . . 38 G9
Udzungwa Range,
  Tanzania 83 D4
Ueckermünde, Germany . . . 18 B10
Ueda, Japan 49 F9
Uedineniya, Os., Russia . . . 4 B12
Uele →, Zaïre 80 D4
Uelen, Russia 45 C19
Uelzen, Germany 18 C6
Ufa, Russia 44 D6
Uffenheim, Germany 19 F6
Ugab →, Namibia 84 C1
Ugalla →, Tanzania 82 D3
Uganda ■, Africa 82 B3
Ugchelen, Neths. 16 D7
Ugento, Italy 35 C11
Ugep, Nigeria 79 D6
Ugie, S. Africa 85 E4
Ugijar, Spain 29 J1
Ugine, France 27 C10
Uglegorsk, Russia 45 E15
Uglich, Russia 42 B4
Ugljane, Croatia 33 E13
Ugolyak, Russia 45 C13
Ugra →, Russia 42 C3
Ugūn Mūsa, Egypt 69 F1
Uğurchin, Bulgaria 38 F7
Uh →, Slovak Rep. 21 G11
Uherské Hradiště, Czech. . . 20 F7
Uhrichsville, U.S.A. 106 F3
Uibhist a Deas = South
  Uist, U.K. 14 D1
Uibhist a Tuath = North
  Uist, U.K. 14 D1
Uíge, Angola 80 F2
Uijŏngbu, S. Korea 51 F14
Uiju, N. Korea 51 D13
Uinta Mts., U.S.A. 110 F8
Uitenhage, S. Africa 84 E4
Uitgeest, Neths. 16 C5
Uithoorn, Neths. 16 D5
Uithuizen, Neths. 16 B9
Uitkerke, Belgium 17 F2
Újfehértó, Hungary 21 H11
Ujhani, India 63 F8
Ujjain, India 62 H6
Ujpest, Hungary 21 H9
Ujszász, Hungary 21 H10
Ujung Pandang, Indonesia . 57 F5
Uka, Russia 45 D17
Ukara I., Tanzania 82 C3
Uke-Shima, Japan 49 K4
Ukerewe □, Tanzania 82 C3
Ukerewe I., Tanzania 82 C3
Ukholovo, Russia 42 D5
Ukhrul, India 61 G19
Ukhta, Russia 44 C6
Ukiah, U.S.A. 112 F3
Ukki Fort, India 63 C7
Ukmerge, Lithuania 9 J21

Ukraine ■, Europe 41 H7
Ukwi, Botswana 84 C3
Ulaanbaatar, Mongolia 45 E11
Ulaangom, Mongolia 54 A4
Ulamba, Zaïre 83 D1
Ulan Bator = Ulaanbaatar,
  Mongolia 45 E11
Ulan Erge, Russia 43 G7
Ulan Khol, Russia 43 H9
Ulan Ude, Russia 45 D11
Ulanga □, Tanzania 83 D4
Ulanów, Poland 20 E12
Ulaş, Turkey 66 C7
Ulaya, Morogoro, Tanzania 82 D4
Ulaya, Tabora, Tanzania . . 82 C3
Ulcinj, Montenegro, Yug. . . 39 H2
Ulco, S. Africa 84 D3
Ulefoss, Norway 9 G13
Ulfborg, Denmark 11 H2
Ulft, Neths. 16 E8
Ulhasnagar, India 60 K8
Uljma, Serbia, Yug. 21 K11
Ulla →, Spain 30 C2
Ulladulla, Australia 91 F5
Ullånger, Sweden 10 B12
Ullapool, U.K. 14 D3
Ullared, Sweden 11 G6
Ulldecona, Spain 28 E5
Ullswater, U.K. 12 C5
Ullung-do, S. Korea 51 F16
Ulm, Germany 19 G5
Ulmarra, Australia 91 D5
Ulmeni, Romania 38 D9
Ulongué, Mozam. 83 E3
Ulricehamn, Sweden 9 H15
Ulrum, Neths. 16 B8
Ulsan, S. Korea 51 G15
Ulsberg, Norway 10 B3
Ulster □, U.K. 15 B5
Ulubaria, India 63 H13
Ulubat Gölü, Turkey 66 B3
Ulubey, Turkey 66 C3
Uluborlu, Turkey 66 C4
Uluçinar, Turkey 66 D6
Uludağ, Turkey 66 B3
Uludere, Turkey 67 D10
Uluguru Mts., Tanzania . . . 82 D4
Ulukışla, Turkey 66 D6
Ulungur He →, China 54 B3
Uluru = Ayers Rock,
  Australia 89 E5
Ulutau, Kazakhstan 44 E7
Ulvenhout, Neths. 17 E5
Ulverston, U.K. 12 C4
Ulverstone, Australia 90 G4
Ulya, Russia 45 D15
Ulyanovsk = Simbirsk,
  Russia 42 C9
Ulyasutay, Mongolia 54 B4
Ulysses, U.S.A. 109 G4
Umag, Croatia 33 C10
Umala, Bolivia 124 D4
Uman, Ukraine 41 H6
Umaria, India 61 H12
Umarkot, Pakistan 60 G6
Umatilla, U.S.A. 110 D4
Umba, Russia 44 C4
Umbértide, Italy 33 E9
Umbrella Mts., N.Z. 87 L2
Umbria □, Italy 33 F9
Ume älv →, Sweden 8 E19
Umeå, Sweden 8 E19
Umera, Indonesia 57 E7
Umfuli →, Zimbabwe 83 F2
Umgusa, Zimbabwe 83 F2
Umka, Serbia, Yug. 21 L10
Umkomaas, S. Africa 85 E5
Umm ad Daraj, J., Jordan . 69 C4
Umm al Qaywayn, U.A.E. . 65 E7
Umm al Qittayn, Jordan . . . 69 C5
Umm Arda, Sudan 77 D3
Umm Bāb, Qatar 65 E6
Umm Bel, Sudan 77 E2
Umm Dubban, Sudan 77 D3
Umm el Fahm, Israel 69 C4
Umm Koweika, Sudan 77 E3
Umm Lajj, Si. Arabia 64 E3
Umm Merwa, Sudan 76 D3
Umm Ruwaba, Sudan 77 E3
Umm Sidr, Sudan 77 E2
Ummanz, Germany 18 A9
Umnak I., U.S.A. 96 C3
Umniati →, Zimbabwe 83 F2
Umpqua →, U.S.A. 110 E1
Umreth, India 62 H5
Umtata, S. Africa 85 E4
Umuahia, Nigeria 79 D6
Umuarama, Brazil 127 A5
Umvukwe Ra., Zimbabwe . 83 F3
Umzimvubu = Port St.
  Johns, S. Africa 85 E4
Umzingwane →,
  Zimbabwe 83 G2
Umzinto, S. Africa 85 E5
Una, India 62 J4
Una →, Bos.-H. 33 C13
Unac →, Bos.-H. 33 D13
Unadilla, U.S.A. 107 D9
Unalaska, U.S.A. 96 C3
'Unāzah, J., Asia 67 F8
Uncastillo, Spain 28 C3
Uncía, Bolivia 124 D4
Uncompahgre Peak, U.S.A. 111 G10
Unden, Sweden 11 F8
Underbool, Australia 91 F3
Undersaker, Sweden 10 A7
Undersvik, Sweden 10 C10

Unecha, *Russia* 41 F7
Uneiuxi, *Brazil* 120 D4
Ungarie, *Australia* 91 E4
Ungarra, *Australia* 91 E2
Ungava B., *Canada* 97 C13
Ungava Pen., *Canada* 97 C12
Ungeny = Ungheni,
  Moldova 41 J4
Unggi, *N. Korea* 51 C16
Ungheni, *Moldova* 41 J4
Ungwatiri, *Sudan* 77 D4
Uni, *Russia* 42 B10
União da Vitória, *Brazil* .. 127 B5
União dos Palmares, *Brazil* 122 C4
Unije, *Croatia* 33 D11
Unimak I., *U.S.A.* 96 C3
Unini →, *Brazil* 121 D5
Union, *Miss., U.S.A.* 109 J10
Union, *Mo., U.S.A.* 108 F9
Union, *S.C., U.S.A.* 105 H5
Union, *Mt., U.S.A.* 111 J7
Union City, *Calif., U.S.A.* 112 H4
Union City, *N.J., U.S.A.* . 107 F10
Union City, *Pa., U.S.A.* .. 106 E5
Union City, *Tenn., U.S.A.* 109 G10
Union Gap, *U.S.A.* 110 C3
Union Springs, *U.S.A.* .. 105 J3
Uniondale, *S. Africa* 84 E3
Uniontown, *U.S.A.* 104 F6
Unionville, *U.S.A.* 108 E8
United Arab Emirates ■,
  Asia 65 F7
United Kingdom ■, *Europe* 7 E5
United States of
  America ■, *N. Amer.* .. 102 C7
Unity, *Canada* 101 C7
Universales, Mtes., *Spain* . 28 E3
Unjha, *India* 62 H5
Unnao, *India* 63 F9
Uno, Ilha, *Guinea-Biss.* .. 78 C1
Unst, *U.K.* 14 A8
Unstrut →, *Germany* 18 D7
Unter-engadin, *Switz.* ... 23 C10
Unterägeri, *Switz.* 23 B7
Unterkulm, *Switz.* 22 B6
Unterseen, *Switz.* 22 C5
Unterwaldner Alpen, *Switz.* 23 C6
Unuk →, *Canada* 100 B2
Ünye, *Turkey* 66 B7
Unzha, *Russia* 42 A7
Unzha →, *Russia* 42 B6
Uors, *Switz.* 23 C8
Uozu, *Japan* 49 F8
Upa →, *Czech.* 20 E6
Upata, *Venezuela* 121 B5
Upemba, L., *Zaïre* 83 D2
Upington, *S. Africa* 84 D3
Upleta, *India* 62 J4
Upolu, *W. Samoa* 87 A13
Upper Alkali Lake, *U.S.A.* 110 F3
Upper Arrow L., *Canada* . 100 C5
Upper Foster L., *Canada* . 101 B7
Upper Hutt, *N.Z.* 87 J5
Upper Klamath L., *U.S.A.* 110 E3
Upper Lake, *U.S.A.* 112 F4
Upper Musquodoboit,
  Canada 99 C7
Upper Red L., *U.S.A.* .. 108 A7
Upper Sandusky, *U.S.A.* . 104 E4
Upper Volta = Burkina
  Faso ■, *Africa* 78 C4
Upphärad, *Sweden* 11 F6
Uppland, *Sweden* 9 F17
Uppsala, *Sweden* 10 E11
Upshi, *India* 63 C7
Upstart, C., *Australia* ... 90 B4
Upton, *U.S.A.* 108 C2
Ur, *Iraq* 64 D5
Urabá, G. de, *Colombia* .. 120 B2
Uracara, *Brazil* 121 D6
Urad Qianqi, *China* 50 D5
Urakawa, *Japan* 48 C11
Ural = Zhayyq →,
  Kazakhstan 44 E6
Ural, *Australia* 91 E4
Ural Mts. = Uralskie Gory,
  Eurasia 44 D6
Uralla, *Australia* 91 E5
Uralsk = Oral, *Kazakhstan* 42 E10
Uralskie Gory, *Eurasia* .. 44 D6
Urambo, *Tanzania* 82 D3
Urambo □, *Tanzania* 82 D3
Urandangi, *Australia* 90 C2
Uranium City, *Canada* ... 101 B7
Uranquinty, *Australia* ... 91 F4
Uraricaá →, *Brazil* 121 C5
Uraricoera →, *Brazil* 121 C5
Urawa, *Japan* 49 G9
Uray, *Russia* 44 C7
'Uray'irah, *Si. Arabia* ... 65 E6
Urbana, *Ill., U.S.A.* 104 E1
Urbana, *Ohio, U.S.A.* ... 104 E4
Urbánia, *Italy* 33 E9
Urbano Santos, *Brazil* .. 122 B3
Urbel →, *Spain* 28 C1
Urbino, *Italy* 33 E9
Urbión, Picos de, *Spain* .. 28 C2
Urcos, *Peru* 124 C3
Urda, *Spain* 31 F7
Urdinarrain, *Argentina* .. 126 C4
Urdos, *France* 26 F3
Urdzhar, *Kazakhstan* 44 E9
Ure →, *U.K.* 12 C6
Ures, *Mexico* 114 B2
Urfa = Sanliurfa, *Turkey* . 67 D8

Urfahr, *Austria* 21 G4
Urganch, *Uzbekistan* 44 E7
Urgench = Urganch,
  Uzbekistan 44 E7
Uri, *India* 63 B6
Uri □, *Switz.* 23 C7
Uribante →, *Venezuela* .. 120 B3
Uribe, *Colombia* 120 C3
Uribia, *Colombia* 120 A3
Uriondo, *Bolivia* 126 A3
Urique, *Mexico* 114 B3
Urique →, *Mexico* 114 B3
Urk, *Neths.* 16 C7
Urla, *Turkey* 66 C2
Urlati, *Romania* 38 E9
Urmia = Orūmīyeh, *Iran* . 67 D11
Urmia, L. = Orūmīyeh,
  Daryācheh-ye, *Iran* ... 67 D11
Urner Alpen, *Switz.* 23 C7
Uroševac, *Serbia, Yug.* .. 21 N11
Urrao, *Colombia* 120 B2
Ursus, *Poland* 20 C10
Uruaçu, *Brazil* 123 D2
Uruana, *Brazil* 123 E2
Uruapan, *Mexico* 114 D4
Uruará →, *Brazil* 121 D7
Urubamba, *Peru* 124 C3
Urubamba →, *Peru* 124 C3
Urubaxi →, *Brazil* 121 D5
Urubu →, *Brazil* 121 D6
Uruçara, *Brazil* 121 D6
Uruçuí, *Brazil* 122 C3
Uruçuí, Serra do, *Brazil* .. 122 C3
Uruçuí Prêto →, *Brazil* .. 122 C3
Urucuia →, *Brazil* 123 E2
Urucurituba, *Brazil* 121 D6
Uruguai →, *Brazil* 127 B5
Uruguaiana, *Brazil* 126 B4
Uruguay ■, *S. Amer.* 126 C4
Uruguay →, *S. Amer.* 126 C4
Urumchi = Ürümqi, *China* 44 E9
Ürümqi, *China* 44 E9
Urup, →, *Russia* 43 H5
Urup, Os., *Russia* 45 E16
Urutaí, *Brazil* 123 E2
Uryupinsk, *Russia* 42 E5
Urzhum, *Russia* 42 B9
Urziceni, *Romania* 38 E9
Uşak, *Turkey* 66 C3
Usakos, *Namibia* 84 C2
Usborne, Mt., *Falk. Is.* .. 128 D5
Ušče, *Serbia, Yug.* 21 M10
Usedom, *Germany* 18 B9
'Usfān, *Si. Arabia* 76 C4
Ush-Tobe, *Kazakhstan* ... 44 E8
Ushakova, Os., *Russia* ... 4 A12
Ushant = Ouessant, I. d',
  France 24 D1
Ushashi, *Tanzania* 82 C3
Ushat, *Sudan* 77 F2
Ushibuka, *Japan* 49 H5
Ushuaia, *Argentina* 128 D3
Ushumun, *Russia* 45 D13
Usk →, *U.K.* 13 F5
Üsküdar, *Turkey* 39 H11
Uslar, *Germany* 18 D5
Usman, *Russia* 42 D4
Usoke, *Tanzania* 82 D3
Usolye Sibirskoye, *Russia* . 45 D11
Usoro, *Nigeria* 79 D6
Uspallata, P. de, *Argentina* 126 C2
Uspenskiy, *Kazakhstan* .. 44 E8
Usquert, *Neths.* 16 B9
Ussel, *France* 26 C6
Ussuri →, *Asia* 48 A7
Ussuriysk, *Russia* 45 E14
Ussurka, *Russia* 48 B6
Ust-Aldan = Batamay,
  Russia 45 C13
Ust Amginskoye =
  Khandyga, *Russia* 45 C14
Ust-Bolsheretsk, *Russia* . 45 D16
Ust Buzulukskaya, *Russia* 42 E6
Ust Chaun, *Russia* 45 C18
Ust-Donetskiy, *Russia* ... 43 G5
Ust'-Ilga, *Russia* 45 D11
Ust Ilimpeya = Yukti,
  Russia 45 C11
Ust-Ilimsk, *Russia* 45 D11
Ust Ishim, *Russia* 44 D8
Ust-Kamchatsk, *Russia* .. 45 D17
Ust-Kamenogorsk =
  Öskemen, *Kazakhstan* . 44 E9
Ust-Karenga, *Russia* 45 D12
Ust Khayryuzovo, *Russia* 45 D16
Ust-Kut, *Russia* 45 D11
Ust Kuyga, *Russia* 45 B14
Ust-Labinsk, *Russia* 43 H4
Ust Luga, *Russia* 40 C5
Ust Maya, *Russia* 45 C14
Ust-Mil, *Russia* 45 D14
Ust Muya, *Russia* 45 D12
Ust-Nera, *Russia* 45 C15
Ust-Nyukzha, *Russia* 45 D13
Ust Olenek, *Russia* 45 B12
Ust-Omchug, *Russia* 45 C15
Ust Port, *Russia* 44 C9
Ust Tsilma, *Russia* 44 C6
Ust-Tungir, *Russia* 45 D13
Ust Urt = Ustyurt,
  Plateau, *Asia* 44 E6
Ust Vorkuta, *Russia* 44 C7
Ustaoset, *Norway* 10 D2
Ustaritz, *France* 26 E2
Úster, *Switz.* 23 B7
Ústí nad Labem, *Czech.* .. 20 E4

Ústí nad Orlicí, *Czech.* ... 20 F6
Ustica, *Italy* 34 E6
Ustinov = Izhevsk, *Russia* 44 D6
Ustka, *Poland* 20 A6
Ustrzyki Dolne, *Poland* .. 20 F12
Ustye, *Russia* 45 D10
Ustyuzhna, *Russia* 40 C9
Usu, *China* 44 E9
Usuki, *Japan* 49 H5
Usulután, *El Salv.* 116 D2
Usumacinta →, *Mexico* .. 115 D6
Usumbura = Bujumbura,
  Burundi 82 C2
Usure, *Tanzania* 82 C3
Uta, *Indonesia* 57 E9
Utah □, *U.S.A.* 100 G8
Utah, L., *U.S.A.* 100 F8
Ute Creek →, *U.S.A.* ... 109 H3
Utena, *Lithuania* 9 J21
Ütersen, *Germany* 18 B5
Utete, *Tanzania* 82 D4
Uthai Thani, *Thailand* .. 58 E3
Uthal, *Pakistan* 62 G2
Utiariti, *Brazil* 125 C6
Utica, *N.Y., U.S.A.* 107 C9
Utica, *Ohio, U.S.A.* 106 F2
Utiel, *Spain* 28 F3
Utik L., *Canada* 101 B9
Utikuma L., *Canada* 100 B5
Utinga, *Brazil* 123 D3
Utrecht, *Neths.* 16 D6
Utrecht, *S. Africa* 85 D5
Utrecht □, *Neths.* 16 D6
Utrera, *Spain* 31 H5
Utsjoki, *Finland* 8 B22
Utsunomiya, *Japan* 49 F9
Uttar Pradesh □, *India* .. 63 F9
Uttaradit, *Thailand* 58 D3
Uttoxeter, *U.K.* 12 E6
Ütze, *Germany* 18 C6
Uummannarsuaq = Farvel,
  Kap, *Greenland* 4 D5
Uusikaarlepyy, *Finland* .. 8 E20
Uusikaupunki, *Finland* .. 9 F19
Uva, *Russia* 42 B11
Uvá →, *Colombia* 120 C3
Uvalde, *U.S.A.* 109 L5
Uvarovo, *Russia* 42 E6
Uvat, *Russia* 44 D7
Uvinza, *Tanzania* 82 D3
Uvira, *Zaïre* 82 C2
Uvs Nuur, *Mongolia* 54 A4
Uwajima, *Japan* 49 H6
Uweinat, Jebel, *Sudan* .. 76 C1
Uxbridge, *Canada* 106 B5
Uxin Qi, *China* 50 E5
Uxmal, *Mexico* 115 C7
Uyandi, *Russia* 45 C15
Uyo, *Nigeria* 79 D6
Uyuni, *Bolivia* 124 E4
Uzbekistan ■, *Asia* 44 E7
Uzen, Bolshoi →,
  Kazakhstan 43 F9
Uzen, Mal →, *Kazakhstan* 43 F9
Uzerche, *France* 26 C5
Uzès, *France* 27 D8
Uzh →, *Ukraine* 41 G6
Uzhgorod = Uzhhorod,
  Ukraine 41 H2
Uzhhorod, *Ukraine* 41 H2
Uzlovaya, *Russia* 42 D4
Uzunköprü, *Turkey* 66 B2
Uzwil, *Switz.* 23 B8

V

Vaal →, *S. Africa* 84 D3
Vaal Dam, *S. Africa* 85 D4
Vaals, *Neths.* 17 G8
Vaalwater, *S. Africa* 85 C4
Vaasa, *Finland* 8 E19
Vaassen, *Neths.* 16 D7
Vabre, *France* 26 E6
Vác, *Hungary* 21 H9
Vacaria, *Brazil* 127 B5
Vacaville, *U.S.A.* 112 G5
Vaccarès, Étang de, *France* 27 E8
Vach = Vakh →, *Russia* . 44 C8
Vache, I.-à-, *Haiti* 117 C5
Vadnagar, *India* 62 H5
Vado Lígure, *Italy* 32 D5
Vadodara, *India* 62 H5
Vadsø, *Norway* 8 A23
Vadstena, *Sweden* 11 F8
Værøy, *Norway* 8 C15
Vágar, *Færoe Is.* 8 E9
Vagney, *France* 25 D13
Vagnhärad, *Sweden* 10 F11
Vagos, *Portugal* 30 E2
Vågsfjorden, *Norway* 8 B17
Váh →, *Slovak Rep.* 21 H8
Vahsel B., *Antarctica* ... 5 D1
Väï, *Greece* 37 D8
Vaigach, *Russia* 44 B6
Vaiges, *France* 24 D6
Vaihingen, *Germany* 19 G4
Vailly-sur-Aisne, *France* . 25 C10
Vaison-la-Romaine, *France* 27 D9
Vakfikebir, *Turkey* 67 B8
Vakh →, *Russia* 44 C8
Vakhtan, *Russia* 42 B8
Val-de-Marne □, *France* .. 25 D9

Val-d'Oise □, *France* 25 C9
Val d'Or, *Canada* 98 C4
Val Marie, *Canada* 101 D7
Valaam, *Russia* 40 B6
Valadares, *Portugal* 30 D2
Valahia, *Romania* 38 E8
Valais □, *Switz.* 22 D5
Valais, Alpes du, *Switz.* . 22 D5
Valandovo, *Macedonia* .. 39 H5
Valcheta, *Argentina* 128 B3
Valdagno, *Italy* 33 C8
Valdahon, *France* 25 E13
Valday, *Russia* 42 B1
Valdayskaya
  Vozvyshennost, *Russia* . 42 B1
Valdeazogues →, *Spain* . 31 G6
Valdemarsvik, *Sweden* .. 11 F10
Valdepeñas, Ciudad Real,
  Spain 31 G7
Valdepeñas, Jaén, *Spain* . 31 H7
Valderaduey →, *Spain* .. 30 D5
Valderrobres, *Spain* 28 E5
Valdés, Pen., *Argentina* .. 128 B4
Valdez, *Ecuador* 120 C2
Valdez, *U.S.A.* 96 B5
Valdivia, *Chile* 128 A2
Valdivia, *Colombia* 120 B2
Valdivia □, *Chile* 128 A2
Valdosta, *U.S.A.* 105 K4
Valdoviño, *Spain* 30 B2
Valdres, *Norway* 10 D3
Vale, *Georgia* 43 K6
Vale, *U.S.A.* 110 E5
Valea lui Mihai, *Romania* . 38 B5
Valença, *Brazil* 123 D4
Valença, *Portugal* 30 C2
Valença do Piauí, *Brazil* . 122 C3
Valençay, *France* 25 E8
Valence, *Drôme, France* . 27 D8
Valence, *Tarn-et-Garonne,
  France* 26 D4
Valencia, *Spain* 29 F4
Valencia, *Venezuela* 120 A4
Valencia □, *Spain* 29 F4
Valencia, G. de, *Spain* ... 29 F5
Valencia de Alcántara,
  Spain 31 F3
Valencia de Don Juan,
  Spain 30 C5
Valencia del Ventoso,
  Spain 31 G4
Valencia Harbour, *Ireland* 15 E1
Valencia I., *Ireland* 15 E1
Valenciennes, *France* 25 B10
Valensole, *France* 27 E9
Valentim, Sa. do, *Brazil* . 122 C3
Valentin, *Russia* 48 C7
Valentine, *Nebr., U.S.A.* . 108 D4
Valentine, *Tex., U.S.A.* .. 109 K2
Valenza, *Italy* 32 C5
Valera, *Venezuela* 120 B3
Valga, *Estonia* 9 H22
Valguarnera Caropepe,
  Italy 35 E7
Valier, *U.S.A.* 110 B7
Valjevo, *Serbia, Yug.* ... 21 L9
Valka, *Latvia* 9 H21
Valkeakoski, *Finland* 9 F20
Valkenburg, *Neths.* 17 G7
Valkenswaard, *Neths.* ... 17 F6
Vall de Uxó, *Spain* 28 F4
Valla, *Sweden* 10 E10
Valladolid, *Mexico* 115 C7
Valladolid, *Spain* 30 D6
Valladolid □, *Spain* 30 D6
Vallata, *Italy* 35 A8
Valldemosa, *Spain* 36 B9
Valle d'Aosta □, *Italy* 32 C4
Valle de Arán, *Spain* 28 C5
Valle de Cabuérniga, *Spain* 30 B6
Valle de la Pascua,
  Venezuela 120 B4
Valle de las Palmas, *Mexico* 113 N10
Valle de Santiago, *Mexico* 114 C4
Valle de Suchil, *Mexico* .. 114 C4
Valle de Zaragoza, *Mexico* 114 B3
Valle del Cauca □,
  Colombia 120 C2
Valle Fértil, Sierra del,
  Argentina 126 C2
Valle Hermoso, *Mexico* .. 115 B5
Vallecas, *Spain* 30 E7
Valledupar, *Colombia* ... 120 A3
Vallehermoso, *Canary Is.* 36 F2
Vallejo, *U.S.A.* 112 G4
Vallenar, *Chile* 126 B1
Valleraugue, *France* 26 D7
Vallet, *France* 24 E5
Valletta, *Malta* 37 D2
Valley Center, *U.S.A.* ... 113 M9
Valley City, *U.S.A.* 108 B6
Valley Falls, *U.S.A.* 110 E3
Valley Springs, *U.S.A.* .. 112 G6
Valley Wells, *U.S.A.* 113 K11
Valleyview, *Canada* 100 B5
Valli di Comácchio, *Italy* . 33 D9
Vallimanca, Arroyo,
  Argentina 126 D4
Vallo della Lucánia, *Italy* . 35 B8
Vallon-Pont-d'Arc, *France* 27 D8
Vallorbe, *Switz.* 22 C2
Valls, *Spain* 28 D6
Vallsta, *Sweden* 10 C10
Valmaseda, *Spain* 28 B1

Valmont, *France* 24 C7
Valmontone, *Italy* 34 A5
Valmy, *France* 25 C11
Valnera, Mte., *Spain* 28 B1
Valognes, *France* 24 C5
Valona = Vlóra, *Albania* . 39 J2
Valongo, *Portugal* 30 D2
Valozhyn, *Belarus* 40 E4
Valpaços, *Portugal* 30 D3
Valparaíso, *Chile* 126 C1
Valparaíso, *Mexico* 114 C4
Valparaíso, *U.S.A.* 104 E2
Valparaíso □, *Chile* 126 C1
Valpovo, *Croatia* 21 K8
Valréas, *France* 27 D8
Vals, *Switz.* 23 C8
Vals →, *S. Africa* 84 D4
Vals, Tanjung, *Indonesia* . 57 F9
Vals-les-Bains, *France* ... 27 D8
Valsad, *India* 60 J8
Valskog, *Sweden* 10 E9
Válta, *Greece* 39 J6
Valtellina, *Italy* 32 B6
Valuyki, *Russia* 42 E4
Valverde, *Canary Is.* 36 G2
Valverde del Camino,
  Spain 31 H4
Valverde del Fresno, *Spain* 30 E4
Vama, *Romania* 38 B8
Vammala, *Finland* 9 F20
Vámos, *Greece* 37 D6
Van, *Turkey* 67 C10
Van, L. = Van Gölü,
  Turkey 67 C10
Van Alstyne, *U.S.A.* 109 J6
Van Bruyssel, *Canada* ... 99 C5
Van Buren, *Canada* 99 C6
Van Buren, *Ark., U.S.A.* . 109 H7
Van Buren, *Maine, U.S.A.* 105 B11
Van Buren, *Mo., U.S.A.* . 109 G9
Van Canh, *Vietnam* 58 F7
Van Diemen, C., *N. Terr.,
  Australia* 88 B5
Van Diemen, C., *Queens.,
  Australia* 90 B2
Van Diemen G., *Australia* 88 B5
Van Gölü, *Turkey* 67 C10
Van Horn, *U.S.A.* 109 K2
Van Ninh, *Vietnam* 58 F7
Van Rees, Pegunungan,
  Indonesia 57 E9
Van Tassell, *U.S.A.* 108 D2
Van Wert, *U.S.A.* 104 E3
Van Yen, *Vietnam* 58 B5
Vanadzor, *Armenia* 43 K7
Vanavara, *Russia* 45 C11
Vancouver, *Canada* 100 D4
Vancouver, *U.S.A.* 112 E4
Vancouver, C., *Australia* . 89 G2
Vancouver I., *Canada* ... 100 D3
Vandalia, *Ill., U.S.A.* 108 F10
Vandalia, *Mo., U.S.A.* ... 108 F9
Vandenburg, *U.S.A.* 113 L6
Vanderbijlpark, *S. Africa* . 85 D4
Vandergrift, *U.S.A.* 106 F5
Vanderhoof, *Canada* 100 C4
Vanderkloof Dam,
  S. Africa 84 E3
Vanderlin I., *Australia* ... 90 B2
Vandyke, *Australia* 90 C4
Vänern, *Sweden* 11 F7
Vänersborg, *Sweden* 11 F6
Vang Vieng, *Laos* 58 C4
Vanga, *Kenya* 82 C4
Vangaindrano, *Madag.* .. 85 C8
Vanguard, *Canada* 101 D7
Vanier, *Canada* 98 C4
Vankleek Hill, *Canada* .. 98 C5
Vanna, *Norway* 8 A18
Vännäs, *Sweden* 8 E18
Vannes, *France* 24 E4
Vanoise, Massif de la,
  France 27 C10
Vanrhynsdorp, *S. Africa* . 84 E2
Vanrook, *Australia* 90 B3
Vansbro, *Sweden* 9 F16
Vansittart B., *Australia* .. 88 B4
Vantaa, *Finland* 9 F21
Vanthli, *India* 62 J4
Vanua Levu, *Fiji* 87 C8
Vanua Mbalavu, *Fiji* 87 C9
Vanuatu ■, *Pac. Oc.* 92 J8
Vanwyksvlei, *S. Africa* .. 84 E3
Vanzylsrus, *S. Africa* ... 84 D3
Vapnyarka, *Ukraine* 41 H5
Var □, *France* 27 E10
Var →, *France* 27 E11
Vara, *Sweden* 11 F6
Varades, *France* 24 E5
Varáita →, *Italy* 32 D4
Varallo, *Italy* 32 C5
Varanasi, *India* 63 G10
Varanger-halvøya, *Norway* 8 A23
Varangerfjorden, *Norway* 8 A23
Varaždin, *Croatia* 33 B13
Varazze, *Italy* 32 D5
Varberg, *Sweden* 11 G6
Vardar = Axiós →, *Greece* 39 J5
Varde, *Denmark* 11 J2
Varde Å →, *Denmark* ... 11 J2
Vardø, *Norway* 8 A24
Varel, *Germany* 18 B4
Varèna, *Lithuania* 9 J21
Varennes-sur-Allier, *France* 26 B7
Vareš, *Bos.-H.* 21 L8
Varese, *Italy* 32 C5

Varese Lígure, *Italy* 32 D6
Vårgårda, *Sweden* 11 F6
Vargem Bonita, *Brazil* ... 123 F2
Vargem Grande, *Brazil* .. 122 B3
Varginha, *Brazil* 127 A6
Vargön, *Sweden* 11 F6
Variadero, *U.S.A.* 109 H2
Varillas, *Chile* 126 A1
Väring, *Sweden* 11 F8
Varkaus, *Finland* 9 E22
Varna, *Bulgaria* 38 F10
Värnamo, *Sweden* 9 H16
Varsseveld, *Neths.* 16 E8
Vars, *Canada* 107 A9
Varto, *Turkey* 67 C9
Varvarin, *Serbia, Yug.* ... 21 M11
Várzea Alegre, *Brazil* ... 122 C4
Várzea da Palma, *Brazil* . 123 E3
Várzea Grande, *Brazil* ... 125 D6
Varzi, *Italy* 32 D6
Varzo, *Italy* 32 B5
Varzy, *France* 25 E10
Vasa Barris →, *Brazil* ... 122 D4
Vascão →, *Portugal* 31 H3
Vașcău, *Romania* 38 C5
Vascongadas = País
   Vasco □, *Spain* 28 C2
Vasht = Khāsh, *Iran* 60 E2
Vasilevichi, *Belarus* 41 F5
Vasilikón, *Greece* 39 L6
Vasilkov = Vasylkiv,
   Ukraine 41 G6
Vaslui, *Romania* 38 C10
Vassar, *Canada* 101 D9
Vassar, *U.S.A.* 104 D4
Västerås, *Sweden* 10 E10
Västerbotten, *Sweden* 8 D18
Västerdalälven →, *Sweden* . 9 F16
Västernorrlands län □,
   Sweden 10 A11
Västervik, *Sweden* 9 H17
Västmanland, *Sweden* 9 G16
Vasto, *Italy* 33 F11
Vasvár, *Hungary* 21 H6
Vasylkiv, *Ukraine* 41 G6
Vatan, *France* 25 E8
Vathí, *Greece* 39 M10
Váthia, *Greece* 39 N5
Vatican City ■, *Europe* .. 33 G9
Vaticano, C., *Italy* 35 D8
Vatili, *Cyprus* 37 D12
Vatnajökull, *Iceland* 8 D5
Vatnås, *Norway* 10 E3
Vatoa, *Fiji* 87 D9
Vatólakkos, *Greece* 37 D5
Vatoloha, *Madag.* 85 B8
Vatomandry, *Madag.* 85 B8
Vatra-Dornei, *Romania* .. 38 B8
Vättern, *Sweden* 11 F8
Vättis, *Switz.* 23 C8
Vaucluse □, *France* 27 E9
Vaucouleurs, *France* 25 D12
Vaud □, *Switz.* 22 C2
Vaughn, *Mont., U.S.A.* ... 110 C8
Vaughn, *N. Mex., U.S.A.* . 111 J11
Vaulruz, *Switz.* 22 C3
Vaupés = Uaupés →,
   Brazil 120 C4
Vaupes □, *Colombia* 120 C3
Vauvert, *France* 27 E8
Vauxhall, *Canada* 100 C6
Vava'u, *Tonga* 87 D11
Vavoua, *Ivory C.* 78 D3
Vawkavysk, *Belarus* 41 F3
Vaxholm, *Sweden* 10 E12
Växjö, *Sweden* 9 H16
Vaygach, Ostrov, *Russia* . 44 C6
Veadeiros, *Brazil* 123 D2
Vechta, *Germany* 18 C4
Vechte →, *Neths.* 16 C8
Vecsés, *Hungary* 21 H9
Veddige, *Sweden* 11 G6
Vedea →, *Romania* 38 F8
Vedia, *Argentina* 126 C3
Vedra, I. del, *Spain* 36 C7
Vedrin, *Belgium* 17 G5
Veendam, *Neths.* 16 B9
Veenendaal, *Neths.* 16 D7
Veerle, *Belgium* 17 F5
Vefsna →, *Norway* 8 D15
Vega, *Norway* 8 D14
Vega, *U.S.A.* 109 H3
Vegadeo, *Spain* 30 B3
Veghel, *Neths.* 17 E7
Vegorritis, Límni, *Greece* . 39 J4
Vegreville, *Canada* 100 C6
Vegusdal, *Norway* 11 F2
Veii, *Italy* 33 F9
Vejen, *Denmark* 11 J3
Vejer de la Frontera, *Spain* . 31 J5
Vejle, *Denmark* 11 J3
Vejle Fjord, *Denmark* 11 J3
Vela Luka, *Croatia* 33 F13
Velas, C., *Costa Rica* ... 116 D2
Velasco, Sierra de,
   Argentina 126 B2
Velay, Mts. du, *France* .. 26 D7
Velddrif, *S. Africa* 84 E2
Veldegem, *Belgium* 17 F2
Velden, *Neths.* 17 F8
Veldhoven, *Neths.* 17 F6
Velebit Planina, *Croatia* . 33 D12
Velebitski Kanal, *Croatia* . 33 D11
Veleka →, *Bulgaria* 38 G10

Velenje, *Slovenia* 33 B12
Velestínon, *Greece* 39 K5
Vélez, *Colombia* 120 B3
Vélez Blanco, *Spain* 29 H2
Vélez Málaga, *Spain* 31 J6
Vélez Rubio, *Spain* 29 H2
Velhas →, *Brazil* 123 E3
Velika, *Croatia* 21 K7
Velika Gorica, *Croatia* .. 33 C13
Velika Kapela, *Croatia* .. 33 C12
Velika Kladuša, *Bos.-H.* . 33 C12
Velika Morava →,
   Serbia, Yug. 21 L11
Velikaya →, *Russia* 40 D5
Velikaya Kema, *Russia* ... 48 B8
Velikaya Lepetikha,
   Ukraine 41 J7
Velike Lašče, *Slovenia* .. 33 C11
Velikiye Luki, *Russia* ... 40 D6
Veliko Tŭrnovo, *Bulgaria* . 38 F8
Velikonda Range, *India* .. 60 M11
Velingrad, *Bulgaria* 39 G6
Velino, Mte., *Italy* 33 F10
Velizh, *Russia* 40 E6
Velke Meziřiči, *Czech.* .. 20 F6
Velletri, *Italy* 34 A5
Vellinge, *Sweden* 11 J7
Vellore, *India* 60 N11
Velp, *Neths.* 16 D7
Velsen-Noord, *Neths.* 16 D5
Velsk, *Russia* 40 B11
Velten, *Germany* 18 C9
Veluwe Meer, *Neths.* 16 D7
Velva, *U.S.A.* 108 A4
Veme, *Norway* 10 D4
Ven, *Sweden* 11 J6
Venaco, *France* 27 F13
Venado Tuerto, *Argentina* . 126 C3
Venafro, *Italy* 35 A7
Venarey-les-Laumes,
   France 25 E11
Venaria, *Italy* 32 C4
Vence, *France* 27 E11
Vendas Novas, *Portugal* .. 31 G2
Vendée □, *France* 24 F5
Vendée →, *France* 24 F5
Vendéen, Bocage, *France* . 26 B2
Vendeuvre-sur-Barse,
   France 25 D11
Vendôme, *France* 24 E8
Vendrell, *Spain* 28 D6
Vendsyssel, *Denmark* 11 G4
Véneta, L., *Italy* 33 C9
Véneto □, *Italy* 33 C8
Venev, *Russia* 42 C4
Venézia, *Italy* 33 C9
Venézia, G. di, *Italy* ... 33 C10
Venezuela ■, *S. Amer.* ... 120 B4
Venezuela, G. de,
   Venezuela 120 A3
Vengurla, *India* 60 M8
Venice = Venézia, *Italy* . 33 C9
Venkatapuram, *India* 61 K12
Venlo, *Neths.* 17 F8
Vennesla, *Norway* 9 G12
Venraij, *Neths.* 17 E7
Venta de Cardeña, *Spain* . 31 G6
Venta de San Rafael, *Spain* . 30 E6
Ventana, Punta de la,
   Mexico 114 C3
Ventana, Sa. de la,
   Argentina 126 D3
Ventersburg, *S. Africa* .. 84 D4
Venterstad, *S. Africa* ... 84 E4
Ventimíglia, *Italy* 32 E4
Ventnor, *U.K.* 13 G6
Ventotene, *Italy* 34 B6
Ventoux, Mt., *France* 27 D9
Ventspils, *Latvia* 9 H19
Ventuarí →, *Venezuela* ... 120 C4
Ventucopa, *U.S.A.* 113 L7
Ventura, *U.S.A.* 113 L7
Venus B., *Australia* 91 F4
Veøy, *Norway* 10 B1
Vera, *Argentina* 126 B3
Vera, *Spain* 29 H3
Veracruz, *Mexico* 115 D5
Veracruz □, *Mexico* 115 D5
Veraval, *India* 62 J4
Verbánia, *Italy* 32 C5
Verbicaro, *Italy* 35 C8
Verbier, *Switz.* 22 D4
Vercelli, *Italy* 32 C5
Verchovchevo, *Ukraine* ... 41 H8
Verdalsøra, *Norway* 8 E14
Verde →, *Argentina* 128 B3
Verde →, *Goiás, Brazil* . 123 E1
Verde →, *Goiás, Brazil* . 123 E1
Verde →, *Mato Grosso,
   Brazil* 125 C6
Verde →,
   *Mato Grosso do Sul,
   Brazil* 125 E7
Verde →, *Chihuahua,
   Mexico* 114 B3
Verde →, *Oaxaca, Mexico* . 115 D5
Verde →, *Veracruz,
   Mexico* 114 C4
Verde →, *Paraguay* 126 A4
Verde, Cay, *Bahamas* 116 B4
Verde Grande →, *Brazil* .. 123 E3
Verde Island Pass, *Phil.* . 55 E4
Verde Pequeno →, *Brazil* . 123 D3
Verden, *Germany* 18 C5
Verdi, *U.S.A.* 112 F7
Verdigre, *U.S.A.* 108 D5

Verdon →, *France* 27 E9
Verdun, *France* 25 C12
Verdun-sur-le-Doubs,
   France 25 F12
Vereeniging, *S. Africa* .. 85 D4
Vérendrye, Parc Prov. de
   la, *Canada* 98 C4
Verga, C., *Guinea* 78 C2
Vergato, *Italy* 32 D8
Vergemont, *Australia* 90 C3
Vergemont Cr. →,
   Australia 90 C3
Vergennes, *U.S.A.* 107 B11
Vergt, *France* 26 C4
Verín, *Spain* 30 D3
Veriña, *Spain* 30 B5
Verkhnedvinsk =
   Vyerkhnyadzvinsk,
   Belarus 40 E4
Verkhnevilyuysk, *Russia* . 45 C13
Verkhneye Kalinino, *Russia* . 45 D11
Verkhniy Baskunchak,
   Russia 43 F8
Verkhnyaya Amga, *Russia* . 45 D13
Verkhovye, *Russia* 42 D3
Verkhoyansk, *Russia* 45 C14
Verkhoyansk Ra. =
   Verkhoyanskiy Khrebet,
   Russia 45 C13
Verkhoyanskiy Khrebet,
   Russia 45 C13
Verlo, *Canada* 101 C7
Verma, *Norway* 10 B2
Vermenton, *France* 25 E10
Vermilion, *Canada* 101 C6
Vermilion →, *Alta.,
   Canada* 101 C6
Vermilion →, *Qué.,
   Canada* 98 C5
Vermilion, B., *U.S.A.* ... 109 L9
Vermilion Bay, *Canada* ... 101 D10
Vermilion Chutes, *Canada* . 100 B6
Vermilion L., *U.S.A.* 108 B8
Vermillion, *U.S.A.* 108 D6
Vermont □, *U.S.A.* 107 C12
Vernal, *U.S.A.* 110 F9
Vernalis, *U.S.A.* 112 H5
Vernayaz, *Switz.* 22 D4
Verner, *Canada* 98 C3
Verneuil-sur-Avre, *France* . 24 D7
Verneukpan, *S. Africa* ... 84 D3
Vernier, *Switz.* 22 D2
Vernon, *Canada* 100 C5
Vernon, *France* 24 C8
Vernon, *U.S.A.* 109 H5
Vernonia, *U.S.A.* 112 E3
Vero Beach, *U.S.A.* 105 M5
Véroia, *Greece* 39 J5
Verolanuova, *Italy* 32 C7
Véroli, *Italy* 34 A6
Verona, *Italy* 32 C8
Versailles, *France* 25 D9
Versailles, *Bolivia* 125 C5
Versoix, *Switz.* 22 D2
Vert, C., *Senegal* 78 C1
Vertou, *France* 24 E5
Vertus, *France* 25 D11
Verulam, *S. Africa* 85 D5
Verviers, *Belgium* 17 G7
Vervins, *France* 25 C10
Verzej, *Slovenia* 33 B13
Vescavoto, *France* 27 F13
Vesdre →, *Belgium* 17 G7
Veselí nad Lužnicí, *Czech.* . 20 F4
Veselovskoye Vdkhr.,
   Russia 43 G5
Veshenskaya, *Russia* 42 F5
Vesle →, *France* 25 C10
Vesoul, *France* 25 E13
Vessigebro, *Sweden* 11 H6
Vesterålen, *Norway* 8 B16
Vestersche Veld, *Neths.* . 16 C8
Vestfjorden, *Norway* 8 C15
Vestmannaeyjar, *Iceland* . 8 E3
Vestmarka, *Norway* 10 E5
Vestone, *Italy* 32 C7
Vestsjællands
   Amtskommune □,
   Denmark 11 J5
Vestspitsbergen, *Svalbard* . 4 B8
Vestvågøy, *Norway* 8 B15
Vesuvio, *Italy* 35 B7
Vesuvius, Mte. = Vesuvio,
   Italy 35 B7
Vesyegonsk, *Russia* 40 C9
Veszprém, *Hungary* 21 H7
Vésztő, *Hungary* 21 J11
Vetlanda, *Sweden* 9 H16
Vetluga, *Russia* 42 B7
Vetlugu →, *Russia* 42 B8
Vetluzhskiy, *Russia* 42 B7
Vetluzhskiy, *Russia* 42 A7
Vetovo, *Bulgaria* 38 F9
Vetralia, *Italy* 33 F9
Vettore, Mte., *Italy* 33 F10
Veurne, *Belgium* 17 F1
Vevey, *Switz.* 22 D3
Veynes, *France* 27 D9
Veys, *France* 21 C9
Vézelise, *France* 25 D13
Vézère →, *France* 26 D4
Vezirköprü, *Turkey* 66 B6
Vi Thanh, *Vietnam* 59 H5
Viacha, *Bolivia* 124 D4
Viadana, *Italy* 32 D7
Viamão, *Brazil* 127 C5
Viana, *Brazil* 122 B3

Viana, *Spain* 28 C2
Viana del Bollo, *Spain* .. 30 C3
Viana do Alentejo,
   Portugal 31 G3
Viana do Castelo, *Portugal* . 30 D2
Vianen, *Neths.* 16 E6
Vianna do Castelo □,
   Portugal 30 D2
Vianópolis, *Brazil* 123 E2
Viar →, *Spain* 31 H5
Viaréggio, *Italy* 32 E7
Viaur →, *France* 26 D5
Vibank, *Canada* 101 C8
Vibo Valéntia, *Italy* 35 D9
Viborg, *Denmark* 11 H3
Vibraye, *France* 24 D7
Vic, Étang de, *France* ... 26 E7
Vic-en-Bigorre, *France* .. 26 E4
Vic-Fézensac, *France* 26 E4
Vic-sur-Cère, *France* 26 D6
Vicenza, *Italy* 33 C8
Vich, *Spain* 28 D7
Vichada □, *Colombia* 120 C4
Vichada →, *Colombia* 120 C4
Vichuga, *Russia* 42 B5
Vichy, *France* 26 B7
Vicksburg, *Ariz., U.S.A.* . 113 M13
Vicksburg, *Mich., U.S.A.* . 104 D3
Vicksburg, *Miss., U.S.A.* . 109 J9
Vico, L. di, *Italy* 33 F9
Vico del Gargano, *Italy* . 35 A8
Vicosoprano, *Switz.* 23 D9
Victor, *India* 62 J4
Victor, *Colo., U.S.A.* ... 108 F2
Victor, *N.Y., U.S.A.* 106 D7
Victor Harbor, *Australia* . 91 F2
Victoria, *Argentina* 126 C3
Victoria, *Canada* 100 D4
Victoria, *Chile* 128 A2
Victoria, *Guinea* 78 C2
Victoria, *Malaysia* 56 C5
Victoria, *Malta* 37 C1
Victoria, *Phil.* 55 D4
Victoria, *Kans., U.S.A.* . 108 F5
Victoria, *Tex., U.S.A.* .. 109 L6
Victoria □, *Australia* ... 91 F3
Victoria →, *Australia* ... 88 C4
Victoria, Grand L., *Canada* . 98 C4
Victoria, L., *Africa* 82 C3
Victoria, L., *Australia* . 91 E3
Victoria Beach, *Canada* .. 101 C9
Victoria de Durango,
   Mexico 114 C4
Victoria de las Tunas, *Cuba* . 116 B4
Victoria Falls, *Zimbabwe* . 83 F2
Victoria Harbour, *Canada* . 98 D4
Victoria I., *Canada* 96 A8
Victoria Ld., *Antarctica* . 5 D11
Victoria Nile →, *Uganda* . 82 B3
Victoria Res., *Canada* ... 99 C8
Victoria River Downs,
   Australia 88 C4
Victoria Taungdeik, *Burma* . 61 J18
Victoria West, *S. Africa* . 84 E3
Victorias, *Phil.* 55 F5
Victoriaville, *Canada* ... 99 C5
Victorica, *Argentina* 126 D2
Victorville, *U.S.A.* 113 L9
Vicuña, *Chile* 126 C1
Vicuña Mackenna,
   Argentina 126 C3
Vidal, *U.S.A.* 113 L12
Vidal Junction, *U.S.A.* .. 113 L12
Vidalia, *U.S.A.* 105 J4
Vidauban, *France* 27 E10
Vídho, *Greece* 37 A3
Vidigueira, *Portugal* 31 G3
Vidin, *Bulgaria* 38 F5
Vidio, C., *Spain* 30 B4
Vidisha, *India* 62 H7
Vidzy, *Belarus* 9 J22
Viechtach, *Germany* 19 F8
Viedma, *Argentina* 128 B4
Viedma, L., *Argentina* ... 128 C2
Vieira, *Portugal* 30 D2
Viella, *Spain* 28 C5
Vielsalm, *Belgium* 17 H7
Vienenburg, *Germany* 18 D6
Vieng Pou Kha, *Laos* 58 B3
Vienna = Wien, *Austria* .. 21 G6
Vienna, *U.S.A.* 109 G10
Vienne, *France* 27 C8
Vienne □, *France* 26 B4
Vienne →, *France* 24 E7
Vientiane, *Laos* 58 D4
Vientos, Paso de los,
   Caribbean 117 C5
Vierlingsbeek, *Neths.* ... 17 E8
Viersen, *Germany* 18 D2
Vierwaldstättersee, *Switz.* . 23 C7
Vierzon, *France* 25 E9
Vieste, *Italy* 35 A9
Vietnam ■, *Asia* 58 C5
Vieux-Boucau-les-Bains,
   France 26 E2
Vif, *France* 27 C9
Vigan, *Phil.* 55 C4
Vigévano, *Italy* 32 C5
Vigia, *Brazil* 122 B2
Vigía Chico, *Mexico* 115 D7
Víglas, Ákra, *Greece* 37 D9
Vignemale, Pic du, *France* . 26 F3
Vigneulles-lès-Hattonchâtel,
   France 25 D12

Vignola, *Italy* 32 D8
Vigo, *Spain* 30 C2
Vigo, Ría de, *Spain* 30 C2
Vihiers, *France* 24 E6
Vijayawada, *India* 61 L12
Vijfhuizen, *Neths.* 16 D5
Vík, *Iceland* 8 E4
Vikeke, *Indonesia* 57 F7
Viken, *Sweden* 11 F8
Viking, *Canada* 100 C6
Vikna, *Norway* 8 D14
Viksjö, *Sweden* 10 B11
Vikulovo, *Russia* 44 D8
Vila da Maganja, *Mozam.* . 83 F4
Vila de João Belo = Xai-
   Xai, *Mozam.* 85 D5
Vila de Rei, *Portugal* ... 31 F2
Vila do Bispo, *Portugal* . 31 H2
Vila do Chibuto, *Mozam.* . 85 C5
Vila do Conde, *Portugal* . 30 D2
Vila Franca de Xira,
   Portugal 31 G2
Vila Gamito, *Mozam.* 83 E3
Vila Gomes da Costa,
   Mozam. 85 C5
Vila Machado, *Mozam.* 83 F3
Vila Mouzinho, *Mozam.* ... 83 E3
Vila Nova de Foscôa,
   Portugal 30 D3
Vila Nova de Ourém,
   Portugal 31 F2
Vila Novo de Gaia,
   Portugal 30 D2
Vila Pouca de Aguiar,
   Portugal 30 D3
Vila Real, *Portugal* 30 D3
Vila Real de Santo
   António, *Portugal* 31 H3
Vila Vasco da Gama,
   Mozam. 83 E3
Vila Velha, *Amapá, Brazil* . 121 C7
Vila Velha, *Espírito Santo,
   Brazil* 123 F3
Vila Viçosa, *Portugal* ... 31 G3
Vilaboa, *Spain* 30 C2
Vilaine →, *France* 24 E4
Vilanandro, Tanjona,
   Madag. 85 B7
Vilanculos, *Mozam.* 85 C6
Vilar Formoso, *Portugal* . 30 E4
Vilareal □, *Portugal* 30 D3
Vilaseca-Salou, *Spain* ... 28 D6
Vilcabamba, Cordillera,
   Peru 124 C3
Vilcanchos, *Peru* 124 C3
Vileyka, *Belarus* 40 E4
Vilhelmina, *Sweden* 8 D17
Vilhena, *Brazil* 125 C5
Viliga, *Russia* 45 C16
Viliya →, *Lithuania* 9 J21
Viljandi, *Estonia* 9 G21
Vilkitskogo, Proliv, *Russia* . 45 B11
Vilkovo = Vylkove,
   Ukraine 41 K5
Villa Abecia, *Bolivia* ... 126 A2
Villa Ahumada, *Mexico* ... 114 A3
Villa Ana, *Argentina* 126 B4
Villa Ángela, *Argentina* . 126 B3
Villa Bella, *Bolivia* 125 C4
Villa Bens = Tarfaya,
   Morocco 74 C2
Villa Cañás, *Argentina* .. 126 C3
Villa Carlos, *Spain* 36 B11
Villa Cisneros = Dakhla,
   W. Sahara 74 D1
Villa Colón, *Argentina* .. 126 C2
Villa Constitución,
   Argentina 126 C3
Villa de Cura, *Venezuela* . 120 A4
Villa de María, *Argentina* . 126 B3
Villa del Rosario,
   Venezuela 120 A3
Villa Dolores, *Argentina* . 126 C2
Villa Frontera, *Mexico* .. 114 B4
Villa Guillermina,
   Argentina 126 B4
Villa Hayes, *Paraguay* ... 126 B4
Villa Iris, *Argentina* ... 126 D3
Villa Juárez, *Mexico* 114 B4
Villa María, *Argentina* .. 126 C3
Villa Mazán, *Argentina* .. 126 B2
Villa Minozzo, *Italy* 32 D7
Villa Montes, *Bolivia* ... 126 A3
Villa Ocampo, *Argentina* . 126 B4
Villa Ocampo, *Mexico* 114 B3
Villa Ojo de Agua,
   Argentina 126 B3
Villa San Giovanni, *Italy* . 35 D8
Villa San José, *Argentina* . 126 C4
Villa San Martín, *Argentina* 126 B3
Villa Unión, *Italy* 33 B9
Villa Unión, *Mexico* 114 C3
Villablino, *Spain* 30 C4
Villacañas, *Spain* 28 F1
Villacarriedo, *Spain* 28 B1
Villacarrillo, *Spain* 29 G1
Villacastín, *Spain* 30 E6
Villach, *Austria* 21 J3
Villacidro, *Italy* 34 C1
Villada, *Spain* 30 C6
Villadiego, *Spain* 30 C7
Villadóssola, *Italy* 32 B5
Villafeliche, *Spain* 28 D3
Villafranca, *Spain* 28 C3
Villafranca de los Barros,
   Spain 31 G4

Villafranca de los Caballeros, *Baleares, Spain* ... 36 B10
Villafranca de los Caballeros, *Toledo, Spain* 29 F1
Villafranca del Bierzo, *Spain* ... 30 C4
Villafranca del Cid, *Spain* . 28 E4
Villafranca del Panadés, *Spain* ... 28 D6
Villafranca di Verona, *Italy* 32 C7
Villagarcía de Arosa, *Spain* 30 C2
Villagrán, *Mexico* ... 115 C5
Villaguay, *Argentina* ... 126 C4
Villaharta, *Spain* ... 31 G6
Villahermosa, *Mexico* ... 115 D6
Villahermosa, *Spain* ... 29 G2
Villaines-la-Juhel, *France* . 24 D6
Villajoyosa, *Spain* ... 29 G4
Villalba, *Spain* ... 30 B3
Villalba de Guardo, *Spain* 30 C6
Villalcampo, Pantano de, *Spain* ... 30 D4
Villalón de Campos, *Spain* 30 C5
Villalpando, *Spain* ... 30 D5
Villaluenga, *Spain* ... 30 E7
Villamanán, *Spain* ... 30 C5
Villamartín, *Spain* ... 31 J5
Villamblard, *France* ... 26 C4
Villanova Monteleone, *Italy* 34 B1
Villanueva, *Colombia* ... 120 A3
Villanueva, *U.S.A.* ... 111 J11
Villanueva de Castellón, *Spain* ... 29 F4
Villanueva de Córdoba, *Spain* ... 31 G6
Villanueva de la Fuente, *Spain* ... 29 G2
Villanueva de la Serena, *Spain* ... 31 G5
Villanueva de la Sierra, *Spain* ... 30 E4
Villanueva de los Castillejos, *Spain* ... 31 H3
Villanueva del Arzobispo, *Spain* ... 29 G1
Villanueva del Duque, *Spain* ... 31 G5
Villanueva del Fresno, *Spain* ... 31 G3
Villanueva y Geltrú, *Spain* 28 D6
Villaodrid, *Spain* ... 30 B3
Villaputzu, *Italy* ... 34 C2
Villar del Arzobispo, *Spain* 28 F4
Villar del Rey, *Spain* ... 31 F4
Villarcayo, *Spain* ... 28 C1
Villard-Bonnot, *France* ... 27 C9
Villard-de-Lans, *France* ... 27 C9
Villarino de los Aires, *Spain* ... 30 D4
Villarosa, *Italy* ... 35 E7
Villarramiel, *Spain* ... 30 C6
Villarreal, *Spain* ... 28 F4
Villarrica, *Chile* ... 128 A2
Villarrica, *Paraguay* ... 126 B4
Villarrobledo, *Spain* ... 29 F2
Villarroya de la Sierra, *Spain* ... 28 D3
Villars-les-Dombes, *France* 27 B9
Villarta de San Juan, *Spain* 29 F1
Villasayas, *Spain* ... 28 D2
Villaseca de los Gamitos, *Spain* ... 30 D4
Villastar, *Spain* ... 28 E3
Villatobas, *Spain* ... 28 F1
Villavicencio, *Argentina* ... 126 C2
Villavicencio, *Colombia* ... 120 C3
Villaviciosa, *Spain* ... 30 B5
Villazón, *Bolivia* ... 126 A2
Ville-Marie, *Canada* ... 98 C4
Ville Platte, *U.S.A.* ... 109 K8
Villedieu-les-Poêlles, *France* ... 24 D5
Villefort, *France* ... 26 D7
Villefranche-de-Lauragais, *France* ... 26 E5
Villefranche-de-Rouergue, *France* ... 26 D6
Villefranche-du-Périgord, *France* ... 26 D5
Villefranche-sur-Cher, *France* ... 25 E8
Villefranche-sur-Saône, *France* ... 27 C8
Villegrande, *Bolivia* ... 125 D5
Villel, *Spain* ... 28 E3
Villemaur-sur-Vanne, *France* ... 25 D10
Villemur-sur-Tarn, *France* 26 E5
Villena, *Spain* ... 29 G4
Villenauxe-la-Grande, *France* ... 25 D10
Villeneuve-d'Ornon, *France* 26 D3
Villeneuve, *Italy* ... 32 C4
Villeneuve, *Switz.* ... 22 D3
Villeneuve-l'Archevêque, *France* ... 25 D10
Villeneuve-lès-Avignon, *France* ... 27 E8
Villeneuve-St.-Georges, *France* ... 25 D9
Villeneuve-sur-Allier, *France* ... 26 B7
Villeneuve-sur-Lot, *France* 26 D4

Villeréal, *France* ... 26 D4
Villers-Bocage, *France* ... 24 C6
Villers-Bretonneux, *France* 25 C9
Villers-Cotterêts, *France* . 25 C10
Villers-le-Bouillet, *Belgium* 17 G6
Villers-le-Gambon, *Belgium* 17 H5
Villers-sur-Mer, *France* ... 24 C6
Villersexel, *France* ... 25 E13
Villerupt, *France* ... 25 C12
Villerville, *France* ... 24 C7
Villiers, *S. Africa* ... 85 D4
Villingen-Schwenningen, *Germany* ... 19 G4
Villisca, *U.S.A.* ... 108 E7
Vilna, *Canada* ... 100 C6
Vilnius, *Lithuania* ... 9 J21
Vils, *Germany* ... 19 G9
Vilsbiburg, *Germany* ... 19 G8
Vilshofen, *Germany* ... 19 G9
Vilusi, *Montenegro, Yug.* . 21 N8
Vilvoorde, *Belgium* ... 17 G4
Vilyuy →, *Russia* ... 45 C13
Vilyuysk, *Russia* ... 45 C13
Vimercate, *Italy* ... 32 C6
Vimioso, *Portugal* ... 30 D4
Vimoutiers, *France* ... 24 D7
Vimperk, *Czech.* ... 20 F3
Viña del Mar, *Chile* ... 126 C1
Vinaroz, *Spain* ... 28 E5
Vincennes, *U.S.A.* ... 104 F2
Vincent, *U.S.A.* ... 113 L8
Vinces, *Ecuador* ... 120 D2
Vinchina, *Argentina* ... 126 B2
Vindelälven →, *Sweden* .. 8 E18
Vindeln, *Sweden* ... 8 D18
Vinderup, *Denmark* ... 11 H2
Vindhya Ra., *India* ... 62 H7
Vineland, *U.S.A.* ... 104 F8
Vinga, *Romania* ... 38 D4
Vingnes, *Norway* ... 10 C4
Vinh, *Vietnam* ... 58 C5
Vinh Linh, *Vietnam* ... 58 D6
Vinh Long, *Vietnam* ... 59 G5
Vinh Yen, *Vietnam* ... 58 B5
Vinhais, *Portugal* ... 30 D3
Vinica, *Croatia* ... 33 B13
Vinica, *Slovenia* ... 33 C12
Vinita, *U.S.A.* ... 109 G7
Vinkeveen, *Neths.* ... 16 D5
Vinkovci, *Croatia* ... 21 K8
Vinnitsa = Vinnytsya, *Ukraine* ... 41 H5
Vinnytsya, *Ukraine* ... 41 H5
Vinstra, *Norway* ... 10 C3
Vinton, *Calif., U.S.A.* ... 112 F6
Vinton, *Iowa, U.S.A.* ... 108 D8
Vinton, *La., U.S.A.* ... 109 K8
Vințu de Jos, *Romania* ... 38 D6
Viöl, *Germany* ... 18 A5
Vipava, *Slovenia* ... 33 C10
Vipiteno, *Italy* ... 33 B8
Vir, *Croatia* ... 33 D12
Virac, *Phil.* ... 55 E6
Virachei, *Cambodia* ... 58 F6
Virago Sd., *Canada* ... 100 C2
Viramgam, *India* ... 62 H5
Viranşehir, *Turkey* ... 67 D8
Virden, *Canada* ... 101 D8
Vire, *France* ... 24 D6
Vire →, *France* ... 24 C5
Virgem da Lapa, *Brazil* ... 123 E3
Vírgenes, C., *Argentina* ... 128 D3
Virgin →, *Canada* ... 101 B7
Virgin →, *U.S.A.* ... 111 H6
Virgin Gorda, *Virgin Is.* ... 117 C7
Virgin Is. (British) ■, *W. Indies* ... 117 C7
Virgin Is. (U.S.) ■, *W. Indies* ... 117 C7
Virginia, *S. Africa* ... 84 D4
Virginia, *U.S.A.* ... 108 B8
Virginia □, *U.S.A.* ... 104 G7
Virginia Beach, *U.S.A.* ... 104 G8
Virginia City, *Mont., U.S.A.* ... 110 D8
Virginia City, *Nev., U.S.A.* 112 F7
Virginia Falls, *Canada* ... 100 A3
Virginiatown, *Canada* ... 98 C4
Virieu-le-Grand, *France* .. 27 C9
Viroqua, *U.S.A.* ... 108 D9
Virovitica, *Croatia* ... 21 K7
Virton, *Belgium* ... 17 J7
Virú, *Peru* ... 124 B2
Virudunagar, *India* ... 60 Q10
Vis, *Croatia* ... 33 E13
Vis Kanal, *Croatia* ... 33 E13
Visalia, *U.S.A.* ... 111 H4
Visayan Sea, *Phil.* ... 55 F5
Visby, *Sweden* ... 9 H18
Viscount Melville Sd., *Canada* ... 4 B2
Visé, *Belgium* ... 17 G7
Višegrad, *Bos.-H.* ... 21 M9
Viseu, *Brazil* ... 122 B2
Viseu, *Portugal* ... 30 E3
Viseu □, *Portugal* ... 30 E3
Vișeu de Sus, *Romania* ... 38 B7
Vishakhapatnam, *India* ... 61 L13
Viskafors, *Sweden* ... 11 G6
Visnagar, *India* ... 62 H5
Višnja Gora, *Slovenia* ... 33 C11
Viso, Mte., *Italy* ... 32 D4
Viso del Marqués, *Spain* .. 29 G1
Visoko, *Bos.-H.* ... 21 M8
Visokoi I., *Antarctica* ... 5 B1
Visp, *Switz.* ... 22 D5
Vispa →, *Switz.* ... 22 D5

Visselhövede, *Germany* ... 18 C5
Vissoie, *Switz.* ... 22 D5
Vista, *U.S.A.* ... 113 M9
Vistula = Wisła →, *Poland* 20 A8
Vit →, *Bulgaria* ... 38 F7
Vitanje, *Slovenia* ... 33 B12
Vitebsk = Vitsyebsk, *Belarus* ... 40 E6
Viterbo, *Italy* ... 33 F9
Viti Levu, *Fiji* ... 87 C7
Vitigudino, *Spain* ... 30 D4
Vitim, *Russia* ... 45 D12
Vitim →, *Russia* ... 45 D12
Vitória, *Brazil* ... 123 F3
Vitoria, *Spain* ... 28 C2
Vitória da Conquista, *Brazil* ... 123 D3
Vitória de São Antão, *Brazil* ... 122 C4
Vitorino Friere, *Brazil* ... 122 B2
Vitré, *France* ... 24 D5
Vitry-le-François, *France* . 25 D11
Vitsi, Óros, *Greece* ... 39 J4
Vitsyebsk, *Belarus* ... 40 E6
Vitteaux, *France* ... 25 E11
Vittel, *France* ... 25 D12
Vittória, *Italy* ... 35 F7
Vittório Véneto, *Italy* ... 33 C9
Vivario, *France* ... 27 F13
Vivegnis, *Belgium* ... 17 G7
Viver, *Spain* ... 28 F4
Vivero, *Spain* ... 30 B3
Viviers, *France* ... 27 D8
Vivonne, *France* ... 26 B4
Vizcaíno, Desierto de, *Mexico* ... 114 B2
Vizcaíno, Sierra, *Mexico* ... 114 B2
Vizcaya □, *Spain* ... 28 B2
Vize, *Turkey* ... 66 B2
Vizianagaram, *India* ... 61 K13
Vizille, *France* ... 27 C9
Viziňada, *Croatia* ... 33 C10
Viziru, *Romania* ... 38 E10
Vizovice, *Czech.* ... 20 F7
Vizzini, *Italy* ... 35 E7
Vlaardingen, *Neths.* ... 16 E4
Vlădeasa, *Romania* ... 38 C5
Vladikavkaz, *Russia* ... 43 J7
Vladimir, *Russia* ... 42 B5
Vladimir Volynskiy = Volodymyr-Volynskyy, *Ukraine* ... 41 G3
Vladimirovac, *Serbia, Yug.* 21 K10
Vladimirovka, *Russia* ... 43 F8
Vladimorvka, *Kazakhstan* . 42 E10
Vladislavovka, *Ukraine* ... 41 K8
Vladivostok, *Russia* ... 45 E14
Vlamertinge, *Belgium* ... 17 G1
Vlasenica, *Bos.-H.* ... 21 L8
Vlasinsko Jezero, *Serbia, Yug.* ... 21 N12
Vleuten, *Neths.* ... 16 D6
Vlieland, *Neths.* ... 16 B5
Vliestroom, *Neths.* ... 16 B6
Vlijmen, *Neths.* ... 17 E6
Vlissingen, *Neths.* ... 17 F3
Vlóra, *Albania* ... 39 J2
Vlorës, Gjiri i, *Albania* ... 39 J2
Vltava →, *Czech.* ... 20 E4
Vo Dat, *Vietnam* ... 59 G6
Vobarno, *Italy* ... 32 C7
Voćin, *Croatia* ... 21 K7
Vodice, *Croatia* ... 33 E12
Vodnjan, *Croatia* ... 33 D10
Vogelkop = Doberai, Jazirah, *Indonesia* ... 57 E8
Vogelsberg, *Germany* ... 18 E5
Voghera, *Italy* ... 32 D6
Vohibinany, *Madag.* ... 85 B8
Vohimarina, *Madag.* ... 85 A9
Vohimena, Tanjon' i, *Madag.* ... 85 D8
Vohipeno, *Madag.* ... 85 C8
Voi, *Kenya* ... 82 C4
Void, *France* ... 25 D12
Voiron, *France* ... 27 C9
Voisey B., *Canada* ... 99 A7
Voitsberg, *Austria* ... 21 H5
Voiviis Límni, *Greece* ... 39 K5
Vojens, *Denmark* ... 11 J3
Vojmsjön, *Sweden* ... 8 D17
Vojnić, *Croatia* ... 33 C12
Vojnik, *Italy* ... 33 B12
Vojvodina □, *Serbia, Yug.* 40 C11
Volcano Is. = Kazan-Rettō, *Pac. Oc.* ... 92 E6
Volchansk = Vovchansk, *Ukraine* ... 41 G9
Volchayevka, *Russia* ... 45 E14
Volchya →, *Ukraine* ... 41 H8
Volda, *Norway* ... 9 E12
Volendam, *Neths.* ... 16 D6
Volga →, *Russia* ... 42 A4
Volga →, *Russia* ... 43 G9
Volga Hts. = Privolzhskaya Vozvyshennost, *Russia* 42 E7
Volgo-Baltiyskiy Kanal, *Russia* ... 40 B9
Volgo-Donskoy Kanal, *Russia* ... 43 F7
Volgodonsk, *Russia* ... 43 G6
Volgograd, *Russia* ... 43 F7
Volgogradskoye Vdkhr., *Russia* ... 42 E8
Volgorechensk, *Russia* ... 42 B5
Volkach, *Germany* ... 19 F6

Volkerak, *Neths.* ... 17 E4
Volkhov, *Russia* ... 40 C7
Volkhov →, *Russia* ... 40 B7
Völklingen, *Germany* ... 19 F2
Volkovysk = Vawkavysk, *Belarus* ... 41 F3
Volksrust, *S. Africa* ... 85 D4
Vollenhove, *Neths.* ... 16 C7
Volnansk, *Ukraine* ... 41 H8
Volnovakha, *Ukraine* ... 41 J9
Volochanka, *Russia* ... 45 B10
Volodarsk, *Russia* ... 42 B6
Volodymyr-Volynskyy, *Ukraine* ... 41 G3
Vologda, *Russia* ... 40 C10
Volokolamsk, *Russia* ... 42 B8
Volokonovka, *Russia* ... 42 E3
Vólos, *Greece* ... 39 K5
Volosovo, *Russia* ... 40 C5
Volovets, *Ukraine* ... 41 H2
Volovo, *Russia* ... 42 D4
Volozhin = Valozhyn, *Belarus* ... 40 E4
Volsk, *Russia* ... 42 D8
Volta →, *Ghana* ... 79 D5
Volta, L., *Ghana* ... 79 D5
Volta Blanche = White Volta →, *Ghana* ... 79 D4
Volta Redonda, *Brazil* ... 123 F3
Voltaire, C., *Australia* ... 88 B4
Volterra, *Italy* ... 32 E7
Voltri, *Italy* ... 32 D5
Volturara Appula, *Italy* ... 35 A8
Volturno →, *Italy* ... 34 A6
Volubilis, *Morocco* ... 74 B3
Volvo, *Australia* ... 91 E3
Volzhsk, *Russia* ... 42 C9
Volzhskiy, *Russia* ... 43 F7
Vondrozo, *Madag.* ... 85 C8
Voorburg, *Neths.* ... 16 D4
Voorne Putten, *Neths.* ... 16 E4
Voorst, *Neths.* ... 16 D8
Voorthuizen, *Neths.* ... 16 D7
Vopnafjörður, *Iceland* ... 8 D6
Vóras Óros, *Greece* ... 39 J4
Vorbasse, *Denmark* ... 11 J3
Vorden, *Neths.* ... 16 D8
Vorderrhein →, *Switz.* ... 23 C8
Vordingborg, *Denmark* ... 11 K5
Voreppe, *France* ... 27 C9
Voríai Sporádhes, *Greece* . 39 K6
Vórios Evvoïkos Kólpos, *Greece* ... 39 L6
Vorkuta, *Russia* ... 44 C7
Vorma →, *Norway* ... 10 D5
Vormsi, *Estonia* ... 9 G20
Vorona →, *Russia* ... 42 E6
Voronezh, *Russia* ... 42 E4
Voronezh, *Ukraine* ... 41 G7
Voronezh →, *Russia* ... 42 E4
Vorontsovo-Aleksandrovskoye = Zelenokumsk, *Russia* ... 43 H6
Voroshilovgrad = Luhansk, *Ukraine* ... 41 H10
Voroshilovsk = Alchevsk, *Ukraine* ... 41 H10
Vorovskoye, *Russia* ... 45 D16
Vorselaar, *Belgium* ... 17 F5
Vorskla →, *Ukraine* ... 41 H8
Võrts Järv, *Estonia* ... 9 G22
Võru, *Estonia* ... 9 H22
Vorupør, *Denmark* ... 11 H2
Vosges, *France* ... 25 D14
Vosges □, *France* ... 25 D13
Voskopoja, *Albania* ... 39 J3
Voskresensk, *Russia* ... 42 C4
Voskresenskoye, *Russia* ... 42 B7
Voss, *Norway* ... 9 F12
Vosselaar, *Belgium* ... 17 F5
Vostok I., *Kiribati* ... 93 J12
Vouga →, *Portugal* ... 30 E2
Vouillé, *France* ... 24 F7
Vouvray, *France* ... 24 E7
Vouvry, *Switz.* ... 22 D3
Vouziers, *France* ... 25 C11
Vovchansk, *Ukraine* ... 41 G9
Voves, *France* ... 25 D8
Voxna, *Sweden* ... 10 C9
Vozhe Ozero, *Russia* ... 40 B10
Vozhega, *Russia* ... 40 B11
Voznesenka, *Russia* ... 45 D10
Voznesensk, *Ukraine* ... 41 J6
Voznesenye, *Russia* ... 40 B8
Vrådal, *Norway* ... 10 E3
Vrakhnéïka, *Greece* ... 39 L4
Vrancea, Munții, *Romania* . 38 D9
Vranica, *Bos.-H.* ... 21 M7
Vranje, *Serbia, Yug.* ... 21 N11
Vransko, *Slovenia* ... 33 B11
Vratsa, *Bulgaria* ... 38 F6
Vrbas, *Serbia, Yug.* ... 21 K9
Vrbas →, *Bos.-H.* ... 21 K7
Vrbnik, *Croatia* ... 33 C11
Vrbovec, *Croatia* ... 33 C13
Vrbovsko, *Croatia* ... 33 C12
Vrchlabí, *Czech.* ... 20 E5
Vrede, *S. Africa* ... 85 D4
Vredefort, *S. Africa* ... 84 D4
Vredenburg, *S. Africa* ... 84 E2
Vredendal, *S. Africa* ... 84 E2
Vreeswijk, *Neths.* ... 16 D6
Vrena, *Sweden* ... 11 F10
Vrgorac, *Croatia* ... 21 M7

Vrhnika, *Slovenia* ... 33 C11
Vřídi, *Ivory C.* ... 78 D4
Vries, *Neths.* ... 16 B9
Vriezenveen, *Neths.* ... 16 D9
Vrindavan, *India* ... 62 F7
Vríses, *Greece* ... 37 D6
Vrnograč, *Bos.-H.* ... 33 C12
Vroomshoop, *Neths.* ... 16 D9
Vršac, *Serbia, Yug.* ... 21 K11
Vrsacki Kanal, *Serbia, Yug.* 21 K11
Vryburg, *S. Africa* ... 84 D3
Vryheid, *S. Africa* ... 85 D5
Vsetín, *Czech.* ... 20 F8
Vu Liet, *Vietnam* ... 58 C5
Vucha →, *Bulgaria* ... 39 G7
Vught, *Neths.* ... 17 E6
Vukovar, *Croatia* ... 21 K8
Vulcan, *Canada* ... 100 C6
Vulcan, *U.S.A.* ... 104 C2
Vulcanești, *Moldova* ... 41 K5
Vulcano, *Italy* ... 35 D7
Vulchedruma, *Bulgaria* ... 38 F6
Vulci, *Italy* ... 33 F8
Vulkaneshty = Vulcanești, *Moldova* ... 41 K5
Vunduzi →, *Mozam.* ... 83 F3
Vung Tau, *Vietnam* ... 59 G6
Vŭrbitsa, *Bulgaria* ... 38 G9
Vyartsilya, *Russia* ... 40 A6
Vyatka = Kirov, *Russia* .. 44 D5
Vyatka →, *Russia* ... 42 C10
Vyatskiye Polyany, *Russia* 42 B10
Vyazemskiy, *Russia* ... 45 E14
Vyazma, *Russia* ... 42 C2
Vyazniki, *Russia* ... 42 B6
Vyborg, *Russia* ... 40 B5
Vychegda →, *Russia* ... 44 C7
Vychodné Beskydy, *Europe* 41 H2
Vyerkhnyadzvinsk, *Belarus* 40 E4
Vyksa, *Russia* ... 42 C6
Vylkove, *Ukraine* ... 41 K5
Vynohradiv, *Ukraine* ... 41 H2
Vyrnwy, L., *U.K.* ... 12 E4
Vyshniy Volochek, *Russia* 42 B2
Vyškov, *Czech.* ... 20 F6
Vysoké Mýto, *Czech.* ... 20 F6
Vysokovsk, *Russia* ... 42 B3
Vytegra, *Russia* ... 40 B9

W

W.A.C. Bennett Dam, *Canada* ... 100 B4
Wa, *Ghana* ... 78 C4
Waal →, *Neths.* ... 16 E6
Waalwijk, *Neths.* ... 17 E6
Waarschoot, *Belgium* ... 17 F3
Waasmunster, *Belgium* ... 17 F4
Wabakimi L., *Canada* ... 98 B2
Wabana, *Canada* ... 99 C9
Wabasca, *Canada* ... 100 B6
Wabash, *U.S.A.* ... 104 E3
Wabash →, *U.S.A.* ... 104 G1
Wabeno, *U.S.A.* ... 104 C1
Wabi →, *Ethiopia* ... 77 F5
Wabigoon L., *Canada* ... 101 D10
Wabowden, *Canada* ... 101 C9
Wąbrzeźno, *Poland* ... 20 B8
Wabu Hu, *China* ... 53 A11
Wabuk Pt., *Canada* ... 98 A2
Wabush, *Canada* ... 99 B6
Wabuska, *U.S.A.* ... 110 G4
Wachtebeke, *Belgium* ... 17 F3
Wächtersbach, *Germany* .. 19 E5
Waco, *U.S.A.* ... 109 K6
Waconichi, L., *Canada* ... 98 B5
Wad Ban Naqa, *Sudan* ... 77 D3
Wad Banda, *Sudan* ... 77 E2
Wad el Haddad, *Sudan* ... 77 E3
Wad en Nau, *Sudan* ... 77 E3
Wad Hamid, *Sudan* ... 77 D3
Wâd Medanî, *Sudan* ... 77 E3
Wad Thana, *Pakistan* ... 62 F2
Wadayama, *Japan* ... 49 G7
Waddeneilanden, *Neths.* ... 16 B6
Waddenzee, *Neths.* ... 16 B6
Wadderin Hill, *Australia* .. 89 F2
Waddington, *U.S.A.* ... 107 B9
Waddington, Mt., *Canada* 100 C3
Waddinxveen, *Neths.* ... 16 D5
Waddy Pt., *Australia* ... 91 C5
Wadena, *Canada* ... 101 C8
Wadena, *U.S.A.* ... 108 B7
Wädenswil, *Switz.* ... 23 B7
Wadesboro, *U.S.A.* ... 105 H5
Wadhams, *Canada* ... 100 C3
Wādī as Sīr, *Jordan* ... 69 D4
Wadi Gemâl, *Egypt* ... 76 C4
Wadi Halfa, *Sudan* ... 76 C3
Wadian, *China* ... 53 A9
Wadowice, *Poland* ... 20 F9
Wadsworth, *U.S.A.* ... 110 G4
Waegwan, *S. Korea* ... 51 G15
Wafrah, *Si. Arabia* ... 64 D5
Wageningen, *Neths.* ... 16 E7
Wageningen, *Surinam* ... 121 B6
Wager B., *Canada* ... 97 B11
Wager Bay, *Canada* ... 97 B10
Wagga Wagga, *Australia* .. 91 F4
Waghete, *Indonesia* ... 57 E9
Wagin, *Australia* ... 89 F2
Wagon Mound, *U.S.A.* ... 109 G2
Wagoner, *U.S.A.* ... 109 G7

Wagrowiec, Poland 20 C7
Wah, Pakistan 62 C5
Wahai, Indonesia 57 E7
Wahiawa, U.S.A. 102 H15
Wâhid, Egypt 69 E1
Wahnai, Afghan. 62 C1
Wahoo, U.S.A. 108 E6
Wahpeton, U.S.A. 108 B6
Wai, Koh, Cambodia 59 H4
Waiau →, N.Z. 87 K4
Waibeem, Indonesia 57 E8
Waiblingen, Germany ... 19 G5
Waidhofen,
  Niederösterreich, Austria 20 G5
Waidhofen,
  Niederösterreich, Austria 21 H4
Waigeo, Indonesia 57 E8
Waihi, N.Z. 87 G5
Waihou →, N.Z. 87 G5
Waika, Zaïre 82 C2
Waikabubak, Indonesia ... 57 F5
Waikari, N.Z. 87 K4
Waikato →, N.Z. 87 G5
Waikerie, Australia ... 91 E2
Waikokopu, N.Z. 87 H6
Waikouaiti, N.Z. 87 L3
Waimakariri →, N.Z. ... 87 K4
Waimate, N.Z. 87 L3
Waimes, Belgium 17 H8
Wainganga →, India 60 K11
Waingapu, Indonesia ... 57 F6
Waini →, Guyana 121 B6
Wainwright, Canada 101 C6
Wainwright, U.S.A. 96 A3
Waiouru, N.Z. 87 H5
Waipara, N.Z. 87 K4
Waipawa, N.Z. 87 H6
Waipiro, N.Z. 87 H7
Waipu, N.Z. 87 F5
Waipukurau, N.Z. 87 J6
Wairakei, N.Z. 87 H6
Wairarapa, L., N.Z. ... 87 J5
Wairoa, N.Z. 87 H6
Waitaki →, N.Z. 87 L3
Waitara, N.Z. 87 H5
Waitsburg, U.S.A. 110 C5
Waiuku, N.Z. 87 G5
Wajima, Japan 49 F8
Wajir, Kenya 82 B5
Wajir □, Kenya 82 B5
Wakasa, Japan 49 G7
Wakasa-Wan, Japan 49 G7
Wakatipu, L., N.Z. 87 L2
Wakaw, Canada 101 C7
Wakayama, Japan 49 G7
Wakayama-ken □, Japan . 49 H7
Wake Forest, U.S.A. ... 105 H6
Wake I., Pac. Oc. 92 F8
Wakefield, N.Z. 87 J4
Wakefield, U.K. 12 D6
Wakefield, Mass., U.S.A. 107 D13
Wakefield, Mich., U.S.A. 108 B10
Wakeham Bay =
  Maricourt, Canada 97 C12
Wakema, Burma 61 L19
Wakkanai, Japan 48 B10
Wakkerstroom, S. Africa . 85 D5
Wakool, Australia 91 F3
Wakool →, Australia ... 91 F3
Wakre, Indonesia 57 E8
Wakuach L., Canada 99 A6
Walamba, Zambia 83 E2
Wałbrzych, Poland 20 E6
Walbury Hill, U.K. 13 F6
Walcha, Australia 91 E5
Walcheren, Neths. 17 E3
Walcott, U.S.A. 110 F10
Wałcz, Poland 20 B6
Wald, Switz. 23 B7
Waldbröl, Germany 18 E3
Waldburg Ra., Australia . 88 D2
Waldeck, Germany 18 D5
Walden, Colo., U.S.A. . 110 F10
Walden, N.Y., U.S.A. .. 107 E10
Waldenburg, Switz. 22 B5
Waldport, U.S.A. 110 D1
Waldron, U.S.A. 109 H7
Waldshut, Germany 19 H4
Walembele, Ghana 78 C4
Walensee, Switz. 23 B8
Walenstadt, Switz. 23 B8
Wales □, U.K. 13 E4
Walewale, Ghana 79 C4
Walgett, Australia 91 E4
Walgreen Coast, Antarctica 5 D15
Walhalla, Australia ... 91 F4
Walhalla, U.S.A. 101 D9
Walker, U.S.A. 108 B7
Walker L., Man., Canada . 101 C9
Walker L., Qué., Canada . 99 B6
Walker L., U.S.A. 110 G4
Walkerston, Australia . 90 C4
Walkerton, Canada 106 B3
Wall, U.S.A. 108 C3
Walla Walla, U.S.A. ... 110 C4
Wallabadah, Australia . 90 B3
Wallace, Idaho, U.S.A. . 110 C6
Wallace, N.C., U.S.A. . 105 H7
Wallace, Nebr., U.S.A. . 108 E4
Wallaceburg, Canada ... 98 D3
Wallachia = Valahia,
  Romania 38 E8
Wallal, Australia 91 D4
Wallal Downs, Australia . 88 C3
Wallambin, L., Australia . 89 F2
Wallaroo, Australia ... 91 E2
Wallasey, U.K. 12 D4

Walldürn, Germany 19 F5
Wallerawang, Australia . 91 E5
Wallhallow, Australia . 90 B2
Wallingford, U.S.A. ... 107 E12
Wallis & Futuna, Is.,
  Pac. Oc. 92 J10
Wallisellen, Switz. ... 23 B7
Wallowa, U.S.A. 110 D5
Wallowa Mts., U.S.A. .. 110 D5
Wallsend, Australia ... 91 E5
Wallsend, U.K. 12 C6
Wallula, U.S.A. 110 C4
Wallumbilla, Australia . 91 D4
Walmsley, L., Canada .. 101 A7
Walney, I. of, U.K. ... 12 C4
Walnut Creek, U.S.A. .. 112 H4
Walnut Ridge, U.S.A. .. 109 G9
Walsall, U.K. 13 E6
Walsenburg, U.S.A. 109 G2
Walsh, U.S.A. 109 G3
Walsh →, Australia 90 B3
Walsh P.O., Australia . 90 B3
Walshoutem, Belgium ... 17 G6
Walsrode, Germany 18 C5
Walterboro, U.S.A. 105 J5
Walters, U.S.A. 109 H5
Waltershausen, Germany . 18 E6
Waltham, U.S.A. 107 D13
Waltham Station, Canada . 98 C4
Waltman, U.S.A. 110 E10
Walton, U.S.A. 107 D9
Walvisbaai, Namibia ... 84 C1
Wamba, Kenya 82 B4
Wamba, Zaïre 82 B2
Wamego, U.S.A. 108 F6
Wamena, Indonesia 57 E9
Wamulan, Indonesia 57 E7
Wan Xian, China 50 E8
Wana, Pakistan 62 C3
Wanaaring, Australia .. 91 D3
Wanaka, N.Z. 87 L2
Wanaka L., N.Z. 87 L2
Wan'an, China 53 D10
Wanapiri, Indonesia ... 57 E9
Wanapitei L., Canada .. 98 C3
Wanbi, Australia 91 E3
Wandaik, Guyana 121 C6
Wandarrie, Australia .. 89 E2
Wandel Sea = McKinley
  Sea, Arctic 4 A7
Wanderer, Zimbabwe 83 F3
Wandoan, Australia 91 D4
Wandre, Belgium 17 G7
Wanfercée-Baulet, Belgium 17 H5
Wanfu, China 51 D12
Wang →, Thailand 58 D2
Wang Kai, Sudan 77 F2
Wang Noi, Thailand 58 E3
Wang Saphung, Thailand . 58 D3
Wang Thong, Thailand .. 58 D3
Wanga, Zaïre 82 B2
Wangal, Indonesia 57 F8
Wanganella, Australia . 91 F3
Wanganui, N.Z. 87 H5
Wangaratta, Australia . 91 F4
Wangary, Australia 91 E2
Wangcang, China 52 A6
Wangdu, China 50 E8
Wangerooge, Germany ... 18 B3
Wangi, Kenya 82 C5
Wangiwangi, Indonesia . 57 F6
Wangjiang, China 53 B11
Wangmo, China 52 E6
Wangqing, China 51 C15
Wankaner, India 62 H4
Wanless, Canada 101 C8
Wannian, China 53 C11
Wanon Niwat, Thailand . 58 D4
Wanquan, China 50 D8
Wanrong, China 50 G6
Wanshan, China 52 D7
Wanshengchang, China .. 52 C6
Wanssum, Neths. 17 E8
Wanxian, China 52 B7
Wanyuan, China 52 A7
Wanzai, China 53 C10
Wanze, Belgium 17 G6
Wapakoneta, U.S.A. 104 E3
Wapato, U.S.A. 110 C3
Wapawekka L., Canada .. 101 C8
Wapikopa L., Canada ... 98 B2
Wappingers Falls, U.S.A. . 107 E11
Wapsipinicon →, U.S.A. . 108 E9
Warangal, India 60 L11
Waratah, Australia 90 G4
Waratah B., Australia . 91 F4
Warburg, Germany 18 D5
Warburton, Vic., Australia 91 F4
Warburton, W. Austral.,
  Australia 89 E4
Warburton Ra., Australia . 89 E4
Ward, N.Z. 87 J5
Ward →, Australia 91 D4
Ward Cove, U.S.A. 100 B2
Ward Mt., U.S.A. 112 H8
Warden, S. Africa 85 D4
Wardha, India 60 J11
Wardha →, India 60 K11
Wardlow, Canada 100 C6
Ware, Canada 100 B3
Ware, U.S.A. 107 D12
Waregem, Belgium 17 G2
Wareham, U.S.A. 107 E14
Waremme, Belgium 17 G6
Waren, Germany 18 B8
Warendorf, Germany 18 D3
Warialda, Australia ... 91 D5

Wariap, Indonesia 57 E8
Warin Chamrap, Thailand 58 E5
Warkopi, Indonesia 57 E8
Warley, U.K. 13 E6
Warm Springs, U.S.A. .. 111 G5
Warman, Canada 101 C7
Warmbad, Namibia 84 D2
Warmbad, S. Africa 85 C4
Warmenhuizen, Neths. .. 16 C5
Warmeriville, France .. 25 C11
Warmond, Neths. 16 D5
Warnambool Downs,
  Australia 90 C3
Warnemünde, Germany ... 18 A8
Warner, Canada 100 D6
Warner Mts., U.S.A. ... 110 F3
Warner Robins, U.S.A. . 105 J4
Warnes, Bolivia 125 D5
Warneton, Belgium 17 G1
Warnow →, Germany 18 A8
Warnsveld, Neths. 16 D8
Waroona, Australia 89 F2
Warracknabeal, Australia 91 F3
Warragul, Australia ... 91 F4
Warrawagine, Australia . 88 D3
Warrego →, Australia .. 91 E4
Warrego Ra., Australia . 90 C4
Warren, Australia 91 E4
Warren, Ark., U.S.A. .. 109 J8
Warren, Mich., U.S.A. . 104 D4
Warren, Minn., U.S.A. . 108 A6
Warren, Ohio, U.S.A. .. 106 E4
Warren, Pa., U.S.A. ... 106 E5
Warrenpoint, U.K. 15 B5
Warrensburg, U.S.A. ... 108 F8
Warrenton, S. Africa .. 84 D3
Warrenton, U.S.A. 112 D3
Warrenville, Australia . 91 D4
Warri, Nigeria 79 D6
Warrina, Australia 91 D2
Warrington, U.K. 12 D5
Warrington, U.S.A. 105 K2
Warrnambool, Australia . 91 F3
Warroad, U.S.A. 108 A7
Warsa, Indonesia 57 E9
Warsaw = Warszawa,
  Poland 20 C11
Warsaw, Ind., U.S.A. .. 104 E3
Warsaw, N.Y., U.S.A. .. 106 D6
Warsaw, Ohio, U.S.A. .. 106 F2
Warstein, Germany 18 D4
Warszawa, Poland 20 C11
Warta →, Poland 20 C4
Warthe = Warta →,
  Poland 20 C4
Waru, Indonesia 57 E8
Warwick, Australia 91 D5
Warwick, U.K. 13 E6
Warwick, U.S.A. 107 E13
Warwickshire □, U.K. .. 13 E6
Wasaga Beach, Canada .. 106 B4
Wasatch Ra., U.S.A. ... 110 F8
Wasbank, S. Africa 85 D5
Wasco, Calif., U.S.A. . 113 K7
Wasco, Oreg., U.S.A. .. 110 D3
Waseca, U.S.A. 108 C8
Wasekamio L., Canada .. 101 B7
Wash, The, U.K. 12 E8
Washago, Canada 106 B5
Washburn, N. Dak.,
  U.S.A. 108 B4
Washburn, Wis., U.S.A. . 108 B9
Washim, India 60 J10
Washington, D.C., U.S.A. 104 F7
Washington, Ga., U.S.A. 105 J4
Washington, Ind., U.S.A. 104 F2
Washington, Iowa, U.S.A. 108 E9
Washington, Mo., U.S.A. 108 F9
Washington, N.C., U.S.A. 105 H7
Washington, N.J., U.S.A. 107 F10
Washington, Pa., U.S.A. 106 F4
Washington, Utah, U.S.A. 111 H7
Washington □, U.S.A. .. 110 C3
Washington, Mt., U.S.A. 107 B13
Washington I., U.S.A. . 104 C2
Washougal, U.S.A. 112 E4
Wasian, Indonesia 57 E8
Wasior, Indonesia 57 E8
Waskaganish, Canada ... 98 B4
Waskaiowaka, L., Canada 101 B9
Waskesiu Lake, Canada . 101 C7
Wasmes, Belgium 17 H3
Waspik, Neths. 17 E5
Wassen, Switz. 23 C7
Wassenaar, Neths. 16 D4
Wasserburg, Germany ... 19 G8
Wasserkuppe, Germany .. 18 E5
Wassy, France 25 D11
Waswanipi, Canada 98 C4
Waswanipi, L., Canada . 98 C4
Watangpone, Indonesia . 57 E6
Water Park Pt., Australia 90 C5
Water Valley, U.S.A. .. 109 H10
Waterberge, S. Africa . 85 C4
Waterbury, Conn., U.S.A. 107 E11
Waterbury, Vt., U.S.A. . 107 B12
Waterbury L., Canada .. 101 B8
Waterdown, Canada 106 C5
Waterford, Canada 106 D4
Waterford, Ireland 15 D4
Waterford, U.S.A. 112 H6
Waterford □, Ireland .. 15 D4
Waterford Harbour, Ireland 15 D5
Waterhen L., Man.,
  Canada 101 C9
Waterhen L., Sask.,
  Canada 101 C7

Wateringen, Neths. 16 D4
Waterloo, Belgium 17 G4
Waterloo, Ont., Canada . 98 D3
Waterloo, Qué., Canada . 107 A12
Waterloo, S. Leone 78 D2
Waterloo, Ill., U.S.A. . 108 F9
Waterloo, Iowa, U.S.A. . 108 D8
Waterloo, N.Y., U.S.A. . 106 D8
Watermeal-Boitsford,
  Belgium 17 G4
Watermeet, U.S.A. 108 B10
Waterton-Glacier
  International Peace Park,
  U.S.A. 110 B7
Watertown, Conn., U.S.A. 107 E11
Watertown, N.Y., U.S.A. 107 C9
Watertown, S. Dak.,
  U.S.A. 108 C6
Watertown, Wis., U.S.A. 108 D10
Waterval-Boven, S. Africa 85 D5
Waterville, Canada 107 A13
Waterville, Maine, U.S.A. 99 D6
Waterville, N.Y., U.S.A. 107 D9
Waterville, Pa., U.S.A. . 106 E7
Waterville, Wash., U.S.A. 110 C3
Watervliet, Belgium ... 17 F3
Watervliet, U.S.A. 107 D11
Wates, Indonesia 57 G14
Watford, Canada 106 D3
Watford, U.K. 13 F7
Watford City, U.S.A. .. 108 B3
Watham →, Canada 101 B8
Watheroo, Australia ... 89 F2
Wating, China 50 G4
Watkins Glen, U.S.A. .. 106 D8
Watling I. = San Salvador,
  Bahamas 117 B5
Watonga, U.S.A. 109 H5
Watou, Belgium 17 G1
Watrous, Canada 101 C7
Watrous, U.S.A. 109 H2
Watsa, Zaïre 82 B2
Watseka, U.S.A. 104 E2
Watson, Australia 89 F5
Watson, Canada 101 C8
Watson Lake, Canada ... 100 A3
Watsonville, U.S.A. ... 111 H3
Wattenwil, Switz. 22 C5
Wattiwarriganna Cr. →,
  Australia 91 D2
Wattwil, Switz. 23 B8
Watuata = Batuata,
  Indonesia 57 F6
Watubela, Kepulauan,
  Indonesia 57 E8
Watubela Is. = Watubela,
  Kepulauan, Indonesia . 57 E8
Waubach, Neths. 17 G8
Waubamik, Canada 106 A4
Waubay, U.S.A. 108 C6
Waubra, Australia 91 F3
Wauchope, Australia ... 91 E5
Wauchula, U.S.A. 105 M5
Waugh, Canada 101 D9
Waukarlycarly, L.,
  Australia 88 D3
Waukegan, U.S.A. 104 D2
Waukesha, U.S.A. 104 D1
Waukon, U.S.A. 108 D9
Wauneta, U.S.A. 108 E4
Waupaca, U.S.A. 108 C10
Waupun, U.S.A. 108 D10
Waurika, U.S.A. 109 H6
Wausau, U.S.A. 108 C10
Wautoma, U.S.A. 108 C10
Wauwatosa, U.S.A. 104 D2
Wave Hill, Australia .. 88 C5
Waveney →, U.K. 13 E9
Waverley, N.Z. 87 H5
Waverly, Iowa, U.S.A. . 108 D8
Waverly, N.Y., U.S.A. . 107 D8
Wavre, Belgium 17 G5
Wavreille, Belgium 17 H6
Wâw, Sudan 77 F2
Wāw al Kabīr, Libya ... 73 C8
Wawa, Canada 98 C3
Wawa, Nigeria 79 D5
Wawa, Sudan 76 C3
Wawanesa, Canada 101 D9
Wawona, U.S.A. 112 H7
Waxahachie, U.S.A. 109 J6
Way, L., Australia 89 E3
Wayabula Rau, Indonesia 57 D7
Wayatinah, Australia .. 90 G4
Waycross, U.S.A. 105 K4
Wayi, Sudan 77 F3
Wayne, Nebr., U.S.A. .. 108 D6
Wayne, W. Va., U.S.A. . 104 F4
Waynesboro, Ga., U.S.A. 105 J4
Waynesboro, Miss., U.S.A. 105 K1
Waynesboro, Pa., U.S.A. 104 F7
Waynesboro, Va., U.S.A. 104 F6
Waynesburg, U.S.A. 104 F5
Waynesville, U.S.A. ... 105 H4
Waynoka, U.S.A. 109 G5
Wazirabad, Pakistan ... 62 C6
We, Indonesia 56 C1
Weald, The, U.K. 13 F8
Wear →, U.K. 12 C6
Weatherford, Okla.,
  U.S.A. 109 H5
Weatherford, Tex., U.S.A. 109 J6
Weaverville, U.S.A. ... 110 F2
Webb City, U.S.A. 109 G7
Webo = Nyaake, Liberia 78 E3
Webster, Mass., U.S.A. . 107 D13

Webster, N.Y., U.S.A. . 106 C7
Webster, S. Dak., U.S.A. 108 C6
Webster, Wis., U.S.A. . 108 C8
Webster City, U.S.A. .. 108 D8
Webster Green, U.S.A. . 108 F9
Webster Springs, U.S.A. 104 F5
Weda, Indonesia 57 D7
Weda, Teluk, Indonesia 57 D7
Weddell I., Falk. Is. . 128 D4
Weddell Sea, Antarctica 5 D1
Wedderburn, Australia . 91 F3
Wedel, Germany 18 B5
Wedgeport, Canada 99 D6
Wedza, Zimbabwe 83 F3
Wee Waa, Australia 91 E4
Weed, U.S.A. 110 F2
Weed Heights, U.S.A. .. 112 G7
Weedsport, U.S.A. 107 C8
Weedville, U.S.A. 106 E6
Weemelah, Australia ... 91 D4
Weenen, S. Africa 85 D5
Weener, Germany 18 B3
Weert, Neths. 17 F7
Weesp, Neths. 16 D6
Weggis, Switz. 23 B6
Wegliniec, Poland 20 D5
Wegorzewo, Poland 20 A11
Wegrów, Poland 20 C12
Wehl, Neths. 16 E8
Wei He →, Hebei, China 50 F8
Wei He →, Shaanxi, China 50 G6
Weichang, China 51 D9
Weichuan, China 50 G7
Weida, Germany 18 E8
Weiden, Germany 19 F8
Weifang, China 51 F10
Weihai, China 51 F12
Weilburg, Germany 18 E4
Weilheim, Germany 19 H7
Weimar, Germany 18 E7
Weinan, China 50 G5
Weinfelden, Switz. 23 A8
Weingarten, Germany ... 19 H5
Weinheim, Germany 19 F4
Weining, China 52 D5
Weipa, Australia 90 A3
Weir →, Australia 91 D4
Weir →, Canada 101 B10
Weir River, Canada 101 B10
Weirton, U.S.A. 106 F4
Weisen, Switz. 23 C9
Weiser, U.S.A. 110 D5
Weishan, Shandong, China 51 G9
Weishan, Yunnan, China 52 E3
Weissenburg, Germany .. 19 F6
Weissenfels, Germany .. 18 D8
Weisshorn, Switz. 22 D5
Weissmies, Switz. 22 D6
Weisstannen, Switz. ... 23 C8
Weisswasser, Germany .. 18 D10
Weiswampach, Belgium .. 17 H8
Weixi, China 52 D2
Weixin, China 52 D5
Weiyuan, China 50 G3
Weiz, Austria 21 H5
Weizhou Dao, China 52 G7
Wejherowo, Poland 20 A8
Wekusko L., Canada 101 C9
Welbourn Hill, Australia 91 D1
Welch, U.S.A. 104 G5
Weldya, Ethiopia 77 E4
Welega □, Ethiopia 77 F3
Welkenraedt, Belgium .. 17 G7
Welkite, Ethiopia 77 F4
Welkom, S. Africa 84 D4
Welland, Canada 98 D4
Welland →, U.K. 12 E7
Wellen, Belgium 17 G6
Wellesley Is., Australia 90 B2
Wellin, Belgium 17 H6
Wellingborough, U.K. .. 13 E7
Wellington, Australia . 91 E4
Wellington, Canada 98 D4
Wellington, N.Z. 87 J5
Wellington, S. Africa . 84 E2
Wellington, Shrops., U.K. 13 E5
Wellington, Somst., U.K. 13 G4
Wellington, Colo., U.S.A. 108 E2
Wellington, Kans., U.S.A. 109 G6
Wellington, Nev., U.S.A. 112 G7
Wellington, Ohio, U.S.A. 106 E2
Wellington, Tex., U.S.A. 109 H4
Wellington, I., Chile .. 128 C2
Wellington, L., Australia 91 F4
Wells, U.K. 13 F5
Wells, Maine, U.S.A. .. 107 C14
Wells, Minn., U.S.A. .. 108 D8
Wells, Nev., U.S.A. ... 110 F6
Wells, L., Australia .. 89 E3
Wells Gray Prov. Park,
  Canada 100 C4
Wells-next-the-Sea, U.K. 12 E8
Wells River, U.S.A. ... 107 B12
Wellsboro, U.S.A. 106 E7
Wellsburg, U.S.A. 106 F4
Wellsville, Mo., U.S.A. 108 F9
Wellsville, N.Y., U.S.A. 106 D7
Wellsville, Ohio, U.S.A. 106 F4
Wellsville, Utah, U.S.A. 110 F8
Wellton, U.S.A. 111 K6
Welmel, Wabi →, Ethiopia 77 F5
Welo □, Ethiopia 77 E4
Wels, Austria 21 G4
Welshpool, U.K. 13 E4
Wem, U.K. 12 E5
Wembere →, Tanzania ... 82 C3
Wemindji, Canada 98 B4

Wemmel, *Belgium* 17 G4
Wen Xian, *Gansu, China* . 50 H3
Wen Xian, *Henan, China* . 50 G7
Wenatchee, *U.S.A.* 110 C3
Wenchang, *China* 58 C8
Wencheng, *China* 53 D13
Wenchi, *Ghana* 78 D4
Wenchow = Wenzhou,
  China 53 C13
Wenchuan, *China* 52 B4
Wendell, *U.S.A.* 110 E6
Wenden, *U.S.A.* 113 M13
Wendeng, *China* 51 F12
Wendesi, *Indonesia* 57 E8
Wendo, *Ethiopia* 77 F4
Wendover, *U.S.A.* 110 F6
Wenduine, *Belgium* 17 F2
Weng'an, *China* 52 D6
Wengcheng, *China* 53 E9
Wengen, *Switz.* 22 C5
Wengyuan, *China* 53 E10
Wenjiang, *China* 52 B4
Wenling, *China* 53 C13
Wenlock →, *Australia* ... 90 A3
Wenshan, *China* 52 F5
Wenshang, *China* 50 G9
Wenshui, *Guizhou, China* 52 C6
Wenshui, *Shanxi, China* . 50 F7
Wensu, *China* 54 B3
Wentworth, *Australia* ... 91 E3
Wenut, *Indonesia* 57 E8
Wenxi, *China* 50 G6
Wenzhou, *China* 53 C13
Weott, *U.S.A.* 110 F2
Wepener, *S. Africa* 84 D4
Werbomont, *Belgium* ... 17 H7
Werda, *Botswana* 84 D3
Werdau, *Germany* 18 E8
Werder, *Ethiopia* 68 F4
Werder, *Germany* 18 C8
Werdohl, *Germany* 18 D3
Wereilu, *Ethiopia* 77 E4
Weri, *Indonesia* 57 E8
Werkendam, *Neths.* 16 E5
Werne, *Germany* 18 D3
Werneck, *Germany* 19 F6
Wernigerode, *Germany* .. 18 D6
Werra →, *Germany* 18 D5
Werribee, *Australia* 91 F3
Werrimull, *Australia* ... 91 E3
Werris Creek, *Australia* . 91 E5
Wersar, *Indonesia* 57 E8
Wertach →, *Germany* .. 19 G6
Wertheim, *Germany* ... 19 F5
Wertingen, *Germany* ... 19 G6
Wervershoof, *Neths.* ... 16 C6
Wervik, *Belgium* 17 G2
Wesel, *Germany* 18 D2
Weser →, *Germany* 18 B4
Wesiri, *Indonesia* 57 F7
Wesley Vale, *U.S.A.* 111 J10
Wesleyville, *Canada* 99 C9
Wesleyville, *U.S.A.* 106 D4
Wessel, C., *Australia* ... 90 A2
Wessel Is., *Australia* ... 90 A2
Wesselburen, *Germany* . 18 A4
Wessem, *Neths.* 17 F7
Wessington, *U.S.A.* 108 C5
Wessington Springs, *U.S.A.* 108 C5
West, *U.S.A.* 109 K6
West B., *U.S.A.* 109 L10
West Baines →, *Australia* 88 C4
West Bank □, *Asia* 69 C4
West Bend, *U.S.A.* 104 D1
West Bengal □, *India* ... 63 H12
West Beskids = Západné
  Beskydy, *Europe* 20 F9
West Branch, *U.S.A.* 104 C3
West Bromwich, *U.K.* ... 13 E5
West Cape Howe, *Australia* 89 G2
West Chazy, *U.S.A.* 107 B11
West Chester, *U.S.A.* ... 104 F8
West Columbia, *U.S.A.* . 109 L7
West Covina, *U.S.A.* ... 113 L9
West Des Moines, *U.S.A.* 108 E8
West End, *Bahamas* 116 A4
West Falkland, *Falk. Is.* . 128 D4
West Fjord = Vestfjorden,
  Norway 8 C15
West Frankfort, *U.S.A.* .. 108 G10
West Glamorgan □, *U.K.* 13 F4
West Hartford, *U.S.A.* .. 107 E12
West Haven, *U.S.A.* 107 E12
West Helena, *U.S.A.* ... 109 H9
West Ice Shelf, *Antarctica* 5 C7
West Indies, *Cent. Amer.* 117 C7
West Lorne, *Canada* 106 D3
West Lunga →, *Zambia* . 83 E1
West Memphis, *U.S.A.* .. 109 H9
West Midlands □, *U.K.* . 13 E6
West Mifflin, *U.S.A.* 106 F5
West Monroe, *U.S.A.* ... 109 J8
West Newton, *U.S.A.* ... 106 F5
West Nicholson, *Zimbabwe* 83 G2
West Palm Beach, *U.S.A.* 105 M5
West Plains, *U.S.A.* 109 G9
West Point, *Ga., U.S.A.* . 105 J3
West Point, *Miss., U.S.A.* 105 J1
West Point, *Nebr., U.S.A.* 108 E6
West Point, *N.Y., U.S.A.* 104 G7
West Pokot □, *Kenya* ... 82 B4
West Pt. = Ouest, Pte.,
  Canada 99 C7
West Pt., *Australia* 91 F2
West Road →, *Canada* .. 100 C4
West Rutland, *U.S.A.* ... 107 C11

West Schelde =
  Westerschelde →, *Neths.* 17 F2
West Seneca, *U.S.A.* ... 106 D6
West Siberian Plain, *Russia* 46 C11
West Sussex □, *U.K.* ... 13 G7
West-Terschelling, *Neths.* 16 B6
West Virginia □, *U.S.A.* . 104 F5
West-Vlaanderen □,
  Belgium 17 G2
West Walker →, *U.S.A.* . 112 G7
West Wyalong, *Australia* . 91 E4
West Yellowstone, *U.S.A.* 110 D8
West Yorkshire □, *U.K.* . 12 D6
Westall Pt., *Australia* ... 91 E1
Westbrook, *Maine, U.S.A.* 105 D10
Westbrook, *Tex., U.S.A.* 109 J4
Westbury, *Australia* 90 G4
Westby, *U.S.A.* 108 A2
Westend, *U.S.A.* 113 K9
Westerbork, *Neths.* 16 C9
Westerland, *Germany* ... 9 J13
Western □, *Kenya* 82 B3
Western □, *Uganda* 82 B3
Western □, *Zambia* 83 F1
Western Australia □,
  Australia 89 E2
Western Cape □, *S. Africa* 84 E3
Western Ghats, *India* ... 60 N9
Western Isles □, *U.K.* .. 14 D1
Western Sahara ■, *Africa* 74 D2
Western Samoa ■,
  Pac. Oc. 87 A13
Westernport, *U.S.A.* 104 F6
Westerschelde →, *Neths.* 17 F2
Westerstede, *Germany* .. 18 B3
Westervoort, *Neths.* 16 E7
Westerwald, *Germany* ... 18 E4
Westfield, *Mass., U.S.A.* . 107 D12
Westfield, *N.Y., U.S.A.* . 106 D5
Westfield, *Pa., U.S.A.* .. 106 E7
Westgat, *Neths.* 17 E3
Westhope, *U.S.A.* 108 A4
Westkapelle, *Belgium* ... 17 F2
Westkapelle, *Neths.* 17 E2
Westland Bight, *N.Z.* ... 87 K3
Westlock, *Canada* 100 C6
Westmalle, *Belgium* 17 F5
Westmeath □, *Ireland* .. 15 C4
Westminster, *U.S.A.* ... 104 F7
Westmorland, *U.S.A.* ... 111 K6
Weston, *Malaysia* 56 C5
Weston, *Oreg., U.S.A.* .. 110 D4
Weston, *W. Va., U.S.A.* . 104 F5
Weston I., *Canada* 98 B4
Weston-super-Mare, *U.K.* 13 F5
Westport, *Canada* 107 B8
Westport, *Ireland* 15 C2
Westport, *N.Z.* 87 J3
Westport, *Oreg., U.S.A.* . 112 D3
Westport, *Wash., U.S.A.* 110 C1
Westray, *Canada* 101 C8
Westray, *U.K.* 14 B6
Westree, *Canada* 98 C3
Westville, *Calif., U.S.A.* . 112 F6
Westville, *Ill., U.S.A.* ... 104 E2
Westville, *Okla., U.S.A.* . 109 G7
Westwood, *U.S.A.* 110 F3
Wetar, *Indonesia* 57 F7
Wetaskiwin, *Canada* ... 100 C6
Wethersfield, *U.S.A.* ... 107 E12
Wetteren, *Belgium* 17 G3
Wettingen, *Switz.* 23 B6
Wetzikon, *Switz.* 23 B7
Wetzlar, *Germany* 18 E4
Wevelgem, *Belgium* 17 G2
Wewoka, *U.S.A.* 109 H6
Wexford, *Ireland* 15 D5
Wexford □, *Ireland* 15 D5
Wexford Harbour, *Ireland* 15 D5
Weyburn, *Canada* 101 D8
Weyburn L., *Canada* ... 100 A5
Weyer, *Austria* 21 H4
Weyib →, *Ethiopia* 77 F5
Weymouth, *Canada* 99 D6
Weymouth, *U.K.* 13 G5
Weymouth, *U.S.A.* 107 D14
Weymouth, C., *Australia* 90 A3
Wezemaal, *Belgium* 17 G5
Wezep, *Neths.* 16 D7
Whakatane, *N.Z.* 87 G6
Whale →, *Canada* 99 A6
Whale Cove, *Canada* ... 101 A10
Whales, B. of, *Antarctica* 5 D12
Whalsay, *U.K.* 14 A7
Whangamomona, *N.Z.* .. 87 H5
Whangarei, *N.Z.* 87 F5
Whangarei Harb., *N.Z.* . 87 F5
Wharfe →, *U.K.* 12 D6
Wharfedale, *U.K.* 12 C5
Wharton, *N.J., U.S.A.* .. 107 F10
Wharton, *Pa., U.S.A.* ... 106 E6
Wharton, *Tex., U.S.A.* .. 109 L6
Wheatland, *Calif., U.S.A.* 112 F5
Wheatland, *Wyo., U.S.A.* 108 D2
Wheatley, *Canada* 106 D2
Wheaton, *U.S.A.* 108 C6
Wheelbarrow Pk., *U.S.A.* 112 H10
Wheeler, *Oreg., U.S.A.* . 110 D2
Wheeler, *Tex., U.S.A.* .. 109 H4
Wheeler →, *Canada* 101 B7
Wheeler Pk., *N. Mex.,*
  U.S.A. 111 H11
Wheeler Pk., *Nev., U.S.A.* 111 G6
Wheeler Ridge, *U.S.A.* .. 113 L8
Wheeling, *U.S.A.* 106 F4
Whernside, *U.K.* 12 C5
Whidbey I., *U.S.A.* 100 D4

Whiskey Gap, *Canada* ... 100 D6
Whiskey Jack L., *Canada* 101 B8
Whistleduck Cr. →,
  Australia 90 C2
Whitby, *Canada* 106 C6
Whitby, *U.K.* 12 C7
White →, *Ark., U.S.A.* .. 109 J9
White →, *Ind., U.S.A.* .. 104 F2
White →, *S. Dak., U.S.A.* 108 D5
White →, *Utah, U.S.A.* . 110 F9
White →, *Wash., U.S.A.* 112 C4
White, L., *Australia* 88 D4
White B., *Canada* 99 B8
White Bear Res., *Canada* . 99 C8
White Bird, *U.S.A.* 110 D5
White Butte, *U.S.A.* 108 B3
White City, *U.S.A.* 108 F6
White Cliffs, *Australia* .. 91 E3
White Deer, *U.S.A.* 109 H4
White Hall, *U.S.A.* 108 F9
White Haven, *U.S.A.* ... 107 E9
White Horse, Vale of, *U.K.* 13 F6
White I., *N.Z.* 87 G6
White L., *Canada* 107 A8
White L., *U.S.A.* 109 L8
White Mts., *Calif., U.S.A.* 111 H4
White Mts., *N.H., U.S.A.* 107 B13
White Nile = Nîl el
  Abyad →, *Sudan* 77 D3
White Nile Dam =
  Khazzân Jabal el Awliyâ,
  Sudan 77 D3
White Otter L., *Canada* .. 98 C1
White Pass, *Canada* 100 B1
White Pass, *U.S.A.* 112 D5
White Plains, *U.S.A.* ... 107 E11
White River, *Canada* ... 98 C2
White River, *S. Africa* .. 85 D5
White River, *U.S.A.* 108 D4
White Russia = Belarus ■,
  Europe 40 F4
White Sea = Beloye More,
  Russia 44 C4
White Sulphur Springs,
  Mont., U.S.A. 110 C8
White Sulphur Springs,
  W. Va., U.S.A. 104 G5
White Swan, *U.S.A.* 112 D6
White Volta →, *Ghana* . 79 D4
Whitecliffs, *N.Z.* 87 K3
Whitecourt, *Canada* 100 C5
Whiteface, *U.S.A.* 109 J3
Whitefield, *U.S.A.* 107 B13
Whitefish, *U.S.A.* 110 A6
Whitefish L., *Canada* ... 101 A7
Whitefish Point, *U.S.A.* . 104 B3
Whitegull, L., *Canada* ... 99 A7
Whitehall, *Mich., U.S.A.* 104 D2
Whitehall, *Mont., U.S.A.* 110 D7
Whitehall, *N.Y., U.S.A.* . 107 C11
Whitehall, *Wis., U.S.A.* . 108 C9
Whitehaven, *U.K.* 12 C4
Whitehorse, *Canada* ... 100 A1
Whitemark, *Australia* ... 90 G4
Whitemouth, *Canada* ... 101 D9
Whiteplains, *Liberia* ... 78 D2
Whitesboro, *N.Y., U.S.A.* 107 C9
Whitesboro, *Tex., U.S.A.* 109 J6
Whiteshell Prov. Park,
  Canada 101 C9
Whiteside, Canal, *Chile* . 128 D2
Whitetail, *U.S.A.* 108 A2
Whiteville, *U.S.A.* 105 H6
Whitewater, *U.S.A.* 104 D1
Whitewater Baldy, *U.S.A.* 111 K9
Whitewater L., *Canada* . 98 B2
Whitewood, *Australia* .. 90 C3
Whitewood, *Canada* ... 101 C8
Whitfield, *Australia* 91 F4
Whithorn, *U.K.* 14 G4
Whitianga, *N.Z.* 87 G5
Whitman, *U.S.A.* 107 D14
Whitmire, *U.S.A.* 105 H5
Whitney, *Canada* 98 C4
Whitney, Mt., *U.S.A.* ... 111 H4
Whitney Point, *U.S.A.* .. 107 D9
Whitstable, *U.K.* 13 F9
Whitsunday I., *Australia* 90 C4
Whittier, *U.S.A.* 113 M8
Whittlesea, *Australia* ... 91 F4
Whitwell, *U.S.A.* 105 H3
Wholdaia L., *Canada* ... 101 A8
Whyalla, *Australia* 91 E2
Whyjonta, *Australia* 91 D3
Wiarton, *Canada* 98 D3
Wiawso, *Ghana* 78 D4
Wibaux, *U.S.A.* 108 B2
Wichabai, *Guyana* 121 C6
Wichian Buri, *Thailand* . 58 E3
Wichita, *U.S.A.* 109 G6
Wichita Falls, *U.S.A.* ... 109 J5
Wick, *U.K.* 14 C5
Wickenburg, *U.S.A.* ... 111 K7
Wickepin, *Australia* 89 F2
Wickham, C., *Australia* . 90 F3
Wicklow, *Ireland* 15 D5
Wicklow □, *Ireland* 15 D5
Wicklow Hd., *Ireland* .. 15 D5
Widgiemooltha, *Australia* 89 F3
Widnes, *U.K.* 12 D5
Wiedenbrück, *Germany* . 18 D4
Wiehl, *Germany* 18 E3
Wiek, *Germany* 18 A9
Wielbark, *Poland* 20 B10
Wieliczka, *Poland* 20 F10
Wieluń, *Poland* 20 D8

Wien, *Austria* 21 G6
Wiener Neustadt, *Austria* 21 H6
Wieprz →, *Koszalin,*
  Poland 20 A6
Wieprz →, *Lublin, Poland* 20 D11
Wierden, *Neths.* 16 D9
Wiers, *Belgium* 17 H3
Wiesbaden, *Germany* ... 19 E4
Wiesental, *Germany* 19 F4
Wigan, *U.K.* 12 D5
Wiggins, *Colo., U.S.A.* .. 108 E2
Wiggins, *Miss., U.S.A.* .. 109 K10
Wight, I. of □, *U.K.* ... 13 G6
Wigtown, *U.K.* 14 G4
Wigtown B., *U.K.* 14 G4
Wijchen, *Neths.* 16 E7
Wijhe, *Neths.* 16 D8
Wijk bij Duurstede, *Neths.* 16 E6
Wil, *Switz.* 23 B8
Wilber, *U.S.A.* 108 E6
Wilberforce, *Canada* ... 106 A6
Wilberforce, C., *Australia* 90 A2
Wilburton, *U.S.A.* 109 H7
Wilcannia, *Australia* ... 91 E3
Wilcox, *U.S.A.* 106 E6
Wildbad, *Germany* 19 G4
Wildervank, *Neths.* 16 B9
Wildeshausen, *Germany* 18 C4
Wildhorn, *Switz.* 22 D4
Wildrose, *Calif., U.S.A.* . 113 J9
Wildrose, *N. Dak., U.S.A.* 108 A3
Wildspitze, *Austria* 19 J6
Wildstrubel, *Switz.* 22 D5
Wildwood, *U.S.A.* 104 F8
Wilge →, *S. Africa* 85 D4
Wilhelm II Coast,
  Antarctica 5 C7
Wilhelm-Pieck-Stadt-
  Guben, *Germany* 18 D10
Wilhelmina, Geb., *Surinam* 121 C6
Wilhelmina Kanaal, *Neths.* 17 E6
Wilhelmsburg, *Austria* .. 21 G5
Wilhelmshaven, *Germany* 18 B4
Wilhelmstal, *Namibia* .. 84 C2
Wilkes-Barre, *U.S.A.* ... 107 E9
Wilkesboro, *U.S.A.* 105 G5
Wilkie, *Canada* 101 C7
Wilkinsburg, *U.S.A.* ... 106 F5
Wilkinson Lakes, *Australia* 89 E5
Willamina, *U.S.A.* 110 D2
Willandra Billabong
  Creek →, *Australia* .. 91 E4
Willapa B., *U.S.A.* 110 C2
Willapa Hills, *U.S.A.* ... 112 D3
Willard, *N. Mex., U.S.A.* 111 J10
Willard, *Utah, U.S.A.* .. 110 F7
Willcox, *U.S.A.* 111 K9
Willebroek, *Belgium* ... 17 F4
Willemstad, *Neth. Ant.* . 117 D6
Willeroo, *Australia* 88 C5
William →, *Canada* 101 B7
William Creek, *Australia* 91 D2
Williambury, *Australia* .. 89 D2
Williams, *Australia* 89 F2
Williams, *Ariz., U.S.A.* . 111 J7
Williams, *Calif., U.S.A.* . 112 F4
Williams Lake, *Canada* . 100 C4
Williamsburg, *Ky., U.S.A.* 105 G3
Williamsburg, *Pa., U.S.A.* 106 F6
Williamsburg, *Va., U.S.A.* 104 G7
Williamson, *N.Y., U.S.A.* 106 C7
Williamson, *W. Va.,*
  U.S.A. 104 G4
Williamsport, *U.S.A.* ... 106 E7
Williamston, *U.S.A.* ... 105 H7
Williamstown, *Australia* . 91 F3
Williamstown, *Mass.,*
  U.S.A. 107 D11
Williamstown, *N.Y.,*
  U.S.A. 107 C9
Williamsville, *U.S.A.* ... 109 G9
Willimantic, *U.S.A.* 107 E12
Willis Group, *Australia* . 90 B5
Willisau, *Switz.* 22 B6
Williston, *S. Africa* 84 E3
Williston, *Fla., U.S.A.* .. 105 L4
Williston, *N. Dak., U.S.A.* 108 A3
Williston L., *Canada* ... 100 B4
Willits, *U.S.A.* 110 G2
Willmar, *U.S.A.* 108 C7
Willoughby, *U.S.A.* 106 E3
Willow Bunch, *Canada* . 101 D7
Willow L., *Canada* 100 A5
Willow Lake, *U.S.A.* ... 108 C6
Willow Springs, *U.S.A.* . 109 G8
Willow Wall, The, *China* 51 C12
Willowlake →, *Canada* . 100 A4
Willowmore, *S. Africa* .. 84 E3
Willows, *Australia* 90 C4
Willows, *U.S.A.* 112 F4
Willowvale = Gatyana,
  S. Africa 85 E4
Wills, L., *Australia* 88 D4
Wills Cr. →, *Australia* .. 90 C3
Wills Point, *U.S.A.* 109 J7
Willunga, *Australia* 91 F2
Wilmette, *U.S.A.* 104 D2
Wilmington, *Australia* .. 91 E2
Wilmington, *Del., U.S.A.* 104 F8
Wilmington, *Ill., U.S.A.* 104 E1
Wilmington, *N.C., U.S.A.* 105 H7
Wilmington, *Ohio, U.S.A.* 104 F4
Wilpena Cr. →, *Australia* 91 E2
Wilrijk, *Belgium* 17 F4
Wilsall, *U.S.A.* 110 D8
Wilson, *U.S.A.* 105 H7

Wilson →, *Queens.,*
  Australia 91 D3
Wilson →, *W. Austral.,*
  Australia 88 C4
Wilson Bluff, *Australia* .. 89 F4
Wilsons Promontory,
  Australia 91 F4
Wilster, *Germany* 18 B5
Wilton, *U.K.* 13 F6
Wilton, *U.S.A.* 108 B4
Wilton →, *Australia* 90 A1
Wiltshire □, *U.K.* 13 F6
Wiltz, *Lux.* 17 J7
Wiluna, *Australia* 89 E3
Wimereux, *France* 25 B8
Wimmera →, *Australia* . 91 F3
Winam G., *Kenya* 82 C3
Winburg, *S. Africa* 84 D4
Winchendon, *U.S.A.* ... 107 D12
Winchester, *U.K.* 13 F6
Winchester, *Conn., U.S.A.* 107 E11
Winchester, *Idaho, U.S.A.* 110 C5
Winchester, *Ind., U.S.A.* 104 E3
Winchester, *Ky., U.S.A.* 104 G3
Winchester, *N.H., U.S.A.* 107 D12
Winchester, *Nev., U.S.A.* 113 J11
Winchester, *Tenn., U.S.A.* 105 H2
Winchester, *Va., U.S.A.* . 104 F6
Wind →, *U.S.A.* 110 E9
Wind River Range, *U.S.A.* 110 E9
Windau = Ventspils, *Latvia* 9 H19
Windber, *U.S.A.* 106 F6
Windermere, L., *U.K.* .. 12 C5
Windfall, *Canada* 100 C5
Windflower L., *Canada* . 100 A5
Windhoek, *Namibia* 84 C2
Windom, *U.S.A.* 108 D7
Windorah, *Australia* ... 90 D3
Window Rock, *U.S.A.* .. 111 J9
Windrush →, *U.K.* 13 F6
Windsor, *Australia* 91 E5
Windsor, *N.S., Canada* . 99 D7
Windsor, *Nfld., Canada* . 99 C8
Windsor, *Ont., Canada* . 98 D3
Windsor, *U.K.* 13 F7
Windsor, *Colo., U.S.A.* . 108 E2
Windsor, *Conn., U.S.A.* . 107 E12
Windsor, *Mo., U.S.A.* .. 108 F8
Windsor, *N.Y., U.S.A.* .. 107 D9
Windsor, *Vt., U.S.A.* ... 107 C12
Windsorton, *S. Africa* .. 84 D3
Windward Is., *W. Indies* 117 D7
Windward Passage =
  Vientos, Paso de los,
  Caribbean 117 C5
Windy L., *Canada* 101 A8
Winefred L., *Canada* ... 101 B6
Winejok, *Sudan* 77 F2
Winfield, *U.S.A.* 109 G6
Wingate Mts., *Australia* . 88 B5
Wingen, *Australia* 91 E5
Wingene, *Belgium* 17 F2
Wingham, *Australia* 91 E5
Wingham, *Canada* 98 D3
Winifred, *U.S.A.* 110 C9
Winisk, *Canada* 98 A2
Winisk →, *Canada* 98 A2
Winisk L., *Canada* 98 B2
Wink, *U.S.A.* 109 K3
Winkler, *Canada* 101 D9
Winlock, *U.S.A.* 112 D4
Winneba, *Ghana* 79 D4
Winnebago, *U.S.A.* 108 D7
Winnebago, L., *U.S.A.* . 104 D1
Winnecke Cr. →, *Australia* 88 C5
Winnemucca, *U.S.A.* ... 110 F5
Winnemucca L., *U.S.A.* 110 F4
Winner, *U.S.A.* 108 D5
Winnett, *U.S.A.* 110 C9
Winnfield, *U.S.A.* 109 K8
Winnibigoshish, L., *U.S.A.* 108 B7
Winning, *Australia* 88 D1
Winnipeg, *Canada* 101 D9
Winnipeg →, *Canada* .. 101 C9
Winnipeg, L., *Canada* .. 101 C9
Winnipeg Beach, *Canada* 101 C9
Winnipegosis, *Canada* .. 101 C9
Winnipegosis L., *Canada* 101 C9
Winnipesaukee, L., *U.S.A.* 107 C13
Winnsboro, *La., U.S.A.* . 109 J9
Winnsboro, *S.C., U.S.A.* 105 H5
Winnsboro, *Tex., U.S.A.* 109 J7
Winokapau, L., *Canada* . 99 B7
Winona, *Minn., U.S.A.* . 108 C9
Winona, *Miss., U.S.A.* .. 109 J10
Winooski, *U.S.A.* 107 B11
Winschoten, *Neths.* 16 B10
Winsen, *Germany* 18 B6
Winslow, *Ariz., U.S.A.* . 111 J8
Winslow, *Wash., U.S.A.* 112 C4
Winsted, *U.S.A.* 107 E11
Winston-Salem, *U.S.A.* . 105 G5
Winsum, *Neths.* 16 B9
Winter Garden, *U.S.A.* . 105 L5
Winter Haven, *U.S.A.* .. 105 M5
Winter Park, *U.S.A.* ... 105 L5
Winterberg, *Germany* .. 18 D4
Winterhaven, *U.S.A.* ... 113 N12
Winters, *Calif., U.S.A.* . 112 G5
Winters, *Tex., U.S.A.* .. 109 K5
Winterset, *U.S.A.* 108 E7
Wintersville, *U.S.A.* ... 106 F4
Winterswijk, *Neths.* 16 E9
Winterthur, *Switz.* 23 B7
Winthrop, *Minn., U.S.A.* 108 C7
Winthrop, *Wash., U.S.A.* 110 B3
Winton, *Australia* 90 C3

Winton, N.Z. ... 87 M2
Winton, U.S.A. ... 105 G7
Wintzenheim, France ... 25 D14
Wipper →, Germany ... 18 D7
Wirral, U.K. ... 12 D4
Wirrulla, Australia ... 91 E1
Wisbech, U.K. ... 12 E8
Wisconsin □, U.S.A. ... 108 C10
Wisconsin →, U.S.A. ... 108 D9
Wisconsin Dells, U.S.A. ... 108 D10
Wisconsin Rapids, U.S.A. ... 108 C10
Wisdom, U.S.A. ... 110 D7
Wishaw, U.K. ... 14 F5
Wishek, U.S.A. ... 108 B5
Wisła, Poland ... 20 F8
Wisła →, Poland ... 20 A8
Wisłok →, Poland ... 20 E12
Wisłoka →, Poland ... 20 E11
Wismar, Germany ... 18 B7
Wismar, Guyana ... 121 B6
Wisner, U.S.A. ... 108 E6
Wissant, France ... 25 B8
Wissembourg, France ... 25 C14
Wissenkerke, Neths. ... 17 E3
Witbank, S. Africa ... 85 D4
Witdraai, S. Africa ... 84 D3
Witham →, U.K. ... 12 D7
Withernsea, U.K. ... 12 D8
Witmarsum, Neths. ... 16 B6
Witney, U.K. ... 13 F6
Witnossob →, Namibia ... 84 D3
Wittdün, Germany ... 18 A4
Witten, Germany ... 17 F10
Wittenberg, Germany ... 18 D8
Wittenberge, Germany ... 18 B7
Wittenburg, Germany ... 18 B7
Wittenoom, Australia ... 88 D2
Wittingen, Germany ... 18 C6
Wittlich, Germany ... 19 F2
Wittmund, Germany ... 18 B3
Wittow, Germany ... 18 A9
Wittstock, Germany ... 18 B8
Witzenhausen, Germany ... 18 D5
Wlingi, Indonesia ... 57 H15
Włocławek, Poland ... 20 C9
Włodawa, Poland ... 20 D13
Włoszczowa, Poland ... 20 E9
Woburn, U.S.A. ... 107 D13
Wodian, China ... 50 H7
Wodonga, Australia ... 91 F4
Woerden, Neths. ... 16 D5
Woerth, France ... 25 D14
Woëvre, France ... 25 C12
Wognum, Neths. ... 16 C6
Wohlen, Switz. ... 23 B6
Woinbogoin, China ... 52 A2
Wokam, Indonesia ... 57 F8
Wolbrom, Poland ... 20 E9
Woldegk, Germany ... 18 B9
Wolf →, Canada ... 100 A2
Wolf Creek, U.S.A. ... 110 C7
Wolf L., Canada ... 100 A2
Wolf Point, U.S.A. ... 108 A2
Wolfe I., Canada ... 98 D4
Wolfenbüttel, Germany ... 18 C6
Wolfheze, Neths. ... 16 D7
Wolfsberg, Austria ... 21 J4
Wolfsburg, Germany ... 18 C6
Wolgast, Germany ... 18 A9
Wolhusen, Switz. ... 22 B6
Wolin, Poland ... 20 B8
Wollaston, Is., Chile ... 128 E3
Wollaston, Is., Canada ... 101 B8
Wollaston Pen., Canada ... 96 B8
Wollogorang, Australia ... 90 B2
Wollongong, Australia ... 91 E5
Wolmaransstad, S. Africa ... 84 D4
Wolmirstedt, Germany ... 18 C7
Wolseley, Australia ... 91 F3
Wolseley, Canada ... 101 C8
Wolseley, S. Africa ... 84 E2
Wolstenholme, C., Canada ... 94 C12
Wolsztyn, Poland ... 20 C6
Wolvega, Neths. ... 16 C7
Wolverhampton, U.K. ... 13 E5
Wommels, Neths. ... 16 B7
Wonarah, Australia ... 90 B2
Wonck, Belgium ... 17 G7
Wondai, Australia ... 91 D5
Wondelgem, Belgium ... 17 F3
Wongalarroo L., Australia ... 91 E3
Wongan Hills, Australia ... 89 F2
Wongawol, Australia ... 89 E3
Wŏnju, S. Korea ... 51 F14
Wonosari, Indonesia ... 57 G14
Wŏnsan, N. Korea ... 51 E14
Wonthaggi, Australia ... 91 F4
Woocalla, Australia ... 91 E2
Wood Buffalo Nat. Park, Canada ... 100 B6
Wood Is., Australia ... 88 C3
Wood L., Canada ... 101 B8
Wood Lake, U.S.A. ... 108 D4
Woodah I., Australia ... 90 A2
Woodanilling, Australia ... 89 F2
Woodbridge, Canada ... 106 C5
Woodburn, Australia ... 91 D5
Woodenbong, Australia ... 91 D5
Woodend, Australia ... 91 F3
Woodfords, U.S.A. ... 112 G7
Woodgreen, Australia ... 90 C1
Woodlake, U.S.A. ... 112 J7
Woodland, U.S.A. ... 112 G5
Woodlands, Australia ... 88 D2
Woodpecker, Canada ... 100 C4
Woodridge, Canada ... 101 D9
Woodroffe, Mt., Australia ... 89 E5

Woodruff, Ariz., U.S.A. ... 111 J8
Woodruff, Utah, U.S.A. ... 110 F8
Woods, L., Australia ... 90 B1
Woods, L., Canada ... 99 B6
Woods, L. of the, Canada ... 101 D10
Woodstock, Queens., Australia ... 90 B4
Woodstock, W. Austral., Australia ... 88 D2
Woodstock, N.B., Canada ... 99 C6
Woodstock, Ont., Canada ... 98 D3
Woodstock, U.K. ... 13 F6
Woodstock, Ill., U.S.A. ... 108 D10
Woodstock, Vt., U.S.A. ... 107 C12
Woodsville, U.S.A. ... 107 B13
Woodville, N.Z. ... 87 J5
Woodville, U.S.A. ... 109 K7
Woodward, U.S.A. ... 109 G5
Woody, U.S.A. ... 113 K8
Woolamai, C., Australia ... 91 F4
Woolgoolga, Australia ... 91 E5
Woombye, Australia ... 91 D5
Woomera, Australia ... 91 E2
Woonsocket, R.I., U.S.A. ... 107 D13
Woonsocket, S. Dak., U.S.A. ... 108 C5
Wooramel, Australia ... 89 E1
Wooramel →, Australia ... 89 E1
Wooroloo, Australia ... 89 F2
Wooster, U.S.A. ... 106 F3
Worb, Switz. ... 22 C5
Worcester, S. Africa ... 84 E2
Worcester, U.K. ... 13 E5
Worcester, Mass., U.S.A. ... 107 D13
Worcester, N.Y., U.S.A. ... 107 D10
Wörgl, Austria ... 19 H8
Workington, U.K. ... 12 C4
Worksop, U.K. ... 12 D6
Workum, Neths. ... 16 C6
Worland, U.S.A. ... 110 D10
Wormerveer, Neths. ... 16 D5
Wormhoudt, France ... 25 B9
Worms, Germany ... 19 F4
Wörth, Germany ... 19 F8
Wortham, U.S.A. ... 109 K6
Wörther See, Austria ... 21 J4
Worthing, U.K. ... 13 G7
Worthington, U.S.A. ... 108 D7
Wosi, Indonesia ... 57 E7
Wou-han = Wuhan, China ... 53 B10
Woubrugge, Neths. ... 16 D5
Woudenberg, Neths. ... 16 D6
Woudsend, Neths. ... 16 C7
Wour, Chad ... 73 D8
Wousi = Wuxi, China ... 53 B13
Wouw, Neths. ... 17 F4
Wowoni, Indonesia ... 57 E6
Woy Woy, Australia ... 91 E5
Wrangel I. = Vrangelya, Ostrov, Russia ... 45 B19
Wrangell, U.S.A. ... 96 C6
Wrangell I., U.S.A. ... 100 B2
Wrangell Mts., U.S.A. ... 96 B5
Wrath, C., U.K. ... 14 C3
Wray, U.S.A. ... 108 E3
Wrekin, The, U.K. ... 12 E5
Wrens, U.S.A. ... 105 J4
Wrexham, U.K. ... 12 D4
Wriezen, Germany ... 18 C10
Wright, Canada ... 100 C4
Wright, Phil. ... 55 F6
Wrightson Mt., U.S.A. ... 111 L8
Wrightwood, U.S.A. ... 113 L9
Wrigley, Canada ... 96 B7
Wrocław, Poland ... 20 D7
Września, Poland ... 20 C7
Wschowa, Poland ... 20 D6
Wu Jiang →, China ... 52 C6
Wu'an, China ... 50 F8
Wubin, Australia ... 89 F2
Wubu, China ... 50 F6
Wuchang, China ... 51 B14
Wucheng, China ... 50 F9
Wuchuan, Guangdong, China ... 53 G8
Wuchuan, Guizhou, China ... 52 C7
Wuchuan, Nei Mongol Zizhiqu, China ... 50 D6
Wudi, China ... 51 F9
Wuding, China ... 52 E4
Wuding He →, China ... 50 F6
Wudu, China ... 50 H3
Wufeng, China ... 53 B8
Wugang, China ... 53 D8
Wugong Shan, China ... 53 D9
Wuhan, China ... 53 B10
Wuhe, China ... 51 H9
Wuhsi = Wuxi, China ... 53 B13
Wuhu, China ... 53 B12
Wujiang, China ... 53 B13
Wukari, Nigeria ... 79 D6
Wulajie, China ... 51 B14
Wulanbulang, China ... 50 D6
Wulehe, Ghana ... 79 D4
Wulian, China ... 51 G10
Wuliang Shan, China ... 52 E3
Wuliaru, Indonesia ... 57 F8
Wulumuchi = Ürümqi, China ... 44 E9
Wum, Cameroon ... 79 D7
Wuming, China ... 52 F7
Wuning, China ... 53 C10
Wunnummin L., Canada ... 98 B2
Wunsiedel, Germany ... 19 E8
Wunstorf, Germany ... 18 C5
Wuntho, Burma ... 61 H19

Wuping, China ... 53 E11
Wuppertal, Germany ... 18 D3
Wuppertal, S. Africa ... 84 E2
Wuqing, China ... 51 E9
Würenlingen, Switz. ... 23 A6
Wurung, Australia ... 90 B3
Würzburg, Germany ... 19 F5
Wushan, Gansu, China ... 50 G3
Wushan, Sichuan, China ... 52 B7
Wusuli Jiang = Ussuri →, Asia ... 48 A7
Wutach →, Germany ... 19 H4
Wutai, China ... 50 E7
Wuting = Huimin, China ... 51 F9
Wutong, China ... 53 E8
Wutonghaolai, China ... 51 C11
Wutongqiao, China ... 52 C4
Wuustwezel, Belgium ... 17 F5
Wuwei, Anhui, China ... 53 B11
Wuwei, Gansu, China ... 54 C5
Wuxi, Jiangsu, China ... 53 B13
Wuxi, Sichuan, China ... 52 B7
Wuxiang, China ... 50 F7
Wuxing, China ... 53 B13
Wuxuan, China ... 52 F7
Wuyang, China ... 50 H7
Wuyi, Hebei, China ... 50 F8
Wuyi, Zhejiang, China ... 53 C12
Wuyi Shan, China ... 53 D11
Wuyo, Nigeria ... 79 C7
Wuyuan, Jiangxi, China ... 53 C11
Wuyuan, Nei Mongol Zizhiqu, China ... 50 D5
Wuzhai, China ... 50 E6
Wuzhi Shan, China ... 54 E5
Wuzhong, China ... 50 E4
Wuzhou, China ... 53 F8
Wyaaba Cr. →, Australia ... 90 B3
Wyalkatchem, Australia ... 89 F2
Wyalusing, U.S.A. ... 107 E8
Wyandotte, U.S.A. ... 104 D4
Wyandra, Australia ... 91 D4
Wyangala Res., Australia ... 91 E4
Wyara, L., Australia ... 91 D3
Wycheproof, Australia ... 91 F3
Wye →, U.K. ... 13 F5
Wyemandoo, Australia ... 89 E2
Wyk, Germany ... 18 A4
Wymondham, U.K. ... 13 E7
Wymore, U.S.A. ... 108 E6
Wynbring, Australia ... 91 E1
Wyndham, Australia ... 88 C4
Wyndham, N.Z. ... 87 M2
Wyndmere, U.S.A. ... 108 B6
Wynne, U.S.A. ... 109 H9
Wynnum, Australia ... 91 D5
Wynyard, Australia ... 90 G4
Wynyard, Canada ... 101 C8
Wyola, L., Australia ... 89 E5
Wyoming □, U.S.A. ... 110 E10
Wyong, Australia ... 91 E5
Wyszków, Poland ... 20 C11
Wyszogród, Poland ... 20 C10
Wytheville, U.S.A. ... 104 G5

X

Xaçmaz, Azerbaijan ... 43 K9
Xai-Xai, Mozam. ... 85 D5
Xainza, China ... 54 C3
Xambioá, Brazil ... 122 C2
Xangongo, Angola ... 84 B2
Xankändi, Azerbaijan ... 67 C12
Xanlar, Azerbaijan ... 43 K8
Xanten, Germany ... 18 D2
Xánthi, Greece ... 39 H7
Xanthos, Turkey ... 66 D3
Xapuri, Brazil ... 124 C4
Xar Moron He →, China ... 51 C11
Xau, L., Botswana ... 84 C3
Xavantina, Brazil ... 127 A5
Xenia, U.S.A. ... 104 F4
Xeropotamos →, Cyprus ... 37 E11
Xhora, S. Africa ... 85 E4
Xhumo, Botswana ... 84 C3
Xi Jiang →, China ... 53 F9
Xi Xian, Henan, China ... 53 A10
Xi Xian, Shanxi, China ... 50 F6
Xia Xian, China ... 50 G6
Xiachengzi, China ... 51 B16
Xiachuan Dao, China ... 53 G9
Xiaguan, China ... 52 E3
Xiajiang, China ... 53 D10
Xiajin, China ... 50 F8
Xiamen, China ... 53 E12
Xi'an, China ... 50 G5
Xian Xian, China ... 50 E9
Xianfeng, China ... 52 C7
Xiang Jiang →, China ... 53 C9
Xiangcheng, Henan, China ... 50 H8
Xiangcheng, Henan, China ... 50 H7
Xiangcheng, Sichuan, China ... 52 C2
Xiangdu, China ... 52 F6
Xiangfan, China ... 53 A9
Xianghuang Qi, China ... 50 C7
Xiangning, China ... 50 G6
Xiangquan, China ... 50 F7
Xiangshan, China ... 53 C13
Xiangshui, China ... 51 G10
Xiangtan, China ... 53 D9
Xiangxiang, China ... 53 D9

Xiangyin, China ... 53 C9
Xiangyun, China ... 52 E3
Xiangzhou, China ... 52 F7
Xianju, China ... 53 C13
Xianning, China ... 53 C10
Xianshui He →, China ... 52 B3
Xianyang, China ... 50 G5
Xianyou, China ... 53 E12
Xiao Hinggan Ling, China ... 54 B7
Xiao Xian, China ... 50 G9
Xiaofeng, China ... 53 B12
Xiaogan, China ... 53 B9
Xiaojin, China ... 52 B4
Xiaolan, China ... 53 F9
Xiaoshan, China ... 53 B13
Xiaoyi, China ... 50 F6
Xiapu, China ... 53 D12
Xiawa, China ... 51 C11
Xiayi, China ... 50 G9
Xichang, China ... 52 D4
Xichong, China ... 52 B5
Xichuan, China ... 50 H6
Xiemahe, China ... 53 B8
Xieng Khouang, Laos ... 58 C4
Xifei He →, China ... 50 H9
Xifeng, Guizhou, China ... 52 D6
Xifeng, Liaoning, China ... 51 C13
Xifengzhen, China ... 50 G4
Xigazê, China ... 54 D3
Xihe, China ... 50 G3
Xihua, China ... 50 H8
Xiliao He →, China ... 51 C12
Xilin, China ... 52 E5
Xilókastron, Greece ... 39 L5
Xin Jiang →, China ... 53 C11
Xin Xian, China ... 50 E7
Xinavane, Mozam. ... 85 D5
Xinbin, China ... 51 D13
Xincai, China ... 53 A10
Xinchang, China ... 53 C13
Xincheng, Guangxi Zhuangzu, China ... 52 E7
Xincheng, Jiangxi, China ... 53 D10
Xinfeng, Guangdong, China ... 53 E10
Xinfeng, Jiangxi, China ... 53 D11
Xinfeng, Jiangxi, China ... 53 E10
Xing Xian, China ... 50 E6
Xing'an, Guangxi Zhuangzu, China ... 53 E8
Xingan, Jiangxi, China ... 53 D10
Xingcheng, China ... 51 D11
Xingguo, China ... 53 D10
Xinghe, China ... 50 D7
Xinghua, China ... 51 H10
Xinghua Wan, China ... 53 E12
Xinglong, China ... 51 D9
Xingning, China ... 53 E10
Xingping, China ... 50 G5
Xingren, China ... 52 E5
Xingshan, China ... 53 B8
Xingtai, China ... 50 F8
Xingu →, Brazil ... 121 D7
Xingyang, China ... 50 G7
Xinhe, China ... 50 F8
Xinhua, China ... 53 D8
Xinhuang, China ... 52 D7
Xinhui, China ... 53 F9
Xining, China ... 54 C5
Xinjiang, China ... 50 G6
Xinjiang Uygur Zizhiqu □, China ... 54 B3
Xinjie, China ... 52 D3
Xinjin, Liaoning, China ... 51 E11
Xinjin, Sichuan, China ... 52 B4
Xinkai He →, China ... 51 C12
Xinle, China ... 50 E8
Xinlitun, China ... 51 D12
Xinlong, China ... 52 B3
Xinmin, China ... 51 D12
Xinning, China ... 53 D8
Xinping, China ... 52 E3
Xinshao, China ... 53 D8
Xintai, China ... 51 G9
Xintian, China ... 53 E9
Xinxiang, China ... 50 G7
Xinxing, China ... 53 F9
Xinyang, China ... 53 A10
Xinye, China ... 53 A9
Xinyi, China ... 53 F8
Xinyu, China ... 53 D10
Xinzhan, China ... 51 C14
Xinzheng, China ... 50 G7
Xinzhou, China ... 53 B10
Xinzhu, Taiwan ... 53 E13
Xiong Xian, China ... 50 E9
Xiongyuecheng, China ... 51 D12
Xiping, Henan, China ... 50 H8
Xiping, Henan, China ... 50 H6
Xiping, Zhejiang, China ... 53 C12
Xique-Xique, Brazil ... 122 D3
Xiruá →, Brazil ... 124 B4
Xisha Qundao = Hsisha Chuntao, Pac. Oc. ... 56 A4
Xishui, China ... 53 B10
Xituozhen, China ... 52 B7
Xiuning, China ... 53 C12
Xiuren, China ... 53 E8
Xiushan, China ... 52 C7
Xiushui, China ... 53 C10
Xiuwen, China ... 52 D6
Xiuyan, China ... 51 D12
Xixabangma Feng, China ... 61 E14
Xixia, China ... 50 H6
Xixiang, China ... 50 H4

Xiyang, China ... 50 F7
Xizang □, China ... 54 C3
Xlendi, Malta ... 37 C1
Xu Jiang →, China ... 53 D11
Xuan Loc, Vietnam ... 59 G6
Xuancheng, China ... 53 B12
Xuan'en, China ... 52 C7
Xuanhan, China ... 52 B6
Xuanhua, China ... 50 D8
Xuchang, China ... 50 G7
Xudat, Azerbaijan ... 43 K9
Xuefeng Shan, China ... 53 D8
Xuejiaping, China ... 53 B8
Xun Jiang →, China ... 53 F8
Xun Xian, China ... 50 G8
Xundian, China ... 52 E4
Xunwu, China ... 53 E10
Xunyang, China ... 50 H5
Xunyi, China ... 50 G5
Xupu, China ... 53 D8
Xushui, China ... 50 E8
Xuwen, China ... 53 G8
Xuyong, China ... 52 C5
Xuzhou, China ... 51 G9
Xylophagou, Cyprus ... 37 E12

Y

Ya Xian, China ... 58 C7
Yaamba, Australia ... 90 C5
Ya'an, China ... 52 C4
Yaapeet, Australia ... 91 F3
Yabassi, Cameroon ... 79 E6
Yabelo, Ethiopia ... 77 G4
Yablonovy Ra. = Yablonovyy Khrebet, Russia ... 45 D12
Yablonovyy Khrebet, Russia ... 45 D12
Yabrai Shan, China ... 50 E2
Yabrūd, Syria ... 69 B5
Yacuiba, Bolivia ... 126 A3
Yacuma →, Bolivia ... 125 C4
Yadgir, India ... 60 L10
Yadkin →, U.S.A. ... 105 H5
Yadrin, Russia ... 42 C8
Yagaba, Ghana ... 79 C4
Yagodnoye, Russia ... 45 C15
Yagoua, Cameroon ... 80 B3
Yaguas →, Peru ... 120 D4
Yaha, Thailand ... 59 J3
Yahila, Zaïre ... 82 B1
Yahk, Canada ... 100 D5
Yahotyn, Ukraine ... 41 G6
Yahuma, Zaïre ... 80 D4
Yahyalı, Turkey ... 66 C6
Yaita, Japan ... 49 F9
Yaiza, Canary Is. ... 36 F6
Yajiang, China ... 52 B3
Yajua, Nigeria ... 79 C7
Yakima, U.S.A. ... 110 C3
Yakima →, U.S.A. ... 110 C3
Yako, Burkina Faso ... 78 C4
Yakoruda, Bulgaria ... 39 G6
Yakovlevka, Russia ... 48 B6
Yaku-Shima, Japan ... 49 J5
Yakut, U.S.A. ... 96 C6
Yakutia = Sakha □, Russia ... 45 C13
Yakutsk, Russia ... 45 C13
Yala, Thailand ... 59 J3
Yalbalgo, Australia ... 89 E1
Yalboroo, Australia ... 90 C4
Yale, U.S.A. ... 106 C4
Yalgoo, Australia ... 89 E2
Yalinga, C.A.R. ... 73 C9
Yalkubul, Punta, Mexico ... 115 C7
Yalleroi, Australia ... 90 C4
Yalobusha →, U.S.A. ... 109 J9
Yalong Jiang →, China ... 52 D3
Yalova, Turkey ... 66 B3
Yalpuh, Ozero, Ukraine ... 38 D11
Yalta, Ukraine ... 41 K8
Yalu Jiang →, China ... 51 E13
Yalutorovsk, Russia ... 44 D7
Yalvaç, Turkey ... 66 C4
Yam Ha Melah = Dead Sea, Asia ... 69 D4
Yam Kinneret, Israel ... 69 C4
Yamada, Japan ... 49 H5
Yamagata, Japan ... 48 E10
Yamagata □, Japan ... 48 E10
Yamaguchi, Japan ... 49 G5
Yamaguchi □, Japan ... 49 G5
Yamal, Poluostrov, Russia ... 44 B8
Yamal Pen. = Yamal, Poluostrov, Russia ... 44 B8
Yamanashi □, Japan ... 49 G9
Yamantau, Gora, Russia ... 44 D6
Yamba, N.S.W., Australia ... 91 D5
Yamba, S. Austral., Australia ... 91 E3
Yambah, Australia ... 90 C1
Yambarran Ra., Australia ... 88 C5
Yâmbiô, Sudan ... 77 G2
Yambol, Bulgaria ... 38 G9
Yamdena, Indonesia ... 57 F8
Yame, Japan ... 49 H5
Yamethin, Burma ... 61 J20
Yami, Nigeria ... 79 C6
Yamma-Yamma, L., Australia ... 91 D3
Yamoussoukro, Ivory C. ... 78 D4
Yampa →, U.S.A. ... 110 F9

Yampi Sd., Australia 88 C3
Yampil, Moldova 41 H5
Yampol = Yampil, Moldova 41 H5
Yamrat, Nigeria 79 C6
Yamrukchal, Bulgaria 38 G7
Yamuna →, India 63 G9
Yamzho Yumco, China .. 54 D4
Yan, Nigeria 79 C7
Yana →, Russia 45 B14
Yanac, Australia 91 F3
Yanagawa, Japan 49 H5
Yanai, Japan 49 H6
Yan'an, China 50 F5
Yanbian, China 52 D3
Yanbu 'al Baḥr, Si. Arabia 64 F3
Yancannia, Australia 91 E3
Yanchang, China 50 F6
Yancheng, Henan, China . 50 H7
Yancheng, Jiangsu, China 51 H11
Yanchi, China 50 F4
Yanchuan, China 50 F6
Yanco Cr. →, Australia . 91 F4
Yandal, Australia 89 E3
Yandanooka, Australia .. 89 E2
Yandaran, Australia 90 C5
Yandoon, Burma 61 L19
Yanfeng, China 52 E3
Yanfolila, Mali 78 C3
Yang Xian, China 50 H4
Yangambi, Zaïre 82 B1
Yangbi, China 52 E2
Yangcheng, China 50 G7
Yangch'ü = Taiyuan, China 50 F7
Yangchun, China 53 F8
Yanggao, China 50 D7
Yanggu, China 50 F8
Yangjiang, China 53 G8
Yangliuqing, China 51 E9
Yangon = Rangoon, Burma 61 L20
Yangping, China 53 B8
Yangpingguan, China ... 50 H4
Yangquan, China 50 F7
Yangshan, China 53 E9
Yangshuo, China 53 E8
Yangtze Kiang = Chang Jiang →, China .. 53 B13
Yangxin, China 53 C10
Yangyang, S. Korea 51 E15
Yangyuan, China 50 D8
Yangzhou, China 53 A12
Yanhe, China 52 C7
Yanji, China 51 C15
Yanjin, China 52 C5
Yanjing, China 52 C2
Yankton, U.S.A. 108 D6
Yanna, Australia 91 D4
Yanonge, Zaïre 82 B1
Yanqi, China 54 B3
Yanqing, China 50 D8
Yanshan, Hebei, China . 51 E9
Yanshan, Jiangxi, China 53 C11
Yanshan, Yunnan, China . 52 F5
Yanshou, China 51 B15
Yantabulla, Australia 91 D4
Yantai, China 51 F11
Yanting, China 52 B5
Yantra →, Bulgaria ... 38 F8
Yanwa, China 52 D2
Yanykurgan, Kazakhstan . 44 E7
Yanyuan, China 52 D3
Yanzhou, China 50 G9
Yao, Chad 73 F8
Yao Xian, China 50 G5
Yao Yai, Ko, Thailand .. 59 J2
Yao'an, China 52 E3
Yaodu, China 52 A5
Yaoundé, Cameroon 79 E7
Yaowan, China 51 G10
Yap I., Pac. Oc. 92 G5
Yapen, Indonesia 57 E9
Yapen, Selat, Indonesia . 57 E9
Yappar →, Australia .. 90 B3
Yaqui →, Mexico 114 B2
Yar-Sale, Russia 44 C8
Yaracuy □, Venezuela . 120 A4
Yaracuy →, Venezuela . 120 A4
Yaraka, Australia 90 C3
Yaransk, Russia 42 B8
Yardea P.O., Australia . 91 E2
Yare →, U.K. 13 E9
Yaremcha, Ukraine 41 H3
Yarensk, Russia 44 C5
Yarí →, Colombia 120 C3
Yaritagua, Venezuela 120 A4
Yarkand = Shache, China 54 C2
Yarker, Canada 107 B8
Yarkhun →, Pakistan . 63 A5
Yarmouth, Canada 99 D6
Yarmūk →, Syria 69 C4
Yaroslavl, Russia 42 B4
Yarqa, W. →, Egypt .. 69 F2
Yarra Yarra Lakes, Australia 89 E2
Yarraden, Australia 90 A3
Yarraloola, Australia ... 88 D2
Yarram, Australia 91 F4
Yarraman, Australia 91 D5
Yarranvale, Australia ... 91 D4
Yarras, Australia 91 E5
Yarrowmere, Australia . 90 C4
Yartsevo, Russia 40 E7
Yartsevo, Russia 45 C10
Yarumal, Colombia 120 B2
Yasawa Group, Fiji 87 C7

Yaselda, Belarus 41 F4
Yashi, Nigeria 79 C6
Yashkul, Russia 43 G7
Yasin, Pakistan 63 A5
Yasinovataya, Ukraine .. 41 H9
Yasinski, L., Canada 98 B4
Yasinya, Ukraine 41 H3
Yasothon, Thailand 58 E5
Yass, Australia 91 E4
Yata →, Bolivia 125 C4
Yatağan, Turkey 66 D3
Yates Center, U.S.A. ... 109 G7
Yathkyed L., Canada ... 101 A9
Yatsushiro, Japan 49 H5
Yatta Plateau, Kenya ... 82 C4
Yauca, Peru 124 D3
Yauya, Peru 124 B2
Yauyos, Peru 124 C2
Yavari →, Peru 124 A3
Yavatmal, India 60 J11
Yavne, Israel 69 D3
Yavoriv, Ukraine 41 H2
Yavorov = Yavoriv, Ukraine 41 H2
Yavuzeli, Turkey 66 D7
Yawatahama, Japan 49 H6
Yawri B., S. Leone 78 D2
Yaxi, China 52 D6
Yayama-Rettō, Japan .. 49 M1
Yazd, Iran 65 D7
Yazd □, Iran 65 D7
Yazoo →, U.S.A. 109 J9
Yazoo City, U.S.A. 109 J9
Yding Skovhøj, Denmark . 9 J13
Ye Xian, Henan, China .. 50 H7
Ye Xian, Shandong, China 51 F10
Yealering, Australia 89 F2
Yechŏn, S. Korea 51 F15
Yecla, Spain 29 G3
Yécora, Mexico 114 B3
Yedintsy = Edinița, Moldova 41 H4
Yeeda, Australia 88 C3
Yeelanna, Australia 91 E2
Yefremov, Russia 42 D4
Yegorlyk →, Russia .. 43 G5
Yegorlykskaya, Russia .. 43 G5
Yegoryevsk, Russia 42 C4
Yegros, Paraguay 126 B4
Yehuda, Midbar, Israel . 69 D4
Yei, Sudan 77 G3
Yei, Nahr →, Sudan .. 77 F3
Yejmiadzin, Armenia ... 43 K7
Yekaterinburg, Russia .. 44 D7
Yekaterinodar = Krasnodar, Russia ... 43 H4
Yekhegnadzor, Armenia . 67 C11
Yelabuga, Russia 42 C11
Yelan, Russia 42 E6
Yelanskoye, Russia 45 C13
Yelarbon, Australia 91 D5
Yelatma, Russia 42 C5
Yelcho, L., Chile 128 B2
Yelets, Russia 42 D4
Yélimané, Mali 78 B2
Yelizavetgrad = Kirovohrad, Ukraine ... 41 H7
Yell, U.K. 14 A7
Yell Sd., U.K. 14 A7
Yellow Sea, China 51 G12
Yellowhead Pass, Canada . 100 C5
Yellowknife, Canada ... 100 A6
Yellowknife →, Canada . 100 A6
Yellowstone →, U.S.A. 108 B3
Yellowstone L., U.S.A. . 110 D8
Yellowstone National Park, U.S.A. 110 D8
Yellowtail Res., U.S.A. . 110 D9
Yelnya, Russia 40 E7
Yelsk, Belarus 41 G5
Yelvertoft, Australia ... 90 C2
Yelwa, Nigeria 79 C5
Yemen ■, Asia 68 E3
Yen Bai, Vietnam 58 B5
Yenakiyeve, Ukraine ... 41 H10
Yenakiyevo = Yenakiyeve, Ukraine 41 H10
Yenangyaung, Burma ... 61 J19
Yenbo = Yanbu 'al Baḥr, Si. Arabia 64 F3
Yenda, Australia 91 E4
Yendéré, Ivory C. 78 C4
Yendi, Ghana 79 D4
Yenice, Ankara, Turkey . 66 C5
Yenice, Çanakkale, Turkey 66 C2
Yenice →, Turkey 66 D6
Yenisaía, Greece 39 H7
Yenişehir, Turkey 66 B3
Yenisey →, Russia ... 44 B9
Yeniseysk, Russia 45 D10
Yeniseyskiy Zaliv, Russia . 44 B9
Yennádhi, Greece 37 C9
Yenne, France 27 C9
Yenotayevka, Russia ... 43 G8
Yenyuka, Russia 45 D13
Yeo, L., Australia 89 E3
Yeola, India 60 J9
Yeoryioúpolis, Greece .. 37 D6
Yeovil, U.K. 13 G5
Yepes, Spain 28 F1
Yeppoon, Australia 90 C5
Yeráki, Greece 39 N4
Yerbent, Turkmenistan . 44 F6
Yerbogachen, Russia ... 45 C11
Yerevan, Armenia 43 K7

Yerilla, Australia 89 E3
Yerköy, Turkey 66 C6
Yermak, Kazakhstan ... 44 D8
Yermakovo, Russia 45 D13
Yermo, U.S.A. 113 L10
Yerofey Pavlovich, Russia 45 D13
Yerólakkos, Cyprus 37 D12
Yeropol, Russia 45 C17
Yeropótamos →, Greece 37 D6
Yeroskipos, Cyprus 37 E11
Yerushalayim = Jerusalem, Israel 69 D4
Yerville, France 24 C7
Yes Tor, U.K. 13 G4
Yesan, S. Korea 51 F14
Yeşilhisar, Turkey 66 C6
Yeşilırmak →, Turkey . 66 B7
Yeşilkent, Turkey 66 D7
Yesnogorsk, Russia 42 C3
Yeso, U.S.A. 109 H2
Yessentuki, Russia 43 H6
Yessey, Russia 45 C11
Yeste, Spain 29 G2
Yeu, I. d', France 24 F4
Yevlakh = Yevlax, Azerbaijan 43 K8
Yevlax, Azerbaijan 43 K8
Yevpatoriya, Ukraine .. 41 K7
Yeya →, Russia 43 G4
Yeysk, Russia 43 G4
Yezd = Yazd, Iran 65 D7
Yezerishche, Belarus ... 40 E5
Yhati, Paraguay 126 B4
Yhú, Paraguay 127 B4
Yi →, Uruguay 126 C4
Yi 'Allaq, G., Egypt ... 69 E2
Yi He →, China 51 G10
Yi Xian, Anhui, China . 53 C11
Yi Xian, Hebei, China .. 50 E8
Yi Xian, Liaoning, China . 51 D11
Yialí, Greece 39 N10
Yialiás →, Cyprus 37 D12
Yi'allaq, G., Egypt 76 H8
Yialousa, Cyprus 37 D13
Yiáltra, Greece 39 L5
Yianisádhes, Greece ... 37 D8
Yiannitsa, Greece 39 J5
Yibin, China 52 C5
Yichang, China 53 B8
Yicheng, Henan, China . 53 B9
Yicheng, Shanxi, China . 50 G6
Yichuan, China 50 F6
Yichun, Heilongjiang, China 54 B7
Yichun, Jiangxi, China . 53 D10
Yidu, Hubei, China 53 B8
Yidu, Shandong, China . 51 F10
Yidun, China 52 B2
Yihuang, China 53 D11
Yijun, China 50 G5
Yilan, China 54 B7
Yilan, Taiwan 53 E13
Yildizeli, Turkey 66 C7
Yiliang, Yunnan, China . 52 D5
Yiliang, Yunnan, China . 52 E4
Yilong, China 52 B6
Yimen, China 52 E4
Yimianpo, China 51 B15
Yinchuan, China 50 E4
Yindarlgooda, L., Australia 89 F3
Ying He →, China 53 H9
Ying Xian, China 50 E7
Yingcheng, China 53 B9
Yingde, China 53 E9
Yingjiang, China 52 E1
Yingjing, China 52 C4
Yingkou, China 51 D12
Yingshan, Henan, China 53 B9
Yingshan, Hubei, China . 53 B10
Yingshan, Sichuan, China 52 B6
Yingshang, China 53 A11
Yingtan, China 53 D6
Yining, China 44 E9
Yinmabin, Burma 61 H19
Yinnietharra, Australia . 88 D2
Yiofiros →, Greece ... 37 D7
Yioúra, Greece 39 K7
Yipinglang, China 52 E3
Yirga Alem, Ethiopia .. 77 F4
Yishan, China 52 E7
Yishui, China 51 G10
Yíthion, Greece 39 N5
Yitiaoshan, China 50 F3
Yitong, China 51 C13
Yiwu, China 53 C13
Yixing, China 53 B12
Yiyang, Henan, China . 50 G7
Yiyang, Hunan, China . 53 C9
Yiyang, Jiangxi, China . 53 C11
Yizhang, China 53 E9
Yizheng, China 53 A12
Yli-Kitka, Finland 8 C23
Ylitornio, Finland 8 C20
Ylivieska, Finland 8 D21
Yngaren, Sweden 11 F10
Ynykchanskiy, Russia .. 45 C14
Yoakum, U.S.A. 109 L6
Yobe □, Nigeria 79 C7
Yog Pt., Phil. 57 B6
Yogan, Togo 79 D5
Yogyakarta, Indonesia . 57 G14
Yoho Nat. Park, Canada 100 C5
Yojoa, L. de, Honduras . 116 D2

Yŏju, S. Korea 51 F14
Yokadouma, Cameroon . 80 D2
Yokkaichi, Japan 49 G8
Yoko, Cameroon 79 D7
Yokohama, Japan 49 G9
Yokosuka, Japan 49 G9
Yokote, Japan 48 E10
Yola, Nigeria 79 D7
Yolaina, Cordillera de, Nic. 116 D3
Yonago, Japan 49 G6
Yonaguni-Jima, Japan .. 49 M1
Yŏnan, N. Korea 51 F14
Yonezawa, Japan 48 F10
Yong Peng, Malaysia .. 59 L4
Yong Sata, Thailand ... 59 J2
Yongampo, N. Korea .. 51 E13
Yong'an, China 53 E11
Yongcheng, China 50 H9
Yŏngch'ŏn, S. Korea .. 51 G15
Yongchuan, China 52 C5
Yongdeng, China 50 F2
Yongding, China 53 E11
Yŏngdŏk, S. Korea 51 F15
Yŏngdŭngp'o, S. Korea . 51 F14
Yongfeng, China 53 D10
Yongfu, China 52 E7
Yonghe, China 50 F6
Yŏnghŭng, N. Korea .. 51 E14
Yongji, China 50 G6
Yŏngju, S. Korea 51 F15
Yongkang, Yunnan, China 52 E2
Yongkang, Zhejiang, China 53 C13
Yongnian, China 50 F8
Yongning, Guangxi Zhuangzu, China 52 F7
Yongning, Ningxia Huizu, China 50 E4
Yongping, China 52 E2
Yongqing, China 50 E9
Yongren, China 52 D3
Yongshan, China 52 C4
Yongsheng, China 52 D3
Yongshun, China 52 C7
Yongtai, China 53 E12
Yongxin, China 53 D10
Yongxing, China 53 D9
Yongxiu, China 53 C10
Yonibana, S. Leone ... 78 D2
Yonkers, U.S.A. 107 F11
Yonne □, France 25 E10
Yonne →, France 25 D9
York, Australia 89 F2
York, U.K. 12 D6
York, Ala., U.S.A. 105 J1
York, Nebr., U.S.A. ... 108 E6
York, Pa., U.S.A. 104 F7
York, C., Australia 90 A3
York, Kap, Greenland .. 4 B4
York Sd., Australia 88 B4
Yorke Pen., Australia .. 91 E2
Yorkshire Wolds, U.K. . 12 D7
Yorkton, Canada 101 C8
Yorktown, U.S.A. 109 L6
Yorkville, U.S.A. 112 G3
Yornup, Australia 89 F2
Yoro, Honduras 116 C2
Yoron-Jima, Japan 49 L4
Yos Sudarso, Pulau, Indonesia 57 F9
Yosemite National Park, U.S.A. 111 H4
Yosemite Village, U.S.A. 112 H7
Yoshkar Ola, Russia ... 42 B8
Yŏsu, S. Korea 51 G14
Yotala, Bolivia 125 D4
Yotvata, Israel 69 F4
You Xian, China 53 D9
Youbou, Canada 100 D4
Youghal, Ireland 15 E4
Youghal B., Ireland ... 15 E4
Youkounkoun, Guinea . 78 C2
Young, Australia 91 E4
Young, Canada 101 C7
Young, Uruguay 126 C4
Younghusband, L., Australia 91 E2
Younghusband Pen., Australia 91 F2
Youngstown, Canada .. 101 C6
Youngstown, N.Y., U.S.A. 106 C5
Youngstown, Ohio, U.S.A. 106 E4
Youngsville, U.S.A. ... 106 E5
Youssoufia, Morocco .. 74 B3
Youxi, China 53 D12
Youyang, China 52 C7
Youyu, China 50 D7
Yoweragabbie, Australia 89 E2
Yozgat, Turkey 66 C6
Ypané →, Paraguay .. 126 A4
Yport, France 24 C7
Ypres = Ieper, Belgium . 17 G1
Ypsilanti, U.S.A. 104 D4
Yreka, U.S.A. 110 F2
Ysleta, U.S.A. 111 L10
Yssingeaux, France ... 27 C8
Ystad, Sweden 11 J7
Ysyk-Köl, Ozero, Kyrgyzstan 44 E8
Ythan →, U.K. 14 D7
Ytterhogdal, Sweden .. 10 B8
Ytyk Kuyel, Russia ... 45 C14
Yu Jiang →, China ... 54 D6
Yu Shan, Taiwan 53 F13

Yu Xian, Hebei, China ... 50 E8
Yu Xian, Henan, China .. 50 G7
Yu Xian, Shanxi, China . 50 E7
Yuan Jiang →, Hunan, China 53 C8
Yuan Jiang →, Yunnan, China 52 F4
Yuan'an, China 53 B8
Yuanjiang, Hunan, China . 53 C9
Yuanjiang, Yunnan, China 52 F4
Yuanli, Taiwan 53 E13
Yuanlin, Taiwan 53 F13
Yuanling, China 53 C8
Yuanmou, China 52 E3
Yuanquan, China 50 G6
Yuanyang, Henan, China . 50 G7
Yuanyang, Yunnan, China 52 F4
Yuba →, U.S.A. 112 F5
Yuba City, U.S.A. 112 F5
Yūbari, Japan 48 C10
Yūbetsu, Japan 48 B11
Yucatán □, Mexico ... 115 C7
Yucatán, Canal de, Caribbean 116 B2
Yucatan Str. = Yucatán, Canal de, Caribbean 116 B2
Yucca, U.S.A. 113 L12
Yucca Valley, U.S.A. .. 113 L10
Yucheng, China 50 F9
Yuci, China 50 F7
Yudino, Russia 44 D7
Yudu, China 53 E10
Yuendumu, Australia .. 88 D5
Yueqing, China 53 C13
Yueqing Wan, China .. 53 C13
Yuexi, Anhui, China ... 53 B11
Yuexi, Sichuan, China . 52 C4
Yueyang, China 53 C9
Yugan, China 53 C11
Yugoslavia ■, Europe . 21 M10
Yuhuan, China 53 C13
Yujiang, China 53 C11
Yukhnov, Russia 42 C2
Yukon →, U.S.A. 96 B3
Yukon Territory □, Canada 96 B6
Yüksekova, Turkey 67 D11
Yukti, Russia 45 C11
Yukuhashi, Japan 49 H5
Yule →, Australia 88 D2
Yuli, Nigeria 79 D7
Yulin, Guangxi Zhuangzu, China 53 F8
Yulin, Shaanxi, China .. 50 E5
Yuma, Ariz., U.S.A. .. 113 N12
Yuma, Colo., U.S.A. .. 108 E3
Yuma, B. de, Dom. Rep. . 117 C6
Yumbe, Uganda 82 B3
Yumbi, Zaïre 82 C2
Yumbo, Colombia 120 C2
Yumen, China 54 C4
Yumurtalık, Turkey ... 66 D6
Yun Ho →, China 51 E9
Yun Xian, Hubei, China . 53 A8
Yun Xian, Yunnan, China 52 E3
Yunak, Turkey 66 C4
Yunan, China 53 F8
Yuncheng, Henan, China 50 G8
Yuncheng, Shanxi, China 50 G6
Yundamindra, Australia . 89 E3
Yunfu, China 53 F9
Yungas, Bolivia 125 D4
Yungay, Chile 126 D1
Yungay, Peru 124 C2
Yunhe, China 53 C12
Yunlin, Taiwan 53 F13
Yunling, China 52 D2
Yunlong, China 52 E2
Yunmeng, China 53 B9
Yunnan □, China 52 E4
Yunquera de Henares, Spain 28 E1
Yunta, Australia 91 E2
Yunxi, China 50 H6
Yunxiao, China 53 F11
Yunyang, China 52 B7
Yuping, China 52 D7
Yupukarri, Guyana 121 C6
Yupyongdong, N. Korea . 51 D15
Yuqing, China 52 D6
Yur, Russia 45 D14
Yurgao, Russia 44 D9
Yuribei, Russia 44 B8
Yurimaguas, Peru 124 B2
Yuryev-Polskiy, Russia . 42 B4
Yuryevets, Russia 42 B6
Yuryung Kaya, Russia . 45 B12
Yuscarán, Honduras ... 116 D2
Yushanzhen, China 52 C7
Yushe, China 50 F7
Yushu, Jilin, China 51 B14
Yushu, Qinghai, China . 54 C4
Yusufeli, Turkey 67 B9
Yutai, China 50 G9
Yutian, China 51 E9
Yuxarı Qarabağ = Nagorno-Karabakh, Azerbaijan 67 C12
Yuxi, China 52 E4
Yuyao, China 53 B13
Yuzawa, Japan 48 E10
Yuzha, Russia 42 B6
Yuzhno-Sakhalinsk, Russia 45 E15
Yvelines □, France ... 25 D8
Yverdon, Switz. 22 C3
Yvetot, France 24 C7
Yvonand, Switz. 22 C3

Zaamslag

Z

Zaamslag, Neths. 17 F3
Zaan →, Neths. 16 D5
Zaandam, Neths. 16 D5
Zab, Monts du, Algeria 75 B6
Žabalj, Serbia, Yug. 21 K10
Žabari, Serbia, Yug. 21 L11
Zabarjad, Egypt 76 C4
Zabaykalsk, Russia 45 E12
Zabid, Yemen 68 E3
Ząbkowice Śląskie, Poland 20 E6
Zabłudów, Poland 20 B13
Zābol, Iran 65 D9
Zābolī, Iran 65 E9
Zabré, Burkina Faso 79 C4
Zabrze, Poland 20 E8
Zacapa, Guatemala 116 D2
Zacapu, Mexico 114 D4
Zacatecas, Mexico 114 C4
Zacatecas □, Mexico 114 C4
Zacatecoluca, El Salv. 116 D2
Zacoalco, Mexico 114 C4
Zacualtipán, Mexico 115 C5
Zadar, Croatia 33 D12
Zadawa, Nigeria 79 C7
Zadetkyi Kyun, Burma 59 H2
Zadonsk, Russia 42 D4
Zafarqand, Iran 65 C7
Zafra, Spain 31 G4
Żagań, Poland 20 D5
Zagazig, Egypt 76 H7
Zāgheh, Iran 65 C6
Zaghouan, Tunisia 75 A7
Zaglivérion, Greece 39 J6
Zaglou, Algeria 75 C4
Zagnanado, Benin 79 D5
Zagorá, Greece 39 K6
Zagora, Morocco 74 B3
Zagorsk = Sergiyev Posad, Russia 42 B4
Zagreb, Croatia 33 C12
Zāgros, Kūhhā-ye, Iran 65 C6
Zagros Mts. = Zāgros, Kūhhā-ye, Iran 65 C6
Zaguinaso, Ivory C. 78 C3
Zāhedān, Fārs, Iran 65 D7
Zāhedān, Sīstān va Balūchestān, Iran 65 D9
Zahlah, Lebanon 69 B4
Zahna, Germany 18 D8
Zahrez Chergui, Algeria 75 A5
Zahrez Rharbi, Algeria 75 B5
Zainsk, Russia 42 C11
Zaïre ■, Africa 80 E4
Zaïre →, Africa 80 F2
Zaječar, Serbia, Yug. 21 M12
Zakamensk, Russia 45 D11
Zakataly = Zaqatala, Azerbaijan 43 K8
Zakhodnaya Dzvina = Daugava →, Latvia 9 H21
Zākhū, Iraq 67 D10
Zákinthos, Greece 39 M3
Zakopane, Poland 20 F9
Zákros, Greece 37 D8
Zala →, Hungary 21 J7
Zalaegerszeg, Hungary 21 J6
Zalalövö, Hungary 21 J6
Zalamea de la Serena, Spain 31 G5
Zalamea la Real, Spain 31 H4
Žalec, Slovenia 33 B12
Zaleshchiki = Zalishchyky, Ukraine 41 H3
Zalingei, Sudan 73 F9
Zalishchyky, Ukraine 41 H3
Zaltbommel, Neths. 16 E6
Zambeke, Zaïre 82 B2
Zambeze →, Africa 83 F4
Zambezi = Zambeze →, Africa 83 F4
Zambezi, Zambia 81 G4
Zambezia □, Mozam. 83 F4
Zambia ■, Africa 83 E2
Zamboanga, Phil. 55 H5
Zamboanguita, Phil. 55 G5
Zambrano, Colombia 120 B3
Zambrów, Poland 20 C12
Zametchino, Russia 42 D6
Zamora, Ecuador 120 D2
Zamora, Mexico 114 C4
Zamora, Spain 30 D5
Zamora □, Spain 30 D5
Zamora-Chinchipe □, Ecuador 120 D2
Zamość, Poland 20 E13
Zamuro, Sierra del, Venezuela 121 C5
Zan, Ghana 79 D4
Zanaga, Congo 80 E2
Záncara →, Spain 29 F1
Zandijk, Neths. 16 D5
Zandvoort, Neths. 16 D5
Zanesville, U.S.A. 106 G2
Zangābād, Iran 64 B5
Zangue →, Mozam. 83 F4
Zanjān, Iran 67 D13
Zanjān □, Iran 65 B6
Zannone, Italy 34 B6
Zante = Zákinthos, Greece 39 M3
Zanthus, Australia 89 F3
Zanzibar, Tanzania 82 D4
Zanzūr, Libya 75 B7
Zaouiet El-Kala = Bordj Omar Driss, Algeria 75 C6
Zaouiet Reggane, Algeria 75 C5
Zaoyang, China 53 A9
Zaozhuang, China 51 G9
Zap Suyu = Kabīr, Zab al →, Iraq 67 D10
Zapadna Morava →, Serbia, Yug. 21 M11
Zapadnaya Dvina, Russia 40 D7
Zapadnaya Dvina = Daugava →, Latvia 9 H21
Západné Beskydy, Europe 20 F9
Zapala, Argentina 128 A2
Zapaleri, Cerro, Bolivia 126 A2
Zapata, U.S.A. 109 M5
Zapatón →, Spain 31 G4
Zapiga, Chile 124 D4
Zaporizhzhya, Ukraine 41 J8
Zaporozhye = Zaporizhzhya, Ukraine 41 J8
Zapponeta, Italy 35 A8
Zaqatala, Azerbaijan 43 K8
Zara, Turkey 66 C7
Zaragoza, Colombia 120 B3
Zaragoza, Coahuila, Mexico 114 B4
Zaragoza, Nuevo León, Mexico 115 C5
Zaragoza, Spain 28 D4
Zaragoza □, Spain 28 D4
Zarand, Kermān, Iran 65 D8
Zarand, Markazī, Iran 65 C6
Zărandului, Munţii, Romania 38 C5
Zaranj, Afghan. 60 D2
Zarasai, Lithuania 9 J22
Zarate, Argentina 126 C4
Zaraysk, Russia 42 C4
Zaraza, Venezuela 121 B4
Zāreh, Iran 65 C6
Zarembo I., U.S.A. 100 B2
Zaria, Nigeria 79 C6
Zarneh, Iran 64 C5
Zarós, Greece 37 D6
Zarqā' →, Jordan 69 C4
Zarrīn, Iran 65 C7
Zaruma, Ecuador 120 D2
Żary, Poland 20 D5
Zarza de Alange, Spain 31 G4
Zarza de Granadilla, Spain 30 E4
Zarzaïtine, Algeria 75 C6
Zarzal, Colombia 120 C2
Zarzis, Tunisia 75 B7
Zas, Spain 30 B2
Zashiversk, Russia 45 C15
Zaskar →, India 63 B7
Zaskar Mts., India 63 C7
Zastron, S. Africa 84 E4
Zaterechnyy, Russia 43 H7
Zavāreh, Iran 65 C7
Zaventem, Belgium 17 G4
Zavetnoye, Russia 43 G6
Zavidovići, Bos.-H. 21 L8
Zavitinsk, Russia 45 D13
Zavodovski, I., Antarctica 5 B1
Zavolzhsk, Russia 42 B6
Zavolzhye, Russia 42 B6
Zawiercie, Poland 20 E9
Zawyet Shammâs, Egypt 76 A2
Zâwyet Um el Rakham, Egypt 76 A2
Zâwyet Ungeîla, Egypt 76 A2
Zāyā, Iraq 64 C5
Zayarsk, Russia 45 D11
Zaysan, Kazakhstan 44 E9
Zaysan, Oz., Kazakhstan 44 E9
Zayü, China 52 C1
Zazir, O. →, Algeria 75 D6
Zbarazh, Ukraine 41 H3
Zbąszyń, Poland 20 C5
Zblewo, Poland 20 B8
Zdolbuniv, Ukraine 41 G4
Ždrelo, Serbia, Yug. 21 L11
Zduńska Wola, Poland 20 D8
Zeballos, Canada 100 D3
Zebediela, S. Africa 85 C4
Zedelgem, Belgium 17 F2
Zeebrugge, Belgium 17 F2
Zeehan, Australia 90 G4
Zeeland, Neths. 17 E7
Zeeland □, Neths. 17 F3
Zeelst, Neths. 17 F6
Zeerust, S. Africa 84 D4
Zefat, Israel 69 C4
Zegdou, Algeria 74 C4
Zege, Ethiopia 77 E4
Zegelsem, Belgium 17 G3
Zégoua, Mali 78 C3
Zehdenick, Germany 18 C9
Zeil, Mt., Australia 88 D5
Zeila, Somali Rep. 68 E3
Zeist, Neths. 16 D6
Zeitz, Germany 18 D8
Zele, Belgium 17 F4
Zelenodolsk, Russia 42 C9
Zelenogorsk, Russia 40 B5
Zelenograd, Russia 42 B3
Zelenogradsk, Russia 9 J19
Zelenokumsk, Russia 43 H6
Zelhem, Neths. 16 D8
Zell, Baden-W., Germany 19 H3
Zell, Rhld-Pfz., Germany 19 E3
Zell am See, Austria 21 H2
Zella-Mehlis, Germany 18 E6
Zelzate, Belgium 17 F3
Zembra, I., Tunisia 75 A7
Zémio, C.A.R. 82 A2
Zemmora, Algeria 75 A5
Zemmur, W. Sahara 74 C2
Zemoul, O. →, Algeria 74 C3
Zemst, Belgium 17 G4
Zemun, Serbia, Yug. 21 L10
Zengbe, Cameroon 79 D7
Zengcheng, China 53 F9
Zenica, Bos.-H. 21 L7
Žepce, Bos.-H. 21 L8
Zeraf, Bahr ez →, Sudan 77 F3
Zerbst, Germany 18 D8
Zermatt, Switz. 22 D5
Zernez, Switz. 23 C10
Zernograd, Russia 43 G5
Zerqani, Albania 39 H3
Zestaponi, Georgia 43 J6
Zetel, Germany 18 B3
Zetten, Neths. 16 E7
Zeulenroda, Germany 18 E7
Zeven, Germany 18 B5
Zevenaar, Neths. 16 E8
Zevenbergen, Neths. 17 E5
Zévio, Italy 32 C8
Zeya, Russia 45 D13
Zeya →, Russia 45 D13
Zêzere →, Portugal 31 F2
Zghartā, Lebanon 69 A4
Zgierz, Poland 20 D9
Zgorzelec, Poland 20 D5
Zhabinka, Belarus 41 F3
Zhailma, Kazakhstan 44 D7
Zhambyl, Kazakhstan 44 E8
Zhangaly, Kazakhstan 43 G10
Zhangaqazaly, Kazakhstan 44 E7
Zhangbei, China 50 D8
Zhangguangcai Ling, China 51 B15
Zhanghua, Taiwan 53 E13
Zhangjiakou, China 50 D8
Zhangping, China 53 E11
Zhangpu, China 53 E11
Zhangwu, China 51 C12
Zhangye, China 54 C5
Zhangzhou, China 53 E11
Zhanhua, China 51 F10
Zhanjiang, China 53 G8
Zhanyi, China 52 E4
Zhanyu, China 51 B12
Zhao Xian, China 50 F8
Zhao'an, China 53 F11
Zhaocheng, China 50 F6
Zhaojue, China 52 C4
Zhaoping, China 53 E8
Zhaoqing, China 53 F9
Zhaotong, China 52 D4
Zhaoyuan, Heilongjiang, China 51 B13
Zhaoyuan, Shandong, China 51 F11
Zharkovskiy, Russia 40 E7
Zhashkiv, Ukraine 41 H6
Zhashui, China 50 H5
Zhayyq →, Kazakhstan 44 E6
Zhdanov = Mariupol, Ukraine 41 J9
Zhecheng, China 50 G8
Zhegao, China 53 B11
Zhejiang □, China 53 C13
Zheleznogorsk, Russia 42 D2
Zheleznogorsk-Ilimskiy, Russia 45 D11
Zheltyye Vody = Zhovti Vody, Ukraine 41 H7
Zhen'an, China 50 H5
Zhenfeng, China 52 E5
Zheng'an, China 52 C6
Zhengding, China 50 E8
Zhenghe, China 53 D12
Zhengyang, China 53 A10
Zhengyangguan, China 53 A11
Zhengzhou, China 50 G7
Zhenhai, China 53 C13
Zhenjiang, China 53 A12
Zhenlai, China 51 B12
Zhenning, China 52 D5
Zhenping, Henan, China 50 H7
Zhenping, Shaanxi, China 52 B7
Zhenxiong, China 52 D5
Zhenyuan, Gansu, China 50 G4
Zhenyuan, Guizhou, China 52 D7
Zherdevka, Russia 42 E5
Zherong, China 53 D12
Zhetiqara, Kazakhstan 44 D7
Zhezqazghan, Kazakhstan 44 E7
Zhidan, China 50 F5
Zhigansk, Russia 45 C13
Zhigulevsk, Russia 42 D9
Zhijiang, Hubei, China 53 B8
Zhijiang, Hunan, China 52 D7
Zhijin, China 52 D5
Zhilinda, Russia 45 C12
Zhirnovsk, Russia 42 E7
Zhitomir = Zhytomyr, Ukraine 41 G5
Zhizdra, Russia 42 D2
Zhlobin, Belarus 41 F6
Zhmerinka = Zhmerynka, Ukraine 41 H5
Zhmerynka, Ukraine 41 H5
Zhodino = Zhodzina, Belarus 40 E5
Zhodzina, Belarus 40 E5
Zhokhova, Ostrov, Russia 45 B16
Zhong Xian, China 52 B7
Zhongdian, China 52 D2
Zhongdong, China 52 F6
Zhongdu, China 52 E7
Zhongning, China 50 F3
Zhongshan, Guangdong, China 53 F9
Zhongshan, Guangxi Zhuangzu, China 53 E8
Zhongtiao Shan, China 50 G6
Zhongwei, China 50 F3
Zhongxiang, China 53 B9
Zhongyang, China 50 F6
Zhoucun, China 51 F9
Zhouning, China 53 D12
Zhoushan Dao, China 53 C14
Zhouzhi, China 50 G5
Zhovti Vody, Ukraine 41 H7
Zhovtneve, Ukraine 41 J7
Zhovtnevoye = Zhovtneve, Ukraine 41 J7
Zhuanghe, China 51 E12
Zhucheng, China 51 G10
Zhugqu, China 50 H3
Zhuhai, China 53 F9
Zhuji, China 53 C13
Zhukovka, Russia 42 D1
Zhumadian, China 50 H8
Zhuo Xian, China 50 E8
Zhuolu, China 50 D8
Zhuozi, China 50 D7
Zhupanovo, Russia 45 D16
Zhushan, China 53 A8
Zhuxi, China 52 A7
Zhuzhou, China 53 D9
Zhytomyr, Ukraine 41 G5
Zi Shui →, China 53 C9
Zīārān, Iran 65 B6
Ziarat, Pakistan 62 D2
Zibo, China 51 F10
Zichang, China 50 F5
Zichem, Belgium 17 F5
Zielona Góra, Poland 20 D5
Zierikzee, Neths. 17 E3
Ziesar, Germany 18 C8
Zifta, Egypt 76 H7
Zigey, Chad 73 F8
Zigong, China 52 C5
Zigui, China 53 B8
Ziguinchor, Senegal 78 C1
Zihuatanejo, Mexico 114 D4
Zijin, China 53 F10
Zile, Turkey 66 B6
Žilina, Slovak Rep. 20 F8
Zillah, Libya 73 C8
Zillertaler Alpen, Austria 19 H7
Zima, Russia 45 D11
Zimane, Adrar in, Algeria 75 D5
Zimapán, Mexico 115 C5
Zimba, Zambia 83 F2
Zimbabwe, Zimbabwe 83 G3
Zimbabwe ■, Africa 83 F2
Zimovniki, Russia 43 G6
Zinal, Switz. 22 D5
Zinder, Niger 79 C6
Zinga, Tanzania 83 D4
Zingem, Belgium 17 G3
Zingst, Germany 18 A8
Ziniaré, Burkina Faso 79 C4
Zinkgruvan, Sweden 11 F9
Zinnowitz, Germany 18 A9
Zion National Park, U.S.A. 111 H7
Zipaquirá, Colombia 120 C3
Zirc, Hungary 21 H7
Žiri, Slovenia 33 B11
Žirje, Croatia 33 E12
Zirl, Austria 19 H7
Ziros, Greece 37 D8
Zitácuaro, Mexico 114 D4
Zitava →, Slovak Rep. 21 G8
Zittau, Germany 18 E10
Zitundo, Mozam. 85 D5
Živinice, Bos.-H. 21 L8
Ziway, L., Ethiopia 77 F4
Zixi, China 53 D11
Zixing, China 53 E9
Ziyang, Shaanxi, China 50 H5
Ziyang, Sichuan, China 52 B5
Ziyun, China 52 E6
Ziz, Oued →, Morocco 74 B4
Zizhixian, China 53 E8
Zizhong, China 52 C5
Zlarin, Croatia 33 E12
Zlatar, Croatia 33 B13
Zlataritsa, Bulgaria 38 F8
Zlatitsa, Bulgaria 38 G7
Zlatograd, Bulgaria 39 H8
Zlatoust, Russia 44 D6
Zletovo, Macedonia 39 H5
Zlin, Czech. 20 F7
Zlītan, Libya 73 B7
Złocieniec, Poland 20 B6
Złoczew, Poland 20 D8
Złotoryja, Poland 20 D5
Złotów, Poland 20 B7
Zmeinogorsk, Kazakhstan 44 D9
Żmigród, Poland 20 D6
Zmiyev, Ukraine 41 H9
Znamenka = Znamyanka, Ukraine 41 H7
Znamyanka, Ukraine 41 H7
Żnin, Poland 20 C7
Znojmo, Czech. 20 G6
Zobeyrī, Iran 64 C5
Zobia, Zaïre 82 B2
Zoetermeer, Neths. 16 D5
Zofingen, Switz. 22 B5
Zogang, China 52 C1
Zogno, Italy 32 C6
Zogqên, China 52 A2
Zolder, Belgium 17 F6
Zollikofen, Switz. 22 C4
Zollikon, Switz. 23 B7
Zolochev = Zolochiv, Ukraine 41 H3
Zolochiv, Ukraine 41 H3
Zolotonosha, Ukraine 41 H7
Zomba, Malawi 83 F4
Zomergem, Belgium 17 F3
Zongo, Zaïre 80 D3
Zonguldak, Turkey 66 B4
Zonhoven, Belgium 17 G6
Zonqor Pt., Malta 37 D2
Zonza, France 27 G13
Zorgo, Burkina Faso 79 C4
Zorita, Spain 31 F5
Zorritos, Peru 124 A1
Zorzor, Liberia 78 D3
Zossen, Germany 18 C9
Zottegem, Belgium 17 G3
Zou Xiang, China 50 G9
Zouar, Chad 73 D8
Zouérate, Mauritania 74 D2
Zousfana, O. →, Algeria 75 B4
Zoushan Dao, China 53 B14
Zoutkamp, Neths. 16 B8
Zrenjanin, Serbia, Yug. 21 K10
Zuarungu, Ghana 79 C4
Zuba, Nigeria 79 D6
Zubayr, Yemen 77 D5
Zubia, Spain 31 H7
Zubtsov, Russia 42 B2
Zudáñez, Bolivia 125 D5
Zuénoula, Ivory C. 78 D3
Zuera, Spain 28 D4
Zuetina = Az Zuwaytīnah, Libya 73 B9
Zufar, Oman 68 D5
Zug, Switz. 23 B7
Zug □, Switz. 23 B7
Zugdidi, Georgia 43 J5
Zugersee, Switz. 23 B7
Zugspitze, Germany 19 H6
Zuid-Holland □, Neths. 16 E5
Zuidbeveland, Neths. 17 F3
Zuidbroek, Neths. 16 B9
Zuidelijk-Flevoland, Neths. 16 D6
Zuidhorn, Neths. 16 B8
Zuidlaarder meer, Neths. 16 B9
Zuidlaren, Neths. 16 B9
Zuidwolde, Neths. 16 C8
Zújar, Spain 29 H2
Zújar →, Spain 31 F5
Zújar, Pantano del, Spain 31 G5
Zula, Eritrea 77 D4
Zulia □, Venezuela 120 B3
Zülpich, Germany 18 E2
Zumaya, Spain 28 B2
Zumbo, Mozam. 83 F3
Zummo, Nigeria 79 D7
Zumpango, Mexico 115 D5
Zundert, Neths. 17 F5
Zungeru, Nigeria 79 D6
Zunhua, China 51 D9
Zuni, U.S.A. 111 J9
Zunyi, China 52 D6
Zuoquan, China 50 F7
Zuozhou, China 52 F6
Županja, Croatia 21 K8
Zurbātīyah, Iraq 67 F12
Zürich, Switz. 23 B7
Zürich □, Switz. 23 B7
Zürichsee, Switz. 23 B7
Zuromin, Poland 20 B9
Zuru, Nigeria 79 C6
Zurzach, Switz. 23 A6
Žut, Croatia 33 E12
Zutendaal, Belgium 17 G7
Zutphen, Neths. 16 D8
Zuwārah, Libya 75 B7
Zūzan, Iran 65 C8
Žužemberk, Slovenia 33 C11
Zvenigorodka = Zvenyhorodka, Ukraine 41 H6
Zvenyhorodka, Ukraine 41 H6
Zverinogolovskoye, Russia 44 D7
Zvezdets, Bulgaria 38 G10
Zvishavane, Zimbabwe 83 G3
Zvolen, Slovak Rep. 20 G9
Zvonce, Serbia, Yug. 21 N12
Zvornik, Bos.-H. 21 L9
Zwaag, Neths. 16 C6
Zwanenburg, Neths. 16 D5
Zwarte Meer, Neths. 16 C7
Zwarte Waler, Neths. 16 C8
Zwartemeer, Neths. 16 C10
Zwartsluis, Neths. 16 C8
Zwedru = Tchien, Liberia 78 D3
Zweibrücken, Germany 19 F3
Zwenkau, Germany 18 D8
Zwevegem, Belgium 17 G2
Zwickau, Germany 18 E8
Zwiesel, Germany 19 F9
Zwijnaarde, Belgium 17 F3
Zwijndrecht, Belgium 17 F4
Zwijndrecht, Neths. 16 E5
Zwischenahn, Germany 18 B4
Zwolle, Neths. 16 C8
Zwolle, U.S.A. 109 K8
Zymoetz →, Canada 100 C3
Żyrardów, Poland 20 C10
Zyryan, Kazakhstan 44 E9
Zyryanka, Russia 45 C16
Zyryanovsk = Zyryan, Kazakhstan 44 E9
Zyyi, Cyprus 37 E12

KEY TO WORLD MAP PAGES

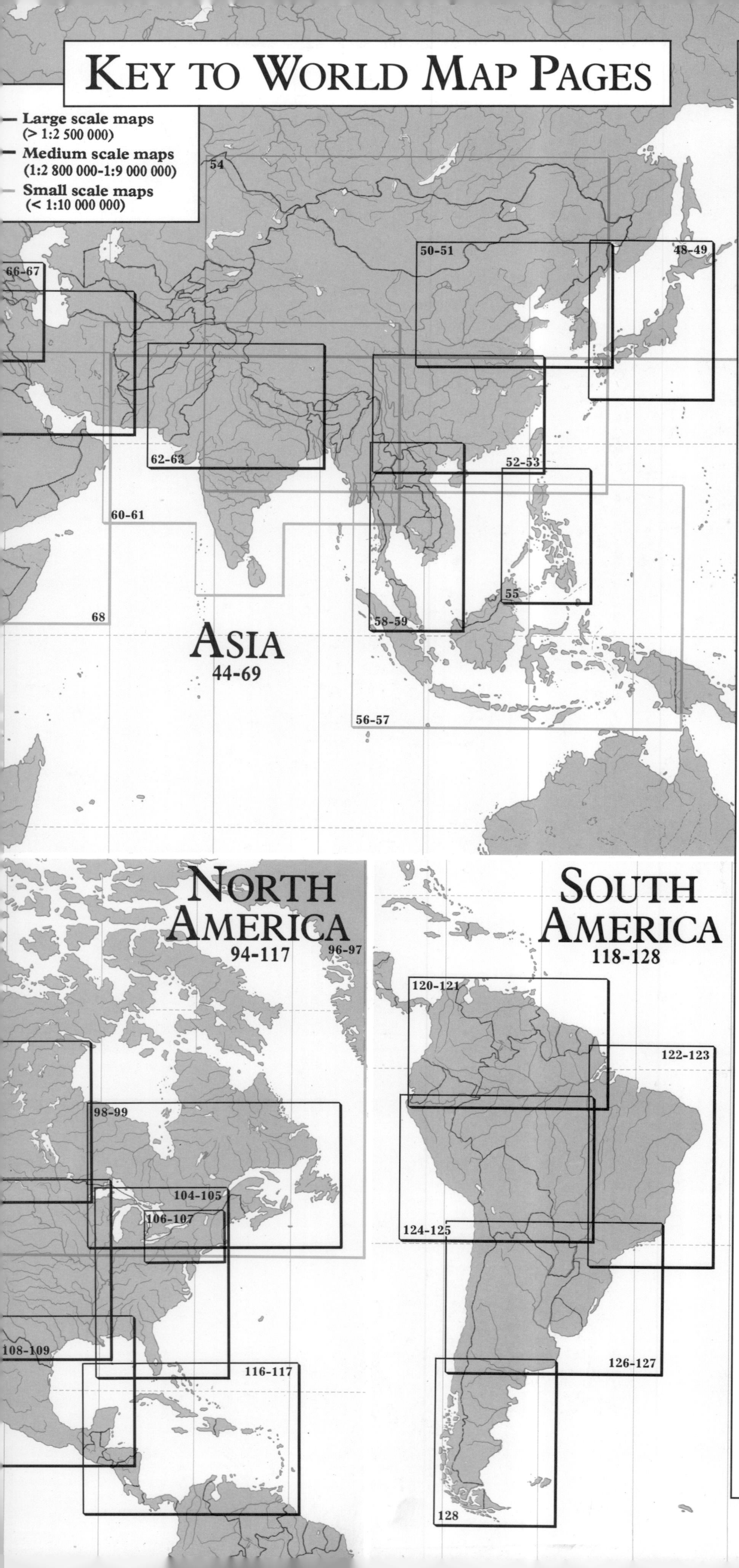

- ▬ **Large scale maps**
  (> 1:2 500 000)
- ▬ **Medium scale maps**
  (1:2 800 000-1:9 000 000)
- ▬ **Small scale maps**
  (< 1:10 000 000)

54

66-67

50-51

48-49

62-63

52-53

60-61

55

68

58-59

56-57

ASIA
44-69

NORTH AMERICA
94-117

96-97

98-99

104-105

106-107

108-109

116-117

SOUTH AMERICA
118-128

120-121

122-123

124-125

126-127

128

COUNTRY INDEX

Afghanistan	60	Kyrgyzstan	44
Albania	38–39		
Algeria	74–75	Laos	58
Angola	80–81	Latvia	40
Argentina	126, 128	Lebanon	69
Armenia	67	Lesotho	85
Australia	88–91	Liberia	78
Austria	19, 20–21	Libya	73
Azerbaijan	67	Lithuania	40
		Luxembourg	17
Bahamas	116–117		
Bahrain	65	Macedonia	38–39
Bangladesh	61	Madagascar	85
Barbados	117	Malawi	83
Belarus	40	Malaysia	55–56
Belgium	17	Mali	78–79
Belize	116	Malta	37
Benin	79	Mauritania	78
Bhutan	61	Mauritius	71
Bolivia	124–125	Mexico	114–115
Bosnia-		Moldova	41
Herzegovina	21	Mongolia	54
Botswana	84–85	Morocco	74
Brazil	120–127	Mozambique	83
Brunei	56		
Bulgaria	38–39	Namibia	84
Burkina Faso	78–79	Nepal	63
Burma	61	Netherlands	16–17
Burundi	82	New Zealand	87
		Nicaragua	116
Cambodia	58–59	Niger	79
Cameroon	82	Nigeria	79
Canada	96–101	Northern Ireland	15
Central African		Norway	8–9
Republic	82		
Chad	73	Oman	68
Chile	126, 128		
China	50–54	Pakistan	62
Colombia	120	Panama	116
Congo	80	Papua New Guinea	86
Costa Rica	116	Paraguay	126–127
Croatia	21	Peru	124
Cuba	116–117	Philippines	55
Cyprus	37	Poland	20
Czech Republic	20–21	Portugal	30–31
		Puerto Rico	117
Denmark	11		
Djibouti	68	Qatar	65
Dominican			
Republic	117	Romania	38
		Russia	40–45
Ecuador	120	Rwanda	82
Egypt	76		
El Salvador	116	Saudi Arabia	68
England	12–13	Scotland	14
Equatorial Guinea	80	Senegal	78
Eritrea	76–77	Sierra Leone	78
Estonia	40	Singapore	59
Ethiopia	68, 77	Slovak Republic	20–21
		Slovenia	33
Fiji	87	Somali Republic	68
Finland	8–9	South Africa	84–85
France	24–27	Spain	28–31
French Guiana	121	Sri Lanka	60
		Sudan	77
Gabon	80	Surinam	121
Gambia	78	Swaziland	85
Georgia	43	Sweden	8–9
Germany	18–19	Switzerland	22–23
Ghana	78–79	Syria	67
Greece	39		
Greenland	4	Taiwan	53
Guatemala	116	Tajikistan	44
Guinea	78	Tanzania	82–83
Guinea-Bissau	78	Thailand	58–59
Guyana	121	Togo	79
		Trinidad and	
Haiti	117	Tobago	117
Honduras	116	Tunisia	75
Hong Kong	53	Turkey	66–67
Hungary	21	Turkmenistan	44
Iceland	8	Uganda	82
India	60–63	Ukraine	41
Indonesia	56–57	United Arab Emirates	65
Iran	64–65	United Kingdom	12–15
Iraq	64–65	USA	102–113
Irish Republic	15	Uruguay	126–127
Israel	69	Uzbekistan	44
Italy	32–35		
Ivory Coast	78	Venezuela	120–121
		Vietnam	58–59
Jamaica	116		
Japan	48–49	Wales	12–13
Jordan	69		
		Yemen	68
Kazakhstan	44	Yugoslavia	38–39
Kenya	82		
Korea, North	51	Zaïre	80–81
Korea, South	51	Zambia	83
Kuwait	64–65	Zimbabwe	83